*"Your word is a lamp
to my feet and a
light to my path."
Psalm 119:105*

This
***Precious Moments*™**
***One Year*® Bible**

Presented to

_____

_____

By _____

_____

_____

Date _____

THE
PRECIOUS MOMENTS™
ONE YEAR® BIBLE

NEW KING JAMES VERSION

THE

PRECIOUS MOMENTS™

ONE YEAR® BIBLE

Arranged in 365 Daily Readings

New King James Version

Tyndale House Publishers, Inc.
WHEATON, ILLINOIS

Library of Congress Cataloging-in-Publication Data

Bible. English. New King James. 1991.
    The Precious moments one year Bible : arranged in 365 daily
    readings : New King James Version.
        p.   cm.
    Illustrated with Precious moments artwork by Samuel Butcher.
    Includes index.
    ISBN 0-8423-2610-3   —   ISBN 0-8423-2611-1 (pbk.)
    1. Devotional calendars.   I. Butcher, Samuel J. (Samuel John),
date . II. Title.
BS195.N38   1991
220.5′2034—dc20   91-32630

The Precious Moments
One Year Bible
New King James Version

Printed in the United States of America

97   96   95   94   93   92   91
7   6   5   4   3   2   1

INDEX
TO THE BOOKS OF THE BIBLE

ALPHABETICAL INDEX
TO THE BOOKS OF THE BIBLE

PUBLISHER'S NOTE

The One Year Bible has been prepared especially for regular Bible readers who wish to read through the entire Bible in one year.

Each day you will read a passage from the Old Testament and one from the New, along with a psalm and one or two proverbs. This gives variety and freshness to your daily reading.

Instead of following a Bible reading chart and experiencing the delay of turning from place to place, you will find the text here in sequence, ready for your quiet reading and meditation.

In this edition of *The One Year Bible* you will find bracketed noun insertions at the beginning of readings where the primary speakers and actors are only referred to by pronouns. These bracketed nouns are not part of the New King James Version text, but they will ensure clarity as you begin each new day's reading.

May this year and every year be enriched as you enjoy daily portions from God's Word!

WAYS TO USE *THE ONE YEAR BIBLE*

The One Year Bible is divided into daily readings. For each day there is a portion of the Old Testament, the New Testament, Psalms, and Proverbs. These four separate daily readings are grouped on consecutive pages, giving diversity to each day's reading. This also makes it easy to use *The One Year Bible* in a variety of ways.

The One Year Bible has led thousands of readers through the Bible in one year. Its arrangement, however, is equally useful for guiding a reader through the Bible in two, or even three, years. If you feel too rushed or want to spend more time on each day's selections, here are a few other suggested reading plans:

The Revised One-Year Plan
Schedule some time both in the morning and evening. Read the New Testament and Psalms selections in the morning and the Old Testament and Proverbs selections in the evening.

The Two-Year Plan
During the first year, read only the Old Testament and Proverbs selections. Then during the second year, read the portions from the New Testament and Psalms.

The Three-Year Plan
Read the Old Testament selections the first year, the New Testament the second year, and the Psalms and Proverbs portions during the third.

Words of Praise and Wisdom in One Year
Read the Psalms and Proverbs selections for each day. This will take you through the Psalms twice and Proverbs once during the year, giving you words of praise and wisdom to live by each day.

And you need not limit yourself to these suggested plans, either. The arrangement of *The One Year Bible* makes it easy to devise any number of Bible reading plans to meet your particular needs.

Preface to the New King James Version

Purpose

In the preface to the 1611 edition, the translators of the King James Bible state that it was not their purpose "to make a new translation . . . but to make a good one better." Indebted to the earlier work of William Tyndale and others, they saw their best contribution to consist in revising and enhancing the excellence of the English versions which had sprung from the Reformation of the sixteenth century. In harmony with the purpose of the King James scholars, the translators and editors of the New King James Version have perceived their work as a continuation of the labors of the earlier translators, thus unlocking for today's readers the spiritual treasures of the King James tradition.

A Living Legacy

For nearly four hundred years, and throughout several revisions, the King James Bible has been deeply revered among the English-speaking peoples of the world. The quality of translation for which it is historically renowned, and its majesty of style, have enabled that monumental version of the Word of God to make a unique contribution to the religion and language of the English-speaking world.

Although the Elizabethan period and our own era share in zeal for technical advance, the former period was more aggressively devoted to classical learning. Along with this awakened concern for the classics came a flourishing companion interest in the Scriptures as the inspired Word of God. The King James translators were committed to producing an English Bible that would be a precise translation, and by no means a paraphrase or a broadly approximate rendering. On the one hand, the scholars were fully familiar with the original languages of the Bible and were especially gifted in their use of their native English. On the other hand, their reverence for the divine Author and His Word assured a translation of the Scriptures in which only a principle of utmost accuracy could be accepted.

In 1786 the Catholic scholar Alexander Geddes said of the King James Bible, "If accuracy and strictest attention to the letter of the text be supposed to constitute an excellent version, this is of all versions the most excellent." George Bernard Shaw became a literary legend in our century because of his severe and often humorous criticisms of our most cherished values. Surprisingly, however, Shaw pays the following tribute to the scholars commissioned by King James: "The translation was extraordinarily well done because to the translators what they were translating was not merely a curious collection of ancient books written by different authors in different stages of culture, but the Word of God divinely revealed through His chosen and expressly inspired scribes. In this conviction they carried out their work with boundless reverence and care and achieved a beautifully artistic result." History agrees with these estimates. Therefore, while seeking to unveil the excellent *form* of the traditional English Bible, special care has also been taken in the New King James Version to preserve the work of *precision* which is the legacy of the 1611 translators.

Devotional Quality

The King James scholars readily appreciated the intrinsic beauty of divine revelation. They accordingly disciplined their talents to render well-chosen English words of their time, as well as a graceful, often musical arrangement of language, which has stirred the hearts of Bible readers through the years. The translators, the committees, and the editors of the New King James Version, while sensitive to the late-twentieth-century English idiom, and while adhering faithfully to the Hebrew, Aramaic, and Greek texts, have sought to maintain that lyrical quality which is so highly regarded in the King James Bible. This devotional quality is especially apparent in the poetic and prophetic books, although even the relatively plain style of the Gospels and Epistles cannot strictly be likened to modern newspaper style.

The Style

Students of the Bible applaud the timeless devotional character of our historic Bible. Yet it is also universally understood that our language, like all living languages, has undergone profound change since 1611. Subsequent revisions of the King James Bible have sought to keep abreast of changes in English speech. The New King James Version is a further step toward this objective. Where obsolescence and other reading difficulties exist, present-day vocabulary, punctuation, and grammar have been carefully integrated. Words representing ancient objects, such as *chariot* and *phylactery*, have no modern substitutes and are therefore retained.

A special feature of the New King James Version is its conformity to the thought flow of the 1611 Bible. The reader discovers that the sequence and selection of words, phrases, and clauses of the new edition, while much clearer, are so close to the traditional that there is remarkable ease in listening to the reading of either edition while following with the other.

In the discipline of translating biblical and other ancient languages, a standard method of transliteration, that is, the English spelling of untranslated words, such as names of persons and places, has never been commonly adopted. In keeping with the design of the New King James Version, the King James spelling of untranslated words is retained, although made uniform throughout. For example, instead of the spellings *Isaiah* and *Elijah* in the Old Testament, and *Esaias* and *Elias* in the New Testament, *Isaiah* and *Elijah* now appear in both Testaments.

Standard doctrinal and theological terms used in the King James Bible, such as *propitiation, justification*, and *sanctification*, have been retained, except where the original language indicates need for a more precise translation.

Readers of the King James Bible will immediately be struck by the absence of several pronouns: *thee, thou,* and *ye* are replaced by the simple *you,* while *your* and *yours* are substituted for *thy* and *thine* as applicable. *Thee, thou, thy* and *thine* were once forms of address to express a special relationship to human as well as divine persons. These pronouns are no longer part of our language. However, pronouns referring to God in the present work are capitalized. Capitalization of these pronouns benefits the reader by clearly distinguishing divine and human persons referred to in a passage. Without such capitalization the distinction may be obscure, because the antecedent of a pronoun is not always clear from the English.

In addition to the pronoun usages of the seventeenth century, the *-eth* and *-est* verb endings so familiar in the earlier King James editions are now obsolete.

Unless a speaker is schooled in these verb endings, there is common difficulty in selecting the correct form to be used with a given subject of the verb in vocal prayer. That is, should we use *love, loveth,* or *lovest? do, doeth, doest,* or *dost? have, hath,* or *hast?* Therefore, contemporary English usage has been substituted for the previous verb endings.

In older editions of the King James Bible, the frequency of the connective *and* far exceeded the limits of present English usage. Also, biblical linguists agree that the Hebrew and Greek original words for this conjunction may commonly be translated otherwise, depending on the immediate context. Therefore, instead of *and,* alternatives such as *also, but, however, now, so, then,* and *thus* are accordingly rendered in the present edition, when the original language permits.

The real character of the King James Bible does not reside in its archaic pronouns or verbs or other grammatical forms of the seventeenth century, but rather in the care taken by its scholars to impart the letter and spirit of the original text in a majestic and reverent style.

The Format

The format of the New King James Version is designed to enhance the vividness and devotional quality of the Holy Scriptures:

- Words or phrases in *italics* indicate expressions in the original language which require clarification by additional English words.
- *Oblique type* in the New Testament indicates a quotation from the Old Testament.
- Prose is divided into paragraphs to indicate the structure of thought.
- Poetry is structured as contemporary verse to reflect the poetic form and beauty of the passage in the original language.
- The covenant name of God was usually translated from the Hebrew as "LORD" or "GOD" (using capital letters as shown) in the King James Old Testament. This tradition is maintained. In the present edition the name is so capitalized whenever the covenant name is quoted in the New Testament from a passage in the Old Testament.
- Significant explanatory notes, alternate translations, textual variants, and cross-references, as well as New Testament citations of Old Testament passages, are supplied in notes placed at the end of the Bible text. Asterisks in the Bible text key the reader to applicable notes.

The Old Testament Text

The Hebrew Bible has come down to us through the scrupulous care of ancient scribes who copied the original text in successive generations. By the sixth century A.D. the scribes were succeeded by a group known as the Masoretes, who continued to preserve the sacred Scriptures for another five hundred years in a form known as the Masoretic Text. Babylonia, Palestine, and Tiberias were the main centers of Masoretic activity; but by the tenth century A.D. the Masoretes of Tiberias, led by the family of ben Asher, gained the ascendancy. Through subsequent editions, the ben Asher text became in the twelfth century the only recognized form of the Hebrew Scriptures.

Daniel Bomberg printed the first Rabbinic Bible in 1516–17; that work was followed in 1524–25 by a second edition prepared by Jacob ben Chayyim and also published by Bomberg. The text of ben Chayyim was adopted in most subsequent Hebrew Bibles, including those used by the King James translators. The ben Chayyim text was also used for the first two editions of Rudolph Kittel's

Biblia Hebraica of 1906 and 1912. In 1937 Paul Kahle published a third edition of *Biblia Hebraica*. This edition was based on the oldest dated manuscript of the ben Asher text, the Leningrad Manuscript B19a (A.D. 1008), which Kahle regarded as superior to that used by ben Chayyim.

For the New King James Version the text used was the 1967/1977 Stuttgart edition of the *Biblia Hebraica*, with frequent comparisons being made with the Bomberg edition of 1524–25. The Septuagint (Greek) Version of the Old Testament and the Latin Vulgate also were consulted. In addition to referring to a variety of ancient versions of the Hebrew Scriptures, the New King James Version draws on the resources of relevant manuscripts from the Dead Sea caves. In the few places where the Hebrew was so obscure that the 1611 King James followed one of the versions, but where information is now available to resolve these problems, the New King James Version follows the Hebrew text.

The New Testament Text

There is more manuscript support for the New Testament than for any other body of ancient literature. Over five thousand Greek, eight thousand Latin, and many more manuscripts in other languages attest to the integrity of the New Testament. There is only one basic New Testament used by Protestants, Roman Catholics, and Orthodox. Minor variations in hand copying have appeared through the centuries, before mechanical printing began about A.D. 1450.

Some variations exist in the spelling of Greek words, in word order, and in similar details. These ordinarily do not show up in translation and do not affect the sense of the text in any way.

Other manuscript differences, regarding the omission or inclusion of a word or a clause, as well as two paragraphs in the Gospels, should not overshadow the overwhelming degree of *agreement* which exists among the ancient records. Bible readers may be assured that the most important differences in English New Testaments of today are due, not to manuscript divergence, but to the way in which translators view the task of translation. The New King James Version follows the historic precedent of the King James Bible in maintaining a literal approach to translation, except where the idiom of the original language occasionally cannot be translated directly into our tongue.

The King James New Testament was based on the traditional text of the Greek-speaking churches, first published in 1516, and later called the Textus Receptus or Received Text. Although based on the relatively few available manuscripts, these were representative of many more which existed at the time but only became known later. Because the New King James Version is the fifth revision of this historic document translated from specific Greek texts, the editors decided to retain the traditional text in the body of the New Testament.

Endnotes

Where significant variations occur in the New Testament Greek manuscripts, textual information can be found among the notes at the end of the Bible text. The textual notes are classified as follows:

1. NU-Text

   These variations from the traditional text generally represent the Alexandrian or Egyptian type of text, as found in the twenty-sixth edition of the Nestle-Aland Greek New Testament (N) and in the United Bible Societies' third edition (U), hence the acronym, "NU-Text."

2. M-Text

These variations from the traditional text represent readings as found in the first edition of *The Greek New Testament According to the Majority Text*, whether supported by overwhelming, strong, or only a divided majority textual tradition.

In closing, let readers be encouraged to approach the Bible "not *as* the word of men, but as it is in truth, the Word of God, which also effectively works in you who believe" (1 Thessalonians 2:13). The same Holy Spirit who originated the Scriptures must also make them clear to the reader, for the truths they contain "are spiritually discerned" (1 Corinthians 2:14). It is through the work of the Spirit of life that the Word of life accomplishes its purposes in human hearts and minds. May God teach us His life-giving truth as we submit to Him, that He alone may be glorified.

JANUARY 1

GENESIS 1:1–2:25

IN the beginning God created the heavens and the earth. ²The earth was without form, and void; and darkness *was** on the face of the deep. And the Spirit of God was hovering over the face of the waters.

³Then God said, "Let there be light"; and there was light. ⁴And God saw the light, that *it was* good; and God divided the light from the darkness. ⁵God called the light Day, and the darkness He called Night. So the evening and the morning were the first day.

⁶Then God said, "Let there be a firmament in the midst of the waters, and let it divide the waters from the waters." ⁷Thus God made the firmament, and divided the waters which *were* under the firmament from the waters which *were* above the firmament; and it was so. ⁸And God called the firmament Heaven. So the evening and the morning were the second day.

⁹Then God said, "Let the waters under the heavens be gathered together into one place, and let the dry *land* appear"; and it was so. ¹⁰And God called the dry *land* Earth, and the gathering together of the waters He called Seas. And God saw that *it was* good.

¹¹Then God said, "Let the earth bring forth grass, the herb *that* yields seed, *and* the fruit tree *that* yields fruit according to its kind, whose seed *is* in itself, on the earth"; and it was so. ¹²And the earth brought forth grass, the herb *that* yields seed according to its kind, and the tree *that* yields fruit, whose seed *is* in itself according to its kind. And God saw that *it was* good. ¹³So the evening and the morning were the third day.

¹⁴Then God said, "Let there be lights in the firmament of the heavens to divide the day from the night; and let them be for signs and seasons, and for days and years; ¹⁵and let them be for lights in the firmament of the heavens to give light on the earth"; and it was so. ¹⁶Then God made two great lights: the greater light to rule the day, and the lesser light to rule the night. *He made* the stars also. ¹⁷God set them in the firmament of the heavens to give light on the earth, ¹⁸and to rule over

the day and over the night, and to divide the light from the darkness. And God saw that *it was* good. ¹⁹So the evening and the morning were the fourth day.

²⁰Then God said, "Let the waters abound with an abundance of living creatures, and let birds fly above the earth across the face of the firmament of the heavens." ²¹So God created great sea creatures and every living thing that moves, with which the waters abounded, according to their kind, and every winged bird according to its kind. And God saw that *it was* good. ²²And God blessed them, saying, "Be fruitful and multiply, and fill the waters in the seas, and let birds multiply on the earth." ²³So the evening and the morning were the fifth day.

²⁴Then God said, "Let the earth bring forth the living creature according to its kind: cattle and creeping thing and beast of the earth, *each* according to its kind"; and it was so. ²⁵And God made the beast of the earth according to its kind, cattle according to its kind, and everything that creeps on the earth according to its kind. And God saw that *it was* good.

²⁶Then God said, "Let Us make man in Our image, according to Our likeness; let them have dominion over the fish of the sea, over the birds of the air, and over the cattle, over all* the earth and over every creeping thing that creeps on the earth." ²⁷So God created man in His *own* image; in the image of God He created him; male and female He created them. ²⁸Then God blessed them, and God said to them, "Be fruitful and multiply; fill the earth and subdue it; have dominion over the fish of the sea, over the birds of the air, and over every living thing that moves on the earth."

²⁹And God said, "See, I have given you every herb *that* yields seed which *is* on the face of all the earth, and every tree whose fruit yields seed; to you it

shall be for food. ³⁰Also, to every beast of the earth, to every bird of the air, and to everything that creeps on the earth, in which *there is* life, *I have given* every green herb for food"; and it was so. ³¹Then God saw everything that He had made, and indeed *it was* very good. So the evening and the morning were the sixth day.

Thus the heavens and the earth, and all the host of them, were finished. ²And on the seventh day God ended His work which He had done, and He rested on the seventh day from all His work which He had done. ³Then God blessed the seventh day and sanctified it, because in it He rested from all His work which God had created and made.

⁴This *is* the history* of the heavens and the earth when they were created, in the day that the Lord God made the earth and the heavens, ⁵before any plant of the field was in the earth and before any herb of the field had grown. For the Lord God had not caused it to rain on the earth, and *there was* no man to till the ground; ⁶but a mist went up from the earth and watered the whole face of the ground.

⁷And the Lord God formed man *of* the dust of the ground, and breathed into his nostrils the breath of life; and man became a living being.

⁸The Lord God planted a garden eastward in Eden, and there He put the man whom He had formed. ⁹And out of the ground the Lord God made every tree grow that is pleasant to the sight and good for food. The tree of life *was* also in the midst of the garden, and the tree of the knowledge of good and evil.

¹⁰Now a river went out of Eden to water the garden, and from there it parted and became four riverheads. ¹¹The name of the first *is* Pishon; it *is* the one which skirts the whole land of Havilah, where *there is* gold. ¹²And the gold of that land *is* good. Bdellium and

the onyx stone *are* there. ¹³The name of the second river *is* Gihon; it *is* the one which goes around the whole land of Cush. ¹⁴The name of the third river *is* Hiddekel;* it *is* the one which goes toward the east of Assyria. The fourth river *is* the Euphrates.

¹⁵Then the Lord God took the man and put him in the garden of Eden to tend and keep it. ¹⁶And the Lord God commanded the man, saying, "Of every tree of the garden you may freely eat; ¹⁷but of the tree of the knowledge of good and evil you shall not eat, for in the day that you eat of it you shall surely die."

¹⁸And the Lord God said, "*It is* not good that man should be alone; I will make him a helper comparable to him." ¹⁹Out of the ground the Lord God formed every beast of the field and every bird of the air, and brought *them* to Adam to see what he would call them. And whatever Adam called each living creature, that *was* its name. ²⁰So Adam gave names to all cattle, to the birds of the air, and to every beast of the field. But for Adam there was not found a helper comparable to him.

²¹And the Lord God caused a deep sleep to fall on Adam, and he slept; and He took one of his ribs, and closed up the flesh in its place. ²²Then the rib which the Lord God had taken from man He made into a woman, and He brought her to the man.

²³And Adam said:

"This *is* now bone of my bones
And flesh of my flesh;
She shall be called Woman,
Because she was taken out of Man."

²⁴Therefore a man shall leave his father and mother and be joined to his wife, and they shall become one flesh. ²⁵And they were both naked, the man and his wife, and were not ashamed.

MATTHEW 1:1–2:12

THE book of the genealogy of Jesus Christ, the Son of David, the Son of Abraham:

²Abraham begot Isaac, Isaac begot Jacob, and Jacob begot Judah and his brothers. ³Judah begot Perez and Zerah by Tamar, Perez begot Hezron, and Hezron begot Ram. ⁴Ram begot Amminadab, Amminadab begot Nahshon, and Nahshon begot Salmon. ⁵Salmon begot Boaz by Rahab, Boaz begot Obed by Ruth, Obed begot Jesse, ⁶and Jesse begot David the king.

David the king begot Solomon by her *who had been the wife** of Uriah. ⁷Solomon begot Rehoboam, Rehoboam begot Abijah, and Abijah begot Asa.* ⁸Asa begot Jehoshaphat, Jehoshaphat begot Joram, and Joram begot Uzziah. ⁹Uzziah begot Jotham, Jotham begot Ahaz, and Ahaz begot Hezekiah. ¹⁰Hezekiah begot Manasseh, Manasseh begot Amon,* and Amon begot Josiah. ¹¹Josiah begot Jeconiah and his brothers about the time they were carried away to Babylon.

¹²And after they were brought to Babylon, Jeconiah begot Shealtiel, and Shealtiel begot Zerubbabel. ¹³Zerubbabel begot Abiud, Abiud begot Eliakim, and Eliakim begot Azor. ¹⁴Azor begot Zadok, Zadok begot Achim, and Achim begot Eliud. ¹⁵Eliud begot Eleazar, Eleazar begot Matthan, and Matthan begot Jacob. ¹⁶And Jacob begot Joseph the husband of Mary, of whom was born Jesus who is called Christ.

¹⁷So all the generations from Abraham to David *are* fourteen generations, from David until the captivity in Babylon *are* fourteen generations, and from the captivity in Babylon until the Christ *are* fourteen generations.

¹⁸Now the birth of Jesus Christ was as follows: After His mother Mary

was betrothed to Joseph, before they came together, she was found with child of the Holy Spirit. ¹⁹Then Joseph her husband, being a just *man,* and not wanting to make her a public example, was minded to put her away secretly. ²⁰But while he thought about these things, behold, an angel of the Lord appeared to him in a dream, saying, "Joseph, son of David, do not be afraid to take to you Mary your wife, for that which is conceived in her is of the Holy Spirit. ²¹And she will bring forth a Son, and you shall call His name Jesus, for He will save His people from their sins."

²²So all this was done that it might be fulfilled which was spoken by the Lord through the prophet, saying: ²³*"Behold, the virgin shall be with child, and bear a Son, and they shall call His name Immanuel,"** which is translated, "God with us."

²⁴Then Joseph, being aroused from sleep, did as the angel of the Lord commanded him and took to him his wife, ²⁵and did not know her till she had brought forth her firstborn Son.* And he called His name Jesus.

Now after Jesus was born in Bethlehem of Judea in the days of Herod the king, behold, wise men from the East came to Jerusalem, ²saying, "Where is He who has been born King of the Jews? For we have seen His star in the East and have come to worship Him."

³When Herod the king heard *this,* he was troubled, and all Jerusalem with him. ⁴And when he had gathered all the chief priests and scribes of the people together, he inquired of them where the Christ was to be born.

⁵So they said to him, "In Bethlehem of Judea, for thus it is written by the prophet:

⁶   'But you, Bethlehem, in the
        land of Judah,

Are not the least among the
    rulers of Judah;
For out of you shall come a
    Ruler
Who will shepherd My people
    Israel.'"*

⁷Then Herod, when he had secretly called the wise men, determined from them what time the star appeared. ⁸And he sent them to Bethlehem and said, "Go and search carefully for the young Child, and when you have found *Him,* bring back word to me, that I may come and worship Him also."

⁹When they heard the king, they departed; and behold, the star which they had seen in the East went before them, till it came and stood over where the young Child was. ¹⁰When they saw the star, they rejoiced with exceedingly great joy. ¹¹And when they had come into the house, they saw the young Child with Mary His mother, and fell down and worshiped Him. And when they had opened their treasures, they presented gifts to Him: gold, frankincense, and myrrh.

¹²Then, being divinely warned in a dream that they should not return to Herod, they departed for their own country another way.

PSALM 1:1-6

Blessed *is* the man
Who walks not in the counsel
of the ungodly,
    Nor stands in the path of
        sinners,
    Nor sits in the seat of the
        scornful;
2   But his delight *is* in the law of
        the Lord,
    And in His law he
        meditates day and night.
3   He shall be like a tree
        Planted by the rivers of
            water,

That brings forth its fruit in
its season,
Whose leaf also shall not
wither;
And whatever he does shall
prosper.

4   The ungodly *are* not so,
But *are* like the chaff which
the wind drives away.

5   Therefore the ungodly shall
not stand in the
judgment,
Nor sinners in the congregation of the righteous.

6   For the LORD knows the way
of the righteous,
But the way of the ungodly
shall perish.

PROVERBS FOR TODAY/ 1:1-6

*The proverbs of Solomon the son of David, king of Israel: To know wisdom and
instruction, to perceive the words of understanding, to receive the instruction of
wisdom, justice, judgment, and equity; to give prudence to the simple, to the young
man knowledge and discretion—a wise* man *will hear and increase learning, and
a man of understanding will attain wise counsel, to understand a proverb and an
enigma, the words of the wise and their riddles.*

JANUARY 2

GENESIS 3:1–4:26

Now the serpent was more cunning than any beast of the field
which the LORD God had made.
And he said to the woman, "Has God
indeed said, 'You shall not eat of every
tree of the garden'?"

2And the woman said to the serpent,
"We may eat the fruit of the trees of the
garden; 3but of the fruit of the tree
which *is* in the midst of the garden,
God has said, 'You shall not eat it, nor
shall you touch it, lest you die.' "

4Then the serpent said to the
woman, "You will not surely die. 5For
God knows that in the day you eat of it
your eyes will be opened, and you will
be like God, knowing good and evil."

6So when the woman saw that the
tree *was* good for food, that it *was*
pleasant to the eyes, and a tree desirable to make *one* wise, she took of its
fruit and ate. She also gave to her husband with her, and he ate. 7Then the
eyes of both of them were opened, and
they knew that they *were* naked; and
they sewed fig leaves together and
made themselves coverings.

8And they heard the sound of the
LORD God walking in the garden in the
cool of the day, and Adam and his wife
hid themselves from the presence of
the LORD God among the trees of the
garden.

9Then the LORD God called to Adam
and said to him, "Where *are* you?"

10So he said, "I heard Your voice in
the garden, and I was afraid because I
was naked; and I hid myself."

11And He said, "Who told you that
you *were* naked? Have you eaten from
the tree of which I commanded you
that you should not eat?"

12Then the man said, "The woman
whom You gave *to be* with me, she
gave me of the tree, and I ate."

13And the LORD God said to the woman, "What *is* this you have done?" The woman said, "The serpent deceived me, and I ate."

14So the LORD God said to the serpent:

> "Because you have done this,
> You *are* cursed more than all cattle,
> And more than every beast of the field;
> On your belly you shall go,
> And you shall eat dust
> All the days of your life.
> 15 And I will put enmity
> Between you and the woman,
> And between your seed and her Seed;
> He shall bruise your head,
> And you shall bruise His heel."

16To the woman He said:

> "I will greatly multiply your sorrow and your conception;
> In pain you shall bring forth children;
> Your desire *shall be* for your husband,
> And he shall rule over you."

17Then to Adam He said, "Because you have heeded the voice of your wife, and have eaten from the tree of which I commanded you, saying, 'You shall not eat of it':

> "Cursed *is* the ground for your sake;
> In toil you shall eat *of* it
> All the days of your life.
> 18 Both thorns and thistles it shall bring forth for you,
> And you shall eat the herb of the field.
> 19 In the sweat of your face you shall eat bread
> Till you return to the ground,
> For out of it you were taken;
> For dust you *are,*
> And to dust you shall return."

20And Adam called his wife's name Eve, because she was the mother of all living.

21Also for Adam and his wife the LORD God made tunics of skin, and clothed them.

22Then the LORD God said, "Behold, the man has become like one of Us, to know good and evil. And now, lest he put out his hand and take also of the tree of life, and eat, and live forever"— 23therefore the LORD God sent him out of the garden of Eden to till the ground from which he was taken. 24So He drove out the man; and He placed cherubim at the east of the garden of Eden, and a flaming sword which turned every way, to guard the way to the tree of life.

Now Adam knew Eve his wife, and she conceived and bore Cain, and said, "I have acquired a man from the LORD." 2Then she bore again, this time his brother Abel. Now Abel was a keeper of sheep, but Cain was a tiller of the ground. 3And in the process of time it came to pass that Cain brought an offering of the fruit of the ground to the LORD. 4Abel also brought of the firstborn of his flock and of their fat. And the LORD respected Abel and his offering, 5but He did not respect Cain and his offering. And Cain was very angry, and his countenance fell.

6So the LORD said to Cain, "Why are you angry? And why has your countenance fallen? 7If you do well, will you not be accepted? And if you do not do well, sin lies at the door. And its desire *is* for you, but you should rule over it."

8Now Cain talked with Abel his brother;* and it came to pass, when they were in the field, that Cain rose up against Abel his brother and killed him.

⁹Then the LORD said to Cain, "Where *is* Abel your brother?"

He said, "I do not know. *Am* I my brother's keeper?"

¹⁰And He said, "What have you done? The voice of your brother's blood cries out to Me from the ground. ¹¹So now you *are* cursed from the earth, which has opened its mouth to receive your brother's blood from your hand. ¹²When you till the ground, it shall no longer yield its strength to you. A fugitive and a vagabond you shall be on the earth."

¹³And Cain said to the LORD, "My punishment *is* greater than I can bear! ¹⁴Surely You have driven me out this day from the face of the ground; I shall be hidden from Your face; I shall be a fugitive and a vagabond on the earth, and it will happen *that* anyone who finds me will kill me."

¹⁵And the LORD said to him, "Therefore,* whoever kills Cain, vengeance shall be taken on him sevenfold." And the LORD set a mark on Cain, lest anyone finding him should kill him.

¹⁶Then Cain went out from the presence of the LORD and dwelt in the land of Nod on the east of Eden. ¹⁷And Cain knew his wife, and she conceived and bore Enoch. And he built a city, and called the name of the city after the name of his son—Enoch. ¹⁸To Enoch was born Irad; and Irad begot Mehujael, and Mehujael begot Methushael, and Methushael begot Lamech.

¹⁹Then Lamech took for himself two wives: the name of one *was* Adah, and the name of the second *was* Zillah. ²⁰And Adah bore Jabal. He was the father of those who dwell in tents and have livestock. ²¹His brother's name *was* Jubal. He was the father of all those who play the harp and flute. ²²And as for Zillah, she also bore Tubal-Cain, an instructor of every craftsman in bronze and iron. And the sister of Tubal-Cain *was* Naamah.

²³Then Lamech said to his wives:

"Adah and Zillah, hear my voice;
Wives of Lamech, listen to my speech!
For I have killed a man for wounding me,
Even a young man for hurting me.
24　If Cain shall be avenged sevenfold,
Then Lamech seventy-sevenfold."

²⁵And Adam knew his wife again, and she bore a son and named him Seth, "For God has appointed another seed for me instead of Abel, whom Cain killed." ²⁶And as for Seth, to him also a son was born; and he named him Enosh.* Then *men* began to call on the name of the LORD.

MATTHEW 2:13–3:6

Now when they [the wise men] had departed, behold, an angel of the Lord appeared to Joseph in a dream, saying, "Arise, take the young Child and His mother, flee to Egypt, and stay there until I bring you word; for Herod will seek the young Child to destroy Him."

¹⁴When he arose, he took the young Child and His mother by night and departed for Egypt, ¹⁵and was there until the death of Herod, that it might be fulfilled which was spoken by the Lord through the prophet, saying, *"Out of Egypt I called My Son."*

¹⁶Then Herod, when he saw that he was deceived by the wise men, was exceedingly angry; and he sent forth and put to death all the male children who were in Bethlehem and in all its districts, from two years old and under, according to the time which he had determined from the wise men. ¹⁷Then was fulfilled what was spoken by Jeremiah the prophet, saying:

18 "A *voice was heard in Ramah,*
 Lamentation, weeping, and
 great mourning,
 Rachel weeping for her
 children,
 Refusing to be comforted,
 Because they are no more.'"*

19Now when Herod was dead, behold, an angel of the Lord appeared in a dream to Joseph in Egypt, 20saying, "Arise, take the young Child and His mother, and go to the land of Israel, for those who sought the young Child's life are dead." 21Then he arose, took the young Child and His mother, and came into the land of Israel.

22But when he heard that Archelaus was reigning over Judea instead of his father Herod, he was afraid to go there. And being warned by God in a dream, he turned aside into the region of Galilee. 23And he came and dwelt in a city called Nazareth, that it might be fulfilled which was spoken by the prophets, "He shall be called a Nazarene."

In those days John the Baptist came preaching in the wilderness of Judea, 2and saying, "Repent, for the kingdom of heaven is at hand!" 3For this is he who was spoken of by the prophet Isaiah, saying:

 "The voice of one crying in the
 wilderness:
 'Prepare the way of the Lord;
 Make His paths straight.' "*

4Now John himself was clothed in camel's hair, with a leather belt around his waist; and his food was locusts and wild honey. 5Then Jerusalem, all Judea, and all the region around the Jordan went out to him 6and were baptized by him in the Jordan, confessing their sins.

PSALM 2:1-12

WHY do the nations rage,
 And the people plot a vain
 thing?
2 The kings of the earth set
 themselves,
 And the rulers take counsel
 together,
 Against the Lord and against
 His Anointed, *saying,*
3 "Let us break Their bonds in
 pieces
 And cast away Their cords
 from us."

4 He who sits in the heavens
 shall laugh;
 The Lord shall hold them in
 derision.
5 Then He shall speak to them
 in His wrath,
 And distress them in His deep
 displeasure:
6 "Yet I have set My King
 On My holy hill of Zion."

7 "I will declare the decree:
 The Lord has said to Me,
 'You *are* My Son,
 Today I have begotten You.
8 Ask of Me, and I will give *You*
 The nations *for* Your
 inheritance,
 And the ends of the earth *for*
 Your possession.
9 You shall break* them with a
 rod of iron;
 You shall dash them to pieces
 like a potter's vessel.' "

10 Now therefore, be wise,
 O kings;
 Be instructed, you judges of
 the earth.
11 Serve the Lord with fear,
 And rejoice with trembling.
12 Kiss the Son,* lest He* be
 angry,
 And you perish *in* the way,

When His wrath is kindled
but a little.

Blessed *are* all those who put
their trust in Him.

PROVERBS FOR TODAY/ 1:7-9

The fear of the LORD *is the beginning of knowledge, but fools despise wisdom and instruction.* □ *My son, hear the instruction of your father, and do not forsake the law of your mother; for they will be a graceful ornament on your head, and chains about your neck.*

JANUARY 3

GENESIS 5:1–7:24

THIS is the book of the genealogy of Adam. In the day that God created man, He made him in the likeness of God. ²He created them male and female, and blessed them and called them Mankind in the day they were created. ³And Adam lived one hundred and thirty years, and begot *a son* in his own likeness, after his image, and named him Seth. ⁴After he begot Seth, the days of Adam were eight hundred years; and he had sons and daughters. ⁵So all the days that Adam lived were nine hundred and thirty years; and he died.

⁶Seth lived one hundred and five years, and begot Enosh. ⁷After he begot Enosh, Seth lived eight hundred and seven years, and had sons and daughters. ⁸So all the days of Seth were nine hundred and twelve years; and he died.

⁹Enosh lived ninety years, and begot Cainan.* ¹⁰After he begot Cainan, Enosh lived eight hundred and fifteen years, and had sons and daughters. ¹¹So all the days of Enosh were nine hundred and five years; and he died.

¹²Cainan lived seventy years, and begot Mahalalel. ¹³After he begot Mahalalel, Cainan lived eight hundred and forty years, and had sons and daugh-

ters. ¹⁴So all the days of Cainan were nine hundred and ten years; and he died.

¹⁵Mahalalel lived sixty-five years, and begot Jared. ¹⁶After he begot Jared, Mahalalel lived eight hundred and thirty years, and had sons and daughters. ¹⁷So all the days of Mahalalel were eight hundred and ninety-five years; and he died.

¹⁸Jared lived one hundred and sixty-two years, and begot Enoch. ¹⁹After he begot Enoch, Jared lived eight hundred years, and had sons and daughters. ²⁰So all the days of Jared were nine hundred and sixty-two years; and he died.

²¹Enoch lived sixty-five years, and begot Methuselah. ²²After he begot Methuselah, Enoch walked with God three hundred years, and had sons and daughters. ²³So all the days of Enoch were three hundred and sixty-five years. ²⁴And Enoch walked with God; and he *was* not, for God took him.

²⁵Methuselah lived one hundred and eighty-seven years, and begot Lamech. ²⁶After he begot Lamech, Methuselah lived seven hundred and eighty-two years, and had sons and daughters. ²⁷So all the days of Methuselah were nine hundred and sixty-nine years; and he died.

²⁸Lamech lived one hundred and

eighty-two years, and had a son. ²⁹And he called his name Noah, saying, "This *one* will comfort us concerning our work and the toil of our hands, because of the ground which the LORD has cursed." ³⁰After he begot Noah, Lamech lived five hundred and ninety-five years, and had sons and daughters. ³¹So all the days of Lamech were seven hundred and seventy-seven years; and he died.

³²And Noah was five hundred years old, and Noah begot Shem, Ham, and Japheth.

Now it came to pass, when men began to multiply on the face of the earth, and daughters were born to them, ²that the sons of God saw the daughters of men, that they *were* beautiful; and they took wives for themselves of all whom they chose.

³And the LORD said, "My Spirit shall not strive* with man forever, for he *is* indeed flesh; yet his days shall be one hundred and twenty years." ⁴There were giants on the earth in those days, and also afterward, when the sons of God came in to the daughters of men and they bore *children* to them. Those *were* the mighty men who *were* of old, men of renown.

⁵Then the LORD* saw that the wickedness of man *was* great in the earth, and *that* every intent of the thoughts of his heart *was* only evil continually. ⁶And the LORD was sorry that He had made man on the earth, and He was grieved in His heart. ⁷So the LORD said, "I will destroy man whom I have created from the face of the earth, both man and beast, creeping thing and birds of the air, for I am sorry that I have made them." ⁸But Noah found grace in the eyes of the LORD.

⁹This is the genealogy of Noah. Noah was a just man, perfect in his generations. Noah walked with God. ¹⁰And Noah begot three sons: Shem, Ham, and Japheth.

¹¹The earth also was corrupt before God, and the earth was filled with violence. ¹²So God looked upon the earth, and indeed it was corrupt; for all flesh had corrupted their way on the earth.

¹³And God said to Noah, "The end of all flesh has come before Me, for the earth is filled with violence through them; and behold, I will destroy them with the earth. ¹⁴Make yourself an ark of gopherwood; make rooms in the ark, and cover it inside and outside with pitch. ¹⁵And this is how you shall make it: The length of the ark *shall be* three hundred cubits, its width fifty cubits, and its height thirty cubits. ¹⁶You shall make a window for the ark, and you shall finish it to a cubit from above; and set the door of the ark in its side. You shall make it *with* lower, second, and third *decks.* ¹⁷And behold, I Myself am bringing floodwaters on the earth, to destroy from under heaven all flesh in which *is* the breath of life; everything that *is* on the earth shall die. ¹⁸But I will establish My covenant with you; and you shall go into the ark— you, your sons, your wife, and your sons' wives with you. ¹⁹And of every living thing of all flesh you shall bring two of every *sort* into the ark, to keep *them* alive with you; they shall be male and female. ²⁰Of the birds after their kind, of animals after their kind, and of every creeping thing of the earth after its kind, two of every *kind* will come to you to keep *them* alive. ²¹And you shall take for yourself of all food that is eaten, and you shall gather *it* to yourself; and it shall be food for you and for them."

²²Thus Noah did; according to all that God commanded him, so he did.

THEN the LORD said to Noah, "Come into the ark, you and all your household, because I have seen *that* you *are* righteous before Me in this generation. ²You shall take with you seven each of every clean animal, a male and his female; two each of animals that *are* unclean, a male and his female; [3]also seven each of birds of the air, male and female, to keep the species alive on the face of all the earth. [4]For after seven more days I will cause it to rain on the earth forty days and forty nights, and I will destroy from the face of the earth all living things that I have made." [5]And Noah did according to all that the LORD commanded him. [6]Noah *was* six hundred years old when the floodwaters were on the earth.

[7]So Noah, with his sons, his wife, and his sons' wives, went into the ark because of the waters of the flood. [8]Of clean animals, of animals that *are* unclean, of birds, and of everything that creeps on the earth, [9]two by two they went into the ark to Noah, male and female, as God had commanded Noah. [10]And it came to pass after seven days that the waters of the flood were on the earth. [11]In the six hundredth year of Noah's life, in the second month, the seventeenth day of the month, on that day all the fountains of the great deep were broken up, and the windows of heaven were opened. [12]And the rain was on the earth forty days and forty nights.

[13]On the very same day Noah and Noah's sons, Shem, Ham, and Japheth, and Noah's wife and the three wives of his sons with them, entered the ark— [14]they and every beast after its kind, all cattle after their kind, every creeping thing that creeps on the earth after its kind, and every bird after its kind, every bird of every sort. [15]And they went into the ark to Noah, two by two, of all flesh in which *is* the breath of life. [16]So those that entered, male and female of all flesh, went in as God had commanded him; and the LORD shut him in.

[17]Now the flood was on the earth forty days. The waters increased and lifted up the ark, and it rose high above the earth. [18]The waters prevailed and greatly increased on the earth, and the ark moved about on the surface of the waters. [19]And the waters prevailed exceedingly on the earth, and all the high hills under the whole heaven were covered. [20]The waters prevailed fifteen cubits upward, and the mountains were covered. [21]And all flesh died that moved on the earth: birds and cattle and beasts and every creeping thing that creeps on the earth, and every man. [22]All in whose nostrils *was* the breath of the spirit* of life, all that *was* on the dry *land,* died. [23]So He destroyed all living things which were on the face of the ground: both man and cattle, creeping thing and bird of the air. They were destroyed from the earth. Only Noah and those who *were* with him in the ark remained *alive.* [24]And the waters prevailed on the earth one hundred and fifty days.

MATTHEW 3:7–4:11

BUT when he [John the Baptist] saw many of the Pharisees and Sadducees coming to his baptism, he said to them, "Brood of vipers! Who warned you to flee from the wrath to come? [8]Therefore bear fruits worthy of repentance, [9]and do not think to say to yourselves, 'We have Abraham as *our* father.' For I say to you that God is able to raise up children to Abraham from these stones. [10]And even now the ax is laid to the root of the trees. Therefore every tree which does not bear good fruit is cut down and thrown into the fire. [11]I indeed baptize you with water unto repentance, but He who is coming after me is mightier than I, whose sandals I am not worthy to carry. He will baptize you with the Holy Spirit and fire.* [12]His winnowing fan *is* in His hand, and He will thoroughly clean out His threshing floor, and gather His wheat into the barn; but He will burn up the chaff with unquenchable fire."

¹³Then Jesus came from Galilee to John at the Jordan to be baptized by him. ¹⁴And John *tried to* prevent Him, saying, "I need to be baptized by You, and are You coming to me?"

¹⁵But Jesus answered and said to him, "Permit *it to be so* now, for thus it is fitting for us to fulfill all righteousness." Then he allowed Him.

¹⁶When He had been baptized, Jesus came up immediately from the water; and behold, the heavens were opened to Him, and He* saw the Spirit of God descending like a dove and alighting upon Him. ¹⁷And suddenly a voice *came* from heaven, saying, "This is My beloved Son, in whom I am well pleased."

THEN Jesus was led up by the Spirit into the wilderness to be tempted by the devil. ²And when He had fasted forty days and forty nights, afterward He was hungry. ³Now when the tempter came to Him, he said, "If You are the Son of God, command that these stones become bread."

⁴But He answered and said, "It is written, *'Man shall not live by bread alone, but by every word that proceeds from the mouth of God.'"* *

⁵Then the devil took Him up into the holy city, set Him on the pinnacle of the temple, ⁶and said to Him, "If You are the Son of God, throw Yourself down. For it is written:

'He shall give His angels charge over you,'

and,

*'In their hands they shall bear you up,
Lest you dash your foot against a stone.'"* *

⁷Jesus said to him, "It is written again, *'You shall not tempt the LORD your God.'"* *

⁸Again, the devil took Him up on an exceedingly high mountain, and showed Him all the kingdoms of the world and their glory. ⁹And he said to Him, "All these things I will give You if You will fall down and worship me."

¹⁰Then Jesus said to him, "Away with you,* Satan! For it is written, *'You shall worship the LORD your God, and Him only you shall serve.'"* *

¹¹Then the devil left Him, and behold, angels came and ministered to Him.

PSALM 3:1-8

A Psalm of David when he fled from Absalom his son.

L ORD, how they have increased who trouble me!
Many *are* they who rise up against me.

2   Many *are* they who say of me,
"There is no help for him in God."   Selah

3   But You, O LORD, *are* a shield for me,
My glory and the One who lifts up my head.

4   I cried to the LORD with my voice,
And He heard me from His holy hill.   Selah

5   I lay down and slept;
I awoke, for the LORD sustained me.

6   I will not be afraid of ten thousands of people
Who have set *themselves* against me all around.

7   Arise, O LORD;
Save me, O my God!
For You have struck all my enemies on the cheekbone;
You have broken the teeth of the ungodly.

8   Salvation *belongs* to the LORD.
Your blessing *is* upon Your people.   Selah

PROVERBS FOR TODAY/ 1:10-19

My son, if sinners entice you, do not consent. If they say, "Come with us, let us lie in wait to shed blood; let us lurk secretly for the innocent without cause; let us swallow them alive like Sheol,* and whole, like those who go down to the pit; we shall find all kinds of precious possessions, we shall fill our houses with spoil; cast in your lot among us, let us all have one purse"—My son, do not walk in the way with them, keep your foot from their path; for their feet run to evil, and they make haste to shed blood. Surely, in vain the net is spread in the sight of any bird; but they lie in wait for their own blood, they lurk secretly for their own lives. So are the ways of everyone who is greedy for gain; it takes away the life of its owners.

JANUARY 4

GENESIS 8:1–10:32

THEN God remembered Noah, and every living thing, and all the animals that *were* with him in the ark. And God made a wind to pass over the earth, and the waters subsided. ²The fountains of the deep and the windows of heaven were also stopped, and the rain from heaven was restrained. ³And the waters receded continually from the earth. At the end of the hundred and fifty days the waters decreased. ⁴Then the ark rested in the seventh month, the seventeenth day of the month, on the mountains of Ararat. ⁵And the waters decreased continually until the tenth month. In the tenth *month,* on the first *day* of the month, the tops of the mountains were seen.

⁶So it came to pass, at the end of forty days, that Noah opened the window of the ark which he had made. ⁷Then he sent out a raven, which kept going to and fro until the waters had dried up from the earth. ⁸He also sent out from himself a dove, to see if the waters had receded from the face of the ground. ⁹But the dove found no resting place for the sole of her foot, and she returned into the ark to him, for the waters *were* on the face of the whole earth. So he put out his hand

and took her, and drew her into the ark to himself. ¹⁰And he waited yet another seven days, and again he sent the dove out from the ark. ¹¹Then the dove came to him in the evening, and behold, a freshly plucked olive leaf *was* in her mouth; and Noah knew that the waters had receded from the earth. ¹²So he waited yet another seven days and sent out the dove, which did not return again to him anymore.

¹³And it came to pass in the six hundred and first year, in the first *month,* the first *day* of the month, that the waters were dried up from the earth; and Noah removed the covering of the ark and looked, and indeed the surface of the ground was dry. ¹⁴And in the second month, on the twenty-seventh day of the month, the earth was dried.

¹⁵Then God spoke to Noah, saying, ¹⁶"Go out of the ark, you and your wife, and your sons and your sons' wives with you. ¹⁷Bring out with you every living thing of all flesh that *is* with you: birds and cattle and every creeping thing that creeps on the earth, so that they may abound on the earth, and be fruitful and multiply on the earth." ¹⁸So Noah went out, and his sons and his wife and his sons' wives with him. ¹⁹Every animal, every

creeping thing, every bird, *and* whatever creeps on the earth, according to their families, went out of the ark.

²⁰Then Noah built an altar to the LORD, and took of every clean animal and of every clean bird, and offered burnt offerings on the altar. ²¹And the LORD smelled a soothing aroma. Then the LORD said in His heart, "I will never again curse the ground for man's sake, although the imagination of man's heart *is* evil from his youth; nor will I again destroy every living thing as I have done.

22 "While the earth remains,
Seedtime and harvest,
Cold and heat,
Winter and summer,
And day and night
Shall not cease."

So God blessed Noah and his sons, and said to them: "Be fruitful and multiply, and fill the earth.* ²And the fear of you and the dread of you shall be on every beast of the earth, on every bird of the air, on all that move *on* the earth, and on all the fish of the sea. They are given into your hand. ³Every moving thing that lives shall be food for you. I have given you all things, even as the green herbs. ⁴But you shall not eat flesh with its life, *that is,* its blood. ⁵Surely for your lifeblood I will demand *a reckoning;* from the hand of every beast I will require it, and from the hand of man. From the hand of every man's brother I will require the life of man.

6 "Whoever sheds man's blood,
By man his blood shall be
shed;
For in the image of God
He made man.
7 And as for you, be fruitful and
multiply;
Bring forth abundantly in the
earth
And multiply in it."

⁸Then God spoke to Noah and to his sons with him, saying: ⁹"And as for Me, behold, I establish My covenant with you and with your descendants* after you, ¹⁰and with every living creature that *is* with you: the birds, the cattle, and every beast of the earth with you, of all that go out of the ark, every beast of the earth. ¹¹Thus I establish My covenant with you: Never again shall all flesh be cut off by the waters of the flood; never again shall there be a flood to destroy the earth."

¹²And God said: "This *is* the sign of the covenant which I make between Me and you, and every living creature that *is* with you, for perpetual generations: ¹³I set My rainbow in the cloud, and it shall be for the sign of the covenant between Me and the earth. ¹⁴It shall be, when I bring a cloud over the earth, that the rainbow shall be seen in the cloud; ¹⁵and I will remember My covenant which *is* between Me and you and every living creature of all flesh; the waters shall never again become a flood to destroy all flesh. ¹⁶The rainbow shall be in the cloud, and I will look on it to remember the everlasting covenant between God and every living creature of all flesh that *is* on the earth." ¹⁷And God said to Noah, "This *is* the sign of the covenant which I have established between Me and all flesh that *is* on the earth."

¹⁸Now the sons of Noah who went out of the ark were Shem, Ham, and Japheth. And Ham *was* the father of Canaan. ¹⁹These three *were* the sons of Noah, and from these the whole earth was populated.

²⁰And Noah began *to be* a farmer, and he planted a vineyard. ²¹Then he drank of the wine and was drunk, and became uncovered in his tent. ²²And Ham, the father of Canaan, saw the nakedness of his father, and told his two brothers outside. ²³But Shem and Japheth took a garment, laid *it* on both their shoulders, and went backward

and covered the nakedness of their father. Their faces *were* turned away, and they did not see their father's nakedness.

24So Noah awoke from his wine, and knew what his younger son had done to him. 25Then he said:

"Cursed *be* Canaan;
A servant of servants
He shall be to his brethren."

26And he said:

"Blessed *be* the LORD,
The God of Shem,
And may Canaan be his
servant.
27 May God enlarge Japheth,
And may he dwell in the tents
of Shem;
And may Canaan be his
servant."

28And Noah lived after the flood three hundred and fifty years. 29So all the days of Noah were nine hundred and fifty years; and he died.

Now this *is* the genealogy of the sons of Noah: Shem, Ham, and Japheth. And sons were born to them after the flood.

2The sons of Japheth *were* Gomer, Magog, Madai, Javan, Tubal, Meshech, and Tiras. 3The sons of Gomer *were* Ashkenaz, Riphath,* and Togarmah. 4The sons of Javan *were* Elishah, Tarshish, Kittim, and Dodanim.* 5From these the coastland *peoples* of the Gentiles were separated into their lands, everyone according to his language, according to their families, into their nations.

6The sons of Ham *were* Cush, Mizraim, Put,* and Canaan. 7The sons of Cush *were* Seba, Havilah, Sabtah, Raamah, and Sabtechah; and the sons of Raamah *were* Sheba and Dedan.

8Cush begot Nimrod; he began to be a mighty one on the earth. 9He was a mighty hunter before the LORD; therefore it is said, "Like Nimrod the mighty hunter before the LORD." 10And the beginning of his kingdom was Babel, Erech, Accad, and Calneh, in the land of Shinar. 11From that land he went to Assyria and built Nineveh, Rehoboth Ir, Calah, 12and Resen between Nineveh and Calah (that *is* the principal city).

13Mizraim begot Ludim, Anamim, Lehabim, Naphtuhim, 14Pathrusim, and Casluhim (from whom came the Philistines and Caphtorim).

15Canaan begot Sidon his firstborn, and Heth; 16the Jebusite, the Amorite, and the Girgashite; 17the Hivite, the Arkite, and the Sinite; 18the Arvadite, the Zemarite, and the Hamathite. Afterward the families of the Canaanites were dispersed. 19And the border of the Canaanites was from Sidon as you go toward Gerar, as far as Gaza; then as you go toward Sodom, Gomorrah, Admah, and Zeboiim, as far as Lasha. 20These *were* the sons of Ham, according to their families, according to their languages, in their lands *and* in their nations.

21And *children* were born also to Shem, the father of all the children of Eber, the brother of Japheth the elder. 22The sons of Shem *were* Elam, Asshur, Arphaxad, Lud, and Aram. 23The sons of Aram *were* Uz, Hul, Gether, and Mash.* 24Arphaxad begot Salah,* and Salah begot Eber. 25To Eber were born two sons: the name of one *was* Peleg, for in his days the earth was divided; and his brother's name *was* Joktan. 26Joktan begot Almodad, Sheleph, Hazarmaveth, Jerah, 27Hadoram, Uzal, Diklah, 28Obal,* Abimael, Sheba, 29Ophir, Havilah, and Jobab. All these *were* the sons of Joktan. 30And their dwelling place was from Mesha as you go toward Sephar, the mountain of the east. 31These *were* the sons of Shem, according to their families, according to their languages, in their lands, according to their nations.

³²These *were* the families of the sons of Noah, according to their generations, in their nations; and from these the nations were divided on the earth after the flood.

MATTHEW 4:12-25

Now when Jesus heard that John had been put in prison, He departed to Galilee. ¹³And leaving Nazareth, He came and dwelt in Capernaum, which is by the sea, in the regions of Zebulun and Naphtali, ¹⁴that it might be fulfilled which was spoken by Isaiah the prophet, saying:

¹⁵ *"The land of Zebulun and the*
land of Naphtali,
By the way of the sea, beyond
the Jordan,
Galilee of the Gentiles:
¹⁶ *The people who sat in dark-*
ness have seen a great light,
And upon those who sat in the
region and shadow of death
Light has dawned."*

¹⁷From that time Jesus began to preach and to say, "Repent, for the kingdom of heaven is at hand."

¹⁸And Jesus, walking by the Sea of Galilee, saw two brothers, Simon called Peter, and Andrew his brother, casting a net into the sea; for they were fishermen. ¹⁹Then He said to them, "Follow Me, and I will make you fishers of men." ²⁰They immediately left *their* nets and followed Him.

²¹Going on from there, He saw two other brothers, James *the son* of Zebedee, and John his brother, in the boat with Zebedee their father, mending their nets. He called them, ²²and immediately they left the boat and their father, and followed Him.

²³And Jesus went about all Galilee, teaching in their synagogues, preaching the gospel of the kingdom, and healing all kinds of sickness and all kinds of disease among the people. ²⁴Then His fame went throughout all Syria; and they brought to Him all sick people who were afflicted with various diseases and torments, and those who were demon-possessed, epileptics, and paralytics; and He healed them. ²⁵Great multitudes followed Him—from Galilee, and *from* Decapolis, Jerusalem, Judea, and beyond the Jordan.

PSALM 4:1-8

To the Chief Musician. With stringed instruments. A Psalm of David.

Hear me when I call, O God of my righteousness!
You have relieved me in *my* distress;
Have mercy on me, and hear my prayer.

2 How long, O you sons of men,
Will you turn my glory to shame?
How long will you love worthlessness
And seek falsehood? Selah
3 But know that the LORD has set apart* for Himself him who is godly;
The LORD will hear when I call to Him.

4 Be angry, and do not sin.
Meditate within your heart on your bed, and be still. Selah
5 Offer the sacrifices of righteousness,
And put your trust in the LORD.

6 *There are* many who say,
"Who will show us *any* good?"
LORD, lift up the light of Your countenance upon us.
7 You have put gladness in my heart,
More than in the season that

their grain and wine
increased.

8 I will both lie down in peace,
and sleep;

For You alone, O LORD, make
me dwell in safety.

PROVERBS FOR TODAY / 1:20-23

*Wisdom calls aloud outside; she raises her voice in the open squares. She cries out in the chief concourses, * at the openings of the gates in the city she speaks her words: "How long, you simple ones, will you love simplicity? For scorners delight in their scorning, and fools hate knowledge. Turn at my rebuke; surely I will pour out my spirit on you; I will make my words known to you."*

JANUARY 5

GENESIS 11:1–13:4

Now the whole earth had one language and one speech. ²And it came to pass, as they journeyed from the east, that they found a plain in the land of Shinar, and they dwelt there. ³Then they said to one another, "Come, let us make bricks and bake *them* thoroughly." They had brick for stone, and they had asphalt for mortar. ⁴And they said, "Come, let us build ourselves a city, and a tower whose top *is* in the heavens; let us make a name for ourselves, lest we be scattered abroad over the face of the whole earth."

⁵But the LORD came down to see the city and the tower which the sons of men had built. ⁶And the LORD said, "Indeed the people *are* one and they all have one language, and this is what they begin to do; now nothing that they propose to do will be withheld from them. ⁷Come, let Us go down and there confuse their language, that they may not understand one another's speech." ⁸So the LORD scattered them abroad from there over the face of all the earth, and they ceased building the city. ⁹Therefore

its name is called Babel, because there the LORD confused the language of all the earth; and from there the LORD scattered them abroad over the face of all the earth.

¹⁰This *is* the genealogy of Shem: Shem *was* one hundred years old, and begot Arphaxad two years after the flood. ¹¹After he begot Arphaxad, Shem lived five hundred years, and begot sons and daughters.

¹²Arphaxad lived thirty-five years, and begot Salah. ¹³After he begot Salah, Arphaxad lived four hundred and three years, and begot sons and daughters.

¹⁴Salah lived thirty years, and begot Eber. ¹⁵After he begot Eber, Salah lived four hundred and three years, and begot sons and daughters.

¹⁶Eber lived thirty-four years, and begot Peleg. ¹⁷After he begot Peleg, Eber lived four hundred and thirty years, and begot sons and daughters.

¹⁸Peleg lived thirty years, and begot Reu. ¹⁹After he begot Reu, Peleg lived two hundred and nine years, and begot sons and daughters.

²⁰Reu lived thirty-two years, and begot Serug. ²¹After he begot Serug, Reu

lived two hundred and seven years, and begot sons and daughters.

²²Serug lived thirty years, and begot Nahor. ²³After he begot Nahor, Serug lived two hundred years, and begot sons and daughters.

²⁴Nahor lived twenty-nine years, and begot Terah. ²⁵After he begot Terah, Nahor lived one hundred and nineteen years, and begot sons and daughters.

²⁶Now Terah lived seventy years, and begot Abram, Nahor, and Haran.

²⁷This *is* the genealogy of Terah: Terah begot Abram, Nahor, and Haran. Haran begot Lot. ²⁸And Haran died before his father Terah in his native land, in Ur of the Chaldeans. ²⁹Then Abram and Nahor took wives: the name of Abram's wife *was* Sarai, and the name of Nahor's wife, Milcah, the daughter of Haran the father of Milcah and the father of Iscah. ³⁰But Sarai was barren; she had no child.

³¹And Terah took his son Abram and his grandson Lot, the son of Haran, and his daughter-in-law Sarai, his son Abram's wife, and they went out with them from Ur of the Chaldeans to go to the land of Canaan; and they came to Haran and dwelt there. ³²So the days of Terah were two hundred and five years, and Terah died in Haran.

Now the Lord had said to Abram:

"Get out of your country,
From your family
And from your father's house,
To a land that I will show you.
2   I will make you a great nation;
I will bless you
And make your name great;
And you shall be a blessing.
3   I will bless those who bless
you,
And I will curse him who
curses you;
And in you all the families of
the earth shall be blessed."

⁴So Abram departed as the Lord had spoken to him, and Lot went with him. And Abram *was* seventy-five years old when he departed from Haran. ⁵Then Abram took Sarai his wife and Lot his brother's son, and all their possessions that they had gathered, and the people whom they had acquired in Haran, and they departed to go to the land of Canaan. So they came to the land of Canaan. ⁶Abram passed through the land to the place of Shechem, as far as the terebinth tree of Moreh.* And the Canaanites *were* then in the land.

⁷Then the Lord appeared to Abram and said, "To your descendants I will give this land." And there he built an altar to the Lord, who had appeared to him. ⁸And he moved from there to the mountain east of Bethel, and he pitched his tent *with* Bethel on the west and Ai on the east; there he built an altar to the Lord and called on the name of the Lord. ⁹So Abram journeyed, going on still toward the South.*

¹⁰Now there was a famine in the land, and Abram went down to Egypt to dwell there, for the famine *was* severe in the land. ¹¹And it came to pass, when he was close to entering Egypt, that he said to Sarai his wife, "Indeed I know that you *are* a woman of beautiful countenance. ¹²Therefore it will happen, when the Egyptians see you, that they will say, 'This *is* his wife'; and they will kill me, but they will let you live. ¹³Please say you *are* my sister, that it may be well with me for your sake, and that I* may live because of you."

¹⁴So it was, when Abram came into Egypt, that the Egyptians saw the woman, that she *was* very beautiful. ¹⁵The princes of Pharaoh also saw her and commended her to Pharaoh. And the woman was taken to Pharaoh's house. ¹⁶He treated Abram well for her sake. He had sheep, oxen, male donkeys, male and female servants, female donkeys, and camels.

¹⁷But the Lord plagued Pharaoh and

his house with great plagues because of Sarai, Abram's wife. ¹⁸And Pharaoh called Abram and said, "What *is* this you have done to me? Why did you not tell me that she *was* your wife? ¹⁹Why did you say, 'She *is* my sister'? I might have taken her as my wife. Now therefore, here is your wife; take *her* and go your way." ²⁰So Pharaoh commanded *his* men concerning him; and they sent him away, with his wife and all that he had.

THEN Abram went up from Egypt, he and his wife and all that he had, and Lot with him, to the South.* ²Abram *was* very rich in livestock, in silver, and in gold. ³And he went on his journey from the South as far as Bethel, to the place where his tent had been at the beginning, between Bethel and Ai, ⁴to the place of the altar which he had made there at first. And there Abram called on the name of the LORD.

MATTHEW 5:1-26

AND seeing the multitudes, He [Jesus] went up on a mountain, and when He was seated His disciples came to Him. ²Then He opened His mouth and taught them, saying:

3   "Blessed *are* the poor in spirit,
        For theirs is the kingdom of
        heaven.
4   Blessed *are* those who mourn,
        For they shall be comforted.
5   Blessed *are* the meek,
        For they shall inherit the
        earth.
6   Blessed *are* those who
        hunger and thirst for
        righteousness,
        For they shall be filled.
7   Blessed *are* the merciful,
        For they shall obtain mercy.
8   Blessed *are* the pure in heart,
        For they shall see God.
9   Blessed *are* the peacemakers,

        For they shall be called
        sons of God.
10   Blessed are those who are
        persecuted for
        righteousness' sake,
        For theirs is the kingdom of
        heaven.

¹¹"Blessed are you when they revile and persecute you, and say all kinds of evil against you falsely for My sake. ¹²Rejoice and be exceedingly glad, for great *is* your reward in heaven, for so they persecuted the prophets who were before you.

¹³"You are the salt of the earth; but if the salt loses its flavor, how shall it be seasoned? It is then good for nothing but to be thrown out and trampled underfoot by men.

¹⁴"You are the light of the world. A city that is set on a hill cannot be hidden. ¹⁵Nor do they light a lamp and put it under a basket, but on a lampstand, and it gives light to all *who are* in the house. ¹⁶Let your light so shine before men, that they may see your good works and glorify your Father in heaven.

¹⁷"Do not think that I came to destroy the Law or the Prophets. I did not come to destroy but to fulfill. ¹⁸For assuredly, I say to you, till heaven and earth pass away, one jot or one tittle will by no means pass from the law till all is fulfilled. ¹⁹Whoever therefore breaks one of the least of these commandments, and teaches men so, shall be called least in the kingdom of heaven; but whoever does and teaches *them,* he shall be called great in the kingdom of heaven. ²⁰For I say to you, that unless your righteousness exceeds *the righteousness* of the scribes and Pharisees, you will by no means enter the kingdom of heaven.

²¹"You have heard that it was said to those of old, *'You shall not murder,*** and whoever murders will be in danger of the judgment.' ²²But I say to you

that whoever is angry with his brother without a cause* shall be in danger of the judgment. And whoever says to his brother, 'Raca!' shall be in danger of the council. But whoever says, 'You fool!' shall be in danger of hell fire. ²³Therefore if you bring your gift to the altar, and there remember that your brother has something against you, ²⁴leave your gift there before the altar, and go your way. First be reconciled to your brother, and then come and offer your gift. ²⁵Agree with your adversary quickly, while you are on the way with him, lest your adversary deliver you to the judge, the judge hand you over to the officer, and you be thrown into prison. ²⁶Assuredly, I say to you, you will by no means get out of there till you have paid the last penny."

PSALM 5:1-12

To the Chief Musician. With flutes. * A Psalm of David.

GIVE ear to my words, O LORD,
Consider my meditation.
²Give heed to the voice of my cry,
My King and my God,
For to You I will pray.
³ My voice You shall hear in the morning, O LORD;
In the morning I will direct *it* to You,
And I will look up.

⁴ For You *are* not a God who takes pleasure in wickedness,
Nor shall evil dwell with You.
⁵ The boastful shall not stand in Your sight;

You hate all workers of iniquity.
⁶ You shall destroy those who speak falsehood;
The LORD abhors the bloodthirsty and deceitful man.

⁷ But as for me, I will come into Your house in the multitude of Your mercy;
In fear of You I will worship toward Your holy temple.
⁸ Lead me, O LORD, in Your righteousness because of my enemies;
Make Your way straight before my face.

⁹ For *there is* no faithfulness in their mouth;
Their inward part *is* destruction;
Their throat *is* an open tomb;
They flatter with their tongue.
¹⁰ Pronounce them guilty, O God!
Let them fall by their own counsels;
Cast them out in the multitude of their transgressions,
For they have rebelled against You.

¹¹ But let all those rejoice who put their trust in You;
Let them ever shout for joy, because You defend them;
Let those also who love Your name
Be joyful in You.
¹² For You, O LORD, will bless the righteous;
With favor You will surround him as *with* a shield.

PROVERBS FOR TODAY/ 1:24-28

"Because I [Wisdom] have called and you refused, I have stretched out my hand and no one regarded, because you disdained all my counsel, and would have none of my rebuke, I also will laugh at your calamity; I will mock when your terror

comes, when your terror comes like a storm, and your destruction comes like a whirlwind, when distress and anguish come upon you. Then they will call on me, but I will not answer; they will seek me diligently, but they will not find me."

JANUARY 6

GENESIS 13:5–15:21

Lot also, who went with Abram, had flocks and herds and tents. 6Now the land was not able to support them, that they might dwell together, for their possessions were so great that they could not dwell together. 7And there was strife between the herdsmen of Abram's livestock and the herdsmen of Lot's livestock. The Canaanites and the Perizzites then dwelt in the land.

8So Abram said to Lot, "Please let there be no strife between you and me, and between my herdsmen and your herdsmen; for we *are* brethren. 9*Is* not the whole land before you? Please separate from me. If *you take* the left, then I will go to the right; or, if *you go* to the right, then I will go to the left."

10And Lot lifted his eyes and saw all the plain of Jordan, that it *was* well watered everywhere (before the LORD destroyed Sodom and Gomorrah) like the garden of the LORD, like the land of Egypt as you go toward Zoar. 11Then Lot chose for himself all the plain of Jordan, and Lot journeyed east. And they separated from each other. 12Abram dwelt in the land of Canaan, and Lot dwelt in the cities of the plain and pitched *his* tent even as far as Sodom. 13But the men of Sodom *were* exceedingly wicked and sinful against the LORD.

14And the LORD said to Abram, after Lot had separated from him: "Lift your eyes now and look from the place where you are—northward, southward, eastward, and westward; 15for all the land which you see I give to you and your descendants* forever. 16And I will make your descendants as the dust of the earth; so that if a man could number the dust of the earth, *then* your descendants also could be numbered. 17Arise, walk in the land through its length and its width, for I give it to you."

18Then Abram moved *his* tent, and went and dwelt by the terebinth trees of Mamre,* which *are* in Hebron, and built an altar there to the LORD.

And it came to pass in the days of Amraphel king of Shinar, Arioch king of Ellasar, Chedorlaomer king of Elam, and Tidal king of nations,* 2*that* they made war with Bera king of Sodom, Birsha king of Gomorrah, Shinab king of Admah, Shemeber king of Zeboiim, and the king of Bela (that is, Zoar). 3All these joined together in the Valley of Siddim (that is, the Salt Sea). 4Twelve years they served Chedorlaomer, and in the thirteenth year they rebelled.

5In the fourteenth year Chedorlaomer and the kings that *were* with him came and attacked the Rephaim in Ashteroth Karnaim, the Zuzim in Ham, the Emim in Shaveh Kiriathaim, 6and the Horites in their mountain of Seir, as far as El Paran, which *is* by the wilderness. 7Then they turned back and came to En Mishpat (that *is,* Kadesh), and attacked all the country of the Amalekites, and also the Amorites who dwelt in Hazezon Tamar.

8And the king of Sodom, the king of

Gomorrah, the king of Admah, the king of Zeboiim, and the king of Bela (that *is,* Zoar) went out and joined together in battle in the Valley of Siddim ⁹against Chedorlaomer king of Elam, Tidal king of nations,* Amraphel king of Shinar, and Arioch king of Ellasar— four kings against five. ¹⁰Now the Valley of Siddim *was full of* asphalt pits; and the kings of Sodom and Gomorrah fled; *some* fell there, and the remainder fled to the mountains. ¹¹Then they took all the goods of Sodom and Gomorrah, and all their provisions, and went their way. ¹²They also took Lot, Abram's brother's son who dwelt in Sodom, and his goods, and departed.

¹³Then one who had escaped came and told Abram the Hebrew, for he dwelt by the terebinth trees of Mamre* the Amorite, brother of Eshcol and brother of Aner; and they *were* allies with Abram. ¹⁴Now when Abram heard that his brother was taken captive, he armed his three hundred and eighteen trained *servants* who were born in his own house, and went in pursuit as far as Dan. ¹⁵He divided his forces against them by night, and he and his servants attacked them and pursued them as far as Hobah, which *is* north of Damascus. ¹⁶So he brought back all the goods, and also brought back his brother Lot and his goods, as well as the women and the people.

¹⁷And the king of Sodom went out to meet him at the Valley of Shaveh (that *is,* the King's Valley), after his return from the defeat of Chedorlaomer and the kings who *were* with him.

¹⁸Then Melchizedek king of Salem brought out bread and wine; he *was* the priest of God Most High. ¹⁹And he blessed him and said:

> "Blessed be Abram of God
>   Most High,
> Possessor of heaven and
>   earth;

20 And blessed be God Most
>   High,
> Who has delivered your
>   enemies into your hand."

And he gave him a tithe of all.

²¹Now the king of Sodom said to Abram, "Give me the persons, and take the goods for yourself."

²²But Abram said to the king of Sodom, "I have raised my hand to the LORD, God Most High, the Possessor of heaven and earth, ²³that I *will take* nothing, from a thread to a sandal strap, and that I will not take anything that *is* yours, lest you should say, 'I have made Abram rich'— ²⁴except only what the young men have eaten, and the portion of the men who went with me: Aner, Eshcol, and Mamre; let them take their portion."

AFTER these things the word of the LORD came to Abram in a vision, saying, "Do not be afraid, Abram. I *am* your shield, your exceedingly great reward."

²But Abram said, "Lord GOD, what will You give me, seeing I go childless, and the heir of my house *is* Eliezer of Damascus?" ³Then Abram said, "Look, You have given me no offspring; indeed one born in my house is my heir!"

⁴And behold, the word of the LORD *came* to him, saying, "This one shall not be your heir, but one who will come from your own body shall be your heir." ⁵Then He brought him outside and said, "Look now toward heaven, and count the stars if you are able to number them." And He said to him, "So shall your descendants be."

⁶And he believed in the LORD, and He accounted it to him for righteousness.

⁷Then He said to him, "I *am* the LORD, who brought you out of Ur of the Chaldeans, to give you this land to inherit it."

8And he said, "Lord God, how shall I know that I will inherit it?"

9So He said to him, "Bring Me a three-year-old heifer, a three-year-old female goat, a three-year-old ram, a turtledove, and a young pigeon." 10Then he brought all these to Him and cut them in two, down the middle, and placed each piece opposite the other; but he did not cut the birds in two. 11And when the vultures came down on the carcasses, Abram drove them away.

12Now when the sun was going down, a deep sleep fell upon Abram; and behold, horror *and* great darkness fell upon him. 13Then He said to Abram: "Know certainly that your descendants will be strangers in a land *that is* not theirs, and will serve them, and they will afflict them four hundred years. 14And also the nation whom they serve I will judge; afterward they shall come out with great possessions. 15Now as for you, you shall go to your fathers in peace; you shall be buried at a good old age. 16But in the fourth generation they shall return here, for the iniquity of the Amorites *is* not yet complete."

17And it came to pass, when the sun went down and it was dark, that behold, there appeared a smoking oven and a burning torch that passed between those pieces. 18On the same day the Lord made a covenant with Abram, saying:

"To your descendants I have given this land, from the river of Egypt to the great river, the River Euphrates— 19the Kenites, the Kenezzites, the Kadmonites, 20the Hittites, the Perizzites, the Rephaim, 21the Amorites, the Canaanites, the Girgashites, and the Jebusites."

MATTHEW 5:27-48

"**Y**ou have heard that it was said to those of old,* *'You shall not commit adultery.'** 28But I say to you that whoever looks at a woman to lust for her has already committed adultery with her in his heart. 29If your right eye causes you to sin, pluck it out and cast *it* from you; for it is more profitable for you that one of your members perish, than for your whole body to be cast into hell. 30And if your right hand causes you to sin, cut it off and cast *it* from you; for it is more profitable for you that one of your members perish, than for your whole body to be cast into hell.

31"Furthermore it has been said, 'Whoever divorces his wife, let him give her a certificate of divorce.' 32But I say to you that whoever divorces his wife for any reason except sexual immorality* causes her to commit adultery; and whoever marries a woman who is divorced commits adultery.

33"Again you have heard that it was said to those of old, 'You shall not swear falsely, but shall perform your oaths to the Lord.' 34But I say to you, do not swear at all: neither by heaven, for it is God's throne; 35nor by the earth, for it is His footstool; nor by Jerusalem, for it is the city of the great King. 36Nor shall you swear by your head, because you cannot make one hair white or black. 37But let your 'Yes' be 'Yes,' and your 'No,' 'No.' For whatever is more than these is from the evil one.

38"You have heard that it was said, '*An eye for an eye and a tooth for a tooth.*'* 39But I tell you not to resist an evil person. But whoever slaps you on your right cheek, turn the other to him also. 40If anyone wants to sue you and take away your tunic, let him have *your* cloak also. 41And whoever compels you to go one mile, go with him two. 42Give to him who asks you, and from him who wants to borrow from you do not turn away.

43"You have heard that it was said, '*You shall love your neighbor*'* and hate your enemy.' 44But I say to you, love your enemies, bless those who curse you, do good to those who hate you, and pray for those who spitefully use you and persecute you,* 45that you may be sons of your Father in heaven; for He makes His sun rise on the evil and on the good, and sends rain on the just and on the unjust. 46For if you love those who love you, what reward have you? Do not even the tax collectors do the same? 47And if you greet your brethren* only, what do you do more *than others?* Do not even the tax collectors* do so? 48Therefore you shall be perfect, just as your Father in heaven is perfect."

PSALM 6:1-10

To the Chief Musician. With stringed instruments. On an eight-stringed harp.* A Psalm of David.

O LORD, do not rebuke me in Your anger,
Nor chasten me in Your hot displeasure.
2 Have mercy on me, O LORD, for I *am* weak;
O LORD, heal me, for my bones are troubled.
3 My soul also is greatly troubled;
But You, O LORD—how long?

4 Return, O LORD, deliver me!
Oh, save me for Your mercies' sake!
5 For in death *there is* no remembrance of You;
In the grave who will give You thanks?

6 I am weary with my groaning;
All night I make my bed swim;
I drench my couch with my tears.
7 My eye wastes away because of grief;
It grows old because of all my enemies.

8 Depart from me, all you workers of iniquity;
For the LORD has heard the voice of my weeping.
9 The LORD has heard my supplication;
The LORD will receive my prayer.
10 Let all my enemies be ashamed and greatly troubled;
Let them turn back *and* be ashamed suddenly.

PROVERBS FOR TODAY/ 1:29-33

"Because they hated knowledge and did not choose the fear of the LORD, they would have none of my counsel and despised my every rebuke. Therefore they shall eat the fruit of their own way, and be filled to the full with their own fancies. For the turning away of the simple will slay them, and the complacency of fools will destroy them; but whoever listens to me will dwell safely, and will be secure, without fear of evil."

JANUARY 7

GENESIS 16:1–18:19

Now Sarai, Abram's wife, had borne him no *children*. And she had an Egyptian maidservant whose name was Hagar. ²So Sarai said to Abram, "See now, the Lord has restrained me from bearing *children*. Please, go in to my maid; perhaps I shall obtain children by her." And Abram heeded the voice of Sarai. ³Then Sarai, Abram's wife, took Hagar her maid, the Egyptian, and gave her to her husband Abram to be his wife, after Abram had dwelt ten years in the land of Canaan. ⁴So he went in to Hagar, and she conceived. And when she saw that she had conceived, her mistress became despised in her eyes.

⁵Then Sarai said to Abram, "My wrong *be* upon you! I gave my maid into your embrace; and when she saw that she had conceived, I became despised in her eyes. The Lord judge between you and me."

⁶So Abram said to Sarai, "Indeed your maid *is* in your hand; do to her as you please." And when Sarai dealt harshly with her, she fled from her presence.

⁷Now the Angel of the Lord found her by a spring of water in the wilderness, by the spring on the way to Shur. ⁸And He said, "Hagar, Sarai's maid, where have you come from, and where are you going?"

She said, "I am fleeing from the presence of my mistress Sarai."

⁹The Angel of the Lord said to her, "Return to your mistress, and submit yourself under her hand." ¹⁰Then the Angel of the Lord said to her, "I will multiply your descendants exceedingly, so that they shall not be counted for multitude." ¹¹And the Angel of the Lord said to her:

"Behold, you *are* with child,
And you shall bear a son.
You shall call his name Ishmael,
Because the Lord has heard your affliction.
12 He shall be a wild man;
His hand *shall be* against every man,
And every man's hand against him.
And he shall dwell in the presence of all his brethren."

¹³Then she called the name of the Lord who spoke to her, You-Are-the-God-Who-Sees; for she said, "Have I also here seen Him who sees me?" ¹⁴Therefore the well was called Beer Lahai Roi;* observe, *it is* between Kadesh and Bered.

¹⁵So Hagar bore Abram a son; and Abram named his son, whom Hagar bore, Ishmael. ¹⁶Abram *was* eighty-six years old when Hagar bore Ishmael to Abram.

When Abram was ninety-nine years old, the Lord appeared to Abram and said to him, "I *am* Almighty God; walk before Me and be blameless. ²And I will make My covenant between Me and you, and will multiply you exceedingly." ³Then Abram fell on his face, and God talked with him, saying: ⁴"As for Me, behold, My covenant is with you, and you shall be a father of many nations. ⁵No longer shall your name be called Abram, but your name shall be Abraham; for I have made you a father of many nations. ⁶I will make you exceedingly fruitful; and I will make nations of you, and kings shall come from you. ⁷And I will establish My covenant between Me and you and your descendants after you in their generations, for an everlasting covenant, to be God to you and your descendants after you. 8Also I give to you and your descendants after you the land in which you are a stranger, all the land of Canaan, as an everlasting possession; and I will be their God."

9And God said to Abraham: "As for you, you shall keep My covenant, you and your descendants after you throughout their generations. 10This *is* My covenant which you shall keep, between Me and you and your descendants after you: Every male child among you shall be circumcised; 11and you shall be circumcised in the flesh of your foreskins, and it shall be a sign of the covenant between Me and you. 12He who is eight days old among you shall be circumcised, every male child in your generations, he who is born in your house or bought with money from any foreigner who is not your descendant. 13He who is born in your house and he who is bought with your money must be circumcised, and My covenant shall be in your flesh for an everlasting covenant. 14And the uncircumcised male child, who is not circumcised in the flesh of his foreskin, that person shall be cut off from his people; he has broken My covenant."

15Then God said to Abraham, "As for Sarai your wife, you shall not call her name Sarai, but Sarah *shall be* her name. 16And I will bless her and also give you a son by her; then I will bless her, and she shall be *a mother of* nations; kings of peoples shall be from her."

17Then Abraham fell on his face and laughed, and said in his heart, "Shall *a child* be born to a man who is one hundred years old? And shall Sarah, who is ninety years old, bear *a child?*" 18And Abraham said to God, "Oh, that Ishmael might live before You!"

19Then God said: "No, Sarah your wife shall bear you a son, and you shall call his name Isaac; I will establish My covenant with him for an everlasting covenant, *and* with his descendants after him. 20And as for Ishmael, I have heard you. Behold, I have blessed him, and will make him fruitful, and will multiply him exceedingly. He shall beget twelve princes, and I will make him a great nation. 21But My covenant I will establish with Isaac, whom Sarah shall bear to you at this set time next year." 22Then He finished talking with him, and God went up from Abraham.

23So Abraham took Ishmael his son, all who were born in his house and all who were bought with his money, every male among the men of Abraham's house, and circumcised the flesh of their foreskins that very same day, as God had said to him. 24Abraham *was* ninety-nine years old when he was circumcised in the flesh of his foreskin. 25And Ishmael his son *was* thirteen years old when he was circumcised in the flesh of his foreskin. 26That very same day Abraham was circumcised, and his son Ishmael; 27and all the men of his house, born in the house or bought with money from a foreigner, were circumcised with him.

THEN the LORD appeared to him by the terebinth trees of Mamre,* as he was sitting in the tent door in the heat of the day. 2So he lifted his eyes and looked, and behold, three men were standing by him; and when he saw *them,* he ran from the tent door to meet them, and bowed himself to the ground, 3and said, "My Lord, if I have now found favor in Your sight, do not pass on by Your servant. 4Please let a little water be brought, and wash your feet, and rest yourselves under the tree. 5And I will bring a morsel of bread, that you may refresh your hearts. After that you may pass by, inasmuch as you have come to your servant."

They said, "Do as you have said."

6So Abraham hurried into the tent to

Sarah and said, "Quickly, make ready three measures of fine meal; knead *it* and make cakes." [7]And Abraham ran to the herd, took a tender and good calf, gave *it* to a young man, and he hastened to prepare it. [8]So he took butter and milk and the calf which he had prepared, and set *it* before them; and he stood by them under the tree as they ate.

[9]Then they said to him, "Where *is* Sarah your wife?"

So he said, "Here, in the tent."

[10]And He said, "I will certainly return to you according to the time of life, and behold, Sarah your wife shall have a son."

(Sarah was listening in the tent door which *was* behind him.) [11]Now Abraham and Sarah were old, well advanced in age; *and* Sarah had passed the age of childbearing.* [12]Therefore Sarah laughed within herself, saying, "After I have grown old, shall I have pleasure, my lord being old also?"

[13]And the LORD said to Abraham, "Why did Sarah laugh, saying, 'Shall I surely bear *a child,* since I am old?' [14]Is anything too hard for the LORD? At the appointed time I will return to you, according to the time of life, and Sarah shall have a son."

[15]But Sarah denied *it,* saying, "I did not laugh," for she was afraid.

And He said, "No, but you did laugh!"

[16]Then the men rose from there and looked toward Sodom, and Abraham went with them to send them on the way. [17]And the LORD said, "Shall I hide from Abraham what I am doing, [18]since Abraham shall surely become a great and mighty nation, and all the nations of the earth shall be blessed in him? [19]For I have known him, in order that he may command his children and his household after him, that they keep the way of the LORD, to do righteousness and justice, that the LORD may bring to Abraham what He has spoken to him."

MATTHEW 6:1-24

"TAKE heed that you do not do your charitable deeds before men, to be seen by them. Otherwise you have no reward from your Father in heaven. [2]Therefore, when you do a charitable deed, do not sound a trumpet before you as the hypocrites do in the synagogues and in the streets, that they may have glory from men. Assuredly, I say to you, they have their reward. [3]But when you do a charitable deed, do not let your left hand know what your right hand is doing, [4]that your charitable deed may be in secret; and your Father who sees in secret will Himself reward you openly.*

[5]"And when you pray, you shall not be like the hypocrites. For they love to pray standing in the synagogues and on the corners of the streets, that they may be seen by men. Assuredly, I say to you, they have their reward. [6]But you, when you pray, go into your room, and when you have shut your door, pray to your Father who *is* in the secret *place;* and your Father who sees in secret will reward you openly.* [7]And when you pray, do not use vain repetitions as the heathen *do.* For they think that they will be heard for their many words.

[8]"Therefore do not be like them. For your Father knows the things you have need of before you ask Him. [9]In this manner, therefore, pray:

> Our Father in heaven,
> Hallowed be Your name.
> 10 Your kingdom come.
> Your will be done
> On earth as *it is* in heaven.
> 11 Give us this day our daily
> bread.
> 12 And forgive us our debts,
> As we forgive our debtors.
> 13 And do not lead us into
> temptation,
> But deliver us from the evil
> one.

For Yours is the kingdom and
the power and the glory
forever. Amen.*

14"For if you forgive men their trespasses, your heavenly Father will also
forgive you. 15But if you do not forgive
men their trespasses, neither will your
Father forgive your trespasses.

16"Moreover, when you fast, do not
be like the hypocrites, with a sad countenance. For they disfigure their faces
that they may appear to men to be fasting. Assuredly, I say to you, they have
their reward. 17But you, when you fast,
anoint your head and wash your face,
18so that you do not appear to men to
be fasting, but to your Father who *is* in
the secret *place;* and your Father who
sees in secret will reward you openly.*

19"Do not lay up for yourselves treasures on earth, where moth and rust
destroy and where thieves break in
and steal; 20but lay up for yourselves
treasures in heaven, where neither
moth nor rust destroys and where
thieves do not break in and steal. 21For
where your treasure is, there your
heart will be also.

22"The lamp of the body is the eye. If
therefore your eye is good, your whole
body will be full of light. 23But if your
eye is bad, your whole body will be full
of darkness. If therefore the light that
is in you is darkness, how great *is* that
darkness!

24"No one can serve two masters;
for either he will hate the one and love
the other, or else he will be loyal to the
one and despise the other. You cannot
serve God and mammon."

PSALM 7:1-17

A Meditation * of David, which he sang to the
Lord concerning the words of Cush, a Benjamite.

O Lord my God, in You I put my
trust;
Save me from all those who
persecute me;

And deliver me,
2 Lest they tear me like a lion,
Rending *me* in pieces, while
there is none to deliver.

3 O Lord my God, if I have done
this:
If there is iniquity in my
hands,
4 If I have repaid evil to him
who was at peace with me,
Or have plundered my enemy
without cause,
5 Let the enemy pursue me and
overtake *me;*
Yes, let him trample my life to
the earth,
And lay my honor in the dust.
Selah

6 Arise, O Lord, in Your anger;
Lift Yourself up because of the
rage of my enemies;
Rise up for me* *to* the
judgment You have
commanded!
7 So the congregation of the
peoples shall surround You;
For their sakes, therefore,
return on high.
8 The Lord shall judge the
peoples;
Judge me, O Lord, according
to my righteousness,
And according to my integrity
within me.

9 Oh, let the wickedness of the
wicked come to an end,
But establish the just;
For the righteous God tests
the hearts and minds.
10 My defense *is* of God,
Who saves the upright in
heart.

11 God *is* a just judge,
And God is angry *with the
wicked* every day.
12 If he does not turn back,

He will sharpen His sword;
He bends His bow and makes
it ready.

13 He also prepares for Himself
instruments of death;
He makes His arrows into
fiery shafts.

14 Behold, *the wicked* brings
forth iniquity;
Yes, he conceives trouble and
brings forth falsehood.

15 He made a pit and dug it out,

And has fallen into the ditch
which he made.

16 His trouble shall return upon
his own head,
And his violent dealing shall
come down on his own
crown.

17 I will praise the LORD
according to His
righteousness,
And will sing praise to the
name of the LORD Most
High.

PROVERBS FOR TODAY / 2:1-5

*My son, if you receive my words, and treasure my commands within you, so that
you incline your ear to wisdom,* and *apply your heart to understanding; yes, if you
cry out for discernment,* and *lift up your voice for understanding, if you seek her as
silver, and search for her as* for *hidden treasures, then you will understand the fear
of the LORD, and find the knowledge of God.*

JANUARY 8

GENESIS 18:20–19:38

AND the LORD said, "Because the
outcry against Sodom and Gomorrah is great, and because
their sin is very grave, 21I will go down
now and see whether they have done
altogether according to the outcry
against it that has come to Me; and if
not, I will know."

22Then the men turned away from
there and went toward Sodom, but
Abraham still stood before the LORD.
23And Abraham came near and said,
"Would You also destroy the righteous
with the wicked? 24Suppose there were
fifty righteous within the city; would
You also destroy the place and not
spare *it* for the fifty righteous that
were in it? 25Far be it from You to do
such a thing as this, to slay the righteous with the wicked, so that the righteous should be as the wicked; far be it
from You! Shall not the Judge of all the
earth do right?"

26So the LORD said, "If I find in
Sodom fifty righteous within the city,
then I will spare all the place for their
sakes."

27Then Abraham answered and
said, "Indeed now, I who *am but* dust
and ashes have taken it upon myself to
speak to the Lord: 28Suppose there
were five less than the fifty righteous;
would You destroy all of the city for
lack of five?"

So He said, "If I find there forty-five,
I will not destroy *it.*"

29And he spoke to Him yet again and
said, "Suppose there should be forty
found there?"

So He said, "I will not do *it* for the sake of forty."

³⁰Then he said, "Let not the Lord be angry, and I will speak: Suppose thirty should be found there?"

So He said, "I will not do *it* if I find thirty there."

³¹And he said, "Indeed now, I have taken it upon myself to speak to the Lord: Suppose twenty should be found there?"

So He said, "I will not destroy *it* for the sake of twenty."

³²Then he said, "Let not the Lord be angry, and I will speak but once more: Suppose ten should be found there?"

And He said, "I will not destroy *it* for the sake of ten." ³³So the LORD went His way as soon as He had finished speaking with Abraham; and Abraham returned to his place.

Now the two angels came to Sodom in the evening, and Lot was sitting in the gate of Sodom. When Lot saw *them,* he rose to meet them, and he bowed himself with his face toward the ground. ²And he said, "Here now, my lords, please turn in to your servant's house and spend the night, and wash your feet; then you may rise early and go on your way."

And they said, "No, but we will spend the night in the open square."

³But he insisted strongly; so they turned in to him and entered his house. Then he made them a feast, and baked unleavened bread, and they ate.

⁴Now before they lay down, the men of the city, the men of Sodom, both old and young, all the people from every quarter, surrounded the house. ⁵And they called to Lot and said to him, "Where are the men who came to you tonight? Bring them out to us that we may know them *carnally.*"

⁶So Lot went out to them through the doorway, shut the door behind him, ⁷and said, "Please, my brethren, do not do so wickedly! ⁸See now, I have two daughters who have not known a man; please, let me bring them out to you, and you may do to them as you wish; only do nothing to these men, since this is the reason they have come under the shadow of my roof."

⁹And they said, "Stand back!" Then they said, "This one came in to stay *here,* and he keeps acting as a judge; now we will deal worse with you than with them." So they pressed hard against the man Lot, and came near to break down the door. ¹⁰But the men reached out their hands and pulled Lot into the house with them, and shut the door. ¹¹And they struck the men who *were* at the doorway of the house with blindness, both small and great, so that they became weary *trying* to find the door.

¹²Then the men said to Lot, "Have you anyone else here? Son-in-law, your sons, your daughters, and whomever you have in the city—take *them* out of this place! ¹³For we will destroy this place, because the outcry against them has grown great before the face of the LORD, and the LORD has sent us to destroy it."

¹⁴So Lot went out and spoke to his sons-in-law, who had married his daughters, and said, "Get up, get out of this place; for the LORD will destroy this city!" But to his sons-in-law he seemed to be joking.

¹⁵When the morning dawned, the angels urged Lot to hurry, saying, "Arise, take your wife and your two daughters who are here, lest you be consumed in the punishment of the city." ¹⁶And while he lingered, the men took hold of his hand, his wife's hand, and the hands of his two daughters, the LORD being merciful to him, and they brought him out and set him outside the city. ¹⁷So it came to pass, when they had brought them outside, that he* said, "Escape for your life! Do not look behind you nor stay anywhere in

the plain. Escape to the mountains, lest you be destroyed."

18Then Lot said to them, "Please, no, my lords! 19Indeed now, your servant has found favor in your sight, and you have increased your mercy which you have shown me by saving my life; but I cannot escape to the mountains, lest some evil overtake me and I die. 20See now, this city *is* near *enough* to flee to, and it *is* a little one; please let me escape there (*is* it not a little one?) and my soul shall live."

21And he said to him, "See, I have favored you concerning this thing also, in that I will not overthrow this city for which you have spoken. 22Hurry, escape there. For I cannot do anything until you arrive there."

Therefore the name of the city was called Zoar.

23The sun had risen upon the earth when Lot entered Zoar. 24Then the LORD rained brimstone and fire on Sodom and Gomorrah, from the LORD out of the heavens. 25So He overthrew those cities, all the plain, all the inhabitants of the cities, and what grew on the ground.

26But his wife looked back behind him, and she became a pillar of salt.

27And Abraham went early in the morning to the place where he had stood before the LORD. 28Then he looked toward Sodom and Gomorrah, and toward all the land of the plain; and he saw, and behold, the smoke of the land which went up like the smoke of a furnace. 29And it came to pass, when God destroyed the cities of the plain, that God remembered Abraham, and sent Lot out of the midst of the overthrow, when He overthrew the cities in which Lot had dwelt.

30Then Lot went up out of Zoar and dwelt in the mountains, and his two daughters were with him; for he was afraid to dwell in Zoar. And he and his two daughters dwelt in a cave. 31Now the firstborn said to the younger, "Our

father *is* old, and *there is* no man on the earth to come in to us as is the custom of all the earth. 32Come, let us make our father drink wine, and we will lie with him, that we may preserve the lineage of our father." 33So they made their father drink wine that night. And the firstborn went in and lay with her father, and he did not know when she lay down or when she arose.

34It happened on the next day that the firstborn said to the younger, "Indeed I lay with my father last night; let us make him drink wine tonight also, and you go in *and* lie with him, that we may preserve the lineage of our father." 35Then they made their father drink wine that night also. And the younger arose and lay with him, and he did not know when she lay down or when she arose.

36Thus both the daughters of Lot were with child by their father. 37The firstborn bore a son and called his name Moab; he *is* the father of the Moabites to this day. 38And the younger, she also bore a son and called his name Ben-Ammi; he *is* the father of the people of Ammon to this day.

MATTHEW 6:25–7:14

"**T**HEREFORE I [Jesus] say to you, do not worry about your life, what you will eat or what you will drink; nor about your body, what you will put on. Is not life more than food and the body more than clothing? 26Look at the birds of the air, for they neither sow nor reap nor gather into barns; yet your heavenly Father feeds them. Are you not of more value than they? 27Which of you by worrying can add one cubit to his stature?

28"So why do you worry about clothing? Consider the lilies of the field, how they grow: they neither toil nor spin; 29and yet I say to you that even Solomon in all his glory was not arrayed like one of these. 30Now if God so clothes the grass of the field, which today is, and tomorrow is thrown into the oven, *will He* not much more *clothe* you, O you of little faith?

31"Therefore do not worry, saying, 'What shall we eat?' or 'What shall we drink?' or 'What shall we wear?' 32For after all these things the Gentiles seek. For your heavenly Father knows that you need all these things. 33But seek first the kingdom of God and His righteousness, and all these things shall be added to you. 34Therefore do not worry about tomorrow, for tomorrow will worry about its own things. Sufficient for the day *is* its own trouble.

"JUDGE not, that you be not judged. 2For with what judgment you judge, you will be judged; and with the measure you use, it will be measured back to you. 3And why do you look at the speck in your brother's eye, but do not consider the plank in your own eye? 4Or how can you say to your brother, 'Let me remove the speck from your eye'; and look, a plank *is* in your own eye? 5Hypocrite! First remove the plank from your own eye, and then you will see clearly to remove the speck from your brother's eye.

6"Do not give what is holy to the dogs; nor cast your pearls before swine, lest they trample them under their feet, and turn and tear you in pieces.

7"Ask, and it will be given to you; seek, and you will find; knock, and it will be opened to you. 8For everyone who asks receives, and he who seeks finds, and to him who knocks it will be opened. 9Or what man is there among you who, if his son asks for bread, will give him a stone? 10Or if he asks for a fish, will he give him a serpent? 11If you then, being evil, know how to give good gifts to your children, how much more will your Father who is in heaven give good things to those who ask Him! 12Therefore, whatever you want

men to do to you, do also to them, for this is the Law and the Prophets.

13"Enter by the narrow gate; for wide *is* the gate and broad *is* the way that leads to destruction, and there are many who go in by it. 14Because* narrow *is* the gate and difficult *is* the way which leads to life, and there are few who find it."

PSALM 8:1-9

To the Chief Musician. On the instrument of Gath. A Psalm of David.*

O LORD, our Lord,
How excellent *is* Your name in all the earth,
Who have set Your glory above the heavens!

2 Out of the mouth of babes and nursing infants
You have ordained strength,
Because of Your enemies,
That You may silence the enemy and the avenger.

3 When I consider Your heavens, the work of Your fingers,
The moon and the stars, which You have ordained,

4 What is man that You are mindful of him,
And the son of man that You visit him?

5 For You have made him a little lower than the angels,*
And You have crowned him with glory and honor.

6 You have made him to have dominion over the works of Your hands;
You have put all *things* under his feet,

7 All sheep and oxen—
Even the beasts of the field,

8 The birds of the air,
And the fish of the sea

That pass through the paths
of the seas.

9   O Lord, our Lord,
How excellent *is* Your name in
all the earth!

PROVERBS FOR TODAY/ 2:6-17

For the Lord gives wisdom; from His mouth come knowledge and understanding; He stores up sound wisdom for the upright; He is a shield to those who walk uprightly; He guards the paths of justice, and preserves the way of His saints. Then you will understand righteousness and justice, equity and every good path. When wisdom enters your heart, and knowledge is pleasant to your soul, discretion will preserve you; understanding will keep you, to deliver you from the way of evil, from the man who speaks perverse things, from those who leave the paths of uprightness to walk in the ways of darkness; who rejoice in doing evil, and delight in the perversity of the wicked; whose ways are crooked, and who are devious in their paths; to deliver you from the immoral woman, from the seductress who flatters with her words, who forsakes the companion of her youth, and forgets the covenant of her God.

JANUARY 9

GENESIS 20:1–22:24

A ND Abraham journeyed from there to the South, and dwelt between Kadesh and Shur, and stayed in Gerar. ²Now Abraham said of Sarah his wife, "She *is* my sister." And Abimelech king of Gerar sent and took Sarah.

³But God came to Abimelech in a dream by night, and said to him, "Indeed you *are* a dead man because of the woman whom you have taken, for she *is* a man's wife."

⁴But Abimelech had not come near her; and he said, "Lord, will You slay a righteous nation also? ⁵Did he not say to me, 'She *is* my sister'? And she, even she herself said, 'He *is* my brother.' In the integrity of my heart and innocence of my hands I have done this."

⁶And God said to him in a dream, "Yes, I know that you did this in the integrity of your heart. For I also withheld you from sinning against Me; therefore I did not let you touch her. ⁷Now therefore, restore the man's wife; for he *is* a prophet, and he will pray for you and you shall live. But if you do not restore *her,* know that you shall surely die, you and all who *are* yours."

⁸So Abimelech rose early in the morning, called all his servants, and told all these things in their hearing; and the men were very much afraid. ⁹And Abimelech called Abraham and said to him, "What have you done to us? How have I offended you, that you have brought on me and on my kingdom a great sin? You have done deeds to me that ought not to be done." ¹⁰Then Abimelech said to Abraham, "What did you have in view, that you have done this thing?"

¹¹And Abraham said, "Because I thought, surely the fear of God *is* not in this place; and they will kill me on account of my wife. ¹²But indeed *she is* truly my sister. She *is* the daughter of

my father, but not the daughter of my mother; and she became my wife. ¹³And it came to pass, when God caused me to wander from my father's house, that I said to her, 'This *is* your kindness that you should do for me: in every place, wherever we go, say of me, "He *is* my brother." ' "

¹⁴Then Abimelech took sheep, oxen, and male and female servants, and gave *them* to Abraham; and he restored Sarah his wife to him. ¹⁵And Abimelech said, "See, my land *is* before you; dwell where it pleases you." ¹⁶Then to Sarah he said, "Behold, I have given your brother a thousand *pieces* of silver; indeed this vindicates you* before all who *are* with you and before everybody." Thus she was rebuked.

¹⁷So Abraham prayed to God; and God healed Abimelech, his wife, and his female servants. Then they bore *children;* ¹⁸for the LORD had closed up all the wombs of the house of Abimelech because of Sarah, Abraham's wife.

AND the LORD visited Sarah as He had said, and the LORD did for Sarah as He had spoken. ²For Sarah conceived and bore Abraham a son in his old age, at the set time of which God had spoken to him. ³And Abraham called the name of his son who was born to him— whom Sarah bore to him—Isaac. ⁴Then Abraham circumcised his son Isaac when he was eight days old, as God had commanded him. ⁵Now Abraham was one hundred years old when his son Isaac was born to him. ⁶And Sarah said, "God has made me laugh, *and* all who hear will laugh with me." ⁷She also said, "Who would have said to Abraham that Sarah would nurse children? For I have borne *him* a son in his old age."

⁸So the child grew and was weaned. And Abraham made a great feast on the same day that Isaac was weaned.

⁹And Sarah saw the son of Hagar the Egyptian, whom she had borne to Abraham, scoffing. ¹⁰Therefore she said to Abraham, "Cast out this bondwoman and her son; for the son of this bondwoman shall not be heir with my son, *namely* with Isaac." ¹¹And the matter was very displeasing in Abraham's sight because of his son.

¹²But God said to Abraham, "Do not let it be displeasing in your sight because of the lad or because of your bondwoman. Whatever Sarah has said to you, listen to her voice; for in Isaac your seed shall be called. ¹³Yet I will also make a nation of the son of the bondwoman, because he *is* your seed."

¹⁴So Abraham rose early in the morning, and took bread and a skin of water; and putting *it* on her shoulder, he gave *it* and the boy to Hagar, and sent her away. Then she departed and wandered in the Wilderness of Beersheba. ¹⁵And the water in the skin was used up, and she placed the boy under one of the shrubs. ¹⁶Then she went and sat down across from *him* at a distance of about a bowshot; for she said to herself, "Let me not see the death of the boy." So she sat opposite *him,* and lifted her voice and wept.

¹⁷And God heard the voice of the lad. Then the angel of God called to Hagar out of heaven, and said to her, "What ails you, Hagar? Fear not, for God has heard the voice of the lad where he *is.* ¹⁸Arise, lift up the lad and hold him with your hand, for I will make him a great nation."

¹⁹Then God opened her eyes, and she saw a well of water. And she went and filled the skin with water, and gave the lad a drink. ²⁰So God was with the lad; and he grew and dwelt in the wilderness, and became an archer. ²¹He dwelt in the Wilderness of Paran; and his mother took a wife for him from the land of Egypt.

²²And it came to pass at that time that Abimelech and Phichol, the commander of his army, spoke to Abra-

ham, saying, "God *is* with you in all that you do. ²³Now therefore, swear to me by God that you will not deal falsely with me, with my offspring, or with my posterity; but that according to the kindness that I have done to you, you will do to me and to the land in which you have dwelt."

²⁴And Abraham said, "I will swear."

²⁵Then Abraham rebuked Abimelech because of a well of water which Abimelech's servants had seized. ²⁶And Abimelech said, "I do not know who has done this thing; you did not tell me, nor had I heard *of it* until today." ²⁷So Abraham took sheep and oxen and gave them to Abimelech, and the two of them made a covenant. ²⁸And Abraham set seven ewe lambs of the flock by themselves.

²⁹Then Abimelech asked Abraham, "What *is the meaning of* these seven ewe lambs which you have set by themselves?"

³⁰And he said, "You will take *these* seven ewe lambs from my hand, that they may be my witness that I have dug this well." ³¹Therefore he called that place Beersheba,* because the two of them swore an oath there.

³²Thus they made a covenant at Beersheba. So Abimelech rose with Phichol, the commander of his army, and they returned to the land of the Philistines. ³³Then *Abraham* planted a tamarisk tree in Beersheba, and there called on the name of the LORD, the Everlasting God. ³⁴And Abraham stayed in the land of the Philistines many days.

Now it came to pass after these things that God tested Abraham, and said to him, "Abraham!"

And he said, "Here I am."

²Then He said, "Take now your son, your only *son* Isaac, whom you love, and go to the land of Moriah, and offer him there as a burnt offering on one of the mountains of which I shall tell you."

³So Abraham rose early in the morning and saddled his donkey, and took two of his young men with him, and Isaac his son; and he split the wood for the burnt offering, and arose and went to the place of which God had told him. ⁴Then on the third day Abraham lifted his eyes and saw the place afar off. ⁵And Abraham said to his young men, "Stay here with the donkey; the lad* and I will go yonder and worship, and we will come back to you."

⁶So Abraham took the wood of the burnt offering and laid *it* on Isaac his son; and he took the fire in his hand, and a knife, and the two of them went together. ⁷But Isaac spoke to Abraham his father and said, "My father!"

And he said, "Here I am, my son."

Then he said, "Look, the fire and the wood, but where *is* the lamb for a burnt offering?"

⁸And Abraham said, "My son, God will provide for Himself the lamb for a burnt offering." So the two of them went together.

⁹Then they came to the place of which God had told him. And Abraham built an altar there and placed the wood in order; and he bound Isaac his son and laid him on the altar, upon the wood. ¹⁰And Abraham stretched out his hand and took the knife to slay his son.

¹¹But the Angel of the LORD called to him from heaven and said, "Abraham, Abraham!"

So he said, "Here I am."

¹²And He said, "Do not lay your hand on the lad, or do anything to him; for now I know that you fear God, since you have not withheld your son, your only *son,* from Me."

¹³Then Abraham lifted his eyes and looked, and there behind *him was* a ram caught in a thicket by its horns. So Abraham went and took the ram, and offered it up for a burnt offering instead of his son. ¹⁴And Abraham called the name of the place, The-LORD-Will-Provide;* as it is said *to* this day, "In the Mount of the LORD it shall be provided."

¹⁵Then the Angel of the LORD called to Abraham a second time out of heaven, ¹⁶and said: "By Myself I have sworn, says the LORD, because you have done this thing, and have not withheld your son, your only *son*— ¹⁷blessing I will bless you, and multiplying I will multiply your descendants as the stars of the heaven and as the sand which *is* on the seashore; and your descendants shall possess the gate of their enemies. ¹⁸In your seed all the nations of the earth shall be blessed, because you have obeyed My voice." ¹⁹So Abraham returned to his young men, and they rose and went together to Beersheba; and Abraham dwelt at Beersheba.

²⁰Now it came to pass after these things that it was told Abraham, saying, "Indeed Milcah also has borne children to your brother Nahor: ²¹Huz his firstborn, Buz his brother, Kemuel the father of Aram, ²²Chesed, Hazo, Pildash, Jidlaph, and Bethuel." ²³And Bethuel begot Rebekah.* These eight Milcah bore to Nahor, Abraham's brother. ²⁴His concubine, whose name was Reumah, also bore Tebah, Gaham, Thahash, and Maachah.

MATTHEW 7:15-29

"**B**EWARE of false prophets, who come to you in sheep's clothing, but inwardly they are ravenous wolves. ¹⁶You will know them by their fruits. Do men gather grapes from thornbushes or figs from thistles? ¹⁷Even so, every good tree bears good fruit, but a bad tree bears bad fruit. ¹⁸A good tree cannot bear bad fruit, nor *can* a bad tree bear good fruit. ¹⁹Every tree that does not bear good fruit is cut down and thrown into the fire. ²⁰Therefore by their fruits you will know them.

²¹"Not everyone who says to Me, 'Lord, Lord,' shall enter the kingdom of heaven, but he who does the will of My Father in heaven. ²²Many will say to Me in that day, 'Lord, Lord, have we not prophesied in Your name, cast out demons in Your name, and done many wonders in Your name?' ²³And then I will declare to them, 'I never knew you; depart from Me, you who practice lawlessness!'

²⁴"Therefore whoever hears these sayings of Mine, and does them, I will liken him to a wise man who built his house on the rock: ²⁵and the rain descended, the floods came, and the winds blew and beat on that house; and it did not fall, for it was founded on the rock.

²⁶"But everyone who hears these sayings of Mine, and does not do them, will be like a foolish man who built his house on the sand: ²⁷and the rain descended, the floods came, and the winds blew and beat on that house; and it fell. And great was its fall."

²⁸And so it was, when Jesus had ended these sayings, that the people were astonished at His teaching, ²⁹for He taught them as one having authority, and not as the scribes.

PSALM 9:1-12

To the Chief Musician. To the tune of "Death of the Son." A Psalm of David.*

I WILL praise *You,* O LORD, with my whole heart;
I will tell of all Your marvelous works.
2   I will be glad and rejoice in You;
I will sing praise to Your name, O Most High.

3   When my enemies turn back,
They shall fall and perish at Your presence.
4   For You have maintained my right and my cause;
You sat on the throne judging in righteousness.
5   You have rebuked the nations,

You have destroyed the wicked;
You have blotted out their name forever and ever.

6 O enemy, destructions are finished forever!
And you have destroyed cities;
Even their memory has perished.

7 But the LORD shall endure forever;
He has prepared His throne for judgment.

8 He shall judge the world in righteousness,
And He shall administer judgment for the peoples in uprightness.

9 The LORD also will be a refuge for the oppressed,
A refuge in times of trouble.

10 And those who know Your name will put their trust in You;
For You, LORD, have not forsaken those who seek You.

11 Sing praises to the LORD, who dwells in Zion!
Declare His deeds among the people.

12 "When He avenges blood, He remembers them;
He does not forget the cry of the humble.

PROVERBS FOR TODAY/ 2:18-22

For her [the immoral woman's] house leads down to death, and her paths to the dead; none who go to her return, nor do they regain the paths of life—so you may walk in the way of goodness, and keep to the paths of righteousness. For the upright will dwell in the land, and the blameless will remain in it; but the wicked will be cut off from the earth, and the unfaithful will be uprooted from it.

JANUARY 10

GENESIS 23:1–24:51

SARAH lived one hundred and twenty-seven years; *these were* the years of the life of Sarah. ²So Sarah died in Kirjath Arba (that *is,* Hebron) in the land of Canaan, and Abraham came to mourn for Sarah and to weep for her.

³Then Abraham stood up from before his dead, and spoke to the sons of Heth, saying, ⁴"I *am* a foreigner and a visitor among you. Give me property for a burial place among you, that I may bury my dead out of my sight."

⁵And the sons of Heth answered Abraham, saying to him, ⁶"Hear us, my lord: You *are* a mighty prince among us; bury your dead in the choicest of our burial places. None of us will withhold from you his burial place, that you may bury your dead."

⁷Then Abraham stood up and bowed himself to the people of the land, the sons of Heth. ⁸And he spoke with them, saying, "If it is your wish that I bury my dead out of my sight, hear me, and meet with Ephron the son of Zohar for me, ⁹that he may give me the cave of Machpelah which he has, which *is* at

the end of his field. Let him give it to me at the full price, as property for a burial place among you."

¹⁰Now Ephron dwelt among the sons of Heth; and Ephron the Hittite answered Abraham in the presence of the sons of Heth, all who entered at the gate of his city, saying, ¹¹"No, my lord, hear me: I give you the field and the cave that *is* in it; I give it to you in the presence of the sons of my people. I give it to you. Bury your dead!"

¹²Then Abraham bowed himself down before the people of the land; ¹³and he spoke to Ephron in the hearing of the people of the land, saying, "If you *will give it,* please hear me. I will give you money for the field; take *it* from me and I will bury my dead there."

¹⁴And Ephron answered Abraham, saying to him, ¹⁵"My lord, listen to me; the land *is worth* four hundred shekels of silver. What *is* that between you and me? So bury your dead." ¹⁶And Abraham listened to Ephron; and Abraham weighed out the silver for Ephron which he had named in the hearing of the sons of Heth, four hundred shekels of silver, currency of the merchants.

¹⁷So the field of Ephron which *was* in Machpelah, which *was* before Mamre, the field and the cave which *was* in it, and all the trees that *were* in the field, which *were* within all the surrounding borders, were deeded ¹⁸to Abraham as a possession in the presence of the sons of Heth, before all who went in at the gate of his city.

¹⁹And after this, Abraham buried Sarah his wife in the cave of the field of Machpelah, before Mamre (that *is,* Hebron) in the land of Canaan. ²⁰So the field and the cave that *is* in it were deeded to Abraham by the sons of Heth as property for a burial place.

Now Abraham was old, well advanced in age; and the LORD had blessed Abraham in all things. ²So Abraham said to the oldest servant of his house, who

ruled over all that he had, "Please, put your hand under my thigh, ³and I will make you swear by the LORD, the God of heaven and the God of the earth, that you will not take a wife for my son from the daughters of the Canaanites, among whom I dwell; ⁴but you shall go to my country and to my family, and take a wife for my son Isaac."

⁵And the servant said to him, "Perhaps the woman will not be willing to follow me to this land. Must I take your son back to the land from which you came?"

⁶But Abraham said to him, "Beware that you do not take my son back there. ⁷The LORD God of heaven, who took me from my father's house and from the land of my family, and who spoke to me and swore to me, saying, 'To your descendants* I give this land,' He will send His angel before you, and you shall take a wife for my son from there. ⁸And if the woman is not willing to follow you, then you will be released from this oath; only do not take my son back there." ⁹So the servant put his hand under the thigh of Abraham his master, and swore to him concerning this matter.

¹⁰Then the servant took ten of his master's camels and departed, for all his master's goods *were in* his hand. And he arose and went to Mesopotamia, to the city of Nahor. ¹¹And he made his camels kneel down outside the city by a well of water at evening time, the time when women go out to draw *water.* ¹²Then he said, "O LORD God of my master Abraham, please give me success this day, and show kindness to my master Abraham. ¹³Behold, *here* I stand by the well of water, and the daughters of the men of the city are coming out to draw water. ¹⁴Now let it be that the young woman to whom I say, 'Please let down your pitcher that I may drink,' and she says, 'Drink, and I will also give your camels a drink'—*let* her *be the one* You have appointed for Your servant Isaac. And

by this I will know that You have shown kindness to my master."

15And it happened, before he had finished speaking, that behold, Rebekah, who was born to Bethuel, son of Milcah, the wife of Nahor, Abraham's brother, came out with her pitcher on her shoulder. 16Now the young woman was very beautiful to behold, a virgin; no man had known her. And she went down to the well, filled her pitcher, and came up. 17And the servant ran to meet her and said, "Please let me drink a little water from your pitcher."

18So she said, "Drink, my lord." Then she quickly let her pitcher down to her hand, and gave him a drink. 19And when she had finished giving him a drink, she said, "I will draw water for your camels also, until they have finished drinking." 20Then she quickly emptied her pitcher into the trough, ran back to the well to draw water, and drew for all his camels. 21And the man, wondering at her, remained silent so as to know whether the LORD had made his journey prosperous or not.

22So it was, when the camels had finished drinking, that the man took a golden nose ring weighing half a shekel, and two bracelets for her wrists weighing ten shekels of gold, 23and said, "Whose daughter are you? Tell me, please, is there room in your father's house for us to lodge?"

24So she said to him, "I am the daughter of Bethuel, Milcah's son, whom she bore to Nahor." 25Moreover she said to him, "We have both straw and feed enough, and room to lodge."

26Then the man bowed down his head and worshiped the LORD. 27And he said, "Blessed be the LORD God of my master Abraham, who has not forsaken His mercy and His truth toward my master. As for me, being on the way, the LORD led me to the house of my master's brethren." 28So the young woman ran and told her mother's household these things.

29Now Rebekah had a brother whose name was Laban, and Laban ran out to the man by the well. 30So it came to pass, when he saw the nose ring, and the bracelets on his sister's wrists, and when he heard the words of his sister Rebekah, saying, "Thus the man spoke to me," that he went to the man. And there he stood by the camels at the well. 31And he said, "Come in, O blessed of the LORD! Why do you stand outside? For I have prepared the house, and a place for the camels."

32Then the man came to the house. And he unloaded the camels, and provided straw and feed for the camels, and water to wash his feet and the feet of the men who were with him. 33Food was set before him to eat, but he said, "I will not eat until I have told about my errand."

And he said, "Speak on."

34So he said, "I am Abraham's servant. 35The LORD has blessed my master greatly, and he has become great; and He has given him flocks and herds, silver and gold, male and female servants, and camels and donkeys. 36And Sarah my master's wife bore a son to my master when she was old; and to him he has given all that he has. 37Now my master made me swear, saying, 'You shall not take a wife for my son from the daughters of the Canaanites, in whose land I dwell; 38but you shall go to my father's house and to my family, and take a wife for my son.' 39And I said to my master, 'Perhaps the woman will not follow me.' 40But he said to me, 'The LORD, before whom I walk, will send His angel with you and prosper your way; and you shall take a wife for my son from my family and from my father's house. 41You will be clear from this oath when you arrive among my family; for if they will not give her to you, then you will be released from my oath.' 42"And this day I came to the well and said, 'O LORD God of my master Abraham, if You will now prosper the way in which I go, ⁴³behold, I stand by the well of water; and it shall come to pass that when the virgin comes out to draw *water,* and I say to her, "Please give me a little water from your pitcher to drink," ⁴⁴and she says to me, "Drink, and I will draw for your camels also,"— *let* her *be* the woman whom the LORD has appointed for my master's son.'

⁴⁵"But before I had finished speaking in my heart, there was Rebekah, coming out with her pitcher on her shoulder; and she went down to the well and drew *water.* And I said to her, 'Please let me drink.' ⁴⁶And she made haste and let her pitcher down from her *shoulder,* and said, 'Drink, and I will give your camels a drink also.' So I drank, and she gave the camels a drink also. ⁴⁷Then I asked her, and said, 'Whose daughter *are* you?' And she said, 'The daughter of Bethuel, Nahor's son, whom Milcah bore to him.' So I put the nose ring on her nose and the bracelets on her wrists. ⁴⁸And I bowed my head and worshiped the LORD, and blessed the LORD God of my master Abraham, who had led me in the way of truth to take the daughter of my master's brother for his son. ⁴⁹Now if you will deal kindly and truly with my master, tell me. And if not, tell me, that I may turn to the right hand or to the left."

⁵⁰Then Laban and Bethuel answered and said, "The thing comes from the LORD; we cannot speak to you either bad or good. ⁵¹Here *is* Rebekah before you; take *her* and go, and let her be your master's son's wife, as the LORD has spoken."

MATTHEW 8:1-17

WHEN He [Jesus] had come down from the mountain, great multitudes followed Him. ²And behold, a leper came and worshiped Him, saying, "Lord, if You are willing, You can make me clean."

³Then Jesus put out *His* hand and touched him, saying, "I am willing; be cleansed." Immediately his leprosy was cleansed.

⁴And Jesus said to him, "See that you tell no one; but go your way, show yourself to the priest, and offer the gift that Moses commanded, as a testimony to them."

⁵Now when Jesus had entered Capernaum, a centurion came to Him, pleading with Him, ⁶saying, "Lord, my servant is lying at home paralyzed, dreadfully tormented."

⁷And Jesus said to him, "I will come and heal him."

⁸The centurion answered and said, "Lord, I am not worthy that You should come under my roof. But only speak a word, and my servant will be healed. ⁹For I also am a man under authority, having soldiers under me. And I say to this *one,* 'Go,' and he goes; and to another, 'Come,' and he comes; and to my servant, 'Do this,' and he does *it.*"

¹⁰When Jesus heard *it,* He marveled, and said to those who followed, "Assuredly, I say to you, I have not found such great faith, not even in Israel! ¹¹And I say to you that many will come from east and west, and sit down with Abraham, Isaac, and Jacob in the kingdom of heaven. ¹²But the sons of the kingdom will be cast out into outer darkness. There will be weeping and gnashing of teeth." ¹³Then Jesus said to the centurion, "Go your way; and as you have believed, *so* let it be done for you." And his servant was healed that same hour.

¹⁴Now when Jesus had come into Peter's house, He saw his wife's mother lying sick with a fever. ¹⁵So He touched her hand, and the fever left her. And she arose and served them.*

¹⁶When evening had come, they brought to Him many who were demon-possessed. And He cast out the spirits with a word, and healed all who were sick, ¹⁷that it might be fulfilled

which was spoken by Isaiah the prophet, saying:

"*He Himself took our infirmities And bore our sicknesses.*"*

PSALM 9:13-20

HAVE mercy on me, O LORD! Consider my trouble from those who hate me, You who lift me up from the gates of death,
14 That I may tell of all Your praise In the gates of the daughter of Zion. I will rejoice in Your salvation.

15 The nations have sunk down in the pit *which* they made; In the net which they hid, their own foot is caught.

16 The LORD is known *by* the judgment He executes; The wicked is snared in the work of his own hands.
Meditation.* Selah

17 The wicked shall be turned into hell, *And* all the nations that forget God.
18 For the needy shall not always be forgotten; The expectation of the poor shall *not* perish forever.

19 Arise, O LORD, Do not let man prevail; Let the nations be judged in Your sight.
20 Put them in fear, O LORD, *That* the nations may know themselves *to be but* men.
Selah

PROVERBS FOR TODAY/ 3:1-6

My son, do not forget my law, but let your heart keep my commands; for length of days and long life and peace they will add to you. □*Let not mercy and truth forsake you; bind them around your neck, write them on the tablet of your heart,* and *so find favor and high esteem in the sight of God and man.* □ *Trust in the LORD with all your heart, and lean not on your own understanding; in all your ways acknowledge Him, and He shall direct* * your paths.*

JANUARY 11

GENESIS 24:52–26:16

AND it came to pass, when Abraham's servant heard their [Laban's and Bethuel's] words, that he worshiped the LORD, *bowing himself* to the earth. 53Then the servant brought out jewelry of silver, jewelry of gold, and clothing, and gave *them* to Rebekah. He also gave precious things to her brother and to her mother.

54And he and the men who *were* with him ate and drank and stayed all night. Then they arose in the morning, and he said, "Send me away to my master."

55But her brother and her mother said, "Let the young woman stay with us *a few* days, at least ten; after that she may go."

56And he said to them, "Do not hinder me, since the LORD has prospered my way; send me away so that I may go to my master."

⁵⁷So they said, "We will call the young woman and ask her personally." ⁵⁸Then they called Rebekah and said to her, "Will you go with this man?"

And she said, "I will go."

⁵⁹So they sent away Rebekah their sister and her nurse, and Abraham's servant and his men. ⁶⁰And they blessed Rebekah and said to her:

> "Our sister, *may* you *become*
> *The mother of* thousands of
> ten thousands;
> And may your descendants
> possess
> The gates of those who hate
> them."

⁶¹Then Rebekah and her maids arose, and they rode on the camels and followed the man. So the servant took Rebekah and departed.

⁶²Now Isaac came from the way of Beer Lahai Roi, for he dwelt in the South. ⁶³And Isaac went out to meditate in the field in the evening; and he lifted his eyes and looked, and there, the camels *were* coming. ⁶⁴Then Rebekah lifted her eyes, and when she saw Isaac she dismounted from her camel; ⁶⁵for she had said to the servant, "Who *is* this man walking in the field to meet us?"

The servant said, "It *is* my master." So she took a veil and covered herself.

⁶⁶And the servant told Isaac all the things that he had done. ⁶⁷Then Isaac brought her into his mother Sarah's tent; and he took Rebekah and she became his wife, and he loved her. So Isaac was comforted after his mother's *death.*

ABRAHAM again took a wife, and her name *was* Keturah. ²And she bore him Zimran, Jokshan, Medan, Midian, Ishbak, and Shuah. ³Jokshan begot Sheba and Dedan. And the sons of Dedan were Asshurim, Letushim, and Leummim. ⁴And the sons of Midian *were* Ephah, Epher, Hanoch, Abidah, and Eldaah. All these *were* the children of Keturah.

⁵And Abraham gave all that he had to Isaac. ⁶But Abraham gave gifts to the sons of the concubines which Abraham had; and while he was still living he sent them eastward, away from Isaac his son, to the country of the east.

⁷This *is* the sum of the years of Abraham's life which he lived: one hundred and seventy-five years. ⁸Then Abraham breathed his last and died in a good old age, an old man and full *of years,* and was gathered to his people. ⁹And his sons Isaac and Ishmael buried him in the cave of Machpelah, which *is* before Mamre, in the field of Ephron the son of Zohar the Hittite, ¹⁰the field which Abraham purchased from the sons of Heth. There Abraham was buried, and Sarah his wife. ¹¹And it came to pass, after the death of Abraham, that God blessed his son Isaac. And Isaac dwelt at Beer Lahai Roi.

¹²Now this *is* the genealogy of Ishmael, Abraham's son, whom Hagar the Egyptian, Sarah's maidservant, bore to Abraham. ¹³And these *were* the names of the sons of Ishmael, by their names, according to their generations: The firstborn of Ishmael, Nebajoth; then Kedar, Adbeel, Mibsam, ¹⁴Mishma, Dumah, Massa, ¹⁵Hadar,* Tema, Jetur, Naphish, and Kedemah. ¹⁶These *were* the sons of Ishmael and these *were* their names, by their towns and their settlements, twelve princes according to their nations. ¹⁷These *were* the years of the life of Ishmael: one hundred and thirty-seven years; and he breathed his last and died, and was gathered to his people. ¹⁸(They dwelt from Havilah as far as Shur, which *is* east of Egypt as you go toward Assyria.) He died in the presence of all his brethren.

¹⁹This *is* the genealogy of Isaac,

Abraham's son. Abraham begot Isaac. ²⁰Isaac was forty years old when he took Rebekah as wife, the daughter of Bethuel the Syrian of Padan Aram, the sister of Laban the Syrian. ²¹Now Isaac pleaded with the LORD for his wife, because she *was* barren; and the LORD granted his plea, and Rebekah his wife conceived. ²²But the children struggled together within her; and she said, "If *all is* well, why *am I like* this? " So she went to inquire of the LORD.

²³And the LORD said to her:

> "Two nations *are* in your
>   womb,
> Two peoples shall be
>   separated from your body;
> *One* people shall be stronger
>   than the other,
> And the older shall serve the
>   younger."

²⁴So when her days were fulfilled *for her* to give birth, indeed *there were* twins in her womb. ²⁵And the first came out red. *He was* like a hairy garment all over; so they called his name Esau.* ²⁶Afterward his brother came out, and his hand took hold of Esau's heel; so his name was called Jacob.* Isaac was sixty years old when she bore them.

²⁷So the boys grew. And Esau was a skillful hunter, a man of the field; but Jacob was a mild man, dwelling in tents. ²⁸And Isaac loved Esau because he ate *of his* game, but Rebekah loved Jacob.

²⁹Now Jacob cooked a stew; and Esau came in from the field, and he *was* weary. ³⁰And Esau said to Jacob, "Please feed me with that same red *stew,* for I *am* weary." Therefore his name was called Edom.*

³¹But Jacob said, "Sell me your birthright as of this day."

³²And Esau said, "Look, I *am* about to die; so what *is* this birthright to me?"

³³Then Jacob said, "Swear to me as of this day."

So he swore to him, and sold his birthright to Jacob. ³⁴And Jacob gave Esau bread and stew of lentils; then he ate and drank, arose, and went his way. Thus Esau despised *his* birthright.

THERE was a famine in the land, besides the first famine that was in the days of Abraham. And Isaac went to Abimelech king of the Philistines, in Gerar.

²Then the LORD appeared to him and said: "Do not go down to Egypt; live in the land of which I shall tell you. ³Dwell in this land, and I will be with you and bless you; for to you and your descendants I give all these lands, and I will perform the oath which I swore to Abraham your father. ⁴And I will make your descendants multiply as the stars of heaven; I will give to your descendants all these lands; and in your seed all the nations of the earth shall be blessed; ⁵because Abraham obeyed My voice and kept My charge, My commandments, My statutes, and My laws."

⁶So Isaac dwelt in Gerar. ⁷And the men of the place asked about his wife. And he said, "She *is* my sister"; for he was afraid to say, *"She is* my wife," *because he thought,* lest the men of the place kill me for Rebekah, because she *is* beautiful to behold." ⁸Now it came to pass, when he had been there a long time, that Abimelech king of the Philistines looked through a window, and saw, and there was Isaac, showing endearment to Rebekah his wife. ⁹Then Abimelech called Isaac and said, "Quite obviously she *is* your wife; so how could you say, 'She *is* my sister'?"

Isaac said to him, "Because I said, 'Lest I die on account of her.' "

¹⁰And Abimelech said, "What *is* this you have done to us? One of the people might soon have lain with your wife, and you would have brought guilt on us." ¹¹So Abimelech charged all *his* people, saying, "He who touches this

man or his wife shall surely be put to death."

¹²Then Isaac sowed in that land, and reaped in the same year a hundredfold; and the Lord blessed him. ¹³The man began to prosper, and continued prospering until he became very prosperous; ¹⁴for he had possessions of flocks and possessions of herds and a great number of servants. So the Philistines envied him. ¹⁵Now the Philistines had stopped up all the wells which his father's servants had dug in the days of Abraham his father, and they had filled them with earth. ¹⁶And Abimelech said to Isaac, "Go away from us, for you are much mightier than we."

MATTHEW 8:18-34

AND when Jesus saw great multitudes about Him, He gave a command to depart to the other side. ¹⁹Then a certain scribe came and said to Him, "Teacher, I will follow You wherever You go."

²⁰And Jesus said to him, "Foxes have holes and birds of the air *have* nests, but the Son of Man has nowhere to lay *His* head."

²¹Then another of His disciples said to Him, "Lord, let me first go and bury my father."

²²But Jesus said to him, "Follow Me, and let the dead bury their own dead."

²³Now when He got into a boat, His disciples followed Him. ²⁴And suddenly a great tempest arose on the sea, so that the boat was covered with the waves. But He was asleep. ²⁵Then His disciples came to *Him* and awoke Him, saying, "Lord, save us! We are perishing!"

²⁶But He said to them, "Why are you fearful, O you of little faith?" Then He arose and rebuked the winds and the sea, and there was a great calm. ²⁷So the men marveled, saying, "Who can this be, that even the winds and the sea obey Him?"

²⁸When He had come to the other side, to the country of the Gergesenes,* there met Him two demonpossessed *men,* coming out of the tombs, exceedingly fierce, so that no one could pass that way. ²⁹And suddenly they cried out, saying, "What have we to do with You, Jesus, You Son of God? Have You come here to torment us before the time?"

³⁰Now a good way off from them there was a herd of many swine feeding. ³¹So the demons begged Him, saying, "If You cast us out, permit us to go away* into the herd of swine."

³²And He said to them, "Go." So when they had come out, they went into the herd of swine. And suddenly the whole herd of swine ran violently down the steep place into the sea, and perished in the water.

³³Then those who kept *them* fled; and they went away into the city and told everything, including what *had happened* to the demon-possessed *men.* ³⁴And behold, the whole city came out to meet Jesus. And when they saw Him, they begged *Him* to depart from their region.

PSALM 10:1-15

WHY do You stand afar off, O Lord?
Why do You hide in times of trouble?

2 The wicked in *his* pride persecutes the poor;
Let them be caught in the plots which they have devised.

3 For the wicked boasts of his heart's desire;
He blesses the greedy *and* renounces the Lord.

4 The wicked in his proud

countenance does not seek
  God;
God *is* in none of his thoughts.

5 His ways are always
    prospering;
  Your judgments *are* far above,
    out of his sight;
  As for all his enemies, he
    sneers at them.

6 He has said in his heart, "I
    shall not be moved;
  I shall never be in adversity."

7 His mouth is full of cursing
    and deceit and oppression;
  Under his tongue *is* trouble
    and iniquity.

8 He sits in the lurking places
    of the villages;
  In the secret places he
    murders the innocent;
  His eyes are secretly fixed on
    the helpless.

9 He lies in wait secretly, as a
    lion in his den;
  He lies in wait to catch the
    poor;
  He catches the poor when he
    draws him into his net.

10 So he crouches, he lies low,
  That the helpless may fall by
    his strength.

11 He has said in his heart,
  "God has forgotten;
  He hides His face;
  He will never see."

12 Arise, O LORD!
  O God, lift up Your hand!
  Do not forget the humble.

13 Why do the wicked renounce
    God?
  He has said in his heart,
  "You will not require *an*
    account."

14 But You have seen, for You
      observe trouble and grief,
  To repay *it* by Your hand.
  The helpless commits himself
    to You;
  You are the helper of the
    fatherless.

15 Break the arm of the wicked
    and the evil *man;*
  Seek out his wickedness *until*
  You find none.

PROVERBS FOR TODAY/ 3:7-8

Do not be wise in your own eyes; fear the LORD and depart from evil. It will be health to your flesh, * *and strength* * *to your bones.*

JANUARY 12

GENESIS 26:17–27:46

THEN Isaac departed from there and pitched his tent in the Valley of Gerar, and dwelt there. 18And Isaac dug again the wells of water which they had dug in the days of Abraham his father, for the Philistines

had stopped them up after the death of Abraham. He called them by the names which his father had called them.

19Also Isaac's servants dug in the valley, and found a well of running water there. 20But the herdsmen of Gerar quarreled with Isaac's herdsmen, saying, "The water *is* ours." So he called the name of the well Esek,* because they quarreled with him. 21Then they dug another well, and they quarreled over that *one* also. So he called its name Sitnah.* 22And he moved from there and dug another well, and they did not quarrel over it. So he called its name Rehoboth,* because he said, "For now the LORD has made room for us, and we shall be fruitful in the land."

23Then he went up from there to Beersheba. 24And the LORD appeared to him the same night and said, "I *am* the God of your father Abraham; do not fear, for I *am* with you. I will bless you and multiply your descendants for My servant Abraham's sake." 25So he built an altar there and called on the name of the LORD, and he pitched his tent there; and there Isaac's servants dug a well.

26Then Abimelech came to him from Gerar with Ahuzzath, one of his friends, and Phichol the commander of his army. 27And Isaac said to them, "Why have you come to me, since you hate me and have sent me away from you?"

28But they said, "We have certainly seen that the LORD is with you. So we said, 'Let there now be an oath between us, between you and us; and let us make a covenant with you, 29that you will do us no harm, since we have not touched you, and since we have done nothing to you but good and have sent you away in peace. You *are* now the blessed of the LORD.' "

30So he made them a feast, and they ate and drank. 31Then they arose early in the morning and swore an oath with one another; and Isaac sent them away, and they departed from him in peace.

32It came to pass the same day that Isaac's servants came and told him about the well which they had dug, and said to him, "We have found water." 33So he called it Shebah.* Therefore the name of the city *is* Beersheba* to this day.

34When Esau was forty years old, he took as wives Judith the daughter of Beeri the Hittite, and Basemath the daughter of Elon the Hittite. 35And they were a grief of mind to Isaac and Rebekah.

Now it came to pass, when Isaac was old and his eyes were so dim that he could not see, that he called Esau his older son and said to him, "My son."

And he answered him, "Here I am."

2Then he said, "Behold now, I am old. I do not know the day of my death. 3Now therefore, please take your weapons, your quiver and your bow, and go out to the field and hunt game for me. 4And make me savory food, such as I love, and bring *it* to me that I may eat, that my soul may bless you before I die."

5Now Rebekah was listening when Isaac spoke to Esau his son. And Esau went to the field to hunt game and to bring *it.* 6So Rebekah spoke to Jacob her son, saying, "Indeed I heard your father speak to Esau your brother, saying, 7'Bring me game and make savory food for me, that I may eat it and bless you in the presence of the LORD before my death.' 8Now therefore, my son, obey my voice according to what I command you. 9Go now to the flock and bring me from there two choice kids of the goats, and I will make savory food from them for your father, such as he loves. 10Then you shall take *it* to your father, that he may eat *it,* and that he may bless you before his death."

11And Jacob said to Rebekah his mother, "Look, Esau my brother *is* a hairy man, and I *am* a smooth-*skinned* man. 12Perhaps my father will feel me, and I shall seem to be a deceiver to him; and I shall bring a curse on myself and not a blessing."

13But his mother said to him, "*Let

your curse *be* on me, my son; only obey my voice, and go, get *them* for me." ¹⁴And he went and got *them* and brought *them* to his mother, and his mother made savory food, such as his father loved. ¹⁵Then Rebekah took the choice clothes of her elder son Esau, which *were* with her in the house, and put them on Jacob her younger son. ¹⁶And she put the skins of the kids of the goats on his hands and on the smooth part of his neck. ¹⁷Then she gave the savory food and the bread, which she had prepared, into the hand of her son Jacob.

¹⁸So he went to his father and said, "My father."

And he said, "Here I am. Who *are* you, my son?"

¹⁹Jacob said to his father, "I *am* Esau your firstborn; I have done just as you told me; please arise, sit and eat of my game, that your soul may bless me."

²⁰But Isaac said to his son, "How *is it* that you have found *it* so quickly, my son?"

And he said, "Because the LORD your God brought *it* to me."

²¹Isaac said to Jacob, "Please come near, that I may feel you, my son, whether you *are* really my son Esau or not." ²²So Jacob went near to Isaac his father, and he felt him and said, "The voice *is* Jacob's voice, but the hands *are* the hands of Esau." ²³And he did not recognize him, because his hands were hairy like his brother Esau's hands; so he blessed him.

²⁴Then he said, "*Are* you really my son Esau?"

He said, "I *am.*"

²⁵He said, "Bring *it* near to me, and I will eat of my son's game, so that my soul may bless you." So he brought *it* near to him, and he ate; and he brought him wine, and he drank. ²⁶Then his father Isaac said to him, "Come near now and kiss me, my son." ²⁷And he came near and kissed him; and he smelled the smell of his clothing, and blessed him and said:

> "Surely, the smell of my son
> *Is* like the smell of a field
> Which the LORD has blessed.
> 28 Therefore may God give you
> Of the dew of heaven,
> Of the fatness of the earth,
> And plenty of grain and wine.
> 29 Let peoples serve you,
> And nations bow down to you.
> Be master over your brethren,
> And let your mother's sons
>   bow down to you.
> Cursed *be* everyone who
>   curses you,
> And blessed *be* those who
>   bless you!"

³⁰Now it happened, as soon as Isaac had finished blessing Jacob, and Jacob had scarcely gone out from the presence of Isaac his father, that Esau his brother came in from his hunting. ³¹He also had made savory food, and brought it to his father, and said to his father, "Let my father arise and eat of his son's game, that your soul may bless me."

³²And his father Isaac said to him, "Who *are* you?"

So he said, "I *am* your son, your firstborn, Esau."

³³Then Isaac trembled exceedingly, and said, "Who? Where *is* the one who hunted game and brought *it* to me? I ate all *of it* before you came, and I have blessed him—*and* indeed he shall be blessed."

³⁴When Esau heard the words of his father, he cried with an exceedingly great and bitter cry, and said to his father, "Bless me—me also, O my father!"

³⁵But he said, "Your brother came with deceit and has taken away your blessing."

³⁶And *Esau* said, "Is he not rightly named Jacob? For he has supplanted me these two times. He took away my

birthright, and now look, he has taken away my blessing!" And he said, "Have you not reserved a blessing for me?"

37Then Isaac answered and said to Esau, "Indeed I have made him your master, and all his brethren I have given to him as servants; with grain and wine I have sustained him. What shall I do now for you, my son?"

38And Esau said to his father, "Have you only one blessing, my father? Bless me—me also, O my father!" And Esau lifted up his voice and wept.

39Then Isaac his father answered and said to him:

> "Behold, your dwelling shall
> be of the fatness of the
> earth,
> And of the dew of heaven
> from above.
> 40 By your sword you shall live,
> And you shall serve your
> brother;
> And it shall come to pass,
> when you become restless,
> That you shall break his yoke
> from your neck."

41So Esau hated Jacob because of the blessing with which his father blessed him, and Esau said in his heart, "The days of mourning for my father are at hand; then I will kill my brother Jacob."

42And the words of Esau her older son were told to Rebekah. So she sent and called Jacob her younger son, and said to him, "Surely your brother Esau comforts himself concerning you *by intending* to kill you. 43Now therefore, my son, obey my voice: arise, flee to my brother Laban in Haran. 44And stay with him a few days, until your brother's fury turns away, 45until your brother's anger turns away from you, and he forgets what you have done to him; then I will send and bring you from there. Why should I be bereaved also of you both in one day?"

46And Rebekah said to Isaac, "I am weary of my life because of the daughters of Heth; if Jacob takes a wife of the daughters of Heth, like these *who are* the daughters of the land, what good will my life be to me?"

MATTHEW 9:1-17

So He [Jesus] got into a boat, crossed over, and came to His own city. 2Then behold, they brought to Him a paralytic lying on a bed. When Jesus saw their faith, He said to the paralytic, "Son, be of good cheer; your sins are forgiven you."

3And at once some of the scribes said within themselves, "This Man blasphemes!"

4But Jesus, knowing their thoughts, said, "Why do you think evil in your hearts? 5For which is easier, to say, 'Your sins are forgiven you,' or to say, 'Arise and walk'? 6But that you may know that the Son of Man has power on earth to forgive sins"—then He said to the paralytic, "Arise, take up your bed, and go to your house." 7And he arose and departed to his house.

8Now when the multitudes saw *it,* they marveled* and glorified God, who had given such power to men.

9As Jesus passed on from there, He saw a man named Matthew sitting at the tax office. And He said to him, "Follow Me." So he arose and followed Him.

10Now it happened, as Jesus sat at the table in the house, *that* behold, many tax collectors and sinners came and sat down with Him and His disciples. 11And when the Pharisees saw *it,* they said to His disciples, "Why does your Teacher eat with tax collectors and sinners?"

12When Jesus heard *that,* He said to them, "Those who are well have no need of a physician, but those who are sick. 13But go and learn what *this* means: *'I desire mercy and not sacrifice.'* For I did not come to call the righteous, but sinners, to repentance."*

14Then the disciples of John came to Him, saying, "Why do we and the Pharisees fast often,* but Your disciples do not fast?"

15And Jesus said to them, "Can the friends of the bridegroom mourn as long as the bridegroom is with them? But the days will come when the bridegroom will be taken away from them, and then they will fast. 16No one puts a piece of unshrunk cloth on an old garment; for the patch pulls away from the garment, and the tear is made worse. 17Nor do they put new wine into old wineskins, or else the wineskins break, the wine is spilled, and the wineskins are ruined. But they put new wine into new wineskins, and both are preserved."

PSALM 10:16-18

THE LORD *is* King forever and ever; The nations have perished out of His land.
17   LORD, You have heard the desire of the humble; You will prepare their heart; You will cause Your ear to hear,
18   To do justice to the fatherless and the oppressed, That the man of the earth may oppress no more.

PROVERBS FOR TODAY / 3:9-10

Honor the LORD with your possessions, and with the firstfruits of all your increase; so your barns will be filled with plenty, and your vats will overflow with new wine.

JANUARY 13

GENESIS 28:1–29:35

THEN Isaac called Jacob and blessed him, and charged him, and said to him: "You shall not take a wife from the daughters of Canaan. 2Arise, go to Padan Aram, to the house of Bethuel your mother's father; and take yourself a wife from there of the daughters of Laban your mother's brother.

3   "May God Almighty bless you, And make you fruitful and multiply you, That you may be an assembly of peoples;
4   And give you the blessing of Abraham,

To you and your descendants with you, That you may inherit the land In which you are a stranger, Which God gave to Abraham."

5So Isaac sent Jacob away, and he went to Padan Aram, to Laban the son of Bethuel the Syrian, the brother of Rebekah, the mother of Jacob and Esau.

6Esau saw that Isaac had blessed Jacob and sent him away to Padan Aram to take himself a wife from there, *and that* as he blessed him he gave him a charge, saying, "You shall not take a wife from the daughters of Canaan," 7and that Jacob had obeyed his father and his mother and had gone to Padan Aram. 8Also Esau saw that the daughters of Canaan did not please his father

Isaac. ⁹So Esau went to Ishmael and took Mahalath the daughter of Ishmael, Abraham's son, the sister of Nebajoth, to be his wife in addition to the wives he had.

¹⁰Now Jacob went out from Beersheba and went toward Haran. ¹¹So he came to a certain place and stayed there all night, because the sun had set. And he took one of the stones of that place and put it at his head, and he lay down in that place to sleep. ¹²Then he dreamed, and behold, a ladder *was* set up on the earth, and its top reached to heaven; and there the angels of God were ascending and descending on it.

¹³And behold, the LORD stood above it and said: "I *am* the LORD God of Abraham your father and the God of Isaac; the land on which you lie I will give to you and your descendants. ¹⁴Also your descendants shall be as the dust of the earth; you shall spread abroad to the west and the east, to the north and the south; and in you and in your seed all the families of the earth shall be blessed. ¹⁵Behold, I *am* with you and will keep you wherever you go, and will bring you back to this land; for I will not leave you until I have done what I have spoken to you."

¹⁶Then Jacob awoke from his sleep and said, "Surely the LORD is in this place, and I did not know *it.*" ¹⁷And he was afraid and said, "How awesome *is* this place! This *is* none other than the house of God, and this *is* the gate of heaven!"

¹⁸Then Jacob rose early in the morning, and took the stone that he had put at his head, set it up as a pillar, and poured oil on top of it. ¹⁹And he called the name of that place Bethel;* but the name of that city had been Luz previously. ²⁰Then Jacob made a vow, saying, "If God will be with me, and keep me in this way that I am going, and give me bread to eat and clothing to put on, ²¹so that I come back to my father's house in peace, then the LORD

shall be my God. ²²And this stone which I have set as a pillar shall be God's house, and of all that You give me I will surely give a tenth to You."

So Jacob went on his journey and came to the land of the people of the East. ²And he looked, and saw a well in the field; and behold, there *were* three flocks of sheep lying by it; for out of that well they watered the flocks. A large stone *was* on the well's mouth. ³Now all the flocks would be gathered there; and they would roll the stone from the well's mouth, water the sheep, and put the stone back in its place on the well's mouth.

⁴And Jacob said to them, "My brethren, where *are* you from?"

And they said, "We *are* from Haran."

⁵Then he said to them, "Do you know Laban the son of Nahor?"

And they said, "We know him."

⁶So he said to them, "Is he well?"

And they said, *"He is* well. And look, his daughter Rachel is coming with the sheep."

⁷Then he said, "Look, *it is* still high day; *it is* not time for the cattle to be gathered together. Water the sheep, and go and feed *them.*"

⁸But they said, "We cannot until all the flocks are gathered together, and they have rolled the stone from the well's mouth; then we water the sheep."

⁹Now while he was still speaking with them, Rachel came with her father's sheep, for she was a shepherdess. ¹⁰And it came to pass, when Jacob saw Rachel the daughter of Laban his mother's brother, and the sheep of Laban his mother's brother, that Jacob went near and rolled the stone from the well's mouth, and watered the flock of Laban his mother's brother. ¹¹Then Jacob kissed Rachel, and lifted up his voice and wept. ¹²And Jacob told Rachel that he *was* her father's relative

and that he *was* Rebekah's son. So she ran and told her father.

¹³Then it came to pass, when Laban heard the report about Jacob his sister's son, that he ran to meet him, and embraced him and kissed him, and brought him to his house. So he told Laban all these things. ¹⁴And Laban said to him, "Surely you *are* my bone and my flesh." And he stayed with him for a month.

¹⁵Then Laban said to Jacob, "Because you *are* my relative, should you therefore serve me for nothing? Tell me, what *should* your wages *be?*" ¹⁶Now Laban had two daughters: the name of the elder *was* Leah, and the name of the younger *was* Rachel. ¹⁷Leah's eyes *were* delicate, but Rachel was beautiful of form and appearance.

¹⁸Now Jacob loved Rachel; so he said, "I will serve you seven years for Rachel your younger daughter."

¹⁹And Laban said, "*It is* better that I give her to you than that I should give her to another man. Stay with me." ²⁰So Jacob served seven years for Rachel, and they seemed *only* a few days to him because of the love he had for her.

²¹Then Jacob said to Laban, "Give *me* my wife, for my days are fulfilled, that I may go in to her." ²²And Laban gathered together all the men of the place and made a feast. ²³Now it came to pass in the evening, that he took Leah his daughter and brought her to Jacob; and he went in to her. ²⁴And Laban gave his maid Zilpah to his daughter Leah *as* a maid. ²⁵So it came to pass in the morning, that behold, it *was* Leah. And he said to Laban, "What is this you have done to me? Was it not for Rachel that I served you? Why then have you deceived me?"

²⁶And Laban said, "It must not be done so in our country, to give the younger before the firstborn. ²⁷Fulfill her week, and we will give you this one also for the service which you will

serve with me still another seven years."

²⁸Then Jacob did so and fulfilled her week. So he gave him his daughter Rachel as wife also. ²⁹And Laban gave his maid Bilhah to his daughter Rachel as a maid. ³⁰Then *Jacob* also went in to Rachel, and he also loved Rachel more than Leah. And he served with Laban still another seven years.

³¹When the Lord saw that Leah *was* unloved, He opened her womb; but Rachel *was* barren. ³²So Leah conceived and bore a son, and she called his name Reuben;* for she said, "The Lord has surely looked on my affliction. Now therefore, my husband will love me." ³³Then she conceived again and bore a son, and said, "Because the Lord has heard that I *am* unloved, He has therefore given me this *son* also." And she called his name Simeon.* ³⁴She conceived again and bore a son, and said, "Now this time my husband will become attached to me, because I have borne him three sons." Therefore his name was called Levi.* ³⁵And she conceived again and bore a son, and said, "Now I will praise the Lord." Therefore she called his name Judah.* Then she stopped bearing.

MATTHEW 9:18-38

W HILE He [Jesus] spoke these things to them, behold, a ruler came and worshiped Him, saying, "My daughter has just died, but come and lay Your hand on her and she will live." ¹⁹So Jesus arose and followed him, and so *did* His disciples.

²⁰And suddenly, a woman who had a flow of blood for twelve years came from behind and touched the hem of His garment. ²¹For she said to herself, "If only I may touch His garment, I shall be made well." ²²But Jesus turned around, and when He saw her He said, "Be of good cheer, daughter; your faith

has made you well." And the woman was made well from that hour.

23When Jesus came into the ruler's house, and saw the flute players and the noisy crowd wailing, 24He said to them, "Make room, for the girl is not dead, but sleeping." And they ridiculed Him. 25But when the crowd was put outside, He went in and took her by the hand, and the girl arose. 26And the report of this went out into all that land.

27When Jesus departed from there, two blind men followed Him, crying out and saying, "Son of David, have mercy on us!"

28And when He had come into the house, the blind men came to Him. And Jesus said to them, "Do you believe that I am able to do this?"

They said to Him, "Yes, Lord."

29Then He touched their eyes, saying, "According to your faith let it be to you." 30And their eyes were opened. And Jesus sternly warned them, saying, "See that no one knows it." 31But when they had departed, they spread the news about Him in all that country.

32As they went out, behold, they brought to Him a man, mute and demon-possessed. 33And when the demon was cast out, the mute spoke. And the multitudes marveled, saying, "It was never seen like this in Israel!"

34But the Pharisees said, "He casts out demons by the ruler of the demons."

35Then Jesus went about all the cities and villages, teaching in their synagogues, preaching the gospel of the kingdom, and healing every sickness and every disease among the people.* 36But when He saw the multitudes, He was moved with compassion for them,

because they were weary* and scattered, like sheep having no shepherd. 37Then He said to His disciples, "The harvest truly is plentiful, but the laborers are few. 38Therefore pray the Lord of the harvest to send out laborers into His harvest."

PSALM 11:1-7

To the Chief Musician. A Psalm of David.

IN the LORD I put my trust;
How can you say to my soul,
"Flee as a bird to your mountain"?

2   For look! The wicked bend
       their bow,
     They make ready their arrow
       on the string,
     That they may shoot secretly
       at the upright in heart.

3   If the foundations are
       destroyed,
     What can the righteous do?

4   The LORD is in His holy temple,
     The LORD's throne is in heaven;
     His eyes behold,
     His eyelids test the sons of
       men.

5   The LORD tests the righteous,
     But the wicked and the one
       who loves violence His soul
       hates.

6   Upon the wicked He will rain
       coals;
     Fire and brimstone and a
       burning wind
     Shall be the portion of their
       cup.

7   For the LORD is righteous,
     He loves righteousness;
     His countenance beholds the
       upright.*

PROVERBS FOR TODAY/ 3:11-12

My son, do not despise the chastening of the LORD, nor detest His correction; for whom the LORD loves He corrects, just as a father the son in whom he delights.

GENESIS 30:1–31:16

Now when Rachel saw that she bore Jacob no children, Rachel envied her sister, and said to Jacob, "Give me children, or else I die!"

²And Jacob's anger was aroused against Rachel, and he said, "Am I in the place of God, who has withheld from you the fruit of the womb?"

³So she said, "Here is my maid Bilhah; go in to her, and she will bear a child on my knees, that I also may have children by her." ⁴Then she gave him Bilhah her maid as wife, and Jacob went in to her. ⁵And Bilhah conceived and bore Jacob a son. ⁶Then Rachel said, "God has judged my case; and He has also heard my voice and given me a son." Therefore she called his name Dan.* ⁷And Rachel's maid Bilhah conceived again and bore Jacob a second son. ⁸Then Rachel said, "With great wrestlings I have wrestled with my sister, and indeed I have prevailed." So she called his name Naphtali.*

⁹When Leah saw that she had stopped bearing, she took Zilpah her maid and gave her to Jacob as wife. ¹⁰And Leah's maid Zilpah bore Jacob a son. ¹¹Then Leah said, "A troop comes!"* So she called his name Gad.* ¹²And Leah's maid Zilpah bore Jacob a second son. ¹³Then Leah said, "I am happy, for the daughters will call me blessed." So she called his name Asher.*

¹⁴Now Reuben went in the days of wheat harvest and found mandrakes in the field, and brought them to his mother Leah. Then Rachel said to Leah, "Please give me some of your son's mandrakes."

¹⁵But she said to her, "Is it a small matter that you have taken away my husband? Would you take away my son's mandrakes also?"

And Rachel said, "Therefore he will lie with you tonight for your son's mandrakes."

¹⁶When Jacob came out of the field in the evening, Leah went out to meet him and said, "You must come in to me, for I have surely hired you with my son's mandrakes." And he lay with her that night.

¹⁷And God listened to Leah, and she conceived and bore Jacob a fifth son. ¹⁸Leah said, "God has given me my wages, because I have given my maid to my husband." So she called his name Issachar.* ¹⁹Then Leah conceived again and bore Jacob a sixth son. ²⁰And Leah said, "God has endowed me with a good endowment; now my husband will dwell with me, because I have borne him six sons." So she called his name Zebulun.* ²¹Afterward she bore a daughter, and called her name Dinah.

²²Then God remembered Rachel, and God listened to her and opened her womb. ²³And she conceived and bore a son, and said, "God has taken away my reproach." ²⁴So she called his name Joseph,* and said, "The Lord shall add to me another son."

²⁵And it came to pass, when Rachel had borne Joseph, that Jacob said to Laban, "Send me away, that I may go to my own place and to my country. ²⁶Give me my wives and my children for whom I have served you, and let me go; for you know my service which I have done for you."

²⁷And Laban said to him, "Please stay, if I have found favor in your eyes, for I have learned by experience that the Lord has blessed me for your

sake." 28Then he said, "Name me your wages, and I will give *it*."

29So *Jacob* said to him, "You know how I have served you and how your livestock has been with me. 30For what you had before I *came was* little, and it has increased to a great amount; the LORD has blessed you since my coming. And now, when shall I also provide for my own house?"

31So he said, "What shall I give you?"

And Jacob said, "You shall not give me anything. If you will do this thing for me, I will again feed and keep your flocks: 32Let me pass through all your flock today, removing from there all the speckled and spotted sheep, and all the brown ones among the lambs, and the spotted and speckled among the goats; and *these* shall be my wages. 33So my righteousness will answer for me in time to come, when the subject of my wages comes before you: every one that *is* not speckled and spotted among the goats, and brown among the lambs, will be considered stolen, if *it is* with me."

34And Laban said, "Oh, that it were according to your word!" 35So he removed that day the male goats that were speckled and spotted, all the female goats that were speckled and spotted, every one that had *some* white in it, and all the brown ones among the lambs, and gave *them* into the hand of his sons. 36Then he put three days' journey between himself and Jacob, and Jacob fed the rest of Laban's flocks.

37Now Jacob took for himself rods of green poplar and of the almond and chestnut trees, peeled white strips in them, and exposed the white which *was* in the rods. 38And the rods which he had peeled, he set before the flocks in the gutters, in the watering troughs where the flocks came to drink, so that they should conceive when they came to drink. 39So the flocks conceived before the rods, and the flocks brought forth streaked, speckled, and spotted. 40Then Jacob separated the lambs, and made the flocks face toward the streaked and all the brown in the flock of Laban; but he put his own flocks by themselves and did not put them with Laban's flock.

41And it came to pass, whenever the stronger livestock conceived, that Jacob placed the rods before the eyes of the livestock in the gutters, that they might conceive among the rods. 42But when the flocks were feeble, he did not put *them* in; so the feebler were Laban's and the stronger Jacob's. 43Thus the man became exceedingly prosperous, and had large flocks, female and male servants, and camels and donkeys.

Now *Jacob* heard the words of Laban's sons, saying, "Jacob has taken away all that was our father's, and from what was our father's he has acquired all this wealth." 2And Jacob saw the countenance of Laban, and indeed it *was* not *favorable* toward him as before. 3Then the LORD said to Jacob, "Return to the land of your fathers and to your family, and I will be with you."

4So Jacob sent and called Rachel and Leah to the field, to his flock, 5and said to them, "I see your father's countenance, that it *is* not *favorable* toward me as before; but the God of my father has been with me. 6And you know that with all my might I have served your father. 7Yet your father has deceived me and changed my wages ten times, but God did not allow him to hurt me. 8If he said thus: 'The speckled shall be your wages,' then all the flocks bore speckled. And if he said thus: 'The streaked shall be your wages,' then all the flocks bore streaked. 9So God has taken away the livestock of your father and given *them* to me.

10"And it happened, at the time when the flocks conceived, that I lifted my eyes and saw in a dream, and behold, the rams which leaped upon the flocks *were* streaked, speckled, and gray-spotted. [11]Then the Angel of God spoke to me in a dream, saying, 'Jacob.' And I said, 'Here I am.' [12]And He said, 'Lift your eyes now and see, all the rams which leap on the flocks *are* streaked, speckled, and gray-spotted; for I have seen all that Laban is doing to you. [13]I *am* the God of Bethel, where you anointed the pillar *and* where you made a vow to Me. Now arise, get out of this land, and return to the land of your family.' "

[14]Then Rachel and Leah answered and said to him, "Is there still any portion or inheritance for us in our father's house? [15]Are we not considered strangers by him? For he has sold us, and also completely consumed our money. [16]For all these riches which God has taken from our father are *really* ours and our children's; now then, whatever God has said to you, do it."

MATTHEW 10:1-26

A[ND] when He [Jesus] had called His twelve disciples to *Him,* He gave them power *over* unclean spirits, to cast them out, and to heal all kinds of sickness and all kinds of disease. [2]Now the names of the twelve apostles are these: first, Simon, who is called Peter, and Andrew his brother; James the *son* of Zebedee, and John his brother; [3]Philip and Bartholomew; Thomas and Matthew the tax collector; James the *son* of Alphaeus, and Lebbaeus, whose surname was* Thaddaeus; [4]Simon the Cananite,* and Judas Iscariot, who also betrayed Him.

[5]These twelve Jesus sent out and commanded them, saying: "Do not go into the way of the Gentiles, and do not enter a city of the Samaritans. [6]But go rather to the lost sheep of the house of Israel. [7]And as you go, preach, saying, 'The kingdom of heaven is at hand.' [8]Heal the sick, cleanse the lepers, raise the dead,* cast out demons. Freely you have received, freely give. [9]Provide neither gold nor silver nor copper in your money belts, [10]nor bag for *your* journey, nor two tunics, nor sandals, nor staffs; for a worker is worthy of his food.

[11]"Now whatever city or town you enter, inquire who in it is worthy, and stay there till you go out. [12]And when you go into a household, greet it. [13]If the household is worthy, let your peace come upon it. But if it is not worthy, let your peace return to you. [14]And whoever will not receive you nor hear your words, when you depart from that house or city, shake off the dust from your feet. [15]Assuredly, I say to you, it will be more tolerable for the land of Sodom and Gomorrah in the day of judgment than for that city!

[16]"Behold, I send you out as sheep in the midst of wolves. Therefore be wise as serpents and harmless as doves. [17]But beware of men, for they will deliver you up to councils and scourge you in their synagogues. [18]You will be brought before governors and kings for My sake, as a testimony to them and to the Gentiles. [19]But when they deliver you up, do not worry about how or what you should speak. For it will be given to you in that hour what you should speak; [20]for it is not you who speak, but the Spirit of your Father who speaks in you.

[21]"Now brother will deliver up brother to death, and a father *his* child; and children will rise up against parents and cause them to be put to death. [22]And you will be hated by all for My name's sake. But he who endures to the end will be saved. [23]When they persecute you in this city, flee to another. For assuredly, I say to you, you will not have gone through the cities of Israel before the Son of Man comes.

[24]"A disciple is not above *his* teacher, nor a servant above his master. [25]It is enough for a disciple that he be like his

teacher, and a servant like his master. If they have called the master of the house Beelzebub,* how much more *will they call* those of his household! 26Therefore do not fear them. For there is nothing covered that will not be revealed, and hidden that will not be known."

PSALM 12:1-8

To the Chief Musician. On an eight-stringed harp. A Psalm of David.*

HELP, LORD, for the godly man ceases!
For the faithful disappear from among the sons of men.
2 They speak idly everyone with his neighbor;
With flattering lips *and* a double heart they speak.

3 May the LORD cut off all flattering lips,
And the tongue that speaks proud things,
4 Who have said,

"With our tongue we will prevail;
Our lips *are* our own;
Who *is* lord over us?"

5 "For the oppression of the poor, for the sighing of the needy,
Now I will arise," says the LORD;
"I will set *him* in the safety for which he yearns."

6 The words of the LORD *are* pure words,
Like silver tried in a furnace of earth,
Purified seven times.

7 You shall keep them, O LORD,
You shall preserve them from this generation forever.

8 The wicked prowl on every side,
When vileness is exalted among the sons of men.

PROVERBS FOR TODAY/ 3:13-15

Happy is *the man* who *finds wisdom, and the man* who *gains understanding; for her proceeds* are *better than the profits of silver, and her gain than fine gold. She* is *more precious than rubies, and all the things you may desire cannot compare with her.*

JANUARY 15

GENESIS 31:17–32:12

THEN Jacob rose and set his sons and his wives on camels. 18And he carried away all his livestock and all his possessions which he had gained, his acquired livestock which he had gained in Padan Aram, to go to his father Isaac in the land of Canaan. 19Now Laban had gone to shear his

sheep, and Rachel had stolen the household idols that were her father's. 20And Jacob stole away, unknown to Laban the Syrian, in that he did not tell him that he intended to flee. 21So he fled with all that he had. He arose and crossed the river, and headed toward the mountains of Gilead.

22And Laban was told on the third

day that Jacob had fled. 23Then he took his brethren with him and pursued him for seven days' journey, and he overtook him in the mountains of Gilead. 24But God had come to Laban the Syrian in a dream by night, and said to him, "Be careful that you speak to Jacob neither good nor bad."

25So Laban overtook Jacob. Now Jacob had pitched his tent in the mountains, and Laban with his brethren pitched in the mountains of Gilead.

26And Laban said to Jacob: "What have you done, that you have stolen away unknown to me, and carried away my daughters like captives *taken* with the sword? 27Why did you flee away secretly, and steal away from me, and not tell me; for I might have sent you away with joy and songs, with timbrel and harp? 28And you did not allow me to kiss my sons and my daughters. Now you have done foolishly in *so* doing. 29It is in my power to do you harm, but the God of your father spoke to me last night, saying, 'Be careful that you speak to Jacob neither good nor bad.' 30And now you have surely gone because you greatly long for your father's house, *but* why did you steal my gods?"

31Then Jacob answered and said to Laban, "Because I was afraid, for I said, 'Perhaps you would take your daughters from me by force.' 32With whomever you find your gods, do not let him live. In the presence of our brethren, identify what I have of yours and take *it* with you." For Jacob did not know that Rachel had stolen them.

33And Laban went into Jacob's tent, into Leah's tent, and into the two maids' tents, but he did not find *them.* Then he went out of Leah's tent and entered Rachel's tent. 34Now Rachel had taken the household idols, put them in the camel's saddle, and sat on them. And Laban searched all about the tent but did not find *them.* 35And she said to her father, "Let it not displease my lord that I cannot rise before

you, for the manner of women *is* with me." And he searched but did not find the household idols.

36Then Jacob was angry and rebuked Laban, and Jacob answered and said to Laban: "What *is* my trespass? What *is* my sin, that you have so hotly pursued me? 37Although you have searched all my things, what part of your household things have you found? Set *it* here before my brethren and your brethren, that they may judge between us both! 38These twenty years I *have been* with you; your ewes and your female goats have not miscarried their young, and I have not eaten the rams of your flock. 39That which was torn *by beasts* I did not bring to you; I bore the loss of it. You required it from my hand, *whether* stolen by day or stolen by night. 40*There* I was! In the day the drought consumed me, and the frost by night, and my sleep departed from my eyes. 41Thus I have been in your house twenty years; I served you fourteen years for your two daughters, and six years for your flock, and you have changed my wages ten times. 42Unless the God of my father, the God of Abraham and the Fear of Isaac, had been with me, surely now you would have sent me away empty-handed. God has seen my affliction and the labor of my hands, and rebuked *you* last night."

43And Laban answered and said to Jacob, *"These* daughters *are* my daughters, and *these* children *are* my children, and *this* flock *is* my flock; all that you see *is* mine. But what can I do this day to these my daughters or to their children whom they have borne? 44Now therefore, come, let us make a covenant, you and I, and let it be a witness between you and me."

45So Jacob took a stone and set it up *as* a pillar. 46Then Jacob said to his brethren, "Gather stones." And they took stones and made a heap, and they ate there on the heap. 47Laban called it Jegar Sahadutha,* but Jacob called it

Galeed.* ⁴⁸And Laban said, "This heap *is* a witness between you and me this day." Therefore its name was called Galeed, ⁴⁹also Mizpah,* because he said, "May the LORD watch between you and me when we are absent one from another. ⁵⁰If you afflict my daughters, or if you take *other* wives besides my daughters, *although* no man *is* with us—see, God *is* witness between you and me!"

⁵¹Then Laban said to Jacob, "Here is this heap and here is *this* pillar, which I have placed between you and me. ⁵²This heap *is* a witness, and *this* pillar *is* a witness, that I will not pass beyond this heap to you, and you will not pass beyond this heap and this pillar to me, for harm. ⁵³The God of Abraham, the God of Nahor, and the God of their father judge between us." And Jacob swore by the Fear of his father Isaac. ⁵⁴Then Jacob offered a sacrifice on the mountain, and called his brethren to eat bread. And they ate bread and stayed all night on the mountain. ⁵⁵And early in the morning Laban arose, and kissed his sons and daughters and blessed them. Then Laban departed and returned to his place.

So Jacob went on his way, and the angels of God met him. ²When Jacob saw them, he said, "This *is* God's camp." And he called the name of that place Mahanaim.*

³Then Jacob sent messengers before him to Esau his brother in the land of Seir, the country of Edom. ⁴And he commanded them, saying, "Speak thus to my lord Esau, 'Thus your servant Jacob says: "I have dwelt with Laban and stayed there until now. ⁵I have oxen, donkeys, flocks, and male and female servants; and I have sent to tell my lord, that I may find favor in your sight." ' "

⁶Then the messengers returned to Jacob, saying, "We came to your brother Esau, and he also is coming to meet you, and four hundred men *are* with him." ⁷So Jacob was greatly afraid and distressed; and he divided the people that *were* with him, and the flocks and herds and camels, into two companies. ⁸And he said, "If Esau comes to the one company and attacks it, then the other company which is left will escape."

⁹Then Jacob said, "O God of my father Abraham and God of my father Isaac, the LORD who said to me, 'Return to your country and to your family, and I will deal well with you': ¹⁰I am not worthy of the least of all the mercies and of all the truth which You have shown Your servant; for I crossed over this Jordan with my staff, and now I have become two companies. ¹¹Deliver me, I pray, from the hand of my brother, from the hand of Esau; for I fear him, lest he come and attack me *and* the mother with the children. ¹²For You said, 'I will surely treat you well, and make your descendants as the sand of the sea, which cannot be numbered for multitude.' "

MATTHEW 10:27–11:6

"WHATEVER I [Jesus] tell you in the dark, speak in the light; and what you hear in the ear, preach on the housetops. ²⁸And do not fear those who kill the body but cannot kill the soul. But rather fear Him who is able to destroy both soul and body in hell. ²⁹Are not two sparrows sold for a copper coin? And not one of them falls to the ground apart from your Father's will. ³⁰But the very hairs of your head are all numbered. ³¹Do not fear therefore; you are of more value than many sparrows.

³²"Therefore whoever confesses Me before men, him I will also confess before My Father who is in heaven. ³³But whoever denies Me before men, him I will also deny before My Father who is in heaven.

34"Do not think that I came to bring peace on earth. I did not come to bring peace but a sword. 35For I have come to *set a man against his father, a daughter against her mother, and a daughter-in-law against her mother-in-law*'; 36and *'a man's enemies will be those of his own household.'** 37He who loves father or mother more than Me is not worthy of Me. And he who loves son or daughter more than Me is not worthy of Me. 38And he who does not take his cross and follow after Me is not worthy of Me. 39He who finds his life will lose it, and he who loses his life for My sake will find it.

40"He who receives you receives Me, and he who receives Me receives Him who sent Me. 41He who receives a prophet in the name of a prophet shall receive a prophet's reward. And he who receives a righteous man in the name of a righteous man shall receive a righteous man's reward. 42And whoever gives one of these little ones only a cup of cold *water* in the name of a disciple, assuredly, I say to you, he shall by no means lose his reward."

Now it came to pass, when Jesus finished commanding His twelve disciples, that He departed from there to teach and to preach in their cities.

2And when John had heard in prison about the works of Christ, he sent two of* his disciples 3and said to Him, "Are You the Coming One, or do we look for another?"

4Jesus answered and said to them,

"Go and tell John the things which you hear and see: 5The blind see and *the* lame walk; *the* lepers are cleansed and *the* deaf hear; *the* dead are raised up and *the* poor have the gospel preached to them. 6And blessed is he who is not offended because of Me."

PSALM 13:1-6

To the Chief Musician. A Psalm of David.

How long, O Lord? Will You forget me forever? How long will You hide Your face from me?
2 How long shall I take counsel in my soul,
   Having sorrow in my heart daily?
   How long will my enemy be exalted over me?

3 Consider *and* hear me,
   O Lord my God;
   Enlighten my eyes,
   Lest I sleep the *sleep of* death;
4 Lest my enemy say,
   "I have prevailed against him";
   Lest those who trouble me rejoice when I am moved.

5 But I have trusted in Your mercy;
   My heart shall rejoice in Your salvation.
6 I will sing to the Lord,
   Because He has dealt bountifully with me.

PROVERBS FOR TODAY/ 3:16-18

Length of days is *in her [Wisdom's] right hand, in her left hand riches and honor. Her ways* are *ways of pleasantness, and all her paths* are *peace. She* is *a tree of life to those who take hold of her, and happy* are all *who retain her.*

JANUARY 16

So he [Jacob] lodged there that same night, and took what came to his hand as a present for Esau his brother: 14two hundred female goats and twenty male goats, two hundred ewes and twenty rams, 15thirty milk camels with their colts, forty cows and ten bulls, twenty female donkeys and ten foals. 16Then he delivered *them* to the hand of his servants, every drove by itself, and said to his servants, "Pass over before me, and put some distance between successive droves." 17And he commanded the first one, saying, "When Esau my brother meets you and asks you, saying, 'To whom do you belong, and where are you going? Whose *are* these in front of you?' 18then you shall say, 'They *are* your servant Jacob's. It *is* a present sent to my lord Esau; and behold, he also *is* behind us.' "

19So he commanded the second, the third, and all who followed the droves, saying, "In this manner you shall speak to Esau when you find him; 20and also say, 'Behold, your servant Jacob *is* behind us.' " For he said, "I will appease him with the present that goes before me, and afterward I will see his face; perhaps he will accept me." 21So the present went on over before him, but he himself lodged that night in the camp.

22And he arose that night and took his two wives, his two female servants, and his eleven sons, and crossed over the ford of Jabbok. 23He took them, sent them over the brook, and sent over what he had. 24Then Jacob was left alone; and a Man wrestled with him until the breaking of day. 25Now when He saw that He did not prevail against him, He touched the socket of his hip; and the socket of Jacob's hip was out of joint as He wrestled with him. 26And He said, "Let Me go, for the day breaks."

But he said, "I will not let You go unless You bless me!"

27So He said to him, "What *is* your name?"

He said, "Jacob."

28And He said, "Your name shall no longer be called Jacob, but Israel;* for you have struggled with God and with men, and have prevailed."

29Then Jacob asked, saying, "Tell *me* Your name, I pray."

And He said, "Why *is* it *that* you ask about My name?" And He blessed him there.

30So Jacob called the name of the place Peniel:* "For I have seen God face to face, and my life is preserved." 31Just as he crossed over Penuel* the sun rose on him, and he limped on his hip. 32Therefore to this day the children of Israel do not eat the muscle that shrank, which *is* on the hip socket, because He touched the socket of Jacob's hip in the muscle that shrank.

Now Jacob lifted his eyes and looked, and there, Esau was coming, and with him were four hundred men. So he divided the children among Leah, Rachel, and the two maidservants. 2And he put the maidservants and their children in front, Leah and her children behind, and Rachel and Joseph last. 3Then he crossed over before them and bowed himself to the ground seven times, until he came near to his brother.

4But Esau ran to meet him, and embraced him, and fell on his neck and kissed him, and they wept. 5And he lifted his eyes and saw the women and children, and said, "Who *are* these with you?"

So he said, "The children whom God has graciously given your servant." ⁶Then the maidservants came near, they and their children, and bowed down. ⁷And Leah also came near with her children, and they bowed down. Afterward Joseph and Rachel came near, and they bowed down.

⁸Then Esau said, "What *do* you *mean by* all this company which I met?"

And he said, "*These are* to find favor in the sight of my lord."

⁹But Esau said, "I have enough, my brother; keep what you have for yourself."

¹⁰And Jacob said, "No, please, if I have now found favor in your sight, then receive my present from my hand, inasmuch as I have seen your face as though I had seen the face of God, and you were pleased with me. ¹¹Please, take my blessing that is brought to you, because God has dealt graciously with me, and because I have enough." So he urged him, and he took *it.*

¹²Then Esau said, "Let us take our journey; let us go, and I will go before you."

¹³But Jacob said to him, "My lord knows that the children *are* weak, and the flocks and herds which are nursing *are* with me. And if the men should drive them hard one day, all the flock will die. ¹⁴Please let my lord go on ahead before his servant. I will lead on slowly at a pace which the livestock that go before me, and the children, are able to endure, until I come to my lord in Seir."

¹⁵And Esau said, "Now let me leave with you *some* of the people who *are* with me."

But he said, "What need is there? Let me find favor in the sight of my lord." ¹⁶So Esau returned that day on his way to Seir. ¹⁷And Jacob journeyed to Succoth, built himself a house, and made booths for his livestock. Therefore the name of the place is called Succoth.*

¹⁸Then Jacob came safely to the city of Shechem, which *is* in the land of Canaan, when he came from Padan Aram; and he pitched his tent before the city. ¹⁹And he bought the parcel of land, where he had pitched his tent, from the children of Hamor, Shechem's father, for one hundred pieces of money. ²⁰Then he erected an altar there and called it El Elohe Israel.*

Now Dinah the daughter of Leah, whom she had borne to Jacob, went out to see the daughters of the land. ²And when Shechem the son of Hamor the Hivite, prince of the country, saw her, he took her and lay with her, and violated her. ³His soul was strongly attracted to Dinah the daughter of Jacob, and he loved the young woman and spoke kindly to the young woman. ⁴So Shechem spoke to his father Hamor, saying, "Get me this young woman as a wife."

⁵And Jacob heard that he had defiled Dinah his daughter. Now his sons were with his livestock in the field; so Jacob held his peace until they came. ⁶Then Hamor the father of Shechem went out to Jacob to speak with him. ⁷And the sons of Jacob came in from the field when they heard *it;* and the men were grieved and very angry, because he had done a disgraceful thing in Israel by lying with Jacob's daughter, a thing which ought not to be done. ⁸But Hamor spoke with them, saying, "The soul of my son Shechem longs for your daughter. Please give her to him as a wife. ⁹And make marriages with us; give your daughters to us, and take our daughters to yourselves. ¹⁰So you shall dwell with us, and the land shall be before you. Dwell and trade in it, and acquire possessions for yourselves in it."

¹¹Then Shechem said to her father and her brothers, "Let me find favor in your eyes, and whatever you say to me I will give. ¹²Ask me ever so much dowry and gift, and I will give according to what you say to me; but give me the young woman as a wife."

¹³But the sons of Jacob answered Shechem and Hamor his father, and spoke deceitfully, because he had defiled Dinah their sister. ¹⁴And they said to them, "We cannot do this thing, to give our sister to one who is uncircumcised, for that *would be* a reproach to us. ¹⁵But on this *condition* we will consent to you: If you will become as we *are,* if every male of you is circumcised, ¹⁶then we will give our daughters to you, and we will take your daughters to us; and we will dwell with you, and we will become one people. ¹⁷But if you will not heed us and be circumcised, then we will take our daughter and be gone."

¹⁸And their words pleased Hamor and Shechem, Hamor's son. ¹⁹So the young man did not delay to do the thing, because he delighted in Jacob's daughter. He *was* more honorable than all the household of his father.

²⁰And Hamor and Shechem his son came to the gate of their city, and spoke with the men of their city, saying: ²¹"These men *are* at peace with us. Therefore let them dwell in the land and trade in it. For indeed the land *is* large enough for them. Let us take their daughters to us as wives, and let us give them our daughters. ²²Only on this *condition* will the men consent to dwell with us, to be one people: if every male among us is circumcised as they *are* circumcised. ²³*Will* not their livestock, their property, and every animal of theirs *be* ours? Only let us consent to them, and they will dwell with us." ²⁴And all who went out of the gate of his city heeded Hamor and Shechem his son; every male was circumcised, all who went out of the gate of his city.

²⁵Now it came to pass on the third day, when they were in pain, that two of the sons of Jacob, Simeon and Levi, Dinah's brothers, each took his sword and came boldly upon the city and killed all the males. ²⁶And they killed Hamor and Shechem his son with the edge of the sword, and took Dinah from Shechem's house, and went out. ²⁷The sons of Jacob came upon the slain, and plundered the city, because their sister had been defiled. ²⁸They took their sheep, their oxen, and their donkeys, what *was* in the city and what *was* in the field, ²⁹and all their wealth. All their little ones and their wives they took captive; and they plundered even all that *was* in the houses.

³⁰Then Jacob said to Simeon and Levi, "You have troubled me by making me obnoxious among the inhabitants of the land, among the Canaanites and the Perizzites; and since I *am* few in number, they will gather themselves together against me and kill me. I shall be destroyed, my household and I."

³¹But they said, "Should he treat our sister like a harlot?"

MATTHEW 11:7-30

As they departed, Jesus began to say to the multitudes concerning John: "What did you go out into the wilderness to see? A reed shaken by the wind? ⁸But what did you go out to see? A man clothed in soft garments? Indeed, those who wear soft *clothing* are in kings' houses. ⁹But what did you go out to see? A prophet? Yes, I say to you, and more than a prophet. ¹⁰For this is *he* of whom it is written:

'Behold, I send My messenger
before Your face,

Who will prepare Your way before You.'

11"Assuredly, I say to you, among those born of women there has not risen one greater than John the Baptist; but he who is least in the kingdom of heaven is greater than he. 12And from the days of John the Baptist until now the kingdom of heaven suffers violence, and the violent take it by force. 13For all the prophets and the law prophesied until John. 14And if you are willing to receive *it,* he is Elijah who is to come. 15He who has ears to hear, let him hear!

16"But to what shall I liken this generation? It is like children sitting in the marketplaces and calling to their companions, 17and saying:

> 'We played the flute for you,
> And you did not dance;
> We mourned to you,
> And you did not lament.'

18For John came neither eating nor drinking, and they say, 'He has a demon.' 19The Son of Man came eating and drinking, and they say, 'Look, a glutton and a winebibber, a friend of tax collectors and sinners!' But wisdom is justified by her children."*

20Then He began to rebuke the cities in which most of His mighty works had been done, because they did not repent: 21"Woe to you, Chorazin! Woe to you, Bethsaida! For if the mighty works which were done in you had been done in Tyre and Sidon, they would have repented long ago in sackcloth and ashes. 22But I say to you, it will be more tolerable for Tyre and Sidon in the day of judgment than for you. 23And you, Capernaum, who are exalted to heaven, will be* brought down to Hades; for if the mighty works which were done in you had been done in Sodom, it would have remained until this day. 24But I say to you that it shall be more tolerable for the land of Sodom in the day of judgment than for you."

25At that time Jesus answered and said, "I thank You, Father, Lord of heaven and earth, that You have hidden these things from *the* wise and prudent and have revealed them to babes. 26Even so, Father, for so it seemed good in Your sight. 27All things have been delivered to Me by My Father, and no one knows the Son except the Father. Nor does anyone know the Father except the Son, and *the one* to whom the Son wills to reveal *Him.* 28Come to Me, all *you* who labor and are heavy laden, and I will give you rest. 29Take My yoke upon you and learn from Me, for I am gentle and lowly in heart, and you will find rest for your souls. 30For My yoke *is* easy and My burden is light."

PSALM 14:1-7

To the Chief Musician. A Psalm of David.

THE fool has said in his heart,
    "*There is* no God."
They are corrupt,
    They have done abominable
        works,
    There is none who does good.

2   The LORD looks down from
        heaven upon the children
        of men,
    To see if there are any who
        understand, who seek God.
3   They have all turned aside,
    They have together become
        corrupt;
    There is none who does good,
    No, not one.

4   Have all the workers of
        iniquity no knowledge,
    Who eat up my people *as* they
        eat bread,
    And do not call on the LORD?
5   There they are in great fear,

For God *is* with the
generation of the righteous.
6 You shame the counsel of the
poor,
But the LORD *is* his refuge.

7 Oh, that the salvation of Israel
would come out of Zion!
When the LORD brings back
the captivity of His people,
Let Jacob rejoice *and* Israel
be glad.

PROVERBS FOR TODAY/ 3:19-20

The LORD by wisdom founded the earth; by understanding He established the heavens; by His knowledge the depths were broken up, and clouds drop down the dew.

JANUARY 17

GENESIS 35:1–36:43

THEN God said to Jacob, "Arise, go up to Bethel and dwell there; and make an altar there to God, who appeared to you when you fled from the face of Esau your brother."

2And Jacob said to his household and to all who *were* with him, "Put away the foreign gods that *are* among you, purify yourselves, and change your garments. 3Then let us arise and go up to Bethel; and I will make an altar there to God, who answered me in the day of my distress and has been with me in the way which I have gone." 4So they gave Jacob all the foreign gods which *were* in their hands, and the earrings which *were* in their ears; and Jacob hid them under the terebinth tree which *was* by Shechem.

5And they journeyed, and the terror of God was upon the cities that *were* all around them, and they did not pursue the sons of Jacob. 6So Jacob came to Luz (that *is,* Bethel), which *is* in the land of Canaan, he and all the people who *were* with him. 7And he built an altar there and called the place El Bethel,* because there God appeared

to him when he fled from the face of his brother.

8Now Deborah, Rebekah's nurse, died, and she was buried below Bethel under the terebinth tree. So the name of it was called Allon Bachuth.*

9Then God appeared to Jacob again, when he came from Padan Aram, and blessed him. 10And God said to him, "Your name *is* Jacob; your name shall not be called Jacob anymore, but Israel shall be your name." So He called his name Israel. 11Also God said to him: "I *am* God Almighty. Be fruitful and multiply; a nation and a company of nations shall proceed from you, and kings shall come from your body. 12The land which I gave Abraham and Isaac I give to you; and to your descendants after you I give this land." 13Then God went up from him in the place where He talked with him. 14So Jacob set up a pillar in the place where He talked with him, a pillar of stone; and he poured a drink offering on it, and he poured oil on it. 15And Jacob called the name of the place where God spoke with him, Bethel.

16Then they journeyed from Bethel. And when there was but a little distance to go to Ephrath, Rachel labored *in childbirth,* and she had hard labor. [17]Now it came to pass, when she was in hard labor, that the midwife said to her, "Do not fear; you will have this son also." [18]And so it was, as her soul was departing (for she died), that she called his name Ben-Oni;* but his father called him Benjamin.* [19]So Rachel died and was buried on the way to Ephrath (that *is,* Bethlehem). [20]And Jacob set a pillar on her grave, which *is* the pillar of Rachel's grave to this day.

[21]Then Israel journeyed and pitched his tent beyond the tower of Eder. [22]And it happened, when Israel dwelt in that land, that Reuben went and lay with Bilhah his father's concubine; and Israel heard *about it.*

Now the sons of Jacob were twelve: [23]the sons of Leah *were* Reuben, Jacob's firstborn, and Simeon, Levi, Judah, Issachar, and Zebulun; [24]the sons of Rachel *were* Joseph and Benjamin; [25]the sons of Bilhah, Rachel's maidservant, *were* Dan and Naphtali; [26]and the sons of Zilpah, Leah's maidservant, *were* Gad and Asher. These *were* the sons of Jacob who were born to him in Padan Aram.

[27]Then Jacob came to his father Isaac at Mamre, or Kirjath Arba* (that *is,* Hebron), where Abraham and Isaac had dwelt. [28]Now the days of Isaac were one hundred and eighty years. [29]So Isaac breathed his last and died, and was gathered to his people, *being* old and full of days. And his sons Esau and Jacob buried him.

Now this *is* the genealogy of Esau, who is Edom. [2]Esau took his wives from the daughters of Canaan: Adah the daughter of Elon the Hittite; Aholibamah the daughter of Anah, the daughter of Zibeon the Hivite; [3]and Basemath, Ishmael's daughter, sister of Nebajoth. [4]Now Adah bore Eliphaz to Esau, and Basemath bore Reuel. [5]And Aholibamah bore Jeush, Jaalam, and Korah.

These *were* the sons of Esau who were born to him in the land of Canaan.

[6]Then Esau took his wives, his sons, his daughters, and all the persons of his household, his cattle and all his animals, and all his goods which he had gained in the land of Canaan, and went to a country away from the presence of his brother Jacob. [7]For their possessions were too great for them to dwell together, and the land where they were strangers could not support them because of their livestock. [8]So Esau dwelt in Mount Seir. Esau *is* Edom.

[9]And this *is* the genealogy of Esau the father of the Edomites in Mount Seir. [10]These *were* the names of Esau's sons: Eliphaz the son of Adah the wife of Esau, and Reuel the son of Basemath the wife of Esau. [11]And the sons of Eliphaz were Teman, Omar, Zepho,* Gatam, and Kenaz.

[12]Now Timna was the concubine of Eliphaz, Esau's son, and she bore Amalek to Eliphaz. These *were* the sons of Adah, Esau's wife.

[13]These *were* the sons of Reuel: Nahath, Zerah, Shammah, and Mizzah. These were the sons of Basemath, Esau's wife.

[14]These were the sons of Aholibamah, Esau's wife, the daughter of Anah, the daughter of Zibeon. And she bore to Esau: Jeush, Jaalam, and Korah.

[15]These *were* the chiefs of the sons of Esau. The sons of Eliphaz, the firstborn *son* of Esau, were Chief Teman, Chief Omar, Chief Zepho, Chief Kenaz, [16]Chief Korah,* Chief Gatam, *and* Chief Amalek. These *were* the chiefs of Eliphaz in the land of Edom. They *were* the sons of Adah.

[17]These *were* the sons of Reuel, Esau's son: Chief Nahath, Chief Zerah, Chief Shammah, and Chief Mizzah. These *were* the chiefs of Reuel in the land of Edom. These *were* the sons of Basemath, Esau's wife.

18And these *were* the sons of Aholibamah, Esau's wife: Chief Jeush, Chief Jaalam, and Chief Korah. These *were* the chiefs *who descended* from Aholibamah, Esau's wife, the daughter of Anah. 19These *were* the sons of Esau, who is Edom, and these *were* their chiefs.

20These *were* the sons of Seir the Horite who inhabited the land: Lotan, Shobal, Zibeon, Anah, 21Dishon, Ezer, and Dishan. These *were* the chiefs of the Horites, the sons of Seir, in the land of Edom.

22And the sons of Lotan were Hori and Hemam.* Lotan's sister *was* Timna.

23These *were* the sons of Shobal: Alvan,* Manahath, Ebal, Shepho,* and Onam.

24These *were* the sons of Zibeon: both Ajah and Anah. This *was the* Anah who found the water* in the wilderness as he pastured the donkeys of his father Zibeon. 25These *were* the children of Anah: Dishon and Aholibamah the daughter of Anah.

26These *were* the sons of Dishon:* Hemdan,* Eshban, Ithran, and Cheran. 27These *were* the sons of Ezer: Bilhan, Zaavan, and Akan.* 28These *were* the sons of Dishan: Uz and Aran.

29These *were* the chiefs of the Horites: Chief Lotan, Chief Shobal, Chief Zibeon, Chief Anah, 30Chief Dishon, Chief Ezer, and Chief Dishan. These *were* the chiefs of the Horites, according to their chiefs in the land of Seir.

31Now these *were* the kings who reigned in the land of Edom before any king reigned over the children of Israel: 32Bela the son of Beor reigned in Edom, and the name of his city *was* Dinhabah. 33And when Bela died, Jobab the son of Zerah of Bozrah reigned in his place. 34When Jobab died, Husham of the land of the Temanites reigned in his place. 35And when Husham died, Hadad the son of Bedad, who attacked Midian in the field of Moab, reigned in his place. And the name of his city *was* Avith. 36When Hadad died, Samlah of Masrekah reigned in his place. 37And when Samlah died, Saul of Rehoboth-*by*-the-River reigned in his place. 38When Saul died, Baal-Hanan the son of Achbor reigned in his place. 39And when Baal-Hanan the son of Achbor died, Hadar* reigned in his place; and the name of his city *was* Pau.* His wife's name *was* Mehetabel, the daughter of Matred, the daughter of Mezahab.

40And these *were* the names of the chiefs of Esau, according to their families and their places, by their names: Chief Timnah, Chief Alvah,* Chief Jetheth, 41Chief Aholibamah, Chief Elah, Chief Pinon, 42Chief Kenaz, Chief Teman, Chief Mibzar, 43Chief Magdiel, and Chief Iram. These *were* the chiefs of Edom, according to their dwelling places in the land of their possession. Esau *was* the father of the Edomites.

MATTHEW 12:1-21

A T that time Jesus went through the grainfields on the Sabbath. And His disciples were hungry, and began to pluck heads of grain and to eat. 2And when the Pharisees saw *it,* they said to Him, "Look, Your disciples are doing what is not lawful to do on the Sabbath!"

3But He said to them, "Have you not read what David did when he was hungry, he and those who were with him: 4how he entered the house of God and ate the showbread which was not lawful for him to eat, nor for those who were with him, but only for the priests? 5Or have you not read in the law that on the Sabbath the priests in the temple profane the Sabbath, and are blameless? 6Yet I say to you that in this place there is *One* greater than the temple. 7But if you had known what *this* means, *'I desire mercy and not sac-*

rifice,'* you would not have condemned the guiltless. 8For the Son of Man is Lord even* of the Sabbath."

9Now when He had departed from there, He went into their synagogue. 10And behold, there was a man who had a withered hand. And they asked Him, saying, "Is it lawful to heal on the Sabbath?"—that they might accuse Him.

11Then He said to them, "What man is there among you who has one sheep, and if it falls into a pit on the Sabbath, will not lay hold of it and lift *it* out? 12Of how much more value then is a man than a sheep? Therefore it is lawful to do good on the Sabbath." 13Then He said to the man, "Stretch out your hand." And he stretched *it* out, and it was restored as whole as the other. 14Then the Pharisees went out and plotted against Him, how they might destroy Him.

15But when Jesus knew *it,* He withdrew from there. And great multitudes* followed Him, and He healed them all. 16Yet He warned them not to make Him known, 17that it might be fulfilled which was spoken by Isaiah the prophet, saying:

18 *"Behold! My Servant whom I
have chosen,
My Beloved in whom My soul
is well pleased!
I will put My Spirit upon Him,
And He will declare justice to
the Gentiles.*
19 *He will not quarrel nor cry
out,
Nor will anyone hear His
voice in the streets.*

20 *A bruised reed He will not
break,
And smoking flax He will not
quench,
Till He sends forth justice to
victory;*
21 *And in His name Gentiles will
trust."*

PSALM 15:1-5
A Psalm of David.

Lord, who may abide in Your tabernacle?
Who may dwell in Your holy hill?

2 He who walks uprightly,
And works righteousness,
And speaks the truth in his
heart;
3 He *who* does not backbite
with his tongue,
Nor does evil to his
neighbor,
Nor does he take up a
reproach against his
friend;
4 In whose eyes a vile person is
despised,
But he honors those who
fear the Lord;
He *who* swears to his own
hurt and does not
change;
5 He *who* does not put out his
money at usury,
Nor does he take a bribe
against the innocent.

He who does these *things*
shall never be moved.

PROVERBS FOR TODAY/ 3:21-26
My son, let them [wisdom, understanding, and knowledge] not depart from your eyes—keep sound wisdom and discretion; so they will be life to your soul and grace to your neck. Then you will walk safely in your way, and your foot will not stumble. When you lie down, you will not be afraid; yes, you will lie down and your sleep

will be sweet. Do not be afraid of sudden terror, nor of trouble from the wicked when it comes; for the LORD will be your confidence, and will keep your foot from being caught.

JANUARY 18

GENESIS 37:1–38:30

Now Jacob dwelt in the land where his father was a stranger, in the land of Canaan. ²This *is* the history of Jacob.

Joseph, *being* seventeen years old, was feeding the flock with his brothers. And the lad *was* with the sons of Bilhah and the sons of Zilpah, his father's wives; and Joseph brought a bad report of them to his father.

³Now Israel loved Joseph more than all his children, because he *was* the son of his old age. Also he made him a tunic of *many* colors. ⁴But when his brothers saw that their father loved him more than all his brothers, they hated him and could not speak peaceably to him.

⁵Now Joseph had a dream, and he told *it* to his brothers; and they hated him even more. ⁶So he said to them, "Please hear this dream which I have dreamed: ⁷There we were, binding sheaves in the field. Then behold, my sheaf arose and also stood upright; and indeed your sheaves stood all around and bowed down to my sheaf."

⁸And his brothers said to him, "Shall you indeed reign over us? Or shall you indeed have dominion over us?" So they hated him even more for his dreams and for his words.

⁹Then he dreamed still another dream and told it to his brothers, and said, "Look, I have dreamed another dream. And this time, the sun, the moon, and the eleven stars bowed down to me."

¹⁰So he told *it* to his father and his brothers; and his father rebuked him and said to him, "What *is* this dream that you have dreamed? Shall your mother and I and your brothers indeed come to bow down to the earth before you?" ¹¹And his brothers envied him, but his father kept the matter *in mind.*

¹²Then his brothers went to feed their father's flock in Shechem. ¹³And Israel said to Joseph, "Are not your brothers feeding *the flock* in Shechem? Come, I will send you to them."

So he said to him, "Here I am."

¹⁴Then he said to him, "Please go and see if it is well with your brothers and well with the flocks, and bring back word to me." So he sent him out of the Valley of Hebron, and he went to Shechem.

¹⁵Now a certain man found him, and there he was, wandering in the field. And the man asked him, saying, "What are you seeking?"

¹⁶So he said, "I am seeking my brothers. Please tell me where they are feeding *their flocks.*"

¹⁷And the man said, "They have departed from here, for I heard them say, 'Let us go to Dothan.'" So Joseph went after his brothers and found them in Dothan.

¹⁸Now when they saw him afar off, even before he came near them, they conspired against him to kill him. ¹⁹Then they said to one another, "Look, this dreamer is coming! ²⁰Come therefore, let us now kill him and cast him into some pit; and we

shall say, 'Some wild beast has devoured him.' We shall see what will become of his dreams!"

21But Reuben heard *it,* and he delivered him out of their hands, and said, "Let us not kill him." 22And Reuben said to them, "Shed no blood, *but* cast him into this pit which *is* in the wilderness, and do not lay a hand on him"— that he might deliver him out of their hands, and bring him back to his father.

23So it came to pass, when Joseph had come to his brothers, that they stripped Joseph *of* his tunic, the tunic of *many* colors that *was* on him. 24Then they took him and cast him into a pit. And the pit *was* empty; *there was* no water in it.

25And they sat down to eat a meal. Then they lifted their eyes and looked, and there was a company of Ishmaelites, coming from Gilead with their camels, bearing spices, balm, and myrrh, on their way to carry *them* down to Egypt. 26So Judah said to his brothers, "What profit *is there* if we kill our brother and conceal his blood? 27Come and let us sell him to the Ishmaelites, and let not our hand be upon him, for he *is* our brother *and* our flesh." And his brothers listened. 28Then Midianite traders passed by; so *the brothers* pulled Joseph up and lifted him out of the pit, and sold him to the Ishmaelites for twenty *shekels* of silver. And they took Joseph to Egypt.

29Then Reuben returned to the pit, and indeed Joseph *was* not in the pit; and he tore his clothes. 30And he returned to his brothers and said, "The lad *is* no *more;* and I, where shall I go?" 31So they took Joseph's tunic, killed a kid of the goats, and dipped the tunic in the blood. 32Then they sent the tunic of *many* colors, and they brought *it* to their father and said, "We have found this. Do you know whether it *is* your son's tunic or not?"

33And he recognized it and said, *"It is* my son's tunic. A wild beast has devoured him. Without doubt Joseph is torn to pieces." 34Then Jacob tore his clothes, put sackcloth on his waist, and mourned for his son many days. 35And all his sons and all his daughters arose to comfort him; but he refused to be comforted, and he said, "For I shall go down into the grave to my son in mourning." Thus his father wept for him.

36Now the Midianites* had sold him in Egypt to Potiphar, an officer of Pharaoh *and* captain of the guard.

It came to pass at that time that Judah departed from his brothers, and visited a certain Adullamite whose name *was* Hirah. 2And Judah saw there a daughter of a certain Canaanite whose name *was* Shua, and he married her and went in to her. 3So she conceived and bore a son, and he called his name Er. 4She conceived again and bore a son, and she called his name Onan. 5And she conceived yet again and bore a son, and called his name Shelah. He was at Chezib when she bore him.

6Then Judah took a wife for Er his firstborn, and her name *was* Tamar. 7But Er, Judah's firstborn, was wicked in the sight of the Lord, and the Lord killed him. 8And Judah said to Onan, "Go in to your brother's wife and marry her, and raise up an heir to your brother." 9But Onan knew that the heir would not be his; and it came to pass, when he went in to his brother's wife, that he emitted on the ground, lest he should give an heir to his brother. 10And the thing which he did displeased the Lord; therefore He killed him also.

11Then Judah said to Tamar his daughter-in-law, "Remain a widow in your father's house till my son Shelah is grown." For he said, "Lest he also die like his brothers." And Tamar went and dwelt in her father's house.

¹²Now in the process of time the daughter of Shua, Judah's wife, died; and Judah was comforted, and went up to his sheepshearers at Timnah, he and his friend Hirah the Adullamite. ¹³And it was told Tamar, saying, "Look, your father-in-law is going up to Timnah to shear his sheep." ¹⁴So she took off her widow's garments, covered *herself* with a veil and wrapped herself, and sat in an open place which *was* on the way to Timnah; for she saw that Shelah was grown, and she was not given to him as a wife. ¹⁵When Judah saw her, he thought she *was* a harlot, because she had covered her face. ¹⁶Then he turned to her by the way, and said, "Please let me come in to you"; for he did not know that she *was* his daughter-in-law.

So she said, "What will you give me, that you may come in to me?"

¹⁷And he said, "I will send a young goat from the flock."

So she said, "Will you give *me* a pledge till you send *it?*"

¹⁸Then he said, "What pledge shall I give you?"

So she said, "Your signet and cord, and your staff that *is* in your hand." Then he gave *them* to her, and went in to her, and she conceived by him. ¹⁹So she arose and went away, and laid aside her veil and put on the garments of her widowhood.

²⁰And Judah sent the young goat by the hand of his friend the Adullamite, to receive *his* pledge from the woman's hand, but he did not find her. ²¹Then he asked the men of that place, saying, "Where is the harlot who *was* openly by the roadside?"

And they said, "There was no harlot in this *place.*"

²²So he returned to Judah and said, "I cannot find her. Also, the men of the place said there was no harlot in this *place.*"

²³Then Judah said, "Let her take *them* for herself, lest we be shamed;

for I sent this young goat and you have not found her."

²⁴And it came to pass, about three months after, that Judah was told, saying, "Tamar your daughter-in-law has played the harlot; furthermore she *is* with child by harlotry."

So Judah said, "Bring her out and let her be burned!"

²⁵When she *was* brought out, she sent to her father-in-law, saying, "By the man to whom these belong, I *am* with child." And she said, "Please determine whose these *are*—the signet and cord, and staff."

²⁶So Judah acknowledged *them* and said, "She has been more righteous than I, because I did not give her to Shelah my son." And he never knew her again.

²⁷Now it came to pass, at the time for giving birth, that behold, twins *were* in her womb. ²⁸And so it was, when she was giving birth, that *the one* put out *his* hand; and the midwife took a scarlet *thread* and bound it on his hand, saying, "This one came out first." ²⁹Then it happened, as he drew back his hand, that his brother came out unexpectedly; and she said, "How did you break through? *This* breach *be* upon you!" Therefore his name was called Perez.* ³⁰Afterward his brother came out who had the scarlet *thread* on his hand. And his name was called Zerah.

MATTHEW 12:22-45

THEN one was brought to Him [Jesus] who was demon-possessed, blind and mute; and He healed him, so that the blind and* mute man both spoke and saw. ²³And all the multitudes were amazed and said, "Could this be the Son of David?"

²⁴Now when the Pharisees heard *it* they said, "This *fellow* does not cast out demons except by Beelzebub,* the ruler of the demons."

²⁵But Jesus knew their thoughts, and

said to them: "Every kingdom divided against itself is brought to desolation, and every city or house divided against itself will not stand. 26If Satan casts out Satan, he is divided against himself. How then will his kingdom stand? 27And if I cast out demons by Beelzebub, by whom do your sons cast *them* out? Therefore they shall be your judges. 28But if I cast out demons by the Spirit of God, surely the kingdom of God has come upon you. 29Or how can one enter a strong man's house and plunder his goods, unless he first binds the strong man? And then he will plunder his house. 30He who is not with Me is against Me, and he who does not gather with Me scatters abroad.

31"Therefore I say to you, every sin and blasphemy will be forgiven men, but the blasphemy *against* the Spirit will not be forgiven men. 32Anyone who speaks a word against the Son of Man, it will be forgiven him; but whoever speaks against the Holy Spirit, it will not be forgiven him, either in this age or in the *age* to come.

33"Either make the tree good and its fruit good, or else make the tree bad and its fruit bad; for a tree is known by *its* fruit. 34Brood of vipers! How can you, being evil, speak good things? For out of the abundance of the heart the mouth speaks. 35A good man out of the good treasure of his heart* brings forth good things, and an evil man out of the evil treasure brings forth evil things. 36But I say to you that for every idle word men may speak, they will give account of it in the day of judgment. 37For by your words you will be justified, and by your words you will be condemned."

38Then some of the scribes and Pharisees answered, saying, "Teacher, we want to see a sign from You."

39But He answered and said to them, "An evil and adulterous generation seeks after a sign, and no sign will be given to it except the sign of the prophet Jonah. 40For as Jonah was three days and three nights in the belly of the great fish, so will the Son of Man be three days and three nights in the heart of the earth. 41The men of Nineveh will rise up in the judgment with this generation and condemn it, because they repented at the preaching of Jonah; and indeed a greater than Jonah *is* here. 42The queen of the South will rise up in the judgment with this generation and condemn it, for she came from the ends of the earth to hear the wisdom of Solomon; and indeed a greater than Solomon *is* here.

43"When an unclean spirit goes out of a man, he goes through dry places, seeking rest, and finds none. 44Then he says, 'I will return to my house from which I came.' And when he comes, he finds *it* empty, swept, and put in order. 45Then he goes and takes with him seven other spirits more wicked than himself, and they enter and dwell there; and the last *state* of that man is worse than the first. So shall it also be with this wicked generation."

PSALM 16:1-11

A Michtam of David.

PRESERVE me, O God, for in You I put my trust.

2   *O my soul,* you have said to
         the LORD,
     "You *are* my Lord,
       My goodness is nothing apart
         from You."
3   As for the saints who *are* on
         the earth,
     "They are the excellent ones,
         in whom is all my delight."

4   Their sorrows shall be
         multiplied who hasten *after*
         another *god;*
     Their drink offerings of blood
         I will not offer,

Nor take up their names on
my lips.

5   O Lord, *You are* the portion of
my inheritance and my cup;
You maintain my lot.
6   The lines have fallen to me in
pleasant *places;*
Yes, I have a good inheritance.

7   I will bless the Lord who has
given me counsel;
My heart also instructs me in
the night seasons.
8   I have set the Lord always
before me;

Because *He is* at my right
hand I shall not be moved.

9   Therefore my heart is glad,
and my glory rejoices;
My flesh also will rest in hope.
10 For You will not leave my soul
in Sheol,
Nor will You allow Your Holy
One to see corruption.
11 You will show me the path of
life;
In Your presence *is* fullness of
joy;
At Your right hand *are*
pleasures forevermore.

PROVERBS FOR TODAY/ 3:27-32

*Do not withhold good from those to whom it is due, when it is in the power of your
hand to do so. Do not say to your neighbor, "Go, and come back, and tomorrow I
will give it," when you have it with you. □Do not devise evil against your neighbor,
for he dwells by you for safety's sake. Do not strive with a man without cause, if he
has done you no harm. □Do not envy the oppressor, and choose none of his ways;
for the perverse person is an abomination to the Lord, but His secret counsel is
with the upright.*

JANUARY 19

GENESIS 39:1–41:16

Now Joseph had been taken
down to Egypt. And Potiphar,
an officer of Pharaoh, captain
of the guard, an Egyptian, bought him
from the Ishmaelites who had taken
him down there. [2]The Lord was with
Joseph, and he was a successful man;
and he was in the house of his master
the Egyptian. [3]And his master saw that
the Lord *was* with him and that the
Lord made all he did to prosper in his
hand. [4]So Joseph found favor in his
sight, and served him. Then he made
him overseer of his house, and all *that*
he had he put under his authority. [5]So

it was, from the time *that* he had made
him overseer of his house and all that
he had, that the Lord blessed the
Egyptian's house for Joseph's sake;
and the blessing of the Lord was on all
that he had in the house and in the
field. [6]Thus he left all that he had in
Joseph's hand, and he did not know
what he had except for the bread
which he ate.

Now Joseph was handsome in form
and appearance.

[7]And it came to pass after these
things that his master's wife cast longing eyes on Joseph, and she said, "Lie
with me."

[8]But he refused and said to his mas-

ter's wife, "Look, my master does not know what *is* with me in the house, and he has committed all that he has to my hand. ⁹*There is* no one greater in this house than I, nor has he kept back anything from me but you, because you *are* his wife. How then can I do this great wickedness, and sin against God?"

¹⁰So it was, as she spoke to Joseph day by day, that he did not heed her, to lie with her *or* to be with her.

¹¹But it happened about this time, when Joseph went into the house to do his work, and none of the men of the house *was* inside, ¹²that she caught him by his garment, saying, "Lie with me." But he left his garment in her hand, and fled and ran outside. ¹³And so it was, when she saw that he had left his garment in her hand and fled outside, ¹⁴that she called to the men of her house and spoke to them, saying, "See, he has brought in to us a Hebrew to mock us. He came in to me to lie with me, and I cried out with a loud voice. ¹⁵And it happened, when he heard that I lifted my voice and cried out, that he left his garment with me, and fled and went outside."

¹⁶So she kept his garment with her until his master came home. ¹⁷Then she spoke to him with words like these, saying, "The Hebrew servant whom you brought to us came in to me to mock me; ¹⁸so it happened, as I lifted my voice and cried out, that he left his garment with me and fled outside."

¹⁹So it was, when his master heard the words which his wife spoke to him, saying, "Your servant did to me after this manner," that his anger was aroused. ²⁰Then Joseph's master took him and put him into the prison, a place where the king's prisoners *were* confined. And he was there in the prison. ²¹But the LORD was with Joseph and showed him mercy, and He gave him favor in the sight of the keeper of the prison. ²²And the keeper of the prison committed to Joseph's hand all the prisoners who *were* in the prison; whatever they did there, it was his doing. ²³The keeper of the prison did not look into anything *that was* under *Joseph's* authority,* because the LORD was with him; and whatever he did, the LORD made *it* prosper.

IT came to pass after these things *that* the butler and the baker of the king of Egypt offended their lord, the king of Egypt. ²And Pharaoh was angry with his two officers, the chief butler and the chief baker. ³So he put them in custody in the house of the captain of the guard, in the prison, the place where Joseph *was* confined. ⁴And the captain of the guard charged Joseph with them, and he served them; so they were in custody for a while.

⁵Then the butler and the baker of the king of Egypt, who *were* confined in the prison, had a dream, both of them, each man's dream in one night *and* each man's dream with its *own* interpretation. ⁶And Joseph came in to them in the morning and looked at them, and saw that they *were* sad. ⁷So he asked Pharaoh's officers who *were* with him in the custody of his lord's house, saying, "Why do you look *so* sad today?"

⁸And they said to him, "We each have had a dream, and *there is* no interpreter of it."

So Joseph said to them, "Do not interpretations belong to God? Tell *them* to me, please."

⁹Then the chief butler told his dream to Joseph, and said to him, "Behold, in my dream a vine *was* before me, ¹⁰and in the vine *were* three branches; it *was* as though it budded, its blossoms shot forth, and its clusters brought forth ripe grapes. ¹¹Then Pharaoh's cup *was* in my hand; and I took the grapes and pressed them into Pharaoh's cup, and placed the cup in Pharaoh's hand."

¹²And Joseph said to him, "This *is*

the interpretation of it: The three branches *are* three days. 13Now within three days Pharaoh will lift up your head and restore you to your place, and you will put Pharaoh's cup in his hand according to the former manner, when you were his butler. 14But remember me when it is well with you, and please show kindness to me; make mention of me to Pharaoh, and get me out of this house. 15For indeed I was stolen away from the land of the Hebrews; and also I have done nothing here that they should put me into the dungeon."

16When the chief baker saw that the interpretation was good, he said to Joseph, "I also *was* in my dream, and there *were* three white baskets on my head. 17In the uppermost basket *were* all kinds of baked goods for Pharaoh, and the birds ate them out of the basket on my head."

18So Joseph answered and said, "This *is* the interpretation of it: The three baskets *are* three days. 19Within three days Pharaoh will lift off your head from you and hang you on a tree; and the birds will eat your flesh from you."

20Now it came to pass on the third day, *which was* Pharaoh's birthday, that he made a feast for all his servants; and he lifted up the head of the chief butler and of the chief baker among his servants. 21Then he restored the chief butler to his butlership again, and he placed the cup in Pharaoh's hand. 22But he hanged the chief baker, as Joseph had interpreted to them. 23Yet the chief butler did not remember Joseph, but forgot him.

THEN it came to pass, at the end of two full years, that Pharaoh had a dream; and behold, he stood by the river. 2Suddenly there came up out of the river seven cows, fine looking and fat; and they fed in the meadow. 3Then behold, seven other cows came up after them out of the river, ugly and gaunt, and stood by the *other* cows on the bank of the river. 4And the ugly and gaunt cows ate up the seven fine looking and fat cows. So Pharaoh awoke. 5He slept and dreamed a second time; and suddenly seven heads of grain came up on one stalk, plump and good. 6Then behold, seven thin heads, blighted by the east wind, sprang up after them. 7And the seven thin heads devoured the seven plump and full heads. So Pharaoh awoke, and indeed, *it was* a dream. 8Now it came to pass in the morning that his spirit was troubled, and he sent and called for all the magicians of Egypt and all its wise men. And Pharaoh told them his dreams, but *there was* no one who could interpret them for Pharaoh.

9Then the chief butler spoke to Pharaoh, saying: "I remember my faults this day. 10When Pharaoh was angry with his servants, and put me in custody in the house of the captain of the guard, *both* me and the chief baker, 11we each had a dream in one night, he and I. Each of us dreamed according to the interpretation of his *own* dream. 12Now there *was* a young Hebrew man with us there, a servant of the captain of the guard. And we told him, and he interpreted our dreams for us; to each man he interpreted according to his *own* dream. 13And it came to pass, just as he interpreted for us, so it happened. He restored me to my office, and he hanged him."

14Then Pharaoh sent and called Joseph, and they brought him quickly out of the dungeon; and he shaved, changed his clothing, and came to Pharaoh. 15And Pharaoh said to Joseph, "I have had a dream, and *there is* no one who can interpret it. But I have heard it said of you *that* you can understand a dream, to interpret it."

16So Joseph answered Pharaoh, saying, *"It is* not in me; God will give Pharaoh an answer of peace."

MATTHEW 12:46–13:23

WHILE He [Jesus] was still talking to the multitudes, behold, His mother and brothers stood outside, seeking to speak with Him. 47Then one said to Him, "Look, Your mother and Your brothers are standing outside, seeking to speak with You."

48But He answered and said to the one who told Him, "Who is My mother and who are My brothers?" 49And He stretched out His hand toward His disciples and said, "Here are My mother and My brothers! 50For whoever does the will of My Father in heaven is My brother and sister and mother."

On the same day Jesus went out of the house and sat by the sea. 2And great multitudes were gathered together to Him, so that He got into a boat and sat; and the whole multitude stood on the shore.

3Then He spoke many things to them in parables, saying: "Behold, a sower went out to sow. 4And as he sowed, some *seed* fell by the wayside; and the birds came and devoured them. 5Some fell on stony places, where they did not have much earth; and they immediately sprang up because they had no depth of earth. 6But when the sun was up they were scorched, and because they had no root they withered away. 7And some fell among thorns, and the thorns sprang up and choked them. 8But others fell on good ground and yielded a crop: some a hundredfold, some sixty, some thirty. 9He who has ears to hear, let him hear!"

10And the disciples came and said to Him, "Why do You speak to them in parables?"

11He answered and said to them, "Because it has been given to you to know the mysteries of the kingdom of heaven, but to them it has not been given. 12For whoever has, to him more will be given, and he will have abundance; but whoever does not have, even what he has will be taken away from him. 13Therefore I speak to them in parables, because seeing they do not see, and hearing they do not hear, nor do they understand. 14And in them the prophecy of Isaiah is fulfilled, which says:

> 'Hearing you will hear and
>   shall not understand,
> And seeing you will see and
>   not perceive;
> 15 For the hearts of this people
>   have grown dull.
> Their ears are hard of hearing,
> And their eyes they have
>   closed,
> Lest they should see with
>   their eyes and hear with
>   their ears,
> Lest they should understand
>   with their hearts and turn,
> So that I should* heal them.'*

16But blessed *are* your eyes for they see, and your ears for they hear; 17for assuredly, I say to you that many prophets and righteous *men* desired to see what you see, and did not see *it,* and to hear what you hear, and did not hear *it.*

18"Therefore hear the parable of the sower: 19When anyone hears the word of the kingdom, and does not understand *it,* then the wicked *one* comes and snatches away what was sown in his heart. This is he who received seed by the wayside. 20But he who received the seed on stony places, this is he who hears the word and immediately receives it with joy; 21yet he has no root in himself, but endures only for a while. For when tribulation or persecution arises because of the word, immediately he stumbles. 22Now he who received seed among the thorns is he who hears the word, and the cares of this world and the deceitfulness of riches choke the word, and he becomes unfruitful. ²³But he who received seed on the good ground is he who hears the word and understands *it,* who indeed bears fruit and produces: some a hundredfold, some sixty, some thirty."

PSALM 17:1-15

A Prayer of David.

H EAR a just cause, O LORD,
Attend to my cry;
Give ear to my prayer *which is* not from deceitful lips.

2   Let my vindication come from
    Your presence;
    Let Your eyes look on the
    things that are upright.

3   You have tested my heart;
    You have visited *me* in the
    night;
    You have tried me and have
    found nothing;
    I have purposed that my
    mouth shall not transgress.
4   Concerning the works of men,
    By the word of Your lips,
    I have kept away from the
    paths of the destroyer.
5   Uphold my steps in Your
    paths,
    That my footsteps may not
    slip.

6   I have called upon You, for
    You will hear me, O God;
    Incline Your ear to me, *and*
    hear my speech.
7   Show Your marvelous
    lovingkindness by Your
    right hand,
    O You who save those who
    trust *in You*

From those who rise up
    against them.
8   Keep me as the apple of Your
    eye;
    Hide me under the shadow of
    Your wings,
9   From the wicked who
    oppress me,
    From my deadly enemies who
    surround me.

10   They have closed up their fat
     hearts;
     With their mouths they speak
     proudly.
11   They have now surrounded
     us in our steps;
     They have set their eyes,
     crouching down to the
     earth,
12   As a lion is eager to tear his
     prey,
     And like a young lion lurking
     in secret places.

13   Arise, O LORD,
     Confront him, cast him down;
     Deliver my life from the
     wicked with Your sword,
14   With Your hand from men,
     O LORD,
     From men of the world *who
     have* their portion in *this* life,
     And whose belly You fill with
     Your hidden treasure.
     They are satisfied with
     children,
     And leave the rest of their
     possession for their babes.

15   As for me, I will see Your face
     in righteousness;
     I shall be satisfied when I
     awake in Your likeness.

PROVERBS FOR TODAY/ 3:33-35

The curse of the LORD *is on the house of the wicked, but He blesses the home of the just. Surely He scorns the scornful, but gives grace to the humble. The wise shall inherit glory, but shame shall be the legacy of fools.*

JANUARY 20

GENESIS 41:17–42:17

THEN Pharaoh said to Joseph: "Behold, in my dream I stood on the bank of the river. 18Suddenly seven cows came up out of the river, fine looking and fat; and they fed in the meadow. 19Then behold, seven other cows came up after them, poor and very ugly and gaunt, such ugliness as I have never seen in all the land of Egypt. 20And the gaunt and ugly cows ate up the first seven, the fat cows. 21When they had eaten them up, no one would have known that they had eaten them, for they *were* just as ugly as at the beginning. So I awoke. 22Also I saw in my dream, and suddenly seven heads came up on one stalk, full and good. 23Then behold, seven heads, withered, thin, *and* blighted by the east wind, sprang up after them. 24And the thin heads devoured the seven good heads. So I told *this* to the magicians, but *there was* no one who could explain *it* to me."

25Then Joseph said to Pharaoh, "The dreams of Pharaoh *are* one; God has shown Pharaoh what He *is* about to do: 26The seven good cows *are* seven years, and the seven good heads *are* seven years; the dreams *are* one. 27And the seven thin and ugly cows which came up after them *are* seven years, and the seven empty heads blighted by the east wind are seven years of famine. 28This *is* the thing which I have spoken to Pharaoh. God has shown Pharaoh what He *is* about to do. 29Indeed seven years of great plenty will come throughout all the land of Egypt; 30but after them seven years of famine will arise, and all the plenty will be forgotten in the land of Egypt; and the famine will deplete the land. 31So the plenty will not be known in the land because of the famine following, for it *will be* very severe. 32And the dream was repeated to Pharaoh twice because the thing *is* established by God, and God will shortly bring it to pass.

33"Now therefore, let Pharaoh select a discerning and wise man, and set him over the land of Egypt. 34Let Pharaoh do *this,* and let him appoint officers over the land, to collect one-fifth *of the produce* of the land of Egypt in the seven plentiful years. 35And let them gather all the food of those good years that are coming, and store up grain under the authority of Pharaoh, and let them keep food in the cities. 36Then that food shall be as a reserve for the land for the seven years of famine which shall be in the land of Egypt, that the land may not perish during the famine."

37So the advice was good in the eyes of Pharaoh and in the eyes of all his servants. 38And Pharaoh said to his servants, "Can we find *such a one* as this, a man in whom *is* the Spirit of God?"

39Then Pharaoh said to Joseph, "Inasmuch as God has shown you all this, *there is* no one as discerning and wise as you. 40You shall be over my house, and all my people shall be ruled according to your word; only in regard to the throne will I be greater than you."

⁴¹And Pharaoh said to Joseph, "See, I have set you over all the land of Egypt."

⁴²Then Pharaoh took his signet ring off his hand and put it on Joseph's hand; and he clothed him in garments of fine linen and put a gold chain around his neck. ⁴³And he had him ride in the second chariot which he had; and they cried out before him, "Bow the knee!" So he set him over all the land of Egypt. ⁴⁴Pharaoh also said to Joseph, "I *am* Pharaoh, and without your consent no man may lift his hand or foot in all the land of Egypt." ⁴⁵And Pharaoh called Joseph's name Zaphnath-Paaneah. And he gave him as a wife Asenath, the daughter of Poti-Pherah priest of On. So Joseph went out over *all* the land of Egypt.

⁴⁶Joseph was thirty years old when he stood before Pharaoh king of Egypt. And Joseph went out from the presence of Pharaoh, and went throughout all the land of Egypt. ⁴⁷Now in the seven plentiful years the ground brought forth abundantly. ⁴⁸So he gathered up all the food of the seven years which were in the land of Egypt, and laid up the food in the cities; he laid up in every city the food of the fields which surrounded them. ⁴⁹Joseph gathered very much grain, as the sand of the sea, until he stopped counting, for *it was* immeasurable.

⁵⁰And to Joseph were born two sons before the years of famine came, whom Asenath, the daughter of Poti-Pherah priest of On, bore to him. ⁵¹Joseph called the name of the firstborn Manasseh:* "For God has made me forget all my toil and all my father's house." ⁵²And the name of the second he called Ephraim:* "For God has caused me to be fruitful in the land of my affliction."

⁵³Then the seven years of plenty which were in the land of Egypt ended, ⁵⁴and the seven years of famine began to come, as Joseph had said. The famine was in all lands, but in all the land of Egypt there was bread. ⁵⁵So when all the land of Egypt was famished, the people cried to Pharaoh for bread. Then Pharaoh said to all the Egyptians, "Go to Joseph; whatever he says to you, do." ⁵⁶The famine was over all the face of the earth, and Joseph opened all the storehouses* and sold to the Egyptians. And the famine became severe in the land of Egypt. ⁵⁷So all countries came to Joseph in Egypt to buy *grain,* because the famine was severe in all lands.

WHEN Jacob saw that there was grain in Egypt, Jacob said to his sons, "Why do you look at one another?" ²And he said, "Indeed I have heard that there is grain in Egypt; go down to that place and buy for us there, that we may live and not die."

³So Joseph's ten brothers went down to buy grain in Egypt. ⁴But Jacob did not send Joseph's brother Benjamin with his brothers, for he said, "Lest some calamity befall him." ⁵And the sons of Israel went to buy *grain* among those who journeyed, for the famine was in the land of Canaan.

⁶Now Joseph *was* governor over the land; and it was he who sold to all the people of the land. And Joseph's brothers came and bowed down before him with *their* faces to the earth. ⁷Joseph saw his brothers and recognized them, but he acted as a stranger to them and spoke roughly to them. Then he said to them, "Where do you come from?"

And they said, "From the land of Canaan to buy food."

⁸So Joseph recognized his brothers, but they did not recognize him. ⁹Then Joseph remembered the dreams which he had dreamed about them, and said to them, "You *are* spies! You

have come to see the nakedness of the land!"

¹⁰And they said to him, "No, my lord, but your servants have come to buy food. ¹¹We *are* all one man's sons; we *are* honest *men;* your servants are not spies."

¹²But he said to them, "No, but you have come to see the nakedness of the land."

¹³And they said, "Your servants *are* twelve brothers, the sons of one man in the land of Canaan; and in fact, the youngest *is* with our father today, and one *is* no more."

¹⁴But Joseph said to them, "It *is* as I spoke to you, saying, 'You *are* spies!' ¹⁵In this *manner* you shall be tested: By the life of Pharaoh, you shall not leave this place unless your youngest brother comes here. ¹⁶Send one of you, and let him bring your brother; and you shall be kept in prison, that your words may be tested to see whether *there is* any truth in you; or else, by the life of Pharaoh, surely you *are* spies!" ¹⁷So he put them all together in prison three days.

MATTHEW 13:24-46

ANOTHER parable He [Jesus] put forth to them, saying: "The kingdom of heaven is like a man who sowed good seed in his field; ²⁵but while men slept, his enemy came and sowed tares among the wheat and went his way. ²⁶But when the grain had sprouted and produced a crop, then the tares also appeared. ²⁷So the servants of the owner came and said to him, 'Sir, did you not sow good seed in your field? How then does it have tares?' ²⁸He said to them, 'An enemy has done this.' The servants said to him, 'Do you want us then to go and gather them up?' ²⁹But he said, 'No, lest while you gather up the tares you also uproot the wheat with them. ³⁰Let both grow together until the harvest, and at the time of harvest I will say to the reapers, "First gather together the tares and bind them in bundles to burn them, but gather the wheat into my barn." ' "

³¹Another parable He put forth to them, saying: "The kingdom of heaven is like a mustard seed, which a man took and sowed in his field, ³²which indeed is the least of all the seeds; but when it is grown it is greater than the herbs and becomes a tree, so that the birds of the air come and nest in its branches."

³³Another parable He spoke to them: "The kingdom of heaven is like leaven, which a woman took and hid in three measures* of meal till it was all leavened."

³⁴All these things Jesus spoke to the multitude in parables; and without a parable He did not speak to them, ³⁵that it might be fulfilled which was spoken by the prophet, saying:

> "*I will open My mouth in parables;
> I will utter things kept secret from the foundation of the world.*"*

³⁶Then Jesus sent the multitude away and went into the house. And His disciples came to Him, saying, "Explain to us the parable of the tares of the field."

³⁷He answered and said to them: "He who sows the good seed is the Son of Man. ³⁸The field is the world, the good seeds are the sons of the kingdom, but the tares are the sons of the wicked *one*. ³⁹The enemy who sowed them is the devil, the harvest is the end of the age, and the reapers are the angels. ⁴⁰Therefore as the tares are gathered and burned in the fire, so it will be at the end of this age. ⁴¹The Son of Man will send out His angels, and they will gather out of His king-

dom all things that offend, and those who practice lawlessness, 42and will cast them into the furnace of fire. There will be wailing and gnashing of teeth. 43Then the righteous will shine forth as the sun in the kingdom of their Father. He who has ears to hear, let him hear!

44"Again, the kingdom of heaven is like treasure hidden in a field, which a man found and hid; and for joy over it he goes and sells all that he has and buys that field.

45"Again, the kingdom of heaven is like a merchant seeking beautiful pearls, 46who, when he had found one pearl of great price, went and sold all that he had and bought it.

PSALM 18:1-15

To the Chief Musician. A Psalm of David the servant of the LORD, who spoke to the LORD the words of this song on the day that the LORD delivered him from the hand of all his enemies and from the hand of Saul. And he said:

I WILL love You, O LORD, my strength.
2The LORD is my rock and my fortress and my deliverer;
My God, my strength, in whom I will trust;
My shield and the horn of my salvation, my stronghold.

3 I will call upon the LORD, *who is worthy* to be praised;
So shall I be saved from my enemies.

4 The pangs of death surrounded me,
And the floods of ungodliness made me afraid.

5 The sorrows of Sheol surrounded me;
The snares of death confronted me.

6 In my distress I called upon the LORD,
And cried out to my God;

He heard my voice from His temple,
And my cry came before Him, *even* to His ears.

7 Then the earth shook and trembled;
The foundations of the hills also quaked and were shaken,
Because He was angry.

8 Smoke went up from His nostrils,
And devouring fire from His mouth;
Coals were kindled by it.

9 He bowed the heavens also, and came down
With darkness under His feet.

10 And He rode upon a cherub, and flew;
He flew upon the wings of the wind.

11 He made darkness His secret place;
His canopy around Him *was* dark waters
And thick clouds of the skies.

12 From the brightness before Him,
His thick clouds passed with hailstones and coals of fire.

13 The LORD thundered from heaven,
And the Most High uttered His voice,
Hailstones and coals of fire.*

14 He sent out His arrows and scattered the foe,
Lightnings in abundance, and He vanquished them.

15 Then the channels of the sea were seen,
The foundations of the world were uncovered
At Your rebuke, O LORD,
At the blast of the breath of Your nostrils.

PROVERBS FOR TODAY / 4:1-6

Hear, my children, the instruction of a father, and give attention to know understanding; for I give you good doctrine: Do not forsake my law. When I was my father's son, tender and the only one in the sight of my mother, he also taught me, and said to me: "Let your heart retain my words; keep my commands, and live. Get wisdom! Get understanding! Do not forget, nor turn away from the words of my mouth. Do not forsake her, and she will preserve you; love her, and she will keep you."

JANUARY 21

GENESIS 42:18–43:34

THEN Joseph said to them [his brothers] the third day, "Do this and live, *for* I fear God; ¹⁹If you *are* honest *men,* let one of your brothers be confined to your prison house; but you, go and carry grain for the famine of your houses. ²⁰And bring your youngest brother to me; so your words will be verified, and you shall not die."

And they did so. ²¹Then they said to one another, "We *are* truly guilty concerning our brother, for we saw the anguish of his soul when he pleaded with us, and we would not hear; therefore this distress has come upon us."

²²And Reuben answered them, saying, "Did I not speak to you, saying, 'Do not sin against the boy'; and you would not listen? Therefore behold, his blood is now required of us." ²³But they did not know that Joseph understood *them,* for he spoke to them through an interpreter. ²⁴And he turned himself away from them and wept. Then he returned to them again, and talked with them. And he took Simeon from them and bound him before their eyes.

²⁵Then Joseph gave a command to fill their sacks with grain, to restore every man's money to his sack, and to give them provisions for the journey. Thus he did for them. ²⁶So they loaded their donkeys with the grain and departed from there. ²⁷But as one *of them* opened his sack to give his donkey feed at the encampment, he saw his money; and there it was, in the mouth of his sack. ²⁸So he said to his brothers, "My money has been restored, and there it is, in my sack!" Then their hearts failed *them* and they were afraid, saying to one another, "What *is* this *that* God has done to us?"

²⁹Then they went to Jacob their father in the land of Canaan and told him all that had happened to them, saying: ³⁰"The man *who is* lord of the land spoke roughly to us, and took us for spies of the country. ³¹But we said to him, 'We *are* honest *men;* we are not spies. ³²We *are* twelve brothers, sons of our father; one *is* no *more,* and the youngest *is* with our father this day in the land of Canaan.' ³³Then the man, the lord of the country, said to us, 'By this I will know that you *are* honest *men:* Leave one of your brothers *here* with me, take *food for* the famine of your households, and be gone. ³⁴And bring your youngest brother to me; so I shall know that you *are* not spies, but *that* you *are* honest *men.* I will grant your brother to you, and you may trade in the land.' "

³⁵Then it happened as they emptied their sacks, that surprisingly each

man's bundle of money *was* in his sack; and when they and their father saw the bundles of money, they were afraid. 36And Jacob their father said to them, "You have bereaved me: Joseph is no *more,* Simeon is no *more,* and you want to take Benjamin. All these things are against me."

37Then Reuben spoke to his father, saying, "Kill my two sons if I do not bring him *back* to you; put him in my hands, and I will bring him back to you."

38But he said, "My son shall not go down with you, for his brother is dead, and he is left alone. If any calamity should befall him along the way in which you go, then you would bring down my gray hair with sorrow to the grave."

Now the famine *was* severe in the land. 2And it came to pass, when they had eaten up the grain which they had brought from Egypt, that their father said to them, "Go back, buy us a little food."

3But Judah spoke to him, saying, "The man solemnly warned us, saying, 'You shall not see my face unless your brother *is* with you.' 4If you send our brother with us, we will go down and buy you food. 5But if you will not send *him,* we will not go down; for the man said to us, 'You shall not see my face unless your brother *is* with you.' "

6And Israel said, "Why did you deal *so* wrongfully with me *as* to tell the man whether you had still *another* brother?"

7But they said, "The man asked us pointedly about ourselves and our family, saying, '*Is* your father still alive? Have you *another* brother?' And we told him according to these words. Could we possibly have known that he would say, 'Bring your brother down'?"

8Then Judah said to Israel his father, "Send the lad with me, and we will arise and go, that we may live and not die, both we and you *and* also our little ones. 9I myself will be surety for him; from my hand you shall require him. If I do not bring him *back* to you and set him before you, then let me bear the blame forever. 10For if we had not lingered, surely by now we would have returned this second time."

11And their father Israel said to them, "If *it must be* so, then do this: Take some of the best fruits of the land in your vessels and carry down a present for the man—a little balm and a little honey, spices and myrrh, pistachio nuts and almonds. 12Take double money in your hand, and take back in your hand the money that was returned in the mouth of your sacks; perhaps it was an oversight. 13Take your brother also, and arise, go back to the man. 14And may God Almighty give you mercy before the man, that he may release your other brother and Benjamin. If I am bereaved, I am bereaved!"

15So the men took that present and Benjamin, and they took double money in their hand, and arose and went down to Egypt; and they stood before Joseph. 16When Joseph saw Benjamin with them, he said to the steward of his house, "Take *these* men to my home, and slaughter an animal and make ready; for *these* men will dine with me at noon." 17Then the man did as Joseph ordered, and the man brought the men into Joseph's house.

18Now the men were afraid because they were brought into Joseph's house; and they said, "*It is* because of the money, which was returned in our sacks the first time, that we are brought in, so that he may make a case against us and seize us, to take us as slaves with our donkeys."

19When they drew near to the steward of Joseph's house, they talked with him at the door of the house, 20and said, "O sir, we indeed came down the first time to buy food; 21but it happened, when we came to the encampment, that we opened our sacks, and there, *each* man's money *was* in the mouth of his sack, our money in full weight; so we have brought it back in our hand. 22And we have brought down other money in our hands to buy food. We do not know who put our money in our sacks."

23But he said, "Peace *be* with you, do not be afraid. Your God and the God of your father has given you treasure in your sacks; I had your money." Then he brought Simeon out to them.

24So the man brought the men into Joseph's house and gave *them* water, and they washed their feet; and he gave their donkeys feed. 25Then they made the present ready for Joseph's coming at noon, for they heard that they would eat bread there.

26And when Joseph came home, they brought him the present which *was* in their hand into the house, and bowed down before him to the earth. 27Then he asked them about *their* well-being, and said, "*Is* your father well, the old man of whom you spoke? *Is* he still alive?"

28And they answered, "Your servant our father *is* in good health; he *is* still alive." And they bowed their heads down and prostrated themselves.

29Then he lifted his eyes and saw his brother Benjamin, his mother's son, and said, "*Is* this your younger brother of whom you spoke to me?" And he said, "God be gracious to you, my son." 30Now his heart yearned for his brother; so Joseph made haste and sought *somewhere* to weep. And he went into *his* chamber and wept there. 31Then he washed his face and came out; and he restrained himself, and said, "Serve the bread."

32So they set him a place by himself, and them by themselves, and the Egyptians who ate with him by themselves; because the Egyptians could not eat food with the Hebrews, for that *is* an abomination to the Egyptians. 33And they sat before him, the firstborn according to his birthright and the youngest according to his youth; and the men looked in astonishment at one another. 34Then he took servings to them from before him, but Benjamin's serving was five times as much as any of theirs. So they drank and were merry with him.

MATTHEW 13:47–14:13

"AGAIN, the kingdom of heaven is like a dragnet that was cast into the sea and gathered some of every kind, 48which, when it was full, they drew to shore; and they sat down and gathered the good into vessels, but threw the bad away. 49So it will be at the end of the age. The angels will come forth, separate the wicked from among the just, 50and cast them into the furnace of fire. There will be wailing and gnashing of teeth."

51Jesus said to them,* "Have you understood all these things?"

They said to Him, "Yes, Lord."*

52Then He said to them, "Therefore every scribe instructed concerning* the kingdom of heaven is like a householder who brings out of his treasure *things* new and old."

53Now it came to pass, when Jesus had finished these parables, that He departed from there. 54When He had come to His own country, He taught them in their synagogue, so that they were astonished and said, "Where did this *Man* get this wisdom and *these* mighty works? 55Is this not the carpenter's son? Is not His mother called Mary? And His brothers James, Joses,* Simon, and Judas? 56And His sisters, are they not all with us? Where then did this *Man* get all these things?" 57So they were offended at Him.

But Jesus said to them, "A prophet is not without honor except in his own country and in his own house." 58Now He did not do many mighty works there because of their unbelief.

At that time Herod the tetrarch heard the report about Jesus 2and said to his servants, "This is John the Baptist; he is risen from the dead, and therefore these powers are at work in him." 3For Herod had laid hold of John and bound him, and put *him* in prison for the sake of Herodias, his brother Philip's wife. 4Because John had said to him, "It is not lawful for you to have her." 5And although he wanted to put him to death, he feared the multitude, because they counted him as a prophet.

6But when Herod's birthday was celebrated, the daughter of Herodias danced before them and pleased Herod. 7Therefore he promised with an oath to give her whatever she might ask.

8So she, having been prompted by her mother, said, "Give me John the Baptist's head here on a platter."

9And the king was sorry; nevertheless, because of the oaths and because of those who sat with him, he commanded *it* to be given to *her.* 10So he sent and had John beheaded in prison. 11And his head was brought on a platter and given to the girl, and she brought *it* to her mother. 12Then his disciples came and took away the body and buried it, and went and told Jesus.

13When Jesus heard *it,* He departed from there by boat to a deserted place by Himself. But when the multitudes heard it, they followed Him on foot from the cities.

PSALM 18:16-34

HE sent from above, He took me; He drew me out of many waters.
17 He delivered me from my strong enemy,

From those who hated me,
For they were too strong for me.
18 They confronted me in the day of my calamity,
But the Lord was my support.
19 He also brought me out into a broad place;
He delivered me because He delighted in me.

20 The Lord rewarded me according to my righteousness;
According to the cleanness of my hands
He has recompensed me.
21 For I have kept the ways of the Lord,
And have not wickedly departed from my God.
22 For all His judgments *were* before me,
And I did not put away His statutes from me.
23 I was also blameless before Him,
And I kept myself from my iniquity.
24 Therefore the Lord has recompensed me according to my righteousness,
According to the cleanness of my hands in His sight.

25 With the merciful You will show Yourself merciful;
With a blameless man You will show Yourself blameless;
26 With the pure You will show Yourself pure;
And with the devious You will show Yourself shrewd.
27 For You will save the humble people,
But will bring down haughty looks.
28 For You will light my lamp;

The LORD my God will
enlighten my darkness.
29 For by You I can run against a
troop,
By my God I can leap over a
wall.
30 As for God, His way is perfect;
The word of the LORD is
proven;
He is a shield to all who trust
in Him.

31 For who is God, except the
LORD?

And who is a rock, except our
God?
32 It is God who arms me with
strength,
And makes my way perfect.
33 He makes my feet like the feet
of deer,
And sets me on my high
places.
34 He teaches my hands to make
war,
So that my arms can bend a
bow of bronze.

PROVERBS FOR TODAY / 4:7-10

*"Wisdom is the principal thing; therefore get wisdom. And in all your getting, get
understanding. Exalt her, and she will promote you; she will bring you honor, when
you embrace her. She will place on your head an ornament of grace; a crown of
glory she will deliver to you."* □ *Hear, my son, and receive my sayings, and the
years of your life will be many.*

JANUARY 22

GENESIS 44:1–45:28

AND he [Joseph] commanded
the steward of his house, saying, "Fill the men's sacks with
food, as much as they can carry, and
put each man's money in the mouth of
his sack. 2Also put my cup, the silver
cup, in the mouth of the sack of the
youngest, and his grain money." So he
did according to the word that Joseph
had spoken. 3As soon as the morning
dawned, the men were sent away, they
and their donkeys. 4When they had
gone out of the city, and were not yet
far off, Joseph said to his steward, "Get
up, follow the men; and when you
overtake them, say to them, 'Why
have you repaid evil for good? 5Is not
this the one from which my lord drinks,
and with which he indeed practices

divination? You have done evil in so
doing.' "
6So he overtook them, and he spoke
to them these same words. 7And they
said to him, "Why does my lord say
these words? Far be it from us that
your servants should do such a thing.
8Look, we brought back to you from
the land of Canaan the money which
we found in the mouth of our sacks.
How then could we steal silver or gold
from your lord's house? 9With whomever of your servants it is found, let
him die, and we also will be my lord's
slaves."
10And he said, "Now also let it be according to your words; he with whom
it is found shall be my slave, and you
shall be blameless." 11Then each man
speedily let down his sack to the
ground, and each opened his sack.

¹²So he searched. He began with the oldest and left off with the youngest; and the cup was found in Benjamin's sack. ¹³Then they tore their clothes, and each man loaded his donkey and returned to the city.

¹⁴So Judah and his brothers came to Joseph's house, and he *was* still there; and they fell before him on the ground. ¹⁵And Joseph said to them, "What deed *is* this you have done? Did you not know that such a man as I can certainly practice divination?"

¹⁶Then Judah said, "What shall we say to my lord? What shall we speak? Or how shall we clear ourselves? God has found out the iniquity of your servants; here we are, my lord's slaves, both we and *he* also with whom the cup was found."

¹⁷But he said, "Far be it from me that I should do so; the man in whose hand the cup was found, he shall be my slave. And as for you, go up in peace to your father."

¹⁸Then Judah came near to him and said: "O my lord, please let your servant speak a word in my lord's hearing, and do not let your anger burn against your servant; for you *are* even like Pharaoh. ¹⁹My lord asked his servants, saying, 'Have you a father or a brother?' ²⁰And we said to my lord, 'We have a father, an old man, and a child of *his* old age, *who is* young; his brother is dead, and he alone is left of his mother's children, and his father loves him.' ²¹Then you said to your servants, 'Bring him down to me, that I may set my eyes on him.' ²²And we said to my lord, 'The lad cannot leave his father, for *if* he should leave his father, *his father* would die.' ²³But you said to your servants, 'Unless your youngest brother comes down with you, you shall see my face no more.'

²⁴"So it was, when we went up to your servant my father, that we told him the words of my lord. ²⁵And our father said, 'Go back *and* buy us a little food.' ²⁶But we said, 'We cannot go down; if our youngest brother is with us, then we will go down; for we may not see the man's face unless our youngest brother *is* with us.' ²⁷Then your servant my father said to us, 'You know that my wife bore me two sons; ²⁸and the one went out from me, and I said, "Surely he is torn to pieces"; and I have not seen him since. ²⁹But if you take this one also from me, and calamity befalls him, you shall bring down my gray hair with sorrow to the grave.'

³⁰"Now therefore, when I come to your servant my father, and the lad *is* not with us, since his life is bound up in the lad's life, ³¹it will happen, when he sees that the lad *is* not *with us,* that he will die. So your servants will bring down the gray hair of your servant our father with sorrow to the grave. ³²For your servant became surety for the lad to my father, say-ing, 'If I do not bring him *back* to you, then I shall bear the blame before my father forever.' ³³Now therefore, please let your servant remain instead of the lad as a slave to my lord, and let the lad go up with his brothers. ³⁴For how shall I go up to my father if the lad *is* not with me, lest perhaps I see the evil that would come upon my father?"

THEN Joseph could not restrain himself before all those who stood by him, and he cried out, "Make everyone go out from me!" So no one stood with him while Joseph made himself known to his brothers. ²And he wept aloud, and the Egyptians and the house of Pharaoh heard *it.*

³Then Joseph said to his brothers, "I *am* Joseph; does my father still live?" But his brothers could not answer him, for they were dismayed in his presence. ⁴And Joseph said to his brothers, "Please come near to me." So they came near. Then he said: "I *am* Joseph your brother, whom you sold into Egypt. ⁵But now, do not therefore

be grieved or angry with yourselves because you sold me here; for God sent me before you to preserve life. 6For these two years the famine *has been* in the land, and *there are* still five years in which *there will be* neither plowing nor harvesting. 7And God sent me before you to preserve a posterity for you in the earth, and to save your lives by a great deliverance. 8So now *it was* not you *who* sent me here, but God; and He has made me a father to Pharaoh, and lord of all his house, and a ruler throughout all the land of Egypt.

9"Hurry and go up to my father, and say to him, 'Thus says your son Joseph: "God has made me lord of all Egypt; come down to me, do not tarry. 10You shall dwell in the land of Goshen, and you shall be near to me, you and your children, your children's children, your flocks and your herds, and all that you have. 11There I will provide for you, lest you and your household, and all that you have, come to poverty; for *there are* still five years of famine." '

12"And behold, your eyes and the eyes of my brother Benjamin see that *it is* my mouth that speaks to you. 13So you shall tell my father of all my glory in Egypt, and of all that you have seen; and you shall hurry and bring my father down here."

14Then he fell on his brother Benjamin's neck and wept, and Benjamin wept on his neck. 15Moreover he kissed all his brothers and wept over them, and after that his brothers talked with him.

16Now the report of it was heard in Pharaoh's house, saying, "Joseph's brothers have come." So it pleased Pharaoh and his servants well. 17And Pharaoh said to Joseph, "Say to your brothers, 'Do this: Load your animals and depart; go to the land of Canaan. 18Bring your father and your households and come to me; I will give you the best of the land of Egypt, and you will eat the fat of the land. 19Now you are commanded—do this: Take carts out of the land of Egypt for your little ones and your wives; bring your father and come. 20Also do not be concerned about your goods, for the best of all the land of Egypt *is* yours.' "

21Then the sons of Israel did so; and Joseph gave them carts, according to the command of Pharaoh, and he gave them provisions for the journey. 22He gave to all of them, to each man, changes of garments; but to Benjamin he gave three hundred *pieces* of silver and five changes of garments. 23And he sent to his father these *things:* ten donkeys loaded with the good things of Egypt, and ten female donkeys loaded with grain, bread, and food for his father for the journey. 24So he sent his brothers away, and they departed; and he said to them, "See that you do not become troubled along the way."

25Then they went up out of Egypt, and came to the land of Canaan to Jacob their father. 26And they told him, saying, "Joseph *is* still alive, and he *is* governor over all the land of Egypt." And Jacob's heart stood still, because he did not believe them. 27But when they told him all the words which Joseph had said to them, and when he saw the carts which Joseph had sent to carry him, the spirit of Jacob their father revived. 28Then Israel said, "*It is* enough. Joseph my son *is* still alive. I will go and see him before I die."

MATTHEW 14:14-36

AND when Jesus went out He saw a great multitude; and He was moved with compassion for them, and healed their sick. 15When it was evening, His disciples came to Him, saying, "This is a deserted place, and the hour is already late. Send the multitudes away, that they may go into the villages and buy themselves food."

¹⁶But Jesus said to them, "They do not need to go away. You give them something to eat."

¹⁷And they said to Him, "We have here only five loaves and two fish."

¹⁸He said, "Bring them here to Me." ¹⁹Then He commanded the multitudes to sit down on the grass. And He took the five loaves and the two fish, and looking up to heaven, He blessed and broke and gave the loaves to the disciples; and the disciples gave to the multitudes. ²⁰So they all ate and were filled, and they took up twelve baskets full of the fragments that remained. ²¹Now those who had eaten were about five thousand men, besides women and children.

²²Immediately Jesus made His disciples get into the boat and go before Him to the other side, while He sent the multitudes away. ²³And when He had sent the multitudes away, He went up on the mountain by Himself to pray. Now when evening came, He was alone there. ²⁴But the boat was now in the middle of the sea,* tossed by the waves, for the wind was contrary.

²⁵Now in the fourth watch of the night Jesus went to them, walking on the sea. ²⁶And when the disciples saw Him walking on the sea, they were troubled, saying, "It is a ghost!" And they cried out for fear.

²⁷But immediately Jesus spoke to them, saying, "Be of good cheer! It is I; do not be afraid."

²⁸And Peter answered Him and said, "Lord, if it is You, command me to come to You on the water."

²⁹So He said, "Come." And when Peter had come down out of the boat, he walked on the water to go to Jesus. ³⁰But when he saw that the wind *was* boisterous,* he was afraid; and beginning to sink he cried out, saying, "Lord, save me!"

³¹And immediately Jesus stretched out *His* hand and caught him, and said to him, "O you of little faith, why did you doubt?" ³²And when they got into the boat, the wind ceased.

³³Then those who were in the boat came and* worshiped Him, saying, "Truly You are the Son of God."

³⁴When they had crossed over, they came to the land of* Gennesaret. ³⁵And when the men of that place recognized Him, they sent out into all that surrounding region, brought to Him all who were sick, ³⁶and begged Him that they might only touch the hem of His garment. And as many as touched *it* were made perfectly well.

PSALM 18:35-50

Yᴏᴜ have also given me the shield of Your salvation;
Your right hand has held me up,
Your gentleness has made me great.
36 You enlarged my path under me,
So my feet did not slip.

37 I have pursued my enemies and overtaken them;
Neither did I turn back again till they were destroyed.
38 I have wounded them,
So that they could not rise;
They have fallen under my feet.
39 For You have armed me with strength for the battle;
You have subdued under me those who rose up against me.
40 You have also given me the necks of my enemies,
So that I destroyed those who hated me.
41 They cried out, but *there was* none to save;
Even to the Lᴏʀᴅ, but He did not answer them.
42 Then I beat them as fine as the dust before the wind;

I cast them out like dirt in the
streets.

43 You have delivered me from
the strivings of the people;
You have made me the head
of the nations;
A people I have not known
shall serve me.

44 As soon as they hear of me
they obey me;
The foreigners submit to me.

45 The foreigners fade away,
And come frightened from
their hideouts.

46 The LORD lives!
Blessed be my Rock!
Let the God of my salvation
be exalted.

47 It is God who avenges me,

And subdues the peoples
under me;

48 He delivers me from my
enemies.
You also lift me up above
those who rise against me;
You have delivered me from
the violent man.

49 Therefore I will give thanks to
You, O LORD, among the
Gentiles,
And sing praises to Your
name.

50 Great deliverance He gives to
His king,
And shows mercy to His
anointed,
To David and his descendants
forevermore.

PROVERBS FOR TODAY/ 4:11-13

*I have taught you in the way of wisdom; I have led you in right paths. When you
walk, your steps will not be hindered, and when you run, you will not stumble. Take
firm hold of instruction, do not let go; keep her, for she is your life.*

JANUARY 23

GENESIS 46:1–47:31

So Israel took his journey with all that he had, and came to Beersheba, and offered sacrifices to the God of his father Isaac. ²Then God spoke to Israel in the visions of the night, and said, "Jacob, Jacob!"

And he said, "Here I am."

³So He said, "I *am* God, the God of your father; do not fear to go down to Egypt, for I will make of you a great nation there. ⁴I will go down with you to Egypt, and I will also surely bring you up *again;* and Joseph will put his hand on your eyes."

⁵Then Jacob arose from Beersheba; and the sons of Israel carried their father Jacob, their little ones, and their wives, in the carts which Pharaoh had sent to carry him. ⁶So they took their livestock and their goods, which they had acquired in the land of Canaan, and went to Egypt, Jacob and all his descendants with him. ⁷His sons and his sons' sons, his daughters and his sons' daughters, and all his descendants he brought with him to Egypt.

⁸Now these *were* the names of the children of Israel, Jacob and his sons, who went to Egypt: Reuben *was* Jacob's firstborn. ⁹The sons of Reuben

were Hanoch, Pallu, Hezron, and Carmi. 10The sons of Simeon *were* Jemuel,* Jamin, Ohad, Jachin,* Zohar,* and Shaul, the son of a Canaanite woman. 11The sons of Levi *were* Gershon, Kohath, and Merari. 12The sons of Judah *were* Er, Onan, Shelah, Perez, and Zerah (but Er and Onan died in the land of Canaan). The sons of Perez were Hezron and Hamul. 13The sons of Issachar *were* Tola, Puvah,* Job,* and Shimron. 14The sons of Zebulun *were* Sered, Elon, and Jahleel. 15These *were* the sons of Leah, whom she bore to Jacob in Padan Aram, with his daughter Dinah. All the persons, his sons and his daughters, *were* thirty-three.

16The sons of Gad *were* Ziphion,* Haggi, Shuni, Ezbon,* Eri, Arodi,* and Areli. 17The sons of Asher *were* Jimnah, Ishuah, Isui, Beriah, and Serah, their sister. And the sons of Beriah *were* Heber and Malchiel. 18These *were* the sons of Zilpah, whom Laban gave to Leah his daughter; and these she bore to Jacob: sixteen persons.

19The sons of Rachel, Jacob's wife, *were* Joseph and Benjamin. 20And to Joseph in the land of Egypt were born Manasseh and Ephraim, whom Asenath, the daughter of Poti-Pherah priest of On, bore to him. 21The sons of Benjamin *were* Belah, Becher, Ashbel, Gera, Naaman, Ehi, Rosh, Muppim, Huppim,* and Ard. 22These *were* the sons of Rachel, who were born to Jacob: fourteen persons in all.

23The son of Dan *was* Hushim.* 24The sons of Naphtali *were* Jahzeel,* Guni, Jezer, and Shillem.* 25These *were* the sons of Bilhah, whom Laban gave to Rachel his daughter, and she bore these to Jacob: seven persons in all.

26All the persons who went with Jacob to Egypt, who came from his body, besides Jacob's sons' wives, *were* sixty-six persons in all. 27And the sons of Joseph who were born to him in Egypt *were* two persons. All the persons of the house of Jacob who went to Egypt were seventy.

28Then he sent Judah before him to Joseph, to point out before him *the way* to Goshen. And they came to the land of Goshen. 29So Joseph made ready his chariot and went up to Goshen to meet his father Israel; and he presented himself to him, and fell on his neck and wept on his neck a good while.

30And Israel said to Joseph, "Now let me die, since I have seen your face, because you *are* still alive."

31Then Joseph said to his brothers and to his father's household, "I will go up and tell Pharaoh, and say to him, 'My brothers and those of my father's house, who *were* in the land of Canaan, have come to me. 32And the men *are* shepherds, for their occupation has been to feed livestock; and they have brought their flocks, their herds, and all that they have.' 33So it shall be, when Pharaoh calls you and says, 'What is your occupation?' 34that you shall say, 'Your servants' occupation has been with livestock from our youth even till now, both we *and* also our fathers,' that you may dwell in the land of Goshen; for every shepherd *is* an abomination to the Egyptians."

THEN Joseph went and told Pharaoh, and said, "My father and my brothers, their flocks and their herds and all that they possess, have come from the land of Canaan; and indeed they *are* in the land of Goshen." 2And he took five men from among his brothers and presented them to Pharaoh. 3Then Pharaoh said to his brothers, "What *is* your occupation?"

And they said to Pharaoh, "Your servants *are* shepherds, both we *and* also our fathers." 4And they said to Pharaoh, "We have come to dwell in the land, because your servants have no pasture for their flocks, for the famine *is* severe in the land of Canaan. Now therefore, please let your servants dwell in the land of Goshen."

⁵Then Pharaoh spoke to Joseph, saying, "Your father and your brothers have come to you. ⁶The land of Egypt *is* before you. Have your father and brothers dwell in the best of the land; let them dwell in the land of Goshen. And if you know *any* competent men among them, then make them chief herdsmen over my livestock."

⁷Then Joseph brought in his father Jacob and set him before Pharaoh; and Jacob blessed Pharaoh. ⁸Pharaoh said to Jacob, "How old *are* you?"

⁹And Jacob said to Pharaoh, "The days of the years of my pilgrimage *are* one hundred and thirty years; few and evil have been the days of the years of my life, and they have not attained to the days of the years of the life of my fathers in the days of their pilgrimage." ¹⁰So Jacob blessed Pharaoh, and went out from before Pharaoh.

¹¹And Joseph situated his father and his brothers, and gave them a possession in the land of Egypt, in the best of the land, in the land of Rameses, as Pharaoh had commanded. ¹²Then Joseph provided his father, his brothers, and all his father's household with bread, according to the number in *their* families.

¹³Now *there was* no bread in all the land; for the famine *was* very severe, so that the land of Egypt and the land of Canaan languished because of the famine. ¹⁴And Joseph gathered up all the money that was found in the land of Egypt and in the land of Canaan, for the grain which they bought; and Joseph brought the money into Pharaoh's house.

¹⁵So when the money failed in the land of Egypt and in the land of Canaan, all the Egyptians came to Joseph and said, "Give us bread, for why should we die in your presence? For the money has failed."

¹⁶Then Joseph said, "Give your live-stock, and I will give you *bread* for your livestock, if the money is gone." ¹⁷So they brought their livestock to Joseph, and Joseph gave them bread *in exchange* for the horses, the flocks, the cattle of the herds, and for the donkeys. Thus he fed them with bread *in exchange* for all their livestock that year.

¹⁸When that year had ended, they came to him the next year and said to him, "We will not hide from my lord that our money is gone; my lord also has our herds of livestock. There is nothing left in the sight of my lord but our bodies and our lands. ¹⁹Why should we die before your eyes, both we and our land? Buy us and our land for bread, and we and our land will be servants of Pharaoh; give *us* seed, that we may live and not die, that the land may not be desolate."

²⁰Then Joseph bought all the land of Egypt for Pharaoh; for every man of the Egyptians sold his field, because the famine was severe upon them. So the land became Pharaoh's. ²¹And as for the people, he moved them into the cities,* from *one* end of the borders of Egypt to the *other* end. ²²Only the land of the priests he did not buy; for the priests had rations *allotted to them* by Pharaoh, and they ate their rations which Pharaoh gave them; therefore they did not sell their lands.

²³Then Joseph said to the people, "Indeed I have bought you and your land this day for Pharaoh. Look, *here is* seed for you, and you shall sow the land. ²⁴And it shall come to pass in the harvest that you shall give one-fifth to Pharaoh. Four-fifths shall be your own, as seed for the field and for your food, for those of your households and as food for your little ones."

²⁵So they said, "You have saved our lives; let us find favor in the sight of my lord, and we will be Pharaoh's servants." ²⁶And Joseph made it a law over the land of Egypt to this day, *that* Pharaoh should have one-fifth, except for

the land of the priests only, *which* did not become Pharaoh's.

²⁷So Israel dwelt in the land of Egypt, in the country of Goshen; and they had possessions there and grew and multiplied exceedingly. ²⁸And Jacob lived in the land of Egypt seventeen years. So the length of Jacob's life was one hundred and forty-seven years. ²⁹When the time drew near that Israel must die, he called his son Joseph and said to him, "Now if I have found favor in your sight, please put your hand under my thigh, and deal kindly and truly with me. Please do not bury me in Egypt, ³⁰but let me lie with my fathers; you shall carry me out of Egypt and bury me in their burial place."

And he said, "I will do as you have said."

³¹Then he said, "Swear to me." And he swore to him. So Israel bowed himself on the head of the bed.

MATTHEW 15:1-28

THEN the scribes and Pharisees who were from Jerusalem came to Jesus, saying, ²"Why do Your disciples transgress the tradition of the elders? For they do not wash their hands when they eat bread."

³He answered and said to them, "Why do you also transgress the commandment of God because of your tradition? ⁴For God commanded, saying, *'Honor your father and your mother';** and, *'He who curses father or mother, let him be put to death.'** ⁵But you say, 'Whoever says to his father or mother, "Whatever profit you might have received from me *is* a gift *to God*"— ⁶then he need not honor his father or mother.'* Thus you have made the commandment* of God of no effect by your tradition. ⁷Hypocrites! Well did Isaiah prophesy about you, saying:

⁸   *'These people draw near to*
        Me with their mouth,

And* *honor Me with their lips,*
        But their heart is far from Me.
⁹   *And in vain they worship Me,*
        Teaching as doctrines the
            commandments of men.'*

¹⁰When He had called the multitude to *Himself,* He said to them, "Hear and understand: ¹¹Not what goes into the mouth defiles a man; but what comes out of the mouth, this defiles a man."

¹²Then His disciples came and said to Him, "Do You know that the Pharisees were offended when they heard this saying?"

¹³But He answered and said, "Every plant which My heavenly Father has not planted will be uprooted. ¹⁴Let them alone. They are blind leaders of the blind. And if the blind leads the blind, both will fall into a ditch."

¹⁵Then Peter answered and said to Him, "Explain this parable to us."

¹⁶So Jesus said, "Are you also still without understanding? ¹⁷Do you not yet understand that whatever enters the mouth goes into the stomach and is eliminated? ¹⁸But those things which proceed out of the mouth come from the heart, and they defile a man. ¹⁹For out of the heart proceed evil thoughts, murders, adulteries, fornications, thefts, false witness, blasphemies. ²⁰These are *the things* which defile a man, but to eat with unwashed hands does not defile a man."

²¹Then Jesus went out from there and departed to the region of Tyre and Sidon. ²²And behold, a woman of Canaan came from that region and cried out to Him, saying, "Have mercy on me, O Lord, Son of David! My daughter is severely demon-possessed."

²³But He answered her not a word. And His disciples came and urged Him, saying, "Send her away, for she cries out after us."

²⁴But He answered and said, "I was not sent except to the lost sheep of the house of Israel."

25Then she came and worshiped Him, saying, "Lord, help me!"

26But He answered and said, "It is not good to take the children's bread and throw *it* to the little dogs."

27And she said, "Yes, Lord, yet even the little dogs eat the crumbs which fall from their masters' table."

28Then Jesus answered and said to her, "O woman, great *is* your faith! Let it be to you as you desire." And her daughter was healed from that very hour.

PSALM 19:1-14

To the Chief Musician. A Psalm of David

THE heavens declare the glory of God;
And the firmament shows His handiwork.

2 Day unto day utters speech,
And night unto night reveals knowledge.

3 *There is* no speech nor language
Where their voice is not heard.

4 Their line* has gone out through all the earth,
And their words to the end of the world.

In them He has set a tabernacle for the sun,

5 Which *is* like a bridegroom coming out of his chamber,
And rejoices like a strong man to run its race.

6 Its rising *is* from one end of heaven,
And its circuit to the other end;
And there is nothing hidden from its heat.

7 The law of the LORD *is* perfect, converting the soul;
The testimony of the LORD *is* sure, making wise the simple;

8 The statutes of the LORD *are* right, rejoicing the heart;
The commandment of the LORD *is* pure, enlightening the eyes;

9 The fear of the LORD *is* clean, enduring forever;
The judgments of the LORD *are* true *and* righteous altogether.

10 More to be desired *are they* than gold,
Yea, than much fine gold;
Sweeter also than honey and the honeycomb.

11 Moreover by them Your servant is warned,
And in keeping them *there is* great reward.

12 Who can understand *his* errors?
Cleanse me from secret *faults.*

10 Keep back Your servant also from presumptuous *sins;*
Let them not have dominion over me.
Then I shall be blameless,
And I shall be innocent of great transgression.

14 Let the words of my mouth and the meditation of my heart
Be acceptable in Your sight,
O LORD, my strength and my Redeemer.

PROVERBS FOR TODAY/ 4:14-19

Do not enter the path of the wicked, and do not walk in the way of evil. Avoid it, do not travel on it; turn away from it and pass on. For they do not sleep unless they have done evil; and their sleep is taken away unless they make someone fall. For *they eat the bread of wickedness, and drink the wine of violence. But the path of the just is like the shining sun, * that shines ever brighter unto the perfect day. The way of the wicked is like darkness; they do not know what makes them stumble.*

JANUARY 24

GENESIS 48:1–49:33

Now it came to pass after these things that Joseph was told, "Indeed your father *is* sick"; and he took with him his two sons, Manasseh and Ephraim. ²And Jacob was told, "Look, your son Joseph is coming to you"; and Israel strengthened himself and sat up on the bed. ³Then Jacob said to Joseph: "God Almighty appeared to me at Luz in the land of Canaan and blessed me, ⁴and said to me, 'Behold, I will make you fruitful and multiply you, and I will make of you a multitude of people, and give this land to your descendants after you *as* an everlasting possession.' ⁵And now your two sons, Ephraim and Manasseh, who were born to you in the land of Egypt before I came to you in Egypt, *are* mine; as Reuben and Simeon, they shall be mine. ⁶Your offspring whom you beget after them shall be yours; they will be called by the name of their brothers in their inheritance. ⁷But as for me, when I came from Padan, Rachel died beside me in the land of Canaan on the way, when *there was* but a little distance to go to Ephrath; and I buried her there on the way to Ephrath (that is, Bethlehem)."

⁸Then Israel saw Joseph's sons, and said, "Who *are* these?"

⁹Joseph said to his father, "They *are* my sons, whom God has given me in this *place.*"

And he said, "Please bring them to me, and I will bless them." ¹⁰Now the eyes of Israel were dim with age, *so that* he could not see. Then Joseph brought them near him, and he kissed them and embraced them. ¹¹And Israel said to Joseph, "I had not thought to see your face; but in fact, God has also shown me your offspring!"

¹²So Joseph brought them from beside his knees, and he bowed down with his face to the earth. ¹³And Joseph took them both, Ephraim with his right hand toward Israel's left hand, and Manasseh with his left hand toward Israel's right hand, and brought *them* near him. ¹⁴Then Israel stretched out his right hand and laid *it* on Ephraim's head, who *was* the younger, and his left hand on Manasseh's head, guiding his hands knowingly, for Manasseh *was* the firstborn. ¹⁵And he blessed Joseph, and said:

> "God, before whom my fathers
>   Abraham and Isaac walked,
> The God who has fed me all
>   my life long to this day,
> 16   The Angel who has redeemed
>   me from all evil,
> Bless the lads;
> Let my name be named upon
>   them,
> And the name of my fathers
>   Abraham and Isaac;
> And let them grow into a
>   multitude in the midst of
>   the earth."

¹⁷Now when Joseph saw that his father laid his right hand on the head of Ephraim, it displeased him; so he took hold of his father's hand to re-

move it from Ephraim's head to Manasseh's head. ¹⁸And Joseph said to his father, "Not so, my father, for this *one is* the firstborn; put your right hand on his head."

¹⁹But his father refused and said, "I know, my son, I know. He also shall become a people, and he also shall be great; but truly his younger brother shall be greater than he, and his descendants shall become a multitude of nations."

²⁰So he blessed them that day, saying, "By you Israel will bless, saying, 'May God make you as Ephraim and as Manasseh!' " And thus he set Ephraim before Manasseh.

²¹Then Israel said to Joseph, "Behold, I am dying, but God will be with you and bring you back to the land of your fathers. ²²Moreover I have given to you one portion above your brothers, which I took from the hand of the Amorite with my sword and my bow."

AND Jacob called his sons and said, "Gather together, that I may tell you what shall befall you in the last days:

2   "Gather together and hear, you
        sons of Jacob,
     And listen to Israel your
        father.

3   "Reuben, you are my firstborn,
     My might and the beginning
        of my strength,
     The excellency of dignity and
        the excellency of power.
4   Unstable as water, you shall
        not excel,
     Because you went up to your
        father's bed;
     Then you defiled *it*—
     He went up to my couch.

5   "Simeon and Levi *are* brothers;
     Instruments of cruelty *are in*
        their dwelling place.

6   Let not my soul enter their
        council;
     Let not my honor be united to
        their assembly;
     For in their anger they slew a
        man,
     And in their self-will they
        hamstrung an ox.
7   Cursed *be* their anger, for *it is*
        fierce;
     And their wrath, for it is cruel!
     I will divide them in Jacob
     And scatter them in Israel.

8   "Judah, you *are he* whom your
        brothers shall praise;
     Your hand *shall be* on the
        neck of your enemies;
     Your father's children shall
        bow down before you.
9   Judah *is* a lion's whelp;
     From the prey, my son, you
        have gone up.
     He bows down, he lies down
        as a lion;
     And as a lion, who shall rouse
        him?
10   The scepter shall not depart
        from Judah,
     Nor a lawgiver from between
        his feet,
     Until Shiloh comes;
     And to Him *shall be* the
        obedience of the people.
11   Binding his donkey to the
        vine,
     And his donkey's colt to the
        choice vine,
     He washed his garments in
        wine,
     And his clothes in the blood
        of grapes.
12   His eyes *are* darker than wine,
     And his teeth whiter than
        milk.

13   "Zebulun shall dwell by the
        haven of the sea;
     He *shall become* a haven for
        ships,

And his border shall adjoin
Sidon.

14 "Issachar is a strong donkey,
Lying down between two
burdens;
15 He saw that rest *was* good,
And that the land *was* pleasant;
He bowed his shoulder to
bear *a burden,*
And became a band of slaves.

16 "Dan shall judge his people
As one of the tribes of Israel.
17 Dan shall be a serpent by the
way,
A viper by the path,
That bites the horse's heels
So that its rider shall fall
backward.
18 I have waited for your
salvation, O Lord!

19 "Gad, a troop shall tramp upon
him,
But he shall triumph at last.

20 "Bread from Asher *shall be*
rich,
And he shall yield royal
dainties.

21 "Naphtali *is* a deer let loose;
He uses beautiful words.

22 "Joseph *is* a fruitful bough,
A fruitful bough by a well;
His branches run over the
wall.
23 The archers have bitterly
grieved him,
Shot *at him* and hated him.
24 But his bow remained in
strength,
And the arms of his hands
were made strong
By the hands of the Mighty
God of Jacob
(From there *is* the Shepherd,
the Stone of Israel),

25 By the God of your father
who will help you,
And by the Almighty who will
bless you
With blessings of heaven
above,
Blessings of the deep that lies
beneath,
Blessings of the breasts and
of the womb.
26 The blessings of your father
Have excelled the blessings of
my ancestors,
Up to the utmost bound of the
everlasting hills.
They shall be on the head of
Joseph,
And on the crown of the head
of him who was separate
from his brothers.

27 "Benjamin is a ravenous wolf;
In the morning he shall
devour the prey,
And at night he shall divide
the spoil."

28All these *are* the twelve tribes of Israel, and this *is* what their father spoke to them. And he blessed them; he blessed each one according to his own blessing.
29Then he charged them and said to them: "I am to be gathered to my people; bury me with my fathers in the cave that *is* in the field of Ephron the Hittite, 30in the cave that *is* in the field of Machpelah, which *is* before Mamre in the land of Canaan, which Abraham bought with the field of Ephron the Hittite as a possession for a burial place. 31There they buried Abraham and Sarah his wife, there they buried Isaac and Rebekah his wife, and there I buried Leah. 32The field and the cave that *is* there *were* purchased from the sons of Heth." 33And when Jacob had finished commanding his sons, he drew his feet up into the bed and breathed his last, and was gathered to his people.

MATTHEW 15:29–16:12

JESUS departed from there, skirted the Sea of Galilee, and went up on the mountain and sat down there. 30Then great multitudes came to Him, having with them *the* lame, blind, mute, maimed, and many others; and they laid them down at Jesus' feet, and He healed them. 31So the multitude marveled when they saw *the* mute speaking, *the* maimed made whole, *the* lame walking, and *the* blind seeing; and they glorified the God of Israel.

32Now Jesus called His disciples to *Himself* and said, "I have compassion on the multitude, because they have now continued with Me three days and have nothing to eat. And I do not want to send them away hungry, lest they faint on the way."

33Then His disciples said to Him, "Where could we get enough bread in the wilderness to fill such a great multitude?"

34Jesus said to them, "How many loaves do you have?"

And they said, "Seven, and a few little fish."

35So He commanded the multitude to sit down on the ground. 36And He took the seven loaves and the fish and gave thanks, broke *them* and gave *them* to His disciples; and the disciples *gave* to the multitude. 37So they all ate and were filled, and they took up seven large baskets full of the fragments that were left. 38Now those who ate were four thousand men, besides women and children. 39And He sent away the multitude, got into the boat, and came to the region of Magdala.*

THEN the Pharisees and Sadducees came, and testing Him asked that He would show them a sign from heaven. 2He answered and said to them, "When it is evening you say, *It will be* fair weather, for the sky is red'; 3and in the morning, *It will be* foul weather today, for the sky is red and threatening.' Hypocrites!* You know how to discern the face of the sky, but you cannot *discern* the signs of the times. 4A wicked and adulterous generation seeks after a sign, and no sign shall be given to it except the sign of the prophet* Jonah." And He left them and departed.

5Now when His disciples had come to the other side, they had forgotten to take bread. 6Then Jesus said to them, "Theed and beware of the leaven of the Pharisees and the Sadducees."

7And they reasoned among themselves, saying, *It is* because we have taken no bread."

8But Jesus, being aware of *it*, said to them, "O you of little faith, why do you reason among yourselves because you have brought no bread?* 9Do you not yet understand, or remember the five loaves of the five thousand and how many baskets you took up? 10Nor the seven loaves of the four thousand and how many large baskets you took up? 11How is it you do not understand that I did not speak to you concerning bread?—*but* to beware of the leaven of the Pharisees and Sadducees." 12Then they understood that He did not tell *them* to beware of the leaven of bread, but of the doctrine of the Pharisees and Sadducees.

PSALM 20:1-9

To the Chief Musician. A Psalm of David.

MAY the LORD answer you in the day of trouble;
May the name of the God of Jacob defend you;
2 May He send you help from the sanctuary,
And strengthen you out of Zion;
3 May He remember all your offerings,
And accept your burnt sacrifice.　　Selah

4 May He grant you according
to your heart's *desire,*
And fulfill all your purpose.
5 We will rejoice in your
salvation,
And in the name of our God
we will set up *our* banners!
May the LORD fulfill all your
petitions.

6 Now I know that the LORD
saves His anointed;
He will answer him from His
holy heaven

With the saving strength of
His right hand.
7 Some *trust* in chariots, and
some in horses;
But we will remember the
name of the LORD our God.
8 They have bowed down and
fallen;
But we have risen and stand
upright.

9 Save, LORD!
May the King answer us
when we call.

PROVERBS FOR TODAY/ 4:20-27

*My son, give attention to my words; incline your ear to my sayings. Do not let them
depart from your eyes; keep them in the midst of your heart; for they are life to those
who find them, and health to all their flesh. Keep your heart with all diligence, for
out of it spring the issues of life. Put away from you a deceitful mouth, and put
perverse lips far from you. Let your eyes look straight ahead, and your eyelids look
right before you. Ponder the path of your feet, and let all your ways be established.
Do not turn to the right or the left; remove your foot from evil.*

JANUARY 25

GENESIS 50:1—EXODUS 2:10

THEN Joseph fell on his father's face and wept over him, and kissed him. ²And Joseph commanded his servants the physicians to embalm his father. So the physicians embalmed Israel. ³Forty days were required for him, for such are the days required for those who are embalmed; and the Egyptians mourned for him seventy days.

⁴Now when the days of his mourning were past, Joseph spoke to the household of Pharaoh, saying, "If now I have found favor in your eyes, please speak in the hearing of Pharaoh, saying, ⁵'My father made me swear, saying, "Behold, I am dying; in my grave which I dug for myself in the land of Canaan, there you shall bury me." Now therefore, please let me go up and bury my father, and I will come back.' "

⁶And Pharaoh said, "Go up and bury your father, as he made you swear."

⁷So Joseph went up to bury his father; and with him went up all the servants of Pharaoh, the elders of his house, and all the elders of the land of Egypt, ⁸as well as all the house of Joseph, his brothers, and his father's house. Only their little ones, their flocks, and their herds they left in the land of Goshen. ⁹And there went up with him both chariots and horsemen, and it was a very great gathering.

¹⁰Then they came to the threshing floor of Atad, which *is* beyond the Jor-

dan, and they mourned there with a great and very solemn lamentation. He observed seven days of mourning for his father. [11]And when the inhabitants of the land, the Canaanites, saw the mourning at the threshing floor of Atad, they said, "This *is* a deep mourning of the Egyptians." Therefore its name was called Abel Mizraim,* which *is* beyond the Jordan.

[12]So his sons did for him just as he had commanded them. [13]For his sons carried him to the land of Canaan, and buried him in the cave of the field of Machpelah, before Mamre, which Abraham bought with the field from Ephron the Hittite as property for a burial place. [14]And after he had buried his father, Joseph returned to Egypt, he and his brothers and all who went up with him to bury his father.

[15]When Joseph's brothers saw that their father was dead, they said, "Perhaps Joseph will hate us, and may actually repay us for all the evil which we did to him." [16]So they sent *messengers* to Joseph, saying, "Before your father died he commanded, saying, [17]'Thus you shall say to Joseph: "I beg you, please forgive the trespass of your brothers and their sin; for they did evil to you." ' Now, please, forgive the trespass of the servants of the God of your father." And Joseph wept when they spoke to him.

[18]Then his brothers also went and fell down before his face, and they said, "Behold, we *are* your servants." [19]Joseph said to them, "Do not be afraid, for *am* I in the place of God? [20]But as for you, you meant evil against me; *but* God meant it for good, in order to bring it about as *it is* this day, to save many people alive. [21]Now therefore, do not be afraid; I will provide for you and your little ones." And he comforted them and spoke kindly to them.

[22]So Joseph dwelt in Egypt, he and his father's household. And Joseph lived one hundred and ten years. [23]Jo-seph saw Ephraim's children to the third *generation*. The children of Machir, the son of Manasseh, were also brought up on Joseph's knees.

[24]And Joseph said to his brethren, "I am dying; but God will surely visit you, and bring you out of this land to the land of which He swore to Abraham, to Isaac, and to Jacob." [25]Then Joseph took an oath from the children of Israel, saying, "God will surely visit you, and you shall carry up my bones from here." [26]So Joseph died, *being* one hundred and ten years old; and they embalmed him, and he was put in a coffin in Egypt.

Now these *are* the names of the children of Israel who came to Egypt; each man and his household came with Jacob: [2]Reuben, Simeon, Levi, and Judah; [3]Issachar, Zebulun, and Benjamin; [4]Dan, Naphtali, Gad, and Asher. [5]All those who were descendants* of Jacob were seventy* persons (for Joseph was in Egypt *already*). [6]And Joseph died, all his brothers, and all that generation. [7]But the children of Israel were fruitful and increased abundantly, multiplied and grew exceedingly mighty; and the land was filled with them.

[8]Now there arose a new king over Egypt, who did not know Joseph. [9]And he said to his people, "Look, the people of the children of Israel *are* more and mightier than we; [10]come, let us deal shrewdly with them, lest they multiply, and it happen, in the event of war, that they also join our enemies and fight against us, and *so* go up out of the land." [11]Therefore they set taskmasters over them to afflict them with their burdens. And they built for Pharaoh supply cities, Pithom and Raamses. [12]But the more they afflicted them, the more they multiplied and grew. And they were in dread of the children of Israel. [13]So the Egyptians made the children of Israel serve with rigor. [14]And they made their lives

bitter with hard bondage—in mortar, in brick, and in all manner of service in the field. All their service in which they made them serve *was* with rigor.

15Then the king of Egypt spoke to the Hebrew midwives, of whom the name of one *was* Shiphrah and the name of the other Puah; 16and he said, "When you do the duties of a midwife for the Hebrew women, and see *them* on the birthstools, if it *is* a son, then you shall kill him; but if it *is* a daughter, then she shall live." 17But the midwives feared God, and did not do as the king of Egypt commanded them, but saved the male children alive. 18So the king of Egypt called for the midwives and said to them, "Why have you done this thing, and saved the male children alive?"

19And the midwives said to Pharaoh, "Because the Hebrew women *are* not like the Egyptian women; for they *are* lively and give birth before the midwives come to them."

20Therefore God dealt well with the midwives, and the people multiplied and grew very mighty. 21And so it was, because the midwives feared God, that He provided households for them.

22So Pharaoh commanded all his people, saying, "Every son who is born* you shall cast into the river, and every daughter you shall save alive."

AND a man of the house of Levi went and took *as wife* a daughter of Levi. 2So the woman conceived and bore a son. And when she saw that he *was* a beautiful *child,* she hid him three months. 3But when she could no longer hide him, she took an ark of bulrushes for him, daubed it with asphalt and pitch, put the child in it, and laid *it* in the reeds by the river's bank. 4And his sister stood afar off, to know what would be done to him.

5Then the daughter of Pharaoh came down to bathe at the river. And her maidens walked along the riverside; and when she saw the ark among the reeds, she sent her maid to get it. 6And when she opened *it,* she saw the child, and behold, the baby wept. So she had compassion on him, and said, "This is one of the Hebrews' children."

7Then his sister said to Pharaoh's daughter, "Shall I go and call a nurse for you from the Hebrew women, that she may nurse the child for you?"

8And Pharaoh's daughter said to her, "Go." So the maiden went and called the child's mother. 9Then Pharaoh's daughter said to her, "Take this child away and nurse him for me, and I will give *you* your wages." So the woman took the child and nursed him. 10And the child grew, and she brought him to Pharaoh's daughter, and he became her son. So she called his name Moses,* saying, "Because I drew him out of the water."

MATTHEW 16:13–17:9

WHEN Jesus came into the region of Caesarea Philippi, He asked His disciples, saying, "Who do men say that I, the Son of Man, am?"

14So they said, "Some *say* John the Baptist, some Elijah, and others Jeremiah or one of the prophets."

15He said to them, "But who do you say that I am?"

16Simon Peter answered and said, "You are the Christ, the Son of the living God."

17Jesus answered and said to him, "Blessed are you, Simon Bar-Jonah, for flesh and blood has not revealed *this* to you, but My Father who is in heaven. 18And I also say to you that you are Peter, and on this rock I will build My church, and the gates of Hades shall not prevail against it. 19And I will give you the keys of the kingdom of heaven, and whatever you bind on earth will be bound in heaven, and whatever you loose on earth will be loosed* in heaven."

20Then He commanded His disciples that they should tell no one that He was Jesus the Christ.

21From that time Jesus began to show to His disciples that He must go to Jerusalem, and suffer many things from the elders and chief priests and scribes, and be killed, and be raised the third day.

22Then Peter took Him aside and began to rebuke Him, saying, "Far be it from You, Lord; this shall not happen to You!"

23But He turned and said to Peter, "Get behind Me, Satan! You are an offense to Me, for you are not mindful of the things of God, but the things of men."

24Then Jesus said to His disciples, "If anyone desires to come after Me, let him deny himself, and take up his cross, and follow Me. 25For whoever desires to save his life will lose it, but whoever loses his life for My sake will find it. 26For what profit is it to a man if he gains the whole world, and loses his own soul? Or what will a man give in exchange for his soul? 27For the Son of Man will come in the glory of His Father with His angels, and then He will reward each according to his works. 28Assuredly, I say to you, there are some standing here who shall not taste death till they see the Son of Man coming in His kingdom."

Now after six days Jesus took Peter, James, and John his brother, led them up on a high mountain by themselves; 2and He was transfigured before them. His face shone like the sun, and His clothes became as white as the light. 3And behold, Moses and Elijah appeared to them, talking with Him. 4Then Peter answered and said to Jesus, "Lord, it is good for us to be here; if You wish, let us* make here three tabernacles: one for You, one for Moses, and one for Elijah."

5While he was still speaking, behold, a bright cloud overshadowed them; and suddenly a voice came out of the cloud, saying, "This is My beloved Son, in whom I am well pleased. Hear Him!" 6And when the disciples heard it, they fell on their faces and were greatly afraid. 7But Jesus came and touched them and said, "Arise, and do not be afraid." 8When they had lifted up their eyes, they saw no one but Jesus only.

9Now as they came down from the mountain, Jesus commanded them, saying, "Tell the vision to no one until the Son of Man is risen from the dead."

PSALM 21:1-13

To the Chief Musician. A Psalm of David.

THE king shall have joy in Your strength, O LORD;
And in Your salvation how greatly shall he rejoice!
2 You have given him his heart's desire,
And have not withheld the request of his lips.   Selah

3 For You meet him with the blessings of goodness;
You set a crown of pure gold upon his head.
4 He asked life from You, *and* You gave *it* to him—
Length of days forever and ever.
5 His glory *is* great in Your salvation;
Honor and majesty You have placed upon him.
6 For You have made him most blessed forever;
You have made him exceedingly glad with Your presence.
7 For the king trusts in the LORD,
And through the mercy of the Most High he shall not be moved.

8   Your hand will find all Your
     enemies;
     Your right hand will find those
     who hate You.
9   You shall make them as a
     fiery oven in the time of
     Your anger;
     The LORD shall swallow them
     up in His wrath,
     And the fire shall devour
     them.
10   Their offspring You shall
     destroy from the earth,
     And their descendants from
     among the sons of men.

11   For they intended evil against
     You;
     They devised a plot *which*
     they are not able *to perform.*
12   Therefore You will make
     them turn their back;
     You will make ready *Your*
     arrows on Your string
     toward their faces.

13   Be exalted, O LORD, in Your
     own strength!
     We will sing and praise Your
     power.

PROVERBS FOR TODAY / 5:1-6

*My son, pay attention to my wisdom; lend your ear to my understanding, that you may preserve discretion, and your lips may keep knowledge. For the lips of an immoral woman drip honey, and her mouth is smoother than oil; but in the end she is bitter as wormwood, sharp as a two-edged sword. Her feet go down to death, her steps lay hold of hell. * Lest you ponder her path of life—her ways are unstable; you do not know them.*

JANUARY 26

EXODUS 2:11–3:22

Now it came to pass in those days, when Moses was grown, that he went out to his brethren and looked at their burdens. And he saw an Egyptian beating a Hebrew, one of his brethren. 12So he looked this way and that way, and when he saw no one, he killed the Egyptian and hid him in the sand. 13And when he went out the second day, behold, two Hebrew men were fighting, and he said to the one who did the wrong, "Why are you striking your companion?"

14Then he said, "Who made you a prince and a judge over us? Do you intend to kill me as you killed the Egyptian?"

So Moses feared and said, "Surely this thing is known!" 15When Pharaoh heard of this matter, he sought to kill Moses. But Moses fled from the face of Pharaoh and dwelt in the land of Midian; and he sat down by a well.

16Now the priest of Midian had seven daughters. And they came and drew water, and they filled the troughs to water their father's flock. 17Then the shepherds came and drove them away; but Moses stood up and helped them, and watered their flock.

18When they came to Reuel their father, he said, "How *is it that* you have come so soon today?"

19And they said, "An Egyptian delivered us from the hand of the shepherds, and he also drew enough water for us and watered the flock."

20So he said to his daughters, "And where *is* he? Why *is* it *that* you have left the man? Call him, that he may eat bread."

21Then Moses was content to live with the man, and he gave Zipporah his daughter to Moses. 22And she bore *him* a son. He called his name Gershom,* for he said, "I have been a stranger in a foreign land."

23Now it happened in the process of time that the king of Egypt died. Then the children of Israel groaned because of the bondage, and they cried out; and their cry came up to God because of the bondage. 24So God heard their groaning, and God remembered His covenant with Abraham, with Isaac, and with Jacob. 25And God looked upon the children of Israel, and God acknowledged *them.*

Now Moses was tending the flock of Jethro his father-in-law, the priest of Midian. And he led the flock to the back of the desert, and came to Horeb, the mountain of God. 2And the Angel of the LORD appeared to him in a flame of fire from the midst of a bush. So he looked, and behold, the bush was burning with fire, but the bush *was* not consumed. 3Then Moses said, "I will now turn aside and see this great sight, why the bush does not burn."

4So when the LORD saw that he turned aside to look, God called to him from the midst of the bush and said, "Moses, Moses!"

And he said, "Here I am."

5Then He said, "Do not draw near this place. Take your sandals off your feet, for the place where you stand *is* holy ground." 6Moreover He said, "I *am* the God of your father—the God of Abraham, the God of Isaac, and the God of Jacob." And Moses hid his face, for he was afraid to look upon God.

7And the LORD said: "I have surely seen the oppression of My people who *are* in Egypt, and have heard their cry because of their taskmasters, for I know their sorrows. 8So I have come down to deliver them out of the hand of the Egyptians, and to bring them up from that land to a good and large land, to a land flowing with milk and honey, to the place of the Canaanites and the Hittites and the Amorites and the Perizzites and the Hivites and the Jebusites. 9Now therefore, behold, the cry of the children of Israel has come to Me, and I have also seen the oppression with which the Egyptians oppress them. 10Come now, therefore, and I will send you to Pharaoh that you may bring My people, the children of Israel, out of Egypt."

11But Moses said to God, "Who *am* I that I should go to Pharaoh, and that I should bring the children of Israel out of Egypt?"

12So He said, "I will certainly be with you. And this *shall be* a sign to you that I have sent you: When you have brought the people out of Egypt, you shall serve God on this mountain."

13Then Moses said to God, "Indeed, *when* I come to the children of Israel and say to them, 'The God of your fathers has sent me to you,' and they say to me, 'What *is* His name?' what shall I say to them?"

14And God said to Moses, "I AM WHO I AM." And He said, "Thus you shall say to the children of Israel, 'I AM has sent me to you.' " 15Moreover God said to Moses, "Thus you shall say to the children of Israel: 'The LORD God of your fathers, the God of Abraham, the God of Isaac, and the God of Jacob, has sent me to you. This *is* My name forever, and this *is* My memorial to all generations.' 16Go and gather the elders of Israel together, and say to them, 'The LORD God of your fathers, the God of Abraham, of Isaac, and of Jacob, appeared to me, saying, "I have surely visited you and *seen* what is done to you in Egypt; [17]and I have said I will bring you up out of the affliction of Egypt to the land of the Canaanites and the Hittites and the Amorites and the Perizzites and the Hivites and the Jebusites, to a land flowing with milk and honey.' ' [18]Then they will heed your voice; and you shall come, you and the elders of Israel, to the king of Egypt; and you shall say to him, 'The LORD God of the Hebrews has met with us; and now, please, let us go three days' journey into the wilderness, that we may sacrifice to the LORD our God.' [19]But I am sure that the king of Egypt will not let you go, no, not even by a mighty hand. [20]So I will stretch out My hand and strike Egypt with all My wonders which I will do in its midst; and after that he will let you go. [21]And I will give this people favor in the sight of the Egyptians; and it shall be, when you go, that you shall not go empty-handed. [22]But every woman shall ask of her neighbor, namely, of her who dwells near her house, articles of silver, articles of gold, and clothing; and you shall put *them* on your sons and on your daughters. So you shall plunder the Egyptians."

MATTHEW 17:10-27

AND His disciples asked Him [Jesus], saying, "Why then do the scribes say that Elijah must come first?"

[11]Jesus answered and said to them, "Indeed, Elijah is coming first* and will restore all things. [12]But I say to you that Elijah has come already, and they did not know him but did to him whatever they wished. Likewise the Son of Man is also about to suffer at their hands." [13]Then the disciples understood that He spoke to them of John the Baptist.

[14]And when they had come to the multitude, a man came to Him, kneel-ing down to Him and saying, [15]"Lord, have mercy on my son, for he is an epileptic* and suffers severely; for he often falls into the fire and often into the water. [16]So I brought him to Your disciples, but they could not cure him."

[17]Then Jesus answered and said, "O faithless and perverse generation, how long shall I be with you? How long shall I bear with you? Bring him here to Me." [18]And Jesus rebuked the demon, and it came out of him; and the child was cured from that very hour.

[19]Then the disciples came to Jesus privately and said, "Why could we not cast it out?"

[20]So Jesus said to them, "Because of your unbelief;* for assuredly, I say to you, if you have faith as a mustard seed, you will say to this mountain, 'Move from here to there,' and it will move; and nothing will be impossible for you. [21]However, this kind does not go out except by prayer and fasting."*

[22]Now while they were staying* in Galilee, Jesus said to them, "The Son of Man is about to be betrayed into the hands of men, [23]and they will kill Him, and the third day He will be raised up." And they were exceedingly sorrowful.

[24]When they had come to Capernaum,* those who received the *temple* tax came to Peter and said, "Does your Teacher not pay the *temple* tax?"

[25]He said, "Yes."

And when he had come into the house, Jesus anticipated him, saying, "What do you think, Simon? From whom do the kings of the earth take customs or taxes, from their sons or from strangers?"

[26]Peter said to Him, "From strangers."

Jesus said to him, "Then the sons are free. [27]Nevertheless, lest we offend them, go to the sea, cast in a hook, and take the fish that comes up first. And when you have opened its mouth, you will find a piece of money;* take that and give it to them for Me and you."

PSALM 22:1-18

To the Chief Musician. Set to "The Deer of the Dawn."* A Psalm of David.

M Y God, My God, why have You forsaken Me?
Why are You so far from helping Me,
And from the words of My groaning?

2 O My God, I cry in the daytime, but You do not hear;
And in the night season, and am not silent.

3 But You *are* holy,
Enthroned in the praises of Israel.

4 Our fathers trusted in You;
They trusted, and You delivered them.

5 They cried to You, and were delivered;
They trusted in You, and were not ashamed.

6 But I *am* a worm, and no man;
A reproach of men, and despised by the people.

7 All those who see Me ridicule Me;
They shoot out the lip, they shake the head, *saying,*

8 "He trusted* in the LORD, let Him rescue Him;
Let Him deliver Him, since He delights in Him!"

9 But You *are* He who took Me out of the womb;

You made Me trust *while* on My mother's breasts.

10 I was cast upon You from birth.
From My mother's womb You *have been* My God.

11 Be not far from Me,
For trouble *is* near;
For *there is* none to help.

12 Many bulls have surrounded Me;
Strong *bulls* of Bashan have encircled Me.

13 They gape at Me *with* their mouths,
Like a raging and roaring lion.

14 I am poured out like water,
And all My bones are out of joint;
My heart is like wax;
It has melted within Me.

15 My strength is dried up like a potsherd,
And My tongue clings to My jaws;
You have brought Me to the dust of death.

16 For dogs have surrounded Me;
The congregation of the wicked has enclosed Me.
They pierced* My hands and My feet;

17 I can count all My bones.
They look *and* stare at Me.

18 They divide My garments among them,
And for My clothing they cast lots.

PROVERBS FOR TODAY/ 5:7-14

Therefore hear me now, my *children, and do not depart from the words of my mouth. Remove your way far from her [an immoral woman], and do not go near the door of her house, lest you give your honor to others, and your years to the cruel one; lest aliens be filled with your wealth, and your labors go to the house of a foreigner; and you mourn at last, when your flesh and your body are consumed, and say: "How I have hated instruction, and my heart despised correction! I have not obeyed the voice of my teachers, nor inclined my ear to those who instructed me! I was on the verge of total ruin, in the midst of the assembly and congregation."*

JANUARY 27

EXODUS 4:1–5:21

THEN Moses answered and said, "But suppose they will not believe me or listen to my voice; suppose they say, 'The LORD has not appeared to you.'"

²So the LORD said to him, "What *is* that in your hand?"

He said, "A rod."

³And He said, "Cast it on the ground." So he cast it on the ground, and it became a serpent; and Moses fled from it. ⁴Then the LORD said to Moses, "Reach out your hand and take *it* by the tail" (and he reached out his hand and caught it, and it became a rod in his hand), ⁵"that they may believe that the LORD God of their fathers, the God of Abraham, the God of Isaac, and the God of Jacob, has appeared to you."

⁶Furthermore the LORD said to him, "Now put your hand in your bosom." And he put his hand in his bosom, and when he took it out, behold, his hand *was* leprous, like snow. ⁷And He said, "Put your hand in your bosom again." So he put his hand in his bosom again, and drew it out of his bosom, and behold, it was restored like his *other* flesh. ⁸"Then it will be, if they do not believe you, nor heed the message of the first sign, that they may believe the message of the latter sign. ⁹And it shall be, if they do not believe even these two signs, or listen to your voice, that you shall take water from the river* and pour *it* on the dry *land*. The water which you take from the river will become blood on the dry *land*."

¹⁰Then Moses said to the LORD, "O my Lord, I *am* not eloquent, neither before nor since You have spoken to Your servant; but I *am* slow of speech and slow of tongue."

¹¹So the LORD said to him, "Who has made man's mouth? Or who makes the mute, the deaf, the seeing, or the blind? *Have* not I, the LORD? ¹²Now therefore, go, and I will be with your mouth and teach you what you shall say."

¹³But he said, "O my Lord, please send by the hand of whomever *else* You may send."

¹⁴So the anger of the LORD was kindled against Moses, and He said: "Is not Aaron the Levite your brother? I know that he can speak well. And look, he is also coming out to meet you. When he sees you, he will be glad in his heart. ¹⁵Now you shall speak to him and put the words in his mouth. And I will be with your mouth and with his mouth, and I will teach you what you shall do. ¹⁶So he shall be your spokesman to the people. And he himself shall be as a mouth for you, and you shall be to him as God. ¹⁷And you shall take this rod in your hand, with which you shall do the signs."

¹⁸So Moses went and returned to Jethro his father-in-law, and said to him, "Please let me go and return to my brethren who *are* in Egypt, and see whether they are still alive."

And Jethro said to Moses, "Go in peace."

¹⁹Now the LORD said to Moses in Midian, "Go, return to Egypt; for all the men who sought your life are dead." ²⁰Then Moses took his wife and his sons and set them on a donkey, and he returned to the land of Egypt. And Moses took the rod of God in his hand.

²¹And the LORD said to Moses, "When you go back to Egypt, see that you do all those wonders before Pharaoh which I have put in your hand. But I will harden his heart, so that he will not let the people go. ²²Then you shall say to Pharaoh, 'Thus says the LORD: "Israel *is* My son, My firstborn. ²³So I say to you, let My son go that he may serve Me. But if you refuse to let him go, indeed I will kill your son, your firstborn." ' "

²⁴And it came to pass on the way, at the encampment, that the LORD met him and sought to kill him. ²⁵Then Zipporah took a sharp stone and cut off the foreskin of her son and cast *it* at *Moses'** feet, and said, "Surely you *are* a husband of blood to me!" ²⁶So He let him go. Then she said, *"You are* a husband of blood!"—because of the circumcision.

²⁷And the LORD said to Aaron, "Go into the wilderness to meet Moses." So he went and met him on the mountain of God, and kissed him. ²⁸So Moses told Aaron all the words of the LORD who had sent him, and all the signs which He had commanded him. ²⁹Then Moses and Aaron went and gathered together all the elders of the children of Israel. ³⁰And Aaron spoke all the words which the LORD had spoken to Moses. Then he did the signs in the sight of the people. ³¹So the people believed; and when they heard that the LORD had visited the children of Israel and that He had looked on their affliction, then they bowed their heads and worshiped.

AFTERWARD Moses and Aaron went in and told Pharaoh, "Thus says the LORD God of Israel: 'Let My people go, that they may hold a feast to Me in the wilderness.' "

²And Pharaoh said, "Who *is* the LORD, that I should obey His voice to let Israel go? I do not know the LORD, nor will I let Israel go."

³So they said, "The God of the Hebrews has met with us. Please, let us go three days' journey into the desert and sacrifice to the LORD our God, lest He fall upon us with pestilence or with the sword."

⁴Then the king of Egypt said to them, "Moses and Aaron, why do you take the people from their work? Get *back* to your labor." ⁵And Pharaoh said, "Look, the people of the land *are* many now, and you make them rest from their labor!"

⁶So the same day Pharaoh commanded the taskmasters of the people and their officers, saying, ⁷"You shall no longer give the people straw to make brick as before. Let them go and gather straw for themselves. ⁸And you shall lay on them the quota of bricks which they made before. You shall not reduce it. For they are idle; therefore they cry out, saying, 'Let us go *and* sacrifice to our God.' ⁹Let more work be laid on the men, that they may labor in it, and let them not regard false words."

¹⁰And the taskmasters of the people and their officers went out and spoke to the people, saying, "Thus says Pharaoh: 'I will not give you straw. ¹¹Go, get yourselves straw where you can find it; yet none of your work will be reduced.' " ¹²So the people were scattered abroad throughout all the land of Egypt to gather stubble instead of straw. ¹³And the taskmasters forced *them* to hurry, saying, "Fulfill your work, *your* daily quota, as when there was straw." ¹⁴Also the officers of the children of Israel, whom Pharaoh's

taskmasters had set over them, were beaten *and* were asked, "Why have you not fulfilled your task in making brick both yesterday and today, as before?"

¹⁵Then the officers of the children of Israel came and cried out to Pharaoh, saying, "Why are you dealing thus with your servants? ¹⁶There is no straw given to your servants, and they say to us, 'Make brick!' And indeed your servants *are* beaten, but the fault *is* in your *own* people."

¹⁷But he said, "You *are* idle! Idle! Therefore you say, 'Let us go *and* sacrifice to the LORD.' ¹⁸Therefore go now *and* work; for no straw shall be given you, yet you shall deliver the quota of bricks." ¹⁹And the officers of the children of Israel saw *that* they *were* in trouble after it was said, "You shall not reduce *any* bricks from your daily quota."

²⁰Then, as they came out from Pharaoh, they met Moses and Aaron who stood there to meet them. ²¹And they said to them, "Let the LORD look on you and judge, because you have made us abhorrent in the sight of Pharaoh and in the sight of his servants, to put a sword in their hand to kill us."

MATTHEW 18:1-22

AT that time the disciples came to Jesus, saying, "Who then is greatest in the kingdom of heaven?"

²Then Jesus called a little child to Him, set him in the midst of them, ³and said, "Assuredly, I say to you, unless you are converted and become as little children, you will by no means enter the kingdom of heaven. ⁴Therefore whoever humbles himself as this little child is the greatest in the kingdom of heaven. ⁵Whoever receives one little child like this in My name receives Me.

⁶"Whoever causes one of these little ones who believe in Me to sin, it would be better for him if a millstone were hung around his neck, and he were drowned in the depth of the sea. ⁷Woe to the world because of offenses! For offenses must come, but woe to that man by whom the offense comes!

⁸"If your hand or foot causes you to sin, cut it off and cast *it* from you. It is better for you to enter into life lame or maimed, rather than having two hands or two feet, to be cast into the everlasting fire. ⁹And if your eye causes you to sin, pluck it out and cast *it* from you. It is better for you to enter into life with one eye, rather than having two eyes, to be cast into hell fire.

¹⁰"Take heed that you do not despise one of these little ones, for I say to you that in heaven their angels always see the face of My Father who is in heaven. ¹¹For the Son of Man has come to save that which was lost.*

¹²"What do you think? If a man has a hundred sheep, and one of them goes astray, does he not leave the ninety-nine and go to the mountains to seek the one that is straying? ¹³And if he should find it, assuredly, I say to you, he rejoices more over that *sheep* than over the ninety-nine that did not go astray. ¹⁴Even so it is not the will of your Father who is in heaven that one of these little ones should perish.

¹⁵"Moreover if your brother sins against you, go and tell him his fault between you and him alone. If he hears you, you have gained your brother. ¹⁶But if he will not hear, take with you one or two more, that *'by the mouth of two or three witnesses every word may be established.'** ¹⁷And if he refuses to hear them, tell *it* to the church. But if he refuses even to hear the church, let him be to you like a heathen and a tax collector.

¹⁸"Assuredly, I say to you, whatever you bind on earth will be bound in heaven, and whatever you loose on earth will be loosed in heaven.

¹⁹"Again I say* to you that if two of

you agree on earth concerning anything that they ask, it will be done for them by My Father in heaven. ²⁰For where two or three are gathered together in My name, I am there in the midst of them."

²¹Then Peter came to Him and said, "Lord, how often shall my brother sin against me, and I forgive him? Up to seven times?"

²²Jesus said to him, "I do not say to you, up to seven times, but up to seventy times seven.

PSALM 22:19-31

Bᵁᵀ You, O Lᴏʀᴅ, do not be far from Me;
O My Strength, hasten to help Me!

20 Deliver Me from the sword,
My precious *life* from the power of the dog.

21 Save Me from the lion's mouth
And from the horns of the wild oxen!

You have answered Me.

22 I will declare Your name to My brethren;
In the midst of the assembly I will praise You.

23 You who fear the Lᴏʀᴅ, praise Him!
All you descendants of Jacob, glorify Him,
And fear Him, all you offspring of Israel!

24 For He has not despised nor abhorred the affliction of the afflicted;

Nor has He hidden His face from Him;
But when He cried to Him, He heard.

25 My praise *shall be* of You in the great assembly;
I will pay My vows before those who fear Him.

26 The poor shall eat and be satisfied;
Those who seek Him will praise the Lᴏʀᴅ.
Let your heart live forever!

27 All the ends of the world
Shall remember and turn to the Lᴏʀᴅ,
And all the families of the nations
Shall worship before You.*

28 For the kingdom *is* the Lᴏʀᴅ's,
And He rules over the nations.

29 All the prosperous of the earth
Shall eat and worship;
All those who go down to the dust
Shall bow before Him,
Even he who cannot keep himself alive.

30 A posterity shall serve Him.
It will be recounted of the Lord to the *next* generation,

31 They will come and declare His righteousness to a people who will be born,
That He has done *this*.

PROVERBS FOR TODAY/ 5:15-21

Drink water from your own cistern, and running water from your own well. Should your fountains be dispersed abroad, streams of water in the streets? Let them be only your own, and not for strangers with you. Let your fountain be blessed, and rejoice with the wife of your youth. As a loving deer and a graceful doe, let her breasts satisfy you at all times; and always be enraptured with her love. For why should you, my son, be enraptured by an immoral woman, and be embraced in the arms of a seductress? For the ways of man are before the eyes of the Lord, and He ponders all his paths.

JANUARY 28

EXODUS 5:22–7:25

So Moses returned to the Lord and said, "Lord, why have You brought trouble on this people? Why *is* it You have sent me? ²³For since I came to Pharaoh to speak in Your name, he has done evil to this people; neither have You delivered Your people at all."

Then the Lord said to Moses, "Now you shall see what I will do to Pharaoh. For with a strong hand he will let them go, and with a strong hand he will drive them out of his land."

²And God spoke to Moses and said to him: "I *am* the Lord. ³I appeared to Abraham, to Isaac, and to Jacob, as God Almighty, but *by* My name Lord* I was not known to them. ⁴I have also established My covenant with them, to give them the land of Canaan, the land of their pilgrimage, in which they were strangers. ⁵And I have also heard the groaning of the children of Israel whom the Egyptians keep in bondage, and I have remembered My covenant. ⁶Therefore say to the children of Israel: 'I *am* the Lord; I will bring you out from under the burdens of the Egyptians, I will rescue you from their bondage, and I will redeem you with an outstretched arm and with great judgments. ⁷I will take you as My people, and I will be your God. Then you shall know that I *am* the Lord your God who brings you out from under the burdens of the Egyptians. ⁸And I will bring you into the land which I swore to give to Abraham, Isaac, and Jacob; and I will give it to you *as* a heritage: I *am* the Lord.' "

⁹So Moses spoke thus to the children of Israel; but they did not heed Moses, because of anguish of spirit and cruel bondage.

¹⁰And the Lord spoke to Moses, saying, ¹¹"Go in, tell Pharaoh king of Egypt to let the children of Israel go out of his land."

¹²And Moses spoke before the Lord, saying, "The children of Israel have not heeded me. How then shall Pharaoh heed me, for I *am* of uncircumcised lips?"

¹³Then the Lord spoke to Moses and Aaron, and gave them a command for the children of Israel and for Pharaoh king of Egypt, to bring the children of Israel out of the land of Egypt.

¹⁴These *are* the heads of their fathers' houses: The sons of Reuben, the firstborn of Israel, *were* Hanoch, Pallu, Hezron, and Carmi. These are the families of Reuben. ¹⁵And the sons of Simeon *were* Jemuel,* Jamin, Ohad, Jachin, Zohar, and Shaul the son of a Canaanite woman. These *are* the families of Simeon. ¹⁶These *are* the names of the sons of Levi according to their generations: Gershon, Kohath, and Merari. And the years of the life of Levi *were* one hundred and thirty-seven. ¹⁷The sons of Gershon *were* Libni and Shimi according to their families. ¹⁸And the sons of Kohath *were* Amram, Izhar, Hebron, and Uzziel. And the years of the life of Kohath *were* one

hundred and thirty-three. ¹⁹The sons of Merari *were* Mahli and Mushi. These *are* the families of Levi according to their generations.

²⁰Now Amram took for himself Jochebed, his father's sister, as wife; and she bore him Aaron and Moses. And the years of the life of Amram *were* one hundred and thirty-seven. ²¹The sons of Izhar *were* Korah, Nepheg, and Zichri. ²²And the sons of Uzziel *were* Mishael, Elzaphan, and Zithri. ²³Aaron took to himself Elisheba, daughter of Amminadab, sister of Nahshon, as wife; and she bore him Nadab, Abihu, Eleazar, and Ithamar. ²⁴And the sons of Korah *were* Assir, Elkanah, and Abiasaph. These are the families of the Korahites. ²⁵Eleazar, Aaron's son, took for himself one of the daughters of Putiel as wife; and she bore him Phinehas. These *are* the heads of the fathers' houses of the Levites according to their families.

²⁶These *are the same* Aaron and Moses to whom the Lord said, "Bring out the children of Israel from the land of Egypt according to their armies." ²⁷These *are* the ones who spoke to Pharaoh king of Egypt, to bring out the children of Israel from Egypt. These *are the same* Moses and Aaron.

²⁸And it came to pass, on the day the Lord spoke to Moses in the land of Egypt, ²⁹that the Lord spoke to Moses, saying, "I *am* the Lord. Speak to Pharaoh king of Egypt all that I say to you." ³⁰But Moses said before the Lord, "Behold, I *am* of uncircumcised lips, and how shall Pharaoh heed me?"

So the Lord said to Moses: "See, I have made you *as* God to Pharaoh, and Aaron your brother shall be your prophet. ²You shall speak all that I command you. And Aaron your brother shall tell Pharaoh to send the children of Israel out of his land. ³And I will harden Pharaoh's heart, and multiply My signs and My wonders in the land of Egypt. ⁴But Pharaoh will not heed you, so that I may lay My hand on Egypt and bring My armies *and* My people, the children of Israel, out of the land of Egypt by great judgments. ⁵And the Egyptians shall know that I *am* the Lord, when I stretch out My hand on Egypt and bring out the children of Israel from among them."

⁶Then Moses and Aaron did *so;* just as the Lord commanded them, so they did. ⁷And Moses *was* eighty years old and Aaron eighty-three years old when they spoke to Pharaoh.

⁸Then the Lord spoke to Moses and Aaron, saying, ⁹"When Pharaoh speaks to you, saying, 'Show a miracle for yourselves,' then you shall say to Aaron, 'Take your rod and cast *it* before Pharaoh, *and* let it become a serpent.'" ¹⁰So Moses and Aaron went in to Pharaoh, and they did so, just as the Lord commanded. And Aaron cast down his rod before Pharaoh and before his servants, and it became a serpent.

¹¹But Pharaoh also called the wise men and the sorcerers; so the magicians of Egypt, they also did in like manner with their enchantments. ¹²For every man threw down his rod, and they became serpents. But Aaron's rod swallowed up their rods. ¹³And Pharaoh's heart grew hard, and he did not heed them, as the Lord had said.

¹⁴So the Lord said to Moses: "Pharaoh's heart *is* hard; he refuses to let the people go. ¹⁵Go to Pharaoh in the morning, when he goes out to the water, and you shall stand by the river's bank to meet him; and the rod which was turned to a serpent you shall take in your hand. ¹⁶And you shall say to him, 'The Lord God of the Hebrews has sent me to you, saying, "Let My people go, that they may serve Me in the wilderness"; but indeed, until now you would not hear! ¹⁷Thus says the Lord: "By this you shall know that I *am*

the LORD. Behold, I will strike the waters which *are* in the river with the rod that *is* in my hand, and they shall be turned to blood. [18]And the fish that *are* in the river shall die, the river shall stink, and the Egyptians will loathe to drink the water of the river." ' "

[19]Then the LORD spoke to Moses, "Say to Aaron, 'Take your rod and stretch out your hand over the waters of Egypt, over their streams, over their rivers, over their ponds, and over all their pools of water, that they may become blood. And there shall be blood throughout all the land of Egypt, both in *buckets of* wood and *pitchers of* stone.' " [20]And Moses and Aaron did so, just as the LORD commanded. So he lifted up the rod and struck the waters that *were* in the river, in the sight of Pharaoh and in the sight of his servants. And all the waters that *were* in the river were turned to blood. [21]The fish that *were* in the river died, the river stank, and the Egyptians could not drink the water of the river. So there was blood throughout all the land of Egypt.

[22]Then the magicians of Egypt did so with their enchantments; and Pharaoh's heart grew hard, and he did not heed them, as the LORD had said. [23]And Pharaoh turned and went into his house. Neither was his heart moved by this. [24]So all the Egyptians dug all around the river for water to drink, because they could not drink the water of the river. [25]And seven days passed after the LORD had struck the river.

MATTHEW 18:23–19:12

"THEREFORE the kingdom of heaven is like a certain king who wanted to settle accounts with his servants. [24]And when he had begun to settle accounts, one was brought to him who owed him ten thousand talents. [25]But as he was not able to pay, his master commanded that he be sold, with his wife and children and all that he had, and that payment be made. [26]The servant therefore fell down before him, saying, 'Master, have patience with me, and I will pay you all.' [27]Then the master of that servant was moved with compassion, released him, and forgave him the debt.

[28]"But that servant went out and found one of his fellow servants who owed him a hundred denarii; and he laid hands on him and took *him* by the throat, saying, 'Pay me what you owe!' [29]So his fellow servant fell down at his feet* and begged him, saying, 'Have patience with me, and I will pay you all.'* [30]And he would not, but went and threw him into prison till he should pay the debt. [31]So when his fellow servants saw what had been done, they were very grieved, and came and told their master all that had been done. [32]Then his master, after he had called him, said to him, 'You wicked servant! I forgave you all that debt because you begged me. [33]Should you not also have had compassion on your fellow servant, just as I had pity on you?' [34]And his master was angry, and delivered him to the torturers until he should pay all that was due to him.

[35]"So My heavenly Father also will do to you if each of you, from his heart, does not forgive his brother his trespasses."*

Now it came to pass, when Jesus had finished these sayings, *that* He departed from Galilee and came to the region of Judea beyond the Jordan. [2]And great multitudes followed Him, and He healed them there.

[3]The Pharisees also came to Him, testing Him, and saying to Him, "Is it lawful for a man to divorce his wife for *just* any reason?"

[4]And He answered and said to them, "Have you not read that He who

made* *them* at the beginning *'made them male and female,'** 5and said, *'For this reason a man shall leave his father and mother and be joined to his wife, and the two shall become one flesh'?** 6So then, they are no longer two but one flesh. Therefore what God has joined together, let not man separate."

7They said to Him, "Why then did Moses command to give a certificate of divorce, and to put her away?"

8He said to them, "Moses, because of the hardness of your hearts, permitted you to divorce your wives, but from the beginning it was not so. 9And I say to you, whoever divorces his wife, except for sexual immorality,* and marries another, commits adultery; and whoever marries her who is divorced commits adultery."

10His disciples said to Him, "If such is the case of the man with *his* wife, it is better not to marry."

11But He said to them, "All cannot accept this saying, but only *those* to whom it has been given: 12For there are eunuchs who were born thus from *their* mother's womb, and there are eunuchs who were made eunuchs by men, and there are eunuchs who have made themselves eunuchs for the kingdom of heaven's sake. He who is able to accept *it,* let him accept *it."*

PSALM 23:1-6

A Psalm of David.

THE LORD *is* my shepherd;
I shall not want.
2He makes me to lie down in
green pastures;
He leads me beside the still
waters.

3   He restores my soul;
He leads me in the paths of
righteousness
For His name's sake.

4   Yea, though I walk through
the valley of the shadow of
death,
I will fear no evil;
For You *are* with me;
Your rod and Your staff, they
comfort me.

5   You prepare a table before me
in the presence of my
enemies;
You anoint my head with oil;
My cup runs over.

6   Surely goodness and mercy
shall follow me
All the days of my life;
And I will dwell* in the house
of the LORD
Forever.

PROVERBS FOR TODAY/ 5:22-23

His [a man's] own iniquities entrap the wicked man, *and he is caught in the cords of his sin. He shall die for lack of instruction, and in the greatness of his folly he shall go astray.*

EXODUS 8:1–9:35

AND the LORD spoke to Moses, "Go to Pharaoh and say to him, 'Thus says the LORD: "Let My people go, that they may serve Me. ²But if you refuse to let *them* go, behold, I will smite all your territory with frogs. ³So the river shall bring forth frogs abundantly, which shall go up and come into your house, into your bedroom, on your bed, into the houses of your servants, on your people, into your ovens, and into your kneading bowls. ⁴And the frogs shall come up on you, on your people, and on all your servants." ' "

⁵Then the LORD spoke to Moses, "Say to Aaron, 'Stretch out your hand with your rod over the streams, over the rivers, and over the ponds, and cause frogs to come up on the land of Egypt.' " ⁶So Aaron stretched out his hand over the waters of Egypt, and the frogs came up and covered the land of Egypt. ⁷And the magicians did so with their enchantments, and brought up frogs on the land of Egypt.

⁸Then Pharaoh called for Moses and Aaron, and said, "Entreat the LORD that He may take away the frogs from me and from my people; and I will let the people go, that they may sacrifice to the LORD."

⁹And Moses said to Pharaoh, "Accept the honor of saying when I shall intercede for you, for your servants, and for your people, to destroy the frogs from you and your houses, *that* they may remain in the river only."

¹⁰So he said, "Tomorrow." And he said, *"Let it be* according to your word, that you may know that *there is* no one like the LORD our God. ¹¹And the frogs shall depart from you, from your houses, from your servants, and from your people. They shall remain in the river only."

¹²Then Moses and Aaron went out from Pharaoh. And Moses cried out to the LORD concerning the frogs which He had brought against Pharaoh. ¹³So the LORD did according to the word of Moses. And the frogs died out of the houses, out of the courtyards, and out of the fields. ¹⁴They gathered them together in heaps, and the land stank. ¹⁵But when Pharaoh saw that there was relief, he hardened his heart and did not heed them, as the LORD had said.

¹⁶So the LORD said to Moses, "Say to Aaron, 'Stretch out your rod, and strike the dust of the land, so that it may become lice throughout all the land of Egypt.' " ¹⁷And they did so. For Aaron stretched out his hand with his rod and struck the dust of the earth, and it became lice on man and beast. All the dust of the land became lice throughout all the land of Egypt.

¹⁸Now the magicians so worked with their enchantments to bring forth lice, but they could not. So there were lice on man and beast. ¹⁹Then the magicians said to Pharaoh, "This *is* the finger of God." But Pharaoh's heart grew hard, and he did not heed them, just as the LORD had said.

²⁰And the LORD said to Moses, "Rise early in the morning and stand before Pharaoh as he comes out to the water. Then say to him, 'Thus says the LORD: "Let My people go, that they may serve Me. ²¹Or else, if you will not let My people go, behold, I will send swarms *of flies* on you and your servants, on your people and into your houses. The houses of the Egyptians shall be full of swarms *of flies,* and also the ground on which they *stand.* ²²And

in that day I will set apart the land of Goshen, in which My people dwell, that no swarms *of flies* shall be there, in order that you may know that I *am* the LORD in the midst of the land. ²³I will make a difference* between My people and your people. Tomorrow this sign shall be." ' " ²⁴And the LORD did so. Thick swarms *of flies* came into the house of Pharaoh, *into* his servants' houses, and into all the land of Egypt. The land was corrupted because of the swarms *of flies.*

²⁵Then Pharaoh called for Moses and Aaron, and said, "Go, sacrifice to your God in the land."

²⁶And Moses said, "It is not right to do so, for we would be sacrificing the abomination of the Egyptians to the LORD our God. If we sacrifice the abomination of the Egyptians before their eyes, then will they not stone us? ²⁷We will go three days' journey into the wilderness and sacrifice to the LORD our God as He will command us."

²⁸So Pharaoh said, "I will let you go, that you may sacrifice to the LORD your God in the wilderness; only you shall not go very far away. Intercede for me."

²⁹Then Moses said, "Indeed I am going out from you, and I will entreat the LORD, that the swarms *of flies* may depart tomorrow from Pharaoh, from his servants, and from his people. But let Pharaoh not deal deceitfully anymore in not letting the people go to sacrifice to the LORD."

³⁰So Moses went out from Pharaoh and entreated the LORD. ³¹And the LORD did according to the word of Moses; He removed the swarms *of flies* from Pharaoh, from his servants, and from his people. Not one remained. ³²But Pharaoh hardened his heart at this time also; neither would he let the people go.

THEN the LORD said to Moses, "Go in to Pharaoh and tell him, 'Thus says the LORD God of the Hebrews: "Let My people go, that they may serve Me. ²For if you refuse to let *them* go, and still hold them, ³behold, the hand of the LORD will be on your cattle in the field, on the horses, on the donkeys, on the camels, on the oxen, and on the sheep—a very severe pestilence. ⁴And the LORD will make a difference between the livestock of Israel and the livestock of Egypt. So nothing shall die of all *that* belongs to the children of Israel." ' " ⁵Then the LORD appointed a set time, saying, "Tomorrow the LORD will do this thing in the land."

⁶So the LORD did this thing on the next day, and all the livestock of Egypt died; but of the livestock of the children of Israel, not one died. ⁷Then Pharaoh sent, and indeed, not even one of the livestock of the Israelites was dead. But the heart of Pharaoh became hard, and he did not let the people go.

⁸So the LORD said to Moses and Aaron, "Take for yourselves handfuls of ashes from a furnace, and let Moses scatter it toward the heavens in the sight of Pharaoh. ⁹And it will become fine dust in all the land of Egypt, and it will cause boils that break out in sores on man and beast throughout all the land of Egypt." ¹⁰Then they took ashes from the furnace and stood before Pharaoh, and Moses scattered *them* toward heaven. And *they* caused boils that break out in sores on man and beast. ¹¹And the magicians could not stand before Moses because of the boils, for the boils were on the magicians and on all the Egyptians. ¹²But the LORD hardened the heart of Pharaoh; and he did not heed them, just as the LORD had spoken to Moses.

¹³Then the LORD said to Moses, "Rise early in the morning and stand before Pharaoh, and say to him, 'Thus says the LORD God of the Hebrews: "Let My people go, that they may serve Me, ¹⁴for at this time I will send

all My plagues to your very heart, and on your servants and on your people, that you may know that *there is* none like Me in all the earth. ¹⁵Now if I had stretched out My hand and struck you and your people with pestilence, then you would have been cut off from the earth. ¹⁶But indeed for this *purpose* I have raised you up, that I may show My power *in* you, and that My name may be declared in all the earth. ¹⁷As yet you exalt yourself against My people in that you will not let them go. ¹⁸Behold, tomorrow about this time I will cause very heavy hail to rain down, such as has not been in Egypt since its founding until now. ¹⁹Therefore send now *and* gather your livestock and all that you have in the field, for the hail shall come down on every man and every animal which is found in the field and is not brought home; and they shall die." ' "

²⁰He who feared the word of the LORD among the servants of Pharaoh made his servants and his livestock flee to the houses. ²¹But he who did not regard the word of the LORD left his servants and his livestock in the field.

²²Then the LORD said to Moses, "Stretch out your hand toward heaven, that there may be hail in all the land of Egypt—on man, on beast, and on every herb of the field, throughout the land of Egypt." ²³And Moses stretched out his rod toward heaven; and the LORD sent thunder and hail, and fire darted to the ground. And the LORD rained hail on the land of Egypt. ²⁴So there was hail, and fire mingled with the hail, so very heavy that there was none like it in all the land of Egypt since it became a nation. ²⁵And the hail struck throughout the whole land of Egypt, all that *was* in the field, both man and beast; and the hail struck every herb of the field and broke every tree of the field. ²⁶Only in the land of Goshen, where the children of Israel *were,* there was no hail.

²⁷And Pharaoh sent and called for Moses and Aaron, and said to them, "I have sinned this time. The LORD *is* righteous, and my people and I *are* wicked. ²⁸Entreat the LORD, that there may be no *more* mighty thundering and hail, for *it is* enough. I will let you go, and you shall stay no longer."

²⁹So Moses said to him, "As soon as I have gone out of the city, I will spread out my hands to the LORD; the thunder will cease, and there will be no more hail, that you may know that the earth *is* the LORD's. ³⁰But as for you and your servants, I know that you will not yet fear the LORD God."

³¹Now the flax and the barley were struck, for the barley *was* in the head and the flax *was* in bud. ³²But the wheat and the spelt were not struck, for they *are* late crops.

³³So Moses went out of the city from Pharaoh and spread out his hands to the LORD; then the thunder and the hail ceased, and the rain was not poured on the earth. ³⁴And when Pharaoh saw that the rain, the hail, and the thunder had ceased, he sinned yet more; and he hardened his heart, he and his servants. ³⁵So the heart of Pharaoh was hard; neither would he let the children of Israel go, as the LORD had spoken by Moses.

MATTHEW 19:13-30

THEN little children were brought to Him [Jesus] that He might put *His* hands on them and pray, but the disciples rebuked them. ¹⁴But Jesus said, "Let the little children come to Me, and do not forbid them; for of such is the kingdom of heaven." ¹⁵And He laid *His* hands on them and departed from there.

¹⁶Now behold, one came and said to Him, "Good* Teacher, what good thing shall I do that I may have eternal life?"

¹⁷So He said to him, "Why do you call Me good?* No one *is* good but One, *that is,* God.* But if you want to enter into life, keep the commandments."

¹⁸He said to Him, "Which ones?"

Jesus said, *"'You shall not murder,' 'You shall not commit adultery,' 'You shall not steal,' 'You shall not bear false witness,'* ¹⁹*'Honor your father and your mother,'** and, *'You shall love your neighbor as yourself.'"**

²⁰The young man said to Him, "All these things I have kept from my youth.* What do I still lack?"

²¹Jesus said to him, "If you want to be perfect, go, sell what you have and give to the poor, and you will have treasure in heaven; and come, follow Me."

²²But when the young man heard that saying, he went away sorrowful, for he had great possessions.

²³Then Jesus said to His disciples, "Assuredly, I say to you that it is hard for a rich man to enter the kingdom of heaven. ²⁴And again I say to you, it is easier for a camel to go through the eye of a needle than for a rich man to enter the kingdom of God."

²⁵When His disciples heard *it,* they were greatly astonished, saying, "Who then can be saved?"

²⁶But Jesus looked at *them* and said to them, "With men this is impossible, but with God all things are possible."

²⁷Then Peter answered and said to Him, "See, we have left all and followed You. Therefore what shall we have?"

²⁸So Jesus said to them, "Assuredly I say to you, that in the regeneration, when the Son of Man sits on the throne of His glory, you who have followed Me will also sit on twelve thrones, judging the twelve tribes of Israel. ²⁹And everyone who has left houses or brothers or sisters or father or mother or wife* or children or lands, for My name's sake, shall receive a hundredfold, and inherit eternal life. ³⁰But many *who are* first will be last, and the last first.

PSALM 24:1-10

A Psalm of David.

THE earth *is* the LORD's, and all its fullness,
The world and those who dwell therein.

2 For He has founded it upon the seas,
And established it upon the waters.

3 Who may ascend into the hill of the LORD?
Or who may stand in His holy place?

4 He who has clean hands and a pure heart,
Who has not lifted up his soul to an idol,
Nor sworn deceitfully.

5 He shall receive blessing from the LORD,
And righteousness from the God of his salvation.

6 This *is* Jacob, the generation of those who seek Him,
Who seek Your face.   Selah

7 Lift up your heads, O you gates!
And be lifted up, you everlasting doors!
And the King of glory shall come in.

8 Who *is* this King of glory?
The LORD strong and mighty,
The LORD mighty in battle.

9 Lift up your heads, O you gates!
Lift up, you everlasting doors!
And the King of glory shall come in.

10 Who is this King of glory?
The LORD of hosts,
He *is* the King of glory.   Selah

PROVERBS FOR TODAY/ 6:1-5

My son, if you become surety for your friend, if you have shaken hands in pledge for a stranger, you are snared by the words of your mouth; you are taken by the words of your mouth. So do this, my son, and deliver yourself; for you have come into the hand of your friend: Go and humble yourself; plead with your friend. Give no sleep to your eyes, nor slumber to your eyelids. Deliver yourself like a gazelle from the hand of the hunter, and like a bird from the hand of the fowler. *

JANUARY 30

EXODUS 10:1–12:13

Now the LORD said to Moses, "Go in to Pharaoh; for I have hardened his heart and the hearts of his servants, that I may show these signs of Mine before him, ²and that you may tell in the hearing of your son and your son's son the mighty things I have done in Egypt, and My signs which I have done among them, that you may know that I *am* the LORD."

³So Moses and Aaron came in to Pharaoh and said to him, "Thus says the LORD God of the Hebrews: 'How long will you refuse to humble yourself before Me? Let My people go, that they may serve Me. ⁴Or else, if you refuse to let My people go, behold, tomorrow I will bring locusts into your territory. ⁵And they shall cover the face of the earth, so that no one will be able to see the earth; and they shall eat the residue of what is left, which remains to you from the hail, and they shall eat every tree which grows up for you out of the field. ⁶They shall fill your houses, the houses of all your servants, and the houses of all the Egyptians—which neither your fathers nor your fathers' fathers have seen, since the day that they were on the earth to this day.' " And he turned and went out from Pharaoh.

⁷Then Pharaoh's servants said to him, "How long shall this man be a snare to us? Let the men go, that they may serve the LORD their God. Do you not yet know that Egypt is destroyed?"

⁸So Moses and Aaron were brought again to Pharaoh, and he said to them, "Go, serve the LORD your God. Who *are* the ones that are going?"

⁹And Moses said, "We will go with our young and our old; with our sons and our daughters, with our flocks and our herds we will go, for we must hold a feast to the LORD."

¹⁰Then he said to them, "The LORD had better be with you when I let you and your little ones go! Beware, for evil is ahead of you. ¹¹Not so! Go now, you *who are* men, and serve the LORD, for that is what you desired." And they were driven out from Pharaoh's presence.

¹²Then the LORD said to Moses, "Stretch out your hand over the land of Egypt for the locusts, that they may come upon the land of Egypt, and eat every herb of the land—all that the hail has left." ¹³So Moses stretched out his rod over the land of Egypt, and the LORD brought an east wind on the land all that day and all *that* night. When it was morning, the east wind brought the locusts. ¹⁴And the locusts went up over all the land of Egypt and rested on all the territory of Egypt. *They were* very severe; previously there had been no such locusts as they, nor shall there be such after them. ¹⁵For they

covered the face of the whole earth, so that the land was darkened; and they ate every herb of the land and all the fruit of the trees which the hail had left. So there remained nothing green on the trees or on the plants of the field throughout all the land of Egypt.

16Then Pharaoh called for Moses and Aaron in haste, and said, "I have sinned against the LORD your God and against you. 17Now therefore, please forgive my sin only this once, and entreat the LORD your God, that He may take away from me this death only." 18So he went out from Pharaoh and entreated the LORD. 19And the LORD turned a very strong west wind, which took the locusts away and blew them into the Red Sea. There remained not one locust in all the territory of Egypt. 20But the LORD hardened Pharaoh's heart, and he did not let the children of Israel go.

21Then the LORD said to Moses, "Stretch out your hand toward heaven, that there may be darkness over the land of Egypt, darkness *which* may even be felt." 22So Moses stretched out his hand toward heaven, and there was thick darkness in all the land of Egypt three days. 23They did not see one another; nor did anyone rise from his place for three days. But all the children of Israel had light in their dwellings.

24Then Pharaoh called to Moses and said, "Go, serve the LORD; only let your flocks and your herds be kept back. Let your little ones also go with you."

25But Moses said, "You must also give us sacrifices and burnt offerings, that we may sacrifice to the LORD our God. 26Our livestock also shall go with us; not a hoof shall be left behind. For we must take some of them to serve the LORD our God, and even we do not know with what we must serve the LORD until we arrive there."

27But the LORD hardened Pharaoh's heart, and he would not let them go.

28Then Pharaoh said to him, "Get away from me! Take heed to yourself and see my face no more! For in the day you see my face you shall die!"

29So Moses said, "You have spoken well. I will never see your face again."

AND the LORD said to Moses, "I will bring one more plague on Pharaoh and on Egypt. Afterward he will let you go from here. When he lets *you* go, he will surely drive you out of here altogether. 2Speak now in the hearing of the people, and let every man ask from his neighbor and every woman from her neighbor, articles of silver and articles of gold." 3And the LORD gave the people favor in the sight of the Egyptians. Moreover the man Moses *was* very great in the land of Egypt, in the sight of Pharaoh's servants and in the sight of the people.

4Then Moses said, "Thus says the LORD: 'About midnight I will go out into the midst of Egypt; 5and all the firstborn in the land of Egypt shall die, from the firstborn of Pharaoh who sits on his throne, even to the firstborn of the female servant who *is* behind the handmill, and all the firstborn of the animals. 6Then there shall be a great cry throughout all the land of Egypt, such as was not like it *before,* nor shall be like it again. 7But against none of the children of Israel shall a dog move its tongue, against man or beast, that you may know that the LORD does make a difference between the Egyptians and Israel.' 8And all these your servants shall come down to me and bow down to me, saying, 'Get out, and all the people who follow you!' After that I will go out." Then he went out from Pharaoh in great anger.

9But the LORD said to Moses, "Pharaoh will not heed you, so that My wonders may be multiplied in the land of Egypt." 10So Moses and Aaron did all these wonders before Pharaoh; and the LORD hardened Pharaoh's heart, and he did not let the children of Israel go out of his land.

Now the LORD spoke to Moses and Aaron in the land of Egypt, saying, [2]"This month *shall be* your beginning of months; it *shall be* the first month of the year to you. [3]Speak to all the congregation of Israel, saying: 'On the tenth of this month every man shall take for himself a lamb, according to the house of *his* father, a lamb for a household. [4]And if the household is too small for the lamb, let him and his neighbor next to his house take *it* according to the number of the persons; according to each man's need you shall make your count for the lamb. [5]Your lamb shall be without blemish, a male of the first year. You may take *it* from the sheep or from the goats. [6]Now you shall keep it until the fourteenth day of the same month. Then the whole assembly of the congregation of Israel shall kill it at twilight. [7]And they shall take *some* of the blood and put *it* on the two doorposts and on the lintel of the houses where they eat it. [8]Then they shall eat the flesh on that night; roasted in fire, with unleavened bread *and* with bitter *herbs* they shall eat it. [9]Do not eat it raw, nor boiled at all with water, but roasted in fire—its head with its legs and its entrails. [10]You shall let none of it remain until morning, and what remains of it until morning you shall burn with fire. [11]And thus you shall eat it: *with* a belt on your waist, your sandals on your feet, and your staff in your hand. So you shall eat it in haste. It *is* the LORD's Passover.

[12]"For I will pass through the land of Egypt on that night, and will strike all the firstborn in the land of Egypt, both man and beast; and against all the gods of Egypt I will execute judgment: I *am* the LORD. [13]Now the blood shall be a sign for you on the houses where you *are.* And when I see the blood, I will pass over you; and the plague shall not be on you to destroy *you* when I strike the land of Egypt.' "

MATTHEW 20:1-28

"FOR the kingdom of heaven is like a landowner who went out early in the morning to hire laborers for his vineyard. [2]Now when he had agreed with the laborers for a denarius a day, he sent them into his vineyard. [3]And he went out about the third hour and saw others standing idle in the marketplace, [4]and said to them, 'You also go into the vineyard, and whatever is right I will give you.' So they went. [5]Again he went out about the sixth and the ninth hour, and did likewise. [6]And about the eleventh hour he went out and found others standing idle,* and said to them, 'Why have you been standing here idle all day?' [7]They said to him, 'Because no one hired us.' He said to them, 'You also go into the vineyard, and whatever is right you will receive.'*

[8]"So when evening had come, the owner of the vineyard said to his steward, 'Call the laborers and give them *their* wages, beginning with the last to the first.' [9]And when those came who *were hired* about the eleventh hour, they each received a denarius. [10]But when the first came, they supposed that they would receive more; and they likewise received each a denarius. [11]And when they had received *it,* they complained against the landowner, [12]saying, 'These last *men* have worked *only* one hour, and you made them equal to us who have borne the burden and the heat of the day.' [13]But he answered one of them and said, 'Friend, I am doing you no wrong. Did you not agree with me for a denarius? [14]Take *what is* yours and go your way. I wish to give to this last man *the same* as to you. [15]Is it not lawful for me to do what I wish with my own things? Or is your eye evil because I am good?' [16]So the

last will be first, and the first last. For many are called, but few chosen."*

17Now Jesus, going up to Jerusalem, took the twelve disciples aside on the road and said to them, 18"Behold, we are going up to Jerusalem, and the Son of Man will be betrayed to the chief priests and to the scribes; and they will condemn Him to death, 19and deliver Him to the Gentiles to mock and to scourge and to crucify. And the third day He will rise again."

20Then the mother of Zebedee's sons came to Him with her sons, kneeling down and asking something from Him.

21And He said to her, "What do you wish?"

She said to Him, "Grant that these two sons of mine may sit, one on Your right hand and the other on the left, in Your kingdom."

22But Jesus answered and said, "You do not know what you ask. Are you able to drink the cup that I am about to drink, and be baptized with the baptism that I am baptized with?"*

They said to Him, "We are able."

23So He said to them, "You will indeed drink My cup, and be baptized with the baptism that I am baptized with;* but to sit on My right hand and on My left is not Mine to give, but *it is for those* for whom it is prepared by My Father."

24And when the ten heard *it,* they were greatly displeased with the two brothers. 25But Jesus called them to *Himself* and said, "You know that the rulers of the Gentiles lord it over them, and those who are great exercise authority over them. 26Yet it shall not be so among you; but whoever desires to become great among you, let him be your servant. 27And whoever desires to be first among you, let him be your slave— 28just as the Son of Man did not come to be served, but to serve, and to give His life a ransom for many."

PSALM 25:1-11

A Psalm of David.

To You, O LORD, I lift up my soul.
2 O my God, I trust in You;
Let me not be ashamed;
Let not my enemies triumph
over me.
3 Indeed, let no one who waits
on You be ashamed;
Let those be ashamed who
deal treacherously without
cause.

4 Show me Your ways, O LORD;
Teach me Your paths.
5 Lead me in Your truth and
teach me,
For You *are* the God of my
salvation;
On You I wait all the day.

6 Remember, O LORD, Your
tender mercies and Your
lovingkindnesses,
For they *are* from of old.
7 Do not remember the sins of
my youth, nor my
transgressions;
According to Your mercy
remember me,
For Your goodness' sake,
O LORD.

8 Good and upright *is* the LORD;
Therefore He teaches sinners
in the way.
9 The humble He guides in
justice,
And the humble He teaches
His way.
10 All the paths of the LORD *are*
mercy and truth,
To such as keep His covenant
and His testimonies.
11 For Your name's sake, O LORD,
Pardon my iniquity, for it *is*
great.

PROVERBS FOR TODAY/ 6:6-11

Go to the ant, you sluggard! Consider her ways and be wise, which, having no captain, overseer or ruler, provides her supplies in the summer, and gathers her food in the harvest. ▢How long will you slumber, O sluggard? When will you rise from your sleep? A little sleep, a little slumber, a little folding of the hands to sleep—so shall your poverty come on you like a prowler, and your need like an armed man.

JANUARY 31

EXODUS 12:14–13:16

"**S**o this day shall be to you a memorial; and you shall keep it as a feast to the LORD throughout your generations. You shall keep it as a feast by an everlasting ordinance. ¹⁵Seven days you shall eat unleavened bread. On the first day you shall remove leaven from your houses. For whoever eats leavened bread from the first day until the seventh day, that person shall be cut off from Israel. ¹⁶On the first day *there shall be* a holy convocation, and on the seventh day there shall be a holy convocation for you. No manner of work shall be done on them; but *that* which everyone must eat—that only may be prepared by you. ¹⁷So you shall observe *the Feast of* Unleavened Bread, for on this same day I will have brought your armies out of the land of Egypt. Therefore you shall observe this day throughout your generations as an everlasting ordinance. ¹⁸In the first *month,* on the fourteenth day of the month at evening, you shall eat unleavened bread, until the twenty-first day of the month at evening. ¹⁹For seven days no leaven shall be found in your houses, since whoever eats what is leavened, that same person shall be cut off from the congregation of Israel, whether *he is* a stranger or a native of the land. ²⁰You shall eat nothing leav-ened; in all your dwellings you shall eat unleavened bread.' "

²¹Then Moses called for all the elders of Israel and said to them, "Pick out and take lambs for yourselves according to your families, and kill the Passover *lamb.* ²²And you shall take a bunch of hyssop, dip *it* in the blood that *is* in the basin, and strike the lintel and the two doorposts with the blood that *is* in the basin. And none of you shall go out of the door of his house until morning. ²³For the LORD will pass through to strike the Egyptians; and when He sees the blood on the lintel and on the two doorposts, the LORD will pass over the door and not allow the destroyer to come into your houses to strike *you.* ²⁴And you shall observe this thing as an ordinance for you and your sons forever. ²⁵It will come to pass when you come to the land which the LORD will give you, just as He promised, that you shall keep this service. ²⁶And it shall be, when your children say to you, 'What do you mean by this service?' ²⁷that you shall say, 'It *is* the Passover sacrifice of the LORD, who passed over the houses of the children of Israel in Egypt when He struck the Egyptians and delivered our households.' " So the people bowed their heads and worshiped. ²⁸Then the children of Israel went away and did *so;*

just as the LORD had commanded Moses and Aaron, so they did.

29And it came to pass at midnight that the LORD struck all the firstborn in the land of Egypt, from the firstborn of Pharaoh who sat on his throne to the firstborn of the captive who *was* in the dungeon, and all the firstborn of livestock. 30So Pharaoh rose in the night, he, all his servants, and all the Egyptians; and there was a great cry in Egypt, for *there was* not a house where *there was* not one dead.

31Then he called for Moses and Aaron by night, and said, "Rise, go out from among my people, both you and the children of Israel. And go, serve the LORD as you have said. 32Also take your flocks and your herds, as you have said, and be gone; and bless me also."

33And the Egyptians urged the people, that they might send them out of the land in haste. For they said, "We *shall* all *be* dead." 34So the people took their dough before it was leavened, having their kneading bowls bound up in their clothes on their shoulders. 35Now the children of Israel had done according to the word of Moses, and they had asked from the Egyptians articles of silver, articles of gold, and clothing. 36And the LORD had given the people favor in the sight of the Egyptians, so that they granted them *what they requested.* Thus they plundered the Egyptians.

37Then the children of Israel journeyed from Rameses to Succoth, about six hundred thousand men on foot, besides children. 38A mixed multitude went up with them also, and flocks and herds—a great deal of livestock. 39And they baked unleavened cakes of the dough which they had brought out of Egypt; for it was not leavened, because they were driven out of Egypt and could not wait, nor had they prepared provisions for themselves.

40Now the sojourn of the children of Israel who lived in Egypt* *was* four hundred and thirty years. 41And it came to pass at the end of the four hundred and thirty years—on that very same day—it came to pass that all the armies of the LORD went out from the land of Egypt. 42It *is* a night of solemn observance to the LORD for bringing them out of the land of Egypt. This *is* that night of the LORD, a solemn observance for all the children of Israel throughout their generations.

43And the LORD said to Moses and Aaron, "This *is* the ordinance of the Passover: No foreigner shall eat it. 44But every man's servant who is bought for money, when you have circumcised him, then he may eat it. 45A sojourner and a hired servant shall not eat it. 46In one house it shall be eaten; you shall not carry any of the flesh outside the house, nor shall you break one of its bones. 47All the congregation of Israel shall keep it. 48And when a stranger dwells with you *and wants* to keep the Passover to the LORD, let all his males be circumcised, and then let him come near and keep it; and he shall be as a native of the land. For no uncircumcised person shall eat it. 49One law shall be for the native-born and for the stranger who dwells among you."

50Thus all the children of Israel did; as the LORD commanded Moses and Aaron, so they did. 51And it came to pass, on that very same day, that the LORD brought the children of Israel out of the land of Egypt according to their armies.

THEN the LORD spoke to Moses, saying, 2"Consecrate to Me all the firstborn, whatever opens the womb among the children of Israel, *both* of man and beast; it is Mine."

3And Moses said to the people: "Remember this day in which you went out of Egypt, out of the house of bondage; for by strength of hand the LORD brought you out of this *place.* No leavened bread shall be eaten. ⁴On this day you are going out, in the month Abib. ⁵And it shall be, when the Lᴏʀᴅ brings you into the land of the Canaanites and the Hittites and the Amorites and the Hivites and the Jebusites, which He swore to your fathers to give you, a land flowing with milk and honey, that you shall keep this service in this month. ⁶Seven days you shall eat unleavened bread, and on the seventh day *there shall be* a feast to the Lᴏʀᴅ. ⁷Unleavened bread shall be eaten seven days. And no leavened bread shall be seen among you, nor shall leaven be seen among you in all your quarters. ⁸And you shall tell your son in that day, saying, *'This is done* because of what the Lᴏʀᴅ did for me when I came up from Egypt.' ⁹It shall be as a sign to you on your hand and as a memorial between your eyes, that the Lᴏʀᴅ's law may be in your mouth; for with a strong hand the Lᴏʀᴅ has brought you out of Egypt. ¹⁰You shall therefore keep this ordinance in its season from year to year.

¹¹"And it shall be, when the Lᴏʀᴅ brings you into the land of the Canaanites, as He swore to you and your fathers, and gives it to you, ¹²that you shall set apart to the Lᴏʀᴅ all that open the womb, that is, every firstborn that comes from an animal which you have; the males *shall be* the Lᴏʀᴅ's. ¹³But every firstborn of a donkey you shall redeem with a lamb; and if you will not redeem *it,* then you shall break its neck. And all the firstborn of man among your sons you shall redeem. ¹⁴So it shall be, when your son asks you in time to come, saying, 'What *is* this?' that you shall say to him, 'By strength of hand the Lᴏʀᴅ brought us out of Egypt, out of the house of bondage. ¹⁵And it came to pass, when Pharaoh was stubborn about letting us go, that the Lᴏʀᴅ killed all the firstborn in the land of Egypt, both the firstborn of man and the firstborn of beast. Therefore I sacrifice to the Lᴏʀᴅ all males

that open the womb, but all the firstborn of my sons I redeem.' ¹⁶It shall be as a sign on your hand and as frontlets between your eyes, for by strength of hand the Lᴏʀᴅ brought us out of Egypt."

MATTHEW 20:29–21:22

Nᴏᴡ as they [Jesus and his disciples] went out of Jericho, a great multitude followed Him. ³⁰And behold, two blind men sitting by the road, when they heard that Jesus was passing by, cried out, saying, "Have mercy on us, O Lord, Son of David!"

³¹Then the multitude warned them that they should be quiet; but they cried out all the more, saying, "Have mercy on us, O Lord, Son of David!"

³²So Jesus stood still and called them, and said, "What do you want Me to do for you?"

³³They said to Him, "Lord, that our eyes may be opened." ³⁴So Jesus had compassion and touched their eyes. And immediately their eyes received sight, and they followed Him.

Nᴏᴡ when they drew near Jerusalem, and came to Bethphage,* at the Mount of Olives, then Jesus sent two disciples, ²saying to them, "Go into the village opposite you, and immediately you will find a donkey tied, and a colt with her. Loose *them* and bring *them* to Me. ³And if anyone says anything to you, you shall say, 'The Lord has need of them,' and immediately he will send them."

⁴All* this was done that it might be fulfilled which was spoken by the prophet, saying:

5   *"Tell the daughter of Zion,*
       'Behold, your King is coming
          to you,
       Lowly, and sitting on a donkey,
       A colt, the foal of a donkey.' " *

⁶So the disciples went and did as Jesus commanded them. ⁷They brought the donkey and the colt, laid their clothes on them, and set *Him** on them. ⁸And a very great multitude spread their clothes on the road; others cut down branches from the trees and spread *them* on the road. ⁹Then the multitudes who went before and those who followed cried out, saying:

"Hosanna to the Son of David!
*'Blessed is He who comes in
the name of the Lᴏʀᴅ!'**
Hosanna in the highest!"

¹⁰And when He had come into Jerusalem, all the city was moved, saying, "Who is this?"

¹¹So the multitudes said, "This is Jesus, the prophet from Nazareth of Galilee."

¹²Then Jesus went into the temple of God* and drove out all those who bought and sold in the temple, and overturned the tables of the money changers and the seats of those who sold doves. ¹³And He said to them, "It is written, *'My house shall be called a house of prayer,'** but you have made it a *'den of thieves.'*"*

¹⁴Then *the* blind and *the* lame came to Him in the temple, and He healed them. ¹⁵But when the chief priests and scribes saw the wonderful things that He did, and the children crying out in the temple and saying, "Hosanna to the Son of David!" they were indignant ¹⁶and said to Him, "Do You hear what these are saying?"

And Jesus said to them, "Yes. Have you never read,

*'Out of the mouth of babes
and nursing infants
You have perfected praise'?* "*

¹⁷Then He left them and went out of the city to Bethany, and He lodged there.

¹⁸Now in the morning, as He returned to the city, He was hungry.

¹⁹And seeing a fig tree by the road, He came to it and found nothing on it but leaves, and said to it, "Let no fruit grow on you ever again." Immediately the fig tree withered away.

²⁰And when the disciples saw *it,* they marveled, saying, "How did the fig tree wither away so soon?"

²¹So Jesus answered and said to them, "Assuredly, I say to you, if you have faith and do not doubt, you will not only do what was done to the fig tree, but also if you say to this mountain, 'Be removed and be cast into the sea,' it will be done. ²²And whatever things you ask in prayer, believing, you will receive."

PSALM 25:12-22

Wʜᴏ *is* the man that fears the Lᴏʀᴅ?
Him shall He* teach in the way He* chooses.
13 He himself shall dwell in prosperity,
And his descendants shall inherit the earth.
14 The secret of the Lᴏʀᴅ *is* with those who fear Him,
And He will show them His covenant.
15 My eyes *are* ever toward the Lᴏʀᴅ,
For He shall pluck my feet out of the net.

16 Turn Yourself to me, and have mercy on me,
For I *am* desolate and afflicted.
17 The troubles of my heart have enlarged;
Bring me out of my distresses!
18 Look on my affliction and my pain,
And forgive all my sins.
19 Consider my enemies, for they are many;

And they hate me with cruel
   hatred.
20 Keep my soul, and deliver me;
   Let me not be ashamed, for I
    put my trust in You.

21 Let integrity and uprightness
   preserve me,
For I wait for You.

22 Redeem Israel, O God,
Out of all their troubles!

PROVERBS FOR TODAY/ 6:12-15

A worthless person, a wicked man, walks with a perverse mouth; he winks with his eyes, he shuffles his feet, he points with his fingers; perversity is *in his heart, he devises evil continually, he sows discord. Therefore his calamity shall come suddenly; suddenly he shall be broken without remedy.*

FEBRUARY 1

EXODUS 13:17–15:19

THEN it came to pass, when Pharaoh had let the people go, that God did not lead them *by* way of the land of the Philistines, although that *was* near; for God said, "Lest perhaps the people change their minds when they see war, and return to Egypt." 18So God led the people around *by* way of the wilderness of the Red Sea. And the children of Israel went up in orderly ranks out of the land of Egypt.

19And Moses took the bones of Joseph with him, for he had placed the children of Israel under solemn oath, saying, "God will surely visit you, and you shall carry up my bones from here with you."*

20So they took their journey from Succoth and camped in Etham at the edge of the wilderness. 21And the LORD went before them by day in a pillar of cloud to lead the way, and by night in a pillar of fire to give them light, so as to go by day and night. 22He did not take away the pillar of cloud by day or the pillar of fire by night *from* before the people.

Now the LORD spoke to Moses, saying: 2"Speak to the children of Israel, that they turn and camp before Pi Hahiroth, between Migdol and the sea, opposite Baal Zephon; you shall camp before it by the sea. 3For Pharaoh will say of the children of Israel, 'They *are* bewildered by the land; the wilderness has closed them in.' 4Then I will harden Pharaoh's heart, so that he will pursue them; and I will gain honor over Pharaoh and over all his army, that the Egyptians may know that I *am* the LORD." And they did so.

5Now it was told the king of Egypt that the people had fled, and the heart of Pharaoh and his servants was turned against the people; and they said, "Why have we done this, that we have let Israel go from serving us?" 6So he made ready his chariot and took his people with him. 7Also, he took six hundred choice chariots, and all the chariots of Egypt with captains over every one of them. 8And the LORD hardened the heart of Pharaoh king of Egypt, and he pursued the children of Israel; and the children of Israel went out with boldness. 9So the Egyptians pursued them, all the horses *and* chariots of Pharaoh, his horsemen and his army, and overtook them camping by the sea beside Pi Hahiroth, before Baal Zephon.

¹⁰And when Pharaoh drew near, the children of Israel lifted their eyes, and behold, the Egyptians marched after them. So they were very afraid, and the children of Israel cried out to the LORD. ¹¹Then they said to Moses, "Because *there were* no graves in Egypt, have you taken us away to die in the wilderness? Why have you so dealt with us, to bring us up out of Egypt? ¹²*Is* this not the word that we told you in Egypt, saying, 'Let us alone that we may serve the Egyptians'? For *it would have been* better for us to serve the Egyptians than that we should die in the wilderness."

¹³And Moses said to the people, "Do not be afraid. Stand still, and see the salvation of the LORD, which He will accomplish for you today. For the Egyptians whom you see today, you shall see again no more forever. ¹⁴The LORD will fight for you, and you shall hold your peace."

¹⁵And the LORD said to Moses, "Why do you cry to Me? Tell the children of Israel to go forward. ¹⁶But lift up your rod, and stretch out your hand over the sea and divide it. And the children of Israel shall go on dry *ground* through the midst of the sea. ¹⁷And I indeed will harden the hearts of the Egyptians, and they shall follow them. So I will gain honor over Pharaoh and over all his army, his chariots, and his horsemen. ¹⁸Then the Egyptians shall know that I *am* the LORD, when I have gained honor for Myself over Pharaoh, his chariots, and his horsemen."

¹⁹And the Angel of God, who went before the camp of Israel, moved and went behind them; and the pillar of cloud went from before them and stood behind them. ²⁰So it came between the camp of the Egyptians and the camp of Israel. Thus it was a cloud

and darkness *to the one,* and it gave light by night *to the other,* so that the one did not come near the other all that night.

²¹Then Moses stretched out his hand over the sea; and the LORD caused the sea to go *back* by a strong east wind all that night, and made the sea into dry *land,* and the waters were divided. ²²So the children of Israel went into the midst of the sea on the dry *ground,* and the waters *were* a wall to them on their right hand and on their left. ²³And the Egyptians pursued and went after them into the midst of the sea, all Pharaoh's horses, his chariots, and his horsemen.

²⁴Now it came to pass, in the morning watch, that the LORD looked down upon the army of the Egyptians through the pillar of fire and cloud, and He troubled the army of the Egyptians. ²⁵And He took off* their chariot wheels, so that they drove them with difficulty; and the Egyptians said, "Let us flee from the face of Israel, for the LORD fights for them against the Egyptians."

²⁶Then the LORD said to Moses, "Stretch out your hand over the sea, that the waters may come back upon the Egyptians, on their chariots, and on their horsemen." ²⁷And Moses stretched out his hand over the sea; and when the morning appeared, the sea returned to its full depth, while the Egyptians were fleeing into it. So the LORD overthrew the Egyptians in the midst of the sea. ²⁸Then the waters returned and covered the chariots, the horsemen, *and* all the army of Pharaoh that came into the sea after them. Not so much as one of them remained. ²⁹But the children of Israel had walked on dry *land* in the midst of the sea, and the waters *were* a wall to them on their right hand and on their left.

³⁰So the LORD saved Israel that day out of the hand of the Egyptians, and Israel saw the Egyptians dead on the

seashore. ³¹Thus Israel saw the great work which the LORD had done in Egypt; so the people feared the LORD, and believed the LORD and His servant Moses.

THEN Moses and the children of Israel sang this song to the LORD, and spoke, saying:

"I will sing to the LORD,
For He has triumphed
gloriously!
The horse and its rider
He has thrown into the sea!
2 The LORD *is* my strength and
song,
And He has become my
salvation;
He *is* my God, and I will
praise Him;
My father's God, and I will
exalt Him.
3 The LORD *is* a man of war;
The LORD *is* His name.
4 Pharaoh's chariots and his
army He has cast into the
sea;
His chosen captains also are
drowned in the Red Sea.
5 The depths have covered
them;
They sank to the bottom like
a stone.

6 "Your right hand, O LORD, has
become glorious in power;
Your right hand, O LORD, has
dashed the enemy in pieces.
7 And in the greatness of Your
excellence
You have overthrown those
who rose against You;
You sent forth Your wrath;
It consumed them like
stubble.
8 And with the blast of Your
nostrils
The waters were gathered
together;

The floods stood upright like
a heap;
The depths congealed in the
heart of the sea.
9 The enemy said, 'I will pursue,
I will overtake,
I will divide the spoil;
My desire shall be satisfied
on them.
I will draw my sword,
My hand shall destroy them.'
10 You blew with Your wind,
The sea covered them;
They sank like lead in the
mighty waters.

11 "Who *is* like You, O LORD,
among the gods?
Who *is* like You, glorious in
holiness,
Fearful in praises, doing
wonders?
12 You stretched out Your right
hand;
The earth swallowed them.
13 You in Your mercy have led
forth
The people whom You have
redeemed;
You have guided *them* in Your
strength
To Your holy habitation.

14 "The people will hear *and* be
afraid;
Sorrow will take hold of the
inhabitants of Philistia.
15 Then the chiefs of Edom will
be dismayed;
The mighty men of Moab,
Trembling will take hold of
them;
All the inhabitants of Canaan
will melt away.
16 Fear and dread will fall on
them;
By the greatness of Your arm
They will be *as* still as a stone,
Till Your people pass over,
O LORD,

Till the people pass over
Whom You have purchased.
17 You will bring them in and
plant them
In the mountain of Your
inheritance,
In the place, O LORD, *which*
You have made
For Your own dwelling,
The sanctuary, O LORD, *which*
Your hands have
established.

18 "The LORD shall reign forever
and ever."

19For the horses of Pharaoh went with his chariots and his horsemen into the sea, and the LORD brought back the waters of the sea upon them. But the children of Israel went on dry *land* in the midst of the sea.

MATTHEW 21:23-46

Now when He [Jesus] came into the temple, the chief priests and the elders of the people confronted Him as He was teaching, and said, "By what authority are You doing these things? And who gave You this authority?"

24But Jesus answered and said to them, "I also will ask you one thing, which if you tell Me, I likewise will tell you by what authority I do these things: 25The baptism of John—where was it from? From heaven or from men?"

And they reasoned among themselves, saying, "If we say, 'From heaven,' He will say to us, 'Why then did you not believe him?' 26But if we say, 'From men,' we fear the multitude, for all count John as a prophet." 27So they answered Jesus and said, "We do not know."

And He said to them, "Neither will I tell you by what authority I do these things.

28"But what do you think? A man had two sons, and he came to the first and said, 'Son, go, work today in my vineyard.' 29He answered and said, 'I will not,' but afterward he regretted it and went. 30Then he came to the second and said likewise. And he answered and said, 'I *go,* sir,' but he did not go. 31Which of the two did the will of *his* father?"

They said to Him, "The first."

Jesus said to them, "Assuredly, I say to you that tax collectors and harlots enter the kingdom of God before you. 32For John came to you in the way of righteousness, and you did not believe him; but tax collectors and harlots believed him; and when you saw *it,* you did not afterward relent and believe him.

33"Hear another parable: There was a certain landowner who planted a vineyard and set a hedge around it, dug a winepress in it and built a tower. And he leased it to vinedressers and went into a far country. 34Now when vintage-time drew near, he sent his servants to the vinedressers, that they might receive its fruit. 35And the vinedressers took his servants, beat one, killed one, and stoned another. 36Again he sent other servants, more than the first, and they did likewise to them. 37Then last of all he sent his son to them, saying, 'They will respect my son.' 38But when the vinedressers saw the son, they said among themselves, 'This is the heir. Come, let us kill him and seize his inheritance.' 39So they took him and cast *him* out of the vineyard and killed *him.*

40"Therefore, when the owner of the vineyard comes, what will he do to those vinedressers?"

41They said to Him, "He will destroy those wicked men miserably, and lease *his* vineyard to other vinedressers who will render to him the fruits in their seasons."

42Jesus said to them, "Have you never read in the Scriptures:

> 'The stone which the builders
>   rejected
> Has become the chief
>   cornerstone.
> This was the LORD's doing,
> And it is marvelous in our
>   eyes'?*

43"Therefore I say to you, the kingdom of God will be taken from you and given to a nation bearing the fruits of it. 44And whoever falls on this stone will be broken; but on whomever it falls, it will grind him to powder."

45Now when the chief priests and Pharisees heard His parables, they perceived that He was speaking of them. 46But when they sought to lay hands on Him, they feared the multitudes, because they took Him for a prophet.

PSALM 26:1-12

A Psalm of David.

VINDICATE me, O LORD,
    For I have walked in my integrity.
    I have also trusted in the LORD;
    I shall not slip.
2   Examine me, O LORD, and
        prove me;
    Try my mind and my heart.
3   For Your lovingkindness *is*
        before my eyes,
    And I have walked in Your
        truth.

4   I have not sat with idolatrous
        mortals,
    Nor will I go in with
        hypocrites.
5   I have hated the assembly of
        evildoers,
    And will not sit with the
        wicked.

6   I will wash my hands in
        innocence;
    So I will go about Your altar,
        O LORD,
7   That I may proclaim with the
        voice of thanksgiving,
    And tell of all Your wondrous
        works.
8   LORD, I have loved the
        habitation of Your house,
    And the place where Your
        glory dwells.

9   Do not gather my soul with
        sinners,
    Nor my life with bloodthirsty
        men,
10 In whose hands *is* a sinister
        scheme,
    And whose right hand is full
        of bribes.

11 But as for me, I will walk in
        my integrity;
    Redeem me and be merciful
        to me.
12 My foot stands in an even
        place;
    In the congregations I will
        bless the LORD.

PROVERBS FOR TODAY/ 6:16-19

These six things the LORD hates, yes, seven are an abomination to Him: A proud look, a lying tongue, hands that shed innocent blood, a heart that devises wicked plans, feet that are swift in running to evil, a false witness who speaks lies, and one who sows discord among brethren.

FEBRUARY 2

EXODUS 15:20–17:7

THEN Miriam the prophetess, the sister of Aaron, took the timbrel in her hand; and all the women went out after her with timbrels and with dances. ²¹And Miriam answered them:

"Sing to the LORD,
   For He has triumphed
   gloriously!
The horse and its rider
He has thrown into the sea!"

²²So Moses brought Israel from the Red Sea; then they went out into the Wilderness of Shur. And they went three days in the wilderness and found no water. ²³Now when they came to Marah, they could not drink the waters of Marah, for they *were* bitter. Therefore the name of it was called Marah.* ²⁴And the people complained against Moses, saying, "What shall we drink?" ²⁵So he cried out to the LORD, and the LORD showed him a tree. When he cast *it* into the waters, the waters were made sweet.

There He made a statute and an ordinance for them, and there He tested them, ²⁶and said, "If you diligently heed the voice of the LORD your God and do what is right in His sight, give ear to His commandments and keep all His statutes, I will put none of the diseases on you which I have brought on the Egyptians. For I *am* the LORD who heals you."

²⁷Then they came to Elim, where there *were* twelve wells of water and seventy palm trees; so they camped there by the waters.

AND they journeyed from Elim, and all the congregation of the children of Israel came to the Wilderness of Sin, which is between Elim and Sinai, on the fifteenth day of the second month after they departed from the land of Egypt. ²Then the whole congregation of the children of Israel complained against Moses and Aaron in the wilderness. ³And the children of Israel said to them, "Oh, that we had died by the hand of the LORD in the land of Egypt, when we sat by the pots of meat *and* when we ate bread to the full! For you have brought us out into this wilderness to kill this whole assembly with hunger."

⁴Then the LORD said to Moses, "Behold, I will rain bread from heaven for you. And the people shall go out and gather a certain quota every day, that I may test them, whether they will walk in My law or not. ⁵And it shall be on the sixth day that they shall prepare what they bring in, and it shall be twice as much as they gather daily."

⁶Then Moses and Aaron said to all the children of Israel, "At evening you shall know that the LORD has brought you out of the land of Egypt. ⁷And in the morning you shall see the glory of the LORD; for He hears your complaints against the LORD. But what *are* we, that you complain against us?" ⁸Also Moses said, "*This shall be seen* when the LORD gives you meat to eat in the evening, and in the morning bread to the full; for the LORD hears your complaints which you make against Him. And what *are* we? Your complaints *are* not against us but against the LORD."

⁹Then Moses spoke to Aaron, "Say to all the congregation of the children of Israel, 'Come near before the LORD, for He has heard your complaints.'" ¹⁰Now it came to pass, as Aaron spoke to the whole congregation of the children of Israel, that they looked toward

the wilderness, and behold, the glory of the LORD appeared in the cloud.

[11]And the LORD spoke to Moses, saying, [12]"I have heard the complaints of the children of Israel. Speak to them, saying, 'At twilight you shall eat meat, and in the morning you shall be filled with bread. And you shall know that I *am* the LORD your God.' "

[13]So it was that quails came up at evening and covered the camp, and in the morning the dew lay all around the camp. [14]And when the layer of dew lifted, there, on the surface of the wilderness, was a small round substance, *as* fine as frost on the ground. [15]So when the children of Israel saw *it,* they said to one another, "What is it?" For they did not know what it *was.*

And Moses said to them, "This *is* the bread which the LORD has given you to eat. [16]This is the thing which the LORD has commanded: 'Let every man gather it according to each one's need, one omer for each person, *according to the* number of persons; let every man take for *those* who *are* in his tent.' "

[17]Then the children of Israel did so and gathered, some more, some less. [18]So when they measured *it* by omers, he who gathered much had nothing left over, and he who gathered little had no lack. Every man had gathered according to each man's need. [19]And Moses said, "Let no one leave any of it till morning." [20]Notwithstanding they did not heed Moses. But some of them left part of it until morning, and it bred worms and stank. And Moses was angry with them. [21]So they gathered it every morning, every man according to his need. And when the sun became hot, it melted.

[22]And so it was, on the sixth day, *that* they gathered twice as much bread, two omers for each one. And all the rulers of the congregation came and told Moses. [23]Then he said to them, "This *is what* the LORD has said: 'Tomorrow *is* a Sabbath rest, a holy Sabbath to the LORD. Bake what you will bake *today,* and boil what you will boil; and lay up for yourselves all that remains, to be kept until morning.' " [24]So they laid it up till morning, as Moses commanded; and it did not stink, nor were there any worms in it. [25]Then Moses said, "Eat that today, for today *is* a Sabbath to the LORD; today you will not find it in the field. [26]Six days you shall gather it, but on the seventh day, the Sabbath, there will be none."

[27]Now it happened *that some* of the people went out on the seventh day to gather, but they found none. [28]And the LORD said to Moses, "How long do you refuse to keep My commandments and My laws? [29]See! For the LORD has given you the Sabbath; therefore He gives you on the sixth day bread for two days. Let every man remain in his place; let no man go out of his place on the seventh day." [30]So the people rested on the seventh day.

[31]And the house of Israel called its name Manna.* And it *was* like white coriander seed, and the taste of it *was* like wafers *made* with honey.

[32]Then Moses said, "This *is* the thing which the LORD has commanded: 'Fill an omer with it, to be kept for your generations, that they may see the bread with which I fed you in the wilderness, when I brought you out of the land of Egypt.' " [33]And Moses said to Aaron, "Take a pot and put an omer of manna in it, and lay it up before the LORD, to be kept for your generations." [34]As the LORD commanded Moses, so Aaron laid it up before the Testimony, to be kept. [35]And the children of Israel ate manna forty years, until they came to an inhabited land; they ate manna until they came to the border of the land of Canaan. [36]Now an omer *is* one-tenth of an ephah.

THEN all the congregation of the children of Israel set out on their journey from the Wilderness of Sin, according to the commandment of the LORD, and camped in Rephidim; but *there was* no water for the people to drink. ²Therefore the people contended with Moses, and said, "Give us water, that we may drink."

So Moses said to them, "Why do you contend with me? Why do you tempt the LORD?"

³And the people thirsted there for water, and the people complained against Moses, and said, "Why *is* it you have brought us up out of Egypt, to kill us and our children and our livestock with thirst?"

⁴So Moses cried out to the LORD, saying, "What shall I do with this people? They are almost ready to stone me!"

⁵And the LORD said to Moses, "Go on before the people, and take with you some of the elders of Israel. Also take in your hand your rod with which you struck the river, and go. ⁶Behold, I will stand before you there on the rock in Horeb; and you shall strike the rock, and water will come out of it, that the people may drink."

And Moses did so in the sight of the elders of Israel. ⁷So he called the name of the place Massah* and Meribah,* because of the contention of the children of Israel, and because they tempted the LORD, saying, "Is the LORD among us or not?"

MATTHEW 22:1-33

AND Jesus answered and spoke to them again by parables and said: ²"The kingdom of heaven is like a certain king who arranged a marriage for his son, ³and sent out his servants to call those who were invited to the wedding; and they were not willing to come. ⁴Again, he sent out other servants, saying, 'Tell those who are invited, "See, I have prepared my dinner; my oxen and fatted cattle *are* killed, and all things *are* ready. Come to the wedding." ' ⁵But they made light of

it and went their ways, one to his own farm, another to his business. ⁶And the rest seized his servants, treated *them* spitefully, and killed *them.* ⁷But when the king heard *about it,* he was furious. And he sent out his armies, destroyed those murderers, and burned up their city. ⁸Then he said to his servants, 'The wedding is ready, but those who were invited were not worthy. ⁹Therefore go into the highways, and as many as you find, invite to the wedding.' ¹⁰So those servants went out into the highways and gathered together all whom they found, both bad and good. And the wedding *hall* was filled with guests.

¹¹"But when the king came in to see the guests, he saw a man there who did not have on a wedding garment. ¹²So he said to him, 'Friend, how did you come in here without a wedding garment?' And he was speechless. ¹³Then the king said to the servants, 'Bind him hand and foot, take him away, and* cast *him* into outer darkness; there will be weeping and gnashing of teeth.'

¹⁴"For many are called, but few *are* chosen."

¹⁵Then the Pharisees went and plotted how they might entangle Him in *His* talk. ¹⁶And they sent to Him their disciples with the Herodians, saying, "Teacher, we know that You are true, and teach the way of God in truth; nor do You care about anyone, for You do not regard the person of men. ¹⁷Tell us, therefore, what do You think? Is it lawful to pay taxes to Caesar, or not?"

¹⁸But Jesus perceived their wickedness, and said, "Why do you test Me, *you* hypocrites? ¹⁹Show Me the tax money."

So they brought Him a denarius.

²⁰And He said to them, "Whose image and inscription *is* this?"

²¹They said to Him, "Caesar's."

And He said to them, "Render therefore to Caesar the things that are Caesar's, and to God the things that are

God's." 22When they had heard *these words,* they marveled, and left Him and went their way.

23The same day the Sadducees, who say there is no resurrection, came to Him and asked Him, 24saying: "Teacher, Moses said that if a man dies, having no children, his brother shall marry his wife and raise up offspring for his brother. 25Now there were with us seven brothers. The first died after he had married, and having no offspring, left his wife to his brother. 26Likewise the second also, and the third, even to the seventh. 27Last of all the woman died also. 28Therefore, in the resurrection, whose wife of the seven will she be? For they all had her."

29Jesus answered and said to them, "You are mistaken, not knowing the Scriptures nor the power of God. 30For in the resurrection they neither marry nor are given in marriage, but are like angels of God* in heaven. 31But concerning the resurrection of the dead, have you not read what was spoken to you by God, saying, 32*I am the God of Abraham, the God of Isaac, and the God of Jacob'?** God is not the God of the dead, but of the living." 33And when the multitudes heard *this,* they were astonished at His teaching.

PSALM 27:1-6

A Psalm of David.

T HE LORD *is* my light and my salvation;
Whom shall I fear?
The LORD *is* the strength of my life;

2 Of whom shall I be afraid?
When the wicked came
   against me
To eat up my flesh,
My enemies and foes,
They stumbled and fell.

3 Though an army may encamp
   against me,
My heart shall not fear;
Though war may rise against
   me,
In this I *will be* confident.

4 One *thing* I have desired of
   the LORD,
That will I seek:
That I may dwell in the house
   of the LORD
All the days of my life,
To behold the beauty of the
   LORD,
And to inquire in His temple.

5 For in the time of trouble
He shall hide me in His
   pavilion;
In the secret place of His
   tabernacle
He shall hide me;
He shall set me high upon a
   rock.

6 And now my head shall be
   lifted up above my enemies
   all around me;
Therefore I will offer
   sacrifices of joy in His
   tabernacle;
I will sing, yes, I will sing
   praises to the LORD.

PROVERBS FOR TODAY/ 6:20-26

My son, keep your father's command, and do not forsake the law of your mother. Bind them continually upon your heart; tie them around your neck. When you roam, they* will lead you; when you sleep, they will keep you; and when you awake, they will speak with you. For the commandment is a lamp, and the law a light; reproofs of instruction are the way of life, to keep you from the evil woman, from the flattering tongue of a seductress. Do not lust after her beauty in your heart, nor *let her allure you with her eyelids. For by means of a harlot a man is reduced to a crust of bread; and an adulteress * will prey upon his precious life.*

FEBRUARY 3

EXODUS 17:8–19:15

Now Amalek came and fought with Israel in Rephidim. 9And Moses said to Joshua, "Choose us some men and go out, fight with Amalek. Tomorrow I will stand on the top of the hill with the rod of God in my hand." 10So Joshua did as Moses said to him, and fought with Amalek. And Moses, Aaron, and Hur went up to the top of the hill. 11And so it was, when Moses held up his hand, that Israel prevailed; and when he let down his hand, Amalek prevailed. 12But Moses' hands *became* heavy; so they took a stone and put *it* under him, and he sat on it. And Aaron and Hur supported his hands, one on one side, and the other on the other side; and his hands were steady until the going down of the sun. 13So Joshua defeated Amalek and his people with the edge of the sword.

14Then the LORD said to Moses, "Write this *for* a memorial in the book and recount *it* in the hearing of Joshua, that I will utterly blot out the remembrance of Amalek from under heaven." 15And Moses built an altar and called its name, The-LORD-Is-My-Banner;* 16for he said, "Because the LORD has sworn: the LORD *will have* war with Amalek from generation to generation."

AND Jethro, the priest of Midian, Moses' father-in-law, heard of all that God had done for Moses and for Israel His people—that the LORD had brought Israel out of Egypt. 2Then Jethro, Moses' father-in-law, took Zipporah, Moses' wife, after he had sent her back, 3with her two sons, of whom the name of one *was* Gershom (for he said, "I have been a stranger in a foreign land")* 4and the name of the other *was* Eliezer* (for *he said,* "The God of my father *was* my help, and delivered me from the sword of Pharaoh"); 5and Jethro, Moses' father-in-law, came with his sons and his wife to Moses in the wilderness, where he was encamped at the mountain of God. 6Now he had said to Moses, "I, your father-in-law Jethro, am coming to you with your wife and her two sons with her."

7So Moses went out to meet his father-in-law, bowed down, and kissed him. And they asked each other about *their* well-being, and they went into the tent. 8And Moses told his father-in-law all that the LORD had done to Pharaoh and to the Egyptians for Israel's sake, all the hardship that had come upon them on the way, and *how* the LORD had delivered them. 9Then Jethro rejoiced for all the good which the LORD had done for Israel, whom He had delivered out of the hand of the Egyptians. 10And Jethro said, "Blessed *be* the LORD, who has delivered you out of the hand of the Egyptians and out of the hand of Pharaoh, *and* who has delivered the people from under the hand of the Egyptians. 11Now I know that the LORD *is* greater than all the gods; for in the very thing in which they behaved proudly, *He was* above them." 12Then Jethro, Moses' father-in-law, took* a burnt offering and *other* sacrifices *to offer* to God. And Aaron came with all the elders of Israel to eat bread with Moses' father-in-law before God.

¹³And so it was, on the next day, that Moses sat to judge the people; and the people stood before Moses from morning until evening. ¹⁴So when Moses' father-in-law saw all that he did for the people, he said, "What *is* this thing that you are doing for the people? Why do you alone sit, and all the people stand before you from morning until evening?"

¹⁵And Moses said to his father-in-law, "Because the people come to me to inquire of God. ¹⁶When they have a difficulty, they come to me, and I judge between one and another; and I make known the statutes of God and His laws."

¹⁷So Moses' father-in-law said to him, "The thing that you do *is* not good. ¹⁸Both you and these people who *are* with you will surely wear yourselves out. For this thing *is* too much for you; you are not able to perform it by yourself. ¹⁹Listen now to my voice; I will give you counsel, and God will be with you: Stand before God for the people, so that you may bring the difficulties to God. ²⁰And you shall teach them the statutes and the laws, and show them the way in which they must walk and the work they must do. ²¹Moreover you shall select from all the people able men, such as fear God, men of truth, hating covetousness; and place *such* over them *to be* rulers of thousands, rulers of hundreds, rulers of fifties, and rulers of tens. ²²And let them judge the people at all times. Then it will be *that* every great matter they shall bring to you, but every small matter they themselves shall judge. So it will be easier for you, for they will bear *the burden* with you. ²³If you do this thing, and God *so* commands you, then you will be able to endure, and all this people will also go to their place in peace."

²⁴So Moses heeded the voice of his father-in-law and did all that he had said. ²⁵And Moses chose able men out of all Israel, and made them heads over the people: rulers of thousands, rulers of hundreds, rulers of fifties, and rulers of tens. ²⁶So they judged the people at all times; the hard cases they brought to Moses, but they judged every small case themselves.

²⁷Then Moses let his father-in-law depart, and he went his way to his own land.

IN the third month after the children of Israel had gone out of the land of Egypt, on the same day, they came *to* the Wilderness of Sinai. ²For they had departed from Rephidim, had come *to* the Wilderness of Sinai, and camped in the wilderness. So Israel camped there before the mountain.

³And Moses went up to God, and the LORD called to him from the mountain, saying, "Thus you shall say to the house of Jacob, and tell the children of Israel: ⁴'You have seen what I did to the Egyptians, and *how* I bore you on eagles' wings and brought you to Myself. ⁵Now therefore, if you will indeed obey My voice and keep My covenant, then you shall be a special treasure to Me above all people; for all the earth *is* Mine. ⁶And you shall be to Me a kingdom of priests and a holy nation.' These *are* the words which you shall speak to the children of Israel."

⁷So Moses came and called for the elders of the people, and laid before them all these words which the LORD commanded him. ⁸Then all the people answered together and said, "All that the LORD has spoken we will do." So Moses brought back the words of the people to the LORD. ⁹And the LORD said to Moses, "Behold, I come to you in the thick cloud, that the people may hear when I speak with you, and believe you forever."

So Moses told the words of the people to the LORD.

10Then the LORD said to Moses, "Go to the people and consecrate them today and tomorrow, and let them wash their clothes. 11And let them be ready for the third day. For on the third day the LORD will come down upon Mount Sinai in the sight of all the people. 12You shall set bounds for the people all around, saying, 'Take heed to yourselves *that* you do *not* go up to the mountain or touch its base. Whoever touches the mountain shall surely be put to death. 13Not a hand shall touch him, but he shall surely be stoned or shot *with an arrow;* whether man or beast, he shall not live.' When the trumpet sounds long, they shall come near the mountain."

14So Moses went down from the mountain to the people and sanctified the people, and they washed their clothes. 15And he said to the people, "Be ready for the third day; do not come near *your* wives."

MATTHEW 22:34–23:12

BUT when the Pharisees heard that He [Jesus] had silenced the Sadducees, they gathered together. 35Then one of them, a lawyer, asked *Him a question,* testing Him, and saying, 36"Teacher, which *is* the great commandment in the law?"

37Jesus said to him, " *'You shall love the LORD your God with all your heart, with all your soul, and with all your mind.'** 38This is *the* first and great commandment. 39And *the* second *is* like it: *'You shall love your neighbor as yourself.'** 40On these two commandments hang all the Law and the Prophets."

41While the Pharisees were gathered together, Jesus asked them, 42saying, "What do you think about the Christ? Whose Son is He?" They said to Him, *"The Son* of David."

43He said to them, "How then does David in the Spirit call Him *'Lord,'* saying:

44 *'The LORD said to my Lord,*
"Sit at My right hand,
Till I make Your enemies
Your footstool" '?*

45If David then calls Him *'Lord,'* how is He his Son?" 46And no one was able to answer Him a word, nor from that day on did anyone dare question Him anymore.

THEN Jesus spoke to the multitudes and to His disciples, 2saying: "The scribes and the Pharisees sit in Moses' seat. 3Therefore whatever they tell you to observe,* *that* observe and do, but do not do according to their works; for they say, and do not do. 4For they bind heavy burdens, hard to bear, and lay *them* on men's shoulders; but they *themselves* will not move them with one of their fingers. 5But all their works they do to be seen by men. They make their phylacteries broad and enlarge the borders of their garments. 6They love the best places at feasts, the best seats in the synagogues, 7greetings in the marketplaces, and to be called by men, 'Rabbi, Rabbi.' 8But you, do not be called 'Rabbi'; for One is your Teacher, the Christ,* and you are all brethren. 9Do not call anyone on earth your father; for One is your Father, He who is in heaven. 10And do not be called teachers; for One is your Teacher, the Christ. 11But he who is greatest among you shall be your servant. 12And whoever exalts himself will be humbled, and he who humbles himself will be exalted.

PSALM 27:7-14

HEAR, O LORD, *when* I cry with my voice!
Have mercy also upon me, and answer me.

8 When You said, "Seek My
   face,"
   My heart said to You, "Your
   face, LORD, I will seek."
9 Do not hide Your face from
   me;
   Do not turn Your servant
   away in anger;
   You have been my help;
   Do not leave me nor forsake
   me,
   O God of my salvation.
10 When my father and my
   mother forsake me,
   Then the LORD will take care
   of me.

11 Teach me Your way, O LORD,
   And lead me in a smooth

path, because of my
enemies.
12 Do not deliver me to the will
   of my adversaries;
   For false witnesses have risen
   against me,
   And such as breathe out
   violence.
13 *I would have lost heart,* unless
   I had believed
   That I would see the
   goodness of the LORD
   In the land of the living.

14 Wait on the LORD;
   Be of good courage,
   And He shall strengthen your
   heart;
   Wait, I say, on the LORD!

PROVERBS FOR TODAY / 6:27-35

Can a man take fire to his bosom, and his clothes not be burned? Can one walk on hot coals, and his feet not be seared? So is *he who goes in to his neighbor's wife; whoever touches her shall not be innocent.* People *do not despise a thief if he steals to satisfy himself when he is starving.* Yet when *he is found, he must restore sevenfold; he may have to give up all the substance of his house. Whoever commits adultery with a woman lacks understanding; he* who *does so destroys his own soul. Wounds and dishonor he will get, and his reproach will not be wiped away. For jealousy* is *a husband's fury; therefore he will not spare in the day of vengeance. He will accept no recompense, nor will he be appeased though you give many gifts.*

FEBRUARY 4

EXODUS 19:16–21:21

THEN it came to pass on the third day, in the morning, that there were thunderings and lightnings, and a thick cloud on the mountain; and the sound of the trumpet was very loud, so that all the people who *were* in the camp trembled. [17]And Moses brought the people out of the camp to meet with God, and they stood at the foot of the mountain. [18]Now Mount Sinai *was* completely in smoke, because the LORD descended upon it in fire. Its smoke ascended like the smoke of a furnace, and the whole mountain* quaked greatly. [19]And when the blast of the trumpet sounded long and became louder and louder, Moses spoke, and God answered him by voice. [20]Then the LORD came down upon Mount Sinai, on the top of the mountain. And the LORD called Moses to the top of the mountain, and Moses went up.

21And the LORD said to Moses, "Go down and warn the people, lest they break through to gaze at the LORD, and many of them perish. 22Also let the priests who come near the LORD consecrate themselves, lest the LORD break out against them."

23But Moses said to the LORD, "The people cannot come up to Mount Sinai; for You warned us, saying, 'Set bounds around the mountain and consecrate it.' "

24Then the LORD said to him, "Away! Get down and then come up, you and Aaron with you. But do not let the priests and the people break through to come up to the LORD, lest He break out against them." 25So Moses went down to the people and spoke to them.

AND God spoke all these words, saying:

2 "I *am* the LORD your God, who brought you out of the land of Egypt, out of the house of bondage.

3 "You shall have no other gods before Me.

4 "You shall not make for yourself a carved image—any likeness *of anything* that *is* in heaven above, or that *is* in the earth beneath, or that *is* in the water under the earth; 5you shall not bow down to them nor serve them. For I, the LORD your God, *am* a jealous God, visiting the iniquity of the fathers upon the children to the third and fourth *generations* of those who hate Me, 6but showing mercy to thousands, to those who love Me and keep My commandments.

7 "You shall not take the name of the LORD your God in vain, for the LORD will not hold *him* guiltless who takes His name in vain.

8 "Remember the Sabbath day, to keep it holy. 9Six days you shall labor and do all your work, 10but the seventh day *is* the Sabbath of the LORD your God. *In it* you shall do no work: you, nor your son, nor your daughter, nor your male servant, nor your female servant, nor your cattle, nor your stranger who *is* within your gates. 11For *in* six days the LORD made the heavens and the earth, the sea, and all that *is* in them, and rested the seventh day. Therefore the LORD blessed the Sabbath day and hallowed it.

12 "Honor your father and your mother, that your days may be long upon the land which the LORD your God is giving you.

13 "You shall not murder.

14 "You shall not commit adultery.

15 "You shall not steal.

16 "You shall not bear false witness against your neighbor.

17 "You shall not covet your neighbor's house; you shall not covet your neighbor's wife, nor his male servant, nor his female servant, nor his ox, nor his donkey, nor anything that *is* your neighbor's."

18Now all the people witnessed the thunderings, the lightning flashes, the sound of the trumpet, and the mountain smoking; and when the people saw *it,* they trembled and stood afar off. 19Then they said to Moses, "You speak with us, and we will hear; but let not God speak with us, lest we die."

20And Moses said to the people, "Do not fear; for God has come to test you, and that His fear may be before you, so that you may not sin." 21So the people stood afar off, but Moses drew near the thick darkness where God *was*.

22Then the LORD said to Moses, "Thus you shall say to the children of Israel: 'You have seen that I have talked with you from heaven. 23You shall not make *anything to be* with Me—gods of silver or gods of gold you shall not make for yourselves. 24An altar of earth you shall make for Me, and you shall sacrifice on it your burnt offerings and your peace offerings, your sheep and your oxen. In every place where I record My name I will come to you, and I will bless you. 25And if you make Me an altar of stone, you shall not build it of hewn stone; for if you use your tool on it, you have profaned it. 26Nor shall you go up by steps to My altar, that your nakedness may not be exposed on it.'

"Now these *are* the judgments which you shall set before them: 2If you buy a Hebrew servant, he shall serve six years; and in the seventh he shall go out free and pay nothing. 3If he comes in by himself, he shall go out by himself; if he *comes in* married, then his wife shall go out with him. 4If his master has given him a wife, and she has borne him sons or daughters, the wife and her children shall be her master's, and he shall go out by himself. 5But if the servant plainly says, 'I love my master, my wife, and my children; I will not go out free,' 6then his master shall bring him to the judges. He shall also bring him to the door, or to the doorpost, and his master shall pierce his ear with an awl; and he shall serve him forever.

7"And if a man sells his daughter to be a female slave, she shall not go out as the male slaves do. 8If she does not please her master, who has betrothed her to himself, then he shall let her be redeemed. He shall have no right to sell her to a foreign people, since he has dealt deceitfully with her. 9And if

he has betrothed her to his son, he shall deal with her according to the custom of daughters. 10If he takes another *wife,* he shall not diminish her food, her clothing, and her marriage rights. 11And if he does not do these three for her, then she shall go out free, without *paying* money.

12"He who strikes a man so that he dies shall surely be put to death. 13However, if he did not lie in wait, but God delivered *him* into his hand, then I will appoint for you a place where he may flee.

14"But if a man acts with premeditation against his neighbor, to kill him by treachery, you shall take him from My altar, that he may die.

15"And he who strikes his father or his mother shall surely be put to death.

16"He who kidnaps a man and sells him, or if he is found in his hand, shall surely be put to death.

17"And he who curses his father or his mother shall surely be put to death.

18"If men contend with each other, and one strikes the other with a stone or with *his* fist, and he does not die but is confined to *his* bed, 19if he rises again and walks about outside with his staff, then he who struck *him* shall be acquitted. He shall only pay *for* the loss of his time, and shall provide *for him* to be thoroughly healed.

20"And if a man beats his male or female servant with a rod, so that he dies under his hand, he shall surely be punished. 21Notwithstanding, if he remains alive a day or two, he shall not be punished; for he *is* his property."

MATTHEW 23:13-39

"**B**UT woe to you, scribes and Pharisees, hypocrites! For you shut up the kingdom of heaven against men; for you neither go in *yourselves,* nor do you allow those who are entering to go in. 14Woe to you, scribes and Pharisees, hypocrites! For you devour widows' houses, and for a pretense make long prayers. Therefore you will receive greater condemnation.*

15"Woe to you, scribes and Pharisees, hypocrites! For you travel land and sea to win one proselyte, and when he is won, you make him twice as much a son of hell as yourselves.

16"Woe to you, blind guides, who say, 'Whoever swears by the temple, it is nothing; but whoever swears by the gold of the temple, he is obliged *to perform it.*' 17Fools and blind! For which is greater, the gold or the temple that sanctifies* the gold? 18And, 'Whoever swears by the altar, it is nothing; but whoever swears by the gift that is on it, he is obliged *to perform it.*' 19Fools and blind! For which is greater, the gift or the altar that sanctifies the gift? 20Therefore he who swears by the altar, swears by it and by all things on it. 21He who swears by the temple, swears by it and by Him who dwells* in it. 22And he who swears by heaven, swears by the throne of God and by Him who sits on it.

23"Woe to you, scribes and Pharisees, hypocrites! For you pay tithe of mint and anise and cummin, and have neglected the weightier *matters* of the law: justice and mercy and faith. These you ought to have done, without leaving the others undone. 24Blind guides, who strain out a gnat and swallow a camel!

25"Woe to you, scribes and Pharisees, hypocrites! For you cleanse the outside of the cup and dish, but inside they are full of extortion and self-indulgence.* 26Blind Pharisee, first cleanse the inside of the cup and dish, that the outside of them may be clean also.

27"Woe to you, scribes and Pharisees, hypocrites! For you are like whitewashed tombs which indeed appear beautiful outwardly, but inside are full of dead *men's* bones and all uncleanness. 28Even so you also outwardly appear righteous to men, but inside you are full of hypocrisy and lawlessness.

29"Woe to you, scribes and Pharisees, hypocrites! Because you build the tombs of the prophets and adorn the monuments of the righteous, 30and say, 'If we had lived in the days of our fathers, we would not have been partakers with them in the blood of the prophets.'

31"Therefore you are witnesses against yourselves that you are sons of those who murdered the prophets. 32Fill up, then, the measure of your fathers' *guilt.* 33Serpents, brood of vipers! How can you escape the condemnation of hell? 34Therefore, indeed, I send you prophets, wise men, and scribes: *some* of them you will kill and crucify, and *some* of them you will scourge in your synagogues and persecute from city to city, 35that on you may come all the righteous blood shed on the earth, from the blood of righteous Abel to the blood of Zechariah, son of Berechiah, whom you murdered between the temple and the altar. 36Assuredly, I say to you, all these things will come upon this generation.

37"O Jerusalem, Jerusalem, the one who kills the prophets and stones those who are sent to her! How often I wanted to gather your children together, as a hen gathers her chicks under *her* wings, but you were not willing! 38See! Your house is left to you desolate; 39for I say to you, you shall see Me no more till you say, *'Blessed is He who comes in the name of the LORD!'"* *

PSALM 28:1-9

A Psalm of David.

To You I will cry, O LORD my Rock:
Do not be silent to me,
Lest, if You *are* silent to me,
I become like those who go
down to the pit.

2 Hear the voice of my
supplications
When I cry to You,
When I lift up my hands
toward Your holy sanctuary.

3 Do not take me away with the
wicked
And with the workers of
iniquity,
Who speak peace to their
neighbors,
But evil *is* in their hearts.
4 Give them according to their
deeds,
And according to the
wickedness of their
endeavors;
Give them according to the
work of their hands;
Render to them what they
deserve.
5 Because they do not regard
the works of the LORD,

Nor the operation of His
hands,
He shall destroy them
And not build them up.

6 Blessed *be* the LORD,
Because He has heard the
voice of my supplications!
7 The LORD *is* my strength and
my shield;
My heart trusted in Him, and
I am helped;
Therefore my heart greatly
rejoices,
And with my song I will praise
Him.

8 The LORD *is* their strength,*
And He *is* the saving refuge of
His anointed.
9 Save Your people,
And bless Your inheritance;
Shepherd them also,
And bear them up forever.

PROVERBS FOR TODAY/ 7:1-5

My son, keep my words, and treasure my commands within you. Keep my commands and live, and my law as the apple of your eye. Bind them on your fingers; write them on the tablet of your heart. Say to wisdom, "You are my sister," and call understanding your nearest kin, that they may keep you from the immoral woman, from the seductress who flatters with her words.

FEBRUARY 5

EXODUS 21:22–22:13

"IF men fight, and hurt a woman with child, so that she gives birth prematurely, yet no harm follows, he shall surely be punished accordingly as the woman's husband imposes on him; and he shall pay as the judges *determine*. 23But if *any* harm follows, then you shall give life for life, 24eye for eye, tooth for tooth, hand for hand, foot for foot, 25burn for burn, wound for wound, stripe for stripe.

26"If a man strikes the eye of his male or female servant, and destroys it, he shall let him go free for the sake of his eye. 27And if he knocks out the tooth of his male or female servant, he shall let him go free for the sake of his tooth.

28"If an ox gores a man or a woman to death, then the ox shall surely be stoned, and its flesh shall not be eaten; but the owner of the ox *shall be* acquitted. [29]But if the ox tended to thrust with its horn in times past, and it has been made known to his owner, and he has not kept it confined, so that it has killed a man or a woman, the ox shall be stoned and its owner also shall be put to death. [30]If there is imposed on him a sum of money, then he shall pay to redeem his life, whatever is imposed on him. [31]Whether it has gored a son or gored a daughter, according to this judgment it shall be done to him. [32]If the ox gores a male or female servant, he shall give to their master thirty shekels of silver, and the ox shall be stoned.

[33]"And if a man opens a pit, or if a man digs a pit and does not cover it, and an ox or a donkey falls in it, [34]the owner of the pit shall make *it* good; he shall give money to their owner, but the dead *animal* shall be his.

[35]"If one man's ox hurts another's, so that it dies, then they shall sell the live ox and divide the money from it; and the dead *ox* they shall also divide. [36]Or if it was known that the ox tended to thrust in time past, and its owner has not kept it confined, he shall surely pay ox for ox, and the dead animal shall be his own.

"If a man steals an ox or a sheep, and slaughters it or sells it, he shall restore five oxen for an ox and four sheep for a sheep. [2]If the thief is found breaking in, and he is struck so that he dies, *there shall be* no guilt for his bloodshed. [3]If the sun has risen on him, *there shall be* guilt for his bloodshed. He should make full restitution; if he has nothing, then he shall be sold for his theft. [4]If the theft is certainly found alive in his hand, whether it is an ox or donkey or sheep, he shall restore double.

[5]"If a man causes a field or vineyard to be grazed, and lets loose his animal, and it feeds in another man's field, he shall make restitution from the best of his own field and the best of his own vineyard.

[6]"If fire breaks out and catches in thorns, so that stacked grain, standing grain, or the field is consumed, he who kindled the fire shall surely make restitution.

[7]"If a man delivers to his neighbor money or articles to keep, and it is stolen out of the man's house, if the thief is found, he shall pay double. [8]If the thief is not found, then the master of the house shall be brought to the judges *to see* whether he has put his hand into his neighbor's goods.

[9]"For any kind of trespass, *whether it concerns* an ox, a donkey, a sheep, or clothing, *or* for any kind of lost thing which *another* claims to be his, the cause of both parties shall come before the judges; *and* whomever the judges condemn shall pay double to his neighbor. [10]If a man delivers to his neighbor a donkey, an ox, a sheep, or any animal to keep, and it dies, is hurt, or driven away, no one seeing *it,* [11]*then* an oath of the LORD shall be between them both, that he has not put his hand into his neighbor's goods; and the owner of it shall accept *that,* and he shall not make *it* good. [12]But if, in fact, it is stolen from him, he shall make restitution to the owner of it. [13]If it is torn to pieces *by a beast, then* he shall bring it as evidence, *and* he shall not make good what was torn."

MATTHEW 24:1-28

THEN Jesus went out and departed from the temple, and His disciples came up to show Him the buildings of the temple. [2]And Jesus said to them, "Do you not see all these things? Assuredly, I say to you, not *one* stone shall be left here upon another, that shall not be thrown down."

[3]Now as He sat on the Mount of

Olives, the disciples came to Him privately, saying, "Tell us, when will these things be? And what *will be* the sign of Your coming, and of the end of the age?"

⁴And Jesus answered and said to them: "Take heed that no one deceives you. ⁵For many will come in My name, saying, 'I am the Christ,' and will deceive many. ⁶And you will hear of wars and rumors of wars. See that you are not troubled; for all* *these things* must come to pass, but the end is not yet. ⁷For nation will rise against nation, and kingdom against kingdom. And there will be famines, pestilences,* and earthquakes in various places. ⁸All these *are* the beginning of sorrows.

⁹"Then they will deliver you up to tribulation and kill you, and you will be hated by all nations for My name's sake. ¹⁰And then many will be offended, will betray one another, and will hate one another. ¹¹Then many false prophets will rise up and deceive many. ¹²And because lawlessness will abound, the love of many will grow cold. ¹³But he who endures to the end shall be saved. ¹⁴And this gospel of the kingdom will be preached in all the world as a witness to all the nations, and then the end will come.

¹⁵"Therefore when you see the 'abomination of desolation,'* spoken of by Daniel the prophet, standing in the holy place" (whoever reads, let him understand), ¹⁶"then let those who are in Judea flee to the mountains. ¹⁷Let him who is on the housetop not go down to take anything out of his house. ¹⁸And let him who is in the field not go back to get his clothes. ¹⁹But woe to those who are pregnant and to those who are nursing babies in those days! ²⁰And pray that your flight may not be in winter or on the Sabbath. ²¹For then there will be great tribulation, such as has not been since the beginning of the world until this time, no, nor ever shall be. ²²And unless those days were shortened, no flesh would be saved; but for the elect's sake those days will be shortened.

²³"Then if anyone says to you, 'Look, here *is* the Christ!' or 'There!' do not believe *it.* ²⁴For false christs and false prophets will rise and show great signs and wonders to deceive, if possible, even the elect. ²⁵See, I have told you beforehand.

²⁶"Therefore if they say to you, 'Look, He is in the desert!' do not go out; *or* 'Look, *He is* in the inner rooms!' do not believe *it.* ²⁷For as the lightning comes from the east and flashes to the west, so also will the coming of the Son of Man be. ²⁸For wherever the carcass is, there the eagles will be gathered together."

PSALM 29:1-11

A Psalm of David.

G IVE unto the LORD, O you mighty ones,
Give unto the LORD glory and strength.

2 Give unto the LORD the glory due to His name;
Worship the LORD in the beauty of holiness.

3 The voice of the LORD *is* over the waters;
The God of glory thunders;
The LORD *is* over many waters.

4 The voice of the LORD *is* powerful;
The voice of the LORD *is* full of majesty.

5 The voice of the LORD breaks the cedars,
Yes, the LORD splinters the cedars of Lebanon.

6 He makes them also skip like a calf,
Lebanon and Sirion like a young wild ox.

7   The voice of the LORD divides
      the flames of fire.

8   The voice of the LORD shakes
      the wilderness;
    The LORD shakes the
      Wilderness of Kadesh.

9   The voice of the LORD makes
      the deer give birth,
    And strips the forests bare;

      And in His temple everyone
        says, "Glory!"

10   The LORD sat *enthroned* at the
       Flood,
     And the LORD sits as King
       forever.

11   The LORD will give strength to
       His people;
     The LORD will bless His people
       with peace.

PROVERBS FOR TODAY/ 7:6-23

For at the window of my house I looked through my lattice, and saw among the simple, I perceived among the youths, a young man devoid of understanding, passing along the street near her corner; and he took the path to her house in the twilight, in the evening, in the black and dark night. And there a woman met him, with the attire of a harlot, and a crafty heart. She was loud and rebellious, her feet would not stay at home. At times she was outside, at times in the open square, lurking at every corner. So she caught him and kissed him; with an impudent face she said to him: "I have peace offerings with me; today I have paid my vows. So I came out to meet you, diligently to seek your face, and I have found you. I have spread my bed with tapestry, colored coverings of Egyptian linen. I have perfumed my bed with myrrh, aloes, and cinnamon. Come, let us take our fill of love until morning; let us delight ourselves with love. For my husband is not at home; he has gone on a long journey; he has taken a bag of money with him, and will come home on the appointed day." With her enticing speech she caused him to yield, with her flattering lips she seduced him. Immediately he went after her, as an ox goes to the slaughter, or as a fool to the correction of the stocks, * till an arrow struck his liver. As a bird hastens to the snare, he did not know it would cost his life.

FEBRUARY 6

EXODUS 22:14–25:40

"ND if a man borrows *anything* from his neighbor, and it becomes injured or dies, the owner of it not *being* with it, he shall surely make *it* good. [15]If its owner *was* with it, he shall not make *it* good; if it *was* hired, it came for its hire.

[16]"If a man entices a virgin who is not betrothed, and lies with her, he shall surely pay the bride-price for her

to be his wife. [17]If her father utterly refuses to give her to him, he shall pay money according to the bride-price of virgins.

[18]"You shall not permit a sorceress to live.

[19]"Whoever lies with an animal shall surely be put to death.

[20]"He who sacrifices to *any* god, except to the LORD only, he shall be utterly destroyed.

[21]"You shall neither mistreat a

stranger nor oppress him, for you were strangers in the land of Egypt.

²²"You shall not afflict any widow or fatherless child. ²³If you afflict them in any way, *and* they cry at all to Me, I will surely hear their cry; ²⁴and My wrath will become hot, and I will kill you with the sword; your wives shall be widows, and your children fatherless.

²⁵"If you lend money to *any of* My people *who are* poor among you, you shall not be like a moneylender to him; you shall not charge him interest. ²⁶If you ever take your neighbor's garment as a pledge, you shall return it to him before the sun goes down. ²⁷For that *is* his only covering, it *is* his garment for his skin. What will he sleep in? And it will be that when he cries to Me, I will hear, for I *am* gracious.

²⁸"You shall not revile God, nor curse a ruler of your people.

²⁹"You shall not delay *to offer* the first of your ripe produce and your juices. The firstborn of your sons you shall give to Me. ³⁰Likewise you shall do with your oxen *and* your sheep. It shall be with its mother seven days; on the eighth day you shall give it to Me.

³¹"And you shall be holy men to Me: you shall not eat meat torn *by beasts* in the field; you shall throw it to the dogs.

"You shall not circulate a false report. Do not put your hand with the wicked to be an unrighteous witness. ²You shall not follow a crowd to do evil; nor shall you testify in a dispute so as to turn aside after many to pervert *justice.* ³You shall not show partiality to a poor man in his dispute.

⁴"If you meet your enemy's ox or his donkey going astray, you shall surely bring it back to him again. ⁵If you see the donkey of one who hates you lying under its burden, and you would refrain from helping it, you shall surely help him with it.

⁶"You shall not pervert the judgment of your poor in his dispute. ⁷Keep yourself far from a false matter; do not kill the innocent and righteous. For I will not justify the wicked. ⁸And you shall take no bribe, for a bribe blinds the discerning and perverts the words of the righteous.

⁹"Also you shall not oppress a stranger, for you know the heart of a stranger, because you were strangers in the land of Egypt.

¹⁰"Six years you shall sow your land and gather in its produce, ¹¹but the seventh *year* you shall let it rest and lie fallow, that the poor of your people may eat; and what they leave, the beasts of the field may eat. In like manner you shall do with your vineyard *and* your olive grove. ¹²Six days you shall do your work, and on the seventh day you shall rest, that your ox and your donkey may rest, and the son of your female servant and the stranger may be refreshed.

¹³"And in all that I have said to you, be circumspect and make no mention of the name of other gods, nor let it be heard from your mouth.

¹⁴"Three times you shall keep a feast to Me in the year: ¹⁵You shall keep the Feast of Unleavened Bread (you shall eat unleavened bread seven days, as I commanded you, at the time appointed in the month of Abib, for in it you came out of Egypt; none shall appear before Me empty); ¹⁶and the Feast of Harvest, the firstfruits of your labors which you have sown in the field; and the Feast of Ingathering at the end of the year, when you have gathered in *the fruit of* your labors from the field.

¹⁷"Three times in the year all your males shall appear before the Lord God.*

¹⁸"You shall not offer the blood of My sacrifice with leavened bread; nor shall the fat of My sacrifice remain until morning. ¹⁹The first of the firstfruits of your land you shall bring into the house of the Lord your God. You shall

not boil a young goat in its mother's milk.

20"Behold, I send an Angel before you to keep you in the way and to bring you into the place which I have prepared. 21Beware of Him and obey His voice; do not provoke Him, for He will not pardon your transgressions; for My name *is* in Him. 22But if you indeed obey His voice and do all that I speak, then I will be an enemy to your enemies and an adversary to your adversaries. 23For My Angel will go before you and bring you in to the Amorites and the Hittites and the Perizzites and the Canaanites and the Hivites and the Jebusites; and I will cut them off. 24You shall not bow down to their gods, nor serve them, nor do according to their works; but you shall utterly overthrow them and completely break down their *sacred* pillars.

25"So you shall serve the LORD your God, and He will bless your bread and your water. And I will take sickness away from the midst of you. 26No one shall suffer miscarriage or be barren in your land; I will fulfill the number of your days.

27"I will send My fear before you, I will cause confusion among all the people to whom you come, and will make all your enemies turn *their* backs to you. 28And I will send hornets before you, which shall drive out the Hivite, the Canaanite, and the Hittite from before you. 29I will not drive them out from before you in one year, lest the land become desolate and the beasts of the field become too numerous for you. 30Little by little I will drive them out from before you, until you have increased, and you inherit the land. 31And I will set your bounds from the Red Sea to the sea, Philistia, and from the desert to the River.* For I will deliver the inhabitants of the land into your hand, and you shall drive them out before you. 32You shall make no covenant with them, nor with their gods. 33They shall not dwell in your land, lest they make you sin against Me. For *if* you serve their gods, it will surely be a snare to you."

Now He said to Moses, "Come up to the LORD, you and Aaron, Nadab and Abihu, and seventy of the elders of Israel, and worship from afar. 2And Moses alone shall come near the LORD, but they shall not come near; nor shall the people go up with him."

3So Moses came and told the people all the words of the LORD and all the judgments. And all the people answered with one voice and said, "All the words which the LORD has said we will do." 4And Moses wrote all the words of the LORD. And he rose early in the morning, and built an altar at the foot of the mountain, and twelve pillars according to the twelve tribes of Israel. 5Then he sent young men of the children of Israel, who offered burnt offerings and sacrificed peace offerings of oxen to the LORD. 6And Moses took half the blood and put *it* in basins, and half the blood he sprinkled on the altar. 7Then he took the Book of the Covenant and read in the hearing of the people. And they said, "All that the LORD has said we will do, and be obedient." 8And Moses took the blood, sprinkled *it* on the people, and said, "This is the blood of the covenant which the LORD has made with you according to all these words."

9Then Moses went up, also Aaron, Nadab, and Abihu, and seventy of the elders of Israel, 10and they saw the God of Israel. And *there was* under His feet as it were a paved work of sapphire stone, and it was like the very heavens in *its* clarity. 11But on the nobles of the children of Israel He did not lay His hand. So they saw God, and they ate and drank.

12Then the LORD said to Moses, "Come up to Me on the mountain and be there; and I will give you tablets of stone, and the law and commandments which I have written, that you may teach them."

¹³So Moses arose with his assistant Joshua, and Moses went up to the mountain of God. ¹⁴And he said to the elders, "Wait here for us until we come back to you. Indeed, Aaron and Hur *are* with you. If any man has a difficulty, let him go to them." ¹⁵Then Moses went up into the mountain, and a cloud covered the mountain.

¹⁶Now the glory of the LORD rested on Mount Sinai, and the cloud covered it six days. And on the seventh day He called to Moses out of the midst of the cloud. ¹⁷The sight of the glory of the LORD *was* like a consuming fire on the top of the mountain in the eyes of the children of Israel. ¹⁸So Moses went into the midst of the cloud and went up into the mountain. And Moses was on the mountain forty days and forty nights.

THEN the LORD spoke to Moses, saying: ²"Speak to the children of Israel, that they bring Me an offering. From everyone who gives it willingly with his heart you shall take My offering. ³And this *is* the offering which you shall take from them: gold, silver, and bronze; ⁴blue, purple, and scarlet *thread,* fine linen, and goats' *hair;* ⁵ram skins dyed red, badger skins, and acacia wood; ⁶oil for the light, and spices for the anointing oil and for the sweet incense; ⁷onyx stones, and stones to be set in the ephod and in the breastplate. ⁸And let them make Me a sanctuary, that I may dwell among them. ⁹According to all that I show you, *that is,* the pattern of the tabernacle and the pattern of all its furnishings, just so you shall make *it.*

¹⁰"And they shall make an ark of acacia wood; two and a half cubits *shall be* its length, a cubit and a half its width, and a cubit and a half its height. ¹¹And you shall overlay it with pure gold, inside and out you shall overlay it, and

shall make on it a molding of gold all around. ¹²You shall cast four rings of gold for it, and put *them* in its four corners; two rings *shall be* on one side, and two rings on the other side. ¹³And you shall make poles *of* acacia wood, and overlay them with gold. ¹⁴You shall put the poles into the rings on the sides of the ark, that the ark may be carried by them. ¹⁵The poles shall be in the rings of the ark; they shall not be taken from it. ¹⁶And you shall put into the ark the Testimony which I will give you.

¹⁷"You shall make a mercy seat of pure gold; two and a half cubits *shall be* its length and a cubit and a half its width. ¹⁸And you shall make two cherubim of gold; of hammered work you shall make them at the two ends of the mercy seat. ¹⁹Make one cherub at one end, and the other cherub at the other end; you shall make the cherubim at the two ends of it *of one piece* with the mercy seat. ²⁰And the cherubim shall stretch out *their* wings above, covering the mercy seat with their wings, and they shall face one another; the faces of the cherubim *shall be* toward the mercy seat. ²¹You shall put the mercy seat on top of the ark, and in the ark you shall put the Testimony that I will give you. ²²And there I will meet with you, and I will speak with you from above the mercy seat, from between the two cherubim which *are* on the ark of the Testimony, about everything which I will give you in commandment to the children of Israel.

²³"You shall also make a table of acacia wood; two cubits *shall be* its length, a cubit its width, and a cubit and a half its height. ²⁴And you shall overlay it with pure gold, and make a molding of gold all around. ²⁵You shall make for it a frame of a handbreadth all around, and you shall make a gold molding for the frame all around. ²⁶And you shall make for it four rings of gold, and put the rings on the four corners that *are*

at its four legs. ²⁷The rings shall be close to the frame, as holders for the poles to bear the table. ²⁸And you shall make the poles of acacia wood, and overlay them with gold, that the table may be carried with them. ²⁹You shall make its dishes, its pans, its pitchers, and its bowls for pouring. You shall make them of pure gold. ³⁰And you shall set the showbread on the table before Me always.

³¹"You shall also make a lampstand of pure gold; the lampstand shall be of hammered work. Its shaft, its branches, its bowls, its *ornamental* knobs, and flowers shall be *of one piece.* ³²And six branches shall come out of its sides: three branches of the lampstand out of one side, and three branches of the lampstand out of the other side. ³³Three bowls *shall be* made like almond *blossoms* on one branch, *with* an *ornamental* knob and a flower, and three bowls made like almond *blossoms* on the other branch, *with* an *ornamental* knob and a flower—and so for the six branches that come out of the lampstand. ³⁴On the lampstand itself four bowls *shall be* made like almond *blossoms, each with* its *ornamental* knob and flower. ³⁵And *there shall be* a knob under the *first* two branches of the same, a knob under the *second* two branches of the same, and a knob under the *third* two branches of the same, according to the six branches that extend from the lampstand. ³⁶Their knobs and their branches *shall be of one piece;* all of it *shall be* one hammered piece of pure gold. ³⁷You shall make seven lamps for it, and they shall arrange its lamps so that they give light in front of it. ³⁸And its wick-trimmers and their trays *shall be* of pure gold. ³⁹It shall be made of a talent of pure gold, with all these utensils. ⁴⁰And see to it that you make *them* according to the pattern which was shown you on the mountain."

MATTHEW 24:29-51

"IMMEDIATELY after the tribulation of those days the sun will be darkened, and the moon will not give its light; the stars will fall from heaven, and the powers of the heavens will be shaken. ³⁰Then the sign of the Son of Man will appear in heaven, and then all the tribes of the earth will mourn, and they will see the Son of Man coming on the clouds of heaven with power and great glory. ³¹And He will send His angels with a great sound of a trumpet, and they will gather together His elect from the four winds, from one end of heaven to the other.

³²"Now learn this parable from the fig tree: When its branch has already become tender and puts forth leaves, you know that summer *is* near. ³³So you also, when you see all these things, know that it* is near—at the doors! ³⁴Assuredly, I say to you, this generation will by no means pass away till all these things take place. ³⁵Heaven and earth will pass away, but My words will by no means pass away.

³⁶"But of that day and hour no one knows, not even the angels of heaven,* but My Father only. ³⁷But as the days of Noah *were,* so also will the coming of the Son of Man be. ³⁸For as in the days before the flood, they were eating and drinking, marrying and giving in marriage, until the day that Noah entered the ark, ³⁹and did not know until the flood came and took them all away, so also will the coming of the Son of Man be. ⁴⁰Then two *men* will be in the field: one will be taken and the other left. ⁴¹Two *women will be* grinding at the mill: one will be taken and the other left. ⁴²Watch therefore, for you do not know what hour* your Lord is coming. ⁴³But know this, that if the master of the house had known what hour the thief would come, he would have watched and not allowed his house to be broken into. ⁴⁴Therefore

you also be ready, for the Son of Man is coming at an hour you do not expect.

45"Who then is a faithful and wise servant, whom his master made ruler over his household, to give them food in due season? 46Blessed *is* that servant whom his master, when he comes, will find so doing. 47Assuredly, I say to you that he will make him ruler over all his goods. 48But if that evil servant says in his heart, 'My master is delaying his coming,' * 49and begins to beat *his* fellow servants, and to eat and drink with the drunkards, 50the master of that servant will come on a day when he is not looking for *him* and at an hour that he is not aware of, 51and will cut him in two and appoint *him* his portion with the hypocrites. There shall be weeping and gnashing of teeth."

PSALM 30:1-12

A Psalm. A Song at the dedication of the house of David.

I WILL extol You, O LORD, for You have lifted me up,
And have not let my foes rejoice over me.
2 O LORD my God, I cried out to You,
And You healed me.
3 O LORD, You brought my soul up from the grave;
You have kept me alive, that I should not go down to the pit.*

4 Sing praise to the LORD, you saints of His,
And give thanks at the remembrance of His holy name.*
5 For His anger *is but for* a moment,
His favor *is for* life;
Weeping may endure for a night,
But joy *comes* in the morning.

6 Now in my prosperity I said,
"I shall never be moved."
7 LORD, by Your favor You have made my mountain stand strong;
You hid Your face, *and* I was troubled.

8 I cried out to You, O LORD;
And to the LORD I made supplication:

9 "What profit *is there* in my blood,
When I go down to the pit?
Will the dust praise You?
Will it declare Your truth?
10 Hear, O LORD, and have mercy on me;
LORD, be my helper!"

11 You have turned for me my mourning into dancing;
You have put off my sackcloth and clothed me with gladness,
12 To the end that *my* glory may sing praise to You and not be silent.
O LORD my God, I will give thanks to You forever.

PROVERBS FOR TODAY/ 7:24-27

Now therefore, listen to me, my children; pay attention to the words of my mouth: do not let your heart turn aside to her [a prostitute's] ways, do not stray into her paths; for she has cast down many wounded, and all who were slain by her were strong men. Her house is the way to hell, * *descending to the chambers of death.*

FEBRUARY 7

EXODUS 26:1–27:21

"**M**OREOVER you shall make the tabernacle *with* ten curtains *of* fine woven linen and blue, purple, and scarlet *thread;* with artistic designs of cherubim you shall weave them. ²The length of each curtain *shall be* twenty-eight cubits, and the width of each curtain four cubits. And every one of the curtains shall have the same measurements. ³Five curtains shall be coupled to one another, and *the other* five curtains *shall be* coupled to one another. ⁴And you shall make loops of blue *yarn* on the edge of the curtain on the selvedge of *one* set, and likewise you shall do on the outer edge of *the other* curtain of the second set. ⁵Fifty loops you shall make in the one curtain, and fifty loops you shall make on the edge of the curtain that *is* on the end of the second set, that the loops may be clasped to one another. ⁶And you shall make fifty clasps of gold, and couple the curtains together with the clasps, so that it may be one tabernacle.

⁷"You shall also make curtains of goats' *hair,* to be a tent over the tabernacle. You shall make eleven curtains. ⁸The length of each curtain *shall be* thirty cubits, and the width of each curtain four cubits; and the eleven curtains shall all have the same measurements. ⁹And you shall couple five curtains by themselves and six curtains by themselves, and you shall double over the sixth curtain at the forefront of the tent. ¹⁰You shall make fifty loops on the edge of the curtain that is outermost in *one* set, and fifty loops on the edge of the curtain of the second set. ¹¹And you shall make fifty bronze clasps, put the clasps into the loops, and couple the tent together, that it may be one. ¹²The remnant that remains of the curtains of the tent, the half curtain that remains, shall hang over the back of the tabernacle. ¹³And a cubit on one side and a cubit on the other side, of what remains of the length of the curtains of the tent, shall hang over the sides of the tabernacle, on this side and on that side, to cover it.

¹⁴"You shall also make a covering of ram skins dyed red for the tent, and a covering of badger skins above that.

¹⁵"And for the tabernacle you shall make the boards of acacia wood, standing upright. ¹⁶Ten cubits *shall be* the length of a board, and a cubit and a half *shall be* the width of each board. ¹⁷Two tenons *shall be* in each board for binding one to another. Thus you shall make for all the boards of the tabernacle. ¹⁸And you shall make the boards for the tabernacle, twenty boards for the south side. ¹⁹You shall make forty sockets of silver under the twenty boards: two sockets under each of the boards for its two tenons. ²⁰And for the second side of the tabernacle, the north side, *there shall be* twenty boards ²¹and their forty sockets of silver: two sockets under each of the boards. ²²For the far side of the tabernacle, westward, you shall make six boards. ²³And you shall also make two boards for the two back corners of the tabernacle. ²⁴They shall be coupled together at the bottom and they shall be coupled together at the top by one ring. Thus it shall be for both of them. They shall be for the two corners. ²⁵So there shall be eight boards with their sockets of silver—sixteen sockets—two sockets under each of the boards.

²⁶"And you shall make bars of acacia wood: five for the boards on one side

of the tabernacle, 27five bars for the boards on the other side of the tabernacle, and five bars for the boards of the side of the tabernacle, for the far side westward. 28The middle bar shall pass through the midst of the boards from end to end. 29You shall overlay the boards with gold, make their rings of gold *as* holders for the bars, and overlay the bars with gold. 30And you shall raise up the tabernacle according to its pattern which you were shown on the mountain.

31"You shall make a veil woven of blue, purple, and scarlet *thread,* and fine woven linen. It shall be woven with an artistic design of cherubim. 32You shall hang it upon the four pillars of acacia *wood* overlaid with gold. Their hooks *shall be* gold, upon four sockets of silver. 33And you shall hang the veil from the clasps. Then you shall bring the ark of the Testimony in there, behind the veil. The veil shall be a divider for you between the holy *place* and the Most Holy. 34You shall put the mercy seat upon the ark of the Testimony in the Most Holy. 35You shall set the table outside the veil, and the lampstand across from the table on the side of the tabernacle toward the south; and you shall put the table on the north side.

36"You shall make a screen for the door of the tabernacle, *woven of* blue, purple, and scarlet *thread,* and fine woven linen, made by a weaver. 37And you shall make for the screen five pillars of acacia *wood,* and overlay them with gold; their hooks *shall be* gold, and you shall cast five sockets of bronze for them.

"You shall make an altar of acacia wood, five cubits long and five cubits wide—the altar shall be square—and its height *shall be* three cubits. 2You shall make its horns on its four corners; its horns shall be of one piece with it. And you shall overlay it with bronze. 3Also you shall make its pans to receive its ashes, and its shovels and its basins and its forks and its firepans; you shall make all its utensils of bronze. 4You shall make a grate for it, a network of bronze; and on the network you shall make four bronze rings at its four corners. 5You shall put it under the rim of the altar beneath, that the network may be midway up the altar. 6And you shall make poles for the altar, poles of acacia wood, and overlay them with bronze. 7The poles shall be put in the rings, and the poles shall be on the two sides of the altar to bear it. 8You shall make it hollow with boards; as it was shown you on the mountain, so shall they make *it.*

9"You shall also make the court of the tabernacle. For the south side *there shall be* hangings for the court *made of* fine woven linen, one hundred cubits long for one side. 10And its twenty pillars and their twenty sockets *shall be* bronze. The hooks of the pillars and their bands *shall be* silver. 11Likewise along the length of the north side *there shall be* hangings one hundred *cubits* long, with its twenty pillars and their twenty sockets of bronze, and the hooks of the pillars and their bands of silver.

12"And along the width of the court on the west side *shall be* hangings of fifty cubits, with their ten pillars and their ten sockets. 13The width of the court on the east side *shall be* fifty cubits. 14The hangings on *one* side *of the gate shall be* fifteen cubits, *with* their three pillars and their three sockets. 15And on the other side *shall be* hangings of fifteen *cubits, with* their three pillars and their three sockets.

16"For the gate of the court *there shall be* a screen twenty cubits long, *woven of* blue, purple, and scarlet *thread,* and fine woven linen, made by a weaver. It *shall have* four pillars and four sockets. 17All the pillars around the court shall have bands of silver; their hooks *shall be* of silver and their sockets of bronze. 18The length of the court *shall be* one hundred cubits, the width fifty throughout, and the height five cubits, *made of* fine woven linen, and its sockets of bronze. 19All the utensils of the tabernacle for all its service, all its pegs, and all the pegs of the court, *shall be* of bronze.

20"And you shall command the children of Israel that they bring you pure oil of pressed olives for the light, to cause the lamp to burn continually. 21In the tabernacle of meeting, outside the veil which *is* before the Testimony, Aaron and his sons shall tend it from evening until morning before the LORD. *It shall be* a statute forever to their generations on behalf of the children of Israel."

MATTHEW 25:1-30

"THEN the kingdom of heaven shall be likened to ten virgins who took their lamps and went out to meet the bridegroom. 2Now five of them were wise, and five *were* foolish. 3Those who *were* foolish took their lamps and took no oil with them, 4but the wise took oil in their vessels with their lamps. 5But while the bridegroom was delayed, they all slumbered and slept.

6"And at midnight a cry was *heard:* 'Behold, the bridegroom is coming;* go out to meet him!' 7Then all those virgins arose and trimmed their lamps. 8And the foolish said to the wise, 'Give us *some* of your oil, for our lamps are going out.' 9But the wise answered, saying, '*No,* lest there should not be enough for us and you; but go rather to those who sell, and buy for yourselves.' 10And while they went to buy, the bridegroom came, and those who were ready went in with him to the wedding; and the door was shut.

11"Afterward the other virgins came also, saying, 'Lord, Lord, open to us!' 12But he answered and said, 'Assuredly, I say to you, I do not know you.'

13"Watch therefore, for you know neither the day nor the hour* in which the Son of Man is coming.

14"For *the kingdom of heaven is* like a man traveling to a far country, *who* called his own servants and delivered his goods to them. 15And to one he gave five talents, to another two, and to another one, to each according to his own ability; and immediately he went on a journey. 16Then he who had received the five talents went and traded with them, and made another five talents. 17And likewise he who *had received* two gained two more also. 18But he who had received one went and dug in the ground, and hid his lord's money. 19After a long time the lord of those servants came and settled accounts with them.

20"So he who had received five talents came and brought five other talents, saying, 'Lord, you delivered to me five talents; look, I have gained five more talents besides them.' 21His lord said to him, 'Well *done,* good and faithful servant; you were faithful over a few things, I will make you ruler over many things. Enter into the joy of your lord.' 22He also who had received two talents came and said, 'Lord, you delivered to me two talents; look, I have gained two more talents besides them.' 23His lord said to him, 'Well *done,* good and faithful servant; you have been faithful over a few things, I will make you ruler over many things. Enter into the joy of your lord.'

24"Then he who had received the one talent came and said, 'Lord, I knew you to be a hard man, reaping where you have not sown, and gathering where you have not scattered seed. 25And I was afraid, and went and hid your talent in the ground. Look, *there* you have *what is* yours.'

26"But his lord answered and said to him, 'You wicked and lazy servant, you knew that I reap where I have not sown, and gather where I have not scattered seed. ²⁷So you ought to have deposited my money with the bankers, and at my coming I would have received back my own with interest. ²⁸So take the talent from him, and give *it* to him who has ten talents.

²⁹"For to everyone who has, more will be given, and he will have abundance; but from him who does not have, even what he has will be taken away. ³⁰And cast the unprofitable servant into the outer darkness. There will be weeping and gnashing of teeth.'"

PSALM 31:1-8

To the Chief Musician. A Psalm of David.

I N You, O LORD, I put my trust;
Let me never be ashamed;
Deliver me in Your
    righteousness.
2   Bow down Your ear to me,
    Deliver me speedily;
    Be my rock of refuge,
    A fortress of defense to save
        me.

3   For You *are* my rock and my
        fortress;
    Therefore, for Your name's
        sake,
    Lead me and guide me.
4   Pull me out of the net which
        they have secretly laid for
        me,
    For You *are* my strength.
5   Into Your hand I commit my
        spirit;
    You have redeemed me,
        O LORD God of truth.

6   I have hated those who
        regard useless idols;
    But I trust in the LORD.
7   I will be glad and rejoice in
        Your mercy,
    For You have considered my
        trouble;
    You have known my soul in
        adversities,
8   And have not shut me up into
        the hand of the enemy;
    You have set my feet in a wide
        place.

PROVERBS FOR TODAY/ 8:1-10

Does not wisdom cry out, and understanding lift up her voice? She takes her stand on the top of the high hill, beside the way, where the paths meet. She cries out by the gates, at the entry of the city, at the entrance of the doors: "To you, O men, I call, and my voice is to the sons of men. O you simple ones, understand prudence, and you fools, be of an understanding heart. Listen, for I will speak of excellent things, and from the opening of my lips will come right things; for my mouth will speak truth; wickedness is an abomination to my lips. All the words of my mouth are with righteousness; nothing crooked or perverse is in them. They are all plain to him who understands, and right to those who find knowledge. Receive my instruction, and not silver, and knowledge rather than choice gold."

FEBRUARY 8

EXODUS 28:1-43

"**N**ow take Aaron your brother, and his sons with him, from among the children of Israel, that he may minister to Me as priest, Aaron *and* Aaron's sons: Nadab, Abihu, Eleazar, and Ithamar. ²And you shall make holy garments for Aaron your brother, for glory and for beauty. ³So you shall speak to all *who are* gifted artisans, whom I have filled with the spirit of wisdom, that they may make Aaron's garments, to consecrate him, that he may minister to Me as priest. ⁴And these *are* the garments which they shall make: a breastplate, an ephod,* a robe, a skillfully woven tunic, a turban, and a sash. So they shall make holy garments for Aaron your brother and his sons, that he may minister to Me as priest.

⁵"They shall take the gold, blue, purple, and scarlet *thread,* and the fine linen, ⁶and they shall make the ephod of gold, blue, purple, *and* scarlet *thread,* and fine woven linen, artistically worked. ⁷It shall have two shoulder straps joined at its two edges, and *so* it shall be joined together. ⁸And the intricately woven band of the ephod, which *is* on it, shall be of the same workmanship, *made of* gold, blue, purple, and scarlet *thread,* and fine woven linen.

⁹"Then you shall take two onyx stones and engrave on them the names of the sons of Israel: ¹⁰six of their names on one stone and six names on the other stone, in order of their birth. ¹¹With the work of an engraver in stone, *like* the engravings of a signet, you shall engrave the two stones with the names of the sons of Israel. You shall set them in settings of gold. ¹²And you shall put the two stones on the shoulders of the ephod *as* memorial stones for the sons of Israel. So Aaron shall bear their names before the Lord on his two shoulders as a memorial. ¹³You shall also make settings of gold, ¹⁴and you shall make two chains of pure gold like braided cords, and fasten the braided chains to the settings.

¹⁵"You shall make the breastplate of judgment. Artistically woven according to the workmanship of the ephod you shall make it: of gold, blue, purple, and scarlet *thread,* and fine woven linen, you shall make it. ¹⁶It shall be doubled into a square: a span *shall be* its length, and a span *shall be* its width. ¹⁷And you shall put settings of stones in it, four rows of stones: *The first* row *shall be* a sardius, a topaz, and an emerald; *this shall be* the first row; ¹⁸the second row *shall be* a turquoise, a sapphire, and a diamond; ¹⁹the third row, a jacinth, an agate, and an amethyst; ²⁰and the fourth row, a beryl, an onyx, and a jasper. They shall be set in gold settings. ²¹And the stones shall have the names of the sons of Israel, twelve according to their names, *like* the engravings of a signet, each one with its own name; they shall be according to the twelve tribes.

²²"You shall make chains for the breastplate at the end, like braided cords of pure gold. ²³And you shall make two rings of gold for the breastplate, and put the two rings on the two ends of the breastplate. ²⁴Then you shall put the two braided *chains* of gold in the two rings which are on the ends of the breastplate; ²⁵and the *other* two ends of the two braided *chains* you shall fasten to the two settings, and put them on the shoulder straps of the ephod in the front.

26"You shall make two rings of gold, and put them on the two ends of the breastplate, on the edge of it, which is on the inner side of the ephod. 27And two *other* rings of gold you shall make, and put them on the two shoulder straps, underneath the ephod toward its front, right at the seam above the intricately woven band of the ephod. 28They shall bind the breastplate by means of its rings to the rings of the ephod, using a blue cord, so that it is above the intricately woven band of the ephod, and so that the breastplate does not come loose from the ephod.

29"So Aaron shall bear the names of the sons of Israel on the breastplate of judgment over his heart, when he goes into the holy *place,* as a memorial before the LORD continually. 30And you shall put in the breastplate of judgment the Urim and the Thummim,* and they shall be over Aaron's heart when he goes in before the LORD. So Aaron shall bear the judgment of the children of Israel over his heart before the LORD continually.

31"You shall make the robe of the ephod all of blue. 32There shall be an opening for his head in the middle of it; it shall have a woven binding all around its opening, like the opening in a coat of mail, so that it does not tear. 33And upon its hem you shall make pomegranates of blue, purple, and scarlet, all around its hem, and bells of gold between them all around: 34a golden bell and a pomegranate, a golden bell and a pomegranate, upon the hem of the robe all around. 35And it shall be upon Aaron when he ministers, and its sound will be heard when he goes into the holy *place* before the LORD and when he comes out, that he may not die.

36"You shall also make a plate of pure gold and engrave on it, *like* the engraving of a signet:

HOLINESS TO THE LORD.

37And you shall put it on a blue cord, that it may be on the turban; it shall be on the front of the turban. 38So it shall be on Aaron's forehead, that Aaron may bear the iniquity of the holy things which the children of Israel hallow in all their holy gifts; and it shall always be on his forehead, that they may be accepted before the LORD.

39"You shall skillfully weave the tunic of fine linen *thread,* you shall make the turban of fine linen, and you shall make the sash of woven work.

40"For Aaron's sons you shall make tunics, and you shall make sashes for them. And you shall make hats for them, for glory and beauty. 41So you shall put them on Aaron your brother and on his sons with him. You shall anoint them, consecrate them, and sanctify them, that they may minister to Me as priests. 42And you shall make for them linen trousers to cover their nakedness; they shall reach from the waist to the thighs. 43They shall be on Aaron and on his sons when they come into the tabernacle of meeting, or when they come near the altar to minister in the holy *place,* that they do not incur iniquity and die. *It shall be* a statute forever to him and his descendants after him."

MATTHEW 25:31–26:13

"WHEN the Son of Man comes in His glory, and all the holy* angels with Him, then He will sit on the throne of His glory. 32All the nations will be gathered before Him, and He will separate them one from another, as a shepherd divides *his* sheep from the goats. 33And He will set the sheep on His right hand, but the goats on the left. 34Then the King will say to those on His right hand, 'Come, you blessed of My Father, inherit the kingdom prepared for you from the foundation of the world: 35for I was hungry and you gave Me food; I was thirsty and you gave Me drink; I was a stranger and you took Me in; 36I *was* naked and you clothed Me; I was sick and you visited Me; I was in prison and you came to Me.'

37"Then the righteous will answer Him, saying, 'Lord, when did we see You hungry and feed *You,* or thirsty and give *You* drink? 38When did we see You a stranger and take *You* in, or naked and clothe *You?* 39Or when did we see You sick, or in prison, and come to You?' 40And the King will answer and say to them, 'Assuredly, I say to you, inasmuch as you did *it* to one of the least of these My brethren, you did *it* to Me.'

41"Then He will also say to those on the left hand, 'Depart from Me, you cursed, into the everlasting fire prepared for the devil and his angels: 42for I was hungry and you gave Me no food; I was thirsty and you gave Me no drink; 43I was a stranger and you did not take Me in, naked and you did not clothe Me, sick and in prison and you did not visit Me.'

44"Then they also will answer Him,* saying, 'Lord, when did we see You hungry or thirsty or a stranger or naked or sick or in prison, and did not minister to You?' 45Then He will answer them, saying, 'Assuredly, I say to you, inasmuch as you did not do *it* to one of the least of these, you did not do *it* to Me.' 46And these will go away into everlasting punishment, but the righteous into eternal life."

Now it came to pass, when Jesus had finished all these sayings, *that* He said to His disciples, 2"You know that after two days is the Passover, and the Son of Man will be delivered up to be crucified."

3Then the chief priests, the scribes,* and the elders of the people assembled at the palace of the high priest, who was called Caiaphas, 4and plotted to take Jesus by trickery and kill *Him.* 5But they said, "Not during the feast, lest there be an uproar among the people."

6And when Jesus was in Bethany at the house of Simon the leper, 7a woman came to Him having an alabaster flask of very costly fragrant oil, and she poured *it* on His head as He sat *at the table.* 8But when His disciples saw *it,* they were indignant, saying, "Why this waste? 9For this fragrant oil might have been sold for much and given to *the* poor."

10But when Jesus was aware of *it,* He said to them, "Why do you trouble the woman? For she has done a good work for Me. 11For you have the poor with you always, but Me you do not have always. 12For in pouring this fragrant oil on My body, she did *it* for My burial. 13Assuredly, I say to you, wherever this gospel is preached in the whole world, what this woman has done will also be told as a memorial to her."

PSALM 31:9-18

HAVE mercy on me, O LORD, for I
am in trouble;
My eye wastes away with
grief,
Yes, my soul and my body!
10   For my life is spent with grief,
And my years with sighing;
My strength fails because of
my iniquity,
And my bones waste away.
11   I am a reproach among all my
enemies,
But especially among my
neighbors,
And *am* repulsive to my
acquaintances;
Those who see me outside
flee from me.
12   I am forgotten like a dead
man, out of mind;
I am like a broken vessel.

13 For I hear the slander of
    many;
    Fear *is* on every side;
    While they take counsel
    together against me,
    They scheme to take away my
    life.

14 But as for me, I trust in You,
    O Lᴏʀᴅ;
    I say, "You *are* my God."
15 My times *are* in Your hand;
    Deliver me from the hand of
    my enemies,
    And from those who
    persecute me.

16 Make Your face shine upon
    Your servant;
    Save me for Your mercies'
    sake.
17 Do not let me be ashamed,
    O Lᴏʀᴅ, for I have called
    upon You;
    Let the wicked be ashamed;
    Let them be silent in the
    grave.
18 Let the lying lips be put to
    silence,
    Which speak insolent things
    proudly and
    contemptuously against the
    righteous.

PROVERBS FOR TODAY/ 8:11-13

"For wisdom is *better than rubies, and all the things one may desire cannot be compared with her. I, wisdom, dwell with prudence, and find out knowledge* and *discretion. The fear of the* Lᴏʀᴅ *is to hate evil; pride and arrogance and the evil way and the perverse mouth I hate."*

FEBRUARY 9

EXODUS 29:1–30:10

"Aɴᴅ this is what you shall do to them [Aaron and his sons] to hallow them for ministering to Me as priests: Take one young bull and two rams without blemish, ²and unleavened bread, unleavened cakes mixed with oil, and unleavened wafers anointed with oil (you shall make them of wheat flour). ³You shall put them in one basket and bring them in the basket, with the bull and the two rams.

⁴"And Aaron and his sons you shall bring to the door of the tabernacle of meeting, and you shall wash them with water. ⁵Then you shall take the garments, put the tunic on Aaron, and the robe of the ephod, the ephod, and the breastplate, and gird him with the intri-

cately woven band of the ephod. ⁶You shall put the turban on his head, and put the holy crown on the turban. ⁷And you shall take the anointing oil, pour *it* on his head, and anoint him. ⁸Then you shall bring his sons and put tunics on them. ⁹And you shall gird them with sashes, Aaron and his sons, and put the hats on them. The priesthood shall be theirs for a perpetual statute. So you shall consecrate Aaron and his sons.

¹⁰"You shall also have the bull brought before the tabernacle of meeting, and Aaron and his sons shall put their hands on the head of the bull. ¹¹Then you shall kill the bull before the Lᴏʀᴅ, *by* the door of the tabernacle of meeting. ¹²You shall take *some* of the blood of the bull and put *it* on the horns of the altar with your finger, and

pour all the blood beside the base of the altar. 13And you shall take all the fat that covers the entrails, the fatty lobe *attached* to the liver, and the two kidneys and the fat that *is* on them, and burn *them* on the altar. 14But the flesh of the bull, with its skin and its offal, you shall burn with fire outside the camp. It *is* a sin offering.

15"You shall also take one ram, and Aaron and his sons shall put their hands on the head of the ram; 16and you shall kill the ram, and you shall take its blood and sprinkle *it* all around on the altar. 17Then you shall cut the ram in pieces, wash its entrails and its legs, and put *them* with its pieces and with its head. 18And you shall burn the whole ram on the altar. It *is* a burnt offering to the LORD; it *is* a sweet aroma, an offering made by fire to the LORD.

19"You shall also take the other ram, and Aaron and his sons shall put their hands on the head of the ram. 20Then you shall kill the ram, and take some of its blood and put *it* on the tip of the right ear of Aaron and on the tip of the right ear of his sons, on the thumb of their right hand and on the big toe of their right foot, and sprinkle the blood all around on the altar. 21And you shall take some of the blood that is on the altar, and some of the anointing oil, and sprinkle *it* on Aaron and on his garments, on his sons and on the garments of his sons with him; and he and his garments shall be hallowed, and his sons and his sons' garments with him.

22"Also you shall take the fat of the ram, the fat tail, the fat that covers the entrails, the fatty lobe *attached to* the liver, the two kidneys and the fat on them, the right thigh (for it *is* a ram of consecration), 23one loaf of bread, one cake *made with* oil, and one wafer from the basket of the unleavened bread that *is* before the LORD; 24and you shall put all these in the hands of Aaron and in the hands of his sons, and you shall

wave them *as* a wave offering before the LORD. 25You shall receive them back from their hands and burn *them* on the altar as a burnt offering, as a sweet aroma before the LORD. It *is* an offering made by fire to the LORD.

26"Then you shall take the breast of the ram of Aaron's consecration and wave it *as* a wave offering before the LORD; and it shall be your portion. 27And from the ram of the consecration you shall consecrate the breast of the wave offering which is waved, and the thigh of the heave offering which is raised, of *that* which *is* for Aaron and of *that* which is for his sons. 28It shall be from the children of Israel *for* Aaron and his sons by a statute forever. For it is a heave offering; it shall be a heave offering from the children of Israel from the sacrifices of their peace offerings, *that is,* their heave offering to the LORD.

29"And the holy garments of Aaron shall be his sons' after him, to be anointed in them and to be consecrated in them. 30That son who becomes priest in his place shall put them on for seven days, when he enters the tabernacle of meeting to minister in the holy *place.*

31"And you shall take the ram of the consecration and boil its flesh in the holy place. 32Then Aaron and his sons shall eat the flesh of the ram, and the bread that *is* in the basket, *by* the door of the tabernacle of meeting. 33They shall eat those things with which the atonement was made, to consecrate *and* to sanctify them; but an outsider shall not eat *them,* because they *are* holy. 34And if any of the flesh of the consecration offerings, or of the bread, remains until the morning, then you shall burn the remainder with fire. It shall not be eaten, because it *is* holy.

35"Thus you shall do to Aaron and his sons, according to all that I have commanded you. Seven days you shall consecrate them. 36And you shall offer a bull every day *as* a sin offering for atonement. You shall cleanse the altar when you make atonement for it, and you shall anoint it to sanctify it. 37Seven days you shall make atonement for the altar and sanctify it. And the altar shall be most holy. Whatever touches the altar must be holy.*

38"Now this *is* what you shall offer on the altar: two lambs of the first year, day by day continually. 39One lamb you shall offer in the morning, and the other lamb you shall offer at twilight. 40With the one lamb shall be one-tenth *of an ephah* of flour mixed with one-fourth of a hin of pressed oil, and one-fourth of a hin of wine *as* a drink offering. 41And the other lamb you shall offer at twilight; and you shall offer with it the grain offering and the drink offering, as in the morning, for a sweet aroma, an offering made by fire to the LORD. 42*This shall be* a continual burnt offering throughout your generations *at* the door of the tabernacle of meeting before the LORD, where I will meet you to speak with you. 43And there I will meet with the children of Israel, and *the tabernacle* shall be sanctified by My glory. 44So I will consecrate the tabernacle of meeting and the altar. I will also consecrate both Aaron and his sons to minister to Me as priests. 45I will dwell among the children of Israel and will be their God. 46And they shall know that I *am* the LORD their God, who brought them up out of the land of Egypt, that I may dwell among them. I *am* the LORD their God.

"You shall make an altar to burn incense on; you shall make it of acacia wood. 2A cubit *shall be* its length and a cubit its width—it shall be square—and two cubits *shall be* its height. Its horns *shall be* of one piece with it. 3And you shall overlay its top, its sides all around, and its horns with pure gold; and you shall make for it a molding of gold all around. 4Two gold rings you shall make for it, under the molding on both its sides. You shall place *them* on its two sides, and they will be holders for the poles with which to bear it. 5You shall make the poles of acacia wood, and overlay them with gold. 6And you shall put it before the veil that *is* before the ark of the Testimony, before the mercy seat that *is* over the Testimony, where I will meet with you.

7"Aaron shall burn on it sweet incense every morning; when he tends the lamps, he shall burn incense on it. 8And when Aaron lights the lamps at twilight, he shall burn incense on it, a perpetual incense before the LORD throughout your generations. 9You shall not offer strange incense on it, or a burnt offering, or a grain offering; nor shall you pour a drink offering on it. 10And Aaron shall make atonement upon its horns once a year with the blood of the sin offering of atonement; once a year he shall make atonement upon it throughout your generations. It *is* most holy to the LORD."

MATTHEW 26:14-46

THEN one of the twelve, called Judas Iscariot, went to the chief priests 15and said, "What are you willing to give me if I deliver Him to you?" And they counted out to him thirty pieces of silver. 16So from that time he sought opportunity to betray Him.

17Now on the first *day of the Feast* of Unleavened Bread the disciples came to Jesus, saying to Him, "Where do You want us to prepare for You to eat the Passover?"

18And He said, "Go into the city to a certain man, and say to him, 'The Teacher says, "My time is at hand; I will keep the Passover at your house with My disciples." ' "

19So the disciples did as Jesus had directed them; and they prepared the Passover.

20When evening had come, He sat

down with the twelve. ²¹Now as they were eating, He said, "Assuredly, I say to you, one of you will betray Me."

²²And they were exceedingly sorrowful, and each of them began to say to Him, "Lord, is it I?"

²³He answered and said, "He who dipped *his* hand with Me in the dish will betray Me. ²⁴The Son of Man indeed goes just as it is written of Him, but woe to that man by whom the Son of Man is betrayed! It would have been good for that man if he had not been born."

²⁵Then Judas, who was betraying Him, answered and said, "Rabbi, is it I?"

He said to him, "You have said it."

²⁶And as they were eating, Jesus took bread, blessed* and broke *it,* and gave *it* to the disciples and said, "Take, eat; this is My body."

²⁷Then He took the cup, and gave thanks, and gave *it* to them, saying, "Drink from it, all of you. ²⁸For this is My blood of the new* covenant, which is shed for many for the remission of sins. ²⁹But I say to you, I will not drink of this fruit of the vine from now on until that day when I drink it new with you in My Father's kingdom."

³⁰And when they had sung a hymn, they went out to the Mount of Olives.

³¹Then Jesus said to them, "All of you will be made to stumble because of Me this night, for it is written:

> 'I will strike the Shepherd,
> And the sheep of the flock will
> be scattered.'*

³²But after I have been raised, I will go before you to Galilee."

³³Peter answered and said to Him, "Even if all are made to stumble because of You, I will never be made to stumble."

³⁴Jesus said to him, "Assuredly, I say to you that this night, before the rooster crows, you will deny Me three times."

³⁵Peter said to Him, "Even if I have to die with You, I will not deny You!" And so said all the disciples.

³⁶Then Jesus came with them to a place called Gethsemane, and said to the disciples, "Sit here while I go and pray over there." ³⁷And He took with Him Peter and the two sons of Zebedee, and He began to be sorrowful and deeply distressed. ³⁸Then He said to them, "My soul is exceedingly sorrowful, even to death. Stay here and watch with Me."

³⁹He went a little farther and fell on His face, and prayed, saying, "O My Father, if it is possible, let this cup pass from Me; nevertheless, not as I will, but as You *will.*"

⁴⁰Then He came to the disciples and found them sleeping, and said to Peter, "What! Could you not watch with Me one hour? ⁴¹Watch and pray, lest you enter into temptation. The spirit indeed *is* willing, but the flesh *is* weak."

⁴²Again, a second time, He went away and prayed, saying, "O My Father, if this cup cannot pass away from Me unless* I drink it, Your will be done." ⁴³And He came and found them asleep again, for their eyes were heavy.

⁴⁴So He left them, went away again, and prayed the third time, saying the same words. ⁴⁵Then He came to His disciples and said to them, "Are *you* still sleeping and resting? Behold, the hour is at hand, and the Son of Man is being betrayed into the hands of sinners. ⁴⁶Rise, let us be going. See, My betrayer is at hand."

PSALM 31:19-24

O H, how great *is* Your goodness, Which You have laid up for those who fear You,
Which You have prepared for those who trust in You
In the presence of the sons of men!
20   You shall hide them in the

secret place of Your
presence
From the plots of man;
You shall keep them secretly
in a pavilion
From the strife of tongues.

21 Blessed *be* the LORD,
For He has shown me His
marvelous kindness in a
strong city!
22 For I said in my haste,
"I am cut off from before Your
eyes";

Nevertheless You heard the
voice of my supplications
When I cried out to You.

23 Oh, love the LORD, all you His
saints!
For the LORD preserves the
faithful,
And fully repays the proud
person.
24 Be of good courage,
And He shall strengthen your
heart,
All you who hope in the LORD.

PROVERBS FOR TODAY / 8:14-26

[Wisdom cries out,] "Counsel is mine, and sound wisdom; I am understanding, I have strength. By me kings reign, and rulers decree justice. By me princes rule, and nobles, all the judges of the earth. * I love those who love me, and those who seek me diligently will find me. Riches and honor are with me, enduring riches and righteousness. My fruit is better than gold, yes, than fine gold, and my revenue than choice silver. I traverse the way of righteousness, in the midst of the paths of justice, that I may cause those who love me to inherit wealth, that I may fill their treasuries. The LORD possessed me at the beginning of His way, before His works of old. I have been established from everlasting, from the beginning, before there was ever an earth. When there were no depths I was brought forth, when there were no fountains abounding with water. Before the mountains were settled, before the hills, I was brought forth; while as yet He had not made the earth or the fields, or the primal dust of the world."

FEBRUARY 10

EXODUS 30:11–31:18

THEN the LORD spoke to Moses, saying: 12"When you take the census of the children of Israel for their number, then every man shall give a ransom for himself to the LORD, when you number them, that there may be no plague among them when *you* number them. 13This is what everyone among those who are numbered shall give: half a shekel according to the shekel of the sanctu-

ary (a shekel *is* twenty gerahs). The half-shekel *shall be* an offering to the LORD. 14Everyone included among those who are numbered, from twenty years old and above, shall give an offering to the LORD. 15The rich shall not give more and the poor shall not give less than half a shekel, when *you* give an offering to the LORD, to make atonement for yourselves. 16And you shall take the atonement money of the children of Israel, and shall appoint it for the service of the tabernacle of meeting, that it may be a memorial for the children of Israel before the LORD, to make atonement for yourselves."

17Then the LORD spoke to Moses, saying: 18"You shall also make a laver of bronze, with its base also of bronze, for washing. You shall put it between the tabernacle of meeting and the altar. And you shall put water in it, 19for Aaron and his sons shall wash their hands and their feet in water from it. 20When they go into the tabernacle of meeting, or when they come near the altar to minister, to burn an offering made by fire to the LORD, they shall wash with water, lest they die. 21So they shall wash their hands and their feet, lest they die. And it shall be a statute forever to them—to him and his descendants throughout their generations."

22Moreover the LORD spoke to Moses, saying: 23"Also take for yourself quality spices—five hundred *shekels* of liquid myrrh, half as much sweet-smelling cinnamon (two hundred and fifty *shekels*), two hundred and fifty *shekels* of sweet-smelling cane, 24five hundred *shekels* of cassia, according to the shekel of the sanctuary, and a hin of olive oil. 25And you shall make from these a holy anointing oil, an ointment compounded according to the art of the perfumer. It shall be a holy anointing oil. 26With it you shall anoint the tabernacle of meeting and the ark of the Testimony; 27the table and all its utensils, the lampstand and its utensils, and the altar of incense; 28the altar of burnt offering with all its utensils, and the laver and its base. 29You shall consecrate them, that they may be most holy; whatever touches them must be holy.* 30And you shall anoint Aaron and his sons, and consecrate them, that *they* may minister to Me as priests.

31"And you shall speak to the children of Israel, saying: 'This shall be a holy anointing oil to Me throughout your generations. 32It shall not be poured on man's flesh; nor shall you make *any other* like it, according to its composition. It *is* holy, *and* it shall be holy to you. 33Whoever compounds *any* like it, or whoever puts *any* of it on an outsider, shall be cut off from his people.'"

34And the LORD said to Moses: "Take sweet spices, stacte and onycha and galbanum, and pure frankincense with *these* sweet spices; there shall be equal amounts of each. 35You shall make of these an incense, a compound according to the art of the perfumer, salted, pure, *and* holy. 36And you shall beat *some* of it very fine, and put some of it before the Testimony in the tabernacle of meeting where I will meet with you. It shall be most holy to you. 37But *as for* the incense which you shall make, you shall not make any for yourselves, according to its composition. It shall be to you holy for the LORD. 38Whoever makes *any* like it, to smell it, he shall be cut off from his people."

THEN the LORD spoke to Moses, saying: 2"See, I have called by name Bezalel the son of Uri, the son of Hur, of the tribe of Judah. 3And I have filled him with the Spirit of God, in wisdom, in understanding, in knowledge, and in all *manner of* workmanship, 4to design artistic works, to work in gold, in silver, in bronze, 5in cutting jewels for setting, in carving wood, and to work in all *manner of* workmanship.

6"And I, indeed I, have appointed with him Aholiab the son of Ahisamach, of the tribe of Dan; and I have put wisdom in the hearts of all the gifted artisans, that they may make all that I have commanded you: 7the tabernacle of meeting, the ark of the Testimony and the mercy seat that *is* on it, and all the furniture of the tabernacle— 8the table and its utensils, the pure *gold* lampstand with all its utensils, the altar of incense, 9the altar of burnt offering with all its utensils, and the laver and its base— 10the garments of ministry,* the holy garments for Aaron the priest and the garments of his sons, to minister as priests, 11and the anointing oil and sweet incense for the holy *place*. According to all that I have commanded you they shall do."

12And the LORD spoke to Moses, saying, 13"Speak also to the children of Israel, saying: 'Surely My Sabbaths you shall keep, for it *is* a sign between Me and you throughout your generations, that *you* may know that I *am* the LORD who sanctifies you. 14You shall keep the Sabbath, therefore, for *it is* holy to you. Everyone who profanes it shall surely be put to death; for whoever does *any* work on it, that person shall be cut off from among his people. 15Work shall be done for six days, but the seventh *is* the Sabbath of rest, holy to the LORD. Whoever does *any* work on the Sabbath day, he shall surely be put to death. 16Therefore the children of Israel shall keep the Sabbath, to observe the Sabbath throughout their generations *as* a perpetual covenant. 17It *is* a sign between Me and the children of Israel forever; for *in* six days the LORD made the heavens and the earth, and on the seventh day He rested and was refreshed.' "

18And when He had made an end of speaking with him on Mount Sinai, He gave Moses two tablets of the Testimony, tablets of stone, written with the finger of God.

MATTHEW 26:47-68

AND while He [Jesus] was still speaking, behold, Judas, one of the twelve, with a great multitude with swords and clubs, came from the chief priests and elders of the people.

48Now His betrayer had given them a sign, saying, "Whomever I kiss, He is the One; seize Him." 49Immediately he went up to Jesus and said, "Greetings, Rabbi!" and kissed Him.

50But Jesus said to him, "Friend, why have you come?"

Then they came and laid hands on Jesus and took Him. 51And suddenly, one of those *who were* with Jesus stretched out *his* hand and drew his sword, struck the servant of the high priest, and cut off his ear.

52But Jesus said to him, "Put your sword in its place, for all who take the sword will perish* by the sword. 53Or do you think that I cannot now pray to My Father, and He will provide Me with more than twelve legions of angels? 54How then could the Scriptures be fulfilled, that it must happen thus?"

55In that hour Jesus said to the multitudes, "Have you come out, as against a robber, with swords and clubs to take Me? I sat daily with you, teaching in the temple, and you did not seize Me. 56But all this was done that the Scriptures of the prophets might be fulfilled."

Then all the disciples forsook Him and fled.

57And those who had laid hold of Jesus led *Him* away to Caiaphas the high priest, where the scribes and the elders were assembled. 58But Peter followed Him at a distance to the high priest's courtyard. And he went in and sat with the servants to see the end.

59Now the chief priests, the elders,* and all the council sought false testimony against Jesus to put Him to death, 60but found none. Even though many false witnesses came forward, they found none.* But at last two false witnesses* came forward 61and said, "This *fellow* said, 'I am able to destroy the temple of God and to build it in three days.' "

62And the high priest arose and said to Him, "Do You answer nothing? What *is it* these men testify against You?" 63But Jesus kept silent. And the high priest answered and said to Him,

"I put You under oath by the living God: Tell us if You are the Christ, the Son of God!"

64Jesus said to him, "*It is as* you said. Nevertheless, I say to you, hereafter you will see the Son of Man sitting at the right hand of the Power, and coming on the clouds of heaven."

65Then the high priest tore his clothes, saying, "He has spoken blasphemy! What further need do we have of witnesses? Look, now you have heard His blasphemy! 66What do you think?"

They answered and said, "He is deserving of death."

67Then they spat in His face and beat Him; and others struck *Him* with the palms of their hands, 68saying, "Prophesy to us, Christ! Who is the one who struck You?"

PSALM 32:1-11

A Psalm of David. A Contemplation. *

BLESSED *is he whose* transgression *is* forgiven,
Whose sin *is* covered.
2 Blessed *is* the man to whom the LORD does not impute iniquity,
And in whose spirit *there is* no deceit.

3 When I kept silent, my bones grew old
Through my groaning all the day long.
4 For day and night Your hand was heavy upon me;
My vitality was turned into the drought of summer. Selah

5 I acknowledged my sin to You,
And my iniquity I have not hidden.
I said, "I will confess my transgressions to the LORD,"
And You forgave the iniquity of my sin. Selah

6 For this cause everyone who is godly shall pray to You
In a time when You may be found;
Surely in a flood of great waters
They shall not come near him.
7 You *are* my hiding place;
You shall preserve me from trouble;
You shall surround me with songs of deliverance. Selah

8 I will instruct you and teach you in the way you should go;
I will guide you with My eye.
9 Do not be like the horse *or* like the mule,
Which have no understanding,
Which must be harnessed with bit and bridle,
Else they will not come near you.

10 Many sorrows *shall be* to the wicked;
But he who trusts in the LORD, mercy shall surround him.
11 Be glad in the LORD and rejoice, you righteous;
And shout for joy, all *you* upright in heart!

PROVERBS FOR TODAY/ 8:27-32

"When He prepared the heavens, I [wisdom] was there, when He drew a circle on the face of the deep, when He established the clouds above, when He strengthened the fountains of the deep, when He assigned to the sea its limit, so that the waters would not transgress His command, when He marked out the foundations of the

earth, then I was beside Him as *a master craftsman;* * *and I was daily* His *delight, rejoicing always before Him, rejoicing in His inhabited world, and my delight* was *with the sons of men. Now therefore, listen to me,* my *children, for blessed* are those who *keep my ways."*

FEBRUARY 11

EXODUS 32:1–33:23

Now when the people saw that Moses delayed coming down from the mountain, the people gathered together to Aaron, and said to him, "Come, make us gods that shall go before us; for *as for* this Moses, the man who brought us up out of the land of Egypt, we do not know what has become of him."

²And Aaron said to them, "Break off the golden earrings which *are* in the ears of your wives, your sons, and your daughters, and bring *them* to me." ³So all the people broke off the golden earrings which *were* in their ears, and brought *them* to Aaron. ⁴And he received *the gold* from their hand, and he fashioned it with an engraving tool, and made a molded calf.

Then they said, "This *is* your god, O Israel, that brought you out of the land of Egypt!"

⁵So when Aaron saw *it,* he built an altar before it. And Aaron made a proclamation and said, "Tomorrow *is* a feast to the LORD." ⁶Then they rose early on the next day, offered burnt offerings, and brought peace offerings; and the people sat down to eat and drink, and rose up to play.

⁷And the LORD said to Moses, "Go, get down! For your people whom you brought out of the land of Egypt have corrupted *themselves.* ⁸They have turned aside quickly out of the way which I commanded them. They have made themselves a molded calf, and wor-

shiped it and sacrificed to it, and said, 'This *is* your god, O Israel, that brought you out of the land of Egypt!' " ⁹And the LORD said to Moses, "I have seen this people, and indeed it *is* a stiff-necked people! ¹⁰Now therefore, let Me alone, that My wrath may burn hot against them and I may consume them. And I will make of you a great nation."

¹¹Then Moses pleaded with the LORD his God, and said: "LORD, why does Your wrath burn hot against Your people whom You have brought out of the land of Egypt with great power and with a mighty hand? ¹²Why should the Egyptians speak, and say, 'He brought them out to harm them, to kill them in the mountains, and to consume them from the face of the earth'? Turn from Your fierce wrath, and relent from this harm to Your people. ¹³Remember Abraham, Isaac, and Israel, Your servants, to whom You swore by Your own self, and said to them, 'I will multiply your descendants as the stars of heaven; and all this land that I have spoken of I give to your descendants, and they shall inherit *it* forever.' "* ¹⁴So the LORD relented from the harm which He said He would do to His people.

¹⁵And Moses turned and went down from the mountain, and the two tablets of the Testimony *were* in his hand. The tablets *were* written on both sides; on the one *side* and on the other they were written. ¹⁶Now the tablets *were* the work of God, and the writing *was* the writing of God engraved on the tablets.

17And when Joshua heard the noise of the people as they shouted, he said to Moses, "*There is* a noise of war in the camp."

18But he said:

"*It is* not the noise of the shout
of victory,
Nor the noise of the cry of
defeat,
But the sound of singing I
hear."

19So it was, as soon as he came near the camp, that he saw the calf *and* the dancing. So Moses' anger became hot, and he cast the tablets out of his hands and broke them at the foot of the mountain. 20Then he took the calf which they had made, burned *it* in the fire, and ground *it* to powder; and he scattered *it* on the water and made the children of Israel drink *it.* 21And Moses said to Aaron, "What did this people do to you that you have brought *so* great a sin upon them?"

22So Aaron said, "Do not let the anger of my lord become hot. You know the people, that they *are set* on evil. 23For they said to me, 'Make us gods that shall go before us; *as for* this Moses, the man who brought us out of the land of Egypt, we do not know what has become of him.' 24And I said to them, 'Whoever has any gold, let them break *it* off.' So they gave *it* to me, and I cast it into the fire, and this calf came out."

25Now when Moses saw that the people *were* unrestrained (for Aaron had not restrained them, to *their* shame among their enemies), 26then Moses stood in the entrance of the camp, and said, "Whoever *is* on the Lord's side—*come* to me!" And all the sons of Levi gathered themselves together to him. 27And he said to them, "Thus says the Lord God of Israel: 'Let every man put his sword on his side, and go in and out from entrance to entrance throughout the camp, and let every man kill his brother, every man

his companion, and every man his neighbor.' " 28So the sons of Levi did according to the word of Moses. And about three thousand men of the people fell that day. 29Then Moses said, "Consecrate yourselves today to the Lord, that He may bestow on you a blessing this day, for every man has opposed his son and his brother."

30Now it came to pass on the next day that Moses said to the people, "You have committed a great sin. So now I will go up to the Lord; perhaps I can make atonement for your sin." 31Then Moses returned to the Lord and said, "Oh, these people have committed a great sin, and have made for themselves a god of gold! 32Yet now, if You will forgive their sin—but if not, I pray, blot me out of Your book which You have written."

33And the Lord said to Moses, "Whoever has sinned against Me, I will blot him out of My book. 34Now therefore, go, lead the people to *the place* of which I have spoken to you. Behold, My Angel shall go before you. Nevertheless, in the day when I visit for punishment, I will visit punishment upon them for their sin."

35So the Lord plagued the people because of what they did with the calf which Aaron made.

Then the Lord said to Moses, "Depart *and* go up from here, you and the people whom you have brought out of the land of Egypt, to the land of which I swore to Abraham, Isaac, and Jacob, saying, 'To your descendants I will give it.' 2And I will send *My* Angel before you, and I will drive out the Canaanite and the Amorite and the Hittite and the Perizzite and the Hivite and the Jebusite. 3*Go up* to a land flowing with milk and honey; for I will not go up in your midst, lest I consume you on the way, for you *are* a stiff-necked people."

4And when the people heard this

bad news, they mourned, and no one put on his ornaments. ⁵For the LORD had said to Moses, "Say to the children of Israel, 'You *are* a stiff-necked people. I could come up into your midst in one moment and consume you. Now therefore, take off your ornaments, that I may know what to do to you.' " ⁶So the children of Israel stripped themselves of their ornaments by Mount Horeb.

⁷Moses took his tent and pitched it outside the camp, far from the camp, and called it the tabernacle of meeting. And it came to pass *that* everyone who sought the LORD went out to the tabernacle of meeting which *was* outside the camp. ⁸So it was, whenever Moses went out to the tabernacle, *that* all the people rose, and each man stood *at* his tent door and watched Moses until he had gone into the tabernacle. ⁹And it came to pass, when Moses entered the tabernacle, that the pillar of cloud descended and stood *at* the door of the tabernacle, and *the* LORD talked with Moses. ¹⁰All the people saw the pillar of cloud standing *at* the tabernacle door, and all the people rose and worshiped, each man *in* his tent door. ¹¹So the LORD spoke to Moses face to face, as a man speaks to his friend. And he would return to the camp, but his servant Joshua the son of Nun, a young man, did not depart from the tabernacle.

¹²Then Moses said to the LORD, "See, You say to me, 'Bring up this people.' But You have not let me know whom You will send with me. Yet You have said, 'I know you by name, and you have also found grace in My sight.' ¹³Now therefore, I pray, if I have found grace in Your sight, show me now Your way, that I may know You and that I may find grace in Your sight. And consider that this nation *is* Your people."

¹⁴And He said, "My Presence will go *with you,* and I will give you rest."

¹⁵Then he said to Him, "If Your Presence does not go *with us,* do not bring us up from here. ¹⁶For how then will it be known that Your people and I have found grace in Your sight, except You go with us? So we shall be separate, Your people and I, from all the people who *are* upon the face of the earth."

¹⁷So the LORD said to Moses, "I will also do this thing that you have spoken; for you have found grace in My sight, and I know you by name."

¹⁸And he said, "Please, show me Your glory."

¹⁹Then He said, "I will make all My goodness pass before you, and I will proclaim the name of the LORD before you. I will be gracious to whom I will be gracious, and I will have compassion on whom I will have compassion." ²⁰But He said, "You cannot see My face; for no man shall see Me, and live." ²¹And the LORD said, "Here is a place by Me, and you shall stand on the rock. ²²So it shall be, while My glory passes by, that I will put you in the cleft of the rock, and will cover you with My hand while I pass by. ²³Then I will take away My hand, and you shall see My back; but My face shall not be seen."

MATTHEW 26:69–27:14

Now Peter sat outside in the courtyard. And a servant girl came to him, saying, "You also were with Jesus of Galilee."

⁷⁰But he denied it before *them* all, saying, "I do not know what you are saying."

⁷¹And when he had gone out to the gateway, another *girl* saw him and said to those *who were* there, "This *fellow* also was with Jesus of Nazareth."

⁷²But again he denied with an oath, "I do not know the Man!"

⁷³And a little later those who stood by came up and said to Peter, "Surely you also are *one* of them, for your speech betrays you."

⁷⁴Then he began to curse and swear, *saying,* "I do not know the Man!" Immediately a rooster crowed.

75And Peter remembered the word of Jesus who had said to him, "Before the rooster crows, you will deny Me three times." So he went out and wept bitterly.

WHEN morning came, all the chief priests and elders of the people plotted against Jesus to put Him to death. 2And when they had bound Him, they led Him away and delivered Him to Pontius* Pilate the governor.

3Then Judas, His betrayer, seeing that He had been condemned, was remorseful and brought back the thirty pieces of silver to the chief priests and elders, 4saying, "I have sinned by betraying innocent blood."

And they said, "What is that to us? You see to it!"

5Then he threw down the pieces of silver in the temple and departed, and went and hanged himself.

6But the chief priests took the silver pieces and said, "It is not lawful to put them into the treasury, because they are the price of blood." 7And they consulted together and bought with them the potter's field, to bury strangers in. 8Therefore that field has been called the Field of Blood to this day.

9Then was fulfilled what was spoken by Jeremiah the prophet, saying, *"And they took the thirty pieces of silver, the value of Him who was priced, whom they of the children of Israel priced, 10and gave them for the potter's field, as the LORD directed me."*

11Now Jesus stood before the governor. And the governor asked Him, saying, "Are You the King of the Jews?"

Jesus said to him, "*It is as* you say." 12And while He was being accused by the chief priests and elders, He answered nothing.

13Then Pilate said to Him, "Do You not hear how many things they testify against You?" 14But He answered him not one word, so that the governor marveled greatly.

PSALM 33:1-12

REJOICE in the LORD, O you righteous!
For praise from the upright is beautiful.
2 Praise the LORD with the harp;
Make melody to Him with an instrument of ten strings.
3 Sing to Him a new song;
Play skillfully with a shout of joy.

4 For the word of the LORD *is* right,
And all His work *is done* in truth.
5 He loves righteousness and justice;
The earth is full of the goodness of the LORD.

6 By the word of the LORD the heavens were made,
And all the host of them by the breath of His mouth.
7 He gathers the waters of the sea together as a heap;*
He lays up the deep in storehouses.

8 Let all the earth fear the LORD;
Let all the inhabitants of the world stand in awe of Him.
9 For He spoke, and it was *done;*
He commanded, and it stood fast.

10 The LORD brings the counsel of the nations to nothing;
He makes the plans of the peoples of no effect.
11 The counsel of the LORD stands forever,
The plans of His heart to all generations.
12 Blessed *is* the nation whose God *is* the LORD,
The people He has chosen as His own inheritance.

PROVERBS FOR TODAY/ 8:33-36

"Hear instruction and be wise, and do not disdain it. Blessed is the man who listens to me [wisdom], watching daily at my gates, waiting at the posts of my doors. For whoever finds me finds life, and obtains favor from the LORD; but he who sins against me wrongs his own soul; all those who hate me love death."

FEBRUARY 12

EXODUS 34:1–35:9

AND the LORD said to Moses, "Cut two tablets of stone like the first *ones,* and I will write on *these* tablets the words that were on the first tablets which you broke. ²So be ready in the morning, and come up in the morning to Mount Sinai, and present yourself to Me there on the top of the mountain. ³And no man shall come up with you, and let no man be seen throughout all the mountain; let neither flocks nor herds feed before that mountain."

⁴So he cut two tablets of stone like the first *ones.* Then Moses rose early in the morning and went up Mount Sinai, as the LORD had commanded him; and he took in his hand the two tablets of stone.

⁵Now the LORD descended in the cloud and stood with him there, and proclaimed the name of the LORD. ⁶And the LORD passed before him and proclaimed, "The LORD, the LORD God, merciful and gracious, longsuffering, and abounding in goodness and truth, ⁷keeping mercy for thousands, forgiving iniquity and transgression and sin, by no means clearing *the guilty,* visiting the iniquity of the fathers upon the children and the children's children to the third and the fourth generation."

⁸So Moses made haste and bowed his head toward the earth, and worshiped. ⁹Then he said, "If now I have found grace in Your sight, O Lord, let my Lord, I pray, go among us, even though we *are* a stiff-necked people; and pardon our iniquity and our sin, and take us as Your inheritance."

¹⁰And He said: "Behold, I make a covenant. Before all your people I will do marvels such as have not been done in all the earth, nor in any nation; and all the people among whom you *are* shall see the work of the LORD. For it *is* an awesome thing that I will do with you. ¹¹Observe what I command you this day. Behold, I am driving out from before you the Amorite and the Canaanite and the Hittite and the Perizzite and the Hivite and the Jebusite. ¹²Take heed to yourself, lest you make a covenant with the inhabitants of the land where you are going, lest it be a snare in your midst. ¹³But you shall destroy their altars, break their *sacred* pillars, and cut down their wooden images ¹⁴(for you shall worship no other god, for the LORD, whose name *is* Jealous, *is* a jealous God), ¹⁵lest you make a covenant with the inhabitants of the land, and they play the harlot with their gods and make sacrifice to their gods, and *one of them* invites you and you eat of his sacrifice, ¹⁶and you take of his daughters for your sons, and his daughters play the harlot with their gods and make your sons play the harlot with their gods.

¹⁷"You shall make no molded gods for yourselves.

¹⁸"The Feast of Unleavened Bread

you shall keep. Seven days you shall eat unleavened bread, as I commanded you, in the appointed time of the month of Abib; for in the month of Abib you came out from Egypt.

19"All that open the womb *are* Mine, and every male firstborn among your livestock, *whether* ox or sheep. 20But the firstborn of a donkey you shall redeem with a lamb. And if you will not redeem *him,* then you shall break his neck. All the firstborn of your sons you shall redeem.

"And none shall appear before Me empty-handed.

21"Six days you shall work, but on the seventh day you shall rest; in plowing time and in harvest you shall rest.

22"And you shall observe the Feast of Weeks, of the firstfruits of wheat harvest, and the Feast of Ingathering at the year's end.

23"Three times in the year all your men shall appear before the Lord, the LORD God of Israel. 24For I will cast out the nations before you and enlarge your borders; neither will any man covet your land when you go up to appear before the LORD your God three times in the year.

25"You shall not offer the blood of My sacrifice with leaven, nor shall the sacrifice of the Feast of the Passover be left until morning.

26"The first of the firstfruits of your land you shall bring to the house of the LORD your God. You shall not boil a young goat in its mother's milk."

27Then the LORD said to Moses, "Write these words, for according to the tenor of these words I have made a covenant with you and with Israel." 28So he was there with the LORD forty days and forty nights; he neither ate bread nor drank water. And He wrote on the tablets the words of the covenant, the Ten Commandments.*

29Now it was so, when Moses came down from Mount Sinai (and the two tablets of the Testimony *were* in Moses'

hand when he came down from the mountain), that Moses did not know that the skin of his face shone while he talked with Him. 30So when Aaron and all the children of Israel saw Moses, behold, the skin of his face shone, and they were afraid to come near him. 31Then Moses called to them, and Aaron and all the rulers of the congregation returned to him; and Moses talked with them. 32Afterward all the children of Israel came near, and he gave them as commandments all that the LORD had spoken with him on Mount Sinai. 33And when Moses had finished speaking with them, he put a veil on his face. 34But whenever Moses went in before the LORD to speak with Him, he would take the veil off until he came out; and he would come out and speak to the children of Israel whatever he had been commanded. 35And whenever the children of Israel saw the face of Moses, that the skin of Moses' face shone, then Moses would put the veil on his face again, until he went in to speak with Him.

THEN Moses gathered all the congregation of the children of Israel together, and said to them, "These *are* the words which the LORD has commanded *you* to do: 2Work shall be done for six days, but the seventh day shall be a holy day for you, a Sabbath of rest to the LORD. Whoever does any work on it shall be put to death. 3You shall kindle no fire throughout your dwellings on the Sabbath day."

4And Moses spoke to all the congregation of the children of Israel, saying, "This *is* the thing which the LORD commanded, saying: 5'Take from among you an offering to the LORD. Whoever *is* of a willing heart, let him bring it as an offering to the LORD: gold, silver, and bronze; 6blue, purple, and scarlet *thread,* fine linen, and goats' *hair;* 7ram skins dyed red, badger skins, and acacia wood; 8oil for the light, and spices for the anointing oil and for the sweet incense; ⁹onyx stones, and stones to be set in the ephod and in the breast-plate.' "

MATTHEW 27:15-31

Now at the feast the governor was accustomed to releasing to the multitude one prisoner whom they wished. ¹⁶And at that time they had a notorious prisoner called Barabbas.* ¹⁷Therefore, when they had gathered together, Pilate said to them, "Whom do you want me to release to you? Barabbas, or Jesus who is called Christ?" ¹⁸For he knew that they had handed Him over because of envy.

¹⁹While he was sitting on the judgment seat, his wife sent to him, saying, "Have nothing to do with that just Man, for I have suffered many things today in a dream because of Him."

²⁰But the chief priests and elders persuaded the multitudes that they should ask for Barabbas and destroy Jesus. ²¹The governor answered and said to them, "Which of the two do you want me to release to you?"

They said, "Barabbas!"

²²Pilate said to them, "What then shall I do with Jesus who is called Christ?"

They all said to him, "Let Him be crucified!"

²³Then the governor said, "Why, what evil has He done?"

But they cried out all the more, saying, "Let Him be crucified!"

²⁴When Pilate saw that he could not prevail at all, but rather *that* a tumult was rising, he took water and washed *his* hands before the multitude, saying, "I am innocent of the blood of this just Person.* You see *to it.*"

²⁵And all the people answered and said, "His blood *be* on us and on our children."

²⁶Then he released Barabbas to them; and when he had scourged Jesus, he delivered *Him* to be crucified.

²⁷Then the soldiers of the governor took Jesus into the Praetorium and gathered the whole garrison around Him. ²⁸And they stripped Him and put a scarlet robe on Him. ²⁹When they had twisted a crown of thorns, they put *it* on His head, and a reed in His right hand. And they bowed the knee before Him and mocked Him, saying, "Hail, King of the Jews!" ³⁰Then they spat on Him, and took the reed and struck Him on the head. ³¹And when they had mocked Him, they took the robe off Him, put His *own* clothes on Him, and led Him away to be crucified.

PSALM 33:13-22

The Lord looks from heaven; He sees all the sons of men.
¹⁴From the place of His dwelling He looks On all the inhabitants of the earth;
15　He fashions their hearts individually; He considers all their works.

16　No king *is* saved by the multitude of an army; A mighty man is not delivered by great strength.
17　A horse *is* a vain hope for safety; Neither shall it deliver *any* by its great strength.

18　Behold, the eye of the Lord *is* on those who fear Him, On those who hope in His mercy,
19　To deliver their soul from death, And to keep them alive in famine.

20　Our soul waits for the Lord; He *is* our help and our shield.

21 For our heart shall rejoice in
Him,
Because we have trusted in
His holy name.

22 Let Your mercy, O LORD, be
upon us,
Just as we hope in You.

PROVERBS FOR TODAY/ 9:1-6

Wisdom has built her house, she has hewn out her seven pillars; she has slaughtered her meat, she has mixed her wine, she has also furnished her table. She has sent out her maidens, she cries out from the highest places of the city, "Whoever is simple, let him turn in here!" As for him who lacks understanding, she says to him, "Come, eat of my bread and drink of the wine I have mixed. Forsake foolishness and live, and go in the way of understanding."

FEBRUARY 13

EXODUS 35:10–36:38

"**A**LL *who are* gifted artisans among you shall come and make all that the LORD has commanded: 11the tabernacle, its tent, its covering, its clasps, its boards, its bars, its pillars, and its sockets; 12the ark and its poles, *with* the mercy seat, and the veil of the covering; 13the table and its poles, all its utensils, and the showbread; 14also the lampstand for the light, its utensils, its lamps, and the oil for the light; 15the incense altar, its poles, the anointing oil, the sweet incense, and the screen for the door at the entrance of the tabernacle; 16the altar of burnt offering with its bronze grating, its poles, all its utensils, *and* the laver and its base; 17the hangings of the court, its pillars, their sockets, and the screen for the gate of the court; 18the pegs of the tabernacle, the pegs of the court, and their cords; 19the garments of ministry,* for ministering in the holy *place*—the holy garments for Aaron the priest and the garments of his sons, to minister as priests.'"

20And all the congregation of the children of Israel departed from the presence of Moses. 21Then everyone came whose heart was stirred, and everyone whose spirit was willing, *and* they brought the LORD's offering for the work of the tabernacle of meeting, for all its service, and for the holy garments. 22They came, both men and women, as many as had a willing heart, *and* brought earrings and nose rings, rings and necklaces, all jewelry of gold, that is, every man who *made* an offering of gold to the LORD. 23And every man, with whom was found blue, purple, and scarlet *thread*, fine linen, goats' *hair*, red skins of rams, and badger skins, brought *them*. 24Everyone who offered an offering of silver or bronze brought the LORD's offering. And everyone with whom was found acacia wood for any work of the service, brought *it*. 25All the women *who were* gifted artisans spun yarn with their hands, and brought what they had spun, of blue, purple, *and* scarlet, and fine linen. 26And all the women whose hearts stirred with wisdom spun yarn of goats' *hair.* 27The rulers brought onyx stones, and the stones to be set in the ephod and in the breastplate, 28and spices and oil for the light, for the anointing oil, and for the sweet incense. 29The children of Israel brought a freewill offering to the LORD, all the men and women whose hearts were willing to bring *material* for all kinds of work which the LORD, by the hand of Moses, had commanded to be done.

30And Moses said to the children of Israel, "See, the LORD has called by name Bezalel the son of Uri, the son of Hur, of the tribe of Judah; 31and He has filled him with the Spirit of God, in wisdom and understanding, in knowledge and all manner of workmanship, 32to design artistic works, to work in gold and silver and bronze, 33in cutting jewels for setting, in carving wood, and to work in all manner of artistic workmanship.

34"And He has put in his heart the ability to teach, *in* him and Aholiab the son of Ahisamach, of the tribe of Dan. 35He has filled them with skill to do all manner of work of the engraver and the designer and the tapestry maker, in blue, purple, and scarlet *thread,* and fine linen, and of the weaver—those who do every work and those who design artistic works.

"AND Bezalel and Aholiab, and every gifted artisan in whom the LORD has put wisdom and understanding, to know how to do all manner of work for the service of the sanctuary, shall do according to all that the LORD has commanded."

2Then Moses called Bezalel and Aholiab, and every gifted artisan in whose heart the LORD had put wisdom, everyone whose heart was stirred, to come and do the work. 3And they received from Moses all the offering which the children of Israel had brought for the work of the service of making the sanctuary. So they continued bringing to him freewill offerings every morning. 4Then all the crafts-

men who were doing all the work of the sanctuary came, each from the work he was doing, 5and they spoke to Moses, saying, "The people bring much more than enough for the service of the work which the LORD commanded *us* to do."

6So Moses gave a commandment, and they caused it to be proclaimed throughout the camp, saying, "Let neither man nor woman do any more work for the offering of the sanctuary." And the people were restrained from bringing, 7for the material they had was sufficient for all the work to be done—indeed too much.

8Then all the gifted artisans among them who worked on the tabernacle made ten curtains woven of fine linen, and of blue, purple, and scarlet thread; *with* artistic designs of cherubim they made them. 9The length of each curtain *was* twenty-eight cubits, and the width of each curtain four cubits; the curtains *were* all the same size. 10And he coupled five curtains to one another, and *the other* five curtains he coupled to one another. 11He made loops of blue *yarn* on the edge of the curtain on the selvedge of one set; likewise he did on the outer edge of *the other* curtain of the second set. 12Fifty loops he made on one curtain, and fifty loops he made on the edge of the curtain on the end of the second set; the loops held one *curtain* to another. 13And he made fifty clasps of gold, and coupled the curtains to one another with the clasps, that it might be one tabernacle.

14He made curtains of goats' *hair* for the tent over the tabernacle; he made eleven curtains. 15The length of each curtain *was* thirty cubits, and the width of each curtain four cubits; the eleven curtains *were* the same size. 16He coupled five curtains by themselves and six curtains by themselves. 17And he made fifty loops on the edge of the curtain that is outermost in one set, and fifty loops he made on the edge of the curtain of the second set. 18He also made fifty bronze clasps to couple the tent together, that it might be one. 19Then he made a covering for the tent of ram skins dyed red, and a covering of badger skins above *that.*

20For the tabernacle he made boards of acacia wood, standing upright. 21The length of each board *was* ten cubits, and the width of each board a cubit and a half. 22Each board had two tenons for binding one to another. Thus he made for all the boards of the tabernacle. 23And he made boards for the tabernacle, twenty boards for the south side. 24Forty sockets of silver he made to go under the twenty boards: two sockets under each of the boards for its two tenons. 25And for the other side of the tabernacle, the north side, he made twenty boards 26and their forty sockets of silver: two sockets under each of the boards. 27For the west side of the tabernacle he made six boards. 28He also made two boards for the two back corners of the tabernacle. 29And they were coupled at the bottom and coupled together at the top by one ring. Thus he made both of them for the two corners. 30So there were eight boards and their sockets—sixteen sockets of silver—two sockets under each of the boards.

31And he made bars of acacia wood: five for the boards on one side of the tabernacle, 32five bars for the boards on the other side of the tabernacle, and five bars for the boards of the tabernacle on the far side westward. 33And he made the middle bar to pass through the boards from one end to the other. 34He overlaid the boards with gold, made their rings of gold *to be* holders for the bars, and overlaid the bars with gold.

35And he made a veil of blue, purple, and scarlet *thread,* and fine woven linen; it was worked *with* an artistic design of cherubim. 36He made for it four pillars of acacia *wood,* and overlaid them with gold, with their hooks of gold; and he cast four sockets of silver for them.

37He also made a screen for the tabernacle door, of blue, purple, and scarlet *thread,* and fine woven linen, made by a weaver, 38and its five pillars with their hooks. And he overlaid their capitals and their rings with gold, but their five sockets *were* bronze.

MATTHEW 27:32-66

Now as they [the soldiers] came out, they found a man of Cyrene, Simon by name. Him they compelled to bear His cross. 33And when they had come to a place called Golgotha, that is to say, Place of a Skull, 34they gave Him sour* wine mingled with gall to drink. But when He had tasted *it,* He would not drink.

35Then they crucified Him, and divided His garments, casting lots,* that it might be fulfilled which was spoken by the prophet:

> *"They divided My garments among them,*
> *And for My clothing they cast lots."**

36Sitting down, they kept watch over Him there. 37And they put up over His head the accusation written against Him:

THIS IS JESUS
THE KING OF THE JEWS.

38Then two robbers were crucified with Him, one on the right and another on the left.

39And those who passed by blasphemed Him, wagging their heads 40and saying, "You who destroy the temple and build *it* in three days, save Yourself! If You are the Son of God, come down from the cross." 41Likewise the chief priests also, mocking with the scribes and elders,* said, 42"He saved others; Himself He cannot save. If He is the King of Israel,* let Him now come down from the cross, and we will believe Him.* 43He trusted in God; let Him deliver Him now if He will have Him; for He said, 'I am the Son of God.'"

44Even the robbers who were crucified with Him reviled Him with the same thing.

45Now from the sixth hour until the ninth hour there was darkness over all the land. 46And about the ninth hour Jesus cried out with a loud voice, saying, "Eli, Eli, lama sabachthani?" that is, *My God, My God, why have You forsaken Me?"**

47Some of those who stood there, when they heard *that,* said, "This Man is calling for Elijah!" 48Immediately one of them ran and took a sponge, filled *it* with sour wine and put *it* on a reed, and offered it to Him to drink.

49The rest said, "Let Him alone; let us see if Elijah will come to save Him."

50And Jesus cried out again with a loud voice, and yielded up His spirit.

51Then, behold, the veil of the temple was torn in two from top to bottom; and the earth quaked, and the rocks were split, 52and the graves were opened; and many bodies of the saints who had fallen asleep were raised; 53and coming out of the graves after His resurrection, they went into the holy city and appeared to many.

54So when the centurion and those with him, who were guarding Jesus, saw the earthquake and the things that had happened, they feared greatly, saying, "Truly this was the Son of God!"

55And many women who followed Jesus from Galilee, ministering to Him, were there looking on from afar, 56among whom were Mary Magdalene, Mary the mother of James and Joses,* and the mother of Zebedee's sons.

57Now when evening had come, there came a rich man from Arimathea, named Joseph, who himself had also become a disciple of Jesus. 58This man went to Pilate and asked for the body of Jesus. Then Pilate commanded the body to be given to him. 59When Joseph had taken the body, he wrapped it in a clean linen cloth, 60and laid it in his new tomb which he had hewn out of the rock; and he rolled a large stone against the door of the tomb, and departed. 61And Mary Magdalene was there, and the other Mary, sitting opposite the tomb.

62On the next day, which followed the Day of Preparation, the chief priests and Pharisees gathered together to Pilate, 63saying, "Sir, we remember, while He was still alive, how that deceiver said, 'After three days I will rise.' 64Therefore command that the tomb be made secure until the third day, lest His disciples come by night* and steal Him *away,* and say to the people, 'He has risen from the dead.' So the last deception will be worse than the first."

65Pilate said to them, "You have a guard; go your way, make *it* as secure as you know how." 66So they went and made the tomb secure, sealing the stone and setting the guard.

PSALM 34:1–10

A Psalm of David when he pretended madness before Abimelech, who drove him away, and he departed.

I WILL bless the LORD at all times;
His praise *shall* continually *be* in my mouth.

2 My soul shall make its boast in the LORD;
The humble shall hear *of it* and be glad.

3 Oh, magnify the LORD with me,
And let us exalt His name together.

⁴ I sought the Lord, and He
   heard me,
   And delivered me from all my
   fears.
⁵ They looked to Him and were
   radiant,
   And their faces were not
   ashamed.
⁶ This poor man cried out, and
   the Lord heard *him,*
   And saved him out of all his
   troubles.
⁷ The angel* of the Lord
   encamps all around those
   who fear Him,

And delivers them.
⁸ Oh, taste and see that the
   Lord *is* good;
   Blessed *is* the man *who* trusts
   in Him!
⁹ Oh, fear the Lord, you His
   saints!
   There is no want to those who
   fear Him.
¹⁰ The young lions lack and
   suffer hunger;
   But those who seek the Lord
   shall not lack any good
   thing.

PROVERBS FOR TODAY/ 9:7-8

"He who corrects a scoffer gets shame for himself, and he who rebukes a wicked man only *harms himself. Do not correct a scoffer, lest he hate you; rebuke a wise* man, *and he will love you."*

FEBRUARY 14

EXODUS 37:1–38:31

THEN Bezalel made the ark of acacia wood; two and a half cubits *was* its length, a cubit and a half its width, and a cubit and a half its height. ²He overlaid it with pure gold inside and outside, and made a molding of gold all around it. ³And he cast for it four rings of gold *to be set* in its four corners: two rings on one side, and two rings on the other side of it. ⁴He made poles of acacia wood, and overlaid them with gold. ⁵And he put the poles into the rings at the sides of the ark, to bear the ark. ⁶He also made the mercy seat of pure gold; two and a half cubits *was* its length and a cubit and a half its width. ⁷He made two cherubim of beaten gold; he made them of one piece at the two ends of

the mercy seat: ⁸one cherub at one end on this side, and the other cherub at the *other* end on that side. He made the cherubim at the two ends *of one piece* with the mercy seat. ⁹The cherubim spread out *their* wings above, *and* covered the mercy seat with their wings. They faced one another; the faces of the cherubim were toward the mercy seat.

¹⁰He made the table of acacia wood; two cubits *was* its length, a cubit its width, and a cubit and a half its height. ¹¹And he overlaid it with pure gold, and made a molding of gold all around it. ¹²Also he made a frame of a handbreadth all around it, and made a molding of gold for the frame all around it. ¹³And he cast for it four rings of gold, and put the rings on the four corners that *were* at its four legs. ¹⁴The rings

were close to the frame, as holders for the poles to bear the table. ¹⁵And he made the poles of acacia wood to bear the table, and overlaid them with gold. ¹⁶He made of pure gold the utensils which were on the table: its dishes, its cups, its bowls, and its pitchers for pouring.

¹⁷He also made the lampstand of pure gold; of hammered work he made the lampstand. Its shaft, its branches, its bowls, its *ornamental* knobs, and its flowers were of the same piece. ¹⁸And six branches came out of its sides: three branches of the lampstand out of one side, and three branches of the lampstand out of the other side. ¹⁹There were three bowls made like almond *blossoms* on one branch, with an *ornamental* knob and a flower, and three bowls made like almond *blossoms* on the other branch, with an *ornamental* knob and a flower—and so for the six branches coming out of the lampstand. ²⁰And on the lampstand itself *were* four bowls made like almond *blossoms, each with* its *ornamental* knob and flower. ²¹*There was* a knob under the *first* two branches of the same, a knob under the *second* two branches of the same, and a knob under the *third* two branches of the same, according to the six branches extending from it. ²²Their knobs and their branches were of one piece; all of it *was* one hammered piece of pure gold. ²³And he made its seven lamps, its wick-trimmers, and its trays of pure gold. ²⁴Of a talent of pure gold he made it, with all its utensils.

²⁵He made the incense altar of acacia wood. Its length *was* a cubit and its width a cubit—*it was* square—and two cubits *was* its height. Its horns were *of one piece* with it. ²⁶And he overlaid it with pure gold: its top, its sides all around, and its horns. He also made for it a molding of gold all around it. ²⁷He made two rings of gold for it under its molding, by its two corners on both sides, as holders for the poles with which to bear it. ²⁸And he made the poles of acacia wood, and overlaid them with gold.

²⁹He also made the holy anointing oil and the pure incense of sweet spices, according to the work of the perfumer.

He made the altar of burnt offering of acacia wood; five cubits *was* its length and five cubits its width—*it was* square—and its height *was* three cubits. ²He made its horns on its four corners; the horns were *of one piece* with it. And he overlaid it with bronze. ³He made all the utensils for the altar: the pans, the shovels, the basins, the forks, and the firepans; all its utensils he made of bronze. ⁴And he made a grate of bronze network for the altar, under its rim, midway from the bottom. ⁵He cast four rings for the four corners of the bronze grating, *as* holders for the poles. ⁶And he made the poles of acacia wood, and overlaid them with bronze. ⁷Then he put the poles into the rings on the sides of the altar, with which to bear it. He made the altar hollow with boards.

⁸He made the laver of bronze and its base of bronze, from the bronze mirrors of the serving women who assembled at the door of the tabernacle of meeting.

⁹Then he made the court on the south side; the hangings of the court *were of* fine woven linen, one hundred cubits long. ¹⁰There *were* twenty pillars for them, with twenty bronze sockets. The hooks of the pillars and their bands *were* silver. ¹¹On the north side *the hangings were* one hundred cubits *long,* with twenty pillars and their twenty bronze sockets. The hooks of the pillars and their bands *were* silver. ¹²And on the west side *there were* hangings of fifty cubits, with ten pillars and their ten sockets. The hooks of the pillars and their bands *were* silver. ¹³For

the east side *the hangings were* fifty cubits. ¹⁴The hangings of one side *of the gate were* fifteen cubits *long, with* their three pillars and their three sockets, ¹⁵and the same for the other side of the court gate; on this side and that *were* hangings of fifteen cubits, *with* their three pillars and their three sockets. ¹⁶All the hangings of the court all around *were of* fine woven linen. ¹⁷The sockets for the pillars *were* bronze, the hooks of the pillars and their bands *were* silver, and the overlay of their capitals *was* silver; and all the pillars of the court had bands of silver. ¹⁸The screen for the gate of the court *was* woven of blue, purple, and scarlet *thread,* and of fine woven linen. The length *was* twenty cubits, and the height along its width *was* five cubits, corresponding to the hangings of the court. ¹⁹And *there were* four pillars *with* their four sockets of bronze; their hooks *were* silver, and the overlay of their capitals and their bands *was* silver. ²⁰All the pegs of the tabernacle, and of the court all around, *were* bronze.

²¹This is the inventory of the tabernacle, the tabernacle of the Testimony, which was counted according to the commandment of Moses, for the service of the Levites, by the hand of Ithamar, son of Aaron the priest.

²²Bezalel the son of Uri, the son of Hur, of the tribe of Judah, made all that the Lord had commanded Moses. ²³And with him *was* Aholiab the son of Ahisamach, of the tribe of Dan, an engraver and designer, a weaver of blue, purple, and scarlet *thread,* and of fine linen.

²⁴All the gold that was used in all the work of the holy *place,* that is, the gold of the offering, was twenty-nine talents and seven hundred and thirty shekels, according to the shekel of the sanctuary. ²⁵And the silver from those who were numbered of the congregation *was* one hundred talents and one thousand seven hundred and seventy-five shekels, according to the shekel of the sanctuary: ²⁶a bekah for each man (*that is,* half a shekel, according to the shekel of the sanctuary), for everyone included in the numbering from twenty years old and above, for six hundred and three thousand, five hundred and fifty *men.* ²⁷And from the hundred talents of silver were cast the sockets of the sanctuary and the bases of the veil: one hundred sockets from the hundred talents, one talent for each socket. ²⁸Then from the one thousand seven hundred and seventy-five *shekels* he made hooks for the pillars, overlaid their capitals, and made bands for them.

²⁹The offering of bronze *was* seventy talents and two thousand four hundred shekels. ³⁰And with it he made the sockets for the door of the tabernacle of meeting, the bronze altar, the bronze grating for it, and all the utensils for the altar, ³¹the sockets for the court all around, the bases for the court gate, all the pegs for the tabernacle, and all the pegs for the court all around.

MATTHEW 28:1-20

Now after the Sabbath, as the first *day* of the week began to dawn, Mary Magdalene and the other Mary came to see the tomb. ²And behold, there was a great earthquake; for an angel of the Lord descended from heaven, and came and rolled back the stone from the door,* and sat on it. ³His countenance was like lightning, and his clothing as white as snow. ⁴And the guards shook for fear of him, and became like dead *men.*

⁵But the angel answered and said to the women, "Do not be afraid, for I know that you seek Jesus who was crucified. ⁶He is not here; for He is risen, as He said. Come, see the place where

the Lord lay. [7]And go quickly and tell His disciples that He is risen from the dead, and indeed He is going before you into Galilee; there you will see Him. Behold, I have told you."

[8]So they went out quickly from the tomb with fear and great joy, and ran to bring His disciples word.

[9]And as they went to tell His disciples,* behold, Jesus met them, saying, "Rejoice!" So they came and held Him by the feet and worshiped Him. [10]Then Jesus said to them, "Do not be afraid. Go and tell My brethren to go to Galilee, and there they will see Me."

[11]Now while they were going, behold, some of the guard came into the city and reported to the chief priests all the things that had happened. [12]When they had assembled with the elders and consulted together, they gave a large sum of money to the soldiers, [13]saying, "Tell them, 'His disciples came at night and stole Him away while we slept.' [14]And if this comes to the governor's ears, we will appease him and make you secure." [15]So they took the money and did as they were instructed; and this saying is commonly reported among the Jews until this day.

[16]Then the eleven disciples went away into Galilee, to the mountain which Jesus had appointed for them. [17]When they saw Him, they worshiped Him; but some doubted.

[18]And Jesus came and spoke to them, saying, "All authority has been given to Me in heaven and on earth. [19]Go therefore* and make disciples of all the nations, baptizing them in the name of the Father and of the Son and of the Holy Spirit, [20]teaching them to observe all things that I have commanded you; and lo, I am with you always, even to the end of the age." Amen.*

PSALM 34:11-22

COME, you children, listen to me; I will teach you the fear of the LORD.
12 Who is the man who desires life,
And loves many days, that he may see good?
13 Keep your tongue from evil,
And your lips from speaking deceit.
14 Depart from evil and do good;
Seek peace and pursue it.

15 The eyes of the LORD are on the righteous,
And His ears are open to their cry.
16 The face of the LORD is against those who do evil,
To cut off the remembrance of them from the earth.

17 The righteous cry out, and the LORD hears,
And delivers them out of all their troubles.
18 The LORD is near to those who have a broken heart,
And saves such as have a contrite spirit.

19 Many are the afflictions of the righteous,
But the LORD delivers him out of them all.
20 He guards all his bones;
Not one of them is broken.
21 Evil shall slay the wicked,
And those who hate the righteous shall be condemned.
22 The LORD redeems the soul of His servants,
And none of those who trust in Him shall be condemned.

PROVERBS FOR TODAY/ 9:9-10

"Give instruction to a wise man, and he will be still wiser; teach a just man, and *he will increase in learning. The fear of the L*ORD *is the beginning of wisdom, and the knowledge of the Holy One is understanding."*

FEBRUARY 15

EXODUS 39:1–40:38

O F the blue, purple, and scarlet *thread* they made garments of ministry,* for ministering in the holy *place,* and made the holy garments for Aaron, as the LORD had commanded Moses.

²He made the ephod of gold, blue, purple, and scarlet *thread,* and of fine woven linen. ³And they beat the gold into thin sheets and cut *it into* threads, to work *it* in *with* the blue, purple, and scarlet *thread,* and the fine linen, *into* artistic designs. ⁴They made shoulder straps for it to couple *it* together; it was coupled together at its two edges. ⁵And the intricately woven band of his ephod that *was* on it *was* of the same workmanship, *woven of* gold, blue, purple, and scarlet *thread,* and of fine woven linen, as the LORD had commanded Moses.

⁶And they set onyx stones, enclosed in settings of gold; they were engraved, as signets are engraved, with the names of the sons of Israel. ⁷He put them on the shoulders of the ephod *as* memorial stones for the sons of Israel, as the LORD had commanded Moses.

⁸And he made the breastplate, artistically woven like the workmanship of the ephod, of gold, blue, purple, and scarlet *thread,* and of fine woven linen. ⁹They made the breastplate square by doubling it; a span *was* its length and a span its width when doubled. ¹⁰And they set in it four rows of stones: a row with a sardius, a topaz, and an emerald was the first row; ¹¹the second row,

a turquoise, a sapphire, and a diamond; ¹²the third row, a jacinth, an agate, and an amethyst; ¹³the fourth row, a beryl, an onyx, and a jasper. *They were* enclosed in settings of gold in their mountings. ¹⁴*There were* twelve stones according to the names of the sons of Israel: according to their names, *engraved like* a signet, each one with its own name according to the twelve tribes. ¹⁵And they made chains for the breastplate at the ends, like braided cords of pure gold. ¹⁶They also made two settings of gold and two gold rings, and put the two rings on the two ends of the breastplate. ¹⁷And they put the two braided *chains* of gold in the two rings on the ends of the breastplate. ¹⁸The two ends of the two braided *chains* they fastened in the two settings, and put them on the shoulder straps of the ephod in the front. ¹⁹And they made two rings of gold and put *them* on the two ends of the breastplate, on the edge of it, which *was* on the inward side of the ephod. ²⁰They made two *other* gold rings and put them on the two shoulder straps, underneath the ephod toward its front, right at the seam above the intricately woven band of the ephod. ²¹And they bound the breastplate by means of its rings to the rings of the ephod with a blue cord, so that it would be above the intricately woven band of the ephod, and that the breastplate would not come loose from the ephod, as the LORD had commanded Moses.

²²He made the robe of the ephod of woven work, all of blue. ²³And *there was* an opening in the middle of the robe, like the opening in a coat of mail, *with* a woven binding all around the opening, so that it would not tear. ²⁴They made on the hem of the robe pomegranates of blue, purple, and scarlet, and of fine woven *linen.* ²⁵And they made bells of pure gold, and put the bells between the pomegranates on the hem of the robe all around between the pomegranates: ²⁶a bell and a pomegranate, a bell and a pomegranate, all around the hem of the robe to minister in, as the Lord had commanded Moses.

²⁷They made tunics, artistically woven of fine linen, for Aaron and his sons, ²⁸a turban of fine linen, exquisite hats of fine linen, short trousers of fine woven linen, ²⁹and a sash of fine woven linen with blue, purple, and scarlet *thread,* made by a weaver, as the Lord had commanded Moses.

³⁰Then they made the plate of the holy crown of pure gold, and wrote on it an inscription *like* the engraving of a signet:

HOLINESS TO THE LORD.

³¹And they tied to it a blue cord, to fasten *it* above on the turban, as the Lord had commanded Moses.

³²Thus all the work of the tabernacle of the tent of meeting was finished. And the children of Israel did according to all that the Lord had commanded Moses; so they did. ³³And they brought the tabernacle to Moses, the tent and all its furnishings: its clasps, its boards, its bars, its pillars, and its sockets; ³⁴the covering of ram skins dyed red, the covering of badger skins, and the veil of the covering; ³⁵the ark of the Testimony with its poles, and the mercy seat; ³⁶the table, all its utensils, and the showbread; ³⁷the pure *gold* lampstand with its lamps (the lamps set in order), all its

utensils, and the oil for light; ³⁸the gold altar, the anointing oil, and the sweet incense; the screen for the tabernacle door; ³⁹the bronze altar, its grate of bronze, its poles, and all its utensils; the laver with its base; ⁴⁰the hangings of the court, its pillars and its sockets, the screen for the court gate, its cords, and its pegs; all the utensils for the service of the tabernacle, for the tent of meeting; ⁴¹and the garments of ministry,* to minister in the holy *place:* the holy garments for Aaron the priest, and his sons' garments, to minister as priests.

⁴²According to all that the Lord had commanded Moses, so the children of Israel did all the work. ⁴³Then Moses looked over all the work, and indeed they had done it; as the Lord had commanded, just so they had done it. And Moses blessed them.

Then the Lord spoke to Moses, saying: ²"On the first day of the first month you shall set up the tabernacle of the tent of meeting. ³You shall put in it the ark of the Testimony, and partition off the ark with the veil. ⁴You shall bring in the table and arrange the things that are to be set in order on it; and you shall bring in the lampstand and light its lamps. ⁵You shall also set the altar of gold for the incense before the ark of the Testimony, and put up the screen for the door of the tabernacle. ⁶Then you shall set the altar of the burnt offering before the door of the tabernacle of the tent of meeting. ⁷And you shall set the laver between the tabernacle of meeting and the altar, and put water in it. ⁸You shall set up the court all around, and hang up the screen at the court gate.

⁹"And you shall take the anointing oil, and anoint the tabernacle and all that *is* in it; and you shall hallow it and all its utensils, and it shall be holy. ¹⁰You shall anoint the altar of the burnt offering and all its utensils, and conse-

crate the altar. The altar shall be most holy. ¹¹And you shall anoint the laver and its base, and consecrate it.

¹²"Then you shall bring Aaron and his sons to the door of the tabernacle of meeting and wash them with water. ¹³You shall put the holy garments on Aaron, and anoint him and consecrate him, that he may minister to Me as priest. ¹⁴And you shall bring his sons and clothe them with tunics. ¹⁵You shall anoint them, as you anointed their father, that they may minister to Me as priests; for their anointing shall surely be an everlasting priesthood throughout their generations."

¹⁶Thus Moses did; according to all that the LORD had commanded him, so he did.

¹⁷And it came to pass in the first month of the second year, on the first *day* of the month, *that* the tabernacle was raised up. ¹⁸So Moses raised up the tabernacle, fastened its sockets, set up its boards, put in its bars, and raised up its pillars. ¹⁹And he spread out the tent over the tabernacle and put the covering of the tent on top of it, as the LORD had commanded Moses. ²⁰He took the Testimony and put *it* into the ark, inserted the poles through the rings of the ark, and put the mercy seat on top of the ark. ²¹And he brought the ark into the tabernacle, hung up the veil of the covering, and partitioned off the ark of the Testimony, as the LORD had commanded Moses.

²²He put the table in the tabernacle of meeting, on the north side of the tabernacle, outside the veil; ²³and he set the bread in order upon it before the LORD, as the LORD had commanded Moses. ²⁴He put the lampstand in the tabernacle of meeting, across from the table, on the south side of the tabernacle; ²⁵and he lit the lamps before the LORD, as the LORD had commanded Moses. ²⁶He put the gold altar in the tabernacle of meeting in front of the veil; ²⁷and he burned sweet incense on

it, as the LORD had commanded Moses. ²⁸He hung up the screen *at* the door of the tabernacle. ²⁹And he put the altar of burnt offering *before* the door of the tabernacle of the tent of meeting, and offered upon it the burnt offering and the grain offering, as the LORD had commanded Moses. ³⁰He set the laver between the tabernacle of meeting and the altar, and put water there for washing; ³¹and Moses, Aaron, and his sons would wash their hands and their feet *with water* from it. ³²Whenever they went into the tabernacle of meeting, and when they came near the altar, they washed, as the LORD had commanded Moses. ³³And he raised up the court all around the tabernacle and the altar, and hung up the screen of the court gate. So Moses finished the work.

³⁴Then the cloud covered the tabernacle of meeting, and the glory of the LORD filled the tabernacle. ³⁵And Moses was not able to enter the tabernacle of meeting, because the cloud rested above it, and the glory of the LORD filled the tabernacle. ³⁶Whenever the cloud was taken up from above the tabernacle, the children of Israel would go onward in all their journeys. ³⁷But if the cloud was not taken up, then they did not journey till the day that it was taken up. ³⁸For the cloud of the LORD *was* above the tabernacle by day, and fire was over it by night, in the sight of all the house of Israel, throughout all their journeys.

MARK 1:1-28

THE beginning of the gospel of Jesus Christ, the Son of God. ²As it is written in the Prophets:*

*"Behold, I send My messenger before Your face,
Who will prepare Your way before You." ***

3 *"The voice of one crying in the wilderness:*
'Prepare the way of the LORD;
*Make His paths straight.' " ***

4John came baptizing in the wilderness and preaching a baptism of repentance for the remission of sins. 5Then all the land of Judea, and those from Jerusalem, went out to him and were all baptized by him in the Jordan River, confessing their sins.

6Now John was clothed with camel's hair and with a leather belt around his waist, and he ate locusts and wild honey. 7And he preached, saying, "There comes One after me who is mightier than I, whose sandal strap I am not worthy to stoop down and loose. 8I indeed baptized you with water, but He will baptize you with the Holy Spirit."

9It came to pass in those days *that* Jesus came from Nazareth of Galilee, and was baptized by John in the Jordan. 10And immediately, coming up from* the water, He saw the heavens parting and the Spirit descending upon Him like a dove. 11Then a voice came from heaven, "You are My beloved Son, in whom I am well pleased."

12Immediately the Spirit drove Him into the wilderness. 13And He was there in the wilderness forty days, tempted by Satan, and was with the wild beasts; and the angels ministered to Him.

14Now after John was put in prison, Jesus came to Galilee, preaching the gospel of the kingdom* of God, 15and saying, "The time is fulfilled, and the kingdom of God is at hand. Repent, and believe in the gospel."

16And as He walked by the Sea of Galilee, He saw Simon and Andrew his brother casting a net into the sea; for they were fishermen. 17Then Jesus said to them, "Follow Me, and I will make you become fishers of men."

18They immediately left their nets and followed Him.

19When He had gone a little farther from there, He saw James the *son* of Zebedee, and John his brother, who also *were* in the boat mending their nets. 20And immediately He called them, and they left their father Zebedee in the boat with the hired servants, and went after Him.

21Then they went into Capernaum, and immediately on the Sabbath He entered the synagogue and taught. 22And they were astonished at His teaching, for He taught them as one having authority, and not as the scribes.

23Now there was a man in their synagogue with an unclean spirit. And he cried out, 24saying, "Let *us* alone! What have we to do with You, Jesus of Nazareth? Did You come to destroy us? I know who You are—the Holy One of God!"

25But Jesus rebuked him, saying, "Be quiet, and come out of him!" 26And when the unclean spirit had convulsed him and cried out with a loud voice, he came out of him. 27Then they were all amazed, so that they questioned among themselves, saying, "What is this? What new doctrine *is* this? For with authority* He commands even the unclean spirits, and they obey Him." 28And immediately His fame spread throughout all the region around Galilee.

PSALM 35:1-16

A Psalm of David.

PLEAD *my cause,* O LORD, with those who strive with me;
Fight against those who fight against me.

2 Take hold of shield and buckler,
And stand up for my help.

3 Also draw out the spear,

And stop those who pursue
me.
Say to my soul,
"I *am* your salvation."

4 Let those be put to shame and
brought to dishonor
Who seek after my life;
Let those be turned back and
brought to confusion
Who plot my hurt.
5 Let them be like chaff before
the wind,
And let the angel* of the LORD
chase *them.*
6 Let their way be dark and
slippery,
And let the angel of the LORD
pursue them.
7 For without cause they have
hidden their net for me *in* a
pit,
Which they have dug without
cause for my life.
8 Let destruction come upon
him unexpectedly,
And let his net that he has
hidden catch himself;
Into that very destruction let
him fall.
9 And my soul shall be joyful in
the LORD;
It shall rejoice in His salvation.
10 All my bones shall say,

"LORD, who *is* like You,
Delivering the poor from him
who is too strong for him,
Yes, the poor and the needy
from him who plunders
him?"

11 Fierce witnesses rise up;
They ask me *things* that I do
not know.
12 They reward me evil for good,
To the sorrow of my soul.
13 But as for me, when they
were sick,
My clothing *was* sackcloth;
I humbled myself with fasting;
And my prayer would return
to my own heart.
14 I paced about as though *he
were* my friend *or* brother;
I bowed down heavily, as one
who mourns *for his* mother.

15 But in my adversity they
rejoiced
And gathered together;
Attackers gathered against
me,
And I did not know *it;*
They tore *at me* and did not
cease;
16 With ungodly mockers at
feasts
They gnashed at me with
their teeth.

PROVERBS FOR TODAY/ 9:11-12

*"For by me [wisdom] your days will be multiplied, and years of life will be added
to you. If you are wise, you are wise for yourself, and if you scoff, you will bear it
alone."*

FEBRUARY 16

LEVITICUS 1:1–3:17

Now the LORD called to Moses, and spoke to him from the tabernacle of meeting, saying, 2"Speak to the children of Israel, and say to them: 'When any one of you brings an offering to the LORD, you shall bring your offering of the livestock—of the herd and of the flock.

3'If his offering is a burnt sacrifice of the herd, let him offer a male without blemish; he shall offer it of his own free will at the door of the tabernacle of meeting before the LORD. 4Then he shall put his hand on the head of the burnt offering, and it will be accepted on his behalf to make atonement for him. 5He shall kill the bull before the LORD; and the priests, Aaron's sons, shall bring the blood and sprinkle the blood all around on the altar that is by the door of the tabernacle of meeting. 6And he shall skin the burnt offering and cut it into its pieces. 7The sons of Aaron the priest shall put fire on the altar, and lay the wood in order on the fire. 8Then the priests, Aaron's sons, shall lay the parts, the head, and the fat in order on the wood that is on the fire upon the altar; 9but he shall wash its entrails and its legs with water. And the priest shall burn all on the altar as a burnt sacrifice, an offering made by fire, a sweet aroma to the LORD.

10'If his offering is of the flocks—of the sheep or of the goats—as a burnt sacrifice, he shall bring a male without blemish. 11He shall kill it on the north side of the altar before the LORD; and the priests, Aaron's sons, shall sprinkle its blood all around on the altar. 12And he shall cut it into its pieces, with its head and its fat; and the priest shall lay them in order on the wood that is on the fire upon the altar; 13but he shall wash the entrails and the legs with water. Then the priest shall bring it all and burn it on the altar; it is a burnt sacrifice, an offering made by fire, a sweet aroma to the LORD.

14'And if the burnt sacrifice of his offering to the LORD is of birds, then he shall bring his offering of turtledoves or young pigeons. 15The priest shall bring it to the altar, wring off its head, and burn it on the altar; its blood shall be drained out at the side of the altar. 16And he shall remove its crop with its feathers and cast it beside the altar on the east side, into the place for ashes. 17Then he shall split it at its wings, but shall not divide it completely; and the priest shall burn it on the altar, on the wood that is on the fire. It is a burnt sacrifice, an offering made by fire, a sweet aroma to the LORD.

'WHEN anyone offers a grain offering to the LORD, his offering shall be of fine flour. And he shall pour oil on it, and put frankincense on it. 2He shall bring it to Aaron's sons, the priests, one of whom shall take from it his handful of fine flour and oil with all the frankincense. And the priest shall burn it as a memorial on the altar, an offering made by fire, a sweet aroma to the LORD. 3The rest of the grain offering shall be Aaron's and his sons'. It is most holy of the offerings to the LORD made by fire.

4'And if you bring as an offering a grain offering baked in the oven, it shall be unleavened cakes of fine flour mixed with oil, or unleavened wafers anointed with oil. 5But if your offering is a grain offering baked in a pan, it shall be of fine flour, unleavened, mixed with oil. 6You shall break it in pieces and pour oil on it; it is a grain offering.

7If your offering *is* a grain offering *baked* in a covered pan, it shall be made *of* fine flour with oil. 8You shall bring the grain offering that is made of these things to the LORD. And when it is presented to the priest, he shall bring it to the altar. 9Then the priest shall take from the grain offering a memorial portion, and burn *it* on the altar. *It is* an offering made by fire, a sweet aroma to the LORD. 10And what is left of the grain offering *shall be* Aaron's and his sons'. *It is* most holy of the offerings to the LORD made by fire.

11'No grain offering which you bring to the LORD shall be made with leaven, for you shall burn no leaven nor any honey in any offering to the LORD made by fire. 12As for the offering of the firstfruits, you shall offer them to the LORD, but they shall not be burned on the altar for a sweet aroma. 13And every offering of your grain offering you shall season with salt; you shall not allow the salt of the covenant of your God to be lacking from your grain offering. With all your offerings you shall offer salt.

14'If you offer a grain offering of your firstfruits to the LORD, you shall offer for the grain offering of your firstfruits green heads of grain roasted on the fire, grain beaten from full heads. 15And you shall put oil on it, and lay frankincense on it. It *is* a grain offering. 16Then the priest shall burn the memorial portion: *part* of its beaten grain and *part* of its oil, with all the frankincense, as an offering made by fire to the LORD.

'WHEN his offering *is* a sacrifice of a peace offering, if he offers *it* of the herd, whether male or female, he shall offer it without blemish before the LORD. 2And he shall lay his hand on the head of his offering, and kill it *at* the door of the tabernacle of meeting; and Aaron's sons, the priests, shall sprinkle the blood all around on the altar.

3Then he shall offer from the sacrifice of the peace offering an offering made by fire to the LORD. The fat that covers the entrails and all the fat that *is* on the entrails, 4the two kidneys and the fat that *is* on them by the flanks, and the fatty lobe *attached* to the liver above the kidneys, he shall remove; 5and Aaron's sons shall burn it on the altar upon the burnt sacrifice, which *is* on the wood that *is* on the fire, *as* an offering made by fire, a sweet aroma to the LORD.

6'If his offering as a sacrifice of a peace offering to the LORD *is* of the flock, *whether* male or female, he shall offer it without blemish. 7If he offers a lamb as his offering, then he shall offer it before the LORD. 8And he shall lay his hand on the head of his offering, and kill it before the tabernacle of meeting; and Aaron's sons shall sprinkle its blood all around on the altar.

9'Then he shall offer from the sacrifice of the peace offering, as an offering made by fire to the LORD, its fat *and* the whole fat tail which he shall remove close to the backbone. And the fat that covers the entrails and all the fat that *is* on the entrails, 10the two kidneys and the fat that *is* on them by the flanks, and the fatty lobe *attached* to the liver above the kidneys, he shall remove; 11and the priest shall burn *them* on the altar *as* food, an offering made by fire to the LORD.

12'And if his offering *is* a goat, then he shall offer it before the LORD. 13He shall lay his hand on its head and kill it before the tabernacle of meeting; and the sons of Aaron shall sprinkle its blood all around on the altar. 14Then he shall offer from it his offering, as an offering made by fire to the LORD. The fat that covers the entrails and all the fat that *is* on the entrails, 15the two kidneys and the fat that *is* on them by the flanks, and the fatty lobe *attached* to the liver above the kidneys, he shall remove; 16and the priest shall burn them on the altar *as* food, an offering made by fire for a sweet aroma; all the fat *is* the LORD'S.

17"*This shall be* a perpetual statute throughout your generations in all your dwellings: you shall eat neither fat nor blood.'"

MARK 1:29–2:12

Now as soon as they [Jesus, Simon, and Andrew] had come out of the synagogue, they entered the house of Simon and Andrew, with James and John. 30But Simon's wife's mother lay sick with a fever, and they told Him about her at once. 31So He came and took her by the hand and lifted her up, and immediately the fever left her. And she served them.

32At evening, when the sun had set, they brought to Him all who were sick and those who were demon-possessed. 33And the whole city was gathered together at the door. 34Then He healed many who were sick with various diseases, and cast out many demons; and He did not allow the demons to speak, because they knew Him.

35Now in the morning, having risen a long while before daylight, He went out and departed to a solitary place; and there He prayed. 36And Simon and those *who were* with Him searched for Him. 37When they found Him, they said to Him, "Everyone is looking for You."

38But He said to them, "Let us go into the next towns, that I may preach there also, because for this purpose I have come forth."

39And He was preaching in their synagogues throughout all Galilee, and casting out demons.

40Now a leper came to Him, imploring Him, kneeling down to Him and saying to Him, "If You are willing, You can make me clean."

41Then Jesus, moved with compassion, stretched out *His* hand and touched him, and said to him, "I am willing; be cleansed." 42As soon as He had spoken, immediately the leprosy left him, and he was cleansed. 43And He strictly warned him and sent him away at once, 44and said to him, "See that you say nothing to anyone; but go your way, show yourself to the priest, and offer for your cleansing those things which Moses commanded, as a testimony to them."

45However, he went out and began to proclaim *it* freely, and to spread the matter, so that Jesus could no longer openly enter the city, but was outside in deserted places; and they came to Him from every direction.

And again He entered Capernaum after *some* days, and it was heard that He was in the house. 2Immediately* many gathered together, so that there was no longer room to receive *them,* not even near the door. And He preached the word to them. 3Then they came to Him, bringing a paralytic who was carried by four *men.* 4And when they could not come near Him because of the crowd, they uncovered the roof where He was. So when they had broken through, they let down the bed on which the paralytic was lying.

5When Jesus saw their faith, He said to the paralytic, "Son, your sins are forgiven you."

6And some of the scribes were sitting there and reasoning in their hearts, 7"Why does this *Man* speak blasphemies like this? Who can forgive sins but God alone?"

8But immediately, when Jesus perceived in His spirit that they reasoned thus within themselves, He said to them, "Why do you reason about these things in your hearts? 9Which is easier, to say to the paralytic, '*Your* sins are forgiven you,' or to say, 'Arise, take up your bed and walk'? 10But that you may know that the Son of Man has power on earth to forgive sins"—He said to the paralytic, [11]"I say to you, arise, take up your bed, and go to your house." [12]Immediately he arose, took up the bed, and went out in the presence of them all, so that all were amazed and glorified God, saying, "We never saw *anything* like this!"

PSALM 35:17-28

Lord, how long will You look on? Rescue me from their destructions, My precious *life* from the lions.

[18] I will give You thanks in the great assembly; I will praise You among many people.

[19] Let them not rejoice over me who are wrongfully my enemies; Nor let them wink with the eye who hate me without a cause.

[20] For they do not speak peace, But they devise deceitful matters Against *the* quiet ones in the land.

[21] They also opened their mouth wide against me, *And* said, "Aha, aha! Our eyes have seen *it.*"

[22] *This* You have seen, O Lord; Do not keep silence. O Lord, do not be far from me.

[23] Stir up Yourself, and awake to my vindication, To my cause, my God and my Lord.

[24] Vindicate me, O Lord my God, according to Your righteousness; And let them not rejoice over me.

[25] Let them not say in their hearts, "Ah, so we would have it!" Let them not say, "We have swallowed him up."

[26] Let them be ashamed and brought to mutual confusion Who rejoice at my hurt; Let them be clothed with shame and dishonor Who exalt themselves against me.

[27] Let them shout for joy and be glad, Who favor my righteous cause; And let them say continually, "Let the Lord be magnified, Who has pleasure in the prosperity of His servant."

[28] And my tongue shall speak of Your righteousness *And* of Your praise all the day long.

PROVERBS FOR TODAY/ 9:13-18

A foolish woman is clamorous; she is *simple, and knows nothing. For she sits at the door of her house, on a seat* by *the highest places of the city, to call to those who pass by, who go straight on their way: "Whoever* is *simple, let him turn in here"; and* as for *him who lacks understanding, she says to him, "Stolen water is sweet, and bread* eaten *in secret is pleasant." But he does not know that the dead* are *there,* that *her guests* are *in the depths of hell.* *

LEVITICUS 4:1–5:19

Now the LORD spoke to Moses, saying, ²"Speak to the children of Israel, saying: 'If a person sins unintentionally against any of the commandments of the LORD *in anything* which ought not to be done, and does any of them, ³if the anointed priest sins, bringing guilt on the people, then let him offer to the LORD for his sin which he has sinned a young bull without blemish as a sin offering. ⁴He shall bring the bull to the door of the tabernacle of meeting before the LORD, lay his hand on the bull's head, and kill the bull before the LORD. ⁵Then the anointed priest shall take some of the bull's blood and bring it to the tabernacle of meeting. ⁶The priest shall dip his finger in the blood and sprinkle some of the blood seven times before the LORD, in front of the veil of the sanctuary. ⁷And the priest shall put some of the blood on the horns of the altar of sweet incense before the LORD, which is in the tabernacle of meeting; and he shall pour the remaining blood of the bull at the base of the altar of the burnt offering, which is at the door of the tabernacle of meeting. ⁸He shall take from it all the fat of the bull as the sin offering. The fat that covers the entrails and all the fat which *is* on the entrails, ⁹the two kidneys and the fat that *is* on them by the flanks, and the fatty lobe *attached* to the liver above the kidneys, he shall remove, ¹⁰as it was taken from the bull of the sacrifice of the peace offering; and the priest shall burn them on the altar of the burnt offering. ¹¹But the bull's hide and all its flesh, with its head and legs, its entrails and offal— ¹²the whole bull he shall carry outside the camp to a clean place, where the ashes are poured out, and burn it on wood with fire; where the ashes are poured out it shall be burned.

¹³Now if the whole congregation of Israel sins unintentionally, and the thing is hidden from the eyes of the assembly, and they have done *something against* any of the commandments of the LORD *in anything* which should not be done, and are guilty; ¹⁴when the sin which they have committed becomes known, then the assembly shall offer a young bull for the sin, and bring it before the tabernacle of meeting. ¹⁵And the elders of the congregation shall lay their hands on the head of the bull before the LORD. Then the bull shall be killed before the LORD. ¹⁶The anointed priest shall bring some of the bull's blood to the tabernacle of meeting. ¹⁷Then the priest shall dip his finger in the blood and sprinkle *it* seven times before the LORD, in front of the veil. ¹⁸And he shall put *some* of the blood on the horns of the altar which *is* before the LORD, which *is* in the tabernacle of meeting; and he shall pour the remaining blood at the base of the altar of burnt offering, which is at the door of the tabernacle of meeting. ¹⁹He shall take all the fat from it and burn *it* on the altar. ²⁰And he shall do with the bull as he did with the bull as a sin offering; thus he shall do with it. So the priest shall make atonement for them, and it shall be forgiven them. ²¹Then he shall carry the bull outside the camp, and burn it as he burned the first bull. It *is* a sin offering for the assembly.

²²'When a ruler has sinned, and done *something* unintentionally *against* any of the commandments of the LORD his God *in anything* which should not be done, and is guilty, ²³or if his sin

which he has committed comes to his knowledge, he shall bring as his offering a kid of the goats, a male without blemish. 24And he shall lay his hand on the head of the goat, and kill it at the place where they kill the burnt offering before the LORD. It *is* a sin offering. 25The priest shall take some of the blood of the sin offering with his finger, put *it* on the horns of the altar of burnt offering, and pour its blood at the base of the altar of burnt offering. 26And he shall burn all its fat on the altar, like the fat of the sacrifice of the peace offering. So the priest shall make atonement for him concerning his sin, and it shall be forgiven him.

27'If anyone of the common people sins unintentionally by doing *some thing against* any of the commandments of the LORD *in anything* which ought not to be done, and is guilty, 28or if his sin which he has committed comes to his knowledge, then he shall bring as his offering a kid of the goats, a female without blemish, for his sin which he has committed. 29And he shall lay his hand on the head of the sin offering, and kill the sin offering at the place of the burnt offering. 30Then the priest shall take *some* of its blood with his finger, put *it* on the horns of the altar of burnt offering, and pour all *the remaining* blood at the base of the altar. 31He shall remove all its fat, as fat is removed from the sacrifice of the peace offering; and the priest shall burn it on the altar for a sweet aroma to the LORD. So the priest shall make atonement for him, and it shall be forgiven him.

32'If he brings a lamb as his sin offering, he shall bring a female without blemish. 33Then he shall lay his hand on the head of the sin offering, and kill it as a sin offering at the place where they kill the burnt offering. 34The priest shall take *some* of the blood of the sin offering with his finger, put *it* on the horns of the altar of burnt offering, and pour all *the remaining* blood at the base of the altar. 35He shall remove all its fat, as the fat of the lamb is removed from the sacrifice of the peace offering. Then the priest shall burn it on the altar, according to the offerings made by fire to the LORD. So the priest shall make atonement for his sin that he has committed, and it shall be forgiven him.

'IF a person sins in hearing the utterance of an oath, and *is* a witness, whether he has seen or known *of the matter*—if he does not tell *it,* he bears guilt.

2'Or if a person touches any unclean thing, whether *it is* the carcass of an unclean beast, or the carcass of unclean livestock, or the carcass of unclean creeping things, and he is unaware of it, he also shall be unclean and guilty. 3Or if he touches human uncleanness—whatever uncleanness with which a man may be defiled, and he is unaware of it—when he realizes *it,* then he shall be guilty.

4'Or if a person swears, speaking thoughtlessly with *his* lips to do evil or to do good, whatever *it is* that a man may pronounce by an oath, and he is unaware of it—when he realizes *it,* then he shall be guilty in any of these *matters.*

5'And it shall be, when he is guilty in any of these *matters,* that he shall confess that he has sinned in that *thing;* 6and he shall bring his trespass offering to the LORD for his sin which he has committed, a female from the flock, a lamb or a kid of the goats as a sin offering. So the priest shall make atonement for him concerning his sin.

7'If he is not able to bring a lamb, then he shall bring to the LORD, for his trespass which he has committed, two turtledoves or two young pigeons: one as a sin offering and the other as a burnt offering. 8And he shall bring them to the priest, who shall offer *that* which *is* for the sin offering first, and wring off its head from its neck, but shall not divide *it* completely. ⁹Then he shall sprinkle *some* of the blood of the sin offering on the side of the altar, and the rest of the blood shall be drained out at the base of the altar. It *is* a sin offering. ¹⁰And he shall offer the second *as* a burnt offering according to the prescribed manner. So the priest shall make atonement on his behalf for his sin which he has committed, and it shall be forgiven him.

¹¹'But if he is not able to bring two turtledoves or two young pigeons, then he who sinned shall bring for his offering one-tenth of an ephah of fine flour as a sin offering. He shall put no oil on it, nor shall he put frankincense on it, for it *is* a sin offering. ¹²Then he shall bring it to the priest, and the priest shall take his handful of it as a memorial portion, and burn *it* on the altar according to the offerings made by fire to the LORD. It *is* a sin offering. ¹³The priest shall make atonement for him, for his sin that he has committed in any of these matters; and it shall be forgiven him. *The rest* shall be the priest's as a grain offering.' "

¹⁴Then the LORD spoke to Moses, saying: ¹⁵"If a person commits a trespass, and sins unintentionally in regard to the holy things of the LORD, then he shall bring to the LORD as his trespass offering a ram without blemish from the flocks, with your valuation in shekels of silver according to the shekel of the sanctuary, as a trespass offering. ¹⁶And he shall make restitution for the harm that he has done in regard to the holy thing, and shall add one-fifth to it and give it to the priest. So the priest shall make atonement for him with the ram of the trespass offering, and it shall be forgiven him.

¹⁷"If a person sins, and commits any of these things which are forbidden to be done by the commandments of the LORD, though he does not know *it,* yet he is guilty and shall bear his iniquity. ¹⁸And he shall bring to the priest a ram without blemish from the flock, with your valuation, as a trespass offering. So the priest shall make atonement for him regarding his ignorance in which he erred and did not know *it,* and it shall be forgiven him. ¹⁹It is a trespass offering; he has certainly trespassed against the LORD."

MARK 2:13–3:6

THEN He [Jesus] went out again by the sea; and all the multitude came to Him, and He taught them. ¹⁴As He passed by, He saw Levi the *son* of Alphaeus sitting at the tax office. And He said to him, "Follow Me." So he arose and followed Him.

¹⁵Now it happened, as He was dining in *Levi's* house, that many tax collectors and sinners also sat together with Jesus and His disciples; for there were many, and they followed Him. ¹⁶And when the scribes and* Pharisees saw Him eating with the tax collectors and sinners, they said to His disciples, "How *is it* that He eats and drinks with tax collectors and sinners?"

¹⁷When Jesus heard *it,* He said to them, "Those who are well have no need of a physician, but those who are sick. I did not come to call *the* righteous, but sinners, to repentance."*

¹⁸The disciples of John and of the Pharisees were fasting. Then they came and said to Him, "Why do the disciples of John and of the Pharisees fast, but Your disciples do not fast?"

¹⁹And Jesus said to them, "Can the friends of the bridegroom fast while the bridegroom is with them? As long as they have the bridegroom with them they cannot fast. ²⁰But the days will come when the bridegroom will be taken away from them, and then they will fast in those days. ²¹No one sews a piece of unshrunk cloth on an old gar-

ment; or else the new piece pulls away from the old, and the tear is made worse. 22And no one puts new wine into old wineskins; or else the new wine bursts the wineskins, the wine is spilled, and the wineskins are ruined. But new wine must be put into new wineskins."

23Now it happened that He went through the grainfields on the Sabbath; and as they went His disciples began to pluck the heads of grain. 24And the Pharisees said to Him, "Look, why do they do what is not lawful on the Sabbath?"

25But He said to them, "Have you never read what David did when he was in need and hungry, he and those with him: 26how he went into the house of God in the days of Abiathar the high priest, and ate the showbread, which is not lawful to eat except for the priests, and also gave some to those who were with him?"

27And He said to them, "The Sabbath was made for man, and not man for the Sabbath. 28Therefore the Son of Man is also Lord of the Sabbath."

AND He entered the synagogue again, and a man was there who had a withered hand. 2So they watched Him closely, whether He would heal him on the Sabbath, so that they might accuse Him. 3And He said to the man who had the withered hand, "Step forward." 4Then He said to them, "Is it lawful on the Sabbath to do good or to do evil, to save life or to kill?" But they kept silent. 5And when He had looked around at them with anger, being grieved by the hardness of their hearts, He said to the man, "Stretch out your hand." And he stretched it out, and his hand was restored as whole as the other.* 6Then the Pharisees went out and immediately plotted with the Herodians against Him, how they might destroy Him.

PSALM 36:1-12
To the Chief Musician. A Psalm of David the servant of the LORD.

AN oracle within my heart concerning the transgression of the wicked:
There is no fear of God before his eyes.
2 For he flatters himself in his own eyes,
When he finds out his iniquity *and* when he hates.
3 The words of his mouth *are* wickedness and deceit;
He has ceased to be wise *and* to do good.
4 He devises wickedness on his bed;
He sets himself in a way *that is* not good;
He does not abhor evil.

5 Your mercy, O LORD, *is* in the heavens;
Your faithfulness *reaches* to the clouds.
6 Your righteousness *is* like the great mountains;
Your judgments *are* a great deep;
O LORD, You preserve man and beast.

7 How precious *is* Your lovingkindness, O God!
Therefore the children of men put their trust under the shadow of Your wings.
8 They are abundantly satisfied with the fullness of Your house,
And You give them drink from the river of Your pleasures.
9 For with You *is* the fountain of life;
In Your light we see light.

10 Oh, continue Your

lovingkindness to those
who know You,
And Your righteousness to
the upright in heart.
11 Let not the foot of pride come
against me,

And let not the hand of the
wicked drive me away.
12 There the workers of iniquity
have fallen;
They have been cast down
and are not able to rise.

PROVERBS FOR TODAY / 10:1-2

The proverbs of Solomon: A wise son makes a glad father, but a foolish son is *the grief of his mother.* □ *Treasures of wickedness profit nothing, but righteousness delivers from death.*

FEBRUARY 18

LEVITICUS 6:1–7:27

AND the LORD spoke to Moses, saying: 2"If a person sins and commits a trespass against the LORD by lying to his neighbor about what was delivered to him for safekeeping, or about a pledge, or about a robbery, or if he has extorted from his neighbor, 3or if he has found what was lost and lies concerning it, and swears falsely—in any one of these things that a man may do in which he sins: 4then it shall be, because he has sinned and is guilty, that he shall restore what he has stolen, or the thing which he has extorted, or what was delivered to him for safekeeping, or the lost thing which he found, 5or all that about which he has sworn falsely. He shall restore its full value, add one-fifth more to it, *and* give it to whomever it belongs, on the day of his trespass offering. 6And he shall bring his trespass offering to the LORD, a ram without blemish from the flock, with your valuation, as a trespass offering, to the priest. 7So the priest shall make atonement for him before the LORD, and he shall be forgiven for any one of these things that he may have done in which he trespasses."

8Then the LORD spoke to Moses, saying, 9"Command Aaron and his sons, saying, 'This *is* the law of the burnt offering: The burnt offering *shall be* on the hearth upon the altar all night until morning, and the fire of the altar shall be kept burning on it. 10And the priest shall put on his linen garment, and his linen trousers he shall put on his body, and take up the ashes of the burnt offering which the fire has consumed on the altar, and he shall put them beside the altar. 11Then he shall take off his garments, put on other garments, and carry the ashes outside the camp to a clean place. 12And the fire on the altar shall be kept burning on it; it shall not be put out. And the priest shall burn wood on it every morning, and lay the burnt offering in order on it; and he shall burn on it the fat of the peace offerings. 13A fire shall always be burning on the altar; it shall never go out.

14"This *is* the law of the grain offering: The sons of Aaron shall offer it on the altar before the LORD. 15He shall take from it his handful of the fine flour of the grain offering, with its oil, and all the frankincense which *is* on the grain offering, and shall burn *it* on the altar *for* a sweet aroma, as a memorial to the LORD. 16And the remainder of it Aaron and his sons shall eat; with unleavened bread it shall be eaten in a holy place; in the court of the tabernacle of meeting they shall eat it. 17It shall not be baked with leaven. I have given it *as* their portion of My offerings made by fire; it *is* most holy, like the sin offering and the trespass offering. 18All the males among the children of Aaron may eat it. *It shall be* a statute forever in your generations concerning the offerings made by fire to the LORD. Everyone who touches them must be holy.' "*

19And the LORD spoke to Moses, saying, 20"This *is* the offering of Aaron and his sons, which they shall offer to the LORD, *beginning* on the day when he is anointed: one-tenth of an ephah of fine flour as a daily grain offering, half of it in the morning and half of it at night. 21It shall be made in a pan with oil. *When it is* mixed, you shall bring it in. The baked pieces of the grain offering you shall offer *for* a sweet aroma to the LORD. 22The priest from among his sons, who is anointed in his place, shall offer it. *It is* a statute forever to the LORD. It shall be wholly burned. 23For every grain offering for the priest shall be wholly burned. It shall not be eaten."

24Also the LORD spoke to Moses, saying, 25"Speak to Aaron and to his sons, saying, 'This *is* the law of the sin offering: In the place where the burnt offering is killed, the sin offering shall be killed before the LORD. It *is* most holy. 26The priest who offers it for sin shall eat it. In a holy place it shall be eaten, in the court of the tabernacle of meeting. 27Everyone who touches its flesh must be holy.* And when its blood is sprinkled on any garment, you shall wash that on which it was sprinkled, in a holy place. 28But the earthen vessel in which it is boiled shall be broken.

And if it is boiled in a bronze pot, it shall be both scoured and rinsed in water. 29All the males among the priests may eat it. It *is* most holy. 30But no sin offering from which *any* of the blood is brought into the tabernacle of meeting, to make atonement in the holy *place,** shall be eaten. It shall be burned in the fire.

'LIKEWISE this *is* the law of the trespass offering (it *is* most holy): 2In the place where they kill the burnt offering they shall kill the trespass offering. And its blood he shall sprinkle all around on the altar. 3And he shall offer from it all its fat. The fat tail and the fat that covers the entrails, 4the two kidneys and the fat that *is* on them by the flanks, and the fatty lobe *attached* to the liver above the kidneys, he shall remove; 5and the priest shall burn them on the altar *as* an offering made by fire to the LORD. It *is* a trespass offering. 6Every male among the priests may eat it. It shall be eaten in a holy place. It *is* most holy. 7The trespass offering *is* like the sin offering; *there is* one law for them both: the priest who makes atonement *with* it shall have *it.* 8And the priest who offers anyone's burnt offering, that priest shall have for himself the skin of the burnt offering which he has offered. 9Also every grain offering that is baked in the oven and all that is prepared in the covered pan, or in a pan, shall be the priest's who offers it. 10Every grain offering, *whether* mixed with oil or dry, shall belong to all the sons of Aaron, to one *as much* as the other.

11'This *is* the law of the sacrifice of peace offerings which he shall offer to the LORD: 12If he offers it for a thanksgiving, then he shall offer, with the sacrifice of thanksgiving, unleavened cakes mixed with oil, unleavened wafers anointed with oil, or cakes of blended flour mixed with oil. 13Besides the cakes, *as* his offering he shall offer leavened bread with the sacrifice of thanksgiving of his peace offering. [14]And from it he shall offer one cake from each offering *as* a heave offering to the LORD. It shall belong to the priest who sprinkles the blood of the peace offering.

[15]'The flesh of the sacrifice of his peace offering for thanksgiving shall be eaten the same day it is offered. He shall not leave any of it until morning. [16]But if the sacrifice of his offering *is* a vow or a voluntary offering, it shall be eaten the same day that he offers his sacrifice; but on the next day the remainder of it also may be eaten; [17]the remainder of the flesh of the sacrifice on the third day must be burned with fire. [18]And if *any* of the flesh of the sacrifice of his peace offering is eaten at all on the third day, it shall not be accepted, nor shall it be imputed to him; it shall be an abomination *to* him who offers it, and the person who eats of it shall bear guilt.

[19]'The flesh that touches any unclean thing shall not be eaten. It shall be burned with fire. And as for the *clean* flesh, all who are clean may eat of it. [20]But the person who eats the flesh of the sacrifice of the peace offering that *belongs* to the LORD, while he is unclean, that person shall be cut off from his people. [21]Moreover the person who touches any unclean thing, *such as* human uncleanness, *an* unclean animal, or any abominable unclean thing,* and who eats the flesh of the sacrifice of the peace offering that *belongs* to the LORD, that person shall be cut off from his people.' "

[22]And the LORD spoke to Moses, saying, [23]"Speak to the children of Israel, saying: 'You shall not eat any fat, of ox or sheep or goat. [24]And the fat of an animal that dies *naturally,* and the fat of what is torn by wild beasts, may be used in any other way; but you shall by no means eat it. [25]For whoever eats the fat of the animal of which men offer an offering made by fire to the LORD, the person who eats *it* shall be cut off from his people. [26]Moreover you shall not eat any blood in any of your dwellings, *whether* of bird or beast. [27]Whoever eats any blood, that person shall be cut off from his people.' "

MARK 3:7-30

BUT Jesus withdrew with His disciples to the sea. And a great multitude from Galilee followed Him, and from Judea [8]and Jerusalem and Idumea and beyond the Jordan; and those from Tyre and Sidon, a great multitude, when they heard how many things He was doing, came to Him. [9]So He told His disciples that a small boat should be kept ready for Him because of the multitude, lest they should crush Him. [10]For He healed many, so that as many as had afflictions pressed about Him to touch Him. [11]And the unclean spirits, whenever they saw Him, fell down before Him and cried out, saying, "You are the Son of God." [12]But He sternly warned them that they should not make Him known.

[13]And He went up on the mountain and called to *Him* those He Himself wanted. And they came to Him. [14]Then He appointed twelve,* that they might be with Him and that He might send them out to preach, [15]and to have power to heal sicknesses and* to cast out demons: [16]Simon,* to whom He gave the name Peter; [17]James the *son* of Zebedee and John the brother of James, to whom He gave the name Boanerges, that is, "Sons of Thunder"; [18]Andrew, Philip, Bartholomew, Matthew, Thomas, James the *son* of Alphaeus, Thaddaeus, Simon the Cananite; [19]and Judas Iscariot, who also betrayed Him. And they went into a house.

[20]Then the multitude came together again, so that they could not so much

as eat bread. 21But when His own people heard *about this,* they went out to lay hold of Him, for they said, "He is out of His mind."

22And the scribes who came down from Jerusalem said, "He has Beelzebub," and, "By the ruler of the demons He casts out demons."

23So He called them to *Himself* and said to them in parables: "How can Satan cast out Satan? 24If a kingdom is divided against itself, that kingdom cannot stand. 25And if a house is divided against itself, that house cannot stand. 26And if Satan has risen up against himself, and is divided, he cannot stand, but has an end. 27No one can enter a strong man's house and plunder his goods, unless he first binds the strong man. And then he will plunder his house.

28"Assuredly, I say to you, all sins will be forgiven the sons of men, and whatever blasphemies they may utter; 29but he who blasphemes against the Holy Spirit never has forgiveness, but is subject to eternal condemnation"— 30because they said, "He has an unclean spirit."

PSALM 37:1-11

A Psalm of David.

D o not fret because of evildoers, Nor be envious of the workers of iniquity.
2   For they shall soon be cut down like the grass, And wither as the green herb.

3   Trust in the LORD, and do good;
Dwell in the land, and feed on His faithfulness.
4   Delight yourself also in the LORD,
And He shall give you the desires of your heart.

5   Commit your way to the LORD, Trust also in Him, And He shall bring *it* to pass.
6   He shall bring forth your righteousness as the light, And your justice as the noonday.

7   Rest in the LORD, and wait patiently for Him; Do not fret because of him who prospers in his way, Because of the man who brings wicked schemes to pass.
8   Cease from anger, and forsake wrath; Do not fret—*it* only *causes* harm.

9   For evildoers shall be cut off; But those who wait on the LORD, They shall inherit the earth.
10   For yet a little while and the wicked *shall be* no *more;* Indeed, you will look carefully for his place, But it *shall be* no *more.*
11   But the meek shall inherit the earth, And shall delight themselves in the abundance of peace.

PROVERBS FOR TODAY / 10:3-4

The LORD will not allow the righteous soul to famish, but He casts away the desire of the wicked. □ *He who has a slack hand becomes poor, but the hand of the diligent makes rich.*

FEBRUARY 19

LEVITICUS 7:28–9:6

THEN the LORD spoke to Moses, saying, 29"Speak to the children of Israel, saying: 'He who offers the sacrifice of his peace offering to the LORD shall bring his offering to the LORD from the sacrifice of his peace offering. 30His own hands shall bring the offerings made by fire to the LORD. The fat with the breast he shall bring, that the breast may be waved *as* a wave offering before the LORD. 31And the priest shall burn the fat on the altar, but the breast shall be Aaron's and his sons'. 32Also the right thigh you shall give to the priest *as* a heave offering from the sacrifices of your peace offerings. 33He among the sons of Aaron, who offers the blood of the peace offering and the fat, shall have the right thigh for *his* part. 34For the breast of the wave offering and the thigh of the heave offering I have taken from the children of Israel, from the sacrifices of their peace offerings, and I have given them to Aaron the priest and to his sons from the children of Israel by a statute forever.' "

35This *is* the consecrated portion for Aaron and his sons, from the offerings made by fire to the LORD, on the day when *Moses* presented them to minister to the LORD as priests. 36The LORD commanded this to be given to them by the children of Israel, on the day that He anointed them, *by* a statute forever throughout their generations.

37This *is* the law of the burnt offering, the grain offering, the sin offering, the trespass offering, the consecrations, and the sacrifice of the peace offering, 38which the LORD commanded Moses on Mount Sinai, on the day when He commanded the children of Israel to offer their offerings to the LORD in the Wilderness of Sinai.

AND the LORD spoke to Moses, saying: 2"Take Aaron and his sons with him, and the garments, the anointing oil, a bull as the sin offering, two rams, and a basket of unleavened bread; 3and gather all the congregation together at the door of the tabernacle of meeting."

4So Moses did as the LORD commanded him. And the congregation was gathered together at the door of the tabernacle of meeting. 5And Moses said to the congregation, "This *is* what the LORD commanded to be done."

6Then Moses brought Aaron and his sons and washed them with water. 7And he put the tunic on him, girded him with the sash, clothed him with the robe, and put the ephod on him; and he girded him with the intricately woven band of the ephod, and with it tied *the ephod* on him. 8Then he put the breastplate on him, and he put the Urim and the Thummim* in the breastplate. 9And he put the turban on his head. Also on the turban, on its front, he put the golden plate, the holy crown, as the LORD had commanded Moses.

10Also Moses took the anointing oil, and anointed the tabernacle and all that *was* in it, and consecrated them. 11He sprinkled some of it on the altar seven times, anointed the altar and all its utensils, and the laver and its base, to consecrate them. 12And he poured some of the anointing oil on Aaron's head and anointed him, to consecrate him.

13Then Moses brought Aaron's sons and put tunics on them, girded them with sashes, and put hats on them, as the LORD had commanded Moses.

14And he brought the bull for the sin

offering. Then Aaron and his sons laid their hands on the head of the bull for the sin offering, 15and Moses killed *it.* Then he took the blood, and put *some* on the horns of the altar all around with his finger, and purified the altar. And he poured the blood at the base of the altar, and consecrated it, to make atonement for it. 16Then he took all the fat that *was* on the entrails, the fatty lobe *attached to* the liver, and the two kidneys with their fat, and Moses burned *them* on the altar. 17But the bull, its hide, its flesh, and its offal, he burned with fire outside the camp, as the LORD had commanded Moses.

18Then he brought the ram as the burnt offering. And Aaron and his sons laid their hands on the head of the ram, 19and Moses killed *it.* Then he sprinkled the blood all around on the altar. 20And he cut the ram into pieces; and Moses burned the head, the pieces, and the fat. 21Then he washed the entrails and the legs in water. And Moses burned the whole ram on the altar. It *was* a burnt sacrifice for a sweet aroma, an offering made by fire to the LORD, as the LORD had commanded Moses.

22And he brought the second ram, the ram of consecration. Then Aaron and his sons laid their hands on the head of the ram, 23and Moses killed *it.* Also he took *some* of its blood and put it on the tip of Aaron's right ear, on the thumb of his right hand, and on the big toe of his right foot. 24Then he brought Aaron's sons. And Moses put *some* of the blood on the tips of their right ears, on the thumbs of their right hands, and on the big toes of their right feet. And Moses sprinkled the blood all around on the altar. 25Then he took the fat and the fat tail, all the fat that *was* on the entrails, the fatty lobe *attached to* the liver, the two kidneys and their fat, and the right thigh; 26and from the basket of unleavened bread that was before the LORD he took one unleavened cake, a cake of bread *anointed with* oil, and one

wafer, and put *them* on the fat and on the right thigh; 27and he put all *these* in Aaron's hands and in his sons' hands, and waved them *as* a wave offering before the LORD. 28Then Moses took them from their hands and burned *them* on the altar, on the burnt offering. They *were* consecration offerings for a sweet aroma. That *was* an offering made by fire to the LORD. 29And Moses took the breast and waved it *as* a wave offering before the LORD. It was Moses' part of the ram of consecration, as the LORD had commanded Moses.

30Then Moses took some of the anointing oil and some of the blood which *was* on the altar, and sprinkled *it* on Aaron, on his garments, on his sons, and on the garments of his sons with him; and he consecrated Aaron, his garments, his sons, and the garments of his sons with him.

31And Moses said to Aaron and his sons, "Boil the flesh *at* the door of the tabernacle of meeting, and eat it there with the bread that *is* in the basket of consecration offerings, as I commanded, saying, 'Aaron and his sons shall eat it.' 32What remains of the flesh and of the bread you shall burn with fire. 33And you shall not go outside the door of the tabernacle of meeting *for* seven days, until the days of your consecration are ended. For seven days he shall consecrate you. 34As he has done this day, *so* the LORD has commanded to do, to make atonement for you. 35Therefore you shall stay *at* the door of the tabernacle of meeting day and night for seven days, and keep the charge of the LORD, so that you may not die; for so I have been commanded." 36So Aaron and his sons did all the things that the LORD had commanded by the hand of Moses.

IT came to pass on the eighth day that Moses called Aaron and his sons and the elders of Israel. 2And he said to Aaron, "Take for yourself a young bull as a sin offering and a ram as a burnt offering, without blemish, and offer *them* before the LORD. ³And to the children of Israel you shall speak, saying, 'Take a kid of the goats as a sin offering, and a calf and a lamb, *both* of the first year, without blemish, as a burnt offering, ⁴also a bull and a ram as peace offerings, to sacrifice before the LORD, and a grain offering mixed with oil; for today the LORD will appear to you.' "

⁵So they brought what Moses commanded before the tabernacle of meeting. And all the congregation drew near and stood before the LORD. ⁶Then Moses said, "This *is* the thing which the LORD commanded you to do, and the glory of the LORD will appear to you."

MARK 3:31–4:25

THEN His [Jesus'] brothers and His mother came, and standing outside they sent to Him, calling Him. ³²And a multitude was sitting around Him; and they said to Him, "Look, Your mother and Your brothers* are outside seeking You."

³³But He answered them, saying, "Who is My mother, or My brothers?" ³⁴And He looked around in a circle at those who sat about Him, and said, "Here are My mother and My brothers! ³⁵For whoever does the will of God is My brother and My sister and mother."

AND again He began to teach by the sea. And a great multitude was gathered to Him, so that He got into a boat and sat *in it* on the sea; and the whole multitude was on the land facing the sea. ²Then He taught them many things by parables, and said to them in His teaching:

³"Listen! Behold, a sower went out to sow. ⁴And it happened, as he sowed, *that* some *seed* fell by the wayside; and

the birds of the air* came and devoured it. ⁵Some fell on stony ground, where it did not have much earth; and immediately it sprang up because it had no depth of earth. ⁶But when the sun was up it was scorched, and because it had no root it withered away. ⁷And some *seed* fell among thorns; and the thorns grew up and choked it, and it yielded no crop. ⁸But other *seed* fell on good ground and yielded a crop that sprang up, increased and produced: some thirtyfold, some sixty, and some a hundred."

⁹And He said to them,* "He who has ears to hear, let him hear!"

¹⁰But when He was alone, those around Him with the twelve asked Him about the parable. ¹¹And He said to them, "To you it has been given to know the mystery of the kingdom of God; but to those who are outside, all things come in parables, ¹²so that

'Seeing they may see and not
    perceive,
And hearing they may hear
    and not understand;
Lest they should turn,
And their sins be forgiven
    them.' " *

¹³And He said to them, "Do you not understand this parable? How then will you understand all the parables? ¹⁴The sower sows the word. ¹⁵And these are the ones by the wayside where the word is sown. When they hear, Satan comes immediately and takes away the word that was sown in their hearts. ¹⁶These likewise are the ones sown on stony ground who, when they hear the word, immediately receive it with gladness; ¹⁷and they have no root in themselves, and so endure only for a time. Afterward, when tribulation or persecution arises for the word's sake, immediately they stumble. ¹⁸Now these are the ones sown among thorns; *they are* the ones who

hear the word, 19and the cares of this world, the deceitfulness of riches, and the desires for other things entering in choke the word, and it becomes unfruitful. 20But these are the ones sown on good ground, those who hear the word, accept *it,* and bear fruit: some thirtyfold, some sixty, and some a hundred."

21Also He said to them, "Is a lamp brought to be put under a basket or under a bed? Is it not to be set on a lampstand? 22For there is nothing hidden which will not be revealed, nor has anything been kept secret but that it should come to light. 23If anyone has ears to hear, let him hear."

24Then He said to them, "Take heed what you hear. With the same measure you use, it will be measured to you; and to you who hear, more will be given. 25For whoever has, to him more will be given; but whoever does not have, even what he has will be taken away from him."

PSALM 37:12-29

THE wicked plots against the just,
And gnashes at him with his teeth.

13 The Lord laughs at him,
For He sees that his day is coming.

14 The wicked have drawn the sword
And have bent their bow,
To cast down the poor and needy,
To slay those who are of upright conduct.

15 Their sword shall enter their own heart,
And their bows shall be broken.

16 A little that a righteous man has
Is better than the riches of many wicked.

17 For the arms of the wicked shall be broken,
But the LORD upholds the righteous.

18 The LORD knows the days of the upright,
And their inheritance shall be forever.

19 They shall not be ashamed in the evil time,
And in the days of famine they shall be satisfied.

20 But the wicked shall perish;
And the enemies of the LORD,
Like the splendor of the meadows, shall vanish.
Into smoke they shall vanish away.

21 The wicked borrows and does not repay,
But the righteous shows mercy and gives.

22 For *those* blessed by Him shall inherit the earth,
But *those* cursed by Him shall be cut off.

23 The steps of a *good* man are ordered by the LORD,
And He delights in his way.

24 Though he fall, he shall not be utterly cast down;
For the LORD upholds *him with* His hand.

25 I have been young, and *now* am old;
Yet I have not seen the righteous forsaken,
Nor his descendants begging bread.

26 *He is* ever merciful, and lends;
And his descendants *are* blessed.

27 Depart from evil, and do good;
And dwell forevermore.

28 For the LORD loves justice,

And does not forsake His
saints;
They are preserved forever,
But the descendants of the
wicked shall be cut off.

29   The righteous shall inherit
the land,
And dwell in it forever.

PROVERBS FOR TODAY/ 10:5

He who gathers in summer is *a wise son; he who sleeps in harvest* is *a son who causes shame.*

FEBRUARY 20

LEVITICUS 9:7–10:20

AND Moses said to Aaron, "Go to the altar, offer your sin offering and your burnt offering, and make atonement for yourself and for the people. Offer the offering of the people, and make atonement for them, as the LORD commanded."

⁸Aaron therefore went to the altar and killed the calf of the sin offering, which *was* for himself. ⁹Then the sons of Aaron brought the blood to him. And he dipped his finger in the blood, put *it* on the horns of the altar, and poured the blood at the base of the altar. ¹⁰But the fat, the kidneys, and the fatty lobe from the liver of the sin offering he burned on the altar, as the LORD had commanded Moses. ¹¹The flesh and the hide he burned with fire outside the camp.

¹²And he killed the burnt offering; and Aaron's sons presented to him the blood, which he sprinkled all around on the altar. ¹³Then they presented the burnt offering to him, with its pieces and head, and he burned *them* on the altar. ¹⁴And he washed the entrails and the legs, and burned *them* with the burnt offering on the altar.

¹⁵Then he brought the people's offering, and took the goat, which *was* the sin offering for the people, and killed it and offered it for sin, like the first one. ¹⁶And he brought the burnt offering and offered it according to the prescribed manner. ¹⁷Then he brought the grain offering, took a handful of it, and burned *it* on the altar, besides the burnt sacrifice of the morning.

¹⁸He also killed the bull and the ram *as* sacrifices of peace offerings, which *were* for the people. And Aaron's sons presented to him the blood, which he sprinkled all around on the altar, ¹⁹and the fat from the bull and the ram—the fatty tail, what covers *the entrails* and the kidneys, and the fatty lobe *attached to* the liver; ²⁰and they put the fat on the breasts. Then he burned the fat on the altar; ²¹but the breasts and the right thigh Aaron waved *as* a wave offering before the LORD, as Moses had commanded.

²²Then Aaron lifted his hand toward the people, blessed them, and came down from offering the sin offering, the burnt offering, and peace offerings. ²³And Moses and Aaron went into the tabernacle of meeting, and came out and blessed the people. Then the glory of the LORD appeared to all the people, ²⁴and fire came out from before the LORD and consumed the burnt offering and the fat on the altar. When

all the people saw *it,* they shouted and fell on their faces.

THEN Nadab and Abihu, the sons of Aaron, each took his censer and put fire in it, put incense on it, and offered profane fire before the LORD, which He had not commanded them. ²So fire went out from the LORD and devoured them, and they died before the LORD. ³And Moses said to Aaron, "This is what the LORD spoke, saying:

> 'By those who come near Me
> I must be regarded as holy;
> And before all the people
> I must be glorified.' "

3∪ Aaron held his peace.
⁴Then Moses called Mishael and El zaphan, the sons of Uzziel the uncle of Aaron, and said to them, "Come near, carry your brethren from before the sanctuary out of the camp." ⁵So they went near and carried them by their tunics out of the camp, as Moses had said.
⁶And Moses said to Aaron, and to Eleazar and Ithamar, his sons, "Do not uncover your heads nor tear your clothes, lest you die, and wrath come upon all the people. But let your brethren, the whole house of Israel, bewail the burning which the LORD has kindled. ⁷You shall not go out from the door of the tabernacle of meeting, lest you die, for the anointing oil of the LORD *is* upon you." And they did according to the word of Moses.
⁸Then the LORD spoke to Aaron, saying: ⁹"Do not drink wine or intoxicating drink, you, nor your sons with you, when you go into the tabernacle of meeting, lest you die. *It shall be* a statute forever throughout your generations, ¹⁰that you may distinguish between holy and unholy, and between unclean and clean, ¹¹and that you may teach the children of Israel all the statutes which the LORD has spoken to them by the hand of Moses."

¹²And Moses spoke to Aaron, and to Eleazar and Ithamar, his sons who were left: "Take the grain offering that remains of the offerings made by fire to the LORD, and eat it without leaven beside the altar; for it *is* most holy. ¹³You shall eat it in a holy place, because it *is* your due and your sons' due, of the sacrifices made by fire to the LORD; for so I have been commanded. ¹⁴The breast of the wave offering and the thigh of the heave offering you shall eat in a clean place, you, your sons, and your daughters with you; for *they are* your due and your sons' due, *which* are given from the sacrifices of peace offerings of the children of Israel. ¹⁵The thigh of the heave offering and the breast of the wave offering they shall bring with the offerings of fat made by fire, to offer *as* a wave offering before the LORD. And it shall be yours and your sons' with you, by a statute forever, as the LORD has commanded."

¹⁶Then Moses made careful inquiry about the goat of the sin offering, and there it was—burned up. And he was angry with Eleazar and Ithamar, the sons of Aaron *who were* left, saying, ¹⁷"Why have you not eaten the sin offering in a holy place, since it *is* most holy, and *God* has given it to you to bear the guilt of the congregation, to make atonement for them before the LORD? ¹⁸See! Its blood was not brought inside the holy *place;** indeed you should have eaten it in a holy *place,* as I commanded."

¹⁹And Aaron said to Moses, "Look, this day they have offered their sin offering and their burnt offering before the LORD, and such things have befallen me! *If* I had eaten the sin offering today, would it have been accepted in the sight of the LORD?" ²⁰So when Moses heard *that,* he was content.

MARK 4:26–5:20

AND He [Jesus] said, "The kingdom of God is as if a man should scatter seed on the ground, ²⁷and should sleep by night and rise by day, and the seed should sprout and grow, he himself does not know how. ²⁸For the earth yields crops by itself: first the blade, then the head, after that the full grain in the head. ²⁹But when the grain ripens, immediately he puts in the sickle, because the harvest has come."

³⁰Then He said, "To what shall we liken the kingdom of God? Or with what parable shall we picture it? ³¹*It is* like a mustard seed which, when it is sown on the ground, is smaller than all the seeds on earth; ³²but when it is sown, it grows up and becomes greater than all herbs, and shoots out large branches, so that the birds of the air may nest under its shade."

³³And with many such parables He spoke the word to them as they were able to hear *it.* ³⁴But without a parable He did not speak to them. And when they were alone, He explained all things to His disciples.

³⁵On the same day, when evening had come, He said to them, "Let us cross over to the other side." ³⁶Now when they had left the multitude, they took Him along in the boat as He was. And other little boats were also with Him. ³⁷And a great windstorm arose, and the waves beat into the boat, so that it was already filling. ³⁸But He was in the stern, asleep on a pillow. And they awoke Him and said to Him, "Teacher, do You not care that we are perishing?"

³⁹Then He arose and rebuked the wind, and said to the sea, "Peace, be still!" And the wind ceased and there was a great calm. ⁴⁰But He said to them, "Why are you so fearful? How *is it* that you have no faith?"* ⁴¹And they feared exceedingly, and said to one an-other, "Who can this be, that even the wind and the sea obey Him!"

THEN they came to the other side of the sea, to the country of the Gadarenes.* ²And when He had come out of the boat, immediately there met Him out of the tombs a man with an unclean spirit, ³who had *his* dwelling among the tombs; and no one could bind him,* not even with chains, ⁴because he had often been bound with shackles and chains. And the chains had been pulled apart by him, and the shackles broken in pieces; neither could anyone tame him. ⁵And always, night and day, he was in the mountains and in the tombs, crying out and cutting himself with stones.

⁶When he saw Jesus from afar, he ran and worshiped Him. ⁷And he cried out with a loud voice and said, "What have I to do with You, Jesus, Son of the Most High God? I implore You by God that You do not torment me."

⁸For He said to him, "Come out of the man, unclean spirit!" ⁹Then He asked him, "What *is* your name?"

And he answered, saying, "My name *is* Legion; for we are many." ¹⁰Also he begged Him earnestly that He would not send them out of the country.

¹¹Now a large herd of swine was feeding there near the mountains. ¹²So all the demons begged Him, saying, "Send us to the swine, that we may enter them." ¹³And at once Jesus* gave them permission. Then the unclean spirits went out and entered the swine (there were about two thousand); and the herd ran violently down the steep place into the sea, and drowned in the sea.

¹⁴So those who fed the swine fled, and they told *it* in the city and in the country. And they went out to see what it was that had happened. ¹⁵Then they came to Jesus, and saw the one *who had been* demon-possessed and had

the legion, sitting and clothed and in his right mind. And they were afraid. ¹⁶And those who saw it told them how it happened to him *who had been* demon-possessed, and about the swine. ¹⁷Then they began to plead with Him to depart from their region.

¹⁸And when He got into the boat, he who had been demon-possessed begged Him that he might be with Him. ¹⁹However, Jesus did not permit him, but said to him, "Go home to your friends, and tell them what great things the Lord has done for you, and how He has had compassion on you." ²⁰And he departed and began to proclaim in Decapolis all that Jesus had done for him; and all marveled.

PSALM 37:30-40

THE mouth of the righteous speaks wisdom, And his tongue talks of justice. 31 The law of his God *is* in his heart; None of his steps shall slide.

32 The wicked watches the righteous, And seeks to slay him. 33 The LORD will not leave him in his hand, Nor condemn him when he is judged.

34 Wait on the LORD, And keep His way, And He shall exalt you to inherit the land; When the wicked are cut off, you shall see *it*.

35 I have seen the wicked in great power, And spreading himself like a native green tree. 36 Yet he passed away,* and behold, he *was* no *more;* Indeed I sought him, but he could not be found.

37 Mark the blameless *man,* and observe the upright; For the future of *that* man *is* peace.

38 But the transgressors shall be destroyed together; The future of the wicked shall be cut off.

39 But the salvation of the righteous *is* from the LORD; *He is* their strength in the time of trouble. 40 And the LORD shall help them and deliver them; He shall deliver them from the wicked, And save them, Because they trust in Him.

PROVERBS FOR TODAY/ 10:6-7

Blessings are *on the head of the righteous, but violence covers the mouth of the wicked. The memory of the righteous* is *blessed, but the name of the wicked will rot.*

FEBRUARY 21

LEVITICUS 11:1–12:8

Now the LORD spoke to Moses and Aaron, saying to them, 2"Speak to the children of Israel, saying, 'These *are* the animals which you may eat among all the animals that *are* on the earth: 3Among the animals, whatever divides the hoof, having cloven hooves *and* chewing the cud—that you may eat. 4Nevertheless these you shall not eat among those that chew the cud or those that have cloven hooves: the camel, because it chews the cud but does not have cloven hooves, is unclean to you; 5the rock hyrax, because it chews the cud but does not have cloven hooves, *is* unclean to you; 6the hare, because it chews the cud but does not have cloven hooves, *is* unclean to you; 7and the swine, though it divides the hoof, having cloven hooves, yet does not chew the cud, *is* unclean to you. 8Their flesh you shall not eat, and their carcasses you shall not touch. They *are* unclean to you.

9"These you may eat of all that *are* in the water: whatever in the water has fins and scales, whether in the seas or in the rivers—that you may eat. 10But all in the seas or in the rivers that do not have fins and scales, all that move in the water or any living thing which *is* in the water, they *are* an abomination to you. 11They shall be an abomination to you; you shall not eat their flesh, but you shall regard their carcasses as an abomination. 12Whatever in the water does not have fins or scales—that *shall be* an abomination to you.

13"And these you shall regard as an abomination among the birds; they shall not be eaten, they *are* an abomination: the eagle, the vulture, the buzzard, 14the kite, and the falcon after its kind; 15every raven after its kind, 16the ostrich, the short-eared owl, the sea gull, and the hawk after its kind; 17the little owl, the fisher owl, and the screech owl; 18the white owl, the jackdaw, and the carrion vulture; 19the stork, the heron after its kind, the hoopoe, and the bat.

20"All flying insects that creep on *all* fours *shall be* an abomination to you. 21Yet these you may eat of every flying insect that creeps on *all* fours: those which have jointed legs above their feet with which to leap on the earth. 22These you may eat: the locust after its kind, the destroying locust after its kind, the cricket after its kind, and the grasshopper after its kind. 23But all *other* flying insects which have four feet *shall be* an abomination to you.

24"By these you shall become unclean; whoever touches the carcass of any of them shall be unclean until evening; 25whoever carries part of the carcass of any of them shall wash his clothes and be unclean until evening: 26*The carcass* of any animal which divides the foot, but is not cloven-hoofed or does not chew the cud, *is* unclean to you. Everyone who touches it shall be unclean. 27And whatever goes on its paws, among all kinds of animals that go on *all* fours, those *are* unclean to you. Whoever touches any such carcass shall be unclean until evening. 28Whoever carries *any such* carcass shall wash his clothes and be unclean until evening. It *is* unclean to you.

29"These also *shall be* unclean to you among the creeping things that creep on the earth: the mole, the mouse, and the large lizard after its kind; 30the gecko, the monitor lizard, the sand reptile, the sand lizard, and the chameleon. 31These *are* unclean to you among all that creep. Whoever touches them when they are dead shall be unclean until evening. ³²Anything on which *any* of them falls, when they are dead shall be unclean, whether *it is* any item of wood or clothing or skin or sack, whatever item *it is,* in which *any* work is done, it must be put in water. And it shall be unclean until evening; then it shall be clean. ³³Any earthen vessel into which *any* of them falls you shall break; and whatever *is* in it shall be unclean: ³⁴in such a vessel, any edible food upon which water falls becomes unclean, and any drink that may be drunk from it becomes unclean. ³⁵And everything on which *a part* of *any such* carcass falls shall be unclean, *whether it is* an oven or cooking stove, it shall be broken down; *for* they *are* unclean, and shall be unclean to you. ³⁶Nevertheless a spring or a cistern, *in which there is* plenty of water, shall be clean, but whatever touches any such carcass becomes unclean. ³⁷And if a part of *any such* carcass falls on any planting seed which is to be sown, it *remains* clean. ³⁸But if water is put on the seed, and if *a part* of *any such* carcass falls on it, it *becomes* unclean to you.

³⁹'And if any animal which you may eat dies, he who touches its carcass shall be unclean until evening. ⁴⁰He who eats of its carcass shall wash his clothes and be unclean until evening. He also who carries its carcass shall wash his clothes and be unclean until evening.

⁴¹'And every creeping thing that creeps on the earth *shall be* an abomination. It shall not be eaten. ⁴²Whatever crawls on its belly, whatever goes on *all* fours, or whatever has many feet among all creeping things that creep on the earth—these you shall not eat, for they *are* an abomination. ⁴³You shall not make yourselves abominable with any creeping thing that creeps; nor shall you make yourselves unclean with them, lest you be defiled by them. ⁴⁴For I *am* the LORD your God. You shall therefore consecrate yourselves, and you shall be holy; for I *am* holy. Neither shall you defile yourselves with any creeping thing that creeps on the earth. ⁴⁵For I *am* the LORD who brings you up out of the land of Egypt, to be your God. You shall therefore be holy, for I *am* holy.

⁴⁶'This *is* the law of the animals and the birds and every living creature that moves in the waters, and of every creature that creeps on the earth, ⁴⁷to distinguish between the unclean and the clean, and between the animal that may be eaten and the animal that may not be eaten.' "

THEN the LORD spoke to Moses, saying, ²"Speak to the children of Israel, saying: 'If a woman has conceived, and borne a male child, then she shall be unclean seven days; as in the days of her customary impurity she shall be unclean. ³And on the eighth day the flesh of his foreskin shall be circumcised. ⁴She shall then continue in the blood of *her* purification thirty-three days. She shall not touch any hallowed thing, nor come into the sanctuary until the days of her purification are fulfilled.

⁵'But if she bears a female child, then she shall be unclean two weeks, as in her customary impurity, and she shall continue in the blood of *her* purification sixty-six days.

⁶'When the days of her purification are fulfilled, whether for a son or a daughter, she shall bring to the priest a lamb of the first year as a burnt offering, and a young pigeon or a turtledove as a sin offering, to the door of the tabernacle of meeting. ⁷Then he shall offer it before the LORD, and make atonement for her. And she shall be clean from the flow of her blood. This *is* the law for her who has borne a male or a female.

8"And if she is not able to bring a lamb, then she may bring two turtledoves or two young pigeons—one as a burnt offering and the other as a sin offering. So the priest shall make atonement for her, and she will be clean.' "

MARK 5:21-43

Now when Jesus had crossed over again by boat to the other side, a great multitude gathered to Him; and He was by the sea. 22And behold, one of the rulers of the synagogue came, Jairus by name. And when he saw Him, he fell at His feet 23and begged Him earnestly, saying, "My little daughter lies at the point of death. Come and lay Your hands on her, that she may be healed, and she will live." 24So *Jesus* went with him, and a great multitude followed Him and thronged Him.

25Now a certain woman had a flow of blood for twelve years, 26and had suffered many things from many physicians. She had spent all that she had and was no better, but rather grew worse. 27When she heard about Jesus, she came behind *Him* in the crowd and touched His garment. 28For she said, "If only I may touch His clothes, I shall be made well."

29Immediately the fountain of her blood was dried up, and she felt in *her* body that she was healed of the affliction. 30And Jesus, immediately knowing in Himself that power had gone out of Him, turned around in the crowd and said, "Who touched My clothes?"

31But His disciples said to Him, "You see the multitude thronging You, and You say, 'Who touched Me?' "

32And He looked around to see her who had done this thing. 33But the woman, fearing and trembling, knowing what had happened to her, came and fell down before Him and told Him the whole truth. 34And He said to her, "Daughter, your faith has made you well. Go in peace, and be healed of your affliction."

35While He was still speaking, *some* came from the ruler of the synagogue's *house* who said, "Your daughter is dead. Why trouble the Teacher any further?"

36As soon as Jesus heard the word that was spoken, He said to the ruler of the synagogue, "Do not be afraid; only believe." 37And He permitted no one to follow Him except Peter, James, and John the brother of James. 38Then He came to the house of the ruler of the synagogue, and saw a tumult and those who wept and wailed loudly. 39When He came in, He said to them, "Why make this commotion and weep? The child is not dead, but sleeping."

40And they ridiculed Him. But when He had put them all outside, He took the father and the mother of the child, and those *who were* with Him, and entered where the child was lying. 41Then He took the child by the hand, and said to her, "Talitha, cumi," which is translated, "Little girl, I say to you, arise." 42Immediately the girl arose and walked, for she was twelve years *of age.* And they were overcome with great amazement. 43But He commanded them strictly that no one should know it, and said that *something* should be given her to eat.

PSALM 38:1-22

A Psalm of David. To bring to remembrance.

O LORD, do not rebuke me in Your wrath,
   Nor chasten me in Your hot
   displeasure!
2 For Your arrows pierce me
   deeply,
   And Your hand presses me
   down.

3 *There is* no soundness in my
  flesh
  Because of Your anger,
  Nor *any* health in my bones
  Because of my sin.
4 For my iniquities have gone
  over my head;
  Like a heavy burden they are
  too heavy for me.
5 My wounds are foul *and*
  festering
  Because of my foolishness.

6 I am troubled, I am bowed
  down greatly;
  I go mourning all the day long.
7 For my loins are full of
  inflammation,
  And *there is* no soundness in
  my flesh.
8 I am feeble and severely
  broken;
  I groan because of the turmoil
  of my heart.

9 Lord, all my desire *is* before
  You;
  And my sighing is not hidden
  from You.
10 My heart pants, my strength
   fails me;
   As for the light of my eyes, it
   also has gone from me.

11 My loved ones and my friends
   stand aloof from my plague,
   And my relatives stand afar
   off.
12 Those also who seek my life
   lay snares *for me;*

Those who seek my hurt
  speak of destruction,
And plan deception all the day
  long.

13 But I, like a deaf *man,* do not
   hear;
   And *I am* like a mute *who*
   does not open his mouth.
14 Thus I am like a man who
   does not hear,
   And in whose mouth *is* no
   response.

15 For in You, O LORD, I hope;
   You will hear, O Lord my God.
16 For I said, "Hear me, lest
   they rejoice over me,
   Lest, when my foot slips, they
   exalt *themselves* against me."
17 For I *am* ready to fall,
   And my sorrow *is* continually
   before me.
18 For I will declare my iniquity;
   I will be in anguish over my
   sin.
19 But my enemies *are* vigorous,
   and they are strong;
   And those who hate me
   wrongfully have multiplied.
20 Those also who render evil
   for good,
   They are my adversaries,
   because I follow *what is*
   good.

21 Do not forsake me, O LORD;
   O my God, be not far from me!
22 Make haste to help me,
   O Lord, my salvation!

PROVERBS FOR TODAY/ 10:8-9

The wise in heart will receive commands, but a prating fool will fall. □ *He who walks with integrity walks securely, but he who perverts his ways will become known.*

FEBRUARY 22

LEVITICUS 13:1-59

AND the LORD spoke to Moses and Aaron, saying: [2]"When a man has on the skin of his body a swelling, a scab, or a bright spot, and it becomes on the skin of his body *like* a leprous* sore, then he shall be brought to Aaron the priest or to one of his sons the priests. [3]The priest shall examine the sore on the skin of the body; and if the hair on the sore has turned white, and the sore appears *to be* deeper than the skin of his body, it *is* a leprous sore. Then the priest shall examine him, and pronounce him unclean. [4]But if the bright spot *is* white on the skin of his body, and does not appear *to be* deeper than the skin, and its hair has not turned white, then the priest shall isolate *the one who has* the sore seven days. [5]And the priest shall examine him on the seventh day; and indeed *if* the sore appears to be as it was, *and* the sore has not spread on the skin, then the priest shall isolate him another seven days. [6]Then the priest shall examine him again on the seventh day; and indeed *if* the sore has faded, *and* the sore has not spread on the skin, then the priest shall pronounce him clean; it *is only* a scab, and he shall wash his clothes and be clean. [7]But if the scab should at all spread over the skin, after he has been seen by the priest for his cleansing, he shall be seen by the priest again. [8]And *if* the priest sees that the scab has indeed spread on the skin, then the priest shall pronounce him unclean. It *is* leprosy.

[9]"When the leprous sore is on a person, then he shall be brought to the priest. [10]And the priest shall examine *him;* and indeed *if* the swelling on the skin *is* white, and it has turned the hair white, and *there is* a spot of raw flesh in the swelling, [11]it *is* an old leprosy on the skin of his body. The priest shall pronounce him unclean, and shall not isolate him, for he *is* unclean.

[12]"And if leprosy breaks out all over the skin, and the leprosy covers all the skin of *the one who has* the sore, from his head to his foot, wherever the priest looks, [13]then the priest shall consider; and indeed *if* the leprosy has covered all his body, he shall pronounce *him* clean *who has* the sore. It has all turned white. He *is* clean. [14]But when raw flesh appears on him, he shall be unclean. [15]And the priest shall examine the raw flesh and pronounce him to be unclean; *for* the raw flesh *is* unclean. It *is* leprosy. [16]Or if the raw flesh changes and turns white again, he shall come to the priest. [17]And the priest shall examine him; and indeed *if* the sore has turned white, then the priest shall pronounce *him* clean *who has* the sore. He *is* clean.

[18]"If the body develops a boil in the skin, and it is healed, [19]and in the place of the boil there comes a white swelling or a bright spot, reddish-white, then it shall be shown to the priest; [20]and if, when the priest sees it, it indeed *appears* deeper than the skin, and its hair has turned white, the priest shall pronounce him unclean. It *is* a leprous sore which has broken out of the boil. [21]But if the priest examines it, and indeed *there are* no white hairs in it, and it *is* not deeper than the skin, but has faded, then the priest shall isolate him seven days; [22]and if it should at all spread over the skin, then the priest shall pronounce him unclean. It *is* a leprous sore. [23]But if the bright spot stays in one place, *and* has not spread, it *is* the scar of the boil; and the priest shall pronounce him clean.

24"Or if the body receives a burn on its skin by fire, and the raw *flesh* of the burn becomes a bright spot, reddish-white or white, 25then the priest shall examine it; and indeed *if* the hair of the bright spot has turned white, and it appears deeper than the skin, it *is* leprosy broken out in the burn. Therefore the priest shall pronounce him unclean. It *is* a leprous sore. 26But if the priest examines it, and indeed *there are* no white hairs in the bright spot, and it *is* not deeper than the skin, but has faded, then the priest shall isolate him seven days. 27And the priest shall examine him on the seventh day. If it has at all spread over the skin, then the priest shall pronounce him unclean. It *is* a leprous sore. 28But if the bright spot stays in one place, *and* has not spread on the skin, but has faded, it *is* a swelling from the burn. The priest shall pronounce him clean, for it *is* the scar from the burn.

29"If a man or woman has a sore on the head or the beard, 30then the priest shall examine the sore; and indeed if it appears deeper than the skin, *and there is* in it thin yellow hair, then the priest shall pronounce him unclean. It *is* a scaly leprosy of the head or beard. 31But if the priest examines the scaly sore, and indeed it does not appear deeper than the skin, and *there is* no black hair in it, then the priest shall isolate *the one who has* the scale seven days. 32And on the seventh day the priest shall examine the sore; and indeed *if* the scale has not spread, and there is no yellow hair in it, and the scale does not appear deeper than the skin, 33he shall shave himself, but the scale he shall not shave. And the priest shall isolate *the one who has* the scale another seven days. 34On the seventh day the priest shall examine the scale; and indeed *if* the scale has not spread over the skin, and does not appear deeper than the skin, then the priest shall pronounce him clean. He shall wash his clothes and be clean. 35But if the scale should at all spread over the skin after his cleansing, 36then the priest shall examine him; and indeed *if* the scale has spread over the skin, the priest need not seek for yellow hair. He *is* unclean. 37But if the scale appears to be at a standstill, and there is black hair grown up in it, the scale has healed. He *is* clean, and the priest shall pronounce him clean.

38"If a man or a woman has bright spots on the skin of the body, *specifically* white bright spots, 39then the priest shall look; and indeed *if* the bright spots on the skin of the body *are* dull white, it *is* a white spot *that* grows on the skin. He *is* clean.

40"As for the man whose hair has fallen from his head, he *is* bald, *but* he *is* clean. 41He whose hair has fallen from his forehead, he *is* bald on the forehead, *but* he *is* clean. 42And if there is on the bald head or bald forehead a reddish-white sore, it *is* leprosy breaking out on his bald head or his bald forehead. 43Then the priest shall examine it; and indeed *if* the swelling of the sore *is* reddish-white on his bald head or on his bald forehead, as the appearance of leprosy on the skin of the body, 44he is a leprous man. He *is* unclean. The priest shall surely pronounce him unclean; his sore *is* on his head.

45"Now the leper on whom the sore *is,* his clothes shall be torn and his head bare; and he shall cover his mustache, and cry, 'Unclean! Unclean!' 46He shall be unclean. All the days he has the sore he shall be unclean. He *is* unclean, and he shall dwell alone; his dwelling *shall be* outside the camp.

47"Also, if a garment has a leprous plague* in it, *whether it is* a woolen garment or a linen garment, 48whether *it is* in the warp or woof of linen or wool, whether in leather or in anything made of leather, 49and if the plague is greenish or reddish in the garment or in the leather, whether in the warp or in the woof, or in anything made of leather, it *is* a leprous plague and shall be shown to the priest. ⁵⁰The priest shall examine the plague and isolate *that which has* the plague seven days. ⁵¹And he shall examine the plague on the seventh day. If the plague has spread in the garment, either in the warp or in the woof, in the leather *or* in anything made of leather, the plague *is* an active leprosy. It *is* unclean. ⁵²He shall therefore burn that garment in which is the plague, whether warp or woof, in wool or in linen, or anything of leather, for it *is* an active leprosy; *the garment* shall be burned in the fire.

⁵³"But if the priest examines *it,* and indeed the plague has not spread in the garment, either in the warp or in the woof, or in anything made of leather, ⁵⁴then the priest shall command that they wash *the thing* in which *is* the plague; and he shall isolate it another seven days. ⁵⁵Then the priest shall examine the plague after it has been washed; and indeed *if* the plague has not changed its color, though the plague has not spread, it *is* unclean, and you shall burn it in the fire; it continues eating away, *whether* the damage *is* outside or inside. ⁵⁶If the priest examines *it,* and indeed the plague has faded after washing it, then he shall tear it out of the garment, whether out of the warp or out of the woof, or out of the leather. ⁵⁷But if it appears again in the garment, either in the warp or in the woof, or in anything made of leather, it *is* a spreading *plague;* you shall burn with fire that in which is the plague. ⁵⁸And if you wash the garment, either warp or woof, or whatever is made of leather, if the plague has disappeared from it, then it shall be washed a second time, and shall be clean.

⁵⁹"This *is* the law of the leprous plague in a garment of wool or linen, either in the warp or woof, or in anything made of leather, to pronounce it clean or to pronounce it unclean."

MARK 6:1-29

THEN He [Jesus] went out from there and came to His own country, and His disciples followed Him. ²And when the Sabbath had come, He began to teach in the synagogue. And many hearing *Him* were astonished, saying, "Where *did* this Man *get* these things? And what wisdom *is* this which is given to Him, that such mighty works are performed by His hands! ³Is this not the carpenter, the Son of Mary, and brother of James, Joses, Judas, and Simon? And are not His sisters here with us?" So they were offended at Him.

⁴But Jesus said to them, "A prophet is not without honor except in his own country, among his own relatives, and in his own house." ⁵Now He could do no mighty work there, except that He laid His hands on a few sick people and healed *them.* ⁶And He marveled because of their unbelief. Then He went about the villages in a circuit, teaching.

⁷And He called the twelve to *Himself,* and began to send them out two *by* two, and gave them power over unclean spirits. ⁸He commanded them to take nothing for the journey except a staff—no bag, no bread, no copper in *their* money belts— ⁹but to wear sandals, and not to put on two tunics.

¹⁰Also He said to them, "In whatever place you enter a house, stay there till you depart from that place. ¹¹And whoever* will not receive you nor hear you, when you depart from there, shake off the dust under your feet as a testimony against them.* Assuredly, I say to you, it will be more tolerable for Sodom and Gomorrah in the day of judgment than for that city!"

¹²So they went out and preached that *people* should repent. ¹³And they cast out many demons, and anointed with oil many who were sick, and healed *them.*

¹⁴Now King Herod heard *of Him,* for

His name had become well known. And he said, "John the Baptist is risen from the dead, and therefore these powers are at work in him."

15Others said, "It is Elijah."

And others said, "It is the Prophet, or* like one of the prophets."

16But when Herod heard, he said, "This is John, whom I beheaded; he has been raised from the dead!" 17For Herod himself had sent and laid hold of John, and bound him in prison for the sake of Herodias, his brother Philip's wife; for he had married her. 18Because John had said to Herod, "It is not lawful for you to have your brother's wife."

19Therefore Herodias held it against him and wanted to kill him, but she could not; 20for Herod feared John, knowing that he *was* a just and holy man, and he protected him. And when he heard him, he did many things, and heard him gladly.

21Then an opportune day came when Herod on his birthday gave a feast for his nobles, the high officers, and the chief *men* of Galilee. 22And when Herodias' daughter herself came in and danced, and pleased Herod and those who sat with him, the king said to the girl, "Ask me whatever you want, and I will give *it* to you." 23He also swore to her, "Whatever you ask me, I will give you, up to half my kingdom."

24So she went out and said to her mother, "What shall I ask?"

And she said, "The head of John the Baptist!"

25Immediately she came in with haste to the king and asked, saying, "I want you to give me at once the head of John the Baptist on a platter."

26And the king was exceedingly sorry; *yet,* because of the oaths and because of those who sat with him, he did not want to refuse her. 27Immediately the king sent an executioner and commanded his head to be brought. And he went and beheaded him in prison, 28brought his head on a platter, and gave it to the girl; and the girl gave it to her mother. 29When his disciples heard *of it,* they came and took away his corpse and laid it in a tomb.

PSALM 39:1-13

To the Chief Musician. To Jeduthun. A Psalm of David.

I SAID, "I will guard my ways,
Lest I sin with my tongue;
I will restrain my mouth with a
    muzzle,
    While the wicked are before
    me."
2   I was mute with silence,
    I held my peace *even* from
        good;
    And my sorrow was stirred
        up.
3   My heart was hot within me;
    While I was musing, the fire
        burned.
    Then I spoke with my tongue:

4   "LORD, make me to know my
        end,
    And what *is* the measure of
        my days,
    That I may know how frail I
        am.
5   Indeed, You have made my
        days *as* handbreadths,
    And my age *is* as nothing
        before You;
    Certainly every man at his
        best state *is* but vapor. Selah
6   Surely every man walks about
        like a shadow;
    Surely they busy themselves
        in vain;
    He heaps up *riches,*
    And does not know who will
        gather them.

7   "And now, Lord, what do I wait
        for?
    My hope *is* in You.

8   Deliver me from all my
transgressions;
Do not make me the reproach
of the foolish.

9   I was mute, I did not open my
mouth,
Because it was You who did *it.*

10   Remove Your plague from me;
I am consumed by the blow of
Your hand.

11   When with rebukes You
correct man for iniquity,
You make his beauty melt
away like a moth;

Surely every man *is* vapor.
Selah

12   "Hear my prayer, O Lord,
And give ear to my cry;
Do not be silent at my tears;
For I *am* a stranger with You,
A sojourner, as all my fathers
were.

13   Remove Your gaze from me,
that I may regain strength,
Before I go away and am no
more."

PROVERBS FOR TODAY/ 10:10

He who winks with the eye causes trouble, But a prating fool will fall.

FEBRUARY 23

LEVITICUS 14:1-57

THEN the Lord spoke to Moses, saying, [2]"This shall be the law of the leper for the day of his cleansing: He shall be brought to the priest. [3]And the priest shall go out of the camp, and the priest shall examine *him*; and indeed, *if* the leprosy is healed in the leper, [4]then the priest shall command to take for him who is to be cleansed two living *and* clean birds, cedar wood, scarlet, and hyssop. [5]And the priest shall command that one of the birds be killed in an earthen vessel over running water. [6]As for the living bird, he shall take it, the cedar wood and the scarlet and the hyssop, and dip them and the living bird in the blood of the bird *that was* killed over the running water. [7]And he shall sprinkle it seven times on him who is to be cleansed from the leprosy, and shall pronounce him clean, and shall let the living bird loose in the open field. [8]He

who is to be cleansed shall wash his clothes, shave off all his hair, and wash himself in water, that he may be clean. After that he shall come into the camp, and shall stay outside his tent seven days. [9]But on the seventh day he shall shave all the hair off his head and his beard and his eyebrows—all his hair he shall shave off. He shall wash his clothes and wash his body in water, and he shall be clean.

[10]"And on the eighth day he shall take two male lambs without blemish, one ewe lamb of the first year without blemish, three-tenths *of an ephah* of fine flour mixed with oil as a grain offering, and one log of oil. [11]Then the priest who makes *him* clean shall present the man who is to be made clean, and those things, before the Lord, *at* the door of the tabernacle of meeting. [12]And the priest shall take one male lamb and offer it as a trespass offering, and the log of oil, and wave them *as* a wave offering before the Lord. [13]Then

he shall kill the lamb in the place where he kills the sin offering and the burnt offering, in a holy place; for as the sin offering *is* the priest's, so *is* the trespass offering. It *is* most holy. ¹⁴The priest shall take *some* of the blood of the trespass offering, and the priest shall put *it* on the tip of the right ear of him who is to be cleansed, on the thumb of his right hand, and on the big toe of his right foot. ¹⁵And the priest shall take *some* of the log of oil, and pour *it* into the palm of his own left hand. ¹⁶Then the priest shall dip his right finger in the oil that *is* in his left hand, and shall sprinkle some of the oil with his finger seven times before the LORD. ¹⁷And of the rest of the oil in his hand, the priest shall put *some* on the tip of the right ear of him who is to be cleansed, on the thumb of his right hand, and on the big toe of his right foot, on the blood of the trespass offering. ¹⁸The rest of the oil that *is* in the priest's hand he shall put on the head of him who is to be cleansed. So the priest shall make atonement for him before the LORD.

¹⁹"Then the priest shall offer the sin offering, and make atonement for him who is to be cleansed from his uncleanness. Afterward he shall kill the burnt offering. ²⁰And the priest shall offer the burnt offering and the grain offering on the altar. So the priest shall make atonement for him, and he shall be clean.

²¹"But if he *is* poor and cannot afford it, then he shall take one male lamb *as* a trespass offering to be waved, to make atonement for him, one-tenth *of an ephah* of fine flour mixed with oil as a grain offering, a log of oil, ²²and two turtledoves or two young pigeons, such as he is able to afford: one shall be a sin offering and the other a burnt offering. ²³He shall bring them to the priest on the eighth day for his cleansing, to the door of the tabernacle of meeting, before the LORD. ²⁴And the priest shall take the lamb of the trespass offering and the log of oil, and the priest shall wave them *as* a wave offering before the LORD. ²⁵Then he shall kill the lamb of the trespass offering, and the priest shall take *some* of the blood of the trespass offering and put *it* on the tip of the right ear of him who is to be cleansed, on the thumb of his right hand, and on the big toe of his right foot. ²⁶And the priest shall pour some of the oil into the palm of his own left hand. ²⁷Then the priest shall sprinkle with his right finger *some* of the oil that *is* in his left hand seven times before the LORD. ²⁸And the priest shall put *some* of the oil that *is* in his hand on the tip of the right ear of him who is to be cleansed, on the thumb of the right hand, and on the big toe of his right foot, on the place of the blood of the trespass offering. ²⁹The rest of the oil that *is* in the priest's hand he shall put on the head of him who is to be cleansed, to make atonement for him before the LORD. ³⁰And he shall offer one of the turtledoves or young pigeons, such as he can afford— ³¹such as he is able to afford, the one *as* a sin offering and the other *as* a burnt offering, with the grain offering. So the priest shall make atonement for him who is to be cleansed before the LORD. ³²This *is* the law *for one* who had a leprous sore, who cannot afford the usual cleansing."

³³And the LORD spoke to Moses and Aaron, saying: ³⁴"When you have come into the land of Canaan, which I give you as a possession, and I put the leprous plague* in a house in the land of your possession, ³⁵and he who owns the house comes and tells the priest, saying, 'It seems to me that *there is* some plague in the house,' ³⁶then the priest shall command that they empty the house, before the priest goes *into* it to examine the plague, that all that *is* in the house may not be made unclean; and afterward the priest shall go in to

examine the house. ³⁷And he shall examine the plague; and indeed *if* the plague *is* on the walls of the house with ingrained streaks, greenish or reddish, which appear to be deep in the wall, ³⁸then the priest shall go out of the house, to the door of the house, and shut up the house seven days. ³⁹And the priest shall come again on the seventh day and look; and indeed *if* the plague has spread on the walls of the house, ⁴⁰then the priest shall command that they take away the stones in which *is* the plague, and they shall cast them into an unclean place outside the city. ⁴¹And he shall cause the house to be scraped inside, all around, and the dust that they scrape off they shall pour out in an unclean place outside the city. ⁴²Then they shall take other stones and put *them* in the place of *those* stones, and he shall take other mortar and plaster the house.

⁴³"Now if the plague comes back and breaks out in the house, after he has taken away the stones, after he has scraped the house, and after it is plastered, ⁴⁴then the priest shall come and look; and indeed *if* the plague has spread in the house, it *is* an active leprosy in the house. It *is* unclean. ⁴⁵And he shall break down the house, its stones, its timber, and all the plaster of the house, and he shall carry *them* outside the city to an unclean place. ⁴⁶Moreover he who goes into the house at all while it is shut up shall be unclean until evening. ⁴⁷And he who lies down in the house shall wash his clothes, and he who eats in the house shall wash his clothes.

⁴⁸"But if the priest comes in and examines *it,* and indeed the plague has not spread in the house after the house was plastered, then the priest shall pronounce the house clean, because the plague is healed. ⁴⁹And he shall take, to cleanse the house, two birds, cedar wood, scarlet, and hyssop. ⁵⁰Then he shall kill one of the birds in an earthen vessel over running water; ⁵¹and he shall take the cedar wood, the hyssop, the scarlet, and the living bird, and dip them in the blood of the slain bird and in the running water, and sprinkle the house seven times. ⁵²And he shall cleanse the house with the blood of the bird and the running water and the living bird, with the cedar wood, the hyssop, and the scarlet. ⁵³Then he shall let the living bird loose outside the city in the open field, and make atonement for the house, and it shall be clean.

⁵⁴"This *is* the law for any leprous sore and scale, ⁵⁵for the leprosy of a garment and of a house, ⁵⁶for a swelling and a scab and a bright spot, ⁵⁷to teach when *it is* unclean and when *it is* clean. This *is* the law of leprosy."

MARK 6:30-56

THEN the apostles gathered to Jesus and told Him all things, both what they had done and what they had taught. ³¹And He said to them, "Come aside by yourselves to a deserted place and rest a while." For there were many coming and going, and they did not even have time to eat. ³²So they departed to a deserted place in the boat by themselves.

³³But the multitudes* saw them departing, and many knew Him and ran there on foot from all the cities. They arrived before them and came together to Him. ³⁴And Jesus, when He came out, saw a great multitude and was moved with compassion for them, because they were like sheep not having a shepherd. So He began to teach them many things. ³⁵When the day was now far spent, His disciples came to Him and said, "This is a deserted place, and already the hour *is* late. ³⁶Send them away, that they may go into the surrounding country and villages and buy themselves bread;* for they have nothing to eat."

37But He answered and said to them, "You give them something to eat."

And they said to Him, "Shall we go and buy two hundred denarii worth of bread and give them *something* to eat?"

38But He said to them, "How many loaves do you have? Go and see."

And when they found out they said, "Five, and two fish."

39Then He commanded them to make them all sit down in groups on the green grass. 40So they sat down in ranks, in hundreds and in fifties. 41And when He had taken the five loaves and the two fish, He looked up to heaven, blessed and broke the loaves, and gave *them* to His disciples to set before them; and the two fish He divided among *them* all. 42So they all ate and were filled. 43And they took up twelve baskets full of fragments and of the fish. 44Now those who had eaten the loaves were about* five thousand men.

45Immediately He made His disciples get into the boat and go before Him to the other side, to Bethsaida, while He sent the multitude away. 46And when He had sent them away, He departed to the mountain to pray. 47Now when evening came, the boat was in the middle of the sea; and He *was* alone on the land. 48Then He saw them straining at rowing, for the wind was against them. Now about the fourth watch of the night He came to them, walking on the sea, and would have passed them by. 49And when they saw Him walking on the sea, they supposed it was a ghost, and cried out; 50for they all saw Him and were troubled. But immediately He talked with them and said to them, "Be of good cheer! It is I; do not be afraid." 51Then He went up into the boat to them, and the wind ceased. And they were greatly amazed in themselves beyond measure, and marveled. 52For they had not understood about the loaves, because their heart was hardened.

53When they had crossed over, they came to the land of Gennesaret and anchored there. 54And when they came out of the boat, immediately the people recognized Him, 55ran through that whole surrounding region, and began to carry about on beds those who were sick to wherever they heard He was. 56Wherever He entered, into villages, cities, or the country, they laid the sick in the marketplaces, and begged Him that they might just touch the hem of His garment. And as many as touched Him were made well.

PSALM 40:1-10

To the Chief Musician. A Psalm of David.

I WAITED patiently for the LORD;
And He inclined to me,
And heard my cry.

2 He also brought me up out of
    a horrible pit,
  Out of the miry clay,
  And set my feet upon a rock,
  And established my steps.

3 He has put a new song in my
    mouth—
  Praise to our God;
  Many will see *it* and fear,
  And will trust in the LORD.

4 Blessed *is* that man who
    makes the LORD his trust,
  And does not respect the
    proud, nor such as turn
    aside to lies.

5 Many, O LORD my God, *are*
    Your wonderful works
  Which You have done;
  And Your thoughts toward us
  Cannot be recounted to You
    in order;
  If I would declare and speak *of*
    them,
  They are more than can be
    numbered.

6 Sacrifice and offering You did
    not desire;

My ears You have opened.
Burnt offering and sin
   offering You did not require.

7 Then I said, "Behold, I come;
In the scroll of the book *it is*
   written of me.

8 I delight to do Your will, O my
   God,
And Your law *is* within my
   heart."

9 I have proclaimed the good
   news of righteousness
In the great assembly;

Indeed, I do not restrain my
   lips,
O Lord, You Yourself know.

10 I have not hidden Your
   righteousness within my
   heart;
I have declared Your
   faithfulness and Your
   salvation;
I have not concealed Your
   lovingkindness and Your
   truth
From the great assembly.

PROVERBS FOR TODAY/ 10:11-12

The mouth of the righteous is *a well of life, but violence covers the mouth of the wicked.* ▢ *Hatred stirs up strife, but love covers all sins.*

FEBRUARY 24

LEVITICUS 15:1–16:28

AND the Lord spoke to Moses and Aaron, saying, 2"Speak to the children of Israel, and say to them: 'When any man has a discharge from his body, his discharge *is* unclean. 3And this shall be his uncleanness in regard to his discharge— whether his body runs with his discharge, or his body is stopped up by his discharge, it *is* his uncleanness. 4Every bed is unclean on which he who has the discharge lies, and everything on which he sits shall be unclean. 5And whoever touches his bed shall wash his clothes and bathe in water, and be unclean until evening. 6He who sits on anything on which he who has the discharge sat shall wash his clothes and bathe in water, and be unclean until evening. 7And he who touches the body of him who has the discharge shall wash his clothes and

bathe in water, and be unclean until evening. 8If he who has the discharge spits on him who is clean, then he shall wash his clothes and bathe in water, and be unclean until evening. 9Any saddle on which he who has the discharge rides shall be unclean. 10Whoever touches anything that was under him shall be unclean until evening. He who carries *any of* those things shall wash his clothes and bathe in water, and be unclean until evening. 11And whomever the one who has the discharge touches, and has not rinsed his hands in water, he shall wash his clothes and bathe in water, and be unclean until evening. 12The vessel of earth that he who has the discharge touches shall be broken, and every vessel of wood shall be rinsed in water.
13'And when he who has a discharge is cleansed of his discharge, then he shall count for himself seven days for his cleansing, wash his clothes, and

bathe his body in running water; then he shall be clean. [14]On the eighth day he shall take for himself two turtledoves or two young pigeons, and come before the LORD, to the door of the tabernacle of meeting, and give them to the priest. [15]Then the priest shall offer them, the one *as* a sin offering and the other *as* a burnt offering. So the priest shall make atonement for him before the LORD because of his discharge.

[16]'If any man has an emission of semen, then he shall wash all his body in water, and be unclean until evening. [17]And any garment and any leather on which there is semen, it shall be washed with water, and be unclean until evening. [18]Also, when a woman lies with a man, and *there is* an emission of semen, they shall bathe in water, and be unclean until evening.

[19]'If a woman has a discharge, *and* the discharge from her body is blood, she shall be set apart seven days; and whoever touches her shall be unclean until evening. [20]Everything that she lies on during her impurity shall be unclean; also everything that she sits on shall be unclean. [21]Whoever touches her bed shall wash his clothes and bathe in water, and be unclean until evening. [22]And whoever touches anything that she sat on shall wash his clothes and bathe in water, and be unclean until evening. [23]If *anything* is on *her* bed or on anything on which she sits, when he touches it, he shall be unclean until evening. [24]And if any man lies with her at all, so that her impurity is on him, he shall be unclean seven days; and every bed on which he lies shall be unclean.

[25]'If a woman has a discharge of blood for many days, other than at the time of her *customary* impurity, or if it runs beyond her *usual time of* impurity, all the days of her unclean discharge shall be as the days of her *customary* impurity. She *shall be* unclean. [26]Every bed on which she lies all the days of her discharge shall be to her as the bed of her impurity; and whatever she sits on shall be unclean, as the uncleanness of her impurity. [27]Whoever touches those things shall be unclean; he shall wash his clothes and bathe in water, and be unclean until evening.

[28]'But if she is cleansed of her discharge, then she shall count for herself seven days, and after that she shall be clean. [29]And on the eighth day she shall take for herself two turtledoves or two young pigeons, and bring them to the priest, to the door of the tabernacle of meeting. [30]Then the priest shall offer the one *as* a sin offering and the other *as* a burnt offering, and the priest shall make atonement for her before the LORD for the discharge of her uncleanness.

[31]'Thus you shall separate the children of Israel from their uncleanness, lest they die in their uncleanness when they defile My tabernacle that *is* among them. [32]This *is* the law for one who has a discharge, and *for him* who emits semen and is unclean thereby, [33]and for her who is indisposed because of her *customary* impurity, and for one who has a discharge, either man or woman, and for him who lies with her who is unclean.' "

Now the LORD spoke to Moses after the death of the two sons of Aaron, when they offered *profane fire* before the LORD, and died; [2]and the LORD said to Moses: "Tell Aaron your brother not to come at *just* any time into the Holy *Place* inside the veil, before the mercy seat which *is* on the ark, lest he die; for I will appear in the cloud above the mercy seat.

[3]"Thus Aaron shall come into the Holy *Place:* with *the blood of* a young bull as a sin offering, and *of* a ram as a burnt offering. [4]He shall put the holy linen tunic and the linen trousers on his body; he shall be girded with a linen sash, and with the linen turban he shall be attired. These *are* holy gar-

ments. Therefore he shall wash his body in water, and put them on. 5And he shall take from the congregation of the children of Israel two kids of the goats as a sin offering, and one ram as a burnt offering.

6"Aaron shall offer the bull as a sin offering, which *is* for himself, and make atonement for himself and for his house. 7He shall take the two goats and present them before the LORD *at* the door of the tabernacle of meeting. 8Then Aaron shall cast lots for the two goats: one lot for the LORD and the other lot for the scapegoat. 9And Aaron shall bring the goat on which the LORD's lot fell, and offer it *as* a sin offering. 10But the goat on which the lot fell to be the scapegoat shall be presented alive before the LORD, to make atonement upon it, *and* to let it go as the scapegoat into the wilderness.

11"And Aaron shall bring the bull of the sin offering, which is for himself, and make atonement for himself and for his house, and shall kill the bull as the sin offering which *is* for himself. 12Then he shall take a censer full of burning coals of fire from the altar before the LORD, with his hands full of sweet incense beaten fine, and bring *it* inside the veil. 13And he shall put the incense on the fire before the LORD, that the cloud of incense may cover the mercy seat that *is* on the Testimony, lest he die. 14He shall take some of the blood of the bull and sprinkle *it* with his finger on the mercy seat on the east *side;* and before the mercy seat he shall sprinkle some of the blood with his finger seven times.

15"Then he shall kill the goat of the sin offering, which *is* for the people, bring its blood inside the veil, do with that blood as he did with the blood of the bull, and sprinkle it on the mercy seat and before the mercy seat. 16So he shall make atonement for the Holy *Place,* because of the uncleanness of the children of Israel, and because of

their transgressions, for all their sins; and so he shall do for the tabernacle of meeting which remains among them in the midst of their uncleanness. 17There shall be no man in the tabernacle of meeting when he goes in to make atonement in the Holy *Place,* until he comes out, that he may make atonement for himself, for his household, and for all the assembly of Israel. 18And he shall go out to the altar that *is* before the LORD, and make atonement for it, and shall take some of the blood of the bull and some of the blood of the goat, and put it on the horns of the altar all around. 19Then he shall sprinkle some of the blood on it with his finger seven times, cleanse it, and consecrate it from the uncleanness of the children of Israel.

20"And when he has made an end of atoning for the Holy *Place,* the tabernacle of meeting, and the altar, he shall bring the live goat. 21Aaron shall lay both his hands on the head of the live goat, confess over it all the iniquities of the children of Israel, and all their transgressions, concerning all their sins, putting them on the head of the goat, and shall send *it* away into the wilderness by the hand of a suitable man. 22The goat shall bear on itself all their iniquities to an uninhabited land; and he shall release the goat in the wilderness.

23"Then Aaron shall come into the tabernacle of meeting, shall take off the linen garments which he put on when he went into the Holy *Place,* and shall leave them there. 24And he shall wash his body with water in a holy place, put on his garments, come out and offer his burnt offering and the burnt offering of the people, and make atonement for himself and for the people. 25The fat of the sin offering he shall burn on the altar. 26And he who released the goat as the scapegoat shall wash his clothes and bathe his body in water, and afterward he may come into the camp. ²⁷The bull *for* the sin offering and the goat *for* the sin offering, whose blood was brought in to make atonement in the Holy *Place,* shall be carried outside the camp. And they shall burn in the fire their skins, their flesh, and their offal. ²⁸Then he who burns them shall wash his clothes and bathe his body in water, and afterward he may come into the camp."

MARK 7:1-23

THEN the Pharisees and some of the scribes came together to Him [Jesus], having come from Jerusalem. ²Now when* they saw some of His disciples eat bread with defiled, that is, with unwashed hands, they found fault. ³For the Pharisees and all the Jews do not eat unless they wash *their* hands in a special way, holding the tradition of the elders. ⁴*When they come* from the marketplace, they do not eat unless they wash. And there are many other things which they have received and hold, *like* the washing of cups, pitchers, copper vessels, and couches.

⁵Then the Pharisees and scribes asked Him, "Why do Your disciples not walk according to the tradition of the elders, but eat bread with unwashed hands?"

⁶He answered and said to them, "Well did Isaiah prophesy of you hypocrites, as it is written:

'This people honors Me with
   their lips,
But their heart is far from Me.
7   And in vain they worship Me,
   Teaching as doctrines the
      commandments of men.' *

⁸For laying aside the commandment of God, you hold the tradition of men*—the washing of pitchers and cups, and many other such things you do."

⁹He said to them, "*All too* well you reject the commandment of God, that you may keep your tradition. ¹⁰For Moses said, 'Honor your father and your mother';* and, 'He who curses father or mother, let him be put to death.' * ¹¹But you say, 'If a man says to his father or mother, "Whatever profit you might have received from me *is* Corban"—' (that is, a gift *to God*), ¹²then you no longer let him do anything for his father or his mother, ¹³making the word of God of no effect through your tradition which you have handed down. And many such things you do."

¹⁴When He had called all the multitude to *Himself,* He said to them, "Hear Me, everyone, and understand: ¹⁵There is nothing that enters a man from outside which can defile him; but the things which come out of him, those are the things that defile a man. ¹⁶If anyone has ears to hear, let him hear!"*

¹⁷When He had entered a house away from the crowd, His disciples asked Him concerning the parable. ¹⁸So He said to them, "Are you thus without understanding also? Do you not perceive that whatever enters a man from outside cannot defile him, ¹⁹because it does not enter his heart but his stomach, and is eliminated, *thus* purifying all foods?"* ²⁰And He said, "What comes out of a man, that defiles a man. ²¹For from within, out of the heart of men, proceed evil thoughts, adulteries, fornications, murders, ²²thefts, covetousness, wickedness, deceit, lewdness, an evil eye, blasphemy, pride, foolishness. ²³All these evil things come from within and defile a man."

PSALM 40:11-17

Do not withhold Your tender mercies from me, O LORD; Let Your lovingkindness and Your truth continually preserve me.

12 For innumerable evils have
surrounded me;
My iniquities have overtaken
me, so that I am not able to
look up;
They are more than the hairs
of my head;
Therefore my heart fails me.

13 Be pleased, O LORD, to deliver
me;
O LORD, make haste to help
me!

14 Let them be ashamed and
brought to mutual confusion
Who seek to destroy my life;

Let them be driven backward
and brought to dishonor
Who wish me evil.
15 Let them be confounded
because of their shame,
Who say to me, "Aha, aha!"

16 Let all those who seek You
rejoice and be glad in You;
Let such as love Your
salvation say continually,
"The LORD be magnified!"
17 But I *am* poor and needy;
Yet the LORD thinks upon me.
You *are* my help and my
deliverer;
Do not delay, O my God.

PROVERBS FOR TODAY/ 10:13-14

Wisdom is found on the lips of him who has understanding, but a rod is *for the back of him who is devoid of understanding. Wise* people *store up knowledge, but the mouth of the foolish* is *near destruction.*

FEBRUARY 25

LEVITICUS 16:29–18:30

"**T**HIS shall be a statute forever for you: In the seventh month, on the tenth day of the month, you shall afflict your souls, and do no work at all, *whether* a native of your own country or a stranger who dwells among you. 30For on that day *the priest* shall make atonement for you, to cleanse you, *that* you may be clean from all your sins before the LORD. 31It *is* a sabbath of solemn rest for you, and you shall afflict your souls. *It is* a statute forever. 32And the priest, who is anointed and consecrated to minister as priest in his father's place, shall make atonement, and put on the linen clothes, the holy garments; 33then he shall make atonement for the Holy

Sanctuary,* and he shall make atonement for the tabernacle of meeting and for the altar, and he shall make atonement for the priests and for all the people of the assembly. 34This shall be an everlasting statute for you, to make atonement for the children of Israel, for all their sins, once a year." And he did as the LORD commanded Moses.

AND the LORD spoke to Moses, saying, 2"Speak to Aaron, to his sons, and to all the children of Israel, and say to them, 'This *is* the thing which the LORD has commanded, saying: 3"Whatever man of the house of Israel who kills an ox or lamb or goat in the camp, or who kills *it* outside the camp, 4and does not bring it to the door of the tabernacle of meeting to offer an offering to the LORD before the tabernacle of the Lord, the guilt of bloodshed shall be imputed to that man. He has shed blood; and that man shall be cut off from among his people, 5to the end that the children of Israel may bring their sacrifices which they offer in the open field, that they may bring them to the Lord at the door of the tabernacle of meeting, to the priest, and offer them *as* peace offerings to the Lord. 6And the priest shall sprinkle the blood on the altar of the Lord *at* the door of the tabernacle of meeting, and burn the fat for a sweet aroma to the Lord. 7They shall no more offer their sacrifices to demons, after whom they have played the harlot. This shall be a statute forever for them throughout their generations." '

8"Also you shall say to them: 'Whatever man of the house of Israel, or of the strangers who dwell among you, who offers a burnt offering or sacrifice, 9and does not bring it to the door of the tabernacle of meeting, to offer it to the Lord, that man shall be cut off from among his people.

10'And whatever man of the house of Israel, or of the strangers who dwell among you, who eats any blood, I will set My face against that person who eats blood, and will cut him off from among his people. 11For the life of the flesh *is* in the blood, and I have given it to you upon the altar to make atonement for your souls; for it *is* the blood *that* makes atonement for the soul.' 12Therefore I said to the children of Israel, 'No one among you shall eat blood, nor shall any stranger who dwells among you eat blood.'

13"Whatever man of the children of Israel, or of the strangers who dwell among you, who hunts and catches any animal or bird that may be eaten, he shall pour out its blood and cover it with dust; 14for *it is* the life of all flesh. Its blood sustains its life. Therefore I said to the children of Israel, 'You shall not eat the blood of any flesh, for the life of all flesh is its blood. Whoever eats it shall be cut off.'

15"And every person who eats what died *naturally* or what was torn *by beasts, whether he is* a native of your own country or a stranger, he shall both wash his clothes and bathe in water, and be unclean until evening. Then he shall be clean. 16But if he does not wash *them* or bathe his body, then he shall bear his guilt."

Then the Lord spoke to Moses, saying, 2"Speak to the children of Israel, and say to them: 'I am the Lord your God. 3According to the doings of the land of Egypt, where you dwelt, you shall not do; and according to the doings of the land of Canaan, where I am bringing you, you shall not do; nor shall you walk in their ordinances. 4You shall observe My judgments and keep My ordinances, to walk in them: I *am* the Lord your God. 5You shall therefore keep My statutes and My judgments, which if a man does, he shall live by them: I *am* the Lord.

6'None of you shall approach anyone who is near of kin to him, to uncover his nakedness: I *am* the Lord. 7The nakedness of your father or the nakedness of your mother you shall not uncover. She *is* your mother; you shall not uncover her nakedness. 8The nakedness of your father's wife you shall not uncover; it *is* your father's nakedness. 9The nakedness of your sister, the daughter of your father, or the daughter of your mother, *whether* born at home or elsewhere, their nakedness you shall not uncover. 10The nakedness of your son's daughter or your daughter's daughter, their nakedness you shall not uncover; for theirs *is* your own nakedness. 11The nakedness of your father's wife's daughter, begotten by your father—she *is* your sister—you shall not uncover her nakedness. 12You shall not uncover the nakedness of your father's sister; she *is* near of kin to your father. 13You shall not uncover the nakedness of your mother's sister, for she *is* near of kin to your mother. 14You shall not uncover the nakedness of your father's brother. You shall not approach his wife; she *is* your aunt. 15You shall not uncover the nakedness of your daughter-in-law—she *is* your son's wife—you shall not uncover her nakedness. 16You shall not uncover the nakedness of your brother's wife; it *is* your brother's nakedness. 17You shall not uncover the nakedness of a woman and her daughter, nor shall you take her son's daughter or her daughter's daughter, to uncover her nakedness. They *are* near of kin to her. It *is* wickedness. 18Nor shall you take a woman as a rival to her sister, to uncover her nakedness while the other is alive.

19"Also you shall not approach a woman to uncover her nakedness as long as she is in her *customary* impurity. 20Moreover you shall not lie carnally with your neighbor's wife, to defile yourself with her. 21And you shall not let any of your descendants pass through *the fire* to Molech, nor shall you profane the name of your God: I *am* the Lord. 22You shall not lie with a male as with a woman. It *is* an abomination. 23Nor shall you mate with any animal, to defile yourself with it. Nor shall any woman stand before an animal to mate with it. It *is* perversion.

24"Do not defile yourselves with any of these things; for by all these the nations are defiled, which I am casting out before you. 25For the land is defiled; therefore I visit the punishment of its iniquity upon it, and the land vomits out its inhabitants. 26You shall therefore keep My statutes and My judgments, and shall not commit *any* of these abominations, *either* any of your own nation or any stranger who dwells among you 27(for all these abominations the men of the land have done, who *were* before you, and thus

the land is defiled), 28lest the land vomit you out also when you defile it, as it vomited out the nations that *were* before you. 29For whoever commits any of these abominations, the persons who commit *them* shall be cut off from among their people.

30"Therefore you shall keep My ordinance, so that *you* do not commit *any* of these abominable customs which were committed before you, and that you do not defile yourselves by them: I *am* the Lord your God.' "

MARK 7:24–8:10

From there He [Jesus] arose and went to the region of Tyre and Sidon.* And He entered a house and wanted no one to know *it,* but He could not be hidden. 25For a woman whose young daughter had an unclean spirit heard about Him, and she came and fell at His feet. 26The woman was a Greek, a Syro-Phoenician by birth, and she kept asking Him to cast the demon out of her daughter. 27But Jesus said to her, "Let the children be filled first, for it is not good to take the children's bread and throw *it* to the little dogs."

28And she answered and said to Him, "Yes, Lord, yet even the little dogs under the table eat from the children's crumbs."

29Then He said to her, "For this saying go your way; the demon has gone out of your daughter."

30And when she had come to her house, she found the demon gone out, and her daughter lying on the bed.

31Again, departing from the region of Tyre and Sidon, He came through the midst of the region of Decapolis to the Sea of Galilee. 32Then they brought to Him one who was deaf and had an impediment in his speech, and they begged Him to put His hand on him. 33And He took him aside from the multitude, and put His fingers in his ears, and He spat and touched his tongue. ³⁴Then, looking up to heaven, He sighed, and said to him, "Ephphatha," that is, "Be opened."

³⁵Immediately his ears were opened, and the impediment of his tongue was loosed, and he spoke plainly. ³⁶Then He commanded them that they should tell no one; but the more He commanded them, the more widely they proclaimed it. ³⁷And they were astonished beyond measure, saying, "He has done all things well. He makes both the deaf to hear and the mute to speak."

In those days, the multitude being very great and having nothing to eat, Jesus called His disciples to Him and said to them, ²"I have compassion on the multitude, because they have now continued with Me three days and have nothing to eat. ³And if I send them away hungry to their own houses, they will faint on the way; for some of them have come from afar."

⁴Then His disciples answered Him, "How can one satisfy these people with bread here in the wilderness?"

⁵He asked them, "How many loaves do you have?"

And they said, "Seven."

⁶So He commanded the multitude to sit down on the ground. And He took the seven loaves and gave thanks, broke them and gave them to His disciples to set before them; and they set them before the multitude. ⁷They also had a few small fish; and having blessed them, He said to set them also before them. ⁸So they ate and were filled, and they took up seven large baskets of leftover fragments. ⁹Now those who had eaten were about four thousand. And He sent them away, ¹⁰immediately got into the boat with His disciples, and came to the region of Dalmanutha.

PSALM 41:1-13

To the Chief Musician. A Psalm of David.

B
LESSED *is* he who considers the poor;
The LORD will deliver him in time of trouble.

2 The LORD will preserve him and keep him alive,
And he will be blessed on the earth;
You will not deliver him to the will of his enemies.

3 The LORD will strengthen him on his bed of illness;
You will sustain him on his sickbed.

4 I said, "LORD, be merciful to me;
Heal my soul, for I have sinned against You."

5 My enemies speak evil of me:
"When will he die, and his name perish?"

6 And if he comes to see *me,* he speaks lies;
His heart gathers iniquity to itself;
When he goes out, he tells *it.*

7 All who hate me whisper together against me;
Against me they devise my hurt.

8 "An evil disease," *they say,*
"clings to him.
And *now* that he lies down, he will rise up no more."

9 Even my own familiar friend in whom I trusted,
Who ate my bread,
Has lifted up *his* heel against me.

10 But You, O LORD, be merciful to me, and raise me up,
That I may repay them.

11 By this I know that You are well pleased with me,

Because my enemy does not
triumph over me.

12 As for me, You uphold me in
my integrity,
And set me before Your face
forever.

13 Blessed *be* the Lord God of
Israel
From everlasting to
everlasting!
Amen and Amen.

PROVERBS FOR TODAY/ 10:15-16

The rich man's wealth is *his strong city; the destruction of the poor* is *their poverty.*
□ *The labor of the righteous* leads *to life, the wages of the wicked to sin.*

FEBRUARY 26

LEVITICUS 19:1–20:21

AND the Lord spoke to Moses, saying, 2"Speak to all the congregation of the children of Israel, and say to them: 'You shall be holy, for I the Lord your God *am* holy.

3'Every one of you shall revere his mother and his father, and keep My Sabbaths: I *am* the Lord your God.

4'Do not turn to idols, nor make for yourselves molded gods: I *am* the Lord your God.

5'And if you offer a sacrifice of a peace offering to the Lord, you shall offer it of your own free will. 6It shall be eaten the same day you offer *it,* and on the next day. And if any remains until the third day, it shall be burned in the fire. 7And if it is eaten at all on the third day, it *is* an abomination. It shall not be accepted. 8Therefore *everyone* who eats it shall bear his iniquity, because he has profaned the hallowed *offering* of the Lord; and that person shall be cut off from his people.

9'When you reap the harvest of your land, you shall not wholly reap the corners of your field, nor shall you gather the gleanings of your harvest. 10And you shall not glean your vineyard, nor shall you gather *every* grape of your vineyard; you shall leave them for the poor and the stranger: I *am* the Lord your God.

11'You shall not steal, nor deal falsely, nor lie to one another.12And you shall not swear by My name falsely, nor shall you profane the name of your God: I *am* the Lord.

13'You shall not cheat your neighbor, nor rob *him.* The wages of him who is hired shall not remain with you all night until morning. 14You shall not curse the deaf, nor put a stumbling block before the blind, but shall fear your God: I *am* the Lord.

15'You shall do no injustice in judgment. You shall not be partial to the poor, nor honor the person of the mighty. In righteousness you shall judge your neighbor. 16You shall not go about *as* a talebearer among your people; nor shall you take a stand against the life of your neighbor: I *am* the Lord.

17'You shall not hate your brother in your heart. You shall surely rebuke your neighbor, and not bear sin because of him. 18You shall not take vengeance, nor bear any grudge against the children of your people, but you shall love your neighbor as yourself: I *am* the Lord.

19'You shall keep My statutes. You

shall not let your livestock breed with another kind. You shall not sow your field with mixed seed. Nor shall a garment of mixed linen and wool come upon you.

20"Whoever lies carnally with a woman who *is* betrothed to a man as a concubine, and who has not at all been redeemed nor given her freedom, for this there shall be scourging; *but* they shall not be put to death, because she was not free. 21And he shall bring his trespass offering to the LORD, to the door of the tabernacle of meeting, a ram as a trespass offering. 22The priest shall make atonement for him with the ram of the trespass offering before the LORD for his sin which he has committed. And the sin which he has committed shall be forgiven him.

23"When you come into the land, and have planted all kinds of trees for food, then you shall count their fruit as uncircumcised. Three years it shall be as uncircumcised to you. *It* shall not be eaten. 24But in the fourth year all its fruit shall be holy, a praise to the LORD. 25And in the fifth year you may eat its fruit, that it may yield to you its increase: I *am* the LORD your God.

26"You shall not eat *anything* with the blood, nor shall you practice divination or soothsaying. 27You shall not shave around the sides of your head, nor shall you disfigure the edges of your beard. 28You shall not make any cuttings in your flesh for the dead, nor tattoo any marks on you: I *am* the LORD.

29"Do not prostitute your daughter, to cause her to be a harlot, lest the land fall into harlotry, and the land become full of wickedness.

30"You shall keep My Sabbaths and reverence My sanctuary: I *am* the LORD.

31"Give no regard to mediums and familiar spirits; do not seek after them, to be defiled by them: I *am* the LORD your God.

32"You shall rise before the gray headed and honor the presence of an old man, and fear your God: I *am* the LORD.

33"And if a stranger dwells with you in your land, you shall not mistreat him. 34The stranger who dwells among you shall be to you as one born among you, and you shall love him as yourself; for you were strangers in the land of Egypt: I *am* the LORD your God.

35"You shall do no injustice in judgment, in measurement of length, weight, or volume. 36You shall have honest scales, honest weights, an honest ephah, and an honest hin: I *am* the LORD your God, who brought you out of the land of Egypt.

37"Therefore you shall observe all My statutes and all My judgments, and perform them: I *am* the LORD.' "

THEN the LORD spoke to Moses, saying, 2"Again, you shall say to the children of Israel: 'Whoever of the children of Israel, or of the strangers who dwell in Israel, who gives *any* of his descendants to Molech, he shall surely be put to death. The people of the land shall stone him with stones. 3I will set My face against that man, and will cut him off from his people, because he has given *some* of his descendants to Molech, to defile My sanctuary and profane My holy name. 4And if the people of the land should in any way hide their eyes from the man, when he gives *some* of his descendants to Molech, and they do not kill him, 5then I will set My face against that man and against his family; and I will cut him off from his people, and all who prostitute themselves with him to commit harlotry with Molech.

6"And the person who turns to mediums and familiar spirits, to prostitute himself with them, I will set My face against that person and cut him off from his people. 7Consecrate yourselves therefore, and be holy, for I *am* the LORD your God. 8And you shall keep My statutes, and perform them: I *am* the LORD who sanctifies you.

⁹"For everyone who curses his father or his mother shall surely be put to death. He has cursed his father or his mother. His blood *shall be* upon him.

¹⁰"The man who commits adultery with *another* man's wife, *he* who commits adultery with his neighbor's wife, the adulterer and the adulteress, shall surely be put to death. ¹¹The man who lies with his father's wife has uncovered his father's nakedness; both of them shall surely be put to death. Their blood *shall be* upon them. ¹²If a man lies with his daughter-in-law, both of them shall surely be put to death. They have committed perversion. Their blood *shall be* upon them. ¹³If a man lies with a male as he lies with a woman, both of them have committed an abomination. They shall surely be put to death. Their blood *shall be* upon them. ¹⁴If a man marries a woman and her mother, it *is* wickedness. They shall be burned with fire, both he and they, that there may be no wickedness among you. ¹⁵If a man mates with an animal, he shall surely be put to death, and you shall kill the animal. ¹⁶If a woman approaches any animal and mates with it, you shall kill the woman and the animal. They shall surely be put to death. Their blood *is* upon them.

¹⁷"If a man takes his sister, his father's daughter or his mother's daughter, and sees her nakedness and she sees his nakedness, it *is* a wicked thing. And they shall be cut off in the sight of their people. He has uncovered his sister's nakedness. He shall bear his guilt. ¹⁸If a man lies with a woman during her sickness and uncovers her nakedness, he has exposed her flow, and she has uncovered the flow of her blood. Both of them shall be cut off from their people.

¹⁹"You shall not uncover the nakedness of your mother's sister nor of your father's sister, for that would uncover his near of kin. They shall bear their guilt. ²⁰If a man lies with his uncle's wife, he has uncovered his uncle's nakedness. They shall bear their sin; they shall die childless. ²¹If a man takes his brother's wife, it *is* an unclean thing. He has uncovered his brother's nakedness. They shall be childless.'"

MARK 8:11-38

THEN the Pharisees came out and began to dispute with Him [Jesus], seeking from Him a sign from heaven, testing Him. ¹²But He sighed deeply in His spirit, and said, "Why does this generation seek a sign? Assuredly, I say to you, no sign shall be given to this generation."

¹³And He left them, and getting into the boat again, departed to the other side. ¹⁴Now the disciples* had forgotten to take bread, and they did not have more than one loaf with them in the boat. ¹⁵Then He charged them, saying, "Take heed, beware of the leaven of the Pharisees and the leaven of Herod."

¹⁶And they reasoned among themselves, saying, *"It is* because we have no bread."

¹⁷But Jesus, being aware of *it,* said to them, "Why do you reason because you have no bread? Do you not yet perceive nor understand? Is your heart still* hardened? ¹⁸Having eyes, do you not see? And having ears, do you not hear? And do you not remember? ¹⁹When I broke the five loaves for the five thousand, how many baskets full of fragments did you take up?"

They said to Him, "Twelve."

²⁰"Also, when I broke the seven for the four thousand, how many large baskets full of fragments did you take up?"

And they said, "Seven."

²¹So He said to them, "How *is it* you do not understand?"

²²Then He came to Bethsaida; and they brought a blind man to Him, and begged Him to touch him. ²³So He took the blind man by the hand and led him out of the town. And when He had spit on his eyes and put His hands on him, He asked him if he saw anything.

²⁴And he looked up and said, "I see men like trees, walking."

²⁵Then He put *His* hands on his eyes again and made him look up. And he was restored and saw everyone clearly. ²⁶Then He sent him away to his house, saying, "Neither go into the town, nor tell anyone in the town."*

²⁷Now Jesus and His disciples went out to the towns of Caesarea Philippi; and on the road He asked His disciples, saying to them, "Who do men say that I am?"

²⁸So they answered, "John the Baptist; but some *say,* Elijah; and others, one of the prophets."

²⁹He said to them, "But who do you say that I am?"

Peter answered and said to Him, "You are the Christ."

³⁰Then He strictly warned them that they should tell no one about Him.

³¹And He began to teach them that the Son of Man must suffer many things, and be rejected by the elders and chief priests and scribes, and be killed, and after three days rise again. ³²He spoke this word openly. Then Peter took Him aside and began to rebuke Him. ³³But when He had turned around and looked at His disciples, He rebuked Peter, saying, "Get behind Me, Satan! For you are not mindful of the things of God, but the things of men."

³⁴When He had called the people to *Himself,* with His disciples also, He said to them, "Whoever desires to come after Me, let him deny himself, and take up his cross, and follow Me. ³⁵For whoever desires to save his life will lose it, but whoever loses his life for My sake and the gospel's will save

it. ³⁶For what will it profit a man if he gains the whole world, and loses his own soul? ³⁷Or what will a man give in exchange for his soul? ³⁸For whoever is ashamed of Me and My words in this adulterous and sinful generation, of him the Son of Man also will be ashamed when He comes in the glory of His Father with the holy angels."

PSALM 42:1-11

To the Chief Musician. A Contemplation * *of the sons of Korah.*

A s the deer pants for the water brooks,
So pants my soul for You,
O God.

2 My soul thirsts for God, for the living God.
When shall I come and appear before God?*

3 My tears have been my food day and night,
While they continually say to me,
"Where *is* your God?"

4 When I remember these *things,*
I pour out my soul within me.
For I used to go with the multitude;
I went with them to the house of God,
With the voice of joy and praise,
With a multitude that kept a pilgrim feast.

5 Why are you cast down, O my soul?
And *why* are you disquieted within me?
Hope in God, for I shall yet praise Him
For the help of His countenance.*

6 O my God,* my soul is cast
down within me;
Therefore I will remember
You from the land of the
Jordan,
And from the heights of
Hermon,
From the Hill Mizar.

7 Deep calls unto deep at the
noise of Your waterfalls;
All Your waves and billows
have gone over me.

8 The LORD will command His
lovingkindness in the
daytime,
And in the night His song
shall be with me—
A prayer to the God of my life.

9 I will say to God my Rock,

"Why have You forgotten me?
Why do I go mourning
because of the oppression
of the enemy?"

10 *As* with a breaking of my
bones,
My enemies reproach me,
While they say to me all day
long,
"Where *is* your God?"

11 Why are you cast down, O my
soul?
And why are you disquieted
within me?
Hope in God;
For I shall yet praise Him,
The help of my countenance
and my God.

PROVERBS FOR TODAY/ 10:17

He who keeps instruction is in *the way of life, but he who refuses correction goes astray.*

FEBRUARY 27

LEVITICUS 20:22–22:16

" "You shall therefore keep all My statutes and all My judgments, and perform them, that the land where I am bringing you to dwell may not vomit you out. 23And you shall not walk in the statutes of the nation which I am casting out before you; for they commit all these things, and therefore I abhor them. 24But I have said to you, "You shall inherit their land, and I will give it to you to possess, a land flowing with milk and honey." I *am* the LORD your God, who has separated you from the peoples. 25You shall therefore distinguish between clean animals and unclean, between unclean birds and clean, and you shall not make yourselves abominable by beast or by bird, or by any kind of living thing that creeps on the ground, which I have separated from you as unclean. 26And you shall be holy to Me, for I the LORD *am* holy, and have separated you from the peoples, that you should be Mine.

27'A man or a woman who is a medium, or who has familiar spirits, shall surely be put to death; they shall stone them with stones. Their blood *shall be* upon them.' "

AND the LORD said to Moses, "Speak to the priests, the sons of Aaron, and say to them: 'None shall defile himself for the dead among his people, 2except for his relatives who are nearest to him: his mother, his father, his son, his daughter, and his brother; 3also his virgin sister who is near to him, who has had no husband, for her he may defile himself. 4*Otherwise* he shall not defile himself, *being* a chief man among his people, to profane himself.

5'They shall not make any bald *place* on their heads, nor shall they shave the edges of their beards nor make any cuttings in their flesh. 6They shall be holy to their God and not profane the name of their God, for they offer the offerings of the LORD made by fire, *and* the bread of their God; therefore they shall be holy. 7They shall not take a wife *who is* a harlot or a defiled woman, nor shall they take a woman divorced from her husband; for *the priest** is holy to his God. 8Therefore you shall consecrate him, for he offers the bread of your God. He shall be holy to you, for I the LORD, who sanctify you, *am* holy. 9The daughter of any priest, if she profanes herself by playing the harlot, she profanes her father. She shall be burned with fire.

10'*He who is* the high priest among his brethren, on whose head the anointing oil was poured and who is consecrated to wear the garments, shall not uncover his head nor tear his clothes; 11nor shall he go near any dead body, nor defile himself for his father or his mother; 12nor shall he go out of the sanctuary, nor profane the sanctuary of his God; for the consecration of the anointing oil of his God *is* upon him: I *am* the LORD. 13And he shall take a wife in her virginity. 14A widow or a divorced woman or a defiled woman *or* a harlot—these he shall not marry; but he shall take a virgin of his own people as wife. 15Nor shall he profane his posterity among his people, for I the LORD sanctify him.' "

16And the LORD spoke to Moses, saying, 17"Speak to Aaron, saying: 'No man of your descendants in *succeeding* generations, who has *any* defect, may approach to offer the bread of his God. 18For any man who has a defect shall not approach: a man blind or lame, who has a marred *face* or any *limb* too long, 19a man who has a broken foot or broken hand, 20or is a hunchback or a dwarf, or *a man* who has a defect in his eye, or eczema or scab, or is a eunuch. 21No man of the descendants of Aaron the priest, who has a defect, shall come near to offer the offerings made by fire to the LORD. He has a defect; he shall not come near to offer the bread of his God. 22He may eat the bread of his God, *both* the most holy and the holy; 23only he shall not go near the veil or approach the altar, because he has a defect, lest he profane My sanctuaries; for I the LORD sanctify them.' "

24And Moses told *it* to Aaron and his sons, and to all the children of Israel.

THEN the LORD spoke to Moses, saying, 2"Speak to Aaron and his sons, that they separate themselves from the holy things of the children of Israel, and that they do not profane My holy name *by* what they dedicate to Me: I *am* the LORD. 3Say to them: 'Whoever of all your descendants throughout your generations, who goes near the holy things which the children of Israel dedicate to the LORD, while he has uncleanness upon him, that person shall be cut off from My presence: I *am* the LORD.

4'Whatever man of the descendants of Aaron, who *is* a leper or has a discharge, shall not eat the holy offerings until he is clean. And whoever touches anything made unclean *by* a corpse, or a man who has had an emission of semen, 5or whoever touches any creeping thing by which he would be made unclean, or any person by whom he would become unclean, whatever his uncleanness may be— 6the person who has touched any such thing shall be unclean until evening, and shall not eat the holy *offerings* unless he washes his body with water. [7]And when the sun goes down he shall be clean; and afterward he may eat the holy *offerings,* because it *is* his food. [8]Whatever dies *naturally* or is torn *by beasts* he shall not eat, to defile himself with it: I *am* the LORD.

[9]"They shall therefore keep My ordinance, lest they bear sin for it and die thereby, if they profane it: I the LORD sanctify them.

[10]"No outsider shall eat the holy *offering;* one who dwells with the priest, or a hired servant, shall not eat the holy thing. [11]But if the priest buys a person with his money, he may eat it; and one who is born in his house may eat his food. [12]If the priest's daughter is married to an outsider, she may not eat of the holy offerings. [13]But if the priest's daughter is a widow or divorced, and has no child, and has returned to her father's house as in her youth, she may eat her father's food; but no outsider shall eat it.

[14]"And if a man eats the holy *offering* unintentionally, then he shall restore a holy *offering* to the priest, and add one-fifth to it. [15]They shall not profane the holy *offerings* of the children of Israel, which they offer to the LORD, [16]or allow them to bear the guilt of trespass when they eat their holy *offerings;* for I the LORD sanctify them.' "

MARK 9:1-29

AND He [Jesus] said to them, "Assuredly, I say to you that there are some standing here who will not taste death till they see the kingdom of God present with power."

[2]Now after six days Jesus took Peter, James, and John, and led them up on a high mountain apart by themselves; and He was transfigured before them. [3]His clothes became shining, exceedingly white, like snow, such as no launderer on earth can whiten them. [4]And Elijah appeared to them with Moses, and they were talking with Jesus. [5]Then Peter answered and said to Jesus, "Rabbi, it is good for us to be here; and let us make three tabernacles: one for You, one for Moses, and one for Elijah"— [6]because he did not know what to say, for they were greatly afraid.

[7]And a cloud came and overshadowed them; and a voice came out of the cloud, saying, "This is My beloved Son. Hear Him!" [8]Suddenly, when they had looked around, they saw no one anymore, but only Jesus with themselves.

[9]Now as they came down from the mountain, He commanded them that they should tell no one the things they had seen, till the Son of Man had risen from the dead. [10]So they kept this word to themselves, questioning what the rising from the dead meant.

[11]And they asked Him, saying, "Why do the scribes say that Elijah must come first?"

[12]Then He answered and told them, "Indeed, Elijah is coming first and restores all things. And how is it written concerning the Son of Man, that He must suffer many things and be treated with contempt? [13]But I say to you that Elijah has also come, and they did to him whatever they wished, as it is written of him."

[14]And when He came to the disciples, He saw a great multitude around them, and scribes disputing with them. [15]Immediately, when they saw Him, all the people were greatly amazed, and running to *Him,* greeted Him. [16]And He asked the scribes, "What are you discussing with them?"

[17]Then one of the crowd answered and said, "Teacher, I brought You my son, who has a mute spirit. [18]And wherever it seizes him, it throws him down; he foams at the mouth, gnashes his

teeth, and becomes rigid. So I spoke to Your disciples, that they should cast it out, but they could not."

¹⁹He answered him and said, "O faithless generation, how long shall I be with you? How long shall I bear with you? Bring him to Me." ²⁰Then they brought him to Him. And when he saw Him, immediately the spirit convulsed him, and he fell on the ground and wallowed, foaming at the mouth.

²¹So He asked his father, "How long has this been happening to him?"

And he said, "From childhood. ²²And often he has thrown him both into the fire and into the water to destroy him. But if You can do anything, have compassion on us and help us."

²³Jesus said to him, "If you can believe,* all things are possible to him who believes."

²⁴Immediately the father of the child cried out and said with tears, "Lord, I believe; help my unbelief!"

²⁵When Jesus saw that the people came running together, He rebuked the unclean spirit, saying to it, "Deaf and dumb spirit, I command you, come out of him and enter him no more!" ²⁶Then the spirit cried out, convulsed him greatly, and came out of him. And he became as one dead, so that many said, "He is dead." ²⁷But Jesus took him by the hand and lifted him up, and he arose.

²⁸And when He had come into the house, His disciples asked Him privately, "Why could we not cast it out?"

²⁹So He said to them, "This kind can come out by nothing but prayer and fasting."*

PSALM 43:1-5

VINDICATE me, O God,
And plead my cause against an ungodly nation;
Oh, deliver me from the deceitful and unjust man!
2   For You are the God of my strength;
Why do You cast me off?
Why do I go mourning because of the oppression of the enemy?
3   Oh, send out Your light and Your truth!
Let them lead me;
Let them bring me to Your holy hill
And to Your tabernacle.
4   Then I will go to the altar of God,
To God my exceeding joy;
And on the harp I will praise You,
O God, my God.
5   Why are you cast down, O my soul?
And why are you disquieted within me?
Hope in God;
For I shall yet praise Him,
The help of my countenance and my God.

PROVERBS FOR TODAY/ 10:18

Whoever hides hatred has *lying lips, and whoever spreads slander* is *a fool.*

FEBRUARY 28

LEVITICUS 22:17–23:44

And the LORD spoke to Moses, saying, 18"Speak to Aaron and his sons, and to all the children of Israel, and say to them: 'Whatever man of the house of Israel, or of the strangers in Israel, who offers his sacrifice for any of his vows or for any of his freewill offerings, which they offer to the LORD as a burnt offering— 19*you shall offer* of your own free will a male without blemish from the cattle, from the sheep, or from the goats. 20Whatever has a defect, you shall not offer, for it shall not be acceptable on your behalf. 21And whoever offers a sacrifice of a peace offering to the LORD, to fulfill *his* vow, or a freewill offering from the cattle or the sheep, it must be perfect to be accepted; there shall be no defect in it. 22Those *that are* blind or broken or maimed, or have an ulcer or eczema or scabs, you shall not offer to the LORD, nor make an offering by fire of them on the altar to the LORD. 23Either a bull or a lamb that has any limb too long or too short you may offer *as* a freewill offering, but for a vow it shall not be accepted.

24'You shall not offer to the LORD what is bruised or crushed, or torn or cut; nor shall you make *any offering of them* in your land. 25Nor from a foreigner's hand shall you offer any of these as the bread of your God, because their corruption *is* in them, *and* defects *are* in them. They shall not be accepted on your behalf.' "

26And the LORD spoke to Moses, saying: 27"When a bull or a sheep or a goat is born, it shall be seven days with its mother; and from the eighth day and thereafter it shall be accepted as an offering made by fire to the LORD. 28*Whether it is* a cow or ewe, do not kill both her and her young on the same day. 29And when you offer a sacrifice of thanksgiving to the LORD, offer *it* of your own free will. 30On the same day it shall be eaten; you shall leave none of it until morning: I *am* the LORD.

31"Therefore you shall keep My commandments, and perform them: I *am* the LORD. 32You shall not profane My holy name, but I will be hallowed among the children of Israel. I *am* the LORD who sanctifies you, 33who brought you out of the land of Egypt, to be your God: I *am* the LORD."

And the LORD spoke to Moses, saying, 2"Speak to the children of Israel, and say to them: 'The feasts of the LORD, which you shall proclaim *to be* holy convocations, these *are* My feasts.

3'Six days shall work be done, but the seventh day *is* a Sabbath of solemn rest, a holy convocation. You shall do no work *on it;* it *is* the Sabbath of the LORD in all your dwellings.

4'These *are* the feasts of the LORD, holy convocations which you shall proclaim at their appointed times. 5On the fourteenth *day* of the first month at twilight *is* the LORD's Passover. 6And on the fifteenth day of the same month *is* the Feast of Unleavened Bread to the LORD; seven days you must eat unleavened bread. 7On the first day you shall have a holy convocation; you shall do no customary work on it. 8But you shall offer an offering made by fire to the LORD for seven days. The seventh day *shall be* a holy convocation; you shall do no customary work *on it.*' "

9And the LORD spoke to Moses, saying, 10"Speak to the children of Israel, and say to them: 'When you come into the land which I give to you, and reap its harvest, then you shall bring a sheaf of the firstfruits of your harvest to the priest. [11]He shall wave the sheaf before the LORD, to be accepted on your behalf; on the day after the Sabbath the priest shall wave it. [12]And you shall offer on that day, when you wave the sheaf, a male lamb of the first year, without blemish, as a burnt offering to the LORD. [13]Its grain offering *shall be* two-tenths *of an ephah* of fine flour mixed with oil, an offering made by fire to the LORD, for a sweet aroma; and its drink offering *shall be* of wine, one-fourth of a hin. [14]You shall eat neither bread nor parched grain nor fresh grain until the same day that you have brought an offering to your God; *it shall be* a statute forever throughout your generations in all your dwellings.

[15]'And you shall count for yourselves from the day after the Sabbath, from the day that you brought the sheaf of the wave offering: seven Sabbaths shall be completed. [16]Count fifty days to the day after the seventh Sabbath; then you shall offer a new grain offering to the LORD. [17]You shall bring from your dwellings two wave *loaves* of two-tenths *of an ephah*. They shall be of fine flour; they shall be baked with leaven. *They are* the firstfruits to the LORD. [18]And you shall offer with the bread seven lambs of the first year, without blemish, one young bull, and two rams. They shall be *as* a burnt offering to the LORD, with their grain offering and their drink offerings, an offering made by fire for a sweet aroma to the LORD. [19]Then you shall sacrifice one kid of the goats as a sin offering, and two male lambs of the first year as a sacrifice of a peace offering. [20]The priest shall wave them with the bread of the firstfruits *as* a wave offering before the LORD, with the two lambs. They shall be holy to the LORD for the priest. [21]And you shall proclaim on the same day *that* it is a holy convocation to you. You shall do no customary work *on it. It shall be* a statute

forever in all your dwellings throughout your generations.

[22]'When you reap the harvest of your land, you shall not wholly reap the corners of your field when you reap, nor shall you gather any gleaning from your harvest. You shall leave them for the poor and for the stranger: I *am* the LORD your God.' "

[23]Then the LORD spoke to Moses, saying, [24]"Speak to the children of Israel, saying: 'In the seventh month, on the first *day* of the month, you shall have a sabbath-*rest,* a memorial of blowing of trumpets, a holy convocation. [25]You shall do no customary work *on it;* and you shall offer an offering made by fire to the LORD.' "

[26]And the LORD spoke to Moses, saying: [27]"Also the tenth *day* of this seventh month *shall be* the Day of Atonement. It shall be a holy convocation for you; you shall afflict your souls, and offer an offering made by fire to the LORD. [28]And you shall do no work on that same day, for it *is* the Day of Atonement, to make atonement for you before the LORD your God. [29]For any person who is not afflicted *in soul* on that same day shall be cut off from his people. [30]And any person who does any work on that same day, that person I will destroy from among his people. [31]You shall do no manner of work; *it shall be* a statute forever throughout your generations in all your dwellings. [32]It *shall be* to you a sabbath of *solemn* rest, and you shall afflict your souls; on the ninth *day* of the month at evening, from evening to evening, you shall celebrate your sabbath."

[33]Then the LORD spoke to Moses, saying, [34]"Speak to the children of Israel, saying: 'The fifteenth day of this seventh month *shall be* the Feast of Tabernacles *for* seven days to the LORD. [35]On the first day *there shall be* a holy convocation. You shall do no customary work *on it.* [36]*For* seven days you shall offer an offering made by fire

to the Lord. On the eighth day you shall have a holy convocation, and you shall offer an offering made by fire to the Lord. It *is* a sacred assembly, *and* you shall do no customary work *on it*.

37"These *are* the feasts of the Lord which you shall proclaim *to be* holy convocations, to offer an offering made by fire to the Lord, a burnt offering and a grain offering, a sacrifice and drink offerings, everything on its day— 38besides the Sabbaths of the Lord, besides your gifts, besides all your vows, and besides all your freewill offerings which you give to the Lord.

39"Also on the fifteenth day of the seventh month, when you have gathered in the fruit of the land, you shall keep the feast of the Lord *for* seven days; on the first day *there shall be* a sabbath-*rest,* and on the eighth day a sabbath-*rest.* 40And you shall take for yourselves on the first day the fruit of beautiful trees, branches of palm trees, the boughs of leafy trees, and willows of the brook; and you shall rejoice before the Lord your God for seven days. 41You shall keep it as a feast to the Lord for seven days in the year. *It shall be* a statute forever in your generations. You shall celebrate it in the seventh month. 42You shall dwell in booths for seven days. All who are native Israelites shall dwell in booths, 43that your generations may know that I made the children of Israel dwell in booths when I brought them out of the land of Egypt: I *am* the Lord your God.' "

44So Moses declared to the children of Israel the feasts of the Lord.

MARK 9:30–10:12

THEN they [Jesus and his disciples] departed from there and passed through Galilee, and He did not want anyone to know *it*. 31For He taught His disciples and said to them, "The Son of Man is being betrayed into the hands of men, and they will kill Him. And after He is killed, He will rise the third day." 32But they did not understand this saying, and were afraid to ask Him.

33Then He came to Capernaum. And when He was in the house He asked them, "What was it you disputed among yourselves on the road?" 34But they kept silent, for on the road they had disputed among themselves who *would be the* greatest. 35And He sat down, called the twelve, and said to them, "If anyone desires to be first, he shall be last of all and servant of all." 36Then He took a little child and set him in the midst of them. And when He had taken him in His arms, He said to them, 37"Whoever receives one of these little children in My name receives Me; and whoever receives Me, receives not Me but Him who sent Me."

38Now John answered Him, saying, "Teacher, we saw someone who does not follow us casting out demons in Your name, and we forbade him because he does not follow us."

39But Jesus said, "Do not forbid him, for no one who works a miracle in My name can soon afterward speak evil of Me. 40For he who is not against us is on our* side. 41For whoever gives you a cup of water to drink in My name, because you belong to Christ, assuredly, I say to you, he will by no means lose his reward.

42"But whoever causes one of these little ones who believe in Me to stumble, it would be better for him if a millstone were hung around his neck, and he were thrown into the sea. 43If your hand causes you to sin, cut it off. It is better for you to enter into life maimed, rather than having two hands, to go to hell, into the fire that shall never be quenched— 44where

*'Their worm does not die
And the fire is not quenched.'**

45And if your foot causes you to sin, cut it off. It is better for you to enter life lame, rather than having two feet, to be cast into hell, into the fire that shall never be quenched— 46where

> 'Their worm does not die
> And the fire is not quenched.'*

47And if your eye causes you to sin, pluck it out. It is better for you to enter the kingdom of God with one eye, rather than having two eyes, to be cast into hell fire— 48where

> 'Their worm does not die
> And the fire is not quenched.'*

49"For everyone will be seasoned with fire,* and every sacrifice will be seasoned with salt. 50Salt is good, but if the salt loses its flavor, how will you season it? Have salt in yourselves, and have peace with one another."

THEN He arose from there and came to the region of Judea by the other side of the Jordan. And multitudes gathered to Him again, and as He was accustomed, He taught them again. 2The Pharisees came and asked Him, "Is it lawful for a man to divorce his wife?" testing Him. 3And He answered and said to them, "What did Moses command you?" 4They said, "Moses permitted a man to write a certificate of divorce, and to dismiss her." 5And Jesus answered and said to them, "Because of the hardness of your heart he wrote you this precept. 6But from the beginning of the creation, God 'made them male and female.' * 7'For this reason a man shall leave his father and mother and be joined to his wife, 8and the two shall become one flesh';* so then they are no longer two, but one flesh. 9Therefore what God has joined together, let not man separate." 10In the house His disciples also asked Him again about the same matter.

11So He said to them, "Whoever divorces his wife and marries another commits adultery against her. 12And if a woman divorces her husband and marries another, she commits adultery."

PSALM 44:1-8

To the Chief Musician. A Contemplation of the sons of Korah.*

WE have heard with our ears, O God,
Our fathers have told us,
The deeds You did in their days,
In days of old:
2 You drove out the nations with Your hand,
But them You planted;
You afflicted the peoples, and cast them out.
3 For they did not gain possession of the land by their own sword,
Nor did their own arm save them;
But it was Your right hand, Your arm, and the light of Your countenance,
Because You favored them.

4 You are my King, O God;*
Command* victories for Jacob.
5 Through You we will push down our enemies;
Through Your name we will trample those who rise up against us.
6 For I will not trust in my bow, Nor shall my sword save me.
7 But You have saved us from our enemies,
And have put to shame those who hated us.
8 In God we boast all day long, And praise Your name forever.
Selah

PROVERBS FOR TODAY/ 10:19

In the multitude of words sin is not lacking, but he who restrains his lips is *wise.*

MARCH 1

LEVITICUS 24:1–25:46

THEN the LORD spoke to Moses, saying: [2]"Command the children of Israel that they bring to you pure oil of pressed olives for the light, to make the lamps burn continually. [3]Outside the veil of the Testimony, in the tabernacle of meeting, Aaron shall be in charge of it from evening until morning before the LORD continually; *it shall be* a statute forever in your generations. [4]He shall be in charge of the lamps on the pure *gold* lampstand before the LORD continually.

[5]"And you shall take fine flour and bake twelve cakes with it. Two-tenths *of an ephah* shall be in each cake. [6]You shall set them in two rows, six in a row, on the pure *gold* table before the LORD. [7]And you shall put pure frankincense on *each* row, that it may be on the bread for a memorial, an offering made by fire to the LORD. [8]Every Sabbath he shall set it in order before the LORD continually, *being taken* from the children of Israel by an everlasting covenant. [9]And it shall be for Aaron and his sons, and they shall eat it in a holy place; for it *is* most holy to him from the offerings of the LORD made by fire, by a perpetual statute."

[10]Now the son of an Israelite woman, whose father *was* an Egyptian, went out among the children of Israel; and this Israelite *woman's* son and a man of Israel fought each other in the camp. [11]And the Israelite woman's son blasphemed the name *of the LORD* and cursed; and so they brought him to Moses. (His mother's name *was* Shelo-mith the daughter of Dibri, of the tribe of Dan.) [12]Then they put him in custody, that the mind of the LORD might be shown to them.

[13]And the LORD spoke to Moses, saying, [14]"Take outside the camp him who has cursed; then let all who heard *him* lay their hands on his head, and let all the congregation stone him. [15]"Then you shall speak to the children of Israel, saying: 'Whoever curses his God shall bear his sin. [16]And whoever blasphemes the name of the LORD shall surely be put to death. All the congregation shall certainly stone him, the stranger as well as him who is born in the land. When he blasphemes the name *of the LORD,* he shall be put to death.

[17]'Whoever kills any man shall surely be put to death. [18]Whoever kills an animal shall make it good, animal for animal.

[19]'If a man causes disfigurement of his neighbor, as he has done, so shall it be done to him— [20]fracture for fracture, eye for eye, tooth for tooth; as he has caused disfigurement of a man, so shall it be done to him. [21]And whoever kills an animal shall restore it; but whoever kills a man shall be put to death. [22]You shall have the same law for the stranger and for one from your own country; for I *am* the LORD your God.' "

[23]Then Moses spoke to the children of Israel; and they took outside the camp him who had cursed, and stoned him with stones. So the children of Israel did as the LORD commanded Moses.

"Go into all the world and preach the gospel."

Mark 16:15

"Love . . . bears all things."
1 Corinthians 13:4, 7

AND the LORD spoke to Moses on Mount Sinai, saying, ²"Speak to the children of Israel, and say to them: 'When you come into the land which I give you, then the land shall keep a sabbath to the LORD. ³Six years you shall sow your field, and six years you shall prune your vineyard, and gather its fruit; ⁴but in the seventh year there shall be a sabbath of solemn rest for the land, a sabbath to the LORD. You shall neither sow your field nor prune your vineyard. ⁵What grows of its own accord of your harvest you shall not reap, nor gather the grapes of your untended vine, *for* it is a year of rest for the land. ⁶And the sabbath *produce* of the land shall be food for you: for you, your male and female servants, your hired man, and the stranger who dwells with you, ⁷for your livestock and the beasts that *are* in your land—all its produce shall be for food.

⁸And you shall count seven sabbaths of years for yourself, seven times seven years; and the time of the seven sabbaths of years shall be to you forty-nine years. ⁹Then you shall cause the trumpet of the Jubilee to sound on the tenth *day* of the seventh month; on the Day of Atonement you shall make the trumpet to sound throughout all your land. ¹⁰And you shall consecrate the fiftieth year, and proclaim liberty throughout *all* the land to all its inhabitants. It shall be a Jubilee for you; and each of you shall return to his possession, and each of you shall return to his family. ¹¹That fiftieth year shall be a Jubilee to you; in it you shall neither sow nor reap what grows of its own accord, nor gather *the grapes* of your untended vine. ¹²For it *is* the Jubilee; it shall be holy to you; you shall eat its produce from the field.

¹³In this Year of Jubilee, each of you shall return to his possession. ¹⁴And if you sell anything to your neighbor or buy from your neighbor's hand, you shall not oppress one another. ¹⁵According to the number of years after the Jubilee you shall buy from your neighbor, and according to the number of years of crops he shall sell to you. ¹⁶According to the multitude of years you shall increase its price, and according to the fewer number of years you shall diminish its price; for he sells to you *according* to the number *of the years* of the crops. ¹⁷Therefore you shall not oppress one another, but you shall fear your God; for I *am* the LORD your God.

¹⁸"So you shall observe My statutes and keep My judgments, and perform them; and you will dwell in the land in safety. ¹⁹Then the land will yield its fruit, and you will eat your fill, and dwell there in safety.

²⁰"And if you say, "What shall we eat in the seventh year, since we shall not sow nor gather in our produce?" ²¹Then I will command My blessing on you in the sixth year, and it will bring forth produce enough for three years. ²²And you shall sow in the eighth year, and eat old produce until the ninth year; until its produce comes in, you shall eat *of* the old *harvest*.

²³"The land shall not be sold permanently, for the land *is* Mine; for you *are* strangers and sojourners with Me. ²⁴And in all the land of your possession you shall grant redemption of the land.

²⁵"If one of your brethren becomes poor, and has sold *some* of his possession, and if his redeeming relative comes to redeem it, then he may redeem what his brother sold. ²⁶Or if the man has no one to redeem it, but he himself becomes able to redeem it, ²⁷then let him count the years since its sale, and restore the remainder to the man to whom he sold it, that he may return to his possession. ²⁸But if he is not able to have *it* restored to himself, then what was sold shall remain in the hand of him who bought it until the Year of Jubilee; and in the Jubilee it

shall be released, and he shall return to his possession.

29"If a man sells a house in a walled city, then he may redeem it within a whole year after it is sold; *within* a full year he may redeem it. 30But if it is not redeemed within the space of a full year, then the house in the walled city shall belong permanently to him who bought it, throughout his generations. It shall not be released in the Jubilee. 31However the houses of villages which have no wall around them shall be counted as the fields of the country. They may be redeemed, and they shall be released in the Jubilee. 32Nevertheless the cities of the Levites, *and* the houses in the cities of their possession, the Levites may redeem at any time. 33And if a man purchases a house from the Levites, then the house that was sold in the city of his possession shall be released in the Jubilee; for the houses in the cities of the Levites *are* their possession among the children of Israel. 34But the field of the common-land of their cities may not be sold, for it *is* their perpetual possession.

35"If one of your brethren becomes poor, and falls into poverty among you, then you shall help him, like a stranger or a sojourner, that he may live with you. 36Take no usury or interest from him; but fear your God, that your brother may live with you. 37You shall not lend him your money for usury, nor lend him your food at a profit. 38I *am* the LORD your God, who brought you out of the land of Egypt, to give you the land of Canaan *and* to be your God.

39"And if *one of* your brethren *who dwells* by you becomes poor, and sells himself to you, you shall not compel him to serve as a slave. 40As a hired servant *and* a sojourner he shall be with you, *and* shall serve you until the Year of Jubilee. 41And *then* he shall depart from you—he and his children with him—and shall return to his own family. He shall return to the possession of his fathers. 42For they *are* My servants, whom I brought out of the land of Egypt; they shall not be sold as slaves. 43You shall not rule over him with rigor, but you shall fear your God. 44And as for your male and female slaves whom you may have—from the nations that are around you, from them you may buy male and female slaves. 45Moreover you may buy the children of the strangers who dwell among you, and their families who are with you, which they beget in your land; and they shall become your property. 46And you may take them as an inheritance for your children after you, to inherit *them as* a possession; they shall be your permanent slaves. But regarding your brethren, the children of Israel, you shall not rule over one another with rigor.'"

MARK 10:13-31

THEN they [the people] brought little children to Him, that He might touch them; but the disciples rebuked those who brought *them.* 14But when Jesus saw *it,* He was greatly displeased and said to them, "Let the little children come to Me, and do not forbid them; for of such is the kingdom of God. 15Assuredly, I say to you, whoever does not receive the kingdom of God as a little child will by no means enter it." 16And He took them up in His arms, laid *His* hands on them, and blessed them.

17Now as He was going out on the road, one came running, knelt before Him, and asked Him, "Good Teacher, what shall I do that I may inherit eternal life?"

18So Jesus said to him, "Why do you call Me good? No one *is* good but One, *that is,* God. 19You know the commandments: *'Do not commit adultery,' 'Do* not murder,' 'Do not steal,' 'Do not bear false witness,' 'Do not defraud,' 'Honor your father and your mother.' " *

²⁰And he answered and said to Him, "Teacher, all these things I have kept from my youth."

²¹Then Jesus, looking at him, loved him, and said to him, "One thing you lack: Go your way, sell whatever you have and give to the poor, and you will have treasure in heaven; and come, take up the cross, and follow Me."

²²But he was sad at this word, and went away sorrowful, for he had great possessions.

²³Then Jesus looked around and said to His disciples, "How hard it is for those who have riches to enter the kingdom of God!" ²⁴And the disciples were astonished at His words. But Jesus answered again and said to them, "Children, how hard it is for those who trust in riches* to enter the kingdom of God! ²⁵It is easier for a camel to go through the eye of a needle than for a rich man to enter the kingdom of God."

²⁶And they were greatly astonished, saying among themselves, "Who then can be saved?"

²⁷But Jesus looked at them and said, "With men it is impossible, but not with God; for with God all things are possible."

²⁸Then Peter began to say to Him, "See, we have left all and followed You."

²⁹So Jesus answered and said, "Assuredly, I say to you, there is no one who has left house or brothers or sisters or father or mother or wife* or children or lands, for My sake and the gospel's, ³⁰who shall not receive a hundredfold now in this time—houses and brothers and sisters and mothers and children and lands, with persecutions—and in the age to come, eternal life. ³¹But many who are first will be last, and the last first."

PSALM 44:9-26

BUT You [God] have cast us off and put us to shame, And You do not go out with our armies.

10 You make us turn back from the enemy, And those who hate us have taken spoil for themselves.

11 You have given us up like sheep intended for food, And have scattered us among the nations.

12 You sell Your people for next to nothing, And are not enriched by selling them.

13 You make us a reproach to our neighbors, A scorn and a derision to those all around us.

14 You make us a byword among the nations, A shaking of the head among the peoples.

15 My dishonor is continually before me, And the shame of my face has covered me,

16 Because of the voice of him who reproaches and reviles, Because of the enemy and the avenger.

17 All this has come upon us; But we have not forgotten You, Nor have we dealt falsely with Your covenant.

18 Our heart has not turned back, Nor have our steps departed from Your way;

19 But You have severely broken us in the place of jackals, And covered us with the shadow of death.

20 If we had forgotten the name
of our God,
Or stretched out our hands to
a foreign god,
21 Would not God search this
out?
For He knows the secrets of
the heart.
22 Yet for Your sake we are
killed all day long;
We are accounted as sheep
for the slaughter.

23 Awake! Why do You sleep,
O Lord?
Arise! Do not cast *us* off
forever.
24 Why do You hide Your face,
And forget our affliction and
our oppression?
25 For our soul is bowed down to
the dust;
Our body clings to the ground.
26 Arise for our help,
And redeem us for Your
mercies' sake.

PROVERBS FOR TODAY/ 10:20-21

The tongue of the righteous is *choice silver; the heart of the wicked* is worth *little.*
The lips of the righteous feed many, but fools die for lack of wisdom. *

MARCH 2

LEVITICUS 25:47–27:13

"**N**ow if a sojourner or stranger close to you becomes rich, and *one of* your brethren *who dwells* by him becomes poor, and sells himself to the stranger *or* sojourner close to you, or to a member of the stranger's family, 48after he is sold he may be redeemed again. One of his brothers may redeem him; 49or his uncle or his uncle's son may redeem him; or *anyone* who is near of kin to him in his family may redeem him; or if he is able he may redeem himself. 50Thus he shall reckon with him who bought him: The price of his release shall be according to the number of years, from the year that he was sold to him until the Year of Jubilee; *it shall be* according to the time of a hired servant for him. 51If *there are* still many years *remaining,* according to them he shall repay the price of his

redemption from the money with which he was bought. 52And if there remain but a few years until the Year of Jubilee, then he shall reckon with him, *and* according to his years he shall repay him the price of his redemption. 53He shall be with him as a yearly hired servant, and he shall not rule with rigor over him in your sight. 54And if he is not redeemed in these *years,* then he shall be released in the Year of Jubilee—he and his children with him. 55For the children of Israel *are* servants to Me; they *are* My servants whom I brought out of the land of Egypt: I *am* the LORD your God.

'You shall not make idols for your selves;
neither a carved image nor a *sacred* pillar shall you rear up for yourselves;
nor shall you set up an en-

graved stone in your land, to bow down to it;
for I *am* the LORD your God.

2 You shall keep My Sabbaths and reverence My sanctuary:
I *am* the LORD.

3 'If you walk in My statutes and keep My commandments, and perform them,

4 then I will give you rain in its season, the land shall yield its produce, and the trees of the field shall yield their fruit.

5 Your threshing shall last till the time of vintage, and the vintage shall last till the time of sowing;
you shall eat your bread to the full, and dwell in your land safely.

6 I will give peace in the land, and you shall lie down, and none will make *you* afraid;
I will rid the land of evil beasts, and the sword will not go through your land.

7 You will chase your enemies, and they shall fall by the sword before you.

8 Five of you shall chase a hundred, and a hundred of you shall put ten thousand to flight;
your enemies shall fall by the sword before you.

9 'For I will look on you favorably and make you fruitful, multiply you and confirm My covenant with you.

10 You shall eat the old harvest, and clear out the old because of the new.

11 I will set My tabernacle among you, and My soul shall not abhor you.

12 I will walk among you and be your God, and you shall be My people.

13 I *am* the LORD your God, who brought you out of the land of Egypt, that *you* should not be their slaves;
I have broken the bands of your yoke and made you walk upright.

14 'But if you do not obey Me, and do not observe all these commandments,

15 and if you despise My statutes, or if your soul abhors My judgments, so that you do not perform all My commandments, *but* break My covenant,

16 I also will do this to you:
I will even appoint terror over you, wasting disease and fever which shall consume the eyes and cause sorrow of heart.
And you shall sow your seed in vain, for your enemies shall eat it.

17 I will set My face against you, and you shall be defeated by your enemies.
Those who hate you shall reign over you, and you shall flee when no one pursues you.

18 'And after all this, if you do not obey Me, then I will punish you seven times more for your sins.

19 I will break the pride of your power;
I will make your heavens like iron and your earth like bronze.

20 And your strength shall be spent in vain;
for your land shall not yield its produce, nor shall the trees of the land yield their fruit.

21 'Then, if you walk contrary to Me, and are not willing to obey Me, I will bring on you seven times more plagues, according to your sins.

22 I will also send wild beasts among you, which shall rob you of your children, destroy your livestock, and make you few in number;

and your highways shall be desolate.

23 'And if by these things you are not reformed by Me, but walk contrary to Me,

24 then I also will walk contrary to you, and I will punish you yet seven times for your sins.

25 And I will bring a sword against you that will execute the vengeance of the covenant;

when you are gathered together within your cities I will send pestilence among you;

and you shall be delivered into the hand of the enemy.

26 When I have cut off your supply of bread, ten women shall bake your bread in one oven, and they shall bring back your bread by weight, and you shall eat and not be satisfied.

27 'And after all this, if you do not obey Me, but walk contrary to Me,

28 then I also will walk contrary to you in fury;

and I, even I, will chastise you seven times for your sins.

29 You shall eat the flesh of your sons, and you shall eat the flesh of your daughters.

30 I will destroy your high places, cut down your incense altars, and cast your carcasses on the lifeless forms of your idols;

and My soul shall abhor you.

31 I will lay your cities waste and bring your sanctuaries to desolation, and I will not smell the fragrance of your sweet aromas.

32 I will bring the land to desolation, and your enemies who dwell in it shall be astonished at it.

33 I will scatter you among the nations and draw out a sword after you;

your land shall be desolate and your cities waste.

34 Then the land shall enjoy its sabbaths as long as it lies desolate and you *are* in your enemies' land;

then the land shall rest and enjoy its sabbaths.

35 As long as *it* lies desolate it shall rest—

for the time it did not rest on your sabbaths when you dwelt in it.

36 'And as for those of you who are left, I will send faintness into their hearts in the lands of their enemies;

the sound of a shaken leaf shall cause them to flee;

they shall flee as though fleeing from a sword, and they shall fall when no one pursues.

37 They shall stumble over one another, as it were before a sword, when no one pursues;

and you shall have no *power* to stand before your enemies.

38 You shall perish among the nations, and the land of your enemies shall eat you up.

39 And those of you who are left shall waste away in their iniquity in your enemies' lands;

also in their fathers' iniquities, which are with them, they shall waste away.

40 '*But* if they confess their iniquity and the iniquity of their fathers, with their unfaithfulness in which they were unfaithful to Me, and that they also have walked contrary to Me,

41 and *that* I also have walked contrary to them and have brought them into the land of their enemies; if their uncircumcised hearts are humbled, and they accept their guilt—

42 then I will remember My covenant with Jacob, and My covenant with Isaac and My covenant with Abraham I will remember; I will remember the land.

43 The land also shall be left empty by them, and will enjoy its sabbaths while it lies desolate without them; they will accept their guilt, because they despised My judgments and because their soul abhorred My statutes.

44 Yet for all that, when they are in the land of their enemies, I will not cast them away, nor shall I abhor them, to utterly destroy them and break My covenant with them; for I *am* the LORD their God.

45 But for their sake I will remember the covenant of their ancestors, whom I brought out of the land of Egypt in the sight of the nations, that I might be their God: I *am* the LORD.' "

46These *are* the statutes and judgments and laws which the LORD made between Himself and the children of Israel on Mount Sinai by the hand of Moses.

Now the LORD spoke to Moses, saying, 2"Speak to the children of Israel, and say to them: 'When a man consecrates by a vow certain persons to the LORD, according to your valuation, 3if your valuation is of a male from twenty years old up to sixty years old, then your valuation shall be fifty shekels of silver, according to the shekel of the sanctuary. 4If it *is* a female, then your valuation shall be thirty shekels; 5and if from five years old up to twenty years old, then your valuation for a male shall be twenty shekels, and for a female ten shekels; 6and if from a month old up to five years old, then your valuation for a male shall be five shekels of silver, and for a female your valuation shall be three shekels of silver; 7and if from sixty years old and above, if *it is* a male, then your valuation shall be fifteen shekels, and for a female ten shekels.

8'But if he is too poor to pay your valuation, then he shall present himself before the priest, and the priest shall set a value for him; according to the ability of him who vowed, the priest shall value him.

9'If *it is* an animal that men may bring as an offering to the LORD, all that *anyone* gives to the LORD shall be holy. 10He shall not substitute it or exchange it, good for bad or bad for good; and if he at all exchanges animal for animal, then both it and the one exchanged for it shall be holy. 11If *it is* an unclean animal which they do not offer as a sacrifice to the LORD, then he shall present the animal before the priest; 12and the priest shall set a value for it, whether it is good or bad; as you, the priest, value it, so it shall be. 13But if he *wants* at all *to* redeem it, then he must add one-fifth to your valuation.' "

MARK 10:32-52

Now they [the disciples] were on the road, going up to Jerusalem, and Jesus was going before them; and they were amazed. And as they followed they were afraid. Then He took the twelve aside again and began to tell them the things that would happen to Him: ³³"Behold, we are going up to Jerusalem, and the Son of Man will be betrayed to the chief priests and to the scribes; and they will condemn Him to death and deliver Him to the Gentiles; ³⁴and they will mock Him, and scourge Him, and spit on Him, and kill Him. And the third day He will rise again."

³⁵Then James and John, the sons of Zebedee, came to Him, saying, "Teacher, we want You to do for us whatever we ask."

³⁶And He said to them, "What do you want Me to do for you?"

³⁷They said to Him, "Grant us that we may sit, one on Your right hand and the other on Your left, in Your glory."

³⁸But Jesus said to them, "You do not know what you ask. Are you able to drink the cup that I drink, and be baptized with the baptism that I am baptized with?"

³⁹They said to Him, "We are able."

So Jesus said to them, "You will indeed drink the cup that I drink, and with the baptism I am baptized with you will be baptized; ⁴⁰but to sit on My right hand and on My left is not Mine to give, but *it is for those* for whom it is prepared."

⁴¹And when the ten heard *it,* they began to be greatly displeased with James and John. ⁴²But Jesus called them to *Himself* and said to them, "You know that those who are considered rulers over the Gentiles lord it over them, and their great ones exercise authority over them. ⁴³Yet it shall not be so among you; but whoever desires to become great among you shall be your servant. ⁴⁴And whoever of you desires to be first shall be slave of all. ⁴⁵For even the Son of Man did not come to be served, but to serve, and to give His life a ransom for many."

⁴⁶Now they came to Jericho. As He went out of Jericho with His disciples and a great multitude, blind Bartimaeus, the son of Timaeus, sat by the road begging. ⁴⁷And when he heard that it was Jesus of Nazareth, he began to cry out and say, "Jesus, Son of David, have mercy on me!"

⁴⁸Then many warned him to be quiet; but he cried out all the more, "Son of David, have mercy on me!"

⁴⁹So Jesus stood still and commanded him to be called.

Then they called the blind man, saying to him, "Be of good cheer. Rise, He is calling you."

⁵⁰And throwing aside his garment, he rose and came to Jesus.

⁵¹So Jesus answered and said to him, "What do you want Me to do for you?"

The blind man said to Him, "Rabboni, that I may receive my sight."

⁵²Then Jesus said to him, "Go your way; your faith has made you well." And immediately he received his sight and followed Jesus on the road.

PSALM 45:1-17

To the Chief Musician. Set to "The Lilies." * *A Contemplation* * *of the sons of Korah. A Song of Love.*

My heart is overflowing with a good theme;
    I recite my composition concerning the King;
    My tongue *is* the pen of a ready writer.

2   You are fairer than the sons of men;
    Grace is poured upon Your lips;

Therefore God has blessed
You forever.

3 Gird Your sword upon *Your*
thigh, O Mighty One,
With Your glory and Your
majesty.

4 And in Your majesty ride
prosperously because of
truth, humility, *and*
righteousness;
And Your right hand shall
teach You awesome things.

5 Your arrows *are* sharp in the
heart of the King's enemies;
The peoples fall under You.

6 Your throne, O God, *is* forever
and ever;
A scepter of righteousness *is*
the scepter of Your
kingdom.

7 You love righteousness and
hate wickedness;
Therefore God, Your God, has
anointed You
With the oil of gladness more
than Your companions.

8 All Your garments are scented
with myrrh and aloes *and*
cassia,
Out of the ivory palaces, by
which they have made You
glad.

9 Kings' daughters *are* among
Your honorable women;
At Your right hand stands the
queen in gold from Ophir.

10 Listen, O daughter,
Consider and incline your ear;
Forget your own people also,
and your father's house;

11 So the King will greatly desire
your beauty;
Because He *is* your Lord,
worship Him.

12 And the daughter of Tyre *will
come* with a gift;
The rich among the people
will seek your favor.

13 The royal daughter *is* all
glorious within *the palace;*
Her clothing *is* woven with
gold.

14 She shall be brought to the
King in robes of many
colors;
The virgins, her companions
who follow her, shall be
brought to You.

15 With gladness and rejoicing
they shall be brought;
They shall enter the King's
palace.

16 Instead of Your fathers shall
be Your sons,
Whom You shall make
princes in all the earth.

17 I will make Your name to be
remembered in all
generations;
Therefore the people shall
praise You forever and ever.

PROVERBS FOR TODAY/ 10:22

The blessing of the LORD makes one *rich, and He adds no sorrow with it.*

MARCH 3

LEVITICUS 27:14—NUMBERS 1:54

"**A**ND when a man dedicates his house *to be* holy to the LORD, then the priest shall set a value for it, whether it is good or bad; as the priest values it, so it shall stand. 15If he who dedicated it *wants to* redeem his house, then he must add one-fifth of the money of your valuation to it, and it shall be his.

16'If a man dedicates to the LORD *part* of a field of his possession, then your valuation shall be according to the seed for it. A homer of barley seed *shall be valued* at fifty shekels of silver. 17If he dedicates his field from the Year of Jubilee, according to your valuation it shall stand. 18But if he dedicates his field after the Jubilee, then the priest shall reckon to him the money due according to the years that remain till the Year of Jubilee, and it shall be deducted from your valuation. 19And if he who dedicates the field ever wishes to redeem it, then he must add one-fifth of the money of your valuation to it, and it shall belong to him. 20But if he does not want to redeem the field, or if he has sold the field to another man, it shall not be redeemed anymore; 21but the field, when it is released in the Jubilee, shall be holy to the LORD, as a devoted field; it shall be the possession of the priest.

22'And if a man dedicates to the LORD a field which he has bought, which is not the field of his possession, 23then the priest shall reckon to him the worth of your valuation, up to the Year of Jubilee, and he shall give your valuation on that day *as* a holy *offering* to the LORD. 24In the Year of Jubilee the field shall return to him from whom it was bought, to the one who *owned* the land as a possession. 25And all your valuations shall be according to the shekel of the sanctuary: twenty gerahs to the shekel.

26'But the firstborn of the animals, which should be the LORD's firstborn, no man shall dedicate; whether *it is* an ox or sheep, it *is* the LORD's. 27And if *it is* an unclean animal, then he shall redeem *it* according to your valuation, and shall add one-fifth to it; or if it is not redeemed, then it shall be sold according to your valuation.

28'Nevertheless no devoted *offering* that a man may devote to the LORD of all that he has, *both* man and beast, or the field of his possession, shall be sold or redeemed; every devoted *offering is* most holy to the LORD. 29No person under the ban, who may become doomed to destruction among men, shall be redeemed, *but* shall surely be put to death. 30And all the tithe of the land, *whether* of the seed of the land *or* of the fruit of the tree, *is* the LORD's. It *is* holy to the LORD. 31If a man wants at all to redeem *any* of his tithes, he shall add one-fifth to it. 32And concerning the tithe of the herd or the flock, of whatever passes under the rod, the tenth one shall be holy to the LORD. 33He shall not inquire whether it is good or bad, nor shall he exchange it; and if he exchanges it at all, then both it and the one exchanged for it shall be holy; it shall not be redeemed.' "

34These *are* the commandments which the LORD commanded Moses for the children of Israel on Mount Sinai.

Now the LORD spoke to Moses in the Wilderness of Sinai, in the tabernacle of meeting, on the first *day* of the second month, in the second year after they had come out of the land of Egypt, saying: 2"Take a census of all the congregation of the children of Israel, by their families, by their fathers' houses, according to the number of names, every male individually, 3from twenty years old and above—all who *are able to* go to war in Israel. You and Aaron shall number them by their armies. 4And with you there shall be a man from every tribe, each one the head of his father's house.

5"These are the names of the men who shall stand with you: from Reuben, Elizur the son of Shedeur; 6from Simeon, Shelumiel the son of Zurishaddai; 7from Judah, Nahshon the son of Amminadab; 8from Issachar, Nethanel the son of Zuar; 9from Zebulun, Eliab the son of Helon; 10from the sons of Joseph: from Ephraim, Elishama the son of Ammihud; from Manasseh, Gamaliel the son of Pedahzur; 11from Benjamin, Abidan the son of Gideoni; 12from Dan, Ahiezer the son of Ammishaddai; 13from Asher, Pagiel the son of Ocran; 14from Gad, Eliasaph the son of Deuel;* 15from Naphtali, Ahira the son of Enan." 16These *were* chosen from the congregation, leaders of their fathers' tribes, heads of the divisions in Israel.

17Then Moses and Aaron took these men who had been mentioned by name, 18and they assembled all the congregation together on the first *day* of the second month; and they recited their ancestry by families, by their fathers' houses, according to the number of names, from twenty years old and above, each one individually. 19As the LORD commanded Moses, so he numbered them in the Wilderness of Sinai.

20Now the children of Reuben, Israel's oldest son, their genealogies by their families, by their fathers' house, according to the number of names, every male individually, from twenty years old and above, all who *were able*

to go to war: 21those who were numbered of the tribe of Reuben *were* forty-six thousand five hundred.

22From the children of Simeon, their genealogies by their families, by their fathers' house, of those who were numbered, according to the number of names, every male individually, from twenty years old and above, all who *were able to* go to war: 23those who were numbered of the tribe of Simeon *were* fifty-nine thousand three hundred.

24From the children of Gad, their genealogies by their families, by their fathers' house, according to the number of names, from twenty years old and above, all who *were able to* go to war: 25those who were numbered of the tribe of Gad *were* forty-five thousand six hundred and fifty.

26From the children of Judah, their genealogies by their families, by their fathers' house, according to the number of names, from twenty years old and above, all who *were able to* go to war: 27those who were numbered of the tribe of Judah *were* seventy-four thousand six hundred.

28From the children of Issachar, their genealogies by their families, by their fathers' house, according to the number of names, from twenty years old and above, all who *were able to* go to war: 29those who were numbered of the tribe of Issachar *were* fifty-four thousand four hundred.

30From the children of Zebulun, their genealogies by their families, by their fathers' house, according to the number of names, from twenty years old and above, all who *were able to* go to war: 31those who were numbered of the tribe of Zebulun *were* fifty-seven thousand four hundred.

32From the sons of Joseph, the children of Ephraim, their genealogies by their families, by their fathers' house, according to the number of names, from twenty years old and above, all who *were able to* go to war: 33those who were numbered of the tribe of Ephraim *were* forty thousand five hundred.

³⁴From the children of Manasseh, their genealogies by their families, by their fathers' house, according to the number of names, from twenty years old and above, all who *were able to* go to war: ³⁵those who were numbered of the tribe of Manasseh *were* thirty-two thousand two hundred.

³⁶From the children of Benjamin, their genealogies by their families, by their fathers' house, according to the number of names, from twenty years old and above, all who *were able to* go to war: ³⁷those who were numbered of the tribe of Benjamin *were* thirty-five thousand four hundred.

³⁸From the children of Dan, their genealogies by their families, by their fathers' house, according to the number of names, from twenty years old and above, all who *were able to* go to war: ³⁹those who were numbered of the tribe of Dan *were* sixty-two thousand seven hundred.

⁴⁰From the children of Asher, their genealogies by their families, by their fathers' house, according to the number of names, from twenty years old and above, all who *were able to* go to war: ⁴¹those who were numbered of the tribe of Asher *were* forty-one thousand five hundred.

⁴²From the children of Naphtali, their genealogies by their families, by their fathers' house, according to the number of names, from twenty years old and above, all who *were able to* go to war: ⁴³those who were numbered of the tribe of Naphtali *were* fifty-three thousand four hundred.

⁴⁴These are the ones who were numbered, whom Moses and Aaron numbered, with the leaders of Israel, twelve men, each one representing his father's house. ⁴⁵So all who were numbered of the children of Israel, by their fathers' houses, from twenty years old

and above, all who *were able to* go to war in Israel— ⁴⁶all who were numbered were six hundred and three thousand five hundred and fifty.

⁴⁷But the Levites were not numbered among them by their fathers' tribe; ⁴⁸for the LORD had spoken to Moses, saying: ⁴⁹"Only the tribe of Levi you shall not number, nor take a census of them among the children of Israel; ⁵⁰but you shall appoint the Levites over the tabernacle of the Testimony, over all its furnishings, and over all things that belong to it; they shall carry the tabernacle and all its furnishings; they shall attend to it and camp around the tabernacle. ⁵¹And when the tabernacle is to go forward, the Levites shall take it down; and when the tabernacle is to be set up, the Levites shall set it up. The outsider who comes near shall be put to death. ⁵²The children of Israel shall pitch their tents, everyone by his own camp, everyone by his own standard, according to their armies; ⁵³but the Levites shall camp around the tabernacle of the Testimony, that there may be no wrath on the congregation of the children of Israel; and the Levites shall keep charge of the tabernacle of the Testimony."

⁵⁴Thus the children of Israel did; according to all that the LORD commanded Moses, so they did.

MARK 11:1-26

Now when they [Jesus and his disciples] drew near Jerusalem, to Bethphage* and Bethany, at the Mount of Olives, He sent two of His disciples; ²and He said to them, "Go into the village opposite you; and as soon as you have entered it you will find a colt tied, on which no one has sat. Loose it and bring *it.* ³And if anyone says to you, 'Why are you doing this?' say, 'The Lord has need of it,' and immediately he will send it here."

⁴So they went their way, and found the* colt tied by the door outside on the street, and they loosed it. ⁵But some of those who stood there said to them, "What are you doing, loosing the colt?"

⁶And they spoke to them just as Jesus had commanded. So they let them go. ⁷Then they brought the colt to Jesus and threw their clothes on it, and He sat on it. ⁸And many spread their clothes on the road, and others cut down leafy branches from the trees and spread *them* on the road. ⁹Then those who went before and those who followed cried out, saying:

"Hosanna!
'Blessed is He who comes in
the name of the Lᴏʀᴅ!' *
10   Blessed *is* the kingdom of our
father David
That comes in the name of
the Lord!*
Hosanna in the highest!"

¹¹And Jesus went into Jerusalem and into the temple. So when He had looked around at all things, as the hour was already late, He went out to Bethany with the twelve.

¹²Now the next day, when they had come out from Bethany, He was hungry. ¹³And seeing from afar a fig tree having leaves, He went to see if perhaps He would find something on it. When He came to it, He found nothing but leaves, for it was not the season for figs. ¹⁴In response Jesus said to it, "Let no one eat fruit from you ever again."

And His disciples heard *it.*

¹⁵So they came to Jerusalem. Then Jesus went into the temple and began to drive out those who bought and sold in the temple, and overturned the tables of the money changers and the seats of those who sold doves. ¹⁶And He would not allow anyone to carry wares through the temple. ¹⁷Then He

taught, saying to them, "Is it not written, *'My house shall be called a house of prayer for all nations'?* * But you have made it a *'den of thieves.'"* *

¹⁸And the scribes and chief priests heard it and sought how they might destroy Him; for they feared Him, because all the people were astonished at His teaching. ¹⁹When evening had come, He went out of the city.

²⁰Now in the morning, as they passed by, they saw the fig tree dried up from the roots. ²¹And Peter, remembering, said to Him, "Rabbi, look! The fig tree which You cursed has withered away."

²²So Jesus answered and said to them, "Have faith in God. ²³For assuredly, I say to you, whoever says to this mountain, 'Be removed and be cast into the sea,' and does not doubt in his heart, but believes that those things he says will be done, he will have whatever he says. ²⁴Therefore I say to you, whatever things you ask when you pray, believe that you receive *them,* and you will have *them.*

²⁵"And whenever you stand praying, if you have anything against anyone, forgive him, that your Father in heaven may also forgive you your trespasses. ²⁶But if you do not forgive, neither will your Father in heaven forgive your trespasses."*

PSALM 46:1-11

To the Chief Musician. A Psalm of the sons of Korah. A Song for Alamoth.

Gᴏᴅ *is* our refuge and strength,
A very present help in trouble.
²Therefore we will not fear,
Even though the earth be
removed,
And though the mountains be
carried into the midst of the
sea;
3   *Though* its waters roar *and* be
troubled,

Though the mountains shake
　　with its swelling.　　Selah

4　*There is* a river whose streams
　　shall make glad the city of
　　God,
　The holy *place* of the
　　tabernacle of the Most
　　High.
5　God *is* in the midst of her, she
　　shall not be moved;
　God shall help her, just at the
　　break of dawn.
6　The nations raged, the
　　kingdoms were moved;
　He uttered His voice, the
　　earth melted.

7　The Lord of hosts *is* with us;
　The God of Jacob *is* our
　　refuge.　　Selah

8　Come, behold the works of
　　the Lord,
　Who has made desolations in
　　the earth.
9　He makes wars cease to the
　　end of the earth;
　He breaks the bow and cuts
　　the spear in two;
　He burns the chariot in the
　　fire.

10　Be still, and know that I *am*
　　God;
　I will be exalted among the
　　nations,
　I will be exalted in the earth!

11　The Lord of hosts *is* with us;
　The God of Jacob *is* our
　　refuge.　　Selah

PROVERBS FOR TODAY/ 10:23

To do evil is *like sport to a fool, but a man of understanding has wisdom.*

MARCH 4

NUMBERS 2:1–3:51

AND the Lord spoke to Moses and Aaron, saying: 2"Everyone of the children of Israel shall camp by his own standard, beside the emblems of his father's house; they shall camp some distance from the tabernacle of meeting. 3On the east side, toward the rising of the sun, those of the standard of the forces with Judah shall camp according to their armies; and Nahshon the son of Amminadab *shall be* the leader of the children of Judah." 4And his army was numbered at seventy-four thousand six hundred. 5"Those who camp next to him *shall*

be the tribe of Issachar, and Nethanel the son of Zuar *shall be* the leader of the children of Issachar." 6And his army was numbered at fifty-four thousand four hundred.

7"Then *comes* the tribe of Zebulun, and Eliab the son of Helon *shall be* the leader of the children of Zebulun." 8And his army was numbered at fifty-seven thousand four hundred. 9"All who were numbered according to their armies of the forces with Judah, one hundred and eighty-six thousand four hundred—these shall break camp first.

10"On the south side *shall be* the standard of the forces with Reuben according to their armies, and the leader of the children of Reuben *shall be* Elizur the son of Shedeur." ¹¹And his army was numbered at forty-six thousand five hundred.

¹²"Those who camp next to him *shall be* the tribe of Simeon, and the leader of the children of Simeon *shall be* Shelumiel the son of Zurishaddai." ¹³And his army was numbered at fifty-nine thousand three hundred.

¹⁴"Then *comes* the tribe of Gad, and the leader of the children of Gad *shall be* Eliasaph the son of Reuel."* ¹⁵And his army was numbered at forty-five thousand six hundred and fifty. ¹⁶"All who were numbered according to their armies of the forces with Reuben, one hundred and fifty-one thousand four hundred and fifty—they shall be the second to break camp.

¹⁷"And the tabernacle of meeting shall move out with the camp of the Levites in the middle of the camps; as they camp, so they shall move out, everyone in his place, by their standards.

¹⁸"On the west side *shall be* the standard of the forces with Ephraim according to their armies, and the leader of the children of Ephraim *shall be* Elishama the son of Ammihud." ¹⁹And his army was numbered at forty thousand five hundred.

²⁰"Next to him *comes* the tribe of Manasseh, and the leader of the children of Manasseh *shall be* Gamaliel the son of Pedahzur." ²¹And his army was numbered at thirty-two thousand two hundred.

²²"Then *comes* the tribe of Benjamin, and the leader of the children of Benjamin *shall be* Abidan the son of Gideoni." ²³And his army was numbered at thirty-five thousand four hundred. ²⁴"All who were numbered according to their armies of the forces with Ephraim, one hundred and eight thousand one hundred—they shall be the third to break camp.

²⁵"The standard of the forces with Dan *shall be* on the north side according to their armies, and the leader of the children of Dan *shall be* Ahiezer the son of Ammishaddai." ²⁶And his army was numbered at sixty-two thousand seven hundred.

²⁷"Those who camp next to him *shall be* the tribe of Asher, and the leader of the children of Asher *shall be* Pagiel the son of Ocran." ²⁸And his army was numbered at forty-one thousand five hundred.

²⁹"Then *comes* the tribe of Naphtali, and the leader of the children of Naphtali *shall be* Ahira the son of Enan." ³⁰And his army was numbered at fifty-three thousand four hundred. ³¹"All who were numbered of the forces with Dan, one hundred and fifty-seven thousand six hundred—they shall break camp last, with their standards."

³²These *are* the ones who were numbered of the children of Israel by their fathers' houses. All who were numbered according to their armies of the forces *were* six hundred and three thousand five hundred and fifty. ³³But the Levites were not numbered among the children of Israel, just as the LORD commanded Moses.

³⁴Thus the children of Israel did according to all that the LORD commanded Moses; so they camped by their standards and so they broke camp, each one by his family, according to their fathers' houses.

Now these *are* the records of Aaron and Moses when the LORD spoke with Moses on Mount Sinai. ²And these *are* the names of the sons of Aaron: Nadab, the firstborn, and Abihu, Eleazar, and Ithamar. ³These *are* the names of the sons of Aaron, the anointed priests, whom he consecrated to minister as priests. ⁴Nadab and Abihu had died before the LORD when they offered profane fire before the LORD in the Wilderness of Sinai; and they had no children. So Eleazar and Ithamar ministered as priests in the presence of Aaron their father.

5And the LORD spoke to Moses, saying: 6"Bring the tribe of Levi near, and present them before Aaron the priest, that they may serve him. 7And they shall attend to his needs and the needs of the whole congregation before the tabernacle of meeting, to do the work of the tabernacle. 8Also they shall attend to all the furnishings of the tabernacle of meeting, and to the needs of the children of Israel, to do the work of the tabernacle. 9And you shall give the Levites to Aaron and his sons; they *are* given entirely to him* from among the children of Israel. 10So you shall appoint Aaron and his sons, and they shall attend to their priesthood; but the outsider who comes near shall be put to death."

11Then the LORD spoke to Moses, saying: 12"Now behold, I Myself have taken the Levites from among the children of Israel instead of every firstborn who opens the womb among the children of Israel. Therefore the Levites shall be Mine, 13because all the firstborn *are* Mine. On the day that I struck all the firstborn in the land of Egypt, I sanctified to Myself all the firstborn in Israel, both man and beast. They shall be Mine: I *am* the LORD."

14Then the LORD spoke to Moses in the Wilderness of Sinai, saying: 15"Number the children of Levi by their fathers' houses, by their families; you shall number every male from a month old and above."

16So Moses numbered them according to the word of the LORD, as he was commanded. 17These were the sons of Levi by their names: Gershon, Kohath, and Merari. 18And these *are* the names of the sons of Gershon by their families: Libni and Shimei. 19And the sons of Kohath by their families: Amram, Izehar, Hebron, and Uzziel. 20And the sons of Merari by their families: Mahli

and Mushi. These *are* the families of the Levites by their fathers' houses.

21From Gershon *came* the family of the Libnites and the family of the Shimites; these *were* the families of the Gershonites. 22Those who were numbered, according to the number of all the males from a month old and above—of those who were numbered *there were* seven thousand five hundred. 23The families of the Gershonites were to camp behind the tabernacle westward. 24And the leader of the father's house of the Gershonites *was* Eliasaph the son of Lael. 25The duties of the children of Gershon in the tabernacle of meeting *included* the tabernacle, the tent with its covering, the screen for the door of the tabernacle of meeting, 26the screen for the door of the court, the hangings of the court which *are* around the tabernacle and the altar, and their cords, according to all the work relating to them.

27From Kohath *came* the family of the Amramites, the family of the Izharites, the family of the Hebronites, and the family of the Uzzielites; these *were* the families of the Kohathites. 28According to the number of all the males, from a month old and above, *there were* eight thousand six* hundred keeping charge of the sanctuary. 29The families of the children of Kohath were to camp on the south side of the tabernacle. 30And the leader of the fathers' house of the families of the Kohathites *was* Elizaphan the son of Uzziel. 31Their duty *included* the ark, the table, the lampstand, the altars, the utensils of the sanctuary with which they ministered, the screen, and all the work relating to them.

32And Eleazar the son of Aaron the priest *was to be* chief over the leaders of the Levites, *with* oversight of those who kept charge of the sanctuary.

33From Merari *came* the family of the Mahlites and the family of the Mushites; these *were* the families of

Merari. ³⁴And those who were numbered, according to the number of all the males from a month old and above, *were* six thousand two hundred. ³⁵The leader of the fathers' house of the families of Merari *was* Zuriel the son of Abihail. These *were* to camp on the north side of the tabernacle. ³⁶And the appointed duty of the children of Merari *included* the boards of the tabernacle, its bars, its pillars, its sockets, its utensils, all the work relating to them, ³⁷and the pillars of the court all around, with their sockets, their pegs, and their cords.

³⁸Moreover those who were to camp before the tabernacle on the east, before the tabernacle of meeting, *were* Moses, Aaron, and his sons, keeping charge of the sanctuary, to meet the needs of the children of Israel; but the outsider who came near was to be put to death. ³⁹All who were numbered of the Levites, whom Moses and Aaron numbered at the commandment of the LORD, by their families, all the males from a month old and above, *were* twenty-two thousand.

⁴⁰Then the LORD said to Moses: "Number all the firstborn males of the children of Israel from a month old and above, and take the number of their names. ⁴¹And you shall take the Levites for Me—I *am* the LORD—instead of all the firstborn among the children of Israel, and the livestock of the Levites instead of all the firstborn among the livestock of the children of Israel." ⁴²So Moses numbered all the firstborn among the children of Israel, as the LORD commanded him. ⁴³And all the firstborn males, according to the number of names from a month old and above, of those who were numbered of them, were twenty-two thousand two hundred and seventy-three.

⁴⁴Then the LORD spoke to Moses, saying: ⁴⁵"Take the Levites instead of all the firstborn among the children of Israel, and the livestock of the Levites instead of their livestock. The Levites shall be Mine: I *am* the LORD. ⁴⁶And for the redemption of the two hundred and seventy-three of the firstborn of the children of Israel, who are more than the number of the Levites, ⁴⁷you shall take five shekels for each one individually; you shall take *them* in the currency of the shekel of the sanctuary, the shekel of twenty gerahs. ⁴⁸And you shall give the money, with which the excess number of them is redeemed, to Aaron and his sons."

⁴⁹So Moses took the redemption money from those who were over and above those who were redeemed by the Levites. ⁵⁰From the firstborn of the children of Israel he took the money, one thousand three hundred and sixty-five *shekels,* according to the shekel of the sanctuary. ⁵¹And Moses gave their redemption money to Aaron and his sons, according to the word of the LORD, as the LORD commanded Moses

MARK 11:27–12:17

THEN they [Jesus and his disciples] came again to Jerusalem. And as He was walking in the temple, the chief priests, the scribes, and the elders came to Him. ²⁸And they said to Him, "By what authority are You doing these things? And who gave You this authority to do these things?"

²⁹But Jesus answered and said to them, "I also will ask you one question; then answer Me, and I will tell you by what authority I do these things: ³⁰The baptism of John—was it from heaven or from men? Answer Me."

³¹And they reasoned among themselves, saying, "If we say, 'From heaven,' He will say, 'Why then did you not believe him?' ³²But if we say, 'From men' "—they feared the people, for all counted John to have been a prophet indeed. ³³So they answered and said to Jesus, "We do not know."

And Jesus answered and said to them, "Neither will I tell you by what authority I do these things."

Then He began to speak to them in parables: "A man planted a vineyard and set a hedge around *it,* dug *a place for* the wine vat and built a tower. And he leased it to vinedressers and went into a far country. ²Now at vintage-time he sent a servant to the vinedressers, that he might receive some of the fruit of the vineyard from the vinedressers. ³And they took *him* and beat him and sent *him* away empty-handed. ⁴Again he sent them another servant, and at him they threw stones,* wounded *him* in the head, and sent *him* away shamefully treated. ⁵And again he sent another, and him they killed; and many others, beating some and killing some. ⁶Therefore still having one son, his beloved, he also sent him to them last, saying, 'They will respect my son.' ⁷But those vinedressers said among themselves, 'This is the heir. Come, let us kill him, and the inheritance will be ours.' ⁸So they took him and killed *him* and cast *him* out of the vineyard.

⁹"Therefore what will the owner of the vineyard do? He will come and destroy the vinedressers, and give the vineyard to others. ¹⁰Have you not even read this Scripture:

'The stone which the builders
    rejected
Has become the chief
    cornerstone.
¹¹ This was the Lord's doing,
And it is marvelous in our
    eyes'? " *

¹²And they sought to lay hands on Him, but feared the multitude, for they knew He had spoken the parable against them. So they left Him and went away.

¹³Then they sent to Him some of the Pharisees and the Herodians, to catch Him in *His* words. ¹⁴When they had come, they said to Him, "Teacher, we know that You are true, and care about no one; for You do not regard the person of men, but teach the way of God in truth. Is it lawful to pay taxes to Caesar, or not? ¹⁵Shall we pay, or shall we not pay?"

But He, knowing their hypocrisy, said to them, "Why do you test Me? Bring Me a denarius that I may see *it.*" ¹⁶So they brought *it.*

And He said to them, "Whose image and inscription *is* this?" They said to Him, "Caesar's."

¹⁷And Jesus answered and said to them, "Render to Caesar the things that are Caesar's, and to God the things that are God's."

And they marveled at Him.

PSALM 47:1-9

To the Chief Musician. A Psalm of the sons of Korah.

O H, clap your hands, all you peoples!
    Shout to God with the voice of
        triumph!
2   For the Lord Most High *is*
        awesome;
    He is a great King over all the
        earth.
3   He will subdue the peoples
        under us,
    And the nations under our
        feet.
4   He will choose our
        inheritance for us,
    The excellence of Jacob
        whom He loves.   Selah

5   God has gone up with a shout,
    The Lord with the sound of a
        trumpet.
6   Sing praises to God, sing
        praises!
    Sing praises to our King, sing
        praises!

7 For God *is* the King of all the
earth;
Sing praises with
understanding.

8 God reigns over the nations;
God sits on His holy throne.

9 The princes of the people
have gathered together,
The people of the God of
Abraham.
For the shields of the earth
belong to God;
He is greatly exalted.

PROVERBS FOR TODAY/ 10:24-25

The fear of the wicked will come upon him, and the desire of the righteous will be granted. When the whirlwind passes by, the wicked is *no* more, *but the righteous* has *an everlasting foundation.*

MARCH 5

NUMBERS 4:1–5:31

THEN the LORD spoke to Moses and Aaron, saying: 2"Take a census of the sons of Kohath from among the children of Levi, by their families, by their fathers' house, 3from thirty years old and above, even to fifty years old, all who enter the service to do the work in the tabernacle of meeting.

4"This *is* the service of the sons of Kohath in the tabernacle of meeting, *relating to* the most holy things: 5When the camp prepares to journey, Aaron and his sons shall come, and they shall take down the covering veil and cover the ark of the Testimony with it. 6Then they shall put on it a covering of badger skins, and spread over *that* a cloth entirely of blue; and they shall insert its poles.

7"On the table of showbread they shall spread a blue cloth, and put on it the dishes, the pans, the bowls, and the pitchers for pouring; and the showbread* shall be on it. 8They shall spread over them a scarlet cloth, and cover the same with a covering of badger skins; and they shall insert its

poles. 9And they shall take a blue cloth and cover the lampstand of the light, with its lamps, its wick-trimmers, its trays, and all its oil vessels, with which they service it. 10Then they shall put it with all its utensils in a covering of badger skins, and put *it* on a carrying beam.

11"Over the golden altar they shall spread a blue cloth, and cover it with a covering of badger skins; and they shall insert its poles. 12Then they shall take all the utensils of service with which they minister in the sanctuary, put *them* in a blue cloth, cover them with a covering of badger skins, and put *them* on a carrying beam. 13Also they shall take away the ashes from the altar, and spread a purple cloth over it. 14They shall put on it all its implements with which they minister there—the firepans, the forks, the shovels, the basins, and all the utensils of the altar—and they shall spread on it a covering of badger skins, and insert its poles. 15And when Aaron and his sons have finished covering the sanctuary and all the furnishings of the sanctuary, when the camp is set to go, then the sons of Kohath shall come to carry *them;* but they shall not touch any holy thing, lest they die.

"These *are* the things in the tabernacle of meeting which the sons of Kohath are to carry.

16"The appointed duty of Eleazar the son of Aaron the priest *is* the oil for the light, the sweet incense, the daily grain offering, the anointing oil, the oversight of all the tabernacle, of all that *is* in it, with the sanctuary and its furnishings."

17Then the LORD spoke to Moses and Aaron, saying: 18"Do not cut off the tribe of the families of the Kohathites from among the Levites; 19but do this in regard to them, that they may live and not die when they approach the most holy things: Aaron and his sons shall go in and appoint each of them to his service and his task. 20But they shall not go in to watch while the holy things are being covered, lest they die."

21Then the LORD spoke to Moses, saying: 22"Also take a census of the sons of Gershon, by their fathers' house, by their families. 23From thirty years old and above, even to fifty years old, you shall number them, all who enter to perform the service, to do the work in the tabernacle of meeting. 24This *is* the service of the families of the Gershonites, in serving and carrying: 25They shall carry the curtains of the tabernacle and the tabernacle of meeting *with* its covering, the covering of badger skins that *is* on it, the screen for the door of the tabernacle of meeting, 26the screen for the door of the gate of the court, the hangings of the court which *are* around the tabernacle and altar, and their cords, all the furnishings for their service and all that is made for these things: so shall they serve.

27"Aaron and his sons shall assign all the service of the sons of the Gershonites, all their tasks and all their service. And you shall appoint to them all their tasks as their duty. 28This *is* the service of the families of the sons of Gershon in the tabernacle of meeting. And their duties *shall be* under the authority* of Ithamar the son of Aaron the priest.

29"*As for* the sons of Merari, you shall number them by their families and by their fathers' house. 30From thirty years old and above, even to fifty years old, you shall number them, everyone who enters the service to do the work of the tabernacle of meeting. 31And this *is* what they must carry as all their service for the tabernacle of meeting: the boards of the tabernacle, its bars, its pillars, its sockets, 32and the pillars around the court with their sockets, pegs, and cords, with all their furnishings and all their service; and you shall assign *to each man* by name the items he must carry. 33This *is* the service of the families of the sons of Merari, as all their service for the tabernacle of meeting, under the authority* of Ithamar the son of Aaron the priest."

34And Moses, Aaron, and the leaders of the congregation numbered the sons of the Kohathites by their families and by their fathers' house, 35from thirty years old and above, even to fifty years old, everyone who entered the service for work in the tabernacle of meeting; 36and those who were numbered by their families were two thousand seven hundred and fifty. 37These *were* the ones who were numbered of the families of the Kohathites, all who might serve in the tabernacle of meeting, whom Moses and Aaron numbered according to the commandment of the LORD by the hand of Moses.

38And those who were numbered of the sons of Gershon, by their families and by their fathers' house, 39from thirty years old and above, even to fifty years old, everyone who entered the service for work in the tabernacle of meeting— 40those who were numbered by their families, by their fathers' house, were two thousand six hundred and thirty. ⁴¹These *are* the ones who were numbered of the families of the sons of Gershon, of all who might serve in the tabernacle of meeting, whom Moses and Aaron numbered according to the commandment of the LORD.

⁴²Those of the families of the sons of Merari who were numbered, by their families, by their fathers' house, ⁴³from thirty years old and above, even to fifty years old, everyone who entered the service for work in the tabernacle of meeting— ⁴⁴those who were numbered by their families were three thousand two hundred. ⁴⁵These *are* the ones who were numbered of the families of the sons of Merari, whom Moses and Aaron numbered according to the word of the LORD by the hand of Moses.

⁴⁶All who were numbered of the Levites, whom Moses, Aaron, and the leaders of Israel numbered, by their families and by their fathers' houses, ⁴⁷from thirty years old and above, even to fifty years old, everyone who came to do the work of service and the work of bearing burdens in the tabernacle of meeting— ⁴⁸those who were numbered were eight thousand five hundred and eighty.

⁴⁹According to the commandment of the LORD they were numbered by the hand of Moses, each according to his service and according to his task; thus were they numbered by him, as the LORD commanded Moses.

AND the LORD spoke to Moses, saying: ²"Command the children of Israel that they put out of the camp every leper, everyone who has a discharge, and whoever becomes defiled by a corpse. ³You shall put out both male and female; you shall put them outside the camp, that they may not defile their camps in the midst of which I dwell." ⁴And the children of Israel did so, and put them outside the camp; as the LORD spoke to Moses, so the children of Israel did.

⁵Then the LORD spoke to Moses, saying, ⁶"Speak to the children of Israel: 'When a man or woman commits any sin that men commit in unfaithfulness against the LORD, and that person is guilty, ⁷then he shall confess the sin which he has committed. He shall make restitution for his trespass in full, plus one-fifth of it, and give *it* to the one he has wronged. ⁸But if the man has no relative to whom restitution may be made for the wrong, the restitution for the wrong *must go* to the LORD for the priest, in addition to the ram of the atonement with which atonement is made for him. ⁹Every offering of all the holy things of the children of Israel, which they bring to the priest, shall be his. ¹⁰And every man's holy things shall be his; whatever any man gives the priest shall be his.' "

¹¹And the LORD spoke to Moses, saying, ¹²"Speak to the children of Israel, and say to them: 'If any man's wife goes astray and behaves unfaithfully toward him, ¹³and a man lies with her carnally, and it is hidden from the eyes of her husband, and it is concealed that she has defiled herself, and *there was* no witness against her, nor was she caught— ¹⁴if the spirit of jealousy comes upon him and he becomes jealous of his wife, who has defiled herself; or if the spirit of jealousy comes upon him and he becomes jealous of his wife, although she has not defiled herself— ¹⁵then the man shall bring his wife to the priest. He shall bring the offering required for her, one-tenth of an ephah of barley meal; he shall pour no oil on it and put no frankincense on it, because it *is* a grain offering of jealousy, an offering for remembering, for bringing iniquity to remembrance.

¹⁶'And the priest shall bring her near, and set her before the LORD.

¹⁷The priest shall take holy water in an earthen vessel, and take some of the dust that is on the floor of the tabernacle and put *it* into the water. ¹⁸Then the priest shall stand the woman before the LORD, uncover the woman's head, and put the offering for remembering in her hands, which *is* the grain offering of jealousy. And the priest shall have in his hand the bitter water that brings a curse. ¹⁹And the priest shall put her under oath, and say to the woman, "If no man has lain with you, and if you have not gone astray to uncleanness *while* under your husband's *authority,* be free from this bitter water that brings a curse. ²⁰But if you have gone astray *while* under your husband's *authority,* and if you have defiled yourself and some man other than your husband has lain with you"— ²¹then the priest shall put the woman under the oath of the curse, and he shall say to the woman—"the LORD make you a curse and an oath among your people, when the LORD makes your thigh rot and your belly swell; ²²and may this water that causes the curse go into your stomach, and make *your* belly swell and *your* thigh rot."

'Then the woman shall say, "Amen, so be it."

²³'Then the priest shall write these curses in a book, and he shall scrape *them* off into the bitter water. ²⁴And he shall make the woman drink the bitter water that brings a curse, and the water that brings the curse shall enter her *to become* bitter. ²⁵Then the priest shall take the grain offering of jealousy from the woman's hand, shall wave the offering before the LORD, and bring it to the altar; ²⁶and the priest shall take a handful of the offering, as its memorial portion, burn *it* on the altar, and afterward make the woman drink the water. ²⁷When he has made her drink the water, then it shall be, if she has defiled herself and behaved unfaith-

fully toward her husband, that the water that brings a curse will enter her *and become* bitter, and her belly will swell, her thigh will rot, and the woman will become a curse among her people. ²⁸But if the woman has not defiled herself, and is clean, then she shall be free and may conceive children.

²⁹'This *is* the law of jealousy, when a wife, *while* under her husband's *authority,* goes astray and defiles herself, ³⁰or when the spirit of jealousy comes upon a man, and he becomes jealous of his wife; then he shall stand the woman before the LORD, and the priest shall execute all this law upon her. ³¹Then the man shall be free from iniquity, but that woman shall bear her guilt.' "

MARK 12:18-37

THEN *some* Sadducees, who say there is no resurrection, came to Him [Jesus]; and they asked Him, saying: ¹⁹"Teacher, Moses wrote to us that if a man's brother dies, and leaves *his* wife behind, and leaves no children, his brother should take his wife and raise up offspring for his brother. ²⁰Now there were seven brothers. The first took a wife; and dying, he left no offspring. ²¹And the second took her, and he died; nor did he leave any offspring. And the third likewise. ²²So the seven had her and left no offspring. Last of all the woman died also. ²³Therefore, in the resurrection, when they rise, whose wife will she be? For all seven had her as wife."

²⁴Jesus answered and said to them, "Are you not therefore mistaken, because you do not know the Scriptures nor the power of God? ²⁵For when they rise from the dead, they neither marry nor are given in marriage, but are like angels in heaven. ²⁶But concerning the dead, that they rise, have you not read in the book of Moses, in the *burning*

bush *passage,* how God spoke to him, saying, *'I am the God of Abraham, the God of Isaac, and the God of Jacob'?** ²⁷He is not the God of the dead, but the God of the living. You are therefore greatly mistaken."

²⁸Then one of the scribes came, and having heard them reasoning together, perceiving* that He had answered them well, asked Him, "Which is the first commandment of all?"

²⁹Jesus answered him, "The first of all the commandments *is: 'Hear, O Israel, the* LORD *our God, the* LORD *is one.* ³⁰*And you shall love the* LORD *your God with all your heart, with all your soul, with all your mind, and with all your strength.'** This *is* the first commandment.* ³¹And the second, like *it,* is this: *'You shall love your neighbor as yourself.'** There is no other commandment greater than these."

³²So the scribe said to Him, "Well *said,* Teacher. You have spoken the truth, for there is one God, and there is no other but He. ³³And to love Him with all the heart, with all the understanding, with all the soul,* and with all the strength, and to love one's neighbor as oneself, is more than all the whole burnt offerings and sacrifices."

³⁴Now when Jesus saw that he answered wisely, He said to him, "You are not far from the kingdom of God." But after that no one dared question Him.

³⁵Then Jesus answered and said, while He taught in the temple, "How *is it* that the scribes say that the Christ is the Son of David? ³⁶For David himself said by the Holy Spirit:

> '*The* LORD *said to my Lord,*
> *"Sit at My right hand,*
> *Till I make Your enemies*
> *Your footstool."'**

³⁷Therefore David himself calls Him *'Lord'*; how is He *then* his Son?"

And the common people heard Him gladly.

PSALM 48:1-14

A Song. A Psalm of the sons of Korah.

GREAT *is* the LORD, and greatly to be praised
In the city of our God,
In His holy mountain.
2 Beautiful in elevation,
The joy of the whole earth,
Is Mount Zion *on* the sides of the north,
The city of the great King.
3 God *is* in her palaces;
He is known as her refuge.

4 For behold, the kings assembled,
They passed by together.
5 They saw *it, and* so they marveled;
They were troubled, they hastened away.
6 Fear took hold of them there,
And pain, as of a woman in birth pangs,
7 *As when* You break the ships of Tarshish
With an east wind.

8 As we have heard,
So we have seen
In the city of the LORD of hosts,
In the city of our God:
God will establish it forever.
                                    Selah

9 We have thought, O God, on Your lovingkindness,
In the midst of Your temple.
10 According to Your name, O God,
So *is* Your praise to the ends of the earth;
Your right hand is full of righteousness.
11 Let Mount Zion rejoice,

Let the daughters of Judah be
  glad,
Because of Your judgments.

12 Walk about Zion,
    And go all around her.
    Count her towers;
13 Mark well her bulwarks;

Consider her palaces;
That you may tell *it* to the
  generation following.
14 For this *is* God,
    Our God forever and ever;
    He will be our guide
    Even to death.*

PROVERBS FOR TODAY/ 10:26

As vinegar to the teeth and smoke to the eyes, so is *the lazy* man *to those who send him.*

MARCH 6

NUMBERS 6:1–7:89

THEN the LORD spoke to Moses, saying, 2"Speak to the children of Israel, and say to them: 'When either a man or woman consecrates an offering to take the vow of a Nazirite, to separate himself to the LORD, 3he shall separate himself from wine and *similar* drink; he shall drink neither vinegar made from wine nor vinegar made from *similar* drink; neither shall he drink any grape juice, nor eat fresh grapes or raisins. 4All the days of his separation he shall eat nothing that is produced by the grapevine, from seed to skin.

5All the days of the vow of his separation no razor shall come upon his head; until the days are fulfilled for which he separated himself to the LORD, he shall be holy. *Then* he shall let the locks of the hair of his head grow. 6All the days that he separates himself to the LORD he shall not go near a dead body. 7He shall not make himself unclean even for his father or his mother, for his brother or his sister, when they die, because his separation to God *is*

on his head. 8All the days of his separation he shall be holy to the LORD.

9And if anyone dies very suddenly beside him, and he defiles his consecrated head, then he shall shave his head on the day of his cleansing; on the seventh day he shall shave it. 10Then on the eighth day he shall bring two turtledoves or two young pigeons to the priest, to the door of the tabernacle of meeting; 11and the priest shall offer one as a sin offering and *the* other as a burnt offering, and make atonement for him, because he sinned in regard to the corpse; and he shall sanctify his head that same day. 12He shall consecrate to the LORD the days of his separation, and bring a male lamb in its first year as a trespass offering; but the former days shall be lost, because his separation was defiled.

13'Now this *is* the law of the Nazirite: When the days of his separation are fulfilled, he shall be brought to the door of the tabernacle of meeting. 14And he shall present his offering to the LORD: one male lamb in its first year without blemish as a burnt offering, one ewe lamb in its first year without blemish as a sin offering, one ram without blemish as a peace offering, [15]a basket of unleavened bread, cakes of fine flour mixed with oil, unleavened wafers anointed with oil, and their grain offering with their drink offerings.

[16]"Then the priest shall bring *them* before the LORD and offer his sin offering and his burnt offering; [17]and he shall offer the ram as a sacrifice of a peace offering to the LORD, with the basket of unleavened bread; the priest shall also offer its grain offering and its drink offering. [18]Then the Nazirite shall shave his consecrated head *at* the door of the tabernacle of meeting, and shall take the hair from his consecrated head and put *it* on the fire which is under the sacrifice of the peace offering.

[19]"And the priest shall take the boiled shoulder of the ram, one unleavened cake from the basket, and one unleavened wafer, and put *them* upon the hands of the Nazirite after he has shaved his consecrated *hair,* [20]and the priest shall wave them as a wave offering before the LORD; they *are* holy for the priest, together with the breast of the wave offering and the thigh of the heave offering. After that the Nazirite may drink wine.'

[21]"This is the law of the Nazirite who vows to the LORD the offering for his separation, and besides that, whatever else his hand is able to provide; according to the vow which he takes, so he must do according to the law of his separation."

[22]And the LORD spoke to Moses, saying: [23]"Speak to Aaron and his sons, saying, 'This is the way you shall bless the children of Israel. Say to them:

[24] "The LORD bless you and keep you;
[25] The LORD make His face shine upon you,
And be gracious to you;
[26] The LORD lift up His countenance upon you,
And give you peace." '

[27]"So they shall put My name on the children of Israel, and I will bless them."

Now it came to pass, when Moses had finished setting up the tabernacle, that he anointed it and consecrated it and all its furnishings, and the altar and all its utensils; so he anointed them and consecrated them. [2]Then the leaders of Israel, the heads of their fathers' houses, who *were* the leaders of the tribes and over those who were numbered, made an offering. [3]And they brought their offering before the LORD, six covered carts and twelve oxen, a cart for *every* two of the leaders, and for each one an ox; and they presented them before the tabernacle.

[4]Then the LORD spoke to Moses, saying, [5]"Accept *these* from them, that they may be used in doing the work of the tabernacle of meeting; and you shall give them to the Levites, *to* every man according to his service." [6]So Moses took the carts and the oxen, and gave them to the Levites. [7]Two carts and four oxen he gave to the sons of Gershon, according to their service; [8]and four carts and eight oxen he gave to the sons of Merari, according to their service, under the authority* of Ithamar the son of Aaron the priest. [9]But to the sons of Kohath he gave none, because theirs *was* the service of the holy things, *which* they carried on their shoulders.

[10]Now the leaders offered the dedication *offering* for the altar when it was anointed; so the leaders offered their offering before the altar. [11]For the LORD said to Moses, "They shall offer their offering, one leader each day, for the dedication of the altar."

[12]And the one who offered his offering on the first day *was* Nahshon the

son of Amminadab, from the tribe of Judah. [13]His offering *was* one silver platter, the weight of which *was* one hundred and thirty *shekels,* and one silver bowl of seventy shekels, according to the shekel of the sanctuary, both of them full of fine flour mixed with oil as a grain offering; [14]one gold pan of ten *shekels,* full of incense; [15]one young bull, one ram, and one male lamb in its first year, as a burnt offering; [16]one kid of the goats as a sin offering; [17]and for the sacrifice of peace offerings: two oxen, five rams, five male goats, and five male lambs in their first year. This *was* the offering of Nahshon the son of Amminadab.

[18]On the second day Nethanel the son of Zuar, leader of Issachar, presented *an offering.* [19]*For* his offering he offered one silver platter, the weight of which *was* one hundred and thirty *shekels,* and one silver bowl of seventy shekels, according to the shekel of the sanctuary, both of them full of fine flour mixed with oil as a grain offering; [20]one gold pan of ten *shekels,* full of incense; [21]one young bull, one ram, and one male lamb in its first year, as a burnt offering; [22]one kid of the goats as a sin offering; [23]and as the sacrifice of peace offerings: two oxen, five rams, five male goats, and five male lambs in their first year. This *was* the offering of Nethanel the son of Zuar.

[24]On the third day Eliab the son of Helon, leader of the children of Zebulun, *presented an offering.* [25]His offering *was* one silver platter, the weight of which *was* one hundred and thirty *shekels,* and one silver bowl of seventy shekels, according to the shekel of the sanctuary, both of them full of fine flour mixed with oil as a grain offering; [26]one gold pan of ten *shekels,* full of incense; [27]one young bull, one ram, and one male lamb in its first year, as a burnt offering; [28]one kid of the goats as a sin offering; [29]and for

the sacrifice of peace offerings: two oxen, five rams, five male goats, and five male lambs in their first year. This *was* the offering of Eliab the son of Helon.

[30]On the fourth day Elizur the son of Shedeur, leader of the children of Reuben, *presented an offering.* [31]His offering *was* one silver platter, the weight of which *was* one hundred and thirty *shekels,* and one silver bowl of seventy shekels, according to the shekel of the sanctuary, both of them full of fine flour mixed with oil as a grain offering; [32]one gold pan of ten *shekels,* full of incense; [33]one young bull, one ram, and one male lamb in its first year, as a burnt offering; [34]one kid of the goats as a sin offering; [35]and as the sacrifice of peace offerings: two oxen, five rams, five male goats, and five male lambs in their first year. This *was* the offering of Elizur the son of Shedeur.

[36]On the fifth day Shelumiel the son of Zurishaddai, leader of the children of Simeon, *presented an offering.* [37]His offering *was* one silver platter, the weight of which *was* one hundred and thirty *shekels,* and one silver bowl of seventy shekels, according to the shekel of the sanctuary, both of them full of fine flour mixed with oil as a grain offering; [38]one gold pan of ten *shekels,* full of incense; [39]one young bull, one ram, and one male lamb in its first year, as a burnt offering; [40]one kid of the goats as a sin offering; [41]and as the sacrifice of peace offerings: two oxen, five rams, five male goats, and five male lambs in their first year. This *was* the offering of Shelumiel the son of Zurishaddai.

[42]On the sixth day Eliasaph the son of Deuel,* leader of the children of Gad, *presented an offering.* [43]His offering *was* one silver platter, the weight of which *was* one hundred and thirty *shekels,* and one silver bowl of seventy shekels, according to the shekel of the sanctuary, both of them full of fine

flour mixed with oil as a grain offering; ⁴⁴one gold pan of ten *shekels,* full of incense; ⁴⁵one young bull, one ram, and one male lamb in its first year, as a burnt offering; ⁴⁶one kid of the goats as a sin offering; ⁴⁷and as the sacrifice of peace offerings: two oxen, five rams, five male goats, and five male lambs in their first year. This *was* the offering of Eliasaph the son of Deuel.

⁴⁸On the seventh day Elishama the son of Ammihud, leader of the children of Ephraim, *presented an offering.* ⁴⁹His offering *was* one silver platter, the weight of which *was* one hundred and thirty *shekels,* and one silver bowl of seventy shekels, according to the shekel of the sanctuary, both of them full of fine flour mixed with oil as a grain offering; ⁵⁰one gold pan of ten *shekels,* full of incense; ⁵¹one young bull, one ram, and one male lamb in its first year, as a burnt offering; ⁵²one kid of the goats as a sin offering; ⁵³and as the sacrifice of peace offerings: two oxen, five rams, five male goats, and five male lambs in their first year. This *was* the offering of Elishama the son of Ammihud.

⁵⁴On the eighth day Gamaliel the son of Pedahzur, leader of the children of Manasseh, *presented an offering.* ⁵⁵His offering *was* one silver platter, the weight of which *was* one hundred and thirty *shekels,* and one silver bowl of seventy shekels, according to the shekel of the sanctuary, both of them full of fine flour mixed with oil as a grain offering; ⁵⁶one gold pan of ten *shekels,* full of incense; ⁵⁷one young bull, one ram, and one male lamb in its first year, as a burnt offering; ⁵⁸one kid of the goats as a sin offering; ⁵⁹and as the sacrifice of peace offerings: two oxen, five rams, five male goats, and five male lambs in their first year. This *was* the offering of Gamaliel the son of Pedahzur.

⁶⁰On the ninth day Abidan the son of Gideoni, leader of the children of Ben-jamin, *presented an offering.* ⁶¹His offering *was* one silver platter, the weight of which *was* one hundred and thirty *shekels,* and one silver bowl of seventy shekels, according to the shekel of the sanctuary, both of them full of fine flour mixed with oil as a grain offering; ⁶²one gold pan of ten *shekels,* full of incense; ⁶³one young bull, one ram, and one male lamb in its first year, as a burnt offering; ⁶⁴one kid of the goats as a sin offering; ⁶⁵and as the sacrifice of peace offerings: two oxen, five rams, five male goats, and five male lambs in their first year. This *was* the offering of Abidan the son of Gideoni.

⁶⁶On the tenth day Ahiezer the son of Ammishaddai, leader of the children of Dan, *presented an offering.* ⁶⁷His offering *was* one silver platter, the weight of which *was* one hundred and thirty *shekels,* and one silver bowl of seventy shekels, according to the shekel of the sanctuary, both of them full of fine flour mixed with oil as a grain offering; ⁶⁸one gold pan of ten *shekels,* full of incense; ⁶⁹one young bull, one ram, and one male lamb in its first year, as a burnt offering; ⁷⁰one kid of the goats as a sin offering; ⁷¹and as the sacrifice of peace offerings: two oxen, five rams, five male goats, and five male lambs in their first year. This *was* the offering of Ahiezer the son of Ammishaddai.

⁷²On the eleventh day Pagiel the son of Ocran, leader of the children of Asher, *presented an offering.* ⁷³His offering *was* one silver platter, the weight of which *was* one hundred and thirty *shekels,* and one silver bowl of seventy shekels, according to the shekel of the sanctuary, both of them full of fine flour mixed with oil as a grain offering; ⁷⁴one gold pan of ten *shekels,* full of incense; ⁷⁵one young bull, one ram, and one male lamb in its first year, as a burnt offering; ⁷⁶one kid of the goats as a sin offering; ⁷⁷and as

the sacrifice of peace offerings: two oxen, five rams, five male goats, and five male lambs in their first year. This *was* the offering of Pagiel the son of Ocran.

78On the twelfth day Ahira the son of Enan, leader of the children of Naphtali, *presented an offering.* 79His offering *was* one silver platter, the weight of which *was* one hundred and thirty *shekels,* and one silver bowl of seventy shekels, according to the shekel of the sanctuary, both of them full of fine flour mixed with oil as a grain offering; 80one gold pan of ten *shekels,* full of incense; 81one young bull, one ram, and one male lamb in its first year, as a burnt offering; 82one kid of the goats as a sin offering; 83and as the sacrifice of peace offerings: two oxen, five rams, five male goats, and five male lambs in their first year. This *was* the offering of Ahira the son of Enan.

84This *was* the dedication *offering* for the altar from the leaders of Israel, when it was anointed: twelve silver platters, twelve silver bowls, and twelve gold pans. 85Each silver platter *weighed* one hundred and thirty *shekels* and each bowl seventy *shekels.* All the silver of the vessels *weighed* two thousand four hundred *shekels,* according to the shekel of the sanctuary. 86The twelve gold pans full of incense *weighed* ten *shekels* apiece, according to the shekel of the sanctuary; all the gold of the pans *weighed* one hundred and twenty *shekels.* 87All the oxen for the burnt offering *were* twelve young bulls, the rams twelve, the male lambs in their first year twelve, with their grain offering, and the kids of the goats as a sin offering twelve. 88And all the oxen for the sacrifice of peace offerings were twenty-four bulls, the rams sixty, the male goats sixty, and the lambs in their first year sixty. This *was* the dedication *offering* for the altar after it was anointed.

89Now when Moses went into the tabernacle of meeting to speak with Him, he heard the voice of One speaking to him from above the mercy seat that *was* on the ark of the Testimony, from between the two cherubim; thus He spoke to him.

MARK 12:38–13:13

THEN He [Jesus] said to them in His teaching, "Beware of the scribes, who desire to go around in long robes, *love* greetings in the marketplaces, 39the best seats in the synagogues, and the best places at feasts, 40who devour widows' houses, and for a pretense make long prayers. These will receive greater condemnation."

41Now Jesus sat opposite the treasury and saw how the people put money into the treasury. And many *who were* rich put in much. 42Then one poor widow came and threw in two mites,* which make a quadrans. 43So He called His disciples to *Himself* and said to them, "Assuredly, I say to you that this poor widow has put in more than all those who have given to the treasury; 44for they all put in out of their abundance, but she out of her poverty put in all that she had, her whole livelihood."

THEN as He went out of the temple, one of His disciples said to Him, "Teacher, see what manner of stones and what buildings *are here!*"

2And Jesus answered and said to him, "Do you see these great buildings? Not *one* stone shall be left upon another, that shall not be thrown down."

3Now as He sat on the Mount of Olives opposite the temple, Peter, James, John, and Andrew asked Him privately, 4"Tell us, when will these things be? And what *will be* the sign when all these things will be fulfilled?"

5And Jesus, answering them, began

to say: "Take heed that no one deceives you. ⁶For many will come in My name, saying, 'I am *He,*' and will deceive many. ⁷But when you hear of wars and rumors of wars, do not be troubled; for *such things* must happen, but the end *is* not yet. ⁸For nation will rise against nation, and kingdom against kingdom. And there will be earthquakes in various places, and there will be famines and troubles.* These *are* the beginnings of sorrows.

⁹"But watch out for yourselves, for they will deliver you up to councils, and you will be beaten in the synagogues. You will be brought* before rulers and kings for My sake, for a testimony to them. ¹⁰And the gospel must first be preached to all the nations. ¹¹But when they arrest *you* and deliver you up, do not worry beforehand, or premeditate* what you will speak. But whatever is given you in that hour, speak that; for it is not you who speak, but the Holy Spirit. ¹²Now brother will betray brother to death, and a father *his* child; and children will rise up against parents and cause them to be put to death. ¹³And you will be hated by all for My name's sake. But he who endures to the end shall be saved.' "

PSALM 49:1-20

To the Chief Musician. A Psalm of the sons of Korah.

HEAR this, all peoples;
Give ear, all inhabitants of the world,
2 Both low and high,
Rich and poor together.
3 My mouth shall speak wisdom,
And the meditation of my heart *shall give* understanding.
4 I will incline my ear to a proverb;
I will disclose my dark saying on the harp.

5 Why should I fear in the days of evil,
When the iniquity at my heels surrounds me?
6 Those who trust in their wealth
And boast in the multitude of their riches,
7 None *of them* can by any means redeem *his* brother,
Nor give to God a ransom for him—
8 For the redemption of their souls *is* costly,
And it shall cease forever—
9 That he should continue to live eternally,
And not see the Pit.

10 For he sees wise men die;
Likewise the fool and the senseless person perish,
And leave their wealth to others.
11 Their inner thought *is that* their houses *will last* forever,*
Their dwelling places to all generations;
They call *their* lands after their own names.
12 Nevertheless man, *though* in honor, does not remain;*
He is like the beasts *that* perish.

13 This is the way of those who *are* foolish,
And of their posterity who approve their sayings. Selah
14 Like sheep they are laid in the grave;
Death shall feed on them;
The upright shall have dominion over them in the morning;
And their beauty shall be consumed in the grave, far from their dwelling.

15 But God will redeem my soul
from the power of the grave,
For He shall receive me. Selah

16 Do not be afraid when one
becomes rich,
When the glory of his house
is increased;
17 For when he dies he shall
carry nothing away;
His glory shall not descend
after him.

18 Though while he lives he
blesses himself
(For *men* will praise you when
you do well for yourself),
19 He shall go to the generation
of his fathers;
They shall never see light.
20 A man *who is* in honor, yet
does not understand,
Is like the beasts *that* perish.

PROVERBS FOR TODAY / 10:27-28

The fear of the LORD *prolongs days, but the years of the wicked will be shortened. The hope of the righteous* will be *gladness, but the expectation of the wicked will perish.*

MARCH 7

NUMBERS 8:1–9:23

AND the LORD spoke to Moses, saying: ²"Speak to Aaron, and say to him, 'When you arrange the lamps, the seven lamps shall give light in front of the lampstand.' " ³And Aaron did so; he arranged the lamps to face toward the front of the lampstand, as the LORD commanded Moses. ⁴Now this workmanship of the lampstand *was* hammered gold; from its shaft to its flowers it *was* hammered work. According to the pattern which the LORD had shown Moses, so he made the lampstand.

⁵Then the LORD spoke to Moses, saying: ⁶"Take the Levites from among the children of Israel and cleanse them *ceremonially.* ⁷Thus you shall do to them to cleanse them: Sprinkle water of purification on them, and let them shave all their body, and let them wash their clothes, and *so* make themselves clean. ⁸Then let them take a young bull with its grain offering of fine flour mixed with oil, and you shall take another young bull as a sin offering. ⁹And you shall bring the Levites before the tabernacle of meeting, and you shall gather together the whole congregation of the children of Israel. ¹⁰So you shall bring the Levites before the LORD, and the children of Israel shall lay their hands on the Levites; ¹¹and Aaron shall offer the Levites before the LORD *like* a wave offering from the children of Israel, that they may perform the work of the LORD. ¹²Then the Levites shall lay their hands on the heads of the young bulls, and you shall offer one as a sin offering and the other as a burnt offering to the LORD, to make atonement for the Levites.

¹³"And you shall stand the Levites before Aaron and his sons, and then offer them *like* a wave offering to the LORD. ¹⁴Thus you shall separate the Levites from among the children of Israel, and the Levites shall be Mine.

¹⁵After that the Levites shall go in to service the tabernacle of meeting. So you shall cleanse them and offer them *like* a wave offering. ¹⁶For they *are* wholly given to Me from among the children of Israel; I have taken them for Myself instead of all who open the womb, the firstborn of all the children of Israel. ¹⁷For all the firstborn among the children of Israel *are* Mine, *both* man and beast; on the day that I struck all the firstborn in the land of Egypt I sanctified them to Myself. ¹⁸I have taken the Levites instead of all the firstborn of the children of Israel. ¹⁹And I have given the Levites as a gift to Aaron and his sons from among the children of Israel, to do the work for the children of Israel in the tabernacle of meeting, and to make atonement for the children of Israel, that there be no plague among the children of Israel when the children of Israel come near the sanctuary."

²⁰Thus Moses and Aaron and all the congregation of the children of Israel did to the Levites; according to all that the LORD commanded Moses concerning the Levites, so the children of Israel did to them. ²¹And the Levites purified themselves and washed their clothes; then Aaron presented them *like* a wave offering before the LORD, and Aaron made atonement for them to cleanse them. ²²After that the Levites went in to do their work in the tabernacle of meeting before Aaron and his sons; as the LORD commanded Moses concerning the Levites, so they did to them.

²³Then the LORD spoke to Moses, saying, ²⁴"This *is* what *pertains* to the Levites: From twenty-five years old and above one may enter to perform service in the work of the tabernacle of meeting; ²⁵and at the age of fifty years they must cease performing this work, and shall work no more. ²⁶They may minister with their brethren in the tabernacle of meeting, to attend to needs, but they *themselves* shall do no work. Thus you shall do to the Levites regarding their duties."

Now the LORD spoke to Moses in the Wilderness of Sinai, in the first month of the second year after they had come out of the land of Egypt, saying: ²"Let the children of Israel keep the Passover at its appointed time. ³On the fourteenth day of this month, at twilight, you shall keep it at its appointed time. According to all its rites and ceremonies you shall keep it." ⁴So Moses told the children of Israel that they should keep the Passover. ⁵And they kept the Passover on the fourteenth day of the first month, at twilight, in the Wilderness of Sinai; according to all that the LORD commanded Moses, so the children of Israel did.

⁶Now there were *certain* men who were defiled by a human corpse, so that they could not keep the Passover on that day; and they came before Moses and Aaron that day. ⁷And those men said to him, "We *became* defiled by a human corpse. Why are we kept from presenting the offering of the LORD at its appointed time among the children of Israel?"

⁸And Moses said to them, "Stand still, that I may hear what the LORD will command concerning you."

⁹Then the LORD spoke to Moses, saying, ¹⁰"Speak to the children of Israel, saying: 'If anyone of you or your posterity is unclean because of a corpse, or *is* far away on a journey, he may still keep the LORD's Passover. ¹¹On the fourteenth day of the second month, at twilight, they may keep it. They shall eat it with unleavened bread and bitter herbs. ¹²They shall leave none of it until morning, nor break one of its bones. According to all the ordinances of the Passover they shall keep it. ¹³But the man who *is* clean and is not on a journey, and ceases to keep the Passover, that same person shall be cut off from among his people,

because he did not bring the offering of the Lord at its appointed time; that man shall bear his sin.

14"And if a stranger dwells among you, and would keep the Lord's Passover, he must do so according to the rite of the Passover and according to its ceremony; you shall have one ordinance, both for the stranger and the native of the land.' "

15Now on the day that the tabernacle was raised up, the cloud covered the tabernacle, the tent of the Testimony; from evening until morning it was above the tabernacle like the appearance of fire. 16So it was always: the cloud covered it *by day,* and the appearance of fire by night. 17Whenever the cloud was taken up from above the tabernacle, after that the children of Israel would journey; and in the place where the cloud settled, there the children of Israel would pitch their tents. 18At the command of the Lord the children of Israel would journey, and at the command of the Lord they would camp; as long as the cloud stayed above the tabernacle they remained encamped. 19Even when the cloud continued long, many days above the tabernacle, the children of Israel kept the charge of the Lord and did not journey. 20So it was, when the cloud was above the tabernacle a few days: according to the command of the Lord they would remain encamped, and according to the command of the Lord they would journey. 21So it was, when the cloud remained only from evening until morning: when the cloud was taken up in the morning, then they would journey; whether by day or by night, whenever the cloud was taken up, they would journey. 22*Whether it was* two days, a month, or a year that the cloud remained above the tabernacle, the children of Israel would remain encamped and not journey; but when it was taken up, they would journey. 23At the command of the Lord they remained encamped, and

at the command of the Lord they journeyed; they kept the charge of the Lord, at the command of the Lord by the hand of Moses.

MARK 13:14-37

"So when you see the *'abomination of desolation,'* * spoken of by Daniel the prophet,* standing where it ought not" (let the reader understand), "then let those who are in Judea flee to the mountains. 15Let him who is on the housetop not go down into the house, nor enter to take anything out of his house. 16And let him who is in the field not go back to get his clothes. 17But woe to those who are pregnant and to those who are nursing babies in those days! 18And pray that your flight may not be in winter. 19For *in* those days there will be tribulation, such as has not been since the beginning of the creation which God created until this time, nor ever shall be. 20And unless the Lord had shortened those days, no flesh would be saved; but for the elect's sake, whom He chose, He shortened the days.

21"Then if anyone says to you, 'Look, here *is* the Christ!' or, 'Look, *He is* there!' do not believe it. 22For false christs and false prophets will rise and show signs and wonders to deceive, if possible, even the elect. 23But take heed; see, I have told you all things beforehand.

24"But in those days, after that tribulation, the sun will be darkened, and the moon will not give its light; 25the stars of heaven will fall, and the powers in the heavens will be shaken. 26Then they will see the Son of Man coming in the clouds with great power and glory. 27And then He will send His angels, and gather together His elect from the four winds, from the farthest part of earth to the farthest part of heaven.

28"Now learn this parable from the

fig tree: When its branch has already become tender, and puts forth leaves, you know that summer is near. 29So you also, when you see these things happening, know that it* is near—at the doors! 30Assuredly, I say to you, this generation will by no means pass away till all these things take place. 31Heaven and earth will pass away, but My words will by no means pass away.

32"But of that day and hour no one knows, not even the angels in heaven, nor the Son, but only the Father. 33Take heed, watch and pray; for you do not know when the time is. 34It is like a man going to a far country, who left his house and gave authority to his servants, and to each his work, and commanded the doorkeeper to watch. 35Watch therefore, for you do not know when the master of the house is coming—in the evening, at midnight, at the crowing of the rooster, or in the morning— 36lest, coming suddenly, he find you sleeping. 37And what I say to you, I say to all: Watch!"

PSALM 50:1-23

A Psalm of Asaph.

THE Mighty One, God the LORD,
Has spoken and called the earth
From the rising of the sun to
its going down.
2   Out of Zion, the perfection of
beauty,
God will shine forth.
3   Our God shall come, and shall
not keep silent;
A fire shall devour before Him,
And it shall be very
tempestuous all around
Him.

4   He shall call to the heavens
from above,
And to the earth, that He may
judge His people:
5   "Gather My saints together to
Me,

Those who have made a
covenant with Me by
sacrifice."
6   Let the heavens declare His
righteousness,
For God Himself *is* Judge.
Selah

7   "Hear, O My people, and I will
speak,
O Israel, and I will testify
against you;
I *am* God, your God!
8   I will not rebuke you for your
sacrifices
Or your burnt offerings,
Which are continually before
Me.
9   I will not take a bull from your
house,
Nor goats out of your folds.
10   For every beast of the forest
is Mine,
And the cattle on a thousand
hills.
11   I know all the birds of the
mountains,
And the wild beasts of the
field *are* Mine.

12   "If I were hungry, I would not
tell you;
For the world *is* Mine, and all
its fullness.
13   Will I eat the flesh of bulls,
Or drink the blood of goats?
14   Offer to God thanksgiving,
And pay your vows to the
Most High.
15   Call upon Me in the day of
trouble;
I will deliver you, and you
shall glorify Me."

16   But to the wicked God says:
"What *right* have you to
declare My statutes,
Or take My covenant in your
mouth,
17   Seeing you hate instruction

And cast My words behind
you?

18 When you saw a thief, you
consented* with him,
And have been a partaker
with adulterers.

19 You give your mouth to evil,
And your tongue frames
deceit.

20 You sit *and* speak against
your brother;
You slander your own
mother's son.

21 These *things* you have done,
and I kept silent;

You thought that I was
altogether like you;
But I will rebuke you,
And set *them* in order before
your eyes.

22 "Now consider this, you who
forget God,
Lest I tear *you* in pieces,
And *there be* none to deliver:

23 Whoever offers praise
glorifies Me;
And to him who orders *his*
conduct *aright*
I will show the salvation of
God."

PROVERBS FOR TODAY/ 10:29-30

The way of the Lord *is strength for the upright, but destruction will come to the workers of iniquity. The righteous will never be removed, but the wicked will not inhabit the earth.*

MARCH 8

NUMBERS 10:1–11:23

AND the Lord spoke to Moses, saying: [2]"Make two silver trumpets for yourself; you shall make them of hammered work; you shall use them for calling the congregation and for directing the movement of the camps. [3]When they blow both of them, all the congregation shall gather before you at the door of the tabernacle of meeting. [4]But if they blow *only* one, then the leaders, the heads of the divisions of Israel, shall gather to you. [5]When you sound the advance, the camps that lie on the east side shall then begin their journey. [6]When you sound the advance the second time, then the camps that lie on the south side shall begin their journey; they shall sound the call for them to begin their journeys. [7]And when the assembly is to be gathered together, you shall blow, but not sound the advance. [8]The sons of Aaron, the priests, shall blow the trumpets; and these shall be to you as an ordinance forever throughout your generations.

[9]"When you go to war in your land against the enemy who oppresses you, then you shall sound an alarm with the trumpets, and you will be remembered before the Lord your God, and you will be saved from your enemies. [10]Also in the day of your gladness, in your appointed feasts, and at the beginning of your months, you shall blow the trumpets over your burnt offerings and over the sacrifices of your peace offerings; and they shall be a memorial for you before your God: I *am* the Lord your God."

¹¹Now it came to pass on the twentieth *day* of the second month, in the second year, that the cloud was taken up from above the tabernacle of the Testimony. ¹²And the children of Israel set out from the Wilderness of Sinai on their journeys; then the cloud settled down in the Wilderness of Paran. ¹³So they started out for the first time according to the command of the LORD by the hand of Moses.

¹⁴The standard of the camp of the children of Judah set out first according to their armies; over their army was Nahshon the son of Amminadab. ¹⁵Over the army of the tribe of the children of Issachar *was* Nethanel the son of Zuar. ¹⁶And over the army of the tribe of the children of Zebulun *was* Eliab the son of Helon.

¹⁷Then the tabernacle was taken down; and the sons of Gershon and the sons of Merari set out, carrying the tabernacle.

¹⁸And the standard of the camp of Reuben set out according to their armies; over their army *was* Elizur the son of Shedeur. ¹⁹Over the army of the tribe of the children of Simeon *was* Shelumiel the son of Zurishaddai. ²⁰And over the army of the tribe of the children of Gad *was* Eliasaph the son of Deuel.

²¹Then the Kohathites set out, carrying the holy things. (The tabernacle would be prepared for their arrival.)

²²And the standard of the camp of the children of Ephraim set out according to their armies; over their army *was* Elishama the son of Ammihud. ²³Over the army of the tribe of the children of Manasseh *was* Gamaliel the son of Pedahzur. ²⁴And over the army of the tribe of the children of Benjamin *was* Abidan the son of Gideoni.

²⁵Then the standard of the camp of the children of Dan (the rear guard of all the camps) set out according to their armies; over their army *was* Ahiezer the son of Ammishaddai.

²⁶Over the army of the tribe of the children of Asher *was* Pagiel the son of Ocran. ²⁷And over the army of the tribe of the children of Naphtali *was* Ahira the son of Enan.

²⁸Thus *was* the order of march of the children of Israel, according to their armies, when they began their journey.

²⁹Now Moses said to Hobab the son of Reuel* the Midianite, Moses' father-in-law, "We are setting out for the place of which the LORD said, 'I will give it to you.' Come with us, and we will treat you well; for the LORD has promised good things to Israel."

³⁰And he said to him, "I will not go, but I will depart to my *own* land and to my relatives."

³¹So *Moses* said, "Please do not leave, inasmuch as you know how we are to camp in the wilderness, and you can be our eyes. ³²And it shall be, if you go with us—indeed it shall be—that whatever good the LORD will do to us, the same we will do to you."

³³So they departed from the mountain of the LORD on a journey of three days; and the ark of the covenant of the LORD went before them for the three days' journey, to search out a resting place for them. ³⁴And the cloud of the LORD *was* above them by day when they went out from the camp.

³⁵So it was, whenever the ark set out, that Moses said:

"Rise up, O LORD!
Let Your enemies be scattered,
And let those who hate You flee
before You."

³⁶And when it rested, he said:

"Return, O LORD,
To the many thousands of
Israel."

Now *when* the people complained, it displeased the LORD; for the LORD heard *it,* and His anger was aroused. So the fire of the LORD burned among them, and consumed *some* in the outskirts of the camp. ²Then the people cried out to Moses, and when Moses prayed to the Lord, the fire was quenched. ³So he called the name of the place Taberah,* because the fire of the Lord had burned among them.

⁴Now the mixed multitude who were among them yielded to intense craving; so the children of Israel also wept again and said: "Who will give us meat to eat? ⁵We remember the fish which we ate freely in Egypt, the cucumbers, the melons, the leeks, the onions, and the garlic; ⁶but now our whole being *is* dried up; *there is* nothing at all except this manna *before* our eyes!"

⁷Now the manna *was* like coriander seed, and its color like the color of bdellium. ⁸The people went about and gathered *it,* ground *it* on millstones or beat *it* in the mortar, cooked *it* in pans, and made cakes of it; and its taste was like the taste of pastry prepared with oil. ⁹And when the dew fell on the camp in the night, the manna fell on it.

¹⁰Then Moses heard the people weeping throughout their families, everyone at the door of his tent; and the anger of the Lord was greatly aroused; Moses also was displeased. ¹¹So Moses said to the Lord, "Why have You afflicted Your servant? And why have I not found favor in Your sight, that You have laid the burden of all these people on me? ¹²Did I conceive all these people? Did I beget them, that You should say to me, 'Carry them in your bosom, as a guardian carries a nursing child,' to the land which You swore to their fathers? ¹³Where am I to get meat to give to all these people? For they weep all over me, saying, 'Give us meat, that we may eat.' ¹⁴I am not able to bear all these people alone, because the burden *is* too heavy for me. ¹⁵If You treat me like this, please kill me here and now—if I have found favor in Your sight—and do not let me see my wretchedness!"

¹⁶So the Lord said to Moses: "Gather to Me seventy men of the elders of Israel, whom you know to be the elders of the people and officers over them; bring them to the tabernacle of meeting, that they may stand there with you. ¹⁷Then I will come down and talk with you there. I will take of the Spirit that *is* upon you and will put *the same* upon them; and they shall bear the burden of the people with you, that you may not bear *it* yourself alone. ¹⁸Then you shall say to the people, 'Consecrate yourselves for tomorrow, and you shall eat meat; for you have wept in the hearing of the Lord, saying, "Who will give us meat to eat? For *it was* well with us in Egypt." Therefore the Lord will give you meat, and you shall eat. ¹⁹You shall eat, not one day, nor two days, nor five days, nor ten days, nor twenty days, ²⁰but *for* a whole month, until it comes out of your nostrils and becomes loathsome to you, because you have despised the Lord who is among you, and have wept before Him, saying, "Why did we ever come up out of Egypt?" ' "

²¹And Moses said, "The people whom I *am* among *are* six hundred thousand men on foot; yet You have said, 'I will give them meat, that they may eat *for* a whole month.' ²²Shall flocks and herds be slaughtered for them, to provide enough for them? Or shall all the fish of the sea be gathered together for them, to provide enough for them?"

²³And the Lord said to Moses, "Has the Lord's arm been shortened? Now you shall see whether what I say will happen to you or not."

MARK 14:1-21

AFTER two days it was the Passover and *the Feast* of Unleavened Bread. And the chief priests and the scribes sought how they might take Him [Jesus] by trickery and put *Him* to death. 2But they said, "Not during the feast, lest there be an uproar of the people."

3And being in Bethany at the house of Simon the leper, as He sat at the table, a woman came having an alabaster flask of very costly oil of spikenard. Then she broke the flask and poured *it* on His head. 4But there were some who were indignant among themselves, and said, "Why was this fragrant oil wasted? 5For it might have been sold for more than three hundred denarii and given to the poor." And they criticized her sharply.

6But Jesus said, "Let her alone. Why do you trouble her? She has done a good work for Me. 7For you have the poor with you always, and whenever you wish you may do them good; but Me you do not have always. 8She has done what she could. She has come beforehand to anoint My body for burial. 9Assuredly, I say to you, wherever this gospel is preached in the whole world, what this woman has done will also be told as a memorial to her."

10Then Judas Iscariot, one of the twelve, went to the chief priests to betray Him to them. 11And when they heard *it,* they were glad, and promised to give him money. So he sought how he might conveniently betray Him.

12Now on the first day of Unleavened Bread, when they killed the Passover *lamb,* His disciples said to Him, "Where do You want us to go and prepare, that You may eat the Passover?"

13And He sent out two of His disciples and said to them, "Go into the city, and a man will meet you carrying a pitcher of water; follow him. 14Wherever he goes in, say to the master of the house, 'The Teacher says, "Where is the guest room in which I may eat the Passover with My disciples?" ' 15Then he will show you a large upper room, furnished *and* prepared; there make ready for us."

16So His disciples went out, and came into the city, and found it just as He had said to them; and they prepared the Passover.

17In the evening He came with the twelve. 18Now as they sat and ate, Jesus said, "Assuredly, I say to you, one of you who eats with Me will betray Me."

19And they began to be sorrowful, and to say to Him one by one, "*Is* it I?" And another *said, "Is* it I?"*

20He answered and said to them, "*It is* one of the twelve, who dips with Me in the dish. 21The Son of Man indeed goes just as it is written of Him, but woe to that man by whom the Son of Man is betrayed! It would have been good for that man if he had never been born."

PSALM 51:1-19

To the Chief Musician. A Psalm of David when Nathan the prophet went to him, after he had gone in to Bathsheba.

Have mercy upon me, O God,
According to Your loving kindness;
According to the multitude of
Your tender mercies,
Blot out my transgressions.

2 Wash me thoroughly from my iniquity,
And cleanse me from my sin.

3 For I acknowledge my transgressions,
And my sin *is* always before me.

4 Against You, You only, have I sinned,
And done *this* evil in Your sight—
That You may be found just when You speak,*
And blameless when You judge.

5 Behold, I was brought forth in
iniquity,
And in sin my mother
conceived me.
6 Behold, You desire truth in
the inward parts,
And in the hidden *part* You
will make me to know
wisdom.

7 Purge me with hyssop, and I
shall be clean;
Wash me, and I shall be
whiter than snow.
8 Make me hear joy and
gladness,
That the bones You have
broken may rejoice.
9 Hide Your face from my sins,
And blot out all my iniquities.

10 Create in me a clean heart,
O God,
And renew a steadfast spirit
within me.
11 Do not cast me away from
Your presence,
And do not take Your Holy
Spirit from me.

12 Restore to me the joy of Your
salvation,
And uphold me *by Your*
generous Spirit.
13 *Then* I will teach
transgressors Your ways,
And sinners shall be
converted to You.

14 Deliver me from the guilt of
bloodshed, O God,
The God of my salvation,
And my tongue shall sing
aloud of Your
righteousness.
15 O Lord, open my lips,
And my mouth shall show
forth Your praise.
16 For You do not desire
sacrifice, or else I would
give *it;*
You do not delight in burnt
offering.
17 The sacrifices of God *are* a
broken spirit,
A broken and a contrite
heart—
These, O God, You will not
despise.

18 Do good in Your good
pleasure to Zion;
Build the walls of Jerusalem.
19 Then You shall be pleased
with the sacrifices of
righteousness,
With burnt offering and
whole burnt offering;
Then they shall offer bulls on
Your altar.

PROVERBS FOR TODAY/ 10:31-32

The mouth of the righteous brings forth wisdom, but the perverse tongue will be cut out. The lips of the righteous know what is acceptable, but the mouth of the wicked what is perverse.

MARCH 9

NUMBERS 11:24–13:33

So Moses went out and told the people the words of the LORD, and he gathered the seventy men of the elders of the people and placed them around the tabernacle. ²⁵Then the LORD came down in the cloud, and spoke to him, and took of the Spirit that *was* upon him, and placed *the same* upon the seventy elders; and it happened, when the Spirit rested upon them, that they prophesied, although they never did *so* again.*

²⁶But two men had remained in the camp: the name of one *was* Eldad, and the name of the other Medad. And the Spirit rested upon them. Now they *were* among those listed, but who had not gone out to the tabernacle; yet they prophesied in the camp. ²⁷And a young man ran and told Moses, and said, "Eldad and Medad are prophesying in the camp."

²⁸So Joshua the son of Nun, Moses' assistant, *one* of his choice men, answered and said, "Moses my lord, forbid them!"

²⁹Then Moses said to him, "Are you zealous for my sake? Oh, that all the LORD's people were prophets *and* that the LORD would put His Spirit upon them!" ³⁰And Moses returned to the camp, he and the elders of Israel.

³¹Now a wind went out from the LORD, and it brought quail from the sea and left *them* fluttering near the camp, about a day's journey on this side and about a day's journey on the other side, all around the camp, and about two cubits above the surface of the ground. ³²And the people stayed up all that day, all night, and all the next day, and gathered the quail (he who gathered least gathered ten homers); and

they spread *them* out for themselves all around the camp. ³³But while the meat *was* still between their teeth, before it was chewed, the wrath of the LORD was aroused against the people, and the LORD struck the people with a very great plague. ³⁴So he called the name of that place Kibroth Hattaavah,* because there they buried the people who had yielded to craving.

³⁵From Kibroth Hattaavah the people moved to Hazeroth, and camped at Hazeroth.

THEN Miriam and Aaron spoke against Moses because of the Ethiopian woman whom he had married; for he had married an Ethiopian woman. ²So they said, "Has the LORD indeed spoken only through Moses? Has He not spoken through us also?" And the LORD heard *it*. ³(Now the man Moses *was* very humble, more than all men who *were* on the face of the earth.)

⁴Suddenly the LORD said to Moses, Aaron, and Miriam, "Come out, you three, to the tabernacle of meeting!" So the three came out. ⁵Then the LORD came down in the pillar of cloud and stood *in* the door of the tabernacle, and called Aaron and Miriam. And they both went forward. ⁶Then He said,

"Hear now My words:
If there is a prophet among you,
I, the LORD, make Myself known to him in a vision;
I speak to him in a dream.
7 Not so with My servant Moses;
He *is* faithful in all My house.
8 I speak with him face to face,

Even plainly, and not in dark
sayings;
And he sees the form of the
LORD.
Why then were you not afraid
To speak against My servant
Moses?"

9So the anger of the LORD was aroused against them, and He departed. 10And when the cloud departed from above the tabernacle, suddenly Miriam *became* leprous, as *white as* snow. Then Aaron turned toward Miriam, and there she was, a leper. 11So Aaron said to Moses, "Oh, my lord! Please do not lay *this* sin on us, in which we have done foolishly and in which we have sinned. 12Please do not let her be as one dead, whose flesh is half consumed when he comes out of his mother's womb!"

13So Moses cried out to the LORD, saying, "Please heal her, O God, I pray!"

14Then the LORD said to Moses, "If her father had but spit in her face, would she not be shamed seven days? Let her be shut out of the camp seven days, and afterward she may be received *again*." 15So Miriam was shut out of the camp seven days, and the people did not journey till Miriam was brought in *again*. 16And afterward the people moved from Hazeroth and camped in the Wilderness of Paran.

AND the LORD spoke to Moses, saying, 2"Send men to spy out the land of Canaan, which I am giving to the children of Israel; from each tribe of their fathers you shall send a man, every one a leader among them."

3So Moses sent them from the Wilderness of Paran according to the command of the LORD, all of them men who *were* heads of the children of Israel. 4Now these *were* their names: from the tribe of Reuben, Shammua the son of Zaccur; 5from the tribe of

Simeon, Shaphat the son of Hori; 6from the tribe of Judah, Caleb the son of Jephunneh; 7from the tribe of Issachar, Igal the son of Joseph; 8from the tribe of Ephraim, Hoshea* the son of Nun; 9from the tribe of Benjamin, Palti the son of Raphu; 10from the tribe of Zebulun, Gaddiel the son of Sodi; 11from the tribe of Joseph, *that is,* from the tribe of Manasseh, Gaddi the son of Susi; 12from the tribe of Dan, Ammiel the son of Gemalli; 13from the tribe of Asher, Sethur the son of Michael; 14from the tribe of Naphtali, Nahbi the son of Vophsi; 15from the tribe of Gad, Geuel the son of Machi.

16These *are* the names of the men whom Moses sent to spy out the land. And Moses called Hoshea* the son of Nun, Joshua.

17Then Moses sent them to spy out the land of Canaan, and said to them, "Go up this *way* into the South, and go up to the mountains, 18and see what the land is like: whether the people who dwell in it *are* strong or weak, few or many; 19whether the land they dwell in *is* good or bad; whether the cities they inhabit *are* like camps or strongholds; 20whether the land *is* rich or poor; and whether there are forests there or not. Be of good courage. And bring some of the fruit of the land." Now the time *was* the season of the first ripe grapes.

21So they went up and spied out the land from the Wilderness of Zin as far as Rehob, near the entrance of Hamath. 22And they went up through the South and came to Hebron; Ahiman, Sheshai, and Talmai, the descendants of Anak, *were* there. (Now Hebron was built seven years before Zoan in Egypt.) 23Then they came to the Valley of Eshcol, and there cut down a branch with one cluster of grapes; they carried it between two of them on a pole. *They* also *brought* some of the pomegranates and figs. 24The place was called the Valley of Eshcol,* because of the cluster which the men of Israel cut down there. ²⁵And they returned from spying out the land after forty days.

²⁶Now they departed and came back to Moses and Aaron and all the congregation of the children of Israel in the Wilderness of Paran, at Kadesh; they brought back word to them and to all the congregation, and showed them the fruit of the land. ²⁷Then they told him, and said: "We went to the land where you sent us. It truly flows with milk and honey, and this *is* its fruit. ²⁸Nevertheless the people who dwell in the land *are* strong; the cities *are* fortified *and* very large; moreover we saw the descendants of Anak there. ³⁰The Amalekites dwell in the land of the South; the Hittites, the Jebusites, and the Amorites dwell in the mountains; and the Canaanites dwell by the sea and along the banks of the Jordan."

³⁰Then Caleb quieted the people before Moses, and said, "Let us go up at once and take possession, for we are well able to overcome it."

³¹But the men who had gone up with him said, "We are not able to go up against the people, for they are stronger than we." ³²And they gave the children of Israel a bad report of the land which they had spied out, saying, "The land through which we have gone as spies *is* a land that devours its inhabitants, and all the people whom we saw in it *are* men of *great* stature. ³³There we saw the giants* (the descendants of Anak came from the giants); and we were like grasshoppers in our own sight, and so we were in their sight."

MARK 14:22-52

AND as they [Jesus and his disciples] were eating, Jesus took bread, blessed and broke *it,* and gave *it* to them and said, "Take, eat;* this is My body."

²³Then He took the cup, and when He had given thanks He gave *it* to them, and they all drank from it. ²⁴And He said to them, "This is My blood of the new* covenant, which is shed for many. ²⁵Assuredly, I say to you, I will no longer drink of the fruit of the vine until that day when I drink it new in the kingdom of God."

²⁶And when they had sung a hymn, they went out to the Mount of Olives.

²⁷Then Jesus said to them, "All of you will be made to stumble because of Me this night,* for it is written:

'*I will strike the Shepherd,
And the sheep will be
scattered.*'*

²⁸"But after I have been raised, I will go before you to Galilee."

²⁹Peter said to Him, "Even if all are made to stumble, yet I *will* not *be.*"

³⁰Jesus said to him, "Assuredly, I say to you that today, *even* this night, before the rooster crows twice, you will deny Me three times."

³¹But he spoke more vehemently, "If I have to die with You, I will not deny You!"

And they all said likewise.

³²Then they came to a place which was named Gethsemane; and He said to His disciples, "Sit here while I pray." ³³And He took Peter, James, and John with Him, and He began to be troubled and deeply distressed. ³⁴Then He said to them, "My soul is exceedingly sorrowful, *even* to death. Stay here and watch."

³⁵He went a little farther, and fell on the ground, and prayed that if it were possible, the hour might pass from Him. ³⁶And He said, "Abba, Father, all things *are* possible for You. Take this cup away from Me; nevertheless, not what I will, but what You *will.*"

³⁷Then He came and found them sleeping, and said to Peter, "Simon, are you sleeping? Could you not watch one hour? ³⁸Watch and pray, lest you enter

into temptation. The spirit indeed *is* willing, but the flesh *is* weak."

³⁹Again He went away and prayed, and spoke the same words. ⁴⁰And when He returned, He found them asleep again, for their eyes were heavy; and they did not know what to answer Him.

⁴¹Then He came the third time and said to them, "Are you still sleeping and resting? It is enough! The hour has come; behold, the Son of Man is being betrayed into the hands of sinners. ⁴²Rise, let us be going. See, My betrayer is at hand."

⁴³And immediately, while He was still speaking, Judas, one of the twelve, with a great multitude with swords and clubs, came from the chief priests and the scribes and the elders. ⁴⁴Now His betrayer had given them a signal, saying, "Whomever I kiss, He is the One; seize Him and lead *Him* away safely."

⁴⁵As soon as He had come, immediately he went up to Him and said to Him, "Rabbi, Rabbi!" and kissed Him.

⁴⁶Then they laid their hands on Him and took Him. ⁴⁷And one of those who stood by drew his sword and struck the servant of the high priest, and cut off his ear.

⁴⁸Then Jesus answered and said to them, "Have you come out, as against a robber, with swords and clubs to take Me? ⁴⁹I was daily with you in the temple teaching, and you did not seize Me. But the Scriptures must be fulfilled."

⁵⁰Then they all forsook Him and fled.

⁵¹Now a certain young man followed Him, having a linen cloth thrown around *his* naked *body*. And the young men laid hold of him, ⁵²and he left the linen cloth and fled from them naked.

PSALM 52:1-9

To the Chief Musician. A Contemplation* of David when Doeg the Edomite went and told Saul, and said to him, "David has gone to the house of Ahimelech."

WHY do you boast in evil, O mighty man?
The goodness of God *endures* continually.

2 Your tongue devises destruction,
Like a sharp razor, working deceitfully.

3 You love evil more than good,
Lying rather than speaking righteousness.   Selah

4 You love all devouring words,
You deceitful tongue.

5 God shall likewise destroy you forever;
He shall take you away, and pluck you out of *your* dwelling place,
And uproot you from the land of the living.   Selah

6 The righteous also shall see and fear,
And shall laugh at him, *saying,*

7 "Here is the man *who* did not make God his strength,
But trusted in the abundance of his riches,
And strengthened himself in his wickedness."

8 But I *am* like a green olive tree in the house of God;
I trust in the mercy of God forever and ever.

9 I will praise You forever,
Because You have done *it;*
And in the presence of Your saints
I will wait on Your name, for *it is* good.

PROVERBS FOR TODAY/ 11:1-3

Dishonest scales are *an abomination to the* Lord, *but a just weight* is *His delight.*

When pride comes, then comes shame; but with the humble is wisdom. The integrity of the upright will guide them, but the perversity of the unfaithful will destroy them.

MARCH 10

NUMBERS 14:1–15:16

So all the congregation lifted up their voices and cried, and the people wept that night. ²And all the children of Israel complained against Moses and Aaron, and the whole congregation said to them, "If only we had died in the land of Egypt! Or if only we had died in this wilderness! ³Why has the LORD brought us to this land to fall by the sword, that our wives and children should become victims? Would it not be better for us to return to Egypt?" ⁴So they said to one another, "Let us select a leader and return to Egypt."

⁵Then Moses and Aaron fell on their faces before all the assembly of the congregation of the children of Israel.

⁶But Joshua the son of Nun and Caleb the son of Jephunneh, *who were* among those who had spied out the land, tore their clothes; ⁷and they spoke to all the congregation of the children of Israel, saying: "The land we passed through to spy out *is* an exceedingly good land. ⁸If the LORD delights in us, then He will bring us into this land and give it to us, 'a land which flows with milk and honey.'* ⁹Only do not rebel against the LORD, nor fear the people of the land, for they *are* our bread; their protection has departed from them, and the LORD *is* with us. Do not fear them."

¹⁰And all the congregation said to stone them with stones. Now the glory of the LORD appeared in the tabernacle of meeting before all the children of Israel.

¹¹Then the LORD said to Moses: "How long will these people reject Me? And how long will they not believe Me, with all the signs which I have performed among them? ¹²I will strike them with the pestilence and disinherit them, and I will make of you a nation greater and mightier than they."

¹³And Moses said to the LORD: "Then the Egyptians will hear *it,* for by Your might You brought these people up from among them, ¹⁴and they will tell *it* to the inhabitants of this land. They have heard that You, LORD, *are* among these people; that You, LORD, are seen face to face and Your cloud stands above them, and You go before them in a pillar of cloud by day and in a pillar of fire by night. ¹⁵Now *if* You kill these people as one man, then the nations which have heard of Your fame will speak, saying, ¹⁶'Because the LORD was not able to bring this people to the land which He swore to give them, therefore He killed them in the wilderness.' ¹⁷And now, I pray, let the power of my Lord be great, just as You have spoken, saying, ¹⁸'The LORD is longsuffering and abundant in mercy, forgiving iniquity and transgression; but He by no means clears *the guilty,* visiting the iniquity of the fathers on the children to the third and fourth *generation.'*＊ ¹⁹Pardon the iniquity of this people, I pray, according to the greatness of Your mercy, just as You have forgiven this people, from Egypt even until now."

²⁰Then the LORD said: "I have pardoned, according to your word; ²¹but

truly, as I live, all the earth shall be filled with the glory of the LORD— 22because all these men who have seen My glory and the signs which I did in Egypt and in the wilderness, and have put Me to the test now these ten times, and have not heeded My voice, 23they certainly shall not see the land of which I swore to their fathers, nor shall any of those who rejected Me see it. 24But My servant Caleb, because he has a different spirit in him and has followed Me fully, I will bring into the land where he went, and his descendants shall inherit it. 25Now the Amalekites and the Canaanites dwell in the valley; tomorrow turn and move out into the wilderness by the Way of the Red Sea."

26And the LORD spoke to Moses and Aaron, saying, 27"How long *shall I bear with* this evil congregation who complain against Me? I have heard the complaints which the children of Israel make against Me. 28Say to them, 'As I live,' says the LORD, 'just as you have spoken in My hearing, so I will do to you: 29The carcasses of you who have complained against Me shall fall in this wilderness, all of you who were numbered, according to your entire number, from twenty years old and above. 30Except for Caleb the son of Jephunneh and Joshua the son of Nun, you shall by no means enter the land which I swore I would make you dwell in. 31But your little ones, whom you said would be victims, I will bring in, and they shall know the land which you have despised. 32But *as for* you, your carcasses shall fall in this wilderness. 33And your sons shall be shepherds in the wilderness forty years, and bear the brunt of your infidelity, until your carcasses are consumed in the wilderness. 34According to the number of the days in which you spied out the land, forty days, for each day you shall bear your guilt one year, *namely* forty years, and you shall know

My rejection. 35I the LORD have spoken this. I will surely do so to all this evil congregation who are gathered together against Me. In this wilderness they shall be consumed, and there they shall die.' "

36Now the men whom Moses sent to spy out the land, who returned and made all the congregation complain against him by bringing a bad report of the land, 37those very men who brought the evil report about the land, died by the plague before the LORD. 38But Joshua the son of Nun and Caleb the son of Jephunneh remained alive, of the men who went to spy out the land.

39Then Moses told these words to all the children of Israel, and the people mourned greatly. 40And they rose early in the morning and went up to the top of the mountain, saying, "Here we are, and we will go up to the place which the LORD has promised, for we have sinned!"

41And Moses said, "Now why do you transgress the command of the LORD? For this will not succeed. 42Do not go up, lest you be defeated by your enemies, for the LORD *is* not among you. 43For the Amalekites and the Canaanites *are* there before you, and you shall fall by the sword; because you have turned away from the LORD, the LORD will not be with you."

44But they presumed to go up to the mountaintop. Nevertheless, neither the ark of the covenant of the LORD nor Moses departed from the camp. 45Then the Amalekites and the Canaanites who dwelt in that mountain came down and attacked them, and drove them back as far as Hormah.

AND the LORD spoke to Moses, saying, 2"Speak to the children of Israel, and say to them: 'When you have come into the land you are to inhabit, which I am giving to you, 3and you make an offering by fire to the LORD, a burnt offering or a sacrifice, to fulfill a vow or as a freewill offering or in your appointed feasts, to make a sweet aroma to the LORD, from the herd or the flock, [4]then he who presents his offering to the LORD shall bring a grain offering of one-tenth *of an ephah* of fine flour mixed with one-fourth of a hin of oil; [5]and one-fourth of a hin of wine as a drink offering you shall prepare with the burnt offering or the sacrifice, for each lamb. [6]Or for a ram you shall prepare as a grain offering two-tenths *of an ephah* of fine flour mixed with one-third of a hin of oil; [7]and as a drink offering you shall offer one-third of a hin of wine as a sweet aroma to the LORD. [8]And when you prepare a young bull as a burnt offering, or as a sacrifice to fulfill a vow, or as a peace offering to the LORD, [9]then shall be offered with the young bull a grain offering of three-tenths *of an ephah* of fine flour mixed with half a hin of oil; [10]and you shall bring as the drink offering half a hin of wine as an offering made by fire, a sweet aroma to the LORD.

[11]"Thus it shall be done for each young bull, for each ram, or for each lamb or young goat. [12]According to the number that you prepare, so you shall do with everyone according to their number. [13]All who are native-born shall do these things in this manner, in presenting an offering made by fire, a sweet aroma to the LORD. [14]And if a stranger dwells with you, or whoever *is* among you throughout your generations, and would present an offering made by fire, a sweet aroma to the LORD, just as you do, so shall he do. [15]One ordinance *shall be* for you of the assembly and for the stranger who dwells *with you,* an ordinance forever throughout your generations; as you are, so shall the stranger be before the LORD. [16]One law and one custom shall be for you and for the stranger who dwells with you.' "*

MARK 14:53-72

AND they led Jesus away to the high priest; and with him were assembled all the chief priests, the elders, and the scribes. [54]But Peter followed Him at a distance, right into the courtyard of the high priest. And he sat with the servants and warmed himself at the fire.

[55]Now the chief priests and all the council sought testimony against Jesus to put Him to death, but found none. [56]For many bore false witness against Him, but their testimonies did not agree.

[57]Then some rose up and bore false witness against Him, saying, [58]"We heard Him say, 'I will destroy this temple made with hands, and within three days I will build another made without hands.' " [59]But not even then did their testimony agree.

[60]And the high priest stood up in the midst and asked Jesus, saying, "Do You answer nothing? What *is it* these men testify against You?" [61]But He kept silent and answered nothing.

Again the high priest asked Him, saying to Him, "Are You the Christ, the Son of the Blessed?"

[62]Jesus said, "I am. And you will see the Son of Man sitting at the right hand of the Power, and coming with the clouds of heaven."

[63]Then the high priest tore his clothes and said, "What further need do we have of witnesses? [64]You have heard the blasphemy! What do you think?"

And they all condemned Him to be deserving of death.

[65]Then some began to spit on Him, and to blindfold Him, and to beat Him, and to say to Him, "Prophesy!" And the officers struck Him with the palms of their hands.*

[66]Now as Peter was below in the courtyard, one of the servant girls of the high priest came. [67]And when she

saw Peter warming himself, she looked at him and said, "You also were with Jesus of Nazareth."

⁶⁸But he denied it, saying, "I neither know nor understand what you are saying." And he went out on the porch, and a rooster crowed.

⁶⁹And the servant girl saw him again, and began to say to those who stood by, "This is one of them." ⁷⁰But he denied it again.

And a little later those who stood by said to Peter again, "Surely you are *one* of them; for you are a Galilean, and your speech shows *it*."*

⁷¹Then he began to curse and swear, "I do not know this Man of whom you speak!"

⁷²A second time *the* rooster crowed. Then Peter called to mind the word that Jesus had said to him, "Before the rooster crows twice, you will deny Me three times." And when he thought about it, he wept.

PSALM 53:1-6

To the Chief Musician. Set to "Mahalath."
A Contemplation of David.*

THE fool has said in his heart,
  "*There is* no God."
  They are corrupt, and have
    done abominable iniquity;

There is none who does good.

2 God looks down from heaven
    upon the children of men,
  To see if there are *any* who
    understand, who seek God.

3 Every one of them has turned
    aside;
  They have together become
    corrupt;
  There is none who does good,
  No, not one.

4 Have the workers of iniquity
    no knowledge,
  Who eat up my people *as* they
    eat bread,
  And do not call upon God?

5 There they are in great fear
  Where no fear was,
  For God has scattered the
    bones of him who encamps
    against you;
  You have put *them* to shame,
  Because God has despised
    them.

6 Oh, that the salvation of Israel
    would come out of Zion!
  When God brings back the
    captivity of His people,
  Let Jacob rejoice *and* Israel
    be glad.

PROVERBS FOR TODAY/ 11:4

Riches do not profit in the day of wrath, but righteousness delivers from death.

MARCH 11

NUMBERS 15:17–16:40

AGAIN the LORD spoke to Moses, saying, ¹⁸"Speak to the children of Israel, and say to them: 'When you come into the land to which

I bring you, ¹⁹then it will be, when you eat of the bread of the land, that you shall offer up a heave offering to the LORD. ²⁰You shall offer up a cake of the first of your ground meal *as* a heave offering; as a heave offering of the threshing floor, so shall you offer it up. ²¹Of the first of your ground meal you shall give to the LORD a heave offering throughout your generations.

²²'If you sin unintentionally, and do not observe all these commandments which the LORD has spoken to Moses— ²³all that the LORD has commanded you by the hand of Moses, from the day the LORD gave commandment and onward throughout your generations— ²⁴then it will be, if it is unintentionally committed, without the knowledge of the congregation, that the whole congregation shall offer one young bull as a burnt offering, as a sweet aroma to the LORD, with its grain offering and its drink offering, according to the ordinance, and one kid of the goats as a sin offering. ²⁵So the priest shall make atonement for the whole congregation of the children of Israel, and it shall be forgiven them, for it was unintentional; they shall bring their offering, an offering made by fire to the LORD, and their sin offering before the LORD, for their unintended sin. ²⁶It shall be forgiven the whole congregation of the children of Israel and the stranger who dwells among them, because all the people *did it* unintentionally.

²⁷'And if a person sins unintentionally, then he shall bring a female goat in its first year as a sin offering. ²⁸So the priest shall make atonement for the person who sins unintentionally, when he sins unintentionally before the LORD, to make atonement for him; and it shall be forgiven him. ²⁹You shall have one law for him who sins unintentionally, *for* him who is native-born among the children of Israel and for the stranger who dwells among them.

³⁰'But the person who does *anything* presumptuously, *whether he is* native-born or a stranger, that one brings reproach on the LORD, and he shall be cut off from among his people. ³¹Because

he has despised the word of the LORD, and has broken His commandment, that person shall be completely cut off; his guilt *shall be* upon him.' "

³²Now while the children of Israel were in the wilderness, they found a man gathering sticks on the Sabbath day. ³³And those who found him gathering sticks brought him to Moses and Aaron, and to all the congregation. ³⁴They put him under guard, because it had not been explained what should be done to him.

³⁵Then the LORD said to Moses, "The man must surely be put to death; all the congregation shall stone him with stones outside the camp." ³⁶So, as the LORD commanded Moses, all the congregation brought him outside the camp and stoned him with stones, and he died.

³⁷Again the LORD spoke to Moses, saying, ³⁸"Speak to the children of Israel: Tell them to make tassels on the corners of their garments throughout their generations, and to put a blue thread in the tassels of the corners. ³⁹And you shall have the tassel, that you may look upon it and remember all the commandments of the LORD and do them, and that you *may* not follow the harlotry to which your own heart and your own eyes are inclined, ⁴⁰and that you may remember and do all My commandments, and be holy for your God. ⁴¹I *am* the LORD your God, who brought you out of the land of Egypt, to be your God: I *am* the LORD your God."

Now Korah the son of Izhar, the son of Kohath, the son of Levi, with Dathan and Abiram the sons of Eliab, and On the son of Peleth, sons of Reuben, took *men;* ²and they rose up before Moses with some of the children of Israel, two hundred and fifty leaders of the congregation, representatives of the congregation, men of renown. ³They gathered together against Moses and

Aaron, and said to them, "*You take* too much upon yourselves, for all the congregation *is* holy, every one of them, and the Lᴏʀᴅ *is* among them. Why then do you exalt yourselves above the assembly of the Lᴏʀᴅ?"

⁴So when Moses heard *it,* he fell on his face; ⁵and he spoke to Korah and all his company, saying, "Tomorrow morning the Lᴏʀᴅ will show who *is* His and *who is* holy, and will cause *him* to come near to Him. That one whom He chooses He will cause to come near to Him. ⁶Do this: Take censers, Korah and all your company; ⁷put fire in them and put incense in them before the Lᴏʀᴅ tomorrow, and it shall be *that* the man whom the Lᴏʀᴅ chooses *is* the holy one. *You take* too much upon yourselves, you sons of Levi!"

⁸Then Moses said to Korah, "Hear now, you sons of Levi: ⁹*Is it* a small thing to you that the God of Israel has separated you from the congregation of Israel, to bring you near to Himself, to do the work of the tabernacle of the Lᴏʀᴅ, and to stand before the congregation to serve them; ¹⁰and that He has brought you near *to Himself,* you and all your brethren, the sons of Levi, with you? And are you seeking the priesthood also? ¹¹Therefore you and all your company *are* gathered together against the Lᴏʀᴅ. And what *is* Aaron that you complain against him?"

¹²And Moses sent to call Dathan and Abiram the sons of Eliab, but they said, "We will not come up! ¹³*Is it* a small thing that you have brought us up out of a land flowing with milk and honey, to kill us in the wilderness, that you should keep acting like a prince over us? ¹⁴Moreover you have not brought us into a land flowing with milk and honey, nor given us inheritance of fields and vineyards. Will you put out the eyes of these men? We will not come up!"

¹⁵Then Moses was very angry, and said to the Lᴏʀᴅ, "Do not respect their offering. I have not taken one donkey from them, nor have I hurt one of them."

¹⁶And Moses said to Korah, "Tomorrow, you and all your company be present before the Lᴏʀᴅ—you and they, as well as Aaron. ¹⁷Let each take his censer and put incense in it, and each of you bring his censer before the Lᴏʀᴅ, two hundred and fifty censers; both you and Aaron, each *with* his censer." ¹⁸So every man took his censer, put fire in it, laid incense on it, and stood at the door of the tabernacle of meeting with Moses and Aaron. ¹⁹And Korah gathered all the congregation against them at the door of the tabernacle of meeting. Then the glory of the Lᴏʀᴅ appeared to all the congregation.

²⁰And the Lᴏʀᴅ spoke to Moses and Aaron, saying, ²¹"Separate yourselves from among this congregation, that I may consume them in a moment."

²²Then they fell on their faces, and said, "O God, the God of the spirits of all flesh, shall one man sin, and You be angry with all the congregation?"

²³So the Lᴏʀᴅ spoke to Moses, saying, ²⁴"Speak to the congregation, saying, 'Get away from the tents of Korah, Dathan, and Abiram.' "

²⁵Then Moses rose and went to Dathan and Abiram, and the elders of Israel followed him. ²⁶And he spoke to the congregation, saying, "Depart now from the tents of these wicked men! Touch nothing of theirs, lest you be consumed in all their sins." ²⁷So they got away from around the tents of Korah, Dathan, and Abiram; and Dathan and Abiram came out and stood at the door of their tents, with their wives, their sons, and their little children.

²⁸And Moses said: "By this you shall know that the Lᴏʀᴅ has sent me to do all these works, for *I have* not *done them* of my own will. ²⁹If these men die naturally like all men, or if they are visited by the common fate of all men,

then the Lord has not sent me. ³⁰But if the Lord creates a new thing, and the earth opens its mouth and swallows them up with all that belongs to them, and they go down alive into the pit, then you will understand that these men have rejected the Lord."

³¹Now it came to pass, as he finished speaking all these words, that the ground split apart under them, ³²and the earth opened its mouth and swallowed them up, with their households and all the men with Korah, with all *their* goods ³³So they and all those with them went down alive into the pit; the earth closed over them, and they perished from among the assembly. ³⁴Then all Israel who *were* around them fled at their cry, for they said, "Lest the earth swallow us up *also!*"

³⁵And a fire came out from the Lord and consumed the two hundred and fifty men who were offering incense.

³⁶Then the Lord spoke to Moses, saying: ³⁷"Tell Eleazar, the son of Aaron the priest, to pick up the censers out of the blaze, for they are holy, and scatter the fire some distance away. ³⁸The censers of these men who sinned against their own souls, let them be made into hammered plates as a covering for the altar. Because they presented them before the Lord, therefore they are holy; and they shall be a sign to the children of Israel." ³⁹So Eleazar the priest took the bronze censers, which those who were burned up had presented, and they were hammered out as a covering on the altar, ⁴⁰*to be* a memorial to the children of Israel that no outsider, who *is* not a descendant of Aaron, should come near to offer incense before the Lord, that he might not become like Korah and his companions, just as the Lord had said to him through Moses.

MARK 15:1-47

Immediately, in the morning, the chief priests held a consultation with the elders and scribes and the whole council; and they bound Jesus, led *Him* away, and delivered *Him* to Pilate. ²Then Pilate asked Him, "Are You the King of the Jews?"

He answered and said to him, "*It is as* you say."

³And the chief priests accused Him of many things, but He answered nothing. ⁴Then Pilate asked Him again, saying, "Do You answer nothing? See how many things they testify against You!"* ⁵But Jesus still answered nothing, so that Pilate marveled.

⁶Now at the feast he was accustomed to releasing one prisoner to them, whomever they requested. ⁷And there was one named Barabbas, *who was* chained with his fellow rebels; they had committed murder in the rebellion. ⁸Then the multitude, crying aloud,* began to ask *him to do* just as he had always done for them. ⁹But Pilate answered them, saying, "Do you want me to release to you the King of the Jews?" ¹⁰For he knew that the chief priests had handed Him over because of envy.

¹¹But the chief priests stirred up the crowd, so that he should rather release Barabbas to them. ¹²Pilate answered and said to them again, "What then do you want me to do *with Him* whom you call the King of the Jews?"

¹³So they cried out again, "Crucify Him!"

¹⁴Then Pilate said to them, "Why, what evil has He done?"

But they cried out all the more, "Crucify Him!"

¹⁵So Pilate, wanting to gratify the crowd, released Barabbas to them; and he delivered Jesus, after he had scourged *Him,* to be crucified.

¹⁶Then the soldiers led Him away into the hall called Praetorium, and

they called together the whole garrison. ¹⁷And they clothed Him with purple; and they twisted a crown of thorns, put it on His *head,* ¹⁸and began to salute Him, "Hail, King of the Jews!" ¹⁹Then they struck Him on the head with a reed and spat on Him; and bowing the knee, they worshiped Him. ²⁰And when they had mocked Him, they took the purple off Him, put His own clothes on Him, and led Him out to crucify Him.

²¹Then they compelled a certain man, Simon a Cyrenian, the father of Alexander and Rufus, as he was coming out of the country and passing by, to bear His cross. ²²And they brought Him to the place Golgotha, which is translated, Place of a Skull. ²³Then they gave Him wine mingled with myrrh to drink, but He did not take *it.* ²⁴And when they crucified Him, they divided His garments, casting lots for them to determine what every man should take.

²⁵Now it was the third hour, and they crucified Him. ²⁶And the inscription of His accusation was written above:

THE KING OF THE JEWS.

²⁷With Him they also crucified two robbers, one on His right and the other on His left. ²⁸So the Scripture was fulfilled* which says, *"And He was numbered with the transgressors."* *

²⁹And those who passed by blasphemed Him, wagging their heads and saying, "Aha! *You* who destroy the temple and build *it* in three days, ³⁰save Yourself, and come down from the cross!"

³¹Likewise the chief priests also, mocking among themselves with the scribes, said, "He saved others; Himself He cannot save. ³²Let the Christ, the King of Israel, descend now from the cross, that we may see and believe."*

Even those who were crucified with Him reviled Him.

³³Now when the sixth hour had come, there was darkness over the whole land until the ninth hour. ³⁴And at the ninth hour Jesus cried out with a loud voice, saying, "Eloi, Eloi, lama sabachthani?" which is translated, *"My God, My God, why have You forsaken Me?"* *

³⁵Some of those who stood by, when they heard *that,* said, "Look, He is calling for Elijah!" ³⁶Then someone ran and filled a sponge full of sour wine, put *it* on a reed, and offered *it* to Him to drink, saying, "Let Him alone; let us see if Elijah will come to take Him down."

³⁷And Jesus cried out with a loud voice, and breathed His last.

³⁸Then the veil of the temple was torn in two from top to bottom. ³⁹So when the centurion, who stood opposite Him, saw that He cried out like this and breathed His last,* he said, "Truly this Man was the Son of God!"

⁴⁰There were also women looking on from afar, among whom were Mary Magdalene, Mary the mother of James the Less and of Joses, and Salome, ⁴¹who also followed Him and ministered to Him when He was in Galilee, and many other women who came up with Him to Jerusalem.

⁴²Now when evening had come, because it was the Preparation Day, that is, the day before the Sabbath, ⁴³Joseph of Arimathea, a prominent council member, who was himself waiting for the kingdom of God, coming and taking courage, went in to Pilate and asked for the body of Jesus. ⁴⁴Pilate marveled that He was already dead; and summoning the centurion, he asked him if He had been dead for some time. ⁴⁵So when he found out from the centurion, he granted the body to Joseph. ⁴⁶Then he bought fine linen, took Him down, and wrapped Him in the linen. And he laid Him in a tomb which had been hewn out of the rock, and rolled a stone against the

door of the tomb. ⁴⁷And Mary Magdalene and Mary *the mother* of Joses observed where He was laid.

PSALM 54:1-7

To the Chief Musician. With stringed instruments.* A Contemplation* of David when the Ziphites went and said to Saul, "Is David not hiding with us?"

SAVE me, O God, by Your name,
And vindicate me by Your
strength.
2   Hear my prayer, O God;
Give ear to the words of my
mouth.
3   For strangers have risen up
against me,

And oppressors have sought
after my life;
They have not set God before
them.   Selah

4   Behold, God *is* my helper;
The Lord *is* with those who
uphold my life.
5   He will repay my enemies for
their evil.
Cut them off in Your truth.

6   I will freely sacrifice to You;
I will praise Your name,
O LORD, for *it is* good.
7   For He has delivered me out
of all trouble;
And my eye has seen *its desire*
upon my enemies.

PROVERBS FOR TODAY / 11:5-6

The righteousness of the blameless will direct* his way aright, but the wicked will fall by his own wickedness. The righteousness of the upright will deliver them, but the unfaithful will be caught by their *lust.*

MARCH 12

NUMBERS 16:41–18:32

ON the next day all the congregation of the children of Israel complained against Moses and Aaron, saying, "You have killed the people of the LORD." ⁴²Now it happened, when the congregation had gathered against Moses and Aaron, that they turned toward the tabernacle of meeting; and suddenly the cloud covered it, and the glory of the LORD appeared. ⁴³Then Moses and Aaron came before the tabernacle of meeting.

⁴⁴And the LORD spoke to Moses, saying, ⁴⁵"Get away from among this congregation, that I may consume them in a moment."

And they fell on their faces.

⁴⁶So Moses said to Aaron, "Take a censer and put fire in it from the altar, put incense *on it,* and take it quickly to the congregation and make atonement for them; for wrath has gone out from the LORD. The plague has begun." ⁴⁷Then Aaron took *it* as Moses commanded, and ran into the midst of the assembly; and already the plague had begun among the people. So he put in the incense and made atonement for the people. ⁴⁸And he stood between the dead and the living; so the plague was stopped. ⁴⁹Now those who died in the plague were fourteen thousand seven hundred, besides those who died in the Korah incident. ⁵⁰So Aaron

returned to Moses at the door of the tabernacle of meeting, for the plague had stopped.

AND the LORD spoke to Moses, saying: [2]"Speak to the children of Israel, and get from them a rod from each father's house, all their leaders according to their fathers' houses—twelve rods. Write each man's name on his rod. [3]And you shall write Aaron's name on the rod of Levi. For there shall be one rod for the head of *each* father's house. [4]Then you shall place them in the tabernacle of meeting before the Testimony, where I meet with you. [5]And it shall be *that* the rod of the man whom I choose will blossom; thus I will rid Myself of the complaints of the children of Israel, which they make against you."

[6]So Moses spoke to the children of Israel, and each of their leaders gave him a rod apiece, for each leader according to their fathers' houses, twelve rods; and the rod of Aaron *was* among their rods. [7]And Moses placed the rods before the LORD in the tabernacle of witness.

[8]Now it came to pass on the next day that Moses went into the tabernacle of witness, and behold, the rod of Aaron, of the house of Levi, had sprouted and put forth buds, had produced blossoms and yielded ripe almonds. [9]Then Moses brought out all the rods from before the LORD to all the children of Israel; and they looked, and each man took his rod.

[10]And the LORD said to Moses, "Bring Aaron's rod back before the Testimony, to be kept as a sign against the rebels, that you may put their complaints away from Me, lest they die." [11]Thus did Moses; just as the LORD had commanded him, so he did.

[12]So the children of Israel spoke to Moses, saying, "Surely we die, we perish, we all perish! [13]Whoever even comes near the tabernacle of the LORD must die. Shall we all utterly die?"

THEN the LORD said to Aaron: "You and your sons and your father's house with you shall bear the iniquity *related to* the sanctuary, and you and your sons with you shall bear the iniquity *associated with* your priesthood. [2]Also bring with you your brethren of the tribe of Levi, the tribe of your father, that they may be joined with you and serve you while you and your sons *are* with you before the tabernacle of witness. [3]They shall attend to your needs and all the needs of the tabernacle; but they shall not come near the articles of the sanctuary and the altar, lest they die—they and you also. [4]They shall be joined with you and attend to the needs of the tabernacle of meeting, for all the work of the tabernacle; but an outsider shall not come near you. [5]And you shall attend to the duties of the sanctuary and the duties of the altar, that there *may* be no more wrath on the children of Israel. [6]Behold, I Myself have taken your brethren the Levites from among the children of Israel; *they are* a gift to you, given by the LORD, to do the work of the tabernacle of meeting. [7]Therefore you and your sons with you shall attend to your priesthood for everything at the altar and behind the veil; and you shall serve. I give your priesthood *to you* as a gift for service, but the outsider who comes near shall be put to death."

[8]And the LORD spoke to Aaron: "Here, I Myself have also given you charge of My heave offerings, all the holy gifts of the children of Israel; I have given them as a portion to you and your sons, as an ordinance forever. [9]This shall be yours of the most holy things *reserved* from the fire: every offering of theirs, every grain offering and every sin offering and every trespass offering which they render to Me, *shall be* most holy for

you and your sons. [10]In a most holy *place* you shall eat it; every male shall eat it. It shall be holy to you.

[11]"This also *is* yours: the heave offering of their gift, with all the wave offerings of the children of Israel; I have given them to you, and your sons and daughters with you, as an ordinance forever. Everyone who is clean in your house may eat it.

[12]"All the best of the oil, all the best of the new wine and the grain, their firstfruits which they offer to the Lord, I have given them to you. [13]Whatever first ripe fruit is in their land, which they bring to the Lord, shall be yours. Everyone who is clean in your house may eat it.

[14]"Every devoted thing in Israel shall be yours.

[15]"Everything that first opens the womb of all flesh, which they bring to the Lord, whether man or beast, shall be yours; nevertheless the firstborn of man you shall surely redeem, and the firstborn of unclean animals you shall redeem. [16]And those redeemed of the devoted things you shall redeem when one month old, according to your valuation, for five shekels of silver, according to the shekel of the sanctuary, which *is* twenty gerahs. [17]But the firstborn of a cow, the firstborn of a sheep, or the firstborn of a goat you shall not redeem; they *are* holy. You shall sprinkle their blood on the altar, and burn their fat *as* an offering made by fire for a sweet aroma to the Lord. [18]And their flesh shall be yours, just as the wave breast and the right thigh are yours.

[19]"All the heave offerings of the holy things, which the children of Israel offer to the Lord, I have given to you and your sons and daughters with you as an ordinance forever; it *is* a covenant of salt forever before the Lord with you and your descendants with you."

[20]Then the Lord said to Aaron: "You shall have no inheritance in their land, nor shall you have any portion among them; I *am* your portion and your inheritance among the children of Israel.

[21]"Behold, I have given the children of Levi all the tithes in Israel as an inheritance in return for the work which they perform, the work of the tabernacle of meeting. [22]Hereafter the children of Israel shall not come near the tabernacle of meeting, lest they bear sin and die. [23]But the Levites shall perform the work of the tabernacle of meeting, and they shall bear their iniquity; *it shall be* a statute forever, throughout your generations, that among the children of Israel they shall have no inheritance. [24]For the tithes of the children of Israel, which they offer up *as* a heave offering to the Lord, I have given to the Levites as an inheritance; therefore I have said to them, 'Among the children of Israel they shall have no inheritance.' "

[25]Then the Lord spoke to Moses, saying, [26]"Speak thus to the Levites, and say to them: 'When you take from the children of Israel the tithes which I have given you from them as your inheritance, then you shall offer up a heave offering of it to the Lord, a tenth of the tithe. [27]And your heave offering shall be reckoned to you as though *it were* the grain of the threshing floor and as the fullness of the winepress. [28]Thus you shall also offer a heave offering to the Lord from all your tithes which you receive from the children of Israel, and you shall give the Lord's heave offering from it to Aaron the priest. [29]Of all your gifts you shall offer up every heave offering due to the Lord, from all the best of them, the consecrated part of them.' [30]Therefore you shall say to them: 'When you have lifted up the best of it, then *the rest* shall be accounted to the Levites as the produce of the threshing floor and as the produce of the winepress. [31]You may eat it in any place, you and your households, for it *is* your reward for your work in the tabernacle of meeting.

32And you shall bear no sin because of it, when you have lifted up the best of it. But you shall not profane the holy gifts of the children of Israel, lest you die.' "

MARK 16:1-20

Now when the Sabbath was past, Mary Magdalene, Mary *the mother* of James, and Salome bought spices, that they might come and anoint Him [Jesus]. 2Very early in the morning, on the first *day* of the week, they came to the tomb when the sun had risen. 3And they said among themselves, "l roll away the stone from the door of the tomb for us?" 4But when they looked up, they saw that the stone had been rolled away—for it was very large. 5And entering the tomb, they saw a young man clothed in a long white robe sitting on the right side; and they were alarmed.

6But he said to them, "Do not be alarmed. You seek Jesus of Nazareth, who was crucified. He is risen! He is not here. See the place where they laid Him. 7But go, tell His disciples—and Peter—that He is going before you into Galilee; there you will see Him, as He said to you."

8So they went out quickly* and fled from the tomb, for they trembled and were amazed. And they said nothing to anyone, for they were afraid.

9Now when *He* rose early on the first *day* of the week, He appeared first to Mary Magdalene, out of whom He had cast seven demons. 10She went and told those who had been with Him, as they mourned and wept. 11And when they heard that He was alive and had been seen by her, they did not believe.

12After that, He appeared in another form to two of them as they walked and went into the country. 13And they went and told *it* to the rest, *but* they did not believe them either.

14Later He appeared to the eleven as they sat at the table; and He rebuked their unbelief and hardness of heart, because they did not believe those who had seen Him after He had risen. 15And He said to them, "Go into all the world and preach the gospel to every creature. 16He who believes and is baptized will be saved; but he who does not believe will be condemned. 17And these signs will follow those who believe: In My name they will cast out demons; they will speak with new tongues; 18they* will take up serpents; and if they drink anything deadly, it will by no means hurt them; they will lay hands on the sick, and they will recover."

19So then, after the Lord had spoken to them, He was received up into heaven, and sat down at the right hand of God. 20And they went out and preached everywhere, the Lord working with *them* and confirming the word through the accompanying signs. Amen.*

PSALM 55:1-23

To the Chief Musician. With stringed instruments. A Contemplation* of David.*

Give ear to my prayer, O God, And do not hide Yourself from my supplication.
2 Attend to me, and hear me;
    I am restless in my complaint,
       and moan noisily,
3 Because of the voice of the
       enemy,
    Because of the oppression of
       the wicked;
    For they bring down trouble
       upon me,
    And in wrath they hate me.

4 My heart is severely pained
       within me,
    And the terrors of death have
       fallen upon me.
5 Fearfulness and trembling
       have come upon me,

And horror has overwhelmed
me.
6 So I said, "Oh, that I had
wings like a dove!
I would fly away and be at rest.
7 Indeed, I would wander far off,
And remain in the wilderness.
Selah
8 I would hasten my escape
From the windy storm *and*
tempest."

9 Destroy, O Lord, *and* divide
their tongues,
For I have seen violence and
strife in the city.
10 Day and night they go around
it on its walls;
Iniquity and trouble *are* also
in the midst of it.
11 Destruction *is* in its midst;
Oppression and deceit do not
depart from its streets.

12 For *it is* not an enemy *who*
reproaches me;
Then I could bear *it.*
Nor *is it* one *who* hates me
who has exalted *himself*
against me;
Then I could hide from him.
13 But *it was* you, a man my
equal,
My companion and my
acquaintance.
14 We took sweet counsel
together,
And walked to the house of
God in the throng.

15 Let death seize them;
Let them go down alive into
hell,

For wickedness *is* in their
dwellings *and* among them.

16 As for me, I will call upon God,
And the LORD shall save me.
17 Evening and morning and at
noon
I will pray, and cry aloud,
And He shall hear my voice.
18 He has redeemed my soul in
peace from the battle *that
was* against me,
For there were many against
me.
19 God will hear, and afflict them,
Even He who abides from of
old. Selah
Because they do not change,
Therefore they do not fear
God.

20 He has put forth his hands
against those who were at
peace with him;
He has broken his covenant.
21 *The words* of his mouth were
smoother than butter,
But war *was* in his heart;
His words were softer than oil,
Yet they *were* drawn swords.

22 Cast your burden on the LORD,
And He shall sustain you;
He shall never permit the
righteous to be moved.

23 But You, O God, shall bring
them down to the pit of
destruction;
Bloodthirsty and deceitful
men shall not live out half
their days;
But I will trust in You.

PROVERBS FOR TODAY/ 11:7

When a wicked man dies, his *expectation will perish, and the hope of the unjust
perishes.*

MARCH 13

Now the LORD spoke to Moses and Aaron, saying, 2"This *is* the ordinance of the law which the LORD has commanded, saying: 'Speak to the children of Israel, that they bring you a red heifer without blemish, in which there *is* no defect *and* on which a yoke has never come. 3You shall give it to Eleazar the priest, that he may take it outside the camp, and it shall be slaughtered before him; 4and Eleazar the priest shall take some of its blood with his finger, and sprinkle some of its blood seven times directly in front of the tabernacle of meeting. 5Then the heifer shall be burned in his sight: its hide, its flesh, its blood, and its offal shall be burned. 6And the priest shall take cedar wood and hyssop and scarlet, and cast *them* into the midst of the fire burning the heifer. 7Then the priest shall wash his clothes, he shall bathe in water, and afterward he shall come into the camp; the priest shall be unclean until evening. 8And the one who burns it shall wash his clothes in water, bathe in water, and shall be unclean until evening. 9Then a man *who is* clean shall gather up the ashes of the heifer, and store *them* outside the camp in a clean place; and they shall be kept for the congregation of the children of Israel for the water of purification;* it *is* for purifying from sin. 10And the one who gathers the ashes of the heifer shall wash his clothes, and be unclean until evening. It shall be a statute forever to the children of Israel and to the stranger who dwells among them.

11"He who touches the dead body of anyone shall be unclean seven days. 12He shall purify himself with the water on the third day and on the seventh day; *then* he will be clean. But if he does not purify himself on the third day and on the seventh day, he will not be clean. 13Whoever touches the body of anyone who has died, and does not purify himself, defiles the tabernacle of the LORD. That person shall be cut off from Israel. He shall be unclean, because the water of purification was not sprinkled on him; his uncleanness *is* still on him.

14"This *is* the law when a man dies in a tent: All who come into the tent and all who *are* in the tent shall be unclean seven days; 15and every open vessel, which has no cover fastened on it, *is* unclean. 16Whoever in the open field touches one who is slain by a sword or who has died, or a bone of a man, or a grave, shall be unclean seven days.

17"And for an unclean *person* they shall take some of the ashes of the heifer burnt for purification from sin, and running water shall be put on them in a vessel. 18A clean person shall take hyssop and dip *it* in the water, sprinkle *it* on the tent, on all the vessels, on the persons who were there, or on the one who touched a bone, the slain, the dead, or a grave. 19The clean *person* shall sprinkle the unclean on the third day and on the seventh day; and on the seventh day he shall purify himself, wash his clothes, and bathe in water; and at evening he shall be clean.

20"But the man who is unclean and does not purify himself, that person shall be cut off from among the assembly, because he has defiled the sanctuary of the LORD. The water of purification has not been sprinkled on him; he *is* unclean. 21It shall be a perpetual statute for them. He who sprinkles the water of purification shall wash his clothes; and he who touches the water of purification shall be unclean until evening. ²²Whatever the unclean *person* touches shall be unclean; and the person who touches *it* shall be unclean until evening.' "

THEN the children of Israel, the whole congregation, came into the Wilderness of Zin in the first month, and the people stayed in Kadesh; and Miriam died there and was buried there.

²Now there was no water for the congregation; so they gathered together against Moses and Aaron. ³And the people contended with Moses and spoke, saying: "If only we had died when our brethren died before the LORD! ⁴Why have you brought up the assembly of the LORD into this wilderness, that we and our animals should die here? ⁵And why have you made us come up out of Egypt, to bring us to this evil place? It *is* not a place of grain or figs or vines or pomegranates; nor *is* there any water to drink." ⁶So Moses and Aaron went from the presence of the assembly to the door of the tabernacle of meeting, and they fell on their faces. And the glory of the LORD appeared to them.

⁷Then the LORD spoke to Moses, saying, ⁸"Take the rod; you and your brother Aaron gather the congregation together. Speak to the rock before their eyes, and it will yield its water; thus you shall bring water for them out of the rock, and give drink to the congregation and their animals." ⁹So Moses took the rod from before the LORD as He commanded him.

¹⁰And Moses and Aaron gathered the assembly together before the rock; and he said to them, "Hear now, you rebels! Must we bring water for you out of this rock?" ¹¹Then Moses lifted his hand and struck the rock twice with his rod; and water came out abundantly, and the congregation and their animals drank.

¹²Then the LORD spoke to Moses and Aaron, "Because you did not believe Me, to hallow Me in the eyes of the children of Israel, therefore you shall not bring this assembly into the land which I have given them."

¹³This *was* the water of Meribah,* because the children of Israel contended with the LORD, and He was hallowed among them.

¹⁴Now Moses sent messengers from Kadesh to the king of Edom. "Thus says your brother Israel: 'You know all the hardship that has befallen us, ¹⁵how our fathers went down to Egypt, and we dwelt in Egypt a long time, and the Egyptians afflicted us and our fathers. ¹⁶When we cried out to the LORD, He heard our voice and sent the Angel and brought us up out of Egypt; now here we are in Kadesh, a city on the edge of your border. ¹⁷Please let us pass through your country. We will not pass through fields or vineyards, nor will we drink water from wells; we will go along the King's Highway; we will not turn aside to the right hand or to the left until we have passed through your territory.' "

¹⁸Then Edom said to him, "You shall not pass through my *land,* lest I come out against you with the sword."

¹⁹So the children of Israel said to him, "We will go by the Highway, and if I or my livestock drink any of your water, then I will pay for it; let me only pass through on foot, nothing *more.*"

²⁰Then he said, "You shall not pass through." So Edom came out against them with many men and with a strong hand. ²¹Thus Edom refused to give Israel passage through his territory; so Israel turned away from him.

²²Now the children of Israel, the whole congregation, journeyed from Kadesh and came to Mount Hor. ²³And the LORD spoke to Moses and Aaron in Mount Hor by the border of the land of Edom, saying: ²⁴"Aaron shall be gathered to his people, for he shall not enter the land which I have given to the

children of Israel, because you rebelled against My word at the water of Meribah. 25Take Aaron and Eleazar his son, and bring them up to Mount Hor; 26and strip Aaron of his garments and put them on Eleazar his son; for Aaron shall be gathered *to his people* and die there." 27So Moses did just as the LORD commanded, and they went up to Mount Hor in the sight of all the congregation. 28Moses stripped Aaron of his garments and put them on Eleazar his son; and Aaron died there on the top of the mountain. Then Moses and Eleazar came down from the mountain. 29Now when all the congregation saw that Aaron was dead, all the house of Israel mourned for Aaron thirty days.

LUKE 1:1-25

INASMUCH as many have taken in hand to set in order a narrative of those things which have been fulfilled* among us, 2just as those who from the beginning were eyewitnesses and ministers of the word delivered them to us, 3it seemed good to me also, having had perfect understanding of all things from the very first, to write to you an orderly account, most excellent Theophilus, 4that you may know the certainty of those things in which you were instructed.

5There was in the days of Herod, the king of Judea, a certain priest named Zacharias, of the division of Abijah. His wife *was* of the daughters of Aaron, and her name *was* Elizabeth. 6And they were both righteous before God, walking in all the commandments and ordinances of the Lord blameless. 7But they had no child, because Elizabeth was barren, and they were both well advanced in years.

8So it was, that while he was serving as priest before God in the order of his division, 9according to the custom of the priesthood, his lot fell to burn incense when he went into the temple of the Lord. 10And the whole multitude of the people was praying outside at the hour of incense. 11Then an angel of the Lord appeared to him, standing on the right side of the altar of incense. 12And when Zacharias saw *him,* he was troubled, and fear fell upon him.

13But the angel said to him, "Do not be afraid, Zacharias, for your prayer is heard; and your wife Elizabeth will bear you a son, and you shall call his name John. 14And you will have joy and gladness, and many will rejoice at his birth. 15For he will be great in the sight of the Lord, and shall drink neither wine nor strong drink. He will also be filled with the Holy Spirit, even from his mother's womb. 16And he will turn many of the children of Israel to the Lord their God. 17He will also go before Him in the spirit and power of Elijah, *'to turn the hearts of the fathers to the children,'* * and the disobedient to the wisdom of the just, to make ready a people prepared for the Lord."

18And Zacharias said to the angel, "How shall I know this? For I am an old man, and my wife is well advanced in years."

19And the angel answered and said to him, "I am Gabriel, who stands in the presence of God, and was sent to speak to you and bring you these glad tidings. 20But behold, you will be mute and not able to speak until the day these things take place, because you did not believe my words which will be fulfilled in their own time."

21And the people waited for Zacharias, and marveled that he lingered so long in the temple. 22But when he came out, he could not speak to them; and they perceived that he had seen a vision in the temple, for he beckoned to them and remained speechless.

23So it was, as soon as the days of his service were completed, that he departed to his own house. 24Now after those days his wife Elizabeth conceived; and she hid herself five months, saying, 25"Thus the Lord has dealt with me, in the days when He looked on *me,* to take away my reproach among people."

PSALM 56:1-13

To the Chief Musician. Set to "The Silent Dove in Distant Lands." * A Michtam of David when the Philistines captured him in Gath.

E merciful to me, O God, for man would swallow me up; Fighting all day he oppresses me.

2 My enemies would hound *me* all day,
For *there are* many who fight against me, O Most High.

3 Whenever I am afraid,
I will trust in You.

4 In God (I will praise His word),
In God I have put my trust;
I will not fear.
What can flesh do to me?

5 All day they twist my words;
All their thoughts *are* against me for evil.

6 They gather together,

They hide, they mark my steps,
When they lie in wait for my life.

7 Shall they escape by iniquity?
In anger cast down the peoples, O God!

8 You number my wanderings;
Put my tears into Your bottle;
Are they not in Your book?

9 When I cry out *to You,*
Then my enemies will turn back;
This I know, because God *is* for me.

10 In God (I will praise *His* word),
In the LORD (I will praise *His* word),

11 In God I have put my trust;
I will not be afraid.
What can man do to me?

12 Vows *made* to You *are binding* upon me, O God;
I will render praises to You,

13 For You have delivered my soul from death.
Have You not *kept* my feet from falling,
That I may walk before God
In the light of the living?

PROVERBS FOR TODAY/ 11:8

The righteous is delivered from trouble, and it comes to the wicked instead.

MARCH 14

NUMBERS 21:1–22:20

THE king of Arad, the Canaanite, who dwelt in the South, heard that Israel was coming on the road to Atharim. Then he fought against Israel and took *some* of them prisoners. 2So Israel made a vow to the LORD, and said, "If You will indeed deliver this people into my hand, then I will utterly destroy their cities." 3And the LORD listened to the voice of Israel and delivered up the Canaanites, and they utterly destroyed them and their cities. So the name of that place was called Hormah.*

⁴Then they journeyed from Mount Hor by the Way of the Red Sea, to go around the land of Edom; and the soul of the people became very discouraged on the way. ⁵And the people spoke against God and against Moses: "Why have you brought us up out of Egypt to die in the wilderness? For *there is* no food and no water, and our soul loathes this worthless bread." ⁶So the LORD sent fiery serpents among the people, and they bit the people; and many of the people of Israel died.

⁷Therefore the people came to Moses, and said, "We have sinned, for we have spoken against the LORD and against you; pray to the LORD that He take away the serpents from us." So Moses prayed for the people.

⁸Then the LORD said to Moses, "Make a fiery *serpent,* and set it on a pole; and it shall be that everyone who is bitten, when he looks at it, shall live." ⁹So Moses made a bronze serpent, and put it on a pole; and so it was, if a serpent had bitten anyone, when he looked at the bronze serpent, he lived.

¹⁰Now the children of Israel moved on and camped in Oboth. ¹¹And they journeyed from Oboth and camped at Ije Abarim, in the wilderness which *is* east of Moab, toward the sunrise. ¹²From there they moved and camped in the Valley of Zered. ¹³From there they moved and camped on the other side of the Arnon, which *is* in the wilderness that extends from the border of the Amorites; for the Arnon *is* the border of Moab, between Moab and the Amorites. ¹⁴Therefore it is said in the Book of the Wars of the LORD:

> "Waheb in Suphah,*
> The brooks of the Arnon,

15   And the slope of the brooks
>   That reaches to the dwelling
>   of Ar,
>   And lies on the border of
>   Moab."

¹⁶From there *they went* to Beer, which *is* the well where the LORD said to Moses, "Gather the people together, and I will give them water." ¹⁷Then Israel sang this song:

> "Spring up, O well!
>   All of you sing to it—
18   The well the leaders sank,
>   Dug by the nation's nobles,
>   By the lawgiver, with their
>   staves."

And from the wilderness *they went* to Mattanah, ¹⁹from Mattanah to Nahaliel, from Nahaliel to Bamoth, ²⁰and from Bamoth, *in* the valley that *is* in the country of Moab, to the top of Pisgah which looks down on the wasteland.*

²¹Then Israel sent messengers to Sihon king of the Amorites, saying, ²²"Let me pass through your land. We will not turn aside into fields or vineyards; we will not drink water from wells. We will go by the King's Highway until we have passed through your territory." ²³But Sihon would not allow Israel to pass through his territory. So Sihon gathered all his people together and went out against Israel in the wilderness, and he came to Jahaz and fought against Israel. ²⁴Then Israel defeated him with the edge of the sword, and took possession of his land from the Arnon to the Jabbok, as far as the people of Ammon; for the border of the people of Ammon *was* fortified. ²⁵So Israel took all these cities, and Israel dwelt in all the cities of the Amorites, in Heshbon and in all its villages. ²⁶For Heshbon *was* the city of Sihon king of the Amorites, who had fought against the former king of Moab, and had

taken all his land from his hand as far as the Arnon. 27Therefore those who speak in proverbs say:

"Come to Heshbon, let it be
    built;
Let the city of Sihon be
    repaired.

28 "For fire went out from
    Heshbon,
A flame from the city of Sihon;
It consumed Ar of Moab,
The lords of the heights of the
    Arnon.
29 Woe to you, Moab!
You have perished, O people
    of Chemosh!
He has given his sons as
    fugitives,
And his daughters into
    captivity,
To Sihon king of the Amorites.

30 "But we have shot at them;
Heshbon has perished as far
    as Dibon.
Then we laid waste as far as
    Nophah,
Which reaches to Medeba."

31Thus Israel dwelt in the land of the Amorites. 32Then Moses sent to spy out Jazer; and they took its villages and drove out the Amorites who were there.

33And they turned and went up by the way to Bashan. So Og king of Bashan went out against them, he and all his people, to battle at Edrei. 34Then the Lord said to Moses, "Do not fear him, for I have delivered him into your hand, with all his people and his land; and you shall do to him as you did to Sihon king of the Amorites, who dwelt at Heshbon." 35So they defeated him, his sons, and all his people, until there was no survivor left him; and they took possession of his land.

Then the children of Israel moved, and camped in the plains of Moab on the side of the Jordan across from Jericho.

2Now Balak the son of Zippor saw all that Israel had done to the Amorites. 3And Moab was exceedingly afraid of the people because they were many, and Moab was sick with dread because of the children of Israel. 4So Moab said to the elders of Midian, "Now this company will lick up everything around us, as an ox licks up the grass of the field." And Balak the son of Zippor was king of the Moabites at that time. 5Then he sent messengers to Balaam the son of Beor at Pethor, which is near the River* in the land of the sons of his people,* to call him, saying: "Look, a people has come from Egypt. See, they cover the face of the earth, and are settling next to me! 6Therefore please come at once, curse this people for me, for they are too mighty for me. Perhaps I shall be able to defeat them and drive them out of the land, for I know that he whom you bless is blessed, and he whom you curse is cursed."

7So the elders of Moab and the elders of Midian departed with the diviner's fee in their hand, and they came to Balaam and spoke to him the words of Balak. 8And he said to them, "Lodge here tonight, and I will bring back word to you, as the Lord speaks to me." So the princes of Moab stayed with Balaam.

9Then God came to Balaam and said, "Who are these men with you?"

10So Balaam said to God, "Balak the son of Zippor, king of Moab, has sent to me, saying, 11'Look, a people has come out of Egypt, and they cover the face of the earth. Come now, curse them for me; perhaps I shall be able to overpower them and drive them out.' "

12And God said to Balaam, "You shall not go with them; you shall not curse the people, for they are blessed."

13So Balaam rose in the morning and said to the princes of Balak, "Go back to your land, for the LORD has refused to give me permission to go with you."

¹⁴And the princes of Moab rose and went to Balak, and said, "Balaam refuses to come with us."

¹⁵Then Balak again sent princes, more numerous and more honorable than they. ¹⁶And they came to Balaam and said to him, "Thus says Balak the son of Zippor: 'Please let nothing hinder you from coming to me; ¹⁷for I will certainly honor you greatly, and I will do whatever you say to me. Therefore please come, curse this people for me.' "

¹⁸Then Balaam answered and said to the servants of Balak, "Though Balak were to give me his house full of silver and gold, I could not go beyond the word of the LORD my God, to do less or more. ¹⁹Now therefore, please, you also stay here tonight, that I may know what more the LORD will say to me."

²⁰And God came to Balaam at night and said to him, "If the men come to call you, rise *and* go with them; but only the word which I speak to you— that you shall do."

LUKE 1:26-56

Now in the sixth month the angel Gabriel was sent by God to a city of Galilee named Nazareth, ²⁷to a virgin betrothed to a man whose name was Joseph, of the house of David. The virgin's name *was* Mary. ²⁸And having come in, the angel said to her, "Rejoice, highly favored *one,* the Lord *is* with you; blessed *are* you among women!"*

²⁹But when she saw *him,* * she was troubled at his saying, and considered what manner of greeting this was. ³⁰Then the angel said to her, "Do not be afraid, Mary, for you have found favor with God. ³¹And behold, you will conceive in your womb and bring forth

a Son, and shall call His name JESUS. ³²He will be great, and will be called the Son of the Highest; and the Lord God will give Him the throne of His father David. ³³And He will reign over the house of Jacob forever, and of His kingdom there will be no end."

³⁴Then Mary said to the angel, "How can this be, since I do not know a man?"

³⁵And the angel answered and said to her, "*The* Holy Spirit will come upon you, and the power of the Highest will overshadow you; therefore, also, that Holy One who is to be born will be called the Son of God. ³⁶Now indeed, Elizabeth your relative has also conceived a son in her old age; and this is now the sixth month for her who was called barren. ³⁷For with God nothing will be impossible."

³⁸Then Mary said, "Behold the maidservant of the Lord! Let it be to me according to your word." And the angel departed from her.

³⁹Now Mary arose in those days and went into the hill country with haste, to a city of Judah, ⁴⁰and entered the house of Zacharias and greeted Elizabeth. ⁴¹And it happened, when Elizabeth heard the greeting of Mary, that the babe leaped in her womb; and Elizabeth was filled with the Holy Spirit. ⁴²Then she spoke out with a loud voice and said, "Blessed *are* you among women, and blessed *is* the fruit of your womb! ⁴³But why *is* this *granted* to me, that the mother of my Lord should come to me? ⁴⁴For indeed, as soon as the voice of your greeting sounded in my ears, the babe leaped in my womb for joy. ⁴⁵Blessed *is* she who believed, for there will be a fulfillment of those things which were told her from the Lord."

⁴⁶And Mary said:

" My soul magnifies the Lord,
⁴⁷   And my spirit has rejoiced in
          God my Savior.
⁴⁸   For He has regarded the

lowly state of His maidservant;
For behold, henceforth all generations will call me blessed.

49 For He who is mighty has done great things for me,
And holy *is* His name.

50 And His mercy *is* on those who fear Him
From generation to generation.

51 He has shown strength with His arm;
He has scattered *the* proud in the imagination of their hearts.

52 He has put down the mighty from *their* thrones,
And exalted *the* lowly.

53 He has filled *the* hungry with good things,
And *the* rich He has sent away empty.

54 He has helped His servant Israel,
In remembrance of *His* mercy,

55 As He spoke to our fathers,
To Abraham and to his seed forever."

56And Mary remained with her about three months, and returned to her house.

PSALM 57:1-11

*To the Chief Musician. Set to "Do Not Destroy."**
A Michtam of David when he fled from Saul into the cave.

E merciful to me, O God, be merciful to me!
For my soul trusts in You;
And in the shadow of Your wings I will make my refuge,
Until *these* calamities have passed by.

2 I will cry out to God Most High,

To God who performs *all things* for me.

3 He shall send from heaven and save me;
He reproaches the one who would swallow me up.
      Selah
God shall send forth His mercy and His truth.

4 My soul *is* among lions;
I lie *among* the sons of men
Who are set on fire,
Whose teeth *are* spears and arrows,
And their tongue a sharp sword.

5 Be exalted, O God, above the heavens;
Let Your glory *be* above all the earth.

6 They have prepared a net for my steps;
My soul is bowed down;
They have dug a pit before me;
Into the midst of it they *themselves* have fallen. Selah

7 My heart is steadfast, O God, my heart is steadfast;
I will sing and give praise.

8 Awake, my glory!
Awake, lute and harp!
I will awaken the dawn.

9 I will praise You, O Lord, among the peoples;
I will sing to You among the nations.

10 For Your mercy reaches unto the heavens,
And Your truth unto the clouds.

11 Be exalted, O God, above the heavens;
Let Your glory *be* above all the earth.

PROVERBS FOR TODAY/ 11:9-11

The hypocrite with his *mouth destroys his neighbor, but through knowledge the righteous will be delivered. When it goes well with the righteous, the city rejoices; and when the wicked perish,* there is *jubilation. By the blessing of the upright the city is exalted, but it is overthrown by the mouth of the wicked.*

MARCH 15

NUMBERS 22:21–23:30

So Balaam rose in the morning, saddled his donkey, and went with the princes of Moab.

²²Then God's anger was aroused because he went, and the Angel of the LORD took His stand in the way as an adversary against him. And he was riding on his donkey, and his two servants *were* with him. ²³Now the donkey saw the Angel of the LORD standing in the way with His drawn sword in His hand, and the donkey turned aside out of the way and went into the field. So Balaam struck the donkey to turn her back onto the road. ²⁴Then the Angel of the LORD stood in a narrow path between the vineyards, *with* a wall on this side and a wall on that side. ²⁵And when the donkey saw the Angel of the LORD, she pushed herself against the wall and crushed Balaam's foot against the wall; so he struck her again. ²⁶Then the Angel of the LORD went further, and stood in a narrow place where there *was* no way to turn either to the right hand or to the left. ²⁷And when the donkey saw the Angel of the LORD, she lay down under Balaam; so Balaam's anger was aroused, and he struck the donkey with his staff.

²⁸Then the LORD opened the mouth of the donkey, and she said to Balaam, "What have I done to you, that you have struck me these three times?"

²⁹And Balaam said to the donkey, "Because you have abused me. I wish there were a sword in my hand, for now I would kill you!"

³⁰So the donkey said to Balaam, "*Am* I not your donkey on which you have ridden, ever since *I became* yours, to this day? Was I ever disposed to do this to you?"

And he said, "No."

³¹Then the LORD opened Balaam's eyes, and he saw the Angel of the LORD standing in the way with His drawn sword in His hand; and he bowed his head and fell flat on his face. ³²And the Angel of the LORD said to him, "Why have you struck your donkey these three times? Behold, I have come out to stand against you, because *your* way is perverse before Me. ³³The donkey saw Me and turned aside from Me these three times. If she had not turned aside from Me, surely I would also have killed you by now, and let her live."

³⁴And Balaam said to the Angel of the LORD, "I have sinned, for I did not know You stood in the way against me. Now therefore, if it displeases You, I will turn back."

³⁵Then the Angel of the LORD said to Balaam, "Go with the men, but only the word that I speak to you, that you shall speak." So Balaam went with the princes of Balak.

³⁶Now when Balak heard that Balaam was coming, he went out to meet him at the city of Moab, which *is* on the border at the Arnon, the boundary of the territory. ³⁷Then Balak said

to Balaam, "Did I not earnestly send to you, calling for you? Why did you not come to me? Am I not able to honor you?"

38And Balaam said to Balak, "Look, I have come to you! Now, have I any power at all to say anything? The word that God puts in my mouth, that I must speak." 39So Balaam went with Balak, and they came to Kirjath Huzoth. 40Then Balak offered oxen and sheep, and he sent *some* to Balaam and to the princes who *were* with him.

41So it was, the next day, that Balak took Balaam and brought him up to the high places of Baal, that from there he might observe the extent of the people.

THEN Balaam said to Balak, "Build seven altars for me here, and prepare for me here seven bulls and seven rams."

2And Balak did just as Balaam had spoken, and Balak and Balaam offered a bull and a ram on *each* altar. 3Then Balaam said to Balak, "Stand by your burnt offering, and I will go; perhaps the LORD will come to meet me, and whatever He shows me I will tell you." So he went to a desolate height. 4And God met Balaam, and he said to Him, "I have prepared the seven altars, and I have offered on *each* altar a bull and a ram."

5Then the LORD put a word in Balaam's mouth, and said, "Return to Balak, and thus you shall speak." 6So he returned to him, and there he was, standing by his burnt offering, he and all the princes of Moab.

7And he took up his oracle and said:

"Balak the king of Moab has
brought me from Aram,
From the mountains of the
east.
'Come, curse Jacob for me,
And come, denounce Israel!'

8 "How shall I curse whom God
has not cursed?
And how shall I denounce
whom the LORD has not
denounced?

9 For from the top of the rocks I
see him,
And from the hills I behold
him;
There! A people dwelling
alone,
Not reckoning itself among
the nations.

10 "Who can count the dust* of
Jacob,
Or number one-fourth of
Israel?
Let me die the death of the
righteous,
And let my end be like his!"

11Then Balak said to Balaam, "What have you done to me? I took you to curse my enemies, and look, you have blessed *them* bountifully!"

12So he answered and said, "Must I not take heed to speak what the LORD has put in my mouth?"

13Then Balak said to him, "Please come with me to another place from which you may see them; you shall see only the outer part of them, and shall not see them all; curse them for me from there." 14So he brought him to the field of Zophim, to the top of Pisgah, and built seven altars, and offered a bull and a ram on *each* altar.

15And he said to Balak, "Stand here by your burnt offering while I meet* *the LORD* over there."

16Then the LORD met Balaam, and put a word in his mouth, and said, "Go back to Balak, and thus you shall speak." 17So he came to him, and there he was, standing by his burnt offering, and the princes of Moab were with him. And Balak said to him, "What has the LORD spoken?"

¹⁸Then he took up his oracle and said:

> "Rise up, Balak, and hear!
> Listen to me, son of Zippor!

19 "God *is* not a man, that He
>   should lie,
>   Nor a son of man, that He
>   should repent.
>   Has He said, and will He not
>   do?
>   Or has He spoken, and will
>   He not make it good?

20 Behold, I have received *a*
>   *command* to bless;
>   He has blessed, and I cannot
>   reverse it.

21 "He has not observed iniquity
>   in Jacob,
>   Nor has He seen wickedness
>   in Israel.
>   The Lᴏʀᴅ his God *is* with him,
>   And the shout of a King *is*
>   among them.

22 God brings them out of Egypt;
>   He has strength like a wild ox.

23 "For *there is* no sorcery against
>   Jacob,
>   Nor any divination against
>   Israel.
>   It now must be said of Jacob
>   And of Israel, 'Oh, what God
>   has done!'

24 Look, a people rises like a
>   lioness,
>   And lifts itself up like a lion;
>   It shall not lie down until it
>   devours the prey,
>   And drinks the blood of the
>   slain."

²⁵Then Balak said to Balaam, "Neither curse them at all, nor bless them at all!"

²⁶So Balaam answered and said to Balak, "Did I not tell you, saying, 'All that the Lᴏʀᴅ speaks, that I must do'?"

²⁷Then Balak said to Balaam, "Please come, I will take you to another place; perhaps it will please God that you may curse them for me from there." ²⁸So Balak took Balaam to the top of Peor, that overlooks the wasteland.* ²⁹Then Balaam said to Balak, "Build for me here seven altars, and prepare for me here seven bulls and seven rams." ³⁰And Balak did as Balaam had said, and offered a bull and a ram on *every* altar.

LUKE 1:57-80

Now Elizabeth's full time came for her to be delivered, and she brought forth a son. ⁵⁸When her neighbors and relatives heard how the Lord had shown great mercy to her, they rejoiced with her.

⁵⁹So it was, on the eighth day, that they came to circumcise the child; and they would have called him by the name of his father, Zacharias. ⁶⁰His mother answered and said, "No; he shall be called John."

⁶¹But they said to her, "There is no one among your relatives who is called by this name." ⁶²So they made signs to his father—what he would have him called.

⁶³And he asked for a writing tablet, and wrote, saying, "His name is John." So they all marveled. ⁶⁴Immediately his mouth was opened and his tongue *loosed,* and he spoke, praising God. ⁶⁵Then fear came on all who dwelt around them; and all these sayings were discussed throughout all the hill country of Judea. ⁶⁶And all those who heard *them* kept *them* in their hearts, saying, "What kind of child will this be?" And the hand of the Lord was with him.

⁶⁷Now his father Zacharias was filled with the Holy Spirit, and prophesied, saying:

68 "Blessed *is* the Lord God of
>   Israel,

For He has visited and
redeemed His people,

69 And has raised up a horn of
salvation for us
In the house of His servant
David,

70 As He spoke by the mouth of
His holy prophets,
Who *have been* since the
world began,

71 That we should be saved from
our enemies
And from the hand of all who
hate us,

72 To perform the mercy
promised to our fathers
And to remember His holy
covenant,

73 The oath which He swore to
our father Abraham:

74 To grant us that we,
Being delivered from the
hand of our enemies,
Might serve Him without fear,

75 In holiness and righteousness
before Him all the days of
our life.

76 "And you, child, will be called
the prophet of the Highest,
For you will go before the
face of the Lord to prepare
His ways,

77 To give knowledge of
salvation to His people
By the remission of their sins,

78 Through the tender mercy of
our God,
With which the Dayspring
from on high has visited*
us;

79 To give light to those who sit
in darkness and the shadow
of death,
To guide our feet into the way
of peace."

80So the child grew and became
strong in spirit, and was in the deserts
till the day of his manifestation to Israel.

PSALM 58:1-11

To the Chief Musician. Set to "Do Not Destroy." *
A Michtam of David.

Do you indeed speak righteousness, you silent ones?
Do you judge uprightly, you
sons of men?

2 No, in heart you work
wickedness;
You weigh out the violence of
your hands in the earth.

3 The wicked are estranged
from the womb;
They go astray as soon as
they are born, speaking lies.

4 Their poison *is* like the poison
of a serpent;
They are like the deaf cobra
that stops its ear,

5 Which will not heed the voice
of charmers,
Charming ever so skillfully.

6 Break their teeth in their
mouth, O God!
Break out the fangs of the
young lions, O LORD!

7 Let them flow away as waters
which run continually;
When he bends *his bow,*
Let his arrows be as if cut in
pieces.

8 *Let them be* like a snail which
melts away as it goes,
Like a stillborn child of a
woman, that they may not
see the sun.

9 Before your pots can feel *the
burning* thorns,
He shall take them away as
with a whirlwind,
As in His living and burning
wrath.

10 The righteous shall rejoice

when he sees the
vengeance;
He shall wash his feet in the
blood of the wicked,
11 So that men will say,

"Surely *there is* a reward for
the righteous;
Surely He is God who judges
in the earth."

PROVERBS FOR TODAY/ 11:12-13

He who is devoid of wisdom despises his neighbor, but a man of understanding holds his peace. A talebearer reveals secrets, but he who is of a faithful spirit conceals a matter.

MARCH 16

NUMBERS 24:1–25:18

Now when Balaam saw that it pleased the LORD to bless Israel, he did not go as at other times, to seek to use sorcery, but he set his face toward the wilderness. 2And Balaam raised his eyes, and saw Israel encamped according to their tribes; and the Spirit of God came upon him.

3Then he took up his oracle and said:

"The utterance of Balaam the
son of Beor,
The utterance of the man
whose eyes are opened,
4 The utterance of him who
hears the words of God,
Who sees the vision of the
Almighty,
Who falls down, with eyes
wide open:

5 "How lovely are your tents,
O Jacob!
Your dwellings, O Israel!
6 Like valleys that stretch out,
Like gardens by the riverside,
Like aloes planted by the LORD,
Like cedars beside the waters.
7 He shall pour water from his
buckets,
And his seed *shall be* in many
waters.

"His king shall be higher than
Agag,
And his kingdom shall be
exalted.

8 "God brings him out of Egypt;
He has strength like a wild ox;
He shall consume the nations,
his enemies;
He shall break their bones
And pierce *them* with his
arrows.
9 'He bows down, he lies down
as a lion;
And as a lion, who shall rouse
him?'*

"Blessed *is* he who blesses you,
And cursed *is* he who curses
you."

10Then Balak's anger was aroused against Balaam, and he struck his hands together; and Balak said to Balaam, "I called you to curse my enemies, and look, you have bountifully blessed *them* these three times! ¹¹Now therefore, flee to your place. I said I would greatly honor you, but in fact, the LORD has kept you back from honor."

¹²So Balaam said to Balak, "Did I not also speak to your messengers whom you sent to me, saying, ¹³'If Balak were to give me his house full of silver and gold, I could not go beyond the word of the LORD, to do good or bad of my own will. What the LORD says, that I must speak'? ¹⁴And now, indeed, I am going to my people. Come, I will advise you what this people will do to your people in the latter days."

¹⁵So he took up his oracle and said:

" The utterance of Balaam the
son of Beor,
And the utterance of the man
whose eyes are opened;
16   The utterance of him who
hears the words of God,
And has the knowledge of the
Most High,
Who sees the vision of the
Almighty,
Who falls down, with eyes
wide open:

17   "I see Him, but not now;
I behold Him, but not near;
A Star shall come out of Jacob;
A Scepter shall rise out of
Israel,
And batter the brow of Moab,
And destroy all the sons of
tumult.*

18   "And Edom shall be a
possession;
Seir also, his enemies, shall
be a possession,
While Israel does valiantly.
19   Out of Jacob One shall have
dominion,
And destroy the remains of
the city."

²⁰Then he looked on Amalek, and he took up his oracle and said:

"Amalek *was* first among the
nations,
But *shall be* last until he
perishes."

²¹Then he looked on the Kenites, and he took up his oracle and said:

"Firm is your dwelling place,
And your nest is set in the
rock;
22   Nevertheless Kain shall be
burned.
How long until Asshur carries
you away captive?"

²³Then he took up his oracle and said:

"Alas! Who shall live when
God does this?
24   But ships *shall come* from the
coasts of Cyprus,*
And they shall afflict Asshur
and afflict Eber,
And so shall *Amalek,** until he
perishes."

²⁵So Balaam rose and departed and returned to his place; Balak also went his way.

Now Israel remained in Acacia Grove,* and the people began to commit harlotry with the women of Moab. ²They invited the people to the sacrifices of their gods, and the people ate and bowed down to their gods. ³So Israel was joined to Baal of Peor, and the anger of the LORD was aroused against Israel.

⁴Then the LORD said to Moses, "Take all the leaders of the people and hang the offenders before the LORD, out in the sun, that the fierce anger of the LORD may turn away from Israel."

⁵So Moses said to the judges of Is-

rael, "Every one of you kill his men who were joined to Baal of Peor."

6And indeed, one of the children of Israel came and presented to his brethren a Midianite woman in the sight of Moses and in the sight of all the congregation of the children of Israel, who *were* weeping at the door of the tabernacle of meeting. 7Now when Phinehas the son of Eleazar, the son of Aaron the priest, saw *it,* he rose from among the congregation and took a javelin in his hand; 8and he went after the man of Israel into the tent and thrust both of them through, the man of Israel, and the woman through her body. So the plague was stopped among the children of Israel. 9And those who died in the plague were twenty-four thousand.

10Then the Lord spoke to Moses, saying: 11"Phinehas the son of Eleazar, the son of Aaron the priest, has turned back My wrath from the children of Israel, because he was zealous with My zeal among them, so that I did not consume the children of Israel in My zeal. 12Therefore say, 'Behold, I give to him My covenant of peace; 13and it shall be to him and his descendants after him a covenant of an everlasting priesthood, because he was zealous for his God, and made atonement for the children of Israel.' "

14Now the name of the Israelite who was killed, who was killed with the Midianite woman, *was* Zimri the son of Salu, a leader of a father's house among the Simeonites. 15And the name of the Midianite woman who was killed *was* Cozbi the daughter of Zur; he *was* head of the people of a father's house in Midian.

16Then the Lord spoke to Moses, saying: 17"Harass the Midianites, and attack them; 18for they harassed you with their schemes by which they seduced you in the matter of Peor and in the matter of Cozbi, the daughter of a leader of Midian, their sister, who was

killed in the day of the plague because of Peor."

LUKE 2:1-35

And it came to pass in those days *that* a decree went out from Caesar Augustus that all the world should be registered. 2This census first took place while Quirinius was governing Syria. 3So all went to be registered, everyone to his own city.

4Joseph also went up from Galilee, out of the city of Nazareth, into Judea, to the city of David, which is called Bethlehem, because he was of the house and lineage of David, 5to be registered with Mary, his betrothed wife,* who was with child. 6So it was, that while they were there, the days were completed for her to be delivered. 7And she brought forth her firstborn Son, and wrapped Him in swaddling cloths, and laid Him in a manger, because there was no room for them in the inn.

8Now there were in the same country shepherds living out in the fields, keeping watch over their flock by night. 9And behold,* an angel of the Lord stood before them, and the glory of the Lord shone around them, and they were greatly afraid. 10Then the angel said to them, "Do not be afraid, for behold, I bring you good tidings of great joy which will be to all people. 11For there is born to you this day in the city of David a Savior, who is Christ the Lord. 12And this *will be* the sign to you: You will find a Babe wrapped in swaddling cloths, lying in a manger."

13And suddenly there was with the angel a multitude of the heavenly host praising God and saying:

14 "Glory to God in the highest,
   And on earth peace, goodwill
      toward men!"*

¹⁵So it was, when the angels had gone away from them into heaven, that the shepherds said to one another, "Let us now go to Bethlehem and see this thing that has come to pass, which the Lord has made known to us." ¹⁶And they came with haste and found Mary and Joseph, and the Babe lying in a manger. ¹⁷Now when they had seen *Him,* they made widely* known the saying which was told them concerning this Child. ¹⁸And all those who heard *it* marveled at those things which were told them by the shepherds. ¹⁹But Mary kept all these things and pondered *them* in her heart. ²⁰Then the shepherds returned, glorifying and praising God for all the things that they had heard and seen, as it was told them.

²¹And when eight days were completed for the circumcision of the Child,* His name was called JESUS, the name given by the angel before He was conceived in the womb.

²²Now when the days of her purification according to the law of Moses were completed, they brought Him to Jerusalem to present *Him* to the Lord ²³(as it is written in the law of the Lord, *"Every male who opens the womb shall be called holy to the LORD"),* ²⁴and to offer a sacrifice according to what is said in the law of the Lord, *"A pair of turtledoves or two young pigeons."* *

²⁵And behold, there was a man in Jerusalem whose name was Simeon, and this man was just and devout, waiting for the Consolation of Israel, and the Holy Spirit was upon him. ²⁶And it had been revealed to him by the Holy Spirit that he would not see death before he had seen the Lord's Christ. ²⁷So he came by the Spirit into the temple. And when the parents brought in the Child Jesus, to do for Him according to the custom of the law, ²⁸he took Him up in his arms and blessed God and said:

²⁹ "Lord, now You are letting
  Your servant depart in
  peace,
  According to Your word;
³⁰ For my eyes have seen Your
  salvation
³¹ Which You have prepared
  before the face of all
  peoples,
³² A light to *bring* revelation to
  the Gentiles,
  And the glory of Your people
  Israel."

³³And Joseph and His mother* marveled at those things which were spoken of Him. ³⁴Then Simeon blessed them, and said to Mary His mother, "Behold, this *Child* is destined for the fall and rising of many in Israel, and for a sign which will be spoken against ³⁵(yes, a sword will pierce through your own soul also), that the thoughts of many hearts may be revealed."

PSALM 59:1-17

To the Chief Musician. Set to "Do Not Destroy." *
A Michtam of David when Saul sent men, and
they watched the house in order to kill him.

DELIVER me from my enemies,
  O my God;
  Defend me from those who
  rise up against me.
2 Deliver me from the workers
  of iniquity,
  And save me from
  bloodthirsty men.

3 For look, they lie in wait for
  my life;
  The mighty gather against me,
  Not *for* my transgression nor
  for my sin, O LORD.
4 They run and prepare
  themselves through no
  fault *of mine.*

  Awake to help me, and behold!
5 You therefore, O LORD God of
  hosts, the God of Israel,

Awake to punish all the
nations;
Do not be merciful to any
wicked transgressors.
Selah

6   At evening they return,
They growl like a dog,
And go all around the city.
7   Indeed, they belch with their
mouth;
Swords *are* in their lips;
For *they say,* "Who hears?"

8   But You, O Lord, shall laugh
at them;
You shall have all the nations
in derision.
9   I will wait for You, O You his
Strength;*
For God *is* my defense.
10 My God of mercy* shall come
to meet me;
God shall let me see *my desire*
on my enemies.

11 Do not slay them, lest my
people forget;
Scatter them by Your power,
And bring them down,
O Lord our shield.

12 *For* the sin of their mouth *and*
the words of their lips,
Let them even be taken in
their pride,
And for the cursing and lying
which they speak.
13 Consume *them* in wrath,
consume *them,*
That they *may* not *be;*
And let them know that God
rules in Jacob
To the ends of the earth.
Selah

14 And at evening they return,
They growl like a dog,
And go all around the city.
15 They wander up and down for
food,
And howl* if they are not
satisfied.

16 But I will sing of Your power;
Yes, I will sing aloud of Your
mercy in the morning;
For You have been my defense
And refuge in the day of my
trouble.
17 To You, O my Strength, I will
sing praises;
For God *is* my defense,
My God of mercy.

PROVERBS FOR TODAY/ 11:14

Where there is *no counsel, the people fall; but in the multitude of counselors* there
is *safety.*

MARCH 17

NUMBERS 26:1-51

A ND it came to pass, after the
plague, that the Lord spoke to
Moses and Eleazar the son of
Aaron the priest, saying: 2"Take a census of all the congregation of the children of Israel from twenty years old
and above, by their fathers' houses, all
who are able to go to war in Israel." 3So
Moses and Eleazar the priest spoke

with them in the plains of Moab by the Jordan, *across from* Jericho, saying: 4*"Take a census of the people* from twenty years old and above, just as the LORD commanded Moses and the children of Israel who came out of the land of Egypt."

5Reuben *was* the firstborn of Israel. The children of Reuben *were: of* Hanoch, the family of the Hanochites; *of* Pallu, the family of the Palluites; 6*of* Hezron, the family of the Hezronites; *of* Carmi, the family of the Carmites. 7These *are* the families of the Reubenites: those who were numbered of them were forty-three thousand seven hundred and thirty. 8And the son of Pallu *was* Eliab. 9The sons of Eliab *were* Nemuel, Dathan, and Abiram. These *are* the Dathan and Abiram, representatives of the congregation, who contended against Moses and Aaron in the company of Korah, when they contended against the LORD; 10and the earth opened its mouth and swallowed them up together with Korah when that company died, when the fire devoured two hundred and fifty men; and they became a sign. 11Nevertheless the children of Korah did not die.

12The sons of Simeon according to their families *were: of* Nemuel,* the family of the Nemuelites; *of* Jamin, the family of the Jaminites; *of* Jachin,* the family of the Jachinites; 13*of* Zerah,* the family of the Zarhites; *of* Shaul, the family of the Shaulites. 14These *are* the families of the Simeonites: twenty-two thousand two hundred.

15The sons of Gad according to their families *were: of* Zephon,* the family of the Zephonites; *of* Haggi, the family of the Haggites; *of* Shuni, the family of the Shunites; 16*of* Ozni,* the family of the Oznites; *of* Eri, the family of the Erites; 17*of* Arod,* the family of the Arodites; *of* Areli, the family of the Arelites. 18These *are* the families of the sons of Gad according to those who

were numbered of them: forty thousand five hundred.

19The sons of Judah *were* Er and Onan; and Er and Onan died in the land of Canaan. 20And the sons of Judah according to their families were: *of* Shelah, the family of the Shelanites; *of* Perez, the family of the Parzites; *of* Zerah, the family of the Zarhites. 21And the sons of Perez were: *of* Hezron, the family of the Hezronites; *of* Hamul, the family of the Hamulites. 22These *are* the families of Judah according to those who were numbered of them: seventy-six thousand five hundred.

23The sons of Issachar according to their families *were: of* Tola, the family of the Tolaites; of Puah,* the family of the Punites;* 24*of* Jashub, the family of the Jashubites; of Shimron, the family of the Shimronites. 25These *are* the families of Issachar according to those who were numbered of them: sixty-four thousand three hundred.

26The sons of Zebulun according to their families *were: of* Sered, the family of the Sardites; of Elon, the family of the Elonites; of Jahleel, the family of the Jahleelites. 27These *are* the families of the Zebulunites according to those who were numbered of them: sixty thousand five hundred.

28The sons of Joseph according to their families, by Manasseh and Ephraim, *were:* 29The sons of Manasseh: of Machir, the family of the Machirites; and Machir begot Gilead; of Gilead, the family of the Gileadites. 30These *are* the sons of Gilead: *of* Jeezer,* the family of the Jeezerites; of Helek, the family of the Helekites; 31*of* Asriel, the family of the Asrielites; *of* Shechem, the family of the Shechemites; 32*of* Shemida, the family of the Shemidaites; *of* Hepher, the family of the Hepherites. 33Now Zelophehad the son of Hepher had no sons, but daughters; and the names of the daughters of Zelophehad *were* Mahlah, Noah, Hoglah, Milcah, and Tirzah. 34These *are* the families of Manasseh; and those who were numbered of them *were* fifty-two thousand seven hundred.

35These *are* the sons of Ephraim according to their families: of Shuthelah, the family of the Shuthalhites; of Becher,* the family of the Bachrites; of Tahan, the family of the Tahanites. 36And these *are* the sons of Shuthelah: of Eran, the family of the Eranites. 37These *are* the families of the sons of Ephraim according to those who were numbered of them: thirty-two thousand five hundred.

These *are* the sons of Joseph according to their families.

38The sons of Benjamin according to their families were: of Bela, the family of the Belaites; of Ashbel, the family of the Ashbelites; of Ahiram, the family of the Ahiramites; 39of Shupham,* the family of the Shuphamites; of Hupham,* the family of the Huphamites. 40And the sons of Bela were Ard* and Naaman: *of Ard,* the family of the Ardites; of Naaman, the family of the Naamites. 41These *are* the sons of Benjamin according to their families; and those who were numbered of them *were* forty-five thousand six hundred.

42These *are* the sons of Dan according to their families: of Shuham,* the family of the Shuhamites. These *are* the families of Dan according to their families. 43All the families of the Shuhamites, according to those who were numbered of them, *were* sixty-four thousand four hundred.

44The sons of Asher according to their families *were:* of Jimna, the family of the Jimnites; of Jesui, the family of the Jesuites; of Beriah, the family of the Beriites. 45Of the sons of Beriah: of Heber, the family of the Heberites; of Malchiel, the family of the Malchielites. 46And the name of the daughter of Asher *was* Serah. 47These *are* the families of the sons of Asher according

to those who were numbered of them: fifty-three thousand four hundred.

48The sons of Naphtali according to their families *were:* of Jahzeel,* the family of the Jahzeelites; of Guni, the family of the Gunites; 49of Jezer, the family of the Jezerites; of Shillem, the family of the Shillemites. 50These *are* the families of Naphtali according to their families; and those who were numbered of them *were* forty-five thousand four hundred.

51These *are* those who were numbered of the children of Israel: six hundred and one thousand seven hundred and thirty.

LUKE 2:36-52

Now there was one, Anna, a prophetess, the daughter of Phanuel, of the tribe of Asher. She was of a great age, and had lived with a husband seven years from her virginity; 37and this woman *was* a widow of about eighty-four years,* who did not depart from the temple, but served *God* with fastings and prayers night and day. 38And coming in that instant she gave thanks to the Lord,* and spoke of Him to all those who looked for redemption in Jerusalem.

39So when they had performed all things according to the law of the Lord, they returned to Galilee, to their *own* city, Nazareth. 40And the Child grew and became strong in spirit,* filled with wisdom; and the grace of God was upon Him.

41His parents went to Jerusalem every year at the Feast of the Passover. 42And when He was twelve years old, they went up to Jerusalem according to the custom of the feast. 43When they had finished the days, as they returned, the Boy Jesus lingered behind in Jerusalem. And Joseph and His mother* did not know *it;* 44but supposing Him to have been in the company, they went a day's journey, and sought

Him among *their* relatives and acquaintances. 45So when they did not find Him, they returned to Jerusalem, seeking Him. 46Now so it was *that* after three days they found Him in the temple, sitting in the midst of the teachers, both listening to them and asking them questions. 47And all who heard Him were astonished at His understanding and answers. 48So when they saw Him, they were amazed; and His mother said to Him, "Son, why have You done this to us? Look, Your father and I have sought You anxiously."

49And He said to them, "Why did you seek Me? Did you not know that I must be about My Father's business?" 50But they did not understand the statement which He spoke to them.

51Then He went down with them and came to Nazareth, and was subject to them, but His mother kept all these things in her heart. 52And Jesus increased in wisdom and stature, and in favor with God and men.

PSALM 60:1-12

To the Chief Musician. Set to "Lily of the Testimony." A Michtam *of David. For teaching. When he fought against Mesopotamia and Syria of Zobah, and Joab returned and killed twelve thousand Edomites in the Valley of Salt.*

O GOD, You have cast us off;
You have broken us down;
You have been displeased;
Oh, restore us again!
2 You have made the earth
    tremble;
You have broken it;
Heal its breaches, for it is
    shaking.
3 You have shown Your people
    hard things;

You have made us drink the
    wine of confusion.

4 You have given a banner to
    those who fear You,
That it may be displayed
    because of the truth.   Selah
5 That Your beloved may be
    delivered,
Save *with* Your right hand,
    and hear me.

6 God has spoken in His
    holiness:
"I will rejoice;
I will divide Shechem
And measure out the Valley of
    Succoth.
7 Gilead *is* Mine, and Manasseh
    is Mine;
Ephraim also *is* the helmet for
    My head;
Judah *is* My lawgiver.
8 Moab *is* My washpot;
Over Edom I will cast My
    shoe;
Philistia, shout in triumph
    because of Me."

9 Who will bring me *to* the
    strong city?
Who will lead me to Edom?
10 *Is it* not You, O God, *who* cast
    us off?
And You, O God, *who* did not
    go out with our armies?
11 Give us help from trouble,
For the help of man *is* useless.
12 Through God we will do
    valiantly,
For *it is* He *who* shall tread
    down our enemies.*

PROVERBS FOR TODAY/ 11:15

He who is surety for a stranger will suffer, but one who hates being surety is secure.

MARCH 18

NUMBERS 26:52–28:15

THEN the LORD spoke to Moses, saying: 53"To these the land shall be divided as an inheritance, according to the number of names. 54To a large *tribe* you shall give a larger inheritance, and to a small *tribe* you shall give a smaller inheritance. Each shall be given its inheritance according to those who were numbered of them. 55But the land shall be divided by lot; they shall inherit according to the names of the tribes of their fathers. 56According to the lot their inheritance shall be divided between the larger and the smaller."

57And these *are* those who were numbered of the Levites according to their families: of Gershon, the family of the Gershonites; of Kohath, the family of the Kohathites; of Merari, the family of the Merarites. 58These *are* the families of the Levites: the family of the Libnites, the family of the Hebronites, the family of the Mahlites, the family of the Mushites, and the family of the Korathites. And Kohath begot Amram. 59The name of Amram's wife *was* Jochebed the daughter of Levi, who was born to Levi in Egypt; and to Amram she bore Aaron and Moses and their sister Miriam. 60To Aaron were born Nadab and Abihu, Eleazar and Ithamar. 61And Nadab and Abihu died when they offered profane fire before the LORD.

62Now those who were numbered of them were twenty-three thousand, every male from a month old and above; for they were not numbered among the other children of Israel, because there was no inheritance given to them among the children of Israel.

63These *are* those who were numbered by Moses and Eleazar the priest, who numbered the children of Israel in the plains of Moab by the Jordan, *across from* Jericho. 64But among these there was not a man of those who were numbered by Moses and Aaron the priest when they numbered the children of Israel in the Wilderness of Sinai. 65For the LORD had said of them, "They shall surely die in the wilderness." So there was not left a man of them, except Caleb the son of Jephunneh and Joshua the son of Nun.

THEN came the daughters of Zelophehad the son of Hepher, the son of Gilead, the son of Machir, the son of Manasseh, from the families of Manasseh the son of Joseph; and these *were* the names of his daughters: Mahlah, Noah, Hoglah, Milcah, and Tirzah. 2And they stood before Moses, before Eleazar the priest, and before the leaders and all the congregation, *by* the doorway of the tabernacle of meeting, saying: 3"Our father died in the wilderness; but he was not in the company of those who gathered together against the LORD, in company with Korah, but he died in his own sin; and he had no sons. 4Why should the name of our father be removed from among his family because he had no son? Give us a possession among our father's brothers."

5So Moses brought their case before the LORD.

6And the LORD spoke to Moses, saying: 7"The daughters of Zelophehad speak *what is* right; you shall surely give them a possession of inheritance among their father's brothers, and cause the inheritance of their father to pass to them. 8And you shall speak to the children of Israel, saying: 'If a man dies and has no son, then you shall cause his inheritance to pass to his daughter. 9If he has no daughter, then you shall give his inheritance to his brothers. 10If he has no brothers, then you shall give his inheritance to his father's brothers. 11And if his father has no brothers, then you shall give his inheritance to the relative closest to him in his family, and he shall possess it.' " And it shall be to the children of Israel a statute of judgment, just as the LORD commanded Moses.

12Now the LORD said to Moses: "Go up into this Mount Abarim, and see the land which I have given to the children of Israel. 13And when you have seen it, you also shall be gathered to your people, as Aaron your brother was gathered. 14For in the Wilderness of Zin, during the strife of the congregation, you rebelled against My command to hallow Me at the waters before their eyes." (These *are* the waters of Meribah, at Kadesh in the Wilderness of Zin.)

15Then Moses spoke to the LORD, saying: 16"Let the LORD, the God of the spirits of all flesh, set a man over the congregation, 17who may go out before them and go in before them, who may lead them out and bring them in, that the congregation of the LORD may not be like sheep which have no shepherd."

18And the LORD said to Moses: "Take Joshua the son of Nun with you, a man in whom *is* the Spirit, and lay your hand on him; 19set him before Eleazar the priest and before all the congregation, and inaugurate him in their sight. 20And you shall give *some* of your authority to him, that all the congregation of the children of Israel may be obedient. 21He shall stand before Eleazar the priest, who shall inquire before the LORD for him by the judgment of the Urim. At his word they shall go out, and at his word they shall come in, he and all the children of Israel with him—all the congregation."

22So Moses did as the LORD commanded him. He took Joshua and set him before Eleazar the priest and before all the congregation. 23And he laid his hands on him and inaugurated him, just as the LORD commanded by the hand of Moses.

Now the LORD spoke to Moses, saying, 2"Command the children of Israel, and say to them, 'My offering, My food for My offerings made by fire as a sweet aroma to Me, you shall be careful to offer to Me at their appointed time.'

3"And you shall say to them, 'This *is* the offering made by fire which you shall offer to the LORD: two male lambs in their first year without blemish, day by day, as a regular burnt offering. 4The one lamb you shall offer in the morning, the other lamb you shall offer in the evening, 5and one-tenth of an ephah of fine flour as a grain offering mixed with one-fourth of a hin of pressed oil. 6It is a regular burnt offering which was ordained at Mount Sinai for a sweet aroma, an offering made by fire to the LORD. 7And its drink offering *shall be* one-fourth of a hin for each lamb; in a holy *place* you shall pour out the drink to the LORD as an offering. 8The other lamb you shall offer in the evening; as the morning grain offering and its drink offering, you shall offer *it* as an offering made by fire, a sweet aroma to the LORD.

9"And on the Sabbath day two lambs in their first year, without blemish, and two-tenths *of an ephah* of fine flour as a grain offering, mixed with oil, with its drink offering— 10*this is* the burnt offering for every Sabbath, besides the regular burnt offering with its drink offering.

11"At the beginnings of your months you shall present a burnt offering to the LORD: two young bulls, one ram, and seven lambs in their first year, without blemish; 12three-tenths *of an ephah* of fine flour as a grain offering, mixed with oil, for each bull; two-tenths *of an ephah* of fine flour as a grain offering, mixed with oil, for the one ram; [13]and one-tenth *of an ephah* of fine flour, mixed with oil, as a grain offering for each lamb, as a burnt offering of sweet aroma, an offering made by fire to the LORD. [14]Their drink offering shall be half a hin of wine for a bull, one-third of a hin for a ram, and one-fourth of a hin for a lamb; this *is* the burnt offering for each month throughout the months of the year. [15]Also one kid of the goats as a sin offering to the LORD shall be offered, besides the regular burnt offering and its drink offering.'"

LUKE 3:1-22

Now in the fifteenth year of the reign of Tiberius Caesar, Pontius Pilate being governor of Judea, Herod being tetrarch of Galilee, his brother Philip tetrarch of Iturea and the region of Trachonitis, and Lysanias tetrarch of Abilene, [2]while Annas and Caiaphas were high priests,* the word of God came to John the son of Zacharias in the wilderness. [3]And he went into all the region around the Jordan, preaching a baptism of repentance for the remission of sins, [4]as it is written in the book of the words of Isaiah the prophet, saying:

> "The voice of one crying in the
>   wilderness:
> 'Prepare the way of the LORD;
> Make His paths straight.
> 5   Every valley shall be filled
>   And every mountain and hill
>   brought low;
>   The crooked places shall be
>   made straight
>   And the rough ways smooth;
> 6   And all flesh shall see the
>   salvation of God.' " *

[7]Then he said to the multitudes that came out to be baptized by him,

"Brood of vipers! Who warned you to flee from the wrath to come? [8]Therefore bear fruits worthy of repentance, and do not begin to say to yourselves, 'We have Abraham as *our* father.' For I say to you that God is able to raise up children to Abraham from these stones. [9]And even now the ax is laid to the root of the trees. Therefore every tree which does not bear good fruit is cut down and thrown into the fire."

[10]So the people asked him, saying, "What shall we do then?"

[11]He answered and said to them, "He who has two tunics, let him give to him who has none; and he who has food, let him do likewise."

[12]Then tax collectors also came to be baptized, and said to him, "Teacher, what shall we do?"

[13]And he said to them, "Collect no more than what is appointed for you."

[14]Likewise the soldiers asked him, saying, "And what shall we do?"

So he said to them, "Do not intimidate anyone or accuse falsely, and be content with your wages."

[15]Now as the people were in expectation, and all reasoned in their hearts about John, whether he was the Christ *or* not, [16]John answered, saying to all, "I indeed baptize you with water; but One mightier than I is coming, whose sandal strap I am not worthy to loose. He will baptize you with the Holy Spirit and fire. [17]His winnowing fan *is* in His hand, and He will thoroughly clean out His threshing floor, and gather the wheat into His barn; but the chaff He will burn with unquenchable fire."

[18]And with many other exhortations he preached to the people. [19]But Herod the tetrarch, being rebuked by him concerning Herodias, his brother Philip's wife,* and for all the evils which Herod had done, [20]also added this, above all, that he shut John up in prison.

[21]When all the people were baptized, it came to pass that Jesus also

was baptized; and while He prayed, the heaven was opened. 22And the Holy Spirit descended in bodily form like a dove upon Him, and a voice came from heaven which said, "You are My beloved Son; in You I am well pleased."

PSALM 61:1-8

To the Chief Musician. On a stringed instrument. A Psalm of David.*

HEAR my cry, O God; Attend to my prayer. 2From the end of the earth I will cry to You, When my heart is overwhelmed; Lead me to the rock that is higher than I.

3 For You have been a shelter for me, A strong tower from the enemy.

4 I will abide in Your tabernacle forever; I will trust in the shelter of Your wings.   Selah

5 For You, O God, have heard my vows; You have given *me* the heritage of those who fear Your name.

6 You will prolong the king's life, His years as many generations.

7 He shall abide before God forever. Oh, prepare mercy and truth, *which* may preserve him!

8 So I will sing praise to Your name forever, That I may daily perform my vows.

PROVERBS FOR TODAY/ 11:16-17

A gracious woman retains honor, but ruthless men *retain riches. The merciful man does good for his own soul, but* he who is *cruel troubles his own flesh.*

MARCH 19

NUMBERS 28:16—29:40

"ON the fourteenth day of the first month *is* the Passover of the LORD. 17And on the fifteenth day of this month *is* the feast; unleavened bread shall be eaten for seven days. 18On the first day *you shall have* a holy convocation. You shall do no customary work. 19And you shall present an offering made by fire as a burnt offering to the LORD: two young bulls, one ram, and seven lambs in their first year. Be sure they are without blemish. 20Their grain offering shall be of fine flour mixed with oil: three-tenths *of an ephah* you shall offer for a bull, and two-tenths for a ram; 21you shall offer one-tenth *of an ephah* for each of the seven lambs; 22also one goat *as* a sin offering, to make atonement for you. 23You shall offer these besides the burnt offering of the morning, which *is* for a regular burnt offering. 24In this manner you shall offer the food of the offering made by fire daily for seven days, as a sweet aroma to the LORD; it shall be offered besides the regular burnt offering and its drink offering.

25And on the seventh day you shall have a holy convocation. You shall do no customary work.

26'Also on the day of the firstfruits, when you bring a new grain offering to the LORD at your *Feast of* Weeks, you shall have a holy convocation. You shall do no customary work. 27You shall present a burnt offering as a sweet aroma to the LORD: two young bulls, one ram, and seven lambs in their first year, 28with their grain offering of fine flour mixed with oil: three-tenths *of an ephah* for each bull, two-tenths for the one ram, 29and one-tenth for each of the seven lambs; 30*also* one kid of the goats, to make atonement for you. 31Be sure they are without blemish. You shall present *them* with their drink offerings, besides the regular burnt offering with its grain offering.

'AND in the seventh month, on the first *day* of the month, you shall have a holy convocation. You shall do no customary work. For you it is a day of blowing the trumpets. 2You shall offer a burnt offering as a sweet aroma to the LORD: one young bull, one ram, *and* seven lambs in their first year, without blemish. 3Their grain offering *shall be* fine flour mixed with oil: three-tenths *of an ephah* for the bull, two-tenths for the ram, 4and one-tenth for each of the seven lambs; 5also one kid of the goats *as* a sin offering, to make atonement for you; 6besides the burnt offering with its grain offering for the New Moon, the regular burnt offering with its grain offering, and their drink offerings, according to their ordinance, as a sweet aroma, an offering made by fire to the LORD.

7'On the tenth *day* of this seventh month you shall have a holy convocation. You shall afflict your souls; you shall not do any work. 8You shall present a burnt offering to the LORD *as* a sweet aroma: one young bull, one ram,

and seven lambs in their first year. Be sure they are without blemish. 9Their grain offering *shall be of* fine flour mixed with oil: three-tenths *of an ephah* for the bull, two-tenths for the one ram, 10and one-tenth for each of the seven lambs; 11also one kid of the goats *as* a sin offering, besides the sin offering for atonement, the regular burnt offering with its grain offering, and their drink offerings.

12'On the fifteenth day of the seventh month you shall have a holy convocation. You shall do no customary work, and you shall keep a feast to the LORD seven days. 13You shall present a burnt offering, an offering made by fire as a sweet aroma to the LORD: thirteen young bulls, two rams, *and* fourteen lambs in their first year. They shall be without blemish. 14Their grain offering *shall be of* fine flour mixed with oil: three-tenths *of an ephah* for each of the thirteen bulls, two-tenths for each of the two rams, 15and one-tenth for each of the fourteen lambs; 16also one kid of the goats *as* a sin offering, besides the regular burnt offering, its grain offering, and its drink offering.

17'On the second day *present* twelve young bulls, two rams, fourteen lambs in their first year without blemish, 18and their grain offering and their drink offerings for the bulls, for the rams, and for the lambs, by their number, according to the ordinance; 19also one kid of the goats *as* a sin offering, besides the regular burnt offering with its grain offering, and their drink offerings.

20'On the third day *present* eleven bulls, two rams, fourteen lambs in their first year without blemish, 21and their grain offering and their drink offerings for the bulls, for the rams, and for the lambs, by their number, according to the ordinance; 22also one goat *as* a sin offering, besides the regular burnt offering, its grain offering, and its drink offering.

23'On the fourth day *present* ten bulls, two rams, *and* fourteen lambs in their first year, without blemish, 24and their grain offering and their drink offerings for the bulls, for the rams, and for the lambs, by their number, according to the ordinance; 25also one kid of the goats *as* a sin offering, besides the regular burnt offering, its grain offering, and its drink offering.

26'On the fifth day *present* nine bulls, two rams, *and* fourteen lambs in their first year without blemish, 27and their grain offering and their drink offerings for the bulls, for the rams, and for the lambs, by their number, according to the ordinance; 28also one goat *as* a sin offering, besides the regular burnt offering, its grain offering, and its drink offering.

29'On the sixth day *present* eight bulls, two rams, *and* fourteen lambs in their first year without blemish, 30and their grain offering and their drink offerings for the bulls, for the rams, and for the lambs, by their number, according to the ordinance; 31also one goat *as* a sin offering, besides the regular burnt offering, its grain offering, and its drink offering.

32'On the seventh day *present* seven bulls, two rams, *and* fourteen lambs in their first year without blemish, 33and their grain offering and their drink offerings for the bulls, for the rams, and for the lambs, by their number, according to the ordinance; 34also one goat *as* a sin offering, besides the regular burnt offering, its grain offering, and its drink offering.

35'On the eighth day you shall have a sacred assembly. You shall do no customary work. 36You shall present a burnt offering, an offering made by fire as a sweet aroma to the LORD: one bull, one ram, seven lambs in their first year without blemish, 37and their grain offering and their drink offerings for the bull, for the ram, and for the lambs, by their number, according to the ordi-

nance; 38also one goat *as* a sin offering, besides the regular burnt offering, its grain offering, and its drink offering.

39'These you shall present to the LORD at your appointed feasts (besides your vowed offerings and your freewill offerings) as your burnt offerings and your grain offerings, as your drink offerings and your peace offerings.' "

40So Moses told the children of Israel everything, just as the LORD commanded Moses.

LUKE 3:23-38

Now Jesus Himself began *His ministry at* about thirty years of age, being (as was supposed) *the* son of Joseph, *the son* of Heli, 24*the son* of Matthat,* *the son* of Levi, *the son* of Melchi, *the son* of Janna, *the son* of Joseph, 25*the son* of Mattathiah, *the son* of Amos, *the son* of Nahum, *the son* of Esli, *the son* of Naggai, 26*the son* of Maath, *the son* of Mattathiah, *the son* of Semei, *the son* of Joseph, *the son* of Judah, 27*the son* of Joannas, *the son* of Rhesa, *the son* of Zerubbabel, *the son* of Shealtiel, *the son* of Neri, 28*the son* of Melchi, *the son* of Addi, *the son* of Cosam, *the son* of Elmodam, *the son* of Er, 29*the son* of Jose, *the son* of Eliezer, *the son* of Jorim, *the son* of Matthat, *the son* of Levi, 30*the son* of Simeon, *the son* of Judah, *the son* of Joseph, *the son* of Jonan, *the son* of Eliakim, 31*the son* of Melea, *the son* of Menan, *the son* of Mattathah, *the son* of Nathan, *the son* of David, 32*the son* of Jesse, *the son* of Obed, *the son* of Boaz, *the son* of Salmon, *the son* of Nahshon, 33*the son* of Amminadab, *the son* of Ram, *the son* of Hezron, *the son* of Perez, *the son* of Judah, 34*the son* of Jacob, *the son* of Isaac, *the son* of Abraham, *the son* of Terah, *the son* of Nahor, 35*the son* of Serug, *the son* of Reu, *the son* of Peleg, *the son* of Eber, *the son* of Shelah, 36*the son* of Cainan, *the son* of Arphaxad, *the son* of Shem, *the son* of

Noah, *the son* of Lamech, [37]*the son* of Methuselah, *the son* of Enoch, *the son* of Jared, *the son* of Mahalalel, *the son* of Cainan, [38]*the son* of Enosh, *the son* of Seth, *the son* of Adam, *the son* of God.

PSALM 62:1-12

To the Chief Musician. To Jeduthun. A Psalm of David.

T RULY my soul silently *waits* for God;
From Him *comes* my salvation.
2   He only *is* my rock and my salvation;
He is my defense;
I shall not be greatly moved.

3   How long will you attack a man?
You shall be slain, all of you,
Like a leaning wall and a tottering fence.
4   They only consult to cast *him* down from his high position;
They delight in lies;
They bless with their mouth,
But they curse inwardly. Selah

5   My soul, wait silently for God alone,
For my expectation *is* from Him.

6   He only *is* my rock and my salvation;
He is my defense;
I shall not be moved.
7   In God *is* my salvation and my glory;
The rock of my strength,
And my refuge, *is* in God.

8   Trust in Him at all times, you people;
Pour out your heart before Him;
God *is* a refuge for us.   Selah

9   Surely men of low degree *are* a vapor,
Men of high degree *are* a lie;
If they are weighed on the scales,
They *are* altogether *lighter* than vapor.
10   Do not trust in oppression,
Nor vainly hope in robbery;
If riches increase,
Do not set *your* heart *on them.*

11   God has spoken once,
Twice I have heard this:
That power *belongs* to God.
12   Also to You, O Lord, *belongs* mercy;
For You render to each one according to his work.

PROVERBS FOR TODAY/ 11:18-19

The wicked man *does deceptive work, but he who sows righteousness* will have *a sure reward. As righteousness* leads *to life, so he who pursues evil* pursues it *to his own death.*

MARCH 20

NUMBERS 30:1–31:54

THEN Moses spoke to the heads of the tribes concerning the children of Israel, saying, "This *is* the thing which the LORD has commanded: ²If a man makes a vow to the LORD, or swears an oath to bind himself by some agreement, he shall not break his word; he shall do according to all that proceeds out of his mouth.

³"Or if a woman makes a vow to the LORD, and binds *herself* by some agreement while in her father's house in her youth, ⁴and her father hears her vow and the agreement by which she has bound herself, and her father holds his peace, then all her vows shall stand, and every agreement with which she has bound herself shall stand. ⁵But if her father overrules her on the day that he hears, then none of her vows nor her agreements by which she has bound herself shall stand; and the LORD will release her, because her father overruled her.

⁶"If indeed she takes a husband, while bound by her vows or by a rash utterance from her lips by which she bound herself, ⁷and her husband hears *it,* and makes no response to her on the day that he hears, then her vows shall stand, and her agreements by which she bound herself shall stand. ⁸But if her husband overrules her on the day that he hears *it,* he shall make void her vow which she took and what she uttered with her lips, by which she bound herself, and the LORD will release her.

⁹"Also any vow of a widow or a divorced woman, by which she has bound herself, shall stand against her.

¹⁰"If she vowed in her husband's house, or bound herself by an agreement with an oath, ¹¹and her husband heard *it,* and made no response to her *and* did not overrule her, then all her vows shall stand, and every agreement by which she bound herself shall stand. ¹²But if her husband truly made them void on the day he heard *them,* then whatever proceeded from her lips concerning her vows or concerning the agreement binding her, it shall not stand; her husband has made them void, and the LORD will release her. ¹³Every vow and every binding oath to afflict her soul, her husband may confirm it, or her husband may make it void. ¹⁴Now if her husband makes no response whatever to her from day to day, then he confirms all her vows or all the agreements that bind her; he confirms them, because he made no response to her on the day that he heard *them.* ¹⁵But if he does make them void after he has heard *them,* then he shall bear her guilt."

¹⁶These *are* the statutes which the LORD commanded Moses, between a man and his wife, and between a father and his daughter in her youth in her father's house.

AND the LORD spoke to Moses, saying: ²"Take vengeance on the Midianites for the children of Israel. Afterward you shall be gathered to your people."

³So Moses spoke to the people, saying, "Arm some of yourselves for war, and let them go against the Midianites to take vengeance for the LORD on Midian. ⁴A thousand from each tribe of all the tribes of Israel you shall send to the war."

⁵So there were recruited from the divisions of Israel one thousand from *each* tribe, twelve thousand armed for war. ⁶Then Moses sent them to the

war, one thousand from *each* tribe; he sent them to the war with Phinehas the son of Eleazar the priest, with the holy articles and the signal trumpets in his hand. ⁷And they warred against the Midianites, just as the Lord commanded Moses, and they killed all the males. ⁸They killed the kings of Midian with *the rest of* those who were killed—Evi, Rekem, Zur, Hur, and Reba, the five kings of Midian. Balaam the son of Beor they also killed with the sword.

⁹And the children of Israel took the women of Midian captive, with their little ones, and took as spoil all their cattle, all their flocks, and all their goods. ¹⁰They also burned with fire all the cities where they dwelt, and all their forts. ¹¹And they took all the spoil and all the booty—of man and beast.

¹²Then they brought the captives, the booty, and the spoil to Moses, to Eleazar the priest, and to the congregation of the children of Israel, to the camp in the plains of Moab by the Jordan, *across from* Jericho. ¹³And Moses, Eleazar the priest, and all the leaders of the congregation, went to meet them outside the camp. ¹⁴But Moses was angry with the officers of the army, *with* the captains over thousands and captains over hundreds, who had come from the battle.

¹⁵And Moses said to them: "Have you kept all the women alive? ¹⁶Look, these *women* caused the children of Israel, through the counsel of Balaam, to trespass against the Lord in the incident of Peor, and there was a plague among the congregation of the Lord. ¹⁷Now therefore, kill every male among the little ones, and kill every woman who has known a man intimately. ¹⁸But keep alive for yourselves all the young girls who have not known a man intimately. ¹⁹And as for you, remain outside the camp seven days; whoever has killed any person, and whoever has touched any slain, purify yourselves and your captives on the third day and on the seventh day. ²⁰Purify every garment, everything made of leather, everything woven of goats' *hair,* and everything made of wood."

²¹Then Eleazar the priest said to the men of war who had gone to the battle, "This *is* the ordinance of the law which the Lord commanded Moses: ²²"Only the gold, the silver, the bronze, the iron, the tin, and the lead, ²³everything that can endure fire, you shall put through the fire, and it shall be clean; and it shall be purified with the water of purification. But all that cannot endure fire you shall put through water. ²⁴And you shall wash your clothes on the seventh day and be clean, and afterward you may come into the camp."

²⁵Now the Lord spoke to Moses, saying: ²⁶"Count up the plunder that was taken—of man and beast—you and Eleazar the priest and the chief fathers of the congregation; ²⁷and divide the plunder into two parts, between those who took part in the war, who went out to battle, and all the congregation. ²⁸And levy a tribute for the Lord on the men of war who went out to battle: one of every five hundred of the persons, the cattle, the donkeys, and the sheep; ²⁹take *it* from their half, and give *it* to Eleazar the priest as a heave offering to the Lord. ³⁰And from the children of Israel's half you shall take one of every fifty, drawn from the persons, the cattle, the donkeys, and the sheep, from all the livestock, and give them to the Levites who keep charge of the tabernacle of the Lord." ³¹So Moses and Eleazar the priest did as the Lord commanded Moses.

³²The booty remaining from the plunder, which the men of war had taken, was six hundred and seventy-five thousand sheep, ³³seventy-two thousand cattle, ³⁴sixty-one thousand donkeys, ³⁵and thirty-two thousand

persons in all, of women who had not known a man intimately. 36And the half, the portion for those who had gone out to war, was in number three hundred and thirty-seven thousand five hundred sheep; 37and the LORD's tribute of the sheep was six hundred and seventy-five. 38The cattle *were* thirty-six thousand, of which the LORD's tribute *was* seventy-two. 39The donkeys *were* thirty thousand five hundred, of which the LORD's tribute *was* sixty-one. 40The persons *were* sixteen thousand, of which the LORD's tribute *was* thirty-two persons. 41So Moses gave the tribute *which was* the LORD's heave offering to Eleazar the priest, as the LORD commanded Moses.

42And from the children of Israel's half, which Moses separated from the men who fought— 43now the half belonging to the congregation was three hundred and thirty-seven thousand five hundred sheep, 44thirty-six thousand cattle, 45thirty thousand five hundred donkeys, 46and sixteen thousand persons— 47and from the children of Israel's half Moses took one of every fifty, drawn from man and beast, and gave them to the Levites, who kept charge of the tabernacle of the LORD, as the LORD commanded Moses.

48Then the officers who *were* over thousands of the army, the captains of thousands and captains of hundreds, came near to Moses; 49and they said to Moses, "Your servants have taken a count of the men of war who *are* under our command, and not a man of us is missing. 50Therefore we have brought an offering for the LORD, what every man found of ornaments of gold: armlets and bracelets and signet rings and earrings and necklaces, to make atonement for ourselves before the LORD." 51So Moses and Eleazar the priest received the gold from them, all the fashioned ornaments. 52And all the gold of the offering that they offered to the LORD, from the captains of thousands and captains of hundreds, was sixteen thousand seven hundred and fifty shekels. 53(The men of war had taken spoil, every man for himself.) 54And Moses and Eleazar the priest received the gold from the captains of thousands and of hundreds, and brought it into the tabernacle of meeting as a memorial for the children of Israel before the LORD.

LUKE 4:1-30

THEN Jesus, being filled with the Holy Spirit, returned from the Jordan and was led by the Spirit into* the wilderness, 2being tempted for forty days by the devil. And in those days He ate nothing, and afterward, when they had ended, He was hungry

3And the devil said to Him, "If You are the Son of God, command this stone to become bread."

4But Jesus answered him, saying,* "It is written, *'Man shall not live by bread alone, but by every word of God.'"* *

5Then the devil, taking Him up on a high mountain, showed Him* all the kingdoms of the world in a moment of time. 6And the devil said to Him, "All this authority I will give You, and their glory; for *this* has been delivered to me, and I give it to whomever I wish. 7Therefore, if You will worship before me, all will be Yours."

8And Jesus answered and said to him, "Get behind Me, Satan!* For* it is written, *'You shall worship the LORD your God, and Him only you shall serve.'"* *

9Then he brought Him to Jerusalem, set Him on the pinnacle of the temple, and said to Him, "If You are the Son of God, throw Yourself down from here. 10For it is written:

*'He shall give His angels
    charge over you,
To keep you,'*

[11]and,

> 'In their hands they shall bear
> you up,
> Lest you dash your foot
> against a stone.'" *

[12]And Jesus answered and said to him, "It has been said, 'You shall not tempt the LORD your God.'" *

[13]Now when the devil had ended every temptation, he departed from Him until an opportune time.

[14]Then Jesus returned in the power of the Spirit to Galilee, and news of Him went out through all the surrounding region. [15]And He taught in their synagogues, being glorified by all.

[16]So He came to Nazareth, where He had been brought up. And as His custom was, He went into the synagogue on the Sabbath day, and stood up to read. [17]And He was handed the book of the prophet Isaiah. And when He had opened the book, He found the place where it was written:

[18]   "The Spirit of the LORD is upon Me,
> Because He has anointed Me
> To preach the gospel to the poor;
> He has sent Me to heal the brokenhearted, *
> To proclaim liberty to the captives
> And recovery of sight to the blind,
> To set at liberty those who are oppressed;
[19]   To proclaim the acceptable year of the LORD." *

[20]Then He closed the book, and gave it back to the attendant and sat down. And the eyes of all who were in the synagogue were fixed on Him. [21]And He began to say to them, "Today this Scripture is fulfilled in your hearing." [22]So all bore witness to Him, and marveled at the gracious words which proceeded out of His mouth. And they said, "Is this not Joseph's son?"

[23]He said to them, "You will surely say this proverb to Me, 'Physician, heal yourself! Whatever we have heard done in Capernaum,* do also here in Your country.'" [24]Then He said, "Assuredly, I say to you, no prophet is accepted in his own country. [25]But I tell you truly, many widows were in Israel in the days of Elijah, when the heaven was shut up three years and six months, and there was a great famine throughout all the land; [26]but to none of them was Elijah sent except to Zarephath,* in the region of Sidon, to a woman who was a widow. [27]And many lepers were in Israel in the time of Elisha the prophet, and none of them was cleansed except Naaman the Syrian."

[28]So all those in the synagogue, when they heard these things, were filled with wrath, [29]and rose up and thrust Him out of the city; and they led Him to the brow of the hill on which their city was built, that they might throw Him down over the cliff. [30]Then passing through the midst of them, He went His way.

PSALM 63:1-11

A Psalm of David when he was in the wilderness of Judah.

O GOD, You are my God;
> Early will I seek You;
> My soul thirsts for You;
> My flesh longs for You
> In a dry and thirsty land
> Where there is no water.
[2]   So I have looked for You in the sanctuary,
> To see Your power and Your glory.

[3]   Because Your lovingkindness is better than life,
> My lips shall praise You.

4 Thus I will bless You while I
 live;
 I will lift up my hands in Your
 name.
5 My soul shall be satisfied as
 with marrow and fatness,
 And my mouth shall praise
 You with joyful lips.

6 When I remember You on my
 bed,
 I meditate on You in the *night*
 watches.
7 Because You have been my
 help,
 Therefore in the shadow of
 Your wings I will rejoice.

8 My soul follows close behind
 You;
 Your right hand upholds me.
9 But those *who* seek my life, to
 destroy *it,*
 Shall go into the lower parts
 of the earth.
10 They shall fall by the sword;
 They shall be a portion for
 jackals.

11 But the king shall rejoice in
 God;
 Everyone who swears by Him
 shall glory;
 But the mouth of those who
 speak lies shall be stopped.

PROVERBS FOR TODAY/ 11:20-21

Those who are of a perverse heart are *an abomination to the LORD, but* the *blameless in their ways* are *His delight.* Though they join *forces,* * *the wicked will not go unpunished; but the posterity of the righteous will be delivered.*

MARCH 21

NUMBERS 32:1–33:39

Now the children of Reuben and the children of Gad had a very great multitude of livestock; and when they saw the land of Jazer and the land of Gilead, that indeed the region *was* a place for livestock, [2]the children of Gad and the children of Reuben came and spoke to Moses, to Eleazar the priest, and to the leaders of the congregation, saying, [3]"Ataroth, Dibon, Jazer, Nimrah, Heshbon, Elealeh, Shebam, Nebo, and Beon, [4]the country which the LORD defeated before the congregation of Israel, *is* a land for livestock, and your servants have livestock." [5]Therefore they said, "If we have found favor in your sight,

let this land be given to your servants as a possession. Do not take us over the Jordan."

[6]And Moses said to the children of Gad and to the children of Reuben: "Shall your brethren go to war while you sit here? [7]Now why will you discourage the heart of the children of Israel from going over into the land which the LORD has given them? [8]Thus your fathers did when I sent them away from Kadesh Barnea to see the land. [9]For when they went up to the Valley of Eshcol and saw the land, they discouraged the heart of the children of Israel, so that they did not go into the land which the LORD had given them. [10]So the LORD's anger was aroused on that day, and He swore an

oath, saying, [11]'Surely none of the men who came up from Egypt, from twenty years old and above, shall see the land of which I swore to Abraham, Isaac, and Jacob, because they have not wholly followed Me, [12]except Caleb the son of Jephunneh, the Kenizzite, and Joshua the son of Nun, for they have wholly followed the LORD.' [13]So the LORD's anger was aroused against Israel, and He made them wander in the wilderness forty years, until all the generation that had done evil in the sight of the LORD was gone. [14]And look! You have risen in your fathers' place, a brood of sinful men, to increase still more the fierce anger of the LORD against Israel. [15]For if you turn away from following Him, He will once again leave them in the wilderness, and you will destroy all these people."

[16]Then they came near to him and said: "We will build sheepfolds here for our livestock, and cities for our little ones, [17]but we ourselves will be armed, ready *to go* before the children of Israel until we have brought them to their place; and our little ones will dwell in the fortified cities because of the inhabitants of the land. [18]We will not return to our homes until every one of the children of Israel has received his inheritance. [19]For we will not inherit with them on the other side of the Jordan and beyond, because our inheritance has fallen to us on this eastern side of the Jordan."

[20]Then Moses said to them: "If you do this thing, if you arm yourselves before the LORD for the war, [21]and all your armed men cross over the Jordan before the LORD until He has driven out His enemies from before Him, [22]and the land is subdued before the LORD, then afterward you may return and be blameless before the LORD and before Israel; and this land shall be your possession before the LORD. [23]But if you do not do so, then take note, you have sinned against the LORD; and be sure your sin will find you out. [24]Build cities for your little ones and folds for your sheep, and do what has proceeded out of your mouth."

[25]And the children of Gad and the children of Reuben spoke to Moses, saying: "Your servants will do as my lord commands. [26]Our little ones, our wives, our flocks, and all our livestock will be there in the cities of Gilead; [27]but your servants will cross over, every man armed for war, before the LORD to battle, just as my lord says."

[28]So Moses gave command concerning them to Eleazar the priest, to Joshua the son of Nun, and to the chief fathers of the tribes of the children of Israel. [29]And Moses said to them: "If the children of Gad and the children of Reuben cross over the Jordan with you, every man armed for battle before the LORD, and the land is subdued before you, then you shall give them the land of Gilead as a possession. [30]But if they do not cross over armed with you, they shall have possessions among you in the land of Canaan."

[31]Then the children of Gad and the children of Reuben answered, saying: "As the LORD has said to your servants, so we will do. [32]We will cross over armed before the LORD into the land of Canaan, but the possession of our inheritance *shall remain* with us on this side of the Jordan."

[33]So Moses gave to the children of Gad, to the children of Reuben, and to half the tribe of Manasseh the son of Joseph, the kingdom of Sihon king of the Amorites and the kingdom of Og king of Bashan, the land with its cities within the borders, the cities of the surrounding country. [34]And the children of Gad built Dibon and Ataroth and Aroer, [35]Atroth and Shophan and Jazer and Jogbehah, [36]Beth Nimrah and Beth Haran, fortified cities, and folds for sheep. [37]And the children of Reuben built Heshbon and Elealeh and Kirjathaim, [38]Nebo and Baal Meon

(*their* names being changed) and Shibmah; and they gave *other* names to the cities which they built.

39And the children of Machir the son of Manasseh went to Gilead and took it, and dispossessed the Amorites who *were* in it. 40So Moses gave Gilead to Machir the son of Manasseh, and he dwelt in it. 41Also Jair the son of Manasseh went and took its small towns, and called them Havoth Jair.* 42Then Nobah went and took Kenath and its villages, and he called it Nobah, after his own name.

THESE *are* the journeys of the children of Israel, who went out of the land of Egypt by their armies under the hand of Moses and Aaron 2Now Moses wrote down the starting points of their journeys at the command of the LORD. And these *are* their journeys according to their starting points:

3They departed from Rameses in the first month, on the fifteenth day of the first month; on the day after the Passover the children of Israel went out with boldness in the sight of all the Egyptians. 4For the Egyptians were burying all *their* firstborn, whom the LORD had killed among them. Also on their gods the LORD had executed judgments.

5Then the children of Israel moved from Rameses and camped at Succoth. 6They departed from Succoth and camped at Etham, which *is* on the edge of the wilderness. 7They moved from Etham and turned back to Pi Hahiroth, which *is* east of Baal Zephon; and they camped near Migdol. 8They departed from before Hahiroth* and passed through the midst of the sea into the wilderness, went three days' journey in the Wilderness of Etham, and camped at Marah. 9They moved from Marah and came to Elim. At Elim *were* twelve springs of water and seventy palm trees; so they camped there.

10They moved from Elim and camped by the Red Sea. 11They moved from the Red Sea and camped in the Wilderness of Sin. 12They journeyed from the Wilderness of Sin and camped at Dophkah. 13They departed from Dophkah and camped at Alush. 14They moved from Alush and camped at Rephidim, where there was no water for the people to drink.

15They departed from Rephidim and camped in the Wilderness of Sinai. 16They moved from the Wilderness of Sinai and camped at Kibroth Hattaavah. 17They departed from Kibroth Hattaavah and camped at Hazeroth. 18They departed from Hazeroth and camped at Rithmah. 19They departed from Rithmah and camped at Rimmon Perez. 20They departed from Rimmon Perez and camped at Libnah. 21They moved from Libnah and camped at Rissah. 22They journeyed from Rissah and camped at Kehelathah. 23They went from Kehelathah and camped at Mount Shepher. 24They moved from Mount Shepher and camped at Haradah. 25They moved from Haradah and camped at Makheloth. 26They moved from Makheloth and camped at Tahath. 27They departed from Tahath and camped at Terah. 28They moved from Terah and camped at Mithkah. 29They went from Mithkah and camped at Hashmonah. 30They departed from Hashmonah and camped at Moseroth. 31They departed from Moseroth and camped at Bene Jaakan. 32They moved from Bene Jaakan and camped at Hor Hagidgad. 33They went from Hor Hagidgad and camped at Jotbathah. 34They moved from Jotbathah and camped at Abronah. 35They departed from Abronah and camped at Ezion Geber. 36They moved from Ezion Geber and camped in the Wilderness of Zin, which *is* Kadesh. 37They moved from Kadesh and camped at Mount Hor, on the boundary of the land of Edom.

38Then Aaron the priest went up to

Mount Hor at the command of the LORD, and died there in the fortieth year after the children of Israel had come out of the land of Egypt, on the first *day* of the fifth month. ³⁹Aaron *was* one hundred and twenty-three years old when he died on Mount Hor.

LUKE 4:31–5:11

THEN He [Jesus] went down to Capernaum, a city of Galilee, and was teaching them on the Sabbaths. ³²And they were astonished at His teaching, for His word was with authority. ³³Now in the synagogue there was a man who had a spirit of an unclean demon. And he cried out with a loud voice, ³⁴saying, "Let *us* alone! What have we to do with You, Jesus of Nazareth? Did You come to destroy us? I know who You are—the Holy One of God!"

³⁵But Jesus rebuked him, saying, "Be quiet, and come out of him!" And when the demon had thrown him in *their* midst, it came out of him and did not hurt him. ³⁶Then they were all amazed and spoke among themselves, saying, "What a word this *is!* For with authority and power He commands the unclean spirits, and they come out." ³⁷And the report about Him went out into every place in the surrounding region.

³⁸Now He arose from the synagogue and entered Simon's house. But Simon's wife's mother was sick with a high fever, and they made request of Him concerning her. ³⁹So He stood over her and rebuked the fever, and it left her. And immediately she arose and served them.

⁴⁰When the sun was setting, all those who had any that were sick with various diseases brought them to Him; and He laid His hands on every one of them and healed them. ⁴¹And demons also came out of many, crying out and saying, "You are the Christ,* the Son of God!"

And He, rebuking *them,* did not allow them to speak, for they knew that He was the Christ.

⁴²Now when it was day, He departed and went into a deserted place. And the crowd sought Him and came to Him, and tried to keep Him from leaving them; ⁴³but He said to them, "I must preach the kingdom of God to the other cities also, because for this purpose I have been sent." ⁴⁴And He was preaching in the synagogues of Galilee.*

So it was, as the multitude pressed about Him to hear the word of God, that He stood by the Lake of Gennesaret, ²and saw two boats standing by the lake; but the fishermen had gone from them and were washing *their* nets. ³Then He got into one of the boats, which was Simon's, and asked him to put out a little from the land. And He sat down and taught the multitudes from the boat.

⁴When He had stopped speaking, He said to Simon, "Launch out into the deep and let down your nets for a catch."

⁵But Simon answered and said to Him, "Master, we have toiled all night and caught nothing; nevertheless at Your word I will let down the net." ⁶And when they had done this, they caught a great number of fish, and their net was breaking. ⁷So they signaled to *their* partners in the other boat to come and help them. And they came and filled both the boats, so that they began to sink. ⁸When Simon Peter saw *it,* he fell down at Jesus' knees, saying, "Depart from me, for I am a sinful man, O Lord!"

⁹For he and all who were with him were astonished at the catch of fish which they had taken; ¹⁰and so also *were* James and John, the sons of Zebedee, who were partners with Si-

mon. And Jesus said to Simon, "Do not be afraid. From now on you will catch men." ¹¹So when they had brought their boats to land, they forsook all and followed Him.

PSALM 64:1-10

To the Chief Musician. A Psalm of David.

Hear my voice, O God, in my meditation;
Preserve my life from fear of the enemy.

2 Hide me from the secret plots of the wicked,
From the rebellion of the workers of iniquity,

3 Who sharpen their tongue like a sword,
And bend *their bows to shoot* their arrows—bitter words,

4 That they may shoot in secret at the blameless;
Suddenly they shoot at him and do not fear.

5 They encourage themselves *in* an evil matter;

They talk of laying snares secretly;
They say, "Who will see them?"

6 They devise iniquities:
"We have perfected a shrewd scheme."
Both the inward thought and the heart of man are deep.

7 But God shall shoot at them *with* an arrow;
Suddenly they shall be wounded.

8 So He will make them stumble over their own tongue;
All who see them shall flee away.

9 All men shall fear,
And shall declare the work of God;
For they shall wisely consider His doing.

10 The righteous shall be glad in the LORD, and trust in Him.
And all the upright in heart shall glory.

PROVERBS FOR TODAY / 11:22

As *a ring of gold in a swine's snout,* so is *a lovely woman who lacks discretion.*

MARCH 22

NUMBERS 33:40–35:34

Now the king of Arad, the Canaanite, who dwelt in the South in the land of Canaan, heard of the coming of the children of Israel.

⁴¹So they departed from Mount Hor and camped at Zalmonah. ⁴²They departed from Zalmonah and camped at Punon. ⁴³They departed from Punon and camped at Oboth. ⁴⁴They departed from Oboth and camped at Ije Abarim, at the border of Moab. ⁴⁵They departed from Ijim* and camped at Dibon Gad. ⁴⁶They moved from Dibon Gad and camped at Almon Diblathaim. ⁴⁷They moved from Almon Diblathaim and camped in the mountains of Abarim, before Nebo. ⁴⁸They departed

from the mountains of Abarim and camped in the plains of Moab by the Jordan, *across from* Jericho. ⁴⁹They camped by the Jordan, from Beth Jesimoth as far as the Abel Acacia Grove* in the plains of Moab.

⁵⁰Now the LORD spoke to Moses in the plains of Moab by the Jordan, *across from* Jericho, saying, ⁵¹"Speak to the children of Israel, and say to them: 'When you have crossed the Jordan into the land of Canaan, ⁵²then you shall drive out all the inhabitants of the land from before you, destroy all their engraved stones, destroy all their molded images, and demolish all their high places; ⁵³you shall dispossess *the inhabitants of* the land and dwell in it, for I have given you the land to possess. ⁵⁴And you shall divide the land by lot as an inheritance among your families; to the larger you shall give a larger inheritance, and to the smaller you shall give a smaller inheritance; there everyone's *inheritance* shall be whatever falls to him by lot. You shall inherit according to the tribes of your fathers. ⁵⁵But if you do not drive out the inhabitants of the land from before you, then it shall be that those whom you let remain *shall be* irritants in your eyes and thorns in your sides, and they shall harass you in the land where you dwell. ⁵⁶Moreover it shall be *that* I will do to you as I thought to do to them.' "

THEN the LORD spoke to Moses, saying, ²"Command the children of Israel, and say to them: 'When you come into the land of Canaan, this *is* the land that shall fall to you as an inheritance—the land of Canaan to its boundaries. ³Your southern border shall be from the Wilderness of Zin along the border of Edom; then your southern border shall extend eastward to the end of the Salt Sea; ⁴your border shall turn from the southern side of the Ascent of Akrabbim, continue to Zin, and be on the south of Kadesh Barnea; then it

shall go on to Hazar Addar, and continue to Azmon; ⁵the border shall turn from Azmon to the Brook of Egypt, and it shall end at the Sea.

⁶'As for the western border, you shall have the Great Sea for a border; this shall be your western border.

⁷'And this shall be your northern border: From the Great Sea you shall mark out your *border* line to Mount Hor; ⁸from Mount Hor you shall mark out *your border* to the entrance of Hamath; then the direction of the border shall be toward Zedad; ⁹the border shall proceed to Ziphron, and it shall end at Hazar Enan. This shall be your northern border.

¹⁰'You shall mark out your eastern border from Hazar Enan to Shepham; ¹¹the border shall go down from Shepham to Riblah on the east side of Ain; the border shall go down and reach to the eastern side of the Sea of Chinnereth; ¹²the border shall go down along the Jordan, and it shall end at the Salt Sea. This shall be your land with its surrounding boundaries.' "

¹³Then Moses commanded the children of Israel, saying: "This *is* the land which you shall inherit by lot, which the LORD has commanded to give to the nine tribes and to the half-tribe. ¹⁴For the tribe of the children of Reuben according to the house of their fathers, and the tribe of the children of Gad according to the house of their fathers, have received *their inheritance;* and the half-tribe of Manasseh has received its inheritance. ¹⁵The two tribes and the half-tribe have received their inheritance on this side of the Jordan, *across from* Jericho eastward, toward the sunrise."

¹⁶And the LORD spoke to Moses, saying, ¹⁷"These *are* the names of the men who shall divide the land among you as an inheritance: Eleazar the priest and Joshua the son of Nun. ¹⁸And you shall take one leader of every tribe to divide the land for the inheritance.

19These *are* the names of the men: from the tribe of Judah, Caleb the son of Jephunneh; 20from the tribe of the children of Simeon, Shemuel the son of Ammihud; 21from the tribe of Benjamin, Elidad the son of Chislon; 22a leader from the tribe of the children of Dan, Bukki the son of Jogli; 23from the sons of Joseph: a leader from the tribe of the children of Manasseh, Hanniel the son of Ephod, 24and a leader from the tribe of the children of Ephraim, Kemuel the son of Shiphtan; 25a leader from the tribe of the children of Zebulun, Elizaphan the son of Parnach; 26a leader from the tribe of the children of Issachar, Paltiel the son of Azzan; 27a leader from the tribe of the children of Asher, Ahihud the son of Shelomi; 28and a leader from the tribe of the children of Naphtali, Pedahel the son of Ammihud."

29These *are* the ones the LORD commanded to divide the inheritance among the children of Israel in the land of Canaan.

AND the LORD spoke to Moses in the plains of Moab by the Jordan *across from* Jericho, saying: 2"Command the children of Israel that they give the Levites cities to dwell in from the inheritance of their possession, and you shall *also* give the Levites commonland around the cities. 3They shall have the cities to dwell in; and their common-land shall be for their cattle, for their herds, and for all their animals. 4The common-land of the cities which you will give the Levites *shall extend* from the wall of the city outward a thousand cubits all around. 5And you shall measure outside the city on the east side two thousand cubits, on the south side two thousand cubits, on the west side two thousand cubits, and on the north side two thousand cubits. The city *shall be* in the middle. This shall belong to them as common-land for the cities.

6"Now among the cities which you will give to the Levites *you shall appoint* six cities of refuge, to which a manslayer may flee. And to these you shall add forty-two cities. 7So all the cities you will give to the Levites *shall be* forty-eight; these *you shall give* with their common-land. 8And the cities which you will give *shall be* from the possession of the children of Israel; from the larger *tribe* you shall give many, from the smaller you shall give few. Each shall give some of its cities to the Levites, in proportion to the inheritance that each receives."

9Then the LORD spoke to Moses, saying, 10"Speak to the children of Israel, and say to them: 'When you cross the Jordan into the land of Canaan, 11then you shall appoint cities to be cities of refuge for you, that the manslayer who kills any person accidentally may flee there. 12They shall be cities of refuge for you from the avenger, that the manslayer may not die until he stands before the congregation in judgment. 13And of the cities which you give, you shall have six cities of refuge. 14You shall appoint three cities on this side of the Jordan, and three cities you shall appoint in the land of Canaan, *which* will be cities of refuge. 15These six cities shall be for refuge for the children of Israel, for the stranger, and for the sojourner among them, that anyone who kills a person accidentally may flee there.

16'But if he strikes him with an iron implement, so that he dies, he *is* a murderer; the murderer shall surely be put to death. 17And if he strikes him with a stone in the hand, by which one could die, and he does die, he *is* a murderer; the murderer shall surely be put to death. 18Or *if* he strikes him with a wooden hand weapon, by which one could die, and he does die, he *is* a murderer; the murderer shall surely be put to death. 19The avenger of blood himself shall put the murderer to death;

when he meets him, he shall put him to death. 20If he pushes him out of hatred or, while lying in wait, hurls something at him so that he dies, 21or in enmity he strikes him with his hand so that he dies, the one who struck *him* shall surely be put to death. He *is* a murderer. The avenger of blood shall put the murderer to death when he meets him.

22'However, if he pushes him suddenly without enmity, or throws anything at him without lying in wait, 23or uses a stone, by which a man could die, throwing *it* at him without seeing *him,* so that he dies, while he was not his enemy or seeking his harm, 24then the congregation shall judge between the manslayer and the avenger of blood according to these judgments. 25So the congregation shall deliver the manslayer from the hand of the avenger of blood, and the congregation shall return him to the city of refuge where he had fled, and he shall remain there until the death of the high priest who was anointed with the holy oil. 26But if the manslayer at any time goes outside the limits of the city of refuge where he fled, 27and the avenger of blood finds him outside the limits of his city of refuge, and the avenger of blood kills the manslayer, he shall not be guilty of blood, 28because he should have remained in his city of refuge until the death of the high priest. But after the death of the high priest the manslayer may return to the land of his possession.

29'And these *things* shall be a statute of judgment to you throughout your generations in all your dwellings. 30Whoever kills a person, the murderer shall be put to death on the testimony of witnesses; but one witness is not *sufficient* testimony against a person for the death *penalty.* 31Moreover you shall take no ransom for the life of a murderer who *is* guilty of death, but he shall surely be put to death. 32And you shall take no ransom for him who has fled to

his city of refuge, that he may return to dwell in the land before the death of the priest. 33So you shall not pollute the land where you *are;* for blood defiles the land, and no atonement can be made for the land, for the blood that is shed on it, except by the blood of him who shed it. 34Therefore do not defile the land which you inhabit, in the midst of which I dwell; for I the LORD dwell among the children of Israel.' "

LUKE 5:12-28

AND it happened when He [Jesus] was in a certain city, that behold, a man who was full of leprosy saw Jesus; and he fell on *his* face and implored Him, saying, "Lord, if You are willing, You can make me clean."

13Then He put out *His* hand and touched him, saying, "I am willing; be cleansed." Immediately the leprosy left him. 14And He charged him to tell no one, "But go and show yourself to the priest, and make an offering for your cleansing, as a testimony to them, just as Moses commanded."

15However, the report went around concerning Him all the more; and great multitudes came together to hear, and to be healed by Him of their infirmities. 16So He Himself *often* withdrew into the wilderness and prayed.

17Now it happened on a certain day, as He was teaching, that there were Pharisees and teachers of the law sitting by, who had come out of every town of Galilee, Judea, and Jerusalem. And the power of the Lord was *present* to heal them.* 18Then behold, men brought on a bed a man who was paralyzed, whom they sought to bring in and lay before Him. 19And when they could not find how they might bring him in, because of the crowd, they went up on the housetop and let him down with *his* bed through the tiling into the midst before Jesus.

20When He saw their faith, He said to him, "Man, your sins are forgiven you."

21And the scribes and the Pharisees began to reason, saying, "Who is this who speaks blasphemies? Who can forgive sins but God alone?"

22But when Jesus perceived their thoughts, He answered and said to them, "Why are you reasoning in your hearts? 23Which is easier, to say, 'Your sins are forgiven you,' or to say, 'Rise up and walk'? 24But that you may know that the Son of Man has power on earth to forgive sins"—He said to the man who was paralyzed, "I say to you, arise, take up your bed, and go to your house."

25Immediately he rose up before them, took up what he had been lying on, and departed to his own house, glorifying God. 26And they were all amazed, and they glorified God and were filled with fear, saying, "We have seen strange things today!"

27After these things He went out and saw a tax collector named Levi, sitting at the tax office. And He said to him, "Follow Me." 28So he left all, rose up, and followed Him.

PSALM 65:1-13

To the Chief Musician. A Psalm of David. A Song.

PRAISE is awaiting You, O God, in Zion;
    And to You the vow shall be performed.
2 O You who hear prayer,
    To You all flesh will come.
3 Iniquities prevail against me;
    As for our transgressions,
    You will provide atonement for them.

4 Blessed *is the man* You choose,
    And cause to approach *You,*
That he may dwell in Your courts.
We shall be satisfied with the goodness of Your house,
Of Your holy temple.

5 *By* awesome deeds in righteousness You will answer us,
O God of our salvation,
You who are the confidence of all the ends of the earth,
And of the far-off seas;
6 Who established the mountains by His strength,
Being clothed with power;
7 You who still the noise of the seas,
The noise of their waves,
And the tumult of the peoples.
8 They also who dwell in the farthest parts are afraid of Your signs;
You make the outgoings of the morning and evening rejoice.

9 You visit the earth and water it,
You greatly enrich it;
The river of God is full of water;
You provide their grain,
For so You have prepared it.
10 You water its ridges abundantly,
You settle its furrows;
You make it soft with showers,
You bless its growth.

11 You crown the year with Your goodness,
And Your paths drip *with* abundance.
12 They drop *on* the pastures of the wilderness,
And the little hills rejoice on every side.
13 The pastures are clothed with flocks;

The valleys also are covered
with grain;

They shout for joy, they also
sing.

PROVERBS FOR TODAY/ 11:23

The desire of the righteous is *only good,* but *the expectation of the wicked* is *wrath.*

MARCH 23

NUMBERS 36:1—DEUTERONOMY 1:46

Now the chief fathers of the families of the children of Gilead the son of Machir, the son of Manasseh, of the families of the sons of Joseph, came near and spoke before Moses and before the leaders, the chief fathers of the children of Israel. ²And they said: "The Lord commanded my lord *Moses* to give the land as an inheritance by lot to the children of Israel, and my lord was commanded by the Lord to give the inheritance of our brother Zelophehad to his daughters. ³Now if they are married to any of the sons of the *other* tribes of the children of Israel, then their inheritance will be taken from the inheritance of our fathers, and it will be added to the inheritance of the tribe into which they marry; so it will be taken from the lot of our inheritance. ⁴And when the Jubilee of the children of Israel comes, then their inheritance will be added to the inheritance of the tribe into which they marry; so their inheritance will be taken away from the inheritance of the tribe of our fathers."

⁵Then Moses commanded the children of Israel according to the word of the Lord, saying: "What the tribe of the sons of Joseph speaks is right. ⁶This *is* what the Lord commands concerning the daughters of Zelophehad, saying, 'Let them marry whom they think best, but they may marry only within

the family of their father's tribe.' ⁷So the inheritance of the children of Israel shall not change hands from tribe to tribe, for every one of the children of Israel shall keep the inheritance of the tribe of his fathers. ⁸And every daughter who possesses an inheritance in any tribe of the children of Israel shall be the wife of one of the family of her father's tribe, so that the children of Israel each may possess the inheritance of his fathers. ⁹Thus no inheritance shall change hands from *one* tribe to another, but every tribe of the children of Israel shall keep its own inheritance."

¹⁰Just as the Lord commanded Moses, so did the daughters of Zelophehad; ¹¹for Mahlah, Tirzah, Hoglah, Milcah, and Noah, the daughters of Zelophehad, were married to the sons of their father's brothers. ¹²They were married into the families of the children of Manasseh the son of Joseph, and their inheritance remained in the tribe of their father's family.

¹³These *are* the commandments and the judgments which the Lord commanded the children of Israel by the hand of Moses in the plains of Moab by the Jordan, *across from* Jericho.

These *are* the words which Moses spoke to all Israel on this side of the Jordan in the wilderness, in the plain* opposite Suph,* between Paran, Tophel, Laban, Hazeroth, and Dizahab. ²*It is* eleven days' *journey* from Horeb by way of Mount Seir to Kadesh Barnea. ³Now it came to pass in the fortieth year, in the eleventh month, on the first *day* of the month, *that* Moses spoke to the children of Israel according to all that the LORD had given him as commandments to them, ⁴after he had killed Sihon king of the Amorites, who dwelt in Heshbon, and Og king of Bashan, who dwelt at Ashtaroth in* Edrei.

⁵On this side of the Jordan in the land of Moab, Moses began to explain this law, saying, ⁶"The LORD our God spoke to us in Horeb, saying: 'You have dwelt long enough at this mountain. ⁷Turn and take your journey, and go to the mountains of the Amorites, to all the neighboring *places* in the plain,* in the mountains and in the lowland, in the South and on the seacoast, to the land of the Canaanites and to Lebanon, as far as the great river, the River Euphrates. ⁸See, I have set the land before you; go in and possess the land which the LORD swore to your fathers—to Abraham, Isaac, and Jacob—to give to them and their descendants after them.'

⁹"And I spoke to you at that time, saying: 'I alone am not able to bear you. ¹⁰The LORD your God has multiplied you, and here you *are* today, as the stars of heaven in multitude. ¹¹May the LORD God of your fathers make you a thousand times more numerous than you are, and bless you as He has promised you! ¹²How can I alone bear your problems and your burdens and your complaints? ¹³Choose wise, understanding, and knowledgeable men from among your tribes, and I will make them heads over you.' ¹⁴And you answered me and said, 'The thing which you have told *us* to do *is* good.' ¹⁵So I took the heads of your tribes, wise and knowledgeable men, and made them heads over you, leaders of thousands, leaders of hundreds, leaders of fifties, leaders of tens, and officers for your tribes.

¹⁶"Then I commanded your judges at that time, saying, 'Hear *the cases* between your brethren, and judge righteously between a man and his brother or the stranger who is with him. ¹⁷You shall not show partiality in judgment; you shall hear the small as well as the great; you shall not be afraid in any man's presence, for the judgment *is* God's. The case that is too hard for you, bring to me, and I will hear it.' ¹⁸And I commanded you at that time all the things which you should do.

¹⁹"So we departed from Horeb, and went through all that great and terrible wilderness which you saw on the way to the mountains of the Amorites, as the LORD our God had commanded us. Then we came to Kadesh Barnea. ²⁰And I said to you, 'You have come to the mountains of the Amorites, which the LORD our God is giving us. ²¹Look, the LORD your God has set the land before you; go up *and* possess *it,* as the LORD God of your fathers has spoken to you; do not fear or be discouraged.'

²²"And every one of you came near to me and said, 'Let us send men before us, and let them search out the land for us, and bring back word to us of the way by which we should go up, and of the cities into which we shall come.'

²³"The plan pleased me well; so I took twelve of your men, one man from *each* tribe. ²⁴And they departed and went up into the mountains, and came to the Valley of Eshcol, and spied it out. ²⁵They also took *some* of the fruit of the land in their hands and brought *it* down to us; and they brought back word to us, saying, '*It is* a good land which the LORD our God is giving us.'

²⁶"Nevertheless you would not go up, but rebelled against the command

of the Lord your God; 27and you complained in your tents, and said, 'Because the Lord hates us, He has brought us out of the land of Egypt to deliver us into the hand of the Amorites, to destroy us. 28Where can we go up? Our brethren have discouraged our hearts, saying, "The people *are* greater and taller than we; the cities *are* great and fortified up to heaven; moreover we have seen the sons of the Anakim there." '

29"Then I said to you, 'Do not be terrified, or afraid of them. 30The Lord your God, who goes before you, He will fight for you, according to all He did for you in Egypt before your eyes, 31and in the wilderness where you saw how the Lord your God carried you, as a man carries his son, in all the way that you went until you came to this place.' 32Yet, for all that, you did not believe the Lord your God, 33who went in the way before you to search out a place for you to pitch your tents, to show you the way you should go, in the fire by night and in the cloud by day.

34"And the Lord heard the sound of your words, and was angry, and took an oath, saying, 35'Surely not one of these men of this evil generation shall see that good land of which I swore to give to your fathers, 36except Caleb the son of Jephunneh; he shall see it, and to him and his children I am giving the land on which he walked, because he wholly followed the Lord.' 37The Lord was also angry with me for your sakes, saying, 'Even you shall not go in there. 38Joshua the son of Nun, who stands before you, he shall go in there. Encourage him, for he shall cause Israel to inherit it.

39'Moreover your little ones and your children, who you say will be victims, who today have no knowledge of good and evil, they shall go in there; to them I will give it, and they shall possess it. 40But *as for* you, turn and take your journey into the wilderness by the Way of the Red Sea.'

41"Then you answered and said to me, 'We have sinned against the Lord; we will go up and fight, just as the Lord our God commanded us.' And when everyone of you had girded on his weapons of war, you were ready to go up into the mountain.

42"And the Lord said to me, 'Tell them, "Do not go up nor fight, for I *am* not among you; lest you be defeated before your enemies." ' 43So I spoke to you; yet you would not listen, but rebelled against the command of the Lord, and presumptuously went up into the mountain. 44And the Amorites who dwelt in that mountain came out against you and chased you as bees do, and drove you back from Seir to Hormah. 45Then you returned and wept before the Lord, but the Lord would not listen to your voice nor give ear to you.

46"So you remained in Kadesh many days, according to the days that you spent *there.*"

LUKE 5:29–6:11

THEN Levi gave Him [Jesus] a great feast in his own house. And there were a great number of tax collectors and others who sat down with them. 30And their scribes and the Pharisees* complained against His disciples, saying, "Why do You eat and drink with tax collectors and sinners?"

31Jesus answered and said to them, "Those who are well have no need of a physician, but those who are sick. 32I have not come to call *the* righteous, but sinners, to repentance."

33Then they said to Him, "Why do* the disciples of John fast often and make prayers, and likewise those of the Pharisees, but Yours eat and drink?"

34And He said to them, "Can you make the friends of the bridegroom fast while the bridegroom is with them? 35But the days will come when the bridegroom will be taken away from them; then they will fast in those days."

36Then He spoke a parable to them: "No one puts a piece from a new garment on an old one;* otherwise the new makes a tear, and also the piece that was *taken* out of the new does not match the old. 37And no one puts new wine into old wineskins; or else the new wine will burst the wineskins and be spilled, and the wineskins will be ruined. 38But new wine must be put into new wineskins, and both are preserved.* 39And no one, having drunk old *wine,* immediately* desires new; for he says, 'The old is better.' "*

Now it happened on the second Sabbath after the first* that He went through the grainfields. And His disciples plucked the heads of grain and ate *them,* rubbing *them* in *their* hands. 2And some of the Pharisees said to them, "Why are you doing what is not lawful to do on the Sabbath?"

3But Jesus answering them said, "Have you not even read this, what David did when he was hungry, he and those who were with him: 4how he went into the house of God, took and ate the showbread, and also gave some to those with him, which is not lawful for any but the priests to eat?" 5And He said to them, "The Son of Man is also Lord of the Sabbath."

6Now it happened on another Sabbath, also, that He entered the synagogue and taught. And a man was there whose right hand was withered. 7So the scribes and Pharisees watched Him closely, whether He would heal on the Sabbath, that they might find an accusation against Him. 8But He knew their thoughts, and said to the man who had the withered hand, "Arise and stand here." And he arose and stood. 9Then Jesus said to them, "I will ask you one thing: Is it lawful on the Sabbath to do good or to do evil, to save life or to destroy?"* 10And when He had looked around at them all, He said to the man,* "Stretch out your hand." And he did so, and his hand was restored as whole as the other.* 11But they were filled with rage, and discussed with one another what they might do to Jesus.

PSALM 66:1-20

To the Chief Musician. A Song. A Psalm.

MAKE a joyful shout to God, all the earth!
  2Sing out the honor of His name;
  Make His praise glorious.
3 Say to God,
  "How awesome are Your works!
  Through the greatness of Your power
  Your enemies shall submit themselves to You.
4 All the earth shall worship You
  And sing praises to You;
  They shall sing praises *to* Your name."   Selah

5 Come and see the works of God;
  He is awesome *in His* doing toward the sons of men.
6 He turned the sea into dry *land;*
  They went through the river on foot.
  There we will rejoice in Him.
7 He rules by His power forever;
  His eyes observe the nations;
  Do not let the rebellious exalt themselves.   Selah

8 Oh, bless our God, you peoples!

And make the voice of His
praise to be heard,

9 Who keeps our soul among
the living,
And does not allow our feet to
be moved.

10 For You, O God, have tested
us;
You have refined us as silver
is refined.

11 You brought us into the net;
You laid affliction on our
backs.

12 You have caused men to ride
over our heads;
We went through fire and
through water;
But You brought us out to
rich *fulfillment*.

13 I will go into Your house with
burnt offerings;
I will pay You my vows,

14 Which my lips have uttered
And my mouth has spoken
when I was in trouble.

15 I will offer You burnt
sacrifices of fat animals,
With the sweet aroma of rams;
I will offer bulls with goats.
Selah

16 Come *and* hear, all you who
fear God,
And I will declare what He
has done for my soul.

17 I cried to Him with my mouth,
And He was extolled with my
tongue.

18 If I regard iniquity in my
heart,
The Lord will not hear.

19 *But* certainly God has heard
me;
He has attended to the voice
of my prayer.

20 Blessed *be* God,
Who has not turned away my
prayer,
Nor His mercy from me!

PROVERBS FOR TODAY/ 11:24-26

There is one *who scatters, yet increases more; and there is* one *who withholds more than is right, but it* leads *to poverty. The generous soul will be made rich, and he who waters will also be watered himself. The people will curse him who withholds grain, but blessing* will be *on the head of him who sells* it.

MARCH 24

DEUTERONOMY 2:1–3:29

"THEN we [Moses and the Israelites] turned and journeyed into the wilderness of the Way of the Red Sea, as the LORD spoke to me, and we skirted Mount Seir for many days.

2"And the LORD spoke to me, saying: 3"You have skirted this mountain long enough; turn northward. 4And command the people, saying, "You *are about to* pass through the territory of your brethren, the descendants of Esau, who live in Seir; and they will be afraid of you. Therefore watch yourselves carefully. 5Do not meddle with them, for I will not give you *any* of their land, no, not so much as one footstep, because I have given Mount Seir to

Esau *as* a possession. 6You shall buy food from them with money, that you may eat; and you shall also buy water from them with money, that you may drink.

7"For the LORD your God has blessed you in all the work of your hand. He knows your trudging through this great wilderness. These forty years the LORD your God *has been* with you; you have lacked nothing." '

8"And when we passed beyond our brethren, the descendants of Esau who dwell in Seir, away from the road of the plain, away from Elath and Ezion Geber, we turned and passed by way of the Wilderness of Moab. 9Then the LORD said to me, 'Do not harass Moab, nor contend with them in battle, for I will not give you *any* of their land *as* a possession, because I have given Ar to the descendants of Lot *as* a possession.' "

10(The Emim had dwelt there in times past, a people as great and numerous and tall as the Anakim. 11They were also regarded as giants,* like the Anakim, but the Moabites call them Emim. 12The Horites formerly dwelt in Seir, but the descendants of Esau dispossessed them and destroyed them from before them, and dwelt in their place, just as Israel did to the land of their possession which the LORD gave them.)

13" 'Now rise and cross over the Valley of the Zered.' So we crossed over the Valley of the Zered. 14And the time we took to come from Kadesh Barnea until we crossed over the Valley of the Zered *was* thirty-eight years, until all the generation of the men of war was consumed from the midst of the camp, just as the LORD had sworn to them. 15For indeed the hand of the LORD was against them, to destroy them from the midst of the camp until they were consumed.

16"So it was, when all the men of war had finally perished from among the people, 17that the LORD spoke to me, saying: 18"This day you are to cross over at Ar, the boundary of Moab. 19And *when* you come near the people of Ammon, do not harass them or meddle with them, for I will not give you *any* of the land of the people of Ammon *as* a possession, because I have given it to the descendants of Lot *as* a possession.' "

20(That was also regarded as a land of giants;* giants formerly dwelt there. But the Ammonites call them Zamzummim, 21a people as great and numerous and tall as the Anakim. But the LORD destroyed them before them, and they dispossessed them and dwelt in their place, 22just as He had done for the descendants of Esau, who dwelt in Seir, when He destroyed the Horites from before them. They dispossessed them and dwelt in their place, even to this day. 23And the Avim, who dwelt in villages as far as Gaza—the Caphtorim, who came from Caphtor, destroyed them and dwelt in their place.)

24" 'Rise, take your journey, and cross over the River Arnon. Look, I have given into your hand Sihon the Amorite, king of Heshbon, and his land. Begin to possess *it,* and engage him in battle. 25This day I will begin to put the dread and fear of you upon the nations under the whole heaven, who shall hear the report of you, and shall tremble and be in anguish because of you.'

26"And I sent messengers from the Wilderness of Kedemoth to Sihon king of Heshbon, with words of peace, saying, 27'Let me pass through your land; I will keep strictly to the road, and I will turn neither to the right nor to the left. 28You shall sell me food for money, that I may eat, and give me water for money, that I may drink; only let me pass through on foot, 29just as the descendants of Esau who dwell in Seir and the Moabites who dwell in Ar did for me, until I cross the Jordan to the land which the LORD our God is giving us.'

30"But Sihon king of Heshbon would not let us pass through, for the LORD your God hardened his spirit and made his heart obstinate, that He might deliver him into your hand, as *it is* this day.

31"And the LORD said to me, 'See, I have begun to give Sihon and his land over to you. Begin to possess *it,* that you may inherit his land.' 32Then Sihon and all his people came out against us to fight at Jahaz. 33And the LORD our God delivered him over to us; so we defeated him, his sons, and all his people. 34We took all his cities at that time, and we utterly destroyed the men, women, and little ones of every city; we left none remaining. 35We took only the livestock as plunder for ourselves, with the spoil of the cities which we took. 36From Aroer, which *is* on the bank of the River Arnon, and *from* the city that *is* in the ravine, as far as Gilead, there was not one city too strong for us; the LORD our God delivered all to us. 37Only you did not go near the land of the people of Ammon—anywhere along the River Jabbok, or to the cities of the mountains, or wherever the LORD our God had forbidden us.

"THEN we turned and went up the road to Bashan; and Og king of Bashan came out against us, he and all his people, to battle at Edrei. 2And the LORD said to me, 'Do not fear him, for I have delivered him and all his people and his land into your hand; you shall do to him as you did to Sihon king of the Amorites, who dwelt at Heshbon.'

3"So the LORD our God also delivered into our hands Og king of Bashan, with all his people, and we attacked him until he had no survivors remaining. 4And we took all his cities at that time; there was not a city which we did not take from them: sixty cities, all the region of Argob, the kingdom of Og in

Bashan. 5All these cities *were* fortified with high walls, gates, and bars, besides a great many rural towns. 6And we utterly destroyed them, as we did to Sihon king of Heshbon, utterly destroying the men, women, and children of every city. 7But all the livestock and the spoil of the cities we took as booty for ourselves.

8"And at that time we took the land from the hand of the two kings of the Amorites who *were* on this side of the Jordan, from the River Arnon to Mount Hermon 9(the Sidonians call Hermon Sirion, and the Amorites call it Senir), 10all the cities of the plain, all Gilead, and all Bashan, as far as Salcah and Edrei, cities of the kingdom of Og in Bashan.

11"For only Og king of Bashan remained of the remnant of the giants.* Indeed his bedstead *was* an iron bedstead. (*Is* it not in Rabbah of the people of Ammon?) Nine cubits *is* its length and four cubits its width, according to the standard cubit.

12"And this land, *which* we possessed at that time, from Aroer, which *is* by the River Arnon, and half the mountains of Gilead and its cities, I gave to the Reubenites and the Gadites. 13The rest of Gilead, and all Bashan, the kingdom of Og, I gave to half the tribe of Manasseh. (All the region of Argob, with all Bashan, was called the land of the giants.* 14Jair the son of Manasseh took all the region of Argob, as far as the border of the Geshurites and the Maachathites, and called Bashan after his own name, Havoth Jair,* to this day.)

15"Also I gave Gilead to Machir. 16And to the Reubenites and the Gadites I gave from Gilead as far as the River Arnon, the middle of the river as *the* border, as far as the River Jabbok, the border of the people of Ammon; 17the plain also, with the Jordan as *the* border, from Chinnereth as far as the east side of the Sea of the Arabah (the Salt Sea), below the slopes of Pisgah.

18"Then I commanded you at that time, saying: 'The LORD your God has given you this land to possess. All you men of valor shall cross over armed before your brethren, the children of Israel. 19But your wives, your little ones, and your livestock (I know that you have much livestock) shall stay in your cities which I have given you, 20until the LORD has given rest to your brethren as to you, and they also possess the land which the LORD your God is giving them beyond the Jordan. Then each of you may return to his possession which I have given you.'

21"And I commanded Joshua at that time, saying, 'Your eyes have seen all that the LORD your God has done to these two kings; so will the LORD do to all the kingdoms through which you pass. 22You must not fear them, for the LORD your God Himself fights for you.'

23"Then I pleaded with the LORD at that time, saying: 24'O Lord GOD, You have begun to show Your servant Your greatness and Your mighty hand, for what god *is there* in heaven or on earth who can do *anything* like Your works and Your mighty *deeds?* 25I pray, let me cross over and see the good land beyond the Jordan, those pleasant mountains, and Lebanon.'

26"But the LORD was angry with me on your account, and would not listen to me. So the LORD said to me: 'Enough of that! Speak no more to Me of this matter. 27Go up to the top of Pisgah, and lift your eyes toward the west, the north, the south, and the east; behold *it* with your eyes, for you shall not cross over this Jordan. 28But command Joshua, and encourage him and strengthen him; for he shall go over before this people, and he shall cause them to inherit the land which you will see.'

29"So we stayed in the valley opposite Beth Peor."

LUKE 6:12-38

Now it came to pass in those days that He [Jesus] went out to the mountain to pray, and continued all night in prayer to God. 13And when it was day, He called His disciples to *Himself;* and from them He chose twelve whom He also named apostles: 14Simon, whom He also named Peter, and Andrew his brother; James and John; Philip and Bartholomew; 15Matthew and Thomas; James the *son* of Alphaeus, and Simon called the Zealot; 16Judas *the son* of James, and Judas Iscariot who also became a traitor.

17And He came down with them and stood on a level place with a crowd of His disciples and a great multitude of people from all Judea and Jerusalem, and from the seacoast of Tyre and Sidon, who came to hear Him and be healed of their diseases, 18as well as those who were tormented with unclean spirits. And they were healed. 19And the whole multitude sought to touch Him, for power went out from Him and healed *them* all.

20Then He lifted up His eyes toward His disciples, and said:

"Blessed *are you* poor,
For yours is the kingdom of God.
21 Blessed *are you* who hunger now,
For you shall be filled.
Blessed *are you* who weep now,
For you shall laugh.
22 Blessed are you when men hate you,
And when they exclude you,
And revile *you,* and cast out your name as evil,
For the Son of Man's sake.
23 Rejoice in that day and leap for joy!
For indeed your reward *is* great in heaven,

For in like manner their fathers did to the prophets.

24 "But woe to you who are rich,
For you have received your consolation.
25 Woe to you who are full,
For you shall hunger.
Woe to you who laugh now,
For you shall mourn and weep.
26 Woe to you* when all* men speak well of you,
For so did their fathers to the false prophets.

27"But I say to you who hear: Love your enemies, do good to those who hate you, 28bless those who curse you, and pray for those who spitefully use you. 29To him who strikes you on the *one* cheek, offer the other also. And from him who takes away your cloak, do not withhold *your* tunic either. 30Give to everyone who asks of you. And from him who takes away your goods do not ask *them* back. 31And just as you want men to do to you, you also do to them likewise.

32"But if you love those who love you, what credit is that to you? For even sinners love those who love them. 33And if you do good to those who do good to you, what credit is that to you? For even sinners do the same. 34And if you lend *to those* from whom you hope to receive back, what credit is that to you? For even sinners lend to sinners to receive as much back. 35But love your enemies, do good, and lend, hoping for nothing in return; and your reward will be great, and you will be sons of the Most High. For He is kind to the unthankful and evil. 36Therefore be merciful, just as your Father also is merciful.

37"Judge not, and you shall not be judged. Condemn not, and you shall not be condemned. Forgive, and you will be forgiven. 38Give, and it will be given to you: good measure, pressed down, shaken together, and running over will be put into your bosom. For with the same measure that you use, it will be measured back to you."

PSALM 67:1-7

To the Chief Musician. On stringed instruments. *
A Psalm. A Song.

G OD be merciful to us and bless us,
  And cause His face to shine upon us,   Selah
2 That Your way may be known on earth,
Your salvation among all nations.

3 Let the peoples praise You,
  O God;
Let all the peoples praise You.
4 Oh, let the nations be glad and sing for joy!
For You shall judge the people righteously,
And govern the nations on earth.   Selah

5 Let the peoples praise You,
  O God;
Let all the peoples praise You.
6 *Then* the earth shall yield her increase;
God, our own God, shall bless us.
7 God shall bless us,
And all the ends of the earth shall fear Him.

PROVERBS FOR TODAY/ 11:27

He who earnestly seeks good finds favor, but trouble will come to him who seeks evil.

DEUTERONOMY 4:1-49

"**N**ow, O Israel, listen to the statutes and the judgments which I [Moses] teach you to observe, that you may live, and go in and possess the land which the LORD God of your fathers is giving you. ²You shall not add to the word which I command you, nor take from it, that you may keep the commandments of the LORD your God which I command you. ³Your eyes have seen what the LORD did at Baal Peor; for the LORD your God has destroyed from among you all the men who followed Baal of Peor. ⁴But you who held fast to the LORD your God *are* alive today, every one of you.

⁵"Surely I have taught you statutes and judgments, just as the LORD my God commanded me, that you should act according *to them* in the land which you go to possess. ⁶Therefore be careful to observe *them;* for this *is* your wisdom and your understanding in the sight of the peoples who will hear all these statutes, and say, 'Surely this great nation *is* a wise and understanding people.'

⁷"For what great nation *is there* that has God *so* near to it, as the LORD our God *is* to us, for whatever *reason* we may call upon Him? ⁸And what great nation *is there* that has *such* statutes and righteous judgments as are in all this law which I set before you this day? ⁹Only take heed to yourself, and diligently keep yourself, lest you forget the things your eyes have seen, and lest they depart from your heart all the days of your life. And teach them to your children and your grandchildren, ¹⁰*especially concerning* the day you stood before the LORD your God in Horeb, when the LORD said to me, 'Gather the people to Me, and I will let them hear My words, that they may learn to fear Me all the days they live on the earth, and *that* they may teach their children.'

¹¹"Then you came near and stood at the foot of the mountain, and the mountain burned with fire to the midst of heaven, with darkness, cloud, and thick darkness. ¹²And the LORD spoke to you out of the midst of the fire. You heard the sound of the words, but saw no form; *you* only *heard* a voice. ¹³So He declared to you His covenant which He commanded you to perform, the Ten Commandments; and He wrote them on two tablets of stone. ¹⁴And the LORD commanded me at that time to teach you statutes and judgments, that you might observe them in the land which you cross over to possess.

¹⁵"Take careful heed to yourselves, for you saw no form when the LORD spoke to you at Horeb out of the midst of the fire, ¹⁶lest you act corruptly and make for yourselves a carved image in the form of any figure: the likeness of male or female, ¹⁷the likeness of any animal that *is* on the earth or the likeness of any winged bird that flies in the air, ¹⁸the likeness of anything that creeps on the ground or the likeness of any fish that *is* in the water beneath the earth. ¹⁹And *take heed,* lest you lift your eyes to heaven, and *when* you see the sun, the moon, and the stars, all the host of heaven, you feel driven to worship them and serve them, which the LORD your God has given to all the peoples under the whole heaven as a heritage. ²⁰But the LORD has taken you and brought you out of the iron furnace, out of Egypt, to be His people, an inheritance, as you are this day. ²¹Furthermore the LORD was angry with me for your sakes, and swore that I would

not cross over the Jordan, and that I would not enter the good land which the LORD your God is giving you as an inheritance. 22But I must die in this land, I must not cross over the Jordan; but you shall cross over and possess that good land. 23Take heed to yourselves, lest you forget the covenant of the LORD your God which He made with you, and make for yourselves a carved image in the form of anything which the LORD your God has forbidden you. 24For the LORD your God is a consuming fire, a jealous God.

25"When you beget children and grandchildren and have grown old in the land, and act corruptly and make a carved image in the form of anything, and do evil in the sight of the LORD your God to provoke Him to anger, 26I call heaven and earth to witness against you this day, that you will soon utterly perish from the land which you cross over the Jordan to possess; you will not prolong *your* days in it, but will be utterly destroyed. 27And the LORD will scatter you among the peoples, and you will be left few in number among the nations where the LORD will drive you. 28And there you will serve gods, the work of men's hands, wood and stone, which neither see nor hear nor eat nor smell. 29But from there you will seek the LORD your God, and you will find *Him* if you seek Him with all your heart and with all your soul. 30When you are in distress, and all these things come upon you in the latter days, when you turn to the LORD your God and obey His voice 31(for the LORD your God *is* a merciful God), He will not forsake you nor destroy you, nor forget the covenant of your fathers which He swore to them.

32"For ask now concerning the days that are past, which were before you, since the day that God created man on the earth, and *ask* from one end of heaven to the other, whether *any* great *thing* like this has happened, or *anything* like it has been heard. 33Did *any* people *ever* hear the voice of God speaking out of the midst of the fire, as you have heard, and live? 34Or did God *ever* try to go *and* take for Himself a nation from the midst of *another* nation, by trials, by signs, by wonders, by war, by a mighty hand and an outstretched arm, and by great terrors, according to all that the LORD your God did for you in Egypt before your eyes? 35To you it was shown, that you might know that the LORD Himself *is* God; *there is* none other besides Him. 36Out of heaven He let you hear His voice, that He might instruct you; on earth He showed you His great fire, and you heard His words out of the midst of the fire. 37And because He loved your fathers, therefore He chose their descendants after them; and He brought you out of Egypt with His Presence, with His mighty power, 38driving out from before you nations greater and mightier than you, to bring you in, to give you their land *as* an inheritance, as *it is* this day. 39Therefore know this day, and consider *it* in your heart, that the LORD Himself *is* God in heaven above and on the earth beneath; *there is* no other. 40You shall therefore keep His statutes and His commandments which I command you today, that it may go well with you and with your children after you, and that you may prolong *your* days in the land which the LORD your God is giving you for all time."

41Then Moses set apart three cities on this side of the Jordan, toward the rising of the sun, 42that the manslayer might flee there, who kills his neighbor unintentionally, without having hated him in time past, and that by fleeing to one of these cities he might live: 43Bezer in the wilderness on the plateau for the Reubenites, Ramoth in Gilead for the Gadites, and Golan in Bashan for the Manassites.

44Now this *is* the law which Moses set before the children of Israel. 45These *are* the testimonies, the statutes, and the judgments which Moses spoke to the children of Israel after they came out of Egypt, 46on this side of the Jordan, in the valley opposite Beth Peor, in the land of Sihon king of the Amorites, who dwelt at Heshbon, whom Moses and the children of Israel defeated after they came out of Egypt. 47And they took possession of his land and the land of Og king of Bashan, two kings of the Amorites, who *were* on this side of the Jordan, toward the rising of the sun, 48from Aroer, which *is* on the bank of the River Arnon, even to Mount Sion* (that is, Hermon), 49and all the plain on the east side of the Jordan as far as the Sea of the Arabah, below the slopes of Pisgah.

LUKE 6:39–7:10

A ND He [Jesus] spoke a parable to them: "Can the blind lead the blind? Will they not both fall into the ditch? 40A disciple is not above his teacher, but everyone who is perfectly trained will be like his teacher. 41And why do you look at the speck in your brother's eye, but do not perceive the plank in your own eye? 42Or how can you say to your brother, 'Brother, let me remove the speck that *is* in your eye,' when you yourself do not see the plank that *is* in your own eye? Hypocrite! First remove the plank from your own eye, and then you will see clearly to remove the speck that is in your brother's eye.

43"For a good tree does not bear bad fruit, nor does a bad tree bear good fruit. 44For every tree is known by its own fruit. For *men* do not gather figs from thorns, nor do they gather grapes from a bramble bush. 45A good man out of the good treasure of his heart brings forth good; and an evil man out of the evil treasure of his heart* brings forth evil. For out of the abundance of the heart his mouth speaks.

46"But why do you call Me 'Lord, Lord,' and not do the things which I say? 47Whoever comes to Me, and hears My sayings and does them, I will show you whom he is like: 48He is like a man building a house, who dug deep and laid the foundation on the rock. And when the flood arose, the stream beat vehemently against that house, and could not shake it, for it was founded on the rock.* 49But he who heard and did nothing is like a man who built a house on the earth without a foundation, against which the stream beat vehemently; and immediately it fell.* And the ruin of that house was great."

Now when He concluded all His sayings in the hearing of the people, He entered Capernaum. 2And a certain centurion's servant, who was dear to him, was sick and ready to die. 3So when he heard about Jesus, he sent elders of the Jews to Him, pleading with Him to come and heal his servant. 4And when they came to Jesus, they begged Him earnestly, saying that the one for whom He should do this was deserving, 5"for he loves our nation, and has built us a synagogue."

6Then Jesus went with them. And when He was already not far from the house, the centurion sent friends to Him, saying to Him, "Lord, do not trouble Yourself, for I am not worthy that You should enter under my roof. 7Therefore I did not even think myself worthy to come to You. But say the word, and my servant will be healed. 8For I also am a man placed under authority, having soldiers under me. And I say to one, 'Go,' and he goes; and to another, 'Come,' and he comes; and to my servant, 'Do this,' and he does *it.*"

9When Jesus heard these things, He marveled at him, and turned around and said to the crowd that followed Him, "I say to you, I have not found such great faith, not even in Israel!"

¹⁰And those who were sent, returning to the house, found the servant well who had been sick.*

PSALM 68:1-18

To the Chief Musician. A Psalm of David. A Song.

L ET God arise,
Let His enemies be scattered;
Let those also who hate Him
flee before Him.

2 As smoke is driven away,
So drive *them* away;
As wax melts before the fire,
So let the wicked perish at the
presence of God.

3 But let the righteous be glad;
Let them rejoice before God;
Yes, let them rejoice
exceedingly.

4 Sing to God, sing praises to
His name;
Extol Him who rides on the
clouds,*
By His name YAH,
And rejoice before Him.

5 A father of the fatherless, a
defender of widows,
Is God in His holy habitation.

6 God sets the solitary in
families;
He brings out those who are
bound into prosperity;
But the rebellious dwell in a
dry *land.*

7 O God, when You went out
before Your people,
When You marched through
the wilderness,   Selah

8 The earth shook;
The heavens also dropped
rain at the presence of God;
Sinai itself *was moved* at the
presence of God, the God
of Israel.

9 You, O God, sent a plentiful
rain,
Whereby You confirmed Your
inheritance,
When it was weary.

10 Your congregation dwelt in it;
You, O God, provided from
Your goodness for the poor.

11 The Lord gave the word;
Great *was* the company of
those who proclaimed *it:*

12 "Kings of armies flee, they flee,
And she who remains at
home divides the spoil.

13 Though you lie down among
the sheepfolds,
You will be like the wings of a
dove covered with silver,
And her feathers with yellow
gold."

14 When the Almighty scattered
kings in it,
It was *white* as snow in
Zalmon.

15 A mountain of God *is* the
mountain of Bashan;
A mountain *of many* peaks *is*
the mountain of Bashan.

16 Why do you fume with envy,
you mountains of *many*
peaks?
This is the mountain *which*
God desires to dwell in;
Yes, the LORD will dwell *in it*
forever.

17 The chariots of God *are*
twenty thousand,
Even thousands of thousands;
The Lord is among them *as in*
Sinai, in the Holy *Place.*

18 You have ascended on high,
You have led captivity captive;
You have received gifts
among men,
Even *from* the rebellious,
That the LORD God might
dwell *there.*

PROVERBS FOR TODAY/ 11:28

He who trusts in his riches will fall, but the righteous will flourish like foliage.

MARCH 26

DEUTERONOMY 5:1–6:25

AND Moses called all Israel, and said to them: "Hear, O Israel, the statutes and judgments which I speak in your hearing today, that you may learn them and be careful to observe them. ²The LORD our God made a covenant with us in Horeb. ³The LORD did not make this covenant with our fathers, but with us, those who *are* here today, all of us who *are* alive. ⁴The LORD talked with you face to face on the mountain from the midst of the fire. ⁵I stood between the LORD and you at that time, to declare to you the word of the LORD; for you were afraid because of the fire, and you did not go up the mountain. *He* said:

6 'I *am* the LORD your God who brought you out of the land of Egypt, out of the house of bondage.

7 'You shall have no other gods before Me.

8 'You shall not make for yourself a carved image—any likeness *of anything* that *is* in heaven above, or that *is* in the earth beneath, or that *is* in the water under the earth; ⁹you shall not bow down to them nor serve them. For I, the LORD your God, *am* a jealous God, visiting the iniquity of the fathers upon the children to the third and fourth *generations* of those who hate Me, ¹⁰but showing mercy to thousands, to those who love Me and keep My commandments.

11 'You shall not take the name of the LORD your God in vain, for the LORD will not hold *him* guiltless who takes His name in vain.

12 'Observe the Sabbath day, to keep it holy, as the LORD your God commanded you. ¹³Six days you shall labor and do all your work, ¹⁴but the seventh day *is* the Sabbath of the LORD your God. *In it* you shall do no work: you, nor your son, nor your daughter, nor your male servant, nor your female servant, nor your ox, nor your donkey, nor any of your cattle, nor your stranger who *is* within your gates, that your male servant and your female servant may rest as well as you. ¹⁵And remember that you were a slave in the land of Egypt, and the LORD your God brought you out from there by a mighty hand and by an outstretched arm; therefore the LORD your God commanded you to keep the Sabbath day.

16 'Honor your father and your mother, as the LORD your God has commanded you, that your days may be long, and that it may be well with you in the land which the

LORD your God is giving you.

17 'You shall not murder.

18 'You shall not commit adultery.

19 'You shall not steal.

20 'You shall not bear false witness against your neighbor.

21 'You shall not covet your neighbor's wife; and you shall not desire your neighbor's house, his field, his male servant, his female servant, his ox, his donkey, or anything that *is* your neighbor's.'

22 "These words the LORD spoke to all your assembly, in the mountain from the midst of the fire, the cloud, and the thick darkness, with a loud voice; and He added no more. And He wrote them on two tablets of stone and gave them to me.

23 "So it was, when you heard the voice from the midst of the darkness, while the mountain was burning with fire, that you came near to me, all the heads of your tribes and your elders. 24 And you said: 'Surely the LORD our God has shown us His glory and His greatness, and we have heard His voice from the midst of the fire. We have seen this day that God speaks with man; yet he *still* lives. 25 Now therefore, why should we die? For this great fire will consume us; if we hear the voice of the LORD our God anymore, then we shall die. 26 For who *is there* of all flesh who has heard the voice of the living God speaking from the midst of the fire, as we *have,* and lived? 27 You go near and hear all that the LORD our God may say, and tell us all that the LORD our God says to you, and we will hear and do *it.*'

28 "Then the LORD heard the voice of your words when you spoke to me, and the LORD said to me: 'I have heard the voice of the words of this people which they have spoken to you. They are right *in* all that they have spoken.

29 Oh, that they had such a heart in them that they would fear Me and always keep all My commandments, that it might be well with them and with their children forever! 30 Go and say to them, "Return to your tents." 31 But as for you, stand here by Me, and I will speak to you all the commandments, the statutes, and the judgments which you shall teach them, that they may observe *them* in the land which I am giving them to possess.'

32 "Therefore you shall be careful to do as the LORD your God has commanded you; you shall not turn aside to the right hand or to the left. 33 You shall walk in all the ways which the LORD your God has commanded you, that you may live and *that it may be* well with you, and *that* you may prolong *your* days in the land which you shall possess.

"Now this *is* the commandment, *and these are* the statutes and judgments which the LORD your God has commanded to teach you, that you may observe *them* in the land which you are crossing over to possess, 2 that you may fear the LORD your God, to keep all His statutes and His commandments which I command you, you and your son and your grandson, all the days of your life, and that your days may be prolonged. 3 Therefore hear, O Israel, and be careful to observe *it,* that it may be well with you, and that you may multiply greatly as the LORD God of your fathers has promised you—'a land flowing with milk and honey.'*

4 "Hear, O Israel: The LORD our God, the LORD *is* one!* 5 You shall love the LORD your God with all your heart, with all your soul, and with all your strength.

6 "And these words which I command you today shall be in your heart. 7 You shall teach them diligently to your children, and shall talk of them when you sit in your house, when you walk by the way, when you lie down,

and when you rise up. 8You shall bind them as a sign on your hand, and they shall be as frontlets between your eyes. 9You shall write them on the doorposts of your house and on your gates.

10"It shall be, when the LORD your God brings you into the land of which He swore to your fathers, to Abraham, Isaac, and Jacob, to give you large and beautiful cities which you did not build, 11houses full of all good things, which you did not fill, hewn-out wells which you did not dig, vineyards and olive trees which you did not plant—when you have eaten and are full 12then beware, lest you forget the LORD who brought you out of the land of Egypt, from the house of bondage. 13You shall fear the LORD your God and serve Him, and shall take oaths in His name. 14You shall not go after other gods, the gods of the peoples who *are* all around you 15(for the LORD your God *is* a jealous God among you), lest the anger of the LORD your God be aroused against you and destroy you from the face of the earth.

16"You shall not tempt the LORD your God as you tempted *Him* in Massah. 17You shall diligently keep the commandments of the LORD your God, His testimonies, and His statutes which He has commanded you. 18And you shall do *what is* right and good in the sight of the LORD, that it may be well with you, and that you may go in and possess the good land of which the LORD swore to your fathers, 19to cast out all your enemies from before you, as the LORD has spoken.

20"When your son asks you in time to come, saying, 'What *is the meaning of* the testimonies, the statutes, and the judgments which the LORD our God has commanded you?' 21then you shall say to your son: 'We were slaves of Pharaoh in Egypt, and the LORD brought us out of Egypt with a mighty hand; 22and the LORD showed signs and wonders before our eyes, great and severe, against Egypt, Pharaoh, and all his household. 23Then He brought us out from there, that He might bring us in, to give us the land of which He swore to our fathers. 24And the LORD commanded us to observe all these statutes, to fear the LORD our God, for our good always, that He might preserve us alive, as *it is* this day. 25Then it will be righteousness for us, if we are careful to observe all these commandments before the LORD our God, as He has commanded us.'"

LUKE 7:11-35

Now it happened, the day after, *that* He [Jesus] went into a city called Nain; and many of His disciples went with Him, and a large crowd. 12And when He came near the gate of the city, behold, a dead man was being carried out, the only son of his mother; and she was a widow. And a large crowd from the city was with her. 13When the Lord saw her, He had compassion on her and said to her, "Do not weep." 14Then He came and touched the open coffin, and those who carried *him* stood still. And He said, "Young man, I say to you, arise." 15So he who was dead sat up and began to speak. And He presented him to his mother.

16Then fear came upon all, and they glorified God, saying, "A great prophet has risen up among us"; and, "God has visited His people." 17And this report about Him went throughout all Judea and all the surrounding region.

18Then the disciples of John reported to him concerning all these things. 19And John, calling two of his disciples to *him,* sent *them* to Jesus,* saying, "Are You the Coming One, or do we look for another?"

20When the men had come to Him, they said, "John the Baptist has sent us to You, saying, 'Are You the Coming

One, or do we look for another?' "
²¹And that very hour He cured many of infirmities, afflictions, and evil spirits; and to many blind He gave sight.

²²Jesus answered and said to them, "Go and tell John the things you have seen and heard: that *the* blind see, *the* lame walk, *the* lepers are cleansed, *the* deaf hear, *the* dead are raised, *the* poor have the gospel preached to them. ²³And blessed is *he* who is not offended because of Me."

²⁴When the messengers of John had departed, He began to speak to the multitudes concerning John: "What did you go out into the wilderness to see? A reed shaken by the wind? ²⁵But what did you go out to see? A man clothed in soft garments? Indeed those who are gorgeously appareled and live in luxury are in kings' courts. ²⁶But what did you go out to see? A prophet? Yes, I say to you, and more than a prophet. ²⁷This is *he* of whom it is written:

> 'Behold, I send My messenger
> before Your face,
> Who will prepare Your way
> before You.' *

²⁸For I say to you, among those born of women there is not a greater prophet than John the Baptist;* but he who is least in the kingdom of God is greater than he."

²⁹And when all the people heard *Him,* even the tax collectors justified God, having been baptized with the baptism of John. ³⁰But the Pharisees and lawyers rejected the will of God for themselves, not having been baptized by him.

³¹And the Lord said,* "To what then shall I liken the men of this generation, and what are they like? ³²They are like children sitting in the marketplace and calling to one another, saying:

> 'We played the flute for you,
> And you did not dance;

> We mourned to you,
> And you did not weep.'

³³For John the Baptist came neither eating bread nor drinking wine, and you say, 'He has a demon.' ³⁴The Son of Man has come eating and drinking, and you say, 'Look, a glutton and a winebibber, a friend of tax collectors and sinners!' ³⁵But wisdom is justified by all her children."

PSALM 68:19-35

BLESSED *be* the Lord,
Who daily loads us *with benefits,*
The God of our salvation!
Selah

20 Our God *is* the God of
    salvation;
And to GOD the Lord *belong*
    escapes from death.

21 But God will wound the head
    of His enemies,
The hairy scalp of the one
    who still goes on in his
    trespasses.

22 The Lord said, "I will bring
    back from Bashan,
I will bring *them* back from
    the depths of the sea,

23 That your foot may crush
    *them** in blood,
And the tongues of your dogs
    may have their portion from
    your enemies."

24 They have seen Your
    procession, O God,
The procession of my God,
    my King, into the sanctuary.

25 The singers went before, the
    players on instruments
    followed after;
Among *them were* the
    maidens playing timbrels.

26 Bless God in the
    congregations,

The Lord, from the fountain
of Israel.

27 There *is* little Benjamin, their
leader,
The princes of Judah *and*
their company,
The princes of Zebulun *and*
the princes of Naphtali.

28 Your God has commanded*
your strength;
Strengthen, O God, what You
have done for us.

29 Because of Your temple at
Jerusalem,
Kings will bring presents to
You.

30 Rebuke the beasts of the
reeds,
The herd of bulls with the
calves of the peoples,
Till everyone submits himself
with pieces of silver.
Scatter the peoples *who*
delight in war.

31 Envoys will come out of Egypt;
Ethiopia will quickly stretch
out her hands to God.

32 Sing to God, you kingdoms of
the earth;
Oh, sing praises to the Lord,
Selah

33 To Him who rides on the
heaven of heavens, *which*
were of old!
Indeed, He sends out His
voice, a mighty voice.

34 Ascribe strength to God;
His excellence *is* over Israel,
And His strength *is* in the
clouds.

35 O God, *You are* more
awesome than Your holy
places.
The God of Israel *is* He who
gives strength and power to
His people.
Blessed *be* God!

PROVERBS FOR TODAY / 11:29-31

He who troubles his own house will inherit the wind, and the fool will be *servant*
to the wise of heart. □ *The fruit of the righteous* is a *tree of life, and he who wins*
souls is *wise.* □ *If the righteous will be recompensed on the earth, how much more*
the ungodly and the sinner.

MARCH 27

DEUTERONOMY 7:1–8:20

"**W**HEN the LORD your God
brings you [the Israelites]
into the land which you go
to possess, and has cast out many nations before you, the Hittites and the
Girgashites and the Amorites and the
Canaanites and the Perizzites and the
Hivites and the Jebusites, seven nations greater and mightier than you,

²and when the LORD your God delivers
them over to you, you shall conquer
them *and* utterly destroy them. You
shall make no covenant with them nor
show mercy to them. ³Nor shall you
make marriages with them. You shall
not give your daughter to their son,
nor take their daughter for your son.
⁴For they will turn your sons away
from following Me, to serve other
gods; so the anger of the LORD will be

aroused against you and destroy you suddenly. [5]But thus you shall deal with them: you shall destroy their altars, and break down their *sacred* pillars, and cut down their wooden images,* and burn their carved images with fire.

[6]"For you *are* a holy people to the LORD your God; the LORD your God has chosen you to be a people for Himself, a special treasure above all the peoples on the face of the earth. [7]The LORD did not set His love on you nor choose you because you were more in number than any other people, for you were the least of all peoples; [8]but because the LORD loves you, and because He would keep the oath which He swore to your fathers, the LORD has brought you out with a mighty hand, and redeemed you from the house of bondage, from the hand of Pharaoh king of Egypt.

[9]"Therefore know that the LORD your God, He *is* God, the faithful God who keeps covenant and mercy for a thousand generations with those who love Him and keep His commandments; [10]and He repays those who hate Him to their face, to destroy them. He will not be slack with him who hates Him; He will repay him to his face. [11]Therefore you shall keep the commandment, the statutes, and the judgments which I command you today, to observe them.

[12]"Then it shall come to pass, because you listen to these judgments, and keep and do them, that the LORD your God will keep with you the covenant and the mercy which He swore to your fathers. [13]And He will love you and bless you and multiply you; He will also bless the fruit of your womb and the fruit of your land, your grain and your new wine and your oil, the increase of your cattle and the offspring of your flock, in the land of which He swore to your fathers to give you. [14]You shall be blessed above all peoples; there shall not be a male or female barren among you or among your livestock. [15]And the LORD will take away from you all sickness, and will afflict you with none of the terrible diseases of Egypt which you have known, but will lay *them* on all those who hate you. [16]Also you shall destroy all the peoples whom the LORD your God delivers over to you; your eye shall have no pity on them; nor shall you serve their gods, for that *will be* a snare to you.

[17]"If you should say in your heart, 'These nations are greater than I; how can I dispossess them?'— [18]you shall not be afraid of them, *but* you shall remember well what the LORD your God did to Pharaoh and to all Egypt: [19]the great trials which your eyes saw, the signs and the wonders, the mighty hand and the outstretched arm, by which the LORD your God brought you out. So shall the LORD your God do to all the peoples of whom you are afraid. [20]Moreover the LORD your God will send the hornet among them until those who are left, who hide themselves from you, are destroyed. [21]You shall not be terrified of them; for the LORD your God, the great and awesome God, *is* among you. [22]And the LORD your God will drive out those nations before you little by little; you will be unable to destroy them at once, lest the beasts of the field become *too* numerous for you. [23]But the LORD your God will deliver them over to you, and will inflict defeat upon them until they are destroyed. [24]And He will deliver their kings into your hand, and you will destroy their name from under heaven; no one shall be able to stand against you until you have destroyed them. [25]You shall burn the carved images of their gods with fire; you shall not covet the silver or gold *that is* on them, nor take *it* for yourselves, lest you be snared by it; for it *is* an abomination to the LORD your God. [26]Nor

shall you bring an abomination into your house, lest you be doomed to destruction like it. You shall utterly detest it and utterly abhor it, for it *is* an accursed thing.

"Every commandment which I command you today you must be careful to observe, that you may live and multiply, and go in and possess the land of which the Lord swore to your fathers. 2And you shall remember that the Lord your God led you all the way these forty years in the wilderness, to humble you *and* test you, to know what *was* in your heart, whether you would keep His commandments or not. 3So He humbled you, allowed you to hunger, and fed you with manna which you did not know nor did your fathers know, that He might make you know that man shall not live by bread alone; but man lives by every *word* that proceeds from the mouth of the Lord. 4Your garments did not wear out on you, nor did your foot swell these forty years. 5You should know in your heart that as a man chastens his son, *so* the Lord your God chastens you.

6"Therefore you shall keep the commandments of the Lord your God, to walk in His ways and to fear Him. 7For the Lord your God is bringing you into a good land, a land of brooks of water, of fountains and springs, that flow out of valleys and hills; 8a land of wheat and barley, of vines and fig trees and pomegranates, a land of olive oil and honey; 9a land in which you will eat bread without scarcity, in which you will lack nothing; a land whose stones *are* iron and out of whose hills you can dig copper. 10When you have eaten and are full, then you shall bless the Lord your God for the good land which He has given you.

11"Beware that you do not forget the Lord your God by not keeping His commandments, His judgments, and His statutes which I command you to-day, 12lest—*when* you have eaten and are full, and have built beautiful houses and dwell *in them;* 13and *when* your herds and your flocks multiply, and your silver and your gold are multiplied, and all that you have is multiplied; 14when your heart is lifted up, and you forget the Lord your God who brought you out of the land of Egypt, from the house of bondage; 15who led you through that great and terrible wilderness, *in which were* fiery serpents and scorpions and thirsty land where there was no water; who brought water for you out of the flinty rock; 16who fed you in the wilderness with manna, which your fathers did not know, that He might humble you and that He might test you, to do you good in the end— 17then you say in your heart, 'My power and the might of my hand have gained me this wealth.'

18"And you shall remember the Lord your God, for *it is* He who gives you power to get wealth, that He may establish His covenant which He swore to your fathers, as *it is* this day. 19Then it shall be, if you by any means forget the Lord your God, and follow other gods, and serve them and worship them, I testify against you this day that you shall surely perish. 20As the nations which the Lord destroys before you, so you shall perish, because you would not be obedient to the voice of the Lord your God."

LUKE 7:36–8:3

THEN one of the Pharisees asked Him [Jesus] to eat with him. And He went to the Pharisee's house, and sat down to eat. 37And behold, a woman in the city who was a sinner, when she knew that *Jesus* sat at the table in the Pharisee's house, brought an alabaster flask of fragrant oil, 38and stood at His feet behind *Him* weeping; and she began to wash His feet with her tears, and wiped *them* with the hair of her head; and she kissed His feet and anointed *them* with the fragrant oil. ³⁹Now when the Pharisee who had invited Him saw *this,* he spoke to himself, saying, "This Man, if He were a prophet, would know who and what manner of woman *this is* who is touching Him, for she is a sinner."

⁴⁰And Jesus answered and said to him, "Simon, I have something to say to you."

So he said, "Teacher, say it."

⁴¹"There was a certain creditor who had two debtors. One owed five hundred denarii, and the other fifty. ⁴²And when they had nothing with which to repay, he freely forgave them both. Tell Me, therefore, which of them will love him more?"

⁴³Simon answered and said, "I suppose the *one* whom he forgave more."

And He said to him, "You have rightly judged." ⁴⁴Then He turned to the woman and said to Simon, "Do you see this woman? I entered your house; you gave Me no water for My feet, but she has washed My feet with her tears and wiped *them* with the hair of her head. ⁴⁵You gave Me no kiss, but this woman has not ceased to kiss My feet since the time I came in. ⁴⁶You did not anoint My head with oil, but this woman has anointed My feet with fragrant oil. ⁴⁷Therefore I say to you, her sins, *which are* many, are forgiven, for she loved much. But to whom little is forgiven, *the same* loves little."

⁴⁸Then He said to her, "Your sins are forgiven."

⁴⁹And those who sat at the table with Him began to say to themselves, "Who is this who even forgives sins?"

⁵⁰Then He said to the woman, "Your faith has saved you. Go in peace."

Now it came to pass, afterward, that He went through every city and village, preaching and bringing the glad tidings of the kingdom of God. And the twelve *were* with Him, ²and certain women who had been healed of evil spirits and infirmities—Mary called Magdalene, out of whom had come seven demons, ³and Joanna the wife of Chuza, Herod's steward, and Susanna, and many others who provided for Him* from their substance.

PSALM 69:1-18

To the Chief Musician. Set to "The Lilies." *
A Psalm of David.

S AVE me, O God!
　　For the waters have come up to *my* neck.
2　　I sink in deep mire,
　　Where *there is* no standing;
　　I have come into deep waters,
　　Where the floods overflow
　　　me.
3　　I am weary with my crying;
　　My throat is dry;
　　My eyes fail while I wait for
　　　my God.

4　　Those who hate me without a
　　　cause
　　Are more than the hairs of my
　　　head;
　　They are mighty who would
　　　destroy me,
　　Being my enemies wrongfully;
　　Though I have stolen nothing,
　　I *still* must restore *it.*

5　　O God, You know my
　　　foolishness;
　　And my sins are not hidden
　　　from You.
6　　Let not those who wait for
　　　You, O Lord GOD of hosts,
　　　be ashamed because of me;
　　Let not those who seek You
　　　be confounded because of
　　　me, O God of Israel.
7　　Because for Your sake I have
　　　borne reproach;

Shame has covered my face.

8 I have become a stranger to
my brothers,
And an alien to my mother's
children;

9 Because zeal for Your house
has eaten me up,
And the reproaches of those
who reproach You have
fallen on me.

10 When I wept *and chastened*
my soul with fasting,
That became my reproach.

11 I also made sackcloth my
garment;
I became a byword to them.

12 Those who sit in the gate
speak against me,
And I *am* the song of the
drunkards.

13 But as for me, my prayer *is* to
You,
O Lord, *in* the acceptable time;
O God, in the multitude of
Your mercy,
Hear me in the truth of Your
salvation.

14 Deliver me out of the mire,
And let me not sink;
Let me be delivered from
those who hate me,
And out of the deep waters.

15 Let not the floodwater
overflow me,
Nor let the deep swallow me
up;
And let not the pit shut its
mouth on me.

16 Hear me, O Lord, for Your
lovingkindness *is* good;
Turn to me according to the
multitude of Your tender
mercies.

17 And do not hide Your face
from Your servant,
For I am in trouble;
Hear me speedily.

18 Draw near to my soul, *and*
redeem it;
Deliver me because of my
enemies.

PROVERBS FOR TODAY/ 12:1

Whoever loves instruction loves knowledge, but he who hates correction is *stupid.*

MARCH 28

DEUTERONOMY 9:1–10:22

"**H**EAR, O Israel: You *are* to cross over the Jordan today, and go in to dispossess nations greater and mightier than yourself, cities great and fortified up to heaven, [2]a people great and tall, the descendants of the Anakim, whom you know, and *of whom* you heard *it said,* 'Who can stand before the descendants of Anak?' [3]Therefore understand today that the Lord your God *is* He who goes over before you *as* a consuming fire. He will destroy them and bring them down before you; so you shall drive them out and destroy them quickly, as the Lord has said to you.

[4]"Do not think in your heart, after the Lord your God has cast them out before you, saying, 'Because of my righteousness the Lord has brought

me in to possess this land'; but *it is* because of the wickedness of these nations *that* the Lᴏʀᴅ is driving them out from before you. ⁵*It is* not because of your righteousness or the uprightness of your heart *that* you go in to possess their land, but because of the wickedness of these nations *that* the Lᴏʀᴅ your God drives them out from before you, and that He may fulfill the word which the Lᴏʀᴅ swore to your fathers, to Abraham, Isaac, and Jacob. ⁶Therefore understand that the Lᴏʀᴅ your God is not giving you this good land to possess because of your righteousness, for you *are* a stiff-necked people.

⁷"Remember! Do not forget how you provoked the Lᴏʀᴅ your God to wrath in the wilderness. From the day that you departed from the land of Egypt until you came to this place, you have been rebellious against the Lᴏʀᴅ. ⁸Also in Horeb you provoked the Lᴏʀᴅ to wrath, so that the Lᴏʀᴅ was angry *enough* with you to have destroyed you. ⁹When I went up into the mountain to receive the tablets of stone, the tablets of the covenant which the Lᴏʀᴅ made with you, then I stayed on the mountain forty days and forty nights. I neither ate bread nor drank water. ¹⁰Then the Lᴏʀᴅ delivered to me two tablets of stone written with the finger of God, and on them *were* all the words which the Lᴏʀᴅ had spoken to you on the mountain from the midst of the fire in the day of the assembly. ¹¹And it came to pass, at the end of forty days and forty nights, *that* the Lᴏʀᴅ gave me the two tablets of stone, the tablets of the covenant.

¹²"Then the Lᴏʀᴅ said to me, 'Arise, go down quickly from here, for your people whom you brought out of Egypt have acted corruptly; they have quickly turned aside from the way which I commanded them; they have made themselves a molded image.'

¹³"Furthermore the Lᴏʀᴅ spoke to me, saying, 'I have seen this people,

and indeed they are a stiff-necked people. ¹⁴Let Me alone, that I may destroy them and blot out their name from under heaven; and I will make of you a nation mightier and greater than they.'

¹⁵"So I turned and came down from the mountain, and the mountain burned with fire; and the two tablets of the covenant *were* in my two hands. ¹⁶And I looked, and behold, you had sinned against the Lᴏʀᴅ your God— had made for yourselves a molded calf! You had turned aside quickly from the way which the Lᴏʀᴅ had commanded you. ¹⁷Then I took the two tablets and threw them out of my two hands and broke them before your eyes. ¹⁸And I fell down before the Lᴏʀᴅ, as at the first, forty days and forty nights; I neither ate bread nor drank water, because of all your sin which you committed in doing wickedly in the sight of the Lᴏʀᴅ, to provoke Him to anger. ¹⁹For I was afraid of the anger and hot displeasure with which the Lᴏʀᴅ was angry with you, to destroy you. But the Lᴏʀᴅ listened to me at that time also. ²⁰And the Lᴏʀᴅ was very angry with Aaron *and* would have destroyed him; so I prayed for Aaron also at the same time. ²¹Then I took your sin, the calf which you had made, and burned it with fire and crushed it *and* ground *it* very small, until it was as fine as dust; and I threw its dust into the brook that descended from the mountain.

²²"Also at Taberah and Massah and Kibroth Hattaavah you provoked the Lᴏʀᴅ to wrath. ²³Likewise, when the Lᴏʀᴅ sent you from Kadesh Barnea, saying, 'Go up and possess the land which I have given you,' then you rebelled against the commandment of the Lᴏʀᴅ your God, and you did not believe Him nor obey His voice. ²⁴You have been rebellious against the Lᴏʀᴅ from the day that I knew you.

²⁵"Thus I prostrated myself before

the LORD; forty days and forty nights I kept prostrating myself, because the LORD had said He would destroy you. ²⁶Therefore I prayed to the LORD, and said: 'O Lord GOD, do not destroy Your people and Your inheritance whom You have redeemed through Your greatness, whom You have brought out of Egypt with a mighty hand. ²⁷Remember Your servants, Abraham, Isaac, and Jacob; do not look on the stubbornness of this people, or on their wickedness or their sin, ²⁸lest the land from which You brought us should say, "Because the LORD was not able to bring them to the land which He promised them, and because He hated them, He has brought them out to kill them in the wilderness." ²⁹Yet they *are* Your people and Your inheritance, whom You brought out by Your mighty power and by Your outstretched arm.'

"AT that time the LORD said to me, 'Hew for yourself two tablets of stone like the first, and come up to Me on the mountain and make yourself an ark of wood. ²And I will write on the tablets the words that were on the first tablets, which you broke; and you shall put them in the ark.'

³"So I made an ark of acacia wood, hewed two tablets of stone like the first, and went up the mountain, having the two tablets in my hand. ⁴And He wrote on the tablets according to the first writing, the Ten Commandments, which the LORD had spoken to you in the mountain from the midst of the fire in the day of the assembly; and the LORD gave them to me. ⁵Then I turned and came down from the mountain, and put the tablets in the ark which I had made; and there they are, just as the LORD commanded me."

⁶(Now the children of Israel journeyed from the wells of Bene Jaakan to Moserah, where Aaron died, and where he was buried; and Eleazar his son ministered as priest in his stead. ⁷From there they journeyed to Gudgodah, and from Gudgodah to Jotbathah, a land of rivers of water. ⁸At that time the LORD separated the tribe of Levi to bear the ark of the covenant of the LORD, to stand before the LORD to minister to Him and to bless in His name, to this day. ⁹Therefore Levi has no portion nor inheritance with his brethren; the LORD *is* his inheritance, just as the LORD your God promised him.)

¹⁰"As at the first time, I stayed in the mountain forty days and forty nights; the LORD also heard me at that time, *and* the LORD chose not to destroy you. ¹¹Then the LORD said to me, 'Arise, begin *your* journey before the people, that they may go in and possess the land which I swore to their fathers to give them.'

¹²"And now, Israel, what does the LORD your God require of you, but to fear the LORD your God, to walk in all His ways and to love Him, to serve the LORD your God with all your heart and with all your soul, ¹³*and* to keep the commandments of the LORD and His statutes which I command you today for your good? ¹⁴Indeed heaven and the highest heavens belong to the LORD your God, *also* the earth with all that *is* in it. ¹⁵The LORD delighted only in your fathers, to love them; and He chose their descendants after them, you above all peoples, as *it is* this day. ¹⁶Therefore circumcise the foreskin of your heart, and be stiff-necked no longer. ¹⁷For the LORD your God *is* God of gods and Lord of lords, the great God, mighty and awesome, who shows no partiality nor takes a bribe. ¹⁸He administers justice for the fatherless and the widow, and loves the stranger, giving him food and clothing. ¹⁹Therefore love the stranger, for you were strangers in the land of Egypt. ²⁰You shall fear the LORD your God; you shall serve Him, and to Him you shall hold fast, and take oaths in His name.

²¹He *is* your praise, and He *is* your God, who has done for you these great and awesome things which your eyes have seen. ²²Your fathers went down to Egypt with seventy persons, and now the LORD your God has made you as the stars of heaven in multitude."

LUKE 8:4-21

AND when a great multitude had gathered, and they had come to Him from every city, He [Jesus] spoke by a parable: ⁵"A sower went out to sow his seed. And as he sowed, some fell by the wayside; and it was trampled down, and the birds of the air devoured it. ⁶Some fell on rock; and as soon as it sprang up, it withered away because it lacked moisture. ⁷And some fell among thorns, and the thorns sprang up with it and choked it. ⁸But others fell on good ground, sprang up, and yielded a crop a hundredfold." When He had said these things He cried, "He who has ears to hear, let him hear!"

⁹Then His disciples asked Him, saying, "What does this parable mean?" ¹⁰And He said, "To you it has been given to know the mysteries of the kingdom of God, but to the rest *it is given* in parables, that

> '*Seeing they may not see,*
> *And hearing they may not*
> *understand.'* *

¹¹"Now the parable is this: The seed is the word of God. ¹²Those by the wayside are the ones who hear; then the devil comes and takes away the word out of their hearts, lest they should believe and be saved. ¹³But the ones on the rock *are those* who, when they hear, receive the word with joy; and these have no root, who believe for a while and in time of temptation fall away. ¹⁴Now the ones *that* fell among thorns are those who, when they have heard, go out and are choked with

cares, riches, and pleasures of life, and bring no fruit to maturity. ¹⁵But the ones *that* fell on the good ground are those who, having heard the word with a noble and good heart, keep *it* and bear fruit with patience.

¹⁶"No one, when he has lit a lamp, covers it with a vessel or puts *it* under a bed, but sets *it* on a lampstand, that those who enter may see the light. ¹⁷For nothing is secret that will not be revealed, nor *anything* hidden that will not be known and come to light. ¹⁸Therefore take heed how you hear. For whoever has, to him *more* will be given; and whoever does not have, even what he seems to have will be taken from him."

¹⁹Then His mother and brothers came to Him, and could not approach Him because of the crowd. ²⁰And it was told Him *by some,* who said, "Your mother and Your brothers are standing outside, desiring to see You."

²¹But He answered and said to them, "My mother and My brothers are these who hear the word of God and do it."

PSALM 69:19-36

YOU know my reproach, my shame, and my dishonor;
My adversaries *are* all before You.
20 Reproach has broken my heart,
And I am full of heaviness;
I looked *for someone* to take pity, but *there was* none;
And for comforters, but I found none.
21 They also gave me gall for my food,
And for my thirst they gave me vinegar to drink.

22 Let their table become a snare before them,
And their well-being a trap.

23 Let their eyes be darkened, so
   that they do not see;
   And make their loins shake
   continually.
24 Pour out Your indignation
   upon them,
   And let Your wrathful anger
   take hold of them.
25 Let their dwelling place be
   desolate;
   Let no one live in their tents.
26 For they persecute the *ones*
   You have struck,
   And talk of the grief of those
   You have wounded.
27 Add iniquity to their iniquity,
   And let them not come into
   Your righteousness.
28 Let them be blotted out of the
   book of the living,
   And not be written with the
   righteous.
29 But I *am* poor and sorrowful;
   Let Your salvation, O God, set
   me up on high.

30 I will praise the name of God
   with a song,
   And will magnify Him with
   thanksgiving.
31 *This* also shall please the LORD
   better than an ox *or* bull,
   Which has horns and hooves.
32 The humble shall see *this and*
   be glad;
   And you who seek God, your
   hearts shall live.
33 For the LORD hears the poor,
   And does not despise His
   prisoners.
34 Let heaven and earth praise
   Him,
   The seas and everything that
   moves in them.
35 For God will save Zion
   And build the cities of Judah,
   That they may dwell there
   and possess it.
36 Also, the descendants of His
   servants shall inherit it,
   And those who love His name
   shall dwell in it.

PROVERBS FOR TODAY/ 12:2-3

A good man *obtains favor from the* LORD, *but a man of wicked intentions He will* condemn. □ *A man is not established by wickedness, but the root of the righteous cannot be moved.*

MARCH 29

DEUTERONOMY 11:1–12:32

"THEREFORE you shall love the LORD your God, and keep His charge, His statutes, His judgments, and His commandments always. ²Know today that *I do* not *speak* with your children, who have not known and who have not seen the chastening of the LORD your God, His greatness and His mighty hand and His outstretched arm— ³His signs and His acts which He did in the midst of Egypt, to Pharaoh king of Egypt, and to all his land; ⁴what He did to the army of Egypt, to their horses and their chariots: how He made the waters of the Red Sea overflow them as they pursued you, and *how* the LORD has destroyed them to this day; ⁵what He did for you in the wilderness until you came to this place; 6and what He did to Dathan and Abiram the sons of Eliab, the son of Reuben: how the earth opened its mouth and swallowed them up, their households, their tents, and all the substance that *was* in their possession, in the midst of all Israel— 7but your eyes have seen every great act of the LORD which He did.

8"Therefore you shall keep every commandment which I command you today, that you may be strong, and go in and possess the land which you cross over to possess, 9and that you may prolong *your* days in the land which the LORD swore to give your fathers, to them and their descendants, 'a land flowing with milk and honey.'* 10For the land which you go to possess *is* not like the land of Egypt from which you have come, where you sowed your seed and watered *it* by foot, as a vegetable garden; 11but the land which you cross over to possess *is* a land of hills and valleys, which drinks water from the rain of heaven, 12a land for which the LORD your God cares; the eyes of the LORD your God *are* always on it, from the beginning of the year to the very end of the year.

13"And it shall be that if you earnestly obey My commandments which I command you today, to love the LORD your God and serve Him with all your heart and with all your soul, 14then I* will give *you* the rain for your land in its season, the early rain and the latter rain, that you may gather in your grain, your new wine, and your oil. 15And I will send grass in your fields for your livestock, that you may eat and be filled.' 16Take heed to yourselves, lest your heart be deceived, and you turn aside and serve other gods and worship them, 17lest the LORD's anger be aroused against you, and He shut up the heavens so that there be no rain, and the land yield no produce, and you

perish quickly from the good land which the LORD is giving you.

18"Therefore you shall lay up these words of mine in your heart and in your soul, and bind them as a sign on your hand, and they shall be as frontlets between your eyes. 19You shall teach them to your children, speaking of them when you sit in your house, when you walk by the way, when you lie down, and when you rise up. 20And you shall write them on the doorposts of your house and on your gates, 21that your days and the days of your children may be multiplied in the land of which the LORD swore to your fathers to give them, like the days of the heavens above the earth.

22"For if you carefully keep all these commandments which I command you to do—to love the LORD your God, to walk in all His ways, and to hold fast to Him— 23then the LORD will drive out all these nations from before you, and you will dispossess greater and mightier nations than yourselves. 24Every place on which the sole of your foot treads shall be yours: from the wilderness and Lebanon, from the river, the River Euphrates, even to the Western Sea,* shall be your territory. 25No man shall be able to stand against you; the LORD your God will put the dread of you and the fear of you upon all the land where you tread, just as He has said to you.

26"Behold, I set before you today a blessing and a curse: 27the blessing, if you obey the commandments of the LORD your God which I command you today; 28and the curse, if you do not obey the commandments of the LORD your God, but turn aside from the way which I command you today, to go after other gods which you have not known. 29Now it shall be, when the LORD your God has brought you into the land which you go to possess, that you shall put the blessing on Mount Gerizim and the curse on Mount Ebal.

³⁰*Are* they not on the other side of the Jordan, toward the setting sun, in the land of the Canaanites who dwell in the plain opposite Gilgal, beside the terebinth trees of Moreh? ³¹For you will cross over the Jordan and go in to possess the land which the LORD your God is giving you, and you will possess it and dwell in it. ³²And you shall be careful to observe all the statutes and judgments which I set before you today.

"THESE *are* the statutes and judgments which you shall be careful to observe in the land which the LORD God of your fathers is giving you to possess, all the days that you live on the earth. ²You shall utterly destroy all the places where the nations which you shall dispossess served their gods, on the high mountains and on the hills and under every green tree. ³And you shall destroy their altars, break their *sacred* pillars, and burn their wooden images with fire; you shall cut down the carved images of their gods and destroy their names from that place. ⁴You shall not worship the LORD your God *with* such *things*.

⁵"But you shall seek the place where the LORD your God chooses, out of all your tribes, to put His name for His dwelling place; and there you shall go. ⁶There you shall take your burnt offerings, your sacrifices, your tithes, the heave offerings of your hand, your vowed offerings, your freewill offerings, and the firstborn of your herds and flocks. ⁷And there you shall eat before the LORD your God, and you shall rejoice in all to which you have put your hand, you and your households, in which the LORD your God has blessed you.

⁸"You shall not at all do as we are doing here today—every man doing whatever *is* right in his own eyes— ⁹for as yet you have not come to the rest and the inheritance which the LORD your God is giving you. ¹⁰But *when* you cross over the Jordan and dwell in the land which the LORD your God is giving you to inherit, and He gives you rest from all your enemies round about, so that you dwell in safety, ¹¹then there will be the place where the LORD your God chooses to make His name abide. There you shall bring all that I command you: your burnt offerings, your sacrifices, your tithes, the heave offerings of your hand, and all your choice offerings which you vow to the LORD. ¹²And you shall rejoice before the LORD your God, you and your sons and your daughters, your male and female servants, and the Levite who *is* within your gates, since he has no portion nor inheritance with you. ¹³Take heed to yourself that you do not offer your burnt offerings in every place that you see; ¹⁴but in the place which the LORD chooses, in one of your tribes, there you shall offer your burnt offerings, and there you shall do all that I command you.

¹⁵"However, you may slaughter and eat meat within all your gates, whatever your heart desires, according to the blessing of the LORD your God which He has given you; the unclean and the clean may eat of it, of the gazelle and the deer alike. ¹⁶Only you shall not eat the blood; you shall pour it on the earth like water. ¹⁷You may not eat within your gates the tithe of your grain or your new wine or your oil, of the firstborn of your herd or your flock, of any of your offerings which you vow, of your freewill offerings, or of the heave offering of your hand. ¹⁸But you must eat them before the LORD your God in the place which the LORD your God chooses, you and your son and your daughter, your male servant and your female servant, and the Levite who *is* within your gates; and you shall rejoice before the LORD your God in all to which you put your hands. ¹⁹Take heed to yourself that

you do not forsake the Levite as long as you live in your land.

20"When the LORD your God enlarges your border as He has promised you, and you say, 'Let me eat meat,' because you long to eat meat, you may eat as much meat as your heart desires. 21If the place where the LORD your God chooses to put His name is too far from you, then you may slaughter from your herd and from your flock which the LORD has given you, just as I have commanded you, and you may eat within your gates as much as your heart desires. 22Just as the gazelle and the deer are eaten, so you may eat them; the unclean and the clean alike may eat them. 23Only be sure that you do not eat the blood, for the blood *is* the life; you may not eat the life with the meat. 24You shall not eat it; you shall pour it on the earth like water. 25You shall not eat it, that it may go well with you and your children after you, when you do *what is* right in the sight of the LORD. 26Only the holy things which you have, and your vowed offerings, you shall take and go to the place which the LORD chooses. 27And you shall offer your burnt offerings, the meat and the blood, on the altar of the LORD your God; and the blood of your sacrifices shall be poured out on the altar of the LORD your God, and you shall eat the meat. 28Observe and obey all these words which I command you, that it may go well with you and your children after you forever, when you do *what is* good and right in the sight of the LORD your God.

29"When the LORD your God cuts off from before you the nations which you go to dispossess, and you displace them and dwell in their land, 30take heed to yourself that you are not ensnared to follow them, after they are destroyed from before you, and that you do not inquire after their gods, saying, 'How did these nations serve their gods? I also will do likewise.' 31You shall not worship the LORD your God in that way; for every abomination to the LORD which He hates they have done to their gods; for they burn even their sons and daughters in the fire to their gods.

32"Whatever I command you, be careful to observe it; you shall not add to it nor take away from it."

LUKE 8:22-39

Now it happened, on a certain day, that He [Jesus] got into a boat with His disciples. And He said to them, "Let us cross over to the other side of the lake." And they launched out. 23But as they sailed He fell asleep. And a windstorm came down on the lake, and they were filling *with water,* and were in jeopardy. 24And they came to Him and awoke Him, saying, "Master, Master, we are perishing!"

Then He arose and rebuked the wind and the raging of the water. And they ceased, and there was a calm. 25But He said to them, "Where is your faith?"

And they were afraid, and marveled, saying to one another, "Who can this be? For He commands even the winds and water, and they obey Him!"

26Then they sailed to the country of the Gadarenes,* which is opposite Galilee. 27And when He stepped out on the land, there met Him a certain man from the city who had demons for a long time. And he wore no clothes,* nor did he live in a house but in the tombs. 28When he saw Jesus, he cried out, fell down before Him, and with a loud voice said, "What have I to do with You, Jesus, Son of the Most High God? I beg You, do not torment me!" 29For He had commanded the unclean spirit to come out of the man. For it had often seized him, and he was kept under guard, bound with chains and shackles; and he broke the bonds and was driven by the demon into the wilderness.

³⁰Jesus asked him, saying, "What is your name?"

And he said, "Legion," because many demons had entered him. ³¹And they begged Him that He would not command them to go out into the abyss.

³²Now a herd of many swine was feeding there on the mountain. So they begged Him that He would permit them to enter them. And He permitted them. ³³Then the demons went out of the man and entered the swine, and the herd ran violently down the steep place into the lake and drowned.

³⁴When those who fed *them* saw what had happened, they fled and told *it* in the city and in the country. ³⁵Then they went out to see what had happened, and came to Jesus, and found the man from whom the demons had departed, sitting at the feet of Jesus, clothed and in his right mind. And they were afraid. ³⁶They also who had seen *it* told them by what means he who had been demon-possessed was healed. ³⁷Then the whole multitude of the surrounding region of the Gadarenes* asked Him to depart from them, for they were seized with great fear. And He got into the boat and returned.

³⁸Now the man from whom the demons had departed begged Him that he might be with Him. But Jesus sent him away, saying, ³⁹"Return to your own house, and tell what great things God has done for you." And he went his way and proclaimed throughout the whole city what great things Jesus had done for him.

PSALM 70:1-5

To the Chief Musician. A Psalm *of David. To bring to remembrance.*

MAKE *haste,* O God, to deliver me!
Make haste to help me,
O Lᴏʀᴅ!

2   Let them be ashamed and confounded
Who seek my life;
Let them be turned back* and confused
Who desire my hurt.

3   Let them be turned back because of their shame,
Who say, "Aha, aha!"

4   Let all those who seek You rejoice and be glad in You;
And let those who love Your salvation say continually,
"Let God be magnified!"

5   But I *am* poor and needy;
Make haste to me, O God!
You *are* my help and my deliverer;
O Lᴏʀᴅ, do not delay.

PROVERBS FOR TODAY / 12:4

An excellent wife* is *the crown of her husband, but she who causes shame* is *like rottenness in his bones.*

MARCH 30

DEUTERONOMY 13:1–15:23

"**I**F there arises among you a prophet or a dreamer of dreams, and he gives you a sign or a wonder, ²and the sign or the wonder comes to pass, of which he spoke to you, saying, 'Let us go after other gods'—which you have not known—'and let us serve them,' ³you shall not listen to the words of that prophet or that dreamer of dreams, for the LORD your God is testing you to know whether you love the LORD your God with all your heart and with all your soul. ⁴You shall walk after the LORD your God and fear Him, and keep His commandments and obey His voice; you shall serve Him and hold fast to Him. ⁵But that prophet or that dreamer of dreams shall be put to death, because he has spoken in order to turn *you* away from the LORD your God, who brought you out of the land of Egypt and redeemed you from the house of bondage, to entice you from the way in which the LORD your God commanded you to walk. So you shall put away the evil from your midst.

⁶"If your brother, the son of your mother, your son or your daughter, the wife of your bosom, or your friend who is as your own soul, secretly entices you, saying, 'Let us go and serve other gods,' which you have not known, neither you nor your fathers, ⁷of the gods of the people which *are* all around you, near to you or far off from you, from *one* end of the earth to the *other* end of the earth, ⁸you shall not consent to him or listen to him, nor shall your eye pity him, nor shall you spare him or conceal him; ⁹but you shall surely kill him; your hand shall be first against him to put him to death, and afterward the hand of all the people. ¹⁰And you shall stone him with stones until he dies, because he sought to entice you away from the LORD your God, who brought you out of the land of Egypt, from the house of bondage. ¹¹So all Israel shall hear and fear, and not again do such wickedness as this among you.

¹²"If you hear someone in one of your cities, which the LORD your God gives you to dwell in, saying, ¹³'Corrupt men have gone out from among you and enticed the inhabitants of their city, saying, "Let us go and serve other gods"'—which you have not known— ¹⁴then you shall inquire, search out, and ask diligently. And *if it is* indeed true *and* certain *that* such an abomination was committed among you, ¹⁵you shall surely strike the inhabitants of that city with the edge of the sword, utterly destroying it, all that is in it and its livestock—with the edge of the sword. ¹⁶And you shall gather all its plunder into the middle of the street, and completely burn with fire the city and all its plunder, for the LORD your God. It shall be a heap forever; it shall not be built again. ¹⁷So none of the accursed things shall remain in your hand, that the LORD may turn from the fierceness of His anger and show you mercy, have compassion on you and multiply you, just as He swore to your fathers, ¹⁸because you have listened to the voice of the LORD your God, to keep all His commandments which I command you today, to do *what is* right in the eyes of the LORD your God.

"You *are* the children of the LORD your God; you shall not cut yourselves nor shave the front of your head for the dead. ²For you *are* a holy people to the LORD your God, and the LORD has chosen you to be a people for Himself, a special treasure above all the peoples who *are* on the face of the earth.

³"You shall not eat any detestable thing. ⁴These *are* the animals which you may eat: the ox, the sheep, the goat, ⁵the deer, the gazelle, the roe deer, the wild goat, the mountain goat,* the antelope, and the mountain sheep. ⁶And you may eat every animal with cloven hooves, having the hoof split into two parts, *and that* chews the cud, among the animals. ⁷Nevertheless, of those that chew the cud or have cloven hooves, you shall not eat, *such as* these: the camel, the hare, and the rock hyrax; for they chew the cud but do not have cloven hooves; they *are* unclean for you. ⁸Also the swine is unclean for you, because it has cloven hooves, yet *does* not *chew* the cud; you shall not eat their flesh or touch their dead carcasses.

⁹"These you may eat of all that *are* in the waters: you may eat all that have fins and scales. ¹⁰And whatever does not have fins and scales you shall not eat; it *is* unclean for you.

¹¹"All clean birds you may eat. ¹²But these you shall not eat: the eagle, the vulture, the buzzard, ¹³the red kite, the falcon, and the kite after their kinds; ¹⁴every raven after its kind; ¹⁵the ostrich, the short-eared owl, the sea gull, and the hawk after their kinds; ¹⁶the little owl, the screech owl, the white owl, ¹⁷the jackdaw, the carrion vulture, the fisher owl, ¹⁸the stork, the heron after its kind, and the hoopoe and the bat.

¹⁹"Also every creeping thing that flies is unclean for you; they shall not be eaten.

²⁰"You may eat all clean birds.

²¹"You shall not eat anything that dies *of itself;* you may give it to the alien who *is* within your gates, that he may eat it, or you may sell it to a foreigner;

for you *are* a holy people to the LORD your God.

"You shall not boil a young goat in its mother's milk.

²²"You shall truly tithe all the increase of your grain that the field produces year by year. ²³And you shall eat before the LORD your God, in the place where He chooses to make His name abide, the tithe of your grain and your new wine and your oil, of the firstborn of your herds and your flocks, that you may learn to fear the LORD your God always. ²⁴But if the journey is too long for you, so that you are not able to carry *the tithe, or* if the place where the LORD your God chooses to put His name is too far from you, when the LORD your God has blessed you, ²⁵then you shall exchange *it* for money, take the money in your hand, and go to the place which the LORD your God chooses. ²⁶And you shall spend that money for whatever your heart desires: for oxen or sheep, for wine or similar drink, for whatever your heart desires; you shall eat there before the LORD your God, and you shall rejoice, you and your household. ²⁷You shall not forsake the Levite who *is* within your gates, for he has no part nor inheritance with you.

²⁸"At the end of *every* third year you shall bring out the tithe of your produce of that year and store *it* up within your gates. ²⁹And the Levite, because he has no portion nor inheritance with you, and the stranger and the fatherless and the widow who *are* within your gates, may come and eat and be satisfied, that the LORD your God may bless you in all the work of your hand which you do.

"AT the end of *every* seven years you shall grant a release *of debts.* ²And this *is* the form of the release: Every creditor who has lent *anything* to his neighbor shall release *it;* he shall not require *it* of his neighbor or his brother, because it is called the LORD's release. ³Of a foreigner you may require *it;* but you shall give up your claim to what is owed by your brother, ⁴except when there may be no poor among you; for the LORD will greatly bless you in the land which the LORD your God is giving you to possess *as* an inheritance— ⁵only if you carefully obey the voice of the LORD your God, to observe with care all these commandments which I command you today. ⁶For the LORD your God will bless you just as He promised you; you shall lend to many nations, but you shall not borrow; you shall reign over many nations, but they shall not reign over you.

⁷"If there is among you a poor man of your brethren, within any of the gates in your land which the LORD your God is giving you, you shall not harden your heart nor shut your hand from your poor brother, ⁸but you shall open your hand wide to him and willingly lend him sufficient for his need, whatever he needs. ⁹Beware lest there be a wicked thought in your heart, saying, 'The seventh year, the year of release, is at hand,' and your eye be evil against your poor brother and you give him nothing, and he cry out to the LORD against you, and it become sin among you. ¹⁰You shall surely give to him, and your heart should not be grieved when you give to him, because for this thing the LORD your God will bless you in all your works and in all to which you put your hand. ¹¹For the poor will never cease from the land; therefore I command you, saying, 'You shall open your hand wide to your brother, to your poor and your needy, in your land.'

¹²"If your brother, a Hebrew man, or a Hebrew woman, is sold to you and serves you six years, then in the seventh year you shall let him go free from you. ¹³And when you send him away free from you, you shall not let him go away empty-handed; ¹⁴you

shall supply him liberally from your flock, from your threshing floor, and from your winepress. *From what* the LORD has blessed you with, you shall give to him. ¹⁵You shall remember that you were a slave in the land of Egypt, and the LORD your God redeemed you; therefore I command you this thing today. ¹⁶And if it happens that he says to you, 'I will not go away from you,' because he loves you and your house, since he prospers with you, ¹⁷then you shall take an awl and thrust *it* through his ear to the door, and he shall be your servant forever. Also to your female servant you shall do likewise. ¹⁸It shall not seem hard to you when you send him away free from you; for he has been worth a double hired servant in serving you six years. Then the LORD your God will bless you in all that you do.

¹⁹"All the firstborn males that come from your herd and your flock you shall sanctify to the LORD your God; you shall do no work with the firstborn of your herd, nor shear the firstborn of your flock. ²⁰You and your household shall eat *it* before the LORD your God year by year in the place which the LORD chooses. ²¹But if there is a defect in it, *if it is* lame or blind *or has* any serious defect, you shall not sacrifice it to the LORD your God. ²²You may eat it within your gates; the unclean and the clean *person* alike *may eat it,* as *if it were* a gazelle or a deer. ²³Only you shall not eat its blood; you shall pour it on the ground like water."

LUKE 8:40–9:6

So it was, when Jesus returned, that the multitude welcomed Him, for they were all waiting for Him. ⁴¹And behold, there came a man named Jairus, and he was a ruler of the synagogue. And he fell down at Jesus' feet and begged Him to come to his house, ⁴²for he had an only daugh-

"The LORD is good to all."

Psalm 145:9

"This is *the day the* L*ORD* *has made;*
we will rejoice and be glad in it."
    Psalm 118:24

ter about twelve years of age, and she was dying.

But as He went, the multitudes thronged Him. 43Now a woman, having a flow of blood for twelve years, who had spent all her livelihood on physicians and could not be healed by any, 44came from behind and touched the border of His garment. And immediately her flow of blood stopped.

45And Jesus said, "Who touched Me?"

When all denied it, Peter and those with him* said, "Master, the multitudes throng and press You, and You say, 'Who touched Me?' "*

46But Jesus said, "Somebody touched Me, for I perceived power going out from Me." 47Now when the woman saw that she was not hidden, she came trembling; and falling down before Him, she declared to Him in the presence of all the people the reason she had touched Him and how she was healed immediately.

48And He said to her, "Daughter, be of good cheer;* your faith has made you well. Go in peace."

49While He was still speaking, someone came from the ruler of the synagogue's *house,* saying to him, "Your daughter is dead. Do not trouble the Teacher."*

50But when Jesus heard *it,* He answered him, saying, "Do not be afraid; only believe, and she will be made well." 51When He came into the house, He permitted no one to go in* except Peter, James, and John,* and the father and mother of the girl. 52Now all wept and mourned for her; but He said, "Do not weep; she is not dead, but sleeping." 53And they ridiculed Him, knowing that she was dead.

54But He put them all outside,* took her by the hand and called, saying, "Little girl, arise." 55Then her spirit returned, and she arose immediately. And He commanded that she be given *something* to eat. 56And her parents

were astonished, but He charged them to tell no one what had happened.

THEN He called His twelve disciples together and gave them power and authority over all demons, and to cure diseases. 2He sent them to preach the kingdom of God and to heal the sick. 3And He said to them, "Take nothing for the journey, neither staffs nor bag nor bread nor money; and do not have two tunics apiece.

4"Whatever house you enter, stay there, and from there depart. 5And whoever will not receive you, when you go out of that city, shake off the very dust from your feet as a testimony against them."

6So they departed and went through the towns, preaching the gospel and healing everywhere.

PSALM 71:1-24

IN You, O LORD, I put my trust;
Let me never be put to shame.
2Deliver me in Your righteousness, and cause me to
    escape;
Incline Your ear to me, and
    save me.
3   Be my strong refuge,
To which I may resort
    continually;
You have given the
    commandment to save me,
For You *are* my rock and my
    fortress.

4   Deliver me, O my God, out of
    the hand of the wicked,
Out of the hand of the
    unrighteous and cruel man.
5   For You are my hope, O Lord
    GOD;
You are my trust from my
    youth.
6   By You I have been upheld
    from birth;

You are He who took me out
of my mother's womb.
My praise *shall be* continually
of You.

7   I have become as a wonder to
    many,
    But You *are* my strong refuge.
8   Let my mouth be filled *with*
    Your praise
    And with Your glory all the
    day.

9   Do not cast me off in the time
    of old age;
    Do not forsake me when my
    strength fails.
10 For my enemies speak
    against me;
    And those who lie in wait for
    my life take counsel
    together,
11 Saying, "God has forsaken
    him;
    Pursue and take him, for *there
    is* none to deliver *him."*

12 O God, do not be far from me;
    O my God, make haste to
    help me!
13 Let them be confounded *and*
    consumed
    Who are adversaries of my
    life;
    Let them be covered *with*
    reproach and dishonor
    Who seek my hurt.

14 But I will hope continually,
    And will praise You yet more
    and more.
15 My mouth shall tell of Your
    righteousness
    And Your salvation all the day,
    For I do not know *their* limits.
16 I will go in the strength of the
    Lord God;

I will make mention of Your
righteousness, of Yours
only.

17 O God, You have taught me
    from my youth;
    And to this *day* I declare Your
    wondrous works.
18 Now also when *I am* old and
    grayheaded,
    O God, do not forsake me,
    Until I declare Your strength
    to *this* generation,
    Your power to everyone *who*
    is to come.

19 Also Your righteousness,
    O God, *is* very high,
    You who have done great
    things;
    O God, who *is* like You?
20 *You,* who have shown me
    great and severe troubles,
    Shall revive me again,
    And bring me up again from
    the depths of the earth.
21 You shall increase my
    greatness,
    And comfort me on every
    side.

22 Also with the lute I will praise
    You—
    And Your faithfulness, O my
    God!
    To You I will sing with the
    harp,
    O Holy One of Israel.
23 My lips shall greatly rejoice
    when I sing to You,
    And my soul, which You have
    redeemed.
24 My tongue also shall talk of
    Your righteousness all the
    day long;
    For they are confounded,
    For they are brought to shame
    Who seek my hurt.

PROVERBS FOR TODAY/ 12:5-7

The thoughts of the righteous are *right,* but *the counsels of the wicked* are *deceitful. The words of the wicked* are, *"Lie in wait for blood," but the mouth of the upright will deliver them. The wicked are overthrown and* are *no more, but the house of the righteous will stand.*

MARCH 31

DEUTERONOMY 16:1–17:20

"**O**BSERVE the month of Abib, and keep the Passover to the LORD your God, for in the month of Abib the LORD your God brought you out of Egypt by night. ²Therefore you shall sacrifice the Passover to the LORD your God, from the flock and the herd, in the place where the LORD chooses to put His name. ³You shall eat no leavened bread with it; seven days you shall eat unleavened bread with it, *that is,* the bread of affliction (for you came out of the land of Egypt in haste), that you may remember the day in which you came out of the land of Egypt all the days of your life. ⁴And no leaven shall be seen among you in all your territory for seven days, nor shall *any* of the meat which you sacrifice the first day at twilight remain overnight until morning.

⁵"You may not sacrifice the Passover within any of your gates which the LORD your God gives you; ⁶but at the place where the LORD your God chooses to make His name abide, there you shall sacrifice the Passover at twilight, at the going down of the sun, at the time you came out of Egypt. ⁷And you shall roast and eat *it* in the place which the LORD your God chooses, and in the morning you shall turn and go to your tents. ⁸Six days you shall eat unleavened bread, and on the seventh day there *shall be* a sacred as-

sembly to the LORD your God. You shall do no work *on it.*

⁹"You shall count seven weeks for yourself; begin to count the seven weeks from *the time* you begin *to put* the sickle to the grain. ¹⁰Then you shall keep the Feast of Weeks to the LORD your God with the tribute of a freewill offering from your hand, which you shall give as the LORD your God blesses you. ¹¹You shall rejoice before the LORD your God, you and your son and your daughter, your male servant and your female servant, the Levite who *is* within your gates, the stranger and the fatherless and the widow who *are* among you, at the place where the LORD your God chooses to make His name abide. ¹²And you shall remember that you were a slave in Egypt, and you shall be careful to observe these statutes.

¹³"You shall observe the Feast of Tabernacles seven days, when you have gathered from your threshing floor and from your winepress. ¹⁴And you shall rejoice in your feast, you and your son and your daughter, your male servant and your female servant and the Levite, the stranger and the fatherless and the widow, who *are* within your gates. ¹⁵Seven days you shall keep a sacred feast to the LORD your God in the place which the LORD chooses, because the LORD your God will bless you in all your produce and

in all the work of your hands, so that you surely rejoice.

16"Three times a year all your males shall appear before the LORD your God in the place which He chooses: at the Feast of Unleavened Bread, at the Feast of Weeks, and at the Feast of Tabernacles; and they shall not appear before the LORD empty-handed. 17Every man *shall give* as he is able, according to the blessing of the LORD your God which He has given you.

18"You shall appoint judges and officers in all your gates, which the LORD your God gives you, according to your tribes, and they shall judge the people with just judgment. 19You shall not pervert justice; you shall not show partiality, nor take a bribe, for a bribe blinds the eyes of the wise and twists the words of the righteous. 20You shall follow what is altogether just, that you may live and inherit the land which the LORD your God is giving you.

21"You shall not plant for yourself any tree, as a wooden image, near the altar which you build for yourself to the LORD your God. 22You shall not set up a sacred pillar, which the LORD your God hates.

"YOU shall not sacrifice to the LORD your God a bull or sheep which has any blemish *or* defect, for that *is* an abomination to the LORD your God.

2"If there is found among you, within any of your gates which the LORD your God gives you, a man or a woman who has been wicked in the sight of the LORD your God, in transgressing His covenant, 3who has gone and served other gods and worshiped them, either the sun or moon or any of the host of heaven, which I have not commanded, 4and it is told you, and you hear *of it,* then you shall inquire diligently. And if *it is* indeed true *and* certain that such an abomination has been committed in Israel, 5then you shall bring out to your gates that man or woman who has committed that wicked thing, and shall stone to death that man or woman with stones. 6Whoever is deserving of death shall be put to death on the testimony of two or three witnesses; he shall not be put to death on the testimony of one witness. 7The hands of the witnesses shall be the first against him to put him to death, and afterward the hands of all the people. So you shall put away the evil from among you.

8"If a matter arises which is too hard for you to judge, between degrees of guilt for bloodshed, between one judgment or another, or between one punishment or another, matters of controversy within your gates, then you shall arise and go up to the place which the LORD your God chooses. 9And you shall come to the priests, the Levites, and to the judge *there* in those days, and inquire *of them;* they shall pronounce upon you the sentence of judgment. 10You shall do according to the sentence which they pronounce upon you in that place which the LORD chooses. And you shall be careful to do according to all that they order you. 11According to the sentence of the law in which they instruct you, according to the judgment which they tell you, you shall do; you shall not turn aside *to* the right hand or *to* the left from the sentence which they pronounce upon you. 12Now the man who acts presumptuously and will not heed the priest who stands to minister there before the LORD your God, or the judge, that man shall die. So you shall put away the evil from Israel. 13And all the people shall hear and fear, and no longer act presumptuously.

14"When you come to the land which the LORD your God is giving you, and possess it and dwell in it, and say, 'I will set a king over me like all the nations that *are* around me,' 15you shall surely set a king over you whom the LORD your God chooses; *one* from among your brethren you shall set as king over you; you may not set a foreigner over you, who *is* not your brother. [16]But he shall not multiply horses for himself, nor cause the people to return to Egypt to multiply horses, for the LORD has said to you, 'You shall not return that way again.' [17]Neither shall he multiply wives for himself, lest his heart turn away; nor shall he greatly multiply silver and gold for himself.

[18]"Also it shall be, when he sits on the throne of his kingdom, that he shall write for himself a copy of this law in a book, from *the one* before the priests, the Levites. [19]And it shall be with him, and he shall read it all the days of his life, that he may learn to fear the LORD his God and be careful to observe all the words of this law and these statutes, [20]that his heart may not be lifted above his brethren, that he may not turn aside from the commandment *to* the right hand or *to* the left, and that he may prolong *his* days in his kingdom, he and his children in the midst of Israel."

LUKE 9:7-27

Now Herod the tetrarch heard of all that was done by Him [Jesus]; and he was perplexed, because it was said by some that John had risen from the dead, [8]and by some that Elijah had appeared, and by others that one of the old prophets had risen again. [9]Herod said, "John I have beheaded, but who is this of whom I hear such things?" So he sought to see Him.

[10]And the apostles, when they had returned, told Him all that they had done. Then He took them and went aside privately into a deserted place belonging to the city called Bethsaida. [11]But when the multitudes knew *it,* they followed Him; and He received them and spoke to them about the kingdom of God, and healed those who had need of healing. [12]When the day began to wear away, the twelve came and said to Him, "Send the multitude away, that they may go into the surrounding towns and country, and lodge and get provisions; for we are in a deserted place here."

[13]But He said to them, "You give them something to eat."

And they said, "We have no more than five loaves and two fish, unless we go and buy food for all these people." [14]For there were about five thousand men.

Then He said to His disciples, "Make them sit down in groups of fifty." [15]And they did so, and made them all sit down.

[16]Then He took the five loaves and the two fish, and looking up to heaven, He blessed and broke *them,* and gave *them* to the disciples to set before the multitude. [17]So they all ate and were filled, and twelve baskets of the leftover fragments were taken up by them.

[18]And it happened, as He was alone praying, *that* His disciples joined Him, and He asked them, saying, "Who do the crowds say that I am?"

[19]So they answered and said, "John the Baptist; but some *say* Elijah; and others *say* that one of the old prophets has risen again."

[20]He said to them, "But who do you say that I am?"

Peter answered and said, "The Christ of God."

[21]And He strictly warned and commanded them to tell this to no one, [22]saying, "The Son of Man must suffer many things, and be rejected by the elders and chief priests and scribes, and be killed, and be raised the third day."

[23]Then He said to *them* all, "If anyone desires to come after Me, let him deny himself, and take up his cross daily,* and follow Me. [24]For whoever desires to save his life will lose it, but

whoever loses his life for My sake will save it. 25For what profit is it to a man if he gains the whole world, and is himself destroyed or lost? 26For whoever is ashamed of Me and My words, of him the Son of Man will be ashamed when He comes in His *own* glory, and *in His* Father's, and of the holy angels. 27But I tell you truly, there are some standing here who shall not taste death till they see the kingdom of God."

PSALM 72:1-20

A Psalm of Solomon.

GIVE the king Your judgments, O God,
   And Your righteousness to
      the king's Son.
2   He will judge Your people
      with righteousness,
   And Your poor with justice.
3   The mountains will bring
      peace to the people,
   And the little hills, by
      righteousness.
4   He will bring justice to the
      poor of the people;
   He will save the children of
      the needy,
   And will break in pieces the
      oppressor.

5   They shall fear You*
   As long as the sun and moon
      endure,
   Throughout all generations.
6   He shall come down like rain
      upon the grass before
      mowing,
   Like showers *that* water the
      earth.
7   In His days the righteous
      shall flourish,
   And abundance of peace,
   Until the moon is no more.

8   He shall have dominion also
      from sea to sea,

And from the River to the
   ends of the earth.
9   Those who dwell in the
      wilderness will bow before
      Him,
   And His enemies will lick the
      dust.
10   The kings of Tarshish and of
      the isles
   Will bring presents;
   The kings of Sheba and Seba
   Will offer gifts.
11   Yes, all kings shall fall down
      before Him;
   All nations shall serve Him.

12   For He will deliver the needy
      when he cries,
   The poor also, and *him* who
      has no helper.
13   He will spare the poor and
      needy,
   And will save the souls of the
      needy.
14   He will redeem their life from
      oppression and violence;
   And precious shall be their
      blood in His sight.

15   And He shall live;
   And the gold of Sheba will be
      given to Him;
   Prayer also will be made for
      Him continually,
   And daily He shall be praised.

16   There will be an abundance of
      grain in the earth,
   On the top of the mountains;
   Its fruit shall wave like
      Lebanon;
   And *those* of the city shall
      flourish like grass of the
      earth.

17   His name shall endure forever;
   His name shall continue as
      long as the sun.
   And *men* shall be blessed in
      Him;

All nations shall call Him
blessed.

18 Blessed *be* the Lord God, the
God of Israel,
Who only does wondrous
things!

19 And blessed *be* His glorious
name forever!
And let the whole earth be
filled *with* His glory.
Amen and Amen.

20 The prayers of David the son
of Jesse are ended.

PROVERBS FOR TODAY / 12:8-9

A man will be commended according to his wisdom, but he who is of a perverse heart will be despised. □ *Better* is the one *who is slighted but has a servant, than he who honors himself but lacks bread.*

APRIL 1

DEUTERONOMY 18:1–20:20

"THE priests, the Levites—all the tribe of Levi—shall have no part nor inheritance with Israel; they shall eat the offerings of the Lord made by fire, and His portion. ²Therefore they shall have no inheritance among their brethren; the Lord is their inheritance, as He said to them.

³"And this shall be the priest's due from the people, from those who offer a sacrifice, whether *it is* bull or sheep: they shall give to the priest the shoulder, the cheeks, and the stomach. ⁴The firstfruits of your grain and your new wine and your oil, and the first of the fleece of your sheep, you shall give him. ⁵For the Lord your God has chosen him out of all your tribes to stand to minister in the name of the Lord, him and his sons forever.

⁶"So if a Levite comes from any of your gates, from where he dwells among all Israel, and comes with all the desire of his mind to the place which the Lord chooses, ⁷then he may serve in the name of the Lord his God as all his brethren the Levites *do,* who

stand there before the Lord. ⁸They shall have equal portions to eat, besides what comes from the sale of his inheritance.

⁹"When you come into the land which the Lord your God is giving you, you shall not learn to follow the abominations of those nations. ¹⁰There shall not be found among you *anyone* who makes his son or his daughter pass through the fire, *or one* who practices witchcraft, *or* a soothsayer, or one who interprets omens, or a sorcerer, ¹¹or one who conjures spells, or a medium, or a spiritist, or one who calls up the dead. ¹²For all who do these things *are* an abomination to the Lord, and because of these abominations the Lord your God drives them out from before you. ¹³You shall be blameless before the Lord your God. ¹⁴For these nations which you will dispossess listened to soothsayers and diviners; but as for you, the Lord your God has not appointed such for you.

¹⁵"The Lord your God will raise up for you a Prophet like me from your midst, from your brethren. Him you shall hear, ¹⁶according to all you de-

sired of the LORD your God in Horeb in the day of the assembly, saying, 'Let me not hear again the voice of the LORD my God, nor let me see this great fire anymore, lest I die.'

¹⁷"And the LORD said to me: 'What they have spoken is good. ¹⁸I will raise up for them a Prophet like you from among their brethren, and will put My words in His mouth, and He shall speak to them all that I command Him. ¹⁹And it shall be *that* whoever will not hear My words, which He speaks in My name, I will require *it* of him. ²⁰But the prophet who presumes to speak a word in My name, which I have not commanded him to speak, or who speaks in the name of other gods, that prophet shall die.' ²¹And if you say in your heart, 'How shall we know the word which the LORD has not spoken?'— ²²when a prophet speaks in the name of the LORD, if the thing does not happen or come to pass, that *is* the thing which the LORD has not spoken; the prophet has spoken it presumptuously; you shall not be afraid of him.

"WHEN the LORD your God has cut off the nations whose land the LORD your God is giving you, and you dispossess them and dwell in their cities and in their houses, ²you shall separate three cities for yourself in the midst of your land which the LORD your God is giving you to possess. ³You shall prepare roads for yourself, and divide into three parts the territory of your land which the LORD your God is giving you to inherit, that any manslayer may flee there.

⁴"And this *is* the case of the manslayer who flees there, that he may live: Whoever kills his neighbor unintentionally, not having hated him in time past— ⁵as when *a man* goes to the woods with his neighbor to cut timber, and his hand swings a stroke with the ax to cut down the tree, and the head slips from the handle and strikes his neighbor so that he dies—he shall flee to one of these cities and live; ⁶lest the avenger of blood, while his anger is hot, pursue the manslayer and overtake him, because the way is long, and kill him, though he *was* not deserving of death, since he had not hated the victim in time past. ⁷Therefore I command you, saying, 'You shall separate three cities for yourself.'

⁸"Now if the LORD your God enlarges your territory, as He swore to your fathers, and gives you the land which He promised to give to your fathers, ⁹and if you keep all these commandments and do them, which I command you today, to love the LORD your God and to walk always in His ways, then you shall add three more cities for yourself besides these three, ¹⁰lest innocent blood be shed in the midst of your land which the LORD your God is giving you *as* an inheritance, and *thus* guilt of bloodshed be upon you.

¹¹"But if anyone hates his neighbor, lies in wait for him, rises against him and strikes him mortally, so that he dies, and he flees to one of these cities, ¹²then the elders of his city shall send and bring him from there, and deliver him over to the hand of the avenger of blood, that he may die. ¹³Your eye shall not pity him, but you shall put away *the guilt of* innocent blood from Israel, that it may go well with you.

¹⁴"You shall not remove your neighbor's landmark, which the men of old have set, in your inheritance which you will inherit in the land that the LORD your God is giving you to possess.

¹⁵"One witness shall not rise against a man concerning any iniquity or any sin that he commits; by the mouth of two or three witnesses the matter shall be established. ¹⁶If a false witness rises against any man to testify against him of wrongdoing, ¹⁷then both men in the controversy shall

stand before the LORD, before the priests and the judges who serve in those days. 18And the judges shall make careful inquiry, and indeed, *if* the witness *is* a false witness, who has testified falsely against his brother, 19then you shall do to him as he thought to have done to his brother; so you shall put away the evil from among you. 20And those who remain shall hear and fear, and hereafter they shall not again commit such evil among you. 21Your eye shall not pity: life *shall be* for life, eye for eye, tooth for tooth, hand for hand, foot for foot.

"WHEN you go out to battle against your enemies, and see horses and chariots *and* people more numerous than you, do not be afraid of them, for the LORD your God *is* with you, who brought you up from the land of Egypt. 2So it shall be, when you are on the verge of battle, that the priest shall approach and speak to the people. 3And he shall say to them, 'Hear, O Israel: Today you are on the verge of battle with your enemies. Do not let your heart faint, do not be afraid, and do not tremble or be terrified because of them; 4for the LORD your God *is* He who goes with you, to fight for you against your enemies, to save you.'

5"Then the officers shall speak to the people, saying: 'What man *is there* who has built a new house and has not dedicated it? Let him go and return to his house, lest he die in the battle and another man dedicate it. 6Also what man *is there* who has planted a vineyard and has not eaten of it? Let him go and return to his house, lest he die in the battle and another man eat of it. 7And what man *is there* who is betrothed to a woman and has not married her? Let him go and return to his house, lest he die in the battle and another man marry her.'

8"The officers shall speak further to the people, and say, 'What man *is there*

who *is* fearful and fainthearted? Let him go and return to his house, lest the heart of his brethren faint* like his heart.' 9And so it shall be, when the officers have finished speaking to the people, that they shall make captains of the armies to lead the people.

10"When you go near a city to fight against it, then proclaim an offer of peace to it. 11And it shall be that if they accept your offer of peace, and open to you, then all the people *who are* found in it shall be placed under tribute to you, and serve you. 12Now if *the city* will not make peace with you, but war against you, then you shall besiege it. 13And when the LORD your God delivers it into your hands, you shall strike every male in it with the edge of the sword. 14But the women, the little ones, the livestock, and all that is in the city, all its spoil, you shall plunder for yourself; and you shall eat the enemies' plunder which the LORD your God gives you. 15Thus you shall do to all the cities *which are* very far from you, which *are* not of the cities of these nations.

16"But of the cities of these peoples which the LORD your God gives you *as* an inheritance, you shall let nothing that breathes remain alive, 17but you shall utterly destroy them: the Hittite and the Amorite and the Canaanite and the Perizzite and the Hivite and the Jebusite, just as the LORD your God has commanded you, 18lest they teach you to do according to all their abominations which they have done for their gods, and you sin against the LORD your God.

19"When you besiege a city for a long time, while making war against it to take it, you shall not destroy its trees by wielding an ax against them; if you can eat of them, do not cut them down to use in the siege, for the tree of the field *is* man's *food.* 20Only the trees which you know *are* not trees for food you may destroy and cut down, to build siegeworks against the city that makes war with you, until it is subdued."

LUKE 9:28-50

Now it came to pass, about eight days after these sayings, that He [Jesus] took Peter, John, and James and went up on the mountain to pray. 29As He prayed, the appearance of His face was altered, and His robe *became* white *and* glistening. 30And behold, two men talked with Him, who were Moses and Elijah, 31who appeared in glory and spoke of His decease which He was about to accomplish at Jerusalem. 32But Peter and those with him were heavy with sleep; and when they were fully awake, they saw His glory and the two men who stood with Him. 33Then it happened, as they were parting from Him, *that* Peter said to Jesus, "Master, it is good for us to be here; and let us make three tabernacles: one for You, one for Moses, and one for Elijah"—not knowing what he said.

34While he was saying this, a cloud came and overshadowed them; and they were fearful as they entered the cloud. 35And a voice came out of the cloud, saying, "This is My beloved Son.* Hear Him!" 36When the voice had ceased, Jesus was found alone. But they kept quiet, and told no one in those days any of the things they had seen.

37Now it happened on the next day, when they had come down from the mountain, that a great multitude met Him. 38Suddenly a man from the multitude cried out, saying, "Teacher, I implore You, look on my son, for he is my only child. 39And behold, a spirit seizes him, and he suddenly cries out; it convulses him so that he foams *at the mouth;* and it departs from him with great difficulty, bruising him. 40So I im-plored Your disciples to cast it out, but they could not."

41Then Jesus answered and said, "O faithless and perverse generation, how long shall I be with you and bear with you? Bring your son here." 42And as he was still coming, the demon threw him down and convulsed *him.* Then Jesus rebuked the unclean spirit, healed the child, and gave him back to his father.

43And they were all amazed at the majesty of God.

But while everyone marveled at all the things which Jesus did, He said to His disciples, 44"Let these words sink down into your ears, for the Son of Man is about to be betrayed into the hands of men." 45But they did not understand this saying, and it was hidden from them so that they did not perceive it; and they were afraid to ask Him about this saying.

46Then a dispute arose among them as to which of them would be greatest. 47And Jesus, perceiving the thought of their heart, took a little child and set him by Him, 48and said to them, "Whoever receives this little child in My name receives Me; and whoever receives Me receives Him who sent Me. For he who is least among you all will be great."

49Now John answered and said, "Master, we saw someone casting out demons in Your name, and we forbade him because he does not follow with us."

50But Jesus said to him, "Do not forbid *him,* for he who is not against us* is on our* side."

PSALM 73:1-28

A Psalm of Asaph.

Truly God *is* good to Israel,
To such as are pure in heart.
2But as for me, my feet had
almost stumbled;
My steps had nearly slipped.

3 For I *was* envious of the
    boastful,
  When I saw the prosperity of
    the wicked.

4 For *there are* no pangs in their
    death,
  But their strength *is* firm.

5 They *are* not in trouble *as
    other* men,
  Nor are they plagued like
    other men.

6 Therefore pride serves as
    their necklace;
  Violence covers them *like* a
    garment.

7 Their eyes bulge* with
    abundance;
  They have more than heart
    could wish.

8 They scoff and speak
    wickedly *concerning*
    oppression;
  They speak loftily.

9 They set their mouth against
    the heavens,
  And their tongue walks
    through the earth.

10 Therefore his people return
    here,
  And waters of a full *cup* are
    drained by them.

11 And they say, "How does God
    know?
  And is there knowledge in the
    Most High?"

12 Behold, these *are* the ungodly,
  Who are always at ease;
  They increase *in* riches.

13 Surely I have cleansed my
    heart *in* vain,
  And washed my hands in
    innocence.

14 For all day long I have been
    plagued,
  And chastened every
    morning.

15 If I had said, "I will speak
    thus,"
  Behold, I would have been
    untrue to the generation of
    Your children.

16 When I thought *how* to
    understand this,
  It *was* too painful for me—

17 Until I went into the
    sanctuary of God;
  Then I understood their end.

18 Surely You set them in
    slippery places;
  You cast them down to
    destruction.

19 Oh, how they are *brought* to
    desolation, as in a moment!
  They are utterly consumed
    with terrors.

20 As a dream when *one* awakes,
  So, Lord, when You awake,
  You shall despise their image.

21 Thus my heart was grieved,
  And I was vexed in my mind.

22 I *was* so foolish and ignorant;
  I was *like* a beast before You.

23 Nevertheless I *am* continually
    with You;
  You hold *me* by my right hand.

24 You will guide me with Your
    counsel,
  And afterward receive me *to*
    glory.

25 Whom have I in heaven *but
    You?*
  And *there is* none upon earth
    that I desire besides You.

26 My flesh and my heart fail;
  But God *is* the strength of my
    heart and my portion
    forever.

27 For indeed, those who are far
    from You shall perish;
  You have destroyed all those
    who desert You for harlotry.

²⁸ But *it is* good for me to draw
near to God;
I have put my trust in the
Lord GOD,

That I may declare all Your
works.

PROVERBS FOR TODAY/ 12:10

A righteous man *regards the life of his animal, but the tender mercies of the wicked*
are *cruel.*

APRIL 2

DEUTERONOMY 21:1–22:30

"I F *anyone* is found slain, lying in
the field in the land which the
LORD your God is giving you to
possess, *and* it is not known who killed
him, ²then your elders and your judges
shall go out and measure *the distance*
from the slain man to the surrounding
cities. ³And it shall be *that* the elders of
the city nearest to the slain man will
take a heifer which has not been
worked *and* which has not pulled with
a yoke. ⁴The elders of that city shall
bring the heifer down to a valley with
flowing water, which is neither plowed
nor sown, and they shall break the
heifer's neck there in the valley. ⁵Then
the priests, the sons of Levi, shall
come near, for the LORD your God has
chosen them to minister to Him and to
bless in the name of the LORD; by their
word every controversy and every as-
sault shall be *settled.* ⁶And all the elders
of that city nearest to the slain *man*
shall wash their hands over the heifer
whose neck was broken in the valley.
⁷Then they shall answer and say, 'Our
hands have not shed this blood, nor
have our eyes seen *it.* ⁸Provide atonement, O LORD, for Your people Israel,
whom You have redeemed, and do not
lay innocent blood to the charge of
Your people Israel.' And atonement

shall be provided on their behalf for
the blood. ⁹So you shall put away the
guilt of innocent blood from among
you when you do *what is* right in the
sight of the LORD.

¹⁰"When you go out to war against
your enemies, and the LORD your God
delivers them into your hand, and you
take them captive, ¹¹and you see
among the captives a beautiful woman,
and desire her and would take her for
your wife, ¹²then you shall bring her
home to your house, and she shall
shave her head and trim her nails.
¹³She shall put off the clothes of her
captivity, remain in your house, and
mourn her father and her mother a full
month; after that you may go in to her
and be her husband, and she shall be
your wife. ¹⁴And it shall be, if you have
no delight in her, then you shall set her
free, but you certainly shall not sell her
for money; you shall not treat her bru-
tally, because you have humbled her.

¹⁵"If a man has two wives, one loved
and the other unloved, and they have
borne him children, *both* the loved and
the unloved, and *if* the firstborn son is
of her who is unloved, ¹⁶then it shall
be, on the day he bequeaths his possessions to his sons, *that* he must not
bestow firstborn status on the son of
the loved wife in preference to the son
of the unloved, the *true* firstborn. ¹⁷But

he shall acknowledge the son of the unloved wife *as* the firstborn by giving him a double portion of all that he has, for he *is* the beginning of his strength; the right of the firstborn *is* his.

18"If a man has a stubborn and rebellious son who will not obey the voice of his father or the voice of his mother, and *who,* when they have chastened him, will not heed them, 19then his father and his mother shall take hold of him and bring him out to the elders of his city, to the gate of his city. 20And they shall say to the elders of his city, 'This son of ours is stubborn and rebellious; he will not obey our voice; he is a glutton and a drunkard.' 21Then all the men of his city shall stone him to death with stones; so you shall put away the evil from among you, and all Israel shall hear and fear.

22"If a man has committed a sin deserving of death, and he is put to death, and you hang him on a tree, 23his body shall not remain overnight on the tree, but you shall surely bury him that day, so that you do not defile the land which the LORD your God is giving you *as* an inheritance; for he who is hanged *is* accursed of God.

"You shall not see your brother's ox or his sheep going astray, and hide yourself from them; you shall certainly bring them back to your brother. 2And if your brother *is* not near you, or if you do not know him, then you shall bring it to your own house, and it shall remain with you until your brother seeks it; then you shall restore it to him. 3You shall do the same with his donkey, and so shall you do with his garment; with any lost thing of your brother's, which he has lost and you have found, you shall do likewise; you must not hide yourself.

4"You shall not see your brother's donkey or his ox fall down along the road, and hide yourself from them; you shall surely help him lift *them* up again.

5"A woman shall not wear anything that pertains to a man, nor shall a man put on a woman's garment, for all who do so *are* an abomination to the LORD your God.

6"If a bird's nest happens to be before you along the way, in any tree or on the ground, with young ones or eggs, with the mother sitting on the young or on the eggs, you shall not take the mother with the young; 7you shall surely let the mother go, and take the young for yourself, that it may be well with you and *that* you may prolong *your* days.

8"When you build a new house, then you shall make a parapet for your roof, that you may not bring guilt of bloodshed on your household if anyone falls from it.

9"You shall not sow your vineyard with different kinds of seed, lest the yield of the seed which you have sown and the fruit of your vineyard be defiled.

10"You shall not plow with an ox and a donkey together.

11"You shall not wear a garment of different sorts, *such as* wool and linen mixed together.

12"You shall make tassels on the four corners of the clothing with which you cover *yourself.*

13"If any man takes a wife, and goes in to her, and detests her, 14and charges her with shameful conduct, and brings a bad name on her, and says, 'I took this woman, and when I came to her I found she *was* not a virgin,' 15then the father and mother of the young woman shall take and bring out *the evidence of* the young woman's virginity to the elders of the city at the gate. 16And the young woman's father shall say to the elders, 'I gave my daughter to this man as wife, and he detests her. 17Now he has charged her with shameful conduct, saying, "I found your daughter *was* not a virgin," and yet these *are the evidences of* my daughter's virginity.' And they shall spread the cloth before the elders of the city. [18]Then the elders of that city shall take that man and punish him; [19]and they shall fine him one hundred *shekels* of silver and give *them* to the father of the young woman, because he has brought a bad name on a virgin of Israel. And she shall be his wife; he cannot divorce her all his days.

[20]"But if the thing is true, *and evidences of* virginity are not found for the young woman, [21]then they shall bring out the young woman to the door of her father's house, and the men of her city shall stone her to death with stones, because she has done a disgraceful thing in Israel, to play the harlot in her father's house. So you shall put away the evil from among you.

[22]"If a man is found lying with a woman married to a husband, then both of them shall die—the man that lay with the woman, and the woman; so you shall put away the evil from Israel.

[23]"If a young woman *who is* a virgin is betrothed to a husband, and a man finds her in the city and lies with her, [24]then you shall bring them both out to the gate of that city, and you shall stone them to death with stones, the young woman because she did not cry out in the city, and the man because he humbled his neighbor's wife; so you shall put away the evil from among you.

[25]"But if a man finds a betrothed young woman in the countryside, and the man forces her and lies with her, then only the man who lay with her shall die. [26]But you shall do nothing to the young woman; *there is* in the young woman no sin *deserving* of death, for just as when a man rises against his neighbor and kills him, even so *is* this matter. [27]For he found her in the countryside, *and* the betrothed young woman cried out, but *there was* no one to save her.

[28]"If a man finds a young woman *who is* a virgin, who is not betrothed, and he seizes her and lies with her, and they are found out, [29]then the man who lay with her shall give to the young woman's father fifty *shekels* of silver, and she shall be his wife because he has humbled her; he shall not be permitted to divorce her all his days.

[30]"A man shall not take his father's wife, nor uncover his father's bed."

LUKE 9:51–10:12

Now it came to pass, when the time had come for Him [Jesus] to be received up, that He steadfastly set His face to go to Jerusalem, [52]and sent messengers before His face. And as they went, they entered a village of the Samaritans, to prepare for Him. [53]But they did not receive Him, because His face was *set* for the journey to Jerusalem. [54]And when His disciples James and John saw *this,* they said, "Lord, do You want us to command fire to come down from heaven and consume them, just as Elijah did?"*

[55]But He turned and rebuked them,* and said, "You do not know what manner of spirit you are of. [56]For the Son of Man did not come to destroy men's lives but to save *them.*"* And they went to another village.

[57]Now it happened as they journeyed on the road, *that* someone said to Him, "Lord, I will follow You wherever You go."

[58]And Jesus said to him, "Foxes have holes and birds of the air *have* nests, but the Son of Man has nowhere to lay *His* head."

[59]Then He said to another, "Follow Me."

But he said, "Lord, let me first go and bury my father."

[60]Jesus said to him, "Let the dead bury their own dead, but you go and preach the kingdom of God."

[61]And another also said, "Lord, I will

follow You, but let me first go *and* bid them farewell who are at my house."

⁶²But Jesus said to him, "No one, having put his hand to the plow, and looking back, is fit for the kingdom of God."

AFTER these things the Lord appointed seventy others also,* and sent them two by two before His face into every city and place where He Himself was about to go. ²Then He said to them, "The harvest truly *is* great, but the laborers *are* few; therefore pray the Lord of the harvest to send out laborers into His harvest. ³Go your way; behold, I send you out as lambs among wolves. ⁴Carry neither money bag, knapsack, nor sandals; and greet no one along the road. ⁵But whatever house you enter, first say, 'Peace to this house.' ⁶And if a son of peace is there, your peace will rest on it; if not, it will return to you. ⁷And remain in the same house, eating and drinking such things as they give, for the laborer is worthy of his wages. Do not go from house to house. ⁸Whatever city you enter, and they receive you, eat such things as are set before you. ⁹And heal the sick there, and say to them, 'The kingdom of God has come near to you.' ¹⁰But whatever city you enter, and they do not receive you, go out into its streets and say, ¹¹'The very dust of your city which clings to us* we wipe off against you. Nevertheless know this, that the kingdom of God has come near you.' ¹²But* I say to you that it will be more tolerable in that Day for Sodom than for that city."

PSALM 74:1-23

A Contemplation * *of Asaph.*

O GOD, why have You cast *us* off forever?
Why does Your anger smoke against the sheep of Your pasture?

2 Remember Your congregation, *which* You have purchased of old,
The tribe of Your inheritance, *which* You have redeemed—
This Mount Zion where You have dwelt.

3 Lift up Your feet to the perpetual desolations.
The enemy has damaged everything in the sanctuary.

4 Your enemies roar in the midst of Your meeting place;
They set up their banners *for* signs.

5 They seem like men who lift up
Axes among the thick trees.

6 And now they break down its carved work, all at once,
With axes and hammers.

7 They have set fire to Your sanctuary;
They have defiled the dwelling place of Your name to the ground.

8 They said in their hearts,
"Let us destroy them altogether."
They have burned up all the meeting places of God in the land.

9 We do not see our signs;
There is no longer any prophet;
Nor *is there* any among us who knows how long.

10 O God, how long will the adversary reproach?
Will the enemy blaspheme Your name forever?

11 Why do You withdraw Your hand, even Your right hand?
Take it out of Your bosom and destroy *them.*

12 For God *is* my King from of old,

Working salvation in the
midst of the earth.
13 You divided the sea by Your
strength;
You broke the heads of the
sea serpents in the waters.
14 You broke the heads of
Leviathan in pieces,
And gave him *as* food to the
people inhabiting the
wilderness.
15 You broke open the fountain
and the flood;
You dried up mighty rivers.
16 The day *is* Yours, the night
also *is* Yours;
You have prepared the light
and the sun.
17 You have set all the borders of
the earth;
You have made summer and
winter.

18 Remember this, *that* the
enemy has reproached,
O Lord,

And *that* a foolish people has
blasphemed Your name.
19 Oh, do not deliver the life of
Your turtledove to the wild
beast!
Do not forget the life of Your
poor forever.
20 Have respect to the covenant;
For the dark places of the
earth are full of the haunts
of cruelty.
21 Oh, do not let the oppressed
return ashamed!
Let the poor and needy praise
Your name.

22 Arise, O God, plead Your own
cause;
Remember how the foolish
man reproaches You daily.
23 Do not forget the voice of
Your enemies;
The tumult of those who rise
up against You increases
continually.

PROVERBS FOR TODAY/ 12:11

He who tills his land will be satisfied with bread, but he who follows frivolity is
devoid of understanding. *

APRIL 3

DEUTERONOMY 23:1–25:19

"**H**E who is emasculated by crushing or mutilation shall not enter the assembly of the Lord.

2"One of illegitimate birth shall not enter the assembly of the Lord; even to the tenth generation none of his *descendants* shall enter the assembly of the Lord.

3"An Ammonite or Moabite shall not enter the assembly of the Lord; even to the tenth generation none of his *descendants* shall enter the assembly of the Lord forever, 4because they did not meet you with bread and water on the road when you came out of Egypt, and because they hired against you Balaam the son of Beor from Pethor of Mesopotamia,* to curse you. 5Nevertheless the Lord your God would not listen to Balaam, but the LORD your God turned the curse into a blessing for you, because the LORD your God loves you. ⁶You shall not seek their peace nor their prosperity all your days forever.

⁷"You shall not abhor an Edomite, for he *is* your brother. You shall not abhor an Egyptian, because you were an alien in his land. ⁸The children of the third generation born to them may enter the assembly of the LORD.

⁹"When the army goes out against your enemies, then keep yourself from every wicked thing. ¹⁰If there is any man among you who becomes unclean by some occurrence in the night, then he shall go outside the camp; he shall not come inside the camp. ¹¹But it shall be, when evening comes, that he shall wash with water; and when the sun sets, he may come into the camp.

¹²"Also you shall have a place outside the camp, where you may go out; ¹³and you shall have an implement among your equipment, and when you sit down outside, you shall dig with it and turn and cover your refuse. ¹⁴For the LORD your God walks in the midst of your camp, to deliver you and give your enemies over to you; therefore your camp shall be holy, that He may see no unclean thing among you, and turn away from you.

¹⁵"You shall not give back to his master the slave who has escaped from his master to you. ¹⁶He may dwell with you in your midst, in the place which he chooses within one of your gates, where it seems best to him; you shall not oppress him.

¹⁷"There shall be no *ritual* harlot* of the daughters of Israel, or a perverted* one of the sons of Israel. ¹⁸You shall not bring the wages of a harlot or the price of a dog to the house of the LORD your God for any vowed offering, for both of these *are* an abomination to the LORD your God.

¹⁹"You shall not charge interest to your brother—interest on money *or* food *or* anything that is lent out at interest. ²⁰To a foreigner you may charge interest, but to your brother you shall not charge interest, that the LORD your God may bless you in all to which you set your hand in the land which you are entering to possess.

²¹"When you make a vow to the LORD your God, you shall not delay to pay it; for the LORD your God will surely require it of you, and it would be sin to you. ²²But if you abstain from vowing, it shall not be sin to you. ²³That which has gone from your lips you shall keep and perform, for you voluntarily vowed to the LORD your God what you have promised with your mouth.

²⁴"When you come into your neighbor's vineyard, you may eat your fill of grapes at your pleasure, but you shall not put *any* in your container. ²⁵When you come into your neighbor's standing grain, you may pluck the heads with your hand, but you shall not use a sickle on your neighbor's standing grain.

"WHEN a man takes a wife and marries her, and it happens that she finds no favor in his eyes because he has found some uncleanness in her, and he writes her a certificate of divorce, puts *it* in her hand, and sends her out of his house, ²when she has departed from his house, and goes and becomes another man's *wife,* ³if the latter husband detests her and writes her a certificate of divorce, puts *it* in her hand, and sends her out of his house, or if the latter husband dies who took her as his wife, ⁴then her former husband who divorced her must not take her back to be his wife after she has been defiled; for that *is* an abomination before the LORD, and you shall not bring sin on the land which the LORD your God is giving you *as* an inheritance.

⁵"When a man has taken a new wife, he shall not go out to war or be

charged with any business; he shall be free at home one year, and bring happiness to his wife whom he has taken.

⁶"No man shall take the lower or the upper millstone in pledge, for he takes *one's* living in pledge.

⁷"If a man is found kidnapping any of his brethren of the children of Israel, and mistreats him or sells him, then that kidnapper shall die; and you shall put away the evil from among you.

⁸"Take heed in an outbreak of leprosy, that you carefully observe and do according to all that the priests, the Levites, shall teach you; just as I commanded them, *so* you shall be careful to do. ⁹Remember what the Lord your God did to Miriam on the way when you came out of Egypt!

¹⁰"When you lend your brother anything, you shall not go into his house to get his pledge. ¹¹You shall stand outside, and the man to whom you lend shall bring the pledge out to you. ¹²And if the man *is* poor, you shall not keep his pledge overnight. ¹³You shall in any case return the pledge to him again when the sun goes down, that he may sleep in his own garment and bless you; and it shall be righteousness to you before the Lord your God.

¹⁴"You shall not oppress a hired servant *who is* poor and needy, *whether* one of your brethren or one of the aliens who *is* in your land within your gates. ¹⁵Each day you shall give *him* his wages, and not let the sun go down on it, for he *is* poor and has set his heart on it; lest he cry out against you to the Lord, and it be sin to you.

¹⁶"Fathers shall not be put to death for *their* children, nor shall children be put to death for *their* fathers; a person shall be put to death for his own sin.

¹⁷"You shall not pervert justice due the stranger or the fatherless, nor take a widow's garment as a pledge. ¹⁸But you shall remember that you were a slave in Egypt, and the Lord your God

redeemed you from there; therefore I command you to do this thing.

¹⁹"When you reap your harvest in your field, and forget a sheaf in the field, you shall not go back to get it; it shall be for the stranger, the fatherless, and the widow, that the Lord your God may bless you in all the work of your hands. ²⁰When you beat your olive trees, you shall not go over the boughs again; it shall be for the stranger, the fatherless, and the widow. ²¹When you gather the grapes of your vineyard, you shall not glean *it* afterward; it shall be for the stranger, the fatherless, and the widow. ²²And you shall remember that you were a slave in the land of Egypt; therefore I command you to do this thing.

"If there is a dispute between men, and they come to court, that *the judges* may judge them, and they justify the righteous and condemn the wicked, ²then it shall be, if the wicked man deserves to be beaten, that the judge will cause him to lie down and be beaten in his presence, according to his guilt, with a certain number of blows. ³Forty blows he may give him *and* no more, lest he should exceed this and beat him with many blows above these, and your brother be humiliated in your sight.

⁴"You shall not muzzle an ox while it treads out *the grain.*

⁵"If brothers dwell together, and one of them dies and has no son, the widow of the dead man shall not be *married* to a stranger outside *the family;* her husband's brother shall go in to her, take her as his wife, and perform the duty of a husband's brother to her. ⁶And it shall be *that* the firstborn son which she bears will succeed to the name of his dead brother, that his name may not be blotted out of Israel. ⁷But if the man does not want to take his brother's wife, then let his brother's wife go up to the gate to the elders, and say, 'My husband's brother refuses to

raise up a name to his brother in Israel; he will not perform the duty of my husband's brother.' 8Then the elders of his city shall call him and speak to him. But *if* he stands firm and says, 'I do not want to take her,' 9then his brother's wife shall come to him in the presence of the elders, remove his sandal from his foot, spit in his face, and answer and say, 'So shall it be done to the man who will not build up his brother's house.' 10And his name shall be called in Israel, 'The house of him who had his sandal removed.'

11"If *two* men fight together, and the wife of one draws near to rescue her husband from the hand of the one attacking him, and puts out her hand and seizes him by the genitals, 12then you shall cut off her hand; your eye shall not pity *her.*

13"You shall not have in your bag differing weights, a heavy and a light. 14You shall not have in your house differing measures, a large and a small. 15You shall have a perfect and just weight, a perfect and just measure, that your days may be lengthened in the land which the LORD your God is giving you. 16For all who do such things, all who behave unrighteously, *are* an abomination to the LORD your God.

17"Remember what Amalek did to you on the way as you were coming out of Egypt, 18how he met you on the way and attacked your rear ranks, all the stragglers at your rear, when you *were* tired and weary; and he did not fear God. 19Therefore it shall be, when the LORD your God has given you rest from your enemies all around, in the land which the LORD your God is giving you to possess *as* an inheritance, *that* you will blot out the remembrance of Amalek from under heaven. You shall not forget."

LUKE 10:13-37

"**W**OE to you, Chorazin! Woe to you, Bethsaida! For if the mighty works which were done in you had been done in Tyre and Sidon, they would have repented long ago, sitting in sackcloth and ashes. 14But it will be more tolerable for Tyre and Sidon at the judgment than for you. 15And you, Capernaum, who are exalted to heaven, will be brought down to Hades.* 16He who hears you hears Me, he who rejects you rejects Me, and he who rejects Me rejects Him who sent Me."

17Then the seventy* returned with joy, saying, "Lord, even the demons are subject to us in Your name."

18And He said to them, "I saw Satan fall like lightning from heaven. 19Behold, I give you the authority to trample on serpents and scorpions, and over all the power of the enemy, and nothing shall by any means hurt you. 20Nevertheless do not rejoice in this, that the spirits are subject to you, but rather* rejoice because your names are written in heaven."

21In that hour Jesus rejoiced in the Spirit and said, "I thank You, Father, Lord of heaven and earth, that You have hidden these things from *the* wise and prudent and revealed them to babes. Even so, Father, for so it seemed good in Your sight. 22All* things have been delivered to Me by My Father, and no one knows who the Son is except the Father, and who the Father is except the Son, and *the one* to whom the Son wills to reveal *Him.*"

23Then He turned to *His* disciples and said privately, "Blessed *are* the eyes which see the things you see; 24for I tell you that many prophets and kings have desired to see what you see, and have not seen *it,* and to hear what you hear, and have not heard *it.*"

²⁵And behold, a certain lawyer stood up and tested Him, saying, "Teacher, what shall I do to inherit eternal life?"

²⁶He said to him, "What is written in the law? What is your reading *of it?*"

²⁷So he answered and said, " *'You shall love the* LORD *your God with all your heart, with all your soul, with all your strength, and with all your mind,'* * and *'your neighbor as yourself.'"* *

²⁸And He said to him, "You have answered rightly; do this and you will live."

²⁹But he, wanting to justify himself, said to Jesus, "And who is my neighbor?"

³⁰Then Jesus answered and said: "A certain *man* went down from Jerusalem to Jericho, and fell among thieves, who stripped him of his clothing, wounded *him,* and departed, leaving *him* half dead. ³¹Now by chance a certain priest came down that road. And when he saw him, he passed by on the other side. ³²Likewise a Levite, when he arrived at the place, came and looked, and passed by on the other side. ³³But a certain Samaritan, as he journeyed, came where he was. And when he saw him, he had compassion. ³⁴So he went to *him* and bandaged his wounds, pouring on oil and wine; and he set him on his own animal, brought him to an inn, and took care of him. ³⁵On the next day, when he departed,* he took out two denarii, gave *them* to the innkeeper, and said to him, 'Take care of him; and whatever more you spend, when I come again, I will repay you.' ³⁶So which of these three do you think was neighbor to him who fell among the thieves?"

³⁷And he said, "He who showed mercy on him."

Then Jesus said to him, "Go and do likewise."

PSALM 75:1-10

To the Chief Musician. Set to "Do Not Destroy." *
A Psalm of Asaph. A Song.

WE give thanks to You, O God, we give thanks!
For Your wondrous works declare *that* Your name is near.

2 "When I choose the proper time,
I will judge uprightly.
3 The earth and all its inhabitants are dissolved;
I set up its pillars firmly. Selah

4 "I said to the boastful, 'Do not deal boastfully,'
And to the wicked, 'Do not lift up the horn.
5 Do not lift up your horn on high;
Do *not* speak with a stiff neck.' "

6 For exaltation *comes* neither from the east
Nor from the west nor from the south.
7 But God *is* the Judge:
He puts down one,
And exalts another.
8 For in the hand of the LORD *there is* a cup,
And the wine is red;
It is fully mixed, and He pours it out;
Surely its dregs shall all the wicked of the earth
Drain *and* drink down.

9 But I will declare forever,
I will sing praises to the God of Jacob.

10 "All the horns of the wicked I will also cut off,
But the horns of the righteous shall be exalted."

PROVERBS FOR TODAY/ 12:12-14

The wicked covet the catch of evil men, but the root of the righteous yields fruit. The wicked is ensnared by the transgression of his lips, but the righteous will come through trouble. A man will be satisfied with good by the fruit of his mouth, and the recompense of a man's hands will be rendered to him.

APRIL 4

DEUTERONOMY 26:1–27:26

"**A**ND it shall be, when you [the Israelites] come into the land which the LORD your God is giving you *as* an inheritance, and you possess it and dwell in it, ²that you shall take some of the first of all the produce of the ground, which you shall bring from your land that the LORD your God is giving you, and put *it* in a basket and go to the place where the LORD your God chooses to make His name abide. ³And you shall go to the one who is priest in those days, and say to him, 'I declare today to the LORD your* God that I have come to the country which the LORD swore to our fathers to give us.'

⁴"Then the priest shall take the basket out of your hand and set it down before the altar of the LORD your God. ⁵And you shall answer and say before the LORD your God: 'My father *was* a Syrian,* about to perish, and he went down to Egypt and dwelt there, few in number; and there he became a nation, great, mighty, and populous. ⁶But the Egyptians mistreated us, afflicted us, and laid hard bondage on us. ⁷Then we cried out to the LORD God of our fathers, and the LORD heard our voice and looked on our affliction and our labor and our oppression. ⁸So the LORD brought us out of Egypt with a mighty hand and with an outstretched arm, with great terror and with signs and

wonders. ⁹He has brought us to this place and has given us this land, "a land flowing with milk and honey";* ¹⁰and now, behold, I have brought the firstfruits of the land which you, O LORD, have given me.'

"Then you shall set it before the LORD your God, and worship before the LORD your God. ¹¹So you shall rejoice in every good *thing* which the LORD your God has given to you and your house, you and the Levite and the stranger who *is* among you.

¹²"When you have finished laying aside all the tithe of your increase in the third year—the year of tithing—and have given *it* to the Levite, the stranger, the fatherless, and the widow, so that they may eat within your gates and be filled, ¹³then you shall say before the LORD your God: 'I have removed the holy *tithe* from *my* house, and also have given them to the Levite, the stranger, the fatherless, and the widow, according to all Your commandments which You have commanded me; I have not transgressed Your commandments, nor have I forgotten *them.* ¹⁴I have not eaten any of it when in mourning, nor have I removed *any* of it for an unclean *use,* nor given *any* of it for the dead. I have obeyed the voice of the LORD my God, and have done according to all that You have commanded me. ¹⁵Look down from Your holy habitation, from heaven, and bless Your people Israel

and the land which You have given us, just as You swore to our fathers, "a land flowing with milk and honey." '*

16"This day the LORD your God commands you to observe these statutes and judgments; therefore you shall be careful to observe them with all your heart and with all your soul. 17Today you have proclaimed the LORD to be your God, and that you will walk in His ways and keep His statutes, His commandments, and His judgments, and that you will obey His voice. 18Also today the LORD has proclaimed you to be His special people, just as He promised you, that *you* should keep all His commandments, 19and that He will set you high above all nations which He has made, in praise, in name, and in honor, and that you may be a holy people to the LORD your God, just as He has spoken."

Now Moses, with the elders of Israel, commanded the people, saying: "Keep all the commandments which I command you today. 2And it shall be, on the day when you cross over the Jordan to the land which the LORD your God is giving you, that you shall set up for yourselves large stones, and whitewash them with lime. 3You shall write on them all the words of this law, when you have crossed over, that you may enter the land which the LORD your God is giving you, 'a land flowing with milk and honey,'* just as the LORD God of your fathers promised you. 4Therefore it shall be, when you have crossed over the Jordan, *that* on Mount Ebal you shall set up these stones, which I command you today, and you shall whitewash them with lime. 5And there you shall build an altar to the LORD your God, an altar of stones; you shall not use an iron *tool* on them. 6You shall build with whole stones the altar of the LORD your God, and offer burnt offerings on it to the LORD your God. 7You shall offer peace offerings, and shall eat

there, and rejoice before the LORD your God. 8And you shall write very plainly on the stones all the words of this law."

9Then Moses and the priests, the Levites, spoke to all Israel, saying, "Take heed and listen, O Israel: This day you have become the people of the LORD your God. 10Therefore you shall obey the voice of the LORD your God, and observe His commandments and His statutes which I command you today."

11And Moses commanded the people on the same day, saying, 12"These shall stand on Mount Gerizim to bless the people, when you have crossed over the Jordan: Simeon, Levi, Judah, Issachar, Joseph, and Benjamin; 13and these shall stand on Mount Ebal to curse: Reuben, Gad, Asher, Zebulun, Dan, and Naphtali.

14"And the Levites shall speak with a loud voice and say to all the men of Israel: 15'Cursed *is* the one who makes a carved or molded image, an abomination to the LORD, the work of the hands of the craftsman, and sets *it* up in secret.'

"And all the people shall answer and say, 'Amen!'

16'Cursed *is* the one who treats his father or his mother with contempt.'

"And all the people shall say, 'Amen!'

17'Cursed *is* the one who moves his neighbor's landmark.'

"And all the people shall say, 'Amen!'

18'Cursed *is* the one who makes the blind to wander off the road.'

"And all the people shall say, 'Amen!'

19'Cursed *is* the one who perverts the justice due the stranger, the fatherless, and widow.'

"And all the people shall say, 'Amen!'

20'Cursed *is* the one who lies with his father's wife, because he has uncovered his father's bed.'

"And all the people shall say, 'Amen!'

21'Cursed *is* the one who lies with any kind of animal.'

"And all the people shall say, 'Amen!'

22'Cursed *is* the one who lies with his sister, the daughter of his father or the daughter of his mother.'

"And all the people shall say, 'Amen!'

23'Cursed *is* the one who lies with his mother-in-law.'

"And all the people shall say, 'Amen!'

24'Cursed *is* the one who attacks his neighbor secretly.'

"And all the people shall say, 'Amen!'

25'Cursed *is* the one who takes a bribe to slay an innocent person.'

"And all the people shall say, 'Amen!'

26'Cursed *is* the one who does not confirm *all* the words of this law.'

"And all the people shall say, 'Amen!' "

LUKE 10:38–11:13

Now it happened as they [Jesus and his disciples] went that He [Jesus] entered a certain village; and a certain woman named Martha welcomed Him into her house. 39And she had a sister called Mary, who also sat at Jesus'* feet and heard His word. 40But Martha was distracted with much serving, and she approached Him and said, "Lord, do You not care that my sister has left me to serve alone? Therefore tell her to help me."

41And Jesus* answered and said to her, "Martha, Martha, you are worried and troubled about many things. 42But one thing is needed, and Mary has chosen that good part, which will not be taken away from her."

Now it came to pass, as He was praying in a certain place, when He ceased, *that* one of His disciples said to Him, "Lord, teach us to pray, as John also taught his disciples."

2So He said to them, "When you pray, say:

Our Father in heaven,*
Hallowed be Your name.
Your kingdom come.*
Your will be done

On earth as *it is* in heaven.
3   Give us day by day our daily
    bread.
4   And forgive us our sins,
    For we also forgive everyone
        who is indebted to us.
    And do not lead us into
        temptation,
    But deliver us from the evil
        one." *

5And He said to them, "Which of you shall have a friend, and go to him at midnight and say to him, 'Friend, lend me three loaves; 6for a friend of mine has come to me on his journey, and I have nothing to set before him'; 7and he will answer from within and say, 'Do not trouble me; the door is now shut, and my children are with me in bed; I cannot rise and give to you'? 8I say to you, though he will not rise and give to him because he is his friend, yet because of his persistence he will rise and give him as many as he needs.

9"So I say to you, ask, and it will be given to you; seek, and you will find; knock, and it will be opened to you. 10For everyone who asks receives, and he who seeks finds, and to him who knocks it will be opened. 11If a son asks for bread* from any father among you, will he give him a stone? Or if *he asks* for a fish, will he give him a serpent instead of a fish? 12Or if he asks for an egg, will he offer him a scorpion? 13If you then, being evil, know how to give good gifts to your children, how much more will *your* heavenly Father give the Holy Spirit to those who ask Him!"

PSALM 76:1-12

To the Chief Musician. On stringed instruments. A Psalm of Asaph. A Song.*

In Judah God *is* known;
His name *is* great in Israel.
2In Salem* also is His tabernacle,
    And His dwelling place in
        Zion.

3 There He broke the arrows of
   the bow,
   The shield and sword of battle.
                              Selah

4 You *are* more glorious and
   excellent
   Than the mountains of prey.
5 The stouthearted were
   plundered;
   They have sunk into their
   sleep;
   And none of the mighty men
   have found the use of their
   hands.
6 At Your rebuke, O God of
   Jacob,
   Both the chariot and horse
   were cast into a dead sleep.

7 You, Yourself, *are* to be feared;
   And who may stand in Your
   presence

When once You are angry?
8 You caused judgment to be
   heard from heaven;
   The earth feared and was still,
9 When God arose to judgment,
   To deliver all the oppressed of
   the earth.   Selah

10 Surely the wrath of man shall
   praise You;
   With the remainder of wrath
   You shall gird Yourself.

11 Make vows to the LORD your
   God, and pay *them;*
   Let all who are around Him
   bring presents to Him who
   ought to be feared.
12 He shall cut off the spirit of
   princes;
   He is awesome to the kings of
   the earth.

PROVERBS FOR TODAY / 12:15-17

The way of a fool is *right in his own eyes, but he who heeds counsel* is *wise. A fool's wrath is known at once, but a prudent* man *covers shame. He* who *speaks truth declares righteousness, but a false witness, deceit.*

APRIL 5

DEUTERONOMY 28:1-68

"**N**ow it shall come to pass, if you diligently obey the voice of the LORD your God, to observe carefully all His commandments which I command you today, that the LORD your God will set you high above all nations of the earth. ²And all these blessings shall come upon you and overtake you, because you obey the voice of the LORD your God:

³"Blessed *shall* you *be* in the city, and blessed *shall* you *be* in the country.

⁴"Blessed *shall be* the fruit of your body, the produce of your ground and the increase of your herds, the increase of your cattle and the offspring of your flocks.

⁵"Blessed *shall be* your basket and your kneading bowl.

⁶"Blessed *shall* you *be* when you come in, and blessed *shall* you *be* when you go out.

⁷"The LORD will cause your enemies who rise against you to be defeated before your face; they shall come out

against you one way and flee before you seven ways.

8"The LORD will command the blessing on you in your storehouses and in all to which you set your hand, and He will bless you in the land which the LORD your God is giving you.

9"The LORD will establish you as a holy people to Himself, just as He has sworn to you, if you keep the commandments of the LORD your God and walk in His ways. 10Then all peoples of the earth shall see that you are called by the name of the LORD, and they shall be afraid of you. 11And the LORD will grant you plenty of goods, in the fruit of your body, in the increase of your livestock, and in the produce of your ground, in the land of which the LORD swore to your fathers to give you. 12The LORD will open to you His good treasure, the heavens, to give the rain to your land in its season, and to bless all the work of your hand. You shall lend to many nations, but you shall not borrow. 13And the LORD will make you the head and not the tail; you shall be above only, and not be beneath, if you heed the commandments of the LORD your God, which I command you today, and are careful to observe *them.* 14So you shall not turn aside from any of the words which I command you this day, *to* the right or the left, to go after other gods to serve them.

15"But it shall come to pass, if you do not obey the voice of the LORD your God, to observe carefully all His commandments and His statutes which I command you today, that all these curses will come upon you and overtake you:

16"Cursed *shall* you *be* in the city, and cursed *shall* you *be* in the country.

17"Cursed *shall be* your basket and your kneading bowl.

18"Cursed *shall be* the fruit of your body and the produce of your land, the increase of your cattle and the offspring of your flocks.

19"Cursed *shall* you *be* when you come in, and cursed *shall* you *be* when you go out.

20"The LORD will send on you cursing, confusion, and rebuke in all that you set your hand to do, until you are destroyed and until you perish quickly, because of the wickedness of your doings in which you have forsaken Me. 21The LORD will make the plague cling to you until He has consumed you from the land which you are going to possess. 22The LORD will strike you with consumption, with fever, with inflammation, with severe burning fever, with the sword, with scorching, and with mildew; they shall pursue you until you perish. 23And your heavens which *are* over your head shall be bronze, and the earth which is under you *shall be* iron. 24The LORD will change the rain of your land to powder and dust; from the heaven it shall come down on you until you are destroyed.

25"The LORD will cause you to be defeated before your enemies; you shall go out one way against them and flee seven ways before them; and you shall become troublesome to all the kingdoms of the earth. 26Your carcasses shall be food for all the birds of the air and the beasts of the earth, and no one shall frighten *them* away. 27The LORD will strike you with the boils of Egypt, with tumors, with the scab, and with the itch, from which you cannot be healed. 28The LORD will strike you with madness and blindness and confusion of heart. 29And you shall grope at noonday, as a blind man gropes in darkness; you shall not prosper in your ways; you shall be only oppressed and plundered continually, and no one shall save *you.*

30"You shall betroth a wife, but another man shall lie with her; you shall build a house, but you shall not dwell in it; you shall plant a vineyard, but shall not gather its grapes. 31Your ox *shall be* slaughtered before your eyes, but you shall not eat of it; your donkey *shall be* violently taken away from before you, and shall not be restored to you; your sheep *shall be* given to your enemies, and you shall have no one to rescue *them*. ³²Your sons and your daughters *shall be* given to another people, and your eyes shall look and fail *with longing* for them all day long; and *there shall be* no strength in your hand. ³³A nation whom you have not known shall eat the fruit of your land and the produce of your labor, and you shall be only oppressed and crushed continually. ³⁴So you shall be driven mad because of the sight which your eyes see. ³⁵The LORD will strike you in the knees and on the legs with severe boils which cannot be healed, and from the sole of your foot to the top of your head.

³⁶"The LORD will bring you and the king whom you set over you to a nation which neither you nor your fathers have known, and there you shall serve other gods—wood and stone. ³⁷And you shall become an astonishment, a proverb, and a byword among all nations where the LORD will drive you.

³⁸"You shall carry much seed out to the field but gather little in, for the locust shall consume it. ³⁹You shall plant vineyards and tend *them,* but you shall neither drink *of* the wine nor gather the *grapes;* for the worms shall eat them. ⁴⁰You shall have olive trees throughout all your territory, but you shall not anoint *yourself* with the oil; for your olives shall drop off. ⁴¹You shall beget sons and daughters, but they shall not be yours; for they shall go into captivity. ⁴²Locusts shall consume all your trees and the produce of your land.

⁴³"The alien who *is* among you shall rise higher and higher above you, and you shall come down lower and lower. ⁴⁴He shall lend to you, but you shall not lend to him; he shall be the head, and you shall be the tail.

⁴⁵"Moreover all these curses shall come upon you and pursue and overtake you, until you are destroyed, because you did not obey the voice of the LORD your God, to keep His commandments and His statutes which He commanded you. ⁴⁶And they shall be upon you for a sign and a wonder, and on your descendants forever.

⁴⁷"Because you did not serve the LORD your God with joy and gladness of heart, for the abundance of everything, ⁴⁸therefore you shall serve your enemies, whom the LORD will send against you, in hunger, in thirst, in nakedness, and in need of everything; and He will put a yoke of iron on your neck until He has destroyed you. ⁴⁹The LORD will bring a nation against you from afar, from the end of the earth, *as swift* as the eagle flies, a nation whose language you will not understand, ⁵⁰a nation of fierce countenance, which does not respect the elderly nor show favor to the young. ⁵¹And they shall eat the increase of your livestock and the produce of your land, until you are destroyed; they shall not leave you grain or new wine or oil, *or* the increase of your cattle or the offspring of your flocks, until they have destroyed you.

⁵²"They shall besiege you at all your gates until your high and fortified walls, in which you trust, come down throughout all your land; and they shall besiege you at all your gates throughout all your land which the LORD your God has given you. ⁵³You shall eat the fruit of your own body, the flesh of your sons and your daughters whom the LORD your God has given you, in the siege and desperate straits in which your enemy shall distress you. ⁵⁴The sensitive and very refined man among you will be hostile toward his brother, toward the wife of his bosom, and toward the rest of his children whom he leaves behind, ⁵⁵so that he will not give any of them the flesh of his children whom he will eat, because

he has nothing left in the siege and desperate straits in which your enemy shall distress you at all your gates. 56The tender and delicate woman among you, who would not venture to set the sole of her foot on the ground because of her delicateness and sensitivity, will refuse* to the husband of her bosom, and to her son and her daughter, 57her placenta which comes out from between her feet and her children whom she bears; for she will eat them secretly for lack of everything in the siege and desperate straits in which your enemy shall distress you at all your gates.

58"If you do not carefully observe all the words of this law that are written in this book, that you may fear this glorious and awesome name, THE LORD YOUR GOD, 59then the LORD will bring upon you and your descendants extraordinary plagues—great and prolonged plagues—and serious and prolonged sicknesses. 60Moreover He will bring back on you all the diseases of Egypt, of which you were afraid, and they shall cling to you. 61Also every sickness and every plague, which is not written in this Book of the Law, will the LORD bring upon you until you are destroyed. 62You shall be left few in number, whereas you were as the stars of heaven in multitude, because you would not obey the voice of the LORD your God. 63And it shall be, that just as the LORD rejoiced over you to do you good and multiply you, so the LORD will rejoice over you to destroy you and bring you to nothing; and you shall be plucked from off the land which you go to possess.

64"Then the LORD will scatter you among all peoples, from one end of the earth to the other, and there you shall serve other gods, which neither you nor your fathers have known—wood and stone. 65And among those nations you shall find no rest, nor shall the sole of your foot have a resting place; but there the LORD will give you a trembling heart, failing eyes, and anguish of soul. 66Your life shall hang in doubt before you; you shall fear day and night, and have no assurance of life. 67In the morning you shall say, 'Oh, that it were evening!' And at evening you shall say, 'Oh, that it were morning!' because of the fear which terrifies your heart, and because of the sight which your eyes see.

68"And the LORD will take you back to Egypt in ships, by the way of which I said to you, 'You shall never see it again.' And there you shall be offered for sale to your enemies as male and female slaves, but no one will buy you."

LUKE 11:14-36

And He [Jesus] was casting out a demon, and it was mute. So it was, when the demon had gone out, that the mute spoke; and the multitudes marveled. 15But some of them said, "He casts out demons by Beelzebub,* the ruler of the demons."

16Others, testing Him, sought from Him a sign from heaven. 17But He, knowing their thoughts, said to them: "Every kingdom divided against itself is brought to desolation, and a house divided against a house falls. 18If Satan also is divided against himself, how will his kingdom stand? Because you say I cast out demons by Beelzebub. 19And if I cast out demons by Beelzebub, by whom do your sons cast them out? Therefore they will be your judges. 20But if I cast out demons with the finger of God, surely the kingdom of God has come upon you. 21When a strong man, fully armed, guards his own palace, his goods are in peace. 22But when a stronger than he comes upon him and overcomes him, he takes from him all his armor in which he trusted, and divides his spoils. 23He who is not with Me is against Me, and he who does not gather with Me scatters.

24"When an unclean spirit goes out of a man, he goes through dry places, seeking rest; and finding none, he says, 'I will return to my house from which I came.' 25And when he comes, he finds *it* swept and put in order. 26Then he goes and takes with *him* seven other spirits more wicked than himself, and they enter and dwell there; and the last *state* of that man is worse than the first."

27And it happened, as He spoke these things, that a certain woman from the crowd raised her voice and said to Him, "Blessed *is* the womb that bore You, and *the* breasts which nursed You!"

28But He said, "More than that, blessed *are* those who hear the word of God and keep it!"

29And while the crowds were thickly gathered together, He began to say, "This is an evil generation. It seeks a sign, and no sign will be given to it except the sign of Jonah the prophet.* 30For as Jonah became a sign to the Ninevites, so also the Son of Man will be to this generation. 31The queen of the South will rise up in the judgment with the men of this generation and condemn them, for she came from the ends of the earth to hear the wisdom of Solomon; and indeed a greater than Solomon *is* here. 32The men of Nineveh will rise up in the judgment with this generation and condemn it, for they repented at the preaching of Jonah; and indeed a greater than Jonah *is* here.

33"No one, when he has lit a lamp, puts *it* in a secret place or under a basket, but on a lampstand, that those who come in may see the light. 34The lamp of the body is the eye. Therefore, when your eye is good, your whole body also is full of light. But when *your eye* is bad, your body also *is* full of darkness. 35Therefore take heed that the light which is in you is not darkness. 36If then your whole body *is* full of light, having no part dark, *the* whole *body* will be full of light, as when the bright shining of a lamp gives you light."

PSALM 77:1-20

To the Chief Musician. To Jeduthun. A Psalm of Asaph.

I CRIED out to God with my voice—
To God with my voice;
And He gave ear to me.
2   In the day of my trouble I
        sought the Lord;
    My hand was stretched out in
        the night without ceasing;
    My soul refused to be
        comforted.
3   I remembered God, and was
        troubled;
    I complained, and my spirit
        was overwhelmed.   Selah

4   You hold my eyelids *open;*
    I am so troubled that I cannot
        speak.
5   I have considered the days of
        old,
    The years of ancient times.
6   I call to remembrance my
        song in the night;
    I meditate within my heart,
    And my spirit makes diligent
        search.

7   Will the Lord cast off forever?
    And will He be favorable no
        more?
8   Has His mercy ceased
        forever?
    Has *His* promise failed
        forevermore?
9   Has God forgotten to be
        gracious?
    Has He in anger shut up His
        tender mercies?   Selah

10   And I said, "This *is* my
        anguish;

But I will remember the years
of the right hand of the
Most High."
11 I will remember the works of
the LORD;
Surely I will remember Your
wonders of old.
12 I will also meditate on all Your
work,
And talk of Your deeds.
13 Your way, O God, *is* in the
sanctuary;
Who *is* so great a God as *our*
God?
14 You *are* the God who does
wonders;
You have declared Your
strength among the
peoples.
15 You have with *Your* arm
redeemed Your people,
The sons of Jacob and Joseph.
Selah

16 The waters saw You, O God;
The waters saw You, they
were afraid;
The depths also trembled.
17 The clouds poured out water;
The skies sent out a sound;
Your arrows also flashed
about.
18 The voice of Your thunder
was in the whirlwind;
The lightnings lit up the world;
The earth trembled and
shook.
19 Your way *was* in the sea,
Your path in the great waters,
And Your footsteps were not
known.
20 You led Your people like a
flock
By the hand of Moses and
Aaron.

PROVERBS FOR TODAY/ 12:18

There is one who speaks like the piercings of a sword, but the tongue of the wise
promotes *health.*

APRIL 6

DEUTERONOMY 29:1–30:20

THESE *are* the words of the covenant which the LORD commanded Moses to make with the children of Israel in the land of Moab, besides the covenant which He made with them in Horeb.

2Now Moses called all Israel and said to them: "You have seen all that the LORD did before your eyes in the land of Egypt, to Pharaoh and to all his servants and to all his land— 3the great trials which your eyes have seen,

the signs, and those great wonders. 4Yet the LORD has not given you a heart to perceive and eyes to see and ears to hear, to this *very* day. 5And I have led you forty years in the wilderness. Your clothes have not worn out on you, and your sandals have not worn out on your feet. 6You have not eaten bread, nor have you drunk wine or *similar* drink, that you may know that I *am* the LORD your God. 7And when you came to this place, Sihon king of Heshbon and Og king of Bashan came out against us to battle, and we conquered them. 8We took their land and gave it as an inheritance to the Reubenites, to the Gadites, and to half the tribe of Manasseh. 9Therefore keep the words of this covenant, and do them, that you may prosper in all that you do.

10"All of you stand today before the LORD your God: your leaders and your tribes and your elders and your officers, all the men of Israel, 11your little ones and your wives—also the stranger who *is* in your camp, from the one who cuts your wood to the one who draws your water— 12that you may enter into covenant with the LORD your God, and into His oath, which the LORD your God makes with you today, 13that He may establish you today as a people for Himself, and *that* He may be God to you, just as He has spoken to you, and just as He has sworn to your fathers, to Abraham, Isaac, and Jacob.

14"I make this covenant and this oath, not with you alone, 15but with *him* who stands here with us today before the LORD our God, as well as with *him* who *is* not here with us today 16(for you know that we dwelt in the land of Egypt and that we came through the nations which you passed by, 17and you saw their abominations and their idols which *were* among them—wood and stone and silver and gold); 18so that there may not be among you man or woman or family or tribe, whose heart turns away today from the LORD our God, to go *and* serve the gods of these nations, and that there may not be among you a root bearing bitterness or wormwood; 19and so it may not happen, when he hears the words of this curse, that he blesses himself in his heart, saying, 'I shall have peace, even though I follow the dictates* of my heart'—as though the drunkard could be included with the sober.

20"The LORD would not spare him; for then the anger of the LORD and His jealousy would burn against that man, and every curse that is written in this book would settle on him, and the LORD would blot out his name from under heaven. 21And the LORD would separate him from all the tribes of Israel for adversity, according to all the curses of the covenant that are written in this Book of the Law, 22so that the coming generation of your children who rise up after you, and the foreigner who comes from a far land, would say, when they see the plagues of that land and the sicknesses which the LORD has laid on it:

23'The whole land *is* brimstone, salt, and burning; it is not sown, nor does it bear, nor does any grass grow there, like the overthrow of Sodom and Gomorrah, Admah, and Zeboiim, which the LORD overthrew in His anger and His wrath.' 24All nations would say, 'Why has the LORD done so to this land? What does the heat of this great anger mean?' 25Then *people* would say: 'Because they have forsaken the covenant of the LORD God of their fathers, which He made with them when He brought them out of the land of Egypt; 26for they went and served other gods and worshiped them, gods that they did not know and that He had not given to them. 27Then the anger of the LORD was aroused against this land, to bring on it every curse that is written in this book. 28And the LORD uprooted them from their land in anger, in wrath, and in great indignation, and cast them into another land, as *it is* this day.'

29"The secret *things belong* to the LORD our God, but those *things which are* revealed *belong* to us and to our children forever, that *we* may do all the words of this law.

"Now it shall come to pass, when all these things come upon you, the blessing and the curse which I have set before you, and you call *them* to mind among all the nations where the LORD your God drives you, 2and you return to the LORD your God and obey His voice, according to all that I command you today, you and your children, with all your heart and with all your soul, ³that the LORD your God will bring you back from captivity, and have compassion on you, and gather you again from all the nations where the LORD your God has scattered you. ⁴If *any* of you are driven out to the farthest *parts* under heaven, from there the LORD your God will gather you, and from there He will bring you. ⁵Then the LORD your God will bring you to the land which your fathers possessed, and you shall possess it. He will prosper you and multiply you more than your fathers. ⁶And the LORD your God will circumcise your heart and the heart of your descendants, to love the LORD your God with all your heart and with all your soul, that you may live.

⁷"Also the LORD your God will put all these curses on your enemies and on those who hate you, who persecuted you. ⁸And you will again obey the voice of the LORD and do all His commandments which I command you today. ⁹The LORD your God will make you abound in all the work of your hand, in the fruit of your body, in the increase of your livestock, and in the produce of your land for good. For the LORD will again rejoice over you for good as He rejoiced over your fathers, ¹⁰if you obey the voice of the LORD your God, to keep His commandments and His statutes which are written in this Book of the Law, *and* if you turn to the LORD your God with all your heart and with all your soul.

¹¹"For this commandment which I command you today *is* not *too* mysterious for you, nor *is* it far off. ¹²It *is* not in heaven, that you should say, 'Who will ascend into heaven for us and bring it to us, that we may hear it and do it?' ¹³Nor *is* it beyond the sea, that you should say, 'Who will go over the sea for us and bring it to us, that we may hear it and do it?' ¹⁴But the word *is* very near you, in your mouth and in your heart, that you may do it.

¹⁵"See, I have set before you today life and good, death and evil, ¹⁶in that I command you today to love the LORD your God, to walk in His ways, and to keep His commandments, His statutes, and His judgments, that you may live and multiply; and the LORD your God will bless you in the land which you go to possess. ¹⁷But if your heart turns away so that you do not hear, and are drawn away, and worship other gods and serve them, ¹⁸I announce to you today that you shall surely perish; you shall not prolong *your* days in the land which you cross over the Jordan to go in and possess. ¹⁹I call heaven and earth as witnesses today against you, *that* I have set before you life and death, blessing and cursing; therefore choose life, that both you and your descendants may live; ²⁰that you may love the LORD your God, that you may obey His voice, and that you may cling to Him, for He *is* your life and the length of your days; and that you may dwell in the land which the LORD swore to your fathers, to Abraham, Isaac, and Jacob, to give them."

LUKE 11:37–12:7

AND as He [Jesus] spoke, a certain Pharisee asked Him to dine with him. So He went in and sat down to eat. ³⁸When the Pharisee saw *it,* he marveled that He had not first washed before dinner.

³⁹Then the Lord said to him, "you Pharisees make the outside of the cup and dish clean, but your inward part is full of greed and wickedness. ⁴⁰Foolish ones! Did not He who made the outside make the inside also? ⁴¹But rather give alms of such things as you have; then indeed all things are clean to you.

⁴²"But woe to you Pharisees! For you tithe mint and rue and all manner of herbs, and pass by justice and the

love of God. These you ought to have done, without leaving the others undone. ⁴³Woe to you Pharisees! For you love the best seats in the synagogues and greetings in the marketplaces. ⁴⁴Woe to you, scribes and Pharisees, hypocrites!* For you are like graves which are not seen, and the men who walk over *them* are not aware *of them.*"

⁴⁵Then one of the lawyers answered and said to Him, "Teacher, by saying these things You reproach us also."

⁴⁶And He said, "Woe to you also, lawyers! For you load men with burdens hard to bear, and you yourselves do not touch the burdens with one of your fingers. ⁴⁷Woe to you! For you build the tombs of the prophets, and your fathers killed them. ⁴⁸In fact, you bear witness that you approve the deeds of your fathers; for they indeed killed them, and you build their tombs. ⁴⁹Therefore the wisdom of God also said, 'I will send them prophets and apostles, and *some* of them they will kill and persecute,' ⁵⁰that the blood of all the prophets which was shed from the foundation of the world may be required of this generation, ⁵¹from the blood of Abel to the blood of Zechariah who perished between the altar and the temple. Yes, I say to you, it shall be required of this generation.

⁵²"Woe to you lawyers! For you have taken away the key of knowledge. You did not enter in yourselves, and those who were entering in you hindered."

⁵³And as He said these things to them,* the scribes and the Pharisees began to assail *Him* vehemently, and to cross-examine Him about many things, ⁵⁴lying in wait for Him, and seeking to catch Him in something He might say, that they might accuse Him.*

IN the meantime, when an innumerable multitude of people had gathered together, so that they trampled one another, He began to say to His disciples first *of all,* "Beware of the leaven of the Pharisees, which is hypocrisy. ²For there is nothing covered that will not be revealed, nor hidden that will not be known. ³Therefore whatever you have spoken in the dark will be heard in the light, and what you have spoken in the ear in inner rooms will be proclaimed on the housetops.

⁴"And I say to you, My friends, do not be afraid of those who kill the body, and after that have no more that they can do. ⁵But I will show you whom you should fear: Fear Him who, after He has killed, has power to cast into hell; yes, I say to you, fear Him! ⁶"Are not five sparrows sold for two copper coins?* And not one of them is forgotten before God. ⁷But the very hairs of your head are all numbered. Do not fear therefore; you are of more value than many sparrows."

PSALM 78:1-31
A Contemplation of Asaph.*

G IVE ear, O my people, *to* my law;
   Incline your ears to the words of my mouth.
2   I will open my mouth in a parable;
   I will utter dark sayings of old,
3   Which we have heard and known,
   And our fathers have told us.
4   We will not hide *them* from their children,
   Telling to the generation to come the praises of the LORD,
   And His strength and His wonderful works that He has done.

5   For He established a testimony in Jacob,
   And appointed a law in Israel,
   Which He commanded our fathers,

That they should make them
known to their children;

6 That the generation to come
might know *them,*
The children *who* would be
born,
That they may arise and
declare *them* to their
children,

7 That they may set their hope
in God,
And not forget the works of
God,
But keep His commandments;

8 And may not be like their
fathers,
A stubborn and rebellious
generation,
A generation *that* did not set
its heart aright,
And whose spirit was not
faithful to God.

9 The children of Ephraim,
being armed *and* carrying
bows,
Turned back in the day of
battle.

10 They did not keep the
covenant of God;
They refused to walk in His
law,

11 And forgot His works
And His wonders that He had
shown them.

12 Marvelous things He did in
the sight of their fathers,
In the land of Egypt, *in* the
field of Zoan.

13 He divided the sea and
caused them to pass
through;
And He made the waters
stand up like a heap.

14 In the daytime also He led
them with the cloud,
And all the night with a light
of fire.

15 He split the rocks in the
wilderness,
And gave *them* drink in
abundance like the depths.

16 He also brought streams out
of the rock,
And caused waters to run
down like rivers.

17 But they sinned even more
against Him
By rebelling against the Most
High in the wilderness.

18 And they tested God in their
heart
By asking for the food of their
fancy.

19 Yes, they spoke against God:
They said, "Can God prepare
a table in the wilderness?

20 Behold, He struck the rock,
So that the waters gushed out,
And the streams overflowed.
Can He give bread also?
Can He provide meat for His
people? "

21 Therefore the LORD heard *this*
and was furious;
So a fire was kindled against
Jacob,
And anger also came up
against Israel,

22 Because they did not believe
in God,
And did not trust in His
salvation.

23 Yet He had commanded the
clouds above,
And opened the doors of
heaven,

24 Had rained down manna on
them to eat,
And given them of the bread
of heaven.

25 Men ate angels' food;
He sent them food to the full.

26 He caused an east wind to
blow in the heavens;

And by His power He brought
in the south wind.
27 He also rained meat on them
like the dust,
Feathered fowl like the sand
of the seas;
28 And He let *them* fall in the
midst of their camp,
All around their dwellings.
29 So they ate and were well
filled,

For He gave them their own
desire.
30 They were not deprived of
their craving;
But while their food *was* still
in their mouths,
31 The wrath of God came
against them,
And slew the stoutest of them,
And struck down the choice
men of Israel.

PROVERBS FOR TODAY/ 12:19-20

The truthful lip shall be established forever, but a lying tongue is *but for a moment.
Deceit is in the heart of those who devise evil, but counselors of peace have joy.*

APRIL 7

DEUTERONOMY 31:1–32:27

THEN Moses went and spoke these words to all Israel. ²And he said to them: "I *am* one hundred and twenty years old today. I can no longer go out and come in. Also the LORD has said to me, 'You shall not cross over this Jordan.' ³The LORD your God Himself crosses over before you; He will destroy these nations from before you, and you shall dispossess them. Joshua himself crosses over before you, just as the LORD has said. ⁴And the LORD will do to them as He did to Sihon and Og, the kings of the Amorites and their land, when He destroyed them. ⁵The LORD will give them over to you, that you may do to them according to every commandment which I have commanded you. ⁶Be strong and of good courage, do not fear nor be afraid of them; for the LORD your God, He *is* the One who goes with you. He will not leave you nor forsake you."

⁷Then Moses called Joshua and said to him in the sight of all Israel, "Be strong and of good courage, for you must go with this people to the land which the LORD has sworn to their fathers to give them, and you shall cause them to inherit it. ⁸And the LORD, He *is* the One who goes before you. He will be with you, He will not leave you nor forsake you; do not fear nor be dismayed."

⁹So Moses wrote this law and delivered it to the priests, the sons of Levi, who bore the ark of the covenant of the LORD, and to all the elders of Israel. ¹⁰And Moses commanded them, saying: "At the end of *every* seven years, at the appointed time in the year of release, at the Feast of Tabernacles, ¹¹when all Israel comes to appear before the LORD your God in the place which He chooses, you shall read this law before all Israel in their hearing. ¹²Gather the people together, men and women and little ones, and the stranger who *is* within your gates, that they may hear and that they may learn to fear the LORD your God and carefully

observe all the words of this law, ¹³and *that* their children, who have not known it, may hear and learn to fear the LORD your God as long as you live in the land which you cross the Jordan to possess."

¹⁴Then the LORD said to Moses, "Behold, the days approach when you must die; call Joshua, and present yourselves in the tabernacle of meeting, that I may inaugurate him."

So Moses and Joshua went and presented themselves in the tabernacle of meeting. ¹⁵Now the LORD appeared at the tabernacle in a pillar of cloud, and the pillar of cloud stood above the door of the tabernacle.

¹⁶And the LORD said to Moses: "Behold, you will rest with your fathers; and this people will rise and play the harlot with the gods of the foreigners of the land, where they go *to be* among them, and they will forsake Me and break My covenant which I have made with them. ¹⁷Then My anger shall be aroused against them in that day, and I will forsake them, and I will hide My face from them, and they shall be devoured. And many evils and troubles shall befall them, so that they will say in that day, 'Have not these evils come upon us because our God *is* not among us?' ¹⁸And I will surely hide My face in that day because of all the evil which they have done, in that they have turned to other gods.

¹⁹"Now therefore, write down this song for yourselves, and teach it to the children of Israel; put it in their mouths, that this song may be a witness for Me against the children of Israel. ²⁰When I have brought them to the land flowing with milk and honey, of which I swore to their fathers, and they have eaten and filled themselves and grown fat, then they will turn to other gods and serve them; and they will provoke Me and break My covenant. ²¹Then it shall be, when many evils and troubles have come upon

them, that this song will testify against them as a witness; for it will not be forgotten in the mouths of their descendants, for I know the inclination of their behavior today, even before I have brought them to the land of which I swore *to give them.*"

²²Therefore Moses wrote this song the same day, and taught it to the children of Israel. ²³Then He inaugurated Joshua the son of Nun, and said, "Be strong and of good courage; for you shall bring the children of Israel into the land of which I swore to them, and I will be with you."

²⁴So it was, when Moses had completed writing the words of this law in a book, when they were finished, ²⁵that Moses commanded the Levites, who bore the ark of the covenant of the LORD, saying: ²⁶"Take this Book of the Law, and put it beside the ark of the covenant of the LORD your God, that it may be there as a witness against you; ²⁷for I know your rebellion and your stiff neck. *If* today, while I am yet alive with you, you have been rebellious against the LORD, then how much more after my death? ²⁸Gather to me all the elders of your tribes, and your officers, that I may speak these words in their hearing and call heaven and earth to witness against them. ²⁹For I know that after my death you will become utterly corrupt, and turn aside from the way which I have commanded you. And evil will befall you in the latter days, because you will do evil in the sight of the LORD, to provoke Him to anger through the work of your hands."

³⁰Then Moses spoke in the hearing of all the assembly of Israel the words of this song until they were ended:

"GIVE ear, O heavens, and I will speak;
And hear, O earth, the words
of my mouth.

2   Let my teaching drop as the
    rain,
    My speech distill as the dew,
    As raindrops on the tender
    herb,
    And as showers on the grass.
3   For I proclaim the name of
    the LORD:
    Ascribe greatness to our God.
4   *He is* the Rock, His work *is*
    perfect;
    For all His ways *are* justice,
    A God of truth and without
    injustice;
    Righteous and upright *is* He.

5   "They have corrupted
    themselves;
    They are not His children,
    Because of their blemish:
    A perverse and crooked
    generation.
6   Do you thus deal with the
    LORD,
    O foolish and unwise people?
    Is He not your Father, *who*
    bought you?
    Has He not made you and
    established you?

7   "Remember the days of old,
    Consider the years of many
    generations.
    Ask your father, and he will
    show you;
    Your elders, and they will tell
    you:
8   When the Most High divided
    their inheritance to the
    nations,
    When He separated the sons
    of Adam,
    He set the boundaries of the
    peoples
    According to the number of
    the children of Israel.
9   For the LORD's portion *is* His
    people;
    Jacob *is* the place of His
    inheritance.

10 "He found him in a desert land
    And in the wasteland, a
    howling wilderness;
    He encircled him, He
    instructed him,
    He kept him as the apple of
    His eye.
11 As an eagle stirs up its nest,
    Hovers over its young,
    Spreading out its wings,
    taking them up,
    Carrying them on its wings,
12 *So* the LORD alone led him,
    And *there was* no foreign god
    with him.

13 "He made him ride in the
    heights of the earth,
    That he might eat the
    produce of the fields;
    He made him draw honey
    from the rock,
    And oil from the flinty rock;
14 Curds from the cattle, and
    milk of the flock,
    With fat of lambs;
    And rams of the breed of
    Bashan, and goats,
    With the choicest wheat;
    And you drank wine, the
    blood of the grapes.

15 "But Jeshurun grew fat and
    kicked;
    You grew fat, you grew thick,
    You are obese!
    Then he forsook God *who*
    made him,
    And scornfully esteemed the
    Rock of his salvation.
16 They provoked Him to
    jealousy with foreign *gods;*
    With abominations they
    provoked Him to anger.
17 They sacrificed to demons,
    not to God,
    To gods they did not know,
    To new *gods,* new arrivals
    That your fathers did not fear.

18 Of the Rock *who* begot you,
you are unmindful,
And have forgotten the God
who fathered you.

19 "And when the Lord saw *it,* He
spurned *them,*
Because of the provocation of
His sons and His daughters.

20 And He said: 'I will hide My
face from them,
I will see what their end *will
be,*
For they *are* a perverse
generation,
Children in whom *is* no faith.

21 They have provoked Me to
jealousy by *what* is not God;
They have moved Me to
anger by their foolish idols.
But I will provoke them to
jealousy by *those who are*
not a nation;
I will move them to anger by a
foolish nation.

22 For a fire is kindled in My
anger,
And shall burn to the lowest
hell;
It shall consume the earth
with her increase,
And set on fire the
foundations of the
mountains.

23 'I will heap disasters on them;
I will spend My arrows on
them.

24 *They shall be* wasted with
hunger,
Devoured by pestilence and
bitter destruction;
I will also send against them
the teeth of beasts,
With the poison of serpents of
the dust.

25 The sword shall destroy
outside;
There shall be terror within
For the young man and virgin,

The nursing child with the
man of gray hairs.

26 I would have said, "I will dash
them in pieces,
I will make the memory of
them to cease from among
men,"

27 Had I not feared the wrath of
the enemy,
Lest their adversaries should
misunderstand,
Lest they should say, "Our
hand *is* high;
And it is not the Lord who has
done all this." '"

LUKE 12:8-34

"Also I [Jesus] say to you, whoever confesses Me before men, him the Son of Man also will confess before the angels of God. 9But he who denies Me before men will be denied before the angels of God.

10"And anyone who speaks a word against the Son of Man, it will be forgiven him; but to him who blasphemes against the Holy Spirit, it will not be forgiven.

11"Now when they bring you to the synagogues and magistrates and authorities, do not worry about how or what you should answer, or what you should say. 12For the Holy Spirit will teach you in that very hour what you ought to say."

13Then one from the crowd said to Him, "Teacher, tell my brother to divide the inheritance with me."

14But He said to him, "Man, who made Me a judge or an arbitrator over you?" 15And He said to them, "Take heed and beware of covetousness,* for one's life does not consist in the abundance of the things he possesses."

16Then He spoke a parable to them, saying: "The ground of a certain rich man yielded plentifully. 17And he thought within himself, saying, 'What shall I do, since I have no room to store my crops?' ¹⁸So he said, 'I will do this: I will pull down my barns and build greater, and there I will store all my crops and my goods. ¹⁹And I will say to my soul, "Soul, you have many goods laid up for many years; take your ease; eat, drink, *and* be merry." ' ²⁰But God said to him, 'Fool! This night your soul will be required of you; then whose will those things be which you have provided?'

²¹"So *is* he who lays up treasure for himself, and is not rich toward God."

²²Then He said to His disciples, "Therefore I say to you, do not worry about your life, what you will eat; nor about the body, what you will put on. ²³Life is more than food, and the body *is more* than clothing. ²⁴Consider the ravens, for they neither sow nor reap, which have neither storehouse nor barn; and God feeds them. Of how much more value are you than the birds? ²⁵And which of you by worrying can add one cubit to his stature? ²⁶If you then are not able to do *the* least, why are you anxious for the rest? ²⁷Consider the lilies, how they grow: they neither toil nor spin; and yet I say to you, even Solomon in all his glory was not arrayed like one of these. ²⁸If then God so clothes the grass, which today is in the field and tomorrow is thrown into the oven, how much more *will He clothe* you, O *you* of little faith?

²⁹"And do not seek what you should eat or what you should drink, nor have an anxious mind. ³⁰For all these things the nations of the world seek after, and your Father knows that you need these things. ³¹But seek the kingdom of God, and all these things* shall be added to you.

³²"Do not fear, little flock, for it is your Father's good pleasure to give you the kingdom. ³³Sell what you have and give alms; provide yourselves money bags which do not grow old, a treasure in the heavens that does not fail, where no thief approaches nor moth destroys. ³⁴For where your treasure is, there your heart will be also."

PSALM 78:32-55

Iᴺ spite of this they still sinned,
And did not believe in His
wondrous works.
33   Therefore their days He
         consumed in futility,
      And their years in fear.

34   When He slew them, then
         they sought Him;
      And they returned and sought
         earnestly for God.
35   Then they remembered that
         God *was* their rock,
      And the Most High God their
         Redeemer.
36   Nevertheless they flattered
         Him with their mouth,
      And they lied to Him with
         their tongue;
37   For their heart was not
         steadfast with Him,
      Nor were they faithful in His
         covenant.
38   But He, *being* full of
         compassion, forgave *their*
         iniquity,
      And did not destroy *them.*
      Yes, many a time He turned
         His anger away,
      And did not stir up all His
         wrath;
39   For He remembered that they
         were but flesh,
      A breath that passes away and
         does not come again.

40   How often they provoked Him
         in the wilderness,
      And grieved Him in the
         desert!
41   Yes, again and again they
         tempted God,
      And limited the Holy One of
         Israel.

42 They did not remember His
    power:
    The day when He redeemed
    them from the enemy,
43 When He worked His signs in
    Egypt,
    And His wonders in the field
    of Zoan;
44 Turned their rivers into blood,
    And their streams, that they
    could not drink.
45 He sent swarms of flies
    among them, which
    devoured them,
    And frogs, which destroyed
    them.
46 He also gave their crops to
    the caterpillar,
    And their labor to the locust.
47 He destroyed their vines with
    hail,
    And their sycamore trees with
    frost.
48 He also gave up their cattle to
    the hail,
    And their flocks to fiery
    lightning.
49 He cast on them the
    fierceness of His anger,
    Wrath, indignation, and
    trouble,
    By sending angels of
    destruction *among them*.
50 He made a path for His anger;
    He did not spare their soul
    from death,
    But gave their life over to the
    plague,
51 And destroyed all the
    firstborn in Egypt,
    The first of *their* strength in
    the tents of Ham.
52 But He made His own people
    go forth like sheep,
    And guided them in the
    wilderness like a flock;
53 And He led them on safely, so
    that they did not fear;
    But the sea overwhelmed
    their enemies.
54 And He brought them to His
    holy border,
    This mountain *which* His right
    hand had acquired.
55 He also drove out the nations
    before them,
    Allotted them an inheritance
    by survey,
    And made the tribes of Israel
    dwell in their tents.

PROVERBS FOR TODAY/ 12:21-23

No grave trouble will overtake the righteous, but the wicked shall be filled with evil.
□ *Lying lips* are *an abomination to the LORD, but those who deal truthfully* are *His delight. A prudent man conceals knowledge, but the heart of fools proclaims foolishness.*

APRIL 8

DEUTERONOMY 32:28-52

"FOR they [the Israelites] *are* a
nation void of counsel,
Nor *is there any*
understanding in them.

29 Oh, that they were wise, *that*
    they understood this,
    That they would consider
    their latter end!

30 How could one chase a
thousand,
And two put ten thousand to
flight,
Unless their Rock had sold
them,
And the LORD had
surrendered them?

31 For their rock *is* not like our
Rock,
Even our enemies themselves
being judges.

32 For their vine *is* of the vine of
Sodom
And of the fields of Gomorrah;
Their grapes *are* grapes of
gall,
Their clusters *are* bitter.

33 Their wine *is* the poison of
serpents,
And the cruel venom of
cobras.

34 '*Is* this not laid up in store with
Me,
Sealed up among My
treasures?

35 Vengeance is Mine, and
recompense;
Their foot shall slip in *due*
time;
For the day of their calamity
is at hand,
And the things to come
hasten upon them.'

36 "For the LORD will judge His
people
And have compassion on His
servants,
When He sees that *their*
power is gone,
And *there is* no one
remaining, bond or free.

37 He will say: 'Where *are* their
gods,
The rock in which they
sought refuge?

38 Who ate the fat of their
sacrifices,

And drank the wine of their
drink offering?
Let them rise and help you,
And be your refuge.

39 'Now see that I, *even* I, *am* He,
And *there is* no God besides
Me;
I kill and I make alive;
I wound and I heal;
Nor *is there any* who can
deliver from My hand.

40 For I raise My hand to heaven,
And say, "*As* I live forever,

41 If I whet My glittering sword,
And My hand takes hold on
judgment,
I will render vengeance to My
enemies,
And repay those who hate Me.

42 I will make My arrows drunk
with blood,
And My sword shall devour
flesh,
With the blood of the slain
and the captives,
From the heads of the leaders
of the enemy." '

43 "Rejoice, O Gentiles, *with* His
people;*
For He will avenge the blood
of His servants,
And render vengeance to His
adversaries;
He will provide atonement for
His land *and* His people."

44So Moses came with Joshua* the
son of Nun and spoke all the words of
this song in the hearing of the people.
45Moses finished speaking all these
words to all Israel, 46and he said to
them: "Set your hearts on all the words
which I testify among you today, which
you shall command your children to
be careful to observe—all the words of
this law. 47For it *is* not a futile thing for
you, because it *is* your life, and by this
word you shall prolong *your* days in

the land which you cross over the Jordan to possess."

48Then the LORD spoke to Moses that very same day, saying: 49"Go up this mountain of the Abarim, Mount Nebo, which *is* in the land of Moab, across from Jericho; view the land of Canaan, which I give to the children of Israel as a possession; 50and die on the mountain which you ascend, and be gathered to your people, just as Aaron your brother died on Mount Hor and was gathered to his people; 51because you trespassed against Me among the children of Israel at the waters of Meribah Kadesh, in the Wilderness of Zin, because you did not hallow Me in the midst of the children of Israel. 52Yet you shall see the land before *you,* though you shall not go there, into the land which I am giving to the children of Israel."

LUKE 12:35-59

"LET your waist be girded and *your* lamps burning; 36and you yourselves be like men who wait for their master, when he will return from the wedding, that when he comes and knocks they may open to him immediately. 37Blessed *are* those servants whom the master, when he comes, will find watching. Assuredly, I say to you that he will gird himself and have them sit down *to eat,* and will come and serve them. 38And if he should come in the second watch, or come in the third watch, and find *them* so, blessed are those servants. 39But know this, that if the master of the house had known what hour the thief would come, he would have watched and* not allowed his house to be broken into. 40Therefore you also be ready, for the Son of Man is coming at an hour you do not expect."

41Then Peter said to Him, "Lord, do You speak this parable *only* to us, or to all *people?"*

42And the Lord said, "Who then is that faithful and wise steward, whom *his* master will make ruler over his household, to give *them their* portion of food in due season? 43Blessed *is* that servant whom his master will find so doing when he comes. 44Truly, I say to you that he will make him ruler over all that he has. 45But if that servant says in his heart, 'My master is delaying his coming,' and begins to beat the male and female servants, and to eat and drink and be drunk, 46the master of that servant will come on a day when he is not looking for *him,* and at an hour when he is not aware, and will cut him in two and appoint *him* his portion with the unbelievers. 47And that servant who knew his master's will, and did not prepare *himself* or do according to his will, shall be beaten with many *stripes.* 48But he who did not know, yet committed things deserving of stripes, shall be beaten with few. For everyone to whom much is given, from him much will be required; and to whom much has been committed, of him they will ask the more.

49"I came to send fire on the earth, and how I wish it were already kindled! 50But I have a baptism to be baptized with, and how distressed I am till it is accomplished! 51Do *you* suppose that I came to give peace on earth? I tell you, not at all, but rather division. 52For from now on five in one house will be divided: three against two, and two against three. 53Father will be divided against son and son against father, mother against daughter and daughter against mother, mother-in-law against her daughter-in-law and daughter-in-law against her mother-in-law."

54Then He also said to the multitudes, "Whenever *you see* a cloud rising out of the west, immediately you say, 'A shower is coming'; and so it is. 55And when you see the south wind blow, you say, 'There will be hot weather'; and there is. 56Hypocrites!

You can discern the face of the sky and of the earth, but how *is it* you do not discern this time?

⁵⁷"Yes, and why, even of yourselves, do you not judge what is right? ⁵⁸When you go with your adversary to the magistrate, make every effort along the way to settle with him, lest he drag you to the judge, the judge deliver you to the officer, and the officer throw you into prison. ⁵⁹I tell you, you shall not depart from there till you have paid the very last mite."

PSALM 78:56-64

Yᴇᴛ they tested and provoked the Most High God,
And did not keep His testimonies,
57 But turned back and acted unfaithfully like their fathers;
They were turned aside like a deceitful bow.
58 For they provoked Him to anger with their high places,
And moved Him to jealousy with their carved images.
59 When God heard *this,* He was furious,
And greatly abhorred Israel,
60 So that He forsook the tabernacle of Shiloh,
The tent He had placed among men,
61 And delivered His strength into captivity,
And His glory into the enemy's hand.
62 He also gave His people over to the sword,
And was furious with His inheritance.
63 The fire consumed their young men,
And their maidens were not given in marriage.
64 Their priests fell by the sword,
And their widows made no lamentation.

PROVERBS FOR TODAY/ 12:24

The hand of the diligent will rule, but the lazy man *will be put to forced labor.*

APRIL 9

DEUTERONOMY 33:1-29

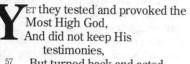Nᴏᴡ this *is* the blessing with which Moses the man of God blessed the children of Israel before his death. ²And he said:

"The Lᴏʀᴅ came from Sinai,
And dawned on them from Seir;
He shone forth from Mount Paran,
And He came with ten thousands of saints;
From His right hand
Came a fiery law for them.
3 Yes, He loves the people;
All His saints *are* in Your hand;
They sit down at Your feet;
Everyone receives Your words.
4 Moses commanded a law for us,
A heritage of the congregation of Jacob.

5   And He was King in Jeshurun,
     When the leaders of the
          people were gathered,
     All the tribes of Israel
          together.

6   "Let Reuben live, and not die,
     Nor let his men be few."

7And this he said of Judah:

     "Hear, LORD, the voice of Judah,
     And bring him to his people;
     Let his hands be sufficient for
          him,
     And may You be a help
          against his enemies."

8And of Levi he said:

     "*Let* Your Thummim and Your
          Urim *be* with Your holy one,
     Whom You tested at Massah,
     And with whom You
          contended at the waters of
          Meribah,
9   Who says of his father and
          mother,
     'I have not seen them';
     Nor did he acknowledge his
          brothers,
     Or know his own children;
     For they have observed Your
          word
     And kept Your covenant.
10   They shall teach Jacob Your
          judgments,
     And Israel Your law.
     They shall put incense before
          You,
     And a whole burnt sacrifice
          on Your altar.
11   Bless his substance, LORD,
     And accept the work of his
          hands;
     Strike the loins of those who
          rise against him,
     And of those who hate him,
          that they rise not again."

12Of Benjamin he said:

     "The beloved of the LORD shall
          dwell in safety by Him,
     Who shelters him all the day
          long;
     And he shall dwell between
          His shoulders."

13And of Joseph he said:

     "Blessed of the LORD *is* his land,
     With the precious things of
          heaven, with the dew,
     And the deep lying beneath,
14   With the precious fruits of the
          sun,
     With the precious produce of
          the months,
15   With the best things of the
          ancient mountains,
     With the precious things of
          the everlasting hills,
16   With the precious things of
          the earth and its fullness,
     And the favor of Him who
          dwelt in the bush.
     Let *the blessing* come 'on the
          head of Joseph,
     And on the crown of the head
          of him *who was* separate
          from his brothers.'*
17   His glory *is like* a firstborn
          bull,
     And his horns *like* the horns
          of the wild ox;
     Together with them
     He shall push the peoples
     To the ends of the earth;
     They *are* the ten thousands of
          Ephraim,
     And they *are* the thousands of
          Manasseh."

18And of Zebulun he said:

     "Rejoice, Zebulun, in your
          going out,
     And Issachar in your tents!

19 They shall call the peoples *to* the mountain;
There they shall offer sacrifices of righteousness;
For they shall partake *of* the abundance of the seas
And *of* treasures hidden in the sand."

20And of Gad he said:

"Blessed *is* he who enlarges Gad;
He dwells as a lion,
And tears the arm and the crown of his head.
21 He provided the first *part* for himself,
Because a lawgiver's portion was reserved there.
He came *with* the heads of the people;
He administered the justice of the LORD,
And His judgments with Israel."

22And of Dan he said:

"Dan *is* a lion's whelp;
He shall leap from Bashan."

23And of Naphtali he said:

"O Naphtali, satisfied with favor,
And full of the blessing of the LORD,
Possess the west and the south."

24And of Asher he said:

"Asher *is* most blessed of sons;
Let him be favored by his brothers,
And let him dip his foot in oil.
25 Your sandals *shall be* iron and bronze;

As your days, *so shall* your strength *be.*

26 "*There is* no one like the God of Jeshurun,
Who rides the heavens to help you,
And in His excellency on the clouds.
27 The eternal God *is your* refuge,
And underneath *are* the everlasting arms;
He will thrust out the enemy from before you,
And will say, 'Destroy!'
28 Then Israel shall dwell in safety,
The fountain of Jacob alone,
In a land of grain and new wine;
His heavens shall also drop dew.
29 Happy *are* you, O Israel!
Who *is* like you, a people saved by the LORD,
The shield of your help
And the sword of your majesty!
Your enemies shall submit to you,
And you shall tread down their high places."

LUKE 13:1-21

THERE were present at that season some who told Him [Jesus] about the Galileans whose blood Pilate had mingled with their sacrifices. 2And Jesus answered and said to them, "Do you suppose that these Galileans were worse sinners than all *other* Galileans, because they suffered such things? 3I tell you, no; but unless you repent you will all likewise perish. 4Or those eighteen on whom the tower in Siloam fell and killed them, do you think that they were worse sinners than all *other* men who dwelt in Jerusalem? ⁵I tell you, no; but unless you repent you will all likewise perish."

⁶He also spoke this parable: "A certain *man* had a fig tree planted in his vineyard, and he came seeking fruit on it and found none. ⁷Then he said to the keeper of his vineyard, 'Look, for three years I have come seeking fruit on this fig tree and find none. Cut it down; why does it use up the ground?' ⁸But he answered and said to him, 'Sir, let it alone this year also, until I dig around it and fertilize *it.* ⁹And if it bears fruit, *well.* But if not, after that* you can cut it down.' "

¹⁰Now He was teaching in one of the synagogues on the Sabbath. ¹¹And behold, there was a woman who had a spirit of infirmity eighteen years, and was bent over and could in no way raise *herself* up. ¹²But when Jesus saw her, He called *her* to *Him* and said to her, "Woman, you are loosed from your infirmity." ¹³And He laid *His* hands on her, and immediately she was made straight, and glorified God.

¹⁴But the ruler of the synagogue answered with indignation, because Jesus had healed on the Sabbath; and he said to the crowd, "There are six days on which men ought to work; therefore come and be healed on them, and not on the Sabbath day."

¹⁵The Lord then answered him and said, "Hypocrite!* Does not each one of you on the Sabbath loose his ox or donkey from the stall, and lead *it* away to water it? ¹⁶So ought not this woman, being a daughter of Abraham, whom Satan has bound—think of it—for eighteen years, be loosed from this bond on the Sabbath?" ¹⁷And when He said these things, all His adversaries were put to shame; and all the multitude rejoiced for all the glorious things that were done by Him.

¹⁸Then He said, "What is the king-dom of God like? And to what shall I compare it? ¹⁹It is like a mustard seed, which a man took and put in his garden; and it grew and became a large* tree, and the birds of the air nested in its branches."

²⁰And again He said, "To what shall I liken the kingdom of God? ²¹It is like leaven, which a woman took and hid in three measures* of meal till it was all leavened."

PSALM 78:65-72

THEN the Lord awoke as *from* sleep,
Like a mighty man who shouts because of wine.

66 And He beat back His enemies;
He put them to a perpetual reproach.

67 Moreover He rejected the tent of Joseph,
And did not choose the tribe of Ephraim,

68 But chose the tribe of Judah,
Mount Zion which He loved.

69 And He built His sanctuary like the heights,
Like the earth which He has established forever.

70 He also chose David His servant,
And took him from the sheepfolds;

71 From following the ewes that had young He brought him,
To shepherd Jacob His people,
And Israel His inheritance.

72 So he shepherded them according to the integrity of his heart,
And guided them by the skillfulness of his hands.

PROVERBS FOR TODAY/ 12:25

Anxiety in the heart of man causes depression, but a good word makes it glad.

APRIL 10

DEUTERONOMY 34:1—JOSHUA 2:24

THEN Moses went up from the plains of Moab to Mount Nebo, to the top of Pisgah, which is across from Jericho. And the LORD showed him all the land of Gilead as far as Dan, ²all Naphtali and the land of Ephraim and Manasseh, all the land of Judah as far as the Western Sea,* ³the South, and the plain of the Valley of Jericho, the city of palm trees, as far as Zoar. ⁴Then the LORD said to him, "This *is* the land of which I swore to give Abraham, Isaac, and Jacob, saying, 'I will give it to your descendants.' I have caused you to see *it* with your eyes, but you shall not cross over there."

⁵So Moses the servant of the LORD died there in the land of Moab, according to the word of the LORD. ⁶And He buried him in a valley in the land of Moab, opposite Beth Peor; but no one knows his grave to this day. ⁷Moses *was* one hundred and twenty years old when he died. His eyes were not dim nor his natural vigor diminished. ⁸And the children of Israel wept for Moses in the plains of Moab thirty days. So the days of weeping *and* mourning for Moses ended.

⁹Now Joshua the son of Nun was full of the spirit of wisdom, for Moses had laid his hands on him; so the children of Israel heeded him, and did as the LORD had commanded Moses.

¹⁰But since then there has not arisen in Israel a prophet like Moses, whom the LORD knew face to face, ¹¹in all the signs and wonders which the LORD sent him to do in the land of Egypt, before Pharaoh, before all his servants, and in all his land, ¹²and by all that mighty power and all the great terror which Moses performed in the sight of all Israel.

AFTER the death of Moses the servant of the LORD, it came to pass that the LORD spoke to Joshua the son of Nun, Moses' assistant, saying: ²"Moses My servant is dead. Now therefore, arise, go over this Jordan, you and all this people, to the land which I am giving to them—the children of Israel. ³Every place that the sole of your foot will tread upon I have given you, as I said to Moses. ⁴From the wilderness and this Lebanon as far as the great river, the River Euphrates, all the land of the Hittites, and to the Great Sea toward the going down of the sun, shall be your territory. ⁵No man shall *be able to* stand before you all the days of your life; as I was with Moses, *so* I will be with you. I will not leave you nor forsake you. ⁶Be strong and of good courage, for to this people you shall divide as an inheritance the land which I swore to their fathers to give them. ⁷Only be strong and very courageous, that you may observe to do according to all the law which Moses My servant commanded you; do not turn from it to the right hand or to the left, that you may prosper wherever you go. ⁸This Book of the Law shall not depart from your mouth, but you shall meditate in it day and night, that you may observe to do according to all that is written in it. For then you will make your way prosperous, and then you will have good success. ⁹Have I not commanded you? Be strong and of good courage; do not be afraid, nor be dismayed, for the LORD your God *is* with you wherever you go."

¹⁰Then Joshua commanded the officers of the people, saying, ¹¹"Pass through the camp and command the

people, saying, 'Prepare provisions for yourselves, for within three days you will cross over this Jordan, to go in to possess the land which the LORD your God is giving you to possess.' "

12And to the Reubenites, the Gadites, and half the tribe of Manasseh Joshua spoke, saying, 13"Remember the word which Moses the servant of the LORD commanded you, saying, 'The LORD your God is giving you rest and is giving you this land.' 14Your wives, your little ones, and your livestock shall remain in the land which Moses gave you on this side of the Jordan. But you shall pass before your brethren armed, all your mighty men of valor, and help them, 15until the LORD has given your brethren rest, as He gave you, and they also have taken possession of the land which the LORD your God is giving them. Then you shall return to the land of your possession and enjoy it, which Moses the LORD's servant gave you on this side of the Jordan toward the sunrise."

16So they answered Joshua, saying, "All that you command us we will do, and wherever you send us we will go. 17Just as we heeded Moses in all things, so we will heed you. Only the LORD your God be with you, as He was with Moses. 18Whoever rebels against your command and does not heed your words, in all that you command him, shall be put to death. Only be strong and of good courage."

Now Joshua the son of Nun sent out two men from Acacia Grove* to spy secretly, saying, "Go, view the land, especially Jericho."

So they went, and came to the house of a harlot named Rahab, and lodged there. 2And it was told the king of Jericho, saying, "Behold, men have come here tonight from the children of Israel to search out the country."

3So the king of Jericho sent to Rahab, saying, "Bring out the men who have come to you, who have entered your house, for they have come to search out all the country."

4Then the woman took the two men and hid them. So she said, "Yes, the men came to me, but I did not know where they were from. 5And it happened as the gate was being shut, when it was dark, that the men went out. Where the men went I do not know; pursue them quickly, for you may overtake them." 6(But she had brought them up to the roof and hidden them with the stalks of flax, which she had laid in order on the roof.) 7Then the men pursued them by the road to the Jordan, to the fords. And as soon as those who pursued them had gone out, they shut the gate.

8Now before they lay down, she came up to them on the roof, 9and said to the men: "I know that the LORD has given you the land, that the terror of you has fallen on us, and that all the inhabitants of the land are fainthearted because of you. 10For we have heard how the LORD dried up the water of the Red Sea for you when you came out of Egypt, and what you did to the two kings of the Amorites who were on the other side of the Jordan, Sihon and Og, whom you utterly destroyed. 11And as soon as we heard these things, our hearts melted; neither did there remain any more courage in anyone because of you, for the LORD your God, He is God in heaven above and on earth beneath. 12Now therefore, I beg you, swear to me by the LORD, since I have shown you kindness, that you also will show kindness to my father's house, and give me a true token, 13and spare my father, my mother, my brothers, my sisters, and all that they have, and deliver our lives from death."

14So the men answered her, "Our lives for yours, if none of you tell this business of ours. And it shall be, when the LORD has given us the land, that we will deal kindly and truly with you."

¹⁵Then she let them down by a rope through the window, for her house *was* on the city wall; she dwelt on the wall. ¹⁶And she said to them, "Get to the mountain, lest the pursuers meet you. Hide there three days, until the pursuers have returned. Afterward you may go your way."

¹⁷So the men said to her: "We *will be* blameless of this oath of yours which you have made us swear, ¹⁸unless, *when* we come into the land, you bind this line of scarlet cord in the window through which you let us down, and unless you bring your father, your mother, your brothers, and all your father's household to your own home. ¹⁹So it shall be *that* whoever goes outside the doors of your house into the street, his blood *shall be* on his own head, and we *will be* guiltless. And whoever is with you in the house, his blood *shall be* on our head if a hand is laid on him. ²⁰And if you tell this business of ours, then we will be free from your oath which you made us swear."

²¹Then she said, "According to your words, so *be* it." And she sent them away, and they departed. And she bound the scarlet cord in the window.

²²They departed and went to the mountain, and stayed there three days until the pursuers returned. The pursuers sought *them* all along the way, but did not find *them*. ²³So the two men returned, descended from the mountain, and crossed over; and they came to Joshua the son of Nun, and told him all that had befallen them. ²⁴And they said to Joshua, "Truly the LORD has delivered all the land into our hands, for indeed all the inhabitants of the country are fainthearted because of us."

LUKE 13:22–14:6

AND He [Jesus] went through the cities and villages, teaching, and journeying toward Jerusalem. ²³Then one said to Him, "Lord, are there few who are saved?"

And He said to them, ²⁴"Strive to enter through the narrow gate, for many, I say to you, will seek to enter and will not be able. ²⁵When once the Master of the house has risen up and shut the door, and you begin to stand outside and knock at the door, saying, 'Lord, Lord, open for us,' and He will answer and say to you, 'I do not know you, where you are from,' ²⁶then you will begin to say, 'We ate and drank in Your presence, and You taught in our streets.' ²⁷But He will say, 'I tell you I do not know you, where you are from. Depart from Me, all you workers of iniquity.' ²⁸There will be weeping and gnashing of teeth, when you see Abraham and Isaac and Jacob and all the prophets in the kingdom of God, and yourselves thrust out. ²⁹They will come from the east and the west, from the north and the south, and sit down in the kingdom of God. ³⁰And indeed there are last who will be first, and there are first who will be last."

³¹On that very day* some Pharisees came, saying to Him, "Get out and depart from here, for Herod wants to kill You."

³²And He said to them, "Go, tell that fox, 'Behold, I cast out demons and perform cures today and tomorrow, and the third *day* I shall be perfected.' ³³Nevertheless I must journey today, tomorrow, and the *day* following; for it cannot be that a prophet should perish outside of Jerusalem.

³⁴"O Jerusalem, Jerusalem, the one who kills the prophets and stones those who are sent to her! How often I wanted to gather your children together, as a hen *gathers* her brood under *her* wings, but you were not

willing! ³⁵See! Your house is left to you desolate; and assuredly,* I say to you, you shall not see Me until *the time* comes when you say, *'Blessed is He who comes in the name of the* Lord!' "*

Now it happened, as He went into the house of one of the rulers of the Pharisees to eat bread on the Sabbath, that they watched Him closely. ²And behold, there was a certain man before Him who had dropsy. ³And Jesus, answering, spoke to the lawyers and Pharisees, saying, "Is it lawful to heal on the Sabbath?"*

⁴But they kept silent. And He took *him* and healed him, and let him go. ⁵Then He answered them, saying, "Which of you, having a donkey* or an ox that has fallen into a pit, will not immediately pull him out on the Sabbath day?" ⁶And they could not answer Him regarding these things.

PSALM 79:1-13

A Psalm of Asaph.

O God, the nations have come into Your inheritance;
Your holy temple they have defiled;
They have laid Jerusalem in heaps.
2 The dead bodies of Your servants
They have given *as* food for the birds of the heavens,
The flesh of Your saints to the beasts of the earth.
3 Their blood they have shed like water all around Jerusalem,
And *there was* no one to bury *them.*
4 We have become a reproach to our neighbors,
A scorn and derision to those who are around us.

5 How long, Lord?
Will You be angry forever?
Will Your jealousy burn like fire?
6 Pour out Your wrath on the nations that do not know You,
And on the kingdoms that do not call on Your name.
7 For they have devoured Jacob,
And laid waste his dwelling place.

8 Oh, do not remember former iniquities against us!
Let Your tender mercies come speedily to meet us,
For we have been brought very low.
9 Help us, O God of our salvation,
For the glory of Your name;
And deliver us, and provide atonement for our sins,
For Your name's sake!
10 Why should the nations say,
"Where *is* their God?"
Let there be known among the nations in our sight
The avenging of the blood of Your servants *which has been* shed.

11 Let the groaning of the prisoner come before You;
According to the greatness of Your power
Preserve those who are appointed to die;
12 And return to our neighbors sevenfold into their bosom
Their reproach with which they have reproached You, O Lord.

13 So we, Your people and sheep of Your pasture,
Will give You thanks forever;
We will show forth Your praise to all generations.

PROVERBS FOR TODAY/ 12:26

The righteous should choose his friends carefully, for the way of the wicked leads them astray.

APRIL 11

JOSHUA 3:1–4:24

THEN Joshua rose early in the morning; and they set out from Acacia Grove* and came to the Jordan, he and all the children of Israel, and lodged there before they crossed over. ²So it was, after three days, that the officers went through the camp; ³and they commanded the people, saying, "When you see the ark of the covenant of the LORD your God, and the priests, the Levites, bearing it, then you shall set out from your place and go after it. ⁴Yet there shall be a space between you and it, about two thousand cubits by measure. Do not come near it, that you may know the way by which you must go, for you have not passed *this* way before."

⁵And Joshua said to the people, "Sanctify yourselves, for tomorrow the LORD will do wonders among you." ⁶Then Joshua spoke to the priests, saying, "Take up the ark of the covenant and cross over before the people."

So they took up the ark of the covenant and went before the people.

⁷And the LORD said to Joshua, "This day I will begin to exalt you in the sight of all Israel, that they may know that, as I was with Moses, *so* I will be with you. ⁸You shall command the priests who bear the ark of the covenant, saying, 'When you have come to the edge of the water of the Jordan, you shall stand in the Jordan.'"

⁹So Joshua said to the children of Israel, "Come here, and hear the words of the LORD your God." ¹⁰And

Joshua said, "By this you shall know that the living God *is* among you, and *that* He will without fail drive out from before you the Canaanites and the Hittites and the Hivites and the Perizzites and the Girgashites and the Amorites and the Jebusites: ¹¹Behold, the ark of the covenant of the Lord of all the earth is crossing over before you into the Jordan. ¹²Now therefore, take for yourselves twelve men from the tribes of Israel, one man from every tribe. ¹³And it shall come to pass, as soon as the soles of the feet of the priests who bear the ark of the LORD, the Lord of all the earth, shall rest in the waters of the Jordan, *that* the waters of the Jordan shall be cut off, the waters that come down from upstream, and they shall stand as a heap."

¹⁴So it was, when the people set out from their camp to cross over the Jordan, with the priests bearing the ark of the covenant before the people, ¹⁵and as those who bore the ark came to the Jordan, and the feet of the priests who bore the ark dipped in the edge of the water (for the Jordan overflows all its banks during the whole time of harvest), ¹⁶that the waters which came down from upstream stood *still, and* rose in a heap very far away at Adam, the city that *is* beside Zaretan. So the waters that went down into the Sea of the Arabah, the Salt Sea, failed, *and* were cut off; and the people crossed over opposite Jericho. ¹⁷Then the priests who bore the ark of the covenant of the LORD stood firm on dry

ground in the midst of the Jordan; and all Israel crossed over on dry ground, until all the people had crossed completely over the Jordan.

AND it came to pass, when all the people had completely crossed over the Jordan, that the LORD spoke to Joshua, saying: [2]"Take for yourselves twelve men from the people, one man from every tribe, [3]and command them, saying, 'Take for yourselves twelve stones from here, out of the midst of the Jordan, from the place where the priests' feet stood firm. You shall carry them over with you and leave them in the lodging place where you lodge tonight.'"

[4]Then Joshua called the twelve men whom he had appointed from the children of Israel, one man from every tribe; [5]and Joshua said to them: "Cross over before the ark of the LORD your God into the midst of the Jordan, and each one of you take up a stone on his shoulder, according to the number of the tribes of the children of Israel, [6]that this may be a sign among you when your children ask in time to come, saying, 'What do these stones mean to you?' [7]Then you shall answer them that the waters of the Jordan were cut off before the ark of the covenant of the LORD; when it crossed over the Jordan, the waters of the Jordan were cut off. And these stones shall be for a memorial to the children of Israel forever."

[8]And the children of Israel did so, just as Joshua commanded, and took up twelve stones from the midst of the Jordan, as the LORD had spoken to Joshua, according to the number of the tribes of the children of Israel, and carried them over with them to the place where they lodged, and laid them down there. [9]Then Joshua set up twelve stones in the midst of the Jordan, in the place where the feet of the priests who bore the ark of the cov-

enant stood; and they are there to this day.

[10]So the priests who bore the ark stood in the midst of the Jordan until everything was finished that the LORD had commanded Joshua to speak to the people, according to all that Moses had commanded Joshua; and the people hurried and crossed over. [11]Then it came to pass, when all the people had completely crossed over, that the ark of the LORD and the priests crossed over in the presence of the people. [12]And the men of Reuben, the men of Gad, and half the tribe of Manasseh crossed over armed before the children of Israel, as Moses had spoken to them. [13]About forty thousand prepared for war crossed over before the LORD for battle, to the plains of Jericho. [14]On that day the LORD exalted Joshua in the sight of all Israel; and they feared him, as they had feared Moses, all the days of his life.

[15]Then the LORD spoke to Joshua, saying, [16]"Command the priests who bear the ark of the Testimony to come up from the Jordan." [17]Joshua therefore commanded the priests, saying, "Come up from the Jordan." [18]And it came to pass, when the priests who bore the ark of the covenant of the LORD had come from the midst of the Jordan, and the soles of the priests' feet touched the dry land, that the waters of the Jordan returned to their place and overflowed all its banks as before.

[19]Now the people came up from the Jordan on the tenth day of the first month, and they camped in Gilgal on the east border of Jericho. [20]And those twelve stones which they took out of the Jordan, Joshua set up in Gilgal. [21]Then he spoke to the children of Israel, saying: "When your children ask their fathers in time to come, saying, 'What are these stones?' [22]then you shall let your children know, saying, 'Israel crossed over this Jordan on dry

land'; [23]for the LORD your God dried up the waters of the Jordan before you until you had crossed over, as the LORD your God did to the Red Sea, which He dried up before us until we had crossed over, [24]that all the peoples of the earth may know the hand of the LORD, that it *is* mighty, that you may fear the LORD your God forever."

LUKE 14:7-35

So He [Jesus] told a parable to those who were invited, when He noted how they chose the best places, saying to them: [8]"When you are invited by anyone to a wedding feast, do not sit down in the best place, lest one more honorable than you be invited by him; [9]and he who invited you and him come and say to you, 'Give place to this man,' and then you begin with shame to take the lowest place. [10]But when you are invited, go and sit down in the lowest place, so that when he who invited you comes he may say to you, 'Friend, go up higher.' Then you will have glory in the presence of those who sit at the table with you. [11]For whoever exalts himself will be humbled, and he who humbles himself will be exalted."

[12]Then He also said to him who invited Him, "When you give a dinner or a supper, do not ask your friends, your brothers, your relatives, nor rich neighbors, lest they also invite you back, and you be repaid. [13]But when you give a feast, invite *the* poor, *the* maimed, *the* lame, *the* blind. [14]And you will be blessed, because they cannot repay you; for you shall be repaid at the resurrection of the just."

[15]Now when one of those who sat at the table with Him heard these things, he said to Him, "Blessed *is* he who shall eat bread* in the kingdom of God!"

[16]Then He said to him, "A certain man gave a great supper and invited many, [17]and sent his servant at supper time to say to those who were invited, 'Come, for all things are now ready.' [18]But they all with one *accord* began to make excuses. The first said to him, 'I have bought a piece of ground, and I must go and see it. I ask you to have me excused.' [19]And another said, 'I have bought five yoke of oxen, and I am going to test them. I ask you to have me excused.' [20]Still another said, 'I have married a wife, and therefore I cannot come.' [21]So that servant came and reported these things to his master. Then the master of the house, being angry, said to his servant, 'Go out quickly into the streets and lanes of the city, and bring in here *the* poor and *the* maimed and *the* lame and *the* blind.' [22]And the servant said, 'Master, it is done as you commanded, and still there is room.' [23]Then the master said to the servant, 'Go out into the highways and hedges, and compel *them* to come in, that my house may be filled. [24]For I say to you that none of those men who were invited shall taste my supper.' "

[25]Now great multitudes went with Him. And He turned and said to them, [26]"If anyone comes to Me and does not hate his father and mother, wife and children, brothers and sisters, yes, and his own life also, he cannot be My disciple. [27]And whoever does not bear his cross and come after Me cannot be My disciple. [28]For which of you, intending to build a tower, does not sit down first and count the cost, whether he has *enough* to finish *it*— [29]lest, after he has laid the foundation, and is not able to finish, all who see *it* begin to mock him, [30]saying, 'This man began to build and was not able to finish.' [31]Or what king, going to make war against another king, does not sit down first and consider whether he is able with ten thousand to meet him who comes against him with twenty thousand? [32]Or else, while the other is still a great

way off, he sends a delegation and asks conditions of peace. ³³So likewise, whoever of you does not forsake all that he has cannot be My disciple.

³⁴"Salt *is* good; but if the salt has lost its flavor, how shall it be seasoned? ³⁵It is neither fit for the land nor for the dunghill, *but* men throw it out. He who has ears to hear, let him hear!"

PSALM 80:1-19

To the Chief Musician. Set to "The Lilies." *
A Testimony of Asaph. A Psalm.*

GIVE ear, O Shepherd of Israel,
You who lead Joseph like a flock;
You who dwell between the cherubim, shine forth!

2 Before Ephraim, Benjamin, and Manasseh,
Stir up Your strength,
And come *and* save us!

3 Restore us, O God;
Cause Your face to shine,
And we shall be saved!

4 O LORD God of hosts,
How long will You be angry
Against the prayer of Your people?

5 You have fed them with the bread of tears,
And given them tears to drink in great measure.

6 You have made us a strife to our neighbors,
And our enemies laugh among themselves.

7 Restore us, O God of hosts;
Cause Your face to shine,
And we shall be saved!

8 You have brought a vine out of Egypt;
You have cast out the nations, and planted it.

9 You prepared *room* for it,
And caused it to take deep root,
And it filled the land.

10 The hills were covered with its shadow,
And the mighty cedars with its boughs.

11 She sent out her boughs to the Sea,*
And her branches to the River.*

12 Why have You broken down her hedges,
So that all who pass by the way pluck her *fruit?*

13 The boar out of the woods uproots it,
And the wild beast of the field devours it.

14 Return, we beseech You, O God of hosts;
Look down from heaven and see,
And visit this vine

15 And the vineyard which Your right hand has planted,
And the branch *that* You made strong for Yourself.

16 *It is* burned with fire, *it is* cut down;
They perish at the rebuke of Your countenance.

17 Let Your hand be upon the man of Your right hand,
Upon the son of man *whom* You made strong for Yourself.

18 Then we will not turn back from You;
Revive us, and we will call upon Your name.

19 Restore us, O LORD God of hosts;
Cause Your face to shine,
And we shall be saved!

PROVERBS FOR TODAY/ 12:27-28

The lazy man *does not roast what he took in hunting, but diligence* is *man's precious possession.* □ *In the way of righteousness* is *life, and in* its *pathway* there is *no death.*

APRIL 12

JOSHUA 5:1–7:15

So it was, when all the kings of the Amorites who *were* on the west side of the Jordan, and all the kings of the Canaanites who *were* by the sea, heard that the LORD had dried up the waters of the Jordan from before the children of Israel until we* had crossed over, that their heart melted; and there was no spirit in them any longer because of the children of Israel.

²At that time the LORD said to Joshua, "Make flint knives for yourself, and circumcise the sons of Israel again the second time." ³So Joshua made flint knives for himself, and circumcised the sons of Israel at the hill of the fore-skins.* ⁴And this *is* the reason why Joshua circumcised them: All the people who came out of Egypt *who were* males, all the men of war, had died in the wilderness on the way, after they had come out of Egypt. ⁵For all the people who came out had been circumcised, but all the people born in the wilderness, on the way as they came out of Egypt, had not been circumcised. ⁶For the children of Israel walked forty years in the wilderness, till all the people *who were* men of war, who came out of Egypt, were consumed, because they did not obey the voice of the LORD—to whom the LORD swore that He would not show them the land which the LORD had sworn to their fathers that He would give us, "a land flowing with milk and honey."*

⁷Then Joshua circumcised their sons *whom* He raised up in their place; for they were uncircumcised, because they had not been circumcised on the way.

⁸So it was, when they had finished circumcising all the people, that they stayed in their places in the camp till they were healed. ⁹Then the LORD said to Joshua, "This day I have rolled away the reproach of Egypt from you." Therefore the name of the place is called Gilgal* to this day.

¹⁰Now the children of Israel camped in Gilgal, and kept the Passover on the fourteenth day of the month at twilight on the plains of Jericho. ¹¹And they ate of the produce of the land on the day after the Passover, unleavened bread and parched grain, on the very same day. ¹²Then the manna ceased on the day after they had eaten the produce of the land; and the children of Israel no longer had manna, but they ate the food of the land of Canaan that year.

¹³And it came to pass, when Joshua was by Jericho, that he lifted his eyes and looked, and behold, a Man stood opposite him with His sword drawn in His hand. And Joshua went to Him and said to Him, "*Are* You for us or for our adversaries?"

¹⁴So He said, "No, but *as* Commander of the army of the LORD I have now come."

And Joshua fell on his face to the earth and worshiped, and said to Him,

"What does my Lord say to His servant?"

¹⁵Then the Commander of the LORD's army said to Joshua, "Take your sandal off your foot, for the place where you stand *is* holy." And Joshua did so.

Now Jericho was securely shut up because of the children of Israel; none went out, and none came in. ²And the LORD said to Joshua: "See! I have given Jericho into your hand, its king, *and* the mighty men of valor. ³You shall march around the city, all *you* men of war; you shall go all around the city once. This you shall do six days. ⁴And seven priests shall bear seven trumpets of rams' horns before the ark. But the seventh day you shall march around the city seven times, and the priests shall blow the trumpets. ⁵It shall come to pass, when they make a long *blast* with the ram's horn, *and* when you hear the sound of the trumpet, that all the people shall shout with a great shout; then the wall of the city will fall down flat. And the people shall go up every man straight before him."

⁶Then Joshua the son of Nun called the priests and said to them, "Take up the ark of the covenant, and let seven priests bear seven trumpets of rams' horns before the ark of the LORD." ⁷And he said to the people, "Proceed, and march around the city, and let him who is armed advance before the ark of the LORD."

⁸So it was, when Joshua had spoken to the people, that the seven priests bearing the seven trumpets of rams' horns before the LORD advanced and blew the trumpets, and the ark of the covenant of the LORD followed them. ⁹The armed men went before the priests who blew the trumpets, and the rear guard came after the ark, while *the priests* continued blowing the trumpets. ¹⁰Now Joshua had commanded the people, saying, "You shall not shout or make any noise with your voice, nor shall a word proceed out of your mouth, until the day I say to you, 'Shout!' Then you shall shout." ¹¹So he had the ark of the LORD circle the city, going around *it* once. Then they came into the camp and lodged in the camp.

¹²And Joshua rose early in the morning, and the priests took up the ark of the LORD. ¹³Then seven priests bearing seven trumpets of rams' horns before the ark of the LORD went on continually and blew with the trumpets. And the armed men went before them. But the rear guard came after the ark of the LORD, while *the priests* continued blowing the trumpets. ¹⁴And the second day they marched around the city once and returned to the camp. So they did six days.

¹⁵But it came to pass on the seventh day that they rose early, about the dawning of the day, and marched around the city seven times in the same manner. On that day only they marched around the city seven times. ¹⁶And the seventh time it happened, when the priests blew the trumpets, that Joshua said to the people: "Shout, for the LORD has given you the city! ¹⁷Now the city shall be doomed by the LORD to destruction, it and all who *are* in it. Only Rahab the harlot shall live, she and all who *are* with her in the house, because she hid the messengers that we sent. ¹⁸And you, by all means abstain from the accursed things, lest you become accursed when you take of the accursed things, and make the camp of Israel a curse, and trouble it. ¹⁹But all the silver and gold, and vessels of bronze and iron, *are* consecrated to the LORD; they shall come into the treasury of the LORD."

²⁰So the people shouted when *the priests* blew the trumpets. And it happened when the people heard the sound of the trumpet, and the people shouted with a great shout, that the wall fell down flat. Then the people

went up into the city, every man straight before him, and they took the city. ²¹And they utterly destroyed all that *was* in the city, both man and woman, young and old, ox and sheep and donkey, with the edge of the sword.

²²But Joshua had said to the two men who had spied out the country, "Go into the harlot's house, and from there bring out the woman and all that she has, as you swore to her." ²³And the young men who had been spies went in and brought out Rahab, her father, her mother, her brothers, and all that she had. So they brought out all her relatives and left them outside the camp of Israel. ²⁴But they burned the city and all that *was* in it with fire. Only the silver and gold, and the vessels of bronze and iron, they put into the treasury of the house of the Lᴏʀᴅ. ²⁵And Joshua spared Rahab the harlot, her father's household, and all that she had. So she dwells in Israel to this day, because she hid the messengers whom Joshua sent to spy out Jericho.

²⁶Then Joshua charged *them* at that time, saying, "Cursed *be* the man before the Lᴏʀᴅ who rises up and builds this city Jericho; he shall lay its foundation with his firstborn, and with his youngest he shall set up its gates."

²⁷So the Lᴏʀᴅ was with Joshua, and his fame spread throughout all the country.

Bᴜᴛ the children of Israel committed a trespass regarding the accursed things, for Achan the son of Carmi, the son of Zabdi,* the son of Zerah, of the tribe of Judah, took of the accursed things; so the anger of the Lᴏʀᴅ burned against the children of Israel.

²Now Joshua sent men from Jericho to Ai, which *is* beside Beth Aven, on the east side of Bethel, and spoke to them, saying, "Go up and spy out the country." So the men went up and spied out Ai. ³And they returned to Joshua and said to him, "Do not let all the people go up, but let about two or three thousand men go up and attack Ai. Do not weary all the people there, for *the people of Ai are* few." ⁴So about three thousand men went up there from the people, but they fled before the men of Ai. ⁵And the men of Ai struck down about thirty-six men, for they chased them *from* before the gate as far as Shebarim, and struck them down on the descent; therefore the hearts of the people melted and became like water.

⁶Then Joshua tore his clothes, and fell to the earth on his face before the ark of the Lᴏʀᴅ until evening, he and the elders of Israel; and they put dust on their heads. ⁷And Joshua said, "Alas, Lord Gᴏᴅ, why have You brought this people over the Jordan at all—to deliver us into the hand of the Amorites, to destroy us? Oh, that we had been content, and dwelt on the other side of the Jordan! ⁸O Lord, what shall I say when Israel turns its back before its enemies? ⁹For the Canaanites and all the inhabitants of the land will hear *it,* and surround us, and cut off our name from the earth. Then what will You do for Your great name?"

¹⁰So the Lᴏʀᴅ said to Joshua: "Get up! Why do you lie thus on your face? ¹¹Israel has sinned, and they have also transgressed My covenant which I commanded them. For they have even taken some of the accursed things, and have both stolen and deceived; and they have also put *it* among their own stuff. ¹²Therefore the children of Israel could not stand before their enemies, *but* turned *their* backs before their enemies, because they have become doomed to destruction. Neither will I be with you anymore, unless you destroy the accursed from among you. ¹³Get up, sanctify the people, and say, 'Sanctify yourselves for tomorrow, because thus says the Lᴏʀᴅ God of Israel:

"*There is* an accursed thing in your midst, O Israel; you cannot stand before your enemies until you take away the accursed thing from among you." [14]In the morning therefore you shall be brought according to your tribes. And it shall be *that* the tribe which the LORD takes shall come according to families; and the family which the LORD takes shall come by households; and the household which the LORD takes shall come man by man. [15]Then it shall be *that* he who is taken with the accursed thing shall be burned with fire, he and all that he has, because he has transgressed the covenant of the LORD, and because he has done a disgraceful thing in Israel.' "

LUKE 15:1-32

THEN all the tax collectors and the sinners drew near to Him [Jesus] to hear Him. [2]And the Pharisees and scribes complained, saying, "This Man receives sinners and eats with them." [3]So He spoke this parable to them, saying:

[4]"What man of you, having a hundred sheep, if he loses one of them, does not leave the ninety-nine in the wilderness, and go after the one which is lost until he finds it? [5]And when he has found *it,* he lays *it* on his shoulders, rejoicing. [6]And when he comes home, he calls together *his* friends and neighbors, saying to them, 'Rejoice with me, for I have found my sheep which was lost!' [7]I say to you that likewise there will be more joy in heaven over one sinner who repents than over ninety-nine just persons who need no repentance.

[8]"Or what woman, having ten silver coins,* if she loses one coin, does not light a lamp, sweep the house, and search carefully until she finds *it?* [9]And when she has found *it,* she calls *her* friends and neighbors together, saying, 'Rejoice with me, for I have found the piece which I lost!' [10]Likewise, I say to you, there is joy in the presence of the angels of God over one sinner who repents."

[11]Then He said: "A certain man had two sons. [12]And the younger of them said to *his* father, 'Father, give me the portion of goods that falls *to me.*' So he divided to them *his* livelihood. [13]And not many days after, the younger son gathered all together, journeyed to a far country, and there wasted his possessions with prodigal living. [14]But when he had spent all, there arose a severe famine in that land, and he began to be in want. [15]Then he went and joined himself to a citizen of that country, and he sent him into his fields to feed swine. [16]And he would gladly have filled his stomach with the pods that the swine ate, and no one gave him *anything.*

[17]"But when he came to himself, he said, 'How many of my father's hired servants have bread enough and to spare, and I perish with hunger! [18]I will arise and go to my father, and will say to him, "Father, I have sinned against heaven and before you, [19]and I am no longer worthy to be called your son. Make me like one of your hired servants." '

[20]"And he arose and came to his father. But when he was still a great way off, his father saw him and had compassion, and ran and fell on his neck and kissed him. [21]And the son said to him, 'Father, I have sinned against heaven and in your sight, and am no longer worthy to be called your son.'

[22]"But the father said to his servants, 'Bring* out the best robe and put *it* on him, and put a ring on his hand and sandals on *his* feet. [23]And bring the fatted calf here and kill *it,* and let us eat and be merry; [24]for this my son was dead and is alive again; he was lost and is found.' And they began to be merry.

25"Now his older son was in the field. And as he came and drew near to the house, he heard music and dancing. 26So he called one of the servants and asked what these things meant. 27And he said to him, 'Your brother has come, and because he has received him safe and sound, your father has killed the fatted calf.'

28"But he was angry and would not go in. Therefore his father came out and pleaded with him. 29So he answered and said to *his* father, 'Lo, these many years I have been serving you; I never transgressed your commandment at any time; and yet you never gave me a young goat, that I might make merry with my friends. 30But as soon as this son of yours came, who has devoured your livelihood with harlots, you killed the fatted calf for him.'

31"And he said to him, 'Son, you are always with me, and all that I have is yours. 32It was right that we should make merry and be glad, for your brother was dead and is alive again, and was lost and is found.' "

PSALM 81:1-16

To the Chief Musician. On an instrument of Gath. * *A Psalm of Asaph.*

S ING aloud to God our strength;
Make a joyful shout to the God of Jacob.
2   Raise a song and strike the timbrel,
The pleasant harp with the lute.

3   Blow the trumpet at the time of the New Moon,
At the full moon, on our solemn feast day.
4   For this *is* a statute for Israel,
A law of the God of Jacob.
5   This He established in Joseph *as* a testimony,

When He went throughout the land of Egypt,
Where I heard a language I did not understand.

6   "I removed his shoulder from the burden;
His hands were freed from the baskets.
7   You called in trouble, and I delivered you;
I answered you in the secret place of thunder;
I tested you at the waters of Meribah.   Selah

8   "Hear, O My people, and I will admonish you!
O Israel, if you will listen to Me!
9   There shall be no foreign god among you;
Nor shall you worship any foreign god.
10   I *am* the LORD your God,
Who brought you out of the land of Egypt;
Open your mouth wide, and I will fill it.

11   "But My people would not heed My voice,
And Israel would *have* none of Me.
12   So I gave them over to their own stubborn heart,
To walk in their own counsels.

13   "Oh, that My people would listen to Me,
That Israel would walk in My ways!
14   I would soon subdue their enemies,
And turn My hand against their adversaries.
15   The haters of the LORD would pretend submission to Him,
But their fate would endure forever.

16 He would have fed them also
with the finest of wheat;

And with honey from the rock
I would have satisfied you."

PROVERBS FOR TODAY/ 13:1

A wise son heeds *his father's instruction, but a scoffer does not listen to rebuke.*

APRIL 13

JOSHUA 7:16–9:2

So Joshua rose early in the morning and brought Israel by their tribes, and the tribe of Judah was taken. 17He brought the clan of Judah, and he took the family of the Zarhites; and he brought the family of the Zarhites man by man, and Zabdi was taken. 18Then he brought his household man by man, and Achan the son of Carmi, the son of Zabdi, the son of Zerah, of the tribe of Judah, was taken.

19Now Joshua said to Achan, "My son, I beg you, give glory to the LORD God of Israel, and make confession to Him, and tell me now what you have done; do not hide *it* from me."

20And Achan answered Joshua and said, "Indeed I have sinned against the LORD God of Israel, and this is what I have done: 21When I saw among the spoils a beautiful Babylonian garment, two hundred shekels of silver, and a wedge of gold weighing fifty shekels, I coveted them and took them. And there they are, hidden in the earth in the midst of my tent, with the silver under it."

22So Joshua sent messengers, and they ran to the tent; and there it was, hidden in his tent, with the silver under it. 23And they took them from the midst of the tent, brought them to Joshua and to all the children of Israel, and laid them out before the LORD.

24Then Joshua, and all Israel with him, took Achan the son of Zerah, the silver, the garment, the wedge of gold, his sons, his daughters, his oxen, his donkeys, his sheep, his tent, and all that he had, and they brought them to the Valley of Achor. 25And Joshua said, "Why have you troubled us? The LORD will trouble you this day." So all Israel stoned him with stones; and they burned them with fire after they had stoned them with stones.

26Then they raised over him a great heap of stones, still there to this day. So the LORD turned from the fierceness of His anger. Therefore the name of that place has been called the Valley of Achor* to this day.

Now the LORD said to Joshua: "Do not be afraid, nor be dismayed; take all the people of war with you, and arise, go up to Ai. See, I have given into your hand the king of Ai, his people, his city, and his land. 2And you shall do to Ai and its king as you did to Jericho and its king. Only its spoil and its cattle you shall take as booty for yourselves. Lay an ambush for the city behind it."

3So Joshua arose, and all the people of war, to go up against Ai; and Joshua chose thirty thousand mighty men of valor and sent them away by night. 4And he commanded them, saying: "Behold, you shall lie in ambush against the city, behind the city. Do not go very far from the city, but all of you be ready. ⁵Then I and all the people who *are* with me will approach the city; and it will come about, when they come out against us as at the first, that we shall flee before them. ⁶For they will come out after us till we have drawn them from the city, for they will say, '*They are* fleeing before us as at the first.' Therefore we will flee before them. ⁷Then you shall rise from the ambush and seize the city, for the LORD your God will deliver it into your hand. ⁸And it will be, when you have taken the city, *that* you shall set the city on fire. According to the commandment of the LORD you shall do. See, I have commanded you."

⁹Joshua therefore sent them out; and they went to lie in ambush, and stayed between Bethel and Ai, on the west side of Ai; but Joshua lodged that night among the people. ¹⁰Then Joshua rose up early in the morning and mustered the people, and went up, he and the elders of Israel, before the people to Ai. ¹¹And all the people of war who *were* with him went up and drew near; and they came before the city and camped on the north side of Ai. Now a valley *lay* between them and Ai. ¹²So he took about five thousand men and set them in ambush between Bethel and Ai, on the west side of the city. ¹³And when they had set the people, all the army that *was* on the north of the city, and its rear guard on the west of the city, Joshua went that night into the midst of the valley.

¹⁴Now it happened, when the king of Ai saw *it,* that the men of the city hurried and rose early and went out against Israel to battle, he and all his people, at an appointed place before the plain. But he did not know that *there was* an ambush against him behind the city. ¹⁵And Joshua and all Israel made as if they were beaten before them, and fled by the way of the wilderness. ¹⁶So all the people who

were in Ai were called together to pursue them. And they pursued Joshua and were drawn away from the city. ¹⁷There was not a man left in Ai or Bethel who did not go out after Israel. So they left the city open and pursued Israel.

¹⁸Then the LORD said to Joshua, "Stretch out the spear that *is* in your hand toward Ai, for I will give it into your hand." And Joshua stretched out the spear that *was* in his hand toward the city. ¹⁹So *those in* ambush arose quickly out of their place; they ran as soon as he had stretched out his hand, and they entered the city and took it, and hurried to set the city on fire. ²⁰And when the men of Ai looked behind them, they saw, and behold, the smoke of the city ascended to heaven. So they had no power to flee this way or that way, and the people who had fled to the wilderness turned back on the pursuers. ²¹Now when Joshua and all Israel saw that the ambush had taken the city and that the smoke of the city ascended, they turned back and struck down the men of Ai. ²²Then the others came out of the city against them; so they were *caught* in the midst of Israel, some on this side and some on that side. And they struck them down, so that they let none of them remain or escape. ²³But the king of Ai they took alive, and brought him to Joshua.

²⁴And it came to pass when Israel had made an end of slaying all the inhabitants of Ai in the field, in the wilderness where they pursued them, and when they all had fallen by the edge of the sword until they were consumed, that all the Israelites returned to Ai and struck it with the edge of the sword. ²⁵So it was *that* all who fell that day, both men and women, *were* twelve thousand—all the people of Ai. ²⁶For Joshua did not draw back his hand, with which he stretched out the spear, until he had utterly destroyed

all the inhabitants of Ai. ²⁷Only the livestock and the spoil of that city Israel took as booty for themselves, according to the word of the Lᴏʀᴅ which He had commanded Joshua. ²⁸So Joshua burned Ai and made it a heap forever, a desolation to this day. ²⁹And the king of Ai he hanged on a tree until evening. And as soon as the sun was down, Joshua commanded that they should take his corpse down from the tree, cast it at the entrance of the gate of the city, and raise over it a great heap of stones *that remains* to this day.

³⁰Now Joshua built an altar to the Lᴏʀᴅ God of Israel in Mount Ebal, ³¹as Moses the servant of the Lᴏʀᴅ had commanded the children of Israel, as it is written in the Book of the Law of Moses: "an altar of whole stones over which no man has wielded an iron *tool.*"* And they offered on it burnt offerings to the Lᴏʀᴅ, and sacrificed peace offerings. ³²And there, in the presence of the children of Israel, he wrote on the stones a copy of the law of Moses, which he had written. ³³Then all Israel, with their elders and officers and judges, stood on either side of the ark before the priests, the Levites, who bore the ark of the covenant of the Lᴏʀᴅ, the stranger as well as he who was born among them. Half of them *were* in front of Mount Gerizim and half of them in front of Mount Ebal, as Moses the servant of the Lᴏʀᴅ had commanded before, that they should bless the people of Israel. ³⁴And afterward he read all the words of the law, the blessings and the cursings, according to all that is written in the Book of the Law. ³⁵There was not a word of all that Moses had commanded which Joshua did not read before all the assembly of Israel, with the women, the little ones, and the strangers who were living among them.

Aɴᴅ it came to pass when all the kings who *were* on this side of the Jordan, in the hills and in the lowland and in all the coasts of the Great Sea toward Lebanon—the Hittite, the Amorite, the Canaanite, the Perizzite, the Hivite, and the Jebusite—heard *about it,* ²that they gathered together to fight with Joshua and Israel with one accord.

LUKE 16:1-18

Hᴇ [Jesus] also said to His disciples: "There was a certain rich man who had a steward, and an accusation was brought to him that this man was wasting his goods. ²So he called him and said to him, 'What is this I hear about you? Give an account of your stewardship, for you can no longer be steward.'

³"Then the steward said within himself, 'What shall I do? For my master is taking the stewardship away from me. I cannot dig; I am ashamed to beg. ⁴I have resolved what to do, that when I am put out of the stewardship, they may receive me into their houses.'

⁵"So he called every one of his master's debtors to *him,* and said to the first, 'How much do you owe my master?' ⁶And he said, 'A hundred measures* of oil.' So he said to him, 'Take your bill, and sit down quickly and write fifty.' ⁷Then he said to another, 'And how much do you owe?' So he said, 'A hundred measures* of wheat.' And he said to him, 'Take your bill, and write eighty.' ⁸So the master commended the unjust steward because he had dealt shrewdly. For the sons of this world are more shrewd in their generation than the sons of light.

⁹"And I say to you, make friends for yourselves by unrighteous mammon, that when you fail,* they may receive you into an everlasting home. ¹⁰He who *is* faithful in *what is* least is faithful also in much; and he who is unjust in *what is* least is unjust also in much.

11Therefore if you have not been faithful in the unrighteous mammon, who will commit to your trust the true *riches?* 12And if you have not been faithful in what is another man's, who will give you what is your own?

13"No servant can serve two masters; for either he will hate the one and love the other, or else he will be loyal to the one and despise the other. You cannot serve God and mammon."

14Now the Pharisees, who were lovers of money, also heard all these things, and they derided Him. 15And He said to them, "You are those who justify yourselves before men, but God knows your hearts. For what is highly esteemed among men is an abomination in the sight of God.

16"The law and the prophets *were* until John. Since that time the kingdom of God has been preached, and everyone is pressing into it. 17And it is easier for heaven and earth to pass away than for one tittle of the law to fail.

18"Whoever divorces his wife and marries another commits adultery; and whoever marries her who is divorced from *her* husband commits adultery."

PSALM 82:1-8

A Psalm of Asaph.

G OD stands in the congregation of the mighty;
He judges among the gods.*

2 How long will you judge unjustly,
And show partiality to the wicked?   Selah

3 Defend the poor and fatherless;
Do justice to the afflicted and needy.

4 Deliver the poor and needy;
Free *them* from the hand of the wicked.

5 They do not know, nor do they understand;
They walk about in darkness;
All the foundations of the earth are unstable.

6 I said, "You *are* gods,*
And all of you *are* children of the Most High.

7 But you shall die like men,
And fall like one of the princes."

8 Arise, O God, judge the earth;
For You shall inherit all nations.

PROVERBS FOR TODAY/ 13:2-3

A man shall eat well by the fruit of his *mouth, but the soul of the unfaithful feeds on violence. He who guards his mouth preserves his life,* but *he who opens wide his lips shall have destruction.*

JOSHUA 9:3–10:43

BUT when the inhabitants of Gibeon heard what Joshua had done to Jericho and Ai, ⁴they worked craftily, and went and pretended to be ambassadors. And they took old sacks on their donkeys, old wineskins torn and mended, ⁵old and patched sandals on their feet, and old garments on themselves; and all the bread of their provision was dry *and* moldy. ⁶And they went to Joshua, to the camp at Gilgal, and said to him and to the men of Israel, "We have come from a far country; now therefore, make a covenant with us."

⁷Then the men of Israel said to the Hivites, "Perhaps you dwell among us; so how can we make a covenant with you?"

⁸But they said to Joshua, "We *are* your servants."

And Joshua said to them, "Who *are* you, and where do you come from?"

⁹So they said to him: "From a very far country your servants have come, because of the name of the LORD your God; for we have heard of His fame, and all that He did in Egypt, ¹⁰and all that He did to the two kings of the Amorites who *were* beyond the Jordan— to Sihon king of Heshbon, and Og king of Bashan, who was at Ashtaroth. ¹¹Therefore our elders and all the inhabitants of our country spoke to us, saying, 'Take provisions with you for the journey, and go to meet them, and say to them, "We *are* your servants; now therefore, make a covenant with us." ' ¹²This bread of ours we took hot *for* our provision from our houses on the day we departed to come to you. But now look, it is dry and moldy. ¹³And these wineskins which we filled *were* new, and see, they are torn; and

these our garments and our sandals have become old because of the very long journey."

¹⁴Then the men of Israel took some of their provisions; but they did not ask counsel of the LORD. ¹⁵So Joshua made peace with them, and made a covenant with them to let them live; and the rulers of the congregation swore to them.

¹⁶And it happened at the end of three days, after they had made a covenant with them, that they heard that they *were* their neighbors who dwelt near them. ¹⁷Then the children of Israel journeyed and came to their cities on the third day. Now their cities *were* Gibeon, Chephirah, Beeroth, and Kirjath Jearim. ¹⁸But the children of Israel did not attack them, because the rulers of the congregation had sworn to them by the LORD God of Israel. And all the congregation complained against the rulers.

¹⁹Then all the rulers said to all the congregation, "We have sworn to them by the LORD God of Israel; now therefore, we may not touch them. ²⁰This we will do to them: We will let them live, lest wrath be upon us because of the oath which we swore to them." ²¹And the rulers said to them, "Let them live, but let them be woodcutters and water carriers for all the congregation, as the rulers had promised them."

²²Then Joshua called for them, and he spoke to them, saying, "Why have you deceived us, saying, 'We *are* very far from you,' when you dwell near us? ²³Now therefore, you *are* cursed, and none of you shall be freed from being slaves—woodcutters and water carriers for the house of my God."

²⁴So they answered Joshua and said, "Because your servants were clearly

told that the LORD your God commanded His servant Moses to give you all the land, and to destroy all the inhabitants of the land from before you; therefore we were very much afraid for our lives because of you, and have done this thing. 25And now, here we are, in your hands; do with us as it seems good and right to do to us." 26So he did to them, and delivered them out of the hand of the children of Israel, so that they did not kill them. 27And that day Joshua made them woodcutters and water carriers for the congregation and for the altar of the LORD, in the place which He would choose, even to this day.

NOW it came to pass when Adoni-Zedek king of Jerusalem heard how Joshua had taken Ai and had utterly destroyed it—as he had done to Jericho and its king, so he had done to Ai and its king—and how the inhabitants of Gibeon had made peace with Israel and were among them, 2that they feared greatly, because Gibeon *was* a great city, like one of the royal cities, and because it *was* greater than Ai, and all its men *were* mighty. 3Therefore Adoni-Zedek king of Jerusalem sent to Hoham king of Hebron, Piram king of Jarmuth, Japhia king of Lachish, and Debir king of Eglon, saying, 4"Come up to me and help me, that we may attack Gibeon, for it has made peace with Joshua and with the children of Israel." 5Therefore the five kings of the Amorites, the king of Jerusalem, the king of Hebron, the king of Jarmuth, the king of Lachish, *and* the king of Eglon, gathered together and went up, they and all their armies, and camped before Gibeon and made war against it.

6And the men of Gibeon sent to Joshua at the camp at Gilgal, saying, "Do not forsake your servants; come up to us quickly, save us and help us, for all the kings of the Amorites who dwell in the mountains have gathered together against us."

7So Joshua ascended from Gilgal, he and all the people of war with him, and all the mighty men of valor. 8And the LORD said to Joshua, "Do not fear them, for I have delivered them into your hand; not a man of them shall stand before you." 9Joshua therefore came upon them suddenly, having marched all night from Gilgal. 10So the LORD routed them before Israel, killed them with a great slaughter at Gibeon, chased them along the road that goes to Beth Horon, and struck them down as far as Azekah and Makkedah. 11And it happened, as they fled before Israel *and* were on the descent of Beth Horon, that the LORD cast down large hailstones from heaven on them as far as Azekah, and they died. *There were* more who died from the hailstones than the children of Israel killed with the sword.

12Then Joshua spoke to the LORD in the day when the LORD delivered up the Amorites before the children of Israel, and he said in the sight of Israel:

> "Sun, stand still over Gibeon;
> And Moon, in the Valley of
>   Aijalon."
> 13   So the sun stood still,
>   And the moon stopped,
>   Till the people had revenge
>   Upon their enemies.

Is this not written in the Book of Jasher? So the sun stood still in the midst of heaven, and did not hasten to go *down* for about a whole day. 14And there has been no day like that, before it or after it, that the LORD heeded the voice of a man; for the LORD fought for Israel.

15Then Joshua returned, and all Israel with him, to the camp at Gilgal.

16But these five kings had fled and hidden themselves in a cave at Makkedah. 17And it was told Joshua, saying,

"The five kings have been found hidden in the cave at Makkedah."

¹⁸So Joshua said, "Roll large stones against the mouth of the cave, and set men by it to guard them. ¹⁹And do not stay *there* yourselves, *but* pursue your enemies, and attack their rear *guard.* Do not allow them to enter their cities, for the Lord your God has delivered them into your hand." ²⁰Then it happened, while Joshua and the children of Israel made an end of slaying them with a very great slaughter, till they had finished, that those who escaped entered fortified cities. ²¹And all the people returned to the camp, to Joshua at Makkedah, in peace.

No one moved his tongue against any of the children of Israel.

²²Then Joshua said, "Open the mouth of the cave, and bring out those five kings to me from the cave." ²³And they did so, and brought out those five kings to him from the cave: the king of Jerusalem, the king of Hebron, the king of Jarmuth, the king of Lachish, *and* the king of Eglon.

²⁴So it was, when they brought out those kings to Joshua, that Joshua called for all the men of Israel, and said to the captains of the men of war who went with him, "Come near, put your feet on the necks of these kings." And they drew near and put their feet on their necks. ²⁵Then Joshua said to them, "Do not be afraid, nor be dismayed; be strong and of good courage, for thus the Lord will do to all your enemies against whom you fight." ²⁶And afterward Joshua struck them and killed them, and hanged them on five trees; and they were hanging on the trees until evening. ²⁷So it was at the time of the going down of the sun *that* Joshua commanded, and they took them down from the trees, cast them into the cave where they had been hidden, and laid large stones against the cave's mouth, *which remain* until this very day.

²⁸On that day Joshua took Makkedah, and struck it and its king with the edge of the sword. He utterly destroyed them*—all the people who *were* in it. He let none remain. He also did to the king of Makkedah as he had done to the king of Jericho.

²⁹Then Joshua passed from Makkedah, and all Israel with him, to Libnah; and they fought against Libnah. ³⁰And the Lord also delivered it and its king into the hand of Israel; he struck it and all the people who *were* in it with the edge of the sword. He let none remain in it, but did to its king as he had done to the king of Jericho.

³¹Then Joshua passed from Libnah, and all Israel with him, to Lachish; and they encamped against it and fought against it. ³²And the Lord delivered Lachish into the hand of Israel, who took it on the second day, and struck it and all the people who *were* in it with the edge of the sword, according to all that he had done to Libnah. ³³Then Horam king of Gezer came up to help Lachish; and Joshua struck him and his people, until he left him none remaining.

³⁴From Lachish Joshua passed to Eglon, and all Israel with him; and they encamped against it and fought against it. ³⁵They took it on that day and struck it with the edge of the sword; all the people who *were* in it he utterly destroyed that day, according to all that he had done to Lachish.

³⁶So Joshua went up from Eglon, and all Israel with him, to Hebron; and they fought against it. ³⁷And they took it and struck it with the edge of the sword—its king, all its cities, and all the people who *were* in it; he left none remaining, according to all that he had done to Eglon, but utterly destroyed it and all the people who *were* in it.

³⁸Then Joshua returned, and all Israel with him, to Debir; and they fought against it. ³⁹And he took it and its king and all its cities; they struck them with the edge of the sword and

utterly destroyed all the people who *were* in it. He left none remaining; as he had done to Hebron, so he did to Debir and its king, as he had done also to Libnah and its king.

⁴⁰So Joshua conquered all the land: the mountain country and the South* and the lowland and the wilderness slopes, and all their kings; he left none remaining, but utterly destroyed all that breathed, as the LORD God of Israel had commanded. ⁴¹And Joshua conquered them from Kadesh Barnea as far as Gaza, and all the country of Goshen, even as far as Gibeon. ⁴²All these kings and their land Joshua took at one time, because the LORD God of Israel fought for Israel. ⁴³Then Joshua returned, and all Israel with him, to the camp at Gilgal.

LUKE 16:19–17:10

"**T**HERE was a certain rich man who was clothed in purple and fine linen and fared sumptuously every day. ²⁰But there was a certain beggar named Lazarus, full of sores, who was laid at his gate, ²¹desiring to be fed with the crumbs which fell* from the rich man's table. Moreover the dogs came and licked his sores. ²²So it was that the beggar died, and was carried by the angels to Abraham's bosom. The rich man also died and was buried. ²³And being in torments in Hades, he lifted up his eyes and saw Abraham afar off, and Lazarus in his bosom.

²⁴"Then he cried and said, 'Father Abraham, have mercy on me, and send Lazarus that he may dip the tip of his finger in water and cool my tongue; for I am tormented in this flame.' ²⁵But Abraham said, 'Son, remember that in your lifetime you received your good things, and likewise Lazarus evil things; but now he is comforted and you are tormented. ²⁶And besides all this, between us and you there is a great gulf fixed, so that those who want to pass from here to you cannot, nor can those from there pass to us.'

²⁷"Then he said, 'I beg you therefore, father, that you would send him to my father's house, ²⁸for I have five brothers, that he may testify to them, lest they also come to this place of torment.' ²⁹Abraham said to him, 'They have Moses and the prophets; let them hear them.' ³⁰And he said, 'No, father Abraham; but if one goes to them from the dead, they will repent.' ³¹But he said to him, 'If they do not hear Moses and the prophets, neither will they be persuaded though one rise from the dead.'"

THEN He said to the disciples, "It is impossible that no offenses should come, but woe *to him* through whom they do come! ²It would be better for him if a millstone were hung around his neck, and he were thrown into the sea, than that he should offend one of these little ones. ³Take heed to yourselves. If your brother sins against you,* rebuke him; and if he repents, forgive him. ⁴And if he sins against you seven times in a day, and seven times in a day returns to you,* saying, 'I repent,' you shall forgive him."

⁵And the apostles said to the Lord, "Increase our faith."

⁶So the Lord said, "If you have faith as a mustard seed, you can say to this mulberry tree, 'Be pulled up by the roots and be planted in the sea,' and it would obey you. ⁷And which of you, having a servant plowing or tending sheep, will say to him when he has come in from the field, 'Come at once and sit down to eat'? ⁸But will he not rather say to him, 'Prepare something for my supper, and gird yourself and serve me till I have eaten and drunk, and afterward you will eat and drink'? ⁹Does he thank that servant because he did the things that were com-

manded him? I think not.* [10]So likewise you, when you have done all
those things which you are commanded, say, 'We are unprofitable servants. We have done what was our
duty to do.' "

PSALM 83:1-18

A Song. A Psalm of Asaph.

D o not keep silent, O God!
Do not hold Your peace,
And do not be still, O God!

2 For behold, Your enemies
make a tumult;
And those who hate You have
lifted up their head.

3 They have taken crafty
counsel against Your
people,
And consulted together
against Your sheltered ones.

4 They have said, "Come, and
let us cut them off from
being a nation,
That the name of Israel may
be remembered no more."

5 For they have consulted
together with one consent;
They form a confederacy
against You:

6 The tents of Edom and the
Ishmaelites;
Moab and the Hagrites;

7 Gebal, Ammon, and Amalek;
Philistia with the inhabitants
of Tyre;

8 Assyria also has joined with
them;
They have helped the
children of Lot.   Selah

9 Deal with them as *with*
Midian,
As *with* Sisera,
As *with* Jabin at the Brook
Kishon,

10 Who perished at En Dor,
Who became *as* refuse on the
earth.

11 Make their nobles like Oreb
and like Zeeb,
Yes, all their princes like
Zebah and Zalmunna,

12 Who said, "Let us take for
ourselves
The pastures of God for a
possession."

13 O my God, make them like
the whirling dust,
Like the chaff before the wind!

14 As the fire burns the woods,
And as the flame sets the
mountains on fire,

15 So pursue them with Your
tempest,
And frighten them with Your
storm.

16 Fill their faces with shame,
That they may seek Your
name, O LORD.

17 Let them be confounded and
dismayed forever;
Yes, let them be put to shame
and perish,

18 That they may know that You,
whose name alone *is* the
LORD,
Are the Most High over all
the earth.

PROVERBS FOR TODAY/ 13:4

*The soul of a lazy man desires, and has nothing; but the soul of the diligent shall
be made rich.*

APRIL 15

JOSHUA 11:1–12:24

AND it came to pass, when Jabin king of Hazor heard *these things,* that he sent to Jobab king of Madon, to the king of Shimron, to the king of Achshaph, [2]and to the kings who *were* from the north, in the mountains, in the plain south of Chinneroth, in the lowland, and in the heights of Dor on the west, [3]to the Canaanites in the east and in the west, the Amorite, the Hittite, the Perizzite, the Jebusite in the mountains, and the Hivite below Hermon in the land of Mizpah. [4]So they went out, they and all their armies with them, *as* many people *as* the sand that *is* on the seashore in multitude, with very many horses and chariots. [5]And when all these kings had met together, they came and camped together at the waters of Merom to fight against Israel.

[6]But the Lord said to Joshua, "Do not be afraid because of them, for tomorrow about this time I will deliver all of them slain before Israel. You shall hamstring their horses and burn their chariots with fire." [7]So Joshua and all the people of war with him came against them suddenly by the waters of Merom, and they attacked them. [8]And the Lord delivered them into the hand of Israel, who defeated them and chased them to Greater Sidon, to the Brook Misrephoth,* and to the Valley of Mizpah eastward; they attacked them until they left none of them remaining. [9]So Joshua did to them as the Lord had told him: he hamstrung their horses and burned their chariots with fire.

[10]Joshua turned back at that time and took Hazor, and struck its king with the sword; for Hazor was formerly the head of all those kingdoms. [11]And they struck all the people who *were* in it with the edge of the sword, utterly destroying *them.* There was none left breathing. Then he burned Hazor with fire.

[12]So all the cities of those kings, and all their kings, Joshua took and struck with the edge of the sword. He utterly destroyed them, as Moses the servant of the Lord had commanded. [13]But *as for* the cities that stood on their mounds,* Israel burned none of them, except Hazor only, *which* Joshua burned. [14]And all the spoil of these cities and the livestock, the children of Israel took as booty for themselves; but they struck every man with the edge of the sword until they had destroyed them, and they left none breathing. [15]As the Lord had commanded Moses his servant, so Moses commanded Joshua, and so Joshua did. He left nothing undone of all that the Lord had commanded Moses.

[16]Thus Joshua took all this land: the mountain country, all the South, all the land of Goshen, the lowland, and the Jordan plain*—the mountains of Israel and its lowlands, [17]from Mount Halak and the ascent to Seir, even as far as Baal Gad in the Valley of Lebanon below Mount Hermon. He captured all their kings, and struck them down and killed them. [18]Joshua made war a long time with all those kings. [19]There was not a city that made peace with the children of Israel, except the Hivites, the inhabitants of Gibeon. All *the others* they took in battle. [20]For it was of the Lord to harden their hearts, that they should come against Israel in battle, that He might utterly destroy them, *and* that they might receive no

mercy, but that He might destroy them, as the LORD had commanded Moses.

²¹And at that time Joshua came and cut off the Anakim from the mountains: from Hebron, from Debir, from Anab, from all the mountains of Judah, and from all the mountains of Israel; Joshua utterly destroyed them with their cities. ²²None of the Anakim were left in the land of the children of Israel; they remained only in Gaza, in Gath, and in Ashdod.

²³So Joshua took the whole land, according to all that the LORD had said to Moses; and Joshua gave it as an inheritance to Israel according to their divisions by their tribes. Then the land rested from war.

THESE *are* the kings of the land whom the children of Israel defeated, and whose land they possessed on the other side of the Jordan toward the rising of the sun, from the River Arnon to Mount Hermon, and all the eastern Jordan plain: ²*One king was* Sihon king of the Amorites, who dwelt in Heshbon *and* ruled half of Gilead, from Aroer, which is on the bank of the River Arnon, from the middle of that river, even as far as the River Jabbok, *which is* the border of the Ammonites, ³and the eastern Jordan plain from the Sea of Chinneroth as far as the Sea of the Arabah (the Salt Sea), the road to Beth Jeshimoth, and southward below the slopes of Pisgah. ⁴*The other king was* Og king of Bashan and his territory, *who was* of the remnant of the giants, who dwelt at Ashtaroth and at Edrei, ⁵and reigned over Mount Hermon, over Salcah, over all Bashan, as far as the border of the Geshurites and the Maachathites, and over half of Gilead *to* the border of Sihon king of Heshbon. ⁶These Moses the servant of the LORD and the children of Israel had conquered; and Moses the servant of

the LORD had given it *as* a possession to the Reubenites, the Gadites, and half the tribe of Manasseh.

⁷And these *are* the kings of the country which Joshua and the children of Israel conquered on this side of the Jordan, on the west, from Baal Gad in the Valley of Lebanon as far as Mount Halak and the ascent to Seir, which Joshua gave to the tribes of Israel *as* a possession according to their divisions, ⁸in the mountain country, in the lowlands, in the *Jordan* plain, in the slopes, in the wilderness, and in the South—the Hittites, the Amorites, the Canaanites, the Perizzites, the Hivites, and the Jebusites: ⁹the king of Jericho, one; the king of Ai, which *is* beside Bethel, one; ¹⁰the king of Jerusalem, one; the king of Hebron, one; ¹¹the king of Jarmuth, one; the king of Lachish, one; ¹²the king of Eglon, one; the king of Gezer, one; ¹³the king of Debir, one; the king of Geder, one; ¹⁴the king of Hormah, one; the king of Arad, one; ¹⁵the king of Libnah, one; the king of Adullam, one; ¹⁶the king of Makkedah, one; the king of Bethel, one; ¹⁷the king of Tappuah, one; the king of Hepher, one; ¹⁸the king of Aphek, one; the king of Lasharon, one; ¹⁹the king of Madon, one; the king of Hazor, one; ²⁰the king of Shimron Meron, one; the king of Achshaph, one; ²¹the king of Taanach, one; the king of Megiddo, one; ²²the king of Kedesh, one; the king of Jokneam in Carmel, one; ²³the king of Dor in the heights of Dor, one; the king of the people of Gilgal, one; ²⁴the king of Tirzah, one—all the kings, thirty-one.

LUKE 17:11-37

Now it happened as He [Jesus] went to Jerusalem that He passed through the midst of Samaria and Galilee. ¹²Then as He entered a certain village, there met Him ten men who were lepers, who stood afar off. 13And they lifted up *their* voices and said, "Jesus, Master, have mercy on us!"

14So when He saw *them,* He said to them, "Go, show yourselves to the priests." And so it was that as they went, they were cleansed.

15And one of them, when he saw that he was healed, returned, and with a loud voice glorified God, 16and fell down on *his* face at His feet, giving Him thanks. And he was a Samaritan.

17So Jesus answered and said, "Were there not ten cleansed? But where *are* the nine? 18Were there not any found who returned to give glory to God except this foreigner?" 19And He said to him, "Arise, go your way. Your faith has made you well."

20Now when He was asked by the Pharisees when the kingdom of God would come, He answered them and said, "The kingdom of God does not come with observation; 21nor will they say, 'See here!' or 'See there!'* For indeed, the kingdom of God is within you."

22Then He said to the disciples, "The days will come when you will desire to see one of the days of the Son of Man, and you will not see *it.* 23And they will say to you, 'Look here!' or 'Look there!'* Do not go after *them* or follow *them.* 24For as the lightning that flashes out of one *part* under heaven shines to the other *part* under heaven, so also the Son of Man will be in His day. 25But first He must suffer many things and be rejected by this generation. 26And as it was in the days of Noah, so it will be also in the days of the Son of Man: 27They ate, they drank, they married wives, they were given in marriage, until the day that Noah entered the ark, and the flood came and destroyed them all. 28Likewise as it was also in the days of Lot: They ate, they drank, they bought, they sold, they planted, they built;

29but on the day that Lot went out of Sodom it rained fire and brimstone from heaven and destroyed *them* all. 30Even so will it be in the day when the Son of Man is revealed.

31"In that day, he who is on the housetop, and his goods *are* in the house, let him not come down to take them away. And likewise the one who is in the field, let him not turn back. 32Remember Lot's wife. 33Whoever seeks to save his life will lose it, and whoever loses his life will preserve it. 34I tell you, in that night there will be two *men* in one bed: the one will be taken and the other will be left. 35Two *women* will be grinding together: the one will be taken and the other left. 36Two *men* will be in the field: the one will be taken and the other left."*

37And they answered and said to Him, "Where, Lord?"

So He said to them, "Wherever the body is, there the eagles will be gathered together."

PSALM 84:1-12

To the Chief Musician. On an instrument of Gath. A Psalm of the sons of Korah.*

How lovely *is* Your tabernacle,
O Lord of hosts!
2My soul longs, yes, even
faints
For the courts of the Lord;
My heart and my flesh cry
out for the living God.

3   Even the sparrow has found a
home,
And the swallow a nest for
herself,
Where she may lay her
young—
Even Your altars, O Lord of
hosts,
My King and my God.
4   Blessed *are* those who dwell
in Your house;

They will still be praising You.
Selah

5 Blessed *is* the man whose
strength *is* in You,
Whose heart *is* set on
pilgrimage.
6 *As they* pass through the
Valley of Baca,
They make it a spring;
The rain also covers it with
pools.
7 They go from strength to
strength;
Each one appears before God
in Zion.*

8 O Lord God of hosts, hear my
prayer;
Give ear, O God of Jacob!
Selah
9 O God, behold our shield,

And look upon the face of
Your anointed.

10 For a day in Your courts *is*
better than a thousand.
I would rather be a
doorkeeper in the house of
my God
Than dwell in the tents of
wickedness.
11 For the Lord God *is* a sun and
shield;
The Lord will give grace and
glory;
No good *thing* will He
withhold
From those who walk
uprightly.

12 O Lord of hosts,
Blessed *is* the man who trusts
in You!

PROVERBS FOR TODAY/ 13:5-6

A righteous man *hates lying, but a wicked* man *is loathsome and comes to shame.
Righteousness guards* him whose *way is blameless, but wickedness overthrows the
sinner.*

APRIL 16

JOSHUA 13:1–14:15

Now Joshua was old, advanced in years. And the Lord said to him: "You are old, advanced in years, and there remains very much land yet to be possessed. ²This is the land that yet remains: all the territory of the Philistines and all *that of* the Geshurites, ³from Sihor, which *is* east of Egypt, as far as the border of Ekron northward (*which* is counted as Canaanite); the five lords of the Philistines—the Gazites, the Ashdodites, the Ashkelonites, the Gittites, and the Ekronites; also the Avites; ⁴from the south, all the land of the Canaanites, and Mearah that belongs to the Sidonians as far as Aphek, to the border of the Amorites; ⁵the land of the Gebalites,* and all Lebanon, toward the sunrise, from Baal Gad below Mount Hermon as far as the entrance to Hamath; ⁶all the inhabitants of the mountains from Lebanon as far as the Brook Misrephoth,* *and* all the Sidonians—them I will drive out from before the children of Israel; only divide it by lot to Israel as an inheritance, as I have commanded you. ⁷Now therefore, divide this land as an inheritance to the nine tribes and half the tribe of Manasseh."

⁸With the other half-tribe the Reubenites and the Gadites received their inheritance, which Moses had given them, beyond the Jordan eastward, as Moses the servant of the LORD had given them: ⁹from Aroer which *is* on the bank of the River Arnon, and the town that *is* in the midst of the ravine, and all the plain of Medeba as far as Dibon; ¹⁰all the cities of Sihon king of the Amorites, who reigned in Heshbon, as far as the border of the children of Ammon; ¹¹Gilead, and the border of the Geshurites and Maachathites, all Mount Hermon, and all Bashan as far as Salcah; ¹²all the kingdom of Og in Bashan, who reigned in Ashtaroth and Edrei, who remained of the remnant of the giants; for Moses had defeated and cast out these.

¹³Nevertheless the children of Israel did not drive out the Geshurites or the Maachathites, but the Geshurites and the Maachathites dwell among the Israelites until this day.

¹⁴Only to the tribe of Levi he had given no inheritance; the sacrifices of the LORD God of Israel made by fire *are* their inheritance, as He said to them.

¹⁵And Moses had given to the tribe of the children of Reuben *an inheritance* according to their families. ¹⁶Their territory was from Aroer, which *is* on the bank of the River Arnon, and the city that *is* in the midst of the ravine, and all the plain by Medeba; ¹⁷Heshbon and all its cities that *are* in the plain: Dibon, Bamoth Baal, Beth Baal Meon, ¹⁸Jahaza, Kedemoth, Mephaath, ¹⁹Kirjathaim, Sibmah, Zereth Shahar on the mountain of the valley, ²⁰Beth Peor, the slopes of Pisgah, and Beth Jeshimoth— ²¹all the cities of the plain and all the kingdom of Sihon king of the Amorites, who reigned in Heshbon, whom Moses had struck with the princes of Midian:

Evi, Rekem, Zur, Hur, and Reba, who *were* princes of Sihon dwelling in the country. ²²The children of Israel also killed with the sword Balaam the son of Beor, the soothsayer, among those who were killed by them. ²³And the border of the children of Reuben was the bank of the Jordan. This *was* the inheritance of the children of Reuben according to their families, the cities and their villages.

²⁴Moses also had given *an inheritance* to the tribe of Gad, to the children of Gad according to their families. ²⁵Their territory was Jazer, and all the cities of Gilead, and half the land of the Ammonites as far as Aroer, which *is* before Rabbah, ²⁶and from Heshbon to Ramath Mizpah and Betonim, and from Mahanaim to the border of Debir, ²⁷and in the valley Beth Haram, Beth Nimrah, Succoth, and Zaphon, the rest of the kingdom of Sihon king of Heshbon, with the Jordan as *its* border, as far as the edge of the Sea of Chinnereth, on the other side of the Jordan eastward. ²⁸This *is* the inheritance of the children of Gad according to their families, the cities and their villages.

²⁹Moses also had given *an inheritance* to half the tribe of Manasseh; it was for half the tribe of the children of Manasseh according to their families: ³⁰Their territory was from Mahanaim, all Bashan, all the kingdom of Og king of Bashan, and all the towns of Jair which are in Bashan, sixty cities; ³¹half of Gilead, and Ashtaroth and Edrei, cities of the kingdom of Og in Bashan, *were* for the children of Machir the son of Manasseh, for half of the children of Machir according to their families.

³²These *are the areas* which Moses had distributed as an inheritance in the plains of Moab on the other side of the Jordan, by Jericho eastward. ³³But to the tribe of Levi Moses had given no inheritance; the LORD God of Israel *was*

their inheritance, as He had said to them.

THESE *are the areas* which the children of Israel inherited in the land of Canaan, which Eleazar the priest, Joshua the son of Nun, and the heads of the fathers of the tribes of the children of Israel distributed as an inheritance to them. ²Their inheritance *was* by lot, as the LORD had commanded by the hand of Moses, for the nine tribes and the half-tribe. ³For Moses had given the inheritance of the two tribes and the half-tribe on the other side of the Jordan; but to the Levites he had given no inheritance among them. ⁴For the children of Joseph were two tribes: Manasseh and Ephraim. And they gave no part to the Levites in the land, except cities to dwell *in,* with their common-lands for their livestock and their property. ⁵As the LORD had commanded Moses, so the children of Israel did; and they divided the land.

⁶Then the children of Judah came to Joshua in Gilgal. And Caleb the son of Jephunneh the Kenizzite said to him: "You know the word which the LORD said to Moses the man of God concerning you and me in Kadesh Barnea. ⁷I *was* forty years old when Moses the servant of the LORD sent me from Kadesh Barnea to spy out the land, and I brought back word to him as *it was* in my heart. ⁸Nevertheless my brethren who went up with me made the heart of the people melt, but I wholly followed the LORD my God. ⁹So Moses swore on that day, saying, 'Surely the land where your foot has trodden shall be your inheritance and your children's forever, because you have wholly followed the LORD my God.' ¹⁰And now, behold, the LORD has kept me alive, as He said, these forty-five years, ever since the LORD spoke this word to Moses while Israel wandered in the wilderness; and now, here I am this day, eighty-five years old. ¹¹As yet I *am as* strong this day as on the day that Moses sent me; just as my strength *was* then, so now *is* my strength for war, both for going out and for coming in. ¹²Now therefore, give me this mountain of which the LORD spoke in that day; for you heard in that day how the Anakim *were* there, and *that* the cities *were* great *and* fortified. It may be that the LORD *will be* with me, and I shall be able to drive them out as the LORD said."

¹³And Joshua blessed him, and gave Hebron to Caleb the son of Jephunneh as an inheritance. ¹⁴Hebron therefore became the inheritance of Caleb the son of Jephunneh the Kenizzite to this day, because he wholly followed the LORD God of Israel. ¹⁵And the name of Hebron formerly was Kirjath Arba (*Arba was* the greatest man among the Anakim).

Then the land had rest from war.

LUKE 18:1-17

THEN He [Jesus] spoke a parable to them, that men always ought to pray and not lose heart, ²saying: "There was in a certain city a judge who did not fear God nor regard man. ³Now there was a widow in that city; and she came to him, saying, 'Get justice for me from my adversary.' ⁴And he would not for a while; but afterward he said within himself, 'Though I do not fear God nor regard man, ⁵yet because this widow troubles me I will avenge her, lest by her continual coming she weary me.' "

⁶Then the Lord said, "Hear what the unjust judge said. ⁷And shall God not avenge His own elect who cry out day and night to Him, though He bears long with them? ⁸I tell you that He will avenge them speedily. Nevertheless, when the Son of Man comes, will He really find faith on the earth?"

⁹Also He spoke this parable to some

who trusted in themselves that they were righteous, and despised others: [10]"Two men went up to the temple to pray, one a Pharisee and the other a tax collector. [11]The Pharisee stood and prayed thus with himself, 'God, I thank You that I am not like other men—extortioners, unjust, adulterers, or even as this tax collector. [12]I fast twice a week; I give tithes of all that I possess.' [13]And the tax collector, standing afar off, would not so much as raise *his* eyes to heaven, but beat his breast, saying, 'God, be merciful to me a sinner!' [14]I tell you, this man went down to his house justified *rather* than the other; for everyone who exalts himself will be humbled, and he who humbles himself will be exalted."

[15]Then they also brought infants to Him that He might touch them; but when the disciples saw *it,* they rebuked them. [16]But Jesus called them to *Him* and said, "Let the little children come to Me, and do not forbid them; for of such is the kingdom of God. [17]Assuredly, I say to you, whoever does not receive the kingdom of God as a little child will by no means enter it."

PSALM 85:1-13

To the Chief Musician. A Psalm of the sons of Korah.

L ORD, You have been favorable to Your land;
　You have brought back the captivity of Jacob.
2　You have forgiven the iniquity of Your people;
　You have covered all their sin.
　　　　　　　Selah
3　You have taken away all Your wrath;

You have turned from the fierceness of Your anger.

4　Restore us, O God of our salvation,
　And cause Your anger toward us to cease.
5　Will You be angry with us forever?
　Will You prolong Your anger to all generations?
6　Will You not revive us again,
　That Your people may rejoice in You?
7　Show us Your mercy, LORD,
　And grant us Your salvation.

8　I will hear what God the LORD will speak,
　For He will speak peace To His people and to His saints;
　But let them not turn back to folly.
9　Surely His salvation *is* near to those who fear Him,
　That glory may dwell in our land.

10　Mercy and truth have met together;
　Righteousness and peace have kissed.
11　Truth shall spring out of the earth,
　And righteousness shall look down from heaven.
12　Yes, the LORD will give *what is* good;
　And our land will yield its increase.
13　Righteousness will go before Him,
　And shall make His footsteps *our* pathway.

PROVERBS FOR TODAY/ 13:7-8

There is one who makes himself rich, yet has *nothing; and one who makes himself poor, yet* has *great riches.*   □ *The ransom of a man's life* is *his riches, but the poor does not hear rebuke.*

APRIL 17

JOSHUA 15:1-63

So *this* was the lot of the tribe of the children of Judah according to their families:

The border of Edom at the Wilderness of Zin southward *was* the extreme southern boundary. [2]And their southern border began at the shore of the Salt Sea, from the bay that faces southward. [3]Then it went out to the south ern side of the Ascent of Akrabbim, passed along to Zin, ascended on the south side of Kadesh Barnea, passed along to Hezron, went up to Adar, and went around to Karkaa. [4]*From there* it passed toward Azmon and went out to the Brook of Egypt; and the border ended at the sea. This shall be your southern border.

[5]The east border *was* the Salt Sea as far as the mouth of the Jordan.

And the border on the northern quarter *began* at the bay of the sea at the mouth of the Jordan. [6]The border went up to Beth Hoglah and passed north of Beth Arabah; and the border went up to the stone of Bohan the son of Reuben. [7]Then the border went up toward Debir from the Valley of Achor, and it turned northward toward Gilgal, which *is* before the Ascent of Adummim, which *is* on the south side of the valley. The border continued toward the waters of En Shemesh and ended at En Rogel. [8]And the border went up by the Valley of the Son of Hinnom to the southern slope of the Jebusite *city* (which *is* Jerusalem). The border went up to the top of the mountain that *lies* before the Valley of Hinnom westward,

which *is* at the end of the Valley of Rephaim* northward. [9]Then the border went around from the top of the hill to the fountain of the water of Nephtoah, and extended to the cities of Mount Ephron. And the border went around to Baalah (which *is* Kirjath Jearim). [10]Then the border turned westward from Baalah to Mount Seir, passed along to the side of Mount Jearim on the north (which *is* Chesalon), went down to Beth Shemesh, and passed on to Timnah. [11]And the border went out to the side of Ekron northward. Then the border went around to Shicron, passed along to Mount Baalah, and extended to Jabneel; and the border ended at the sea.

[12]The west border *was* the coastline of the Great Sea. This *is* the boundary of the children of Judah all around according to their families.

[13]Now to Caleb the son of Jephunneh he gave a share among the children of Judah, according to the commandment of the LORD to Joshua, *namely,* Kirjath Arba, which *is* Hebron (*Arba was* the father of Anak). [14]Caleb drove out the three sons of Anak from there: Sheshai, Ahiman, and Talmai, the children of Anak. [15]Then he went up from there to the inhabitants of Debir (formerly the name of Debir *was* Kirjath Sepher).

[16]And Caleb said, "He who attacks Kirjath Sepher and takes it, to him I will give Achsah my daughter as wife." [17]So Othniel the son of Kenaz, the brother of Caleb, took it; and he gave him Achsah his daughter as wife.

¹⁸Now it was so, when she came *to him,* that she persuaded him to ask her father for a field. So she dismounted from *her* donkey, and Caleb said to her, "What do you wish?" ¹⁹She answered, "Give me a blessing; since you have given me land in the South, give me also springs of water." So he gave her the upper springs and the lower springs.

²⁰This *was* the inheritance of the tribe of the children of Judah according to their families:

²¹The cities at the limits of the tribe of the children of Judah, toward the border of Edom in the South, were Kabzeel, Eder, Jagur, ²²Kinah, Dimonah, Adadah, ²³Kedesh, Hazor, Ithnan, ²⁴Ziph, Telem, Bealoth, ²⁵Hazor, Hadattah, Kerioth, Hezron (which *is* Hazor), ²⁶Amam, Shema, Moladah, ²⁷Hazar Gaddah, Heshmon, Beth Pelet, ²⁸Hazar Shual, Beersheba, Bizjothjah, ²⁹Baalah, Ijim, Ezem, ³⁰Eltolad, Chesil, Hormah, ³¹Ziklag, Madmannah, Sansannah, ³²Lebaoth, Shilhim, Ain, and Rimmon: all the cities *are* twenty-nine, with their villages.

³³In the lowland: Eshtaol, Zorah, Ashnah, ³⁴Zanoah, En Gannim, Tappuah, Enam, ³⁵Jarmuth, Adullam, Socoh, Azekah, ³⁶Sharaim, Adithaim, Gederah, and Gederothaim: fourteen cities with their villages; ³⁷Zenan, Hadashah, Migdal Gad, ³⁸Dilean, Mizpah, Joktheel, ³⁹Lachish, Bozkath, Eglon, ⁴⁰Cabbon, Lahmas,* Kithlish, ⁴¹Gederoth, Beth Dagon, Naamah, and Makkedah: sixteen cities with their villages; ⁴²Libnah, Ether, Ashan, ⁴³Jiphtah, Ashnah, Nezib, ⁴⁴Keilah, Achzib, and Mareshah: nine cities with their villages; ⁴⁵Ekron, with its towns and villages; ⁴⁶from Ekron to the sea, all that *lay* near Ashdod, with their villages; ⁴⁷Ashdod with its towns and villages, Gaza with its towns and villages—as far as the Brook of Egypt and the Great Sea with *its* coastline.

⁴⁸And in the mountain country:

Shamir, Jattir, Sochoh, ⁴⁹Dannah, Kirjath Sannah (which *is* Debir), ⁵⁰Anab, Eshtemoh, Anim, ⁵¹Goshen, Holon, and Giloh: eleven cities with their villages; ⁵²Arab, Dumah, Eshean, ⁵³Janum, Beth Tappuah, Aphekah, ⁵⁴Humtah, Kirjath Arba (which *is* Hebron), and Zior: nine cities with their villages; ⁵⁵Maon, Carmel, Ziph, Juttah, ⁵⁶Jezreel, Jokdeam, Zanoah, ⁵⁷Kain, Gibeah, and Timnah: ten cities with their villages; ⁵⁸Halhul, Beth Zur, Gedor, ⁵⁹Maarath, Beth Anoth, and Eltekon: six cities with their villages; ⁶⁰Kirjath Baal (which *is* Kirjath Jearim) and Rabbah: two cities with their villages.

⁶¹In the wilderness: Beth Arabah, Middin, Secacah, ⁶²Nibshan, the City of Salt, and En Gedi: six cities with their villages.

⁶³As for the Jebusites, the inhabitants of Jerusalem, the children of Judah could not drive them out; but the Jebusites dwell with the children of Judah at Jerusalem to this day.

LUKE 18:18-43

Now a certain ruler asked Him [Jesus], saying, "Good Teacher, what shall I do to inherit eternal life?"

¹⁹So Jesus said to him, "Why do you call Me good? No one *is* good but One, *that is,* God. ²⁰You know the commandments: *'Do not commit adultery,' 'Do not murder,' 'Do not steal,' 'Do not bear false witness,' 'Honor your father and your mother.'"*

²¹And he said, "All these things I have kept from my youth."

²²So when Jesus heard these things, He said to him, "You still lack one thing. Sell all that you have and distribute to the poor, and you will have treasure in heaven; and come, follow Me."

²³But when he heard this, he became very sorrowful, for he was very rich.

24And when Jesus saw that he became very sorrowful, He said, "How hard it is for those who have riches to enter the kingdom of God! 25For it is easier for a camel to go through the eye of a needle than for a rich man to enter the kingdom of God."

26And those who heard it said, "Who then can be saved?"

27But He said, "The things which are impossible with men are possible with God."

28Then Peter said, "See, we have left all* and followed You."

29So He said to them, "Assuredly, I say to you, there is no one who has left house or parents or brothers or wife or children, for the sake of the kingdom of God, 30who shall not receive many times more in this present time, and in the age to come eternal life."

31Then He took the twelve aside and said to them, "Behold, we are going up to Jerusalem, and all things that are written by the prophets concerning the Son of Man will be accomplished. 32For He will be delivered to the Gentiles and will be mocked and insulted and spit upon. 33They will scourge *Him* and kill Him. And the third day He will rise again."

34But they understood none of these things; this saying was hidden from them, and they did not know the things which were spoken.

35Then it happened, as He was coming near Jericho, that a certain blind man sat by the road begging. 36And hearing a multitude passing by, he asked what it meant. 37So they told him that Jesus of Nazareth was passing by. 38And he cried out, saying, "Jesus, Son of David, have mercy on me!"

39Then those who went before warned him that he should be quiet; but he cried out all the more, "Son of David, have mercy on me!"

40So Jesus stood still and commanded him to be brought to Him. And when he had come near, He asked him, 41saying, "What do you want Me to do for you?"

He said, "Lord, that I may receive my sight."

42Then Jesus said to him, "Receive your sight; your faith has made you well." 43And immediately he received his sight, and followed Him, glorifying God. And all the people, when they saw *it,* gave praise to God.

PSALM 86:1-17

A Prayer of David.

Bow down Your ear, O LORD, hear me;
For I *am* poor and needy.
2 Preserve my life, for I *am*
      holy;
   You are my God,
   Save Your servant who trusts
      in You!
3 Be merciful to me, O Lord,
   For I cry to You all day long.
4 Rejoice the soul of Your
      servant,
   For to You, O Lord, I lift up
      my soul.
5 For You, Lord, *are* good, and
      ready to forgive,
   And abundant in mercy to all
      those who call upon You.

6 Give ear, O LORD, to my
      prayer;
   And attend to the voice of my
      supplications.
7 In the day of my trouble I will
      call upon You,
   For You will answer me.

8 Among the gods *there is* none
      like You, O Lord;
   Nor *are there any works* like
      Your works.
9 All nations whom You have
      made
   Shall come and worship
      before You, O Lord,
   And shall glorify Your name.

10 For You *are* great, and do
    wondrous things;
    You alone *are* God.

11 Teach me Your way, O LORD;
    I will walk in Your truth;
    Unite my heart to fear Your
    name.

12 I will praise You, O Lord my
    God, with all my heart,
    And I will glorify Your name
    forevermore.

13 For great *is* Your mercy
    toward me,
    And You have delivered my
    soul from the depths of
    Sheol.

14 O God, the proud have risen
    against me,
    And a mob of violent *men*
    have sought my life,

And have not set You before
    them.

15 But You, O Lord, *are* a God
    full of compassion, and
    gracious,
    Longsuffering and abundant
    in mercy and truth.

16 Oh, turn to me, and have
    mercy on me!
    Give Your strength to Your
    servant,
    And save the son of Your
    maidservant.

17 Show me a sign for good,
    That those who hate me may
    see *it* and be ashamed,
    Because You, LORD, have
    helped me and comforted
    me.

PROVERBS FOR TODAY/ 13:9-10

The light of the righteous rejoices, but the lamp of the wicked will be put out. □ *By pride comes nothing but strife, but with the well-advised* is *wisdom.*

APRIL 18

JOSHUA 16:1–18:28

THE lot fell to the children of Joseph from the Jordan, by Jericho, to the waters of Jericho on the east, to the wilderness that goes up from Jericho through the mountains to Bethel, ²then went out from Bethel to Luz,* passed along to the border of the Archites at Ataroth, ³and went down westward to the boundary of the Japhletites, as far as the boundary of Lower Beth Horon to Gezer; and it ended at the sea.

⁴So the children of Joseph, Manasseh and Ephraim, took their inheritance.

⁵The border of the children of Ephraim, according to their families, was *thus:* The border of their inheritance on the east side was Ataroth Addar as far as Upper Beth Horon.

⁶And the border went out toward the sea on the north side of Michmethath; then the border went around eastward to Taanath Shiloh, and passed by it on the east of Janohah. ⁷Then it went down from Janohah to Ataroth and Naarah,* reached to Jericho, and came out at the Jordan.

⁸The border went out from Tappuah westward to the Brook Kanah, and it ended at the sea. This *was* the inheri-

tance of the tribe of the children of Ephraim according to their families. 9The separate cities for the children of Ephraim *were* among the inheritance of the children of Manasseh, all the cities with their villages.

10And they did not drive out the Canaanites who dwelt in Gezer; but the Canaanites dwell among the Ephraimites to this day and have become forced laborers.

THERE was also a lot for the tribe of Manasseh, for he *was* the firstborn of Joseph: *namely* for Machir the firstborn of Manasseh, the father of Gilead, because he was a man of war; therefore he was given Gilead and Bashan. 2And there was *a lot* for the rest of the children of Manasseh according to their families: for the children of Abiezer,* the children of Helek, the children of Asriel, the children of Shechem, the children of Hepher, and the children of Shemida; these *were* the male children of Manasseh the son of Joseph according to their families.

3But Zelophehad the son of Hepher, the son of Gilead, the son of Machir, the son of Manasseh, had no sons, but only daughters. And these *are* the names of his daughters: Mahlah, Noah, Hoglah, Milcah, and Tirzah. 4And they came near before Eleazar the priest, before Joshua the son of Nun, and before the rulers, saying, "The LORD commanded Moses to give us an inheritance among our brothers." Therefore, according to the commandment of the LORD, he gave them an inheritance among their father's brothers. 5Ten shares fell to Manasseh, besides the land of Gilead and Bashan, which *were* on the other side of the Jordan, 6because the daughters of Manasseh received an inheritance among his sons; and the rest of Manasseh's sons had the land of Gilead.

7And the territory of Manasseh was from Asher to Michmethath, that *lies*

east of Shechem; and the border went along south to the inhabitants of En Tappuah. 8Manasseh had the land of Tappuah, but Tappuah on the border of Manasseh *belonged* to the children of Ephraim. 9And the border descended to the Brook Kanah, southward to the brook. These cities of Ephraim *are* among the cities of Manasseh. The border of Manasseh *was* on the north side of the brook; and it ended at the sea.

10Southward *it was* Ephraim's, northward *it was* Manasseh's, and the sea was its border. Manasseh's territory was adjoining Asher on the north and Issachar on the east. 11And in Issachar and in Asher, Manasseh had Beth Shean and its towns, Ibleam and its towns, the inhabitants of Dor and its towns, the inhabitants of En Dor and its towns, the inhabitants of Taanach and its towns, and the inhabitants of Megiddo and its towns—three hilly regions. 12Yet the children of Manasseh could not drive out *the inhabitants of* those cities, but the Canaanites were determined to dwell in that land. 13And it happened, when the children of Israel grew strong, that they put the Canaanites to forced labor, but did not utterly drive them out.

14Then the children of Joseph spoke to Joshua, saying, "Why have you given us *only* one lot and one share to inherit, since we *are* a great people, inasmuch as the LORD has blessed us until now?"

15So Joshua answered them, "If you *are* a great people, *then* go up to the forest *country* and clear a place for yourself there in the land of the Perizzites and the giants, since the mountains of Ephraim are too confined for you."

16But the children of Joseph said, "The mountain country is not enough for us; and all the Canaanites who dwell in the land of the valley have chariots of iron, *both those* who *are* of

Beth Shean and its towns and *those* who *are* of the Valley of Jezreel."

¹⁷And Joshua spoke to the house of Joseph—to Ephraim and Manasseh—saying, "You *are* a great people and have great power; you shall not have *only* one lot, ¹⁸but the mountain country shall be yours. Although it *is* wooded, you shall cut it down, and its farthest extent shall be yours; for you shall drive out the Canaanites, though they have iron chariots *and* are strong."

Now the whole congregation of the children of Israel assembled together at Shiloh, and set up the tabernacle of meeting there. And the land was subdued before them. ²But there remained among the children of Israel seven tribes which had not yet received their inheritance.

³Then Joshua said to the children of Israel: "How long will you neglect to go and possess the land which the Lord God of your fathers has given you? ⁴Pick out from among you three men for *each* tribe, and I will send them; they shall rise and go through the land, survey it according to their inheritance, and come *back* to me. ⁵And they shall divide it into seven parts. Judah shall remain in their territory on the south, and the house of Joseph shall remain in their territory on the north. ⁶You shall therefore survey the land in seven parts and bring *the survey* here to me, that I may cast lots for you here before the Lord our God. ⁷But the Levites have no part among you, for the priesthood of the Lord *is* their inheritance. And Gad, Reuben, and half the tribe of Manasseh have received their inheritance beyond the Jordan on the east, which Moses the servant of the Lord gave them."

⁸Then the men arose to go away; and Joshua charged those who went to survey the land, saying, "Go, walk through the land, survey it, and come back to me, that I may cast lots for you here before the Lord in Shiloh." ⁹So the men went, passed through the land, and wrote the survey in a book in seven parts by cities; and they came to Joshua at the camp in Shiloh. ¹⁰Then Joshua cast lots for them in Shiloh before the Lord, and there Joshua divided the land to the children of Israel according to their divisions.

¹¹Now the lot of the tribe of the children of Benjamin came up according to their families, and the territory of their lot came out between the children of Judah and the children of Joseph. ¹²Their border on the north side began at the Jordan, and the border went up to the side of Jericho on the north, and went up through the mountains westward; it ended at the Wilderness of Beth Aven. ¹³The border went over from there toward Luz, to the side of Luz (which *is* Bethel) southward; and the border descended to Ataroth Addar, near the hill that *lies* on the south side of Lower Beth Horon.

¹⁴Then the border extended around the west side to the south, from the hill that *lies* before Beth Horon southward; and it ended at Kirjath Baal (which *is* Kirjath Jearim), a city of the children of Judah. This *was* the west side.

¹⁵The south side *began* at the end of Kirjath Jearim, and the border extended on the west and went out to the spring of the waters of Nephtoah. ¹⁶Then the border came down to the end of the mountain that *lies* before the Valley of the Son of Hinnom, which *is* in the Valley of the Rephaim* on the north, descended to the Valley of Hinnom, to the side of the Jebusite *city* on the south, and descended to En Rogel. ¹⁷And it went around from the north, went out to En Shemesh, and extended toward Geliloth, which is before the Ascent of Adummim, and descended to the stone of Bohan the son of Reuben. ¹⁸Then it passed along toward the north side of Arabah,* and went down to Arabah. ¹⁹And the border passed along to the north side of

Beth Hoglah; then the border ended at the north bay at the Salt Sea, at the south end of the Jordan. This *was* the southern boundary.

20The Jordan was its border on the east side. This *was* the inheritance of the children of Benjamin, according to its boundaries all around, according to their families.

21Now the cities of the tribe of the children of Benjamin, according to their families, were Jericho, Beth Hoglah, Emek Keziz, 22Beth Arabah, Zemaraim, Bethel, 23Avim, Parah, Ophrah, 24Chephar Haammoni, Ophni, and Gaba: twelve cities with their villages; 25Gibeon, Ramah, Beeroth, 26Mizpah, Chephirah, Mozah, 27Rekem, Irpeel, Taralah, 28Zelah, Eleph, Jebus (which *is* Jerusalem), Gibeath, *and* Kirjath: fourteen cities with their villages. This was the inheritance of the children of Benjamin according to their families.

LUKE 19:1-27

THEN *Jesus* entered and passed through Jericho. 2Now behold, *there was* a man named Zacchaeus who was a chief tax collector, and he was rich. 3And he sought to see who Jesus was, but could not because of the crowd, for he was of short stature. 4So he ran ahead and climbed up into a sycamore tree to see Him, for He was going to pass that *way.* 5And when Jesus came to the place, He looked up and saw him,* and said to him, "Zacchaeus, make haste and come down, for today I must stay at your house." 6So he made haste and came down, and received Him joyfully. 7But when they saw *it,* they all complained, saying, "He has gone to be a guest with a man who is a sinner."

8Then Zacchaeus stood and said to the Lord, "Look, Lord, I give half of my goods to the poor; and if I have taken anything from anyone by false accusation, I restore fourfold."

9And Jesus said to him, "Today salvation has come to this house, because he also is a son of Abraham; 10for the Son of Man has come to seek and to save that which was lost."

11Now as they heard these things, He spoke another parable, because He was near Jerusalem and because they thought the kingdom of God would appear immediately. 12Therefore He said: "A certain nobleman went into a far country to receive for himself a kingdom and to return. 13So he called ten of his servants, delivered to them ten minas,* and said to them, 'Do business till I come.' 14But his citizens hated him, and sent a delegation after him, saying, 'We will not have this *man* to reign over us.'

15"And so it was that when he returned, having received the kingdom, he then commanded these servants, to whom he had given the money, to be called to him, that he might know how much every man had gained by trading. 16Then came the first, saying, 'Master, your mina has earned ten minas.' 17And he said to him, 'Well done, good servant; because you were faithful in a very little, have authority over ten cities.' 18And the second came, saying, 'Master, your mina has earned five minas.' 19Likewise he said to him, 'You also be over five cities.'

20"Then another came, saying, 'Master, here is your mina, which I have kept put away in a handkerchief. 21For I feared you, because you are an austere man. You collect what you did not deposit, and reap what you did not sow.' 22And he said to him, 'Out of your own mouth I will judge you, *you* wicked servant. You knew that I was an austere man, collecting what I did not deposit and reaping what I did not sow. 23Why then did you not put my money in the bank, that at my coming I might have collected it with interest?' 24"And he said to those who stood by, 'Take the mina from him, and give *it* to him who has ten minas.' 25(But they said to him, 'Master, he has ten minas.') 26'For I say to you, that to everyone who has will be given; and from him who does not have, even what he has will be taken away from him. 27But bring here those enemies of mine, who did not want me to reign over them, and slay *them* before me.' "

PSALM 87:1-7

A Psalm of the sons of Korah. A Song.

HIS foundation *is* in the holy mountains.
2The LORD loves the gates of Zion
More than all the dwellings of Jacob.
3 Glorious things are spoken of you,

O city of God!   Selah

4 "I will make mention of Rahab and Babylon to those who know Me;
Behold, O Philistia and Tyre, with Ethiopia:
'This *one* was born there.' "

5 And of Zion it will be said, "This *one* and that *one* were born in her;
And the Most High Himself shall establish her."
6 The LORD will record, When He registers the peoples:
"This *one* was born there."
       Selah

7 Both the singers and the players on instruments *say,*
"All my springs *are* in you."

PROVERBS FOR TODAY/ 13:11

Wealth gained by *dishonesty will be diminished, but he who gathers by labor will increase.*

APRIL 19

JOSHUA 19:1–20:9

THE second lot came out for Simeon, for the tribe of the children of Simeon according to their families. And their inheritance was within the inheritance of the children of Judah. 2They had in their inheritance Beersheba (Sheba), Moladah, 3Hazar Shual, Balah, Ezem, 4Eltolad, Bethul, Hormah, 5Ziklag, Beth Marcaboth, Hazar Susah, 6Beth Lebaoth, and Sharuhen: thirteen cities and their villages; 7Ain, Rimmon, Ether, and Ashan: four cities and their villages; 8and all the villages that *were* all around these cities as far as Baalath Beer, Ramah of the South. This *was* the inheritance of the tribe of the children of Simeon according to their families.

9The inheritance of the children of Simeon *was included* in the share of the children of Judah, for the share of the children of Judah was too much for them. Therefore the children of Simeon had *their* inheritance within the inheritance of that people.

10The third lot came out for the children of Zebulun according to their families, and the border of their inheritance was as far as Sarid. 11Their border went toward the west and to Maralah, went to Dabbasheth, and extended along the brook that is east of Jokneam. 12Then from Sarid it went eastward toward the sunrise along the border of Chisloth Tabor, and went out toward Daberath, bypassing Japhia. 13And from there it passed along on the east of Gath Hepher, toward Eth Kazin, and extended to Rimmon, which borders on Neah. 14Then the border went around it on the north side of Hannathon, and it ended in the Valley of Jiphthah El. 15Included were Kattath, Nahallal, Shimron, Idalah, and Bethlehem: twelve cities with their villages. 16This *was* the inheritance of the children of Zebulun according to their families, these cities with their villages.

17The fourth lot came out to Issachar, for the children of Issachar according to their families. 18And their territory went to Jezreel, and *included* Chesulloth, Shunem, 19Haphraim, Shion, Anaharath, 20Rabbith, Kishion, Abez, 21Remeth, En Gannim, En Haddah, and Beth Pazzez. 22And the border reached to Tabor, Shahazimah, and Beth Shemesh; their border ended at the Jordan: sixteen cities with their villages. 23This *was* the inheritance of the tribe of the children of Issachar according to their families, the cities and their villages.

24The fifth lot came out for the tribe of the children of Asher according to their families. 25And their territory included Helkath, Hali, Beten, Achshaph, 26Alammelech, Amad, and Mishal; it reached to Mount Carmel westward, along *the Brook* Shihor Lib-

nath. 27It turned toward the sunrise to Beth Dagon; and it reached to Zebulun and to the Valley of Jiphthah El, then northward beyond Beth Emek and Neiel, bypassing Cabul *which was* on the left, 28including Ebron,* Rehob, Hammon, and Kanah, as far as Greater Sidon. 29And the border turned to Ramah and to the fortified city of Tyre; then the border turned to Hosah, and ended at the sea by the region of Achzib. 30Also Ummah, Aphek, and Rehob *were included:* twenty-two cities with their villages. 31This *was* the inheritance of the tribe of the children of Asher according to their families, these cities with their villages.

32The sixth lot came out to the children of Naphtali, for the children of Naphtali according to their families. 33And their border began at Heleph, enclosing the territory from the terebinth tree in Zaanannim, Adami Nekeb, and Jabneel, as far as Lakkum; it ended at the Jordan. 34From Heleph the border extended westward to Aznoth Tabor, and went out from there toward Hukkok; it adjoined Zebulun on the south side and Asher on the west side, and ended at Judah by the Jordan toward the sunrise. 35And the fortified cities *are* Ziddim, Zer, Hammath, Rakkath, Chinnereth, 36Adamah, Ramah, Hazor, 37Kedesh, Edrei, En Hazor, 38Iron, Migdal El, Horem, Beth Anath, and Beth Shemesh: nineteen cities with their villages. 39This *was* the inheritance of the tribe of the children of Naphtali according to their families, the cities and their villages.

40The seventh lot came out for the tribe of the children of Dan according to their families. 41And the territory of their inheritance was Zorah, Eshtaol, Ir Shemesh, 42Shaalabbin, Aijalon, Jethlah, 43Elon, Timnah, Ekron, 44Eltekeh, Gibbethon, Baalath, 45Jehud, Bene Berak, Gath Rimmon, 46Me Jarkon, and Rakkon, with the region near Joppa. 47And the border of the children of Dan went beyond these, because the children of Dan went up to fight against Leshem and took it; and they struck it with the edge of the sword, took possession of it, and dwelt in it. They called Leshem, Dan, after the name of Dan their father. ⁴⁸This *is* the inheritance of the tribe of the children of Dan according to their families, these cities with their villages.

⁴⁹When they had made an end of dividing the land as an inheritance according to their borders, the children of Israel gave an inheritance among them to Joshua the son of Nun. ⁵⁰According to the word of the Lᴏʀᴅ they gave him the city which he asked for, Timnath Serah in the mountains of Ephraim; and he built the city and dwelt in it.

⁵¹These *were* the inheritances which Eleazar the priest, Joshua the son of Nun, and the heads of the fathers of the tribes of the children of Israel divided as an inheritance by lot in Shiloh before the Lᴏʀᴅ, at the door of the tabernacle of meeting. So they made an end of dividing the country.

Tʜᴇ Lᴏʀᴅ also spoke to Joshua, saying, ²"Speak to the children of Israel, saying: 'Appoint for yourselves cities of refuge, of which I spoke to you through Moses, ³that the slayer who kills a person accidentally *or* unintentionally may flee there; and they shall be your refuge from the avenger of blood. ⁴And when he flees to one of those cities, and stands at the entrance of the gate of the city, and declares his case in the hearing of the elders of that city, they shall take him into the city as one of them, and give him a place, that he may dwell among them. ⁵Then if the avenger of blood pursues him, they shall not deliver the slayer into his hand, because he struck his neighbor unintentionally, but did not hate him beforehand. ⁶And he shall dwell in that city until he stands before the con-

gregation for judgment, *and* until the death of the one who is high priest in those days. Then the slayer may return and come to his own city and his own house, to the city from which he fled.' "

⁷So they appointed Kedesh in Galilee, in the mountains of Naphtali, Shechem in the mountains of Ephraim, and Kirjath Arba (which *is* Hebron) in the mountains of Judah. ⁸And on the other side of the Jordan, by Jericho eastward, they assigned Bezer in the wilderness on the plain, from the tribe of Reuben, Ramoth in Gilead, from the tribe of Gad, and Golan in Bashan, from the tribe of Manasseh. ⁹These were the cities appointed for all the children of Israel and for the stranger who dwelt among them, that whoever killed a person accidentally might flee there, and not die by the hand of the avenger of blood until he stood before the congregation.

LUKE 19:28-48

Wʜᴇɴ He [Jesus] had said this, He went on ahead, going up to Jerusalem. ²⁹And it came to pass, when He drew near to Bethphage* and Bethany, at the mountain called Olivet, *that* He sent two of His disciples, ³⁰saying, "Go into the village opposite *you,* where as you enter you will find a colt tied, on which no one has ever sat. Loose it and bring *it here.* ³¹And if anyone asks you, 'Why are you loosing *it?* ' thus you shall say to him, 'Because the Lord has need of it.' "

³²So those who were sent went their way and found *it* just as He had said to them. ³³But as they were loosing the colt, the owners of it said to them, "Why are you loosing the colt?"

³⁴And they said, "The Lord has need of him." ³⁵Then they brought him to Jesus. And they threw their own clothes on the colt, and they set Jesus

on him. ³⁶And as He went, *many* spread their clothes on the road.

³⁷Then, as He was now drawing near the descent of the Mount of Olives, the whole multitude of the disciples began to rejoice and praise God with a loud voice for all the mighty works they had seen, ³⁸saying:

> " *'Blessed is the King who comes in the name of the* LORD*!'* *
> Peace in heaven and glory in the highest!"

³⁹And some of the Pharisees called to Him from the crowd, "Teacher, rebuke Your disciples."

⁴⁰But He answered and said to them, "I tell you that if these should keep silent, the stones would immediately cry out."

⁴¹Now as He drew near, He saw the city and wept over it, ⁴²saying, "If you had known, even you, especially in this your day, the things *that make* for your peace! But now they are hidden from your eyes. ⁴³For days will come upon you when your enemies will build an embankment around you, surround you and close you in on every side, ⁴⁴and level you, and your children within you, to the ground; and they will not leave in you one stone upon another, because you did not know the time of your visitation."

⁴⁵Then He went into the temple and began to drive out those who bought and sold in it,* ⁴⁶saying to them, "It is written, *'My house is* * *a house of prayer,'* * but you have made it a *'den of thieves.'"* *

⁴⁷And He was teaching daily in the temple. But the chief priests, the scribes, and the leaders of the people sought to destroy Him, ⁴⁸and were unable to do anything; for all the people were very attentive to hear Him.

PSALM 88:1-18

*A Song. A Psalm of the sons of Korah. To the Chief Musician. Set to "Mahalath Leannoth." A Contemplation * of Heman the Ezrahite.*

O LORD, God of my salvation,
    I have cried out day and night
    before You.
2   Let my prayer come before
        You;
    Incline Your ear to my cry.

3   For my soul is full of troubles,
    And my life draws near to the
        grave.
4   I am counted with those who
        go down to the pit;
    I am like a man *who has* no
        strength,
5   Adrift among the dead,
    Like the slain who lie in the
        grave,
    Whom You remember no
        more,
    And who are cut off from
        Your hand.

6   You have laid me in the lowest
        pit,
    In darkness, in the depths.
7   Your wrath lies heavy upon
        me,
    And You have afflicted *me*
        with all Your waves.   Selah
8   You have put away my
        acquaintances far from me;
    You have made me an
        abomination to them;
    I am shut up, and I cannot get
        out;
9   My eye wastes away because
        of affliction.

    LORD, I have called daily upon
        You;
    I have stretched out my hands
        to You.
10 Will You work wonders for
        the dead?
    Shall the dead arise *and*
        praise You?   Selah

11 Shall Your lovingkindness be
    declared in the grave?
    Or Your faithfulness in the
    place of destruction?
12 Shall Your wonders be known
    in the dark?
    And Your righteousness in
    the land of forgetfulness?

13 But to You I have cried out,
    O LORD,
    And in the morning my
    prayer comes before You.
14 LORD, why do You cast off my
    soul?

Why do You hide Your face
    from me?
15 I *have been* afflicted and ready
    to die from *my* youth;
    I suffer Your terrors;
    I am distraught.
16 Your fierce wrath has gone
    over me;
    Your terrors have cut me off.
17 They came around me all day
    long like water;
    They engulfed me altogether.
18 Loved one and friend You
    have put far from me,
    And my acquaintances into
    darkness.

PROVERBS FOR TODAY/ 13:12-14

Hope deferred makes the heart sick, but when *the desire comes,* it is *a tree of life.*
□ *He who despises the word will be destroyed, but he who fears the commandment will be rewarded.* □ *The law of the wise* is *a fountain of life, to turn* one *away from the snares of death.*

APRIL 20

JOSHUA 21:1–22:20

THEN the heads of the fathers' *houses* of the Levites came near to Eleazar the priest, to Joshua the son of Nun, and to the heads of the fathers' *houses* of the tribes of the children of Israel. [2]And they spoke to them at Shiloh in the land of Canaan, saying, "The LORD commanded through Moses to give us cities to dwell in, with their common-lands for our livestock." [3]So the children of Israel gave to the Levites from their inheritance, at the commandment of the LORD, these cities and their common-lands:

[4]Now the lot came out for the families of the Kohathites. And the children of Aaron the priest, *who were* of the Levites, had thirteen cities by lot from the tribe of Judah, from the tribe of Simeon, and from the tribe of Benjamin. [5]The rest of the children of Kohath had ten cities by lot from the families of the tribe of Ephraim, from the tribe of Dan, and from the half-tribe of Manasseh.

[6]And the children of Gershon had thirteen cities by lot from the families of the tribe of Issachar, from the tribe of Asher, from the tribe of Naphtali, and from the half-tribe of Manasseh in Bashan.

[7]The children of Merari according to their families had twelve cities from the tribe of Reuben, from the tribe of Gad, and from the tribe of Zebulun.

[8]And the children of Israel gave these cities with their common-lands

by lot to the Levites, as the LORD had commanded by the hand of Moses.

⁹So they gave from the tribe of the children of Judah and from the tribe of the children of Simeon these cities which are designated by name, ¹⁰which were for the children of Aaron, one of the families of the Kohathites, *who were* of the children of Levi; for the lot was theirs first. ¹¹And they gave them Kirjath Arba (*Arba was* the father of Anak), which *is* Hebron, in the mountains of Judah, with the common-land surrounding it. ¹²But the fields of the city and its villages they gave to Caleb the son of Jephunnch as his possession.

¹³Thus to the children of Aaron the priest they gave Hebron with its common-land (a city of refuge for the slayer), Libnah with its common-land, ¹⁴Jattir with its common-land, Eshtemoa with its common-land, ¹⁵Holon with its common-land, Debir with its common-land, ¹⁶Ain with its common-land, Juttah with its common-land, and Beth Shemesh with its common-land: nine cities from those two tribes; ¹⁷and from the tribe of Benjamin, Gibeon with its common-land, Geba with its common-land, ¹⁸Anathoth with its common-land, and Almon with its common-land: four cities. ¹⁹All the cities of the children of Aaron, the priests, *were* thirteen cities with their common-lands.

²⁰And the families of the children of Kohath, the Levites, the rest of the children of Kohath, even they had the cities of their lot from the tribe of Ephraim. ²¹For they gave them Shechem with its common-land in the mountains of Ephraim (a city of refuge for the slayer), Gezer with its common-land, ²²Kibzaim with its common-land, and Beth Horon with its common-land: four cities; ²³and from the tribe of Dan, Eltekeh with its common-land, Gibbethon with its common-land, ²⁴Aijalon with its common-land, *and* Gath Rimmon with its common-land: four cities; ²⁵and from the half-tribe of Manasseh, Tanach with its common-land and Gath Rimmon with its common-land: two cities. ²⁶All the ten cities with their common-lands were for the rest of the families of the children of Kohath.

²⁷Also to the children of Gershon, of the families of the Levites, from the *other* half-tribe of Manasseh, *they gave* Golan in Bashan with its common-land (a city of refuge for the slayer), and Be Eshterah with its common-land: two cities; ²⁸and from the tribe of Issachar, Kishion with its common-land, Daberath with its common-land, ²⁹Jarmuth with its common-land, *and* En Gannim with its common-land: four cities; ³⁰and from the tribe of Asher, Mishal with its common-land, Abdon with its common-land, ³¹Helkath with its common-land, and Rehob with its common-land: four cities; ³²and from the tribe of Naphtali, Kedesh in Galilee with its common-land (a city of refuge for the slayer), Hammoth Dor with its common-land, and Kartan with its common-land: three cities. ³³All the cities of the Gershonites according to their families *were* thirteen cities with their common-lands.

³⁴And to the families of the children of Merari, the rest of the Levites, from the tribe of Zebulun, Jokneam with its common-land, Kartah with its common-land, ³⁵Dimnah with its common-land, *and* Nahalal with its common-land: four cities; ³⁶and from the tribe of Reuben, Bezer with its common-land, Jahaz with its common-land, ³⁷Kedemoth with its common-land, and Mephaath with its common-land: four cities;* ³⁸and from the tribe of Gad, Ramoth in Gilead with its common-land (a city of refuge for the slayer), Mahanaim with its common-land, ³⁹Heshbon with its common-land, *and* Jazer with its common-land: four cities in all. ⁴⁰So all the cities for

the children of Merari according to their families, the rest of the families of the Levites, were *by* their lot twelve cities.

⁴¹All the cities of the Levites within the possession of the children of Israel *were* forty-eight cities with their common-lands. ⁴²Every one of these cities had its common-land surrounding it; thus *were* all these cities.

⁴³So the LORD gave to Israel all the land of which He had sworn to give to their fathers, and they took possession of it and dwelt in it. ⁴⁴The LORD gave them rest all around, according to all that He had sworn to their fathers. And not a man of all their enemies stood against them; the LORD delivered all their enemies into their hand. ⁴⁵Not a word failed of any good thing which the LORD had spoken to the house of Israel. All came to pass.

THEN Joshua called the Reubenites, the Gadites, and half the tribe of Manasseh, ²and said to them: "You have kept all that Moses the servant of the LORD commanded you, and have obeyed my voice in all that I commanded you. ³You have not left your brethren these many days, up to this day, but have kept the charge of the commandment of the LORD your God. ⁴And now the LORD your God has given rest to your brethren, as He promised them; now therefore, return and go to your tents *and* to the land of your possession, which Moses the servant of the LORD gave you on the other side of the Jordan. ⁵But take careful heed to do the commandment and the law which Moses the servant of the LORD commanded you, to love the LORD your God, to walk in all His ways, to keep His commandments, to hold fast to Him, and to serve Him with all your heart and with all your soul." ⁶So Joshua blessed them and sent them away, and they went to their tents.

⁷Now to half the tribe of Manasseh Moses had given a possession in Bashan, but to the *other* half of it Joshua gave *a possession* among their brethren on this side of the Jordan, westward. And indeed, when Joshua sent them away to their tents, he blessed them, ⁸and spoke to them, saying, "Return with much riches to your tents, with very much livestock, with silver, with gold, with bronze, with iron, and with very much clothing. Divide the spoil of your enemies with your brethren."

⁹So the children of Reuben, the children of Gad, and half the tribe of Manasseh returned, and departed from the children of Israel at Shiloh, which *is* in the land of Canaan, to go to the country of Gilead, to the land of their possession, which they had obtained according to the word of the LORD by the hand of Moses.

¹⁰And when they came to the region of the Jordan which *is* in the land of Canaan, the children of Reuben, the children of Gad, and half the tribe of Manasseh built an altar there by the Jordan—a great, impressive altar. ¹¹Now the children of Israel heard *someone* say, "Behold, the children of Reuben, the children of Gad, and half the tribe of Manasseh have built an altar on the frontier of the land of Canaan, in the region of the Jordan—on the children of Israel's side." ¹²And when the children of Israel heard *of it,* the whole congregation of the children of Israel gathered together at Shiloh to go to war against them.

¹³Then the children of Israel sent Phinehas the son of Eleazar the priest to the children of Reuben, to the children of Gad, and to half the tribe of Manasseh, into the land of Gilead, ¹⁴and with him ten rulers, one ruler each from the chief house of every tribe of Israel; and each one *was* the head of the house of his father among the divisions* of Israel. ¹⁵Then they

came to the children of Reuben, to the children of Gad, and to half the tribe of Manasseh, to the land of Gilead, and they spoke with them, saying, 16"Thus says the whole congregation of the LORD: 'What treachery *is* this that you have committed against the God of Israel, to turn away this day from following the LORD, in that you have built for yourselves an altar, that you might rebel this day against the LORD? 17*Is* the iniquity of Peor not enough for us, from which we are not cleansed till this day, although there was a plague in the congregation of the LORD, 18but that you must turn away this day from following the LORD? And it shall be, if you rebel today against the LORD, that tomorrow He will be angry with the whole congregation of Israel. 19Nevertheless, if the land of your possession *is* unclean, *then* cross over to the land of the possession of the LORD, where the LORD's tabernacle stands, and take possession among us; but do not rebel against the LORD, nor rebel against us, by building yourselves an altar besides the altar of the LORD our God. 20Did not Achan the son of Zerah commit a trespass in the accursed thing, and wrath fell on all the congregation of Israel? And that man did not perish alone in his iniquity.' "

LUKE 20:1-26

Now it happened on one of those days, as He [Jesus] taught the people in the temple and preached the gospel, *that* the chief priests and the scribes, together with the elders, confronted Him 2and spoke to Him, saying, "Tell us, by what authority are You doing these things? Or who is he who gave You this authority?"

3But He answered and said to them, "I also will ask you one thing, and an-swer Me: 4The baptism of John—was it from heaven or from men?"

5And they reasoned among themselves, saying, "If we say, 'From heaven,' He will say, 'Why then* did you not believe him?' 6But if we say, 'From men,' all the people will stone us, for they are persuaded that John was a prophet." 7So they answered that they did not know where *it was* from.

8And Jesus said to them, "Neither will I tell you by what authority I do these things."

9Then He began to tell the people this parable: "A certain man planted a vineyard, leased it to vinedressers, and went into a far country for a long time. 10Now at vintage-time he sent a servant to the vinedressers, that they might give him some of the fruit of the vineyard. But the vinedressers beat him and sent *him* away empty-handed. 11Again he sent another servant; and they beat him also, treated *him* shamefully, and sent *him* away empty-handed. 12And again he sent a third; and they wounded him also and cast *him* out.

13"Then the owner of the vineyard said, 'What shall I do? I will send my beloved son. Probably they will respect *him* when they see him.' 14But when the vinedressers saw him, they reasoned among themselves, saying, 'This is the heir. Come, let us kill him, that the inheritance may be ours.' 15So they cast him out of the vineyard and killed *him*. Therefore what will the owner of the vineyard do to them? 16He will come and destroy those vinedressers and give the vineyard to others."

And when they heard *it* they said, "Certainly not!"

17Then He looked at them and said, "What then is this that is written:

'*The stone which the builders rejected*

*Has become the chief
cornerstone'?* *

18Whoever falls on that stone will be broken; but on whomever it falls, it will grind him to powder."

19And the chief priests and the scribes that very hour sought to lay hands on Him, but they feared the people*—for they knew He had spoken this parable against them.

20So they watched *Him,* and sent spies who pretended to be righteous, that they might seize on His words, in order to deliver Him to the power and the authority of the governor.

21Then they asked Him, saying, "Teacher, we know that You say and teach rightly, and You do not show personal favoritism, but teach the way of God in truth: 22Is it lawful for us to pay taxes to Caesar or not?"

23But He perceived their craftiness, and said to them, "Why do you test Me?* 24Show Me a denarius. Whose image and inscription does it have?"

They answered and said, "Caesar's."

25And He said to them, "Render therefore to Caesar the things that are Caesar's, and to God the things that are God's."

26But they could not catch Him in His words in the presence of the people. And they marveled at His answer and kept silent.

PSALM 89:1-13

A Contemplation * *of Ethan the Ezrahite.*

I WILL sing of the mercies of the LORD forever;
With my mouth will I make known Your faithfulness to all generations.
2 For I have said, "Mercy shall be built up forever;
Your faithfulness You shall establish in the very heavens."

3 "I have made a covenant with My chosen,
I have sworn to My servant David:
4 'Your seed I will establish forever,
And build up your throne to all generations.'" Selah

5 And the heavens will praise Your wonders, O LORD;
Your faithfulness also in the assembly of the saints.
6 For who in the heavens can be compared to the LORD?
Who among the sons of the mighty can be likened to the LORD?
7 God is greatly to be feared in the assembly of the saints,
And to be held in reverence by all *those* around Him.
8 O LORD God of hosts,
Who *is* mighty like You, O LORD?
Your faithfulness also surrounds You.
9 You rule the raging of the sea;
When its waves rise, You still them.
10 You have broken Rahab in pieces, as one who is slain;
You have scattered Your enemies with Your mighty arm.
11 The heavens *are* Yours, the earth also *is* Yours;
The world and all its fullness, You have founded them.
12 The north and the south, You have created them;
Tabor and Hermon rejoice in Your name.
13 You have a mighty arm;
Strong is Your hand, *and* high is Your right hand.

PROVERBS FOR TODAY/ 13:15-16

Good understanding gains favor, but the way of the unfaithful is *hard. Every prudent man acts with knowledge, but a fool lays open his folly.*

APRIL 21

JOSHUA 22:21–23:16

THEN the children of Reuben, the children of Gad, and half the tribe of Manasseh answered and said to the heads of the divisions* of Israel: 22"The Lord God of gods, the Lord God of gods, He knows, and let Israel itself know—if *it is* in rebellion, or if in treachery against the Lord, do not save us this day. 23If we have built ourselves an altar to turn from following the Lord, or if to offer on it burnt offerings or grain offerings, or if to offer peace offerings on it, let the Lord Himself require *an account.* 24But in fact we have done it for fear, for a reason, saying, 'In time to come your descendants may speak to our descendants, saying, "What have you to do with the Lord God of Israel? 25For the Lord has made the Jordan a border between you and us, *you* children of Reuben and children of Gad. You have no part in the Lord." So your descendants would make our descendants cease fearing the Lord.' 26Therefore we said, 'Let us now prepare to build ourselves an altar, not for burnt offering nor for sacrifice, 27but *that* it *may be* a witness between you and us and our generations after us, that we may perform the service of the Lord before Him with our burnt offerings, with our sacrifices, and with our peace offerings; that your descendants may not say to our descendants in time to come, "You have no part in the Lord." ' 28Therefore we said that it will be, when they say *this* to us or to our gen-

erations in time to come, that we may say, 'Here is the replica of the altar of the Lord which our fathers made, though not for burnt offerings nor for sacrifices; but it *is* a witness between you and us.' 29Far be it from us that we should rebel against the Lord, and turn from following the Lord this day, to build an altar for burnt offerings, for grain offerings, or for sacrifices, besides the altar of the Lord our God which *is* before His tabernacle."

30Now when Phinehas the priest and the rulers of the congregation, the heads of the divisions* of Israel who *were* with him, heard the words that the children of Reuben, the children of Gad, and the children of Manasseh spoke, it pleased them. 31Then Phinehas the son of Eleazar the priest said to the children of Reuben, the children of Gad, and the children of Manasseh, "This day we perceive that the Lord *is* among us, because you have not committed this treachery against the Lord. Now you have delivered the children of Israel out of the hand of the Lord."

32And Phinehas the son of Eleazar the priest, and the rulers, returned from the children of Reuben and the children of Gad, from the land of Gilead to the land of Canaan, to the children of Israel, and brought back word to them. 33So the thing pleased the children of Israel, and the children of Israel blessed God; they spoke no more of going against them in battle, to destroy the land where the children of Reuben and Gad dwelt.

³⁴The children of Reuben and the children of Gad* called the altar, *Witness,* "For *it is* a witness between us that the LORD *is* God."

Now it came to pass, a long time after the LORD had given rest to Israel from all their enemies round about, that Joshua was old, advanced in age. ²And Joshua called for all Israel, for their elders, for their heads, for their judges, and for their officers, and said to them:

"I am old, advanced in age. ³You have seen all that the LORD your God has done to all these nations because of you, for the LORD your God *is* He who has fought for you. ⁴See, I have divided to you by lot these nations that remain, to be an inheritance for your tribes, from the Jordan, with all the nations that I have cut off, as far as the Great Sea westward. ⁵And the LORD your God will expel them from before you and drive them out of your sight. So you shall possess their land, as the LORD your God promised you. ⁶Therefore be very courageous to keep and to do all that is written in the Book of the Law of Moses, lest you turn aside from it to the right hand or to the left, ⁷*and* lest you go among these nations, these who remain among you. You shall not make mention of the name of their gods, nor cause *anyone* to swear *by them;* you shall not serve them nor bow down to them, ⁸but you shall hold fast to the LORD your God, as you have done to this day. ⁹For the LORD has driven out from before you great and strong nations; but *as for* you, no one has been able to stand against you to this day. ¹⁰One man of you shall chase a thousand, for the LORD your God *is* He who fights for you, as He promised you. ¹¹Therefore take careful heed to yourselves, that you love the LORD your God. ¹²Or else, if indeed you do go back, and cling to the remnant of these nations—these that remain among you—and make marriages with them, and go in to them and they to you, ¹³know for certain that the LORD your God will no longer drive out these nations from before you. But they shall be snares and traps to you, and scourges on your sides and thorns in your eyes, until you perish from this good land which the LORD your God has given you.

¹⁴"Behold, this day I *am* going the way of all the earth. And you know in all your hearts and in all your souls that not one thing has failed of all the good things which the LORD your God spoke concerning you. All have come to pass for you; not one word of them has failed. ¹⁵Therefore it shall come to pass, that as all the good things have come upon you which the LORD your God promised you, so the LORD will bring upon you all harmful things, until He has destroyed you from this good land which the LORD your God has given you. ¹⁶When you have transgressed the covenant of the LORD your God, which He commanded you, and have gone and served other gods, and bowed down to them, then the anger of the LORD will burn against you, and you shall perish quickly from the good land which He has given you."

LUKE 20:27-47

THEN some of the Sadducees, who deny that there is a resurrection, came to *Him* [Jesus] and asked Him, ²⁸saying: "Teacher, Moses wrote to us *that* if a man's brother dies, having a wife, and he dies without children, his brother should take his wife and raise up offspring for his brother. ²⁹Now there were seven brothers. And the first took a wife, and died without children. ³⁰And the second* took her as wife, and he died childless. ³¹Then the third took her, and in like manner the seven also; and they left no children,* and died. ³²Last of all the woman died also. ³³Therefore, in the resurrection, whose wife does she become? For all seven had her as wife."

³⁴Jesus answered and said to them, "The sons of this age marry and are given in marriage. ³⁵But those who are counted worthy to attain that age, and the resurrection from the dead, neither marry nor are given in marriage; ³⁶nor can they die anymore, for they are equal to the angels and are sons of God, being sons of the resurrection. ³⁷But even Moses showed in the *burning* bush *passage* that the dead are raised, when he called the Lord '*the God of Abraham, the God of Isaac, and the God of Jacob.*'* ³⁸For He is not the God of the dead but of the living, for all live to Him."

³⁹Then some of the scribes answered and said, "Teacher, You have spoken well." ⁴⁰But after that they dared not question Him anymore.

⁴¹And He said to them, "How can they say that the Christ is the Son of David? ⁴²Now David himself said in the Book of Psalms:

> '*The Lord said to my Lord,*
> "*Sit at My right hand,*
> ⁴³   *Till I make Your enemies*
>   *Your footstool.*" ' *

⁴⁴Therefore David calls Him '*Lord*'; how is He then his Son?"

⁴⁵Then, in the hearing of all the people, He said to His disciples, ⁴⁶"Beware of the scribes, who desire to go around in long robes, love greetings in the marketplaces, the best seats in the synagogues, and the best places at feasts, ⁴⁷who devour widows' houses, and for a pretense make long prayers. These will receive greater condemnation."

PSALM 89:14-37

R IGHTEOUSNESS and justice *are* the foundation of Your throne; Mercy and truth go before Your face.

15 Blessed *are* the people who know the joyful sound! They walk, O Lord, in the light of Your countenance.

16 In Your name they rejoice all day long, And in Your righteousness they are exalted.

17 For You *are* the glory of their strength, And in Your favor our horn is exalted.

18 For our shield *belongs* to the Lord, And our king to the Holy One of Israel.

19 Then You spoke in a vision to Your holy one,* And said: "I have given help to *one who is* mighty; I have exalted one chosen from the people.

20 I have found My servant David; With My holy oil I have anointed him,

21 With whom My hand shall be established; Also My arm shall strengthen him.

22 The enemy shall not outwit him, Nor the son of wickedness afflict him.

23 I will beat down his foes before his face, And plague those who hate him.

24 "But My faithfulness and My mercy *shall be* with him, And in My name his horn shall be exalted.

25 Also I will set his hand over the sea, And his right hand over the rivers.

26 He shall cry to Me, 'You *are* my Father,

My God, and the rock of my
salvation.'
27 Also I will make him *My*
firstborn,
The highest of the kings of
the earth.
28 My mercy I will keep for him
forever,
And My covenant shall stand
firm with him.
29 His seed also I will make *to
endure* forever,
And his throne as the days of
heaven.

30 "If his sons forsake My law
And do not walk in My
judgments,
31 If they break My statutes
And do not keep My
commandments,

32 Then I will punish their
transgression with the rod,
And their iniquity with stripes.
33 Nevertheless My
lovingkindness I will not
utterly take from him,
Nor allow My faithfulness to
fail.
34 My covenant I will not break,
Nor alter the word that has
gone out of My lips.
35 Once I have sworn by My
holiness;
I will not lie to David:
36 His seed shall endure forever,
And his throne as the sun
before Me;
37 It shall be established forever
like the moon,
Even *like* the faithful witness
in the sky." Selah

PROVERBS FOR TODAY/ 13:17-19

A wicked messenger falls into trouble, but a faithful ambassador brings *health.*
□ *Poverty and shame* will come *to him who disdains correction, but he who regards
a rebuke will be honored.* □ *A desire accomplished is sweet to the soul, but* it is *an
abomination to fools to depart from evil.*

APRIL 22

JOSHUA 24:1-33

THEN Joshua gathered all the
tribes of Israel to Shechem and
called for the elders of Israel, for
their heads, for their judges, and for
their officers; and they presented
themselves before God. ²And Joshua
said to all the people, "Thus says the
Lord God of Israel: 'Your fathers, *including* Terah, the father of Abraham
and the father of Nahor, dwelt on the
other side of the River* in old times;
and they served other gods. ³Then I
took your father Abraham from the
other side of the River, led him
throughout all the land of Canaan, and
multiplied his descendants and gave
him Isaac. ⁴To Isaac I gave Jacob and
Esau. To Esau I gave the mountains of
Seir to possess, but Jacob and his children went down to Egypt. ⁵Also I sent
Moses and Aaron, and I plagued
Egypt, according to what I did among
them. Afterward I brought you out.
⁶'Then I brought your fathers out of
Egypt, and you came to the sea; and
the Egyptians pursued your fathers
with chariots and horsemen to the Red
Sea. ⁷So they cried out to the Lord; and

He put darkness between you and the Egyptians, brought the sea upon them, and covered them. And your eyes saw what I did in Egypt. Then you dwelt in the wilderness a long time. 8And I brought you into the land of the Amorites, who dwelt on the other side of the Jordan, and they fought with you. But I gave them into your hand, that you might possess their land, and I destroyed them from before you. 9Then Balak the son of Zippor, king of Moab, arose to make war against Israel, and sent and called Balaam the son of Beor to curse you. 10But I would not listen to Balaam; therefore he continued to bless you. So I delivered you out of his hand. 11Then you went over the Jordan and came to Jericho. And the men of Jericho fought against you—*also* the Amorites, the Perizzites, the Canaanites, the Hittites, the Girgashites, the Hivites, and the Jebusites. But I delivered them into your hand. 12I sent the hornet before you which drove them out from before you, *also* the two kings of the Amorites, *but* not with your sword or with your bow. 13I have given you a land for which you did not labor, and cities which you did not build, and you dwell in them; you eat of the vineyards and olive groves which you did not plant.'

14"Now therefore, fear the LORD, serve Him in sincerity and in truth, and put away the gods which your fathers served on the other side of the River and in Egypt. Serve the LORD! 15And if it seems evil to you to serve the LORD, choose for yourselves this day whom you will serve, whether the gods which your fathers served that *were* on the other side of the River, or the gods of the Amorites, in whose land you dwell. But as for me and my house, we will serve the LORD."

16So the people answered and said: "Far be it from us that we should forsake the LORD to serve other gods; 17for the LORD our God *is* He who brought us and our fathers up out of the land of Egypt, from the house of bondage, who did those great signs in our sight, and preserved us in all the way that we went and among all the people through whom we passed. 18And the LORD drove out from before us all the people, including the Amorites who dwelt in the land. We also will serve the LORD, for He *is* our God."

19But Joshua said to the people, "You cannot serve the LORD, for He *is* a holy God. He *is* a jealous God; He will not forgive your transgressions nor your sins. 20If you forsake the LORD and serve foreign gods, then He will turn and do you harm and consume you, after He has done you good."

21And the people said to Joshua, "No, but we will serve the LORD!"

22So Joshua said to the people, "You *are* witnesses against yourselves that you have chosen the LORD for yourselves, to serve Him."

And they said, "*We are* witnesses!"

23"Now therefore," *he said,* "put away the foreign gods which *are* among you, and incline your heart to the LORD God of Israel."

24And the people said to Joshua, "The LORD our God we will serve, and His voice we will obey!"

25So Joshua made a covenant with the people that day, and made for them a statute and an ordinance in Shechem.

26Then Joshua wrote these words in the Book of the Law of God. And he took a large stone, and set it up there under the oak that *was* by the sanctuary of the LORD. 27And Joshua said to all the people, "Behold, this stone shall be a witness to us, for it has heard all the words of the LORD which He spoke to us. It shall therefore be a witness to you, lest you deny your God." 28So Joshua let the people depart, each to his own inheritance.

29Now it came to pass after these things that Joshua the son of Nun, the servant of the LORD, died, *being* one hundred and ten years old. [30]And they buried him within the border of his inheritance at Timnath Serah, which *is* in the mountains of Ephraim, on the north side of Mount Gaash.

[31]Israel served the LORD all the days of Joshua, and all the days of the elders who outlived Joshua, who had known all the works of the LORD which He had done for Israel.

[32]The bones of Joseph, which the children of Israel had brought up out of Egypt, they buried at Shechem, in the plot of ground which Jacob had bought from the sons of Hamor the father of Shechem for one hundred pieces of silver, and which had become an inheritance of the children of Joseph.

[33]And Eleazar the son of Aaron died. They buried him in a hill *belonging to* Phinehas his son, which was given to him in the mountains of Ephraim.

LUKE 21:1-28

A[ND] He [Jesus] looked up and saw the rich putting their gifts into the treasury, [2]and He saw also a certain poor widow putting in two mites. [3]So He said, "Truly I say to you that this poor widow has put in more than all; [4]for all these out of their abundance have put in offerings for God,* but she out of her poverty put in all the livelihood that she had."

[5]Then, as some spoke of the temple, how it was adorned with beautiful stones and donations, He said, [6]"These things which you see—the days will come in which not *one* stone shall be left upon another that shall not be thrown down."

[7]So they asked Him, saying, "Teacher, but when will these things be? And what sign *will there be* when these things are about to take place?"

[8]And He said: "Take heed that you not be deceived. For many will come in My name, saying, 'I am *He*,' and, 'The time has drawn near.' Therefore* do not go after them. [9]But when you hear of wars and commotions, do not be terrified; for these things must come to pass first, but the end *will not come* immediately."

[10]Then He said to them, "Nation will rise against nation, and kingdom against kingdom. [11]And there will be great earthquakes in various places, and famines and pestilences; and there will be fearful sights and great signs from heaven. [12]But before all these things, they will lay their hands on you and persecute *you*, delivering *you* up to the synagogues and prisons. You will be brought before kings and rulers for My name's sake. [13]But it will turn out for you as an occasion for testimony. [14]Therefore settle *it* in your hearts not to meditate beforehand on what you will answer; [15]for I will give you a mouth and wisdom which all your adversaries will not be able to contradict or resist. [16]You will be betrayed even by parents and brothers, relatives and friends; and they will put *some* of you to death. [17]And you will be hated by all for My name's sake. [18]But not a hair of your head shall be lost. [19]By your patience possess your souls.

[20]"But when you see Jerusalem surrounded by armies, then know that its desolation is near. [21]Then let those who are in Judea flee to the mountains, let those who are in the midst of her depart, and let not those who are in the country enter her. [22]For these are the days of vengeance, that all things which are written may be fulfilled. [23]But woe to those who are pregnant and to those who are nursing babies in those days! For there will be great distress in the land and wrath upon this people. [24]And they will fall by the edge of the sword, and be led away captive into all nations. And Jerusalem will be trampled by Gentiles until the times of the Gentiles are fulfilled.

25"And there will be signs in the sun, in the moon, and in the stars; and on the earth distress of nations, with perplexity, the sea and the waves roaring; 26men's hearts failing them from fear and the expectation of those things which are coming on the earth, for the powers of the heavens will be shaken. 27Then they will see the Son of Man coming in a cloud with power and great glory. 28Now when these things begin to happen, look up and lift up your heads, because your redemption draws near."

PSALM 89:38-52

BUT You have cast off and abhorred,
You have been furious with Your anointed.
39 You have renounced the covenant of Your servant;
You have profaned his crown *by casting it* to the ground.
40 You have broken down all his hedges;
You have brought his strongholds to ruin.
41 All who pass by the way plunder him;
He is a reproach to his neighbors.
42 You have exalted the right hand of his adversaries;
You have made all his enemies rejoice.
43 You have also turned back the edge of his sword,
And have not sustained him in the battle.

44 You have made his glory cease,
And cast his throne down to the ground.
45 The days of his youth You have shortened;
You have covered him with shame. Selah

46 How long, LORD?
Will You hide Yourself forever?
Will Your wrath burn like fire?
47 Remember how short my time is;
For what futility have You created all the children of men?
48 What man can live and not see death?
Can he deliver his life from the power of the grave? Selah

49 Lord, where *are* Your former lovingkindnesses,
Which You swore to David in Your truth?
50 Remember, Lord, the reproach of Your servants—
How I bear in my bosom *the reproach of* all the many peoples,
51 With which Your enemies have reproached, O LORD,
With which they have reproached the footsteps of Your anointed.

52 Blessed *be* the LORD forevermore!
Amen and Amen.

PROVERBS FOR TODAY/ 13:20-23

He who walks with wise men *will be wise, but the companion of fools will be destroyed.* □ *Evil pursues sinners, but to the righteous, good shall be repaid.* □ *A good* man *leaves an inheritance to his children's children, but the wealth of the sinner is stored up for the righteous.* □ *Much food* is in *the fallow* ground *of the poor, and for lack of justice there is waste.* *

JUDGES 1:1–2:9

Now after the death of Joshua it came to pass that the children of Israel asked the LORD, saying, "Who shall be first to go up for us against the Canaanites to fight against them?"

²And the LORD said, "Judah shall go up. Indeed I have delivered the land into his hand."

³So Judah said to Simeon his brother, "Come up with me to my allotted territory, that we may fight against the Canaanites; and I will likewise go with you to your allotted territory." And Simeon went with him. ⁴Then Judah went up, and the LORD delivered the Canaanites and the Perizzites into their hand; and they killed ten thousand men at Bezek. ⁵And they found Adoni-Bezek in Bezek, and fought against him; and they defeated the Canaanites and the Perizzites. ⁶Then Adoni-Bezek fled, and they pursued him and caught him and cut off his thumbs and big toes. ⁷And Adoni-Bezek said, "Seventy kings with their thumbs and big toes cut off used to gather *scraps* under my table; as I have done, so God has repaid me." Then they brought him to Jerusalem, and there he died.

⁸Now the children of Judah fought against Jerusalem and took it; they struck it with the edge of the sword and set the city on fire. ⁹And afterward the children of Judah went down to fight against the Canaanites who dwelt in the mountains, in the South,* and in the lowland. ¹⁰Then Judah went against the Canaanites who dwelt in Hebron. (Now the name of Hebron *was* formerly Kirjath Arba.) And they killed Sheshai, Ahiman, and Talmai.

¹¹From there they went against the inhabitants of Debir. (The name of Debir *was* formerly Kirjath Sepher.)

¹²Then Caleb said, "Whoever attacks Kirjath Sepher and takes it, to him I will give my daughter Achsah as wife." ¹³And Othniel the son of Kenaz, Caleb's younger brother, took it; so he gave him his daughter Achsah as wife. ¹⁴Now it happened, when she came *to him*, that she urged him* to ask her father for a field. And she dismounted from *her* donkey, and Caleb said to her, "What do you wish?" ¹⁵So she said to him, "Give me a blessing; since you have given me land in the South, give me also springs of water."

And Caleb gave her the upper springs and the lower springs.

¹⁶Now the children of the Kenite, Moses' father-in-law, went up from the City of Palms with the children of Judah into the Wilderness of Judah, which *lies* in the South *near* Arad; and they went and dwelt among the people. ¹⁷And Judah went with his brother Simeon, and they attacked the Canaanites who inhabited Zephath, and utterly destroyed it. So the name of the city was called Hormah. ¹⁸Also Judah took Gaza with its territory, Ashkelon with its territory, and Ekron with its territory. ¹⁹So the LORD was with Judah. And they drove out the mountaineers, but they could not drive out the inhabitants of the lowland, because they had chariots of iron. ²⁰And they gave Hebron to Caleb, as Moses had said. Then he expelled from there the three sons of Anak. ²¹But the children of Benjamin did not drive out the Jebusites who inhabited Jerusalem; so the Jebusites dwell with the children of Benjamin in Jerusalem to this day.

²²And the house of Joseph also went up against Bethel, and the LORD *was*

with them. ²³So the house of Joseph sent men to spy out Bethel. (The name of the city *was* formerly Luz.) ²⁴And when the spies saw a man coming out of the city, they said to him, "Please show us the entrance to the city, and we will show you mercy." ²⁵So he showed them the entrance to the city, and they struck the city with the edge of the sword; but they let the man and all his family go. ²⁶And the man went to the land of the Hittites, built a city, and called its name Luz, which *is* its name to this day.

²⁷However, Manasseh did not drive out *the inhabitants of* Beth Shean and its villages, or Taanach and its villages, or the inhabitants of Dor and its villages, or the inhabitants of Ibleam and its villages, or the inhabitants of Megiddo and its villages; for the Canaanites were determined to dwell in that land. ²⁸And it came to pass, when Israel was strong, that they put the Canaanites under tribute, but did not completely drive them out.

²⁹Nor did Ephraim drive out the Canaanites who dwelt in Gezer; so the Canaanites dwelt in Gezer among them.

³⁰Nor did Zebulun drive out the inhabitants of Kitron or the inhabitants of Nahalol; so the Canaanites dwelt among them, and were put under tribute.

³¹Nor did Asher drive out the inhabitants of Acco or the inhabitants of Sidon, or of Ahlab, Achzib, Helbah, Aphik, or Rehob. ³²So the Asherites dwelt among the Canaanites, the inhabitants of the land; for they did not drive them out.

³³Nor did Naphtali drive out the inhabitants of Beth Shemesh or the inhabitants of Beth Anath; but they dwelt among the Canaanites, the inhabitants of the land. Nevertheless the inhabitants of Beth Shemesh and Beth Anath were put under tribute to them.

³⁴And the Amorites forced the children of Dan into the mountains, for they would not allow them to come down to the valley; ³⁵and the Amorites were determined to dwell in Mount Heres, in Aijalon, and in Shaalbim;* yet when the strength of the house of Joseph became greater, they were put under tribute.

³⁶Now the boundary of the Amorites *was* from the Ascent of Akrabbim, from Sela, and upward.

Then the Angel of the Lord came up from Gilgal to Bochim, and said: "I led you up from Egypt and brought you to the land of which I swore to your fathers; and I said, 'I will never break My covenant with you. ²And you shall make no covenant with the inhabitants of this land; you shall tear down their altars.' But you have not obeyed My voice. Why have you done this? ³Therefore I also said, 'I will not drive them out before you; but they shall be *thorns* in your side,* and their gods shall be a snare to you.' " ⁴So it was, when the Angel of the Lord spoke these words to all the children of Israel, that the people lifted up their voices and wept.

⁵Then they called the name of that place Bochim;* and they sacrificed there to the Lord. ⁶And when Joshua had dismissed the people, the children of Israel went each to his own inheritance to possess the land.

⁷So the people served the Lord all the days of Joshua, and all the days of the elders who outlived Joshua, who had seen all the great works of the Lord which He had done for Israel. ⁸Now Joshua the son of Nun, the servant of the Lord, died *when he was* one hundred and ten years old. ⁹And they buried him within the border of his inheritance at Timnath Heres, in the mountains of Ephraim, on the north side of Mount Gaash.

LUKE 21:29–22:13

THEN He [Jesus] spoke to them a parable: "Look at the fig tree, and all the trees. ³⁰When they are already budding, you see and know for yourselves that summer is now near. ³¹So you also, when you see these things happening, know that the kingdom of God is near. ³²Assuredly, I say to you, this generation will by no means pass away till all things take place. ³³Heaven and earth will pass away, but My words will by no means pass away.

³⁴"But take heed to yourselves, lest your hearts be weighed down with carousing, drunkenness, and cares of this life, and that Day come on you unexpectedly. ³⁵For it will come as a snare on all those who dwell on the face of the whole earth. ³⁶Watch therefore, and pray always that you may be counted worthy* to escape all these things that will come to pass, and to stand before the Son of Man."

³⁷And in the daytime He was teaching in the temple, but at night He went out and stayed on the mountain called Olivet. ³⁸Then early in the morning all the people came to Him in the temple to hear Him.

Now the Feast of Unleavened Bread drew near, which is called Passover. ²And the chief priests and the scribes sought how they might kill Him, for they feared the people.

³Then Satan entered Judas, surnamed Iscariot, who was numbered among the twelve. ⁴So he went his way and conferred with the chief priests and captains, how he might betray Him to them. ⁵And they were glad, and agreed to give him money. ⁶So he promised and sought opportunity to betray Him to them in the absence of the multitude.

⁷Then came the Day of Unleavened Bread, when the Passover must be killed. ⁸And He sent Peter and John, saying, "Go and prepare the Passover for us, that we may eat."

⁹So they said to Him, "Where do You want us to prepare?"

¹⁰And He said to them, "Behold, when you have entered the city, a man will meet you carrying a pitcher of water; follow him into the house which he enters. ¹¹Then you shall say to the master of the house, 'The Teacher says to you, "Where is the guest room where I may eat the Passover with My disciples?"' ¹²Then he will show you a large, furnished upper room; there make ready."

¹³So they went and found it just as He had said to them, and they prepared the Passover.

PSALM 90:1–91:16

A Prayer of Moses the man of God.

LORD, You have been our dwelling place* in all generations.
²Before the mountains were
    brought forth,
Or ever You had formed the
    earth and the world,
Even from everlasting to
    everlasting, You *are* God.

3   You turn man to destruction,
    And say, "Return, O children
        of men."
4   For a thousand years in Your
        sight
    Are like yesterday when it is
        past,
    And *like* a watch in the night.
5   You carry them away *like* a
        flood;
    They are like a sleep.
    In the morning they are like
        grass *which* grows up:
6   In the morning it flourishes
        and grows up;
    In the evening it is cut down
        and withers.

7 For we have been consumed
by Your anger,
And by Your wrath we are
terrified.

8 You have set our iniquities
before You,
Our secret *sins* in the light of
Your countenance.

9 For all our days have passed
away in Your wrath;
We finish our years like a sigh.

10 The days of our lives *are*
seventy years;
And if by reason of strength
they are eighty years,
Yet their boast *is* only labor
and sorrow;
For it is soon cut off, and we
fly away.

11 Who knows the power of Your
anger?
For as the fear of You, *so is*
Your wrath.

12 So teach *us* to number our
days,
That we may gain a heart of
wisdom.

13 Return, O Lord!
How long?
And have compassion on Your
servants.

14 Oh, satisfy us early with Your
mercy,
That we may rejoice and be
glad all our days!

15 Make us glad according to
the days *in which* You have
afflicted us,
The years *in which* we have
seen evil.

16 Let Your work appear to Your
servants,
And Your glory to their
children.

17 And let the beauty of the Lord
our God be upon us,
And establish the work of our
hands for us;

Yes, establish the work of our
hands.

He who dwells in the secret place of
the Most High
Shall abide under the shadow
of the Almighty.

2 I will say of the Lord, "He is
my refuge and my fortress;
My God, in Him I will trust."

3 Surely He shall deliver you
from the snare of the
fowler*
And from the perilous
pestilence.

4 He shall cover you with His
feathers,
And under His wings you
shall take refuge;
His truth *shall be your* shield
and buckler.

5 You shall not be afraid of the
terror by night,
Nor of the arrow *that* flies by
day,

6 *Nor* of the pestilence *that*
walks in darkness,
Nor of the destruction *that*
lays waste at noonday.

7 A thousand may fall at your
side,
And ten thousand at your
right hand;
But it shall not come near you.

8 Only with your eyes shall you
look,
And see the reward of the
wicked.

9 Because you have made the
Lord, *who is* my refuge,
Even the Most High, your
dwelling place,

10 No evil shall befall you,
Nor shall any plague come
near your dwelling;

11 For He shall give His angels
charge over you,

To keep you in all your ways.
12 In *their* hands they shall bear
you up,
Lest you dash your foot
against a stone.
13 You shall tread upon the lion
and the cobra,
The young lion and the
serpent you shall trample
underfoot.

14 "Because he has set his love

upon Me, therefore I will
deliver him;
I will set him on high,
because he has known My
name.
15 He shall call upon Me, and I
will answer him;
I *will be* with him in trouble;
I will deliver him and honor
him.
16 With long life I will satisfy
him,
And show him My salvation."

PROVERBS FOR TODAY/ 13:24-25

He who spares his rod hates his son, but he who loves him disciplines him promptly.
□ *The righteous eats to the satisfying of his soul, but the stomach of the wicked shall*
be in want.

APRIL 24

JUDGES 2:10–3:31

WHEN all that generation had been gathered to their fathers, another generation arose after them who did not know the LORD nor the work which He had done for Israel.

11Then the children of Israel did evil in the sight of the LORD, and served the Baals; 12and they forsook the LORD God of their fathers, who had brought them out of the land of Egypt; and they followed other gods from *among* the gods of the people who *were* all around them, and they bowed down to them; and they provoked the LORD to anger. 13They forsook the LORD and served Baal and the Ashtoreths.* 14And the anger of the LORD was hot against Israel. So He delivered them into the hands of plunderers who despoiled them; and He sold them into the hands of their enemies all around, so that

they could no longer stand before their enemies. 15Wherever they went out, the hand of the LORD was against them for calamity, as the LORD had said, and as the LORD had sworn to them. And they were greatly distressed.

16Nevertheless, the LORD raised up judges who delivered them out of the hand of those who plundered them. 17Yet they would not listen to their judges, but they played the harlot with other gods, and bowed down to them. They turned quickly from the way in which their fathers walked, in obeying the commandments of the LORD; they did not do so. 18And when the LORD raised up judges for them, the LORD was with the judge and delivered them out of the hand of their enemies all the days of the judge; for the LORD was moved to pity by their groaning because of those who oppressed them and harassed them. 19And it came to pass, when the judge was dead, that they reverted and behaved more corruptly than their fathers, by following other gods, to serve them and bow down to them. They did not cease from their own doings nor from their stubborn way.

20Then the anger of the LORD was hot against Israel; and He said, "Because this nation has transgressed My covenant which I commanded their fathers, and has not heeded My voice, 21I also will no longer drive out before them any of the nations which Joshua left when he died, 22so that through them I may test Israel, whether they will keep the ways of the LORD, to walk in them as their fathers kept *them,* or not." 23Therefore the LORD left those nations, without driving them out immediately; nor did He deliver them into the hand of Joshua.

Now these *are* the nations which the LORD left, that He might test Israel by them, *that is,* all who had not known any of the wars in Canaan 2(*this was* only so that the generations of the children of Israel might be taught to know war, at least those who had not formerly known it), 3*namely,* five lords of the Philistines, all the Canaanites, the Sidonians, and the Hivites who dwelt in Mount Lebanon, from Mount Baal Hermon to the entrance of Hamath. 4And they were *left, that He might* test Israel by them, to know whether they would obey the commandments of the LORD, which He had commanded their fathers by the hand of Moses.

5Thus the children of Israel dwelt among the Canaanites, the Hittites, the Amorites, the Perizzites, the Hivites, and the Jebusites. 6And they took their daughters to be their wives, and gave their daughters to their sons; and they served their gods.

7So the children of Israel did evil in the sight of the LORD. They forgot the LORD their God, and served the Baals and Asherahs.* 8Therefore the anger of the LORD was hot against Israel, and He sold them into the hand of Cushan-Rishathaim king of Mesopotamia; and the children of Israel served Cushan-Rishathaim eight years. 9When the children of Israel cried out to the LORD, the LORD raised up a deliverer for the children of Israel, who delivered them: Othniel the son of Kenaz, Caleb's younger brother. 10The Spirit of the LORD came upon him, and he judged Israel. He went out to war, and the LORD delivered Cushan-Rishathaim king of Mesopotamia into his hand; and his hand prevailed over Cushan-Rishathaim. 11So the land had rest for forty years. Then Othniel the son of Kenaz died.

12And the children of Israel again did evil in the sight of the LORD. So the LORD strengthened Eglon king of Moab against Israel, because they had done evil in the sight of the LORD. 13Then he gathered to himself the people of Ammon and Amalek, went and defeated Israel, and took possession of the City of Palms. 14So the children of Israel served Eglon king of Moab eighteen years.

15But when the children of Israel cried out to the LORD, the LORD raised up a deliverer for them: Ehud the son of Gera, the Benjamite, a left-handed man. By him the children of Israel sent tribute to Eglon king of Moab. 16Now Ehud made himself a dagger (it was double-edged and a cubit in length) and fastened it under his clothes on his right thigh. 17So he brought the tribute to Eglon king of Moab. (Now Eglon *was* a very fat man.) 18And when he had finished presenting the tribute, he sent away the people who had carried the tribute. 19But he himself turned back from the stone images that *were* at Gilgal, and said, "I have a secret message for you, O king."

He said, "Keep silence!" And all who attended him went out from him.

20So Ehud came to him (now he was

sitting upstairs in his cool private chamber). Then Ehud said, "I have a message from God for you." So he arose from *his* seat. ²¹Then Ehud reached with his left hand, took the dagger from his right thigh, and thrust it into his belly. ²²Even the hilt went in after the blade, and the fat closed over the blade, for he did not draw the dagger out of his belly; and his entrails came out. ²³Then Ehud went out through the porch and shut the doors of the upper room behind him and locked them.

²⁴When he had gone out, *Eglon's** servants came to look, and *to their* surprise, the doors of the upper room were locked. So they said, "He is probably attending to his needs in the cool chamber." ²⁵So they waited till they were embarrassed, and still he had not opened the doors of the upper room. Therefore they took the key and opened *them*. And there was their master, fallen dead on the floor.

²⁶But Ehud had escaped while they delayed, and passed beyond the stone images and escaped to Seirah. ²⁷And it happened, when he arrived, that he blew the trumpet in the mountains of Ephraim, and the children of Israel went down with him from the mountains; and he led them. ²⁸Then he said to them, "Follow *me,* for the LORD has delivered your enemies the Moabites into your hand." So they went down after him, seized the fords of the Jordan leading to Moab, and did not allow anyone to cross over. ²⁹And at that time they killed about ten thousand men of Moab, all stout men of valor; not a man escaped. ³⁰So Moab was subdued that day under the hand of Israel. And the land had rest for eighty years.

³¹After him was Shamgar the son of Anath, who killed six hundred men of the Philistines with an ox goad; and he also delivered Israel.

LUKE 22:14-34

WHEN the hour had come, He [Jesus] sat down, and the twelve* apostles with Him. ¹⁵Then He said to them, "With *fervent* desire I have desired to eat this Passover with you before I suffer; ¹⁶for I say to you, I will no longer eat of it until it is fulfilled in the kingdom of God."

¹⁷Then He took the cup, and gave thanks, and said, "Take this and divide *it* among yourselves; ¹⁸for I say to you,* I will not drink of the fruit of the vine until the kingdom of God comes."

¹⁹And He took bread, gave thanks and broke *it,* and gave *it* to them, saying, "This is My body which is given for you; do this in remembrance of Me."

²⁰Likewise He also *took* the cup after supper, saying, "This cup *is* the new covenant in My blood, which is shed for you. ²¹But behold, the hand of My betrayer *is* with Me on the table. ²²And truly the Son of Man goes as it has been determined, but woe to that man by whom He is betrayed!"

²³Then they began to question among themselves, which of them it was who would do this thing.

²⁴Now there was also a dispute among them, as to which of them should be considered the greatest. ²⁵And He said to them, "The kings of the Gentiles exercise lordship over them, and those who exercise authority over them are called 'benefactors.' ²⁶But not so *among* you; on the contrary, he who is greatest among you, let him be as the younger, and he who governs as he who serves. ²⁷For who *is* greater, he who sits at the table, or he who serves? *Is* it not he who sits at the table? Yet I am among you as the One who serves.

²⁸"But you are those who have continued with Me in My trials. ²⁹And I bestow upon you a kingdom, just as My Father bestowed *one* upon Me,

30that you may eat and drink at My table in My kingdom, and sit on thrones judging the twelve tribes of Israel."

31And the Lord said,* "Simon, Simon! Indeed, Satan has asked for you, that he may sift *you* as wheat. 32But I have prayed for you, that your faith should not fail; and when you have returned to *Me,* strengthen your brethren."

33But he said to Him, "Lord, I am ready to go with You, both to prison and to death."

34Then He said, "I tell you, Peter, the rooster shall not crow this day before you will deny three times that you know Me."

PSALM 92:1–93:5

A Psalm. A Song for the Sabbath day.

IT is good to give thanks to the LORD,
And to sing praises to Your name, O Most High;
2 To declare Your
lovingkindness in the
morning,
And Your faithfulness every
night,
3 On an instrument of ten
strings,
On the lute,
And on the harp,
With harmonious sound.
4 For You, LORD, have made me
glad through Your work;
I will triumph in the works of
Your hands.

5 O LORD, how great are Your
works!
Your thoughts are very deep.
6 A senseless man does not
know,
Nor does a fool understand
this.
7 When the wicked spring up
like grass,

And when all the workers of
iniquity flourish,
It is that they may be
destroyed forever.

8 But You, LORD, *are* on high
forevermore.
9 For behold, Your enemies,
O LORD,
For behold, Your enemies
shall perish;
All the workers of iniquity
shall be scattered.

10 But my horn You have
exalted like a wild ox;
I have been anointed with
fresh oil.
11 My eye also has seen *my*
desire on my enemies;
My ears hear *my desire* on the
wicked
Who rise up against me.

12 The righteous shall flourish
like a palm tree,
He shall grow like a cedar in
Lebanon.
13 Those who are planted in the
house of the LORD
Shall flourish in the courts of
our God.
14 They shall still bear fruit in
old age;
They shall be fresh and
flourishing,
15 To declare that the LORD is
upright;
He is my rock, and *there is* no
unrighteousness in Him.

THE LORD reigns, He is clothed with
majesty;
The LORD is clothed,
He has girded Himself with
strength.
Surely the world is
established, so that it
cannot be moved.

2   Your throne *is* established
          from of old;
     You *are* from everlasting.

3   The floods have lifted up,
          O LORD,
     The floods have lifted up their
          voice;
     The floods lift up their waves.

4   The LORD on high *is* mightier

Than the noise of many
     waters,
Than the mighty waves of the
     sea.

5   Your testimonies are very
          sure;
     Holiness adorns Your house,
          O LORD, forever.

PROVERBS FOR TODAY/ 14:1-2

The wise woman builds her house, but the foolish pulls it down with her hands.
□ *He who walks in his uprightness fears the LORD, but* he who is *perverse in his ways despises Him.*

APRIL 25

JUDGES 4:1–5:31

WHEN Ehud was dead, the children of Israel again did evil in the sight of the LORD. ²So the LORD sold them into the hand of Jabin king of Canaan, who reigned in Hazor. The commander of his army *was* Sisera, who dwelt in Harosheth Hagoyim. ³And the children of Israel cried out to the LORD; for Jabin had nine hundred chariots of iron, and for twenty years he had harshly oppressed the children of Israel.

⁴Now Deborah, a prophetess, the wife of Lapidoth, was judging Israel at that time. ⁵And she would sit under the palm tree of Deborah between Ramah and Bethel in the mountains of Ephraim. And the children of Israel came up to her for judgment. ⁶Then she sent and called for Barak the son of Abinoam from Kedesh in Naphtali, and said to him, "Has not the LORD God of Israel commanded, 'Go and deploy *troops* at Mount Tabor; take with you ten thousand men of the sons of

Naphtali and of the sons of Zebulun; ⁷and against you I will deploy Sisera, the commander of Jabin's army, with his chariots and his multitude at the River Kishon; and I will deliver him into your hand'?"

⁸And Barak said to her, "If you will go with me, then I will go; but if you will not go with me, I will not go!"

⁹So she said, "I will surely go with you; nevertheless there will be no glory for you in the journey you are taking, for the LORD will sell Sisera into the hand of a woman." Then Deborah arose and went with Barak to Kedesh. ¹⁰And Barak called Zebulun and Naphtali to Kedesh; he went up with ten thousand men under his command,* and Deborah went up with him.

¹¹Now Heber the Kenite, of the children of Hobab the father-in-law of Moses, had separated himself from the Kenites and pitched his tent near the terebinth tree at Zaanaim, which *is* beside Kedesh.

¹²And they reported to Sisera that Barak the son of Abinoam had gone up

to Mount Tabor. 13So Sisera gathered together all his chariots, nine hundred chariots of iron, and all the people who *were* with him, from Harosheth Hagoyim to the River Kishon.

14Then Deborah said to Barak, "Up! For this *is* the day in which the LORD has delivered Sisera into your hand. Has not the LORD gone out before you?" So Barak went down from Mount Tabor with ten thousand men following him. 15And the LORD routed Sisera and all *his* chariots and all *his* army with the edge of the sword before Barak; and Sisera alighted from *his* chariot and fled away on foot. 16But Barak pursued the chariots and the army as far as Harosheth Hagoyim, and all the army of Sisera fell by the edge of the sword; not a man was left.

17However, Sisera had fled away on foot to the tent of Jael, the wife of Heber the Kenite; for *there was* peace between Jabin king of Hazor and the house of Heber the Kenite. 18And Jael went out to meet Sisera, and said to him, "Turn aside, my lord, turn aside to me; do not fear." And when he had turned aside with her into the tent, she covered him with a blanket.

19Then he said to her, "Please give me a little water to drink, for I am thirsty." So she opened a jug of milk, gave him a drink, and covered him. 20And he said to her, "Stand at the door of the tent, and if any man comes and inquires of you, and says, 'Is there any man here?' you shall say, 'No.'"

21Then Jael, Heber's wife, took a tent peg and took a hammer in her hand, and went softly to him and drove the peg into his temple, and it went down into the ground; for he was fast asleep and weary. So he died. 22And then, as Barak pursued Sisera, Jael came out to meet him, and said to him, "Come, I will show you the man whom you seek." And when he went into her *tent,* there lay Sisera, dead with the peg in his temple.

23So on that day God subdued Jabin king of Canaan in the presence of the children of Israel. 24And the hand of the children of Israel grew stronger and stronger against Jabin king of Canaan, until they had destroyed Jabin king of Canaan.

THEN Deborah and Barak the son of Abinoam sang on that day, saying:

2   "When leaders lead in Israel,
        When the people willingly
            offer themselves,
        Bless the LORD!

3   "Hear, O kings! Give ear,
            O princes!
        I, *even* I, will sing to the LORD;
        I will sing praise to the LORD
            God of Israel.

4   "LORD, when You went out from
            Seir,
        When You marched from the
            field of Edom,
        The earth trembled and the
            heavens poured,
        The clouds also poured water;
5   The mountains gushed
            before the LORD,
        This Sinai, before the LORD
            God of Israel.

6   "In the days of Shamgar, son of
            Anath,
        In the days of Jael,
        The highways were deserted,
        And the travelers walked
            along the byways.
7   Village life ceased, it ceased
            in Israel,
        Until I, Deborah, arose,
        Arose a mother in Israel.
8   They chose new gods;
        Then *there was* war in the
            gates;
        Not a shield or spear was
            seen among forty thousand
            in Israel.

9 My heart *is* with the rulers of
   Israel
   Who offered themselves
   willingly with the people.
   Bless the LORD!

10 "Speak, you who ride on white
   donkeys,
   Who sit in judges' attire,
   And who walk along the road.
11 Far from the noise of the
   archers, among the
   watering places,
   There they shall recount the
   righteous acts of the LORD,
   The righteous acts *for* His
   villagers in Israel;
   Then the people of the LORD
   shall go down to the gates.

12 "Awake, awake, Deborah!
   Awake, awake, sing a song!
   Arise, Barak, and lead your
   captives away,
   O son of Abinoam!

13 "Then the survivors came
   down, the people against
   the nobles;
   The LORD came down for me
   against the mighty.
14 From Ephraim *were* those
   whose roots were in
   Amalek.
   After you, Benjamin, with
   your peoples,
   From Machir rulers came
   down,
   And from Zebulun those who
   bear the recruiter's staff.
15 And the princes of Issachar*
   were with Deborah;
   As Issachar, so *was* Barak
   Sent into the valley under his
   command;*
   Among the divisions of
   Reuben
   There were great resolves of
   heart.

16 Why did you sit among the
   sheepfolds,
   To hear the pipings for the
   flocks?
   The divisions of Reuben have
   great searchings of heart.
17 Gilead stayed beyond the
   Jordan,
   And why did Dan remain on
   ships?*
   Asher continued at the
   seashore,
   And stayed by his inlets.
18 Zebulun *is* a people *who*
   jeopardized their lives to
   the point of death,
   Naphtali also, on the heights
   of the battlefield.

19 "The kings came *and* fought,
   Then the kings of Canaan
   fought
   In Taanach, by the waters of
   Megiddo;
   They took no spoils of silver.
20 They fought from the heavens;
   The stars from their courses
   fought against Sisera.
21 The torrent of Kishon swept
   them away,
   That ancient torrent, the
   torrent of Kishon.
   O my soul, march on in
   strength!
22 Then the horses' hooves
   pounded,
   The galloping, galloping of his
   steeds.
23 'Curse Meroz,' said the angel*
   of the LORD,
   'Curse its inhabitants bitterly,
   Because they did not come to
   the help of the LORD,
   To the help of the LORD
   against the mighty.'

24 "Most blessed among women
   is Jael,
   The wife of Heber the Kenite;

Blessed is she among women
in tents.

25 He asked for water, she gave
milk;
She brought out cream in a
lordly bowl.

26 She stretched her hand to the
tent peg,
Her right hand to the
workmen's hammer;
She pounded Sisera, she
pierced his head,
She split and struck through
his temple.

27 At her feet he sank, he fell, he
lay still,
At her feet he sank, he fell;
Where he sank, there he fell
dead.

28 "The mother of Sisera looked
through the window,
And cried out through the
lattice,
'Why is his chariot so long in
coming?
Why tarries the clatter of his
chariots?'

29 Her wisest ladies answered
her,
Yes, she answered herself,

30 'Are they not finding and
dividing the spoil:
To every man a girl or two;
For Sisera, plunder of dyed
garments,
Plunder of garments
embroidered and dyed,
Two pieces of dyed
embroidery for the neck of
the looter?'

31 "Thus let all Your enemies
perish, O LORD!
But let those who love Him be
like the sun
When it comes out in full
strength."

So the land had rest for forty years.

LUKE 22:35-53

AND He [Jesus] said to them [his disciples], "When I sent you without money bag, knapsack, and sandals, did you lack anything?"
So they said, "Nothing."

36Then He said to them, "But now, he who has a money bag, let him take it, and likewise a knapsack; and he who has no sword, let him sell his garment and buy one. 37For I say to you that this which is written must still be accomplished in Me: 'And He was numbered with the transgressors.'* For the things concerning Me have an end."

38So they said, "Lord, look, here are two swords."

And He said to them, "It is enough."

39Coming out, He went to the Mount of Olives, as He was accustomed, and His disciples also followed Him. 40When He came to the place, He said to them, "Pray that you may not enter into temptation."

41And He was withdrawn from them about a stone's throw, and He knelt down and prayed, 42saying, "Father, if it is Your will, take this cup away from Me; nevertheless not My will, but Yours, be done." 43Then an angel appeared to Him from heaven, strengthening Him. 44And being in agony, He prayed more earnestly. Then His sweat became like great drops of blood falling down to the ground.*

45When He rose up from prayer, and had come to His disciples, He found them sleeping from sorrow. 46Then He said to them, "Why do you sleep? Rise and pray, lest you enter into temptation."

47And while He was still speaking, behold, a multitude; and he who was called Judas, one of the twelve, went before them and drew near to Jesus to kiss Him. 48But Jesus said to him, "Judas, are you betraying the Son of Man with a kiss?"

⁴⁹When those around Him saw what was going to happen, they said to Him, "Lord, shall we strike with the sword?" ⁵⁰And one of them struck the servant of the high priest and cut off his right ear.

⁵¹But Jesus answered and said, "Permit even this." And He touched his ear and healed him.

⁵²Then Jesus said to the chief priests, captains of the temple, and the elders who had come to Him, "Have you come out, as against a robber, with swords and clubs? ⁵³When I was with you daily in the temple, you did not try to seize Me. But this is your hour, and the power of darkness."

PSALM 94:1-23

O LORD God, to whom vengeance belongs—
O God, to whom vengeance belongs, shine forth!
2 Rise up, O Judge of the earth;
Render punishment to the proud.
3 LORD, how long will the wicked,
How long will the wicked triumph?

4 They utter speech, *and* speak insolent things;
All the workers of iniquity boast in themselves.
5 They break in pieces Your people, O LORD,
And afflict Your heritage.
6 They slay the widow and the stranger,
And murder the fatherless.
7 Yet they say, "The LORD does not see,
Nor does the God of Jacob understand."

8 Understand, you senseless among the people;

And *you* fools, when will you be wise?
9 He who planted the ear, shall He not hear?
He who formed the eye, shall He not see?
10 He who instructs the nations, shall He not correct,
He who teaches man knowledge?
11 The LORD knows the thoughts of man,
That they *are* futile.

12 Blessed *is* the man whom You instruct, O LORD,
And teach out of Your law,
13 That You may give him rest from the days of adversity,
Until the pit is dug for the wicked.
14 For the LORD will not cast off His people,
Nor will He forsake His inheritance.
15 But judgment will return to righteousness,
And all the upright in heart will follow it.

16 Who will rise up for me against the evildoers?
Who will stand up for me against the workers of iniquity?
17 Unless the LORD *had been* my help,
My soul would soon have settled in silence.
18 If I say, "My foot slips,"
Your mercy, O LORD, will hold me up.
19 In the multitude of my anxieties within me,
Your comforts delight my soul.

20 Shall the throne of iniquity, which devises evil by law,
Have fellowship with You?

21 They gather together against
the life of the righteous,
And condemn innocent blood.
22 But the LORD has been my
defense,
And my God the rock of my
refuge.

23 He has brought on them their
own iniquity,
And shall cut them off in their
own wickedness;
The LORD our God shall cut
them off.

PROVERBS FOR TODAY/ 14:3-4

In the mouth of a fool is *a rod of pride, but the lips of the wise will preserve them.*
□ *Where no oxen* are, *the trough* is *clean; but much increase* comes *by the strength of an ox.*

APRIL 26

JUDGES 6:1-40

THEN the children of Israel did evil in the sight of the LORD. So the LORD delivered them into the hand of Midian for seven years, 2and the hand of Midian prevailed against Israel. Because of the Midianites, the children of Israel made for themselves the dens, the caves, and the strongholds which *are* in the mountains. 3So it was, whenever Israel had sown, Midianites would come up; also Amalekites and the people of the East would come up against them. 4Then they would encamp against them and destroy the produce of the earth as far as Gaza, and leave no sustenance for Israel, neither sheep nor ox nor donkey. 5For they would come up with their livestock and their tents, coming in as numerous as locusts; both they and their camels were without number; and they would enter the land to destroy it. 6So Israel was greatly impoverished because of the Midianites, and the children of Israel cried out to the LORD.

7And it came to pass, when the children of Israel cried out to the LORD because of the Midianites, 8that the LORD sent a prophet to the children of Israel, who said to them, "Thus says the LORD God of Israel: 'I brought you up from Egypt and brought you out of the house of bondage; 9and I delivered you out of the hand of the Egyptians and out of the hand of all who oppressed you, and drove them out before you and gave you their land. 10Also I said to you, "I am the LORD your God; do not fear the gods of the Amorites, in whose land you dwell." But you have not obeyed My voice.' "

11Now the Angel of the LORD came and sat under the terebinth tree which *was* in Ophrah, which *belonged* to Joash the Abiezrite, while his son Gideon threshed wheat in the winepress, in order to hide *it* from the Midianites. 12And the Angel of the LORD appeared to him, and said to him, "The LORD *is* with you, you mighty man of valor!"

13Gideon said to Him, "O my lord,* if the LORD is with us, why then has all this happened to us? And where *are* all His miracles which our fathers told us about, saying, 'Did not the LORD bring us up from Egypt?' But now the LORD has forsaken us and delivered us into the hands of the Midianites."

¹⁴Then the LORD turned to him and said, "Go in this might of yours, and you shall save Israel from the hand of the Midianites. Have I not sent you?"

¹⁵So he said to Him, "O my Lord,* how can I save Israel? Indeed my clan *is* the weakest in Manasseh, and I *am* the least in my father's house."

¹⁶And the LORD said to him, "Surely I will be with you, and you shall defeat the Midianites as one man."

¹⁷Then he said to Him, "If now I have found favor in Your sight, then show me a sign that it is You who talk with me. ¹⁸Do not depart from here, I pray, until I come to You and bring out my offering and set *it* before You."

And He said, "I will wait until you come back."

¹⁹So Gideon went in and prepared a young goat, and unleavened bread from an ephah of flour. The meat he put in a basket, and he put the broth in a pot; and he brought *them* out to Him under the terebinth tree and presented *them*. ²⁰The Angel of God said to him, "Take the meat and the unleavened bread and lay *them* on this rock, and pour out the broth." And he did so.

²¹Then the Angel of the LORD put out the end of the staff that *was* in His hand, and touched the meat and the unleavened bread; and fire rose out of the rock and consumed the meat and the unleavened bread. And the Angel of the LORD departed out of his sight.

²²Now Gideon perceived that He *was* the Angel of the LORD. So Gideon said, "Alas, O Lord GOD! For I have seen the Angel of the LORD face to face."

²³Then the LORD said to him, "Peace *be* with you; do not fear, you shall not die." ²⁴So Gideon built an altar there to the LORD, and called it The-LORD-*Is-*Peace.* To this day it *is* still in Ophrah of the Abiezrites.

²⁵Now it came to pass the same night that the LORD said to him, "Take your father's young bull, the second

bull of seven years old, and tear down the altar of Baal that your father has, and cut down the wooden image* that *is* beside it; ²⁶and build an altar to the LORD your God on top of this rock in the proper arrangement, and take the second bull and offer a burnt sacrifice with the wood of the image which you shall cut down." ²⁷So Gideon took ten men from among his servants and did as the LORD had said to him. But because he feared his father's household and the men of the city too much to do *it* by day, he did *it* by night.

²⁸And when the men of the city arose early in the morning, there was the altar of Baal, torn down; and the wooden image that *was* beside it was cut down, and the second bull was being offered on the altar *which had been* built. ²⁹So they said to one another, "Who has done this thing?" And when they had inquired and asked, they said, "Gideon the son of Joash has done this thing." ³⁰Then the men of the city said to Joash, "Bring out your son, that he may die, because he has torn down the altar of Baal, and because he has cut down the wooden image that *was* beside it."

³¹But Joash said to all who stood against him, "Would you plead for Baal? Would you save him? Let the one who would plead for him be put to death by morning! If he *is* a god, let him plead for himself, because his altar has been torn down!" ³²Therefore on that day he called him Jerubbaal,* saying, "Let Baal plead against him, because he has torn down his altar."

³³Then all the Midianites and Amalekites, the people of the East, gathered together; and they crossed over and encamped in the Valley of Jezreel. ³⁴But the Spirit of the LORD came upon Gideon; then he blew the trumpet, and the Abiezrites gathered behind him. ³⁵And he sent messengers throughout all Manasseh, who also gathered behind him. He also sent messengers to

Asher, Zebulun, and Naphtali; and they came up to meet them.

³⁶So Gideon said to God, "If You will save Israel by my hand as You have said— ³⁷look, I shall put a fleece of wool on the threshing floor; if there is dew on the fleece only, and *it is* dry on all the ground, then I shall know that You will save Israel by my hand, as You have said." ³⁸And it was so. When he rose early the next morning and squeezed the fleece together, he wrung the dew out of the fleece, a bowlful of water. ³⁹Then Gideon said to God, "Do not be angry with me, but let me speak just once more: Let me test, I pray, just once more with the fleece; let it now be dry only on the fleece, but on all the ground let there be dew." ⁴⁰And God did so that night. It was dry on the fleece only, but there was dew on all the ground.

LUKE 22:54–23:12

HAVING arrested Him [Jesus], they led *Him* and brought Him into the high priest's house. But Peter followed at a distance. ⁵⁵Now when they had kindled a fire in the midst of the courtyard and sat down together, Peter sat among them. ⁵⁶And a certain servant girl, seeing him as he sat by the fire, looked intently at him and said, "This man was also with Him."

⁵⁷But he denied Him,* saying, "Woman, I do not know Him."

⁵⁸And after a little while another saw him and said, "You also are of them."

But Peter said, "Man, I am not!"

⁵⁹Then after about an hour had passed, another confidently affirmed, saying, "Surely this *fellow* also was with Him, for he is a Galilean."

⁶⁰But Peter said, "Man, I do not know what you are saying!"

Immediately, while he was still speaking, the rooster* crowed. ⁶¹And the Lord turned and looked at Peter.

Then Peter remembered the word of the Lord, how He had said to him, "Before the rooster crows,* you will deny Me three times." ⁶²So Peter went out and wept bitterly.

⁶³Now the men who held Jesus mocked Him and beat Him. ⁶⁴And having blindfolded Him, they struck Him on the face and asked Him,* saying, "Prophesy! Who is the one who struck You?" ⁶⁵And many other things they blasphemously spoke against Him.

⁶⁶As soon as it was day, the elders of the people, both chief priests and scribes, came together and led Him into their council, saying, ⁶⁷"If You are the Christ, tell us."

But He said to them, "If I tell you, you will by no means believe. ⁶⁸And if I also ask *you,* you will by no means answer Me or let *Me* go.* ⁶⁹Hereafter the Son of Man will sit on the right hand of the power of God."

⁷⁰Then they all said, "Are You then the Son of God?"

So He said to them, "You *rightly* say that I am."

⁷¹And they said, "What further testimony do we need? For we have heard it ourselves from His own mouth."

THEN the whole multitude of them arose and led Him to Pilate. ²And they began to accuse Him, saying, "We found this *fellow* perverting the* nation, and forbidding to pay taxes to Caesar, saying that He Himself is Christ, a King."

³Then Pilate asked Him, saying, "Are You the King of the Jews?"

He answered him and said, "*It is as* you say."

⁴So Pilate said to the chief priests and the crowd, "I find no fault in this Man."

⁵But they were the more fierce, saying, "He stirs up the people, teaching throughout all Judea, beginning from Galilee to this place."

⁶When Pilate heard of Galilee,* he

asked if the Man were a Galilean. ⁷And as soon as he knew that He belonged to Herod's jurisdiction, he sent Him to Herod, who was also in Jerusalem at that time. ⁸Now when Herod saw Jesus, he was exceedingly glad; for he had desired for a long *time* to see Him, because he had heard many things about Him, and he hoped to see some miracle done by Him. ⁹Then he questioned Him with many words, but He answered him nothing. ¹⁰And the chief priests and scribes stood and vehemently accused Him. ¹¹Then Herod, with his men of war, treated Him with contempt and mocked *Him,* arrayed Him in a gorgeous robe, and sent Him back to Pilate. ¹²That very day Pilate and Herod became friends with each other, for previously they had been at enmity with each other.

PSALM 95:1–96:13

O H come, let us sing to the Lord! Let us shout joyfully to the Rock of our salvation.
2 Let us come before His
presence with thanksgiving;
Let us shout joyfully to Him
with psalms.
3 For the Lord *is* the great God,
And the great King above all
gods.
4 In His hand *are* the deep
places of the earth;
The heights of the hills *are*
His also.
5 The sea *is* His, for He made it;
And His hands formed the
dry *land.*

6 Oh come, let us worship and
bow down;
Let us kneel before the Lord
our Maker.
7 For He *is* our God,
And we *are* the people of His
pasture,
And the sheep of His hand.

Today, if you will hear His
voice:
8 "Do not harden your hearts, as
in the rebellion,*
As *in* the day of trial* in the
wilderness,
9 When your fathers tested Me;
They tried Me, though they
saw My work.
10 For forty years I was grieved
with *that* generation,
And said, 'It *is* a people who
go astray in their hearts,
And they do not know My
ways.'
11 So I swore in My wrath,
'They shall not enter My rest.' "

O H, sing to the Lord a new song!
Sing to the Lord, all the earth.
2 Sing to the Lord, bless His
name;
Proclaim the good news of
His salvation from day to
day.
3 Declare His glory among the
nations,
His wonders among all
peoples.
4 For the Lord *is* great and
greatly to be praised;
He *is* to be feared above all
gods.
5 For all the gods of the peoples
are idols,
But the Lord made the
heavens.
6 Honor and majesty *are* before
Him;
Strength and beauty *are* in
His sanctuary.
7 Give to the Lord, O families of
the peoples,
Give to the Lord glory and
strength.
8 Give to the Lord the glory *due*
His name;

Bring an offering, and come
into His courts.
9 Oh, worship the LORD in the
beauty of holiness!
Tremble before Him, all the
earth.

10 Say among the nations, "The
LORD reigns;
The world also is firmly
established,
It shall not be moved;
He shall judge the peoples
righteously."

11 Let the heavens rejoice, and
let the earth be glad;
Let the sea roar, and all its
fullness;
12 Let the field be joyful, and all
that *is* in it.
Then all the trees of the
woods will rejoice before
the LORD.
13 For He is coming, for He is
coming to judge the earth.
He shall judge the world with
righteousness,
And the peoples with His
truth.

PROVERBS FOR TODAY/ 14:5-6

A faithful witness does not lie, but a false witness will utter lies. □ *A scoffer seeks
wisdom and does not find it, but knowledge is easy to him who understands.*

APRIL 27

JUDGES 7:1–8:17

THEN Jerubbaal (that *is,* Gideon)
and all the people who *were* with
him rose early and encamped
beside the well of Harod, so that the
camp of the Midianites was on the
north side of them by the hill of Moreh
in the valley.

2And the LORD said to Gideon, "The
people who *are* with you *are* too many
for Me to give the Midianites into their
hands, lest Israel claim glory for itself
against Me, saying, 'My own hand has
saved me.' 3Now therefore, proclaim in
the hearing of the people, saying,
'Whoever *is* fearful and afraid, let him
turn and depart at once from Mount Gilead.' " And twenty-two thousand of the
people returned, and ten thousand remained.

4But the LORD said to Gideon, "The
people *are* still *too* many; bring them

down to the water, and I will test them
for you there. Then it will be, *that* of
whom I say to you, 'This one shall go
with you,' the same shall go with you;
and of whomever I say to you, 'This
one shall not go with you,' the same
shall not go." 5So he brought the
people down to the water. And the
LORD said to Gideon, "Everyone who
laps from the water with his tongue, as
a dog laps, you shall set apart by himself; likewise everyone who gets down
on his knees to drink." 6And the number of those who lapped, *putting* their
hand to their mouth, was three hundred men; but all the rest of the people
got down on their knees to drink water.
7Then the LORD said to Gideon, "By the
three hundred men who lapped I will
save you, and deliver the Midianites
into your hand. Let all the *other* people
go, every man to his place." 8So the
people took provisions and their trum-

pets in their hands. And he sent away all *the rest of* Israel, every man to his tent, and retained those three hundred men. Now the camp of Midian was below him in the valley.

9It happened on the same night that the LORD said to him, "Arise, go down against the camp, for I have delivered it into your hand. 10But if you are afraid to go down, go down to the camp with Purah your servant, 11and you shall hear what they say; and afterward your hands shall be strengthened to go down against the camp." Then he went down with Purah his servant to the outpost of the armed men who *were* in the camp. 12Now the Midianites and Amalekites, all the people of the East, were lying in the valley as numerous as locusts; and their camels *were* without number, as the sand by the seashore in multitude.

13And when Gideon had come, there was a man telling a dream to his companion. He said, "I have had a dream: *To my* surprise, a loaf of barley bread tumbled into the camp of Midian; it came to a tent and struck it so that it fell and overturned, and the tent collapsed."

14Then his companion answered and said, "This *is* nothing else but the sword of Gideon the son of Joash, a man of Israel! Into his hand God has delivered Midian and the whole camp."

15And so it was, when Gideon heard the telling of the dream and its interpretation, that he worshiped. He returned to the camp of Israel, and said, "Arise, for the LORD has delivered the camp of Midian into your hand." 16Then he divided the three hundred men *into* three companies, and he put a trumpet into every man's hand, with empty pitchers, and torches inside the pitchers. 17And he said to them, "Look at me and do likewise; watch, and when I come to the edge of the camp you shall do as I do: 18When I blow the trumpet, I and all

who *are* with me, then you also blow the trumpets on every side of the whole camp, and say, '*The sword of* the LORD and of Gideon!'"

19So Gideon and the hundred men who *were* with him came to the outpost of the camp at the beginning of the middle watch, just as they had posted the watch; and they blew the trumpets and broke the pitchers that *were* in their hands. 20Then the three companies blew the trumpets and broke the pitchers—they held the torches in their left hands and the trumpets in their right hands for blowing—and they cried, "The sword of the LORD and of Gideon!" 21And every man stood in his place all around the camp; and the whole army ran and cried out and fled. 22When the three hundred blew the trumpets, the LORD set every man's sword against his companion throughout the whole camp; and the army fled to Beth Acacia,* toward Zererah, as far as the border of Abel Meholah, by Tabbath.

23And the men of Israel gathered together from Naphtali, Asher, and all Manasseh, and pursued the Midianites.

24Then Gideon sent messengers throughout all the mountains of Ephraim, saying, "Come down against the Midianites, and seize from them the watering places as far as Beth Barah and the Jordan." Then all the men of Ephraim gathered together and seized the watering places as far as Beth Barah and the Jordan. 25And they captured two princes of the Midianites, Oreb and Zeeb. They killed Oreb at the rock of Oreb, and Zeeb they killed at the winepress of Zeeb. They pursued Midian and brought the heads of Oreb and Zeeb to Gideon on the other side of the Jordan.

Now the men of Ephraim said to him, "Why have you done this to us by not calling us when you went to fight with the Midianites?" And they reprimanded him sharply.

²So he said to them, "What have I done now in comparison with you? *Is* not the gleaning *of the grapes* of Ephraim better than the vintage of Abiezer? ³God has delivered into your hands the princes of Midian, Oreb and Zeeb. And what was I able to do in comparison with you?" Then their anger toward him subsided when he said that.

⁴When Gideon came to the Jordan, he and the three hundred men who *were* with him crossed over, exhausted but still in pursuit. ⁵Then he said to the men of Succoth, "Please give loaves of bread to the people who follow me, for they are exhausted, and I am pursuing Zebah and Zalmunna, kings of Midian."

⁶And the leaders of Succoth said, "*Are* the hands of Zebah and Zalmunna now in your hand, that we should give bread to your army?"

⁷So Gideon said, "For this cause, when the LORD has delivered Zebah and Zalmunna into my hand, then I will tear your flesh with the thorns of the wilderness and with briers!" ⁸Then he went up from there to Penuel and spoke to them in the same way. And the men of Penuel answered him as the men of Succoth had answered. ⁹So he also spoke to the men of Penuel, saying, "When I come back in peace, I will tear down this tower!"

¹⁰Now Zebah and Zalmunna *were* at Karkor, and their armies with them, about fifteen thousand, all who were left of all the army of the people of the East; for one hundred and twenty thousand men who drew the sword had fallen. ¹¹Then Gideon went up by the road of those who dwell in tents on the east of Nobah and Jogbehah; and he attacked the army while the camp felt secure. ¹²When Zebah and Zalmunna fled, he pursued them; and he took the two kings of Midian, Zebah and Zalmunna, and routed the whole army.

¹³Then Gideon the son of Joash returned from battle, from the Ascent of Heres. ¹⁴And he caught a young man of the men of Succoth and interrogated him; and he wrote down for him the leaders of Succoth and its elders, seventy-seven men. ¹⁵Then he came to the men of Succoth and said, "Here are Zebah and Zalmunna, about whom you ridiculed me, saying, '*Are* the hands of Zebah and Zalmunna now in your hand, that we should give bread to your weary men?' " ¹⁶And he took the elders of the city, and thorns of the wilderness and briers, and with them he taught the men of Succoth. ¹⁷Then he tore down the tower of Penuel and killed the men of the city.

LUKE 23:13-43

THEN Pilate, when he had called together the chief priests, the rulers, and the people, ¹⁴said to them, "You have brought this Man [Jesus] to me, as one who misleads the people. And indeed, having examined *Him* in your presence, I have found no fault in this Man concerning those things of which you accuse Him; ¹⁵no, neither did Herod, for I sent you back to him;* and indeed nothing deserving of death has been done by Him. ¹⁶I will therefore chastise Him and release *Him*" ¹⁷(for it was necessary for him to release one to them at the feast).*

¹⁸And they all cried out at once, saying, "Away with this *Man,* and release to us Barabbas"— ¹⁹who had been thrown into prison for a certain rebellion made in the city, and for murder.

²⁰Pilate, therefore, wishing to release Jesus, again called out to them. ²¹But they shouted, saying, "Crucify *Him,* crucify Him!"

²²Then he said to them the third time, "Why, what evil has He done? I have found no reason for death in Him. I will therefore chastise Him and let *Him* go."

²³But they were insistent, demanding with loud voices that He be crucified. And the voices of these men and of the chief priests prevailed.* ²⁴So Pilate gave sentence that it should be as they requested. ²⁵And he released to them* the one they requested, who for rebellion and murder had been thrown into prison; but he delivered Jesus to their will.

²⁶Now as they led Him away, they laid hold of a certain man, Simon a Cyrenian, who was coming from the country, and on him they laid the cross that he might bear *it* after Jesus.

²⁷And a great multitude of the people followed Him, and women who also mourned and lamented Him. ²⁸But Jesus, turning to them, said, "Daughters of Jerusalem, do not weep for Me, but weep for yourselves and for your children. ²⁹For indeed the days are coming in which they will say, 'Blessed *are* the barren, wombs that never bore, and breasts which never nursed!' ³⁰Then they will begin *'to say to the mountains, "Fall on us!" and to the hills, "Cover us!"'* * ³¹For if they do these things in the green wood, what will be done in the dry?"

³²There were also two others, criminals, led with Him to be put to death. ³³And when they had come to the place called Calvary, there they crucified Him, and the criminals, one on the right hand and the other on the left. ³⁴Then Jesus said, "Father, forgive them, for they do not know what they do."*

And they divided His garments and cast lots. ³⁵And the people stood looking on. But even the rulers with them sneered, saying, "He saved others; let Him save Himself if He is the Christ, the chosen of God."

³⁶The soldiers also mocked Him, coming and offering Him sour wine, ³⁷and saying, "If You are the King of the Jews, save Yourself."

³⁸And an inscription also was written over Him in letters of Greek, Latin, and Hebrew:*

THIS IS THE KING OF THE JEWS.

³⁹Then one of the criminals who were hanged blasphemed Him, saying, "If You are the Christ,* save Yourself and us."

⁴⁰But the other, answering, rebuked him, saying, "Do you not even fear God, seeing you are under the same condemnation? ⁴¹And we indeed justly, for we receive the due reward of our deeds; but this Man has done nothing wrong." ⁴²Then he said to Jesus, "Lord,* remember me when You come into Your kingdom."

⁴³And Jesus said to him, "Assuredly, I say to you, today you will be with Me in Paradise."

PSALM 97:1–98:9

THE LORD reigns;
Let the earth rejoice;
Let the multitude of isles be
glad!

2   Clouds and darkness
surround Him;
Righteousness and justice *are*
the foundation of His
throne.
3   A fire goes before Him,
And burns up His enemies
round about.
4   His lightnings light the world;
The earth sees and trembles.
5   The mountains melt like wax
at the presence of the LORD,
At the presence of the Lord of
the whole earth.
6   The heavens declare His
righteousness,
And all the peoples see His
glory.

7   Let all be put to shame who
serve carved images,
Who boast of idols.

Worship Him, all *you* gods.
8 Zion hears and is glad,
And the daughters of Judah
rejoice
Because of Your judgments,
O LORD.
9 For You, LORD, *are* most high
above all the earth;
You are exalted far above all
gods.

10 You who love the LORD, hate
evil!
He preserves the souls of His
saints;
He delivers them out of the
hand of the wicked.
11 Light is sown for the
righteous,
And gladness for the upright
in heart.
12 Rejoice in the LORD, you
righteous,
And give thanks at the
remembrance of His holy
name.*

A Psalm.
OH, sing to the LORD a new song!
For He has done marvelous
things;
His right hand and His holy
arm have gained Him the
victory.
2 The LORD has made known
His salvation;

His righteousness He has
revealed in the sight of the
nations.
3 He has remembered His
mercy and His faithfulness
to the house of Israel;
All the ends of the earth have
seen the salvation of our
God.

4 Shout joyfully to the LORD, all
the earth;
Break forth in song, rejoice,
and sing praises.
5 Sing to the LORD with the harp,
With the harp and the sound
of a psalm,
6 With trumpets and the sound
of a horn;
Shout joyfully before the
LORD, the King.

7 Let the sea roar, and all its
fullness,
The world and those who
dwell in it;
8 Let the rivers clap *their* hands;
Let the hills be joyful together
before the LORD,
9 For He is coming to judge the
earth.
With righteousness He shall
judge the world,
And the peoples with equity.

PROVERBS FOR TODAY/ 14:7-8

Go from the presence of a foolish man, when you do not perceive in him *the lips of knowledge. The wisdom of the prudent* is *to understand his way, but the folly of fools* is *deceit.*

JUDGES 8:18–9:21

A ND he [Gideon] said to Zebah and Zalmunna, "What kind of men *were they* whom you killed at Tabor?"

So they answered, "As you *are,* so *were* they; each one resembled the son of a king."

¹⁹Then he said, "They *were* my brothers, the sons of my mother. *As* the LORD lives, if you had let them live, I would not kill you." ²⁰And he said to Jether his firstborn, "Rise, kill them!" But the youth would not draw his sword; for he was afraid, because he *was* still a youth.

²¹So Zebah and Zalmunna said, "Rise yourself, and kill us; for as a man *is, so is* his strength." So Gideon arose and killed Zebah and Zalmunna, and took the crescent ornaments that *were* on their camels' necks.

²²Then the men of Israel said to Gideon, "Rule over us, both you and your son, and your grandson also; for you have delivered us from the hand of Midian."

²³But Gideon said to them, "I will not rule over you, nor shall my son rule over you; the LORD shall rule over you." ²⁴Then Gideon said to them, "I would like to make a request of you, that each of you would give me the earrings from his plunder." For they had golden earrings, because they *were* Ishmaelites.

²⁵So they answered, "We will gladly give *them.*" And they spread out a garment, and each man threw into it the earrings from his plunder. ²⁶Now the weight of the gold earrings that he requested was one thousand seven hundred *shekels* of gold, besides the crescent ornaments, pendants, and purple robes which *were* on the kings of Midian, and besides the chains that *were* around their camels' necks. ²⁷Then Gideon made it into an ephod and set it up in his city, Ophrah. And all Israel played the harlot with it there. It became a snare to Gideon and to his house.

²⁸Thus Midian was subdued before the children of Israel, so that they lifted their heads no more. And the country was quiet for forty years in the days of Gideon.

²⁹Then Jerubbaal the son of Joash went and dwelt in his own house. ³⁰Gideon had seventy sons who were his own offspring, for he had many wives. ³¹And his concubine who *was* in Shechem also bore him a son, whose name he called Abimelech. ³²Now Gideon the son of Joash died at a good old age, and was buried in the tomb of Joash his father, in Ophrah of the Abiezrites.

³³So it was, as soon as Gideon was dead, that the children of Israel again played the harlot with the Baals, and made Baal-Berith their god. ³⁴Thus the children of Israel did not remember the LORD their God, who had delivered them from the hands of all their enemies on every side; ³⁵nor did they show kindness to the house of Jerubbaal (Gideon) in accordance with the good he had done for Israel.

THEN Abimelech the son of Jerubbaal went to Shechem, to his mother's brothers, and spoke with them and with all the family of the house of his mother's father, saying, ²"Please speak in the hearing of all the men of Shechem: 'Which is better for you, that all seventy of the sons of Jerubbaal reign over you, or that one reign over you?' Remember that I *am* your own flesh and bone."

³And his mother's brothers spoke all

these words concerning him in the hearing of all the men of Shechem; and their heart was inclined to follow Abimelech, for they said, "He is our brother." 4So they gave him seventy *shekels* of silver from the temple of Baal-Berith, with which Abimelech hired worthless and reckless men; and they followed him. 5Then he went to his father's house at Ophrah and killed his brothers, the seventy sons of Jerubbaal, on one stone. But Jotham the youngest son of Jerubbaal was left, because he hid himself. 6And all the men of Shechem gathered together, all of Beth Millo, and they went and made Abimelech king beside the terebinth tree at the pillar that *was* in Shechem.

7Now when they told Jotham, he went and stood on top of Mount Gerizim, and lifted his voice and cried out. And he said to them:

> "Listen to me, you men of
>   Shechem,
> That God may listen to you!
>
> 8 "The trees once went forth to
>   anoint a king over them.
>   And they said to the olive tree,
>   'Reign over us!'
> 9 But the olive tree said to them,
>   'Should I cease giving my oil,
>   With which they honor God
>   and men,
>   And go to sway over trees?'
>
> 10 "Then the trees said to the fig
>   tree,
>   'You come *and* reign over us!'
> 11 But the fig tree said to them,
>   'Should I cease my sweetness
>   and my good fruit,
>   And go to sway over trees?'
>
> 12 "Then the trees said to the
>   vine,
>   'You come *and* reign over us!'
> 13 But the vine said to them,
>   'Should I cease my new wine,

> Which cheers *both* God and
>   men,
> And go to sway over trees?'
>
> 14 "Then all the trees said to the
>   bramble,
>   'You come *and* reign over us!'
> 15 And the bramble said to the
>   trees,
>   'If in truth you anoint me as
>   king over you,
>   *Then* come *and* take shelter in
>   my shade;
>   But if not, let fire come out of
>   the bramble
>   And devour the cedars of
>   Lebanon!'

16"Now therefore, if you have acted in truth and sincerity in making Abimelech king, and if you have dealt well with Jerubbaal and his house, and have done to him as he deserves— 17for my father fought for you, risked his life, and delivered you out of the hand of Midian; 18but you have risen up against my father's house this day, and killed his seventy sons on one stone, and made Abimelech, the son of his female servant, king over the men of Shechem, because he is your brother— 19if then you have acted in truth and sincerity with Jerubbaal and with his house this day, *then* rejoice in Abimelech, and let him also rejoice in you. 20But if not, let fire come from Abimelech and devour the men of Shechem and Beth Millo; and let fire come from the men of Shechem and from Beth Millo and devour Abimelech!" 21And Jotham ran away and fled; and he went to Beer and dwelt there, for fear of Abimelech his brother.

LUKE 23:44–24:12

Now it was* about the sixth hour, and there was darkness over all the earth until the ninth hour. 45Then the sun was darkened,* and the veil of the temple was torn in two. ⁴⁶And when Jesus had cried out with a loud voice, He said, "Father, *'into Your hands I commit My spirit.'* "* Having said this, He breathed His last.

⁴⁷So when the centurion saw what had happened, he glorified God, saying, "Certainly this was a righteous Man!"

⁴⁸And the whole crowd who came together to that sight, seeing what had been done, beat their breasts and returned. ⁴⁹But all His acquaintances, and the women who followed Him from Galilee, stood at a distance, watching these things.

⁵⁰Now behold, *there was* a man named Joseph, a council member, a good and just man. ⁵¹He had not consented to their decision and deed. *He was* from Arimathea, a city of the Jews, who himself was also waiting* for the kingdom of God. ⁵²This man went to Pilate and asked for the body of Jesus. ⁵³Then he took it down, wrapped it in linen, and laid it in a tomb *that was* hewn out of the rock, where no one had ever lain before. ⁵⁴That day was the Preparation, and the Sabbath drew near.

⁵⁵And the women who had come with Him from Galilee followed after, and they observed the tomb and how His body was laid. ⁵⁶Then they returned and prepared spices and fragrant oils. And they rested on the Sabbath according to the commandment.

Now on the first *day* of the week, very early in the morning, they, and certain *other women* with them,* came to the tomb bringing the spices which they had prepared. ²But they found the stone rolled away from the tomb. ³Then they went in and did not find the body of the Lord Jesus. ⁴And it happened, as they were greatly* perplexed about this, that behold, two men stood by them in shining gar-

ments. ⁵Then, as they were afraid and bowed *their* faces to the earth, they said to them, "Why do you seek the living among the dead? ⁶He is not here, but is risen! Remember how He spoke to you when He was still in Galilee, ⁷saying, 'The Son of Man must be delivered into the hands of sinful men, and be crucified, and the third day rise again.' "

⁸And they remembered His words. ⁹Then they returned from the tomb and told all these things to the eleven and to all the rest. ¹⁰It was Mary Magdalene, Joanna, Mary *the mother* of James, and the other *women* with them, who told these things to the apostles. ¹¹And their words seemed to them like idle tales, and they did not believe them. ¹²But Peter arose and ran to the tomb; and stooping down, he saw the linen cloths lying* by themselves; and he departed, marveling to himself at what had happened.

PSALM 99:1-9

THE LORD reigns;
    Let the peoples tremble!
    He dwells *between* the
        cherubim;
    Let the earth be moved!
2   The LORD *is* great in Zion,
    And He *is* high above all the
        peoples.
3   Let them praise Your great
        and awesome name—
    He *is* holy.

4   The King's strength also loves
        justice;
    You have established equity;
    You have executed justice and
        righteousness in Jacob.
5   Exalt the LORD our God,
    And worship at His footstool—
    He *is* holy.

6   Moses and Aaron were
        among His priests,

And Samuel was among those
who called upon His name;
They called upon the LORD,
and He answered them.
7   He spoke to them in the
cloudy pillar;
They kept His testimonies
and the ordinance He gave
them.

8   You answered them, O LORD
our God;
You were to them
God-Who-Forgives,
Though You took vengeance
on their deeds.
9   Exalt the LORD our God,
And worship at His holy hill;
For the LORD our God *is* holy.

PROVERBS FOR TODAY/ 14:9-10

Fools mock at sin, but among the upright there is *favor.* □ *The heart knows its own bitterness, and a stranger does not share its joy.*

APRIL 29

JUDGES 9:22–10:18

AFTER Abimelech had reigned over Israel three years, 23God sent a spirit of ill will between Abimelech and the men of Shechem; and the men of Shechem dealt treacherously with Abimelech, 24that the crime *done* to the seventy sons of Jerubbaal might be settled and their blood be laid on Abimelech their brother, who killed them, and on the men of Shechem, who aided him in the killing of his brothers. 25And the men of Shechem set men in ambush against him on the tops of the mountains, and they robbed all who passed by them along that way; and it was told Abimelech.

26Now Gaal the son of Ebed came with his brothers and went over to Shechem; and the men of Shechem put their confidence in him. 27So they went out into the fields, and gathered *grapes* from their vineyards and trod *them,* and made merry. And they went into the house of their god, and ate and drank, and cursed Abimelech. 28Then

Gaal the son of Ebed said, "Who *is* Abimelech, and who *is* Shechem, that we should serve him? *Is he* not the son of Jerubbaal, and *is not* Zebul his officer? Serve the men of Hamor the father of Shechem; but why should we serve him? 29If only this people were under my authority!* Then I would remove Abimelech." So he* said to Abimelech, "Increase your army and come out!"

30When Zebul, the ruler of the city, heard the words of Gaal the son of Ebed, his anger was aroused. 31And he sent messengers to Abimelech secretly, saying, "Take note! Gaal the son of Ebed and his brothers have come to Shechem; and here they are, fortifying the city against you. 32Now therefore, get up by night, you and the people who *are* with you, and lie in wait in the field. 33And it shall be, as soon as the sun is up in the morning, *that* you shall rise early and rush upon the city; and *when* he and the people who are with him come out against you, you may then do to them as you find opportunity."

34So Abimelech and all the people

who *were* with him rose by night, and lay in wait against Shechem in four companies. ³⁵When Gaal the son of Ebed went out and stood in the entrance to the city gate, Abimelech and the people who *were* with him rose from lying in wait. ³⁶And when Gaal saw the people, he said to Zebul, "Look, people are coming down from the tops of the mountains!"

But Zebul said to him, "You see the shadows of the mountains as *if they were* men."

³⁷So Gaal spoke again and said, "See, people are coming down from the center of the land, and another company is coming from the Diviners'* Terebinth Tree."

³⁸Then Zebul said to him, "Where indeed *is* your mouth now, with which you said, 'Who is Abimelech, that we should serve him?' *Are* not these the people whom you despised? Go out, if you will, and fight with them now."

³⁹So Gaal went out, leading the men of Shechem, and fought with Abimelech. ⁴⁰And Abimelech chased him, and he fled from him; and many fell wounded, to the *very* entrance of the gate. ⁴¹Then Abimelech dwelt at Arumah, and Zebul drove out Gaal and his brothers, so that they would not dwell in Shechem.

⁴²And it came about on the next day that the people went out into the field, and they told Abimelech. ⁴³So he took his people, divided them into three companies, and lay in wait in the field. And he looked, and there were the people, coming out of the city; and he rose against them and attacked them. ⁴⁴Then Abimelech and the company that *was* with him rushed forward and stood at the entrance of the gate of the city; and the *other* two companies rushed upon all who *were* in the fields and killed them. ⁴⁵So Abimelech fought against the city all that day; he took the city and killed the people who

were in it; and he demolished the city and sowed it with salt.

⁴⁶Now when all the men of the tower of Shechem had heard *that,* they entered the stronghold of the temple of the god Berith. ⁴⁷And it was told Abimelech that all the men of the tower of Shechem were gathered together. ⁴⁸Then Abimelech went up to Mount Zalmon, he and all the people who *were* with him. And Abimelech took an ax in his hand and cut down a bough from the trees, and took it and laid *it* on his shoulder; then he said to the people who were with him, "What you have seen me do, make haste *and* do as I *have done.*" ⁴⁹So each of the people likewise cut down his own bough and followed Abimelech, put *them* against the stronghold, and set the stronghold on fire above them, so that all the people of the tower of Shechem died, about a thousand men and women.

⁵⁰Then Abimelech went to Thebez, and he encamped against Thebez and took it. ⁵¹But there was a strong tower in the city, and all the men and women—all the people of the city— fled there and shut themselves in; then they went up to the top of the tower. ⁵²So Abimelech came as far as the tower and fought against it; and he drew near the door of the tower to burn it with fire. ⁵³But a certain woman dropped an upper millstone on Abimelech's head and crushed his skull. ⁵⁴Then he called quickly to the young man, his armorbearer, and said to him, "Draw your sword and kill me, lest men say of me, 'A woman killed him.' " So his young man thrust him through, and he died. ⁵⁵And when the men of Israel saw that Abimelech was dead, they departed, every man to his place.

⁵⁶Thus God repaid the wickedness of Abimelech, which he had done to his father by killing his seventy brothers. ⁵⁷And all the evil of the men of Shechem God returned on their own

heads, and on them came the curse of Jotham the son of Jerubbaal.

AFTER Abimelech there arose to save Israel Tola the son of Puah, the son of Dodo, a man of Issachar; and he dwelt in Shamir in the mountains of Ephraim. ²He judged Israel twenty-three years; and he died and was buried in Shamir.

³After him arose Jair, a Gileadite; and he judged Israel twenty-two years. ⁴Now he had thirty sons who rode on thirty donkeys; they also had thirty towns, which are called "Havoth Jair"* to this day, which *are* in the land of Gilead. ⁵And Jair died and was buried in Camon.

⁶Then the children of Israel again did evil in the sight of the LORD, and served the Baals and the Ashtoreths, the gods of Syria, the gods of Sidon, the gods of Moab, the gods of the people of Ammon, and the gods of the Philistines; and they forsook the LORD and did not serve Him. ⁷So the anger of the LORD was hot against Israel; and He sold them into the hands of the Philistines and into the hands of the people of Ammon. ⁸From that year they harassed and oppressed the children of Israel for eighteen years—all the children of Israel who *were* on the other side of the Jordan in the land of the Amorites, in Gilead. ⁹Moreover the people of Ammon crossed over the Jordan to fight against Judah also, against Benjamin, and against the house of Ephraim, so that Israel was severely distressed.

¹⁰And the children of Israel cried out to the LORD, saying, "We have sinned against You, because we have both forsaken our God and served the Baals!" ¹¹So the LORD said to the children of Israel, *"Did I* not *deliver you* from the Egyptians and from the Amorites and from the people of Ammon and from the Philistines? ¹²Also the Sidonians and Amalekites and Maonites* op-

pressed you; and you cried out to Me, and I delivered you from their hand. ¹³Yet you have forsaken Me and served other gods. Therefore I will deliver you no more. ¹⁴Go and cry out to the gods which you have chosen; let them deliver you in your time of distress."

¹⁵And the children of Israel said to the LORD, "We have sinned! Do to us whatever seems best to You; only deliver us this day, we pray." ¹⁶So they put away the foreign gods from among them and served the LORD. And His soul could no longer endure the misery of Israel.

¹⁷Then the people of Ammon gathered together and encamped in Gilead. And the children of Israel assembled together and encamped in Mizpah. ¹⁸And the people, the leaders of Gilead, said to one another, "Who *is* the man who will begin the fight against the people of Ammon? He shall be head over all the inhabitants of Gilead."

LUKE 24:13-53

Now behold, two of them were traveling that same day to a village called Emmaus, which was seven miles* from Jerusalem. ¹⁴And they talked together of all these things which had happened. ¹⁵So it was, while they conversed and reasoned, that Jesus Himself drew near and went with them. ¹⁶But their eyes were restrained, so that they did not know Him.

¹⁷And He said to them, "What kind of conversation *is* this that you have with one another as you walk and are sad?"*

¹⁸Then the one whose name was Cleopas answered and said to Him, "Are You the only stranger in Jerusalem, and have You not known the things which have happened there in these days?"

¹⁹And He said to them, "What things?"

So they said to Him, "The things concerning Jesus of Nazareth, who was a Prophet mighty in deed and word before God and all the people, ²⁰and how the chief priests and our rulers delivered Him to be condemned to death, and crucified Him. ²¹But we were hoping that it was He who was going to redeem Israel. Indeed, besides all this, today is the third day since these things happened. ²²Yes, and certain women of our company, who arrived at the tomb early, astonished us. ²³When they did not find His body, they came saying that they had also seen a vision of angels who said He was alive. ²⁴And certain of those *who were* with us went to the tomb and found *it* just as the women had said; but Him they did not see."

²⁵Then He said to them, "O foolish ones, and slow of heart to believe in all that the prophets have spoken! ²⁶Ought not the Christ to have suffered these things and to enter into His glory?" ²⁷And beginning at Moses and all the Prophets, He expounded to them in all the Scriptures the things concerning Himself.

²⁸Then they drew near to the village where they were going, and He indicated that He would have gone farther. ²⁹But they constrained Him, saying, "Abide with us, for it is toward evening, and the day is far spent." And He went in to stay with them.

³⁰Now it came to pass, as He sat at the table with them, that He took bread, blessed and broke *it,* and gave it to them. ³¹Then their eyes were opened and they knew Him; and He vanished from their sight.

³²And they said to one another, "Did not our heart burn within us while He talked with us on the road, and while He opened the Scriptures to us?" ³³So they rose up that very hour and returned to Jerusalem, and found the eleven and those *who were* with them gathered together, ³⁴saying, "The Lord is risen indeed, and has appeared to Simon!" ³⁵And they told about the things *that had happened* on the road, and how He was known to them in the breaking of bread.

³⁶Now as they said these things, Jesus Himself stood in the midst of them, and said to them, "Peace to you." ³⁷But they were terrified and frightened, and supposed they had seen a spirit. ³⁸And He said to them, "Why are you troubled? And why do doubts arise in your hearts? ³⁹Behold My hands and My feet, that it is I Myself. Handle Me and see, for a spirit does not have flesh and bones as you see I have."

⁴⁰When He had said this, He showed them His hands and His feet.* ⁴¹But while they still did not believe for joy, and marveled, He said to them, "Have you any food here?" ⁴²So they gave Him a piece of a broiled fish and some honeycomb.* ⁴³And He took *it* and ate in their presence.

⁴⁴Then He said to them, "These *are* the words which I spoke to you while I was still with you, that all things must be fulfilled which were written in the Law of Moses and *the* Prophets and *the* Psalms concerning Me." ⁴⁵And He opened their understanding, that they might comprehend the Scriptures.

⁴⁶Then He said to them, "Thus it is written, and thus it was necessary for the Christ to suffer and to rise* from the dead the third day, ⁴⁷and that repentance and remission of sins should be preached in His name to all nations, beginning at Jerusalem. ⁴⁸And you are witnesses of these things. ⁴⁹Behold, I send the Promise of My Father upon you; but tarry in the city of Jerusalem* until you are endued with power from on high."

⁵⁰And He led them out as far as Bethany, and He lifted up His hands and blessed them. ⁵¹Now it came to

pass, while He blessed them, that He was parted from them and carried up into heaven. ⁵²And they worshiped Him, and returned to Jerusalem with great joy, ⁵³and were continually in the temple praising and* blessing God. Amen.*

PSALM 100:1-5

A Psalm of Thanksgiving.

MAKE a joyful shout to the LORD, all you lands!
²Serve the LORD with gladness;
Come before His presence with singing.

³ Know that the LORD, He *is* God;
It is He *who* has made us, and not we ourselves;*
We are His people and the sheep of His pasture.

⁴ Enter into His gates with thanksgiving,
And into His courts with praise.
Be thankful to Him, *and* bless His name.
⁵ For the LORD *is* good;
His mercy *is* everlasting,
And His truth *endures* to all generations.

PROVERBS FOR TODAY/ 14:11-12

The house of the wicked will be overthrown, but the tent of the upright will flourish.
▢ *There is a way* that seems *right to a man, but its end* is *the way of death.*

APRIL 30

JUDGES 11:1–12:15

Now Jephthah the Gileadite was a mighty man of valor, but he *was* the son of a harlot; and Gilead begot Jephthah. ²Gilead's wife bore sons; and when his wife's sons grew up, they drove Jephthah out, and said to him, "You shall have no inheritance in our father's house, for you *are* the son of another woman." ³Then Jephthah fled from his brothers and dwelt in the land of Tob; and worthless men banded together with Jephthah and went out *raiding* with him.

⁴It came to pass after a time that the people of Ammon made war against Israel. ⁵And so it was, when the people of Ammon made war against Israel, that the elders of Gilead went to get Jephthah from the land of Tob. ⁶Then they said to Jephthah, "Come and be our commander, that we may fight against the people of Ammon."

⁷So Jephthah said to the elders of Gilead, "Did you not hate me, and expel me from my father's house? Why have you come to me now when you are in distress?"

⁸And the elders of Gilead said to Jephthah, "That is why we have turned again to you now, that you may go with us and fight against the people of Ammon, and be our head over all the inhabitants of Gilead."

⁹So Jephthah said to the elders of Gilead, "If you take me back home to fight against the people of Ammon, and the LORD delivers them to me, shall I be your head?"

¹⁰And the elders of Gilead said to Jephthah, "The LORD will be a witness between us, if we do not do according to your words." ¹¹Then Jephthah went with the elders of Gilead, and the people made him head and commander over them; and Jephthah spoke all his words before the LORD in Mizpah.

¹²Now Jephthah sent messengers to the king of the people of Ammon, saying, "What do you have against me, that you have come to fight against me in my land?"

¹³And the king of the people of Ammon answered the messengers of Jephthah, "Because Israel took away my land when they came up out of Egypt, from the Arnon as far as the Jabbok, and to the Jordan. Now therefore, restore those *lands* peaceably."

¹⁴So Jephthah again sent messengers to the king of the people of Ammon, ¹⁵and said to him, "Thus says Jephthah: 'Israel did not take away the land of Moab, nor the land of the people of Ammon; ¹⁶for when Israel came up from Egypt, they walked through the wilderness as far as the Red Sea and came to Kadesh. ¹⁷Then Israel sent messengers to the king of Edom, saying, "Please let me pass through your land." But the king of Edom would not heed. And in like manner they sent to the king of Moab, but he would not *consent.* So Israel remained in Kadesh. ¹⁸And they went along through the wilderness and bypassed the land of Edom and the land of Moab, came to the east side of the land of Moab, and encamped on the other side of the Arnon. But they did not enter the border of Moab, for the Arnon *was* the border of Moab. ¹⁹Then Israel sent messengers to Sihon king of the Amorites, king of Heshbon; and Israel said to him, "Please let us pass through your land into our place." ²⁰But Sihon did not trust Israel to pass through his territory. So Sihon gathered all his people together, encamped in Jahaz, and fought against Israel. ²¹And the LORD God of Israel delivered Sihon and all his people into the hand of Israel, and they defeated them. Thus Israel gained possession of all the land of the Amorites, who inhabited that country. ²²They took possession of all the territory of the Amorites, from the Arnon to the Jabbok and from the wilderness to the Jordan.

²³'And now the LORD God of Israel has dispossessed the Amorites from before His people Israel; should you then possess it? ²⁴Will you not possess whatever Chemosh your god gives you to possess? So whatever the LORD our God takes possession of before us, we will possess. ²⁵And now, *are* you any better than Balak the son of Zippor, king of Moab? Did he ever strive against Israel? Did he ever fight against them? ²⁶While Israel dwelt in Heshbon and its villages, in Aroer and its villages, and in all the cities along the banks of the Arnon, for three hundred years, why did you not recover *them* within that time? ²⁷Therefore I have not sinned against you, but you wronged me by fighting against me. May the LORD, the Judge, render judgment this day between the children of Israel and the people of Ammon.' " ²⁸However, the king of the people of Ammon did not heed the words which Jephthah sent him.

²⁹Then the Spirit of the LORD came upon Jephthah, and he passed through Gilead and Manasseh, and passed through Mizpah of Gilead; and from Mizpah of Gilead he advanced *toward* the people of Ammon. ³⁰And Jephthah made a vow to the LORD, and said, "If You will indeed deliver the people of Ammon into my hands, ³¹then it will be that whatever comes out of the doors of my house to meet me, when I return in peace from the people of Ammon, shall surely be the LORD's, and I will offer it up as a burnt offering." ³²So Jephthah advanced toward the

"Praise the LORD, for the LORD is good; sing praises to His name."
Psalm 135:3

"As for me and my house,
we will serve the LORD."

Joshua 24:15

"The LORD bless you and keep you; the LORD make His face shine upon you."

Numbers 6:24-25

people of Ammon to fight against them, and the LORD delivered them into his hands. ³³And he defeated them from Aroer as far as Minnith—twenty cities—and to Abel Keramim,* with a very great slaughter. Thus the people of Ammon were subdued before the children of Israel.

³⁴When Jephthah came to his house at Mizpah, there was his daughter, coming out to meet him with timbrels and dancing; and she *was his* only child. Besides her he had neither son nor daughter. ³⁵And it came to pass, when he saw her, that he tore his clothes, and said, "Alas, my daughter! You have brought me very low! You are among those who trouble me! For I have given my word to the LORD, and I cannot go back on it."

³⁶So she said to him, "My father, *if* you have given your word to the LORD, do to me according to what has gone out of your mouth, because the LORD has avenged you of your enemies, the people of Ammon." ³⁷Then she said to her father, "Let this thing be done for me: let me alone for two months, that I may go and wander on the mountains and bewail my virginity, my friends and I."

³⁸So he said, "Go." And he sent her away *for* two months; and she went with her friends, and bewailed her virginity on the mountains. ³⁹And it was so at the end of two months that she returned to her father, and he carried out his vow with her which he had vowed. She knew no man.

And it became a custom in Israel ⁴⁰*that* the daughters of Israel went four days each year to lament the daughter of Jephthah the Gileadite.

THEN the men of Ephraim gathered together, crossed over toward Zaphon, and said to Jephthah, "Why did you cross over to fight against the people of Ammon, and did not call us to go with you? We will burn your house down on you with fire!"

²And Jephthah said to them, "My people and I were in a great struggle with the people of Ammon; and when I called you, you did not deliver me out of their hands. ³So when I saw that you would not deliver *me,* I took my life in my hands and crossed over against the people of Ammon; and the LORD delivered them into my hand. Why then have you come up to me this day to fight against me?" ⁴Now Jephthah gathered together all the men of Gilead and fought against Ephraim. And the men of Gilead defeated Ephraim, because they said, "You Gileadites *are* fugitives of Ephraim among the Ephraimites *and* among the Manassites." ⁵The Gileadites seized the fords of the Jordan before the Ephraimites *arrived.* And when *any* Ephraimite who escaped said, "Let me cross over," the men of Gilead would say to him, "*Are* you an Ephraimite?" If he said, "No," ⁶then they would say to him, "Then say, 'Shibboleth'!" And he would say, "Sibboleth," for he could not pronounce *it* right. Then they would take him and kill him at the fords of the Jordan. There fell at that time forty-two thousand Ephraimites.

⁷And Jephthah judged Israel six years. Then Jephthah the Gileadite died and was buried among the cities of Gilead.

⁸After him, Ibzan of Bethlehem judged Israel. ⁹He had thirty sons. And he gave away thirty daughters in marriage, and brought in thirty daughters from elsewhere for his sons. He judged Israel seven years. ¹⁰Then Ibzan died and was buried at Bethlehem.

¹¹After him, Elon the Zebulunite judged Israel. He judged Israel ten years. ¹²And Elon the Zebulunite died and was buried at Aijalon in the country of Zebulun.

¹³After him, Abdon the son of Hillel the Pirathonite judged Israel. ¹⁴He had forty sons and thirty grandsons, who

rode on seventy young donkeys. He judged Israel eight years. ¹⁵Then Abdon the son of Hillel the Pirathonite died and was buried in Pirathon in the land of Ephraim, in the mountains of the Amalekites.

JOHN 1:1-28

Iɴ the beginning was the Word, and the Word was with God, and the Word was God. ²He was in the beginning with God. ³All things were made through Him, and without Him nothing was made that was made. ⁴In Him was life, and the life was the light of men. ⁵And the light shines in the darkness, and the darkness did not comprehend* it.

⁶There was a man sent from God, whose name *was* John. ⁷This man came for a witness, to bear witness of the Light, that all through him might believe. ⁸He was not that Light, but *was sent* to bear witness of that Light. ⁹That was the true Light which gives light to every man coming into the world.*

¹⁰He was in the world, and the world was made through Him, and the world did not know Him. ¹¹He came to His own,* and His own* did not receive Him. ¹²But as many as received Him, to them He gave the right to become children of God, to those who believe in His name: ¹³who were born, not of blood, nor of the will of the flesh, nor of the will of man, but of God.

¹⁴And the Word became flesh and dwelt among us, and we beheld His glory, the glory as of the only begotten of the Father, full of grace and truth.

¹⁵John bore witness of Him and cried out, saying, "This was He of whom I said, 'He who comes after me is preferred before me, for He was before me.' "

¹⁶And* of His fullness we have all received, and grace for grace. ¹⁷For the law was given through Moses, *but* grace and truth came through Jesus Christ. ¹⁸No one has seen God at any time. The only begotten Son,* who is in the bosom of the Father, He has declared *Him.*

¹⁹Now this is the testimony of John, when the Jews sent priests and Levites from Jerusalem to ask him, "Who are you?"

²⁰He confessed, and did not deny, but confessed, "I am not the Christ."

²¹And they asked him, "What then? Are you Elijah?"

He said, "I am not."

"Are you the Prophet?"

And he answered, "No."

²²Then they said to him, "Who are you, that we may give an answer to those who sent us? What do you say about yourself?"

²³He said: "I *am*

> '*The voice of one crying in the wilderness:*
> "*Make straight the way of the* Lᴏʀᴅ," ' *

as the prophet Isaiah said."

²⁴Now those who were sent were from the Pharisees. ²⁵And they asked him, saying, "Why then do you baptize if you are not the Christ, nor Elijah, nor the Prophet?"

²⁶John answered them, saying, "I baptize with water, but there stands One among you whom you do not know. ²⁷It is He who, coming after me, is preferred before me, whose sandal strap I am not worthy to loose."

²⁸These things were done in Bethabara* beyond the Jordan, where John was baptizing.

PSALM 101:1-8

A Psalm of David.

I ᴡɪʟʟ sing of mercy and justice; To You, O Lᴏʀᴅ, I will sing praises.

2   I will behave wisely in a perfect way.

Oh, when will You come to
me?
I will walk within my house
with a perfect heart.

3 I will set nothing wicked
before my eyes;
I hate the work of those who
fall away;
It shall not cling to me.

4 A perverse heart shall depart
from me;
I will not know wickedness.

5 Whoever secretly slanders his
neighbor,
Him I will destroy;

The one who has a haughty
look and a proud heart,
Him I will not endure.

6 My eyes *shall be* on the
faithful of the land,
That they may dwell with me;
He who walks in a perfect way,
He shall serve me.

7 He who works deceit shall not
dwell within my house;
He who tells lies shall not
continue in my presence.

8 Early I will destroy all the
wicked of the land,
That I may cut off all the
evildoers from the city of
the LORD.

PROVERBS FOR TODAY/ 14:13-14

Even in laughter the heart may sorrow, and the end of mirth may be *grief.* □ *The*
backslider in heart will be filled with his own ways, but a good man will be satisfied
from above. *

MAY 1

JUDGES 13:1–14:20

A GAIN the children of Israel did
evil in the sight of the LORD,
and the LORD delivered them
into the hand of the Philistines for
forty years.

2Now there was a certain man from
Zorah, of the family of the Danites,
whose name *was* Manoah; and his wife
was barren and had no children. 3And
the Angel of the LORD appeared to the
woman and said to her, "Indeed now,
you are barren and have borne no children, but you shall conceive and bear
a son. 4Now therefore, please be careful not to drink wine or *similar* drink,
and not to eat anything unclean. 5For
behold, you shall conceive and bear a

son. And no razor shall come upon his
head, for the child shall be a Nazirite to
God from the womb; and he shall begin to deliver Israel out of the hand of
the Philistines."

6So the woman came and told her
husband, saying, "A Man of God came
to me, and His countenance *was* like
the countenance of the Angel of God,
very awesome; but I did not ask Him
where He *was* from, and He did not tell
me His name. 7And He said to me, 'Behold, you shall conceive and bear a
son. Now drink no wine or *similar*
drink, nor eat anything unclean, for the
child shall be a Nazirite to God from
the womb to the day of his death.' ".

8Then Manoah prayed to the LORD,
and said, "O my Lord, please let the

Man of God whom You sent come to us again and teach us what we shall do for the child who will be born."

⁹And God listened to the voice of Manoah, and the Angel of God came to the woman again as she was sitting in the field; but Manoah her husband *was* not with her. ¹⁰Then the woman ran in haste and told her husband, and said to him, "Look, the Man who came to me the *other* day has just now appeared to me!"

¹¹So Manoah arose and followed his wife. When he came to the Man, he said to Him, "Are You the Man who spoke to this woman?"

And He said, "I *am.*"

¹²Manoah said, "Now let Your words come *to pass!* What will be the boy's rule of life, and his work?"

¹³So the Angel of the LORD said to Manoah, "Of all that I said to the woman let her be careful. ¹⁴She may not eat anything that comes from the vine, nor may she drink wine or *similar* drink, nor eat anything unclean. All that I commanded her let her observe."

¹⁵Then Manoah said to the Angel of the LORD, "Please let us detain You, and we will prepare a young goat for You."

¹⁶And the Angel of the LORD said to Manoah, "Though you detain Me, I will not eat your food. But if you offer a burnt offering, you must offer it to the LORD." (For Manoah did not know He *was* the Angel of the LORD.)

¹⁷Then Manoah said to the Angel of the LORD, "What *is* Your name, that when Your words come *to pass* we may honor You?"

¹⁸And the Angel of the LORD said to him, "Why do you ask My name, seeing it *is* wonderful?"

¹⁹So Manoah took the young goat with the grain offering, and offered it upon the rock to the LORD. And He did a wondrous thing while Manoah and his wife looked on— ²⁰it happened as the flame went up toward heaven from the altar—the Angel of the LORD ascended in the flame of the altar! When Manoah and his wife saw *this,* they fell on their faces to the ground. ²¹When the Angel of the LORD appeared no more to Manoah and his wife, then Manoah knew that He *was* the Angel of the LORD.

²²And Manoah said to his wife, "We shall surely die, because we have seen God!"

²³But his wife said to him, "If the LORD had desired to kill us, He would not have accepted a burnt offering and a grain offering from our hands, nor would He have shown us all these *things,* nor would He have told us *such things* as these at this time."

²⁴So the woman bore a son and called his name Samson; and the child grew, and the LORD blessed him. ²⁵And the Spirit of the LORD began to move upon him at Mahaneh Dan* between Zorah and Eshtaol.

Now Samson went down to Timnah, and saw a woman in Timnah of the daughters of the Philistines. ²So he went up and told his father and mother, saying, "I have seen a woman in Timnah of the daughters of the Philistines; now therefore, get her for me as a wife."

³Then his father and mother said to him, "*Is there* no woman among the daughters of your brethren, or among all my people, that you must go and get a wife from the uncircumcised Philistines?"

And Samson said to his father, "Get her for me, for she pleases me well."

⁴But his father and mother did not know that it was of the LORD—that He was seeking an occasion to move against the Philistines. For at that time the Philistines had dominion over Israel.

⁵So Samson went down to Timnah with his father and mother, and came to the vineyards of Timnah.

Now *to his* surprise, a young lion *came* roaring against him. 6And the Spirit of the LORD came mightily upon him, and he tore the lion apart as one would have torn apart a young goat, though *he had* nothing in his hand. But he did not tell his father or his mother what he had done.

7Then he went down and talked with the woman; and she pleased Samson well. 8After some time, when he returned to get her, he turned aside to see the carcass of the lion. And behold, a swarm of bees and honey *were* in the carcass of the lion. 9He took some of it in his hands and went along, eating When he came to his father and mother, he gave *some* to them, and they also ate. But he did not tell them that he had taken the honey out of the carcass of the lion.

10So his father went down to the woman. And Samson gave a feast there, for young men used to do so. 11And it happened, when they saw him, that they brought thirty companions to be with him.

12Then Samson said to them, "Let me pose a riddle to you. If you can correctly solve and explain it to me within the seven days of the feast, then I will give you thirty linen garments and thirty changes of clothing. 13But if you cannot explain *it* to me, then you shall give me thirty linen garments and thirty changes of clothing."

And they said to him, "Pose your riddle, that we may hear it."

14So he said to them:

> "Out of the eater came
>   something to eat,
> And out of the strong came
>   something sweet."

Now for three days they could not explain the riddle.

15But it came to pass on the seventh* day that they said to Samson's wife, "Entice your husband, that he may explain the riddle to us, or else we will burn you and your father's house with fire. Have you invited us in order to take what is ours? *Is that* not *so?*"

16Then Samson's wife wept on him, and said, "You only hate me! You do not love me! You have posed a riddle to the sons of my people, but you have not explained *it* to me."

And he said to her, "Look, I have not explained *it* to my father or my mother; so should I explain *it* to you?" 17Now she had wept on him the seven days while their feast lasted. And it happened on the seventh day that he told her, because she pressed him so much. Then she explained the riddle to the sons of her people. 18So the men of the city said to him on the seventh day before the sun went down:

> "What *is* sweeter than honey?
> And what *is* stronger than a
>   lion?"

And he said to them:

> "If you had not plowed with my
>   heifer,
> You would not have solved my
>   riddle!"

19Then the Spirit of the LORD came upon him mightily, and he went down to Ashkelon and killed thirty of their men, took their apparel, and gave the changes *of clothing* to those who had explained the riddle. So his anger was aroused, and he went back up to his father's house. 20And Samson's wife was *given* to his companion, who had been his best man.

JOHN 1:29-51

THE next day John [the Baptist] saw Jesus coming toward him, and said, "Behold! The Lamb of God who takes away the sin of the world! 30This is He of whom I said, 'After me comes a Man who is preferred before me, for He was before me.' 31I did not know Him; but that He should be revealed to Israel, therefore I came baptizing with water."

³²And John bore witness, saying, "I saw the Spirit descending from heaven like a dove, and He remained upon Him. ³³I did not know Him, but He who sent me to baptize with water said to me, 'Upon whom you see the Spirit descending, and remaining on Him, this is He who baptizes with the Holy Spirit.' ³⁴And I have seen and testified that this is the Son of God."

³⁵Again, the next day, John stood with two of his disciples. ³⁶And looking at Jesus as He walked, he said, "Behold the Lamb of God!"

³⁷The two disciples heard him speak, and they followed Jesus. ³⁸Then Jesus turned, and seeing them following, said to them, "What do you seek?"

They said to Him, "Rabbi" (which is to say, when translated, Teacher), "where are You staying?"

³⁹He said to them, "Come and see." They came and saw where He was staying, and remained with Him that day (now it was about the tenth hour).

⁴⁰One of the two who heard John *speak,* and followed Him, was Andrew, Simon Peter's brother. ⁴¹He first found his own brother Simon, and said to him, "We have found the Messiah" (which is translated, the Christ). ⁴²And he brought him to Jesus.

Now when Jesus looked at him, He said, "You are Simon the son of Jonah.* You shall be called Cephas" (which is translated, A Stone).

⁴³The following day Jesus wanted to go to Galilee, and He found Philip and said to him, "Follow Me." ⁴⁴Now Philip was from Bethsaida, the city of Andrew and Peter. ⁴⁵Philip found Nathanael and said to him, "We have found Him of whom Moses in the law, and also the prophets, wrote—Jesus of Nazareth, the son of Joseph."

⁴⁶And Nathanael said to him, "Can anything good come out of Nazareth?" Philip said to him, "Come and see."

⁴⁷Jesus saw Nathanael coming toward Him, and said of him, "Behold, an Israelite indeed, in whom is no deceit!"

⁴⁸Nathanael said to Him, "How do You know me?"

Jesus answered and said to him, "Before Philip called you, when you were under the fig tree, I saw you."

⁴⁹Nathanael answered and said to Him, "Rabbi, You are the Son of God! You are the King of Israel!"

⁵⁰Jesus answered and said to him, "Because I said to you, 'I saw you under the fig tree,' do you believe? You will see greater things than these." ⁵¹And He said to him, "Most assuredly, I say to you, hereafter* you shall see heaven open, and the angels of God ascending and descending upon the Son of Man."

PSALM 102:1-28

A Prayer of the afflicted, when he is overwhelmed and pours out his complaint before the LORD.

HEAR my prayer, O LORD,
And let my cry come to You.
²Do not hide Your face from
    me in the day of my trouble;
Incline Your ear to me;
In the day that I call, answer
    me speedily.

3   For my days are consumed
        like smoke,
    And my bones are burned
        like a hearth.
4   My heart is stricken and
        withered like grass,
    So that I forget to eat my
        bread.
5   Because of the sound of my
        groaning
    My bones cling to my skin.
6   I am like a pelican of the
        wilderness;
    I am like an owl of the desert.
7   I lie awake,
    And am like a sparrow alone
        on the housetop.

8 My enemies reproach me all
day long;
Those who deride me swear
an oath against me.

9 For I have eaten ashes like
bread,
And mingled my drink with
weeping,

10 Because of Your indignation
and Your wrath;
For You have lifted me up and
cast me away.

11 My days *are* like a shadow
that lengthens,
And I wither away like grass.

12 But You, O LORD, shall endure
forever,
And the remembrance of
Your name to all
generations.

13 You will arise *and* have mercy
on Zion;
For the time to favor her,
Yes, the set time, has come.

14 For Your servants take
pleasure in her stones,
And show favor to her dust.

15 So the nations shall fear the
name of the LORD,
And all the kings of the earth
Your glory.

16 For the LORD shall build up
Zion;
He shall appear in His glory.

17 He shall regard the prayer of
the destitute,
And shall not despise their
prayer.

18 This will be written for the
generation to come,
That a people yet to be

created may praise the
LORD.

19 For He looked down from the
height of His sanctuary;
From heaven the LORD viewed
the earth,

20 To hear the groaning of the
prisoner,
To release those appointed to
death,

21 To declare the name of the
LORD in Zion,
And His praise in Jerusalem,

22 When the peoples are
gathered together,
And the kingdoms, to serve
the LORD.

23 He weakened my strength in
the way;
He shortened my days.

24 I said, "O my God,
Do not take me away in the
midst of my days;
Your years *are* throughout all
generations.

25 Of old You laid the foundation
of the earth,
And the heavens *are* the work
of Your hands.

26 They will perish, but You will
endure;
Yes, they will all grow old like
a garment;
Like a cloak You will change
them,
And they will be changed.

27 But You *are* the same,
And Your years will have no
end.

28 The children of Your servants
will continue,
And their descendants will be
established before You."

PROVERBS FOR TODAY / 14:15-16

The simple believes every word, but the prudent considers well his steps. A wise
man *fears and departs from evil, but a fool rages and is self-confident.*

MAY 2

JUDGES 15:1–16:31

AFTER a while, in the time of wheat harvest, it happened that Samson visited his wife with a young goat. And he said, "Let me go in to my wife, into *her* room." But her father would not permit him to go in.

2Her father said, "I really thought that you thoroughly hated her; therefore I gave her to your companion. *Is* not her younger sister better than she? Please, take her instead."

3And Samson said to them, "This time I shall be blameless regarding the Philistines if I harm them!" 4Then Samson went and caught three hundred foxes; and he took torches, turned *the foxes* tail to tail, and put a torch between each pair of tails. 5When he had set the torches on fire, he let *the foxes* go into the standing grain of the Philistines, and burned up both the shocks and the standing grain, as well as the vineyards *and* olive groves.

6Then the Philistines said, "Who has done this?"

And they answered, "Samson, the son-in-law of the Timnite, because he has taken his wife and given her to his companion." So the Philistines came up and burned her and her father with fire.

7Samson said to them, "Since you would do a thing like this, I will surely take revenge on you, and after that I will cease." 8So he attacked them hip and thigh with a great slaughter; then he went down and dwelt in the cleft of the rock of Etam.

9Now the Philistines went up, encamped in Judah, and deployed themselves against Lehi. 10And the men of Judah said, "Why have you come up against us?"

So they answered, "We have come up to arrest Samson, to do to him as he has done to us."

11Then three thousand men of Judah went down to the cleft of the rock of Etam, and said to Samson, "Do you not know that the Philistines rule over us? What *is* this you have done to us?"

And he said to them, "As they did to me, so I have done to them."

12But they said to him, "We have come down to arrest you, that we may deliver you into the hand of the Philistines."

Then Samson said to them, "Swear to me that you will not kill me yourselves."

13So they spoke to him, saying, "No, but we will tie you securely and deliver you into their hand; but we will surely not kill you." And they bound him with two new ropes and brought him up from the rock.

14When he came to Lehi, the Philistines came shouting against him. Then the Spirit of the LORD came mightily upon him; and the ropes that *were* on his arms became like flax that is burned with fire, and his bonds broke loose from his hands. 15He found a fresh jawbone of a donkey, reached out his hand and took it, and killed a thousand men with it. 16Then Samson said:

> "With the jawbone of a donkey,
> Heaps upon heaps,
> With the jawbone of a donkey
> I have slain a thousand men!"

17And so it was, when he had finished speaking, that he threw the jawbone from his hand, and called that place Ramath Lehi.*

18Then he became very thirsty; so

he cried out to the LORD and said, "You have given this great deliverance by the hand of Your servant; and now shall I die of thirst and fall into the hand of the uncircumcised?" [19]So God split the hollow place that *is* in Lehi,* and water came out, and he drank; and his spirit returned, and he revived. Therefore he called its name En Hakkore,* which is in Lehi to this day. [20]And he judged Israel twenty years in the days of the Philistines.

Now Samson went to Gaza and saw a harlot there, and went in to her. [2]*When* the Gazites *were told,* "Samson has come here!" they surrounded *the place* and lay in wait for him all night at the gate of the city. They were quiet all night, saying, "In the morning, when it is daylight, we will kill him." [3]And Samson lay *low* till midnight; then he arose at midnight, took hold of the doors of the gate of the city and the two gateposts, pulled them up, bar and all, put *them* on his shoulders, and carried them to the top of the hill that faces Hebron.

[4]Afterward it happened that he loved a woman in the Valley of Sorek, whose name *was* Delilah. [5]And the lords of the Philistines came up to her and said to her, "Entice him, and find out where his great strength *lies,* and by what *means* we may overpower him, that we may bind him to afflict him; and every one of us will give you eleven hundred *pieces* of silver."

[6]So Delilah said to Samson, "Please tell me where your great strength *lies,* and with what you may be bound to afflict you."

[7]And Samson said to her, "If they bind me with seven fresh bowstrings, not yet dried, then I shall become weak, and be like any *other* man."

[8]So the lords of the Philistines brought up to her seven fresh bowstrings, not yet dried, and she bound him with them. [9]Now *men were* lying in wait, staying with her in the room. And she said to him, "The Philistines *are* upon you, Samson!" But he broke the bowstrings as a strand of yarn breaks when it touches fire. So the secret of his strength was not known.

[10]Then Delilah said to Samson, "Look, you have mocked me and told me lies. Now, please tell me what you may be bound with."

[11]So he said to her, "If they bind me securely with new ropes that have never been used, then I shall become weak, and be like any *other* man."

[12]Therefore Delilah took new ropes and bound him with them, and said to him, "The Philistines *are* upon you, Samson!" And *men were* lying in wait, staying in the room. But he broke them off his arms like a thread.

[13]Delilah said to Samson, "Until now you have mocked me and told me lies. Tell me what you may be bound with."

And he said to her, "If you weave the seven locks of my head into the web of the loom"—

[14]So she wove *it* tightly with the batten of the loom, and said to him, "The Philistines *are* upon you, Samson!" But he awoke from his sleep, and pulled out the batten and the web from the loom.

[15]Then she said to him, "How can you say, 'I love you,' when your heart *is* not with me? You have mocked me these three times, and have not told me where your great strength *lies.*" [16]And it came to pass, when she pestered him daily with her words and pressed him, *so* that his soul was vexed to death, [17]that he told her all his heart, and said to her, "No razor has ever come upon my head, for I *have been* a Nazirite to God from my mother's womb. If I am shaven, then my strength will leave me, and I shall become weak, and be like any *other* man."

[18]When Delilah saw that he had told her all his heart, she sent and called

for the lords of the Philistines, saying, "Come up once more, for he has told me all his heart." So the lords of the Philistines came up to her and brought the money in their hand. ¹⁹Then she lulled him to sleep on her knees, and called for a man and had him shave off the seven locks of his head. Then she began to torment him,* and his strength left him. ²⁰And she said, "The Philistines *are* upon you, Samson!" So he awoke from his sleep, and said, "I will go out as before, at other times, and shake myself free!" But he did not know that the LORD had departed from him.

²¹Then the Philistines took him and put out his eyes, and brought him down to Gaza. They bound him with bronze fetters, and he became a grinder in the prison. ²²However, the hair of his head began to grow again after it had been shaven.

²³Now the lords of the Philistines gathered together to offer a great sacrifice to Dagon their god, and to rejoice. And they said:

> "Our god has delivered into
> our hands
> Samson our enemy!"

²⁴When the people saw him, they praised their god; for they said:

> "Our god has delivered into
> our hands our enemy,
> The destroyer of our land,
> And the one who multiplied
> our dead."

²⁵So it happened, when their hearts were merry, that they said, "Call for Samson, that he may perform for us." So they called for Samson from the prison, and he performed for them. And they stationed him between the pillars. ²⁶Then Samson said to the lad who held him by the hand, "Let me feel the pillars which support the temple, so that I can lean on them." ²⁷Now the temple was full of men and women. All

the lords of the Philistines *were* there—about three thousand men and women on the roof watching while Samson performed.

²⁸Then Samson called to the LORD, saying, "O Lord GOD, remember me, I pray! Strengthen me, I pray, just this once, O God, that I may with one *blow* take vengeance on the Philistines for my two eyes!" ²⁹And Samson took hold of the two middle pillars which supported the temple, and he braced himself against them, one on his right and the other on his left. ³⁰Then Samson said, "Let me die with the Philistines!" And he pushed with *all his* might, and the temple fell on the lords and all the people who *were* in it. So the dead that he killed at his death were more than he had killed in his life.

³¹And his brothers and all his father's household came down and took him, and brought *him* up and buried him between Zorah and Eshtaol in the tomb of his father Manoah. He had judged Israel twenty years.

JOHN 2:1-25

ON the third day there was a wedding in Cana of Galilee, and the mother of Jesus was there. ²Now both Jesus and His disciples were invited to the wedding. ³And when they ran out of wine, the mother of Jesus said to Him, "They have no wine."

⁴Jesus said to her, "Woman, what does your concern have to do with Me? My hour has not yet come."

⁵His mother said to the servants, "Whatever He says to you, do *it*."

⁶Now there were set there six waterpots of stone, according to the manner of purification of the Jews, containing twenty or thirty gallons apiece. ⁷Jesus said to them, "Fill the waterpots with water." And they filled them up to the brim. ⁸And He said to them, "Draw *some* out now, and take *it*

to the master of the feast." And they took *it*. ⁹When the master of the feast had tasted the water that was made wine, and did not know where it came from (but the servants who had drawn the water knew), the master of the feast called the bridegroom. ¹⁰And he said to him, "Every man at the beginning sets out the good wine, and when the *guests* have well drunk, then the inferior. You have kept the good wine until now!"

¹¹This beginning of signs Jesus did in Cana of Galilee, and manifested His glory; and His disciples believed in Him.

¹²After this He went down to Capernaum, He, His mother, His brothers, and His disciples; and they did not stay there many days.

¹³Now the Passover of the Jews was at hand, and Jesus went up to Jerusalem. ¹⁴And He found in the temple those who sold oxen and sheep and doves, and the money changers doing business. ¹⁵When He had made a whip of cords, He drove them all out of the temple, with the sheep and the oxen, and poured out the changers' money and overturned the tables. ¹⁶And He said to those who sold doves, "Take these things away! Do not make My Father's house a house of merchandise!" ¹⁷Then His disciples remembered that it was written, *"Zeal for Your house has eaten * Me up." *

¹⁸So the Jews answered and said to Him, "What sign do You show to us, since You do these things?"

¹⁹Jesus answered and said to them, "Destroy this temple, and in three days I will raise it up."

²⁰Then the Jews said, "It has taken forty-six years to build this temple, and will You raise it up in three days?"

²¹But He was speaking of the temple of His body. ²²Therefore, when He had risen from the dead, His disciples remembered that He had said this to them;* and they believed the Scripture and the word which Jesus had said.

²³Now when He was in Jerusalem at the Passover, during the feast, many believed in His name when they saw the signs which He did. ²⁴But Jesus did not commit Himself to them, because He knew all *men*, ²⁵and had no need that anyone should testify of man, for He knew what was in man.

PSALM 103:1-22

A Psalm *of David*.

BLESS the LORD, O my soul;
And all that is within me, *bless*
His holy name!

2 Bless the LORD, O my soul,
And forget not all His benefits:

3 Who forgives all your
iniquities,
Who heals all your diseases,

4 Who redeems your life from
destruction,
Who crowns you with
lovingkindness and tender
mercies,

5 Who satisfies your mouth
with good *things*,
So that your youth is renewed
like the eagle's.

6 The LORD executes
righteousness
And justice for all who are
oppressed.

7 He made known His ways to
Moses,
His acts to the children of
Israel.

8 The LORD *is* merciful and
gracious,
Slow to anger, and abounding
in mercy.

9 He will not always strive *with
us,*
Nor will He keep *His anger*
forever.

10 He has not dealt with us
according to our sins,

Nor punished us according to
our iniquities.

11 For as the heavens are high
above the earth,
So great is His mercy toward
those who fear Him;

12 As far as the east is from the
west,
So far has He removed our
transgressions from us.

13 As a father pities *his* children,
So the LORD pities those who
fear Him.

14 For He knows our frame;
He remembers that we *are*
dust.

15 *As for* man, his days *are* like
grass;
As a flower of the field, so he
flourishes.

16 For the wind passes over it,
and it is gone,
And its place remembers it no
more.*

17 But the mercy of the LORD *is*
from everlasting to
everlasting

On those who fear Him,
And His righteousness to
children's children,

18 To such as keep His covenant,
And to those who remember
His commandments to do
them.

19 The LORD has established His
throne in heaven,
And His kingdom rules over
all.

20 Bless the LORD, you His
angels,
Who excel in strength, who
do His word,
Heeding the voice of His
word.

21 Bless the LORD, all *you* His
hosts,
You ministers of His, who do
His pleasure.

22 Bless the LORD, all His works,
In all places of His dominion.

Bless the LORD, O my soul!

PROVERBS FOR TODAY/ 14:17-19

A quick-tempered man acts foolishly, and a man of wicked intentions is hated.
□ *The simple inherit folly, but the prudent are crowned with knowledge.* □ *The evil
will bow before the good, and the wicked at the gates of the righteous.*

MAY 3

JUDGES 17:1–18:31

Now there was a man from the
mountains of Ephraim, whose
name *was* Micah. ²And he said
to his mother, "The eleven hundred
shekels of silver that were taken from
you, and on which you put a curse,
even saying it in my ears—here *is* the
silver with me; I took it."

And his mother said, "*May you be
blessed* by the LORD, my son!" ³So
when he had returned the eleven hundred *shekels* of silver to his mother, his
mother said, "I had wholly dedicated

the silver from my hand to the LORD for my son, to make a carved image and a molded image; now therefore, I will return it to you." ⁴Thus he returned the silver to his mother. Then his mother took two hundred *shekels* of silver and gave them to the silversmith, and he made it into a carved image and a molded image; and they were in the house of Micah.

⁵The man Micah had a shrine, and made an ephod and household idols;* and he consecrated one of his sons, who became his priest. ⁶In those days *there was* no king in Israel; everyone did *what was* right in his own eyes.

⁷Now there was a young man from Bethlehem in Judah, of the family of Judah; he *was* a Levite, and was staying there. ⁸The man departed from the city of Bethlehem in Judah to stay wherever he could find *a place.* Then he came to the mountains of Ephraim, to the house of Micah, as he journeyed. ⁹And Micah said to him, "Where do you come from?"

So he said to him, "I *am* a Levite from Bethlehem in Judah, and I am on my way to find *a place* to stay."

¹⁰Micah said to him, "Dwell with me, and be a father and a priest to me, and I will give you ten *shekels* of silver per year, a suit of clothes, and your sustenance." So the Levite went in. ¹¹Then the Levite was content to dwell with the man; and the young man became like one of his sons to him. ¹²So Micah consecrated the Levite, and the young man became his priest, and lived in the house of Micah. ¹³Then Micah said, "Now I know that the LORD will be good to me, since I have a Levite as priest!"

IN those days *there was* no king in Israel. And in those days the tribe of the Danites was seeking an inheritance for itself to dwell in; for until that day *their* inheritance among the tribes of Israel had not fallen to them. ²So the children of Dan sent five men of their family from their territory, men of valor from Zorah and Eshtaol, to spy out the land and search it. They said to them, "Go, search the land." So they went to the mountains of Ephraim, to the house of Micah, and lodged there. ³While they *were* at the house of Micah, they recognized the voice of the young Levite. They turned aside and said to him, "Who brought you here? What are you doing in this *place?* What do you have here?"

⁴He said to them, "Thus and so Micah did for me. He has hired me, and I have become his priest."

⁵So they said to him, "Please inquire of God, that we may know whether the journey on which we go will be prosperous."

⁶And the priest said to them, "Go in peace. The presence of the LORD *be* with you on your way."

⁷So the five men departed and went to Laish. They saw the people who *were* there, how they dwelt safely, in the manner of the Sidonians, quiet and secure. *There were* no rulers in the land who might put *them* to shame for anything. They *were* far from the Sidonians, and they had no ties with anyone.*

⁸Then *the spies* came back to their brethren at Zorah and Eshtaol, and their brethren said to them, "What *is* your *report?*"

⁹So they said, "Arise, let us go up against them. For we have seen the land, and indeed it *is* very good. *Would* you *do* nothing? Do not hesitate to go, *and* enter to possess the land. ¹⁰When you go, you will come to a secure people and a large land. For God has given it into your hands, a place where *there is* no lack of anything that *is* on the earth."

¹¹And six hundred men of the family of the Danites went from there, from Zorah and Eshtaol, armed with weapons of war. ¹²Then they went up and encamped in Kirjath Jearim in Judah.

(Therefore they call that place Mahaneh Dan* to this day. There *it is,* west of Kirjath Jearim.) ¹³And they passed from there to the mountains of Ephraim, and came to the house of Micah.

¹⁴Then the five men who had gone to spy out the country of Laish answered and said to their brethren, "Do you know that there are in these houses an ephod, household idols, a carved image, and a molded image? Now therefore, consider what you should do." ¹⁵So they turned aside there, and came to the house of the young Levite man—to the house of Micah—and greeted him. ¹⁶The six hundred men armed with their weapons of war, who *were* of the children of Dan, stood by the entrance of the gate. ¹⁷Then the five men who had gone to spy out the land went up. Entering there, they took the carved image, the ephod, the household idols, and the molded image. The priest stood at the entrance of the gate with the six hundred men *who were* armed with weapons of war.

¹⁸When these went into Micah's house and took the carved image, the ephod, the household idols, and the molded image, the priest said to them, "What are you doing?"

¹⁹And they said to him, "Be quiet, put your hand over your mouth, and come with us; be a father and a priest to us. *Is it* better for you to be a priest to the household of one man, or that you be a priest to a tribe and a family in Israel?" ²⁰So the priest's heart was glad; and he took the ephod, the household idols, and the carved image, and took his place among the people.

²¹Then they turned and departed, and put the little ones, the livestock, and the goods in front of them. ²²When they were a good way from the house of Micah, the men who *were* in the houses near Micah's house gathered together and overtook the children of

Dan. ²³And they called out to the children of Dan. So they turned around and said to Micah, "What ails you, that you have gathered such a company?"

²⁴So he said, "You have taken away my gods which I made, and the priest, and you have gone away. Now what more do I have? How can you say to me, 'What ails you?' "

²⁵And the children of Dan said to him, "Do not let your voice be heard among us, lest angry men fall upon you, and you lose your life, with the lives of your household!" ²⁶Then the children of Dan went their way. And when Micah saw that they *were* too strong for him, he turned and went back to his house.

²⁷So they took *the things* Micah had made, and the priest who had belonged to him, and went to Laish, to a people quiet and secure; and they struck them with the edge of the sword and burned the city with fire. ²⁸*There was* no deliverer, because it *was* far from Sidon, and they had no ties with anyone. It was in the valley that belongs to Beth Rehob. So they rebuilt the city and dwelt there. ²⁹And they called the name of the city Dan, after the name of Dan their father, who was born to Israel. However, the name of the city formerly *was* Laish.

³⁰Then the children of Dan set up for themselves the carved image; and Jonathan the son of Gershom, the son of Manasseh,* and his sons were priests to the tribe of Dan until the day of the captivity of the land. ³¹So they set up for themselves Micah's carved image which he made, all the time that the house of God was in Shiloh.

JOHN 3:1-21

THERE was a man of the Pharisees named Nicodemus, a ruler of the Jews. ²This man came to Jesus by night and said to Him, "Rabbi, we know that You are a teacher come from God; for no one can do these signs that You do unless God is with him."

3Jesus answered and said to him, "Most assuredly, I say to you, unless one is born again, he cannot see the kingdom of God."

4Nicodemus said to Him, "How can a man be born when he is old? Can he enter a second time into his mother's womb and be born?"

5Jesus answered, "Most assuredly, I say to you, unless one is born of water and the Spirit, he cannot enter the kingdom of God. 6That which is born of the flesh is flesh, and that which is born of the Spirit is spirit. 7Do not marvel that I said to you, 'You must be born again.' 8The wind blows where it wishes, and you hear the sound of it, but cannot tell where it comes from and where it goes. So is everyone who is born of the Spirit."

9Nicodemus answered and said to Him, "How can these things be?"

10Jesus answered and said to him, "Are you the teacher of Israel, and do not know these things? 11Most assuredly, I say to you, We speak what We know and testify what We have seen, and you do not receive Our witness. 12If I have told you earthly things and you do not believe, how will you believe if I tell you heavenly things? 13No one has ascended to heaven but He who came down from heaven, *that is,* the Son of Man who is in heaven.* 14And as Moses lifted up the serpent in the wilderness, even so must the Son of Man be lifted up, 15that whoever believes in Him should not perish but* have eternal life. 16For God so loved the world that He gave His only begotten Son, that whoever believes in Him should not perish but have everlasting life. 17For God did not send His Son into the world to condemn the world, but that the world through Him might be saved.

18"He who believes in Him is not condemned; but he who does not believe is condemned already, because he has not believed in the name of the only begotten Son of God. 19And this is the condemnation, that the light has come into the world, and men loved darkness rather than light, because their deeds were evil. 20For everyone practicing evil hates the light and does not come to the light, lest his deeds should be exposed. 21But he who does the truth comes to the light, that his deeds may be clearly seen, that they have been done in God."

PSALM 104:1-23

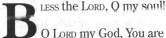

LESS the LORD, O my soul!

O LORD my God, You are very
   great:
You are clothed with honor
   and majesty,
2 Who cover *Yourself* with light
   as *with* a garment,
Who stretch out the heavens
   like a curtain.

3 He lays the beams of His
   upper chambers in the
   waters,
Who makes the clouds His
   chariot,
Who walks on the wings of
   the wind,
4 Who makes His angels spirits,
   His ministers a flame of fire.

5 *You who* laid the foundations
   of the earth,
So *that* it should not be
   moved forever,
6 You covered it with the deep
   as *with* a garment;
The waters stood above the
   mountains.
7 At Your rebuke they fled;
At the voice of Your thunder
   they hastened away.

8 They went up over the
mountains;
They went down into the
valleys,
To the place which You
founded for them.
9 You have set a boundary that
they may not pass over,
That they may not return to
cover the earth.

10 He sends the springs into the
valleys;
They flow among the hills.
11 They give drink to every
beast of the field;
The wild donkeys quench
their thirst.
12 By them the birds of the
heavens have their home;
They sing among the
branches.
13 He waters the hills from His
upper chambers;
The earth is satisfied with the
fruit of Your works.

14 He causes the grass to grow
for the cattle,
And vegetation for the service
of man,
That he may bring forth food
from the earth,
15 And wine *that* makes glad the
heart of man,

Oil to make *his* face shine,
And bread *which* strengthens
man's heart.
16 The trees of the Lord are full
of sap,
The cedars of Lebanon which
He planted,
17 Where the birds make their
nests;
The stork has her home in
the fir trees.
18 The high hills *are* for the wild
goats;
The cliffs are a refuge for the
rock badgers.*

19 He appointed the moon for
seasons;
The sun knows its going
down.
20 You make darkness, and it is
night,
In which all the beasts of the
forest creep about.
21 The young lions roar after
their prey,
And seek their food from God.
22 *When* the sun rises, they
gather together
And lie down in their dens.
23 Man goes out to his work
And to his labor until the
evening.

PROVERBS FOR TODAY/ 14:20-21

The poor man *is hated even by his own neighbor, but the rich* has *many friends. He
who despises his neighbor sins; but he who has mercy on the poor, happy* is *he.*

JUDGES 19:1–20:48

AND it came to pass in those days, when *there was* no king in Israel, that there was a certain Levite staying in the remote mountains of Ephraim. He took for himself a concubine from Bethlehem in Judah. ²But his concubine played the harlot against him, and went away from him to her father's house at Bethlehem in Judah, and was there four whole months. ³Then her husband arose and went after her, to speak kindly to her *and* bring her back, having his servant and a couple of donkeys with him. So she brought him into her father's house; and when the father of the young woman saw him, he was glad to meet him. ⁴Now his father-in-law, the young woman's father, detained him; and he stayed with him three days. So they ate and drank and lodged there.

⁵Then it came to pass on the fourth day that they arose early in the morning, and he stood to depart; but the young woman's father said to his son-in-law, "Refresh your heart with a morsel of bread, and afterward go your way."

⁶So they sat down, and the two of them ate and drank together. Then the young woman's father said to the man, "Please be content to stay all night, and let your heart be merry." ⁷And when the man stood to depart, his father-in-law urged him; so he lodged there again. ⁸Then he arose early in the morning on the fifth day to depart, but the young woman's father said, "Please refresh your heart." So they delayed until afternoon; and both of them ate.

⁹And when the man stood to depart—he and his concubine and his servant—his father-in-law, the young woman's father, said to him, "Look, the day is now drawing toward evening; please spend the night. See, the day is coming to an end; lodge here, that your heart may be merry. Tomorrow go your way early, so that you may get home."

¹⁰However, the man was not willing to spend that night; so he rose and departed, and came opposite Jebus (that *is,* Jerusalem). With him were the two saddled donkeys; his concubine *was* also with him. ¹¹They *were* near Jebus, and the day was far spent, and the servant said to his master, "Come, please, and let us turn aside into this city of the Jebusites and lodge in it."

¹²But his master said to him, "We will not turn aside here into a city of foreigners, who *are* not of the children of Israel; we will go on to Gibeah." ¹³So he said to his servant, "Come, let us draw near to one of these places, and spend the night in Gibeah or in Ramah." ¹⁴And they passed by and went their way; and the sun went down on them near Gibeah, which belongs to Benjamin. ¹⁵They turned aside there to go in to lodge in Gibeah. And when he went in, he sat down in the open square of the city, for no one would take them into *his* house to spend the night.

¹⁶Just then an old man came in from his work in the field at evening, who also *was* from the mountains of Ephraim; he was staying in Gibeah, whereas the men of the place *were* Benjamites. ¹⁷And when he raised his eyes, he saw the traveler in the open square of the city; and the old man said, "Where are you going, and where do you come from?"

¹⁸So he said to him, "We *are* passing

from Bethlehem in Judah toward the remote mountains of Ephraim; I *am* from there. I went to Bethlehem in Judah; *now* I am going to the house of the LORD. But there *is* no one who will take me into his house, ¹⁹although we have both straw and fodder for our donkeys, and bread and wine for myself, for your female servant, and for the young man *who is* with your servant; *there is* no lack of anything."

²⁰And the old man said, "Peace *be* with you! However, *let* all your needs *be* my responsibility; only do not spend the night in the open square." ²¹So he brought him into his house, and gave fodder to the donkeys. And they washed their feet, and ate and drank.

²²As they were enjoying themselves, suddenly certain men of the city, perverted men,* surrounded the house *and* beat on the door. They spoke to the master of the house, the old man, saying, "Bring out the man who came to your house, that we may know him *carnally!*"

²³But the man, the master of the house, went out to them and said to them, "No, my brethren! I beg you, do not act *so* wickedly! Seeing this man has come into my house, do not commit this outrage. ²⁴Look, *here is* my virgin daughter and *the man's** concubine; let me bring them out now. Humble them, and do with them as you please; but to this man do not do such a vile thing!" ²⁵But the men would not heed him. So the man took his concubine and brought *her* out to them. And they knew her and abused her all night until morning; and when the day began to break, they let her go.

²⁶Then the woman came as the day was dawning, and fell down at the door of the man's house where her master *was,* till it was light.

²⁷When her master arose in the morning, and opened the doors of the house and went out to go his way, there was his concubine, fallen *at* the door of the house with her hands on the threshold. ²⁸And he said to her, "Get up and let us be going." But there was no answer. So the man lifted her onto the donkey; and the man got up and went to his place.

²⁹When he entered his house he took a knife, laid hold of his concubine, and divided her into twelve pieces, limb by limb,* and sent her throughout all the territory of Israel. ³⁰And so it was that all who saw it said, "No such deed has been done or seen from the day that the children of Israel came up from the land of Egypt until this day. Consider it, confer, and speak up!"

So all the children of Israel came out, from Dan to Beersheba, as well as from the land of Gilead, and the congregation gathered together as one man before the LORD at Mizpah. ²And the leaders of all the people, all the tribes of Israel, presented themselves in the assembly of the people of God, four hundred thousand foot soldiers who drew the sword. ³(Now the children of Benjamin heard that the children of Israel had gone up to Mizpah.)

Then the children of Israel said, "Tell *us,* how did this wicked deed happen?"

⁴So the Levite, the husband of the woman who was murdered, answered and said, "My concubine and I went into Gibeah, which belongs to Benjamin, to spend the night. ⁵And the men of Gibeah rose against me, and surrounded the house at night because of me. They intended to kill me, but instead they ravished my concubine so that she died. ⁶So I took hold of my concubine, cut her in pieces, and sent her throughout all the territory of the inheritance of Israel, because they committed lewdness and outrage in Israel. ⁷Look! All of you *are* children of Israel; give your advice and counsel here and now!"

⁸So all the people arose as one man,

saying, "None *of us* will go to his tent, nor will any turn back to his house; [9]but now this *is* the thing which we will do to Gibeah: *We will go up* against it by lot. [10]We will take ten men out of *every* hundred throughout all the tribes of Israel, a hundred out of *every* thousand, and a thousand out of *every* ten thousand, to make provisions for the people, that when they come to Gibeah in Benjamin, they may repay all the vileness that they have done in Israel." [11]So all the men of Israel were gathered against the city, united together as one man.

[12]Then the tribes of Israel sent men through all the tribe of Benjamin, saying, "What *is* this wickedness that has occurred among you? [13]Now therefore, deliver up the men, the perverted men* who *are* in Gibeah, that we may put them to death and remove the evil from Israel!" But the children of Benjamin would not listen to the voice of their brethren, the children of Israel. [14]Instead, the children of Benjamin gathered together from their cities to Gibeah, to go to battle against the children of Israel. [15]And from their cities at that time the children of Benjamin numbered twenty-six thousand men who drew the sword, besides the inhabitants of Gibeah, who numbered seven hundred select men. [16]Among all this people *were* seven hundred select men *who were* left-handed; every one could sling a stone at a hair's *breadth* and not miss. [17]Now besides Benjamin, the men of Israel numbered four hundred thousand men who drew the sword; all of these *were* men of war.

[18]Then the children of Israel arose and went up to the house of God* to inquire of God. They said, "Which of us shall go up first to battle against the children of Benjamin?"

The LORD said, "Judah first!"

[19]So the children of Israel rose in the morning and encamped against Gibeah. [20]And the men of Israel went out to battle against Benjamin, and the men of Israel put themselves in battle array to fight against them at Gibeah. [21]Then the children of Benjamin came out of Gibeah, and on that day cut down to the ground twenty-two thousand men of the Israelites. [22]And the people, that is, the men of Israel, encouraged themselves and again formed the battle line at the place where they had put themselves in array on the first day. [23]Then the children of Israel went up and wept before the LORD until evening, and asked counsel of the LORD, saying, "Shall I again draw near for battle against the children of my brother Benjamin?"

And the LORD said, "Go up against him."

[24]So the children of Israel approached the children of Benjamin on the second day. [25]And Benjamin went out against them from Gibeah on the second day, and cut down to the ground eighteen thousand more of the children of Israel; all these drew the sword.

[26]Then all the children of Israel, that is, all the people, went up and came to the house of God* and wept. They sat there before the LORD and fasted that day until evening; and they offered burnt offerings and peace offerings before the LORD. [27]So the children of Israel inquired of the LORD (the ark of the covenant of God *was* there in those days, [28]and Phinehas the son of Eleazar, the son of Aaron, stood before it in those days), saying, "Shall I yet again go out to battle against the children of my brother Benjamin, or shall I cease?"

And the LORD said, "Go up, for tomorrow I will deliver them into your hand."

[29]Then Israel set men in ambush all around Gibeah. [30]And the children of Israel went up against the children of Benjamin on the third day, and put themselves in battle array against

Gibeah as at the other times. ³¹So the children of Benjamin went out against the people, *and* were drawn away from the city. They began to strike down *and* kill some of the people, as at the other times, in the highways (one of which goes up to Bethel and the other to Gibeah) and in the field, about thirty men of Israel. ³²And the children of Benjamin said, "They *are* defeated before us, as at first."

But the children of Israel said, "Let us flee and draw them away from the city to the highways." ³³So all the men of Israel rose from their place and put themselves in battle array at Baal Tamar. Then Israel's men in ambush burst forth from their position in the plain of Geba. ³⁴And ten thousand select men from all Israel came against Gibeah, and the battle was fierce. But *the Benjamites** did not know that disaster *was* upon them. ³⁵The LORD defeated Benjamin before Israel. And the children of Israel destroyed that day twenty-five thousand one hundred Benjamites; all these drew the sword.

³⁶So the children of Benjamin saw that they were defeated. The men of Israel had given ground to the Benjamites, because they relied on the men in ambush whom they had set against Gibeah. ³⁷And the men in ambush quickly rushed upon Gibeah; the men in ambush spread out and struck the whole city with the edge of the sword. ³⁸Now the appointed signal between the men of Israel and the men in ambush was that they would make a great cloud of smoke rise up from the city, ³⁹whereupon the men of Israel would turn in battle. Now Benjamin had begun to strike *and* kill about thirty of the men of Israel. For they said, "Surely they are defeated before us, as *in* the first battle." ⁴⁰But when the cloud began to rise from the city in a column of smoke, the Benjamites looked behind them, and there was the whole city going up *in smoke* to heaven. ⁴¹And when the men of Israel turned back, the men of Benjamin panicked, for they saw that disaster had come upon them. ⁴²Therefore they turned *their backs* before the men of Israel in the direction of the wilderness; but the battle overtook them, and whoever *came* out of the cities they destroyed in their midst. ⁴³They surrounded the Benjamites, chased them, *and* easily trampled them down as far as the front of Gibeah toward the east. ⁴⁴And eighteen thousand men of Benjamin fell; all these *were* men of valor. ⁴⁵Then they* turned and fled toward the wilderness to the rock of Rimmon; and they cut down five thousand of them on the highways. Then they pursued them relentlessly up to Gidom, and killed two thousand of them. ⁴⁶So all who fell of Benjamin that day were twenty-five thousand men who drew the sword; all these *were* men of valor.

⁴⁷But six hundred men turned and fled toward the wilderness to the rock of Rimmon, and they stayed at the rock of Rimmon for four months. ⁴⁸And the men of Israel turned back against the children of Benjamin, and struck them down with the edge of the sword—from *every* city, men and beasts, all who were found. They also set fire to all the cities they came to.

JOHN 3:22–4:4

AFTER these things Jesus and His disciples came into the land of Judea, and there He remained with them and baptized. ²³Now John also was baptizing in Aenon near Salim, because there was much water there. And they came and were baptized. ²⁴For John had not yet been thrown into prison.

²⁵Then there arose a dispute between *some* of John's disciples and the Jews about purification. ²⁶And they came to John and said to him, "Rabbi,

He who was with you beyond the Jordan, to whom you have testified—behold, He is baptizing, and all are coming to Him!"

27John answered and said, "A man can receive nothing unless it has been given to him from heaven. 28You yourselves bear me witness, that I said, 'I am not the Christ,' but, 'I have been sent before Him.' 29He who has the bride is the bridegroom; but the friend of the bridegroom, who stands and hears him, rejoices greatly because of the bridegroom's voice. Therefore this joy of mine is fulfilled. 30He must increase, but I *must* decrease. 31He who comes from above is above all; he who is of the earth is earthly and speaks of the earth. He who comes from heaven is above all. 32And what He has seen and heard, that He testifies; and no one receives His testimony. 33He who has received His testimony has certified that God is true. 34For He whom God has sent speaks the words of God, for God does not give the Spirit by measure. 35The Father loves the Son, and has given all things into His hand. 36He who believes in the Son has everlasting life; and he who does not believe the Son shall not see life, but the wrath of God abides on him."

THEREFORE, when the Lord knew that the Pharisees had heard that Jesus made and baptized more disciples than John 2(though Jesus Himself did not baptize, but His disciples), 3He left Judea and departed again to Galilee. 4But He needed to go through Samaria.

PSALM 104:24-35

O LORD, how manifold are Your works!
In wisdom You have made them all.
The earth is full of Your possessions—

25 This great and wide sea,
In which *are* innumerable teeming things,
Living things both small and great.
26 There the ships sail about;
There is that Leviathan
Which You have made to play there.

27 These all wait for You,
That You may give *them* their food in due season.
28 *What* You give them they gather in;
You open Your hand, they are filled with good.
29 You hide Your face, they are troubled;
You take away their breath, they die and return to their dust.
30 You send forth Your Spirit, they are created;
And You renew the face of the earth.

31 May the glory of the LORD endure forever;
May the LORD rejoice in His works.
32 He looks on the earth, and it trembles;
He touches the hills, and they smoke.

33 I will sing to the LORD as long as I live;
I will sing praise to my God while I have my being.
34 May my meditation be sweet to Him;
I will be glad in the LORD.
35 May sinners be consumed from the earth,
And the wicked be no more.

Bless the LORD, O my soul!
Praise the LORD!

PROVERBS FOR TODAY/ 14:22-24

Do they not go astray who devise evil? But mercy and truth belong to those who devise good. ▢ *In all labor there is profit, but idle chatter* leads only to poverty.* ▢ *The crown of the wise is their riches,* but *the foolishness of fools is folly.*

MAY 5

JUDGES 21:1—RUTH 1:22

Now the men of Israel had sworn an oath at Mizpah, saying, "None of us shall give his daughter to Benjamin as a wife." ²Then the people came to the house of God,* and remained there before God till evening. They lifted up their voices and wept bitterly, ³and said, "O LORD God of Israel, why has this come to pass in Israel, that today there should be one tribe *missing* in Israel?"

⁴So it was, on the next morning, that the people rose early and built an altar there, and offered burnt offerings and peace offerings. ⁵The children of Israel said, "Who *is there* among all the tribes of Israel who did not come up with the assembly to the LORD?" For they had made a great oath concerning anyone who had not come up to the LORD at Mizpah, saying, "He shall surely be put to death." ⁶And the children of Israel grieved for Benjamin their brother, and said, "One tribe is cut off from Israel today. ⁷What shall we do for wives for those who remain, seeing we have sworn by the LORD that we will not give them our daughters as wives?"

⁸And they said, "What one *is there* from the tribes of Israel who did not come up to Mizpah to the LORD?" And, in fact, no one had come to the camp from Jabesh Gilead to the assembly. ⁹For when the people were counted, indeed, not one of the inhabitants of Jabesh Gilead *was* there. ¹⁰So the congregation sent out there twelve thousand of their most valiant men, and commanded them, saying, "Go and strike the inhabitants of Jabesh Gilead with the edge of the sword, including the women and children. ¹¹And this *is* the thing that you shall do: You shall utterly destroy every male, and every woman who has known a man intimately." ¹²So they found among the inhabitants of Jabesh Gilead four hundred young virgins who had not known a man intimately; and they brought them to the camp at Shiloh, which is in the land of Canaan.

¹³Then the whole congregation sent *word* to the children of Benjamin who *were* at the rock of Rimmon, and announced peace to them. ¹⁴So Benjamin came back at that time, and they gave them the women whom they had saved alive of the women of Jabesh Gilead; and yet they had not found enough for them.

¹⁵And the people grieved for Benjamin, because the LORD had made a void in the tribes of Israel.

¹⁶Then the elders of the congregation said, "What shall we do for wives for those who remain, since the women of Benjamin have been destroyed?" ¹⁷And they said, "*There must be* an inheritance for the survivors of Benjamin, that a tribe may not be destroyed from Israel. ¹⁸However, we cannot give them wives from our daughters, for the children of Israel have sworn an oath, saying, 'Cursed *be* the one who gives a wife to Benjamin.'" ¹⁹Then they said,

"In fact, *there is* a yearly feast of the LORD in Shiloh, which *is* north of Bethel, on the east side of the highway that goes up from Bethel to Shechem, and south of Lebonah."

20Therefore they instructed the children of Benjamin, saying, "Go, lie in wait in the vineyards, 21and watch; and just when the daughters of Shiloh come out to perform their dances, then come out from the vineyards, and every man catch a wife for himself from the daughters of Shiloh; then go to the land of Benjamin. 22Then it shall be, when their fathers or their brothers come to us to complain, that we will say to them, 'Be kind to them for our sakes, because we did not take a wife for any of them in the war; for *it is* not *as though* you have given the *women* to them at this time, making yourselves guilty of your oath.' "

23And the children of Benjamin did so; they took enough wives for their number from those who danced, whom they caught. Then they went and returned to their inheritance, and they rebuilt the cities and dwelt in them. 24So the children of Israel departed from there at that time every man to his tribe and family; they went out from there, every man to his inheritance.

25In those days *there was* no king in Israel; everyone did *what was* right in his own eyes.

Now it came to pass, in the days when the judges ruled, that there was a famine in the land. And a certain man of Bethlehem, Judah, went to dwell in the country of Moab, he and his wife and his two sons. 2The name of the man *was* Elimelech, the name of his wife *was* Naomi, and the names of his two sons *were* Mahlon and Chilion—Ephrathites of Bethlehem, Judah. And they went to the country of Moab and remained there. 3Then Elimelech, Naomi's husband, died; and she was left,

and her two sons. 4Now they took wives of the women of Moab: the name of the one *was* Orpah, and the name of the other Ruth. And they dwelt there about ten years. 5Then both Mahlon and Chilion also died; so the woman survived her two sons and her husband.

6Then she arose with her daughters-in-law that she might return from the country of Moab, for she had heard in the country of Moab that the LORD had visited His people by giving them bread. 7Therefore she went out from the place where she was, and her two daughters in law with her; and they went on the way to return to the land of Judah. 8And Naomi said to her two daughters-in-law, "Go, return each to her mother's house. The LORD deal kindly with you, as you have dealt with the dead and with me. 9The LORD grant that you may find rest, each in the house of her husband."

So she kissed them, and they lifted up their voices and wept. 10And they said to her, "Surely we will return with you to your people."

11But Naomi said, "Turn back, my daughters; why will you go with me? *Are* there still sons in my womb, that they may be your husbands? 12Turn back, my daughters, go—for I am too old to have a husband. If I should say I have hope, *if* I should have a husband tonight and should also bear sons, 13would you wait for them till they were grown? Would you restrain yourselves from having husbands? No, my daughters; for it grieves me very much for your sakes that the hand of the LORD has gone out against me!"

14Then they lifted up their voices and wept again; and Orpah kissed her mother-in-law, but Ruth clung to her.

15And she said, "Look, your sister-in-law has gone back to her people and to her gods; return after your sister-in-law."

16But Ruth said:

"Entreat me not to leave you,
  Or to turn back from
    following after you;
  For wherever you go, I will go;
  And wherever you lodge, I
    will lodge;
  Your people *shall be* my
    people,
  And your God, my God.
17 Where you die, I will die,
  And there will I be buried.
  The LORD do so to me, and
    more also,
  If *anything but* death parts
    you and me."

18When she saw that she was determined to go with her, she stopped speaking to her.

19Now the two of them went until they came to Bethlehem. And it happened, when they had come to Bethlehem, that all the city was excited because of them; and the women said, "*Is* this Naomi?"

20But she said to them, "Do not call me Naomi;* call me Mara,* for the Almighty has dealt very bitterly with me. 21I went out full, and the LORD has brought me home again empty. Why do you call me Naomi, since the LORD has testified against me, and the Almighty has afflicted me?"

22So Naomi returned, and Ruth the Moabitess her daughter-in-law with her, who returned from the country of Moab. Now they came to Bethlehem at the beginning of barley harvest.

JOHN 4:5-42

So He [Jesus] came to a city of Samaria which is called Sychar, near the plot of ground that Jacob gave to his son Joseph. 6Now Jacob's well was there. Jesus therefore, being wearied from *His* journey, sat thus by the well. It was about the sixth hour.

7A woman of Samaria came to draw water. Jesus said to her, "Give Me a drink." 8For His disciples had gone away into the city to buy food.

9Then the woman of Samaria said to Him, "How is it that You, being a Jew, ask a drink from me, a Samaritan woman?" For Jews have no dealings with Samaritans.

10Jesus answered and said to her, "If you knew the gift of God, and who it is who says to you, 'Give Me a drink,' you would have asked Him, and He would have given you living water."

11The woman said to Him, "Sir, You have nothing to draw with, and the well is deep. Where then do You get that living water? 12Are You greater than our father Jacob, who gave us the well, and drank from it himself, as well as his sons and his livestock?"

13Jesus answered and said to her, "Whoever drinks of this water will thirst again, 14but whoever drinks of the water that I shall give him will never thirst. But the water that I shall give him will become in him a fountain of water springing up into everlasting life."

15The woman said to Him, "Sir, give me this water, that I may not thirst, nor come here to draw."

16Jesus said to her, "Go, call your husband, and come here."

17The woman answered and said, "I have no husband."

Jesus said to her, "You have well said, 'I have no husband,' 18for you have had five husbands, and the one whom you now have is not your husband; in that you spoke truly."

19The woman said to Him, "Sir, I perceive that You are a prophet. 20Our fathers worshiped on this mountain, and you *Jews* say that in Jerusalem is the place where one ought to worship."

21Jesus said to her, "Woman, believe Me, the hour is coming when you will neither on this mountain, nor in Jerusalem, worship the Father. 22You worship what you do not know; we know what we worship, for salvation is of the Jews. 23But the hour is coming, and now is, when the true worshipers will worship the Father in spirit and truth; for the Father is seeking such to worship Him. 24God *is* Spirit, and those who worship Him must worship in spirit and truth."

25The woman said to Him, "I know that Messiah is coming" (who is called Christ). "When He comes, He will tell us all things."

26Jesus said to her, "I who speak to you am *He*."

27And at this *point* His disciples came, and they marveled that He talked with a woman; yet no one said, "What do You seek?" or, "Why are You talking with her?"

28The woman then left her waterpot, went her way into the city, and said to the men, 29"Come, see a Man who told me all things that I ever did. Could this be the Christ?" 30Then they went out of the city and came to Him.

31In the meantime His disciples urged Him, saying, "Rabbi, eat."

32But He said to them, "I have food to eat of which you do not know."

33Therefore the disciples said to one another, "Has anyone brought Him *anything* to eat?"

34Jesus said to them, "My food is to do the will of Him who sent Me, and to finish His work. 35Do you not say, 'There are still four months and *then* comes the harvest'? Behold, I say to you, lift up your eyes and look at the fields, for they are already white for harvest! 36And he who reaps receives wages, and gathers fruit for eternal life, that both he who sows and he who reaps may rejoice together. 37For in this the saying is true: 'One sows and another reaps.' 38I sent you to reap that for which you have not labored; others have labored, and you have entered into their labors."

39And many of the Samaritans of that city believed in Him because of the word of the woman who testified, "He told me all that I *ever* did." 40So when the Samaritans had come to Him, they urged Him to stay with them; and He stayed there two days. 41And many more believed because of His own word.

42Then they said to the woman, "Now we believe, not because of what you said, for we ourselves have heard *Him* and we know that this is indeed the Christ,* the Savior of the world."

PSALM 105:1-15

Oh, give thanks to the LORD!
Call upon His name;
Make known His deeds
    among the peoples!
2 Sing to Him, sing psalms to
    Him;
    Talk of all His wondrous
    works!
3 Glory in His holy name;
    Let the hearts of those rejoice
    who seek the LORD!
4 Seek the LORD and His
    strength;
    Seek His face evermore!
5 Remember His marvelous
    works which He has done,
    His wonders, and the
    judgments of His mouth,
6 O seed of Abraham His
    servant,
    You children of Jacob, His
    chosen ones!

7 He *is* the LORD our God;
    His judgments *are* in all the
    earth.
8 He remembers His covenant
    forever,
    The word *which* He
    commanded, for a thousand
    generations,
9 *The covenant* which He made
    with Abraham,
    And His oath to Isaac,

10 And confirmed it to Jacob for
       a statute,
     To Israel *as* an everlasting
       covenant,
11 Saying, "To you I will give the
       land of Canaan
     As the allotment of your
       inheritance,"
12 When they were few in
       number,
     Indeed very few, and
       strangers in it.

13 When they went from one
       nation to another,
     From *one* kingdom to another
       people,
14 He permitted no one to do
       them wrong;
     Yes, He rebuked kings for
       their sakes,
15 Saying, "Do not touch My
       anointed ones,
     And do My prophets no
       harm."

PROVERBS FOR TODAY/ 14:25

A true witness delivers souls, but a deceitful witness *speaks lies.*

MAY 6

RUTH 2:1–4:22

THERE was a relative of Naomi's husband, a man of great wealth, of the family of Elimelech. His name *was* Boaz. ²So Ruth the Moabitess said to Naomi, "Please let me go to the field, and glean heads of grain after *him* in whose sight I may find favor."

And she said to her, "Go, my daughter."

³Then she left, and went and gleaned in the field after the reapers. And she happened to come to the part of the field *belonging* to Boaz, who *was* of the family of Elimelech.

⁴Now behold, Boaz came from Bethlehem, and said to the reapers, "The LORD *be* with you!"

And they answered him, "The LORD bless you!"

⁵Then Boaz said to his servant who was in charge of the reapers, "Whose young woman *is* this?"

⁶So the servant who was in charge of the reapers answered and said, "It *is* the young Moabite woman who came back with Naomi from the country of Moab. ⁷And she said, 'Please let me glean and gather after the reapers among the sheaves.' So she came and has continued from morning until now, though she rested a little in the house."

⁸Then Boaz said to Ruth, "You will listen, my daughter, will you not? Do not go to glean in another field, nor go from here, but stay close by my young women. ⁹*Let* your eyes *be* on the field which they reap, and go after them. Have I not commanded the young men not to touch you? And when you are thirsty, go to the vessels and drink from what the young men have drawn."

¹⁰So she fell on her face, bowed down to the ground, and said to him, "Why have I found favor in your eyes, that you should take notice of me, since I *am* a foreigner?"

¹¹And Boaz answered and said to her, "It has been fully reported to me, all that you have done for your mother-

in-law since the death of your husband, and *how* you have left your father and your mother and the land of your birth, and have come to a people whom you did not know before. [12]The LORD repay your work, and a full reward be given you by the LORD God of Israel, under whose wings you have come for refuge."

[13]Then she said, "Let me find favor in your sight, my lord; for you have comforted me, and have spoken kindly to your maidservant, though I am not like one of your maidservants."

[14]Now Boaz said to her at mealtime, "Come here, and eat of the bread, and dip your piece of bread in the vinegar." So she sat beside the reapers, and he passed parched *grain* to her; and she ate and was satisfied, and kept some back. [15]And when she rose up to glean, Boaz commanded his young men, saying, "Let her glean even among the sheaves, and do not reproach her. [16]Also let *grain* from the bundles fall purposely for her; leave *it* that she may glean, and do not rebuke her."

[17]So she gleaned in the field until evening, and beat out what she had gleaned, and it was about an ephah of barley. [18]Then she took *it* up and went into the city, and her mother-in-law saw what she had gleaned. So she brought out and gave to her what she had kept back after she had been satisfied.

[19]And her mother-in-law said to her, "Where have you gleaned today? And where did you work? Blessed be the one who took notice of you."

So she told her mother-in-law with whom she had worked, and said, "The man's name with whom I worked today *is* Boaz."

[20]Then Naomi said to her daughter-in-law, "Blessed *be* he of the LORD, who has not forsaken His kindness to the living and the dead!" And Naomi said to her, "This man *is* a relation of ours, one of our close relatives."

[21]Ruth the Moabitess said, "He also said to me, 'You shall stay close by my young men until they have finished all my harvest.'"

[22]And Naomi said to Ruth her daughter-in-law, "*It is* good, my daughter, that you go out with his young women, and that people do not meet you in any other field." [23]So she stayed close by the young women of Boaz, to glean until the end of barley harvest and wheat harvest; and she dwelt with her mother-in-law.

THEN Naomi her mother-in-law said to her, "My daughter, shall I not seek security for you, that it may be well with you? [2]Now Boaz, whose young women you were with, *is he* not our relative? In fact, he is winnowing barley tonight at the threshing floor. [3]Therefore wash yourself and anoint yourself, put on your *best* garment and go down to the threshing floor; *but* do not make yourself known to the man until he has finished eating and drinking. [4]Then it shall be, when he lies down, that you shall notice the place where he lies; and you shall go in, uncover his feet, and lie down; and he will tell you what you should do."

[5]And she said to her, "All that you say to me I will do."

[6]So she went down to the threshing floor and did according to all that her mother-in-law instructed her. [7]And after Boaz had eaten and drunk, and his heart was cheerful, he went to lie down at the end of the heap of grain; and she came softly, uncovered his feet, and lay down.

[8]Now it happened at midnight that the man was startled, and turned himself; and there, a woman was lying at his feet. [9]And he said, "Who *are* you?"

So she answered, "I *am* Ruth, your maidservant. Take your maidservant under your wing,* for you are a close relative."

[10]Then he said, "Blessed *are* you of the LORD, my daughter! For you have

shown more kindness at the end than at the beginning, in that you did not go after young men, whether poor or rich. ¹¹And now, my daughter, do not fear. I will do for you all that you request, for all the people of my town know that you *are* a virtuous woman. ¹²Now it is true that I *am* a close relative; however, there is a relative closer than I. ¹³Stay this night, and in the morning it shall be *that* if he will perform the duty of a close relative for you—good; let him do it. But if he does not want to perform the duty for you, then I will perform the duty for you, *as* the Lord lives! Lie down until morning."

¹⁴So she lay at his feet until morning, and she arose before one could recognize another. Then he said, "Do not let it be known that the woman came to the threshing floor." ¹⁵Also he said, "Bring the shawl that *is* on you and hold it." And when she held it, he measured six *ephahs* of barley, and laid *it* on her. Then she* went into the city.

¹⁶When she came to her mother-in-law, she said, "*Is* that you, my daughter?"

Then she told her all that the man had done for her. ¹⁷And she said, "These six *ephahs* of barley he gave me; for he said to me, 'Do not go empty-handed to your mother-in-law.' "

¹⁸Then she said, "Sit still, my daughter, until you know how the matter will turn out; for the man will not rest until he has concluded the matter this day."

Now Boaz went up to the gate and sat down there; and behold, the close relative of whom Boaz had spoken came by. So Boaz said, "Come aside, friend,* sit down here." So he came aside and sat down. ²And he took ten men of the elders of the city, and said, "Sit down here." So they sat down. ³Then he said to the close relative, "Naomi, who has come back from the country of Moab, sold the piece of land which *belonged* to our brother Elimelech. ⁴And I thought

to inform you, saying, 'Buy *it* back in the presence of the inhabitants and the elders of my people. If you will redeem *it*, redeem *it;* but if you* will not redeem *it, then* tell me, that I may know; for *there is* no one but you to redeem *it*, and I *am* next after you.' "

And he said, "I will redeem *it*."

⁵Then Boaz said, "On the day you buy the field from the hand of Naomi, you must also buy *it* from Ruth the Moabitess, the wife of the dead, to perpetuate* the name of the dead through his inheritance."

⁶And the close relative said, "I cannot redeem *it* for myself, lest I ruin my own inheritance. You redeem my right of redemption for yourself, for I cannot redeem *it*."

⁷Now this *was the custom* in former times in Israel concerning redeeming and exchanging, to confirm anything: one man took off his sandal and gave *it* to the other, and this *was* a confirmation in Israel.

⁸Therefore the close relative said to Boaz, "Buy *it* for yourself." So he took off his sandal. ⁹And Boaz said to the elders and all the people, "You *are* witnesses this day that I have bought all that was Elimelech's, and all that *was* Chilion's and Mahlon's, from the hand of Naomi. ¹⁰Moreover, Ruth the Moabitess, the widow of Mahlon, I have acquired as my wife, to perpetuate the name of the dead through his inheritance, that the name of the dead may not be cut off from among his brethren and from his position at the gate.* You *are* witnesses this day."

¹¹And all the people who *were* at the gate, and the elders, said, "*We are* witnesses. The Lord make the woman who is coming to your house like Rachel and Leah, the two who built the house of Israel; and may you prosper in Ephrathah and be famous in Bethlehem. ¹²May your house be like the house of Perez, whom Tamar bore to Judah, because of the offspring which

the LORD will give you from this young woman."

13So Boaz took Ruth and she became his wife; and when he went in to her, the LORD gave her conception, and she bore a son. 14Then the women said to Naomi, "Blessed be the LORD, who has not left you this day without a close relative; and may his name be famous in Israel! 15And may he be to you a restorer of life and a nourisher of your old age; for your daughter-in-law, who loves you, who is better to you than seven sons, has borne him." 16Then Naomi took the child and laid him on her bosom, and became a nurse to him. 17Also the neighbor women gave him a name, saying, "There is a son born to Naomi." And they called his name Obed. He is the father of Jesse, the father of David.

18Now this is the genealogy of Perez: Perez begot Hezron; 19Hezron begot Ram, and Ram begot Amminadab; 20Amminadab begot Nahshon, and Nahshon begot Salmon;* 21Salmon begot Boaz, and Boaz begot Obed; 22Obed begot Jesse, and Jesse begot David.

JOHN 4:43-54

Now after the two days He [Jesus] departed from there and went to Galilee. 44For Jesus Himself testified that a prophet has no honor in his own country. 45So when He came to Galilee, the Galileans received Him, having seen all the things He did in Jerusalem at the feast; for they also had gone to the feast.

46So Jesus came again to Cana of Galilee where He had made the water wine. And there was a certain nobleman whose son was sick at Capernaum. 47When he heard that Jesus had come out of Judea into Galilee, he went to Him and implored Him to come down and heal his son, for he was at the point of death. 48Then Jesus said to him, "Unless you people see signs and wonders, you will by no means believe."

49The nobleman said to Him, "Sir, come down before my child dies!"

50Jesus said to him, "Go your way; your son lives." So the man believed the word that Jesus spoke to him, and he went his way. 51And as he was now going down, his servants met him and told him, saying, "Your son lives!"

52Then he inquired of them the hour when he got better. And they said to him, "Yesterday at the seventh hour the fever left him." 53So the father knew that it was at the same hour in which Jesus said to him, "Your son lives." And he himself believed, and his whole household.

54This again is the second sign Jesus did when He had come out of Judea into Galilee.

PSALM 105:16-36

Moreover He called for a famine in the land;
He destroyed all the provision of bread.
17 He sent a man before them—
Joseph—who was sold as a slave.
18 They hurt his feet with fetters,
He was laid in irons.
19 Until the time that his word came to pass,
The word of the LORD tested him.
20 The king sent and released him,
The ruler of the people let him go free.
21 He made him lord of his house,
And ruler of all his possessions,
22 To bind his princes at his pleasure,
And teach his elders wisdom.

23 Israel also came into Egypt,

And Jacob dwelt in the land of
Ham.
24 He increased His people
greatly,
And made them stronger than
their enemies.
25 He turned their heart to hate
His people,
To deal craftily with His
servants.

26 He sent Moses His servant,
And Aaron whom He had
chosen.
27 They performed His signs
among them,
And wonders in the land of
Ham.
28 He sent darkness, and made
it dark;
And they did not rebel against
His word.
29 He turned their waters into
blood,

And killed their fish.
30 Their land abounded with
frogs,
Even in the chambers of their
kings.
31 He spoke, and there came
swarms of flies,
And lice in all their territory.
32 He gave them hail for rain,
And flaming fire in their land.
33 He struck their vines also,
and their fig trees,
And splintered the trees of
their territory.
34 He spoke, and locusts came,
Young locusts without
number,
35 And ate up all the vegetation
in their land,
And devoured the fruit of
their ground.
36 He also destroyed all the
firstborn in their land,
The first of all their strength.

PROVERBS FOR TODAY/ 14:26-27

In the fear of the LORD there is strong confidence, and His children will have a place of refuge. The fear of the LORD is a fountain of life, to turn one away from the snares of death.

MAY 7

1 SAMUEL 1:1–2:21

Now there was a certain man of Ramathaim Zophim, of the mountains of Ephraim, and his name *was* Elkanah the son of Jeroham, the son of Elihu,* the son of Tohu,* the son of Zuph, an Ephraimite. 2And he had two wives: the name of one *was* Hannah, and the name of the other Peninnah. Peninnah had children, but Hannah had no children. 3This man went up from his city yearly to worship and sacrifice to the LORD of hosts in Shiloh. Also the two sons of Eli, Hophni and Phinehas, the priests of the LORD, *were* there. 4And whenever the time came for Elkanah to make an offering, he would give portions to Peninnah his wife and to all her sons and daughters. 5But to Hannah he would give a double portion, for he loved Hannah, although the LORD had closed her womb. 6And her rival also provoked her severely, to make her miserable, because the LORD had closed her womb. 7So it was, year by year, when she went up to the house of the LORD, that she provoked her; therefore she wept and did not eat.

8Then Elkanah her husband said to her, "Hannah, why do you weep? Why do you not eat? And why is your heart grieved? *Am* I not better to you than ten sons?"

9So Hannah arose after they had finished eating and drinking in Shiloh. Now Eli the priest was sitting on the seat by the doorpost of the tabernacle* of the LORD. 10And she *was* in bitterness of soul, and prayed to the LORD and wept in anguish. 11Then she made a vow and said, "O LORD of hosts, if You will indeed look on the affliction of Your maidservant and remember me, and not forget Your maidservant, but will give Your maidservant a male child, then I will give him to the LORD all the days of his life, and no razor shall come upon his head."

12And it happened, as she continued praying before the LORD, that Eli watched her mouth. 13Now Hannah spoke in her heart; only her lips moved, but her voice was not heard. Therefore Eli thought she was drunk. 14So Eli said to her, "How long will you be drunk? Put your wine away from you!"

15But Hannah answered and said, "No, my lord, I *am* a woman of sorrowful spirit. I have drunk neither wine nor intoxicating drink, but have poured out my soul before the LORD. 16Do not consider your maidservant a wicked woman,* for out of the abundance of my complaint and grief I have spoken until now."

17Then Eli answered and said, "Go in peace, and the God of Israel grant your petition which you have asked of Him."

18And she said, "Let your maidservant find favor in your sight." So the woman went her way and ate, and her face was no longer *sad*.

19Then they rose early in the morning and worshiped before the LORD, and returned and came to their house at Ramah. And Elkanah knew Hannah his wife, and the LORD remembered her. 20So it came to pass in the process of time that Hannah conceived and bore a son, and called his name Samuel,* *saying*, "Because I have asked for him from the LORD."

21Now the man Elkanah and all his house went up to offer to the LORD the yearly sacrifice and his vow. 22But Hannah did not go up, for she said to her husband, "*Not* until the child is weaned; then I will take him, that he may appear before the LORD and remain there forever."

23So Elkanah her husband said to her, "Do what seems best to you; wait until you have weaned him. Only let the LORD establish His* word." Then the woman stayed and nursed her son until she had weaned him.

24Now when she had weaned him, she took him up with her, with three bulls,* one ephah of flour, and a skin of wine, and brought him to the house of the LORD in Shiloh. And the child *was* young. 25Then they slaughtered a bull, and brought the child to Eli. 26And she said, "O my lord! As your soul lives, my lord, I *am* the woman who stood by you here, praying to the LORD. 27For this child I prayed, and the LORD has granted me my petition which I asked of Him. 28Therefore I also have lent him to the LORD; as long as he lives he shall be lent to the LORD." So they worshiped the LORD there.

AND Hannah prayed and said:

> "My heart rejoices in the LORD;
> My horn* is exalted in the
>   LORD.
> I smile at my enemies,
> Because I rejoice in Your
>   salvation.

2   "No one is holy like the LORD,
> For *there is* none besides You,

Nor *is there* any rock like our
God.

3 "Talk no more so very proudly;
Let no arrogance come from
your mouth,
For the LORD *is* the God of
knowledge;
And by Him actions are
weighed.

4 "The bows of the mighty men
are broken,
And those who stumbled are
girded with strength.
5 *Those who were* full have hired
themselves out for bread,
And the hungry have ceased
to hunger.
Even the barren has borne
seven,
And she who has many
children has become feeble.

6 "The LORD kills and makes
alive;
He brings down to the grave
and brings up.
7 The LORD makes poor and
makes rich;
He brings low and lifts up.
8 He raises the poor from the
dust
And lifts the beggar from the
ash heap,
To set *them* among princes
And make them inherit the
throne of glory.

"For the pillars of the earth *are*
the LORD'S,
And He has set the world
upon them.
9 He will guard the feet of His
saints,
But the wicked shall be silent
in darkness.

"For by strength no man shall
prevail.

10 The adversaries of the LORD
shall be broken in pieces;
From heaven He will thunder
against them.
The LORD will judge the ends
of the earth.

"He will give strength to His
king,
And exalt the horn of His
anointed."

11Then Elkanah went to his house at
Ramah. But the child ministered to the
LORD before Eli the priest.

12Now the sons of Eli *were* corrupt;*
they did not know the LORD. 13And the
priests' custom with the people *was
that* when any man offered a sacrifice,
the priest's servant would come with a
three-pronged fleshhook in his hand
while the meat was boiling. 14Then he
would thrust *it* into the pan, or kettle,
or caldron, or pot; and the priest would
take for himself all that the fleshhook
brought up. So they did in Shiloh to all
the Israelites who came there. 15Also,
before they burned the fat, the priest's
servant would come and say to the
man who sacrificed, "Give meat for
roasting to the priest, for he will not
take boiled meat from you, but raw."

16And *if* the man said to him, "They
should really burn the fat first; *then*
you may take *as much* as your heart
desires," he would then answer him,
"*No,* but you must give *it* now; and if
not, I will take *it* by force."

17Therefore the sin of the young men
was very great before the LORD, for men
abhorred the offering of the LORD.

18But Samuel ministered before the
LORD, *even as* a child, wearing a linen
ephod. 19Moreover his mother used to
make him a little robe, and bring *it* to
him year by year when she came up
with her husband to offer the yearly
sacrifice. 20And Eli would bless Elkanah and his wife, and say, "The LORD
give you descendants from this

woman for the loan that was given to the LORD." Then they would go to their own home.

21And the LORD visited Hannah, so that she conceived and bore three sons and two daughters. Meanwhile the child Samuel grew before the LORD.

JOHN 5:1-23

AFTER this there was a feast of the Jews, and Jesus went up to Jerusalem. 2Now there is in Jerusalem by the Sheep *Gate* a pool, which is called in Hebrew, Bethesda,* having five porches. 3In these lay a great multitude of sick people, blind, lame, paralyzed, waiting for the moving of the water. 4For an angel went down at a certain time into the pool and stirred up the water; then whoever stepped in first, after the stirring of the water, was made well of whatever disease he had.* 5Now a certain man was there who had an infirmity thirty-eight years. 6When Jesus saw him lying there, and knew that he already had been *in that condition* a long time, He said to him, "Do you want to be made well?"

7The sick man answered Him, "Sir, I have no man to put me into the pool when the water is stirred up; but while I am coming, another steps down before me."

8Jesus said to him, "Rise, take up your bed and walk." 9And immediately the man was made well, took up his bed, and walked.

And that day was the Sabbath. 10The Jews therefore said to him who was cured, "It is the Sabbath; it is not lawful for you to carry your bed."

11He answered them, "He who made me well said to me, 'Take up your bed and walk.'"

12Then they asked him, "Who is the Man who said to you, 'Take up your bed and walk'?" 13But the one who was healed did not know who it was, for Jesus had withdrawn, a multitude be-

ing in *that* place. 14Afterward Jesus found him in the temple, and said to him, "See, you have been made well. Sin no more, lest a worse thing come upon you."

15The man departed and told the Jews that it was Jesus who had made him well.

16For this reason the Jews persecuted Jesus, and sought to kill Him,* because He had done these things on the Sabbath. 17But Jesus answered them, "My Father has been working until now, and I have been working."

18Therefore the Jews sought all the more to kill Him, because He not only broke the Sabbath, but also said that God was His Father, making Himself equal with God. 19Then Jesus answered and said to them, "Most assuredly, I say to you, the Son can do nothing of Himself, but what He sees the Father do; for whatever He does, the Son also does in like manner. 20For the Father loves the Son, and shows Him all things that He Himself does; and He will show Him greater works than these, that you may marvel. 21For as the Father raises the dead and gives life to *them,* even so the Son gives life to whom He will. 22For the Father judges no one, but has committed all judgment to the Son, 23that all should honor the Son just as they honor the Father. He who does not honor the Son does not honor the Father who sent Him."

PSALM 105:37-45

HE also brought them out with silver and gold,
And *there was* none feeble among His tribes.
38 Egypt was glad when they departed,
For the fear of them had fallen upon them.
39 He spread a cloud for a covering,

And fire to give light in the
night.
40 *The people* asked, and He
brought quail,
And satisfied them with the
bread of heaven.
41 He opened the rock, and
water gushed out;
It ran in the dry places *like* a
river.

42 For He remembered His holy
promise,
And Abraham His servant.

43 He brought out His people
with joy,
His chosen ones with
gladness.
44 He gave them the lands of the
Gentiles,
And they inherited the labor
of the nations,
45 That they might observe His
statutes
And keep His laws.

Praise the LORD!

PROVERBS FOR TODAY/ 14:28-29

In a multitude of people is *a king's honor, but in the lack of people* is *the downfall of a prince.* □ He who is *slow to wrath has great understanding, but* he who is *impulsive* * exalts folly.*

MAY 8

1 SAMUEL 2:22–4:22

Now Eli was very old; and he heard everything his sons did to all Israel,* and how they lay with the women who assembled at the door of the tabernacle of meeting. 23So he said to them, "Why do you do such things? For I hear of your evil dealings from all the people. 24No, my sons! For *it is* not a good report that I hear. You make the LORD's people transgress. 25If one man sins against another, God will judge him. But if a man sins against the LORD, who will intercede for him?" Nevertheless they did not heed the voice of their father, because the LORD desired to kill them.

26And the child Samuel grew in stature, and in favor both with the LORD and men.

27Then a man of God came to Eli and said to him, "Thus says the LORD: 'Did

I not clearly reveal Myself to the house of your father when they were in Egypt in Pharaoh's house? 28Did I not choose him out of all the tribes of Israel *to be* My priest, to offer upon My altar, to burn incense, and to wear an ephod before Me? And did I not give to the house of your father all the offerings of the children of Israel made by fire? 29Why do you kick at My sacrifice and My offering which I have commanded *in My* dwelling place, and honor your sons more than Me, to make yourselves fat with the best of all the offerings of Israel My people?' 30Therefore the LORD God of Israel says: 'I said indeed *that* your house and the house of your father would walk before Me forever.' But now the LORD says: 'Far be it from Me; for those who honor Me I will honor, and those who despise Me shall be lightly esteemed. 31Behold, the days are coming that I will cut off your arm and the arm of your father's house, so that there will not be an old man in your house. ³²And you will see an enemy *in My* dwelling place, *despite* all the good which God does for Israel. And there shall not be an old man in your house forever. ³³But any of your men *whom* I do not cut off from My altar shall consume your eyes and grieve your heart. And all the descendants of your house shall die in the flower of their age. ³⁴Now this *shall be* a sign to you that will come upon your two sons, on Hophni and Phinehas: in one day they shall die, both of them. ³⁵Then I will raise up for Myself a faithful priest *who* shall do according to what *is* in My heart and in My mind. I will build him a sure house, and he shall walk before My anointed forever. ³⁶And it shall come to pass that everyone who is left in your house will come *and* bow down to him for a piece of silver and a morsel of bread, and say, "Please, put me in one of the priestly positions, that I may eat a piece of bread." ' "

Now the boy Samuel ministered to the Lord before Eli. And the word of the Lord was rare in those days; *there was* no widespread revelation. ²And it came to pass at that time, while Eli *was* lying down in his place, and when his eyes had begun to grow so dim that he could not see, ³and before the lamp of God went out in the tabernacle* of the Lord where the ark of God *was,* and while Samuel was lying down, ⁴that the Lord called Samuel. And he answered, "Here I am!" ⁵So he ran to Eli and said, "Here I am, for you called me."

And he said, "I did not call; lie down again." And he went and lay down.

⁶Then the Lord called yet again, "Samuel!"

So Samuel arose and went to Eli, and said, "Here I am, for you called me." He answered, "I did not call, my son; lie down again." ⁷(Now Samuel did not yet know the Lord, nor was the word of the Lord yet revealed to him.)

⁸And the Lord called Samuel again the third time. So he arose and went to Eli, and said, "Here I am, for you did call me."

Then Eli perceived that the Lord had called the boy. ⁹Therefore Eli said to Samuel, "Go, lie down; and it shall be, if He calls you, that you must say, 'Speak, Lord, for Your servant hears.' " So Samuel went and lay down in his place.

¹⁰Now the Lord came and stood and called as at other times, "Samuel! Samuel!"

And Samuel answered, "Speak, for Your servant hears."

¹¹Then the Lord said to Samuel: "Behold, I will do something in Israel at which both ears of everyone who hears it will tingle. ¹²In that day I will perform against Eli all that I have spoken concerning his house, from beginning to end. ¹³For I have told him that I will judge his house forever for the iniquity which he knows, because his sons made themselves vile, and he did not restrain them. ¹⁴And therefore I have sworn to the house of Eli that the iniquity of Eli's house shall not be atoned for by sacrifice or offering forever."

¹⁵So Samuel lay down until morning,* and opened the doors of the house of the Lord. And Samuel was afraid to tell Eli the vision. ¹⁶Then Eli called Samuel and said, "Samuel, my son!"

He answered, "Here I am."

¹⁷And he said, "What *is* the word that *the Lord* spoke to you? Please do not hide *it* from me. God do so to you, and more also, if you hide anything from me of all the things that He said to you." ¹⁸Then Samuel told him everything, and hid nothing from him. And he said, "It *is* the Lord. Let Him do what seems good to Him."

¹⁹So Samuel grew, and the Lord was with him and let none of his words fall

to the ground. ²⁰And all Israel from Dan to Beersheba knew that Samuel *had been* established as a prophet of the LORD. ²¹Then the LORD appeared again in Shiloh. For the LORD revealed Himself to Samuel in Shiloh by the word of the LORD.

AND the word of Samuel came to all Israel.*

Now Israel went out to battle against the Philistines, and encamped beside Ebenezer; and the Philistines encamped in Aphek. ²Then the Philistines put themselves in battle array against Israel. And when they joined battle, Israel was defeated by the Philistines, who killed about four thousand men of the army in the field. ³And when the people had come into the camp, the elders of Israel said, "Why has the LORD defeated us today before the Philistines? Let us bring the ark of the covenant of the LORD from Shiloh to us, that when it comes among us it may save us from the hand of our enemies." ⁴So the people sent to Shiloh, that they might bring from there the ark of the covenant of the LORD of hosts, who dwells *between* the cherubim. And the two sons of Eli, Hophni and Phinehas, *were* there with the ark of the covenant of God.

⁵And when the ark of the covenant of the LORD came into the camp, all Israel shouted so loudly that the earth shook. ⁶Now when the Philistines heard the noise of the shout, they said, "What *does* the sound of this great shout in the camp of the Hebrews *mean?*" Then they understood that the ark of the LORD had come into the camp. ⁷So the Philistines were afraid, for they said, "God has come into the camp!" And they said, "Woe to us! For such a thing has never happened before. ⁸Woe to us! Who will deliver us from the hand of these mighty gods? These *are* the gods who struck the Egyptians with all the plagues in the wilderness. ⁹Be strong

and conduct yourselves like men, you Philistines, that you do not become servants of the Hebrews, as they have been to you. Conduct yourselves like men, and fight!"

¹⁰So the Philistines fought, and Israel was defeated, and every man fled to his tent. There was a very great slaughter, and there fell of Israel thirty thousand foot soldiers. ¹¹Also the ark of God was captured; and the two sons of Eli, Hophni and Phinehas, died.

¹²Then a man of Benjamin ran from the battle line the same day, and came to Shiloh with his clothes torn and dirt on his head. ¹³Now when he came, there was Eli, sitting on a seat by the wayside watching,* for his heart trembled for the ark of God. And when the man came into the city and told *it,* all the city cried out. ¹⁴When Eli heard the noise of the outcry, he said, "What *does* the sound of this tumult *mean?*" And the man came quickly and told Eli. ¹⁵Eli was ninety-eight years old, and his eyes were so dim that he could not see.

¹⁶Then the man said to Eli, "I *am* he who came from the battle. And I fled today from the battle line."

And he said, "What happened, my son?"

¹⁷So the messenger answered and said, "Israel has fled before the Philistines, and there has been a great slaughter among the people. Also your two sons, Hophni and Phinehas, are dead; and the ark of God has been captured."

¹⁸Then it happened, when he made mention of the ark of God, that Eli fell off the seat backward by the side of the gate; and his neck was broken and he died, for the man was old and heavy. And he had judged Israel forty years.

¹⁹Now his daughter-in-law, Phinehas' wife, was with child, *due* to be delivered; and when she heard the news that the ark of God was captured, and that her father-in-law and her husband

were dead, she bowed herself and gave birth, for her labor pains came upon her. [20]And about the time of her death the women who stood by her said to her, "Do not fear, for you have borne a son." But she did not answer, nor did she regard it. [21]Then she named the child Ichabod,* saying, "The glory has departed from Israel!" because the ark of God had been captured and because of her father-in-law and her husband. [22]And she said, "The glory has departed from Israel, for the ark of God has been captured."

JOHN 5:24-47

"**M**OST assuredly, I [Jesus] say to you, he who hears My word and believes in Him who sent Me has everlasting life, and shall not come into judgment, but has passed from death into life. [25]Most assuredly, I say to you, the hour is coming, and now is, when the dead will hear the voice of the Son of God; and those who hear will live. [26]For as the Father has life in Himself, so He has granted the Son to have life in Himself, [27]and has given Him authority to execute judgment also, because He is the Son of Man. [28]Do not marvel at this; for the hour is coming in which all who are in the graves will hear His voice [29]and come forth—those who have done good, to the resurrection of life, and those who have done evil, to the resurrection of condemnation. [30]I can of Myself do nothing. As I hear, I judge; and My judgment is righteous, because I do not seek My own will but the will of the Father who sent Me.

[31]"If I bear witness of Myself, My witness is not true. [32]There is another who bears witness of Me, and I know that the witness which He witnesses of Me is true. [33]You have sent to John, and he has borne witness to the truth. [34]Yet I do not receive testimony from man, but I say these things that you

may be saved. [35]He was the burning and shining lamp, and you were willing for a time to rejoice in his light. [36]But I have a greater witness than John's; for the works which the Father has given Me to finish—the very works that I do—bear witness of Me, that the Father has sent Me. [37]And the Father Himself, who sent Me, has testified of Me. You have neither heard His voice at any time, nor seen His form. [38]But you do not have His word abiding in you, because whom He sent, Him you do not believe. [39]You search the Scriptures, for in them you think you have eternal life; and these are they which testify of Me. [40]But you are not willing to come to Me that you may have life.

[41]"I do not receive honor from men. [42]But I know you, that you do not have the love of God in you. [43]I have come in My Father's name, and you do not receive Me; if another comes in his own name, him you will receive. [44]How can you believe, who receive honor from one another, and do not seek the honor that *comes* from the only God? [45]Do not think that I shall accuse you to the Father; there is *one* who accuses you—Moses, in whom you trust. [46]For if you believed Moses, you would believe Me; for he wrote about Me. [47]But if you do not believe his writings, how will you believe My words?"

PSALM 106:1-12

PRAISE the LORD!

Oh, give thanks to the LORD,
    for *He is* good!
For His mercy *endures* forever.

2   Who can utter the mighty acts
        of the LORD?
    Who can declare all His
        praise?
3   Blessed *are* those who keep
        justice,

And he who does*
righteousness at all times!

4 Remember me, O LORD, with
the favor *You have toward*
Your people.
Oh, visit me with Your
salvation,
5 That I may see the benefit of
Your chosen ones,
That I may rejoice in the
gladness of Your nation,
That I may glory with Your
inheritance.

6 We have sinned with our
fathers,
We have committed iniquity,
We have done wickedly.
7 Our fathers in Egypt did not
understand Your wonders;
They did not remember the
multitude of Your mercies,

But rebelled by the sea—the
Red Sea.

8 Nevertheless He saved them
for His name's sake,
That He might make His
mighty power known.
9 He rebuked the Red Sea also,
and it dried up;
So He led them through the
depths,
As through the wilderness.
10 He saved them from the hand
of him who hated *them,*
And redeemed them from the
hand of the enemy.
11 The waters covered their
enemies;
There was not one of them
left.
12 Then they believed His words;
They sang His praise.

PROVERBS FOR TODAY/ 14:30-31

A sound heart is *life to the body, but envy* is *rottenness to the bones.* □ *He who oppresses the poor reproaches his Maker, but he who honors Him has mercy on the needy.*

MAY 9

1 SAMUEL 5:1–7:17

THEN the Philistines took the ark of God and brought it from Ebenezer to Ashdod. 2When the Philistines took the ark of God, they brought it into the house of Dagon* and set it by Dagon. 3And when the people of Ashdod arose early in the morning, there was Dagon, fallen on its face to the earth before the ark of the LORD. So they took Dagon and set it in its place again. 4And when they arose early the next morning, there

was Dagon, fallen on its face to the ground before the ark of the LORD. The head of Dagon and both the palms of its hands *were* broken off on the threshold; only Dagon's torso* was left of it. 5Therefore neither the priests of Dagon nor any who come into Dagon's house tread on the threshold of Dagon in Ashdod to this day.

6But the hand of the LORD was heavy on the people of Ashdod, and He ravaged them and struck them with tumors,* *both* Ashdod and its territory. 7And when the men of Ashdod saw how *it was,* they said, "The ark of the God of Israel must not remain with us, for His hand is harsh toward us and Dagon our god." ⁸Therefore they sent and gathered to themselves all the lords of the Philistines, and said, "What shall we do with the ark of the God of Israel?"

And they answered, "Let the ark of the God of Israel be carried away to Gath." So they carried the ark of the God of Israel away. ⁹So it was, after they had carried it away, that the hand of the LORD was against the city with a very great destruction; and He struck the men of the city, both small and great, and tumors broke out on them.

¹⁰Therefore they sent the ark of God to Ekron. So it was, as the ark of God came to Ekron, that the Ekronites cried out, saying, "They have brought the ark of the God of Israel to us, to kill us and our people!" ¹¹So they sent and gathered together all the lords of the Philistines, and said, "Send away the ark of the God of Israel, and let it go back to its own place, so that it does not kill us and our people." For there was a deadly destruction throughout all the city; the hand of God was very heavy there. ¹²And the men who did not die were stricken with the tumors, and the cry of the city went up to heaven.

Now the ark of the LORD was in the country of the Philistines seven months. ²And the Philistines called for the priests and the diviners, saying, "What shall we do with the ark of the LORD? Tell us how we should send it to its place."

³So they said, "If you send away the ark of the God of Israel, do not send it empty; but by all means return *it* to Him *with* a trespass offering. Then you will be healed, and it will be known to you why His hand is not removed from you."

⁴Then they said, "What *is* the tres- pass offering which we shall return to Him?"

They answered, "Five golden tumors and five golden rats, *according to* the number of the lords of the Philistines. For the same plague *was* on all of you and on your lords. ⁵Therefore you shall make images of your tumors and images of your rats that ravage the land, and you shall give glory to the God of Israel; perhaps He will lighten His hand from you, from your gods, and from your land. ⁶Why then do you harden your hearts as the Egyptians and Pharaoh hardened their hearts? When He did mighty things among them, did they not let the people go, that they might depart? ⁷Now there- fore, make a new cart, take two milk cows which have never been yoked, and hitch the cows to the cart; and take their calves home, away from them. ⁸Then take the ark of the LORD and set it on the cart; and put the articles of gold which you are returning to Him *as* a trespass offering in a chest by its side. Then send it away, and let it go. ⁹And watch: if it goes up the road to its own territory, to Beth Shemesh, *then* He has done us this great evil. But if not, then we shall know that *it is* not His hand *that* struck us—it happened to us by chance."

¹⁰Then the men did so; they took two milk cows and hitched them to the cart, and shut up their calves at home. ¹¹And they set the ark of the LORD on the cart, and the chest with the gold rats and the images of their tumors. ¹²Then the cows headed straight for the road to Beth Shemesh, *and* went along the highway, lowing as they went, and did not turn aside to the right hand or the left. And the lords of the Philistines went after them to the border of Beth Shemesh.

¹³Now *the people of* Beth Shemesh *were* reaping their wheat harvest in the valley; and they lifted their eyes and saw the ark, and rejoiced to see *it.*

¹⁴Then the cart came into the field of Joshua of Beth Shemesh, and stood there; a large stone *was* there. So they split the wood of the cart and offered the cows as a burnt offering to the LORD. ¹⁵The Levites took down the ark of the LORD and the chest that *was* with it, in which *were* the articles of gold, and put *them* on the large stone. Then the men of Beth Shemesh offered burnt offerings and made sacrifices the same day to the LORD. ¹⁶So when the five lords of the Philistines had seen *it,* they returned to Ekron the same day.

¹⁷These *are* the golden tumors which the Philistines returned *as* a trespass offering to the LORD: one for Ashdod, one for Gaza, one for Ashkelon, one for Gath, one for Ekron; ¹⁸and the golden rats, *according to* the number of all the cities of the Philistines *belonging* to the five lords, *both* fortified cities and country villages, even as far as the large *stone of* Abel on which they set the ark of the LORD, *which stone remains* to this day in the field of Joshua of Beth Shemesh.

¹⁹Then He struck the men of Beth Shemesh, because they had looked into the ark of the LORD. He struck fifty thousand and seventy men* of the people, and the people lamented because the LORD had struck the people with a great slaughter.

²⁰And the men of Beth Shemesh said, "Who is able to stand before this holy LORD God? And to whom shall it go up from us?" ²¹So they sent messengers to the inhabitants of Kirjath Jearim, saying, "The Philistines have brought back the ark of the LORD; come down *and* take it up with you."

THEN the men of Kirjath Jearim came and took the ark of the LORD, and brought it into the house of Abinadab on the hill, and consecrated Eleazar his son to keep the ark of the LORD.

²So it was that the ark remained in Kirjath Jearim a long time; it was there twenty years. And all the house of Israel lamented after the LORD.

³Then Samuel spoke to all the house of Israel, saying, "If you return to the LORD with all your hearts, *then* put away the foreign gods and the Ashtoreths* from among you, and prepare your hearts for the LORD, and serve Him only; and He will deliver you from the hand of the Philistines." ⁴So the children of Israel put away the Baals and the Ashtoreths,* and served the LORD only.

⁵And Samuel said, "Gather all Israel to Mizpah, and I will pray to the LORD for you." ⁶So they gathered together at Mizpah, drew water, and poured *it* out before the LORD. And they fasted that day, and said there, "We have sinned against the LORD." And Samuel judged the children of Israel at Mizpah.

⁷Now when the Philistines heard that the children of Israel had gathered together at Mizpah, the lords of the Philistines went up against Israel. And when the children of Israel heard *of it,* they were afraid of the Philistines. ⁸So the children of Israel said to Samuel, "Do not cease to cry out to the LORD our God for us, that He may save us from the hand of the Philistines."

⁹And Samuel took a suckling lamb and offered *it as* a whole burnt offering to the LORD. Then Samuel cried out to the LORD for Israel, and the LORD answered him. ¹⁰Now as Samuel was offering up the burnt offering, the Philistines drew near to battle against Israel. But the LORD thundered with a loud thunder upon the Philistines that day, and so confused them that they were overcome before Israel. ¹¹And the men of Israel went out of Mizpah and pursued the Philistines, and drove them back as far as below Beth Car. ¹²Then Samuel took a stone and set *it* up between Mizpah and Shen, and called its name Ebenezer,* saying, "Thus far the LORD has helped us."

¹³So the Philistines were subdued, and they did not come anymore into the territory of Israel. And the hand of the LORD was against the Philistines all the days of Samuel. ¹⁴Then the cities which the Philistines had taken from Israel were restored to Israel, from Ekron to Gath; and Israel recovered its territory from the hands of the Philistines. Also there was peace between Israel and the Amorites.

¹⁵And Samuel judged Israel all the days of his life. ¹⁶He went from year to year on a circuit to Bethel, Gilgal, and Mizpah, and judged Israel in all those places. ¹⁷But he always returned to Ramah, for his home was there. There he judged Israel, and there he built an altar to the LORD.

JOHN 6:1-21

AFTER these things Jesus went over the Sea of Galilee, which is the Sea of Tiberias. ²Then a great multitude followed Him, because they saw His signs which He performed on those who were diseased. ³And Jesus went up on the mountain, and there He sat with His disciples.

⁴Now the Passover, a feast of the Jews, was near. ⁵Then Jesus lifted up His eyes, and seeing a great multitude coming toward Him, He said to Philip, "Where shall we buy bread, that these may eat?" ⁶But this He said to test him, for He Himself knew what He would do.

⁷Philip answered Him, "Two hundred denarii worth of bread is not sufficient for them, that every one of them may have a little."

⁸One of His disciples, Andrew, Simon Peter's brother, said to Him, ⁹"There is a lad here who has five barley loaves and two small fish, but what are they among so many?"

¹⁰Then Jesus said, "Make the people sit down." Now there was much grass in the place. So the men sat down, in number about five thousand. ¹¹And Jesus took the loaves, and when He had given thanks He distributed them to the disciples, and the disciples* to those sitting down; and likewise of the fish, as much as they wanted. ¹²So when they were filled, He said to His disciples, "Gather up the fragments that remain, so that nothing is lost." ¹³Therefore they gathered them up, and filled twelve baskets with the fragments of the five barley loaves which were left over by those who had eaten. ¹⁴Then those men, when they had seen the sign that Jesus did, said, "This is truly the Prophet who is to come into the world."

¹⁵Therefore when Jesus perceived that they were about to come and take Him by force to make Him king, He departed again to the mountain by Himself alone.

¹⁶Now when evening came, His disciples went down to the sea, ¹⁷got into the boat, and went over the sea toward Capernaum. And it was already dark, and Jesus had not come to them. ¹⁸Then the sea arose because of a great wind was blowing. ¹⁹So when they had rowed about three or four miles,* they saw Jesus walking on the sea and drawing near the boat; and they were afraid. ²⁰But He said to them, "It is I; do not be afraid." ²¹Then they willingly received Him into the boat, and immediately the boat was at the land where they were going.

PSALM 106:13-31

THEY soon forgot His works;
They did not wait for His counsel,
14   But lusted exceedingly in the
        wilderness,
        And tested God in the desert.
15   And He gave them their
        request,
        But sent leanness into their
        soul.

16 When they envied Moses in
the camp,
And Aaron the saint of the
Lord,
17 The earth opened up and
swallowed Dathan,
And covered the faction of
Abiram.
18 A fire was kindled in their
company;
The flame burned up the
wicked.

19 They made a calf in Horeb,
And worshiped the molded
image.
20 Thus they changed their glory
Into the image of an ox that
eats grass.
21 They forgot God their Savior,
Who had done great things in
Egypt,
22 Wondrous works in the land
of Ham,
Awesome things by the Red
Sea.
23 Therefore He said that He
would destroy them,
Had not Moses His chosen
one stood before Him in
the breach,
To turn away His wrath, lest
He destroy *them.*

24 Then they despised the
pleasant land;
They did not believe His word,
25 But complained in their tents,
And did not heed the voice of
the Lord.
26 Therefore He raised His hand
in an oath against them,
To overthrow them in the
wilderness,
27 To overthrow their
descendants among the
nations,
And to scatter them in the
lands.

28 They joined themselves also
to Baal of Peor,
And ate sacrifices made to the
dead.
29 Thus they provoked *Him* to
anger with their deeds,
And the plague broke out
among them.
30 Then Phinehas stood up and
intervened,
And the plague was stopped.
31 And that was accounted to
him for righteousness
To all generations
forevermore.

PROVERBS FOR TODAY/ 14:32-33

The wicked is banished in his wickedness, but the righteous has a refuge in his death. □ *Wisdom rests in the heart of him who has understanding, but* what is in *the heart of fools is made known.*

MAY 10

1 SAMUEL 8:1–9:27

Now it came to pass when Samuel was old that he made his sons judges over Israel. ²The name of his firstborn was Joel, and the name of his second, Abijah; *they were* judges in Beersheba. ³But his sons did not walk in his ways; they turned aside after dishonest gain, took bribes, and perverted justice.

⁴Then all the elders of Israel gathered together and came to Samuel at Ramah, ⁵and said to him, "Look, you are old, and your sons do not walk in your ways. Now make us a king to judge us like all the nations."

⁶But the thing displeased Samuel when they said, "Give us a king to judge us." So Samuel prayed to the LORD. ⁷And the LORD said to Samuel, "Heed the voice of the people in all that they say to you; for they have not rejected you, but they have rejected Me, that I should not reign over them. ⁸According to all the works which they have done since the day that I brought them up out of Egypt, even to this day—with which they have forsaken Me and served other gods—so they are doing to you also. ⁹Now therefore, heed their voice. However, you shall solemnly forewarn them, and show them the behavior of the king who will reign over them."

¹⁰So Samuel told all the words of the LORD to the people who asked him for a king. ¹¹And he said, "This will be the behavior of the king who will reign over you: He will take your sons and appoint *them* for his own chariots and *to be* his horsemen, and *some* will run before his chariots. ¹²He will appoint captains over his thousands and captains over his fifties, *will set some* to plow his ground and reap his harvest, and *some* to make his weapons of war and equipment for his chariots. ¹³He will take your daughters *to be* perfumers, cooks, and bakers. ¹⁴And he will take the best of your fields, your vineyards, and your olive groves, and give *them* to his servants. ¹⁵He will take a tenth of your grain and your vintage, and give it to his officers and servants. ¹⁶And he will take your male servants, your female servants, your finest young men,* and your donkeys, and put *them* to his work. ¹⁷He will take a tenth of your sheep. And you will be his servants. ¹⁸And you will cry out in that day because of your king whom you have chosen for yourselves, and the LORD will not hear you in that day."

¹⁹Nevertheless the people refused to obey the voice of Samuel; and they said, "No, but we will have a king over us, ²⁰that we also may be like all the nations, and that our king may judge us and go out before us and fight our battles."

²¹And Samuel heard all the words of the people, and he repeated them in the hearing of the LORD. ²²So the LORD said to Samuel, "Heed their voice, and make them a king."

And Samuel said to the men of Israel, "Every man go to his city."

THERE was a man of Benjamin whose name *was* Kish the son of Abiel, the son of Zeror, the son of Bechorath, the son of Aphiah, a Benjamite, a mighty man of power. ²And he had a choice and handsome son whose name *was* Saul. *There was* not a more handsome person than he among the children of Israel. From his shoulders upward *he was* taller than any of the people.

³Now the donkeys of Kish, Saul's father, were lost. And Kish said to his

son Saul, "Please take one of the servants with you, and arise, go and look for the donkeys." ⁴So he passed through the mountains of Ephraim and through the land of Shalisha, but they did not find *them.* Then they passed through the land of Shaalim, and *they were* not *there.* Then he passed through the land of the Benjamites, but they did not find *them.*

⁵When they had come to the land of Zuph, Saul said to his servant who *was* with him, "Come, let us return, lest my father cease *caring* about the donkeys and become worried about us."

⁶And he said to him, "Look now, *there is* in this city a man of God, and *he is* an honorable man; all that he says surely comes to pass. So let us go there; perhaps he can show us the way that we should go."

⁷Then Saul said to his servant, "But look, *if* we go, what shall we bring the man? For the bread in our vessels is all gone, and *there is* no present to bring to the man of God. What do we have?"

⁸And the servant answered Saul again and said, "Look, I have here at hand one-fourth of a shekel of silver. I will give *that* to the man of God, to tell us our way." ⁹(Formerly in Israel, when a man went to inquire of God, he spoke thus: "Come, let us go to the seer"; for *he who is* now *called* a prophet was formerly called a seer.)

¹⁰Then Saul said to his servant, "Well said; come, let us go." So they went to the city where the man of God *was.*

¹¹As they went up the hill to the city, they met some young women going out to draw water, and said to them, "Is the seer here?"

¹²And they answered them and said, "Yes, there he is, just ahead of you. Hurry now; for today he came to this city, because there is a sacrifice of the people today on the high place. ¹³As soon as you come into the city, you will surely find him before he goes up to the

high place to eat. For the people will not eat until he comes, because he must bless the sacrifice; afterward those who are invited will eat. Now therefore, go up, for about this time you will find him." ¹⁴So they went up to the city. As they were coming into the city, there was Samuel, coming out toward them on his way up to the high place.

¹⁵Now the LORD had told Samuel in his ear the day before Saul came, saying, ¹⁶"Tomorrow about this time I will send you a man from the land of Benjamin, and you shall anoint him commander over My people Israel, that he may save My people from the hand of the Philistines; for I have looked upon My people, because their cry has come to Me."

¹⁷So when Samuel saw Saul, the LORD said to him, "There he is, the man of whom I spoke to you. This one shall reign over My people." ¹⁸Then Saul drew near to Samuel in the gate, and said, "Please tell me, where *is* the seer's house?"

¹⁹Samuel answered Saul and said, "I *am* the seer. Go up before me to the high place, for you shall eat with me today; and tomorrow I will let you go and will tell you all that *is* in your heart. ²⁰But as for your donkeys that were lost three days ago, do not be anxious about them, for they have been found. And on whom *is* all the desire of Israel? *Is it* not on you and on all your father's house?"

²¹And Saul answered and said, "*Am* I not a Benjamite, of the smallest of the tribes of Israel, and my family the least of all the families of the tribe* of Benjamin? Why then do you speak like this to me?"

²²Now Samuel took Saul and his servant and brought them into the hall, and had them sit in the place of honor among those who were invited; there *were* about thirty persons. ²³And Samuel said to the cook, "Bring the portion which I gave you, of which I said to

you, 'Set it apart.' " [24]So the cook took up the thigh with its upper part and set *it* before Saul. And *Samuel* said, "Here it is, what was kept back. *It* was set apart for you. Eat; for until this time it has been kept for you, since I said I invited the people." So Saul ate with Samuel that day.

[25]When they had come down from the high place into the city, *Samuel* spoke with Saul on the top of the house.* [26]They arose early; and it was about the dawning of the day that Samuel called to Saul on the top of the house, saying, "Get up, that I may send you on your way." And Saul arose, and both of them went outside, he and Samuel.

[27]As they were going down to the outskirts of the city, Samuel said to Saul, "Tell the servant to go on ahead of us." And he went on. "But you stand here awhile, that I may announce to you the word of God."

JOHN 6:22-42

ON the following day, when the people who were standing on the other side of the sea saw that there was no other boat there, except that one which His disciples had entered,* and that Jesus had not entered the boat with His disciples, but His disciples had gone away alone— [23]however, other boats came from Tiberias, near the place where they ate bread after the Lord had given thanks— [24]when the people therefore saw that Jesus was not there, nor His disciples, they also got into boats and came to Capernaum, seeking Jesus. [25]And when they found Him on the other side of the sea, they said to Him, "Rabbi, when did You come here?"

[26]Jesus answered them and said, "Most assuredly, I say to you, you seek Me, not because you saw the signs, but because you ate of the loaves and were filled. [27]Do not labor for the food which perishes, but for the food which endures to everlasting life, which the Son of Man will give you, because God the Father has set His seal on Him."

[28]Then they said to Him, "What shall we do, that we may work the works of God?"

[29]Jesus answered and said to them, "This is the work of God, that you believe in Him whom He sent."

[30]Therefore they said to Him, "What sign will You perform then, that we may see it and believe You? What work will You do? [31]Our fathers ate the manna in the desert; as it is written, 'He gave them bread from heaven to eat.' " *

[32]Then Jesus said to them, "Most assuredly, I say to you, Moses did not give you the bread from heaven, but My Father gives you the true bread from heaven. [33]For the bread of God is He who comes down from heaven and gives life to the world."

[34]Then they said to Him, "Lord, give us this bread always."

[35]And Jesus said to them, "I am the bread of life. He who comes to Me shall never hunger, and he who believes in Me shall never thirst. [36]But I said to you that you have seen Me and yet do not believe. [37]All that the Father gives Me will come to Me, and the one who comes to Me I will by no means cast out. [38]For I have come down from heaven, not to do My own will, but the will of Him who sent Me. [39]This is the will of the Father who sent Me, that of all He has given Me I should lose nothing, but should raise it up at the last day. [40]And this is the will of Him who sent Me, that everyone who sees the Son and believes in Him may have everlasting life; and I will raise him up at the last day."

[41]The Jews then complained about Him, because He said, "I am the bread which came down from heaven." [42]And they said, "Is not this Jesus, the son of Joseph, whose father and

mother we know? How is it then that He says, 'I have come down from heaven'?"

PSALM 106:32-48

They angered *Him* also at the waters of strife,*
So that it went ill with Moses on account of them;

33 Because they rebelled against His Spirit,
So that he spoke rashly with his lips.

34 They did not destroy the peoples,
Concerning whom the LORD had commanded them,
35 But they mingled with the Gentiles
And learned their works;
36 They served their idols,
Which became a snare to them.
37 They even sacrificed their sons
And their daughters to demons,
38 And shed innocent blood,
The blood of their sons and daughters,
Whom they sacrificed to the idols of Canaan;
And the land was polluted with blood.
39 Thus they were defiled by their own works,
And played the harlot by their own deeds.

40 Therefore the wrath of the LORD was kindled against His people,
So that He abhorred His own inheritance.
41 And He gave them into the hand of the Gentiles,
And those who hated them ruled over them.
42 Their enemies also oppressed them,
And they were brought into subjection under their hand.
43 Many times He delivered them;
But they rebelled in their counsel,
And were brought low for their iniquity.

44 Nevertheless He regarded their affliction,
When He heard their cry;
45 And for their sake He remembered His covenant,
And relented according to the multitude of His mercies.
46 He also made them to be pitied
By all those who carried them away captive.

47 Save us, O LORD our God,
And gather us from among the Gentiles,
To give thanks to Your holy name,
To triumph in Your praise.

48 Blessed *be* the LORD God of Israel
From everlasting to everlasting!
And let all the people say, "Amen!"

Praise the LORD!

PROVERBS FOR TODAY/ 14:34-35

Righteousness exalts a nation, but sin is *a reproach to* any *people.* □ *The king's favor* is *toward a wise servant, but his wrath* is against *him who causes shame.*

MAY 11

1 SAMUEL 10:1–11:15

THEN Samuel took a flask of oil and poured *it* on his [Saul's] head, and kissed him and said: "*Is it* not because the LORD has anointed you commander over His inheritance?* 2When you have departed from me today, you will find two men by Rachel's tomb in the territory of Benjamin at Zelzah; and they will say to you, 'The donkeys which you went to look for have been found. And now your father has ceased caring about the donkeys and is worrying about you, saying, "What shall I do about my son?" ' 3Then you shall go on forward from there and come to the terebinth tree of Tabor. There three men going up to God at Bethel will meet you, one carrying three young goats, another carrying three loaves of bread, and another carrying a skin of wine. 4And they will greet you and give you two *loaves* of bread, which you shall receive from their hands. 5After that you shall come to the hill of God where the Philistine garrison *is*. And it will happen, when you have come there to the city, that you will meet a group of prophets coming down from the high place with a stringed instrument, a tambourine, a flute, and a harp before them; and they will be prophesying. 6Then the Spirit of the LORD will come upon you, and you will prophesy with them and be turned into another man. 7And let it be, when these signs come to you, *that* you do as the occasion demands; for God *is* with you. 8You shall go down before me to Gilgal; and surely I will come down to you to offer burnt offerings *and* make sacrifices of peace offerings. Seven days you shall wait, till I come to you and show you what you should do."

9So it was, when he had turned his back to go from Samuel, that God gave him another heart; and all those signs came to pass that day. 10When they came there to the hill, there was a group of prophets to meet him; then the Spirit of God came upon him, and he prophesied among them. 11And it happened, when all who knew him formerly saw that he indeed prophesied among the prophets, that the people said to one another, "What *is* this *that* has come upon the son of Kish? *Is* Saul also among the prophets?" 12Then a man from there answered and said, "But who *is* their father?" Therefore it became a proverb: "*Is* Saul also among the prophets?" 13And when he had finished prophesying, he went to the high place.

14Then Saul's uncle said to him and his servant, "Where did you go?"

So he said, "To look for the donkeys. When we saw that *they were* nowhere *to be found, we* went to Samuel."

15And Saul's uncle said, "Tell me, please, what Samuel said to you."

16So Saul said to his uncle, "He told us plainly that the donkeys had been found." But about the matter of the kingdom, he did not tell him what Samuel had said.

17Then Samuel called the people together to the LORD at Mizpah, 18and said to the children of Israel, "Thus says the LORD God of Israel: 'I brought up Israel out of Egypt, and delivered you from the hand of the Egyptians *and* from the hand of all kingdoms and from those who oppressed you.' 19But you have today rejected your God, who Himself saved you from all your adversities and your tribulations; and you have said to Him, 'No, set a king over us!' Now therefore, present yourselves before the LORD by your tribes and by your clans."*

²⁰And when Samuel had caused all the tribes of Israel to come near, the tribe of Benjamin was chosen. ²¹When he had caused the tribe of Benjamin to come near by their families, the family of Matri was chosen. And Saul the son of Kish was chosen. But when they sought him, he could not be found. ²²Therefore they inquired of the LORD further, "Has the man come here yet?"

And the LORD answered, "There he is, hidden among the equipment."

²³So they ran and brought him from there; and when he stood among the people, he was taller than any of the people from his shoulders upward. ²⁴And Samuel said to all the people, "Do you see him whom the LORD has chosen, that *there is* no one like him among all the people?"

So all the people shouted and said, "Long live the king!"

²⁵Then Samuel explained to the people the behavior of royalty, and wrote *it* in a book and laid *it* up before the LORD. And Samuel sent all the people away, every man to his house. ²⁶And Saul also went home to Gibeah; and valiant *men* went with him, whose hearts God had touched. ²⁷But some rebels said, "How can this man save us?" So they despised him, and brought him no presents. But he held his peace.

THEN Nahash the Ammonite came up and encamped against Jabesh Gilead; and all the men of Jabesh said to Nahash, "Make a covenant with us, and we will serve you."

²And Nahash the Ammonite answered them, "On this *condition* I will make *a covenant* with you, that I may put out all your right eyes, and bring reproach on all Israel."

³Then the elders of Jabesh said to him, "Hold off for seven days, that we may send messengers to all the terri-

tory of Israel. And then, if *there is* no one to save us, we will come out to you."

⁴So the messengers came to Gibeah of Saul and told the news in the hearing of the people. And all the people lifted up their voices and wept. ⁵Now there was Saul, coming behind the herd from the field; and Saul said, "What *troubles* the people, that they weep?" And they told him the words of the men of Jabesh. ⁶Then the Spirit of God came upon Saul when he heard this news, and his anger was greatly aroused. ⁷So he took a yoke of oxen and cut them in pieces, and sent *them* throughout all the territory of Israel by the hands of messengers, saying, "Whoever does not go out with Saul and Samuel to battle, so it shall be done to his oxen."

And the fear of the LORD fell on the people, and they came out with one consent. ⁸When he numbered them in Bezek, the children of Israel were three hundred thousand, and the men of Judah thirty thousand. ⁹And they said to the messengers who came, "Thus you shall say to the men of Jabesh Gilead: 'Tomorrow, by *the time* the sun is hot, you shall have help.'" Then the messengers came and reported *it* to the men of Jabesh, and they were glad. ¹⁰Therefore the men of Jabesh said, "Tomorrow we will come out to you, and you may do with us whatever seems good to you."

¹¹So it was, on the next day, that Saul put the people in three companies; and they came into the midst of the camp in the morning watch, and killed Ammonites until the heat of the day. And it happened that those who survived were scattered, so that no two of them were left together.

¹²Then the people said to Samuel, "Who *is* he who said, 'Shall Saul reign over us?' Bring the men, that we may put them to death."

¹³But Saul said, "Not a man shall be

put to death this day, for today the LORD has accomplished salvation in Israel."

[14]Then Samuel said to the people, "Come, let us go to Gilgal and renew the kingdom there." [15]So all the people went to Gilgal, and there they made Saul king before the LORD in Gilgal. There they made sacrifices of peace offerings before the LORD, and there Saul and all the men of Israel rejoiced greatly.

JOHN 6:43-71

JESUS therefore answered and said to them, "Do not murmur among yourselves. [44]No one can come to Me unless the Father who sent Me draws him; and I will raise him up at the last day. [45]It is written in the prophets, *'And they shall all be taught by God.'* * Therefore everyone who has heard and learned* from the Father comes to Me. [46]Not that anyone has seen the Father, except He who is from God; He has seen the Father. [47]Most assuredly, I say to you, he who believes in Me* has everlasting life. [48]I am the bread of life. [49]Your fathers ate the manna in the wilderness, and are dead. [50]This is the bread which comes down from heaven, that one may eat of it and not die. [51]I am the living bread which came down from heaven. If anyone eats of this bread, he will live forever; and the bread that I shall give is My flesh, which I shall give for the life of the world."

[52]The Jews therefore quarreled among themselves, saying, "How can this Man give us *His* flesh to eat?"

[53]Then Jesus said to them, "Most assuredly, I say to you, unless you eat the flesh of the Son of Man and drink His blood, you have no life in you. [54]Whoever eats My flesh and drinks My blood has eternal life, and I will raise him up at the last day. [55]For My flesh is food indeed,* and My blood is drink indeed. [56]He who eats My flesh and drinks My blood abides in Me, and I in him. [57]As the living Father sent Me, and I live because of the Father, so he who feeds on Me will live because of Me. [58]This is the bread which came down from heaven—not as your fathers ate the manna, and are dead. He who eats this bread will live forever."

[59]These things He said in the synagogue as He taught in Capernaum.

[60]Therefore many of His disciples, when they heard *this,* said, "This is a hard saying; who can understand it?"

[61]When Jesus knew in Himself that His disciples complained about this, He said to them, "Does this offend you? [62]*What* then if you should see the Son of Man ascend where He was before? [63]It is the Spirit who gives life; the flesh profits nothing. The words that I speak to you are spirit, and *they* are life. [64]But there are some of you who do not believe." For Jesus knew from the beginning who they were who did not believe, and who would betray Him. [65]And He said, "Therefore I have said to you that no one can come to Me unless it has been granted to him by My Father."

[66]From that *time* many of His disciples went back and walked with Him no more. [67]Then Jesus said to the twelve, "Do you also want to go away?"

[68]But Simon Peter answered Him, "Lord, to whom shall we go? You have the words of eternal life. [69]Also we have come to believe and know that You are the Christ, the Son of the living God."*

[70]Jesus answered them, "Did I not choose you, the twelve, and one of you is a devil?" [71]He spoke of Judas Iscariot, *the son* of Simon, for it was he who would betray Him, being one of the twelve.

PSALM 107:1-43

O H, give thanks to the LORD, for
He is good!
For His mercy *endures*
forever.

2 Let the redeemed of the LORD
say *so,*
Whom He has redeemed
from the hand of the enemy,

3 And gathered out of the lands,
From the east and from the
west,
From the north and from the
south.

4 They wandered in the
wilderness in a desolate
way;
They found no city to dwell in.

5 Hungry and thirsty,
Their soul fainted in them.

6 Then they cried out to the
LORD in their trouble,
And He delivered them out of
their distresses.

7 And He led them forth by the
right way,
That they might go to a city
for a dwelling place.

8 Oh, that *men* would give
thanks to the LORD *for* His
goodness,
And *for* His wonderful works
to the children of men!

9 For He satisfies the longing
soul,
And fills the hungry soul with
goodness.

10 Those who sat in darkness
and in the shadow of death,
Bound in affliction and irons—

11 Because they rebelled against
the words of God,
And despised the counsel of
the Most High,

12 Therefore He brought down
their heart with labor;
They fell down, and *there was*
none to help.

13 Then they cried out to the
LORD in their trouble,
And He saved them out of
their distresses.

14 He brought them out of
darkness and the shadow of
death,
And broke their chains in
pieces.

15 Oh, that *men* would give
thanks to the LORD *for* His
goodness,
And *for* His wonderful works
to the children of men!

16 For He has broken the gates
of bronze,
And cut the bars of iron in two.

17 Fools, because of their
transgression,
And because of their
iniquities, were afflicted.

18 Their soul abhorred all
manner of food,
And they drew near to the
gates of death.

19 Then they cried out to the
LORD in their trouble,
And He saved them out of
their distresses.

20 He sent His word and healed
them,
And delivered *them* from their
destructions.

21 Oh, that *men* would give
thanks to the LORD *for* His
goodness,
And *for* His wonderful works
to the children of men!

22 Let them sacrifice the
sacrifices of thanksgiving,
And declare His works with
rejoicing.

23 Those who go down to the
sea in ships,
Who do business on great
waters,

24 They see the works of the LORD,
And His wonders in the deep.
25 For He commands and raises the stormy wind,
Which lifts up the waves of the sea.
26 They mount up to the heavens,
They go down again to the depths;
Their soul melts because of trouble.
27 They reel to and fro, and stagger like a drunken man,
And are at their wits' end.
28 Then they cry out to the LORD in their trouble,
And He brings them out of their distresses.
29 He calms the storm,
So that its waves are still.
30 Then they are glad because they are quiet;
So He guides them to their desired haven.
31 Oh, that *men* would give thanks to the LORD *for* His goodness,
And *for* His wonderful works to the children of men!
32 Let them exalt Him also in the assembly of the people,
And praise Him in the company of the elders.

33 He turns rivers into a wilderness,
And the watersprings into dry ground;
34 A fruitful land into barrenness,
For the wickedness of those who dwell in it.
35 He turns a wilderness into pools of water,
And dry land into watersprings.
36 There He makes the hungry dwell,
That they may establish a city for a dwelling place,
37 And sow fields and plant vineyards,
That they may yield a fruitful harvest.
38 He also blesses them, and they multiply greatly;
And He does not let their cattle decrease.

39 When they are diminished and brought low
Through oppression, affliction and sorrow,
40 He pours contempt on princes,
And causes them to wander in the wilderness *where there is* no way;
41 Yet He sets the poor on high, far from affliction,
And makes *their* families like a flock.
42 The righteous see *it* and rejoice,
And all iniquity stops its mouth.

43 Whoever *is* wise will observe these *things,*
And they will understand the lovingkindness of the LORD.

PROVERBS FOR TODAY/ 15:1-3

A soft answer turns away wrath, but a harsh word stirs up anger. The tongue of the wise uses knowledge rightly, but the mouth of fools pours forth foolishness. □ *The eyes of the LORD are in every place, keeping watch on the evil and the good.*

MAY 12

1 SAMUEL 12:1–13:23

Now Samuel said to all Israel: "Indeed I have heeded your voice in all that you said to me, and have made a king over you. ²And now here is the king, walking before you; and I am old and grayheaded, and look, my sons *are* with you. I have walked before you from my childhood to this day. ³Here I am. Witness against me before the LORD and before His anointed: Whose ox have I taken, or whose donkey have I taken, or whom have I cheated? Whom have I oppressed, or from whose hand have I received *any* bribe with which to blind my eyes? I will restore *it* to you."

⁴And they said, "You have not cheated us or oppressed us, nor have you taken anything from any man's hand."

⁵Then he said to them, "The LORD *is* witness against you, and His anointed *is* witness this day, that you have not found anything in my hand."

And they answered, "*He is* witness."

⁶Then Samuel said to the people, "*It is* the LORD who raised up Moses and Aaron, and who brought your fathers up from the land of Egypt. ⁷Now therefore, stand still, that I may reason with you before the LORD concerning all the righteous acts of the LORD which He did to you and your fathers: ⁸When Jacob had gone into Egypt,* and your fathers cried out to the LORD, then the LORD sent Moses and Aaron, who brought your fathers out of Egypt and made them dwell in this place. ⁹And when they forgot the LORD their God, He sold them into the hand of Sisera, commander of the army of Hazor, into the hand of the Philistines, and into the hand of the king of Moab; and they fought against them. ¹⁰Then they cried

out to the LORD, and said, 'We have sinned, because we have forsaken the LORD and served the Baals and Ashtoreths;* but now deliver us from the hand of our enemies, and we will serve You.' ¹¹And the LORD sent Jerubbaal,* Bedan,* Jephthah, and Samuel,* and delivered you out of the hand of your enemies on every side; and you dwelt in safety. ¹²And when you saw that Nahash king of the Ammonites came against you, you said to me, 'No, but a king shall reign over us,' when the LORD your God *was* your king.

¹³"Now therefore, here is the king whom you have chosen *and* whom you have desired. And take note, the LORD has set a king over you. ¹⁴If you fear the LORD and serve Him and obey His voice, and do not rebel against the commandment of the LORD, then both you and the king who reigns over you will continue following the LORD your God. ¹⁵However, if you do not obey the voice of the LORD, but rebel against the commandment of the LORD, then the hand of the LORD will be against you, as *it was* against your fathers.

¹⁶"Now therefore, stand and see this great thing which the LORD will do before your eyes: ¹⁷*Is* today not the wheat harvest? I will call to the LORD, and He will send thunder and rain, that you may perceive and see that your wickedness *is* great, which you have done in the sight of the LORD, in asking a king for yourselves."

¹⁸So Samuel called to the LORD, and the LORD sent thunder and rain that day; and all the people greatly feared the LORD and Samuel.

¹⁹And all the people said to Samuel, "Pray for your servants to the LORD your God, that we may not die; for we

have added to all our sins the evil of asking a king for ourselves."

20Then Samuel said to the people, "Do not fear. You have done all this wickedness; yet do not turn aside from following the LORD, but serve the LORD with all your heart. 21And do not turn aside; for *then you would go* after empty things which cannot profit or deliver, for they *are* nothing. 22For the LORD will not forsake His people, for His great name's sake, because it has pleased the LORD to make you His people. 23Moreover, as for me, far be it from me that I should sin against the LORD in ceasing to pray for you; but I will teach you the good and the right way. 24Only fear the LORD, and serve Him in truth with all your heart; for consider what great things He has done for you. 25But if you still do wickedly, you shall be swept away, both you and your king."

SAUL reigned one year; and when he had reigned two years over Israel,* 2Saul chose for himself three thousand *men* of Israel. Two thousand were with Saul in Michmash and in the mountains of Bethel, and a thousand were with Jonathan in Gibeah of Benjamin. The rest of the people he sent away, every man to his tent.

3And Jonathan attacked the garrison of the Philistines that *was* in Geba, and the Philistines heard *of it.* Then Saul blew the trumpet throughout all the land, saying, "Let the Hebrews hear!" 4Now all Israel heard it said *that* Saul had attacked a garrison of the Philistines, and *that* Israel had also become an abomination to the Philistines. And the people were called together to Saul at Gilgal.

5Then the Philistines gathered together to fight with Israel, thirty* thousand chariots and six thousand horsemen, and people as the sand which *is* on the seashore in multitude. And they came up and encamped in Michmash, to the east of Beth Aven.

6When the men of Israel saw that they were in danger (for the people were distressed), then the people hid in caves, in thickets, in rocks, in holes, and in pits. 7And *some of* the Hebrews crossed over the Jordan to the land of Gad and Gilead.

As for Saul, he *was* still in Gilgal, and all the people followed him trembling. 8Then he waited seven days, according to the time set by Samuel. But Samuel did not come to Gilgal; and the people were scattered from him. 9So Saul said, "Bring a burnt offering and peace offerings here to me." And he offered the burnt offering. 10Now it happened, as soon as he had finished presenting the burnt offering, that Samuel came, and Saul went out to meet him, that he might greet him.

11And Samuel said, "What have you done?"

Saul said, "When I saw that the people were scattered from me, and *that* you did not come within the days appointed, and *that* the Philistines gathered together at Michmash, 12then I said, 'The Philistines will now come down on me at Gilgal, and I have not made supplication to the LORD.' Therefore I felt compelled, and offered a burnt offering."

13And Samuel said to Saul, "You have done foolishly. You have not kept the commandment of the LORD your God, which He commanded you. For now the LORD would have established your kingdom over Israel forever. 14But now your kingdom shall not continue. The LORD has sought for Himself a man after His own heart, and the LORD has commanded him *to be* commander over His people, because you have not kept what the LORD commanded you."

15Then Samuel arose and went up from Gilgal to Gibeah of Benjamin.* And Saul numbered the people present with him, about six hundred men.

16Saul, Jonathan his son, and the

people present with them remained in Gibeah of Benjamin. But the Philistines encamped in Michmash. 17Then raiders came out of the camp of the Philistines in three companies. One company turned onto the road to Ophrah, to the land of Shual, 18another company turned to the road *to* Beth Horon, and another company turned *to* the road of the border that overlooks the Valley of Zeboim toward the wilderness.

19Now there was no blacksmith to be found throughout all the land of Israel, for the Philistines said, "Lest the Hebrews make swords or spears." 20But all the Israelites would go down to the Philistines to sharpen each man's plowshare, his mattock, his ax, and his sickle; 21and the charge for a sharpening was a pim* for the plowshares, the mattocks, the forks, and the axes, and to set the points of the goads. 22So it came about, on the day of battle, that there was neither sword nor spear found in the hand of any of the people who *were* with Saul and Jonathan. But they were found with Saul and Jonathan his son.

23And the garrison of the Philistines went out to the pass of Michmash.

JOHN 7:1-29

AFTER these things Jesus walked in Galilee; for He did not want to walk in Judea, because the Jews* sought to kill Him. 2Now the Jews' Feast of Tabernacles was at hand. 3His brothers therefore said to Him, "Depart from here and go into Judea, that Your disciples also may see the works that You are doing. 4For no one does anything in secret while he himself seeks to be known openly. If You do these things, show Yourself to the world." 5For even His brothers did not believe in Him.

6Then Jesus said to them, "My time has not yet come, but your time is always ready. 7The world cannot hate you, but it hates Me because I testify of it that its works are evil. 8You go up to this feast. I am not yet* going up to this feast, for My time has not yet fully come." 9When He had said these things to them, He remained in Galilee.

10But when His brothers had gone up, then He also went up to the feast, not openly, but as it were in secret. 11Then the Jews sought Him at the feast, and said, "Where is He?" 12And there was much complaining among the people concerning Him. Some said, "He is good"; others said, "No, on the contrary, He deceives the people." 13However, no one spoke openly of Him for fear of the Jews.

14Now about the middle of the feast Jesus went up into the temple and taught. 15And the Jews marveled, saying, "How does this Man know letters, having never studied?"

16Jesus* answered them and said, "My doctrine is not Mine, but His who sent Me. 17If anyone wills to do His will, he shall know concerning the doctrine, whether it is from God or *whether* I speak on My own *authority.* 18He who speaks from himself seeks his own glory; but He who seeks the glory of the One who sent Him is true, and no unrighteousness is in Him. 19Did not Moses give you the law, yet none of you keeps the law? Why do you seek to kill Me?"

20The people answered and said, "You have a demon. Who is seeking to kill You?"

21Jesus answered and said to them, "I did one work, and you all marvel. 22Moses therefore gave you circumcision (not that it is from Moses, but from the fathers), and you circumcise a man on the Sabbath. 23If a man receives circumcision on the Sabbath, so that the law of Moses should not be broken, are you angry with Me because I made a man completely well on the Sabbath? 24Do not judge according to appearance, but judge with righteous judgment."

25Now some of them from Jerusalem said, "Is this not He whom they seek to kill? 26But look! He speaks boldly, and they say nothing to Him. Do the rulers know indeed that this is truly* the Christ? 27However, we know where this Man is from; but when the Christ comes, no one knows where He is from."

28Then Jesus cried out, as He taught in the temple, saying, "You both know Me, and you know where I am from; and I have not come of Myself, but He who sent Me is true, whom you do not know. 29But* I know Him, for I am from Him, and He sent Me."

PSALM 108:1-13

A Song. A Psalm of David.

O GOD, my heart is steadfast;
I will sing and give praise, even with my glory.
2 Awake, lute and harp!
I will awaken the dawn.
3 I will praise You, O LORD,
among the peoples,
And I will sing praises to You
among the nations.
4 For Your mercy *is* great above
the heavens,
And Your truth *reaches* to the
clouds.
5 Be exalted, O God, above the
heavens,
And Your glory above all the
earth;
6 That Your beloved may be
delivered,
Save *with* Your right hand,
and hear me.

7 God has spoken in His
holiness:
"I will rejoice;
I will divide Shechem
And measure out the Valley of
Succoth.
8 Gilead *is* Mine; Manasseh *is*
Mine;
Ephraim also *is* the helmet for
My head;
Judah *is* My lawgiver
9 Moab *is* My washpot;
Over Edom I will cast My
shoe;
Over Philistia I will triumph."

10 Who will bring me *into* the
strong city?
Who will lead me to Edom?
11 *Is it* not *You,* O God, *who* cast
us off?
And *You,* O God, *who* did not
go out with our armies?
12 Give us help from trouble,
For the help of man is useless.
13 Through God we will do
valiantly,
For *it is* He *who* shall tread
down our enemies.*

PROVERBS FOR TODAY/ 15:4

A wholesome tongue is *a tree of life, but perverseness in it breaks the spirit.*

MAY 13

1 SAMUEL 14:1–14:52

Now it happened one day that Jonathan the son of Saul said to the young man who bore his armor, "Come, let us go over to the Philistines' garrison that *is* on the other side." But he did not tell his father. ²And Saul was sitting in the outskirts of Gibeah under a pomegranate tree which *is* in Migron. The people who *were* with him *were* about six hundred men. ³Ahijah the son of Ahitub, Ichabod's brother, the son of Phinehas, the son of Eli, the LORD's priest in Shiloh, was wearing an ephod. But the people did not know that Jonathan had gone.

⁴Between the passes, by which Jonathan sought to go over to the Philistines' garrison, *there was* a sharp rock on one side and a sharp rock on the other side. And the name of one *was* Bozez, and the name of the other Seneh. ⁵The front of one faced northward opposite Michmash, and the other southward opposite Gibeah.

⁶Then Jonathan said to the young man who bore his armor, "Come, let us go over to the garrison of these uncircumcised; it may be that the LORD will work for us. For nothing restrains the LORD from saving by many or by few."

⁷So his armorbearer said to him, "Do all that is in your heart. Go then; here I am with you, according to your heart."

⁸Then Jonathan said, "Very well, let us cross over to *these* men, and we will show ourselves to them. ⁹If they say thus to us, 'Wait until we come to you,' then we will stand still in our place and not go up to them. ¹⁰But if they say thus, 'Come up to us,' then we will go up. For the LORD has delivered them into our hand, and this *will be* a sign to us."

¹¹So both of them showed themselves to the garrison of the Philistines. And the Philistines said, "Look, the Hebrews are coming out of the holes where they have hidden." ¹²Then the men of the garrison called to Jonathan and his armorbearer, and said, "Come up to us, and we will show you something."

Jonathan said to his armorbearer, "Come up after me, for the LORD has delivered them into the hand of Israel." ¹³And Jonathan climbed up on his hands and knees with his armorbearer after him; and they fell before Jonathan. And as he came after him, his armorbearer killed them. ¹⁴That first slaughter which Jonathan and his armorbearer made was about twenty men within about half an acre of land.*

¹⁵And there was trembling in the camp, in the field, and among all the people. The garrison and the raiders also trembled; and the earth quaked, so that it was a very great trembling. ¹⁶Now the watchmen of Saul in Gibeah of Benjamin looked, and *there* was the multitude, melting away; and they went here and there. ¹⁷Then Saul said to the people who *were* with him, "Now call the roll and see who has gone from us." And when they had called the roll, surprisingly, Jonathan and his armorbearer *were* not *there*. ¹⁸And Saul said to Ahijah, "Bring the ark* of God here" (for at that time the ark* of God was with the children of Israel). ¹⁹Now it happened, while Saul talked to the priest, that the noise which *was* in the camp of the Philistines continued to increase; so Saul said to the priest, "Withdraw your hand." ²⁰Then Saul and all the people who *were* with him assembled, and they went to the battle; and indeed every man's sword was

against his neighbor, *and there was* very great confusion. ²¹Moreover the Hebrews *who* were with the Philistines before that time, who went up with them into the camp *from the* surrounding *country,* they also joined the Israelites who *were* with Saul and Jonathan. ²²Likewise all the men of Israel who had hidden in the mountains of Ephraim, *when* they heard that the Philistines fled, they also followed hard after them in the battle. ²³So the LORD saved Israel that day, and the battle shifted to Beth Aven.

²⁴And the men of Israel were distressed that day, for Saul had placed the people under oath, saying, "Cursed *is* the man who eats *any* food until evening, before I have taken vengeance on my enemies." So none of the people tasted food. ²⁵Now all *the people* of the land came to a forest; and there was honey on the ground. ²⁶And when the people had come into the woods, there was the honey, dripping; but no one put his hand to his mouth, for the people feared the oath. ²⁷But Jonathan had not heard his father charge the people with the oath; therefore he stretched out the end of the rod that *was* in his hand and dipped it in a honeycomb, and put his hand to his mouth; and his countenance brightened. ²⁸Then one of the people said, "Your father strictly charged the people with an oath, saying, 'Cursed *is* the man who eats food this day.' " And the people were faint.

²⁹But Jonathan said, "My father has troubled the land. Look now, how my countenance has brightened because I tasted a little of this honey. ³⁰How much better if the people had eaten freely today of the spoil of their enemies which they found! For now would there not have been a much greater slaughter among the Philistines?"

³¹Now they had driven back the Philistines that day from Michmash to Aijalon. So the people were very faint.

³²And the people rushed on the spoil, and took sheep, oxen, and calves, and slaughtered *them* on the ground; and the people ate *them* with the blood. ³³Then they told Saul, saying, "Look, the people are sinning against the LORD by eating with the blood!"

So he said, "You have dealt treacherously; roll a large stone to me this day." ³⁴Then Saul said, "Disperse yourselves among the people, and say to them, 'Bring me here every man's ox and every man's sheep, slaughter *them* here, and eat; and do not sin against the LORD by eating with the blood.' " So every one of the people brought his ox with him that night, and slaughtered *it* there. ³⁵Then Saul built an altar to the LORD. This was the first altar that he built to the LORD.

³⁶Now Saul said, "Let us go down after the Philistines by night, and plunder them until the morning light; and let us not leave a man of them."

And they said, "Do whatever seems good to you."

Then the priest said, "Let us draw near to God here."

³⁷So Saul asked counsel of God, "Shall I go down after the Philistines? Will You deliver them into the hand of Israel?" But He did not answer him that day. ³⁸And Saul said, "Come over here, all you chiefs of the people, and know and see what this sin was today. ³⁹For *as* the LORD lives, who saves Israel, though it be in Jonathan my son, he shall surely die." But not a man among all the people answered him. ⁴⁰Then he said to all Israel, "You be on one side, and my son Jonathan and I will be on the other side."

And the people said to Saul, "Do what seems good to you."

⁴¹Therefore Saul said to the LORD God of Israel, "Give a perfect *lot.*"* So Saul and Jonathan were taken, but the people escaped. ⁴²And Saul said, "Cast *lots* between my son Jonathan and me." So Jonathan was taken. ⁴³Then

Saul said to Jonathan, "Tell me what you have done."

And Jonathan told him, and said, "I only tasted a little honey with the end of the rod that *was* in my hand. So now I must die!"

44Saul answered, "God do so and more also; for you shall surely die, Jonathan."

45But the people said to Saul, "Shall Jonathan die, who has accomplished this great deliverance in Israel? Certainly not! *As* the LORD lives, not one hair of his head shall fall to the ground, for he has worked with God this day." So the people rescued Jonathan, and he did not die.

46Then Saul returned from pursuing the Philistines, and the Philistines went to their own place.

47So Saul established his sovereignty over Israel, and fought against all his enemies on every side, against Moab, against the people of Ammon, against Edom, against the kings of Zobah, and against the Philistines. Wherever he turned, he harassed *them.** 48And he gathered an army and attacked the Amalekites, and delivered Israel from the hands of those who plundered them.

49The sons of Saul were Jonathan, Jishui,* and Malchishua. And the names of his two daughters *were these:* the name of the firstborn Merab, and the name of the younger Michal. 50The name of Saul's wife *was* Ahinoam the daughter of Ahimaaz. And the name of the commander of his army *was* Abner the son of Ner, Saul's uncle. 51Kish *was* the father of Saul, and Ner the father of Abner *was* the son of Abiel.

52Now there was fierce war with the Philistines all the days of Saul. And when Saul saw any strong man or any valiant man, he took him for himself.

JOHN 7:30-53

THEREFORE they sought to take Him [Jesus]; but no one laid a hand on Him, because His hour had not yet come. 31And many of the people believed in Him, and said, "When the Christ comes, will He do more signs than these which this *Man* has done?"

32The Pharisees heard the crowd murmuring these things concerning Him, and the Pharisees and the chief priests sent officers to take Him. 33Then Jesus said to them,* "I shall be with you a little while longer, and *then* I go to Him who sent Me. 34You will seek Me and not find *Me,* and where I am you cannot come."

35Then the Jews said among themselves, "Where does He intend to go that we shall not find Him? Does He intend to go to the Dispersion among the Greeks and teach the Greeks? 36What is this thing that He said, 'You will seek Me and not find Me, and where I am you cannot come'?"

37On the last day, that great *day* of the feast, Jesus stood and cried out, saying, "If anyone thirsts, let him come to Me and drink. 38He who believes in Me, as the Scripture has said, out of his heart will flow rivers of living water." 39But this He spoke concerning the Spirit, whom those believing* in Him would receive; for the Holy* Spirit was not yet *given,* because Jesus was not yet glorified.

40Therefore many* from the crowd, when they heard this saying, said, "Truly this is the Prophet." 41Others said, "This is the Christ."

But some said, "Will the Christ come out of Galilee? 42Has not the Scripture said that the Christ comes from the seed of David and from the town of Bethlehem, where David was?" 43So there was a division among the people because of Him. 44Now some of them wanted to take Him, but no one laid hands on Him.

⁴⁵Then the officers came to the chief priests and Pharisees, who said to them, "Why have you not brought Him?"

⁴⁶The officers answered, "No man ever spoke like this Man!"

⁴⁷Then the Pharisees answered them, "Are you also deceived? ⁴⁸Have any of the rulers or the Pharisees believed in Him? ⁴⁹But this crowd that does not know the law is accursed."

⁵⁰Nicodemus (he who came to Jesus by night,* being one of them) said to them, ⁵¹"Does our law judge a man before it hears him and knows what he is doing?"

⁵²They answered and said to him, "Are you also from Galilee? Search and look, for no prophet has arisen* out of Galilee."

⁵³And everyone went to his *own* house.*

PSALM 109:1-31

To the Chief Musician. A Psalm of David.

Do not keep silent,
O God of my praise!
²For the mouth of the wicked
and the mouth of the
deceitful
Have opened against me;
They have spoken against me
with a lying tongue.
³ They have also surrounded
me with words of hatred,
And fought against me
without a cause.
⁴ In return for my love they are
my accusers,
But I *give myself to* prayer.
⁵ Thus they have rewarded me
evil for good,
And hatred for my love.

⁶ Set a wicked man over him,
And let an accuser* stand at
his right hand.

⁷ When he is judged, let him be
found guilty,
And let his prayer become sin.
⁸ Let his days be few,
And let another take his office.
⁹ Let his children be fatherless,
And his wife a widow.
¹⁰ Let his children continually be
vagabonds, and beg;
Let them seek *their bread*
also from their desolate
places.
¹¹ Let the creditor seize all that
he has,
And let strangers plunder his
labor.
¹² Let there be none to extend
mercy to him,
Nor let there be any to favor
his fatherless children.
¹³ Let his posterity be cut off,
And in the generation
following let their name be
blotted out.

¹⁴ Let the iniquity of his fathers
be remembered before the
LORD,
And let not the sin of his
mother be blotted out.
¹⁵ Let them be continually
before the LORD,
That He may cut off the
memory of them from the
earth;
¹⁶ Because he did not remember
to show mercy,
But persecuted the poor and
needy man,
That he might even slay the
broken in heart.
¹⁷ As he loved cursing, so let it
come to him;
As he did not delight in
blessing, so let it be far
from him.
¹⁸ As he clothed himself with
cursing as with his garment,
So let it enter his body like
water,

And like oil into his bones.

19 Let it be to him like the
garment which covers him,
And for a belt with which he
girds himself continually.

20 *Let* this *be* the LORD's reward
to my accusers,
And to those who speak evil
against my person.

21 But You, O GOD the Lord,
Deal with me for Your name's
sake;
Because Your mercy *is* good,
deliver me.

22 For I *am* poor and needy,
And my heart is wounded
within me.

23 I am gone like a shadow when
it lengthens;
I am shaken off like a locust.

24 My knees are weak through
fasting,
And my flesh is feeble from
lack of fatness.

25 I also have become a
reproach to them;

When they look at me, they
shake their heads.

26 Help me, O LORD my God!
Oh, save me according to
Your mercy,

27 That they may know that this
is Your hand—
That You, LORD, have done it!

28 Let them curse, but You bless;
When they arise, let them be
ashamed,
But let Your servant rejoice.

29 Let my accusers be clothed
with shame,
And let them cover
themselves with their own
disgrace as with a mantle.

30 I will greatly praise the LORD
with my mouth;
Yes, I will praise Him among
the multitude.

31 For He shall stand at the right
hand of the poor,
To save *him* from those who
condemn him.

PROVERBS FOR TODAY/ 15:5-7

A fool despises his father's instruction, but he who receives correction is prudent.
□ In *the house of the righteous* there is *much treasure, but in the revenue of the
wicked is trouble.* □ *The lips of the wise disperse knowledge, but the heart of the
fool* does *not* do *so.*

MAY 14

1 SAMUEL 15:1–16:23

SAMUEL also said to Saul, "The LORD
sent me to anoint you king over
His people, over Israel. Now
therefore, heed the voice of the words
of the LORD. ²Thus says the LORD of
hosts: 'I will punish Amalek *for* what he
did to Israel, how he ambushed him on

the way when he came up from Egypt.
³Now go and attack Amalek, and utterly
destroy all that they have, and do not
spare them. But kill both man and
woman, infant and nursing child, ox and
sheep, camel and donkey.' "

⁴So Saul gathered the people together and numbered them in Telaim,
two hundred thousand foot soldiers

and ten thousand men of Judah. ⁵And Saul came to a city of Amalek, and lay in wait in the valley.

⁶Then Saul said to the Kenites, "Go, depart, get down from among the Amalekites, lest I destroy you with them. For you showed kindness to all the children of Israel when they came up out of Egypt." So the Kenites departed from among the Amalekites. ⁷And Saul attacked the Amalekites, from Havilah all the way to Shur, which is east of Egypt. ⁸He also took Agag king of the Amalekites alive, and utterly destroyed all the people with the edge of the sword. ⁹But Saul and the people spared Agag and the best of the sheep, the oxen, the fatlings, the lambs, and all *that was* good, and were unwilling to utterly destroy them. But everything despised and worthless, that they utterly destroyed.

¹⁰Now the word of the Lᴏʀᴅ came to Samuel, saying, ¹¹"I greatly regret that I have set up Saul *as* king, for he has turned back from following Me, and has not performed My commandments." And it grieved Samuel, and he cried out to the Lᴏʀᴅ all night. ¹²So when Samuel rose early in the morning to meet Saul, it was told Samuel, saying, "Saul went to Carmel, and indeed, he set up a monument for himself; and he has gone on around, passed by, and gone down to Gilgal." ¹³Then Samuel went to Saul, and Saul said to him, "Blessed *are* you of the Lᴏʀᴅ! I have performed the commandment of the Lᴏʀᴅ."

¹⁴But Samuel said, "What then *is* this bleating of the sheep in my ears, and the lowing of the oxen which I hear?"

¹⁵And Saul said, "They have brought them from the Amalekites; for the people spared the best of the sheep and the oxen, to sacrifice to the Lᴏʀᴅ your God; and the rest we have utterly destroyed."

¹⁶Then Samuel said to Saul, "Be quiet! And I will tell you what the Lᴏʀᴅ said to me last night."

And he said to him, "Speak on."

¹⁷So Samuel said, "When you *were* little in your own eyes, *were* you not head of the tribes of Israel? And did not the Lᴏʀᴅ anoint you king over Israel? ¹⁸Now the Lᴏʀᴅ sent you on a mission, and said, 'Go, and utterly destroy the sinners, the Amalekites, and fight against them until they are consumed.' ¹⁹Why then did you not obey the voice of the Lᴏʀᴅ? Why did you swoop down on the spoil, and do evil in the sight of the Lᴏʀᴅ?"

²⁰And Saul said to Samuel, "But I have obeyed the voice of the Lᴏʀᴅ, and gone on the mission on which the Lᴏʀᴅ sent me, and brought back Agag king of Amalek; I have utterly destroyed the Amalekites. ²¹But the people took of the plunder, sheep and oxen, the best of the things which should have been utterly destroyed, to sacrifice to the Lᴏʀᴅ your God in Gilgal."

²²So Samuel said:

> "Has the Lᴏʀᴅ *as great* delight
>   in burnt offerings and
>   sacrifices,
> As in obeying the voice of the
>   Lᴏʀᴅ?
> Behold, to obey is better than
>   sacrifice,
> *And* to heed than the fat of
>   rams.
> 23   For rebellion *is as* the sin of
>   witchcraft,
> And stubbornness *is as*
>   iniquity and idolatry.
> Because you have rejected
>   the word of the Lᴏʀᴅ,
> He also has rejected you from
>   *being* king."

²⁴Then Saul said to Samuel, "I have sinned, for I have transgressed the commandment of the Lᴏʀᴅ and your words, because I feared the people and obeyed their voice. ²⁵Now therefore,

please pardon my sin, and return with me, that I may worship the Lord."

26But Samuel said to Saul, "I will not return with you, for you have rejected the word of the Lord, and the Lord has rejected you from being king over Israel."

27And as Samuel turned around to go away, *Saul* seized the edge of his robe, and it tore. 28So Samuel said to him, "The Lord has torn the kingdom of Israel from you today, and has given it to a neighbor of yours, *who is* better than you. 29And also the Strength of Israel will not lie nor relent. For He *is* not a man, that He should relent."

30Then he said, "I have sinned; *yet* honor me now, please, before the elders of my people and before Israel, and return with me, that I may worship the Lord your God." 31So Samuel turned back after Saul, and Saul worshiped the Lord.

32Then Samuel said, "Bring Agag king of the Amalekites here to me." So Agag came to him cautiously.

And Agag said, "Surely the bitterness of death is past."

33But Samuel said, "As your sword has made women childless, so shall your mother be childless among women." And Samuel hacked Agag in pieces before the Lord in Gilgal.

34Then Samuel went to Ramah, and Saul went up to his house at Gibeah of Saul. 35And Samuel went no more to see Saul until the day of his death. Nevertheless Samuel mourned for Saul, and the Lord regretted that He had made Saul king over Israel.

Now the Lord said to Samuel, "How long will you mourn for Saul, seeing I have rejected him from reigning over Israel? Fill your horn with oil, and go; I am sending you to Jesse the Bethlehemite. For I have provided Myself a king among his sons."

2And Samuel said, "How can I go? If Saul hears *it,* he will kill me."

But the Lord said, "Take a heifer with you, and say, 'I have come to sacrifice to the Lord.' 3Then invite Jesse to the sacrifice, and I will show you what you shall do; you shall anoint for Me the one I name to you."

4So Samuel did what the Lord said, and went to Bethlehem. And the elders of the town trembled at his coming, and said, "Do you come peaceably?"

5And he said, "Peaceably; I have come to sacrifice to the Lord. Sanctify yourselves, and come with me to the sacrifice." Then he consecrated Jesse and his sons, and invited them to the sacrifice.

6So it was, when they came, that he looked at Eliab and said, "Surely the Lord's anointed *is* before Him!"

7But the Lord said to Samuel, "Do not look at his appearance or at his physical stature, because I have refused him. For *the Lord does* not *see* as man sees;* for man looks at the outward appearance, but the Lord looks at the heart."

8So Jesse called Abinadab, and made him pass before Samuel. And he said, "Neither has the Lord chosen this one." 9Then Jesse made Shammah pass by. And he said, "Neither has the Lord chosen this one." 10Thus Jesse made seven of his sons pass before Samuel. And Samuel said to Jesse, "The Lord has not chosen these." 11And Samuel said to Jesse, "Are all the young men here?" Then he said, "There remains yet the youngest, and there he is, keeping the sheep."

And Samuel said to Jesse, "Send and bring him. For we will not sit down* till he comes here." 12So he sent and brought him in. Now he *was* ruddy, with bright eyes, and good-looking. And the Lord said, "Arise, anoint him; for this *is* the one!" 13Then Samuel took the horn of oil and anointed him in the midst of his brothers; and the Spirit of the Lord came upon David from that day forward. So Samuel arose and went to Ramah.

14But the Spirit of the LORD departed from Saul, and a distressing spirit from the LORD troubled him. 15And Saul's servants said to him, "Surely, a distressing spirit from God is troubling you. 16Let our master now command your servants, *who are* before you, to seek out a man *who is* a skillful player on the harp. And it shall be that he will play it with his hand when the distressing spirit from God is upon you, and you shall be well."

17So Saul said to his servants, "Provide me now a man who can play well, and bring *him* to me."

18Then one of the servants answered and said, "Look, I have seen a son of Jesse the Bethlehemite, *who is* skillful in playing, a mighty man of valor, a man of war, prudent in speech, and a handsome person; and the LORD *is* with him."

19Therefore Saul sent messengers to Jesse, and said, "Send me your son David, who *is* with the sheep." 20And Jesse took a donkey *loaded with* bread, a skin of wine, and a young goat, and sent *them* by his son David to Saul. 21So David came to Saul and stood before him. And he loved him greatly, and he became his armorbearer. 22Then Saul sent to Jesse, saying, "Please let David stand before me, for he has found favor in my sight." 23And so it was, whenever the spirit from God was upon Saul, that David would take a harp and play *it* with his hand. Then Saul would become refreshed and well, and the distressing spirit would depart from him.

JOHN 8:1-20

BUT Jesus went to the Mount of Olives.
2Now early* in the morning He came again into the temple, and all the people came to Him; and He sat down and taught them. 3Then the scribes and Pharisees brought to Him a woman caught in adultery. And when they had set her in the midst, 4they said to Him, "Teacher, this woman was caught* in adultery, in the very act. 5Now Moses, in the law, commanded* us that such should be stoned.* But what do You say?"* 6This they said, testing Him, that they might have *something* of which to accuse Him. But Jesus stooped down and wrote on the ground with *His* finger, as though He did not hear.*

7So when they continued asking Him, He raised Himself up* and said to them, "He who is without sin among you, let him throw a stone at her first." 8And again He stooped down and wrote on the ground. 9Then those who heard *it,* being convicted by *their* conscience,* went out one by one, beginning with the oldest *even* to the last. And Jesus was left alone, and the woman standing in the midst. 10When Jesus had raised Himself up and saw no one but the woman, He said to her,* "Woman, where are those accusers of yours?* Has no one condemned you?"

11She said, "No one, Lord."

And Jesus said to her, "Neither do I condemn you; go and* sin no more."

12Then Jesus spoke to them again, saying, "I am the light of the world. He who follows Me shall not walk in darkness, but have the light of life."

13The Pharisees therefore said to Him, "You bear witness of Yourself; Your witness is not true."

14Jesus answered and said to them, "Even if I bear witness of Myself, My witness is true, for I know where I came from and where I am going; but you do not know where I come from and where I am going. 15You judge according to the flesh; I judge no one. 16And yet if I do judge, My judgment is true; for I am not alone, but I *am* with the Father who sent Me. 17It is also written in your law that the testimony of two men is true. 18I am One who bears witness of Myself, and the Father who sent Me bears witness of Me." ¹⁹Then they said to Him, "Where is Your Father?"

Jesus answered, "You know neither Me nor My Father. If you had known Me, you would have known My Father also."

²⁰These words Jesus spoke in the treasury, as He taught in the temple; and no one laid hands on Him, for His hour had not yet come.

PSALM 110:1-7

A Psalm of David.

THE LORD said to my Lord,
"Sit at My right hand,
Till I make Your enemies Your
footstool."
2   The LORD shall send the rod of
Your strength out of Zion.
Rule in the midst of Your
enemies!

3   Your people *shall be* volunteers
In the day of Your power;
In the beauties of holiness,
from the womb of the
morning,
You have the dew of Your
youth.
4   The LORD has sworn
And will not relent,
"You *are* a priest forever
According to the order of
Melchizedek."

5   The Lord *is* at Your right hand;
He shall execute kings in the
day of His wrath.
6   He shall judge among the
nations,
He shall fill *the places* with
dead bodies,
He shall execute the heads of
many countries.
7   He shall drink of the brook by
the wayside;
Therefore He shall lift up the
head.

PROVERBS FOR TODAY/ 15:8-10

The sacrifice of the wicked is *an abomination to the LORD, but the prayer of the upright* is *His delight. The way of the wicked* is *an abomination to the LORD, but He loves him who follows righteousness. Harsh discipline* is *for him who forsakes the way,* and *he who hates correction will die.*

MAY 15

1 SAMUEL 17:1–18:4

Now the Philistines gathered their armies together to battle, and were gathered at Sochoh, which *belongs* to Judah; they encamped between Sochoh and Azekah, in Ephes Dammim. ²And Saul and the men of Israel were gathered together, and they encamped in the Valley of Elah, and drew up in battle array against the Philistines. ³The Philistines stood on a mountain on one side, and Israel stood on a mountain on the other side, with a valley between them.

⁴And a champion went out from the camp of the Philistines, named Goliath, from Gath, whose height *was* six cubits and a span. ⁵*He had* a bronze helmet on his head, and he *was* armed with a coat

of mail, and the weight of the coat *was* five thousand shekels of bronze. ⁶And *he had* bronze armor on his legs and a bronze javelin between his shoulders. ⁷Now the staff of his spear *was* like a weaver's beam, and his iron spearhead *weighed* six hundred shekels; and a shield-bearer went before him. ⁸Then he stood and cried out to the armies of Israel, and said to them, "Why have you come out to line up for battle? *Am* I not a Philistine, and you the servants of Saul? Choose a man for yourselves, and let him come down to me. ⁹If he is able to fight with me and kill me, then we will be your servants. But if I prevail against him and kill him, then you shall be our servants and serve us." ¹⁰And the Philistine said, "I defy the armies of Israel this day; give me a man, that we may fight together." ¹¹When Saul and all Israel heard these words of the Philistine, they were dismayed and greatly afraid.

¹²Now David *was* the son of that Ephrathite of Bethlehem Judah, whose name *was* Jesse, and who had eight sons. And the man was old, advanced *in years,* in the days of Saul. ¹³The three oldest sons of Jesse had gone to follow Saul to the battle. The names of his three sons who went to the battle *were* Eliab the firstborn, next to him Abinadab, and the third Shammah. ¹⁴David *was* the youngest. And the three oldest followed Saul. ¹⁵But David occasionally went and returned from Saul to feed his father's sheep at Bethlehem.

¹⁶And the Philistine drew near and presented himself forty days, morning and evening.

¹⁷Then Jesse said to his son David, "Take now for your brothers an ephah of this dried *grain* and these ten loaves, and run to your brothers at the camp. ¹⁸And carry these ten cheeses to the captain of *their* thousand, and see how your brothers fare, and bring back news of them." ¹⁹Now Saul and

they and all the men of Israel *were* in the Valley of Elah, fighting with the Philistines.

²⁰So David rose early in the morning, left the sheep with a keeper, and took *the things* and went as Jesse had commanded him. And he came to the camp as the army was going out to the fight and shouting for the battle. ²¹For Israel and the Philistines had drawn up in battle array, army against army. ²²And David left his supplies in the hand of the supply keeper, ran to the army, and came and greeted his brothers. ²³Then as he talked with them, there was the champion, the Philistine of Gath, Goliath by name, coming up from the armies of the Philistines; and he spoke according to the same words. So David heard *them.* ²⁴And all the men of Israel, when they saw the man, fled from him and were dreadfully afraid. ²⁵So the men of Israel said, "Have you seen this man who has come up? Surely he has come up to defy Israel; and it shall be *that* the man who kills him the king will enrich with great riches, will give him his daughter, and give his father's house exemption *from taxes* in Israel."

²⁶Then David spoke to the men who stood by him, saying, "What shall be done for the man who kills this Philistine and takes away the reproach from Israel? For who *is* this uncircumcised Philistine, that he should defy the armies of the living God?"

²⁷And the people answered him in this manner, saying, "So shall it be done for the man who kills him."

²⁸Now Eliab his oldest brother heard when he spoke to the men; and Eliab's anger was aroused against David, and he said, "Why did you come down here? And with whom have you left those few sheep in the wilderness? I know your pride and the insolence of your heart, for you have come down to see the battle."

²⁹And David said, "What have I done

now? *Is there* not a cause?" ³⁰Then he turned from him toward another and said the same thing; and these people answered him as the first ones *did*.

³¹Now when the words which David spoke were heard, they reported *them* to Saul; and he sent for him. ³²Then David said to Saul, "Let no man's heart fail because of him; your servant will go and fight with this Philistine."

³³And Saul said to David, "You are not able to go against this Philistine to fight with him; for you *are* a youth, and he a man of war from his youth."

³⁴But David said to Saul, "Your servant used to keep his father's sheep, and when a lion or a bear came and took a lamb out of the flock, ³⁵I went out after it and struck it, and delivered *the lamb* from its mouth; and when it arose against me, I caught *it* by its beard, and struck and killed it. ³⁶Your servant has killed both lion and bear; and this uncircumcised Philistine will be like one of them, seeing he has defied the armies of the living God." ³⁷Moreover David said, "The LORD, who delivered me from the paw of the lion and from the paw of the bear, He will deliver me from the hand of this Philistine."

And Saul said to David, "Go, and the LORD be with you!"

³⁸So Saul clothed David with his armor, and he put a bronze helmet on his head; he also clothed him with a coat of mail. ³⁹David fastened his sword to his armor and tried to walk, for he had not tested *them*. And David said to Saul, "I cannot walk with these, for I have not tested *them*." So David took them off.

⁴⁰Then he took his staff in his hand; and he chose for himself five smooth stones from the brook, and put them in a shepherd's bag, in a pouch which he had, and his sling was in his hand. And he drew near to the Philistine. ⁴¹So the Philistine came, and began drawing near to David, and the man who bore

the shield *went* before him. ⁴²And when the Philistine looked about and saw David, he disdained him; for he was *only* a youth, ruddy and good-looking. ⁴³So the Philistine said to David, "*Am* I a dog, that you come to me with sticks?" And the Philistine cursed David by his gods. ⁴⁴And the Philistine said to David, "Come to me, and I will give your flesh to the birds of the air and the beasts of the field!"

⁴⁵Then David said to the Philistine, "You come to me with a sword, with a spear, and with a javelin. But I come to you in the name of the LORD of hosts, the God of the armies of Israel, whom you have defied. ⁴⁶This day the LORD will deliver you into my hand, and I will strike you and take your head from you. And this day I will give the carcasses of the camp of the Philistines to the birds of the air and the wild beasts of the earth, that all the earth may know that there is a God in Israel. ⁴⁷Then all this assembly shall know that the LORD does not save with sword and spear; for the battle *is* the LORD's, and He will give you into our hands."

⁴⁸So it was, when the Philistine arose and came and drew near to meet David, that David hurried and ran toward the army to meet the Philistine. ⁴⁹Then David put his hand in his bag and took out a stone; and he slung *it* and struck the Philistine in his forehead, so that the stone sank into his forehead, and he fell on his face to the earth. ⁵⁰So David prevailed over the Philistine with a sling and a stone, and struck the Philistine and killed him. But *there was* no sword in the hand of David. ⁵¹Therefore David ran and stood over the Philistine, took his sword and drew it out of its sheath and killed him, and cut off his head with it.

And when the Philistines saw that their champion was dead, they fled. ⁵²Now the men of Israel and Judah arose and shouted, and pursued the Philistines as far as the entrance of the valley* and to the gates of Ekron. And the wounded of the Philistines fell along the road to Shaaraim, even as far as Gath and Ekron. ⁵³Then the children of Israel returned from chasing the Philistines, and they plundered their tents. ⁵⁴And David took the head of the Philistine and brought it to Jerusalem, but he put his armor in his tent.

⁵⁵When Saul saw David going out against the Philistine, he said to Abner, the commander of the army, "Abner, whose son *is* this youth?"

And Abner said, "As your soul lives, O king, I do not know."

⁵⁶So the king said, "Inquire whose son this young man *is.*"

⁵⁷Then, as David returned from the slaughter of the Philistine, Abner took him and brought him before Saul with the head of the Philistine in his hand. ⁵⁸And Saul said to him, "Whose son *are* you, young man?"

So David answered, "*I am* the son of your servant Jesse the Bethlehemite."

Now when he had finished speaking to Saul, the soul of Jonathan was knit to the soul of David, and Jonathan loved him as his own soul. ²Saul took him that day, and would not let him go home to his father's house anymore. ³Then Jonathan and David made a covenant, because he loved him as his own soul. ⁴And Jonathan took off the robe that *was* on him and gave it to David, with his armor, even to his sword and his bow and his belt.

JOHN 8:21-30

THEN Jesus said to them again, "I am going away, and you will seek Me, and will die in your sin. Where I go you cannot come."

²²So the Jews said, "Will He kill Himself, because He says, 'Where I go you cannot come'?"

²³And He said to them, "You are from beneath; I am from above. You are of this world; I am not of this world. ²⁴Therefore I said to you that you will die in your sins; for if you do not believe that I am *He,* you will die in your sins."

²⁵Then they said to Him, "Who are You?"

And Jesus said to them, "Just what I have been saying to you from the beginning. ²⁶I have many things to say and to judge concerning you, but He who sent Me is true; and I speak to the world those things which I heard from Him."

²⁷They did not understand that He spoke to them of the Father.

²⁸Then Jesus said to them, "When you lift up the Son of Man, then you will know that I am *He,* and *that* I do nothing of Myself; but as My Father taught Me, I speak these things. ²⁹And He who sent Me is with Me. The Father has not left Me alone, for I always do those things that please Him." ³⁰As He spoke these words, many believed in Him.

PSALM 111:1-10

PRAISE the LORD!
I will praise the LORD with *my* whole heart,
In the assembly of the upright and *in* the congregation.

2 The works of the LORD *are* great,
Studied by all who have pleasure in them.

3 His work *is* honorable and glorious,
And His righteousness endures forever.

4 He has made His wonderful works to be remembered;
The LORD *is* gracious and full of compassion.

5 He has given food to those who fear Him;

He will ever be mindful of His
covenant.
6   He has declared to His people
the power of His works,
In giving them the heritage of
the nations.

7   The works of His hands *are*
verity and justice;
All His precepts *are* sure.
8   They stand fast forever and
ever,
And are done in truth and
uprightness.

9   He has sent redemption to
His people;
He has commanded His
covenant forever:
Holy and awesome *is* His
name.

10   The fear of the LORD *is* the
beginning of wisdom;
A good understanding have
all those who do *His
commandments.*
His praise endures forever.

PROVERBS FOR TODAY/ 15:11

Hell * *and Destruction* * are *before the* LORD; *so how much more the hearts of the
sons of men.*

MAY 16

1 SAMUEL 18:5–19:24

So David went out wherever Saul
sent him, *and* behaved wisely.
And Saul set him over the men
of war, and he was accepted in the
sight of all the people and also in the
sight of Saul's servants. 6Now it had
happened as they were coming *home,*
when David was returning from the
slaughter of the Philistine, that the
women had come out of all the cities of
Israel, singing and dancing, to meet
King Saul, with tambourines, with joy,
and with musical instruments. 7So the
women sang as they danced, and said:

"Saul has slain his thousands,
And David his ten thousands."

8Then Saul was very angry, and the
saying displeased him; and he said,
"They have ascribed to David ten thousands, and to me they have ascribed

only thousands. Now *what* more can
he have but the kingdom?" 9So Saul
eyed David from that day forward.

10And it happened on the next day
that the distressing spirit from God
came upon Saul, and he prophesied inside the house. So David played *music*
with his hand, as at other times; but
there was a spear in Saul's hand. 11And
Saul cast the spear, for he said, "I will
pin David to the wall!" But David escaped his presence twice.

12Now Saul was afraid of David, because the LORD was with him, but had
departed from Saul. 13Therefore Saul
removed him from his presence, and
made him his captain over a thousand;
and he went out and came in before
the people. 14And David behaved
wisely in all his ways, and the LORD *was*
with him. 15Therefore, when Saul saw
that he behaved very wisely, he was
afraid of him. 16But all Israel and Judah

loved David, because he went out and came in before them.

17Then Saul said to David, "Here is my older daughter Merab; I will give her to you as a wife. Only be valiant for me, and fight the LORD's battles." For Saul thought, "Let my hand not be against him, but let the hand of the Philistines be against him."

18So David said to Saul, "Who *am* I, and what *is* my life *or* my father's family in Israel, that I should be son-in-law to the king?" 19But it happened at the time when Merab, Saul's daughter, should have been given to David, that she was given to Adriel the Meholathite as a wife.

20Now Michal, Saul's daughter, loved David. And they told Saul, and the thing pleased him. 21So Saul said, "I will give her to him, that she may be a snare to him, and that the hand of the Philistines may be against him." Therefore Saul said to David a second time, "You shall be my son-in-law today."

22And Saul commanded his servants, "Communicate with David secretly, and say, 'Look, the king has delight in you, and all his servants love you. Now therefore, become the king's son-in-law.' "

23So Saul's servants spoke those words in the hearing of David. And David said, "Does it seem to you *a* light *thing* to be a king's son-in-law, seeing I *am* a poor and lightly esteemed man?" 24And the servants of Saul told him, saying, "In this manner David spoke."

25Then Saul said, "Thus you shall say to David: 'The king does not desire any dowry but one hundred foreskins of the Philistines, to take vengeance on the king's enemies.' " But Saul thought to make David fall by the hand of the Philistines. 26So when his servants told David these words, it pleased David well to become the king's son-in-law. Now the days had not expired; 27therefore David arose and went, he and his

men, and killed two hundred men of the Philistines. And David brought their foreskins, and they gave them in full count to the king, that he might become the king's son-in-law. Then Saul gave him Michal his daughter as a wife.

28Thus Saul saw and knew that the LORD *was* with David, and *that* Michal, Saul's daughter, loved him; 29and Saul was still more afraid of David. So Saul became David's enemy continually. 30Then the princes of the Philistines went out *to war.* And so it was, whenever they went out, *that* David behaved more wisely than all the servants of Saul, so that his name became highly esteemed.

Now Saul spoke to Jonathan his son and to all his servants, that they should kill David; but Jonathan, Saul's son, delighted greatly in David. 2So Jonathan told David, saying, "My father Saul seeks to kill you. Therefore please be on your guard until morning, and stay in a secret *place* and hide. 3And I will go out and stand beside my father in the field where you *are,* and I will speak with my father about you. Then what I observe, I will tell you."

4Thus Jonathan spoke well of David to Saul his father, and said to him, "Let not the king sin against his servant, against David, because he has not sinned against you, and because his works *have been* very good toward you. 5For he took his life in his hands and killed the Philistine, and the LORD brought about a great deliverance for all Israel. You saw *it* and rejoiced. Why then will you sin against innocent blood, to kill David without a cause?"

6So Saul heeded the voice of Jonathan, and Saul swore, "*As* the LORD lives, he shall not be killed." 7Then Jonathan called David, and Jonathan told him all these things. So Jonathan brought David to Saul, and he was in his presence as in times past.

8And there was war again; and David

went out and fought with the Philistines, and struck them with a mighty blow, and they fled from him.

⁹Now the distressing spirit from the LORD came upon Saul as he sat in his house with his spear in his hand. And David was playing *music* with *his* hand. ¹⁰Then Saul sought to pin David to the wall with the spear, but he slipped away from Saul's presence; and he drove the spear into the wall. So David fled and escaped that night.

¹¹Saul also sent messengers to David's house to watch him and to kill him in the morning. And Michal, David's wife, told him, saying, "If you do not save your life tonight, tomorrow you will be killed." ¹²So Michal let David down through a window. And he went and fled and escaped. ¹³And Michal took an image and laid *it* in the bed, put a cover of goats' *hair* for his head, and covered *it* with clothes. ¹⁴So when Saul sent messengers to take David, she said, "He *is* sick."

¹⁵Then Saul sent the messengers *back* to see David, saying, "Bring him up to me in the bed, that I may kill him." ¹⁶And when the messengers had come in, there was the image in the bed, with a cover of goats' *hair* for his head. ¹⁷Then Saul said to Michal, "Why have you deceived me like this, and sent my enemy away, so that he has escaped?"

And Michal answered Saul, "He said to me, 'Let me go! Why should I kill you?' "

¹⁸So David fled and escaped, and went to Samuel at Ramah, and told him all that Saul had done to him. And he and Samuel went and stayed in Naioth. ¹⁹Now it was told Saul, saying, "Take note, David *is* at Naioth in Ramah!" ²⁰Then Saul sent messengers to take David. And when they saw the group of prophets prophesying, and Samuel standing *as* leader over them, the Spirit of God came upon the messengers of Saul, and they also prophesied.

²¹And when Saul was told, he sent other messengers, and they prophesied likewise. Then Saul sent messengers again the third time, and they prophesied also. ²²Then he also went to Ramah, and came to the great well that *is* at Sechu. So he asked, and said, "Where *are* Samuel and David?"

And *someone* said, "Indeed *they are* at Naioth in Ramah." ²³So he went there to Naioth in Ramah. Then the Spirit of God was upon him also, and he went on and prophesied until he came to Naioth in Ramah. ²⁴And he also stripped off his clothes and prophesied before Samuel in like manner, and lay down naked all that day and all that night. Therefore they say, "*Is* Saul also among the prophets?"*

JOHN 8:31-59

THEN Jesus said to those Jews who believed Him, "If you abide in My word, you are My disciples indeed. ³²And you shall know the truth, and the truth shall make you free."

³³They answered Him, "We are Abraham's descendants, and have never been in bondage to anyone. How *can* you say, 'You will be made free'?"

³⁴Jesus answered them, "Most assuredly, I say to you, whoever commits sin is a slave of sin. ³⁵And a slave does not abide in the house forever, *but* a son abides forever. ³⁶Therefore if the Son makes you free, you shall be free indeed.

³⁷"I know that you are Abraham's descendants, but you seek to kill Me, because My word has no place in you. ³⁸I speak what I have seen with My Father, and you do what you have seen with* your father."

³⁹They answered and said to Him, "Abraham is our father."

Jesus said to them, "If you were Abraham's children, you would do the works of Abraham. ⁴⁰But now you seek to kill Me, a Man who has told you the truth which I heard from God. Abraham did not do this. ⁴¹You do the deeds of your father."

Then they said to Him, "We were not born of fornication; we have one Father—God."

⁴²Jesus said to them, "If God were your Father, you would love Me, for I proceeded forth and came from God; nor have I come of Myself, but He sent Me. ⁴³Why do you not understand My speech? Because you are not able to listen to My word. ⁴⁴You are of *your* father the devil, and the desires of your father you want to do. He was a murderer from the beginning, and *does not* stand in the truth, because there is no truth in him. When he speaks a lie, he speaks from his own *resources,* for he is a liar and the father of it. ⁴⁵But because I tell the truth, you do not believe Me. ⁴⁶Which of you convicts Me of sin? And if I tell the truth, why do you not believe Me? ⁴⁷He who is of God hears God's words; therefore you do not hear, because you are not of God."

⁴⁸Then the Jews answered and said to Him, "Do we not say rightly that You are a Samaritan and have a demon?"

⁴⁹Jesus answered, "I do not have a demon; but I honor My Father, and you dishonor Me. ⁵⁰And I do not seek My *own* glory; there is One who seeks and judges. ⁵¹Most assuredly, I say to you, if anyone keeps My word he shall never see death."

⁵²Then the Jews said to Him, "Now we know that You have a demon! Abraham is dead, and the prophets; and You say, 'If anyone keeps My word he shall never taste death.' ⁵³Are You greater than our father Abraham, who is dead? And the prophets are dead. Who do You make Yourself out to be?"

⁵⁴Jesus answered, "If I honor Myself, My honor is nothing. It is My Father who honors Me, of whom you say that He is your* God. ⁵⁵Yet you

have not known Him, but I know Him. And if I say, 'I do not know Him,' I shall be a liar like you; but I do know Him and keep His word. ⁵⁶Your father Abraham rejoiced to see My day, and he saw *it* and was glad."

⁵⁷Then the Jews said to Him, "You are not yet fifty years old, and have You seen Abraham?"

⁵⁸Jesus said to them, "Most assuredly, I say to you, before Abraham was, I AM."

⁵⁹Then they took up stones to throw at Him; but Jesus hid Himself and went out of the temple,* going through the midst of them, and so passed by.

PSALM 112:1-10

PRAISE the Lord!

Blessed *is* the man *who* fears
the Lord,
Who delights greatly in His
commandments.

2 His descendants will be
mighty on earth;
The generation of the upright
will be blessed.
3 Wealth and riches *will be* in
his house,
And his righteousness
endures forever.
4 Unto the upright there arises
light in the darkness;
He is gracious, and full of
compassion, and righteous.
5 A good man deals graciously
and lends;
He will guide his affairs with
discretion.
6 Surely he will never be
shaken;
The righteous will be in
everlasting remembrance.
7 He will not be afraid of evil
tidings;
His heart is steadfast, trusting
in the Lord.

8 His heart *is* established;
He will not be afraid,
Until he sees *his desire* upon
his enemies.

9 He has dispersed abroad,
He has given to the poor;
His righteousness endures
forever;

His horn will be exalted with
honor.
10 The wicked will see *it* and be
grieved;
He will gnash his teeth and
melt away;
The desire of the wicked shall
perish.

PROVERBS FOR TODAY/ 15:12-14

A scoffer does not love one who corrects him, nor will he go to the wise. ▢ A merry heart makes a cheerful countenance, but by sorrow of the heart the spirit is broken. ▢ The heart of him who has understanding seeks knowledge, but the mouth of fools feeds on foolishness.

MAY 17

1 SAMUEL 20:1–21:15

THEN David fled from Naioth in Ramah, and went and said to Jonathan, "What have I done? What *is* my iniquity, and what *is* my sin before your father, that he seeks my life?"

²So Jonathan said to him, "By no means! You shall not die! Indeed, my father will do nothing either great or small without first telling me. And why should my father hide this thing from me? It *is* not *so!*"

³Then David took an oath again, and said, "Your father certainly knows that I have found favor in your eyes, and he has said, 'Do not let Jonathan know this, lest he be grieved.' But truly, *as* the LORD lives and *as* your soul lives, *there is* but a step between me and death."

⁴So Jonathan said to David, "Whatever you yourself desire, I will do *it* for you."

⁵And David said to Jonathan, "Indeed tomorrow *is* the New Moon, and I should not fail to sit with the king to eat. But let me go, that I may hide in the field until the third *day* at evening. ⁶If your father misses me at all, then say, 'David earnestly asked *permission* of me that he might run over to Bethlehem, his city, for *there is* a yearly sacrifice there for all the family.' ⁷If he says thus: '*It is* well,' your servant will be safe. But if he is very angry, be sure that evil is determined by him. ⁸Therefore you shall deal kindly with your servant, for you have brought your servant into a covenant of the LORD with you. Nevertheless, if there is iniquity in me, kill me yourself, for why should you bring me to your father?"

⁹But Jonathan said, "Far be it from you! For if I knew certainly that evil was determined by my father to come upon you, then would I not tell you?"

¹⁰Then David said to Jonathan, "Who will tell me, or what *if* your father answers you roughly?"

¹¹And Jonathan said to David, "Come, let us go out into the field." So both of them went out into the field.

¹²Then Jonathan said to David: "The LORD God of Israel *is witness!* When I have sounded out my father sometime tomorrow, *or* the third *day,* and indeed *there is* good toward David, and I do not send to you and tell you, ¹³may the LORD do so and much more to Jonathan. But if it pleases my father *to do* you evil, then I will report it to you and send you away, that you may go in safety. And the LORD be with you as He has been with my father. ¹⁴And you shall not only show me the kindness of the LORD while I still live, that I may not die; ¹⁵but you shall not cut off your kindness from my house forever, no, not when the LORD has cut off every one of the enemies of David from the face of the earth." ¹⁶So Jonathan made *a covenant* with the house of David, *saying,* "Let the LORD require *it* at the hand of David's enemies."

¹⁷Now Jonathan again caused David to vow, because he loved him; for he loved him as he loved his own soul. ¹⁸Then Jonathan said to David, "Tomorrow *is* the New Moon; and you will be missed, because your seat will be empty. ¹⁹And *when* you have stayed three days, go down quickly and come to the place where you hid on the day of the deed; and remain by the stone Ezel. ²⁰Then I will shoot three arrows to the side, as though I shot at a target; ²¹and there I will send a lad, *saying,* 'Go, find the arrows.' If I expressly say to the lad, 'Look, the arrows *are* on this side of you; get them and come'— then, as the LORD lives, *there is* safety for you and no harm. ²²But if I say thus to the young man, 'Look, the arrows *are* beyond you'—go your way, for the LORD has sent you away. ²³And as for the matter which you and I have spoken of, indeed the LORD *be* between you and me forever."

²⁴Then David hid in the field. And when the New Moon had come, the king sat down to eat the feast. ²⁵Now the king sat on his seat, as at other times, on a seat by the wall. And Jonathan arose,* and Abner sat by Saul's side, but David's place was empty. ²⁶Nevertheless Saul did not say anything that day, for he thought, "Something has happened to him; he *is* unclean, surely he *is* unclean." ²⁷And it happened the next day, the second *day* of the month, that David's place was empty. And Saul said to Jonathan his son, "Why has the son of Jesse not come to eat, either yesterday or today?"

²⁸So Jonathan answered Saul, "David earnestly asked *permission* of me *to go* to Bethlehem. ²⁹And he said, 'Please let me go, for our family has a sacrifice in the city, and my brother has commanded me *to be there.* And now, if I have found favor in your eyes, please let me get away and see my brothers.' Therefore he has not come to the king's table."

³⁰Then Saul's anger was aroused against Jonathan, and he said to him, "You son of a perverse, rebellious *woman!* Do I not know that you have chosen the son of Jesse to your own shame and to the shame of your mother's nakedness? ³¹For as long as the son of Jesse lives on the earth, you shall not be established, nor your kingdom. Now therefore, send and bring him to me, for he shall surely die."

³²And Jonathan answered Saul his father, and said to him, "Why should he be killed? What has he done?" ³³Then Saul cast a spear at him to kill him, by which Jonathan knew that it was determined by his father to kill David.

³⁴So Jonathan arose from the table in fierce anger, and ate no food the second day of the month, for he was grieved for David, because his father had treated him shamefully.

³⁵And so it was, in the morning, that Jonathan went out into the field at the time appointed with David, and a little lad *was* with him. ³⁶Then he said to his lad, "Now run, find the arrows which I

shoot." As the lad ran, he shot an arrow beyond him. 37When the lad had come to the place where the arrow was which Jonathan had shot, Jonathan cried out after the lad and said, "*Is* not the arrow beyond you?" 38And Jonathan cried out after the lad, "Make haste, hurry, do not delay!" So Jonathan's lad gathered up the arrows and came back to his master. 39But the lad did not know anything. Only Jonathan and David knew of the matter. 40Then Jonathan gave his weapons to his lad, and said to him, "Go, carry *them* to the city."

41As soon as the lad had gone, David arose from *a place* toward the south, fell on his face to the ground, and bowed down three times. And they kissed one another; and they wept together, but David more so. 42Then Jonathan said to David, "Go in peace, since we have both sworn in the name of the LORD, saying, 'May the LORD be between you and me, and between your descendants and my descendants, forever.' " So he arose and departed, and Jonathan went into the city.

Now David came to Nob, to Ahimelech the priest. And Ahimelech was afraid when he met David, and said to him, "Why *are* you alone, and no one is with you?"

2So David said to Ahimelech the priest, "The king has ordered me on some business, and said to me, 'Do not let anyone know anything about the business on which I send you, or what I have commanded you.' And I have directed *my* young men to such and such a place. 3Now therefore, what have you on hand? Give *me* five *loaves of* bread in my hand, or whatever can be found."

4And the priest answered David and said, "*There is* no common bread on hand; but there is holy bread, if the young men have at least kept themselves from women."

5Then David answered the priest, and said to him, "Truly, women *have been* kept from us about three days since I came out. And the vessels of the young men are holy, and *the bread is* in effect common, even though it was consecrated in the vessel this day."

6So the priest gave him holy *bread;* for there was no bread there but the showbread which had been taken from before the LORD, in order to put hot bread *in its place* on the day when it was taken away.

7Now a certain man of the servants of Saul *was* there that day, detained before the LORD. And his name *was* Doeg, an Edomite, the chief of the herdsmen who *belonged* to Saul.

8And David said to Ahimelech, "Is there not here on hand a spear or a sword? For I have brought neither my sword nor my weapons with me, because the king's business required haste."

9So the priest said, "The sword of Goliath the Philistine, whom you killed in the Valley of Elah, there it is, wrapped in a cloth behind the ephod. If you will take that, take *it.* For *there is* no other except that one here."

And David said, "*There is* none like it; give it to me."

10Then David arose and fled that day from before Saul, and went to Achish the king of Gath. 11And the servants of Achish said to him, "*Is* this not David the king of the land? Did they not sing of him to one another in dances, saying:

> 'Saul has slain his thousands,
> And David his ten
> thousands'?"*

12Now David took these words to heart, and was very much afraid of Achish the king of Gath. 13So he changed his behavior before them, pretended madness in their hands, scratched on the doors of the gate, and let his saliva fall down on his beard. 14Then Achish said to his servants, "Look, you see the man is insane. Why have you brought him to me? [15]Have I need of madmen, that you have brought this *fellow* to play the madman in my presence? Shall this *fellow* come into my house?"

JOHN 9:1-41

Now as *Jesus* passed by, He saw a man who was blind from birth. [2]And His disciples asked Him, saying, "Rabbi, who sinned, this man or his parents, that he was born blind?"

[3]Jesus answered, "Neither this man nor his parents sinned, but that the works of God should be revealed in him. [4]I* must work the works of Him who sent Me while it is day; *the* night is coming when no one can work. [5]As long as I am in the world, I am the light of the world."

[6]When He had said these things, He spat on the ground and made clay with the saliva; and He anointed the eyes of the blind man with the clay. [7]And He said to him, "Go, wash in the pool of Siloam" (which is translated, Sent). So he went and washed, and came back seeing.

[8]Therefore the neighbors and those who previously had seen that he was blind* said, "Is not this he who sat and begged?"

[9]Some said, "This is he." Others *said,* "He is like him."*

He said, "I am *he.*"

[10]Therefore they said to him, "How were your eyes opened?"

[11]He answered and said, "A Man called Jesus made clay and anointed my eyes and said to me, 'Go to the pool of* Siloam and wash.' So I went and washed, and I received sight."

[12]Then they said to him, "Where is He?"

He said, "I do not know."

[13]They brought him who formerly was blind to the Pharisees. [14]Now it was a Sabbath when Jesus made the clay and opened his eyes. [15]Then the Pharisees also asked him again how he had received his sight. He said to them, "He put clay on my eyes, and I washed, and I see."

[16]Therefore some of the Pharisees said, "This Man is not from God, because He does not keep the Sabbath." Others said, "How can a man who is a sinner do such signs?" And there was a division among them.

[17]They said to the blind man again, "What do you say about Him because He opened your eyes?"

He said, "He is a prophet."

[18]But the Jews did not believe concerning him, that he had been blind and received his sight, until they called the parents of him who had received his sight. [19]And they asked them, saying, "Is this your son, who you say was born blind? How then does he now see?"

[20]His parents answered them and said, "We know that this is our son, and that he was born blind; [21]but by what means he now sees we do not know, or who opened his eyes we do not know. He is of age; ask him. He will speak for himself." [22]His parents said these *things* because they feared the Jews, for the Jews had agreed already that if anyone confessed *that* He *was* Christ, he would be put out of the synagogue. [23]Therefore his parents said, "He is of age; ask him."

[24]So they again called the man who was blind, and said to him, "Give God the glory! We know that this Man is a sinner."

[25]He answered and said, "Whether He is a sinner *or not* I do not know. One thing I know: that though I was blind, now I see."

[26]Then they said to him again, "What did He do to you? How did He open your eyes?"

[27]He answered them, "I told you already, and you did not listen. Why do you want to hear *it* again? Do you also want to become His disciples?"

²⁸Then they reviled him and said, "You are His disciple, but we are Moses' disciples. ²⁹We know that God spoke to Moses; *as for* this *fellow,* we do not know where He is from."

³⁰The man answered and said to them, "Why, this is a marvelous thing, that you do not know where He is from; yet He has opened my eyes! ³¹Now we know that God does not hear sinners; but if anyone is a worshiper of God and does His will, He hears him. ³²Since the world began it has been unheard of that anyone opened the eyes of one who was born blind. ³³If this Man were not from God, He could do nothing."

³⁴They answered and said to him, "You were completely born in sins, and are you teaching us?" And they cast him out.

³⁵Jesus heard that they had cast him out; and when He had found him, He said to him, "Do you believe in the Son of God?"*

³⁶He answered and said, "Who is He, Lord, that I may believe in Him?"

³⁷And Jesus said to him, "You have both seen Him and it is He who is talking with you."

³⁸Then he said, "Lord, I believe!" And he worshiped Him.

³⁹And Jesus said, "For judgment I have come into this world, that those who do not see may see, and that those who see may be made blind."

⁴⁰Then *some* of the Pharisees who were with Him heard these words, and said to Him, "Are we blind also?"

⁴¹Jesus said to them, "If you were blind, you would have no sin; but now you say, 'We see.' Therefore your sin remains."

PSALM 113:1–114:8

P RAISE the LORD!

Praise, O servants of the LORD,
Praise the name of the LORD!

2   Blessed be the name of the
    LORD
From this time forth and
    forevermore!
3   From the rising of the sun to
    its going down
The LORD's name *is* to be
    praised.

4   The LORD *is* high above all
    nations,
His glory above the heavens.
5   Who *is* like the LORD our God,
Who dwells on high,
6   Who humbles Himself to
    behold
The things that are in the
    heavens and in the earth?

7   He raises the poor out of the
    dust,
And lifts the needy out of the
    ash heap,
8   That He may seat *him* with
    princes—
With the princes of His
    people.
9   He grants the barren woman
    a home,
Like a joyful mother of
    children.

Praise the LORD!

WHEN Israel went out of Egypt,
The house of Jacob from a
    people of strange language,
2   Judah became His sanctuary,
And Israel His dominion.

3   The sea saw *it* and fled;
Jordan turned back.
4   The mountains skipped like
    rams,
The little hills like lambs.
5   What ails you, O sea, that you
    fled?
O Jordan, *that* you turned
    back?

6   O mountains, *that* you
        skipped like rams?
      O little hills, like lambs?

7   Tremble, O earth, at the
        presence of the Lord,

At the presence of the God of
  Jacob,

8   Who turned the rock *into* a
        pool of water,
      The flint into a fountain of
        waters.

PROVERBS FOR TODAY/ 15:15-17

All the days of the afflicted are *evil, but he who is of a merry heart* has *a continual feast. Better* is *a little with the fear of the* LORD, *than great treasure with trouble. Better* is *a dinner of herbs* * *where love is, than a fatted calf with hatred.*

MAY 18

1 SAMUEL 22:1–23:29

DAVID therefore departed from there and escaped to the cave of Adullam. So when his brothers and all his father's house heard *it,* they went down there to him. ²And everyone *who was* in distress, everyone who *was* in debt, and everyone *who was* discontented gathered to him. So he became captain over them. And there were about four hundred men with him.

³Then David went from there to Mizpah of Moab; and he said to the king of Moab, "Please let my father and mother come here with you, till I know what God will do for me." ⁴So he brought them before the king of Moab, and they dwelt with him all the time that David was in the stronghold.

⁵Now the prophet Gad said to David, "Do not stay in the stronghold; depart, and go to the land of Judah." So David departed and went into the forest of Hereth.

⁶When Saul heard that David and the men who *were* with him had been discovered—now Saul was staying in Gibeah under a tamarisk tree in Ramah, with his spear in his hand, and all his servants standing about him— ⁷then Saul said to his servants who stood about him, "Hear now, you Benjamites! Will the son of Jesse give every one of you fields and vineyards, *and* make you all captains of thousands and captains of hundreds? ⁸All of you have conspired against me, and *there is* no one who reveals to me that my son has made a covenant with the son of Jesse; and *there is* not one of you who is sorry for me or reveals to me that my son has stirred up my servant against me, to lie in wait, as *it is* this day."

⁹Then answered Doeg the Edomite, who was set over the servants of Saul, and said, "I saw the son of Jesse going to Nob, to Ahimelech the son of Ahitub. ¹⁰And he inquired of the LORD for him, gave him provisions, and gave him the sword of Goliath the Philistine."

¹¹So the king sent to call Ahimelech the priest, the son of Ahitub, and all his father's house, the priests who *were* in Nob. And they all came to the king. ¹²And Saul said, "Hear now, son of Ahitub!"

He answered, "Here I am, my lord." ¹³Then Saul said to him, "Why have you conspired against me, you and the son of Jesse, in that you have given him bread and a sword, and have inquired of God for him, that he should rise against me, to lie in wait, as it is this day?"

¹⁴So Ahimelech answered the king and said, "And who among all your servants *is as* faithful as David, who is the king's son-in-law, who goes at your bidding, and is honorable in your house? ¹⁵Did I then begin to inquire of God for him? Far be it from me! Let not the king impute anything to his servant, *or* to any in the house of my father. For your servant knew nothing of all this, little or much."

¹⁶And the king said, "You shall surely die, Ahimelech, you and all your father's house!" ¹⁷Then the king said to the guards who stood about him, "Turn and kill the priests of the Lord, because their hand also *is* with David, and because they knew when he fled and did not tell it to me." But the servants of the king would not lift their hands to strike the priests of the Lord. ¹⁸And the king said to Doeg, "You turn and kill the priests!" So Doeg the Edomite turned and struck the priests, and killed on that day eighty-five men who wore a linen ephod. ¹⁹Also Nob, the city of the priests, he struck with the edge of the sword, both men and women, children and nursing infants, oxen and donkeys and sheep—with the edge of the sword.

²⁰Now one of the sons of Ahimelech the son of Ahitub, named Abiathar, escaped and fled after David. ²¹And Abiathar told David that Saul had killed the Lord's priests. ²²So David said to Abiathar, "I knew that day, when Doeg the Edomite *was* there, that he would surely tell Saul. I have caused *the death* of all the persons of your father's house. ²³Stay with me; do not fear. For he who seeks my life seeks your life, but with me you *shall be* safe."

Then they told David, saying, "Look, the Philistines are fighting against Keilah, and they are robbing the threshing floors."

²Therefore David inquired of the Lord, saying, "Shall I go and attack these Philistines?"

And the Lord said to David, "Go and attack the Philistines, and save Keilah."

³But David's men said to him, "Look, we are afraid here in Judah. How much more then if we go to Keilah against the armies of the Philistines?" ⁴Then David inquired of the Lord once again.

And the Lord answered him and said, "Arise, go down to Keilah. For I will deliver the Philistines into your hand." ⁵And David and his men went to Keilah and fought with the Philistines, struck them with a mighty blow, and took away their livestock. So David saved the inhabitants of Keilah.

⁶Now it happened, when Abiathar the son of Ahimelech fled to David at Keilah, *that* he went down *with* an ephod in his hand.

⁷And Saul was told that David had gone to Keilah. So Saul said, "God has delivered him into my hand, for he has shut himself in by entering a town that has gates and bars." ⁸Then Saul called all the people together for war, to go down to Keilah to besiege David and his men.

⁹When David knew that Saul plotted evil against him, he said to Abiathar the priest, "Bring the ephod here." ¹⁰Then David said, "O Lord God of Israel, Your servant has certainly heard that Saul seeks to come to Keilah to destroy the city for my sake. ¹¹Will the men of Keilah deliver me into his hand? Will Saul come down, as Your servant has heard? O Lord God of Israel, I pray, tell Your servant."

And the Lord said, "He will come down."

¹²Then David said, "Will the men of

Keilah deliver me and my men into the hand of Saul?"

And the Lord said, "They will deliver *you.*"

13So David and his men, about six hundred, arose and departed from Keilah and went wherever they could go. Then it was told Saul that David had escaped from Keilah; so he halted the expedition.

14And David stayed in strongholds in the wilderness, and remained in the mountains in the Wilderness of Ziph. Saul sought him every day, but God did not deliver him into his hand. 15So David saw that Saul had come out to seek his life. And David *was* in the Wilderness of Ziph in a forest.* 16Then Jonathan, Saul's son, arose and went to David in the woods and strengthened his hand in God. 17And he said to him, "Do not fear, for the hand of Saul my father shall not find you. You shall be king over Israel, and I shall be next to you. Even my father Saul knows that." 18So the two of them made a covenant before the Lord. And David stayed in the woods, and Jonathan went to his own house.

19Then the Ziphites came up to Saul at Gibeah, saying, "Is David not hiding with us in strongholds in the woods, in the hill of Hachilah, which *is* on the south of Jeshimon? 20Now therefore, O king, come down according to all the desire of your soul to come down; and our part *shall be* to deliver him into the king's hand."

21And Saul said, "Blessed *are* you of the Lord, for you have compassion on me. 22Please go and find out for sure, and see the place where his hideout is, *and* who has seen him there. For I am told he is very crafty. 23See therefore, and take knowledge of all the lurking places where he hides; and come back to me with certainty, and I will go with you. And it shall be, if he is in the land, that I will search for him throughout all the clans* of Judah."

24So they arose and went to Ziph before Saul. But David and his men *were* in the Wilderness of Maon, in the plain on the south of Jeshimon. 25When Saul and his men went to seek *him,* they told David. Therefore he went down to the rock, and stayed in the Wilderness of Maon. And when Saul heard *that,* he pursued David in the Wilderness of Maon. 26Then Saul went on one side of the mountain, and David and his men on the other side of the mountain. So David made haste to get away from Saul, for Saul and his men were encircling David and his men to take them. 27But a messenger came to Saul, saying, "Hurry and come, for the Philistines have invaded the land!" 28Therefore Saul returned from pursuing David, and went against the Philistines; so they called that place the Rock of Escape.* 29Then David went up from there and dwelt in strongholds at En Gedi.

JOHN 10:1-21

"**M**ost assuredly, I [Jesus] say to you, he who does not enter the sheepfold by the door, but climbs up some other way, the same is a thief and a robber. 2But he who enters by the door is the shepherd of the sheep. 3To him the doorkeeper opens, and the sheep hear his voice; and he calls his own sheep by name and leads them out. 4And when he brings out his own sheep, he goes before them; and the sheep follow him, for they know his voice. 5Yet they will by no means follow a stranger, but will flee from him, for they do not know the voice of strangers." 6Jesus used this illustration, but they did not understand the things which He spoke to them.

7Then Jesus said to them again, "Most assuredly, I say to you, I am the door of the sheep. 8All who *ever* came before Me* are thieves and robbers, but the sheep did not hear them. ⁹I am the door. If anyone enters by Me, he will be saved, and will go in and out and find pasture. ¹⁰The thief does not come except to steal, and to kill, and to destroy. I have come that they may have life, and that they may have *it* more abundantly.

¹¹"I am the good shepherd. The good shepherd gives His life for the sheep. ¹²But a hireling, *he who is* not the shepherd, one who does not own the sheep, sees the wolf coming and leaves the sheep and flees; and the wolf catches the sheep and scatters them. ¹³The hireling flees because he is a hireling and does not care about the sheep. ¹⁴I am the good shepherd; and I know My *sheep,* and am known by My own. ¹⁵As the Father knows Me, even so I know the Father; and I lay down My life for the sheep. ¹⁶And other sheep I have which are not of this fold; them also I must bring, and they will hear My voice; and there will be one flock *and* one shepherd.

¹⁷"Therefore My Father loves Me, because I lay down My life that I may take it again. ¹⁸No one takes it from Me, but I lay it down of Myself. I have power to lay it down, and I have power to take it again. This command I have received from My Father."

¹⁹Therefore there was a division again among the Jews because of these sayings. ²⁰And many of them said, "He has a demon and is mad. Why do you listen to Him?"

²¹Others said, "These are not the words of one who has a demon. Can a demon open the eyes of the blind?"

PSALM 115:1-18

OT unto us, O LORD, not unto us, But to Your name give glory, Because of Your mercy, Because of Your truth.
2   Why should the Gentiles say, "So where *is* their God?"

3   But our God *is* in heaven;
He does whatever He pleases.
4   Their idols *are* silver and gold,
The work of men's hands.
5   They have mouths, but they
do not speak;
Eyes they have, but they do
not see;
6   They have ears, but they do
not hear;
Noses they have, but they do
not smell;
7   They have hands, but they do
not handle;
Feet they have, but they do
not walk;
Nor do they mutter through
their throat.
8   Those who make them are
like them;
So is everyone who trusts in
them.

9   O Israel, trust in the LORD;
He *is* their help and their
shield.
10 O house of Aaron, trust in the
LORD;
He *is* their help and their
shield.
11 You who fear the LORD, trust
in the LORD;
He *is* their help and their
shield.

12 The LORD has been mindful
of *us;*
He will bless us;
He will bless the house of
Israel;
He will bless the house of
Aaron.
13 He will bless those who fear
the LORD,
Both small and great.

14 May the LORD give you
increase more and more,
You and your children.

15 *May* you *be* blessed by the
LORD,
Who made heaven and earth.

16 The heaven, *even* the
heavens, *are* the LORD'S;
But the earth He has given to
the children of men.

17 The dead do not praise the
LORD,
Nor any who go down into
silence.

18 But we will bless the LORD
From this time forth and
forevermore.

Praise the LORD!

PROVERBS FOR TODAY/ 15:18-19

A wrathful man stirs up strife, but he who is *slow to anger allays contention.*
□ *The way of the lazy* man is *like a hedge of thorns, but the way of the upright* is *a highway.*

MAY 19

1 SAMUEL 24:1–25:44

Now it happened, when Saul had returned from following the Philistines, that it was told him, saying, "Take note! David *is* in the Wilderness of En Gedi." ²Then Saul took three thousand chosen men from all Israel, and went to seek David and his men on the Rocks of the Wild Goats. ³So he came to the sheepfolds by the road, where there *was* a cave; and Saul went in to attend to his needs. (David and his men were staying in the recesses of the cave.) ⁴Then the men of David said to him, "This is the day of which the LORD said to you, 'Behold, I will deliver your enemy into your hand, that you may do to him as it seems good to you.' " And David arose and secretly cut off a corner of Saul's robe. ⁵Now it happened afterward that David's heart troubled him because he had cut Saul's *robe*. ⁶And he said to his men, "The LORD forbid that I should do this thing to my master, the LORD's anointed, to stretch out my hand against him, seeing he *is* the anointed

of the LORD." ⁷So David restrained his servants with *these* words, and did not allow them to rise against Saul. And Saul got up from the cave and went on *his* way.

⁸David also arose afterward, went out of the cave, and called out to Saul, saying, "My lord the king!" And when Saul looked behind him, David stooped with his face to the earth, and bowed down. ⁹And David said to Saul: "Why do you listen to the words of men who say, 'Indeed David seeks your harm'? ¹⁰Look, this day your eyes have seen that the LORD delivered you today into my hand in the cave, and *someone* urged *me* to kill you. But *my eye* spared you, and I said, 'I will not stretch out my hand against my lord, for he *is* the LORD's anointed.' ¹¹Moreover, my father, see! Yes, see the corner of your robe in my hand! For in that I cut off the corner of your robe, and did not kill you, know and see that *there is* neither evil nor rebellion in my hand, and I have not sinned against you. Yet you hunt my life to take it. ¹²Let the LORD judge between you and

me, and let the LORD avenge me on you. But my hand shall not be against you. 13As the proverb of the ancients says, 'Wickedness proceeds from the wicked.' But my hand shall not be against you. 14After whom has the king of Israel come out? Whom do you pursue? A dead dog? A flea? 15Therefore let the LORD be judge, and judge between you and me, and see and plead my case, and deliver me out of your hand."

16So it was, when David had finished speaking these words to Saul, that Saul said, "Is this your voice, my son David?" And Saul lifted up his voice and wept. 17Then he said to David: "You are more righteous than I; for you have rewarded me with good, whereas I have rewarded you with evil. 18And you have shown this day how you have dealt well with me; for when the LORD delivered me into your hand, you did not kill me. 19For if a man finds his enemy, will he let him get away safely? Therefore may the LORD reward you with good for what you have done to me this day. 20And now I know indeed that you shall surely be king, and that the kingdom of Israel shall be established in your hand. 21Therefore swear now to me by the LORD that you will not cut off my descendants after me, and that you will not destroy my name from my father's house."

22So David swore to Saul. And Saul went home, but David and his men went up to the stronghold.

THEN Samuel died; and the Israelites gathered together and lamented for him, and buried him at his home in Ramah. And David arose and went down to the Wilderness of Paran.*
2Now there was a man in Maon whose business was in Carmel, and the man was very rich. He had three thousand sheep and a thousand goats. And he was shearing his sheep in Carmel. 3The name of the man was Nabal,

and the name of his wife Abigail. And she was a woman of good understanding and beautiful appearance; but the man was harsh and evil in his doings. He was of the house of Caleb.

4When David heard in the wilderness that Nabal was shearing his sheep, 5David sent ten young men; and David said to the young men, "Go up to Carmel, go to Nabal, and greet him in my name. 6And thus you shall say to him who lives in prosperity: 'Peace be to you, peace to your house, and peace to all that you have! 7Now I have heard that you have shearers. Your shepherds were with us, and we did not hurt them, nor was there anything missing from them all the while they were in Carmel. 8Ask your young men, and they will tell you. Therefore let my young men find favor in your eyes, for we come on a feast day. Please give whatever comes to your hand to your servants and to your son David.' "

9So when David's young men came, they spoke to Nabal according to all these words in the name of David, and waited.

10Then Nabal answered David's servants, and said, "Who is David, and who is the son of Jesse? There are many servants nowadays who break away each one from his master. 11Shall I then take my bread and my water and my meat that I have killed for my shearers, and give it to men when I do not know where they are from?"

12So David's young men turned on their heels and went back; and they came and told him all these words. 13Then David said to his men, "Every man gird on his sword." So every man girded on his sword, and David also girded on his sword. And about four hundred men went with David, and two hundred stayed with the supplies.

14Now one of the young men told Abigail, Nabal's wife, saying, "Look, David sent messengers from the wilderness to greet our master; and he reviled them. [15]But the men *were* very good to us, and we were not hurt, nor did we miss anything as long as we accompanied them, when we were in the fields. [16]They were a wall to us both by night and day, all the time we were with them keeping the sheep. [17]Now therefore, know and consider what you will do, for harm is determined against our master and against all his household. For he *is such* a scoundrel* that *one* cannot speak to him."

[18]Then Abigail made haste and took two hundred *loaves* of bread, two skins of wine, five sheep already dressed, five seahs of roasted *grain,* one hundred clusters of raisins, and two hundred cakes of figs, and loaded *them* on donkeys. [19]And she said to her servants, "Go on before me; see, I am coming after you." But she did not tell her husband Nabal.

[20]So it was, *as* she rode on the donkey, that she went down under cover of the hill; and there were David and his men, coming down toward her, and she met them. [21]Now David had said, "Surely in vain I have protected all that this *fellow* has in the wilderness, so that nothing was missed of all that *belongs* to him. And he has repaid me evil for good. [22]May God do so, and more also, to the enemies of David, if I leave one male of all who *belong* to him by morning light."

[23]Now when Abigail saw David, she dismounted quickly from the donkey, fell on her face before David, and bowed down to the ground. [24]So she fell at his feet and said: "On me, my lord, *on* me *let* this iniquity *be!* And please let your maidservant speak in your ears, and hear the words of your maidservant. [25]Please, let not my lord regard this scoundrel Nabal. For as his name *is,* so *is* he: Nabal* *is* his name, and folly *is* with him! But I, your maidservant, did not see the young men of my lord whom you sent. [26]Now therefore, my lord, *as* the LORD lives and *as*

your soul lives, since the LORD has held you back from coming to bloodshed and from avenging yourself with your own hand, now then, let your enemies and those who seek harm for my lord be as Nabal. [27]And now this present which your maidservant has brought to my lord, let it be given to the young men who follow my lord. [28]Please forgive the trespass of your maidservant. For the LORD will certainly make for my lord an enduring house, because my lord fights the battles of the LORD, and evil is not found in you throughout your days. [29]Yet a man has risen to pursue you and seek your life, but the life of my lord shall be bound in the bundle of the living with the LORD your God; and the lives of your enemies He shall sling out, *as from* the pocket of a sling. [30]And it shall come to pass, when the LORD has done for my lord according to all the good that He has spoken concerning you, and has appointed you ruler over Israel, [31]that this will be no grief to you, nor offense of heart to my lord, either that you have shed blood without cause, or that my lord has avenged himself. But when the LORD has dealt well with my lord, then remember your maidservant."

[32]Then David said to Abigail: "Blessed *is* the LORD God of Israel, who sent you this day to meet me! [33]And blessed *is* your advice and blessed *are* you, because you have kept me this day from coming to bloodshed and from avenging myself with my own hand. [34]For indeed, *as* the LORD God of Israel lives, who has kept me back from hurting you, unless you had hurried and come to meet me, surely by morning light no males would have been left to Nabal!" [35]So David received from her hand what she had brought him, and said to her, "Go up in peace to your house. See, I have heeded your voice and respected your person."

[36]Now Abigail went to Nabal, and

there he was, holding a feast in his house, like the feast of a king. And Nabal's heart *was* merry within him, for he *was* very drunk; therefore she told him nothing, little or much, until morning light. 37So it was, in the morning, when the wine had gone from Nabal, and his wife had told him these things, that his heart died within him, and he became *like* a stone. 38Then it happened, *after* about ten days, that the LORD struck Nabal, and he died.

39So when David heard that Nabal was dead, he said, "Blessed *be* the LORD, who has pleaded the cause of my reproach from the hand of Nabal, and has kept His servant from evil! For the LORD has returned the wickedness of Nabal on his own head."

And David sent and proposed to Abigail, to take her as his wife. 40When the servants of David had come to Abigail at Carmel, they spoke to her saying, "David sent us to you, to ask you to become his wife."

41Then she arose, bowed her face to the earth, and said, "Here is your maidservant, a servant to wash the feet of the servants of my lord." 42So Abigail rose in haste and rode on a donkey, attended by five of her maidens; and she followed the messengers of David, and became his wife. 43David also took Ahinoam of Jezreel, and so both of them were his wives.

44But Saul had given Michal his daughter, David's wife, to Palti* the son of Laish, who *was* from Gallim.

JOHN 10:22-42

Now it was the Feast of Dedication in Jerusalem, and it was winter. 23And Jesus walked in the temple, in Solomon's porch. 24Then the Jews surrounded Him and said to Him, "How long do You keep us in doubt? If You are the Christ, tell us plainly."

25Jesus answered them, "I told you, and you do not believe. The works that I do in My Father's name, they bear witness of Me. 26But you do not believe, because you are not of My sheep, as I said to you.* 27My sheep hear My voice, and I know them, and they follow Me. 28And I give them eternal life, and they shall never perish; neither shall anyone snatch them out of My hand. 29My Father, who has given *them* to Me, is greater than all; and no one is able to snatch *them* out of My Father's hand. 30I and *My* Father are one."

31Then the Jews took up stones again to stone Him. 32Jesus answered them, "Many good works I have shown you from My Father. For which of those works do you stone Me?"

33The Jews answered Him, saying, "For a good work we do not stone You, but for blasphemy, and because You, being a Man, make Yourself God."

34Jesus answered them, "Is it not written in your law, *'I* said, "You are gods" '?* 35If He called them gods, to whom the word of God came (and the Scripture cannot be broken), 36do you say of Him whom the Father sanctified and sent into the world, 'You are blaspheming,' because I said, 'I am the Son of God'? 37If I do not do the works of My Father, do not believe Me; 38but if I do, though you do not believe Me, believe the works, that you may know and believe* that the Father *is* in Me, and I in Him." 39Therefore they sought again to seize Him, but He escaped out of their hand.

40And He went away again beyond the Jordan to the place where John was baptizing at first, and there He stayed. 41Then many came to Him and said, "John performed no sign, but all the things that John spoke about this Man were true." 42And many believed in Him there.

PSALM 116:1-19

I LOVE the LORD, because He has heard
My voice *and* my supplications.

2 Because He has inclined His ear to me,
Therefore I will call *upon Him* as long as I live.

3 The pains of death surrounded me,
And the pangs of Sheol laid hold of me;
I found trouble and sorrow.

4 Then I called upon the name of the LORD:
"O LORD, I implore You, deliver my soul!"

5 Gracious *is* the LORD, and righteous;
Yes, our God *is* merciful.

6 The LORD preserves the simple;
I was brought low, and He saved me.

7 Return to your rest, O my soul,
For the LORD has dealt bountifully with you.

8 For You have delivered my soul from death,
My eyes from tears,
And my feet from falling.

9 I will walk before the LORD
In the land of the living.

10 I believed, therefore I spoke,
"I am greatly afflicted."

11 I said in my haste,
"All men *are* liars."

12 What shall I render to the LORD
For all His benefits toward me?

13 I will take up the cup of salvation,
And call upon the name of the LORD.

14 I will pay my vows to the LORD
Now in the presence of all His people.

15 Precious in the sight of the LORD
Is the death of His saints.

16 O LORD, truly I *am* Your servant;
I *am* Your servant, the son of Your maidservant;
You have loosed my bonds.

17 I will offer to You the sacrifice of thanksgiving,
And will call upon the name of the LORD.

18 I will pay my vows to the LORD
Now in the presence of all His people,

19 In the courts of the LORD's house,
In the midst of you,
O Jerusalem.

Praise the LORD!

PROVERBS FOR TODAY/ 15:20-21

A wise son makes a father glad, but a foolish man despises his mother. □ *Folly is joy to him who is destitute of discernment, but a man of understanding walks uprightly.*

1 SAMUEL 26:1–28:25

Now the Ziphites came to Saul at Gibeah, saying, "Is David not hiding in the hill of Hachilah, opposite Jeshimon?" ²Then Saul arose and went down to the Wilderness of Ziph, having three thousand chosen men of Israel with him, to seek David in the Wilderness of Ziph. ³And Saul encamped in the hill of Hachilah, which *is* opposite Jeshimon, by the road. But David stayed in the wilderness, and he saw that Saul came after him into the wilderness. ⁴David therefore sent out spies, and understood that Saul had indeed come.

⁵So David arose and came to the place where Saul had encamped. And David saw the place where Saul lay, and Abner the son of Ner, the commander of his army. Now Saul lay within the camp, with the people encamped all around him. ⁶Then David answered, and said to Ahimelech the Hittite and to Abishai the son of Zeruiah, brother of Joab, saying, "Who will go down with me to Saul in the camp?"

And Abishai said, "I will go down with you."

⁷So David and Abishai came to the people by night; and there Saul lay sleeping within the camp, with his spear stuck in the ground by his head. And Abner and the people lay all around him. ⁸Then Abishai said to David, "God has delivered your enemy into your hand this day. Now therefore, please, let me strike him at once with the spear, right to the earth; and I will not *have to strike* him a second time!"

⁹But David said to Abishai, "Do not destroy him; for who can stretch out his hand against the Lord's anointed, and be guiltless?" ¹⁰David said furthermore, "*As* the Lord lives, the Lord shall strike him, or his day shall come to die, or he shall go out to battle and perish. ¹¹The Lord forbid that I should stretch out my hand against the Lord's anointed. But please, take now the spear and the jug of water that *are* by his head, and let us go." ¹²So David took the spear and the jug of water *by* Saul's head, and they got away; and no man saw or knew *it* or awoke. For they *were* all asleep, because a deep sleep from the Lord had fallen on them.

¹³Now David went over to the other side, and stood on the top of a hill afar off, a great distance *being* between them. ¹⁴And David called out to the people and to Abner the son of Ner, saying, "Do you not answer, Abner?"

Then Abner answered and said, "Who *are* you, calling out to the king?"

¹⁵So David said to Abner, "*Are* you not a man? And who *is* like you in Israel? Why then have you not guarded your lord the king? For one of the people came in to destroy your lord the king. ¹⁶This thing that you have done *is* not good. *As* the Lord lives, you deserve to die, because you have not guarded your master, the Lord's anointed. And now see where the king's spear *is,* and the jug of water that *was* by his head."

¹⁷Then Saul knew David's voice, and said, "*Is* that your voice, my son David?"

David said, "*It is* my voice, my lord, O king." ¹⁸And he said, "Why does my lord thus pursue his servant? For what have I done, or what evil *is* in my hand? ¹⁹Now therefore, please, let my lord the king hear the words of his servant: If the Lord has stirred you up against me, let Him accept an offering. But if *it* is the children of men, *may* they *be* cursed before the LORD, for they have driven me out this day from sharing in the inheritance of the LORD, saying, 'Go, serve other gods.' ²⁰So now, do not let my blood fall to the earth before the face of the LORD. For the king of Israel has come out to seek a flea, as when one hunts a partridge in the mountains."

²¹Then Saul said, "I have sinned. Return, my son David. For I will harm you no more, because my life was precious in your eyes this day. Indeed I have played the fool and erred exceedingly."

²²And David answered and said, "Here is the king's spear. Let one of the young men come over and get it. ²³May the LORD repay every man *for* his righteousness and his faithfulness; for the LORD delivered you into *my* hand today, but I would not stretch out my hand against the LORD's anointed. ²⁴And indeed, as your life was valued much this day in my eyes, so let my life be valued much in the eyes of the LORD, and let Him deliver me out of all tribulation."

²⁵Then Saul said to David, "*May* you *be* blessed, my son David! You shall both do great things and also still prevail."

So David went on his way, and Saul returned to his place.

AND David said in his heart, "Now I shall perish someday by the hand of Saul. *There is* nothing better for me than that I should speedily escape to the land of the Philistines; and Saul will despair of me, to seek me anymore in any part of Israel. So I shall escape out of his hand." ²Then David arose and went over with the six hundred men who *were* with him to Achish the son of Maoch, king of Gath. ³So David dwelt with Achish at Gath, he and his men, each man with his household, *and* David with his two wives, Ahinoam the Jezreelitess, and Abigail the Carmelitess, Nabal's widow. ⁴And it was told Saul that David had fled to Gath; so he sought him no more.

⁵Then David said to Achish, "If I have now found favor in your eyes, let them give me a place in some town in the country, that I may dwell there. For why should your servant dwell in the royal city with you?" ⁶So Achish gave him Ziklag that day. Therefore Ziklag has belonged to the kings of Judah to this day. ⁷Now the time that David dwelt in the country of the Philistines was one full year and four months.

⁸And David and his men went up and raided the Geshurites, the Girzites,* and the Amalekites. For those nations were the inhabitants of the land from of old, as you go to Shur, even as far as the land of Egypt. ⁹Whenever David attacked the land, he left neither man nor woman alive, but took away the sheep, the oxen, the donkeys, the camels, and the apparel, and returned and came to Achish. ¹⁰Then Achish would say, "Where have you made a raid today?" And David would say, "Against the southern *area* of Judah, or against the southern *area* of the Jerahmeelites, or against the southern *area* of the Kenites." ¹¹David would save neither man nor woman alive, to bring *news* to Gath, saying, "Lest they should inform on us, saying, 'Thus David did.' " And thus *was* his behavior all the time he dwelt in the country of the Philistines. ¹²So Achish believed David, saying, "He has made his people Israel utterly abhor him; therefore he will be my servant forever."

Now it happened in those days that the Philistines gathered their armies together for war, to fight with Israel. And Achish said to David, "You assuredly know that you will go out with me to battle, you and your men."

²So David said to Achish, "Surely you know what your servant can do."

And Achish said to David, "Therefore I will make you one of my chief guardians forever."

³Now Samuel had died, and all Israel had lamented for him and buried him in Ramah, in his own city. And Saul had put the mediums and the spiritists out of the land.

⁴Then the Philistines gathered together, and came and encamped at Shunem. So Saul gathered all Israel together, and they encamped at Gilboa. ⁵When Saul saw the army of the Philistines, he was afraid, and his heart trembled greatly. ⁶And when Saul inquired of the LORD, the LORD did not answer him, either by dreams or by Urim or by the prophets.

⁷Then Saul said to his servants, "Find me a woman who is a medium, that I may go to her and inquire of her."

And his servants said to him, "In fact, *there is* a woman who is a medium at En Dor."

⁸So Saul disguised himself and put on other clothes, and he went, and two men with him; and they came to the woman by night. And he said, "Please conduct a séance for me, and bring up for me the one I shall name to you."

⁹Then the woman said to him, "Look, you know what Saul has done, how he has cut off the mediums and the spiritists from the land. Why then do you lay a snare for my life, to cause me to die?"

¹⁰And Saul swore to her by the LORD, saying, "*As* the LORD lives, no punishment shall come upon you for this thing."

¹¹Then the woman said, "Whom shall I bring up for you?"

And he said, "Bring up Samuel for me."

¹²When the woman saw Samuel, she cried out with a loud voice. And the woman spoke to Saul, saying, "Why have you deceived me? For you *are* Saul!"

¹³And the king said to her, "Do not be afraid. What did you see?"

And the woman said to Saul, "I saw a spirit* ascending out of the earth."

¹⁴So he said to her, "What *is* his form?"

And she said, "An old man is coming up, and he *is* covered with a mantle." And Saul perceived that it *was* Samuel, and he stooped with *his* face to the ground and bowed down.

¹⁵Now Samuel said to Saul, "Why have you disturbed me by bringing me up?"

And Saul answered, "I am deeply distressed; for the Philistines make war against me, and God has departed from me and does not answer me anymore, neither by prophets nor by dreams. Therefore I have called you, that you may reveal to me what I should do."

¹⁶Then Samuel said: "So why do you ask me, seeing the LORD has departed from you and has become your enemy? ¹⁷And the LORD has done for Himself* as He spoke by me. For the LORD has torn the kingdom out of your hand and given it to your neighbor, David. ¹⁸Because you did not obey the voice of the LORD nor execute His fierce wrath upon Amalek, therefore the LORD has done this thing to you this day. ¹⁹Moreover the LORD will also deliver Israel with you into the hand of the Philistines. And tomorrow you and your sons *will be* with me. The LORD will also deliver the army of Israel into the hand of the Philistines."

²⁰Immediately Saul fell full length on the ground, and was dreadfully afraid because of the words of Samuel. And there was no strength in him, for he had eaten no food all day or all night.

²¹And the woman came to Saul and saw that he was severely troubled, and said to him, "Look, your maidservant has obeyed your voice, and I have put

my life in my hands and heeded the words which you spoke to me. ²²Now therefore, please, heed also the voice of your maidservant, and let me set a piece of bread before you; and eat, that you may have strength when you go on *your* way."

²³But he refused and said, "I will not eat."

So his servants, together with the woman, urged him; and he heeded their voice. Then he arose from the ground and sat on the bed. ²⁴Now the woman had a fatted calf in the house, and she hastened to kill it. And she took flour and kneaded *it,* and baked unleavened bread from it. ²⁵So she brought *it* before Saul and his servants, and they ate. Then they rose and went away that night.

JOHN 11:1-54

Now a certain *man* was sick, Lazarus of Bethany, the town of Mary and her sister Martha. ²It was *that* Mary who anointed the Lord with fragrant oil and wiped His feet with her hair, whose brother Lazarus was sick. Therefore the sisters sent to Him, saying, "Lord, behold, he whom You love is sick."

⁴When Jesus heard *that,* He said, "This sickness is not unto death, but for the glory of God, that the Son of God may be glorified through it."

⁵Now Jesus loved Martha and her sister and Lazarus. ⁶So, when He heard that he was sick, He stayed two more days in the place where He was. ⁷Then after this He said to *the* disciples, "Let us go to Judea again."

⁸*The* disciples said to Him, "Rabbi, lately the Jews sought to stone You, and are You going there again?"

⁹Jesus answered, "Are there not twelve hours in the day? If anyone walks in the day, he does not stumble, because he sees the light of this world. ¹⁰But if one walks in the night, he stumbles, because the light is not in him." ¹¹These things He said, and after that He said to them, "Our friend Lazarus sleeps, but I go that I may wake him up."

¹²Then His disciples said, "Lord, if he sleeps he will get well." ¹³However, Jesus spoke of his death, but they thought that He was speaking about taking rest in sleep.

¹⁴Then Jesus said to them plainly, "Lazarus is dead. ¹⁵And I am glad for your sakes that I was not there, that you may believe. Nevertheless let us go to him."

¹⁶Then Thomas, who is called the Twin, said to his fellow disciples, "Let us also go, that we may die with Him."

¹⁷So when Jesus came, He found that he had already been in the tomb four days. ¹⁸Now Bethany was near Jerusalem, about two miles* away. ¹⁹And many of the Jews had joined the women around Martha and Mary, to comfort them concerning their brother.

²⁰Now Martha, as soon as she heard that Jesus was coming, went and met Him, but Mary was sitting in the house. ²¹Now Martha said to Jesus, "Lord, if You had been here, my brother would not have died. ²²But even now I know that whatever You ask of God, God will give You."

²³Jesus said to her, "Your brother will rise again."

²⁴Martha said to Him, "I know that he will rise again in the resurrection at the last day."

²⁵Jesus said to her, "I am the resurrection and the life. He who believes in Me, though he may die, he shall live. ²⁶And whoever lives and believes in Me shall never die. Do you believe this?"

²⁷She said to Him, "Yes, Lord, I believe that You are the Christ, the Son of God, who is to come into the world."

²⁸And when she had said these things, she went her way and secretly

called Mary her sister, saying, "The Teacher has come and is calling for you." 29As soon as she heard *that,* she arose quickly and came to Him. 30Now Jesus had not yet come into the town, but was* in the place where Martha met Him. 31Then the Jews who were with her in the house, and comforting her, when they saw that Mary rose up quickly and went out, followed her, saying, "She is going to the tomb to weep there."*

32Then, when Mary came where Jesus was, and saw Him, she fell down at His feet, saying to Him, "Lord, if You had been here, my brother would not have died."

33Therefore, when Jesus saw her weeping, and the Jews who came with her weeping, He groaned in the spirit and was troubled. 34And He said, "Where have you laid him?"

They said to Him, "Lord, come and see."

35Jesus wept. 36Then the Jews said, "See how He loved him!"

37And some of them said, "Could not this Man, who opened the eyes of the blind, also have kept this man from dying?"

38Then Jesus, again groaning in Himself, came to the tomb. It was a cave, and a stone lay against it. 39Jesus said, "Take away the stone."

Martha, the sister of him who was dead, said to Him, "Lord, by this time there is a stench, for he has been *dead* four days."

40Jesus said to her, "Did I not say to you that if you would believe you would see the glory of God?" 41Then they took away the stone *from the place* where the dead man was lying.* And Jesus lifted up *His* eyes and said, "Father, I thank You that You have heard Me. 42And I know that You always hear Me, but because of the people who are standing by I said *this,* that they may believe that You sent Me." 43Now when He had said these

things, He cried with a loud voice, "Lazarus, come forth!" 44And he who had died came out bound hand and foot with graveclothes, and his face was wrapped with a cloth. Jesus said to them, "Loose him, and let him go."

45Then many of the Jews who had come to Mary, and had seen the things Jesus did, believed in Him. 46But some of them went away to the Pharisees and told them the things Jesus did. 47Then the chief priests and the Pharisees gathered a council and said, "What shall we do? For this Man works many signs. 48If we let Him alone like this, everyone will believe in Him, and the Romans will come and take away both our place and nation."

49And one of them, Caiaphas, being high priest that year, said to them, "You know nothing at all, 50nor do you consider that it is expedient for us* that one man should die for the people, and not that the whole nation should perish." 51Now this he did not say on his own *authority;* but being high priest that year he prophesied that Jesus would die for the nation, 52and not for that nation only, but also that He would gather together in one the children of God who were scattered abroad.

53Then, from that day on, they plotted to put Him to death. 54Therefore Jesus no longer walked openly among the Jews, but went from there into the country near the wilderness, to a city called Ephraim, and there remained with His disciples.

PSALM 117:1-2

Praise the Lord, all you Gentiles! Laud Him, all you peoples! 2For His merciful kindness is great toward us, And the truth of the Lord *endures* forever.

Praise the Lord!

MAY 21

1 SAMUEL 29:1–31:13

THEN the Philistines gathered together all their armies at Aphek, and the Israelites encamped by a fountain which *is* in Jezreel. ²And the lords of the Philistines passed in review by hundreds and by thousands, but David and his men passed in review at the rear with Achish. ³Then the princes of the Philistines said, "What *are* these Hebrews *doing here?*"

And Achish said to the princes of the Philistines, "*Is* this not David, the servant of Saul king of Israel, who has been with me these days, or these years? And to this day I have found no fault in him since he defected *to me.*"

⁴But the princes of the Philistines were angry with him; so the princes of the Philistines said to him, "Make this fellow return, that he may go back to the place which you have appointed for him, and do not let him go down with us to battle, lest in the battle he become our adversary. For with what could he reconcile himself to his master, if not with the heads of these men? ⁵*Is* this not David, of whom they sang to one another in dances, saying:

'Saul has slain his thousands,
And David his ten
thousands'?"*

⁶Then Achish called David and said to him, "Surely, *as* the LORD lives, you have been upright, and your going out and your coming in with me in the army *is* good in my sight. For to this day I have not found evil in you since the day of your coming to me. Nevertheless the lords do not favor you. ⁷Therefore return now, and go in peace, that you may not displease the lords of the Philistines."

⁸So David said to Achish, "But what have I done? And to this day what have you found in your servant as long as I have been with you, that I may not go and fight against the enemies of my lord the king?"

⁹Then Achish answered and said to David, "I know that you *are* as good in my sight as an angel of God; nevertheless the princes of the Philistines have said, 'He shall not go up with us to the battle.' ¹⁰Now therefore, rise early in the morning with your master's servants who have come with you.* And as soon as you are up early in the morning and have light, depart."

¹¹So David and his men rose early to depart in the morning, to return to the land of the Philistines. And the Philistines went up to Jezreel.

Now it happened, when David and his men came to Ziklag, on the third day, that the Amalekites had invaded the South and Ziklag, attacked Ziklag and burned it with fire, ²and had taken captive the women and those who *were* there, from small to great; they did not kill anyone, but carried *them* away and went their way. ³So David and his men came to the city, and there it was, burned with fire; and their wives, their sons, and their daughters had been taken captive. ⁴Then David and the people who *were* with him lifted up their voices and wept, until they had no more power to weep. ⁵And David's two wives, Ahinoam the Jezreelitess, and Abigail the widow of Nabal the Carmelite, had been taken captive. ⁶Now David was greatly distressed, for the people spoke of stoning him, because the soul of all the people was grieved, every man for his sons and his daughters. But David strengthened himself in the Lord his God.

⁷Then David said to Abiathar the priest, Ahimelech's son, "Please bring the ephod here to me." And Abiathar brought the ephod to David. ⁸So David inquired of the Lord, saying, "Shall I pursue this troop? Shall I overtake them?"

And He answered him, "Pursue, for you shall surely overtake *them* and without fail recover *all.*"

⁹So David went, he and the six hundred men who *were* with him, and came to the Brook Besor, where those stayed who were left behind. ¹⁰But David pursued, he and four hundred men; for two hundred stayed *behind,* who were so weary that they could not cross the Brook Besor.

¹¹Then they found an Egyptian in the field, and brought him to David; and they gave him bread and he ate, and they let him drink water. ¹²And they gave him a piece of a cake of figs and two clusters of raisins. So when he had eaten, his strength came back to him; for he had eaten no bread nor drunk water for three days and three nights. ¹³Then David said to him, "To whom do you *belong,* and where *are* you from?"

And he said, "I *am* a young man from Egypt, servant of an Amalekite; and my master left me behind, because three days ago I fell sick. ¹⁴We made an invasion of the southern *area* of the Cherethites, in the *territory*

which *belongs* to Judah, and of the southern *area* of Caleb; and we burned Ziklag with fire."

¹⁵And David said to him, "Can you take me down to this troop?"

So he said, "Swear to me by God that you will neither kill me nor deliver me into the hands of my master, and I will take you down to this troop."

¹⁶And when he had brought him down, there they were, spread out over all the land, eating and drinking and dancing, because of all the great spoil which they had taken from the land of the Philistines and from the land of Judah. ¹⁷Then David attacked them from twilight until the evening of the next day. Not a man of them escaped, except four hundred young men who rode on camels and fled. ¹⁸So David recovered all that the Amalekites had carried away, and David rescued his two wives. ¹⁹And nothing of theirs was lacking, either small or great, sons or daughters, spoil or anything which they had taken from them; David recovered all. ²⁰Then David took all the flocks and herds they had driven before those *other* livestock, and said, "This *is* David's spoil."

²¹Now David came to the two hundred men who had been so weary that they could not follow David, whom they also had made to stay at the Brook Besor. So they went out to meet David and to meet the people who *were* with him. And when David came near the people, he greeted them. ²²Then all the wicked and worthless men* of those who went with David answered and said, "Because they did not go with us, we will not give them *any* of the spoil that we have recovered, except for every man's wife and children, that they may lead *them* away and depart."

²³But David said, "My brethren, you shall not do so with what the Lord has given us, who has preserved us and delivered into our hand the troop that

came against us. 24For who will heed you in this matter? But as his part *is* who goes down to the battle, so *shall* his part *be* who stays by the supplies; they shall share alike." 25So it was, from that day forward; he made it a statute and an ordinance for Israel to this day.

26Now when David came to Ziklag, he sent *some* of the spoil to the elders of Judah, to his friends, saying, "Here is a present for you from the spoil of the enemies of the LORD"— 27to *those* who *were* in Bethel, *those* who *were* in Ramoth of the South, *those* who *were* in Jattir, 28*those* who *were* in Aroer, *those* who *were* in Siphmoth, *those* who *were* in Eshtemoa, 29*those* who *were* in Rachal, *those* who *were* in the cities of the Jerahmeelites, *those* who *were* in the cities of the Kenites, 30*those* who *were* in Hormah, *those* who *were* in Chorashan,* *those* who *were* in Athach, 31*those* who *were* in Hebron, and to all the places where David himself and his men were accustomed to rove.

Now the Philistines fought against Israel; and the men of Israel fled from before the Philistines, and fell slain on Mount Gilboa. 2Then the Philistines followed hard after Saul and his sons. And the Philistines killed Jonathan, Abinadab, and Malchishua, Saul's sons. 3The battle became fierce against Saul. The archers hit him, and he was severely wounded by the archers.

4Then Saul said to his armorbearer, "Draw your sword, and thrust me through with it, lest these uncircumcised men come and thrust me through and abuse me."

But his armorbearer would not, for he was greatly afraid. Therefore Saul took a sword and fell on it. 5And when his armorbearer saw that Saul was dead, he also fell on his sword, and died with him. 6So Saul, his three sons,

his armorbearer, and all his men died together that same day.

7And when the men of Israel who *were* on the other side of the valley, and *those* who *were* on the other side of the Jordan, saw that the men of Israel had fled and that Saul and his sons were dead, they forsook the cities and fled; and the Philistines came and dwelt in them. 8So it happened the next day, when the Philistines came to strip the slain, that they found Saul and his three sons fallen on Mount Gilboa. 9And they cut off his head and stripped off his armor, and sent *word* throughout the land of the Philistines, to proclaim *it in* the temple of their idols and among the people. 10Then they put his armor in the temple of the Ashtoreths, and they fastened his body to the wall of Beth Shan.*

11Now when the inhabitants of Jabesh Gilead heard what the Philistines had done to Saul, 12all the valiant men arose and traveled all night, and took the body of Saul and the bodies of his sons from the wall of Beth Shan; and they came to Jabesh and burned them there. 13Then they took their bones and buried *them* under the tamarisk tree at Jabesh, and fasted seven days.

JOHN 11:55–12:19

AND the Passover of the Jews was near, and many went from the country up to Jerusalem before the Passover, to purify themselves. 56Then they sought Jesus, and spoke among themselves as they stood in the temple, "What do you think—that He will not come to the feast?" 57Now both the chief priests and the Pharisees had given a command, that if anyone knew where He was, he should report *it,* that they might seize Him.

THEN, six days before the Passover, Jesus came to Bethany, where Lazarus was who had been dead,* whom He had raised from the dead. ²There they made Him a supper; and Martha served, but Lazarus was one of those who sat at the table with Him. ³Then Mary took a pound of very costly oil of spikenard, anointed the feet of Jesus, and wiped His feet with her hair. And the house was filled with the fragrance of the oil.

⁴But one of His disciples, Judas Iscariot, Simon's *son,* who would betray Him, said, ⁵"Why was this fragrant oil not sold for three hundred denarii* and given to the poor?" ⁶This he said, not that he cared for the poor, but because he was a thief, and had the money box; and he used to take what was put in it.

⁷But Jesus said, "Let her alone; she has kept* this for the day of My burial. ⁸For the poor you have with you always, but Me you do not have always."

⁹Now a great many of the Jews knew that He was there; and they came, not for Jesus' sake only, but that they might also see Lazarus, whom He had raised from the dead. ¹⁰But the chief priests plotted to put Lazarus to death also, ¹¹because on account of him many of the Jews went away and believed in Jesus.

¹²The next day a great multitude that had come to the feast, when they heard that Jesus was coming to Jerusalem, ¹³took branches of palm trees and went out to meet Him, and cried out:

> "Hosanna!
> '*Blessed is He who comes in
>   the name of the LORD!*' *
> The King of Israel!"

¹⁴Then Jesus, when He had found a young donkey, sat on it; as it is written:

15 "*Fear not, daughter of Zion;
>   Behold, your King is coming,
>   Sitting on a donkey's colt.*" *

¹⁶His disciples did not understand these things at first; but when Jesus was glorified, then they remembered that these things were written about Him and *that* they had done these things to Him.

¹⁷Therefore the people, who were with Him when He called Lazarus out of his tomb and raised him from the dead, bore witness. ¹⁸For this reason the people also met Him, because they heard that He had done this sign. ¹⁹The Pharisees therefore said among themselves, "You see that you are accomplishing nothing. Look, the world has gone after Him!"

PSALM 118:1-18

O H, give thanks to the LORD, for
He is good!
For His mercy *endures*
forever.

2 Let Israel now say,
>   "His mercy *endures* forever."
3 Let the house of Aaron now
>   say,
>   "His mercy *endures* forever."
4 Let those who fear the LORD
>   now say,
>   "His mercy *endures* forever."

5 I called on the LORD in distress;
>   The LORD answered me *and
>   set me* in a broad place.
6 The LORD *is* on my side;
>   I will not fear.
>   What can man do to me?
7 The LORD is for me among
>   those who help me;
>   Therefore I shall see *my
>   desire* on those who hate
>   me.
8 *It is* better to trust in the LORD
>   Than to put confidence in
>   man.
9 *It is* better to trust in the LORD

Than to put confidence in
princes.

10 All nations surrounded me,
But in the name of the LORD I
will destroy them.
11 They surrounded me,
Yes, they surrounded me;
But in the name of the LORD I
will destroy them.
12 They surrounded me like
bees;
They were quenched like a
fire of thorns;
For in the name of the LORD I
will destroy them.
13 You pushed me violently, that
I might fall,
But the LORD helped me.
14 The LORD is my strength and
song,

And He has become my
salvation.*

15 The voice of rejoicing and
salvation
Is in the tents of the righteous;
The right hand of the LORD
does valiantly.
16 The right hand of the LORD is
exalted;
The right hand of the LORD
does valiantly.
17 I shall not die, but live,
And declare the works of the
LORD.
18 The LORD has chastened me
severely,
But He has not given me over
to death.

PROVERBS FOR TODAY/ 15:24-26

The way of life winds *upward for the wise, that he may turn away from hell** below.*
□ *The* LORD *will destroy the house of the proud, but He will establish the boundary
of the widow.* □ *The thoughts of the wicked* are *an abomination to the* LORD, *but*
the words *of the pure* are *pleasant.*

MAY 22

2 SAMUEL 1:1–2:11

Now it came to pass after the
death of Saul, when David had
returned from the slaughter of
the Amalekites, and David had stayed
two days in Ziklag, 2on the third day,
behold, it happened that a man came
from Saul's camp with his clothes torn
and dust on his head. So it was, when
he came to David, that he fell to the
ground and prostrated himself.
3And David said to him, "Where
have you come from?"

So he said to him, "I have escaped
from the camp of Israel."
4Then David said to him, "How did
the matter go? Please tell me."
And he answered, "The people have
fled from the battle, many of the
people are fallen and dead, and Saul
and Jonathan his son are dead also."
5So David said to the young man
who told him, "How do you know that
Saul and Jonathan his son are dead?"
6Then the young man who told him
said, "As I happened by chance to be on
Mount Gilboa, there was Saul, leaning

on his spear; and indeed the chariots and horsemen followed hard after him. 7Now when he looked behind him, he saw me and called to me. And I answered, 'Here I am.' 8And he said to me, 'Who *are* you?' So I answered him, 'I *am* an Amalekite.' 9He said to me again, 'Please stand over me and kill me, for anguish has come upon me, but my life still *remains* in me.' 10So I stood over him and killed him, because I was sure that he could not live after he had fallen. And I took the crown that *was* on his head and the bracelet that *was* on his arm, and have brought them here to my lord."

11Therefore David took hold of his own clothes and tore them, and *so did* all the men who *were* with him. 12And they mourned and wept and fasted until evening for Saul and for Jonathan his son, for the people of the LORD and for the house of Israel, because they had fallen by the sword.

13Then David said to the young man who told him, "Where *are* you from?"

And he answered, "I *am* the son of an alien, an Amalekite."

14So David said to him, "How was it you were not afraid to put forth your hand to destroy the LORD's anointed?" 15Then David called one of the young men and said, "Go near, *and* execute him!" And he struck him so that he died. 16So David said to him, "Your blood *is* on your own head, for your own mouth has testified against you, saying, 'I have killed the LORD's anointed.' "

17Then David lamented with this lamentation over Saul and over Jonathan his son, 18and he told *them* to teach the children of Judah *the Song of* the Bow; indeed *it is* written in the Book of Jasher:

19 "The beauty of Israel is slain
  on your high places!
 How the mighty have fallen!

20 Tell *it* not in Gath,
 Proclaim *it* not in the streets
  of Ashkelon—
 Lest the daughters of the
  Philistines rejoice,
 Lest the daughters of the
  uncircumcised triumph.

21 "O mountains of Gilboa,
 Let there be no dew nor rain
  upon you,
 Nor fields of offerings.
 For the shield of the mighty is
  cast away there!
 The shield of Saul, not
  anointed with oil.

22 From the blood of the slain,
 From the fat of the mighty,
 The bow of Jonathan did not
  turn back,
 And the sword of Saul did not
  return empty.

23 "Saul and Jonathan *were*
  beloved and pleasant in
  their lives,
 And in their death they were
  not divided;
 They were swifter than eagles,
 They were stronger than lions.

24 "O daughters of Israel, weep
  over Saul,
 Who clothed you in scarlet,
  with luxury;
 Who put ornaments of gold
  on your apparel.

25 "How the mighty have fallen in
  the midst of the battle!
 Jonathan *was* slain in your
  high places.

26 I am distressed for you, my
  brother Jonathan;
 You have been very pleasant
  to me;
 Your love to me was
  wonderful,
 Surpassing the love of women.

²⁷ "How the mighty have fallen,
And the weapons of war
perished!"

Iᴛ happened after this that David inquired of the Lᴏʀᴅ, saying, "Shall I go up to any of the cities of Judah?"

And the Lᴏʀᴅ said to him, "Go up."
David said, "Where shall I go up?"
And He said, "To Hebron."

²So David went up there, and his two wives also, Ahinoam the Jezreelitess, and Abigail the widow of Nabal the Carmelite. ³And David brought up the men who *were* with him, every man with his household. So they dwelt in the cities of Hebron.

⁴Then the men of Judah came, and there they anointed David king over the house of Judah. And they told David, saying, "The men of Jabesh Gilead *were the ones* who buried Saul." ⁵So David sent messengers to the men of Jabesh Gilead, and said to them, "You *are* blessed of the Lᴏʀᴅ, for you have shown this kindness to your lord, to Saul, and have buried him. ⁶And now may the Lᴏʀᴅ show kindness and truth to you. I also will repay you this kindness, because you have done this thing. ⁷Now therefore, let your hands be strengthened, and be valiant; for your master Saul is dead, and also the house of Judah has anointed me king over them."

⁸But Abner the son of Ner, commander of Saul's army, took Ishbosheth* the son of Saul and brought him over to Mahanaim; ⁹and he made him king over Gilead, over the Ashurites, over Jezreel, over Ephraim, over Benjamin, and over all Israel. ¹⁰Ishbosheth, Saul's son, *was* forty years old when he began to reign over Israel, and he reigned two years. Only the house of Judah followed David. ¹¹And the time that David was king in Hebron over the house of Judah was seven years and six months.

JOHN 12:20-50

Now there were certain Greeks among those who came up to worship at the feast. ²¹Then they came to Philip, who was from Bethsaida of Galilee, and asked him, saying, "Sir, we wish to see Jesus."

²²Philip came and told Andrew, and in turn Andrew and Philip told Jesus.

²³But Jesus answered them, saying, "The hour has come that the Son of Man should be glorified. ²⁴Most assuredly, I say to you, unless a grain of wheat falls into the ground and dies, it remains alone; but if it dies, it produces much grain. ²⁵He who loves his life will lose it, and he who hates his life in this world will keep it for eternal life. ²⁶If anyone serves Me, let him follow Me; and where I am, there My servant will be also. If anyone serves Me, him *My* Father will honor.

²⁷"Now My soul is troubled, and what shall I say? 'Father, save Me from this hour'? But for this purpose I came to this hour. ²⁸Father, glorify Your name."

Then a voice came from heaven, *saying,* "I have both glorified *it* and will glorify *it* again."

²⁹Therefore the people who stood by and heard *it* said that it had thundered. Others said, "An angel has spoken to Him."

³⁰Jesus answered and said, "This voice did not come because of Me, but for your sake. ³¹Now is the judgment of this world; now the ruler of this world will be cast out. ³²And I, if I am lifted up from the earth, will draw all *peoples* to Myself." ³³This He said, signifying by what death He would die.

³⁴The people answered Him, "We have heard from the law that the Christ remains forever; and how *can* You say, 'The Son of Man must be lifted up'? Who is this Son of Man?"

³⁵Then Jesus said to them, "A little while longer the light is with you. Walk

while you have the light, lest darkness overtake you; he who walks in darkness does not know where he is going. [36]While you have the light, believe in the light, that you may become sons of light." These things Jesus spoke, and departed, and was hidden from them.

[37]But although He had done so many signs before them, they did not believe in Him, [38]that the word of Isaiah the prophet might be fulfilled, which he spoke:

> "Lord, who has believed our
> report?
> And to whom has the arm of
> the LORD been revealed?" *

[39]Therefore they could not believe, because Isaiah said again:

[40] "He has blinded their eyes and
> hardened their hearts,
> Lest they should see with
> their eyes,
> Lest they should understand
> with their hearts and turn,
> So that I should heal them." *

[41]These things Isaiah said when* he saw His glory and spoke of Him.

[42]Nevertheless even among the rulers many believed in Him, but because of the Pharisees they did not confess Him, lest they should be put out of the synagogue; [43]for they loved the praise of men more than the praise of God.

[44]Then Jesus cried out and said, "He who believes in Me, believes not in Me but in Him who sent Me. [45]And he who sees Me sees Him who sent Me. [46]I have come as a light into the world, that whoever believes in Me should not abide in darkness. [47]And if anyone hears My words and does not believe,* I do not judge him; for I did not come to judge the world but to save the world. [48]He who rejects Me, and does not receive My words, has that which judges him—the word that I have spoken will judge him in the last day. [49]For I have not spoken on My own author-

ity; but the Father who sent Me gave Me a command, what I should say and what I should speak. [50]And I know that His command is everlasting life. Therefore, whatever I speak, just as the Father has told Me, so I speak."

PSALM 118:19-29

OPEN to me the gates of righteousness;
> I will go through them,
> And I will praise the LORD.
20 This is the gate of the LORD,
> Through which the righteous
> shall enter.

21 I will praise You,
> For You have answered me,
> And have become my
> salvation.

22 The stone which the builders
> rejected
> Has become the chief
> cornerstone.
23 This was the LORD's doing;
> It is marvelous in our eyes.
24 This is the day the LORD has
> made;
> We will rejoice and be glad
> in it.

25 Save now, I pray, O LORD;
> O LORD, I pray, send now
> prosperity.
26 Blessed is he who comes in
> the name of the LORD!
> We have blessed you from the
> house of the LORD.
27 God is the LORD,
> And He has given us light;
> Bind the sacrifice with cords
> to the horns of the altar.
28 You are my God, and I will
> praise You;
> You are my God, I will exalt
> You.

29   Oh, give thanks to the Lord,
      for *He is* good!

For His mercy *endures* forever.

PROVERBS FOR TODAY/ 15:27-28

He who is greedy for gain troubles his own house, but he who hates bribes will live.
☐ *The heart of the righteous studies how to answer, but the mouth of the wicked pours forth evil.*

MAY 23

2 SAMUEL 2:12–3:39

Now Abner the son of Ner, and the servants of Ishbosheth the son of Saul, went out from Mahanaim to Gibeon. 13And Joab the son of Zeruiah, and the servants of David, went out and met them by the pool of Gibeon. So they sat down, one on one side of the pool and the other on the other side of the pool. 14Then Abner said to Joab, "Let the young men now arise and compete before us."

And Joab said, "Let them arise."

15So they arose and went over by number, twelve from Benjamin, *followers* of Ishbosheth the son of Saul, and twelve from the servants of David. 16And each one grasped his opponent by the head and *thrust* his sword in his opponent's side; so they fell down together. Therefore that place was called the Field of Sharp Swords,* which *is* in Gibeon. 17So there was a very fierce battle that day, and Abner and the men of Israel were beaten before the servants of David.

18Now the three sons of Zeruiah were there: Joab and Abishai and Asahel. And Asahel *was as* fleet of foot as a wild gazelle. 19So Asahel pursued Abner, and in going he did not turn to the right hand or to the left from following Abner.

20Then Abner looked behind him and said, "*Are* you Asahel?"

He answered, "I *am.*"

21And Abner said to him, "Turn aside to your right hand or to your left, and lay hold on one of the young men and take his armor for yourself." But Asahel would not turn aside from following him. 22So Abner said again to Asahel, "Turn aside from following me. Why should I strike you to the ground? How then could I face your brother Joab?" 23However, he refused to turn aside. Therefore Abner struck him in the stomach with the blunt end of the spear, so that the spear came out of his back; and he fell down there and died on the spot. So it was *that* as many as came to the place where Asahel fell down and died, stood still.

24Joab and Abishai also pursued Abner. And the sun was going down when they came to the hill of Ammah, which *is* before Giah by the road to the Wilderness of Gibeon. 25Now the children of Benjamin gathered together behind Abner and became a unit, and took their stand on top of a hill. 26Then Abner called to Joab and said, "Shall the sword devour forever? Do you not know that it will be bitter in the latter end? How long will it be then until you tell the people to return from pursuing their brethren?"

27And Joab said, "*As* God lives, unless you had spoken, surely then by morning all the people would have given up pursuing their brethren." 28So Joab blew a trumpet; and all the people stood still and did not pursue Israel anymore, nor did they fight anymore. 29Then Abner and his men went on all that night through the plain, crossed over the Jordan, and went through all Bithron; and they came to Mahanaim.

30So Joab returned from pursuing Abner. And when he had gathered all the people together, there were missing of David's servants nineteen men and Asahel. 31But the servants of David had struck down, of Benjamin and Abner's men, three hundred and sixty men who died. 32Then they took up Asahel and buried him in his father's tomb, which *was in* Bethlehem. And Joab and his men went all night, and they came to Hebron at daybreak.

Now there was a long war between the house of Saul and the house of David. But David grew stronger and stronger, and the house of Saul grew weaker and weaker.

2Sons were born to David in Hebron: His firstborn was Amnon by Ahinoam the Jezreelitess; 3his second, Chileab, by Abigail the widow of Nabal the Carmelite; the third, Absalom the son of Maacah, the daughter of Talmai, king of Geshur; 4the fourth, Adonijah the son of Haggith; the fifth, Shephatiah the son of Abital; 5and the sixth, Ithream, by David's wife Eglah. These were born to David in Hebron.

6Now it was so, while there was war between the house of Saul and the house of David, that Abner was strengthening *his hold* on the house of Saul.

7And Saul had a concubine, whose name *was* Rizpah, the daughter of Aiah. So *Ishbosheth* said to Abner, "Why have you gone in to my father's concubine?"

8Then Abner became very angry at the words of Ishbosheth, and said, "*Am* I a dog's head that belongs to Judah? Today I show loyalty to the house of Saul your father, to his brothers, and to his friends, and have not delivered you into the hand of David; and you charge me today with a fault concerning this woman? 9May God do so to Abner, and more also, if I do not do for David as the LORD has sworn to him— 10to transfer the kingdom from the house of Saul, and set up the throne of David over Israel and over Judah, from Dan to Beersheba." 11And he could not answer Abner another word, because he feared him.

12Then Abner sent messengers on his behalf to David, saying, "Whose *is* the land?" saying *also,* "Make your covenant with me, and indeed my hand *shall be* with you to bring all Israel to you."

13And *David* said, "Good, I will make a covenant with you. But one thing I require of you: you shall not see my face unless you first bring Michal, Saul's daughter, when you come to see my face." 14So David sent messengers to Ishbosheth, Saul's son, saying, "Give *me* my wife Michal, whom I betrothed to myself for a hundred foreskins of the Philistines." 15And Ishbosheth sent and took her from *her* husband, from Paltiel* the son of Laish. 16Then her husband went along with her to Bahurim, weeping behind her. So Abner said to him, "Go, return!" And he returned.

17Now Abner had communicated with the elders of Israel, saying, "In time past you were seeking for David *to be* king over you. 18Now then, do *it!* For the LORD has spoken of David, saying, 'By the hand of My servant David, I* will save My people Israel from the hand of the Philistines and the hand of all their enemies.' " 19And Abner also spoke in the hearing of Benjamin. Then Abner also went to speak in the hearing of David in Hebron all that seemed good to Israel and the whole house of Benjamin.

²⁰So Abner and twenty men with him came to David at Hebron. And David made a feast for Abner and the men who *were* with him. ²¹Then Abner said to David, "I will arise and go, and gather all Israel to my lord the king, that they may make a covenant with you, and that you may reign over all that your heart desires." So David sent Abner away, and he went in peace.

²²At that moment the servants of David and Joab came from a raid and brought much spoil with them. But Abner *was* not with David in Hebron, for he had sent him away, and he had gone in peace. ²³When Joab and all the troops that *were* with him had come, they told Joab, saying, "Abner the son of Ner came to the king, and he sent him away, and he has gone in peace." ²⁴Then Joab came to the king and said, "What have you done? Look, Abner came to you; why *is* it *that* you sent him away, and he has already gone? ²⁵Surely you realize that Abner the son of Ner came to deceive you, to know your going out and your coming in, and to know all that you are doing."

²⁶And when Joab had gone from David's presence, he sent messengers after Abner, who brought him back from the well of Sirah. But David did not know *it*. ²⁷Now when Abner had returned to Hebron, Joab took him aside in the gate to speak with him privately, and there stabbed him in the stomach, so that he died for the blood of Asahel his brother.

²⁸Afterward, when David heard *it,* he said, "My kingdom and I *are* guiltless before the LORD forever of the blood of Abner the son of Ner. ²⁹Let it rest on the head of Joab and on all his father's house; and let there never fail to be in the house of Joab one who has a discharge or is a leper, who leans on a staff or falls by the sword, or who lacks bread." ³⁰So Joab and Abishai his brother killed Abner, because he had killed their brother Asahel at Gibeon in the battle.

³¹Then David said to Joab and to all the people who were with him, "Tear your clothes, gird yourselves with sackcloth, and mourn for Abner." And King David followed the coffin. ³²So they buried Abner in Hebron; and the king lifted up his voice and wept at the grave of Abner, and all the people wept. ³³And the king sang *a lament* over Abner and said:

> "Should Abner die as a fool
>   dies?
> 34 Your hands were not bound
>   Nor your feet put into fetters;
>   As a man falls before wicked
>   men, *so* you fell."

Then all the people wept over him again.

³⁵And when all the people came to persuade David to eat food while it was still day, David took an oath, saying, "God do so to me, and more also, if I taste bread or anything else till the sun goes down!" ³⁶Now all the people took note *of it,* and it pleased them, since whatever the king did pleased all the people. ³⁷For all the people and all Israel understood that day that it had not been the king's *intent* to kill Abner the son of Ner. ³⁸Then the king said to his servants, "Do you not know that a prince and a great man has fallen this day in Israel? ³⁹And I *am* weak today, though anointed king; and these men, the sons of Zeruiah, *are* too harsh for me. The LORD shall repay the evildoer according to his wickedness."

JOHN 13:1-30

Now before the Feast of the Passover, when Jesus knew that His hour had come that He should depart from this world to the Father, having loved His own who were in the world, He loved them to the end.

²And supper being ended,* the devil having already put it into the heart of Judas Iscariot, Simon's *son,* to betray Him, ³Jesus, knowing that the Father had given all things into His hands, and that He had come from God and was going to God, ⁴rose from supper and laid aside His garments, took a towel and girded Himself. ⁵After that, He poured water into a basin and began to wash the disciples' feet, and to wipe *them* with the towel with which He was girded. ⁶Then He came to Simon Peter. And *Peter* said to Him, "Lord, are You washing my feet?"

⁷Jesus answered and said to him, "What I am doing you do not understand now, but you will know after this."

⁸Peter said to Him, "You shall never wash my feet!"

Jesus answered him, "If I do not wash you, you have no part with Me."

⁹Simon Peter said to Him, "Lord, not my feet only, but also *my* hands and *my* head!"

¹⁰Jesus said to him, "He who is bathed needs only to wash *his* feet, but is completely clean; and you are clean, but not all of you." ¹¹For He knew who would betray Him; therefore He said, "You are not all clean."

¹²So when He had washed their feet, taken His garments, and sat down again, He said to them, "Do you know what I have done to you? ¹³You call Me Teacher and Lord, and you say well, for *so* I am. ¹⁴If I then, *your* Lord and Teacher, have washed your feet, you also ought to wash one another's feet. ¹⁵For I have given you an example, that you should do as I have done to you. ¹⁶Most assuredly, I say to you, a servant is not greater than his master; nor is he who is sent greater than he who sent him. ¹⁷If you know these things, blessed are you if you do them. ¹⁸"I do not speak concerning all of you. I know whom I have chosen; but that the Scripture may be fulfilled, *'He who eats bread with Me * has lifted up his heel against Me.'* * ¹⁹Now I tell you before it comes, that when it does come to pass, you may believe that I am *He.* ²⁰Most assuredly, I say to you, he who receives whomever I send receives Me; and he who receives Me receives Him who sent Me."

²¹When Jesus had said these things, He was troubled in spirit, and testified and said, "Most assuredly, I say to you, one of you will betray Me." ²²Then the disciples looked at one another, perplexed about whom He spoke.

²³Now there was leaning on Jesus' bosom one of His disciples, whom Jesus loved. ²⁴Simon Peter therefore motioned to him to ask who it was of whom He spoke.

²⁵Then, leaning back* on Jesus' breast, he said to Him, "Lord, who is it?"

²⁶Jesus answered, "It is he to whom I shall give a piece of bread when I have dipped *it.*" And having dipped the bread, He gave *it* to Judas Iscariot, *the son* of Simon. ²⁷Now after the piece of bread, Satan entered him. Then Jesus said to him, "What you do, do quickly." ²⁸But no one at the table knew for what reason He said this to him. ²⁹For some thought, because Judas had the money box, that Jesus had said to him, "Buy *those things* we need for the feast," or that he should give something to the poor.

³⁰Having received the piece of bread, he then went out immediately. And it was night.

PSALM 119:1-16

א   ALEPH

BLESSED *are* the undefiled in the way,
Who walk in the law of the Lᴏʀᴅ!

2 Blessed *are* those who keep
  His testimonies,
  Who seek Him with the whole
  heart!
3 They also do no iniquity;
  They walk in His ways.
4 You have commanded *us*
  To keep Your precepts
  diligently.
5 Oh, that my ways were
  directed
  To keep Your statutes!
6 Then I would not be ashamed,
  When I look into all Your
  commandments.
7 I will praise You with
  uprightness of heart,
  When I learn Your righteous
  judgments.
8 I will keep Your statutes;
  Oh, do not forsake me utterly!

ב BETH

9 How can a young man cleanse
  his way?

By taking heed according to
  Your word.
10 With my whole heart I have
  sought You;
  Oh, let me not wander from
  Your commandments!
11 Your word I have hidden in
  my heart,
  That I might not sin against
  You.
12 Blessed *are* You, O LORD!
  Teach me Your statutes.
13 With my lips I have declared
  All the judgments of Your
  mouth.
14 I have rejoiced in the way of
  Your testimonies,
  As *much as* in all riches.
15 I will meditate on Your
  precepts,
  And contemplate Your ways.
16 I will delight myself in Your
  statutes;
  I will not forget Your word.

PROVERBS FOR TODAY/ 15:29-30

The LORD is far from the wicked, but He hears the prayer of the righteous. □ *The light of the eyes rejoices the heart,* and *a good report makes the bones healthy.* *

MAY 24

2 SAMUEL 4:1–6:23

WHEN Saul's son* heard that Abner had died in Hebron, he lost heart, and all Israel was troubled. 2Now Saul's son *had* two men *who were* captains of troops. The name of one *was* Baanah and the name of the other Rechab, the sons of Rimmon the Beerothite, of the children of Benjamin. (For Beeroth also was *part* of Benjamin, 3because the Be-

erothites fled to Gittaim and have been sojourners there until this day.)

4Jonathan, Saul's son, had a son *who was* lame in *his* feet. He was five years old when the news about Saul and Jonathan came from Jezreel; and his nurse took him up and fled. And it happened, as she made haste to flee, that he fell and became lame. His name *was* Mephibosheth.*

5Then the sons of Rimmon the Beerothite, Rechab and Baanah, set out and came at about the heat of the day to the house of Ishbosheth, who was lying on his bed at noon. 6And they came there, all the way into the house, *as though* to get wheat, and they stabbed him in the stomach. Then Rechab and Baanah his brother escaped. 7For when they came into the house, he was lying on his bed in his bedroom; then they struck him and killed him, beheaded him and took his head, and were all night escaping through the plain. 8And they brought the head of Ishbosheth to David at Hebron, and said to the king, "Here is the head of Ishbosheth, the son of Saul your enemy, who sought your life; and the LORD has avenged my lord the king this day of Saul and his descendants."

9But David answered Rechab and Baanah his brother, the sons of Rimmon the Beerothite, and said to them, "*As* the LORD lives, who has redeemed my life from all adversity, 10when someone told me, saying, 'Look, Saul is dead,' thinking to have brought good news, I arrested him and had him executed in Ziklag—the one who *thought* I would give him a reward for *his* news. 11How much more, when wicked men have killed a righteous person in his own house on his bed? Therefore, shall I not now require his blood at your hand and remove you from the earth?" 12So David commanded his young men, and they executed them, cut off their hands and feet, and hanged *them* by the pool in Hebron. But they took the head of Ishbosheth and buried *it* in the tomb of Abner in Hebron.

THEN all the tribes of Israel came to David at Hebron and spoke, saying, "Indeed we *are* your bone and your flesh. 2Also, in time past, when Saul was king over us, you were the one who led Israel out and brought them in; and the LORD said to you, 'You shall shepherd My people Israel, and be ruler over Israel.' " 3Therefore all the elders of Israel came to the king at Hebron, and King David made a covenant with them at Hebron before the LORD. And they anointed David king over Israel. 4David *was* thirty years old when he began to reign, *and* he reigned forty years. 5In Hebron he reigned over Judah seven years and six months, and in Jerusalem he reigned thirty-three years over all Israel and Judah.

6And the king and his men went to Jerusalem against the Jebusites, the inhabitants of the land, who spoke to David, saying, "You shall not come in here; but the blind and the lame will repel you," thinking, "David cannot come in here." 7Nevertheless David took the stronghold of Zion (that *is,* the City of David).

8Now David said on that day, "Whoever climbs up by way of the water shaft and defeats the Jebusites (the lame and the blind, *who are* hated by David's soul), *he shall be chief and captain.*"* Therefore they say, "The blind and the lame shall not come into the house."

9Then David dwelt in the stronghold, and called it the City of David. And David built all around from the Millo* and inward. 10So David went on and became great, and the LORD God of hosts *was* with him.

11Then Hiram king of Tyre sent messengers to David, and cedar trees, and carpenters and masons. And they built David a house. 12So David knew that the LORD had established him as king over Israel, and that He had exalted His kingdom for the sake of His people Israel.

13And David took more concubines and wives from Jerusalem, after he had come from Hebron. Also more sons and daughters were born to David. 14Now these *are* the names of those who were born to him in Jerusalem: Shammua,* Shobab, Nathan, Solomon,

15Ibhar, Elishua,* Nepheg, Japhia, 16Elishama, Eliada, and Eliphelet.

17Now when the Philistines heard that they had anointed David king over Israel, all the Philistines went up to search for David. And David heard *of it* and went down to the stronghold. 18The Philistines also went and deployed themselves in the Valley of Rephaim. 19So David inquired of the LORD, saying, "Shall I go up against the Philistines? Will You deliver them into my hand?"

And the LORD said to David, "Go up, for I will doubtless deliver the Philistines into your hand."

20So David went to Baal Perazim, and David defeated them there; and he said, "The LORD has broken through my enemies before me, like a breakthrough of water." Therefore he called the name of that place Baal Perazim.* 21And they left their images there, and David and his men carried them away.

22Then the Philistines went up once again and deployed themselves in the Valley of Rephaim. 23Therefore David inquired of the LORD, and He said, "You shall not go up; circle around behind them, and come upon them in front of the mulberry trees. 24And it shall be, when you hear the sound of marching in the tops of the mulberry trees, then you shall advance quickly. For then the LORD will go out before you to strike the camp of the Philistines." 25And David did so, as the LORD commanded him; and he drove back the Philistines from Geba* as far as Gezer.

AGAIN David gathered all *the* choice *men* of Israel, thirty thousand. 2And David arose and went with all the people who *were* with him from Baale Judah to bring up from there the ark of God, whose name is called by the Name,* the LORD of Hosts, who dwells *between* the cherubim. 3So they set the ark of God on a new cart, and brought it out of the house of Abinadab, which *was* on the hill; and Uzzah and Ahio, the sons of Abinadab, drove the new cart.* 4And they brought it out of the house of Abinadab, which *was* on the hill, accompanying the ark of God; and Ahio went before the ark. 5Then David and all the house of Israel played *music* before the LORD on all kinds of *instruments of* fir wood, on harps, on stringed instruments, on tambourines, on sistrums, and on cymbals.

6And when they came to Nachon's threshing floor, Uzzah put out *his hand* to the ark of God and took hold of it, for the oxen stumbled. 7Then the anger of the LORD was aroused against Uzzah, and God struck him there for *his* error; and he died there by the ark of God. 8And David became angry because of the LORD's outbreak against Uzzah; and he called the name of the place Perez Uzzah* to this day.

9David was afraid of the LORD that day; and he said, "How can the ark of the LORD come to me?" 10So David would not move the ark of the LORD with him into the City of David; but David took it aside into the house of Obed-Edom the Gittite. 11The ark of the LORD remained in the house of Obed-Edom the Gittite three months. And the LORD blessed Obed-Edom and all his household.

12Now it was told King David, saying, "The LORD has blessed the house of Obed-Edom and all that *belongs* to him, because of the ark of God." So David went and brought up the ark of God from the house of Obed-Edom to the City of David with gladness. 13And so it was, when those bearing the ark of the LORD had gone six paces, that he sacrificed oxen and fatted sheep. 14Then David danced before the LORD with all *his* might; and David *was* wearing a linen ephod. 15So David and all the house of Israel brought up the ark of the LORD with shouting and with the sound of the trumpet.

16Now as the ark of the LORD came

into the City of David, Michal, Saul's daughter, looked through a window and saw King David leaping and whirling before the Lord; and she despised him in her heart. [17]So they brought the ark of the Lord, and set it in its place in the midst of the tabernacle that David had erected for it. Then David offered burnt offerings and peace offerings before the Lord. [18]And when David had finished offering burnt offerings and peace offerings, he blessed the people in the name of the Lord of hosts. [19]Then he distributed among all the people, among the whole multitude of Israel, both the women and the men, to everyone a loaf of bread, a piece *of meat,* and a cake of raisins. So all the people departed, everyone to his house.

[20]Then David returned to bless his household. And Michal the daughter of Saul came out to meet David, and said, "How glorious was the king of Israel today, uncovering himself today in the eyes of the maids of his servants, as one of the base fellows shamelessly uncovers himself!"

[21]So David said to Michal, "*It was* before the Lord, who chose me instead of your father and all his house, to appoint me ruler over the people of the Lord, over Israel. Therefore I will play *music* before the Lord. [22]And I will be even more undignified than this, and will be humble in my own sight. But as for the maidservants of whom you have spoken, by them I will be held in honor."

[23]Therefore Michal the daughter of Saul had no children to the day of her death.

JOHN 13:31–14:14

So, when he [Judas Iscariot] had gone out, Jesus said, "Now the Son of Man is glorified, and God is glorified in Him. [32]If God is glorified in Him, God will also glorify Him in Himself, and glorify Him immediately. [33]Little children, I shall be with you a little while longer. You will seek Me; and as I said to the Jews, 'Where I am going, you cannot come,' so now I say to you. [34]A new commandment I give to you, that you love one another; as I have loved you, that you also love one another. [35]By this all will know that you are My disciples, if you have love for one another."

[36]Simon Peter said to Him, "Lord, where are You going?"

Jesus answered him, "Where I am going you cannot follow Me now, but you shall follow Me afterward."

[37]Peter said to Him, "Lord, why can I not follow You now? I will lay down my life for Your sake."

[38]Jesus answered him, "Will you lay down your life for My sake? Most assuredly, I say to you, the rooster shall not crow till you have denied Me three times.

"Let not your heart be troubled; you believe in God, believe also in Me. [2]In My Father's house are many mansions;* if *it were* not *so,* I would have told you. I go to prepare a place for you.* [3]And if I go and prepare a place for you, I will come again and receive you to Myself; that where I am, *there* you may be also. [4]And where I go you know, and the way you know."

[5]Thomas said to Him, "Lord, we do not know where You are going, and how can we know the way?"

[6]Jesus said to him, "I am the way, the truth, and the life. No one comes to the Father except through Me.

[7]"If you had known Me, you would have known My Father also; and from now on you know Him and have seen Him."

[8]Philip said to Him, "Lord, show us the Father, and it is sufficient for us."

[9]Jesus said to him, "Have I been with you so long, and yet you have not known Me, Philip? He who has seen

Me has seen the Father; so how can you say, 'Show us the Father'? [10]Do you not believe that I am in the Father, and the Father in Me? The words that I speak to you I do not speak on My own *authority;* but the Father who dwells in Me does the works. [11]Believe Me that I *am* in the Father and the Father in Me, or else believe Me for the sake of the works themselves.

[12]"Most assuredly, I say to you, he who believes in Me, the works that I do he will do also; and greater *works* than these he will do, because I go to My Father. [13]And whatever you ask in My name, that I will do, that the Father may be glorified in the Son. [14]If you ask* anything in My name, I will do *it.*"

PSALM 119:17-32

ℷ GIMEL

DEAL bountifully with Your servant,
   That I may live and keep Your word.
18   Open my eyes, that I may see Wondrous things from Your law.
19   I *am* a stranger in the earth; Do not hide Your commandments from me.
20   My soul breaks with longing For Your judgments at all times.
21   You rebuke the proud—the cursed, Who stray from Your commandments.

22   Remove from me reproach and contempt, For I have kept Your testimonies.
23   Princes also sit *and* speak against me, *But* Your servant meditates on Your statutes.
24   Your testimonies also *are* my delight *And* my counselors.

ר DALETH

25   My soul clings to the dust; Revive me according to Your word.
26   I have declared my ways, and You answered me; Teach me Your statutes.
27   Make me understand the way of Your precepts; So shall I meditate on Your wonderful works.
28   My soul melts from heaviness; Strengthen me according to Your word.
29   Remove from me the way of lying, And grant me Your law graciously.
30   I have chosen the way of truth; Your judgments I have laid *before me.*
31   I cling to Your testimonies; O LORD, do not put me to shame!
32   I will run the course of Your commandments, For You shall enlarge my heart.

PROVERBS FOR TODAY/ 15:31-32

The ear that hears the rebukes of life will abide among the wise. He who disdains instruction despises his own soul, but he who heeds rebuke gets understanding.

MAY 25

2 SAMUEL 7:1–8:18

Now it came to pass when the king [David] was dwelling in his house, and the LORD had given him rest from all his enemies all around, ²that the king said to Nathan the prophet, "See now, I dwell in a house of cedar, but the ark of God dwells inside tent curtains."

³Then Nathan said to the king, "Go, do all that *is* in your heart, for the LORD *is* with you."

⁴But it happened that night that the word of the LORD came to Nathan, saying, ⁵"Go and tell My servant David, 'Thus says the LORD: "Would you build a house for Me to dwell in? ⁶For I have not dwelt in a house since the time that I brought the children of Israel up from Egypt, even to this day, but have moved about in a tent and in a tabernacle. ⁷Wherever I have moved about with all the children of Israel, have I ever spoken a word to anyone from the tribes of Israel, whom I commanded to shepherd My people Israel, saying, 'Why have you not built Me a house of cedar?' " ' ⁸Now therefore, thus shall you say to My servant David, 'Thus says the LORD of hosts: "I took you from the sheepfold, from following the sheep, to be ruler over My people, over Israel. ⁹And I have been with you wherever you have gone, and have cut off all your enemies from before you, and have made you a great name, like the name of the great men who *are* on the earth. ¹⁰Moreover I will appoint a place for My people Israel, and will plant them, that they may dwell in a place of their own and move no more; nor shall the sons of wickedness oppress them anymore, as previously, ¹¹since the time that I commanded judges *to be* over My people Israel, and have caused you to rest from all your enemies. Also the LORD tells you that He will make you a house.*

¹²"When your days are fulfilled and you rest with your fathers, I will set up your seed after you, who will come from your body, and I will establish his kingdom. ¹³He shall build a house for My name, and I will establish the throne of his kingdom forever. ¹⁴I will be his Father, and he shall be My son. If he commits iniquity, I will chasten him with the rod of men and with the blows of the sons of men. ¹⁵But My mercy shall not depart from him, as I took *it* from Saul, whom I removed from before you. ¹⁶And your house and your kingdom shall be established forever before you.* Your throne shall be established forever." ' "

¹⁷According to all these words and according to all this vision, so Nathan spoke to David.

¹⁸Then King David went in and sat before the LORD; and he said: "Who *am* I, O Lord GOD? And what is my house, that You have brought me this far? ¹⁹And yet this was a small thing in Your sight, O Lord GOD; and You have also spoken of Your servant's house for a great while to come. *Is* this the manner of man, O Lord GOD? ²⁰Now what more can David say to You? For You, Lord GOD, know Your servant. ²¹For Your word's sake, and according to Your own heart, You have done all these great things, to make Your servant know *them*. ²²Therefore You are great, O Lord GOD.* For *there is* none like You, nor *is there any* God besides You, according to all that we have heard with our ears. ²³And who *is* like Your people, like Israel, the one nation on the earth whom God went to re-

deem for Himself as a people, to make for Himself a name—and to do for Yourself great and awesome deeds for Your land—before Your people whom You redeemed for Yourself from Egypt, the nations, and their gods? 24For You have made Your people Israel Your very own people forever; and You, LORD, have become their God.

25"Now, O LORD God, the word which You have spoken concerning Your servant and concerning his house, establish it forever and do as You have said. 26So let Your name be magnified forever, saying, 'The LORD of hosts is the God over Israel.' And let the house of Your servant David be established before You. 27For You, O LORD of hosts, God of Israel, have revealed this to Your servant, saying, 'I will build you a house.' Therefore Your servant has found it in his heart to pray this prayer to You.

28"And now, O Lord GOD, You are God, and Your words are true, and You have promised this goodness to Your servant. 29Now therefore, let it please You to bless the house of Your servant, that it may continue before You forever; for You, O Lord GOD, have spoken it, and with Your blessing let the house of Your servant be blessed forever."

AFTER this it came to pass that David attacked the Philistines and subdued them. And David took Metheg Ammah from the hand of the Philistines.

2Then he defeated Moab. Forcing them down to the ground, he measured them off with a line. With two lines he measured off those to be put to death, and with one full line those to be kept alive. So the Moabites became David's servants, and brought tribute.

3David also defeated Hadadezer the son of Rehob, king of Zobah, as he went to recover his territory at the River Euphrates. 4David took from him one thousand chariots, seven hundred* horsemen, and twenty thousand foot soldiers. Also David hamstrung all the chariot horses, except that he spared enough of them for one hundred chariots.

5When the Syrians of Damascus came to help Hadadezer king of Zobah, David killed twenty-two thousand of the Syrians. 6Then David put garrisons in Syria of Damascus; and the Syrians became David's servants, and brought tribute. So the LORD preserved David wherever he went. 7And David took the shields of gold that had belonged to the servants of Hadadezer, and brought them to Jerusalem. 8Also from Betah* and from Berothai, cities of Hadadezer, King David took a large amount of bronze.

9When Toi* king of Hamath heard that David had defeated all the army of Hadadezer, 10then Toi sent Joram* his son to King David, to greet him and bless him, because he had fought against Hadadezer and defeated him (for Hadadezer had been at war with Toi); and Joram brought with him articles of silver, articles of gold, and articles of bronze. 11King David also dedicated these to the LORD, along with the silver and gold that he had dedicated from all the nations which he had subdued— 12from Syria,* from Moab, from the people of Ammon, from the Philistines, from Amalek, and from the spoil of Hadadezer the son of Rehob, king of Zobah.

13And David made himself a name when he returned from killing eighteen thousand Syrians* in the Valley of Salt. 14He also put garrisons in Edom; throughout all Edom he put garrisons, and all the Edomites became David's servants. And the LORD preserved David wherever he went.

15So David reigned over all Israel; and David administered judgment and justice to all his people. 16Joab the son of Zeruiah *was* over the army; Jehoshaphat the son of Ahilud *was* recorder; [17]Zadok the son of Ahitub and Ahimelech the son of Abiathar *were* the priests; Seraiah* *was* the scribe; [18]Benaiah the son of Jehoiada *was over* both the Cherethites and the Pelethites; and David's sons were chief ministers.

JOHN 14:15-31

"**I**F you love Me, keep* My commandments. [16]And I will pray the Father, and He will give you another Helper, that He may abide with you forever— [17]the Spirit of truth, whom the world cannot receive, because it neither sees Him nor knows Him; but you know Him, for He dwells with you and will be in you. [18]I will not leave you orphans; I will come to you.

[19]"A little while longer and the world will see Me no more, but you will see Me. Because I live, you will live also. [20]At that day you will know that I *am* in My Father, and you in Me, and I in you. [21]He who has My commandments and keeps them, it is he who loves Me. And he who loves Me will be loved by My Father, and I will love him and manifest Myself to him."

[22]Judas (not Iscariot) said to Him, "Lord, how is it that You will manifest Yourself to us, and not to the world?"

[23]Jesus answered and said to him, "If anyone loves Me, he will keep* My word; and My Father will love him, and We will come to him and make Our home with him. [24]He who does not love Me does not keep My words; and the word which you hear is not Mine but the Father's who sent Me.

[25]"These things I have spoken to you while being present with you. [26]But the Helper, the Holy Spirit, whom the Father will send in My name, He will teach you all things, and bring to your remembrance all things that I said to you. [27]Peace I leave with you, My peace I give to you; not as the world gives do I give to you. Let not your heart be troubled, neither let it be afraid. [28]You have heard Me say to you, 'I am going away and coming *back* to you.' If you loved Me, you would rejoice because I said,* 'I am going to the Father,' for My Father is greater than I.

[29]"And now I have told you before it comes, that when it does come to pass, you may believe. [30]I will no longer talk much with you, for the ruler of this world is coming, and he has nothing in Me. [31]But that the world may know that I love the Father, and as the Father gave Me commandment, so I do. Arise, let us go from here."

PSALM 119:33-48

ה HE

TEACH me, O LORD, the way of Your statutes,
And I shall keep it *to* the end.
34 Give me understanding, and I shall keep Your law;
Indeed, I shall observe it with *my* whole heart.
35 Make me walk in the path of Your commandments,
For I delight in it.
36 Incline my heart to Your testimonies,
And not to covetousness.
37 Turn away my eyes from looking at worthless things,
And revive me in Your way.*
38 Establish Your word to Your servant,
Who *is devoted* to fearing You.
39 Turn away my reproach which I dread,
For Your judgments *are* good.
40 Behold, I long for Your precepts;
Revive me in Your righteousness.

ו WAW

41 Let Your mercies come also to
me, O LORD—
Your salvation according to
Your word.
42 So shall I have an answer for
him who reproaches me,
For I trust in Your word.
43 And take not the word of
truth utterly out of my
mouth,
For I have hoped in Your
ordinances.
44 So shall I keep Your law
continually,

Forever and ever.
45 And I will walk at liberty,
For I seek Your precepts.
46 I will speak of Your
testimonies also before
kings,
And will not be ashamed.
47 And I will delight myself in
Your commandments,
Which I love.
48 My hands also I will lift up to
Your commandments,
Which I love,
And I will meditate on Your
statutes.

PROVERBS FOR TODAY / 15:33

The fear of the LORD is the instruction of wisdom, and before honor is humility.

MAY 26

2 SAMUEL 9:1–11:27

Now David said, "Is there still anyone who is left of the house of Saul, that I may show him kindness for Jonathan's sake?"

2And *there was* a servant of the house of Saul whose name *was* Ziba. So when they had called him to David, the king said to him, "*Are* you Ziba?"

He said, "At your service!"

3Then the king said, "*Is* there not still someone of the house of Saul, to whom I may show the kindness of God?"

And Ziba said to the king, "There is still a son of Jonathan *who is* lame in *his* feet."

4So the king said to him, "Where *is* he?"

And Ziba said to the king, "Indeed he *is* in the house of Machir the son of Ammiel, in Lo Debar."

5Then King David sent and brought him out of the house of Machir the son of Ammiel, from Lo Debar.

6Now when Mephibosheth the son of Jonathan, the son of Saul, had come to David, he fell on his face and prostrated himself. Then David said, "Mephibosheth?"

And he answered, "Here is your servant!"

7So David said to him, "Do not fear, for I will surely show you kindness for Jonathan your father's sake, and will restore to you all the land of Saul your grandfather; and you shall eat bread at my table continually."

8Then he bowed himself, and said, "What *is* your servant, that you should look upon such a dead dog as I?"

9And the king called to Ziba, Saul's servant, and said to him, "I have given to your master's son all that belonged to Saul and to all his house. 10You therefore, and your sons and your servants, shall work the land for him, and you shall bring in *the harvest,* that your master's son may have food to eat. But Mephibosheth your master's son shall eat bread at my table always." Now Ziba had fifteen sons and twenty servants.

¹¹Then Ziba said to the king, "According to all that my lord the king has commanded his servant, so will your servant do."

"As for Mephibosheth," *said the king,* "he shall eat at my table* like one of the king's sons." ¹²Mephibosheth had a young son whose name *was* Micha. And all who dwelt in the house of Ziba *were* servants of Mephibosheth. ¹³So Mephibosheth dwelt in Jerusalem, for he ate continually at the king's table. And he was lame in both his feet.

It happened after this that the king of the people of Ammon died, and Hanun his son reigned in his place. ²Then David said, "I will show kindness to Hanun the son of Nahash, as his father showed kindness to me."

So David sent by the hand of his servants to comfort him concerning his father. And David's servants came into the land of the people of Ammon. ³And the princes of the people of Ammon said to Hanun their lord, "Do you think that David really honors your father because he has sent comforters to you? Has David not *rather* sent his servants to you to search the city, to spy it out, and to overthrow it?"

⁴Therefore Hanun took David's servants, shaved off half of their beards, cut off their garments in the middle, at their buttocks, and sent them away. ⁵When they told David, he sent to meet them, because the men were greatly ashamed. And the king said, "Wait at Jericho until your beards have grown, and *then* return."

⁶When the people of Ammon saw that they had made themselves repul-

sive to David, the people of Ammon sent and hired the Syrians of Beth Rehob and the Syrians of Zoba, twenty thousand foot soldiers; and from the king of Maacah one thousand men, and from Ish-Tob twelve thousand men. ⁷Now when David heard *of it,* he sent Joab and all the army of the mighty men. ⁸Then the people of Ammon came out and put themselves in battle array at the entrance of the gate. And the Syrians of Zoba, Beth Rehob, Ish-Tob, and Maacah *were* by themselves in the field.

⁹When Joab saw that the battle line was against him before and behind, he chose some of Israel's best and put *them* in battle array against the Syrians. ¹⁰And the rest of the people he put under the command of Abishai his brother, that he might set *them* in battle array against the people of Ammon. ¹¹Then he said, "If the Syrians are too strong for me, then you shall help me; but if the people of Ammon are too strong for you, then I will come and help you. ¹²Be of good courage, and let us be strong for our people and for the cities of our God. And may the Lord do *what is* good in His sight."

¹³So Joab and the people who *were* with him drew near for the battle against the Syrians, and they fled before him. ¹⁴When the people of Ammon saw that the Syrians were fleeing, they also fled before Abishai, and entered the city. So Joab returned from the people of Ammon and went to Jerusalem.

¹⁵When the Syrians saw that they had been defeated by Israel, they gathered together. ¹⁶Then Hadadezer* sent and brought out the Syrians who *were* beyond the River,* and they came to Helam. And Shobach the commander of Hadadezer's army *went* before them. ¹⁷When it was told David, he gathered all Israel, crossed over the Jordan, and came to Helam. And the Syrians set themselves in battle array

against David and fought with him. [18]Then the Syrians fled before Israel; and David killed seven hundred charioteers and forty thousand horsemen of the Syrians, and struck Shobach the commander of their army, who died there. [19]And when all the kings *who were* servants to Hadadezer* saw that they were defeated by Israel, they made peace with Israel and served them. So the Syrians were afraid to help the people of Ammon anymore.

It happened in the spring of the year, at the time when kings go out *to battle,* that David sent Joab and his servants with him, and all Israel; and they destroyed the people of Ammon and besieged Rabbah. But David remained at Jerusalem.

[2]Then it happened one evening that David arose from his bed and walked on the roof of the king's house. And from the roof he saw a woman bathing, and the woman *was* very beautiful to behold. [3]So David sent and inquired about the woman. And *someone* said, "*Is* this not Bathsheba, the daughter of Eliam, the wife of Uriah the Hittite?" [4]Then David sent messengers, and took her; and she came to him, and he lay with her, for she was cleansed from her impurity; and she returned to her house. [5]And the woman conceived; so she sent and told David, and said, "I *am* with child."

[6]Then David sent to Joab, *saying,* "Send me Uriah the Hittite." And Joab sent Uriah to David. [7]When Uriah had come to him, David asked how Joab was doing, and how the people were doing, and how the war prospered. [8]And David said to Uriah, "Go down to your house and wash your feet." So Uriah departed from the king's house, and a gift *of food* from the king followed him. [9]But Uriah slept at the door of the king's house with all the servants of his lord, and did not go down to his house. [10]So when they told David, say-

ing, "Uriah did not go down to his house," David said to Uriah, "Did you not come from a journey? Why did you not go down to your house?"

[11]And Uriah said to David, "The ark and Israel and Judah are dwelling in tents, and my lord Joab and the servants of my lord are encamped in the open fields. Shall I then go to my house to eat and drink, and to lie with my wife? *As* you live, and *as* your soul lives, I will not do this thing."

[12]Then David said to Uriah, "Wait here today also, and tomorrow I will let you depart." So Uriah remained in Jerusalem that day and the next. [13]Now when David called him, he ate and drank before him; and he made him drunk. And at evening he went out to lie on his bed with the servants of his lord, but he did not go down to his house.

[14]In the morning it happened that David wrote a letter to Joab and sent *it* by the hand of Uriah. [15]And he wrote in the letter, saying, "Set Uriah in the forefront of the hottest battle, and retreat from him, that he may be struck down and die." [16]So it was, while Joab besieged the city, that he assigned Uriah to a place where he knew there *were* valiant men. [17]Then the men of the city came out and fought with Joab. And *some* of the people of the servants of David fell; and Uriah the Hittite died also.

[18]Then Joab sent and told David all the things concerning the war, [19]and charged the messenger, saying, "When you have finished telling the matters of the war to the king, [20]if it happens that the king's wrath rises, and he says to you: 'Why did you approach so near to the city when you fought? Did you not know that they would shoot from the wall? [21]Who struck Abimelech the son of Jerubbesheth?* Was it not a woman who cast a piece of a millstone on him from the wall, so that he died in Thebez? Why did you go near the wall?'—then

you shall say, 'Your servant Uriah the Hittite is dead also.' "

²²So the messenger went, and came and told David all that Joab had sent by him. ²³And the messenger said to David, "Surely the men prevailed against us and came out to us in the field; then we drove them back as far as the entrance of the gate. ²⁴The archers shot from the wall at your servants; and *some* of the king's servants are dead, and your servant Uriah the Hittite is dead also."

²⁵Then David said to the messenger, "Thus you shall say to Joab: 'Do not let this thing displease you, for the sword devours one as well as another. Strengthen your attack against the city, and overthrow it.' So encourage him."

²⁶When the wife of Uriah heard that Uriah her husband was dead, she mourned for her husband. ²⁷And when her mourning was over, David sent and brought her to his house, and she became his wife and bore him a son. But the thing that David had done displeased the Lord.

JOHN 15:1-27

"**I** AM the true vine, and My Father is the vinedresser. ²Every branch in Me that does not bear fruit He takes away;* and every *branch* that bears fruit He prunes, that it may bear more fruit. ³You are already clean because of the word which I have spoken to you. ⁴Abide in Me, and I in you. As the branch cannot bear fruit of itself, unless it abides in the vine, neither can you, unless you abide in Me.

⁵"I am the vine, you *are* the branches. He who abides in Me, and I in him, bears much fruit; for without Me you can do nothing. ⁶If anyone does not abide in Me, he is cast out as a branch and is withered; and they gather them and throw *them* into the fire, and they are burned. ⁷If you abide in Me, and My words abide in you, you will* ask what you desire, and it shall be done for you. ⁸By this My Father is glorified, that you bear much fruit; so you will be My disciples.

⁹"As the Father loved Me, I also have loved you; abide in My love. ¹⁰If you keep My commandments, you will abide in My love, just as I have kept My Father's commandments and abide in His love.

¹¹"These things I have spoken to you, that My joy may remain in you, and *that* your joy may be full. ¹²This is My commandment, that you love one another as I have loved you. ¹³Greater love has no one than this, than to lay down one's life for his friends. ¹⁴You are My friends if you do whatever I command you. ¹⁵No longer do I call you servants, for a servant does not know what his master is doing; but I have called you friends, for all things that I heard from My Father I have made known to you. ¹⁶You did not choose Me, but I chose you and appointed you that you should go and bear fruit, and *that* your fruit should remain, that whatever you ask the Father in My name He may give you. ¹⁷These things I command you, that you love one another.

¹⁸"If the world hates you, you know that it hated Me before *it hated* you. ¹⁹If you were of the world, the world would love its own. Yet because you are not of the world, but I chose you out of the world, therefore the world hates you. ²⁰Remember the word that I said to you, 'A servant is not greater than his master.' If they persecuted Me, they will also persecute you. If they kept My word, they will keep yours also. ²¹But all these things they will do to you for My name's sake, because they do not know Him who sent Me. ²²If I had not come and spoken to them, they would have no sin, but now they have no excuse for their sin. ²³He who hates Me hates My Father also. ²⁴If I had not

done among them the works which no one else did, they would have no sin; but now they have seen and also hated both Me and My Father. 25But *this happened* that the word might be fulfilled which is written in their law, *'They hated Me without a cause.'* *

26"But when the Helper comes, whom I shall send to you from the Father, the Spirit of truth who proceeds from the Father, He will testify of Me. 27And you also will bear witness, because you have been with Me from the beginning."

PSALM 119:49-64

ז ZAYIN

REMEMBER the word to Your servant, Upon which You have caused me to hope.

50 This *is* my comfort in my affliction, For Your word has given me life.

51 The proud have me in great derision, *Yet* I do not turn aside from Your law.

52 I remembered Your judgments of old, O LORD, And have comforted myself.

53 Indignation has taken hold of me Because of the wicked, who forsake Your law.

54 Your statutes have been my songs In the house of my pilgrimage.

55 I remember Your name in the night, O LORD, And I keep Your law.

56 This has become mine, Because I kept Your precepts.

ח HETH

57 *You are* my portion, O LORD; I have said that I would keep Your words.

58 I entreated Your favor with *my* whole heart; Be merciful to me according to Your word.

59 I thought about my ways, And turned my feet to Your testimonies.

60 I made haste, and did not delay To keep Your commandments.

61 The cords of the wicked have bound me, *But* I have not forgotten Your law.

62 At midnight I will rise to give thanks to You, Because of Your righteous judgments.

63 I *am* a companion of all who fear You, And of those who keep Your precepts.

64 The earth, O LORD, is full of Your mercy; Teach me Your statutes.

PROVERBS FOR TODAY/ 16:1-3

The preparations of the heart belong to man, but the answer of the tongue is from the LORD. All the ways of a man are pure in his own eyes, but the LORD weighs the spirits. Commit your works to the LORD, and your thoughts will be established.

MAY 27

2 SAMUEL 12:1-31

THEN the LORD sent Nathan to David. And he came to him, and said to him: "There were two men in one city, one rich and the other poor. ²The rich *man* had exceedingly many flocks and herds. ³But the poor *man* had nothing, except one little ewe lamb which he had bought and nourished; and it grew up together with him and with his children. It ate of his own food and drank from his own cup and lay in his bosom; and it was like a daughter to him. ⁴And a traveler came to the rich man, who refused to take from his own flock and from his own herd to prepare one for the wayfaring man who had come to him; but he took the poor man's lamb and prepared it for the man who had come to him."

⁵So David's anger was greatly aroused against the man, and he said to Nathan, "*As* the LORD lives, the man who has done this shall surely die! ⁶And he shall restore fourfold for the lamb, because he did this thing and because he had no pity."

⁷Then Nathan said to David, "You *are* the man! Thus says the LORD God of Israel: 'I anointed you king over Israel, and I delivered you from the hand of Saul. ⁸I gave you your master's house and your master's wives into your keeping, and gave you the house of Israel and Judah. And if *that had been* too little, I also would have given you much more! ⁹Why have you despised the commandment of the LORD, to do evil in His sight? You have killed Uriah the Hittite with the sword; you have taken his wife *to be* your wife, and have killed him with the sword of the people of Ammon. ¹⁰Now therefore, the sword shall never depart from your house, because you have despised Me, and have taken the wife of Uriah the Hittite to be your wife.' ¹¹Thus says the LORD: 'Behold, I will raise up adversity against you from your own house; and I will take your wives before your eyes and give *them* to your neighbor, and he shall lie with your wives in the sight of this sun. ¹²For you did *it* secretly, but I will do this thing before all Israel, before the sun.' "

¹³So David said to Nathan, "I have sinned against the LORD."

And Nathan said to David, "The LORD also has put away your sin; you shall not die. ¹⁴However, because by this deed you have given great occasion to the enemies of the LORD to blaspheme, the child also *who is* born to you shall surely die." ¹⁵Then Nathan departed to his house.

And the LORD struck the child that Uriah's wife bore to David, and it became ill. ¹⁶David therefore pleaded with God for the child, and David fasted and went in and lay all night on the ground. ¹⁷So the elders of his house arose *and went* to him, to raise him up from the ground. But he would not, nor did he eat food with them. ¹⁸Then on the seventh day it came to pass that the child died. And the servants of David were afraid to tell him that the child was dead. For they said, "Indeed, while the child was alive, we spoke to him, and he would not heed our voice. How can we tell him that the child is dead? He may do some harm!"

¹⁹When David saw that his servants were whispering, David perceived that the child was dead. Therefore David said to his servants, "Is the child dead?"

And they said, "He is dead."

²⁰So David arose from the ground, washed and anointed himself, and

changed his clothes; and he went into the house of the Lord and worshiped. Then he went to his own house; and when he requested, they set food before him, and he ate. ²¹Then his servants said to him, "What *is* this that you have done? You fasted and wept for the child *while he was* alive, but when the child died, you arose and ate food."

²²And he said, "While the child was alive, I fasted and wept; for I said, 'Who can tell *whether* the Lord* will be gracious to me, that the child may live?' ²³But now he is dead; why should I fast? Can I bring him back again? I shall go to him, but he shall not return to me."

²⁴Then David comforted Bathsheba his wife, and went in to her and lay with her. So she bore a son, and he* called his name Solomon. Now the Lord loved him, ²⁵and He sent *word* by the hand of Nathan the prophet: So he* called his name Jedidiah,* because of the Lord.

²⁶Now Joab fought against Rabbah of the people of Ammon, and took the royal city. ²⁷And Joab sent messengers to David, and said, "I have fought against Rabbah, and I have taken the city's water *supply.* ²⁸Now therefore, gather the rest of the people together and encamp against the city and take it, lest I take the city and it be called after my name." ²⁹So David gathered all the people together and went to Rabbah, fought against it, and took it. ³⁰Then he took their king's crown from his head. Its weight *was* a talent of gold, with precious stones. And it was *set* on David's head. Also he brought out the spoil of the city in great abundance. ³¹And he brought out the people who *were* in it, and put *them to work* with saws and iron picks and iron axes, and made them cross over to the brick works. So he did to all the cities of the people of Ammon. Then David and all the people returned to Jerusalem.

JOHN 16:1-33

"**T**HESE things I [Jesus] have spoken to you, that you should not be made to stumble. ²They will put you out of the synagogues; yes, the time is coming that whoever kills you will think that he offers God service. ³And these things they will do to you* because they have not known the Father nor Me. ⁴But these things I have told you, that when the* time comes, you may remember that I told you of them.

"And these things I did not say to you at the beginning, because I was with you.

⁵"But now I go away to Him who sent Me, and none of you asks Me, 'Where are You going?' ⁶But because I have said these things to you, sorrow has filled your heart. ⁷Nevertheless I tell you the truth. It is to your advantage that I go away; for if I do not go away, the Helper will not come to you; but if I depart, I will send Him to you. ⁸And when He has come, He will convict the world of sin, and of righteousness, and of judgment: ⁹of sin, because they do not believe in Me; ¹⁰of righteousness, because I go to My Father and you see Me no more; ¹¹of judgment, because the ruler of this world is judged.

¹²"I still have many things to say to you, but you cannot bear *them* now. ¹³However, when He, the Spirit of truth, has come, He will guide you into all truth; for He will not speak on His own *authority,* but whatever He hears He will speak; and He will tell you things to come. ¹⁴He will glorify Me, for He will take of what is Mine and declare *it* to you. ¹⁵All things that the Father has are Mine. Therefore I said that He will take of Mine and declare *it* to you.*

¹⁶"A little while, and you will not see Me; and again a little while, and you

will see Me, because I go to the Father."

¹⁷Then *some* of His disciples said among themselves, "What is this that He says to us, 'A little while, and you will not see Me; and again a little while, and you will see Me'; and, 'because I go to the Father'?" ¹⁸They said therefore, "What is this that He says, 'A little while'? We do not know what He is saying."

¹⁹Now Jesus knew that they desired to ask Him, and He said to them, "Are you inquiring among yourselves about what I said, 'A little while, and you will not see Me; and again a little while, and you will see Me'? ²⁰Most assuredly, I say to you that you will weep and lament, but the world will rejoice; and you will be sorrowful, but your sorrow will be turned into joy. ²¹A woman, when she is in labor, has sorrow because her hour has come; but as soon as she has given birth to the child, she no longer remembers the anguish, for joy that a human being has been born into the world. ²²Therefore you now have sorrow; but I will see you again and your heart will rejoice, and your joy no one will take from you.

²³"And in that day you will ask Me nothing. Most assuredly, I say to you, whatever you ask the Father in My name He will give you. ²⁴Until now you have asked nothing in My name. Ask, and you will receive, that your joy may be full.

²⁵"These things I have spoken to you in figurative language; but the time is coming when I will no longer speak to you in figurative language, but I will tell you plainly about the Father. ²⁶In that day you will ask in My name, and I do not say to you that I shall pray the Father for you; ²⁷for the Father Himself loves you, because you have loved Me, and have believed that I came forth from God. ²⁸I came forth from the Father and have come into the world. Again, I leave the world and go to the Father."

²⁹His disciples said to Him, "See, now You are speaking plainly, and using no figure of speech! ³⁰Now we are sure that You know all things, and have no need that anyone should question You. By this we believe that You came forth from God."

³¹Jesus answered them, "Do you now believe? ³²Indeed the hour is coming, yes, has now come, that you will be scattered, each to his own, and will leave Me alone. And yet I am not alone, because the Father is with Me. ³³These things I have spoken to you, that in Me you may have peace. In the world you will* have tribulation; but be of good cheer, I have overcome the world."

PSALM 119:65–80

ט TETH

YOU have dealt well with Your servant,
O LORD, according to Your word.
66 Teach me good judgment and knowledge,
For I believe Your commandments.
67 Before I was afflicted I went astray,
But now I keep Your word.
68 You *are* good, and do good;
Teach me Your statutes.
69 The proud have forged a lie against me,
But I will keep Your precepts with *my* whole heart.
70 Their heart is as fat as grease,
But I delight in Your law.
71 *It is* good for me that I have been afflicted,
That I may learn Your statutes.
72 The law of Your mouth *is* better to me

Than thousands of *coins of*
gold and silver.

` YOD

73 Your hands have made me
and fashioned me;
Give me understanding, that I
may learn Your
commandments.
74 Those who fear You will be
glad when they see me,
Because I have hoped in Your
word.
75 I know, O LORD, that Your
judgments *are* right,
And *that* in faithfulness You
have afflicted me.

76 Let, I pray, Your merciful
kindness be for my comfort,
According to Your word to
Your servant.
77 Let Your tender mercies come
to me, that I may live;
For Your law *is* my delight.
78 Let the proud be ashamed,
For they treated me
wrongfully with falsehood;
But I will meditate on Your
precepts.
79 Let those who fear You turn
to me,
Those who know Your
testimonies.
80 Let my heart be blameless
regarding Your statutes,
That I may not be ashamed.

PROVERBS FOR TODAY/ 16:4-5

The LORD has made all for Himself, yes, even the wicked for the day of doom.
□ *Everyone proud in heart is an abomination to the LORD; though they join
forces,* * *none will go unpunished.*

MAY 28

2 SAMUEL 13:1-39

AFTER this Absalom the son of
David had a lovely sister,
whose name *was* Tamar; and
Amnon the son of David loved her.
²Amnon was so distressed over his sister Tamar that he became sick; for she
was a virgin. And it was improper for
Amnon to do anything to her. ³But
Amnon had a friend whose name *was*
Jonadab the son of Shimeah, David's
brother. Now Jonadab *was* a very
crafty man. ⁴And he said to him, "Why
are you, the king's son, becoming thin-
ner day after day? Will you not tell
me?"

Amnon said to him, "I love Tamar,
my brother Absalom's sister."
⁵So Jonadab said to him, "Lie down
on your bed and pretend to be ill. And
when your father comes to see you,
say to him, 'Please let my sister Tamar
come and give me food, and prepare
the food in my sight, that I may see *it*
and eat it from her hand.' " ⁶Then
Amnon lay down and pretended to be
ill; and when the king came to see him,
Amnon said to the king, "Please let
Tamar my sister come and make a
couple of cakes for me in my sight, that
I may eat from her hand."
⁷And David sent home to Tamar,
saying, "Now go to your brother
Amnon's house, and prepare food for

him." ⁸So Tamar went to her brother Amnon's house; and he was lying down. Then she took flour and kneaded *it,* made cakes in his sight, and baked the cakes. ⁹And she took the pan and placed *them* out before him, but he refused to eat. Then Amnon said, "Have everyone go out from me." And they all went out from him. ¹⁰Then Amnon said to Tamar, "Bring the food into the bedroom, that I may eat from your hand." And Tamar took the cakes which she had made, and brought *them* to Amnon her brother in the bedroom. ¹¹Now when she had brought *them* to him to eat, he took hold of her and said to her, "Come, lie with me, my sister."

¹²But she answered him, "No, my brother, do not force me, for no such thing should be done in Israel. Do not do this disgraceful thing! ¹³And I, where could I take my shame? And as for you, you would be like one of the fools in Israel. Now therefore, please speak to the king; for he will not withhold me from you." ¹⁴However, he would not heed her voice; and being stronger than she, he forced her and lay with her.

¹⁵Then Amnon hated her exceedingly, so that the hatred with which he hated her *was* greater than the love with which he had loved her. And Amnon said to her, "Arise, be gone!"

¹⁶So she said to him, "No, indeed! This evil of sending me away *is* worse than the other that you did to me."

But he would not listen to her. ¹⁷Then he called his servant who attended him, and said, "Here! Put this *woman* out, away from me, and bolt the door behind her." ¹⁸Now she had on a robe of many colors, for the king's virgin daughters wore such apparel. And his servant put her out and bolted the door behind her.

¹⁹Then Tamar put ashes on her head, and tore her robe of many colors

that *was* on her, and laid her hand on her head and went away crying bitterly. ²⁰And Absalom her brother said to her, "Has Amnon your brother been with you? But now hold your peace, my sister. He *is* your brother; do not take this thing to heart." So Tamar remained desolate in her brother Absalom's house.

²¹But when King David heard of all these things, he was very angry. ²²And Absalom spoke to his brother Amnon neither good nor bad. For Absalom hated Amnon, because he had forced his sister Tamar.

²³And it came to pass, after two full years, that Absalom had sheepshearers in Baal Hazor, which *is* near Ephraim; so Absalom invited all the king's sons. ²⁴Then Absalom came to the king and said, "Kindly note, your servant has sheepshearers; please, let the king and his servants go with your servant."

²⁵But the king said to Absalom, "No, my son, let us not all go now, lest we be a burden to you." Then he urged him, but he would not go; and he blessed him.

²⁶Then Absalom said, "If not, please let my brother Amnon go with us."

And the king said to him, "Why should he go with you?" ²⁷But Absalom urged him; so he let Amnon and all the king's sons go with him.

²⁸Now Absalom had commanded his servants, saying, "Watch now, when Amnon's heart is merry with wine, and when I say to you, 'Strike Amnon!' then kill him. Do not be afraid. Have I not commanded you? Be courageous and valiant." ²⁹So the servants of Absalom did to Amnon as Absalom had commanded. Then all the king's sons arose, and each one got on his mule and fled.

³⁰And it came to pass, while they were on the way, that news came to David, saying, "Absalom has killed all the king's sons, and not one of them is

left!" 31So the king arose and tore his garments and lay on the ground, and all his servants stood by with their clothes torn. 32Then Jonadab the son of Shimeah, David's brother, answered and said, "Let not my lord suppose they have killed all the young men, the king's sons, for only Amnon is dead. For by the command of Absalom this has been determined from the day that he forced his sister Tamar. 33Now therefore, let not my lord the king take the thing to his heart, to think that all the king's sons are dead. For only Amnon is dead."

34Then Absalom fled. And the young man who was keeping watch lifted his eyes and looked, and there, many people were coming from the road on the hillside behind him.* 35And Jonadab said to the king, "Look, the king's sons are coming; as your servant said, so it is." 36So it was, as soon as he had finished speaking, that the king's sons indeed came, and they lifted up their voice and wept. Also the king and all his servants wept very bitterly.

37But Absalom fled and went to Talmai the son of Ammihud, king of Geshur. And *David* mourned for his son every day. 38So Absalom fled and went to Geshur, and was there three years. 39And King David* longed to go to* Absalom. For he had been comforted concerning Amnon, because he was dead.

JOHN 17:1-26

JESUS spoke these words, lifted up His eyes to heaven, and said: "Father, the hour has come. Glorify Your Son, that Your Son also may glorify You, 2as You have given Him authority over all flesh, that He should* give eternal life to as many as You have given Him. 3And this is eternal life, that they may know You, the only true God, and Jesus Christ whom

You have sent. 4I have glorified You on the earth. I have finished the work which You have given Me to do. 5And now, O Father, glorify Me together with Yourself, with the glory which I had with You before the world was.

6"I have manifested Your name to the men whom You have given Me out of the world. They were Yours, You gave them to Me, and they have kept Your word. 7Now they have known that all things which You have given Me are from You. 8For I have given to them the words which You have given Me; and they have received *them,* and have known surely that I came forth from You; and they have believed that You sent Me.

9"I pray for them. I do not pray for the world but for those whom You have given Me, for they are Yours. 10And all Mine are Yours, and Yours are Mine, and I am glorified in them. 11Now I am no longer in the world, but these are in the world, and I come to You. Holy Father, keep through Your name those whom You have given Me,* that they may be one as We *are.* 12While I was with them in the world,* I kept them in Your name. Those whom You gave Me I have kept;* and none of them is lost except the son of perdition, that the Scripture might be fulfilled. 13But now I come to You, and these things I speak in the world, that they may have My joy fulfilled in themselves. 14I have given them Your word; and the world has hated them because they are not of the world, just as I am not of the world. 15I do not pray that You should take them out of the world, but that You should keep them from the evil one. 16They are not of the world, just as I am not of the world. 17Sanctify them by Your truth. Your word is truth. 18As You sent Me into the world, I also have sent them into the world. 19And for their sakes I sanctify Myself, that they also may be sanctified by the truth.

20"I do not pray for these alone, but also for those who will* believe in Me through their word; 21that they all may be one, as You, Father, *are* in Me, and I in You; that they also may be one in Us, that the world may believe that You sent Me. 22And the glory which You gave Me I have given them, that they may be one just as We are one: 23I in them, and You in Me; that they may be made perfect in one, and that the world may know that You have sent Me, and have loved them as You have loved Me.

24"Father, I desire that they also whom You gave Me may be with Me where I am, that they may behold My glory which You have given Me; for You loved Me before the foundation of the world. 25O righteous Father! The world has not known You, but I have known You; and these have known that You sent Me. 26And I have declared to them Your name, and will declare *it,* that the love with which You loved Me may be in them, and I in them."

PSALM 119:81-96

 כ KAPH

MY soul faints for Your salvation,
But I hope in Your word.
82 My eyes fail *from searching* Your word,
Saying, "When will You comfort me?"
83 For I have become like a wineskin in smoke,
Yet I do not forget Your statutes.
84 How many *are* the days of Your servant?
When will You execute judgment on those who persecute me?
85 The proud have dug pits for me,

Which *is* not according to Your law.
86 All Your commandments *are* faithful;
They persecute me wrongfully;
Help me!
87 They almost made an end of me on earth,
But I did not forsake Your precepts.
88 Revive me according to Your lovingkindness,
So that I may keep the testimony of Your mouth.

ל LAMED

89 Forever, O Lord,
Your word is settled in heaven.
90 Your faithfulness *endures* to all generations;
You established the earth, and it abides.
91 They continue this day according to Your ordinances,
For all *are* Your servants.
92 Unless Your law *had been* my delight,
I would then have perished in my affliction.
93 I will never forget Your precepts,
For by them You have given me life.
94 I *am* Yours, save me;
For I have sought Your precepts.
95 The wicked wait for me to destroy me,
But I will consider Your testimonies.
96 I have seen the consummation of all perfection,
But Your commandment *is* exceedingly broad.

PROVERBS FOR TODAY/ 16:6-7

In mercy and truth atonement is provided for iniquity; and by the fear of the LORD *one departs from evil.* □ *When a man's ways please the* LORD, *he makes even his enemies to be at peace with him.*

MAY 29

2 SAMUEL 14:1–15:21

So Joab the son of Zeruiah perceived that the king's heart *was* concerned about Absalom. ²And Joab sent to Tekoa and brought from there a wise woman, and said to her, "Please pretend to be a mourner, and put on mourning apparel; do not anoint yourself with oil, but act like a woman who has been mourning a long time for the dead. ³Go to the king and speak to him in this manner." So Joab put the words in her mouth.

⁴And when the woman of Tekoa spoke* to the king, she fell on her face to the ground and prostrated herself, and said, "Help, O king!"

⁵Then the king said to her, "What troubles you?"

And she answered, "Indeed I *am* a widow, my husband is dead. ⁶Now your maidservant had two sons; and the two fought with each other in the field, and *there was* no one to part them, but the one struck the other and killed him. ⁷And now the whole family has risen up against your maidservant, and they said, 'Deliver him who struck his brother, that we may execute him for the life of his brother whom he killed; and we will destroy the heir also.' So they would extinguish my ember that is left, and leave to my husband *neither* name nor remnant on the earth."

⁸Then the king said to the woman, "Go to your house, and I will give orders concerning you."

⁹And the woman of Tekoa said to the king, "My lord, O king, *let* the iniquity *be* on me and on my father's house, and the king and his throne *be* guiltless."

¹⁰So the king said, "Whoever says *anything* to you, bring him to me, and he shall not touch you anymore."

¹¹Then she said, "Please let the king remember the LORD your God, and do not permit the avenger of blood to destroy anymore, lest they destroy my son."

And he said, "*As* the LORD lives, not one hair of your son shall fall to the ground."

¹²Therefore the woman said, "Please, let your maidservant speak *another* word to my lord the king."

And he said, "Say on."

¹³So the woman said: "Why then have you schemed such a thing against the people of God? For the king speaks this thing as one who is guilty, *in that* the king does not bring his banished one home again. ¹⁴For we will surely die and *become* like water spilled on the ground, which cannot be gathered up again. Yet God does not take away a life; but He devises means, so that His banished ones are not expelled from Him. ¹⁵Now therefore, I have come to speak of this thing to my lord the king because the people have made me afraid. And your maidservant said, 'I will now speak to the king; it may be that the king will perform the request of his maidservant. ¹⁶For the king will hear and deliver his maidser-

vant from the hand of the man *who would* destroy me and my son together from the inheritance of God.' ¹⁷Your maidservant said, 'The word of my lord the king will now be comforting; for as the angel of God, so *is* my lord the king in discerning good and evil. And may the LORD your God be with you.' "

¹⁸Then the king answered and said to the woman, "Please do not hide from me anything that I ask you."

And the woman said, "Please, let my lord the king speak."

¹⁹So the king said, "*Is* the hand of Joab with you in all this?" And the woman answered and said, "*As* you live, my lord the king, no one can turn to the right hand or to the left from anything that my lord the king has spoken. For your servant Joab commanded me, and he put all these words in the mouth of your maidservant. ²⁰To bring about this change of affairs your servant Joab has done this thing; but my lord *is* wise, according to the wisdom of the angel of God, to know everything that *is* in the earth."

²¹And the king said to Joab, "All right, I have granted this thing. Go therefore, bring back the young man Absalom."

²²Then Joab fell to the ground on his face and bowed himself, and thanked the king. And Joab said, "Today your servant knows that I have found favor in your sight, my lord, O king, in that the king has fulfilled the request of his servant." ²³So Joab arose and went to Geshur, and brought Absalom to Jerusalem. ²⁴And the king said, "Let him return to his own house, but do not let him see my face." So Absalom returned to his own house, but did not see the king's face.

²⁵Now in all Israel there was no one who was praised as much as Absalom for his good looks. From the sole of his foot to the crown of his head there was no blemish in him. ²⁶And when he cut the hair of his head—at the end of every year he cut *it* because it was heavy on him—when he cut it, he weighed the hair of his head at two hundred shekels according to the king's standard. ²⁷To Absalom were born three sons, and one daughter whose name *was* Tamar. She was a woman of beautiful appearance.

²⁸And Absalom dwelt two full years in Jerusalem, but did not see the king's face. ²⁹Therefore Absalom sent for Joab, to send him to the king, but he would not come to him. And when he sent again the second time, he would not come. ³⁰So he said to his servants, "See, Joab's field is near mine, and he has barley there; go and set it on fire." And Absalom's servants set the field on fire.

³¹Then Joab arose and came to Absalom's house, and said to him, "Why have your servants set my field on fire?"

³²And Absalom answered Joab, "Look, I sent to you, saying, 'Come here, so that I may send you to the king, to say, "Why have I come from Geshur? *It would be* better for me *to be* there still." ' Now therefore, let me see the king's face; but if there is iniquity in me, let him execute me."

³³So Joab went to the king and told him. And when he had called for Absalom, he came to the king and bowed himself on his face to the ground before the king. Then the king kissed Absalom.

AFTER this it happened that Absalom provided himself with chariots and horses, and fifty men to run before him. ²Now Absalom would rise early and stand beside the way to the gate. *So* it was, whenever anyone who had a lawsuit came to the king for a decision, that Absalom would call to him and say, "What city *are* you from?" And he would say, "Your servant *is* from such and such a tribe of Israel." ³Then Absalom would say to him, "Look, your case *is* good and right; but *there is* no deputy of the king to hear you." [4]Moreover Absalom would say, "Oh, that I were made judge in the land, and everyone who has any suit or cause would come to me; then I would give him justice." [5]And *so* it was, whenever anyone came near to bow down to him, that he would put out his hand and take him and kiss him. [6]In this manner Absalom acted toward all Israel who came to the king for judgment. So Absalom stole the hearts of the men of Israel.

[7]Now it came to pass after forty* years that Absalom said to the king, "Please, let me go to Hebron and pay the vow which I made to the LORD. [8]For your servant took a vow while I dwelt at Geshur in Syria, saying, 'If the LORD indeed brings me back to Jerusalem, then I will serve the LORD.' "

[9]And the king said to him, "Go in peace." So he arose and went to Hebron.

[10]Then Absalom sent spies throughout all the tribes of Israel, saying, "As soon as you hear the sound of the trumpet, then you shall say, 'Absalom reigns in Hebron!' " [11]And with Absalom went two hundred men invited from Jerusalem, and they went along innocently and did not know anything. [12]Then Absalom sent for Ahithophel the Gilonite, David's counselor, from his city—from Giloh—while he offered sacrifices. And the conspiracy grew strong, for the people with Absalom continually increased in number.

[13]Now a messenger came to David, saying, "The hearts of the men of Israel are with Absalom."

[14]So David said to all his servants who *were* with him at Jerusalem, "Arise, and let us flee, or we shall not escape from Absalom. Make haste to depart, lest he overtake us suddenly and bring disaster upon us, and strike the city with the edge of the sword."

[15]And the king's servants said to the king, "We *are* your servants, *ready to do* whatever my lord the king commands." [16]Then the king went out with all his household after him. But the king left ten women, concubines, to keep the house. [17]And the king went out with all the people after him, and stopped at the outskirts. [18]Then all his servants passed before him; and all the Cherethites, all the Pelethites, and all the Gittites, six hundred men who had followed him from Gath, passed before the king.

[19]Then the king said to Ittai the Gittite, "Why are you also going with us? Return and remain with the king. For you *are* a foreigner and also an exile from your own place. [20]In fact, you came *only* yesterday. Should I make you wander up and down with us today, since I go I know not where? Return, and take your brethren back. Mercy and truth *be* with you."

[21]But Ittai answered the king and said, "*As* the LORD lives, and *as* my lord the king lives, surely in whatever place my lord the king shall be, whether in death or life, even there also your servant will be."

JOHN 18:1-24

WHEN Jesus had spoken these words, He went out with His disciples over the Brook Kidron, where there was a garden, which He and His disciples entered. [2]And Judas, who betrayed Him, also knew the place; for Jesus often met there with His disciples. [3]Then Judas, having received a detachment *of troops,* and officers from the chief priests and Pharisees, came there with lanterns, torches, and weapons. [4]Jesus therefore, knowing all things that would come upon Him, went forward and said to them, "Whom are you seeking?"

[5]They answered Him, "Jesus of Nazareth."

Jesus said to them, "I am *He*." And Judas, who betrayed Him, also stood with them. 6Now when He said to them, "I am *He*," they drew back and fell to the ground.

7Then He asked them again, "Whom are you seeking?"

And they said, "Jesus of Nazareth."

8Jesus answered, "I have told you that I am *He*. Therefore, if you seek Me, let these go their way," 9that the saying might be fulfilled which He spoke, "Of those whom You gave Me I have lost none."

10Then Simon Peter, having a sword, drew it and struck the high priest's servant, and cut off his right ear. The servant's name was Malchus.

11So Jesus said to Peter, "Put your sword into the sheath. Shall I not drink the cup which My Father has given Me?"

12Then the detachment *of troops* and the captain and the officers of the Jews arrested Jesus and bound Him. 13And they led Him away to Annas first, for he was the father-in-law of Caiaphas who was high priest that year. 14Now it was Caiaphas who advised the Jews that it was expedient that one man should die for the people.

15And Simon Peter followed Jesus, and so *did* another* disciple. Now that disciple was known to the high priest, and went with Jesus into the courtyard of the high priest. 16But Peter stood at the door outside. Then the other disciple, who was known to the high priest, went out and spoke to her who kept the door, and brought Peter in. 17Then the servant girl who kept the door said to Peter, "You are not also *one* of this Man's disciples, are you?"

He said, "I am not."

18Now the servants and officers who had made a fire of coals stood there, for it was cold, and they warmed themselves. And Peter stood with them and warmed himself.

19The high priest then asked Jesus about His disciples and His doctrine. 20Jesus answered him, "I spoke openly to the world. I always taught in synagogues and in the temple, where the Jews always meet,* and in secret I have said nothing. 21Why do you ask Me? Ask those who have heard Me what I said to them. Indeed they know what I said."

22And when He had said these things, one of the officers who stood by struck Jesus with the palm of his hand, saying, "Do You answer the high priest like that?"

23Jesus answered him, "If I have spoken evil, bear witness of the evil; but if well, why do you strike Me?"

24Then Annas sent Him bound to Caiaphas the high priest.

PSALM 119:97-112

מ   MEM

O H, how I love Your law!
It *is* my meditation all the day.
98You, through Your
commandments, make me
wiser than my enemies;
For they *are* ever with me.

99   I have more understanding
than all my teachers,
For Your testimonies *are* my
meditation.

100   I understand more than the
ancients,
Because I keep Your precepts.

101   I have restrained my feet from
every evil way,
That I may keep Your word.

102   I have not departed from Your
judgments,
For You Yourself have taught
me.

103   How sweet are Your words to
my taste,
Sweeter than honey to my
mouth!

104 Through Your precepts I get
   understanding;
   Therefore I hate every false
   way.

ב NUN

105 Your word *is* a lamp to my feet
   And a light to my path.
106 I have sworn and confirmed
   That I will keep Your
      righteous judgments.
107 I am afflicted very much;
   Revive me, O Lord, according
      to Your word.
108 Accept, I pray, the freewill

offerings of my mouth,
   O Lord,
   And teach me Your judgments.
109 My life *is* continually in my
      hand,
   Yet I do not forget Your law.
110 The wicked have laid a snare
      for me,
   Yet I have not strayed from
      Your precepts.
111 Your testimonies I have taken
      as a heritage forever,
   For they *are* the rejoicing of
      my heart.
112 I have inclined my heart to
      perform Your statutes
   Forever, to the very end.

PROVERBS FOR TODAY/ 16:8-9

Better is *a little with righteousness, than vast revenues without justice.* ▢ *A man's heart plans his way, but the Lord directs his steps.*

MAY 30

2 SAMUEL 15:22–16:23

So David said to Ittai, "Go, and cross over." Then Ittai the Gittite and all his men and all the little ones who *were* with him crossed over. 23And all the country wept with a loud voice, and all the people crossed over. The king himself also crossed over the Brook Kidron, and all the people crossed over toward the way of the wilderness.

24There was Zadok also, and all the Levites with him, bearing the ark of the covenant of God. And they set down the ark of God, and Abiathar went up until all the people had finished crossing over from the city. 25Then the king said to Zadok, "Carry the ark of God back into the city. If I find favor in the eyes of the Lord, He

will bring me back and show me *both* it and His dwelling place. 26But if He says thus: 'I have no delight in you,' here I am, let Him do to me as seems good to Him." 27The king also said to Zadok the priest, "*Are* you *not* a seer? Return to the city in peace, and your two sons with you, Ahimaaz your son, and Jonathan the son of Abiathar. 28See, I will wait in the plains of the wilderness until word comes from you to inform me." 29Therefore Zadok and Abiathar carried the ark of God back to Jerusalem. And they remained there.

30So David went up by the Ascent of the *Mount of* Olives, and wept as he went up; and he had his head covered and went barefoot. And all the people who *were* with him covered their heads and went up, weeping as they went up. ³¹Then *someone* told David, saying, "Ahithophel *is* among the conspirators with Absalom." And David said, "O LORD, I pray, turn the counsel of Ahithophel into foolishness!"

³²Now it happened when David had come to the top *of the mountain,* where he worshiped God—there was Hushai the Archite coming to meet him with his robe torn and dust on his head. ³³David said to him, "If you go on with me, then you will become a burden to me. ³⁴But if you return to the city, and say to Absalom, 'I will be your servant, O king; *as* I *was* your father's servant previously, so I *will* now also *be* your servant,' then you may defeat the counsel of Ahithophel for me. ³⁵And *do* you not *have* Zadok and Abiathar the priests with you there? Therefore it will be *that* whatever you hear from the king's house, you shall tell to Zadok and Abiathar the priests. ³⁶Indeed *they have* there with them their two sons, Ahimaaz, Zadok's *son,* and Jonathan, Abiathar's *son;* and by them you shall send me everything you hear."

³⁷So Hushai, David's friend, went into the city. And Absalom came into Jerusalem.

WHEN David was a little past the top *of the mountain,* there was Ziba the servant of Mephibosheth, who met him with a couple of saddled donkeys, and on them two hundred *loaves* of bread, one hundred clusters of raisins, one hundred summer fruits, and a skin of wine. ²And the king said to Ziba, "What do you mean to do with these?"

So Ziba said, "The donkeys *are* for the king's household to ride on, the bread and summer fruit for the young men to eat, and the wine for those who are faint in the wilderness to drink."

³Then the king said, "And where *is* your master's son?"

And Ziba said to the king, "Indeed he is staying in Jerusalem, for he said,

'Today the house of Israel will restore the kingdom of my father to me.' "

⁴So the king said to Ziba, "Here, all that *belongs* to Mephibosheth *is* yours."

And Ziba said, "I humbly bow before you, *that* I may find favor in your sight, my lord, O king!"

⁵Now when King David came to Bahurim, there was a man from the family of the house of Saul, whose name *was* Shimei the son of Gera, coming from there. He came out, cursing continuously as he came. ⁶And he threw stones at David and at all the servants of King David. And all the people and all the mighty men *were* on his right hand and on his left. ⁷Also Shimei said thus when he cursed: "Come out! Come out! You bloodthirsty man, you rogue! ⁸The LORD has brought upon you all the blood of the house of Saul, in whose place you have reigned; and the LORD has delivered the kingdom into the hand of Absalom your son. So now you *are caught* in your own evil, because you are a bloodthirsty man!"

⁹Then Abishai the son of Zeruiah said to the king, "Why should this dead dog curse my lord the king? Please, let me go over and take off his head!"

¹⁰But the king said, "What have I to do with you, you sons of Zeruiah? So let him curse, because the LORD has said to him, 'Curse David.' Who then shall say, 'Why have you done so?' "

¹¹And David said to Abishai and all his servants, "See how my son who came from my own body seeks my life. How much more now *may this* Benjamite? Let him alone, and let him curse; for so the LORD has ordered him. ¹²It may be that the LORD will look on my affliction,* and that the LORD will repay me with good for his cursing this day." ¹³And as David and his men went along the road, Shimei went along the hillside opposite him and cursed as he went, threw stones at him and kicked

"For you are all one in Christ Jesus."
Galatians 3:28

"Her children rise up and call her blessed."
Proverbs 31:28

up dust. [14]Now the king and all the people who *were* with him became weary; so they refreshed themselves there.

[15]Meanwhile Absalom and all the people, the men of Israel, came to Jerusalem; and Ahithophel *was* with him. [16]And so it was, when Hushai the Archite, David's friend, came to Absalom, that Hushai said to Absalom, "*Long* live the king! *Long* live the king!"

[17]So Absalom said to Hushai, "*Is* this your loyalty to your friend? Why did you not go with your friend?"

[18]And Hushai said to Absalom, "No, but whom the Lord and this people and all the men of Israel choose, his I will be, and with him I will remain. [19]"Furthermore, whom should I serve? *Should I* not *serve* in the presence of his son? As I have served in your father's presence, so will I be in your presence."

[20]Then Absalom said to Ahithophel, "Give advice as to what we should do."

[21]And Ahithophel said to Absalom, "Go in to your father's concubines, whom he has left to keep the house; and all Israel will hear that you are abhorred by your father. Then the hands of all who are with you will be strong." [22]So they pitched a tent for Absalom on the top of the house, and Absalom went in to his father's concubines in the sight of all Israel.

[23]Now the advice of Ahithophel, which he gave in those days, *was* as if one had inquired at the oracle of God. So *was* all the advice of Ahithophel both with David and with Absalom.

JOHN 18:25–19:22

Now Simon Peter stood and warmed himself. Therefore they said to him, "You are not also *one* of His disciples, are you?"

He denied *it* and said, "I am not!"

[26]One of the servants of the high priest, a relative *of him* whose ear Peter cut off, said, "Did I not see you in the garden with Him?" [27]Peter then denied again; and immediately a rooster crowed.

[28]Then they led Jesus from Caiaphas to the Praetorium, and it was early morning. But they themselves did not go into the Praetorium, lest they should be defiled, but that they might eat the Passover. [29]Pilate then went out to them and said, "What accusation do you bring against this Man?"

[30]They answered and said to him, "If He were not an evildoer, we would not have delivered Him up to you."

[31]Then Pilate said to them, "You take Him and judge Him according to your law."

Therefore the Jews said to him, "It is not lawful for us to put anyone to death," [32]that the saying of Jesus might be fulfilled which He spoke, signifying by what death He would die.

[33]Then Pilate entered the Praetorium again, called Jesus, and said to Him, "Are You the King of the Jews?"

[34]Jesus answered him, "Are you speaking for yourself about this, or did others tell you this concerning Me?"

[35]Pilate answered, "Am I a Jew? Your own nation and the chief priests have delivered You to me. What have You done?"

[36]Jesus answered, "My kingdom is not of this world. If My kingdom were of this world, My servants would fight, so that I should not be delivered to the Jews; but now My kingdom is not from here."

[37]Pilate therefore said to Him, "Are You a king then?"

Jesus answered, "You say *rightly* that I am a king. For this cause I was born, and for this cause I have come into the world, that I should bear witness to the truth. Everyone who is of the truth hears My voice."

[38]Pilate said to Him, "What is truth?" And when he had said this, he went out

again to the Jews, and said to them, "I find no fault in Him at all.

³⁹"But you have a custom that I should release someone to you at the Passover. Do you therefore want me to release to you the King of the Jews?"

⁴⁰Then they all cried again, saying, "Not this Man, but Barabbas!" Now Barabbas was a robber.

So then Pilate took Jesus and scourged *Him.* ²And the soldiers twisted a crown of thorns and put *it* on His head, and they put on Him a purple robe. ³Then they said,* "Hail, King of the Jews!" And they struck Him with their hands.

⁴Pilate then went out again, and said to them, "Behold, I am bringing Him out to you, that you may know that I find no fault in Him."

⁵Then Jesus came out, wearing the crown of thorns and the purple robe. And *Pilate* said to them, "Behold the Man!"

⁶Therefore, when the chief priests and officers saw Him, they cried out, saying, "Crucify *Him,* crucify *Him!*"

Pilate said to them, "You take Him and crucify *Him,* for I find no fault in Him."

⁷The Jews answered him, "We have a law, and according to our* law He ought to die, because He made Himself the Son of God."

⁸Therefore, when Pilate heard that saying, he was the more afraid, ⁹and went again into the Praetorium, and said to Jesus, "Where are You from?" But Jesus gave him no answer.

¹⁰Then Pilate said to Him, "Are You not speaking to me? Do You not know that I have power to crucify You, and power to release You?"

¹¹Jesus answered, "You could have no power at all against Me unless it had been given you from above. Therefore the one who delivered Me to you has the greater sin."

¹²From then on Pilate sought to release Him, but the Jews cried out, say-

ing, "If you let this Man go, you are not Caesar's friend. Whoever makes himself a king speaks against Caesar."

¹³When Pilate therefore heard that saying, he brought Jesus out and sat down in the judgment seat in a place that is called *The* Pavement, but in Hebrew, Gabbatha. ¹⁴Now it was the Preparation Day of the Passover, and about the sixth hour. And he said to the Jews, "Behold your King!"

¹⁵But they cried out, "Away with *Him,* away with *Him!* Crucify Him!"

Pilate said to them, "Shall I crucify your King?"

The chief priests answered, "We have no king but Caesar!"

¹⁶Then he delivered Him to them to be crucified. Then they took Jesus and led *Him* away.*

¹⁷And He, bearing His cross, went out to a place called *the Place* of a Skull, which is called in Hebrew, Golgotha, ¹⁸where they crucified Him, and two others with Him, one on either side, and Jesus in the center. ¹⁹Now Pilate wrote a title and put *it* on the cross. And the writing was:

JESUS OF NAZARETH,
THE KING OF THE JEWS.

²⁰Then many of the Jews read this title, for the place where Jesus was crucified was near the city; and it was written in Hebrew, Greek, *and* Latin.

²¹Therefore the chief priests of the Jews said to Pilate, "Do not write, 'The King of the Jews,' but, 'He said, "I am the King of the Jews." ' "

²²Pilate answered, "What I have written, I have written."

PSALM 119:113-128

ם   SAMEK

I HATE the double-minded,
But I love Your law.
¹¹⁴You *are* my hiding place and
my shield;

I hope in Your word.
115 Depart from me, you
evildoers,
For I will keep the
commandments of my God!
116 Uphold me according to Your
word, that I may live;
And do not let me be
ashamed of my hope.
117 Hold me up, and I shall be
safe,
And I shall observe Your
statutes continually.
118 You reject all those who stray
from Your statutes,
For their deceit *is* falsehood.
119 You put away all the wicked of
the earth *like* dross;
Therefore I love Your
testimonies.
120 My flesh trembles for fear of
You,
And I am afraid of Your
judgments.

ע   AYIN

121 I have done justice and
righteousness;

Do not leave me to my
oppressors.
122 Be surety for Your servant for
good;
Do not let the proud oppress
me.
123 My eyes fail *from seeking* Your
salvation
And Your righteous word.
124 Deal with Your servant
according to Your mercy,
And teach me Your statutes.
125 I *am* Your servant;
Give me understanding,
That I may know Your
testimonies.
126 *It is* time for *You* to act,
O LORD,
For they have regarded Your
law as void.
127 Therefore I love Your
commandments
More than gold, yes, than fine
gold!
128 Therefore all *Your* precepts
concerning all *things*
I consider *to be* right;
I hate every false way.

PROVERBS FOR TODAY/ 16:10-11

Divination is *on the lips of the king; his mouth must not transgress in judgment.*
□ *Honest weights and scales* are *the LORD'S; all the weights in the bag* are *His work.*

MAY 31

2 SAMUEL 17:1-29

MOREOVER Ahithophel said to Absalom, "Now let me choose twelve thousand men, and I will arise and pursue David tonight. ²I will come upon him while he *is* weary and weak, and make him afraid. And all the people who *are* with him will flee, and I will strike only the king. ³Then I will bring back all the people to you. When all return except the man whom you seek, all the people will be at peace." ⁴And the saying pleased Absalom and all the elders of Israel.

⁵Then Absalom said, "Now call Hushai the Archite also, and let us hear what he says too." ⁶And when

Hushai came to Absalom, Absalom spoke to him, saying, "Ahithophel has spoken in this manner. Shall we do as he says? If not, speak up."

7So Hushai said to Absalom: "The advice that Ahithophel has given *is* not good at this time. 8For," said Hushai, "you know your father and his men, that they *are* mighty men, and they *are* enraged in their minds, like a bear robbed of her cubs in the field; and your father *is* a man of war, and will not camp with the people. 9Surely by now he is hidden in some pit, or in some *other* place. And it will be, when some of them are overthrown at the first, that whoever hears *it* will say, 'There is a slaughter among the people who follow Absalom.' 10And even he *who is* valiant, whose heart *is* like the heart of a lion, will melt completely. For all Israel knows that your father *is* a mighty man, and *those* who *are* with him *are* valiant men. 11Therefore I advise that all Israel be fully gathered to you, from Dan to Beersheba, like the sand that *is* by the sea for multitude, and that you go to battle in person. 12So we will come upon him in some place where he may be found, and we will fall on him as the dew falls on the ground. And of him and all the men who *are* with him there shall not be left so much as one. 13Moreover, if he has withdrawn into a city, then all Israel shall bring ropes to that city; and we will pull it into the river, until there is not one small stone found there."

14So Absalom and all the men of Israel said, "The advice of Hushai the Archite *is* better than the advice of Ahithophel." For the LORD had purposed to defeat the good advice of Ahithophel, to the intent that the LORD might bring disaster on Absalom.

15Then Hushai said to Zadok and Abiathar the priests, "Thus and so Ahithophel advised Absalom and the elders of Israel, and thus and so I have advised. 16Now therefore, send quickly and tell David, saying, 'Do not spend this night in the plains of the wilderness, but speedily cross over, lest the king and all the people who *are* with him be swallowed up.' " 17Now Jonathan and Ahimaaz stayed at En Rogel, for they dared not be seen coming into the city; so a female servant would come and tell them, and they would go and tell King David. 18Nevertheless a lad saw them, and told Absalom. But both of them went away quickly and came to a man's house in Bahurim, who had a well in his court; and they went down into it. 19Then the woman took and spread a covering over the well's mouth, and spread ground grain on it; and the thing was not known. 20And when Absalom's servants came to the woman at the house, they said, "Where *are* Ahimaaz and Jonathan?"

So the woman said to them, "They have gone over the water brook."

And when they had searched and could not find *them,* they returned to Jerusalem. 21Now it came to pass, after they had departed, that they came up out of the well and went and told King David, and said to David, "Arise and cross over the water quickly. For thus has Ahithophel advised against you." 22So David and all the people who *were* with him arose and crossed over the Jordan. By morning light not one of them was left who had not gone over the Jordan.

23Now when Ahithophel saw that his advice was not followed, he saddled a donkey, and arose and went home to his house, to his city. Then he put his household in order, and hanged himself, and died; and he was buried in his father's tomb.

24Then David went to Mahanaim. And Absalom crossed over the Jordan, he and all the men of Israel with him. 25And Absalom made Amasa captain of the army instead of Joab. This Amasa was the son of a man whose name was Jithra,* an Israelite,* who had gone in to Abigail the daughter of Nahash, sister of Zeruiah, Joab's mother. 26So Israel and Absalom encamped in the land of Gilead.

27Now it happened, when David had come to Mahanaim, that Shobi the son of Nahash from Rabbah of the people of Ammon, Machir the son of Ammiel from Lo Debar, and Barzillai the Gileadite from Rogelim, 28brought beds and basins, earthen vessels and wheat, barley and flour, parched *grain* and beans, lentils and parched *seeds,* 29honey and curds, sheep and cheese of the herd, for David and the people who *were* with him to eat. For they said, "The people are hungry and weary and thirsty in the wilderness."

JOHN 19:23-42

THEN the soldiers, when they had crucified Jesus, took His garments and made four parts, to each soldier a part, and also the tunic. Now the tunic was without seam, woven from the top in one piece. 24They said therefore among themselves, "Let us not tear it, but cast lots for it, whose it shall be," that the Scripture might be fulfilled which says:

> "They divided My garments
>   among them,
> And for My clothing they cast
>   lots." *

Therefore the soldiers did these things.

25Now there stood by the cross of Jesus His mother, and His mother's sister, Mary the *wife* of Clopas, and Mary Magdalene. 26When Jesus therefore saw His mother, and the disciple whom He loved standing by, He said to His mother, "Woman, behold your son!" 27Then He said to the disciple, "Behold your mother!" And from that

hour that disciple took her to his own *home.*

28After this, Jesus, knowing* that all things were now accomplished, that the Scripture might be fulfilled, said, "I thirst!" 29Now a vessel full of sour wine was sitting there; and they filled a sponge with sour wine, put *it* on hyssop, and put *it* to His mouth. 30So when Jesus had received the sour wine, He said, "It is finished!" And bowing His head, He gave up His spirit.

31Therefore, because it was the Preparation *Day,* that the bodies should not remain on the cross on the Sabbath (for that Sabbath was a high day), the Jews asked Pilate that their legs might be broken, and *that* they might be taken away. 32Then the soldiers came and broke the legs of the first and of the other who was crucified with Him. 33But when they came to Jesus and saw that He was already dead, they did not break His legs. 34But one of the soldiers pierced His side with a spear, and immediately blood and water came out. 35And he who has seen has testified, and his testimony is true; and he knows that he is telling the truth, so that you may believe. 36For these things were done that the Scripture should be fulfilled, *"Not one of His bones shall be broken."* * 37And again another Scripture says, *"They shall look on Him whom they pierced."* *

38After this, Joseph of Arimathea, being a disciple of Jesus, but secretly, for fear of the Jews, asked Pilate that he might take away the body of Jesus; and Pilate gave *him* permission. So he came and took the body of Jesus. 39And Nicodemus, who at first came to Jesus by night, also came, bringing a mixture of myrrh and aloes, about a hundred pounds. 40Then they took the body of Jesus, and bound it in strips of linen with the spices, as the custom of the Jews is to bury. 41Now in the place where He was crucified there was a garden, and in the garden a new tomb in which no one had yet been laid. ⁴²So there they laid Jesus, because of the Jews' Preparation *Day,* for the tomb was nearby.

PSALM 119:129-152

YOUR testimonies are wonderful; Therefore my soul keeps them.
¹³⁰ The entrance of Your words gives light;
It gives understanding to the simple.
¹³¹ I opened my mouth and panted,
For I longed for Your commandments.
¹³² Look upon me and be merciful to me,
As Your custom *is* toward those who love Your name.
¹³³ Direct my steps by Your word,
And let no iniquity have dominion over me.
¹³⁴ Redeem me from the oppression of man,
That I may keep Your precepts.
¹³⁵ Make Your face shine upon Your servant,
And teach me Your statutes.
¹³⁶ Rivers of water run down from my eyes,
Because *men* do not keep Your law.

צ TSADDE

¹³⁷ Righteous *are* You, O LORD,
And upright *are* Your judgments.
¹³⁸ Your testimonies, *which* You have commanded,
Are righteous and very faithful.
¹³⁹ My zeal has consumed me,
Because my enemies have forgotten Your words.
¹⁴⁰ Your word *is* very pure;
Therefore Your servant loves it.
¹⁴¹ I *am* small and despised,
Yet I do not forget Your precepts.
¹⁴² Your righteousness *is* an everlasting righteousness,
And Your law *is* truth.
¹⁴³ Trouble and anguish have overtaken me,
Yet Your commandments *are* my delights.
¹⁴⁴ The righteousness of Your testimonies *is* everlasting;
Give me understanding, and I shall live.

ק QOPH

¹⁴⁵ I cry out with *my* whole heart;
Hear me, O LORD!
I will keep Your statutes.
¹⁴⁶ I cry out to You;
Save me, and I will keep Your testimonies.
¹⁴⁷ I rise before the dawning of the morning,
And cry for help;
I hope in Your word.
¹⁴⁸ My eyes are awake through the *night* watches,
That I may meditate on Your word.
¹⁴⁹ Hear my voice according to Your lovingkindness;
O LORD, revive me according to Your justice.
¹⁵⁰ They draw near who follow after wickedness;
They are far from Your law.
¹⁵¹ You *are* near, O LORD,
And all Your commandments *are* truth.
¹⁵² Concerning Your testimonies,
I have known of old that You have founded them forever.

PROVERBS FOR TODAY/ 16:12-13

It is *an abomination for kings to commit wickedness, for a throne is established by righteousness. Righteous lips* are *the delight of kings, and they love him who speaks* what is *right.*

JUNE 1

2 SAMUEL 18:1–19:10

AND David numbered the people who *were* with him, and set captains of thousands and captains of hundreds over them. ²Then David sent out one third of the people under the hand of Joab, one third under the hand of Abishai the son of Zeruiah, Joab's brother, and one third under the hand of Ittai the Gittite. And the king said to the people, "I also will surely go out with you myself."

³But the people answered, "You shall not go out! For if we flee away, they will not care about us; nor if half of us die, will they care about us. But *you are* worth ten thousand of us now. For you are now more help to us in the city."

⁴Then the king said to them, "Whatever seems best to you I will do." So the king stood beside the gate, and all the people went out by hundreds and by thousands. ⁵Now the king had commanded Joab, Abishai, and Ittai, saying, "*Deal* gently for my sake with the young man Absalom." And all the people heard when the king gave all the captains orders concerning Absalom.

⁶So the people went out into the field of battle against Israel. And the battle was in the woods of Ephraim. ⁷The people of Israel were overthrown there before the servants of David, and a great slaughter of twenty thousand took place there that day. ⁸For the battle there was scattered over the face of the whole countryside, and the woods devoured more people that day than the sword devoured.

⁹Then Absalom met the servants of David. Absalom rode on a mule. The mule went under the thick boughs of a great terebinth tree, and his head caught in the terebinth; so he was left hanging between heaven and earth. And the mule which *was* under him went on. ¹⁰Now a certain man saw *it* and told Joab, and said, "I just saw Absalom hanging in a terebinth tree!"

¹¹So Joab said to the man who told him, "You just saw *him!* And why did you not strike him there to the ground? I would have given you ten *shekels* of silver and a belt."

¹²But the man said to Joab, "Though I were to receive a thousand *shekels* of silver in my hand, I would not raise my hand against the king's son. For in our hearing the king commanded you and Abishai and Ittai, saying, 'Beware lest anyone *touch* the young man Absalom!'* ¹³Otherwise I would have dealt falsely against my own life. For there is nothing hidden from the king, and you yourself would have set yourself against *me.*"

¹⁴Then Joab said, "I cannot linger with you." And he took three spears in his hand and thrust them through Absalom's heart, while he was *still* alive in the midst of the terebinth tree. ¹⁵And ten young men who bore Joab's armor surrounded Absalom, and struck and killed him.

¹⁶So Joab blew the trumpet, and the people returned from pursuing Israel. For Joab held back the people. ¹⁷And they took Absalom and cast him into a large pit in the woods, and laid a very large heap of stones over him. Then all Israel fled, everyone to his tent.

¹⁸Now Absalom in his lifetime had taken and set up a pillar for himself, which *is* in the King's Valley. For he said, "I have no son to keep my name in remembrance." He called the pillar after his own name. And to this day it is called Absalom's Monument.

¹⁹Then Ahimaaz the son of Zadok said, "Let me run now and take the news to the king, how the LORD has avenged him of his enemies."

²⁰And Joab said to him, "You shall not take the news this day, for you shall take the news another day. But today you shall take no news, because the king's son is dead." ²¹Then Joab said to the Cushite, "Go, tell the king what you have seen." So the Cushite bowed himself to Joab and ran.

²²And Ahimaaz the son of Zadok said again to Joab, "But whatever happens, please let me also run after the Cushite."

So Joab said, "Why will you run, my son, since you have no news ready?"

²³"But whatever happens," *he said,* "let me run."

So he said to him, "Run." Then Ahimaaz ran by way of the plain, and outran the Cushite.

²⁴Now David was sitting between the two gates. And the watchman went up to the roof over the gate, to the wall, lifted his eyes and looked, and there was a man, running alone. ²⁵Then the watchman cried out and told the king. And the king said, "If he *is* alone, *there is* news in his mouth." And he came rapidly and drew near.

²⁶Then the watchman saw *another* man running, and the watchman called to the gatekeeper and said, "There is *another* man, running alone!"

And the king said, "He also brings news."

²⁷So the watchman said, "I think the running of the first is like the running of Ahimaaz the son of Zadok."

And the king said, "He *is* a good man, and comes with good news."

²⁸So Ahimaaz called out and said to the king, "All is well!" Then he bowed down with his face to the earth before the king, and said, "Blessed *be* the LORD your God, who has delivered up the men who raised their hand against my lord the king!"

²⁹The king said, "Is the young man Absalom safe?"

Ahimaaz answered, "When Joab sent the king's servant and *me* your servant, I saw a great tumult, but I did not know what *it was about.*"

³⁰And the king said, "Turn aside *and* stand here." So he turned aside and stood still.

³¹Just then the Cushite came, and the Cushite said, "There is good news, my lord the king! For the LORD has avenged you this day of all those who rose against you."

³²And the king said to the Cushite, "Is the young man Absalom safe?"

So the Cushite answered, "May the enemies of my lord the king, and all who rise against you to do harm, be like *that* young man!"

³³Then the king was deeply moved, and went up to the chamber over the gate, and wept. And as he went, he said thus: "O my son Absalom—my son, my son Absalom—if only I had died in your place! O Absalom my son, my son!"

AND Joab was told, "Behold, the king is weeping and mourning for Absalom." ²So the victory that day was *turned* into mourning for all the people. For the people heard it said that day, "The king is grieved for his son." ³And the people stole back into the city that day, as people who are ashamed steal away when they flee in battle. ⁴But the king covered his face, and the king cried out with a loud voice, "O my son Absalom! O Absalom, my son, my son!"

⁵Then Joab came into the house to the king, and said, "Today you have disgraced all your servants who today have saved your life, the lives of your sons and daughters, the lives of your wives and the lives of your concubines, ⁶in that you love your enemies and hate your friends. For you have declared today that you regard neither princes nor servants; for today I perceive that if Absalom had lived and all of us had died today, then it would have pleased you well. ⁷Now therefore, arise, go out and speak comfort to your servants. For I swear by the LORD, if you do not go out, not one will stay with you this night. And that will be worse for you than all the evil that has befallen you from your youth until now." ⁸Then the king arose and sat in the gate. And they told all the people, saying, "There is the king, sitting in the gate." So all the people came before the king.

For everyone of Israel had fled to his tent.

⁹Now all the people were in a dispute throughout all the tribes of Israel, saying, "The king saved us from the hand of our enemies, he delivered us from the hand of the Philistines, and now he has fled from the land because of Absalom. ¹⁰But Absalom, whom we anointed over us, has died in battle. Now therefore, why do you say nothing about bringing back the king?"

JOHN 20:1-31

Now the first *day* of the week Mary Magdalene went to the tomb early, while it was still dark, and saw *that* the stone had been taken away from the tomb. ²Then she ran and came to Simon Peter, and to the other disciple, whom Jesus loved, and said to them, "They have taken away the Lord out of the tomb, and we do not know where they have laid Him."

³Peter therefore went out, and the other disciple, and were going to the tomb. ⁴So they both ran together, and the other disciple outran Peter and came to the tomb first. ⁵And he, stooping down and looking in, saw the linen cloths lying *there;* yet he did not go in. ⁶Then Simon Peter came, following him, and went into the tomb; and he saw the linen cloths lying *there,* ⁷and the handkerchief that had been around His head, not lying with the linen cloths, but folded together in a place by itself. ⁸Then the other disciple, who came to the tomb first, went in also; and he saw and believed. ⁹For as yet they did not know the Scripture, that He must rise again from the dead. ¹⁰Then the disciples went away again to their own homes.

¹¹But Mary stood outside by the tomb weeping, and as she wept she stooped down *and looked* into the tomb. ¹²And she saw two angels in white sitting, one at the head and the other at the feet, where the body of Jesus had lain. ¹³Then they said to her, "Woman, why are you weeping?"

She said to them, "Because they have taken away my Lord, and I do not know where they have laid Him."

¹⁴Now when she had said this, she turned around and saw Jesus standing *there,* and did not know that it was Jesus. ¹⁵Jesus said to her, "Woman, why are you weeping? Whom are you seeking?"

She, supposing Him to be the gardener, said to Him, "Sir, if You have carried Him away, tell me where You have laid Him, and I will take Him away."

¹⁶Jesus said to her, "Mary!"

She turned and said to Him,* "Rabboni!" (which is to say, Teacher).

¹⁷Jesus said to her, "Do not cling to Me, for I have not yet ascended to My Father; but go to My brethren and say to them, 'I am ascending to My Father and your Father, and *to* My God and your God.'"

¹⁸Mary Magdalene came and told the disciples that she had seen the Lord,* and *that* He had spoken these things to her.

¹⁹Then, the same day at evening, being the first *day* of the week, when the doors were shut where the disciples were assembled,* for fear of the Jews, Jesus came and stood in the midst, and said to them, "Peace *be* with you." ²⁰When He had said this, He showed them *His* hands and His side. Then the disciples were glad when they saw the Lord.

²¹So Jesus said to them again, "Peace to you! As the Father has sent Me, I also send you." ²²And when He had said this, He breathed on *them,* and said to them, "Receive the Holy Spirit. ²³If you forgive the sins of any, they are forgiven them; if you retain the *sins* of any, they are retained."

²⁴Now Thomas, called the Twin, one of the twelve, was not with them when Jesus came. ²⁵The other disciples therefore said to him, "We have seen the Lord."

So he said to them, "Unless I see in His hands the print of the nails, and put my finger into the print of the nails, and put my hand into His side, I will not believe."

²⁶And after eight days His disciples were again inside, and Thomas with them. Jesus came, the doors being shut, and stood in the midst, and said, "Peace to you!" ²⁷Then He said to Thomas, "Reach your finger here, and look at My hands; and reach your hand *here,* and put *it* into My side. Do not be unbelieving, but believing."

²⁸And Thomas answered and said to Him, "My Lord and my God!"

²⁹Jesus said to him, "Thomas,* because you have seen Me, you have believed. Blessed *are* those who have not seen and *yet* have believed."

³⁰And truly Jesus did many other signs in the presence of His disciples, which are not written in this book; ³¹but these are written that you may believe that Jesus is the Christ, the Son of God, and that believing you may have life in His name.

PSALM 119:153-176

ר RESH

Consider my affliction and deliver me,
For I do not forget Your law.

154 Plead my cause and redeem me;
Revive me according to Your word.

155 Salvation *is* far from the wicked,
For they do not seek Your statutes.

156 Great *are* Your tender mercies, O Lord;
Revive me according to Your judgments.

157 Many *are* my persecutors and my enemies,
Yet I do not turn from Your testimonies.

158 I see the treacherous, and am disgusted,
Because they do not keep Your word.

159 Consider how I love Your precepts;
Revive me, O Lord, according to Your lovingkindness.

160 The entirety of Your word *is* truth,
And every one of Your

righteous judgments *endures* forever.

ש   SHIN

161 Princes persecute me without a cause,
But my heart stands in awe of Your word.
162 I rejoice at Your word
As one who finds great treasure.
163 I hate and abhor lying,
But I love Your law.
164 Seven times a day I praise You,
Because of Your righteous judgments.
165 Great peace have those who love Your law,
And nothing causes them to stumble.
166 LORD, I hope for Your salvation,
And I do Your commandments.
167 My soul keeps Your testimonies,
And I love them exceedingly.
168 I keep Your precepts and Your testimonies,
For all my ways *are* before You.

ת   TAU

169 Let my cry come before You, O LORD;
Give me understanding according to Your word.
170 Let my supplication come before You;
Deliver me according to Your word.
171 My lips shall utter praise,
For You teach me Your statutes.
172 My tongue shall speak of Your word,
For all Your commandments *are* righteousness.
173 Let Your hand become my help,
For I have chosen Your precepts.
174 I long for Your salvation, O LORD,
And Your law *is* my delight.
175 Let my soul live, and it shall praise You;
And let Your judgments help me.
176 I have gone astray like a lost sheep;
Seek Your servant,
For I do not forget Your commandments.

PROVERBS FOR TODAY / 16:14-15

As messengers of death is *the king's wrath, but a wise man will appease it. In the light of the king's face* is *life, and his favor* is *like a cloud of the latter rain.*

JUNE 2

2 SAMUEL 19:11–20:13

So King David sent to Zadok and Abiathar the priests, saying, "Speak to the elders of Judah, saying, 'Why are you the last to bring the king back to his house, since the words of all Israel have come to the king, to his *very* house? 12You *are* my brethren, you *are* my bone and my flesh. Why then are you the last to bring back the king?' ¹³And say to Amasa, '*Are* you not my bone and my flesh? God do so to me, and more also, if you are not commander of the army before me continually in place of Joab.' " ¹⁴So he swayed the hearts of all the men of Judah, just as *the heart of* one man, so that they sent *this word* to the king: "Return, you and all your servants!"

¹⁵Then the king returned and came to the Jordan. And Judah came to Gilgal, to go to meet the king, to escort the king across the Jordan. ¹⁶And Shimei the son of Gera, a Benjamite, who *was* from Bahurim, hurried and came down with the men of Judah to meet King David. ¹⁷*There were* a thousand men of Benjamin with him, and Ziba the servant of the house of Saul, and his fifteen sons and his twenty servants with him; and they went over the Jordan before the king. ¹⁸Then a ferryboat went across to carry over the king's household, and to do what he thought good.

Now Shimei the son of Gera fell down before the king when he had crossed the Jordan. ¹⁹Then he said to the king, "Do not let my lord impute iniquity to me, or remember what wrong your servant did on the day that my lord the king left Jerusalem, that the king should take *it* to heart. ²⁰For I, your servant, know that I have sinned. Therefore here I am, the first to come today of all the house of Joseph to go down to meet my lord the king."

²¹But Abishai the son of Zeruiah answered and said, "Shall not Shimei be put to death for this, because he cursed the Lord's anointed?"

²²And David said, "What have I to do with you, you sons of Zeruiah, that you should be adversaries to me today? Shall any man be put to death today in Israel? For do I not know that today I *am* king over Israel?" ²³Therefore the

king said to Shimei, "You shall not die." And the king swore to him.

²⁴Now Mephibosheth the son of Saul came down to meet the king. And he had not cared for his feet, nor trimmed his mustache, nor washed his clothes, from the day the king departed until the day he returned in peace. ²⁵So it was, when he had come to Jerusalem to meet the king, that the king said to him, "Why did you not go with me, Mephibosheth?"

²⁶And he answered, "My lord, O king, my servant deceived me. For your servant said, 'I will saddle a donkey for myself, that I may ride on it and go to the king,' because your servant *is* lame. ²⁷And he has slandered your servant to my lord the king, but my lord the king *is* like the angel of God. Therefore do *what is* good in your eyes. ²⁸For all my father's house were but dead men before my lord the king. Yet you set your servant among those who eat at your own table. Therefore what right have I still to cry out anymore to the king?"

²⁹So the king said to him, "Why do you speak anymore of your matters? I have said, 'You and Ziba divide the land.' "

³⁰Then Mephibosheth said to the king, "Rather, let him take it all, inasmuch as my lord the king has come back in peace to his own house."

³¹And Barzillai the Gileadite came down from Rogelim and went across the Jordan with the king, to escort him across the Jordan. ³²Now Barzillai was a very aged man, eighty years old. And he had provided the king with supplies while he stayed at Mahanaim, for he *was* a very rich man. ³³And the king said to Barzillai, "Come across with me, and I will provide for you while you are with me in Jerusalem."

³⁴But Barzillai said to the king, "How long have I to live, that I should go up with the king to Jerusalem? ³⁵I *am* today eighty years old. Can I discern be-

tween the good and bad? Can your servant taste what I eat or what I drink? Can I hear any longer the voice of singing men and singing women? Why then should your servant be a further burden to my lord the king? 36Your servant will go a little way across the Jordan with the king. And why should the king repay me *with* such a reward? 37Please let your servant turn back again, that I may die in my own city, near the grave of my father and mother. But here is your servant Chimham; let him cross over with my lord the king, and do for him what seems good to you."

38And the king answered, "Chimham shall cross over with me, and I will do for him what seems good to you. Now whatever you request of me, I will do for you." 39Then all the people went over the Jordan. And when the king had crossed over, the king kissed Barzillai and blessed him, and he returned to his own place.

40Now the king went on to Gilgal, and Chimham* went on with him. And all the people of Judah escorted the king, and also half the people of Israel. 41Just then all the men of Israel came to the king, and said to the king, "Why have our brethren, the men of Judah, stolen you away and brought the king, his household, and all David's men with him across the Jordan?"

42So all the men of Judah answered the men of Israel, "Because the king *is* a close relative of ours. Why then are you angry over this matter? Have we ever eaten at the king's *expense?* Or has he given us any gift?"

43And the men of Israel answered the men of Judah, and said, "We have ten shares in the king; therefore we also have more *right* to David than you. Why then do you despise us—were we not the first to advise bringing back our king?"

Yet the words of the men of Judah

were fiercer than the words of the men of Israel.

AND there happened to be there a rebel,* whose name *was* Sheba the son of Bichri, a Benjamite. And he blew a trumpet, and said:

> "We have no share in David,
> Nor do we have inheritance in
> the son of Jesse;
> Every man to his tents,
> O Israel!"

2So every man of Israel deserted David, *and* followed Sheba the son of Bichri. But the men of Judah, from the Jordan as far as Jerusalem, remained loyal to their king.

3Now David came to his house at Jerusalem. And the king took the ten women, his concubines whom he had left to keep the house, and put them in seclusion and supported them, but did not go in to them. So they were shut up to the day of their death, living in widowhood.

4And the king said to Amasa, "Assemble the men of Judah for me within three days, and be present here yourself." 5So Amasa went to assemble the men of Judah. But he delayed longer than the set time which David had appointed him. 6And David said to Abishai, "Now Sheba the son of Bichri will do us more harm than Absalom. Take your lord's servants and pursue him, lest he find for himself fortified cities, and escape us." 7So Joab's men, with the Cherethites, the Pelethites, and all the mighty men, went out after him. And they went out of Jerusalem to pursue Sheba the son of Bichri. 8When they *were* at the large stone which *is* in Gibeon, Amasa came before them. Now Joab was dressed in battle armor; on it was a belt *with* a sword fastened in its sheath at his hips; and as he was going forward, it fell out. 9Then Joab said to Amasa, "*Are* you in health, my brother?" And Joab took

Amasa by the beard with his right hand to kiss him. [10]But Amasa did not notice the sword that *was* in Joab's hand. And he struck him with it in the stomach, and his entrails poured out on the ground; and he did not *strike* him again. Thus he died.

Then Joab and Abishai his brother pursued Sheba the son of Bichri. [11]Meanwhile one of Joab's men stood near Amasa, and said, "Whoever favors Joab and whoever *is* for David— follow Joab!" [12]But Amasa wallowed in *his* blood in the middle of the highway. And when the man saw that all the people stood still, he moved Amasa from the highway to the field and threw a garment over him, when he saw that everyone who came upon him halted. [13]When he was removed from the highway, all the people went on after Joab to pursue Sheba the son of Bichri.

JOHN 21:1-25

AFTER these things Jesus showed Himself again to the disciples at the Sea of Tiberias, and in this way He showed *Himself*: [2]Simon Peter, Thomas called the Twin, Nathanael of Cana in Galilee, the *sons* of Zebedee, and two others of His disciples were together. [3]Simon Peter said to them, "I am going fishing."

They said to him, "We are going with you also." They went out and immediately* got into the boat, and that night they caught nothing. [4]But when the morning had now come, Jesus stood on the shore; yet the disciples did not know that it was Jesus. [5]Then Jesus said to them, "Children, have you any food?"

They answered Him, "No."

[6]And He said to them, "Cast the net on the right side of the boat, and you will find *some*." So they cast, and now they were not able to draw it in because of the multitude of fish.

[7]Therefore that disciple whom Jesus loved said to Peter, "It is the Lord!" Now when Simon Peter heard that it was the Lord, he put on *his* outer garment (for he had removed it), and plunged into the sea. [8]But the other disciples came in the little boat (for they were not far from land, but about two hundred cubits), dragging the net with fish. [9]Then, as soon as they had come to land, they saw a fire of coals there, and fish laid on it, and bread. [10]Jesus said to them, "Bring some of the fish which you have just caught."

[11]Simon Peter went up and dragged the net to land, full of large fish, one hundred and fifty-three; and although there were so many, the net was not broken. [12]Jesus said to them, "Come *and* eat breakfast." Yet none of the disciples dared ask Him, "Who are You?"—knowing that it was the Lord. [13]Jesus then came and took the bread and gave it to them, and likewise the fish.

[14]This *is* now the third time Jesus showed Himself to His disciples after He was raised from the dead.

[15]So when they had eaten breakfast, Jesus said to Simon Peter, "Simon, *son* of Jonah,* do you love Me more than these?"

He said to Him, "Yes, Lord; You know that I love You."

He said to him, "Feed My lambs."

[16]He said to him again a second time, "Simon, *son* of Jonah,* do you love Me?"

He said to Him, "Yes, Lord; You know that I love You."

He said to him, "Tend My sheep."

[17]He said to him the third time, "Simon, *son* of Jonah,* do you love Me?" Peter was grieved because He said to him the third time, "Do you love Me?"

And he said to Him, "Lord, You know all things; You know that I love You."

Jesus said to him, "Feed My sheep. [18]Most assuredly, I say to you, when you were younger, you girded yourself and walked where you wished; but when you are old, you will stretch out your hands, and another will gird you and carry *you* where you do not wish." ¹⁹This He spoke, signifying by what death he would glorify God. And when He had spoken this, He said to him, "Follow Me."

²⁰Then Peter, turning around, saw the disciple whom Jesus loved following, who also had leaned on His breast at the supper, and said, "Lord, who is the one who betrays You?" ²¹Peter, seeing him, said to Jesus, "But Lord, what *about* this man?"

²²Jesus said to him, "If I will that he remain till I come, what *is that* to you? You follow Me."

²³Then this saying went out among the brethren that this disciple would not die. Yet Jesus did not say to him that he would not die, but, "If I will that he remain till I come, what *is that* to you?"

²⁴This is the disciple who testifies of these things, and wrote these things; and we know that his testimony is true.

²⁵And there are also many other things that Jesus did, which if they were written one by one, I suppose that even the world itself could not contain the books that would be written. Amen.

PSALM 120:1-7

A Song of Ascents.

I
N my distress I cried to the LORD,
And He heard me.
²Deliver my soul, O LORD, from
lying lips
And from a deceitful tongue.

3 What shall be given to you,
Or what shall be done to you,
You false tongue?
4 Sharp arrows of the warrior,
With coals of the broom tree!

5 Woe is me, that I dwell in
Meshech,
That I dwell among the tents
of Kedar!
6 My soul has dwelt too long
With one who hates peace.
7 I *am for* peace;
But when I speak, they *are* for
war.

PROVERBS FOR TODAY/ 16:16-17

How much better to get wisdom than gold! And to get understanding is to be chosen rather than silver. □ *The highway of the upright* is *to depart from evil; he who keeps his way preserves his soul.*

JUNE 3

2 SAMUEL 20:14–22:20

A
ND he [Sheba] went through all the tribes of Israel to Abel and Beth Maachah and all the Berites. So they were gathered together and also went after *Sheba.**

¹⁵Then they came and besieged him in Abel of Beth Maachah; and they cast up a siege mound against the city, and it stood by the rampart. And all the people who *were* with Joab battered the wall to throw it down.

[16]Then a wise woman cried out from the city, "Hear, hear! Please say to Joab, 'Come nearby, that I may speak with you.'" [17]When he had come near to her, the woman said, "*Are* you Joab?"

He answered, "I *am.*"

Then she said to him, "Hear the words of your maidservant."

And he answered, "I am listening."

[18]So she spoke, saying, "They used to talk in former times, saying, 'They shall surely seek *guidance* at Abel,' and so they would end *disputes.* [19]I *am among the* peaceable *and* faithful in Israel. You seek to destroy a city and a mother in Israel. Why would you swallow up the inheritance of the LORD?"

[20]And Joab answered and said, "Far be it, far be it from me, that I should swallow up or destroy! [21]That *is* not so. But a man from the mountains of Ephraim, Sheba the son of Bichri by name, has raised his hand against the king, against David. Deliver him only, and I will depart from the city."

So the woman said to Joab, "Watch, his head will be thrown to you over the wall." [22]Then the woman in her wisdom went to all the people. And they cut off the head of Sheba the son of Bichri, and threw *it* out to Joab. Then he blew a trumpet, and they withdrew from the city, every man to his tent. So Joab returned to the king at Jerusalem.

[23]And Joab *was* over all the army of Israel; Benaiah the son of Jehoiada *was* over the Cherethites and the Pelethites; [24]Adoram *was* in charge of revenue; Jehoshaphat the son of Ahilud *was* recorder; [25]Sheva *was* scribe; Zadok and Abiathar *were* the priests; [26]and Ira the Jairite was a chief minister under David.

Now there was a famine in the days of David for three years, year after year; and David inquired of the LORD. And the LORD answered, "*It is* because of Saul and *his* bloodthirsty house, be-

cause he killed the Gibeonites." [2]So the king called the Gibeonites and spoke to them. Now the Gibeonites *were* not of the children of Israel, but of the remnant of the Amorites; the children of Israel had sworn protection to them, but Saul had sought to kill them in his zeal for the children of Israel and Judah.

[3]Therefore David said to the Gibeonites, "What shall I do for you? And with what shall I make atonement, that you may bless the inheritance of the LORD?"

[4]And the Gibeonites said to him, "We will have no silver or gold from Saul or from his house, nor shall you kill any man in Israel for us."

So he said, "Whatever you say, I will do for you."

[5]Then they answered the king, "As for the man who consumed us and plotted against us, *that* we should be destroyed from remaining in any of the territories of Israel, [6]let seven men of his descendants be delivered to us, and we will hang them before the LORD in Gibeah of Saul, *whom* the LORD chose."

And the king said, "I will give *them.*"

[7]But the king spared Mephibosheth the son of Jonathan, the son of Saul, because of the LORD's oath that *was* between them, between David and Jonathan the son of Saul. [8]So the king took Armoni and Mephibosheth, the two sons of Rizpah the daughter of Aiah, whom she bore to Saul, and the five sons of Michal* the daughter of Saul, whom she brought up for Adriel the son of Barzillai the Meholathite; [9]and he delivered them into the hands of the Gibeonites, and they hanged them on the hill before the LORD. So they fell, *all* seven together, and were put to death in the days of harvest, in the first *days,* in the beginning of barley harvest.

[10]Now Rizpah the daughter of Aiah took sackcloth and spread it for herself on the rock, from the beginning of har-

vest until the late rains poured on them from heaven. And she did not allow the birds of the air to rest on them by day nor the beasts of the field by night.

11And David was told what Rizpah the daughter of Aiah, the concubine of Saul, had done. 12Then David went and took the bones of Saul, and the bones of Jonathan his son, from the men of Jabesh Gilead who had stolen them from the street of Beth Shan,* where the Philistines had hung them up, after the Philistines had struck down Saul in Gilboa. 13So he brought up the bones of Saul and the bones of Jonathan his son from there; and they gathered the bones of those who had been hanged. 14They buried the bones of Saul and Jonathan his son in the country of Benjamin in Zelah, in the tomb of Kish his father. So they performed all that the king commanded. And after that God heeded the prayer for the land.

15When the Philistines were at war again with Israel, David and his servants with him went down and fought against the Philistines; and David grew faint. 16Then Ishbi-Benob, who *was* one of the sons of the giant, the weight of whose bronze spear *was* three hundred *shekels,* who was bearing a new *sword,* thought he could kill David. 17But Abishai the son of Zeruiah came to his aid, and struck the Philistine and killed him. Then the men of David swore to him, saying, "You shall go out no more with us to battle, lest you quench the lamp of Israel."

18Now it happened afterward that there was again a battle with the Philistines at Gob. Then Sibbechai the Hushathite killed Saph,* who *was* one of the sons of the giant. 19Again there was war at Gob with the Philistines, where Elhanan the son of Jaare-Oregim* the Bethlehemite killed *the brother of* Goliath the Gittite, the shaft of whose spear *was* like a weaver's beam.

20Yet again there was war at Gath, where there was a man of *great* stat-ure, who had six fingers on each hand and six toes on each foot, twenty-four in number; and he also was born to the giant. 21So when he defied Israel, Jonathan the son of Shimea,* David's brother, killed him.

22These four were born to the giant in Gath, and fell by the hand of David and by the hand of his servants.

THEN David spoke to the LORD the words of this song, on the day when the LORD had delivered him from the hand of all his enemies, and from the hand of Saul. 2And he said:*

> "The LORD *is* my rock and my
>   fortress and my deliverer;
> 3 The God of my strength, in
>   whom I will trust;
> My shield and the horn of my
>   salvation,
> My stronghold and my refuge;
> My Savior, You save me from
>   violence.
> 4 I will call upon the LORD, *who*
>   *is worthy* to be praised;
> So shall I be saved from my
>   enemies.
>
> 5 "When the waves of death
>   surrounded me,
> The floods of ungodliness
>   made me afraid.
> 6 The sorrows of Sheol
>   surrounded me;
> The snares of death
>   confronted me.
> 7 In my distress I called upon
>   the LORD,
> And cried out to my God;
> He heard my voice from His
>   temple,
> And my cry *entered* His ears.
>
> 8 "Then the earth shook and
>   trembled;
> The foundations of heaven*
>   quaked and were shaken,
> Because He was angry.

9 Smoke went up from His
    nostrils,
   And devouring fire from His
    mouth;
   Coals were kindled by it.
10 He bowed the heavens also,
    and came down
   With darkness under His feet.
11 He rode upon a cherub, and
    flew;
   And He was seen* upon the
    wings of the wind.
12 He made darkness canopies
    around Him,
   Dark waters *and* thick clouds
    of the skies.
13 From the brightness before
    Him
   Coals of fire were kindled.

14 "The LORD thundered from
    heaven,
   And the Most High uttered
    His voice.
15 He sent out arrows and
    scattered them;
   Lightning bolts, and He
    vanquished them.
16 Then the channels of the sea
    were seen,
   The foundations of the world
    were uncovered,
   At the rebuke of the LORD,
   At the blast of the breath of
    His nostrils.

17 "He sent from above, He took
    me,
   He drew me out of many
    waters.
18 He delivered me from my
    strong enemy,
   From those who hated me;
   For they were too strong for
    me.
19 They confronted me in the
    day of my calamity,
   But the LORD was my support.
20 He also brought me out into a
    broad place;

He delivered me because He
 delighted in me."

ACTS 1:1-26

THE former account I made,
O Theophilus, of all that Jesus
began both to do and teach, 2until the day in which He was taken up, after He through the Holy Spirit had given commandments to the apostles whom He had chosen, 3to whom He also presented Himself alive after His suffering by many infallible proofs, being seen by them during forty days and speaking of the things pertaining to the kingdom of God.

4And being assembled together with *them,* He commanded them not to depart from Jerusalem, but to wait for the Promise of the Father, "which," *He said,* "you have heard from Me; 5for John truly baptized with water, but you shall be baptized with the Holy Spirit not many days from now." 6Therefore, when they had come together, they asked Him, saying, "Lord, will You at this time restore the kingdom to Israel?" 7And He said to them, "It is not for you to know times or seasons which the Father has put in His own authority. 8But you shall receive power when the Holy Spirit has come upon you; and you shall be witnesses to Me* in Jerusalem, and in all Judea and Samaria, and to the end of the earth."

9Now when He had spoken these things, while they watched, He was taken up, and a cloud received Him out of their sight. 10And while they looked steadfastly toward heaven as He went up, behold, two men stood by them in white apparel, 11who also said, "Men of Galilee, why do you stand gazing up into heaven? This *same* Jesus, who was taken up from you into heaven, will so come in like manner as you saw Him go into heaven."

12Then they returned to Jerusalem from the mount called Olivet, which is near Jerusalem, a Sabbath day's journey. 13And when they had entered, they went up into the upper room where they were staying: Peter, James, John, and Andrew; Philip and Thomas; Bartholomew and Matthew; James *the son* of Alphaeus and Simon the Zealot; and Judas *the son* of James. 14These all continued with one accord in prayer and supplication,* with the women and Mary the mother of Jesus, and with His brothers.

15And in those days Peter stood up in the midst of the disciples* (altogether the number of names was about a hundred and twenty), and said, 16"Men *and* brethren, this Scripture had to be fulfilled, which the Holy Spirit spoke before by the mouth of David concerning Judas, who became a guide to those who arrested Jesus; 17for he was numbered with us and obtained a part in this ministry."

18(Now this man purchased a field with the wages of iniquity; and falling headlong, he burst open in the middle and all his entrails gushed out. 19And it became known to all those dwelling in Jerusalem; so that field is called in their own language, Akel Dama, that is, Field of Blood.)

20"For it is written in the Book of Psalms:

> 'Let his dwelling place be desolate,
> And let no one live in it';*

and,

> 'Let * another take his office.'*

21"Therefore, of these men who have accompanied us all the time that the Lord Jesus went in and out among us, 22beginning from the baptism of John to that day when He was taken up from us, one of these must become a witness with us of His resurrection."

23And they proposed two: Joseph called Barsabas, who was surnamed Justus, and Matthias. 24And they prayed and said, "You, O Lord, who know the hearts of all, show which of these two You have chosen 25to take part in this ministry and apostleship from which Judas by transgression fell, that he might go to his own place." 26And they cast their lots, and the lot fell on Matthias. And he was numbered with the eleven apostles.

PSALM 121:1-8

A Song of Ascents.

I will lift up my eyes to the hills—
From whence comes my help?
2My help *comes* from the LORD,
Who made heaven and earth.

3 He will not allow your foot to
   be moved;
   He who keeps you will not
   slumber.
4 Behold, He who keeps Israel
   Shall neither slumber nor
   sleep.

5 The LORD *is* your keeper;
   The LORD *is* your shade at
   your right hand.
6 The sun shall not strike you
   by day,
   Nor the moon by night.

7 The LORD shall preserve you
   from all evil;
   He shall preserve your soul.
8 The LORD shall preserve your
   going out and your coming
   in
   From this time forth, and
   even forevermore.

PROVERBS FOR TODAY/ 16:18

Pride goes *before destruction, and a haughty spirit before a fall.*

2 SAMUEL 22:21–23:23

"THE LORD rewarded me [David]
according to my righteousness;
According to the cleanness of
my hands
He has recompensed me.

22 For I have kept the ways of
the LORD,
And have not wickedly
departed from my God.

23 For all His judgments *were*
before me;
And *as for* His statutes, I did
not depart from them.

24 I was also blameless before
Him,
And I kept myself from my
iniquity.

25 Therefore the LORD has
recompensed me according
to my righteousness,
According to my cleanness in
His eyes.*

26 "With the merciful You will
show Yourself merciful;
With a blameless man You
will show Yourself
blameless;

27 With the pure You will show
Yourself pure;
And with the devious You will
show Yourself shrewd.

28 You will save the humble
people;
But Your eyes *are* on the
haughty, *that* You may
bring *them* down.

29 "For You *are* my lamp, O LORD;
The LORD shall enlighten my
darkness.

30 For by You I can run against a
troop;

By my God I can leap over a
wall.

31 *As for* God, His way *is* perfect;
The word of the LORD *is*
proven;
He *is* a shield to all who trust
in Him.

32 "For who *is* God, except the
LORD?
And who *is* a rock, except our
God?

33 God *is* my strength *and*
power,*
And He makes my* way
perfect.

34 He makes my* feet like the
feet of deer,
And sets me on my high
places.

35 He teaches my hands to make
war,
So that my arms can bend a
bow of bronze.

36 "You have also given me the
shield of Your salvation;
Your gentleness has made me
great.

37 You enlarged my path under
me;
So my feet did not slip.

38 "I have pursued my enemies
and destroyed them;
Neither did I turn back again
till they were destroyed.

39 And I have destroyed them
and wounded them,
So that they could not rise;
They have fallen under my
feet.

40 For You have armed me with
strength for the battle;

You have subdued under me
    those who rose against me.
41 You have also given me the
    necks of my enemies,
So that I destroyed those who
    hated me.
42 They looked, but *there was*
    none to save;
Even to the LORD, but He did
    not answer them.
43 Then I beat them as fine as
    the dust of the earth;
I trod them like dirt in the
    streets,
And I spread them out.

44 "You have also delivered me
    from the strivings of my
    people;
You have kept me as the head
    of the nations.
A people I have not known
    shall serve me.
45 The foreigners submit to me;
As soon as they hear, they
    obey me.
46 The foreigners fade away,
And come frightened* from
    their hideouts.

47 "The LORD lives!
Blessed *be* my Rock!
Let God be exalted,
The Rock of my salvation!
48 *It is* God who avenges me,
And subdues the peoples
    under me;
49 He delivers me from my
    enemies.
You also lift me up above
    those who rise against me;
You have delivered me from
    the violent man.
50 Therefore I will give thanks to
    You, O LORD, among the
    Gentiles,
And sing praises to Your
    name.

51 "*He is* the tower of salvation to
    His king,
And shows mercy to His
    anointed,
To David and his descendants
    forevermore."

Now these *are* the last words of David.

Thus says David the son of
    Jesse;
Thus says the man raised up
    on high,
The anointed of the God of
    Jacob,
And the sweet psalmist of
    Israel:

2 "The Spirit of the LORD spoke
    by me,
And His word *was* on my
    tongue.
3 The God of Israel said,
The Rock of Israel spoke to
    me:

'He who rules over men *must
    be* just,
Ruling in the fear of God.
4 And *he shall be* like the light of
    the morning *when* the sun
    rises,
A morning without clouds,
Like the tender grass
    springing out of the earth,
By clear shining after rain.'

5 "Although my house *is* not so
    with God,
Yet He has made with me an
    everlasting covenant,
Ordered in all *things* and
    secure.
For *this is* all my salvation and
    all *my* desire;
Will He not make *it* increase?
6 But *the sons* of rebellion *shall*
    all *be* as thorns thrust away,
Because they cannot be taken
    with hands.

7 But the man *who* touches them
Must be armed with iron and the shaft of a spear,
And they shall be utterly burned with fire in *their* place."

8These *are* the names of the mighty men whom David had: Josheb-Basshebeth* the Tachmonite, chief among the captains.* He was called Adino the Eznite, because he had killed eight hundred men at one time. 9And after him *was* Eleazar the son of Dodo,* the Ahohite, *one* of the three mighty men with David when they defied the Philistines *who* were gathered there for battle, and the men of Israel had retreated. 10He arose and attacked the Philistines until his hand was weary, and his hand stuck to the sword. The LORD brought about a great victory that day; and the people returned after him only to plunder. 11And after him *was* Shammah the son of Agee the Hararite. The Philistines had gathered together into a troop where there was a piece of ground full of lentils. So the people fled from the Philistines. 12But he stationed himself in the middle of the field, defended it, and killed the Philistines. So the LORD brought about a great victory.

13Then three of the thirty chief men went down at harvest time and came to David at the cave of Adullam. And the troop of Philistines encamped in the Valley of Rephaim. 14David *was* then in the stronghold, and the garrison of the Philistines *was* then *in* Bethlehem. 15And David said with longing, "Oh, that someone would give me a drink of the water from the well of Bethlehem, which *is* by the gate!" 16So the three mighty men broke through the camp of the Philistines, drew water from the well of Bethlehem that *was* by the gate, and took it and brought *it* to David. Nevertheless he would not drink it, but poured it out to the LORD. 17And he

said, "Far be it from me, O LORD, that I should do this! Is *this not* the blood of the men who went in *jeopardy of* their lives?" Therefore he would not drink it.

These things were done by the three mighty men.

18Now Abishai the brother of Joab, the son of Zeruiah, was chief of *another* three.* He lifted his spear against three hundred *men,* killed *them,* and won a name among *these* three. 19Was he not the most honored of three? Therefore he became their captain. However, he did not attain to the *first* three.

20Benaiah *was* the son of Jehoiada, the son of a valiant man from Kabzeel, who had done many deeds. He had killed two lion-like heroes of Moab. He also had gone down and killed a lion in the midst of a pit on a snowy day. 21And he killed an Egyptian, a spectacular man. The Egyptian *had* a spear in his hand; so he went down to him with a staff, wrested the spear out of the Egyptian's hand, and killed him with his own spear. 22These *things* Benaiah the son of Jehoiada did, and won a name among three mighty men. 23He was more honored than the thirty, but he did not attain to the *first* three. And David appointed him over his guard.

ACTS 2:1-47

WHEN the Day of Pentecost had fully come, they [the believers] were all with one accord* in one place. 2And suddenly there came a sound from heaven, as of a rushing mighty wind, and it filled the whole house where they were sitting. 3Then there appeared to them divided tongues, as of fire, and *one* sat upon each of them. 4And they were all filled with the Holy Spirit and began to speak with other tongues, as the Spirit gave them utterance.

5And there were dwelling in Jerusalem Jews, devout men, from every nation under heaven. ⁶And when this sound occurred, the multitude came together, and were confused, because everyone heard them speak in his own language. ⁷Then they were all amazed and marveled, saying to one another, "Look, are not all these who speak Galileans? ⁸And how *is it that* we hear, each in our own language in which we were born? ⁹Parthians and Medes and Elamites, those dwelling in Mesopotamia, Judea and Cappadocia, Pontus and Asia, ¹⁰Phrygia and Pamphylia, Egypt and the parts of Libya adjoining Cyrene, visitors from Rome, both Jews and proselytes, ¹¹Cretans and Arabs—we hear them speaking in our own tongues the wonderful works of God." ¹²So they were all amazed and perplexed, saying to one another, "Whatever could this mean?"

¹³Others mocking said, "They are full of new wine."

¹⁴But Peter, standing up with the eleven, raised his voice and said to them, "Men of Judea and all who dwell in Jerusalem, let this be known to you, and heed my words. ¹⁵For these are not drunk, as you suppose, since it is *only* the third hour of the day. ¹⁶But this is what was spoken by the prophet Joel:

17 'And it shall come to pass in
      the last days, says God,
    That I will pour out of My
      Spirit on all flesh;
    Your sons and your daughters
      shall prophesy,
    Your young men shall see
      visions,
    Your old men shall dream
      dreams.
18 And on My menservants and
      on My maidservants
    I will pour out My Spirit in
      those days;
    And they shall prophesy.
19 I will show wonders in heaven
      above

    And signs in the earth
      beneath:
    Blood and fire and vapor of
      smoke.
20 The sun shall be turned into
      darkness,
    And the moon into blood,
    Before the coming of the
      great and awesome day of
      the LORD.
21 And it shall come to pass
    That whoever calls on the
      name of the LORD
    Shall be saved.' *

²²"Men of Israel, hear these words. Jesus of Nazareth, a Man attested by God to you by miracles, wonders, and signs which God did through Him in your midst, as you yourselves also know— ²³Him, being delivered by the determined purpose and foreknowledge of God, you have taken* by lawless hands, have crucified, and put to death; ²⁴whom God raised up, having loosed the pains of death, because it was not possible that He should be held by it. ²⁵For David says concerning Him:

    'I foresaw the LORD always
      before my face,
    For He is at my right hand,
      that I may not be shaken.
26 Therefore my heart rejoiced,
      and my tongue was glad;
    Moreover my flesh also will
      rest in hope.
27 For You will not leave my soul
      in Hades,
    Nor will You allow Your Holy
      One to see corruption.
28 You have made known to me
      the ways of life;
    You will make me full of joy in
      Your presence.' *

²⁹"Men *and* brethren, let *me* speak freely to you of the patriarch David, that he is both dead and buried, and his tomb is with us to this day. ³⁰There-

fore, being a prophet, and knowing that God had sworn with an oath to him that of the fruit of his body, according to the flesh, He would raise up the Christ to sit on his throne,* ³¹he, foreseeing this, spoke concerning the resurrection of the Christ, that His soul was not left in Hades, nor did His flesh see corruption. ³²This Jesus God has raised up, of which we are all witnesses. ³³Therefore being exalted to the right hand of God, and having received from the Father the promise of the Holy Spirit, He poured out this which you now see and hear.

³⁴"For David did not ascend into the heavens, but he says himself:

> 'The LORD said to my Lord,
> "Sit at My right hand,
> ³⁵ Till I make Your enemies
> Your footstool." '*

³⁶"Therefore let all the house of Israel know assuredly that God has made this Jesus, whom you crucified, both Lord and Christ."

³⁷Now when they heard *this,* they were cut to the heart, and said to Peter and the rest of the apostles, "Men *and* brethren, what shall we do?"

³⁸Then Peter said to them, "Repent, and let every one of you be baptized in the name of Jesus Christ for the remission of sins; and you shall receive the gift of the Holy Spirit. ³⁹For the promise is to you and to your children, and to all who are afar off, as many as the Lord our God will call."

⁴⁰And with many other words he testified and exhorted them, saying, "Be saved from this perverse generation." ⁴¹Then those who gladly* received his word were baptized; and that day about three thousand souls were added *to them.* ⁴²And they continued steadfastly in the apostles' doctrine and fellowship, in the breaking of bread, and in prayers. ⁴³Then fear came upon every soul, and many wonders and signs were done through the apostles. ⁴⁴Now all who believed were together, and had all things in common, ⁴⁵and sold their possessions and goods, and divided them among all, as anyone had need.

⁴⁶So continuing daily with one accord in the temple, and breaking bread from house to house, they ate their food with gladness and simplicity of heart, ⁴⁷praising God and having favor with all the people. And the Lord added to the church* daily those who were being saved.

PSALM 122:1-9

A Song of Ascents. Of David.

I WAS glad when they said to me, "Let us go into the house of the LORD."
2 Our feet have been standing
  Within your gates,
    O Jerusalem!

3 Jerusalem is built
  As a city that is compact together,
4 Where the tribes go up,
  The tribes of the LORD,
  To the Testimony of Israel,
  To give thanks to the name of the LORD.
5 For thrones are set there for judgment,
  The thrones of the house of David.

6 Pray for the peace of Jerusalem:
  "May they prosper who love you.
7 Peace be within your walls,
  Prosperity within your palaces."
8 For the sake of my brethren and companions,
  I will now say, "Peace *be* within you."
9 Because of the house of the LORD our God
  I will seek your good.

PROVERBS FOR TODAY/ 16:19-20

Better to be of a humble spirit with the lowly, than to divide the spoil with the proud. □ *He who heeds the word wisely will find good, and whoever trusts in the* LORD, *happy* is *he.*

JUNE 5

2 SAMUEL 23:24–24:25

ASAHEL the brother of Joab *was* one of the thirty; Elhanan the son of Dodo of Bethlehem, 25Shammah the Harodite, Elika the Harodite, 26Helez the Paltite, Ira the son of Ikkesh the Tekoite, 27Abiezer the Anathothite, Mebunnai the Hushathite, 28Zalmon the Ahohite, Maharai the Netophathite, 29Heleb the son of Baanah (the Netophathite), Ittai the son of Ribai from Gibeah of the children of Benjamin, 30Benaiah a Pirathonite, Hiddai from the brooks of Gaash, 31Abi-Albon the Arbathite, Azmaveth the Barhumite, 32Eliahba the Shaalbonite (of the sons of Jashen), Jonathan, 33Shammah the Hararite, Ahiam the son of Sharar the Hararite, 34Eliphelet the son of Ahasbai, the son of the Maachathite, Eliam the son of Ahithophel the Gilonite, 35Hezrai* the Carmelite, Paarai the Arbite, 36Igal the son of Nathan of Zobah, Bani the Gadite, 37Zelek the Ammonite, Naharai the Beerothite (armorbearer of Joab the son of Zeruiah), 38Ira the Ithrite, Gareb the Ithrite, 39*and* Uriah the Hittite: thirty-seven in all.

AGAIN the anger of the LORD was aroused against Israel, and He moved David against them to say, "Go, number Israel and Judah."

2So the king said to Joab the commander of the army who *was* with him, "Now go throughout all the tribes of Israel, from Dan to Beersheba, and count the people, that I may know the number of the people."

3And Joab said to the king, "Now may the LORD your God add to the people a hundred times more than there are, and may the eyes of my lord the king see *it*. But why does my lord the king desire this thing?" 4Nevertheless the king's word prevailed against Joab and against the captains of the army. Therefore Joab and the captains of the army went out from the presence of the king to count the people of Israel.

5And they crossed over the Jordan and camped in Aroer, on the right side of the town which *is* in the midst of the ravine of Gad, and toward Jazer. 6Then they came to Gilead and to the land of Tahtim Hodshi; they came to Dan Jaan and around to Sidon; 7and they came to the stronghold of Tyre and to all the cities of the Hivites and the Canaanites. Then they went out to South Judah *as far as* Beersheba. 8So when they had gone through all the land, they came to Jerusalem at the end of nine months and twenty days. 9Then Joab gave the sum of the number of the people to the king. And there were in Israel eight hundred thousand valiant men who drew the sword, and the men of Judah were five hundred thousand men.

10And David's heart condemned him after he had numbered the people. So David said to the LORD, "I have sinned greatly in what I have done; but now, I pray, O LORD, take away the iniquity of Your servant, for I have done very foolishly."

¹¹Now when David arose in the morning, the word of the LORD came to the prophet Gad, David's seer, saying, ¹²"Go and tell David, 'Thus says the LORD: "I offer you three *things;* choose one of them for yourself, that I may do *it* to you." ' " ¹³So Gad came to David and told him; and he said to him, "Shall seven* years of famine come to you in your land? Or shall you flee three months before your enemies, while they pursue you? Or shall there be three days' plague in your land? Now consider and see what answer I should take back to Him who sent me."

¹⁴And David said to Gad, "I am in great distress. Please let us fall into the hand of the LORD, for His mercies *are* great; but do not let me fall into the hand of man."

¹⁵So the LORD sent a plague upon Israel from the morning till the appointed time. From Dan to Beersheba seventy thousand men of the people died. ¹⁶And when the angel* stretched out His hand over Jerusalem to destroy it, the LORD relented from the destruction, and said to the angel who was destroying the people, "It is enough; now restrain your hand." And the angel of the LORD was by the threshing floor of Araunah* the Jebusite.

¹⁷Then David spoke to the LORD when he saw the angel who was striking the people, and said, "Surely I have sinned, and I have done wickedly; but these sheep, what have they done? Let Your hand, I pray, be against me and against my father's house."

¹⁸And Gad came that day to David and said to him, "Go up, erect an altar to the LORD on the threshing floor of Araunah the Jebusite." ¹⁹So David, according to the word of Gad, went up as the LORD commanded. ²⁰Now Araunah looked, and saw the king and his servants coming toward him. So Araunah

went out and bowed before the king with his face to the ground.

²¹Then Araunah said, "Why has my lord the king come to his servant?"

And David said, "To buy the threshing floor from you, to build an altar to the LORD, that the plague may be withdrawn from the people."

²²Now Araunah said to David, "Let my lord the king take and offer up whatever *seems* good to him. Look, *here are* oxen for burnt sacrifice, and threshing implements and the yokes of the oxen for wood. ²³All these, O king, Araunah has given to the king."

And Araunah said to the king, "May the LORD your God accept you."

²⁴Then the king said to Araunah, "No, but I will surely buy *it* from you for a price; nor will I offer burnt offerings to the LORD my God with that which costs me nothing." So David bought the threshing floor and the oxen for fifty shekels of silver. ²⁵And David built there an altar to the LORD, and offered burnt offerings and peace offerings. So the LORD heeded the prayers for the land, and the plague was withdrawn from Israel.

ACTS 3:1-26

Now Peter and John went up together to the temple at the hour of prayer, the ninth *hour.* ²And a certain man lame from his mother's womb was carried, whom they laid daily at the gate of the temple which is called Beautiful, to ask alms from those who entered the temple; ³who, seeing Peter and John about to go into the temple, asked for alms. ⁴And fixing his eyes on him, with John, Peter said, "Look at us." ⁵So he gave them his attention, expecting to receive something from them. ⁶Then Peter said, "Silver and gold I do not have, but what I do have I give you: In the name of Jesus Christ of Nazareth, rise up and walk." ⁷And he took him by the right hand and lifted *him* up, and immediately his feet and ankle bones received strength. ⁸So he, leaping up, stood and walked and entered the temple with them—walking, leaping, and praising God. ⁹And all the people saw him walking and praising God. ¹⁰Then they knew that it was he who sat begging alms at the Beautiful Gate of the temple; and they were filled with wonder and amazement at what had happened to him.

¹¹Now as the lame man who was healed held on to Peter and John, all the people ran together to them in the porch which is called Solomon's, greatly amazed. ¹²So when Peter saw *it,* he responded to the people: "Men of Israel, why do you marvel at this? Or why look so intently at us, as though by our own power or godliness we had made this man walk? ¹³The God of Abraham, Isaac, and Jacob, the God of our fathers, glorified His Servant Jesus, whom you delivered up and denied in the presence of Pilate, when he was determined to let *Him* go. ¹⁴But you denied the Holy One and the Just, and asked for a murderer to be granted to you, ¹⁵and killed the Prince of life, whom God raised from the dead, of which we are witnesses. ¹⁶And His name, through faith in His name, has made this man strong, whom you see and know. Yes, the faith which *comes* through Him has given him this perfect soundness in the presence of you all.

¹⁷"Yet now, brethren, I know that you did *it* in ignorance, as *did* also your rulers. ¹⁸But those things which God foretold by the mouth of all His prophets, that the Christ would suffer, He has thus fulfilled. ¹⁹Repent therefore and be converted, that your sins may be blotted out, so that times of refreshing may come from the presence of the Lord, ²⁰and that He may send Jesus Christ, who was preached to you be-fore,* ²¹whom heaven must receive until the times of restoration of all things, which God has spoken by the mouth of all His holy prophets since the world began. ²²For Moses truly said to the fathers, *'The Lᴏʀᴅ your God will raise up for you a Prophet like me from your brethren. Him you shall hear in all things, whatever He says to you. ²³And it shall be that every soul who will not hear that Prophet shall be utterly destroyed from among the people.'* * ²⁴Yes, and all the prophets, from Samuel and those who follow, as many as have spoken, have also fore-told* these days. ²⁵You are sons of the prophets, and of the covenant which God made with our fathers, saying to Abraham, *'And in your seed all the families of the earth shall be blessed.'* * ²⁶To you first, God, having raised up His Servant Jesus, sent Him to bless you, in turning away every one *of you* from your iniquities."

PSALM 123:1-4

A Song of Ascents.

U NTO You I lift up my eyes,
O You who dwell in the
heavens.
2   Behold, as the eyes of
servants *look* to the hand of
their masters,
As the eyes of a maid to the
hand of her mistress,
So our eyes *look* to the Lᴏʀᴅ
our God,
Until He has mercy on us.

3   Have mercy on us, O Lᴏʀᴅ,
have mercy on us!
For we are exceedingly filled
with contempt.
4   Our soul is exceedingly filled
With the scorn of those who
are at ease,
With the contempt of the
proud.

PROVERBS FOR TODAY/ 16:21-23

The wise in heart will be called prudent, and sweetness of the lips increases learning. Understanding is a wellspring of life to him who has it. But the correction of fools is folly. The heart of the wise teaches his mouth, and adds learning to his lips.

JUNE 6

1 KINGS 1:1-53

Now King David was old, advanced in years; and they put covers on him, but he could not get warm. ²Therefore his servants said to him, "Let a young woman, a virgin, be sought for our lord the king, and let her stand before the king, and let her care for him; and let her lie in your bosom, that our lord the king may be warm." ³So they sought for a lovely young woman throughout all the territory of Israel, and found Abishag the Shunammite, and brought her to the king. ⁴The young woman *was* very lovely; and she cared for the king, and served him; but the king did not know her.

⁵Then Adonijah the son of Haggith exalted himself, saying, "I will be king"; and he prepared for himself chariots and horsemen, and fifty men to run before him. ⁶(And his father had not rebuked him at any time by saying, "Why have you done so?" He *was* also very good-looking. *His mother* had borne him after Absalom.) ⁷Then he conferred with Joab the son of Zeruiah and with Abiathar the priest, and they followed and helped Adonijah. ⁸But Zadok the priest, Benaiah the son of Jehoiada, Nathan the prophet, Shimei, Rei, and the mighty men who *belonged* to David were not with Adonijah.

⁹And Adonijah sacrificed sheep and oxen and fattened cattle by the stone of Zoheleth, which *is* by En Rogel; he also invited all his brothers, the king's sons, and all the men of Judah, the king's servants. ¹⁰But he did not invite Nathan the prophet, Benaiah, the mighty men, or Solomon his brother.

¹¹So Nathan spoke to Bathsheba the mother of Solomon, saying, "Have you not heard that Adonijah the son of Haggith has become king, and David our lord does not know *it?* ¹²Come, please, let me now give you advice, that you may save your own life and the life of your son Solomon. ¹³Go immediately to King David and say to him, 'Did you not, my lord, O king, swear to your maidservant, saying, "Assuredly your son Solomon shall reign after me, and he shall sit on my throne"? Why then has Adonijah become king?' ¹⁴Then, while you are still talking there with the king, I also will come in after you and confirm your words."

¹⁵So Bathsheba went into the chamber to the king. (Now the king was very old, and Abishag the Shunammite was serving the king.) ¹⁶And Bathsheba bowed and did homage to the king. Then the king said, "What is your wish?"

¹⁷Then she said to him, "My lord, you swore by the LORD your God to your maidservant, *saying,* 'Assuredly Solomon your son shall reign after me, and he shall sit on my throne.' ¹⁸So now, look! Adonijah has become king; and now, my lord the king, you do not

know about *it.* ¹⁹He has sacrificed oxen and fattened cattle and sheep in abundance, and has invited all the sons of the king, Abiathar the priest, and Joab the commander of the army; but Solomon your servant he has not invited. ²⁰And as for you, my lord, O king, the eyes of all Israel *are* on you, that you should tell them who will sit on the throne of my lord the king after him. ²¹Otherwise it will happen, when my lord the king rests with his fathers, that I and my son Solomon will be counted as offenders."

²²And just then, while she was still talking with the king, Nathan the prophet also came in. ²³So they told the king, saying, "Here is Nathan the prophet." And when he came in before the king, he bowed down before the king with his face to the ground. ²⁴And Nathan said, "My lord, O king, have you said, 'Adonijah shall reign after me, and he shall sit on my throne'? ²⁵For he has gone down today, and has sacrificed oxen and fattened cattle and sheep in abundance, and has invited all the king's sons, and the commanders of the army, and Abiathar the priest; and look! They are eating and drinking before him; and they say, '*Long* live King Adonijah!' ²⁶But he has not invited me—me your servant—nor Zadok the priest, nor Benaiah the son of Jehoiada, nor your servant Solomon. ²⁷Has this thing been done by my lord the king, and you have not told your servant who should sit on the throne of my lord the king after him?"

²⁸Then King David answered and said, "Call Bathsheba to me." So she came into the king's presence and stood before the king. ²⁹And the king took an oath and said, "*As* the Lord lives, who has redeemed my life from every distress, ³⁰just as I swore to you by the Lord God of Israel, saying, 'Assuredly Solomon your son shall be king after me, and he shall sit on my

throne in my place,' so I certainly will do this day."

³¹Then Bathsheba bowed with *her* face to the earth, and paid homage to the king, and said, "Let my lord King David live forever!"

³²And King David said, "Call to me Zadok the priest, Nathan the prophet, and Benaiah the son of Jehoiada." So they came before the king. ³³The king also said to them, "Take with you the servants of your lord, and have Solomon my son ride on my own mule, and take him down to Gihon. ³⁴There let Zadok the priest and Nathan the prophet anoint him king over Israel; and blow the horn, and say, '*Long* live King Solomon!' ³⁵Then you shall come up after him, and he shall come and sit on my throne, and he shall be king in my place. For I have appointed him to be ruler over Israel and Judah."

³⁶Benaiah the son of Jehoiada answered the king and said, "Amen! May the Lord God of my lord the king say so *too.* ³⁷As the Lord has been with my lord the king, even so may He be with Solomon, and make his throne greater than the throne of my lord King David."

³⁸So Zadok the priest, Nathan the prophet, Benaiah the son of Jehoiada, the Cherethites, and the Pelethites went down and had Solomon ride on King David's mule, and took him to Gihon. ³⁹Then Zadok the priest took a horn of oil from the tabernacle and anointed Solomon. And they blew the horn, and all the people said, "*Long* live King Solomon!" ⁴⁰And all the people went up after him; and the people played the flutes and rejoiced with great joy, so that the earth *seemed to* split with their sound.

⁴¹Now Adonijah and all the guests who *were* with him heard *it* as they finished eating. And when Joab heard the sound of the horn, he said, "Why *is* the city in such a noisy uproar?" ⁴²While he was still speaking, there

came Jonathan, the son of Abiathar the priest. And Adonijah said to him, "Come in, for you *are* a prominent man, and bring good news."

⁴³Then Jonathan answered and said to Adonijah, "No! Our lord King David has made Solomon king. ⁴⁴The king has sent with him Zadok the priest, Nathan the prophet, Benaiah the son of Jehoiada, the Cherethites, and the Pelethites; and they have made him ride on the king's mule. ⁴⁵So Zadok the priest and Nathan the prophet have anointed him king at Gihon; and they have gone up from there rejoicing, so that the city is in an uproar. This *is* the noise that you have heard. ⁴⁶Also Solomon sits on the throne of the kingdom. ⁴⁷And moreover the king's servants have gone to bless our lord King David, saying, 'May God make the name of Solomon better than your name, and may He make his throne greater than your throne.' Then the king bowed himself on the bed. ⁴⁸Also the king said thus, 'Blessed *be* the LORD God of Israel, who has given *one* to sit on my throne this day, while my eyes see *it!*' "

⁴⁹So all the guests who were with Adonijah were afraid, and arose, and each one went his way.

⁵⁰Now Adonijah was afraid of Solomon; so he arose, and went and took hold of the horns of the altar. ⁵¹And it was told Solomon, saying, "Indeed Adonijah is afraid of King Solomon; for look, he has taken hold of the horns of the altar, saying, 'Let King Solomon swear to me today that he will not put his servant to death with the sword.' "

⁵²Then Solomon said, "If he proves himself a worthy man, not one hair of him shall fall to the earth; but if wickedness is found in him, he shall die." ⁵³So King Solomon sent them to bring him down from the altar. And he came and fell down before King Solomon; and Solomon said to him, "Go to your house."

ACTS 4:1-37

Now as they [Peter and John] spoke to the people, the priests, the captain of the temple, and the Sadducees came upon them, ²being greatly disturbed that they taught the people and preached in Jesus the resurrection from the dead. ³And they laid hands on them, and put *them* in custody until the next day, for it was already evening. ⁴However, many of those who heard the word believed; and the number of the men came to be about five thousand.

⁵And it came to pass, on the next day, that their rulers, elders, and scribes, ⁶as well as Annas the high priest, Caiaphas, John, and Alexander, and as many as were of the family of the high priest, were gathered together at Jerusalem. ⁷And when they had set them in the midst, they asked, "By what power or by what name have you done this?"

⁸Then Peter, filled with the Holy Spirit, said to them, "Rulers of the people and elders of Israel: ⁹If we this day are judged for a good deed *done* to a helpless man, by what means he has been made well, ¹⁰let it be known to you all, and to all the people of Israel, that by the name of Jesus Christ of Nazareth, whom you crucified, whom God raised from the dead, by Him this man stands here before you whole. ¹¹This is the *'stone which was rejected by you builders, which has become the chief cornerstone.'* * ¹²Nor is there salvation in any other, for there is no other name under heaven given among men by which we must be saved."

¹³Now when they saw the boldness of Peter and John, and perceived that they were uneducated and untrained men, they marveled. And they realized that they had been with Jesus. ¹⁴And seeing the man who had been healed standing with them, they could say

nothing against it. [15]But when they had commanded them to go aside out of the council, they conferred among themselves, [16]saying, "What shall we do to these men? For, indeed, that a notable miracle has been done through them *is* evident to all who dwell in Jerusalem, and we cannot deny it. [17]But so that it spreads no further among the people, let us severely threaten them, that from now on they speak to no man in this name."

[18]So they called them and commanded them not to speak at all nor teach in the name of Jesus. [19]But Peter and John answered and said to them, "Whether it is right in the sight of God to listen to you more than to God, you judge. [20]For we cannot but speak the things which we have seen and heard." [21]So when they had further threatened them, they let them go, finding no way of punishing them, because of the people, since they all glorified God for what had been done. [22]For the man was over forty years old on whom this miracle of healing had been performed.

[23]And being let go, they went to their own *companions* and reported all that the chief priests and elders had said to them. [24]So when they heard that, they raised their voice to God with one accord and said: "Lord, You *are* God, who made heaven and earth and the sea, and all that is in them, [25]who by the mouth of Your servant David* have said:

> 'Why did the nations rage,
>   And the people plot vain
>   things?
> [26] The kings of the earth took
>   their stand,
>   And the rulers were gathered
>   together
>   Against the LORD and against
>   His Christ.'*

[27]"For truly against Your holy Servant Jesus, whom You anointed, both Herod and Pontius Pilate, with the Gentiles and the people of Israel, were gathered together [28]to do whatever Your hand and Your purpose determined before to be done. [29]Now, Lord, look on their threats, and grant to Your servants that with all boldness they may speak Your word, [30]by stretching out Your hand to heal, and that signs and wonders may be done through the name of Your holy Servant Jesus."

[31]And when they had prayed, the place where they were assembled together was shaken; and they were all filled with the Holy Spirit, and they spoke the word of God with boldness.

[32]Now the multitude of those who believed were of one heart and one soul; neither did anyone say that any of the things he possessed was his own, but they had all things in common. [33]And with great power the apostles gave witness to the resurrection of the Lord Jesus. And great grace was upon them all. [34]Nor was there anyone among them who lacked; for all who were possessors of lands or houses sold them, and brought the proceeds of the things that were sold, [35]and laid *them* at the apostles' feet; and they distributed to each as anyone had need.

[36]And Joses,* who was also named Barnabas by the apostles (which is translated Son of Encouragement), a Levite of the country of Cyprus, [37]having land, sold *it,* and brought the money and laid *it* at the apostles' feet.

PSALM 124:1-8

A Song of Ascents. Of David.

"IF it had not been the LORD who
        was on our side,"
    Let Israel now say—
[2] "If it had not been the LORD
        who was on our side,
    When men rose up against us,
[3] Then they would have
        swallowed us alive,

When their wrath was kindled
against us;

4 Then the waters would have
overwhelmed us,
The stream would have gone
over our soul;

5 Then the swollen waters
Would have gone over our
soul."

6 Blessed *be* the LORD,

Who has not given us *as* prey
to their teeth.

7 Our soul has escaped as a
bird from the snare of the
fowlers;*
The snare is broken, and we
have escaped.

8 Our help *is* in the name of the
LORD,
Who made heaven and earth.

PROVERBS FOR TODAY/ 16:24

Pleasant words are like *a honeycomb, sweetness to the soul and health to the bones.*

JUNE 7

1 KINGS 2:1–3:3

Now the days of David drew near that he should die, and he charged Solomon his son, saying: ²"I go the way of all the earth; be strong, therefore, and prove yourself a man. ³And keep the charge of the LORD your God: to walk in His ways, to keep His statutes, His commandments, His judgments, and His testimonies, as it is written in the Law of Moses, that you may prosper in all that you do and wherever you turn; ⁴that the LORD may fulfill His word which He spoke concerning me, saying, 'If your sons take heed to their way, to walk before Me in truth with all their heart and with all their soul,' He said, 'you shall not lack a man on the throne of Israel.'

⁵"Moreover you know also what Joab the son of Zeruiah did to me, *and* what he did to the two commanders of the armies of Israel, to Abner the son of Ner and Amasa the son of Jether, whom he killed. And he shed the blood of war in peacetime, and put the blood of war on his belt that *was* around his waist, and on his sandals that *were* on his feet. ⁶Therefore do according to your wisdom, and do not let his gray hair go down to the grave in peace.

⁷"But show kindness to the sons of Barzillai the Gileadite, and let them be among those who eat at your table, for so they came to me when I fled from Absalom your brother.

⁸"And see, *you have* with you Shimei the son of Gera, a Benjamite from Bahurim, who cursed me with a malicious curse in the day when I went to Mahanaim. But he came down to meet me at the Jordan, and I swore to him by the LORD, saying, 'I will not put you to death with the sword.' ⁹Now therefore, do not hold him guiltless, for you *are* a wise man and know what you ought to do to him; but bring his gray hair down to the grave with blood."

¹⁰So David rested with his fathers, and was buried in the City of David. ¹¹The period that David reigned over Israel *was* forty years; seven years he reigned in Hebron, and in Jerusalem he reigned thirty-three years. ¹²Then Solomon sat on the throne of his father

David; and his kingdom was firmly established.

¹³Now Adonijah the son of Haggith came to Bathsheba the mother of Solomon. So she said, "Do you come peaceably?"

And he said, "Peaceably." ¹⁴Moreover he said, "I have something *to say* to you."

And she said, "Say it."

¹⁵Then he said, "You know that the kingdom was mine, and all Israel had set their expectations on me, that I should reign. However, the kingdom has been turned over, and has become my brother's; for it was his from the Lord. ¹⁶Now I ask one petition of you; do not deny me."

And she said to him, "Say it."

¹⁷Then he said, "Please speak to King Solomon, for he will not refuse you, that he may give me Abishag the Shunammite as wife."

¹⁸So Bathsheba said, "Very well, I will speak for you to the king."

¹⁹Bathsheba therefore went to King Solomon, to speak to him for Adonijah. And the king rose up to meet her and bowed down to her, and sat down on his throne and had a throne set for the king's mother; so she sat at his right hand. ²⁰Then she said, "I desire one small petition of you; do not refuse me."

And the king said to her, "Ask it, my mother, for I will not refuse you."

²¹So she said, "Let Abishag the Shunammite be given to Adonijah your brother as wife."

²²And King Solomon answered and said to his mother, "Now why do you ask Abishag the Shunammite for Adonijah? Ask for him the kingdom also— for he *is* my older brother—for him, and for Abiathar the priest, and for Joab the son of Zeruiah." ²³Then King Solomon swore by the Lord, saying, "May God do so to me, and more also, if Adonijah has not spoken this word against his own life! ²⁴Now therefore, *as* the Lord lives, who has confirmed me and set me on the throne of David my father, and who has established a house* for me, as He promised, Adonijah shall be put to death today!"

²⁵So King Solomon sent by the hand of Benaiah the son of Jehoiada; and he struck him down, and he died.

²⁶And to Abiathar the priest the king said, "Go to Anathoth, to your own fields, for you *are* deserving of death; but I will not put you to death at this time, because you carried the ark of the Lord God before my father David, and because you were afflicted every time my father was afflicted." ²⁷So Solomon removed Abiathar from being priest to the Lord, that he might fulfill the word of the Lord which He spoke concerning the house of Eli at Shiloh.

²⁸Then news came to Joab, for Joab had defected to Adonijah, though he had not defected to Absalom. So Joab fled to the tabernacle of the Lord, and took hold of the horns of the altar. ²⁹And King Solomon was told, "Joab has fled to the tabernacle of the Lord; there *he is,* by the altar." Then Solomon sent Benaiah the son of Jehoiada, saying, "Go, strike him down." ³⁰So Benaiah went to the tabernacle of the Lord, and said to him, "Thus says the king, 'Come out!' "

And he said, "No, but I will die here." And Benaiah brought back word to the king, saying, "Thus said Joab, and thus he answered me."

³¹Then the king said to him, "Do as he has said, and strike him down and bury him, that you may take away from me and from the house of my father the innocent blood which Joab shed. ³²So the Lord will return his blood on his head, because he struck down two men more righteous and better than he, and killed them with the sword—Abner the son of Ner, the commander of the army of Israel, and Amasa the son of Jether, the commander of the army of Judah—though my father David did not know *it.*

³³Their blood shall therefore return upon the head of Joab and upon the head of his descendants forever. But upon David and his descendants, upon his house and his throne, there shall be peace forever from the LORD."

³⁴So Benaiah the son of Jehoiada went up and struck and killed him; and he was buried in his own house in the wilderness. ³⁵The king put Benaiah the son of Jehoiada in his place over the army, and the king put Zadok the priest in the place of Abiathar.

³⁶Then the king sent and called for Shimei, and said to him, "Build yourself a house in Jerusalem and dwell there, and do not go out from there anywhere. ³⁷For it shall be, on the day you go out and cross the Brook Kidron, know for certain you shall surely die; your blood shall be on your own head."

³⁸And Shimei said to the king, "The saying *is* good. As my lord the king has said, so your servant will do." So Shimei dwelt in Jerusalem many days.

³⁹Now it happened at the end of three years, that two slaves of Shimei ran away to Achish the son of Maachah, king of Gath. And they told Shimei, saying, "Look, your slaves *are* in Gath!" ⁴⁰So Shimei arose, saddled his donkey, and went to Achish at Gath to seek his slaves. And Shimei went and brought his slaves from Gath. ⁴¹And Solomon was told that Shimei had gone from Jerusalem to Gath and had come back. ⁴²Then the king sent and called for Shimei, and said to him, "Did I not make you swear by the LORD, and warn you, saying, 'Know for certain that on the day you go out and travel anywhere, you shall surely die'? And you said to me, 'The word I have heard *is* good.' ⁴³Why then have you not kept the oath of the LORD and the commandment that I gave you?" ⁴⁴The king said moreover to Shimei, "You know, as your heart acknowledges, all the wickedness that you did to my father David; therefore the LORD will return your wickedness on your own head. ⁴⁵But King Solomon *shall be* blessed, and the throne of David shall be established before the LORD forever."

⁴⁶So the king commanded Benaiah the son of Jehoiada; and he went out and struck him down, and he died. Thus the kingdom was established in the hand of Solomon.

Now Solomon made a treaty with Pharaoh king of Egypt, and married Pharaoh's daughter; then he brought her to the City of David until he had finished building his own house, and the house of the LORD, and the wall all around Jerusalem. ²Meanwhile the people sacrificed at the high places, because there was no house built for the name of the LORD until those days. ³And Solomon loved the LORD, walking in the statutes of his father David, except that he sacrificed and burned incense at the high places.

ACTS 5:1-42

BUT a certain man named Ananias, with Sapphira his wife, sold a possession. ²And he kept back *part* of the proceeds, his wife also being aware *of it,* and brought a certain part and laid *it* at the apostles' feet. ³But Peter said, "Ananias, why has Satan filled your heart to lie to the Holy Spirit and keep back *part* of the price of the land for yourself? ⁴While it remained, was it not your own? And after it was sold, was it not in your own control? Why have you conceived this thing in your heart? You have not lied to men but to God."

⁵Then Ananias, hearing these words, fell down and breathed his last. So great fear came upon all those who heard these things. ⁶And the young men arose and wrapped him up, carried *him* out, and buried *him.*

7Now it was about three hours later when his wife came in, not knowing what had happened. 8And Peter answered her, "Tell me whether you sold the land for so much?"

She said, "Yes, for so much."

9Then Peter said to her, "How is it that you have agreed together to test the Spirit of the Lord? Look, the feet of those who have buried your husband *are* at the door, and they will carry you out." 10Then immediately she fell down at his feet and breathed her last. And the young men came in and found her dead, and carrying *her* out, buried *her* by her husband. 11So great fear came upon all the church and upon all who heard these things.

12And through the hands of the apostles many signs and wonders were done among the people. And they were all with one accord in Solomon's Porch. 13Yet none of the rest dared join them, but the people esteemed them highly. 14And believers were increasingly added to the Lord, multitudes of both men and women, 15so that they brought the sick out into the streets and laid *them* on beds and couches, that at least the shadow of Peter passing by might fall on some of them. 16Also a multitude gathered from the surrounding cities to Jerusalem, bringing sick people and those who were tormented by unclean spirits, and they were all healed.

17Then the high priest rose up, and all those who *were* with him (which is the sect of the Sadducees), and they were filled with indignation, 18and laid their hands on the apostles and put them in the common prison. 19But at night an angel of the Lord opened the prison doors and brought them out, and said, 20"Go, stand in the temple and speak to the people all the words of this life."

21And when they heard *that,* they entered the temple early in the morning and taught. But the high priest and those with him came and called the council together, with all the elders of the children of Israel, and sent to the prison to have them brought.

22But when the officers came and did not find them in the prison, they returned and reported, 23saying, "Indeed we found the prison shut securely, and the guards standing outside* before the doors; but when we opened them, we found no one inside!" 24Now when the high priest,* the captain of the temple, and the chief priests heard these things, they wondered what the outcome would be. 25So one came and told them, saying,* "Look, the men whom you put in prison are standing in the temple and teaching the people!"

26Then the captain went with the officers and brought them without violence, for they feared the people, lest they should be stoned. 27And when they had brought them, they set *them* before the council. And the high priest asked them, 28saying, "Did we not strictly command you not to teach in this name? And look, you have filled Jerusalem with your doctrine, and intend to bring this Man's blood on us!"

29But Peter and the *other* apostles answered and said: "We ought to obey God rather than men. 30The God of our fathers raised up Jesus whom you murdered by hanging on a tree. 31Him God has exalted to His right hand *to be* Prince and Savior, to give repentance to Israel and forgiveness of sins. 32And we are His witnesses to these things, and *so* also *is* the Holy Spirit whom God has given to those who obey Him."

33When they heard *this,* they were furious and plotted to kill them. 34Then one in the council stood up, a Pharisee named Gamaliel, a teacher of the law held in respect by all the people, and commanded them to put the apostles outside for a little while. 35And he said to them: "Men of Israel, take heed to yourselves what you intend to do regarding these men. ³⁶For some time ago Theudas rose up, claiming to be somebody. A number of men, about four hundred, joined him. He was slain, and all who obeyed him were scattered and came to nothing. ³⁷After this man, Judas of Galilee rose up in the days of the census, and drew away many people after him. He also perished, and all who obeyed him were dispersed. ³⁸And now I say to you, keep away from these men and let them alone; for if this plan or this work is of men, it will come to nothing; ³⁹but if it is of God, you cannot overthrow it—lest you even be found to fight against God."

⁴⁰And they agreed with him, and when they had called for the apostles and beaten *them,* they commanded that they should not speak in the name of Jesus, and let them go. ⁴¹So they departed from the presence of the council, rejoicing that they were counted worthy to suffer shame for His* name. ⁴²And daily in the temple, and in every house, they did not cease teaching and preaching Jesus *as* the Christ.

PSALM 125:1-5
A Song of Ascents.

THOSE who trust in the LORD
  Are like Mount Zion,
  Which cannot be moved, *but*
    abides forever.
2 As the mountains surround
    Jerusalem,
  So the LORD surrounds His
    people
  From this time forth and
    forever.

3 For the scepter of wickedness
    shall not rest
  On the land allotted to the
    righteous,
  Lest the righteous reach out
    their hands to iniquity.

4 Do good, O LORD, to *those who
    are* good,
  And to *those who are* upright
    in their hearts.

5 As for such as turn aside to
    their crooked ways,
  The LORD shall lead them away
  With the workers of iniquity.
  Peace *be* upon Israel!

PROVERBS FOR TODAY/ 16:25

There is a way that seems *right to a man, but its end* is *the way of death.*

JUNE 8

1 KINGS 3:4–4:34

NOW the king went to Gibeon to sacrifice there, for that *was* the great high place: Solomon offered a thousand burnt offerings on that altar. ⁵At Gibeon the LORD appeared to Solomon in a dream by night; and God said, "Ask! What shall I give you?"

⁶And Solomon said: "You have shown great mercy to Your servant David my father, because he walked before You in truth, in righteousness, and in uprightness of heart with You; You

have continued this great kindness for him, and You have given him a son to sit on his throne, as *it is* this day. 7Now, O Lord my God, You have made Your servant king instead of my father David, but I *am* a little child; I do not know *how* to go out or come in. 8And Your servant *is* in the midst of Your people whom You have chosen, a great people, too numerous to be numbered or counted. 9Therefore give to Your servant an understanding heart to judge Your people, that I may discern between good and evil. For who is able to judge this great people of Yours?"

10The speech pleased the Lord, that Solomon had asked this thing. 11Then God said to him: "Because you have asked this thing, and have not asked long life for yourself, nor have asked riches for yourself, nor have asked the life of your enemies, but have asked for yourself understanding to discern justice, 12behold, I have done according to your words; see, I have given you a wise and understanding heart, so that there has not been anyone like you before you, nor shall any like you arise after you. 13And I have also given you what you have not asked: both riches and honor, so that there shall not be anyone like you among the kings all your days. 14So if you walk in My ways, to keep My statutes and My commandments, as your father David walked, then I will lengthen your days."

15Then Solomon awoke; and indeed it had been a dream. And he came to Jerusalem and stood before the ark of the covenant of the Lord, offered up burnt offerings, offered peace offerings, and made a feast for all his servants.

16Now two women *who were* harlots came to the king, and stood before him. 17And one woman said, "O my lord, this woman and I dwell in the same house; and I gave birth while she *was* in the house. 18Then it happened, the third day after I had given birth, that this woman also gave birth. And we *were* together; no one *was* with us in the house, except the two of us in the house. 19And this woman's son died in the night, because she lay on him. 20So she arose in the middle of the night and took my son from my side, while your maidservant slept, and laid him in her bosom, and laid her dead child in my bosom. 21And when I rose in the morning to nurse my son, there he was, dead. But when I had examined him in the morning, indeed, he was not my son whom I had borne."

22Then the other woman said, "No! But the living one *is* my son, and the dead one *is* your son."

And the first woman said, "No! But the dead one *is* your son, and the living one *is* my son."

Thus they spoke before the king.

23And the king said, "The one says, 'This *is* my son, who lives, and your son *is* the dead one'; and the other says, 'No! But your son *is* the dead one, and my son *is* the living one.' " 24Then the king said, "Bring me a sword." So they brought a sword before the king. 25And the king said, "Divide the living child in two, and give half to one, and half to the other."

26Then the woman whose son *was* living spoke to the king, for she yearned with compassion for her son; and she said, "O my lord, give her the living child, and by no means kill him!"

But the other said, "Let him be neither mine nor yours, *but* divide *him.*"

27So the king answered and said, "Give the first woman the living child, and by no means kill him; she *is* his mother."

28And all Israel heard of the judgment which the king had rendered; and they feared the king, for they saw that the wisdom of God *was* in him to administer justice.

So King Solomon was king over all Israel. 2And these *were* his officials: Azariah the son of Zadok, the priest; ³Elihoreph and Ahijah, the sons of Shisha, scribes; Jehoshaphat the son of Ahilud, the recorder; ⁴Benaiah the son of Jehoiada, over the army; Zadok and Abiathar, the priests; ⁵Azariah the son of Nathan, over the officers; Zabud the son of Nathan, a priest *and* the king's friend; ⁶Ahishar, over the household; and Adoniram the son of Abda, over the labor force.

⁷And Solomon had twelve governors over all Israel, who provided food for the king and his household; each one made provision for one month of the year. ⁸These *are* their names: Ben-Hur,* in the mountains of Ephraim; ⁹Ben-Deker,* in Makaz, Shaalbim, Beth Shemesh, and Elon Beth Hanan; ¹⁰Ben-Hesed,* in Arubboth; to him *belonged* Sochoh and all the land of Hepher; ¹¹Ben-Abinadab,* *in* all the regions of Dor; he had Taphath the daughter of Solomon as wife; ¹²Baana the son of Ahilud, *in* Taanach, Megiddo, and all Beth Shean, which *is* beside Zaretan below Jezreel, from Beth Shean to Abel Meholah, as far as the other side of Jokneam; ¹³Ben-Geber,* in Ramoth Gilead; to him *belonged* the towns of Jair the son of Manasseh, in Gilead; to him *also belonged* the region of Argob in Bashan—sixty large cities with walls and bronze gate-bars; ¹⁴Ahinadab the son of Iddo, *in* Mahanaim; ¹⁵Ahimaaz, in Naphtali; he also took Basemath the daughter of Solomon as wife; ¹⁶Baanah the son of Hushai, in Asher and Aloth; ¹⁷Jehoshaphat the son of Paruah, in Issachar; ¹⁸Shimei the son of Elah, in Benjamin; ¹⁹Geber the son of Uri, in the land of Gilead, *in* the country of Sihon king of the Amorites, and of Og king of Bashan. *He was* the only governor who *was* in the land.

²⁰Judah and Israel *were* as numerous as the sand by the sea in multitude, eating and drinking and rejoicing. ²¹So Solomon reigned over all kingdoms from the River* *to* the land of the Philistines, as far as the border of Egypt. *They* brought tribute and served Solomon all the days of his life.

²²Now Solomon's provision for one day was thirty kors of fine flour, sixty kors of meal, ²³ten fatted oxen, twenty oxen from the pastures, and one hundred sheep, besides deer, gazelles, roebucks, and fatted fowl.

²⁴For he had dominion over all *the region* on this side of the River* from Tiphsah even to Gaza, namely over all the kings on this side of the River; and he had peace on every side all around him. ²⁵And Judah and Israel dwelt safely, each man under his vine and his fig tree, from Dan as far as Beersheba, all the days of Solomon.

²⁶Solomon had forty* thousand stalls of horses for his chariots, and twelve thousand horsemen. ²⁷And these governors, each man in his month, provided food for King Solomon and for all who came to King Solomon's table. There was no lack in their supply. ²⁸They also brought barley and straw to the proper place, for the horses and steeds, each man according to his charge.

²⁹And God gave Solomon wisdom and exceedingly great understanding, and largeness of heart like the sand on the seashore. ³⁰Thus Solomon's wisdom excelled the wisdom of all the men of the East and all the wisdom of Egypt. ³¹For he was wiser than all men—than Ethan the Ezrahite, and Heman, Chalcol, and Darda, the sons of Mahol; and his fame was in all the surrounding nations. ³²He spoke three thousand proverbs, and his songs were one thousand and five. ³³Also he spoke of trees, from the cedar tree of Lebanon even to the hyssop that springs out of the wall; he spoke also of animals, of birds, of creeping things, and of fish. ³⁴And men of all nations, from all the kings of the earth who had heard of his wisdom, came to hear the wisdom of Solomon.

ACTS 6:1-15

Now in those days, when *the number of* the disciples was multiplying, there arose a complaint against the Hebrews by the Hellenists,* because their widows were neglected in the daily distribution. ²Then the twelve summoned the multitude of the disciples and said, "It is not desirable that we should leave the word of God and serve tables. ³Therefore, brethren, seek out from among you seven men of *good* reputation, full of the Holy Spirit and wisdom, whom we may appoint over this business; ⁴but we will give ourselves continually to prayer and to the ministry of the word."

⁵And the saying pleased the whole multitude. And they chose Stephen, a man full of faith and the Holy Spirit, and Philip, Prochorus, Nicanor, Timon, Parmenas, and Nicolas, a proselyte from Antioch, ⁶whom they set before the apostles; and when they had prayed, they laid hands on them.

⁷Then the word of God spread, and the number of the disciples multiplied greatly in Jerusalem, and a great many of the priests were obedient to the faith.

⁸And Stephen, full of faith* and power, did great wonders and signs among the people. ⁹Then there arose some from what is called the Synagogue of the Freedmen (Cyrenians, Alexandrians, and those from Cilicia and Asia), disputing with Stephen. ¹⁰And they were not able to resist the wisdom and the Spirit by which he spoke. ¹¹Then they secretly induced men to say, "We have heard him speak blasphemous words against Moses and God." ¹²And they stirred up the people, the elders, and the scribes; and they came upon *him,* seized him, and brought *him* to the council. ¹³They also set up false witnesses who said, "This man does not cease to speak blasphemous* words against this holy place and the law; ¹⁴for we have heard him say that this Jesus of Nazareth will destroy this place and change the customs which Moses delivered to us." ¹⁵And all who sat in the council, looking steadfastly at him, saw his face as the face of an angel.

PSALM 126:1-6

A Song of Ascents.

When the Lord brought back the captivity of Zion,
We were like those who dream.
2   Then our mouth was filled
with laughter,
And our tongue with singing.
Then they said among the
nations,
"The Lord has done great
things for them."
3   The Lord has done great
things for us,
And we are glad.

4   Bring back our captivity,
O Lord,
As the streams in the South.

5   Those who sow in tears
Shall reap in joy.
6   He who continually goes forth
weeping,
Bearing seed for sowing,
Shall doubtless come again
with rejoicing,
Bringing his sheaves *with him.*

PROVERBS FOR TODAY/ 16:26-27

The person who labors, labors for himself, for his hungry *mouth drives him* on.
□ *An ungodly man digs up evil, and* it is *on his lips like a burning fire.*

JUNE 9

1 KINGS 5:1–6:38

Now Hiram king of Tyre sent his servants to Solomon, because he heard that they had anointed him king in place of his father, for Hiram had always loved David. ²Then Solomon sent to Hiram, saying:

3   You know how my father David could not build a house for the name of the LORD his God because of the wars which were fought against him on every side, until the LORD put *his foes** under the soles of his feet.
4   But now the LORD my God has given me rest on every side; *there is* neither adversary nor evil occurrence.
5   And behold, I propose to build a house for the name of the LORD my God, as the LORD spoke to my father David, saying, "Your son, whom I will set on your throne in your place, he shall build the house for My name."
6   Now therefore, command that they cut down cedars for me from Lebanon; and my servants will be with your servants, and I will pay you wages for your servants according to whatever you say. For you know *there is* none among us who has skill to cut timber like the Sidonians.

⁷So it was, when Hiram heard the words of Solomon, that he rejoiced greatly and said,

Blessed *be* the LORD this day, for He has given David a wise son over this great people!

⁸Then Hiram sent to Solomon, saying:

I have considered *the message* which you sent me, *and* I will do all you desire concerning the cedar and cypress logs.
9   My servants shall bring *them* down from Lebanon to the sea; I will float them in rafts by sea to the place you indicate to me, and will have them broken apart there; then you can take *them* away. And you shall fulfill my desire by giving food for my household.

¹⁰Then Hiram gave Solomon cedar and cypress logs *according to* all his desire. ¹¹And Solomon gave Hiram twenty thousand kors of wheat *as* food for his household, and twenty* kors of pressed oil. Thus Solomon gave to Hiram year by year.

¹²So the LORD gave Solomon wisdom, as He had promised him; and there was peace between Hiram and Solomon, and the two of them made a treaty together.

¹³Then King Solomon raised up a labor force out of all Israel; and the labor force was thirty thousand men. ¹⁴And he sent them to Lebanon, ten thousand a month in shifts: they were one month in Lebanon *and* two months at home; Adoniram *was* in charge of the labor force. ¹⁵Solomon had seventy thousand who carried burdens, and eighty thousand who quarried *stone* in the mountains, ¹⁶besides three thousand three hundred* from the chiefs

of Solomon's deputies, who supervised the people who labored in the work. [17]And the king commanded them to quarry large stones, costly stones, *and* hewn stones, to lay the foundation of the temple.* [18]So Solomon's builders, Hiram's builders, and the Gebalites quarried *them;* and they prepared timber and stones to build the temple.

AND it came to pass in the four hundred and eightieth* year after the children of Israel had come out of the land of Egypt, in the fourth year of Solomon's reign over Israel, in the month of Ziv, which *is* the second month, that he began to build the house of the LORD. [2]Now the house which King Solomon built for the LORD, its length *was* sixty cubits, its width twenty, and its height thirty cubits. [3]The vestibule in front of the sanctuary* of the house *was* twenty cubits long across the width of the house, *and* the width of *the vestibule* * *extended* ten cubits from the front of the house. [4]And he made for the house windows with beveled frames.

[5]Against the wall of the temple he built chambers all around, *against* the walls of the temple, all around the sanctuary and the inner sanctuary.* Thus he made side chambers all around it. [6]The lowest chamber *was* five cubits wide, the middle *was* six cubits wide, and the third *was* seven cubits wide; for he made narrow ledges around the outside of the temple, so that *the support beams* would not be fastened into the walls of the temple. [7]And the temple, when it was being built, was built with stone finished at the quarry, so that no hammer or chisel *or* any iron tool was heard in the temple while it was being built. [8]The doorway for the middle story* *was* on the right side of the temple. They went up by stairs to the middle *story,* and from the middle to the third.

[9]So he built the temple and finished it, and he paneled the temple with beams and boards of cedar. [10]And he built side chambers against the entire temple, each five cubits high; they were attached to the temple with cedar beams.

[11]Then the word of the LORD came to Solomon, saying: [12]"*Concerning* this temple which you are building, if you walk in My statutes, execute My judgments, keep all My commandments, and walk in them, then I will perform My word with you, which I spoke to your father David. [13]And I will dwell among the children of Israel, and will not forsake My people Israel."

[14]So Solomon built the temple and finished it. [15]And he built the inside walls of the temple with cedar boards; from the floor of the temple to the ceiling he paneled the inside with wood; and he covered the floor of the temple with planks of cypress. [16]Then he built the twenty-cubit room at the rear of the temple, from floor to ceiling, with cedar boards; he built *it* inside as the inner sanctuary, as the Most Holy *Place.* [17]And in front of it the temple sanctuary was forty cubits *long.* [18]The inside of the temple was cedar, carved with ornamental buds and open flowers. All *was* cedar; there was no stone *to be* seen.

[19]And he prepared the inner sanctuary inside the temple, to set the ark of the covenant of the LORD there. [20]The inner sanctuary *was* twenty cubits long, twenty cubits wide, and twenty cubits high. He overlaid it with pure gold, and overlaid the altar of cedar. [21]So Solomon overlaid the inside of the temple with pure gold. He stretched gold chains across the front of the inner sanctuary, and overlaid it with gold. [22]The whole temple he overlaid with gold, until he had finished all the temple; also he overlaid with gold the entire altar that *was* by the inner sanctuary.

²³Inside the inner sanctuary he made two cherubim *of* olive wood, *each* ten cubits high. ²⁴One wing of the cherub *was* five cubits, and the other wing of the cherub five cubits: ten cubits from the tip of one wing to the tip of the other. ²⁵And the other cherub *was* ten cubits; both cherubim *were* of the same size and shape. ²⁶The height of one cherub *was* ten cubits, and so *was* the other cherub. ²⁷Then he set the cherubim inside the inner room;* and they stretched out the wings of the cherubim so that the wing of the one touched *one* wall, and the wing of the other cherub touched the other wall. And their wings touched each other in the middle of the room. ²⁸Also he overlaid the cherubim with gold.

²⁹Then he carved all the walls of the temple all around, both the inner and outer *sanctuaries,* with carved figures of cherubim, palm trees, and open flowers. ³⁰And the floor of the temple he overlaid with gold, both the inner and outer *sanctuaries.*

³¹For the entrance of the inner sanctuary he made doors *of* olive wood; the lintel *and* doorposts *were* one-fifth *of the wall.* ³²The two doors *were of* olive wood; and he carved on them figures of cherubim, palm trees, and open flowers, and overlaid *them* with gold; and he spread gold on the cherubim and on the palm trees. ³³So for the door of the sanctuary he also made doorposts *of* olive wood, one-fourth *of the wall.* ³⁴And the two doors *were of* cypress wood; two panels *comprised* one folding door, and two panels *comprised* the other folding door. ³⁵Then he carved cherubim, palm trees, and open flowers *on them,* and overlaid *them* with gold applied evenly on the carved work.

³⁶And he built the inner court with three rows of hewn stone and a row of cedar beams.

³⁷In the fourth year the foundation of the house of the LORD was laid, in the month of Ziv. ³⁸And in the eleventh year, in the month of Bul, which is the eighth month, the house was finished in all its details and according to all its plans. So he was seven years in building it.

ACTS 7:1-29

THEN the high priest said, "Are these things so?"

²And he said, "Brethren and fathers, listen: The God of glory appeared to our father Abraham when he was in Mesopotamia, before he dwelt in Haran, ³and said to him, *'Get out of your country and from your relatives, and come to a land that I will show you.'** ⁴Then he came out of the land of the Chaldeans and dwelt in Haran. And from there, when his father was dead, He moved him to this land in which you now dwell. ⁵And *God* gave him no inheritance in it, not even *enough* to set his foot on. But even when *Abraham* had no child, He promised to give it to him for a possession, and to his descendants after him. ⁶But God spoke in this way: that his descendants would dwell in a foreign land, and that they would bring them into bondage and oppress *them* four hundred years. ⁷*'And the nation to whom they will be in bondage I will judge,'** said God, *'and after that they shall come out and serve Me in this place.'** ⁸Then He gave him the covenant of circumcision; and so *Abraham* begot Isaac and circumcised him on the eighth day; and Isaac *begot* Jacob, and Jacob *begot* the twelve patriarchs.

⁹"And the patriarchs, becoming envious, sold Joseph into Egypt. But God was with him ¹⁰and delivered him out of all his troubles, and gave him favor and wisdom in the presence of Pharaoh, king of Egypt; and he made him governor over Egypt and all his house. ¹¹Now a famine and great trouble came over all the land of Egypt and

Canaan, and our fathers found no sustenance. [12]But when Jacob heard that there was grain in Egypt, he sent out our fathers first. [13]And the second *time* Joseph was made known to his brothers, and Joseph's family became known to the Pharaoh. [14]Then Joseph sent and called his father Jacob and all his relatives to *him,* seventy-five* people. [15]So Jacob went down to Egypt; and he died, he and our fathers. [16]And they were carried back to Shechem and laid in the tomb that Abraham bought for a sum of money from the sons of Hamor, *the father* of Shechem.

[17]"But when the time of the promise drew near which God had sworn to Abraham, the people grew and multiplied in Egypt [18]till another king arose who did not know Joseph. [19]This man dealt treacherously with our people, and oppressed our forefathers, making them expose their babies, so that they might not live. [20]At this time Moses was born, and was well pleasing to God; and he was brought up in his father's house for three months. [21]But when he was set out, Pharaoh's daughter took him away and brought him up as her own son. [22]And Moses was learned in all the wisdom of the Egyptians, and was mighty in words and deeds.

[23]"Now when he was forty years old, it came into his heart to visit his brethren, the children of Israel. [24]And seeing one of *them* suffer wrong, he defended and avenged him who was oppressed, and struck down the Egyptian. [25]For he supposed that his brethren would have understood that God would deliver them by his hand, but they did not understand. [26]And the next day he appeared to two of them as they were fighting, and *tried to* reconcile them, saying, 'Men, you are brethren; why do you wrong one another?' [27]But he who did his neighbor wrong pushed him away, saying, '*Who made you a ruler and a judge over us?* [28]*Do you want to kill me as you did the Egyptian yesterday?'* * [29]Then, at this saying, Moses fled and became a dweller in the land of Midian, where he had two sons."

PSALM 127:1-5

A Song of Ascents Of Solomon.

UNLESS the LORD builds the house,
They labor in vain who build it;
Unless the LORD guards the city,
The watchman stays awake in vain.

2   *It is* vain for you to rise up early,
To sit up late,
To eat the bread of sorrows;
For so He gives His beloved sleep.

3   Behold, children *are* a heritage from the LORD,
The fruit of the womb *is* a reward.

4   Like arrows in the hand of a warrior,
So *are* the children of one's youth.

5   Happy *is* the man who has his quiver full of them;
They shall not be ashamed,
But shall speak with their enemies in the gate.

PROVERBS FOR TODAY/ 16:28-30

A perverse man sows strife, and a whisperer separates the best of friends. A violent man entices his neighbor, and leads him in a way that is *not good. He winks his eye to devise perverse things; he purses his lips* and *brings about evil.*

JUNE 10

1 KINGS 7:1-51

BUT Solomon took thirteen years to build his own house; so he finished all his house.

²He also built the House of the Forest of Lebanon; its length *was* one hundred cubits, its width fifty cubits, and its height thirty cubits, with four rows of cedar pillars, and cedar beams on the pillars. ³And *it was* paneled with cedar above the beams that *were* on forty-five pillars, fifteen *to* a row. ⁴*There were* windows *with beveled frames in* three rows, and window *was* opposite window *in* three tiers. ⁵And all the doorways and doorposts *had* rectangular frames; and window *was* opposite window *in* three tiers.

⁶He also made the Hall of Pillars: its length *was* fifty cubits, and its width thirty cubits; and in front of them *was* a portico with pillars, and a canopy *was* in front of them.

⁷Then he made a hall for the throne, the Hall of Judgment, where he might judge; and *it was* paneled with cedar from floor to ceiling.*

⁸And the house where he dwelt *had* another court inside the hall, of like workmanship. Solomon also made a house like this hall for Pharaoh's daughter, whom he had taken *as wife.*

⁹All these *were of* costly stones cut to size, trimmed with saws, inside and out, from the foundation to the eaves, and also on the outside to the great court. ¹⁰The foundation *was of* costly stones, large stones, some ten cubits and some eight cubits. ¹¹And above *were* costly stones, hewn to size, and cedar wood. ¹²The great court *was* enclosed with three rows of hewn stones and a row of cedar beams. So were the inner court of the house of the LORD and the vestibule of the temple.

¹³Now King Solomon sent and brought Huram* from Tyre. ¹⁴He *was* the son of a widow from the tribe of Naphtali, and his father *was* a man of Tyre, a bronze worker; he was filled with wisdom and understanding and skill in working with all kinds of bronze work. So he came to King Solomon and did all his work.

¹⁵And he cast two pillars of bronze, each one eighteen cubits high, and a line of twelve cubits measured the circumference of each. ¹⁶Then he made two capitals *of* cast bronze, to set on the tops of the pillars. The height of one capital *was* five cubits, and the height of the other capital *was* five cubits. ¹⁷*He made* a lattice network, with wreaths of chainwork, for the capitals which *were* on top of the pillars: seven chains for one capital and seven for the other capital. ¹⁸So he made the pillars, and two rows of pomegranates above the network all around to cover the capitals that *were* on top; and thus he did for the other capital.

¹⁹The capitals which *were* on top of the pillars in the hall *were* in the shape of lilies, four cubits. ²⁰The capitals on the two pillars also *had pomegranates* above, by the convex surface which *was* next to the network; and there *were* two hundred such pomegranates in rows on each of the capitals all around.

²¹Then he set up the pillars by the vestibule of the temple; he set up the pillar on the right and called its name Jachin, and he set up the pillar on the left and called its name Boaz. ²²The tops of the pillars were in the shape of lilies. So the work of the pillars was finished.

²³And he made the Sea of cast bronze, ten cubits from one brim to the

other; *it was* completely round. Its height *was* five cubits, and a line of thirty cubits measured its circumference.

²⁴Below its brim *were* ornamental buds encircling it all around, ten to a cubit, all the way around the Sea. The ornamental buds *were* cast in two rows when it was cast. ²⁵It stood on twelve oxen: three looking toward the north, three looking toward the west, three looking toward the south, and three looking toward the east; the Sea *was set* upon them, and all their back parts *pointed* inward. ²⁶It *was* a handbreadth thick; and its brim was shaped like the brim of a cup, *like* a lily blossom. It contained two thousand* baths.

²⁷He also made ten carts of bronze; four cubits *was* the length of each cart, four cubits its width, and three cubits its height. ²⁸And this *was* the design of the carts: They had panels, and the panels *were* between frames; ²⁹on the panels that *were* between the frames *were* lions, oxen, and cherubim. And on the frames *was* a pedestal on top. Below the lions and oxen *were* wreaths of plaited work. ³⁰Every cart had four bronze wheels and axles of bronze, and its four feet had supports. Under the laver *were* supports of cast *bronze* beside each wreath. ³¹Its opening inside the crown at the top *was* one cubit in diameter; and the opening *was* round, shaped *like* a pedestal, one and a half cubits in outside diameter; and also on the opening *were* engravings, but the panels were square, not round. ³²Under the panels *were* the four wheels, and the axles of the wheels *were joined* to the cart. The height of a wheel *was* one and a half cubits. ³³The workmanship of the wheels *was* like the workmanship of a chariot wheel; their axle pins, their rims, their spokes, and their hubs *were* all of cast *bronze.* ³⁴And *there were* four supports at the four corners of each cart; its supports *were* part of the cart itself. ³⁵On the top of the cart, at the height of half a cubit, *it was* perfectly round. And on the top of the cart, its flanges and its panels *were* of the same casting. ³⁶On the plates of its flanges and on its panels he engraved cherubim, lions, and palm trees, wherever there was a clear space on each, with wreaths all around. ³⁷Thus he made the ten carts. All of them were of the same mold, one measure, *and* one shape.

³⁸Then he made ten lavers of bronze; each laver contained forty baths, *and* each laver *was* four cubits. On each of the ten carts *was* a laver. ³⁹And he put five carts on the right side of the house, and five on the left side of the house. He set the Sea on the right side of the house, toward the south east.

⁴⁰Huram* made the lavers and the shovels and the bowls. So Huram finished doing all the work that he was to do for King Solomon *for* the house of the LORD: ⁴¹the two pillars, the *two* bowl-shaped capitals that *were* on top of the two pillars; the two networks covering the two bowl-shaped capitals which *were* on top of the pillars; ⁴²four hundred pomegranates for the two networks (two rows of pomegranates for each network, to cover the two bowl-shaped capitals that *were* on top of the pillars); ⁴³the ten carts, and ten lavers on the carts; ⁴⁴one Sea, and twelve oxen under the Sea; ⁴⁵the pots, the shovels, and the bowls.

All these articles which Huram* made for King Solomon *for* the house of the LORD *were of* burnished bronze. ⁴⁶In the plain of Jordan the king had them cast in clay molds, between Succoth and Zaretan. ⁴⁷And Solomon did not weigh all the articles, because *there were* so many; the weight of the bronze was not determined.

⁴⁸Thus Solomon had all the furnishings made for the house of the LORD: the altar of gold, and the table of gold on which *was* the showbread; ⁴⁹the

lampstands of pure gold, five on the right *side* and five on the left in front of the inner sanctuary, with the flowers and the lamps and the wick-trimmers of gold; 50the basins, the trimmers, the bowls, the ladles, and the censers of pure gold; and the hinges of gold, *both* for the doors of the inner room (the Most Holy *Place*) *and* for the doors of the main hall of the temple.

51So all the work that King Solomon had done for the house of the LORD was finished; and Solomon brought in the things which his father David had dedicated: the silver and the gold and the furnishings. He put them in the treasuries of the house of the LORD.

ACTS 7:30-50

"AND when forty years had passed, an Angel of the Lord* appeared to him [Moses] in a flame of fire in a bush, in the wilderness of Mount Sinai. 31When Moses saw *it,* he marveled at the sight; and as he drew near to observe, the voice of the Lord came to him, 32*saying, 'I am the God of your fathers—the God of Abraham, the God of Isaac, and the God of Jacob.'* * And Moses trembled and dared not look. 33*'Then the LORD said to him, "Take your sandals off your feet, for the place where you stand is holy ground. 34I have surely seen the oppression of My people who are in Egypt; I have heard their groan ing and have come down to deliver them. And now come, I will send you to Egypt." '* *

35"This Moses whom they rejected, saying, *'Who made you a ruler and a judge?'* * is the one God sent *to be* a ruler and a deliverer by the hand of the Angel who appeared to him in the bush. 36He brought them out, after he had shown wonders and signs in the land of Egypt, and in the Red Sea, and in the wilderness forty years.

37"This is that Moses who said to the children of Israel,* *'The LORD your God will raise up for you a Prophet like me from your brethren. Him you shall hear.'* *

38"This is he who was in the congregation in the wilderness with the Angel who spoke to him on Mount Sinai, and *with* our fathers, the one who received the living oracles to give to us, 39whom our fathers would not obey, but rejected. And in their hearts they turned back to Egypt, 40saying to Aaron, *'Make us gods to go before us; as for this Moses who brought us out of the land of Egypt, we do not know what has become of him.'* * 41And they made a calf in those days, offered sacrifices to the idol, and rejoiced in the works of their own hands. 42Then God turned and gave them up to worship the host of heaven, as it is written in the book of the Prophets:

> *'Did you offer Me slaughtered animals and sacrifices during forty years in the wilderness, O house of Israel?*
> 43 *You also took up the tabernacle of Moloch, And the star of your god Remphan, Images which you made to worship; And I will carry you away beyond Babylon.'* *

44"Our fathers had the tabernacle of witness in the wilderness, as He appointed, instructing Moses to make it according to the pattern that he had seen, 45which our fathers, having received it in turn, also brought with Joshua into the land possessed by the Gentiles, whom God drove out before the face of our fathers until the days of David, 46who found favor before God and asked to find a dwelling for the God of Jacob. 47But Solomon built Him a house.

48"However, the Most High does not

dwell in temples made with hands, as the prophet says:

49 'Heaven is My throne,
   And earth is My footstool.
   What house will you build for
      Me? says the LORD,
   Or what is the place of My
      rest?
50 Has My hand not made all
   these things?'*"

PSALM 128:1-6

A Song of Ascents.

BLESSED *is* every one who fears
the LORD,
Who walks in His ways.

2   When you eat the labor of
    your hands,

You *shall be* happy, and *it shall
   be* well with you.
3 Your wife *shall be* like a
   fruitful vine
   In the very heart of your
      house,
   Your children like olive plants
   All around your table.
4 Behold, thus shall the man be
      blessed
   Who fears the LORD.

5 The LORD bless you out of
      Zion,
   And may you see the good of
      Jerusalem
   All the days of your life.
6 Yes, may you see your
      children's children.

   Peace *be* upon Israel!

PROVERBS FOR TODAY/ 16:31-33

The silver-haired head is *a crown of glory,* if *it is found in the way of righteousness.*
□ He who is *slow to anger* is *better than the mighty, and he who rules his spirit
than he who takes a city.* □ *The lot is cast into the lap, but its every decision* is
from the LORD.

JUNE 11

1 KINGS 8:1-66

Now Solomon assembled the elders of Israel and all the heads of the tribes, the chief fathers of the children of Israel, to King Solomon in Jerusalem, that they might bring up the ark of the covenant of the LORD from the City of David, which *is* Zion. 2Therefore all the men of Israel assembled with King Solomon at the feast in the month of Ethanim, which *is* the seventh month. 3So all the elders of Israel came, and the priests took up the ark. 4Then they brought up the ark of the LORD, the tabernacle of meeting, and all the holy furnishings that *were* in the tabernacle. The priests and the Levites brought them up. 5Also King Solomon, and all the congregation of Israel who were assembled with him, *were* with him before the ark, sacrificing sheep and oxen that could not be counted or numbered for multitude. 6Then the priests brought in the ark of the covenant of the LORD to its place, into the inner sanctuary of the temple, to the Most Holy *Place,* under the wings of the cherubim. 7For the cherubim spread *their* two wings over the place of the ark, and the cherubim overshadowed the ark and its poles. [8]The poles extended so that the ends of the poles could be seen from the holy *place,* in front of the inner sanctuary; but they could not be seen from outside. And they are there to this day. [9]Nothing *was* in the ark except the two tablets of stone which Moses put there at Horeb, when the LORD made *a covenant* with the children of Israel, when they came out of the land of Egypt.

[10]And it came to pass, when the priests came out of the holy *place,* that the cloud filled the house of the LORD, [11]so that the priests could not continue ministering because of the cloud; for the glory of the LORD filled the house of the LORD.

[12]Then Solomon spoke:

> "The LORD said He would dwell
>   in the dark cloud.
> [13]   I have surely built You an
>   exalted house,
>   And a place for You to dwell in
>   forever."

[14]Then the king turned around and blessed the whole assembly of Israel, while all the assembly of Israel was standing. [15]And he said: "Blessed *be* the LORD God of Israel, who spoke with His mouth to my father David, and with His hand has fulfilled *it,* saying, [16]'Since the day that I brought My people Israel out of Egypt, I have chosen no city from any tribe of Israel *in which* to build a house, that My name might be there; but I chose David to be over My people Israel.' [17]Now it was in the heart of my father David to build a temple* for the name of the LORD God of Israel. [18]But the LORD said to my father David, 'Whereas it was in your heart to build a temple for My name, you did well that it was in your heart. [19]Nevertheless you shall not build the temple, but your son who will come from your body, he shall build the

temple for My name.' [20]So the LORD has fulfilled His word which He spoke; and I have filled the position of my father David, and sit on the throne of Israel, as the LORD promised; and I have built a temple for the name of the LORD God of Israel. [21]And there I have made a place for the ark, in which *is* the covenant of the LORD which He made with our fathers, when He brought them out of the land of Egypt."

[22]Then Solomon stood before the altar of the LORD in the presence of all the assembly of Israel, and spread out his hands toward heaven; [23]and he said: "LORD God of Israel, *there is* no God in heaven above or on earth below like You, who keep *Your* covenant and mercy with Your servants who walk before You with all their hearts. [24]You have kept what You promised Your servant David my father; You have both spoken with Your mouth and fulfilled *it* with Your hand, as *it is* this day. [25]Therefore, LORD God of Israel, now keep what You promised Your servant David my father, saying, 'You shall not fail to have a man sit before Me on the throne of Israel, only if your sons take heed to their way, that they walk before Me as you have walked before Me.' [26]And now I pray, O God of Israel, let Your word come true, which You have spoken to Your servant David my father.

[27]"But will God indeed dwell on the earth? Behold, heaven and the heaven of heavens cannot contain You. How much less this temple which I have built! [28]Yet regard the prayer of Your servant and his supplication, O LORD my God, and listen to the cry and the prayer which Your servant is praying before You today: [29]that Your eyes may be open toward this temple night and day, toward the place of which You said, 'My name shall be there,' that You may hear the prayer which Your servant makes toward this place. [30]And may You hear the supplication of

Your servant and of Your people Israel, when they pray toward this place. Hear in heaven Your dwelling place; and when You hear, forgive.

31"When anyone sins against his neighbor, and is forced to take an oath, and comes *and* takes an oath before Your altar in this temple, 32then hear in heaven, and act, and judge Your servants, condemning the wicked, bringing his way on his head, and justifying the righteous by giving him according to his righteousness.

33"When Your people Israel are defeated before an enemy because they have sinned against You, and when they turn back to You and confess Your name, and pray and make supplication to You in this temple, 34then hear in heaven, and forgive the sin of Your people Israel, and bring them back to the land which You gave to their fathers.

35"When the heavens are shut up and there is no rain because they have sinned against You, when they pray toward this place and confess Your name, and turn from their sin because You afflict them, 36then hear in heaven, and forgive the sin of Your servants, Your people Israel, that You may teach them the good way in which they should walk; and send rain on Your land which You have given to Your people as an inheritance.

37"When there is famine in the land, pestilence *or* blight *or* mildew, locusts *or* grasshoppers; when their enemy besieges them in the land of their cities; whatever plague or whatever sickness *there is;* 38whatever prayer, whatever supplication is made by anyone, *or* by all Your people Israel, when each one knows the plague of his own heart, and spreads out his hands toward this temple: 39then hear in heaven Your dwelling place, and forgive, and act, and give to everyone according to all his ways, whose heart You know (for You alone know the hearts of all the sons of men), 40that they may fear You all the days that they live in the land which You gave to our fathers.

41"Moreover, concerning a foreigner, who *is* not of Your people Israel, but has come from a far country for Your name's sake 42(for they will hear of Your great name and Your strong hand and Your outstretched arm), when he comes and prays toward this temple, 43hear in heaven Your dwelling place, and do according to all for which the foreigner calls to You, that all peoples of the earth may know Your name and fear You, as *do* Your people Israel, and that they may know that this temple which I have built is called by Your name.

44"When Your people go out to battle against their enemy, wherever You send them, and when they pray to the LORD toward the city which You have chosen and the temple which I have built for Your name, 45then hear in heaven their prayer and their supplication, and maintain their cause.

46"When they sin against You (for *there is* no one who does not sin), and You become angry with them and deliver them to the enemy, and they take them captive to the land of the enemy, far or near; 47yet when they come to themselves in the land where they were carried captive, and repent, and make supplication to You in the land of those who took them captive, saying, 'We have sinned and done wrong, we have committed wickedness'; 48and *when* they return to You with all their heart and with all their soul in the land of their enemies who led them away captive, and pray to You toward their land which You gave to their fathers, the city which You have chosen and the temple which I have built for Your name: 49then hear in heaven Your dwelling place their prayer and their supplication, and maintain their cause, 50and forgive Your people who have sinned against You, and all their transgressions which they have transgressed against You; and grant them compassion before those who took them captive, that they may have compassion on them ⁵¹(for they *are* Your people and Your inheritance, whom You brought out of Egypt, out of the iron furnace), ⁵²that Your eyes may be open to the supplication of Your servant and the supplication of Your people Israel, to listen to them whenever they call to You. ⁵³For You separated them from among all the peoples of the earth *to be* Your inheritance, as You spoke by Your servant Moses, when You brought our fathers out of Egypt, O Lord God."

⁵⁴And so it was, when Solomon had finished praying all this prayer and supplication to the Lord, that he arose from before the altar of the Lord, from kneeling on his knees with his hands spread up to heaven. ⁵⁵Then he stood and blessed all the assembly of Israel with a loud voice, saying: ⁵⁶"Blessed *be* the Lord, who has given rest to His people Israel, according to all that He promised. There has not failed one word of all His good promise, which He promised through His servant Moses. ⁵⁷May the Lord our God be with us, as He was with our fathers. May He not leave us nor forsake us, ⁵⁸that He may incline our hearts to Himself, to walk in all His ways, and to keep His commandments and His statutes and His judgments, which He commanded our fathers. ⁵⁹And may these words of mine, with which I have made supplication before the Lord, be near the Lord our God day and night, that He may maintain the cause of His servant and the cause of His people Israel, as each day may require, ⁶⁰that all the peoples of the earth may know that the Lord *is* God; *there is* no other. ⁶¹Let your heart therefore be loyal to the Lord our God, to walk in His stat-

utes and keep His commandments, as at this day."

⁶²Then the king and all Israel with him offered sacrifices before the Lord. ⁶³And Solomon offered a sacrifice of peace offerings, which he offered to the Lord, twenty-two thousand bulls and one hundred and twenty thousand sheep. So the king and all the children of Israel dedicated the house of the Lord. ⁶⁴On the same day the king consecrated the middle of the court that *was* in front of the house of the Lord; for there he offered burnt offerings, grain offerings, and the fat of the peace offerings, because the bronze altar that *was* before the Lord *was* too small to receive the burnt offerings, the grain offerings, and the fat of the peace offerings.

⁶⁵At that time Solomon held a feast, and all Israel with him, a great assembly from the entrance of Hamath to the Brook of Egypt, before the Lord our God, seven days and seven *more* days—fourteen days. ⁶⁶On the eighth day he sent the people away; and they blessed the king, and went to their tents joyful and glad of heart for all the good that the Lord had done for His servant David, and for Israel His people.

ACTS 7:51–8:13

"**Y**ou stiff-necked and uncircumcised in heart and ears! You always resist the Holy Spirit; as your fathers *did,* so *do* you. ⁵²Which of the prophets did your fathers not persecute? And they killed those who foretold the coming of the Just One, of whom you now have become the betrayers and murderers, ⁵³who have received the law by the direction of angels and have not kept *it.*"

⁵⁴When they heard these things they were cut to the heart, and they gnashed at him with *their* teeth. ⁵⁵But he, being full of the Holy Spirit, gazed

into heaven and saw the glory of God, and Jesus standing at the right hand of God, [56]and said, "Look! I see the heavens opened and the Son of Man standing at the right hand of God!"

[57]Then they cried out with a loud voice, stopped their ears, and ran at him with one accord; [58]and they cast *him* out of the city and stoned *him*. And the witnesses laid down their clothes at the feet of a young man named Saul. [59]And they stoned Stephen as he was calling on *God* and saying, "Lord Jesus, receive my spirit." [60]Then he knelt down and cried out with a loud voice, "Lord, do not charge them with this sin." And when he had said this, he fell asleep.

Now Saul was consenting to his death.

At that time a great persecution arose against the church which was at Jerusalem; and they were all scattered throughout the regions of Judea and Samaria, except the apostles. [2]And devout men carried Stephen *to his burial,* and made great lamentation over him.

[3]As for Saul, he made havoc of the church, entering every house, and dragging off men and women, committing *them* to prison.

[4]Therefore those who were scattered went everywhere preaching the word. [5]Then Philip went down to the* city of Samaria and preached Christ to them. [6]And the multitudes with one accord heeded the things spoken by Philip, hearing and seeing the miracles which he did. [7]For unclean spirits, crying with a loud voice, came out of many who were possessed; and many who were paralyzed and lame were healed. [8]And there was great joy in that city.

[9]But there was a certain man called Simon, who previously practiced sorcery in the city and astonished the people of Samaria, claiming that he was someone great, [10]to whom they all gave heed, from the least to the great-est, saying, "This man is the great power of God." [11]And they heeded him because he had astonished them with his sorceries for a long time. [12]But when they believed Philip as he preached the things concerning the kingdom of God and the name of Jesus Christ, both men and women were baptized. [13]Then Simon himself also believed; and when he was baptized he continued with Philip, and was amazed, seeing the miracles and signs which were done.

PSALM 129:1-8

A Song of Ascents

"**M**ANY a time they have afflicted me from my youth,"
Let Israel now say—

2 "Many a time they have
afflicted me from my youth;
Yet they have not prevailed
against me.

3 The plowers plowed on my
back;
They made their furrows
long."

4 The Lord *is* righteous;
He has cut in pieces the cords
of the wicked.

5 Let all those who hate Zion
Be put to shame and turned
back.

6 Let them be as the grass *on*
the housetops,
Which withers before it grows
up,

7 With which the reaper does
not fill his hand,
Nor he who binds sheaves,
his arms.

8 Neither let those who pass by
them say,
"The blessing of the Lord *be*
upon you;
We bless you in the name of
the Lord!"

PROVERBS FOR TODAY/ 17:1
Better is *a dry morsel with quietness, than a house full of feasting* * with *strife.*

JUNE 12

1 KINGS 9:1–10:29

ND it came to pass, when Solomon had finished building the house of the LORD and the king's house, and all Solomon's desire which he wanted to do, ²that the LORD appeared to Solomon the second time, as He had appeared to him at Gibeon. ³And the LORD said to him: "I have heard your prayer and your supplication that you have made before Me; I have consecrated this house which you have built to put My name there forever, and My eyes and My heart will be there perpetually. ⁴Now if you walk before Me as your father David walked, in integrity of heart and in uprightness, to do according to all that I have commanded you, *and* if you keep My statutes and My judgments, ⁵then I will establish the throne of your kingdom over Israel forever, as I promised David your father, saying, 'You shall not fail to have a man on the throne of Israel.' ⁶*But* if you or your sons at all turn from following Me, and do not keep My commandments *and* My statutes which I have set before you, but go and serve other gods and worship them, ⁷then I will cut off Israel from the land which I have given them; and this house which I have consecrated for My name I will cast out of My sight. Israel will be a proverb and a byword among all peoples. ⁸And *as for* this house, *which* is exalted, everyone who passes by it will be astonished and will hiss, and say, 'Why has the LORD done thus to this land and to this house?' ⁹Then they will answer, 'Because they

forsook the LORD their God, who brought their fathers out of the land of Egypt, and have embraced other gods, and worshiped them and served them; therefore the LORD has brought all this calamity on them.' "

¹⁰Now it happened at the end of twenty years, when Solomon had built the two houses, the house of the LORD and the king's house ¹¹(Hiram the king of Tyre had supplied Solomon with cedar and cypress and gold, as much as he desired), *that* King Solomon then gave Hiram twenty cities in the land of Galilee. ¹²Then Hiram went from Tyre to see the cities which Solomon had given him, but they did not please him. ¹³So he said, "What *kind of* cities *are* these which you have given me, my brother?" And he called them the land of Cabul,* as they are to this day. ¹⁴Then Hiram sent the king one hundred and twenty talents of gold.

¹⁵And this *is* the reason for the labor force which King Solomon raised: to build the house of the LORD, his own house, the Millo,* the wall of Jerusalem, Hazor, Megiddo, and Gezer. ¹⁶(Pharaoh king of Egypt had gone up and taken Gezer and burned it with fire, had killed the Canaanites who dwelt in the city, and had given it *as* a dowry to his daughter, Solomon's wife.) ¹⁷And Solomon built Gezer, Lower Beth Horon, ¹⁸Baalath, and Tadmor in the wilderness, in the land *of Judah,* ¹⁹all the storage cities that Solomon had, cities for his chariots and cities for his cavalry, and whatever Solomon desired to build in Jeru-

salem, in Lebanon, and in all the land of his dominion.

20All the people *who were* left of the Amorites, Hittites, Perizzites, Hivites, and Jebusites, who *were* not of the children of Israel— 21that is, their descendants who were left in the land after them, whom the children of Israel had not been able to destroy completely— from these Solomon raised forced labor, as it is to this day. 22But of the children of Israel Solomon made no forced laborers, because they *were* men of war and his servants: his officers, his captains, commanders of his chariots, and his cavalry.

23Others *were* chiefs of the officials who *were* over Solomon's work: five hundred and fifty, who ruled over the people who did the work.

24But Pharaoh's daughter came up from the City of David to her house which *Solomon** had built for her. Then he built the Millo.

25Now three times a year Solomon offered burnt offerings and peace offerings on the altar which he had built for the Lord, and he burned incense with them *on the altar* that *was* before the Lord. So he finished the temple.

26King Solomon also built a fleet of ships at Ezion Geber, which *is* near Elath* on the shore of the Red Sea, in the land of Edom. 27Then Hiram sent his servants with the fleet, seamen who knew the sea, to work with the servants of Solomon. 28And they went to Ophir, and acquired four hundred and twenty talents of gold from there, and brought *it* to King Solomon.

Now when the queen of Sheba heard of the fame of Solomon concerning the name of the Lord, she came to test him with hard questions. 2She came to Jerusalem with a very great retinue, with camels that bore spices, very much gold, and precious stones; and when she came to Solomon, she spoke with him about all that was in her heart. 3So Solomon answered all her questions; there was nothing so difficult for the king that he could not explain *it* to her. 4And when the queen of Sheba had seen all the wisdom of Solomon, the house that he had built, 5the food on his table, the seating of his servants, the service of his waiters and their apparel, his cupbearers, and his entryway by which he went up to the house of the Lord, there was no more spirit in her. 6Then she said to the king: "It was a true report which I heard in my own land about your words and your wisdom. 7However I did not believe the words until I came and saw with my own eyes; and indeed the half was not told me. Your wisdom and prosperity exceed the fame of which I heard. 8Happy *are* your men and happy *are* these your servants, who stand continually before you *and* hear your wisdom! 9Blessed be the Lord your God, who delighted in you, setting you on the throne of Israel! Because the Lord has loved Israel forever, therefore He made you king, to do justice and righteousness."

10Then she gave the king one hundred and twenty talents of gold, spices in great quantity, and precious stones. There never again came such abundance of spices as the queen of Sheba gave to King Solomon. 11Also, the ships of Hiram, which brought gold from Ophir, brought great *quantities* of almug* wood and precious stones from Ophir. 12And the king made steps of the almug wood for the house of the Lord and for the king's house, also harps and stringed instruments for singers. There never again came such almug wood, nor has the like been seen to this day.

13Now King Solomon gave the queen of Sheba all she desired, whatever she asked, besides what Solomon had given her according to the royal generosity. So she turned and went to her own country, she and her servants.

14The weight of gold that came to Solomon yearly was six hundred and sixty-six talents of gold, 15besides *that* from the traveling merchants, from the income of traders, from all the kings of Arabia, and from the governors of the country.

16And King Solomon made two hundred large shields *of* hammered gold; six hundred *shekels* of gold went into each shield. 17He also *made* three hundred shields *of* hammered gold; three minas of gold went into each shield. The king put them in the House of the Forest of Lebanon.

18Moreover the king made a great throne of ivory, and overlaid it with pure gold. 19The throne had six steps, and the top of the throne *was* round at the back; *there were* armrests on either side of the place of the seat, and two lions stood beside the armrests. 20Twelve lions stood there, one on each side of the six steps; nothing like *this* had been made for any *other* kingdom.

21All King Solomon's drinking vessels *were* gold, and all the vessels of the House of the Forest of Lebanon *were* pure gold. Not *one was* silver, for this was accounted as nothing in the days of Solomon. 22For the king had merchant ships* at sea with the fleet of Hiram. Once every three years the merchant ships came bringing gold, silver, ivory, apes, and monkeys.* 23So King Solomon surpassed all the kings of the earth in riches and wisdom.

24Now all the earth sought the presence of Solomon to hear his wisdom, which God had put in his heart. 25Each man brought his present: articles of silver and gold, garments, armor, spices, horses, and mules, at a set rate year by year.

26And Solomon gathered chariots and horsemen; he had one thousand four hundred chariots and twelve thousand horsemen, whom he stationed* in the chariot cities and with the king at Jerusalem. 27The king made silver *as common* in Jerusalem as stones, and he made cedar trees as abundant as the sycamores which *are* in the lowland.

28Also Solomon had horses imported from Egypt and Keveh; the king's merchants bought them in Keveh at the *current* price. 29Now a chariot that was imported from Egypt cost six hundred *shekels* of silver, and a horse one hundred and fifty; and thus, through their agents,* they exported *them* to all the kings of the Hittites and the kings of Syria.

ACTS 8:14-40

Now when the apostles who were at Jerusalem heard that Samaria had received the word of God, they sent Peter and John to them, 15who, when they had come down, prayed for them that they might receive the Holy Spirit. 16For as yet He had fallen upon none of them. They had only been baptized in the name of the Lord Jesus. 17Then they laid hands on them, and they received the Holy Spirit.

18And when Simon saw that through the laying on of the apostles' hands the Holy Spirit was given, he offered them money, 19saying, "Give me this power also, that anyone on whom I lay hands may receive the Holy Spirit."

20But Peter said to him, "Your money perish with you, because you thought that the gift of God could be purchased with money! 21You have neither part nor portion in this matter, for your heart is not right in the sight of God. 22Repent therefore of this your wickedness, and pray God if perhaps the thought of your heart may be forgiven you. 23For I see that you are poisoned by bitterness and bound by iniquity."

24Then Simon answered and said, "Pray to the Lord for me, that none of the things which you have spoken may come upon me."

25So when they had testified and preached the word of the Lord, they returned to Jerusalem, preaching the gospel in many villages of the Samaritans.

26Now an angel of the Lord spoke to Philip, saying, "Arise and go toward the south along the road which goes down from Jerusalem to Gaza." This is desert. 27So he arose and went. And behold, a man of Ethiopia, a eunuch of great authority under Candace the queen of the Ethiopians, who had charge of all her treasury, and had come to Jerusalem to worship, 28was returning. And sitting in his chariot, he was reading Isaiah the prophet. 29Then the Spirit said to Philip, "Go near and overtake this chariot."

30So Philip ran to him, and heard him reading the prophet Isaiah, and said, "Do you understand what you are reading?"

31And he said, "How can I, unless someone guides me?" And he asked Philip to come up and sit with him. 32The place in the Scripture which he read was this:

> "He was led as a sheep to the
>   slaughter;
> And as a lamb before its
>   shearer is silent,
> So He opened not His mouth.
> 33   In His humiliation His justice
>   was taken away,
> And who will declare His
>   generation?
> For His life is taken from the
>   earth." *

34So the eunuch answered Philip and said, "I ask you, of whom does the prophet say this, of himself or of some other man?" 35Then Philip opened his mouth, and beginning at this Scripture, preached Jesus to him. 36Now as they went down the road, they came to some water. And the eunuch said, "See, *here is* water. What hinders me from being baptized?"

37Then Philip said, "If you believe with all your heart, you may."

And he answered and said, "I believe that Jesus Christ is the Son of God." *

38So he commanded the chariot to stand still. And both Philip and the eunuch went down into the water, and he baptized him. 39Now when they came up out of the water, the Spirit of the Lord caught Philip away, so that the eunuch saw him no more; and he went on his way rejoicing. 40But Philip was found at Azotus. And passing through, he preached in all the cities till he came to Caesarea.

PSALM 130:1-8

A Song of Ascents.

Out of the depths I have cried to You, O LORD;
2Lord, hear my voice!
Let Your ears be attentive
To the voice of my
    supplications.

3   If You, LORD, should mark
        iniquities,
    O Lord, who could stand?
4   But *there is* forgiveness with
        You,
    That You may be feared.

5   I wait for the LORD, my soul
        waits,
    And in His word I do hope.
6   My soul *waits* for the Lord
    More than those who watch
        for the morning—
    Yes, more than those who
        watch for the morning.

7   O Israel, hope in the LORD;
    For with the LORD *there is*
        mercy,

	And with Him *is* abundant redemption.	8	And He shall redeem Israel From all his iniquities.

PROVERBS FOR TODAY/ 17:2-3

A wise servant will rule over a son who causes shame, and will share an inheritance among the brothers. □ *The refining pot* is *for silver and the furnace for gold, but the* LORD *tests the hearts.*

JUNE 13

1 KINGS 11:1–12:19

BUT King Solomon loved many foreign women, as well as the daughter of Pharaoh: women of the Moabites, Ammonites, Edomites, Sidonians, *and* Hittites— 2from the nations of whom the LORD had said to the children of Israel, "You shall not intermarry with them, nor they with you. Surely they will turn away your hearts after their gods." Solomon clung to these in love. 3And he had seven hundred wives, princesses, and three hundred concubines; and his wives turned away his heart. 4For it was so, when Solomon was old, that his wives turned his heart after other gods; and his heart was not loyal to the LORD his God, as *was* the heart of his father David. 5For Solomon went after Ashtoreth the goddess of the Sidonians, and after Milcom the abomination of the Ammonites. 6Solomon did evil in the sight of the LORD, and did not fully follow the LORD, as *did* his father David. 7Then Solomon built a high place for Chemosh the abomination of Moab, on the hill that *is* east of Jerusalem, and for Molech the abomination of the people of Ammon. 8And he did likewise for all his foreign wives, who burned incense and sacrificed to their gods.

9So the LORD became angry with Solomon, because his heart had turned from the LORD God of Israel, who had appeared to him twice, 10and had commanded him concerning this thing, that he should not go after other gods; but he did not keep what the LORD had commanded. 11Therefore the LORD said to Solomon, "Because you have done this, and have not kept My covenant and My statutes, which I have commanded you, I will surely tear the kingdom away from you and give it to your servant. 12Nevertheless I will not do it in your days, for the sake of your father David; I will tear it out of the hand of your son. 13However I will not tear away the whole kingdom; I will give one tribe to your son for the sake of my servant David, and for the sake of Jerusalem which I have chosen."

14Now the LORD raised up an adversary against Solomon, Hadad the Edomite; he *was* a descendant of the king in Edom. 15For it happened, when David was in Edom, and Joab the commander of the army had gone up to bury the slain, after he had killed every male in Edom 16(because for six months Joab remained there with all Israel, until he had cut down every male in Edom), 17that Hadad fled to go to Egypt, he and certain Edomites of his father's servants with him. Hadad *was* still a little child. 18Then they arose from Midian and came to Paran; and they took men with them from Paran and came to Egypt, to Pharaoh king of Egypt, who gave him a house, apportioned food for him, and gave him land. ¹⁹And Hadad found great favor in the sight of Pharaoh, so that he gave him as wife the sister of his own wife, that is, the sister of Queen Tahpenes. ²⁰Then the sister of Tahpenes bore him Genubath his son, whom Tahpenes weaned in Pharaoh's house. And Genubath was in Pharaoh's household among the sons of Pharaoh.

²¹So when Hadad heard in Egypt that David rested with his fathers, and that Joab the commander of the army was dead, Hadad said to Pharaoh, "Let me depart, that I may go to my own country."

²²Then Pharaoh said to him, "But what have you lacked with me, that suddenly you seek to go to your own country?"

So he answered, "Nothing, but do let me go anyway."

²³And God raised up *another* adversary against him, Rezon the son of Eliadah, who had fled from his lord, Hadadezer king of Zobah. ²⁴So he gathered men to him and became captain over a band *of raiders,* when David killed those *of Zobah.* And they went to Damascus and dwelt there, and reigned in Damascus. ²⁵He was an adversary of Israel all the days of Solomon (besides the trouble that Hadad *caused*); and he abhorred Israel, and reigned over Syria.

²⁶Then Solomon's servant, Jeroboam the son of Nebat, an Ephraimite from Zereda, whose mother's name *was* Zeruah, a widow, also rebelled against the king.

²⁷And this *is* what caused him to rebel against the king: Solomon had built the Millo *and* repaired the damages to the City of David his father. ²⁸The man Jeroboam *was* a mighty man of valor; and Solomon, seeing that the young man was industrious, made him the officer over all the labor force of the house of Joseph.

²⁹Now it happened at that time, when Jeroboam went out of Jerusalem, that the prophet Ahijah the Shilonite met him on the way; and he had clothed himself with a new garment, and the two *were* alone in the field. ³⁰Then Ahijah took hold of the new garment that *was* on him, and tore it *into* twelve pieces. ³¹And he said to Jeroboam, "Take for yourself ten pieces, for thus says the LORD, the God of Israel: 'Behold, I will tear the kingdom out of the hand of Solomon and will give ten tribes to you ³²(but he shall have one tribe for the sake of My servant David, and for the sake of Jerusalem, the city which I have chosen out of all the tribes of Israel), ³³because they have* forsaken Me, and worshiped Ashtoreth the goddess of the Sidonians, Chemosh the god of the Moabites, and Milcom the god of the people of Ammon, and have not walked in My ways to do *what is* right in My eyes and *keep* My statutes and My judgments, as *did* his father David. ³⁴However I will not take the whole kingdom out of his hand, because I have made him ruler all the days of his life for the sake of My servant David, whom I chose because he kept My commandments and My statutes. ³⁵But I will take the kingdom out of his son's hand and give it to you—ten tribes. ³⁶And to his son I will give one tribe, that My servant David may always have a lamp before Me in Jerusalem, the city which I have chosen for Myself, to put My name there. ³⁷So I will take you, and you shall reign over all your heart desires, and you shall be king over Israel. ³⁸Then it shall be, if you heed all that I command you, walk in My ways, and do *what is* right in My sight, to keep My statutes and My commandments, as My servant David did, then I will be with you and build for you an enduring house, as I

built for David, and will give Israel to you. ³⁹And I will afflict the descendants of David because of this, but not forever.' "

⁴⁰Solomon therefore sought to kill Jeroboam. But Jeroboam arose and fled to Egypt, to Shishak king of Egypt, and was in Egypt until the death of Solomon.

⁴¹Now the rest of the acts of Solomon, all that he did, and his wisdom, *are* they not written in the book of the acts of Solomon? ⁴²And the period that Solomon reigned in Jerusalem over all Israel *was* forty years. ⁴³Then Solomon rested with his fathers, and was buried in the City of David his father. And Rehoboam his son reigned in his place.

AND Rehoboam went to Shechem, for all Israel had gone to Shechem to make him king. ²So it happened, when Jeroboam the son of Nebat heard *it* (he was still in Egypt, for he had fled from the presence of King Solomon and had been dwelling in Egypt), ³that they sent and called him. Then Jeroboam and the whole assembly of Israel came and spoke to Rehoboam, saying, ⁴"Your father made our yoke heavy; now therefore, lighten the burdensome service of your father, and his heavy yoke which he put on us, and we will serve you."

⁵So he said to them, "Depart *for* three days, then come back to me." And the people departed.

⁶Then King Rehoboam consulted the elders who stood before his father Solomon while he still lived, and he said, "How do you advise *me* to answer these people?"

⁷And they spoke to him, saying, "If you will be a servant to these people today, and serve them, and answer them, and speak good words to them, then they will be your servants forever."

⁸But he rejected the advice which the elders had given him, and consulted the young men who had grown up with him, who stood before him. ⁹And he said to them, "What advice do you give? How should we answer this people who have spoken to me, saying, 'Lighten the yoke which your father put on us'?"

¹⁰Then the young men who had grown up with him spoke to him, saying, "Thus you should speak to this people who have spoken to you, saying, 'Your father made our yoke heavy, but you make *it* lighter on us'—thus you shall say to them: 'My little *finger* shall be thicker than my father's waist! ¹¹And now, whereas my father put a heavy yoke on you, I will add to your yoke; my father chastised you with whips, but I will chastise you with scourges!' "*

¹²So Jeroboam and all the people came to Rehoboam the third day, as the king had directed, saying, "Come back to me the third day." ¹³Then the king answered the people roughly, and rejected the advice which the elders had given him; ¹⁴and he spoke to them according to the advice of the young men, saying, "My father made your yoke heavy, but I will add to your yoke; my father chastised you with whips, but I will chastise you with scourges!"*

¹⁵So the king did not listen to the people; for the turn *of events* was from the LORD, that He might fulfill His word, which the LORD had spoken by Ahijah the Shilonite to Jeroboam the son of Nebat.

¹⁶Now when all Israel saw that the king did not listen to them, the people answered the king, saying:

"What share have we in David?
We have no inheritance in the
    son of Jesse.
To your tents, O Israel!
Now, see to your own house,
    O David!"

So Israel departed to their tents. ¹⁷But Rehoboam reigned over the children of Israel who dwelt in the cities of Judah.

¹⁸Then King Rehoboam sent Adoram, who *was* in charge of the revenue; but all Israel stoned him with stones, and he died. Therefore King Rehoboam mounted his chariot in haste to flee to Jerusalem. ¹⁹So Israel has been in rebellion against the house of David to this day.

ACTS 9:1-25

THEN Saul, still breathing threats and murder against the disciples of the Lord, went to the high priest ²and asked letters from him to the synagogues of Damascus, so that if he found any who were of the Way, whether men or women, he might bring them bound to Jerusalem.

³As he journeyed he came near Damascus, and suddenly a light shone around him from heaven. ⁴Then he fell to the ground, and heard a voice saying to him, "Saul, Saul, why are you persecuting Me?"

⁵And he said, "Who are You, Lord?"

Then the Lord said, "I am Jesus, whom you are persecuting.* It *is* hard for you to kick against the goads."

⁶So he, trembling and astonished, said, "Lord, what do You want me to do?"

Then the Lord *said* to him, "Arise and go into the city, and you will be told what you must do."

⁷And the men who journeyed with him stood speechless, hearing a voice but seeing no one. ⁸Then Saul arose from the ground, and when his eyes were opened he saw no one. But they led him by the hand and brought *him* into Damascus. ⁹And he was three days without sight, and neither ate nor drank.

¹⁰Now there was a certain disciple at Damascus named Ananias; and to him the Lord said in a vision, "Ananias."

And he said, "Here I am, Lord."

¹¹So the Lord *said* to him, "Arise and go to the street called Straight, and inquire at the house of Judas for *one* called Saul of Tarsus, for behold, he is praying. ¹²And in a vision he has seen a man named Ananias coming in and putting *his* hand on him, so that he might receive his sight."

¹³Then Ananias answered, "Lord, I have heard from many about this man, how much harm he has done to Your saints in Jerusalem. ¹⁴And here he has authority from the chief priests to bind all who call on Your name."

¹⁵But the Lord said to him, "Go, for he is a chosen vessel of Mine to bear My name before Gentiles, kings, and the children of Israel. ¹⁶For I will show him how many things he must suffer for My name's sake."

¹⁷And Ananias went his way and entered the house; and laying his hands on him he said, "Brother Saul, the Lord Jesus,* who appeared to you on the road as you came, has sent me that you may receive your sight and be filled with the Holy Spirit." ¹⁸Immediately there fell from his eyes *something* like scales, and he received his sight at once; and he arose and was baptized.

¹⁹So when he had received food, he was strengthened. Then Saul spent some days with the disciples at Damascus.

²⁰Immediately he preached the Christ* in the synagogues, that He is the Son of God.

²¹Then all who heard were amazed, and said, "Is this not he who destroyed those who called on this name in Jerusalem, and has come here for that purpose, so that he might bring them bound to the chief priests?"

²²But Saul increased all the more in strength, and confounded the Jews who dwelt in Damascus, proving that this *Jesus* is the Christ.

²³Now after many days were past, the Jews plotted to kill him. ²⁴But their plot became known to Saul. And they

watched the gates day and night, to kill him. 25Then the disciples took him by night and let *him* down through the wall in a large basket.

PSALM 131:1-3
A Song of Ascents. Of David.

L ORD, my heart is not haughty,
Nor my eyes lofty,
Neither do I concern myself
with great matters,

Nor with things too profound
for me.

2 Surely I have calmed and
quieted my soul,
Like a weaned child with his
mother;
Like a weaned child *is* my
soul within me.

3 O Israel, hope in the LORD
From this time forth and
forever.

PROVERBS FOR TODAY/ 17:4-5

An evildoer gives heed to false lips; a liar listens eagerly to a spiteful tongue. ▫ He who mocks the poor reproaches his Maker; he who is glad at calamity will not go unpunished.

JUNE 14

1 KINGS 12:20–13:34

N ow it came to pass when all Israel heard that Jeroboam had come back, they sent for him and called him to the congregation, and made him king over all Israel. There was none who followed the house of David, but the tribe of Judah only.

21And when Rehoboam came to Jerusalem, he assembled all the house of Judah with the tribe of Benjamin, one hundred and eighty thousand chosen *men* who were warriors, to fight against the house of Israel, that he might restore the kingdom to Rehoboam the son of Solomon. 22But the word of God came to Shemaiah the man of God, saying, 23"Speak to Rehoboam the son of Solomon, king of Judah, to all the house of Judah and Benjamin, and to the rest of the people, saying, 24"Thus says the LORD: "You

shall not go up nor fight against your brethren the children of Israel. Let every man return to his house, for this thing is from Me." ' " Therefore they obeyed the word of the LORD, and turned back, according to the word of the LORD.

25Then Jeroboam built Shechem in the mountains of Ephraim, and dwelt there. Also he went out from there and built Penuel. 26And Jeroboam said in his heart, "Now the kingdom may return to the house of David: 27If these people go up to offer sacrifices in the house of the LORD at Jerusalem, then the heart of this people will turn back to their lord, Rehoboam king of Judah, and they will kill me and go back to Rehoboam king of Judah."

28Therefore the king asked advice, made two calves of gold, and said to the people, "It is too much for you to go up to Jerusalem. Here are your gods, O Israel, which brought you up from the land of Egypt!" ²⁹And he set up one in Bethel, and the other he put in Dan. ³⁰Now this thing became a sin, for the people went *to worship* before the one as far as Dan. ³¹He made shrines* on the high places, and made priests from every class of people, who were not of the sons of Levi.

³²Jeroboam ordained a feast on the fifteenth day of the eighth month, like the feast that *was* in Judah, and offered sacrifices on the altar. So he did at Bethel, sacrificing to the calves that he had made. And at Bethel he installed the priests of the high places which he had made. ³³So he made offerings on the altar which he had made at Bethel on the fifteenth day of the eighth month, in the month which he had devised in his own heart. And he ordained a feast for the children of Israel, and offered sacrifices on the altar and burned incense.

AND behold, a man of God went from Judah to Bethel by the word of the LORD, and Jeroboam stood by the altar to burn incense. ²Then he cried out against the altar by the word of the LORD, and said, "O altar, altar! Thus says the LORD: 'Behold, a child, Josiah by name, shall be born to the house of David; and on you he shall sacrifice the priests of the high places who burn incense on you, and men's bones shall be burned on you.' " ³And he gave a sign the same day, saying, "This *is* the sign which the LORD has spoken: Surely the altar shall split apart, and the ashes on it shall be poured out."

⁴So it came to pass when King Jeroboam heard the saying of the man of God, who cried out against the altar in Bethel, that he stretched out his hand from the altar, saying, "Arrest him!" Then his hand, which he stretched out toward him, withered, so that he could not pull it back to himself. ⁵The altar also was split apart, and the ashes poured out from the altar, according to the sign which the man of God had given by the word of the LORD. ⁶Then the king answered and said to the man of God, "Please entreat the favor of the LORD your God, and pray for me, that my hand may be restored to me."

So the man of God entreated the LORD, and the king's hand was restored to him, and became as before. ⁷Then the king said to the man of God, "Come home with me and refresh yourself, and I will give you a reward."

⁸But the man of God said to the king, "If you were to give me half your house, I would not go in with you; nor would I eat bread nor drink water in this place. ⁹For so it was commanded me by the word of the LORD, saying, 'You shall not eat bread, nor drink water, nor return by the same way you came.' " ¹⁰So he went another way and did not return by the way he came to Bethel.

¹¹Now an old prophet dwelt in Bethel, and his sons came and told him all the works that the man of God had done that day in Bethel; they also told their father the words which he had spoken to the king. ¹²And their father said to them, "Which way did he go?" For his sons had seen* which way the man of God went who came from Judah. ¹³Then he said to his sons, "Saddle the donkey for me." So they saddled the donkey for him; and he rode on it, ¹⁴and went after the man of God, and found him sitting under an oak. Then he said to him, "*Are* you the man of God who came from Judah?"

And he said, "I *am.*"

¹⁵Then he said to him, "Come home with me and eat bread."

¹⁶And he said, "I cannot return with you nor go in with you; neither can I eat bread nor drink water with you in this place. ¹⁷For I have been told by the word of the LORD, 'You shall not eat bread nor drink water there, nor return by going the way you came.' "

18He said to him, "I too *am* a prophet as you *are,* and an angel spoke to me by the word of the LORD, saying, 'Bring him back with you to your house, that he may eat bread and drink water.'" (He was lying to him.) 19So he went back with him, and ate bread in his house, and drank water.

20Now it happened, as they sat at the table, that the word of the LORD came to the prophet who had brought him back; 21and he cried out to the man of God who came from Judah, saying, "Thus says the LORD: 'Because you have disobeyed the word of the LORD, and have not kept the commandment which the LORD your God commanded you, 22but you came back, ate bread, and drank water in the place of which *the* LORD said to you, "Eat no bread and drink no water," your corpse shall not come to the tomb of your fathers.'"

23So it was, after he had eaten bread and after he had drunk, that he saddled the donkey for him, the prophet whom he had brought back. 24When he was gone, a lion met him on the road and killed him. And his corpse was thrown on the road, and the donkey stood by it. The lion also stood by the corpse. 25And there, men passed by and saw the corpse thrown on the road, and the lion standing by the corpse. Then they went and told *it* in the city where the old prophet dwelt.

26Now when the prophet who had brought him back from the way heard *it,* he said, "It *is* the man of God who was disobedient to the word of the LORD. Therefore the LORD has delivered him to the lion, which has torn him and killed him, according to the word of the LORD which He spoke to him." 27And he spoke to his sons, saying, "Saddle the donkey for me." So they saddled *it.* 28Then he went and found his corpse thrown on the road, and the donkey and the lion standing by the corpse. The lion had not eaten the corpse nor torn the donkey. 29And the prophet took up the corpse of the man of God, laid it on the donkey, and brought it back. So the old prophet came to the city to mourn, and to bury him. 30Then he laid the corpse in his own tomb; and they mourned over him, *saying,* "Alas, my brother!" 31So it was, after he had buried him, that he spoke to his sons, saying, "When I am dead, then bury me in the tomb where the man of God *is* buried; lay my bones beside his bones. 32For the saying which he cried out by the word of the LORD against the altar in Bethel, and against all the shrines* on the high places which *are* in the cities of Samaria, will surely come to pass."

33After this event Jeroboam did not turn from his evil way, but again he made priests from every class of people for the high places; whoever wished, he consecrated him, and he became *one* of the priests of the high places. 34And this thing was the sin of the house of Jeroboam, so as to exterminate and destroy *it* from the face of the earth.

ACTS 9:26-43

AND when Saul had come to Jerusalem, he tried to join the disciples; but they were all afraid of him, and did not believe that he was a disciple. 27But Barnabas took him and brought *him* to the apostles. And he declared to them how he had seen the Lord on the road, and that He had spoken to him, and how he had preached boldly at Damascus in the name of Jesus. 28So he was with them at Jerusalem, coming in and going out. 29And he spoke boldly in the name of the Lord Jesus and disputed against the Hellenists, but they attempted to kill him. 30When the brethren found out, they brought him down to Caesarea and sent him out to Tarsus.

³¹Then the churches* throughout all Judea, Galilee, and Samaria had peace and were edified. And walking in the fear of the Lord and in the comfort of the Holy Spirit, they were multiplied.

³²Now it came to pass, as Peter went through all *parts of the country,* that he also came down to the saints who dwelt in Lydda. ³³There he found a certain man named Aeneas, who had been bedridden eight years and was paralyzed. ³⁴And Peter said to him, "Aeneas, Jesus the Christ heals you. Arise and make your bed." Then he arose immediately. ³⁵So all who dwelt at Lydda and Sharon saw him and turned to the Lord.

³⁶At Joppa there was a certain disciple named Tabitha, which is translated Dorcas. This woman was full of good works and charitable deeds which she did. ³⁷But it happened in those days that she became sick and died. When they had washed her, they laid *her* in an upper room. ³⁸And since Lydda was near Joppa, and the disciples had heard that Peter was there, they sent two men to him, imploring *him* not to delay in coming to them. ³⁹Then Peter arose and went with them. When he had come, they brought *him* to the upper room. And all the widows stood by him weeping, showing the tunics and garments which Dorcas had made while she was with them. ⁴⁰But Peter put them all out, and knelt down and prayed. And turning to the body he said, "Tabitha, arise." And she opened her eyes, and when she saw Peter she sat up. ⁴¹Then he gave her *his* hand and lifted her up; and when he had called the saints and widows, he presented her alive. ⁴²And it became known throughout all Joppa, and many believed on the Lord. ⁴³So it was that he stayed many days in Joppa with Simon, a tanner.

PSALM 132:1-18

A Song of Ascents.

L ORD, remember David
And all his afflictions;
²How he swore to the LORD,
And vowed to the Mighty One of Jacob:

3   "Surely I will not go into the chamber of my house,
Or go up to the comfort of my bed;

4   I will not give sleep to my eyes
Or slumber to my eyelids,

5   Until I find a place for the LORD,
A dwelling place for the Mighty One of Jacob."

6   Behold, we heard of it in Ephrathah;
We found it in the fields of the woods.*

7   Let us go into His tabernacle;
Let us worship at His footstool.

8   Arise, O LORD, to Your resting place,
You and the ark of Your strength.

9   Let Your priests be clothed with righteousness,
And let Your saints shout for joy.

10   For Your servant David's sake,
Do not turn away the face of Your Anointed.

11   The LORD has sworn *in* truth to David;
He will not turn from it:
"I will set upon your throne the fruit of your body.

12   If your sons will keep My covenant
And My testimony which I shall teach them,
Their sons also shall sit upon your throne forevermore."

13 For the LORD has chosen Zion;
    He has desired *it* for His
        dwelling place:
14 "This *is* My resting place
        forever;
    Here I will dwell, for I have
        desired it.
15 I will abundantly bless her
        provision;
    I will satisfy her poor with
        bread.
16 I will also clothe her priests
        with salvation,
    And her saints shall shout
        aloud for joy.
17 There I will make the horn of
        David grow;
    I will prepare a lamp for My
        Anointed.
18 His enemies I will clothe with
        shame,
    But upon Himself His crown
        shall flourish."

PROVERBS FOR TODAY/ 17:6

Children's children are *the crown of old men, and the glory of children* is *their father.*

JUNE 15

1 KINGS 14:1–15:24

AT that time Abijah the son of Jeroboam became sick. ²And Jeroboam said to his wife, "Please arise, and disguise yourself, that they may not recognize you as the wife of Jeroboam, and go to Shiloh. Indeed, Ahijah the prophet *is* there, who told me that *I would be* king over this people. ³Also take with you ten loaves, *some* cakes, and a jar of honey, and go to him; he will tell you what will become of the child." ⁴And Jeroboam's wife did so; she arose and went to Shiloh, and came to the house of Ahijah. But Ahijah could not see, for his eyes were glazed by reason of his age.

⁵Now the LORD had said to Ahijah, "Here is the wife of Jeroboam, coming to ask you something about her son, for he *is* sick. Thus and thus you shall say to her; for it will be, when she comes in, that she will pretend *to be* another *woman*."

⁶And so it was, when Ahijah heard the sound of her footsteps as she came through the door, he said, "Come in, wife of Jeroboam. Why do you pretend *to be* another *person?* For I *have been* sent to you *with* bad *news.* ⁷Go, tell Jeroboam, 'Thus says the LORD God of Israel: "Because I exalted you from among the people, and made you ruler over My people Israel, ⁸and tore the kingdom away from thc house of David, and gave it to you; and *yet* you have not been as My servant David, who kept My commandments and who followed Me with all his heart, to do only *what was* right in My eyes; ⁹but you have done more evil than all who were before you, for you have gone and made for yourself other gods and molded images to provoke Me to anger, and have cast Me behind your back—¹⁰therefore behold! I will bring disaster on the house of Jeroboam, and will cut off from Jeroboam every

male in Israel, bond and free; I will take away the remnant of the house of Jeroboam, as one takes away refuse until it is all gone. ¹¹The dogs shall eat whoever belongs to Jeroboam and dies in the city, and the birds of the air shall eat whoever dies in the field; for the Lord has spoken!"' ¹²Arise therefore, go to your own house. When your feet enter the city, the child shall die. ¹³And all Israel shall mourn for him and bury him, for he is the only one of Jeroboam who shall come to the grave, because in him there is found something good toward the Lord God of Israel in the house of Jeroboam.

¹⁴"Moreover the Lord will raise up for Himself a king over Israel who shall cut off the house of Jeroboam; this is the day. What? Even now! ¹⁵For the Lord will strike Israel, as a reed is shaken in the water. He will uproot Israel from this good land which He gave to their fathers, and will scatter them beyond the River,* because they have made their wooden images,* provoking the Lord to anger. ¹⁶And He will give Israel up because of the sins of Jeroboam, who sinned and who made Israel sin."

¹⁷Then Jeroboam's wife arose and departed, and came to Tirzah. When she came to the threshold of the house, the child died. ¹⁸And they buried him; and all Israel mourned for him, according to the word of the Lord which He spoke through His servant Ahijah the prophet.

¹⁹Now the rest of the acts of Jeroboam, how he made war and how he reigned, indeed they *are* written in the book of the chronicles of the kings of Israel. ²⁰The period that Jeroboam reigned *was* twenty-two years. So he rested with his fathers. Then Nadab his son reigned in his place.

²¹And Rehoboam the son of Solomon reigned in Judah. Rehoboam *was* forty-one years old when he became king. He reigned seventeen years in Jerusalem, the city which the Lord had chosen out of all the tribes of Israel, to put His name there. His mother's name *was* Naamah, an Ammonitess. ²²Now Judah did evil in the sight of the Lord, and they provoked Him to jealousy with their sins which they committed, more than all that their fathers had done. ²³For they also built for themselves high places, *sacred* pillars, and wooden images on every high hill and under every green tree. ²⁴And there were also perverted persons* in the land. They did according to all the abominations of the nations which the Lord had cast out before the children of Israel.

²⁵It happened in the fifth year of King Rehoboam *that* Shishak king of Egypt came up against Jerusalem. ²⁶And he took away the treasures of the house of the Lord and the treasures of the king's house; he took away everything. He also took away all the gold shields which Solomon had made. ²⁷Then King Rehoboam made bronze shields in their place, and committed *them* to the hands of the captains of the guard, who guarded the doorway of the king's house. ²⁸And whenever the king entered the house of the Lord, the guards carried them, then brought them back into the guardroom.

²⁹Now the rest of the acts of Rehoboam, and all that he did, *are* they not written in the book of the chronicles of the kings of Judah? ³⁰And there was war between Rehoboam and Jeroboam all *their* days. ³¹So Rehoboam rested with his fathers, and was buried with his fathers in the City of David. His mother's name *was* Naamah, an Ammonitess. Then Abijam* his son reigned in his place.

In the eighteenth year of King Jeroboam the son of Nebat, Abijam became king over Judah. ²He reigned three years in Jerusalem. His mother's name *was* Maachah the granddaughter of Abishalom. ³And he walked in all the sins of his father, which he had done before him; his heart was not loyal to the LORD his God, as was the heart of his father David. ⁴Nevertheless for David's sake the LORD his God gave him a lamp in Jerusalem, by setting up his son after him and by establishing Jerusalem; ⁵because David did *what was* right in the eyes of the LORD, and had not turned aside from anything that He commanded him all the days of his life, except in the matter of Uriah the Hittite. ⁶And there was war between Rehoboam* and Jeroboam all the days of his life. ⁷Now the rest of the acts of Abijam, and all that he did, *are* they not written in the book of the chronicles of the kings of Judah? And there was war between Abijam and Jeroboam.

⁸So Abijam rested with his fathers, and they buried him in the City of David. Then Asa his son reigned in his place.

⁹In the twentieth year of Jeroboam king of Israel, Asa became king over Judah. ¹⁰And he reigned forty-one years in Jerusalem. His grandmother's name *was* Maachah the granddaughter of Abishalom. ¹¹Asa did *what was* right in the eyes of the LORD, as *did* his father David. ¹²And he banished the perverted persons* from the land, and removed all the idols that his fathers had made. ¹³Also he removed Maachah his grandmother from *being* queen mother, because she had made an obscene image of Asherah.* And Asa cut down her obscene image and burned *it* by the Brook Kidron. ¹⁴But the high places were not removed. Nevertheless Asa's heart was loyal to the LORD all his days. ¹⁵He also brought into the house of the LORD the things which his father had dedicated, and the things which he himself had dedicated: silver and gold and utensils.

¹⁶Now there was war between Asa and Baasha king of Israel all their days. ¹⁷And Baasha king of Israel came up against Judah, and built Ramah, that he might let none go out or come in to Asa king of Judah. ¹⁸Then Asa took all the silver and gold *that was* left in the treasuries of the house of the LORD and the treasuries of the king's house, and delivered them into the hand of his servants. And King Asa sent them to Ben-Hadad the son of Tabrimmon, the son of Hezion, king of Syria, who dwelt in Damascus, saying, ¹⁹"*Let there be* a treaty between you and me, as there was between my father and your father. See, I have sent you a present of silver and gold. Come and break your treaty with Baasha king of Israel, so that he will withdraw from me."

²⁰So Ben-Hadad heeded King Asa, and sent the captains of his armies against the cities of Israel. He attacked Ijon, Dan, Abel Beth Maachah, and all Chinneroth, with all the land of Naphtali. ²¹Now it happened, when Baasha heard *it,* that he stopped building Ramah, and remained in Tirzah.

²²Then King Asa made a proclamation throughout all Judah; none *was* exempted. And they took away the stones and timber of Ramah, which Baasha had used for building; and with them King Asa built Geba of Benjamin, and Mizpah.

²³The rest of all the acts of Asa, all his might, all that he did, and the cities which he built, *are* they not written in the book of the chronicles of the kings of Judah? But in the time of his old age he was diseased in his feet. ²⁴So Asa rested with his fathers, and was buried with his fathers in the City of David his father. Then Jehoshaphat his son reigned in his place.

ACTS 10:1–23a

THERE was a certain man in Caesarea called Cornelius, a centurion of what was called the Italian Regiment, ²a devout *man* and one who feared God with all his household, who gave alms generously to the people, and prayed to God always. ³About the ninth hour of the day he saw clearly in a vision an angel of God coming in and saying to him, "Cornelius!"

⁴And when he observed him, he was afraid, and said, "What is it, lord?"

So he said to him, "Your prayers and your alms have come up for a memorial before God. ⁵Now send men to Joppa, and send for Simon whose surname is Peter. ⁶He is lodging with Simon, a tanner, whose house is by the sea.* He will tell you what you must do." ⁷And when the angel who spoke to him had departed, Cornelius called two of his household servants and a devout soldier from among those who waited on him continually. ⁸So when he had explained all *these* things to them, he sent them to Joppa.

⁹The next day, as they went on their journey and drew near the city, Peter went up on the housetop to pray, about the sixth hour. ¹⁰Then he became very hungry and wanted to eat; but while they made ready, he fell into a trance ¹¹and saw heaven opened and an object like a great sheet bound at the four corners, descending to him and let down to the earth. ¹²In it were all kinds of four-footed animals of the earth, wild beasts, creeping things, and birds of the air. ¹³And a voice came to him, "Rise, Peter; kill and eat."

¹⁴But Peter said, "Not so, Lord! For I have never eaten anything common or unclean."

¹⁵And a voice *spoke* to him again the second time, "What God has cleansed you must not call common." ¹⁶This was done three times. And the object was taken up into heaven again.

¹⁷Now while Peter wondered within himself what this vision which he had seen meant, behold, the men who had been sent from Cornelius had made inquiry for Simon's house, and stood before the gate. ¹⁸And they called and asked whether Simon, whose surname was Peter, was lodging there.

¹⁹While Peter thought about the vision, the Spirit said to him, "Behold, three men are seeking you. ²⁰Arise therefore, go down and go with them, doubting nothing; for I have sent them."

²¹Then Peter went down to the men who had been sent to him from Cornelius,* and said, "Yes, I am he whom you seek. For what reason have you come?"

²²And they said, "Cornelius *the* centurion, a just man, one who fears God and has a good reputation among all the nation of the Jews, was divinely instructed by a holy angel to summon you to his house, and to hear words from you." ²³Then he invited them in and lodged *them.*

PSALM 133:1-3

A Song of Ascents. Of David.

BEHOLD, how good and how pleasant *it is*
For brethren to dwell
together in unity!

2   *It is* like the precious oil upon
the head,
Running down on the beard,
The beard of Aaron,
Running down on the edge of
his garments.

3   *It is* like the dew of Hermon,
Descending upon the
mountains of Zion;
For there the LORD
commanded the blessing—
Life forevermore.

PROVERBS FOR TODAY/ 17:7-8

Excellent speech is not becoming to a fool, much less lying lips to a prince. □ *A present* is *a precious stone in the eyes of its possessor; wherever he turns, he prospers.*

JUNE 16

1 KINGS 15:25–17:24

Now Nadab the son of Jeroboam became king over Israel in the second year of Asa king of Judah, and he reigned over Israel two years. 26And he did evil in the sight of the LORD, and walked in the way of his father, and in his sin by which he had made Israel sin.

27Then Baasha the son of Ahijah, of the house of Issachar, conspired against him. And Baasha killed him at Gibbethon, which *belonged* to the Philistines, while Nadab and all Israel laid siege to Gibbethon. 28Baasha killed him in the third year of Asa king of Judah, and reigned in his place. 29And it was so, when he became king, *that* he killed all the house of Jeroboam. He did not leave to Jeroboam anyone that breathed, until he had destroyed him, according to the word of the LORD which He had spoken by His servant Ahijah the Shilonite, 30because of the sins of Jeroboam, which he had sinned and by which he had made Israel sin, because of his provocation with which he had provoked the LORD God of Israel to anger.

31Now the rest of the acts of Nadab, and all that he did, *are* they not written in the book of the chronicles of the kings of Israel? 32And there was war between Asa and Baasha king of Israel all their days.

33In the third year of Asa king of Judah, Baasha the son of Ahijah became king over all Israel in Tirzah, and *reigned* twenty-four years. 34He did evil in the sight of the LORD, and walked in the way of Jeroboam, and in his sin by which he had made Israel sin.

THEN the word of the LORD came to Jehu the son of Hanani, against Baasha, saying: 2"Inasmuch as I lifted you out of the dust and made you ruler over My people Israel, and you have walked in the way of Jeroboam, and have made My people Israel sin, to provoke Me to anger with their sins, 3surely I will take away the posterity of Baasha and the posterity of his house, and I will make your house like the house of Jeroboam the son of Nebat. 4The dogs shall eat whoever belongs to Baasha and dies in the city, and the birds of the air shall eat whoever dies in the fields."

5Now the rest of the acts of Baasha, what he did, and his might, *are* they not written in the book of the chronicles of the kings of Israel? 6So Baasha rested with his fathers and was buried in Tirzah. Then Elah his son reigned in his place.

7And also the word of the LORD came by the prophet Jehu the son of Hanani against Baasha and his house, because of all the evil that he did in the sight of the LORD in provoking Him to anger with the work of his hands, in being like the house of Jeroboam, and because he killed them.

8In the twenty-sixth year of Asa king of Judah, Elah the son of Baasha became king over Israel, *and reigned* two years in Tirzah. ⁹Now his servant Zimri, commander of half *his* chariots, conspired against him as he was in Tirzah drinking himself drunk in the house of Arza, steward of *his* house in Tirzah. ¹⁰And Zimri went in and struck him and killed him in the twenty-seventh year of Asa king of Judah, and reigned in his place.

¹¹Then it came to pass, when he began to reign, as soon as he was seated on his throne, *that* he killed all the household of Baasha; he did not leave him one male, neither of his relatives nor of his friends. ¹²Thus Zimri destroyed all the household of Baasha, according to the word of the Lord, which He spoke against Baasha by Jehu the prophet, ¹³for all the sins of Baasha and the sins of Elah his son, by which they had sinned and by which they had made Israel sin, in provoking the Lord God of Israel to anger with their idols.

¹⁴Now the rest of the acts of Elah, and all that he did, *are* they not written in the book of the chronicles of the kings of Israel?

¹⁵In the twenty-seventh year of Asa king of Judah, Zimri had reigned in Tirzah seven days. And the people *were* encamped against Gibbethon, which *belonged* to the Philistines. ¹⁶Now the people *who were* encamped heard it said, "Zimri has conspired and also has killed the king." So all Israel made Omri, the commander of the army, king over Israel that day in the camp. ¹⁷Then Omri and all Israel with him went up from Gibbethon, and they besieged Tirzah. ¹⁸And it happened, when Zimri saw that the city was taken, that he went into the citadel of the king's house and burned the king's house down upon himself with fire, and died, ¹⁹because of the sins which he had committed in doing evil in the sight of the Lord, in walking in the way of Jeroboam, and in his sin which he had committed to make Israel sin.

²⁰Now the rest of the acts of Zimri, and the treason he committed, *are* they not written in the book of the chronicles of the kings of Israel?

²¹Then the people of Israel were divided into two parts: half of the people followed Tibni the son of Ginath, to make him king, and half followed Omri. ²²But the people who followed Omri prevailed over the people who followed Tibni the son of Ginath. So Tibni died and Omri reigned. ²³In the thirty-first year of Asa king of Judah, Omri became king over Israel, *and reigned* twelve years. Six years he reigned in Tirzah. ²⁴And he bought the hill of Samaria from Shemer for two talents of silver; then he built on the hill, and called the name of the city which he built, Samaria, after the name of Shemer, owner of the hill. ²⁵Omri did evil in the eyes of the Lord, and did worse than all who *were* before him. ²⁶For he walked in all the ways of Jeroboam the son of Nebat, and in his sin by which he had made Israel sin, provoking the Lord God of Israel to anger with their idols.

²⁷Now the rest of the acts of Omri which he did, and the might that he showed, *are* they not written in the book of the chronicles of the kings of Israel?

²⁸So Omri rested with his fathers and was buried in Samaria. Then Ahab his son reigned in his place.

²⁹In the thirty-eighth year of Asa king of Judah, Ahab the son of Omri became king over Israel; and Ahab the son of Omri reigned over Israel in Samaria twenty-two years. ³⁰Now Ahab the son of Omri did evil in the sight of the Lord, more than all who *were* before him. ³¹And it came to pass, as though it had been a trivial thing for him to walk in the sins of Jeroboam the son of Nebat, that he took as wife Jezebel the daughter of Ethbaal, king of the Sidoni-

ans; and he went and served Baal and worshiped him. ³²Then he set up an altar for Baal in the temple of Baal, which he had built in Samaria. ³³And Ahab made a wooden image.* Ahab did more to provoke the LORD God of Israel to anger than all the kings of Israel who were before him. ³⁴In his days Hiel of Bethel built Jericho. He laid its foundation with Abiram his firstborn, and with his youngest *son* Segub he set up its gates, according to the word of the LORD, which He had spoken through Joshua the son of Nun.*

AND Elijah the Tishbite, of the inhabitants of Gilead, said to Ahab, "*As* the LORD God of Israel lives, before whom I stand, there shall not be dew nor rain these years, except at my word."

²Then the word of the LORD came to him, saying, ³"Get away from here and turn eastward, and hide by the Brook Cherith, which flows into the Jordan. ⁴And it will be *that* you shall drink from the brook, and I have commanded the ravens to feed you there."

⁵So he went and did according to the word of the LORD, for he went and stayed by the Brook Cherith, which flows into the Jordan. ⁶The ravens brought him bread and meat in the morning, and bread and meat in the evening; and he drank from the brook. ⁷And it happened after a while that the brook dried up, because there had been no rain in the land.

⁸Then the word of the LORD came to him, saying, ⁹"Arise, go to Zarephath, which *belongs* to Sidon, and dwell there. See, I have commanded a widow there to provide for you." ¹⁰So he arose and went to Zarephath. And when he came to the gate of the city, indeed a widow *was* there gathering sticks. And he called to her and said, "Please bring me a little water in a cup, that I may drink." ¹¹And as she was going to get *it,* he called to her and said, "Please

bring me a morsel of bread in your hand."

¹²So she said, "As the LORD your God lives, I do not have bread, only a handful of flour in a bin, and a little oil in a jar; and see, I *am* gathering a couple of sticks that I may go in and prepare it for myself and my son, that we may eat it, and die."

¹³And Elijah said to her, "Do not fear; go *and* do as you have said, but make me a small cake from it first, and bring *it* to me; and afterward make *some* for yourself and your son. ¹⁴For thus says the LORD God of Israel: 'The bin of flour shall not be used up, nor shall the jar of oil run dry, until the day the LORD sends rain on the earth.' "

¹⁵So she went away and did according to the word of Elijah; and she and he and her household ate for *many* days. ¹⁶The bin of flour was not used up, nor did the jar of oil run dry, according to the word of the LORD which He spoke by Elijah.

¹⁷Now it happened after these things *that* the son of the woman who owned the house became sick. And his sickness was so serious that there was no breath left in him. ¹⁸So she said to Elijah, "What have I to do with you, O man of God? Have you come to me to bring my sin to remembrance, and to kill my son?"

¹⁹And he said to her, "Give me your son." So he took him out of her arms and carried him to the upper room where he was staying, and laid him on his own bed. ²⁰Then he cried out to the LORD and said, "O LORD my God, have You also brought tragedy on the widow with whom I lodge, by killing her son?" ²¹And he stretched himself out on the child three times, and cried out to the LORD and said, "O LORD my God, I pray, let this child's soul come back to him." ²²Then the LORD heard the voice of Elijah; and the soul of the child came back to him, and he revived.

23And Elijah took the child and brought him down from the upper room into the house, and gave him to his mother. And Elijah said, "See, your son lives!"

24Then the woman said to Elijah, "Now by this I know that you *are* a man of God, *and* that the word of the LORD in your mouth *is* the truth."

ACTS 10:23b–48

ON the next day Peter went away with them [the men sent from Cornelius], and some brethren from Joppa accompanied him.

24And the following day they entered Caesarea. Now Cornelius was waiting for them, and had called together his relatives and close friends. 25As Peter was coming in, Cornelius met him and fell down at his feet and worshiped *him*. 26But Peter lifted him up, saying, "Stand up; I myself am also a man." 27And as he talked with him, he went in and found many who had come together. 28Then he said to them, "You know how unlawful it is for a Jewish man to keep company with or go to one of another nation. But God has shown me that I should not call any man common or unclean. 29Therefore I came without objection as soon as I was sent for. I ask, then, for what reason have you sent for me?"

30So Cornelius said, "Four days ago I was fasting until this hour; and at the ninth hour* I prayed in my house, and behold, a man stood before me in bright clothing, 31and said, 'Cornelius, your prayer has been heard, and your alms are remembered in the sight of God. 32Send therefore to Joppa and call Simon here, whose surname is Peter. He is lodging in the house of Simon, a tanner, by the sea.* When he comes, he will speak to you.' 33So I sent to you immediately, and you have done well to come. Now therefore, we are all present before God, to hear all the things commanded you by God."

34Then Peter opened *his* mouth and said: "In truth I perceive that God shows no partiality. 35But in every nation whoever fears Him and works righteousness is accepted by Him. 36The word which *God* sent to the children of Israel, preaching peace through Jesus Christ—He is Lord of all— 37that word you know, which was proclaimed throughout all Judea, and began from Galilee after the baptism which John preached: 38how God anointed Jesus of Nazareth with the Holy Spirit and with power, who went about doing good and healing all who were oppressed by the devil, for God was with Him. 39And we are witnesses of all things which He did both in the land of the Jews and in Jerusalem, whom they* killed by hanging on a tree. 40Him God raised up on the third day, and showed Him openly, 41not to all the people, but to witnesses chosen before by God, *even* to us who ate and drank with Him after He arose from the dead. 42And He commanded us to preach to the people, and to testify that it is He who was ordained by God *to be* Judge of the living and the dead. 43To Him all the prophets witness that, through His name, whoever believes in Him will receive remission of sins."

44While Peter was still speaking these words, the Holy Spirit fell upon all those who heard the word. 45And those of the circumcision who believed were astonished, as many as came with Peter, because the gift of the Holy Spirit had been poured out on the Gentiles also. 46For they heard them speak with tongues and magnify God.

Then Peter answered, 47"Can anyone forbid water, that these should not be baptized who have received the Holy Spirit just as we *have?*" 48And he commanded them to be baptized in the name of the Lord. Then they asked him to stay a few days.

PSALM 134:1-3
A Song of Ascents.

BEHOLD, bless the LORD,
All *you* servants of the LORD,
Who by night stand in the
house of the LORD!

2 Lift up your hands *in* the
sanctuary,
And bless the LORD.

3 The LORD who made heaven
and earth
Bless you from Zion!

PROVERBS FOR TODAY/ 17:9-11

He who covers a transgression seeks love, but he who repeats a matter separates friends. ▫ Rebuke is more effective for a wise man *than a hundred blows on a fool. ▫ An evil* man *seeks only rebellion; therefore a cruel messenger will be sent against him.*

JUNE 17

1 KINGS 18:1-46

AND it came to pass *after* many days that the word of the LORD came to Elijah, in the third year, saying, "Go, present yourself to Ahab, and I will send rain on the earth."

2So Elijah went to present himself to Ahab; and *there was* a severe famine in Samaria. 3And Ahab had called Obadiah, who *was* in charge of *his* house. (Now Obadiah feared the LORD greatly. 4For so it was, while Jezebel massacred the prophets of the LORD, that Obadiah had taken one hundred prophets and hidden them, fifty to a cave, and had fed them with bread and water.) 5And Ahab had said to Obadiah, "Go into the land to all the springs of water and to all the brooks; perhaps we may find grass to keep the horses and mules alive, so that we will not have to kill any livestock." 6So they divided the land between them to explore it; Ahab went one way by himself, and Obadiah went another way by himself.

7Now as Obadiah was on his way, suddenly Elijah met him; and he rec-ognized him, and fell on his face, and said, "*Is* that you, my lord Elijah?"

8And he answered him, "*It is* I. Go, tell your master, 'Elijah *is here.*' "

9So he said, "How have I sinned, that you are delivering your servant into the hand of Ahab, to kill me? 10*As* the LORD your God lives, there is no nation or kingdom where my master has not sent someone to hunt for you; and when they said, '*He is* not *here,*' he took an oath from the kingdom or nation that they could not find you. 11And now you say, 'Go, tell your master, "Elijah *is here*" '! 12And it shall come to pass, *as soon as* I am gone from you, that the Spirit of the LORD will carry you to a place I do not know; so when I go and tell Ahab, and he cannot find you, he will kill me. But I your servant have feared the LORD from my youth. 13Was it not reported to my lord what I did when Jezebel killed the prophets of the LORD, how I hid one hundred men of the LORD's prophets, fifty to a cave, and fed them with bread and water? 14And now you say, 'Go, tell your mas-ter, "Elijah *is here.*" ' He will kill me!"

¹⁵Then Elijah said, "*As* the Lᴏʀᴅ of hosts lives, before whom I stand, I will surely present myself to him today."

¹⁶So Obadiah went to meet Ahab, and told him; and Ahab went to meet Elijah.

¹⁷Then it happened, when Ahab saw Elijah, that Ahab said to him, "*Is that* you, O troubler of Israel?"

¹⁸And he answered, "I have not troubled Israel, but you and your father's house *have,* in that you have forsaken the commandments of the Lᴏʀᴅ and have followed the Baals. ¹⁹Now therefore, send *and* gather all Israel to me on Mount Carmel, the four hundred and fifty prophets of Baal, and the four hundred prophets of Asherah,* who eat at Jezebel's table."

²⁰So Ahab sent for all the children of Israel, and gathered the prophets together on Mount Carmel. ²¹And Elijah came to all the people, and said, "How long will you falter between two opinions? If the Lᴏʀᴅ *is* God, follow Him; but if Baal, follow him." But the people answered him not a word. ²²Then Elijah said to the people, "I alone am left a prophet of the Lᴏʀᴅ; but Baal's prophets *are* four hundred and fifty men. ²³Therefore let them give us two bulls; and let them choose one bull for themselves, cut it in pieces, and lay *it* on the wood, but put no fire *under it;* and I will prepare the other bull, and lay *it* on the wood, but put no fire *under it.* ²⁴Then you call on the name of your gods, and I will call on the name of the Lᴏʀᴅ; and the God who answers by fire, He is God."

So all the people answered and said, "It is well spoken."

²⁵Now Elijah said to the prophets of Baal, "Choose one bull for yourselves and prepare *it* first, for you *are* many; and call on the name of your god, but put no fire *under it.*"

²⁶So they took the bull which was given them, and they prepared *it,* and called on the name of Baal from morn-ing even till noon, saying, "O Baal, hear us!" But *there was* no voice; no one answered. Then they leaped about the altar which they had made.

²⁷And so it was, at noon, that Elijah mocked them and said, "Cry aloud, for he *is* a god; either he is meditating, or he is busy, or he is on a journey, *or* perhaps he is sleeping and must be awakened." ²⁸So they cried aloud, and cut themselves, as was their custom, with knives and lances, until the blood gushed out on them. ²⁹And when midday was past, they prophesied until the *time* of the offering of the *evening* sacrifice. But *there was* no voice; no one answered, no one paid attention.

³⁰Then Elijah said to all the people, "Come near to me." So all the people came near to him. And he repaired the altar of the Lᴏʀᴅ *that was* broken down. ³¹And Elijah took twelve stones, according to the number of the tribes of the sons of Jacob, to whom the word of the Lᴏʀᴅ had come, saying, "Israel shall be your name."* ³²Then with the stones he built an altar in the name of the Lᴏʀᴅ; and he made a trench around the altar large enough to hold two seahs of seed. ³³And he put the wood in order, cut the bull in pieces, and laid *it* on the wood, and said, "Fill four waterpots with water, and pour *it* on the burnt sacrifice and on the wood." ³⁴Then he said, "Do *it* a second time," and they did *it* a second time; and he said, "Do *it* a third time," and they did *it* a third time. ³⁵So the water ran all around the altar; and he also filled the trench with water.

³⁶And it came to pass, at *the time of* the offering of the *evening* sacrifice, that Elijah the prophet came near and said, "Lᴏʀᴅ God of Abraham, Isaac, and Israel, let it be known this day that You *are* God in Israel and I *am* Your servant, and *that* I have done all these things at Your word. ³⁷Hear me, O Lᴏʀᴅ, hear me, that this people may know that You *are* the Lᴏʀᴅ God, and

that You have turned their hearts back *to You* again."

38Then the fire of the LORD fell and consumed the burnt sacrifice, and the wood and the stones and the dust, and it licked up the water that *was* in the trench. 39Now when all the people saw *it,* they fell on their faces; and they said, "The LORD, He *is* God! The LORD, He *is* God!"

40And Elijah said to them, "Seize the prophets of Baal! Do not let one of them escape!" So they seized them; and Elijah brought them down to the Brook Kishon and executed them there.

41Then Elijah said to Ahab, "Go up, eat and drink; for *there is* the sound of abundance of rain." 42So Ahab went up to eat and drink. And Elijah went up to the top of Carmel; then he bowed down on the ground, and put his face between his knees, 43and said to his servant, "Go up now, look toward the sea."

So he went up and looked, and said, "*There is* nothing." And seven times he said, "Go again."

44Then it came to pass the seventh *time,* that he said, "There is a cloud, as small as a man's hand, rising out of the sea!" So he said, "Go up, say to Ahab, 'Prepare *your chariot,* and go down before the rain stops you.'"

45Now it happened in the meantime that the sky became black with clouds and wind, and there was a heavy rain. So Ahab rode away and went to Jezreel. 46Then the hand of the LORD came upon Elijah; and he girded up his loins and ran ahead of Ahab to the entrance of Jezreel.

ACTS 11:1-30

Now the apostles and brethren who were in Judea heard that the Gentiles had also received the word of God. 2And when Peter came up to Jerusalem, those of the circumcision contended with him, 3saying, "You went in to uncircumcised men and ate with them!"

4But Peter explained *it* to them in order from the beginning, saying: 5"I was in the city of Joppa praying; and in a trance I saw a vision, an object descending like a great sheet, let down from heaven by four corners; and it came to me. 6When I observed it intently and considered, I saw four-footed animals of the earth, wild beasts, creeping things, and birds of the air. 7And I heard a voice saying to me, 'Rise, Peter; kill and eat.' 8But I said, 'Not so, Lord! For nothing common or unclean has at any time entered my mouth.' 9But the voice answered me again from heaven, 'What God has cleansed you must not call common.' 10Now this was done three times, and all were drawn up again into heaven. 11At that very moment, three men stood before the house where I was, having been sent to me from Caesarea. 12Then the Spirit told me to go with them, doubting nothing. Moreover these six brethren accompanied me, and we entered the man's house. 13And he told us how he had seen an angel standing in his house, who said to him, 'Send men to Joppa, and call for Simon whose surname is Peter, 14who will tell you words by which you and all your household will be saved.' 15And as I began to speak, the Holy Spirit fell upon them, as upon us at the beginning. 16Then I remembered the word of the Lord, how He said, 'John indeed baptized with water, but you shall be baptized with the Holy Spirit.' 17If therefore God gave them the same gift as *He gave* us when we believed on the Lord Jesus Christ, who was I that I could withstand God?"

18When they heard these things they became silent; and they glorified God, saying, "Then God has also granted to the Gentiles repentance to life."

¹⁹Now those who were scattered after the persecution that arose over Stephen traveled as far as Phoenicia, Cyprus, and Antioch, preaching the word to no one but the Jews only. ²⁰But some of them were men from Cyprus and Cyrene, who, when they had come to Antioch, spoke to the Hellenists, preaching the Lord Jesus. ²¹And the hand of the Lord was with them, and a great number believed and turned to the Lord.

²²Then news of these things came to the ears of the church in Jerusalem, and they sent out Barnabas to go as far as Antioch. ²³When he came and had seen the grace of God, he was glad, and encouraged them all that with purpose of heart they should continue with the Lord. ²⁴For he was a good man, full of the Holy Spirit and of faith. And a great many people were added to the Lord.

²⁵Then Barnabas departed for Tarsus to seek Saul. ²⁶And when he had found him, he brought him to Antioch. So it was that for a whole year they assembled with the church and taught a great many people. And the disciples were first called Christians in Antioch.

²⁷And in these days prophets came from Jerusalem to Antioch. ²⁸Then one of them, named Agabus, stood up and showed by the Spirit that there was going to be a great famine throughout all the world, which also happened in the days of Claudius Caesar. ²⁹Then the disciples, each according to his ability, determined to send relief to the brethren dwelling in Judea. ³⁰This they also did, and sent it to the elders by the hands of Barnabas and Saul.

PSALM 135:1-21

Praise the Lord!

Praise the name of the Lord;
Praise *Him,* O you servants of
the Lord!

2 You who stand in the house of
the Lord,
In the courts of the house of
our God,
3 Praise the Lord, for the Lord
is good;
Sing praises to His name, for
it is pleasant.
4 For the Lord has chosen
Jacob for Himself,
Israel for His special treasure.

5 For I know that the Lord *is*
great,
And our Lord *is* above all
gods.
6 Whatever the Lord pleases
He does,
In heaven and in earth,
In the seas and in all deep
places.
7 He causes the vapors to
ascend from the ends of the
earth;
He makes lightning for the
rain;
He brings the wind out of His
treasuries.

8 He destroyed the firstborn of
Egypt,
Both of man and beast.
9 He sent signs and wonders
into the midst of you,
O Egypt,
Upon Pharaoh and all his
servants.
10 He defeated many nations
And slew mighty kings—
11 Sihon king of the Amorites,
Og king of Bashan,
And all the kingdoms of
Canaan—
12 And gave their land *as* a
heritage,
A heritage to Israel His
people.

13 Your name, O Lord, *endures*
forever,

Your fame, O LORD,
throughout all generations.
14 For the LORD will judge His
people,
And He will have compassion
on His servants.

15 The idols of the nations *are*
silver and gold,
The work of men's hands.
16 They have mouths, but they
do not speak;
Eyes they have, but they do
not see;
17 They have ears, but they do
not hear;
Nor is there *any* breath in
their mouths.

18 Those who make them are
like them;
So is everyone who trusts in
them.

19 Bless the LORD, O house of
Israel!
Bless the LORD, O house of
Aaron!
20 Bless the LORD, O house of
Levi!
You who fear the LORD, bless
the LORD!
21 Blessed be the LORD out of
Zion,
Who dwells in Jerusalem!
Praise the LORD!

PROVERBS FOR TODAY/ 17:12-13

Let a man meet a bear robbed of her cubs, rather than a fool in his folly. ☐ *Whoever rewards evil for good, evil will not depart from his house.*

JUNE 18

1 KINGS 19:1-21

AND Ahab told Jezebel all that Elijah had done, also how he had executed all the prophets with the sword. ²Then Jezebel sent a messenger to Elijah, saying, "So let the gods do *to me,* and more also, if I do not make your life as the life of one of them by tomorrow about this time." ³And when he saw *that,* he arose and ran for his life, and went to Beersheba, which *belongs* to Judah, and left his servant there.

⁴But he himself went a day's journey into the wilderness, and came and sat down under a broom tree. And he prayed that he might die, and said, "It is enough! Now, LORD, take my life, for I *am* no better than my fathers!"

⁵Then as he lay and slept under a broom tree, suddenly an angel* touched him, and said to him, "Arise *and* eat." ⁶Then he looked, and there by his head *was* a cake baked on coals, and a jar of water. So he ate and drank, and lay down again. ⁷And the angel* of the LORD came back the second time, and touched him, and said, "Arise *and* eat, because the journey *is* too great for you." ⁸So he arose, and ate and drank; and he went in the strength of that food forty days and forty nights as far as Horeb, the mountain of God.

⁹And there he went into a cave, and spent the night in that place; and behold, the word of the LORD *came* to him, and He said to him, "What are you doing here, Elijah?"

¹⁰So he said, "I have been very zeal-

ous for the LORD God of hosts; for the children of Israel have forsaken Your covenant, torn down Your altars, and killed Your prophets with the sword. I alone am left; and they seek to take my life."

¹¹Then He said, "Go out, and stand on the mountain before the LORD." And behold, the LORD passed by, and a great and strong wind tore into the mountains and broke the rocks in pieces before the LORD, *but* the LORD *was* not in the wind; and after the wind an earthquake, *but* the LORD *was* not in the earthquake; ¹²and after the earthquake a fire, *but* the LORD *was* not in the fire; and after the fire a still small voice.

¹³So it was, when Elijah heard *it,* that he wrapped his face in his mantle and went out and stood in the entrance of the cave. Suddenly a voice *came* to him, and said, "What are you doing here, Elijah?"

¹⁴And he said, "I have been very zealous for the LORD God of hosts; because the children of Israel have forsaken Your covenant, torn down Your altars, and killed Your prophets with the sword. I alone am left; and they seek to take my life."

¹⁵Then the LORD said to him: "Go, return on your way to the Wilderness of Damascus; and when you arrive, anoint Hazael *as* king over Syria. ¹⁶Also you shall anoint Jehu the son of Nimshi *as* king over Israel. And Elisha the son of Shaphat of Abel Meholah you shall anoint *as* prophet in your place. ¹⁷It shall be *that* whoever escapes the sword of Hazael, Jehu will kill; and whoever escapes the sword of Jehu, Elisha will kill. ¹⁸Yet I have reserved seven thousand in Israel, all whose knees have not bowed to Baal, and every mouth that has not kissed him."

¹⁹So he departed from there, and found Elisha the son of Shaphat, who *was* plowing *with* twelve yoke *of* oxen before him, and he was with the twelfth. Then Elijah passed by him and threw his mantle on him. ²⁰And he left the oxen and ran after Elijah, and said, "Please let me kiss my father and my mother, and *then* I will follow you."

And he said to him, "Go back again, for what have I done to you?"

²¹So *Elisha* turned back from him, and took a yoke of oxen and slaughtered them and boiled their flesh, using the oxen's equipment, and gave it to the people, and they ate. Then he arose and followed Elijah, and became his servant.

ACTS 12:1-23

Now about that time Herod the king stretched out *his* hand to harass some from the church. ²Then he killed James the brother of John with the sword. ³And because he saw that it pleased the Jews, he proceeded further to seize Peter also. Now it was *during* the Days of Unleavened Bread. ⁴So when he had arrested him, he put *him* in prison, and delivered *him* to four squads of soldiers to keep him, intending to bring him before the people after Passover.

⁵Peter was therefore kept in prison, but constant* prayer was offered to God for him by the church. ⁶And when Herod was about to bring him out, that night Peter was sleeping, bound with two chains between two soldiers; and the guards before the door were keeping the prison. ⁷Now behold, an angel of the Lord stood by *him,* and a light shone in the prison; and he struck Peter on the side and raised him up, saying, "Arise quickly!" And his chains fell off *his* hands. ⁸Then the angel said to him, "Gird yourself and tie on your sandals"; and so he did. And he said to him, "Put on your garment and follow me." ⁹So he went out and followed him, and did not know that what was done by the angel was real, but thought he was seeing a vision. ¹⁰When they were

past the first and the second guard posts, they came to the iron gate that leads to the city, which opened to them of its own accord; and they went out and went down one street, and immediately the angel departed from him.

¹¹And when Peter had come to himself, he said, "Now I know for certain that the Lord has sent His angel, and has delivered me from the hand of Herod and *from* all the expectation of the Jewish people."

¹²So, when he had considered *this,* he came to the house of Mary, the mother of John whose surname was Mark, where many were gathered together praying. ¹³And as Peter knocked at the door of the gate, a girl named Rhoda came to answer. ¹⁴When she recognized Peter's voice, because of *her* gladness she did not open the gate, but ran in and announced that Peter stood before the gate. ¹⁵But they said to her, "You are beside yourself!" Yet she kept insisting that it was so. So they said, "It is his angel."

¹⁶Now Peter continued knocking; and when they opened *the door* and saw him, they were astonished. ¹⁷But motioning to them with his hand to keep silent, he declared to them how the Lord had brought him out of the prison. And he said, "Go, tell these things to James and to the brethren." And he departed and went to another place.

¹⁸Then, as soon as it was day, there was no small stir among the soldiers about what had become of Peter. ¹⁹But when Herod had searched for him and not found him, he examined the guards and commanded that *they* should be put to death.

And he went down from Judea to Caesarea, and stayed *there.*

²⁰Now Herod had been very angry with the people of Tyre and Sidon; but they came to him with one accord, and having made Blastus the king's personal aide their friend, they asked for peace, because their country was supplied with food by the king's *country.*

²¹So on a set day Herod, arrayed in royal apparel, sat on his throne and gave an oration to them. ²²And the people kept shouting, "The voice of a god and not of a man!" ²³Then immediately an angel of the Lord struck him, because he did not give glory to God. And he was eaten by worms and died.

PSALM 136:1-26

OH, give thanks to the LORD, for *He is* good!
For His mercy *endures*
forever.

2 Oh, give thanks to the God of
gods!
For His mercy *endures*
forever.

3 Oh, give thanks to the Lord of
lords!
For His mercy *endures*
forever:

4 To Him who alone does great
wonders,
For His mercy *endures*
forever;

5 To Him who by wisdom made
the heavens,
For His mercy *endures*
forever;

6 To Him who laid out the earth
above the waters,
For His mercy *endures*
forever;

7 To Him who made great
lights,
For His mercy *endures*
forever—

8 The sun to rule by day,
For His mercy *endures*
forever;

9 The moon and stars to rule by
night,
For His mercy *endures*
forever.

10 To Him who struck Egypt in
their firstborn,
For His mercy *endures*
forever;

11 And brought out Israel from
among them,
For His mercy *endures*
forever;

12 With a strong hand, and with
an outstretched arm,
For His mercy *endures*
forever;

13 To Him who divided the Red
Sea in two,
For His mercy *endures*
forever;

14 And made Israel pass through
the midst of it,
For His mercy *endures*
forever;

15 But overthrew Pharaoh and
his army in the Red Sea,
For His mercy *endures*
forever;

16 To Him who led His people
through the wilderness,
For His mercy *endures*
forever;

17 To Him who struck down
great kings,
For His mercy *endures*
forever;

18 And slew famous kings,

For His mercy *endures*
forever—

19 Sihon king of the Amorites,
For His mercy *endures*
forever;

20 And Og king of Bashan,
For His mercy *endures*
forever—

21 And gave their land as a
heritage,
For His mercy *endures*
forever;

22 A heritage to Israel His
servant,
For His mercy *endures*
forever.

23 Who remembered us in our
lowly state,
For His mercy *endures*
forever;

24 And rescued us from our
enemies,
For His mercy *endures*
forever;

25 Who gives food to all flesh,
For His mercy *endures*
forever.

26 Oh, give thanks to the God of
heaven!
For His mercy *endures*
forever.

PROVERBS FOR TODAY/ 17:14-15

The beginning of strife is like *releasing water; therefore stop contention before a quarrel starts.* □ *He who justifies the wicked, and he who condemns the just, both of them alike* are *an abomination to the* LORD.

1 KINGS 20:1–21:29

Now Ben-Hadad the king of Syria gathered all his forces together; thirty-two kings *were* with him, with horses and chariots. And he went up and besieged Samaria, and made war against it. ²Then he sent messengers into the city to Ahab king of Israel, and said to him, "Thus says Ben-Hadad: ³'Your silver and your gold *are* mine; your loveliest wives and children are mine.' "

⁴And the king of Israel answered and said, "My lord, O king, just as you say, I and all that I have *are* yours."

⁵Then the messengers came back and said, "Thus speaks Ben-Hadad, saying, 'Indeed I have sent to you, saying, "You shall deliver to me your silver and your gold, your wives and your children"; ⁶but I will send my servants to you tomorrow about this time, and they shall search your house and the houses of your servants. And it shall be, *that* whatever is pleasant in your eyes, they will put *it* in their hands and take *it*.' "

⁷So the king of Israel called all the elders of the land, and said, "Notice, please, and see how this *man* seeks trouble, for he sent to me for my wives, my children, my silver, and my gold; and I did not deny him."

⁸And all the elders and all the people said to him, "Do not listen or consent."

⁹Therefore he said to the messengers of Ben-Hadad, "Tell my lord the king, 'All that you sent for to your servant the first time I will do, but this thing I cannot do.' "

And the messengers departed and brought back word to him.

¹⁰Then Ben-Hadad sent to him and said, "The gods do so to me, and more also, if enough dust is left of Samaria for a handful for each of the people who follow me."

¹¹So the king of Israel answered and said, "Tell *him,* 'Let not the one who puts on *his armor* boast like the one who takes *it off.'* "

¹²And it happened when *Ben-Hadad* heard this message, as he and the kings *were* drinking at the command post, that he said to his servants, "Get ready." And they got ready to attack the city.

¹³Suddenly a prophet approached Ahab king of Israel, saying, "Thus says the Lord: 'Have you seen all this great multitude? Behold, I will deliver it into your hand today, and you shall know that I *am* the Lord.' "

¹⁴So Ahab said, "By whom?"

And he said, "Thus says the Lord: 'By the young leaders of the provinces.' "

Then he said, "Who will set the battle in order?"

And he answered, "You."

¹⁵Then he mustered the young leaders of the provinces, and there were two hundred and thirty-two; and after them he mustered all the people, all the children of Israel—seven thousand.

¹⁶So they went out at noon. Meanwhile Ben-Hadad and the thirty-two kings helping him were getting drunk at the command post. ¹⁷The young leaders of the provinces went out first. And Ben-Hadad sent out *a patrol,* and they told him, saying, "Men are coming out of Samaria!" ¹⁸So he said, "If they have come out for peace, take them alive; and if they have come out for war, take them alive."

¹⁹Then these young leaders of the provinces went out of the city with the army which followed them. ²⁰And each

one killed his man; so the Syrians fled, and Israel pursued them; and Ben-Hadad the king of Syria escaped on a horse with the cavalry. ²¹Then the king of Israel went out and attacked the horses and chariots, and killed the Syrians with a great slaughter.

²²And the prophet came to the king of Israel and said to him, "Go, strengthen yourself; take note, and see what you should do, for in the spring of the year the king of Syria will come up against you."

²³Then the servants of the king of Syria said to him, "Their gods *are* gods of the hills. Therefore they were stronger than we; but if we fight against them in the plain, surely we will be stronger than they. ²⁴So do this thing: Dismiss the kings, each from his position, and put captains in their places; ²⁵and you shall muster an army like the army that you have lost, horse for horse and chariot for chariot. Then we will fight against them in the plain; surely we will be stronger than they."

And he listened to their voice and did so.

²⁶So it was, in the spring of the year, that Ben-Hadad mustered the Syrians and went up to Aphek to fight against Israel. ²⁷And the children of Israel were mustered and given provisions, and they went against them. Now the children of Israel encamped before them like two little flocks of goats, while the Syrians filled the countryside.

²⁸Then a man of God came and spoke to the king of Israel, and said, "Thus says the LORD: 'Because the Syrians have said, "The LORD *is* God of the hills, but He *is* not God of the valleys," therefore I will deliver all this great multitude into your hand, and you shall know that I *am* the LORD.'" ²⁹And they encamped opposite each other for seven days. So it was that on the seventh day the battle was joined; and the children of Israel killed one hundred thousand foot soldiers *of* the Syrians in one day. ³⁰But the rest fled to Aphek, into the city; then a wall fell on twenty-seven thousand of the men *who were* left.

And Ben-Hadad fled and went into the city, into an inner chamber.

³¹Then his servants said to him, "Look now, we have heard that the kings of the house of Israel *are* merciful kings. Please, let us put sackcloth around our waists and ropes around our heads, and go out to the king of Israel; perhaps he will spare your life." ³²So they wore sackcloth around their waists and *put* ropes around their heads, and came to the king of Israel and said, "Your servant Ben-Hadad says, 'Please let me live.'"

And he said, "*Is* he still alive? He *is* my brother."

³³Now the men were watching closely to see whether *any sign of mercy would come* from him; and they quickly grasped *at this word* and said, "Your brother Ben-Hadad."

So he said, "Go, bring him." Then Ben-Hadad came out to him; and he had him come up into the chariot.

³⁴So *Ben-Hadad* said to him, "The cities which my father took from your father I will restore; and you may set up marketplaces for yourself in Damascus, as my father did in Samaria."

Then *Ahab said,* "I will send you away with this treaty." So he made a treaty with him and sent him away.

³⁵Now a certain man of the sons of the prophets said to his neighbor by the word of the LORD, "Strike me, please." And the man refused to strike him. ³⁶Then he said to him, "Because you have not obeyed the voice of the LORD, surely, as soon as you depart from me, a lion shall kill you." And as soon as he left him, a lion found him and killed him.

³⁷And he found another man, and said, "Strike me, please." So the man struck him, inflicting a wound. ³⁸Then the prophet departed and waited for the king by the road, and disguised

himself with a bandage over his eyes. [39]Now as the king passed by, he cried out to the king and said, "Your servant went out into the midst of the battle; and there, a man came over and brought a man to me, and said, 'Guard this man; if by any means he is missing, your life shall be for his life, or else you shall pay a talent of silver.' [40]While your servant was busy here and there, he was gone."

Then the king of Israel said to him, "So *shall* your judgment *be;* you yourself have decided *it.*"

[41]And he hastened to take the bandage away from his eyes; and the king of Israel recognized him as one of the prophets. [42]Then he said to him, "Thus says the Lord: 'Because you have let slip out of *your* hand a man whom I appointed to utter destruction, therefore your life shall go for his life, and your people for his people.' "

[43]So the king of Israel went to his house sullen and displeased, and came to Samaria.

And it came to pass after these things *that* Naboth the Jezreelite had a vineyard which *was* in Jezreel, next to the palace of Ahab king of Samaria. [2]So Ahab spoke to Naboth, saying, "Give me your vineyard, that I may have it for a vegetable garden, because it *is* near, next to my house; and for it I will give you a vineyard better than it. *Or,* if it seems good to you, I will give you its worth in money."

[3]But Naboth said to Ahab, "The Lord forbid that I should give the inheritance of my fathers to you!"

[4]So Ahab went into his house sullen and displeased because of the word which Naboth the Jezreelite had spoken to him; for he had said, "I will not give you the inheritance of my fathers." And he lay down on his bed, and turned away his face, and would eat no food. [5]But Jezebel his wife came to him, and said to him, "Why is your spirit so sullen that you eat no food?"

[6]He said to her, "Because I spoke to Naboth the Jezreelite, and said to him, 'Give me your vineyard for money; or else, if it pleases you, I will give you *another* vineyard for it.' And he answered, 'I will not give you my vineyard.' "

[7]Then Jezebel his wife said to him, "You now exercise authority over Israel! Arise, eat food, and let your heart be cheerful; I will give you the vineyard of Naboth the Jezreelite."

[8]And she wrote letters in Ahab's name, sealed *them* with his seal, and sent the letters to the elders and the nobles who *were* dwelling in the city with Naboth. [9]She wrote in the letters, saying,

> Proclaim a fast, and seat Naboth with high honor among the people; [10]and seat two men, scoundrels, before him to bear witness against him, saying, You have blasphemed God and the king. *Then* take him out, and stone him, that he may die.

[11]So the men of his city, the elders and nobles who were inhabitants of his city, did as Jezebel had sent to them, as it *was* written in the letters which she had sent to them. [12]They proclaimed a fast, and seated Naboth with high honor among the people. [13]And two men, scoundrels, came in and sat before him; and the scoundrels witnessed against him, against Naboth, in the presence of the people, saying, "Naboth has blasphemed God and the king!" Then they took him outside the city and stoned him with stones, so that he died. [14]Then they sent to Jezebel, saying, "Naboth has been stoned and is dead."

[15]And it came to pass, when Jezebel heard that Naboth had been stoned

and was dead, that Jezebel said to Ahab, "Arise, take possession of the vineyard of Naboth the Jezreelite, which he refused to give you for money; for Naboth is not alive, but dead." 16So it was, when Ahab heard that Naboth was dead, that Ahab got up and went down to take possession of the vineyard of Naboth the Jezreelite.

17Then the word of the LORD came to Elijah the Tishbite, saying, 18"Arise, go down to meet Ahab king of Israel, who *lives* in Samaria. There *he is,* in the vineyard of Naboth, where he has gone down to take possession of it. 19You shall speak to him, saying, 'Thus says the LORD: "Have you murdered and also taken possession?" ' And you shall speak to him, saying, 'Thus says the LORD: "In the place where dogs licked the blood of Naboth, dogs shall lick your blood, even yours." ' "

20So Ahab said to Elijah, "Have you found me, O my enemy?"

And he answered, "I have found *you,* because you have sold yourself to do evil in the sight of the LORD: 21'Behold, I will bring calamity on you. I will take away your posterity, and will cut off from Ahab every male in Israel, both bond and free. 22I will make your house like the house of Jeroboam the son of Nebat, and like the house of Baasha the son of Ahijah, because of the provocation with which you have provoked *Me* to anger, and made Israel sin.' 23And concerning Jezebel the LORD also spoke, saying, 'The dogs shall eat Jezebel by the wall* of Jezreel.' 24The dogs shall eat whoever belongs to Ahab and dies in the city, and the birds of the air shall eat whoever dies in the field."

25But there was no one like Ahab who sold himself to do wickedness in the sight of the LORD, because Jezebel his wife stirred him up. 26And he behaved very abominably in following idols, according to all *that* the Amorites had done, whom the LORD had cast out before the children of Israel.

27So it was, when Ahab heard those words, that he tore his clothes and put sackcloth on his body, and fasted and lay in sackcloth, and went about mourning.

28And the word of the LORD came to Elijah the Tishbite, saying, 29"See how Ahab has humbled himself before Me? Because he has humbled himself before Me, I will not bring the calamity in his days. In the days of his son I will bring the calamity on his house."

ACTS 12:24–13:15

Bᴜᴛ the word of God grew and multiplied. 25And Barnabas and Saul returned from* Jerusalem when they had fulfilled *their* ministry, and they also took with them John whose surname was Mark.

Now in the church that was at Antioch there were certain prophets and teachers: Barnabas, Simeon who was called Niger, Lucius of Cyrene, Manaen who had been brought up with Herod the tetrarch, and Saul. 2As they ministered to the Lord and fasted, the Holy Spirit said, "Now separate to Me Barnabas and Saul for the work to which I have called them." 3Then, having fasted and prayed, and laid hands on them, they sent *them* away.

4So, being sent out by the Holy Spirit, they went down to Seleucia, and from there they sailed to Cyprus. 5And when they arrived in Salamis, they preached the word of God in the synagogues of the Jews. They also had John as *their* assistant.

6Now when they had gone through the island* to Paphos, they found a certain sorcerer, a false prophet, a Jew whose name *was* Bar-Jesus, 7who was with the proconsul, Sergius Paulus, an intelligent man. This man called for Barnabas and Saul and sought to hear the word of God. 8But Elymas the sorcerer (for so his name is translated) withstood them, seeking to turn the proconsul away from the faith. ⁹Then Saul, who also *is called* Paul, filled with the Holy Spirit, looked intently at him ¹⁰and said, "O full of all deceit and all fraud, *you* son of the devil, *you* enemy of all righteousness, will you not cease perverting the straight ways of the Lord? ¹¹And now, indeed, the hand of the Lord *is* upon you, and you shall be blind, not seeing the sun for a time."

And immediately a dark mist fell on him, and he went around seeking someone to lead him by the hand. ¹²Then the proconsul believed, when he saw what had been done, being astonished at the teaching of the Lord.

¹³Now when Paul and his party set sail from Paphos, they came to Perga in Pamphylia; and John, departing from them, returned to Jerusalem. ¹⁴But when they departed from Perga, they came to Antioch in Pisidia, and went into the synagogue on the Sabbath day and sat down. ¹⁵And after the reading of the Law and the Prophets, the rulers of the synagogue sent to them, saying, "Men *and* brethren, if you have any word of exhortation for the people, say on."

PSALM 137:1-9

B Y the rivers of Babylon,
There we sat down, yea, we
wept
When we remembered Zion.

2 We hung our harps
Upon the willows in the midst
of it.

3 For there those who carried
us away captive asked of us
a song,
And those who plundered us
requested mirth,
Saying, "Sing us *one* of the
songs of Zion!"

4 How shall we sing the LORD's
song
In a foreign land?

5 If I forget you, O Jerusalem,
Let my right hand forget *its*
skill!

6 If I do not remember you,
Let my tongue cling to the
roof of my mouth—
If I do not exalt Jerusalem
Above my chief joy.

7 Remember, O LORD, against
the sons of Edom
The day of Jerusalem,
Who said, "Raze *it,* raze *it,*
To its very foundation!"

8 O daughter of Babylon, who
are to be destroyed,
Happy the one who repays
you as you have served us!

9 Happy the one who takes and
dashes
Your little ones against the
rock!

PROVERBS FOR TODAY/ 17:16

Why is there *in the hand of a fool the purchase price of wisdom, since* he has *no heart* for it?

JUNE 20

1 KINGS 22:1-53

Now three years passed without war between Syria and Israel. ²Then it came to pass, in the third year, that Jehoshaphat the king of Judah went down to *visit* the king of Israel.

³And the king of Israel said to his servants, "Do you know that Ramoth in Gilead *is* ours, but we hesitate to take it out of the hand of the king of Syria?" ⁴So he said to Jehoshaphat, "Will you go with me to fight at Ramoth Gilead?"

Jehoshaphat said to the king of Israel, "I *am* as you *are,* my people as your people, my horses as your horses." ⁵Also Jehoshaphat said to the king of Israel, "Please inquire for the word of the LORD today."

⁶Then the king of Israel gathered the prophets together, about four hundred men, and said to them, "Shall I go against Ramoth Gilead to fight, or shall I refrain?"

So they said, "Go up, for the Lord will deliver *it* into the hand of the king."

⁷And Jehoshaphat said, "*Is there* not still a prophet of the LORD here, that we may inquire of Him?"*

⁸So the king of Israel said to Jehoshaphat, "*There is* still one man, Micaiah the son of Imlah, by whom we may inquire of the LORD; but I hate him, because he does not prophesy good concerning me, but evil."

And Jehoshaphat said, "Let not the king say such things!"

⁹Then the king of Israel called an officer and said, "Bring Micaiah the son of Imlah quickly!"

¹⁰The king of Israel and Jehoshaphat the king of Judah, having put on *their* robes, sat each on his throne, at a threshing floor at the entrance of the gate of Samaria; and all the prophets prophesied before them. ¹¹Now Zedekiah the son of Chenaanah had made horns of iron for himself; and he said, "Thus says the LORD: 'With these you shall gore the Syrians until they are destroyed.' " ¹²And all the prophets prophesied so, saying, "Go up to Ramoth Gilead and prosper, for the LORD will deliver *it* into the king's hand."

¹³Then the messenger who had gone to call Micaiah spoke to him, saying, "Now listen, the words of the prophets with one accord encourage the king. Please, let your word be like the word of one of them, and speak encouragement."

¹⁴And Micaiah said, "*As* the LORD lives, whatever the LORD says to me, that I will speak."

¹⁵Then he came to the king; and the king said to him, "Micaiah, shall we go to war against Ramoth Gilead, or shall we refrain?"

And he answered him, "Go and prosper, for the LORD will deliver *it* into the hand of the king!"

¹⁶So the king said to him, "How many times shall I make you swear that you tell me nothing but the truth in the name of the LORD?"

¹⁷Then he said, "I saw all Israel scattered on the mountains, as sheep that have no shepherd. And the LORD said, 'These have no master. Let each return to his house in peace.' "

¹⁸And the king of Israel said to Jehoshaphat, "Did I not tell you he would not prophesy good concerning me, but evil?"

¹⁹Then *Micaiah* said, "Therefore hear the word of the LORD: I saw the LORD sitting on His throne, and all the

host of heaven standing by, on His right hand and on His left. 20And the LORD said, 'Who will persuade Ahab to go up, that he may fall at Ramoth Gilead?' So one spoke in this manner, and another spoke in that manner. 21Then a spirit came forward and stood before the LORD, and said, 'I will persuade him.' 22The LORD said to him, 'In what way?' So he said, 'I will go out and be a lying spirit in the mouth of all his prophets.' And the LORD said, 'You shall persuade *him,* and also prevail. Go out and do so.' 23Therefore look! The LORD has put a lying spirit in the mouth of all these prophets of yours, and the LORD has declared disaster against you."

24Now Zedekiah the son of Chenaanah went near and struck Micaiah on the cheek, and said, "Which way did the spirit from the LORD go from me to speak to you?"

25And Micaiah said, "Indeed, you shall see on that day when you go into an inner chamber to hide!"

26So the king of Israel said, "Take Micaiah, and return him to Amon the governor of the city and to Joash the king's son; 27and say, 'Thus says the king: "Put this *fellow* in prison, and feed him with bread of affliction and water of affliction, until I come in peace." ' "

28But Micaiah said, "If you ever return in peace, the LORD has not spoken by me." And he said, "Take heed, all you people!"

29So the king of Israel and Jehoshaphat the king of Judah went up to Ramoth Gilead. 30And the king of Israel said to Jehoshaphat, "I will disguise myself and go into battle; but you put on your robes." So the king of Israel disguised himself and went into battle.

31Now the king of Syria had commanded the thirty-two captains of his chariots, saying, "Fight with no one small or great, but only with the king of Israel." 32So it was, when the cap-

tains of the chariots saw Jehoshaphat, that they said, "Surely it *is* the king of Israel!" Therefore they turned aside to fight against him, and Jehoshaphat cried out. 33And it happened, when the captains of the chariots saw that it *was* not the king of Israel, that they turned back from pursuing him. 34Now a *certain* man drew a bow at random, and struck the king of Israel between the joints of his armor. So he said to the driver of his chariot, "Turn around and take me out of the battle, for I am wounded."

35The battle increased that day; and the king was propped up in his chariot, facing the Syrians, and died at evening. The blood ran out from the wound onto the floor of the chariot. 36Then, as the sun was going down, a shout went throughout the army, saying, "Every man to his city, and every man to his own country!"

37So the king died, and was brought to Samaria. And they buried the king in Samaria. 38Then *someone* washed the chariot at a pool in Samaria, and the dogs licked up his blood while the harlots bathed,* according to the word of the LORD which He had spoken.

39Now the rest of the acts of Ahab, and all that he did, the ivory house which he built and all the cities that he built, *are* they not written in the book of the chronicles of the kings of Israel? 40So Ahab rested with his fathers. Then Ahaziah his son reigned in his place.

41Jehoshaphat the son of Asa had become king over Judah in the fourth year of Ahab king of Israel. 42Jehoshaphat *was* thirty-five years old when he became king, and he reigned twenty-five years in Jerusalem. His mother's name *was* Azubah the daughter of Shilhi. 43And he walked in all the ways of his father Asa. He did not turn aside from them, doing *what was* right in the eyes of the LORD. Nevertheless the high places were not taken away, *for* the people offered sacrifices and burned incense on the high places. ⁴⁴Also Jehoshaphat made peace with the king of Israel.

⁴⁵Now the rest of the acts of Jehoshaphat, the might that he showed, and how he made war, *are* they not written in the book of the chronicles of the kings of Judah? ⁴⁶And the rest of the perverted persons,* who remained in the days of his father Asa, he banished from the land. ⁴⁷*There was* then no king in Edom, only a deputy of the king.

⁴⁸Jehoshaphat made merchant ships* to go to Ophir for gold; but they never sailed, for the ships were wrecked at Ezion Geber. ⁴⁹Then Ahaziah the son of Ahab said to Jehoshaphat, "Let my servants go with your servants in the ships." But Jehoshaphat would not.

⁵⁰And Jehoshaphat rested with his fathers, and was buried with his fathers in the City of David his father. Then Jehoram his son reigned in his place.

⁵¹Ahaziah the son of Ahab became king over Israel in Samaria in the seventeenth year of Jehoshaphat king of Judah, and reigned two years over Israel. ⁵²He did evil in the sight of the Lord, and walked in the way of his father and in the way of his mother and in the way of Jeroboam the son of Nebat, who had made Israel sin; ⁵³for he served Baal and worshiped him, and provoked the Lord God of Israel to anger, according to all that his father had done.

ACTS 13:16-41

THEN Paul stood up, and motioning with *his* hand said, "Men of Israel, and you who fear God, listen: ¹⁷The God of this people Israel* chose our fathers, and exalted the people when they dwelt as strangers in the land of Egypt, and with an uplifted arm He brought them out of it. ¹⁸Now for a time of about forty years He put up with their ways in the wilderness. ¹⁹And when He had destroyed seven nations in the land of Canaan, He distributed their land to them by allotment.

²⁰"After that He gave *them* judges for about four hundred and fifty years, until Samuel the prophet. ²¹And afterward they asked for a king; so God gave them Saul the son of Kish, a man of the tribe of Benjamin, for forty years. ²²And when He had removed him, He raised up for them David as king, to whom also He gave testimony and said, '*I have found David* * the *son* of Jesse, *a man after My own heart*, who will do all My will.' * ²³From this man's seed, according to *the* promise, God raised up for Israel a Savior— Jesus*— ²⁴after John had first preached, before His coming, the baptism of repentance to all the people of Israel. ²⁵And as John was finishing his course, he said, 'Who do you think I am? I am not *He.* But behold, there comes One after me, the sandals of whose feet I am not worthy to loose.'

²⁶"Men *and* brethren, sons of the family of Abraham, and those among you who fear God, to you the word of this salvation has been sent. ²⁷For those who dwell in Jerusalem, and their rulers, because they did not know Him, nor even the voices of the Prophets which are read every Sabbath, have fulfilled *them* in condemning *Him.* ²⁸And though they found no cause for death *in Him,* they asked Pilate that He should be put to death. ²⁹Now when they had fulfilled all that was written concerning Him, they took *Him* down from the tree and laid *Him* in a tomb. ³⁰But God raised Him from the dead. ³¹He was seen for many days by those who came up with Him from Galilee to Jerusalem, who are His witnesses to the people. ³²And we declare to you glad tidings—that

promise which was made to the fathers. 33God has fulfilled this for us their children, in that He has raised up Jesus. As it is also written in the second Psalm:

> 'You are My Son,
> Today I have begotten You.' *

34And that He raised Him from the dead, no more to return to corruption, He has spoken thus:

> 'I will give you the sure
> mercies of David.' *

35Therefore He also says in another *Psalm:*

> 'You will not allow Your Holy
> One to see corruption.' *

36"For David, after he had served his own generation by the will of God, fell asleep, was buried with his fathers, and saw corruption; 37but He whom God raised up saw no corruption. 38Therefore let it be known to you, brethren, that through this Man is preached to you the forgiveness of sins; 39and by Him everyone who believes is justified from all things from which you could not be justified by the law of Moses. 40Beware therefore, lest what has been spoken in the prophets come upon you:

> 41 'Behold, you despisers,
> Marvel and perish!
> For I work a work in your
> days,
> A work which you will by no
> means believe,
> Though one were to declare it
> to you.'" *

PSALM 138:1-8

A Psalm *of David.*

I WILL praise You with my whole heart;
Before the gods I will sing
praises to You.
2 I will worship toward Your
holy temple,
And praise Your name
For Your lovingkindness and
Your truth;
For You have magnified Your
word above all Your name.
3 In the day when I cried out,
You answered me,
And made me bold *with*
strength in my soul.

4 All the kings of the earth shall
praise You, O LORD,
When they hear the words of
Your mouth.
5 Yes, they shall sing of the
ways of the LORD,
For great *is* the glory of the
LORD.
6 Though the LORD *is* on high,
Yet He regards the lowly;
But the proud He knows from
afar.

7 Though I walk in the midst of
trouble, You will revive me;
You will stretch out Your hand
Against the wrath of my
enemies,
And Your right hand will save
me.
8 The LORD will perfect *that
which* concerns me;
Your mercy, O LORD, *endures*
forever;
Do not forsake the works of
Your hands.

PROVERBS FOR TODAY/ 17:17-18

A friend loves at all times, and a brother is born for adversity. □ *A man devoid of understanding shakes hands in a pledge,* and *becomes surety for his friend.*

JUNE 21

2 KINGS 1:1–2:25

MOAB rebelled against Israel after the death of Ahab. [2]Now Ahaziah fell through the lattice of his upper room in Samaria, and was injured; so he sent messengers and said to them, "Go, inquire of Baal-Zebub, the god of Ekron, whether I shall recover from this injury." [3]But the angel* of the LORD said to Elijah the Tishbite, "Arise, go up to meet the messengers of the king of Samaria, and say to them, '*Is it* because *there is* no God in Israel *that* you are going to inquire of Baal-Zebub, the god of Ekron?' [4]Now therefore, thus says the LORD: 'You shall not come down from the bed to which you have gone up, but you shall surely die.'" So Elijah departed.

[5]And when the messengers returned to him, he said to them, "Why have you come back?"

[6]So they said to him, "A man came up to meet us, and said to us, 'Go, return to the king who sent you, and say to him, "Thus says the LORD: '*Is it* because *there is* no God in Israel *that* you are sending to inquire of Baal-Zebub, the god of Ekron? Therefore you shall not come down from the bed to which you have gone up, but you shall surely die.'"'"

[7]Then he said to them, "What kind of man *was it* who came up to meet you and told you these words?"

[8]So they answered him, "A hairy man wearing a leather belt around his waist."

And he said, "It *is* Elijah the Tishbite."

[9]Then the king sent to him a captain of fifty with his fifty men. So he went up to him; and there he was, sitting on the top of a hill. And he spoke to him: "Man of God, the king has said, 'Come down!'"

[10]So Elijah answered and said to the captain of fifty, "If I *am* a man of God, then let fire come down from heaven and consume you and your fifty men." And fire came down from heaven and consumed him and his fifty. [11]Then he sent to him another captain of fifty with his fifty men.

And he answered and said to him: "Man of God, thus has the king said, 'Come down quickly!'"

[12]So Elijah answered and said to them, "If I *am* a man of God, let fire come down from heaven and consume you and your fifty men." And the fire of God came down from heaven and consumed him and his fifty.

[13]Again, he sent a third captain of fifty with his fifty men. And the third captain of fifty went up, and came and fell on his knees before Elijah, and pleaded with him, and said to him: "Man of God, please let my life and the life of these fifty servants of yours be precious in your sight. [14]Look, fire has come down from heaven and burned up the first two captains of fifties with their fifties. But let my life now be precious in your sight."

[15]And the angel* of the LORD said to Elijah, "Go down with him; do not be afraid of him." So he arose and went down with him to the king. [16]Then he said to him, "Thus says the LORD: 'Because you have sent messengers to inquire of Baal-Zebub, the god of Ekron, *is it* because *there is* no God in Israel to inquire of His word? Therefore you shall not come down from the bed to which you have gone up, but you shall surely die.'"

[17]So *Ahaziah* died according to the word of the LORD which Elijah had spo-

ken. Because he had no son, Jehoram* became king in his place, in the second year of Jehoram the son of Jehoshaphat, king of Judah.

¹⁸Now the rest of the acts of Ahaziah which he did, *are* they not written in the book of the chronicles of the kings of Israel?

AND it came to pass, when the LORD was about to take up Elijah into heaven by a whirlwind, that Elijah went with Elisha from Gilgal. ²Then Elijah said to Elisha, "Stay here, please, for the LORD has sent me on to Bethel."

But Elisha said, "*As* the LORD lives, and *as* your soul lives, I will not leave you!" So they went down to Bethel.

³Now the sons of the prophets who *were* at Bethel came out to Elisha, and said to him, "Do you know that the LORD will take away your master from over you today?"

And he said, "Yes, I know; keep silent!"

⁴Then Elijah said to him, "Elisha, stay here, please, for the LORD has sent me on to Jericho."

But he said, "*As* the LORD lives, and *as* your soul lives, I will not leave you!" So they came to Jericho.

⁵Now the sons of the prophets who *were* at Jericho came to Elisha and said to him, "Do you know that the LORD will take away your master from over you today?"

So he answered, "Yes, I know; keep silent!"

⁶Then Elijah said to him, "Stay here, please, for the LORD has sent me on to the Jordan."

But he said, "*As* the LORD lives, and *as* your soul lives, I will not leave you!" So the two of them went on. ⁷And fifty men of the sons of the prophets went and stood facing *them* at a distance, while the two of them stood by the Jordan. ⁸Now Elijah took his mantle, rolled *it* up, and struck the water; and it was divided this way and that, so that the two of them crossed over on dry ground.

⁹And so it was, when they had crossed over, that Elijah said to Elisha, "Ask! What may I do for you, before I am taken away from you?"

Elisha said, "Please let a double portion of your spirit be upon me."

¹⁰So he said, "You have asked a hard thing. *Nevertheless,* if you see me *when I am* taken from you, it shall be so for you; but if not, it shall not be *so.*" ¹¹Then it happened, as they continued on and talked, that suddenly a chariot of fire *appeared* with horses of fire, and separated the two of them; and Elijah went up by a whirlwind into heaven.

¹²And Elisha saw *it,* and he cried out, "My father, my father, the chariot of Israel and its horsemen!" So he saw him no more. And he took hold of his own clothes and tore them into two pieces. ¹³He also took up the mantle of Elijah that had fallen from him, and went back and stood by the bank of the Jordan. ¹⁴Then he took the mantle of Elijah that had fallen from him, and struck the water, and said, "Where *is* the LORD God of Elijah?" And when he also had struck the water, it was divided this way and that; and Elisha crossed over.

¹⁵Now when the sons of the prophets who *were* from Jericho saw him, they said, "The spirit of Elijah rests on Elisha." And they came to meet him, and bowed to the ground before him. ¹⁶Then they said to him, "Look now, there are fifty strong men with your servants. Please let them go and search for your master, lest perhaps the Spirit of the LORD has taken him up and cast him upon some mountain or into some valley."

And he said, "You shall not send anyone."

¹⁷But when they urged him till he was ashamed, he said, "Send *them!*" Therefore they sent fifty men, and they searched for three days but did not

find him. ¹⁸And when they came back to him, for he had stayed in Jericho, he said to them, "Did I not say to you, 'Do not go'?"

¹⁹Then the men of the city said to Elisha, "Please notice, the situation of this city *is* pleasant, as my lord sees; but the water *is* bad, and the ground barren."

²⁰And he said, "Bring me a new bowl, and put salt in it." So they brought *it* to him. ²¹Then he went out to the source of the water, and cast in the salt there, and said, "Thus says the Lord: 'I have healed this water; from it there shall be no more death or barrenness.' " ²²So the water remains healed to this day, according to the word of Elisha which he spoke.

²³Then he went up from there to Bethel; and as he was going up the road, some youths came from the city and mocked him, and said to him, "Go up, you baldhead! Go up, you baldhead!"

²⁴So he turned around and looked at them, and pronounced a curse on them in the name of the Lord. And two female bears came out of the woods and mauled forty-two of the youths.

²⁵Then he went from there to Mount Carmel, and from there he returned to Samaria.

ACTS 13:42–14:7

So when the Jews went out of the synagogue,* the Gentiles begged that these words might be preached to them the next Sabbath. ⁴³Now when the congregation had broken up, many of the Jews and devout proselytes followed Paul and Barnabas, who, speaking to them, persuaded them to continue in the grace of God.

⁴⁴On the next Sabbath almost the whole city came together to hear the word of God. ⁴⁵But when the Jews saw the multitudes, they were filled with envy; and contradicting and blaspheming, they opposed the things spoken by Paul. ⁴⁶Then Paul and Barnabas grew bold and said, "It was necessary that the word of God should be spoken to you first; but since you reject it, and judge yourselves unworthy of everlasting life, behold, we turn to the Gentiles. ⁴⁷For so the Lord has commanded us:

'I have set you as a light to the Gentiles,
That you should be for salvation to the ends of the earth.' " *

⁴⁸Now when the Gentiles heard this, they were glad and glorified the word of the Lord. And as many as had been appointed to eternal life believed.

⁴⁹And the word of the Lord was being spread throughout all the region. ⁵⁰But the Jews stirred up the devout and prominent women and the chief men of the city, raised up persecution against Paul and Barnabas, and expelled them from their region. ⁵¹But they shook off the dust from their feet against them, and came to Iconium. ⁵²And the disciples were filled with joy and with the Holy Spirit.

Now it happened in Iconium that they went together to the synagogue of the Jews, and so spoke that a great multitude both of the Jews and of the Greeks believed. ²But the unbelieving Jews stirred up the Gentiles and poisoned their minds against the brethren. ³Therefore they stayed there a long time, speaking boldly in the Lord, who was bearing witness to the word of His grace, granting signs and wonders to be done by their hands.

⁴But the multitude of the city was divided: part sided with the Jews, and part with the apostles. ⁵And when a violent attempt was made by both the Gentiles and Jews, with their rulers, to

abuse and stone them, [6]they became aware of it and fled to Lystra and Derbe, cities of Lycaonia, and to the surrounding region. [7]And they were preaching the gospel there.

PSALM 139:1-24

For the Chief Musician. A Psalm of David.

O LORD, You have searched me and known *me.*
[2]You know my sitting down and my rising up;
You understand my thought afar off.

[3] You comprehend my path and my lying down,
And are acquainted with all my ways.

[4] For *there is* not a word on my tongue,
But behold, O LORD, You know it altogether.

[5] You have hedged me behind and before,
And laid Your hand upon me.

[6] *Such* knowledge *is* too wonderful for me;
It is high, I cannot *attain* it.

[7] Where can I go from Your Spirit?
Or where can I flee from Your presence?

[8] If I ascend into heaven, You *are* there;
If I make my bed in hell, behold, You *are there.*

[9] *If* I take the wings of the morning,
And dwell in the uttermost parts of the sea,

[10] Even there Your hand shall lead me,
And Your right hand shall hold me.

[11] If I say, "Surely the darkness shall fall* on me,"
Even the night shall be light about me;

[12] Indeed, the darkness shall not hide from You,
But the night shines as the day;
The darkness and the light *are* both alike *to You.*

[13] For You formed my inward parts;
You covered me in my mother's womb.

[14] I will praise You, for I am fearfully *and* wonderfully made;*
Marvelous are Your works,
And *that* my soul knows very well.

[15] My frame was not hidden from You,
When I was made in secret,
And skillfully wrought in the lowest parts of the earth.

[16] Your eyes saw my substance, being yet unformed.
And in Your book they all were written,
The days fashioned for me,
When *as yet there were* none of them.

[17] How precious also are Your thoughts to me, O God!
How great is the sum of them!

[18] *If* I should count them, they would be more in number than the sand;
When I awake, I am still with You.

[19] Oh, that You would slay the wicked, O God!
Depart from me, therefore, you bloodthirsty men.

[20] For they speak against You wickedly;
Your enemies take *Your name* in vain.*

[21] Do I not hate them, O LORD, who hate You?

And do I not loathe those who
rise up against You?
22 I hate them with perfect
hatred;
I count them my enemies.

23 Search me, O God, and know
my heart;

Try me, and know my
anxieties;
24 And see if *there is any* wicked
way in me,
And lead me in the way
everlasting.

PROVERBS FOR TODAY/ 17:19-21

*He who loves transgression loves strife, and he who exalts his gate seeks destruction.
He who has a deceitful heart finds no good, and he who has a perverse tongue falls
into evil. He who begets a scoffer does so to his sorrow, and the father of a fool has
no joy.*

JUNE 22

2 KINGS 3:1–4:17

Now Jehoram the son of Ahab became king over Israel at Samaria in the eighteenth year of Jehoshaphat king of Judah, and reigned twelve years. 2And he did evil in the sight of the LORD, but not like his father and mother; for he put away the *sacred* pillar of Baal that his father had made. 3Nevertheless he persisted in the sins of Jeroboam the son of Nebat, who had made Israel sin; he did not depart from them.

4Now Mesha king of Moab was a sheepbreeder, and he regularly paid the king of Israel one hundred thousand lambs and the wool of one hundred thousand rams. 5But it happened, when Ahab died, that the king of Moab rebelled against the king of Israel.

6So King Jehoram went out of Samaria at that time and mustered all Israel. 7Then he went and sent to Jehoshaphat king of Judah, saying, "The king of Moab has rebelled against me. Will you go with me to fight against Moab?"

And he said, "I will go up; I *am* as you *are,* my people as your people, my horses as your horses." 8Then he said, "Which way shall we go up?"

And he answered, "By way of the Wilderness of Edom."

9So the king of Israel went with the king of Judah and the king of Edom, and they marched on that roundabout route seven days; and there was no water for the army, nor for the animals that followed them. 10And the king of Israel said, "Alas! For the LORD has called these three kings together to deliver them into the hand of Moab."

11But Jehoshaphat said, "*Is there* no prophet of the LORD here, that we may inquire of the LORD by him?"

So one of the servants of the king of Israel answered and said, "Elisha the son of Shaphat *is* here, who poured water on the hands of Elijah."

12And Jehoshaphat said, "The word of the LORD is with him." So the king of

Israel and Jehoshaphat and the king of Edom went down to him.

13Then Elisha said to the king of Israel, "What have I to do with you? Go to the prophets of your father and the prophets of your mother."

But the king of Israel said to him, "No, for the LORD has called these three kings *together* to deliver them into the hand of Moab."

14And Elisha said, "*As* the LORD of hosts lives, before whom I stand, surely were it not that I regard the presence of Jehoshaphat king of Judah, I would not look at you, nor see you. 15But now bring me a musician."

Then it happened, when the musician played, that the hand of the LORD came upon him. 16And he said, "Thus says the LORD: 'Make this valley full of ditches.' 17For thus says the LORD: 'You shall not see wind, nor shall you see rain; yet that valley shall be filled with water, so that you, your cattle, and your animals may drink.' 18And this is a simple matter in the sight of the LORD; He will also deliver the Moabites into your hand. 19Also you shall attack every fortified city and every choice city, and shall cut down every good tree, and stop up every spring of water, and ruin every good piece of land with stones."

20Now it happened in the morning, when the grain offering was offered, that suddenly water came by way of Edom, and the land was filled with water.

21And when all the Moabites heard that the kings had come up to fight against them, all who were able to bear arms and older were gathered; and they stood at the border. 22Then they rose up early in the morning, and the sun was shining on the water; and the Moabites saw the water on the other side *as* red as blood. 23And they said, "This is blood; the kings have surely struck swords and have killed one an-other; now therefore, Moab, to the spoil!"

24So when they came to the camp of Israel, Israel rose up and attacked the Moabites, so that they fled before them; and they entered *their* land, killing the Moabites. 25Then they destroyed the cities, and each man threw a stone on every good piece of land and filled it; and they stopped up all the springs of water and cut down all the good trees. But they left the stones of Kir Haraseth *intact.* However the slingers surrounded and attacked it.

26And when the king of Moab saw that the battle was too fierce for him, he took with him seven hundred men who drew swords, to break through to the king of Edom, but they could not. 27Then he took his eldest son who would have reigned in his place, and offered him *as* a burnt offering upon the wall; and there was great indignation against Israel. So they departed from him and returned to *their own* land.

A CERTAIN woman of the wives of the sons of the prophets cried out to Elisha, saying, "Your servant my husband is dead, and you know that your servant feared the LORD. And the creditor is coming to take my two sons to be his slaves."

2So Elisha said to her, "What shall I do for you? Tell me, what do you have in the house?" And she said, "Your maidservant has nothing in the house but a jar of oil."

3Then he said, "Go, borrow vessels from everywhere, from all your neighbors—empty vessels; do not gather just a few. 4And when you have come in, you shall shut the door behind you and your sons; then pour it into all those vessels, and set aside the full ones."

5So she went from him and shut the door behind her and her sons, who brought *the vessels* to her; and she poured *it* out. [6]Now it came to pass, when the vessels were full, that she said to her son, "Bring me another vessel."

And he said to her, "*There is* not another vessel." So the oil ceased. [7]Then she came and told the man of God. And he said, "Go, sell the oil and pay your debt; and you *and* your sons live on the rest."

[8]Now it happened one day that Elisha went to Shunem, where there *was* a notable woman, and she persuaded him to eat some food. So it was, as often as he passed by, he would turn in there to eat some food. [9]And she said to her husband, "Look now, I know that this *is* a holy man of God, who passes by us regularly. [10]Please, let us make a small upper room on the wall; and let us put a bed for him there, and a table and a chair and a lampstand; so it will be, whenever he comes to us, he can turn in there."

[11]And it happened one day that he came there, and he turned in to the upper room and lay down there. [12]Then he said to Gehazi his servant, "Call this Shunammite woman." When he had called her, she stood before him. [13]And he said to him, "Say now to her, 'Look, you have been concerned for us with all this care. What *can I* do for you? Do you want me to speak on your behalf to the king or to the commander of the army?' "

She answered, "I dwell among my own people."

[14]So he said, "What then *is* to be done for her?"

And Gehazi answered, "Actually, she has no son, and her husband is old."

[15]So he said, "Call her." When he had called her, she stood in the doorway. [16]Then he said, "About this time next year you shall embrace a son."

And she said, "No, my lord. Man of God, do not lie to your maidservant!"

[17]But the woman conceived, and bore a son when the appointed time had come, of which Elisha had told her.

ACTS 14:8-28

AND in Lystra a certain man without strength in his feet was sitting, a cripple from his mother's womb, who had never walked. [9]*This* man heard Paul speaking. Paul, observing him intently and seeing that he had faith to be healed, [10]said with a loud voice, "Stand up straight on your feet!" And he leaped and walked. [11]Now when the people saw what Paul had done, they raised their voices, saying in the Lycaonian *language,* "The gods have come down to us in the likeness of men!" [12]And Barnabas they called Zeus, and Paul, Hermes, because he was the chief speaker. [13]Then the priest of Zeus, whose temple was in front of their city, brought oxen and garlands to the gates, intending to sacrifice with the multitudes.

[14]But when the apostles Barnabas and Paul heard this, they tore their clothes and ran in among the multitude, crying out [15]and saying, "Men, why are you doing these things? We also are men with the same nature as you, and preach to you that you should turn from these useless things to the living God, who made the heaven, the earth, the sea, and all things that are in them, [16]who in bygone generations allowed all nations to walk in their own ways. [17]Nevertheless He did not leave Himself without witness, in that He did good, gave us rain from heaven and fruitful seasons, filling our hearts with food and gladness." [18]And with these sayings they could scarcely restrain the multitudes from sacrificing to them.

[19]Then Jews from Antioch and Iconium came there; and having per-

suaded the multitudes, they stoned Paul *and* dragged *him* out of the city, supposing him to be dead. ²⁰However, when the disciples gathered around him, he rose up and went into the city. And the next day he departed with Barnabas to Derbe.

²¹And when they had preached the gospel to that city and made many disciples, they returned to Lystra, Iconium, and Antioch, ²²strengthening the souls of the disciples, exhorting *them* to continue in the faith, and *saying,* "We must through many tribulations enter the kingdom of God." ²³So when they had appointed elders in every church, and prayed with fasting, they commended them to the Lord in whom they had believed. ²⁴And after they had passed through Pisidia, they came to Pamphylia. ²⁵Now when they had preached the word in Perga, they went down to Attalia. ²⁶From there they sailed to Antioch, where they had been commended to the grace of God for the work which they had completed.

²⁷Now when they had come and gathered the church together, they reported all that God had done with them, and that He had opened the door of faith to the Gentiles. ²⁸So they stayed there a long time with the disciples.

PSALM 140:1-13

To the Chief Musician. A Psalm of David.

DELIVER me, O LORD, from evil men;
Preserve me from violent men,
2   Who plan evil things in *their* hearts;
They continually gather together *for* war.
3   They sharpen their tongues like a serpent;
The poison of asps *is* under their lips.   Selah

4   Keep me, O LORD, from the hands of the wicked;
Preserve me from violent men,
Who have purposed to make my steps stumble.
5   The proud have hidden a snare for me, and cords;
They have spread a net by the wayside;
They have set traps for me.   Selah

6   I said to the LORD: "You *are* my God;
Hear the voice of my supplications, O LORD.
7   O GOD the Lord, the strength of my salvation,
You have covered my head in the day of battle.
8   Do not grant, O LORD, the desires of the wicked;
Do not further his *wicked* scheme,
Lest they be exalted.   Selah

9   "*As for* the head of those who surround me,
Let the evil of their lips cover them;
10   Let burning coals fall upon them;
Let them be cast into the fire,
Into deep pits, that they rise not up again.
11   Let not a slanderer be established in the earth;
Let evil hunt the violent man to overthrow *him*."

12   I know that the LORD will maintain
The cause of the afflicted,
And justice for the poor.
13   Surely the righteous shall give thanks to Your name;
The upright shall dwell in Your presence.

PROVERBS FOR TODAY/ 17:22

A merry heart does good, like *medicine,* * *but a broken spirit dries the bones.*

JUNE 23

2 KINGS 4:18–5:27

AND the child [of the Shunammite woman] grew. Now it happened one day that he went out to his father, to the reapers. ¹⁹And he said to his father, "My head, my head!"

So he said to a servant, "Carry him to his mother." ²⁰When he had taken him and brought him to his mother, he sat on her knees till noon, and *then* died. ²¹And she went up and laid him on the bed of the man of God, shut *the door* upon him, and went out. ²²Then she called to her husband, and said, "Please send me one of the young men and one of the donkeys, that I may run to the man of God and come back."

²³So he said, "Why are you going to him today? *It is* neither the New Moon nor the Sabbath."

And she said, "*It is* well." ²⁴Then she saddled a donkey, and said to her servant, "Drive, and go forward; do not slacken the pace for me unless I tell you." ²⁵And so she departed, and went to the man of God at Mount Carmel.

So it was, when the man of God saw her afar off, that he said to his servant Gehazi, "Look, the Shunammite woman! ²⁶Please run now to meet her, and say to her, '*Is it* well with you? *Is it* well with your husband? *Is it* well with the child?' "

And she answered, "*It is* well." ²⁷Now when she came to the man of God at the hill, she caught him by the feet, but Gehazi came near to push her away. But the man of God said, "Let her alone; for her soul *is* in deep distress, and the LORD has hidden *it* from me, and has not told me."

²⁸So she said, "Did I ask a son of my lord? Did I not say, 'Do not deceive me'?"

²⁹Then he said to Gehazi, "Get yourself ready, and take my staff in your hand, and be on your way. If you meet anyone, do not greet him; and if anyone greets you, do not answer him; but lay my staff on the face of the child."

³⁰And the mother of the child said, "*As* the LORD lives, and *as* your soul lives, I will not leave you." So he arose and followed her. ³¹Now Gehazi went on ahead of them, and laid the staff on the face of the child; but *there was* neither voice nor hearing. Therefore he went back to meet him, and told him, saying, "The child has not awakened."

³²When Elisha came into the house, there was the child, lying dead on his bed. ³³He went in therefore, shut the door behind the two of them, and prayed to the LORD. ³⁴And he went up and lay on the child, and put his mouth on his mouth, his eyes on his eyes, and his hands on his hands; and he stretched himself out on the child, and the flesh of the child became warm. ³⁵He returned and walked back and forth in the house, and again went up and stretched himself out on him; then the child sneezed seven times, and the child opened his eyes. ³⁶And he called Gehazi and said, "Call this Shunammite woman." So he called her. And when she came in to him, he said, "Pick up your son." ³⁷So she went in, fell at his feet, and bowed to the

ground; then she picked up her son and went out.

38And Elisha returned to Gilgal, and *there was* a famine in the land. Now the sons of the prophets *were* sitting before him; and he said to his servant, "Put on the large pot, and boil stew for the sons of the prophets." 39So one went out into the field to gather herbs, and found a wild vine, and gathered from it a lapful of wild gourds, and came and sliced *them* into the pot of stew, though they did not know *what they were.* 40Then they served it to the men to eat. Now it happened, as they were eating the stew, that they cried out and said, "Man of God, *there is* death in the pot!" And they could not eat *it.*

41So he said, "Then bring some flour." And he put *it* into the pot, and said, "Serve *it* to the people, that they may eat." And there was nothing harmful in the pot.

42Then a man came from Baal Shalisha, and brought the man of God bread of the firstfruits, twenty loaves of barley bread, and newly ripened grain in his knapsack. And he said, "Give *it* to the people, that they may eat."

43But his servant said, "What? Shall I set this before one hundred men?"

He said again, "Give it to the people, that they may eat; for thus says the LORD: 'They shall eat and have *some* left over.' " 44So he set *it* before them; and they ate and had *some* left over, according to the word of the LORD.

Now Naaman, commander of the army of the king of Syria, was a great and honorable man in the eyes of his master, because by him the LORD had given victory to Syria. He was also a mighty man of valor, *but* a leper. 2And the Syrians had gone out on raids, and had brought back captive a young girl from the land of Israel. She waited on Naaman's wife. 3Then she said to her

mistress, "If only my master *were* with the prophet who *is* in Samaria! For he would heal him of his leprosy." 4And *Naaman* went in and told his master, saying, "Thus and thus said the girl who *is* from the land of Israel."

5Then the king of Syria said, "Go now, and I will send a letter to the king of Israel."

So he departed and took with him ten talents of silver, six thousand *shekels* of gold, and ten changes of clothing. 6Then he brought the letter to the king of Israel, which said,

> Now be advised, when this letter comes to you, that I have sent Naaman my servant to you, that you may heal him of his leprosy.

7And it happened, when the king of Israel read the letter, that he tore his clothes and said, "*Am* I God, to kill and make alive, that this man sends a man to me to heal him of his leprosy? Therefore please consider, and see how he seeks a quarrel with me."

8So it was, when Elisha the man of God heard that the king of Israel had torn his clothes, that he sent to the king, saying, "Why have you torn your clothes? Please let him come to me, and he shall know that there is a prophet in Israel."

9Then Naaman went with his horses and chariot, and he stood at the door of Elisha's house. 10And Elisha sent a messenger to him, saying, "Go and wash in the Jordan seven times, and your flesh shall be restored to you, and *you shall* be clean." 11But Naaman became furious, and went away and said, "Indeed, I said to myself, 'He will surely come out *to me,* and stand and call on the name of the LORD his God, and wave his hand over the place, and heal the leprosy.' 12*Are* not the Abanah* and the Pharpar, the rivers of Damascus, better than all the waters of

Israel? Could I not wash in them and be clean?" So he turned and went away in a rage. [13]And his servants came near and spoke to him, and said, "My father, *if* the prophet had told you *to do* something great, would you not have done *it?* How much more then, when he says to you, 'Wash, and be clean'?" [14]So he went down and dipped seven times in the Jordan, according to the saying of the man of God; and his flesh was restored like the flesh of a little child, and he was clean.

[15]And he returned to the man of God, he and all his aides, and came and stood before him; and he said, "Indeed, now I know that *there is* no God in all the earth, except in Israel; now therefore, please take a gift from your servant."

[16]But he said, "*As* the Lord lives, before whom I stand, I will receive nothing." And he urged him to take *it,* but he refused.

[17]So Naaman said, "Then, if not, please let your servant be given two mule-loads of earth; for your servant will no longer offer either burnt offering or sacrifice to other gods, but to the Lord. [18]Yet in this thing may the Lord pardon your servant: when my master goes into the temple of Rimmon to worship there, and he leans on my hand, and I bow down in the temple of Rimmon—when I bow down in the temple of Rimmon, may the Lord please pardon your servant in this thing."

[19]Then he said to him, "Go in peace." So he departed from him a short distance.

[20]But Gehazi, the servant of Elisha the man of God, said, "Look, my master has spared Naaman this Syrian, while not receiving from his hands what he brought; but *as* the Lord lives, I will run after him and take something from him." [21]So Gehazi pursued Naaman. When Naaman saw *him* running after him, he got down from the chariot to meet him, and said, "*Is* all well?"

[22]And he said, "All *is* well. My master has sent me, saying, 'Indeed, just now two young men of the sons of the prophets have come to me from the mountains of Ephraim. Please give them a talent of silver and two changes of garments.' "

[23]So Naaman said, "Please, take two talents." And he urged him, and bound two talents of silver in two bags, with two changes of garments, and handed *them* to two of his servants; and they carried *them* on ahead of him. [24]When he came to the citadel, he took *them* from their hand, and stored *them* away in the house; then he let the men go, and they departed. [25]Now he went in and stood before his master. Elisha said to him, "Where *did you go,* Gehazi?"

And he said, "Your servant did not go anywhere."

[26]Then he said to him, "Did not my heart go *with you* when the man turned back from his chariot to meet you? *Is it* time to receive money and to receive clothing, olive groves and vineyards, sheep and oxen, male and female servants? [27]Therefore the leprosy of Naaman shall cling to you and your descendants forever." And he went out from his presence leprous, *as white* as snow.

ACTS 15:1-35

AND certain *men* came down from Judea and taught the brethren, "Unless you are circumcised according to the custom of Moses, you cannot be saved." [2]Therefore, when Paul and Barnabas had no small dissension and dispute with them, they determined that Paul and Barnabas and certain others of them should go up to Jerusalem, to the apostles and elders, about this question.

[3]So, being sent on their way by the

church, they passed through Phoenicia and Samaria, describing the conversion of the Gentiles; and they caused great joy to all the brethren. 4And when they had come to Jerusalem, they were received by the church and the apostles and the elders; and they reported all things that God had done with them. 5But some of the sect of the Pharisees who believed rose up, saying, "It is necessary to circumcise them, and to command *them* to keep the law of Moses."

6Now the apostles and elders came together to consider this matter. 7And when there had been much dispute, Peter rose up and said to them: "Men and brethren, you know that a good while ago God chose among us, that by my mouth the Gentiles should hear the word of the gospel and believe. 8So God, who knows the heart, acknowledged them by giving them the Holy Spirit, just as *He did* to us, 9and made no distinction between us and them, purifying their hearts by faith. 10Now therefore, why do you test God by putting a yoke on the neck of the disciples which neither our fathers nor we were able to bear? 11But we believe that through the grace of the Lord Jesus Christ* we shall be saved in the same manner as they."

12Then all the multitude kept silent and listened to Barnabas and Paul declaring how many miracles and wonders God had worked through them among the Gentiles. 13And after they had become silent, James answered, saying, "Men *and* brethren, listen to me: 14Simon has declared how God at the first visited the Gentiles to take out of them a people for His name. 15And with this the words of the prophets agree, just as it is written:

16 *'After this I will return*
   And will rebuild the
      tabernacle of David, which
      has fallen down;

I will rebuild its ruins,
And I will set it up;
17 *So that the rest of mankind*
      may seek the Lord,
Even all the Gentiles who are
      called by My name,
Says the Lord who does all
      *these things.' ***

18"Known to God from eternity are all His works.* 19Therefore I judge that we should not trouble those from among the Gentiles who are turning to God, 20but that we write to them to abstain from things polluted by idols, *from* sexual immorality,* *from* things strangled, and *from* blood. 21For Moses has had throughout many generations those who preach him in every city, being read in the synagogues every Sabbath."

22Then it pleased the apostles and elders, with the whole church, to send chosen men of their own company to Antioch with Paul and Barnabas, *namely,* Judas who was also named Barsabas,* and Silas, leading men among the brethren.

23They wrote this *letter* by them:

The apostles, the elders, and the brethren,

To the brethren who are of the Gentiles in Antioch, Syria, and Cilicia:

Greetings.

24 Since we have heard that some who went out from us have troubled you with words, unsettling your souls, saying, *"You must* be circumcised and keep the law"*—to whom we gave no *such* commandment— 25it seemed good to us, being assembled with one accord, to send chosen men to you with our beloved Barnabas and

Paul, 26men who have risked their lives for the name of our Lord Jesus Christ. 27We have therefore sent Judas and Silas, who will also report the same things by word of mouth. 28For it seemed good to the Holy Spirit, and to us, to lay upon you no greater burden than these necessary things: 29that you abstain from things offered to idols, from blood, from things strangled, and from sexual immorality.* If you keep yourselves from these, you will do well.

Farewell.

30So when they were sent off, they came to Antioch; and when they had gathered the multitude together, they delivered the letter. 31When they had read it, they rejoiced over its encouragement. 32Now Judas and Silas, themselves being prophets also, exhorted and strengthened the brethren with many words. 33And after they had stayed *there* for a time, they were sent back with greetings from the brethren to the apostles.*

34However, it seemed good to Silas to remain there.* 35Paul and Barnabas also remained in Antioch, teaching and preaching the word of the Lord, with many others also.

PSALM 141:1-10

A Psalm of David.

L ORD, I cry out to You;
Make haste to me!
Give ear to my voice when I
cry out to You.

2 Let my prayer be set before
You *as* incense,
The lifting up of my hands *as*
the evening sacrifice.

3 Set a guard, O LORD, over my
mouth;
Keep watch over the door of
my lips.

4 Do not incline my heart to
any evil thing,
To practice wicked works
With men who work iniquity;
And do not let me eat of their
delicacies.

5 Let the righteous strike me;
It shall be a kindness.
And let him rebuke me;
It shall be as excellent oil;
Let my head not refuse it.
For still my prayer *is* against
the deeds of the wicked.

6 Their judges are overthrown
by the sides of the cliff,
And they hear my words, for
they are sweet.

7 Our bones are scattered at
the mouth of the grave,
As when one plows and
breaks up the earth.

8 But my eyes *are* upon You,
O GOD the Lord;
In You I take refuge;
Do not leave my soul destitute.

9 Keep me from the snares they
have laid for me,
And from the traps of the
workers of iniquity.

10 Let the wicked fall into their
own nets,
While I escape safely.

PROVERBS FOR TODAY/ 17:23

A wicked man accepts a bribe behind the back to pervert the ways of justice.*

JUNE 24

2 KINGS 6:1–7:20

AND the sons of the prophets said to Elisha, "See now, the place where we dwell with you is too small for us. ²Please, let us go to the Jordan, and let every man take a beam from there, and let us make there a place where we may dwell."

So he answered, "Go."

³Then one said, "Please consent to go with your servants."

And he answered, "I will go." ⁴So he went with them. And when they came to the Jordan, they cut down trees. ⁵But as one was cutting down a tree, the iron *ax head* fell into the water; and he cried out and said, "Alas, master! For it was borrowed."

⁶So the man of God said, "Where did it fall?" And he showed him the place. So he cut off a stick, and threw *it* in there; and he made the iron float. ⁷Therefore he said, "Pick *it* up for yourself." So he reached out his hand and took it.

⁸Now the king of Syria was making war against Israel; and he consulted with his servants, saying, "My camp *will be* in such and such a place." ⁹And the man of God sent to the king of Israel, saying, "Beware that you do not pass this place, for the Syrians are coming down there." ¹⁰Then the king of Israel sent *someone* to the place of which the man of God had told him. Thus he warned him, and he was watchful there, not just once or twice.

¹¹Therefore the heart of the king of Syria was greatly troubled by this thing; and he called his servants and said to them, "Will you not show me which of us *is* for the king of Israel?"

¹²And one of his servants said, "None, my lord, O king; but Elisha, the prophet who *is* in Israel, tells the king

of Israel the words that you speak in your bedroom."

¹³So he said, "Go and see where he *is,* that I may send and get him."

And it was told him, saying, "Surely *he is* in Dothan."

¹⁴Therefore he sent horses and chariots and a great army there, and they came by night and surrounded the city. ¹⁵And when the servant of the man of God arose early and went out, there was an army, surrounding the city with horses and chariots. And his servant said to him, "Alas, my master! What shall we do?"

¹⁶So he answered, "Do not fear, for those who *are* with us *are* more than those who *are* with them." ¹⁷And Elisha prayed, and said, "Lᴏʀᴅ, I pray, open his eyes that he may see." Then the Lᴏʀᴅ opened the eyes of the young man, and he saw. And behold, the mountain *was* full of horses and chariots of fire all around Elisha. ¹⁸So when *the Syrians* came down to him, Elisha prayed to the Lᴏʀᴅ, and said, "Strike this people, I pray, with blindness." And He struck them with blindness according to the word of Elisha.

¹⁹Now Elisha said to them, "This *is* not the way, nor *is* this the city. Follow me, and I will bring you to the man whom you seek." But he led them to Samaria.

²⁰So it was, when they had come to Samaria, that Elisha said, "Lᴏʀᴅ, open the eyes of these *men,* that they may see." And the Lᴏʀᴅ opened their eyes, and they saw; and there *they were,* inside Samaria!

²¹Now when the king of Israel saw them, he said to Elisha, "My father, shall I kill *them?* Shall I kill *them?*"

²²But he answered, "You shall not

kill *them*. Would you kill those whom you have taken captive with your sword and your bow? Set food and water before them, that they may eat and drink and go to their master." 23Then he prepared a great feast for them; and after they ate and drank, he sent them away and they went to their master. So the bands of Syrian *raiders* came no more into the land of Israel.

24And it happened after this that Ben-Hadad king of Syria gathered all his army, and went up and besieged Samaria. 25And there was a great famine in Samaria; and indeed they besieged it until a donkey's head was *sold* for eighty *shekels* of silver, and one-fourth of a kab of dove droppings for five *shekels* of silver.

26Then, as the king of Israel was passing by on the wall, a woman cried out to him, saying, "Help, my lord, O king!"

27And he said, "If the LORD does not help you, where can I find help for you? From the threshing floor or from the winepress?" 28Then the king said to her, "What is troubling you?"

And she answered, "This woman said to me, 'Give your son, that we may eat him today, and we will eat my son tomorrow.' 29So we boiled my son, and ate him. And I said to her on the next day, 'Give your son, that we may eat him'; but she has hidden her son."

30Now it happened, when the king heard the words of the woman, that he tore his clothes; and as he passed by on the wall, the people looked, and there underneath *he had* sackcloth on his body. 31Then he said, "God do so to me and more also, if the head of Elisha the son of Shaphat remains on him today!"

32But Elisha was sitting in his house, and the elders were sitting with him. And *the king* sent a man ahead of him, but before the messenger came to him, he said to the elders, "Do you see how this son of a murderer has sent

someone to take away my head? Look, when the messenger comes, shut the door, and hold him fast at the door. *Is* not the sound of his master's feet behind him?" 33And while he was still talking with them, there was the messenger, coming down to him; and then *the king* said, "Surely this calamity *is* from the LORD; why should I wait for the LORD any longer?"

THEN Elisha said, "Hear the word of the LORD. Thus says the LORD: 'Tomorrow about this time a seah of fine flour *shall be sold* for a shekel, and two seahs of barley for a shekel, at the gate of Samaria.'"

2So an officer on whose hand the king leaned answered the man of God and said, "Look, *if* the LORD would make windows in heaven, could this thing be?"

And he said, "In fact, you shall see *it* with your eyes, but you shall not eat of it."

3Now there were four leprous men at the entrance of the gate; and they said to one another, "Why are we sitting here until we die? 4If we say, 'We will enter the city,' the famine *is* in the city, and we shall die there. And if we sit here, we die also. Now therefore, come, let us surrender to the army of the Syrians. If they keep us alive, we shall live; and if they kill us, we shall only die." 5And they rose at twilight to go to the camp of the Syrians; and when they had come to the outskirts of the Syrian camp, to their surprise no one *was* there. 6For the LORD had caused the army of the Syrians to hear the noise of chariots and the noise of horses—the noise of a great army; so they said to one another, "Look, the king of Israel has hired against us the kings of the Hittites and the kings of the Egyptians to attack us!" 7Therefore they arose and fled at twilight, and left the camp intact—their tents, their horses, and their donkeys—and they fled for their lives. 8And when these lepers came to the outskirts of the camp, they went into one tent and ate and drank, and carried from it silver and gold and clothing, and went and hid *them;* then they came back and entered another tent, and carried *some* from there *also,* and went and hid *it.*

9Then they said to one another, "We are not doing right. This day *is* a day of good news, and we remain silent. If we wait until morning light, some punishment will come upon us. Now therefore, come, let us go and tell the king's household." 10So they went and called to the gatekeepers of the city, and told them, saying, "We went to the Syrian camp, and surprisingly no one *was* there, not a human sound—only horses and donkeys tied, and the tents intact." 11And the gatekeepers called out, and they told *it* to the king's household inside.

12So the king arose in the night and said to his servants, "Let me now tell you what the Syrians have done to us. They know that we *are* hungry; therefore they have gone out of the camp to hide themselves in the field, saying, 'When they come out of the city, we shall catch them alive, and get into the city.' "

13And one of his servants answered and said, "Please, let several *men* take five of the remaining horses which are left in the city. Look, they *may either become* like all the multitude of Israel that are left in it; or indeed, *I say,* they *may become* like all the multitude of Israel left from those who are consumed; so let us send them and see." 14Therefore they took two chariots with horses; and the king sent them in the direction of the Syrian army, saying, "Go and see." 15And they went after them to the Jordan; and indeed all the road *was* full of garments and weapons which the Syrians had thrown away in their haste. So the

messengers returned and told the king. 16Then the people went out and plundered the tents of the Syrians. So a seah of fine flour was *sold* for a shekel, and two seahs of barley for a shekel, according to the word of the LORD.

17Now the king had appointed the officer on whose hand he leaned to have charge of the gate. But the people trampled him in the gate, and he died, just as the man of God had said, who spoke when the king came down to him. 18So it happened just as the man of God had spoken to the king, saying, "Two seahs of barley for a shekel, and a seah of fine flour for a shekel, shall be *sold* tomorrow about this time in the gate of Samaria."

19Then that officer had answered the man of God, and said, "Now look, *if* the LORD would make windows in heaven, could such a thing be?"

And he had said, "In fact, you shall see *it* with your eyes, but you shall not eat of it." 20And so it happened to him, for the people trampled him in the gate, and he died.

ACTS 15:36–16:15

THEN after some days Paul said to Barnabas, "Let us now go back and visit our brethren in every city where we have preached the word of the Lord, *and see* how they are doing." 37Now Barnabas was determined to take with them John called Mark. 38But Paul insisted that they should not take with them the one who had departed from them in Pamphylia, and had not gone with them to the work. 39Then the contention became so sharp that they parted from one another. And so Barnabas took Mark and sailed to Cyprus; 40but Paul chose Silas and departed, being commended by the brethren to the grace of God. 41And he went through Syria and Cilicia, strengthening the churches.

THEN he came to Derbe and Lystra. And behold, a certain disciple was there, named Timothy, *the* son of a certain Jewish woman who believed, but his father *was* Greek. ²He was well spoken of by the brethren who were at Lystra and Iconium. ³Paul wanted to have him go on with him. And he took *him* and circumcised him because of the Jews who were in that region, for they all knew that his father was Greek. ⁴And as they went through the cities, they delivered to them the decrees to keep, which were determined by the apostles and elders at Jerusalem. ⁵So the churches were strengthened in the faith, and increased in number daily.

⁶Now when they had gone through Phrygia and the region of Galatia, they were forbidden by the Holy Spirit to preach the word in Asia. ⁷After they had come to Mysia, they tried to go into Bithynia, but the Spirit* did not permit them. ⁸So passing by Mysia, they came down to Troas. ⁹And a vision appeared to Paul in the night. A man of Macedonia stood and pleaded with him, saying, "Come over to Macedonia and help us." ¹⁰Now after he had seen the vision, immediately we sought to go to Macedonia, concluding that the Lord had called us to preach the gospel to them.

¹¹Therefore, sailing from Troas, we ran a straight course to Samothrace, and the next *day* came to Neapolis, ¹²and from there to Philippi, which is the foremost city of that part of Macedonia, a colony. And we were staying in that city for some days. ¹³And on the Sabbath day we went out of the city to the riverside, where prayer was customarily made; and we sat down and spoke to the women who met *there*. ¹⁴Now a certain woman named Lydia heard *us*. She was a seller of purple from the city of Thyatira, who worshiped God. The Lord opened her heart to heed the things spoken by Paul. ¹⁵And when she and her household were baptized, she begged *us,* saying, "If you have judged me to be faithful to the Lord, come to my house and stay." So she persuaded us.

PSALM 142:1-7

A Contemplation* of David. A Prayer when he was in the cave.

I CRY out to the LORD with my voice;
With my voice to the LORD I make my supplication.
2   I pour out my complaint
        before Him;
    I declare before Him my
        trouble.

3   When my spirit was
        overwhelmed within me,
    Then You knew my path.
    In the way in which I walk
    They have secretly set a snare
        for me.
4   Look on *my* right hand and
        see,
    For *there is* no one who
        acknowledges me;
    Refuge has failed me;
    No one cares for my soul.

5   I cried out to You, O LORD:
    I said, "You *are* my refuge,
    My portion in the land of the
        living.
6   Attend to my cry,
    For I am brought very low;
    Deliver me from my
        persecutors,
    For they are stronger than I.
7   Bring my soul out of prison,
    That I may praise Your name;
    The righteous shall surround
        me,
    For You shall deal bountifully
        with me."

Wisdom is *in the sight of him who has understanding, but the eyes of a fool* are *on the ends of the earth. A foolish son* is *a grief to his father, and bitterness to her who bore him.*

JUNE 25

2 KINGS 8:1–9:13

THEN Elisha spoke to the woman whose son he had restored to life, saying, "Arise and go, you and your household, and stay wherever you can; for the LORD has called for a famine, and furthermore, it will come upon the land for seven years." ²So the woman arose and did according to the saying of the man of God, and she went with her household and dwelt in the land of the Philistines seven years.

³It came to pass, at the end of seven years, that the woman returned from the land of the Philistines; and she went to make an appeal to the king for her house and for her land. ⁴Then the king talked with Gehazi, the servant of the man of God, saying, "Tell me, please, all the great things Elisha has done." ⁵Now it happened, as he was telling the king how he had restored the dead to life, that there was the woman whose son he had restored to life, appealing to the king for her house and for her land. And Gehazi said, "My lord, O king, this *is* the woman, and this *is* her son whom Elisha restored to life." ⁶And when the king asked the woman, she told him.

So the king appointed a certain officer for her, saying, "Restore all that *was* hers, and all the proceeds of the field from the day that she left the land until now."

⁷Then Elisha went to Damascus, and Ben-Hadad king of Syria was sick; and it was told him, saying, "The man of God has come here." ⁸And the king said to Hazael, "Take a present in your hand, and go to meet the man of God, and inquire of the LORD by him, saying, 'Shall I recover from this disease?' " ⁹So Hazael went to meet him and took a present with him, of every good thing of Damascus, forty camel-loads; and he came and stood before him, and said, "Your son Ben-Hadad king of Syria has sent me to you, saying, 'Shall I recover from this disease?' "

¹⁰And Elisha said to him, "Go, say to him, 'You shall certainly recover.' However the LORD has shown me that he will really die." ¹¹Then he set his countenance in a stare until he was ashamed; and the man of God wept. ¹²And Hazael said, "Why is my lord weeping?"

He answered, "Because I know the evil that you will do to the children of Israel: Their strongholds you will set on fire, and their young men you will kill with the sword; and you will dash their children, and rip open their women with child."

¹³So Hazael said, "But what *is* your servant—a dog, that he should do this gross thing?"

And Elisha answered, "The LORD has shown me that you *will become* king over Syria."

¹⁴Then he departed from Elisha, and came to his master, who said to him, "What did Elisha say to you?" And he answered, "He told me you would

surely recover." ¹⁵But it happened on the next day that he took a thick cloth and dipped *it* in water, and spread *it* over his face so that he died; and Hazael reigned in his place.

¹⁶Now in the fifth year of Joram the son of Ahab, king of Israel, Jehoshaphat *having been* king of Judah, Jehoram the son of Jehoshaphat began to reign as king of Judah. ¹⁷He was thirty-two years old when he became king, and he reigned eight years in Jerusalem. ¹⁸And he walked in the way of the kings of Israel, just as the house of Ahab had done, for the daughter of Ahab was his wife; and he did evil in the sight of the LORD. ¹⁹Yet the LORD would not destroy Judah, for the sake of his servant David, as He promised him to give a lamp to him *and* his sons forever.

²⁰In his days Edom revolted against Judah's authority, and made a king over themselves. ²¹So Joram* went to Zair, and all his chariots with him. Then he rose by night and attacked the Edomites who had surrounded him and the captains of the chariots; and the troops fled to their tents. ²²Thus Edom has been in revolt against Judah's authority to this day. And Libnah revolted at that time.

²³Now the rest of the acts of Joram, and all that he did, *are* they not written in the book of the chronicles of the kings of Judah? ²⁴So Joram rested with his fathers, and was buried with his fathers in the City of David. Then Ahaziah his son reigned in his place.

²⁵In the twelfth year of Joram the son of Ahab, king of Israel, Ahaziah the son of Jehoram, king of Judah, began to reign. ²⁶Ahaziah *was* twenty-two years old when he became king, and he reigned one year in Jerusalem. His mother's name *was* Athaliah the granddaughter of Omri, king of Israel. ²⁷And he walked in the way of the house of Ahab, and did evil in the sight of the LORD, like the house of Ahab, for he *was* the son-in-law of the house of Ahab.

²⁸Now he went with Joram the son of Ahab to war against Hazael king of Syria at Ramoth Gilead; and the Syrians wounded Joram. ²⁹Then King Joram went back to Jezreel to recover from the wounds which the Syrians had inflicted on him at Ramah, when he fought against Hazael king of Syria. And Ahaziah the son of Jehoram, king of Judah, went down to see Joram the son of Ahab in Jezreel, because he was sick.

AND Elisha the prophet called one of the sons of the prophets, and said to him, "Get yourself ready, take this flask of oil in your hand, and go to Ramoth Gilead. ²Now when you arrive at that place, look there for Jehu the son of Jehoshaphat, the son of Nimshi, and go in and make him rise up from among his associates, and take him to an inner room. ³Then take the flask of oil, and pour *it* on his head, and say, 'Thus says the LORD: "I have anointed you king over Israel." ' Then open the door and flee, and do not delay."

⁴So the young man, the servant of the prophet, went to Ramoth Gilead. ⁵And when he arrived, there *were* the captains of the army sitting; and he said, "I have a message for you, Commander."

Jehu said, "For which *one* of us?"

And he said, "For you, Commander." ⁶Then he arose and went into the house. And he poured the oil on his head, and said to him, "Thus says the LORD God of Israel: 'I have anointed you king over the people of the LORD, over Israel. ⁷You shall strike down the house of Ahab your master, that I may avenge the blood of My servants the prophets, and the blood of all the servants of the LORD, at the hand of Jezebel. ⁸For the whole house of Ahab shall perish; and I will cut off from Ahab all the males in Israel, both bond and free.

⁹So I will make the house of Ahab like the house of Jeroboam the son of Nebat, and like the house of Baasha the son of Ahijah. ¹⁰The dogs shall eat Jezebel on the plot *of ground* at Jezreel, and *there shall be* none to bury *her.*'" And he opened the door and fled.

¹¹Then Jehu came out to the servants of his master, and *one* said to him, "*Is* all well? Why did this madman come to you?"

And he said to them, "You know the man and his babble."

¹²And they said, "A lie! Tell us now."

So he said, "Thus and thus he spoke to me, saying, 'Thus says the Lord: "I have anointed you king over Israel."'"

¹³Then each man hastened to take his garment and put *it* under him on the top of the steps; and they blew trumpets, saying, "Jehu is king!"

ACTS 16:16-40

Now it happened, as we [Luke, Paul, and companions] went to prayer, that a certain slave girl possessed with a spirit of divination met us, who brought her masters much profit by fortune-telling. ¹⁷This girl followed Paul and us, and cried out, saying, "These men are the servants of the Most High God, who proclaim to us the way of salvation." ¹⁸And this she did for many days.

But Paul, greatly annoyed, turned and said to the spirit, "I command you in the name of Jesus Christ to come out of her." And he came out that very hour. ¹⁹But when her masters saw that their hope of profit was gone, they seized Paul and Silas and dragged *them* into the marketplace to the authorities.

²⁰And they brought them to the magistrates, and said, "These men, being Jews, exceedingly trouble our city; ²¹and they teach customs which are not lawful for us, being Romans, to receive or observe." ²²Then the multitude rose up together against them; and the magistrates tore off their clothes and commanded *them* to be beaten with rods. ²³And when they had laid many stripes on them, they threw *them* into prison, commanding the jailer to keep them securely. ²⁴Having received such a charge, he put them into the inner prison and fastened their feet in the stocks.

²⁵But at midnight Paul and Silas were praying and singing hymns to God, and the prisoners were listening to them. ²⁶Suddenly there was a great earthquake, so that the foundations of the prison were shaken; and immediately all the doors were opened and everyone's chains were loosed. ²⁷And the keeper of the prison, awaking from sleep and seeing the prison doors open, supposing the prisoners had fled, drew his sword and was about to kill himself. ²⁸But Paul called with a loud voice, saying, "Do yourself no harm, for we are all here."

²⁹Then he called for a light, ran in, and fell down trembling before Paul and Silas. ³⁰And he brought them out and said, "Sirs, what must I do to be saved?"

³¹So they said, "Believe on the Lord Jesus Christ, and you will be saved, you and your household." ³²Then they spoke the word of the Lord to him and to all who were in his house. ³³And he took them the same hour of the night and washed *their* stripes. And immediately he and all his family were baptized. ³⁴Now when he had brought them into his house, he set food before them; and he rejoiced, having believed in God with all his household.

³⁵And when it was day, the magistrates sent the officers, saying, "Let those men go."

³⁶So the keeper of the prison reported these words to Paul, saying, "The magistrates have sent to let you go. Now therefore depart, and go in peace."

37But Paul said to them, "They have beaten us openly, uncondemned Romans, *and* have thrown *us* into prison. And now do they put us out secretly? No indeed! Let them come themselves and get us out."

38And the officers told these words to the magistrates, and they were afraid when they heard that they were Romans. 39Then they came and pleaded with them and brought *them* out, and asked *them* to depart from the city. 40So they went out of the prison and entered *the house of* Lydia; and when they had seen the brethren, they encouraged them and departed.

PSALM 143:1-12

A Psalm of David.

HEAR my prayer, O LORD,
Give ear to my supplications!
In Your faithfulness answer
me,
And in Your righteousness.
2 Do not enter into judgment
with Your servant,
For in Your sight no one living
is righteous.

3 For the enemy has
persecuted my soul;
He has crushed my life to the
ground;
He has made me dwell in
darkness,
Like those who have long
been dead.
4 Therefore my spirit is
overwhelmed within me;
My heart within me is
distressed.

5 I remember the days of old;
I meditate on all Your works;
I muse on the work of Your
hands.
6 I spread out my hands to You;
My soul *longs* for You like a
thirsty land.   Selah

7 Answer me speedily, O LORD;
My spirit fails!
Do not hide Your face from
me,
Lest I be like those who go
down into the pit.
8 Cause me to hear Your
lovingkindness in the
morning,
For in You do I trust;
Cause me to know the way in
which I should walk,
For I lift up my soul to You.

9 Deliver me, O LORD, from my
enemies;
In You I take shelter.*
10 Teach me to do Your will,
For You *are* my God;
Your Spirit *is* good.
Lead me in the land of
uprightness.

11 Revive me, O LORD, for Your
name's sake!
For Your righteousness' sake
bring my soul out of trouble.
12 In Your mercy cut off my
enemies,
And destroy all those who
afflict my soul;
For I *am* Your servant.

PROVERBS FOR TODAY/ 17:26

Also, to punish the righteous is *not good,* nor *to strike princes for* their *uprightness.*

JUNE 26

2 KINGS 9:14–10:31

So Jehu the son of Jehoshaphat, the son of Nimshi, conspired against Joram. (Now Joram had been defending Ramoth Gilead, he and all Israel, against Hazael king of Syria. 15But King Joram had returned to Jezreel to recover from the wounds which the Syrians had inflicted on him when he fought with Hazael king of Syria.) And Jehu said, "If you are so minded, let no one leave or escape from the city to go and tell it in Jezreel." 16So Jehu rode in a chariot and went to Jezreel, for Joram was laid up there; and Ahaziah king of Judah had come down to see Joram.

17Now a watchman stood on the tower in Jezreel, and he saw the company of Jehu as he came, and said, "I see a company of men."

And Joram said, "Get a horseman and send him to meet them, and let him say, 'Is it peace?' "

18So the horseman went to meet him, and said, "Thus says the king: 'Is it peace?' "

And Jehu said, "What have you to do with peace? Turn around and follow me."

So the watchman reported, saying, "The messenger went to them, but is not coming back."

19Then he sent out a second horseman who came to them, and said, "Thus says the king: 'Is it peace?' "

And Jehu answered, "What have you to do with peace? Turn around and follow me."

20So the watchman reported, saying, "He went up to them and is not coming back; and the driving is like the driving of Jehu the son of Nimshi, for he drives furiously!"

21Then Joram said, "Make ready."

And his chariot was made ready. Then Joram king of Israel and Ahaziah king of Judah went out, each in his chariot; and they went out to meet Jehu, and met him on the property of Naboth the Jezreelite. 22Now it happened, when Joram saw Jehu, that he said, "Is it peace, Jehu?"

So he answered, "What peace, as long as the harlotries of your mother Jezebel and her witchcraft are so many?"

23Then Joram turned around and fled, and said to Ahaziah, "Treachery, Ahaziah!" 24Now Jehu drew his bow with full strength and shot Jehoram between his arms; and the arrow came out at his heart, and he sank down in his chariot. 25Then *Jehu* said to Bidkar his captain, "Pick *him* up, *and* throw him into the tract of the field of Naboth the Jezreelite; for remember, when you and I were riding together behind Ahab his father, that the Lord laid this burden upon him: 26'Surely I saw yesterday the blood of Naboth and the blood of his sons,' says the Lord, 'and I will repay you in this plot,' says the Lord. Now therefore, take *and* throw him on the plot *of ground,* according to the word of the Lord."

27But when Ahaziah king of Judah saw *this,* he fled by the road to Beth Haggan.* So Jehu pursued him, and said, "Shoot him also in the chariot." *And they shot him* at the Ascent of Gur, which is by Ibleam. Then he fled to Megiddo, and died there. 28And his servants carried him in the chariot to Jerusalem, and buried him in his tomb with his fathers in the City of David. 29In the eleventh year of Joram the son of Ahab, Ahaziah had become king over Judah.

30Now when Jehu had come to Jezreel, Jezebel heard *of it;* and she put paint on her eyes and adorned her head, and looked through a window. ³¹Then, as Jehu entered at the gate, she said, *"Is it* peace, Zimri, murderer of your master?"

³²And he looked up at the window, and said, "Who *is* on my side? Who?" So two *or* three eunuchs looked out at him. ³³Then he said, "Throw her down." So they threw her down, and *some* of her blood spattered on the wall and on the horses; and he trampled her underfoot. ³⁴And when he had gone in, he ate and drank. Then he said, "Go now, see to this accursed *woman,* and bury her, for she was a king's daughter." ³⁵So they went to bury her, but they found no more of her than the skull and the feet and the palms of *her* hands. ³⁶Therefore they came back and told him. And he said, "This *is* the word of the LORD, which He spoke by His servant Elijah the Tishbite, saying, 'On the plot *of ground* at Jezreel dogs shall eat the flesh of Jezebel;* ³⁷and the corpse of Jezebel shall be as refuse on the surface of the field, in the plot at Jezreel, so that they shall not say, "Here *lies* Jezebel." ' "

Now Ahab had seventy sons in Samaria. And Jehu wrote and sent letters to Samaria, to the rulers of Jezreel,* to the elders, and to those who reared Ahab's *sons,* saying:

2   Now as soon as this letter comes to you, since your master's sons *are* with you, and you have chariots and horses, a fortified city also, and weapons, ³choose the best qualified of your master's sons, set *him* on his father's throne, and fight for your master's house.

⁴But they were exceedingly afraid, and said, "Look, two kings could not stand up to him; how then can we stand?" ⁵And he who *was* in charge of the house, and he who *was* in charge of the city, the elders also, and those who reared *the sons,* sent to Jehu, saying, "We *are* your servants, we will do all you tell us; but we will not make anyone king. Do *what is* good in your sight." ⁶Then he wrote a second letter to them, saying:

If you *are* for me and will obey my voice, take the heads of the men, your master's sons, and come to me at Jezreel by this time tomorrow.

Now the king's sons, seventy persons, *were* with the great men of the city, *who* were rearing them. ⁷So it was, when the letter came to them, that they took the king's sons and slaughtered seventy persons, put their heads in baskets and sent *them* to him at Jezreel.

⁸Then a messenger came and told him, saying, "They have brought the heads of the king's sons."

And he said, "Lay them in two heaps at the entrance of the gate until morning."

⁹So it was, in the morning, that he went out and stood, and said to all the people, "You *are* righteous. Indeed I conspired against my master and killed him; but who killed all these? ¹⁰Know now that nothing shall fall to the earth of the word of the LORD which the LORD spoke concerning the house of Ahab; for the LORD has done what He spoke by His servant Elijah." ¹¹So Jehu killed all who remained of the house of Ahab in Jezreel, and all his great men and his close acquaintances and his priests, until he left him none remaining.

¹²And he arose and departed and went to Samaria. On the way, at Beth Eked* of the Shepherds, ¹³Jehu met

with the brothers of Ahaziah king of Judah, and said, "Who *are* you?"

So they answered, "We *are* the brothers of Ahaziah; we have come down to greet the sons of the king and the sons of the queen mother."

¹⁴And he said, "Take them alive!" So they took them alive, and killed them at the well of Beth Eked, forty-two men; and he left none of them.

¹⁵Now when he departed from there, he met Jehonadab the son of Rechab, *coming* to meet him; and he greeted him and said to him, "Is your heart right, as my heart *is* toward your heart?"

And Jehonadab answered, "It is."

Jehu said, "If it is, give *me* your hand." So he gave *him* his hand, and he took him up to him into the chariot. ¹⁶Then he said, "Come with me, and see my zeal for the LORD." So they had him ride in his chariot. ¹⁷And when he came to Samaria, he killed all who remained to Ahab in Samaria, till he had destroyed them, according to the word of the LORD which He spoke to Elijah.

¹⁸Then Jehu gathered all the people together, and said to them, "Ahab served Baal a little, Jehu will serve him much. ¹⁹Now therefore, call to me all the prophets of Baal, all his servants, and all his priests. Let no one be missing, for I have a great sacrifice for Baal. Whoever is missing shall not live." But Jehu acted deceptively, with the intent of destroying the worshipers of Baal. ²⁰And Jehu said, "Proclaim a solemn assembly for Baal." So they proclaimed *it.* ²¹Then Jehu sent throughout all Israel; and all the worshipers of Baal came, so that there was not a man left who did not come. So they came into the temple* of Baal, and the temple of Baal was full from one end to the other. ²²And he said to the one in charge of the wardrobe, "Bring out vestments for all the worshipers of Baal." So he brought out vestments for them. ²³Then Jehu and Jehonadab the

son of Rechab went into the temple of Baal, and said to the worshipers of Baal, "Search and see that no servants of the LORD are here with you, but only the worshipers of Baal." ²⁴So they went in to offer sacrifices and burnt offerings. Now Jehu had appointed for himself eighty men on the outside, and had said, "*If* any of the men whom I have brought into your hands escapes, *whoever lets him escape, it shall be* his life for the life of the other."

²⁵Now it happened, as soon as he had made an end of offering the burnt offering, that Jehu said to the guard and to the captains, "Go in *and* kill them; let no one come out!" And they killed them with the edge of the sword; then the guards and the officers threw *them* out, and went into the inner room of the temple of Baal. ²⁶And they brought the *sacred* pillars out of the temple of Baal and burned them. ²⁷Then they broke down the *sacred* pillar of Baal, and tore down the temple of Baal and made it a refuse dump to this day. ²⁸Thus Jehu destroyed Baal from Israel.

²⁹However Jehu did not turn away from the sins of Jeroboam the son of Nebat, who had made Israel sin, *that is,* from the golden calves that *were* at Bethel and Dan. ³⁰And the LORD said to Jehu, "Because you have done well in doing *what is* right in My sight, *and* have done to the house of Ahab all that *was* in My heart, your sons shall sit on the throne of Israel to the fourth *generation.*" ³¹But Jehu took no heed to walk in the law of the LORD God of Israel with all his heart; for he did not depart from the sins of Jeroboam, who had made Israel sin.

ACTS 17:1-34

Now when they [Paul and Silas] had passed through Amphipolis and Apollonia, they came to Thessalonica, where there was a synagogue of the Jews. ²Then Paul, as his custom was, went in to them, and for three Sabbaths reasoned with them from the Scriptures, ³explaining and demonstrating that the Christ had to suffer and rise again from the dead, and *saying,* "This Jesus whom I preach to you is the Christ." ⁴And some of them were persuaded; and a great multitude of the devout Greeks, and not a few of the leading women, joined Paul and Silas.

⁵But the Jews who were not persuaded, becoming envious,* took some of the evil men from the marketplace, and gathering a mob, set all the city in an uproar and attacked the house of Jason, and sought to bring them out to the people. ⁶But when they did not find them, they dragged Jason and some brethren to the rulers of the city, crying out, "These who have turned the world upside down have come here too. ⁷Jason has harbored them, and these are all acting contrary to the decrees of Caesar, saying there is another king—Jesus." ⁸And they troubled the crowd and the rulers of the city when they heard these things. ⁹So when they had taken security from Jason and the rest, they let them go.

¹⁰Then the brethren immediately sent Paul and Silas away by night to Berea. When they arrived, they went into the synagogue of the Jews. ¹¹These were more fair-minded than those in Thessalonica, in that they received the word with all readiness, and searched the Scriptures daily *to find out* whether these things were so. ¹²Therefore many of them believed, and also not a few of the Greeks, prominent women as well as men. ¹³But when the Jews from Thessalonica learned that the word of God was preached by Paul at Berea, they came there also and stirred up the crowds. ¹⁴Then immediately the brethren sent Paul away, to go to the sea; but both Silas and Timothy remained there.

¹⁵So those who conducted Paul brought him to Athens; and receiving a command for Silas and Timothy to come to him with all speed, they departed.

¹⁶Now while Paul waited for them at Athens, his spirit was provoked within him when he saw that the city was given over to idols. ¹⁷Therefore he reasoned in the synagogue with the Jews and with the *Gentile* worshipers, and in the marketplace daily with those who happened to be there. ¹⁸Then* certain Epicurean and Stoic philosophers encountered him. And some said, "What does this babbler want to say?"

Others said, "He seems to be a proclaimer of foreign gods," because he preached to them Jesus and the resurrection.

¹⁹And they took him and brought him to the Areopagus, saying, "May we know what this new doctrine *is* of which you speak? ²⁰For you are bringing some strange things to our ears. Therefore we want to know what these things mean." ²¹For all the Athenians and the foreigners who were there spent their time in nothing else but either to tell or to hear some new thing.

²²Then Paul stood in the midst of the Areopagus and said, "Men of Athens, I perceive that in all things you are very religious; ²³for as I was passing through and considering the objects of your worship, I even found an altar with this inscription:

TO THE UNKNOWN GOD.

Therefore, the One whom you worship without knowing, Him I proclaim to you: ²⁴God, who made the world and everything in it, since He is Lord of heaven and earth, does not dwell in temples made with hands. ²⁵Nor is He worshiped with men's hands, as though He needed anything, since He gives to all life, breath, and all things. ²⁶And He has made from one blood* every nation of men to dwell on all the face of the earth, and has determined their preappointed times and the boundaries of their dwellings, [27]so that they should seek the Lord, in the hope that they might grope for Him and find Him, though He is not far from each one of us; [28]for in Him we live and move and have our being, as also some of your own poets have said, 'For we are also His offspring.' [29]Therefore, since we are the offspring of God, we ought not to think that the Divine Nature is like gold or silver or stone, something shaped by art and man's devising. [30]Truly, these times of ignorance God overlooked, but now commands all men everywhere to repent, [31]because He has appointed a day on which He will judge the world in righteousness by the Man whom He has ordained. He has given assurance of this to all by raising Him from the dead."

[32]And when they heard of the resurrection of the dead, some mocked, while others said, "We will hear you again on this *matter.*" [33]So Paul departed from among them. [34]However, some men joined him and believed, among them Dionysius the Areopagite, a woman named Damaris, and others with them.

PSALM 144:1-15

A Psalm of David.

BLESSED *be* the LORD my Rock, Who trains my hands for war, *And* my fingers for battle—

2 My lovingkindness and my fortress,
My high tower and my deliverer,
My shield and *the One* in whom I take refuge,
Who subdues my people* under me.

3 LORD, what *is* man, that You take knowledge of him?

Or the son of man, that You are mindful of him?

4 Man is like a breath;
His days *are* like a passing shadow.

5 Bow down Your heavens, O LORD, and come down;
Touch the mountains, and they shall smoke.

6 Flash forth lightning and scatter them;
Shoot out Your arrows and destroy them.

7 Stretch out Your hand from above;
Rescue me and deliver me out of great waters,
From the hand of foreigners,

8 Whose mouth speaks lying words,
And whose right hand *is* a right hand of falsehood.

9 I will sing a new song to You, O God;
On a harp of ten strings I will sing praises to You,

10 *The One* who gives salvation to kings,
Who delivers David His servant
From the deadly sword.

11 Rescue me and deliver me from the hand of foreigners,
Whose mouth speaks lying words,
And whose right hand *is* a right hand of falsehood—

12 That our sons *may be* as plants grown up in their youth;
That our daughters *may be* as pillars,
Sculptured in palace style;

13 *That* our barns *may be* full, Supplying all kinds of produce;
That our sheep may bring forth thousands

And ten thousands in our
fields;
14 *That* our oxen *may be*
well-laden;
That there be no breaking in
or going out;

That there be no outcry in our
streets.
15 Happy *are* the people who are
in such a state;
Happy *are* the people whose
God *is* the LORD!

PROVERBS FOR TODAY/ 17:27-28

He who has knowledge spares his words, and a man of understanding is of a calm spirit. Even a fool is counted wise when he holds his peace; when he shuts his lips, he is considered perceptive.

JUNE 27

2 KINGS 10:32–12:21

I N those days the LORD began to cut off *parts* of Israel; and Hazael conquered them in all the territory of Israel 33from the Jordan eastward: all the land of Gilead—Gad, Reuben, and Manasseh—from Aroer, which *is* by the River Arnon, including Gilead and Bashan.

34Now the rest of the acts of Jehu, all that he did, and all his might, *are* they not written in the book of the chronicles of the kings of Israel? 35So Jehu rested with his fathers, and they buried him in Samaria. Then Jehoahaz his son reigned in his place. 36And the period that Jehu reigned over Israel in Samaria *was* twenty-eight years.

WHEN Athaliah the mother of Ahaziah saw that her son was dead, she arose and destroyed all the royal heirs. 2But Jehosheba, the daughter of King Joram, sister of Ahaziah, took Joash the son of Ahaziah, and stole him away from among the king's sons *who were* being murdered; and they hid him and his nurse in the bedroom, from Athaliah, so that he was not killed. 3So he was hidden with her in the house of

the LORD for six years, while Athaliah reigned over the land.

4In the seventh year Jehoiada sent and brought the captains of hundreds—of the bodyguards and the escorts—and brought them into the house of the LORD to him. And he made a covenant with them and took an oath from them in the house of the LORD, and showed them the king's son. 5Then he commanded them, saying, "This *is* what you shall do: One-third of you who come on duty on the Sabbath shall be keeping watch over the king's house, 6one-third *shall be* at the gate of Sur, and one-third at the gate behind the escorts. You shall keep the watch of the house, lest it be broken down. 7The two contingents of you who go off duty on the Sabbath shall keep the watch of the house of the LORD for the king. 8But you shall surround the king on all sides, every man with his weapons in his hand; and whoever comes within range, let him be put to death. You are to be with the king as he goes out and as he comes in."

9So the captains of the hundreds did according to all that Jehoiada the priest commanded. Each of them took his men who were to be on duty on the

Sabbath, with those who were going off duty on the Sabbath, and came to Jehoiada the priest. ¹⁰And the priest gave the captains of hundreds the spears and shields which *had belonged* to King David, that were in the temple of the LORD. ¹¹Then the escorts stood, every man with his weapons in his hand, all around the king, from the right side of the temple to the left side of the temple, by the altar and the house. ¹²And he brought out the king's son, put the crown on him, and *gave him* the Testimony;* they made him king and anointed him, and they clapped their hands and said, "Long live the king!"

¹³Now when Athaliah heard the noise of the escorts *and* the people, she came to the people *in* the temple of the LORD. ¹⁴When she looked, there was the king standing by a pillar according to custom; and the leaders and the trumpeters were by the king. All the people of the land were rejoicing and blowing trumpets. So Athaliah tore her clothes and cried out, "Treason! Treason!"

¹⁵And Jehoiada the priest commanded the captains of the hundreds, the officers of the army, and said to them, "Take her outside under guard, and slay with the sword whoever follows her." For the priest had said, "Do not let her be killed in the house of the LORD." ¹⁶So they seized her; and she went by way of the horses' entrance *into* the king's house, and there she was killed.

¹⁷Then Jehoiada made a covenant between the LORD, the king, and the people, that they should be the LORD's people, and *also* between the king and the people. ¹⁸And all the people of the land went to the temple of Baal, and tore it down. They thoroughly broke in pieces its altars and images, and killed Mattan the priest of Baal before the altars. And the priest appointed officers over the house of the LORD. ¹⁹Then

he took the captains of hundreds, the bodyguards, the escorts, and all the people of the land; and they brought the king down from the house of the LORD, and went by way of the gate of the escorts to the king's house. Then he sat on the throne of the kings. ²⁰So all the people of the land rejoiced; and the city was quiet, for they had slain Athaliah with the sword *in* the king's house. ²¹Jehoash *was* seven years old when he became king.

In the seventh year of Jehu, Jehoash* became king, and he reigned forty years in Jerusalem. His mother's name *was* Zibiah of Beersheba. ²Jehoash did *what was* right in the sight of the LORD all the days in which Jehoiada the priest instructed him. ³But the high places were not taken away; the people still sacrificed and burned incense on the high places.

⁴And Jehoash said to the priests, "All the money of the dedicated gifts that are brought into the house of the LORD—each man's census money, each man's assessment money*—*and all the money that a man purposes in his heart to bring into the house of the LORD, ⁵let the priests take *it* themselves, each from his constituency; and let them repair the damages of the temple, wherever any dilapidation is found."

⁶Now it was so, by the twenty-third year of King Jehoash, *that* the priests had not repaired the damages of the temple. ⁷So King Jehoash called Jehoiada the priest and the *other* priests, and said to them, "Why have you not repaired the damages of the temple? Now therefore, do not take *more* money from your constituency, but deliver it for repairing the damages of the temple." ⁸And the priests agreed that they would neither receive *more* money from the people, nor repair the damages of the temple.

⁹Then Jehoiada the priest took a

chest, bored a hole in its lid, and set it beside the altar, on the right side as one comes into the house of the LORD; and the priests who kept the door put there all the money brought into the house of the LORD. 10So it was, whenever they saw that *there was* much money in the chest, that the king's scribe and the high priest came up and put it in bags, and counted the money that was found in the house of the LORD. 11Then they gave the money, which had been apportioned, into the hands of those who did the work, who had the oversight of the house of the LORD; and they paid it out to the carpenters and builders who worked on the house of the LORD, 12and to masons and stonecutters, and for buying timber and hewn stone, to repair the damage of the house of the LORD, and for all that was paid out to repair the temple. 13However there were not made for the house of the LORD basins of silver, trimmers, sprinkling-bowls, trumpets, any articles of gold or articles of silver, from the money brought into the house of the LORD. 14But they gave that to the workmen, and they repaired the house of the LORD with it. 15Moreover they did not require an account from the men into whose hand they delivered the money to be paid to workmen, for they dealt faithfully. 16The money from the trespass offerings and the money from the sin offerings was not brought into the house of the LORD. It belonged to the priests.

17Hazael king of Syria went up and fought against Gath, and took it; then Hazael set his face to go up to Jerusalem. 18And Jehoash king of Judah took all the sacred things that his fathers, Jehoshaphat and Jehoram and Ahaziah, kings of Judah, had dedicated, and his own sacred things, and all the gold found in the treasuries of the house of the LORD and in the king's house, and sent *them* to Hazael king of Syria. Then he went away from Jerusalem.

19Now the rest of the acts of Joash,* and all that he did, *are* they not written in the book of the chronicles of the kings of Judah?

20And his servants arose and formed a conspiracy, and killed Joash in the house of the Millo,* which goes down to Silla. 21For Jozachar* the son of Shimeath and Jehozabad the son of Shomer,* his servants, struck him. So he died, and they buried him with his fathers in the City of David. Then Amaziah his son reigned in his place.

ACTS 18:1-23

AFTER these things Paul departed from Athens and went to Corinth. 2And he found a certain Jew named Aquila, born in Pontus, who had recently come from Italy with his wife Priscilla (because Claudius had commanded all the Jews to depart from Rome); and he came to them. 3So, because he was of the same trade, he stayed with them and worked; for by occupation they were tentmakers. 4And he reasoned in the synagogue every Sabbath, and persuaded both Jews and Greeks.

5When Silas and Timothy had come from Macedonia, Paul was compelled by the Spirit, and testified to the Jews *that* Jesus *is* the Christ. 6But when they opposed him and blasphemed, he shook *his* garments and said to them, "Your blood *be* upon your *own* heads; I *am* clean. From now on I will go to the Gentiles." 7And he departed from there and entered the house of a certain *man* named Justus,* *one* who worshiped God, whose house was next door to the synagogue. 8Then Crispus, the ruler of the synagogue, believed on the Lord with all his household. And many of the Corinthians, hearing, believed and were baptized.

9Now the Lord spoke to Paul in the

night by a vision, "Do not be afraid, but speak, and do not keep silent; ¹⁰for I am with you, and no one will attack you to hurt you; for I have many people in this city." ¹¹And he continued *there* a year and six months, teaching the word of God among them.

¹²When Gallio was proconsul of Achaia, the Jews with one accord rose up against Paul and brought him to the judgment seat, ¹³saying, "This *fellow* persuades men to worship God contrary to the law."

¹⁴And when Paul was about to open *his* mouth, Gallio said to the Jews, "If it were a matter of wrongdoing or wicked crimes, O Jews, there would be reason why I should bear with you. ¹⁵But if it is a question of words and names and your own law, look *to it* yourselves; for I do not want to be a judge of such *matters*." ¹⁶And he drove them from the judgment seat. ¹⁷Then all the Greeks* took Sosthenes, the ruler of the synagogue, and beat *him* before the judgment seat. But Gallio took no notice of these things.

¹⁸So Paul still remained a good while. Then he took leave of the brethren and sailed for Syria, and Priscilla and Aquila *were* with him. He had *his* hair cut off at Cenchrea, for he had taken a vow. ¹⁹And he came to Ephesus, and left them there; but he himself entered the synagogue and reasoned with the Jews. ²⁰When they asked *him* to stay a longer time with them, he did not consent, ²¹but took leave of them, saying, "I must by all means keep this coming feast in Jerusalem;* but I will return again to you, God willing." And he sailed from Ephesus.

²²And when he had landed at Caesarea, and gone up and greeted the church, he went down to Antioch. ²³After he had spent some time *there,* he departed and went over the region of Galatia and Phrygia in order, strengthening all the disciples.

PSALM 145:1-21
A Praise of David.

I WILL extol You, my God, O King;
And I will bless Your name forever
and ever.

2 Every day I will bless You,
And I will praise Your name
forever and ever.

3 Great *is* the LORD, and greatly
to be praised;
And His greatness *is*
unsearchable.

4 One generation shall praise
Your works to another,
And shall declare Your mighty
acts.

5 I* will meditate on the
glorious splendor of Your
majesty,
And on Your wondrous
works.*

6 *Men* shall speak of the might
of Your awesome acts,
And I will declare Your
greatness.

7 They shall utter the memory
of Your great goodness,
And shall sing of Your
righteousness.

8 The LORD *is* gracious and full
of compassion,
Slow to anger and great in
mercy.

9 The LORD *is* good to all,
And His tender mercies *are*
over all His works.

10 All Your works shall praise
You, O LORD,
And Your saints shall bless
You.

11 They shall speak of the glory
of Your kingdom,
And talk of Your power,

12 To make known to the sons of
men His mighty acts,

And the glorious majesty of
His kingdom.
13 Your kingdom *is* an
everlasting kingdom,
And Your dominion *endures*
throughout all generations.*

14 The LORD upholds all who fall,
And raises up all *who are*
bowed down.
15 The eyes of all look
expectantly to You,
And You give them their food
in due season.
16 You open Your hand
And satisfy the desire of
every living thing.

17 The LORD *is* righteous in all
His ways,

Gracious in all His works.
18 The LORD *is* near to all who
call upon Him,
To all who call upon Him in
truth.
19 He will fulfill the desire of
those who fear Him;
He also will hear their cry and
save them.
20 The LORD preserves all who
love Him,
But all the wicked He will
destroy.
21 My mouth shall speak the
praise of the LORD,
And all flesh shall bless His
holy name
Forever and ever.

PROVERBS FOR TODAY/ 18:1

A man who isolates himself seeks his own desire; he rages against all wise judgment.

JUNE 28

2 KINGS 13:1–14:29

IN the twenty-third year of Joash*
the son of Ahaziah, king of Judah,
Jehoahaz the son of Jehu became
king over Israel in Samaria, *and
reigned* seventeen years. 2And he did
evil in the sight of the LORD, and followed the sins of Jeroboam the son of
Nebat, who had made Israel sin. He
did not depart from them.

3Then the anger of the LORD was
aroused against Israel, and He delivered them into the hand of Hazael king
of Syria, and into the hand of Ben-
Hadad the son of Hazael, all *their* days.
4So Jehoahaz pleaded with the LORD,
and the LORD listened to him; for He

saw the oppression of Israel, because
the king of Syria oppressed them.
5Then the LORD gave Israel a deliverer,
so that they escaped from under the
hand of the Syrians; and the children
of Israel dwelt in their tents as before.
6Nevertheless they did not depart
from the sins of the house of Jeroboam, who had made Israel sin, *but*
walked in them; and the wooden image* also remained in Samaria. 7For
He left of the army of Jehoahaz only
fifty horsemen, ten chariots, and ten
thousand foot soldiers; for the king of
Syria had destroyed them and made
them like the dust at threshing.

8Now the rest of the acts of Jehoahaz, all that he did, and his might, *are*

they not written in the book of the chronicles of the kings of Israel? ⁹So Jehoahaz rested with his fathers, and they buried him in Samaria. Then Joash his son reigned in his place.

¹⁰In the thirty-seventh year of Joash king of Judah, Jehoash* the son of Jehoahaz became king over Israel in Samaria, *and reigned* sixteen years. ¹¹And he did evil in the sight of the LORD. He did not depart from all the sins of Jeroboam the son of Nebat, who made Israel sin, *but* walked in them.

¹²Now the rest of the acts of Joash, all that he did, and his might with which he fought against Amaziah king of Judah, *are* they not written in the book of the chronicles of the kings of Israel? ¹³So Joash rested with his fathers. Then Jeroboam sat on his throne. And Joash was buried in Samaria with the kings of Israel.

¹⁴Elisha had become sick with the illness of which he would die. Then Joash the king of Israel came down to him, and wept over his face, and said, "O my father, my father, the chariots of Israel and their horsemen!"

¹⁵And Elisha said to him, "Take a bow and some arrows." So he took himself a bow and some arrows. ¹⁶Then he said to the king of Israel, "Put your hand on the bow." So he put his hand *on it,* and Elisha put his hands on the king's hands. ¹⁷And he said, "Open the east window"; and he opened *it.* Then Elisha said, "Shoot"; and he shot. And he said, "The arrow of the LORD's deliverance and the arrow of deliverance from Syria; for you must strike the Syrians at Aphek till you have destroyed *them.*" ¹⁸Then he said, "Take the arrows"; so he took *them.* And he said to the king of Israel, "Strike the ground"; so he struck three times, and stopped. ¹⁹And the man of God was angry with him, and said, "You should have struck five or six times; then you would have struck

Syria till you had destroyed *it!* But now you will strike Syria *only* three times."

²⁰Then Elisha died, and they buried him. And the *raiding* bands from Moab invaded the land in the spring of the year. ²¹So it was, as they were burying a man, that suddenly they spied a band *of raiders;* and they put the man in the tomb of Elisha; and when the man was let down and touched the bones of Elisha, he revived and stood on his feet.

²²And Hazael king of Syria oppressed Israel all the days of Jehoahaz. ²³But the LORD was gracious to them, had compassion on them, and regarded them, because of His covenant with Abraham, Isaac, and Jacob, and would not yet destroy them or cast them from His presence.

²⁴Now Hazael king of Syria died. Then Ben-Hadad his son reigned in his place. ²⁵And Jehoash* the son of Jehoahaz recaptured from the hand of Ben-Hadad, the son of Hazael, the cities which he had taken out of the hand of Jehoahaz his father by war. Three times Joash defeated him and recaptured the cities of Israel.

IN the second year of Joash the son of Jehoahaz, king of Israel, Amaziah the son of Joash, king of Judah, became king. ²He was twenty-five years old when he became king, and he reigned twenty-nine years in Jerusalem. His mother's name was Jehoaddan of Jerusalem. ³And he did *what was* right in the sight of the LORD, yet not like his father David; he did everything as his father Joash had done. ⁴However the high places were not taken away, and the people still sacrificed and burned incense on the high places.

⁵Now it happened, as soon as the kingdom was established in his hand, that he executed his servants who had murdered his father the king. ⁶But the children of the murderers he did not execute, according to what is written

in the Book of the Law of Moses, in which the LORD commanded, saying, "Fathers shall not be put to death for their children, nor shall children be put to death for their fathers; but a person shall be put to death for his own sin."*

7He killed ten thousand Edomites in the Valley of Salt, and took Sela by war, and called its name Joktheel to this day.

8Then Amaziah sent messengers to Jehoash* the son of Jehoahaz, the son of Jehu, king of Israel, saying, "Come, let us face one another *in battle.*" 9And Jehoash king of Israel sent to Amaziah king of Judah, saying, "The thistle that *was* in Lebanon sent to the cedar that *was* in Lebanon, saying, 'Give your daughter to my son as wife'; and a wild beast that *was* in Lebanon passed by and trampled the thistle. 10You have indeed defeated Edom, and your heart has lifted you up. Glory *in that,* and stay at home; for why should you meddle with trouble so that you fall—you and Judah with you?"

11But Amaziah would not heed. Therefore Jehoash king of Israel went out; so he and Amaziah king of Judah faced one another at Beth Shemesh, which *belongs* to Judah. 12And Judah was defeated by Israel, and every man fled to his tent. 13Then Jehoash king of Israel captured Amaziah king of Judah, the son of Jehoash, the son of Ahaziah, at Beth Shemesh; and he went to Jerusalem, and broke down the wall of Jerusalem from the Gate of Ephraim to the Corner Gate—four hundred cubits. 14And he took all the gold and silver, all the articles that were found in the house of the LORD and in the treasuries of the king's house, and hostages, and returned to Samaria.

15Now the rest of the acts of Jehoash which he did—his might, and how he fought with Amaziah king of Judah—*are* they not written in the book of the chronicles of the kings of Israel? 16So Jehoash rested with his fathers, and was buried in Samaria with the kings of Israel. Then Jeroboam his son reigned in his place.

17Amaziah the son of Joash, king of Judah, lived fifteen years after the death of Jehoash the son of Jehoahaz, king of Israel. 18Now the rest of the acts of Amaziah, *are* they not written in the book of the chronicles of the kings of Judah? 19And they formed a conspiracy against him in Jerusalem, and he fled to Lachish; but they sent after him to Lachish and killed him there. 20Then they brought him on horses, and he was buried at Jerusalem with his fathers in the City of David.

21And all the people of Judah took Azariah,* who *was* sixteen years old, and made him king instead of his father Amaziah. 22He built Elath and restored it to Judah, after the king rested with his fathers.

23In the fifteenth year of Amaziah the son of Joash, king of Judah, Jeroboam the son of Joash, king of Israel, became king in Samaria, *and reigned* forty-one years. 24And he did evil in the sight of the LORD; he did not depart from all the sins of Jeroboam the son of Nebat, who had made Israel sin. 25He restored the territory of Israel from the entrance of Hamath to the Sea of the Arabah, according to the word of the LORD God of Israel, which He had spoken through His servant Jonah the son of Amittai, the prophet who *was* from Gath Hepher. 26For the LORD saw *that* the affliction of Israel *was* very bitter; and whether bond or free, there was no helper for Israel. 27And the LORD did not say that He would blot out the name of Israel from under heaven; but He saved them by the hand of Jeroboam the son of Joash.

28Now the rest of the acts of Jeroboam, and all that he did—his might, how he made war, and how he recaptured for Israel, from Damascus and

Hamath, *what had belonged* to Judah—*are* they not written in the book of the chronicles of the kings of Israel? ²⁹So Jeroboam rested with his fathers, the kings of Israel. Then Zechariah his son reigned in his place.

ACTS 18:24–19:12

Now a certain Jew named Apollos, born at Alexandria, an eloquent man *and* mighty in the Scriptures, came to Ephesus. ²⁵This man had been instructed in the way of the Lord; and being fervent in spirit, he spoke and taught accurately the things of the Lord, though he knew only the baptism of John. ²⁶So he began to speak boldly in the synagogue. When Aquila and Priscilla heard him, they took him aside and explained to him the way of God more accurately. ²⁷And when he desired to cross to Achaia, the brethren wrote, exhorting the disciples to receive him; and when he arrived, he greatly helped those who had believed through grace; ²⁸for he vigorously refuted the Jews publicly, showing from the Scriptures that Jesus is the Christ.

And it happened, while Apollos was at Corinth, that Paul, having passed through the upper regions, came to Ephesus. And finding some disciples ²he said to them, "Did you receive the Holy Spirit when you believed?"

So they said to him, "We have not so much as heard whether there is a Holy Spirit."

³And he said to them, "Into what then were you baptized?"

So they said, "Into John's baptism."

⁴Then Paul said, "John indeed baptized with a baptism of repentance, saying to the people that they should believe on Him who would come after him, that is, on Christ Jesus."

⁵When they heard *this,* they were baptized in the name of the Lord Jesus.

⁶And when Paul had laid hands on them, the Holy Spirit came upon them, and they spoke with tongues and prophesied. ⁷Now the men were about twelve in all.

⁸And he went into the synagogue and spoke boldly for three months, reasoning and persuading concerning the things of the kingdom of God. ⁹But when some were hardened and did not believe, but spoke evil of the Way before the multitude, he departed from them and withdrew the disciples, reasoning daily in the school of Tyrannus. ¹⁰And this continued for two years, so that all who dwelt in Asia heard the word of the Lord Jesus, both Jews and Greeks.

¹¹Now God worked unusual miracles by the hands of Paul, ¹²so that even handkerchiefs or aprons were brought from his body to the sick, and the diseases left them and the evil spirits went out of them.

PSALM 146:1-10

Praise the Lord!

Praise the Lord, O my soul!
²While I live I will praise the Lord;
I will sing praises to my God while I have my being.

3   Do not put your trust in princes,
Nor in a son of man, in whom *there is* no help.

4   His spirit departs, he returns to his earth;
In that very day his plans perish.

5   Happy *is he* who *has* the God of Jacob for his help,
Whose hope *is* in the Lord his God,

6   Who made heaven and earth,

The sea, and all that *is* in
  them;
Who keeps truth forever,
7 Who executes justice for the
  oppressed,
Who gives food to the hungry.
The LORD gives freedom to
  the prisoners.

8 The LORD opens *the eyes of* the
  blind;
The LORD raises those who
  are bowed down;

The LORD loves the righteous.
9 The LORD watches over the
  strangers;
He relieves the fatherless and
  widow;
But the way of the wicked He
  turns upside down.

10 The LORD shall reign forever—
Your God, O Zion, to all
  generations.

Praise the LORD!

PROVERBS FOR TODAY/ 18:2-3

A fool has no delight in understanding, but in expressing his own heart. □ *When the wicked comes, contempt comes also; and with dishonor comes reproach.*

JUNE 29

2 KINGS 15:1–16:20

Iɴ the twenty-seventh year of Jeroboam king of Israel, Azariah the son of Amaziah, king of Judah, became king. 2He was sixteen years old when he became king, and he reigned fifty-two years in Jerusalem. His mother's name *was* Jecholiah of Jerusalem. 3And he did *what was* right in the sight of the LORD, according to all that his father Amaziah had done, 4except that the high places were not removed; the people still sacrificed and burned incense on the high places. 5Then the LORD struck the king, so that he was a leper until the day of his death; so he dwelt in an isolated house. And Jotham the king's son *was* over the *royal* house, judging the people of the land.

6Now the rest of the acts of Azariah, and all that he did, *are* they not written in the book of the chronicles of the kings of Judah? 7So Azariah rested with his fathers, and they buried him with his fathers in the City of David. Then Jotham his son reigned in his place.

8In the thirty-eighth year of Azariah king of Judah, Zechariah the son of Jeroboam reigned over Israel in Samaria six months. 9And he did evil in the sight of the LORD, as his fathers had done; he did not depart from the sins of Jeroboam the son of Nebat, who had made Israel sin. 10Then Shallum the son of Jabesh conspired against him, and struck and killed him in front of the people; and he reigned in his place.

11Now the rest of the acts of Zechariah, indeed they *are* written in the book of the chronicles of the kings of Israel.

12This *was* the word of the LORD which He spoke to Jehu, saying, "Your sons shall sit on the throne of Israel to the fourth *generation.*"* And so it was.

13Shallum the son of Jabesh became king in the thirty-ninth year of Uzziah*

king of Judah; and he reigned a full month in Samaria. ¹⁴For Menahem the son of Gadi went up from Tirzah, came to Samaria, and struck Shallum the son of Jabesh in Samaria and killed him; and he reigned in his place.

¹⁵Now the rest of the acts of Shallum, and the conspiracy which he led, indeed they *are* written in the book of the chronicles of the kings of Israel. ¹⁶Then from Tirzah, Menahem attacked Tiphsah, all who *were* there, and its territory. Because they did not surrender, therefore he attacked *it*. All the women there who were with child he ripped open.

¹⁷In the thirty-ninth year of Azariah king of Judah, Menahem the son of Gadi became king over Israel, *and reigned* ten years in Samaria. ¹⁸And he did evil in the sight of the LORD; he did not depart all his days from the sins of Jeroboam the son of Nebat, who had made Israel sin. ¹⁹Pul* king of Assyria came against the land; and Menahem gave Pul a thousand talents of silver, that his hand might be with him to strengthen the kingdom under his control. ²⁰And Menahem exacted the money from Israel, from all the very wealthy, from each man fifty shekels of silver, to give to the king of Assyria. So the king of Assyria turned back, and did not stay there in the land.

²¹Now the rest of the acts of Menahem, and all that he did, *are* they not written in the book of the chronicles of the kings of Israel? ²²So Menahem rested with his fathers. Then Pekahiah his son reigned in his place.

²³In the fiftieth year of Azariah king of Judah, Pekahiah the son of Menahem became king over Israel in Samaria, *and reigned* two years. ²⁴And he did evil in the sight of the LORD; he did not depart from the sins of Jeroboam the son of Nebat, who had made Israel sin. ²⁵Then Pekah the son of Remaliah, an officer of his, conspired

against him and killed him in Samaria, in the citadel of the king's house, along with Argob and Arieh; and with him were fifty men of Gilead. He killed him and reigned in his place.

²⁶Now the rest of the acts of Pekahiah, and all that he did, indeed they *are* written in the book of the chronicles of the kings of Israel.

²⁷In the fifty-second year of Azariah king of Judah, Pekah the son of Remaliah became king over Israel in Samaria, *and reigned* twenty years. ²⁸And he did evil in the sight of the LORD; he did not depart from the sins of Jeroboam the son of Nebat, who had made Israel sin. ²⁹In the days of Pekah king of Israel, Tiglath-Pileser king of Assyria came and took Ijon, Abel Beth Maachah, Janoah, Kedesh, Hazor, Gilead, and Galilee, all the land of Naphtali; and he carried them captive to Assyria. ³⁰Then Hoshea the son of Elah led a conspiracy against Pekah the son of Remaliah, and struck and killed him; so he reigned in his place in the twentieth year of Jotham the son of Uzziah.

³¹Now the rest of the acts of Pekah, and all that he did, indeed they *are* written in the book of the chronicles of the kings of Israel.

³²In the second year of Pekah the son of Remaliah, king of Israel, Jotham the son of Uzziah, king of Judah, began to reign. ³³He was twenty-five years old when he became king, and he reigned sixteen years in Jerusalem. His mother's name *was* Jerusha* the daughter of Zadok. ³⁴And he did *what was* right in the sight of the LORD; he did according to all that his father Uzziah had done. ³⁵However the high places were not removed; the people still sacrificed and burned incense on the high places. He built the Upper Gate of the house of the LORD.

³⁶Now the rest of the acts of Jotham, and all that he did, *are* they not written in the book of the chronicles of the

kings of Judah? ³⁷In those days the Lord began to send Rezin king of Syria and Pekah the son of Remaliah against Judah. ³⁸So Jotham rested with his fathers, and was buried with his fathers in the City of David his father. Then Ahaz his son reigned in his place.

In the seventeenth year of Pekah the son of Remaliah, Ahaz the son of Jotham, king of Judah, began to reign. ²Ahaz *was* twenty years old when he became king, and he reigned sixteen years in Jerusalem; and he did not do *what was* right in the sight of the Lord his God, as his father David *had done.* ³But he walked in the way of the kings of Israel; indeed he made his son pass through the fire, according to the abominations of the nations whom the Lord had cast out from before the children of Israel. ⁴And he sacrificed and burned incense on the high places, on the hills, and under every green tree.

⁵Then Rezin king of Syria and Pekah the son of Remaliah, king of Israel, came up to Jerusalem to *make* war; and they besieged Ahaz but could not overcome *him.* ⁶At that time Rezin king of Syria captured Elath for Syria, and drove the men of Judah from Elath. Then the Edomites* went to Elath, and dwell there to this day.

⁷So Ahaz sent messengers to Tiglath-Pileser king of Assyria, saying, "I *am* your servant and your son. Come up and save me from the hand of the king of Syria and from the hand of the king of Israel, who rise up against me." ⁸And Ahaz took the silver and gold that was found in the house of the Lord, and in the treasuries of the king's house, and sent *it as* a present to the king of Assyria. ⁹So the king of Assyria heeded him; for the king of Assyria went up against Damascus and took it, carried *its people* captive to Kir, and killed Rezin.

¹⁰Now King Ahaz went to Damascus to meet Tiglath-Pileser king of Assyria, and saw an altar that *was* at Damascus; and King Ahaz sent to Urijah the priest the design of the altar and its pattern, according to all its workmanship. ¹¹Then Urijah the priest built an altar according to all that King Ahaz had sent from Damascus. So Urijah the priest made *it* before King Ahaz came back from Damascus. ¹²And when the king came back from Damascus, the king saw the altar; and the king approached the altar and made offerings on it. ¹³So he burned his burnt offering and his grain offering; and he poured his drink offering and sprinkled the blood of his peace offerings on the altar. ¹⁴He also brought the bronze altar which *was* before the Lord, from the front of the temple—from between the *new* altar and the house of the Lord—and put it on the north side of the *new* altar. ¹⁵Then King Ahaz commanded Urijah the priest, saying, "On the great *new* altar burn the morning burnt offering, the evening grain offering, the king's burnt sacrifice, and his grain offering, with the burnt offering of all the people of the land, their grain offering, and their drink offerings; and sprinkle on it all the blood of the burnt offering and all the blood of the sacrifice. And the bronze altar shall be for me to inquire *by.*" ¹⁶Thus did Urijah the priest, according to all that King Ahaz commanded.

¹⁷And King Ahaz cut off the panels of the carts, and removed the lavers from them; and he took down the Sea from the bronze oxen that *were* under it, and put it on a pavement of stones. ¹⁸Also he removed the Sabbath pavilion which they had built in the temple, and he removed the king's outer entrance from the house of the Lord, on account of the king of Assyria.

¹⁹Now the rest of the acts of Ahaz which he did, *are* they not written in the book of the chronicles of the kings of Judah? ²⁰So Ahaz rested with his

fathers, and was buried with his fathers in the City of David. Then Hezekiah his son reigned in his place.

ACTS 19:13-41

THEN some of the itinerant Jewish exorcists took it upon themselves to call the name of the Lord Jesus over those who had evil spirits, saying, "We* exorcise you by the Jesus whom Paul preaches." 14Also there were seven sons of Sceva, a Jewish chief priest, who did so.

15And the evil spirit answered and said, "Jesus I know, and Paul I know; but who are you?"

16Then the man in whom the evil spirit was leaped on them, overpowered* them, and prevailed against them,* so that they fled out of that house naked and wounded. 17This became known both to all Jews and Greeks dwelling in Ephesus; and fear fell on them all, and the name of the Lord Jesus was magnified. 18And many who had believed came confessing and telling their deeds. 19Also, many of those who had practiced magic brought their books together and burned *them* in the sight of all. And they counted up the value of them, and *it* totaled fifty thousand *pieces* of silver. 20So the word of the Lord grew mightily and prevailed.

21When these things were accomplished, Paul purposed in the Spirit, when he had passed through Macedonia and Achaia, to go to Jerusalem, saying, "After I have been there, I must also see Rome." 22So he sent into Macedonia two of those who ministered to him, Timothy and Erastus, but he himself stayed in Asia for a time.

23And about that time there arose a great commotion about the Way. 24For a certain man named Demetrius, a silversmith, who made silver shrines of Diana,* brought no small profit to the craftsmen. 25He called them together with the workers of similar occupation, and said: "Men, you know that we have our prosperity by this trade. 26Moreover you see and hear that not only at Ephesus, but throughout almost all Asia, this Paul has persuaded and turned away many people, saying that they are not gods which are made with hands. 27So not only is this trade of ours in danger of falling into disrepute, but also the temple of the great goddess Diana may be despised and her magnificence destroyed,* whom all Asia and the world worship."

28Now when they heard *this,* they were full of wrath and cried out, saying, "Great *is* Diana of the Ephesians!" 29So the whole city was filled with confusion, and rushed into the theater with one accord, having seized Gaius and Aristarchus, Macedonians, Paul's travel companions. 30And when Paul wanted to go in to the people, the disciples would not allow him. 31Then some of the officials of Asia, who were his friends, sent to him pleading that he would not venture into the theater. 32Some therefore cried one thing and some another, for the assembly was confused, and most of them did not know why they had come together. 33And they drew Alexander out of the multitude, the Jews putting him forward. And Alexander motioned with his hand, and wanted to make his defense to the people. 34But when they found out that he was a Jew, all with one voice cried out for about two hours, "Great *is* Diana of the Ephesians!"

35And when the city clerk had quieted the crowd, he said: "Men of Ephesus, what man is there who does not know that the city of the Ephesians is temple guardian of the great goddess Diana, and of the *image* which fell down from Zeus? 36Therefore, since these things cannot be denied, you ought to be quiet and do nothing rashly. 37For you have brought these men here who are neither robbers of temples nor blasphemers of your* goddess. 38Therefore, if Demetrius and his fellow craftsmen have a case against anyone, the courts are open and there are proconsuls. Let them bring charges against one another. 39But if you have any other inquiry to make, it shall be determined in the lawful assembly. 40For we are in danger of being called in question for today's uproar, there being no reason which we may give to account for this disorderly gathering." 41And when he had said these things, he dismissed the assembly.

PSALM 147:1-20

PRAISE the LORD!
For *it is* good to sing praises to our God;
For *it is* pleasant, *and* praise is beautiful.

2 The LORD builds up Jerusalem;
He gathers together the outcasts of Israel.
3 He heals the brokenhearted
And binds up their wounds.
4 He counts the number of the stars;
He calls them all by name.
5 Great *is* our Lord, and mighty in power;
His understanding *is* infinite.
6 The LORD lifts up the humble;
He casts the wicked down to the ground.

7 Sing to the LORD with thanksgiving;
Sing praises on the harp to our God,
8 Who covers the heavens with clouds,
Who prepares rain for the earth,
Who makes grass to grow on the mountains.

9 He gives to the beast its food,
And to the young ravens that cry.

10 He does not delight in the strength of the horse;
He takes no pleasure in the legs of a man.
11 The LORD takes pleasure in those who fear Him,
In those who hope in His mercy.

12 Praise the LORD, O Jerusalem!
Praise your God, O Zion!
13 For He has strengthened the bars of your gates;
He has blessed your children within you.
14 He makes peace *in* your borders,
And fills you with the finest wheat.

15 He sends out His command *to the* earth;
His word runs very swiftly.
16 He gives snow like wool;
He scatters the frost like ashes;
17 He casts out His hail like morsels;
Who can stand before His cold?
18 He sends out His word and melts them;
He causes His wind to blow, *and* the waters flow.

19 He declares His word to Jacob,
His statutes and His judgments to Israel.
20 He has not dealt thus with any nation;
And *as for His* judgments, they have not known them.

Praise the LORD!

PROVERBS FOR TODAY/ 18:4-5

The words of a man's mouth are *deep waters; the wellspring of wisdom* is *a flowing brook.* ☐ It is *not good to show partiality to the wicked,* or *to overthrow the righteous in judgment.*

JUNE 30

2 KINGS 17:1–18:12

IN the twelfth year of Ahaz king of Judah, Hoshea the son of Elah became king of Israel in Samaria, *and he reigned* nine years. ²And he did evil in the sight of the LORD, but not as the kings of Israel who were before him. ³Shalmaneser king of Assyria came up against him; and Hoshea became his vassal, and paid him tribute money. ⁴And the king of Assyria uncovered a conspiracy by Hoshea; for he had sent messengers to So, king of Egypt, and brought no tribute to the king of Assyria, as *he had done* year by year. Therefore the king of Assyria shut him up, and bound him in prison.

⁵Now the king of Assyria went throughout all the land, and went up to Samaria and besieged it for three years. ⁶In the ninth year of Hoshea, the king of Assyria took Samaria and carried Israel away to Assyria, and placed them in Halah and by the Habor, the River of Gozan, and in the cities of the Medes.

⁷For so it was that the children of Israel had sinned against the LORD their God, who had brought them up out of the land of Egypt, from under the hand of Pharaoh king of Egypt; and they had feared other gods, ⁸and had walked in the statutes of the nations whom the LORD had cast out from before the children of Israel, and of the kings of Israel, which they had made. ⁹Also the children of Israel secretly did against the LORD their God things that

were not right, and they built for themselves high places in all their cities, from watchtower to fortified city. ¹⁰They set up for themselves *sacred* pillars and wooden images* on every high hill and under every green tree. ¹¹There they burned incense on all the high places, like the nations whom the LORD had carried away before them; and they did wicked things to provoke the LORD to anger, ¹²for they served idols, of which the LORD had said to them, "You shall not do this thing."

¹³Yet the LORD testified against Israel and against Judah, by all of His prophets, every seer, saying, "Turn from your evil ways, and keep My commandments *and* My statutes, according to all the law which I commanded your fathers, and which I sent to you by My servants the prophets." ¹⁴Nevertheless they would not hear, but stiffened their necks, like the necks of their fathers, who did not believe in the LORD their God. ¹⁵And they rejected His statutes and His covenant that He had made with their fathers, and His testimonies which He had testified against them; they followed idols, became idolaters, and *went* after the nations who *were* all around them, *concerning* whom the LORD had charged them that they should not do like them. ¹⁶So they left all the commandments of the LORD their God, made for themselves a molded image *and* two calves, made a wooden image and worshiped all the host of heaven,

"He who keeps you
will not slumber."
Psalm 121:3

"The fruit of the Spirit is love."
  Galatians 5:22

and served Baal. ¹⁷And they caused their sons and daughters to pass through the fire, practiced witchcraft and soothsaying, and sold themselves to do evil in the sight of the LORD, to provoke Him to anger. ¹⁸Therefore the LORD was very angry with Israel, and removed them from His sight; there was none left but the tribe of Judah alone.

¹⁹Also Judah did not keep the commandments of the LORD their God, but walked in the statutes of Israel which they made. ²⁰And the LORD rejected all the descendants of Israel, afflicted them, and delivered them into the hand of plunderers, until He had cast them from His sight. ²¹For He tore Israel from the house of David, and they made Jeroboam the son of Nebat king. Then Jeroboam drove Israel from following the LORD, and made them commit a great sin. ²²For the children of Israel walked in all the sins of Jeroboam which he did; they did not depart from them, ²³until the LORD removed Israel out of His sight, as He had said by all His servants the prophets. So Israel was carried away from their own land to Assyria, as it is to this day.

²⁴Then the king of Assyria brought *people* from Babylon, Cuthah, Ava, Hamath, and from Sepharvaim, and placed *them* in the cities of Samaria instead of the children of Israel; and they took possession of Samaria and dwelt in its cities. ²⁵And it was so, at the beginning of their dwelling there, *that* they did not fear the LORD; therefore the LORD sent lions among them, which killed *some* of them. ²⁶So they spoke to the king of Assyria, saying, "The nations whom you have removed and placed in the cities of Samaria do not know the rituals of the God of the land; therefore He has sent lions among them, and indeed, they are killing them because they do not know the rituals of the God of the land."

²⁷Then the king of Assyria commanded, saying, "Send there one of the priests whom you brought from there; let him go and dwell there, and let him teach them the rituals of the God of the land." ²⁸Then one of the priests whom they had carried away from Samaria came and dwelt in Bethel, and taught them how they should fear the LORD.

²⁹However every nation continued to make gods of its own, and put *them* in the shrines on the high places which the Samaritans had made, *every* nation in the cities where they dwelt. ³⁰The men of Babylon made Succoth Benoth, the men of Cuth made Nergal, the men of Hamath made Ashima, ³¹and the Avites made Nibhaz and Tartak; and the Sepharvites burned their children in fire to Adrammelech and Anammelech, the gods of Sepharvaim. ³²So they feared the LORD, and from every class they appointed for themselves priests of the high places, who sacrificed for them in the shrines of the high places. ³³They feared the LORD, yet served their own gods—according to the rituals of the nations from among whom they were carried away.

³⁴To this day they continue practicing the former rituals; they do not fear the LORD, nor do they follow their statutes or their ordinances, or the law and commandment which the LORD had commanded the children of Jacob, whom He named Israel, ³⁵with whom the LORD had made a covenant and charged them, saying: "You shall not fear other gods, nor bow down to them nor serve them nor sacrifice to them; ³⁶but the LORD, who brought you up from the land of Egypt with great power and an outstretched arm, Him you shall fear, Him you shall worship, and to Him you shall offer sacrifice. ³⁷And the statutes, the ordinances, the law, and the commandment which He wrote for you, you shall be careful to

observe forever; you shall not fear other gods. ³⁸And the covenant that I have made with you, you shall not forget, nor shall you fear other gods. ³⁹But the LORD your God you shall fear; and He will deliver you from the hand of all your enemies." ⁴⁰However they did not obey, but they followed their former rituals. ⁴¹So these nations feared the LORD, yet served their carved images; also their children and their children's children have continued doing as their fathers did, even to this day.

Now it came to pass in the third year of Hoshea the son of Elah, king of Israel, *that* Hezekiah the son of Ahaz, king of Judah, began to reign. ²He was twenty-five years old when he became king, and he reigned twenty-nine years in Jerusalem. His mother's name *was* Abi* the daughter of Zechariah. ³And he did *what was* right in the sight of the LORD, according to all that his father David had done.

⁴He removed the high places and broke the *sacred* pillars, cut down the wooden image* and broke in pieces the bronze serpent that Moses had made; for until those days the children of Israel burned incense to it, and called it Nehushtan.* ⁵He trusted in the LORD God of Israel, so that after him was none like him among all the kings of Judah, nor who were before him. ⁶For he held fast to the LORD; he did not depart from following Him, but kept His commandments, which the LORD had commanded Moses. ⁷The LORD was with him; he prospered wherever he went. And he rebelled against the king of Assyria and did not serve him. ⁸He subdued the Philistines, as far as Gaza and its territory, from watchtower to fortified city.

⁹Now it came to pass in the fourth year of King Hezekiah, which *was* the seventh year of Hoshea the son of Elah, king of Israel, *that* Shalmaneser king of Assyria came up against Samaria and besieged it. ¹⁰And at the end of three years they took it. In the sixth year of Hezekiah, that *is,* the ninth year of Hoshea king of Israel, Samaria was taken. ¹¹Then the king of Assyria carried Israel away captive to Assyria, and put them in Halah and by the Habor, the River of Gozan, and in the cities of the Medes, ¹²because they did not obey the voice of the LORD their God, but transgressed His covenant *and* all that Moses the servant of the LORD had commanded; and they would neither hear nor do *them.*

ACTS 20:1-38

AFTER the uproar had ceased, Paul called the disciples to *himself,* embraced *them,* and departed to go to Macedonia. ²Now when he had gone over that region and encouraged them with many words, he came to Greece ³and stayed three months. And when the Jews plotted against him as he was about to sail to Syria, he decided to return through Macedonia. ⁴And Sopater of Berea accompanied him to Asia—also Aristarchus and Secundus of the Thessalonians, and Gaius of Derbe, and Timothy, and Tychicus and Trophimus of Asia. ⁵These men, going ahead, waited for us at Troas. ⁶But we sailed away from Philippi after the Days of Unleavened Bread, and in five days joined them at Troas, where we stayed seven days.

⁷Now on the first *day* of the week, when the disciples came together to break bread, Paul, ready to depart the next day, spoke to them and continued his message until midnight. ⁸There were many lamps in the upper room where they* were gathered together. ⁹And in a window sat a certain young man named Eutychus, who was sinking into a deep sleep. He was overcome by sleep; and as Paul continued

speaking, he fell down from the third story and was taken up dead. [10]But Paul went down, fell on him, and embracing *him* said, "Do not trouble yourselves, for his life is in him." [11]Now when he had come up, had broken bread and eaten, and talked a long while, even till daybreak, he departed. [12]And they brought the young man in alive, and they were not a little comforted.

[13]Then we went ahead to the ship and sailed to Assos, there intending to take Paul on board; for so he had given orders, intending himself to go on foot. [14]And when he met us at Assos, we took him on board and came to Mitylene. [15]We sailed from there, and the next *day* came opposite Chios. The following *day* we arrived at Samos and stayed at Trogyllium. The next *day* we came to Miletus. [16]For Paul had decided to sail past Ephesus, so that he would not have to spend time in Asia; for he was hurrying to be at Jerusalem, if possible, on the Day of Pentecost.

[17]From Miletus he sent to Ephesus and called for the elders of the church. [18]And when they had come to him, he said to them: "You know, from the first day that I came to Asia, in what manner I always lived among you, [19]serving the Lord with all humility, with many tears and trials which happened to me by the plotting of the Jews; [20]how I kept back nothing that was helpful, but proclaimed it to you, and taught you publicly and from house to house, [21]testifying to Jews, and also to Greeks, repentance toward God and faith toward our Lord Jesus Christ. [22]And see, now I go bound in the spirit to Jerusalem, not knowing the things that will happen to me there, [23]except that the Holy Spirit testifies in every city, saying that chains and tribulations await me. [24]But none of these things move me; nor do I count my life dear to myself,* so that I may finish my race

with joy, and the ministry which I received from the Lord Jesus, to testify to the gospel of the grace of God.

[25]"And indeed, now I know that you all, among whom I have gone preaching the kingdom of God, will see my face no more. [26]Therefore I testify to you this day that I *am* innocent of the blood of all *men*. [27]For I have not shunned to declare to you the whole counsel of God. [28]Therefore take heed to yourselves and to all the flock, among which the Holy Spirit has made you overseers, to shepherd the church of God* which He purchased with His own blood. [29]For I know this, that after my departure savage wolves will come in among you, not sparing the flock. [30]Also from among yourselves men will rise up, speaking perverse things, to draw away the disciples after themselves. [31]Therefore watch, and remember that for three years I did not cease to warn everyone night and day with tears.

[32]"So now, brethren, I commend you to God and to the word of His grace, which is able to build you up and give you an inheritance among all those who are sanctified. [33]I have coveted no one's silver or gold or apparel. [34]Yes,* you yourselves know that these hands have provided for my necessities, and for those who were with me. [35]I have shown you in every way, by laboring like this, that you must support the weak. And remember the words of the Lord Jesus, that He said, 'It is more blessed to give than to receive.' "

[36]And when he had said these things, he knelt down and prayed with them all. [37]Then they all wept freely, and fell on Paul's neck and kissed him, [38]sorrowing most of all for the words which he spoke, that they would see his face no more. And they accompanied him to the ship.

PSALM 148:1-14

PRAISE the LORD!

Praise the LORD from the
heavens;
Praise Him in the heights!
2 Praise Him, all His angels;
Praise Him, all His hosts!
3 Praise Him, sun and moon;
Praise Him, all you stars of
light!
4 Praise Him, you heavens of
heavens,
And you waters above the
heavens!

5 Let them praise the name of
the LORD,
For He commanded and they
were created.
6 He also established them
forever and ever;
He made a decree which shall
not pass away.

7 Praise the LORD from the
earth,
You great sea creatures and
all the depths;

8 Fire and hail, snow and
clouds;
Stormy wind, fulfilling His
word;
9 Mountains and all hills;
Fruitful trees and all cedars;
10 Beasts and all cattle;
Creeping things and flying
fowl;
11 Kings of the earth and all
peoples;
Princes and all judges of the
earth;
12 Both young men and maidens;
Old men and children.

13 Let them praise the name of
the LORD,
For His name alone is exalted;
His glory *is* above the earth
and heaven.
14 And He has exalted the horn
of His people,
The praise of all His saints—
Of the children of Israel,
A people near to Him.

Praise the LORD!

PROVERBS FOR TODAY/ 18:6-7

A fool's lips enter into contention, and his mouth calls for blows. A fool's mouth is
his destruction, and his lips are *the snare of his soul.*

JULY 1

2 KINGS 18:13–19:37

AND in the fourteenth year of
King Hezekiah, Sennacherib
king of Assyria came up
against all the fortified cities of Judah
and took them. 14Then Hezekiah king
of Judah sent to the king of Assyria at
Lachish, saying, "I have done wrong;
turn away from me; whatever you impose on me I will pay." And the king of
Assyria assessed Hezekiah king of
Judah three hundred talents of silver
and thirty talents of gold. 15So Hezekiah gave *him* all the silver that was
found in the house of the LORD and in
the treasuries of the king's house. 16At

that time Hezekiah stripped *the gold from* the doors of the temple of the LORD, and *from* the pillars which Hezekiah king of Judah had overlaid, and gave it to the king of Assyria.

¹⁷Then the king of Assyria sent *the* Tartan,* *the* Rabsaris,* *and the* Rabshakeh* from Lachish, with a great army against Jerusalem, to King Hezekiah. And they went up and came to Jerusalem. When they had come up, they went and stood by the aqueduct from the upper pool, which *was* on the highway to the Fuller's Field. ¹⁸And when they had called to the king, Eliakim the son of Hilkiah, who *was* over the household, Shebna the scribe, and Joah the son of Asaph, the recorder, came out to them. ¹⁹Then *the* Rabshakeh said to them, "Say now to Hezekiah, 'Thus says the great king, the king of Assyria: "What confidence *is* this in which you trust? ²⁰You speak of *having* plans and power for war; but *they are* mere words. And in whom do you trust, that you rebel against me? ²¹Now look! You are trusting in the staff of this broken reed, Egypt, on which if a man leans, it will go into his hand and pierce it. So *is* Pharaoh king of Egypt to all who trust in him. ²²But if you say to me, 'We trust in the LORD our God,' *is* it not He whose high places and whose altars Hezekiah has taken away, and said to Judah and Jerusalem, 'You shall worship before this altar in Jerusalem'?" ' ²³Now therefore, I urge you, give a pledge to my master the king of Assyria, and I will give you two thousand horses—if you are able on your part to put riders on them! ²⁴How then will you repel one captain of the least of my master's servants, and put your trust in Egypt for chariots and horsemen? ²⁵Have I now come up without the LORD against this place to destroy it? The LORD said to me, 'Go up against this land, and destroy it.' "

²⁶Then Eliakim the son of Hilkiah, Shebna, and Joah said to *the* Rabshakeh, "Please speak to your servants in Aramaic, for we understand *it;* and do not speak to us in Hebrew* in the hearing of the people who *are* on the wall."

²⁷But *the* Rabshakeh said to them, "Has my master sent me to your master and to you to speak these words, and not to the men who sit on the wall, who will eat and drink their own waste with you?"

²⁸Then *the* Rabshakeh stood and called out with a loud voice in Hebrew, and spoke, saying, "Hear the word of the great king, the king of Assyria! ²⁹Thus says the king: 'Do not let Hezekiah deceive you, for he shall not be able to deliver you from his hand; ³⁰nor let Hezekiah make you trust in the LORD, saying, "The LORD will surely deliver us; this city shall not be given into the hand of the king of Assyria." ' ³¹Do not listen to Hezekiah; for thus says the king of Assyria: 'Make *peace* with me by a present and come out to me; and every one of you eat from his own vine and every one from his own fig tree, and every one of you drink the waters of his own cistern; ³²until I come and take you away to a land like your own land, a land of grain and new wine, a land of bread and vineyards, a land of olive groves and honey, that you may live and not die. But do not listen to Hezekiah, lest he persuade you, saying, "The LORD will deliver us." ³³Has any of the gods of the nations at all delivered its land from the hand of the king of Assyria? ³⁴Where *are* the gods of Hamath and Arpad? Where *are* the gods of Sepharvaim and Hena and Ivah? Indeed, have they delivered Samaria from my hand? ³⁵Who among all the gods of the lands have delivered their countries from my hand, that the LORD should deliver Jerusalem from my hand?' "

³⁶But the people held their peace and answered him not a word; for the

king's commandment was, "Do not answer him." ³⁷Then Eliakim the son of Hilkiah, who *was* over the household, Shebna the scribe, and Joah the son of Asaph, the recorder, came to Hezekiah with *their* clothes torn, and told him the words of *the* Rabshakeh.

AND so it was, when King Hezekiah heard *it,* that he tore his clothes, covered himself with sackcloth, and went into the house of the LORD. ²Then he sent Eliakim, who *was* over the household, Shebna the scribe, and the elders of the priests, covered with sackcloth, to Isaiah the prophet, the son of Amoz. ³And they said to him, "Thus says Hezekiah: 'This day *is* a day of trouble, and rebuke, and blasphemy; for the children have come to birth, but *there is* no strength to bring them forth. ⁴It may be that the LORD your God will hear all the words of *the* Rabshakeh, whom his master the king of Assyria has sent to reproach the living God, and will rebuke the words which the LORD your God has heard. Therefore lift up *your* prayer for the remnant that is left.' "

⁵So the servants of King Hezekiah came to Isaiah. ⁶And Isaiah said to them, "Thus you shall say to your master, 'Thus says the LORD: "Do not be afraid of the words which you have heard, with which the servants of the king of Assyria have blasphemed Me. ⁷Surely I will send a spirit upon him, and he shall hear a rumor and return to his own land; and I will cause him to fall by the sword in his own land." ' "

⁸Then *the* Rabshakeh returned and found the king of Assyria warring against Libnah, for he heard that he had departed from Lachish. ⁹And the king heard concerning Tirhakah king of Ethiopia, "Look, he has come out to make war with you." So he again sent messengers to Hezekiah, saying, ¹⁰"Thus you shall speak to Hezekiah king of Judah, saying: 'Do not let your God in whom you trust deceive you,

saying, "Jerusalem shall not be given into the hand of the king of Assyria." ¹¹Look! You have heard what the kings of Assyria have done to all lands by utterly destroying them; and shall you be delivered? ¹²Have the gods of the nations delivered those whom my fathers have destroyed, Gozan and Haran and Rezeph, and the people of Eden who *were* in Telassar? ¹³Where *is* the king of Hamath, the king of Arpad, and the king of the city of Sepharvaim, Hena, and Ivah?' "

¹⁴And Hezekiah received the letter from the hand of the messengers, and read it; and Hezekiah went up to the house of the LORD, and spread it before the LORD. ¹⁵Then Hezekiah prayed before the LORD, and said: "O LORD God of Israel, *the One* who dwells *between* the cherubim, You are God, You alone, of all the kingdoms of the earth. You have made heaven and earth. ¹⁶Incline Your ear, O LORD, and hear; open Your eyes, O LORD, and see; and hear the words of Sennacherib, which he has sent to reproach the living God. ¹⁷Truly, LORD, the kings of Assyria have laid waste the nations and their lands, ¹⁸and have cast their gods into the fire; for they *were* not gods, but the work of men's hands—wood and stone. Therefore they destroyed them. ¹⁹Now therefore, O LORD our God, I pray, save us from his hand, that all the kingdoms of the earth may know that You *are* the LORD God, You alone."

²⁰Then Isaiah the son of Amoz sent to Hezekiah, saying, "Thus says the LORD God of Israel: 'Because you have prayed to Me against Sennacherib king of Assyria, I have heard.' ²¹This *is* the word which the LORD has spoken concerning him:

'The virgin, the daughter of
   Zion,
Has despised you, laughed
   you to scorn;
The daughter of Jerusalem

Has shaken *her* head behind
   your back!

22   'Whom have you reproached
      and blasphemed?
   Against whom have you
      raised *your* voice,
   And lifted up your eyes on
      high?
   Against the Holy *One* of Israel.

23   By your messengers you have
      reproached the Lord,
   And said: "By the multitude of
      my chariots
   I have come up to the height
      of the mountains,
   To the limits of Lebanon;
   I will cut down its tall cedars
   And its choice cypress trees;
   I will enter the extremity of its
      borders,
   To its fruitful forest.

24   I have dug and drunk strange
      water,
   And with the soles of my feet I
      have dried up
   All the brooks of defense."

25   'Did you not hear long ago
   How I made it,
   From ancient times that I
      formed it?
   Now I have brought it to pass,
   That you should be
   For crushing fortified cities
      into heaps of ruins.

26   Therefore their inhabitants
      had little power;
   They were dismayed and
      confounded;
   They were *as* the grass of the
      field
   And the green herb,
   As the grass on the housetops
   And *grain* blighted before it is
      grown.

27   'But I know your dwelling
      place,

Your going out and your
   coming in,
And your rage against Me.

28   Because your rage against
      Me and your tumult
   Have come up to My ears,
   Therefore I will put My hook
      in your nose
   And My bridle in your lips,
   And I will turn you back
   By the way which you came.

29"This *shall be* a sign to you:

   You shall eat this year such as
      grows of itself,
   And in the second year what
      springs from the same;
   Also in the third year sow and
      reap,
   Plant vineyards and eat the
      fruit of them.

30   And the remnant who have
      escaped of the house of
      Judah
   Shall again take root
      downward,
   And bear fruit upward.

31   For out of Jerusalem shall go
      a remnant,
   And those who escape from
      Mount Zion.
   The zeal of the Lord of hosts*
      will do this.'

32"Therefore thus says the Lord concerning the king of Assyria:

   'He shall not come into this
      city,
   Nor shoot an arrow there,
   Nor come before it with
      shield,
   Nor build a siege mound
      against it.

33   By the way that he came,
   By the same shall he return;
   And he shall not come into
      this city,'
   Says the Lord.

³⁴ 'For I will defend this city, to
    save it
  For My own sake and for My
    servant David's sake.' "

³⁵And it came to pass on a certain night that the angel* of the LORD went out, and killed in the camp of the Assyrians one hundred and eighty-five thousand; and when *people* arose early in the morning, there were the corpses—all dead. ³⁶So Sennacherib king of Assyria departed and went away, returned *home,* and remained at Nineveh. ³⁷Now it came to pass, as he was worshiping in the temple of Nisroch his god, that his sons Adrammelech and Sharezer struck him down with the sword; and they escaped into the land of Ararat. Then Esarhaddon his son reigned in his place.

ACTS 21:1-16

Now it came to pass, that when we [Luke, Paul, and companions] had departed from them and set sail, running a straight course we came to Cos, the following *day* to Rhodes, and from there to Patara. ²And finding a ship sailing over to Phoenicia, we went aboard and set sail. ³When we had sighted Cyprus, we passed it on the left, sailed to Syria, and landed at Tyre; for there the ship was to unload her cargo. ⁴And finding disciples,* we stayed there seven days. They told Paul through the Spirit not to go up to Jerusalem. ⁵When we had come to the end of those days, we departed and went on our way; and they all accompanied us, with wives and children, till *we were* out of the city. And we knelt down on the shore and prayed. ⁶When we had taken our leave of one another, we boarded the ship, and they returned home.

⁷And when we had finished *our* voyage from Tyre, we came to Ptolemais, greeted the brethren, and stayed with

them one day. ⁸On the next *day* we who were Paul's companions* departed and came to Caesarea, and entered the house of Philip the evangelist, who was *one* of the seven, and stayed with him. ⁹Now this man had four virgin daughters who prophesied. ¹⁰And as we stayed many days, a certain prophet named Agabus came down from Judea. ¹¹When he had come to us, he took Paul's belt, bound his *own* hands and feet, and said, "Thus says the Holy Spirit, 'So shall the Jews at Jerusalem bind the man who owns this belt, and deliver *him* into the hands of the Gentiles.' "

¹²Now when we heard these things, both we and those from that place pleaded with him not to go up to Jerusalem. ¹³Then Paul answered, "What do you mean by weeping and breaking my heart? For I am ready not only to be bound, but also to die at Jerusalem for the name of the Lord Jesus."

¹⁴So when he would not be persuaded, we ceased, saying, "The will of the Lord be done."

¹⁵And after those days we packed and went up to Jerusalem. ¹⁶Also some of the disciples from Caesarea went with us and brought with them a certain Mnason of Cyprus, an early disciple, with whom we were to lodge.

PSALM 149:1-9

PRAISE the LORD!

Sing to the LORD a new song,
And His praise in the
    assembly of saints.

2 Let Israel rejoice in their
    Maker;
  Let the children of Zion be
    joyful in their King.
3 Let them praise His name
    with the dance;
  Let them sing praises to Him
    with the timbrel and harp.

4   For the Lord takes pleasure in
    His people;
    He will beautify the humble
    with salvation.

5   Let the saints be joyful in
    glory;
    Let them sing aloud on their
    beds.

6   *Let* the high praises of God *be*
    in their mouth,
    And a two-edged sword in
    their hand,

7   To execute vengeance on the
    nations,
    And punishments on the
    peoples;

8   To bind their kings with
    chains,
    And their nobles with fetters
    of iron;

9   To execute on them the
    written judgment—
    This honor have all His saints.

    Praise the Lord!

PROVERBS FOR TODAY/ 18:8

The words of a talebearer are like tasty trifles, * *and they go down into the inmost body.*

JULY 2

2 KINGS 20:1–22:2

In those days Hezekiah was sick and near death. And Isaiah the prophet, the son of Amoz, went to him and said to him, "Thus says the Lord: 'Set your house in order, for you shall die, and not live.' "

2Then he turned his face toward the wall, and prayed to the Lord, saying, 3"Remember now, O Lord, I pray, how I have walked before You in truth and with a loyal heart, and have done *what was* good in Your sight." And Hezekiah wept bitterly.

4And it happened, before Isaiah had gone out into the middle court, that the word of the Lord came to him, saying, 5"Return and tell Hezekiah the leader of My people, 'Thus says the Lord, the God of David your father: "I have heard your prayer, I have seen your tears; surely I will heal you. On the third day you shall go up to the house of the Lord. 6And I will add to your days fifteen years. I will deliver you and this city from the hand of the king of Assyria; and I will defend this city for My own sake, and for the sake of My servant David." ' "

7Then Isaiah said, "Take a lump of figs." So they took and laid *it* on the boil, and he recovered.

8And Hezekiah said to Isaiah, "What *is* the sign that the Lord will heal me, and that I shall go up to the house of the Lord the third day?"

9Then Isaiah said, "Tis is the sign to you from the Lord, that the Lord will do the thing which He has spoken: *shall* the shadow go forward ten degrees or go backward ten degrees?"

10And Hezekiah answered, "It is an easy thing for the shadow to go down ten degrees; no, but let the shadow go backward ten degrees."

11So Isaiah the prophet cried out to the Lord, and He brought the shadow ten degrees backward, by which it had gone down on the sundial of Ahaz.

¹²At that time Berodach-Baladan* the son of Baladan, king of Babylon, sent letters and a present to Hezekiah, for he heard that Hezekiah had been sick. ¹³And Hezekiah was attentive to them, and showed them all the house of his treasures—the silver and gold, the spices and precious ointment, and all* his armory—all that was found among his treasures. There was nothing in his house or in all his dominion that Hezekiah did not show them.

¹⁴Then Isaiah the prophet went to King Hezekiah, and said to him, "What did these men say, and from where did they come to you?"

So Hezekiah said, "They came from a far country, from Babylon."

¹⁵And he said, "What have they seen in your house?"

So Hezekiah answered, "They have seen all that *is* in my house; there is nothing among my treasures that I have not shown them."

¹⁶Then Isaiah said to Hezekiah, "Hear the word of the LORD: ¹⁷'Behold, the days are coming when all that *is* in your house, and what your fathers have accumulated until this day, shall be carried to Babylon; nothing shall be left,' says the LORD. ¹⁸'And they shall take away some of your sons who will descend from you, whom you will beget; and they shall be eunuchs in the palace of the king of Babylon.' "

¹⁹So Hezekiah said to Isaiah, "The word of the LORD which you have spoken *is* good!" For he said, "Will there not be peace and truth at least in my days?"

²⁰Now the rest of the acts of Hezekiah—all his might, and how he made a pool and a tunnel and brought water into the city—*are* they not written in the book of the chronicles of the kings of Judah? ²¹So Hezekiah rested with his fathers. Then Manasseh his son reigned in his place.

MANASSEH *was* twelve years old when he became king, and he reigned fifty-five years in Jerusalem. His mother's name *was* Hephzibah. ²And he did evil in the sight of the LORD, according to the abominations of the nations whom the LORD had cast out before the children of Israel. ³For he rebuilt the high places which Hezekiah his father had destroyed; he raised up altars for Baal, and made a wooden image,* as Ahab king of Israel had done; and he worshiped all the host of heaven* and served them. ⁴He also built altars in the house of the LORD, of which the LORD had said, "In Jerusalem I will put My name." ⁵And he built altars for all the host of heaven in the two courts of the house of the LORD. ⁶Also he made his son pass through the fire, practiced soothsaying, used witchcraft, and consulted spiritists and mediums. He did much evil in the sight of the LORD, to provoke *Him* to anger. ⁷He even set a carved image of Asherah* that he had made, in the house of which the LORD had said to David and to Solomon his son, "In this house and in Jerusalem, which I have chosen out of all the tribes of Israel, I will put My name forever; ⁸and I will not make the feet of Israel wander anymore from the land which I gave their fathers—only if they are careful to do according to all that I have commanded them, and according to all the law that My servant Moses commanded them." ⁹But they paid no attention, and Manasseh seduced them to do more evil than the nations whom the LORD had destroyed before the children of Israel.

¹⁰And the LORD spoke by His servants the prophets, saying, ¹¹"Because Manasseh king of Judah has done these abominations (he has acted more wickedly than all the Amorites who *were* before him, and has also made Judah sin with his idols), ¹²therefore thus says the LORD God of Israel: 'Behold, *I* am bringing *such* calamity

upon Jerusalem and Judah, that whoever hears of it, both his ears will tingle. ¹³And I will stretch over Jerusalem the measuring line of Samaria and the plummet of the house of Ahab; I will wipe Jerusalem as *one* wipes a dish, wiping *it* and turning *it* upside down. ¹⁴So I will forsake the remnant of My inheritance and deliver them into the hand of their enemies; and they shall become victims of plunder to all their enemies, ¹⁵because they have done evil in My sight, and have provoked Me to anger since the day their fathers came out of Egypt, even to this day.' "

¹⁶Moreover Manasseh shed very much innocent blood, till he had filled Jerusalem from one end to another, besides his sin by which he made Judah sin, in doing evil in the sight of the LORD.

¹⁷Now the rest of the acts of Manasseh—all that he did, and the sin that he committed—*are* they not written in the book of the chronicles of the kings of Judah? ¹⁸So Manasseh rested with his fathers, and was buried in the garden of his own house, in the garden of Uzza. Then his son Amon reigned in his place.

¹⁹Amon *was* twenty-two years old when he became king, and he reigned two years in Jerusalem. His mother's name *was* Meshullemeth the daughter of Haruz of Jotbah. ²⁰And he did evil in the sight of the LORD, as his father Manasseh had done. ²¹So he walked in all the ways that his father had walked; and he served the idols that his father had served, and worshiped them. ²²He forsook the LORD God of his fathers, and did not walk in the way of the LORD.

²³Then the servants of Amon conspired against him, and killed the king in his own house. ²⁴But the people of the land executed all those who had conspired against King Amon. Then the people of the land made his son Josiah king in his place.

²⁵Now the rest of the acts of Amon which he did, *are* they not written in the book of the chronicles of the kings of Judah? ²⁶And he was buried in his tomb in the garden of Uzza. Then Josiah his son reigned in his place.

JOSIAH *was* eight years old when he became king, and he reigned thirty-one years in Jerusalem. His mother's name *was* Jedidah the daughter of Adaiah of Bozkath. ²And he did *what was* right in the sight of the LORD, and walked in all the ways of his father David; he did not turn aside to the right hand or to the left.

ACTS 21:17-36

AND when we [Luke, Paul, and companions] had come to Jerusalem, the brethren received us gladly. ¹⁸On the following *day* Paul went in with us to James, and all the elders were present. ¹⁹When he had greeted them, he told in detail those things which God had done among the Gentiles through his ministry. ²⁰And when they heard *it,* they glorified the Lord. And they said to him, "You see, brother, how many myriads of Jews there are who have believed, and they are all zealous for the law; ²¹but they have been informed about you that you teach all the Jews who are among the Gentiles to forsake Moses, saying that they ought not to circumcise *their* children nor to walk according to the customs. ²²What then? The assembly must certainly meet, for they will* hear that you have come. ²³Therefore do what we tell you: We have four men who have taken a vow. ²⁴Take them and be purified with them, and pay their expenses so that they may shave *their* heads, and that all may know that those things of which they were informed concerning you are nothing, but *that* you yourself also walk orderly and keep the law. ²⁵But concerning the Gentiles who believe, we have written *and* decided that they should observe no such thing,* except that they should keep themselves from *things* offered to idols, from blood, from things strangled, and from sexual immorality."

26Then Paul took the men, and the next day, having been purified with them, entered the temple to announce the expiration of the days of purification, at which time an offering should be made for each one of them.

27Now when the seven days were almost ended, the Jews from Asia, seeing him in the temple, stirred up the whole crowd and laid hands on him, 28crying out, "Men of Israel, help! This is the man who teaches all *men* everywhere against the people, the law, and this place; and furthermore he also brought Greeks into the temple and has defiled this holy place." 29(For they had previously* seen Trophimus the Ephesian with him in the city, whom they supposed that Paul had brought into the temple.)

30And all the city was disturbed; and the people ran together, seized Paul, and dragged him out of the temple; and immediately the doors were shut. 31Now as they were seeking to kill him, news came to the commander of the garrison that all Jerusalem was in an uproar. 32He immediately took soldiers and centurions, and ran down to them. And when they saw the commander and the soldiers, they stopped beating Paul. 33Then the commander came near and took him, and commanded *him* to be bound with two chains; and he asked who he was and what he had done. 34And some among the multitude cried one thing and some another.

So when he could not ascertain the truth because of the tumult, he commanded him to be taken into the barracks. 35When he reached the stairs, he had to be carried by the soldiers because of the violence of the mob. 36For the multitude of the people followed after, crying out, "Away with him!"

PSALM 150:1-6

PRAISE the LORD!

Praise God in His sanctuary;
Praise Him in His mighty
firmament!

2   Praise Him for His mighty
acts;
Praise Him according to His
excellent greatness!

3   Praise Him with the sound of
the trumpet;
Praise Him with the lute and
harp!

4   Praise Him with the timbrel
and dance;
Praise Him with stringed
instruments and flutes!

5   Praise Him with loud cymbals;
Praise Him with clashing
cymbals!

6   Let everything that has
breath praise the LORD.

Praise the LORD!

PROVERBS FOR TODAY/ 18:9-10

He who is slothful in his work is a brother to him who is a great destroyer. □ *The name of the LORD is a strong tower; the righteous run to it and are safe.*

JULY 3

2 KINGS 22:3–23:30

Now it came to pass, in the eighteenth year of King Josiah, *that* the king sent Shaphan the scribe, the son of Azaliah, the son of Meshullam, to the house of the LORD, saying: 4"Go up to Hilkiah the high priest, that he may count the money which has been brought into the house of the LORD, which the doorkeepers have gathered from the people. 5And let them deliver it into the hand of those doing the work, who are the overseers in the house of the LORD; let them give it to those who *are* in the house of the LORD doing the work, to repair the damages of the house— 6to carpenters and builders and masons— and to buy timber and hewn stone to repair the house. 7However there need be no accounting made with them of the money delivered into their hand, because they deal faithfully."

8Then Hilkiah the high priest said to Shaphan the scribe, "I have found the Book of the Law in the house of the LORD." And Hilkiah gave the book to Shaphan, and he read it. 9So Shaphan the scribe went to the king, bringing the king word, saying, "Your servants have gathered the money that was found in the house, and have delivered it into the hand of those who do the work, who oversee the house of the LORD." 10Then Shaphan the scribe showed the king, saying, "Hilkiah the priest has given me a book." And Shaphan read it before the king.

11Now it happened, when the king heard the words of the Book of the Law, that he tore his clothes. 12Then the king commanded Hilkiah the priest, Ahikam the son of Shaphan, Achbor* the son of Michaiah, Shaphan the scribe, and Asaiah a servant of the king, saying, 13"Go, inquire of the LORD for me, for the people and for all Judah, concerning the words of this book that has been found; for great *is* the wrath of the LORD that is aroused against us, because our fathers have not obeyed the words of this book, to do according to all that is written concerning us."

14So Hilkiah the priest, Ahikam, Achbor, Shaphan, and Asaiah went to Huldah the prophetess, the wife of Shallum the son of Tikvah, the son of Harhas, keeper of the wardrobe. (She dwelt in Jerusalem in the Second Quarter.) And they spoke with her. 15Then she said to them, "Thus says the LORD God of Israel, 'Tell the man who sent you to Me, 16"Thus says the LORD: 'Behold, I will bring calamity on this place and on its inhabitants—all the words of the book which the king of Judah has read— 17because they have forsaken Me and burned incense to other gods, that they might provoke Me to anger with all the works of their hands. Therefore My wrath shall be aroused against this place and shall not be quenched.' " ' 18But as for the king of Judah, who sent you to inquire of the LORD, in this manner you shall speak to him, 'Thus says the LORD God of Israel: "*Concerning* the words which you have heard— 19because your heart was tender, and you humbled yourself before the LORD when you heard what I spoke against this place and against its inhabitants, that they would become a desolation and a curse, and you tore your clothes and wept before Me, I also have heard *you,*" says the LORD. 20Surely, therefore, I will gather you to your fathers, and you shall be gathered to your grave in peace; and your eyes shall not see all the calamity which I will bring on this place." ' " So they brought back word to the king.

Now the king sent them to gather all the elders of Judah and Jerusalem to him. ²The king went up to the house of the LORD with all the men of Judah, and with him all the inhabitants of Jerusalem—the priests and the prophets and all the people, both small and great. And he read in their hearing all the words of the Book of the Covenant which had been found in the house of the LORD.

³Then the king stood by a pillar and made a covenant before the LORD, to follow the LORD and to keep His commandments and His testimonies and His statutes, with all *his* heart and all *his* soul, to perform the words of this covenant that were written in this book. And all the people took a stand for the covenant. ⁴And the king commanded Hilkiah the high priest, the priests of the second order, and the doorkeepers, to bring out of the temple of the LORD all the articles that were made for Baal, for Asherah,* and for all the host of heaven;* and he burned them outside Jerusalem in the fields of Kidron, and carried their ashes to Bethel. ⁵Then he removed the idolatrous priests whom the kings of Judah had ordained to burn incense on the high places in the cities of Judah and in the places all around Jerusalem, and those who burned incense to Baal, to the sun, to the moon, to the constellations, and to all the host of heaven. ⁶And he brought out the wooden image* from the house of the LORD, to the Brook Kidron outside Jerusalem, burned it at the Brook Kidron and ground *it* to ashes, and threw its ashes on the graves of the common people. ⁷Then he tore down the *ritual* booths of the perverted persons* that *were* in the house of the LORD, where the women wove hangings for the wooden

image. ⁸And he brought all the priests from the cities of Judah, and defiled the high places where the priests had burned incense, from Geba to Beersheba; also he broke down the high places at the gates which *were* at the entrance of the Gate of Joshua the governor of the city, which *were* to the left of the city gate. ⁹Nevertheless the priests of the high places did not come up to the altar of the LORD in Jerusalem, but they ate unleavened bread among their brethren.

¹⁰And he defiled Topheth, which *is* in the Valley of the Son* of Hinnom, that no man might make his son or his daughter pass through the fire to Molech. ¹¹Then he removed the horses that the kings of Judah had dedicated to the sun, at the entrance to the house of the LORD, by the chamber of Nathan-Melech, the officer who *was* in the court; and he burned the chariots of the sun with fire. ¹²The altars that *were* on the roof, the upper chamber of Ahaz, which the kings of Judah had made, and the altars which Manasseh had made in the two courts of the house of the LORD, the king broke down and pulverized there, and threw their dust into the Brook Kidron. ¹³Then the king defiled the high places that *were* east of Jerusalem, which *were* on the south of the Mount of Corruption, which Solomon king of Israel had built for Ashtoreth the abomination of the Sidonians, for Chemosh the abomination of the Moabites, and for Milcom the abomination of the people of Ammon. ¹⁴And he broke in pieces the *sacred* pillars and cut down the wooden images, and filled their places with the bones of men.

¹⁵Moreover the altar that *was* at Bethel, *and* the high place which Jeroboam the son of Nebat, who made Israel sin, had made, both that altar and the high place he broke down; and he burned the high place *and* crushed *it* to powder, and burned the wooden im-

age. ¹⁶As Josiah turned, he saw the tombs that *were* there on the mountain. And he sent and took the bones out of the tombs and burned *them* on the altar, and defiled it according to the word of the LORD which the man of God proclaimed, who proclaimed these words. ¹⁷Then he said, "What gravestone *is* this that I see?"

So the men of the city told him, "*It is* the tomb of the man of God who came from Judah and proclaimed these things which you have done against the altar of Bethel."

¹⁸And he said, "Let him alone; let no one move his bones." So they let his bones alone, with the bones of the prophet who came from Samaria.

¹⁹Now Josiah also took away all the shrines of the high places that *were* in the cities of Samaria, which the kings of Israel had made to provoke the LORD* to anger; and he did to them according to all the deeds he had done in Bethel. ²⁰He executed all the priests of the high places who *were* there, on the altars, and burned men's bones on them; and he returned to Jerusalem.

²¹Then the king commanded all the people, saying, "Keep the Passover to the LORD your God, as *it is* written in this Book of the Covenant." ²²Such a Passover surely had never been held since the days of the judges who judged Israel, nor in all the days of the kings of Israel and the kings of Judah. ²³But in the eighteenth year of King Josiah this Passover was held before the LORD in Jerusalem. ²⁴Moreover Josiah put away those who consulted mediums and spiritists, the household gods and idols, all the abominations that were seen in the land of Judah and in Jerusalem, that he might perform the words of the law which were written in the book that Hilkiah the priest found in the house of the LORD. ²⁵Now before him there was no king like him, who turned to the LORD with all his heart, with all his soul, and with all his

might, according to all the Law of Moses; nor after him did *any* arise like him.

²⁶Nevertheless the LORD did not turn from the fierceness of His great wrath, with which His anger was aroused against Judah, because of all the provocations with which Manasseh had provoked Him. ²⁷And the LORD said, "I will also remove Judah from My sight, as I have removed Israel, and will cast off this city Jerusalem which I have chosen, and the house of which I said, 'My name shall be there.' "*

²⁸Now the rest of the acts of Josiah, and all that he did, *are* they not written in the book of the chronicles of the kings of Judah? ²⁹In his days Pharaoh Necho king of Egypt went to the aid of the king of Assyria, to the River Euphrates; and King Josiah went against him. And *Pharaoh Necho* killed him at Megiddo when he confronted him. ³⁰Then his servants moved his body in a chariot from Megiddo, brought him to Jerusalem, and buried him in his own tomb. And the people of the land took Jehoahaz the son of Josiah, anointed him, and made him king in his father's place.

ACTS 21:37–22:16

THEN as Paul was about to be led into the barracks, he said to the commander, "May I speak to you?"

He replied, "Can you speak Greek? ³⁸Are you not the Egyptian who some time ago stirred up a rebellion and led the four thousand assassins out into the wilderness?"

³⁹But Paul said, "I am a Jew from Tarsus, in Cilicia, a citizen of no mean city; and I implore you, permit me to speak to the people."

⁴⁰So when he had given him permission, Paul stood on the stairs and motioned with his hand to the people. And when there was a great silence, he

spoke to *them* in the Hebrew language, saying,

"BRETHREN and fathers, hear my defense before you now." ²And when they heard that he spoke to them in the Hebrew language, they kept all the more silent.

Then he said: ³"I am indeed a Jew, born in Tarsus of Cilicia, but brought up in this city at the feet of Gamaliel, taught according to the strictness of our fathers' law, and was zealous toward God as you all are today. ⁴I persecuted this Way to the death, binding and delivering into prisons both men and women, ⁵as also the high priest bears me witness, and all the council of the elders, from whom I also received letters to the brethren, and went to Damascus to bring in chains even those who were there to Jerusalem to be punished.

⁶"Now it happened, as I journeyed and came near Damascus at about noon, suddenly a great light from heaven shone around me. ⁷And I fell to the ground and heard a voice saying to me, 'Saul, Saul, why are you persecuting Me?' ⁸So I answered, 'Who are You, Lord?' And He said to me, 'I am Jesus of Nazareth, whom you are persecuting.'

⁹"And those who were with me indeed saw the light and were afraid,* but they did not hear the voice of Him who spoke to me. ¹⁰So I said, 'What shall I do, Lord?' And the Lord said to me, 'Arise and go into Damascus, and there you will be told all things which are appointed for you to do.' ¹¹And since I could not see for the glory of that light, being led by the hand of those who were with me, I came into Damascus.

¹²"Then a certain Ananias, a devout man according to the law, having a good testimony with all the Jews who dwelt *there,* ¹³came to me; and he stood and said to me, 'Brother Saul, receive your sight.' And at that same hour I looked up at him. ¹⁴Then he said, 'The God of our fathers has chosen you that you should know His will, and see the Just One, and hear the voice of His mouth. ¹⁵For you will be His witness to all men of what you have seen and heard. ¹⁶And now why are you waiting? Arise and be baptized, and wash away your sins, calling on the name of the Lord.' "

PSALM 1:1-6

BLESSED *is* the man
Who walks not in the counsel of the ungodly,
    Nor stands in the path of sinners,
    Nor sits in the seat of the scornful;
2 But his delight *is* in the law of the LORD,
    And in His law he meditates day and night.
3 He shall be like a tree
    Planted by the rivers of water,
    That brings forth its fruit in its season,
    Whose leaf also shall not wither;
    And whatever he does shall prosper.

4 The ungodly *are* not so,
    But *are* like the chaff which the wind drives away.
5 Therefore the ungodly shall not stand in the judgment,
    Nor sinners in the congregation of the righteous.

6 For the LORD knows the way of the righteous,
    But the way of the ungodly shall perish.

PROVERBS FOR TODAY/ 18:11-12

The rich man's wealth is *his strong city, and like a high wall in his own esteem.*
□ *Before destruction the heart of a man is haughty, and before honor* is *humility.*

JULY 4

2 KINGS 23:31–25:30

JEHOAHAZ *was* twenty-three years old when he became king, and he reigned three months in Jerusalem. His mother's name *was* Hamutal the daughter of Jeremiah of Libnah. 32And he did evil in the sight of the LORD, according to all that his fathers had done. 33Now Pharaoh Necho put him in prison at Riblah in the land of Hamath, that he might not reign in Jerusalem; and he imposed on the land a tribute of one hundred talents of silver and a talent of gold. 34Then Pharaoh Necho made Eliakim the son of Josiah king in place of his father Josiah, and changed his name to Jehoiakim. And *Pharaoh* took Jehoahaz and went to Egypt, and he* died there.

35So Jehoiakim gave the silver and gold to Pharaoh; but he taxed the land to give money according to the command of Pharaoh; he exacted the silver and gold from the people of the land, from every one according to his assessment, to give *it* to Pharaoh Necho. 36Jehoiakim *was* twenty-five years old when he became king, and he reigned eleven years in Jerusalem. His mother's name *was* Zebudah the daughter of Pedaiah of Rumah. 37And he did evil in the sight of the LORD, according to all that his fathers had done.

IN his days Nebuchadnezzar king of Babylon came up, and Jehoiakim became his vassal *for* three years. Then he turned and rebelled against him. 2And the LORD sent against him *raiding* bands

of Chaldeans, bands of Syrians, bands of Moabites, and bands of the people of Ammon; He sent them against Judah to destroy it, according to the word of the LORD which He had spoken by His servants the prophets. 3Surely at the commandment of the LORD *this* came upon Judah, to remove *them* from His sight because of the sins of Manasseh, according to all that he had done, 4and also because of the innocent blood that he had shed; for he had filled Jerusalem with innocent blood, which the LORD would not pardon.

5Now the rest of the acts of Jehoiakim, and all that he did, *are* they not written in the book of the chronicles of the kings of Judah? 6So Jehoiakim rested with his fathers. Then Jehoiachin his son reigned in his place.

7And the king of Egypt did not come out of his land anymore, for the king of Babylon had taken all that belonged to the king of Egypt from the Brook of Egypt to the River Euphrates.

8Jehoiachin *was* eighteen years old when he became king, and he reigned in Jerusalem three months. His mother's name *was* Nehushta the daughter of Elnathan of Jerusalem. 9And he did evil in the sight of the LORD, according to all that his father had done.

10At that time the servants of Nebuchadnezzar king of Babylon came up against Jerusalem, and the city was besieged. 11And Nebuchadnezzar king of Babylon came against the city, as his servants were besieging it. 12Then Jehoiachin king of Judah, his mother, his servants, his princes, and his officers went out to the king of Babylon; and the king of Babylon, in the eighth year of his reign, took him prisoner.

13And he carried out from there all the treasures of the house of the LORD and the treasures of the king's house, and he cut in pieces all the articles of gold which Solomon king of Israel had made in the temple of the LORD, as the LORD had said. 14Also he carried into captivity all Jerusalem: all the captains and all the mighty men of valor, ten thousand captives, and all the craftsmen and smiths. None remained except the poorest people of the land. 15And he carried Jehoiachin captive to Babylon. The king's mother, the king's wives, his officers, and the mighty of the land he carried into captivity from Jerusalem to Babylon. 16All the valiant men, seven thousand, and craftsmen and smiths, one thousand, all who were strong and fit for war, these the king of Babylon brought captive to Babylon. 17Then the king of Babylon made Mattaniah, Jehoiachin's* uncle, king in his place, and changed his name to Zedekiah.

18Zedekiah was twenty-one years old when he became king, and he reigned eleven years in Jerusalem. His mother's name was Hamutal the daughter of Jeremiah of Libnah. 19He also did evil in the sight of the LORD, according to all that Jehoiakim had done. 20For because of the anger of the LORD this happened in Jerusalem and Judah, that He finally cast them out from His presence. Then Zedekiah rebelled against the king of Babylon.

Now it came to pass in the ninth year of his reign, in the tenth month, on the tenth day of the month, that Nebuchadnezzar king of Babylon and all his army came against Jerusalem and encamped against it; and they built a siege wall against it all around. 2So the city was besieged until the eleventh year of King Zedekiah. 3By the ninth day of the fourth month the famine had become so severe in the city that there was no food for the people of the land.

4Then the city wall was broken through, and all the men of war fled at night by way of the gate between two walls, which was by the king's garden, even though the Chaldeans were still encamped all around against the city. And the king* went by way of the plain.* 5But the army of the Chaldeans pursued the king, and they overtook him in the plains of Jericho. All his army was scattered from him. 6So they took the king and brought him up to the king of Babylon at Riblah, and they pronounced judgment on him. 7Then they killed the sons of Zedekiah before his eyes, put out the eyes of Zedekiah, bound him with bronze fetters, and took him to Babylon.

8And in the fifth month, on the seventh day of the month (which was the nineteenth year of King Nebuchadnezzar king of Babylon), Nebuzaradan the captain of the guard, a servant of the king of Babylon, came to Jerusalem. 9He burned the house of the LORD and the king's house; all the houses of Jerusalem, that is, all the houses of the great, he burned with fire. 10And all the army of the Chaldeans who were with the captain of the guard broke down the walls of Jerusalem all around. 11Then Nebuzaradan the captain of the guard carried away captive the rest of the people who remained in the city and the defectors who had deserted to the king of Babylon, with the rest of the multitude. 12But the captain of the guard left some of the poor of the land as vinedressers and farmers. 13The bronze pillars that were in the house of the LORD, and the carts and the bronze Sea that were in the house of the LORD, the Chaldeans broke in pieces, and carried their bronze to Babylon. 14They also took away the pots, the shovels, the trimmers, the spoons, and all the bronze utensils with which the priests ministered. [15]The firepans and the basins, the things of solid gold and solid silver, the captain of the guard took away. [16]The two pillars, one Sea, and the carts, which Solomon had made for the house of the LORD, the bronze of all these articles was beyond measure. [17]The height of one pillar *was* eighteen cubits, and the capital on it *was* of bronze. The height of the capital was three cubits, and the network and pomegranates all around the capital were all of bronze. The second pillar was the same, with a network.

[18]And the captain of the guard took Seraiah the chief priest, Zephaniah the second priest, and the three doorkeepers. [19]He also took out of the city an officer who had charge of the men of war, five men of the king's close associates who were found in the city, the chief recruiting officer of the army, who mustered the people of the land, and sixty men of the people of the land *who were* found in the city. [20]So Nebuzaradan, captain of the guard, took these and brought them to the king of Babylon at Riblah. [21]Then the king of Babylon struck them and put them to death at Riblah in the land of Hamath. Thus Judah was carried away captive from its own land.

[22]Then he made Gedaliah the son of Ahikam, the son of Shaphan, governor over the people who remained in the land of Judah, whom Nebuchadnezzar king of Babylon had left. [23]Now when all the captains of the armies, they and *their* men, heard that the king of Babylon had made Gedaliah governor, they came to Gedaliah at Mizpah—Ishmael the son of Nethaniah, Johanan the son of Careah, Seraiah the son of Tanhumeth the Netophathite, and Jaazaniah* the son of a Maachathite, they and their men. [24]And Gedaliah took an oath before them and their men, and said to them, "Do not be afraid of the servants of the Chaldeans. Dwell in the land and

serve the king of Babylon, and it shall be well with you."

[25]But it happened in the seventh month that Ishmael the son of Nethaniah, the son of Elishama, of the royal family, came with ten men and struck and killed Gedaliah, the Jews, as well as the Chaldeans who were with him at Mizpah. [26]And all the people, small and great, and the captains of the armies, arose and went to Egypt; for they were afraid of the Chaldeans.

[27]Now it came to pass in the thirty-seventh year of the captivity of Jehoiachin king of Judah, in the twelfth month, on the twenty-seventh *day* of the month, *that* Evil-Merodach* king of Babylon, in the year that he began to reign, released Jehoiachin king of Judah from prison. [28]He spoke kindly to him, and gave him a more prominent seat than those of the kings who *were* with him in Babylon. [29]So Jehoiachin changed from his prison garments, and he ate bread regularly before the king all the days of his life. [30]And as for his provisions, *there was* a regular ration given him by the king, a portion for each day, all the days of his life.

ACTS 22:17–23:10

"**N**ow it happened, when I [Paul] returned to Jerusalem and was praying in the temple, that I was in a trance [18]and saw Him saying to me, 'Make haste and get out of Jerusalem quickly, for they will not receive your testimony concerning Me.' [19]So I said, 'Lord, they know that in every synagogue I imprisoned and beat those who believe on You. [20]And when the blood of Your martyr Stephen was shed, I also was standing by consenting to his death,* and guarding the clothes of those who were killing him.' [21]Then He said to me, 'Depart, for I will send you far from here to the Gentiles.' "

[22]And they listened to him until this

word, and *then* they raised their voices and said, "Away with such a *fellow* from the earth, for he is not fit to live!" 23Then, as they cried out and tore off *their* clothes and threw dust into the air, 24the commander ordered him to be brought into the barracks, and said that he should be examined under scourging, so that he might know why they shouted so against him. 25And as they bound him with thongs, Paul said to the centurion who stood by, "Is it lawful for you to scourge a man who is a Roman, and uncondemned?"

26When the centurion heard *that,* he went and told the commander, saying, "Take care what you do, for this man is a Roman."

27Then the commander came and said to him, "Tell me, are you a Roman?"

He said, "Yes."

28The commander answered, "With a large sum I obtained this citizenship."

And Paul said, "But I was born *a citizen.*"

29Then immediately those who were about to examine him withdrew from him; and the commander was also afraid after he found out that he was a Roman, and because he had bound him.

30The next day, because he wanted to know for certain why he was accused by the Jews, he released him from *his* bonds, and commanded the chief priests and all their council to appear, and brought Paul down and set him before them.

THEN Paul, looking earnestly at the council, said, "Men *and* brethren, I have lived in all good conscience before God until this day." 2And the high priest Ananias commanded those who stood by him to strike him on the mouth. 3Then Paul said to him, "God will strike you, *you* whitewashed wall! For you sit to judge me according to

the law, and do you command me to be struck contrary to the law?"

4And those who stood by said, "Do you revile God's high priest?"

5Then Paul said, "I did not know, brethren, that he was the high priest; for it is written, *'You shall not speak evil of a ruler of your people.'*" *

6But when Paul perceived that one part were Sadducees and the other Pharisees, he cried out in the council, "Men *and* brethren, I am a Pharisee, the son of a Pharisee; concerning the hope and resurrection of the dead I am being judged!"

7And when he had said this, a dissension arose between the Pharisees and the Sadducees; and the assembly was divided. 8For Sadducees say that there is no resurrection—and no angel or spirit; but the Pharisees confess both. 9Then there arose a loud outcry. And the scribes of the Pharisees' party arose and protested, saying, "We find no evil in this man; but if a spirit or an angel has spoken to him, let us not fight against God."*

10Now when there arose a great dissension, the commander, fearing lest Paul might be pulled to pieces by them, commanded the soldiers to go down and take him by force from among them, and bring *him* into the barracks.

PSALM 2:1-12

WHY do the nations rage,
And the people plot a vain thing?
2   The kings of the earth set themselves,
And the rulers take counsel together,
Against the LORD and against His Anointed, *saying,*
3   "Let us break Their bonds in pieces
And cast away Their cords from us."

4 He who sits in the heavens
    shall laugh;
  The LORD shall hold them in
    derision.
5 Then He shall speak to them
    in His wrath,
  And distress them in His deep
    displeasure:
6 "Yet I have set My King
  On My holy hill of Zion."

7 "I will declare the decree:
  The LORD has said to Me,
  'You *are* My Son,
  Today I have begotten You.
8 Ask of Me, and I will give *You*
  The nations *for* Your
    inheritance,
  And the ends of the earth *for*
    Your possession.

9 You shall break* them with a
    rod of iron;
  You shall dash them to pieces
    like a potter's vessel.' "

10 Now therefore, be wise,
    O kings;
  Be instructed, you judges of
    the earth.
11 Serve the LORD with fear,
  And rejoice with trembling.
12 Kiss the Son,* lest He* be
    angry,
  And you perish *in* the way,
  When His wrath is kindled
    but a little.
  Blessed *are* all those who put
    their trust in Him.

PROVERBS FOR TODAY/ 18:13

He who answers a matter before he hears it, *it* is *folly and shame to him.*

JULY 5

1 CHRONICLES 1:1–2:17

ADAM, Seth, Enosh, [2]Cainan,*
Mahalalel, Jared, [3]Enoch,
Methuselah, Lamech, [4]Noah,*
Shem, Ham, and Japheth.

[5]The sons of Japheth *were* Gomer,
Magog, Madai, Javan, Tubal, Meshech, and Tiras. [6]The sons of Gomer
were Ashkenaz, Diphath,* and Togarmah. [7]The sons of Javan *were* Elishah,
Tarshishah,* Kittim, and Rodanim.*

[8]The sons of Ham *were* Cush, Mizraim, Put, and Canaan. [9]The sons of
Cush *were* Seba, Havilah, Sabta,*
Raama,* and Sabtecha. The sons of
Raama *were* Sheba and Dedan. [10]Cush
begot Nimrod; he began to be a mighty
one on the earth. [11]Mizraim begot

Ludim, Anamim, Lehabim, Naphtuhim,
[12]Pathrusim, Casluhim (from whom
came the Philistines and the Caphtorim). [13]Canaan begot Sidon, his firstborn, and Heth; [14]the Jebusite, the
Amorite, and the Girgashite; [15]the
Hivite, the Arkite, and the Sinite; [16]the
Arvadite, the Zemarite, and the Hamathite.

[17]The sons of Shem *were* Elam,
Asshur, Arphaxad, Lud, Aram, Uz,
Hul, Gether, and Meshech.* [18]Arphaxad begot Shelah, and Shelah begot Eber. [19]To Eber were born two
sons: the name of one *was* Peleg,* for
in his days the earth was divided; and
his brother's name *was* Joktan.
[20]Joktan begot Almodad, Sheleph, Hazarmaveth, Jerah, [21]Hadoram, Uzal,

Diklah, ²²Ebal,* Abimael, Sheba, ²³Ophir, Havilah, and Jobab. All these *were* the sons of Joktan.

²⁴Shem, Arphaxad, Shelah, ²⁵Eber, Peleg, Reu, ²⁶Serug, Nahor, Terah, ²⁷and Abram, who *is* Abraham. ²⁸The sons of Abraham *were* Isaac and Ishmael.

²⁹These *are* their genealogies: The firstborn of Ishmael *was* Nebajoth; then Kedar, Adbeel, Mibsam, ³⁰Mishma, Dumah, Massa, Hadad,* Tema, ³¹Jetur, Naphish, and Kedemah. These *were* the sons of Ishmael.

³²Now the sons born to Keturah, Abraham's concubine, *were* Zimran, Jokshan, Medan, Midian, Ishbak, and Shuah. The sons of Jokshan *were* Sheba and Dedan. ³³The sons of Midian *were* Ephah, Epher, Hanoch, Abida, and Eldaah. All these were the children of Keturah.

³⁴And Abraham begot Isaac. The sons of Isaac *were* Esau and Israel. ³⁵The sons of Esau *were* Eliphaz, Reuel, Jeush, Jaalam, and Korah. ³⁶And the sons of Eliphaz *were* Teman, Omar, Zephi,* Gatam, *and* Kenaz; and *by* Timna,* Amalek. ³⁷The sons of Reuel *were* Nahath, Zerah, Shammah, and Mizzah.

³⁸The sons of Seir *were* Lotan, Shobal, Zibeon, Anah, Dishon, Ezer, and Dishan. ³⁹And the sons of Lotan *were* Hori and Homam; Lotan's sister *was* Timna. ⁴⁰The sons of Shobal *were* Alian,* Manahath, Ebal, Shephi,* and Onam. The sons of Zibeon *were* Ajah and Anah. ⁴¹The son of Anah *was* Dishon. The sons of Dishon *were* Hamran,* Eshban, Ithran, and Cheran. ⁴²The sons of Ezer *were* Bilhan, Zaavan, *and* Jaakan.* The sons of Dishan *were* Uz and Aran.

⁴³Now these *were* the kings who reigned in the land of Edom before a king reigned over the children of Israel: Bela the son of Beor, and the name of his city was Dinhabah. ⁴⁴And when Bela died, Jobab the son of Zerah of Bozrah reigned in his place. ⁴⁵When Jobab died, Husham of the land of the Temanites reigned in his place. ⁴⁶And when Husham died, Hadad the son of Bedad, who attacked Midian in the field of Moab, reigned in his place. The name of his city *was* Avith. ⁴⁷When Hadad died, Samlah of Masrekah reigned in his place. ⁴⁸And when Samlah died, Saul of Rehoboth-by-the-River reigned in his place. ⁴⁹When Saul died, Baal-Hanan the son of Achbor reigned in his place. ⁵⁰And when Baal-Hanan died, Hadad* reigned in his place; and the name of his city was Pai.* His wife's name was Mehetabel the daughter of Matred, the daughter of Mezahab. ⁵¹Hadad died also. And the chiefs of Edom were Chief Timnah, Chief Aliah,* Chief Jetheth, ⁵²Chief Aholibamah, Chief Elah, Chief Pinon, ⁵³Chief Kenaz, Chief Teman, Chief Mibzar, ⁵⁴Chief Magdiel, and Chief Iram. These *were* the chiefs of Edom.

THESE *were* the sons of Israel: Reuben, Simeon, Levi, Judah, Issachar, Zebulun, ²Dan, Joseph, Benjamin, Naphtali, Gad, and Asher.

³The sons of Judah *were* Er, Onan, and Shelah. *These* three were born to him by the daughter of Shua, the Canaanitess. Er, the firstborn of Judah, was wicked in the sight of the LORD; so He killed him. ⁴And Tamar, his daughter-in-law, bore him Perez and Zerah. All the sons of Judah *were* five.

⁵The sons of Perez *were* Hezron and Hamul. ⁶The sons of Zerah *were* Zimri, Ethan, Heman, Calcol, and Dara—five of them in all.

⁷The son of Carmi *was* Achar,* the troubler of Israel, who transgressed in the accursed thing.

⁸The son of Ethan *was* Azariah.

⁹Also the sons of Hezron who were born to him *were* Jerahmeel, Ram, and Chelubai.* ¹⁰Ram begot Amminadab, and Amminadab begot Nahshon, leader of the children of Judah; ¹¹Nah-

shon begot Salma,* and Salma begot Boaz; 12Boaz begot Obed, and Obed begot Jesse; 13Jesse begot Eliab his firstborn, Abinadab the second, Shimea* the third, 14Nethanel the fourth, Raddai the fifth, 15Ozem the sixth, *and* David the seventh.

16Now their sisters *were* Zeruiah and Abigail. And the sons of Zeruiah *were* Abishai, Joab, and Asahel—three. 17Abigail bore Amasa; and the father of Amasa *was* Jether the Ishmaelite.*

ACTS 23:11-35

But the following night the Lord stood by him [Paul] and said, "Be of good cheer, Paul; for as you have testified for Me in Jerusalem, so you must also bear witness at Rome."

12And when it was day, some of the Jews banded together and bound themselves under an oath, saying that they would neither eat nor drink till they had killed Paul. 13Now there were more than forty who had formed this conspiracy. 14They came to the chief priests and elders, and said, "We have bound ourselves under a great oath that we will eat nothing until we have killed Paul. 15Now you, therefore, together with the council, suggest to the commander that he be brought down to you tomorrow,* as though you were going to make further inquiries concerning him; but we are ready to kill him before he comes near."

16So when Paul's sister's son heard of their ambush, he went and entered the barracks and told Paul. 17Then Paul called one of the centurions to *him* and said, "Take this young man to the commander, for he has something to tell him." 18So he took him and brought *him* to the commander and said, "Paul the prisoner called me to *him* and asked *me* to bring this young man to you. He has something to say to you."

19Then the commander took him by the hand, went aside, and asked privately, "What is it that you have to tell me?"

20And he said, "The Jews have agreed to ask that you bring Paul down to the council tomorrow, as though they were going to inquire more fully about him. 21But do not yield to them, for more than forty of them lie in wait for him, men who have bound themselves by an oath that they will neither eat nor drink till they have killed him; and now they are ready, waiting for the promise from you."

22So the commander let the young man depart, and commanded *him,* "Tell no one that you have revealed these things to me."

23And he called for two centurions, saying, "Prepare two hundred soldiers, seventy horsemen, and two hundred spearmen to go to Caesarea at the third hour of the night; 24and provide mounts to set Paul on, and bring *him* safely to Felix the governor." 25He wrote a letter in the following manner:

26 Claudius Lysias,

To the most excellent governor Felix:

Greetings.

27 This man was seized by the Jews and was about to be killed by them. Coming with the troops I rescued him, having learned that he was a Roman. 28And when I wanted to know the reason they accused him, I brought him before their council. 29I found out that he was accused concerning questions of their law, but had nothing charged against him deserving of death or chains. 30And when it was told me that the Jews lay in wait for the man,* I sent

him immediately to you, and also commanded his accusers to state before you the charges against him.

Farewell.

[31]Then the soldiers, as they were commanded, took Paul and brought *him* by night to Antipatris. [32]The next day they left the horsemen to go on with him, and returned to the barracks. [33]When they came to Caesarea and had delivered the letter to the governor, they also presented Paul to him. [34]And when the governor had read *it,* he asked what province he was from. And when he understood that *he was* from Cilicia, [35]he said, "I will hear you when your accusers also have come." And he commanded him to be kept in Herod's Praetorium.

PSALM 3:1-8

A Psalm of David when he fled from Absalom his son.

L ORD, how they have increased who trouble me! Many *are* they who rise up against me.

2 Many *are* they who say of me, *"There is* no help for him in God." Selah

3 But You, O LORD, *are* a shield for me, My glory and the One who lifts up my head.
4 I cried to the LORD with my voice, And He heard me from His holy hill. Selah

5 I lay down and slept; I awoke, for the LORD sustained me.
6 I will not be afraid of ten thousands of people Who have set *themselves* against me all around.

7 Arise, O LORD; Save me, O my God! For You have struck all my enemies on the cheekbone; You have broken the teeth of the ungodly.
8 Salvation *belongs* to the LORD. Your blessing *is* upon Your people. Selah

PROVERBS FOR TODAY/ 18:14-15

The spirit of a man will sustain him in sickness, but who can bear a broken spirit? The heart of the prudent acquires knowledge, and the ear of the wise seeks knowledge.

JULY 6

1 CHRONICLES 2:18–4:4

C ALEB the son of Hezron had children by Azubah, *his* wife, and by Jerioth. Now these were her sons: Jesher, Shobab, and Ardon. [19]When Azubah died, Caleb took Eph-

rath* as his wife, who bore him Hur. [20]And Hur begot Uri, and Uri begot Bezalel.

[21]Now afterward Hezron went in to the daughter of Machir the father of Gilead, whom he married when he *was*

sixty years old; and she bore him Segub. 22Segub begot Jair, who had twenty-three cities in the land of Gilead. 23(Geshur and Syria took from them the towns of Jair, with Kenath and its towns—sixty towns.) All these *belonged to* the sons of Machir the father of Gilead. 24After Hezron died in Caleb Ephrathah, Hezron's wife Abijah bore him Ashhur the father of Tekoa.

25The sons of Jerahmeel, the firstborn of Hezron, *were* Ram, the firstborn, and Bunah, Oren, Ozem, *and* Ahijah. 26Jerahmeel had another wife, whose name was Atarah; she was the mother of Onam. 27The sons of Ram, the firstborn of Jerahmeel, were Maaz, Jamin, and Eker. 28The sons of Onam were Shammai and Jada. The sons of Shammai *were* Nadab and Abishur.

29And the name of the wife of Abishur *was* Abihail, and she bore him Ahban and Molid. 30The sons of Nadab *were* Seled and Appaim; Seled died without children. 31The son of Appaim *was* Ishi, the son of Ishi *was* Sheshan, and Sheshan's son *was* Ahlai. 32The sons of Jada, the brother of Shammai, *were* Jether and Jonathan; Jether died without children. 33The sons of Jonathan *were* Peleth and Zaza. These were the sons of Jerahmeel.

34Now Sheshan had no sons, only daughters. And Sheshan had an Egyptian servant whose name *was* Jarha. 35Sheshan gave his daughter to Jarha his servant as wife, and she bore him Attai. 36Attai begot Nathan, and Nathan begot Zabad; 37Zabad begot Ephlal, and Ephlal begot Obed; 38Obed begot Jehu, and Jehu begot Azariah; 39Azariah begot Helez, and Helez begot Eleasah; 40Eleasah begot Sismai, and Sismai begot Shallum; 41Shallum begot Jekamiah, and Jekamiah begot Elishama.

42The descendants of Caleb the brother of Jerahmeel *were* Mesha, his firstborn, who was the father of Ziph, and the sons of Mareshah the father of Hebron. 43The sons of Hebron *were* Korah, Tappuah, Rekem, and Shema. 44Shema begot Raham the father of Jorkoam, and Rekem begot Shammai. 45And the son of Shammai *was* Maon, and Maon *was* the father of Beth Zur.

46Ephah, Caleb's concubine, bore Haran, Moza, and Gazez; and Haran begot Gazez. 47And the sons of Jahdai *were* Regem, Jotham, Geshan, Pelet, Ephah, and Shaaph.

48Maachah, Caleb's concubine, bore Sheber and Tirhanah. 49She also bore Shaaph the father of Madmannah, Sheva the father of Machbenah and the father of Gibea. And the daughter of Caleb *was* Achsah.

50These were the descendants of Caleb: The sons of Hur, the firstborn of Ephrathah, *were* Shobal the father of Kirjath Jearim, 51Salma the father of Bethlehem, *and* Hareph the father of Beth Gader.

52And Shobal the father of Kirjath Jearim had descendants: Haroeh, *and* half of the families of Manuhoth.* 53The families of Kirjath Jearim *were* the Ithrites, the Puthites, the Shumathites, and the Mishraites. From these came the Zorathites and the Eshtaolites.

54The sons of Salma *were* Bethlehem, the Netophathites, Atroth Beth Joab, half of the Manahethites, and the Zorites. 55And the families of the scribes who dwelt at Jabez *were* the Tirathites, the Shimeathites, *and* the Suchathites. These *were* the Kenites who came from Hammath, the father of the house of Rechab.

Now these were the sons of David who were born to him in Hebron: The firstborn *was* Amnon, by Ahinoam the Jezreelitess; the second, Daniel,* by Abigail the Carmelitess; 2the third, Absalom the son of Maacah, the daughter of Talmai, king of Geshur; the fourth,

Adonijah the son of Haggith; ³the fifth, Shephatiah, by Abital; the sixth, Ithream, by his wife Eglah.

⁴*These* six were born to him in Hebron. There he reigned seven years and six months, and in Jerusalem he reigned thirty-three years. ⁵And these were born to him in Jerusalem: Shimea,* Shobab, Nathan, and Solomon—four by Bathshua* the daughter of Ammiel.* ⁶Also *there* were Ibhar, Elishama,* Eliphelet,* ⁷Nogah, Nepheg, Japhia, ⁸Elishama, Eliada,* and Eliphelet—nine *in all.* ⁹*These were* all the sons of David, besides the sons of the concubines, and Tamar their sister.

¹⁰Solomon's son *was* Rehoboam; Abijah* *was* his son, Asa his son, Jehoshaphat his son, ¹¹Joram* his son, Ahaziah his son, Joash* his son, ¹²Amaziah his son, Azariah* his son, Jotham his son, ¹³Ahaz his son, Hezekiah his son, Manasseh his son, ¹⁴Amon his son, *and* Josiah his son. ¹⁵The sons of Josiah *were* Johanan the firstborn, the second Jehoiakim, the third Zedekiah, and the fourth Shallum.* ¹⁶The sons of Jehoiakim *were* Jeconiah his son *and* Zedekiah* his son.

¹⁷And the sons of Jeconiah* *were* Assir,* Shealtiel his son, ¹⁸*and* Malchiram, Pedaiah, Shenazzar, Jecamiah, Hoshama, and Nedabiah. ¹⁹The sons of Pedaiah *were* Zerubbabel and Shimei. The sons of Zerubbabel *were* Meshullam, Hananiah, Shelomith their sister, ²⁰and Hashubah, Ohel, Berechiah, Hasadiah, and Jushab-Hesed—five *in all.*

²¹The sons of Hananiah *were* Pelatiah and Jeshaiah, the sons of Rephaiah, the sons of Arnan, the sons of Obadiah, and the sons of Shechaniah. ²²The son of Shechaniah was Shemaiah. The sons of Shemaiah *were* Hattush, Igal, Bariah, Neariah, and Shaphat—six *in all.* ²³The sons of Neariah *were* Elioenai, Hezekiah, and Azrikam—three *in all.* ²⁴The sons of Elioenai *were* Hodaviah, Eliashib, Pela-

iah, Akkub, Johanan, Delaiah, and Anani—seven *in all.*

THE sons of Judah *were* Perez, Hezron, Carmi, Hur, and Shobal. ²And Reaiah the son of Shobal begot Jahath, and Jahath begot Ahumai and Lahad. These *were* the families of the Zorathites. ³These *were* the sons *of the father* of Etam: Jezreel, Ishma, and Idbash; and the name of their sister *was* Hazelelponi; ⁴and Penuel *was* the father of Gedor, and Ezer *was* the father of Hushah.

These *were* the sons of Hur, the firstborn of Ephrathah the father of Bethlehem.

ACTS 24:1-27

N ow after five days Ananias the high priest came down with the elders and a certain orator *named* Tertullus. These gave evidence to the governor against Paul.

²And when he was called upon, Tertullus began his accusation, saying: "Seeing that through you we enjoy great peace, and prosperity is being brought to this nation by your foresight, ³we accept *it* always and in all places, most noble Felix, with all thankfulness. ⁴Nevertheless, not to be tedious to you any further, I beg you to hear, by your courtesy, a few words from us. ⁵For we have found this man a plague, a creator of dissension among all the Jews throughout the world, and a ringleader of the sect of the Nazarenes. ⁶He even tried to profane the temple, and we seized him,* and wanted to judge him according to our law. ⁷But the commander Lysias came by and with great violence took *him* out of our hands, ⁸commanding his accusers to come to you. By examining him yourself you may ascertain all these things of which we accuse him." ⁹And the Jews also assented,* maintaining that these things were so.

¹⁰Then Paul, after the governor had nodded to him to speak, answered: "Inasmuch as I know that you have been for many years a judge of this nation, I do the more cheerfully answer for myself, ¹¹because you may ascertain that it is no more than twelve days since I went up to Jerusalem to worship. ¹²And they neither found me in the temple disputing with anyone nor inciting the crowd, either in the synagogues or in the city. ¹³Nor can they prove the things of which they now accuse me. ¹⁴But this I confess to you, that according to the Way which they call a sect, so I worship the God of my fathers, believing all things which are written in the Law and in the Prophets, ¹⁵I have hope in God, which they themselves also accept, that there will be a resurrection of *the* dead,* both of *the* just and *the* unjust. ¹⁶This *being* so, I myself always strive to have a conscience without offense toward God and men.

¹⁷"Now after many years I came to bring alms and offerings to my nation, ¹⁸in the midst of which some Jews from Asia found me purified in the temple, neither with a mob nor with tumult. ¹⁹They ought to have been here before you to object if they had anything against me. ²⁰Or else let those who are *here* themselves say if they found any wrongdoing* in me while I stood before the council, ²¹unless *it is* for this one statement which I cried out, standing among them, 'Concerning the resurrection of the dead I am being judged by you this day.' "

²²But when Felix heard these things, having more accurate knowledge of *the* Way, he adjourned the proceedings and said, "When Lysias the commander comes down, I will make a decision on your case." ²³So he commanded the centurion to keep Paul and to let *him* have liberty, and told him not to forbid any of his friends to provide for or visit him.

²⁴And after some days, when Felix came with his wife Drusilla, who was Jewish, he sent for Paul and heard him concerning the faith in Christ. ²⁵Now as he reasoned about righteousness, self-control, and the judgment to come, Felix was afraid and answered, "Go away for now; when I have a convenient time I will call for you." ²⁶Meanwhile he also hoped that money would be given him by Paul, that he might release him.* Therefore he sent for him more often and conversed with him.

²⁷But after two years Porcius Festus succeeded Felix; and Felix, wanting to do the Jews a favor, left Paul bound.

PSALM 4:1-8

To the Chief Musician. With stringed instruments. A Psalm of David.

Hear me when I call, O God of
    my righteousness!
You have relieved me in *my*
    distress;
Have mercy on me, and hear
    my prayer.

2   How long, O you sons of men,
    Will you turn my glory to
        shame?
    How long will you love
        worthlessness
    And seek falsehood?   Selah

3   But know that the LORD has
        set apart* for Himself him
        who is godly;
    The LORD will hear when I call
        to Him.

4   Be angry, and do not sin.
    Meditate within your heart on
        your bed, and be still. Selah
5   Offer the sacrifices of
        righteousness,
    And put your trust in the LORD.

6   *There are* many who say,
    "Who will show us *any* good?"

LORD, lift up the light of Your
countenance upon us.
7 You have put gladness in my
heart,
More than in the season that

their grain and wine
increased.
8 I will both lie down in peace,
and sleep;
For You alone, O LORD, make
me dwell in safety.

PROVERBS FOR TODAY/ 18:16-18

A man's gift makes room for him, and brings him before great men. □ *The first one to plead his cause seems right, until his neighbor comes and examines him.* □ *Casting lots causes contentions to cease, and keeps the mighty apart.*

JULY 7

1 CHRONICLES 4:5–5:17

AND Ashhur the father of Tekoa had two wives, Helah and Naarah. 6Naarah bore him Ahuzzam, Hepher, Temeni, and Haahashtari. These *were* the sons of Naarah. 7The sons of Helah *were* Zereth, Zohar, and Ethnan; 8and Koz begot Anub, Zobebah, and the families of Aharhel the son of Harum.

9Now Jabez was more honorable than his brothers, and his mother called his name Jabez,* saying, "Because I bore *him* in pain." 10And Jabez called on the God of Israel saying, "Oh, that You would bless me indeed, and enlarge my territory, that Your hand would be with me, and that You would keep *me* from evil, that I may not cause pain!" So God granted him what he requested.

11Chelub the brother of Shuhah begot Mehir, who *was* the father of Eshton. 12And Eshton begot Beth-Rapha, Paseah, and Tehinnah the father of Ir-Nahash. These *were* the men of Rechah.

13The sons of Kenaz *were* Othniel and Seraiah. The sons of Othniel *were* Hathath,* 14and Meonothai *who* begot

Ophrah. Seraiah begot Joab the father of Ge Harashim,* for they were craftsmen. 15The sons of Caleb the son of Jephunneh *were* Iru, Elah, and Naam. The son of Elah *was* Kenaz. 16The sons of Jehallelel *were* Ziph, Ziphah, Tiria, and Asarel. 17The sons of Ezrah *were* Jether, Mered, Epher, and Jalon. And *Mered's wife** *bore* Miriam, Shammai, and Ishbah the father of Eshtemoa. 18(His wife Jehudijah* bore Jered the father of Gedor, Heber the father of Sochoh, and Jekuthiel the father of Zanoah.) And these were the sons of Bithiah the daughter of Pharaoh, whom Mered took.

19The sons of Hodiah's wife, the sister of Naham, *were* the fathers of Keilah the Garmite and of Eshtemoa the Maachathite. 20And the sons of Shimon *were* Amnon, Rinnah, Ben-Hanan, and Tilon. And the sons of Ishi *were* Zoheth and Ben-Zoheth.

21The sons of Shelah the son of Judah *were* Er the father of Lecah, Laadah the father of Mareshah, and the families of the house of the linen workers of the house of Ashbea; 22also Jokim, the men of Chozeba, and Joash; Saraph, who ruled in Moab, and Jashubi-Lehem. Now the records are ancient. 23These *were* the potters and those who dwell at Netaim* and Gederah;* there they dwelt with the king for his work.

24The sons of Simeon *were* Nemuel, Jamin, Jarib,* Zerah,* *and* Shaul, 25Shallum his son, Mibsam his son, and Mishma his son. 26And the sons of Mishma *were* Hamuel his son, Zacchur his son, and Shimei his son. 27Shimei had sixteen sons and six daughters; but his brothers did not have many children, nor did any of their families multiply as much as the children of Judah.

28They dwelt at Beersheba, Moladah, Hazar Shual, 29Bilhah, Ezem, Tolad, 30Bethuel, Hormah, Ziklag, 31Beth Marcaboth, Hazar Susim, Beth Biri, and at Shaaraim. These *were* their cities until the reign of David. 32And their villages *were* Etam, Ain, Rimmon, Tochen, and Ashan—five cities— 33and all the villages that *were* around these cities as far as Baal.* These *were* their dwelling places, and they maintained their genealogy: 34Meshobab, Jamlech, and Joshah the son of Amaziah, 35Joel, and Jehu the son of Joshibiah, the son of Seraiah, the son of Asiel; 36Elioenai, Jaakobah, Jeshohaiah, Asaiah, Adiel, Jesimiel, and Benaiah; 37Ziza the son of Shiphi, the son of Allon, the son of Jedaiah, the son of Shimri, the son of Shemaiah— 38these mentioned by name *were* leaders in their families, and their father's house increased greatly.

39So they went to the entrance of Gedor, as far as the east side of the valley, to seek pasture for their flocks. 40And they found rich, good pasture, and the land *was* broad, quiet, and peaceful; for some Hamites formerly lived there.

41These recorded by name came in the days of Hezekiah king of Judah; and they attacked their tents and the Meunites who were found there, and utterly destroyed them, as it is to this day. So they dwelt in their place, because *there was* pasture for their flocks there. 42Now *some* of them, five hundred men of the sons of Simeon, went to Mount Seir, having as their captains Pelatiah, Neariah, Rephaiah, and Uzziel, the sons of Ishi. 43And they defeated the rest of the Amalekites who had escaped. They have dwelt there to this day.

Now the sons of Reuben the firstborn of Israel—he *was* indeed the firstborn, but because he defiled his father's bed, his birthright was given to the sons of Joseph, the son of Israel, so that the genealogy is not listed according to the birthright; 2yet Judah prevailed over his brothers, and from him *came* a ruler, although the birthright was Joseph's— 3the sons of Reuben the firstborn of Israel were Hanoch, Pallu, Hezron, and Carmi.

4The sons of Joel *were* Shemaiah his son, Gog his son, Shimei his son, 5Micah his son, Reaiah his son, Baal his son, 6and Beerah his son, whom Tiglath-Pileser* king of Assyria carried into captivity. He *was* leader of the Reubenites. 7And his brethren by their families, when the genealogy of their generations was registered: the chief, Jeiel, and Zechariah, 8and Bela the son of Azaz, the son of Shema, the son of Joel, who dwelt in Aroer, as far as Nebo and Baal Meon. 9Eastward they settled as far as the entrance of the wilderness this side of the River Euphrates, because their cattle had multiplied in the land of Gilead.

10Now in the days of Saul they made war with the Hagrites, who fell by their hand; and they dwelt in their tents throughout the entire *area* east of Gilead.

11And the children of Gad dwelt next to them in the land of Bashan as far as Salcah: 12Joel *was* the chief, Shapham the next, then Jaanai and Shaphat in Bashan, 13and their brethren of their father's house: Michael, Meshullam, Sheba, Jorai, Jachan, Zia, and Eber—seven *in all.* 14These *were* the children of Abihail the son of Huri, the son of Jaroah, the son of Gilead, the son of Michael, the son of Jeshishai, the son of Jahdo, the son of Buz; 15Ahi the son of Abdiel, the son of Guni, *was* chief of their father's house. 16And *the Gadites* dwelt in Gilead, in Bashan and in its villages, and in all the common-lands of Sharon within their borders. 17All these were registered by genealogies in the days of Jotham king of Judah, and in the days of Jeroboam king of Israel.

ACTS 25:1-27

Now when Festus had come to the province, after three days he went up from Caesarea to Jerusalem. 2Then the high priest* and the chief men of the Jews informed him against Paul; and they petitioned him, 3asking a favor against him, that he would summon him to Jerusalem—while *they* lay in ambush along the road to kill him. 4But Festus answered that Paul should be kept at Caesarea, and that he himself was going *there* shortly. 5"Therefore," he said, "let those who have authority among you go down with *me* and accuse this man, to see if there is any fault in him."

6And when he had remained among them more than ten days, he went down to Caesarea. And the next day, sitting on the judgment seat, he commanded Paul to be brought. 7When he had come, the Jews who had come down from Jerusalem stood about and laid many serious complaints against Paul, which they could not prove, 8while he answered for himself, "Neither against the law of the Jews, nor against the temple, nor against Caesar have I offended in anything at all."

9But Festus, wanting to do the Jews a favor, answered Paul and said, "Are you willing to go up to Jerusalem and there be judged before me concerning these things?"

10So Paul said, "I stand at Caesar's judgment seat, where I ought to be judged. To the Jews I have done no wrong, as you very well know. 11For if I am an offender, or have committed anything deserving of death, I do not object to dying; but if there is nothing in these things of which these men accuse me, no one can deliver me to them. I appeal to Caesar."

12Then Festus, when he had conferred with the council, answered, "You have appealed to Caesar? To Caesar you shall go!"

13And after some days King Agrippa and Bernice came to Caesarea to greet Festus. 14When they had been there many days, Festus laid Paul's case before the king, saying: "There is a certain man left a prisoner by Felix, 15about whom the chief priests and the elders of the Jews informed *me,* when I was in Jerusalem, asking for a judgment against him. 16To them I answered, 'It is not the custom of the Romans to deliver any man to destruction* before the accused meets the accusers face to face, and has opportunity to answer for himself concerning the charge against him.' 17Therefore when they had come together, without any delay, the next day I sat on the judgment seat and commanded the man to be brought in. 18When the accusers stood up, they brought no accusation against him of such things as I supposed, 19but had some questions against him about their own religion and about a certain Jesus, who had died, whom Paul affirmed to be alive. 20And because I was uncertain of such questions, I asked whether he was willing to go to Jerusalem and there be judged concerning these matters. 21But when Paul appealed to be reserved for the decision of Augustus, I commanded him to be kept till I could send him to Caesar."

²²Then Agrippa said to Festus, "I also would like to hear the man myself."

"Tomorrow," he said, "you shall hear him."

²³So the next day, when Agrippa and Bernice had come with great pomp, and had entered the auditorium with the commanders and the prominent men of the city, at Festus' command Paul was brought in. ²⁴And Festus said: "King Agrippa and all the men who are here present with us, you see this man about whom the whole assembly of the Jews petitioned me, both at Jerusalem and here, crying out that he was not fit to live any longer. ²⁵But when I found that he had committed nothing deserving of death, and that he himself had appealed to Augustus, I decided to send him. ²⁶I have nothing certain to write to my lord concerning him. Therefore I have brought him out before you, and especially before you, King Agrippa, so that after the examination has taken place I may have something to write. ²⁷For it seems to me unreasonable to send a prisoner and not to specify the charges against him."

PSALM 5:1-12

To the Chief Musician. With flutes.* A Psalm of David.

GIVE ear to my words, O LORD,
Consider my meditation.
²Give heed to the voice of my
cry,
My King and my God,
For to You I will pray.
3 My voice You shall hear in the
morning, O LORD;
In the morning I will direct *it*
to You,
And I will look up.

4 For You *are* not a God who
takes pleasure in
wickedness,

Nor shall evil dwell with You.
5 The boastful shall not stand in
Your sight;
You hate all workers of
iniquity.
6 You shall destroy those who
speak falsehood;
The LORD abhors the
bloodthirsty and deceitful
man.

7 But as for me, I will come into
Your house in the multitude
of Your mercy;
In fear of You I will worship
toward Your holy temple.
8 Lead me, O LORD, in Your
righteousness because of
my enemies;
Make Your way straight
before my face.

9 For *there is* no faithfulness in
their mouth;
Their inward part *is*
destruction;
Their throat *is* an open tomb;
They flatter with their tongue.
10 Pronounce them guilty,
O God!
Let them fall by their own
counsels;
Cast them out in the
multitude of their
transgressions,
For they have rebelled
against You.

11 But let all those rejoice who
put their trust in You;
Let them ever shout for joy,
because You defend them;
Let those also who love Your
name
Be joyful in You.
12 For You, O LORD, will bless the
righteous;
With favor You will surround
him as *with* a shield.

PROVERBS FOR TODAY/ 18:19

A brother offended is harder to win *than a strong city, and contentions* are *like the bars of a castle.*

JULY 8

1 CHRONICLES 5:18–6:81

THE sons of Reuben, the Gadites, and half the tribe of Manasseh *had* forty-four thousand seven hundred and sixty valiant men, men able to bear shield and sword, to shoot with the bow, and skillful in war, who went to war. 19They made war with the Hagrites, Jetur, Naphish, and Nodab. 20And they were helped against them, and the Hagrites were delivered into their hand, and all who *were* with them, for they cried out to God in the battle. He heeded their prayer, because they put their trust in Him. 21Then they took away their livestock—fifty thousand of their camels, two hundred and fifty thousand of their sheep, and two thousand of their donkeys—also one hundred thousand of their men; 22for many fell dead, because the war *was* God's. And they dwelt in their place until the captivity.

23So the children of the half-tribe of Manasseh dwelt in the land. Their *numbers* increased from Bashan to Baal Hermon, that is, to Senir, or Mount Hermon. 24These *were* the heads of their fathers' houses: Epher, Ishi, Eliel, Azriel, Jeremiah, Hodaviah, and Jahdiel. They were mighty men of valor, famous men, *and* heads of their fathers' houses.

25And they were unfaithful to the God of their fathers, and played the harlot after the gods of the peoples of the land, whom God had destroyed before them. 26So the God of Israel stirred up the spirit of Pul king of As-syria, that is, Tiglath-Pileser* king of Assyria. He carried the Reubenites, the Gadites, and the half-tribe of Manasseh into captivity. He took them to Halah, Habor, Hara, and the river of Gozan to this day.

THE sons of Levi *were* Gershon, Kohath, and Merari. 2The sons of Kohath *were* Amram, Izhar, Hebron, and Uzziel. 3The children of Amram *were* Aaron, Moses, and Miriam. And the sons of Aaron *were* Nadab, Abihu, Eleazar, and Ithamar. 4Eleazar begot Phinehas, *and* Phinehas begot Abishua; 5Abishua begot Bukki, and Bukki begot Uzzi; 6Uzzi begot Zera-hiah, and Zerahiah begot Meraioth; 7Meraioth begot Amariah, and Ama-riah begot Ahitub; 8Ahitub begot Zadok, and Zadok begot Ahimaaz; 9Ahimaaz begot Azariah, and Azariah begot Johanan; 10Johanan begot Aza-riah (it was he who ministered as priest in the temple that Solomon built in Jerusalem); 11Azariah begot Ama-riah, and Amariah begot Ahitub; 12Ahitub begot Zadok, and Zadok be-got Shallum; 13Shallum begot Hilkiah, and Hilkiah begot Azariah; 14Azariah begot Seraiah, and Seraiah begot Je-hozadak. 15Jehozadak went *into captiv-ity* when the LORD carried Judah and Jerusalem into captivity by the hand of Nebuchadnezzar.

16The sons of Levi *were* Gershon,* Kohath, and Merari. 17These are the names of the sons of Gershon: Libni and Shimei. 18The sons of Kohath *were*

Amram, Izhar, Hebron, and Uzziel. ¹⁹The sons of Merari *were* Mahli and Mushi. Now these *are* the families of the Levites according to their fathers: ²⁰Of Gershon *were* Libni his son, Jahath his son, Zimmah his son, ²¹Joah his son, Iddo his son, Zerah his son, *and* Jeatherai his son. ²²The sons of Kohath *were* Amminadab his son, Korah his son, Assir his son, ²³Elkanah his son, Ebiasaph his son, Assir his son, ²⁴Tahath his son, Uriel his son, Uzziah his son, and Shaul his son. ²⁵The sons of Elkanah *were* Amasai and Ahimoth. ²⁶*As for* Elkanah,* the sons of Elkanah *were* Zophai* his son, Nahath* his son, ²⁷Eliab* his son, Jeroham his son, *and* Elkanah his son. ²⁸The sons of Samuel *were Joel** the firstborn, and Abijah the second.* ²⁹The sons of Merari *were* Mahli, Libni his son, Shimei his son, Uzzah his son, ³⁰Shimea his son, Haggiah his son, *and* Asaiah his son.

³¹Now these are the men whom David appointed over the service of song in the house of the LORD, after the ark came to rest. ³²They were ministering with music before the dwelling place of the tabernacle of meeting, until Solomon had built the house of the LORD in Jerusalem, and they served in their office according to their order.

³³And these *are* the ones who ministered with their sons: Of the sons of the Kohathites *were* Heman the singer, the son of Joel, the son of Samuel, ³⁴the son of Elkanah, the son of Jeroham, the son of Eliel,* the son of Toah,* ³⁵the son of Zuph, the son of Elkanah, the son of Mahath, the son of Amasai, ³⁶the son of Elkanah, the son of Joel, the son of Azariah, the son of Zephaniah, ³⁷the son of Tahath, the son of Assir, the son of Ebiasaph, the son of Korah, ³⁸the son of Izhar, the son of Kohath, the son of Levi, the son of Israel. ³⁹And his brother Asaph, who stood at his right hand, *was* Asaph the son of Berachiah, the son of Shimea,

⁴⁰the son of Michael, the son of Baaseiah, the son of Malchijah, ⁴¹the son of Ethni, the son of Zerah, the son of Adaiah, ⁴²the son of Ethan, the son of Zimmah, the son of Shimei, ⁴³the son of Jahath, the son of Gershon, the son of Levi.

⁴⁴Their brethren, the sons of Merari, on the left hand, *were* Ethan the son of Kishi, the son of Abdi, the son of Malluch, ⁴⁵the son of Hashabiah, the son of Amaziah, the son of Hilkiah, ⁴⁶the son of Amzi, the son of Bani, the son of Shamer, ⁴⁷the son of Mahli, the son of Mushi, the son of Merari, the son of Levi.

⁴⁸And their brethren, the Levites, *were* appointed to every kind of service of the tabernacle of the house of God.

⁴⁹But Aaron and his sons offered sacrifices on the altar of burnt offering and on the altar of incense, for all the work of the Most Holy *Place,* and to make atonement for Israel, according to all that Moses the servant of God had commanded. ⁵⁰Now these *are* the sons of Aaron: Eleazar his son, Phinehas his son, Abishua his son, ⁵¹Bukki his son, Uzzi his son, Zerahiah his son, ⁵²Meraioth his son, Amariah his son, Ahitub his son, ⁵³Zadok his son, *and* Ahimaaz his son.

⁵⁴Now these *are* their dwelling places throughout their settlements in their territory, for they were *given* by lot to the sons of Aaron, of the family of the Kohathites: ⁵⁵They gave them Hebron in the land of Judah, with its surrounding common-lands. ⁵⁶But the fields of the city and its villages they gave to Caleb the son of Jephunneh. ⁵⁷And to the sons of Aaron they gave *one of* the cities of refuge, Hebron; also Libnah with its common-lands, Jattir, Eshtemoa with its common-lands, ⁵⁸Hilen* with its common-lands, Debir with its common-lands, ⁵⁹Ashan* with its common-lands, and Beth Shemesh with its common-lands. ⁶⁰And from the

tribe of Benjamin: Geba with its common-lands, Alemeth* with its common-lands, and Anathoth with its common-lands. All their cities among their families *were* thirteen.

⁶¹To the rest of the family of the tribe of the Kohathites *they gave* by lot ten cities from half the tribe of Manasseh. ⁶²And to the sons of Gershon, throughout their families, *they gave* thirteen cities from the tribe of Issachar, from the tribe of Asher, from the tribe of Naphtali, and from the tribe of Manasseh in Bashan. ⁶³To the sons of Merari, throughout their families, *they gave* twelve cities from the tribe of Reuben, from the tribe of Gad, and from the tribe of Zebulun. ⁶⁴So the children of Israel gave *these* cities with their common-lands to the Levites. ⁶⁵And they gave by lot from the tribe of the children of Judah, from the tribe of the children of Simeon, and from the tribe of the children of Benjamin these cities which are called by *their* names.

⁶⁶Now some of the families of the sons of Kohath *were given* cities as their territory from the tribe of Ephraim. ⁶⁷And they gave them *one of* the cities of refuge, Shechem with its common-lands, in the mountains of Ephraim, also Gezer with its common-lands, ⁶⁸Jokmeam with its common-lands, Beth Horon with its common-lands, ⁶⁹Aijalon with its common-lands, and Gath Rimmon with its common-lands. ⁷⁰And from the half-tribe of Manasseh: Aner with its common-lands and Bileam with its common-lands, for the rest of the family of the sons of Kohath.

⁷¹From the family of the half-tribe of Manasseh the sons of Gershon *were given* Golan in Bashan with its common-lands and Ashtaroth with its common-lands. ⁷²And from the tribe of Issachar: Kedesh with its common-lands, Daberath with its common-lands, ⁷³Ramoth with its common-lands, and Anem with its common-lands.

⁷⁴And from the tribe of Asher: Mashal with its common-lands, Abdon with its common-lands, ⁷⁵Hukok with its common-lands, and Rehob with its common-lands. ⁷⁶And from the tribe of Naphtali: Kedesh in Galilee with its common-lands, Hammon with its common-lands, and Kirjathaim with its common-lands.

⁷⁷From the tribe of Zebulun the rest of the children of Merari *were given* Rimmon* with its common-lands and Tabor with its common-lands. ⁷⁸And on the other side of the Jordan, across from Jericho, on the east side of the Jordan, *they were given* from the tribe of Reuben: Bezer in the wilderness with its common-lands, Jahzah with its common-lands, ⁷⁹Kedemoth with its common-lands, and Mephaath with its common-lands. ⁸⁰And from the tribe of Gad: Ramoth in Gilead with its common-lands, Mahanaim with its common-lands, ⁸¹Heshbon with its common-lands, and Jazer with its common-lands.

ACTS 26:1-32

THEN Agrippa said to Paul, "You are permitted to speak for yourself."

So Paul stretched out his hand and answered for himself: ²"I think myself happy, King Agrippa, because today I shall answer for myself before you concerning all the things of which I am accused by the Jews, ³especially because you are expert in all customs and questions which have to do with the Jews. Therefore I beg you to hear me patiently.

⁴"My manner of life from my youth, which was spent from the beginning among my own nation at Jerusalem, all the Jews know. ⁵They knew me from the first, if they were willing to testify, that according to the strictest sect of our religion I lived a Pharisee. ⁶And now I stand and am judged for the

hope of the promise made by God to our fathers. 7To this *promise* our twelve tribes, earnestly serving *God* night and day, hope to attain. For this hope's sake, King Agrippa, I am accused by the Jews. 8Why should it be thought incredible by you that God raises the dead?

9"Indeed, I myself thought I must do many things contrary to the name of Jesus of Nazareth. 10This I also did in Jerusalem, and many of the saints I shut up in prison, having received authority from the chief priests; and when they were put to death, I cast my vote against *them*. 11And I punished them often in every synagogue and compelled *them* to blaspheme; and being exceedingly enraged against them, I persecuted *them* even to foreign cities.

12"While thus occupied, as I journeyed to Damascus with authority and commission from the chief priests, 13at midday, O king, along the road I saw a light from heaven, brighter than the sun, shining around me and those who journeyed with me. 14And when we all had fallen to the ground, I heard a voice speaking to me and saying in the Hebrew language, 'Saul, Saul, why are you persecuting Me? *It is* hard for you to kick against the goads.' 15So I said, 'Who are You, Lord?' And He said, 'I am Jesus, whom you are persecuting. 16But rise and stand on your feet; for I have appeared to you for this purpose, to make you a minister and a witness both of the things which you have seen and of the things which I will yet reveal to you. 17I will deliver you from the *Jewish* people, as well as *from* the Gentiles, to whom I now* send you, 18to open their eyes, *in order* to turn *them* from darkness to light, and *from* the power of Satan to God, that they may receive forgiveness of sins and an inheritance among those who are sanctified by faith in Me.'

19"Therefore, King Agrippa, I was not disobedient to the heavenly vision, 20but declared first to those in Damascus and in Jerusalem, and throughout all the region of Judea, and *then* to the Gentiles, that they should repent, turn to God, and do works befitting repentance. 21For these reasons the Jews seized me in the temple and tried to kill *me*. 22Therefore, having obtained help from God, to this day I stand, witnessing both to small and great, saying no other things than those which the prophets and Moses said would come— 23that the Christ would suffer, that He would be the first to rise from the dead, and would proclaim light to the *Jewish* people and to the Gentiles."

24Now as he thus made his defense, Festus said with a loud voice, "Paul, you are beside yourself! Much learning is driving you mad!"

25But he said, "I am not mad, most noble Festus, but speak the words of truth and reason. 26For the king, before whom I also speak freely, knows these things; for I am convinced that none of these things escapes his attention, since this thing was not done in a corner, 27King Agrippa, do you believe the prophets? I know that you do believe."

28Then Agrippa said to Paul, "You almost persuade me to become a Christian."

29And Paul said, "I would to God that not only you, but also all who hear me today, might become both almost and altogether such as I am, except for these chains."

30When he had said these things, the king stood up, as well as the governor and Bernice and those who sat with them; 31and when they had gone aside, they talked among themselves, saying, "This man is doing nothing deserving of death or chains."

32Then Agrippa said to Festus, "This man might have been set free if he had not appealed to Caesar."

PSALM 6:1-10

To the Chief Musician. With stringed instruments. On an eight-stringed harp. *A Psalm of David.*

O LORD, do not rebuke me in Your anger,
Nor chasten me in Your hot displeasure.

2 Have mercy on me, O LORD, for I *am* weak;
O LORD, heal me, for my bones are troubled.

3 My soul also is greatly troubled;
But You, O LORD—how long?

4 Return, O LORD, deliver me!
Oh, save me for Your mercies' sake!

5 For in death *there is* no remembrance of You;
In the grave who will give You thanks?

6 I am weary with my groaning;
All night I make my bed swim;
I drench my couch with my tears.

7 My eye wastes away because of grief;
It grows old because of all my enemies.

8 Depart from me, all you workers of iniquity;
For the LORD has heard the voice of my weeping.

9 The LORD has heard my supplication;
The LORD will receive my prayer.

10 Let all my enemies be ashamed and greatly troubled;
Let them turn back *and* be ashamed suddenly.

PROVERBS FOR TODAY/ 18:20-21

A man's stomach shall be satisfied from the fruit of his mouth; from *the produce of his lips he shall be filled. Death and life are in the power of the tongue, and those who love it will eat its fruit.*

JULY 9

1 CHRONICLES 7:1–8:40

THE sons of Issachar *were* Tola, Puah,* Jashub, and Shimron—four *in all.* 2The sons of Tola *were* Uzzi, Rephaiah, Jeriel, Jahmai, Jibsam, and Shemuel, heads of their father's house. *The sons* of Tola *were* mighty men of valor in their generations; their number in the days of David *was* twenty-two thousand six hundred. 3The son of Uzzi *was* Izrahiah, and the sons of Izrahiah *were* Michael, Obadiah, Joel, and Ishiah. All five of them *were* chief men. 4And with them, by their generations, according to their fathers' houses, *were* thirty-six thousand troops ready for war; for they had many wives and sons.

5Now their brethren among all the families of Issachar *were* mighty men of valor, listed by their genealogies, eighty-seven thousand in all.

6*The sons* of Benjamin *were* Bela, Becher, and Jediael—three *in all.* 7The sons of Bela were Ezbon, Uzzi, Uzziel,

Jerimoth, and Iri—five *in all*. They *were* heads of *their* fathers' houses, and they were listed by their genealogies, twenty-two thousand and thirty-four mighty men of valor.

8The sons of Becher *were* Zemirah, Joash, Eliezer, Elioenai, Omri, Jerimoth, Abijah, Anathoth, and Alemeth. All these *are* the sons of Becher. 9And they were recorded by genealogy according to their generations, heads of their fathers' houses, twenty thousand two hundred mighty men of valor. 10The son of Jediael *was* Bilhan, and the sons of Bilhan *were* Jeush, Benjamin, Ehud, Chenaanah, Zethan, Tharshish, and Ahishahar.

11All these sons of Jediael *were* heads of their fathers' houses; *there were* seventeen thousand two hundred mighty men of valor fit to go out for war *and* battle. 12Shuppim and Huppim* *were* the sons of Ir, *and* Hushim *was* the son of Aher.

13The sons of Naphtali *were* Jahziel,* Guni, Jezer, and Shallum,* the sons of Bilhah.

14The descendants of Manasseh: his Syrian concubine bore him Machir the father of Gilead, the father of Asriel.* 15Machir took as his wife *the sister* of Huppim and Shuppim,* whose name *was* Maachah. The name of *Gilead's* grandson* *was* Zelophehad,* but Zelophehad begot only daughters. 16(Maachah the wife of Machir bore a son, and she called his name Peresh. The name of his brother *was* Sheresh, and his sons *were* Ulam and Rakem. 17The son of Ulam *was* Bedan.) These *were* the descendants of Gilead the son of Machir, the son of Manasseh.

18His sister Hammoleketh bore Ishhod, Abiezer, and Mahlah.

19And the sons of Shemida were Ahian, Shechem, Likhi, and Aniam.

20The sons of Ephraim *were* Shuthelah, Bered his son, Tahath his son, Eladah his son, Tahath his son, 21Zabad his son, Shuthelah his son, and Ezer and Elead. The men of Gath who were born in *that* land killed *them* because they came down to take away their cattle. 22Then Ephraim their father mourned many days, and his brethren came to comfort him.

23And when he went in to his wife, she conceived and bore a son; and he called his name Beriah,* because tragedy had come upon his house. 24Now his daughter *was* Sheerah, who built Lower and Upper Beth Horon and Uzzen Sheerah; 25and Rephah *was* his son, *as well* as Resheph, and Telah his son, Tahan his son, 26Laadan his son, Ammihud his son, Elishama his son, 27Nun* his son, and Joshua his son.

28Now their possessions and dwelling places *were* Bethel and its towns; to the east Naaran, to the west Gezer and its towns, and Shechem and its towns, as far as Ayyah* and its towns; 29and by the borders of the children of Manasseh *were* Beth Shean and its towns, Taanach and its towns, Megiddo and its towns, Dor and its towns. In these dwelt the children of Joseph, the son of Israel.

30The sons of Asher *were* Imnah, Ishvah, Ishvi, Beriah, and their sister Serah. 31The sons of Beriah *were* Heber and Malchiel, who was the father of Birzaith.* 32And Heber begot Japhlet, Shomer,* Hotham,* and their sister Shua. 33The sons of Japhlet *were* Pasach, Bimhal, and Ashvath. These *were* the children of Japhlet. 34The sons of Shemer *were* Ahi, Rohgah, Jehubbah, and Aram. 35And the sons of his brother Helem *were* Zophah, Imna, Shelesh, and Amal. 36The sons of Zophah *were* Suah, Harnepher, Shual, Beri, Imrah, 37Bezer, Hod, Shamma, Shilshah, Jithran,* and Beera. 38The sons of Jether *were* Jephunneh, Pispah, and Ara. 39The sons of Ulla *were* Arah, Haniel, and Rizia.

40All these *were* the children of Asher, heads of *their* fathers' houses, choice men, mighty men of valor, chief leaders. And they were recorded by genealogies among the army fit for battle; their number *was* twenty-six thousand.

Now Benjamin begot Bela his firstborn, Ashbel the second, Aharah* the third, ²Nohah the fourth, and Rapha the fifth. ³The sons of Bela *were* Addar,* Gera, Abihud, ⁴Abishua, Naaman, Ahoah, ⁵Gera, Shephuphan, and Huram.

⁶These *are* the sons of Ehud, who were the heads of the fathers' *houses* of the inhabitants of Geba, and who forced them to move to Manahath: ⁷Naaman, Ahijah, and Gera who forced them to move. He begot Uzza and Ahihud.

⁸Also Shaharaim had children in the country of Moab, after he had sent away Hushim and Baara his wives. ⁹By Hodesh his wife he begot Jobab, Zibia, Mesha, Malcam, ¹⁰Jeuz, Sachiah, and Mirmah. These *were* his sons, heads of their fathers' *houses.*

¹¹And by Hushim he begot Abitub and Elpaal. ¹²The sons of Elpaal *were* Eber, Misham, and Shemed, who built Ono and Lod with its towns; ¹³and Beriah and Shema, who *were* heads of their fathers' *houses* of the inhabitants of Aijalon, who drove out the inhabitants of Gath. ¹⁴Ahio, Shashak, Jeremoth, ¹⁵Zebadiah, Arad, Eder, ¹⁶Michael, Ispah, and Joha *were* the sons of Beriah. ¹⁷Zebadiah, Meshullam, Hizki, Heber, ¹⁸Ishmerai, Jizliah, and Jobab *were* the sons of Elpaal. ¹⁹Jakim, Zichri, Zabdi, ²⁰Elienai, Zillethai, Eliel, ²¹Adaiah, Beraiah, and Shimrath *were* the sons of Shimei. ²²Ishpan, Eber, Eliel, ²³Abdon, Zichri, Hanan, ²⁴Hananiah, Elam, Antothijah, ²⁵Iphdeiah, and Penuel *were* the sons of Shashak. ²⁶Shamsherai, Shehariah, Athaliah, ²⁷Jaareshiah, Elijah, and Zichri *were* the sons of Jeroham.

²⁸These *were* heads of the fathers' *houses* by their generations, chief men. These dwelt in Jerusalem.

²⁹Now the father of Gibeon, whose wife's name *was* Maachah, dwelt at Gibeon. ³⁰And his firstborn son *was* Abdon, then Zur, Kish, Baal, Nadab, ³¹Gedor, Ahio, Zecher, ³²and Mikloth, *who* begot Shimeah.* They also dwelt alongside their relatives in Jerusalem, with their brethren. ³³Ner* begot Kish, Kish begot Saul, and Saul begot Jonathan, Malchishua, Abinadab,* and Esh-Baal.* ³⁴The son of Jonathan *was* Merib-Baal,* and Merib-Baal begot Micah. ³⁵The sons of Micah *were* Pithon, Melech, Tarea, and Ahaz. ³⁶And Ahaz begot Jehoaddah;* Jehoaddah begot Alemeth, Azmaveth, and Zimri; and Zimri begot Moza. ³⁷Moza begot Binea, Raphah* his son, Eleasah his son, *and* Azel his son.

³⁸Azel had six sons whose names *were* these: Azrikam, Bocheru, Ishmael, Sheariah, Obadiah, and Hanan. All these *were* the sons of Azel. ³⁹And the sons of Eshek his brother *were* Ulam his firstborn, Jeush the second, and Eliphelet the third.

⁴⁰The sons of Ulam were mighty men of valor—archers. *They* had many sons and grandsons, one hundred and fifty *in all.* These *were* all sons of Benjamin.

ACTS 27:1-20

AND when it was decided that we [Luke, Paul, and companions] should sail to Italy, they delivered Paul and some other prisoners to *one* named Julius, a centurion of the Augustan Regiment. ²So, entering a ship of Adramyttium, we put to sea, meaning to sail along the coasts of Asia. Aristarchus, a Macedonian of Thessalonica, was with us. ³And the next *day* we landed at Sidon. And Julius treated Paul kindly and gave *him* liberty to go to his friends and receive care. ⁴When we had put to sea from there, we sailed under *the shelter of* Cyprus, because the winds were contrary. 5And when we had sailed over the sea which is off Cilicia and Pamphylia, we came to Myra, *a city* of Lycia. 6There the centurion found an Alexandrian ship sailing to Italy, and he put us on board.

7When we had sailed slowly many days, and arrived with difficulty off Cnidus, the wind not permitting us to proceed, we sailed under *the shelter of* Crete off Salmone. 8Passing it with difficulty, we came to a place called Fair Havens, near the city *of* Lasea.

9Now when much time had been spent, and sailing was now dangerous because the Fast was already over, Paul advised them, 10saying, "Men, I perceive that this voyage will end with disaster and much loss, not only of the cargo and ship, but also our lives." 11Nevertheless the centurion was more persuaded by the helmsman and the owner of the ship than by the things spoken by Paul. 12And because the harbor was not suitable to winter in, the majority advised to set sail from there also, if by any means they could reach Phoenix, a harbor of Crete opening toward the southwest and northwest, *and* winter *there.*

13When the south wind blew softly, supposing that they had obtained *their* desire, putting out to sea, they sailed close by Crete. 14But not long after, a tempestuous head wind arose, called Euroclydon.* 15So when the ship was caught, and could not head into the wind, we let *her* drive. 16And running under *the shelter of* an island called Clauda,* we secured the skiff with difficulty. 17When they had taken it on board, they used cables to undergird the ship; and fearing lest they should run aground on the Syrtis* *Sands,* they struck sail and so were driven. 18And because we were exceedingly tempest-tossed, the next *day* they lightened the ship. 19On the third *day*

we threw the ship's tackle overboard with our own hands. 20Now when neither sun nor stars appeared for many days, and no small tempest beat on *us,* all hope that we would be saved was finally given up.

PSALM 7:1-17

*A Meditation * of David, which he sang to the* LORD *concerning the words of Cush, a Benjamite.*

O LORD my God, in You I put my trust;
Save me from all those who persecute me;
And deliver me,

2 Lest they tear me like a lion,
Rending *me* in pieces, while
there is none to deliver.

3 O LORD my God, if I have done this:
If there is iniquity in my hands,

4 If I have repaid evil to him who was at peace with me,
Or have plundered my enemy without cause,

5 Let the enemy pursue me and overtake *me;*
Yes, let him trample my life to the earth,
And lay my honor in the dust.
Selah

6 Arise, O LORD, in Your anger;
Lift Yourself up because of the rage of my enemies;
Rise up for me* *to* the judgment You have commanded!

7 So the congregation of the peoples shall surround You;
For their sakes, therefore, return on high.

8 The LORD shall judge the peoples;
Judge me, O LORD, according to my righteousness,

And according to my integrity
within me.

9 Oh, let the wickedness of the
wicked come to an end,
But establish the just;
For the righteous God tests
the hearts and minds.

10 My defense *is* of God,
Who saves the upright in
heart.

11 God *is* a just judge,
And God is angry *with the
wicked* every day.

12 If he does not turn back,
He will sharpen His sword;
He bends His bow and makes
it ready.

13 He also prepares for Himself
instruments of death;

He makes His arrows into
fiery shafts.

14 Behold, *the wicked* brings
forth iniquity;
Yes, he conceives trouble and
brings forth falsehood.

15 He made a pit and dug it out,
And has fallen into the ditch
which he made.

16 His trouble shall return upon
his own head,
And his violent dealing shall
come down on his own
crown.

17 I will praise the LORD
according to His
righteousness,
And will sing praise to the
name of the LORD Most
High.

PROVERBS FOR TODAY/ 18:22

He who *finds a wife finds a good* thing, *and obtains favor from the LORD.*

JULY 10

1 CHRONICLES 9:1–10:14

So all Israel was recorded by genealogies, and indeed, they *were* inscribed in the book of the kings of Israel. But Judah was carried away captive to Babylon because of their unfaithfulness. 2And the first inhabitants who *dwelt* in their possessions in their cities *were* Israelites, priests, Levites, and the Nethinim.

3Now in Jerusalem the children of Judah dwelt, and some of the children of Benjamin, and of the children of Ephraim and Manasseh: 4Uthai the son of Ammihud, the son of Omri, the son of Imri, the son of Bani, of the descendants of Perez, the son of Judah. 5Of the Shilonites: Asaiah the firstborn and his sons. 6Of the sons of Zerah: Jeuel, and their brethren—six hundred and ninety. 7Of the sons of Benjamin: Sallu the son of Meshullam, the son of Hodaviah, the son of Hassenuah; 8Ibneiah the son of Jeroham; Elah the son of Uzzi, the son of Michri; Meshullam the son of Shephatiah, the son of Reuel, the son of Ibnijah; 9and their brethren, according to their generations—nine hundred and fifty-six. All these men *were* heads of a father's *house* in their fathers' houses.

10Of the priests: Jedaiah, Jehoiarib, and Jachin; 11Azariah the son of Hilkiah, the son of Meshullam, the son of Zadok, the son of Meraioth, the son of Ahitub, the officer over the house of God; [12]Adaiah the son of Jeroham, the son of Pashur, the son of Malchijah; Maasai the son of Adiel, the son of Jahzerah, the son of Meshullam, the son of Meshillemith, the son of Immer; [13]and their brethren, heads of their fathers' *houses*—one thousand seven hundred and sixty. *They were* very able men for the work of the service of the house of God.

[14]Of the Levites: Shemaiah the son of Hasshub, the son of Azrikam, the son of Hashabiah, of the sons of Merari; [15]Bakbakkar, Heresh, Galal, and Mattaniah the son of Micah, the son of Zichri, the son of Asaph; [16]Obadiah the son of Shemaiah, the son of Galal, the son of Jeduthun; and Berechiah the son of Asa, the son of Elkanah, who lived in the villages of the Netophathites.

[17]And the gatekeepers *were* Shallum, Akkub, Talmon, Ahiman, and their brethren. Shallum *was* the chief. [18]Until then *they had been* gatekeepers for the camps of the children of Levi at the King's Gate on the east.

[19]Shallum the son of Kore, the son of Ebiasaph, the son of Korah, and his brethren, from his father's house, the Korahites, *were* in charge of the work of the service, gatekeepers of the tabernacle. Their fathers had been keepers of the entrance to the camp of the LORD. [20]And Phinehas the son of Eleazar had been the officer over them in time past; the LORD *was* with him. [21]Zechariah the son of Meshelemiah *was* keeper of the door of the tabernacle of meeting.

[22]All those chosen as gatekeepers *were* two hundred and twelve. They were recorded by their genealogy, in their villages. David and Samuel the seer had appointed them to their trusted office. [23]So they and their children *were* in charge of the gates of the house of the LORD, the house of the tabernacle, by assignment. [24]The gatekeepers were assigned to the four directions: the east, west, north, and south. [25]And their brethren in their villages *had* to come with them from time to time for seven days. [26]For in this trusted office *were* four chief gatekeepers; they were Levites. And they had charge over the chambers and treasuries of the house of God. [27]And they lodged *all* around the house of God because they *had* the responsibility, and they *were* in charge of opening *it* every morning.

[28]Now *some* of them were in charge of the serving vessels, for they brought them in and took them out by count. [29]*Some* of them *were* appointed over the furnishings and over all the implements of the sanctuary, and over the fine flour and the wine and the oil and the incense and the spices. [30]And *some* of the sons of the priests made the ointment of the spices.

[31]Mattithiah of the Levites, the firstborn of Shallum the Korahite, had the trusted office over the things that were baked in the pans. [32]And some of their brethren of the sons of the Kohathites *were* in charge of preparing the showbread for every Sabbath.

[33]These are the singers, heads of the fathers' *houses* of the Levites, *who lodged* in the chambers, *and were* free *from other duties;* for they were employed in *that* work day and night. [34]These heads of the fathers' *houses* of the Levites *were* heads throughout their generations. They dwelt at Jerusalem.

[35]Jeiel the father of Gibeon, whose wife's name *was* Maacah, dwelt at Gibeon. [36]His firstborn son *was* Abdon, then Zur, Kish, Baal, Ner, Nadab, [37]Gedor, Ahio, Zechariah,* and Mikloth. [38]And Mikloth begot Shimeam.* They also dwelt alongside their relatives in Jerusalem, with their brethren. [39]Ner begot Kish, Kish begot Saul, and

Saul begot Jonathan, Malchishua, Abinadab, and Esh-Baal. 40The son of Jonathan *was* Merib-Baal, and Merib-Baal begot Micah. 41The sons of Micah *were* Pithon, Melech, Tahrea,* *and Ahaz.* 42And Ahaz begot Jarah;* Jarah begot Alemeth, Azmaveth, and Zimri; and Zimri begot Moza; 43Moza begot Binea, Rephaiah* his son, Eleasah his son, and Azel his son.

44And Azel had six sons whose names *were* these: Azrikam, Bocheru, Ishmael, Sheariah, Obadiah, and Hanan; these *were* the sons of Azel.

Now the Philistines fought against Israel; and the men of Israel fled from before the Philistines, and fell slain on Mount Gilboa. 2Then the Philistines followed hard after Saul and his sons. And the Philistines killed Jonathan, Abinadab, and Malchishua, Saul's sons. 3The battle became fierce against Saul. The archers hit him, and he was wounded by the archers. 4Then Saul said to his armorbearer, "Draw your sword, and thrust me through with it, lest these uncircumcised men come and abuse me." But his armorbearer would not, for he was greatly afraid. Therefore Saul took a sword and fell on it. 5And when his armorbearer saw that Saul was dead, he also fell on his sword and died. 6So Saul and his three sons died, and all his house died together. 7And when all the men of Israel who *were* in the valley saw that they had fled and that Saul and his sons were dead, they forsook their cities and fled; then the Philistines came and dwelt in them.

8So it happened the next day, when the Philistines came to strip the slain, that they found Saul and his sons fallen on Mount Gilboa. 9And they stripped him and took his head and his armor, and sent word *throughout* the land of the Philistines to proclaim the news *in the temple* of their idols and among the people. 10Then they put his armor in the temple of their gods, and fastened his head in the temple of Dagon.

11And when all Jabesh Gilead heard all that the Philistines had done to Saul, 12all the valiant men arose and took the body of Saul and the bodies of his sons; and they brought them to Jabesh, and buried their bones under the tamarisk tree at Jabesh, and fasted seven days.

13So Saul died for his unfaithfulness which he had committed against the LORD, because he did not keep the word of the LORD, and also because he consulted a medium for guidance. 14But *he* did not inquire of the LORD; therefore He killed him, and turned the kingdom over to David the son of Jesse.

ACTS 27:21-44

BUT after long abstinence from food, then Paul stood in the midst of them [the sailors] and said, "Men, you should have listened to me, and not have sailed from Crete and incurred this disaster and loss. 22And now I urge you to take heart, for there will be no loss of life among you, but only of the ship. 23For there stood by me this night an angel of the God to whom I belong and whom I serve, 24saying, 'Do not be afraid, Paul; you must be brought before Caesar; and indeed God has granted you all those who sail with you.' 25Therefore take heart, men, for I believe God that it will be just as it was told me. 26However, we must run aground on a certain island."

27Now when the fourteenth night had come, as we were driven up and down in the Adriatic *Sea,* about midnight the sailors sensed that they were drawing near some land. 28And they took soundings and found *it* to be twenty fathoms; and when they had gone a little farther, they took soundings again and found *it* to be fifteen fathoms. 29Then, fearing lest we should run aground on the rocks, they dropped four anchors from the stern, and prayed for day to come. ³⁰And as the sailors were seeking to escape from the ship, when they had let down the skiff into the sea, under pretense of putting out anchors from the prow, ³¹Paul said to the centurion and the soldiers, "Unless these men stay in the ship, you cannot be saved." ³²Then the soldiers cut away the ropes of the skiff and let it fall off.

³³And as day was about to dawn, Paul implored *them* all to take food, saying, "Today is the fourteenth day you have waited and continued without food, and eaten nothing. ³⁴Therefore I urge you to take nourishment, for this is for your survival, since not a hair will fall from the head of any of you." ³⁵And when he had said these things, he took bread and gave thanks to God in the presence of them all; and when he had broken *it* he began to eat. ³⁶Then they were all encouraged, and also took food themselves. ³⁷And in all we were two hundred and seventy-six persons on the ship. ³⁸So when they had eaten enough, they lightened the ship and threw out the wheat into the sea.

³⁹When it was day, they did not recognize the land; but they observed a bay with a beach, onto which they planned to run the ship if possible. ⁴⁰And they let go the anchors and left *them* in the sea, meanwhile loosing the rudder ropes; and they hoisted the mainsail to the wind and made for shore. ⁴¹But striking a place where two seas met, they ran the ship aground; and the prow stuck fast and remained immovable, but the stern was being broken up by the violence of the waves.

⁴²And the soldiers' plan was to kill the prisoners, lest any of them should swim away and escape. ⁴³But the centurion, wanting to save Paul, kept them from *their* purpose, and commanded that those who could swim should jump *overboard* first and get to land, ⁴⁴and the rest, some on boards and some on *parts* of the ship. And so it was that they all escaped safely to land.

PSALM 8:1-9

To the Chief Musician. On the instrument of Gath.* A Psalm of David.

O Lord, our Lord,
    How excellent *is* Your name in
        all the earth,
    Who have set Your glory
        above the heavens!

2   Out of the mouth of babes
        and nursing infants
    You have ordained strength,
    Because of Your enemies,
    That You may silence the
        enemy and the avenger.

3   When I consider Your
        heavens, the work of Your
        fingers,
    The moon and the stars,
        which You have ordained,
4   What is man that You are
        mindful of him,
    And the son of man that You
        visit him?
5   For You have made him a
        little lower than the angels,*
    And You have crowned him
        with glory and honor.

6   You have made him to have
        dominion over the works of
        Your hands;
    You have put all *things* under
        his feet,
7   All sheep and oxen—
    Even the beasts of the field,
8   The birds of the air,
    And the fish of the sea
    That pass through the paths
        of the seas.

9   O Lord, our Lord,
    How excellent *is* Your name in
        all the earth!

PROVERBS FOR TODAY/ 18:23-24

The poor man *uses entreaties, but the rich answers roughly.* □ *A man* who has *friends must himself be friendly,* * *but there is a friend* who *sticks closer than a brother.*

JULY 11

1 CHRONICLES 11:1–12:18

T HEN all Israel came together to David at Hebron, saying, "Indeed we *are* your bone and your flesh. ²Also, in time past, even when Saul was king, you *were* the one who led Israel out and brought them in; and the LORD your God said to you, 'You shall shepherd My people Israel, and be ruler over My people Israel.' " ³Therefore all the elders of Israel came to the king at Hebron, and David made a covenant with them at Hebron before the LORD. And they anointed David king over Israel, according to the word of the LORD by Samuel.

⁴And David and all Israel went to Jerusalem, which is Jebus, where the Jebusites *were,* the inhabitants of the land. ⁵But the inhabitants of Jebus said to David, "You shall not come in here!" Nevertheless David took the stronghold of Zion (that is, the City of David). ⁶Now David said, "Whoever attacks the Jebusites first shall be chief and captain." And Joab the son of Zeruiah went up first, and became chief. ⁷Then David dwelt in the stronghold; therefore they called it the City of David. ⁸And he built the city around it, from the Millo* to the surrounding area. Joab repaired the rest of the city. ⁹So David went on and became great, and the LORD of hosts *was* with him.

¹⁰Now these *were* the heads of the mighty men whom David had, who strengthened themselves with him in his kingdom, with all Israel, to make

him king, according to the word of the LORD concerning Israel.

¹¹And this *is* the number of the mighty men whom David had: Jashobeam the son of a Hachmonite, chief of the captains;* he had lifted up his spear against three hundred, killed *by him* at one time.

¹²After him *was* Eleazar the son of Dodo, the Ahohite, who *was one* of the three mighty men. ¹³He was with David at Pasdammim. Now there the Philistines were gathered for battle, and there was a piece of ground full of barley. So the people fled from the Philistines. ¹⁴But they stationed themselves in the middle of *that* field, defended it, and killed the Philistines. So the LORD brought about a great victory.

¹⁵Now three of the thirty chief men went down to the rock to David, into the cave of Adullam; and the army of the Philistines encamped in the Valley of Rephaim. ¹⁶David *was* then in the stronghold, and the garrison of the Philistines *was* then in Bethlehem. ¹⁷And David said with longing, "Oh, that someone would give me a drink of water from the well of Bethlehem, which is by the gate!" ¹⁸So the three broke through the camp of the Philistines, drew water from the well of Bethlehem that *was* by the gate, and took *it* and brought *it* to David. Nevertheless David would not drink it, but poured it out to the LORD. ¹⁹And he said, "Far be it from me, O my God, that I should do this! Shall I drink the

blood of these men *who have put* their lives *in jeopardy?* For at the risk of their lives they brought it." Therefore he would not drink it. These things were done by the three mighty men.

20Abishai the brother of Joab was chief of *another* three.* He had lifted up his spear against three hundred *men,* killed *them,* and won a name among *these* three. 21Of the three he was more honored than the other two men. Therefore he became their captain. However he did not attain to the *first* three.

22Benaiah was the son of Jehoiada, the son of a valiant man from Kabzeel, who had done many deeds. He had killed two lion-like heroes of Moab. He also had gone down and killed a lion in the midst of a pit on a snowy day. 23And he killed an Egyptian, a man of *great* height, five cubits tall. In the Egyptian's hand *there was* a spear like a weaver's beam; and he went down to him with a staff, wrested the spear out of the Egyptian's hand, and killed him with his own spear. 24These *things* Benaiah the son of Jehoiada did, and won a name among three mighty men. 25Indeed he was more honored than the thirty, but he did not attain to the *first* three. And David appointed him over his guard.

26Also the mighty warriors *were* Asahel the brother of Joab, Elhanan the son of Dodo of Bethlehem, 27Shammoth the Harorite,* Helez the Pelonite,* 28Ira the son of Ikkesh the Tekoite, Abiezer the Anathothite, 29Sibbechai the Hushathite, Ilai the Ahohite, 30Maharai the Netophathite, Heled* the son of Baanah the Netophathite, 31Ithai* the son of Ribai of Gibeah, of the sons of Benjamin, Benaiah the Pirathonite, 32Hurai* of the brooks of Gaash, Abiel* the Arbathite, 33Azmaveth the Baharumite,* Eliahba the Shaalbonite, 34the sons of Hashem the Gizonite, Jonathan the son of Shageh the Hararite, 35Ahiam the son

of Sacar the Hararite, Eliphal the son of Ur, 36Hepher the Mecherathite, Ahijah the Pelonite, 37Hezro the Carmelite, Naarai the son of Ezbai, 38Joel the brother of Nathan, Mibhar the son of Hagri, 39Zelek the Ammonite, Naharai the Berothite* (the armorbearer of Joab the son of Zeruiah), 40Ira the Ithrite, Gareb the Ithrite, 41Uriah the Hittite, Zabad the son of Ahlai, 42Adina the son of Shiza the Reubenite (a chief of the Reubenites) and thirty with him, 43Hanan the son of Maachah, Joshaphat the Mithnite, 44Uzzia the Ashterathite, Shama and Jeiel the sons of Hotham the Aroerite, 45Jediael the son of Shimri, and Joha his brother, the Tizite, 46Eliel the Mahavite, Jeribai and Joshaviah the sons of Elnaam, Ithmah the Moabite, 47Eliel, Obed, and Jaasiel the Mezobaite.

Now these *were* the men who came to David at Ziklag while he was still a fugitive from Saul the son of Kish; and they *were* among the mighty men, helpers in the war, 2armed with bows, using both the right hand and the left in *hurling* stones and *shooting* arrows with the bow. *They were* of Benjamin, Saul's brethren.

3The chief *was* Ahiezer, then Joash, the sons of Shemaah the Gibeathite; Jeziel and Pelet the sons of Azmaveth; Berachah, and Jehu the Anathothite; 4Ishmaiah the Gibeonite, a mighty man among the thirty, and over the thirty; Jeremiah, Jahaziel, Johanan, and Jozabad the Gederathite; 5Eluzai, Jerimoth, Bealiah, Shemariah, and Shephatiah the Haruphite; 6Elkanah, Jisshiah, Azarel, Joezer, and Jashobeam, the Korahites; 7and Joelah and Zebadiah the sons of Jeroham of Gedor.

8*Some* Gadites joined David at the stronghold in the wilderness, mighty men of valor, men trained for battle, who could handle shield and spear, whose faces *were like* the faces of lions, and *were* as swift as gazelles on the mountains: 9Ezer the first, Obadiah the second, Eliab the third, 10Mishmannah the fourth, Jeremiah the fifth, 11Attai the sixth, Eliel the seventh, 12Johanan the eighth, Elzabad the ninth, 13Jeremiah the tenth, and Machbanai the eleventh. 14These *were* from the sons of Gad, captains of the army; the least was over a hundred, and the greatest was over a thousand. 15These *are* the ones who crossed the Jordan in the first month, when it had overflowed all its banks; and they put to flight all *those* in the valleys, to the east and to the west.

16Then some of the sons of Benjamin and Judah came to David at the stronghold. 17And David went out to meet them, and answered and said to them, "If you have come peaceably to me to help me, my heart will be united with you; but if to betray me to my enemies, since *there is* no wrong in my hands, may the God of our fathers look and bring judgment." 18Then the Spirit came upon Amasai, chief of the captains, *and he said:*

> "*We are* yours, O David;
> We *are* on your side, O son of Jesse!
> Peace, peace to you,
> And peace to your helpers!
> For your God helps you."

So David received them, and made them captains of the troop.

ACTS 28:1-31

Now when they [Paul and his shipmates] had escaped, they then found out that the island was called Malta. 2And the natives showed us unusual kindness; for they kindled a fire and made us all welcome, because of the rain that was falling and because of the cold. 3But when Paul had gathered a bundle of sticks and laid *them* on the fire, a viper came out because of the heat, and fastened on his hand. 4So when the natives saw the creature hanging from his hand, they said to one another, "No doubt this man is a murderer, whom, though he has escaped the sea, yet justice does not allow to live." 5But he shook off the creature into the fire and suffered no harm. 6However, they were expecting that he would swell up or suddenly fall down dead. But after they had looked for a long time and saw no harm come to him, they changed their minds and said that he was a god.

7In that region there was an estate of the leading citizen of the island, whose name was Publius, who received us and entertained us courteously for three days. 8And it happened that the father of Publius lay sick of a fever and dysentery. Paul went in to him and prayed, and he laid his hands on him and healed him. 9So when this was done, the rest of those on the island who had diseases also came and were healed. 10They also honored us in many ways; and when we departed, they provided such things as were necessary.

11After three months we sailed in an Alexandrian ship whose figurehead was the Twin Brothers, which had wintered at the island. 12And landing at Syracuse, we stayed three days. 13From there we circled round and reached Rhegium. And after one day the south wind blew; and the next day we came to Puteoli, 14where we found brethren, and were invited to stay with them seven days. And so we went toward Rome. 15And from there, when the brethren heard about us, they came to meet us as far as Appii Forum and Three Inns. When Paul saw them, he thanked God and took courage.

16Now when we came to Rome, the centurion delivered the prisoners to the captain of the guard; but Paul was permitted to dwell by himself with the soldier who guarded him.

¹⁷And it came to pass after three days that Paul called the leaders of the Jews together. So when they had come together, he said to them: "Men *and* brethren, though I have done nothing against our people or the customs of our fathers, yet I was delivered as a prisoner from Jerusalem into the hands of the Romans, ¹⁸who, when they had examined me, wanted to let *me* go, because there was no cause for putting me to death. ¹⁹But when the Jews* spoke against *it,* I was compelled to appeal to Caesar, not that I had anything of which to accuse my nation. ²⁰For this reason therefore I have called for you, to see *you* and speak with *you,* because for the hope of Israel I am bound with this chain."

²¹Then they said to him, "We neither received letters from Judea concerning you, nor have any of the brethren who came reported or spoken any evil of you. ²²But we desire to hear from you what you think; for concerning this sect, we know that it is spoken against everywhere."

²³So when they had appointed him a day, many came to him at *his* lodging, to whom he explained and solemnly testified of the kingdom of God, persuading them concerning Jesus from both the Law of Moses and the Prophets, from morning till evening. ²⁴And some were persuaded by the things which were spoken, and some disbelieved. ²⁵So when they did not agree among themselves, they departed after Paul had said one word: "The Holy Spirit spoke rightly through Isaiah the prophet to our* fathers, ²⁶saying,

'Go to this people and say:
"Hearing you will hear, and
    shall not understand;
And seeing you will see, and
    not perceive;
²⁷   For the hearts of this people
    have grown dull.
Their ears are hard of hearing,
And their eyes they have
    closed,
Lest they should see with
    their eyes and hear with
    their ears,
Lest they should understand
    with their hearts and turn,
So that I should heal them." ' *

²⁸"Therefore let it be known to you that the salvation of God has been sent to the Gentiles, and they will hear it!" ²⁹And when he had said these words, the Jews departed and had a great dispute among themselves.*

³⁰Then Paul dwelt two whole years in his own rented house, and received all who came to him, ³¹preaching the kingdom of God and teaching the things which concern the Lord Jesus Christ with all confidence, no one forbidding him.

PSALM 9:1-12

To the Chief Musician. To the tune of "Death of the Son." A Psalm of David.*

I WILL praise *You,* O LORD, with
    my whole heart;
I will tell of all Your marvelous
        works.
2   I will be glad and rejoice in
        You;
    I will sing praise to Your
        name, O Most High.

3   When my enemies turn back,
    They shall fall and perish at
        Your presence.
4   For You have maintained my
        right and my cause;
    You sat on the throne judging
        in righteousness.
5   You have rebuked the nations,
    You have destroyed the
        wicked;
    You have blotted out their
        name forever and ever.

6   O enemy, destructions are
        finished forever!

And you have destroyed cities;
Even their memory has
perished.
7 But the LORD shall endure
forever;
He has prepared His throne
for judgment.
8 He shall judge the world in
righteousness,
And He shall administer
judgment for the peoples in
uprightness.

9 The LORD also will be a refuge
for the oppressed,
A refuge in times of trouble.

10 And those who know Your
name will put their trust in
You;
For You, LORD, have not
forsaken those who seek
You.

11 Sing praises to the LORD, who
dwells in Zion!
Declare His deeds among the
people.
12 When He avenges blood, He
remembers them;
He does not forget the cry of
the humble.

PROVERBS FOR TODAY/ 19:1-3

Better is *the poor who walks in his integrity than* one who is *perverse in his lips, and is a fool. Also it is not good* for *a soul* to be *without knowledge, and he sins who hastens with* his *feet. The foolishness of a man twists his way, and his heart frets against the LORD.*

JULY 12

1 CHRONICLES 12:19–14:17

ND *some* from Manasseh defected to David when he was going with the Philistines to battle against Saul; but they did not help them, for the lords of the Philistines sent him away by agreement, saying, "He may defect to his master Saul *and endanger* our heads." 20When he went to Ziklag, those of Manasseh who defected to him were Adnah, Jozabad, Jediael, Michael, Jozabad, Elihu, and Zillethai, captains of the thousands who *were* from Manasseh. 21And they helped David against the bands *of raiders,* for they *were* all mighty men of valor, and they were captains in the army. 22For at *that* time they came to David day by day to help him, until *it was* a great army, like the army of God.

23Now these *were* the numbers of the divisions *that were* equipped for war, *and* came to David at Hebron to turn *over* the kingdom of Saul to him, according to the word of the LORD: 24of the sons of Judah bearing shield and spear, six thousand eight hundred armed for war; 25of the sons of Simeon, mighty men of valor fit for war, seven thousand one hundred; 26of the sons of Levi four thousand six hundred; 27Jehoiada, the leader of the Aaronites, and with him three thousand seven hundred; 28Zadok, a young man, a valiant warrior, and from his father's house twenty-two captains; 29of the sons of Benjamin, relatives of Saul, three thousand (until then the greatest part of them had remained loyal to the house of Saul); ³⁰of the sons of Ephraim twenty thousand eight hundred, mighty men of valor, famous men throughout their father's house; ³¹of the half-tribe of Manasseh eighteen thousand, who were designated by name to come and make David king; ³²of the sons of Issachar who had understanding of the times, to know what Israel ought to do, their chiefs were two hundred; and all their brethren were at their command; ³³of Zebulun there were fifty thousand who went out to battle, expert in war with all weapons of war, stouthearted men who could keep ranks; ³⁴of Naphtali one thousand captains, and with them thirty-seven thousand with shield and spear; ³⁵of the Danites who could keep battle formation, twenty-eight thousand six hundred; ³⁶of Asher, those who could go out to war, able to keep battle formation, forty thousand; ³⁷of the Reubenites and the Gadites and the half-tribe of Manasseh, from the other side of the Jordan, one hundred and twenty thousand armed for battle with every *kind* of weapon of war.

³⁸All these men of war, who could keep ranks, came to Hebron with a loyal heart, to make David king over all Israel; and all the rest of Israel *were* of one mind to make David king. ³⁹And they were there with David three days, eating and drinking, for their brethren had prepared for them. ⁴⁰Moreover those who were near to them, from as far away as Issachar and Zebulun and Naphtali, were bringing food on donkeys and camels, on mules and oxen—provisions of flour and cakes of figs and cakes of raisins, wine and oil and oxen and sheep abundantly, for *there was* joy in Israel.

THEN David consulted with the captains of thousands and hundreds, *and* with every leader. ²And David said to all the assembly of Israel, "If *it seems* good to you, and if it is of the LORD our God, let us send out to our brethren everywhere *who are* left in all the land of Israel, and with them to the priests and Levites *who are* in their cities *and* their common-lands, that they may gather together to us; ³and let us bring the ark of our God back to us, for we have not inquired at it since the days of Saul." ⁴Then all the assembly said that they would do so, for the thing was right in the eyes of all the people.

⁵So David gathered all Israel together, from Shihor in Egypt to as far as the entrance of Hamath, to bring the ark of God from Kirjath Jearim. ⁶And David and all Israel went up to Baalah,* to Kirjath Jearim, which belonged to Judah, to bring up from there the ark of God the LORD, who dwells *between* the cherubim, where *His* name is proclaimed. ⁷So they carried the ark of God on a new cart from the house of Abinadab, and Uzza and Ahio drove the cart. ⁸Then David and all Israel played *music* before God with all *their* might, with singing, on harps, on stringed instruments, on tambourines, on cymbals, and with trumpets.

⁹And when they came to Chidon's* threshing floor, Uzza put out his hand to hold the ark, for the oxen stumbled. ¹⁰Then the anger of the LORD was aroused against Uzza, and He struck him because he put his hand to the ark; and he died there before God. ¹¹And David became angry because of the LORD's outbreak against Uzza; therefore that place is called Perez Uzza* to this day. ¹²David was afraid of God that day, saying, "How can I bring the ark of God to me?"

¹³So David would not move the ark with him into the City of David, but took it aside into the house of Obed-Edom the Gittite. ¹⁴The ark of God remained with the family of Obed-Edom in his house three months. And the LORD blessed the house of Obed-Edom and all that he had.

Now Hiram king of Tyre sent messengers to David, and cedar trees, with masons and carpenters, to build him a house. ²So David knew that the LORD had established him as king over Israel, for his kingdom was highly exalted for the sake of His people Israel.

³Then David took more wives in Jerusalem, and David begot more sons and daughters. ⁴And these are the names of his children whom he had in Jerusalem: Shammua,* Shobab, Nathan, Solomon, ⁵Ibhar, Elishua,* Elpelet,* ⁶Nogah, Nepheg, Japhia, ⁷Elishama, Beeliada,* and Eliphelet.

⁸Now when the Philistines heard that David had been anointed king over all Israel, all the Philistines went up to search for David. And David heard *of it* and went out against them. ⁹Then the Philistines went and made a raid on the Valley of Rephaim. ¹⁰And David inquired of God, saying, "Shall I go up against the Philistines? Will You deliver them into my hand?"

The LORD said to him, "Go up, for I will deliver them into your hand."

¹¹So they went up to Baal Perazim, and David defeated them there. Then David said, "God has broken through my enemies by my hand like a breakthrough of water." Therefore they called the name of that place Baal Perazim.* ¹²And when they left their gods there, David gave a commandment, and they were burned with fire.

¹³Then the Philistines once again made a raid on the valley. ¹⁴Therefore David inquired again of God, and God said to him, "You shall not go up after them; circle around them, and come upon them in front of the mulberry trees. ¹⁵And it shall be, when you hear a sound of marching in the tops of the mulberry trees, then you shall go out to battle, for God has gone out before you to strike the camp of the Philistines." ¹⁶So David did as God commanded him, and they drove back the army of the Philistines from Gibeon as far as Gezer. ¹⁷Then the fame of David went out into all lands, and the LORD brought the fear of him upon all nations.

ROMANS 1:1-17

PAUL, a bondservant of Jesus Christ, called *to be* an apostle, separated to the gospel of God ²which He promised before through His prophets in the Holy Scriptures, ³concerning His Son Jesus Christ our Lord, who was born of the seed of David according to the flesh, ⁴*and* declared *to be* the Son of God with power according to the Spirit of holiness, by the resurrection from the dead. ⁵Through Him we have received grace and apostleship for obedience to the faith among all nations for His name, ⁶among whom you also are the called of Jesus Christ;

⁷To all who are in Rome, beloved of God, called *to be* saints:

Grace to you and peace from God our Father and the Lord Jesus Christ.

⁸First, I thank my God through Jesus Christ for you all, that your faith is spoken of throughout the whole world. ⁹For God is my witness, whom I serve with my spirit in the gospel of His Son, that without ceasing I make mention of you always in my prayers, ¹⁰making request if, by some means, now at last I may find a way in the will of God to come to you. ¹¹For I long to see you, that I may impart to you some spiritual gift, so that you may be established— ¹²that is, that I may be encouraged together with you by the mutual faith both of you and me.

¹³Now I do not want you to be unaware, brethren, that I often planned to come to you (but was hindered until now), that I might have some fruit among you also, just as among the

other Gentiles. [14]I am a debtor both to Greeks and to barbarians, both to wise and to unwise. [15]So, as much as is in me, *I am* ready to preach the gospel to you who are in Rome also.

[16]For I am not ashamed of the gospel of Christ,* for it is the power of God to salvation for everyone who believes, for the Jew first and also for the Greek. [17]For in it the righteousness of God is revealed from faith to faith; as it is written, *"The just shall live by faith."* *

PSALM 9:13-20

Have mercy on me, O LORD! Consider my trouble from those who hate me, You who lift me up from the gates of death,

14 That I may tell of all Your praise In the gates of the daughter of Zion. I will rejoice in Your salvation.

15 The nations have sunk down in the pit *which* they made; In the net which they hid, their own foot is caught.

16 The LORD is known *by* the judgment He executes; The wicked is snared in the work of his own hands. Meditation.* Selah

17 The wicked shall be turned into hell, *And* all the nations that forget God.

18 For the needy shall not always be forgotten; The expectation of the poor shall *not* perish forever.

19 Arise, O LORD, Do not let man prevail; Let the nations be judged in Your sight.

20 Put them in fear, O LORD, *That* the nations may know themselves *to be but* men. Selah

PROVERBS FOR TODAY / 19:4-5

Wealth makes many friends, but the poor is separated from his friend. ◻ *A false witness will not go unpunished, and* he *who speaks lies will not escape.*

JULY 13

1 CHRONICLES 15:1–16:36

DAVID built houses for himself in the City of David; and he prepared a place for the ark of God, and pitched a tent for it. [2]Then David said, "No one may carry the ark of God but the Levites, for the LORD has chosen them to carry the ark of God and to minister before Him forever." [3]And David gathered all Israel together at Jerusalem, to bring up the ark of the LORD to its place, which he had prepared for it. [4]Then David assembled the children of Aaron and the Levites: [5]of the sons of Kohath, Uriel the chief, and one hundred and twenty of his brethren; [6]of the sons of Merari, Asaiah the chief, and two hundred and twenty of his brethren; [7]of the sons of Gershom, Joel the chief, and one hundred and thirty of his brethren; [8]of the sons of Elizaphan, Shemaiah the chief, and two hundred of his brethren; 9of the sons of Hebron, Eliel the chief, and eighty of his brethren; 10of the sons of Uzziel, Amminadab the chief, and one hundred and twelve of his brethren.

11And David called for Zadok and Abiathar the priests, and for the Levites: for Uriel, Asaiah, Joel, Shemaiah, Eliel, and Amminadab. 12He said to them, "You *are* the heads of the fathers' *houses* of the Levites; sanctify yourselves, you and your brethren, that you may bring up the ark of the Lord God of Israel to *the place* I have prepared for it. 13For because you *did* not *do it* the first *time,* the Lord our God broke out against us, because we did not consult Him about the proper order."

14So the priests and the Levites sanctified themselves to bring up the ark of the Lord God of Israel. 15And the children of the Levites bore the ark of God on their shoulders, by its poles, as Moses had commanded according to the word of the Lord.

16Then David spoke to the leaders of the Levites to appoint their brethren *to be* the singers accompanied by instruments of music, stringed instruments, harps, and cymbals, by raising the voice with resounding joy. 17So the Levites appointed Heman the son of Joel; and of his brethren, Asaph the son of Berechiah; and of their brethren, the sons of Merari, Ethan the son of Kushaiah; 18and with them their brethren of the second *rank:* Zechariah, Ben,* Jaaziel, Shemiramoth, Jehiel, Unni, Eliab, Benaiah, Maaseiah, Mattithiah, Elipheleh, Mikneiah, Obed-Edom, and Jeiel, the gatekeepers; 19the singers, Heman, Asaph, and Ethan, *were* to sound the cymbals of bronze; 20Zechariah, Aziel, Shemiramoth, Jehiel, Unni, Eliab, Maaseiah, and Benaiah, with strings according to Alamoth; 21Mattithiah, Elipheleh, Mikneiah, Obed-Edom, Jeiel, and Azaziah, to direct with

harps on the Sheminith; 22Chenaniah, leader of the Levites, was instructor *in charge of* the music, because he *was* skillful; 23Berechiah and Elkanah *were* doorkeepers for the ark; 24Shebaniah, Joshaphat, Nethanel, Amasai, Zechariah, Benaiah, and Eliezer, the priests, were to blow the trumpets before the ark of God; and Obed-Edom and Jehiah, doorkeepers for the ark.

25So David, the elders of Israel, and the captains over thousands went to bring up the ark of the covenant of the Lord from the house of Obed-Edom with joy. 26And so it was, when God helped the Levites who bore the ark of the covenant of the Lord, that they offered seven bulls and seven rams. 27David was clothed with a robe of fine linen, as were all the Levites who bore the ark, the singers, and Chenaniah the music master *with* the singers. David also wore a linen ephod. 28Thus all Israel brought up the ark of the covenant of the Lord with shouting and with the sound of the horn, with trumpets and with cymbals, making music with stringed instruments and harps.

29And it happened, *as* the ark of the covenant of the Lord came to the City of David, that Michal, Saul's daughter, looked through a window and saw King David whirling and playing music; and she despised him in her heart.

So they brought the ark of God, and set it in the midst of the tabernacle that David had erected for it. Then they offered burnt offerings and peace offerings before God. 2And when David had finished offering the burnt offerings and the peace offerings, he blessed the people in the name of the Lord. 3Then he distributed to everyone of Israel, both man and woman, to everyone a loaf of bread, a piece *of meat,* and a cake of raisins.

4And he appointed some of the Levites to minister before the ark of the Lord, to commemorate, to thank, and to praise the Lord God of Israel: ⁵Asaph the chief, and next to him Zechariah, *then* Jeiel, Shemiramoth, Jehiel, Mattithiah, Eliab, Benaiah, and Obed-Edom: Jeiel with stringed instruments and harps, but Asaph made music with cymbals; ⁶Benaiah and Jahaziel the priests regularly *blew* the trumpets before the ark of the covenant of God.

⁷On that day David first delivered *this psalm* into the hand of Asaph and his brethren, to thank the Lord:

8 Oh, give thanks to the Lord!
 Call upon His name;
 Make known His deeds
  among the peoples!
9 Sing to Him, sing psalms to
  Him;
 Talk of all His wondrous
  works!
10 Glory in His holy name;
 Let the hearts of those rejoice
  who seek the Lord!
11 Seek the Lord and His
  strength;
 Seek His face evermore!
12 Remember His marvelous
  works which He has done,
 His wonders, and the
  judgments of His mouth,
13 O seed of Israel His servant,
 You children of Jacob, His
  chosen ones!

14 He *is* the Lord our God;
 His judgments *are* in all the
  earth.
15 Remember His covenant
  forever,
 The word which He
  commanded, for a thousand
  generations,
16 *The covenant which* He made
  with Abraham,
 And His oath to Isaac,
17 And confirmed it to Jacob for
  a statute,
 To Israel *for* an everlasting
  covenant,

18 Saying, "To you I will give the
  land of Canaan
 As the allotment of your
  inheritance,"
19 When you were few in
  number,
 Indeed very few, and
  strangers in it.

20 When they went from one
  nation to another,
 And from *one* kingdom to
  another people,
21 He permitted no man to do
  them wrong;
 Yes, He rebuked kings for
  their sakes,
22 *Saying,* "Do not touch My
  anointed ones,
 And do My prophets no
  harm."*

23 Sing to the Lord, all the earth;
 Proclaim the good news of
  His salvation from day to
  day.
24 Declare His glory among the
  nations,
 His wonders among all
  peoples.

25 For the Lord *is* great and
  greatly to be praised;
 He *is* also to be feared above
  all gods.
26 For all the gods of the peoples
  are idols,
 But the Lord made the
  heavens.
27 Honor and majesty *are* before
  Him;
 Strength and gladness are in
  His place.

28 Give to the Lord, O families of
  the peoples,
 Give to the Lord glory and
  strength.
29 Give to the Lord the glory *due*
  His name;

Bring an offering, and come
before Him.
Oh, worship the LORD in the
beauty of holiness!
30 Tremble before Him, all the
earth.
The world also is firmly
established,
It shall not be moved.

31 Let the heavens rejoice, and
let the earth be glad;
And let them say among the
nations, "The LORD reigns."
32 Let the sea roar, and all its
fullness;
Let the field rejoice, and all
that *is* in it.
33 Then the trees of the woods
shall rejoice before the
LORD,
For He is coming to judge the
earth.*

34 Oh, give thanks to the LORD,
for *He is* good!
For His mercy *endures*
forever.*
35 And say, "Save us, O God of
our salvation;
Gather us together, and
deliver us from the Gentiles,
To give thanks to Your holy
name,
To triumph in Your praise."

36 Blessed *be* the LORD God of
Israel
From everlasting to
everlasting!*

And all the people said, "Amen!" and
praised the LORD.

ROMANS 1:18-32

FOR the wrath of God is revealed
from heaven against all ungodliness and unrighteousness of
men, who suppress the truth in unrighteousness, 19because what may be
known of God is manifest in them, for
God has shown *it* to them. 20For since
the creation of the world His invisible
attributes are clearly seen, being understood by the things that are made,
even His eternal power and Godhead,
so that they are without excuse, 21be-
cause, although they knew God, they
did not glorify *Him* as God, nor were
thankful, but became futile in their
thoughts, and their foolish hearts
were darkened. 22Professing to be
wise, they became fools, 23and
changed the glory of the incorruptible
God into an image made like corruptible man—and birds and four-footed
animals and creeping things.

24Therefore God also gave them up
to uncleanness, in the lusts of their
hearts, to dishonor their bodies
among themselves, 25who exchanged
the truth of God for the lie, and worshiped and served the creature rather
than the Creator, who is blessed forever. Amen.

26For this reason God gave them up
to vile passions. For even their women
exchanged the natural use for what is
against nature. 27Likewise also the
men, leaving the natural use of the
woman, burned in their lust for one
another, men with men committing
what is shameful, and receiving in
themselves the penalty of their error
which was due.

28And even as they did not like to
retain God in *their* knowledge, God
gave them over to a debased mind, to
do those things which are not fitting;
29being filled with all unrighteousness,
sexual immorality,* wickedness, covetousness, maliciousness; full of envy,
murder, strife, deceit, evil-minded-
ness; *they are* whisperers, 30backbit-
ers, haters of God, violent, proud,
boasters, inventors of evil things, disobedient to parents, 31undiscerning,
untrustworthy, unloving, unforgiving,* unmerciful; 32who, knowing the

righteous judgment of God, that those who practice such things are deserving of death, not only do the same but also approve of those who practice them.

PSALM 10:1-15

WHY do You stand afar off, O LORD?
Why do You hide in times of trouble?

2 The wicked in *his* pride persecutes the poor;
Let them be caught in the plots which they have devised.

3 For the wicked boasts of his heart's desire;
He blesses the greedy *and* renounces the LORD.

4 The wicked in his proud countenance does not seek *God;*
God *is* in none of his thoughts.

5 His ways are always prospering;
Your judgments *are* far above, out of his sight;
As for all his enemies, he sneers at them.

6 He has said in his heart, "I shall not be moved;
I shall never be in adversity."

7 His mouth is full of cursing and deceit and oppression;
Under his tongue *is* trouble and iniquity.

8 He sits in the lurking places of the villages;
In the secret places he murders the innocent;
His eyes are secretly fixed on the helpless.

9 He lies in wait secretly, as a lion in his den;
He lies in wait to catch the poor;
He catches the poor when he draws him into his net.

10 So he crouches, he lies low,
That the helpless may fall by his strength.

11 He has said in his heart,
"God has forgotten;
He hides His face;
He will never see."

12 Arise, O LORD!
O God, lift up Your hand!
Do not forget the humble.

13 Why do the wicked renounce God?
He has said in his heart,
"You will not require *an account.*"

14 But You have seen, for You observe trouble and grief,
To repay *it* by Your hand.
The helpless commits himself to You;
You are the helper of the fatherless.

15 Break the arm of the wicked and the evil *man;*
Seek out his wickedness *until* You find none.

PROVERBS FOR TODAY/ 19:6-7

Many entreat the favor of the nobility, and every man is *a friend to one who gives gifts.* □ *All the brothers of the poor hate him; how much more do his friends go far from him! He may pursue* them *with words,* yet *they abandon* him.

1 CHRONICLES 16:37–18:17

So he [David] left Asaph and his brothers there before the ark of the covenant of the LORD to minister before the ark regularly, as every day's work required; 38and Obed-Edom with his sixty-eight brethren, including Obed-Edom the son of Jeduthun, and Hosah, *to be* gatekeepers; 39and Zadok the priest and his brethren the priests, before the tabernacle of the LORD at the high place that *was* at Gibeon, 40to offer burnt offerings to the LORD on the altar of burnt offering regularly morning and evening, and *to do* according to all that is written in the Law of the LORD which He commanded Israel; 41and with them Heman and Jeduthun and the rest who were chosen, who were designated by name, to give thanks to the LORD, because His mercy *endures* forever; 42and with them Heman and Jeduthun, to sound aloud with trumpets and cymbals and the musical instruments of God. Now the sons of Jeduthun *were* gatekeepers.

43Then all the people departed, every man to his house; and David returned to bless his house.

Now it came to pass, when David was dwelling in his house, that David said to Nathan the prophet, "See now, I dwell in a house of cedar, but the ark of the covenant of the LORD *is* under tent curtains."

2Then Nathan said to David, "Do all that *is* in your heart, for God *is* with you."

3But it happened that night that the word of God came to Nathan, saying, 4"Go and tell My servant David, 'Thus says the LORD: "You shall not build Me a house to dwell in. 5For I have not dwelt in a house since the time that I brought up Israel, even to this day, but have gone from tent to tent, and from *one* tabernacle *to another.* 6Wherever I have moved about with all Israel, have I ever spoken a word to any of the judges of Israel, whom I commanded to shepherd My people, saying, 'Why have you not built Me a house of cedar?' " ' 7Now therefore, thus shall you say to My servant David, 'Thus says the LORD of hosts: "I took you from the sheepfold, from following the sheep, to be ruler over My people Israel. 8And I have been with you wherever you have gone, and have cut off all your enemies from before you, and have made you a name like the name of the great men who *are* on the earth. 9Moreover I will appoint a place for My people Israel, and will plant them, that they may dwell in a place of their own and move no more; nor shall the sons of wickedness oppress them anymore, as previously, 10since the time that I commanded judges *to be* over My people Israel. Also I will subdue all your enemies. Furthermore I tell you that the LORD will build you a house.* 11And it shall be, when your days are fulfilled, when you must go *to be* with your fathers, that I will set up your seed after you, who will be of your sons; and I will establish his kingdom. 12He shall build Me a house, and I will establish his throne forever. 13I will be his Father, and he shall be My son; and I will not take My mercy away from him, as I took *it* from *him* who was before you. 14And I will establish him in My house and in My kingdom forever; and his throne shall be established forever." ' "

15According to all these words and

according to all this vision, so Nathan spoke to David.

16Then King David went in and sat before the LORD; and he said: "Who *am* I, O LORD God? And what is my house, that You have brought me this far? 17And *yet* this was a small thing in Your sight, O God; and You have *also* spoken of Your servant's house for a great while to come, and have regarded me according to the rank of a man of high degree, O LORD God. 18What more can David *say* to You for the honor of Your servant? For You know Your servant. 19O LORD, for Your servant's sake, and according to Your own heart, You have done all this greatness, in making known all these great things. 20O LORD, *there is* none like You, nor *is there any* God besides You, according to all that we have heard with our ears. 21And who *is* like Your people Israel, the one nation on the earth whom God went to redeem for Himself *as* a people—to make for Yourself a name by great and awesome deeds, by driving out nations from before Your people whom You redeemed from Egypt? 22For You have made Your people Israel Your very own people forever; and You, LORD, have become their God.

23"And now, O LORD, the word which You have spoken concerning Your servant and concerning his house, *let it* be established forever, and do as You have said. 24So let it be established, that Your name may be magnified forever, saying, 'The LORD of hosts, the God of Israel, *is* Israel's God.' And let the house of Your servant David be established before You. 25For You, O my God, have revealed to Your servant that You will build him a house. Therefore Your servant has found it *in his heart* to pray before You. 26And now, LORD, You are God, and have promised this goodness to Your servant. 27Now You have been pleased to bless the house of Your servant, that it may continue before You forever; for

You have blessed it, O LORD, and *it shall be* blessed forever."

AFTER this it came to pass that David attacked the Philistines, subdued them, and took Gath and its towns from the hand of the Philistines. 2Then he defeated Moab, and the Moabites became David's servants, *and* brought tribute.

3And David defeated Hadadezer* king of Zobah *as far as* Hamath, as he went to establish his power by the River Euphrates. 4David took from him one thousand chariots, seven thousand* horsemen, and twenty thousand foot soldiers. Also David hamstrung all the chariot *horses,* except that he spared enough of them for one hundred chariots.

5When the Syrians of Damascus came to help Hadadezer king of Zobah, David killed twenty-two thousand of the Syrians. 6Then David put *garrisons* in Syria of Damascus; and the Syrians became David's servants, *and* brought tribute. So the LORD preserved David wherever he went. 7And David took the shields of gold that were on the servants of Hadadezer, and brought them to Jerusalem. 8Also from Tibhath* and from Chun, cities of Hadadezer, David brought a large amount of bronze, with which Solomon made the bronze Sea, the pillars, and the articles of bronze.

9Now when Tou* king of Hamath heard that David had defeated all the army of Hadadezer king of Zobah, 10he sent Hadoram* his son to King David, to greet him and bless him, because he had fought against Hadadezer and defeated him (for Hadadezer had been at war with Tou); and *Hadoram brought with him* all kinds of articles of gold, silver, and bronze. 11King David also dedicated these to the LORD, along with the silver and gold that he had brought from all *these* nations—from Edom, from Moab, from the people of

Ammon, from the Philistines, and from Amalek.

¹²Moreover Abishai the son of Zeruiah killed eighteen thousand Edomites* in the Valley of Salt. ¹³He also put garrisons in Edom, and all the Edomites became David's servants. And the LORD preserved David wherever he went.

¹⁴So David reigned over all Israel, and administered judgment and justice to all his people. ¹⁵Joab the son of Zeruiah *was* over the army; Jehoshaphat the son of Ahilud *was* recorder; ¹⁶Zadok the son of Ahitub and Abimelech the son of Abiathar *were* the priests; Shavsha* *was* the scribe; ¹⁷Benaiah the son of Jehoiada *was* over the Cherethites and the Pelethites; and David's sons *were* chief ministers at the king's side.

ROMANS 2:1-24

THEREFORE you are inexcusable, O man, whoever you are who judge, for in whatever you judge another you condemn yourself; for you who judge practice the same things. ²But we know that the judgment of God is according to truth against those who practice such things. ³And do you think this, O man, you who judge those practicing such things, and doing the same, that you will escape the judgment of God? ⁴Or do you despise the riches of His goodness, forbearance, and longsuffering, not knowing that the goodness of God leads you to repentance? ⁵But in accordance with your hardness and your impenitent heart you are treasuring up for yourself wrath in the day of wrath and revelation of the righteous judgment of God, ⁶who *"will render to each one according to his deeds":** ⁷eternal life to those who by patient continuance in doing good seek for glory, honor, and immortality; ⁸but to those who are self-seeking and do not obey the truth, but

obey unrighteousness—indignation and wrath, ⁹tribulation and anguish, on every soul of man who does evil, of the Jew first and also of the Greek; ¹⁰but glory, honor, and peace to everyone who works what is good, to the Jew first and also to the Greek. ¹¹For there is no partiality with God.

¹²For as many as have sinned without law will also perish without law, and as many as have sinned in the law will be judged by the law ¹³(for not the hearers of the law *are* just in the sight of God, but the doers of the law will be justified; ¹⁴for when Gentiles, who do not have the law, by nature do the things in the law, these, although not having the law, are a law to themselves, ¹⁵who show the work of the law written in their hearts, their conscience also bearing witness, and between themselves *their* thoughts accusing or else excusing *them*) ¹⁶in the day when God will judge the secrets of men by Jesus Christ, according to my gospel.

¹⁷Indeed* you are called a Jew, and rest on the law, and make your boast in God, ¹⁸and know *His* will, and approve the things that are excellent, being instructed out of the law, ¹⁹and are confident that you yourself are a guide to the blind, a light to those who are in darkness, ²⁰an instructor of the foolish, a teacher of babes, having the form of knowledge and truth in the law. ²¹You, therefore, who teach another, do you not teach yourself? You who preach that a man should not steal, do you steal? ²²You who say, "Do not commit adultery," do you commit adultery? You who abhor idols, do you rob temples? ²³You who make your boast in the law, do you dishonor God through breaking the law? ²⁴For *"the name of God is blasphemed among the Gentiles because of you,"** as it is written.

PSALM 10:16-18

THE LORD *is* King forever and ever;
The nations have perished out of
His land.
17 LORD, You have heard the
desire of the humble;
You will prepare their heart;

You will cause Your ear to
hear,
18 To do justice to the fatherless
and the oppressed,
That the man of the earth
may oppress no more.

PROVERBS FOR TODAY/ 19:8-9

He who gets wisdom loves his own soul; he who keeps understanding will find good.
□ *A false witness will not go unpunished, and* he who *speaks lies shall perish.*

JULY 15

1 CHRONICLES 19:1–21:30

IT happened after this that Nahash the king of the people of Ammon died, and his son reigned in his place. 2Then David said, "I will show kindness to Hanun the son of Nahash, because his father showed kindness to me." So David sent messengers to comfort him concerning his father. And David's servants came to Hanun in the land of the people of Ammon to comfort him.

3And the princes of the people of Ammon said to Hanun, "Do you think that David really honors your father because he has sent comforters to you? Did his servants not come to you to search and to overthrow and to spy out the land?"

4Therefore Hanun took David's servants, shaved them, and cut off their garments in the middle, at their buttocks, and sent them away. 5Then *some* went and told David about the men; and he sent to meet them, because the men were greatly ashamed. And the king said, "Wait at Jericho until your beards have grown, and *then* return."

6When the people of Ammon saw that they had made themselves repul-

sive to David, Hanun and the people of Ammon sent a thousand talents of silver to hire for themselves chariots and horsemen from Mesopotamia,* from Syrian Maacah, and from Zobah.* 7So they hired for themselves thirty-two thousand chariots, with the king of Maacah and his people, who came and encamped before Medeba. Also the people of Ammon gathered together from their cities, and came to battle.

8Now when David heard *of it,* he sent Joab and all the army of the mighty men. 9Then the people of Ammon came out and put themselves in battle array before the gate of the city, and the kings who had come *were* by themselves in the field.

10When Joab saw that the battle line was against him before and behind, he chose some of Israel's best, and put *them* in battle array against the Syrians. 11And the rest of the people he put under the command of Abishai his brother, and they set *themselves* in battle array against the people of Ammon. 12Then he said, "If the Syrians are too strong for me, then you shall help me; but if the people of Ammon are too strong for you, then I will help you. ¹³Be of good courage, and let us be strong for our people and for the cities of our God. And may the LORD do *what is* good in His sight."

¹⁴So Joab and the people who *were* with him drew near for the battle against the Syrians, and they fled before him. ¹⁵When the people of Ammon saw that the Syrians were fleeing, they also fled before Abishai his brother, and entered the city. So Joab went to Jerusalem.

¹⁶Now when the Syrians saw that they had been defeated by Israel, they sent messengers and brought the Syrians who were beyond the River,* and Shophach* the commander of Hadadezer's army *went* before them. ¹⁷When it was told David, he gathered all Israel, crossed over the Jordan and came upon them, and set up in battle array against them. So when David had set up in *battle* array against the Syrians, they fought with him. ¹⁸Then the Syrians fled before Israel; and David killed seven thousand* charioteers and forty thousand foot soldiers* of the Syrians, and killed Shophach the commander of the army. ¹⁹And when the servants of Hadadezer saw that they were defeated by Israel, they made peace with David and became his servants. So the Syrians were not willing to help the people of Ammon anymore.

IT happened in the spring of the year, at the time kings go out *to battle*, that Joab led out the armed forces and ravaged the country of the people of Ammon, and came and besieged Rabbah. But David stayed at Jerusalem. And Joab defeated Rabbah and overthrew it. ²Then David took their king's crown from his head, and found it to weigh a talent of gold, and *there were* precious stones in it. And it was set on David's head. Also he brought out the spoil of the city in great abundance. ³And he brought out the people who *were* in it, and put *them* to work*

with saws, with iron picks, and with axes. So David did to all the cities of the people of Ammon. Then David and all the people returned *to* Jerusalem.

⁴Now it happened afterward that war broke out at Gezer with the Philistines, at which time Sibbechai the Hushathite killed Sippai,* *who was one* of the sons of the giant. And they were subdued.

⁵Again there was war with the Philistines, and Elhanan the son of Jair* killed Lahmi the brother of Goliath the Gittite, the shaft of whose spear *was* like a weaver's beam.

⁶Yet again there was war at Gath, where there was a man of *great* stature, with twenty-four fingers and toes, six *on each hand* and six *on each foot;* and he also was born to the giant. ⁷So when he defied Israel, Jonathan the son of Shimea,* David's brother, killed him.

⁸These were born to the giant in Gath, and they fell by the hand of David and by the hand of his servants.

Now Satan stood up against Israel, and moved David to number Israel. ²So David said to Joab and to the leaders of the people, "Go, number Israel from Beersheba to Dan, and bring the number of them to me that I may know *it.*"

³And Joab answered, "May the LORD make His people a hundred times more than they are. But, my lord the king, *are* they not all my lord's servants? Why then does my lord require this thing? Why should he be a cause of guilt in Israel?"

⁴Nevertheless the king's word prevailed against Joab. Therefore Joab departed and went throughout all Israel and came to Jerusalem. ⁵Then Joab gave the sum of the number of the people to David. All Israel *had* one million one hundred thousand men who drew the sword, and Judah *had* four hundred and seventy thousand men who drew the sword. ⁶But he did not

count Levi and Benjamin among them, for the king's word was abominable to Joab.

⁷And God was displeased with this thing; therefore He struck Israel. ⁸So David said to God, "I have sinned greatly, because I have done this thing; but now, I pray, take away the iniquity of Your servant, for I have done very foolishly."

⁹Then the LORD spoke to Gad, David's seer, saying, ¹⁰"Go and tell David, saying, 'Thus says the LORD: "I offer you three *things,* choose one of them for yourself, that I may do *it* to you." ' "

¹¹So Gad came to David and said to him, "Thus says the LORD: 'Choose for yourself, ¹²either three* years of famine, or three months to be defeated by your foes with the sword of your enemies overtaking *you,* or else for three days the sword of the LORD—the plague in the land, with the angel* of the LORD destroying throughout all the territory of Israel.' Now consider what answer I should take back to Him who sent me."

¹³And David said to Gad, "I am in great distress. Please let me fall into the hand of the LORD, for His mercies *are* very great; but do not let me fall into the hand of man."

¹⁴So the LORD sent a plague upon Israel, and seventy thousand men of Israel fell. ¹⁵And God sent an angel to Jerusalem to destroy it. As he* was destroying, the LORD looked and relented of the disaster, and said to the angel who was destroying, "It is enough; now restrain your* hand." And the angel of the LORD stood by the threshing floor of Ornan* the Jebusite.

¹⁶Then David lifted his eyes and saw the angel of the LORD standing between earth and heaven, having in his hand a drawn sword stretched out over Jerusalem. So David and the elders, clothed in sackcloth, fell on their faces. ¹⁷And David said to God, "Was it not I who commanded the people to be numbered? I am the one who has sinned and done evil indeed; but these sheep, what have they done? Let Your hand, I pray, O LORD my God, be against me and my father's house, but not against Your people that they should be plagued."

¹⁸Therefore, the angel of the LORD commanded Gad to say to David that David should go and erect an altar to the LORD on the threshing floor of Ornan the Jebusite. ¹⁹So David went up at the word of Gad, which he had spoken in the name of the LORD. ²⁰Now Ornan turned and saw the angel; and his four sons *who were* with him hid themselves, but Ornan continued threshing wheat. ²¹So David came to Ornan, and Ornan looked and saw David. And he went out from the threshing floor, and bowed before David with *his* face to the ground. ²²Then David said to Ornan, "Grant me the place of *this* threshing floor, that I may build an altar on it to the LORD. You shall grant it to me at the full price, that the plague may be withdrawn from the people."

²³But Ornan said to David, "Take *it* to yourself, and let my lord the king do *what is* good in his eyes. Look, I *also* give *you* the oxen for burnt offerings, the threshing implements for wood, and the wheat for the grain offering; I give *it* all."

²⁴Then King David said to Ornan, "No, but I will surely buy *it* for the full price, for I will not take what is yours for the LORD, nor offer burnt offerings with *that which* costs *me* nothing." ²⁵So David gave Ornan six hundred shekels of gold by weight for the place. ²⁶And David built there an altar to the LORD, and offered burnt offerings and peace offerings, and called on the LORD; and He answered him from heaven by fire on the altar of burnt offering.

²⁷So the LORD commanded the an-

gel, and he returned his sword to its sheath.

28At that time, when David saw that the LORD had answered him on the threshing floor of Ornan the Jebusite, he sacrificed there. 29For the tabernacle of the LORD and the altar of the burnt offering, which Moses had made in the wilderness, *were* at that time at the high place in Gibeon. 30But David could not go before it to inquire of God, for he was afraid of the sword of the angel of the LORD.

ROMANS 2:25–3:8

FOR circumcision is indeed profitable if you keep the law; but if you are a breaker of the law, your circumcision has become uncircumcision. 26Therefore, if an uncircumcised man keeps the righteous requirements of the law, will not his uncircumcision be counted as circumcision? 27And will not the physically uncircumcised, if he fulfills the law, judge you who, *even* with *your* written *code* and circumcision, *are* a transgressor of the law? 28For he is not a Jew who *is* one outwardly, nor *is* circumcision that which *is* outward in the flesh; 29but *he is* a Jew who *is one* inwardly; and circumcision *is that* of the heart, in the Spirit, not in the letter; whose praise *is* not from men but from God.

WHAT advantage then has the Jew, or what *is* the profit of circumcision? 2Much in every way! Chiefly because to them were committed the oracles of God. 3For what if some did not believe? Will their unbelief make the faithfulness of God without effect? 4Certainly not! Indeed, let God be true but every man a liar. As it is written:

> "That You may be justified in
> Your words,
> And may overcome when You
> are judged." *

5But if our unrighteousness demonstrates the righteousness of God, what shall we say? *Is* God unjust who inflicts wrath? (I speak as a man.) 6Certainly not! For then how will God judge the world?

7For if the truth of God has increased through my lie to His glory, why am I also still judged as a sinner? 8And *why* not *say*, "Let us do evil that good may come"?—as we are slanderously reported and as some affirm that we say. Their condemnation is just.

PSALM 11:1-7

To the Chief Musician. A Psalm of David.

IN the LORD I put my trust;
How can you say to my soul,
"Flee *as* a bird to your mountain"?

2   For look! The wicked bend
       their bow,
    They make ready their arrow
       on the string,
    That they may shoot secretly
       at the upright in heart.

3   If the foundations are
       destroyed,
    What can the righteous do?

4   The LORD *is* in His holy temple,
    The LORD's throne *is* in heaven;
    His eyes behold,
    His eyelids test the sons of
       men.

5   The LORD tests the righteous,
    But the wicked and the one
       who loves violence His soul
       hates.

6   Upon the wicked He will rain
       coals;
    Fire and brimstone and a
       burning wind
    Shall be the portion of their
       cup.

7   For the LORD *is* righteous,
    He loves righteousness;
    His countenance beholds the
       upright.*

PROVERBS FOR TODAY/ 19:10-12

Luxury is not fitting for a fool, much less for a servant to rule over princes. □ *The discretion of a man makes him slow to anger, and his glory* is *to overlook a transgression.* □ *The king's wrath* is *like the roaring of a lion, but his favor* is *like dew on the grass.*

JULY 16

1 CHRONICLES 22:1–23:32

THEN David said, "This *is* the house of the LORD God, and this *is* the altar of burnt offering for Israel." ²So David commanded to gather the aliens who *were* in the land of Israel; and he appointed masons to cut hewn stones to build the house of God. ³And David prepared iron in abundance for the nails of the doors of the gates and for the joints, and bronze in abundance beyond measure, ⁴and cedar trees in abundance; for the Sidonians and those from Tyre brought much cedar wood to David.

⁵Now David said, "Solomon my son *is* young and inexperienced, and the house to be built for the LORD *must be* exceedingly magnificent, famous and glorious throughout all countries. I will now make preparation for it." So David made abundant preparations before his death.

⁶Then he called for his son Solomon, and charged him to build a house for the LORD God of Israel. ⁷And David said to Solomon: "My son, as for me, it was in my mind to build a house to the name of the LORD my God; ⁸but the word of the LORD came to me, saying, 'You have shed much blood and have made great wars; you shall not build a house for My name, because you have shed much blood on the earth in My sight. ⁹Behold, a son shall be born to you, who shall be a man of rest; and I will give him rest from all his enemies all around. His name shall be Solomon,* for I will give peace and quietness to Israel in his days. ¹⁰He shall build a house for My name, and he shall be My son, and I *will be* his Father; and I will establish the throne of his kingdom over Israel forever.' ¹¹Now, my son, may the LORD be with you; and may you prosper, and build the house of the LORD your God, as He has said to you. ¹²Only may the LORD give you wisdom and understanding, and give you charge concerning Israel, that you may keep the law of the LORD your God. ¹³Then you will prosper, if you take care to fulfill the statutes and judgments with which the LORD charged Moses concerning Israel. Be strong and of good courage; do not fear nor be dismayed. ¹⁴Indeed I have taken much trouble to prepare for the house of the LORD one hundred thousand talents of gold and one million talents of silver, and bronze and iron beyond measure, for it is so abundant. I have prepared timber and stone also, and you may add to them. ¹⁵Moreover *there are* workmen with you in abundance: woodsmen and stonecutters, and all types of skillful men for every kind of work. ¹⁶Of gold and silver and bronze and iron *there is* no limit. Arise and begin working, and the LORD be with you."

¹⁷David also commanded all the leaders of Israel to help Solomon his son, *saying,* ¹⁸"*Is* not the LORD your God

with you? And has He *not* given you rest on every side? For He has given the inhabitants of the land into my hand, and the land is subdued before the Lord and before His people. 19Now set your heart and your soul to seek the Lord your God. Therefore arise and build the sanctuary of the Lord God, to bring the ark of the covenant of the Lord and the holy articles of God into the house that is to be built for the name of the Lord."

So when David was old and full of days, he made his son Solomon king over Israel.

2And he gathered together all the leaders of Israel, with the priests and the Levites. 3Now the Levites were numbered from the age of thirty years and above; and the number of individual males was thirty-eight thousand. 4Of these, twenty-four thousand *were* to look after the work of the house of the Lord, six thousand *were* officers and judges, 5four thousand *were* gatekeepers, and four thousand praised the Lord with *musical* instruments, "which I made," *said David,* "for giving praise."

6Also David separated them into divisions among the sons of Levi: Gershon, Kohath, and Merari.

7Of the Gershonites: Laadan* and Shimei. 8The sons of Laadan: the first Jehiel, then Zetham and Joel—three *in all.* 9The sons of Shimei: Shelomith, Haziel, and Haran—three *in all.* These were the heads of the fathers' *houses* of Laadan. 10And the sons of Shimei: Jahath, Zina,* Jeush, and Beriah. These *were* the four sons of Shimei. 11Jahath was the first and Zizah the second. But Jeush and Beriah did not have many sons; therefore they were assigned as one father's house.

12The sons of Kohath: Amram, Izhar, Hebron, and Uzziel—four *in all.* 13The sons of Amram: Aaron and Moses; and Aaron was set apart, he and his sons forever, that he should sanctify the most holy things, to burn incense before the Lord, to minister to Him, and to give the blessing in His name forever. 14Now the sons of Moses the man of God were reckoned to the tribe of Levi. 15The sons of Moses *were* Gershon* and Eliezer. 16Of the sons of Gershon, Shebuel* *was* the first. 17Of the descendants of Eliezer, Rehabiah was the first. And Eliezer had no other sons, but the sons of Rehabiah were very many. 18Of the sons of Izhar, Shelomith *was* the first. 19Of the sons of Hebron, Jeriah *was* the first, Amariah the second, Jahaziel the third, and Jekameam the fourth. 20Of the sons of Uzziel, Michah *was* the first and Jesshiah the second.

21The sons of Merari *were* Mahli and Mushi. The sons of Mahli *were* Eleazar and Kish. 22And Eleazar died, and had no sons, but only daughters; and their brethren, the sons of Kish, took them *as wives.* 23The sons of Mushi *were* Mahli, Eder, and Jeremoth—three *in all.*

24These *were* the sons of Levi by their fathers' houses—the heads of the fathers' *houses* as they were counted individually by the number of their names, who did the work for the service of the house of the Lord, from the age of twenty years and above.

25For David said, "The Lord God of Israel has given rest to His people, that they may dwell in Jerusalem forever"; 26and also to the Levites, "They shall no longer carry the tabernacle, or any of the articles for its service." 27For by the last words of David the Levites *were* numbered from twenty years old and above; 28because their duty *was* to help the sons of Aaron in the service of the house of the Lord, in the courts and in the chambers, in the purifying of all holy things and the work of the service of the house of God, 29both with the showbread and the fine flour for the grain offering, with the unleavened cakes and *what is baked in* the pan, with what is mixed and with all kinds of measures and sizes; 30to stand every morning to thank and praise the LORD, and likewise at evening; 31and at every presentation of a burnt offering to the LORD on the Sabbaths and on the New Moons and on the set feasts, by number according to the ordinance governing them, regularly before the LORD; 32and that they should attend to the needs of the tabernacle of meeting, the needs of the holy *place,* and the needs of the sons of Aaron their brethren in the work of the house of the LORD.

ROMANS 3:9-31

WHAT then? Are we better *than they?* Not at all. For we have previously charged both Jews and Greeks that they are all under sin.

10As it is written:

> "There is none righteous, no,
> not one;
> 11 There is none who
> understands;
> There is none who seeks after
> God.
> 12 They have all turned aside;
> They have together become
> unprofitable;
> There is none who does good,
> no, not one." *
> 13 "Their throat is an open tomb;
> With their tongues they have
> practiced deceit"; *
> "The poison of asps is under
> their lips"; *
> 14 "Whose mouth is full of
> cursing and bitterness." *
> 15 "Their feet are swift to shed
> blood;
> 16 Destruction and misery are in
> their ways;
> 17 And the way of peace they
> have not known." *
> 18 "There is no fear of God before
> their eyes." *

19Now we know that whatever the law says, it says to those who are under the law, that every mouth may be stopped, and all the world may become guilty before God. 20Therefore by the deeds of the law no flesh will be justified in His sight, for by the law *is* the knowledge of sin.

21But now the righteousness of God apart from the law is revealed, being witnessed by the Law and the Prophets, 22even the righteousness of God, through faith in Jesus Christ, to all and on all* who believe. For there is no difference; 23for all have sinned and fall short of the glory of God, 24being justified freely by His grace through the redemption that is in Christ Jesus, 25whom God set forth as a propitiation by His blood, through faith, to demonstrate His righteousness, because in His forbearance God had passed over the sins that were previously committed, 26to demonstrate at the present time His righteousness, that He might be just and the justifier of the one who has faith in Jesus.

27Where *is* boasting then? It is excluded. By what law? Of works? No, but by the law of faith. 28Therefore we conclude that a man is justified by faith apart from the deeds of the law. 29Or *is* He the God of the Jews only? *Is He* not also the God of the Gentiles? Yes, of the Gentiles also, 30since *there is* one God who will justify the circumcised by faith and the uncircumcised through faith. 31Do we then make void the law through faith? Certainly not! On the contrary, we establish the law.

PSALM 12:1-8

*To the Chief Musician. On an eight-stringed harp. * A Psalm of David.*

HELP, LORD, for the godly man ceases!
For the faithful disappear from
among the sons of men.

2   They speak idly everyone
        with his neighbor;
     With flattering lips *and* a
        double heart they speak.

3   May the LORD cut off all
        flattering lips,
     And the tongue that speaks
        proud things,
4   Who have said,
     "With our tongue we will
        prevail;
     Our lips *are* our own;
     Who *is* lord over us?"

5   "For the oppression of the
        poor, for the sighing of the
        needy,

     Now I will arise," says the
        LORD;
     "I will set *him* in the safety for
        which he yearns."

6   The words of the LORD *are*
        pure words,
     Like silver tried in a furnace of
        earth,
     Purified seven times.
7   You shall keep them, O LORD,
     You shall preserve them from
        this generation forever.

8   The wicked prowl on every
        side,
     When vileness is exalted
        among the sons of men.

PROVERBS FOR TODAY/ 19:13-14

A foolish son is *the ruin of his father, and the contentions of a wife* are *a continual
dripping.* □ *Houses and riches* are *an inheritance from fathers, but a prudent wife*
is *from the LORD.*

JULY 17

1 CHRONICLES 24:1–26:11

Now *these are* the divisions of the sons of Aaron. The sons of Aaron *were* Nadab, Abihu, Eleazar, and Ithamar. 2And Nadab and Abihu died before their father, and had no children; therefore Eleazar and Ithamar ministered as priests. 3Then David with Zadok of the sons of Eleazar, and Ahimelech of the sons of Ithamar, divided them according to the schedule of their service.

4There were more leaders found of the sons of Eleazar than of the sons of Ithamar, and *thus* they were divided. Among the sons of Eleazar *were* sixteen heads of *their* fathers' houses, and

eight heads of their fathers' houses among the sons of Ithamar. 5Thus they were divided by lot, one group as another, for there were officials of the sanctuary and officials *of the house* of God, from the sons of Eleazar and from the sons of Ithamar. 6And the scribe, Shemaiah the son of Nethanel, *one of* the Levites, wrote them down before the king, the leaders, Zadok the priest, Ahimelech the son of Abiathar, and the heads of the fathers' *houses* of the priests and Levites, one father's house taken for Eleazar and *one* for Ithamar.

7Now the first lot fell to Jehoiarib, the second to Jedaiah, 8the third to Harim, the fourth to Seorim, 9the fifth to

Malchijah, the sixth to Mijamin, [10]the seventh to Hakkoz, the eighth to Abijah, [11]the ninth to Jeshua, the tenth to Shecaniah, [12]the eleventh to Eliashib, the twelfth to Jakim, [13]the thirteenth to Huppah, the fourteenth to Jeshebeab, [14]the fifteenth to Bilgah, the sixteenth to Immer, [15]the seventeenth to Hezir, the eighteenth to Happizzez,* [16]the nineteenth to Pethahiah, the twentieth to Jehezekel,* [17]the twenty-first to Jachin, the twenty-second to Gamul, [18]the twenty-third to Delaiah, the twenty-fourth to Maaziah.

[19]This *was* the schedule of their service for coming into the house of the LORD according to their ordinance by the hand of Aaron their father, as the LORD God of Israel had commanded him.

[20]And the rest of the sons of Levi: of the sons of Amram, Shubael;* of the sons of Shubael, Jehdeiah. [21]Concerning Rehabiah, of the sons of Rehabiah, the first *was* Isshiah. [22]Of the Izharites, Shelomoth;* of the sons of Shelomoth, Jahath. [23]Of the sons *of Hebron,** Jeriah *was the first,** Amariah the second, Jahaziel the third, *and* Jekameam the fourth. [24]*Of* the sons of Uzziel, Michah; of the sons of Michah, Shamir. [25]The brother of Michah, Isshiah; of the sons of Isshiah, Zechariah. [26]The sons of Merari *were* Mahli and Mushi; the son of Jaaziah, Beno. [27]The sons of Merari by Jaaziah *were* Beno, Shoham, Zaccur, and Ibri. [28]Of Mahli: Eleazar, who had no sons. [29]Of Kish: the son of Kish, Jerahmeel.

[30]Also the sons of Mushi *were* Mahli, Eder, and Jerimoth. These *were* the sons of the Levites according to their fathers' houses.

[31]These also cast lots just as their brothers the sons of Aaron did, in the presence of King David, Zadok, Ahimelech, and the heads of the fathers' *houses* of the priests and Levites. The chief fathers *did* just as their younger brethren.

MOREOVER David and the captains of the army separated for the service *some* of the sons of Asaph, of Heman, and of Jeduthun, who *should* prophesy with harps, stringed instruments, and cymbals. And the number of the skilled men performing their service was: [2]Of the sons of Asaph: Zaccur, Joseph, Nethaniah, and Asharelah;* the sons of Asaph *were* under the direction of Asaph, who prophesied according to the order of the king. [3]Of Jeduthun, the sons of Jeduthun: Gedaliah, Zeri,* Jeshaiah, Shimei, Hashabiah, and Mattithiah, six,* under the direction of their father Jeduthun, who prophesied with a harp to give thanks and to praise the LORD. [4]Of Heman, the sons of Heman: Bukkiah, Mattaniah, Uzziel,* Shebuel,* Jerimoth,* Hananiah, Hanani, Eliathah, Giddalti, Romamti-Ezer, Joshbekashah, Mallothi, Hothir, *and* Mahazioth. [5]All these *were* the sons of Heman the king's seer in the words of God, to exalt his horn.* For God gave Heman fourteen sons and three daughters.

[6]All these *were* under the direction of their father for the music *in* the house of the LORD, with cymbals, stringed instruments, and harps, for the service of the house of God. Asaph, Jeduthun, and Heman *were* under the authority of the king. [7]So the number of them, with their brethren who were instructed in the songs of the LORD, all who were skillful, *was* two hundred and eighty-eight.

[8]And they cast lots for their duty, the small as well as the great, the teacher with the student.

[9]Now the first lot for Asaph came out for Joseph; the second for Gedaliah, him with his brethren and sons, twelve; [10]the third for Zaccur, his sons and his brethren, twelve; [11]the fourth for Jizri,* his sons and his brethren, twelve; [12]the fifth for Nethaniah, his sons and his brethren, twelve; [13]the sixth for Bukkiah, his sons and his

brethren, twelve; [14]the seventh for Jesharelah,* his sons and his brethren, twelve; [15]the eighth for Jeshaiah, his sons and his brethren, twelve; [16]the ninth for Mattaniah, his sons and his brethren, twelve; [17]the tenth for Shimei, his sons and his brethren, twelve; [18]the eleventh for Azarel,* his sons and his brethren, twelve; [19]the twelfth for Hashabiah, his sons and his brethren, twelve; [20]the thirteenth for Shubael,* his sons and his brethren, twelve; [21]the fourteenth for Mattithiah, his sons and his brethren, twelve; [22]the fifteenth for Jeremoth,* his sons and his brethren, twelve; [23]the sixteenth for Hananiah, his sons and his brethren, twelve; [24]the seventeenth for Joshbekashah, his sons and his brethren, twelve; [25]the eighteenth for Hanani, his sons and his brethren, twelve; [26]the nineteenth for Mallothi, his sons and his brethren, twelve; [27]the twentieth for Eliathah, his sons and his brethren, twelve; [28]the twenty-first for Hothir, his sons and his brethren, twelve; [29]the twenty-second for Giddalti, his sons and his brethren, twelve; [30]the twenty-third for Mahazioth, his sons and his brethren, twelve; [31]the twenty-fourth for Romamti-Ezer, his sons and his brethren, twelve.

CONCERNING the divisions of the gatekeepers: of the Korahites, Meshelemiah the son of Kore, of the sons of Asaph. [2]And the sons of Meshelemiah were Zechariah the firstborn, Jediael the second, Zebadiah the third, Jathniel the fourth, [3]Elam the fifth, Jehohanan the sixth, Eliehoenai the seventh.

[4]Moreover the sons of Obed-Edom were Shemaiah the firstborn, Jehozabad the second, Joah the third, Sacar the fourth, Nethanel the fifth, [5]Ammiel the sixth, Issachar the seventh, Peulthai the eighth; for God blessed him.

[6]Also to Shemaiah his son were sons born who governed their fathers' houses, because they were men of great ability. [7]The sons of Shemaiah were Othni, Rephael, Obed, and Elzabad, whose brothers Elihu and Semachiah were able men.

[8]All these were of the sons of Obed-Edom, they and their sons and their brethren, able men with strength for the work: sixty-two of Obed-Edom.

[9]And Meshelemiah had sons and brethren, eighteen able men.

[10]Also Hosah, of the children of Merari, had sons: Shimri the first (for though he was not the firstborn, his father made him the first), [11]Hilkiah the second, Tebaliah the third, Zechariah the fourth; all the sons and brethren of Hosah were thirteen.

ROMANS 4:1-12

WHAT then shall we say that Abraham our father has found according to the flesh?* [2]For if Abraham was justified by works, he has something to boast about, but not before God. [3]For what does the Scripture say? *"Abraham believed God, and it was accounted to him for righteousness."* * [4]Now to him who works, the wages are not counted as grace but as debt.

[5]But to him who does not work but believes on Him who justifies the ungodly, his faith is accounted for righteousness, [6]just as David also describes the blessedness of the man to whom God imputes righteousness apart from works:

7   *"Blessed are those whose*
        lawless deeds are forgiven,
      And whose sins are covered;
8   *Blessed is the man to whom*
        the LORD shall not impute
        sin." *

[9]*Does* this blessedness then *come* upon the circumcised *only,* or upon the uncircumcised also? For we say that

faith was accounted to Abraham for righteousness. [10]How then was it accounted? While he was circumcised, or uncircumcised? Not while circumcised, but while uncircumcised. [11]And he received the sign of circumcision, a seal of the righteousness of the faith which *he had while still* uncircumcised, that he might be the father of all those who believe, though they are uncircumcised, that righteousness might be imputed to them also, [12]and the father of circumcision to those who not only *are* of the circumcision, but who also walk in the steps of the faith which our father Abraham *had while still* uncircumcised.

PSALM 13:1-6
To the Chief Musician. A Psalm of David.

How long, O LORD? Will You forget me forever? How long will You hide Your face from me?

2 How long shall I take counsel in my soul, *Having* sorrow in my heart daily? How long will my enemy be exalted over me?

3 Consider *and* hear me, O LORD my God; Enlighten my eyes, Lest I sleep the *sleep of* death;

4 Lest my enemy say, "I have prevailed against him"; *Lest* those who trouble me rejoice when I am moved.

5 But I have trusted in Your mercy; My heart shall rejoice in Your salvation.

6 I will sing to the LORD, Because He has dealt bountifully with me.

PROVERBS FOR TODAY/ 19:15-16

Laziness casts one into a deep sleep, and an idle person will suffer hunger. □ *He who keeps the commandment keeps his soul, but he who is careless * of his ways will die.*

JULY 18

1 CHRONICLES 26:12–27:34

Among these *were* the divisions of the gatekeepers, among the chief men, *having* duties just like their brethren, to serve in the house of the LORD. [13]And they cast lots for each gate, the small as well as the great, according to their father's house. [14]The lot for the East *Gate* fell to Shelemiah. Then they cast lots *for* his son Zechariah, a wise counselor, and his lot came out for the North Gate; [15]to Obed-Edom the South Gate, and to his sons the storehouse.* [16]To Shuppim and Hosah *the lot came out* for the West Gate, with the Shallecheth Gate on the ascending highway—watchman opposite watchman. [17]On the east were *six* Levites, on the north four each day, on the south four each day, and for the storehouse* two by two. [18]As for the Parbar* on the west, *there were* four on the highway *and* two at the Parbar. ¹⁹These were the divisions of the gatekeepers among the sons of Korah and among the sons of Merari.

²⁰Of the Levites, Ahijah *was* over the treasuries of the house of God and over the treasuries of the dedicated things. ²¹The sons of Laadan, the descendants of the Gershonites of Laadan, heads of their fathers' *houses,* of Laadan the Gershonite: Jehieli. ²²The sons of Jehieli, Zetham and Joel his brother, *were* over the treasuries of the house of the LORD. ²³Of the Amramites, the Izharites, the Hebronites, and the Uzzielites: ²⁴Shebuel the son of Gershom, the son of Moses, *was* overseer of the treasuries. ²⁵And his brethren by Eliezer *were* Rehabiah his son, Jeshaiah his son, Joram his son, Zichri his son, and Shelomith his son.

²⁶This Shelomith and his brethren *were* over all the treasuries of the dedicated things which King David and the heads of fathers' *houses,* the captains over thousands and hundreds, and the captains of the army, had dedicated. ²⁷Some of the spoils won in battles they dedicated to maintain the house of the LORD. ²⁸And all that Samuel the seer, Saul the son of Kish, Abner the son of Ner, and Joab the son of Zeruiah had dedicated, every dedicated *thing,* was under the hand of Shelomith and his brethren.

²⁹Of the Izharites, Chenaniah and his sons *performed* duties as officials and judges over Israel outside Jerusalem.

³⁰Of the Hebronites, Hashabiah and his brethren, one thousand seven hundred able men, had the oversight of Israel on the west side of the Jordan for all the business of the LORD, and in the service of the king. ³¹Among the Hebronites, Jerijah *was* head of the Hebronites according to his genealogy of the fathers. In the fortieth year of the reign of David they were sought, and there were found among them ca-

pable men at Jazer of Gilead. ³²And his brethren *were* two thousand seven hundred able men, heads of fathers' *houses,* whom King David made officials over the Reubenites, the Gadites, and the half-tribe of Manasseh, for every matter pertaining to God and the affairs of the king.

AND the children of Israel, according to their number, the heads of fathers' *houses,* the captains of thousands and hundreds and their officers, served the king in every matter of the *military* divisions. *These divisions* came in and went out month by month throughout all the months of the year, each division *having* twenty-four thousand.

²Over the first division for the first month *was* Jashobeam the son of Zabdiel, and in his division *were* twenty-four thousand; ³*he was* of the children of Perez, and the chief of all the captains of the army for the first month. ⁴Over the division of the second month *was* Dodai* an Ahohite, and of his division Mikloth also *was* the leader; in his division *were* twenty-four thousand. ⁵The third captain of the army for the third month *was* Benaiah, the son of Jehoiada the priest, who was chief; in his division *were* twenty-four thousand. ⁶This was the Benaiah *who was* mighty *among* the thirty, and was over the thirty; in his division *was* Ammizabad his son. ⁷The fourth *captain* for the fourth month *was* Asahel the brother of Joab, and Zebadiah his son after him; in his division *were* twenty-four thousand. ⁸The fifth *captain* for the fifth month *was* Shamhuth* the Izrahite; in his division were twenty-four thousand. ⁹The sixth *captain* for the sixth month *was* Ira the son of Ikkesh the Tekoite; in his division *were* twenty-four thousand. ¹⁰The seventh *captain* for the seventh month *was* Helez the Pelonite, of the children of Ephraim; in his division *were* twenty-four thousand. ¹¹The eighth *captain*

for the eighth month *was* Sibbechai the Hushathite, of the Zarhites; in his division *were* twenty-four thousand. [12]The ninth *captain* for the ninth month *was* Abiezer the Anathothite, of the Benjamites; in his division *were* twenty-four thousand. [13]The tenth *captain* for the tenth month *was* Maharai the Netophathite, of the Zarhites; in his division *were* twenty-four thousand. [14]The eleventh *captain* for the eleventh month *was* Benaiah the Pirathonite, of the children of Ephraim; in his division *were* twenty-four thousand. [15]The twelfth *captain* for the twelfth month *was* Heldai* the Netophathite, of Othniel; in his division *were* twenty-four thousand.

[16]Furthermore, over the tribes of Israel: the officer over the Reubenites *was* Eliezer the son of Zichri; over the Simeonites, Shephatiah the son of Maachah; [17]*over* the Levites, Hashabiah the son of Kemuel; over the Aaronites, Zadok; [18]*over* Judah, Elihu, *one* of David's brothers; *over* Issachar, Omri the son of Michael; [19]*over* Zebulun, Ishmaiah the son of Obadiah; *over* Naphtali, Jerimoth the son of Azriel; [20]*over* the children of Ephraim, Hoshea the son of Azaziah; *over* the half-tribe of Manasseh, Joel the son of Pedaiah; [21]*over* the half-*tribe* of Manasseh in Gilead, Iddo the son of Zechariah; *over* Benjamin, Jaasiel the son of Abner; [22]*over* Dan, Azarel the son of Jeroham. These *were* the leaders of the tribes of Israel.

[23]But David did not take the number of those twenty years old and under, because the LORD had said He would multiply Israel like the stars of the heavens. [24]Joab the son of Zeruiah began a census, but he did not finish, for wrath came upon Israel because of this census; nor was the number recorded in the account of the chronicles of King David.

[25]And Azmaveth the son of Adiel *was* over the king's treasuries; and Jehonathan the son of Uzziah was over the storehouses in the field, in the cities, in the villages, and in the fortresses. [26]Ezri the son of Chelub was over those who did the work of the field for tilling the ground. [27]And Shimei the Ramathite *was* over the vineyards, and Zabdi the Shiphmite was over the produce of the vineyards for the supply of wine. [28]Baal-Hanan the Gederite was over the olive trees and the sycamore trees that *were* in the lowlands, and Joash *was* over the store of oil. [29]And Shitrai the Sharonite *was* over the herds that fed in Sharon, and Shaphat the son of Adlai was over the herds *that were* in the valleys. [30]Obil the Ishmaelite *was* over the camels, Jehdeiah the Meronothite *was* over the donkeys, [31]and Jaziz the Hagrite *was* over the flocks. All these *were* the officials over King David's property.

[32]Also Jehonathan, David's uncle, *was* a counselor, a wise man, and a scribe; and Jehiel the son of Hachmoni *was* with the king's sons. [33]Ahithophel *was* the king's counselor, and Hushai the Archite *was* the king's companion. [34]After Ahithophel *was* Jehoiada the son of Benaiah, then Abiathar. And the general of the king's army *was* Joab.

ROMANS 4:13–5:5

FOR the promise that he [Abraham] would be the heir of the world *was* not to Abraham or to his seed through the law, but through the righteousness of faith. [14]For if those who are of the law *are* heirs, faith is made void and the promise made of no effect, [15]because the law brings about wrath; for where there is no law *there is* no transgression.

[16]Therefore *it is* of faith that *it might be* according to grace, so that the promise might be sure to all the seed, not only to those who are of the law, but also to those who are of the faith of Abraham, who is the father of us all

¹⁷(as it is written, *"I have made you a father of many nations"* *) in the presence of Him whom he believed—God, who gives life to the dead and calls those things which do not exist as though they did; ¹⁸who, contrary to hope, in hope believed, so that he became the father of many nations, according to what was spoken, *"So shall your descendants be."* * ¹⁹And not being weak in faith, he did not consider his own body, already dead (since he was about a hundred years old), and the deadness of Sarah's womb. ²⁰He did not waver at the promise of God through unbelief, but was strengthened in faith, giving glory to God, ²¹and being fully convinced that what He had promised He was also able to perform. ²²And therefore *"it was accounted to him for righteousness."* *

²³Now it was not written for his sake alone that it was imputed to him, ²⁴but also for us. It shall be imputed to us who believe in Him who raised up Jesus our Lord from the dead, ²⁵who was delivered up because of our offenses, and was raised because of our justification.

THEREFORE, having been justified by faith, we have* peace with God through our Lord Jesus Christ, ²through whom also we have access by faith into this grace in which we stand, and rejoice in hope of the glory of God. ³And not only *that,* but we also glory in tribulations, knowing that tribulation produces perseverance; ⁴and perseverance, character; and character, hope. ⁵Now hope does not disappoint, because the love of God has been poured out in our hearts by the Holy Spirit who was given to us.

PSALM 14:1-7
To the Chief Musician. A Psalm of David.

T HE fool has said in his heart,
    "There is no God."
They are corrupt,
    They have done abominable works,
    There is none who does good.

2   The LORD looks down from
        heaven upon the children
        of men,
    To see if there are any who
        understand, who seek God.
3   They have all turned aside,
    They have together become
        corrupt;
    There is none who does good,
    No, not one.

4   Have all the workers of
        iniquity no knowledge,
    Who eat up my people *as* they
        eat bread,
    And do not call on the LORD?
5   There they are in great fear,
    For God *is* with the
        generation of the righteous.
6   You shame the counsel of the
        poor,
    But the LORD *is* his refuge.

7   Oh, that the salvation of Israel
        would come out of Zion!
    When the LORD brings back
        the captivity of His people,
    Let Jacob rejoice *and* Israel
        be glad.

PROVERBS FOR TODAY/ 19:17
He who has pity on the poor lends to the LORD, and He will pay back what he has given.

1 CHRONICLES 28:1–29:30

Now David assembled at Jerusalem all the leaders of Israel: the officers of the tribes and the captains of the divisions who served the king, the captains over thousands and captains over hundreds, and the stewards over all the substance and possessions of the king and of his sons, with the officials, the valiant men, and all the mighty men of valor.

7Then King David rose to his feet and said, "Hear me, my brethren and my people: I *had* it in my heart to build a house of rest for the ark of the covenant of the LORD, and for the footstool of our God, and had made preparations to build it. 3But God said to me, 'You shall not build a house for My name, because you *have been* a man of war and have shed blood.' 4However the LORD God of Israel chose me above all the house of my father to be king over Israel forever, for He has chosen Judah *to be* the ruler. And of the house of Judah, the house of my father, and among the sons of my father, He was pleased with me to make *me* king over all Israel. 5And of all my sons (for the LORD has given me many sons) He has chosen my son Solomon to sit on the throne of the kingdom of the LORD over Israel. 6Now He said to me, 'It is your son Solomon *who* shall build My house and My courts; for I have chosen him *to be* My son, and I will be his Father. 7Moreover I will establish his kingdom forever, if he is steadfast to observe My commandments and My judgments, as it is this day.' 8Now therefore, in the sight of all Israel, the assembly of the LORD, and in the hearing of our God, be careful to seek out all the commandments of the LORD your God, that you may possess this good land, and leave *it* as an inheritance for your children after you forever.

9"As for you, my son Solomon, know the God of your father, and serve Him with a loyal heart and with a willing mind; for the LORD searches all hearts and understands all the intent of the thoughts. If you seek Him, He will be found by you; but if you forsake Him, He will cast you off forever. 10Consider now, for the LORD has chosen you to build a house for the sanctuary; be strong, and do it."

11Then David gave his son Solomon the plans for the vestibule, its houses, its treasuries, its upper chambers, its inner chambers, and the place of the mercy seat; 12and the plans for all that he had by the Spirit, of the courts of the house of the LORD, of all the chambers all around, of the treasuries of the house of God, and of the treasuries for the dedicated things; 13also for the division of the priests and the Levites, for all the work of the service of the house of the LORD, and for all the articles of service in the house of the LORD. 14*He gave* gold by weight for *things* of gold, for all articles used in every kind of service; also *silver* for all articles of silver by weight, for all articles used in every kind of service; 15the weight for the lampstands of gold, and their lamps of gold, by weight for each lampstand and its lamps; for the lampstands of silver by weight, for the lampstand and its lamps, according to the use of each lampstand. 16And by weight *he gave* gold for the tables of the showbread, for each table, and silver for the tables of silver; 17also pure gold for the forks, the basins, the pitchers of pure gold, and the golden bowls—*he gave gold* by weight for every bowl; and for the silver bowls, *silver* by weight for every bowl; ¹⁸and refined gold by weight for the altar of incense, and for the construction of the chariot, that is, the gold cherubim that spread *their wings* and overshadowed the ark of the covenant of the LORD. ¹⁹"All *this*," *said David,* "the LORD made me understand in writing, by *His* hand upon me, all the works of these plans."

²⁰And David said to his son Solomon, "Be strong and of good courage, and do *it;* do not fear nor be dismayed, for the LORD God—my God—*will be* with you. He will not leave you nor forsake you, until you have finished all the work for the service of the house of the LORD. ²¹*Here are* the divisions of the priests and the Levites for all the service of the house of God; and every willing craftsman *will be* with you for all manner of workmanship, for every kind of service; also the leaders and all the people *will be* completely at your command."

FURTHERMORE King David said to all the assembly: "My son Solomon, whom alone God has chosen, *is* young and inexperienced; and the work *is* great, because the temple* *is* not for man but for the LORD God. ²Now for the house of my God I have prepared with all my might: gold for *things to be made of* gold, silver for *things of* silver, bronze for *things of* bronze, iron for *things of* iron, wood for *things of* wood, onyx stones, *stones* to be set, glistening stones of various colors, all kinds of precious stones, and marble slabs in abundance. ³Moreover, because I have set my affection on the house of my God, I have given to the house of my God, over and above all that I have prepared for the holy house, my own special treasure of gold and silver: ⁴three thousand talents of gold, of the gold of Ophir, and seven thousand talents of

refined silver, to overlay the walls of the houses; ⁵the gold for *things of* gold and the silver for *things of* silver, and for all kinds of work *to be done* by the hands of craftsmen. Who *then* is willing to consecrate himself this day to the LORD?"

⁶Then the leaders of the fathers' *houses,* leaders of the tribes of Israel, the captains of thousands and of hundreds, with the officers over the king's work, offered willingly. ⁷They gave for the work of the house of God five thousand talents and ten thousand darics of gold, ten thousand talents of silver, eighteen thousand talents of bronze, and one hundred thousand talents of iron. ⁸And whoever had *precious* stones gave *them* to the treasury of the house of the LORD, into the hand of Jehiel* the Gershonite. ⁹Then the people rejoiced, for they had offered willingly, because with a loyal heart they had offered willingly to the LORD; and King David also rejoiced greatly.

¹⁰Therefore David blessed the LORD before all the assembly; and David said:

"Blessed are You, LORD God of
　　Israel, our Father, forever
　　and ever.
11　Yours, O LORD, *is* the
　　greatness,
　　The power and the glory,
　　The victory and the majesty;
　　For all *that is* in heaven and in
　　　earth *is Yours;*
　　Yours *is* the kingdom, O LORD,
　　And You are exalted as head
　　　over all.
12　Both riches and honor *come*
　　from You,
　　And You reign over all.
　　In Your hand *is* power and
　　might;
　　In Your hand *it is* to make
　　great
　　And to give strength to all.

13 "Now therefore, our God,
We thank You
And praise Your glorious
name.
14 But who *am* I, and who *are*
my people,
That we should be able to
offer so willingly as this?
For all things *come* from You,
And of Your own we have
given You.
15 For we *are* aliens and pilgrims
before You,
As *were* all our fathers;
Our days on earth *are* as a
shadow,
And without hope.

16"O Lord our God, all this abundance that we have prepared to build You a house for Your holy name is from Your hand, and *is* all Your own. 17I know also, my God, that You test the heart and have pleasure in uprightness. As for me, in the uprightness of my heart I have willingly offered all these *things;* and now with joy I have seen Your people, who are present here to offer willingly to You. 18O Lord God of Abraham, Isaac, and Israel, our fathers, keep this forever in the intent of the thoughts of the heart of Your people, and fix their heart toward You. 19And give my son Solomon a loyal heart to keep Your commandments and Your testimonies and Your statutes, to do all *these things,* and to build the temple* for which I have made provision."

20Then David said to all the assembly, "Now bless the Lord your God." So all the assembly blessed the Lord God of their fathers, and bowed their heads and prostrated themselves before the Lord and the king.

21And they made sacrifices to the Lord and offered burnt offerings to the Lord on the next day: a thousand bulls, a thousand rams, a thousand lambs, with their drink offerings, and sacrifices in abundance for all Israel. 22So they ate and drank before the Lord with great gladness on that day. And they made Solomon the son of David king the second time, and anointed *him* before the Lord *to be* the leader, and Zadok *to be* priest. 23Then Solomon sat on the throne of the Lord as king instead of David his father, and prospered; and all Israel obeyed him. 24All the leaders and the mighty men, and also all the sons of King David, submitted themselves to King Solomon. 25So the Lord exalted Solomon exceedingly in the sight of all Israel, and bestowed on him *such* royal majesty as had not been on any king before him in Israel.

26Thus David the son of Jesse reigned over all Israel. 27And the period that he reigned over Israel *was* forty years; seven years he reigned in Hebron, and thirty-three *years* he reigned in Jerusalem. 28So he died in a good old age, full of days and riches and honor; and Solomon his son reigned in his place. 29Now the acts of King David, first and last, indeed they *are* written in the book of Samuel the seer, in the book of Nathan the prophet, and in the book of Gad the seer, 30with all his reign and his might, and the events that happened to him, to Israel, and to all the kingdoms of the lands.

ROMANS 5:6-21

FOR when we were still without strength, in due time Christ died for the ungodly. 7For scarcely for a righteous man will one die; yet perhaps for a good man someone would even dare to die. 8But God demonstrates His own love toward us, in that while we were still sinners, Christ died for us. 9Much more then, having now been justified by His blood, we shall be saved from wrath through Him. 10For if when we were enemies we were reconciled to God through the death of His Son, much more, having been reconciled, we shall be saved by His life. [11]And not only *that,* but we also rejoice in God through our Lord Jesus Christ, through whom we have now received the reconciliation.

[12]Therefore, just as through one man sin entered the world, and death through sin, and thus death spread to all men, because all sinned— [13](For until the law sin was in the world, but sin is not imputed when there is no law. [14]Nevertheless death reigned from Adam to Moses, even over those who had not sinned according to the likeness of the transgression of Adam, who is a type of Him who was to come. [15]But the free gift *is* not like the offense. For if by the one man's offense many died, much more the grace of God and the gift by the grace of the one Man, Jesus Christ, abounded to many. [16]And the gift *is* not like *that which came* through the one who sinned. For the judgment *which came* from one *offense resulted* in condemnation, but the free gift *which came* from many offenses *resulted* in justification. [17]For if by the one man's offense death reigned through the one, much more those who receive abundance of grace and of the gift of righteousness will reign in life through the One, Jesus Christ.)

[18]Therefore, as through one man's offense *judgment* came to all men, resulting in condemnation, even so through one Man's righteous act *the free gift came* to all men, resulting in justification of life. [19]For as by one man's disobedience many were made

sinners, so also by one Man's obedience many will be made righteous.

[20]Moreover the law entered that the offense might abound. But where sin abounded, grace abounded much more, [21]so that as sin reigned in death, even so grace might reign through righteousness to eternal life through Jesus Christ our Lord.

PSALM 15:1-5
A Psalm of David.

L ORD, who may abide in Your tabernacle?
Who may dwell in Your holy hill?

2 He who walks uprightly,
And works righteousness,
And speaks the truth in his heart;

3 He *who* does not backbite with his tongue,
Nor does evil to his neighbor,
Nor does he take up a reproach against his friend;

4 In whose eyes a vile person is despised,
But he honors those who fear the LORD;
He *who* swears to his own hurt and does not change;

5 He *who* does not put out his money at usury,
Nor does he take a bribe against the innocent.

He who does these *things* shall never be moved.

PROVERBS FOR TODAY/ 19:18-19

Chasten your son while there is hope, and do not set your heart on his destruction. *
□ *A man of great wrath will suffer punishment; for if you rescue* him, *you will have to do it again.*

JULY 20

2 CHRONICLES 1:1–3:17

Now Solomon the son of David was strengthened in his kingdom, and the Lord his God *was* with him and exalted him exceedingly.

2And Solomon spoke to all Israel, to the captains of thousands and of hundreds, to the judges, and to every leader in all Israel, the heads of the fathers' *houses.* 3Then Solomon, and all the assembly with him, went to the high place that *was* at Gibeon; for the tabernacle of meeting with God was there, which Moses the servant of the Lord had made in the wilderness. 4But David had brought up the ark of God from Kirjath Jearim to *the place* David had prepared for it, for he had pitched a tent for it at Jerusalem. 5Now the bronze altar that Bezalel the son of Uri, the son of Hur, had made, he put* before the tabernacle of the Lord; Solomon and the assembly sought Him *there.* 6And Solomon went up there to the bronze altar before the Lord, which *was* at the tabernacle of meeting, and offered a thousand burnt offerings on it.

7On that night God appeared to Solomon, and said to him, "Ask! What shall I give you?"

8And Solomon said to God: "You have shown great mercy to David my father, and have made me king in his place. 9Now, O Lord God, let Your promise to David my father be established, for You have made me king over a people like the dust of the earth in multitude. 10Now give me wisdom and knowledge, that I may go out and come in before this people; for who can judge this great people of Yours?"

11Then God said to Solomon: "Because this was in your heart, and you have not asked riches or wealth or honor or the life of your enemies, nor have you asked long life—but have asked wisdom and knowledge for yourself, that you may judge My people over whom I have made you king— 12wisdom and knowledge *are* granted to you; and I will give you riches and wealth and honor, such as none of the kings have had who *were* before you, nor shall any after you have the like."

13So Solomon came to Jerusalem from the high place that *was* at Gibeon, from before the tabernacle of meeting, and reigned over Israel. 14And Solomon gathered chariots and horsemen; he had one thousand four hundred chariots and twelve thousand horsemen, whom he stationed in the chariot cities and with the king in Jerusalem. 15Also the king made silver and gold as common in Jerusalem as stones, and he made cedars as abundant as the sycamores which *are* in the lowland. 16And Solomon had horses imported from Egypt and Keveh; the king's merchants bought them in Keveh at the *current* price. 17They also acquired and imported from Egypt a chariot for six hundred *shekels* of silver, and a horse for one hundred and fifty; thus, through their agents,* they exported them to all the kings of the Hittites and the kings of Syria.

Then Solomon determined to build a temple for the name of the Lord, and a royal house for himself. 2Solomon selected seventy thousand men to bear burdens, eighty thousand to quarry *stone* in the mountains, and three thousand six hundred to oversee them.

³Then Solomon sent to Hiram* king of Tyre, saying:

> As you have dealt with David my father, and sent him cedars to build himself a house to dwell in, *so deal with me.* ⁴Behold, I am building a temple for the name of the LORD my God, to dedicate *it* to Him, to burn before Him sweet incense, for the continual showbread, for the burnt offerings morning and evening, on the Sabbaths, on the New Moons, and on the set feasts of the LORD our God. This *is an ordinance* forever to Israel.
>
> 5 And the temple which I build *will be* great, for our God is greater than all gods. ⁶But who is able to build Him a temple, since heaven and the heaven of heavens cannot contain Him? Who *am* I then, that I should build Him a temple, except to burn sacrifice before Him?
>
> 7 Therefore send me at once a man skillful to work in gold and silver, in bronze and iron, in purple and crimson and blue, who has skill to engrave with the skillful men who are with me in Judah and Jerusalem, whom David my father provided. ⁸Also send me cedar and cypress and algum logs from Lebanon, for I know that your servants have skill to cut timber in Lebanon; and indeed my servants *will be* with your servants, ⁹to prepare timber for me in abundance, for the temple which I am about to build *shall be* great and wonderful.
>
> 10 And indeed I will give to your servants, the woodsmen who cut timber, twenty thousand kors of ground wheat, twenty thousand kors of barley, twenty thousand baths of wine, and twenty thousand baths of oil.

¹¹Then Hiram king of Tyre answered in writing, which he sent to Solomon:

> Because the LORD loves His people, He has made you king over them.

¹²Hiram* also said:

> Blessed *be* the LORD God of Israel, who made heaven and earth, for He has given King David a wise son, endowed with prudence and understanding, who will build a temple for the LORD and a royal house for himself!
>
> 13 And now I have sent a skillful man, endowed with understanding, Huram* my master* *craftsman* ¹⁴(the son of a woman of the daughters of Dan, and his father was a man of Tyre), skilled to work in gold and silver, bronze and iron, stone and wood, purple and blue, fine linen and crimson, and to make any engraving and to accomplish any plan which may be given to him, with your skillful men and with the skillful men of my lord David your father.
>
> 15 Now therefore, the wheat, the barley, the oil, and the wine

which my lord has spoken of, let him send to his servants. ¹⁶And we will cut wood from Lebanon, as much as you need; we will bring it to you in rafts by sea to Joppa, and you will carry it up to Jerusalem.

¹⁷Then Solomon numbered all the aliens who *were* in the land of Israel, after the census in which David his father had numbered them; and there were found to be one hundred and fifty-three thousand six hundred. ¹⁸And he made seventy thousand of them bearers of burdens, eighty thousand stonecutters in the mountain, and three thousand six hundred overseers to make the people work.

Now Solomon began to build the house of the Lᴏʀᴅ at Jerusalem on Mount Moriah, where *the Lᴏʀᴅ** had appeared to his father David, at the place that David had prepared on the threshing floor of Ornan* the Jebusite. ²And he began to build on the second *day* of the second month in the fourth year of his reign.

³This is the foundation which Solomon laid for building the house of God: The length *was* sixty cubits (by cubits according to the former measure) and the width twenty cubits. ⁴And the vestibule that *was* in front *of the sanctuary** was twenty cubits long across the width of the house, and the height *was* one hundred and* twenty. He overlaid the inside with pure gold. ⁵The larger room* he paneled with cypress which he overlaid with fine gold, and he carved palm trees and chainwork on it. ⁶And he decorated the house with precious stones for beauty, and the gold *was* gold from Parvaim. ⁷He also overlaid the house—the beams and doorposts, its walls and doors—with gold; and he carved cherubim on the walls.

⁸And he made the Most Holy Place. Its length was according to the width of the house, twenty cubits, and its width twenty cubits. He overlaid it with six hundred talents of fine gold. ⁹The weight of the nails *was* fifty shekels of gold; and he overlaid the upper area with gold. ¹⁰In the Most Holy Place he made two cherubim, fashioned by carving, and overlaid them with gold. ¹¹The wings of the cherubim *were* twenty cubits in *overall* length: one wing *of the one cherub was* five cubits, touching the wall of the room, and the other wing *was* five cubits, touching the wing of the other cherub; ¹²one wing of the other cherub *was* five cubits, touching the wall of the room, and the other wing *also was* five cubits, touching the wing of the other cherub. ¹³The wings of these cherubim spanned twenty cubits overall. They stood on their feet, and they faced inward. ¹⁴And he made the veil of blue, purple, crimson, and fine linen, and wove cherubim into it.

¹⁵Also he made in front of the temple* two pillars thirty-five* cubits high, and the capital that *was* on the top of each of *them* was five cubits. ¹⁶He made wreaths of chainwork, as in the inner sanctuary, and put *them* on top of the pillars; and he made one hundred pomegranates, and put *them* on the wreaths of chainwork. ¹⁷Then he set up the pillars before the temple, one on the right hand and the other on the left; he called the name of the one on the right hand Jachin, and the name of the one on the left Boaz.

ROMANS 6:1-23

WHAT shall we say then? Shall we continue in sin that grace may abound? ²Certainly not! How shall we who died to sin live any longer in it? ³Or do you not know that as many of us as were baptized into Christ Jesus were baptized into His death? ⁴Therefore we were buried with Him through baptism into death, that just as

Christ was raised from the dead by the glory of the Father, even so we also should walk in newness of life.

5For if we have been united together in the likeness of His death, certainly we also shall be *in the likeness* of *His* resurrection, 6knowing this, that our old man was crucified with *Him,* that the body of sin might be done away with, that we should no longer be slaves of sin. 7For he who has died has been freed from sin. 8Now if we died with Christ, we believe that we shall also live with Him, 9knowing that Christ, having been raised from the dead, dies no more. Death no longer has dominion over Him. 10For *the death* that He died, He died to sin once for all; but *the life* that He lives, He lives to God. 11Likewise you also, reckon yourselves to be dead indeed to sin, but alive to God in Christ Jesus our Lord.

12Therefore do not let sin reign in your mortal body, that you should obey it in its lusts. 13And do not present your members *as* instruments of unrighteousness to sin, but present yourselves to God as being alive from the dead, and your members *as* instruments of righteousness to God. 14For sin shall not have dominion over you, for you are not under law but under grace.

15What then? Shall we sin because we are not under law but under grace? Certainly not! 16Do you not know that to whom you present yourselves slaves to obey, you are that one's slaves whom you obey, whether of sin *leading* to death, or of obedience *leading* to righteousness? 17But God be thanked that *though* you were slaves of sin, yet you obeyed from the heart that form of doctrine to which you were delivered. 18And having been set free from sin, you became slaves of righteousness. 19I speak in human *terms* because of the weakness of your flesh. For just as you presented your members *as* slaves of uncleanness,

and of lawlessness *leading* to *more* lawlessness, so now present your members *as* slaves *of* righteousness for holiness.

20For when you were slaves of sin, you were free in regard to righteousness. 21What fruit did you have then in the things of which you are now ashamed? For the end of those things *is* death. 22But now having been set free from sin, and having become slaves of God, you have your fruit to holiness, and the end, everlasting life. 23For the wages of sin *is* death, but the gift of God *is* eternal life in Christ Jesus our Lord.

PSALM 16:1-11

A Michtam of David.

PRESERVE me, O God, for in You I put my trust.

2   *O my soul,* you have said to
        the LORD,
    "You *are* my Lord,
        My goodness is nothing apart
        from You."
3   As for the saints who *are* on
        the earth,
    "They are the excellent ones,
        in whom is all my delight."

4   Their sorrows shall be
        multiplied who hasten *after*
        another *god;*
    Their drink offerings of blood
        I will not offer,
    Nor take up their names on
        my lips.

5   O LORD, *You are* the portion of
        my inheritance and my cup;
    You maintain my lot.
6   The lines have fallen to me in
        pleasant *places;*
    Yes, I have a good inheritance.

7   I will bless the LORD who has
        given me counsel;

My heart also instructs me in
the night seasons.

8   I have set the LORD always
before me;
Because *He is* at my right
hand I shall not be moved.

9   Therefore my heart is glad,
and my glory rejoices;
My flesh also will rest in hope.

10   For You will not leave my soul
in Sheol,
Nor will You allow Your Holy
One to see corruption.

11   You will show me the path of
life;
In Your presence *is* fullness of
joy;
At Your right hand *are*
pleasures forevermore.

PROVERBS FOR TODAY/ 19:20-21

Listen to counsel and receive instruction, that you may be wise in your latter days. There are many plans in a man's heart, nevertheless the LORD's counsel—that will stand.

JULY 21

2 CHRONICLES 4:1–6:11

MOREOVER he [Solomon] made a bronze altar: twenty cubits was its length, twenty cubits its width, and ten cubits its height.

2Then he made the Sea of cast *bronze,* ten cubits from one brim to the other; *it was* completely round. Its height *was* five cubits, and a line of thirty cubits measured its circumference. 3And under it *was* the likeness of oxen encircling it all around, ten to a cubit, all the way around the Sea. The oxen *were* cast in two rows, when it was cast. 4It stood on twelve oxen: three looking toward the north, three looking toward the west, three looking toward the south, and three looking toward the east; the Sea *was set* upon them, and all their back parts *pointed* inward. 5It *was* a handbreadth thick; and its brim was shaped like the brim of a cup, *like* a lily blossom. It contained three thousand* baths.

6He also made ten lavers, and put five on the right side and five on the

left, to wash in them; such things as they offered for the burnt offering they would wash in them, but the Sea *was* for the priests to wash in. 7And he made ten lampstands of gold according to their design, and set *them* in the temple, five on the right side and five on the left. 8He also made ten tables, and placed *them* in the temple, five on the right side and five on the left. And he made one hundred bowls of gold.

9Furthermore he made the court of the priests, and the great court and doors for the court; and he overlaid these doors with bronze. 10He set the Sea on the right side, toward the southeast.

11Then Huram made the pots and the shovels and the bowls. So Huram finished doing the work that he was to do for King Solomon for the house of God: 12the two pillars and the bowl-shaped capitals *that were* on top of the two pillars; the two networks covering the two bowl-shaped capitals which *were* on top of the pillars; 13four hundred pomegranates for the two networks (two rows of pomegranates for each network, to cover the two bowl-shaped capitals that *were* on the pillars); 14he also made carts and the lavers on the carts; 15one Sea and twelve oxen under it; 16also the pots, the shovels, the forks—and all their articles Huram his master* *craftsman* made of burnished bronze for King Solomon for the house of the LORD.

17In the plain of Jordan the king had them cast in clay molds, between Succoth and Zeredah.* 18And Solomon had all these articles made in such great abundance that the weight of the bronze was not determined.

19Thus Solomon had all the furnishings made for the house of God: the altar of gold and the tables on which *was* the showbread; 20the lampstands with their lamps of pure gold, to burn in the prescribed manner in front of the inner sanctuary, 21with the flowers and the lamps and the wick-trimmers of gold, of purest gold; 22the trimmers, the bowls, the ladles, and the censers of pure gold. As for the entry of the sanctuary, its inner doors to the Most Holy *Place,* and the doors of the main hall of the temple, *were* gold.

So all the work that Solomon had done for the house of the LORD was finished; and Solomon brought in the things which his father David had dedicated: the silver and the gold and all the furnishings. And he put *them* in the treasuries of the house of God.

2Now Solomon assembled the elders of Israel and all the heads of the tribes, the chief fathers of the children of Israel, in Jerusalem, that they might bring the ark of the covenant of the LORD up from the City of David, which *is* Zion. 3Therefore all the men of Israel assembled with the king at the feast, which *was* in the seventh month. 4So all the elders of Israel came, and the Levites took up the ark. 5Then they brought up the ark, the tabernacle of

meeting, and all the holy furnishings that *were* in the tabernacle. The priests and the Levites brought them up. 6Also King Solomon, and all the congregation of Israel who were assembled with him before the ark, were sacrificing sheep and oxen that could not be counted or numbered for multitude. 7Then the priests brought in the ark of the covenant of the LORD to its place, into the inner sanctuary of the temple,* to the Most Holy *Place,* under the wings of the cherubim. 8For the cherubim spread *their* wings over the place of the ark, and the cherubim overshadowed the ark and its poles. 9The poles extended so that the ends of the poles of the ark could be seen from *the holy place,* in front of the inner sanctuary; but they could not be seen from outside. And they are there to this day. 10Nothing was in the ark except the two tablets which Moses put *there* at Horeb, when the LORD made *a covenant* with the children of Israel, when they had come out of Egypt.

11And it came to pass when the priests came out of the *Most* Holy *Place* (for all the priests who *were* present had sanctified themselves, without keeping to their divisions), 12and the Levites *who were* the singers, all those of Asaph and Heman and Jeduthun, with their sons and their brethren, stood at the east end of the altar, clothed in white linen, having cymbals, stringed instruments and harps, and with them one hundred and twenty priests sounding with trumpets— 13indeed it came to pass, when the trumpeters and singers *were* as one, to make one sound to be heard in praising and thanking the LORD, and when they lifted up their voice with the trumpets and cymbals and instruments of music, and praised the LORD, *saying:*

"*For He is* good,
For His mercy *endures*
forever,"*

that the house, the house of the LORD, was filled with a cloud, [14]so that the priests could not continue ministering because of the cloud; for the glory of the LORD filled the house of God.

THEN Solomon spoke:

> "The LORD said
> He would dwell in the dark cloud.
> [2]   I have surely built You an exalted house,
> And a place for You to dwell in forever."

[3]Then the king turned around and blessed the whole assembly of Israel, while all the assembly of Israel was standing. [4]And he said: "Blessed *be* the LORD God of Israel, who has fulfilled with His hands *what* He spoke with His mouth to my father David, saying, [5]'Since the day that I brought My people out of the land of Egypt, I have chosen no city from any tribe of Israel *in which* to build a house, that My name might be there, nor did I choose any man to be a ruler over My people Israel. [6]Yet I have chosen Jerusalem, that My name may be there, and I have chosen David to be over My people Israel.' [7]Now it was in the heart of my father David to build a temple* for the name of the LORD God of Israel. [8]But the LORD said to my father David, 'Whereas it was in your heart to build a temple for My name, you did well in that it was in your heart. [9]Nevertheless you shall not build the temple, but your son who will come from your body, he shall build the temple for My name.' [10]So the LORD has fulfilled His word which He spoke, and I have filled the position of my father David, and sit on the throne of Israel, as the LORD promised; and I have built the temple for the name of the LORD God of Israel. [11]And there I have put the ark, in which *is* the covenant of the LORD which He made with the children of Israel."

ROMANS 7:1-13

OR do you not know, brethren (for I speak to those who know the law), that the law has dominion over a man as long as he lives? [2]For the woman who has a husband is bound by the law to *her* husband as long as he lives. But if the husband dies, she is released from the law of *her* husband. [3]So then if, while *her* husband lives, she marries another man, she will be called an adulteress; but if her husband dies, she is free from that law, so that she is no adulteress, though she has married another man. [4]Therefore, my brethren, you also have become dead to the law through the body of Christ, that you may be married to another—to Him who was raised from the dead, that we should bear fruit to God. [5]For when we were in the flesh, the sinful passions which were aroused by the law were at work in our members to bear fruit to death. [6]But now we have been delivered from the law, having died to what we were held by, so that we should serve in the newness of the Spirit and not *in* the oldness of the letter.

[7]What shall we say then? *Is* the law sin? Certainly not! On the contrary, I would not have known sin except through the law. For I would not have known covetousness unless the law had said, *"You shall not covet."* * [8]But sin, taking opportunity by the commandment, produced in me all *manner of evil* desire. For apart from the law sin *was* dead. [9]I was alive once without the law, but when the commandment came, sin revived and I died. [10]And the commandment, which *was* to *bring* life, I found to *bring* death. [11]For sin, taking occasion by the commandment, deceived me, and by it killed *me*. [12]Therefore the law *is* holy, and the commandment holy and just and good.

[13]Has then what is good become death to me? Certainly not! But sin,

that it might appear sin, was producing death in me through what is good, so that sin through the commandment might become exceedingly sinful.

PSALM 17:1-15

A Prayer of David.

Hᴇᴀʀ a just cause, O Lᴏʀᴅ,
Attend to my cry;
Give ear to my prayer *which is* not from deceitful lips.
2 Let my vindication come from Your presence;
Let Your eyes look on the things that are upright.

3 You have tested my heart;
You have visited *me* in the night;
You have tried me and have found nothing;
I have purposed that my mouth shall not transgress.
4 Concerning the works of men, By the word of Your lips,
I have kept away from the paths of the destroyer.
5 Uphold my steps in Your paths,
That my footsteps may not slip.

6 I have called upon You, for You will hear me, O God;
Incline Your ear to me, *and* hear my speech.
7 Show Your marvelous lovingkindness by Your right hand,
O You who save those who trust *in You*
From those who rise up *against them.*

8 Keep me as the apple of Your eye;
Hide me under the shadow of Your wings,
9 From the wicked who oppress me,
From my deadly enemies who surround me.

10 They have closed up their fat *hearts;*
With their mouths they speak proudly.
11 They have now surrounded us in our steps;
They have set their eyes, crouching down to the earth,
12 As a lion is eager to tear his prey,
And like a young lion lurking in secret places.

13 Arise, O Lᴏʀᴅ,
Confront him, cast him down;
Deliver my life from the wicked with Your sword,
14 With Your hand from men, O Lᴏʀᴅ,
From men of the world *who have* their portion in *this* life,
And whose belly You fill with Your hidden treasure.
They are satisfied with children,
And leave the rest of their *possession* for their babes.

15 As for me, I will see Your face in righteousness;
I shall be satisfied when I awake in Your likeness.

PROVERBS FOR TODAY/ 19:22-23

What is desired in a man is kindness, and a poor man is better than a liar. □ *The fear of the Lᴏʀᴅ leads to life, and he who has it will abide in satisfaction; he will not be visited with evil.*

JULY 22

2 CHRONICLES 6:12–8:10

THEN *Solomon** stood before the altar of the LORD in the presence of all the assembly of Israel, and spread out his hands [13](for Solomon had made a bronze platform five cubits long, five cubits wide, and three cubits high, and had set it in the midst of the court; and he stood on it, knelt down on his knees before all the assembly of Israel, and spread out his hands toward heaven); [14]and he said: "LORD God of Israel, *there is* no God in heaven or on earth like You, who keep *Your* covenant and mercy with Your servants who walk before You with all their hearts. [15]You have kept what You promised Your servant David my father; You have both spoken with Your mouth and fulfilled *it* with Your hand, as *it is* this day. [16]Therefore, LORD God of Israel, now keep what You promised Your servant David my father, saying, 'You shall not fail to have a man sit before Me on the throne of Israel, only if your sons take heed to their way, that they walk in My law as you have walked before Me.' [17]And now, O LORD God of Israel, let Your word come true, which You have spoken to Your servant David.

[18]"But will God indeed dwell with men on the earth? Behold, heaven and the heaven of heavens cannot contain You. How much less this temple* which I have built! [19]Yet regard the prayer of Your servant and his supplication, O LORD my God, and listen to the cry and the prayer which Your servant is praying before You: [20]that Your eyes may be open toward this temple day and night, toward the place where *You* said *You would* put Your name, that You may hear the prayer which Your servant makes toward this place.

[21]And may You hear the supplications of Your servant and of Your people Israel, when they pray toward this place. Hear from heaven Your dwelling place, and when You hear, forgive.

[22]"If anyone sins against his neighbor, and is forced to take an oath, and comes *and* takes an oath before Your altar in this temple, [23]then hear from heaven, and act, and judge Your servants, bringing retribution on the wicked by bringing his way on his own head, and justifying the righteous by giving him according to his righteousness.

[24]"Or if Your people Israel are defeated before an enemy because they have sinned against You, and return and confess Your name, and pray and make supplication before You in this temple, [25]then hear from heaven and forgive the sin of Your people Israel, and bring them back to the land which You gave to them and their fathers.

[26]"When the heavens are shut up and there is no rain because they have sinned against You, when they pray toward this place and confess Your name, and turn from their sin because You afflict them, [27]then hear *in* heaven, and forgive the sin of Your servants, Your people Israel, that You may teach them the good way in which they should walk; and send rain on Your land which You have given to Your people as an inheritance.

[28]"When there is famine in the land, pestilence or blight or mildew, locusts or grasshoppers; when their enemies besiege them in the land of their cities; whatever plague or whatever sickness *there is;* [29]whatever prayer, whatever supplication is *made* by anyone, or by all Your people Israel, when each one knows his own burden and his own

grief, and spreads out his hands to this temple: ³⁰then hear from heaven Your dwelling place, and forgive, and give to everyone according to all his ways, whose heart You know (for You alone know the hearts of the sons of men), ³¹that they may fear You, to walk in Your ways as long as they live in the land which You gave to our fathers.

³²"Moreover, concerning a foreigner, who is not of Your people Israel, but has come from a far country for the sake of Your great name and Your mighty hand and Your outstretched arm, when they come and pray in this temple; ³³then hear from heaven Your dwelling place, and do according to all for which the foreigner calls to You, that all peoples of the earth may know Your name and fear You, as *do* Your people Israel, and that they may know that this temple which I have built is called by Your name.

³⁴"When Your people go out to battle against their enemies, wherever You send them, and when they pray to You toward this city which You have chosen and the temple which I have built for Your name, ³⁵then hear from heaven their prayer and their supplication, and maintain their cause.

³⁶"When they sin against You (for *there is* no one who does not sin), and You become angry with them and deliver them to the enemy, and they take them captive to a land far or near; ³⁷yet when they come to themselves in the land where they were carried captive, and repent, and make supplication to You in the land of their captivity, saying, 'We have sinned, we have done wrong, and have committed wickedness'; ³⁸and *when* they return to You with all their heart and with all their soul in the land of their captivity, where they have been carried captive, and pray toward their land which You gave to their fathers, the city which You have chosen, and toward the temple which I have built for Your

name: ³⁹then hear from heaven Your dwelling place their prayer and their supplications, and maintain their cause, and forgive Your people who have sinned against You. ⁴⁰Now, my God, I pray, let Your eyes be open and *let* Your ears *be* attentive to the prayer *made* in this place.

41 "Now therefore,
　　Arise, O Lord God, to Your
　　　resting place,
　　You and the ark of Your
　　　strength.
　　Let Your priests, O Lord God,
　　　be clothed with salvation,
　　And let Your saints rejoice in
　　　goodness.

42 "O Lord God, do not turn away
　　　the face of Your Anointed;
　　Remember the mercies of
　　　Your servant David."*

When Solomon had finished praying, fire came down from heaven and consumed the burnt offering and the sacrifices; and the glory of the Lord filled the temple.* ²And the priests could not enter the house of the Lord, because the glory of the Lord had filled the Lord's house. ³When all the children of Israel saw how the fire came down, and the glory of the Lord on the temple, they bowed their faces to the ground on the pavement, and worshiped and praised the Lord, *saying:*

　"For *He is* good,
　　For His mercy *endures*
　　　forever."*

⁴Then the king and all the people offered sacrifices before the Lord. ⁵King Solomon offered a sacrifice of twenty-two thousand bulls and one hundred and twenty thousand sheep. So the king and all the people dedicated the house of God. ⁶And the priests attended to their services; the Levites also with instruments of the

music of the LORD, which King David had made to praise the LORD, saying, "For His mercy *endures* forever,"* whenever David offered praise by their ministry. The priests sounded trumpets opposite them, while all Israel stood.

⁷Furthermore Solomon consecrated the middle of the court that *was* in front of the house of the LORD; for there he offered burnt offerings and the fat of the peace offerings, because the bronze altar which Solomon had made was not able to receive the burnt offerings, the grain offerings, and the fat.

⁸At that time Solomon kept the feast seven days, and all Israel with him, a very great assembly from the entrance of Hamath to the Brook of Egypt.* ⁹And on the eighth day they held a sacred assembly, for they observed the dedication of the altar seven days, and the feast seven days. ¹⁰On the twenty-third day of the seventh month he sent the people away to their tents, joyful and glad of heart for the good that the LORD had done for David, for Solomon, and for His people Israel. ¹¹Thus Solomon finished the house of the LORD and the king's house; and Solomon successfully accomplished all that came into his heart to make in the house of the LORD and in his own house.

¹²Then the LORD appeared to Solomon by night, and said to him: "I have heard your prayer, and have chosen this place for Myself as a house of sacrifice. ¹³When I shut up heaven and there is no rain, or command the locusts to devour the land, or send pestilence among My people, ¹⁴if My people who are called by My name will humble themselves, and pray and seek My face, and turn from their wicked ways, then I will hear from heaven, and will forgive their sin and heal their land. ¹⁵Now My eyes will be open and My ears attentive to prayer

made in this place. ¹⁶For now I have chosen and sanctified this house, that My name may be there forever; and My eyes and My heart will be there perpetually. ¹⁷As for you, if you walk before Me as your father David walked, and do according to all that I have commanded you, and if you keep My statutes and My judgments, ¹⁸then I will establish the throne of your kingdom, as I covenanted with David your father, saying, 'You shall not fail *to have* a man as ruler in Israel.'

¹⁹"But if you turn away and forsake My statutes and My commandments which I have set before you, and go and serve other gods, and worship them, ²⁰then I will uproot them from My land which I have given them; and this house which I have sanctified for My name I will cast out of My sight, and will make it a proverb and a byword among all peoples.

²¹"And *as for* this house, which is exalted, everyone who passes by it will be astonished and say, 'Why has the LORD done thus to this land and this house?' ²²Then they will answer, 'Because they forsook the LORD God of their fathers, who brought them out of the land of Egypt, and embraced other gods, and worshiped them and served them; therefore He has brought all this calamity on them.' "

Iᴛ came to pass at the end of twenty years, when Solomon had built the house of the LORD and his own house, ²that the cities which Hiram* had given to Solomon, Solomon built them; and he settled the children of Israel there. ³And Solomon went to Hamath Zobah and seized it. ⁴He also built Tadmor in the wilderness, and all the storage cities which he built in Hamath. ⁵He built Upper Beth Horon and Lower Beth Horon, fortified cities *with* walls, gates, and bars, ⁶also Baalath and all the storage cities that Solomon had, and all the chariot cities and the cities of the cavalry, and all that Solomon desired to build in Jerusalem, in Lebanon, and in all the land of his dominion. ⁷All the people *who were* left of the Hittites, Amorites, Perizzites, Hivites, and Jebusites, who *were* not of Israel— ⁸that is, their descendants who were left in the land after them, whom the children of Israel did not destroy— from these Solomon raised forced labor, as it is to this day. ⁹But Solomon did not make the children of Israel servants for his work. Some *were* men of war, captains of his officers, captains of his chariots, and his cavalry. ¹⁰And others *were* chiefs of the officials of King Solomon: two hundred and fifty, who ruled over the people.

ROMANS 7:14–8:8

FOR we know that the law is spiritual, but I am carnal, sold under sin. ¹⁵For what I am doing, I do not understand. For what I will to do, that I do not practice; but what I hate, that I do. ¹⁶If, then, I do what I will not to do, I agree with the law that *it is* good. ¹⁷But now, *it is* no longer I who do it, but sin that dwells in me. ¹⁸For I know that in me (that is, in my flesh) nothing good dwells; for to will is present with me, but *how* to perform what is good I do not find. ¹⁹For the good that I will *to do,* I do not do; but the evil I will not *to do,* that I practice. ²⁰Now if I do what I will not *to do,* it is no longer I who do it, but sin that dwells in me.

²¹I find then a law, that evil is present with me, the one who wills to do good. ²²For I delight in the law of God according to the inward man. ²³But I see another law in my members, warring against the law of my mind, and bringing me into captivity to the law of sin which is in my members. ²⁴O wretched man that I am! Who will deliver me from this body of death? ²⁵I thank God—through Jesus Christ our Lord!

So then, with the mind I myself serve the law of God, but with the flesh the law of sin.

THERE *is* therefore now no condemnation to those who are in Christ Jesus,* who do not walk according to the flesh, but according to the Spirit. ²For the law of the Spirit of life in Christ Jesus has made me free from the law of sin and death. ³For what the law could not do in that it was weak through the flesh, God *did* by sending His own Son in the likeness of sinful flesh, on account of sin: He condemned sin in the flesh, ⁴that the righteous requirement of the law might be fulfilled in us who do not walk according to the flesh but according to the Spirit. ⁵For those who live according to the flesh set their minds on the things of the flesh, but those *who live* according to the Spirit, the things of the Spirit. ⁶For to be carnally minded *is* death, but to be spiritually minded *is* life and peace. ⁷Because the carnal mind *is* enmity against God; for it is not subject to the law of God, nor indeed can be. ⁸So then, those who are in the flesh cannot please God.

PSALM 18:1-15

To the Chief Musician. A Psalm of David the servant of the LORD, who spoke to the LORD the words of this song on the day that the LORD delivered him from the hand of all his enemies and from the hand of Saul. And he said:

I WILL love You, O LORD, my strength. ²The LORD is my rock and my fortress and my deliverer;
My God, my strength, in whom I will trust;
My shield and the horn of my salvation, my stronghold.
3   I will call upon the LORD, *who is worthy* to be praised;
So shall I be saved from my enemies.

4   The pangs of death surrounded me,

And the floods of ungodliness
   made me afraid.
5   The sorrows of Sheol
      surrounded me;
   The snares of death
      confronted me.
6   In my distress I called upon
      the LORD,
   And cried out to my God;
   He heard my voice from His
      temple,
   And my cry came before Him,
      even to His ears.

7   Then the earth shook and
      trembled;
   The foundations of the hills
      also quaked and were
      shaken,
   Because He was angry.
8   Smoke went up from His
      nostrils,
   And devouring fire from His
      mouth;
   Coals were kindled by it.
9   He bowed the heavens also,
      and came down
   With darkness under His feet.
10 And He rode upon a cherub,
      and flew;

He flew upon the wings of the
   wind.
11 He made darkness His secret
      place;
   His canopy around Him *was*
      dark waters
   And thick clouds of the skies.
12 From the brightness before
      Him,
   His thick clouds passed with
      hailstones and coals of fire.

13 The LORD thundered from
      heaven,
   And the Most High uttered
      His voice,
   Hailstones and coals of fire.*
14 He sent out His arrows and
      scattered the foe,
   Lightnings in abundance, and
      He vanquished them.
15 Then the channels of the sea
      were seen,
   The foundations of the world
      were uncovered
   At Your rebuke, O LORD,
   At the blast of the breath of
      Your nostrils.

PROVERBS FOR TODAY/ 19:24-25

A lazy man buries his hand in the bowl, and will not so much as bring it to his mouth again.* □ *Strike a scoffer, and the simple will become wary; rebuke one who has understanding,* and *he will discern knowledge.*

JULY 23

2 CHRONICLES 8:11–10:19

Now Solomon brought the daughter of Pharaoh up from the City of David to the house he had built for her, for he said, "My wife shall not dwell in the house of David king of Israel, because *the places* to which the ark of the LORD has come are holy."

12Then Solomon offered burnt offerings to the LORD on the altar of the LORD which he had built before the vestibule, 13according to the daily rate, offering according to the commandment of Moses, for the Sabbaths, the New Moons, and the three appointed yearly feasts—the Feast of Unleavened Bread, the Feast of Weeks, and the Feast of Tabernacles. 14And, according to the order of David his father, he appointed the divisions of the priests for their service, the Levites for their duties (to praise and serve before the priests) as the duty of each day required, and the gatekeepers by their divisions at each gate; for so David the man of God had commanded. 15They did not depart from the command of the king to the priests and Levites concerning any matter or concerning the treasuries.

16Now all the work of Solomon was well-ordered from* the day of the foundation of the house of the LORD until it was finished. So the house of the LORD was completed.

17Then Solomon went to Ezion Geber and Elath* on the seacoast, in the land of Edom. 18And Hiram sent him ships by the hand of his servants, and servants who knew the sea. They went with the servants of Solomon to Ophir, and acquired four hundred and fifty talents of gold from there, and brought it to King Solomon.

Now when the queen of Sheba heard of the fame of Solomon, she came to Jerusalem to test Solomon with hard questions, *having* a very great retinue, camels that bore spices, gold in abundance, and precious stones; and when she came to Solomon, she spoke with him about all that was in her heart. 2So Solomon answered all her questions; there was nothing so difficult for Solomon that he could not explain it to her. 3And when the queen of Sheba had seen the wisdom of Solomon, the house that he had built, 4the food on his table, the seating of his servants, the service of his waiters and their apparel, his cupbearers and their apparel, and his entryway by which he went up to the house of the LORD, there was no more spirit in her.

5Then she said to the king: "*It was* a true report which I heard in my own land about your words and your wisdom. 6However I did not believe their words until I came and saw with my own eyes; and indeed the half of the greatness of your wisdom was not told me. You exceed the fame of which I heard. 7Happy *are* your men and happy *are* these your servants, who stand continually before you and hear your wisdom! 8Blessed be the LORD your God, who delighted in you, setting you on His throne *to be* king for the LORD your God! Because your God has loved Israel, to establish them forever, therefore He made you king over them, to do justice and righteousness."

9And she gave the king one hundred and twenty talents of gold, spices in great abundance, and precious stones; there never were any spices such as those the queen of Sheba gave to King Solomon.

10Also, the servants of Hiram and the servants of Solomon, who brought gold from Ophir, brought algum* wood and precious stones. 11And the king made walkways *of* the algum* wood for the house of the LORD and for the king's house, also harps and stringed instruments for singers; and there were none such *as these* seen before in the land of Judah.

12Now King Solomon gave to the queen of Sheba all she desired, whatever she asked, *much more* than she had brought to the king. So she turned and went to her own country, she and her servants.

13The weight of gold that came to Solomon yearly was six hundred and sixty-six talents of gold, 14besides *what* the traveling merchants and traders brought. And all the kings of Arabia and governors of the country brought gold and silver to Solomon. 15And King Solomon made two hundred large shields of hammered gold; six hundred *shekels* of hammered gold went into each shield. 16*He* also *made* three hundred shields of hammered gold; three hundred *shekels** of gold went into each shield. The king put them in the House of the Forest of Lebanon.

17Moreover the king made a great throne of ivory, and overlaid it with pure gold. 18The throne *had* six steps, with a footstool of gold, *which were* fastened to the throne; there were armrests on either side of the place of the seat, and two lions stood beside the armrests. 19Twelve lions stood there, one on each side of the six steps; nothing like *this* had been made for any *other* kingdom.

20All King Solomon's drinking vessels *were* gold, and all the vessels of the House of the Forest of Lebanon *were* pure gold. Not *one was* silver, for this was accounted as nothing in the days of Solomon. 21For the king's ships went to Tarshish with the servants of Hiram.* Once every three years the merchant ships* came, bringing gold, silver, ivory, apes, and monkeys.*

22So King Solomon surpassed all the kings of the earth in riches and wisdom. 23And all the kings of the earth sought the presence of Solomon to hear his wisdom, which God had put in his heart. 24Each man brought his present: articles of silver and gold, garments, armor, spices, horses, and mules, at a set rate year by year.

25Solomon had four thousand stalls for horses and chariots, and twelve thousand horsemen whom he stationed in the chariot cities and with the king at Jerusalem.

26So he reigned over all the kings from the River* to the land of the Philistines, as far as the border of Egypt. 27The king made silver *as common* in Jerusalem as stones, and he made cedar trees as abundant as the sycamores which *are* in the lowland. 28And they brought horses to Solomon from Egypt and from all lands.

29Now the rest of the acts of Solomon, first and last, *are* they not written in the book of Nathan the prophet, in the prophecy of Ahijah the Shilonite, and in the visions of Iddo the seer concerning Jeroboam the son of Nebat? 30Solomon reigned in Jerusalem over all Israel forty years. 31Then Solomon rested with his fathers, and was buried in the City of David his father. And Rehoboam his son reigned in his place.

AND Rehoboam went to Shechem, for all Israel had gone to Shechem to make him king. 2So it happened, when Jeroboam the son of Nebat heard *it* (he was in Egypt, where he had fled from the presence of King Solomon), that Jeroboam returned from Egypt. 3Then they sent for him and called him. And Jeroboam and all Israel came and spoke to Rehoboam, saying, 4"Your father made our yoke heavy; now therefore, lighten the burdensome service of your father and his heavy yoke which he put on us, and we will serve you."

5So he said to them, "Come back to me after three days." And the people departed.

6Then King Rehoboam consulted the elders who stood before his father Solomon while he still lived, saying, "How do you advise *me* to answer these people?"

7And they spoke to him, saying, "If you are kind to these people, and please them, and speak good words to them, they will be your servants forever."

8But he rejected the advice which the elders had given him, and consulted the young men who had grown up with him, who stood before him. 9And he said to them, "What advice do you give? How should we answer this people who have spoken to me, saying, 'Lighten the yoke which your father put on us'?"

¹⁰Then the young men who had grown up with him spoke to him, saying, "Thus you should speak to the people who have spoken to you, saying, 'Your father made our yoke heavy, but you make *it* lighter on us'—thus you shall say to them: 'My little *finger* shall be thicker than my father's waist! ¹¹And now, whereas my father put a heavy yoke on you, I will add to your yoke; my father chastised you with whips, but I *will chastise you* with scourges!' "*

¹²So Jeroboam and all the people came to Rehoboam on the third day, as the king had directed, saying, "Come back to me the third day." ¹³Then the king answered them roughly. King Rehoboam rejected the advice of the elders, ¹⁴and he spoke to them according to the advice of the young men, saying, "My father* made your yoke heavy, but I will add to it; my father chastised you with whips, but I *will chastise you* with scourges!"* ¹⁵So the king did not listen to the people; for the turn *of events* was from God, that the Lᴏʀᴅ might fulfill His word, which He had spoken by the hand of Ahijah the Shilonite to Jeroboam the son of Nebat.

¹⁶Now when all Israel *saw* that the king did not listen to them, the people answered the king, saying:

"What share have we in David?
We have no inheritance in the
son of Jesse.
Every man to your tents,
O Israel!
Now see to your own house,
O David!"

So all Israel departed to their tents. ¹⁷But Rehoboam reigned over the children of Israel who dwelt in the cities of Judah.

¹⁸Then King Rehoboam sent Hado-ram, who *was* in charge of revenue; but the children of Israel stoned him with stones, and he died. Therefore King Rehoboam mounted *his* chariot in haste to flee to Jerusalem. ¹⁹So Israel has been in rebellion against the house of David to this day.

ROMANS 8:9-21

Bᴜᴛ you are not in the flesh but in the Spirit, if indeed the Spirit of God dwells in you. Now if anyone does not have the Spirit of Christ, he is not His. ¹⁰And if Christ *is* in you, the body *is* dead because of sin, but the Spirit *is* life because of righteousness. ¹¹But if the Spirit of Him who raised Jesus from the dead dwells in you, He who raised Christ from the dead will also give life to your mortal bodies through His Spirit who dwells in you.

¹²Therefore, brethren, we are debtors—not to the flesh, to live according to the flesh. ¹³For if you live according to the flesh you will die; but if by the Spirit you put to death the deeds of the body, you will live. ¹⁴For as many as are led by the Spirit of God, these are sons of God. ¹⁵For you did not receive the spirit of bondage again to fear, but you received the Spirit of adoption by whom we cry out, "Abba, Father." ¹⁶The Spirit Himself bears witness with our spirit that we are children of God, ¹⁷and if children, then heirs—heirs of God and joint heirs with Christ, if indeed we suffer with *Him,* that we may also be glorified together.

¹⁸For I consider that the sufferings of this present time are not worthy *to be compared* with the glory which shall be revealed in us. ¹⁹For the earnest expectation of the creation eagerly waits for the revealing of the sons of God. ²⁰For the creation was subjected to futility, not willingly, but because of Him who subjected *it* in hope; ²¹be-

cause the creation itself also will be delivered from the bondage of corruption into the glorious liberty of the children of God.

PSALM 18:16-36

H E sent from above, He took me;
He drew me out of many waters.

17 He delivered me from my strong enemy,
From those who hated me,
For they were too strong for me.

18 They confronted me in the day of my calamity,
But the LORD was my support.

19 He also brought me out into a broad place;
He delivered me because He delighted in me.

20 The LORD rewarded me according to my righteousness;
According to the cleanness of my hands
He has recompensed me.

21 For I have kept the ways of the LORD,
And have not wickedly departed from my God.

22 For all His judgments *were* before me,
And I did not put away His statutes from me.

23 I was also blameless before Him,
And I kept myself from my iniquity.

24 Therefore the LORD has recompensed me according to my righteousness,
According to the cleanness of my hands in His sight.

25 With the merciful You will show Yourself merciful;
With a blameless man You will show Yourself blameless;

26 With the pure You will show Yourself pure;
And with the devious You will show Yourself shrewd.

27 For You will save the humble people,
But will bring down haughty looks.

28 For You will light my lamp;
The LORD my God will enlighten my darkness.

29 For by You I can run against a troop,
By my God I can leap over a wall.

30 *As for* God, His way *is* perfect;
The word of the LORD is proven;
He *is* a shield to all who trust in Him.

31 For who *is* God, except the LORD?
And who *is* a rock, except our God?

32 *It is* God who arms me with strength,
And makes my way perfect.

33 He makes my feet like the *feet of* deer,
And sets me on my high places.

34 He teaches my hands to make war,
So that my arms can bend a bow of bronze.

35 You have also given me the shield of Your salvation;
Your right hand has held me up,
Your gentleness has made me great.

36 You enlarged my path under me,
So my feet did not slip.

PROVERBS FOR TODAY/ 19:26

He who mistreats his father and chases away his mother is a son who causes shame and brings reproach.

JULY 24

2 CHRONICLES 11:1–13:22

Now when Rehoboam came to Jerusalem, he assembled from the house of Judah and Benjamin one hundred and eighty thousand chosen *men* who were warriors, to fight against Israel, that he might restore the kingdom to Rehoboam.

2But the word of the LORD came to Shemaiah the man of God, saying, 3"Speak to Rehoboam the son of Solomon, king of Judah, and to all Israel in Judah and Benjamin, saying, 4"Thus says the LORD: "You shall not go up or fight against your brethren! Let every man return to his house, for this thing is from Me." ' " Therefore they obeyed the words of the LORD, and turned back from attacking Jeroboam.

5So Rehoboam dwelt in Jerusalem, and built cities for defense in Judah. 6And he built Bethlehem, Etam, Tekoa, 7Beth Zur, Sochoh, Adullam, 8Gath, Mareshah, Ziph, 9Adoraim, Lachish, Azekah, 10Zorah, Aijalon, and Hebron, which are in Judah and Benjamin, for tified cities. 11And he fortified the strongholds, and put captains in them, and stores of food, oil, and wine. 12Also in every city *he put* shields and spears, and made them very strong, having Judah and Benjamin on his side.

13And from all their territories the priests and the Levites who *were* in all Israel took their stand with him. 14For the Levites left their common-lands and their possessions and came to Judah and Jerusalem, for Jeroboam

and his sons had rejected them from serving as priests to the LORD. 15Then he appointed for himself priests for the high places, for the demons, and the calf idols which he had made. 16And after *the Levites left,** those from all the tribes of Israel, such as set their heart to seek the LORD God of Israel, came to Jerusalem to sacrifice to the LORD God of their fathers. 17So they strengthened the kingdom of Judah, and made Rehoboam the son of Solomon strong for three years, because they walked in the way of David and Solomon for three years.

18Then Rehoboam took for himself as wife Mahalath the daughter of Jerimoth the son of David, *and of* Abihail the daughter of Eliah the son of Jesse. 19And she bore him children: Jeush, Shamariah, and Zaham. 20After her he took Maachah the granddaughter* of Absalom; and she bore him Abijah, Attai, Ziza, and Shelomith. 21Now Rehoboam loved Maachah the granddaughter of Absalom more than all his wives and his concubines; for he took eighteen wives and sixty concubines, and begot twenty-eight sons and sixty daughters. 22And Rehoboam appointed Abijah the son of Maachah as chief, *to be* leader among his brothers; for he *intended* to make him king. 23He dealt wisely, and dispersed some of his sons throughout all the territories of Judah and Benjamin, to every fortified city; and he gave them provisions in abundance. He also sought many wives *for them.*

Now it came to pass, when Rehoboam had established the kingdom and had strengthened himself, that he forsook the law of the LORD, and all Israel along with him. 2And it happened in the fifth year of King Rehoboam *that* Shishak king of Egypt came up against Jerusalem, because they had transgressed against the LORD, 3with twelve hundred chariots, sixty thousand horsemen, and people without number who came with him out of Egypt—the Lubim and the Sukkiim and the Ethiopians. 4And he took the fortified cities of Judah and came to Jerusalem.

5Then Shemaiah the prophet came to Rehoboam and the leaders of Judah, who were gathered together in Jerusalem because of Shishak, and said to them, "Thus says the LORD: 'You have forsaken Me, and therefore I also have left you in the hand of Shishak.' "

6So the leaders of Israel and the king humbled themselves; and they said, "The LORD *is* righteous."

7Now when the LORD saw that they humbled themselves, the word of the LORD came to Shemaiah, saying, "They have humbled themselves; *therefore* I will not destroy them, but I will grant them some deliverance. My wrath shall not be poured out on Jerusalem by the hand of Shishak. 8Nevertheless they will be his servants, that they may distinguish My service from the service of the kingdoms of the nations."

9So Shishak king of Egypt came up against Jerusalem, and took away the treasures of the house of the LORD and the treasures of the king's house; he took everything. He also carried away the gold shields which Solomon had made. 10Then King Rehoboam made bronze shields in their place, and committed *them* to the hands of the captains of the guard, who guarded the doorway of the king's house. 11And whenever the king entered the house of the LORD, the guard would go and bring them out; then they would take them back into the guardroom. 12When he humbled himself, the wrath of the LORD turned from him, so as not to destroy *him* completely; and things also went well in Judah.

13Thus King Rehoboam strengthened himself in Jerusalem and reigned. Now Rehoboam *was* forty-one years old when he became king; and he reigned seventeen years in Jerusalem, the city which the LORD had chosen out of all the tribes of Israel, to put His name there. His mother's name *was* Naamah, an Ammonitess. 14And he did evil, because he did not prepare his heart to seek the LORD.

15The acts of Rehoboam, first and last, *are* they not written in the book of Shemaiah the prophet, and of Iddo the seer concerning genealogies? And *there were* wars between Rehoboam and Jeroboam all their days. 16So Rehoboam rested with his fathers, and was buried in the City of David. Then Abijah* his son reigned in his place.

In the eighteenth year of King Jeroboam, Abijah became king over Judah. 2He reigned three years in Jerusalem. His mother's name *was* Michaiah* the daughter of Uriel of Gibeah.

And there was war between Abijah and Jeroboam. 3Abijah set the battle in order with an army of valiant warriors, four hundred thousand choice men. Jeroboam also drew up in battle formation against him with eight hundred thousand choice men, mighty men of valor.

4Then Abijah stood on Mount Zemaraim, which *is* in the mountains of Ephraim, and said, "Hear me, Jeroboam and all Israel: 5Should you not know that the LORD God of Israel gave the dominion over Israel to David forever, to him and his sons, by a covenant of salt? 6Yet Jeroboam the son of Nebat, the servant of Solomon the son of David, rose up and rebelled against his lord. 7Then worthless rogues gathered to him, and strengthened themselves against Rehoboam the son of Solomon, when Rehoboam was young and inexperienced and could not withstand them. 8And now you think to withstand the kingdom of the LORD, which is in the hand of the sons of David; and you *are* a great multitude, and with you are the gold calves which Jeroboam made for you as gods. 9Have you not cast out the priests of the LORD, the sons of Aaron, and the Levites, and made for yourselves priests, like the peoples of *other* lands, so that whoever comes to consecrate himself with a young bull and seven rams may be a priest of *things that are* not gods? 10But as for us, the LORD *is* our God, and we have not forsaken Him; and the priests who minister to the LORD *are* the sons of Aaron, and the Levites *attend* to *their* duties. 11And they burn to the LORD every morning and every evening burnt sacrifices and sweet incense; *they* also *set* the showbread *in order on* the pure *gold* table, and the lampstand of gold with its lamps to burn every evening; for we keep the command of the LORD our God, but you have forsaken Him. 12Now look, God Himself is with us as *our* head, and His priests with sounding trumpets to sound the alarm against you. O children of Israel, do not fight against the LORD God of your fathers, for you shall not prosper!"

13But Jeroboam caused an ambush to go around behind them; so they were in front of Judah, and the ambush *was* behind them. 14And when Judah looked around, to their surprise the battle line *was* at both front and rear; and they cried out to the LORD, and the priests sounded the trumpets. 15Then the men of Judah gave a shout; and as the men of Judah shouted, it happened that God struck Jeroboam and all Israel before Abijah and Judah. 16And the children of Israel fled before Judah, and God delivered them into their hand. 17Then Abijah and his

people struck them with a great slaughter; so five hundred thousand choice men of Israel fell slain. 18Thus the children of Israel were subdued at that time; and the children of Judah prevailed, because they relied on the LORD God of their fathers.

19And Abijah pursued Jeroboam and took cities from him: Bethel with its villages, Jeshanah with its villages, and Ephrain* with its villages. 20So Jeroboam did not recover strength again in the days of Abijah; and the LORD struck him, and he died.

21But Abijah grew mighty, married fourteen wives, and begot twenty-two sons and sixteen daughters. 22Now the rest of the acts of Abijah, his ways, and his sayings *are* written in the annals of the prophet Iddo.

ROMANS 8:22-39

FOR we know that the whole creation groans and labors with birth pangs together until now. 23Not only *that,* but we also who have the firstfruits of the Spirit, even we ourselves groan within ourselves, eagerly waiting for the adoption, the redemption of our body. 24For we were saved in this hope, but hope that is seen is not hope; for why does one still hope for what he sees? 25But if we hope for what we do not see, we eagerly wait for *it* with perseverance.

26Likewise the Spirit also helps in our weaknesses. For we do not know what we should pray for as we ought, but the Spirit Himself makes intercession for us* with groanings which cannot be uttered. 27Now He who searches the hearts knows what the mind of the Spirit *is,* because He makes intercession for the saints according to *the will of* God.

28And we know that all things work together for good to those who love God, to those who are the called according to *His* purpose. 29For whom

He foreknew, He also predestined *to be* conformed to the image of His Son, that He might be the firstborn among many brethren. [30]Moreover whom He predestined, these He also called; whom He called, these He also justified; and whom He justified, these He also glorified.

[31]What then shall we say to these things? If God *is* for us, who *can be* against us? [32]He who did not spare His own Son, but delivered Him up for us all, how shall He not with Him also freely give us all things? [33]Who shall bring a charge against God's elect? *It is* God who justifies. [34]Who *is* he who condemns? *It is* Christ who died, and furthermore is also risen, who is even at the right hand of God, who also makes intercession for us. [35]Who shall separate us from the love of Christ? *Shall* tribulation, or distress, or persecution, or famine, or nakedness, or peril, or sword? [36]As it is written:

> *"For Your sake we are killed all day long;*
> *We are accounted as sheep for the slaughter."* *

[37]Yet in all these things we are more than conquerors through Him who loved us. [38]For I am persuaded that neither death nor life, nor angels nor principalities nor powers, nor things present nor things to come, [39]nor height nor depth, nor any other created thing, shall be able to separate us from the love of God which is in Christ Jesus our Lord.

PSALM 18:37-50

I HAVE pursued my enemies and overtaken them;
Neither did I turn back again till they were destroyed.
[38] I have wounded them,
So that they could not rise;
They have fallen under my feet.

[39] For You have armed me with strength for the battle;
You have subdued under me those who rose up against me.

[40] You have also given me the necks of my enemies,
So that I destroyed those who hated me.

[41] They cried out, but *there was* none to save;
Even to the LORD, but He did not answer them.

[42] Then I beat them as fine as the dust before the wind;
I cast them out like dirt in the streets.

[43] You have delivered me from the strivings of the people;
You have made me the head of the nations;
A people I have not known shall serve me.

[44] As soon as they hear of me they obey me;
The foreigners submit to me.

[45] The foreigners fade away,
And come frightened from their hideouts.

[46] The LORD lives!
Blessed *be* my Rock!
Let the God of my salvation be exalted.

[47] *It is* God who avenges me,
And subdues the peoples under me;

[48] He delivers me from my enemies.
You also lift me up above those who rise against me;
You have delivered me from the violent man.

[49] Therefore I will give thanks to You, O LORD, among the Gentiles,
And sing praises to Your name.

50 Great deliverance He gives to
His king,
And shows mercy to His
anointed,

To David and his descendants
forevermore.

PROVERBS FOR TODAY/ 19:27-29

Cease listening to instruction, my son, and you will stray from the words of knowledge. □ *A disreputable witness scorns justice, and the mouth of the wicked devours iniquity.* □ *Judgments are prepared for scoffers, and beatings for the backs of fools.*

JULY 25

2 CHRONICLES 14:1–16:14

So Abijah rested with his fathers, and they buried him in the City of David. Then Asa his son reigned in his place. In his days the land was quiet for ten years.

2Asa did *what was* good and right in the eyes of the LORD his God, 3for he removed the altars of the foreign *gods* and the high places, and broke down the *sacred* pillars and cut down the wooden images. 4He commanded Judah to seek the LORD God of their fathers, and to observe the law and the commandment. 5He also removed the high places and the incense altars from all the cities of Judah, and the kingdom was quiet under him. 6And he built fortified cities in Judah, for the land had rest; he had no war in those years, because the LORD had given him rest. 7Therefore he said to Judah, "Let us build these cities and make walls around *them,* and towers, gates, and bars, *while* the land *is* yet before us, because we have sought the LORD our God; we have sought *Him,* and He has given us rest on every side." So they built and prospered. 8And Asa had an army of three hundred thousand from Judah who carried shields and spears,

and from Benjamin two hundred and eighty thousand men who carried shields and drew bows; all these *were* mighty men of valor.

9Then Zerah the Ethiopian came out against them with an army of a million men and three hundred chariots, and he came to Mareshah. 10So Asa went out against him, and they set the troops in battle array in the Valley of Zephathah at Mareshah. 11And Asa cried out to the LORD his God, and said, "LORD, *it is* nothing for You to help, whether with many or with those who have no power; help us, O LORD our God, for we rest on You, and in Your name we go against this multitude. O LORD, You *are* our God; do not let man prevail against You!"

12So the LORD struck the Ethiopians before Asa and Judah, and the Ethiopians fled. 13And Asa and the people who *were* with him pursued them to Gerar. So the Ethiopians were overthrown, and they could not recover, for they were broken before the LORD and His army. And they carried away very much spoil. 14Then they defeated all the cities around Gerar, for the fear of the LORD came upon them; and they plundered all the cities, for there was exceedingly much spoil in them. 15They also attacked the livestock enclosures, and carried off sheep and camels in abundance, and returned to Jerusalem.

Now the Spirit of God came upon Azariah the son of Oded. [2]And he went out to meet Asa, and said to him: "Hear me, Asa, and all Judah and Benjamin. The Lord *is* with you while you are with Him. If you seek Him, He will be found by you; but if you forsake Him, He will forsake you. [3]For a long time Israel *has been* without the true God, without a teaching priest, and without law; [4]but when in their trouble they turned to the Lord God of Israel, and sought Him, He was found by them. [5]And in those times *there was* no peace to the one who went out, nor to the one who came in, but great turmoil *was* on all the inhabitants of the lands. [6]So nation was destroyed by nation, and city by city, for God troubled them with every adversity. [7]But you, be strong and do not let your hands be weak, for your work shall be rewarded!"

[8]And when Asa heard these words and the prophecy of Oded* the prophet, he took courage, and removed the abominable idols from all the land of Judah and Benjamin and from the cities which he had taken in the mountains of Ephraim; and he restored the altar of the Lord that *was* before the vestibule of the Lord. [9]Then he gathered all Judah and Benjamin, and those who dwelt with them from Ephraim, Manasseh, and Simeon, for they came over to him in great numbers from Israel when they saw that the Lord his God was with him.

[10]So they gathered together at Jerusalem in the third month, in the fifteenth year of the reign of Asa. [11]And they offered to the Lord at that time seven hundred bulls and seven thousand sheep from the spoil they had brought. [12]Then they entered into a covenant to seek the Lord God of their fathers with all their heart and with all

their soul; [13]and whoever would not seek the Lord God of Israel was to be put to death, whether small or great, whether man or woman. [14]Then they took an oath before the Lord with a loud voice, with shouting and trumpets and rams' horns. [15]And all Judah rejoiced at the oath, for they had sworn with all their heart and sought Him with all their soul; and He was found by them, and the Lord gave them rest all around.

[16]Also he removed Maachah, the mother of Asa the king, from *being* queen mother, because she had made an obscene image of Asherah;* and Asa cut down her obscene image, then crushed and burned *it* by the Brook Kidron. [17]But the high places were not removed from Israel. Nevertheless the heart of Asa was loyal all his days.

[18]He also brought into the house of God the things that his father had dedicated and that he himself had dedicated: silver and gold and utensils. [19]And there was no war until the thirty-fifth year of the reign of Asa.

In the thirty-sixth year of the reign of Asa, Baasha king of Israel came up against Judah and built Ramah, that he might let none go out or come in to Asa king of Judah. [2]Then Asa brought silver and gold from the treasuries of the house of the Lord and of the king's house, and sent to Ben-Hadad king of Syria, who dwelt in Damascus, saying, [3]"Let there be a treaty between you and me, as there was between my father and your father. See, I have sent you silver and gold; come, break your treaty with Baasha king of Israel, so that he will withdraw from me."

[4]So Ben-Hadad heeded King Asa, and sent the captains of his armies against the cities of Israel. They attacked Ijon, Dan, Abel Maim, and all the storage cities of Naphtali. [5]Now it happened, when Baasha heard *it,* that he stopped building Ramah and

ceased his work. [6]Then King Asa took all Judah, and they carried away the stones and timber of Ramah, which Baasha had used for building; and with them he built Geba and Mizpah.

[7]And at that time Hanani the seer came to Asa king of Judah, and said to him: "Because you have relied on the king of Syria, and have not relied on the LORD your God, therefore the army of the king of Syria has escaped from your hand. [8]Were the Ethiopians and the Lubim not a huge army with very many chariots and horsemen? Yet, because you relied on the LORD, He delivered them into your hand. [9]For the eyes of the LORD run to and fro throughout the whole earth, to show Himself strong on behalf of *those* whose heart *is* loyal to Him. In this you have done foolishly; therefore from now on you shall have wars." [10]Then Asa was angry with the seer, and put him in prison, for *he was* enraged at him because of this. And Asa oppressed *some* of the people at that time.

[11]Note that the acts of Asa, first and last, are indeed written in the book of the kings of Judah and Israel. [12]And in the thirty-ninth year of his reign, Asa became diseased in his feet, and his malady was severe; yet in his disease he did not seek the LORD, but the physicians.

[13]So Asa rested with his fathers; he died in the forty-first year of his reign. [14]They buried him in his own tomb, which he had made for himself in the City of David; and they laid him in the bed which was filled with spices and various ingredients prepared in a mixture of ointments. They made a very great burning for him.

ROMANS 9:1-21

I TELL the truth in Christ, I am not lying, my conscience also bearing me witness in the Holy Spirit, [2]that I have great sorrow and continual grief in my heart. [3]For I could wish that I myself were accursed from Christ for my brethren, my countrymen* according to the flesh, [4]who are Israelites, to whom *pertain* the adoption, the glory, the covenants, the giving of the law, the service *of God,* and the promises; [5]of whom *are* the fathers and from whom, according to the flesh, Christ *came,* who is over all, *the* eternally blessed God. Amen.

[6]But it is not that the word of God has taken no effect. For they *are* not all Israel who *are* of Israel, [7]nor *are they* all children because they are the seed of Abraham; but, *"In Isaac your seed shall be called."* * [8]That is, those who *are* the children of the flesh, these *are* not the children of God; but the children of the promise are counted as the seed. [9]For this *is* the word of promise: *"At this time I will come and Sarah shall have a son."* *

[10]And not only *this,* but when Rebecca also had conceived by one man, *even* by our father Isaac [11](for *the children* not yet being born, nor having done any good or evil, that the purpose of God according to election might stand, not of works but of Him who calls), [12]it was said to her, *"The older shall serve the younger."* * [13]As it is written, *"Jacob I have loved, but Esau I have hated."* *

[14]What shall we say then? *Is there* unrighteousness with God? Certainly not! [15]For He says to Moses, *"I will have mercy on whomever I will have mercy, and I will have compassion on whomever I will have compassion."* * [16]So then *it is* not of him who wills, nor of him who runs, but of God who shows mercy. [17]For the Scripture says to the Pharaoh, *"For this very purpose I have raised you up, that I may show My power in you, and that My name may be declared in all the earth."* * [18]Therefore He has mercy on whom He wills, and whom He wills He hardens.

¹⁹You will say to me then, "Why does He still find fault? For who has resisted His will?" ²⁰But indeed, O man, who are you to reply against God? Will the thing formed say to him who formed it, "Why have you made me like this?" ²¹Does not the potter have power over the clay, from the same lump to make one vessel for honor and another for dishonor?

PSALM 19:1-14

To the Chief Musician. A Psalm of David.

THE heavens declare the glory of God;
And the firmament shows His handiwork.
2 Day unto day utters speech,
And night unto night reveals knowledge.
3 *There is* no speech nor language
Where their voice is not heard.
4 Their line* has gone out through all the earth,
And their words to the end of the world.

In them He has set a tabernacle for the sun,
5 Which *is* like a bridegroom coming out of his chamber,
And rejoices like a strong man to run its race.
6 Its rising *is* from one end of heaven,
And its circuit to the other end;
And there is nothing hidden from its heat.

7 The law of the LORD *is* perfect, converting the soul;
The testimony of the LORD *is* sure, making wise the simple;
8 The statutes of the LORD *are* right, rejoicing the heart;
The commandment of the LORD *is* pure, enlightening the eyes;
9 The fear of the LORD *is* clean, enduring forever;
The judgments of the LORD *are* true *and* righteous altogether.
10 More to be desired *are they* than gold,
Yea, than much fine gold;
Sweeter also than honey and the honeycomb.
11 Moreover by them Your servant is warned,
And in keeping them *there is* great reward.

12 Who can understand *his* errors?
Cleanse me from secret *faults.*
13 Keep back Your servant also from presumptuous *sins;*
Let them not have dominion over me.
Then I shall be blameless,
And I shall be innocent of great transgression.

14 Let the words of my mouth and the meditation of my heart
Be acceptable in Your sight,
O LORD, my strength and my Redeemer.

PROVERBS FOR TODAY/ 20:1

Wine is *a mocker, strong drink* is *a brawler, and whoever is led astray by it is not wise.*

JULY 26

2 CHRONICLES 17:1–18:34

THEN Jehoshaphat his [Asa's] son reigned in his place, and strengthened himself against Israel. ²And he placed troops in all the fortified cities of Judah, and set garrisons in the land of Judah and in the cities of Ephraim which Asa his father had taken. ³Now the LORD was with Jehoshaphat, because he walked in the former ways of his father David; he did not seek the Baals, ⁴but sought the God* of his father, and walked in His commandments and not according to the acts of Israel. ⁵Therefore the LORD established the kingdom in his hand; and all Judah gave presents to Jehoshaphat, and he had riches and honor in abundance. ⁶And his heart took delight in the ways of the LORD; moreover he removed the high places and wooden images from Judah.

⁷Also in the third year of his reign he sent his leaders, Ben-Hail, Obadiah, Zechariah, Nethanel, and Michaiah, to teach in the cities of Judah. ⁸And with them *he sent* Levites: Shemaiah, Nethaniah, Zebadiah, Asahel, Shemiramoth, Jehonathan, Adonijah, Tobijah, and Tobadonijah—the Levites; and with them Elishama and Jehoram, the priests. ⁹So they taught in Judah, and *had* the Book of the Law of the LORD with them; they went throughout all the cities of Judah and taught the people.

¹⁰And the fear of the LORD fell on all the kingdoms of the lands that *were* around Judah, so that they did not make war against Jehoshaphat. ¹¹Also *some* of the Philistines brought Jehoshaphat presents and silver as tribute; and the Arabians brought him flocks, seven thousand seven hundred rams and seven thousand seven hundred male goats.

¹²So Jehoshaphat became increasingly powerful, and he built fortresses and storage cities in Judah. ¹³He had much property in the cities of Judah; and the men of war, mighty men of valor, *were* in Jerusalem.

¹⁴These *are* their numbers, according to their fathers' houses. Of Judah, the captains of thousands: Adnah the captain, and with him three hundred thousand mighty men of valor; ¹⁵and next to him *was* Jehohanan the captain, and with him two hundred and eighty thousand; ¹⁶and next to him *was* Amasiah the son of Zichri, who willingly offered himself to the LORD, and with him two hundred thousand mighty men of valor. ¹⁷Of Benjamin: Eliada a mighty man of valor, and with him two hundred thousand men armed with bow and shield; ¹⁸and next to him *was* Jehozabad, and with him one hundred and eighty thousand prepared for war. ¹⁹These served the king, besides those the king put in the fortified cities throughout all Judah.

JEHOSHAPHAT had riches and honor in abundance; and by marriage he allied himself with Ahab. ²After some years he went down to *visit* Ahab in Samaria; and Ahab killed sheep and oxen in abundance for him and the people who were with him, and persuaded him to go up *with him* to Ramoth Gilead. ³So Ahab king of Israel said to Jehoshaphat king of Judah, "Will you go with me *against* Ramoth Gilead?"

And he answered him, "I *am* as you *are,* and my people as your people; *we will be* with you in the war."

⁴Also Jehoshaphat said to the king

of Israel, "Please inquire for the word of the LORD today."

5Then the king of Israel gathered the prophets together, four hundred men, and said to them, "Shall we go to war against Ramoth Gilead, or shall I refrain?"

So they said, "Go up, for God will deliver it into the king's hand."

6But Jehoshaphat said, "*Is there* not still a prophet of the LORD here, that we may inquire of Him?"*

7So the king of Israel said to Jehoshaphat, "*There is* still one man by whom we may inquire of the LORD; but I hate him, because he never prophesies good concerning me, but always evil. He *is* Micaiah the son of Imla."

And Jehoshaphat said, "Let not the king say such things!"

8Then the king of Israel called one *of his* officers and said, "Bring Micaiah the son of Imla quickly!"

9The king of Israel and Jehoshaphat king of Judah, clothed in *their* robes, sat each on his throne; and they sat at a threshing floor at the entrance of the gate of Samaria; and all the prophets prophesied before them. 10Now Zedekiah the son of Chenaanah had made horns of iron for himself; and he said, "Thus says the LORD: 'With these you shall gore the Syrians until they are destroyed.' "

11And all the prophets prophesied so, saying, "Go up to Ramoth Gilead and prosper, for the LORD will deliver *it* into the king's hand."

12Then the messenger who had gone to call Micaiah spoke to him, saying, "Now listen, the words of the prophets with one accord encourage the king. Therefore please let your word be like *the word of* one of them, and speak encouragement."

13And Micaiah said, "*As* the LORD lives, whatever my God says, that I will speak."

14Then he came to the king; and the king said to him, "Micaiah, shall we go to war against Ramoth Gilead, or shall I refrain?"

And he said, "Go and prosper, and they shall be delivered into your hand!"

15So the king said to him, "How many times shall I make you swear that you tell me nothing but the truth in the name of the LORD?"

16Then he said, "I saw all Israel scattered on the mountains, as sheep that have no shepherd. And the LORD said, 'These have no master. Let each return to his house in peace.' "

17And the king of Israel said to Jehoshaphat, "Did I not tell you he would not prophesy good concerning me, but evil?"

18Then *Micaiah* said, "Therefore hear the word of the LORD: I saw the LORD sitting on His throne, and all the host of heaven standing on His right hand and His left. 19And the LORD said, 'Who will persuade Ahab king of Israel to go up, that he may fall at Ramoth Gilead?' So one spoke in this manner, and another spoke in that manner. 20Then a spirit came forward and stood before the LORD, and said, 'I will persuade him.' The LORD said to him, 'In what way?' 21So he said, 'I will go out and be a lying spirit in the mouth of all his prophets.' And *the LORD* said, 'You shall persuade *him* and also prevail; go out and do so.' 22Therefore look! The LORD has put a lying spirit in the mouth of these prophets of yours, and the LORD has declared disaster against you."

23Then Zedekiah the son of Chenaanah went near and struck Micaiah on the cheek, and said, "Which way did the spirit from the LORD go from me to speak to you?"

24And Micaiah said, "Indeed you shall see on that day when you go into an inner chamber to hide!"

25Then the king of Israel said, "Take Micaiah, and return him to Amon the governor of the city and to Joash the king's son; 26and say, 'Thus says the king: "Put this *fellow* in prison, and feed him with bread of affliction and water of affliction, until I return in peace."' "

27But Micaiah said, "If you ever return in peace, the LORD has not spoken by me." And he said, "Take heed, all you people!"

28So the king of Israel and Jehoshaphat the king of Judah went up to Ramoth Gilead. 29And the king of Israel said to Jehoshaphat, "I will disguise myself and go into battle; but you put on your robes." So the king of Israel disguised himself, and they went into battle.

30Now the king of Syria had commanded the captains of the chariots who *were* with him, saying, "Fight with no one small or great, but only with the king of Israel."

31So it was, when the captains of the chariots saw Jehoshaphat, that they said, "It *is* the king of Israel!" Therefore they surrounded him to attack; but Jehoshaphat cried out, and the LORD helped him, and God diverted them from him. 32For so it was, when the captains of the chariots saw that it was not the king of Israel, that they turned back from pursuing him. 33Now a certain man drew a bow at random, and struck the king of Israel between the joints of his armor. So he said to the driver of his chariot, "Turn around and take me out of the battle, for I am wounded." 34The battle increased that day, and the king of Israel propped *himself* up in *his* chariot facing the Syrians until evening; and about the time of sunset he died.

ROMANS 9:22–10:13

WHAT if God, wanting to show His wrath and to make His power known, endured with much longsuffering the vessels of wrath prepared for destruction, 23and

that He might make known the riches of His glory on the vessels of mercy, which He had prepared beforehand for glory, 24*even* us whom He called, not of the Jews only, but also of the Gentiles?

25As He says also in Hosea:

> "I will call them My people,
> who were not My people,
> And her beloved, who was not
> beloved." *
> 26 "And it shall come to pass in
> the place where it was said
> to them,
> 'You are not My people,'
> There they shall be called
> sons of the living God." *

27Isaiah also cries out concerning Israel:*

> "Though the number of the
> children of Israel be as the
> sand of the sea,
> The remnant will be saved.
> 28 For He will finish the work
> and cut it short in
> righteousness,
> Because the LORD will make a
> short work upon the
> earth." *

29And as Isaiah said before:

> "Unless the LORD of Sabaoth*
> had left us a seed,
> We would have become like
> Sodom,
> And we would have been
> made like Gomorrah." *

30What shall we say then? That Gentiles, who did not pursue righteousness, have attained to righteousness, even the righteousness of faith; 31but Israel, pursuing the law of righteousness, has not attained to the law of righteousness.* 32Why? Because *they did* not *seek it* by faith, but as it were, by the works of the law.* For they stumbled at that stumbling stone. 33As it is written:

*"Behold, I lay in Zion a
stumbling stone and rock of
offense,
And whoever believes on Him
will not be put to shame."* *

BRETHREN, my heart's desire and prayer
to God for Israel* is that they may be
saved. ²For I bear them witness that
they have a zeal for God, but not according to knowledge. ³For they being
ignorant of God's righteousness, and
seeking to establish their own righteousness, have not submitted to the
righteousness of God. ⁴For Christ *is*
the end of the law for righteousness to
everyone who believes.

⁵For Moses writes about the righteousness which is of the law, *"The
man who does those things shall live
by them."* * ⁶But the righteousness of
faith speaks in this way, *"Do not say in
your heart, 'Who will ascend into
heaven?'"* * (that is, to bring Christ
down *from above*) ⁷or, *" 'Who will descend into the abyss?'"* * (that is, to
bring Christ up from the dead). ⁸But
what does it say? *"The word is near
you, in your mouth and in your heart"* *
(that is, the word of faith which we
preach): ⁹that if you confess with your
mouth the Lord Jesus and believe in
your heart that God has raised Him
from the dead, you will be saved. ¹⁰For
with the heart one believes unto righteousness, and with the mouth confession is made unto salvation. ¹¹For the
Scripture says, *"Whoever believes on
Him will not be put to shame."* * ¹²For
there is no distinction between Jew
and Greek, for the same Lord over all
is rich to all who call upon Him. ¹³For
*"whoever calls on the name of the LORD
shall be saved."* *

PSALM 20:1-9

To the Chief Musician. A Psalm of David.

MAY the LORD answer you in the
day of trouble;
May the name of the God of
Jacob defend you;
2 May He send you help from
the sanctuary,
And strengthen you out of
Zion;
3 May He remember all your
offerings,
And accept your burnt
sacrifice.   Selah

4 May He grant you according
to your heart's *desire,*
And fulfill all your purpose.
5 We will rejoice in your
salvation,
And in the name of our God
we will set up *our* banners!
May the LORD fulfill all your
petitions.

6 Now I know that the LORD
saves His anointed;
He will answer him from His
holy heaven
With the saving strength of
His right hand.

7 Some *trust* in chariots, and
some in horses;
But we will remember the
name of the LORD our God.
8 They have bowed down and
fallen;
But we have risen and stand
upright.

9 Save, LORD!
May the King answer us
when we call.

PROVERBS FOR TODAY/ 20:2-3

The wrath * *of a king is like the roaring of a lion; whoever provokes him to anger* *sins* against *his own life.* □ It is *honorable for a man to stop striving, since any fool can start a quarrel.*

JULY 27

2 CHRONICLES 19:1–20:37

THEN Jehoshaphat the king of Judah returned safely to his house in Jerusalem. ²And Jehu the son of Hanani the seer went out to meet him, and said to King Jehoshaphat, "Should you help the wicked and love those who hate the LORD? Therefore the wrath of the LORD *is* upon you. ³Nevertheless good things are found in you, in that you have removed the wooden images from the land, and have prepared your heart to seek God."

⁴So Jehoshaphat dwelt at Jerusalem; and he went out again among the people from Beersheba to the mountains of Ephraim, and brought them back to the LORD God of their fathers. ⁵Then he set judges in the land throughout all the fortified cities of Judah, city by city, ⁶and said to the judges, "Take heed to what you are doing, for you do not judge for man but for the LORD, who *is* with you in the judgment. ⁷Now therefore, let the fear of the LORD be upon you; take care and do *it,* for *there is* no iniquity with the LORD our God, no partiality, nor taking of bribes."

⁸Moreover in Jerusalem, for the judgment of the LORD and for controversies, Jehoshaphat appointed some of the Levites and priests, and some of the chief fathers of Israel, when they returned to Jerusalem.* ⁹And he commanded them, saying, "Thus you shall act in the fear of the LORD, faithfully and with a loyal heart: ¹⁰Whatever case comes to you from your brethren who dwell in their cities, whether of bloodshed or offenses against law or commandment, against statutes or ordinances, you shall warn them, lest they trespass against the LORD and wrath come upon you and your brethren. Do this, and you will not be guilty. ¹¹And take notice: Amariah the chief priest *is* over you in all matters of the LORD; and Zebadiah the son of Ishmael, the ruler of the house of Judah, for all the king's matters; also the Levites *will be* officials before you. Behave courageously, and the LORD will be with the good."

IT happened after this *that* the people of Moab with the people of Ammon, and *others* with them besides the Ammonites,* came to battle against Jehoshaphat. ²Then some came and told Jehoshaphat, saying, "A great multitude is coming against you from beyond the sea, from Syria;* and they are in Hazazon Tamar" (which *is* En Gedi). ³And Jehoshaphat feared, and set himself to seek the LORD, and proclaimed a fast throughout all Judah. ⁴So Judah gathered together to ask *help* from the LORD; and from all the cities of Judah they came to seek the LORD.

⁵Then Jehoshaphat stood in the assembly of Judah and Jerusalem, in the house of the LORD, before the new court, ⁶and said: "O LORD God of our fathers, *are* You not God in heaven, and do You *not* rule over all the kingdoms of the nations, and in Your hand *is there not* power and might, so that no

one is able to withstand You? ⁷*Are* You not our God, *who* drove out the inhabitants of this land before Your people Israel, and gave it to the descendants of Abraham Your friend forever? ⁸And they dwell in it, and have built You a sanctuary in it for Your name, saying, ⁹'If disaster comes upon us—sword, judgment, pestilence, or famine—we will stand before this temple and in Your presence (for Your name *is* in this temple), and cry out to You in our affliction, and You will hear and save.' ¹⁰And now, here are the people of Ammon, Moab, and Mount Seir— whom You would not let Israel invade when they came out of the land of Egypt, but they turned from them and did not destroy them— ¹¹here they are, rewarding us by coming to throw us out of Your possession which You have given us to inherit. ¹²O our God, will You not judge them? For we have no power against this great multitude that is coming against us; nor do we know what to do, but our eyes *are* upon You."

¹³Now all Judah, with their little ones, their wives, and their children, stood before the LORD.

¹⁴Then the Spirit of the LORD came upon Jahaziel the son of Zechariah, the son of Benaiah, the son of Jeiel, the son of Mattaniah, a Levite of the sons of Asaph, in the midst of the assembly. ¹⁵And he said, "Listen, all you of Judah and you inhabitants of Jerusalem, and you, King Jehoshaphat! Thus says the LORD to you: 'Do not be afraid nor dismayed because of this great multitude, for the battle *is* not yours, but God's. ¹⁶Tomorrow go down against them. They will surely come up by the Ascent of Ziz, and you will find them at the end of the brook before the Wilderness of Jeruel. ¹⁷You will not *need* to fight in this *battle.* Position yourselves, stand still and see the salvation of the LORD, who is with you, O Judah and Jerusalem!' Do not fear or be dis-

mayed; tomorrow go out against them, for the LORD *is* with you."

¹⁸And Jehoshaphat bowed his head with *his* face to the ground, and all Judah and the inhabitants of Jerusalem bowed before the LORD, worshiping the LORD. ¹⁹Then the Levites of the children of the Kohathites and of the children of the Korahites stood up to praise the LORD God of Israel with voices loud and high.

²⁰So they rose early in the morning and went out into the Wilderness of Tekoa; and as they went out, Jehoshaphat stood and said, "Hear me, O Judah and you inhabitants of Jerusalem: Believe in the LORD your God, and you shall be established; believe His prophets, and you shall prosper." ²¹And when he had consulted with the people, he appointed those who should sing to the LORD, and who should praise the beauty of holiness, as they went out before the army and were saying:

"Praise the LORD,
For His mercy *endures*
    forever."*

²²Now when they began to sing and to praise, the LORD set ambushes against the people of Ammon, Moab, and Mount Seir, who had come against Judah; and they were defeated. ²³For the people of Ammon and Moab stood up against the inhabitants of Mount Seir to utterly kill and destroy *them.* And when they had made an end of the inhabitants of Seir, they helped to destroy one another.

²⁴So when Judah came to a place overlooking the wilderness, they looked toward the multitude; and there *were* their dead bodies, fallen on the earth. No one had escaped.

²⁵When Jehoshaphat and his people came to take away their spoil, they found among them an abundance of valuables on the dead bodies,* and precious jewelry, which they stripped

off for themselves, more than they could carry away; and they were three days gathering the spoil because there was so much. 26And on the fourth day they assembled in the Valley of Berachah, for there they blessed the LORD; therefore the name of that place was called The Valley of Berachah* until this day. 27Then they returned, every man of Judah and Jerusalem, with Jehoshaphat in front of them, to go back to Jerusalem with joy, for the LORD had made them rejoice over their enemies. 28So they came to Jerusalem, with stringed instruments and harps and trumpets, to the house of the LORD. 29And the fear of God was on all the kingdoms of *those* countries when they heard that the LORD had fought against the enemies of Israel. 30Then the realm of Jehoshaphat was quiet, for his God gave him rest all around.

31So Jehoshaphat was king over Judah. *He was* thirty-five years old when he became king, and he reigned twenty-five years in Jerusalem. His mother's name *was* Azubah the daughter of Shilhi. 32And he walked in the way of his father Asa, and did not turn aside from it, doing *what was* right in the sight of the LORD. 33Nevertheless the high places were not taken away, for as yet the people had not directed their hearts to the God of their fathers.

34Now the rest of the acts of Jehoshaphat, first and last, indeed they *are* written in the book of Jehu the son of Hanani, which *is* mentioned in the book of the kings of Israel.

35After this Jehoshaphat king of Judah allied himself with Ahaziah king of Israel, who acted very wickedly. 36And he allied himself with him to make ships to go to Tarshish, and they made the ships in Ezion Geber. 37But Eliezer the son of Dodavah of Mareshah prophesied against Jehoshaphat, saying, "Because you have allied yourself with Ahaziah, the LORD has destroyed your works." Then the ships were wrecked, so that they were not able to go to Tarshish.

ROMANS 10:14–11:12

How then shall they call on Him in whom they have not believed? And how shall they believe in Him of whom they have not heard? And how shall they hear without a preacher? 15And how shall they preach unless they are sent? As it is written:

> *"How beautiful are the feet of those who preach the gospel of peace,* *
> *Who bring glad tidings of good things!"* *

16But they have not all obeyed the gospel. For Isaiah says, *"Lord, who has believed our report?"* * 17So then faith *comes* by hearing, and hearing by the word of God.

18But I say, have they not heard? Yes indeed:

> *"Their sound has gone out to all the earth,*
> *And their words to the ends of the world."* *

19But I say, did Israel not know? First Moses says:

> *"I will provoke you to jealousy by those who are not a nation,*
> *I will move you to anger by a foolish nation."* *

20But Isaiah is very bold and says:

> *"I was found by those who did not seek Me;*
> *I was made manifest to those who did not ask for Me."* *

21But to Israel he says:

> *"All day long I have stretched out My hands*

*To a disobedient and contrary
people."* *

I say then, has God cast away His people? Certainly not! For I also am an Israelite, of the seed of Abraham, *of* the tribe of Benjamin. ²God has not cast away His people whom He foreknew. Or do you not know what the Scripture says of Elijah, how he pleads with God against Israel, saying, ³*"Lord, they have killed Your prophets and torn down Your altars, and I alone am left, and they seek my life"?* * ⁴But what does the divine response say to him? *"I have reserved for Myself seven thousand men who have not bowed the knee to Baal"* * ⁵Even so then, at this present time there is a remnant according to the election of grace. ⁶And if by grace, then *it is* no longer of works; otherwise grace is no longer grace.* But if *it is* of works, it is no longer grace; otherwise work is no longer work.

⁷What then? Israel has not obtained what it seeks; but the elect have obtained it, and the rest were blinded. ⁸Just as it is written:

*"God has given them a spirit of
stupor,
Eyes that they should not see
And ears that they should not
hear,
To this very day."* *

⁹And David says:

*"Let their table become a snare
and a trap,
A stumbling block and a
recompense to them.*
10 *Let their eyes be darkened, so
that they do not see,
And bow down their back
always."* *

¹¹I say then, have they stumbled that they should fall? Certainly not! But through their fall, to provoke them to jealousy, salvation *has come* to the Gen-

tiles. ¹²Now if their fall *is* riches for the world, and their failure riches for the Gentiles, how much more their fullness!

PSALM 21:1-13
To the Chief Musician. A Psalm of David.

THE king shall have joy in Your strength, O Lord;
And in Your salvation how greatly shall he rejoice!
2   You have given him his heart's desire,
And have not withheld the request of his lips.   Selah

3   For You meet him with the blessings of goodness;
You set a crown of pure gold upon his head.
4   He asked life from You, *and* You gave *it* to him—
Length of days forever and ever.
5   His glory *is* great in Your salvation;
Honor and majesty You have placed upon him
6   For You have made him most blessed forever;
You have made him exceedingly glad with Your presence.
7   For the king trusts in the Lord,
And through the mercy of the Most High he shall not be moved.

8   Your hand will find all Your enemies;
Your right hand will find those who hate You.
9   You shall make them as a fiery oven in the time of Your anger;
The Lord shall swallow them up in His wrath,

And the fire shall devour
them.
10 Their offspring You shall
destroy from the earth,
And their descendants from
among the sons of men.
11 For they intended evil against
You;
They devised a plot *which*
they are not able *to perform.*

12 Therefore You will make
them turn their back;
You will make ready *Your*
arrows on Your string
toward their faces.

13 Be exalted, O Lord, in Your
own strength!
We will sing and praise Your
power.

PROVERBS FOR TODAY / 20:4-6

The lazy man will not plow because of winter; he will beg during harvest and have
nothing. □ *Counsel in the heart of man is like deep water, but a man of under-*
standing will draw it out. □ *Most men will proclaim each his own goodness, but*
who can find a faithful man?

JULY 28

2 CHRONICLES 21:1–23:21

A ND Jehoshaphat rested with
his fathers, and was buried
with his fathers in the City of
David. Then Jehoram his son reigned
in his place. ²He had brothers, the sons
of Jehoshaphat: Azariah, Jehiel, Zechariah, Azaryahu, Michael, and Shephatiah; all these *were* the sons of
Jehoshaphat king of Israel. ³Their
father gave them great gifts of silver
and gold and precious things, with fortified cities in Judah; but he gave the
kingdom to Jehoram, because he *was*
the firstborn.

⁴Now when Jehoram was established over the kingdom of his father,
he strengthened himself and killed all
his brothers with the sword, and also
others of the princes of Israel.

⁵Jehoram *was* thirty-two years old
when he became king, and he reigned
eight years in Jerusalem. ⁶And he
walked in the way of the kings of Israel, just as the house of Ahab had

done, for he had the daughter of Ahab
as a wife; and he did evil in the sight of
the Lord. ⁷Yet the Lord would not destroy the house of David, because of
the covenant that He had made with
David, and since He had promised to
give a lamp to him and to his sons forever.

⁸In his days Edom revolted against
Judah's authority, and made a king
over themselves. ⁹So Jehoram went
out with his officers, and all his chariots with him. And he rose by night and
attacked the Edomites who had surrounded him and the captains of the
chariots. ¹⁰Thus Edom has been in revolt against Judah's authority to this
day. At that time Libnah revolted
against his rule, because he had forsaken the Lord God of his fathers.
¹¹Moreover he made high places in the
mountains of Judah, and caused the
inhabitants of Jerusalem to commit
harlotry, and led Judah astray.

¹²And a letter came to him from
Elijah the prophet, saying,

Thus says the LORD God of your father David: Because you have not walked in the ways of Jehoshaphat your father, or in the ways of Asa king of Judah, 13but have walked in the way of the kings of Israel, and have made Judah and the inhabitants of Jerusalem to play the harlot like the harlotry of the house of Ahab, and also have killed your brothers, those of your father's household, *who were* better than yourself, 14behold, the LORD will strike your people with a serious affliction—your children, your wives, and all your possessions; 15and you *will become* very sick with a disease of your intestines, until your intestines come out by reason of the sickness, day by day.

16Moreover the LORD stirred up against Jehoram the spirit of the Philistines and the Arabians who *were* near the Ethiopians. 17And they came up into Judah and invaded it, and carried away all the possessions that were found in the king's house, and also his sons and his wives, so that there was not a son left to him except Jehoahaz,* the youngest of his sons.

18After all this the LORD struck him in his intestines with an incurable disease. 19Then it happened in the course of time, after the end of two years, that his intestines came out because of his sickness; so he died in severe pain. And his people made no burning for him, like the burning for his fathers.

20He was thirty-two years old when he became king. He reigned in Jerusalem eight years and, to no one's sorrow, departed. However they buried him in the City of David, but not in the tombs of the kings.

THEN the inhabitants of Jerusalem made Ahaziah his youngest son king in his place, for the raiders who came with the Arabians into the camp had killed all the older *sons*. So Ahaziah the son of Jehoram, king of Judah, reigned. 2Ahaziah *was* forty-two* years old when he became king, and he reigned one year in Jerusalem. His mother's name *was* Athaliah the granddaughter of Omri. 3He also walked in the ways of the house of Ahab, for his mother advised him to do wickedly. 4Therefore he did evil in the sight of the LORD, like the house of Ahab; for they were his counselors after the death of his father, to his destruction. 5He also followed their advice, and went with Jehoram* the son of Ahab king of Israel to war against Hazael king of Syria at Ramoth Gilead; and the Syrians wounded Joram. 6Then he returned to Jezreel to recover from the wounds which he had received at Ramah, when he fought against Hazael king of Syria. And Azariah* the son of Jehoram, king of Judah, went down to see Jehoram the son of Ahab in Jezreel, because he was sick.

7His going to Joram was God's occasion for Ahaziah's downfall; for when he arrived, he went out with Jehoram against Jehu the son of Nimshi, whom the LORD had anointed to cut off the house of Ahab. 8And it happened, when Jehu was executing judgment on the house of Ahab, and found the princes of Judah and the sons of Ahaziah's brothers who served Ahaziah, that he killed them. 9Then he searched for Ahaziah; and they caught him (he was hiding in Samaria), and brought him to Jehu. When they had killed him, they buried him, "because," they said, "he is the son of Jehoshaphat, who sought the LORD with all his heart."

So the house of Ahaziah had no one to assume power over the kingdom.

10Now when Athaliah the mother of Ahaziah saw that her son was dead, she arose and destroyed all the royal heirs of the house of Judah. ¹¹But Jehoshabeath,* the daughter of the king, took Joash the son of Ahaziah, and stole him away from among the king's sons who were being murdered, and put him and his nurse in a bedroom. So Jehoshabeath, the daughter of King Jehoram, the wife of Jehoiada the priest (for she was the sister of Ahaziah), hid him from Athaliah so that she did not kill him. ¹²And he was hidden with them in the house of God for six years, while Athaliah reigned over the land.

In the seventh year Jehoiada strengthened himself, *and made a* covenant with the captains of hundreds: Azariah the son of Jeroham, Ishmael the son of Jehohanan, Azariah the son of Obed, Maaseiah the son of Adaiah, and Elishaphat the son of Zichri. ²And they went throughout Judah and gathered the Levites from all the cities of Judah, and the chief fathers of Israel, and they came to Jerusalem.

³Then all the assembly made a covenant with the king in the house of God. And he said to them, "Behold, the king's son shall reign, as the Lord has said of the sons of David. ⁴This *is* what you shall do: One-third of you entering on the Sabbath, of the priests and the Levites, *shall be* keeping watch over the doors; ⁵one-third *shall be* at the king's house; and one-third at the Gate of the Foundation. All the people *shall be* in the courts of the house of the Lord. ⁶But let no one come into the house of the Lord except the priests and those of the Levites who serve. They may go in, for they *are* holy; but all the people shall keep the watch of the Lord. ⁷And the Levites shall surround the king on all sides, every man with his weapons in his hand; and whoever comes into the house, let him be put to death. You are to be with the king when he comes in and when he goes out."

⁸So the Levites and all Judah did according to all that Jehoiada the priest commanded. And each man took his men who were to be on duty on the Sabbath, with those who were going *off duty* on the Sabbath; for Jehoiada the priest had not dismissed the divisions. ⁹And Jehoiada the priest gave to the captains of hundreds the spears and the large and small shields which *had belonged* to King David, that *were* in the temple of God. ¹⁰Then he set all the people, every man with his weapon in his hand, from the right side of the temple to the left side of the temple, along by the altar and by the temple, all around the king. ¹¹And they brought out the king's son, put the crown on him, *gave him* the Testimony,* and made him king. Then Jehoiada and his sons anointed him, and said, "*Long* live the king!"

¹²Now when Athaliah heard the noise of the people running and praising the king, she came to the people *in* the temple of the Lord. ¹³*When* she looked, there was the king standing by his pillar at the entrance; and the leaders and the trumpeters *were* by the king. All the people of the land were rejoicing and blowing trumpets, also the singers with musical instruments, and those who led in praise. So Athaliah tore her clothes and said, "Treason! Treason!"

¹⁴And Jehoiada the priest brought out the captains of hundreds who were set over the army, and said to them, "Take her outside under guard, and slay with the sword whoever follows her." For the priest had said, "Do not kill her in the house of the Lord."

¹⁵So they seized her; and she went by way of the entrance of the Horse Gate *into* the king's house, and they killed her there.

¹⁶Then Jehoiada made a covenant between himself, the people, and the king, that they should be the Lord's people. ¹⁷And all the people went to the

temple* of Baal, and tore it down. They broke in pieces its altars and images, and killed Mattan the priest of Baal before the altars. [18]Also Jehoiada appointed the oversight of the house of the Lord to the hand of the priests, the Levites, whom David had assigned in the house of the Lord, to offer the burnt offerings of the Lord, as *it is* written in the Law of Moses, with rejoicing and with singing, *as it was established* by David. [19]And he set the gatekeepers at the gates of the house of the Lord, so that no one *who was* in any way unclean should enter.

[20]Then he took the captains of hundreds, the nobles, the governors of the people, and all the people of the land, and brought the king down from the house of the Lord; and they went through the Upper Gate to the king's house, and set the king on the throne of the kingdom. [21]So all the people of the land rejoiced; and the city was quiet, for they had slain Athaliah with the sword.

ROMANS 11:13-36

FOR I speak to you Gentiles; inasmuch as I am an apostle to the Gentiles, I magnify my ministry, [14]if by any means I may provoke to jealousy *those who are* my flesh and save some of them. [15]For if their being cast away *is* the reconciling of the world, what *will* their acceptance *be* but life from the dead?

[16]For if the firstfruit *is* holy, the lump *is* also *holy;* and if the root *is* holy, so *are* the branches. [17]And if some of the branches were broken off, and you, being a wild olive tree, were grafted in among them, and with them became a partaker of the root and fatness of the olive tree, [18]do not boast against the branches. But if you do boast, *remember that* you do not support the root, but the root supports you.

[19]You will say then, "Branches were broken off that I might be grafted in." [20]Well *said.* Because of unbelief they were broken off, and you stand by faith. Do not be haughty, but fear. [21]For if God did not spare the natural branches, He may not spare you either. [22]Therefore consider the goodness and severity of God: on those who fell, severity; but toward you, goodness,* if you continue in *His* goodness. Otherwise you also will be cut off. [23]And they also, if they do not continue in unbelief, will be grafted in, for God is able to graft them in again. [24]For if you were cut out of the olive tree which is wild by nature, and were grafted contrary to nature into a cultivated olive tree, how much more will these, who *are* natural *branches,* be grafted into their own olive tree?

[25]For I do not desire, brethren, that you should be ignorant of this mystery, lest you should be wise in your own opinion, that blindness in part has happened to Israel until the fullness of the Gentiles has come in. [26]And so all Israel will be saved,* as it is written:

*"The Deliverer will come out of Zion,
And He will turn away ungodliness from Jacob;*
[27] *For this is My covenant with them,
When I take away their sins."* *

[28]Concerning the gospel *they are* enemies for your sake, but concerning the election *they are* beloved for the sake of the fathers. [29]For the gifts and the calling of God *are* irrevocable. [30]For as you were once disobedient to God, yet have now obtained mercy through their disobedience, [31]even so these also have now been disobedient, that through the mercy shown you they also may obtain mercy. [32]For God has committed them all to disobedience, that He might have mercy on all.

[33]Oh, the depth of the riches both of

the wisdom and knowledge of God! How unsearchable *are* His judgments and His ways past finding out!

34 *"For who has known the mind of the Lord?*
Or who has become His counselor?" *
35 *"Or who has first given to Him And it shall be repaid to him?"* *

36For of Him and through Him and to Him *are* all things, to whom *be* glory forever. Amen.

PSALM 22:1-18

To the Chief Musician. Set to "The Deer of the Dawn." * A Psalm of David.*

MY God, My God, why have You forsaken Me?
Why are You so far from helping Me,
And from the words of My groaning?
2 O My God, I cry in the daytime, but You do not hear;
And in the night season, and am not silent.

3 But You *are* holy,
Enthroned in the praises of Israel.
4 Our fathers trusted in You;
They trusted, and You delivered them.
5 They cried to You, and were delivered;
They trusted in You, and were not ashamed.

6 But I *am* a worm, and no man;
A reproach of men, and despised by the people.
7 All those who see Me ridicule Me;
They shoot out the lip, they shake the head, *saying,*

8 "He trusted* in the Lord, let Him rescue Him;
Let Him deliver Him, since He delights in Him!"

9 But You *are* He who took Me out of the womb;
You made Me trust *while* on My mother's breasts.
10 I was cast upon You from birth.
From My mother's womb You *have been* My God.
11 Be not far from Me,
For trouble *is* near;
For *there is* none to help.

12 Many bulls have surrounded Me;
Strong *bulls* of Bashan have encircled Me.
13 They gape at Me *with* their mouths,
Like a raging and roaring lion.

14 I am poured out like water,
And all My bones are out of joint;
My heart is like wax;
It has melted within Me.
15 My strength is dried up like a potsherd,
And My tongue clings to My jaws;
You have brought Me to the dust of death.

16 For dogs have surrounded Me;
The congregation of the wicked has enclosed Me.
They pierced* My hands and My feet;
17 I can count all My bones.
They look *and* stare at Me.
18 They divide My garments among them,
And for My clothing they cast lots.

PROVERBS FOR TODAY/ 20:7
The righteous man *walks in his integrity; his children* are *blessed after him.*

JULY 29

2 CHRONICLES 24:1–25:28

JOASH *was* seven years old when he became king, and he reigned forty years in Jerusalem. His mother's name *was* Zibiah of Beersheba. ²Joash did *what was* right in the sight of the LORD all the days of Jehoiada the priest. ³And Jehoiada took two wives for him, and he had sons and daughters.

⁴Now it happened after this *that* Joash set his heart on repairing the house of the LORD. ⁵Then he gathered the priests and the Levites, and said to them, "Go out to the cities of Judah, and gather from all Israel money to repair the house of your God from year to year, and see that you do it quickly."

However the Levites did not do it quickly. ⁶So the king called Jehoiada the chief *priest,* and said to him, "Why have you not required the Levites to bring in from Judah and from Jerusalem the collection, *according to the commandment* of Moses the servant of the LORD and of the assembly of Israel, for the tabernacle of witness?" ⁷For the sons of Athaliah, that wicked woman, had broken into the house of God, and had also presented all the dedicated things of the house of the LORD to the Baals.

⁸Then at the king's command they made a chest, and set it outside at the gate of the house of the LORD. ⁹And they made a proclamation throughout Judah and Jerusalem to bring to the LORD the collection *that* Moses the servant of God *had imposed* on Israel in the wilderness. ¹⁰Then all the leaders and all the people rejoiced, brought their contributions, and put *them* into the chest until all had given. ¹¹So it was, at that time, when the chest was brought to the king's official by the hand of the Levites, and when they saw that *there was* much money, that the king's scribe and the high priest's officer came and emptied the chest, and took it and returned it to its place. Thus they did day by day, and gathered money in abundance.

¹²The king and Jehoiada gave it to those who did the work of the service of the house of the LORD; and they hired masons and carpenters to repair the house of the LORD, and also those who worked in iron and bronze to restore the house of the LORD. ¹³So the workmen labored, and the work was completed by them; they restored the house of God to its original condition and reinforced it. ¹⁴When they had finished, they brought the rest of the money before the king and Jehoiada; they made from it articles for the house of the LORD, articles for serving and offering, spoons and vessels of gold and silver. And they offered burnt offerings in the house of the LORD continually all the days of Jehoiada.

¹⁵But Jehoiada grew old and was full of days, and he died; *he was* one hundred and thirty years old when he died. ¹⁶And they buried him in the City of David among the kings, because he had done good in Israel, both toward God and His house.

¹⁷Now after the death of Jehoiada the leaders of Judah came and bowed

down to the king. And the king listened to them. 18Therefore they left the house of the LORD God of their fathers, and served wooden images and idols; and wrath came upon Judah and Jerusalem because of their trespass. 19Yet He sent prophets to them, to bring them back to the LORD; and they testified against them, but they would not listen.

20Then the Spirit of God came upon Zechariah the son of Jehoiada the priest, who stood above the people, and said to them, "Thus says God: 'Why do you transgress the commandments of the LORD, so that you cannot prosper? Because you have forsaken the LORD, He also has forsaken you.' " 21So they conspired against him, and at the command of the king they stoned him with stones in the court of the house of the LORD. 22Thus Joash the king did not remember the kindness which Jehoiada his father had done to him, but killed his son; and as he died, he said, "The LORD look on it, and repay!"

23So it happened in the spring of the year that the army of Syria came up against him; and they came to Judah and Jerusalem, and destroyed all the leaders of the people from among the people, and sent all their spoil to the king of Damascus. 24For the army of the Syrians came with a small company of men; but the LORD delivered a very great army into their hand, because they had forsaken the LORD God of their fathers. So they executed judgment against Joash. 25And when they had withdrawn from him (for they left him severely wounded), his own servants conspired against him because of the blood of the sons* of Jehoiada the priest, and killed him on his bed. So he died. And they buried him in the City of David, but they did not bury him in the tombs of the kings.

26These are the ones who conspired against him: Zabad* the son of Shime-

ath the Ammonitess, and Jehozabad the son of Shimrith* the Moabitess. 27Now concerning his sons, and the many oracles about him, and the repairing of the house of God, indeed they are written in the annals of the book of the kings. Then Amaziah his son reigned in his place.

AMAZIAH was twenty-five years old when he became king, and he reigned twenty-nine years in Jerusalem. His mother's name was Jehoaddan of Jerusalem. 2And he did what was right in the sight of the LORD, but not with a loyal heart.

3Now it happened, as soon as the kingdom was established for him, that he executed his servants who had murdered his father the king. 4However he did not execute their children, but did as it is written in the Law in the Book of Moses, where the LORD commanded, saying, "The fathers shall not be put to death for their children, nor shall the children be put to death for their fathers; but a person shall die for his own sin."*

5Moreover Amaziah gathered Judah together and set over them captains of thousands and captains of hundreds, according to their fathers' houses, throughout all Judah and Benjamin; and he numbered them from twenty years old and above, and found them to be three hundred thousand choice men, able to go to war, who could handle spear and shield. 6He also hired one hundred thousand mighty men of valor from Israel for one hundred talents of silver. 7But a man of God came to him, saying, "O king, do not let the army of Israel go with you, for the LORD is not with Israel—not with any of the children of Ephraim. 8But if you go, be gone! Be strong in battle! Even so, God shall make you fall before the enemy; for God has power to help and to overthrow."

⁹Then Amaziah said to the man of God, "But what *shall we* do about the hundred talents which I have given to the troops of Israel?"

And the man of God answered, "The LORD is able to give you much more than this." ¹⁰So Amaziah discharged the troops that had come to him from Ephraim, to go back home. Therefore their anger was greatly aroused against Judah, and they returned home in great anger.

¹¹Then Amaziah strengthened himself, and leading his people, he went to the Valley of Salt and killed ten thousand of the people of Seir. ¹²Also the children of Judah took captive ten thousand alive, brought them to the top of the rock, and cast them down from the top of the rock, so that they all were dashed in pieces.

¹³But as for the soldiers of the army which Amaziah had discharged, so that they would not go with him to battle, they raided the cities of Judah from Samaria to Beth Horon, killed three thousand in them, and took much spoil.

¹⁴Now it was so, after Amaziah came from the slaughter of the Edomites, that he brought the gods of the people of Seir, set them up *to be* his gods, and bowed down before them and burned incense to them. ¹⁵Therefore the anger of the LORD was aroused against Amaziah, and He sent him a prophet who said to him, "Why have you sought the gods of the people, which could not rescue their own people from your hand?"

¹⁶So it was, as he talked with him, that *the king* said to him, "Have we made you the king's counselor? Cease! Why should you be killed?"

Then the prophet ceased, and said, "I know that God has determined to destroy you, because you have done this and have not heeded my advice."

¹⁷Now Amaziah king of Judah asked advice and sent to Joash* the son of Jehoahaz, the son of Jehu, king of Israel, saying, "Come, let us face one another *in battle.*"

¹⁸And Joash king of Israel sent to Amaziah king of Judah, saying, "The thistle that *was* in Lebanon sent to the cedar that was in Lebanon, saying, 'Give your daughter to my son as wife'; and a wild beast that *was* in Lebanon passed by and trampled the thistle. ¹⁹Indeed you say that you have defeated the Edomites, and your heart is lifted up to boast. Stay at home now; why should you meddle with trouble, that you should fall—you and Judah with you?"

²⁰But Amaziah would not heed, for it *came* from God, that He might give them into the hand *of their enemies,* because they sought the gods of Edom. ²¹So Joash king of Israel went out; and he and Amaziah king of Judah faced one another at Beth Shemesh, which *belongs* to Judah. ²²And Judah was defeated by Israel, and every man fled to his tent. ²³Then Joash the king of Israel captured Amaziah king of Judah, the son of Joash, the son of Jehoahaz, at Beth Shemesh; and he brought him to Jerusalem, and broke down the wall of Jerusalem from the Gate of Ephraim to the Corner Gate—four hundred cubits. ²⁴And *he took* all the gold and silver, all the articles that were found in the house of God with Obed-Edom, the treasures of the king's house, and hostages, and returned to Samaria.

²⁵Amaziah the son of Joash, king of Judah, lived fifteen years after the death of Joash the son of Jehoahaz, king of Israel. ²⁶Now the rest of the acts of Amaziah, from first to last, indeed *are* they not written in the book of the kings of Judah and Israel? ²⁷After the time that Amaziah turned away from following the LORD, they made a conspiracy against him in Jerusalem, and he fled to Lachish; but they sent after him to Lachish and killed him

there. ²⁸Then they brought him on horses and buried him with his fathers in the City of Judah.

ROMANS 12:1-21

I BESEECH you therefore, brethren, by the mercies of God, that you present your bodies a living sacrifice, holy, acceptable to God, *which is* your reasonable service. ²And do not be conformed to this world, but be transformed by the renewing of your mind, that you may prove what *is* that good and acceptable and perfect will of God.

³For I say, through the grace given to me, to everyone who is among you, not to think *of himself* more highly than he ought to think, but to think soberly, as God has dealt to each one a measure of faith. ⁴For as we have many members in one body, but all the members do not have the same function, ⁵so we, *being* many, are one body in Christ, and individually members of one another. ⁶Having then gifts differing according to the grace that is given to us, *let us use them:* if prophecy, *let us prophesy* in proportion to our faith; ⁷or ministry, *let us use it* in *our* ministering; he who teaches, in teaching; ⁸he who exhorts, in exhortation; he who gives, with liberality; he who leads, with diligence; he who shows mercy, with cheerfulness.

⁹*Let* love *be* without hypocrisy. Abhor what is evil. Cling to what is good. ¹⁰*Be* kindly affectionate to one another with brotherly love, in honor giving preference to one another; ¹¹not lagging in diligence, fervent in spirit, serving the Lord; ¹²rejoicing in hope, patient in tribulation, continuing steadfastly in prayer; ¹³distributing to the needs of the saints, given to hospitality.

¹⁴Bless those who persecute you; bless and do not curse. ¹⁵Rejoice with those who rejoice, and weep with those who weep. ¹⁶Be of the same mind toward one another. Do not set your mind on high things, but associate with the humble. Do not be wise in your own opinion.

¹⁷Repay no one evil for evil. Have regard for good things in the sight of all men. ¹⁸If it is possible, as much as depends on you, live peaceably with all men. ¹⁹Beloved, do not avenge yourselves, but *rather* give place to wrath; for it is written, *"Vengeance is Mine, I will repay,"* * says the Lord. ²⁰Therefore

> *"If your enemy is hungry, feed him;*
> *If he is thirsty, give him a drink;*
> *For in so doing you will heap coals of fire on his head."* *

²¹Do not be overcome by evil, but overcome evil with good.

PSALM 22:19-31

B UT You, O LORD, do not be far from Me;
O My Strength, hasten to help Me!
20 Deliver Me from the sword,
My precious *life* from the power of the dog.
21 Save Me from the lion's mouth
And from the horns of the wild oxen!

You have answered Me.

22 I will declare Your name to My brethren;
In the midst of the assembly I will praise You.
23 You who fear the LORD, praise Him!
All you descendants of Jacob, glorify Him,
And fear Him, all you offspring of Israel!
24 For He has not despised nor

abhorred the affliction of
the afflicted;
Nor has He hidden His face
from Him;
But when He cried to Him,
He heard.

25 My praise *shall be* of You in
the great assembly;
I will pay My vows before
those who fear Him.
26 The poor shall eat and be
satisfied;
Those who seek Him will
praise the LORD.
Let your heart live forever!

27 All the ends of the world
Shall remember and turn to
the LORD,

And all the families of the
nations
Shall worship before You.*
28 For the kingdom *is* the LORD'S,
And He rules over the nations.

29 All the prosperous of the earth
Shall eat and worship;
All those who go down to the
dust
Shall bow before Him,
Even he who cannot keep
himself alive.

30 A posterity shall serve Him.
It will be recounted of the
Lord to the *next* generation,
31 They will come and declare
His righteousness to a
people who will be born,
That He has done *this*.

PROVERBS FOR TODAY/ 20:8-10

A king who sits on the throne of judgment scatters all evil with his eyes. □ *Who can say, "I have made my heart clean, I am pure from my sin"?* □ *Diverse weights* and *diverse measures, they* are *both alike, an abomination to the* LORD.

JULY 30

2 CHRONICLES 26:1–28:27

Now all the people of Judah took Uzziah,* who *was* sixteen years old, and made him king instead of his father Amaziah. ²He built Elath* and restored it to Judah, after the king rested with his fathers.

³Uzziah *was* sixteen years old when he became king, and he reigned fifty-two years in Jerusalem. His mother's name was Jecholiah of Jerusalem. ⁴And he did *what was* right in the sight of the LORD, according to all that his father Amaziah had done. ⁵He sought God in the days of Zechariah, who had

understanding in the visions* of God; and as long as he sought the LORD, God made him prosper.

⁶Now he went out and made war against the Philistines, and broke down the wall of Gath, the wall of Jabneh, and the wall of Ashdod; and he built cities *around* Ashdod and among the Philistines. ⁷God helped him against the Philistines, against the Arabians who lived in Gur Baal, and against the Meunites. ⁸Also the Ammonites brought tribute to Uzziah. His fame spread as far as the entrance of Egypt, for he became exceedingly strong.

⁹And Uzziah built towers in Jerusalem at the Corner Gate, at the Valley Gate, and at the corner buttress of the wall; then he fortified them. ¹⁰Also he built towers in the desert. He dug many wells, for he had much livestock, both in the lowlands and in the plains; *he also had* farmers and vinedressers in the mountains and in Carmel, for he loved the soil.

¹¹Moreover Uzziah had an army of fighting men who went out to war by companies, according to the number on their roll as prepared by Jeiel the scribe and Maaseiah the officer, under the hand of Hananiah, *one* of the king's captains. ¹²The total number of chief officers* of the mighty men of valor *was* two thousand six hundred. ¹³And under their authority *was* an army of three hundred and seven thousand five hundred, that made war with mighty power, to help the king against the enemy. ¹⁴Then Uzziah prepared for them, for the entire army, shields, spears, helmets, body armor, bows, and slings *to cast* stones. ¹⁵And he made devices in Jerusalem, invented by skillful men, to be on the towers and the corners, to shoot arrows and large stones. So his fame spread far and wide, for he was marvelously helped till he became strong.

¹⁶But when he was strong his heart was lifted up, to *his* destruction, for he transgressed against the LORD his God by entering the temple of the LORD to burn incense on the altar of incense. ¹⁷So Azariah the priest went in after him, and with him were eighty priests of the LORD—valiant men. ¹⁸And they withstood King Uzziah, and said to him, "*It is* not for you, Uzziah, to burn incense to the LORD, but for the priests, the sons of Aaron, who are consecrated to burn incense. Get out of the sanctuary, for you have trespassed! You *shall have* no honor from the LORD God."

¹⁹Then Uzziah became furious; and he *had* a censer in his hand to burn incense. And while he was angry with the priests, leprosy broke out on his forehead, before the priests in the house of the LORD, beside the incense altar. ²⁰And Azariah the chief priest and all the priests looked at him, and there, on his forehead, he *was* leprous; so they thrust him out of that place. Indeed he also hurried to get out, because the LORD had struck him.

²¹King Uzziah was a leper until the day of his death. He dwelt in an isolated house, because he was a leper; for he was cut off from the house of the LORD. Then Jotham his son *was* over the king's house, judging the people of the land.

²²Now the rest of the acts of Uzziah, from first to last, the prophet Isaiah the son of Amoz wrote. ²³So Uzziah rested with his fathers, and they buried him with his fathers in the field of burial which *belonged* to the kings, for they said, "He is a leper." Then Jotham his son reigned in his place.

JOTHAM *was* twenty-five years old when he became king, and he reigned sixteen years in Jerusalem. His mother's name *was* Jerushah* the daughter of Zadok. ²And he did *what was* right in the sight of the LORD, according to all that his father Uzziah had done (although he did not enter the temple of the LORD). But still the people acted corruptly.

³He built the Upper Gate of the house of the LORD, and he built extensively on the wall of Ophel. ⁴Moreover he built cities in the mountains of Judah, and in the forests he built fortresses and towers. ⁵He also fought with the king of the Ammonites and defeated them. And the people of Ammon gave him in that year one hundred talents of silver, ten thousand kors of wheat, and ten thousand of barley. The people of Ammon paid this to him in the second and third years also.

⁶So Jotham became mighty, because he prepared his ways before the Lord his God.

⁷Now the rest of the acts of Jotham, and all his wars and his ways, indeed they *are* written in the book of the kings of Israel and Judah. ⁸He was twenty-five years old when he became king, and he reigned sixteen years in Jerusalem. ⁹So Jotham rested with his fathers, and they buried him in the City of David. Then Ahaz his son reigned in his place.

Ahaz *was* twenty years old when he became king, and he reigned sixteen years in Jerusalem; and he did not do *what was* right in the sight of the Lord, as his father David *had done*. ²For he walked in the ways of the kings of Israel, and made molded images for the Baals. ³He burned incense in the Valley of the Son of Hinnom, and burned his children in the fire, according to the abominations of the nations whom the Lord had cast out before the children of Israel. ⁴And he sacrificed and burned incense on the high places, on the hills, and under every green tree.

⁵Therefore the Lord his God delivered him into the hand of the king of Syria. They defeated him, and carried away a great multitude of them as captives, and brought *them* to Damascus. Then he was also delivered into the hand of the king of Israel, who defeated him with a great slaughter. ⁶For Pekah the son of Remaliah killed one hundred and twenty thousand in Judah in one day, all valiant men, because they had forsaken the Lord God of their fathers. ⁷Zichri, a mighty man of Ephraim, killed Maaseiah the king's son, Azrikam the officer over the house, and Elkanah *who was* second to the king. ⁸And the children of Israel carried away captive of their brethren two hundred thousand women, sons, and daughters; and they also took away much spoil from them, and brought the spoil to Samaria.

⁹But a prophet of the Lord was there, whose name *was* Oded; and he went out before the army that came to Samaria, and said to them: "Look, because the Lord God of your fathers was angry with Judah, He has delivered them into your hand; but you have killed them in a rage *that* reaches up to heaven. ¹⁰And now you propose to force the children of Judah and Jerusalem to be your male and female slaves; *but are* you not also guilty before the Lord your God? ¹¹Now hear me, therefore, and return the captives, whom you have taken captive from your brethren, for the fierce wrath of the Lord *is* upon you."

¹²Then some of the heads of the children of Ephraim, Azariah the son of Johanan, Berechiah the son of Meshillemoth, Jehizkiah the son of Shallum, and Amasa the son of Hadlai, stood up against those who came from the war, ¹³and said to them, "You shall not bring the captives here, for we *already* have offended the Lord. You intend to add to our sins and to our guilt; for our guilt is great, and *there is* fierce wrath against Israel." ¹⁴So the armed men left the captives and the spoil before the leaders and all the assembly. ¹⁵Then the men who were designated by name rose up and took the captives, and from the spoil they clothed all who were naked among them, dressed them and gave them sandals, gave them food and drink, and anointed them; and they let all the feeble ones ride on donkeys. So they brought them to their brethren at Jericho, the city of palm trees. Then they returned to Samaria.

¹⁶At the same time King Ahaz sent to the kings* of Assyria to help him. ¹⁷For again the Edomites had come, attacked Judah, and carried away captives. ¹⁸The Philistines also had invaded the cities of the lowland and of the South of

Judah, and had taken Beth Shemesh, Aijalon, Gederoth, Sochoh with its villages, Timnah with its villages, and Gimzo with its villages; and they dwelt there. 19For the LORD brought Judah low because of Ahaz king of Israel, for he had encouraged moral decline in Judah and had been continually unfaithful to the LORD. 20Also Tiglath-Pileser* king of Assyria came to him and distressed him, and did not assist him. 21For Ahaz took part *of the treasures* from the house of the LORD, from the house of the king, and from the leaders, and he gave *it* to the king of Assyria; but he did not help him.

22Now in the time of his distress King Ahaz became increasingly unfaithful to the LORD. This *is that* King Ahaz. 23For he sacrificed to the gods of Damascus which had defeated him, saying, "Because the gods of the kings of Syria help them, I will sacrifice to them that they may help me." But they were the ruin of him and of all Israel. 24So Ahaz gathered the articles of the house of God, cut in pieces the articles of the house of God, shut up the doors of the house of the LORD, and made for himself altars in every corner of Jerusalem. 25And in every single city of Judah he made high places to burn incense to other gods, and provoked to anger the LORD God of his fathers.

26Now the rest of his acts and all his ways, from first to last, indeed they *are* written in the book of the kings of Judah and Israel. 27So Ahaz rested with his fathers, and they buried him in the city, in Jerusalem; but they did not bring him into the tombs of the kings of Israel. Then Hezekiah his son reigned in his place.

ROMANS 13:1-14

LET every soul be subject to the governing authorities. For there is no authority except from God, and the authorities that ex-ist are appointed by God. 2Therefore whoever resists the authority resists the ordinance of God, and those who resist will bring judgment on themselves. 3For rulers are not a terror to good works, but to evil. Do you want to be unafraid of the authority? Do what is good, and you will have praise from the same. 4For he is God's minister to you for good. But if you do evil, be afraid; for he does not bear the sword in vain; for he is God's minister, an avenger to *execute* wrath on him who practices evil. 5Therefore *you* must be subject, not only because of wrath but also for conscience' sake. 6For because of this you also pay taxes, for they are God's ministers attending continually to this very thing. 7Render therefore to all their due: taxes to whom taxes *are due,* customs to whom customs, fear to whom fear, honor to whom honor.

8Owe no one anything except to love one another, for he who loves another has fulfilled the law. 9For the commandments, *"You shall not commit adultery," "You shall not murder," "You shall not steal," "You shall not bear false witness,"* * *"You shall not covet,"* * and if *there is* any other commandment, are *all* summed up in this saying, namely, *"You shall love your neighbor as yourself."* * 10Love does no harm to a neighbor; therefore love *is* the fulfillment of the law.

11And *do* this, knowing the time, that now *it is* high time to awake out of sleep; for now our salvation *is* nearer than when we *first* believed. 12The night is far spent, the day is at hand. Therefore let us cast off the works of darkness, and let us put on the armor of light. 13Let us walk properly, as in the day, not in revelry and drunkenness, not in lewdness and lust, not in strife and envy. 14But put on the Lord Jesus Christ, and make no provision for the flesh, to *fulfill its* lusts.

PSALM 23:1-6
A Psalm of David.

THE LORD *is* my shepherd;
I shall not want.
²He makes me to lie down in
    green pastures;
He leads me beside the still
    waters.
³ He restores my soul;
He leads me in the paths of
    righteousness
For His name's sake.

4 Yea, though I walk through
    the valley of the shadow of
    death,

I will fear no evil;
For You *are* with me;
Your rod and Your staff, they
    comfort me.

5 You prepare a table before me
    in the presence of my
    enemies;
You anoint my head with oil;
My cup runs over.

6 Surely goodness and mercy
    shall follow me
All the days of my life;
And I will dwell* in the house
    of the LORD
Forever.

PROVERBS FOR TODAY / 20:11
Even a child is known by his deeds, whether what he does is *pure and right.*

JULY 31

2 CHRONICLES 29:1-36

HEZEKIAH became king *when he was* twenty-five years old, and he reigned twenty-nine years in Jerusalem. His mother's name *was* Abijah* the daughter of Zechariah. ²And he did *what was* right in the sight of the LORD, according to all that his father David had done.

³In the first year of his reign, in the first month, he opened the doors of the house of the LORD and repaired them. ⁴Then he brought in the priests and the Levites, and gathered them in the East Square, ⁵and said to them: "Hear me, Levites! Now sanctify yourselves, sanctify the house of the LORD God of your fathers, and carry out the rubbish from the holy *place.* ⁶For our fathers have trespassed and done evil in the eyes of the LORD our God; they have forsaken Him, have turned their

faces away from the dwelling place of the LORD, and turned *their* backs *on Him.* ⁷They have also shut up the doors of the vestibule, put out the lamps, and have not burned incense or offered burnt offerings in the holy *place* to the God of Israel. ⁸Therefore the wrath of the LORD fell upon Judah and Jerusalem, and He has given them up to trouble, to desolation, and to jeering, as you see with your eyes. ⁹For indeed, because of this our fathers have fallen by the sword; and our sons, our daughters, and our wives *are* in captivity.

¹⁰"Now *it is* in my heart to make a covenant with the LORD God of Israel, that His fierce wrath may turn away from us. ¹¹My sons, do not be negligent now, for the LORD has chosen you to stand before Him, to serve Him, and

that you should minister to Him and burn incense."

¹²Then these Levites arose: Mahath the son of Amasai and Joel the son of Azariah, of the sons of the Kohathites; of the sons of Merari, Kish the son of Abdi and Azariah the son of Jehallelel; of the Gershonites, Joah the son of Zimmah and Eden the son of Joah; ¹³of the sons of Elizaphan, Shimri and Jeiel; of the sons of Asaph, Zechariah and Mattaniah; ¹⁴of the sons of Heman, Jehiel and Shimei; and of the sons of Jeduthun, Shemaiah and Uzziel.

¹⁵And they gathered their brethren, sanctified themselves, and went according to the commandment of the king, at the words of the LORD, to cleanse the house of the LORD. ¹⁶Then the priests went into the inner part of the house of the LORD to cleanse *it,* and brought out all the debris that they found in the temple of the LORD to the court of the house of the LORD. And the Levites took *it* out and carried *it* to the Brook Kidron.

¹⁷Now they began to sanctify on the first *day* of the first month, and on the eighth day of the month they came to the vestibule of the LORD. So they sanctified the house of the LORD in eight days, and on the sixteenth day of the first month they finished.

¹⁸Then they went in to King Hezekiah and said, "We have cleansed all the house of the LORD, the altar of burnt offerings with all its articles, and the table of the showbread with all its articles. ¹⁹Moreover all the articles which King Ahaz in his reign had cast aside in his transgression we have prepared and sanctified; and there they *are,* before the altar of the LORD."

²⁰Then King Hezekiah rose early, gathered the rulers of the city, and went up to the house of the LORD. ²¹And they brought seven bulls, seven rams, seven lambs, and seven male goats for a sin offering for the kingdom, for the sanctuary, and for Judah. Then he commanded the priests, the sons of Aaron, to offer *them* on the altar of the LORD. ²²So they killed the bulls, and the priests received the blood and sprinkled *it* on the altar. Likewise they killed the rams and sprinkled the blood on the altar. They also killed the lambs and sprinkled the blood on the altar. ²³Then they brought out the male goats *for* the sin offering before the king and the assembly, and they laid their hands on them. ²⁴And the priests killed them; and they presented their blood on the altar as a sin offering to make an atonement for all Israel, for the king commanded *that* the burnt offering and the sin offering *be made* for all Israel.

²⁵And he stationed the Levites in the house of the LORD with cymbals, with stringed instruments, and with harps, according to the commandment of David, of Gad the king's seer, and of Nathan the prophet; for thus *was* the commandment of the LORD by his prophets. ²⁶The Levites stood with the instruments of David, and the priests with the trumpets. ²⁷Then Hezekiah commanded *them* to offer the burnt offering on the altar. And when the burnt offering began, the song of the LORD *also* began, with the trumpets and with the instruments of David king of Israel. ²⁸So all the assembly worshiped, the singers sang, and the trumpeters sounded; all *this continued* until the burnt offering was finished. ²⁹And when they had finished offering, the king and all who were present with him bowed and worshiped. ³⁰Moreover King Hezekiah and the leaders commanded the Levites to sing praise to the LORD with the words of David and of Asaph the seer. So they sang praises with gladness, and they bowed their heads and worshiped.

³¹Then Hezekiah answered and said, "Now *that* you have consecrated yourselves to the LORD, come near, and bring sacrifices and thank offerings

into the house of the LORD." So the assembly brought in sacrifices and thank offerings, and as many as were of a willing heart *brought* burnt offerings. ³²And the number of the burnt offerings which the assembly brought was seventy bulls, one hundred rams, *and* two hundred lambs; all these *were* for a burnt offering to the LORD. ³³The consecrated things *were* six hundred bulls and three thousand sheep. ³⁴But the priests were too few, so that they could not skin all the burnt offerings; therefore their brethren the Levites helped them until the work was ended and until the *other* priests had sanctified themselves, for the Levites were more diligent in sanctifying themselves than the priests. ³⁵Also the burnt offerings *were* in abundance, with the fat of the peace offerings and *with* the drink offerings for *every* burnt offering.

So the service of the house of the LORD was set in order. ³⁶Then Hezekiah and all the people rejoiced that God had prepared the people, since the events took place so suddenly.

ROMANS 14:1-23

RECEIVE one who is weak in the faith, *but* not to disputes over doubtful things. ²For one believes he may eat all things, but he who is weak eats *only* vegetables. ³Let not him who eats despise him who does not eat, and let not him who does not eat judge him who eats; for God has received him. ⁴Who are you to judge another's servant? To his own master he stands or falls. Indeed, he will be made to stand, for God is able to make him stand.

⁵One person esteems *one* day above another; another esteems every day *alike.* Let each be fully convinced in his own mind. ⁶He who observes the day, observes *it* to the Lord;* and he who does not observe the day, to the Lord he does not observe *it.* He who eats,

eats to the Lord, for he gives God thanks; and he who does not eat, to the Lord he does not eat, and gives God thanks. ⁷For none of us lives to himself, and no one dies to himself. ⁸For if we live, we live to the Lord; and if we die, we die to the Lord. Therefore, whether we live or die, we are the Lord's. ⁹For to this end Christ died and rose* and lived again, that He might be Lord of both the dead and the living. ¹⁰But why do you judge your brother? Or why do you show contempt for your brother? For we shall all stand before the judgment seat of Christ.* ¹¹For it is written:

> *"As I live, says the LORD,*
> *Every knee shall bow to Me,*
> *And every tongue shall*
> *confess to God."* *

¹²So then each of us shall give account of himself to God. ¹³Therefore let us not judge one another anymore, but rather resolve this, not to put a stumbling block or a cause to fall in *our* brother's way.

¹⁴I know and am convinced by the Lord Jesus that *there is* nothing unclean of itself; but to him who considers anything to be unclean, to him *it is* unclean. ¹⁵Yet if your brother is grieved because of *your* food, you are no longer walking in love. Do not destroy with your food the one for whom Christ died. ¹⁶Therefore do not let your good be spoken of as evil; ¹⁷for the kingdom of God is not eating and drinking, but righteousness and peace and joy in the Holy Spirit. ¹⁸For he who serves Christ in these things* *is* acceptable to God and approved by men.

¹⁹Therefore let us pursue the things *which make* for peace and the things by which one may edify another. ²⁰Do not destroy the work of God for the sake of food. All things indeed *are* pure, but *it is* evil for the man who eats with offense. ²¹*It is* good neither to eat meat nor drink wine nor *do anything* by

which your brother stumbles or is offended or is made weak.* 22Do you have faith?* Have *it* to yourself before God. Happy *is* he who does not condemn himself in what he approves. 23But he who doubts is condemned if he eats, because *he does* not *eat* from faith; for whatever *is* not from faith is sin.*

PSALM 24:1-10
A Psalm of David.

T HE earth *is* the LORD's, and all its fullness,
The world and those who dwell therein.
2   For He has founded it upon the seas,
And established it upon the waters.

3   Who may ascend into the hill of the LORD?
Or who may stand in His holy place?
4   He who has clean hands and a pure heart,

Who has not lifted up his soul to an idol,
Nor sworn deceitfully.
5   He shall receive blessing from the LORD,
And righteousness from the God of his salvation.
6   This *is* Jacob, the generation of those who seek Him,
Who seek Your face.   Selah

7   Lift up your heads, O you gates!
And be lifted up, you everlasting doors!
And the King of glory shall come in.
8   Who *is* this King of glory?
The LORD strong and mighty,
The LORD mighty in battle.
9   Lift up your heads, O you gates!
Lift up, you everlasting doors!
And the King of glory shall come in.
10   Who is this King of glory?
The LORD of hosts,
He *is* the King of glory.   Selah

PROVERBS FOR TODAY/ 20:12
The hearing ear and the seeing eye, the LORD has made them both.

AUGUST 1

2 CHRONICLES 30:1–31:21

A ND Hezekiah sent to all Israel and Judah, and also wrote letters to Ephraim and Manasseh, that they should come to the house of the LORD at Jerusalem, to keep the Passover to the LORD God of Israel. 2For the king and his leaders and all the assembly in Jerusalem had agreed to keep the Passover in the second month. 3For they could not keep it at the regular time,* because a sufficient number of priests had not consecrated themselves, nor had the people gathered together at Jerusalem. 4And the matter pleased the king and all the assembly. 5So they resolved to make a proclamation throughout all Israel, from Beersheba to Dan, that they should come to keep the Passover to the LORD God of Israel at Jerusalem, since they had not done *it* for a long *time* in the *prescribed* manner.

⁶Then the runners went throughout all Israel and Judah with the letters from the king and his leaders, and spoke according to the command of the king: "Children of Israel, return to the LORD God of Abraham, Isaac, and Israel; then He will return to the remnant of you who have escaped from the hand of the kings of Assyria. ⁷And do not be like your fathers and your brethren, who trespassed against the LORD God of their fathers, so that He gave them up to desolation, as you see. ⁸Now do not be stiff-necked, as your fathers *were, but* yield yourselves to the LORD; and enter His sanctuary, which He has sanctified forever, and serve the LORD your God, that the fierceness of His wrath may turn away from you. ⁹For if you return to the LORD, your brethren and your children *will be treated* with compassion by those who lead them captive, so that they may come back to this land; for the LORD your God *is* gracious and merciful, and will not turn *His* face from you if you return to Him."

¹⁰So the runners passed from city to city through the country of Ephraim and Manasseh, as far as Zebulun; but they laughed at them and mocked them. ¹¹Nevertheless some from Asher, Manasseh, and Zebulun humbled themselves and came to Jerusalem. ¹²Also the hand of God was on Judah to give them singleness of heart to obey the command of the king and the leaders, at the word of the LORD.

¹³Now many people, a very great assembly, gathered at Jerusalem to keep the Feast of Unleavened Bread in the second month. ¹⁴They arose and took away the altars that *were* in Jerusalem, and they took away all the incense altars and cast *them* into the Brook Kidron. ¹⁵Then they slaughtered the Passover *lambs* on the fourteenth *day* of the second month. The priests and the Levites were ashamed, and sanctified themselves, and brought the burnt offerings to the house of the LORD. ¹⁶They stood in their place according to their custom, according to the Law of Moses the man of God; the priests sprinkled the blood *received* from the hand of the Levites. ¹⁷For *there were* many in the assembly who had not sanctified themselves; therefore the Levites had charge of the slaughter of the Passover *lambs* for everyone *who was* not clean, to sanctify *them* to the LORD. ¹⁸For a multitude of the people, many from Ephraim, Manasseh, Issachar, and Zebulun, had not cleansed themselves, yet they ate the Passover contrary to what was written. But Hezekiah prayed for them, saying, "May the good LORD provide atonement for everyone ¹⁹*who* prepares his heart to seek God, the LORD God of his fathers, though *he is* not *cleansed* according to the purification of the sanctuary." ²⁰And the LORD listened to Hezekiah and healed the people.

²¹So the children of Israel who were present at Jerusalem kept the Feast of Unleavened Bread seven days with great gladness; and the Levites and the priests praised the LORD day by day, *singing* to the LORD, accompanied by loud instruments. ²²And Hezekiah gave encouragement to all the Levites who taught the good knowledge of the LORD; and they ate throughout the feast seven days, offering peace offerings and making confession to the LORD God of their fathers.

²³Then the whole assembly agreed to keep *the feast* another seven days, and they kept it *another* seven days with gladness. ²⁴For Hezekiah king of Judah gave to the assembly a thousand bulls and seven thousand sheep, and the leaders gave to the assembly a thousand bulls and ten thousand

sheep; and a great number of priests sanctified themselves. 25The whole assembly of Judah rejoiced, also the priests and Levites, all the assembly that came from Israel, the sojourners who came from the land of Israel, and those who dwelt in Judah. 26So there was great joy in Jerusalem, for since the time of Solomon the son of David, king of Israel, *there had* been nothing like this in Jerusalem. 27Then the priests, the Levites, arose and blessed the people, and their voice was heard; and their prayer came *up* to His holy dwelling place, to heaven.

Now when all this was finished, all Israel who were present went out to the cities of Judah and broke the sacred pillars in pieces, cut down the wooden images, and threw down the high places and the altars—from all Judah, Benjamin, Ephraim, and Manasseh—until they had utterly destroyed them all. Then all the children of Israel returned to their own cities, every man to his possession.

2And Hezekiah appointed the divisions of the priests and the Levites according to their divisions, each man according to his service, the priests and Levites for burnt offerings and peace offerings, to serve, to give thanks, and to praise in the gates of the camp* of the LORD. 3The king also *appointed* a portion of his possessions for the burnt offerings: for the morning and evening burnt offerings, the burnt offerings for the Sabbaths and the New Moons and the set feasts, as *it is* written in the Law of the LORD.

4Moreover he commanded the people who dwelt in Jerusalem to contribute support for the priests and the Levites, that they might devote themselves to the Law of the LORD.

5As soon as the commandment was circulated, the children of Israel brought in abundance the firstfruits of grain and wine, oil and honey, and of all the produce of the field; and they brought in abundantly the tithe of everything. 6And the children of Israel and Judah, who dwelt in the cities of Judah, brought the tithe of oxen and sheep; also the tithe of holy things which were consecrated to the LORD their God they laid in heaps.

7In the third month they began laying them in heaps, and they finished in the seventh month. 8And when Hezekiah and the leaders came and saw the heaps, they blessed the LORD and His people Israel. 9Then Hezekiah questioned the priests and the Levites concerning the heaps. 10And Azariah the chief priest, from the house of Zadok, answered him and said, "Since *the people* began to bring the offerings into the house of the LORD, we have had enough to eat and have plenty left, for the LORD has blessed His people; and what is left *is* this great abundance."

11Now Hezekiah commanded *them* to prepare rooms in the house of the LORD, and they prepared them. 12Then they faithfully brought in the offerings, the tithes, and the dedicated things; Cononiah the Levite had charge of them, and Shimei his brother *was* the next. 13Jehiel, Azaziah, Nahath, Asahel, Jerimoth, Jozabad, Eliel, Ismachiah, Mahath, and Benaiah *were* overseers under the hand of Cononiah and Shimei his brother, at the commandment of Hezekiah the king and Azariah the ruler of the house of God. 14Kore the son of Imnah the Levite, the keeper of the East Gate, *was* over the freewill offerings to God, to distribute the offerings of the LORD and the most holy things. 15And under him *were* Eden, Miniamin, Jeshua, Shemaiah, Amariah, and Shecaniah, *his* faithful assistants in the cities of the priests, to distribute allotments to their brethren by divisions, to the great as well as the small.

16Besides those males from three years old and up who were written in

"And God will wipe away every tear from their eyes."

Revelation 21:4

"Go therefore and make disciples of all the nations."

Matthew 28:19

the genealogy, they distributed to everyone who entered the house of the LORD his daily portion for the work of his service, by his division, [17]and to the priests who were written in the genealogy according to their father's house, and to the Levites from twenty years old and up according to their work, by their divisions, [18]and to all who were written in the genealogy—their little ones and their wives, their sons and daughters, the whole company of them—for in their faithfulness they sanctified themselves in holiness.

[19]Also for the sons of Aaron the priests, *who were* in the fields of the common-lands of their cities, in every single city, *there were* men who were designated by name to distribute portions to all the males among the priests and to all who were listed by genealogies among the Levites.

[20]Thus Hezekiah did throughout all Judah, and he did what *was* good and right and true before the LORD his God. [21]And in every work that he began in the service of the house of God, in the law and in the commandment, to seek his God, he did *it* with all his heart. So he prospered.

ROMANS 15:1-22

WE then who are strong ought to bear with the scruples of the weak, and not to please ourselves. [2]Let each of us please *his* neighbor for *his* good, leading to edification. [3]For even Christ did not please Himself; but as it is written, *"The reproaches of those who reproached You fell on Me."* * [4]For whatever things were written before were written for our learning, that we through the patience and comfort of the Scriptures might have hope. [5]Now may the God of patience and comfort grant you to be like-minded toward one another, according to Christ Jesus, [6]that you may with one mind *and* one mouth glorify the God and Father of our Lord Jesus Christ.

[7]Therefore receive one another, just as Christ also received us,* to the glory of God. [8]Now I say that Jesus Christ has become a servant to the circumcision for the truth of God, to confirm the promises *made* to the fathers, [9]and that the Gentiles might glorify God for *His* mercy, as it is written:

> *"For this reason I will confess*
> *to You among the Gentiles,*
> *And sing to Your name."* *

[10]And again he says:

> *"Rejoice, O Gentiles, with His*
> *people!"* *

[11]And again:

> *"Praise the LORD, all you*
> *Gentiles!*
> *Laud Him, all you peoples!"* *

[12]And again, Isaiah says:

> *"There shall be a root of Jesse;*
> *And He who shall rise to*
> *reign over the Gentiles,*
> *In Him the Gentiles shall*
> *hope."* *

[13]Now may the God of hope fill you with all joy and peace in believing, that you may abound in hope by the power of the Holy Spirit.

[14]Now I myself am confident concerning you, my brethren, that you also are full of goodness, filled with all knowledge, able also to admonish one another.* [15]Nevertheless, brethren, I have written more boldly to you on *some* points, as reminding you, because of the grace given to me by God, [16]that I might be a minister of Jesus Christ to the Gentiles, ministering the gospel of God, that the offering of the Gentiles might be acceptable, sanctified by the Holy Spirit. [17]Therefore I have reason to glory in Christ Jesus in the things *which pertain* to God. [18]For I will not dare to speak of any of those

things which Christ has not accomplished through me, in word and deed, to make the Gentiles obedient— 19in mighty signs and wonders, by the power of the Spirit of God, so that from Jerusalem and round about to Illyricum I have fully preached the gospel of Christ. 20And so I have made it my aim to preach the gospel, not where Christ was named, lest I should build on another man's foundation, 21but as it is written:

*"To whom He was not
announced, they shall see;
And those who have not
heard shall understand."* *

22For this reason I also have been much hindered from coming to you.

PSALM 25:1-15

A Psalm of David.

To You, O LORD, I lift up my soul. 2O my God, I trust in You;
Let me not be ashamed;
Let not my enemies triumph
over me.
3 Indeed, let no one who waits
on You be ashamed;
Let those be ashamed who
deal treacherously without
cause.

4 Show me Your ways, O LORD;
Teach me Your paths.
5 Lead me in Your truth and
teach me,
For You *are* the God of my
salvation;
On You I wait all the day.

6 Remember, O LORD, Your
tender mercies and Your
lovingkindnesses,
For they *are* from of old.
7 Do not remember the sins of
my youth, nor my
transgressions;
According to Your mercy
remember me,
For Your goodness' sake,
O LORD.

8 Good and upright *is* the LORD;
Therefore He teaches sinners
in the way.
9 The humble He guides in
justice,
And the humble He teaches
His way.
10 All the paths of the LORD *are*
mercy and truth,
To such as keep His covenant
and His testimonies.
11 For Your name's sake, O LORD,
Pardon my iniquity, for it *is*
great.

12 Who *is* the man that fears the
LORD?
Him shall He* teach in the
way He* chooses.
13 He himself shall dwell in
prosperity,
And his descendants shall
inherit the earth.
14 The secret of the LORD *is* with
those who fear Him,
And He will show them His
covenant.
15 My eyes *are* ever toward the
LORD,
For He shall pluck my feet out
of the net.

PROVERBS FOR TODAY/ 20:13-15

Do not love sleep, lest you come to poverty; open your eyes, and you will be satisfied with bread. ☐ *"It is good for nothing,"* * *cries the buyer; but when he has gone his way, then he boasts.* ☐ *There is gold and a multitude of rubies, but the lips of knowledge* are *a precious jewel.*

2 CHRONICLES 32:1–33:13

After these deeds of faithfulness, Sennacherib king of Assyria came and entered Judah; he encamped against the fortified cities, thinking to win them over to himself. 2And when Hezekiah saw that Sennacherib had come, and that his purpose was to make war against Jerusalem, 3he consulted with his leaders and commanders* to stop the water from the springs which *were* outside the city; and they helped him. 4Thus many people gathered together who stopped all the springs and the brook that ran through the land, saying, "Why should the kings* of Assyria come and find much water?" 5And he strengthened himself, built up all the wall that was broken, raised *it* up to the towers, and *built* another wall outside; also he repaired the Millo* *in* the City of David, and made weapons and shields in abundance. 6Then he set military captains over the people, gathered them together to him in the open square of the city gate, and gave them encouragement, saying, 7"Be strong and courageous; do not be afraid nor dismayed before the king of Assyria, nor before all the multitude that *is* with him; for *there are* more with us than with him. 8With him *is* an arm of flesh; but with us *is* the LORD our God, to help us and to fight our battles." And the people were strengthened by the words of Hezekiah king of Judah.

9After this Sennacherib king of Assyria sent his servants to Jerusalem (but he and all the forces with him *laid siege* against Lachish), to Hezekiah king of Judah, and to all Judah who *were* in Jerusalem, saying, 10"Thus says Sennacherib king of Assyria: 'In what do you trust, that you remain under siege in Jerusalem? 11Does not Hezekiah persuade you to give yourselves over to die by famine and by thirst, saying, "The LORD our God will deliver us from the hand of the king of Assyria"? 12Has not the same Hezekiah taken away His high places and His altars, and commanded Judah and Jerusalem, saying, "You shall worship before one altar and burn incense on it"? 13Do you not know what I and my fathers have done to all the peoples of *other* lands? Were the gods of the nations of those lands in any way able to deliver their lands out of my hand? 14Who *was there* among all the gods of those nations that my fathers utterly destroyed that could deliver his people from my hand, that your God should be able to deliver you from my hand? 15Now therefore, do not let Hezekiah deceive you or persuade you like this, and do not believe him; for no god of any nation or kingdom was able to deliver his people from my hand or the hand of my fathers. How much less will your God deliver you from my hand?' "

16Furthermore, his servants spoke against the LORD God and against His servant Hezekiah.

17He also wrote letters to revile the LORD God of Israel, and to speak against Him, saying, "As the gods of the nations of *other* lands have not delivered their people from my hand, so the God of Hezekiah will not deliver His people from my hand." 18Then they called out with a loud voice in Hebrew* to the people of Jerusalem who *were* on the wall, to frighten them and trouble them, that they might take the city. 19And they spoke against the God of Jerusalem, as against the gods of the people of the earth—the work of men's hands.

²⁰Now because of this King Hezekiah and the prophet Isaiah, the son of Amoz, prayed and cried out to heaven. ²¹Then the Lord sent an angel who cut down every mighty man of valor, leader, and captain in the camp of the king of Assyria. So he returned shamefaced to his own land. And when he had gone into the temple of his god, some of his own offspring struck him down with the sword there.

²²Thus the Lord saved Hezekiah and the inhabitants of Jerusalem from the hand of Sennacherib the king of Assyria, and from the hand of all *others,* and guided them* on every side. ²³And many brought gifts to the Lord at Jerusalem, and presents to Hezekiah king of Judah, so that he was exalted in the sight of all nations thereafter.

²⁴In those days Hezekiah was sick and near death, and he prayed to the Lord; and He spoke to him and gave him a sign. ²⁵But Hezekiah did not repay according to the favor *shown* him, for his heart was lifted up; therefore wrath was looming over him and over Judah and Jerusalem. ²⁶Then Hezekiah humbled himself for the pride of his heart, he and the inhabitants of Jerusalem, so that the wrath of the Lord did not come upon them in the days of Hezekiah.

²⁷Hezekiah had very great riches and honor. And he made himself treasuries for silver, for gold, for precious stones, for spices, for shields, and for all kinds of desirable items; ²⁸storehouses for the harvest of grain, wine, and oil; and stalls for all kinds of livestock, and folds for flocks.* ²⁹Moreover he provided cities for himself, and possessions of flocks and herds in abundance; for God had given him very much property. ³⁰This same Hezekiah also stopped the water outlet of Upper Gihon, and brought the water by tunnel* to the west side of the City of David. Hezekiah prospered in all his works.

³¹However, *regarding* the ambassadors of the princes of Babylon, whom they sent to him to inquire about the wonder that was *done* in the land, God withdrew from him, in order to test him, that He might know all *that was* in his heart.

³²Now the rest of the acts of Hezekiah, and his goodness, indeed they *are* written in the vision of Isaiah the prophet, the son of Amoz, *and* in the book of the kings of Judah and Israel. ³³So Hezekiah rested with his fathers, and they buried him in the upper tombs of the sons of David; and all Judah and the inhabitants of Jerusalem honored him at his death. Then Manasseh his son reigned in his place.

Manasseh *was* twelve years old when he became king, and he reigned fifty-five years in Jerusalem. ²But he did evil in the sight of the Lord, according to the abominations of the nations whom the Lord had cast out before the children of Israel. ³For he rebuilt the high places which Hezekiah his father had broken down; he raised up altars for the Baals, and made wooden images; and he worshiped all the host of heaven* and served them. ⁴He also built altars in the house of the Lord, of which the Lord had said, "In Jerusalem shall My name be forever." ⁵And he built altars for all the host of heaven in the two courts of the house of the Lord. ⁶Also he caused his sons to pass through the fire in the Valley of the Son of Hinnom; he practiced soothsaying, used witchcraft and sorcery, and consulted mediums and spiritists. He did much evil in the sight of the Lord, to provoke Him to anger. ⁷He even set a carved image, the idol which he had made, in the house of God, of which God had said to David and to Solomon his son, "In this house and in Jerusalem, which I have chosen out of all the tribes of Israel, I will put

My name forever; [8]and I will not again remove the foot of Israel from the land which I have appointed for your fathers—only if they are careful to do all that I have commanded them, according to the whole law and the statutes and the ordinances by the hand of Moses." [9]So Manasseh seduced Judah and the inhabitants of Jerusalem to do more evil than the nations whom the LORD had destroyed before the children of Israel.

[10]And the LORD spoke to Manasseh and his people, but they would not listen. [11]Therefore the LORD brought upon them the captains of the army of the king of Assyria, who took Manasseh with hooks,* bound him with bronze fetters, and carried him off to Babylon. [12]Now when he was in affliction, he implored the LORD his God, and humbled himself greatly before the God of his fathers, [13]and prayed to Him; and He received his entreaty, heard his supplication, and brought him back to Jerusalem into his kingdom. Then Manasseh knew that the LORD was God.

ROMANS 15:23–16:7

BUT now no longer having a place in these parts, and having a great desire these many years to come to you, [24]whenever I [Paul] journey to Spain, I shall come to you.* For I hope to see you on my journey, and to be helped on my way there by you, if first I may enjoy your company for a while. [25]But now I am going to Jerusalem to minister to the saints. [26]For it pleased those from Macedonia and Achaia to make a certain contribution for the poor among the saints who are in Jerusalem. [27]It pleased them indeed, and they are their debtors. For if the Gentiles have been partakers of their spiritual things, their duty is also to minister to them in material things. [28]Therefore, when I have performed this and have sealed to them this fruit, I shall go by way of you to Spain. [29]But I know that when I come to you, I shall come in the fullness of the blessing of the gospel* of Christ.

[30]Now I beg you, brethren, through the Lord Jesus Christ, and through the love of the Spirit, that you strive together with me in prayers to God for me, [31]that I may be delivered from those in Judea who do not believe, and that my service for Jerusalem may be acceptable to the saints, [32]that I may come to you with joy by the will of God, and may be refreshed together with you. [33]Now the God of peace be with you all. Amen.

I COMMEND to you Phoebe our sister, who is a servant of the church in Cenchrea, [2]that you may receive her in the Lord in a manner worthy of the saints, and assist her in whatever business she has need of you; for indeed she has been a helper of many and of myself also.

[3]Greet Priscilla and Aquila, my fellow workers in Christ Jesus, [4]who risked their own necks for my life, to whom not only I give thanks, but also all the churches of the Gentiles. [5]Likewise greet the church that is in their house.

Greet my beloved Epaenetus, who is the firstfruits of Achaia* to Christ. [6]Greet Mary, who labored much for us. [7]Greet Andronicus and Junia, my countrymen and my fellow prisoners, who are of note among the apostles, who also were in Christ before me.

PSALM 25:16-22

TURN Yourself to me, and have mercy on me,
    For I am desolate and afflicted.
[17]   The troubles of my heart have enlarged;
    Bring me out of my distresses!

18 Look on my affliction and my
pain,
And forgive all my sins.
19 Consider my enemies, for
they are many;
And they hate me with cruel
hatred.
20 Keep my soul, and deliver me;

Let me not be ashamed, for I
put my trust in You.
21 Let integrity and uprightness
preserve me,
For I wait for You.

22 Redeem Israel, O God,
Out of all their troubles!

PROVERBS FOR TODAY/ 20:16-18

Take the garment of one who is surety for *a stranger, and hold it as a pledge* when it *is for a seductress.* ▫ *Bread gained by deceit* is *sweet to a man, but afterward his mouth will be filled with gravel.* ▫ *Plans are established by counsel; by wise counsel wage war.*

AUGUST 3

2 CHRONICLES 33:14–34:33

AFTER this he [Manasseh] built a wall outside the City of David on the west side of Gihon, in the valley, as far as the entrance of the Fish Gate; and *it* enclosed Ophel, and he raised it to a very great height. Then he put military captains in all the fortified cities of Judah. 15He took away the foreign gods and the idol from the house of the LORD, and all the altars that he had built in the mount of the house of the LORD and in Jerusalem; and he cast *them* out of the city. 16He also repaired the altar of the LORD, sacrificed peace offerings and thank offerings on it, and commanded Judah to serve the LORD God of Israel. 17Nevertheless the people still sacrificed on the high places, *but* only to the LORD their God.

18Now the rest of the acts of Manasseh, his prayer to his God, and the words of the seers who spoke to him in the name of the LORD God of Israel, indeed they *are written* in the book* of the kings of Israel. 19Also his prayer

and *how God* received his entreaty, and all his sin and trespass, and the sites where he built high places and set up wooden images and carved images, before he was humbled, indeed they *are* written among the sayings of Hozai.* 20So Manasseh rested with his fathers, and they buried him in his own house. Then his son Amon reigned in his place.

21Amon *was* twenty-two years old when he became king, and he reigned two years in Jerusalem. 22But he did evil in the sight of the LORD, as his father Manasseh had done; for Amon sacrificed to all the carved images which his father Manasseh had made, and served them. 23And he did not humble himself before the LORD, as his father Manasseh had humbled himself; but Amon trespassed more and more.

24Then his servants conspired against him, and killed him in his own house. 25But the people of the land executed all those who had conspired against King Amon. Then the people of the land made his son Josiah king in his place.

JOSIAH *was* eight years old when he became king, and he reigned thirty-one years in Jerusalem. ²And he did *what was* right in the sight of the LORD, and walked in the ways of his father David; *he* did *not* turn aside to the right hand or to the left.

³For in the eighth year of his reign, while he was still young, he began to seek the God of his father David; and in the twelfth year he began to purge Judah and Jerusalem of the high places, the wooden images, the carved images, and the molded images. ⁴They broke down the altars of the Baals in his presence, and the incense altars which *were* above them he cut down; and the wooden images, the carved images, and the molded images he broke in pieces, and made dust of them and scattered *it* on the graves of those who had sacrificed to them. ⁵He also burned the bones of the priests on their altars, and cleansed Judah and Jerusalem. ⁶And *so he did* in the cities of Manasseh, Ephraim, and Simeon, as far as Naphtali and all around, with axes.* ⁷When he had broken down the altars and the wooden images, had beaten the carved images into powder, and cut down all the incense altars throughout all the land of Israel, he returned to Jerusalem.

⁸In the eighteenth year of his reign, when he had purged the land and the temple,* he sent Shaphan the son of Azaliah, Maaseiah the governor of the city, and Joah the son of Joahaz the recorder, to repair the house of the LORD his God. ⁹When they came to Hilkiah the high priest, they delivered the money that was brought into the house of God, which the Levites who kept the doors had gathered from the hand of Manasseh and Ephraim, from all the remnant of Israel, from all Judah and Benjamin, and *which* they had brought back to Jerusalem. ¹⁰Then they put *it* in the hand of the foremen who had the oversight of the house of

the LORD; and they gave it to the workmen who worked in the house of the LORD, to repair and restore the house. ¹¹They gave *it* to the craftsmen and builders to buy hewn stone and timber for beams, and to floor the houses which the kings of Judah had destroyed. ¹²And the men did the work faithfully. Their overseers *were* Jahath and Obadiah the Levites, of the sons of Merari, and Zechariah and Meshullam, of the sons of the Kohathites, to supervise. *Others of* the Levites, all of whom were skillful with instruments of music, ¹³*were* over the burden bearers and *were* overseers of all who did work in any kind of service. And *some* of the Levites *were* scribes, officers, and gatekeepers.

¹⁴Now when they brought out the money that was brought into the house of the LORD, Hilkiah the priest found the Book of the Law of the LORD *given* by Moses. ¹⁵Then Hilkiah answered and said to Shaphan the scribe, "I have found the Book of the Law in the house of the LORD." And Hilkiah gave the book to Shaphan. ¹⁶So Shaphan carried the book to the king, bringing the king word, saying, "All that was committed to your servants they are doing. ¹⁷And they have gathered the money that was found in the house of the LORD, and have delivered it into the hand of the overseers and the workmen." ¹⁸Then Shaphan the scribe told the king, saying, "Hilkiah the priest has given me a book." And Shaphan read it before the king.

¹⁹Thus it happened, when the king heard the words of the Law, that he tore his clothes. ²⁰Then the king commanded Hilkiah, Ahikam the son of Shaphan, Abdon* the son of Micah, Shaphan the scribe, and Asaiah a servant of the king, saying, ²¹"Go, inquire of the LORD for me, and for those who are left in Israel and Judah, concerning the words of the book that is found; for great *is* the wrath of the LORD that is

poured out on us, because our fathers have not kept the word of the LORD, to do according to all that is written in this book."

²²So Hilkiah and those the king *had appointed* went to Huldah the prophetess, the wife of Shallum the son of Tokhath,* the son of Hasrah,* keeper of the wardrobe. (She dwelt in Jerusalem in the Second Quarter.) And they spoke to her to that *effect.*

²³Then she answered them, "Thus says the LORD God of Israel, 'Tell the man who sent you to Me, ²⁴"Thus says the LORD: 'Behold, I will bring calamity on this place and on its inhabitants, all the curses that are written in the book which they have read before the king of Judah, ²⁵because they have forsaken Me and burned incense to other gods, that they might provoke Me to anger with all the works of their hands. Therefore My wrath will be poured out on this place, and not be quenched.' " ' ²⁶But as for the king of Judah, who sent you to inquire of the LORD, in this manner you shall speak to him, 'Thus says the LORD God of Israel: "*Concerning* the words which you have heard— ²⁷because your heart was tender, and you humbled yourself before God when you heard His words against this place and against its inhabitants, and you humbled yourself before Me, and you tore your clothes and wept before Me, I also have heard *you,*" says the LORD. ²⁸"Surely I will gather you to your fathers, and you shall be gathered to your grave in peace; and your eyes shall not see all the calamity which I will bring on this place and its inhabitants." ' " So they brought back word to the king.

²⁹Then the king sent and gathered all the elders of Judah and Jerusalem. ³⁰The king went up to the house of the LORD, with all the men of Judah and the inhabitants of Jerusalem—the priests and the Levites, and all the people, great and small. And he read in their hearing all the words of the Book of the Covenant which had been found in the house of the LORD. ³¹Then the king stood in his place and made a covenant before the LORD, to follow the LORD, and to keep His commandments and His testimonies and His statutes with all his heart and all his soul, to perform the words of the covenant that were written in this book. ³²And he made all who were present in Jerusalem and Benjamin take a stand. So the inhabitants of Jerusalem did according to the covenant of God, the God of their fathers. ³³Thus Josiah removed all the abominations from all the country that *belonged* to the children of Israel, and made all who were present in Israel diligently serve the LORD their God. All his days they did not depart from following the LORD God of their fathers.

ROMANS 16:8-27

GREET Amplias, my beloved in the Lord. ⁹Greet Urbanus, our fellow worker in Christ, and Stachys, my beloved. ¹⁰Greet Apelles, approved in Christ. Greet those who are of the *household* of Aristobulus. ¹¹Greet Herodion, my countryman.* Greet those who are of the *household* of Narcissus who are in the Lord.

¹²Greet Tryphena and Tryphosa, who have labored in the Lord. Greet the beloved Persis, who labored much in the Lord. ¹³Greet Rufus, chosen in the Lord, and his mother and mine. ¹⁴Greet Asyncritus, Phlegon, Hermas, Patrobas, Hermes, and the brethren who are with them. ¹⁵Greet Philologus and Julia, Nereus and his sister, and Olympas, and all the saints who are with them.

¹⁶Greet one another with a holy kiss. The* churches of Christ greet you.

¹⁷Now I urge you, brethren, note those who cause divisions and offenses, contrary to the doctrine which you learned, and avoid them. ¹⁸For those who are such do not serve our

Lord Jesus* Christ, but their own belly, and by smooth words and flattering speech deceive the hearts of the simple. ¹⁹For your obedience has become known to all. Therefore I am glad on your behalf; but I want you to be wise in what is good, and simple concerning evil. ²⁰And the God of peace will crush Satan under your feet shortly.

The grace of our Lord Jesus Christ *be* with you. Amen.

²¹Timothy, my fellow worker, and Lucius, Jason, and Sosipater, my countrymen, greet you.

²²I, Tertius, who wrote *this* epistle, greet you in the Lord.

²³Gaius, my host and *the host* of the whole church, greets you. Erastus, the treasurer of the city, greets you, and Quartus, a brother. ²⁴The grace of our Lord Jesus Christ *be* with you all. Amen.*

²⁵Now to Him who is able to establish you according to my gospel and the preaching of Jesus Christ, according to the revelation of the mystery kept secret since the world began ²⁶but now made manifest, and by the prophetic Scriptures made known to all nations, according to the commandment of the everlasting God, for obedience to the faith— ²⁷to God, alone wise, *be* glory through Jesus Christ forever. Amen.*

PSALM 26:1-12

A Psalm of David.

VINDICATE me, O LORD,
For I have walked in my
integrity.
I have also trusted in the LORD;
I shall not slip.
2 Examine me, O LORD, and
prove me;
Try my mind and my heart.
3 For Your lovingkindness *is*
before my eyes,
And I have walked in Your
truth.
4 I have not sat with idolatrous
mortals,
Nor will I go in with
hypocrites.
5 I have hated the assembly of
evildoers,
And will not sit with the
wicked.
6 I will wash my hands in
innocence;
So I will go about Your altar,
O LORD,
7 That I may proclaim with the
voice of thanksgiving,
And tell of all Your wondrous
works.
8 LORD, I have loved the
habitation of Your house,
And the place where Your
glory dwells.
9 Do not gather my soul with
sinners,
Nor my life with bloodthirsty
men,
10 In whose hands *is* a sinister
scheme,
And whose right hand is full
of bribes.
11 But as for me, I will walk in
my integrity;
Redeem me and be merciful
to me.
12 My foot stands in an even
place;
In the congregations I will
bless the LORD.

PROVERBS FOR TODAY/ 20:19

He who goes about as *a talebearer reveals secrets; therefore do not associate with one who flatters with his lips.*

AUGUST 4

2 CHRONICLES 35:1–36:23

Now Josiah kept a Passover to the LORD in Jerusalem, and they slaughtered the Passover *lambs* on the fourteenth *day* of the first month. ²And he set the priests in their duties and encouraged them for the service of the house of the LORD. ³Then he said to the Levites who taught all Israel, who were holy to the LORD: "Put the holy ark in the house which Solomon the son of David, king of Israel, built. *It shall* no longer *be* a burden on *your* shoulders. Now serve the LORD your God and His people Israel. ⁴Prepare *yourselves* according to your fathers' houses, according to your divisions, following the written instruction of David king of Israel and the written instruction of Solomon his son. ⁵And stand in the holy *place* according to the divisions of the fathers' houses of your brethren the *lay* people, and *according to* the division of the father's house of the Levites. ⁶So slaughter the Passover *offerings,* consecrate yourselves, and prepare *them* for your brethren, that *they* may do according to the word of the LORD by the hand of Moses."

⁷Then Josiah gave the *lay* people lambs and young goats from the flock, all for Passover *offerings* for all who were present, to the number of thirty thousand, as well as three thousand cattle; these *were* from the king's possessions. ⁸And his leaders gave willingly to the people, to the priests, and to the Levites. Hilkiah, Zechariah, and Jehiel, rulers of the house of God, gave to the priests for the Passover *offerings* two thousand six hundred *from the flock,* and three hundred cattle. ⁹Also Conaniah, his brothers Shemaiah and Nethanel, and Hashabiah and Jeiel and Jozabad, chief of the Levites, gave to the Levites for Passover *offerings* five thousand *from the flock* and five hundred cattle.

¹⁰So the service was prepared, and the priests stood in their places, and the Levites in their divisions, according to the king's command. ¹¹And they slaughtered the Passover *offerings;* and the priests sprinkled *the blood* with their hands, while the Levites skinned *the animals.* ¹²Then they removed the burnt offerings that *they* might give them to the divisions of the fathers' houses of the *lay* people, to offer to the LORD, as *it is* written in the Book of Moses. And so *they did* with the cattle. ¹³Also they roasted the Passover *offerings* with fire according to the ordinance; but the *other* holy *offerings* they boiled in pots, in caldrons, and in pans, and divided *them* quickly among all the *lay* people. ¹⁴Then afterward they prepared portions for themselves and for the priests, because the priests, the sons of Aaron, *were busy* in offering burnt offerings and fat until night; therefore the Levites prepared portions for themselves and for the priests, the sons of Aaron. ¹⁵And the singers, the sons of Asaph, *were* in their places, according to the command of David, Asaph, Heman, and Jeduthun the king's seer. Also the gatekeepers were at each gate; they did not have to leave their position, because their brethren the Levites prepared portions for them.

¹⁶So all the service of the LORD was prepared the same day, to keep the Passover and to offer burnt offerings on the altar of the LORD, according to the command of King Josiah. ¹⁷And the children of Israel who were present kept the Passover at that time, and the Feast of Unleavened Bread for

seven days. 18There had been no Passover kept in Israel like that since the days of Samuel the prophet; and none of the kings of Israel had kept such a Passover as Josiah kept, with the priests and the Levites, all Judah and Israel who were present, and the inhabitants of Jerusalem. 19In the eighteenth year of the reign of Josiah this Passover was kept.

20After all this, when Josiah had prepared the temple, Necho king of Egypt came up to fight against Carchemish by the Euphrates; and Josiah went out against him. 21But he sent messengers to him, saying, "What have I to do with you, king of Judah? *I have* not *come* against you this day, but against the house with which I have war; for God commanded me to make haste. Refrain *from meddling with* God, who *is* with me, lest He destroy you." 22Nevertheless Josiah would not turn his face from him, but disguised himself so that he might fight with him, and did not heed the words of Necho from the mouth of God. So he came to fight in the Valley of Megiddo.

23And the archers shot King Josiah; and the king said to his servants, "Take me away, for I am severely wounded." 24His servants therefore took him out of that chariot and put him in the second chariot that he had, and they brought him to Jerusalem. So he died, and was buried in *one of* the tombs of his fathers. And all Judah and Jerusalem mourned for Josiah.

25Jeremiah also lamented for Josiah. And to this day all the singing men and the singing women speak of Josiah in their lamentations. They made it a custom in Israel; and indeed they *are* written in the Laments.

26Now the rest of the acts of Josiah and his goodness, according to *what was* written in the Law of the LORD, 27and his deeds from first to last, indeed they *are* written in the book of the kings of Israel and Judah.

THEN the people of the land took Jehoahaz the son of Josiah, and made him king in his father's place in Jerusalem. 2Jehoahaz* *was* twenty-three years old when he became king, and he reigned three months in Jerusalem. 3Now the king of Egypt deposed him at Jerusalem; and he imposed on the land a tribute of one hundred talents of silver and a talent of gold. 4Then the king of Egypt made *Jehoahaz's** brother Eliakim king over Judah and Jerusalem, and changed his name to Jehoiakim. And Necho took Jehoahaz* his brother and carried him off to Egypt.

5Jehoiakim *was* twenty-five years old when he became king, and he reigned eleven years in Jerusalem. And he did evil in the sight of the LORD his God. 6Nebuchadnezzar king of Babylon came up against him, and bound him in bronze *fetters* to carry him off to Babylon. 7Nebuchadnezzar also carried off *some* of the articles from the house of the LORD to Babylon, and put them in his temple at Babylon. 8Now the rest of the acts of Jehoiakim, the abominations which he did, and what was found against him, indeed they *are* written in the book of the kings of Israel and Judah. Then Jehoiachin his son reigned in his place.

9Jehoiachin *was* eight* years old when he became king, and he reigned in Jerusalem three months and ten days. And he did evil in the sight of the LORD. 10At the turn of the year King Nebuchadnezzar summoned *him* and took him to Babylon, with the costly articles from the house of the LORD, and made Zedekiah, *Jehoiakim's** brother, king over Judah and Jerusalem.

11Zedekiah *was* twenty-one years old when he became king, and he reigned eleven years in Jerusalem. 12He did evil in the sight of the LORD his God, *and* did not humble himself before Jeremiah the prophet, *who spoke* from the mouth of the LORD. 13And he also rebelled against King Nebuchadnezzar, who had made him swear *an oath* by God; but he stiffened his neck and hardened his heart against turning to the LORD God of Israel. [14]Moreover all the leaders of the priests and the people transgressed more and more, *according* to all the abominations of the nations, and defiled the house of the LORD which He had consecrated in Jerusalem.

[15]And the LORD God of their fathers sent *warnings* to them by His messengers, rising up early and sending *them,* because He had compassion on His people and on His dwelling place. [16]But they mocked the messengers of God, despised His words, and scoffed at His prophets, until the wrath of the LORD arose against His people, till *there was* no remedy.

[17]Therefore He brought against them the king of the Chaldeans, who killed their young men with the sword in the house of their sanctuary, and had no compassion on young man or virgin, on the aged or the weak; He gave *them* all into his hand. [18]And all the articles from the house of God, great and small, the treasures of the house of the LORD, and the treasures of the king and of his leaders, all *these* he took to Babylon. [19]Then they burned the house of God, broke down the wall of Jerusalem, burned all its palaces with fire, and destroyed all its precious possessions. [20]And those who escaped from the sword he carried away to Babylon, where they became servants to him and his sons until the rule of the kingdom of Persia, [21]to fulfill the word of the LORD by the mouth of Jeremiah, until the land had enjoyed her Sabbaths. As long as she lay desolate she kept Sabbath, to fulfill seventy years.

[22]Now in the first year of Cyrus king of Persia, that the word of the LORD by the mouth of Jeremiah might be fulfilled, the LORD stirred up the spirit of Cyrus king of Persia, so that he made a proclamation throughout all his kingdom, and also *put it* in writing, saying,

[23]   Thus says Cyrus king of
       Persia:

All the kingdoms of the earth the LORD God of heaven has given me. And He has commanded me to build Him a house at Jerusalem which is in Judah. Who *is* among you of all His people? May the LORD his God *be* with him, and let him go up!

1 CORINTHIANS 1:1-17

PAUL, called *to be* an apostle of Jesus Christ through the will of God, and Sosthenes *our* brother,

[2]To the church of God which is at Corinth, to those who are sanctified in Christ Jesus, called *to be* saints, with all who in every place call on the name of Jesus Christ our Lord, both theirs and ours:

[3]Grace to you and peace from God our Father and the Lord Jesus Christ.

[4]I thank my God always concerning you for the grace of God which was given to you by Christ Jesus, [5]that you were enriched in everything by Him in all utterance and all knowledge, [6]even as the testimony of Christ was confirmed in you, [7]so that you come short in no gift, eagerly waiting for the revelation of our Lord Jesus Christ, [8]who will also confirm you to the end, *that you may be* blameless in the day of our Lord Jesus Christ. [9]God *is* faithful, by whom you were called into the fellowship of His Son, Jesus Christ our Lord.

[10]Now I plead with you, brethren, by the name of our Lord Jesus Christ, that you all speak the same thing, and *that*

there be no divisions among you, but *that* you be perfectly joined together in the same mind and in the same judgment. [11]For it has been declared to me concerning you, my brethren, by those of Chloe's *household,* that there are contentions among you. [12]Now I say this, that each of you says, "I am of Paul," or "I am of Apollos," or "I am of Cephas," or "I am of Christ." [13]Is Christ divided? Was Paul crucified for you? Or were you baptized in the name of Paul?

[14]I thank God that I baptized none of you except Crispus and Gaius, [15]lest anyone should say that I had baptized in my own name. [16]Yes, I also baptized the household of Stephanas. Besides, I do not know whether I baptized any other. [17]For Christ did not send me to baptize, but to preach the gospel, not with wisdom of words, lest the cross of Christ should be made of no effect.

PSALM 27:1-6

A Psalm of David.

THE LORD *is* my light and my salvation;
Whom shall I fear?
The LORD *is* the strength of my life;
Of whom shall I be afraid?
2 When the wicked came against me
To eat up my flesh,
My enemies and foes,
They stumbled and fell.
3 Though an army may encamp against me,
My heart shall not fear;
Though war may rise against me,
In this I *will be* confident.

4 One *thing* I have desired of the LORD,
That will I seek:
That I may dwell in the house of the LORD
All the days of my life,
To behold the beauty of the LORD,
And to inquire in His temple.
5 For in the time of trouble
He shall hide me in His pavilion;
In the secret place of His tabernacle
He shall hide me;
He shall set me high upon a rock.

6 And now my head shall be lifted up above my enemies all around me;
Therefore I will offer sacrifices of joy in His tabernacle;
I will sing, yes, I will sing praises to the LORD.

PROVERBS FOR TODAY / 20:20-21

Whoever curses his father or his mother, his lamp will be put out in deep darkness.
□ *An inheritance gained hastily at the beginning will not be blessed at the end.*

AUGUST 5

EZRA 1:1–2:70

Now in the first year of Cyrus king of Persia, that the word of the LORD by the mouth of Jeremiah might be fulfilled, the LORD stirred up the spirit of Cyrus king of Persia, so that he made a proclamation throughout all his kingdom, and also *put it* in writing, saying,

2 Thus says Cyrus king of Persia: All the kingdoms of the earth the LORD God of heaven has given me. And He has commanded me to build Him a house at Jerusalem which *is* in Judah. ³Who *is* among you of all His people? May his God be with him, and let him go up to Jerusalem which *is* in Judah, and build the house of the LORD God of Israel (He *is* God), which *is* in Jerusalem. ⁴And whoever is left in any place where he dwells, let the men of his place help him with silver and gold, with goods and livestock, besides the freewill offerings for the house of God which *is* in Jerusalem.

⁵Then the heads of the fathers' *houses* of Judah and Benjamin, and the priests and the Levites, with all whose spirits God had moved, arose to go up and build the house of the LORD which *is* in Jerusalem. ⁶And all those who *were* around them encouraged them with articles of silver and gold, with goods and livestock, and with precious things, besides all *that* was willingly offered.

⁷King Cyrus also brought out the articles of the house of the LORD, which Nebuchadnezzar had taken from Jerusalem and put in the temple of his gods; ⁸and Cyrus king of Persia brought them out by the hand of Mithredath the treasurer, and counted them out to Sheshbazzar the prince of Judah. ⁹This *is* the number of them: thirty gold platters, one thousand silver platters, twenty-nine knives, ¹⁰thirty gold basins, four hundred and ten silver basins of a similar *kind, and* one thousand other articles. ¹¹All the articles of gold and silver *were* five thousand four hundred. All *these* Sheshbazzar took with the captives who were brought from Babylon to Jerusalem.

Now* these *are* the people of the province who came back from the captivity, of those who had been carried away, whom Nebuchadnezzar the king of Babylon had carried away to Babylon, and who returned to Jerusalem and Judah, everyone to his *own* city. ²*Those* who came with Zerubbabel *were* Jeshua, Nehemiah, Seraiah, Reelaiah, Mordecai, Bilshan, Mispar,* Bigvai, Rehum,* *and* Baanah. The number of the men of the people of Israel: ³the people of Parosh, two thousand one hundred and seventy-two; ⁴the people of Shephatiah, three hundred and seventy-two; ⁵the people of Arah, seven hundred and seventy-five; ⁶the people of Pahath-Moab, of the people of Jeshua *and* Joab, two thousand eight hundred and twelve; ⁷the people of Elam, one thousand two hundred and fifty-four; ⁸the people of Zattu, nine hundred and forty-five; ⁹the people of Zaccai, seven hundred and sixty; ¹⁰the people of Bani,* six hundred and forty-two; ¹¹the people of Bebai, six hundred and twenty-three;

12the people of Azgad, one thousand two hundred and twenty-two; 13the people of Adonikam, six hundred and sixty-six; 14the people of Bigvai, two thousand and fifty-six; 15the people of Adin, four hundred and fifty-four; 16the people of Ater of Hezekiah, ninety-eight; 17the people of Bezai, three hundred and twenty-three; 18the people of Jorah,* one hundred and twelve; 19the people of Hashum, two hundred and twenty-three; 20the people of Gibbar,* ninety-five; 21the people of Bethlehem, one hundred and twenty-three; 22the men of Netophah, fifty-six; 23the men of Anathoth, one hundred and twenty-eight; 24the people of Azmaveth,* forty-two; 25the people of Kirjath Arim,* Chephirah, and Beeroth, seven hundred and forty-three; 26the people of Ramah and Geba, six hundred and twenty-one; 27the men of Michmas, one hundred and twenty-two; 28the men of Bethel and Ai, two hundred and twenty-three; 29the people of Nebo, fifty-two; 30the people of Magbish, one hundred and fifty-six; 31the people of the other Elam, one thousand two hundred and fifty-four; 32the people of Harim, three hundred and twenty; 33the people of Lod, Hadid, and Ono, seven hundred and twenty-five; 34the people of Jericho, three hundred and forty-five; 35the people of Senaah, three thousand six hundred and thirty.

36The priests: the sons of Jedaiah, of the house of Jeshua, nine hundred and seventy-three; 37the sons of Immer, one thousand and fifty-two; 38the sons of Pashhur, one thousand two hundred and forty-seven; 39the sons of Harim, one thousand and seventeen.

40The Levites: the sons of Jeshua and Kadmiel, of the sons of Hodaviah,* seventy-four.

41The singers: the sons of Asaph, one hundred and twenty-eight.

42The sons of the gatekeepers: the sons of Shallum, the sons of Ater, the sons of Talmon, the sons of Akkub, the sons of Hatita, and the sons of Shobai, one hundred and thirty-nine *in* all.

43The Nethinim: the sons of Ziha, the sons of Hasupha, the sons of Tabbaoth, 44the sons of Keros, the sons of Siaha,* the sons of Padon, 45the sons of Lebanah, the sons of Hagabah, the sons of Akkub, 46the sons of Hagab, the sons of Shalmai, the sons of Hanan, 47the sons of Giddel, the sons of Gahar, the sons of Reaiah, 48the sons of Rezin, the sons of Nekoda, the sons of Gazzam, 49the sons of Uzza, the sons of Paseah, the sons of Besai, 50the sons of Asnah, the sons of Meunim, the sons of Nephusim,* 51the sons of Bakbuk, the sons of Hakupha, the sons of Harhur, 52the sons of Bazluth,* the sons of Mehida, the sons of Harsha, 53the sons of Barkos, the sons of Sisera, the sons of Tamah, 54the sons of Neziah, and the sons of Hatipha.

55The sons of Solomon's servants: the sons of Sotai, the sons of Sophereth, the sons of Peruda,* 56the sons of Jaala, the sons of Darkon, the sons of Giddel, 57the sons of Shephatiah, the sons of Hattil, the sons of Pochereth of Zebaim, and the sons of Ami.* 58All the Nethinim and the children of Solomon's servants were three hundred and ninety-two.

59And these *were* the ones who came up from Tel Melah, Tel Harsha, Cherub, Addan,* and Immer; but they could not identify their father's house or their genealogy,* whether they *were* of Israel: 60the sons of Delaiah, the sons of Tobiah, and the sons of Nekoda, six hundred and fifty-two; 61and of the sons of the priests: the sons of Habaiah, the sons of Koz,* and the sons of Barzillai, who took a wife of the daughters of Barzillai the Gileadite, and was called by their name. 62These sought their listing *among* those who were registered by genealogy, but they were not found; therefore they *were excluded* from the priesthood as defiled. 63And the governor* said to them that they should not eat of the most holy things till a priest could consult with the Urim and Thummim.

64The whole assembly together *was* forty-two thousand three hundred *and* sixty, 65besides their male and female servants, of whom *there were* seven thousand three hundred and thirty-seven; and they had two hundred men and women singers. 66Their horses *were* seven hundred and thirty-six, their mules two hundred and forty-five, 67their camels four hundred and thirty-five, and *their* donkeys six thousand seven hundred and twenty.

68*Some* of the heads of the fathers' *houses,* when they came to the house of the LORD which *is* in Jerusalem, offered freely for the house of God, to erect it in its place: 69According to their ability, they gave to the treasury for the work sixty-one thousand gold drachmas, five thousand minas of silver, and one hundred priestly garments.

70So the priests and the Levites, *some* of the people, the singers, the gatekeepers, and the Nethinim, dwelt in their cities, and all Israel in their cities.

1 CORINTHIANS 1:18–2:5

FOR the message of the cross is foolishness to those who are perishing, but to us who are being saved it is the power of God. 19For it is written:

> *"I will destroy the wisdom of the wise,*
> *And bring to nothing the understanding of the prudent."* *

20Where *is* the wise? Where *is* the scribe? Where *is* the disputer of this age? Has not God made foolish the wisdom of this world? 21For since, in the wisdom of God, the world through wisdom did not know God, it pleased God through the foolishness of the message preached to save those who believe. 22For Jews request a sign, and Greeks seek after wisdom; 23but we preach Christ crucified, to the Jews a stumbling block and to the Greeks* foolishness, 24but to those who are called, both Jews and Greeks, Christ the power of God and the wisdom of God. 25Because the foolishness of God is wiser than men, and the weakness of God is stronger than men.

26For you see your calling, brethren, that not many wise according to the flesh, not many mighty, not many noble, *are called.* 27But God has chosen the foolish things of the world to put to shame the wise, and God has chosen the weak things of the world to put to shame the things which are mighty; 28and the base things of the world and the things which are despised God has chosen, and the things which are not, to bring to nothing the things that are, 29that no flesh should glory in His presence. 30But of Him you are in Christ Jesus, who became for us wisdom from God—and righteousness and sanctification and redemption— 31that, as it is written, *"He who glories, let him glory in the LORD."* *

AND I, brethren, when I came to you, did not come with excellence of speech or of wisdom declaring to you the testimony* of God. 2For I determined not to know anything among you except Jesus Christ and Him crucified. 3I was with you in weakness, in fear, and in much trembling. 4And my speech and my preaching *were* not with persuasive words of human* wisdom, but in demonstration of the Spirit and of power, 5that your faith should not be in the wisdom of men but in the power of God.

PSALM 27:7-14

HEAR, O LORD, *when* I cry with my voice!
Have mercy also upon me, and answer me.

8 *When You said,* "Seek My face,"
My heart said to You, "Your face, LORD, I will seek."

9 Do not hide Your face from me;
Do not turn Your servant away in anger;
You have been my help;
Do not leave me nor forsake me,
O God of my salvation.

10 When my father and my mother forsake me,
Then the LORD will take care of me.

11 Teach me Your way, O LORD,
And lead me in a smooth path, because of my enemies.

12 Do not deliver me to the will of my adversaries;
For false witnesses have risen against me,
And such as breathe out violence.

13 *I would have lost heart,* unless I had believed
That I would see the goodness of the LORD
In the land of the living.

14 Wait on the LORD;
Be of good courage,
And He shall strengthen your heart;
Wait, I say, on the LORD!

PROVERBS FOR TODAY/ 20:22-23

Do not say, "I will recompense evil"; wait for the LORD, and He will save you. □ *Diverse weights* are *an abomination to the LORD, and dishonest scales* are *not good.*

AUGUST 6

EZRA 3:1–4:24

AND when the seventh month had come, and the children of Israel *were* in the cities, the people gathered together as one man to Jerusalem. ²Then Jeshua the son of Jozadak* and his brethren the priests, and Zerubbabel the son of Shealtiel and his brethren, arose and built the altar of the God of Israel, to offer burnt offerings on it, as *it is* written in the Law of Moses the man of God. ³Though fear *had come* upon them because of the people of those countries, they set the altar on its bases; and they offered burnt offerings on it to the LORD, *both* the morning and evening burnt offerings. ⁴They also kept the Feast of Tabernacles, as *it is* written, and *offered* the daily burnt offerings in the number required by ordinance for each day. ⁵Afterwards *they offered* the regular burnt offering, and *those* for New Moons and for all the appointed feasts of the LORD that were consecrated, and *those* of everyone who willingly offered a freewill offering to the LORD. ⁶From the first day of the seventh month they began to offer burnt offerings to the Lord, although the foundation of the temple of the Lord had not been laid. ⁷They also gave money to the masons and the carpenters, and food, drink, and oil to the people of Sidon and Tyre to bring cedar logs from Lebanon to the sea, to Joppa, according to the permission which they had from Cyrus king of Persia.

⁸Now in the second month of the second year of their coming to the house of God at Jerusalem, Zerubbabel the son of Shealtiel, Jeshua the son of Jozadak,* and the rest of their brethren the priests and the Levites, and all those who had come out of the captivity to Jerusalem, began *work* and appointed the Levites from twenty years old and above to oversee the work of the house of the Lord. ⁹Then Jeshua *with* his sons and brothers, Kadmiel *with* his sons, and the sons of Judah,* arose as one to oversee those working on the house of God: the sons of Henadad *with* their sons and their brethren the Levites.

¹⁰When the builders laid the foundation of the temple of the Lord, the priests stood* in their apparel with trumpets, and the Levites, the sons of Asaph, with cymbals, to praise the Lord, according to the ordinance of David king of Israel. ¹¹And they sang responsively, praising and giving thanks to the Lord:

"For *He is* good,
    For His mercy *endures*
        forever toward Israel."*

Then all the people shouted with a great shout, when they praised the Lord, because the foundation of the house of the Lord was laid.

¹²But many of the priests and Levites and heads of the fathers' *houses,* old men who had seen the first temple, wept with a loud voice when the foundation of this temple was laid

before their eyes. Yet many shouted aloud for joy, ¹³so that the people could not discern the noise of the shout of joy from the noise of the weeping of the people, for the people shouted with a loud shout, and the sound was heard afar off.

Now when the adversaries of Judah and Benjamin heard that the descendants of the captivity were building the temple of the Lord God of Israel, ²they came to Zerubbabel and the heads of the fathers' *houses,* and said to them, "Let us build with you, for we seek your God as you *do;* and we have sacrificed to Him since the days of Esarhaddon king of Assyria, who brought us here." ³But Zerubbabel and Jeshua and the rest of the heads of the fathers' *houses* of Israel said to them, "You may do nothing with us to build a house for our God; but we alone will build to the Lord God of Israel, as King Cyrus the king of Persia has commanded us." ⁴Then the people of the land tried to discourage the people of Judah. They troubled them in building, ⁵and hired counselors against them to frustrate their purpose all the days of Cyrus king of Persia, even until the reign of Darius king of Persia.

⁶In the reign of Ahasuerus, in the beginning of his reign, they wrote an accusation against the inhabitants of Judah and Jerusalem.

⁷In the days of Artaxerxes also, Bishlam, Mithredath, Tabel, and the rest of their companions wrote to Artaxerxes king of Persia; and the letter *was* written in Aramaic script, and translated into the Aramaic language. ⁸Rehum* the commander and Shimshai the scribe wrote a letter against Jerusalem to King Artaxerxes in this fashion:

9   From* Rehum the commander, Shimshai the scribe, and the rest of their compan-

ions—*representatives* of the Dinaites, the Apharsathchites, the Tarpelites, the people of Persia and Erech and Babylon and Shushan,* the Dehavites, the Elamites, 10and the rest of the nations whom the great and noble Osnapper took captive and settled in the cities of Samaria and the remainder beyond the River*—and so forth.*

11(This *is* a copy of the letter that they sent him)

To King Artaxerxes from your servants, the men *of the region* beyond the River, and so forth:*

12 Let it be known to the king that the Jews who came up from you have come to us at Jerusalem, and are building the rebellious and evil city, and are finishing *its* walls and repairing the foundations. 13Let it now be known to the king that, if this city is built and the walls completed, they will not pay tax, tribute, or custom, and the king's treasury will be diminished. 14Now because we receive support from the palace, it was not proper for us to see the king's dishonor; therefore we have sent and informed the king, 15that search may be made in the book of the records of your fathers. And you will find in the book of the records and know that this city *is* a rebellious city, harmful to kings and provinces, and that they have incited sedition within the city in former times, for which cause this city was destroyed.

16 We inform the king that if this city is rebuilt and its walls are completed, the result will be that you will have no dominion beyond the River.

17The king sent an answer:

To Rehum the commander, *to* Shimshai the scribe, *to* the rest of their companions who dwell in Samaria, and *to* the remainder beyond the River:

Peace, and so forth.*

18 The letter which you sent to us has been clearly read before me. 19And I gave the command, and a search has been made, and it was found that this city in former times has revolted against kings, and rebellion and sedition have been fostered in it. 20There have also been mighty kings over Jerusalem, who have ruled over all *the region* beyond the River; and tax, tribute, and custom were paid to them. 21Now give the command to make these men cease, that this city may not be built until the command is given by me.

22 Take heed now that you do not fail to do this. Why should damage increase to the hurt of the kings?

23Now when the copy of King Artaxerxes' letter *was* read before Rehum, Shimshai the scribe, and their companions, they went up in haste to Jerusalem against the Jews, and by force of arms made them cease. 24Thus the work of the house of God which *is* at Jerusalem ceased, and it was discontinued until the second year of the reign of Darius king of Persia.

1 CORINTHIANS 2:6–3:4

However, we speak wisdom among those who are mature, yet not the wisdom of this age, nor of the rulers of this age, who are coming to nothing. 7But we speak the wisdom of God in a mystery, the hidden *wisdom* which God ordained before the ages for our glory, 8which none of the rulers of this age knew; for had they known, they would not have crucified the Lord of glory.

9But as it is written:

> "Eye has not seen, nor ear heard,
> Nor have entered into the heart of man
> The things which God has prepared for those who love Him." *

10But God has revealed *them* to us through His Spirit. For the Spirit searches all things, yes, the deep things of God. 11For what man knows the things of a man except the spirit of the man which is in him? Even so no one knows the things of God except the Spirit of God. 12Now we have received, not the spirit of the world, but the Spirit who is from God, that we might know the things that have been freely given to us by God.

13These things we also speak, not in words which man's wisdom teaches but which the Holy* Spirit teaches, comparing spiritual things with spiritual. 14But the natural man does not receive the things of the Spirit of God, for they are foolishness to him; nor can he know *them,* because they are spiritually discerned. 15But he who is spiritual judges all things, yet he himself is *rightly* judged by no one. 16For *"who has known the mind of the Lord that*

he may instruct Him?" * But we have the mind of Christ.

And I, brethren, could not speak to you as to spiritual *people* but as to carnal, as to babes in Christ. 2I fed you with milk and not with solid food; for until now you were not able *to receive it,* and even now you are still not able; 3for you are still carnal. For where *there are* envy, strife, and divisions among you, are you not carnal and behaving like *mere* men? 4For when one says, "I am of Paul," and another, "I *am* of Apollos," are you not carnal?

PSALM 28:1-9

A Psalm of David.

To You I will cry, O Lord my Rock:
Do not be silent to me,
Lest, if You *are* silent to me,
I become like those who go
down to the pit.
2 Hear the voice of my
supplications
When I cry to You,
When I lift up my hands
toward Your holy sanctuary.

3 Do not take me away with the
wicked
And with the workers of
iniquity,
Who speak peace to their
neighbors,
But evil *is* in their hearts.
4 Give them according to their
deeds,
And according to the
wickedness of their
endeavors;
Give them according to the
work of their hands;
Render to them what they
deserve.
5 Because they do not regard
the works of the Lord,
Nor the operation of His
hands,

He shall destroy them
And not build them up.

6   Blessed *be* the Lord,
    Because He has heard the
        voice of my supplications!
7   The Lord *is* my strength and
        my shield;
    My heart trusted in Him, and
        I am helped;
    Therefore my heart greatly
        rejoices,

And with my song I will praise
    Him.

8   The Lord *is* their strength,*
    And He *is* the saving refuge of
        His anointed.
9   Save Your people,
    And bless Your inheritance;
    Shepherd them also,
    And bear them up forever.

PROVERBS FOR TODAY / 20:24-25

A man's steps are *of the Lord; how then can a man understand his own way?* □ It
is *a snare for a man to devote rashly* something as *holy, and afterward to
reconsider* his *vows.*

AUGUST 7

EZRA 5:1–6:22

THEN the prophet Haggai and
Zechariah the son of Iddo,
prophets, prophesied to the
Jews who *were* in Judah and Jerusalem, in the name of the God of Israel,
who was over them. ²So Zerubbabel
the son of Shealtiel and Jeshua the son
of Jozadak* rose up and began to build
the house of God which *is* in Jerusalem; and the prophets of God *were*
with them, helping them.

³At the same time Tattenai the governor of *the region* beyond the River*
and Shethar-Boznai and their companions came to them and spoke thus to
them: "Who has commanded you to
build this temple and finish this wall?"
⁴Then, accordingly, we told them the
names of the men who were construct-
ing this building. ⁵But the eye of their
God was upon the elders of the Jews,
so that they could not make them
cease till a report could go to Darius.

Then a written answer was returned
concerning this *matter.* ⁶This is a copy
of the letter that Tattenai sent:

The governor of *the region*
beyond the River, and
Shethar-Boznai, and his
companions, the Persians
who *were in the region* beyond
the River, to Darius the king.

⁷(They sent a letter to him, in which
was written thus)

To Darius the king:

All peace.

8   Let it be known to the king
    that we went into the province
    of Judea, to the temple of the
    great God, which is being
    built with heavy stones, and
    timber is being laid in the
    walls; and this work goes on

diligently and prospers in their hands.

9 Then we asked those elders, *and* spoke thus to them: "Who commanded you to build this temple and to finish these walls?" ¹⁰We also asked them their names to inform you, that we might write the names of the men who *were* chief among them.

11 And thus they returned us an answer, saying: "We are the servants of the God of heaven and earth, and we are rebuilding the temple that was built many years ago, which a great king of Israel built and completed. ¹²But because our fathers provoked the God of heaven to wrath, He gave them into the hand of Nebuchadnezzar king of Babylon, the Chaldean, *who* destroyed this temple and carried the people away to Babylon. ¹³However, in the first year of Cyrus king of Babylon, King Cyrus issued a decree to build this house of God. ¹⁴Also, the gold and silver articles of the house of God, which Nebuchadnezzar had taken from the temple that *was* in Jerusalem and carried into the temple of Babylon—those King Cyrus took from the temple of Babylon, and they were given to one named Sheshbazzar, whom he had made governor. ¹⁵And he said to him, 'Take these articles; go, carry them to the temple *site* that *is* in Jerusalem, and let the house of God be rebuilt on its former site.' ¹⁶Then the same Sheshbazzar came *and* laid the foundation of the house of God which *is* in Jerusalem; but from that time even until now it has been under construction, and it is not finished."

17 Now therefore, if *it seems* good to the king, let a search be made in the king's treasure house, which *is* there in Babylon, whether it is *so* that a decree was issued by King Cyrus to build this house of God at Jerusalem, and let the king send us his pleasure concerning this *matter.*

Then King Darius issued a decree, and a search was made in the archives,* where the treasures were stored in Babylon. ²And at Achmetha,* in the palace that *is* in the province of Media, a scroll was found, and in it a record *was* written thus:

3 In the first year of King Cyrus, King Cyrus issued a decree *concerning* the house of God at Jerusalem: "Let the house be rebuilt, the place where they offered sacrifices; and let the foundations of it be firmly laid, its height sixty cubits *and* its width sixty cubits, ⁴*with* three rows of heavy stones and one row of new timber. Let the expenses be paid from the king's treasury. ⁵Also let the gold and silver articles of the house of God, which Nebuchadnezzar took from the temple which *is* in Jerusalem and brought to Babylon, be restored and taken back to the temple which *is* in Jerusalem, *each* to its place; and deposit *them* in the house of God"—

6 Now *therefore,* Tattenai, governor of *the region* beyond the River, and Shethar-Boznai, and your companions the Persians who *are* beyond the River, keep yourselves far from there. 7Let the work of this house of God alone; let the governor of the Jews and the elders of the Jews build this house of God on its site.

8 Moreover I issue a decree *as to* what you shall do for the elders of these Jews, for the building of this house of God: Let the cost be paid at the king's expense from taxes *on the region* beyond the River; this is to be given immediately to these men, so that they are not hindered. 9And whatever they need—young bulls, rams, and lambs for the burnt offerings of the God of heaven, wheat, salt, wine, and oil, according to the request of the priests who *are* in Jerusalem—let it be given them day by day without fail, 10that they may offer sacrifices of sweet aroma to the God of heaven, and pray for the life of the king and his sons.

11 Also I issue a decree that whoever alters this edict, let a timber be pulled from his house and erected, and let him be hanged on it; and let his house be made a refuse heap because of this. 12And may the God who causes His name to dwell there destroy any king or people who put their hand to alter it, or to destroy this house of God which is in Jerusalem. I

Darius issue a decree; let it be done diligently.

13Then Tattenai, governor of *the region* beyond the River, Shethar-Boznai, and their companions diligently did according to what King Darius had sent. 14So the elders of the Jews built, and they prospered through the prophesying of Haggai the prophet and Zechariah the son of Iddo. And they built and finished *it,* according to the commandment of the God of Israel, and according to the command of Cyrus, Darius, and Artaxerxes king of Persia. 15Now the temple was finished on the third day of the month of Adar, which was in the sixth year of the reign of King Darius 16Then the children of Israel, the priests and the Levites and the rest of the descendants of the captivity, celebrated the dedication of this house of God with joy. 17And they offered sacrifices at the dedication of this house of God, one hundred bulls, two hundred rams, four hundred lambs, and as a sin offering for all Israel twelve male goats, according to the number of the tribes of Israel. 18They assigned the priests to their divisions and the Levites to their divisions, over the service of God in Jerusalem, as it is written in the Book of Moses.

19And the descendants of the captivity kept the Passover on the fourteenth *day* of the first month. 20For the priests and the Levites had purified themselves; all of them *were ritually* clean. And they slaughtered the Passover *lambs* for all the descendants of the captivity, for their brethren the priests, and for themselves. 21Then the children of Israel who had returned from the captivity ate together with all who had separated themselves from the filth of the nations of the land in order to seek the Lord God of Israel. 22And they kept the Feast of Unleavened Bread seven days with joy; for the Lord made them joyful, and turned the heart of the king of Assyria toward them, to strengthen their hands in the work of the house of God, the God of Israel.

1 CORINTHIANS 3:5-23

WHO then is Paul, and who is Apollos, but ministers through whom you believed, as the Lord gave to each one? 6I planted, Apollos watered, but God gave the increase. 7So then neither he who plants is anything, nor he who waters, but God who gives the increase. 8Now he who plants and he who waters are one, and each one will receive his own reward according to his own labor.

9For we are God's fellow workers; you are God's field, *you are* God's building. 10According to the grace of God which was given to me, as a wise master builder I have laid the foundation, and another builds on it. But let each one take heed how he builds on it. 11For no other foundation can anyone lay than that which is laid, which is Jesus Christ. 12Now if anyone builds on this foundation *with* gold, silver, precious stones, wood, hay, straw, 13each one's work will become clear; for the Day will declare it, because it will be revealed by fire; and the fire will test each one's work, of what sort it is. 14If anyone's work which he has built on *it* endures, he will receive a reward. 15If anyone's work is burned, he will suffer loss; but he himself will be saved, yet so as through fire.

16Do you not know that you are the temple of God and *that* the Spirit of God dwells in you? 17If anyone defiles the temple of God, God will destroy him. For the temple of God is holy, which *temple* you are.

18Let no one deceive himself. If anyone among you seems to be wise in this age, let him become a fool that he may become wise. 19For the wisdom of this world is foolishness with God. For it is written, *"He catches the wise in their own craftiness";* * 20and again, *"The* Lord *knows the thoughts of the wise, that they are futile."* * 21Therefore let no one boast in men. For all things are yours: 22whether Paul or Apollos or Cephas, or the world or life or death, or things present or things to come—all are yours. 23And you *are* Christ's, and Christ *is* God's.

PSALM 29:1-11

A Psalm of David.

GIVE unto the Lord, O you mighty ones,
Give unto the Lord glory and
strength.
2   Give unto the Lord the glory
due to His name;
Worship the Lord in the
beauty of holiness.

3   The voice of the Lord *is* over
the waters;
The God of glory thunders;
The Lord *is* over many waters.
4   The voice of the Lord *is*
powerful;
The voice of the Lord *is* full of
majesty.

5   The voice of the Lord breaks
the cedars,
Yes, the Lord splinters the
cedars of Lebanon.
6   He makes them also skip like
a calf,
Lebanon and Sirion like a
young wild ox.
7   The voice of the Lord divides
the flames of fire.

8   The voice of the Lord shakes
the wilderness;
The Lord shakes the
Wilderness of Kadesh.
9   The voice of the Lord makes
the deer give birth,

And strips the forests bare;
And in His temple everyone
  says, "Glory!"

10 The LORD sat *enthroned* at the
  Flood,

And the LORD sits as King
  forever.
11 The LORD will give strength to
  His people;
The LORD will bless His people
  with peace.

PROVERBS FOR TODAY/ 20:26-27

A wise king sifts out the wicked, and brings the threshing wheel over them. □ *The spirit of a man* is *the lamp of the LORD, searching all the inner depths of his heart.* *

AUGUST 8

EZRA 7:1–8:20

Now after these things, in the reign of Artaxerxes king of Persia, Ezra the son of Seraiah, the son of Azariah, the son of Hilkiah, ²the son of Shallum, the son of Zadok, the son of Ahitub, ³the son of Amariah, the son of Azariah, the son of Meraioth, ⁴the son of Zerahiah, the son of Uzzi, the son of Bukki, ⁵the son of Abishua, the son of Phinehas, the son of Eleazar, the son of Aaron the chief priest— ⁶this Ezra came up from Babylon; and he *was* a skilled scribe in the Law of Moses, which the LORD God of Israel had given. The king granted him all his request, according to the hand of the LORD his God upon him. ⁷*Some* of the children of Israel, the priests, the Levites, the singers, the gatekeepers, and the Nethinim came up to Jerusalem in the seventh year of King Artaxerxes. ⁸And Ezra came to Jerusalem in the fifth month, which *was* in the seventh year of the king. ⁹On the first *day* of the first month he began *his* journey from Babylon, and on the first *day* of the fifth month he came to Jerusalem, according to the good hand of his God upon him. ¹⁰For Ezra had prepared his heart to seek the Law of the LORD, and

to do *it,* and to teach statutes and ordinances in Israel.

¹¹This *is* a copy of the letter that King Artaxerxes gave Ezra the priest, the scribe, expert in the words of the commandments of the LORD, and of His statutes to Israel:

12 Artaxerxes,* king of kings,

To Ezra the priest, a scribe of the Law of the God of heaven:

Perfect *peace,* and so forth.*

13 I issue a decree that all those of the people of Israel and the priests and Levites in my realm, who volunteer to go up to Jerusalem, may go with you. ¹⁴And whereas you are being sent by the king and his seven counselors to inquire concerning Judah and Jerusalem, with regard to the Law of your God which *is* in your hand; ¹⁵and *whereas you are* to carry the silver and gold which the king and his counselors have freely offered to the God of Israel, whose dwelling *is* in

Jerusalem; ¹⁶and *whereas* all the silver and gold that you may find in all the province of Babylon, along with the freewill offering of the people and the priests, *are to be* freely offered for the house of their God in Jerusalem— ¹⁷now therefore, be careful to buy with this money bulls, rams, and lambs, with their grain offerings and their drink offerings, and offer them on the altar of the house of your God in Jerusalem.

¹⁸ And whatever seems good to you and your brethren to do with the rest of the silver and the gold, do it according to the will of your God. ¹⁹Also the articles that are given to you for the service of the house of your God, deliver in full before the God of Jerusalem. ²⁰And whatever more may be needed for the house of your God, which you may have occasion to provide, pay *for it* from the king's treasury.

²¹ And I, *even* I, Artaxerxes the king, issue a decree to all the treasurers who *are in the region* beyond the River, that whatever Ezra the priest, the scribe of the Law of the God of heaven, may require of you, let it be done diligently, ²²up to one hundred talents of silver, one hundred kors of wheat, one hundred baths of wine, one hundred baths of oil, and salt without pre-scribed limit. ²³Whatever is commanded by the God of heaven, let it diligently be done for the house of the God of heaven. For why should

there be wrath against the realm of the king and his sons?

²⁴ Also we inform you that it shall not be lawful to impose tax, tribute, or custom *on* any of the priests, Levites, singers, gatekeepers, Nethinim, or servants of this house of God. ²⁵And you, Ezra, according to your God-given wisdom, set magistrates and judges who may judge all the people who *are in the region* beyond the River, all such as know the laws of your God; and teach those who do not know *them.* ²⁶Whoever will not observe the law of your God and the law of the king, let judgment be executed speedily on him, whether *it be* death, or banishment, or confiscation of goods, or imprisonment.

²⁷Blessed *be* the LORD God of our fathers, who has put *such a thing* as this in the king's heart, to beautify the house of the LORD which *is* in Jeru-salem, ²⁸and has extended mercy to me before the king and his counselors, and before all the king's mighty princes.

So I was encouraged, as the hand of the LORD my God *was* upon me; and I gathered leading men of Israel to go up with me.

THESE *are* the heads of their fathers' *houses,* and *this is* the genealogy of those who went up with me from Bab-ylon, in the reign of King Artaxerxes: ²of the sons of Phinehas, Gershom; of the sons of Ithamar, Daniel; of the sons of David, Hattush; ³of the sons of Shecaniah, of the sons of Parosh, Zechariah; and registered with him *were* one hundred and fifty males; ⁴of the sons of Pahath-Moab, Eliehoenai the son of Zerahiah, and with him two hundred males; [5]of the sons of Shechaniah,* Ben-Jahaziel, and with him three hundred males; [6]of the sons of Adin, Ebed the son of Jonathan, and with him fifty males; [7]of the sons of Elam, Jeshaiah the son of Athaliah, and with him seventy males; [8]of the sons of Shephatiah, Zebadiah the son of Michael, and with him eighty males; [9]of the sons of Joab, Obadiah the son of Jehiel, and with him two hundred and eighteen males; [10]of the sons of Shelomith,* Ben-Josiphiah, and with him one hundred and sixty males; [11]of the sons of Bebai, Zechariah the son of Bebai, and with him twenty-eight males; [12]of the sons of Azgad, Johanan the son of Hakkatan, and with him one hundred and ten males; [13]of the last sons of Adonikam, whose names *are* these—Eliphelet, Jeiel, and Shemaiah—and with them sixty males; [14]also of the sons of Bigvai, Uthai and Zabbud, and with them seventy males.

[15]Now I gathered them by the river that flows to Ahava, and we camped there three days. And I looked among the people and the priests, and found none of the sons of Levi there. [16]Then I sent for Eliezer, Ariel, Shemaiah, Elnathan, Jarib, Elnathan, Nathan, Zechariah, and Meshullam, leaders; also for Joiarib and Elnathan, men of understanding. [17]And I gave them a command for Iddo the chief man at the place Casiphia, and I told them what they should say to Iddo *and* his brethren* the Nethinim at the place Casiphia—that they should bring us servants for the house of our God. [18]Then, by the good hand of our God upon us, they brought us a man of understanding, of the sons of Mahli the son of Levi, the son of Israel, namely Sherebiah, with his sons and brothers, eighteen men; [19]and Hashabiah, and with him Jeshaiah of the sons of Merari, his brothers and their sons, twenty men; [20]also of the Nethinim,

whom David and the leaders had appointed for the service of the Levites, two hundred and twenty Nethinim. All of them were designated by name.

1 CORINTHIANS 4:1-21

LET a man so consider us, as servants of Christ and stewards of the mysteries of God. [2]Moreover it is required in stewards that one be found faithful. [3]But with me it is a very small thing that I should be judged by you or by a human court.* In fact, I do not even judge myself. [4]For I know of nothing against myself, yet I am not justified by this; but He who judges me is the Lord. [5]Therefore judge nothing before the time, until the Lord comes, who will both bring to light the hidden things of darkness and reveal the counsels of the hearts. Then each one's praise will come from God.

[6]Now these things, brethren, I have figuratively transferred to myself and Apollos for your sakes, that you may learn in us not to think beyond what is written, that none of you may be puffed up on behalf of one against the other. [7]For who makes you differ *from another?* And what do you have that you did not receive? Now if you did indeed receive *it,* why do you boast as if you had not received *it?*

[8]You are already full! You are already rich! You have reigned as kings without us—and indeed I could wish you did reign, that we also might reign with you! [9]For I think that God has displayed us, the apostles, last, as men condemned to death; for we have been made a spectacle to the world, both to angels and to men. [10]We *are* fools for Christ's sake, but you *are* wise in Christ! We *are* weak, but you *are* strong! You *are* distinguished, but we *are* dishonored! [11]To the present hour we both hunger and thirst, and we are poorly clothed, and beaten, and homeless. [12]And we labor, working with our

own hands. Being reviled, we bless; being persecuted, we endure; [13]being defamed, we entreat. We have been made as the filth of the world, the offscouring of all things until now.

[14]I do not write these things to shame you, but as my beloved children I warn *you*. [15]For though you might have ten thousand instructors in Christ, yet *you do* not *have* many fathers; for in Christ Jesus I have begotten you through the gospel. [16]Therefore I urge you, imitate me. [17]For this reason I have sent Timothy to you, who is my beloved and faithful son in the Lord, who will remind you of my ways in Christ, as I teach everywhere in every church.

[18]Now some are puffed up, as though I were not coming to you. [19]But I will come to you shortly, if the Lord wills, and I will know, not the word of those who are puffed up, but the power. [20]For the kingdom of God *is* not in word but in power. [21]What do you want? Shall I come to you with a rod, or in love and a spirit of gentleness?

PSALM 30:1-12

A Psalm. A Song at the dedication of the house of David.

I WILL extol You, O LORD, for You have lifted me up,
And have not let my foes rejoice over me.
2 O LORD my God, I cried out to You,
And You healed me.
3 O LORD, You brought my soul up from the grave;
You have kept me alive, that I should not go down to the pit.*

4 Sing praise to the LORD, you saints of His,
And give thanks at the remembrance of His holy name.*
5 For His anger *is but for* a moment,
His favor *is for* life;
Weeping may endure for a night,
But joy *comes* in the morning.

6 Now in my prosperity I said,
"I shall never be moved."
7 LORD, by Your favor You have made my mountain stand strong;
You hid Your face, *and* I was troubled.

8 I cried out to You, O LORD;
And to the LORD I made supplication:

9 "What profit *is there* in my blood,
When I go down to the pit?
Will the dust praise You?
Will it declare Your truth?
10 Hear, O LORD, and have mercy on me;
LORD, be my helper!"

11 You have turned for me my mourning into dancing;
You have put off my sackcloth and clothed me with gladness,
12 To the end that *my* glory may sing praise to You and not be silent.
O LORD my God, I will give thanks to You forever.

PROVERBS FOR TODAY/ 20:28-30

Mercy and truth preserve the king, and by lovingkindness he upholds his throne.
□ *The glory of young men is their strength, and the splendor of old men is their gray*

head.   □ Blows that hurt cleanse away evil, as do *stripes the inner depths of the* heart. *

AUGUST 9

EZRA 8:21–9:15

T HEN I [Ezra] proclaimed a fast there at the river of Ahava, that we might humble ourselves before our God, to seek from Him the right way for us and our little ones and all our possessions. 22For I was ashamed to request of the king an escort of soldiers and horsemen to help us against the enemy on the road, because we had spoken to the king, saying, "The hand of our God *is* upon all those for good who seek Him, but His power and His wrath *are* against all those who forsake Him." 23So we fasted and entreated our God for this, and He answered our prayer.

24And I separated twelve of the leaders of the priests—Sherebiah, Hashabiah, and ten of their brethren with them— 25and weighed out to them the silver, the gold, and the articles, the offering for the house of our God which the king and his counselors and his princes, and all Israel *who were* present, had offered. 26I weighed into their hand six hundred and fifty talents of silver, silver articles *weighing* one hundred talents, one hundred talents of gold, 27twenty gold basins *worth* a thousand drachmas, and two vessels of fine polished bronze, precious as gold. 28And I said to them, "You *are* holy to the LORD; the articles *are* holy also; and the silver and the gold *are* a freewill offering to the LORD God of your fathers. 29Watch and keep *them* until you weigh *them* before the leaders of the priests and the Levites and

heads of the fathers' *houses* of Israel in Jerusalem, *in* the chambers of the house of the LORD." 30So the priests and the Levites received the silver and the gold and the articles by weight, to bring *them* to Jerusalem to the house of our God.

31Then we departed from the river of Ahava on the twelfth *day* of the first month, to go to Jerusalem. And the hand of our God was upon us, and He delivered us from the hand of the enemy and from ambush along the road. 32So we came to Jerusalem, and stayed there three days.

33Now on the fourth day the silver and the gold and the articles were weighed in the house of our God by the hand of Meremoth the son of Uriah the priest, and with him *was* Eleazar the son of Phinehas; with them *were* the Levites, Jozabad the son of Jeshua and Noadiah the son of Binnui, 34with the number *and* weight of everything. All the weight was written down at that time.

35The children of those who had been carried away captive, who had come from the captivity, offered burnt offerings to the God of Israel: twelve bulls for all Israel, ninety-six rams, seventy-seven lambs, and twelve male goats *as* a sin offering. All *this was* a burnt offering to the LORD.

36And they delivered the king's orders to the king's satraps and the governors *in the region* beyond the River. So they gave support to the people and the house of God.

WHEN these things were done, the leaders came to me, saying, "The people of Israel and the priests and the Levites have not separated themselves from the peoples of the lands, with respect to the abominations of the Canaanites, the Hittites, the Perizzites, the Jebusites, the Ammonites, the Moabites, the Egyptians, and the Amorites. ²For they have taken some of their daughters *as wives* for themselves and their sons, so that the holy seed is mixed with the peoples of *those* lands. Indeed, the hand of the leaders and rulers has been foremost in this trespass." ³So when I heard this thing, I tore my garment and my robe, and plucked out some of the hair of my head and beard, and sat down astonished. ⁴Then everyone who trembled at the words of the God of Israel assembled to me, because of the transgression of those who had been carried away captive, and I sat astonished until the evening sacrifice.

⁵At the evening sacrifice I arose from my fasting; and having torn my garment and my robe, I fell on my knees and spread out my hands to the LORD my God. ⁶And I said: "O my God, I am too ashamed and humiliated to lift up my face to You, my God; for our iniquities have risen higher than *our* heads, and our guilt has grown up to the heavens. ⁷Since the days of our fathers to this day we *have been* very guilty, and for our iniquities we, our kings, *and* our priests have been delivered into the hand of the kings of the lands, to the sword, to captivity, to plunder, and to humiliation, as *it is* this day. ⁸And now for a little while grace has been *shown* from the LORD our God, to leave us a remnant to escape, and to give us a peg in His holy place, that our God may enlighten our eyes and give us a measure of revival in our bondage. ⁹For we *were* slaves. Yet our God did not forsake us in our bondage; but He extended mercy to us in the sight of the kings of Persia, to revive us, to repair the house of our God, to rebuild its ruins, and to give us a wall in Judah and Jerusalem. ¹⁰And now, O our God, what shall we say after this? For we have forsaken Your commandments, ¹¹which You commanded by Your servants the prophets, saying, 'The land which you are entering to possess is an unclean land, with the uncleanness of the peoples of the lands, with their abominations which have filled it from one end to another with their impurity. ¹²Now therefore, do not give your daughters as wives for their sons, nor take their daughters to your sons; and never seek their peace or prosperity, that you may be strong and eat the good of the land, and leave *it* as an inheritance to your children forever.' ¹³And after all that has come upon us for our evil deeds and for our great guilt, since You our God have punished us less than our iniquities *deserve,* and have given us such deliverance as this, ¹⁴should we again break Your commandments, and join in marriage with the people *committing* these abominations? Would You not be angry with us until You had consumed *us,* so that *there would be* no remnant or survivor? ¹⁵O LORD God of Israel, You *are* righteous, for we are left as a remnant, as *it is* this day. Here we *are* before You, in our guilt, though no one can stand before You because of this!"

1 CORINTHIANS 5:1-13

IT is actually reported *that there is* sexual immorality among you, and such sexual immorality as is not even named* among the Gentiles— that a man has his father's wife! ²And you are puffed up, and have not rather mourned, that he who has done this deed might be taken away from among you. ³For I indeed, as absent in body but present in spirit, have already judged (as though I were present) him who has so done this deed. 4In the name of our Lord Jesus Christ, when you are gathered together, along with my spirit, with the power of our Lord Jesus Christ, 5deliver such a one to Satan for the destruction of the flesh, that his spirit may be saved in the day of the Lord Jesus.*

6Your glorying *is* not good. Do you not know that a little leaven leavens the whole lump? 7Therefore purge out the old leaven, that you may be a new lump, since you truly are unleavened. For indeed Christ, our Passover, was sacrificed for us.* 8Therefore let us keep the feast, not with old leaven, nor with the leaven of malice and wickedness, but with the unleavened *bread* of sincerity and truth.

9I wrote to you in my epistle not to keep company with sexually immoral people. 10Yet *I* certainly *did* not *mean* with the sexually immoral people of this world, or with the covetous, or extortioners, or idolaters, since then you would need to go out of the world. 11But now I have written to you not to keep company with anyone named a brother, who is sexually immoral, or covetous, or an idolater, or a reviler, or a drunkard, or an extortioner—not even to eat with such a person.

12For what *have* I *to do* with judging those also who are outside? Do you not judge those who are inside? 13But those who are outside God judges. Therefore *"put away from yourselves the evil person."* *

PSALM 31:1-8

To the Chief Musician. A Psalm of David.

I N You, O LORD, I put my trust;
Let me never be ashamed;
Deliver me in Your
righteousness.
2 Bow down Your ear to me,
Deliver me speedily;
Be my rock of refuge,
A fortress of defense to save
me.

3 For You *are* my rock and my
fortress;
Therefore, for Your name's
sake,
Lead me and guide me.
4 Pull me out of the net which
they have secretly laid for
me,
For You *are* my strength.
5 Into Your hand I commit my
spirit;
You have redeemed me,
O LORD God of truth.

6 I have hated those who
regard useless idols;
But I trust in the LORD.
7 I will be glad and rejoice in
Your mercy,
For You have considered my
trouble;
You have known my soul in
adversities,
8 And have not shut me up into
the hand of the enemy;
You have set my feet in a wide
place.

PROVERBS FOR TODAY/ 21:1-2

The king's heart is *in the hand of the LORD,* like *the rivers of water; He turns it wherever He wishes.* ☐ *Every way of a man* is *right in his own eyes, but the LORD weighs the hearts.*

AUGUST 10

EZRA 10:1-44

Now while Ezra was praying, and while he was confessing, weeping, and bowing down before the house of God, a very large assembly of men, women, and children gathered to him from Israel; for the people wept very bitterly. ²And Shechaniah the son of Jehiel, *one* of the sons of Elam, spoke up and said to Ezra, "We have trespassed against our God, and have taken pagan wives from the peoples of the land; yet now there is hope in Israel in spite of this. ³Now therefore, let us make a covenant with our God to put away all these wives and those who have been born to them, according to the advice of my master and of those who tremble at the commandment of our God; and let it be done according to the law. ⁴Arise, for *this* matter *is* your *responsibility.* We also *are* with you. Be of good courage, and do *it.*"

⁵Then Ezra arose, and made the leaders of the priests, the Levites, and all Israel swear an oath that they would do according to this word. So they swore an oath. ⁶Then Ezra rose up from before the house of God, and went into the chamber of Jehohanan the son of Eliashib; and *when* he came there, he ate no bread and drank no water, for he mourned because of the guilt of those from the captivity.

⁷And they issued a proclamation throughout Judah and Jerusalem to all the descendants of the captivity, that they must gather at Jerusalem, ⁸and that whoever would not come within three days, according to the instructions of the leaders and elders, all his property would be confiscated, and he himself would be separated from the assembly of those from the captivity.

⁹So all the men of Judah and Benjamin gathered at Jerusalem within three days. It *was* the ninth month, on the twentieth of the month; and all the people sat in the open square of the house of God, trembling because of *this* matter and because of heavy rain. ¹⁰Then Ezra the priest stood up and said to them, "You have transgressed and have taken pagan wives, adding to the guilt of Israel. ¹¹Now therefore, make confession to the LORD God of your fathers, and do His will; separate yourselves from the peoples of the land, and from the pagan wives."

¹²Then all the assembly answered and said with a loud voice, "Yes! As you have said, so we must do. ¹³But *there are* many people; *it is* the season for heavy rain, and we are not able to stand outside. Nor *is this* the work of one or two days, for *there are* many of us who have transgressed in this matter. ¹⁴Please, let the leaders of our entire assembly stand; and let all those in our cities who have taken pagan wives come at appointed times, together with the elders and judges of their cities, until the fierce wrath of our God is turned away from us in this matter." ¹⁵Only Jonathan the son of Asahel and Jahaziah the son of Tikvah opposed this, and Meshullam and Shabbethai the Levite gave them support.

¹⁶Then the descendants of the captivity did so. And Ezra the priest, *with* certain heads of the fathers' *households,* were set apart by the fathers' *households,* each of them by name; and they sat down on the first day of the tenth month to examine the matter. ¹⁷By the first day of the first month they finished *questioning* all the men who had taken pagan wives.

¹⁸And among the sons of the priests

who had taken pagan wives *the following* were found of the sons of Jeshua the son of Jozadak,* and his brothers: Maaseiah, Eliezer, Jarib, and Gedaliah. 19And they gave their promise that they would put away their wives; and *being* guilty, *they presented* a ram of the flock as their trespass offering.

20Also of the sons of Immer: Hanani and Zebadiah; 21of the sons of Harim: Maaseiah, Elijah, Shemaiah, Jehiel, and Uzziah; 22of the sons of Pashhur: Elioenai, Maaseiah, Ishmael, Nethanel, Jozabad, and Elasah.

23Also of the Levites: Jozabad, Shimei, Kelalah (the same *is* Kelita), Pethahiah, Judah, and Eliezer.

24Also of the singers: Eliashib; and of the gatekeepers: Shallum, Telem, and Uri.

25And others of Israel: of the sons of Parosh: Ramiah, Jeziah, Malchiah, Mijamin, Eleazar, Malchijah, and Benaiah; 26of the sons of Elam: Mattaniah, Zechariah, Jehiel, Abdi, Jeremoth, and Eliah; 27of the sons of Zattu: Elioenai, Eliashib, Mattaniah, Jeremoth, Zabad, and Aziza; 28of the sons of Bebai: Jehohanan, Hananiah, Zabbai, *and* Athlai; 29of the sons of Bani: Meshullam, Malluch, Adaiah, Jashub, Sheal, *and* Ramoth;* 30of the sons of Pahath-Moab: Adna, Chelal, Benaiah, Maaseiah, Mattaniah, Bezalel, Binnui, and Manasseh; 31of the sons of Harim: Eliezer, Ishijah, Malchijah, Shemaiah, Shimeon, 32Benjamin, Malluch, *and* Shemariah; 33of the sons of Hashum: Mattenai, Mattattah, Zabad, Eliphelet, Jeremai, Manasseh, *and* Shimei; 34of the sons of Bani: Maadai, Amram, Uel, 35Benaiah, Bedeiah, Cheluh,* 36Vaniah, Meremoth, Eliashib, 37Mattaniah, Mattenai, Jaasai,* 38Bani, Binnui, Shimei, 39Shelemiah, Nathan, Adaiah, 40Machnadebai, Shashai, Sharai, 41Azarel, Shelemiah, Shemariah, 42Shallum, Amariah, *and* Joseph; 43of the sons of Nebo: Jeiel,

Mattithiah, Zabad, Zebina, Jaddai,* Joel, *and* Benaiah.

44All these had taken pagan wives, and *some* of them had wives *by whom* they had children.

1 CORINTHIANS 6:1-20

DARE any of you, having a matter against another, go to law before the unrighteous, and not before the saints? 2Do you not know that the saints will judge the world? And if the world will be judged by you, are you unworthy to judge the smallest matters? 3Do you not know that we shall judge angels? How much more, things that pertain to this life? 4If then you have judgments concerning things pertaining to this life, do you appoint those who are least esteemed by the church to judge? 5I say this to your shame. Is it so, that there is not a wise man among you, not even one, who will be able to judge between his brethren? 6But brother goes to law against brother, and that before unbelievers!

7Now therefore, it is already an utter failure for you that you go to law against one another. Why do you not rather accept wrong? Why do you not rather *let yourselves* be cheated? 8No, you yourselves do wrong and cheat, and *you do* these things *to your* brethren! 9Do you not know that the unrighteous will not inherit the kingdom of God? Do not be deceived. Neither fornicators, nor idolaters, nor adulterers, nor homosexuals,* nor sodomites, 10nor thieves, nor covetous, nor drunkards, nor revilers, nor extortioners will inherit the kingdom of God. 11And such were some of you. But you were washed, but you were sanctified, but you were justified in the name of the Lord Jesus and by the Spirit of our God.

12All things are lawful for me, but all things are not helpful. All things are lawful for me, but I will not be brought under the power of any. [13]Foods for the stomach and the stomach for foods, but God will destroy both it and them. Now the body *is* not for sexual immorality but for the Lord, and the Lord for the body. [14]And God both raised up the Lord and will also raise us up by His power.

[15]Do you not know that your bodies are members of Christ? Shall I then take the members of Christ and make *them* members of a harlot? Certainly not! [16]Or do you not know that he who is joined to a harlot is one body *with her?* For *"the two,"* He says, *"shall become one flesh."** [17]But he who is joined to the Lord is one spirit *with Him.*

[18]Flee sexual immorality. Every sin that a man does is outside the body, but he who commits sexual immorality sins against his own body. [19]Or do you not know that your body is the temple of the Holy Spirit *who is* in you, whom you have from God, and you are not your own? [20]For you were bought at a price; therefore glorify God in your body* and in your spirit, which are God's.

PSALM 31:9-18

Have mercy on me, O Lord, for I am in trouble;
My eye wastes away with grief,
Yes, my soul and my body!
[10] For my life is spent with grief,
And my years with sighing;
My strength fails because of my iniquity,
And my bones waste away.

[11] I am a reproach among all my enemies,
But especially among my neighbors,
And *am* repulsive to my acquaintances;
Those who see me outside flee from me.
[12] I am forgotten like a dead man, out of mind;
I am like a broken vessel.
[13] For I hear the slander of many;
Fear *is* on every side;
While they take counsel together against me,
They scheme to take away my life.

[14] But as for me, I trust in You, O Lord;
I say, "You *are* my God."
[15] My times *are* in Your hand;
Deliver me from the hand of my enemies,
And from those who persecute me.
[16] Make Your face shine upon Your servant;
Save me for Your mercies' sake.
[17] Do not let me be ashamed, O Lord, for I have called upon You;
Let the wicked be ashamed;
Let them be silent in the grave.
[18] Let the lying lips be put to silence,
Which speak insolent things proudly and contemptuously against the righteous.

PROVERBS FOR TODAY/ 21:3

To do righteousness and justice is *more acceptable to the Lord than sacrifice.*

AUGUST 11

NEHEMIAH 1:1–3:14

THE words of Nehemiah the son of Hachaliah.

It came to pass in the month of Chislev, *in* the twentieth year, as I was in Shushan* the citadel, ²that Hanani one of my brethren came with men from Judah; and I asked them concerning the Jews who had escaped, who had survived the captivity, and concerning Jerusalem. ³And they said to me, "The survivors who are left from the captivity in the province *are* there in great distress and reproach. The wall of Jerusalem *is* also broken down, and its gates *are* burned with fire."

⁴So it was, when I heard these words, that I sat down and wept, and mourned *for many* days; I was fasting and praying before the God of heaven. ⁵And I said: "I pray, LORD God of heaven, O great and awesome God, *You* who keep *Your* covenant and mercy with those who love You* and observe Your* commandments, ⁶please let Your ear be attentive and Your eyes open, that You may hear the prayer of Your servant which I pray before You now, day and night, for the children of Israel Your servants, and confess the sins of the children of Israel which we have sinned against You. Both my father's house and I have sinned. ⁷We have acted very corruptly against You, and have not kept the commandments, the statutes, nor the ordinances which You commanded Your servant Moses. ⁸Remember, I pray, the word that You commanded Your servant Moses, saying, '*If* you are unfaithful, I will scatter you among the nations;* ⁹but *if* you return to Me, and keep My commandments and do them, though some of you were cast out to the farthest part of the heavens, *yet* I will gather them from there, and bring them to the place which I have chosen as a dwelling for My name.'* ¹⁰Now these *are* Your servants and Your people, whom You have redeemed by Your great power, and by Your strong hand. ¹¹O Lord, I pray, please let Your ear be attentive to the prayer of Your servant, and to the prayer of Your servants who desire to fear Your name; and let Your servant prosper this day, I pray, and grant him mercy in the sight of this man."

For I was the king's cupbearer.

AND it came to pass in the month of Nisan, in the twentieth year of King Artaxerxes, *when* wine *was* before him, that I took the wine and gave it to the king. Now I had never been sad in his presence before. ²Therefore the king said to me, "Why *is* your face sad, since you *are* not sick? This *is* nothing but sorrow of heart."

So I became dreadfully afraid, ³and said to the king, "May the king live forever! Why should my face not be sad, when the city, the place of my fathers' tombs, *lies* waste, and its gates are burned with fire?"

⁴Then the king said to me, "What do you request?"

So I prayed to the God of heaven. ⁵And I said to the king, "If it pleases the king, and if your servant has found favor in your sight, I ask that you send me to Judah, to the city of my fathers' tombs, that I may rebuild it."

⁶Then the king said to me (the queen also sitting beside him), "How long will your journey be? And when will you return?" So it pleased the king to send me; and I set him a time.

⁷Furthermore I said to the king, "If

it pleases the king, let letters be given to me for the governors *of the region* beyond the River,* that they must permit me to pass through till I come to Judah, 8and a letter to Asaph the keeper of the king's forest, that he must give me timber to make beams for the gates of the citadel which *pertains* to the temple,* for the city wall, and for the house that I will occupy." And the king granted *them* to me according to the good hand of my God upon me.

9Then I went to the governors *in the region* beyond the River, and gave them the king's letters. Now the king had sent captains of the army and horsemen with me. 10When Sanballat the Horonite and Tobiah the Ammonite official* heard *of it,* they were deeply disturbed that a man had come to seek the well-being of the children of Israel.

11So I came to Jerusalem and was there three days. 12Then I arose in the night, I and a few men with me; I told no one what my God had put in my heart to do at Jerusalem; nor was there any animal with me, except the one on which I rode. 13And I went out by night through the Valley Gate to the Serpent Well and the Refuse Gate, and viewed the walls of Jerusalem which were broken down and its gates which were burned with fire. 14Then I went on to the Fountain Gate and to the King's Pool, but *there was* no room for the animal under me to pass. 15So I went up in the night by the valley, and viewed the wall; then I turned back and entered by the Valley Gate, and so returned. 16And the officials did not know where I had gone or what I had done; I had not yet told the Jews, the priests, the nobles, the officials, or the others who did the work.

17Then I said to them, "You see the distress that we *are* in, how Jerusalem *lies* waste, and its gates are burned with fire. Come and let us build the wall of Jerusalem, that we may no longer be a reproach." 18And I told them of the hand of my God which had been good upon me, and also of the king's words that he had spoken to me.

So they said, "Let us rise up and build." Then they set their hands to *this* good *work.*

19But when Sanballat the Horonite, Tobiah the Ammonite official, and Geshem the Arab heard *of it,* they laughed at us and despised us, and said, "What *is* this thing that you are doing? Will you rebel against the king?"

20So I answered them, and said to them, "The God of heaven Himself will prosper us; therefore we His servants will arise and build, but you have no heritage or right or memorial in Jerusalem."

THEN Eliashib the high priest rose up with his brethren the priests and built the Sheep Gate; they consecrated it and hung its doors. They built as far as the Tower of the Hundred,* *and* consecrated it, then as far as the Tower of Hananel. 2Next to *Eliashib** the men of Jericho built. And next to them Zaccur the son of Imri built.

3Also the sons of Hassenaah built the Fish Gate; they laid its beams and hung its doors with its bolts and bars. 4And next to them Meremoth the son of Urijah, the son of Koz,* made repairs. Next to them Meshullam the son of Berechiah, the son of Meshezabel, made repairs. Next to them Zadok the son of Baana made repairs. 5Next to them the Tekoites made repairs; but their nobles did not put their shoulders* to the work of their Lord.

6Moreover Jehoiada the son of Paseah and Meshullam the son of Besodeiah repaired the Old Gate; they laid its beams and hung its doors, with its bolts and bars. 7And next to them Melatiah the Gibeonite, Jadon the Meronothite, the men of Gibeon and Mizpah, repaired the residence* of the governor *of the region* beyond the River. [8]Next to him Uzziel the son of Harhaiah, one of the goldsmiths, made repairs. Also next to him Hananiah, one* of the perfumers, made repairs; and they fortified Jerusalem as far as the Broad Wall. [9]And next to them Rephaiah the son of Hur, leader of half the district of Jerusalem, made repairs. [10]Next to them Jedaiah the son of Harumaph made repairs in front of his house. And next to him Hattush the son of Hashabniah made repairs.

[11]Malchijah the son of Harim and Hashub the son of Pahath-Moab repaired another section, as well as the Tower of the Ovens. [12]And next to him was Shallum the son of Hallohesh, leader of half the district of Jerusalem; he and his daughters made repairs.

[13]Hanun and the inhabitants of Zanoah repaired the Valley Gate. They built it, hung its doors with its bolts and bars, and *repaired* a thousand cubits of the wall as far as the Refuse Gate.

[14]Malchijah the son of Rechab, leader of the district of Beth Haccerem, repaired the Refuse Gate; he built it and hung its doors with its bolts and bars.

1 CORINTHIANS 7:1-24

Now concerning the things of which you wrote to me:
It is good for a man not to touch a woman. [2]Nevertheless, because of sexual immorality, let each man have his own wife, and let each woman have her own husband. [3]Let the husband render to his wife the affection due her, and likewise also the wife to her husband. [4]The wife does not have authority over her own body, but the husband *does.* And likewise the husband does not have authority over his own body, but the wife *does.* [5]Do not deprive one another except with consent for a

time, that you may give yourselves to fasting and prayer; and come together again so that Satan does not tempt you because of your lack of self-control. [6]But I say this as a concession, not as a commandment. [7]For I wish that all men were even as I myself. But each one has his own gift from God, one in this manner and another in that.

[8]But I say to the unmarried and to the widows: It is good for them if they remain even as I am; [9]but if they cannot exercise self-control, let them marry. For it is better to marry than to burn *with passion.*

[10]Now to the married I command, *yet* not I but the Lord: A wife is not to depart from *her* husband. [11]But even if she does depart, let her remain unmarried or be reconciled to *her* husband. And a husband is not to divorce *his* wife.

[12]But to the rest I, not the Lord, say: If any brother has a wife who does not believe, and she is willing to live with him, let him not divorce her. [13]And a woman who has a husband who does not believe, if he is willing to live with her, let her not divorce him. [14]For the unbelieving husband is sanctified by the wife, and the unbelieving wife is sanctified by the husband; otherwise your children would be unclean, but now they are holy. [15]But if the unbeliever departs, let him depart; a brother or a sister is not under bondage in such *cases.* But God has called us to peace. [16]For how do you know, O wife, whether you will save *your* husband? Or how do you know, O husband, whether you will save *your* wife?

[17]But as God has distributed to each one, as the Lord has called each one, so let him walk. And so I ordain in all the churches. [18]Was anyone called while circumcised? Let him not become uncircumcised. Was anyone called while uncircumcised? Let him not be circumcised. [19]Circumcision is nothing and uncircumcision is noth-

ing, but keeping the commandments of God *is what matters.* [20]Let each one remain in the same calling in which he was called. [21]Were you called *while* a slave? Do not be concerned about it; but if you can be made free, rather use *it.* [22]For he who is called in the Lord *while* a slave is the Lord's freedman. Likewise he who is called *while* free is Christ's slave. [23]You were bought at a price; do not become slaves of men. [24]Brethren, let each one remain with God in that *state* in which he was called.

PSALM 31:19-24

O H, how great *is* Your goodness,
Which You have laid up for
those who fear You,
Which You have prepared for
those who trust in You
In the presence of the sons of
men!
[20] You shall hide them in the
secret place of Your
presence

From the plots of man;
You shall keep them secretly
in a pavilion
From the strife of tongues.

[21] Blessed *be* the LORD,
For He has shown me His
marvelous kindness in a
strong city!
[22] For I said in my haste,
"I am cut off from before Your
eyes";
Nevertheless You heard the
voice of my supplications
When I cried out to You.

[23] Oh, love the LORD, all you His
saints!
For the LORD preserves the
faithful,
And fully repays the proud
person.
[24] Be of good courage,
And He shall strengthen your
heart,
All you who hope in the LORD.

PROVERBS FOR TODAY/ 21:4

A haughty look, a proud heart, and *the plowing* of the wicked* are *sin.*

AUGUST 12

NEHEMIAH 3:15–5:13

S HALLUN the son of Col-Hozeh, leader of the district of Mizpah, repaired the Fountain Gate; he built it, covered it, hung its doors with its bolts and bars, and repaired the wall of the Pool of Shelah by the King's Garden, as far as the stairs that go down from the City of David. [16]After him Nehemiah the son of Azbuk, leader of half the district of Beth Zur, made repairs as far as *the place* in front of the tombs* of David, to the man-made pool, and as far as the House of the Mighty.

[17]After him the Levites, *under* Rehum the son of Bani, made repairs. Next to him Hashabiah, leader of half the district of Keilah, made repairs for his district. [18]After him their brethren, *under* Bavai* the son of Henadad, leader of the *other* half of the district of Keilah, made repairs. [19]And next to him Ezer the son of Jeshua, the leader

of Mizpah, repaired another section in front of the Ascent to the Armory at the buttress. 20After him Baruch the son of Zabbai* carefully repaired the other section, from the buttress to the door of the house of Eliashib the high priest. 21After him Meremoth the son of Urijah, the son of Koz,* repaired another section, from the door of the house of Eliashib to the end of the house of Eliashib.

22And after him the priests, the men of the plain, made repairs. 23After him Benjamin and Hasshub made repairs opposite their house. After them Azariah the son of Maaseiah, the son of Ananiah, made repairs by his house. 24After him Binnui the son of Henadad repaired another section, from the house of Azariah to the buttress, even as far as the corner. 25Palal the son of Uzai *made repairs* opposite the buttress, and on the tower which projects from the king's upper house that *was* by the court of the prison. After him Pedaiah the son of Parosh *made repairs.*

26Moreover the Nethinim who dwelt in Ophel *made repairs* as far as *the place* in front of the Water Gate toward the east, and on the projecting tower. 27After them the Tekoites repaired another section, next to the great projecting tower, and as far as the wall of Ophel.

28Beyond the Horse Gate the priests made repairs, each in front of his *own* house. 29After them Zadok the son of Immer made repairs in front of his *own* house. After him Shemaiah the son of Shechaniah, the keeper of the East Gate, made repairs. 30After him Hananiah the son of Shelemiah, and Hanun, the sixth son of Zalaph, repaired another section. After him Meshullam the son of Berechiah made repairs in front of his dwelling. 31After him Malchijah, one of the goldsmiths, made repairs as far as the house of the Nethinim and of the merchants, in front of the Miphkad* Gate, and as far as the upper room at the corner. 32And between the upper room at the corner, as far as the Sheep Gate, the goldsmiths and the merchants made repairs.

But it so happened, when Sanballat heard that we were rebuilding the wall, that he was furious and very indignant, and mocked the Jews. 2And he spoke before his brethren and the army of Samaria, and said, "What are these feeble Jews doing? Will they fortify themselves? Will they offer sacrifices? Will they complete it in a day? Will they revive the stones from the heaps of rubbish—*stones* that are burned?"

3Now Tobiah the Ammonite *was* beside him, and he said, "Whatever they build, if even a fox goes up *on it,* he will break down their stone wall."

4Hear, O our God, for we are despised; turn their reproach on their own heads, and give them as plunder to a land of captivity! 5Do not cover their iniquity, and do not let their sin be blotted out from before You; for they have provoked *You* to anger before the builders.

6So we built the wall, and the entire wall was joined together up to half its *height,* for the people had a mind to work.

7Now it happened, when Sanballat, Tobiah, the Arabs, the Ammonites, and the Ashdodites heard that the walls of Jerusalem were being restored and the gaps were beginning to be closed, that they became very angry, 8and all of them conspired together to come *and* attack Jerusalem and create confusion. 9Nevertheless we made our prayer to our God, and because of them we set a watch against them day and night.

10Then Judah said, "The strength of the laborers is failing, and *there is* so much rubbish that we are not able to build the wall."

¹¹And our adversaries said, "They will neither know nor see anything, till we come into their midst and kill them and cause the work to cease."

¹²So it was, when the Jews who dwelt near them came, that they told us ten times, "From whatever place you turn, *they will be* upon us."

¹³Therefore I positioned *men* behind the lower parts of the wall, at the openings; and I set the people according to their families, with their swords, their spears, and their bows. ¹⁴And I looked, and arose and said to the nobles, to the leaders, and to the rest of the people, "Do not be afraid of them. Remember the Lord, great and awesome, and fight for your brethren, your sons, your daughters, your wives, and your houses."

¹⁵And it happened, when our enemies heard that it was known to us, and *that* God had brought their plot to nothing, that all of us returned to the wall, everyone to his work. ¹⁶So it was, from that time on, *that* half of my servants worked at construction, while the other half held the spears, the shields, the bows, and *wore* armor; and the leaders *were* behind all the house of Judah. ¹⁷Those who built on the wall, and those who carried burdens, loaded themselves so that with one hand they worked at construction, and with the other held a weapon. ¹⁸Every one of the builders had his sword girded at his side as he built. And the one who sounded the trumpet *was* beside me.

¹⁹Then I said to the nobles, the rulers, and the rest of the people, "The work *is* great and extensive, and we are separated far from one another on the wall. ²⁰Wherever you hear the sound of the trumpet, rally to us there. Our God will fight for us."

²¹So we labored in the work, and half of *the men** held the spears from daybreak until the stars appeared. ²²At the same time I also said to the people,

"Let each man and his servant stay at night in Jerusalem, that they may be our guard by night and a working party by day." ²³So neither I, my brethren, my servants, nor the men of the guard who followed me took off our clothes, *except* that everyone took them off for washing.

AND there was a great outcry of the people and their wives against their Jewish brethren. ²For there were those who said, "We, our sons, and our daughters *are* many; therefore let us get grain, that we may eat and live."

³There were also *some* who said, "We have mortgaged our lands and vineyards and houses, that we might buy grain because of the famine."

⁴There were also those who said, "We have borrowed money for the king's tax *on* our lands and vineyards. ⁵Yet now our flesh *is* as the flesh of our brethren, our children as their children; and indeed we are forcing our sons and our daughters to be slaves, and *some* of our daughters have been brought into slavery. *It is* not in our power *to redeem them,* for other men have our lands and vineyards."

⁶And I became very angry when I heard their outcry and these words. ⁷After serious thought, I rebuked the nobles and rulers, and said to them, "Each of you is exacting usury from his brother." So I called a great assembly against them. ⁸And I said to them, "According to our ability we have redeemed our Jewish brethren who were sold to the nations. Now indeed, will you even sell your brethren? Or should they be sold to us?"

Then they were silenced and found nothing *to say.* ⁹Then I said, "What you are doing *is* not good. Should you not walk in the fear of our God because of the reproach of the nations, our enemies? ¹⁰I also, *with* my brethren and my servants, am lending them money and grain. Please, let us stop this usury! ¹¹Restore now to them, even this day, their lands, their vineyards, their olive groves, and their houses, also a hundredth of the money and the grain, the new wine and the oil, that you have charged them."

¹²So they said, "We will restore *it,* and will require nothing from them; we will do as you say."

Then I called the priests, and required an oath from them that they would do according to this promise. ¹³Then I shook out the fold of my garment* and said, "So may God shake out each man from his house, and from his property, who does not perform this promise. Even thus may he be shaken out and emptied."

And all the assembly said, "Amen!" and praised the LORD. Then the people did according to this promise.

1 CORINTHIANS 7:25-40

Now concerning virgins: I have no commandment from the Lord; yet I give judgment as one whom the Lord in His mercy *has made* trustworthy. ²⁶I suppose therefore that this is good because of the present distress—that *it is* good for a man to remain as he is: ²⁷Are you bound to a wife? Do not seek to be loosed. Are you loosed from a wife? Do not seek a wife. ²⁸But even if you do marry, you have not sinned; and if a virgin marries, she has not sinned. Nevertheless such will have trouble in the flesh, but I would spare you.

²⁹But this I say, brethren, the time *is* short, so that from now on even those who have wives should be as though they had none, ³⁰those who weep as though they did not weep, those who rejoice as though they did not rejoice, those who buy as though they did not possess, ³¹and those who use this world as not misusing *it.* For the form of this world is passing away.

³²But I want you to be without care.

He who is unmarried cares for the things of the Lord—how he may please the Lord. ³³But he who is married cares about the things of the world—how he may please *his* wife. ³⁴There is* a difference between a wife and a virgin. The unmarried woman cares about the things of the Lord, that she may be holy both in body and in spirit. But she who is married cares about the things of the world—how she may please *her* husband. ³⁵And this I say for your own profit, not that I may put a leash on you, but for what is proper, and that you may serve the Lord without distraction.

³⁶But if any man thinks he is behaving improperly toward his virgin, if she is past the flower of youth, and thus it must be, let him do what he wishes. He does not sin; let them marry. ³⁷Nevertheless he who stands steadfast in his heart, having no necessity, but has power over his own will, and has so determined in his heart that he will keep his virgin,* does well. ³⁸So then he who gives *her** in marriage does well, but he who does not give *her* in marriage does better.

³⁹A wife is bound by law as long as her husband lives; but if her husband dies, she is at liberty to be married to whom she wishes, only in the Lord. ⁴⁰But she is happier if she remains as she is, according to my judgment—and I think I also have the Spirit of God.

PSALM 32:1-11

*A Psalm of David. A Contemplation.**

BLESSED *is he whose* transgression *is* forgiven,
  Whose sin *is* covered.
2 Blessed *is* the man to whom the LORD does not impute iniquity,
  And in whose spirit *there is* no deceit.

3   When I kept silent, my bones
    grew old
  Through my groaning all the
    day long.

4   For day and night Your hand
    was heavy upon me;
  My vitality was turned into
    the drought of summer.
                Selah

5   I acknowledged my sin to You,
  And my iniquity I have not
    hidden.

  I said, "I will confess my
    transgressions to the LORD,"
  And You forgave the iniquity
    of my sin.   Selah

6   For this cause everyone who
    is godly shall pray to You
  In a time when You may be
    found;
  Surely in a flood of great
    waters
  They shall not come near him.

7   You *are* my hiding place;

  You shall preserve me from
    trouble;
  You shall surround me with
    songs of deliverance.   Selah

8   I will instruct you and teach
    you in the way you should
    go;
  I will guide you with My eye.

9   Do not be like the horse *or*
    like the mule,
  Which have no understanding,
  Which must be harnessed
    with bit and bridle,
  Else they will not come near
    you.

10   Many sorrows *shall be* to the
    wicked;
  But he who trusts in the LORD,
    mercy shall surround him.

11   Be glad in the LORD and
    rejoice, you righteous;
  And shout for joy, all *you*
    upright in heart!

PROVERBS FOR TODAY/ 21:5-7

The plans of the diligent lead *surely to plenty, but* those of *everyone* who is *hasty, surely to poverty.* □ *Getting treasures by a lying tongue* is *the fleeting fantasy of those who seek death.* * □ *The violence of the wicked will destroy them,* * *because they refuse to do justice.*

AUGUST 13

NEHEMIAH 5:14–7:60

MOREOVER, from the time that I [Nehemiah] was appointed to be their governor in the land of Judah, from the twentieth year until the thirty-second year of King Artaxerxes, twelve years, neither I nor my brothers ate the governor's provisions. [15]But the former governors who *were* before me laid burdens on the people, and took from them bread and wine, besides forty shekels of silver. Yes, even their servants bore rule over the people, but I did not do so, because of the fear of God. [16]Indeed, I also continued the work on this wall, and we* did not buy any land. All my servants *were* gathered there for the work.

¹⁷And at my table *were* one hundred and fifty Jews and rulers, besides those who came to us from the nations around us. ¹⁸Now *that* which was prepared daily *was* one ox *and* six choice sheep. Also fowl were prepared for me, and once every ten days an abundance of all kinds of wine. Yet in spite of this I did not demand the governor's provisions, because the bondage was heavy on this people.

¹⁹Remember me, my God, for good, *according to* all that I have done for this people.

Now it happened when Sanballat, Tobiah, Geshem the Arab, and the rest of our enemies heard that I had rebuilt the wall, and *that* there were no breaks left in it (though at that time I had not hung the doors in the gates), ²that Sanballat and Geshem sent to me, saying, "Come, let us meet together among the villages in the plain of Ono." But they thought to do me harm.

³So I sent messengers to them, saying, "I *am* doing a great work, so that I cannot come down. Why should the work cease while I leave it and go down to you?"

⁴But they sent me this message four times, and I answered them in the same manner.

⁵Then Sanballat sent his servant to me as before, the fifth time, with an open letter in his hand. ⁶In it *was* written:

It is reported among the nations, and Geshem* says, *that* you and the Jews plan to rebel; therefore, according to these rumors, you are rebuilding the wall, that you may be their king. ⁷And you have also appointed prophets to proclaim concerning you at Jerusalem, saying, "*There is* a king in Judah!" Now these matters will be reported to the king. So come, therefore, and let us consult together.

⁸Then I sent to him, saying, "No such things as you say are being done, but you invent them in your own heart."

⁹For they all *were trying to* make us afraid, saying, "Their hands will be weakened in the work, and it will not be done."

Now therefore, *O God,* strengthen my hands.

¹⁰Afterward I came to the house of Shemaiah the son of Delaiah, the son of Mehetabel, who *was* a secret informer; and he said, "Let us meet together in the house of God, within the temple, and let us close the doors of the temple, for they are coming to kill you; indeed, at night they will come to kill you."

¹¹And I said, "Should such a man as I flee? And who *is there* such as I who would go into the temple to save his life? I will not go in!" ¹²Then I perceived that God had not sent him at all, but that he pronounced *this* prophecy against me because Tobiah and Sanballat had hired him. ¹³For this reason he *was* hired, that I should be afraid and act that way and sin, so *that* they might have *cause* for an evil report, that they might reproach me.

¹⁴My God, remember Tobiah and Sanballat, according to these their works, and the prophetess Noadiah and the rest of the prophets who would have made me afraid.

¹⁵So the wall was finished on the twenty-fifth *day* of Elul, in fifty-two days. ¹⁶And it happened, when all our enemies heard *of it,* and all the nations around us saw *these things,* that they were very disheartened in their own eyes; for they perceived that this work was done by our God.

¹⁷Also in those days the nobles of Judah sent many letters to Tobiah, and *the letters of* Tobiah came to them.

18For many in Judah were pledged to him, because he was the son-in-law of Shechaniah the son of Arah, and his son Jehohanan had married the daughter of Meshullam the son of Berechiah. 19Also they reported his good deeds before me, and reported my words to him. Tobiah sent letters to frighten me.

THEN it was, when the wall was built and I had hung the doors, when the gatekeepers, the singers, and the Levites had been appointed, 2that I gave the charge of Jerusalem to my brother Hanani, and Hananiah the leader of the citadel, for he *was* a faithful man and feared God more than many.

3And I said to them, "Do not let the gates of Jerusalem be opened until the sun is hot; and while they stand *guard,* let them shut and bar the doors; and appoint guards from among the inhabitants of Jerusalem, one at his watch station and another in front of his own house."

4Now the city *was* large and spacious, but the people in it *were* few, and the houses *were* not rebuilt. 5Then my God put it into my heart to gather the nobles, the rulers, and the people, that they might be registered by genealogy. And I found a register of the genealogy of those who had come up in the first *return,* and found written in it:

6 These* *are* the people of the province who came back from the captivity, of those who had been carried away, whom Nebuchadnezzar the king of Babylon had carried away, and who returned to Jerusalem and Judah, everyone to his city.

7 Those who came with Zerubbabel *were* Jeshua, Nehemiah, Azariah, Raamiah, Nahamani, Mordecai, Bilshan, Mispereth,* Bigvai, Nehum, and Baanah.

The number of the men of the people of Israel: 8the sons of Parosh, two thousand one hundred and seventy-two; 9the sons of Shephatiah, three hundred and seventy-two; 10the sons of Arah, six hundred and fifty-two; 11the sons of Pahath-Moab, of the sons of Jeshua and Joab, two thousand eight hundred and eighteen; 12the sons of Elam, one thousand two hundred and fifty-four; 13the sons of Zattu, eight hundred and forty-five; 14the sons of Zaccai, seven hundred and sixty; 15the sons of Binnui,* six hundred and forty-eight; 16the sons of Bebai, six hundred and twenty-eight; 17the sons of Azgad, two thousand three hundred and twenty-two; 18the sons of Adonikam, six hundred and sixty-seven; 19the sons of Bigvai, two thousand and sixty-seven; 20the sons of Adin, six hundred and fifty-five; 21the sons of Ater of Hezekiah, ninety-eight; 22the sons of Hashum, three hundred and twenty-eight; 23the sons of Bezai, three hundred and twenty-four; 24the sons of Hariph,* one hundred and twelve; 25the sons of Gibeon,* ninety-five; 26the men of Bethlehem and Netophah, one hundred and eighty-eight;

27the men of Anathoth, one hundred and twenty-eight;
28the men of Beth Azmaveth,* forty-two;
29the men of Kirjath Jearim, Chephirah, and Beeroth, seven hundred and forty-three;
30the men of Ramah and Geba, six hundred and twenty-one;
31the men of Michmas, one hundred and twenty-two;
32the men of Bethel and Ai, one hundred and twenty-three;
33the men of the other Nebo, fifty-two;
34the sons of the other Elam, one thousand two hundred and fifty-four;
35the sons of Harim, three hundred and twenty;
36the sons of Jericho, three hundred and forty-five;
37the sons of Lod, Hadid, and Ono, seven hundred and twenty-one;
38the sons of Senaah, three thousand nine hundred and thirty.

39 The priests: the sons of Jedaiah, of the house of Jeshua, nine hundred and seventy-three;
40the sons of Immer, one thousand and fifty-two;
41the sons of Pashhur, one thousand two hundred and forty-seven;
42the sons of Harim, one thousand and seventeen.

43 The Levites: the sons of Jeshua, of Kadmiel, *and* of the sons of Hodevah,* seventy-four.

44 The singers: the sons of Asaph, one hundred and forty-eight.

45 The gatekeepers: the sons of Shallum,
the sons of Ater,
the sons of Talmon,
the sons of Akkub,
the sons of Hatita,
the sons of Shobai, one hundred and thirty-eight.

46 The Nethinim: the sons of Ziha,
the sons of Hasupha,
the sons of Tabbaoth,
47the sons of Keros,
the sons of Sia,*
the sons of Padon,
48the sons of Lebana,*
the sons of Hagaba,*
the sons of Salmai,*
49the sons of Hanan,
the sons of Giddel,
the sons of Gahar,
50the sons of Reaiah,
the sons of Rezin,
the sons of Nekoda,
51the sons of Gazzam,
the sons of Uzza,
the sons of Paseah,
52the sons of Besai,
the sons of Meunim,
the sons of Nephishesim,*
53the sons of Bakbuk,
the sons of Hakupha,
the sons of Harhur,
54the sons of Bazlith,*
the sons of Mehida,
the sons of Harsha,
55the sons of Barkos,
the sons of Sisera,
the sons of Tamah,
56the sons of Neziah,
and the sons of Hatipha.

57 The sons of Solomon's servants: the sons of Sotai, the sons of Sophereth,

the sons of Perida,*
⁵⁸the sons of Jaala,
the sons of Darkon,
the sons of Giddel,
⁵⁹the sons of Shephatiah,
the sons of Hattil,
the sons of Pochereth of
Zebaim,
and the children of Amon.*
⁶⁰All the Nethinim, and the
sons of Solomon's servants,
were three hundred and
ninety-two.

1 CORINTHIANS 8:1-13

Now concerning things offered
to idols: We know that we all
have knowledge. Knowledge
puffs up, but love edifies. ²And if anyone thinks that he knows anything, he
knows nothing yet as he ought to
know. ³But if anyone loves God, this
one is known by Him.

⁴Therefore concerning the eating of
things offered to idols, we know that
an idol *is* nothing in the world, and that
there is no other God but one. ⁵For
even if there are so-called gods,
whether in heaven or on earth (as
there are many gods and many lords),
⁶yet for us *there is* one God, the Father,
of whom *are* all things, and we for Him;
and one Lord Jesus Christ, through
whom *are* all things, and through
whom we *live.*

⁷However, *there is* not in everyone
that knowledge; for some, with consciousness of the idol, until now eat *it*
as a thing offered to an idol; and their
conscience, being weak, is defiled.
⁸But food does not commend us to
God; for neither if we eat are we the
better, nor if we do not eat are we the
worse.

⁹But beware lest somehow this lib-
erty of yours become a stumbling
block to those who are weak. ¹⁰For if
anyone sees you who have knowledge
eating in an idol's temple, will not the
conscience of him who is weak be em-
boldened to eat those things offered to
idols? ¹¹And because of your knowledge shall the weak brother perish, for
whom Christ died? ¹²But when you
thus sin against the brethren, and
wound their weak conscience, you sin
against Christ. ¹³Therefore, if food
makes my brother stumble, I will
never again eat meat, lest I make my
brother stumble.

PSALM 33:1-12

REJOICE in the LORD, O you
righteous!
For praise from the upright is
beautiful.

2   Praise the LORD with the harp;
Make melody to Him with an
instrument of ten strings.

3   Sing to Him a new song;
Play skillfully with a shout of
joy.

4   For the word of the LORD *is*
right,
And all His work *is done* in
truth.

5   He loves righteousness and
justice;
The earth is full of the
goodness of the LORD.

6   By the word of the LORD the
heavens were made,
And all the host of them by
the breath of His mouth.

7   He gathers the waters of the
sea together as a heap;*
He lays up the deep in
storehouses.

8   Let all the earth fear the LORD;
Let all the inhabitants of the
world stand in awe of Him.

9   For He spoke, and it was *done;*
He commanded, and it stood
fast.

10 The LORD brings the counsel
of the nations to nothing;
He makes the plans of the
peoples of no effect.
11 The counsel of the LORD
stands forever,

The plans of His heart to all
generations.
12 Blessed *is* the nation whose
God *is* the LORD,
The people He has chosen as
His own inheritance.

PROVERBS FOR TODAY/ 21:8-10

The way of a guilty man is *perverse;* * *but* as for *the pure, his work* is *right.*
□ *Better to dwell in a corner of a housetop, than in a house shared with a contentious woman.* □ *The soul of the wicked desires evil; his neighbor finds no favor in his eyes.*

AUGUST 14

NEHEMIAH 7:61–9:21

AND these *were* the ones who came up from Tel Melah, Tel Harsha, Cherub, Addon,* and Immer, but they could not identify their father's house nor their lineage, whether they *were* of Israel: 62the sons of Delaiah, the sons of Tobiah, the sons of Nekoda, six hundred and forty-two; 63and of the priests: the sons of Habaiah, the sons of Koz,* the sons of Barzillai, who took a wife of the daughters of Barzillai the Gileadite, and was called by their name. 64These sought their listing *among* those who were registered by genealogy, but it was not found; therefore they were excluded from the priesthood as defiled. 65And the governor* said to them that they should not eat of the most holy things till a priest could consult with the Urim and Thummim.

66 Altogether the whole assembly *was* forty-two thousand three hundred and sixty, 67besides their male and female servants, of whom *there were* seven thousand three hundred and thirty-seven; and they had two hundred and forty-five men and women singers. 68Their horses were seven hundred and thirty-six, their mules two hundred and forty-five, 69*their* camels four hundred and thirty-five, *and* donkeys six thousand seven hundred and twenty.

70 And some of the heads of the fathers' houses gave to the work. The governor* gave to the treasury one thousand gold drachmas, fifty basins, and five hundred and thirty priestly garments. 71Some of the heads of the fathers' *houses* gave to the treasury of the work twenty thousand gold drachmas, and two thousand two hundred silver

minas. [72]And that which the rest of the people gave *was* twenty thousand gold drachmas, two thousand silver minas, and sixty-seven priestly garments.

[73]So the priests, the Levites, the gatekeepers, the singers, *some* of the people, the Nethinim, and all Israel dwelt in their cities.

When the seventh month came, the children of Israel *were* in their cities.

Now all the people gathered together as one man in the open square that *was* in front of the Water Gate; and they told Ezra the scribe to bring the Book of the Law of Moses, which the Lord had commanded Israel. [2]So Ezra the priest brought the Law before the assembly of men and women and all who *could* hear with understanding on the first day of the seventh month. [3]Then he read from it in the open square that *was* in front of the Water Gate from morning until midday, before the men and women and those who could understand; and the ears of all the people *were attentive* to the Book of the Law.

[4]So Ezra the scribe stood on a platform of wood which they had made for the purpose; and beside him, at his right hand, stood Mattithiah, Shema, Anaiah, Urijah, Hilkiah, and Maaseiah; and at his left hand Pedaiah, Mishael, Malchijah, Hashum, Hashbadana, Zechariah, *and* Meshullam. [5]And Ezra opened the book in the sight of all the people, for he was *standing* above all the people; and when he opened it, all the people stood up. [6]And Ezra blessed the Lord, the great God.

Then all the people answered, "Amen, Amen!" while lifting up their hands. And they bowed their heads and worshiped the Lord with *their* faces to the ground.

[7]Also Jeshua, Bani, Sherebiah, Jamin, Akkub, Shabbethai, Hodijah, Maaseiah, Kelita, Azariah, Jozabad, Hanan, Pelaiah, and the Levites, helped the people to understand the Law; and the people *stood* in their place. [8]So they read distinctly from the book, in the Law of God; and they gave the sense, and helped *them* to understand the reading.

[9]And Nehemiah, who *was* the governor,* Ezra the priest *and* scribe, and the Levites who taught the people said to all the people, "This day *is* holy to the Lord your God; do not mourn nor weep." For all the people wept, when they heard the words of the Law.

[10]Then he said to them, "Go your way, eat the fat, drink the sweet, and send portions to those for whom nothing is prepared; for *this* day *is* holy to our Lord. Do not sorrow, for the joy of the Lord is your strength."

[11]So the Levites quieted all the people, saying, "Be still, for the day *is* holy; do not be grieved." [12]And all the people went their way to eat and drink, to send portions and rejoice greatly, because they understood the words that were declared to them.

[13]Now on the second day the heads of the fathers' *houses* of all the people, with the priests and Levites, were gathered to Ezra the scribe, in order to understand the words of the Law. [14]And they found written in the Law, which the Lord had commanded by Moses, that the children of Israel should dwell in booths during the feast of the seventh month, [15]and that they should announce and proclaim in all their cities and in Jerusalem, saying, "Go out to the mountain, and bring olive branches, branches of oil trees, myrtle branches, palm branches, and branches of leafy trees, to make booths, as *it is* written."

[16]Then the people went out and brought *them* and made themselves booths, each one on the roof of his house, or in their courtyards or the

courts of the house of God, and in the open square of the Water Gate and in the open square of the Gate of Ephraim. [17]So the whole assembly of those who had returned from the captivity made booths and sat under the booths; for since the days of Joshua the son of Nun until that day the children of Israel had not done so. And there was very great gladness. [18]Also day by day, from the first day until the last day, he read from the Book of the Law of God. And they kept the feast seven days; and on the eighth day *there was* a sacred assembly, according to the *prescribed* manner.

Now on the twenty-fourth day of this month the children of Israel were assembled with fasting, in sackcloth, and with dust on their heads.* [2]Then those of Israelite lineage separated themselves from all foreigners; and they stood and confessed their sins and the iniquities of their fathers. [3]And they stood up in their place and read from the Book of the Law of the LORD their God *for one*-fourth of the day; and *for another* fourth they confessed and worshiped the LORD their God.

[4]Then Jeshua, Bani, Kadmiel, Shebaniah, Bunni, Sherebiah, Bani, *and* Chenani stood on the stairs of the Levites and cried out with a loud voice to the LORD their God. [5]And the Levites, Jeshua, Kadmiel, Bani, Hashabniah, Sherebiah, Hodijah,* Shebaniah, *and* Pethahiah, said:

"Stand up *and* bless the LORD
    your God
Forever and ever!

"Blessed be Your glorious
    name,
Which is exalted above all
    blessing and praise!
[6]   You alone *are* the LORD;
You have made heaven,

The heaven of heavens, with
    all their host,
The earth and everything on
    it,
The seas and all that is in
    them,
And You preserve them all.
The host of heaven worships
    You.

[7]   "You *are* the LORD God,
Who chose Abram,
And brought him out of Ur of
    the Chaldeans,
And gave him the name
    Abraham;
[8]   You found his heart faithful
    before You,
And made a covenant with him
To give the land of the
    Canaanites,
The Hittites, the Amorites,
The Perizzites, the Jebusites,
And the Girgashites—
To give *it* to his descendants.
You have performed Your
    words,
For You *are* righteous.

[9]   "You saw the affliction of our
    fathers in Egypt,
And heard their cry by the
    Red Sea.
[10] You showed signs and
    wonders against Pharaoh,
Against all his servants,
And against all the people of
    his land.
For You knew that they acted
    proudly against them.
So You made a name for
    Yourself, as *it is* this day.
[11] And You divided the sea
    before them,
So that they went through the
    midst of the sea on the dry
    land;
And their persecutors You
    threw into the deep,

As a stone into the mighty
waters.
12 Moreover You led them by
day with a cloudy pillar,
And by night with a pillar of
fire,
To give them light on the road
Which they should travel.

13 "You came down also on
Mount Sinai,
And spoke with them from
heaven,
And gave them just
ordinances and true laws,
Good statutes and
commandments.
14 You made known to them
Your holy Sabbath,
And commanded them
precepts, statutes and laws,
By the hand of Moses Your
servant.
15 You gave them bread from
heaven for their hunger,
And brought them water out
of the rock for their thirst,
And told them to go in to
possess the land
Which You had sworn to give
them.

16 "But they and our fathers acted
proudly,
Hardened their necks,
And did not heed Your
commandments.
17 They refused to obey,
And they were not mindful of
Your wonders
That You did among them.
But they hardened their
necks,
And in their rebellion*
They appointed a leader
To return to their bondage.
But You are God,
Ready to pardon,
Gracious and merciful,
Slow to anger,

Abundant in kindness,
And did not forsake them.

18 "Even when they made a
molded calf for themselves,
And said, 'This is your god
That brought you up out of
Egypt,'
And worked great
provocations,
19 Yet in Your manifold mercies
You did not forsake them in
the wilderness.
The pillar of the cloud did not
depart from them by day,
To lead them on the road;
Nor the pillar of fire by night,
To show them light,
And the way they should go.
20 You also gave Your good
Spirit to instruct them,
And did not withhold Your
manna from their mouth,
And gave them water for their
thirst.
21 Forty years You sustained
them in the wilderness;
They lacked nothing;
Their clothes did not wear
out*
And their feet did not swell."

1 CORINTHIANS 9:1-18

AM I not an apostle? Am I not
free? Have I not seen Jesus
Christ our Lord? Are you not
my work in the Lord? 2If I am not an
apostle to others, yet doubtless I am to
you. For you are the seal of my apostleship in the Lord.

3My defense to those who examine
me is this: 4Do we have no right to eat
and drink? 5Do we have no right to
take along a believing wife, as do also
the other apostles, the brothers of the
Lord, and Cephas? 6Or is it only Barnabas and I who have no right to refrain
from working? 7Who ever goes to war
at his own expense? Who plants a vine-

yard and does not eat of its fruit? Or who tends a flock and does not drink of the milk of the flock?

⁸Do I say these things as a *mere man*? Or does not the law say the same also? ⁹For it is written in the law of Moses, *"You shall not muzzle an ox while it treads out the grain."* * Is it oxen God is concerned about? ¹⁰Or does He say *it* altogether for our sakes? For our sakes, no doubt, *this* is written, that he who plows should plow in hope, and he who threshes in hope should be partaker of his hope. ¹¹If we have sown spiritual things for you, *is it* a great thing if we reap your material things? ¹²If others are partakers of *this* right over you, *are* we not even more?

Nevertheless we have not used this right, but endure all things lest we hinder the gospel of Christ. ¹³Do you not know that those who minister the holy things eat *of the things* of the temple, and those who serve at the altar partake of *the offerings of* the altar? ¹⁴Even so the Lord has commanded that those who preach the gospel should live from the gospel.

¹⁵But I have used none of these things, nor have I written these things that it should be done so to me; for it *would be* better for me to die than that anyone should make my boasting void. ¹⁶For if I preach the gospel, I have nothing to boast of, for necessity is laid upon me; yes, woe is me if I do not preach the gospel! ¹⁷For if I do this willingly, I have a reward; but if against my will, I have been entrusted with a stewardship. ¹⁸What is my reward then? That when I preach the gospel, I may present the gospel of Christ*

without charge, that I may not abuse my authority in the gospel.

PSALM 33:13-22

Tʜᴇ Lᴏʀᴅ looks from heaven;
He sees all the sons of men.
¹⁴From the place of His
  dwelling He looks
On all the inhabitants of the
  earth;
15 He fashions their hearts
  individually;
He considers all their works.

16 No king *is* saved by the
  multitude of an army;
A mighty man is not delivered
  by great strength.
17 A horse *is* a vain hope for
  safety;
Neither shall it deliver *any* by
  its great strength.

18 Behold, the eye of the Lᴏʀᴅ *is*
  on those who fear Him,
On those who hope in His
  mercy,
19 To deliver their soul from
  death,
And to keep them alive in
  famine.

20 Our soul waits for the Lᴏʀᴅ;
He *is* our help and our shield.
21 For our heart shall rejoice in
  Him,
Because we have trusted in
  His holy name.
22 Let Your mercy, O Lᴏʀᴅ, be
  upon us,
Just as we hope in You.

PROVERBS FOR TODAY/ 21:11-12

When the scoffer is punished, the simple is made wise; but when the wise is instructed, he receives knowledge. □ *The righteous* God *wisely considers the house of the wicked, overthrowing the wicked for* their *wickedness.*

AUGUST 15

NEHEMIAH 9:22–10:39

"**M**OREOVER You gave them [the Israelites] kingdoms and nations,
And divided them into districts.*
So they took possession of the land of Sihon,
The land of* the king of Heshbon,
And the land of Og king of Bashan.

23 You also multiplied their children as the stars of heaven,
And brought them into the land
Which You had told their fathers
To go in and possess.

24 So the people went in
And possessed the land;
You subdued before them the inhabitants of the land,
The Canaanites,
And gave them into their hands,
With their kings
And the people of the land,
That they might do with them as they wished.

25 And they took strong cities and a rich land,
And possessed houses full of all goods,
Cisterns *already* dug, vineyards, olive groves,
And fruit trees in abundance.
So they ate and were filled and grew fat,
And delighted themselves in Your great goodness.

26 "Nevertheless they were disobedient
And rebelled against You,
Cast Your law behind their backs
And killed Your prophets, who testified against them
To turn them to Yourself;
And they worked great provocations.

27 Therefore You delivered them into the hand of their enemies,
Who oppressed them;
And in the time of their trouble,
When they cried to You,
You heard from heaven;
And according to Your abundant mercies
You gave them deliverers who saved them
From the hand of their enemies.

28 "But after they had rest,
They again did evil before You.
Therefore You left them in the hand of their enemies,
So that they had dominion over them;
Yet when they returned and cried out to You,
You heard from heaven;
And many times You delivered them according to Your mercies,

29 And testified against them,
That You might bring them back to Your law.
Yet they acted proudly,
And did not heed Your commandments,
But sinned against Your judgments,

'Which if a man does, he shall
live by them.'*
And they shrugged their
shoulders,
Stiffened their necks,
And would not hear.
30 Yet for many years You had
patience with them,
And testified against them by
Your Spirit in Your prophets.
Yet they would not listen;
Therefore You gave them into
the hand of the peoples of
the lands.
31 Nevertheless in Your great
mercy
You did not utterly consume
them nor forsake them;
For You *are* God, gracious
and merciful.

32 "Now therefore, our God,
The great, the mighty, and
awesome God,
Who keeps covenant and
mercy:
Do not let all the trouble seem
small before You
That has come upon us,
Our kings and our princes,
Our priests and our prophets,
Our fathers and on all Your
people,
From the days of the kings of
Assyria until this day.
33 However You *are* just in all
that has befallen us;
For You have dealt faithfully,
But we have done wickedly.
34 Neither our kings nor our
princes,
Our priests nor our fathers,
Have kept Your law,
Nor heeded Your
commandments and Your
testimonies,
With which You testified
against them.
35 For they have not served You
in their kingdom,

Or in the many good *things*
that You gave them,
Or in the large and rich land
which You set before them;
Nor did they turn from their
wicked works.

36 "Here we *are,* servants today!
And the land that You gave to
our fathers,
To eat its fruit and its bounty,
Here we *are,* servants in it!
37 And it yields much increase to
the kings
You have set over us,
Because of our sins;
Also they have dominion over
our bodies and our cattle
At their pleasure;
And we *are* in great distress.

38 "And because of all this,
We make a sure *covenant* and
write *it;*
Our leaders, our Levites, *and*
our priests seal *it.*"

Now those who placed *their* seal on *the
document were:*

Nehemiah the governor, the
son of Hacaliah, and
Zedekiah, 2Seraiah, Azariah,
Jeremiah, 3Pashhur, Amariah,
Malchijah, 4Hattush,
Shebaniah, Malluch, 5Harim,
Meremoth, Obadiah, 6Daniel,
Ginnethon, Baruch,
7Meshullam, Abijah, Mijamin,
8Maaziah, Bilgai, *and*
Shemaiah. These *were* the
priests.

9 The Levites: Jeshua the son of
Azaniah, Binnui of the sons of
Henadad, *and* Kadmiel.

10 Their brethren: Shebaniah,
Hodijah, Kelita, Pelaiah,
Hanan, 11Micha, Rehob,

Hashabiah, 12Zaccur, Sherebiah, Shebaniah, 13Hodijah, Bani, *and* Beninu.

14 The leaders of the people: Parosh, Pahath-Moab, Elam, Zattu, Bani, 15Bunni, Azgad, Bebai, 16Adonijah, Bigvai, Adin, 17Ater, Hezekiah, Azzur, 18Hodijah, Hashum, Bezai, 19Hariph, Anathoth, Nebai, 20Magpiash, Meshullam, Hezir, 21Meshezabel, Zadok, Jaddua, 22Pelatiah, Hanan, Anaiah, 23Hoshea, Hananiah, Hasshub, 24Hallohesh, Pilha, Shobek, 25Rehum, Hashabnah, Maaseiah, 26Ahijah, Hanan, Anan, 27Malluch, Harim, *and* Baanah.

28Now the rest of the people—the priests, the Levites, the gatekeepers, the singers, the Nethinim, and all those who had separated themselves from the peoples of the lands to the Law of God, their wives, their sons, and their daughters, everyone who had knowledge and understanding— 29these joined with their brethren, their nobles, and entered into a curse and an oath to walk in God's Law, which was given by Moses the servant of God, and to observe and do all the commandments of the LORD our Lord, and His ordinances and His statutes: 30We would not give our daughters as wives to the peoples of the land, nor take their daughters for our sons; 31*if* the peoples of the land brought wares or any grain to sell on the Sabbath day, we would not buy it from them on the Sabbath, or on a holy day; and we would forego the seventh year's *produce* and the exacting of every debt. 32Also we made ordinances for ourselves, to exact from ourselves yearly one-third of a shekel for the service of the house of our God: 33for the

showbread, for the regular grain offering, for the regular burnt offering of the Sabbaths, the New Moons, and the set feasts; for the holy things, for the sin offerings to make atonement for Israel, and all the work of the house of our God. 34We cast lots among the priests, the Levites, and the people, for *bringing* the wood offering into the house of our God, according to our fathers' houses, at the appointed times year by year, to burn on the altar of the LORD our God as *it is* written in the Law.

35And *we made ordinances* to bring the firstfruits of our ground and the firstfruits of all fruit of all trees, year by year, to the house of the LORD; 36to bring the firstborn of our sons and our cattle, as *it is* written in the Law, and the firstborn of our herds and our flocks, to the house of our God, to the priests who minister in the house of our God; 37to bring the firstfruits of our dough, our offerings, the fruit from all kinds of trees, *the* new wine and oil, to the priests, to the storerooms of the house of our God; and to bring the tithes of our land to the Levites, for the Levites should receive the tithes in all our farming communities. 38And the priest, the descendant of Aaron, shall be with the Levites when the Levites receive tithes; and the Levites shall bring up a tenth of the tithes to the house of our God, to the rooms of the storehouse. 39For the children of Israel and the children of Levi shall bring the offering of the grain, of the new wine and the oil, to the storerooms where the articles of the sanctuary *are, where* the priests who minister and the gatekeepers and the singers *are;* and we will not neglect the house of our God.

1 CORINTHIANS 9:19–10:13

FOR though I am free from all *men,* I have made myself a servant to all, that I might win the more; 20and to the Jews I became as a Jew, that

I might win Jews; to those *who are* under the law, as under the law,* that I might win those *who are* under the law; [21]to those *who are* without law, as without law (not being without law toward God,* but under law toward Christ*), that I might win those *who are* without law; [22]to the weak I became as* weak, that I might win the weak. I have become all things to all *men,* that I might by all means save some. [23]Now this I do for the gospel's sake, that I may be partaker of it with *you.*

[24]Do you not know that those who run in a race all run, but one receives the prize? Run in such a way that you may obtain *it.* [25]And everyone who competes *for the prize* is temperate in all things. Now they *do it* to obtain a perishable crown, but we *for* an imperishable *crown.* [26]Therefore I run thus: not with uncertainty. Thus I fight: not as *one who* beats the air. [27]But I discipline my body and bring *it* into subjection, lest, when I have preached to others, I myself should become disqualified.

MOREOVER, brethren, I do not want you to be unaware that all our fathers were under the cloud, all passed through the sea, [2]all were baptized into Moses in the cloud and in the sea, [3]all ate the same spiritual food, [4]and all drank the same spiritual drink. For they drank of that spiritual Rock that followed them, and that Rock was Christ. [5]But with most of them God was not well pleased, for *their bodies* were scattered in the wilderness.

[6]Now these things became our examples, to the intent that we should not lust after evil things as they also lusted. [7]And do not become idolaters as *were* some of them. As it is written, *"The people sat down to eat and drink, and rose up to play."* * [8]Nor let us commit sexual immorality, as some of them did, and in one day twenty-three thousand fell; [9]nor let us tempt Christ, as some of them also tempted, and were destroyed by serpents; [10]nor complain, as some of them also complained, and were destroyed by the destroyer. [11]Now all* these things happened to them as examples, and they were written for our admonition, upon whom the ends of the ages have come.

[12]Therefore let him who thinks he stands take heed lest he fall. [13]No temptation has overtaken you except such as is common to man; but God *is* faithful, who will not allow you to be tempted beyond what you are able, but with the temptation will also make the way of escape, that you may be able to bear *it.*

PSALM 34:1 10

A Psalm of David when he pretended madness before Abimelech, who drove him away, and he departed.

I WILL bless the LORD at all times;
His praise *shall* continually *be* in
my mouth.
2   My soul shall make its boast
         in the LORD;
     The humble shall hear *of it*
         and be glad.
3   Oh, magnify the LORD with me,
     And let us exalt His name
         together.

4   I sought the LORD, and He
         heard me,
     And delivered me from all my
         fears.
5   They looked to Him and were
         radiant,
     And their faces were not
         ashamed.
6   This poor man cried out, and
         the LORD heard *him,*
     And saved him out of all his
         troubles.
7   The angel* of the LORD
         encamps all around those
         who fear Him,
     And delivers them.

8 Oh, taste and see that the
  LORD *is* good;
  Blessed *is* the man *who* trusts
  in Him!
9 Oh, fear the LORD, you His
  saints!

  There is no want to those who
  fear Him.
10 The young lions lack and
  suffer hunger;
  But those who seek the LORD
  shall not lack any good
  thing.

PROVERBS FOR TODAY/ 21:13

Whoever shuts his ears to the cry of the poor will also cry himself and not be heard.

AUGUST 16

NEHEMIAH 11:1–12:26

Now the leaders of the people dwelt at Jerusalem; the rest of the people cast lots to bring one out of ten to dwell in Jerusalem, the holy city, and nine-tenths *were to dwell* in *other* cities. ²And the people blessed all the men who willingly offered themselves to dwell at Jerusalem.

³These *are* the heads of the province who dwelt in Jerusalem. (But in the cities of Judah everyone dwelt in his own possession in their cities—Israelites, priests, Levites, Nethinim, and descendants of Solomon's servants.) ⁴Also in Jerusalem dwelt *some* of the children of Judah and of the children of Benjamin.

The children of Judah: Athaiah the son of Uzziah, the son of Zechariah, the son of Amariah, the son of Shephatiah, the son of Mahalalel, of the children of Perez; ⁵and Maaseiah the son of Baruch, the son of Col-Hozeh, the son of Hazaiah, the son of Adaiah, the son of Joiarib, the son of Zechariah, the son of Shiloni. ⁶All the sons of Perez who dwelt at Jerusalem *were* four hundred and sixty-eight valiant men.

⁷And these are the sons of Benjamin: Sallu the son of Meshullam, the son of Joed, the son of Pedaiah, the son of Kolaiah, the son of Maaseiah, the son of Ithiel, the son of Jeshaiah; ⁸and after him Gabbai *and* Sallai, nine hundred and twenty-eight. ⁹Joel the son of Zichri *was* their overseer, and Judah the son of Senuah* *was* second over the city.

¹⁰Of the priests: Jedaiah the son of Joiarib, and Jachin; ¹¹Seraiah the son of Hilkiah, the son of Meshullam, the son of Zadok, the son of Meraioth, the son of Ahitub, *was* the leader of the house of God. ¹²Their brethren who did the work of the house *were* eight hundred and twenty-two; and Adaiah the son of Jeroham, the son of Pelaliah, the son of Amzi, the son of Zechariah, the son of Pashhur, the son of Malchijah, ¹³and his brethren, heads of the fathers' *houses, were* two hundred and forty-two; and Amashai the son of Azarel, the son of Ahzai, the son of Meshillemoth, the son of Immer, ¹⁴and their brethren, mighty men of valor, *were* one hundred and twenty-eight. Their overseer *was* Zabdiel the son of *one of* the great men.*

¹⁵Also of the Levites: Shemaiah the son of Hasshub, the son of Azrikam,

the son of Hashabiah, the son of Bunni; [16]Shabbethai and Jozabad, of the heads of the Levites, *had* the oversight of the business outside of the house of God; [17]Mattaniah the son of Micha,* the son of Zabdi, the son of Asaph, the leader *who* began the thanksgiving with prayer; Bakbukiah, the second among his brethren; and Abda the son of Shammua, the son of Galal, the son of Jeduthun. [18]All the Levites in the holy city *were* two hundred and eighty-four.

[19]Moreover the gatekeepers, Akkub, Talmon, and their brethren who kept the gates, *were* one hundred and seventy-two.

[20]And the rest of Israel, of the priests *and* Levites, *were* in all the cities of Judah, everyone in his inheritance. [21]But the Nethinim dwelt in Ophel. And Ziha and Gishpa *were* over the Nethinim.

[22]Also the overseer of the Levites at Jerusalem *was* Uzzi the son of Bani, the son of Hashabiah, the son of Mattaniah, the son of Micha, of the sons of Asaph, the singers in charge of the service of the house of God. [23]For *it was* the king's command concerning them that a certain portion should be for the singers, a quota day by day. [24]Pethahiah the son of Meshezabel, of the children of Zerah the son of Judah, *was* the king's deputy* in all matters concerning the people.

[25]And as for the villages with their fields, *some* of the children of Judah dwelt in Kirjath Arba and its villages, Dibon and its villages, Jekabzeel and its villages; [26]in Jeshua, Moladah, Beth Pelet, [27]Hazar Shual, and Beersheba and its villages; [28]in Ziklag and Meconah and its villages; [29]in En Rimmon, Zorah, Jarmuth, [30]Zanoah, Adullam, and their villages; in Lachish and its fields; in Azekah and its villages. They dwelt from Beersheba to the Valley of Hinnom.

[31]Also the children of Benjamin from Geba *dwelt* in Michmash, Aija, and Bethel, and their villages; [32]in Anathoth, Nob, Ananiah; [33]in Hazor, Ramah, Gittaim; [34]in Hadid, Zeboim, Neballat; [35]in Lod, Ono, *and* the Valley of Craftsmen. [36]Some of the Judean divisions of Levites *were* in Benjamin.

Now these *are* the priests and the Levites who came up with Zerubbabel the son of Shealtiel, and Jeshua: Seraiah, Jeremiah, Ezra, [2]Amariah, Malluch, Hattush, [3]Shechaniah, Rehum, Meremoth, [4]Iddo, Ginnethoi,* Abijah, [5]Mijamin, Maadiah, Bilgah, [6]Shemaiah, Joiarib, Jedaiah, [7]Sallu, Amok, Hilkiah, *and* Jedaiah.

These *were* the heads of the priests and their brethren in the days of Jeshua.

[8]Moreover the Levites *were* Jeshua, Binnui, Kadmiel, Sherebiah, Judah, *and* Mattaniah *who led* the thanksgiving *psalms,* he and his brethren. [9]Also Bakbukiah and Unni, their brethren, *stood* across from them in *their* duties.

[10]Jeshua begot Joiakim, Joiakim begot Eliashib, Eliashib begot Joiada, [11]Joiada begot Jonathan, and Jonathan begot Jaddua.

[12]Now in the days of Joiakim, the priests, the heads of the fathers' *houses were:* of Seraiah, Meraiah; of Jeremiah, Hananiah; [13]of Ezra, Meshullam; of Amariah, Jehohanan; [14]of Melichu,* Jonathan; of Shebaniah,* Joseph; [15]of Harim,* Adna; of Meraioth,* Helkai; [16]of Iddo, Zechariah; of Ginnethon, Meshullam; [17]of Abijah, Zichri; *the son* of Minjamin;* of Moadiah,* Piltai; [18]of Bilgah, Shammua; of Shemaiah, Jehonathan; [19]of Joiarib, Mattenai; of Jedaiah, Uzzi; [20]of Sallai,* Kallai; of Amok, Eber; [21]of Hilkiah, Hashabiah; *and* of Jedaiah, Nethanel.

[22]During the reign of Darius the Persian, a record *was also kept* of the Levites and priests *who had been* heads of their fathers' *houses* in the days of Eliashib, Joiada, Johanan, and Jaddua.

²³The sons of Levi, the heads of the fathers' *houses* until the days of Johanan the son of Eliashib, *were* written in the book of the chronicles.

²⁴And the heads of the Levites *were* Hashabiah, Sherebiah, and Jeshua the son of Kadmiel, with their brothers across from them, to praise *and* give thanks, group alternating with group, according to the command of David the man of God. ²⁵Mattaniah, Bakbukiah, Obadiah, Meshullam, Talmon, and Akkub *were* gatekeepers keeping the watch at the storerooms of the gates. ²⁶These *lived* in the days of Joiakim the son of Jeshua, the son of Jozadak,* and in the days of Nehemiah the governor, and of Ezra the priest, the scribe.

1 CORINTHIANS 10:14–11:2

Therefore, my beloved, flee from idolatry. ¹⁵I speak as to wise men; judge for yourselves what I say. ¹⁶The cup of blessing which we bless, is it not the communion of the blood of Christ? The bread which we break, is it not the communion of the body of Christ? ¹⁷For we, *though* many, are one bread *and* one body; for we all partake of that one bread.

¹⁸Observe Israel after the flesh: Are not those who eat of the sacrifices partakers of the altar? ¹⁹What am I saying then? That an idol is anything, or what is offered to idols is anything? ²⁰Rather, that the things which the Gentiles sacrifice they sacrifice to demons and not to God, and I do not want you to have fellowship with demons. ²¹You cannot drink the cup of the Lord and the cup of demons; you cannot partake of the Lord's table and of the table of demons. ²²Or do we provoke the Lord to jealousy? Are we stronger than He?

²³All things are lawful for me,* but not all things are helpful; all things are lawful for me,* but not all things edify.

²⁴Let no one seek his own, but each one the other's *well-being.*

²⁵Eat whatever is sold in the meat market, asking no questions for conscience' sake; ²⁶for *"the earth is the Lord's, and all its fullness."* *

²⁷If any of those who do not believe invites you *to dinner,* and you desire to go, eat whatever is set before you, asking no question for conscience' sake. ²⁸But if anyone says to you, "This was offered to idols," do not eat it for the sake of the one who told you, and for conscience' sake;* for *"the earth is the Lord's, and all its fullness."* * ²⁹"Conscience," I say, not your own, but that of the other. For why is my liberty judged by another *man's* conscience? ³⁰But if I partake with thanks, why am I evil spoken of for *the food* over which I give thanks?

³¹Therefore, whether you eat or drink, or whatever you do, do all to the glory of God. ³²Give no offense, either to the Jews or to the Greeks or to the church of God, ³³just as I also please all *men* in all *things,* not seeking my own profit, but the *profit* of many, that they may be saved.

Imitate me, just as I also *imitate* Christ.

²Now I praise you, brethren, that you remember me in all things and keep the traditions just as I delivered *them* to you.

PSALM 34:11-22

Come, you children, listen to me; I will teach you the fear of the Lord.
12   Who *is* the man *who* desires life,
      And loves *many* days, that he may see good?
13   Keep your tongue from evil,
      And your lips from speaking deceit.
14   Depart from evil and do good;
      Seek peace and pursue it.

15 The eyes of the LORD *are* on
the righteous,
And His ears *are open* to their
cry.
16 The face of the LORD *is* against
those who do evil,
To cut off the remembrance
of them from the earth.

17 *The righteous* cry out, and the
LORD hears,
And delivers them out of all
their troubles.
18 The LORD *is* near to those who
have a broken heart,
And saves such as have a
contrite spirit.

19 Many *are* the afflictions of the
righteous,
But the LORD delivers him out
of them all.
20 He guards all his bones;
Not one of them is broken.
21 Evil shall slay the wicked,
And those who hate the
righteous shall be
condemned.
22 The LORD redeems the soul of
His servants,
And none of those who trust
in Him shall be condemned.

PROVERBS FOR TODAY/ 21:14-16

A gift in secret pacifies anger, and a bribe behind the back, * strong wrath.* ☐ *It is a joy for the just to do justice, but destruction* will come *to the workers of iniquity.* ☐ *A man who wanders from the way of understanding will rest in the assembly of the dead.*

AUGUST 17

NEHEMIAH 12:27–13:31

N ow at the dedication of the wall of Jerusalem they sought out the Levites in all their places, to bring them to Jerusalem to celebrate the dedication with gladness, both with thanksgivings and singing, *with* cymbals and stringed instruments and harps. 28And the sons of the singers gathered together from the countryside around Jerusalem, from the villages of the Netophathites, 29from the house of Gilgal, and from the fields of Geba and Azmaveth; for the singers had built themselves villages all around Jerusalem. 30Then the priests and Levites purified them-

selves, and purified the people, the gates, and the wall.

31So I brought the leaders of Judah up on the wall, and appointed two large thanksgiving choirs. *One* went to the right hand on the wall toward the Refuse Gate. 32After them went Hoshaiah and half of the leaders of Judah, 33and Azariah, Ezra, Meshullam, 34Judah, Benjamin, Shemaiah, Jeremiah, 35and some of the priests' sons with trumpets—Zechariah the son of Jonathan, the son of Shemaiah, the son of Mattaniah, the son of Michaiah, the son of Zaccur, the son of Asaph, 36and his brethren, Shemaiah, Azarel, Milalai, Gilalai, Maai, Nethanel, Judah, *and* Hanani, with the musical instruments of David the man of God. And Ezra the scribe *went* before them. 37By the Fountain Gate, in front of them, they went up the stairs of the City of David, on the stairway of the wall, beyond the house of David, as far as the Water Gate eastward.

38The other thanksgiving choir went the opposite *way,* and I *was* behind them with half of the people on the wall, going past the Tower of the Ovens as far as the Broad Wall, 39and above the Gate of Ephraim, above the Old Gate, above the Fish Gate, the Tower of Hananel, the Tower of the Hundred, as far as the Sheep Gate; and they stopped by the Gate of the Prison.

40So the two thanksgiving choirs stood in the house of God, likewise I and the half of the rulers with me; 41and the priests, Eliakim, Maaseiah, Minjamin,* Michaiah, Elioenai, Zechariah, *and* Hananiah, with trumpets; 42also Maaseiah, Shemaiah, Eleazar, Uzzi, Jehohanan, Malchijah, Elam, and Ezer. The singers sang loudly with Jezrahiah the director.

43Also that day they offered great sacrifices, and rejoiced, for God had made them rejoice with great joy; the women and the children also rejoiced, so that the joy of Jerusalem was heard afar off.

44And at the same time some were appointed over the rooms of the storehouse for the offerings, the firstfruits, and the tithes, to gather into them from the fields of the cities the portions specified by the Law for the priests and Levites; for Judah rejoiced over the priests and Levites who ministered. 45Both the singers and the gatekeepers kept the charge of their God and the charge of the purification, according to the command of David *and* Solomon his son. 46For in the days of David and Asaph of old *there were* chiefs of the singers, and songs of praise and thanksgiving to God. 47In the days of Zerubbabel and in the days of Nehemiah all Israel gave the portions for the singers and the gatekeepers, a portion for each day. They also consecrated *holy things* for the Levites, and the Levites consecrated *them* for the children of Aaron.

On that day they read from the Book of Moses in the hearing of the people, and in it was found written that no Ammonite or Moabite should ever come into the assembly of God, 2because they had not met the children of Israel with bread and water, but hired Balaam against them to curse them. However, our God turned the curse into a blessing. 3So it was, when they had heard the Law, that they separated all the mixed multitude from Israel.

4Now before this, Eliashib the priest, having authority over the storerooms of the house of our God, *was* allied with Tobiah. 5And he had prepared for him a large room, where previously they had stored the grain offerings, the frankincense, the articles, the tithes of grain, the new wine and oil, which were commanded *to be given* to the Levites and singers and gatekeepers, and the offerings for the priests. 6But during all this I was not in Jerusalem, for in the thirty-second year of Artaxerxes king of Babylon I had returned to the king. Then after certain days I obtained leave from the king, 7and I came to Jerusalem and discovered the evil that Eliashib had done for Tobiah, in preparing a room for him in the courts of the house of God. 8And it grieved me bitterly; therefore I threw all the household goods of Tobiah out of the room. 9Then I commanded them to cleanse the rooms; and I brought back into them the articles of the house of God, with the grain offering and the frankincense.

10I also realized that the portions for the Levites had not been given *them;* for each of the Levites and the singers who did the work had gone back to his field. ¹¹So I contended with the rulers, and said, "Why is the house of God forsaken?" And I gathered them together and set them in their place. ¹²Then all Judah brought the tithe of the grain and the new wine and the oil to the storehouse. ¹³And I appointed as treasurers over the storehouse Shelemiah the priest and Zadok the scribe, and of the Levites, Pedaiah; and next to them *was* Hanan the son of Zaccur, the son of Mattaniah; for they were considered faithful, and their task *was* to distribute to their brethren.

¹⁴Remember me, O my God, concerning this, and do not wipe out my good deeds that I have done for the house of my God, and for its services!

¹⁵In those days I saw *people* in Judah treading wine presses on the Sabbath, and bringing in sheaves, and loading donkeys with wine, grapes, figs, and all *kinds of* burdens, which they brought into Jerusalem on the Sabbath day. And I warned *them* about the day on which they were selling provisions. ¹⁶Men of Tyre dwelt there also, who brought in fish and all kinds of goods, and sold *them* on the Sabbath to the children of Judah, and in Jerusalem.

¹⁷Then I contended with the nobles of Judah, and said to them, "What evil thing *is* this that you do, by which you profane the Sabbath day? ¹⁸Did not your fathers do thus, and did not our God bring all this disaster on us and on this city? Yet you bring added wrath on Israel by profaning the Sabbath."

¹⁹So it was, at the gates of Jerusalem, as it began to be dark before the Sabbath, that I commanded the gates to be shut, and charged that they must not be opened till after the Sabbath. Then I posted *some* of my servants at the gates, *so that* no burdens would be brought in on the Sabbath day. ²⁰Now the merchants and sellers of all kinds of wares lodged outside Jerusalem once or twice.

²¹Then I warned them, and said to them, "Why do you spend the night around the wall? If you do *so* again, I will lay hands on you!" From that time on they came no *more* on the Sabbath. ²²And I commanded the Levites that they should cleanse themselves, and that they should go and guard the gates, to sanctify the Sabbath day.

Remember me, O my God, *concerning* this also, and spare me according to the greatness of Your mercy!

²³In those days I also saw Jews *who* had married women of Ashdod, Ammon, *and* Moab. ²⁴And half of their children spoke the language of Ashdod, and could not speak the language of Judah, but spoke according to the language of one or the other people.

²⁵So I contended with them and cursed them, struck some of them and pulled out their hair, and made them swear by God, *saying,* "You shall not give your daughters as wives to their sons, nor take their daughters for your sons or yourselves. ²⁶Did not Solomon king of Israel sin by these things? Yet among many nations there was no king like him, who was beloved of his God; and God made him king over all Israel. Nevertheless pagan women caused even him to sin. ²⁷Should we then hear of your doing all this great evil, transgressing against our God by marrying pagan women?"

²⁸And *one* of the sons of Joiada, the son of Eliashib the high priest, *was* a son-in-law of Sanballat the Horonite; therefore I drove him from me.

²⁹Remember them, O my God, because they have defiled the priesthood and the covenant of the priesthood and the Levites.

³⁰Thus I cleansed them of everything pagan. I also assigned duties to the priests and the Levites, each to his service, ³¹and *to bringing* the wood offering and the firstfruits at appointed times.

Remember me, O my God, for good!

1 CORINTHIANS 11:3-16

Bᴜᴛ I want you to know that the head of every man is Christ, the head of woman *is* man, and the head of Christ *is* God. ⁴Every man praying or prophesying, having *his* head covered, dishonors his head. ⁵But every woman who prays or prophesies with *her* head uncovered dishonors her head, for that is one and the same as if her head were shaved. ⁶For if a woman is not covered, let her also be shorn. But if it is shameful for a woman to be shorn or shaved, let her be covered. ⁷For a man indeed ought not to cover *his* head, since he is the image and glory of God; but woman is the glory of man. ⁸For man is not from woman, but woman from man. ⁹Nor was man created for the woman, but woman for the man. ¹⁰For this reason the woman ought to have *a symbol of* authority on *her* head, because of the angels. ¹¹Nevertheless, neither *is* man independent of woman, nor woman independent of man, in the Lord. ¹²For as woman *came* from man, even so man also *comes* through woman; but all things are from God.

¹³Judge among yourselves. Is it proper for a woman to pray to God with her head uncovered? ¹⁴Does not even nature itself teach you that if a man has long hair, it is a dishonor to him? ¹⁵But if a woman has long hair, it is a glory to her; for *her* hair is given to her* for a covering. ¹⁶But if anyone seems to be contentious, we have no such custom, nor *do* the churches of God.

PSALM 35:1-16

A Psalm of David.

Pʟᴇᴀᴅ *my cause,* O Lᴏʀᴅ, with those who strive with me; Fight against those who fight against me.

2 Take hold of shield and buckler,
And stand up for my help.
3 Also draw out the spear,
And stop those who pursue me.
Say to my soul,
"I *am* your salvation."

4 Let those be put to shame and brought to dishonor
Who seek after my life;
Let those be turned back and brought to confusion
Who plot my hurt.
5 Let them be like chaff before the wind,
And let the angel* of the Lᴏʀᴅ chase *them.*
6 Let their way be dark and slippery,
And let the angel of the Lᴏʀᴅ pursue them.
7 For without cause they have hidden their net for me *in* a pit,
Which they have dug without cause for my life.
8 Let destruction come upon him unexpectedly,
And let his net that he has hidden catch himself;
Into that very destruction let him fall.

9 And my soul shall be joyful in the Lᴏʀᴅ;
It shall rejoice in His salvation.
10 All my bones shall say,
"Lᴏʀᴅ, who *is* like You,
Delivering the poor from him who is too strong for him,
Yes, the poor and the needy from him who plunders him?"

11 Fierce witnesses rise up;
They ask me *things* that I do not know.
12 They reward me evil for good,

To the sorrow of my soul.
13 But as for me, when they
were sick,
My clothing *was* sackcloth;
I humbled myself with fasting;
And my prayer would return
to my own heart.
14 I paced about as though *he*
were my friend *or* brother;
I bowed down heavily, as one
who mourns *for his* mother.

15 But in my adversity they
rejoiced
And gathered together;
Attackers gathered against
me,
And I did not know *it;*
They tore *at me* and did not
cease;
16 With ungodly mockers at
feasts
They gnashed at me with
their teeth.

PROVERBS FOR TODAY/ 21:17-18

He who loves pleasure will be *a poor man; he who loves wine and oil will not be*
rich. The wicked shall be *a ransom for the righteous, and the unfaithful for the*
upright.

AUGUST 18

ESTHER 1:1–3:15

Now it came to pass in the days of Ahasuerus* (this *was* the Ahasuerus who reigned over one hundred and twenty-seven provinces, from India to Ethiopia), ²in those days when King Ahasuerus sat on the throne of his kingdom, which *was* in Shushan* the citadel, ³*that* in the third year of his reign he made a feast for all his officials and servants— the powers of Persia and Media, the nobles, and the princes of the provinces *being* before him— ⁴when he showed the riches of his glorious kingdom and the splendor of his excellent majesty for many days, one hundred and eighty days *in all.*

⁵And when these days were completed, the king made a feast lasting seven days for all the people who were present in Shushan the citadel, from great to small, in the court of the garden of the king's palace. ⁶*There were* white and blue linen *curtains* fastened with cords of fine linen and purple on silver rods and marble pillars; *and the* couches *were* of gold and silver on a *mosaic* pavement of alabaster, turquoise, and white and black marble. ⁷And they served drinks in golden vessels, each vessel being different from the other, with royal wine in abundance, according to the generosity of the king. ⁸In accordance with the law, the drinking was not compulsory; for so the king had ordered all the officers of his household, that they should do according to each man's pleasure.

⁹Queen Vashti also made a feast for the women *in* the royal palace which *belonged* to King Ahasuerus.

¹⁰On the seventh day, when the heart of the king was merry with wine, he commanded Mehuman, Biztha, Harbona, Bigtha, Abagtha, Zethar, and Carcas, seven eunuchs who served in the presence of King Ahasuerus, ¹¹to bring Queen Vashti before the king,

wearing her royal crown, in order to show her beauty to the people and the officials, for she *was* beautiful to behold. [12]But Queen Vashti refused to come at the king's command *brought* by *his* eunuchs; therefore the king was furious, and his anger burned within him.

[13]Then the king said to the wise men who understood the times (for this *was* the king's manner toward all who knew law and justice, [14]those closest to him *being* Carshena, Shethar, Admatha, Tarshish, Meres, Marsena, and Memucan, the seven princes of Persia and Media, who had access to the king's presence, *and* who ranked highest in the kingdom): [15]"What *shall we* do to Queen Vashti, according to law, because she did not obey the command of King Ahasuerus *brought to her* by the eunuchs?"

[16]And Memucan answered before the king and the princes: "Queen Vashti has not only wronged the king, but also all the princes, and all the people who *are* in all the provinces of King Ahasuerus. [17]For the queen's behavior will become known to all women, so that they will despise their husbands in their eyes, when they report, 'King Ahasuerus commanded Queen Vashti to be brought in before him, but she did not come.' [18]This very day the *noble* ladies of Persia and Media will say to all the king's officials that they have heard of the behavior of the queen. Thus *there will be* excessive contempt and wrath. [19]If it pleases the king, let a royal decree go out from him, and let it be recorded in the laws of the Persians and the Medes, so that it will not be altered, that Vashti shall come no more before King Ahasuerus; and let the king give her royal position to another who is better than she. [20]When the king's decree which he will make is proclaimed throughout all his empire (for it is great), all wives will honor their husbands, both great and small."

[21]And the reply pleased the king and the princes, and the king did according to the word of Memucan. [22]Then he sent letters to all the king's provinces, to each province in its own script, and to every people in their own language, that each man should be master in his own house, and speak in the language of his own people.

AFTER these things, when the wrath of King Ahasuerus subsided, he remembered Vashti, what she had done, and what had been decreed against her. [2]Then the king's servants who attended him said: "Let beautiful young virgins be sought for the king; [3]and let the king appoint officers in all the provinces of his kingdom, that they may gather all the beautiful young virgins to Shushan the citadel, into the women's quarters, under the custody of Hegai* the king's eunuch, custodian of the women. And let beauty preparations be given *them.* [4]Then let the young woman who pleases the king be queen instead of Vashti."

This thing pleased the king, and he did so.

[5]In Shushan the citadel there was a certain Jew whose name *was* Mordecai the son of Jair, the son of Shimei, the son of Kish, a Benjamite. [6]*Kish** had been carried away from Jerusalem with the captives who had been captured with Jeconiah* king of Judah, whom Nebuchadnezzar the king of Babylon had carried away. [7]And *Mordecai* had brought up Hadassah, that *is,* Esther, his uncle's daughter, for she had neither father nor mother. The young woman *was* lovely and beautiful. When her father and mother died, Mordecai took her as his own daughter.

[8]So it was, when the king's command and decree were heard, and when many young women were gath-

ered at Shushan the citadel, *under* the custody of Hegai, that Esther also was taken to the king's palace, into the care of Hegai the custodian of the women. 9Now the young woman pleased him, and she obtained his favor; so he readily gave beauty preparations to her, besides her allowance. Then seven choice maidservants were provided for her from the king's palace, and he moved her and her maidservants to the best *place* in the house of the women.

10Esther had not revealed her people or family, for Mordecai had charged her not to reveal *it.* 11And every day Mordecai paced in front of the court of the women's quarters, to learn of Esther's welfare and what was happening to her.

12Each young woman's turn came to go in to King Ahasuerus after she had completed twelve months' preparation, according to the regulations for the women, for thus were the days of their preparation apportioned: six months with oil of myrrh, and six months with perfumes and preparations for beautifying women. 13Thus *prepared, each* young woman went to the king, and she was given whatever she desired to take with her from the women's quarters to the king's palace. 14In the evening she went, and in the morning she returned to the second house of the women, to the custody of Shaashgaz, the king's eunuch who kept the concubines. She would not go in to the king again unless the king delighted in her and called for her by name.

15Now when the turn came for Esther the daughter of Abihail the uncle of Mordecai, who had taken her as his daughter, to go in to the king, she requested nothing but what Hegai the king's eunuch, the custodian of the women, advised. And Esther obtained favor in the sight of all who saw her. 16So Esther was taken to King Aha-

suerus, into his royal palace, in the tenth month, which *is* the month of Tebeth, in the seventh year of his reign. 17The king loved Esther more than all the *other* women, and she obtained grace and favor in his sight more than all the virgins; so he set the royal crown upon her head and made her queen instead of Vashti. 18Then the king made a great feast, the Feast of Esther, for all his officials and servants; and he proclaimed a holiday in the provinces and gave gifts according to the generosity of a king.

19When virgins were gathered together a second time, Mordecai sat within the king's gate. 20*Now* Esther had not revealed her family and her people, just as Mordecai had charged her, for Esther obeyed the command of Mordecai as when she was brought up by him.

21In those days, while Mordecai sat within the king's gate, two of the king's eunuchs, Bigthan and Teresh, doorkeepers, became furious and sought to lay hands on King Ahasuerus. 22So the matter became known to Mordecai, who told Queen Esther, and Esther informed the king in Mordecai's name. 23And when an inquiry was made into the matter, it was confirmed, and both were hanged on a gallows; and it was written in the book of the chronicles in the presence of the king.

AFTER these things King Ahasuerus promoted Haman, the son of Hammedatha the Agagite, and advanced him and set his seat above all the princes who *were* with him. 2And all the king's servants who *were* within the king's gate bowed and paid homage to Haman, for so the king had commanded concerning him. But Mordecai would not bow or pay homage. 3Then the king's servants who *were* within the king's gate said to Mordecai, "Why do you transgress the king's command?" 4Now it happened, when they spoke to him daily and he would not listen to them, that they told *it* to Haman, to see whether Mordecai's words would stand; for *Mordecai* had told them that he *was* a Jew. ⁵When Haman saw that Mordecai did not bow or pay him homage, Haman was filled with wrath. ⁶But he disdained to lay hands on Mordecai alone, for they had told him of the people of Mordecai. Instead, Haman sought to destroy all the Jews who *were* throughout the whole kingdom of Ahasuerus—the people of Mordecai.

⁷In the first month, which is the month of Nisan, in the twelfth year of King Ahasuerus, they cast Pur (that *is,* the lot), before Haman to determine the day and the month,* until *it fell on the* twelfth *month,** which *is* the month of Adar.

⁸Then Haman said to King Ahasuerus, "There is a certain people scattered and dispersed among the people in all the provinces of your kingdom; their laws *are* different from all *other* people's, and they do not keep the king's laws. Therefore it *is* not fitting for the king to let them remain. ⁹If it pleases the king, let *a decree* be written that they be destroyed, and I will pay ten thousand talents of silver into the hands of those who do the work, to bring *it* into the king's treasuries."

¹⁰So the king took his signet ring from his hand and gave it to Haman, the son of Hammedatha the Agagite, the enemy of the Jews. ¹¹And the king said to Haman, "The money and the people *are* given to you, to do with them as seems good to you."

¹²Then the king's scribes were called on the thirteenth day of the first month, and *a decree* was written according to all that Haman commanded—to the king's satraps, to the governors who *were* over each province, to the officials of all people, to every province according to its script, and to every people in their language.

In the name of King Ahasuerus it was written, and sealed with the king's signet ring. ¹³And the letters were sent by couriers into all the king's provinces, to destroy, to kill, and to annihilate all the Jews, both young and old, little children and women, in one day, on the thirteenth *day* of the twelfth *month,* which *is* the month of Adar, and to plunder their possessions.* ¹⁴A copy of the document was to be issued as law in every province, being published for all people, that they should be ready for that day. ¹⁵The couriers went out, hastened by the king's command; and the decree was proclaimed in Shushan the citadel. So the king and Haman sat down to drink, but the city of Shushan was perplexed.

1 CORINTHIANS 11:17-34

Now in giving these instructions I do not praise *you,* since you come together not for the better but for the worse. ¹⁸For first of all, when you come together as a church, I hear that there are divisions among you, and in part I believe it. ¹⁹For there must also be factions among you, that those who are approved may be recognized among you. ²⁰Therefore when you come together in one place, it is not to eat the Lord's Supper. ²¹For in eating, each one takes his own supper ahead of *others;* and one is hungry and another is drunk. ²²What! Do you not have houses to eat and drink in? Or do you despise the church of God and shame those who have nothing? What shall I say to you? Shall I praise you in this? I do not praise *you.*

²³For I received from the Lord that which I also delivered to you: that the Lord Jesus on the *same* night in which He was betrayed took bread; ²⁴and when He had given thanks, He broke *it* and said, "Take, eat;* this is My body which is broken* for you; do this in remembrance of Me." ²⁵In the

same manner *He* also *took* the cup after supper, saying, "This cup is the new covenant in My blood. This do, as often as you drink *it,* in remembrance of Me."

²⁶For as often as you eat this bread and drink this cup, you proclaim the Lord's death till He comes.

²⁷Therefore whoever eats this bread or drinks *this* cup of the Lord in an unworthy manner will be guilty of the body and blood* of the Lord. ²⁸But let a man examine himself, and so let him eat of the bread and drink of the cup. ²⁹For he who eats and drinks in an unworthy manner* eats and drinks judgment to himself, not discerning the Lord's* body. ³⁰For this reason many *are* weak and sick among you, and many sleep. ³¹For if we would judge ourselves, we would not be judged. ³²But when we are judged, we are chastened by the Lord, that we may not be condemned with the world.

³³Therefore, my brethren, when you come together to eat, wait for one another. ³⁴But if anyone is hungry, let him eat at home, lest you come together for judgment. And the rest I will set in order when I come.

PSALM 35:17-28

L ORD, how long will You look on? Rescue me from their destructions,
My precious *life* from the lions.

18 I will give You thanks in the great assembly;
I will praise You among many people.

19 Let them not rejoice over me who are wrongfully my enemies;
Nor let them wink with the eye who hate me without a cause.

20 For they do not speak peace,
But they devise deceitful matters
Against *the* quiet ones in the land.

21 They also opened their mouth wide against me,
And said, "Aha, aha!
Our eyes have seen *it.*"

22 *This* You have seen, O LORD;
Do not keep silence.
O Lord, do not be far from me.

23 Stir up Yourself, and awake to my vindication,
To my cause, my God and my Lord.

24 Vindicate me, O LORD my God, according to Your righteousness;
And let them not rejoice over me.

25 Let them not say in their hearts, "Ah, so we would have it!"
Let them not say, "We have swallowed him up."

26 Let them be ashamed and brought to mutual confusion
Who rejoice at my hurt;
Let them be clothed with shame and dishonor
Who exalt themselves against me.

27 Let them shout for joy and be glad,
Who favor my righteous cause;
And let them say continually,
"Let the LORD be magnified,
Who has pleasure in the prosperity of His servant."

28 And my tongue shall speak of Your righteousness
And of Your praise all the day long.

PROVERBS FOR TODAY/ 21:19-20

Better to dwell in the wilderness, than with a contentious and angry woman.
There is *desirable treasure, and oil in the dwelling of the wise, but a foolish man*
squanders it.

AUGUST 19

ESTHER 4:1–7:10

WHEN Mordecai learned all that had happened, he tore his clothes and put on sackcloth and ashes, and went out into the midst of the city. He cried out with a loud and bitter cry. ²He went as far as the front of the king's gate, for no one *might* enter the king's gate clothed with sackcloth. ³And in every province where the king's command and decree arrived, *there was* great mourning among the Jews, with fasting, weeping, and wailing; and many lay in sackcloth and ashes.

⁴So Esther's maids and eunuchs came and told her, and the queen was deeply distressed. Then she sent garments to clothe Mordecai and take his sackcloth away from him, but he would not accept *them.* ⁵Then Esther called Hathach, *one* of the king's eunuchs whom he had appointed to attend her, and she gave him a command concerning Mordecai, to learn what and why this *was.* ⁶So Hathach went out to Mordecai in the city square that *was* in front of the king's gate. ⁷And Mordecai told him all that had happened to him, and the sum of money that Haman had promised to pay into the king's treasuries to destroy the Jews. ⁸He also gave him a copy of the written decree for their destruction, which was given at Shushan, that he might show it to Esther and explain it to her, and that he might command her to go in to the king to make supplication to him and plead before him for her people. ⁹So Hathach returned and told Esther the words of Mordecai.

¹⁰Then Esther spoke to Hathach, and gave him a command for Mordecai: ¹¹"All the king's servants and the people of the king's provinces know that any man or woman who goes into the inner court to the king, who has not been called, *he has* but one law: put *all* to death, except the one to whom the king holds out the golden scepter, that he may live. Yet I myself have not been called to go in to the king these thirty days." ¹²So they told Mordecai Esther's words.

¹³And Mordecai told *them* to answer Esther: "Do not think in your heart that you will escape in the king's palace any more than all the other Jews. ¹⁴For if you remain completely silent at this time, relief and deliverance will arise for the Jews from another place, but you and your father's house will perish. Yet who knows whether you have come to the kingdom for *such* a time as this?"

¹⁵Then Esther told *them* to reply to Mordecai: ¹⁶"Go, gather all the Jews who are present in Shushan, and fast for me; neither eat nor drink for three days, night or day. My maids and I will fast likewise. And so I will go to the king, which *is* against the law; and if I perish, I perish!"

¹⁷So Mordecai went his way and did according to all that Esther commanded him.*

Now it happened on the third day that Esther put on *her* royal *robes* and stood in the inner court of the king's palace, across from the king's house, while the king sat on his royal throne in the royal house, facing the entrance of the house.* ²So it was, when the king saw Queen Esther standing in the court, *that* she found favor in his sight, and the king held out to Esther the golden scepter that *was* in his hand. Then Esther went near and touched the top of the scepter.

³And the king said to her, "What do you wish, Queen Esther? What *is* your request? It shall be given to you—up to half the kingdom!"

⁴So Esther answered, "If it pleases the king, let the king and Haman come today to the banquet that I have prepared for him."

⁵Then the king said, "Bring Haman quickly, that he may do as Esther has said." So the king and Haman went to the banquet that Esther had prepared.

⁶At the banquet of wine the king said to Esther, "What *is* your petition? It shall be granted you. What *is* your request, up to half the kingdom? It shall be done!"

⁷Then Esther answered and said, "My petition and request *is this:* ⁸If I have found favor in the sight of the king, and if it pleases the king to grant my petition and fulfill my request, then let the king and Haman come to the banquet which I will prepare for them, and tomorrow I will do as the king has said."

⁹So Haman went out that day joyful and with a glad heart; but when Haman saw Mordecai in the king's gate, and that he did not stand or tremble before him, he was filled with indignation against Mordecai. ¹⁰Nevertheless Haman restrained himself and went home, and he sent and called for his friends and his wife Zeresh. ¹¹Then Haman told them of his great riches, the multitude of his children,

everything in which the king had promoted him, and how he had advanced him above the officials and servants of the king.

¹²Moreover Haman said, "Besides, Queen Esther invited no one but me to come in with the king to the banquet that she prepared; and tomorrow I am again invited by her, along with the king. ¹³Yet all this avails me nothing, so long as I see Mordecai the Jew sitting at the king's gate."

¹⁴Then his wife Zeresh and all his friends said to him, "Let a gallows be made, fifty cubits high, and in the morning suggest to the king that Mordecai be hanged on it; then go merrily with the king to the banquet."

And the thing pleased Haman; so he had the gallows made.

THAT night the king could not sleep. So one was commanded to bring the book of the records of the chronicles; and they were read before the king. ²And it was found written that Mordecai had told of Bigthana and Teresh, two of the king's eunuchs, the doorkeepers who had sought to lay hands on King Ahasuerus. ³Then the king said, "What honor or dignity has been bestowed on Mordecai for this?"

And the king's servants who attended him said, "Nothing has been done for him."

⁴So the king said, "Who *is* in the court?" Now Haman had *just* entered the outer court of the king's palace to suggest that the king hang Mordecai on the gallows that he had prepared for him.

⁵The king's servants said to him, "Haman is there, standing in the court."

And the king said, "Let him come in."

⁶So Haman came in, and the king asked him, "What shall be done for the man whom the king delights to honor?"

Now Haman thought in his heart, "Whom would the king delight to honor more than me?" ⁷And Haman answered the king, "*For* the man whom the king delights to honor, ⁸let a royal robe be brought which the king has worn, and a horse on which the king has ridden, which has a royal crest placed on its head. ⁹Then let this robe and horse be delivered to the hand of one of the king's most noble princes, that he may array the man whom the king delights to honor. Then parade him on horseback through the city square, and proclaim before him: 'Thus shall it be done to the man whom the king delights to honor!' "

¹⁰Then the king said to Haman, "Hurry, take the robe and the horse, as you have suggested, and do so for Mordecai the Jew who sits within the king's gate! Leave nothing undone of all that you have spoken."

¹¹So Haman took the robe and the horse, arrayed Mordecai and led him on horseback through the city square, and proclaimed before him, "Thus shall it be done to the man whom the king delights to honor!"

¹²Afterward Mordecai went back to the king's gate. But Haman hurried to his house, mourning and with his head covered. ¹³When Haman told his wife Zeresh and all his friends everything that had happened to him, his wise men and his wife Zeresh said to him, "If Mordecai, before whom you have begun to fall, is of Jewish descent, you will not prevail against him but will surely fall before him."

¹⁴While they *were* still talking with him, the king's eunuchs came, and hastened to bring Haman to the banquet which Esther had prepared.

So the king and Haman went to dine with Queen Esther. ²And on the second day, at the banquet of wine, the king again said to Esther, "What *is* your petition, Queen Esther? It shall be granted you. And what *is* your request, up to half the kingdom? It shall be done!"

³Then Queen Esther answered and said, "If I have found favor in your sight, O king, and if it pleases the king, let my life be given me at my petition, and my people at my request. ⁴For we have been sold, my people and I, to be destroyed, to be killed, and to be annihilated. Had we been sold as male and female slaves, I would have held my tongue, although the enemy could never compensate for the king's loss."

⁵So King Ahasuerus answered and said to Queen Esther, "Who is he, and where is he, who would dare presume in his heart to do such a thing?"

⁶And Esther said, "The adversary and enemy *is* this wicked Haman!"

So Haman was terrified before the king and queen.

⁷Then the king arose in his wrath from the banquet of wine *and went* into the palace garden; but Haman stood before Queen Esther, pleading for his life, for he saw that evil was determined against him by the king. ⁸When the king returned from the palace garden to the place of the banquet of wine, Haman had fallen across the couch where Esther *was*. Then the king said, "Will he also assault the queen while I *am* in the house?"

As the word left the king's mouth, they covered Haman's face. ⁹Now Harbonah, one of the eunuchs, said to the king, "Look! The gallows, fifty cubits high, which Haman made for Mordecai, who spoke good on the king's behalf, is standing at the house of Haman."

Then the king said, "Hang him on it!"

¹⁰So they hanged Haman on the gallows that he had prepared for Mordecai. Then the king's wrath subsided.

1 CORINTHIANS 12:1-26

Now concerning spiritual *gifts,* brethren, I do not want you to be ignorant: [2]You know that* you were Gentiles, carried away to these dumb idols, however you were led. [3]Therefore I make known to you that no one speaking by the Spirit of God calls Jesus accursed, and no one can say that Jesus is Lord except by the Holy Spirit.

[4]There are diversities of gifts, but the same Spirit. [5]There are differences of ministries, but the same Lord. [6]And there are diversities of activities, but it is the same God who works all in all. [7]But the manifestation of the Spirit is given to each one for the profit *of all:* [8]for to one is given the word of wisdom through the Spirit, to another the word of knowledge through the same Spirit, [9]to another faith by the same Spirit, to another gifts of healings by the same* Spirit, [10]to another the working of miracles, to another prophecy, to another discerning of spirits, to another *different* kinds of tongues, to another the interpretation of tongues. [11]But one and the same Spirit works all these things, distributing to each one individually as He wills.

[12]For as the body is one and has many members, but all the members of that one body, being many, are one body, so also *is* Christ. [13]For by one Spirit we were all baptized into one body—whether Jews or Greeks, whether slaves or free—and have all been made to drink into* one Spirit. [14]For in fact the body is not one member but many.

[15]If the foot should say, "Because I am not a hand, I am not of the body," is it therefore not of the body? [16]And if the ear should say, "Because I am not an eye, I am not of the body," is it therefore not of the body? [17]If the whole body *were* an eye, where *would be* the hearing? If the whole *were* hearing, where *would be* the smelling? [18]But now God has set the members, each one of them, in the body just as He pleased. [19]And if they *were* all one member, where *would* the body *be?*

[20]But now indeed *there are* many members, yet one body. [21]And the eye cannot say to the hand, "I have no need of you"; nor again the head to the feet, "I have no need of you." [22]No, much rather, those members of the body which seem to be weaker are necessary. [23]And those *members* of the body which we think to be less honorable, on these we bestow greater honor; and our unpresentable *parts* have greater modesty, [24]but our presentable *parts* have no need. But God composed the body, having given greater honor to that *part* which lacks it, [25]that there should be no schism in the body, but *that* the members should have the same care for one another. [26]And if one member suffers, all the members suffer with *it;* or if one member is honored, all the members rejoice with *it.*

PSALM 36:1-12

To the Chief Musician. A Psalm of David the servant of the LORD.

AN oracle within my heart concerning the transgression of the wicked:
There is no fear of God before his eyes.

2 For he flatters himself in his own eyes,
When he finds out his iniquity *and* when he hates.

3 The words of his mouth *are* wickedness and deceit;
He has ceased to be wise *and* to do good.

4 He devises wickedness on his bed;
He sets himself in a way *that is* not good;
He does not abhor evil.

5 Your mercy, O Lord, *is* in the
heavens;
Your faithfulness *reaches* to
the clouds.
6 Your righteousness *is* like the
great mountains;
Your judgments *are* a great
deep;
O Lord, You preserve man
and beast.

7 How precious *is* Your
lovingkindness, O God!
Therefore the children of men
put their trust under the
shadow of Your wings.
8 They are abundantly satisfied
with the fullness of Your
house,
And You give them drink

from the river of Your
pleasures.
9 For with You *is* the fountain of
life;
In Your light we see light.

10 Oh, continue Your
lovingkindness to those
who know You,
And Your righteousness to
the upright in heart.
11 Let not the foot of pride come
against me,
And let not the hand of the
wicked drive me away.
12 There the workers of iniquity
have fallen;
They have been cast down
and are not able to rise.

PROVERBS FOR TODAY/ 21:21-22

He who follows righteousness and mercy finds life, righteousness and honor. A wise
man *scales the city of the mighty, and brings down the trusted stronghold.*

AUGUST 20

ESTHER 8:1–10:3

ON that day King Ahasuerus
gave Queen Esther the house
of Haman, the enemy of the
Jews. And Mordecai came before the
king, for Esther had told how he *was
related* to her. [2]So the king took off his
signet ring, which he had taken from
Haman, and gave it to Mordecai; and
Esther appointed Mordecai over the
house of Haman.

[3]Now Esther spoke again to the
king, fell down at his feet, and implored him with tears to counteract the
evil of Haman the Agagite, and the
scheme which he had devised against
the Jews. [4]And the king held out the

golden scepter toward Esther. So Esther arose and stood before the king,
[5]and said, "If it pleases the king, and if
I have found favor in his sight and if
the thing *seems* right to the king and I am
pleasing in his eyes, let it be written to
revoke the letters devised by Haman,
the son of Hammedatha the Agagite,
which he wrote to annihilate the Jews
who *are* in all the king's provinces.
[6]For how can I endure to see the evil
that will come to my people? Or how
can I endure to see the destruction of
my countrymen?"

[7]Then King Ahasuerus said to
Queen Esther and Mordecai the Jew,
"Indeed, I have given Esther the house
of Haman, and they have hanged him

on the gallows because he *tried to* lay his hand on the Jews. ⁸You yourselves write *a decree* concerning the Jews, as you please, in the king's name, and seal *it* with the king's signet ring; for whatever is written in the king's name and sealed with the king's signet ring no one can revoke."

⁹So the king's scribes were called at that time, in the third month, which *is* the month of Sivan, on the twenty-third *day;* and it was written, according to all that Mordecai commanded, to the Jews, the satraps, the governors, and the princes of the provinces from India to Ethiopia, one hundred and twenty-seven provinces *in all,* to every province in its own script, to every people in their own language, and to the Jews in their own script and language. ¹⁰And he wrote in the name of King Ahasuerus, sealed *it* with the king's signet ring, and sent letters by couriers on horseback, riding on royal horses bred from swift steeds.*

¹¹By these letters the king permitted the Jews who *were* in every city to gather together and protect their lives—to destroy, kill, and annihilate all the forces of any people or province that would assault them, *both* little children and women, and to plunder their possessions, ¹²on one day in all the provinces of King Ahasuerus, on the thirteenth *day* of the twelfth month, which *is* the month of Adar.* ¹³A copy of the document was to be issued as a decree in every province and published for all people, so that the Jews would be ready on that day to avenge themselves on their enemies. ¹⁴The couriers who rode on royal horses went out, hastened and pressed on by the king's command. And the decree was issued in Shushan the citadel.

¹⁵So Mordecai went out from the presence of the king in royal apparel of blue and white, with a great crown of gold and a garment of fine linen and purple; and the city of Shushan rejoiced and was glad. ¹⁶The Jews had light and gladness, joy and honor. ¹⁷And in every province and city, wherever the king's command and decree came, the Jews had joy and gladness, a feast and a holiday. Then many of the people of the land became Jews, because fear of the Jews fell upon them.

Now in the twelfth month, that *is,* the month of Adar, on the thirteenth day, *the time* came for the king's command and his decree to be executed. On the day that the enemies of the Jews had hoped to overpower them, the opposite occurred, in that the Jews themselves overpowered those who hated them. ²The Jews gathered together in their cities throughout all the provinces of King Ahasuerus to lay hands on those who sought their harm. And no one could withstand them, because fear of them fell upon all people. ³And all the officials of the provinces, the satraps, the governors, and all those doing the king's work, helped the Jews, because the fear of Mordecai fell upon them. ⁴For Mordecai *was* great in the king's palace, and his fame spread throughout all the provinces; for this man Mordecai became increasingly prominent. ⁵Thus the Jews defeated all their enemies with the stroke of the sword, with slaughter and destruction, and did what they pleased with those who hated them.

⁶And in Shushan the citadel the Jews killed and destroyed five hundred men. ⁷Also Parshandatha, Dalphon, Aspatha, ⁸Poratha, Adalia, Aridatha, ⁹Parmashta, Arisai, Aridai, and Vajezatha— ¹⁰the ten sons of Haman the son of Hammedatha, the enemy of the Jews—they killed; but they did not lay a hand on the plunder.

¹¹On that day the number of those who were killed in Shushan the citadel was brought to the king. ¹²And the king said to Queen Esther, "The Jews have killed and destroyed five hun-

dred men in Shushan the citadel, and the ten sons of Haman. What have they done in the rest of the king's provinces? Now what *is* your petition? It shall be granted to you. Or what *is* your further request? It shall be done."

¹³Then Esther said, "If it pleases the king, let it be granted to the Jews who *are* in Shushan to do again tomorrow according to today's decree, and let Haman's ten sons be hanged on the gallows."

¹⁴So the king commanded this to be done; the decree was issued in Shushan, and they hanged Haman's ten sons.

¹⁵And the Jews who *were* in Shushan gathered together again on the fourteenth day of the month of Adar and killed three hundred men at Shushan; but they did not lay a hand on the plunder.

¹⁶The remainder of the Jews in the king's provinces gathered together and protected their lives, had rest from their enemies, and killed seventy-five thousand of their enemies; but they did not lay a hand on the plunder. ¹⁷*This was* on the thirteenth day of the month of Adar. And on the fourteenth of *the month** they rested and made it a day of feasting and gladness.

¹⁸But the Jews who *were* at Shushan assembled together on the thirteenth *day,* as well as on the fourteenth; and on the fifteenth of *the month** they rested, and made it a day of feasting and gladness. ¹⁹Therefore the Jews of the villages who dwelt in the unwalled towns celebrated the fourteenth day of the month of Adar *with* gladness and feasting, as a holiday, and for sending presents to one another.

²⁰And Mordecai wrote these things and sent letters to all the Jews, near and far, who *were* in all the provinces of King Ahasuerus, ²¹to establish among them that they should celebrate yearly the fourteenth and fifteenth days of the month of Adar, ²²as the days on

which the Jews had rest from their enemies, as the month which was turned from sorrow to joy for them, and from mourning to a holiday; that they should make them days of feasting and joy, of sending presents to one another and gifts to the poor. ²³So the Jews accepted the custom which they had begun, as Mordecai had written to them, ²⁴because Haman, the son of Hammedatha the Agagite, the enemy of all the Jews, had plotted against the Jews to annihilate them, and had cast Pur (that *is,* the lot), to consume them and destroy them; ²⁵but when *Esther** came before the king, he commanded by letter that this* wicked plot which *Haman* had devised against the Jews should return on his own head, and that he and his sons should be hanged on the gallows.

²⁶So they called these days Purim, after the name Pur. Therefore, because of all the words of this letter, what they had seen concerning this matter, and what had happened to them, ²⁷the Jews established and imposed it upon themselves and their descendants and all who would join them, that without fail they should celebrate these two days every year, according to the written *instructions* and according to the *prescribed* time, ²⁸*that* these days *should be* remembered and kept throughout every generation, every family, every province, and every city, that these days of Purim should not fail *to be observed* among the Jews, and *that* the memory of them should not perish among their descendants.

²⁹Then Queen Esther, the daughter of Abihail, with Mordecai the Jew, wrote with full authority to confirm this second letter about Purim. ³⁰And *Mordecai* sent letters to all the Jews, to the one hundred and twenty-seven provinces of the kingdom of Ahasuerus, *with* words of peace and truth, ³¹to confirm these days of Purim at their *appointed* time, as Mordecai the

Jew and Queen Esther had prescribed for them, and as they had decreed for themselves and their descendants concerning matters of their fasting and lamenting. 32So the decree of Esther confirmed these matters of Purim, and it was written in the book.

AND King Ahasuerus imposed tribute on the land and *on* the islands of the sea. 2Now all the acts of his power and his might, and the account of the greatness of Mordecai, to which the king advanced him, *are* they not written in the book of the chronicles of the kings of Media and Persia? 3For Mordecai the Jew *was* second to King Ahasuerus, and was great among the Jews and well received by the multitude of his brethren, seeking the good of his people and speaking peace to all his countrymen.*

1 CORINTHIANS 12:27–13:13

Now you are the body of Christ, and members individually. 28And God has appointed these in the church: first apostles, second prophets, third teachers, after that miracles, then gifts of healings, helps, administrations, varieties of tongues. 29*Are* all apostles? *Are* all prophets? *Are* all teachers? *Are* all workers of miracles? 30Do all have gifts of healings? Do all speak with tongues? Do all interpret? 31But earnestly desire the best* gifts. And yet I show you a more excellent way.

THOUGH I speak with the tongues of men and of angels, but have not love, I have become sounding brass or a clanging cymbal. 2And though I have *the gift of* prophecy, and understand all mysteries and all knowledge, and though I have all faith, so that I could remove mountains, but have not love, I am nothing. 3And though I bestow all my goods to feed *the poor,* and though

I give my body to be burned,* but have not love, it profits me nothing.

4Love suffers long *and* is kind; love does not envy; love does not parade itself, is not puffed up; 5does not behave rudely, does not seek its own, is not provoked, thinks no evil; 6does not rejoice in iniquity, but rejoices in the truth; 7bears all things, believes all things, hopes all things, endures all things.

8Love never fails. But whether *there are* prophecies, they will fail; whether *there are* tongues, they will cease; whether *there is* knowledge, it will vanish away. 9For we know in part and we prophesy in part. 10But when that which is perfect has come, then that which is in part will be done away.

11When I was a child, I spoke as a child, I understood as a child, I thought as a child; but when I became a man, I put away childish things. 12For now we see in a mirror, dimly, but then face to face. Now I know in part, but then I shall know just as I also am known.

13And now abide faith, hope, love, these three; but the greatest of these *is* love.

PSALM 37:1-11

A Psalm of David.

Do not fret because of evildoers,
Nor be envious of the workers of iniquity.

2   For they shall soon be cut
        down like the grass,
     And wither as the green herb.

3   Trust in the LORD, and do
        good;
     Dwell in the land, and feed on
        His faithfulness.

4   Delight yourself also in the
        LORD,
     And He shall give you the
        desires of your heart.

5 Commit your way to the LORD,
Trust also in Him,
And He shall bring *it* to pass.
6 He shall bring forth your
righteousness as the light,
And your justice as the
noonday.

7 Rest in the LORD, and wait
patiently for Him;
Do not fret because of him
who prospers in his way,
Because of the man who
brings wicked schemes to
pass.
8 Cease from anger, and
forsake wrath;

Do not fret—*it* only *causes*
harm.

9 For evildoers shall be cut off;
But those who wait on the
LORD,
They shall inherit the earth.
10 For yet a little while and the
wicked *shall be* no *more;*
Indeed, you will look carefully
for his place,
But it *shall be* no *more.*
11 But the meek shall inherit the
earth,
And shall delight themselves
in the abundance of peace.

PROVERBS FOR TODAY/ 21:23-24

Whoever guards his mouth and tongue keeps his soul from troubles. A proud and
haughty man—*"Scoffer"* is *his name; he acts with arrogant pride.*

AUGUST 21

JOB 1:1–3:26

THERE was a man in the land of Uz, whose name *was* Job; and that man was blameless and upright, and one who feared God and shunned evil. 2And seven sons and three daughters were born to him. 3Also, his possessions were seven thousand sheep, three thousand camels, five hundred yoke of oxen, five hundred female donkeys, and a very large household, so that this man was the greatest of all the people of the East.

4And his sons would go and feast *in their* houses, each on his *appointed* day, and would send and invite their three sisters to eat and drink with them. 5So it was, when the days of feasting had run their course, that Job would send and sanctify them, and he would rise early in the morning and offer burnt offerings *according to* the number of them all. For Job said, "It may be that my sons have sinned and cursed* God in their hearts." Thus Job did regularly.

6Now there was a day when the sons of God came to present themselves before the LORD, and Satan* also came among them. 7And the LORD said to Satan, "From where do you come?"

So Satan answered the LORD and said, "From going to and fro on the earth, and from walking back and forth on it."

8Then the LORD said to Satan, "Have you considered My servant Job, that *there is* none like him on the earth, a blameless and upright man, one who fears God and shuns evil?"

9So Satan answered the LORD and

said, "Does Job fear God for nothing? [10]Have You not made a hedge around him, around his household, and around all that he has on every side? You have blessed the work of his hands, and his possessions have increased in the land. [11]But now, stretch out Your hand and touch all that he has, and he will surely curse You to Your face!"

[12]And the LORD said to Satan, "Behold, all that he has *is* in your power; only do not lay a hand on his *person.*"

So Satan went out from the presence of the LORD.

[13]Now there was a day when his sons and daughters *were* eating and drinking wine in their oldest brother's house; [14]and a messenger came to Job and said, "The oxen were plowing and the donkeys feeding beside them, [15]when the Sabeans* raided *them* and took them away—indeed they have killed the servants with the edge of the sword; and I alone have escaped to tell you!"

[16]While he *was* still speaking, another also came and said, "The fire of God fell from heaven and burned up the sheep and the servants, and consumed them; and I alone have escaped to tell you!"

[17]While he *was* still speaking, another also came and said, "The Chaldeans formed three bands, raided the camels and took them away, yes, and killed the servants with the edge of the sword; and I alone have escaped to tell you!"

[18]While he *was* still speaking, another also came and said, "Your sons and daughters *were* eating and drinking wine in their oldest brother's house, [19]and suddenly a great wind came from across* the wilderness and struck the four corners of the house, and it fell on the young people, and they are dead; and I alone have escaped to tell you!"

[20]Then Job arose, tore his robe, and shaved his head; and he fell to the ground and worshiped. [21]And he said:

> "Naked I came from my
>   mother's womb,
> And naked shall I return
>   there.
> The LORD gave, and the LORD
>   has taken away;
> Blessed be the name of the
>   LORD."

[22]In all this Job did not sin nor charge God with wrong.

AGAIN there was a day when the sons of God came to present themselves before the LORD, and Satan came also among them to present himself before the LORD. [2]And the LORD said to Satan, "From where do you come?"

Satan answered the LORD and said, "From going to and fro on the earth, and from walking back and forth on it."

[3]Then the LORD said to Satan, "Have you considered My servant Job, that *there is* none like him on the earth, a blameless and upright man, one who fears God and shuns evil? And still he holds fast to his integrity, although you incited Me against him, to destroy him without cause."

[4]So Satan answered the LORD and said, "Skin for skin! Yes, all that a man has he will give for his life. [5]But stretch out Your hand now, and touch his bone and his flesh, and he will surely curse You to Your face!"

[6]And the LORD said to Satan, "Behold, he *is* in your hand, but spare his life."

[7]So Satan went out from the presence of the LORD, and struck Job with painful boils from the sole of his foot to the crown of his head. [8]And he took for himself a potsherd with which to scrape himself while he sat in the midst of the ashes.

[9]Then his wife said to him, "Do you still hold fast to your integrity? Curse God and die!"

[10]But he said to her, "You speak as one of the foolish women speaks. Shall we indeed accept good from God, and shall we not accept adversity?" In all this Job did not sin with his lips.

[11]Now when Job's three friends heard of all this adversity that had come upon him, each one came from his own place—Eliphaz the Temanite, Bildad the Shuhite, and Zophar the Naamathite. For they had made an appointment together to come and mourn with him, and to comfort him. [12]And when they raised their eyes from afar, and did not recognize him, they lifted their voices and wept; and each one tore his robe and sprinkled dust on his head toward heaven. [13]So they sat down with him on the ground seven days and seven nights, and no one spoke a word to him, for they saw that *his* grief was very great.

AFTER this Job opened his mouth and cursed the day of his *birth*. [2]And Job spoke, and said:

3 "May the day perish on which
    I was born,
  And the night *in which* it was
    said,
  'A male child is conceived.'
4 May that day be darkness;
  May God above not seek it,
  Nor the light shine upon it.
5 May darkness and the
    shadow of death claim it;
  May a cloud settle on it;
  May the blackness of the day
    terrify it.
6 *As for* that night, may
    darkness seize it;
  May it not rejoice* among the
    days of the year,
  May it not come into the
    number of the months.
7 Oh, may that night be barren!
  May no joyful shout come
    into it!

8 May those curse it who curse
    the day,
  Those who are ready to
    arouse Leviathan.
9 May the stars of its morning
    be dark;
  May it look for light, but *have*
    none,
  And not see the dawning of
    the day;
10 Because it did not shut up
    the doors of my *mother's*
    womb,
  Nor hide sorrow from my
    eyes.

11 "Why did I not die at birth?
  Why did I *not* perish when I
    came from the womb?
12 Why did the knees receive
    me?
  Or why the breasts, that I
    should nurse?
13 For now I would have lain still
    and been quiet,
  I would have been asleep;
  Then I would have been at rest
14 With kings and counselors of
    the earth,
  Who built ruins for
    themselves,
15 Or with princes who had gold,
  Who filled their houses *with*
    silver;
16 Or *why* was I not hidden like
    a stillborn child,
  Like infants who never saw
    light?
17 There the wicked cease *from*
    troubling,
  And there the weary are at
    rest.
18 *There* the prisoners rest
    together;
  They do not hear the voice of
    the oppressor.
19 The small and great are there,
  And the servant *is* free from
    his master.

20 "Why is light given to him who
      is in misery,
   And life to the bitter of soul,
21 Who long for death, but it
      does not *come,*
   And search for it more than
      hidden treasures;
22 Who rejoice exceedingly,
   And are glad when they can
      find the grave?
23 *Why is light given* to a man
      whose way is hidden,
   And whom God has hedged
      in?
24 For my sighing comes before
      I eat,*
   And my groanings pour out
      like water.
25 For the thing I greatly feared
      has come upon me,
   And what I dreaded has
      happened to me.
26 I am not at ease, nor am I
      quiet;
   I have no rest, for trouble
      comes."

1 CORINTHIANS 14:1-17

PURSUE love, and desire spiritual
gifts, but especially that you
may prophesy. ²For he who
speaks in a tongue does not speak to
men but to God, for no one understands *him;* however, in the spirit he
speaks mysteries. ³But he who prophesies speaks edification and exhortation and comfort to men. ⁴He who
speaks in a tongue edifies himself, but
he who prophesies edifies the church.
⁵I wish you all spoke with tongues, but
even more that you prophesied; for*
he who prophesies *is* greater than he
who speaks with tongues, unless indeed he interprets, that the church
may receive edification.

⁶But now, brethren, if I come to you
speaking with tongues, what shall I
profit you unless I speak to you either
by revelation, by knowledge, by proph-

esying, or by teaching? ⁷Even things
without life, whether flute or harp,
when they make a sound, unless they
make a distinction in the sounds, how
will it be known what is piped or
played? ⁸For if the trumpet makes an
uncertain sound, who will prepare for
battle? ⁹So likewise you, unless you utter by the tongue words easy to understand, how will it be known what is
spoken? For you will be speaking into
the air. ¹⁰There are, it may be, so many
kinds of languages in the world, and
none of them *is* without significance.
¹¹Therefore, if I do not know the meaning of the language, I shall be a foreigner to him who speaks, and he who
speaks *will be* a foreigner to me. ¹²Even
so you, since you are zealous for spiritual *gifts, let it be* for the edification of
the church *that* you seek to excel.

¹³Therefore let him who speaks in a
tongue pray that he may interpret.
¹⁴For if I pray in a tongue, my spirit
prays, but my understanding is unfruitful. ¹⁵What is *the conclusion* then?
I will pray with the spirit, and I will also
pray with the understanding. I will sing
with the spirit, and I will also sing with
the understanding. ¹⁶Otherwise, if you
bless with the spirit, how will he who
occupies the place of the uninformed
say "Amen" at your giving of thanks,
since he does not understand what you
say? ¹⁷For you indeed give thanks well,
but the other is not edified.

PSALM 37:12-29

THE wicked plots against the just,
   And gnashes at him with his
   teeth.
13 The Lord laughs at him,
   For He sees that his day is
      coming.
14 The wicked have drawn the
      sword
   And have bent their bow,
   To cast down the poor and
      needy,

To slay those who are of
upright conduct.
15 Their sword shall enter their
own heart,
And their bows shall be
broken.

16 A little that a righteous man
has
Is better than the riches of
many wicked.
17 For the arms of the wicked
shall be broken,
But the Lord upholds the
righteous.

18 The Lord knows the days of
the upright,
And their inheritance shall be
forever.
19 They shall not be ashamed in
the evil time,
And in the days of famine
they shall be satisfied.
20 But the wicked shall perish;
And the enemies of the Lord,
Like the splendor of the
meadows, shall vanish.
Into smoke they shall vanish
away.

21 The wicked borrows and does
not repay,
But the righteous shows
mercy and gives.

22 For *those* blessed by Him
shall inherit the earth,
But *those* cursed by Him shall
be cut off.

23 The steps of a *good* man are
ordered by the Lord,
And He delights in his way.
24 Though he fall, he shall not
be utterly cast down;
For the Lord upholds *him*
with His hand.

25 I have been young, and *now*
am old;
Yet I have not seen the
righteous forsaken,
Nor his descendants begging
bread.
26 *He is* ever merciful, and lends;
And his descendants *are*
blessed.

27 Depart from evil, and do good;
And dwell forevermore.
28 For the Lord loves justice,
And does not forsake His
saints;
They are preserved forever,
But the descendants of the
wicked shall be cut off.
29 The righteous shall inherit
the land,
And dwell in it forever.

PROVERBS FOR TODAY/ 21:25-26

The desire of the lazy man kills him, for his hands refuse to labor. He covets greedily all day long, but the righteous gives and does not spare.

AUGUST 22

JOB 4:1–7:21

THEN Eliphaz the Temanite answered and said:

2   "*If* one attempts a word with
      you, will you become
      weary?
    But who can withhold himself
      from speaking?

3   Surely you have instructed
      many,
    And you have strengthened
      weak hands.

4   Your words have upheld him
      who was stumbling,
    And you have strengthened
      the feeble knees;

5   But now it comes upon you,
      and you are weary;
    It touches you, and you are
      troubled.

6   *Is* not your reverence your
      confidence?
    And the integrity of your ways
      your hope?

7   "Remember now, who *ever*
      perished being innocent?
    Or where were the upright
      ever cut off?

8   Even as I have seen,
    Those who plow iniquity
    And sow trouble reap the
      same.

9   By the blast of God they
      perish,
    And by the breath of His
      anger they are consumed.

10   The roaring of the lion,
    The voice of the fierce lion,
    And the teeth of the young
      lions are broken.

11   The old lion perishes for lack
      of prey,

    And the cubs of the lioness
      are scattered.

12   "Now a word was secretly
      brought to me,
    And my ear received a
      whisper of it.

13   In disquieting thoughts from
      the visions of the night,
    When deep sleep falls on men,

14   Fear came upon me, and
      trembling,
    Which made all my bones
      shake.

15   Then a spirit passed before
      my face;
    The hair on my body stood up.

16   It stood still,
    But I could not discern its
      appearance.
    A form *was* before my eyes;
    There was silence;
    Then I heard a voice *saying:*

17   'Can a mortal be more
      righteous than God?
    Can a man be more pure than
      his Maker?

18   If He puts no trust in His
      servants,
    If He charges His angels with
      error,

19   How much more those who
      dwell in houses of clay,
    Whose foundation is in the
      dust,
    Who are crushed before a
      moth?

20   They are broken in pieces
      from morning till evening;
    They perish forever, with no
      one regarding.

21   Does not their own excellence
      go away?
    They die, even without
      wisdom.'

"CALL out now;
Is there anyone who will
answer you?
And to which of the holy ones
will you turn?
2 For wrath kills a foolish man,
And envy slays a simple one.
3 I have seen the foolish taking
root,
But suddenly I cursed his
dwelling place.
4 His sons are far from safety,
They are crushed in the gate,
And *there is* no deliverer.
5 Because the hungry eat up
his harvest,
Taking it even from the
thorns,*
And a snare snatches their
substance.*
6 For affliction does not come
from the dust,
Nor does trouble spring from
the ground;
7 Yet man is born to trouble,
As the sparks fly upward.

8 "But as for me, I would seek
God,
And to God I would commit
my cause—
9 Who does great things, and
unsearchable,
Marvelous things without
number.
10 He gives rain on the earth,
And sends waters on the
fields.
11 He sets on high those who
are lowly,
And those who mourn are
lifted to safety.
12 He frustrates the devices of
the crafty,
So that their hands cannot
carry out their plans.
13 He catches the wise in their
own craftiness,
And the counsel of the

cunning comes quickly
upon them.
14 They meet with darkness in
the daytime,
And grope at noontime as in
the night.
15 But He saves the needy from
the sword,
From the mouth of the mighty,
And from their hand.
16 So the poor have hope,
And injustice shuts her mouth.

17 "Behold, happy *is* the man
whom God corrects;
Therefore do not despise the
chastening of the Almighty.
18 For He bruises, but He binds
up;
He wounds, but His hands
make whole.
19 He shall deliver you in six
troubles,
Yes, in seven no evil shall
touch you.
20 In famine He shall redeem
you from death,
And in war from the power of
the sword.
21 You shall be hidden from the
scourge of the tongue,
And you shall not be afraid of
destruction when it comes.
22 You shall laugh at destruction
and famine,
And you shall not be afraid of
the beasts of the earth.
23 For you shall have a covenant
with the stones of the field,
And the beasts of the field
shall be at peace with you.
24 You shall know that your tent
is in peace;
You shall visit your dwelling
and find nothing amiss.
25 You shall also know that your
descendants *shall be* many,
And your offspring like the
grass of the earth.

26 You shall come to the grave at
a full age,
As a sheaf of grain ripens in
its season.
27 Behold, this we have
searched out;
It *is* true.
Hear it, and know for
yourself."

THEN Job answered and said:

2 "Oh, that my grief were fully
weighed,
And my calamity laid with it
on the scales!
3 For then it would be heavier
than the sand of the sea—
Therefore my words have
been rash.
4 For the arrows of the
Almighty *are* within me;
My spirit drinks in their
poison;
The terrors of God are
arrayed against me.
5 Does the wild donkey bray
when it has grass,
Or does the ox low over its
fodder?
6 Can flavorless food be eaten
without salt?
Or is there *any* taste in the
white of an egg?
7 My soul refuses to touch
them;
They *are* as loathsome food to
me.

8 "Oh, that I might have my
request,
That God would grant *me* the
thing that I long for!
9 That it would please God to
crush me,
That He would loose His hand
and cut me off!
10 Then I would still have
comfort;

Though in anguish I would
exult,
He will not spare;
For I have not concealed the
words of the Holy One.

11 "What strength do I have, that
I should hope?
And what *is* my end, that I
should prolong my life?
12 *Is* my strength the strength of
stones?
Or is my flesh bronze?
13 *Is* my help not within me?
And is success driven from
me?

14 "To him who is afflicted,
kindness *should be shown*
by his friend,
Even though he forsakes the
fear of the Almighty.
15 My brothers have dealt
deceitfully like a brook,
Like the streams of the
brooks that pass away,
16 Which are dark because of
the ice,
And into which the snow
vanishes.
17 When it is warm, they cease
to flow;
When it is hot, they vanish
from their place.
18 The paths of their way turn
aside,
They go nowhere and perish.
19 The caravans of Tema look,
The travelers of Sheba hope
for them.
20 They are disappointed
because they were
confident;
They come there and are
confused.
21 For now you are nothing,
You see terror and are afraid.
22 Did I ever say, 'Bring
something to me'?

Or, 'Offer a bribe for me from
your wealth'?
23   Or, 'Deliver me from the
enemy's hand'?
Or, 'Redeem me from the
hand of oppressors'?

24   "Teach me, and I will hold my
tongue;
Cause me to understand
wherein I have erred.
25   How forceful are right words!
But what does your arguing
prove?
26   Do you intend to rebuke *my*
words,
And the speeches of a
desperate one, *which are* as
wind?
27   Yes, you overwhelm the
fatherless,
And you undermine your
friend.
28   Now therefore, be pleased to
look at me;
For I would never lie to your
face.
29   Yield now, let there be no
injustice!
Yes, concede, my
righteousness still stands!
30   Is there injustice on my
tongue?
Cannot my taste discern the
unsavory?

"*Is* there not a time of hard service for
man on earth?
Are not his days also like the
days of a hired man?
2   Like a servant who earnestly
desires the shade,
And like a hired man who
eagerly looks for his wages,
3   So I have been allotted
months of futility,
And wearisome nights have
been appointed to me.
4   When I lie down, I say, 'When
shall I arise,

And the night be ended?'
For I have had my fill of
tossing till dawn.
5   My flesh is caked with worms
and dust,
My skin is cracked and
breaks out afresh.

6   "My days are swifter than a
weaver's shuttle,
And are spent without hope.
7   Oh, remember that my life *is*
a breath!
My eye will never again see
good.
8   The eye of him who sees me
will see me no *more;*
While your *eyes* are upon me, I
shall no longer *be.*
9   *As* the cloud disappears and
vanishes away,
So he who goes down to the
grave does not come up.
10   He shall never return to his
house,
Nor shall his place know him
anymore.

11   "Therefore I will not restrain
my mouth;
I will speak in the anguish of
my spirit;
I will complain in the
bitterness of my soul.
12   *Am* I a sea, or a sea serpent,
That You set a guard over me?
13   When I say, 'My bed will
comfort me,
My couch will ease my
complaint,'
14   Then You scare me with
dreams
And terrify me with visions,
15   So that my soul chooses
strangling
And death rather than my
body.*
16   I loathe *my life;*
I would not live forever.
Let me alone,

For my days *are but* a breath.

17 "What *is* man, that You should
exalt him,
That You should set Your
heart on him,
18 That You should visit him
every morning,
And test him every moment?
19 How long?
Will You not look away from
me,
And let me alone till I swallow
my saliva?
20 Have I sinned?
What have I done to You,
O watcher of men?
Why have You set me as Your
target,
So that I am a burden to
myself?*
21 Why then do You not pardon
my transgression,
And take away my iniquity?
For now I will lie down in the
dust,
And You will seek me
diligently,
But I *will* no longer *be.*"

1 CORINTHIANS 14:18-40

I THANK my God I speak with
tongues more than you all; [19]yet in
the church I would rather speak
five words with my understanding,
that I may teach others also, than ten
thousand words in a tongue.

[20]Brethren, do not be children in
understanding; however, in malice be
babes, but in understanding be mature. [21]In the law it is written:

"With men of other tongues
and other lips
I will speak to this people;
And yet, for all that, they will
*not hear Me,"**

says the Lord.

[22]Therefore tongues are for a sign,
not to those who believe but to unbelievers; but prophesying is not for unbelievers but for those who believe.
[23]Therefore if the whole church comes
together in one place, and all speak
with tongues, and there come in *those*
who are uninformed or unbelievers,
will they not say that you are out of
your mind? [24]But if all prophesy, and
an unbeliever or an uninformed person comes in, he is convinced by all, he
is convicted by all. [25]And thus* the secrets of his heart are revealed; and so,
falling down on *his* face, he will worship God and report that God is truly
among you.

[26]How is it then, brethren? Whenever you come together, each of you
has a psalm, has a teaching, has a
tongue, has a revelation, has an interpretation. Let all things be done for edification. [27]If anyone speaks in a
tongue, *let there be* two or at the most
three, *each* in turn, and let one interpret. [28]But if there is no interpreter, let
him keep silent in church, and let him
speak to himself and to God. [29]Let two
or three prophets speak, and let the
others judge. [30]But if *anything* is revealed to another who sits by, let the
first keep silent. [31]For you can all
prophesy one by one, that all may
learn and all may be encouraged.
[32]And the spirits of the prophets are
subject to the prophets. [33]For God is
not *the author* of confusion but of
peace, as in all the churches of the
saints.

[34]Let your* women keep silent in
the churches, for they are not permitted to speak; but *they are* to be submissive, as the law also says. [35]And if they
want to learn something, let them ask
their own husbands at home; for it is
shameful for women to speak in
church.

[36]Or did the word of God come *orig-*
inally from you? Or *was it* you only that
it reached? [37]If anyone thinks himself

to be a prophet or spiritual, let him acknowledge that the things which I write to you are the commandments of the Lord. 38But if anyone is ignorant, let him be ignorant. *

39Therefore, brethren, desire earnestly to prophesy, and do not forbid to speak with tongues. 40Let all things be done decently and in order.

PSALM 37:30-40

T HE mouth of the righteous speaks wisdom,
And his tongue talks of justice.
31 The law of his God *is* in his heart;
None of his steps shall slide.

32 The wicked watches the righteous,
And seeks to slay him.
33 The LORD will not leave him in his hand,
Nor condemn him when he is judged.

34 Wait on the LORD,
And keep His way,
And He shall exalt you to inherit the land;

When the wicked are cut off, you shall see *it*.
35 I have seen the wicked in great power,
And spreading himself like a native green tree.
36 Yet he passed away,* and behold, he *was* no *more;*
Indeed I sought him, but he could not be found.

37 Mark the blameless *man,* and observe the upright;
For the future of *that* man *is* peace.
38 But the transgressors shall be destroyed together;
The future of the wicked shall be cut off.

39 But the salvation of the righteous *is* from the LORD;
He is their strength in the time of trouble.
40 And the LORD shall help them and deliver them;
He shall deliver them from the wicked,
And save them,
Because they trust in Him.

PROVERBS FOR TODAY/ 21:27

The sacrifice of the wicked is *an abomination; how much more* when *he brings it with wicked intent!*

AUGUST 23

JOB 8:1–11:20

T HEN Bildad the Shuhite answered and said:

2 "How long will you speak these *things,*

And the words of your mouth *be like* a strong wind?
3 Does God subvert judgment?
Or does the Almighty pervert justice?

4 If your sons have sinned against Him,
He has cast them away for their transgression.
5 If you would earnestly seek God
And make your supplication to the Almighty,
6 If you *were* pure and upright,
Surely now He would awake for you,
And prosper your rightful dwelling place.
7 Though your beginning was small,
Yet your latter end would increase abundantly.

8 "For inquire, please, of the former age,
And consider the things discovered by their fathers;
9 For we *were born* yesterday, and know nothing,
Because our days on earth *are* a shadow.
10 Will they not teach you and tell you,
And utter words from their heart?

11 "Can the papyrus grow up without a marsh?
Can the reeds flourish without water?
12 While it *is* yet green *and* not cut down,
It withers before any *other* plant.
13 So *are* the paths of all who forget God;
And the hope of the hypocrite shall perish,
14 Whose confidence shall be cut off,
And whose trust *is* a spider's web.
15 He leans on his house, but it does not stand.

He holds it fast, but it does not endure.
16 He grows green in the sun,
And his branches spread out in his garden.
17 His roots wrap around the rock heap,
And look for a place in the stones.
18 If he is destroyed from his place,
Then *it* will deny him, *saying,* 'I have not seen you.'

19 "Behold, this is the joy of His way,
And out of the earth others will grow.
20 Behold, God will not cast away the blameless,
Nor will He uphold the evildoers.
21 He will yet fill your mouth with laughing,
And your lips with rejoicing.
22 Those who hate you will be clothed with shame,
And the dwelling place of the wicked will come to nothing."*

THEN Job answered and said:

2 "Truly I know *it is* so,
But how can a man be righteous before God?
3 If one wished to contend with Him,
He could not answer Him one time out of a thousand.
4 *God is* wise in heart and mighty in strength.
Who has hardened *himself* against Him and prospered?
5 He removes the mountains, and they do not know
When He overturns them in His anger;
6 He shakes the earth out of its place,

And its pillars tremble;
7   He commands the sun, and it
        does not rise;
    He seals off the stars;
8   He alone spreads out the
        heavens,
    And treads on the waves of
        the sea;
9   He made the Bear, Orion, and
        the Pleiades,
    And the chambers of the
        south;
10 He does great things past
        finding out,
    Yes, wonders without number.
11 If He goes by me, I do not see
        Him;
    If He moves past, I do not
        perceive Him;
12 If He takes away, who can
        hinder Him?
    Who can say to Him, 'What
        are You doing?'
13 God will not withdraw His
        anger,
    The allies of the proud* lie
        prostrate beneath Him.

14 "How then can I answer Him,
        And choose my words *to
        reason* with Him?
15 For though I were righteous, I
        could not answer Him;
    I would beg mercy of my
        Judge.
16 If I called and He answered
        me,
    I would not believe that He
        was listening to my voice.
17 For He crushes me with a
        tempest,
    And multiplies my wounds
        without cause.
18 He will not allow me to catch
        my breath,
    But fills me with bitterness.
19 If *it is a matter* of strength,
        indeed *He is* strong;
    And if of justice, who will
        appoint my day *in court?*

20 Though I were righteous, my
        own mouth would condemn
        me;
    Though I *were* blameless, it
        would prove me perverse.

21 "I am blameless, yet I do not
        know myself;
    I despise my life.
22 It *is* all one *thing;*
    Therefore I say, 'He destroys
        the blameless and the
        wicked.'
23 If the scourge slays suddenly,
    He laughs at the plight of the
        innocent.
24 The earth is given into the
        hand of the wicked.
    He covers the faces of its
        judges.
    If it is not *He,* who else could
        it be?

25 "Now my days are swifter than
        a runner;
    They flee away, they see no
        good.
26 They pass by like swift ships,
    Like an eagle swooping on its
        prey.
27 If I say, 'I will forget my
        complaint,
    I will put off my sad face and
        wear a smile,'
28 I am afraid of all my
        sufferings;
    I know that You will not hold
        me innocent.
29 *If* I am condemned,
    Why then do I labor in vain?
30 If I wash myself with snow
        water,
    And cleanse my hands with
        soap,
31 Yet You will plunge me into
        the pit,
    And my own clothes will
        abhor me.

32 "For *He is* not a man, as I *am,*
That I may answer Him,
And that we should go to
court together.
33 Nor is there any mediator
between us,
Who may lay his hand on us
both.
34 Let Him take His rod away
from me,
And do not let dread of Him
terrify me.
35 *Then* I would speak and not
fear Him,
But it is not so with me.

"My soul loathes my life;
I will give free course to my
complaint,
I will speak in the bitterness
of my soul.
2 I will say to God,
'Do not condemn me;
Show me why You contend
with me.
3 *Does it* seem good to You that
You should oppress,
That You should despise the
work of Your hands,
And smile on the counsel of
the wicked?
4 Do You have eyes of flesh?
Or do You see as man sees?
5 *Are* Your days like the days of
a mortal man?
Are Your years like the days
of a mighty man,
6 That You should seek for my
iniquity
And search out my sin,
7 Although You know that I am
not wicked,
And *there is* no one who can
deliver from Your hand?

8 'Your hands have made me
and fashioned me,
An intricate unity;
Yet You would destroy me.

9 Remember, I pray, that You
have made me like clay.
And will You turn me into
dust again?
10 Did You not pour me out like
milk,
And curdle me like cheese,
11 Clothe me with skin and flesh,
And knit me together with
bones and sinews?
12 You have granted me life and
favor,
And Your care has preserved
my spirit.

13 'And these *things* You have
hidden in Your heart;
I know that this *was* with You:
14 If I sin, then You mark me,
And will not acquit me of my
iniquity.
15 If I am wicked, woe to me;
Even *if* I am righteous, I
cannot lift up my head.
I am full of disgrace;
See my misery!
16 If *my head* is exalted,
You hunt me like a fierce lion,
And again You show Yourself
awesome against me.
17 You renew Your witnesses
against me,
And increase Your indignation
toward me;
Changes and war are *ever*
with me.

18 'Why then have You brought
me out of the womb?
Oh, that I had perished and
no eye had seen me!
19 I would have been as though I
had not been.
I would have been carried
from the womb to the grave.
20 Are not my days few?
Cease! Leave me alone, that I
may take a little comfort,
21 Before I go *to the place from
which* I shall not return,

To the land of darkness and
the shadow of death,

22 A land as dark as darkness
itself,
As the shadow of death,
without any order,
Where even the light *is* like
darkness.' "

THEN Zophar the Naamathite answered and said:

2 "Should not the multitude of
words be answered?
And should a man full of talk
be vindicated?

3 Should your empty talk make
men hold their peace?
And when you mock, should
no one rebuke you?

4 For you have said,
'My doctrine *is* pure,
And I am clean in your eyes.'

5 But oh, that God would speak,
And open His lips against you,

6 That He would show you the
secrets of wisdom!
For *they would* double *your*
prudence.
Know therefore that God
exacts from you
Less than your iniquity
deserves.

7 "Can you search out the deep
things of God?
Can you find out the limits of
the Almighty?

8 *They are* higher than
heaven— what can you do?
Deeper than Sheol— what
can you know?

9 Their measure *is* longer than
the earth
And broader than the sea.

10 "If He passes by, imprisons,
and gathers *to judgment,*
Then who can hinder Him?

11 For He knows deceitful men;

He sees wickedness also.
Will He not then consider *it?*

12 For an empty-headed man will
be wise,
When a wild donkey's colt is
born a man.

13 "If you would prepare your
heart,
And stretch out your hands
toward Him;

14 If iniquity *were* in your hand,
and you put it far away,
And would not let wickedness
dwell in your tents;

15 Then surely you could lift up
your face without spot;
Yes, you could be steadfast,
and not fear;

16 Because you would forget
your misery,
And remember *it* as waters
that have passed away,

17 And *your* life would be
brighter than noonday.
Though you were dark, you
would be like the morning.

18 And you would be secure,
because there is hope;
Yes, you would dig *around
you, and* take your rest in
safety.

19 You would also lie down, and
no one would make *you*
afraid;
Yes, many would court your
favor.

20 But the eyes of the wicked
will fail,
And they shall not escape,
And their hope—loss of life!"

1 CORINTHIANS 15:1-28

MOREOVER, brethren, I declare
to you the gospel which I
preached to you, which also
you received and in which you stand,
²by which also you are saved, if you

hold fast that word which I preached to you—unless you believed in vain.

3For I delivered to you first of all that which I also received: that Christ died for our sins according to the Scriptures, 4and that He was buried, and that He rose again the third day according to the Scriptures, 5and that He was seen by Cephas, then by the twelve. 6After that He was seen by over five hundred brethren at once, of whom the greater part remain to the present, but some have fallen asleep. 7After that He was seen by James, then by all the apostles. 8Then last of all He was seen by me also, as by one born out of due time.

9For I am the least of the apostles, who am not worthy to be called an apostle, because I persecuted the church of God. 10But by the grace of God I am what I am, and His grace toward me was not in vain; but I labored more abundantly than they all, yet not I, but the grace of God which was with me. 11Therefore, whether it was I or they, so we preach and so you believed.

12Now if Christ is preached that He has been raised from the dead, how do some among you say that there is no resurrection of the dead? 13But if there is no resurrection of the dead, then Christ is not risen. 14And if Christ is not risen, then our preaching is empty and your faith is also empty. 15Yes, and we are found false witnesses of God, because we have testified of God that He raised up Christ, whom He did not raise up—if in fact the dead do not rise. 16For if the dead do not rise, then Christ is not risen. 17And if Christ is not risen, your faith is futile; you are still in your sins! 18Then also those who have fallen asleep in Christ have perished. 19If in this life only we have hope in Christ, we are of all men the most pitiable.

20But now Christ is risen from the dead, and has become the firstfruits of those who have fallen asleep. 21For since by man came death, by Man also came the resurrection of the dead. 22For as in Adam all die, even so in Christ all shall be made alive. 23But each one in his own order: Christ the firstfruits, afterward those who are Christ's at His coming. 24Then comes the end, when He delivers the kingdom to God the Father, when He puts an end to all rule and all authority and power. 25For He must reign till He has put all enemies under His feet. 26The last enemy that will be destroyed is death. 27For "He has put all things under His feet." * But when He says "all things are put under Him," it is evident that He who put all things under Him is excepted. 28Now when all things are made subject to Him, then the Son Himself will also be subject to Him who put all things under Him, that God may be all in all.

PSALM 38:1-22

A Psalm of David. To bring to remembrance.

O LORD, do not rebuke me in Your wrath,
Nor chasten me in Your hot displeasure!
2 For Your arrows pierce me deeply,
And Your hand presses me down.

3 *There is* no soundness in my flesh
Because of Your anger,
Nor *any* health in my bones
Because of my sin.
4 For my iniquities have gone over my head;
Like a heavy burden they are too heavy for me.
5 My wounds are foul *and* festering
Because of my foolishness.

6 I am troubled, I am bowed
down greatly;
I go mourning all the day long.
7 For my loins are full of
inflammation,
And *there is* no soundness in
my flesh.
8 I am feeble and severely
broken;
I groan because of the turmoil
of my heart.

9 Lord, all my desire *is* before
You;
And my sighing is not hidden
from You.
10 My heart pants, my strength
fails me;
As for the light of my eyes, it
also has gone from me.

11 My loved ones and my friends
stand aloof from my plague,
And my relatives stand afar
off.
12 Those also who seek my life
lay snares *for me;*
Those who seek my hurt
speak of destruction,
And plan deception all the day
long.

13 But I, like a deaf *man,* do not
hear;

14 And *I am* like a mute *who*
does not open his mouth.
Thus I am like a man who
does not hear,
And in whose mouth *is* no
response.

15 For in You, O LORD, I hope;
You will hear, O Lord my God.
16 For I said, *"Hear me,* lest they
rejoice over me,
Lest, when my foot slips, they
exalt *themselves* against me."

17 For I *am* ready to fall,
And my sorrow *is* continually
before me.
18 For I will declare my iniquity;
I will be in anguish over my
sin.
19 But my enemies *are* vigorous,
and they are strong;
And those who hate me
wrongfully have multiplied.
20 Those also who render evil
for good,
They are my adversaries,
because I follow *what is*
good.

21 Do not forsake me, O LORD;
O my God, be not far from me!
22 Make haste to help me,
O Lord, my salvation!

PROVERBS FOR TODAY/ 21:28-29

A false witness shall perish, but the man who hears him *will speak endlessly.*
□ *A wicked man hardens his face, but* as for *the upright, he establishes* his way.*

AUGUST 24

JOB 12:1–15:35

THEN Job answered and said:

2 "No doubt you *are* the people,
And wisdom will die with you!
3 But I have understanding as
well as you;
I *am* not inferior to you.
Indeed, who does not *know*
such things as these?

4 "I am one mocked by his
friends,
Who called on God, and He
answered him,
The just and blameless *who is*
ridiculed.
5 A lamp* is despised in the
thought of one who is at
ease;
It is made ready for those
whose feet slip.
6 The tents of robbers prosper,
And those who provoke God
are secure—
In what God provides by His
hand.

7 "But now ask the beasts, and
they will teach you;
And the birds of the air, and
they will tell you;
8 Or speak to the earth, and it
will teach you;
And the fish of the sea will
explain to you.
9 Who among all these does not
know
That the hand of the LORD has
done this,
10 In whose hand *is* the life of
every living thing,
And the breath of all mankind?
11 Does not the ear test words
And the mouth taste its food?

12 Wisdom *is* with aged men,
And with length of days,
understanding.

13 "With Him *are* wisdom and
strength,
He has counsel and
understanding.
14 If He breaks *a thing* down, it
cannot be rebuilt;
If He imprisons a man, there
can be no release.
15 If He withholds the waters,
they dry up;
If He sends them out, they
overwhelm the earth.
16 With Him *are* strength and
prudence.
The deceived and the
deceiver *are* His.
17 He leads counselors away
plundered,
And makes fools of the judges.
18 He loosens the bonds of kings,
And binds their waist with a
belt.
19 He leads princes* away
plundered,
And overthrows the mighty.
20 He deprives the trusted ones
of speech,
And takes away the
discernment of the elders.
21 He pours contempt on princes,
And disarms the mighty.
22 He uncovers deep things out
of darkness,
And brings the shadow of
death to light.
23 He makes nations great, and
destroys them;
He enlarges nations, and
guides them.
24 He takes away the
understanding* of the

chiefs of the people of the
earth,
And makes them wander in a
pathless wilderness.
25 They grope in the dark
without light,
And He makes them stagger
like a drunken *man*.

"Behold, my eye has seen all *this*,
My ear has heard and
understood it.
2 What you know, I also know;
I *am* not inferior to you.
3 But I would speak to the
Almighty,
And I desire to reason with
God.
4 But you forgers of lies,
You *are* all worthless
physicians.
5 Oh, that you would be silent,
And it would be your wisdom!
6 Now hear my reasoning,
And heed the pleadings of my
lips.
7 Will you speak wickedly for
God,
And talk deceitfully for Him?
8 Will you show partiality for
Him?
Will you contend for God?
9 Will it be well when He
searches you out?
Or can you mock Him as one
mocks a man?
10 He will surely rebuke you
If you secretly show partiality.
11 Will not His excellence make
you afraid,
And the dread of Him fall
upon you?
12 Your platitudes *are* proverbs
of ashes,
Your defenses are defenses of
clay.

13 "Hold your peace with me, and
let me speak,

Then let come on me what
may!
14 Why do I take my flesh in my
teeth,
And put my life in my hands?
15 Though He slay me, yet will I
trust Him.
Even so, I will defend my own
ways before Him.
16 He also *shall* be my salvation,
For a hypocrite could not
come before Him.
17 Listen carefully to my speech,
And to my declaration with
your ears.
18 See now, I have prepared *my*
case,
I know that I shall be
vindicated.
19 Who *is* he *who* will contend
with me?
If now I hold my tongue, I
perish.

20 "Only two *things* do not do to
me,
Then I will not hide myself
from You:
21 Withdraw Your hand far from
me,
And let not the dread of You
make me afraid.
22 Then call, and I will answer;
Or let me speak, then You
respond to me.
23 How many *are* my iniquities
and sins?
Make me know my
transgression and my sin.
24 Why do You hide Your face,
And regard me as Your
enemy?
25 Will You frighten a leaf driven
to and fro?
And will You pursue dry
stubble?
26 For You write bitter things
against me,
And make me inherit the
iniquities of my youth.

27 You put my feet in the stocks,
And watch closely all my
paths.
You set a limit* for the soles
of my feet.

28 "*Man** decays like a rotten
thing,
Like a garment that is
moth-eaten.

"MAN *who is* born of woman
Is of few days and full of
trouble.
2 He comes forth like a flower
and fades away;
He flees like a shadow and
does not continue.
3 And do You open Your eyes
on such a one,
And bring me* to judgment
with Yourself?
4 Who can bring a clean *thing*
out of an unclean?
No one!
5 Since his days *are* determined,
The number of his months *is*
with You;
You have appointed his limits,
so that he cannot pass.
6 Look away from him that he
may rest,
Till like a hired man he
finishes his day.

7 "For there is hope for a tree,
If it is cut down, that it will
sprout again,
And that its tender shoots will
not cease.
8 Though its root may grow old
in the earth,
And its stump may die in the
ground,
9 *Yet* at the scent of water it will
bud
And bring forth branches like
a plant.
10 But man dies and is laid away;
Indeed he breathes his last

And where *is* he?
11 *As* water disappears from the
sea,
And a river becomes parched
and dries up,
12 So man lies down and does
not rise.
Till the heavens *are* no more,
They will not awake
Nor be roused from their
sleep.

13 "Oh, that You would hide me
in the grave,
That You would conceal me
until Your wrath is past,
That You would appoint me a
set time, and remember me!
14 If a man dies, shall he live
again?
All the days of my hard
service I will wait,
Till my change comes.
15 You shall call, and I will
answer You;
You shall desire the work of
Your hands.
16 For now You number my
steps,
But do not watch over my sin.
17 My transgression *is* sealed up
in a bag,
And You cover* my iniquity.

18 "But *as* a mountain falls *and*
crumbles away,
And *as* a rock is moved from
its place;
19 *As* water wears away stones,
And as torrents wash away
the soil of the earth;
So You destroy the hope of
man.
20 You prevail forever against
him, and he passes on;
You change his countenance
and send him away.
21 His sons come to honor, and
he does not know *it;*

They are brought low, and he
does not perceive *it*.
22 But his flesh will be in pain
over it,
And his soul will mourn over
it."

THEN Eliphaz the Temanite answered
and said:

2 "Should a wise man answer
with empty knowledge,
And fill himself with the east
wind?
3 Should he reason with
unprofitable talk,
Or by speeches with which he
can do no good?
4 Yes, you cast off fear,
And restrain prayer before
God.
5 For your iniquity teaches your
mouth,
And you choose the tongue of
the crafty.
6 Your own mouth condemns
you, and not I;
Yes, your own lips testify
against you.

7 "*Are* you the first man *who* was
born?
Or were you made before the
hills?
8 Have you heard the counsel
of God?
Do you limit wisdom to
yourself?
9 What do you know that we do
not know?
What do you understand that
is not in us?
10 Both the gray-haired and the
aged *are* among us,
Much older than your father.
11 *Are* the consolations of God
too small for you,
And the word *spoken* gently*
with you?

12 Why does your heart carry
you away,
And what do your eyes wink
at,
13 That you turn your spirit
against God,
And let *such* words go out of
your mouth?

14 "What *is* man, that he could be
pure?
And *he who is* born of a
woman, that he could be
righteous?
15 If *God* puts no trust in His
saints,
And the heavens are not pure
in His sight,
16 How much less man, *who is*
abominable and filthy,
Who drinks iniquity like water!

17 "I will tell you, hear me;
What I have seen I will
declare,
18 What wise men have told,
Not hiding *anything received*
from their fathers,
19 To whom alone the land was
given,
And no alien passed among
them:
20 The wicked man writhes with
pain all *his* days,
And the number of years is
hidden from the oppressor.
21 Dreadful sounds *are* in his
ears;
In prosperity the destroyer
comes upon him.
22 He does not believe that he
will return from darkness,
For a sword is waiting for him.
23 He wanders about for bread,
saying, 'Where *is* it?'
He knows that a day of
darkness is ready at his
hand.
24 Trouble and anguish make
him afraid;

They overpower him, like a
king ready for battle.
25 For he stretches out his hand
against God,
And acts defiantly against the
Almighty,
26 Running stubbornly against
Him
With his strong, embossed
shield.

27 "Though he has covered his
face with his fatness,
And made *his* waist heavy
with fat,
28 He dwells in desolate cities,
In houses which no one
inhabits,
Which are destined to
become ruins.
29 He will not be rich,
Nor will his wealth continue,
Nor will his possessions
overspread the earth.
30 He will not depart from
darkness;
The flame will dry out his
branches,
And by the breath of His
mouth he will go away.
31 Let him not trust in futile
things, deceiving himself,
For futility will be his reward.
32 It will be accomplished before
his time,
And his branch will not be
green.
33 He will shake off his unripe
grape like a vine,
And cast off his blossom like
an olive tree.
34 For the company of
hypocrites *will be* barren,
And fire will consume the
tents of bribery.
35 They conceive trouble and
bring forth futility;
Their womb prepares deceit."

1 CORINTHIANS 15:29-58

OTHERWISE, what will they do who
are baptized for the dead, if the
dead do not rise at all? Why
then are they baptized for the dead?
30And why do we stand in jeopardy every hour? 31I affirm, by the boasting in you which I have in Christ Jesus our Lord, I die daily. 32If, in the manner of men, I have fought with beasts at Ephesus, what advantage *is it* to me? If *the* dead do not rise, *"Let us eat and drink, for tomorrow we die!"* *

33Do not be deceived: "Evil company corrupts good habits." 34Awake to righteousness, and do not sin; for some do not have the knowledge of God. I speak *this* to your shame.

35But someone will say, "How are the dead raised up? And with what body do they come?" 36Foolish one, what you sow is not made alive unless it dies. 37And what you sow, you do not sow that body that shall be, but mere grain—perhaps wheat or some other *grain.* 38But God gives it a body as He pleases, and to each seed its own body.

39All flesh *is* not the same flesh, but *there is* one *kind of* flesh* of men, another flesh of animals, another of fish, *and* another of birds.

40*There are* also celestial bodies and terrestrial bodies; but the glory of the celestial *is* one, and the *glory* of the terrestrial *is* another. 41*There is* one glory of the sun, another glory of the moon, and another glory of the stars; for *one* star differs from *another* star in glory.

42So also *is* the resurrection of the dead. *The body* is sown in corruption, it is raised in incorruption. 43It is sown in dishonor, it is raised in glory. It is sown in weakness, it is raised in power. 44It is sown a natural body, it is raised a spiritual body. There is a natural body, and there is a spiritual body. 45And so it is written, *"The first man Adam became a living being."* * The last Adam *became* a life-giving spirit.

⁴⁶However, the spiritual is not first, but the natural, and afterward the spiritual. ⁴⁷The first man *was* of the earth, *made* of dust; the second Man *is* the Lord* from heaven. ⁴⁸As *was* the *man* of dust, so also *are* those *who are made* of dust; and as *is* the heavenly *Man,* so also *are* those *who are* heavenly. ⁴⁹And as we have borne the image of the *man* of dust, we shall also bear* the image of the heavenly *Man.*

⁵⁰Now this I say, brethren, that flesh and blood cannot inherit the kingdom of God; nor does corruption inherit incorruption. ⁵¹Behold, I tell you a mystery: We shall not all sleep, but we shall all be changed— ⁵²in a moment, in the twinkling of an eye, at the last trumpet. For the trumpet will sound, and the dead will be raised incorruptible, and we shall be changed. ⁵³For this corruptible must put on incorruption, and this mortal *must* put on immortality. ⁵⁴So when this corruptible has put on incorruption, and this mortal has put on immortality, then shall be brought to pass the saying that is written: *"Death is swallowed up in victory."* *

55   *"O Death, where is your sting?* *
      O Hades, where is your
          victory?" *

⁵⁶The sting of death *is* sin, and the strength of sin *is* the law. ⁵⁷But thanks *be* to God, who gives us the victory through our Lord Jesus Christ.

⁵⁸Therefore, my beloved brethren, be steadfast, immovable, always abounding in the work of the Lord, knowing that your labor is not in vain in the Lord.

PSALM 39:1-13

To the Chief Musician. To Jeduthun. A Psalm of David.

I SAID, "I will guard my ways,
    Lest I sin with my tongue;
    I will restrain my mouth with a
        muzzle,

While the wicked are before
    me."
2   I was mute with silence,
    I held my peace *even* from
        good;
    And my sorrow was stirred
        up.
3   My heart was hot within me;
    While I was musing, the fire
        burned.
    Then I spoke with my tongue:

4   "LORD, make me to know my
        end,
    And what *is* the measure of
        my days,
    That I may know how frail I
        am.
5   Indeed, You have made my
        days *as* handbreadths,
    And my age *is* as nothing
        before You;
    Certainly every man at his
        best state *is* but vapor.
                                    Selah
6   Surely every man walks about
        like a shadow;
    Surely they busy themselves
        in vain;
    He heaps up *riches,*
    And does not know who will
        gather them.

7   "And now, Lord, what do I wait
        for?
    My hope *is* in You.
8   Deliver me from all my
        transgressions;
    Do not make me the reproach
        of the foolish.
9   I was mute, I did not open my
        mouth,
    Because it was You who did *it.*
10   Remove Your plague from me;
    I am consumed by the blow of
        Your hand.
11   When with rebukes You
        correct man for iniquity,
    You make his beauty melt
        away like a moth;

Surely every man *is* vapor.

Selah

12 "Hear my prayer, O LORD,
And give ear to my cry;
Do not be silent at my tears;
For I *am* a stranger with You,

A sojourner, as all my fathers
were.

13 Remove Your gaze from me,
that I may regain strength,
Before I go away and am no
more."

PROVERBS FOR TODAY/ 21:30-31

There is *no wisdom or understanding or counsel against the* LORD. □ *The horse*
is *prepared for the day of battle, but deliverance* is *of the* LORD.

AUGUST 25

JOB 16:1–19:29

THEN Job answered and said:

2"I have heard many such
things;
Miserable comforters *are* you
all!
3 Shall words of wind have an
end?
Or what provokes you that
you answer?
4 I also could speak as you *do,*
If your soul were in my soul's
place.
I could heap up words against
you,
And shake my head at you;
5 *But* I would strengthen you
with my mouth,
And the comfort of my lips
would relieve *your grief.*

6 "Though I speak, my grief is
not relieved;
And *if* I remain silent, how am
I eased?
7 But now He has worn me out;
You have made desolate all
my company.
8 You have shriveled me up,

And it is a witness *against me;*
My leanness rises up against
me
And bears witness to my face.
9 He tears *me* in His wrath, and
hates me;
He gnashes at me with His
teeth;
My adversary sharpens His
gaze on me.
10 They gape at me with their
mouth,
They strike me reproachfully
on the cheek,
They gather together against
me.
11 God has delivered me to the
ungodly,
And turned me over to the
hands of the wicked.
12 I was at ease, but He has
shattered me;
He also has taken *me* by my
neck, and shaken me to
pieces;
He has set me up for His
target,
13 His archers surround me.
He pierces my heart* and
does not pity;

He pours out my gall on the ground.

14 He breaks me with wound upon wound;
He runs at me like a warrior.*

15 "I have sewn sackcloth over my skin,
And laid my head* in the dust.

16 My face is flushed from weeping,
And on my eyelids *is* the shadow of death;

17 Although no violence *is* in my hands,
And my prayer *is* pure.

18 "O earth, do not cover my blood,
And let my cry have no *resting* place!

19 Surely even now my witness *is* in heaven,
And my evidence *is* on high.

20 My friends scorn me;
My eyes pour out *tears* to God.

21 Oh, that one might plead for a man with God,
As a man *pleads* for his neighbor!

22 For when a few years are finished,
I shall go the way of no return.

"My spirit is broken,
My days are extinguished,
The grave *is ready* for me.

2 *Are* not mockers with me?
And does not my eye dwell on their provocation?

3 "Now put down a pledge for me with Yourself.
Who *is* he *who* will shake hands with me?

4 For You have hidden their heart from understanding;
Therefore You will not exalt *them.*

5 He who speaks flattery to *his* friends,
Even the eyes of his children will fail.

6 "But He has made me a byword of the people,
And I have become one in whose face men spit.

7 My eye has also grown dim because of sorrow,
And all my members *are* like shadows.

8 Upright *men* are astonished at this,
And the innocent stirs himself up against the hypocrite.

9 Yet the righteous will hold to his way,
And he who has clean hands will be stronger and stronger.

10 "But please, come back again, all of you,*
For I shall not find *one* wise *man* among you.

11 My days are past,
My purposes are broken off,
Even the thoughts of my heart.

12 They change the night into day;
'The light *is* near,' *they say,* in the face of darkness.

13 If I wait *for* the grave *as* my house,
If I make my bed in the darkness,

14 If I say to corruption, 'You *are* my father,'
And to the worm, 'You *are* my mother and my sister,'

15 Where then *is* my hope?
As for my hope, who can see it?

16 *Will* they go down to the gates of Sheol?
Shall *we have* rest together in the dust?"

THEN Bildad the Shuhite answered and said:

2 "How long *till* you put an end to words?
Gain understanding, and afterward we will speak.
3 Why are we counted as beasts,
And regarded as stupid in your sight?
4 You who tear yourself in anger,
Shall the earth be forsaken for you?
Or shall the rock be removed from its place?

5 "The light of the wicked indeed goes out,
And the flame of his fire does not shine.
6 The light is dark in his tent,
And his lamp beside him is put out.
7 The steps of his strength are shortened,
And his own counsel casts him down.
8 For he is cast into a net by his own feet,
And he walks into a snare.
9 The net takes *him* by the heel,
And a snare lays hold of him.
10 A noose *is* hidden for him on the ground,
And a trap for him in the road.
11 Terrors frighten him on every side,
And drive him to his feet.
12 His strength is starved,
And destruction *is* ready at his side.
13 It devours patches of his skin;
The firstborn of death devours his limbs.
14 He is uprooted from the shelter of his tent,
And they parade him before the king of terrors.

15 They dwell in his tent *who are* none of his;
Brimstone is scattered on his dwelling.
16 His roots are dried out below,
And his branch withers above.
17 The memory of him perishes from the earth,
And he has no name among the renowned.*
18 He is driven from light into darkness,
And chased out of the world.
19 He has neither son nor posterity among his people,
Nor any remaining in his dwellings.
20 Those in the west are astonished at his day,
As those in the east are frightened.
21 Surely such *are* the dwellings of the wicked,
And this *is* the place *of him who* does not know God."

THEN Job answered and said:

2 "How long will you torment my soul,
And break me in pieces with words?
3 These ten times you have reproached me;
You are not ashamed *that* you have wronged me.*
4 And if indeed I have erred,
My error remains with me.
5 If indeed you exalt *yourselves* against me,
And plead my disgrace against me,
6 Know then that God has wronged me,
And has surrounded me with His net.

7 "If I cry out concerning wrong, I am not heard.

If I cry aloud, *there is* no justice.

8 He has fenced up my way, so that I cannot pass;
And He has set darkness in my paths.

9 He has stripped me of my glory,
And taken the crown *from* my head.

10 He breaks me down on every side,
And I am gone;
My hope He has uprooted like a tree.

11 He has also kindled His wrath against me,
And He counts me as *one of* His enemies.

12 His troops come together
And build up their road against me;
They encamp all around my tent.

13 "He has removed my brothers far from me,
And my acquaintances are completely estranged from me.

14 My relatives have failed,
And my close friends have forgotten me.

15 Those who dwell in my house, and my maidservants,
Count me as a stranger;
I am an alien in their sight.

16 I call my servant, but he gives no answer;
I beg him with my mouth.

17 My breath is offensive to my wife,
And I am repulsive to the children of my own body.

18 Even young children despise me;
I arise, and they speak against me.

19 All my close friends abhor me,
And those whom I love have turned against me.

20 My bone clings to my skin and to my flesh,
And I have escaped by the skin of my teeth.

21 "Have pity on me, have pity on me, O you my friends,
For the hand of God has struck me!

22 Why do you persecute me as God *does,*
And are not satisfied with my flesh?

23 "Oh, that my words were written!
Oh, that they were inscribed in a book!

24 That they were engraved on a rock
With an iron pen and lead, forever!

25 For I know *that* my Redeemer lives,
And He shall stand at last on the earth;

26 And after my skin is destroyed, this *I know,*
That in my flesh I shall see God,

27 Whom I shall see for myself,
And my eyes shall behold, and not another.
How my heart yearns within me!

28 If you should say, 'How shall we persecute him?'—
Since the root of the matter is found in me,

29 Be afraid of the sword for yourselves;
For wrath *brings* the punishment of the sword,
That you may know *there is* a judgment."

1 CORINTHIANS 16:1-24

Now concerning the collection for the saints, as I have given orders to the churches of Galatia, so you must do also: ²On the first *day* of the week let each one of you lay something aside, storing up as he may prosper, that there be no collections when I come. ³And when I come, whomever you approve by *your* letters I will send to bear your gift to Jerusalem. ⁴But if it is fitting that I go also, they will go with me.

⁵Now I will come to you when I pass through Macedonia (for I am passing through Macedonia). ⁶And it may be that I will remain, or even spend the winter with you, that you may send me on my journey, wherever I go. ⁷For I do not wish to see you now on the way; but I hope to stay a while with you, if the Lord permits.

⁸But I will tarry in Ephesus until Pentecost. ⁹For a great and effective door has opened to me, and *there are* many adversaries.

¹⁰And if Timothy comes, see that he may be with you without fear; for he does the work of the Lord, as I also *do*. ¹¹Therefore let no one despise him. But send him on his journey in peace, that he may come to me; for I am waiting for him with the brethren.

¹²Now concerning *our* brother Apollos, I strongly urged him to come to you with the brethren, but he was quite unwilling to come at this time; however, he will come when he has a convenient time.

¹³Watch, stand fast in the faith, be brave, be strong. ¹⁴Let all *that* you *do* be done with love.

¹⁵I urge you, brethren—you know the household of Stephanas, that it is the firstfruits of Achaia, and *that* they have devoted themselves to the ministry of the saints— ¹⁶that you also submit to such, and to everyone who works and labors with *us*.

¹⁷I am glad about the coming of Stephanas, Fortunatus, and Achaicus, for what was lacking on your part they supplied. ¹⁸For they refreshed my spirit and yours. Therefore acknowledge such men.

¹⁹The churches of Asia greet you. Aquila and Priscilla greet you heartily in the Lord, with the church that is in their house. ²⁰All the brethren greet you.

Greet one another with a holy kiss.

²¹The salutation with my own hand—Paul's.

²²If anyone does not love the Lord Jesus Christ, let him be accursed.* O Lord, come!*

²³The grace of our Lord Jesus Christ *be* with you. ²⁴My love *be* with you all in Christ Jesus. Amen.

PSALM 40:1-10

To the Chief Musician. A Psalm of David.

I WAITED patiently for the LORD;
And He inclined to me,
And heard my cry.

2 He also brought me up out of
a horrible pit,
Out of the miry clay,
And set my feet upon a rock,
And established my steps.

3 He has put a new song in my
mouth—
Praise to our God;
Many will see *it* and fear,
And will trust in the LORD.

4 Blessed *is* that man who
makes the LORD his trust,
And does not respect the
proud, nor such as turn
aside to lies.

5 Many, O LORD my God, *are*
Your wonderful works
Which You have done;
And Your thoughts toward us
Cannot be recounted to You
in order;

If I would declare and speak *of them,*
They are more than can be numbered.

6 Sacrifice and offering You did not desire;
My ears You have opened.
Burnt offering and sin offering You did not require.

7 Then I said, "Behold, I come;
In the scroll of the book *it is* written of me.

8 I delight to do Your will, O my God,
And Your law *is* within my heart."

9 I have proclaimed the good news of righteousness
In the great assembly;
Indeed, I do not restrain my lips,
O LORD, You Yourself know.

10 I have not hidden Your righteousness within my heart;
I have declared Your faithfulness and Your salvation;
I have not concealed Your lovingkindness and Your truth
From the great assembly.

PROVERBS FOR TODAY/ 22:1

A good name is to be chosen rather than great riches, loving favor rather than silver and gold.

AUGUST 26

JOB 20:1–22:30

THEN Zophar the Naamathite answered and said:

2 "Therefore my anxious thoughts make me answer,
Because of the turmoil within me.

3 I have heard the rebuke that reproaches me,
And the spirit of my understanding causes me to answer.

4 "Do you *not* know this of old,
Since man was placed on earth,

5 That the triumphing of the wicked is short,

And the joy of the hypocrite is *but* for a moment?

6 Though his haughtiness mounts up to the heavens,
And his head reaches to the clouds,

7 *Yet* he will perish forever like his own refuse;
Those who have seen him will say, 'Where is he?'

8 He will fly away like a dream, and not be found;
Yes, he will be chased away like a vision of the night.

9 The eye *that* saw him will *see him* no more,
Nor will his place behold him anymore.

10 His children will seek the favor of the poor,

And his hands will restore his
wealth.
11 His bones are full of his
youthful vigor,
But it will lie down with him
in the dust.

12 "Though evil is sweet in his
mouth,
And he hides it under his
tongue,
13 *Though* he spares it and does
not forsake it,
But still keeps it in his mouth,
14 *Yet* his food in his stomach
turns sour;
It becomes cobra venom
within him.
15 He swallows down riches
And vomits them up again;
God casts them out of his
belly.
16 He will suck the poison of
cobras;
The viper's tongue will slay
him.
17 He will not see the streams,
The rivers flowing with honey
and cream.
18 He will restore that for which
he labored,
And will not swallow *it* down;
From the proceeds of
business
He will get no enjoyment.
19 For he has oppressed *and*
forsaken the poor,
He has violently seized a
house which he did not
build.

20 "Because he knows no
quietness in his heart,*
He will not save anything he
desires.
21 Nothing is left for him to eat;
Therefore his well-being will
not last.
22 In his self-sufficiency he will
be in distress;

Every hand of misery will
come against him.
23 *When* he is about to fill his
stomach,
God will cast on him the fury
of His wrath,
And will rain *it* on him while
he is eating.
24 He will flee from the iron
weapon;
A bronze bow will pierce him
through.
25 It is drawn, and comes out of
the body;
Yes, the glittering *point comes*
out of his gall.
Terrors *come* upon him;
26 Total darkness *is* reserved for
his treasures.
An unfanned fire will
consume him;
It shall go ill with him who is
left in his tent.
27 The heavens will reveal his
iniquity,
And the earth will rise up
against him.
28 The increase of his house will
depart,
And his goods will flow away in
the day of His wrath.
29 This *is* the portion from God
for a wicked man,
The heritage appointed to
him by God."

THEN Job answered and said:

2 "Listen carefully to my speech,
And let this be your
consolation.
3 Bear with me that I may
speak,
And after I have spoken, keep
mocking.

4 "As for me, *is* my complaint
against man?
And if *it were,* why should I
not be impatient?

5 Look at me and be astonished;
Put *your* hand over *your*
mouth.
6 Even when I remember I am
terrified,
And trembling takes hold of
my flesh.
7 Why do the wicked live *and*
become old,
Yes, become mighty in power?
8 Their descendants are
established with them in
their sight,
And their offspring before
their eyes.
9 Their houses *are* safe from
fear,
Neither *is* the rod of God
upon them.
10 Their bull breeds without
failure;
Their cow calves without
miscarriage.
11 They send forth their little
ones like a flock,
And their children dance.
12 They sing to the tambourine
and harp,
And rejoice to the sound of
the flute.
13 They spend their days in
wealth,
And in a moment go down to
the grave.*
14 Yet they say to God, 'Depart
from us,
For we do not desire the
knowledge of Your ways.
15 Who *is* the Almighty, that we
should serve Him?
And what profit do we have if
we pray to Him?'
16 Indeed their prosperity *is* not
in their hand;
The counsel of the wicked is
far from me.

17 "How often is the lamp of the
wicked put out?
How often does their

destruction come upon
them,
The sorrows *God* distributes
in His anger?
18 They are like straw before the
wind,
And like chaff that a storm
carries away.
19 *They say,* 'God lays up one's*
iniquity for his children';
Let Him recompense him,
that he may know *it.*
20 Let his eyes see his
destruction,
And let him drink of the wrath
of the Almighty.
21 For what does he care about
his household after him,
When the number of his
months is cut in half?

22 "Can *anyone* teach God
knowledge,
Since He judges those on
high?
23 One dies in his full strength,
Being wholly at ease and
secure;
24 His pails* are full of milk,
And the marrow of his bones
is moist.
25 Another man dies in the
bitterness of his soul,
Never having eaten with
pleasure.
26 They lie down alike in the
dust,
And worms cover them.

27 "Look, I know your thoughts,
And the schemes *with which*
you would wrong me.
28 For you say,
'Where *is* the house of the
prince?
And where *is* the tent,*
The dwelling place of the
wicked?'
29 Have you not asked those
who travel the road?

And do you not know their signs?

30 For the wicked are reserved for the day of doom;
They shall be brought out on the day of wrath.

31 Who condemns his way to his face?
And who repays him *for what* he has done?

32 Yet he shall be brought to the grave,
And a vigil kept over the tomb.

33 The clods of the valley shall be sweet to him;
Everyone shall follow him,
As countless *have gone* before him

34 How then can you comfort me with empty words,
Since falsehood remains in your answers?"

THEN Eliphaz the Temanite answered and said:

2 "Can a man be profitable to God,
Though he who is wise may be profitable to himself?

3 *Is it* any pleasure to the Almighty that you are righteous?
Or *is it* gain *to Him* that you make your ways blameless?

4 "Is it because of your fear of Him that He corrects you,
And enters into judgment with you?

5 *Is* not your wickedness great,
And your iniquity without end?

6 For you have taken pledges from your brother for no reason,
And stripped the naked of their clothing.

7 You have not given the weary water to drink,

And you have withheld bread from the hungry.

8 But the mighty man possessed the land,
And the honorable man dwelt in it.

9 You have sent widows away empty,
And the strength of the fatherless was crushed.

10 Therefore snares *are* all around you,
And sudden fear troubles you,

11 Or darkness *so that* you cannot see;
And an abundance of water covers you.

12 "Is not God in the height of heaven?
And see the highest stars, how lofty they are!

13 And you say, 'What does God know?
Can He judge through the deep darkness?

14 Thick clouds cover Him, so that He cannot see,
And He walks above the circle of heaven.'

15 Will you keep to the old way Which wicked men have trod,

16 Who were cut down before their time,
Whose foundations were swept away by a flood?

17 They said to God, 'Depart from us!
What can the Almighty do to them?'*

18 Yet He filled their houses with good *things;*
But the counsel of the wicked is far from me.

19 "The righteous see *it* and are glad,
And the innocent laugh at them:

20 'Surely our adversaries* are
    cut down,
    And the fire consumes their
    remnant.'

21 "Now acquaint yourself with
    Him, and be at peace;
    Thereby good will come to
    you.
22 Receive, please, instruction
    from His mouth,
    And lay up His words in your
    heart.
23 If you return to the Almighty,
    you will be built up;
    You will remove iniquity far
    from your tents.
24 Then you will lay your gold in
    the dust,
    And the *gold* of Ophir among
    the stones of the brooks.
25 Yes, the Almighty will be your
    gold*
    And your precious silver;
26 For then you will have your
    delight in the Almighty,
    And lift up your face to God.
27 You will make your prayer to
    Him,
    He will hear you,
    And you will pay your vows.
28 You will also declare a thing,
    And it will be established for
    you;
    So light will shine on your
    ways.
29 When they cast *you* down, and
    you say, 'Exaltation *will
    come!*'
    Then He will save the humble
    person.
30 He will *even* deliver one who
    is not innocent;
    Yes, he will be delivered by
    the purity of your hands."

2 CORINTHIANS 1:1-11

PAUL, an apostle of Jesus Christ by the will of God, and Timothy *our* brother,

To the church of God which is at Corinth, with all the saints who are in all Achaia:

2Grace to you and peace from God our Father and the Lord Jesus Christ.

3Blessed *be* the God and Father of our Lord Jesus Christ, the Father of mercies and God of all comfort, 4who comforts us in all our tribulation, that we may be able to comfort those who are in any trouble, with the comfort with which we ourselves are comforted by God. 5For as the sufferings of Christ abound in us, so our consolation also abounds through Christ. 6Now if we are afflicted, *it is* for your consolation and salvation, which is effective for enduring the same sufferings which we also suffer. Or if we are comforted, *it is* for your consolation and salvation. 7And our hope for you *is* steadfast, because we know that as you are partakers of the sufferings, so also *you will partake* of the consolation.

8For we do not want you to be ignorant, brethren, of our trouble which came to us in Asia: that we were burdened beyond measure, above strength, so that we despaired even of life. 9Yes, we had the sentence of death in ourselves, that we should not trust in ourselves but in God who raises the dead, 10who delivered us from so great a death, and does* deliver us; in whom we trust that He will still deliver *us,* 11you also helping together in prayer for us, that thanks may be given by many persons on our* behalf for the gift *granted* to us through many.

PSALM 40:11-17

Do not withhold Your tender mercies from me, O LORD;
Let Your lovingkindness and Your truth continually preserve me.

12 For innumerable evils have surrounded me;
My iniquities have overtaken me, so that I am not able to look up;
They are more than the hairs of my head;
Therefore my heart fails me.

13 Be pleased, O LORD, to deliver me;
O LORD, make haste to help me!

14 Let them be ashamed and brought to mutual confusion
Who seek to destroy my life;
Let them be driven backward and brought to dishonor
Who wish me evil.

15 Let them be confounded because of their shame,
Who say to me, "Aha, aha!"

16 Let all those who seek You rejoice and be glad in You;
Let such as love Your salvation say continually,
"The LORD be magnified!"

17 But I *am* poor and needy;
Yet the LORD thinks upon me.
You *are* my help and my deliverer;
Do not delay, O my God.

PROVERBS FOR TODAY/ 22:2-4

*The rich and the poor have this in common, the LORD is the maker of them all.
□ A prudent* man *foresees evil and hides himself, but the simple pass on and are punished.* □ *By humility* and *the fear of the LORD* are *riches and honor and life.*

AUGUST 27

JOB 23:1–27:23

THEN Job answered and said:

2 "Even today my complaint is bitter;
My* hand is listless because of my groaning.

3 Oh, that I knew where I might find Him,
That I might come to His seat!

4 I would present *my* case before Him,
And fill my mouth with arguments.

5 I would know the words *which* He would answer me,

And understand what He would say to me.

6 Would He contend with me in His great power?
No! But He would take *note* of me.

7 There the upright could reason with Him,
And I would be delivered forever from my Judge.

8 "Look, I go forward, but He is not *there,*
And backward, but I cannot perceive Him;

9 When He works on the left
hand, I cannot behold *Him;*
When He turns to the right
hand, I cannot see *Him.*
10 But He knows the way that I
take;
When He has tested me, I
shall come forth as gold.
11 My foot has held fast to His
steps;
I have kept His way and not
turned aside.
12 I have not departed from the
commandment of His lips;
I have treasured the words of
His mouth
More than my necessary *food.*

13 "But He *is* unique, and who
can make Him change?
And *whatever* His soul
desires, *that* He does.
14 For He performs *what is*
appointed for me,
And many such *things are*
with Him.
15 Therefore I am terrified at His
presence;
When I consider *this,* I am
afraid of Him.
16 For God made my heart weak,
And the Almighty terrifies me;
17 Because I was not cut off
from the presence of
darkness,
And He did *not* hide deep
darkness from my face.

"SINCE times are not hidden from the
Almighty,
Why do those who know Him
see not His days?

2 "*Some* remove landmarks;
They seize flocks violently
and feed *on them;*
3 They drive away the donkey
of the fatherless;
They take the widow's ox as a
pledge.

4 They push the needy off the
road;
All the poor of the land are
forced to hide.
5 Indeed, *like* wild donkeys in
the desert,
They go out to their work,
searching for food.
The wilderness *yields* food for
them *and* for *their* children.
6 They gather their fodder in
the field
And glean in the vineyard of
the wicked.
7 They spend the night naked,
without clothing,
And have no covering in the
cold.
8 They are wet with the
showers of the mountains,
And huddle around the rock
for want of shelter.

9 "*Some* snatch the fatherless
from the breast,
And take a pledge from the
poor.
10 They cause *the poor* to go
naked, without clothing;
And they take away the
sheaves from the hungry.
11 They press out oil within their
walls,
And tread winepresses, yet
suffer thirst.
12 The dying groan in the city,
And the souls of the wounded
cry out;
Yet God does not charge *them*
with wrong.

13 "There are those who rebel
against the light;
They do not know its ways
Nor abide in its paths.
14 The murderer rises with the
light;
He kills the poor and needy;
And in the night he is like a
thief.

15 The eye of the adulterer waits
for the twilight,
Saying, 'No eye will see me';
And he disguises *his* face.
16 In the dark they break into
houses
Which they marked for
themselves in the daytime;
They do not know the light.
17 For the morning is the same
to them as the shadow of
death;
If *someone* recognizes *them,*
They are in the terrors of the
shadow of death.

18 "They *should be* swift on the
face of the waters,
Their portion *should be* cursed
in the earth,
So that no *one would* turn into
the way of their vineyards.
19 As drought and heat consume
the snow waters,
So the grave* *consumes those*
who have sinned.
20 The womb *should* forget him,
The worm *should* feed sweetly
on him;
He *should* be remembered no
more,
And wickedness *should* be
broken like a tree.
21 For he preys on the barren
who do not bear,
And does no good for the
widow.

22 "But *God* draws the mighty
away with His power;
He rises up, but no *man* is
sure of life.
23 He gives them security, and
they rely *on it;*
Yet His eyes *are* on their ways.
24 They are exalted for a little
while,
Then they are gone.
They are brought low;

They are taken out of the way
like all *others;*
They dry out like the heads of
grain.

25 "Now if *it is* not *so,* who will
prove me a liar,
And make my speech worth
nothing?"

THEN Bildad the Shuhite answered and
said:

2 "Dominion and fear *belong* to
Him;
He makes peace in His high
places.
3 Is there any number to His
armies?
Upon whom does His light
not rise?
4 How then can man be
righteous before God?
Or how can he be pure *who is*
born of a woman?
5 If even the moon does not
shine,
And the stars are not pure in
His sight,
6 How much less man, *who is* a
maggot,
And a son of man, *who is* a
worm?"

BUT Job answered and said:

2 "How have you helped *him*
who is without power?
How have you saved the arm
that has no strength?
3 How have you counseled *one*
who has no wisdom?
And *how* have you declared
sound advice to many?
4 To whom have you uttered
words?
And whose spirit came from
you?

5 "The dead tremble,
   Those under the waters and
      those inhabiting them.
6 Sheol *is* naked before Him,
   And Destruction has no
      covering.
7 He stretches out the north
      over empty space;
   He hangs the earth on
      nothing.
8 He binds up the water in His
      thick clouds,
   Yet the clouds are not broken
      under it.
9 He covers the face of *His*
      throne,
   And spreads His cloud over it.
10 He drew a circular horizon on
      the face of the waters,
   At the boundary of light and
      darkness.
11 The pillars of heaven tremble,
   And are astonished at His
      rebuke.
12 He stirs up the sea with His
      power,
   And by His understanding He
      breaks up the storm.
13 By His Spirit He adorned the
      heavens;
   His hand pierced the fleeing
      serpent.
14 Indeed these *are* the mere
      edges of His ways,
   And how small a whisper we
      hear of Him!
   But the thunder of His power
      who can understand?"

MOREOVER Job continued his discourse,
and said:

2 "*As* God lives, *who* has taken
      away my justice,
   And the Almighty, *who* has
      made my soul bitter,
3 As long as my breath *is* in me,
   And the breath of God in my
      nostrils,

4 My lips will not speak
      wickedness,
   Nor my tongue utter deceit.
5 Far be it from me
   That I should say you are
      right;
   Till I die I will not put away
      my integrity from me.
6 My righteousness I hold fast,
      and will not let it go;
   My heart shall not reproach
      me as long as I live.

7 "May my enemy be like the
      wicked,
   And he who rises up against
      me like the unrighteous.
8 For what is the hope of the
      hypocrite,
   Though he may gain *much,*
   If God takes away his life?
9 Will God hear his cry
   When trouble comes upon
      him?
10 Will he delight himself in the
      Almighty?
   Will he always call on God?

11 "I will teach you about the
      hand of God;
   What *is* with the Almighty I
      will not conceal.
12 Surely all of you have seen *it;*
   Why then do you behave with
      complete nonsense?

13 "This is the portion of a wicked
      man with God,
   And the heritage of
      oppressors, received from
      the Almighty:
14 If his children are multiplied,
      it is for the sword;
   And his offspring shall not be
      satisfied with bread.
15 Those who survive him shall
      be buried in death,
   And their* widows shall not
      weep,

16 Though he heaps up silver
like dust,
And piles up clothing like
clay—
17 He may pile *it* up, but the just
will wear *it,*
And the innocent will divide
the silver.
18 He builds his house like a
moth,*
Like a booth *which* a
watchman makes.
19 The rich man will lie down,
But not be gathered *up;* *
He opens his eyes,
And he *is* no more.
20 Terrors overtake him like a
flood;
A tempest steals him away in
the night.
21 The east wind carries him
away, and he is gone;
It sweeps him out of his place.
22 It hurls against him and does
not spare;
He flees desperately from its
power.
23 *Men* shall clap their hands at
him,
And shall hiss him out of his
place."

2 CORINTHIANS 1:12–2:11

FOR our boasting is this: the testimony of our conscience that we conducted ourselves in the world in simplicity and godly sincerity, not with fleshly wisdom but by the grace of God, and more abundantly toward you. 13For we are not writing any other things to you than what you read or understand. Now I trust you will understand, even to the end 14(as also you have understood us in part), that we are your boast as you also *are* ours, in the day of the Lord Jesus.

15And in this confidence I intended to come to you before, that you might have a second benefit— 16to pass by way of you to Macedonia, to come again from Macedonia to you, and be helped by you on my way to Judea. 17Therefore, when I was planning this, did I do it lightly? Or the things I plan, do I plan according to the flesh, that with me there should be Yes, Yes, and No, No? 18But *as* God *is* faithful, our word to you was not Yes and No. 19For the Son of God, Jesus Christ, who was preached among you by us—by me, Silvanus, and Timothy—was not Yes and No, but in Him was Yes. 20For all the promises of God in Him *are* Yes, and in Him Amen, to the glory of God through us. 21Now He who establishes us with you in Christ and has anointed us *is* God, 22who also has sealed us and given us the Spirit in our hearts as a guarantee.

23Moreover I call God as witness against my soul, that to spare you I came no more to Corinth. 24Not that we have dominion over your faith, but are fellow workers for your joy; for by faith you stand.

BUT I determined this within myself, that I would not come again to you in sorrow. 2For if I make you sorrowful, then who is he who makes me glad but the one who is made sorrowful by me?

3And I wrote this very thing to you, lest, when I came, I should have sorrow over those from whom I ought to have joy, having confidence in you all that my joy is *the joy* of you all. 4For out of much affliction and anguish of heart I wrote to you, with many tears, not that you should be grieved, but that you might know the love which I have so abundantly for you.

5But if anyone has caused grief, he has not grieved me, but all of you to some extent—not to be too severe. 6This punishment which *was inflicted* by the majority *is* sufficient for such a man, 7so that, on the contrary, you *ought* rather to forgive and comfort *him,* lest perhaps such a one be swallowed up with too much sorrow. ⁸Therefore I urge you to reaffirm *your* love to him. ⁹For to this end I also wrote, that I might put you to the test, whether you are obedient in all things. ¹⁰Now whom you forgive anything, I also *forgive*. For if indeed I have forgiven anything, I have forgiven* that one for your sakes in the presence of Christ, ¹¹lest Satan should take advantage of us; for we are not ignorant of his devices.

PSALM 41:1-13

To the Chief Musician. A Psalm of David.

BLESSED *is* he who considers the poor;
The LORD will deliver him in time of trouble.

2 The LORD will preserve him and keep him alive,
And he will be blessed on the earth;
You will not deliver him to the will of his enemies.

3 The LORD will strengthen him on his bed of illness;
You will sustain him on his sickbed.

4 I said, "LORD, be merciful to me;
Heal my soul, for I have sinned against You."

5 My enemies speak evil of me:
"When will he die, and his name perish?"

6 And if he comes to see *me,* he speaks lies;
His heart gathers iniquity to itself;
When he goes out, he tells *it.*

7 All who hate me whisper together against me;
Against me they devise my hurt.

8 "An evil disease," *they say,*
"clings to him.
And *now* that he lies down, he will rise up no more."

9 Even my own familiar friend in whom I trusted,
Who ate my bread,
Has lifted up *his* heel against me.

10 But You, O LORD, be merciful to me, and raise me up,
That I may repay them.

11 By this I know that You are well pleased with me,
Because my enemy does not triumph over me.

12 As for me, You uphold me in my integrity,
And set me before Your face forever.

13 Blessed *be* the LORD God of Israel
From everlasting to everlasting!
Amen and Amen.

PROVERBS FOR TODAY/ 22:5-6

Thorns and *snares* are *in the way of the perverse; he who guards his soul will be far from them.* □ *Train up a child in the way he should go, and when he is old he will not depart from it.*

AUGUST 28

JOB 28:1–30:31

"SURELY there is a mine for silver,
And a place *where* gold is
refined.

2 Iron is taken from the earth,
And copper *is* smelted *from*
ore.

3 *Man* puts an end to darkness,
And searches every recess
For ore in the darkness and
the shadow of death.

4 He breaks open a shaft away
from people;
In places forgotten by feet
They hang far away from men;
They swing to and fro.

5 *As for* the earth, from it
comes bread,
But underneath it is turned
up as by fire;

6 Its stones *are* the source of
sapphires,
And it contains gold dust.

7 *That* path no bird knows,
Nor has the falcon's eye seen
it.

8 The proud lions* have not
trodden it,
Nor has the fierce lion passed
over it.

9 He puts his hand on the flint;
He overturns the mountains
at the roots.

10 He cuts out channels in the
rocks,
And his eye sees every
precious thing.

11 He dams up the streams from
trickling;
What is hidden he brings
forth to light.

12 "But where can wisdom be
found?

And where *is* the place of
understanding?

13 Man does not know its value,
Nor is it found in the land of
the living.

14 The deep says, '*It is* not in me';
And the sea says, '*It is* not
with me.'

15 It cannot be purchased for
gold,
Nor can silver be weighed *for*
its price.

16 It cannot be valued in the gold
of Ophir,
In precious onyx or sapphire.

17 Neither gold nor crystal can
equal it,
Nor can it be exchanged for
jewelry of fine gold.

18 No mention shall be made of
coral or quartz,
For the price of wisdom *is*
above rubies.

19 The topaz of Ethiopia cannot
equal it,
Nor can it be valued in pure
gold.

20 "From where then does
wisdom come?
And where *is* the place of
understanding?

21 It is hidden from the eyes of
all living,
And concealed from the birds
of the air.

22 Destruction and Death say,
'We have heard a report about
it with our ears.'

23 God understands its way,
And He knows its place.

24 For He looks to the ends of
the earth,
And sees under the whole
heavens,

25 To establish a weight for the wind,
And apportion the waters by measure.

26 When He made a law for the rain,
And a path for the thunderbolt,

27 Then He saw *wisdom** and declared it;
He prepared it, indeed, He searched it out.

28 And to man He said,
'Behold, the fear of the Lord, that *is* wisdom,
And to depart from evil *is* understanding.' "

Job further continued his discourse, and said:

2 "Oh, that I were as *in* months past,
As *in* the days *when* God watched over me;

3 When His lamp shone upon my head,
And when by His light I walked *through* darkness;

4 Just as I was in the days of my prime,
When the friendly counsel of God *was* over my tent;

5 When the Almighty *was* yet with me,
When my children *were* around me;

6 When my steps were bathed with cream,*
And the rock poured out rivers of oil for me!

7 "When I went out to the gate by the city,
When I took my seat in the open square,

8 The young men saw me and hid,
And the aged arose *and* stood;

9 The princes refrained from talking,
And put *their* hand on their mouth;

10 The voice of nobles was hushed,
And their tongue stuck to the roof of their mouth.

11 When the ear heard, then it blessed me,
And when the eye saw, then it approved me;

12 Because I delivered the poor who cried out,
The fatherless and *the one who* had no helper.

13 The blessing of a perishing *man* came upon me,
And I caused the widow's heart to sing for joy.

14 I put on righteousness, and it clothed me;
My justice *was* like a robe and a turban.

15 I *was* eyes to the blind,
And I *was* feet to the lame.

16 I *was* a father to the poor,
And I searched out the case *that* I did not know.

17 I broke the fangs of the wicked,
And plucked the victim from his teeth.

18 "Then I said, 'I shall die in my nest,
And multiply *my* days as the sand.

19 My root *is* spread out to the waters,
And the dew lies all night on my branch.

20 My glory *is* fresh within me,
And my bow is renewed in my hand.'

21 "*Men* listened to me and waited,
And kept silence for my counsel.

22 After my words they did not
speak again,
And my speech settled on
them *as dew.*
23 They waited for me *as* for the
rain,
And they opened their mouth
wide *as* for the spring rain.
24 *If* I mocked at them, they did
not believe *it,*
And the light of my
countenance they did not
cast down.
25 I chose the way for them, and
sat as chief;
So I dwelt as a king in the
army,
As one *who* comforts
mourners

"BUT now they mock at me, men
younger than I,
Whose fathers I disdained to
put with the dogs of my
flock.
2 Indeed, what *profit* is the
strength of their hands to
me?
Their vigor has perished.
3 *They are* gaunt from want and
famine,
Fleeing late to the wilderness,
desolate and waste,
4 Who pluck mallow by the
bushes,
And broom tree roots *for* their
food.
5 They were driven out from
among *men,*
They shouted at them as *at* a
thief.
6 *They had* to live in the clefts of
the valleys,
In caves of the earth and the
rocks.
7 Among the bushes they
brayed,
Under the nettles they nestled.
8 *They were* sons of fools,
Yes, sons of vile men;

They were scourged from the
land.
9 "And now I am their taunting
song;
Yes, I am their byword.
10 They abhor me, they keep far
from me;
They do not hesitate to spit in
my face.
11 Because He has loosed my*
bowstring and afflicted me,
They have cast off restraint
before me.
12 At *my* right *hand* the rabble
arises;
They push away my feet,
And they raise against me
their ways of destruction.
13 They break up my path,
They promote my calamity;
They have no helper.
14 They come as broad breakers;
Under the ruinous storm they
roll along.
15 Terrors are turned upon me;
They pursue my honor as the
wind,
And my prosperity has passed
like a cloud.

16 "And now my soul is poured
out because of my *plight;*
The days of affliction take
hold of me.
17 My bones are pierced in me
at night,
And my gnawing pains take
no rest.
18 By great force my garment is
disfigured;
It binds me about as the collar
of my coat.
19 He has cast me into the mire,
And I have become like dust
and ashes.

20 "I cry out to You, but You do
not answer me;
I stand up, and You regard me.

21 *But* You have become cruel
       to me;
    With the strength of Your
       hand You oppose me.
22 You lift me up to the wind and
       cause me to ride *on it;*
    You spoil my success.
23 For I know *that* You will bring
       me *to* death,
    And *to* the house appointed
       for all living.

24 "Surely He would not stretch
       out *His* hand against a heap
       of ruins,
    If they cry out when He
       destroys *it.*
25 Have I not wept for him who
       was in trouble?
    Has *not* my soul grieved for
       the poor?
26 But when I looked for good,
       evil came *to me;*
    And when I waited for light,
       then came darkness.
27 My heart is in turmoil and
       cannot rest;
    Days of affliction confront me.
28 I go about mourning, but not
       in the sun;
    I stand up in the assembly
       and cry out for help.
29 I am a brother of jackals,
    And a companion of ostriches.
30 My skin grows black and falls
       from me;
    My bones burn with fever.
31 My harp is *turned* to
       mourning,
    And my flute to the voice of
       those who weep."

2 CORINTHIANS 2:12-17

FURTHERMORE, when I [Paul] came
to Troas to *preach* Christ's gospel, and a door was opened to
me by the Lord, 13I had no rest in my
spirit, because I did not find Titus my
brother; but taking my leave of them, I
departed for Macedonia.
14Now thanks *be* to God who always
leads us in triumph in Christ, and
through us diffuses the fragrance of
His knowledge in every place. 15For
we are to God the fragrance of Christ
among those who are being saved and
among those who are perishing. 16To
the one *we are* the aroma of death *leading* to death, and to the other the
aroma of life *leading* to life. And who *is*
sufficient for these things? 17For we
are not, as so many,* peddling the
word of God; but as of sincerity, but as
from God, we speak in the sight of God
in Christ.

PSALM 42:1-11

To the Chief Musician. A Contemplation of the
sons of Korah.*

As the deer pants for the water
      brooks,
      So pants my soul for You,
         O God.
2   My soul thirsts for God, for
         the living God.
      When shall I come and
         appear before God?*
3   My tears have been my food
         day and night,
      While they continually say to
         me,
      "Where *is* your God?"

4   When I remember these
         things,
      I pour out my soul within me.
      For I used to go with the
         multitude;
      I went with them to the house
         of God,
      With the voice of joy and
         praise,
      With a multitude that kept a
         pilgrim feast.

5   Why are you cast down, O my
         soul?

And *why* are you disquieted within me?
Hope in God, for I shall yet praise Him
For the help of His countenance.*

6 O my God,* my soul is cast down within me;
Therefore I will remember You from the land of the Jordan,
And from the heights of Hermon,
From the Hill Mizar.

7 Deep calls unto deep at the noise of Your waterfalls;
All Your waves and billows have gone over me.

8 The LORD will command His lovingkindness in the daytime,
And in the night His song *shall be* with me—

A prayer to the God of my life.

9 I will say to God my Rock, "Why have You forgotten me?
Why do I go mourning because of the oppression of the enemy?"

10 *As* with a breaking of my bones,
My enemies reproach me,
While they say to me all day long,
"Where *is* your God?"

11 Why are you cast down, O my soul?
And why are you disquieted within me?
Hope in God;
For I shall yet praise Him,
The help of my countenance and my God.

PROVERBS FOR TODAY/ 22:7

The rich rules over the poor, and the borrower is *servant to the lender.*

AUGUST 29

JOB 31:1–33:33

"I HAVE made a covenant with my eyes;
Why then should I look upon a young woman?

2 For what *is* the allotment of God from above,
And the inheritance of the Almighty from on high?

3 *Is* it not destruction for the wicked,
And disaster for the workers of iniquity?

4 Does He not see my ways,

And count all my steps?

5 "If I have walked with falsehood,
Or if my foot has hastened to deceit,

6 Let me be weighed on honest scales,
That God may know my integrity.

7 If my step has turned from the way,
Or my heart walked after my eyes,

Or if any spot adheres to my hands,

8 *Then* let me sow, and another eat;
Yes, let my harvest be rooted out.

9 "If my heart has been enticed by a woman,
Or *if* I have lurked at my neighbor's door,

10 *Then* let my wife grind for another,
And let others bow down over her.

11 For that *would be* wickedness;
Yes, it *would be* iniquity *deserving of* judgment.

12 For that *would be* a fire *that* consumes to destruction,
And would root out all my increase.

13 "If I have despised the cause of my male or female servant
When they complained against me,

14 What then shall I do when God rises up?
When He punishes, how shall I answer Him?

15 Did not He who made me in the womb make them?
Did not the same One fashion us in the womb?

16 "If I have kept the poor from *their* desire,
Or caused the eyes of the widow to fail,

17 Or eaten my morsel by myself,
So that the fatherless could not eat of it

18 (But from my youth I reared him as a father,
And from my mother's womb I guided *the widow**);

19 If I have seen anyone perish for lack of clothing,

Or any poor *man* without covering;

20 If his heart* has not blessed me,
And *if* he was *not* warmed with the fleece of my sheep;

21 If I have raised my hand against the fatherless,
When I saw I had help in the gate;

22 *Then* let my arm fall from my shoulder,
Let my arm be torn from the socket.

23 For destruction *from* God *is* a terror to me,
And because of His magnificence I cannot endure.

24 "If I have made gold my hope,
Or said to fine gold, '*You are* my confidence';

25 If I have rejoiced because my wealth *was* great,
And because my hand had gained much;

26 If I have observed the sun* when it shines,
Or the moon moving *in* brightness,

27 So that my heart has been secretly enticed,
And my mouth has kissed my hand;

28 This also *would be* an iniquity *deserving of* judgment,
For I would have denied God *who is* above.

29 "If I have rejoiced at the destruction of him who hated me,
Or lifted myself up when evil found him

30 (Indeed I have not allowed my mouth to sin
By asking for a curse on his soul);

31 If the men of my tent have
      not said,
    'Who is there that has not
      been satisfied with his
      meat?'
32 (*But* no sojourner had to
      lodge in the street,
    For I have opened my doors
      to the traveler*);
33 If I have covered my
      transgressions as Adam,
    By hiding my iniquity in my
      bosom,
34 Because I feared the great
      multitude,
    And dreaded the contempt of
      families,
    So that I kept silence
    And did not go out of the
      door—
35 Oh, that I had one to hear me!
    Here is my mark.
    Oh, that the Almighty would
      answer me,
    That my Prosecutor had
      written a book!
36 Surely I would carry it on my
      shoulder,
    And bind it on me *like* a crown;
37 I would declare to Him the
      number of my steps;
    Like a prince I would
      approach Him.

38 "If my land cries out against
      me,
    And its furrows weep
      together;
39 If I have eaten its fruit*
      without money,
    Or caused its owners to lose
      their lives;
40 *Then* let thistles grow instead
      of wheat,
    And weeds instead of barley."

The words of Job are ended.

So these three men ceased answering
Job, because he *was* righteous in his
own eyes. ²Then the wrath of Elihu,
the son of Barachel the Buzite, of the
family of Ram, was aroused against
Job; his wrath was aroused because he
justified himself rather than God. ³Also
against his three friends his wrath was
aroused, because they had found no
answer, and *yet* had condemned Job.
⁴Now because they *were* years older
than he, Elihu had waited to speak to
Job.* ⁵When Elihu saw that *there was*
no answer in the mouth of these three
men, his wrath was aroused.
⁶So Elihu, the son of Barachel the
Buzite, answered and said:

    "I *am* young in years, and you
      are very old;
    Therefore I was afraid,
    And dared not declare my
      opinion to you.
7   I said, 'Age* should speak,
    And multitude of years should
      teach wisdom.'
8   But *there is* a spirit in man,
    And the breath of the
      Almighty gives him
      understanding.
9   Great men* are not *always*
      wise,
    Nor do the aged *always*
      understand justice.

10 "Therefore I say, 'Listen to me,
    I also will declare my opinion.'
11 Indeed I waited for your
      words,
    I listened to your reasonings,
      while you searched out
      what to say.
12 I paid close attention to you;
    And surely not one of you
      convinced Job,
    Or answered his words—
13 Lest you say,
    'We have found wisdom';
    God will vanquish him, not
      man.
14 Now he has not directed *his*
      words against me;

So I will not answer him with
your words.

15 "They are dismayed and
answer no more;
Words escape them.

16 And I have waited, because
they did not speak,
Because they stood still *and*
answered no more.

17 I also will answer my part,
I too will declare my opinion.

18 For I am full of words;
The spirit within me compels
me.

19 Indeed my belly *is* like wine
that has no vent;
It is ready to burst like new
wineskins.

20 I will speak, that I may find
relief;
I must open my lips and
answer.

21 Let me not, I pray, show
partiality to anyone;
Nor let me flatter any man.

22 For I do not know how to
flatter,
Else my Maker would soon
take me away.

"But please, Job, hear my speech,
And listen to all my words.

2 Now, I open my mouth;
My tongue speaks in my
mouth.

3 My words *come* from my
upright heart;
My lips utter pure knowledge.

4 The Spirit of God has made
me,
And the breath of the
Almighty gives me life.

5 If you can answer me,
Set *your words* in order before
me;
Take your stand.

6 Truly I *am* as your
spokesman* before God;

I also have been formed out of
clay.

7 Surely no fear of me will
terrify you,
Nor will my hand be heavy on
you.

8 "Surely you have spoken in my
hearing,
And I have heard the sound of
your words, *saying,*

9 'I *am* pure, without
transgression;
I *am* innocent, and *there is* no
iniquity in me.

10 Yet He finds occasions against
me,
He counts me as His enemy;

11 He puts my feet in the stocks,
He watches all my paths.'

12 "Look, *in* this you are not
righteous.
I will answer you,
For God is greater than man.

13 Why do you contend with
Him?
For He does not give an
accounting of any of His
words.

14 For God may speak in one
way, or in another,
Yet man does not perceive it.

15 In a dream, in a vision of the
night,
When deep sleep falls upon
men,
While slumbering on their
beds,

16 Then He opens the ears of
men,
And seals their instruction.

17 In order to turn man *from his*
deed,
And conceal pride from man,

18 He keeps back his soul from
the Pit,
And his life from perishing by
the sword.

19 "*Man* is also chastened with
   pain on his bed,
   And with strong *pain* in many
   of his bones,
20 So that his life abhors bread,
   And his soul succulent food.
21 His flesh wastes away from
   sight,
   And his bones stick out *which
   once* were not seen.
22 Yes, his soul draws near the
   Pit,
   And his life to the
   executioners.

23 "If there is a messenger for
   him,
   A mediator, one among a
   thousand,
   To show man His uprightness,
24 Then He is gracious to him,
   and says,
   'Deliver him from going down
   to the Pit;
   I have found a ransom';
25 His flesh shall be young like a
   child's,
   He shall return to the days of
   his youth.
26 He shall pray to God, and He
   will delight in him,
   He shall see His face with joy,
   For He restores to man His
   righteousness.
27 Then he looks at men and
   says,
   'I have sinned, and perverted
   what was right,
   And it did not profit me.'
28 He will redeem his* soul from
   going down to the Pit,
   And his* life shall see the
   light.

29 "Behold, God works all these
   things,
   Twice, *in fact,* three *times*
   with a man,
30 To bring back his soul from
   the Pit,

That he may be enlightened
   with the light of life.

31 "Give ear, Job, listen to me;
   Hold your peace, and I will
   speak.
32 If you have anything to say,
   answer me;
   Speak, for I desire to justify
   you.
33 If not, listen to me;
   Hold your peace, and I will
   teach you wisdom."

2 CORINTHIANS 3:1-18

Do we begin again to commend
ourselves? Or do we need, as
some *others,* epistles of commendation to you or *letters* of
commendation from you? [2]You are our
epistle written in our hearts, known
and read by all men; [3]clearly *you are* an
epistle of Christ, ministered by us,
written not with ink but by the Spirit of
the living God, not on tablets of stone
but on tablets of flesh, *that is,* of the
heart.

[4]And we have such trust through
Christ toward God. [5]Not that we are
sufficient of ourselves to think of anything as *being* from ourselves, but our
sufficiency *is* from God, [6]who also
made us sufficient as ministers of the
new covenant, not of the letter but of
the Spirit;* for the letter kills, but the
Spirit gives life.

[7]But if the ministry of death, written
and engraved on stones, was glorious,
so that the children of Israel could not
look steadily at the face of Moses because of the glory of his countenance,
which *glory* was passing away, [8]how
will the ministry of the Spirit not be
more glorious? [9]For if the ministry of
condemnation *had* glory, the ministry
of righteousness exceeds much more
in glory. [10]For even what was made
glorious had no glory in this respect,
because of the glory that excels. [11]For

if what is passing away *was* glorious, what remains *is* much more glorious.

¹²Therefore, since we have such hope, we use great boldness of speech— ¹³unlike Moses, *who* put a veil over his face so that the children of Israel could not look steadily at the end of what was passing away. ¹⁴But their minds were blinded. For until this day the same veil remains unlifted in the reading of the Old Testament, because the *veil* is taken away in Christ. ¹⁵But even to this day, when Moses is read, a veil lies on their heart. ¹⁶Nevertheless when one turns to the Lord, the veil is taken away. ¹⁷Now the Lord is the Spirit; and where the Spirit of the Lord *is,* there *is* liberty. ¹⁸But we all, with unveiled face, beholding as in a mirror the glory of the Lord, are being transformed into the same image from glory to glory, just as by the Spirit of the Lord.

PSALM 43:1-5

Vindicate me, O God,
    And plead my cause against an
        ungodly nation;
    Oh, deliver me from the
        deceitful and unjust man!

2   For You *are* the God of my
        strength;
    Why do You cast me off?
    Why do I go mourning
        because of the oppression
        of the enemy?

3   Oh, send out Your light and
        Your truth!
    Let them lead me;
    Let them bring me to Your
        holy hill
    And to Your tabernacle.

4   Then I will go to the altar of
        God,
    To God my exceeding joy;
    And on the harp I will praise
        You,
    O God, my God.

5   Why are you cast down, O my
        soul?
    And why are you disquieted
        within me?
    Hope in God;
    For I shall yet praise Him,
    The help of my countenance
        and my God.

PROVERBS FOR TODAY/ 22:8-9

He who sows iniquity will reap sorrow, and the rod of his anger will fail. He who has a generous eye will be blessed, for he gives of his bread to the poor.

AUGUST 30

JOB 34:1–36:33

Elihu further answered and said:

²"Hear my words, you wise
    men;
    Give ear to me, you who have
        knowledge.

3   For the ear tests words
    As the palate tastes food.

4   Let us choose justice for
        ourselves;
    Let us know among ourselves
        what *is* good.

5 "For Job has said, 'I am
righteous,
But God has taken away my
justice;

6 Should I lie concerning my
right?
My wound *is* incurable,
though I am without
transgression.'

7 What man *is* like Job,
Who drinks scorn like water,

8 Who goes in company with
the workers of iniquity,
And walks with wicked men?

9 For he has said,
'It profits a man nothing
That he should delight in
God.'

10 "Therefore listen to me, you
men of understanding:
Far be it from God *to do*
wickedness,
And *from* the Almighty to
commit iniquity.

11 For He repays man *according
to* his work,
And makes man to find a
reward according to *his* way.

12 Surely God will never do
wickedly,
Nor will the Almighty pervert
justice.

13 Who gave Him charge over
the earth?
Or who appointed *Him over*
the whole world?

14 If He should set His heart on
it,
If He should gather to
Himself His Spirit and His
breath,

15 All flesh would perish
together,
And man would return to dust.

16 "If *you have* understanding,
hear this;
Listen to the sound of my
words:

17 Should one who hates justice
govern?
Will you condemn *Him who is*
most just?

18 *Is it fitting* to say to a king,
'*You are* worthless,'
And to nobles, '*You are*
wicked'?

19 Yet He is not partial to princes,
Nor does He regard the rich
more than the poor;
For they *are* all the work of
His hands.

20 In a moment they die, in the
middle of the night;
The people are shaken and
pass away;
The mighty are taken away
without a hand.

21 "For His eyes *are* on the ways
of man,
And He sees all his steps.

22 There is no darkness nor
shadow of death
Where the workers of iniquity
may hide themselves.

23 For He need not further
consider a man,
That he should go before God
in judgment.

24 He breaks in pieces mighty
men without inquiry,
And sets others in their place.

25 Therefore He knows their
works;
He overthrows *them* in the
night,
And they are crushed.

26 He strikes them as wicked
men
In the open sight of others,

27 Because they turned back
from Him,
And would not consider any
of His ways,

28 So that they caused the cry of
the poor to come to Him;
For He hears the cry of the
afflicted.

29 When He gives quietness,
who then can make trouble?
And when He hides *His* face,
who then can see Him,
Whether *it is* against a nation
or a man alone?—

30 That the hypocrite should not
reign,
Lest the people be ensnared.

31 "For has *anyone* said to God,
'I have borne *chastening;*
I will offend no more;

32 Teach me *what* I do not see;
If I have done iniquity, I will
do no more'?

33 Should He repay *it* according
to your *terms,*
Just because you disavow it?
You must choose, and not I;
Therefore speak what you
know.

34 "Men of understanding say to
me,
Wise men who listen to me:

35 'Job speaks without
knowledge,
His words *are* without
wisdom.'

36 Oh, that Job were tried to the
utmost,
Because *his* answers *are like*
those of wicked men!

37 For he adds rebellion to his
sin;
He claps *his hands* among us,
And multiplies his words
against God."

MOREOVER Elihu answered and said:

2 "Do you think this is right?
Do you say,
'My righteousness is more
than God's'?

3 For you say,
'What advantage will it be to
You?

What profit shall I have, more
than *if* I had sinned?'

4 "I will answer you,
And your companions with
you.

5 Look to the heavens and see;
And behold the clouds—
They are higher than you.

6 If you sin, what do you
accomplish against Him?
Or, *if* your transgressions are
multiplied, what do you do
to Him?

7 If you are righteous, what do
you give Him?
Or what does He receive from
your hand?

8 Your wickedness affects a
man such as you,
And your righteousness a son
of man.

9 "Because of the multitude of
oppressions they cry out;
They cry out for help because
of the arm of the mighty.

10 But no one says, 'Where *is*
God my Maker,
Who gives songs in the night,

11 Who teaches us more than
the beasts of the earth,
And makes us wiser than the
birds of heaven?'

12 There they cry out, but He
does not answer,
Because of the pride of evil
men.

13 Surely God will not listen to
empty *talk,*
Nor will the Almighty regard
it.

14 Although you say you do not
see Him,
Yet justice *is* before Him, and
you must wait for Him.

15 And now, because He has not
punished in His anger,
Nor taken much notice of folly,

16 Therefore Job opens his
   mouth in vain;
   He multiplies words without
   knowledge."

ELIHU also proceeded and said:

2 "Bear with me a little, and I will
   show you
   That *there are* yet words to
   speak on God's behalf.
3 I will fetch my knowledge
   from afar;
   I will ascribe righteousness to
   my Maker.
4 For truly my words *are* not
   false;
   One who is perfect in
   knowledge *is* with you.

5 "Behold, God *is* mighty, but
   despises *no one;*
   He is mighty in strength of
   understanding.
6 He does not preserve the life
   of the wicked,
   But gives justice to the
   oppressed.
7 He does not withdraw His
   eyes from the righteous;
   But *they are* on the throne
   with kings,
   For He has seated them
   forever,
   And they are exalted.
8 And if *they are* bound in
   fetters,
   Held in the cords of affliction,
9 Then He tells them their
   work and their
   transgressions—
   That they have acted defiantly.
10 He also opens their ear to
   instruction,
   And commands that they turn
   from iniquity.
11 If they obey and serve *Him,*
   They shall spend their days in
   prosperity,
   And their years in pleasures.

12 But if they do not obey,
   They shall perish by the
   sword,
   And they shall die without
   knowledge.*

13 "But the hypocrites in heart
   store up wrath;
   They do not cry for help
   when He binds them.
14 They die in youth,
   And their life *ends* among the
   perverted persons.*
15 He delivers the poor in their
   affliction,
   And opens their ears in
   oppression.

16 "Indeed He would have
   brought you out of dire
   distress,
   Into a broad place where *there
   is* no restraint;
   And what is set on your table
   would be full of richness.
17 But you are filled with the
   judgment due the wicked;
   Judgment and justice take
   hold *of you.*
18 Because *there is* wrath, *beware*
   lest He take you away with
   one blow;
   For a large ransom would not
   help you avoid *it.*
19 Will your riches,
   Or all the mighty forces,
   Keep you from distress?
20 Do not desire the night,
   When people are cut off in
   their place.
21 Take heed, do not turn to
   iniquity,
   For you have chosen t'
   rather than afflic*

22 "Behold, God i
   power;
   Who teac'
23 Who h
   w'

Or who has said, 'You have
done wrong'?

24 "Remember to magnify His
work,
Of which men have sung.
25 Everyone has seen it;
Man looks on *it* from afar.

26 "Behold, God *is* great, and we
do not know *Him;*
Nor can the number of His
years *be* discovered.
27 For He draws up drops of
water,
Which distill as rain from the
mist,
28 Which the clouds drop down
And pour abundantly on man.
29 Indeed, can *anyone*
understand the spreading
of clouds,
The thunder from His canopy?
30 Look, He scatters His light
upon it,
And covers the depths of the
sea.
31 For by these He judges the
peoples;
He gives food in abundance.
32 He covers *His* hands with
lightning,
And commands it to strike.
33 His thunder declares it,
The cattle also, concerning
the rising *storm.*"

2 CORINTHIANS 4:1-12

THEREFORE, since we have this ministry, as we have received
But cy, we do not lose heart.
ngs c renounced the hidden
s nor h
lly, bu not walking in crafti-
commethe word of God de-
onscienfestation of the
ven if our g yes to every
those wh ht of God.
d, it is
ng,

4whose minds the god of this age has
blinded, who do not believe, lest the
light of the gospel of the glory of
Christ, who is the image of God,
should shine on them. 5For we do not
preach ourselves, but Christ Jesus the
Lord, and ourselves your bondservants for Jesus' sake. 6For it is the
God who commanded light to shine
out of darkness, who has shone in our
hearts to *give* the light of the knowledge of the glory of God in the face of
Jesus Christ.

7But we have this treasure in
earthen vessels, that the excellence of
the power may be of God and not of us.
8*We are* hard-pressed on every side,
yet not crushed; *we are* perplexed, but
not in despair; 9persecuted, but not forsaken; struck down, but not destroyed— 10always carrying about in
the body the dying of the Lord Jesus,
that the life of Jesus also may be manifested in our body. 11For we who live
are always delivered to death for Jesus'
sake, that the life of Jesus also may be
manifested in our mortal flesh. 12So
then death is working in us, but life in
you.

PSALM 44:1-8

To the Chief Musician. A Contemplation of the
sons of Korah.*

WE have heard with our ears,
O God,
Our fathers have told us,
The deeds You did in their
days,
In days of old:
2 You drove out the nations
with Your hand,
But them You planted;
You afflicted the peoples, and
cast them out.
3 For they did not gain
possession of the land by
their own sword,
Nor did their own arm save
them;

"Be steadfast, immovable, always abounding in the work of the Lord."
1 Corinthians 15:58

"To You I will sing with the harp, O Holy One of Israel."

Psalm 71:22

But it was Your right hand,
  Your arm, and the light of
  Your countenance,
Because You favored them.

4 You are my King, O God;*
  Command* victories for
  Jacob.
5 Through You we will push
  down our enemies;
Through Your name we will

  trample those who rise up
  against us.
6 For I will not trust in my bow,
Nor shall my sword save me.
7 But You have saved us from
  our enemies,
And have put to shame those
  who hated us.
8 In God we boast all day long,
And praise Your name forever.
                 Selah

PROVERBS FOR TODAY/ 22:10-12

Cast out the scoffer, and contention will leave; yes, strife and reproach will cease.
□ *He who loves purity of heart* and has *grace on his lips, the king* will be *his friend.*
□ *The eyes of the* LORD *preserve knowledge, but He overthrows the words of the faithless.*

AUGUST 31

JOB 37:1–39:30

"A T this also my heart trembles,
And leaps from its place.
   ²Hear attentively the thunder
  of His voice,
And the rumbling *that* comes
  from His mouth.
3 He sends it forth under the
  whole heaven,
His lightning to the ends of
  the earth.
4 After it a voice roars;
He thunders with His majestic
  voice,
And He does not restrain
  them when His voice is
  heard.
5 God thunders marvelously
  with His voice;
He does great things which
  we cannot comprehend.
6 For He says to the snow,
  'Fall *on* the earth';
Likewise to the gentle rain

  and the heavy rain of His
  strength.
7 He seals the hand of every
  man,
That all men may know His
  work.
8 The beasts go into dens,
And remain in their lairs.
9 From the chamber *of the south*
  comes the whirlwind,
And cold from the scattering
  winds *of the north.*
10 By the breath of God ice is
  given,
And the broad waters are
  frozen.
11 Also with moisture He
  saturates the thick clouds;
He scatters His bright clouds.
12 And they swirl about, being
  turned by His guidance,
That they may do whatever
  He commands them
On the face of the whole
  earth.*

13 He causes it to come,
Whether for correction,
Or for His land,
Or for mercy.

14 "Listen to this, O Job;
Stand still and consider the
wondrous works of God.
15 Do you know when God
dispatches them,
And causes the light of His
cloud to shine?
16 Do you know how the clouds
are balanced,
Those wondrous works of
Him who is perfect in
knowledge?
17 Why *are* your garments hot,
When He quiets the earth by
the south *wind?*
18 With Him, have you spread
out the skies,
Strong as a cast metal mirror?

19 "Teach us what we should say
to Him,
For we can prepare nothing
because of the darkness.
20 Should He be told that I *wish
to* speak?
If a man were to speak, surely
he would be swallowed up.
21 Even now *men* cannot look at
the light *when it is* bright in
the skies,
When the wind has passed
and cleared them.
22 He comes from the north *as*
golden *splendor;*
With God *is* awesome majesty.
23 *As for* the Almighty, we cannot
find Him;
He is excellent in power,
In judgment and abundant
justice;
He does not oppress.
24 Therefore men fear Him;
He shows no partiality to any
who are wise of heart."

THEN the LORD answered Job out of the
whirlwind, and said:

2 "Who *is* this who darkens
counsel
By words without knowledge?
3 Now prepare yourself like a
man;
I will question you, and you
shall answer Me.

4 "Where were you when I laid
the foundations of the
earth?
Tell *Me,* if you have
understanding.
5 Who determined its
measurements?
Surely you know!
Or who stretched the line
upon it?
6 To what were its foundations
fastened?
Or who laid its cornerstone,
7 When the morning stars
sang together,
And all the sons of God
shouted for joy?

8 "Or *who* shut in the sea with
doors,
When it burst forth *and*
issued from the womb;
9 When I made the clouds its
garment,
And thick darkness its
swaddling band;
10 When I fixed My limit for it,
And set bars and doors;
11 When I said,
'This far you may come, but
no farther,
And here your proud waves
must stop!'

12 "Have you commanded the
morning since your days
began,
And caused the dawn to know
its place,

13 That it might take hold of the
      ends of the earth,
   And the wicked be shaken out
      of it?
14 It takes on form like clay
      under a seal,
   And stands out like a garment.
15 From the wicked their light is
      withheld,
   And the upraised arm is
      broken.

16 "Have you entered the springs
      of the sea?
   Or have you walked in search
      of the depths?
17 Have the gates of death been
      revealed to you?
   Or have you seen the doors of
      the shadow of death?
18 Have you comprehended the
      breadth of the earth?
   Tell *Me,* if you know all this.

19 "Where *is* the way *to* the
      dwelling of light?
   And darkness, where *is* its
      place,
20 That you may take it to its
      territory,
   That you may know the paths
      to its home?
21 Do you know *it,* because you
      were born then,
   Or *because* the number of
      your days *is* great?

22 "Have you entered the
      treasury of snow,
   Or have you seen the
      treasury of hail,
23 Which I have reserved for the
      time of trouble,
   For the day of battle and war?
24 By what way is light diffused,
   Or the east wind scattered
      over the earth?

25 "Who has divided a channel
      for the overflowing *water,*

Or a path for the thunderbolt,
26 To cause it to rain on a land
      where there is no one,
   A wilderness in which *there is*
      no man;
27 To satisfy the desolate waste,
   And cause to spring forth the
      growth of tender grass?
28 Has the rain a father?
   Or who has begotten the
      drops of dew?
29 From whose womb comes the
      ice?
   And the frost of heaven, who
      gives it birth?
30 The waters harden like stone,
   And the surface of the deep is
      frozen.

31 "Can you bind the cluster of
      the Pleiades,
   Or loose the belt of Orion?
32 Can you bring out
      Mazzaroth* in its season?
   Or can you guide the Great
      Bear with its cubs?
33 Do you know the ordinances
      of the heavens?
   Can you set their dominion
      over the earth?

34 "Can you lift up your voice to
      the clouds,
   That an abundance of water
      may cover you?
35 Can you send out lightnings,
      that they may go,
   And say to you, 'Here we *are!*'?
36 Who has put wisdom in the
      mind?*
   Or who has given
      understanding to the heart?
37 Who can number the clouds
      by wisdom?
   Or who can pour out the
      bottles of heaven,
38 When the dust hardens in
      clumps,
   And the clods cling together?

39 "Can you hunt the prey for the
lion,
Or satisfy the appetite of the
young lions,
40 When they crouch in *their*
dens,
Or lurk in their lairs to lie in
wait?
41 Who provides food for the
raven,
When its young ones cry to
God,
And wander about for lack of
food?

"Do you know the time when the wild
mountain goats bear young?
Or can you mark when the
deer gives birth?
2 Can you number the months
that they fulfill?
Or do you know the time
when they bear young?
3 They bow down,
They bring forth their young,
They deliver their offspring.*
4 Their young ones are healthy,
They grow strong with grain;
They depart and do not
return to them.

5 "Who set the wild donkey free?
Who loosed the bonds of the
onager,
6 Whose home I have made the
wilderness,
And the barren land his
dwelling?
7 He scorns the tumult of the
city;
He does not heed the shouts
of the driver.
8 The range of the mountains *is*
his pasture,
And he searches after every
green thing.

9 "Will the wild ox be willing to
serve you?
Will he bed by your manger?

10 Can you bind the wild ox in
the furrow with ropes?
Or will he plow the valleys
behind you?
11 Will you trust him because
his strength *is* great?
Or will you leave your labor to
him?
12 Will you trust him to bring
home your grain,
And gather it to your
threshing floor?

13 "The wings of the ostrich wave
proudly,
But are her wings and pinions
like the kindly stork's?
14 For she leaves her eggs on
the ground,
And warms them in the dust;
15 She forgets that a foot may
crush them,
Or that a wild beast may
break them.
16 She treats her young harshly,
as though *they were* not
hers;
Her labor is in vain, without
concern,
17 Because God deprived her of
wisdom,
And did not endow her with
understanding.
18 When she lifts herself on high,
She scorns the horse and its
rider.

19 "Have you given the horse
strength?
Have you clothed his neck
with thunder?*
20 Can you frighten him like a
locust?
His majestic snorting strikes
terror.
21 He paws in the valley, and
rejoices in *his* strength;
He gallops into the clash of
arms.

22 He mocks at fear, and is not
frightened;
Nor does he turn back from
the sword.
23 The quiver rattles against him,
The glittering spear and
javelin.
24 He devours the distance with
fierceness and rage;
Nor does he come to a halt
because the trumpet *has*
sounded.
25 At *the blast of* the trumpet he
says, 'Aha!'
He smells the battle from afar,
The thunder of captains and
shouting.

26 "Does the hawk fly by your
wisdom,
And spread its wings toward
the south?
27 Does the eagle mount up at
your command,
And make its nest on high?
28 On the rock it dwells and
resides,
On the crag of the rock and
the stronghold.
29 From there it spies out the
prey;
Its eyes observe from afar.
30 Its young ones suck up blood;
And where the slain *are,* there
it *is.*"

2 CORINTHIANS 4:13–5:10

AND since we have the same
spirit of faith, according to
what is written, *"I believed and
therefore I spoke,"* * we also believe
and therefore speak, 14knowing that
He who raised up the Lord Jesus will
also raise us up with Jesus, and will
present *us* with you. 15For all things *are*
for your sakes, that grace, having
spread through the many, may cause
thanksgiving to abound to the glory of
God.

16Therefore we do not lose heart.
Even though our outward man is perishing, yet the inward *man* is being
renewed day by day. 17For our light
affliction, which is but for a moment, is
working for us a far more exceeding
and eternal weight of glory, 18while we
do not look at the things which are
seen, but at the things which are not
seen. For the things which are seen
are temporary, but the things which
are not seen *are* eternal.

FOR we know that if our earthly house,
this tent, is destroyed, we have a building from God, a house not made with
hands, eternal in the heavens. 2For in
this we groan, earnestly desiring to be
clothed with our habitation which is
from heaven, 3If indeed, having been
clothed, we shall not be found naked.
4For we who are in *this* tent groan, being burdened, not because we want to
be unclothed, but further clothed, that
mortality may be swallowed up by life.
5Now He who has prepared us for this
very thing *is* God, who also has given
us the Spirit as a guarantee.

6So *we are* always confident, knowing that while we are at home in the
body we are absent from the Lord.
7For we walk by faith, not by sight. 8We
are confident, yes, well pleased rather
to be absent from the body and to be
present with the Lord.

9Therefore we make it our aim,
whether present or absent, to be well
pleasing to Him. 10For we must all appear before the judgment seat of
Christ, that each one may receive the
things *done* in the body, according to
what he has done, whether good or
bad.

PSALM 44:9-26

BUT You have cast *us* off and
put us to shame,
And You do not go out with
our armies.

10 You make us turn back from
the enemy,
And those who hate us have
taken spoil for themselves.
11 You have given us up like
sheep *intended* for food,
And have scattered us among
the nations.
12 You sell Your people for *next
to* nothing,
And are not enriched by
selling them.

13 You make us a reproach to
our neighbors,
A scorn and a derision to
those all around us.
14 You make us a byword among
the nations,
A shaking of the head among
the peoples.
15 My dishonor *is* continually
before me,
And the shame of my face has
covered me,
16 Because of the voice of him
who reproaches and reviles,
Because of the enemy and the
avenger.

17 All this has come upon us;
But we have not forgotten You,
Nor have we dealt falsely with
Your covenant.

18 Our heart has not turned
back,
Nor have our steps departed
from Your way;
19 But You have severely broken
us in the place of jackals,
And covered us with the
shadow of death.

20 If we had forgotten the name
of our God,
Or stretched out our hands to
a foreign god,
21 Would not God search this
out?
For He knows the secrets of
the heart.
22 Yet for Your sake we are
killed all day long;
We are accounted as sheep
for the slaughter.

23 Awake! Why do You sleep,
O Lord?
Arise! Do not cast *us* off
forever.
24 Why do You hide Your face,
And forget our affliction and
our oppression?
25 For our soul is bowed down to
the dust;
Our body clings to the ground.
26 Arise for our help,
And redeem us for Your
mercies' sake.

PROVERBS FOR TODAY/ 22:13

The lazy man *says,* "There is *a lion outside! I shall be slain in the streets!"*

SEPTEMBER 1

JOB 40:1–42:17

MOREOVER the LORD answered Job, and said:

2 "Shall the one who contends
with the Almighty correct
Him?
He who rebukes God, let him
answer it."

³Then Job answered the LORD and said:

4 "Behold, I am vile;
What shall I answer You?
I lay my hand over my mouth.
5 Once I have spoken, but I will
not answer;
Yes, twice, but I will proceed
no further."

⁶Then the LORD answered Job out of the whirlwind, and said:

7 "Now prepare yourself like a
man;
I will question you, and you
shall answer Me:

8 "Would you indeed annul My
judgment?
Would you condemn Me that
you may be justified?
9 Have you an arm like God?
Or can you thunder with a
voice like His?
10 Then adorn yourself *with*
majesty and splendor,
And array yourself with glory
and beauty.
11 Disperse the rage of your
wrath;
Look on everyone *who is*
proud, and humble him.

12 Look on everyone *who is*
proud, *and* bring him low;
Tread down the wicked in
their place.
13 Hide them in the dust
together,
Bind their faces in hidden
darkness.
14 Then I will also confess to you
That your own right hand can
save you.

15 "Look now at the behemoth,*
which I made *along* with
you;
He eats grass like an ox.
16 See now, his strength *is* in his
hips,
And his power *is* in his
stomach muscles.
17 He moves his tail like a cedar;
The sinews of his thighs are
tightly knit.
18 His bones *are like* beams of
bronze,
His ribs like bars of iron.
19 He *is* the first of the ways of
God;
Only He who made him can
bring near His sword.
20 Surely the mountains yield
food for him,
And all the beasts of the field
play there.
21 He lies under the lotus trees,
In a covert of reeds and
marsh.
22 The lotus trees cover him
with their shade;
The willows by the brook
surround him.
23 Indeed the river may rage,
Yet he is not disturbed;
He is confident, though the

Jordan gushes into his mouth,

24 *Though* he takes it in his eyes,
Or one pierces *his* nose with a snare.

"CAN you draw out Leviathan* with a hook,
Or *snare* his tongue with a line *which* you lower?

2 Can you put a reed through his nose,
Or pierce his jaw with a hook?

3 Will he make many supplications to you?
Will he speak softly to you?

4 Will he make a covenant with you?
Will you take him as a servant forever?

5 Will you play with him as *with* a bird,
Or will you leash him for your maidens?

6 Will *your* companions make a banquet* of him?
Will they apportion him among the merchants?

7 Can you fill his skin with harpoons,
Or his head with fishing spears?

8 Lay your hand on him;
Remember the battle—
Never do it again!

9 Indeed, *any* hope of *overcoming* him is false;
Shall *one not* be overwhelmed at the sight of him?

10 No one *is so* fierce that he would dare stir him up.
Who then is able to stand against Me?

11 Who has preceded Me, that I should pay *him?*
Everything under heaven is Mine.

12 "I will not conceal* his limbs,

His mighty power, or his graceful proportions.

13 Who can remove his outer coat?
Who can approach *him* with a double bridle?

14 Who can open the doors of his face,
With his terrible teeth all around?

15 *His* rows of scales are *his* pride,
Shut up tightly *as with* a seal;

16 One is so near another
That no air can come between them;

17 They are joined one to another,
They stick together and cannot be parted.

18 His sneezings flash forth light,
And his eyes *are* like the eyelids of the morning.

19 Out of his mouth go burning lights;
Sparks of fire shoot out.

20 Smoke goes out of his nostrils,
As *from* a boiling pot and burning rushes.

21 His breath kindles coals,
And a flame goes out of his mouth.

22 Strength dwells in his neck,
And sorrow dances before him.

23 The folds of his flesh are joined together;
They are firm on him and cannot be moved.

24 His heart is as hard as stone,
Even as hard as the lower *millstone.*

25 When he raises himself up, the mighty are afraid;
Because of his crashings they are beside* themselves.

26 *Though* the sword reaches him, it cannot avail;
Nor does spear, dart, or javelin.

27 He regards iron as straw,
  And bronze as rotten wood.
28 The arrow cannot make him
  flee;
  Slingstones become like
  stubble to him.
29 Darts are regarded as straw;
  He laughs at the threat of
  javelins.
30 His undersides *are* like sharp
  potsherds;
  He spreads pointed *marks* in
  the mire.
31 He makes the deep boil like a
  pot;
  He makes the sea like a pot of
  ointment.
32 He leaves a shining wake
  behind him;
  One would think the deep had
  white hair.
33 On earth there is nothing like
  him,
  Which is made without fear.
34 He beholds every high *thing;*
  He *is* king over all the
  children of pride."

Then Job answered the Lord and said:

2 "I know that You can do
  everything,
  And that no purpose *of Yours*
  can be withheld from You.
3 You asked, 'Who *is* this who
  hides counsel without
  knowledge?'
  Therefore I have uttered what
  I did not understand,
  Things too wonderful for me,
  which I did not know.
4 Listen, please, and let me
  speak;
  You said, 'I will question you,
  and you shall answer Me.'

5 "I have heard of You by the
  hearing of the ear,
  But now my eye sees You.
6 Therefore I abhor *myself,*

And repent in dust and ashes."

7And so it was, after the Lord had spoken these words to Job, that the Lord said to Eliphaz the Temanite, "My wrath is aroused against you and your two friends, for you have not spoken of Me *what is* right, as My servant Job *has.* 8Now therefore, take for yourselves seven bulls and seven rams, go to My servant Job, and offer up for yourselves a burnt offering; and My servant Job shall pray for you. For I will accept him, lest I deal with you *according to your* folly; because you have not spoken of Me *what is* right, as My servant Job *has."*

9So Eliphaz the Temanite and Bildad the Shuhite *and* Zophar the Naamathite went and did as the Lord commanded them; for the Lord had accepted Job. 10And the Lord restored Job's losses* when he prayed for his friends. Indeed the Lord gave Job twice as much as he had before. 11Then all his brothers, all his sisters, and all those who had been his acquaintances before, came to him and ate food with him in his house; and they consoled him and comforted him for all the adversity that the Lord had brought upon him. Each one gave him a piece of silver and each a ring of gold.

12Now the Lord blessed the latter *days* of Job more than his beginning; for he had fourteen thousand sheep, six thousand camels, one thousand yoke of oxen, and one thousand female donkeys. 13He also had seven sons and three daughters. 14And he called the name of the first Jemimah, the name of the second Keziah, and the name of the third Keren-Happuch. 15In all the land were found no women *so* beautiful as the daughters of Job; and their father gave them an inheritance among their brothers.

16After this Job lived one hundred and forty years, and saw his children and grandchildren *for* four generations. [17]So Job died, old and full of days.

2 CORINTHIANS 5:11-21

KNOWING, therefore, the terror of the Lord, we persuade men; but we are well known to God, and I also trust are well known in your consciences.

[12]For we do not commend ourselves again to you, but give you opportunity to boast on our behalf, that you may have *an answer* for those who boast in appearance and not in heart. [13]For if we are beside ourselves, *it is* for God; or if we are of sound mind, *it is* for you. [14]For the love of Christ compels us, because we judge thus: that if One died for all, then all died; [15]and He died for all, that those who live should live no longer for themselves, but for Him who died for them and rose again.

[16]Therefore, from now on, we regard no one according to the flesh. Even though we have known Christ according to the flesh, yet now we know *Him thus* no longer. [17]Therefore, if anyone *is* in Christ, *he is* a new creation; old things have passed away; behold, all things have become new. [18]Now all things *are* of God, who has reconciled us to Himself through Jesus Christ, and has given us the ministry of reconciliation, [19]that is, that God was in Christ reconciling the world to Himself, not imputing their trespasses to them, and has committed to us the word of reconciliation.

[20]Now then, we are ambassadors for Christ, as though God were pleading through us: we implore *you* on Christ's behalf, be reconciled to God. [21]For He made Him who knew no sin *to be* sin for us, that we might become the righteousness of God in Him.

PSALM 45:1-17

To the Chief Musician. Set to "The Lilies." * *A Contemplation* * *of the sons of Korah. A Song of Love.*

MY heart is overflowing with a good theme;
I recite my composition concerning the King;
My tongue *is* the pen of a ready writer.

2 You are fairer than the sons of men;
Grace is poured upon Your lips;
Therefore God has blessed You forever.

3 Gird Your sword upon *Your* thigh, O Mighty One,
With Your glory and Your majesty.

4 And in Your majesty ride prosperously because of truth, humility, *and* righteousness;
And Your right hand shall teach You awesome things.

5 Your arrows *are* sharp in the heart of the King's enemies;
The peoples fall under You.

6 Your throne, O God, *is* forever and ever;
A scepter of righteousness *is* the scepter of Your kingdom.

7 You love righteousness and hate wickedness;
Therefore God, Your God, has anointed You
With the oil of gladness more than Your companions.

8 All Your garments are scented with myrrh and aloes *and* cassia,
Out of the ivory palaces, by which they have made You glad.

9 Kings' daughters *are* among Your honorable women;

At Your right hand stands the
queen in gold from Ophir.

10 Listen, O daughter,
Consider and incline your ear;
Forget your own people also,
and your father's house;

11 So the King will greatly desire
your beauty;
Because He *is* your Lord,
worship Him.

12 And the daughter of Tyre *will
come* with a gift;
The rich among the people
will seek your favor.

13 The royal daughter *is* all
glorious within *the palace;*
Her clothing *is* woven with
gold.

14 She shall be brought to the
King in robes of many
colors;
The virgins, her companions
who follow her, shall be
brought to You.

15 With gladness and rejoicing
they shall be brought;
They shall enter the King's
palace.

16 Instead of Your fathers shall
be Your sons,
Whom You shall make
princes in all the earth.

17 I will make Your name to be
remembered in all
generations;
Therefore the people shall
praise You forever and ever.

PROVERBS FOR TODAY / 22:14

The mouth of an immoral woman is *a deep pit; he who is abhorred by the* LORD
will fall there.

SEPTEMBER 2

ECCLESIASTES 1:1–3:22

THE words of the Preacher, the
son of David, king in Jerusalem.

2 "Vanity* of vanities," says the
Preacher;
"Vanity of vanities, all *is* vanity."

3 What profit has a man from all
his labor
In which he toils under the
sun?

4 *One* generation passes away,
and *another* generation
comes;
But the earth abides forever.

5 The sun also rises, and the
sun goes down,
And hastens to the place
where it arose.

6 The wind goes toward the
south,
And turns around to the north;
The wind whirls about
continually,
And comes again on its circuit.

7 All the rivers run into the sea,
Yet the sea *is* not full;
To the place from which the
rivers come,
There they return again.

8 All things *are* full of labor;
Man cannot express *it.*

The eye is not satisfied with
    seeing,
Nor the ear filled with hearing.

9   That which has been *is* what
    will be,
    That which *is* done is what
    will be done,
    And *there is* nothing new
    under the sun.

10   Is there anything of which it
    may be said,
    "See, this *is* new"?
    It has already been in ancient
    times before us.

11   *There is* no remembrance of
    former *things,*
    Nor will there be any
    remembrance of *things* that
    are to come
    By *those* who will come after.

12I, the Preacher, was king over Israel in Jerusalem. 13And I set my heart to seek and search out by wisdom concerning all that is done under heaven; this burdensome task God has given to the sons of man, by which they may be exercised. 14I have seen all the works that are done under the sun; and indeed, all *is* vanity and grasping for the wind.

15   *What is* crooked cannot be
    made straight,
    And what is lacking cannot be
    numbered.

16I communed with my heart, saying, "Look, I have attained greatness, and have gained more wisdom than all who were before me in Jerusalem. My heart has understood great wisdom and knowledge." 17And I set my heart to know wisdom and to know madness and folly. I perceived that this also is grasping for the wind.

18   For in much wisdom *is* much
    grief,

And he who increases
    knowledge increases
    sorrow.

I SAID in my heart, "Come now, I will test you with mirth; therefore enjoy pleasure"; but surely, this also *was* vanity. 2I said of laughter—"Madness!"; and of mirth, "What does it accomplish?" 3I searched in my heart *how* to gratify my flesh with wine, while guiding my heart with wisdom, and how to lay hold on folly, till I might see what *was* good for the sons of men to do under heaven all the days of their lives.

4I made my works great, I built myself houses, and planted myself vineyards. 5I made myself gardens and orchards, and I planted all *kinds* of fruit trees in them. 6I made myself water pools from which to water the growing trees of the grove. 7I acquired male and female servants, and had servants born in my house. Yes, I had greater possessions of herds and flocks than all who were in Jerusalem before me. 8I also gathered for myself silver and gold and the special treasures of kings and of the provinces. I acquired male and female singers, the delights of the sons of men, *and* musical instruments* of all kinds.

9So I became great and excelled more than all who were before me in Jerusalem. Also my wisdom remained with me.

10   Whatever my eyes desired I
    did not keep from them.
    I did not withhold my heart
    from any pleasure,
    For my heart rejoiced in all
    my labor;
    And this was my reward from
    all my labor.

11   Then I looked on all the
    works that my hands had
    done
    And on the labor in which I
    had toiled;

And indeed all *was* vanity and grasping for the wind.
There was no profit under the sun.

12 Then I turned myself to consider wisdom and madness and folly;
For what *can* the man *do* who succeeds the king?—
Only what he has already done.

13 Then I saw that wisdom excels folly
As light excels darkness.

14 The wise man's eyes *are* in his head,
But the fool walks in darkness.
Yet I myself perceived
That the same event happens to them all.

15 So I said in my heart,
"As it happens to the fool,
It also happens to me,
And why was I then more wise?"
Then I said in my heart,
"This also *is* vanity."

16 For *there is* no more remembrance of the wise than of the fool forever,
Since all that now *is* will be forgotten in the days to come.
And how does a wise *man* die?
As the fool!

[17]Therefore I hated life because the work that was done under the sun *was* distressing to me, for all *is* vanity and grasping for the wind. [18]Then I hated all my labor in which I had toiled under the sun, because I must leave it to the man who will come after me. [19]And who knows whether he will be wise or a fool? Yet he will rule over all my labor in which I toiled and in which I have shown myself wise under the sun. This also *is* vanity.

[20]Therefore I turned my heart and despaired of all the labor in which I had toiled under the sun. [21]For there is a man whose labor *is* with wisdom, knowledge, and skill; yet he must leave his heritage to a man who has not labored for it. This also *is* vanity and a great evil. [22]For what has man for all his labor, and for the striving of his heart with which he has toiled under the sun? [23]For all his days *are* sorrowful, and his work burdensome; even in the night his heart takes no rest. This also is vanity.

[24]Nothing *is* better for a man *than* that he should eat and drink, and *that* his soul should enjoy good in his labor. This also, I saw, was from the hand of God. [25]For who can eat, or who can have enjoyment, more than I? [26]For *God* gives wisdom and knowledge and joy to a man who *is* good in His sight; but to the sinner He gives the work of gathering and collecting, that he may give to *him who is* good before God. This also *is* vanity and grasping for the wind.

To everything *there is* a season,
A time for every purpose under heaven:

2 A time to be born,
And a time to die;
A time to plant,
And a time to pluck *what is* planted;

3 A time to kill,
And a time to heal;
A time to break down,
And a time to build up;

4 A time to weep,
And a time to laugh;
A time to mourn,
And a time to dance;

5 A time to cast away stones,
And a time to gather stones;
A time to embrace,
And a time to refrain from embracing;

6 A time to gain,
    And a time to lose;
  A time to keep,
    And a time to throw away;
7 A time to tear,
    And a time to sew;
  A time to keep silence,
    And a time to speak;
8 A time to love,
    And a time to hate;
  A time of war,
    And a time of peace.

9What profit has the worker from that in which he labors? 10I have seen the God-given task with which the sons of men are to be occupied. 11He has made everything beautiful in its time. Also He has put eternity in their hearts, except that no one can find out the work that God does from beginning to end.

12I know that nothing *is* better for them than to rejoice, and to do good in their lives, 13and also that every man should eat and drink and enjoy the good of all his labor—it *is* the gift of God.

14 I know that whatever God
    does,
  It shall be forever.
  Nothing can be added to it,
  And nothing taken from it.
  God does *it,* that men should
    fear before Him.
15 That which is has already
    been,
  And what is to be has already
    been;
  And God requires an account
    of what is past.

16Moreover I saw under the sun:

  In the place of judgment,
  Wickedness *was* there;
  And *in* the place of
    righteousness,
  Iniquity *was* there.

17I said in my heart,

  "God shall judge the righteous
    and the wicked,
  For *there is* a time there for
    every purpose and for
    every work."

18I said in my heart, "Concerning the condition of the sons of men, God tests them, that they may see that they themselves are *like* animals." 19For what happens to the sons of men also happens to animals; one thing befalls them: as one dies, so dies the other. Surely, they all have one breath; man has no advantage over animals, for all *is* vanity. 20All go to one place: all are from the dust, and all return to dust. 21Who knows the spirit of the sons of men, which goes upward, and the spirit of the animal, which goes down to the earth?* 22So I perceived that nothing *is* better than that a man should rejoice in his own works, for that *is* his heritage. For who can bring him to see what will happen after him?

2 CORINTHIANS 6:1-13

WE then, *as* workers together *with Him* also plead with *you* not to receive the grace of God in vain. 2For He says:

  *"In an acceptable time I have
    heard you,
  And in the day of salvation I
    have helped you."* *

Behold, now *is* the accepted time; behold, now *is* the day of salvation.

3We give no offense in anything, that our ministry may not be blamed. 4But in all *things* we commend ourselves as ministers of God: in much patience, in tribulations, in needs, in distresses, 5in stripes, in imprisonments, in tumults, in labors, in sleeplessness, in fastings; 6by purity, by knowledge, by long-suffering, by kindness, by the Holy

Spirit, by sincere love, [7]by the word of truth, by the power of God, by the armor of righteousness on the right hand and on the left, [8]by honor and dishonor, by evil report and good report; as deceivers, and *yet* true; [9]as unknown, and *yet* well known; as dying, and behold we live; as chastened, and *yet* not killed; [10]as sorrowful, yet always rejoicing; as poor, yet making many rich; as having nothing, and *yet* possessing all things.

[11]O Corinthians! We have spoken openly to you, our heart is wide open. [12]You are not restricted by us, but you are restricted by your *own* affections. [13]Now in return for the same (I speak as to children), you also be open.

PSALM 46:1-11

To the Chief Musician. A Psalm of the sons of Korah. A Song for Alamoth.

God *is* our refuge and strength, A very present help in trouble. [2]Therefore we will not fear, Even though the earth be removed, And though the mountains be carried into the midst of the sea;
[3] *Though* its waters roar *and* be troubled, *Though* the mountains shake with its swelling.   Selah

[4] *There is* a river whose streams shall make glad the city of God,

The holy *place* of the tabernacle of the Most High.
[5] God *is* in the midst of her, she shall not be moved; God shall help her, just at the break of dawn.
[6] The nations raged, the kingdoms were moved; He uttered His voice, the earth melted.

[7] The LORD of hosts *is* with us; The God of Jacob *is* our refuge.   Selah

[8] Come, behold the works of the LORD, Who has made desolations in the earth.
[9] He makes wars cease to the end of the earth; He breaks the bow and cuts the spear in two; He burns the chariot in the fire.

[10] Be still, and know that I *am* God; I will be exalted among the nations, I will be exalted in the earth!

[11] The LORD of hosts *is* with us; The God of Jacob *is* our refuge.   Selah

PROVERBS FOR TODAY/ 22:15

Foolishness is *bound up in the heart of a child; the rod of correction will drive it far from him.*

SEPTEMBER 3

ECCLESIASTES 4:1–6:12

THEN I [the Preacher] returned and considered all the oppression that is done under the sun:

And look! The tears of the
  oppressed,
But they have no comforter—
On the side of their
  oppressors *there is* power,
But they have no comforter.
2 Therefore I praised the dead
  who were already dead,
More than the living who are
  still alive.
3 Yet, better than both *is he* who
  has never existed,
Who has not seen the evil
  work that is done under the
  sun.

4Again, I saw that for all toil and every skillful work a man is envied by his neighbor. This also *is* vanity and grasping for the wind.

5 The fool folds his hands
And consumes his own flesh.
6 Better a handful *with*
  quietness
Than both hands full, *together
  with* toil and grasping for
  the wind.

7Then I returned, and I saw vanity under the sun:

8 There is one alone, without
  companion:
He has neither son nor
  brother.
Yet *there is* no end to all his
  labors,
Nor is his eye satisfied with
  riches.

But he never asks,
"For whom do I toil and
  deprive myself of good?"
This also *is* vanity and a grave
  misfortune.

9 Two *are* better than one,
Because they have a good
  reward for their labor.
10 For if they fall, one will lift up
  his companion.
But woe to him *who is* alone
  when he falls,
For *he has* no one to help him
  up.
11 Again, if two lie down
  together, they will keep
  warm;
But how can one be warm
  alone?
12 Though one may be
  overpowered by another,
  two can withstand him.
And a threefold cord is not
  quickly broken.

13 Better a poor and wise youth
Than an old and foolish king
  who will be admonished no
  more.
14 For he comes out of prison to
  be king,
Although he was born poor in
  his kingdom.
15 I saw all the living who walk
  under the sun;
They were with the second
  youth who stands in his
  place.
16 *There was* no end of all the
  people over whom he was
  made king;
Yet those who come
  afterward will not rejoice in
  him.

Surely this also *is* vanity and
grasping for the wind.

W<small>ALK</small> prudently when you go to the
house of God; and draw near to hear
rather than to give the sacrifice of
fools, for they do not know that they do
evil.

2   Do not be rash with your
        mouth,
    And let not your heart utter
        anything hastily before God.
    For God *is* in heaven, and you
        on earth;
    Therefore let your words be
        few.
3   For a dream comes through
        much activity,
    And a fool's voice *is known* by
        his many words.

4   When you make a vow to
        God, do not delay to pay it;
    For *He has* no pleasure in
        fools.
    Pay what you have vowed—
5   Better not to vow than to vow
        and not pay.

6Do not let your mouth cause your
flesh to sin, nor say before the messenger *of God* that it *was* an error. Why
should God be angry at your excuse*
and destroy the work of your hands?
7For in the multitude of dreams and
many words *there is* also vanity. But
fear God.

8If you see the oppression of the
poor, and the violent perversion of justice and righteousness in a province,
do not marvel at the matter; for high
official watches over high official, and
higher officials are over them.

9Moreover the profit of the land is
for all; *even* the king is served from the
field.

10   He who loves silver will not
        be satisfied with silver;

Nor he who loves abundance,
    with increase.
This also *is* vanity.

11   When goods increase,
    They increase who eat them;
    So what profit have the owners
    Except to see *them* with their
        eyes?

12   The sleep of a laboring man *is*
        sweet,
    Whether he eats little or
        much;
    But the abundance of the rich
        will not permit him to sleep.

13   There is a severe evil *which* I
        have seen under the sun:
    Riches kept for their owner to
        his hurt.
14   But those riches perish
        through misfortune;
    When he begets a son, *there is*
        nothing in his hand.
15   As he came from his mother's
        womb, naked shall he
        return,
    To go as he came;
    And he shall take nothing
        from his labor
    Which he may carry away in
        his hand.

16   And this also *is* a severe evil—
    Just exactly as he came, so
        shall he go.
    And what profit has he who
        has labored for the wind?
17   All his days he also eats in
        darkness,
    And *he has* much sorrow and
        sickness and anger.

18Here is what I have seen: *It is* good
and fitting *for one* to eat and drink, and
to enjoy the good of all his labor in
which he toils under the sun all the
days of his life which God gives him;
for it *is* his heritage. 19As for every man

to whom God has given riches and wealth, and given him power to eat of it, to receive his heritage and rejoice in his labor—this *is* the gift of God. 20For he will not dwell unduly on the days of his life, because God keeps *him* busy with the joy of his heart.

THERE is an evil which I have seen under the sun, and it *is* common among men: 2A man to whom God has given riches and wealth and honor, so that he lacks nothing for himself of all he desires; yet God does not give him power to eat of it, but a foreigner consumes it. This *is* vanity, and it *is* an evil affliction.

3If a man begets a hundred *children* and lives many years, so that the days of his years are many, but his soul is not satisfied with goodness, or indeed he has no burial, I say *that* a stillborn child *is* better than he— 4for it comes in vanity and departs in darkness, and its name is covered with darkness. 5Though it has not seen the sun or known *anything,* this has more rest than that man, 6even if he lives a thousand years twice—but has not seen goodness. Do not all go to one place?

7   All the labor of man *is* for his mouth,
   And yet the soul is not satisfied.
8   For what more has the wise *man* than the fool?
   What does the poor man have,
   Who knows *how* to walk before the living?
9   Better *is* the sight of the eyes than the wandering of desire.
   This also *is* vanity and grasping for the wind.

10   Whatever one is, he has been named already,
   For it is known that he *is* man;
   And he cannot contend with

   Him who is mightier than he.
11   Since there are many things that increase vanity,
   How *is* man the better?

12For who knows what *is* good for man in life, all the days of his vain life which he passes like a shadow? Who can tell a man what will happen after him under the sun?

2 CORINTHIANS 6:14–7:7

Do not be unequally yoked together with unbelievers. For what fellowship has righteousness with lawlessness? And what communion has light with darkness? 15And what accord has Christ with Belial? Or what part has a believer with an unbeliever? 16And what agreement has the temple of God with idols? For you* are the temple of the living God. As God has said:

   "I will dwell in them
   And walk among them.
   I will be their God,
   And they shall be My people." *

17Therefore

   "Come out from among them
   And be separate, says the Lord.
   Do not touch what is unclean,
   And I will receive you." *
18   *"I will be a Father to you,*
   And you shall be My sons and daughters,
   Says the LORD *Almighty."* *

THEREFORE, having these promises, beloved, let us cleanse ourselves from all filthiness of the flesh and spirit, perfecting holiness in the fear of God.

2Open *your hearts* to us. We have wronged no one, we have corrupted no one, we have cheated no one. 3I do not say *this* to condemn; for I have said before that you are in our hearts, to die together and to live together. ⁴Great *is* my boldness of speech toward you, great *is* my boasting on your behalf. I am filled with comfort. I am exceedingly joyful in all our tribulation.

⁵For indeed, when we came to Macedonia, our bodies had no rest, but we were troubled on every side. Outside *were* conflicts, inside *were* fears. ⁶Nevertheless God, who comforts the downcast, comforted us by the coming of Titus, ⁷and not only by his coming, but also by the consolation with which he was comforted in you, when he told us of your earnest desire, your mourning, your zeal for me, so that I rejoiced even more.

PSALM 47:1-9

To the Chief Musician. A Psalm of the sons of Korah.

O H, clap your hands, all you peoples!
Shout to God with the voice of triumph!
2 For the LORD Most High *is* awesome;
He is a great King over all the earth.

3 He will subdue the peoples under us,
And the nations under our feet.
4 He will choose our inheritance for us,
The excellence of Jacob whom He loves.   Selah

5 God has gone up with a shout,
The LORD with the sound of a trumpet.
6 Sing praises to God, sing praises!
Sing praises to our King, sing praises!
7 For God *is* the King of all the earth;
Sing praises with understanding.

8 God reigns over the nations;
God sits on His holy throne.
9 The princes of the people have gathered together,
The people of the God of Abraham.
For the shields of the earth *belong* to God;
He is greatly exalted.

PROVERBS FOR TODAY/ 22:16

He who oppresses the poor to increase his riches, *and he who gives to the rich,* will *surely* come *to poverty.*

SEPTEMBER 4

ECCLESIASTES 7:1–9:18

A GOOD name *is* better than precious ointment,
And the day of death than the day of one's birth;
2 Better to go to the house of mourning

Than to go to the house of feasting,
For that *is* the end of all men;
And the living will take *it* to heart.
3 Sorrow *is* better than laughter,

For by a sad countenance the
heart is made better.

4 The heart of the wise *is* in the
house of mourning,
But the heart of fools *is* in the
house of mirth.

5 *It is* better to hear the rebuke
of the wise
Than for a man to hear the
song of fools.

6 For like the crackling of
thorns under a pot,
So *is* the laughter of the fool.
This also is vanity.

7 Surely oppression destroys a
wise *man's* reason,
And a bribe debases the heart.

8 The end of a thing *is* better
than its beginning;
The patient in spirit *is* better
than the proud in spirit.

9 Do not hasten in your spirit to
be angry,
For anger rests in the bosom
of fools.

10 Do not say,
"Why were the former days
better than these?"
For you do not inquire wisely
concerning this.

11 Wisdom *is* good with an
inheritance,
And profitable to those who
see the sun.

12 For wisdom *is* a defense *as*
money *is* a defense,
But the excellence of
knowledge *is that* wisdom
gives life to those who
have it.

13 Consider the work of God;
For who can make straight
what He has made crooked?

14 In the day of prosperity be
joyful,
But in the day of adversity
consider:
Surely God has appointed the
one as well as the other,
So that man can find out
nothing *that will come* after
him.

15 I have seen everything in my days
of vanity:

There is a just *man* who
perishes in his
righteousness,
And there is a wicked *man*
who prolongs *life* in his
wickedness.

16 Do not be overly righteous,
Nor be overly wise:
Why should you destroy
yourself?

17 Do not be overly wicked,
Nor be foolish:
Why should you die before
your time?

18 *It is* good that you grasp this,
And also not remove your
hand from the other;
For he who fears God will
escape them all.

19 Wisdom strengthens the wise
More than ten rulers of the
city.

20 For *there is* not a just man on
earth who does good
And does not sin.

21 Also do not take to heart
everything people say,
Lest you hear your servant
cursing you.

22 For many times, also, your
own heart has known
That even you have cursed
others.

23 All this I have proved by
wisdom.
I said, "I will be wise";
But it *was* far from me.
24 As for that which is far off and
exceedingly deep,
Who can find it out?
25 I applied my heart to know,
To search and seek out
wisdom and the reason *of
things,*
To know the wickedness of
folly,
Even of foolishness *and*
madness.
26 And I find more bitter than
death
The woman whose heart *is*
snares and nets,
Whose hands are fetters.
He who pleases God shall
escape from her,
But the sinner shall be
trapped by her.

27 "Here is what I have found,"
says the Preacher,
"*Adding* one thing to the other
to find out the reason,
28 Which my soul still seeks but
I cannot find:
One man among a thousand I
have found,
But a woman among all these
I have not found.
29 Truly, this only I have found:
That God made man upright,
But they have sought out
many schemes."

Who *is* like a wise *man?*
And who knows the
interpretation of a thing?
A man's wisdom makes his
face shine,
And the sternness of his face
is changed.

2I *say,* "Keep the king's commandment for the sake of your oath to God.

3Do not be hasty to go from his presence. Do not take your stand for an evil
thing, for he does whatever pleases
him."

4 Where the word of a king *is,
there is* power;
And who may say to him,
"What are you doing?"
5 He who keeps his command
will experience nothing
harmful;
And a wise man's heart
discerns both time and
judgment,
6 Because for every matter
there is a time and
judgment,
Though the misery of man
increases greatly.
7 For he does not know what
will happen;
So who can tell him when it
will occur?
8 No one has power over the
spirit to retain the spirit,
And no one has power in the
day of death.
There is no release from that
war,
And wickedness will not
deliver those who are given
to it.

9All this I have seen, and applied my
heart to every work that is done under
the sun: *There is* a time in which one
man rules over another to his own
hurt. 10Then I saw the wicked buried, who
had come and gone from the place of
holiness, and they were forgotten* in
the city where they had so done. This
also *is* vanity. 11Because the sentence
against an evil work is not executed
speedily, therefore the heart of the
sons of men is fully set in them to do
evil. 12Though a sinner does evil a hundred *times,* and his *days* are prolonged,
yet I surely know that it will be well

with those who fear God, who fear before Him. ¹³But it will not be well with the wicked; nor will he prolong *his* days, *which are* as a shadow, because he does not fear before God.

¹⁴There is a vanity which occurs on earth, that there are just *men* to whom it happens according to the work of the wicked; again, there are wicked *men* to whom it happens according to the work of the righteous. I said that this also *is* vanity.

¹⁵So I commended enjoyment, because a man has nothing better under the sun than to eat, drink, and be merry; for this will remain with him in his labor *all* the days of his life which God gives him under the sun.

¹⁶When I applied my heart to know wisdom and to see the business that is done on earth, even though one sees no sleep day or night, ¹⁷then I saw all the work of God, that a man cannot find out the work that is done under the sun. For though a man labors to discover *it,* yet he will not find *it;* moreover, though a wise *man* attempts to know *it,* he will not be able to find *it.*

FOR I considered all this in my heart, so that I could declare it all: that the righteous and the wise and their works *are* in the hand of God. People know neither love nor hatred *by* anything *they see* before them. ²All things *come* alike to all:

> One event *happens* to the
>   righteous and the wicked;
> To the good,* the clean, and
>   the unclean;
> To him who sacrifices and
>   him who does not sacrifice.
> As is the good, so *is* the
>   sinner;
> He who takes an oath as *he*
>   who fears an oath.

³This *is* an evil in all that is done under the sun: that one thing *happens* to all.

Truly the hearts of the sons of men are full of evil; madness *is* in their hearts while they live, and after that *they go* to the dead. ⁴But for him who is joined to all the living there is hope, for a living dog is better than a dead lion.

> 5 For the living know that they
>   will die;
>   But the dead know nothing,
>   And they have no more
>   reward,
>   For the memory of them is
>   forgotten.
> 6 Also their love, their hatred,
>   and their envy have now
>   perished;
>   Nevermore will they have a
>   share
>   In anything done under the
>   sun.
>
> 7 Go, eat your bread with joy,
>   And drink your wine with a
>   merry heart;
>   For God has already accepted
>   your works.
> 8 Let your garments always be
>   white,
>   And let your head lack no oil.

⁹Live joyfully with the wife whom you love all the days of your vain life which He has given you under the sun, all your days of vanity; for that *is* your portion in life, and in the labor which you perform under the sun. ¹⁰Whatever your hand finds to do, do *it* with your might; for *there is* no work or device or knowledge or wisdom in the grave where you are going. ¹¹I returned and saw under the sun that—

> The race *is* not to the swift,
> Nor the battle to the strong,
> Nor bread to the wise,
> Nor riches to men of
>   understanding,
> Nor favor to men of skill;

But time and chance happen
to them all.
12 For man also does not know
his time:
Like fish taken in a cruel net,
Like birds caught in a snare,
So the sons of men *are* snared
in an evil time,
When it falls suddenly upon
them.

13This wisdom I have also seen under the sun, and it *seemed* great to me: 14*There was* a little city with few men in it; and a great king came against it, besieged it, and built great snares* around it. 15Now there was found in it a poor wise man, and he by his wisdom delivered the city. Yet no one remembered that same poor man. 16Then I said:

"Wisdom *is* better than
strength.
Nevertheless the poor man's
wisdom *is* despised,
And his words are not heard.
17 Words of the wise, *spoken*
quietly, *should be* heard
Rather than the shout of a
ruler of fools.
18 Wisdom *is* better than
weapons of war;
But one sinner destroys much
good."

2 CORINTHIANS 7:8-16

FOR even if I made you sorry with my letter, I do not regret it; though I did regret it. For I perceive that the same epistle made you sorry, though only for a while. 9Now I rejoice, not that you were made sorry, but that your sorrow led to repentance. For you were made sorry in a godly manner, that you might suffer loss from us in nothing. 10For godly sorrow produces repentance *leading* to salvation, not to be regretted; but the sorrow of the world produces death. 11For observe this very thing, that you sorrowed in a godly manner: What diligence it produced in you, *what* clearing *of yourselves, what* indignation, *what* fear, *what* vehement desire, *what* zeal, *what* vindication! In all *things* you proved yourselves to be clear in this matter. 12Therefore, although I wrote to you, *I did* not *do it* for the sake of him who had done the wrong, nor for the sake of him who suffered wrong, but that our care for you in the sight of God might appear to you.

13Therefore we have been comforted in your comfort. And we rejoiced exceedingly more for the joy of Titus, because his spirit has been refreshed by you all. 14For if in anything I have boasted to him about you, I am not ashamed. But as we spoke all things to you in truth, even so our boasting to Titus was found true. 15And his affections are greater for you as he remembers the obedience of you all, how with fear and trembling you received him. 16Therefore I rejoice that I have confidence in you in everything.

PSALM 48:1-14

A Song. A Psalm of the sons of Korah.

GREAT *is* the LORD, and greatly to
be praised
In the city of our God,
In His holy mountain.
2 Beautiful in elevation,
The joy of the whole earth,
Is Mount Zion *on* the sides of
the north,
The city of the great King.
3 God *is* in her palaces;
He is known as her refuge.

4 For behold, the kings
assembled,
They passed by together.

5 They saw *it, and* so they
   marveled;
   They were troubled, they
   hastened away.
6 Fear took hold of them there,
   And pain, as of a woman in
   birth pangs,
7 *As when* You break the ships
   of Tarshish
   With an east wind.

8 As we have heard,
   So we have seen
   In the city of the LORD of hosts,
   In the city of our God:
   God will establish it forever.
                        Selah

9 We have thought, O God, on
   Your lovingkindness,
   In the midst of Your temple.

10 According to Your name,
    O God,
    So *is* Your praise to the ends
    of the earth;
    Your right hand is full of
    righteousness.
11 Let Mount Zion rejoice,
    Let the daughters of Judah be
    glad,
    Because of Your judgments.

12 Walk about Zion,
    And go all around her.
    Count her towers;
13 Mark well her bulwarks;
    Consider her palaces;
    That you may tell *it* to the
    generation following.
14 For this *is* God,
    Our God forever and ever;
    He will be our guide
    Even to death.*

PROVERBS FOR TODAY/ 22:17-19

Incline your ear and hear the words of the wise, and apply your heart to my knowledge; for it is *a pleasant thing if you keep them within you; let them all be fixed upon your lips, so that your trust may be in the* LORD; *I have instructed you today, even you.*

SEPTEMBER 5

ECCLESIASTES 10:1–12:14

DEAD flies putrefy* the perfumer's ointment,
   And cause it to give off a foul
   odor;
   So does a little folly to one
   respected for wisdom *and*
   honor.
2 A wise man's heart *is* at his
   right hand,
   But a fool's heart at his left.
3 Even when a fool walks along
   the way,

He lacks wisdom,
   And he shows everyone *that*
   he *is* a fool.
4 If the spirit of the ruler rises
   against you,
   Do not leave your post;
   For conciliation pacifies great
   offenses.

5 There is an evil I have seen
   under the sun,
   As an error proceeding from
   the ruler:
6 Folly is set in great dignity,

While the rich sit in a lowly place.

7 I have seen servants on horses,
While princes walk on the ground like servants.

8 He who digs a pit will fall into it,
And whoever breaks through a wall will be bitten by a serpent.

9 He who quarries stones may be hurt by them,
And he who splits wood may be endangered by it.

10 If the ax is dull,
And one does not sharpen the edge,
Then he must use more strength;
But wisdom brings success.

11 A serpent may bite when *it is* not charmed;
The babbler is no different.

12 The words of a wise man's mouth *are* gracious,
But the lips of a fool shall swallow him up;

13 The words of his mouth begin with foolishness,
And the end of his talk *is* raving madness.

14 A fool also multiplies words.
No man knows what is to be;
Who can tell him what will be after him?

15 The labor of fools wearies them,
For they do not even know how to go to the city!

16 Woe to you, O land, when your king *is* a child,
And your princes feast in the morning!

17 Blessed *are* you, O land, when your king *is* the son of nobles,

And your princes feast at the proper time—
For strength and not for drunkenness!

18 Because of laziness the building decays,
And through idleness of hands the house leaks.

19 A feast is made for laughter,
And wine makes merry;
But money answers everything.

20 Do not curse the king, even in your thought;
Do not curse the rich, even in your bedroom;
For a bird of the air may carry your voice,
And a bird in flight may tell the matter.

Cast your bread upon the waters,
For you will find it after many days.

2 Give a serving to seven, and also to eight,
For you do not know what evil will be on the earth.

3 If the clouds are full of rain,
They empty *themselves* upon the earth;
And if a tree falls to the south or the north,
In the place where the tree falls, there it shall lie.

4 He who observes the wind will not sow,
And he who regards the clouds will not reap.

5 As you do not know what *is* the way of the wind,*
Or how the bones *grow* in the womb of her who is with child,
So you do not know the works of God who makes everything.

6 In the morning sow your seed,
And in the evening do not
withhold your hand;
For you do not know which
will prosper,
Either this or that,
Or whether both alike *will be*
good.

7 Truly the light is sweet,
And *it is* pleasant for the eyes
to behold the sun;

8 But if a man lives many years
And rejoices in them all,
Yet let him remember the
days of darkness,
For they will be many.
All that is coming *is* vanity.

9 Rejoice, O young man, in your
youth,
And let your heart cheer you
in the days of your youth;
Walk in the ways of your
heart,
And in the sight of your eyes;
But know that for all these
God will bring you into
judgment.

10 Therefore remove sorrow
from your heart,
And put away evil from your
flesh,
For childhood and youth *are*
vanity.

REMEMBER now your Creator in the
days of your youth,
Before the difficult days come,
And the years draw near
when you say,
"I have no pleasure in them":

2 While the sun and the light,
The moon and the stars,
Are not darkened,
And the clouds do not return
after the rain;

3 In the day when the keepers
of the house tremble,

And the strong men bow
down;
When the grinders cease
because they are few,
And those that look through
the windows grow dim;

4 When the doors are shut in
the streets,
And the sound of grinding is
low;
When one rises up at the
sound of a bird,
And all the daughters of
music are brought low.

5 Also they are afraid of height,
And of terrors in the way;
When the almond tree
blossoms,
The grasshopper is a burden,
And desire fails.
For man goes to his eternal
home,
And the mourners go about
the streets.

6 *Remember your Creator* before
the silver cord is loosed,*
Or the golden bowl is broken,
Or the pitcher shattered at
the fountain,
Or the wheel broken at the
well.

7 Then the dust will return to
the earth as it was,
And the spirit will return to
God who gave it.

8 "Vanity of vanities," says the
Preacher,
"All *is* vanity."

9And moreover, because the
Preacher was wise, he still taught the
people knowledge; yes, he pondered
and sought out *and* set in order many
proverbs. 10The Preacher sought to
find acceptable words; and *what was*
written *was* upright—words of truth.
11The words of the wise are like goads,
and the words of scholars* are like

well-driven nails, given by one Shepherd. ¹²And further, my son, be admonished by these. Of making many books *there is* no end, and much study *is* wearisome to the flesh.

¹³Let us hear the conclusion of the whole matter:

> Fear God and keep His
>   commandments,
> For this is man's all.
>
> 14   For God will bring every
>   work into judgment,
> Including every secret thing,
> Whether good or evil.

2 CORINTHIANS 8:1-15

MOREOVER, brethren, we make known to you the grace of God bestowed on the churches of Macedonia: ²that in a great trial of affliction the abundance of their joy and their deep poverty abounded in the riches of their liberality. ³For I bear witness that according to *their* ability, yes, and beyond *their* ability, *they were* freely willing, ⁴imploring us with much urgency that we would receive* the gift and the fellowship of the ministering to the saints. ⁵And not *only* as we had hoped, but they first gave themselves to the Lord, and *then* to us by the will of God. ⁶So we urged Titus, that as he had begun, so he would also complete this grace in you as well. ⁷But as you abound in everything—in faith, in speech, in knowledge, in all diligence, and in your love for us—*see* that you abound in this grace also.

⁸I speak not by commandment, but I am testing the sincerity of your love by the diligence of others. ⁹For you know the grace of our Lord Jesus Christ, that though He was rich, yet for your sakes He became poor, that you through His poverty might become rich.

¹⁰And in this I give advice: It is to your advantage not only to be doing what you began and were desiring to do a year ago; ¹¹but now you also must complete the doing *of it;* that as *there was* a readiness to desire *it,* so *there* also *may be* a completion out of what *you* have. ¹²For if there is first a willing mind, *it is* accepted according to what one has, *and* not according to what he does not have.

¹³For *I do* not *mean* that others should be eased and you burdened; ¹⁴but by an equality, *that* now at this time your abundance *may supply* their lack, that their abundance also may supply your lack—that there may be equality. ¹⁵As it is written, *"He who gathered much had nothing left over, and he who gathered little had no lack."* *

PSALM 49:1-20

To the Chief Musician. A Psalm of the sons of Korah.

HEAR this, all peoples;
    Give ear, all inhabitants of
    the world,
2   Both low and high,
    Rich and poor together.
3   My mouth shall speak
        wisdom,
    And the meditation of my
        heart *shall give*
        understanding.
4   I will incline my ear to a
        proverb;
    I will disclose my dark saying
        on the harp.

5   Why should I fear in the days
        of evil,
    When the iniquity at my heels
        surrounds me?
6   Those who trust in their
        wealth
    And boast in the multitude of
        their riches,
7   None *of them* can by any
        means redeem *his* brother,

Nor give to God a ransom for
him—
8 For the redemption of their
souls *is* costly,
And it shall cease forever—
9 That he should continue to
live eternally,
And not see the Pit.

10 For he sees wise men die;
Likewise the fool and the
senseless person perish,
And leave their wealth to
others.
11 Their inner thought *is that*
their houses *will last*
forever,*
Their dwelling places to all
generations;
They call *their* lands after
their own names.
12 Nevertheless man, *though* in
honor, does not remain;*
He is like the beasts *that*
perish.

13 This is the way of those who
are foolish,
And of their posterity who
approve their sayings. Selah
14 Like sheep they are laid in the
grave;

Death shall feed on them;
The upright shall have
dominion over them in the
morning;
And their beauty shall be
consumed in the grave, far
from their dwelling.
15 But God will redeem my soul
from the power of the grave,
For He shall receive me.
                                    Selah

16 Do not be afraid when one
becomes rich,
When the glory of his house
is increased;
17 For when he dies he shall
carry nothing away;
His glory shall not descend
after him.
18 Though while he lives he
blesses himself
(For *men* will praise you when
you do well for yourself),
19 He shall go to the generation
of his fathers;
They shall never see light.
20 A man *who is* in honor, yet
does not understand,
Is like the beasts *that* perish.

PROVERBS FOR TODAY/ 22:20-21

*Have I not written to you excellent things of counsels and knowledge, that I may
make you know the certainty of the words of truth, that you may answer words of
truth to those who send to you?*

SEPTEMBER 6

SONG OF SOLOMON 1:1–4:16

THE song of songs, which *is* Solomon's.

*The Shulamite**
2   Let him kiss me with the kisses of his mouth—
     For your* love *is* better than wine.
3   Because of the fragrance of your good ointments,
     Your name *is* ointment poured forth;
     Therefore the virgins love you.
4   Draw me away!

The Daughters of Jerusalem
     We will run after you.*

The Shulamite
     The king has brought me into his chambers.

The Daughters of Jerusalem
     We will be glad and rejoice in you.*
     We will remember your* love more than wine.

The Shulamite
     Rightly do they love you.*

5   I *am* dark, but lovely,
     O daughters of Jerusalem,
     Like the tents of Kedar,
     Like the curtains of Solomon.
6   Do not look upon me,
         because I *am* dark,
     Because the sun has tanned me.
     My mother's sons were angry with me;
     They made me the keeper of the vineyards,

     But my own vineyard I have not kept.

(To Her Beloved)
7   Tell me, O you whom I love,
     Where you feed *your flock,*
     Where you make *it* rest at noon.
     For why should I be as one who veils herself^
     By the flocks of your companions?

The Beloved
8   If you do not know, O fairest among women,
     Follow in the footsteps of the flock,
     And feed your little goats
     Beside the shepherds' tents.
9   I have compared you, my love,
     To my filly among Pharaoh's chariots.
10   Your cheeks are lovely with ornaments,
     Your neck with chains *of gold.*

The Daughters of Jerusalem
11   We will make you* ornaments of gold
     With studs of silver.

The Shulamite
12   While the king *is* at his table,
     My spikenard sends forth its fragrance.
13   A bundle of myrrh *is* my beloved to me,
     That lies all night between my breasts.
14   My beloved *is* to me a cluster of henna *blooms*
     In the vineyards of En Gedi.

The Beloved
15 Behold, you *are* fair, my love!
 Behold, you *are* fair!
 You *have* dove's eyes.

The Shulamite
16 Behold, you *are* handsome,
 my beloved!
 Yes, pleasant!
 Also our bed *is* green.
17 The beams of our houses *are*
 cedar,
 And our rafters of fir.

I *AM* the rose of Sharon,
 And the lily of the valleys.

The Beloved
2 Like a lily among thorns,
 So is my love among the
 daughters.

The Shulamite
3 Like an apple tree among the
 trees of the woods,
 So *is* my beloved among the
 sons.
 I sat down in his shade with
 great delight,
 And his fruit *was* sweet to my
 taste.

*The Shulamite to the Daughters of
Jerusalem*
4 He brought me to the
 banqueting house,
 And his banner over me *was*
 love.
5 Sustain me with cakes of
 raisins,
 Refresh me with apples,
 For I *am* lovesick.

6 His left hand *is* under my
 head,
 And his right hand embraces
 me.
7 I charge you, O daughters of
 Jerusalem,

By the gazelles or by the does
 of the field,
Do not stir up nor awaken love
 Until it pleases.

The Shulamite
8 The voice of my beloved!
 Behold, he comes
 Leaping upon the mountains,
 Skipping upon the hills.
9 My beloved is like a gazelle or
 a young stag.
 Behold, he stands behind our
 wall;
 He is looking through the
 windows,
 Gazing through the lattice.

10 My beloved spoke, and said to
 me:
 "Rise up, my love, my fair one,
 And come away.
11 For lo, the winter is past,
 The rain is over *and* gone.
12 The flowers appear on the
 earth;
 The time of singing has come,
 And the voice of the
 turtledove
 Is heard in our land.
13 The fig tree puts forth her
 green figs,
 And the vines *with* the tender
 grapes
 Give a good smell.
 Rise up, my love, my fair one,
 And come away!

14 "O my dove, in the clefts of the
 rock,
 In the secret *places* of the cliff,
 Let me see your face,
 Let me hear your voice;
 For your voice *is* sweet,
 And your face *is* lovely."

Her Brothers
15 Catch us the foxes,
 The little foxes that spoil the
 vines,

For our vines *have* tender grapes.

The Shulamite

16 My beloved *is* mine, and I *am* his.
He feeds *his flock* among the lilies.

(To Her Beloved)

17 Until the day breaks
And the shadows flee away,
Turn, my beloved,
And be like a gazelle
Or a young stag
Upon the mountains of Bether.*

The Shulamite

By night on my bed I sought the one I love;
I sought him, but I did not find him.

2 "I will rise now," *I said,*
"And go about the city;
In the streets and in the squares
I will seek the one I love."
I sought him, but I did not find him.

3 The watchmen who go about the city found me;
I said,
"Have you seen the one I love?"

4 Scarcely had I passed by them,
When I found the one I love.
I held him and would not let him go,
Until I had brought him to the house of my mother,
And into the chamber of her who conceived me.

5 I charge you, O daughters of Jerusalem,
By the gazelles or by the does of the field,
Do not stir up nor awaken love

Until it pleases.

The Shulamite

6 Who *is* this coming out of the wilderness
Like pillars of smoke,
Perfumed with myrrh and frankincense,
With all the merchant's fragrant powders?

7 Behold, it *is* Solomon's couch,
With sixty valiant men around it,
Of the valiant of Israel.

8 They all hold swords,
Being expert in war.
Every man *has* his sword on his thigh
Because of fear in the night.

9 Of the wood of Lebanon
Solomon the King
Made himself a palanquin:*

10 He made its pillars *of* silver,
Its support *of* gold,
Its seat *of* purple,
Its interior paved *with* love
By the daughters of Jerusalem.

11 Go forth, O daughters of Zion,
And see King Solomon with the crown
With which his mother crowned him
On the day of his wedding,
The day of the gladness of his heart.

The Beloved

BEHOLD, you *are* fair, my love!
Behold, you *are* fair!
You *have* dove's eyes behind your veil.
Your hair *is* like a flock of goats,
Going down from Mount Gilead.

2 Your teeth *are* like a flock of shorn *sheep*

Which have come up from the
 washing,
Every one of which bears
 twins,
And none *is* barren among
 them.
3 Your lips *are* like a strand of
 scarlet,
And your mouth is lovely.
Your temples behind your veil
Are like a piece of
 pomegranate.
4 Your neck *is* like the tower of
 David,
Built for an armory,
On which hang a thousand
 bucklers,
All shields of mighty men.
5 Your two breasts *are* like two
 fawns,
Twins of a gazelle,
Which feed among the lilies.

6 Until the day breaks
And the shadows flee away,
I will go my way to the
 mountain of myrrh
And to the hill of frankincense.

7 You *are* all fair, my love,
And *there is* no spot in you.
8 Come with me from Lebanon,
 my spouse,
With me from Lebanon.
Look from the top of Amana,
From the top of Senir and
 Hermon,
From the lions' dens,
From the mountains of the
 leopards.

9 You have ravished my heart,
My sister, *my* spouse;
You have ravished my heart
With one *look* of your eyes,
With one link of your
 necklace.
10 How fair is your love,
My sister, *my* spouse!

How much better than wine is
 your love,
And the scent of your
 perfumes
Than all spices!
11 Your lips, O *my* spouse,
Drip as the honeycomb;
Honey and milk *are* under
 your tongue;
And the fragrance of your
 garments
Is like the fragrance of
 Lebanon.

12 A garden enclosed
Is my sister, *my* spouse,
A spring shut up,
A fountain sealed.
13 Your plants *are* an orchard of
 pomegranates
With pleasant fruits,
Fragrant henna with
 spikenard,
14 Spikenard and saffron,
Calamus and cinnamon,
With all trees of frankincense,
Myrrh and aloes,
With all the chief spices—
15 A fountain of gardens,
A well of living waters,
And streams from Lebanon.

The Shulamite
16 Awake, O north *wind,*
And come, O south!
Blow upon my garden,
That its spices may flow out.
Let my beloved come to his
 garden
And eat its pleasant fruits.

2 CORINTHIANS 8:16-24

BUT thanks *be* to God who puts*
the same earnest care for you
into the heart of Titus. [17]For he
not only accepted the exhortation, but
being more diligent, he went to you of
his own accord. [18]And we have sent
with him the brother whose praise *is*

in the gospel throughout all the churches, ¹⁹and not only *that,* but who was also chosen by the churches to travel with us with this gift, which is administered by us to the glory of the Lord Himself and *to show* your ready mind, ²⁰avoiding this: that anyone should blame us in this lavish gift which is administered by us— ²¹providing honorable things, not only in the sight of the Lord, but also in the sight of men.

²²And we have sent with them our brother whom we have often proved diligent in many things, but now much more diligent, because of the great confidence which *we have* in you. ²³If *anyone inquires* about Titus, *he is* my partner and fellow worker concerning you. Or if our brethren *are inquired about, they are* messengers of the churches, the glory of Christ. ²⁴Therefore show to them, and* before the churches the proof of your love and of our boasting on your behalf.

PSALM 50:1-23

A Psalm of Asaph.

THE Mighty One, God the LORD,
Has spoken and called the earth
From the rising of the sun to
its going down.
2   Out of Zion, the perfection of
beauty,
God will shine forth.
3   Our God shall come, and shall
not keep silent;
A fire shall devour before Him,
And it shall be very
tempestuous all around
Him.

4   He shall call to the heavens
from above,
And to the earth, that He may
judge His people:
5   "Gather My saints together to
Me,
Those who have made a

covenant with Me by
sacrifice."
6   Let the heavens declare His
righteousness,
For God Himself *is* Judge.
                                        Selah

7   "Hear, O My people, and I will
speak,
O Israel, and I will testify
against you;
I *am* God, your God!
8   I will not rebuke you for your
sacrifices
Or your burnt offerings,
Which are continually before
Me.
9   I will not take a bull from your
house,
Nor goats out of your folds.
10 For every beast of the forest
is Mine,
And the cattle on a thousand
hills.
11 I know all the birds of the
mountains,
And the wild beasts of the
field *are* Mine.

12 "If I were hungry, I would not
tell you;
For the world *is* Mine, and all
its fullness.
13 Will I eat the flesh of bulls,
Or drink the blood of goats?
14 Offer to God thanksgiving,
And pay your vows to the
Most High.
15 Call upon Me in the day of
trouble;
I will deliver you, and you
shall glorify Me."

16 But to the wicked God says:
"What *right* have you to
declare My statutes,
Or take My covenant in your
mouth,
17 Seeing you hate instruction

And cast My words behind
you?

18 When you saw a thief, you
consented* with him,
And have been a partaker
with adulterers.

19 You give your mouth to evil,
And your tongue frames
deceit.

20 You sit *and* speak against
your brother;
You slander your own
mother's son.

21 These *things* you have done,
and I kept silent;

You thought that I was
altogether like you;
But I will rebuke you,
And set *them* in order before
your eyes.

22 "Now consider this, you who
forget God,
Lest I tear *you* in pieces,
And *there be* none to deliver:

23 Whoever offers praise
glorifies Me;
And to him who orders *his*
conduct *aright*
I will show the salvation of
God."

PROVERBS FOR TODAY/ 22:22-23

Do not rob the poor because he is *poor, nor oppress the afflicted at the gate; for the*
LORD *will plead their cause, and plunder the soul of those who plunder them.*

SEPTEMBER 7

SONG OF SOLOMON 5:1–8:14

The Beloved

I HAVE come to my garden, my sister,
my spouse;
I have gathered my myrrh with
my spice;
I have eaten my honeycomb
with my honey;
I have drunk my wine with
my milk.

(To His Friends)

Eat, O friends!
Drink, yes, drink deeply,
O beloved ones!

The Shulamite

2 I sleep, but my heart is awake;
It is the voice of my beloved!
He knocks, *saying,*

"Open for me, my sister, my
love,
My dove, my perfect one;
For my head is covered with
dew,
My locks with the drops of
the night."

3 I have taken off my robe;
How can I put it on *again?*
I have washed my feet;
How can I defile them?

4 My beloved put his hand
By the latch *of the door,*
And my heart yearned for
him.

5 I arose to open for my
beloved,

And my hands dripped *with* myrrh,
My fingers with liquid myrrh,
On the handles of the lock.

6 I opened for my beloved,
But my beloved had turned away *and* was gone.
My heart leaped up when he spoke.
I sought him, but I could not find him;
I called him, but he gave me no answer.

7 The watchmen who went about the city found me.
They struck me, they wounded me;
The keepers of the walls Took my veil away from me.

8 I charge you, O daughters of Jerusalem,
If you find my beloved,
That you tell him I *am* lovesick!

The Daughters of Jerusalem

9 What *is* your beloved More than *another* beloved,
O fairest among women?
What *is* your beloved More than *another* beloved,
That you so charge us?

The Shulamite

10 My beloved *is* white and ruddy,
Chief among ten thousand.

11 His head *is like* the finest gold;
His locks *are* wavy,
And black as a raven.

12 His eyes *are* like doves By the rivers of waters,
Washed with milk,
And fitly set.

13 His cheeks *are* like a bed of spices,
Banks of scented herbs.
His lips *are* lilies,
Dripping liquid myrrh.

14 His hands *are* rods of gold Set with beryl.
His body *is* carved ivory Inlaid *with* sapphires.

15 His legs *are* pillars of marble Set on bases of fine gold.
His countenance *is* like Lebanon,
Excellent as the cedars.

16 His mouth *is* most sweet,
Yes, he *is* altogether lovely.
This *is* my beloved,
And this *is* my friend,
O daughters of Jerusalem!

The Daughters of Jerusalem

WHERE has your beloved gone,
O fairest among women?
Where has your beloved turned aside,
That we may seek him with you?

The Shulamite

2 My beloved has gone to his garden,
To the beds of spices,
To feed *his flock* in the gardens,
And to gather lilies.

3 I *am* my beloved's,
And my beloved *is* mine.
He feeds *his flock* among the lilies.

The Beloved

4 O my love, you *are as* beautiful as Tirzah,
Lovely as Jerusalem,
Awesome as *an army* with banners!

5 Turn your eyes away from me,
For they have overcome me.
Your hair *is* like a flock of goats Going down from Gilead.

6 Your teeth *are* like a flock of sheep Which have come up from the washing;

Every one bears twins,
And none *is* barren among
them.

7 Like a piece of pomegranate
Are your temples behind your
veil.

8 There are sixty queens
And eighty concubines,
And virgins without number.

9 My dove, my perfect one,
Is the only one,
The only one of her mother,
The favorite of the one who
bore her.
The daughters saw her
And called her blessed,
The queens and the
concubines,
And they praised her.

10 Who is she who looks forth as
the morning,
Fair as the moon,
Clear as the sun,
Awesome as *an army* with
banners?

The Shulamite
11 I went down to the garden of
nuts
To see the verdure of the
valley,
To see whether the vine had
budded
And the pomegranates had
bloomed.

12 Before I was even aware,
My soul had made me
As the chariots of my noble
people.*

The Beloved and His Friends
13 Return, return, O Shulamite;
Return, return, that we may
look upon you!

The Shulamite
What would you see in the
Shulamite—

As it were, the dance of the
two camps?*

The Beloved
How beautiful are your feet in sandals,
O prince's daughter!
The curves of your thighs *are*
like jewels,
The work of the hands of a
skillful workman.

2 Your navel *is* a rounded goblet;
It lacks no blended beverage.
Your waist *is* a heap of wheat
Set about with lilies.

3 Your two breasts *are* like two
fawns,
Twins of a gazelle.

4 Your neck *is* like an ivory
tower,
Your eyes *like* the pools in
Heshbon
By the gate of Bath Rabbim.
Your nose *is* like the tower of
Lebanon
Which looks toward
Damascus.

5 Your head *crowns* you like
Mount Carmel,
And the hair of your head *is*
like purple;
A king *is* held captive by *your*
tresses.

6 How fair and how pleasant
you are,
O love, with your delights!

7 This stature of yours is like a
palm tree,
And your breasts *like* its
clusters.

8 I said, "I will go up to the palm
tree,
I will take hold of its
branches."
Let now your breasts be like
clusters of the vine,
The fragrance of your breath
like apples,

9 And the roof of your mouth
like the best wine.

The Shulamite
> *The wine* goes *down* smoothly
> for my beloved,
> Moving gently the lips of
> sleepers.*
10 I *am* my beloved's,
> And his desire *is* toward me.

11 Come, my beloved,
> Let us go forth to the field;
> Let us lodge in the villages.
12 Let us get up early to the
> vineyards;
> Let us see if the vine has
> budded,
> *Whether* the grape blossoms
> are open,
> *And* the pomegranates are in
> bloom.
> There I will give you my love.
13 The mandrakes give off a
> fragrance,
> And at our gates *are* pleasant
> *fruits,*
> All manner, new and old,
> Which I have laid up for you,
> my beloved.

OH, that you were like my brother,
> Who nursed at my mother's
> breasts!
> *If* I should find you outside,
> I would kiss you;
> I would not be despised.
2 I would lead you *and* bring
> you
> Into the house of my mother,
> She *who* used to instruct me.
> I would cause you to drink of
> spiced wine,
> Of the juice of my
> pomegranate.

(To the Daughters of Jerusalem)
3 His left hand *is* under my
> head,
> And his right hand embraces
> me.
4 I charge you, O daughters of
> Jerusalem,

Do not stir up nor awaken love
Until it pleases.

A Relative
5 Who *is* this coming up from
> the wilderness,
> Leaning upon her beloved?

I awakened you under the
> apple tree.
There your mother brought
> you forth;
There she *who* bore you
> brought *you* forth.

The Shulamite to Her Beloved
6 Set me as a seal upon your
> heart,
> As a seal upon your arm;
> For love *is as* strong as death,
> Jealousy *as* cruel as the
> grave;*
> Its flames *are* flames of fire,
> A most vehement* flame.

7 Many waters cannot quench
> love,
> Nor can the floods drown it.
> If a man would give for love
> All the wealth of his house,
> It would be utterly despised.

The Shulamite's Brothers
8 We have a little sister,
> And she has no breasts.
> What shall we do for our sister
> In the day when she is spoken
> for?
9 If she *is* a wall,
> We will build upon her
> A battlement of silver;
> And if she *is* a door,
> We will enclose her
> With boards of cedar.

The Shulamite
10 I *am* a wall,
> And my breasts like towers;
> Then I became in his eyes
> As one who found peace.

¹¹ Solomon had a vineyard at
        Baal Hamon;
     He leased the vineyard to
        keepers;
     Everyone was to bring for its
        fruit
     A thousand silver coins.

(To Solomon)
¹² My own vineyard *is* before me.
     You, O Solomon, *may have* a
        thousand,
     And those who tend its fruit
        two hundred.

The Beloved
¹³ You who dwell in the gardens,
     The companions listen for
        your voice—
     Let me hear it!

The Shulamite
¹⁴ Make haste, my beloved,
     And be like a gazelle
     Or a young stag
     On the mountains of spices.

2 CORINTHIANS 9:1-15

Now concerning the ministering to the saints, it is superfluous for me to write to you; ²for I know your willingness, about which I boast of you to the Macedonians, that Achaia was ready a year ago; and your zeal has stirred up the majority. ³Yet I have sent the brethren, lest our boasting of you should be in vain in this respect, that, as I said, you may be ready; ⁴lest if *some* Macedonians come with me and find you unprepared, we (not to mention you!) should be ashamed of this confident boasting.* ⁵Therefore I thought it necessary to exhort the brethren to go to you ahead of time, and prepare your generous gift beforehand, which *you had* previously promised, that it may be ready

as *a matter of* generosity and not as a grudging obligation.

⁶But this *I say:* He who sows sparingly will also reap sparingly, and he who sows bountifully will also reap bountifully. ⁷So let each one *give* as he purposes in his heart, not grudgingly or of necessity; for God loves a cheerful giver. ⁸And God *is* able to make all grace abound toward you, that you, always having all sufficiency in all *things,* may have an abundance for every good work. ⁹As it is written:

> "He has dispersed abroad,
> He has given to the poor;
> His righteousness endures
>   forever." *

¹⁰Now may* He who supplies seed to the sower, and bread for food, supply and multiply the seed you have *sown* and increase the fruits of your righteousness, ¹¹while *you are* enriched in everything for all liberality, which causes thanksgiving through us to God. ¹²For the administration of this service not only supplies the needs of the saints, but also is abounding through many thanksgivings to God, ¹³while, through the proof of this ministry, they glorify God for the obedience of your confession to the gospel of Christ, and for *your* liberal sharing with them and all *men,* ¹⁴and by their prayer for you, who long for you because of the exceeding grace of God in you. ¹⁵Thanks *be* to God for His indescribable gift!

PSALM 51:1-19

To the Chief Musician. A Psalm of David when Nathan the prophet went to him, after he had gone in to Bathsheba.

Have mercy upon me, O God,
     According to Your
     lovingkindness;
     According to the multitude of
        Your tender mercies,
     Blot out my transgressions.

2   Wash me thoroughly from my
      iniquity,
    And cleanse me from my sin.

3   For I acknowledge my
      transgressions,
    And my sin *is* always before
      me.
4   Against You, You only, have I
      sinned,
    And done *this* evil in Your
      sight—
    That You may be found just
      when You speak,*
    And blameless when You
      judge.

5   Behold, I was brought forth in
      iniquity,
    And in sin my mother
      conceived me.
6   Behold, You desire truth in
      the inward parts,
    And in the hidden *part* You
      will make me to know
      wisdom.

7   Purge me with hyssop, and I
      shall be clean;
    Wash me, and I shall be
      whiter than snow.
8   Make me hear joy and
      gladness,
    That the bones You have
      broken may rejoice.
9   Hide Your face from my sins,
    And blot out all my iniquities.

10 Create in me a clean heart,
      O God,
    And renew a steadfast spirit
      within me.
11 Do not cast me away from
      Your presence,

And do not take Your Holy
  Spirit from me.

12 Restore to me the joy of Your
      salvation,
    And uphold me *by Your*
      generous Spirit.
13 *Then* I will teach
      transgressors Your ways,
    And sinners shall be
      converted to You.

14 Deliver me from the guilt of
      bloodshed, O God,
    The God of my salvation,
    And my tongue shall sing
      aloud of Your
      righteousness.
15 O Lord, open my lips,
    And my mouth shall show
      forth Your praise.
16 For You do not desire
      sacrifice, or else I would
      give *it;*
    You do not delight in burnt
      offering.
17 The sacrifices of God *are* a
      broken spirit,
    A broken and a contrite
      heart—
    These, O God, You will not
      despise.

18 Do good in Your good
      pleasure to Zion;
    Build the walls of Jerusalem.
19 Then You shall be pleased
      with the sacrifices of
      righteousness,
    With burnt offering and
      whole burnt offering;
    Then they shall offer bulls on
      Your altar.

PROVERBS FOR TODAY/ 22:24-25

*Make no friendship with an angry man, and with a furious man do not go, lest you
learn his ways and set a snare for your soul.*

SEPTEMBER 8

ISAIAH 1:1–2:22

THE vision of Isaiah the son of Amoz, which he saw concerning Judah and Jerusalem in the days of Uzziah, Jotham, Ahaz, *and* Hezekiah, kings of Judah.

2 Hear, O heavens, and give ear,
      O earth!
   For the Lord has spoken:
   "I have nourished and brought
      up children,
   And they have rebelled
      against Me;
3 The ox knows its owner
   And the donkey its master's
      crib;
   But Israel does not know,
   My people do not consider."

4 Alas, sinful nation,
   A people laden with iniquity,
   A brood of evildoers,
   Children who are corrupters!
   They have forsaken the Lord,
   They have provoked to anger
   The Holy One of Israel,
   They have turned away
      backward.

5 Why should you be stricken
      again?
   You will revolt more and more.
   The whole head is sick,
   And the whole heart faints.
6 From the sole of the foot even
      to the head,
   There is no soundness in it,
   But wounds and bruises and
      putrefying sores;
   They have not been closed or
      bound up,
   Or soothed with ointment.

7 Your country *is* desolate,
   Your cities *are* burned with
      fire;
   Strangers devour your land in
      your presence;
   And *it is* desolate, as
      overthrown by strangers.
8 So the daughter of Zion is left
      as a booth in a vineyard,
   As a hut in a garden of
      cucumbers,
   As a besieged city.
9 Unless the Lord of hosts
   Had left to us a very small
      remnant,
   We would have become like
      Sodom,
   We would have been made
      like Gomorrah.

10 Hear the word of the Lord,
      You rulers of Sodom;
   Give ear to the law of our God,
      You people of Gomorrah:
11 "To what purpose *is* the
      multitude of your sacrifices
      to Me?"
   Says the Lord.
   "I have had enough of burnt
      offerings of rams
   And the fat of fed cattle.
   I do not delight in the blood of
      bulls,
   Or of lambs or goats.

12 "When you come to appear
      before Me,
   Who has required this from
      your hand,
   To trample My courts?
13 Bring no more futile sacrifices;
   Incense is an abomination
      to Me.
   The New Moons, the
      Sabbaths, and the calling of
      assemblies—

I cannot endure iniquity and
the sacred meeting.

14 Your New Moons and your
appointed feasts
My soul hates;
They are a trouble to Me,
I am weary of bearing *them*.

15 When you spread out your
hands,
I will hide My eyes from you;
Even though you make many
prayers,
I will not hear.
Your hands are full of blood.

16 "Wash yourselves, make
yourselves clean;
Put away the evil of your
doings from before My
eyes.
Cease to do evil,

17 Learn to do good;
Seek justice,
Rebuke the oppressor;*
Defend the fatherless,
Plead for the widow.

18 "Come now, and let us reason
together,"
Says the LORD,
"Though your sins are like
scarlet,
They shall be as white as
snow;
Though they are red like
crimson,
They shall be as wool.

19 If you are willing and obedient,
You shall eat the good of the
land;

20 But if you refuse and rebel,
You shall be devoured by the
sword";
For the mouth of the LORD has
spoken.

21 How the faithful city has
become a harlot!
It was full of justice;
Righteousness lodged in it,

But now murderers.

22 Your silver has become dross,
Your wine mixed with water.

23 Your princes *are* rebellious,
And companions of thieves;
Everyone loves bribes,
And follows after rewards.
They do not defend the
fatherless,
Nor does the cause of the
widow come before them.

24 Therefore the Lord says,
The LORD of hosts, the Mighty
One of Israel,
"Ah, I will rid Myself of My
adversaries,
And take vengeance on My
enemies.

25 I will turn My hand against
you,
And thoroughly purge away
your dross,
And take away all your alloy.

26 I will restore your judges as at
the first,
And your counselors as at the
beginning.
Afterward you shall be called
the city of righteousness,
the faithful city."

27 Zion shall be redeemed with
justice,
And her penitents with
righteousness.

28 The destruction of
transgressors and of
sinners *shall be* together,
And those who forsake the
LORD shall be consumed.

29 For they* shall be ashamed of
the terebinth trees
Which you have desired;
And you shall be
embarrassed because of
the gardens
Which you have chosen.

30 For you shall be as a terebinth
whose leaf fades,

And as a garden that has no
water.
31 The strong shall be as tinder,
And the work of it as a spark;
Both will burn together,
And no one shall quench *them*.

THE word that Isaiah the son of Amoz
saw concerning Judah and Jerusalem.

2 Now it shall come to pass in
the latter days
That the mountain of the
LORD's house
Shall be established on the
top of the mountains,
And shall be exalted above
the hills;
And all nations shall flow to it.
3 Many people shall come and
say,
"Come, and let us go up to the
mountain of the LORD,
To the house of the God of
Jacob;
He will teach us His ways,
And we shall walk in His
paths."
For out of Zion shall go forth
the law,
And the word of the LORD
from Jerusalem.
4 He shall judge between the
nations,
And rebuke many people;
They shall beat their swords
into plowshares,
And their spears into pruning
hooks;
Nation shall not lift up sword
against nation,
Neither shall they learn war
anymore.

5 O house of Jacob, come and
let us walk
In the light of the LORD.

6 For You have forsaken Your
people, the house of Jacob,
Because they are filled with
eastern ways;
They *are* soothsayers like the
Philistines,
And they are pleased with the
children of foreigners.
7 Their land is also full of silver
and gold,
And there is no end to their
treasures;
Their land is also full of
horses,
And there is no end to their
chariots.
8 Their land is also full of idols;
They worship the work of
their own hands,
That which their own fingers
have made.
9 People bow down,
And each man humbles
himself;
Therefore do not forgive
them.

10 Enter into the rock, and hide
in the dust,
From the terror of the LORD
And the glory of His majesty.
11 The lofty looks of man shall
be humbled,
The haughtiness of men shall
be bowed down,
And the LORD alone shall be
exalted in that day.

12 For the day of the LORD of
hosts
Shall come upon everything
proud and lofty,
Upon everything lifted up—
And it shall be brought low—
13 Upon all the cedars of
Lebanon *that are* high and
lifted up,
And upon all the oaks of
Bashan;
14 Upon all the high mountains,
And upon all the hills *that are*
lifted up;

15 Upon every high tower,
And upon every fortified wall;
16 Upon all the ships of Tarshish,
And upon all the beautiful
sloops.
17 The loftiness of man shall be
bowed down,
And the haughtiness of men
shall be brought low;
The LORD alone will be exalted
in that day,
18 But the idols He shall utterly
abolish.

19 They shall go into the holes of
the rocks,
And into the caves of the
earth,
From the terror of the LORD
And the glory of His majesty,
When He arises to shake the
earth mightily.

20 In that day a man will cast
away his idols of silver
And his idols of gold,
Which they made, *each* for
himself to worship,
To the moles and bats,
21 To go into the clefts of the
rocks,
And into the crags of the
rugged rocks,
From the terror of the LORD
And the glory of His majesty,
When He arises to shake the
earth mightily.

22 Sever yourselves from such a
man,
Whose breath *is* in his nostrils;
For of what account is he?

2 CORINTHIANS 10:1-18

Now I, Paul, myself am pleading
with you by the meekness and
gentleness of Christ—who in
presence *am* lowly among you, but being absent am bold toward you. 2But I
beg *you* that when I am present I may
not be bold with that confidence by
which I intend to be bold against some,
who think of us as if we walked according to the flesh. 3For though we walk in
the flesh, we do not war according to
the flesh. 4For the weapons of our warfare *are* not carnal but mighty in God
for pulling down strongholds, 5casting
down arguments and every high thing
that exalts itself against the knowledge
of God, bringing every thought into
captivity to the obedience of Christ,
6and being ready to punish all disobedience when your obedience is fulfilled.

7Do you look at things according to
the outward appearance? If anyone is
convinced in himself that he is Christ's,
let him again consider this in himself,
that just as he *is* Christ's, even so we *are*
Christ's.* 8For even if I should boast
somewhat more about our authority,
which the Lord gave us* for edification
and not for your destruction, I shall not
be ashamed— 9lest I seem to terrify
you by letters. 10"For *his* letters," they
say, "*are* weighty and powerful, but *his*
bodily presence *is* weak, and *his* speech
contemptible." 11Let such a person consider this, that what we are in word by
letters when we are absent, such *we
will* also *be* in deed when we are present.

12For we dare not class ourselves or
compare ourselves with those who
commend themselves. But they, measuring themselves by themselves, and
comparing themselves among themselves, are not wise. 13We, however, will
not boast beyond measure, but within
the limits of the sphere which God appointed us—a sphere which especially
includes you. 14For we are not overex-
tending ourselves (as though *our authority* did not extend to you), for it was
to you that we came with the gospel of
Christ; 15not boasting of things beyond
measure, *that is,* in other men's labors,
but having hope, *that* as your faith is

increased, we shall be greatly enlarged by you in our sphere, [16]to preach the gospel in the *regions* beyond you, *and* not to boast in another man's sphere of accomplishment.

[17]But *"he who glories, let him glory in the Lord."* * [18]For not he who commends himself is approved, but whom the Lord commends.

PSALM 52:1-9

To the Chief Musician. A Contemplation * of David when Doeg the Edomite went and told Saul, and said to him, "David has gone to the house of Ahimelech."*

HY do you boast in evil, O mighty man? The goodness of God *endures* continually.
2 Your tongue devises destruction, Like a sharp razor, working deceitfully.
3 You love evil more than good, Lying rather than speaking righteousness. Selah
4 You love all devouring words, *You* deceitful tongue.

5 God shall likewise destroy you forever; He shall take you away, and pluck you out of *your* dwelling place, And uproot you from the land of the living. Selah
6 The righteous also shall see and fear, And shall laugh at him, *saying,*
7 "Here is the man *who* did not make God his strength, But trusted in the abundance of his riches, *And* strengthened himself in his wickedness."

8 But I *am* like a green olive tree in the house of God; I trust in the mercy of God forever and ever.
9 I will praise You forever, Because You have done *it;* And in the presence of Your saints I will wait on Your name, for *it is* good.

PROVERBS FOR TODAY/ 22:26-27

Do not be one of those who shakes hands in a pledge, one of those who is surety for debts; if you have nothing with which to pay, why should he take away your bed from under you?

SEPTEMBER 9

ISAIAH 3:1–5:30

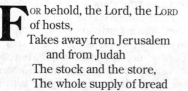OR behold, the Lord, the Lord of hosts, Takes away from Jerusalem and from Judah The stock and the store, The whole supply of bread

and the whole supply of water;
2 The mighty man and the man of war, The judge and the prophet, And the diviner and the elder;

3 The captain of fifty and the
honorable man,
The counselor and the skillful
artisan,
And the expert enchanter.

4 "I will give children *to be* their
princes,
And babes shall rule over
them.

5 The people will be oppressed,
Every one by another and
every one by his neighbor;
The child will be insolent
toward the elder,
And the base toward the
honorable."

6 When a man takes hold of his
brother
In the house of his father,
saying,
"You have clothing;
You be our ruler,
And *let* these ruins *be* under
your power,"*

7 In that day he will protest,
saying,
"I cannot cure *your* ills,
For in my house *is* neither
food nor clothing;
Do not make me a ruler of the
people."

8 For Jerusalem stumbled,
And Judah is fallen,
Because their tongue and
their doings
Are against the LORD,
To provoke the eyes of His
glory.

9 The look on their
countenance witnesses
against them,
And they declare their sin as
Sodom;
They do not hide *it.*
Woe to their soul!
For they have brought evil
upon themselves.

10 "Say to the righteous that *it
shall be* well *with them,*
For they shall eat the fruit of
their doings.

11 Woe to the wicked! *It shall be*
ill *with him,*
For the reward of his hands
shall be given him.

12 *As for* My people, children *are*
their oppressors,
And women rule over them.
O My people! Those who lead
you cause *you* to err,
And destroy the way of your
paths."

13 The LORD stands up to plead,
And stands to judge the
people.

14 The LORD will enter into
judgment
With the elders of His people
And His princes:
"For you have eaten up the
vineyard;
The plunder of the poor *is* in
your houses.

15 What do you mean by
crushing My people
And grinding the faces of the
poor?"
Says the Lord GOD of hosts.

16Moreover the LORD says:

"Because the daughters of
Zion are haughty,
And walk with outstretched
necks
And wanton eyes,
Walking and mincing *as* they
go,
Making a jingling with their
feet,

17 Therefore the Lord will strike
with a scab
The crown of the head of the
daughters of Zion,
And the LORD will uncover
their secret parts."

¹⁸ In that day the Lord will take
away the finery:
The jingling anklets, the
scarves, and the crescents;
¹⁹ The pendants, the bracelets,
and the veils;
²⁰ The headdresses, the leg
ornaments, and the
headbands;
The perfume boxes, the
charms,
²¹ and the rings;
The nose jewels,
²² the festal apparel, and the
mantles;
The outer garments, the
purses,
²³ and the mirrors;
The fine linen, the turbans,
and the robes.

²⁴And so it shall be:

Instead of a sweet smell there
will be a stench;
Instead of a sash, a rope;
Instead of well-set hair,
baldness;
Instead of a rich robe, a
girding of sackcloth;
And branding instead of
beauty.
²⁵ Your men shall fall by the
sword,
And your mighty in the war.

²⁶ Her gates shall lament and
mourn,
And she *being* desolate shall
sit on the ground.

AND in that day seven women shall
take hold of one man, saying,
"We will eat our own food and
wear our own apparel;
Only let us be called by your
name,
To take away our reproach."

² In that day the Branch of the

LORD shall be beautiful and
glorious;
And the fruit of the earth *shall
be* excellent and appealing
For those of Israel who have
escaped.

³And it shall come to pass that *he
who is* left in Zion and remains in
Jerusalem will be called holy—everyone who is recorded among the living
in Jerusalem. ⁴When the Lord has
washed away the filth of the daughters of Zion, and purged the blood of
Jerusalem from her midst, by the
spirit of judgment and by the spirit of
burning, ⁵then the LORD will create
above every dwelling place of Mount
Zion, and above her assemblies, a
cloud and smoke by day and the shining of a flaming fire by night. For over
all the glory there *will be* a covering.
⁶And there will be a tabernacle for
shade in the daytime from the heat,
for a place of refuge, and for a shelter
from storm and rain.

Now let me sing to my Well-beloved
A song of my Beloved
regarding His vineyard:

My Well-beloved has a
vineyard
On a very fruitful hill.
² He dug it up and cleared out
its stones,
And planted it with the
choicest vine.
He built a tower in its midst,
And also made a winepress in
it;
So He expected *it* to bring
forth *good* grapes,
But it brought forth wild
grapes.

³ "And now, O inhabitants of
Jerusalem and men of
Judah,
Judge, please, between Me
and My vineyard.

4 What more could have been
       done to My vineyard
   That I have not done in it?
   Why then, when I expected *it*
       to bring forth *good* grapes,
   Did it bring forth wild grapes?
5 And now, please let Me tell
       you what I will do to My
       vineyard:
   I will take away its hedge, and
       it shall be burned;
   And break down its wall, and
       it shall be trampled down.
6 I will lay it waste;
   It shall not be pruned or dug,
   But there shall come up
       briers and thorns.
   I will also command the clouds
   That they rain no rain on it."

7 For the vineyard of the LORD
       of hosts *is* the house of
       Israel,
   And the men of Judah are His
       pleasant plant.
   He looked for justice, but
       behold, oppression;
   For righteousness, but
       behold, a cry *for help.*

8 Woe to those who join house
       to house;
   They add field to field,
   Till *there is* no place
   Where they may dwell alone
       in the midst of the land!
9 In my hearing the LORD of
       hosts *said,*
   "Truly, many houses shall be
       desolate,
   Great and beautiful ones,
       without inhabitant.
10 For ten acres of vineyard shall
       yield one bath,
   And a homer of seed shall
       yield one ephah."

11 Woe to those who rise early in
       the morning,

That they may follow
       intoxicating drink;
   Who continue until night, *till*
       wine inflames them!
12 The harp and the strings,
   The tambourine and flute,
   And wine are in their feasts;
   But they do not regard the
       work of the LORD,
   Nor consider the operation of
       His hands.

13 Therefore my people have
       gone into captivity,
   Because *they have* no
       knowledge;
   Their honorable men *are*
       famished,
   And their multitude dried up
       with thirst.
14 Therefore Sheol has enlarged
       itself
   And opened its mouth beyond
       measure;
   Their glory and their
       multitude and their pomp,
   And he who is jubilant, shall
       descend into it.
15 People shall be brought down,
   Each man shall be humbled,
   And the eyes of the lofty shall
       be humbled.
16 But the LORD of hosts shall be
       exalted in judgment,
   And God who is holy shall be
       hallowed in righteousness.
17 Then the lambs shall feed in
       their pasture,
   And in the waste places of the
       fat ones strangers shall eat.

18 Woe to those who draw
       iniquity with cords of vanity,
   And sin as if with a cart rope;
19 That say, "Let Him make
       speed *and* hasten His work,
   That we may see *it;*
   And let the counsel of the
       Holy One of Israel draw
       near and come,

That we may know *it*."

20 Woe to those who call evil
good, and good evil;
Who put darkness for light,
and light for darkness;
Who put bitter for sweet, and
sweet for bitter!

21 Woe to *those who are* wise in
their own eyes,
And prudent in their own
sight!

22 Woe to men mighty at
drinking wine,
Woe to men valiant for mixing
intoxicating drink,

23 Who justify the wicked for a
bribe,
And take away justice from
the righteous man!

24 Therefore, as the fire devours
the stubble,
And the flame consumes the
chaff,
So their root will be as
rottenness,
And their blossom will ascend
like dust;
Because they have rejected
the law of the LORD of hosts,
And despised the word of the
Holy One of Israel.

25 Therefore the anger of the
LORD is aroused against His
people;
He has stretched out His
hand against them
And stricken them,
And the hills trembled.
Their carcasses *were* as
refuse in the midst of the
streets.

For all this His anger is not
turned away,
But His hand *is* stretched out
still.

26 He will lift up a banner to the
nations from afar,
And will whistle to them from
the end of the earth;
Surely they shall come with
speed, swiftly.

27 No one will be weary or
stumble among them,
No one will slumber or sleep;
Nor will the belt on their loins
be loosed,
Nor the strap of their sandals
be broken;

28 Whose arrows *are* sharp,
And all their bows bent;
Their horses' hooves will
seem like flint,
And their wheels like a
whirlwind.

29 Their roaring *will be* like a
lion,
They will roar like young
lions;
Yes, they will roar
And lay hold of the prey;
They will carry *it* away safely,
And no one will deliver.

30 In that day they will roar
against them
Like the roaring of the sea.
And if *one* looks to the land,
Behold, darkness *and* sorrow;
And the light is darkened by
the clouds.

2 CORINTHIANS 11:1-15

O H, that you would bear with me
in a little folly—and indeed you
do bear with me. ²For I am jealous for you with godly jealousy. For I
have betrothed you to one husband,
that I may present *you as* a chaste virgin to Christ. ³But I fear, lest somehow,
as the serpent deceived Eve by his
craftiness, so your minds may be corrupted from the simplicity* that is in
Christ. ⁴For if he who comes preaches
another Jesus whom we have not

preached, or *if* you receive a different spirit which you have not received, or a different gospel which you have not accepted—you may well put up with it!

⁵For I consider that I am not at all inferior to the most eminent apostles. ⁶Even though *I am* untrained in speech, yet *I am* not in knowledge. But we have been thoroughly manifested* among you in all things.

⁷Did I commit sin in humbling myself that you might be exalted, because I preached the gospel of God to you free of charge? ⁸I robbed other churches, taking wages *from them* to minister to you. ⁹And when I was present with you, and in need, I was a burden to no one, for what I lacked the brethren who came from Macedonia supplied. And in everything I kept myself from being burdensome to you, and so I will keep *myself*. ¹⁰As the truth of Christ is in me, no one shall stop me from this boasting in the regions of Achaia. ¹¹Why? Because I do not love you? God knows!

¹²But what I do, I will also continue to do, that I may cut off the opportunity from those who desire an opportunity to be regarded just as we are in the things of which they boast. ¹³For such *are* false apostles, deceitful workers, transforming themselves into apostles of Christ. ¹⁴And no wonder! For Satan himself transforms himself into an angel of light. ¹⁵Therefore *it is* no great thing if his ministers also transform themselves into ministers of righteousness, whose end will be according to their works.

PSALM 53:1-6

To the Chief Musician. Set to "Mahalath." A Contemplation* of David.

THE fool has said in his heart, *"There is* no God." They are corrupt, and have done abominable iniquity; *There is* none who does good.

2 God looks down from heaven upon the children of men, To see if there are *any* who understand, who seek God.

3 Every one of them has turned aside; They have together become corrupt; *There is* none who does good, No, not one.

4 Have the workers of iniquity no knowledge, Who eat up my people *as* they eat bread, And do not call upon God?

5 There they are in great fear *Where* no fear was, For God has scattered the bones of him who encamps against you; You have put *them* to shame, Because God has despised them.

6 Oh, that the salvation of Israel would come out of Zion! When God brings back the captivity of His people, Let Jacob rejoice *and* Israel be glad.

PROVERBS FOR TODAY/ 22:28-29

Do not remove the ancient landmark which your fathers have set. □ *Do you see a man* who *excels in his work? He will stand before kings; he will not stand before unknown men.*

SEPTEMBER 10

ISAIAH 6:1–7:25

I N the year that King Uzziah died, I [Isaiah] saw the Lord sitting on a throne, high and lifted up, and the train of His *robe* filled the temple. ²Above it stood seraphim; each one had six wings: with two he covered his face, with two he covered his feet, and with two he flew. ³And one cried to another and said:

> "Holy, holy, holy *is* the LORD of
> hosts;
> The whole earth *is* full of His
> glory!"

⁴And the posts of the door were shaken by the voice of him who cried out, and the house was filled with smoke.
⁵So I said:

> "Woe *is* me, for I am undone!
> Because I *am* a man of
> unclean lips,
> And I dwell in the midst of a
> people of unclean lips;
> For my eyes have seen the
> King,
> The LORD of hosts."

⁶Then one of the seraphim flew to me, having in his hand a live coal *which* he had taken with the tongs from the altar. ⁷And he touched my mouth *with it,* and said:

> "Behold, this has touched your
> lips;
> Your iniquity is taken away,
> And your sin purged."

⁸Also I heard the voice of the Lord, saying:

> "Whom shall I send,
> And who will go for Us?"

Then I said, "Here *am* I! Send me." ⁹And He said, "Go, and tell this people:

> 'Keep on hearing, but do not
> understand;
> Keep on seeing, but do not
> perceive.'

10 "Make the heart of this people
> dull,
> And their ears heavy,
> And shut their eyes;
> Lest they see with their eyes,
> And hear with their ears,
> And understand with their
> heart,
> And return and be healed."

¹¹Then I said, "Lord, how long?" And He answered:

> "Until the cities are laid waste
> and without inhabitant,
> The houses are without a man,
> The land is utterly desolate,
12 The LORD has removed men
> far away,
> And the forsaken places *are*
> many in the midst of the
> land.
13 But yet a tenth *will be* in it,
> And will return and be for
> consuming,
> As a terebinth tree or as an
> oak,
> Whose stump *remains* when it
> is cut down.
> So the holy seed *shall be* its
> stump."

Now it came to pass in the days of Ahaz the son of Jotham, the son of Uzziah, king of Judah, *that* Rezin king of Syria and Pekah the son of Remaliah, king of Israel, went up to Jerusalem to *make* war against it, but could not prevail against it. ²And it was told to the house of David, saying, "Syria's forces are deployed in Ephraim." So his heart and the heart of his people were moved as the trees of the woods are moved with the wind.

³Then the LORD said to Isaiah, "Go out now to meet Ahaz, you and Shear-Jashub* your son, at the end of the aqueduct from the upper pool, on the highway to the Fuller's Field, ⁴and say to him: 'Take heed, and be quiet; do not fear or be fainthearted for these two stubs of smoking firebrands, for the fierce anger of Rezin and Syria, and the son of Remaliah. ⁵Because Syria, Ephraim, and the son of Remaliah have plotted evil against you, saying, ⁶"Let us go up against Judah and trouble it, and let us make a gap in its wall for ourselves, and set a king over them, the son of Tabel"— ⁷thus says the Lord GOD:

"It shall not stand,
Nor shall it come to pass.
8   For the head of Syria *is*
        Damascus,
And the head of Damascus *is*
        Rezin.
Within sixty-five years
        Ephraim will be broken,
So that it will not *be* a people.
9   The head of Ephraim *is*
        Samaria,
And the head of Samaria *is*
        Remaliah's son.
If you will not believe,
Surely you shall not be
        established." ' "

¹⁰Moreover the LORD spoke again to Ahaz, saying, ¹¹"Ask a sign for yourself

from the LORD your God; ask it either in the depth or in the height above."

¹²But Ahaz said, "I will not ask, nor will I test the LORD!"

¹³Then he said, "Hear now, O house of David! *Is it* a small thing for you to weary men, but will you weary my God also? ¹⁴Therefore the Lord Himself will give you a sign: Behold, the virgin shall conceive and bear a Son, and shall call His name Immanuel.* ¹⁵Curds and honey He shall eat, that He may know to refuse the evil and choose the good. ¹⁶For before the Child shall know to refuse the evil and choose the good, the land that you dread will be forsaken by both her kings. ¹⁷The LORD will bring the king of Assyria upon you and your people and your father's house—days that have not come since the day that Ephraim departed from Judah."

18   And it shall come to pass in
        that day
That the LORD will whistle for
        the fly
That *is* in the farthest part of
        the rivers of Egypt,
And for the bee that *is* in the
        land of Assyria.
19   They will come, and all of
        them will rest
In the desolate valleys and in
        the clefts of the rocks,
And on all thorns and in all
        pastures.

20   In the same day the Lord will
        shave with a hired razor,
With those from beyond the
        River,* with the king of
        Assyria,
The head and the hair of the
        legs,
And will also remove the
        beard.

21   It shall be in that day
That a man will keep alive a
        young cow and two sheep;

22 So it shall be, from the
        abundance of milk they
        give,
     That he will eat curds;
     For curds and honey
        everyone will eat who is left
        in the land.

23 It shall happen in that day,
     That wherever there could be
        a thousand vines
     Worth a thousand *shekels* of
        silver,
     It will be for briers and thorns.
24 With arrows and bows men
        will come there,
     Because all the land will
        become briers and thorns.

25 And to any hill which could be
        dug with the hoe,
     You will not go there for fear
        of briers and thorns;
     But it will become a range for
        oxen
     And a place for sheep to roam.

2 CORINTHIANS 11:16-33

I SAY again, let no one think me a
fool. If otherwise, at least receive
me as a fool, that I also may boast
a little. [17]What I speak, I speak not according to the Lord, but as it were,
foolishly, in this confidence of boasting. [18]Seeing that many boast according to the flesh, I also will boast. [19]For
you put up with fools gladly, since you
yourselves are wise! [20]For you put up
with it if one brings you into bondage,
if one devours *you,* if one takes *from
you,* if one exalts himself, if one strikes
you on the face. [21]To *our* shame I say
that we were too weak for that! But in
whatever anyone is bold—I speak foolishly—I am bold also.

[22]Are they Hebrews? So *am* I. Are
they Israelites? So *am* I. Are they the
seed of Abraham? So *am* I. [23]Are they
ministers of Christ?—I speak as a
fool—I *am* more: in labors more abundant, in stripes above measure, in prisons more frequently, in deaths often.
[24]From the Jews five times I received
forty *stripes* minus one. [25]Three times
I was beaten with rods; once I was
stoned; three times I was ship-
wrecked; a night and a day I have been
in the deep; [26]*in* journeys often, *in* perils of waters, *in* perils of robbers, *in*
perils of *my own* countrymen, *in* perils
of the Gentiles, *in* perils in the city, *in*
perils in the wilderness, *in* perils in the
sea, *in* perils among false brethren;
[27]in weariness and toil, in sleeplessness often, in hunger and thirst, in fastings often, in cold and nakedness—
[28]besides the other things, what comes
upon me daily: my deep concern for all
the churches. [29]Who is weak, and I am
not weak? Who is made to stumble,
and I do not burn *with indignation?*

[30]If I must boast, I will boast in the
things which concern my infirmity.
[31]The God and Father of our Lord
Jesus Christ, who is blessed forever,
knows that I am not lying. [32]In Damascus the governor, under Aretas the
king, was guarding the city of the
Damascenes with a garrison, desiring
to arrest me; [33]but I was let down in a
basket through a window in the wall,
and escaped from his hands.

PSALM 54:1-7

*To the Chief Musician. With stringed
instruments. * A Contemplation* of David when
the Ziphites went and said to Saul, "Is David not
hiding with us?"*

S AVE me, O God, by Your name,
        And vindicate me by Your
        strength.
2   Hear my prayer, O God;
        Give ear to the words of my
        mouth.
3   For strangers have risen up
        against me,
     And oppressors have sought
        after my life;

They have not set God before
them.   Selah

4   Behold, God *is* my helper;
    The Lord *is* with those who
        uphold my life.
5   He will repay my enemies for
        their evil.
    Cut them off in Your truth.

6   I will freely sacrifice to You;
    I will praise Your name,
        O LORD, for *it is* good.
7   For He has delivered me out
        of all trouble;
    And my eye has seen *its desire*
        upon my enemies.

PROVERBS FOR TODAY/ 23:1-3

When you sit down to eat with a ruler, consider carefully what is *before you; and put a knife to your throat if you* are *a man given to appetite. Do not desire his delicacies, for they* are *deceptive food.*

SEPTEMBER 11

ISAIAH 8:1–9:21

MOREOVER the LORD said to me [Isaiah], "Take a large scroll, and write on it with a man's pen concerning Maher-Shalal-Hash-Baz.* 2And I will take for Myself faithful witnesses to record, Uriah the priest and Zechariah the son of Jeberechiah."

3Then I went to the prophetess, and she conceived and bore a son. Then the LORD said to me, "Call his name Maher-Shalal-Hash-Baz; 4for before the child shall have knowledge to cry 'My father' and 'My mother,' the riches of Damascus and the spoil of Samaria will be taken away before the king of Assyria."

5The LORD also spoke to me again, saying:

6   "Inasmuch as these people
        refused
    The waters of Shiloah that
        flow softly,

    And rejoice in Rezin and in
        Remaliah's son;
7   Now therefore, behold, the
        Lord brings up over them
    The waters of the River,*
        strong and mighty—
    The king of Assyria and all his
        glory;
    He will go up over all his
        channels
    And go over all his banks.
8   He will pass through Judah,
    He will overflow and pass
        over,
    He will reach up to the neck;
    And the stretching out of his
        wings
    Will fill the breadth of Your
        land, O Immanuel.*

9   "Be shattered, O you peoples,
        and be broken in pieces!
    Give ear, all you from far
        countries.
    Gird yourselves, but be
        broken in pieces;

Gird yourselves, but be
broken in pieces.
10 Take counsel together, but it
will come to nothing;
Speak the word, but it will not
stand,
For God *is* with us."*

11For the LORD spoke thus to me with
a strong hand, and instructed me that
I should not walk in the way of this
people, saying:

12 "Do not say, 'A conspiracy,'
Concerning all that this
people call a conspiracy,
Nor be afraid of their threats,
nor be troubled.
13 The LORD of hosts, Him you
shall hallow;
Let Him *be* your fear,
And *let* Him *be* your dread.
14 He will be as a sanctuary,
But a stone of stumbling and
a rock of offense
To both the houses of Israel,
As a trap and a snare to the
inhabitants of Jerusalem.
15 And many among them shall
stumble;
They shall fall and be broken,
Be snared and taken."

16 Bind up the testimony,
Seal the law among my
disciples.
17 And I will wait on the LORD,
Who hides His face from the
house of Jacob;
And I will hope in Him.
18 Here am I and the children
whom the LORD has given
me!
We are for signs and wonders
in Israel
From the LORD of hosts,
Who dwells in Mount Zion.

19And when they say to you, "Seek
those who are mediums and wizards,
who whisper and mutter," should not a
people seek their God? *Should they
seek* the dead on behalf of the living?
20To the law and to the testimony! If
they do not speak according to this
word, *it is* because *there is* no light in
them.

21They will pass through it hard-
pressed and hungry; and it shall happen, when they are hungry, that they
will be enraged and curse their king
and their God, and look upward.
22Then they will look to the earth, and
see trouble and darkness, gloom of anguish; and *they will be* driven into darkness.

NEVERTHELESS the gloom *will* not *be*
upon her who *is* distressed,
As when at first He lightly
esteemed
The land of Zebulun and the
land of Naphtali,
And afterward more heavily
oppressed *her,*
By the way of the sea, beyond
the Jordan,
In Galilee of the Gentiles.
2 The people who walked in
darkness
Have seen a great light;
Those who dwelt in the land
of the shadow of death,
Upon them a light has shined.

3 You have multiplied the nation
And increased its joy;*
They rejoice before You
According to the joy of
harvest,
As *men* rejoice when they
divide the spoil.
4 For You have broken the yoke
of his burden
And the staff of his shoulder,
The rod of his oppressor,
As in the day of Midian.
5 For every warrior's sandal
from the noisy battle,
And garments rolled in blood,

Will be used for burning *and*
fuel of fire.

6   For unto us a Child is born,
Unto us a Son is given;
And the government will be
upon His shoulder.
And His name will be called
Wonderful, Counselor,
Mighty God,
Everlasting Father, Prince of
Peace.

7   Of the increase of *His*
government and peace
There will be no end,
Upon the throne of David and
over His kingdom,
To order it and establish it
with judgment and justice
From that time forward, even
forever.
The zeal of the Lord of hosts
will perform this.

8   The Lord sent a word against
Jacob,
And it has fallen on Israel.

9   All the people will know—
Ephraim and the inhabitant of
Samaria—
Who say in pride and
arrogance of heart:

10   "The bricks have fallen down,
But we will rebuild with hewn
stones;
The sycamores are cut down,
But we will replace *them* with
cedars."

11   Therefore the Lord shall set
up
The adversaries of Rezin
against him,
And spur his enemies on,

12   The Syrians before and the
Philistines behind;
And they shall devour Israel
with an open mouth.

For all this His anger is not
turned away,

But His hand *is* stretched out
still.

13   For the people do not turn to
Him who strikes them,
Nor do they seek the Lord of
hosts.

14   Therefore the Lord will cut off
head and tail from Israel,
Palm branch and bulrush in
one day.

15   The elder and honorable, he
is the head;
The prophet who teaches lies,
he *is* the tail.

16   For the leaders of this people
cause *them* to err,
And *those who are* led by them
are destroyed.

17   Therefore the Lord will have
no joy in their young men,
Nor have mercy on their
fatherless and widows;
For everyone *is* a hypocrite
and an evildoer,
And every mouth speaks folly.

For all this His anger is not
turned away,
But His hand *is* stretched out
still.

18   For wickedness burns as the
fire;
It shall devour the briers and
thorns,
And kindle in the thickets of
the forest;
They shall mount up *like*
rising smoke.

19   Through the wrath of the
Lord of hosts
The land is burned up,
And the people shall be as
fuel for the fire;
No man shall spare his
brother.

20   And he shall snatch on the
right hand
And be hungry;

He shall devour on the left
hand
And not be satisfied;
Every man shall eat the flesh
of his own arm.
21 Manasseh *shall devour*
Ephraim, and Ephraim
Manasseh;
Together they *shall be* against
Judah.

For all this His anger is not
turned away,
But His hand *is* stretched out
still.

2 CORINTHIANS 12:1-10

IT is doubtless* not profitable for
me to boast. I will come to visions
and revelations of the Lord: 2I
know a man in Christ who fourteen
years ago—whether in the body I do
not know, or whether out of the body I
do not know, God knows—such a one
was caught up to the third heaven.
3And I know such a man—whether in
the body or out of the body I do not
know, God knows— 4how he was
caught up into Paradise and heard inexpressible words, which it is not lawful for a man to utter. 5Of such a one I
will boast; yet of myself I will not boast,
except in my infirmities. 6For though I
might desire to boast, I will not be a
fool; for I will speak the truth. But I
refrain, lest anyone should think of me
above what he sees me *to be* or hears
from me.

7And lest I should be exalted above
measure by the abundance of the revelations, a thorn in the flesh was given
to me, a messenger of Satan to buffet
me, lest I be exalted above measure.
8Concerning this thing I pleaded with
the Lord three times that it might depart from me. 9And He said to me, "My
grace is sufficient for you, for My
strength is made perfect in weakness."
Therefore most gladly I will rather
boast in my infirmities, that the power
of Christ may rest upon me. 10There-
fore I take pleasure in infirmities, in
reproaches, in needs, in persecutions,
in distresses, for Christ's sake. For
when I am weak, then I am strong.

PSALM 55:1-23

*To the Chief Musician. With stringed
instruments.* A Contemplation* of David.*

GIVE ear to my prayer, O God,
And do not hide Yourself from
my supplication.
2 Attend to me, and hear me;
I am restless in my complaint,
and moan noisily,
3 Because of the voice of the
enemy,
Because of the oppression of
the wicked;
For they bring down trouble
upon me,
And in wrath they hate me.

4 My heart is severely pained
within me,
And the terrors of death have
fallen upon me.
5 Fearfulness and trembling
have come upon me,
And horror has overwhelmed
me.
6 So I said, "Oh, that I had
wings like a dove!
I would fly away and be at rest.
7 Indeed, I would wander far off,
And remain in the wilderness.
Selah
8 I would hasten my escape
From the windy storm *and*
tempest."

9 Destroy, O Lord, *and* divide
their tongues,
For I have seen violence and
strife in the city.
10 Day and night they go around
it on its walls;

Iniquity and trouble *are* also
in the midst of it.

11 Destruction *is* in its midst;
Oppression and deceit do not
depart from its streets.

12 For *it is* not an enemy *who*
reproaches me;
Then I could bear *it*.
Nor *is it* one *who* hates me
who has exalted *himself*
against me;
Then I could hide from him.

13 But *it was* you, a man my
equal,
My companion and my
acquaintance.

14 We took sweet counsel
together,
And walked to the house of
God in the throng.

15 Let death seize them;
Let them go down alive into
hell,
For wickedness *is* in their
dwellings *and* among them.

16 As for me, I will call upon God,
And the LORD shall save me.

17 Evening and morning and at
noon
I will pray, and cry aloud,
And He shall hear my voice.

18 He has redeemed my soul in
peace from the battle *that
was* against me,
For there were many against
me.

19 God will hear, and afflict them,
Even He who abides from of
old. Selah
Because they do not change,
Therefore they do not fear
God.

20 He has put forth his hands
against those who were at
peace with him;
He has broken his covenant.

21 *The words* of his mouth were
smoother than butter,
But war *was* in his heart;
His words were softer than oil,
Yet they *were* drawn swords.

22 Cast your burden on the LORD,
And He shall sustain you;
He shall never permit the
righteous to be moved.

23 But You, O God, shall bring
them down to the pit of
destruction;
Bloodthirsty and deceitful
men shall not live out half
their days;
But I will trust in You.

PROVERBS FOR TODAY/ 23:4-5

*Do not overwork to be rich; because of your own understanding, cease! Will you set
your eyes on that which is not? For* riches *certainly make themselves wings; they
fly away like an eagle* toward *heaven.*

SEPTEMBER 12

ISAIAH 10:1–11:16

"**W**OE to those who decree un-
righteous decrees,
Who write misfortune,
Which they have prescribed

2 To rob the needy of justice,
And to take what is right from
the poor of My people,
That widows may be their
prey,
And *that* they may rob the
fatherless.

3 What will you do in the day of
punishment,
And in the desolation *which*
will come from afar?
To whom will you flee for
help?
And where will you leave your
glory?

4 Without Me they shall bow
down among the prisoners,
And they shall fall among the
slain."

For all this His anger is not
turned away,
But His hand *is* stretched out
still.

5 "Woe to Assyria, the rod of My
anger
And the staff in whose hand is
My indignation.

6 I will send him against an
ungodly nation,
And against the people of My
wrath
I will give him charge,
To seize the spoil, to take the
prey,
And to tread them down like
the mire of the streets.

7 Yet he does not mean so,
Nor does his heart think so;

But *it is* in his heart to destroy,
And cut off not a few nations.

8 For he says,
'*Are* not my princes altogether
kings?

9 *Is* not Calno like Carchemish?
Is not Hamath like Arpad?
Is not Samaria like Damascus?

10 As my hand has found the
kingdoms of the idols,
Whose carved images
excelled those of Jerusalem
and Samaria,

11 As I have done to Samaria and
her idols,
Shall I not do also to
Jerusalem and her idols?' "

12Therefore it shall come to pass,
when the Lord has performed all His
work on Mount Zion and on Jerusalem, *that He will say,* "I will punish
the fruit of the arrogant heart of the
king of Assyria, and the glory of his
haughty looks."
13For he says:

"By the strength of my hand I
have done *it,*
And by my wisdom, for I am
prudent;
Also I have removed the
boundaries of the people,
And have robbed their
treasuries;
So I have put down the
inhabitants like a valiant
man.

14 My hand has found like a nest
the riches of the people,
And as one gathers eggs *that
are* left,
I have gathered all the earth;

And there was no one who
moved *his* wing,
Nor opened *his* mouth with
even a peep."

15 Shall the ax boast itself
against him who chops with
it?
Or shall the saw exalt itself
against him who saws with
it?
As if a rod could wield *itself*
against those who lift it up,
Or as if a staff could lift up, *as
if it were* not wood!

16 Therefore the Lord, the Lord*
of hosts,
Will send leanness among his
fat ones;
And under his glory
He will kindle a burning
Like the burning of a fire.

17 So the Light of Israel will be
for a fire,
And his Holy One for a flame;
It will burn and devour
His thorns and his briers in
one day.

18 And it will consume the glory
of his forest and of his
fruitful field,
Both soul and body;
And they will be as when a
sick man wastes away.

19 Then the rest of the trees of
his forest
Will be so few in number
That a child may write them.

20 And it shall come to pass in
that day
That the remnant of Israel,
And such as have escaped of
the house of Jacob,
Will never again depend on
him who defeated them,
But will depend on the LORD,
the Holy One of Israel, in
truth.

21 The remnant will return, the
remnant of Jacob,
To the Mighty God.

22 For though your people,
O Israel, be as the sand of
the sea,
A remnant of them will return;
The destruction decreed shall
overflow with
righteousness.

23 For the Lord GOD of hosts
Will make a determined end
In the midst of all the land.

24Therefore thus says the Lord
GOD of hosts: "O My people, who
dwell in Zion, do not be afraid of the
Assyrian. He shall strike you with a
rod and lift up his staff against you, in
the manner of Egypt. 25For yet a very
little while and the indignation will
cease, as will My anger in their destruction." 26And the LORD of hosts will
stir up a scourge for him like the
slaughter of Midian at the rock of
Oreb; *as* His rod was on the sea, so
will He lift it up in the manner of
Egypt.

27 It shall come to pass in that
day
That his burden will be taken
away from your shoulder,
And his yoke from your neck,
And the yoke will be
destroyed because of the
anointing oil.

28 He has come to Aiath,
He has passed Migron;
At Michmash he has attended
to his equipment.

29 They have gone along the
ridge,
They have taken up lodging at
Geba.
Ramah is afraid,
Gibeah of Saul has fled.

30 Lift up your voice,
O daughter of Gallim!

Cause it to be heard as far as Laish—
O poor Anathoth!*

31 Madmenah has fled,
The inhabitants of Gebim seek refuge.

32 As yet he will remain at Nob that day;
He will shake his fist at the mount of the daughter of Zion,
The hill of Jerusalem.

33 Behold, the Lord,
The LORD of hosts,
Will lop off the bough with terror;
Those of high stature *will be* hewn down,
And the haughty will be humbled.

34 He will cut down the thickets of the forest with iron,
And Lebanon will fall by the Mighty One.

THERE shall come forth a Rod from the stem of Jesse,
And a Branch shall grow out of his roots.

2 The Spirit of the LORD shall rest upon Him,
The Spirit of wisdom and understanding,
The Spirit of counsel and might,
The Spirit of knowledge and of the fear of the LORD.

3 His delight *is* in the fear of the LORD,
And He shall not judge by the sight of His eyes,
Nor decide by the hearing of His ears;

4 But with righteousness He shall judge the poor,
And decide with equity for the meek of the earth;

He shall strike the earth with the rod of His mouth,
And with the breath of His lips He shall slay the wicked.

5 Righteousness shall be the belt of His loins,
And faithfulness the belt of His waist.

6 "The wolf also shall dwell with the lamb,
The leopard shall lie down with the young goat,
The calf and the young lion and the fatling together;
And a little child shall lead them.

7 The cow and the bear shall graze;
Their young ones shall lie down together;
And the lion shall eat straw like the ox.

8 The nursing child shall play by the cobra's hole,
And the weaned child shall put his hand in the viper's den.

9 They shall not hurt nor destroy in all My holy mountain,
For the earth shall be full of the knowledge of the LORD
As the waters cover the sea.

10 "And in that day there shall be a Root of Jesse,
Who shall stand as a banner to the people;
For the Gentiles shall seek Him,
And His resting place shall be glorious."

11 It shall come to pass in that day
That the Lord shall set His hand again the second time

To recover the remnant of His
people who are left,
From Assyria and Egypt,
From Pathros and Cush,
From Elam and Shinar,
From Hamath and the islands
of the sea.

12 He will set up a banner for the
nations,
And will assemble the
outcasts of Israel,
And gather together the
dispersed of Judah
From the four corners of the
earth.

13 Also the envy of Ephraim
shall depart,
And the adversaries of Judah
shall be cut off;
Ephraim shall not envy Judah,
And Judah shall not harass
Ephraim.

14 But they shall fly down upon
the shoulder of the
Philistines toward the west;
Together they shall plunder
the people of the East;
They shall lay their hand on
Edom and Moab;
And the people of Ammon
shall obey them.

15 The Lord will utterly destroy*
the tongue of the Sea of
Egypt;
With His mighty wind He will
shake His fist over the
River,*
And strike it in the seven
streams,
And make men cross over
dryshod.

16 There will be a highway for
the remnant of His people
Who will be left from Assyria,
As it was for Israel
In the day that he came up
from the land of Egypt.

2 CORINTHIANS 12:11-21

I HAVE become a fool in boasting;*
you have compelled me. For I
ought to have been commended
by you; for in nothing was I behind the
most eminent apostles, though I am
nothing. 12Truly the signs of an apostle
were accomplished among you with all
perseverance, in signs and wonders
and mighty deeds. 13For what is it in
which you were inferior to other
churches, except that I myself was not
burdensome to you? Forgive me this
wrong!

14Now for the third time I am ready
to come to you. And I will not be burdensome to you; for I do not seek
yours, but you. For the children ought
not to lay up for the parents, but the
parents for the children. 15And I will
very gladly spend and be spent for
your souls; though the more abundantly I love you, the less I am loved.

16But be that as it may, I did not burden you. Nevertheless, being crafty, I
caught you by cunning! 17Did I take
advantage of you by any of those
whom I sent to you? 18I urged Titus,
and sent our brother with him. Did Titus take advantage of you? Did we not
walk in the same spirit? Did we not
walk in the same steps?

19Again, do you think* that we excuse ourselves to you? We speak before God in Christ. But we do all things,
beloved, for your edification. 20For I
fear lest, when I come, I shall not find
you such as I wish, and that I shall be
found by you such as you do not wish;
lest there be contentions, jealousies,
outbursts of wrath, selfish ambitions,
backbitings, whisperings, conceits, tumults; 21lest, when I come again, my
God will humble me among you, and I
shall mourn for many who have sinned
before and have not repented of the
uncleanness, fornication, and lewdness which they have practiced.

PSALM 56:1-13

To the Chief Musician. Set to "The Silent Dove in Distant Lands."* A Michtam of David when the Philistines captured him in Gath.

B E merciful to me, O God, for man would swallow me up; Fighting all day he oppresses me.

2 My enemies would hound *me* all day,
For *there are* many who fight against me, O Most High.

3 Whenever I am afraid,
I will trust in You.
4 In God (I will praise His word),
In God I have put my trust;
I will not fear.
What can flesh do to me?

5 All day they twist my words;
All their thoughts *are* against me for evil.
6 They gather together,
They hide, they mark my steps,
When they lie in wait for my life.

7 Shall they escape by iniquity?
In anger cast down the peoples, O God!

8 You number my wanderings;
Put my tears into Your bottle;
Are they not in Your book?
9 When I cry out *to You,*
Then my enemies will turn back;
This I know, because God *is* for me.
10 In God (I will praise *His* word),
In the LORD (I will praise *His* word),
11 In God I have put my trust;
I will not be afraid.
What can man do to me?

12 Vows *made* to You *are binding* upon me, O God;
I will render praises to You,
13 For You have delivered my soul from death.
Have You not *kept* my feet from falling,
That I may walk before God
In the light of the living?

PROVERBS FOR TODAY/ 23:6-8

Do not eat the bread of a miser,* nor desire his delicacies; for as he thinks in his heart, so is he. "Eat and drink!" he says to you, but his heart is not with you. The morsel you have eaten, you will vomit up, and waste your pleasant words.

SEPTEMBER 13

ISAIAH 12:1–14:32

A ND in that day you will say:

"O LORD, I will praise You;
Though You were angry with me,

Your anger is turned away,
and You comfort me.
2 Behold, God *is* my salvation,
I will trust and not be afraid;
'For YAH, the LORD, *is* my strength and song;

He also has become my
salvation.' "*

3 Therefore with joy you will
draw water
From the wells of salvation.

⁴And in that day you will say:

"Praise the LORD, call upon His
name;
Declare His deeds among the
peoples,
Make mention that His name
is exalted.
5 Sing to the LORD,
For He has done excellent
things;
This *is* known in all the earth.
6 Cry out and shout,
O inhabitant of Zion,
For great *is* the Holy One of
Israel in your midst!"

THE burden against Babylon which
Isaiah the son of Amoz saw.

2 "Lift up a banner on the high
mountain,
Raise your voice to them;
Wave your hand, that they
may enter the gates of the
nobles.
3 I have commanded My
sanctified ones;
I have also called My mighty
ones for My anger—
Those who rejoice in My
exaltation."

4 The noise of a multitude in
the mountains,
Like that of many people!
A tumultuous noise of the
kingdoms of nations
gathered together!
The LORD of hosts musters
The army for battle.
5 They come from a far country,
From the end of heaven—

The LORD and His weapons of
indignation,
To destroy the whole land.

6 Wail, for the day of the LORD *is*
at hand!
It will come as destruction
from the Almighty.
7 Therefore all hands will be
limp,
Every man's heart will melt,
8 And they will be afraid.
Pangs and sorrows will take
hold of *them;*
They will be in pain as a
woman in childbirth;
They will be amazed at one
another;
Their faces *will be like* flames.

9 Behold, the day of the LORD
comes,
Cruel, with both wrath and
fierce anger,
To lay the land desolate;
And He will destroy its
sinners from it.
10 For the stars of heaven and
their constellations
Will not give their light;
The sun will be darkened in
its going forth,
And the moon will not cause
its light to shine.

11 "I will punish the world for *its*
evil,
And the wicked for their
iniquity;
I will halt the arrogance of the
proud,
And will lay low the
haughtiness of the terrible.
12 I will make a mortal more
rare than fine gold,
A man more than the golden
wedge of Ophir.
13 Therefore I will shake the
heavens,

And the earth will move out of
her place,
In the wrath of the Lord of
hosts
And in the day of His fierce
anger.
14 It shall be as the hunted
gazelle,
And as a sheep that no man
takes up;
Every man will turn to his
own people,
And everyone will flee to his
own land.
15 Everyone who is found will be
thrust through,
And everyone who is
captured will fall by the
sword.
16 Their children also will be
dashed to pieces before
their eyes;
Their houses will be
plundered
And their wives ravished.

17 "Behold, I will stir up the
Medes against them,
Who will not regard silver;
And *as for* gold, they will not
delight in it.
18 Also *their* bows will dash the
young men to pieces,
And they will have no pity on
the fruit of the womb;
Their eye will not spare
children.
19 And Babylon, the glory of
kingdoms,
The beauty of the Chaldeans'
pride,
Will be as when God
overthrew Sodom and
Gomorrah.
20 It will never be inhabited,
Nor will it be settled from
generation to generation;
Nor will the Arabian pitch
tents there,

Nor will the shepherds make
their sheepfolds there.
21 But wild beasts of the desert
will lie there,
And their houses will be full
of owls;
Ostriches will dwell there,
And wild goats will caper
there.
22 The hyenas will howl in their
citadels,
And jackals in their pleasant
palaces.
Her time *is* near to come,
And her days will not be
prolonged."

For the Lord will have mercy on Jacob,
and will still choose Israel, and settle
them in their own land. The strangers
will be joined with them, and they will
cling to the house of Jacob. ²Then
people will take them and bring them
to their place, and the house of Israel
will possess them for servants and
maids in the land of the Lord; they will
take them captive whose captives they
were, and rule over their oppressors.

³It shall come to pass in the day the
Lord gives you rest from your sorrow,
and from your fear and the hard bondage in which you were made to serve,
⁴that you will take up this proverb
against the king of Babylon, and say:

"How the oppressor has
ceased,
The golden* city ceased!
5 The Lord has broken the staff
of the wicked,
The scepter of the rulers;
6 He who struck the people in
wrath with a continual
stroke,
He who ruled the nations in
anger,
Is persecuted *and* no one
hinders.
7 The whole earth is at rest *and*
quiet;

They break forth into singing.

8 Indeed the cypress trees
rejoice over you,
And the cedars of Lebanon,
Saying, 'Since you were cut
down,
No woodsman has come up
against us.'

9 "Hell from beneath is excited
about you,
To meet *you* at your coming;
It stirs up the dead for you,
All the chief ones of the earth;
It has raised up from their
thrones
All the kings of the nations.

10 They all shall speak and say
to you:
'Have you also become as
weak as we?
Have you become like us?

11 Your pomp is brought down
to Sheol,
And the sound of your
stringed instruments;
The maggot is spread under
you,
And worms cover you.'

12 "How you are fallen from
heaven,
O Lucifer,* son of the
morning!
How you are cut down to the
ground,
You who weakened the
nations!

13 For you have said in your
heart:
'I will ascend into heaven,
I will exalt my throne above
the stars of God;
I will also sit on the mount of
the congregation
On the farthest sides of the
north;

14 I will ascend above the
heights of the clouds,
I will be like the Most High.'

15 Yet you shall be brought
down to Sheol,
To the lowest depths of the
Pit.

16 "Those who see you will gaze
at you,
And consider you, *saying:*
'*Is* this the man who made the
earth tremble,
Who shook kingdoms,

17 Who made the world as a
wilderness
And destroyed its cities,
Who did not open the house
of his prisoners?'

18 "All the kings of the nations,
All of them, sleep in glory,
Everyone in his own house;

19 But you are cast out of your
grave
Like an abominable branch,
Like the garment of those
who are slain,
Thrust through with a sword,
Who go down to the stones of
the pit,
Like a corpse trodden
underfoot.

20 You will not be joined with
them in burial,
Because you have destroyed
your land
And slain your people.
The brood of evildoers shall
never be named.

21 Prepare slaughter for his
children
Because of the iniquity of
their fathers,
Lest they rise up and possess
the land,
And fill the face of the world
with cities."

22 "For I will rise up against
them," says the LORD of
hosts,

"And cut off from Babylon the
name and remnant,
And offspring and posterity,"
says the LORD.
23 "I will also make it a
possession for the
porcupine,
And marshes of muddy water;
I will sweep it with the broom
of destruction," says the
LORD of hosts.

24 The LORD of hosts has sworn,
saying,
"Surely, as I have thought, so it
shall come to pass,
And as I have purposed, *so* it
shall stand:
25 That I will break the Assyrian
in My land,
And on My mountains tread
him underfoot.
Then his yoke shall be
removed from them,
And his burden removed
from their shoulders.
26 This *is* the purpose that is
purposed against the whole
earth,
And this *is* the hand that is
stretched out over all the
nations.
27 For the LORD of hosts has
purposed,
And who will annul *it?*
His hand *is* stretched out,
And who will turn it back?"

28This is the burden which came in
the year that King Ahaz died.

29 "Do not rejoice, all you of
Philistia,
Because the rod that struck
you is broken;
For out of the serpent's roots
will come forth a viper,
And its offspring *will be* a
fiery flying serpent.

30 The firstborn of the poor will
feed,
And the needy will lie down in
safety;
I will kill your roots with
famine,
And it will slay your remnant.
31 Wail, O gate! Cry, O city!
All you of Philistia *are*
dissolved;
For smoke will come from the
north,
And no one *will be* alone in his
appointed times."

32 What will they answer the
messengers of the nation?
That the LORD has founded
Zion,
And the poor of His people
shall take refuge in it.

2 CORINTHIANS 13:1-14

THIS *will be* the third *time* I am
coming to you. *"By the mouth of
two or three witnesses every
word shall be established."* * 2I have
told you before, and foretell as if I were
present the second time, and now being absent I write* to those who have
sinned before, and to all the rest, that
if I come again I will not spare— 3since
you seek a proof of Christ speaking in
me, who is not weak toward you, but
mighty in you. 4For though He was
crucified in weakness, yet He lives by
the power of God. For we also are
weak in Him, but we shall live with
Him by the power of God toward you.

5Examine yourselves *as to* whether
you are in the faith. Test yourselves.
Do you not know yourselves, that
Jesus Christ is in you?—unless indeed
you are disqualified. 6But I trust that
you will know that we are not disqualified.

7Now I* pray to God that you do no
evil, not that we should appear approved, but that you should do what is

honorable, though we may seem disqualified. [8]For we can do nothing against the truth, but for the truth. [9]For we are glad when we are weak and you are strong. And this also we pray, that you may be made complete. [10]Therefore I write these things being absent, lest being present I should use sharpness, according to the authority which the Lord has given me for edification and not for destruction.

[11]Finally, brethren, farewell. Become complete. Be of good comfort, be of one mind, live in peace; and the God of love and peace will be with you.

[12]Greet one another with a holy kiss. [13]All the saints greet you.

[14]The grace of the Lord Jesus Christ, and the love of God, and the communion of the Holy Spirit *be* with you all. Amen.

PSALM 57:1-11

*To the Chief Musician. Set to "Do Not Destroy."**
A Michtam of David when he fled from Saul into
the cave.

BE merciful to me, O God, be merciful to me!
For my soul trusts in You;
And in the shadow of Your
    wings I will make my
    refuge,
Until *these* calamities have
    passed by.

2   I will cry out to God Most
        High,
    To God who performs *all*
        things for me.
3   He shall send from heaven
        and save me;
    He reproaches the one who
        would swallow me up. Selah

God shall send forth His
    mercy and His truth.

4   My soul *is* among lions;
    I lie *among* the sons of men
    Who are set on fire,
    Whose teeth *are* spears and
        arrows,
    And their tongue a sharp
        sword.
5   Be exalted, O God, above the
        heavens;
    Let Your glory *be* above all the
        earth.

6   They have prepared a net for
        my steps;
    My soul is bowed down;
    They have dug a pit before
        me;
    Into the midst of it they
        themselves have fallen. Selah

7   My heart is steadfast, O God,
        my heart is steadfast;
    I will sing and give praise.
8   Awake, my glory!
    Awake, lute and harp!
    I will awaken the dawn.

9   I will praise You, O Lord,
        among the peoples;
    I will sing to You among the
        nations.
10   For Your mercy reaches unto
        the heavens,
    And Your truth unto the
        clouds.

11   Be exalted, O God, above the
        heavens;
    Let Your glory *be* above all the
        earth.

PROVERBS FOR TODAY/ 23:9-11

Do not speak in the hearing of a fool, for he will despise the wisdom of your words.
□ *Do not remove the ancient landmark, nor enter the fields of the fatherless; for*
their Redeemer is mighty; He will plead their cause against you.

SEPTEMBER 14

ISAIAH 15:1–18:7

THE burden against Moab.

Because in the night Ar of
    Moab is laid waste
And destroyed,
Because in the night Kir of
    Moab is laid waste
And destroyed,
2 He has gone up to the
    temple* and Dibon,
To the high places to weep.
Moab will wail over Nebo and
    over Medeba;
On all their heads *will be*
    baldness,
And every beard cut off.
3 In their streets they will
    clothe themselves with
    sackcloth;
On the tops of their houses
And in their streets
Everyone will wail, weeping
    bitterly.
4 Heshbon and Elealeh will cry
    out,
Their voice shall be heard as
    far as Jahaz;
Therefore the armed
    soldiers* of Moab will cry
    out;
His life will be burdensome to
    him.

5 "My heart will cry out for
    Moab;
His fugitives *shall flee* to Zoar,
Like a three-year-old heifer.*
For by the Ascent of Luhith
They will go up with weeping;
For in the way of Horonaim
They will raise up a cry of
    destruction,
6 For the waters of Nimrim will
    be desolate,

For the green grass has
    withered away;
The grass fails, there is
    nothing green.
7 Therefore the abundance
    they have gained,
And what they have laid up,
They will carry away to the
    Brook of the Willows.
8 For the cry has gone all
    around the borders of
    Moab,
Its wailing to Eglaim
And its wailing to Beer Elim.
9 For the waters of Dimon* will
    be full of blood;
Because I will bring more
    upon Dimon,*
Lions upon him who escapes
    from Moab,
And on the remnant of the
    land."

SEND the lamb to the ruler of the land,
    From Sela to the wilderness,
    To the mount of the daughter
    of Zion.
2 For it shall be as a wandering
    bird thrown out of the nest;
So shall be the daughters of
    Moab at the fords of the
    Arnon.

3 "Take counsel, execute
    judgment;
Make your shadow like the
    night in the middle of the
    day;
Hide the outcasts,
Do not betray him who
    escapes.
4 Let My outcasts dwell with
    you, O Moab;

Be a shelter to them from the
    face of the spoiler.
For the extortioner is at an
    end,
Devastation ceases,
The oppressors are
    consumed out of the land.
5   In mercy the throne will be
    established;
And One will sit on it in truth,
    in the tabernacle of David,
Judging and seeking justice
    and hastening
    righteousness."

6   We have heard of the pride of
    Moab—
He is very proud—
Of his haughtiness and his
    pride and his wrath;
But his lies *shall* not *be* so.
7   Therefore Moab shall wail for
    Moab;
Everyone shall wail.
For the foundations of Kir
    Hareseth you shall mourn;
Surely *they are* stricken.

8   For the fields of Heshbon
    languish,
And the vine of Sibmah;
The lords of the nations have
    broken down its choice
    plants,
Which have reached to Jazer
And wandered through the
    wilderness.
Her branches are stretched
    out,
They are gone over the sea.
9   Therefore I will bewail the
    vine of Sibmah,
With the weeping of Jazer;
I will drench you with my
    tears,
O Heshbon and Elealeh;
For battle cries have fallen
Over your summer fruits and
    your harvest.

10 Gladness is taken away,
And joy from the plentiful
    field;
In the vineyards there will be
    no singing,
Nor will there be shouting;
No treaders will tread out
    wine in the presses;
I have made their shouting
    cease.
11 Therefore my heart shall
    resound like a harp for
    Moab,
And my inner being for Kir
    Heres.

12 And it shall come to pass,
When it is seen that Moab is
    weary on the high place,
That he will come to his
    sanctuary to pray;
But he will not prevail.

13This *is* the word which the LORD
has spoken concerning Moab since
that time. 14But now the LORD has spoken, saying, "Within three years, as
the years of a hired man, the glory of
Moab will be despised with all that
great multitude, and the remnant *will
be* very small *and* feeble."

THE burden against Damascus.

    "Behold, Damascus will cease
        from *being* a city,
    And it will be a ruinous heap.
2   The cities of Aroer *are*
        forsaken;*
    They will be for flocks
    Which lie down, and no one
        will make *them* afraid.
3   The fortress also will cease
        from Ephraim,
    The kingdom from Damascus,
    And the remnant of Syria;
    They will be as the glory of
        the children of Israel,"
    Says the LORD of hosts.

4 "In that day it shall come to
pass
That the glory of Jacob will
wane,
And the fatness of his flesh
grow lean.
5 It shall be as when the
harvester gathers the grain,
And reaps the heads with his
arm;
It shall be as he who gathers
heads of grain
In the Valley of Rephaim.
6 Yet gleaning grapes will be
left in it,
Like the shaking of an olive
tree,
Two *or* three olives at the top
of the uppermost bough,
Four *or* five in its most fruitful
branches,"
Says the Lord God of Israel.

7 In that day a man will look to
his Maker,
And his eyes will have respect
for the Holy One of Israel.
8 He will not look to the altars,
The work of his hands;
He will not respect what his
fingers have made,
Nor the wooden images* nor
the incense altars.

9 In that day his strong cities
will be as a forsaken bough*
And an uppermost branch,*
Which they left because of
the children of Israel;
And there will be desolation.

10 Because you have forgotten
the God of your salvation,
And have not been mindful of
the Rock of your
stronghold,
Therefore you will plant
pleasant plants
And set out foreign seedlings;

11 In the day you will make your
plant to grow,
And in the morning you will
make your seed to flourish;
But the harvest *will be* a heap
of ruins
In the day of grief and
desperate sorrow.

12 Woe to the multitude of many
people
Who make a noise like the
roar of the seas,
And to the rushing of nations
That make a rushing like the
rushing of mighty waters!
13 The nations will rush like the
rushing of many waters;
But *God* will rebuke them and
they will flee far away,
And be chased like the chaff
of the mountains before the
wind,
Like a rolling thing before the
whirlwind.
14 Then behold, at eventide,
trouble!
And before the morning, he *is*
no more.
This *is* the portion of those
who plunder us,
And the lot of those who rob
us.

Woe to the land shadowed with buzz-
ing wings,
Which *is* beyond the rivers of
Ethiopia,
2 Which sends ambassadors by
sea,
Even in vessels of reed on the
waters, *saying,*
"Go, swift messengers, to a
nation tall and smooth *of
skin,*
To a people terrible from
their beginning onward,
A nation powerful and
treading down,
Whose land the rivers divide."

3 All inhabitants of the world
and dwellers on the earth:
When he lifts up a banner on
the mountains, you see *it;*
And when he blows a
trumpet, you hear *it.*
4 For so the LORD said to me,
"I will take My rest,
And I will look from My
dwelling place
Like clear heat in sunshine,
Like a cloud of dew in the
heat of harvest."
5 For before the harvest, when
the bud is perfect
And the sour grape is
ripening in the flower,
He will both cut off the sprigs
with pruning hooks
And take away *and* cut down
the branches.
6 They will be left together for
the mountain birds of prey
And for the beasts of the
earth;
The birds of prey will summer
on them,
And all the beasts of the earth
will winter on them.

7 In that time a present will be
brought to the LORD of hosts
From* a people tall and
smooth *of skin,*
And from a people terrible
from their beginning
onward,
A nation powerful and
treading down,
Whose land the rivers
divide—
To the place of the name of
the LORD of hosts,
To Mount Zion.

GALATIANS 1:1-24

P AUL, an apostle (not from men
nor through man, but through
Jesus Christ and God the
Father who raised Him from the
dead), ²and all the brethren who are
with me,

To the churches of Galatia:

³Grace to you and peace from God
the Father and our Lord Jesus Christ,
⁴who gave Himself for our sins, that He
might deliver us from this present evil
age, according to the will of our God
and Father, ⁵to whom *be* glory forever
and ever. Amen.

⁶I marvel that you are turning away
so soon from Him who called you in
the grace of Christ, to a different gospel, ⁷which is not another; but there
are some who trouble you and want to
pervert the gospel of Christ. ⁸But even
if we, or an angel from heaven, preach
any other gospel to you than what we
have preached to you, let him be accursed. ⁹As we have said before, so
now I say again, if anyone preaches
any other gospel to you than what you
have received, let him be accursed.
¹⁰For do I now persuade men, or
God? Or do I seek to please men? For
if I still pleased men, I would not be a
bondservant of Christ.
¹¹But I make known to you,
brethren, that the gospel which was
preached by me is not according to
man. ¹²For I neither received it from
man, nor was I taught *it,* but *it came*
through the revelation of Jesus Christ.
¹³For you have heard of my former
conduct in Judaism, how I persecuted
the church of God beyond measure
and *tried to* destroy it. ¹⁴And I advanced in Judaism beyond many of my
contemporaries in my own nation, being more exceedingly zealous for the
traditions of my fathers.
¹⁵But when it pleased God, who separated me from my mother's womb
and called *me* through His grace, ¹⁶to
reveal His Son in me, that I might
preach Him among the Gentiles, I did

not immediately confer with flesh and blood, 17nor did I go up to Jerusalem to those *who were* apostles before me; but I went to Arabia, and returned again to Damascus.

18Then after three years I went up to Jerusalem to see Peter,* and remained with him fifteen days. 19But I saw none of the other apostles except James, the Lord's brother. 20(Now *concerning* the things which I write to you, indeed, before God, I do not lie.)

21Afterward I went into the regions of Syria and Cilicia. 22And I was unknown by face to the churches of Judea which *were* in Christ. 23But they were hearing only, "He who formerly persecuted us now preaches the faith which he once *tried to* destroy." 24And they glorified God in me.

PSALM 58:1-11

To the Chief Musician. Set to "Do Not Destroy." *
A Michtam of David.

Do you indeed speak righteousness, you silent ones? Do you judge uprightly, you sons of men?
2 No, in heart you work wickedness; You weigh out the violence of your hands in the earth.

3 The wicked are estranged from the womb; They go astray as soon as they are born, speaking lies.

4 Their poison *is* like the poison of a serpent; *They are* like the deaf cobra *that* stops its ear,
5 Which will not heed the voice of charmers, Charming ever so skillfully.

6 Break their teeth in their mouth, O God! Break out the fangs of the young lions, O LORD!
7 Let them flow away as waters *which* run continually; *When* he bends *his bow,* Let his arrows be as if cut in pieces.
8 *Let them be* like a snail which melts away as it goes, *Like* a stillborn child of a woman, that they may not see the sun.

9 Before your pots can feel *the burning* thorns, He shall take them away as with a whirlwind, As in His living and burning wrath.
10 The righteous shall rejoice when he sees the vengeance; He shall wash his feet in the blood of the wicked,
11 So that men will say, "Surely *there is* a reward for the righteous; Surely He is God who judges in the earth."

PROVERBS FOR TODAY/ 23:12

Apply your heart to instruction, and your ears to words of knowledge.

SEPTEMBER 15

ISAIAH 19:1–21:17

THE burden against Egypt.

Behold, the LORD rides on a
swift cloud,
And will come into Egypt;
The idols of Egypt will totter
at His presence,
And the heart of Egypt will
melt in its midst.

2 "I will set Egyptians against
Egyptians;
Everyone will fight against his
brother,
And everyone against his
neighbor,
City against city, kingdom
against kingdom.
3 The spirit of Egypt will fail in
its midst;
I will destroy their counsel,
And they will consult the idols
and the charmers,
The mediums and the
sorcerers.
4 And the Egyptians I will give
Into the hand of a cruel
master,
And a fierce king will rule
over them,"
Says the Lord, the LORD of
hosts.

5 The waters will fail from the
sea,
And the river will be wasted
and dried up.
6 The rivers will turn foul;
The brooks of defense will be
emptied and dried up;
The reeds and rushes will
wither.
7 The papyrus reeds by the
River,* by the mouth of the
River,
And everything sown by the
River,
Will wither, be driven away,
and be no more.
8 The fishermen also will
mourn;
All those will lament who cast
hooks into the River,
And they will languish who
spread nets on the waters.
9 Moreover those who work in
fine flax
And those who weave fine
fabric will be ashamed;
10 And its foundations will be
broken.
All who make wages *will be*
troubled of soul.

11 Surely the princes of Zoan *are*
fools;
Pharaoh's wise counselors
give foolish counsel.
How do you say to Pharaoh,
"I *am* the son of the wise,
The son of ancient kings?"
12 Where *are* they?
Where are your wise men?
Let them tell you now,
And let them know what the
LORD of hosts has purposed
against Egypt.
13 The princes of Zoan have
become fools;
The princes of Noph* are
deceived;
They have also deluded Egypt,
Those who are the mainstay of
its tribes.
14 The LORD has mingled a
perverse spirit in her midst;
And they have caused Egypt
to err in all her work,

As a drunken man staggers in
  his vomit.
15 Neither will there be *any*
    work for Egypt,
  Which the head or tail,
  Palm branch or bulrush, may
    do.*

16In that day Egypt will be like women, and will be afraid and fear because of the waving of the hand of the Lord of hosts, which He waves over it. 17And the land of Judah will be a terror to Egypt; everyone who makes mention of it will be afraid in himself, because of the counsel of the Lord of hosts which He has determined against it.

18In that day five cities in the land of Egypt will speak the language of Canaan and swear by the Lord of hosts; one will be called the City of Destruction.*

19In that day there will be an altar to the Lord in the midst of the land of Egypt, and a pillar to the Lord at its border. 20And it will be for a sign and for a witness to the Lord of hosts in the land of Egypt; for they will cry to the Lord because of the oppressors, and He will send them a Savior and a Mighty One, and He will deliver them. 21Then the Lord will be known to Egypt, and the Egyptians will know the Lord in that day, and will make sacrifice and offering; yes, they will make a vow to the Lord and perform *it.* 22And the Lord will strike Egypt, He will strike and heal *it;* they will return to the Lord, and He will be entreated by them and heal them.

23In that day there will be a highway from Egypt to Assyria, and the Assyrian will come into Egypt and the Egyptian into Assyria, and the Egyptians will serve with the Assyrians.

24In that day Israel will be one of three with Egypt and Assyria—a blessing in the midst of the land, 25whom the Lord of hosts shall bless, saying,

"Blessed *is* Egypt My people, and Assyria the work of My hands, and Israel My inheritance."

In the year that Tartan* came to Ashdod, when Sargon the king of Assyria sent him, and he fought against Ashdod and took it, 2at the same time the Lord spoke by Isaiah the son of Amoz, saying, "Go, and remove the sackcloth from your body, and take your sandals off your feet." And he did so, walking naked and barefoot.

3Then the Lord said, "Just as My servant Isaiah has walked naked and barefoot three years *for* a sign and a wonder against Egypt and Ethiopia, 4so shall the king of Assyria lead away the Egyptians as prisoners and the Ethiopians as captives, young and old, naked and barefoot, with their buttocks uncovered, to the shame of Egypt. 5Then they shall be afraid and ashamed of Ethiopia their expectation and Egypt their glory. 6And the inhabitant of this territory will say in that day, 'Surely such *is* our expectation, wherever we flee for help to be delivered from the king of Assyria; and how shall we escape?' "

The burden against the Wilderness of the Sea.

  As whirlwinds in the South
    pass through,
  So it comes from the desert,
    from a terrible land.
2 A distressing vision is
    declared to me;
  The treacherous dealer deals
    treacherously,
  And the plunderer plunders.
  Go up, O Elam!
  Besiege, O Media!
  All its sighing I have made to
    cease.

3 Therefore my loins are filled
    with pain;

Pangs have taken hold of me,
  like the pangs of a woman
    in labor.
I was distressed when *I* heard
  it;
I was dismayed when *I* saw *it.*
4 My heart wavered,
    fearfulness frightened me;
  The night for which I longed
    He turned into fear for me.
5 Prepare the table,
  Set a watchman in the tower,
  Eat and drink.
  Arise, you princes,
  Anoint the shield!

6 For thus has the Lord said to
    me:
  "Go, set a watchman,
  Let him declare what he sees."
7 And he saw a chariot *with* a
    pair of horsemen,
  A chariot of donkeys, *and* a
    chariot of camels,
  And he listened earnestly
    with great care.
8 Then he cried, "A lion,* my
    Lord!
  I stand continually on the
    watchtower in the daytime;
  I have sat at my post every
    night.
9 And look, here comes a
    chariot of men *with* a pair of
    horsemen!"
  Then he answered and said,
  "Babylon is fallen, is fallen!
  And all the carved images of
    her gods
  He has broken to the ground."

10 Oh, my threshing and the
    grain of my floor!
  That which I have heard from
    the LORD of hosts,
  The God of Israel,
  I have declared to you.

11 The burden against Dumah.

He calls to me out of Seir,
"Watchman, what of the night?
  Watchman, what of the night?"
12 The watchman said,
  "The morning comes, and also
    the night.
  If you will inquire, inquire;
  Return! Come back!"

13The burden against Arabia.

  In the forest in Arabia you will
    lodge,
  O you traveling companies of
    Dedanites.
14 O inhabitants of the land of
    Tema,
  Bring water to him who is
    thirsty;
  With their bread they met
    him who fled.
15 For they fled from the
    swords, from the drawn
    sword,
  From the bent bow, and from
    the distress of war.

16For thus the LORD has said to me:
"Within a year, according to the year of
a hired man, all the glory of Kedar will
fail; 17and the remainder of the number
of archers, the mighty men of the
people of Kedar, will be diminished; for
the LORD God of Israel has spoken *it.*"

GALATIANS 2:1-16

THEN after fourteen years I [Paul]
went up again to Jerusalem with
Barnabas, and also took Titus
with *me.* 2And I went up by revelation,
and communicated to them that gospel which I preach among the Gentiles, but privately to those who were of
reputation, lest by any means I might
run, or had run, in vain. 3Yet not even
Titus who *was* with me, being a Greek,
was compelled to be circumcised.
4And *this occurred* because of false
brethren secretly brought in (who

came in by stealth to spy out our liberty which we have in Christ Jesus, that they might bring us into bondage), ⁵to whom we did not yield submission even for an hour, that the truth of the gospel might continue with you.

⁶But from those who seemed to be something—whatever they were, it makes no difference to me; God shows personal favoritism to no man—for those who seemed *to be something* added nothing to me. ⁷But on the contrary, when they saw that the gospel for the uncircumcised had been committed to me, as *the gospel* for the circumcised *was* to Peter ⁸(for He who worked effectively in Peter for the apostleship to the circumcised also worked effectively in me toward the Gentiles), ⁹and when James, Cephas, and John, who seemed to be pillars, perceived the grace that had been given to me, they gave me and Barnabas the right hand of fellowship, that we *should go* to the Gentiles and they to the circumcised. ¹⁰*They desired* only that we should remember the poor, the very thing which I also was eager to do.

¹¹Now when Peter* had come to Antioch, I withstood him to his face, because he was to be blamed; ¹²for before certain men came from James, he would eat with the Gentiles; but when they came, he withdrew and separated himself, fearing those who were of the circumcision. ¹³And the rest of the Jews also played the hypocrite with him, so that even Barnabas was carried away with their hypocrisy.

¹⁴But when I saw that they were not straightforward about the truth of the gospel, I said to Peter before *them* all, "If you, being a Jew, live in the manner of Gentiles and not as the Jews, why do you* compel Gentiles to live as Jews?* ¹⁵We *who are* Jews by nature, and not sinners of the Gentiles, ¹⁶knowing that a man is not justified by the works of the law but by faith in Jesus Christ,

even we have believed in Christ Jesus, that we might be justified by faith in Christ and not by the works of the law; for by the works of the law no flesh shall be justified."

PSALM 59:1-17

*To the Chief Musician. Set to "Do Not Destroy."** *A Michtam of David when Saul sent men, and they watched the house in order to kill him.*

DELIVER me from my enemies, O my God; Defend me from those who rise up against me.
2 Deliver me from the workers of iniquity, And save me from bloodthirsty men.

3 For look, they lie in wait for my life; The mighty gather against me, Not *for* my transgression nor *for* my sin, O LORD.
4 They run and prepare themselves through no fault *of mine.*

Awake to help me, and behold! 5 You therefore, O LORD God of hosts, the God of Israel, Awake to punish all the nations; Do not be merciful to any wicked transgressors. Selah

6 At evening they return, They growl like a dog, And go all around the city.
7 Indeed, they belch with their mouth; Swords *are* in their lips; For *they say,* "Who hears?"

8 But You, O LORD, shall laugh at them; You shall have all the nations in derision.

9 I will wait for You, O You his
Strength;*
For God *is* my defense.

10 My God of mercy* shall come
to meet me;
God shall let me see *my desire*
on my enemies.

11 Do not slay them, lest my
people forget;
Scatter them by Your power,
And bring them down,
O Lord our shield.

12 *For* the sin of their mouth *and*
the words of their lips,
Let them even be taken in
their pride,
And for the cursing and lying
which they speak.

13 Consume *them* in wrath,
consume *them*,
That they *may* not *be;*

And let them know that God
rules in Jacob
To the ends of the earth. Selah

14 And at evening they return,
They growl like a dog,
And go all around the city.

15 They wander up and down for
food,
And howl* if they are not
satisfied.

16 But I will sing of Your power;
Yes, I will sing aloud of Your
mercy in the morning;
For You have been my defense
And refuge in the day of my
trouble.

17 To You, O my Strength, I will
sing praises;
For God *is* my defense,
My God of mercy.

PROVERBS FOR TODAY/ 23:13-14

Do not withhold correction from a child, for if *you beat him with a rod, he will not die. You shall beat him with a rod, and deliver his soul from hell.* *

SEPTEMBER 16

ISAIAH 22:1–24:23

THE burden against the Valley of
Vision.

What ails you now, that you
have all gone up to the
housetops,

2 You who are full of noise,
A tumultuous city, a joyous
city?
Your slain *men are* not slain
with the sword,
Nor dead in battle.

3 All your rulers have fled
together;
They are captured by the
archers.
All who are found in you are
bound together;
They have fled from afar.

4 Therefore I said, "Look away
from me,
I will weep bitterly;
Do not labor to comfort me
Because of the plundering of
the daughter of my people."

5 For *it is* a day of trouble and
treading down and
perplexity
By the Lord GOD of hosts
In the Valley of Vision—
Breaking down the walls
And of crying to the mountain.
6 Elam bore the quiver
With chariots of men *and*
horsemen,
And Kir uncovered the shield.
7 It shall come to pass *that* your
choicest valleys
Shall be full of chariots,
And the horsemen shall set
themselves in array at the
gate.

8 He removed the protection of
Judah.
You looked in that day to the
armor of the House of the
Forest;
9 You also saw the damage to
the city of David,
That it was great;
And you gathered together
the waters of the lower pool.
10 You numbered the houses of
Jerusalem,
And the houses you broke
down
To fortify the wall.
11 You also made a reservoir
between the two walls
For the water of the old pool.
But you did not look to its
Maker,
Nor did you have respect for
Him who fashioned it long
ago.

12 And in that day the Lord GOD
of hosts
Called for weeping and for
mourning,
For baldness and for girding
with sackcloth.
13 But instead, joy and gladness,

Slaying oxen and killing
sheep,
Eating meat and drinking
wine:
"Let us eat and drink, for
tomorrow we die!"

14 Then it was revealed in my
hearing by the LORD of
hosts,
"Surely for this iniquity there
will be no atonement for
you,
Even to your death," says the
Lord GOD of hosts.

15Thus says the Lord GOD of hosts:

"Go, proceed to this steward,
To Shebna, who *is* over the
house, *and say:*
16 'What have you here, and
whom have you here,
That you have hewn a
sepulcher here,
As he who hews himself a
sepulcher on high,
Who carves a tomb for
himself in a rock?
17 Indeed, the LORD will throw
you away violently,
O mighty man,
And will surely seize you.
18 He will surely turn violently
and toss you like a ball
Into a large country;
There you shall die, and there
your glorious chariots
Shall be the shame of your
master's house.
19 So I will drive you out of your
office,
And from your position he will
pull you down.*

20 'Then it shall be in that day,
That I will call My servant
Eliakim the son of Hilkiah;
21 I will clothe him with your
robe

And strengthen him with your
  belt;
I will commit your
  responsibility into his hand.
He shall be a father to the
  inhabitants of Jerusalem
And to the house of Judah.
22 The key of the house of David
  I will lay on his shoulder;
So he shall open, and no one
  shall shut;
And he shall shut, and no one
  shall open.
23 I will fasten him *as* a peg in a
  secure place,
And he will become a glorious
  throne to his father's house.

24'They will hang on him all the
glory of his father's house, the offspring and the posterity, all vessels of
small quantity, from the cups to all the
pitchers. 25In that day,' says the LORD of
hosts, 'the peg that is fastened in the
secure place will be removed and be
cut down and fall, and the burden that
was on it will be cut off; for the LORD
has spoken.' "

THE burden against Tyre.

  Wail, you ships of Tarshish!
  For it is laid waste,
  So that there is no house, no
    harbor;
  From the land of Cyprus* it is
    revealed to them.
2 Be still, you inhabitants of the
    coastland,
  You merchants of Sidon,
  Whom those who cross the
    sea have filled.*
3 And on great waters the grain
    of Shihor,
  The harvest of the River,* *is*
    her revenue;
  And she is a marketplace for
    the nations.

4 Be ashamed, O Sidon;
  For the sea has spoken,
  The strength of the sea,
    saying,
  "I do not labor, nor bring forth
    children;
  Neither do I rear young men,
  Nor bring up virgins."
5 When the report *reaches*
    Egypt,
  They also will be in agony at
    the report of Tyre.

6 Cross over to Tarshish;
  Wail, you inhabitants of the
    coastland!
7 *Is* this your joyous *city,*
  Whose antiquity *is* from
    ancient days,
  Whose feet carried her far off
    to dwell?
8 Who has taken this counsel
    against Tyre, the crowning
    city,
  Whose merchants *are* princes,
  Whose traders *are* the
    honorable of the earth?
9 The LORD of hosts has
    purposed it,
  To bring to dishonor the pride
    of all glory,
  To bring into contempt all the
    honorable of the earth.

10 Overflow through your land
    like the River,*
  O daughter of Tarshish;
  There is no more strength.
11 He stretched out His hand
    over the sea,
  He shook the kingdoms;
  The LORD has given a
    commandment against
    Canaan
  To destroy its strongholds.
12 And He said, "You will rejoice
    no more,
  O you oppressed virgin
    daughter of Sidon.
  Arise, cross over to Cyprus;

There also you will have no
    rest."

13   Behold, the land of the
        Chaldeans,
    This people *which* was not;
    Assyria founded it for wild
        beasts of the desert.
    They set up its towers,
    They raised up its palaces,
    And brought it to ruin.

14   Wail, you ships of Tarshish!
    For your strength is laid
        waste.

15Now it shall come to pass in that
day that Tyre will be forgotten seventy
years, according to the days of one
king. At the end of seventy years it will
happen to Tyre as *in* the song of the
harlot:

16   "Take a harp, go about the city,
    You forgotten harlot;
    Make sweet melody, sing
        many songs,
    That you may be
        remembered."

17And it shall be, at the end of seventy years, that the LORD will deal with
Tyre. She will return to her hire, and
commit fornication with all the kingdoms of the world on the face of the
earth. 18Her gain and her pay will be
set apart for the LORD; it will not be
treasured nor laid up, for her gain will
be for those who dwell before the
LORD, to eat sufficiently, and for fine
clothing.

BEHOLD, the LORD makes the earth
        empty and makes it waste,
    Distorts its surface
    And scatters abroad its
        inhabitants.
2   And it shall be:
    As with the people, so with
        the priest;

As with the servant, so with
    his master;
As with the maid, so with her
    mistress;
As with the buyer, so with the
    seller;
As with the lender, so with the
    borrower;
As with the creditor, so with
    the debtor.
3   The land shall be entirely
        emptied and utterly
        plundered,
    For the LORD has spoken this
        word.

4   The earth mourns *and* fades
        away,
    The world languishes *and*
        fades away;
    The haughty people of the
        earth languish.
5   The earth is also defiled
        under its inhabitants,
    Because they have
        transgressed the laws,
    Changed the ordinance,
    Broken the everlasting
        covenant.
6   Therefore the curse has
        devoured the earth,
    And those who dwell in it are
        desolate.
    Therefore the inhabitants of
        the earth are burned,
    And few men *are* left.

7   The new wine fails, the vine
        languishes,
    All the merry-hearted sigh.
8   The mirth of the tambourine
        ceases,
    The noise of the jubilant ends,
    The joy of the harp ceases.
9   They shall not drink wine
        with a song;
    Strong drink is bitter to those
        who drink it.
10   The city of confusion is
        broken down;

Every house is shut up, so
   that none may go in.
11 *There is* a cry for wine in the
   streets,
All joy is darkened,
The mirth of the land is gone.
12 In the city desolation is left,
And the gate is stricken with
   destruction.
13 When it shall be thus in the
   midst of the land among
   the people,
It shall be like the shaking of
   an olive tree,
Like the gleaning of grapes
   when the vintage is done.

14 They shall lift up their voice,
   they shall sing;
For the majesty of the LORD
They shall cry aloud from the
   sea.
15 Therefore glorify the LORD in
   the dawning light,
The name of the LORD God of
   Israel in the coastlands of
   the sea.
16 From the ends of the earth
   we have heard songs:
"Glory to the righteous!"
But I said, "I am ruined,
   ruined!
Woe to me!
The treacherous dealers have
   dealt treacherously,
Indeed, the treacherous
   dealers have dealt very
   treacherously."

17 Fear and the pit and the snare
Are upon you, O inhabitant of
   the earth.
18 And it shall be
That he who flees from the
   noise of the fear
Shall fall into the pit,
And he who comes up from
   the midst of the pit
Shall be caught in the snare;

For the windows from on
   high are open,
And the foundations of the
   earth are shaken.

19 The earth is violently broken,
The earth is split open,
The earth is shaken
   exceedingly.
20 The earth shall reel to and fro
   like a drunkard,
And shall totter like a hut;
Its transgression shall be
   heavy upon it,
And it will fall, and not rise
   again.

21 It shall come to pass in that
   day
That the LORD will punish on
   high the host of exalted
   ones,
And on the earth the kings of
   the earth.
22 They will be gathered
   together,
As prisoners are gathered in
   the pit,
And will be shut up in the
   prison;
After many days they will be
   punished.
23 Then the moon will be
   disgraced
And the sun ashamed;
For the LORD of hosts will
   reign
On Mount Zion and in
   Jerusalem
And before His elders,
   gloriously.

GALATIANS 2:17–3:9

"**B**UT if, while we seek to be justified by Christ, we ourselves also are found sinners, *is* Christ therefore a minister of sin? Certainly not! [18]For if I build again those things which I destroyed, I make myself a transgressor. ¹⁹For I through the law died to the law that I might live to God. ²⁰I have been crucified with Christ; it is no longer I who live, but Christ lives in me; and the *life* which I now live in the flesh I live by faith in the Son of God, who loved me and gave Himself for me. ²¹I do not set aside the grace of God; for if righteousness *comes* through the law, then Christ died in vain."

O FOOLISH Galatians! Who has bewitched you that you should not obey the truth,* before whose eyes Jesus Christ was clearly portrayed among you* as crucified? ²This only I want to learn from you: Did you receive the Spirit by the works of the law, or by the hearing of faith? ³Are you so foolish? Having begun in the Spirit, are you now being made perfect by the flesh? ⁴Have you suffered so many things in vain—if indeed *it was* in vain?

⁵Therefore He who supplies the Spirit to you and works miracles among you, *does He do it* by the works of the law, or by the hearing of faith?— ⁶just as Abraham *"believed God, and it was accounted to him for righteousness."* * ⁷Therefore know that *only* those who are of faith are sons of Abraham. ⁸And the Scripture, foreseeing that God would justify the Gentiles by faith, preached the gospel to Abraham beforehand, *saying, "In you all the nations shall be blessed."* * ⁹So then those who *are* of faith are blessed with believing Abraham.

PSALM 60:1-12

To the Chief Musician. Set to "Lily of the Testimony." * *A Michtam of David. For teaching. When he fought against Mesopotamia and Syria of Zobah, and Joab returned and killed twelve thousand Edomites in the Valley of Salt.*

O GOD, You have cast us off; You have broken us down; You have been displeased; Oh, restore us again!

2　You have made the earth tremble;
　You have broken it;
　Heal its breaches, for it is shaking.
3　You have shown Your people hard things;
　You have made us drink the wine of confusion.

4　You have given a banner to those who fear You,
　That it may be displayed because of the truth.　Selah
5　That Your beloved may be delivered,
　Save *with* Your right hand, and hear me.

6　God has spoken in His holiness:
　"I will rejoice;
　I will divide Shechem
　And measure out the Valley of Succoth.
7　Gilead *is* Mine, and Manasseh *is* Mine;
　Ephraim also *is* the helmet for My head;
　Judah *is* My lawgiver.
8　Moab *is* My washpot;
　Over Edom I will cast My shoe;
　Philistia, shout in triumph because of Me."

9　Who will bring me *to the* strong city?
　Who will lead me to Edom?
10　*Is it* not You, O God, *who* cast us off?
　And You, O God, *who* did not go out with our armies?
11　Give us help from trouble,
　For the help of man *is* useless.
12　Through God we will do valiantly,
　For *it is* He *who* shall tread down our enemies.*

PROVERBS FOR TODAY/ 23:15-16

My son, if your heart is wise, my heart will rejoice—indeed, I myself, yes, my inmost being will rejoice when your lips speak right things.

SEPTEMBER 17

ISAIAH 25:1–28:13

O LORD, You *are* my God.
   I will exalt You,
   I will praise Your name,
   For You have done wonderful
      things;
   Your counsels of old *are*
      faithfulness *and* truth.
2   For You have made a city a
      ruin,
   A fortified city a ruin,
   A palace of foreigners to be a
      city no more;
   It will never be rebuilt.
3   Therefore the strong people
      will glorify You;
   The city of the terrible
      nations will fear You.
4   For You have been a strength
      to the poor,
   A strength to the needy in his
      distress,
   A refuge from the storm,
   A shade from the heat;
   For the blast of the terrible
      ones *is* as a storm *against*
      the wall.
5   You will reduce the noise of
      aliens,
   As heat in a dry place;
   As heat in the shadow of a
      cloud,
   The song of the terrible ones
      will be diminished.

6   And in this mountain
   The LORD of hosts will make
      for all people

A feast of choice pieces,
A feast of wines on the lees,
Of fat things full of marrow,
Of well-refined wines on the
   lees.
7   And He will destroy on this
      mountain
   The surface of the covering
      cast over all people,
   And the veil that is spread
      over all nations.
8   He will swallow up death
      forever,
   And the Lord GOD will wipe
      away tears from all faces;
   The rebuke of His people
   He will take away from all the
      earth;
   For the LORD has spoken.

9   And it will be said in that day:
   "Behold, this *is* our God;
   We have waited for Him, and
      He will save us.
   This *is* the LORD;
   We have waited for Him;
   We will be glad and rejoice in
      His salvation."

10   For on this mountain the
      hand of the LORD will rest,
   And Moab shall be trampled
      down under Him,
   As straw is trampled down for
      the refuse heap.
11   And He will spread out His
      hands in their midst

As a swimmer reaches out to
swim,
And He will bring down their
pride
Together with the trickery of
their hands.
12 The fortress of the high fort
of your walls
He will bring down, lay low,
And bring to the ground,
down to the dust.

I~n~ that day this song will be sung in the
land of Judah:

"We have a strong city;
God will appoint salvation *for*
walls and bulwarks.
2 Open the gates,
That the righteous nation
which keeps the truth may
enter in.
3 You will keep *him* in perfect
peace,
Whose mind *is* stayed *on You,*
Because he trusts in You.
4 Trust in the LORD forever,
For in YAH, the LORD, *is*
everlasting strength.*
5 For He brings down those
who dwell on high,
The lofty city;
He lays it low,
He lays it low to the ground,
He brings it down to the dust.
6 The foot shall tread it down—
The feet of the poor
And the steps of the needy."

7 The way of the just *is*
uprightness;
O Most Upright,
You weigh the path of the just.
8 Yes, in the way of Your
judgments,
O LORD, we have waited for
You;
The desire of *our* soul *is* for
Your name

And for the remembrance of
You.
9 With my soul I have desired
You in the night,
Yes, by my spirit within me I
will seek You early;
For when Your judgments *are*
in the earth,
The inhabitants of the world
will learn righteousness.

10 Let grace be shown to the
wicked,
Yet he will not learn
righteousness;
In the land of uprightness he
will deal unjustly,
And will not behold the
majesty of the LORD.
11 LORD, *when* Your hand is lifted
up, they will not see.
But they will see and be
ashamed
For *their* envy of people;
Yes, the fire of Your enemies
shall devour them.
12 LORD, You will establish peace
for us,
For You have also done all our
works in us.
13 O LORD our God, masters
besides You
Have had dominion over us;
But by You only we make
mention of Your name.
14 *They are* dead, they will not
live;
They are deceased, they will
not rise.
Therefore You have punished
and destroyed them,
And made all their memory to
perish.
15 You have increased the
nation, O LORD,
You have increased the nation;
You are glorified;
You have expanded all the
borders of the land.

16 LORD, in trouble they have
visited You,
They poured out a prayer
when Your chastening *was*
upon them.
17 As a woman with child
Is in pain and cries out in her
pangs,
When she draws near the time
of her delivery,
So have we been in Your
sight, O LORD.
18 We have been with child, we
have been in pain;
We have, as it were, brought
forth wind;
We have not accomplished
any deliverance in the earth,
Nor have the inhabitants of
the world fallen.

19 Your dead shall live;
Together with my dead body*
they shall arise.
Awake and sing, you who
dwell in dust;
For your dew *is like* the dew
of herbs,
And the earth shall cast out
the dead.

20 Come, my people, enter your
chambers,
And shut your doors behind
you;
Hide yourself, as it were, for a
little moment,
Until the indignation is past.
21 For behold, the LORD comes
out of His place
To punish the inhabitants of
the earth for their iniquity;
The earth will also disclose
her blood,
And will no more cover her
slain.

IN that day the LORD with His severe
sword, great and strong,

Will punish Leviathan the
fleeing serpent,
Leviathan that twisted serpent;
And He will slay the reptile
that *is* in the sea.

2 In that day sing to her,
"A vineyard of red wine!*
3 I, the LORD, keep it,
I water it every moment;
Lest any hurt it,
I keep it night and day.
4 Fury *is* not in Me.
Who would set briers *and*
thorns
Against Me in battle?
I would go through them,
I would burn them together.
5 Or let him take hold of My
strength,
That he may make peace with
Me;
And he shall make peace with
Me."

6 Those who come He shall
cause to take root in Jacob;
Israel shall blossom and bud,
And fill the face of the world
with fruit.

7 Has He struck Israel as He
struck those who struck
him?
Or has He been slain
according to the slaughter
of those who were slain by
Him?
8 In measure, by sending it
away,
You contended with it.
He removes *it* by His rough
wind
In the day of the east wind.
9 Therefore by this the iniquity
of Jacob will be covered;
And this *is* all the fruit of
taking away his sin:
When he makes all the stones
of the altar

Like chalkstones that are
beaten to dust,
Wooden images* and incense
altars shall not stand.

10 Yet the fortified city *will be*
desolate,
The habitation forsaken and
left like a wilderness;
There the calf will feed, and
there it will lie down
And consume its branches.

11 When its boughs are
withered, they will be
broken off;
The women come *and* set
them on fire.
For it *is* a people of no
understanding;
Therefore He who made
them will not have mercy
on them,
And He who formed them will
show them no favor.

12 And it shall come to pass in
that day
That the LORD will thresh,
From the channel of the
River* to the Brook of
Egypt;
And you will be gathered one
by one,
O you children of Israel.

13 So it shall be in that day:
The great trumpet will be
blown;
They will come, who are
about to perish in the land
of Assyria,
And they who are outcasts in
the land of Egypt,
And shall worship the LORD in
the holy mount at
Jerusalem.

WOE to the crown of pride, to the
drunkards of Ephraim,

Whose glorious beauty *is* a
fading flower
Which *is* at the head of the
verdant valleys,
To those who are overcome
with wine!

2 Behold, the Lord has a
mighty and strong one,
Like a tempest of hail and a
destroying storm,
Like a flood of mighty waters
overflowing,
Who will bring *them* down to
the earth with *His* hand.

3 The crown of pride, the
drunkards of Ephraim,
Will be trampled underfoot;

4 And the glorious beauty is a
fading flower
Which *is* at the head of the
verdant valley,
Like the first fruit before the
summer,
Which an observer sees;
He eats it up while it is still in
his hand.

5 In that day the LORD of hosts
will be
For a crown of glory and a
diadem of beauty
To the remnant of His people,

6 For a spirit of justice to him
who sits in judgment,
And for strength to those who
turn back the battle at the
gate.

7 But they also have erred
through wine,
And through intoxicating
drink are out of the way;
The priest and the prophet
have erred through
intoxicating drink,
They are swallowed up by
wine,
They are out of the way
through intoxicating drink;

They err in vision, they
stumble *in* judgment.
8 For all tables are full of vomit
and filth;
No place *is clean.*

9 "Whom will he teach
knowledge?
And whom will he make to
understand the message?
Those *just* weaned from milk?
Those *just* drawn from the
breasts?
10 For precept *must be* upon
precept, precept upon
precept,
Line upon line, line upon line,
Here a little, there a little."

11 For with stammering lips and
another tongue
He will speak to this people,
12 To whom He said, "This *is* the
rest *with which*
You may cause the weary to
rest,"
And, "This *is* the refreshing";
Yet they would not hear.
13 But the word of the LORD was
to them,
"Precept upon precept, precept
upon precept,
Line upon line, line upon line,
Here a little, there a little,"
That they might go and fall
backward, and be broken
And snared and caught.

GALATIANS 3:10-22

FOR as many as are of the works
of the law are under the curse;
for it is written, *"Cursed is everyone who does not continue in all
things which are written in the book of
the law, to do them."* * 11But that no
one is justified by the law in the sight
of God *is* evident, for *"the just shall live
by faith."* * 12Yet the law is not of faith,
but *"the man who does them shall live
by them."* *

13Christ has redeemed us from the
curse of the law, having become a
curse for us (for it is written, *"Cursed
is everyone who hangs on a tree"* *),
14that the blessing of Abraham might
come upon the Gentiles in Christ
Jesus, that we might receive the promise of the Spirit through faith.

15Brethren, I speak in the manner of
men: Though *it is* only a man's covenant, yet *if it is* confirmed, no one an-
nuls or adds to it. 16Now to Abraham and
his Seed were the promises made. He
does not say, "And to seeds," as of many,
but as of one, *"And to your Seed,"* * who
is Christ. 17And this I say, *that* the law,
which was four hundred and thirty
years later, cannot annul the covenant
that was confirmed before by God in
Christ,* that it should make the promise of no effect. 18For if the inheritance
is of the law, *it is* no longer of promise;
but God gave *it* to Abraham by promise.

19What purpose then *does* the law
serve? It was added because of transgressions, till the Seed should come to
whom the promise was made; *and it
was* appointed through angels by the
hand of a mediator. 20Now a mediator
does not *mediate* for one *only,* but God
is one.

21*Is* the law then against the promises of God? Certainly not! For if there
had been a law given which could have
given life, truly righteousness would
have been by the law. 22But the Scripture has confined all under sin, that the
promise by faith in Jesus Christ might
be given to those who believe.

PSALM 61:1-8

*To the Chief Musician. On a stringed
instrument.* * *A Psalm of David.*

HEAR my cry, O God;
Attend to my prayer.
2From the end of the earth I
will cry to You,

When my heart is
overwhelmed;
Lead me to the rock that is
higher than I.

3 For You have been a shelter
for me,
A strong tower from the
enemy.
4 I will abide in Your tabernacle
forever;
I will trust in the shelter of
Your wings.   Selah

5 For You, O God, have heard
my vows;

You have given *me* the
heritage of those who fear
Your name.
6 You will prolong the king's life,
His years as many
generations.
7 He shall abide before God
forever.
Oh, prepare mercy and truth,
which may preserve him!

8 So I will sing praise to Your
name forever,
That I may daily perform my
vows.

PROVERBS FOR TODAY/ 23:17-18

Do not let your heart envy sinners, but be zealous *for the fear of the LORD all the day; for surely there is a hereafter, and your hope will not be cut off.*

SEPTEMBER 18

ISAIAH 28:14–30:11

THEREFORE hear the word of the LORD, you scornful men,
Who rule this people who *are*
in Jerusalem,
15 Because you have said, "We
have made a covenant with
death,
And with Sheol we are in
agreement.
When the overflowing
scourge passes through,
It will not come to us,
For we have made lies our
refuge,
And under falsehood we have
hidden ourselves."

16Therefore thus says the Lord GOD:

"Behold, I lay in Zion a stone
for a foundation,

A tried stone, a precious
cornerstone, a sure
foundation;
Whoever believes will not act
hastily.
17 Also I will make justice the
measuring line,
And righteousness the
plummet;
The hail will sweep away the
refuge of lies,
And the waters will overflow
the hiding place.
18 Your covenant with death will
be annulled,
And your agreement with
Sheol will not stand;
When the overflowing
scourge passes through,
Then you will be trampled
down by it.

19 As often as it goes out it will
    take you;
For morning by morning it
    will pass over,
And by day and by night;
It will be a terror just to
    understand the report."

20 For the bed is too short to
    stretch out *on,*
And the covering so narrow
    that one cannot wrap
    himself *in it.*

21 For the Lord will rise up as *at*
    Mount Perazim,
He will be angry as in the
    Valley of Gibeon—
That He may do His work,
    His awesome work,
And bring to pass His act, His
    unusual act.

22 Now therefore, do not be
    mockers,
Lest your bonds be made
    strong;
For I have heard from the
    Lord God of hosts,
A destruction determined
    even upon the whole earth.

23 Give ear and hear my voice,
Listen and hear my speech.

24 Does the plowman keep
    plowing all day to sow?
Does he keep turning his soil
    and breaking the clods?

25 When he has leveled its
    surface,
Does he not sow the black
    cummin
And scatter the cummin,
Plant the wheat in rows,
The barley in the appointed
    place,
And the spelt in its place?

26 For He instructs him in right
    judgment,
His God teaches him.

27 For the black cummin is not
threshed with a threshing
    sledge,
Nor is a cartwheel rolled over
    the cummin;
But the black cummin is
    beaten out with a stick,
And the cummin with a rod.

28 Bread *flour* must be ground;
Therefore he does not thresh
    it forever,
Break *it with* his cartwheel,
Or crush it *with* his horsemen.

29 This also comes from the
    Lord of hosts,
Who is wonderful in counsel
    and excellent in guidance.

"Woe to Ariel,* to Ariel, the city *where*
    David dwelt!
Add year to year;
Let feasts come around.

2 Yet I will distress Ariel;
There shall be heaviness and
    sorrow,
And it shall be to Me as Ariel.

3 I will encamp against you all
    around,
I will lay siege against you
    with a mound,
And I will raise siegeworks
    against you.

4 You shall be brought down,
You shall speak out of the
    ground;
Your speech shall be low, out
    of the dust;
Your voice shall be like a
    medium's, out of the
    ground;
And your speech shall
    whisper out of the dust.

5 "Moreover the multitude of
    your foes
Shall be like fine dust,
And the multitude of the
    terrible ones
Like chaff that passes away;
Yes, it shall be in an instant,
    suddenly.

6 You will be punished by the
   LORD of hosts
   With thunder and earthquake
   and great noise,
   With storm and tempest
   And the flame of devouring
   fire.
7 The multitude of all the
   nations who fight against
   Ariel,
   Even all who fight against her
   and her fortress,
   And distress her,
   Shall be as a dream of a night
   vision.
8 It shall even be as when a
   hungry man dreams,
   And look—he eats;
   But he awakes, and his soul is
   still empty;
   Or as when a thirsty man
   dreams,
   And look—he drinks;
   But he awakes, and indeed *he
   is* faint,
   And his soul still craves:
   So the multitude of all the
   nations shall be,
   Who fight against Mount
   Zion."

9 Pause and wonder!
   Blind yourselves and be blind!
   They are drunk, but not with
   wine;
   They stagger, but not with
   intoxicating drink.
10 For the LORD has poured out
   on you
   The spirit of deep sleep,
   And has closed your eyes,
   namely, the prophets;
   And He has covered your
   heads, *namely,* the seers.

11The whole vision has become to
you like the words of a book that is
sealed, which *men* deliver to one who
is literate, saying, "Read this, please."

And he says, "I cannot, for it *is*
sealed."
12Then the book is delivered to one
who is illiterate, saying, "Read this,
please."
And he says, "I am not literate."
13Therefore the Lord said:

"Inasmuch as these people
   draw near with their mouths
And honor Me with their lips,
But have removed their
   hearts far from Me,
And their fear toward Me is
   taught by the
   commandment of men,
14 Therefore, behold, I will again
   do a marvelous work
   Among this people,
   A marvelous work and a
   wonder;
   For the wisdom of their wise
   men shall perish,
   And the understanding of
   their prudent *men* shall be
   hidden."

15 Woe to those who seek deep
   to hide their counsel far
   from the LORD,
   And their works are in the
   dark;
   They say, "Who sees us?"
   and, "Who knows us?"
16 Surely you have things turned
   around!
   Shall the potter be esteemed
   as the clay;
   For shall the thing made say
   of him who made it,
   "He did not make me"?
   Or shall the thing formed say
   of him who formed it,
   "He has no understanding"?

17 *Is* it not yet a very little while
   Till Lebanon shall be turned
   into a fruitful field,
   And the fruitful field be
   esteemed as a forest?

18 In that day the deaf shall hear
the words of the book,
And the eyes of the blind shall
see out of obscurity and out
of darkness.
19 The humble also shall
increase *their* joy in the
Lord,
And the poor among men
shall rejoice
In the Holy One of Israel.
20 For the terrible one is
brought to nothing,
The scornful one is consumed,
And all who watch for iniquity
are cut off—
21 Who make a man an offender
by a word,
And lay a snare for him who
reproves in the gate,
And turn aside the just by
empty words.

22Therefore thus says the Lord, who
redeemed Abraham, concerning the
house of Jacob:

"Jacob shall not now be
ashamed,
Nor shall his face now grow
pale;
23 But when he sees his children,
The work of My hands, in his
midst,
They will hallow My name,
And hallow the Holy One of
Jacob,
And fear the God of Israel.
24 These also who erred in spirit
will come to understanding,
And those who complained
will learn doctrine."

"Woe to the rebellious children," says
the Lord,
"Who take counsel, but not of
Me,
And who devise plans, but not
of My Spirit,
That they may add sin to sin;

2 Who walk to go down to
Egypt,
And have not asked My
advice,
To strengthen themselves in
the strength of Pharaoh,
And to trust in the shadow of
Egypt!
3 Therefore the strength of
Pharaoh
Shall be your shame,
And trust in the shadow of
Egypt
Shall be *your* humiliation.
4 For his princes were at Zoan,
And his ambassadors came to
Hanes.
5 They were all ashamed of a
people *who* could not
benefit them,
Or be help or benefit,
But a shame and also a
reproach."

6The burden against the beasts of
the South.

Through a land of trouble and
anguish,
From which *came* the lioness
and lion,
The viper and fiery flying
serpent,
They will carry their riches
on the backs of young
donkeys,
And their treasures on the
humps of camels,
To a people *who* shall not
profit;
7 For the Egyptians shall help
in vain and to no purpose.
Therefore I have called her
Rahab-Hem-Shebeth.*

8 Now go, write it before them
on a tablet,
And note it on a scroll,
That it may be for time to
come,

9 Forever and ever:
   That this *is* a rebellious
     people,
   Lying children,
   Children *who* will not hear the
     law of the LORD;
10 Who say to the seers, "Do not
     see,"
   And to the prophets, "Do not
     prophesy to us right things;
   Speak to us smooth things,
     prophesy deceits.
11 Get out of the way,
   Turn aside from the path,
   Cause the Holy One of Israel
   To cease from before us."

GALATIANS 3:23–4:31

BUT before faith came, we were kept under guard by the law, kept for the faith which would afterward be revealed. 24Therefore the law was our tutor *to bring us* to Christ, that we might be justified by faith. 25But after faith has come, we are no longer under a tutor.

26For you are all sons of God through faith in Christ Jesus. 27For as many of you as were baptized into Christ have put on Christ. 28There is neither Jew nor Greek, there is neither slave nor free, there is neither male nor female; for you are all one in Christ Jesus. 29And if you *are* Christ's, then you are Abraham's seed, and heirs according to the promise.

Now I say *that* the heir, as long as he is a child, does not differ at all from a slave, though he is master of all, 2but is under guardians and stewards until the time appointed by the father. 3Even so we, when we were children, were in bondage under the elements of the world. 4But when the fullness of the time had come, God sent forth His Son, born* of a woman, born under the law, 5to redeem those who were under the law, that we might receive the adoption as sons.

6And because you are sons, God has sent forth the Spirit of His Son into your hearts, crying out, "Abba, Father!" 7Therefore you are no longer a slave but a son, and if a son, then an heir of* God through Christ.

8But then, indeed, when you did not know God, you served those which by nature are not gods. 9But now after you have known God, or rather are known by God, how *is it that* you turn again to the weak and beggarly elements, to which you desire again to be in bondage? 10You observe days and months and seasons and years. 11I am afraid for you, lest I have labored for you in vain.

12Brethren, I urge you to become like me, for I *became* like you. You have not injured me at all. 13You know that because of physical infirmity I preached the gospel to you at the first. 14And my trial which was in my flesh you did not despise or reject, but you received me as an angel of God, *even* as Christ Jesus. 15What* then was the blessing you *enjoyed?* For I bear you witness that, if possible, you would have plucked out your own eyes and given them to me. 16Have I therefore become your enemy because I tell you the truth?

17They zealously court you, *but* for no good; yes, they want to exclude you, that you may be zealous for them. 18But it is good to be zealous in a good thing always, and not only when I am present with you. 19My little children, for whom I labor in birth again until Christ is formed in you, 20I would like to be present with you now and to change my tone; for I have doubts about you.

21Tell me, you who desire to be under the law, do you not hear the law? 22For it is written that Abraham had two sons: the one by a bondwoman, the other by a freewoman. 23But he *who was* of the bondwoman was born according to the flesh, and he of the freewoman through promise, 24which things are symbolic. For these are the* two covenants: the one from Mount Sinai which gives birth to bondage, which is Hagar— 25for this Hagar is Mount Sinai in Arabia, and corresponds to Jerusalem which now is, and is in bondage with her children— 26but the Jerusalem above is free, which is the mother of us all. 27For it is written:

> "Rejoice, O barren,
> *You who do not bear!*
> *Break forth and shout,*
> *You who are not in labor!*
> *For the desolate has many*
>   *more children*
> *Than she who has a*
>   *husband."* *

28Now we, brethren, as Isaac *was,* are children of promise. 29But, as he who was born according to the flesh then persecuted him *who was born* according to the Spirit, even so *it is* now. 30Nevertheless what does the Scripture say? *"Cast out the bondwoman and her son, for the son of the bondwoman shall not be heir with the son of the freewoman."* * 31So then, brethren, we are not children of the bondwoman but of the free.

PSALM 62:1-12

To the Chief Musician. To Jeduthun. A Psalm of David.

TRULY my soul silently *waits* for God;
From Him *comes* my salvation.
2 He only *is* my rock and my salvation;
He is my defense;
I shall not be greatly moved.

3 How long will you attack a man?

You shall be slain, all of you,
Like a leaning wall and a tottering fence.
4 They only consult to cast *him* down from his high position;
They delight in lies;
They bless with their mouth,
But they curse inwardly. Selah

5 My soul, wait silently for God alone,
For my expectation *is* from Him.
6 He only *is* my rock and my salvation;
He is my defense;
I shall not be moved.
7 In God *is* my salvation and my glory;
The rock of my strength,
And my refuge, *is* in God.

8 Trust in Him at all times, you people;
Pour out your heart before Him;
God *is* a refuge for us. Selah

9 Surely men of low degree *are* a vapor,
Men of high degree *are* a lie;
If they are weighed on the scales,
They *are* altogether *lighter* than vapor.
10 Do not trust in oppression,
Nor vainly hope in robbery;
If riches increase,
Do not set *your* heart *on them.*

11 God has spoken once,
Twice I have heard this:
That power *belongs* to God.
12 Also to You, O Lord, *belongs* mercy;
For You render to each one according to his work.

PROVERBS FOR TODAY/ 23:19-21

Hear, my son, and be wise; and guide your heart in the way. Do not mix with winebibbers, or *with gluttonous eaters of meat; for the drunkard and the glutton will come to poverty, and drowsiness will clothe* a man *with rags.*

SEPTEMBER 19

ISAIAH 30:12–33:13

THEREFORE thus says the Holy One of Israel:

"Because you despise this
   word,
And trust in oppression and
   perversity,
And rely on them,
13 Therefore this iniquity shall
   be to you
Like a breach ready to fall,
A bulge in a high wall,
Whose breaking comes
   suddenly, in an instant.
14 And He shall break it like the
   breaking of the potter's
   vessel,
Which is broken in pieces;
He shall not spare.
So there shall not be found
   among its fragments
A shard to take fire from the
   hearth,
Or to take water from the
   cistern."

15For thus says the Lord GOD, the Holy One of Israel:

"In returning and rest you
   shall be saved;
In quietness and confidence
   shall be your strength."
But you would not,
16 And you said, "No, for we will
   flee on horses"—
Therefore you shall flee!

And, "We will ride on swift
   horses"—
Therefore those who pursue
   you shall be swift!

17 One thousand *shall flee* at the
   threat of one,
At the threat of five you shall
   flee,
Till you are left as a pole on
   top of a mountain
And as a banner on a hill.

18 Therefore the LORD will wait,
   that He may be gracious to
   you;
And therefore He will be
   exalted, that He may have
   mercy on you.
For the LORD *is* a God of
   justice;
Blessed *are* all those who wait
   for Him.

19 For the people shall dwell in
   Zion at Jerusalem;
You shall weep no more.
He will be very gracious to
   you at the sound of your
   cry;
When He hears it, He will
   answer you.
20 And *though* the Lord gives you
The bread of adversity and
   the water of affliction,
Yet your teachers will not be
   moved into a corner
   anymore,

But your eyes shall see your teachers.

21 Your ears shall hear a word behind you, saying,
"This *is* the way, walk in it,"
Whenever you turn to the right hand
Or whenever you turn to the left.

22 You will also defile the covering of your images of silver,
And the ornament of your molded images of gold.
You will throw them away as an unclean thing;
You will say to them, "Get away!"

23 Then He will give the rain for your seed
With which you sow the ground,
And bread of the increase of the earth;
It will be fat and plentiful.
In that day your cattle will feed In large pastures.

24 Likewise the oxen and the young donkeys that work the ground
Will eat cured fodder,
Which has been winnowed with the shovel and fan.

25 There will be on every high mountain
And on every high hill
Rivers *and* streams of waters,
In the day of the great slaughter,
When the towers fall.

26 Moreover the light of the moon will be as the light of the sun,
And the light of the sun will be sevenfold,
As the light of seven days,
In the day that the LORD binds up the bruise of His people

And heals the stroke of their wound.

27 Behold, the name of the LORD comes from afar,
Burning *with* His anger,
And *His* burden *is* heavy;
His lips are full of indignation,
And His tongue like a devouring fire.

28 His breath is like an overflowing stream,
Which reaches up to the neck,
To sift the nations with the sieve of futility;
And *there shall be* a bridle in the jaws of the people,
Causing *them* to err.

29 You shall have a song
As in the night *when* a holy festival is kept,
And gladness of heart as when one goes with a flute,
To come into the mountain of the LORD,
To the Mighty One of Israel.

30 The LORD will cause His glorious voice to be heard,
And show the descent of His arm,
With the indignation of *His* anger
And the flame of a devouring fire,
With scattering, tempest, and hailstones.

31 For through the voice of the LORD
Assyria will be beaten down,
As He strikes with the rod.

32 And *in* every place where the staff of punishment passes,
Which the LORD lays on him,
It will be with tambourines and harps;
And in battles of brandishing He will fight with it.

33 For Tophet *was* established of old,

Yes, for the king it is prepared.
He has made *it* deep and
  large;
Its pyre *is* fire with much
  wood;
The breath of the Lord, like a
  stream of brimstone,
Kindles it.

Woe to those who go down to Egypt
  for help,
And rely on horses,
Who trust in chariots because
  they are many,
And in horsemen because
  they are very strong,
But who do not look to the
  Holy One of Israel,
Nor seek the Lord!
2   Yet He also *is* wise and will
      bring disaster,
    And will not call back His
      words,
    But will arise against the
      house of evildoers,
    And against the help of those
      who work iniquity.
3   Now the Egyptians *are* men,
      and not God;
    And their horses are flesh,
      and not spirit.
    When the Lord stretches out
      His hand,
    Both he who helps will fall,
    And he who is helped will fall
      down;
    They all will perish together.

4For thus the Lord has spoken to
me:

  "As a lion roars,
  And a young lion over his prey
  (When a multitude of
    shepherds is summoned
    against him,
  He will not be afraid of their
    voice
  Nor be disturbed by their
    noise),

So the Lord of hosts will come
  down
To fight for Mount Zion and
  for its hill.
5   Like birds flying about,
    So will the Lord of hosts
      defend Jerusalem.
    Defending, He will also
      deliver *it;*
    Passing over, He will preserve
      it."

6Return *to Him* against whom the
children of Israel have deeply revolted. 7For in that day every man shall
throw away his idols of silver and his
idols of gold—sin, which your own
hands have made for yourselves.

8   "Then Assyria shall fall by a
      sword not of man,
    And a sword not of mankind
      shall devour him.
    But he shall flee from the
      sword,
    And his young men shall
      become forced labor.
9   He shall cross over to his
      stronghold for fear,
    And his princes shall be afraid
      of the banner,"
    Says the Lord,
    Whose fire *is* in Zion
    And whose furnace *is* in
      Jerusalem.

Behold, a king will reign in
    righteousness,
  And princes will rule with
    justice.
2   A man will be as a hiding
      place from the wind,
    And a cover from the tempest,
    As rivers of water in a dry
      place,
    As the shadow of a great rock
      in a weary land.
3   The eyes of those who see
      will not be dim,

And the ears of those who
hear will listen.

4 Also the heart of the rash will
understand knowledge,
And the tongue of the
stammerers will be ready to
speak plainly.

5 The foolish person will no
longer be called generous,
Nor the miser said *to be*
bountiful;

6 For the foolish person will
speak foolishness,
And his heart will work
iniquity:
To practice ungodliness,
To utter error against the
LORD,
To keep the hungry
unsatisfied,
And he will cause the drink of
the thirsty to fail.

7 Also the schemes of the
schemer *are* evil;
He devises wicked plans
To destroy the poor with lying
words,
Even when the needy speaks
justice.

8 But a generous man devises
generous things,
And by generosity he shall
stand.

9 Rise up, you women who are
at ease,
Hear my voice;
You complacent daughters,
Give ear to my speech.

10 In a year and *some* days
You will be troubled, you
complacent women;
For the vintage will fail,
The gathering will not come.

11 Tremble, you *women* who are
at ease;
Be troubled, you complacent
ones;

Strip yourselves, make
yourselves bare,
And gird *sackcloth* on *your*
waists.

12 People shall mourn upon
their breasts
For the pleasant fields, for the
fruitful vine.

13 On the land of my people will
come up thorns *and* briers,
Yes, on all the happy homes
in the joyous city;

14 Because the palaces will be
forsaken,
The bustling city will be
deserted.
The forts and towers will
become lairs forever,
A joy of wild donkeys, a
pasture of flocks—

15 Until the Spirit is poured upon
us from on high,
And the wilderness becomes
a fruitful field,
And the fruitful field is
counted as a forest.

16 Then justice will dwell in the
wilderness,
And righteousness remain in
the fruitful field.

17 The work of righteousness
will be peace,
And the effect of
righteousness, quietness
and assurance forever.

18 My people will dwell in a
peaceful habitation,
In secure dwellings, and in
quiet resting places,

19 Though hail comes down on
the forest,
And the city is brought low in
humiliation.

20 Blessed *are* you who sow
beside all waters,
Who send out freely the feet
of the ox and the donkey.

WOE to you who plunder, though you
    have not *been* plundered;
And you who deal
    treacherously, though they
    have not dealt
    treacherously with you!
When you cease plundering,
    You will be plundered;
When you make an end of
    dealing treacherously,
They will deal treacherously
    with you.

2   O LORD, be gracious to us;
    We have waited for You.
    Be their* arm every morning,
    Our salvation also in the time
        of trouble.
3   At the noise of the tumult the
        people shall flee;
    When You lift Yourself up, the
        nations shall be scattered;
4   And Your plunder shall be
        gathered
    Like the gathering of the
        caterpillar;
    As the running to and fro of
        locusts,
    He shall run upon them.

5   The LORD is exalted, for He
        dwells on high;
    He has filled Zion with justice
        and righteousness.
6   Wisdom and knowledge will
        be the stability of your
        times,
    And the strength of salvation;
    The fear of the LORD *is* His
        treasure.

7   Surely their valiant ones shall
        cry outside,
    The ambassadors of peace
        shall weep bitterly.
8   The highways lie waste,
    The traveling man ceases.
    He has broken the covenant,
    He has despised the cities,*
    He regards no man.

9   The earth mourns *and*
        languishes,
    Lebanon is shamed *and*
        shriveled;
    Sharon is like a wilderness,
    And Bashan and Carmel
        shake off *their fruits.*

10   "Now I will rise," says the LORD;
    "Now I will be exalted,
    Now I will lift Myself up.
11   You shall conceive chaff,
    You shall bring forth stubble;
    Your breath, *as* fire, shall
        devour you.
12   And the people shall be *like*
        the burnings of lime;
    Like thorns cut up they shall
        be burned in the fire.
13   Hear, you *who are* afar off,
        what I have done;
    And you *who are* near,
        acknowledge My might."

GALATIANS 5:1-12

STAND fast therefore in the liberty by which Christ has made us free,* and do not be entangled again with a yoke of bondage. ²Indeed I, Paul, say to you that if you become circumcised, Christ will profit you nothing. ³And I testify again to every man who becomes circumcised that he is a debtor to keep the whole law. ⁴You have become estranged from Christ, you who *attempt to* be justified by law; you have fallen from grace. ⁵For we through the Spirit eagerly wait for the hope of righteousness by faith. ⁶For in Christ Jesus neither circumcision nor uncircumcision avails anything, but faith working through love.

⁷You ran well. Who hindered you from obeying the truth? ⁸This persuasion does not *come* from Him who calls you. ⁹A little leaven leavens the whole lump. ¹⁰I have confidence in you, in the Lord, that you will have no other mind;

but he who troubles you shall bear his judgment, whoever he is.

¹¹And I, brethren, if I still preach circumcision, why do I still suffer persecution? Then the offense of the cross has ceased. ¹²I could wish that those who trouble you would even cut themselves off!

PSALM 63:1-11

A Psalm of David when he was in the wilderness of Judah.

O GOD, You *are* my God;
Early will I seek You;
My soul thirsts for You;
My flesh longs for You
In a dry and thirsty land
Where there is no water.

2   So I have looked for You in
the sanctuary,
To see Your power and Your
glory.

3   Because Your lovingkindness
is better than life,
My lips shall praise You.

4   Thus I will bless You while I
live;
I will lift up my hands in Your
name.

5   My soul shall be satisfied as
with marrow and fatness,
And my mouth shall praise
You with joyful lips.

6   When I remember You on my
bed,
I meditate on You in the *night*
watches.

7   Because You have been my
help,
Therefore in the shadow of
Your wings I will rejoice.

8   My soul follows close behind
You;
Your right hand upholds me.

9   But those *who* seek my life, to
destroy *it,*
Shall go into the lower parts
of the earth.

10   They shall fall by the sword;
They shall be a portion for
jackals.

11   But the king shall rejoice in
God;
Everyone who swears by Him
shall glory;
But the mouth of those who
speak lies shall be stopped.

PROVERBS FOR TODAY/ 23:22

Listen to your father who begot you, and do not despise your mother when she is old.

SEPTEMBER 20

ISAIAH 33:14–36:22

THE sinners in Zion are afraid;
Fearfulness has seized the
hypocrites:
"Who among us shall dwell
with the devouring fire?

Who among us shall dwell
with everlasting burnings?"

15   He who walks righteously and
speaks uprightly,
He who despises the gain of
oppressions,

Who gestures with his hands,
    refusing bribes,
Who stops his ears from
    hearing of bloodshed,
And shuts his eyes from
    seeing evil:
16 He will dwell on high;
    His place of defense *will be*
      the fortress of rocks;
    Bread will be given him,
    His water *will be* sure.

17 Your eyes will see the King in
    His beauty;
    They will see the land that is
      very far off.
18 Your heart will meditate on
    terror:
  "Where *is* the scribe?
  Where *is* he who weighs?
  Where *is* he who counts the
    towers?"
19 You will not see a fierce
    people,
    A people of obscure speech,
      beyond perception,
    Of a stammering tongue *that*
      you cannot understand.

20 Look upon Zion, the city of
    our appointed feasts;
    Your eyes will see Jerusalem,
      a quiet home,
    A tabernacle *that* will not be
      taken down;
    Not one of its stakes will ever
      be removed,
    Nor will any of its cords be
      broken.
21 But there the majestic LORD
    will be for us
    A place of broad rivers *and*
      streams,
    In which no galley with oars
      will sail,
    Nor majestic ships pass by
22 (For the LORD *is* our Judge,
    The LORD *is* our Lawgiver,
    The LORD *is* our King;
    He will save us);

23 Your tackle is loosed,
    They could not strengthen
      their mast,
    They could not spread the sail.
    Then the prey of great
      plunder is divided;
    The lame take the prey.
24 And the inhabitant will not
    say, "I am sick";
    The people who dwell in it
      will be forgiven *their*
      iniquity.

COME near, you nations, to hear;
    And heed, you people!
    Let the earth hear, and all that
      is in it,
    The world and all things that
      come forth from it.
2 For the indignation of the
    LORD *is* against all nations,
    And *His* fury against all their
      armies;
    He has utterly destroyed
      them,
    He has given them over to the
      slaughter.
3 Also their slain shall be
    thrown out;
    Their stench shall rise from
      their corpses,
    And the mountains shall be
      melted with their blood.
4 All the host of heaven shall be
    dissolved,
    And the heavens shall be
      rolled up like a scroll;
    All their host shall fall down
    As the leaf falls from the vine,
    And as *fruit* falling from a fig
      tree.

5 "For My sword shall be bathed
    in heaven;
    Indeed it shall come down on
      Edom,
    And on the people of My
      curse, for judgment.
6 The sword of the LORD is filled
    with blood,

It is made overflowing with
fatness,
With the blood of lambs and
goats,
With the fat of the kidneys of
rams.
For the LORD has a sacrifice in
Bozrah,
And a great slaughter in the
land of Edom.

7 The wild oxen shall come
down with them,
And the young bulls with the
mighty bulls;
Their land shall be soaked
with blood,
And their dust saturated with
fatness."

8 For *it is* the day of the LORD's
vengeance,
The year of recompense for
the cause of Zion.

9 Its streams shall be turned
into pitch,
And its dust into brimstone;
Its land shall become burning
pitch.

10 It shall not be quenched night
or day;
Its smoke shall ascend forever.
From generation to
generation it shall lie waste;
No one shall pass through it
forever and ever.

11 But the pelican and the
porcupine shall possess it,
Also the owl and the raven
shall dwell in it.
And He shall stretch out
over it
The line of confusion and the
stones of emptiness.

12 They shall call its nobles to
the kingdom,
But none *shall be* there, and
all its princes shall be
nothing.

13 And thorns shall come up in
its palaces,
Nettles and brambles in its
fortresses;
It shall be a habitation of
jackals,
A courtyard for ostriches.

14 The wild beasts of the desert
shall also meet with the
jackals,
And the wild goat shall bleat
to its companion;
Also the night creature shall
rest there,
And find for herself a place of
rest.

15 There the arrow snake shall
make her nest and lay *eggs*
And hatch, and gather *them*
under her shadow;
There also shall the hawks be
gathered,
Every one with her mate.

16 "Search from the book of the
LORD, and read:
Not one of these shall fail;
Not one shall lack her mate.
For My mouth has
commanded it, and His
Spirit has gathered them.

17 He has cast the lot for them,
And His hand has divided it
among them with a
measuring line.
They shall possess it forever;
From generation to
generation they shall dwell
in it."

THE wilderness and the wasteland
shall be glad for them,
And the desert shall rejoice
and blossom as the rose;

2 It shall blossom abundantly
and rejoice,
Even with joy and singing.
The glory of Lebanon shall be
given to it,

The excellence of Carmel and
Sharon.
They shall see the glory of
the LORD,
The excellency of our God.

3   Strengthen the weak hands,
And make firm the feeble
knees.
4   Say to those *who are*
fearful-hearted,
"Be strong, do not fear!
Behold, your God will come
with vengeance,
With the recompense of God;
He will come and save you."

5   Then the eyes of the blind
shall be opened,
And the ears of the deaf shall
be unstopped.
6   Then the lame shall leap like
a deer,
And the tongue of the dumb
sing.
For waters shall burst forth in
the wilderness,
And streams in the desert.
7   The parched ground shall
become a pool,
And the thirsty land springs of
water;
In the habitation of jackals,
where each lay,
There shall be grass with
reeds and rushes.

8   A highway shall be there, and
a road,
And it shall be called the
Highway of Holiness.
The unclean shall not pass
over it,
But it *shall be* for others.
Whoever walks the road,
although a fool,
Shall not go astray.
9   No lion shall be there,
Nor shall *any* ravenous beast
go up on it;

It shall not be found there.
But the redeemed shall walk
there,
10   And the ransomed of the LORD
shall return,
And come to Zion with
singing,
With everlasting joy on their
heads.
They shall obtain joy and
gladness,
And sorrow and sighing shall
flee away.

Now it came to pass in the fourteenth
year of King Hezekiah *that* Sennacherib king of Assyria came up against all
the fortified cities of Judah and took
them. ²Then the king of Assyria sent
the Rabshakeh* with a great army
from Lachish to King Hezekiah at
Jerusalem. And he stood by the aqueduct from the upper pool, on the highway to the Fuller's Field. ³And Eliakim
the son of Hilkiah, who was over the
household, Shebna the scribe, and
Joah the son of Asaph, the recorder,
came out to him.

⁴Then *the* Rabshakeh said to them,
"Say now to Hezekiah, 'Thus says the
great king, the king of Assyria: "What
confidence is this in which you trust?
⁵I say you speak of having plans and
power for war; but *they are* mere
words. Now in whom do you trust, that
you rebel against me? ⁶Look! You are
trusting in the staff of this broken
reed, Egypt, on which if a man leans, it
will go into his hand and pierce it. So *is*
Pharaoh king of Egypt to all who trust
in him.

⁷"But if you say to me, 'We trust in
the LORD our God,' *is it* not He whose
high places and whose altars Hezekiah
has taken away, and said to Judah and
Jerusalem, 'You shall worship before
this altar'?" ' ⁸Now therefore, I urge
you, give a pledge to my master the
king of Assyria, and I will give you two
thousand horses—if you are able on

your part to put riders on them! ⁹How then will you repel one captain of the least of my master's servants, and put your trust in Egypt for chariots and horsemen? ¹⁰Have I now come up without the LORD against this land to destroy it? The LORD said to me, 'Go up against this land, and destroy it.' "

¹¹Then Eliakim, Shebna, and Joah said to the Rabshakeh, "Please speak to your servants in Aramaic, for we understand it; and do not speak to us in Hebrew* in the hearing of the people who are on the wall."

¹²But the Rabshakeh said, "Has my master sent me to your master and to you to speak these words, and not to the men who sit on the wall, who will eat and drink their own waste with you?"

¹³Then the Rabshakeh stood and called out with a loud voice in Hebrew, and said, "Hear the words of the great king, the king of Assyria! ¹⁴Thus says the king: 'Do not let Hezekiah deceive you, for he will not be able to deliver you; ¹⁵nor let Hezekiah make you trust in the LORD, saying, "The LORD will surely deliver us; this city will not be given into the hand of the king of Assyria." ' ¹⁶Do not listen to Hezekiah; for thus says the king of Assyria: 'Make peace with me by a present and come out to me; and every one of you eat from his own vine and every one from his own fig tree, and every one of you drink the waters of his own cistern; ¹⁷until I come and take you away to a land like your own land, a land of grain and new wine, a land of bread and vineyards. ¹⁸Beware lest Hezekiah persuade you, saying, "The LORD will deliver us." Has any one of the gods of the nations delivered its land from the hand of the king of Assyria? ¹⁹Where are the gods of Hamath and Arpad? Where are the gods of Sepharvaim? Indeed, have they delivered Samaria from my hand? ²⁰Who among all the gods of these lands have delivered

their countries from my hand, that the LORD should deliver Jerusalem from my hand?' "

²¹But they held their peace and answered him not a word; for the king's commandment was, "Do not answer him." ²²Then Eliakim the son of Hilkiah, who was over the household, Shebna the scribe, and Joah the son of Asaph, the recorder, came to Hezekiah with their clothes torn, and told him the words of the Rabshakeh.

GALATIANS 5:13-26

FOR you, brethren, have been called to liberty; only do not use liberty as an opportunity for the flesh, but through love serve one another. ¹⁴For all the law is fulfilled in one word, even in this: "You shall love your neighbor as yourself." * ¹⁵But if you bite and devour one another, beware lest you be consumed by one another!

¹⁶I say then: Walk in the Spirit, and you shall not fulfill the lust of the flesh. ¹⁷For the flesh lusts against the Spirit, and the Spirit against the flesh; and these are contrary to one another, so that you do not do the things that you wish. ¹⁸But if you are led by the Spirit, you are not under the law.

¹⁹Now the works of the flesh are evident, which are: adultery,* fornication, uncleanness, lewdness, ²⁰idolatry, sorcery, hatred, contentions, jealousies, outbursts of wrath, selfish ambitions, dissensions, heresies, ²¹envy, murders,* drunkenness, revelries, and the like; of which I tell you beforehand, just as I also told you in time past, that those who practice such things will not inherit the kingdom of God.

²²But the fruit of the Spirit is love, joy, peace, longsuffering, kindness, goodness, faithfulness, ²³gentleness, self-control. Against such there is no law. ²⁴And those who are Christ's have crucified the flesh with its passions and desires. ²⁵If we live in the Spirit, let

us also walk in the Spirit. 26Let us not become conceited, provoking one another, envying one another.

PSALM 64:1-10

To the Chief Musician. A Psalm of David.

HEAR my voice, O God, in my meditation;
Preserve my life from fear of the enemy.

2 Hide me from the secret plots of the wicked,
From the rebellion of the workers of iniquity,

3 Who sharpen their tongue like a sword,
And bend *their bows to shoot* their arrows—bitter words,

4 That they may shoot in secret at the blameless;
Suddenly they shoot at him and do not fear.

5 They encourage themselves *in* an evil matter;
They talk of laying snares secretly;

They say, "Who will see them?"

6 They devise iniquities:
"We have perfected a shrewd scheme."
Both the inward thought and the heart of man are deep.

7 But God shall shoot at them *with* an arrow;
Suddenly they shall be wounded.

8 So He will make them stumble over their own tongue;
All who see them shall flee away.

9 All men shall fear,
And shall declare the work of God;
For they shall wisely consider His doing.

10 The righteous shall be glad in the LORD, and trust in Him.
And all the upright in heart shall glory.

PROVERBS FOR TODAY/ 23:23

Buy the truth, and do not sell it, also *wisdom and instruction and understanding.*

SEPTEMBER 21

ISAIAH 37:1–38:22

AND so it was, when King Hezekiah heard *it,* that he tore his clothes, covered himself with sackcloth, and went into the house of the LORD. 2Then he sent Eliakim, who *was* over the household, Shebna the scribe, and the elders of the priests, covered with sackcloth, to Isaiah the prophet, the son of Amoz. 3And they

said to him, "Thus says Hezekiah: 'This day *is* a day of trouble and rebuke and blasphemy; for the children have come to birth, but *there is* no strength to bring them forth. 4It may be that the LORD your God will hear the words of *the* Rabshakeh, whom his master the king of Assyria has sent to reproach the living God, and will rebuke the words which the LORD your God has heard. Therefore lift up *your* prayer for the remnant that is left.' "

⁵So the servants of King Hezekiah came to Isaiah. ⁶And Isaiah said to them, "Thus you shall say to your master, 'Thus says the LORD: "Do not be afraid of the words which you have heard, with which the servants of the king of Assyria have blasphemed Me. ⁷Surely I will send a spirit upon him, and he shall hear a rumor and return to his own land; and I will cause him to fall by the sword in his own land." ' "

⁸Then *the* Rabshakeh returned, and found the king of Assyria warring against Libnah, for he heard that he had departed from Lachish. ⁹And the king heard concerning Tirhakah king of Ethiopia, "He has come out to make war with you." So when he heard *it,* he sent messengers to Hezekiah, saying, ¹⁰"Thus you shall speak to Hezekiah king of Judah, saying: 'Do not let your God in whom you trust deceive you, saying, "Jerusalem shall not be given into the hand of the king of Assyria." ¹¹Look! You have heard what the kings of Assyria have done to all lands by utterly destroying them; and shall you be delivered? ¹²Have the gods of the nations delivered those whom my fathers have destroyed, Gozan and Haran and Rezeph, and the people of Eden who *were* in Telassar? ¹³Where *is* the king of Hamath, the king of Arpad, and the king of the city of Sepharvaim, Hena, and Ivah?' "

¹⁴And Hezekiah received the letter from the hand of the messengers, and read it; and Hezekiah went up to the house of the LORD, and spread it before the LORD. ¹⁵Then Hezekiah prayed to the LORD, saying: ¹⁶"O LORD of hosts, God of Israel, *the One* who dwells *between* the cherubim, You *are* God, You alone, of all the kingdoms of the earth. You have made heaven and earth. ¹⁷Incline Your ear, O LORD, and hear; open Your eyes, O LORD, and

see; and hear all the words of Sennacherib, which he has sent to reproach the living God. ¹⁸Truly, LORD, the kings of Assyria have laid waste all the nations and their lands, ¹⁹and have cast their gods into the fire; for they *were* not gods, but the work of men's hands—wood and stone. Therefore they destroyed them. ²⁰Now therefore, O LORD our God, save us from his hand, that all the kingdoms of the earth may know that You *are* the LORD, You alone."

²¹Then Isaiah the son of Amoz sent to Hezekiah, saying, "Thus says the LORD God of Israel, 'Because you have prayed to Me against Sennacherib king of Assyria, ²²this *is* the word which the LORD has spoken concerning him:

> "The virgin, the daughter of Zion,
> Has despised you, laughed you to scorn;
> The daughter of Jerusalem
> Has shaken *her* head behind your back!

23 "Whom have you reproached and blasphemed?
> Against whom have you raised *your* voice,
> And lifted up your eyes on high?
> Against the Holy One of Israel.
24 By your servants you have reproached the Lord,
> And said, 'By the multitude of my chariots
> I have come up to the height of the mountains,
> To the limits of Lebanon;
> I will cut down its tall cedars
> *And* its choice cypress trees;
> I will enter its farthest height,
> To its fruitful forest.
25 I have dug and drunk water,
> And with the soles of my feet I have dried up

All the brooks of defense.'

26 "Did you not hear long ago
How I made it,
From ancient times that I
formed it?
Now I have brought it to pass,
That you should be
For crushing fortified cities
into heaps of ruins.
27 Therefore their inhabitants
had little power;
They were dismayed and
confounded;
They were as the grass of the
field
And the green herb,
As the grass on the housetops
And grain blighted before it is
grown.

28 "But I know your dwelling
place,
Your going out and your
coming in,
And your rage against Me.
29 Because your rage against
Me and your tumult
Have come up to My ears,
Therefore I will put My hook
in your nose
And My bridle in your lips,
And I will turn you back
By the way which you came." '

30 "This shall be a sign to you:

You shall eat this year such as
grows of itself,
And the second year what
springs from the same;
Also in the third year sow and
reap,
Plant vineyards and eat the
fruit of them.
31 And the remnant who have
escaped of the house of
Judah
Shall again take root
downward,

And bear fruit upward.
32 For out of Jerusalem shall go
a remnant,
And those who escape from
Mount Zion.
The zeal of the LORD of hosts
will do this.

33"Therefore thus says the LORD concerning the king of Assyria:

'He shall not come into this
city,
Nor shoot an arrow there,
Nor come before it with
shield,
Nor build a siege mound
against it.
34 By the way that he came,
By the same shall he return;
And he shall not come into
this city,'
Says the LORD.
35 'For I will defend this city, to
save it
For My own sake and for My
servant David's sake.' "

36Then the angel* of the LORD went
out, and killed in the camp of the Assyrians one hundred and eighty-five
thousand; and when people arose early
in the morning, there were the
corpses—all dead. 37So Sennacherib
king of Assyria departed and went
away, returned home, and remained at
Nineveh. 38Now it came to pass, as he
was worshiping in the house of Nisroch his god, that his sons Adrammelech and Sharezer struck him down
with the sword; and they escaped into
the land of Ararat. Then Esarhaddon
his son reigned in his place.

IN those days Hezekiah was sick and
near death. And Isaiah the prophet,
the son of Amoz, went to him and said
to him, "Thus says the LORD: 'Set your
house in order, for you shall die and
not live.' "

²Then Hezekiah turned his face toward the wall, and prayed to the LORD, ³and said, "Remember now, O LORD, I pray, how I have walked before You in truth and with a loyal heart, and have done *what is* good in Your sight." And Hezekiah wept bitterly.

⁴And the word of the LORD came to Isaiah, saying, ⁵"Go and tell Hezekiah, 'Thus says the LORD, the God of David your father: "I have heard your prayer, I have seen your tears; surely I will add to your days fifteen years. ⁶I will deliver you and this city from the hand of the king of Assyria, and I will defend this city." ' ⁷And this *is* the sign to you from the LORD, that the LORD will do this thing which He has spoken: ⁸Behold, I will bring the shadow on the sundial, which has gone down with the sun on the sundial of Ahaz, ten degrees backward." So the sun returned ten degrees on the dial by which it had gone down.

⁹This is the writing of Hezekiah king of Judah, when he had been sick and had recovered from his sickness:

10 I said,
    "In the prime of my life
     I shall go to the gates of Sheol;
     I am deprived of the
        remainder of my years."
11 I said,
    "I shall not see YAH,
     The LORD* in the land of the
        living;
     I shall observe man no more
        among the inhabitants of
        the world.*
12 My life span is gone,
     Taken from me like a
        shepherd's tent;
     I have cut off my life like a
        weaver.
     He cuts me off from the loom;
     From day until night You
        make an end of me.
13 I have considered until
        morning—

Like a lion,
So He breaks all my bones;
From day until night You
   make an end of me.
14 Like a crane *or* a swallow, so I
       chattered;
    I mourned like a dove;
    My eyes fail *from looking*
       upward.
    O LORD,* I am oppressed;
    Undertake for me!

15 "What shall I say?
     He has both spoken to me,*
     And He Himself has done *it*.
     I shall walk carefully all my
        years
     In the bitterness of my soul.
16 O Lord, by these *things men*
        live;
     And in all these *things is* the
        life of my spirit;
     So You will restore me and
        make me live.
17 Indeed *it was* for *my own*
        peace
     That I had great bitterness;
     But You have lovingly
        delivered my soul from the
        pit of corruption,
     For You have cast all my sins
        behind Your back.
18 For Sheol cannot thank You,
     Death cannot praise You;
     Those who go down to the pit
        cannot hope for Your truth.
19 The living, the living man, he
        shall praise You,
     As I *do* this day;
     The father shall make known
        Your truth to the children.

20 "The LORD *was ready* to save
        me;
     Therefore we will sing my
        songs with stringed
        instruments
     All the days of our life, in the
        house of the LORD."

²¹Now Isaiah had said, "Let them take a lump of figs, and apply *it* as a poultice on the boil, and he shall recover."

²²And Hezekiah had said, "What *is* the sign that I shall go up to the house of the LORD?"

GALATIANS 6:1-18

BRETHREN, if a man is overtaken in any trespass, you who *are* spiritual restore such a one in a spirit of gentleness, considering yourself lest you also be tempted. ²Bear one another's burdens, and so fulfill the law of Christ. ³For if anyone thinks himself to be something, when he is nothing, he deceives himself. ⁴But let each one examine his own work, and then he will have rejoicing in himself alone, and not in another. ⁵For each one shall bear his own load.

⁶Let him who is taught the word share in all good things with him who teaches.

⁷Do not be deceived, God is not mocked; for whatever a man sows, that he will also reap. ⁸For he who sows to his flesh will of the flesh reap corruption, but he who sows to the Spirit will of the Spirit reap everlasting life. ⁹And let us not grow weary while doing good, for in due season we shall reap if we do not lose heart. ¹⁰Therefore, as we have opportunity, let us do good to all, especially to those who are of the household of faith.

¹¹See with what large letters I have written to you with my own hand! ¹²As many as desire to make a good showing in the flesh, these *would* compel you to be circumcised, only that they may not suffer persecution for the cross of Christ. ¹³For not even those who are circumcised keep the law, but they desire to have you circumcised that they may boast in your flesh. ¹⁴But God forbid that I should boast except in the cross of our Lord Jesus Christ,

by whom* the world has been crucified to me, and I to the world. ¹⁵For in Christ Jesus neither circumcision nor uncircumcision avails anything, but a new creation.

¹⁶And as many as walk according to this rule, peace and mercy *be* upon them, and upon the Israel of God.

¹⁷From now on let no one trouble me, for I bear in my body the marks of the Lord Jesus.

¹⁸Brethren, the grace of our Lord Jesus Christ *be* with your spirit. Amen.

PSALM 65:1-13

To the Chief Musician. A Psalm of David. A Song.

PRAISE is awaiting You, O God,
   in Zion;
And to You the vow shall be
   performed.
2 O You who hear prayer,
   To You all flesh will come.
3 Iniquities prevail against me;
   As for our transgressions,
   You will provide atonement
     for them.

4 Blessed *is the man* You
     choose,
   And cause to approach *You,*
   That he may dwell in Your
     courts.
   We shall be satisfied with the
     goodness of Your house,
   Of Your holy temple.

5 *By* awesome deeds in
     righteousness You will
     answer us,
   O God of our salvation,
   You who are the confidence of
     all the ends of the earth,
   And of the far-off seas;
6 Who established the
     mountains by His strength,
   Being clothed with power;
7 You who still the noise of the
     seas,

The noise of their waves,
And the tumult of the peoples.
8 They also who dwell in the
farthest parts are afraid of
Your signs;
You make the outgoings of
the morning and evening
rejoice.

9 You visit the earth and water
it,
You greatly enrich it;
The river of God is full of
water;
You provide their grain,
For so You have prepared it.
10 You water its ridges
abundantly,

You settle its furrows;
You make it soft with showers,
You bless its growth.

11 You crown the year with Your
goodness,
And Your paths drip *with*
abundance.
12 They drop *on* the pastures of
the wilderness,
And the little hills rejoice on
every side.
13 The pastures are clothed with
flocks;
The valleys also are covered
with grain;
They shout for joy, they also
sing.

PROVERBS FOR TODAY / 23:24

The father of the righteous will greatly rejoice, and he who begets a wise child *will delight in him.*

SEPTEMBER 22

ISAIAH 39:1–41:16

A T that time Merodach-Baladan* the son of Baladan, king of Babylon, sent letters and a present to Hezekiah, for he heard that he had been sick and had recovered. ²And Hezekiah was pleased with them, and showed them the house of his treasures—the silver and gold, the spices and precious ointment, and all his armory—all that was found among his treasures. There was nothing in his house or in all his dominion that Hezekiah did not show them.

³Then Isaiah the prophet went to King Hezekiah, and said to him, "What did these men say, and from where did they come to you?"

So Hezekiah said, "They came to me from a far country, from Babylon."

⁴And he said, "What have they seen in your house?"

So Hezekiah answered, "They have seen all that *is* in my house; there is nothing among my treasures that I have not shown them."

⁵Then Isaiah said to Hezekiah, "Hear the word of the LORD of hosts: ⁶'Behold, the days are coming when all that *is* in your house, and what your fathers have accumulated until this day, shall be carried to Babylon; nothing shall be left,' says the LORD. ⁷'And they shall take away *some* of your sons who will descend from you, whom you will beget; and they shall be eunuchs in the palace of the king of Babylon.' "

⁸So Hezekiah said to Isaiah, "The

word of the LORD which you have spoken *is* good!" For he said, "At least there will be peace and truth in my days."

"COMFORT, yes, comfort My people!"
　　Says your God.
2　"Speak comfort to Jerusalem,
　　　and cry out to her,
　　That her warfare is ended,
　　That her iniquity is pardoned;
　　For she has received from the
　　　LORD's hand
　　Double for all her sins."

3　The voice of one crying in the
　　　wilderness:
　　"Prepare the way of the LORD;
　　Make straight in the desert*
　　A highway for our God.
4　Every valley shall be exalted
　　And every mountain and hill
　　　brought low;
　　The crooked places shall be
　　　made straight
　　And the rough places smooth;
5　The glory of the LORD shall be
　　　revealed,
　　And all flesh shall see *it*
　　　together;
　　For the mouth of the LORD has
　　　spoken."

6　The voice said, "Cry out!"
　　And he* said, "What shall I
　　　cry?"

　　"All flesh *is* grass,
　　And all its loveliness *is* like
　　　the flower of the field.
7　The grass withers, the flower
　　　fades,
　　Because the breath of the
　　　LORD blows upon it;
　　Surely the people *are* grass.
8　The grass withers, the flower
　　　fades,
　　But the word of our God
　　　stands forever."

9　O Zion,
　　You who bring good tidings,
　　Get up into the high mountain;
　　O Jerusalem,
　　You who bring good tidings,
　　Lift up your voice with
　　　strength,
　　Lift *it* up, be not afraid;
　　Say to the cities of Judah,
　　　"Behold your God!"

10　Behold, the Lord GOD shall
　　　come with a strong *hand,*
　　And His arm shall rule for
　　　Him;
　　Behold, His reward *is* with
　　　Him,
　　And His work before Him.
11　He will feed His flock like a
　　　shepherd;
　　He will gather the lambs with
　　　His arm,
　　And carry *them* in His bosom,
　　And gently lead those who are
　　　with young.

12　Who has measured the
　　　waters* in the hollow of His
　　　hand,
　　Measured heaven with a span
　　And calculated the dust of the
　　　earth in a measure?
　　Weighed the mountains in
　　　scales
　　And the hills in a balance?
13　Who has directed the Spirit of
　　　the LORD,
　　Or *as* His counselor has
　　　taught Him?
14　With whom did He take
　　　counsel, and *who* instructed
　　　Him,
　　And taught Him in the path of
　　　justice?
　　Who taught Him knowledge,
　　And showed Him the way of
　　　understanding?

15　Behold, the nations *are* as a
　　　drop in a bucket,

And are counted as the small
  dust on the scales;
Look, He lifts up the isles as a
  very little thing.
16 And Lebanon *is* not sufficient
    to burn,
  Nor its beasts sufficient for a
    burnt offering.
17 All nations before Him *are* as
    nothing,
  And they are counted by Him
    less than nothing and
    worthless.

18 To whom then will you liken
    God?
  Or what likeness will you
    compare to Him?
19 The workman molds an
    image,
  The goldsmith overspreads it
    with gold,
  And the silversmith casts
    silver chains.
20 Whoever *is* too impoverished
    for *such* a contribution
  Chooses a tree *that* will not
    rot;
  He seeks for himself a skillful
    workman
  To prepare a carved image
    that will not totter.

21 Have you not known?
  Have you not heard?
  Has it not been told you from
    the beginning?
  Have you not understood
    from the foundations of the
    earth?
22 *It is* He who sits above the
    circle of the earth,
  And its inhabitants *are* like
    grasshoppers,
  Who stretches out the
    heavens like a curtain,
  And spreads them out like a
    tent to dwell in.
23 He brings the princes to
    nothing;

He makes the judges of the
  earth useless.

24 Scarcely shall they be planted,
  Scarcely shall they be sown,
  Scarcely shall their stock take
    root in the earth,
  When He will also blow on
    them,
  And they will wither,
  And the whirlwind will take
    them away like stubble.

25 "To whom then will you liken
    Me,
  Or *to whom* shall I be equal?"
    says the Holy One.
26 Lift up your eyes on high,
  And see who has created
    these *things,*
  Who brings out their host by
    number;
  He calls them all by name,
  By the greatness of His might
  And the strength of *His* power;
  Not one is missing.

27 Why do you say, O Jacob,
  And speak, O Israel:
  "My way is hidden from the
    LORD,
  And my just claim is passed
    over by my God"?
28 Have you not known?
  Have you not heard?
  The everlasting God, the LORD,
  The Creator of the ends of the
    earth,
  Neither faints nor is weary.
  His understanding is
    unsearchable.
29 He gives power to the weak,
  And to *those who have* no
    might He increases
    strength.
30 Even the youths shall faint
    and be weary,
  And the young men shall
    utterly fall,

31   But those who wait on the
         LORD
      Shall renew *their* strength;
      They shall mount up with
         wings like eagles,
      They shall run and not be
         weary,
      They shall walk and not faint.

"KEEP silence before Me, O
         coastlands,
      And let the people renew *their*
         strength!
      Let them come near, then let
         them speak;
      Let us come near together for
         judgment.

2   "Who raised up one from the
         east?
      Who in righteousness called
         him to His feet?
      Who gave the nations before
         him,
      And made *him* rule over
         kings?
      Who gave *them* as the dust *to*
         his sword,
      As driven stubble to his bow?
3   Who pursued them, *and*
         passed safely
      By the way *that* he had not
         gone with his feet?
4   Who has performed and
         done *it,*
      Calling the generations from
         the beginning?
      'I, the LORD, am the first;
      And with the last I *am* He.' "

5   The coastlands saw *it* and
         feared,
      The ends of the earth were
         afraid;
      They drew near and came.
6   Everyone helped his neighbor,
      And said to his brother,
      "Be of good courage!"
7   So the craftsman encouraged
         the goldsmith;

He who smooths *with* the
         hammer *inspired* him who
         strikes the anvil,
      Saying, "It *is* ready for the
         soldering";
      Then he fastened it with pegs,
      That it might not totter.

8   "But you, Israel, *are* My
         servant,
      Jacob whom I have chosen,
      The descendants of Abraham
         My friend.
9   *You* whom I have taken from
         the ends of the earth,
      And called from its farthest
         regions,
      And said to you,
      'You *are* My servant,
      I have chosen you and have
         not cast you away:
10   Fear not, for I *am* with you;
      Be not dismayed, for I *am*
         your God.
      I will strengthen you,
      Yes, I will help you,
      I will uphold you with My
         righteous right hand.'

11   "Behold, all those who were
         incensed against you
      Shall be ashamed and
         disgraced;
      They shall be as nothing,
      And those who strive with you
         shall perish.
12   You shall seek them and not
         find them—
      Those who contended with
         you.
      Those who war against you
      Shall be as nothing,
      As a nonexistent thing.
13   For I, the LORD your God, will
         hold your right hand,
      Saying to you, 'Fear not, I will
         help you.'

14   "Fear not, you worm Jacob,
      You men of Israel!

I will help you," says the LORD
And your Redeemer, the Holy
One of Israel.
15 "Behold, I will make you into a
new threshing sledge with
sharp teeth;
You shall thresh the
mountains and beat *them*
small,
And make the hills like chaff.
16 You shall winnow them, the
wind shall carry them away,
And the whirlwind shall
scatter them;
You shall rejoice in the LORD,
And glory in the Holy One of
Israel."

EPHESIANS 1:1-23

PAUL, an apostle of Jesus Christ
by the will of God,

To the saints who are in Ephesus,
and faithful in Christ Jesus:

²Grace to you and peace from God
our Father and the Lord Jesus Christ.

³Blessed *be* the God and Father of
our Lord Jesus Christ, who has
blessed us with every spiritual blessing in the heavenly *places* in Christ,
⁴just as He chose us in Him before the
foundation of the world, that we should
be holy and without blame before Him
in love, ⁵having predestined us to
adoption as sons by Jesus Christ to
Himself, according to the good pleasure of His will, ⁶to the praise of the
glory of His grace, by which He made
us accepted in the Beloved.

⁷In Him we have redemption
through His blood, the forgiveness of
sins, according to the riches of His
grace ⁸which He made to abound toward us in all wisdom and prudence,
⁹having made known to us the mystery of His will, according to His good
pleasure which He purposed in Him-

self, ¹⁰that in the dispensation of the
fullness of the times He might gather
together in one all things in Christ,
both* which are in heaven and which
are on earth—in Him. ¹¹In Him also we
have obtained an inheritance, being
predestined according to the purpose
of Him who works all things according
to the counsel of His will, ¹²that we who
first trusted in Christ should be to the
praise of His glory.

¹³In Him you also *trusted,* after you
heard the word of truth, the gospel of
your salvation; in whom also, having
believed, you were sealed with the
Holy Spirit of promise, ¹⁴who* is the
guarantee of our inheritance until the
redemption of the purchased possession, to the praise of His glory.

¹⁵Therefore I also, after I heard of
your faith in the Lord Jesus and your
love for all the saints, ¹⁶do not cease to
give thanks for you, making mention
of you in my prayers: ¹⁷that the God of
our Lord Jesus Christ, the Father of
glory, may give to you the spirit of wisdom and revelation in the knowledge
of Him, ¹⁸the eyes of your understanding* being enlightened; that you may
know what is the hope of His calling,
what are the riches of the glory of His
inheritance in the saints, ¹⁹and what *is*
the exceeding greatness of His power
toward us who believe, according to
the working of His mighty power
²⁰which He worked in Christ when He
raised Him from the dead and seated
Him at His right hand in the heavenly
places, ²¹far above all principality and
power and might and dominion, and
every name that is named, not only in
this age but also in that which is to
come.

²²And He put all *things* under His
feet, and gave Him *to be* head over all
things to the church, ²³which is His
body, the fullness of Him who fills all
in all.

PSALM 66:1-20

To the Chief Musician. A Song. A Psalm.

MAKE a joyful shout to God, all the earth!
² Sing out the honor of His name;
   Make His praise glorious.
3   Say to God,
   "How awesome are Your works!
   Through the greatness of Your power
   Your enemies shall submit themselves to You.
4   All the earth shall worship You
   And sing praises to You;
   They shall sing praises *to* Your name."   Selah

5   Come and see the works of God;
   He is awesome *in His* doing toward the sons of men.
6   He turned the sea into dry *land;*
   They went through the river on foot.
   There we will rejoice in Him.
7   He rules by His power forever;
   His eyes observe the nations;
   Do not let the rebellious exalt themselves.   Selah

8   Oh, bless our God, you peoples!
   And make the voice of His praise to be heard,
9   Who keeps our soul among the living,
   And does not allow our feet to be moved.
10   For You, O God, have tested us;

11   You have refined us as silver is refined.
   You brought us into the net;
   You laid affliction on our backs.
12   You have caused men to ride over our heads;
   We went through fire and through water;
   But You brought us out to rich *fulfillment.*

13   I will go into Your house with burnt offerings;
   I will pay You my vows,
14   Which my lips have uttered
   And my mouth has spoken when I was in trouble.
15   I will offer You burnt sacrifices of fat animals,
   With the sweet aroma of rams;
   I will offer bulls with goats.   Selah

16   Come *and* hear, all you who fear God,
   And I will declare what He has done for my soul.
17   I cried to Him with my mouth,
   And He was extolled with my tongue.
18   If I regard iniquity in my heart,
   The Lord will not hear.
19   *But* certainly God has heard *me;*
   He has attended to the voice of my prayer.

20   Blessed *be* God,
   Who has not turned away my prayer,
   Nor His mercy from me!

PROVERBS FOR TODAY/ 23:25-28

Let your father and your mother be glad, and let her who bore you rejoice. □ *My son, give me your heart, and let your eyes observe my ways. For a harlot is a deep pit, and a seductress is a narrow well. She also lies in wait as for a victim, and increases the unfaithful among men.*

SEPTEMBER 23

ISAIAH 41:17–43:13

"**T**HE poor and needy seek water,
but *there is* none,
Their tongues fail for thirst.
I, the LORD, will hear them;
I, the God of Israel, will not
forsake them.

18 I will open rivers in desolate
heights,
And fountains in the midst of
the valleys;
I will make the wilderness a
pool of water,
And the dry land springs of
water.

19 I will plant in the wilderness
the cedar and the acacia
tree,
The myrtle and the oil tree;
I will set in the desert the
cypress tree *and* the pine
And the box tree together,

20 That they may see and know,
And consider and understand
together,
That the hand of the LORD has
done this,
And the Holy One of Israel
has created it.

21 "Present your case," says the
LORD.
"Bring forth your strong
reasons," says the King of
Jacob.

22 "Let them bring forth and
show us what will happen;
Let them show the former
things, what they *were,*
That we may consider them,
And know the latter end of
them;
Or declare to us things to
come.

23 Show the things that are to
come hereafter,
That we may know that you
are gods;
Yes, do good or do evil,
That we may be dismayed
and see *it* together.

24 Indeed you *are* nothing,
And your work *is* nothing;
He who chooses you *is* an
abomination.

25 "I have raised up one from the
north,
And he shall come;
From the rising of the sun he
shall call on My name;
And he shall come against
princes as *though* mortar,
As the potter treads clay.

26 Who has declared from the
beginning, that we may
know?
And former times, that we
may say, '*He is* righteous'?
Surely *there is* no one who
shows,
Surely *there is* no one who
declares,
Surely *there is* no one who
hears your words.

27 The first time *I said* to Zion,
'Look, there they are!'
And I will give to Jerusalem
one who brings good
tidings.

28 For I looked, and *there was* no
man;
I looked among them, but
there was no counselor,
Who, when I asked of them,
could answer a word.

29 Indeed they *are* all worthless;*
Their works *are* nothing;

Their molded images *are*
wind and confusion.

"Behold! My Servant whom I uphold,
My Elect One *in whom* My
soul delights!
I have put My Spirit upon
Him;
He will bring forth justice to
the Gentiles.

2 He will not cry out, nor raise
His voice,
Nor cause His voice to be
heard in the street.

3 A bruised reed He will not
break,
And smoking flax He will not
quench;
He will bring forth justice for
truth.

4 He will not fail nor be
discouraged,
Till He has established justice
in the earth;
And the coastlands shall wait
for His law."

5 Thus says God the Lord,
Who created the heavens and
stretched them out,
Who spread forth the earth
and that which comes from
it,
Who gives breath to the
people on it,
And spirit to those who walk
on it:

6 "I, the Lord, have called You in
righteousness,
And will hold Your hand;
I will keep You and give You
as a covenant to the people,
As a light to the Gentiles,

7 To open blind eyes,
To bring out prisoners from
the prison,
Those who sit in darkness
from the prison house.

8 I *am* the Lord, that *is* My
name;

And My glory I will not give
to another,
Nor My praise to carved
images.

9 Behold, the former things
have come to pass,
And new things I declare;
Before they spring forth I tell
you of them."

10 Sing to the Lord a new song,
And His praise from the ends
of the earth,
You who go down to the sea,
and all that is in it,
You coastlands and you
inhabitants of them!

11 Let the wilderness and its
cities lift up *their voice,*
The villages *that* Kedar
inhabits.
Let the inhabitants of Sela
sing,
Let them shout from the top
of the mountains.

12 Let them give glory to the
Lord,
And declare His praise in the
coastlands.

13 The Lord shall go forth like a
mighty man;
He shall stir up *His* zeal like a
man of war.
He shall cry out, yes, shout
aloud;
He shall prevail against His
enemies.

14 "I have held My peace a long
time,
I have been still and
restrained Myself.
Now I will cry like a woman in
labor,
I will pant and gasp at once.

15 I will lay waste the mountains
and hills,
And dry up all their
vegetation;

I will make the rivers
 coastlands,
And I will dry up the pools.
16 I will bring the blind by a way
 they did not know;
I will lead them in paths they
 have not known.
I will make darkness light
 before them,
And crooked places straight.
These things I will do for
 them,
And not forsake them.
17 They shall be turned back,
They shall be greatly
 ashamed,
Who trust in carved images,
Who say to the molded
 images,
'You *are* our gods.'

18 "Hear, you deaf;
And look, you blind, that you
 may see.
19 Who *is* blind but My servant,
Or deaf as My messenger
 whom I send?
Who *is* blind as *he who is*
 perfect,
And blind as the LORD's
 servant?
20 Seeing many things, but you
 do not observe;
Opening the ears, but he does
 not hear."

21 The LORD is well pleased for
 His righteousness' sake;
He will exalt the law and
 make *it* honorable.
22 But this *is* a people robbed
 and plundered;
All of them are snared in
 holes,
And they are hidden in prison
 houses;
They are for prey, and no one
 delivers;
For plunder, and no one says,
 "Restore!"

23 Who among you will give ear
 to this?
Who will listen and hear for
 the time to come?
24 Who gave Jacob for plunder,
 and Israel to the robbers?
Was it not the LORD,
He against whom we have
 sinned?
For they would not walk in
 His ways,
Nor were they obedient to His
 law.
25 Therefore He has poured on
 him the fury of His anger
And the strength of battle;
It has set him on fire all
 around,
Yet he did not know;
And it burned him,
Yet he did not take *it* to heart.

BUT now, thus says the LORD, who
 created you, O Jacob,
And He who formed you,
 O Israel:
"Fear not, for I have redeemed
 you;
I have called *you* by your
 name;
You *are* Mine.
2 When you pass through the
 waters, I *will be* with you;
And through the rivers, they
 shall not overflow you.
When you walk through the
 fire, you shall not be
 burned,
Nor shall the flame scorch
 you.
3 For I *am* the LORD your God,
The Holy One of Israel, your
 Savior;
I gave Egypt for your ransom,
Ethiopia and Seba in your
 place.
4 Since you were precious in
 My sight,
You have been honored,
And I have loved you;

Therefore I will give men for
you,
And people for your life.

5 Fear not, for I *am* with you;
I will bring your descendants
from the east,
And gather you from the west;

6 I will say to the north, 'Give
them up!'
And to the south, 'Do not
keep them back!'
Bring My sons from afar,
And My daughters from the
ends of the earth—

7 Everyone who is called by My
name,
Whom I have created for My
glory;
I have formed him, yes, I have
made him."

8 Bring out the blind people
who have eyes,
And the deaf who have ears.

9 Let all the nations be
gathered together,
And let the people be
assembled.
Who among them can declare
this,
And show us former things?
Let them bring out their
witnesses, that they may be
justified;
Or let them hear and say, "*It
is* truth."

10 "You *are* My witnesses," says
the LORD,
"And My servant whom I have
chosen,
That you may know and
believe Me,
And understand that I *am* He.
Before Me there was no God
formed,
Nor shall there be after Me.

11 I, *even* I, *am* the LORD,
And besides Me *there is* no
savior.

12 I have declared and saved,

I have proclaimed,
And *there was* no foreign *god*
among you;
Therefore you *are* My
witnesses,"
Says the LORD, "that I *am* God.

13 Indeed before the day *was,* I
am He;
And *there is* no one who can
deliver out of My hand;
I work, and who will reverse
it?"

EPHESIANS 2:1-22

AND you *He made alive,* who
were dead in trespasses and
sins, [2]in which you once
walked according to the course of this
world, according to the prince of the
power of the air, the spirit who now
works in the sons of disobedience,
[3]among whom also we all once conducted ourselves in the lusts of our
flesh, fulfilling the desires of the flesh
and of the mind, and were by nature
children of wrath, just as the others.

[4]But God, who is rich in mercy, because of His great love with which He
loved us, [5]even when we were dead in
trespasses, made us alive together
with Christ (by grace you have been
saved), [6]and raised *us* up together, and
made *us* sit together in the heavenly
places in Christ Jesus, [7]that in the ages
to come He might show the exceeding
riches of His grace in *His* kindness toward us in Christ Jesus. [8]For by grace
you have been saved through faith,
and that not of yourselves; *it is* the gift
of God, [9]not of works, lest anyone
should boast. [10]For we are His workmanship, created in Christ Jesus for
good works, which God prepared beforehand that we should walk in them.

[11]Therefore remember that you,
once Gentiles in the flesh—who are
called Uncircumcision by what is
called the Circumcision made in the
flesh by hands— [12]that at that time you

were without Christ, being aliens from the commonwealth of Israel and strangers from the covenants of promise, having no hope and without God in the world. ¹³But now in Christ Jesus you who once were far off have been brought near by the blood of Christ.

¹⁴For He Himself is our peace, who has made both one, and has broken down the middle wall of separation, ¹⁵having abolished in His flesh the enmity, *that is,* the law of commandments *contained* in ordinances, so as to create in Himself one new man *from* the two, *thus* making peace, ¹⁶and that He might reconcile them both to God in one body through the cross, thereby putting to death the enmity. ¹⁷And He came and preached peace to you who were afar off and to those who were near. ¹⁸For through Him we both have access by one Spirit to the Father.

¹⁹Now, therefore, you are no longer strangers and foreigners, but fellow citizens with the saints and members of the household of God, ²⁰having been built on the foundation of the apostles and prophets, Jesus Christ Himself being the chief corner*stone,* ²¹in whom the whole building, being fitted together, grows into a holy temple in the Lord, ²²in whom you also are being built together for a dwelling place of God in the Spirit.

PSALM 67:1-7

To the Chief Musician. On stringed instruments. *
A Psalm. A Song.

G OD be merciful to us and bless us,
And cause His face to shine
upon us, Selah
2 That Your way may be known
on earth,
Your salvation among all
nations.

3 Let the peoples praise You,
O God;
Let all the peoples praise You.
4 Oh, let the nations be glad
and sing for joy!
For You shall judge the
people righteously,
And govern the nations on
earth. Selah

5 Let the peoples praise You,
O God;
Let all the peoples praise You.
6 *Then* the earth shall yield her
increase;
God, our own God, shall
bless us.
7 God shall bless us,
And all the ends of the earth
shall fear Him.

PROVERBS FOR TODAY/ 23:29-35

Who has woe? Who has sorrow? Who has contentions? Who has complaints? Who has wounds without cause? Who has redness of eyes? Those who linger long at the wine, those who go in search of mixed wine. Do not look on the wine when it is red, when it sparkles in the cup, when it swirls around smoothly; at the last it bites like a serpent, and stings like a viper. Your eyes will see strange things, and your heart will utter perverse things. Yes, you will be like one who lies down in the midst of the sea, or like one who lies at the top of the mast, saying: "They have struck me, but I was not hurt; they have beaten me, but I did not feel it. When shall I awake, that I may seek another drink?"

SEPTEMBER 24

ISAIAH 43:14–45:10

THUS says the LORD, your Redeemer,
The Holy One of Israel:
"For your sake I will send to Babylon,
And bring them all down as fugitives—
The Chaldeans, who rejoice in their ships.

15 I *am* the LORD, your Holy One,
The Creator of Israel, your King."

16 Thus says the LORD, who makes a way in the sea
And a path through the mighty waters,

17 Who brings forth the chariot and horse,
The army and the power
(They shall lie down together, they shall not rise;
They are extinguished, they are quenched like a wick):

18 "Do not remember the former things,
Nor consider the things of old.

19 Behold, I will do a new thing,
Now it shall spring forth;
Shall you not know it?
I will even make a road in the wilderness
And rivers in the desert.

20 The beast of the field will honor Me,
The jackals and the ostriches,
Because I give waters in the wilderness
And rivers in the desert,
To give drink to My people, My chosen.

21 This people I have formed for Myself;
They shall declare My praise.

22 "But you have not called upon Me, O Jacob;
And you have been weary of Me, O Israel.

23 You have not brought Me the sheep for your burnt offerings,
Nor have you honored Me with your sacrifices.
I have not caused you to serve with grain offerings,
Nor wearied you with incense.

24 You have bought Me no sweet cane with money,
Nor have you satisfied Me with the fat of your sacrifices;
But you have burdened Me with your sins,
You have wearied Me with your iniquities.

25 "I, *even* I, *am* He who blots out your transgressions for My own sake;
And I will not remember your sins.

26 Put Me in remembrance;
Let us contend together;
State your *case,* that you may be acquitted.

27 Your first father sinned,
And your mediators have transgressed against Me.

28 Therefore I will profane the princes of the sanctuary;
I will give Jacob to the curse,
And Israel to reproaches.

"YET hear me now, O Jacob My servant,
And Israel whom I have chosen.

2 Thus says the LORD who made you

And formed you from the womb, *who* will help you:
'Fear not, O Jacob My servant;
And you, Jeshurun, whom I have chosen.

3 For I will pour water on him who is thirsty,
And floods on the dry ground;
I will pour My Spirit on your descendants,
And My blessing on your offspring;

4 They will spring up among the grass
Like willows by the watercourses.'

5 One will say, 'I *am* the LORD's';
Another will call *himself* by the name of Jacob;
Another will write *with* his hand, 'The LORD's,'
And name *himself* by the name of Israel.

6 "Thus says the LORD, the King of Israel,
And his Redeemer, the LORD of hosts:
'I *am* the First and I *am* the Last;
Besides Me *there is* no God.

7 And who can proclaim as I do?
Then let him declare it and set it in order for Me,
Since I appointed the ancient people.
And the things that are coming and shall come,
Let them show these to them.

8 Do not fear, nor be afraid;
Have I not told you from that time, and declared *it?*
You *are* My witnesses.
Is there a God besides Me?
Indeed *there is* no other Rock;
I know not *one.*'"

9 Those who make an image, all of them *are* useless,
And their precious things shall not profit;
They *are* their own witnesses;
They neither see nor know, that they may be ashamed.

10 Who would form a god or mold an image
That profits him nothing?

11 Surely all his companions would be ashamed;
And the workmen, they *are* mere men.
Let them all be gathered together,
Let them stand up;
Yet they shall fear,
They shall be ashamed together.

12 The blacksmith with the tongs works one in the coals,
Fashions it with hammers,
And works it with the strength of his arms.
Even so, he is hungry, and his strength fails;
He drinks no water and is faint.

13 The craftsman stretches out *his* rule,
He marks one out with chalk;
He fashions it with a plane,
He marks it out with the compass,
And makes it like the figure of a man,
According to the beauty of a man, that it may remain in the house.

14 He cuts down cedars for himself,
And takes the cypress and the oak;
He secures *it* for himself among the trees of the forest.
He plants a pine, and the rain nourishes *it.*

15 Then it shall be for a man to
burn,
For he will take some of it and
warm himself;
Yes, he kindles *it* and bakes
bread;
Indeed he makes a god and
worships *it;*
He makes it a carved image,
and falls down to it.

16 He burns half of it in the fire;
With this half he eats meat;
He roasts a roast, and is
satisfied.
He even warms *himself* and
says,
"Ah! I am warm,
I have seen the fire."

17 And the rest of it he makes
into a god,
His carved image.
He falls down before it and
worships *it,*
Prays to it and says,
"Deliver me, for you *are* my
god!"

18 They do not know nor
understand;
For He has shut their eyes, so
that they cannot see,
And their hearts, so that they
cannot understand.

19 And no one considers in his
heart,
Nor *is there* knowledge nor
understanding to say,
"I have burned half of it in the
fire,
Yes, I have also baked bread
on its coals;
I have roasted meat and eaten
it;
And shall I make the rest of it
an abomination?
Shall I fall down before a
block of wood?"

20 He feeds on ashes;
A deceived heart has turned
him aside;

And he cannot deliver his soul,
Nor say, "*Is there* not a lie in
my right hand?"

21 "Remember these, O Jacob,
And Israel, for you *are* My
servant;
I have formed you, you *are*
My servant;
O Israel, you will not be
forgotten by Me!

22 I have blotted out, like a thick
cloud, your transgressions,
And like a cloud, your sins.
Return to Me, for I have
redeemed you."

23 Sing, O heavens, for the LORD
has done *it!*
Shout, you lower parts of the
earth;
Break forth into singing, you
mountains,
O forest, and every tree in it!
For the LORD has redeemed
Jacob,
And glorified Himself in Israel.

24 Thus says the LORD, your
Redeemer,
And He who formed you from
the womb:
"I *am* the LORD, who makes all
things,
Who stretches out the
heavens all alone,
Who spreads abroad the
earth by Myself;

25 Who frustrates the signs of
the babblers,
And drives diviners mad;
Who turns wise men
backward,
And makes their knowledge
foolishness;

26 Who confirms the word of His
servant,
And performs the counsel of
His messengers;

Who says to Jerusalem, 'You
shall be inhabited,'
To the cities of Judah, 'You
shall be built,'
And I will raise up her waste
places;
27 Who says to the deep, 'Be
dry!
And I will dry up your rivers';
28 Who says of Cyrus, '*He is* My
shepherd,
And he shall perform all My
pleasure,
Saying to Jerusalem, "You
shall be built,"
And to the temple, "Your
foundation shall be laid." '

"Thus says the Lord to His anointed,
To Cyrus, whose right hand I
have held—
To subdue nations before him
And loose the armor of kings,
To open before him the
double doors,
So that the gates will not be
shut:
2 'I will go before you
And make the crooked
places* straight;
I will break in pieces the gates
of bronze
And cut the bars of iron.
3 I will give you the treasures of
darkness
And hidden riches of secret
places,
That you may know that I, the
Lord,
Who call *you* by your name,
Am the God of Israel.
4 For Jacob My servant's sake,
And Israel My elect,
I have even called you by your
name;
I have named you, though
you have not known Me.
5 I *am* the Lord, and *there is* no
other;
There is no God besides Me.

I will gird you, though you
have not known Me,
6 That they may know from the
rising of the sun to its
setting
That *there is* none besides Me.
I *am* the Lord, and *there is* no
other;
7 I form the light and create
darkness,
I make peace and create
calamity;
I, the Lord, do all these *things.*'

8 "Rain down, you heavens, from
above,
And let the skies pour down
righteousness;
Let the earth open, let them
bring forth salvation,
And let righteousness spring
up together.
I, the Lord, have created it.

9 "Woe to him who strives with
his Maker!
Let the potsherd *strive* with
the potsherds of the earth!
Shall the clay say to him who
forms it, 'What are you
making?'
Or shall your handiwork *say,*
'He has no hands'?
10 Woe to him who says to *his*
father, 'What are you
begetting?'
Or to the woman, 'What have
you brought forth?' "

EPHESIANS 3:1-21

For this reason I, Paul, the prisoner of Christ Jesus for you
Gentiles— 2if indeed you have
heard of the dispensation of the grace
of God which was given to me for you,
3how that by revelation He made
known to me the mystery (as I have
briefly written already, 4by which,
when you read, you may understand

my knowledge in the mystery of Christ), [5]which in other ages was not made known to the sons of men, as it has now been revealed by the Spirit to His holy apostles and prophets: [6]that the Gentiles should be fellow heirs, of the same body, and partakers of His promise in Christ through the gospel, [7]of which I became a minister according to the gift of the grace of God given to me by the effective working of His power.

[8]To me, who am less than the least of all the saints, this grace was given, that I should preach among the Gentiles the unsearchable riches of Christ, [9]and to make all see what *is* the fellowship* of the mystery, which from the beginning of the ages has been hidden in God who created all things through Jesus Christ;* [10]to the intent that now the manifold wisdom of God might be made known by the church to the principalities and powers in the heavenly *places,* [11]according to the eternal purpose which He accomplished in Christ Jesus our Lord, [12]in whom we have boldness and access with confidence through faith in Him. [13]Therefore I ask that you do not lose heart at my tribulations for you, which is your glory.

[14]For this reason I bow my knees to the Father of our Lord Jesus Christ,* [15]from whom the whole family in heaven and earth is named, [16]that He would grant you, according to the riches of His glory, to be strengthened with might through His Spirit in the inner man, [17]that Christ may dwell in your hearts through faith; that you, being rooted and grounded in love, [18]may be able to comprehend with all the saints what *is* the width and length and depth and height— [19]to know the love of Christ which passes knowledge; that you may be filled with all the fullness of God.

[20]Now to Him who is able to do exceedingly abundantly above all that we ask or think, according to the power that works in us, [21]to Him *be* glory in the church by Christ Jesus to all generations, forever and ever. Amen.

PSALM 68:1-18

To the Chief Musician. A Psalm of David. A Song.

L ET God arise,
Let His enemies be scattered;
Let those also who hate Him
    flee before Him.
2   As smoke is driven away,
    So drive *them* away;
    As wax melts before the fire,
    So let the wicked perish at the
        presence of God.
3   But let the righteous be glad;
    Let them rejoice before God;
    Yes, let them rejoice
        exceedingly.

4   Sing to God, sing praises to
        His name;
    Extol Him who rides on the
        clouds,*
    By His name YAH,
    And rejoice before Him.

5   A father of the fatherless, a
        defender of widows,
    Is God in His holy habitation.
6   God sets the solitary in
        families;
    He brings out those who are
        bound into prosperity;
    But the rebellious dwell in a
        dry *land.*

7   O God, when You went out
        before Your people,
    When You marched through
        the wilderness,   Selah
8   The earth shook;
    The heavens also dropped
        rain at the presence of God;
    Sinai itself *was moved* at the
        presence of God, the God
        of Israel.

9 You, O God, sent a plentiful
rain,
Whereby You confirmed Your
inheritance,
When it was weary.
10 Your congregation dwelt in it;
You, O God, provided from
Your goodness for the poor.

11 The Lord gave the word;
Great *was* the company of
those who proclaimed *it:*
12 "Kings of armies flee, they flee,
And she who remains at
home divides the spoil.
13 Though you lie down among
the sheepfolds,
You will be like the wings of a
dove covered with silver,
And her feathers with yellow
gold."
14 When the Almighty scattered
kings in it,
It was *white* as snow in
Zalmon.

15 A mountain of God *is* the
mountain of Bashan;
A mountain *of many* peaks *is*
the mountain of Bashan.
16 Why do you fume with envy,
you mountains of *many*
peaks?
This is the mountain *which*
God desires to dwell in;
Yes, the LORD will dwell *in it*
forever.

17 The chariots of God *are*
twenty thousand,
Even thousands of thousands;
The Lord is among them *as in*
Sinai, in the Holy *Place.*
18 You have ascended on high,
You have led captivity captive,
You have received gifts
among men,
Even *from* the rebellious,
That the LORD God might
dwell *there.*

PROVERBS FOR TODAY/ 24:1-2

*Do not be envious of evil men, nor desire to be with them; for their heart devises
violence, and their lips talk of troublemaking.*

SEPTEMBER 25

ISAIAH 45:11–48:11

THUS says the LORD,
The Holy One of Israel, and
his Maker:
"Ask Me of things to come
concerning My sons;
And concerning the work of
My hands, you command
Me.
12 I have made the earth,
And created man on it.

I—My hands—stretched out
the heavens,
And all their host I have
commanded.
13 I have raised him up in
righteousness,
And I will direct all his ways;
He shall build My city
And let My exiles go free,
Not for price nor reward,"
Says the LORD of hosts.

14Thus says the LORD:

"The labor of Egypt and
    merchandise of Cush
And of the Sabeans, men of
    stature,
Shall come over to you, and
    they shall be yours;
They shall walk behind you,
They shall come over in
    chains;
And they shall bow down to
    you.
They will make supplication
    to you, *saying,* 'Surely God
    is in you,
And *there is* no other;
There is no other God.' "

15   Truly You *are* God, who hide
        Yourself,
    O God of Israel, the Savior!
16   They shall be ashamed
    And also disgraced, all of
        them;
    They shall go in confusion
        together,
    Who are makers of idols.
17   *But* Israel shall be saved by
        the LORD
    With an everlasting salvation;
    You shall not be ashamed or
        disgraced
    Forever and ever.

18   For thus says the LORD,
    Who created the heavens,
    Who is God,
    Who formed the earth and
        made it,
    Who has established it,
    Who did not create it in vain,
    Who formed it to be inhabited:
    "I *am* the LORD, and *there is* no
        other.
19   I have not spoken in secret,
    In a dark place of the earth;
    I did not say to the seed of
        Jacob,
    'Seek Me in vain';

I, the LORD, speak
    righteousness,
I declare things that are right.

20   "Assemble yourselves and
        come;
    Draw near together,
    You *who have* escaped from
        the nations.
    They have no knowledge,
    Who carry the wood of their
        carved image,
    And pray to a god *that* cannot
        save.
21   Tell and bring forth *your case;*
    Yes, let them take counsel
        together.
    Who has declared this from
        ancient time?
    Who has told it from that time?
    Have not I, the LORD?
    And *there is* no other God
        besides Me,
    A just God and a Savior;
    There is none besides Me.

22   "Look to Me, and be saved,
    All you ends of the earth!
    For I *am* God, and *there is* no
        other.
23   I have sworn by Myself;
    The word has gone out of My
        mouth *in* righteousness,
    And shall not return,
    That to Me every knee shall
        bow,
    Every tongue shall take an
        oath.
24   He shall say,
    'Surely in the LORD I have
        righteousness and strength.
    To Him *men* shall come,
    And all shall be ashamed
    Who are incensed against
        Him.
25   In the LORD all the
        descendants of Israel
    Shall be justified, and shall
        glory.' "

BEL bows down, Nebo stoops;
Their idols were on the beasts
and on the cattle.
Your carriages *were* heavily
loaded,
A burden to the weary *beast.*

2 They stoop, they bow down
together;
They could not deliver the
burden,
But have themselves gone
into captivity.

3 "Listen to Me, O house of
Jacob,
And all the remnant of the
house of Israel,
Who have been upheld *by Me*
from birth,
Who have been carried from
the womb:

4 Even to *your* old age, I *am* He,
And *even* to gray hairs I will
carry *you!*
I have made, and I will bear;
Even I will carry, and will
deliver *you.*

5 "To whom will you liken Me,
and make *Me* equal
And compare Me, that we
should be alike?

6 They lavish gold out of the
bag,
And weigh silver on the scales;
They hire a goldsmith, and he
makes it a god;
They prostrate themselves,
yes, they worship.

7 They bear it on the shoulder,
they carry it
And set it in its place, and it
stands;
From its place it shall not
move.
Though *one* cries out to it, yet
it cannot answer
Nor save him out of his
trouble.

8 "Remember this, and show
yourselves men;
Recall to mind, O you
transgressors.

9 Remember the former things
of old,
For I *am* God, and *there is* no
other;
I am God, and *there is* none
like Me,

10 Declaring the end from the
beginning,
And from ancient times *things*
that are not *yet* done,
Saying, 'My counsel shall
stand,
And I will do all My pleasure,'

11 Calling a bird of prey from the
east,
The man who executes My
counsel, from a far country.
Indeed I have spoken *it;*
I will also bring it to pass.
I have purposed *it;*
I will also do it.

12 "Listen to Me, you
stubborn-hearted,
Who *are* far from
righteousness:

13 I bring My righteousness
near, it shall not be far off;
My salvation shall not linger.
And I will place salvation in
Zion,
For Israel My glory.

"COME down and sit in the dust,
O virgin daughter of Babylon;
Sit on the ground without a
throne,
O daughter of the Chaldeans!
For you shall no more be
called
Tender and delicate.

2 Take the millstones and grind
meal.
Remove your veil,
Take off the skirt,
Uncover the thigh,

Pass through the rivers.
3 Your nakedness shall be
    uncovered,
Yes, your shame will be seen;
I will take vengeance,
And I will not arbitrate with a
    man."

4 *As for* our Redeemer, the LORD
    of hosts *is* His name,
The Holy One of Israel.

5 "Sit in silence, and go into
    darkness,
O daughter of the Chaldeans;
For you shall no longer be
    called
The Lady of Kingdoms.
6 I was angry with My people;
I have profaned My
    inheritance,
And given them into your
    hand.
You showed them no mercy;
On the elderly you laid your
    yoke very heavily.
7 And you said, 'I shall be a lady
    forever,'
So that you did not take these
    things to heart,
Nor remember the latter end
    of them.

8 "Therefore hear this now, *you
    who are* given to pleasures,
Who dwell securely,
Who say in your heart, 'I *am,*
    and *there is* no one else
    besides me;
I shall not sit *as* a widow,
Nor shall I know the loss of
    children';
9 But these two *things* shall
    come to you
In a moment, in one day:
The loss of children, and
    widowhood.
They shall come upon you in
    their fullness

Because of the multitude of
    your sorceries,
For the great abundance of
    your enchantments.

10 "For you have trusted in your
    wickedness;
You have said, 'No one sees
    me';
Your wisdom and your
    knowledge have warped
    you;
And you have said in your
    heart,
'I *am,* and *there is* no one else
    besides me.'
11 Therefore evil shall come
    upon you;
You shall not know from
    where it arises.
And trouble shall fall upon
    you;
You will not be able to put it
    off.
And desolation shall come
    upon you suddenly,
Which you shall not know.

12 "Stand now with your
    enchantments
And the multitude of your
    sorceries,
In which you have labored
    from your youth—
Perhaps you will be able to
    profit,
Perhaps you will prevail.
13 You are wearied in the
    multitude of your counsels;
Let now the astrologers, the
    stargazers,
And the monthly
    prognosticators
Stand up and save you
From what shall come upon
    you.
14 Behold, they shall be as
    stubble,
The fire shall burn them;

"Behold! The Lamb
of God who takes
away the sin of the
world!"
John 1:29

"Children are *a heritage from the* LORD.*"*
Psalm 127:3

They shall not deliver
 themselves
From the power of the flame;
It shall not *be* a coal to be
 warmed by,
Nor a fire to sit before!
15 Thus shall they be to you
With whom you have labored,
Your merchants from your
 youth;
They shall wander each one
 to his quarter.
No one shall save you.

"HEAR this, O house of Jacob,
Who are called by the name
 of Israel,
And have come forth from the
 wellsprings of Judah;
Who swear by the name of
 the LORD,
And make mention of the God
 of Israel,
But not in truth or in
 righteousness;
2 For they call themselves after
 the holy city,
And lean on the God of Israel;
The LORD of hosts *is* His name:

3 "I have declared the former
 things from the beginning;
They went forth from My
 mouth, and I caused them
 to hear it.
Suddenly I did *them,* and they
 came to pass.
4 Because I knew that you *were*
 obstinate,
And your neck *was* an iron
 sinew,
And your brow bronze,
5 Even from the beginning I
 have declared *it* to you;
Before it came to pass I
 proclaimed *it* to you,
Lest you should say, 'My idol
 has done them,
And my carved image and my
 molded image

Have commanded them.'

6 "You have heard;
See all this.
And will you not declare *it?*
I have made you hear new
 things from this time,
Even hidden things, and you
 did not know them.
7 They are created now and not
 from the beginning;
And before this day you have
 not heard them,
Lest you should say, 'Of
 course I knew them.'
8 Surely you did not hear,
Surely you did not know;
Surely from long ago your ear
 was not opened.
For I knew that you would
 deal very treacherously,
And were called a
 transgressor from the
 womb.

9 "For My name's sake I will
 defer My anger,
And *for* My praise I will
 restrain it from you,
So that I do not cut you off.
10 Behold, I have refined you,
 but not as silver;
I have tested you in the
 furnace of affliction.
11 For My own sake, for My own
 sake, I will do *it;*
For how should *My name* be
 profaned?
And I will not give My glory
 to another."

EPHESIANS 4:1-16

I THEREFORE, the prisoner of the Lord, beseech you to walk worthy of the calling with which you were called, 2with all lowliness and gentleness, with longsuffering, bearing with one another in love, 3endeavoring to keep the unity of the Spirit in the bond of peace.

⁴*There is* one body and one Spirit, just as you were called in one hope of your calling; ⁵one Lord, one faith, one baptism; ⁶one God and Father of all, who *is* above all, and through all, and in you* all.

⁷But to each one of us grace was given according to the measure of Christ's gift. ⁸Therefore He says:

> "When He ascended on high,
> He led captivity captive,
> And gave gifts to men." *

⁹(Now this, *"He ascended"*—what does it mean but that He also first* descended into the lower parts of the earth? ¹⁰He who descended is also the One who ascended far above all the heavens, that He might fill all things.)

¹¹And He Himself gave some *to be* apostles, some prophets, some evangelists, and some pastors and teachers, ¹²for the equipping of the saints for the work of ministry, for the edifying of the body of Christ, ¹³till we all come to the unity of the faith and of the knowledge of the Son of God, to a perfect man, to the measure of the stature of the fullness of Christ; ¹⁴that we should no longer be children, tossed to and fro and carried about with every wind of doctrine, by the trickery of men, in the cunning craftiness of deceitful plotting, ¹⁵but, speaking the truth in love, may grow up in all things into Him who is the head—Christ— ¹⁶from whom the whole body, joined and knit together by what every joint supplies, according to the effective working by which every part does its share, causes growth of the body for the edifying of itself in love.

PSALM 68:19-35

BLESSED *be* the Lord,
Who daily loads us *with benefits,*
The God of our salvation!
Selah

20 Our God *is* the God of
salvation;
And to GOD the Lord *belong*
escapes from death.

21 But God will wound the head
of His enemies,
The hairy scalp of the one
who still goes on in his
trespasses.

22 The Lord said, "I will bring
back from Bashan,
I will bring *them* back from
the depths of the sea,

23 That your foot may crush
them* in blood,
And the tongues of your dogs
may have their portion from
your enemies."

24 They have seen Your
procession, O God,
The procession of my God,
my King, into the sanctuary.

25 The singers went before, the
players on instruments
followed after;
Among *them were* the
maidens playing timbrels.

26 Bless God in the
congregations,
The Lord, from the fountain
of Israel.

27 There *is* little Benjamin, their
leader,
The princes of Judah *and*
their company,
The princes of Zebulun *and*
the princes of Naphtali.

28 Your God has commanded*
your strength;
Strengthen, O God, what You
have done for us.

29 Because of Your temple at
Jerusalem,
Kings will bring presents to
You.

30 Rebuke the beasts of the
reeds,

The herd of bulls with the
calves of the peoples,
Till everyone submits himself
with pieces of silver.
Scatter the peoples *who*
delight in war.
31 Envoys will come out of Egypt;
Ethiopia will quickly stretch
out her hands to God.

32 Sing to God, you kingdoms of
the earth;
Oh, sing praises to the Lord,
Selah

33 To Him who rides on the

heaven of heavens, *which
were* of old!
Indeed, He sends out His
voice, a mighty voice.
34 Ascribe strength to God;
His excellence *is* over Israel,
And His strength *is* in the
clouds.
35 O God, *You are* more
awesome than Your holy
places.
The God of Israel *is* He who
gives strength and power to
His people.

Blessed *be* God!

PROVERBS FOR TODAY/ 24:3-4

*Through wisdom a house is built, and by understanding it is established; by
knowledge the rooms are filled with all precious and pleasant riches.*

SEPTEMBER 26

ISAIAH 48:12–50:11

"Listen to Me, O Jacob,
And Israel, My called:
I *am* He, I *am* the First,
I *am* also the Last.
13 Indeed My hand has laid the
foundation of the earth,
And My right hand has
stretched out the heavens;
When I call to them,
They stand up together.
14 "All of you, assemble
yourselves, and hear!
Who among them has
declared these *things?*
The LORD loves him;
He shall do His pleasure on
Babylon,
And His arm *shall be against*
the Chaldeans.
15 I, *even* I, have spoken;

Yes, I have called him,
I have brought him, and his
way will prosper.

16 "Come near to Me, hear this:
I have not spoken in secret
from the beginning;
From the time that it was, I
was there.
And now the Lord GOD and
His Spirit
Have* sent Me."

17 Thus says the LORD, your
Redeemer,
The Holy One of Israel:
"I *am* the LORD your God,
Who teaches you to profit,
Who leads you by the way
you should go.
18 Oh, that you had heeded My
commandments!

Then your peace would have
　　been like a river,
And your righteousness like
　　the waves of the sea.
19　Your descendants also would
　　have been like the sand,
And the offspring of your
　　body like the grains of sand;
His name would not have
　　been cut off
Nor destroyed from before
　　Me."

20　Go forth from Babylon!
Flee from the Chaldeans!
With a voice of singing,
Declare, proclaim this,
Utter it to the end of the earth;
Say, "The LORD has redeemed
　　His servant Jacob!"
21　And they did not thirst
When He led them through
　　the deserts;
He caused the waters to flow
　　from the rock for them;
He also split the rock, and the
　　waters gushed out.

22　*There is* no peace," says the
　　LORD, "for the wicked.

"LISTEN, O coastlands, to Me,
　　And take heed, you peoples
　　　　from afar!
The LORD has called Me from
　　the womb;
From the matrix of My
　　mother He has made
　　mention of My name.
2　And He has made My mouth
　　like a sharp sword;
In the shadow of His hand He
　　has hidden Me,
And made Me a polished
　　shaft;
In His quiver He has hidden
　　Me."
3　"And He said to me,
　　'You *are* My servant, O Israel,

In whom I will be glorified.'
4　Then I said, 'I have labored in
　　vain,
I have spent my strength for
　　nothing and in vain;
Yet surely my just reward *is*
　　with the LORD,
And my work with my God.' "

5　"And now the LORD says,
Who formed Me from the
　　womb *to be* His Servant,
To bring Jacob back to Him,
So that Israel is gathered to
　　Him*
(For I shall be glorious in the
　　eyes of the LORD,
And My God shall be My
　　strength),
6　Indeed He says,
'It is too small a thing that You
　　should be My Servant
To raise up the tribes of Jacob,
And to restore the preserved
　　ones of Israel;
I will also give You as a light
　　to the Gentiles,
That You should be My
　　salvation to the ends of the
　　earth.' "

7　Thus says the LORD,
The Redeemer of Israel, their
　　Holy One,
To Him whom man despises,
To Him whom the nation
　　abhors,
To the Servant of rulers:
"Kings shall see and arise,
Princes also shall worship,
Because of the LORD who is
　　faithful,
The Holy One of Israel;
And He has chosen You."

8Thus says the LORD:

"In an acceptable time I have
　　heard You,

And in the day of salvation I
have helped You;
I will preserve You and give
You
As a covenant to the people,
To restore the earth,
To cause them to inherit the
desolate heritages;

9 That You may say to the
prisoners, 'Go forth,'
To those who *are* in darkness,
'Show yourselves.'

"They shall feed along the
roads,
And their pastures *shall be* on
all desolate heights.

10 They shall neither hunger nor
thirst,
Neither heat nor sun shall
strike them;
For He who has mercy on
them will lead them,
Even by the springs of water
He will guide them.

11 I will make each of My
mountains a road,
And My highways shall be
elevated.

12 Surely these shall come from
afar;
Look! Those from the north
and the west,
And these from the land of
Sinim."

13 Sing, O heavens!
Be joyful, O earth!
And break out in singing,
O mountains!
For the LORD has comforted
His people,
And will have mercy on His
afflicted.

14 But Zion said,

"The LORD has forsaken me,
And my Lord has forgotten
me."

15 "Can a woman forget her
nursing child,
And not have compassion on
the son of her womb?
Surely they may forget,
Yet I will not forget you.

16 See, I have inscribed you on
the palms *of My hands;*
Your walls *are* continually
before Me.

17 Your sons* shall make haste;
Your destroyers and those
who laid you waste
Shall go away from you.

18 Lift up your eyes, look around
and see;
All these gather together *and*
come to you.
As I live," says the LORD,
"You shall surely clothe
yourselves with them all as
an ornament,
And bind them *on you* as a
bride *does.*

19 "For your waste and desolate
places,
And the land of your
destruction,
Will even now be too small for
the inhabitants;
And those who swallowed you
up will be far away.

20 The children you will have,
After you have lost the others,
Will say again in your ears,
'The place *is* too small for me;
Give me a place where I may
dwell.'

21 Then you will say in your
heart,
'Who has begotten these for
me,
Since I have lost my children
and am desolate,
A captive, and wandering to
and fro?
And who has brought these
up?
There I was, left alone;

But these, where *were* they?' "

²²Thus says the Lord God:

"Behold, I will lift My hand in
an oath to the nations,
And set up My standard for
the peoples;
They shall bring your sons in
their arms,
And your daughters shall be
carried on *their* shoulders;
23 Kings shall be your foster
fathers,
And their queens your
nursing mothers;
They shall bow down to you
with *their* faces to the earth,
And lick up the dust of your
feet.
Then you will know that I *am*
the Lord,
For they shall not be ashamed
who wait for Me."

24 Shall the prey be taken from
the mighty,
Or the captives of the
righteous* be delivered?

²⁵But thus says the Lord:

"Even the captives of the
mighty shall be taken away,
And the prey of the terrible
be delivered;
For I will contend with him
who contends with you,
And I will save your children.
26 I will feed those who oppress
you with their own flesh,
And they shall be drunk with
their own blood as with
sweet wine.
All flesh shall know
That I, the Lord, *am* your
Savior,
And your Redeemer, the
Mighty One of Jacob."

Thus says the Lord:

"Where *is* the certificate of
your mother's divorce,
Whom I have put away?
Or which of My creditors *is it*
to whom I have sold you?
For your iniquities you have
sold yourselves,
And for your transgressions
your mother has been put
away.
2 Why, when I came, *was there*
no man?
Why, when I called, *was there*
none to answer?
Is My hand shortened at all
that it cannot redeem?
Or have I no power to deliver?
Indeed with My rebuke I dry
up the sea,
I make the rivers a wilderness;
Their fish stink because *there
is* no water,
And die of thirst.
3 I clothe the heavens with
blackness,
And I make sackcloth their
covering."

4 "The Lord God has given Me
The tongue of the learned,
That I should know how to
speak
A word in season to *him who
is* weary.
He awakens Me morning by
morning,
He awakens My ear
To hear as the learned.
5 The Lord God has opened My
ear;
And I was not rebellious,
Nor did I turn away.
6 I gave My back to those who
struck *Me,*
And My cheeks to those who
plucked out the beard;
I did not hide My face from
shame and spitting.

7 "For the Lord GOD will help
Me;
Therefore I will not be
disgraced;
Therefore I have set My face
like a flint,
And I know that I will not be
ashamed.
8 *He is* near who justifies Me;
Who will contend with Me?
Let us stand together.
Who *is* My adversary?
Let him come near Me.
9 Surely the Lord GOD will help
Me;
Who *is* he *who* will condemn
Me?
Indeed they will all grow old
like a garment;
The moth will eat them up.

10 "Who among you fears the
LORD?
Who obeys the voice of His
Servant?
Who walks in darkness
And has no light?
Let him trust in the name of
the LORD
And rely upon his God.
11 Look, all you who kindle a fire,
Who encircle *yourselves* with
sparks:
Walk in the light of your fire
and in the sparks you have
kindled—
This you shall have from My
hand:
You shall lie down in torment."

EPHESIANS 4:17-32

THIS I say, therefore, and testify in
the Lord, that you should no
longer walk as the rest of* the
Gentiles walk, in the futility of their
mind, 18having their understanding
darkened, being alienated from the life
of God, because of the ignorance that
is in them, because of the blindness of
their heart; 19who, being past feeling,
have given themselves over to lewdness, to work all uncleanness with
greediness.

20But you have not so learned
Christ, 21if indeed you have heard Him
and have been taught by Him, as the
truth is in Jesus: 22that you put off, concerning your former conduct, the old
man which grows corrupt according
to the deceitful lusts, 23and be renewed
in the spirit of your mind, 24and that
you put on the new man which was
created according to God, in true righteousness and holiness.

25Therefore, putting away lying, *"Let
each one of you speak truth with his
neighbor,"* * for we are members of
one another. 26*"Be angry, and do not
sin":* do not let the sun go down on
your wrath, 27nor give place to the
devil. 28Let him who stole steal no
longer, but rather let him labor, working with *his* hands what is good, that he
may have something to give him who
has need. 29Let no corrupt word proceed out of your mouth, but what is
good for necessary edification, that it
may impart grace to the hearers.
30And do not grieve the Holy Spirit of
God, by whom you were sealed for the
day of redemption. 31Let all bitterness,
wrath, anger, clamor, and evil speaking be put away from you, with all malice. 32And be kind to one another,
tenderhearted, forgiving one another,
even as God in Christ forgave you.

PSALM 69:1-18

To the Chief Musician. Set to "The Lilies." * A
Psalm of David.*

SAVE me, O God!
For the waters have come up
to *my* neck.
2 I sink in deep mire,
Where *there is* no standing;
I have come into deep waters,
Where the floods overflow
me.

3 I am weary with my crying;
My throat is dry;
My eyes fail while I wait for
my God.

4 Those who hate me without a
cause
Are more than the hairs of my
head;
They are mighty who would
destroy me,
Being my enemies wrongfully;
Though I have stolen nothing,
I *still* must restore *it.*

5 O God, You know my
foolishness;
And my sins are not hidden
from You.

6 Let not those who wait for
You, O Lord God of hosts,
be ashamed because of me;
Let not those who seek You
be confounded because of
me, O God of Israel.

7 Because for Your sake I have
borne reproach;
Shame has covered my face.

8 I have become a stranger to
my brothers,
And an alien to my mother's
children;

9 Because zeal for Your house
has eaten me up,
And the reproaches of those
who reproach You have
fallen on me.

10 When I wept *and chastened*
my soul with fasting,
That became my reproach.

11 I also made sackcloth my
garment;
I became a byword to them.

12 Those who sit in the gate
speak against me,
And I *am* the song of the
drunkards.

13 But as for me, my prayer *is* to
You,
O Lord, *in* the acceptable time;
O God, in the multitude of
Your mercy,
Hear me in the truth of Your
salvation.

14 Deliver me out of the mire,
And let me not sink;
Let me be delivered from
those who hate me,
And out of the deep waters.

15 Let not the floodwater
overflow me,
Nor let the deep swallow me
up;
And let not the pit shut its
mouth on me.

16 Hear me, O Lord, for Your
lovingkindness *is* good;
Turn to me according to the
multitude of Your tender
mercies.

17 And do not hide Your face
from Your servant,
For I am in trouble;
Hear me speedily.

18 Draw near to my soul, *and*
redeem it;
Deliver me because of my
enemies.

PROVERBS FOR TODAY/ 24:5-6

A wise man is *strong, yes, a man of knowledge increases strength; for by wise counsel
you will wage your own war, and in a multitude of counselors* there is *safety.*

SEPTEMBER 27

ISAIAH 51:1–53:12

"**L**ISTEN to Me, you who follow
after righteousness,
You who seek the LORD:
Look to the rock *from which*
you were hewn,
And to the hole of the pit *from
which* you were dug.
2 Look to Abraham your father,
And to Sarah *who* bore you;
For I called him alone,
And blessed him and
increased him."

3 For the LORD will comfort Zion,
He will comfort all her waste
places;
He will make her wilderness
like Eden,
And her desert like the
garden of the LORD;
Joy and gladness will be
found in it,
Thanksgiving and the voice of
melody.

4 "Listen to Me, My people;
And give ear to Me, O My
nation:
For law will proceed from Me,
And I will make My justice
rest
As a light of the peoples.
5 My righteousness *is* near,
My salvation has gone forth,
And My arms will judge the
peoples;
The coastlands will wait upon
Me,
And on My arm they will trust.
6 Lift up your eyes to the
heavens,
And look on the earth
beneath.

For the heavens will vanish
away like smoke,
The earth will grow old like a
garment,
And those who dwell in it will
die in like manner;
But My salvation will be
forever,
And My righteousness will
not be abolished.

7 "Listen to Me, you who know
righteousness,
You people in whose heart *is*
My law:
Do not fear the reproach of
men,
Nor be afraid of their insults.
8 For the moth will eat them up
like a garment,
And the worm will eat them
like wool;
But My righteousness will be
forever,
And My salvation from
generation to generation."

9 Awake, awake, put on
strength,
O arm of the LORD!
Awake as in the ancient days,
In the generations of old.
Are You not *the arm* that cut
Rahab apart,
And wounded the serpent?

10 *Are* You not *the One* who
dried up the sea,
The waters of the great deep;
That made the depths of the
sea a road
For the redeemed to cross
over?
11 So the ransomed of the LORD
shall return,

And come to Zion with
    singing,
With everlasting joy on their
    heads.
They shall obtain joy and
    gladness;
Sorrow and sighing shall flee
    away.

12 "I, *even* I, *am* He who comforts
    you.
Who *are* you that you should
    be afraid
Of a man *who* will die,
And of the son of a man *who*
    will be made like grass?
13 And you forget the LORD your
    Maker,
Who stretched out the
    heavens
And laid the foundations of
    the earth;
You have feared continually
    every day
Because of the fury of the
    oppressor,
When *he has* prepared to
    destroy.
And where *is* the fury of the
    oppressor?
14 The captive exile hastens, that
    he may be loosed,
That he should not die in the
    pit,
And that his bread should not
    fail.
15 But I *am* the LORD your God,
Who divided the sea whose
    waves roared—
The LORD of hosts *is* His name.
16 And I have put My words in
    your mouth;
I have covered you with the
    shadow of My hand,
That I may plant the heavens,
Lay the foundations of the
    earth,
And say to Zion, 'You *are* My
    people.' "

17 Awake, awake!
Stand up, O Jerusalem,
You who have drunk at the
    hand of the LORD
The cup of His fury;
You have drunk the dregs of
    the cup of trembling,
And drained *it* out.
18 *There is* no one to guide her
Among all the sons she has
    brought forth;
Nor *is there any* who takes her
    by the hand
Among all the sons she has
    brought up.
19 These two *things* have come
    to you;
Who will be sorry for you?—
Desolation and destruction,
    famine and sword—
By whom will I comfort you?
20 Your sons have fainted,
They lie at the head of all the
    streets,
Like an antelope in a net;
They are full of the fury of the
    LORD,
The rebuke of your God.

21 Therefore please hear this,
    you afflicted,
And drunk but not with wine.
22 Thus says your Lord,
The LORD and your God,
Who pleads the cause of His
    people:
"See, I have taken out of your
    hand
The cup of trembling,
The dregs of the cup of My
    fury;
You shall no longer drink it.
23 But I will put it into the hand
    of those who afflict you,
Who have said to you,*
'Lie down, that we may walk
    over you.'
And you have laid your body
    like the ground,

And as the street, for those
who walk over."

Awake, awake!
Put on your strength, O Zion;
Put on your beautiful
garments,
O Jerusalem, the holy city!
For the uncircumcised and
the unclean
Shall no longer come to you.
2 Shake yourself from the dust,
arise;
Sit down, O Jerusalem!
Loose yourself from the
bonds of your neck,
O captive daughter of Zion!

3For thus says the LORD:

"You have sold yourselves for
nothing,
And you shall be redeemed
without money."

4For thus says the Lord GOD:

"My people went down at first
Into Egypt to dwell there;
Then the Assyrian oppressed
them without cause.
5 Now therefore, what have I
here," says the LORD,
"That My people are taken
away for nothing?
Those who rule over them
Make them wail,"* says the
LORD,
"And My name is blasphemed
continually every day.
6 Therefore My people shall
know My name;
Therefore they shall know in
that day
That I am He who speaks:
'Behold, it is I.' "

7 How beautiful upon the
mountains

Are the feet of him who
brings good news,
Who proclaims peace,
Who brings glad tidings of
good things,
Who proclaims salvation,
Who says to Zion,
"Your God reigns!"
8 Your watchmen shall lift up
their voices,
With their voices they shall
sing together;
For they shall see eye to eye
When the LORD brings back
Zion.
9 Break forth into joy, sing
together,
You waste places of
Jerusalem!
For the LORD has comforted
His people,
He has redeemed Jerusalem.
10 The LORD has made bare His
holy arm
In the eyes of all the nations;
And all the ends of the earth
shall see
The salvation of our God.

11 Depart! Depart! Go out from
there,
Touch no unclean thing;
Go out from the midst of her,
Be clean,
You who bear the vessels of
the LORD.
12 For you shall not go out with
haste,
Nor go by flight;
For the LORD will go before
you,
And the God of Israel will be
your rear guard.

13 Behold, My Servant shall deal
prudently;
He shall be exalted and
extolled and be very high.
14 Just as many were astonished
at you,

So His visage was marred
more than any man,
And His form more than the
sons of men;
15 So shall He sprinkle* many
nations.
Kings shall shut their mouths
at Him;
For what had not been told
them they shall see,
And what they had not heard
they shall consider.

WHO has believed our report?
And to whom has the arm of
the LORD been revealed?
2 For He shall grow up before
Him as a tender plant,
And as a root out of dry
ground.
He has no form or comeliness;
And when we see Him,
There is no beauty that we
should desire Him.
3 He is despised and rejected
by men,
A Man of sorrows and
acquainted with grief.
And we hid, as it were, *our*
faces from Him;
He was despised, and we did
not esteem Him.

4 Surely He has borne our griefs
And carried our sorrows;
Yet we esteemed Him
stricken,
Smitten by God, and afflicted.
5 But He *was* wounded for our
transgressions,
He was bruised for our
iniquities;
The chastisement for our
peace *was* upon Him,
And by His stripes we are
healed.
6 All we like sheep have gone
astray;
We have turned, every one, to
his own way;

And the LORD has laid on Him
the iniquity of us all.

7 He was oppressed and He
was afflicted,
Yet He opened not His mouth;
He was led as a lamb to the
slaughter,
And as a sheep before its
shearers is silent,
So He opened not His mouth.
8 He was taken from prison and
from judgment,
And who will declare His
generation?
For He was cut off from the
land of the living;
For the transgressions of My
people He was stricken.
9 And they* made His grave
with the wicked—
But with the rich at His death,
Because He had done no
violence,
Nor *was any* deceit in His
mouth.

10 Yet it pleased the LORD to
bruise Him;
He has put *Him* to grief.
When You make His soul an
offering for sin,
He shall see *His* seed, He
shall prolong *His* days,
And the pleasure of the LORD
shall prosper in His hand.
11 He shall see the labor of His
soul,* *and* be satisfied.
By His knowledge My
righteous Servant shall
justify many,
For He shall bear their
iniquities.
12 Therefore I will divide Him a
portion with the great,
And He shall divide the spoil
with the strong,
Because He poured out His
soul unto death,

And He was numbered with
the transgressors,
And He bore the sin of many,
And made intercession for the
transgressors.

EPHESIANS 5:1-33

THEREFORE be imitators of God as dear children. ²And walk in love, as Christ also has loved us and given Himself for us, an offering and a sacrifice to God for a sweet-smelling aroma.

³But fornication and all uncleanness or covetousness, let it not even be named among you, as is fitting for saints; ⁴neither filthiness, nor foolish talking, nor coarse jesting, which are not fitting, but rather giving of thanks. ⁵For this you know,* that no fornicator, unclean person, nor covetous man, who is an idolater, has any inheritance in the kingdom of Christ and God. ⁶Let no one deceive you with empty words, for because of these things the wrath of God comes upon the sons of disobedience. ⁷Therefore do not be partakers with them.

⁸For you were once darkness, but now *you are* light in the Lord. Walk as children of light ⁹(for the fruit of the Spirit* *is* in all goodness, righteousness, and truth), ¹⁰finding out what is acceptable to the Lord. ¹¹And have no fellowship with the unfruitful works of darkness, but rather expose *them.* ¹²For it is shameful even to speak of those things which are done by them in secret. ¹³But all things that are exposed are made manifest by the light, for whatever makes manifest is light. ¹⁴Therefore He says:

"Awake, you who sleep,
Arise from the dead,
And Christ will give you light."

¹⁵See then that you walk circumspectly, not as fools but as wise, ¹⁶redeeming the time, because the days are evil.

¹⁷Therefore do not be unwise, but understand what the will of the Lord *is.* ¹⁸And do not be drunk with wine, in which is dissipation; but be filled with the Spirit, ¹⁹speaking to one another in psalms and hymns and spiritual songs, singing and making melody in your heart to the Lord, ²⁰giving thanks always for all things to God the Father in the name of our Lord Jesus Christ, ²¹submitting to one another in the fear of God.*

²²Wives, submit to your own husbands, as to the Lord. ²³For the husband is head of the wife, as also Christ is head of the church; and He is the Savior of the body. ²⁴Therefore, just as the church is subject to Christ, so *let* the wives *be* to their own husbands in everything.

²⁵Husbands, love your wives, just as Christ also loved the church and gave Himself for her, ²⁶that He might sanctify and cleanse her with the washing of water by the word, ²⁷that He might present her to Himself a glorious church, not having spot or wrinkle or any such thing, but that she should be holy and without blemish. ²⁸So husbands ought to love their own wives as their own bodies; he who loves his wife loves himself. ²⁹For no one ever hated his own flesh, but nourishes and cherishes it, just as the Lord *does* the church. ³⁰For we are members of His body,* of His flesh and of His bones. ³¹*"For this reason a man shall leave his father and mother and be joined to his wife, and the two shall become one flesh."* * ³²This is a great mystery, but I speak concerning Christ and the church. ³³Nevertheless let each one of you in particular so love his own wife as himself, and let the wife *see* that she respects *her* husband.

PSALM 69:19-36

YOU know my reproach, my shame, and my dishonor; My adversaries *are* all before You.

20 Reproach has broken my heart,
And I am full of heaviness;
I looked *for someone* to take pity, but *there was* none;
And for comforters, but I found none.

21 They also gave me gall for my food,
And for my thirst they gave me vinegar to drink.

22 Let their table become a snare before them,
And their well-being a trap.

23 Let their eyes be darkened, so that they do not see;
And make their loins shake continually.

24 Pour out Your indignation upon them,
And let Your wrathful anger take hold of them.

25 Let their dwelling place be desolate;
Let no one live in their tents.

26 For they persecute the *ones* You have struck,
And talk of the grief of those You have wounded.

27 Add iniquity to their iniquity,
And let them not come into Your righteousness.

28 Let them be blotted out of the book of the living,
And not be written with the righteous.

29 But I *am* poor and sorrowful;
Let Your salvation, O God, set me up on high.

30 I will praise the name of God with a song,
And will magnify Him with thanksgiving.

31 *This* also shall please the LORD better than an ox *or* bull,
Which has horns and hooves.

32 The humble shall see *this and* be glad;
And you who seek God, your hearts shall live.

33 For the LORD hears the poor,
And does not despise His prisoners.

34 Let heaven and earth praise Him,
The seas and everything that moves in them.

35 For God will save Zion
And build the cities of Judah,
That they may dwell there and possess it.

36 Also, the descendants of His servants shall inherit it,
And those who love His name shall dwell in it.

PROVERBS FOR TODAY/ 24:7

Wisdom is *too lofty for a fool; he does not open his mouth in the gate.*

SEPTEMBER 28

ISAIAH 54:1–57:13

SING, O barren,
You *who* have not borne!
Break forth into singing, and
cry aloud,
You *who* have not labored
with child!
For more *are* the children of
the desolate
Than the children of the
married woman," says the
LORD.

2 "Enlarge the place of your tent,
And let them stretch out the
curtains of your dwellings;
Do not spare;
Lengthen your cords,
And strengthen your stakes.

3 For you shall expand to the
right and to the left,
And your descendants will
inherit the nations,
And make the desolate cities
inhabited.

4 "Do not fear, for you will not be
ashamed;
Neither be disgraced, for you
will not be put to shame;
For you will forget the shame
of your youth,
And will not remember the
reproach of your
widowhood anymore.

5 For your Maker *is* your
husband,
The LORD of hosts *is* His name;
And your Redeemer *is* the
Holy One of Israel;
He is called the God of the
whole earth.

6 For the LORD has called you
Like a woman forsaken and
grieved in spirit,
Like a youthful wife when you
were refused,"
Says your God.

7 "For a mere moment I have
forsaken you,
But with great mercies I will
gather you.

8 With a little wrath I hid My
face from you for a moment;
But with everlasting kindness
I will have mercy on you,"
Says the LORD, your Redeemer.

9 "For this *is* like the waters of
Noah to Me;
For as I have sworn
That the waters of Noah
would no longer cover the
earth,
So have I sworn
That I would not be angry
with you, nor rebuke you.

10 For the mountains shall
depart
And the hills be removed,
But My kindness shall not
depart from you,
Nor shall My covenant of
peace be removed,"
Says the LORD, who has mercy
on you.

11 "O you afflicted one,
Tossed with tempest, *and* not
comforted,
Behold, I will lay your stones
with colorful gems,
And lay your foundations with
sapphires.

12 I will make your pinnacles of
rubies,
Your gates of crystal,
And all your walls of precious
stones.

13 All your children *shall be* taught by the LORD,
And great *shall be* the peace of your children.
14 In righteousness you shall be established;
You shall be far from oppression, for you shall not fear;
And from terror, for it shall not come near you.
15 Indeed they shall surely assemble, *but* not because of Me.
Whoever assembles against you shall fall for your sake.

16 "Behold, I have created the blacksmith
Who blows the coals in the fire,
Who brings forth an instrument for his work;
And I have created the spoiler to destroy.
17 No weapon formed against you shall prosper,
And every tongue *which* rises against you in judgment
You shall condemn.
This *is* the heritage of the servants of the LORD,
And their righteousness *is* from Me,"
Says the LORD.

"Ho! Everyone who thirsts,
Come to the waters;
And you who have no money,
Come, buy and eat.
Yes, come, buy wine and milk
Without money and without price.
2 Why do you spend money for *what is* not bread,
And your wages for *what* does not satisfy?
Listen carefully to Me, and eat *what is* good,

And let your soul delight itself in abundance.
3 Incline your ear, and come to Me.
Hear, and your soul shall live;
And I will make an everlasting covenant with you—
The sure mercies of David.
4 Indeed I have given him *as* a witness to the people,
A leader and commander for the people.
5 Surely you shall call a nation you do not know,
And nations *who* do not know you shall run to you,
Because of the LORD your God,
And the Holy One of Israel;
For He has glorified you."

6 Seek the LORD while He may be found,
Call upon Him while He is near.
7 Let the wicked forsake his way,
And the unrighteous man his thoughts;
Let him return to the LORD,
And He will have mercy on him;
And to our God,
For He will abundantly pardon.

8 "For My thoughts *are* not your thoughts,
Nor *are* your ways My ways," says the LORD.
9 "For *as* the heavens are higher than the earth,
So are My ways higher than your ways,
And My thoughts than your thoughts.

10 "For as the rain comes down, and the snow from heaven,
And do not return there,
But water the earth,

And make it bring forth and
bud,
That it may give seed to the
sower
And bread to the eater,

11 So shall My word be that goes
forth from My mouth;
It shall not return to Me void,
But it shall accomplish what I
please,
And it shall prosper *in the
thing* for which I sent it.

12 "For you shall go out with joy,
And be led out with peace;
The mountains and the hills
Shall break forth into singing
before you,
And all the trees of the field
shall clap *their* hands.

13 Instead of the thorn shall
come up the cypress tree,
And instead of the brier shall
come up the myrtle tree;
And it shall be to the LORD for
a name,
For an everlasting sign *that*
shall not be cut off."

THUS says the LORD:

"Keep justice, and do
righteousness,
For My salvation *is* about to
come,
And My righteousness to be
revealed.

2 Blessed *is* the man *who* does
this,
And the son of man *who* lays
hold on it;
Who keeps from defiling the
Sabbath,
And keeps his hand from
doing any evil."

3 Do not let the son of the
foreigner
Who has joined himself to the
LORD

Speak, saying,
"The LORD has utterly
separated me from His
people";
Nor let the eunuch say,
"Here I am, a dry tree."

4 For thus says the LORD:
"To the eunuchs who keep My
Sabbaths,
And choose what pleases Me,
And hold fast My covenant,

5 Even to them I will give in My
house
And within My walls a place
and a name
Better than that of sons and
daughters;
I will give them* an
everlasting name
That shall not be cut off

6 "Also the sons of the foreigner
Who join themselves to the
LORD, to serve Him,
And to love the name of the
LORD, to be His servants—
Everyone who keeps from
defiling the Sabbath,
And holds fast My covenant—

7 Even them I will bring to My
holy mountain,
And make them joyful in My
house of prayer.
Their burnt offerings and
their sacrifices
Will be accepted on My altar;
For My house shall be called
a house of prayer for all
nations."

8 The Lord GOD, who gathers
the outcasts of Israel, says,
"Yet I will gather to him
Others besides those who are
gathered to him."

9 All you beasts of the field,
come to devour,
All you beasts in the forest.

10 His watchmen *are* blind,
They are all ignorant;

They *are* all dumb dogs,
They cannot bark;
Sleeping, lying down, loving
to slumber.
11 Yes, *they are* greedy dogs
Which never have enough.
And they *are* shepherds
Who cannot understand;
They all look to their own way,
Every one for his own gain,
From his *own* territory.
12 "Come," *one says,* "I will bring
wine,
And we will fill ourselves with
intoxicating drink;
Tomorrow will be as today,
And much more abundant."

THE righteous perishes,
And no man takes *it* to heart;
Merciful men *are* taken away,
While no one considers
That the righteous is taken
away from evil.
2 He shall enter into peace;
They shall rest in their beds,
Each one walking *in* his
uprightness.

3 "But come here,
You sons of the sorceress,
You offspring of the adulterer
and the harlot!
4 Whom do you ridicule?
Against whom do you make a
wide mouth
And stick out the tongue?
Are you not children of
transgression,
Offspring of falsehood,
5 Inflaming yourselves with
gods under every green
tree,
Slaying the children in the
valleys,
Under the clefts of the rocks?
6 Among the smooth *stones* of
the stream
Is your portion;
They, they, *are* your lot!

Even to them you have
poured a drink offering,
You have offered a grain
offering.
Should I receive comfort in
these?

7 "On a lofty and high mountain
You have set your bed;
Even there you went up
To offer sacrifice.
8 Also behind the doors and
their posts
You have set up your
remembrance;
For you have uncovered
yourself *to those other* than
Me,
And have gone up to them;
You have enlarged your bed
And made *a covenant* with
them;
You have loved their bed,
Where you saw *their* nudity.*
9 You went to the king with
ointment,
And increased your perfumes;
You sent your messengers far
off,
And *even* descended to Sheol.
10 You are wearied in the length
of your way;
Yet you did not say, 'There is
no hope.'
You have found the life of
your hand;
Therefore you were not
grieved.

11 "And of whom have you been
afraid, or feared,
That you have lied
And not remembered Me,
Nor taken *it* to your heart?
Is it not because I have held
My peace from of old
That you do not fear Me?
12 I will declare your
righteousness
And your works,

For they will not profit you.
13 When you cry out,
Let your collection *of idols*
deliver you.
But the wind will carry them
all away,
A breath will take *them.*
But he who puts his trust in
Me shall possess the land,
And shall inherit My holy
mountain."

EPHESIANS 6:1-24

CHILDREN, obey your parents in the Lord, for this is right. 2"Honor your father and mother," which is the first commandment with promise: 3"that it may be well with you and you may live long on the earth."

4And you, fathers, do not provoke your children to wrath, but bring them up in the training and admonition of the Lord.

5Bondservants, be obedient to those who are your masters according to the flesh, with fear and trembling, in sincerity of heart, as to Christ; 6not with eye-service, as men-pleasers, but as bondservants of Christ, doing the will of God from the heart, 7with goodwill doing service, as to the Lord, and not to men, 8knowing that whatever good anyone does, he will receive the same from the Lord, whether *he is* a slave or free.

9And you, masters, do the same things to them, giving up threatening, knowing that your own Master also* is in heaven, and there is no partiality with Him.

10Finally, my brethren, be strong in the Lord and in the power of His might. 11Put on the whole armor of God, that you may be able to stand against the wiles of the devil. 12For we do not wrestle against flesh and blood, but against principalities, against powers, against the rulers of the darkness of this age,* against spiritual *hosts* of wickedness in the heavenly *places.* 13Therefore take up the whole armor of God, that you may be able to withstand in the evil day, and having done all, to stand.

14Stand therefore, having girded your waist with truth, having put on the breastplate of righteousness, 15and having shod your feet with the preparation of the gospel of peace; 16above all, taking the shield of faith with which you will be able to quench all the fiery darts of the wicked one. 17And take the helmet of salvation, and the sword of the Spirit, which is the word of God; 18praying always with all prayer and supplication in the Spirit, being watchful to this end with all perseverance and supplication for all the saints— 19and for me, that utterance may be given to me, that I may open my mouth boldly to make known the mystery of the gospel, 20for which I am an ambassador in chains; that in it I may speak boldly, as I ought to speak.

21But that you also may know my affairs *and* how I am doing, Tychicus, a beloved brother and faithful minister in the Lord, will make all things known to you; 22whom I have sent to you for this very purpose, that you may know our affairs, and *that* he may comfort your hearts.

23Peace to the brethren, and love with faith, from God the Father and the Lord Jesus Christ. 24Grace *be* with all those who love our Lord Jesus Christ in sincerity. Amen.

PSALM 70:1-5

To the Chief Musician. A Psalm *of David.* To *bring to remembrance.*

MAKE *haste,* O God, to deliver me!
Make haste to help me,
O LORD!

2 Let them be ashamed and
confounded

Who seek my life;
Let them be turned back* and
confused
Who desire my hurt.
3 Let them be turned back
because of their shame,
Who say, "Aha, aha!"

4 Let all those who seek You
rejoice and be glad in You;

And let those who love Your
salvation say continually,
"Let God be magnified!"

5 But I *am* poor and needy;
Make haste to me, O God!
You *are* my help and my
deliverer;
O LORD, do not delay.

PROVERBS FOR TODAY/ 24:8
He who plots to do evil will be called a schemer.

SEPTEMBER 29

ISAIAH 57:14–59:21

AND one shall say,
"Heap it up! Heap it up!
Prepare the way,
Take the stumbling block out
of the way of My people."

15 For thus says the High and
Lofty One
Who inhabits eternity, whose
name *is* Holy:
"I dwell in the high and holy
place,
With him *who* has a contrite
and humble spirit,
To revive the spirit of the
humble,
And to revive the heart of the
contrite ones.
16 For I will not contend forever,
Nor will I always be angry;
For the spirit would fail before
Me,
And the souls *which* I have
made.
17 For the iniquity of his
covetousness
I was angry and struck him;

I hid and was angry,
And he went on backsliding in
the way of his heart.
18 I have seen his ways, and will
heal him;
I will also lead him,
And restore comforts to him
And to his mourners.

19 "I create the fruit of the lips:
Peace, peace to *him who is* far
off and to *him who is* near,"
Says the LORD,
"And I will heal him."
20 But the wicked *are* like the
troubled sea,
When it cannot rest,
Whose waters cast up mire
and dirt.

21 "*There is* no peace,"
Says my God, "for the
wicked."

"CRY aloud, spare not;
Lift up your voice like a
trumpet;
Tell My people their
transgression,

And the house of Jacob their
    sins.
2   Yet they seek Me daily,
    And delight to know My ways,
    As a nation that did
        righteousness,
    And did not forsake the
        ordinance of their God.
    They ask of Me the
        ordinances of justice;
    They take delight in
        approaching God.
3   'Why have we fasted,' *they say,*
        'and You have not seen?
    Why have we afflicted our
        souls, and You take no
        notice?'

    "In fact, in the day of your fast
        you find pleasure,
    And exploit all your laborers.
4   Indeed you fast for strife and
        debate,
    And to strike with the fist of
        wickedness.
    You will not fast as *you do* this
        day,
    To make your voice heard on
        high.
5   Is it a fast that I have chosen,
    A day for a man to afflict his
        soul?
    Is it to bow down his head like
        a bulrush,
    And to spread out sackcloth
        and ashes?
    Would you call this a fast,
    And an acceptable day to the
        Lord?

6   "*Is* this not the fast that I have
        chosen:
    To loose the bonds of
        wickedness,
    To undo the heavy burdens,
    To let the oppressed go free,
    And that you break every
        yoke?
7   *Is it* not to share your bread
        with the hungry,

And that you bring to your
    house the poor who are
    cast out;
When you see the naked, that
    you cover him,
And not hide yourself from
    your own flesh?
8   Then your light shall break
        forth like the morning,
    Your healing shall spring
        forth speedily,
    And your righteousness shall
        go before you;
    The glory of the Lord shall be
        your rear guard.
9   Then you shall call, and the
        Lord will answer;
    You shall cry, and He will say,
        'Here I *am.*'
    " If you take away the yoke
        from your midst,
    The pointing of the finger, and
        speaking wickedness,
10   *If* you extend your soul to the
        hungry
    And satisfy the afflicted soul,
    Then your light shall dawn in
        the darkness,
    And your darkness shall *be* as
        the noonday.
11   The Lord will guide you
        continually,
    And satisfy your soul in
        drought,
    And strengthen your bones;
    You shall be like a watered
        garden,
    And like a spring of water,
        whose waters do not fail.
12   Those from among you
    Shall build the old waste
        places;
    You shall raise up the
        foundations of many
        generations;
    And you shall be called the
        Repairer of the Breach,
    The Restorer of Streets to
        Dwell In.

13 "If you turn away your foot
from the Sabbath,
From doing your pleasure on
My holy day,
And call the Sabbath a delight,
The holy *day* of the LORD
honorable,
And shall honor Him, not
doing your own ways,
Nor finding your own
pleasure,
Nor speaking *your own* words,

14 Then you shall delight
yourself in the LORD;
And I will cause you to ride on
the high hills of the earth,
And feed you with the
heritage of Jacob your
father.
The mouth of the LORD has
spoken."

BEHOLD, the LORD's hand is not
shortened,
That it cannot save;
Nor His ear heavy,
That it cannot hear.

2 But your iniquities have
separated you from your
God;
And your sins have hidden
His face from you,
So that He will not hear.

3 For your hands are defiled
with blood,
And your fingers with iniquity;
Your lips have spoken lies,
Your tongue has muttered
perversity.

4 No one calls for justice,
Nor does *any* plead for truth.
They trust in empty words
and speak lies;
They conceive evil and bring
forth iniquity.

5 They hatch vipers' eggs and
weave the spider's web;
He who eats of their eggs dies,
And *from* that which is
crushed a viper breaks out.

6 Their webs will not become
garments,
Nor will they cover
themselves with their
works;
Their works *are* works of
iniquity,
And the act of violence *is* in
their hands.

7 Their feet run to evil,
And they make haste to shed
innocent blood;
Their thoughts *are* thoughts
of iniquity;
Wasting and destruction *are*
in their paths.

8 The way of peace they have
not known,
And *there is* no justice in their
ways;
They have made themselves
crooked paths;
Whoever takes that way shall
not know peace.

9 Therefore justice is far from
us,
Nor does righteousness
overtake us;
We look for light, but there is
darkness!
For brightness, *but* we walk in
blackness!

10 We grope for the wall like the
blind,
And we grope as if *we had* no
eyes;
We stumble at noonday as at
twilight;
We are as dead *men* in
desolate places.

11 We all growl like bears,
And moan sadly like doves;
We look for justice, but *there
is* none;
For salvation, *but* it is far from
us.

12 For our transgressions are
multiplied before You,
And our sins testify against us;
For our transgressions *are*
with us,
And *as for* our iniquities, we
know them:
13 In transgressing and lying
against the LORD,
And departing from our God,
Speaking oppression and
revolt,
Conceiving and uttering from
the heart words of
falsehood.
14 Justice is turned back,
And righteousness stands afar
off,
For truth is fallen in the street,
And equity cannot enter.
15 So truth fails,
And he *who* departs from evil
makes himself a prey.

Then the LORD saw *it,* and it
displeased Him
That *there was* no justice.
16 He saw that *there was* no man,
And wondered that *there was*
no intercessor;
Therefore His own arm
brought salvation for Him;
And His own righteousness, it
sustained Him.
17 For He put on righteousness
as a breastplate,
And a helmet of salvation on
His head;
He put on the garments of
vengeance for clothing,
And was clad with zeal as a
cloak.
18 According to *their* deeds,
accordingly He will repay,
Fury to His adversaries,
Recompense to His enemies;
The coastlands He will fully
repay.
19 So shall they fear

The name of the LORD from
the west,
And His glory from the rising
of the sun;
When the enemy comes in
like a flood,
The Spirit of the LORD will lift
up a standard against him.

20 "The Redeemer will come to
Zion,
And to those who turn from
transgression in Jacob,"
Says the LORD.

21"As for Me," says the LORD, "this *is*
My covenant with them: My Spirit who
is upon you, and My words which I
have put in your mouth, shall not depart from your mouth, nor from the
mouth of your descendants, nor from
the mouth of your descendants'
descendants," says the LORD, "from
this time and forevermore."

PHILIPPIANS 1:1-26

PAUL and Timothy, bondservants
of Jesus Christ,

To all the saints in Christ Jesus who
are in Philippi, with the bishops* and
deacons:

2Grace to you and peace from God
our Father and the Lord Jesus Christ.

3I thank my God upon every remembrance of you, 4always in every
prayer of mine making request for you
all with joy, 5for your fellowship in the
gospel from the first day until now, 6be-
ing confident of this very thing, that
He who has begun a good work in you
will complete *it* until the day of Jesus
Christ; 7just as it is right for me to think
this of you all, because I have you in
my heart, inasmuch as both in my
chains and in the defense and confirmation of the gospel, you all are par-

takers with me of grace. 8For God is my witness, how greatly I long for you all with the affection of Jesus Christ.

9And this I pray, that your love may abound still more and more in knowledge and all discernment, 10that you may approve the things that are excellent, that you may be sincere and without offense till the day of Christ, 11being filled with the fruits of righteousness which *are* by Jesus Christ, to the glory and praise of God.

12But I want you to know, brethren, that the things *which happened* to me have actually turned out for the furtherance of the gospel, 13so that it has become evident to the whole palace guard, and to all the rest, that my chains are in Christ; 14and most of the brethren in the Lord, having become confident by my chains, are much more bold to speak the word without fear.

15Some indeed preach Christ even from envy and strife, and some also from goodwill: 16The former* preach Christ from selfish ambition, not sincerely, supposing to add affliction to my chains; 17but the latter out of love, knowing that I am appointed for the defense of the gospel. 18What then? Only *that* in every way, whether in pretense or in truth, Christ is preached; and in this I rejoice, yes, and will rejoice.

19For I know that this will turn out for my deliverance through your prayer and the supply of the Spirit of Jesus Christ, 20according to my earnest expectation and hope that in nothing I shall be ashamed, but with all boldness, as always, so now also Christ will be magnified in my body, whether by life or by death. 21For to me, to live *is* Christ, and to die *is* gain. 22But if *I* live on in the flesh, this *will mean* fruit from *my* labor; yet what I shall choose I cannot tell. 23For* I am hard-pressed between the two, having a desire to depart and be with Christ, *which is* far

better. 24Nevertheless to remain in the flesh *is* more needful for you. 25And being confident of this, I know that I shall remain and continue with you all for your progress and joy of faith, 26that your rejoicing for me may be more abundant in Jesus Christ by my coming to you again.

PSALM 71:1-24

I N You, O LORD, I put my trust;
Let me never be put to shame.
2Deliver me in Your
righteousness, and cause
me to escape;
Incline Your ear to me, and
save me.

3 Be my strong refuge,
To which I may resort
continually;
You have given the
commandment to save me,
For You *are* my rock and my
fortress.

4 Deliver me, O my God, out of
the hand of the wicked,
Out of the hand of the
unrighteous and cruel man.

5 For You are my hope, O Lord
GOD;
You are my trust from my
youth.

6 By You I have been upheld
from birth;
You are He who took me out
of my mother's womb.
My praise *shall be* continually
of You.

7 I have become as a wonder to
many,
But You *are* my strong refuge.

8 Let my mouth be filled *with*
Your praise
And with Your glory all the
day.

9 Do not cast me off in the time
of old age;
Do not forsake me when my
strength fails.
10 For my enemies speak
against me;
And those who lie in wait for
my life take counsel
together,
11 Saying, "God has forsaken
him;
Pursue and take him, for *there
is* none to deliver *him.*"

12 O God, do not be far from me;
O my God, make haste to
help me!
13 Let them be confounded *and*
consumed
Who are adversaries of my
life;
Let them be covered *with*
reproach and dishonor
Who seek my hurt.

14 But I will hope continually,
And will praise You yet more
and more.
15 My mouth shall tell of Your
righteousness
And Your salvation all the day,
For I do not know *their* limits.
16 I will go in the strength of the
Lord God;
I will make mention of Your
righteousness, of Yours
only.

17 O God, You have taught me
from my youth;
And to this *day* I declare Your
wondrous works.

18 Now also when *I am* old and
grayheaded,
O God, do not forsake me,
Until I declare Your strength
to *this* generation,
Your power to everyone *who*
is to come.

19 Also Your righteousness,
O God, *is* very high,
You who have done great
things;
O God, who *is* like You?
20 *You,* who have shown me
great and severe troubles,
Shall revive me again,
And bring me up again from
the depths of the earth.
21 You shall increase my
greatness,
And comfort me on every
side.

22 Also with the lute I will praise
You—
And Your faithfulness, O my
God!
To You I will sing with the
harp,
O Holy One of Israel.
23 My lips shall greatly rejoice
when I sing to You,
And my soul, which You have
redeemed.
24 My tongue also shall talk of
Your righteousness all the
day long;
For they are confounded,
For they are brought to shame
Who seek my hurt.

PROVERBS FOR TODAY/ 24:9-10

*The devising of foolishness is sin, and the scoffer is an abomination to men. If you
faint in the day of adversity, your strength is small.*

SEPTEMBER 30

ISAIAH 60:1–62:5

ARISE, shine;
For your light has come!
And the glory of the LORD is
risen upon you.
2   For behold, the darkness
shall cover the earth,
And deep darkness the people;
But the LORD will arise over
you,
And His glory will be seen
upon you.
3   The Gentiles shall come to
your light,
And kings to the brightness of
your rising.

4   "Lift up your eyes all around,
and see:
They all gather together, they
come to you;
Your sons shall come from
afar,
And your daughters shall be
nursed at *your* side.
5   Then you shall see and
become radiant,
And your heart shall swell
with joy;
Because the abundance of the
sea shall be turned to you,
The wealth of the Gentiles
shall come to you.
6   The multitude of camels shall
cover your *land,*
The dromedaries of Midian
and Ephah;
All those from Sheba shall
come;
They shall bring gold and
incense,
And they shall proclaim the
praises of the LORD.
7   All the flocks of Kedar shall
be gathered together to you,

The rams of Nebaioth shall
minister to you;
They shall ascend with
acceptance on My altar,
And I will glorify the house of
My glory.

8   "Who *are* these *who* fly like a
cloud,
And like doves to their roosts?
9   Surely the coastlands shall
wait for Me;
And the ships of Tarshish *will
come* first,
To bring your sons from afar,
Their silver and their gold
with them,
To the name of the LORD your
God,
And to the Holy One of Israel,
Because He has glorified you.

10   "The sons of foreigners shall
build up your walls,
And their kings shall minister
to you;
For in My wrath I struck you,
But in My favor I have had
mercy on you.
11   Therefore your gates shall be
open continually;
They shall not be shut day or
night,
That *men* may bring to you
the wealth of the Gentiles,
And their kings in procession.
12   For the nation and kingdom
which will not serve you
shall perish,
And *those* nations shall be
utterly ruined.

13   "The glory of Lebanon shall
come to you,

The cypress, the pine, and the
    box tree together,
To beautify the place of My
    sanctuary;
And I will make the place of
    My feet glorious.
14   Also the sons of those who
    afflicted you
Shall come bowing to you,
And all those who despised
    you shall fall prostrate at
    the soles of your feet;
And they shall call you The
    City of the LORD,
Zion of the Holy One of Israel.

15   "Whereas you have been
    forsaken and hated,
So that no one went through
    you,
I will make you an eternal
    excellence,
A joy of many generations.
16   You shall drink the milk of the
    Gentiles,
And milk the breast of kings;
You shall know that I, the
    LORD, *am* your Savior
And your Redeemer, the
    Mighty One of Jacob.

17   "Instead of bronze I will bring
    gold,
Instead of iron I will bring
    silver,
Instead of wood, bronze,
And instead of stones, iron.
I will also make your officers
    peace,
And your magistrates
    righteousness.
18   Violence shall no longer be
    heard in your land,
Neither wasting nor
    destruction within your
    borders;
But you shall call your walls
    Salvation,
And your gates Praise.

19   "The sun shall no longer be
    your light by day,
Nor for brightness shall the
    moon give light to you;
But the LORD will be to you an
    everlasting light,
And your God your glory.
20   Your sun shall no longer go
    down,
Nor shall your moon
    withdraw itself;
For the LORD will be your
    everlasting light,
And the days of your
    mourning shall be ended.
21   Also your people *shall* all *be*
    righteous;
They shall inherit the land
    forever,
The branch of My planting,
The work of My hands,
That I may be glorified.
22   A little one shall become a
    thousand,
And a small one a strong
    nation.
I, the LORD, will hasten it in its
    time.

"THE Spirit of the Lord GOD *is* upon Me,
    Because the LORD has
    anointed Me
To preach good tidings to the
    poor;
He has sent Me to heal the
    brokenhearted,
To proclaim liberty to the
    captives,
And the opening of the prison
    to *those who are* bound;
2   To proclaim the acceptable
    year of the LORD,
And the day of vengeance of
    our God;
To comfort all who mourn,
3   To console those who mourn
    in Zion,
To give them beauty for ashes,
The oil of joy for mourning,

The garment of praise for the spirit of heaviness;
That they may be called trees of righteousness,
The planting of the LORD, that He may be glorified."

4 And they shall rebuild the old ruins,
They shall raise up the former desolations,
And they shall repair the ruined cities,
The desolations of many generations.

5 Strangers shall stand and feed your flocks,
And the sons of the foreigner *Shall be* your plowmen and your vinedressers.

6 But you shall be named the priests of the LORD,
They shall call you the servants of our God.
You shall eat the riches of the Gentiles,
And in their glory you shall boast.

7 Instead of your shame *you shall have* double *honor,*
And *instead of* confusion they shall rejoice in their portion.
Therefore in their land they shall possess double;
Everlasting joy shall be theirs.

8 "For I, the LORD, love justice;
I hate robbery for burnt offering;
I will direct their work in truth,
And will make with them an everlasting covenant.

9 Their descendants shall be known among the Gentiles,
And their offspring among the people.
All who see them shall acknowledge them,
That they *are* the posterity *whom* the LORD has blessed."

10 I will greatly rejoice in the LORD,
My soul shall be joyful in my God;
For He has clothed me with the garments of salvation,
He has covered me with the robe of righteousness,
As a bridegroom decks *himself* with ornaments,
And as a bride adorns *herself* with her jewels.

11 For as the earth brings forth its bud,
As the garden causes the things that are sown in it to spring forth,
So the Lord GOD will cause righteousness and praise to spring forth before all the nations.

FOR Zion's sake I will not hold My peace,
And for Jerusalem's sake I will not rest,
Until her righteousness goes forth as brightness,
And her salvation as a lamp *that* burns.

2 The Gentiles shall see your righteousness,
And all kings your glory.
You shall be called by a new name,
Which the mouth of the LORD will name.

3 You shall also be a crown of glory
In the hand of the LORD,
And a royal diadem
In the hand of your God.

4 You shall no longer be termed Forsaken,
Nor shall your land any more be termed Desolate;
But you shall be called

Hephzibah,* and your land
Beulah;*
For the LORD delights in you,
And your land shall be
married.
5 For *as* a young man marries a
virgin,
So shall your sons marry you;
And *as* the bridegroom
rejoices over the bride,
So shall your God rejoice over
you.

PHILIPPIANS 1:27–2:18

O NLY let your conduct be worthy
of the gospel of Christ, so that
whether I come and see you or
am absent, I may hear of your affairs,
that you stand fast in one spirit, with
one mind striving together for the faith
of the gospel, 28and not in any way terrified by your adversaries, which is to
them a proof of perdition, but to you of
salvation,* and that from God. 29For to
you it has been granted on behalf of
Christ, not only to believe in Him, but
also to suffer for His sake, 30having the
same conflict which you saw in me and
now hear *is* in me.

THEREFORE if *there is* any consolation in
Christ, if any comfort of love, if any
fellowship of the Spirit, if any affection
and mercy, 2fulfill my joy by being like-
minded, having the same love, *being* of
one accord, of one mind. 3*Let* nothing
be done through selfish ambition or
conceit, but in lowliness of mind let
each esteem others better than himself. 4Let each of you look out not only
for his own interests, but also for the
interests of others.

5Let this mind be in you which was
also in Christ Jesus, 6who, being in the
form of God, did not consider it robbery to be equal with God, 7but made
Himself of no reputation, taking the
form of a bondservant, *and* coming in
the likeness of men. 8And being found
in appearance as a man, He humbled
Himself and became obedient to *the
point of* death, even the death of the
cross. 9Therefore God also has highly
exalted Him and given Him the name
which is above every name, 10that at
the name of Jesus every knee should
bow, of those in heaven, and of those
on earth, and of those under the earth,
11and *that* every tongue should confess that Jesus Christ *is* Lord, to the
glory of God the Father.

12Therefore, my beloved, as you
have always obeyed, not as in my presence only, but now much more in my
absence, work out your own salvation
with fear and trembling; 13for it is God
who works in you both to will and to do
for *His* good pleasure.

14Do all things without complaining
and disputing, 15that you may become
blameless and harmless, children of
God without fault in the midst of a
crooked and perverse generation,
among whom you shine as lights in the
world, 16holding fast the word of life, so
that I may rejoice in the day of Christ
that I have not run in vain or labored in
vain.

17Yes, and if I am being poured out *as
a drink offering* on the sacrifice and service of your faith, I am glad and rejoice
with you all. 18For the same reason you
also be glad and rejoice with me.

PSALM 72:1–20

A Psalm of Solomon.

G IVE the king Your judgments,
O God,
And Your righteousness to
the king's Son.
2 He will judge Your people
with righteousness,
And Your poor with justice.
3 The mountains will bring
peace to the people,
And the little hills, by
righteousness.

4 He will bring justice to the
poor of the people;
He will save the children of
the needy,
And will break in pieces the
oppressor.

5 They shall fear You*
As long as the sun and moon
endure,
Throughout all generations.

6 He shall come down like rain
upon the grass before
mowing,
Like showers *that* water the
earth.

7 In His days the righteous
shall flourish,
And abundance of peace,
Until the moon is no more.

8 He shall have dominion also
from sea to sea,
And from the River to the
ends of the earth.

9 Those who dwell in the
wilderness will bow before
Him,
And His enemies will lick the
dust.

10 The kings of Tarshish and of
the isles
Will bring presents;
The kings of Sheba and Seba
Will offer gifts.

11 Yes, all kings shall fall down
before Him;
All nations shall serve Him.

12 For He will deliver the needy
when he cries,
The poor also, and *him* who
has no helper.

13 He will spare the poor and
needy,

And will save the souls of the
needy.

14 He will redeem their life from
oppression and violence;
And precious shall be their
blood in His sight.

15 And He shall live;
And the gold of Sheba will be
given to Him;
Prayer also will be made for
Him continually,
And daily He shall be praised.

16 There will be an abundance of
grain in the earth,
On the top of the mountains;
Its fruit shall wave like
Lebanon;
And *those* of the city shall
flourish like grass of the
earth.

17 His name shall endure forever;
His name shall continue as
long as the sun.
And *men* shall be blessed in
Him;
All nations shall call Him
blessed.

18 Blessed *be* the LORD God, the
God of Israel,
Who only does wondrous
things!

19 And blessed *be* His glorious
name forever!
And let the whole earth be
filled *with* His glory.
Amen and Amen.

20 The prayers of David the son
of Jesse are ended.

PROVERBS FOR TODAY/ 24:11-12

Deliver those who *are drawn toward death, and hold back* those *stumbling to the slaughter. If you say, "Surely we did not know this," does not He who weighs the hearts consider* it? *He who keeps your soul, does He* not *know* it? *And will He* not *render to* each *man according to his deeds?*

OCTOBER 1

ISAIAH 62:6–65:25

I HAVE set watchmen on your walls,
O Jerusalem;
They shall never hold their peace
day or night.
You who make mention of the
LORD, do not keep silent,
7 And give Him no rest till He
establishes
And till He makes Jerusalem
a praise in the earth.

8 The LORD has sworn by His
right hand
And by the arm of His
strength:
"Surely I will no longer give
your grain
As food for your enemies;
And the sons of the foreigner
shall not drink your new
wine,
For which you have labored.
9 But those who have gathered
it shall eat it,
And praise the LORD;
Those who have brought it
together shall drink it in
My holy courts."

10 Go through,
Go through the gates!
Prepare the way for the
people;
Build up,
Build up the highway!
Take out the stones,
Lift up a banner for the
peoples!

11 Indeed the LORD has
proclaimed
To the end of the world:
"Say to the daughter of Zion,
'Surely your salvation is
coming;
Behold, His reward *is* with
Him,
And His work before Him' "
12 And they shall call them The
Holy People,
The Redeemed of the LORD;
And you shall be called
Sought Out,
A City Not Forsaken.

WHO *is* this who comes from Edom,
With dyed garments from
Bozrah,
This *One who is* glorious in
His apparel,
Traveling in the greatness of
His strength?—

"I who speak in righteousness,
mighty to save."

2 Why *is* Your apparel red,
And Your garments like one
who treads in the
winepress?

3 "I have trodden the winepress
alone,
And from the peoples no one
was with Me.
For I have trodden them in
My anger,

And trampled them in My
fury;
Their blood is sprinkled upon
My garments,
And I have stained all My
robes.
4   For the day of vengeance *is* in
My heart,
And the year of My redeemed
has come.
5   I looked, but *there was* no one
to help,
And I wondered
That *there was* no one to
uphold;
Therefore My own arm
brought salvation for Me;
And My own fury, it sustained
Me.
6   I have trodden down the
peoples in My anger,
Made them drunk in My fury,
And brought down their
strength to the earth."

7   I will mention the
lovingkindnesses of the
LORD
And the praises of the LORD,
According to all that the LORD
has bestowed on us,
And the great goodness
toward the house of Israel,
Which He has bestowed on
them according to His
mercies,
According to the multitude of
His lovingkindnesses.
8   For He said, "Surely they *are*
My people,
Children *who* will not lie."
So He became their Savior.
9   In all their affliction He was
afflicted,
And the Angel of His
Presence saved them;
In His love and in His pity He
redeemed them;
And He bore them and
carried them

10   All the days of old.
But they rebelled and grieved
His Holy Spirit;
So He turned Himself against
them as an enemy,
And He fought against them.

11   Then he remembered the
days of old,
Moses *and* his people, *saying:*
"Where *is* He who brought
them up out of the sea
With the shepherd of His
flock?
Where *is* He who put His
Holy Spirit within them,
12   Who led *them* by the right
hand of Moses,
With His glorious arm,
Dividing the water before
them
To make for Himself an
everlasting name,
13   Who led them through the
deep,
As a horse in the wilderness,
That they might not stumble?"

14   As a beast goes down into the
valley,
And the Spirit of the LORD
causes him to rest,
So You lead Your people,
To make Yourself a glorious
name.

15   Look down from heaven,
And see from Your habitation,
holy and glorious.
Where *are* Your zeal and Your
strength,
The yearning of Your heart
and Your mercies toward
me?
Are they restrained?
16   Doubtless You *are* our Father,
Though Abraham was
ignorant of us,
And Israel does not
acknowledge us.

You, O Lord, *are* our Father;
Our Redeemer from
    Everlasting *is* Your name.
17 O Lord, why have You made
    us stray from Your ways,
    And hardened our heart from
        Your fear?
    Return for Your servants'
        sake,
    The tribes of Your inheritance.
18 Your holy people have
    possessed *it* but a little
        while;
    Our adversaries have trodden
        down Your sanctuary.
19 We have become *like* those of
    old, over whom You never
        ruled,
    Those who were never called
        by Your name.

Oh, that You would rend the heavens!
    That You would come down!
    That the mountains might
        shake at Your presence—
2   As fire burns brushwood,
    As fire causes water to boil—
    To make Your name known to
        Your adversaries,
    That the nations may tremble
        at Your presence!
3   When You did awesome
        things *for which* we did not
        look,
    You came down,
    The mountains shook at Your
        presence.
4   For since the beginning of the
        world
    Men have not heard nor
        perceived by the ear,
    Nor has the eye seen any God
        besides You,
    Who acts for the one who
        waits for Him.
5   You meet him who rejoices
        and does righteousness,
    Who remembers You in Your
        ways.

You are indeed angry, for we
    have sinned—
    In these ways we continue;
    And we need to be saved.

6   But we are all like an unclean
        thing,
    And all our righteousnesses
        are like filthy rags;
    We all fade as a leaf,
    And our iniquities, like the
        wind,
    Have taken us away.
7   And *there is* no one who calls
        on Your name,
    Who stirs himself up to take
        hold of You;
    For You have hidden Your
        face from us,
    And have consumed us
        because of our iniquities.

8   But now, O Lord,
    You *are* our Father;
    We *are* the clay, and You our
        potter;
    And all we *are* the work of
        Your hand.
9   Do not be furious, O Lord,
    Nor remember iniquity
        forever;
    Indeed, please look—we all
        are Your people!
10 Your holy cities are a
        wilderness,
    Zion is a wilderness,
    Jerusalem a desolation.
11 Our holy and beautiful temple,
    Where our fathers praised
        You,
    Is burned up with fire;
    And all our pleasant things
        are laid waste.
12 Will You restrain Yourself
        because of these *things,*
        O Lord?
    Will You hold Your peace, and
        afflict us very severely?

"I WAS sought by *those who* did not ask
   for Me;
   I was found by *those who* did
      not seek Me.
   I said, 'Here I am, here I am,'
   To a nation *that* was not called
      by My name.
2   I have stretched out My
      hands all day long to a
      rebellious people,
   Who walk in a way *that is* not
      good,
   According to their own
      thoughts;
3   A people who provoke Me to
      anger continually to My
      face;
   Who sacrifice in gardens,
   And burn incense on altars of
      brick;
4   Who sit among the graves,
   And spend the night in the
      tombs;
   Who eat swine's flesh,
   And the broth of abominable
      things is *in* their vessels;
5   Who say, 'Keep to yourself,
   Do not come near me,
   For I am holier than you!'
   These *are* smoke in My
      nostrils,
   A fire that burns all the day.

6   "Behold, *it is* written before
      Me:
   I will not keep silence, but will
      repay—
   Even repay into their bosom—
7   Your iniquities and the
      iniquities of your fathers
      together,"
   Says the LORD,
   "Who have burned incense on
      the mountains
   And blasphemed Me on the
      hills;
   Therefore I will measure their
      former work into their
      bosom."

8Thus says the LORD:

   "As the new wine is found in
      the cluster,
   And *one* says, 'Do not destroy
      it,
   For a blessing *is* in it,'
   So will I do for My servants'
      sake,
   That I may not destroy them
      all.
9   I will bring forth descendants
      from Jacob,
   And from Judah an heir of My
      mountains;
   My elect shall inherit it,
   And My servants shall dwell
      there.
10   Sharon shall be a fold of
      flocks,
   And the Valley of Achor a
      place for herds to lie down,
   For My people who have
      sought Me.

11   "But you *are* those who
      forsake the LORD,
   Who forget My holy
      mountain,
   Who prepare a table for Gad,*
   And who furnish a drink
      offering for Meni.*
12   Therefore I will number you
      for the sword,
   And you shall all bow down to
      the slaughter;
   Because, when I called, you
      did not answer;
   When I spoke, you did not
      hear,
   But did evil before My eyes,
   And chose *that* in which I do
      not delight."

13Therefore thus says the Lord GOD:

   "Behold, My servants shall eat,
   But you shall be hungry;
   Behold, My servants shall
      drink,

But you shall be thirsty;
Behold, My servants shall
    rejoice,
But you shall be ashamed;
14 Behold, My servants shall
    sing for joy of heart,
But you shall cry for sorrow
    of heart,
And wail for grief of spirit.
15 You shall leave your name as
    a curse to My chosen;
For the Lord God will slay you,
And call His servants by
    another name;
16 So that he who blesses
    himself in the earth
Shall bless himself in the God
    of truth;
And he who swears in the
    earth
Shall swear by the God of
    truth;
Because the former troubles
    are forgotten,
And because they are hidden
    from My eyes.

17 "For behold, I create new
    heavens and a new earth;
And the former shall not be
    remembered or come to
    mind.
18 But be glad and rejoice
    forever in what I create;
For behold, I create
    Jerusalem *as* a rejoicing,
And her people a joy.
19 I will rejoice in Jerusalem,
And joy in My people;
The voice of weeping shall no
    longer be heard in her,
Nor the voice of crying.

20 "No more shall an infant from
    there *live but a few* days,
Nor an old man who has not
    fulfilled his days;
For the child shall die one
    hundred years old,
But the sinner *being* one

hundred years old shall be
    accursed.
21 They shall build houses and
    inhabit *them;*
They shall plant vineyards
    and eat their fruit.
22 They shall not build and
    another inhabit;
They shall not plant and
    another eat;
For as the days of a tree, *so*
    shall be the days of My
    people,
And My elect shall long enjoy
    the work of their hands.
23 They shall not labor in vain,
Nor bring forth children for
    trouble;
For they *shall be* the
    descendants of the blessed
    of the Lord,
And their offspring with them.

24 "It shall come to pass
That before they call, I will
    answer;
And while they are still
    speaking, I will hear.
25 The wolf and the lamb shall
    feed together,
The lion shall eat straw like
    the ox,
And dust *shall be* the serpent's
    food.
They shall not hurt nor
    destroy in all My holy
    mountain,"
Says the Lord.

PHILIPPIANS 2:19–3:4a

BUT I [Paul] trust in the Lord Jesus to send Timothy to you shortly, that I also may be encouraged when I know your state. 20For I have no one like-minded, who will sincerely care for your state. 21For all seek their own, not the things which are of Christ Jesus. 22But you know his proven character, that as a son with *his* father he served with me in the gospel. ²³Therefore I hope to send him at once, as soon as I see how it goes with me. ²⁴But I trust in the Lord that I myself shall also come shortly.

²⁵Yet I considered it necessary to send to you Epaphroditus, my brother, fellow worker, and fellow soldier, but your messenger and the one who ministered to my need; ²⁶since he was longing for you all, and was distressed because you had heard that he was sick. ²⁷For indeed he was sick almost unto death; but God had mercy on him, and not only on him but on me also, lest I should have sorrow upon sorrow. ²⁸Therefore I sent him the more eagerly, that when you see him again you may rejoice, and I may be less sorrowful. ²⁹Receive him therefore in the Lord with all gladness, and hold such men in esteem; ³⁰because for the work of Christ he came close to death, not regarding his life, to supply what was lacking in your service toward me.

FINALLY, my brethren, rejoice in the Lord. For me to write the same things to you *is* not tedious, but for you *it is* safe.

²Beware of dogs, beware of evil workers, beware of the mutilation! ³For we are the circumcision, who worship God in the Spirit,* rejoice in Christ Jesus, and have no confidence in the flesh, ⁴though I also might have confidence in the flesh.

PSALM 73:1-28

A Psalm of Asaph.

TRULY God *is* good to Israel,
To such as are pure in heart.
²But as for me, my feet had almost stumbled;
My steps had nearly slipped.
3   For I *was* envious of the boastful,

When I saw the prosperity of the wicked.

4   For *there are* no pangs in their death,
But their strength *is* firm.
5   They *are* not in trouble *as other* men,
Nor are they plagued like *other* men.
6   Therefore pride serves as their necklace;
Violence covers them *like* a garment.
7   Their eyes bulge* with abundance;
They have more than heart could wish.
8   They scoff and speak wickedly *concerning* oppression;
They speak loftily.
9   They set their mouth against the heavens,
And their tongue walks through the earth.

10   Therefore his people return here,
And waters of a full *cup* are drained by them.
11   And they say, "How does God know?
And is there knowledge in the Most High?"
12   Behold, these *are* the ungodly,
Who are always at ease;
They increase *in* riches.
13   Surely I have cleansed my heart *in* vain,
And washed my hands in innocence.
14   For all day long I have been plagued,
And chastened every morning.

15   If I had said, "I will speak thus,"
Behold, I would have been

untrue to the generation of
Your children.
16 When I thought *how* to
understand this,
It *was* too painful for me—
17 Until I went into the
sanctuary of God;
Then I understood their end.

18 Surely You set them in
slippery places;
You cast them down to
destruction.
19 Oh, how they are *brought* to
desolation, as in a moment!
They are utterly consumed
with terrors.
20 As a dream when *one* awakes,
So, Lord, when You awake,
You shall despise their image.

21 Thus my heart was grieved,
And I was vexed in my mind.
22 I *was* so foolish and ignorant;
I was *like* a beast before You.
23 Nevertheless I *am* continually
with You;

24 You hold *me* by my right hand.
You will guide me with Your
counsel,
And afterward receive me *to*
glory.

25 Whom have I in heaven *but*
You?
And *there is* none upon earth
that I desire besides You.
26 My flesh and my heart fail;
But God *is* the strength of my
heart and my portion
forever.

27 For indeed, those who are far
from You shall perish;
You have destroyed all those
who desert You for harlotry.
28 But *it is* good for me to draw
near to God;
I have put my trust in the
Lord GOD,
That I may declare all Your
works.

PROVERBS FOR TODAY/ 24:13-14

My son, eat honey because it is *good, and the honeycomb* which is *sweet to your
taste; so* shall *the knowledge of wisdom* be *to your soul; if you have found* it, *there
is a prospect, and your hope will not be cut off.*

OCTOBER 2

ISAIAH 66:1-24

THUS says the LORD:

"Heaven *is* My throne,
And earth *is* My footstool.
Where *is* the house that you
will build Me?
And where *is* the place of My
rest?

2 For all those *things* My hand
has made,
And all those *things* exist,"
Says the LORD.
"But on this *one* will I look:
On *him who is* poor and of a
contrite spirit,
And who trembles at My
word.

3 "He who kills a bull *is as if* he
slays a man;
He who sacrifices a lamb, *as if*
he breaks a dog's neck;
He who offers a grain
offering, *as if he offers*
swine's blood;
He who burns incense, *as if*
he blesses an idol.
Just as they have chosen their
own ways,
And their soul delights in
their abominations,

4 So will I choose their
delusions,
And bring their fears on them;
Because, when I called, no
one answered,
When I spoke they did not
hear;
But they did evil before My
eyes,
And chose *that* in which I do
not delight."

5 Hear the word of the LORD,
You who tremble at His word:
"Your brethren who hated you,
Who cast you out for My
name's sake, said,
'Let the LORD be glorified,
That we may see your joy.'
But they shall be ashamed."

6 The sound of noise from the
city!
A voice from the temple!
The voice of the LORD,
Who fully repays His enemies!

7 "Before she was in labor, she
gave birth;
Before her pain came,
She delivered a male child.

8 Who has heard such a thing?
Who has seen such things?
Shall the earth be made to
give birth in one day?
Or shall a nation be born at
once?

For as soon as Zion was in
labor,
She gave birth to her children.

9 Shall I bring to the time of
birth, and not cause
delivery?" says the LORD.
"Shall I who cause delivery
shut up *the womb?*" says
your God.

10 "Rejoice with Jerusalem,
And be glad with her, all you
who love her;
Rejoice for joy with her, all
you who mourn for her;

11 That you may feed and be
satisfied
With the consolation of her
bosom,
That you may drink deeply
and be delighted
With the abundance of her
glory."

12 For thus says the LORD:

"Behold, I will extend peace to
her like a river,
And the glory of the Gentiles
like a flowing stream.
Then you shall feed;
On *her* sides shall you be
carried,
And be dandled on *her* knees.

13 As one whom his mother
comforts,
So I will comfort you;
And you shall be comforted in
Jerusalem."

14 When you see *this,* your heart
shall rejoice,
And your bones shall flourish
like grass;
The hand of the LORD shall be
known to His servants,
And *His* indignation to His
enemies.

15 For behold, the LORD will
come with fire

And with His chariots, like a
whirlwind,
To render His anger with fury,
And His rebuke with flames of
fire.
16 For by fire and by His sword
The LORD will judge all flesh;
And the slain of the LORD shall
be many.

17 "Those who sanctify
themselves and purify
themselves,
To go to the gardens
After an *idol* in the midst,
Eating swine's flesh and the
abomination and the mouse,
Shall be consumed together,"
says the LORD.

18"For I *know* their works and their
thoughts. It shall be that I will gather
all nations and tongues; and they shall
come and see My glory. 19I will set a
sign among them; and those among
them who escape I will send to the nations: *to* Tarshish and Pul* and Lud,
who draw the bow, and Tubal and
Javan, *to* the coastlands afar off who
have not heard My fame nor seen My
glory. And they shall declare My glory
among the Gentiles. 20Then they shall
bring all your brethren for an offering
to the LORD out of all nations, on horses
and in chariots and in litters, on mules
and on camels, to My holy mountain
Jerusalem," says the LORD, "as the children of Israel bring an offering in a
clean vessel into the house of the LORD.
21And I will also take some of them for
priests *and* Levites," says the LORD.

22 "For as the new heavens and
the new earth
Which I will make shall
remain before Me," says
the LORD,
"So shall your descendants and
your name remain.
23 And it shall come to pass

That from one New Moon to
another,
And from one Sabbath to
another,
All flesh shall come to
worship before Me," says
the LORD.

24 "And they shall go forth and
look
Upon the corpses of the men
Who have transgressed
against Me.
For their worm does not die,
And their fire is not quenched.
They shall be an abhorrence
to all flesh."

PHILIPPIANS 3:4b-21

IF anyone else thinks he may have
confidence in the flesh, I [Paul]
more so: 5circumcised the eighth
day, of the stock of Israel, *of* the tribe of
Benjamin, a Hebrew of the Hebrews;
concerning the law, a Pharisee; 6con-
cerning zeal, persecuting the church;
concerning the righteousness which
is in the law, blameless.

7But what things were gain to me,
these I have counted loss for Christ.
8Yet indeed I also count all things loss
for the excellence of the knowledge of
Christ Jesus my Lord, for whom I have
suffered the loss of all things, and
count them as rubbish, that I may gain
Christ 9and be found in Him, not having my own righteousness, which *is*
from the law, but that which *is* through
faith in Christ, the righteousness
which is from God by faith; 10that I may
know Him and the power of His resurrection, and the fellowship of His
sufferings, being conformed to His
death, 11if, by any means, I may attain
to the resurrection from the dead.

12Not that I have already attained, or
am already perfected; but I press on,
that I may lay hold of that for which
Christ Jesus has also laid hold of me.

¹³Brethren, I do not count myself to have apprehended; but one thing *I do,* forgetting those things which are behind and reaching forward to those things which are ahead, ¹⁴I press toward the goal for the prize of the upward call of God in Christ Jesus.

¹⁵Therefore let us, as many as are mature, have this mind; and if in anything you think otherwise, God will reveal even this to you. ¹⁶Nevertheless, to *the degree* that we have already attained, let us walk by the same rule,* let us be of the same mind.

¹⁷Brethren, join in following my example, and note those who so walk, as you have us for a pattern. ¹⁸For many walk, of whom I have told you often, and now tell you even weeping, *that they are* the enemies of the cross of Christ: ¹⁹whose end *is* destruction, whose god *is their* belly, and *whose* glory *is* in their shame—who set their mind on earthly things. ²⁰For our citizenship is in heaven, from which we also eagerly wait for the Savior, the Lord Jesus Christ, ²¹who will transform our lowly body that it may be conformed to His glorious body, according to the working by which He is able even to subdue all things to Himself.

PSALM 74:1-23

A Contemplation of Asaph.*

O GOD, why have You cast *us* off forever?
    Why does Your anger smoke against the sheep of Your pasture?
2   Remember Your congregation, *which* You have purchased of old,
    The tribe of Your inheritance, *which* You have redeemed—
    This Mount Zion where You have dwelt.
3   Lift up Your feet to the perpetual desolations.

    The enemy has damaged everything in the sanctuary.
4   Your enemies roar in the midst of Your meeting place;
    They set up their banners *for* signs.
5   They seem like men who lift up
    Axes among the thick trees.
6   And now they break down its carved work, all at once,
    With axes and hammers.
7   They have set fire to Your sanctuary;
    They have defiled the dwelling place of Your name to the ground.
8   They said in their hearts,
    "Let us destroy them altogether."
    They have burned up all the meeting places of God in the land.

9   We do not see our signs;
    There is no longer any prophet;
    Nor *is there* any among us who knows how long.
10   O God, how long will the adversary reproach?
    Will the enemy blaspheme Your name forever?
11   Why do You withdraw Your hand, even Your right hand?
    Take it out of Your bosom and destroy *them.*
12   For God *is* my King from of old,
    Working salvation in the midst of the earth.
13   You divided the sea by Your strength;
    You broke the heads of the sea serpents in the waters.
14   You broke the heads of Leviathan in pieces,
    And gave him *as* food to the

people inhabiting the
wilderness.

15 You broke open the fountain
and the flood;
You dried up mighty rivers.

16 The day *is* Yours, the night
also *is* Yours;
You have prepared the light
and the sun.

17 You have set all the borders of
the earth;
You have made summer and
winter.

18 Remember this, *that* the
enemy has reproached,
O LORD,
And *that* a foolish people has
blasphemed Your name.

19 Oh, do not deliver the life of
Your turtledove to the wild
beast!

Do not forget the life of Your
poor forever.

20 Have respect to the covenant;
For the dark places of the
earth are full of the haunts
of cruelty.

21 Oh, do not let the oppressed
return ashamed!
Let the poor and needy praise
Your name.

22 Arise, O God, plead Your own
cause;
Remember how the foolish
man reproaches You daily.

23 Do not forget the voice of
Your enemies;
The tumult of those who rise
up against You increases
continually.

PROVERBS FOR TODAY/ 24:15-16

Do not lie in wait, O wicked man, *against the dwelling of the righteous; do not plunder his resting place; for a righteous* man *may fall seven times and rise again, but the wicked shall fall by calamity.*

OCTOBER 3

JEREMIAH 1:1–2:30

THE words of Jeremiah the son of Hilkiah, of the priests who *were* in Anathoth in the land of Benjamin, ²to whom the word of the LORD came in the days of Josiah the son of Amon, king of Judah, in the thirteenth year of his reign. ³It came also in the days of Jehoiakim the son of Josiah, king of Judah, until the end of the eleventh year of Zedekiah the son of Josiah, king of Judah, until the carrying away of Jerusalem captive in the fifth month.

⁴Then the word of the LORD came to me, saying:

5   "Before I formed you in the
womb I knew you;
Before you were born I
sanctified you;
I ordained you a prophet to
the nations."

⁶Then said I:

"Ah, Lord GOD!
Behold, I cannot speak, for I
am a youth."

⁷But the LORD said to me:

"Do not say, 'I *am* a youth,'
For you shall go to all to
whom I send you,
And whatever I command
you, you shall speak.
8 Do not be afraid of their faces,
For I *am* with you to deliver
you," says the LORD.

⁹Then the LORD put forth His hand
and touched my mouth, and the LORD
said to me:

"Behold, I have put My words
in your mouth.
10 See, I have this day set you
over the nations and over
the kingdoms,
To root out and to pull down,
To destroy and to throw down,
To build and to plant."

¹¹Moreover the word of the LORD
came to me, saying, "Jeremiah, what
do you see?"
And I said, "I see a branch of an almond tree."
¹²Then the LORD said to me, "You
have seen well, for I am ready to perform My word."
¹³And the word of the LORD came to
me the second time, saying, "What do
you see?"
And I said, "I see a boiling pot, and it
is facing away from the north."
¹⁴Then the LORD said to me:

"Out of the north calamity
shall break forth
On all the inhabitants of the
land.
15 For behold, I am calling
All the families of the
kingdoms of the north,"
says the LORD;
"They shall come and each one
set his throne

At the entrance of the gates of
Jerusalem,
Against all its walls all around,
And against all the cities of
Judah.
16 I will utter My judgments
Against them concerning all
their wickedness,
Because they have forsaken
Me,
Burned incense to other gods,
And worshiped the works of
their own hands.

17 "Therefore prepare yourself
and arise,
And speak to them all that I
command you.
Do not be dismayed before
their faces,
Lest I dismay you before
them.
18 For behold, I have made you
this day
A fortified city and an iron
pillar,
And bronze walls against the
whole land—
Against the kings of Judah,
Against its princes,
Against its priests,
And against the people of the
land.
19 They will fight against you,
But they shall not prevail
against you.
For I *am* with you," says the
LORD, "to deliver you."

MOREOVER the word of the LORD came to
me, saying, ²"Go and cry in the hearing of Jerusalem, saying, 'Thus says
the LORD:

"I remember you,
The kindness of your youth,
The love of your betrothal,
When you went after Me in
the wilderness,
In a land not sown.

3 Israel *was* holiness to the
Lord,
The firstfruits of His increase.
All that devour him will
offend;
Disaster will come upon
them," says the Lord.' "

4Hear the word of the Lord, O house
of Jacob and all the families of the
house of Israel. 5Thus says the Lord:

"What injustice have your
fathers found in Me,
That they have gone far from
Me,
Have followed idols,
And have become idolaters?

6 Neither did they say, 'Where
is the Lord,
Who brought us up out of the
land of Egypt,
Who led us through the
wilderness,
Through a land of deserts and
pits,
Through a land of drought
and the shadow of death,
Through a land that no one
crossed
And where no one dwelt?'

7 I brought you into a bountiful
country,
To eat its fruit and its
goodness.
But when you entered, you
defiled My land
And made My heritage an
abomination.

8 The priests did not say,
'Where *is* the Lord?'
And those who handle the law
did not know Me;
The rulers also transgressed
against Me;
The prophets prophesied by
Baal,
And walked after *things that*
do not profit.

9 "Therefore I will yet bring
charges against you," says
the Lord,
"And against your children's
children I will bring
charges.

10 For pass beyond the coasts of
Cyprus* and see,
Send to Kedar* and consider
diligently,
And see if there has been
such *a thing*.

11 Has a nation changed *its* gods,
Which *are* not gods?
But My people have changed
their Glory
For *what* does not profit.

12 Be astonished, O heavens, at
this,
And be horribly afraid,
Be very desolate," says the
Lord.

13 "For My people have
committed two evils:
They have forsaken Me, the
fountain of living waters,
And hewn themselves
cisterns—broken cisterns
that can hold no water.

14 "*Is* Israel a servant?
Is he a homeborn *slave?*
Why is he plundered?

15 The young lions roared at
him, *and* growled;
They made his land waste;
His cities are burned, without
inhabitant.

16 Also the people of Noph* and
Tahpanhes
Have broken the crown of
your head.

17 Have you not brought this on
yourself,
In that you have forsaken the
Lord your God
When He led you in the way?

18 And now why take the road to
Egypt,
To drink the waters of Sihor?

Or why take the road to
Assyria,
To drink the waters of the
River?*

19 Your own wickedness will
correct you,
And your backslidings will
rebuke you.
Know therefore and see that
it is an evil and bitter *thing*
That you have forsaken the
LORD your God,
And the fear of Me *is* not in
you,"
Says the Lord GOD of hosts.

20 "For of old I have broken your
yoke *and* burst your bonds;
And you said, 'I will not
transgress,'
When on every high hill and
under every green tree
You lay down, playing the
harlot.

21 Yet I had planted you a noble
vine, a seed of highest
quality.
How then have you turned
before Me
Into the degenerate plant of
an alien vine?

22 For though you wash yourself
with lye, and use much
soap,
Yet your iniquity is marked
before Me," says the Lord
GOD.

23 "How can you say, 'I am not
polluted,
I have not gone after the
Baals'?
See your way in the valley;
Know what you have done:
You are a swift dromedary
breaking loose in her ways,

24 A wild donkey used to the
wilderness,
That sniffs at the wind in her
desire;

In her time of mating, who
can turn her away?
All those who seek her will
not weary themselves;
In her month they will find
her.

25 Withhold your foot from
being unshod, and your
throat from thirst.
But you said, 'There is no
hope.
No! For I have loved aliens,
and after them I will go.'

26 "As the thief is ashamed when
he is found out,
So is the house of Israel
ashamed;
They and their kings and
their princes, and their
priests and their prophets,

27 Saying to a tree, 'You *are* my
father,'
And to a stone, 'You gave
birth to me.'
For they have turned *their*
back to Me, and not *their*
face.
But in the time of their trouble
They will say, 'Arise and save
us.'

28 But where *are* your gods that
you have made for
yourselves?
Let them arise,
If they can save you in the
time of your trouble;
For *according to* the number
of your cities
Are your gods, O Judah.

29 "Why will you plead with Me?
You all have transgressed
against Me," says the LORD.

30 "In vain I have chastened your
children;
They received no correction.
Your sword has devoured
your prophets
Like a destroying lion."

PHILIPPIANS 4:1-23

THEREFORE, my beloved and longed-for brethren, my joy and crown, so stand fast in the Lord, beloved.

²I implore Euodia and I implore Syntyche to be of the same mind in the Lord. ³And* I urge you also, true companion, help these women who labored with me in the gospel, with Clement also, and the rest of my fellow workers, whose names *are* in the Book of Life.

⁴Rejoice in the Lord always. Again I will say, rejoice!

⁵Let your gentleness be known to all men. The Lord *is* at hand.

⁶Be anxious for nothing, but in everything by prayer and supplication, with thanksgiving, let your requests be made known to God; ⁷and the peace of God, which surpasses all understanding, will guard your hearts and minds through Christ Jesus.

⁸Finally, brethren, whatever things are true, whatever things *are* noble, whatever things *are* just, whatever things *are* pure, whatever things *are* lovely, whatever things *are* of good report, if *there is* any virtue and if *there is* anything praiseworthy—meditate on these things. ⁹The things which you learned and received and heard and saw in me, these do, and the God of peace will be with you.

¹⁰But I rejoiced in the Lord greatly that now at last your care for me has flourished again; though you surely did care, but you lacked opportunity. ¹¹Not that I speak in regard to need, for I have learned in whatever state I am, to be content: ¹²I know how to be abased, and I know how to abound. Everywhere and in all things I have learned both to be full and to be hungry, both to abound and to suffer need. ¹³I can do all things through Christ* who strengthens me.

¹⁴Nevertheless you have done well

that you shared in my distress. ¹⁵Now you Philippians know also that in the beginning of the gospel, when I departed from Macedonia, no church shared with me concerning giving and receiving but you only. ¹⁶For even in Thessalonica you sent *aid* once and again for my necessities. ¹⁷Not that I seek the gift, but I seek the fruit that abounds to your account. ¹⁸Indeed I have all and abound. I am full, having received from Epaphroditus the things *sent* from you, a sweet-smelling aroma, an acceptable sacrifice, well pleasing to God. ¹⁹And my God shall supply all your need according to His riches in glory by Christ Jesus. ²⁰Now to our God and Father *be* glory forever and ever. Amen.

²¹Greet every saint in Christ Jesus. The brethren who are with me greet you. ²²All the saints greet you, but especially those who are of Caesar's household.

²³The grace of our Lord Jesus Christ be with you all.* Amen.

PSALM 75:1-10

*To the Chief Musician. Set to "Do Not Destroy."**
A Psalm of Asaph. A Song.

WE give thanks to You, O God, we give thanks!
For Your wondrous works declare *that* Your name is near.

2 "When I choose the proper time,
    I will judge uprightly.
3 The earth and all its
        inhabitants are dissolved;
    I set up its pillars firmly.   Selah

4 "I said to the boastful, 'Do not
        deal boastfully,'
    And to the wicked, 'Do not lift
        up the horn.
5 Do not lift up your horn on
        high;

Do *not* speak with a stiff
neck.' "

6 For exaltation *comes* neither
from the east
Nor from the west nor from
the south.

7 But God *is* the Judge:
He puts down one,
And exalts another.

8 For in the hand of the LORD
there is a cup,
And the wine is red;

It is fully mixed, and He pours
it out;
Surely its dregs shall all the
wicked of the earth
Drain *and* drink down.

9 But I will declare forever,
I will sing praises to the God
of Jacob.

10 "All the horns of the wicked I
will also cut off,
But the horns of the
righteous shall be exalted."

PROVERBS FOR TODAY/ 24:17-20

Do not rejoice when your enemy falls, and do not let your heart be glad when he stumbles; lest the LORD see it, and it displease Him, and He turn away His wrath from him. Do not fret because of evildoers, nor be envious of the wicked; for there will be no prospect for the evil man; the lamp of the wicked will be put out.

OCTOBER 4

JEREMIAH 2:31–4:18

"O GENERATION, see the word
of the LORD!
Have I been a wilderness to
Israel,
Or a land of darkness?
Why do My people say, 'We
are lords;
We will come no more to You'?

32 Can a virgin forget her
ornaments,
Or a bride her attire?
Yet My people have forgotten
Me days without number.

33 "Why do you beautify your
way to seek love?
Therefore you have also
taught
The wicked women your ways.

34 Also on your skirts is found

The blood of the lives of the
poor innocents.
I have not found it by secret
search,
But plainly on all these things.

35 Yet you say, 'Because I am
innocent,
Surely His anger shall turn
from me.'
Behold, I will plead My case
against you,
Because you say, 'I have not
sinned.'

36 Why do you gad about so
much to change your way?
Also you shall be ashamed of
Egypt as you were
ashamed of Assyria.

37 Indeed you will go forth from
him
With your hands on your
head;

For the Lord has rejected
 your trusted allies,
And you will not prosper by
 them.

"They say, 'If a man divorces his wife,
 And she goes from him
 And becomes another man's,
 May he return to her again?'
 Would not that land be greatly
 polluted?
 But you have played the
 harlot with many lovers;
 Yet return to Me," says the
 Lord.

2 "Lift up your eyes to the
 desolate heights and see:
 Where have you not lain *with
 men?*
 By the road you have sat for
 them
 Like an Arabian in the
 wilderness;
 And you have polluted the
 land
 With your harlotries and your
 wickedness.
3 Therefore the showers have
 been withheld,
 And there has been no latter
 rain.
 You have had a harlot's
 forehead;
 You refuse to be ashamed.
4 Will you not from this time
 cry to Me,
 'My Father, You *are* the guide
 of my youth?
5 Will He remain angry forever?
 Will He keep it to the end?'
 Behold, you have spoken and
 done evil things,
 As you were able."

6The Lord said also to me in the days
of Josiah the king: "Have you seen
what backsliding Israel has done? She
has gone up on every high mountain
and under every green tree, and there
played the harlot. 7And I said, after she
had done all these *things,* 'Return to
Me.' But she did not return. And her
treacherous sister Judah saw it. 8Then
I saw that for all the causes for which
backsliding Israel had committed
adultery, I had put her away and given
her a certificate of divorce; yet her
treacherous sister Judah did not fear,
but went and played the harlot also.
9So it came to pass, through her casual
harlotry, that she defiled the land and
committed adultery with stones and
trees. 10And yet for all this her treacherous sister Judah has not turned to
Me with her whole heart, but in pretense," says the Lord.

11Then the Lord said to me, "Backsliding Israel has shown herself more
righteous than treacherous Judah.
12Go and proclaim these words toward
the north, and say:

 'Return, backsliding Israel,'
 says the Lord;
 'I will not cause My anger to
 fall on you.
 For I *am* merciful,' says the
 Lord;
 'I will not remain angry
 forever.
13 Only acknowledge your
 iniquity,
 That you have transgressed
 against the Lord your God,
 And have scattered your
 charms
 To alien deities under every
 green tree,
 And you have not obeyed My
 voice,' says the Lord.

14"Return, O backsliding children,"
says the Lord; "for I am married to you.
I will take you, one from a city and two
from a family, and I will bring you to
Zion. 15And I will give you shepherds
according to My heart, who will feed
you with knowledge and understanding.

¹⁶"Then it shall come to pass, when you are multiplied and increased in the land in those days," says the LORD, "that they will say no more, 'The ark of the covenant of the LORD.' It shall not come to mind, nor shall they remember it, nor shall they visit *it,* nor shall it be made anymore.

¹⁷"At that time Jerusalem shall be called The Throne of the LORD, and all the nations shall be gathered to it, to the name of the LORD, to Jerusalem. No more shall they follow the dictates of their evil hearts.

¹⁸"In those days the house of Judah shall walk with the house of Israel, and they shall come together out of the land of the north to the land that I have given as an inheritance to your fathers.

¹⁹"But I said:

'How can I put you among the
children
And give you a pleasant land,
A beautiful heritage of the
hosts of nations?'

"And I said:

'You shall call Me, "My
Father,"
And not turn away from Me.'
20   Surely, *as* a wife treacherously
departs from her husband,
So have you dealt
treacherously with Me,
O house of Israel," says the
LORD.

21   A voice was heard on the
desolate heights,
Weeping *and* supplications of
the children of Israel.
For they have perverted their
way;
They have forgotten the LORD
their God.

22   "Return, you backsliding
children,

And I will heal your
backslidings."

"Indeed we do come to You,
For You are the LORD our God.
23   Truly, in vain *is salvation
hoped for* from the hills,
And from the multitude of
mountains;
Truly, in the LORD our God
Is the salvation of Israel.
24   For shame has devoured
The labor of our fathers from
our youth—
locks and their herds,
Their sons and their
daughters.
25   We lie down in our shame,
And our reproach covers us.
For we have sinned against
the LORD our God,
We and our fathers,
From our youth even to this
day,
And have not obeyed the
voice of the LORD our God."

"IF you will return, O Israel," says the
LORD,
"Return to Me;
And if you will put away your
abominations out of My
sight,
Then you shall not be moved.
2   And you shall swear, 'The
LORD lives,'
In truth, in judgment, and in
righteousness;
The nations shall bless
themselves in Him,
And in Him they shall glory."

³For thus says the LORD to the men of Judah and Jerusalem:

"Break up your fallow ground,
And do not sow among thorns.
4   Circumcise yourselves to the
LORD,

And take away the foreskins
of your hearts,
You men of Judah and
inhabitants of Jerusalem,
Lest My fury come forth like
fire,
And burn so that no one can
quench *it,*
Because of the evil of your
doings."

5Declare in Judah and proclaim in Jerusalem, and say:

"Blow the trumpet in the land;
Cry, 'Gather together,'
And say, 'Assemble
yourselves,
And let us go into the fortified
cities.'
6 Set up the standard toward
Zion.
Take refuge! Do not delay!
For I will bring disaster from
the north,
And great destruction."

7 The lion has come up from
his thicket,
And the destroyer of nations
is on his way.
He has gone forth from his
place
To make your land desolate.
Your cities will be laid waste,
Without inhabitant.
8 For this, clothe yourself with
sackcloth,
Lament and wail.
For the fierce anger of the
LORD
Has not turned back from us.

9 "And it shall come to pass in
that day," says the LORD,
"*That* the heart of the king
shall perish,
And the heart of the princes;
The priests shall be
astonished,

And the prophets shall
wonder."

10 Then I said, "Ah, Lord GOD!
Surely You have greatly
deceived this people and
Jerusalem,
Saying, 'You shall have peace,'
Whereas the sword reaches
to the heart."

11 At that time it will be said
To this people and to
Jerusalem,
"A dry wind of the desolate
heights *blows* in the
wilderness
Toward the daughter of My
people—
Not to fan or to cleanse—
12 A wind too strong for these
will come for Me;
Now I will also speak
judgment against them."

13 "Behold, he shall come up like
clouds,
And his chariots like a
whirlwind.
His horses are swifter than
eagles.
Woe to us, for we are
plundered!"

14 O Jerusalem, wash your heart
from wickedness,
That you may be saved.
How long shall your evil
thoughts lodge within you?
15 For a voice declares from Dan
And proclaims affliction from
Mount Ephraim:
16 "Make mention to the nations,
Yes, proclaim against
Jerusalem,
That watchers come from a
far country
And raise their voice against
the cities of Judah.

17 Like keepers of a field they
    are against her all around,
  Because she has been
    rebellious against Me,"
    says the LORD.
18 "Your ways and your doings
  Have procured these *things*
    for you.
  This *is* your wickedness,
  Because it is bitter,
  Because it reaches to your
    heart."

COLOSSIANS 1:1-20

PAUL, an apostle of Jesus Christ by the will of God, and Timothy our brother,

2To the saints and faithful brethren in Christ *who are* in Colosse:

Grace to you and peace from God our Father and the Lord Jesus Christ.*

3We give thanks to the God and Father of our Lord Jesus Christ, praying always for you, 4since we heard of your faith in Christ Jesus and of your love for all the saints; 5because of the hope which is laid up for you in heaven, of which you heard before in the word of the truth of the gospel, 6which has come to you, as *it has* also in all the world, and is bringing forth fruit,* as *it is* also among you since the day you heard and knew the grace of God in truth; 7as you also learned from Epaphras, our dear fellow servant, who is a faithful minister of Christ on your behalf, 8who also declared to us your love in the Spirit.

9For this reason we also, since the day we heard it, do not cease to pray for you, and to ask that you may be filled with the knowledge of His will in all wisdom and spiritual understanding; 10that you may walk worthy of the Lord, fully pleasing *Him,* being fruitful in every good work and increasing in

the knowledge of God; 11strengthened with all might, according to His glorious power, for all patience and longsuffering with joy; 12giving thanks to the Father who has qualified us to be partakers of the inheritance of the saints in the light. 13He has delivered us from the power of darkness and conveyed *us* into the kingdom of the Son of His love, 14in whom we have redemption through His blood,* the forgiveness of sins.

15He is the image of the invisible God, the firstborn over all creation. 16For by Him all things were created that are in heaven and that are on earth, visible and invisible, whether thrones or dominions or principalities or powers. All things were created through Him and for Him. 17And He is before all things, and in Him all things consist. 18And He is the head of the body, the church, who is the beginning, the firstborn from the dead, that in all things He may have the preeminence.

19For it pleased *the Father that* in Him all the fullness should dwell, 20and by Him to reconcile all things to Himself, by Him, whether things on earth or things in heaven, having made peace through the blood of His cross.

PSALM 76:1-12

To the Chief Musician. On stringed instruments.
A Psalm of Asaph. A Song.

IN Judah God *is* known;
  His name *is* great in Israel.
2In Salem* also is His tabernacle,
    And His dwelling place in
      Zion.
3 There He broke the arrows of
    the bow,
  The shield and sword of battle.
                              Selah

4 You *are* more glorious and
    excellent
  Than the mountains of prey.

5 The stouthearted were
plundered;
They have sunk into their
sleep;
And none of the mighty men
have found the use of their
hands.
6 At Your rebuke, O God of
Jacob,
Both the chariot and horse
were cast into a dead sleep.

7 You, Yourself, *are* to be feared;
And who may stand in Your
presence
When once You are angry?
8 You caused judgment to be
heard from heaven;
The earth feared and was still,

9 When God arose to judgment,
To deliver all the oppressed of
the earth.   Selah
10 Surely the wrath of man shall
praise You;
With the remainder of wrath
You shall gird Yourself.

11 Make vows to the LORD your
God, and pay *them;*
Let all who are around Him
bring presents to Him who
ought to be feared.
12 He shall cut off the spirit of
princes;
He is awesome to the kings of
the earth.

PROVERBS FOR TODAY/ 24:21-22

My son, fear the LORD and the king; do not associate with those given to change; for their calamity will rise suddenly, and who knows the ruin those two can bring?

OCTOBER 5

JEREMIAH 4:19–6:14

O MY soul, my soul!
I am pained in my very heart!
My heart makes a noise in
me;
I cannot hold my peace,
Because you have heard,
O my soul,
The sound of the trumpet,
The alarm of war.
20 Destruction upon destruction
is cried,
For the whole land is
plundered.
Suddenly my tents are
plundered,
And my curtains in a moment.

21 How long will I see the
standard,
And hear the sound of the
trumpet?

22 "For My people *are* foolish,
They have not known Me.
They *are* silly children,
And they have no
understanding.
They *are* wise to do evil,
But to do good they have no
knowledge."

23 I beheld the earth, and indeed
it was without form, and
void;
And the heavens, they *had* no
light.

24 I beheld the mountains, and
indeed they trembled,
And all the hills moved back
and forth.
25 I beheld, and indeed *there was*
no man,
And all the birds of the
heavens had fled.
26 I beheld, and indeed the
fruitful land *was* a
wilderness,
And all its cities were broken
down
At the presence of the LORD,
By His fierce anger.

27For thus says the LORD:

"The whole land shall be
desolate;
Yet I will not make a full end.
28 For this shall the earth mourn,
And the heavens above be
black,
Because I have spoken.
I have purposed and will not
relent,
Nor will I turn back from it.
29 The whole city shall flee from
the noise of the horsemen
and bowmen.
They shall go into thickets
and climb up on the rocks.
Every city *shall be* forsaken,
And not a man shall dwell in it.

30 "And *when* you *are* plundered,
What will you do?
Though you clothe yourself
with crimson,
Though you adorn *yourself*
with ornaments of gold,
Though you enlarge your
eyes with paint,
In vain you will make yourself
fair;
Your lovers will despise you;
They will seek your life.

31 "For I have heard a voice as of
a woman in labor,
The anguish as of her who
brings forth her first child,
The voice of the daughter of
Zion bewailing herself;
She spreads her hands, *saying,*
'Woe *is* me now, for my soul is
weary
Because of murderers!'

"RUN to and fro through the streets of
Jerusalem;
See now and know;
And seek in her open places
If you can find a man,
If there is *anyone* who
executes judgment,
Who seeks the truth,
And I will pardon her.
2 Though they say, '*As* the LORD
lives,'
Surely they swear falsely."

3 O LORD, *are* not Your eyes on
the truth?
You have stricken them,
But they have not grieved;
You have consumed them,
But they have refused to
receive correction.
They have made their faces
harder than rock;
They have refused to return.

4 Therefore I said, "Surely
these *are* poor.
They are foolish;
For they do not know the way
of the LORD,
The judgment of their God.
5 I will go to the great men and
speak to them,
For they have known the way
of the LORD,
The judgment of their God."

But these have altogether
broken the yoke
And burst the bonds.

6   Therefore a lion from the
       forest shall slay them,
     A wolf of the deserts shall
       destroy them;
     A leopard will watch over
       their cities.
     Everyone who goes out from
       there shall be torn in pieces,
     Because their transgressions
       are many;
     Their backslidings have
       increased.

7   "How shall I pardon you for
       this?
     Your children have forsaken
       Me
     And sworn by *those that are*
       not gods.
     When I had fed them to the
       full,
     Then they committed adultery
     And assembled themselves by
       troops in the harlots'
       houses.
8   They were *like* well-fed lusty
       stallions;
     Every one neighed after his
       neighbor's wife.
9   Shall I not punish *them* for
       these *things?*" says the LORD.
     "And shall I not avenge Myself
       on such a nation as this?

10   "Go up on her walls and
       destroy,
     But do not make a complete
       end.
     Take away her branches,
     For they *are* not the LORD's.
11   For the house of Israel and
       the house of Judah
     Have dealt very treacherously
       with Me," says the LORD.

12   They have lied about the LORD,
     And said, "*It is* not He.
     Neither will evil come upon
       us,
     Nor shall we see sword or
       famine.
13   And the prophets become
       wind,
     For the word *is* not in them.
     Thus shall it be done to them."

14Therefore thus says the LORD God
of hosts:

     "Because you speak this word,
     Behold, I will make My words
       in your mouth fire,
     And this people wood,
     And it shall devour them.
15   Behold, I will bring a nation
       against you from afar,
     O house of Israel," says the
       LORD.
     "It *is* a mighty nation,
     It *is* an ancient nation,
     A nation whose language you
       do not know,
     Nor can you understand what
       they say.
16   Their quiver *is* like an open
       tomb;
     They *are* all mighty men.
17   And they shall eat up your
       harvest and your bread,
     Which your sons and
       daughters should eat.
     They shall eat up your flocks
       and your herds;
     They shall eat up your vines
       and your fig trees;
     They shall destroy your
       fortified cities,
     In which you trust, with the
       sword.

18"Nevertheless in those days," says
the LORD, "I will not make a complete
end of you. 19And it will be when you
say, 'Why does the LORD our God do all
these *things* to us?' then you shall answer them, 'Just as you have forsaken
Me and served foreign gods in your
land, so you shall serve aliens in a land
that is not yours.'

20 "Declare this in the house of
Jacob
And proclaim it in Judah,
saying,
21 'Hear this now, O foolish
people,
Without understanding,
Who have eyes and see not,
And who have ears and hear
not:
22 Do you not fear Me?' says the
LORD.
'Will you not tremble at My
presence,
Who have placed the sand as
the bound of the sea,
By a perpetual decree, that it
cannot pass beyond it?
And though its waves toss to
and fro,
Yet they cannot prevail;
Though they roar, yet they
cannot pass over it.
23 But this people has a defiant
and rebellious heart;
They have revolted and
departed.
24 They do not say in their heart,
"Let us now fear the LORD our
God,
Who gives rain, both the
former and the latter, in its
season.
He reserves for us the
appointed weeks of the
harvest."
25 Your iniquities have turned
these *things* away,
And your sins have withheld
good from you.

26 'For among My people are
found wicked *men;*
They lie in wait as one who
sets snares;
They set a trap;
They catch men.
27 As a cage is full of birds,
So their houses *are* full of
deceit.

Therefore they have become
great and grown rich.
28 They have grown fat, they are
sleek;
Yes, they surpass the deeds of
the wicked;
They do not plead the cause,
The cause of the fatherless;
Yet they prosper,
And the right of the needy
they do not defend.
29 Shall I not punish *them* for
these *things?'* says the LORD.
'Shall I not avenge Myself on
such a nation as this?'

30 "An astonishing and horrible
thing
Has been committed in the
land:
31 The prophets prophesy falsely,
And the priests rule by their
own power;
And My people love *to have it*
so.
But what will you do in the
end?

"O YOU children of Benjamin,
Gather yourselves to flee
from the midst of
Jerusalem!
Blow the trumpet in Tekoa,
And set up a signal-fire in
Beth Haccerem;
For disaster appears out of
the north,
And great destruction.
2 I have likened the daughter of
Zion
To a lovely and delicate
woman.
3 The shepherds with their
flocks shall come to her.
They shall pitch *their* tents
against her all around.
Each one shall pasture in his
own place."
4 "Prepare war against her;

Arise, and let us go up at noon.
Woe to us, for the day goes
    away,
For the shadows of the
    evening are lengthening.
5 Arise, and let us go by night,
And let us destroy her
    palaces."

6For thus has the LORD of hosts said:

"Cut down trees,
    And build a mound against
        Jerusalem.
This *is* the city to be punished.
She *is* full of oppression in her
    midst.
7 As a fountain wells up with
    water,
So she wells up with her
    wickedness.
Violence and plundering are
    heard in her.
Before Me continually *are*
    grief and wounds.
8 Be instructed, O Jerusalem,
Lest My soul depart from you;
Lest I make you desolate,
A land not inhabited."

9Thus says the LORD of hosts:

"They shall thoroughly glean
    as a vine the remnant of
        Israel;
As a grape-gatherer, put your
    hand back into the
        branches."

10 To whom shall I speak and
    give warning,
That they may hear?
Indeed their ear *is*
    uncircumcised,
And they cannot give heed.
Behold, the word of the LORD
    is a reproach to them;
They have no delight in it.
11 Therefore I am full of the fury
    of the LORD.

I am weary of holding *it* in.
"I will pour it out on the
    children outside,
And on the assembly of young
    men together;
For even the husband shall be
    taken with the wife,
The aged with *him who is* full
    of days.
12 And their houses shall be
    turned over to others,
Fields and wives together;
For I will stretch out My hand
    Against the inhabitants of the
        land," says the LORD.
13 "Because from the least of
    them even to the greatest
        of them,
Everyone *is given to*
    covetousness;
And from the prophet even to
    the priest,
Everyone deals falsely.
14 They have also healed the
    hurt of My people slightly,
Saying, 'Peace, peace!'
When *there is* no peace."

COLOSSIANS 1:21–2:7

AND you, who once were alienated and enemies in your mind
by wicked works, yet now He
has reconciled 22in the body of His
flesh through death, to present you
holy, and blameless, and above reproach in His sight— 23if indeed you
continue in the faith, grounded and
steadfast, and are not moved away
from the hope of the gospel which you
heard, which was preached to every
creature under heaven, of which I,
Paul, became a minister.

24I now rejoice in my sufferings for
you, and fill up in my flesh what is lacking in the afflictions of Christ, for the
sake of His body, which is the church,
25of which I became a minister according to the stewardship from God
which was given to me for you, to fulfill

the word of God, 26the mystery which has been hidden from ages and from generations, but now has been revealed to His saints. 27To them God willed to make known what are the riches of the glory of this mystery among the Gentiles: which* is Christ in you, the hope of glory. 28Him we preach, warning every man and teaching every man in all wisdom, that we may present every man perfect in Christ Jesus. 29To this *end* I also labor, striving according to His working which works in me mightily.

For I want you to know what a great conflict I have for you and those in Laodicea, and *for* as many as have not seen my face in the flesh, 2that their hearts may be encouraged, being knit together in love, and *attaining* to all riches of the full assurance of understanding, to the knowledge of the mystery of God, both of the Father and* of Christ, 3in whom are hidden all the treasures of wisdom and knowledge.

4Now this I say lest anyone should deceive you with persuasive words. 5For though I am absent in the flesh, yet I am with you in spirit, rejoicing to see your *good* order and the steadfastness of your faith in Christ.

6As you therefore have received Christ Jesus the Lord, so walk in Him, 7rooted and built up in Him and established in the faith, as you have been taught, abounding in it* with thanksgiving.

PSALM 77:1-20

To the Chief Musician. To Jeduthun. A Psalm of Asaph.

I cried out to God with my voice—
To God with my voice;
And He gave ear to me.
2   In the day of my trouble I
        sought the Lord;

My hand was stretched out in
    the night without ceasing;
My soul refused to be
    comforted.
3   I remembered God, and was
        troubled;
I complained, and my spirit
    was overwhelmed.   Selah

4   You hold my eyelids *open;*
I am so troubled that I cannot
    speak.
5   I have considered the days of
        old,
The years of ancient times.
6   I call to remembrance my
        song in the night;
I meditate within my heart,
And my spirit makes diligent
    search.

7   Will the Lord cast off forever?
And will He be favorable no
    more?
8   Has His mercy ceased
        forever?
Has *His* promise failed
    forevermore?
9   Has God forgotten to be
        gracious?
Has He in anger shut up His
    tender mercies?   Selah

10   And I said, "This *is* my
        anguish;
But I will remember the years
    of the right hand of the
    Most High."
11   I will remember the works of
        the Lord;
Surely I will remember Your
    wonders of old.
12   I will also meditate on all Your
        work,
And talk of Your deeds.
13   Your way, O God, *is* in the
        sanctuary;
Who *is* so great a God as *our*
    God?

14 You *are* the God who does
wonders;
You have declared Your
strength among the
peoples.
15 You have with *Your* arm
redeemed Your people,
The sons of Jacob and Joseph.
Selah

16 The waters saw You, O God;
The waters saw You, they
were afraid;
The depths also trembled.
17 The clouds poured out water;
The skies sent out a sound;

Your arrows also flashed
about.
18 The voice of Your thunder
was in the whirlwind;
The lightnings lit up the world;
The earth trembled and
shook.
19 Your way *was* in the sea,
Your path in the great waters,
And Your footsteps were not
known.
20 You led Your people like a
flock
By the hand of Moses and
Aaron.

PROVERBS FOR TODAY/ 24:23-25

These things also belong to the wise. It is not good to show partiality in judgment.
He who says to the wicked, "You are *righteous," him the people will curse; nations*
will abhor him. But those who rebuke the wicked *will have delight, and a good*
blessing will come upon them.

OCTOBER 6

JEREMIAH 6:15–8:7

"WERE they ashamed when
they had committed abom-
ination?
No! They were not at all
ashamed;
Nor did they know how to
blush.
Therefore they shall fall
among those who fall;
At the time I punish them,
They shall be cast down,"
says the LORD.

16Thus says the LORD:

"Stand in the ways and see,
And ask for the old paths,
where the good way *is,*

And walk in it;
Then you will find rest for
your souls.
But they said, 'We will not
walk *in it.'*
17 Also, I set watchmen over
you, *saying,*
'Listen to the sound of the
trumpet!'
But they said, 'We will not
listen.'
18 Therefore hear, you nations,
And know, O congregation,
what *is* among them.
19 Hear, O earth!
Behold, I will certainly bring
calamity on this people—
The fruit of their thoughts,
Because they have not
heeded My words

Nor My law, but rejected it.
20 For what purpose to Me
Comes frankincense from
Sheba,
And sweet cane from a far
country?
Your burnt offerings *are* not
acceptable,
Nor your sacrifices sweet to
Me."

21Therefore thus says the LORD:

"Behold, I will lay stumbling
blocks before this people,
And the fathers and the sons
together shall fall on them.
The neighbor and his friend
shall perish."

22Thus says the LORD:

"Behold, a people comes from
the north country,
And a great nation will be
raised from the farthest
parts of the earth.
23 They will lay hold on bow and
spear;
They *are* cruel and have no
mercy;
Their voice roars like the sea;
And they ride on horses,
As men of war set in array
against you, O daughter of
Zion."

24 We have heard the report of it;
Our hands grow feeble.
Anguish has taken hold of us,
Pain as of a woman in labor.
25 Do not go out into the field,
Nor walk by the way.
Because of the sword of the
enemy,
Fear *is* on every side.
26 O daughter of my people,
Dress in sackcloth
And roll about in ashes!
Make mourning *as for* an only

son, most bitter
lamentation;
For the plunderer will
suddenly come upon us.

27 "I have set you *as* an assayer
and a fortress among My
people,
That you may know and test
their way.
28 They *are* all stubborn rebels,
walking as slanderers.
They are bronze and iron,
They *are* all corrupters;
29 The bellows blow fiercely,
The lead is consumed by the
fire;
The smelter refines in vain,
For the wicked are not drawn
off.
30 *People* will call them rejected
silver,
Because the LORD has rejected
them."

THE word that came to Jeremiah from the LORD, saying, 2"Stand in the gate of the LORD's house, and proclaim there this word, and say, 'Hear the word of the LORD, all *you of* Judah who enter in at these gates to worship the LORD!' " 3Thus says the LORD of hosts, the God of Israel: "Amend your ways and your doings, and I will cause you to dwell in this place. 4Do not trust in these lying words, saying, 'The temple of the LORD, the temple of the LORD, the temple of the LORD *are* these.'

5"For if you thoroughly amend your ways and your doings, if you thoroughly execute judgment between a man and his neighbor, 6*if* you do not oppress the stranger, the fatherless, and the widow, and do not shed innocent blood in this place, or walk after other gods to your hurt, 7then I will cause you to dwell in this place, in the land that I gave to your fathers forever and ever.

8"Behold, you trust in lying words

that cannot profit. 9Will you steal, murder, commit adultery, swear falsely, burn incense to Baal, and walk after other gods whom you do not know, 10and *then* come and stand before Me in this house which is called by My name, and say, 'We are delivered to do all these abominations'? 11Has this house, which is called by My name, become a den of thieves in your eyes? Behold, I, even I, have seen *it*," says the LORD.

12"But go now to My place which *was* in Shiloh, where I set My name at the first, and see what I did to it because of the wickedness of My people Israel. 13And now, because you have done all these works," says the LORD, "and I spoke to you, rising up early and speaking, but you did not hear, and I called you, but you did not answer, 14therefore I will do to the house which is called by My name, in which you trust, and to this place which I gave to you and your fathers, as I have done to Shiloh. 15And I will cast you out of My sight, as I have cast out all your brethren—the whole posterity of Ephraim.

16"Therefore do not pray for this people, nor lift up a cry or prayer for them, nor make intercession to Me; for I will not hear you. 17Do you not see what they do in the cities of Judah and in the streets of Jerusalem? 18The children gather wood, the fathers kindle the fire, and the women knead dough, to make cakes for the queen of heaven; and *they* pour out drink offerings to other gods, that they may provoke Me to anger. 19Do they provoke Me to anger?" says the LORD. "*Do they* not *provoke* themselves, to the shame of their own faces?"

20Therefore thus says the Lord GOD: "Behold, My anger and My fury will be poured out on this place—on man and on beast, on the trees of the field and on the fruit of the ground. And it will burn and not be quenched."

21Thus says the LORD of hosts, the God of Israel: "Add your burnt offerings to your sacrifices and eat meat. 22For I did not speak to your fathers, or command them in the day that I brought them out of the land of Egypt, concerning burnt offerings or sacrifices. 23But this is what I commanded them, saying, 'Obey My voice, and I will be your God, and you shall be My people. And walk in all the ways that I have commanded you, that it may be well with you.' 24Yet they did not obey or incline their ear, but followed the counsels *and* the dictates of their evil hearts, and went backward and not forward. 25Since the day that your fathers came out of the land of Egypt until this day, I have even sent to you all My servants the prophets, daily rising up early and sending *them.* 26Yet they did not obey Me or incline their ear, but stiffened their neck. They did worse than their fathers.

27"Therefore you shall speak all these words to them, but they will not obey you. You shall also call to them, but they will not answer you.

28"So you shall say to them, 'This *is* a nation that does not obey the voice of the LORD their God nor receive correction. Truth has perished and has been cut off from their mouth. 29Cut off your hair and cast *it* away, and take up a lamentation on the desolate heights; for the LORD has rejected and forsaken the generation of His wrath.' 30For the children of Judah have done evil in My sight," says the LORD. "They have set their abominations in the house which is called by My name, to pollute it. 31And they have built the high places of Tophet, which *is* in the Valley of the Son of Hinnom, to burn their sons and their daughters in the fire, which I did not command, nor did it come into My heart.

32"Therefore behold, the days are coming," says the LORD, "when it will no more be called Tophet, or the Valley of the Son of Hinnom, but the Valley of Slaughter; for they will bury in Tophet until there is no room. ³³The corpses of this people will be food for the birds of the heaven and for the beasts of the earth. And no one will frighten *them away.* ³⁴Then I will cause to cease from the cities of Judah and from the streets of Jerusalem the voice of mirth and the voice of gladness, the voice of the bridegroom and the voice of the bride. For the land shall be desolate.

"At that time," says the Lord, "they shall bring out the bones of the kings of Judah, and the bones of its princes, and the bones of the priests, and the bones of the prophets, and the bones of the inhabitants of Jerusalem, out of their graves. ²They shall spread them before the sun and the moon and all the host of heaven, which they have loved and which they have served and after which they have walked, which they have sought and which they have worshiped. They shall not be gathered nor buried; they shall be like refuse on the face of the earth. ³Then death shall be chosen rather than life by all the residue of those who remain of this evil family, who remain in all the places where I have driven them," says the Lord of hosts.

⁴"Moreover you shall say to them, 'Thus says the Lord:

"Will they fall and not rise?
    Will one turn away and not
        return?
5   Why has this people slidden
        back,
    Jerusalem, in a perpetual
        backsliding?
    They hold fast to deceit,
    They refuse to return.
6   I listened and heard,
    But they do not speak aright.
    No man repented of his
        wickedness,

Saying, 'What have I done?'
    Everyone turned to his own
        course,
    As the horse rushes into the
        battle.

7   "Even the stork in the heavens
        Knows her appointed times;
    And the turtledove, the swift,
        and the swallow
    Observe the time of their
        coming.
    But My people do not know
        the judgment of the Lord."

COLOSSIANS 2:8-23

BEWARE lest anyone cheat you through philosophy and empty deceit, according to the tradition of men, according to the basic principles of the world, and not according to Christ. ⁹For in Him dwells all the fullness of the Godhead bodily; ¹⁰and you are complete in Him, who is the head of all principality and power.

¹¹In Him you were also circumcised with the circumcision made without hands, by putting off the body of the sins* of the flesh, by the circumcision of Christ, ¹²buried with Him in baptism, in which you also were raised with *Him* through faith in the working of God, who raised Him from the dead. ¹³And you, being dead in your trespasses and the uncircumcision of your flesh, He has made alive together with Him, having forgiven you all trespasses, ¹⁴having wiped out the handwriting of requirements that was against us, which was contrary to us. And He has taken it out of the way, having nailed it to the cross. ¹⁵Having disarmed principalities and powers, He made a public spectacle of them, triumphing over them in it.

¹⁶So let no one judge you in food or in drink, or regarding a festival or a new moon or sabbaths, ¹⁷which are a shadow of things to come, but the sub-

stance is of Christ. [18]Let no one cheat you of your reward, taking delight in *false* humility and worship of angels, intruding into those things which he has not* seen, vainly puffed up by his fleshly mind, [19]and not holding fast to the Head, from whom all the body, nourished and knit together by joints and ligaments, grows with the increase *that is* from God.

[20]Therefore,* if you died with Christ from the basic principles of the world, why, as *though* living in the world, do you subject yourselves to regulations— [21]"Do not touch, do not taste, do not handle," [22]which all concern things which perish with the using— according to the commandments and doctrines of men? [23]These things indeed have an appearance of wisdom in self-imposed religion, *false* humility, and neglect of the body, *but are* of no value against the indulgence of the flesh.

PSALM 78:1-31

A Contemplation * of Asaph.*

G IVE ear, O my people, *to* my law;
Incline your ears to the words of my mouth.
2   I will open my mouth in a parable;
I will utter dark sayings of old,
3   Which we have heard and known,
And our fathers have told us.
4   We will not hide *them* from their children,
Telling to the generation to come the praises of the LORD,
And His strength and His wonderful works that He has done.

5   For He established a testimony in Jacob,
And appointed a law in Israel,
Which He commanded our fathers,
That they should make them known to their children;
6   That the generation to come might know *them,*
The children *who* would be born,
That they may arise and declare *them* to their children,
7   That they may set their hope in God,
And not forget the works of God,
But keep His commandments;
8   And may not be like their fathers,
A stubborn and rebellious generation,
A generation *that* did not set its heart aright,
And whose spirit was not faithful to God.

9   The children of Ephraim, *being* armed *and* carrying bows,
Turned back in the day of battle.
10   They did not keep the covenant of God;
They refused to walk in His law,
11   And forgot His works
And His wonders that He had shown them.

12   Marvelous things He did in the sight of their fathers,
In the land of Egypt, *in* the field of Zoan.
13   He divided the sea and caused them to pass through;
And He made the waters stand up like a heap.
14   In the daytime also He led them with the cloud,

And all the night with a light
of fire.

15 He split the rocks in the
wilderness,
And gave *them* drink in
abundance like the depths.

16 He also brought streams out
of the rock,
And caused waters to run
down like rivers.

17 But they sinned even more
against Him
By rebelling against the Most
High in the wilderness.

18 And they tested God in their
heart
By asking for the food of their
fancy.

19 Yes, they spoke against God:
They said, "Can God prepare
a table in the wilderness?

20 Behold, He struck the rock,
So that the waters gushed out,
And the streams overflowed.
Can He give bread also?
Can He provide meat for His
people?"

21 Therefore the LORD heard *this*
and was furious;
So a fire was kindled against
Jacob,
And anger also came up
against Israel,

22 Because they did not believe
in God,

And did not trust in His
salvation.

23 Yet He had commanded the
clouds above,
And opened the doors of
heaven,

24 Had rained down manna on
them to eat,
And given them of the bread
of heaven.

25 Men ate angels' food;
He sent them food to the full.

26 He caused an east wind to
blow in the heavens;
And by His power He brought
in the south wind.

27 He also rained meat on them
like the dust,
Feathered fowl like the sand
of the seas;

28 And He let *them* fall in the
midst of their camp,
All around their dwellings.

29 So they ate and were well
filled,
For He gave them their own
desire.

30 They were not deprived of
their craving;
But while their food *was* still
in their mouths,

31 The wrath of God came
against them,
And slew the stoutest of them,
And struck down the choice
men of Israel.

PROVERBS FOR TODAY / 24:26

He who gives a right answer kisses the lips.

OCTOBER 7

JEREMIAH 8:8–9:26

"**H**ow can you say, 'We *are* wise,
And the law of the LORD *is*
with us'?
Look, the false pen of the
scribe certainly works
falsehood.

9 The wise men are ashamed,
They are dismayed and taken.
Behold, they have rejected
the word of the LORD;
So what wisdom do they have?

10 Therefore I will give their
wives to others,
And their fields to those who
will inherit *them;*
Because from the least even
to the greatest
Everyone is given to
covetousness;
From the prophet even to the
priest
Everyone deals falsely.

11 For they have healed the hurt
of the daughter of My
people slightly,
Saying, 'Peace, peace!'
When *there is* no peace.

12 Were they ashamed when
they had committed
abomination?
No! They were not at all
ashamed,
Nor did they know how to
blush.
Therefore they shall fall
among those who fall;
In the time of their
punishment
They shall be cast down,"
says the LORD.

13 "I will surely consume them,"
says the LORD.
"No grapes *shall be* on the vine,
Nor figs on the fig tree,
And the leaf shall fade;
And *the things* I have given
them shall pass away from
them." ' "

14 "Why do we sit still?
Assemble yourselves,
And let us enter the fortified
cities,
And let us be silent there.
For the LORD our God has put
us to silence
And given us water of gall to
drink,
Because we have sinned
against the LORD.

15 "*We* looked for peace, but no
good *came;*
And for a time of health, and
there was trouble!

16 The snorting of His horses
was heard from Dan.
The whole land trembled at
the sound of the neighing
of His strong ones;
For they have come and
devoured the land and all
that is in it,
The city and those who dwell
in it."

17 "For behold, I will send
serpents among you,
Vipers which cannot be
charmed,
And they shall bite you," says
the LORD.

18 I would comfort myself in
sorrow;
My heart *is* faint in me.

19 Listen! The voice,

The cry of the daughter of my
people
From a far country:
"*Is* not the LORD in Zion?
Is not her King in her?"

"Why have they provoked Me
to anger
With their carved images—
With foreign idols?"

20 "The harvest is past,
The summer is ended,
And we are not saved!"

21 For the hurt of the daughter
of my people I am hurt.
I am mourning;
Astonishment has taken hold
of me.

22 *Is there* no balm in Gilead,
Is there no physician there?
Why then is there no recovery
For the health of the daughter
of my people?

OH, that my head were waters,
And my eyes a fountain of
tears,
That I might weep day and
night
For the slain of the daughter
of my people!

2 Oh, that I had in the
wilderness
A lodging place for travelers;
That I might leave my people,
And go from them!
For they *are* all adulterers,
An assembly of treacherous
men.

3 "And *like* their bow they have
bent their tongues *for* lies.
They are not valiant for the
truth on the earth.
For they proceed from evil to
evil,
And they do not know Me,"
says the LORD.

4 "Everyone take heed to his
neighbor,
And do not trust any brother;
For every brother will utterly
supplant,
And every neighbor will walk
with slanderers.

5 Everyone will deceive his
neighbor,
And will not speak the truth;
They have taught their
tongue to speak lies;
They weary themselves to
commit iniquity.

6 Your dwelling place *is* in the
midst of deceit;
Through deceit they refuse to
know Me," says the LORD.

7Therefore thus says the LORD of
hosts:

"Behold, I will refine them and
try them;
For how shall I deal with the
daughter of My people?

8 Their tongue *is* an arrow shot
out;
It speaks deceit;
One speaks peaceably to his
neighbor with his mouth,
But in his heart he lies in wait.

9 Shall I not punish them for
these *things?*" says the LORD.
"Shall I not avenge Myself on
such a nation as this?"

10 I will take up a weeping and
wailing for the mountains,
And for the dwelling places of
the wilderness a
lamentation,
Because they are burned up,
So that no one can pass
through;
Nor can *men* hear the voice of
the cattle.
Both the birds of the heavens
and the beasts have fled;
They are gone.

11 "I will make Jerusalem a heap
of ruins, a den of jackals.
I will make the cities of Judah
desolate, without an
inhabitant."

12Who *is* the wise man who may understand this? And *who is he* to whom the mouth of the LORD has spoken, that he may declare it? Why does the land perish *and* burn up like a wilderness, so that no one can pass through?

13And the LORD said, "Because they have forsaken My law which I set before them, and have not obeyed My voice, nor walked according to it, 14but they have walked according to the dictates of their own hearts and after the Baals, which their fathers taught them," 15therefore thus says the LORD of hosts, the God of Israel: "Behold, I will feed them, this people, with wormwood, and give them water of gall to drink. 16I will scatter them also among the Gentiles, whom neither they nor their fathers have known. And I will send a sword after them until I have consumed them."

17Thus says the LORD of hosts:

"Consider and call for the
mourning women,
That they may come;
And send for skillful wailing
women,
That they may come.
18 Let them make haste
And take up a wailing for us,
That our eyes may run with
tears,
And our eyelids gush with
water.
19 For a voice of wailing is heard
from Zion:
'How we are plundered!
We are greatly ashamed,
Because we have forsaken the
land,

Because we have been cast
out of our dwellings.' "

20 Yet hear the word of the LORD,
O women,
And let your ear receive the
word of His mouth;
Teach your daughters wailing,
And everyone her neighbor a
lamentation.
21 For death has come through
our windows,
Has entered our palaces,
To kill off the children—*no
longer to be* outside!
And the young men—*no
longer* on the streets!

22 Speak, "Thus says the LORD:

'Even the carcasses of men
shall fall as refuse on the
open field,
Like cuttings after the
harvester,
And no one shall gather *them.*' "

23Thus says the LORD:

"Let not the wise *man* glory in
his wisdom,
Let not the mighty *man* glory
in his might,
Nor let the rich *man* glory in
his riches;
24 But let him who glories glory
in this,
That he understands and
knows Me,
That I *am* the LORD,
exercising lovingkindness,
judgment, and
righteousness in the earth.
For in these I delight," says
the LORD.

25"Behold, the days are coming," says the LORD, "that I will punish all *who are* circumcised with the uncircumcised— 26Egypt, Judah, Edom, the people of Ammon, Moab, and all *who are* in the farthest corners, who dwell in the wilderness. For all *these* nations *are* uncircumcised, and all the house of Israel *are* uncircumcised in the heart."

COLOSSIANS 3:1-17

I F then you were raised with Christ, seek those things which are above, where Christ is, sitting at the right hand of God. ²Set your mind on things above, not on things on the earth. ³For you died, and your life is hidden with Christ in God. ⁴When Christ *who is* our life appears, then you also will appear with Him in glory.

⁵Therefore put to death your members which are on the earth: fornication, uncleanness, passion, evil desire, and covetousness, which is idolatry. ⁶Because of these things the wrath of God is coming upon the sons of disobedience, ⁷in which you yourselves once walked when you lived in them.

⁸But now you yourselves are to put off all these: anger, wrath, malice, blasphemy, filthy language out of your mouth. ⁹Do not lie to one another, since you have put off the old man with his deeds, ¹⁰and have put on the new *man* who is renewed in knowledge according to the image of Him who created him, ¹¹where there is neither Greek nor Jew, circumcised nor uncircumcised, barbarian, Scythian, slave *nor* free, but Christ *is* all and in all.

¹²Therefore, as *the* elect of God, holy and beloved, put on tender mercies, kindness, humility, meekness, longsuffering; ¹³bearing with one another, and forgiving one another, if anyone has a complaint against another; even as Christ forgave you, so you also *must do*. ¹⁴But above all these things put on love, which is the bond of perfection. ¹⁵And let the peace of God rule in your hearts, to which also you were called in one body; and be thankful. ¹⁶Let the word of Christ dwell in you richly in all wisdom, teaching and admonishing one another in psalms and hymns and spiritual songs, singing with grace in your hearts to the Lord. ¹⁷And *whatever* you do in word or deed, *do* all in the name of the Lord Jesus, giving thanks to God the Father through Him.

PSALM 78:32-55

I N spite of this they still sinned, And did not believe in His wondrous works.

33 Therefore their days He consumed in futility, And their years in fear.

34 When He slew them, then they sought Him; And they returned and sought earnestly for God.

35 Then they remembered that God *was* their rock, And the Most High God their Redeemer.

36 Nevertheless they flattered Him with their mouth, And they lied to Him with their tongue;

37 For their heart was not steadfast with Him, Nor were they faithful in His covenant.

38 But He, *being* full of compassion, forgave *their* iniquity, And did not destroy *them*. Yes, many a time He turned His anger away, And did not stir up all His wrath;

39 For He remembered that they *were but* flesh, A breath that passes away and does not come again.

40 How often they provoked Him in the wilderness,

And grieved Him in the desert!

41 Yes, again and again they tempted God,
And limited the Holy One of Israel.

42 They did not remember His power:
The day when He redeemed them from the enemy,

43 When He worked His signs in Egypt,
And His wonders in the field of Zoan;

44 Turned their rivers into blood,
And their streams, that they could not drink.

45 He sent swarms of flies among them, which devoured them,
And frogs, which destroyed them.

46 He also gave their crops to the caterpillar,
And their labor to the locust.

47 He destroyed their vines with hail,
And their sycamore trees with frost.

48 He also gave up their cattle to the hail,
And their flocks to fiery lightning.

49 He cast on them the fierceness of His anger,
Wrath, indignation, and trouble,
By sending angels of destruction *among them*.

50 He made a path for His anger;
He did not spare their soul from death,
But gave their life over to the plague,

51 And destroyed all the firstborn in Egypt,
The first of *their* strength in the tents of Ham.

52 But He made His own people go forth like sheep,
And guided them in the wilderness like a flock;

53 And He led them on safely, so that they did not fear;
But the sea overwhelmed their enemies.

54 And He brought them to His holy border,
This mountain *which* His right hand had acquired.

55 He also drove out the nations before them,
Allotted them an inheritance by survey,
And made the tribes of Israel dwell in their tents.

PROVERBS FOR TODAY/ 24:27

Prepare your outside work, make it fit for yourself in the field; and afterward build your house.

OCTOBER 8

HEAR the word which the LORD speaks to you, O house of Israel.

²Thus says the LORD:

"Do not learn the way of the
  Gentiles;
Do not be dismayed at the
  signs of heaven,
For the Gentiles are dismayed
  at them.

³ For the customs of the
    peoples *are* futile;
For *one* cuts a tree from the
  forest,
The work of the hands of the
  workman, with the ax.

⁴ They decorate it with silver
    and gold;
They fasten it with nails and
  hammers
So that it will not topple.

⁵ They *are* upright, like a palm
    tree,
And they cannot speak;
They must be carried,
Because they cannot go *by
  themselves.*
Do not be afraid of them,
For they cannot do evil,
Nor can they do any good."

⁶ Inasmuch as *there is* none like
    You, O LORD
(You *are* great, and Your
  name *is* great in might),

⁷ Who would not fear You,
    O King of the nations?
For this is Your rightful due.
For among all the wise *men* of
  the nations,
And in all their kingdoms,
There is none like You.

⁸ But they are altogether
    dull-hearted and foolish;
A wooden idol *is* a worthless
  doctrine.

⁹ Silver is beaten into plates;
It is brought from Tarshish,
And gold from Uphaz,
The work of the craftsman
And of the hands of the
  metalsmith;
Blue and purple *are* their
  clothing;
They *are* all the work of
  skillful *men.*

¹⁰ But the LORD *is* the true God;
He *is* the living God and the
  everlasting King.
At His wrath the earth will
  tremble,
And the nations will not be
  able to endure His
  indignation.

¹¹Thus you shall say to them: "The gods that have not made the heavens and the earth shall perish from the earth and from under these heavens."

¹² He has made the earth by His
    power,
He has established the world
  by His wisdom,
And has stretched out the
  heavens at His discretion.

¹³ When He utters His voice,
There is a multitude of waters
  in the heavens:
"And He causes the vapors to
  ascend from the ends of the
  earth.
He makes lightning for the
  rain,
He brings the wind out of His
  treasuries."*

14 Everyone is dull-hearted,
without knowledge;
Every metalsmith is put to
shame by an image;
For his molded image *is*
falsehood,
And *there is* no breath in them.

15 They *are* futile, a work of
errors;
In the time of their
punishment they shall
perish.

16 The Portion of Jacob *is* not
like them,
For He *is* the Maker of all
things,
And Israel *is* the tribe of His
inheritance;
The LORD of hosts *is* His name.

17 Gather up your wares from
the land,
O inhabitant of the fortress!

18For thus says the LORD:

"Behold, I will throw out at this
time
The inhabitants of the land,
And will distress them,
That they may find *it so.*"

19 Woe is me for my hurt!
My wound is severe.
But I say, "Truly this *is* an
infirmity,
And I must bear it."

20 My tent is plundered,
And all my cords are broken;
My children have gone from
me,
And they *are* no more.
There is no one to pitch my
tent anymore,
Or set up my curtains.

21 For the shepherds have
become dull-hearted,
And have not sought the LORD;
Therefore they shall not
prosper,
And all their flocks shall be
scattered.

22 Behold, the noise of the
report has come,
And a great commotion out of
the north country,
To make the cities of Judah
desolate, a den of jackals.

23 O LORD, I know the way of
man *is* not in himself;
It is not in man who walks to
direct his own steps.

24 O LORD, correct me, but with
justice;
Not in Your anger, lest You
bring me to nothing.

25 Pour out Your fury on the
Gentiles, who do not know
You,
And on the families who do
not call on Your name;
For they have eaten up Jacob,
Devoured him and consumed
him,
And made his dwelling place
desolate.

THE word that came to Jeremiah from the LORD, saying, 2"Hear the words of this covenant, and speak to the men of Judah and to the inhabitants of Jerusalem; 3and say to them, 'Thus says the LORD God of Israel: "Cursed *is* the man who does not obey the words of this covenant 4which I commanded your fathers in the day I brought them out of the land of Egypt, from the iron furnace, saying, 'Obey My voice, and do according to all that I command you; so shall you be My people, and I will be your God,' 5that I may establish the oath which I have sworn to your fathers, to give them 'a land flowing with milk and honey,'* as *it is* this day." ' "

And I answered and said, "So be it, LORD."

6Then the LORD said to me, "Proclaim all these words in the cities of

Judah and in the streets of Jerusalem, saying: 'Hear the words of this covenant and do them. ⁷For I earnestly exhorted your fathers in the day I brought them up out of the land of Egypt, until this day, rising early and exhorting, saying, "Obey My voice." ⁸Yet they did not obey or incline their ear, but everyone followed the dictates of his evil heart; therefore I will bring upon them all the words of this covenant, which I commanded *them* to do, but *which* they have not done.' "

⁹And the LORD said to me, "A conspiracy has been found among the men of Judah and among the inhabitants of Jerusalem. ¹⁰They have turned back to the iniquities of their forefathers who refused to hear My words, and they have gone after other gods to serve them; the house of Israel and the house of Judah have broken My covenant which I made with their fathers."

¹¹Therefore thus says the LORD: "Behold, I will surely bring calamity on them which they will not be able to escape; and though they cry out to Me, I will not listen to them. ¹²Then the cities of Judah and the inhabitants of Jerusalem will go and cry out to the gods to whom they offer incense, but they will not save them at all in the time of their trouble. ¹³For *according to* the number of your cities were your gods, O Judah; and *according to* the number of the streets of Jerusalem you have set up altars to *that* shameful thing, altars to burn incense to Baal.

¹⁴"So do not pray for this people, or lift up a cry or prayer for them; for I will not hear *them* in the time that they cry out to Me because of their trouble.

15 "What has My beloved to do in
　　My house,
　　Having done lewd deeds with
　　　many?
　　And the holy flesh has passed
　　　from you.

When you do evil, then you
　　rejoice.
16 The LORD called your name,
　　Green Olive Tree, Lovely *and*
　　　of Good Fruit.
　　With the noise of a great
　　　tumult
　　He has kindled fire on it,
　　And its branches are broken.

¹⁷"For the LORD of hosts, who planted you, has pronounced doom against you for the evil of the house of Israel and of the house of Judah, which they have done against themselves to provoke Me to anger in offering incense to Baal."

¹⁸Now the LORD gave me knowledge *of it,* and I know *it;* for You showed me their doings. ¹⁹But I *was* like a docile lamb brought to the slaughter; and I did not know that they had devised schemes against me, *saying,* "Let us destroy the tree with its fruit, and let us cut him off from the land of the living, that his name may be remembered no more."

20 But, O LORD of hosts,
　　You who judge righteously,
　　Testing the mind and the
　　　heart,
　　Let me see Your vengeance
　　　on them,
　　For to You I have revealed my
　　　cause.

²¹"Therefore thus says the LORD concerning the men of Anathoth who seek your life, saying, 'Do not prophesy in the name of the LORD, lest you die by our hand'— ²²therefore thus says the LORD of hosts: 'Behold, I will punish them. The young men shall die by the sword, their sons and their daughters shall die by famine; ²³and there shall be no remnant of them, for I will bring catastrophe on the men of Anathoth, *even* the year of their punishment.' "

COLOSSIANS 3:18–4:18

WIVES, submit to your own husbands, as is fitting in the Lord.

19Husbands, love your wives and do not be bitter toward them.

20Children, obey your parents in all things, for this is well pleasing to the Lord.

21Fathers, do not provoke your children, lest they become discouraged.

22Bondservants, obey in all things your masters according to the flesh, not with eyeservice, as men-pleasers, but in sincerity of heart, fearing God. 23And whatever you do, do it heartily, as to the Lord and not to men, 24knowing that from the Lord you will receive the reward of the inheritance; for* you serve the Lord Christ. 25But he who does wrong will be repaid for what he has done, and there is no partiality.

MASTERS, give your bondservants what is just and fair, knowing that you also have a Master in heaven.

2Continue earnestly in prayer, being vigilant in it with thanksgiving; 3meanwhile praying also for us, that God would open to us a door for the word, to speak the mystery of Christ, for which I am also in chains, 4that I may make it manifest, as I ought to speak.

5Walk in wisdom toward those *who are* outside, redeeming the time. 6*Let* your speech always *be* with grace, seasoned with salt, that you may know how you ought to answer each one.

7Tychicus, a beloved brother, faithful minister, and fellow servant in the Lord, will tell you all the news about me. 8I am sending him to you for this very purpose, that he* may know your circumstances and comfort your hearts, 9with Onesimus, a faithful and beloved brother, who is *one* of you. They will make known to you all things which *are happening* here.

10Aristarchus my fellow prisoner greets you, with Mark the cousin of Barnabas (about whom you received instructions: if he comes to you, welcome him), 11and Jesus who is called Justus. These *are my* only fellow workers for the kingdom of God who are of the circumcision; they have proved to be a comfort to me.

12Epaphras, who is *one* of you, a bondservant of Christ, greets you, always laboring fervently for you in prayers, that you may stand perfect and complete* in all the will of God. 13For I bear him witness that he has a great zeal* for you, and those who are in Laodicea, and those in Hierapolis. 14Luke the beloved physician and Demas greet you. 15Greet the brethren who are in Laodicea, and Nymphas and the church that *is* in his* house.

16Now when this epistle is read among you, see that it is read also in the church of the Laodiceans, and that you likewise read the epistle from Laodicea. 17And say to Archippus, "Take heed to the ministry which you have received in the Lord, that you may fulfill it."

18This salutation by my own hand—Paul. Remember my chains. Grace *be* with you. Amen.

PSALM 78:56-72

YET they tested and provoked the Most High God,
And did not keep His testimonies,

57 But turned back and acted unfaithfully like their fathers;
They were turned aside like a deceitful bow.

58 For they provoked Him to anger with their high places,
And moved Him to jealousy with their carved images.

59 When God heard *this,* He was furious,

60 And greatly abhorred Israel,
So that He forsook the
tabernacle of Shiloh,
The tent He had placed
among men,
61 And delivered His strength
into captivity,
And His glory into the
enemy's hand.
62 He also gave His people over
to the sword,
And was furious with His
inheritance.
63 The fire consumed their
young men,
And their maidens were not
given in marriage.
64 Their priests fell by the sword,
And their widows made no
lamentation.

65 Then the Lord awoke as *from*
sleep,
Like a mighty man who
shouts because of wine.
66 And He beat back His
enemies;

He put them to a perpetual
reproach.

67 Moreover He rejected the
tent of Joseph,
And did not choose the tribe
of Ephraim,
68 But chose the tribe of Judah,
Mount Zion which He loved.
69 And He built His sanctuary
like the heights,
Like the earth which He has
established forever.
70 He also chose David His
servant,
And took him from the
sheepfolds;
71 From following the ewes that
had young He brought him,
To shepherd Jacob His people,
And Israel His inheritance.
72 So he shepherded them
according to the integrity of
his heart,
And guided them by the
skillfulness of his hands.

PROVERBS FOR TODAY/ 24:28-29

*Do not be a witness against your neighbor without cause, for would you deceive**
with your lips? Do not say, "I will do to him just as he has done to me; I will render
to the man according to his work."

OCTOBER 9

JEREMIAH 12:1–14:10

RIGHTEOUS *are* You, O LORD, when
I plead with You;
Yet let me talk with You about
Your judgments.
Why does the way of the
wicked prosper?
Why are those happy who deal
so treacherously?

2 You have planted them, yes,
they have taken root;
They grow, yes, they bear
fruit.
You *are* near in their mouth
But far from their mind.

3 But You, O LORD, know me;
You have seen me,

And You have tested my heart
  toward You.
Pull them out like sheep for
  the slaughter,
And prepare them for the day
  of slaughter.
4 How long will the land mourn,
  And the herbs of every field
  wither?
The beasts and birds are
  consumed,
For the wickedness of those
  who dwell there,
Because they said, "He will
  not see our final end."

5 "If you have run with the
  footmen, and they have
  wearied you,
Then how can you contend
  with horses?
And *if* in the land of peace,
In which you trusted, *they
  wearied you,*
Then how will you do in the
  floodplain* of the Jordan?
6 For even your brothers, the
  house of your father,
Even they have dealt
  treacherously with you;
Yes, they have called a
  multitude after you.
Do not believe them,
Even though they speak
  smooth words to you.

7 "I have forsaken My house, I
  have left My heritage;
I have given the dearly
  beloved of My soul into the
  hand of her enemies.
8 My heritage is to Me like a
  lion in the forest;
It cries out against Me;
Therefore I have hated it.
9 My heritage *is* to Me *like* a
  speckled vulture;
The vultures all around *are*
  against her.

Come, assemble all the beasts
  of the field,
Bring them to devour!

10 "Many rulers* have destroyed
  My vineyard,
They have trodden My
  portion underfoot;
They have made My pleasant
  portion a desolate
  wilderness.
11 They have made it desolate;
Desolate, it mourns to Me;
The whole land is made
  desolate,
Because no one takes *it* to
  heart.
12 The plunderers have come
On all the desolate heights in
  the wilderness,
For the sword of the LORD
  shall devour
From *one* end of the land to
  the *other* end of the land;
No flesh shall have peace.
13 They have sown wheat but
  reaped thorns;
They have put themselves to
  pain *but* do not profit.
But be ashamed of your
  harvest
Because of the fierce anger of
  the LORD."

14Thus says the LORD: "Against all
My evil neighbors who touch the inheritance which I have caused My
people Israel to inherit—behold, I will
pluck them out of their land and pluck
out the house of Judah from among
them. 15Then it shall be, after I have
plucked them out, that I will return and
have compassion on them and bring
them back, everyone to his heritage
and everyone to his land. 16And it shall
be, if they will learn carefully the ways
of My people, to swear by My name,
'As the LORD lives,' as they taught My
people to swear by Baal, then they
shall be established in the midst of My

people. ¹⁷But if they do not obey, I will utterly pluck up and destroy that nation," says the LORD.

THUS the LORD said to me: "Go and get yourself a linen sash, and put it around your waist, but do not put it in water." ²So I got a sash according to the word of the LORD, and put *it* around my waist.

³And the word of the LORD came to me the second time, saying, ⁴"Take the sash that you acquired, which *is* around your waist, and arise, go to the Euphrates,* and hide it there in a hole in the rock." ⁵So I went and hid it by the Euphrates, as the LORD commanded me.

⁶Now it came to pass after many days that the LORD said to me, "Arise, go to the Euphrates, and take from there the sash which I commanded you to hide there." ⁷Then I went to the Euphrates and dug, and I took the sash from the place where I had hidden it; and there was the sash, ruined. It was profitable for nothing.

⁸Then the word of the LORD came to me, saying, ⁹"Thus says the LORD: 'In this manner I will ruin the pride of Judah and the great pride of Jerusalem. ¹⁰This evil people, who refuse to hear My words, who follow the dictates of their hearts, and walk after other gods to serve them and worship them, shall be just like this sash which is profitable for nothing. ¹¹For as the sash clings to the waist of a man, so I have caused the whole house of Israel and the whole house of Judah to cling to Me,' says the LORD, 'that they may become My people, for renown, for praise, and for glory; but they would not hear.'

¹²"Therefore you shall speak to them this word: 'Thus says the LORD God of Israel: "Every bottle shall be filled with wine." '

"And they will say to you, 'Do we not certainly know that every bottle will be filled with wine?'

¹³"Then you shall say to them, 'Thus says the LORD: "Behold, I will fill all the inhabitants of this land—even the kings who sit on David's throne, the priests, the prophets, and all the inhabitants of Jerusalem—with drunkenness! ¹⁴And I will dash them one against another, even the fathers and the sons together," says the LORD. "I will not pity nor spare nor have mercy, but will destroy them." ' "

15   Hear and give ear:
Do not be proud,
For the LORD has spoken.
16   Give glory to the LORD your
      God
Before He causes darkness,
And before your feet stumble
On the dark mountains,
And while you are looking for
      light,
He turns it into the shadow of
      death
And makes *it* dense darkness.
17   But if you will not hear it,
My soul will weep in secret
      for *your* pride;
My eyes will weep bitterly
And run down with tears,
Because the LORD's flock has
      been taken captive.

18   Say to the king and to the
      queen mother,
"Humble yourselves;
Sit down,
For your rule shall collapse,
      the crown of your glory."
19   The cities of the South shall
      be shut up,
And no one shall open *them;*
Judah shall be carried away
      captive, all of it;
It shall be wholly carried
      away captive.

20   Lift up your eyes and see
Those who come from the
      north.

Where *is* the flock *that* was
given to you,
Your beautiful sheep?
21 What will you say when He
punishes you?
For you have taught them
To be chieftains, to be head
over you.
Will not pangs seize you,
Like a woman in labor?
22 And if you say in your heart,
"Why have these things come
upon me?"
For the greatness of your
iniquity
Your skirts have been
uncovered,
Your heels made bare.
23 Can the Ethiopian change his
skin or the leopard its
spots?
Then may you also do good
who are accustomed to do
evil.

24 "Therefore I will scatter them
like stubble
That passes away by the wind
of the wilderness.
25 This is your lot,
The portion of your measures
from Me," says the Lord,
"Because you have forgotten
Me
And trusted in falsehood.
26 Therefore I will uncover your
skirts over your face,
That your shame may appear.
27 I have seen your adulteries
And your *lustful* neighings,
The lewdness of your harlotry,
Your abominations on the
hills in the fields.
Woe to you, O Jerusalem!
Will you still not be made
clean?"

THE word of the Lord that came to Jeremiah concerning the droughts.

2 "Judah mourns,
And her gates languish;
They mourn for the land,
And the cry of Jerusalem has
gone up.
3 Their nobles have sent their
lads for water;
They went to the cisterns *and*
found no water.
They returned with their
vessels empty;
They were ashamed and
confounded
And covered their heads.
4 Because the ground is
parched,
For there was no rain in the
land,
The plowmen were ashamed;
They covered their heads.
5 Yes, the deer also gave birth
in the field,
But left because there was no
grass.
6 And the wild donkeys stood in
the desolate heights;
They sniffed at the wind like
jackals;
Their eyes failed because
there was no grass."

7 O Lord, though our iniquities
testify against us,
Do it for Your name's sake;
For our backslidings are
many,
We have sinned against You.
8 O the Hope of Israel, his
Savior in time of trouble,
Why should You be like a
stranger in the land,
And like a traveler *who* turns
aside to tarry for a night?
9 Why should You be like a
man astonished,
Like a mighty one *who* cannot
save?
Yet You, O Lord, *are* in our
midst,

And we are called by Your
name;
Do not leave us!

¹⁰Thus says the LORD to this people:

"Thus they have loved to
wander;
They have not restrained
their feet.
Therefore the LORD does not
accept them;
He will remember their
iniquity now,
And punish their sins."

1 THESSALONIANS 1:1–2:9

PAUL, Silvanus, and Timothy,

To the church of the Thessalonians in God the Father and the Lord Jesus Christ:

Grace to you and peace from God our Father and the Lord Jesus Christ.*

²We give thanks to God always for you all, making mention of you in our prayers, ³remembering without ceasing your work of faith, labor of love, and patience of hope in our Lord Jesus Christ in the sight of our God and Father, ⁴knowing, beloved brethren, your election by God. ⁵For our gospel did not come to you in word only, but also in power, and in the Holy Spirit and in much assurance, as you know what kind of men we were among you for your sake.

⁶And you became followers of us and of the Lord, having received the word in much affliction, with joy of the Holy Spirit, ⁷so that you became examples to all in Macedonia and Achaia who believe. ⁸For from you the word of the Lord has sounded forth, not only in Macedonia and Achaia, but also in every place. Your faith toward God has gone out, so that we do not need to say anything. ⁹For they themselves declare concerning us what manner of entry we had to you, and how you turned to God from idols to serve the living and true God, ¹⁰and to wait for His Son from heaven, whom He raised from the dead, *even* Jesus who delivers us from the wrath to come.

FOR you yourselves know, brethren, that our coming to you was not in vain. ²But even* after we had suffered before and were spitefully treated at Philippi, as you know, we were bold in our God to speak to you the gospel of God in much conflict. ³For our exhortation *did* not *come* from error or uncleanness, nor *was it* in deceit.

⁴But as we have been approved by God to be entrusted with the gospel, even so we speak, not as pleasing men, but God who tests our hearts. ⁵For neither at any time did we use flattering words, as you know, nor a cloak for covetousness—God *is* witness. ⁶Nor did we seek glory from men, either from you or from others, when we might have made demands as apostles of Christ. ⁷But we were gentle among you, just as a nursing *mother* cherishes her own children. ⁸So, affectionately longing for you, we were well pleased to impart to you not only the gospel of God, but also our own lives, because you had become dear to us. ⁹For you remember, brethren, our labor and toil; for laboring night and day, that we might not be a burden to any of you, we preached to you the gospel of God.

PSALM 79:1-13

A Psalm of Asaph.

O GOD, the nations have come into Your inheritance;
Your holy temple they have
defiled;
They have laid Jerusalem in
heaps.

2 The dead bodies of Your
servants
They have given *as* food for
the birds of the heavens,
The flesh of Your saints to the
beasts of the earth.
3 Their blood they have shed
like water all around
Jerusalem,
And *there was* no one to bury
them.
4 We have become a reproach
to our neighbors,
A scorn and derision to those
who are around us.

5 How long, LORD?
Will You be angry forever?
Will Your jealousy burn like
fire?
6 Pour out Your wrath on the
nations that do not know
You,
And on the kingdoms that do
not call on Your name.
7 For they have devoured Jacob,
And laid waste his dwelling
place.

8 Oh, do not remember former
iniquities against us!
Let Your tender mercies come
speedily to meet us,

For we have been brought
very low.
9 Help us, O God of our
salvation,
For the glory of Your name;
And deliver us, and provide
atonement for our sins,
For Your name's sake!
10 Why should the nations say,
"Where *is* their God?"
Let there be known among
the nations in our sight
The avenging of the blood of
Your servants *which has
been* shed.

11 Let the groaning of the
prisoner come before You;
According to the greatness of
Your power
Preserve those who are
appointed to die;
12 And return to our neighbors
sevenfold into their bosom
Their reproach with which
they have reproached You,
O Lord.

13 So we, Your people and sheep
of Your pasture,
Will give You thanks forever;
We will show forth Your
praise to all generations.

PROVERBS FOR TODAY/ 24:30-34

I went by the field of the lazy man, *and by the vineyard of the man devoid of understanding; and there it was, all overgrown with thorns; its surface was covered with nettles; its stone wall was broken down. When I saw* it, *I considered it well; I looked on* it and *received instruction: a little sleep, a little slumber, a little folding of the hands to rest; so shall your poverty come* like *a prowler, and your need like an armed man.*

OCTOBER 10

JEREMIAH 14:11–16:15

THEN the LORD said to me, "Do not pray for this people, for *their* good. 12When they fast, I will not hear their cry; and when they offer burnt offering and grain offering, I will not accept them. But I will consume them by the sword, by the famine, and by the pestilence."

13Then I said, "Ah, Lord GOD! Behold, the prophets say to them, 'You shall not see the sword, nor shall you have famine, but I will give you assured peace in this place.' "

14And the LORD said to me, "The prophets prophesy lies in My name. I have not sent them, commanded them, nor spoken to them; they prophesy to you a false vision, divination, a worthless thing, and the deceit of their heart. 15Therefore thus says the LORD concerning the prophets who prophesy in My name, whom I did not send, and who say, 'Sword and famine shall not be in this land'—'By sword and famine those prophets shall be consumed! 16And the people to whom they prophesy shall be cast out in the streets of Jerusalem because of the famine and the sword; they will have no one to bury them—them nor their wives, their sons nor their daughters—for I will pour their wickedness on them.'

17"Therefore you shall say this word to them:

'Let my eyes flow with tears
    night and day,
And let them not cease;
For the virgin daughter of my
    people
Has been broken with a
    mighty stroke, with a very
    severe blow.

18 If I go out to the field,
    Then behold, those slain with
        the sword!
    And if I enter the city,
    Then behold, those sick from
        famine!
    Yes, both prophet and priest
        go about in a land they do
        not know.' "

19 Have You utterly rejected
        Judah?
    Has Your soul loathed Zion?
    Why have You stricken us so
        that *there is* no healing for
        us?
    We looked for peace, but *there
        was* no good;
    And for the time of healing,
        and there was trouble.
20 We acknowledge, O LORD, our
        wickedness
    And the iniquity of our fathers,
    For we have sinned against
        You.
21 Do not abhor *us,* for Your
        name's sake;
    Do not disgrace the throne of
        Your glory.
    Remember, do not break Your
        covenant with us.
22 Are there any among the idols
        of the nations that can
        cause rain?
    Or can the heavens give
        showers?
    Are You not He, O LORD our
        God?
    Therefore we will wait for You,
    Since You have made all these.

THEN the LORD said to me, "*Even* if Moses and Samuel stood before Me, My mind *would* not *be* favorable toward this people. Cast *them* out of My sight, and let them go forth. ²And it shall be, if they say to you, 'Where should we go?' then you shall tell them, 'Thus says the LORD:

> "Such as *are* for death, to
>   death;
> And such as *are* for the
>   sword, to the sword;
> And such as *are* for the
>   famine, to the famine;
> And such as *are* for the
>   captivity, to the captivity." '

³"And I will appoint over them four forms *of destruction,*" says the LORD: "the sword to slay, the dogs to drag, the birds of the heavens and the beasts of the earth to devour and destroy. ⁴I will hand them over to trouble, to all kingdoms of the earth, because of Manasseh the son of Hezekiah, king of Judah, for what he did in Jerusalem.

5   "For who will have pity on you,
>   O Jerusalem?
>   Or who will bemoan you?
>   Or who will turn aside to ask
>   how you are doing?
6   You have forsaken Me," says
>   the LORD,
>   "You have gone backward.
>   Therefore I will stretch out
>   My hand against you and
>   destroy you;
>   I am weary of relenting!
7   And I will winnow them with a
>   winnowing fan in the gates
>   of the land;
>   I will bereave *them* of children;
>   I will destroy My people,
>   *Since* they do not return from
>   their ways.
8   Their widows will be
>   increased to Me more than
>   the sand of the seas;
>   I will bring against them,
>   Against the mother of the
>   young men,
>   A plunderer at noonday;

> I will cause anguish and
>   terror to fall on them
>   suddenly.

9   "She languishes who has
>   borne seven;
>   She has breathed her last;
>   Her sun has gone down
>   While *it was* yet day;
>   She has been ashamed and
>   confounded.
>   And the remnant of them I
>   will deliver to the sword
>   Before their enemies," says
>   the LORD.

10   Woe is me, my mother,
>   That you have borne me,
>   A man of strife and a man of
>   contention to the whole
>   earth!
>   I have neither lent for interest,
>   Nor have men lent to me for
>   interest.
>   Every one of them curses me.

¹¹The LORD said:

> "Surely it will be well with your
>   remnant;
> Surely I will cause the enemy
>   to intercede with you
> In the time of adversity and in
>   the time of affliction.

12   Can anyone break iron,
>   The northern iron and the
>   bronze?
13   Your wealth and your
>   treasures
>   I will give as plunder without
>   price,
>   Because of all your sins,
>   Throughout your territories.
14   And I will make *you* cross
>   over with* your enemies
>   Into a land *which* you do not
>   know;
>   For a fire is kindled in My
>   anger,
>   *Which* shall burn upon you."

15 O Lᴏʀᴅ, You know;
   Remember me and visit me,
   And take vengeance for me
      on my persecutors.
   In Your enduring patience, do
      not take me away.
   Know that for Your sake I
      have suffered rebuke.
16 Your words were found, and I
      ate them,
   And Your word was to me the
      joy and rejoicing of my
      heart;
   For I am called by Your name,
   O Lᴏʀᴅ God of hosts.
17 I did not sit in the assembly of
      the mockers,
   Nor did I rejoice;
   I sat alone because of Your
      hand,
   For You have filled me with
      indignation.
18 Why is my pain perpetual
   And my wound incurable,
   Which refuses to be healed?
   Will You surely be to me like
      an unreliable stream,
   As waters *that* fail?

19Therefore thus says the Lᴏʀᴅ:

   "If you return,
   Then I will bring you back;
   You shall stand before Me;
   If you take out the precious
      from the vile,
   You shall be as My mouth.
   Let them return to you,
   But you must not return to
      them.
20 And I will make you to this
      people a fortified bronze
      wall;
   And they will fight against you,
   But they shall not prevail
      against you;
   For I *am* with you to save you
   And deliver you," says the
   Lᴏʀᴅ.

21 "I will deliver you from the
      hand of the wicked,
   And I will redeem you from
      the grip of the terrible."

Tʜᴇ word of the Lᴏʀᴅ also came to me, saying, 2"You shall not take a wife, nor shall you have sons or daughters in this place." 3For thus says the Lᴏʀᴅ concerning the sons and daughters who are born in this place, and concerning their mothers who bore them and their fathers who begot them in this land: 4"They shall die gruesome deaths; they shall not be lamented nor shall they be buried, *but* they shall be like refuse on the face of the earth. They shall be consumed by the sword and by famine, and their corpses shall be meat for the birds of heaven and for the beasts of the earth."

5For thus says the Lᴏʀᴅ: "Do not enter the house of mourning, nor go to lament or bemoan them; for I have taken away My peace from this people," says the Lᴏʀᴅ, "lovingkindness and mercies. 6Both the great and the small shall die in this land. They shall not be buried; neither shall men lament for them, cut themselves, nor make themselves bald for them. 7Nor shall *men* break *bread* in mourning for them, to comfort them for the dead; nor shall *men* give them the cup of consolation to drink for their father or their mother. 8Also you shall not go into the house of feasting to sit with them, to eat and drink."

9For thus says the Lᴏʀᴅ of hosts, the God of Israel: "Behold, I will cause to cease from this place, before your eyes and in your days, the voice of mirth and the voice of gladness, the voice of the bridegroom and the voice of the bride.

10"And it shall be, when you show this people all these words, and they say to you, 'Why has the Lᴏʀᴅ pronounced all this great disaster against us? Or what *is* our iniquity? Or what *is* our sin that we have committed against the Lord our God?' [11]then you shall say to them, 'Because your fathers have forsaken Me,' says the Lord; 'they have walked after other gods and have served them and worshiped them, and have forsaken Me and not kept My law. [12]And you have done worse than your fathers, for behold, each one follows the dictates of his own evil heart, so that no one listens to Me. [13]Therefore I will cast you out of this land into a land that you do not know, neither you nor your fathers; and there you shall serve other gods day and night, where I will not show you favor.'

[14]"Therefore behold, the days are coming," says the Lord, "that it shall no more be said, 'The Lord lives who brought up the children of Israel from the land of Egypt,' [15]but, 'The Lord lives who brought up the children of Israel from the land of the north and from all the lands where He had driven them.' For I will bring them back into their land which I gave to their fathers."

1 THESSALONIANS 2:10–3:13

YOU *are* witnesses, and God *also,* how devoutly and justly and blamelessly we behaved ourselves among you who believe; [11]as you know how we exhorted, and comforted, and charged* every one of you, as a father *does* his own children, [12]that you would walk worthy of God who calls you into His own kingdom and glory.

[13]For this reason we also thank God without ceasing, because when you received the word of God which you heard from us, you welcomed *it* not *as* the word of men, but as it is in truth, the word of God, which also effectively works in you who believe. [14]For you, brethren, became imitators of the churches of God which are in Judea in Christ Jesus. For you also suffered the same things from your own countrymen, just as they *did* from the Judeans, [15]who killed both the Lord Jesus and their own prophets, and have persecuted us; and they do not please God and are contrary to all men, [16]forbidding us to speak to the Gentiles that they may be saved, so as always to fill up *the measure of* their sins; but wrath has come upon them to the uttermost.

[17]But we, brethren, having been taken away from you for a short time in presence, not in heart, endeavored more eagerly to see your face with great desire. [18]Therefore we wanted to come to you—even I, Paul, time and again—but Satan hindered us. [19]For what *is* our hope, or joy, or crown of rejoicing? *Is it* not even you in the presence of our Lord Jesus Christ at His coming? [20]For you are our glory and joy.

THEREFORE, when we could no longer endure it, we thought it good to be left in Athens alone, [2]and sent Timothy, our brother and minister of God, and our fellow laborer in the gospel of Christ, to establish you and encourage you concerning your faith, [3]that no one should be shaken by these afflictions; for you yourselves know that we are appointed to this. [4]For, in fact, we told you before when we were with you that we would suffer tribulation, just as it happened, and you know. [5]For this reason, when I could no longer endure it, I sent to know your faith, lest by some means the tempter had tempted you, and our labor might be in vain.

[6]But now that Timothy has come to us from you, and brought us good news of your faith and love, and that you always have good remembrance of us, greatly desiring to see us, as we also *to see* you— [7]therefore, brethren, in all our affliction and distress we were comforted concerning you by your faith. [8]For now we live, if you stand fast in the Lord.

⁹For what thanks can we render to God for you, for all the joy with which we rejoice for your sake before our God, ¹⁰night and day praying exceedingly that we may see your face and perfect what is lacking in your faith?

¹¹Now may our God and Father Himself, and our Lord Jesus Christ, direct our way to you. ¹²And may the Lord make you increase and abound in love to one another and to all, just as we *do* to you, ¹³so that He may establish your hearts blameless in holiness before our God and Father at the coming of our Lord Jesus Christ with all His saints.

PSALM 80:1-19

To the Chief Musician. Set to "The Lilies." * A Testimony* of Asaph. A Psalm.*

G IVE ear, O Shepherd of Israel,
You who lead Joseph like
a flock;
You who dwell *between* the
cherubim, shine forth!
2 Before Ephraim, Benjamin,
and Manasseh,
Stir up Your strength,
And come *and* save us!

3 Restore us, O God;
Cause Your face to shine,
And we shall be saved!

4 O Lᴏʀᴅ God of hosts,
How long will You be angry
Against the prayer of Your
people?
5 You have fed them with the
bread of tears,
And given them tears to drink
in great measure.
6 You have made us a strife to
our neighbors,
And our enemies laugh
among themselves.

7 Restore us, O God of hosts;
Cause Your face to shine,

And we shall be saved!

8 You have brought a vine out
of Egypt;
You have cast out the nations,
and planted it.
9 You prepared *room* for it,
And caused it to take deep
root,
And it filled the land.
10 The hills were covered with
its shadow,
And the mighty cedars with
its boughs.
11 She sent out her boughs to
the Sea,*
And her branches to the
River.*

12 Why have You broken down
her hedges,
So that all who pass by the
way pluck her *fruit?*
13 The boar out of the woods
uproots it,
And the wild beast of the field
devours it.

14 Return, we beseech You,
O God of hosts;
Look down from heaven and
see,
And visit this vine
15 And the vineyard which Your
right hand has planted,
And the branch *that* You
made strong for Yourself.
16 *It is* burned with fire, *it is* cut
down;
They perish at the rebuke of
Your countenance.
17 Let Your hand be upon the
man of Your right hand,
Upon the son of man *whom*
You made strong for
Yourself.
18 Then we will not turn back
from You;
Revive us, and we will call
upon Your name.

19 Restore us, O Lᴏʀᴅ God of
        hosts;

Cause Your face to shine,
And we shall be saved!

PROVERBS FOR TODAY/ 25:1-5

These also are *proverbs of Solomon which the men of Hezekiah king of Judah copied:* It is *the glory of God to conceal a matter, but the glory of kings* is *to search out a matter.* As *the heavens for height and the earth for depth, so the heart of kings* is *unsearchable. Take away the dross from silver, and it will go to the silversmith* for *jewelry. Take away the wicked from before the king, and his throne will be established in righteousness.*

OCTOBER 11

JEREMIAH 16:16–18:23

"**B**EHOLD, I will send for many fishermen," says the Lᴏʀᴅ, "and they shall fish them; and afterward I will send for many hunters, and they shall hunt them from every mountain and every hill, and out of the holes of the rocks. ¹⁷For My eyes *are* on all their ways; they are not hidden from My face, nor is their iniquity hidden from My eyes. ¹⁸And first I will repay double for their iniquity and their sin, because they have defiled My land; they have filled My inheritance with the carcasses of their detestable and abominable idols."

19   O Lᴏʀᴅ, my strength and my
          fortress,
       My refuge in the day of
          affliction,
       The Gentiles shall come to
          You
       From the ends of the earth
          and say,
       "Surely our fathers have
          inherited lies,
       Worthlessness and
          unprofitable *things.*"
20   Will a man make gods for
          himself,

Which *are* not gods?

21   "Therefore behold, I will this
          once cause them to know,
       I will cause them to know
       My hand and My might;
       And they shall know that My
          name *is* the Lᴏʀᴅ.

"Tʜᴇ sin of Judah *is* written with a pen
          of iron;
       With the point of a diamond *it*
          is engraved
       On the tablet of their heart,
       And on the horns of your
          altars,
2   While their children
          remember
       Their altars and their wooden
          images*
       By the green trees on the
          high hills.
3   O My mountain in the field,
       I will give as plunder your
          wealth, all your treasures,
       And your high places of sin
          within all your borders.
4   And you, even yourself,
       Shall let go of your heritage
          which I gave you;
       And I will cause you to serve
          your enemies

In the land which you do not
    know;
For you have kindled a fire in
    My anger *which* shall burn
    forever."

5Thus says the Lord:

"Cursed *is* the man who trusts
    in man
And makes flesh his strength,
Whose heart departs from
    the Lord.
6 For he shall be like a shrub in
    the desert,
And shall not see when good
    comes,
But shall inhabit the parched
    places in the wilderness,
In a salt land *which is* not
    inhabited.

7 "Blessed *is* the man who trusts
    in the Lord,
And whose hope is the Lord.
8 For he shall be like a tree
    planted by the waters,
Which spreads out its roots
    by the river,
And will not fear* when heat
    comes;
But its leaf will be green,
And will not be anxious in the
    year of drought,
Nor will cease from yielding
    fruit.

9 "The heart *is* deceitful above
    all *things,*
And desperately wicked;
Who can know it?
10 I, the Lord, search the heart,
I test the mind,
Even to give every man
    according to his ways,
According to the fruit of his
    doings.

11 "*As* a partridge that broods but
    does not hatch,

So is he who gets riches, but
    not by right;
It will leave him in the midst
    of his days,
And at his end he will be a
    fool."

12 A glorious high throne from
    the beginning
Is the place of our sanctuary.
13 O Lord, the hope of Israel,
All who forsake You shall be
    ashamed.

"Those who depart from Me
Shall be written in the earth,
Because they have forsaken
    the Lord,
The fountain of living waters."

14 Heal me, O Lord, and I shall
    be healed;
Save me, and I shall be saved,
For You *are* my praise.
15 Indeed they say to me,
"Where *is* the word of the
    Lord?
Let it come now!"
16 As for me, I have not hurried
    away from *being* a shepherd
    who follows You,
Nor have I desired the woeful
    day;
You know what came out of
    my lips;
It was right there before You.
17 Do not be a terror to me;
You *are* my hope in the day of
    doom.
18 Let them be ashamed who
    persecute me,
But do not let me be put to
    shame;
Let them be dismayed,
But do not let me be
    dismayed.
Bring on them the day of
    doom,
And destroy them with
    double destruction!

¹⁹Thus the LORD said to me: "Go and stand in the gate of the children of the people, by which the kings of Judah come in and by which they go out, and in all the gates of Jerusalem; ²⁰and say to them, 'Hear the word of the LORD, you kings of Judah, and all Judah, and all the inhabitants of Jerusalem, who enter by these gates. ²¹Thus says the LORD: "Take heed to yourselves, and bear no burden on the Sabbath day, nor bring it in by the gates of Jerusalem; ²²nor carry a burden out of your houses on the Sabbath day, nor do any work, but hallow the Sabbath day, as I commanded your fathers. ²³But they did not obey nor incline their ear, but made their neck stiff, that they might not hear nor receive instruction.

²⁴"And it shall be, if you heed Me carefully," says the LORD, "to bring no burden through the gates of this city on the Sabbath day, but hallow the Sabbath day, to do no work in it, ²⁵then shall enter the gates of this city kings and princes sitting on the throne of David, riding in chariots and on horses, they and their princes, accompanied by the men of Judah and the inhabitants of Jerusalem; and this city shall remain forever. ²⁶And they shall come from the cities of Judah and from the places around Jerusalem, from the land of Benjamin and from the lowland, from the mountains and from the South, bringing burnt offerings and sacrifices, grain offerings and incense, bringing sacrifices of praise to the house of the LORD.

²⁷"But if you will not heed Me to hallow the Sabbath day, such as not carrying a burden when entering the gates of Jerusalem on the Sabbath day, then I will kindle a fire in its gates, and it shall devour the palaces of Jerusalem, and it shall not be quenched." ' "

THE word which came to Jeremiah from the LORD, saying: ²"Arise and go down to the potter's house, and there I will cause you to hear My words." ³Then I went down to the potter's house, and there he was, making something at the wheel. ⁴And the vessel that he made of clay was marred in the hand of the potter; so he made it again into another vessel, as it seemed good to the potter to make.

⁵Then the word of the LORD came to me, saying: ⁶"O house of Israel, can I not do with you as this potter?" says the LORD. "Look, as the clay is in the potter's hand, so are you in My hand, O house of Israel! ⁷The instant I speak concerning a nation and concerning a kingdom, to pluck up, to pull down, and to destroy it, ⁸if that nation against whom I have spoken turns from its evil, I will relent of the disaster that I thought to bring upon it. ⁹And the instant I speak concerning a nation and concerning a kingdom, to build and to plant it, ¹⁰if it does evil in My sight so that it does not obey My voice, then I will relent concerning the good with which I said I would benefit it.

¹¹"Now therefore, speak to the men of Judah and to the inhabitants of Jerusalem, saying, 'Thus says the LORD: "Behold, I am fashioning a disaster and devising a plan against you. Return now every one from his evil way, and make your ways and your doings good." ' "

¹²And they said, "That is hopeless! So we will walk according to our own plans, and we will every one obey the dictates of his evil heart."

¹³Therefore thus says the LORD:

"Ask now among the Gentiles,
Who has heard such things?
The virgin of Israel has done
a very horrible thing.
14 Will a man leave the snow
water of Lebanon,
Which comes from the rock of
the field?
Will the cold flowing waters

be forsaken for strange
waters?

15 "Because My people have
forgotten Me,
They have burned incense to
worthless idols.
And they have caused
themselves to stumble in
their ways,
From the ancient paths,
To walk in pathways and not
on a highway,
16 To make their land desolate
and a perpetual hissing;
Everyone who passes by it
will be astonished
And shake his head.
17 I will scatter them as with an
east wind before the enemy;
I will show them* the back
and not the face
In the day of their calamity."

18Then they said, "Come and let us
devise plans against Jeremiah; for the
law shall not perish from the priest,
nor counsel from the wise, nor the
word from the prophet. Come and let
us attack him with the tongue, and let
us not give heed to any of his words."

19 Give heed to me, O Lord,
And listen to the voice of
those who contend with me!
20 Shall evil be repaid for good?
For they have dug a pit for my
life.
Remember that I stood before
You
To speak good for them,
To turn away Your wrath from
them.
21 Therefore deliver up their
children to the famine,
And pour out their *blood*
By the force of the sword;
Let their wives *become* widows
And bereaved of their
children.

Let their men be put to death,
Their young men *be* slain
By the sword in battle.
22 Let a cry be heard from their
houses,
When You bring a troop
suddenly upon them;
For they have dug a pit to
take me,
And hidden snares for my feet.
23 Yet, Lord, You know all their
counsel
Which is against me, to slay
me.
Provide no atonement for
their iniquity,
Nor blot out their sin from
Your sight;
But let them be overthrown
before You.
Deal *thus* with them
In the time of Your anger.

1 THESSALONIANS 4:1–5:3

FINALLY then, brethren, we urge
and exhort in the Lord Jesus that
you should abound more and
more, just as you received from us how
you ought to walk and to please God;
2for you know what commandments we
gave you through the Lord Jesus.

3For this is the will of God, your
sanctification: that you should abstain
from sexual immorality; 4that each of
you should know how to possess his
own vessel in sanctification and honor,
5not in passion of lust, like the Gentiles
who do not know God; 6that no one
should take advantage of and defraud
his brother in this matter, because the
Lord *is* the avenger of all such, as we
also forewarned you and testified. 7For
God did not call us to uncleanness, but
in holiness. 8Therefore he who rejects
this does not reject man, but God, who
has also given* us His Holy Spirit.

9But concerning brotherly love you
have no need that I should write to you,
for you yourselves are taught by God to

love one another; [10]and indeed you do so toward all the brethren who are in all Macedonia. But we urge you, brethren, that you increase more and more; [11]that you also aspire to lead a quiet life, to mind your own business, and to work with your own hands, as we commanded you, [12]that you may walk properly toward those who are outside, and *that* you may lack nothing.

[13]But I do not want you to be ignorant, brethren, concerning those who have fallen asleep, lest you sorrow as others who have no hope. [14]For if we believe that Jesus died and rose again, even so God will bring with Him those who sleep in Jesus.*

[15]For this we say to you by the word of the Lord, that we who are alive *and* remain until the coming of the Lord will by no means precede those who are asleep. [16]For the Lord Himself will descend from heaven with a shout, with the voice of an archangel, and with the trumpet of God. And the dead in Christ will rise first. [17]Then we who are alive *and* remain shall be caught up together with them in the clouds to meet the Lord in the air. And thus we shall always be with the Lord. [18]Therefore comfort one another with these words.

BUT concerning the times and the seasons, brethren, you have no need that I should write to you. [2]For you yourselves know perfectly that the day of the Lord so comes as a thief in the night. [3]For when they say, "Peace and safety!" then sudden destruction comes upon them, as labor pains upon a pregnant woman. And they shall not escape.

PSALM 81:1-16

To the Chief Musician. On an instrument of Gath. * *A Psalm of Asaph.*

SING aloud to God our strength; Make a joyful shout to the God of Jacob.
[2] Raise a song and strike the timbrel,

The pleasant harp with the lute.
[3] Blow the trumpet at the time of the New Moon,
At the full moon, on our solemn feast day.
[4] For this *is* a statute for Israel, A law of the God of Jacob.
[5] This He established in Joseph *as* a testimony,
When He went throughout the land of Egypt,
Where I heard a language I did not understand.

[6] "I removed his shoulder from the burden;
His hands were freed from the baskets.
[7] You called in trouble, and I delivered you;
I answered you in the secret place of thunder;
I tested you at the waters of Meribah. Selah

[8] "Hear, O My people, and I will admonish you!
O Israel, if you will listen to Me!
[9] There shall be no foreign god among you;
Nor shall you worship any foreign god.
[10] I *am* the LORD your God, Who brought you out of the land of Egypt;
Open your mouth wide, and I will fill it.

[11] "But My people would not heed My voice,
And Israel would *have* none of Me.
[12] So I gave them over to their own stubborn heart,
To walk in their own counsels.

13 "Oh, that My people would
    listen to Me,
    That Israel would walk in My
    ways!
14 I would soon subdue their
    enemies,
    And turn My hand against
    their adversaries.

15 The haters of the LORD would
    pretend submission to Him,
    But their fate would endure
    forever.
16 He would have fed them also
    with the finest of wheat;
    And with honey from the rock
    I would have satisfied you."

PROVERBS FOR TODAY / 25:6-7

Do not exalt yourself in the presence of the king, and do not stand in the place of the great; for it is *better that he say to you, "Come up here," than that you should be put lower in the presence of the prince, whom your eyes have seen.*

OCTOBER 12

JEREMIAH 19:1–21:14

THUS says the LORD: "Go and get a potter's earthen flask, and *take* some of the elders of the people and some of the elders of the priests. 2And go out to the Valley of the Son of Hinnom, which *is* by the entry of the Potsherd Gate; and proclaim there the words that I will tell you, 3and say, 'Hear the word of the LORD, O kings of Judah and inhabitants of Jerusalem. Thus says the LORD of hosts, the God of Israel: "Behold, I will bring such a catastrophe on this place, that whoever hears of it, his ears will tingle.

4"Because they have forsaken Me and made this an alien place, because they have burned incense in it to other gods whom neither they, their fathers, nor the kings of Judah have known, and have filled this place with the blood of the innocents 5(they have also built the high places of Baal, to burn their sons with fire *for* burnt offerings to Baal, which I did not command or speak, nor did it come into My mind), 6therefore behold, the days are coming," says the LORD, "that this place

shall no more be called Tophet or the Valley of the Son of Hinnom, but the Valley of Slaughter. 7And I will make void the counsel of Judah and Jerusalem in this place, and I will cause them to fall by the sword before their enemies and by the hands of those who seek their lives; their corpses I will give as meat for the birds of the heaven and for the beasts of the earth. 8I will make this city desolate and a hissing; everyone who passes by it will be astonished and hiss because of all its plagues. 9And I will cause them to eat the flesh of their sons and the flesh of their daughters, and everyone shall eat the flesh of his friend in the siege and in the desperation with which their enemies and those who seek their lives shall drive them to despair." '

10"Then you shall break the flask in the sight of the men who go with you, 11and say to them, 'Thus says the LORD of hosts: "Even so I will break this people and this city, as *one* breaks a potter's vessel, which cannot be made whole again; and they shall bury *them* in Tophet till *there is* no place to bury. 12Thus I will do to this place," says the

LORD, "and to its inhabitants, and make this city like Tophet. ¹³And the houses of Jerusalem and the houses of the kings of Judah shall be defiled like the place of Tophet, because of all the houses on whose roofs they have burned incense to all the host of heaven, and poured out drink offerings to other gods." ' "

¹⁴Then Jeremiah came from Tophet, where the LORD had sent him to prophesy; and he stood in the court of the Lord's house and said to all the people, ¹⁵"Thus says the LORD of hosts, the God of Israel: 'Behold, I will bring on this city and on all her towns all the doom that I have pronounced against it, because they have stiffened their necks that they might not hear My words.' "

Now Pashhur the son of Immer, the priest who *was* also chief governor in the house of the LORD, heard that Jeremiah prophesied these things. ²Then Pashhur struck Jeremiah the prophet, and put him in the stocks that *were* in the high gate of Benjamin, which *was* by the house of the LORD.

³And it happened on the next day that Pashhur brought Jeremiah out of the stocks. Then Jeremiah said to him, "The LORD has not called your name Pashhur, but Magor-Missabib.* ⁴For thus says the LORD: 'Behold, I will make you a terror to yourself and to all your friends; and they shall fall by the sword of their enemies, and your eyes shall see *it.* I will give all Judah into the hand of the king of Babylon, and he shall carry them captive to Babylon and slay them with the sword. ⁵Moreover I will deliver all the wealth of this city, all its produce, and all its precious things; all the treasures of the kings of Judah I will give into the hand of their enemies, who will plunder them, seize them, and carry them to Babylon. ⁶And you, Pashhur, and all who dwell in your house, shall go into captivity.

You shall go to Babylon, and there you shall die, and be buried there, you and all your friends, to whom you have prophesied lies.' "

7   O LORD, You induced me, and
   I was persuaded;
  You are stronger than I, and
   have prevailed.
  I am in derision daily;
  Everyone mocks me.
8   For when I spoke, I cried out;
  I shouted, "Violence and
   plunder!"
  Because the word of the LORD
   was made to me
  A reproach and a derision
   daily.
9   Then I said, "I will not make
   mention of Him,
  Nor speak anymore in His
   name."
  But *His word* was in my heart
   like a burning fire
  Shut up in my bones;
  I was weary of holding *it* back,
  And I could not.
10 For I heard many mocking:
  "Fear on every side!"
  "Report," *they say,* "and we will
   report it!"
  All my acquaintances watched
   for my stumbling, *saying,*
  "Perhaps he can be induced;
  Then we will prevail against
   him,
  And we will take our revenge
   on him."

11 But the LORD *is* with me as a
   mighty, awesome One.
  Therefore my persecutors will
   stumble, and will not
   prevail.
  They will be greatly ashamed,
   for they will not prosper.
  Their everlasting confusion
   will never be forgotten.
12 But, O LORD of hosts,
  You who test the righteous,

And see the mind and heart,
Let me see Your vengeance
on them;
For I have pleaded my cause
before You.

13 Sing to the LORD! Praise the
LORD!
For He has delivered the life
of the poor
From the hand of evildoers.

14 Cursed *be* the day in which I
was born!
Let the day not be blessed in
which my mother bore me!

15 Let the man *be* cursed
Who brought news to my
father, saying,
"A male child has been born to
you!"
Making him very glad.

16 And let that man be like the
cities
Which the LORD overthrew,
and did not relent;
Let him hear the cry in the
morning
And the shouting at noon,

17 Because he did not kill me
from the womb,
That my mother might have
been my grave,
And her womb always
enlarged *with me*.

18 Why did I come forth from
the womb to see labor and
sorrow,
That my days should be
consumed with shame?

THE word which came to Jeremiah
from the LORD when King Zedekiah
sent to him Pashhur the son of
Melchiah, and Zephaniah the son of
Maaseiah, the priest, saying, 2"Please
inquire of the LORD for us, for Nebuchadnezzar* king of Babylon makes
war against us. Perhaps the LORD will
deal with us according to all His wonderful works, that *the king* may go
away from us."

3Then Jeremiah said to them, "Thus
you shall say to Zedekiah, 4"Thus says
the LORD God of Israel: "Behold, I will
turn back the weapons of war that *are*
in your hands, with which you fight
against the king of Babylon and the
Chaldeans* who besiege you outside
the walls; and I will assemble them in
the midst of this city. 5I Myself will
fight against you with an outstretched
hand and with a strong arm, even in
anger and fury and great wrath. 6I will
strike the inhabitants of this city, both
man and beast; they shall die of a great
pestilence. 7And afterward," says the
LORD, "I will deliver Zedekiah king of
Judah, his servants and the people,
and such as are left in this city from the
pestilence and the sword and the famine, into the hand of Nebuchadnezzar
king of Babylon, into the hand of their
enemies, and into the hand of those
who seek their life; and he shall strike
them with the edge of the sword. He
shall not spare them, or have pity or
mercy." '

8"Now you shall say to this people,
'Thus says the LORD: "Behold, I set before you the way of life and the way of
death. 9He who remains in this city
shall die by the sword, by famine, and
by pestilence; but he who goes out and
defects to the Chaldeans who besiege
you, he shall live, and his life shall be
as a prize to him. 10For I have set My
face against this city for adversity and
not for good," says the LORD. "It shall
be given into the hand of the king of
Babylon, and he shall burn it with fire." '

11"And concerning the house of the
king of Judah, *say,* 'Hear the word of
the LORD, 12O house of David! Thus
says the LORD:

"Execute judgment in the
morning;
And deliver *him who is*
plundered

Out of the hand of the
oppressor,
Lest My fury go forth like fire
And burn so that no one can
quench *it,*
Because of the evil of your
doings.

13 "Behold, I *am* against you,
O inhabitant of the valley,
And rock of the plain," says
the LORD,
"Who say, 'Who shall come
down against us?
Or who shall enter our
dwellings?'
14 But I will punish you
according to the fruit of
your doings," says the LORD;
"I will kindle a fire in its forest,
And it shall devour all things
around it." ' "

1 THESSALONIANS 5:4-28

BUT you, brethren, are not in
darkness, so that this Day
should overtake you as a thief.
5You are all sons of light and sons of
the day. We are not of the night nor of
darkness. 6Therefore let us not sleep,
as others *do,* but let us watch and be
sober. 7For those who sleep, sleep at
night, and those who get drunk are
drunk at night. 8But let us who are of
the day be sober, putting on the breastplate of faith and love, and *as* a helmet
the hope of salvation. 9For God did not
appoint us to wrath, but to obtain salvation through our Lord Jesus Christ,
10who died for us, that whether we
wake or sleep, we should live together
with Him.

11Therefore comfort each other and
edify one another, just as you also are
doing.

12And we urge you, brethren, to recognize those who labor among you,
and are over you in the Lord and admonish you, 13and to esteem them

very highly in love for their work's
sake. Be at peace among yourselves.

14Now we exhort you, brethren,
warn those who are unruly, comfort
the fainthearted, uphold the weak, be
patient with all. 15See that no one rend-
ers evil for evil to anyone, but always
pursue what is good both for yourselves and for all.

16Rejoice always, 17pray without
ceasing, 18in everything give thanks;
for this is the will of God in Christ
Jesus for you.

19Do not quench the Spirit. 20Do not
despise prophecies. 21Test all things;
hold fast what is good. 22Abstain from
every form of evil.

23Now may the God of peace Himself sanctify you completely; and may
your whole spirit, soul, and body be
preserved blameless at the coming of
our Lord Jesus Christ. 24He who calls
you *is* faithful, who also will do *it.*

25Brethren, pray for us.

26Greet all the brethren with a holy
kiss.

27I charge you by the Lord that this
epistle be read to all the holy*
brethren.

28The grace of our Lord Jesus Christ
be with you. Amen.

PSALM 82:1-8

A Psalm of Asaph.

GOD stands in the congregation
of the mighty;
He judges among the gods.*
2 How long will you judge
unjustly,
And show partiality to the
wicked?   Selah
3 Defend the poor and
fatherless;
Do justice to the afflicted and
needy.
4 Deliver the poor and needy;
Free *them* from the hand of
the wicked.

5   They do not know, nor do
       they understand;
     They walk about in darkness;
     All the foundations of the
       earth are unstable.

6   I said, "You *are* gods,*
     And all of you *are* children of
     the Most High.

7   But you shall die like men,
     And fall like one of the
       princes."

8   Arise, O God, judge the earth;
     For You shall inherit all
       nations.

PROVERBS FOR TODAY / 25:8-10

Do not go hastily to court; for what will you do in the end, when your neighbor has put you to shame? Debate your case with your neighbor, and do not disclose the secret to another; lest he who hears it expose your shame, and your reputation be ruined.

OCTOBER 13

JEREMIAH 22:1–23:20

THUS says the LORD: "Go down to the house of the king of Judah, and there speak this word, ²and say, 'Hear the word of the LORD, O king of Judah, you who sit on the throne of David, you and your servants and your people who enter these gates! ³Thus says the LORD: "Execute judgment and righteousness, and deliver the plundered out of the hand of the oppressor. Do no wrong and do no violence to the stranger, the fatherless, or the widow, nor shed innocent blood in this place. ⁴For if you indeed do this thing, then shall enter the gates of this house, riding on horses and in chariots, accompanied by servants and people, kings who sit on the throne of David. ⁵But if you will not hear these words, I swear by Myself," says the LORD, "that this house shall become a desolation." ' "

⁶For thus says the LORD to the house of the king of Judah:

     "You *are* Gilead to Me,
     The head of Lebanon;
     Yet I surely will make you a
       wilderness,
     Cities *which* are not inhabited.

7   I will prepare destroyers
       against you,
     Everyone with his weapons;
     They shall cut down your
       choice cedars
     And cast *them* into the fire.

⁸And many nations will pass by this city; and everyone will say to his neighbor, 'Why has the LORD done so to this great city?' ⁹Then they will answer, 'Because they have forsaken the covenant of the LORD their God, and worshiped other gods and served them.' "

10   Weep not for the dead, nor
       bemoan him;
     Weep bitterly for him who
       goes away,
     For he shall return no more,
     Nor see his native country.

¹¹For thus says the Lᴏʀᴅ concerning Shallum* the son of Josiah, king of Judah, who reigned instead of Josiah his father, who went from this place: "He shall not return here anymore, ¹²but he shall die in the place where they have led him captive, and shall see this land no more.

13   "Woe to him who builds his
          house by unrighteousness
      And his chambers by injustice,
      Who uses his neighbor's
          service without wages
      And gives him nothing for his
          work,
14   Who says, 'I will build myself
          a wide house with spacious
          chambers,
      And cut out windows for it,
      Paneling *it* with cedar
      And painting *it* with vermilion.'

15   "Shall you reign because you
          enclose *yourself* in cedar?
      Did not your father eat and
          drink,
      And do justice and
          righteousness?
      Then *it was* well with him.
16   He judged the cause of the
          poor and needy;
      Then *it was* well.
      Was not this knowing Me?"
          says the Lᴏʀᴅ.
17   "Yet your eyes and your heart
          are for nothing but your
          covetousness,
      For shedding innocent blood,
      And practicing oppression
          and violence."

¹⁸Therefore thus says the Lᴏʀᴅ concerning Jehoiakim the son of Josiah, king of Judah:

      "They shall not lament for him,
      Saying, 'Alas, my brother!' or
          'Alas, my sister!'
      They shall not lament for him,

      Saying, 'Alas, master!' or
          'Alas, his glory!'
19   He shall be buried with the
          burial of a donkey,
      Dragged and cast out beyond
          the gates of Jerusalem.

20   "Go up to Lebanon, and cry
          out,
      And lift up your voice in
          Bashan;
      Cry from Abarim,
      For all your lovers are
          destroyed.
21   I spoke to you in your
          prosperity,
      But you said, 'I will not hear.'
      This *has been* your manner
          from your youth,
      That you did not obey My
          voice.
22   The wind shall eat up all your
          rulers,
      And your lovers shall go into
          captivity;
      Surely then you will be
          ashamed and humiliated
      For all your wickedness.
23   O inhabitant of Lebanon,
      Making your nest in the
          cedars,
      How gracious will you be
          when pangs come upon you,
      Like the pain of a woman in
          labor?

²⁴"*As* I live," says the Lᴏʀᴅ, "though Coniah* the son of Jehoiakim, king of Judah, were the signet on My right hand, yet I would pluck you off; ²⁵and I will give you into the hand of those who seek your life, and into the hand *of those* whose face you fear—the hand of Nebuchadnezzar king of Babylon and the hand of the Chaldeans. ²⁶So I will cast you out, and your mother who bore you, into another country where you were not born; and there you shall die. ²⁷But to the land to which they desire to return, there they shall not return.

28 "Is this man Coniah a
despised, broken idol—
A vessel in which *is* no
pleasure?
Why are they cast out, he and
his descendants,
And cast into a land which
they do not know?

29 O earth, earth, earth,
Hear the word of the LORD!

30 Thus says the LORD:
'Write this man down as
childless,
A man *who* shall not prosper
in his days;
For none of his descendants
shall prosper,
Sitting on the throne of David,
And ruling anymore in Judah.' "

"WOE to the shepherds who destroy
and scatter the sheep of My pasture!"
says the LORD. ²Therefore thus says
the LORD God of Israel against the
shepherds who feed My people: "You
have scattered My flock, driven them
away, and not attended to them. Behold, I will attend to you for the evil of
your doings," says the LORD. ³"But I
will gather the remnant of My flock out
of all the countries where I have driven
them, and bring them back to their
folds; and they shall be fruitful and increase. ⁴I will set up shepherds over
them who will feed them; and they
shall fear no more, nor be dismayed,
nor shall they be lacking," says the
LORD.

5 "Behold, *the* days are coming,"
says the LORD,
"That I will raise to David a
Branch of righteousness;
A King shall reign and
prosper,
And execute judgment and
righteousness in the earth.

6 In His days Judah will be
saved,
And Israel will dwell safely;

Now this *is* His name by
which He will be called:

THE LORD OUR
RIGHTEOUSNESS.*

⁷"Therefore, behold, *the* days are
coming," says the LORD, "that they
shall no longer say, 'As the LORD lives
who brought up the children of Israel
from the land of Egypt,' ⁸but, 'As the
LORD lives who brought up and led the
descendants of the house of Israel
from the north country and from all
the countries where I had driven
them.' And they shall dwell in their
own land."

9 My heart within me is broken
Because of the prophets;
All my bones shake.
I am like a drunken man,
And like a man whom wine
has overcome,
Because of the LORD,
And because of His holy
words.

10 For the land is full of
adulterers;
For because of a curse the
land mourns.
The pleasant places of the
wilderness are dried up.
Their course of life is evil,
And their might *is* not right.

11 "For both prophet and priest
are profane;
Yes, in My house I have found
their wickedness," says the
LORD.

12 "Therefore their way shall be
to them
Like slippery *ways;*
In the darkness they shall be
driven on
And fall in them;
For I will bring disaster on
them,

The year of their
punishment," says the LORD.

13 "And I have seen folly in the
prophets of Samaria:
They prophesied by Baal
And caused My people Israel
to err.

14 Also I have seen a horrible
thing in the prophets of
Jerusalem:
They commit adultery and
walk in lies;
They also strengthen the
hands of evildoers,
So that no one turns back
from his wickedness.
All of them are like Sodom to
Me,
And her inhabitants like
Gomorrah.

15"Therefore thus says the LORD of
hosts concerning the prophets:

'Behold, I will feed them with
wormwood,
And make them drink the
water of gall;
For from the prophets of
Jerusalem
Profaneness has gone out into
all the land.' "

16Thus says the LORD of hosts:

"Do not listen to the words of
the prophets who prophesy
to you.
They make you worthless;
They speak a vision of their
own heart,
Not from the mouth of the
LORD.

17 They continually say to those
who despise Me,
The LORD has said, "You shall
have peace" ';
And to everyone who walks
according to the dictates of
his own heart, they say,

'No evil shall come upon you.' "

18 For who has stood in the
counsel of the LORD,
And has perceived and heard
His word?
Who has marked His word
and heard it?

19 Behold, a whirlwind of the
LORD has gone forth in
fury—
A violent whirlwind!
It will fall violently on the
head of the wicked.

20 The anger of the LORD will not
turn back
Until He has executed and
performed the thoughts of
His heart.
In the latter days you will
understand it perfectly.

2 THESSALONIANS 1:1-12

PAUL, Silvanus, and Timothy,

To the church of the Thessalonians in God our Father and the Lord Jesus Christ:

2Grace to you and peace from God our Father and the Lord Jesus Christ.

3We are bound to thank God always for you, brethren, as it is fitting, because your faith grows exceedingly, and the love of every one of you all abounds toward each other, 4so that we ourselves boast of you among the churches of God for your patience and faith in all your persecutions and tribulations that you endure, 5which is manifest evidence of the righteous judgment of God, that you may be counted worthy of the kingdom of God, for which you also suffer; 6since it is a righteous thing with God to repay with tribulation those who trouble you, 7and to give you who are troubled rest with us when the Lord Jesus is revealed from heaven with His mighty angels, 8in flaming fire taking vengeance on those who do not know God, and on those who do not obey the gospel of our Lord Jesus Christ. 9These shall be punished with everlasting destruction from the presence of the Lord and from the glory of His power, 10when He comes, in that Day, to be glorified in His saints and to be admired among all those who believe,* because our testimony among you was believed.

11Therefore we also pray always for you that our God would count you worthy of *this* calling, and fulfill all the good pleasure of *His* goodness and the work of faith with power, 12that the name of our Lord Jesus Christ may be glorified in you, and you in Him, according to the grace of our God and the Lord Jesus Christ.

PSALM 83:1-18

A Song. A Psalm of Asaph.

Do not keep silent, O God!
Do not hold Your peace,
And do not be still, O God!
2 For behold, Your enemies
make a tumult;
And those who hate You have
lifted up their head.
3 They have taken crafty
counsel against Your
people,
And consulted together
against Your sheltered ones.
4 They have said, "Come, and
let us cut them off from
being a nation,
That the name of Israel may
be remembered no more."

5 For they have consulted
together with one consent;
They form a confederacy
against You:

6 The tents of Edom and the
Ishmaelites;
Moab and the Hagrites;
7 Gebal, Ammon, and Amalek;
Philistia with the inhabitants
of Tyre;
8 Assyria also has joined with
them;
They have helped the
children of Lot.   Selah

9 Deal with them as *with*
Midian,
As *with* Sisera,
As *with* Jabin at the Brook
Kishon,
10 Who perished at En Dor,
Who became *as* refuse on the
earth.
11 Make their nobles like Oreb
and like Zeeb,
Yes, all their princes like
Zebah and Zalmunna,
12 Who said, "Let us take for
ourselves
The pastures of God for a
possession."

13 O my God, make them like
the whirling dust,
Like the chaff before the wind!
14 As the fire burns the woods,
And as the flame sets the
mountains on fire,
15 So pursue them with Your
tempest,
And frighten them with Your
storm.
16 Fill their faces with shame,
That they may seek Your
name, O LORD.
17 Let them be confounded and
dismayed forever;
Yes, let them be put to shame
and perish,
18 That they may know that You,
whose name alone *is* the
LORD,
Are the Most High over all
the earth.

PROVERBS FOR TODAY / 25:11-14

A word fitly spoken is like *apples of gold in settings of silver.* Like *an earring of gold and an ornament of fine gold* is *a wise rebuker to an obedient ear. Like the cold of snow in time of harvest* is *a faithful messenger to those who send him, for he refreshes the soul of his masters. Whoever falsely boasts of giving* is like *clouds and wind without rain.*

OCTOBER 14

JEREMIAH 23:21–25:38

"**I** HAVE not sent these prophets,
yet they ran.
I have not spoken to them, yet
they prophesied.

22 But if they had stood in My
counsel,
And had caused My people to
hear My words,
Then they would have turned
them from their evil way
And from the evil of their
doings.

23 "*Am* I a God near at hand,"
says the LORD,
"And not a God afar off?
24 Can anyone hide himself in
secret places,
So I shall not see him?" says
the LORD;
"Do I not fill heaven and
earth?" says the LORD.

25"I have heard what the prophets have said who prophesy lies in My name, saying, 'I have dreamed, I have dreamed!' 26How long will *this* be in the heart of the prophets who prophesy lies? Indeed *they are* prophets of the deceit of their own heart, 27who try to make My people forget My name by their dreams which everyone tells his neighbor, as their fathers forgot My name for Baal.

28 "The prophet who has a
dream, let him tell a dream;
And he who has My word, let
him speak My word
faithfully.
What *is* the chaff to the
wheat?" says the LORD.
29 "*Is* not My word like a fire?"
says the LORD,
"And like a hammer *that*
breaks the rock in pieces?

30"Therefore behold, I *am* against the prophets," says the LORD, "who steal My words every one from his neighbor. 31Behold, I *am* against the prophets," says the LORD, "who use their tongues and say, 'He says.' 32Behold, I *am* against those who prophesy false dreams," says the LORD, "and tell them, and cause My people to err by their lies and by their recklessness. Yet I did not send them or command them; therefore they shall not profit this people at all," says the LORD.

33"So when these people or the prophet or the priest ask you, saying, 'What is the oracle of the LORD?' you shall then say to them, 'What oracle?'* I will even forsake you," says the LORD. 34"And *as for* the prophet and the priest and the people who say, 'The oracle of the LORD!' I will even punish that man and his house. 35Thus every one of you shall say to his neighbor, and every one to his brother, 'What has the LORD answered?' and, 'What has the LORD spoken?' ³⁶And the oracle of the LORD you shall mention no more. For every man's word will be his oracle, for you have perverted the words of the living God, the LORD of hosts, our God. ³⁷Thus you shall say to the prophet, 'What has the LORD answered you?' and, 'What has the LORD spoken?' ³⁸But since you say, 'The oracle of the LORD!' therefore thus says the LORD: 'Because you say this word, "The oracle of the LORD!" and I have sent to you, saying, "Do not say, 'The oracle of the LORD!'" ³⁹therefore behold, I, even I, will utterly forget you and forsake you, and the city that I gave you and your fathers, and *will cast you* out of My presence. ⁴⁰And I will bring an everlasting reproach upon you, and a perpetual shame, which shall not be forgotten.' "

THE LORD showed me, and there were two baskets of figs set before the temple of the LORD, after Nebuchadnezzar king of Babylon had carried away captive Jeconiah the son of Jehoiakim, king of Judah, and the princes of Judah with the craftsmen and smiths, from Jerusalem, and had brought them to Babylon. ²One basket *had* very good figs, like the figs *that are* first ripe; and the other basket *had* very bad figs which could not be eaten, they were so bad. ³Then the LORD said to me, "What do you see, Jeremiah?"

And I said, "Figs, the good figs, very good; and the bad, very bad, which cannot be eaten, they are so bad."

⁴Again the word of the LORD came to me, saying, ⁵"Thus says the LORD, the God of Israel: 'Like these good figs, so will I acknowledge those who are carried away captive from Judah, whom I have sent out of this place for *their own* good, into the land of the Chaldeans. ⁶For I will set My eyes on them for good, and I will bring them back to this land; I will build them and not pull *them*

down, and I will plant them and not pluck *them* up. ⁷Then I will give them a heart to know Me, that I *am* the LORD; and they shall be My people, and I will be their God, for they shall return to Me with their whole heart.

⁸'And as the bad figs which cannot be eaten, they are so bad'—surely thus says the LORD—'so will I give up Zedekiah the king of Judah, his princes, the residue of Jerusalem who remain in this land, and those who dwell in the land of Egypt. ⁹I will deliver them to trouble into all the kingdoms of the earth, for *their* harm, *to be* a reproach and a byword, a taunt and a curse, in all places where I shall drive them. ¹⁰And I will send the sword, the famine, and the pestilence among them, till they are consumed from the land that I gave to them and their fathers.' "

THE word that came to Jeremiah concerning all the people of Judah, in the fourth year of Jehoiakim the son of Josiah, king of Judah (which *was* the first year of Nebuchadnezzar king of Babylon), ²which Jeremiah the prophet spoke to all the people of Judah and to all the inhabitants of Jerusalem, saying: ³"From the thirteenth year of Josiah the son of Amon, king of Judah, even to this day, this *is* the twenty-third year in which the word of the LORD has come to me; and I have spoken to you, rising early and speaking, but you have not listened. ⁴And the LORD has sent to you all His servants the prophets, rising early and sending *them,* but you have not listened nor inclined your ear to hear. ⁵They said, 'Repent now everyone of his evil way and his evil doings, and dwell in the land that the LORD has given to you and your fathers forever and ever. ⁶Do not go after other gods to serve them and worship them, and do not provoke Me to anger with the works of your hands; and I will not harm you.' ⁷Yet you have not listened to Me," says the LORD, "that you might provoke Me to anger with the works of your hands to your own hurt.

8"Therefore thus says the Lord of hosts: 'Because you have not heard My words, 9behold, I will send and take all the families of the north,' says the Lord, 'and Nebuchadnezzar the king of Babylon, My servant, and will bring them against this land, against its inhabitants, and against these nations all around, and will utterly destroy them, and make them an astonishment, a hissing, and perpetual desolations. 10Moreover I will take from them the voice of mirth and the voice of gladness, the voice of the bridegroom and the voice of the bride, the sound of the millstone and the light of the lamp. 11And this whole land shall be a desolation and an astonishment, and these nations shall serve the king of Babylon seventy years.

12"Then it will come to pass, when seventy years are completed, that I will punish the king of Babylon and that nation, the land of the Chaldeans, for their iniquity,' says the Lord; 'and I will make it a perpetual desolation. 13So I will bring on that land all My words which I have pronounced against it, all that is written in this book, which Jeremiah has prophesied concerning all the nations. 14(For many nations and great kings shall be served by them also; and I will repay them according to their deeds and according to the works of their own hands.)' "

15For thus says the Lord God of Israel to me: "Take this wine cup of fury from My hand, and cause all the nations, to whom I send you, to drink it. 16And they will drink and stagger and go mad because of the sword that I will send among them."

17Then I took the cup from the Lord's hand, and made all the nations drink, to whom the Lord had sent me: 18Jerusalem and the cities of Judah, its kings and its princes, to make them a desolation, an astonishment, a hissing, and a curse, as it is this day; 19Pharaoh king of Egypt, his servants, his princes, and all his people; 20all the mixed multitude, all the kings of the land of Uz, all the kings of the land of the Philistines (namely, Ashkelon, Gaza, Ekron, and the remnant of Ashdod); 21Edom, Moab, and the people of Ammon; 22all the kings of Tyre, all the kings of Sidon, and the kings of the coastlands which are across the sea; 23Dedan, Tema, Buz, and all who are in the farthest corners; 24all the kings of Arabia and all the kings of the mixed multitude who dwell in the desert; 25all the kings of Zimri, all the kings of Elam, and all the kings of the Medes; 26all the kings of the north, far and near, one with another; and all the kingdoms of the world which are on the face of the earth. Also the king of Sheshach* shall drink after them.

27"Therefore you shall say to them, 'Thus says the Lord of hosts, the God of Israel: "Drink, be drunk, and vomit! Fall and rise no more, because of the sword which I will send among you." ' 28And it shall be, if they refuse to take the cup from your hand to drink, then you shall say to them, 'Thus says the Lord of hosts: "You shall certainly drink! 29For behold, I begin to bring calamity on the city which is called by My name, and should you be utterly unpunished? You shall not be unpunished, for I will call for a sword on all the inhabitants of the earth," says the Lord of hosts.'

30"Therefore prophesy against them all these words, and say to them:

'The Lord will roar from on high,
And utter His voice from His holy habitation;
He will roar mightily against His fold.

He will give a shout, as those
who tread *the grapes,*
Against all the inhabitants of
the earth.
31 A noise will come to the ends
of the earth—
For the LORD has a
controversy with the
nations;
He will plead His case with all
flesh.
He will give those *who are*
wicked to the sword,' says
the LORD."

32Thus says the LORD of hosts:

"Behold, disaster shall go forth
From nation to nation,
And a great whirlwind shall
be raised up
From the farthest parts of the
earth.

33"And at that day the slain of the LORD shall be from *one* end of the earth even to the *other* end of the earth. They shall not be lamented, or gathered, or buried; they shall become refuse on the ground.

34 "Wail, shepherds, and cry!
Roll about *in the ashes,*
You leaders of the flock!
For the days of your slaughter
and your dispersions are
fulfilled;
You shall fall like a precious
vessel.
35 And the shepherds will have
no way to flee,
Nor the leaders of the flock to
escape.
36 A voice of the cry of the
shepherds,
And a wailing of the leaders to
the flock *will be heard.*
For the LORD has plundered
their pasture,

37 And the peaceful dwellings
are cut down
Because of the fierce anger of
the LORD.
38 He has left His lair like the
lion;
For their land is desolate
Because of the fierceness of
the Oppressor,
And because of His fierce
anger."

2 THESSALONIANS 2:1-17

Now, brethren, concerning the coming of our Lord Jesus Christ and our gathering together to Him, we ask you, 2not to be soon shaken in mind or troubled, either by spirit or by word or by letter, as if from us, as though the day of Christ* had come. 3Let no one deceive you by any means; for *that Day will not come* unless the falling away comes first, and the man of sin* is revealed, the son of perdition, 4who opposes and exalts himself above all that is called God or that is worshiped, so that he sits as God* in the temple of God, showing himself that he is God.

5Do you not remember that when I was still with you I told you these things? 6And now you know what is restraining, that he may be revealed in his own time. 7For the mystery of lawlessness is already at work; only He* who now restrains *will do so* until He* is taken out of the way. 8And then the lawless one will be revealed, whom the Lord will consume with the breath of His mouth and destroy with the brightness of His coming. 9The coming of the *lawless one* is according to the working of Satan, with all power, signs, and lying wonders, 10and with all unrighteous deception among those who perish, because they did not receive the love of the truth, that they might be saved. 11And for this reason God will send them strong delusion, that they should believe the lie, 12that they all may be condemned who did not believe the truth but had pleasure in unrighteousness.

13But we are bound to give thanks to God always for you, brethren beloved by the Lord, because God from the beginning chose you for salvation through sanctification by the Spirit and belief in the truth, 14to which He called you by our gospel, for the obtaining of the glory of our Lord Jesus Christ. 15Therefore, brethren, stand fast and hold the traditions which you were taught, whether by word or our epistle.

16Now may our Lord Jesus Christ Himself, and our God and Father, who has loved us and given *us* everlasting consolation and good hope by grace, 17comfort your hearts and establish you in every good word and work.

PSALM 84:1-12

To the Chief Musician. On an instrument of Gath. * A Psalm of the sons of Korah.

How lovely *is* Your tabernacle,
O LORD of hosts!
2My soul longs, yes, even faints
For the courts of the LORD;
My heart and my flesh cry out for the living God.

3 Even the sparrow has found a home,
And the swallow a nest for herself,
Where she may lay her young—
Even Your altars, O LORD of hosts,
My King and my God.

4 Blessed *are* those who dwell in Your house;
They will still be praising You.
                                    Selah

5 Blessed *is* the man whose strength *is* in You,
Whose heart *is* set on pilgrimage.
6 *As they* pass through the Valley of Baca,
They make it a spring;
The rain also covers it with pools.
7 They go from strength to strength;
Each one appears before God in Zion.*

8 O LORD God of hosts, hear my prayer;
Give ear, O God of Jacob!
                                    Selah
9 O God, behold our shield,
And look upon the face of Your anointed.

10 For a day in Your courts *is* better than a thousand.
I would rather be a doorkeeper in the house of my God
Than dwell in the tents of wickedness.
11 For the LORD God *is* a sun and shield;
The LORD will give grace and glory;
No good *thing* will He withhold
From those who walk uprightly.

12 O LORD of hosts,
Blessed *is* the man who trusts in You!

PROVERBS FOR TODAY/ 25:15
By long forbearance a ruler is persuaded, and a gentle tongue breaks a bone.

OCTOBER 15

JEREMIAH 26:1–27:22

I N the beginning of the reign of Jehoiakim the son of Josiah, king of Judah, this word came from the LORD, saying, [2]"Thus says the LORD: 'Stand in the court of the LORD's house, and speak to all the cities of Judah, which come to worship *in* the LORD's house, all the words that I command you to speak to them. Do not diminish a word. [3]Perhaps everyone will listen and turn from his evil way, that I may relent concerning the calamity which I purpose to bring on them because of the evil of their doings.' [4]And you shall say to them, 'Thus says the LORD: "If you will not listen to Me, to walk in My law which I have set before you, [5]to heed the words of My servants the prophets whom I sent to you, both rising up early and sending *them* (but you have not heeded), [6]then I will make this house like Shiloh, and will make this city a curse to all the nations of the earth." ' "

[7]So the priests and the prophets and all the people heard Jeremiah speaking these words in the house of the LORD. [8]Now it happened, when Jeremiah had made an end of speaking all that the LORD had commanded *him* to speak to all the people, that the priests and the prophets and all the people seized him, saying, "You will surely die! [9]Why have you prophesied in the name of the LORD, saying, 'This house shall be like Shiloh, and this city shall be desolate, without an inhabitant'?" And all the people were gathered against Jeremiah in the house of the LORD.

[10]When the princes of Judah heard these things, they came up from the king's house to the house of the LORD and sat down in the entry of the New Gate of the LORD's *house.* [11]And the priests and the prophets spoke to the princes and all the people, saying, "This man deserves to die! For he has prophesied against this city, as you have heard with your ears."

[12]Then Jeremiah spoke to all the princes and all the people, saying: "The LORD sent me to prophesy against this house and against this city with all the words that you have heard. [13]Now therefore, amend your ways and your doings, and obey the voice of the LORD your God; then the LORD will relent concerning the doom that He has pronounced against you. [14]As for me, here I am, in your hand; do with me as seems good and proper to you. [15]But know for certain that if you put me to death, you will surely bring innocent blood on yourselves, on this city, and on its inhabitants; for truly the LORD has sent me to you to speak all these words in your hearing."

[16]So the princes and all the people said to the priests and the prophets, "This man does not deserve to die. For he has spoken to us in the name of the LORD our God."

[17]Then certain of the elders of the land rose up and spoke to all the assembly of the people, saying: [18]"Micah of Moresheth prophesied in the days of Hezekiah king of Judah, and spoke to all the people of Judah, saying, 'Thus says the LORD of hosts:

> "Zion shall be plowed *like* a
> field,
> Jerusalem shall become
> heaps of ruins,
> And the mountain of the
> temple*
> Like the bare hills of the
> forest." '*

¹⁹Did Hezekiah king of Judah and all Judah ever put him to death? Did he not fear the LORD and seek the LORD's favor? And the LORD relented concerning the doom which He had pronounced against them. But we are doing great evil against ourselves."

²⁰Now there was also a man who prophesied in the name of the LORD, Urijah the son of Shemaiah of Kirjath Jearim, who prophesied against this city and against this land according to all the words of Jeremiah. ²¹And when Jehoiakim the king, with all his mighty men and all the princes, heard his words, the king sought to put him to death; but when Urijah heard *it,* he was afraid and fled, and went to Egypt. ²²Then Jehoiakim the king sent men to Egypt: Elnathan the son of Achbor, and *other* men *who went* with him to Egypt. ²³And they brought Urijah from Egypt and brought him to Jehoiakim the king, who killed him with the sword and cast his dead body into the graves of the common people.

²⁴Nevertheless the hand of Ahikam the son of Shaphan was with Jeremiah, so that they should not give him into the hand of the people to put him to death.

In the beginning of the reign of Jehoiakim* the son of Josiah, king of Judah, this word came to Jeremiah from the LORD, saying,* ²"Thus says the LORD to me: 'Make for yourselves bonds and yokes, and put them on your neck, ³and send them to the king of Edom, the king of Moab, the king of the Ammonites, the king of Tyre, and the king of Sidon, by the hand of the messengers who come to Jerusalem to Zedekiah king of Judah. ⁴And command them to say to their masters, "Thus says the LORD of hosts, the God of Israel—thus you shall say to your masters: ⁵'I have made the earth, the man and the beast that *are* on the ground, by My great power and by My out-

stretched arm, and have given it to whom it seemed proper to Me. ⁶And now I have given all these lands into the hand of Nebuchadnezzar the king of Babylon, My servant; and the beasts of the field I have also given him to serve him. ⁷So all nations shall serve him and his son and his son's son, until the time of his land comes; and then many nations and great kings shall make him serve them. ⁸And it shall be, *that* the nation and kingdom which will not serve Nebuchadnezzar the king of Babylon, and which will not put its neck under the yoke of the king of Babylon, that nation I will punish,' says the LORD, 'with the sword, the famine, and the pestilence, until I have consumed them by his hand. ⁹Therefore do not listen to your prophets, your diviners, your dreamers, your soothsayers, or your sorcerers, who speak to you, saying, "You shall not serve the king of Babylon." ¹⁰For they prophesy a lie to you, to remove you far from your land; and I will drive you out, and you will perish. ¹¹But the nations that bring their necks under the yoke of the king of Babylon and serve him, I will let them remain in their own land,' says the LORD, 'and they shall till it and dwell in it.' " ' "

¹²I also spoke to Zedekiah king of Judah according to all these words, saying, "Bring your necks under the yoke of the king of Babylon, and serve him and his people, and live! ¹³Why will you die, you and your people, by the sword, by the famine, and by the pestilence, as the LORD has spoken against the nation that will not serve the king of Babylon? ¹⁴Therefore do not listen to the words of the prophets who speak to you, saying, 'You shall not serve the king of Babylon,' for they prophesy a lie to you; ¹⁵for I have not sent them," says the LORD, "yet they prophesy a lie in My name, that I may drive you out, and that you may perish,

you and the prophets who prophesy to you."

[16]Also I spoke to the priests and to all this people, saying, "Thus says the LORD: 'Do not listen to the words of your prophets who prophesy to you, saying, "Behold, the vessels of the LORD's house will now shortly be brought back from Babylon"; for they prophesy a lie to you. [17]Do not listen to them; serve the king of Babylon, and live! Why should this city be laid waste? [18]But if they *are* prophets, and if the word of the LORD is with them, let them now make intercession to the LORD of hosts, that the vessels which are left in the house of the LORD, *in* the house of the king of Judah, and at Jerusalem, do not go to Babylon.'

[19]"For thus says the LORD of hosts concerning the pillars, concerning the Sea, concerning the carts, and concerning the remainder of the vessels that remain in this city, [20]which Nebuchadnezzar king of Babylon did not take, when he carried away captive Jeconiah the son of Jehoiakim, king of Judah, from Jerusalem to Babylon, and all the nobles of Judah and Jerusalem— [21]yes, thus says the LORD of hosts, the God of Israel, concerning the vessels that remain in the house of the LORD, and in the house of the king of Judah and of Jerusalem: [22]'They shall be carried to Babylon, and there they shall be until the day that I visit them,' says the LORD. 'Then I will bring them up and restore them to this place.' "

2 THESSALONIANS 3:1-18

FINALLY, brethren, pray for us, that the word of the Lord may run *swiftly* and be glorified, just as *it is* with you, [2]and that we may be delivered from unreasonable and wicked men; for not all have faith.

[3]But the Lord is faithful, who will establish you and guard *you* from the evil one. [4]And we have confidence in the Lord concerning you, both that you do and will do the things we command you.

[5]Now may the Lord direct your hearts into the love of God and into the patience of Christ.

[6]But we command you, brethren, in the name of our Lord Jesus Christ, that you withdraw from every brother who walks disorderly and not according to the tradition which he* received from us. [7]For you yourselves know how you ought to follow us, for we were not disorderly among you; [8]nor did we eat anyone's bread free of charge, but worked with labor and toil night and day, that we might not be a burden to any of you, [9]not because we do not have authority, but to make ourselves an example of how you should follow us.

[10]For even when we were with you, we commanded you this: If anyone will not work, neither shall he eat. [11]For we hear that there are some who walk among you in a disorderly manner, not working at all, but are busybodies. [12]Now those who are such we command and exhort through our Lord Jesus Christ that they work in quietness and eat their own bread.

[13]But *as for* you, brethren, do not grow weary *in* doing good. [14]And if anyone does not obey our word in this epistle, note that person and do not keep company with him, that he may be ashamed. [15]Yet do not count *him* as an enemy, but admonish *him* as a brother.

[16]Now may the Lord of peace Himself give you peace always in every way. The Lord *be* with you all.

[17]The salutation of Paul with my own hand, which is a sign in every epistle; so I write.

[18]The grace of our Lord Jesus Christ *be* with you all. Amen.

PSALM 85:1-13

To the Chief Musician. A Psalm of the sons of Korah.

L ORD, You have been favorable to
Your land;
You have brought back the
captivity of Jacob.

2 You have forgiven the iniquity
of Your people;
You have covered all their sin.
Selah

3 You have taken away all Your
wrath;
You have turned from the
fierceness of Your anger.

4 Restore us, O God of our
salvation,
And cause Your anger toward
us to cease.

5 Will You be angry with us
forever?
Will You prolong Your anger
to all generations?

6 Will You not revive us again,
That Your people may rejoice
in You?

7 Show us Your mercy, LORD,
And grant us Your salvation.

8 I will hear what God the LORD
will speak,
For He will speak peace
To His people and to His
saints;
But let them not turn back to
folly.

9 Surely His salvation *is* near to
those who fear Him,
That glory may dwell in our
land.

10 Mercy and truth have met
together;
Righteousness and peace
have kissed.

11 Truth shall spring out of the
earth,
And righteousness shall look
down from heaven.

12 Yes, the LORD will give *what is*
good;
And our land will yield its
increase.

13 Righteousness will go before
Him,
And shall make His footsteps
our pathway.

PROVERBS FOR TODAY/ 25:16

Have you found honey? Eat only as much as you need, lest you be filled with it and vomit.

OCTOBER 16

JEREMIAH 28:1–29:32

A ND it happened in the same
year, at the beginning of the
reign of Zedekiah king of
Judah, in the fourth year *and* in the
fifth month, *that* Hananiah the son of
Azur the prophet, who *was* from Gibeon, spoke to me in the house of the
LORD in the presence of the priests and
of all the people, saying, 2"Thus speaks
the LORD of hosts, the God of Israel,
saying: 'I have broken the yoke of the
king of Babylon. 3Within two full years
I will bring back to this place all the

vessels of the LORD's house, that Nebuchadnezzar king of Babylon took away from this place and carried to Babylon. ⁴And I will bring back to this place Jeconiah the son of Jehoiakim, king of Judah, with all the captives of Judah who went to Babylon,' says the LORD, 'for I will break the yoke of the king of Babylon.'"

⁵Then the prophet Jeremiah spoke to the prophet Hananiah in the presence of the priests and in the presence of all the people who stood in the house of the LORD, ⁶and the prophet Jeremiah said, "Amen! The LORD do so; the LORD perform your words which you have prophesied, to bring back the vessels of the LORD's house and all who were carried away captive, from Babylon to this place. ⁷Nevertheless hear now this word that I speak in your hearing and in the hearing of all the people: ⁸The prophets who have been before me and before you of old prophesied against many countries and great kingdoms—of war and disaster and pestilence. ⁹As for the prophet who prophesies of peace, when the word of the prophet comes to pass, the prophet will be known *as* one whom the LORD has truly sent."

¹⁰Then Hananiah the prophet took the yoke off the prophet Jeremiah's neck and broke it. ¹¹And Hananiah spoke in the presence of all the people, saying, "Thus says the LORD: 'Even so I will break the yoke of Nebuchadnezzar king of Babylon from the neck of all nations within the space of two full years.'" And the prophet Jeremiah went his way.

¹²Now the word of the LORD came to Jeremiah, after Hananiah the prophet had broken the yoke from the neck of the prophet Jeremiah, saying, ¹³"Go and tell Hananiah, saying, 'Thus says the LORD: "You have broken the yokes of wood, but you have made in their place yokes of iron." ¹⁴For thus says the LORD of hosts, the God of Israel: "I

have put a yoke of iron on the neck of all these nations, that they may serve Nebuchadnezzar king of Babylon; and they shall serve him. I have given him the beasts of the field also." '"

¹⁵Then the prophet Jeremiah said to Hananiah the prophet, "Hear now, Hananiah, the LORD has not sent you, but you make this people trust in a lie. ¹⁶Therefore thus says the LORD: 'Behold, I will cast you from the face of the earth. This year you shall die, because you have taught rebellion against the LORD.'"

¹⁷So Hananiah the prophet died the same year in the seventh month.

Now these *are* the words of the letter that Jeremiah the prophet sent from Jerusalem to the remainder of the elders who were carried away captive—to the priests, the prophets, and all the people whom Nebuchadnezzar had carried away captive from Jerusalem to Babylon. ²(This happened after Jeconiah the king, the queen mother, the eunuchs, the princes of Judah and Jerusalem, the craftsmen, and the smiths had departed from Jerusalem.) ³*The letter was sent* by the hand of Elasah the son of Shaphan, and Gemariah the son of Hilkiah, whom Zedekiah king of Judah sent to Babylon, to Nebuchadnezzar king of Babylon, saying,

4   Thus says the LORD of hosts,
       the God of Israel, to all who
       were carried away captive,
       whom I have caused to be
       carried away from Jerusalem
       to Babylon:

5   Build houses and dwell *in
       them;* plant gardens and eat
       their fruit. ⁶Take wives and
       beget sons and daughters;
       and take wives for your sons
       and give your daughters to
       husbands, so that they may

bear sons and daughters—that you may be increased there, and not diminished. 7And seek the peace of the city where I have caused you to be carried away captive, and pray to the Lord for it; for in its peace you will have peace. 8For thus says the Lord of hosts, the God of Israel: Do not let your prophets and your diviners who are in your midst deceive you, nor listen to your dreams which you cause to be dreamed. 9For they prophesy falsely to you in My name; I have not sent them, says the Lord.

10 For thus says the Lord: After seventy years are completed at Babylon, I will visit you and perform My good word toward you, and cause you to return to this place. 11For I know the thoughts that I think toward you, says the Lord, thoughts of peace and not of evil, to give you a future and a hope. 12Then you will call upon Me and go and pray to Me, and I will listen to you. 13And you will seek Me and find Me, when you search for Me with all your heart. 14I will be found by you, says the Lord, and I will bring you back from your captivity; I will gather you from all the nations and from all the places where I have driven you, says the Lord, and I will bring you to the place from which I cause you to be carried away captive.

15 Because you have said, "The Lord has raised up prophets for us in Babylon"—

16therefore thus says the Lord concerning the king who sits on the throne of David, concerning all the people who dwell in this city, and concerning your brethren who have not gone out with you into captivity— 17thus says the Lord of hosts: Behold, I will send on them the sword, the famine, and the pestilence, and will make them like rotten figs that cannot be eaten, they are so bad. 18And I will pursue them with the sword, with famine, and with pestilence; and I will deliver them to trouble among all the kingdoms of the earth—to be a curse, an astonishment, a hissing, and a reproach among all the nations where I have driven them, 19because they have not heeded My words, says the Lord, which I sent to them by My servants the prophets, rising up early and sending *them;* neither would you heed, says the Lord. 20Therefore hear the word of the Lord, all you of the captivity, whom I have sent from Jerusalem to Babylon.

21 Thus says the Lord of hosts, the God of Israel, concerning Ahab the son of Kolaiah, and Zedekiah the son of Maaseiah, who prophesy a lie to you in My name: Behold, I will deliver them into the hand of Nebuchadnezzar king of Babylon, and he shall slay them before your eyes. 22And because of them a curse shall be taken up by all the captivity of Judah who *are* in Babylon, saying, "The Lord make you like Zedekiah and Ahab,

whom the king of Babylon roasted in the fire"; 23because they have done disgraceful things in Israel, have committed adultery with their neighbors' wives, and have spoken lying words in My name, which I have not commanded them. Indeed I know, and *am* a witness, says the LORD.

24 You shall also speak to Shemaiah the Nehelamite, saying, 25Thus speaks the LORD of hosts, the God of Israel, saying: You have sent letters in your name to all the people who *are* at Jerusalem, to Zephaniah the son of Maaseiah the priest, and to all the priests, saying, 26"The LORD has made you priest instead of Jehoiada the priest, so that there should be officers *in* the house of the LORD over every man *who* is demented and considers himself a prophet, that you should put him in prison and in the stocks. 27Now therefore, why have you not rebuked Jeremiah of Anathoth who makes himself a prophet to you? 28For he has sent to us *in* Babylon, saying, 'This *captivity is* long; build houses and dwell *in them,* and plant gardens and eat their fruit.' "

29 Now Zephaniah the priest read this letter in the hearing of Jeremiah the prophet. 30Then the word of the LORD came to Jeremiah, saying: 31Send to all those in captivity, saying, Thus says the LORD concerning Shemaiah the Nehelamite: Because

Shemaiah has prophesied to you, and I have not sent him, and he has caused you to trust in a lie— 32therefore thus says the LORD: Behold, I will punish Shemaiah the Nehelamite and his family: he shall not have anyone to dwell among this people, nor shall he see the good that I will do for My people, says the LORD, because he has taught rebellion against the LORD.

1 TIMOTHY 1:1-20

PAUL, an apostle of Jesus Christ, by the commandment of God our Savior and the Lord Jesus Christ, our hope,

2To Timothy, a true son in the faith:

Grace, mercy, *and* peace from God our Father and Jesus Christ our Lord.

3As I urged you when I went into Macedonia—remain in Ephesus that you may charge some that they teach no other doctrine, 4nor give heed to fables and endless genealogies, which cause disputes rather than godly edification which is in faith. 5Now the purpose of the commandment is love from a pure heart, *from* a good conscience, and *from* sincere faith, 6from which some, having strayed, have turned aside to idle talk, 7desiring to be teachers of the law, understanding neither what they say nor the things which they affirm.

8But we know that the law *is* good if one uses it lawfully, 9knowing this: that the law is not made for a righteous person, but for *the* lawless and insubordinate, for *the* ungodly and for sinners, for *the* unholy and profane, for murderers of fathers and murderers of mothers, for manslayers, 10for fornicators, for sodomites, for kidnappers, for liars, for perjurers, and if there is any other thing that is contrary to sound doctrine, [11]according to the glorious gospel of the blessed God which was committed to my trust.

[12]And I thank Christ Jesus our Lord who has enabled me, because He counted me faithful, putting *me* into the ministry, [13]although I was formerly a blasphemer, a persecutor, and an insolent man; but I obtained mercy because I did *it* ignorantly in unbelief. [14]And the grace of our Lord was exceedingly abundant, with faith and love which are in Christ Jesus. [15]This *is* a faithful saying and worthy of all acceptance, that Christ Jesus came into the world to save sinners, of whom I am chief. [16]However, for this reason I obtained mercy, that in me first Jesus Christ might show all longsuffering, as a pattern to those who are going to believe on Him for everlasting life. [17]Now to the King eternal, immortal, invisible, to God who alone is wise,* *be* honor and glory forever and ever. Amen.

[18]This charge I commit to you, son Timothy, according to the prophecies previously made concerning you, that by them you may wage the good warfare, [19]having faith and a good conscience, which some having rejected, concerning the faith have suffered shipwreck, [20]of whom are Hymenaeus and Alexander, whom I delivered to Satan that they may learn not to blaspheme.

PSALM 86:1-17

A Prayer of David.

Bow down Your ear, O LORD, hear me;
For I *am* poor and needy.
2   Preserve my life, for I *am* holy;
You are my God;
Save Your servant who trusts in You!

3   Be merciful to me, O Lord,
For I cry to You all day long.
4   Rejoice the soul of Your servant,
For to You, O Lord, I lift up my soul.
5   For You, Lord, *are* good, and ready to forgive,
And abundant in mercy to all those who call upon You.

6   Give ear, O LORD, to my prayer;
And attend to the voice of my supplications.
7   In the day of my trouble I will call upon You,
For You will answer me.

8   Among the gods *there is* none like You, O Lord;
Nor *are there any works* like Your works.
9   All nations whom You have made
Shall come and worship before You, O Lord,
And shall glorify Your name.
10   For You *are* great, and do wondrous things;
You alone *are* God.

11   Teach me Your way, O LORD;
I will walk in Your truth;
Unite my heart to fear Your name.
12   I will praise You, O Lord my God, with all my heart,
And I will glorify Your name forevermore.
13   For great *is* Your mercy toward me,
And You have delivered my soul from the depths of Sheol.

14   O God, the proud have risen against me,
And a mob of violent *men* have sought my life,

And have not set You before them.

15 But You, O Lord, *are* a God full of compassion, and gracious, Longsuffering and abundant in mercy and truth.

16 Oh, turn to me, and have mercy on me!

Give Your strength to Your servant, And save the son of Your maidservant.

17 Show me a sign for good, That those who hate me may see *it* and be ashamed, Because You, LORD, have helped me and comforted me.

PROVERBS FOR TODAY/ 25:17

Seldom set foot in your neighbor's house, lest he become weary of you and hate you.

OCTOBER 17

JEREMIAH 30:1–31:26

THE word that came to Jeremiah from the LORD, saying, ²"Thus speaks the LORD God of Israel, saying: 'Write in a book for yourself all the words that I have spoken to you. ³For behold, the days are coming,' says the LORD, 'that I will bring back from captivity My people Israel and Judah,' says the LORD. 'And I will cause them to return to the land that I gave to their fathers, and they shall possess it.' "

⁴Now these *are* the words that the LORD spoke concerning Israel and Judah.

⁵"For thus says the LORD:

'We have heard a voice of trembling, Of fear, and not of peace.
6 Ask now, and see, Whether a man is ever in labor with child? So why do I see every man *with* his hands on his loins Like a woman in labor,

And all faces turned pale?
7 Alas! For that day *is* great, So that none *is* like it; And it *is* the time of Jacob's trouble, But he shall be saved out of it.

8 'For it shall come to pass in that day,' Says the LORD of hosts, '*That* I will break his yoke from your neck, And will burst your bonds; Foreigners shall no more enslave them.
9 But they shall serve the LORD their God, And David their king, Whom I will raise up for them.

10 'Therefore do not fear, O My servant Jacob,' says the LORD, 'Nor be dismayed, O Israel; For behold, I will save you from afar, And your seed from the land of their captivity.

Jacob shall return, have rest
and be quiet,
And no one shall make *him*
afraid.
11 For I *am* with you,' says the
Lord, 'to save you;
Though I make a full end of
all nations where I have
scattered you,
Yet I will not make a complete
end of you.
But I will correct you in
justice,
And will not let you go
altogether unpunished.'

12 "For thus says the Lord:

'Your affliction *is* incurable,
Your wound *is* severe.
13 *There is* no one to plead your
cause,
That you may be bound up;
You have no healing
medicines.
14 All your lovers have forgotten
you;
They do not seek you;
For I have wounded you with
the wound of an enemy,
With the chastisement of a
cruel one,
For the multitude of your
iniquities,
Because your sins have
increased.
15 Why do you cry about your
affliction?
Your sorrow *is* incurable.
Because of the multitude of
your iniquities,
Because your sins have
increased,
I have done these things to
you.

16 'Therefore all those who
devour you shall be
devoured;
And all your adversaries,

every one of them, shall go
into captivity;
Those who plunder you shall
become plunder,
And all who prey upon you I
will make a prey.
17 For I will restore health to you
And heal you of your wounds,'
says the Lord,
'Because they called you an
outcast *saying:*
"This *is* Zion;
No one seeks her." '

18 "Thus says the Lord:

'Behold, I will bring back the
captivity of Jacob's tents,
And have mercy on his
dwelling places;
The city shall be built upon its
own mound,
And the palace shall remain
according to its own plan.
19 Then out of them shall
proceed thanksgiving
And the voice of those who
make merry;
I will multiply them, and they
shall not diminish;
I will also glorify them, and
they shall not be small.
20 Their children also shall be as
before,
And their congregation shall
be established before Me;
And I will punish all who
oppress them.
21 Their nobles shall be from
among them,
And their governor shall
come from their midst;
Then I will cause him to draw
near,
And he shall approach Me;
For who *is* this who pledged
his heart to approach Me?'
says the Lord.
22 'You shall be My people,
And I will be your God.' "

23 Behold, the whirlwind of the Lord
Goes forth with fury,
A continuing whirlwind;
It will fall violently on the head of the wicked.

24 The fierce anger of the Lord will not return until He has done it,
And until He has performed the intents of His heart.

In the latter days you will consider it.

"At the same time," says the Lord, "I will be the God of all the families of Israel, and they shall be My people."

2Thus says the Lord:

"The people who survived the sword
Found grace in the wilderness—
Israel, when I went to give him rest."

3 The Lord has appeared of old to me, *saying:*
"Yes, I have loved you with an everlasting love;
Therefore with lovingkindness I have drawn you.

4 Again I will build you, and you shall be rebuilt,
O virgin of Israel!
You shall again be adorned with your tambourines,
And shall go forth in the dances of those who rejoice.

5 You shall yet plant vines on the mountains of Samaria;
The planters shall plant and eat *them* as ordinary food.

6 For there shall be a day
When the watchmen will cry on Mount Ephraim,
'Arise, and let us go up *to* Zion,
To the Lord our God.'"

7For thus says the Lord:

"Sing with gladness for Jacob,
And shout among the chief of the nations;
Proclaim, give praise, and say,
'O Lord, save Your people,
The remnant of Israel!'

8 Behold, I will bring them from the north country,
And gather them from the ends of the earth,
Among them the blind and the lame,
The woman with child
And the one who labors with child, together;
A great throng shall return there.

9 They shall come with weeping,
And with supplications I will lead them.
I will cause them to walk by the rivers of waters,
In a straight way in which they shall not stumble;
For I am a Father to Israel,
And Ephraim *is* My firstborn.

10 "Hear the word of the Lord,
O nations,
And declare *it* in the isles afar off, and say,
'He who scattered Israel will gather him,
And keep him as a shepherd *does* his flock.'

11 For the Lord has redeemed Jacob,
And ransomed him from the hand of one stronger than he.

12 Therefore they shall come and sing in the height of Zion,
Streaming to the goodness of the Lord—
For wheat and new wine and oil,

For the young of the flock and
the herd;
Their souls shall be like a
well-watered garden,
And they shall sorrow no
more at all.

13 "Then shall the virgin rejoice
in the dance,
And the young men and the
old, together;
For I will turn their mourning
to joy,
Will comfort them,
And make them rejoice rather
than sorrow.
14 I will satiate the soul of the
priests with abundance,
And My people shall be
satisfied with My goodness,
says the LORD."

15Thus says the LORD:

"A voice was heard in Ramah,
Lamentation and bitter
weeping,
Rachel weeping for her
children,
Refusing to be comforted for
her children,
Because they are no more."

16Thus says the LORD:

"Refrain your voice from
weeping,
And your eyes from tears;
For your work shall be
rewarded, says the LORD,
And they shall come back
from the land of the enemy.
17 There is hope in your future,
says the LORD,
That your children shall come
back to their own border.

18 "I have surely heard Ephraim
bemoaning himself:

'You have chastised me, and I
was chastised,
Like an untrained bull;
Restore me, and I will return,
For You are the LORD my God.
19 Surely, after my turning, I
repented;
And after I was instructed, I
struck myself on the thigh;
I was ashamed, yes, even
humiliated,
Because I bore the reproach
of my youth.'
20 Is Ephraim My dear son?
Is he a pleasant child?
For though I spoke against
him,
I earnestly remember him
still;
Therefore My heart yearns
for him;
I will surely have mercy on
him, says the LORD.

21 "Set up signposts,
Make landmarks;
Set your heart toward the
highway,
The way in which you went.
Turn back, O virgin of Israel,
Turn back to these your cities.
22 How long will you gad about,
O you backsliding daughter?
For the LORD has created a
new thing in the earth—
A woman shall encompass a
man."

23Thus says the LORD of hosts, the
God of Israel: "They shall again use
this speech in the land of Judah and in
its cities, when I bring back their captivity: 'The LORD bless you, O home of
justice, and mountain of holiness!'
24And there shall dwell in Judah itself,
and in all its cities together, farmers
and those going out with flocks. 25For
I have satiated the weary soul, and I
have replenished every sorrowful
soul."

26After this I awoke and looked around, and my sleep was sweet to me.

1 TIMOTHY 2:1-15

THEREFORE I [Paul] exhort first of all that supplications, prayers, intercessions, *and* giving of thanks be made for all men, 2for kings and all who are in authority, that we may lead a quiet and peaceable life in all godliness and reverence. 3For this *is* good and acceptable in the sight of God our Savior, 4who desires all men to be saved and to come to the knowledge of the truth. 5For *there is* one God and one Mediator between God and men, *the* Man Christ Jesus, 6who gave Himself a ransom for all, to be testified in due time, 7for which I was appointed a preacher and an apostle—I am speaking the truth in Christ* *and* not lying—a teacher of the Gentiles in faith and truth.

8I desire therefore that the men pray everywhere, lifting up holy hands, without wrath and doubting; 9in like manner also, that the women adorn themselves in modest apparel, with propriety and moderation, not with braided hair or gold or pearls or costly clothing, 10but, which is proper for women professing godliness, with good works. 11Let a woman learn in silence with all submission. 12And I do not permit a woman to teach or to have authority over a man, but to be in silence. 13For Adam was formed first, then Eve. 14And Adam was not deceived, but the woman being deceived, fell into transgression. 15Nevertheless she will be saved in childbearing if they continue in faith, love, and holiness, with self-control.

PSALM 87:1-7

A Psalm of the sons of Korah. A Song.

HIS foundation *is* in the holy mountains.
2The LORD loves the gates of Zion
More than all the dwellings of Jacob.
3 Glorious things are spoken of you,
O city of God!   Selah

4 "I will make mention of Rahab and Babylon to those who know Me;
Behold, O Philistia and Tyre, with Ethiopia:
'This *one* was born there.' "

5 And of Zion it will be said,
"This *one* and that *one* were born in her;
And the Most High Himself shall establish her."
6 The LORD will record,
When He registers the peoples:
"This *one* was born there."   Selah

7 Both the singers and the players on instruments *say,*
"All my springs *are* in you."

PROVERBS FOR TODAY/ 25:18-19

A man who bears false witness against his neighbor is like *a club, a sword, and a sharp arrow. Confidence in an unfaithful* man *in time of trouble* is like *a bad tooth and a foot out of joint.*

OCTOBER 18

JEREMIAH 31:27–32:44

"**B**EHOLD, the days are coming, says the LORD, that I will sow the house of Israel and the house of Judah with the seed of man and the seed of beast. 28And it shall come to pass, *that* as I have watched over them to pluck up, to break down, to throw down, to destroy, and to afflict, so I will watch over them to build and to plant, says the LORD. 29In those days they shall say no more:

'The fathers have eaten sour grapes,
And the children's teeth are set on edge.'

30But every one shall die for his own iniquity; every man who eats the sour grapes, his teeth shall be set on edge. 31"Behold, the days are coming, says the LORD, when I will make a new covenant with the house of Israel and with the house of Judah— 32not according to the covenant that I made with their fathers in the day *that* I took them by the hand to lead them out of the land of Egypt, My covenant which they broke, though I was a husband to them,* says the LORD. 33But this *is* the covenant that I will make with the house of Israel after those days, says the LORD: I will put My law in their minds, and write it on their hearts; and I will be their God, and they shall be My people. 34No more shall every man teach his neighbor, and every man his brother, saying, 'Know the LORD,' for they all shall know Me, from the least of them to the greatest of them, says the LORD. For I will forgive their iniquity, and their sin I will remember no more."

35 Thus says the LORD,
Who gives the sun for a light by day,
The ordinances of the moon and the stars for a light by night,
Who disturbs the sea,
And its waves roar
(The LORD of hosts *is* His name):

36 "If those ordinances depart
From before Me, says the LORD,
Then the seed of Israel shall also cease
From being a nation before Me forever."

37Thus says the LORD:

"If heaven above can be measured,
And the foundations of the earth searched out beneath,
I will also cast off all the seed of Israel
For all that they have done, says the LORD.

38"Behold, the days are coming, says the LORD, that the city shall be built for the LORD from the Tower of Hananel to the Corner Gate. 39The surveyor's line shall again extend straight forward over the hill Gareb; then it shall turn toward Goath. 40And the whole valley of the dead bodies and of the ashes, and all the fields as far as the Brook Kidron, to the corner of the Horse Gate toward the east, *shall be* holy to the LORD. It shall not be plucked up or thrown down anymore forever."

THE word that came to Jeremiah from the LORD in the tenth year of Zedekiah king of Judah, which was the eighteenth year of Nebuchadnezzar. ²For then the king of Babylon's army besieged Jerusalem, and Jeremiah the prophet was shut up in the court of the prison, which *was in* the king of Judah's house. ³For Zedekiah king of Judah had shut him up, saying, "Why do you prophesy and say, 'Thus says the LORD: "Behold, I will give this city into the hand of the king of Babylon, and he shall take it; ⁴and Zedekiah king of Judah shall not escape from the hand of the Chaldeans, but shall surely be delivered into the hand of the king of Babylon, and shall speak with him face to face,* and see him eye to eye; ⁵then he shall lead Zedekiah to Babylon, and there he shall be until I visit him," says the LORD; "though you fight with the Chaldeans, you shall not succeed" '?"

⁶And Jeremiah said, "The word of the LORD came to me, saying, ⁷'Behold, Hanamel the son of Shallum your uncle will come to you, saying, "Buy my field which *is* in Anathoth, for the right of redemption *is* yours to buy *it.*" ' ⁸Then Hanamel my uncle's son came to me in the court of the prison according to the word of the LORD, and said to me, 'Please buy my field that *is* in Anathoth, which *is* in the country of Benjamin; for the right of inheritance *is* yours, and the redemption yours; buy *it* for yourself.' Then I knew that this was the word of the LORD. ⁹So I bought the field from Hanamel, the son of my uncle who *was* in Anathoth, and weighed *out to* him the money—seventeen shekels of silver. ¹⁰And I signed the deed and sealed *it,* took witnesses, and weighed the money on the scales. ¹¹So I took the purchase deed, *both* that which was sealed *according* to the law and custom, and that which was open; ¹²and I gave the purchase deed to Baruch the son of Neriah, son of Mahseiah, in the presence of Hanamel my uncle's *son,* and in the presence of the witnesses who signed the purchase deed, before all the Jews who sat in the court of the prison.

¹³"Then I charged Baruch before them, saying, ¹⁴"Thus says the LORD of hosts, the God of Israel: "Take these deeds, both this purchase deed which is sealed and this deed which is open, and put them in an earthen vessel, that they may last many days." ¹⁵For thus says the LORD of hosts, the God of Israel: "Houses and fields and vineyards shall be possessed again in this land." '

¹⁶"Now when I had delivered the purchase deed to Baruch the son of Neriah, I prayed to the LORD, saying: ¹⁷'Ah, Lord GOD! Behold, You have made the heavens and the earth by Your great power and outstretched arm. There is nothing too hard for You. ¹⁸*You* show lovingkindness to thousands, and repay the iniquity of the fathers into the bosom of their children after them—the Great, the Mighty God, whose name *is* the LORD of hosts. ¹⁹*You are* great in counsel and mighty in work, for your eyes *are* open to all the ways of the sons of men, to give everyone according to his ways and according to the fruit of his doings. ²⁰You have set signs and wonders in the land of Egypt, to this day, and in Israel and among *other* men; and You have made Yourself a name, as it is this day. ²¹You have brought Your people Israel out of the land of Egypt with signs and wonders, with a strong hand and an outstretched arm, and with great terror; ²²You have given them this land, of which You swore to their fathers to give them—"a land flowing with milk and honey."* ²³And they came in and took possession of it, but they have not obeyed Your voice or walked in Your law. They have done nothing of all that You commanded them to do; therefore You have caused all this calamity to come upon them.

²⁴"Look, the siege mounds! They have come to the city to take it; and the city has been given into the hand of the Chaldeans who fight against it, because of the sword and famine and pestilence. What You have spoken has happened; there You see *it!* ²⁵And You have said to me, O Lord GOD, "Buy the field for money, and take witnesses"!— yet the city has been given into the hand of the Chaldeans.' "

²⁶Then the word of the LORD came to Jeremiah, saying, ²⁷"Behold, I *am* the LORD, the God of all flesh. Is there anything too hard for Me? ²⁸Therefore thus says the LORD: 'Behold, I will give this city into the hand of the Chaldeans, into the hand of Nebuchadnezzar king of Babylon, and he shall take it. ²⁹And the Chaldeans who fight against this city shall come and set fire to this city and burn it, with the houses on whose roofs they have offered incense to Baal and poured out drink offerings to other gods, to provoke Me to anger; ³⁰because the children of Israel and the children of Judah have done only evil before Me from their youth. For the children of Israel have provoked Me only to anger with the work of their hands,' says the LORD. ³¹'For this city has been to Me *a provocation of* My anger and My fury from the day that they built it, even to this day; so I will remove it from before My face ³²because of all the evil of the children of Israel and the children of Judah, which they have done to provoke Me to anger—they, their kings, their princes, their priests, their prophets, the men of Judah, and the inhabitants of Jerusalem. ³³And they have turned to Me the back, and not the face; though I taught them, rising up early and teaching *them,* yet they have not listened to receive instruction. ³⁴But they set their abominations in the house which is called by My name, to defile it. ³⁵And they built the high places of Baal which *are* in the Valley of the Son of Hinnom, to cause their sons and their daughters to pass through *the fire* to Molech, which I did not command them, nor did it come into My mind that they should do this abomination, to cause Judah to sin.'

³⁶"Now therefore, thus says the LORD, the God of Israel, concerning this city of which you say, 'It shall be delivered into the hand of the king of Babylon by the sword, by the famine, and by the pestilence: ³⁷Behold, I will gather them out of all countries where I have driven them in My anger, in My fury, and in great wrath; I will bring them back to this place, and I will cause them to dwell safely. ³⁸They shall be My people, and I will be their God; ³⁹then I will give them one heart and one way, that they may fear Me forever, for the good of them and their children after them. ⁴⁰And I will make an everlasting covenant with them, that I will not turn away from doing them good; but I will put My fear in their hearts so that they will not depart from Me. ⁴¹Yes, I will rejoice over them to do them good, and I will assuredly plant them in this land, with all My heart and with all My soul.'

⁴²"For thus says the LORD: 'Just as I have brought all this great calamity on this people, so I will bring on them all the good that I have promised them. ⁴³And fields will be bought in this land of which you say, "*It is* desolate, without man or beast; it has been given into the hand of the Chaldeans." ⁴⁴Men will buy fields for money, sign deeds and seal *them,* and take witnesses, in the land of Benjamin, in the places around Jerusalem, in the cities of Judah, in the cities of the mountains, in the cities of the lowland, and in the cities of the South; for I will cause their captives to return,' says the LORD."

1 TIMOTHY 3:1-16

THIS *is* a faithful saying: If a man desires the position of a bishop,* he desires a good work. ²A bishop then must be blameless, the husband of one wife, temperate, sober-minded, of good behavior, hospitable, able to teach; ³not given to wine, not violent, not greedy for money,* but gentle, not quarrelsome, not covetous; ⁴one who rules his own house well, having *his* children in submission with all reverence ⁵(for if a man does not know how to rule his own house, how will he take care of the church of God?); ⁶not a novice, lest being puffed up with pride he fall into the *same* condemnation as the devil. ⁷Moreover he must have a good testimony among those who are outside, lest he fall into reproach and the snare of the devil.

⁸Likewise deacons *must be* reverent, not double-tongued, not given to much wine, not greedy for money, ⁹holding the mystery of the faith with a pure conscience. ¹⁰But let these also first be tested; then let them serve as deacons, being *found* blameless. ¹¹Likewise, *their* wives *must be* reverent, not slanderers, temperate, faithful in all things. ¹²Let deacons be the husbands of one wife, ruling *their* children and their own houses well. ¹³For those who have served well as deacons obtain for themselves a good standing and great boldness in the faith which is in Christ Jesus.

¹⁴These things I write to you, though I hope to come to you shortly; ¹⁵but if I am delayed, *I write* so that you may know how you ought to conduct yourself in the house of God, which is the church of the living God, the pillar and ground of the truth. ¹⁶And without controversy great is the mystery of godliness:

> God* was manifested in the
>   flesh,
> Justified in the Spirit,
> Seen by angels,
> Preached among the Gentiles,
> Believed on in the world,
> Received up in glory.

PSALM 88:1-18

A Song. A Psalm of the sons of Korah. To the Chief Musician. Set to "Mahalath Leannoth." A Contemplation* of Heman the Ezrahite.

O LORD, God of my salvation,
I have cried out day and night
before You.
2 Let my prayer come before
    You;
  Incline Your ear to my cry.

3 For my soul is full of troubles,
  And my life draws near to the
    grave.
4 I am counted with those who
    go down to the pit;
  I am like a man *who has* no
    strength,
5 Adrift among the dead,
  Like the slain who lie in the
    grave,
  Whom You remember no
    more,
  And who are cut off from
    Your hand.

6 You have laid me in the lowest
    pit,
  In darkness, in the depths.
7 Your wrath lies heavy upon
    me,
  And You have afflicted *me*
    with all Your waves.   Selah
8 You have put away my
    acquaintances far from me;
  You have made me an
    abomination to them;
  I am shut up, and I cannot get
    out;
9 My eye wastes away because
    of affliction.

LORD, I have called daily upon
You;

I have stretched out my hands
to You.

10 Will You work wonders for
the dead?

Shall the dead arise *and*
praise You?   Selah

11 Shall Your lovingkindness be
declared in the grave?

Or Your faithfulness in the
place of destruction?

12 Shall Your wonders be known
in the dark?

And Your righteousness in
the land of forgetfulness?

13 But to You I have cried out,
O LORD,

And in the morning my
prayer comes before You.

14 LORD, why do You cast off my
soul?

Why do You hide Your face
from me?

15 I *have been* afflicted and ready
to die from *my* youth;

I suffer Your terrors;

I am distraught.

16 Your fierce wrath has gone
over me;

Your terrors have cut me off.

17 They came around me all day
long like water;

They engulfed me altogether.

18 Loved one and friend You
have put far from me,

And my acquaintances into
darkness.

PROVERBS FOR TODAY/ 25:20-22

Like *one who takes away a garment in cold weather,* and like *vinegar on soda,* is
*one who sings songs to a heavy heart. If your enemy is hungry, give him bread to
eat; and if he is thirsty, give him water to drink; for* so *you will heap coals of fire
on his head, and the LORD will reward you.*

OCTOBER 19

JEREMIAH 33:1–34:22

MOREOVER the word of the LORD
came to Jeremiah a second
time, while he was still shut up
in the court of the prison, saying,
2"Thus says the LORD who made it, the
LORD who formed it to establish it (the
LORD *is* His name): 3"Call to Me, and I will
answer you, and show you great and
mighty things, which you do not know.'

4"For thus says the LORD, the God of
Israel, concerning the houses of this
city and the houses of the kings of
Judah, which have been pulled down
to fortify* against the siege mounds

and the sword: 5"They come to fight
with the Chaldeans, but *only* to fill their
places* with the dead bodies of men
whom I will slay in My anger and My
fury, all for whose wickedness I have
hidden My face from this city. 6Behold,
I will bring it health and healing; I will
heal them and reveal to them the abundance of peace and truth. 7And I will
cause the captives of Judah and the
captives of Israel to return, and will
rebuild those places as at the first. 8I
will cleanse them from all their iniquity
by which they have sinned against Me,
and I will pardon all their iniquities by
which they have sinned and by which

they have transgressed against Me. ⁹Then it shall be to Me a name of joy, a praise, and an honor before all nations of the earth, who shall hear all the good that I do to them; they shall fear and tremble for all the goodness and all the prosperity that I provide for it.'

¹⁰"Thus says the LORD: 'Again there shall be heard in this place—of which you say, "It *is* desolate, without man and without beast"—in the cities of Judah, in the streets of Jerusalem that are desolate, without man and without inhabitant and without beast, ¹¹the voice of joy and the voice of gladness, the voice of the bridegroom and the voice of the bride, the voice of those who will say:

"Praise the LORD of hosts,
For the LORD *is* good,
For His mercy *endures*
forever"—

and of those *who will* bring the sacrifice of praise into the house of the LORD. For I will cause the captives of the land to return as at the first,' says the LORD.

¹²"Thus says the LORD of hosts: 'In this place which is desolate, without man and without beast, and in all its cities, there shall again be a dwelling place of shepherds causing *their* flocks to lie down. ¹³In the cities of the mountains, in the cities of the lowland, in the cities of the South, in the land of Benjamin, in the places around Jerusalem, and in the cities of Judah, the flocks shall again pass under the hands of him who counts *them*,' says the LORD.

¹⁴"Behold, the days are coming,' says the LORD, 'that I will perform that good thing which I have promised to the house of Israel and to the house of Judah:

15 'In those days and at that time
I will cause to grow up to
David
A Branch of righteousness;
He shall execute judgment
and righteousness in the
earth.
16 In those days Judah will be
saved,
And Jerusalem will dwell
safely.
And this *is the name* by which
she will be called:

THE LORD OUR
RIGHTEOUSNESS.'*

¹⁷"For thus says the LORD: 'David shall never lack a man to sit on the throne of the house of Israel; ¹⁸nor shall the priests, the Levites, lack a man to offer burnt offerings before Me, to kindle grain offerings, and to sacrifice continually.' "

¹⁹And the word of the LORD came to Jeremiah, saying, ²⁰"Thus says the LORD: 'If you can break My covenant with the day and My covenant with the night, so that there will not be day and night in their season, ²¹then My covenant may also be broken with David My servant, so that he shall not have a son to reign on his throne, and with the Levites, the priests, My ministers. ²²As the host of heaven cannot be numbered, nor the sand of the sea measured, so will I multiply the descendants of David My servant and the Levites who minister to Me.' "

²³Moreover the word of the LORD came to Jeremiah, saying, ²⁴"Have you not considered what these people have spoken, saying, 'The two families which the LORD has chosen, He has also cast them off'? Thus they have despised My people, as if they should no more be a nation before them.

²⁵"Thus says the LORD: 'If My covenant *is* not with day and night, *and if* I have not appointed the ordinances of heaven and earth, ²⁶then I will cast away the descendants of Jacob and David My servant, *so* that I will not

take *any* of his descendants *to be* rulers over the descendants of Abraham, Isaac, and Jacob. For I will cause their captives to return, and will have mercy on them.' "

THE word which came to Jeremiah from the LORD, when Nebuchadnezzar king of Babylon and all his army, all the kingdoms of the earth under his dominion, and all the people, fought against Jerusalem and all its cities, saying, 2"Thus says the LORD, the God of Israel: 'Go and speak to Zedekiah king of Judah and tell him, "Thus says the LORD: 'Behold, I will give this city into the hand of the king of Babylon, and he shall burn it with fire. 3And you shall not escape from his hand, but shall surely be taken and delivered into his hand; your eyes shall see the eyes of the king of Babylon, he shall speak with you face to face,* and you shall go to Babylon.' " ' 4Yet hear the word of the LORD, O Zedekiah king of Judah! Thus says the LORD concerning you: 'You shall not die by the sword. 5You shall die in peace; as in the ceremonies of your fathers, the former kings who were before you, so they shall burn incense for you and lament for you, *saying,* "Alas, lord!" For I have pronounced the word, says the LORD.' "

6Then Jeremiah the prophet spoke all these words to Zedekiah king of Judah in Jerusalem, 7when the king of Babylon's army fought against Jerusalem and all the cities of Judah that were left, against Lachish and Azekah; for *only* these fortified cities remained of the cities of Judah.

8*This is* the word that came to Jeremiah from the LORD, after King Zedekiah had made a covenant with all the people who *were* at Jerusalem to proclaim liberty to them: 9that every man should set free his male and female slave—a Hebrew man or woman— that no one should keep a Jewish brother in bondage. 10Now when all the princes and all the people, who had entered into the covenant, heard that everyone should set free his male and female slaves, that no one should keep them in bondage anymore, they obeyed and let *them* go. 11But afterward they changed their minds and made the male and female slaves return, whom they had set free, and brought them into subjection as male and female slaves.

12Therefore the word of the LORD came to Jeremiah from the LORD, saying, 13"Thus says the LORD, the God of Israel: 'I made a covenant with your fathers in the day that I brought them out of the land of Egypt, out of the house of bondage, saying, 14"At the end of seven years let every man set free his Hebrew brother, who has been sold to him; and when he has served you six years, you shall let him go free from you." But your fathers did not obey Me nor incline their ear. 15Then you recently turned and did what was right in My sight—every man proclaiming liberty to his neighbor; and you made a covenant before Me in the house which is called by My name. 16Then you turned around and profaned My name, and every one of you brought back his male and female slaves, whom he had set at liberty, at their pleasure, and brought them back into subjection, to be your male and female slaves.'

17"Therefore thus says the LORD: 'You have not obeyed Me in proclaiming liberty, every one to his brother and every one to his neighbor. Behold, I proclaim liberty to you,' says the LORD—'to the sword, to pestilence, and to famine! And I will deliver you to trouble among all the kingdoms of the earth. 18And I will give the men who have transgressed My covenant, who have not performed the words of the covenant which they made before Me, when they cut the calf in two and passed between the parts of it— 19the princes of Judah, the princes of Jerusalem, the eunuchs, the priests, and all the people of the land who passed between the parts of the calf— 20I will give them into the hand of their enemies and into the hand of those who seek their life. Their dead bodies shall be for meat for the birds of the heaven and the beasts of the earth. 21And I will give Zedekiah king of Judah and his princes into the hand of their enemies, into the hand of those who seek their life, and into the hand of the king of Babylon's army which has gone back from you. 22Behold, I will command,' says the LORD, 'and cause them to return to this city. They will fight against it and take it and burn it with fire; and I will make the cities of Judah a desolation without inhabitant.' "

1 TIMOTHY 4:1-16

Now the Spirit expressly says that in latter times some will depart from the faith, giving heed to deceiving spirits and doctrines of demons, 2speaking lies in hypocrisy, having their own conscience seared with a hot iron, 3forbidding to marry, *and commanding* to abstain from foods which God created to be received with thanksgiving by those who believe and know the truth. 4For every creature of God *is* good, and nothing is to be refused if it is received with thanksgiving; 5for it is sanctified by the word of God and prayer.

6If you instruct the brethren in these things, you will be a good minister of Jesus Christ, nourished in the words of faith and of the good doctrine which you have carefully followed. 7But reject profane and old wives' fables, and exercise yourself toward godliness. 8For bodily exercise profits a little, but godliness is profitable for all things, having promise of the life that now is and of that which is to come. 9This *is* a faithful saying and worthy of all accep-

tance. 10For to this *end* we both labor and suffer reproach,* because we trust in the living God, who is *the* Savior of all men, especially of those who believe. 11These things command and teach.

12Let no one despise your youth, but be an example to the believers in word, in conduct, in love, in spirit,* in faith, in purity. 13Till I come, give attention to reading, to exhortation, to doctrine. 14Do not neglect the gift that is in you, which was given to you by prophecy with the laying on of the hands of the eldership. 15Meditate on these things; give yourself entirely to them, that your progress may be evident to all. 16Take heed to yourself and to the doctrine. Continue in them, for in doing this you will save both yourself and those who hear you.

PSALM 89:1-13

A Contemplation * *of Ethan the Ezrahite.*

I WILL sing of the mercies of the LORD forever;
　　With my mouth will I make
　　　known Your faithfulness to
　　　all generations.
2　For I have said, "Mercy shall
　　　be built up forever;
　　Your faithfulness You shall
　　　establish in the very
　　　heavens."

3　"I have made a covenant with
　　　My chosen,
　　I have sworn to My servant
　　　David:
4　'Your seed I will establish
　　　forever,
　　And build up your throne to
　　　all generations.' "　　　Selah

5　And the heavens will praise
　　　Your wonders, O LORD;
　　Your faithfulness also in the
　　　assembly of the saints.

6 For who in the heavens can
   be compared to the LORD?
   Who among the sons of the
   mighty can be likened to
   the LORD?
7 God is greatly to be feared in
   the assembly of the saints,
   And to be held in reverence
   by all *those* around Him.
8 O LORD God of hosts,
   Who *is* mighty like You,
   O LORD?
   Your faithfulness also
   surrounds You.
9 You rule the raging of the sea;
   When its waves rise, You still
   them.

10 You have broken Rahab in
   pieces, as one who is slain;
   You have scattered Your
   enemies with Your mighty
   arm.
11 The heavens *are* Yours, the
   earth also *is* Yours;
   The world and all its fullness,
   You have founded them.
12 The north and the south, You
   have created them;
   Tabor and Hermon rejoice in
   Your name.
13 You have a mighty arm;
   Strong is Your hand, *and* high
   is Your right hand.

PROVERBS FOR TODAY/ 25:23-24

The north wind brings forth rain, and a backbiting tongue an angry countenance.
☐ It is *better to dwell in a corner of a housetop, than in a house shared with a
contentious woman.*

OCTOBER 20

JEREMIAH 35:1–36:32

THE word which came to Jeremiah from the LORD in the days of Jehoiakim the son of Josiah, king of Judah, saying, 2"Go to the house of the Rechabites, speak to them, and bring them into the house of the LORD, into one of the chambers, and give them wine to drink."

3Then I took Jaazaniah the son of Jeremiah, the son of Habazziniah, his brothers and all his sons, and the whole house of the Rechabites, 4and I brought them into the house of the LORD, into the chamber of the sons of Hanan the son of Igdaliah, a man of God, which *was* by the chamber of the princes, above the chamber of Maaseiah the son of Shallum, the keeper of the door. 5Then I set before the sons of the house of the Rechabites bowls full of wine, and cups; and I said to them, "Drink wine."

6But they said, "We will drink no wine, for Jonadab the son of Rechab, our father, commanded us, saying, 'You shall drink no wine, you nor your sons, forever. 7You shall not build a house, sow seed, plant a vineyard, nor have *any of these;* but all your days you shall dwell in tents, that you may live many days in the land where you are sojourners.' 8Thus we have obeyed the voice of Jonadab the son of Rechab, our father, in all that he charged us, to drink no wine all our days, we, our wives, our sons, or our daughters, 9nor to build ourselves houses to dwell in; nor do we have vineyard, field, or seed.

¹⁰But we have dwelt in tents, and have obeyed and done according to all that Jonadab our father commanded us. ¹¹But it came to pass, when Nebuchadnezzar king of Babylon came up into the land, that we said, 'Come, let us go to Jerusalem for fear of the army of the Chaldeans and for fear of the army of the Syrians.' So we dwell at Jerusalem."

¹²Then came the word of the LORD to Jeremiah, saying, ¹³"Thus says the LORD of hosts, the God of Israel: 'Go and tell the men of Judah and the inhabitants of Jerusalem, "Will you not receive instruction to obey My words?" says the LORD. ¹⁴"The words of Jonadab the son of Rechab, which he commanded his sons, not to drink wine, are performed; for to this day they drink none, and obey their father's commandment. But although I have spoken to you, rising early and speaking, you did not obey Me. ¹⁵I have also sent to you all My servants the prophets, rising up early and sending *them,* saying, 'Turn now everyone from his evil way, amend your doings, and do not go after other gods to serve them; then you will dwell in the land which I have given you and your fathers.' But you have not inclined your ear, nor obeyed Me. ¹⁶Surely the sons of Jonadab the son of Rechab have performed the commandment of their father, which he commanded them, but this people has not obeyed Me." '

¹⁷"Therefore thus says the LORD God of hosts, the God of Israel: 'Behold, I will bring on Judah and on all the inhabitants of Jerusalem all the doom that I have pronounced against them; because I have spoken to them but they have not heard, and I have called to them but they have not answered.' "

¹⁸And Jeremiah said to the house of the Rechabites, "Thus says the LORD of hosts, the God of Israel: 'Because you have obeyed the commandment of Jonadab your father, and kept all his precepts and done according to all that he commanded you, ¹⁹therefore thus says the LORD of hosts, the God of Israel: "Jonadab the son of Rechab shall not lack a man to stand before Me forever." ' "

Now it came to pass in the fourth year of Jehoiakim the son of Josiah, king of Judah, *that* this word came to Jeremiah from the LORD, saying: ²"Take a scroll of a book and write on it all the words that I have spoken to you against Israel, against Judah, and against all the nations, from the day I spoke to you, from the days of Josiah even to this day. ³It may be that the house of Judah will hear all the adversities which I purpose to bring upon them, that everyone may turn from his evil way, that I may forgive their iniquity and their sin."

⁴Then Jeremiah called Baruch the son of Neriah; and Baruch wrote on a scroll of a book, at the instruction of Jeremiah,* all the words of the LORD which He had spoken to him. ⁵And Jeremiah commanded Baruch, saying, "I *am* confined, I cannot go into the house of the LORD. ⁶You go, therefore, and read from the scroll which you have written at my instruction,* the words of the LORD, in the hearing of the people in the LORD's house on the day of fasting. And you shall also read them in the hearing of all Judah who come from their cities. ⁷It may be that they will present their supplication before the LORD, and everyone will turn from his evil way. For great *is* the anger and the fury that the LORD has pronounced against this people." ⁸And Baruch the son of Neriah did according to all that Jeremiah the prophet commanded him, reading from the book the words of the LORD in the LORD's house.

⁹Now it came to pass in the fifth year

of Jehoiakim the son of Josiah, king of Judah, in the ninth month, *that* they proclaimed a fast before the Lord to all the people in Jerusalem, and to all the people who came from the cities of Judah to Jerusalem. ¹⁰Then Baruch read from the book the words of Jeremiah in the house of the Lord, in the chamber of Gemariah the son of Shaphan the scribe, in the upper court at the entry of the New Gate of the Lord's house, in the hearing of all the people.

¹¹When Michaiah the son of Gemariah, the son of Shaphan, heard all the words of the Lord from the book, ¹²he then went down to the king's house, into the scribe's chamber; and there all the princes were sitting—Elishama the scribe, Delaiah the son of Shemaiah, Elnathan the son of Achbor, Gemariah the son of Shaphan, Zedekiah the son of Hananiah, and all the princes. ¹³Then Michaiah declared to them all the words that he had heard when Baruch read the book in the hearing of the people. ¹⁴Therefore all the princes sent Jehudi the son of Nethaniah, the son of Shelemiah, the son of Cushi, to Baruch, saying, "Take in your hand the scroll from which you have read in the hearing of the people, and come." So Baruch the son of Neriah took the scroll in his hand and came to them. ¹⁵And they said to him, "Sit down now, and read it in our hearing." So Baruch read *it* in their hearing.

¹⁶Now it happened, when they had heard all the words, that they looked in fear from one to another, and said to Baruch, "We will surely tell the king of all these words." ¹⁷And they asked Baruch, saying, "Tell us now, how did you write all these words—at his instruction?"*

¹⁸So Baruch answered them, "He proclaimed with his mouth all these words to me, and I wrote *them* with ink in the book."

¹⁹Then the princes said to Baruch, "Go and hide, you and Jeremiah; and let no one know where you are."

²⁰And they went to the king, into the court; but they stored the scroll in the chamber of Elishama the scribe, and told all the words in the hearing of the king. ²¹So the king sent Jehudi to bring the scroll, and he took it from Elishama the scribe's chamber. And Jehudi read it in the hearing of the king and in the hearing of all the princes who stood beside the king. ²²Now the king was sitting in the winter house in the ninth month, with *a fire* burning on the hearth before him. ²³And it happened, when Jehudi had read three or four columns, *that the king* cut it with the scribe's knife and cast *it* into the fire that *was* on the hearth, until all the scroll was consumed in the fire that *was* on the hearth. ²⁴Yet they were not afraid, nor did they tear their garments, the king nor any of his servants who heard all these words. ²⁵Nevertheless Elnathan, Delaiah, and Gemariah implored the king not to burn the scroll; but he would not listen to them. ²⁶And the king commanded Jerahmeel the king's* son, Seraiah the son of Azriel, and Shelemiah the son of Abdeel, to seize Baruch the scribe and Jeremiah the prophet, but the Lord hid them.

²⁷Now after the king had burned the scroll with the words which Baruch had written at the instruction of Jeremiah,* the word of the Lord came to Jeremiah, saying: ²⁸"Take yet another scroll, and write on it all the former words that were in the first scroll which Jehoiakim the king of Judah has burned. ²⁹And you shall say to Jehoiakim king of Judah, 'Thus says the Lord: "You have burned this scroll, saying, 'Why have you written in it that the king of Babylon will certainly come and destroy this land, and cause man and beast to cease from here?' " ³⁰Therefore thus says the Lord concerning Jehoiakim king of Judah: "He

shall have no one to sit on the throne of David, and his dead body shall be cast out to the heat of the day and the frost of the night. [31]I will punish him, his family, and his servants for their iniquity; and I will bring on them, on the inhabitants of Jerusalem, and on the men of Judah all the doom that I have pronounced against them; but they did not heed." ' "

[32]Then Jeremiah took another scroll and gave it to Baruch the scribe, the son of Neriah, who wrote on it at the instruction of Jeremiah* all the words of the book which Jehoiakim king of Judah had burned in the fire. And besides, there were added to them many similar words.

1 TIMOTHY 5:1-25

Do not rebuke an older man, but exhort *him* as a father, younger men as brothers, [2]older women as mothers, younger women as sisters, with all purity.

[3]Honor widows who are really widows. [4]But if any widow has children or grandchildren, let them first learn to show piety at home and to repay their parents; for this is good and* acceptable before God. [5]Now she who is really a widow, and left alone, trusts in God and continues in supplications and prayers night and day. [6]But she who lives in pleasure is dead while she lives. [7]And these things command, that they may be blameless. [8]But if anyone does not provide for his own, and especially for those of his household, he has denied the faith and is worse than an unbeliever.

[9]Do not let a widow under sixty years old be taken into the number, *and not unless* she has been the wife of one man, [10]well reported for good works: if she has brought up children, if she has lodged strangers, if she has washed the saints' feet, if she has re-

lieved the afflicted, if she has diligently followed every good work.

[11]But refuse *the* younger widows; for when they have begun to grow wanton against Christ, they desire to marry, [12]having condemnation because they have cast off their first faith. [13]And besides they learn *to be* idle, wandering about from house to house, and not only idle but also gossips and busybodies, saying things which they ought not. [14]Therefore I desire that *the* younger *widows* marry, bear children, manage the house, give no opportunity to the adversary to speak reproachfully. [15]For some have already turned aside after Satan. [16]If any believing man or* woman has widows, let them relieve them, and do not let the church be burdened, that it may relieve those who are really widows.

[17]Let the elders who rule well be counted worthy of double honor, especially those who labor in the word and doctrine. [18]For the Scripture says, *"You shall not muzzle an ox while it treads out the grain,"* * and, "The laborer *is* worthy of his wages." * [19]Do not receive an accusation against an elder except from two or three witnesses. [20]Those who are sinning rebuke in the presence of all, that the rest also may fear.

[21]I charge *you* before God and the Lord Jesus Christ and the elect angels that you observe these things without prejudice, doing nothing with partiality. [22]Do not lay hands on anyone hastily, nor share in other people's sins; keep yourself pure.

[23]No longer drink only water, but use a little wine for your stomach's sake and your frequent infirmities.

[24]Some men's sins are clearly evident, preceding *them* to judgment, but those of some *men* follow later. [25]Likewise, the good works *of some* are clearly evident, and those that are otherwise cannot be hidden.

PSALM 89:14-37

R IGHTEOUSNESS and justice *are* the foundation of Your throne; Mercy and truth go before Your face.

15 Blessed *are* the people who know the joyful sound!
They walk, O LORD, in the light of Your countenance.

16 In Your name they rejoice all day long,
And in Your righteousness they are exalted.

17 For You *are* the glory of their strength,
And in Your favor our horn is exalted.

18 For our shield *belongs* to the LORD,
And our king to the Holy One of Israel.

19 Then You spoke in a vision to Your holy one,*
And said: "I have given help to *one who is* mighty;
I have exalted one chosen from the people.

20 I have found My servant David;
With My holy oil I have anointed him,

21 With whom My hand shall be established;
Also My arm shall strengthen him.

22 The enemy shall not outwit him,
Nor the son of wickedness afflict him.

23 I will beat down his foes before his face,
And plague those who hate him.

24 "But My faithfulness and My mercy *shall be* with him,
And in My name his horn shall be exalted.

25 Also I will set his hand over the sea,
And his right hand over the rivers.

26 He shall cry to Me, 'You *are* my Father,
My God, and the rock of my salvation.'

27 Also I will make him *My* firstborn,
The highest of the kings of the earth.

28 My mercy I will keep for him forever,
And My covenant shall stand firm with him.

29 His seed also I will make *to endure* forever,
And his throne as the days of heaven.

30 "If his sons forsake My law And do not walk in My judgments,

31 If they break My statutes And do not keep My commandments,

32 Then I will punish their transgression with the rod,
And their iniquity with stripes.

33 Nevertheless My lovingkindness I will not utterly take from him,
Nor allow My faithfulness to fail.

34 My covenant I will not break,
Nor alter the word that has gone out of My lips.

35 Once I have sworn by My holiness;
I will not lie to David:

36 His seed shall endure forever,
And his throne as the sun before Me;

37 It shall be established forever like the moon,
Even *like* the faithful witness in the sky."   Selah

PROVERBS FOR TODAY / 25:25-27

As *cold water to a weary soul, so* is *good news from a far country. A righteous* man *who falters before the wicked* is like *a murky spring and a polluted well.* ▫ It is *not good to eat much honey; so to seek one's own glory* is not *glory.*

OCTOBER 21

JEREMIAH 37:1–38:28

Now King Zedekiah the son of Josiah reigned instead of Coniah the son of Jehoiakim, whom Nebuchadnezzar king of Babylon made king in the land of Judah. ²But neither he nor his servants nor the people of the land gave heed to the words of the LORD which He spoke by the prophet Jeremiah.

³And Zedekiah the king sent Jehucal the son of Shelemiah, and Zephaniah the son of Maaseiah, the priest, to the prophet Jeremiah, saying, "Pray now to the LORD our God for us." ⁴Now Jeremiah was coming and going among the people, for they had not *yet* put him in prison. ⁵Then Pharaoh's army came up from Egypt; and when the Chaldeans who were besieging Jerusalem heard news of them, they departed from Jerusalem.

⁶Then the word of the LORD came to the prophet Jeremiah, saying, ⁷"Thus says the LORD, the God of Israel, 'Thus you shall say to the king of Judah, who sent you to Me to inquire of Me: "Behold, Pharaoh's army which has come up to help you will return to Egypt, to their own land. ⁸And the Chaldeans shall come back and fight against this city, and take it and burn it with fire." ' ⁹Thus says the LORD: 'Do not deceive yourselves, saying, "The Chaldeans will surely depart from us," for they will not depart. ¹⁰For though you had defeated the whole army of the Chaldeans who fight against you, and there remained *only* wounded men among them, they would rise up, every man in his tent, and burn the city with fire.' "

¹¹And it happened, when the army of the Chaldeans left *the siege* of Jerusalem for fear of Pharaoh's army, ¹²that Jeremiah went out of Jerusalem to go into the land of Benjamin to claim his property there among the people. ¹³And when he was in the Gate of Benjamin, a captain of the guard *was* there whose name *was* Irijah the son of Shelemiah, the son of Hananiah; and he seized Jeremiah the prophet, saying, "You are defecting to the Chaldeans!"

¹⁴Then Jeremiah said, "False! I am not defecting to the Chaldeans." But he did not listen to him.

So Irijah seized Jeremiah and brought him to the princes. ¹⁵Therefore the princes were angry with Jeremiah, and they struck him and put him in prison in the house of Jonathan the scribe. For they had made that the prison.

¹⁶When Jeremiah entered the dungeon and the cells, and Jeremiah had remained there many days, ¹⁷then Zedekiah the king sent and took him *out.* The king asked him secretly in his house, and said, "Is there *any* word from the LORD?"

And Jeremiah said, "There is." Then he said, "You shall be delivered into the hand of the king of Babylon!"

¹⁸Moreover Jeremiah said to King Zedekiah, "What offense have I com-

"This was the LORD's doing;
it is marvelous
in our eyes."
Psalm 118:23

"Blessed are the merciful, for they shall obtain mercy."
Matthew 5:7

mitted against you, against your servants, or against this people, that you have put me in prison? ¹⁹Where now *are* your prophets who prophesied to you, saying, 'The king of Babylon will not come against you or against this land?' ²⁰Therefore please hear now, O my lord the king. Please, let my petition be accepted before you, and do not make me return to the house of Jonathan the scribe, lest I die there."

²¹Then Zedekiah the king commanded that they should commit Jeremiah to the court of the prison, and that they should give him daily a piece of bread from the bakers' street, until all the bread in the city was gone. Thus Jeremiah remained in the court of the prison.

Now Shephatiah the son of Mattan, Gedaliah the son of Pashhur, Jucal* the son of Shelemiah, and Pashhur the son of Malchiah heard the words that Jeremiah had spoken to all the people, saying, ²"Thus says the Lord: 'He who remains in this city shall die by the sword, by famine, and by pestilence; but he who goes over to the Chaldeans shall live; his life shall be as a prize to him, and he shall live.'* ³Thus says the Lord: 'This city shall surely be given into the hand of the king of Babylon's army, which shall take it.' "

⁴Therefore the princes said to the king, "Please, let this man be put to death, for thus he weakens the hands of the men of war who remain in this city, and the hands of all the people, by speaking such words to them. For this man does not seek the welfare of this people, but their harm."

⁵Then Zedekiah the king said, "Look, he *is* in your hand. For the king can *do* nothing against you." ⁶So they took Jeremiah and cast him into the dungeon of Malchiah the king's* son, which *was* in the court of the prison, and they let Jeremiah down with ropes. And in the dungeon *there was*

no water, but mire. So Jeremiah sank in the mire.

⁷Now Ebed-Melech the Ethiopian, one of the eunuchs, who was in the king's house, heard that they had put Jeremiah in the dungeon. When the king was sitting at the Gate of Benjamin, ⁸Ebed-Melech went out of the king's house and spoke to the king, saying: ⁹"My lord the king, these men have done evil in all that they have done to Jeremiah the prophet, whom they have cast into the dungeon, and he is likely to die from hunger in the place where he is. For *there is* no more bread in the city." ¹⁰Then the king commanded Ebed-Melech the Ethiopian, saying, "Take from here thirty men with you, and lift Jeremiah the prophet out of the dungeon before he dies." ¹¹So Ebed-Melech took the men with him and went into the house of the king under the treasury, and took from there old clothes and old rags, and let them down by ropes into the dungeon to Jeremiah. ¹²Then Ebed-Melech the Ethiopian said to Jeremiah, "Please put these old clothes and rags under your armpits, under the ropes." And Jeremiah did so. ¹³So they pulled Jeremiah up with ropes and lifted him out of the dungeon. And Jeremiah remained in the court of the prison.

¹⁴Then Zedekiah the king sent and had Jeremiah the prophet brought to him at the third entrance of the house of the Lord. And the king said to Jeremiah, "I will ask you something. Hide nothing from me."

¹⁵Jeremiah said to Zedekiah, "If I declare *it* to you, will you not surely put me to death? And if I give you advice, you will not listen to me."

¹⁶So Zedekiah the king swore secretly to Jeremiah, saying, "*As* the Lord lives, who made our very souls, I will not put you to death, nor will I give you into the hand of these men who seek your life."

¹⁷Then Jeremiah said to Zedekiah, "Thus says the LORD, the God of hosts, the God of Israel: 'If you surely surrender to the king of Babylon's princes, then your soul shall live; this city shall not be burned with fire, and you and your house shall live. ¹⁸But if you do not surrender to the king of Babylon's princes, then this city shall be given into the hand of the Chaldeans; they shall burn it with fire, and you shall not escape from their hand.' "

¹⁹And Zedekiah the king said to Jeremiah, "I am afraid of the Jews who have defected to the Chaldeans, lest they deliver me into their hand, and they abuse me."

²⁰But Jeremiah said, "They shall not deliver *you*. Please, obey the voice of the LORD which I speak to you. So it shall be well with you, and your soul shall live. ²¹But if you refuse to surrender, this *is* the word that the LORD has shown me: ²²'Now behold, all the women who are left in the king of Judah's house *shall be* surrendered to the king of Babylon's princes, and those *women* shall say:

"Your close friends have set
upon you
And prevailed against you;
Your feet have sunk in the
mire,
And they have turned away
again."

²³'So they shall surrender all your wives and children to the Chaldeans. You shall not escape from their hand, but shall be taken by the hand of the king of Babylon. And you shall cause this city to be burned with fire.' "

²⁴Then Zedekiah said to Jeremiah, "Let no one know of these words, and you shall not die. ²⁵But if the princes hear that I have talked with you, and they come to you and say to you, 'Declare to us now what you have said to the king, and also what the king said to

you; do not hide *it* from us, and we will not put you to death,' ²⁶then you shall say to them, 'I presented my request before the king, that he would not make me return to Jonathan's house to die there.' "

²⁷Then all the princes came to Jeremiah and asked him. And he told them according to all these words that the king had commanded. So they stopped speaking with him, for the conversation had not been heard. ²⁸Now Jeremiah remained in the court of the prison until the day that Jerusalem was taken. And he was *there* when Jerusalem was taken.

1 TIMOTHY 6:1-21

LET as many bondservants as are under the yoke count their own masters worthy of all honor, so that the name of God and *His* doctrine may not be blasphemed. ²And those who have believing masters, let them not despise *them* because they are brethren, but rather serve *them* because those who are benefited are believers and beloved. Teach and exhort these things.

³If anyone teaches otherwise and does not consent to wholesome words, *even* the words of our Lord Jesus Christ, and to the doctrine which accords with godliness, ⁴he is proud, knowing nothing, but is obsessed with disputes and arguments over words, from which come envy, strife, reviling, evil suspicions, ⁵useless wranglings* of men of corrupt minds and destitute of the truth, who suppose that godliness is a *means of* gain. From such withdraw yourself.*

⁶Now godliness with contentment is great gain. ⁷For we brought nothing into *this* world, *and it is* certain* we can carry nothing out. ⁸And having food and clothing, with these we shall be content. ⁹But those who desire to be rich fall into temptation and a snare,

and *into* many foolish and harmful lusts which drown men in destruction and perdition. [10]For the love of money is a root of all *kinds of* evil, for which some have strayed from the faith in their greediness, and pierced themselves through with many sorrows.

[11]But you, O man of God, flee these things and pursue righteousness, godliness, faith, love, patience, gentleness. [12]Fight the good fight of faith, lay hold on eternal life, to which you were also called and have confessed the good confession in the presence of many witnesses. [13]I urge you in the sight of God who gives life to all things, and *before* Christ Jesus who witnessed the good confession before Pontius Pilate, [14]that you keep *this* commandment without spot, blameless until our Lord Jesus Christ's appearing, [15]which He will manifest in His own time, *He who is* the blessed and only Potentate, the King of kings and Lord of lords, [16]who alone has immortality, dwelling in unapproachable light, whom no man has seen or can see, to whom *be* honor and everlasting power. Amen.

[17]Command those who are rich in this present age not to be haughty, nor to trust in uncertain riches but in the living God, who gives us richly all things to enjoy. [18]*Let them* do good, that they be rich in good works, ready to give, willing to share, [19]storing up for themselves a good foundation for the time to come, that they may lay hold on eternal life.

[20]O Timothy! Guard what was committed to your trust, avoiding the profane *and* idle babblings and contradictions of what is falsely called knowledge— [21]by professing it some have strayed concerning the faith.

Grace *be* with you. Amen.

PSALM 89:38-52

BUT You have cast off and abhorred,
You have been furious with Your anointed.

39 You have renounced the covenant of Your servant;
You have profaned his crown *by casting it* to the ground.

40 You have broken down all his hedges;
You have brought his strongholds to ruin.

41 All who pass by the way plunder him;
He is a reproach to his neighbors.

42 You have exalted the right hand of his adversaries,
You have made all his enemies rejoice.

43 You have also turned back the edge of his sword,
And have not sustained him in the battle.

44 You have made his glory cease,
And cast his throne down to the ground.

45 The days of his youth You have shortened;
You have covered him with shame.   Selah

46 How long, LORD?
Will You hide Yourself forever?
Will Your wrath burn like fire?

47 Remember how short my time is;
For what futility have You created all the children of men?

48 What man can live and not see death?
Can he deliver his life from the power of the grave?   Selah

49 Lord, where *are* Your former
   lovingkindnesses,
   Which You swore to David in
   Your truth?
50 Remember, Lord, the
   reproach of Your servants—
   How I bear in my bosom *the
   reproach of* all the many
   peoples,

51 With which Your enemies
   have reproached, O Lord,
   With which they have
   reproached the footsteps of
   Your anointed.

52 Blessed *be* the Lord
   forevermore!
   Amen and Amen.

PROVERBS FOR TODAY/ 25:28

Whoever has *no rule over his own spirit* is like *a city broken down, without walls.*

OCTOBER 22

JEREMIAH 39:1–41:18

IN the ninth year of Zedekiah king of Judah, in the tenth month, Nebuchadnezzar king of Babylon and all his army came against Jerusalem, and besieged it. ²In the eleventh year of Zedekiah, in the fourth month, on the ninth *day* of the month, the city was penetrated.

³Then all the princes of the king of Babylon came in and sat in the Middle Gate: Nergal-Sharezer, Samgar-Nebo, Sarsechim, Rabsaris,* Nergal-Sarezer, Rabmag,* with the rest of the princes of the king of Babylon.

⁴So it was, when Zedekiah the king of Judah and all the men of war saw them, that they fled and went out of the city by night, by way of the king's garden, by the gate between the two walls. And he went out by way of the plain.* ⁵But the Chaldean army pursued them and overtook Zedekiah in the plains of Jericho. And when they had captured him, they brought him up to Nebuchadnezzar king of Babylon, to Riblah in the land of Hamath, where he pronounced judgment on him. ⁶Then the king of Babylon killed the sons of Zedekiah before his eyes in Riblah; the king of Babylon also killed all the nobles of Judah. ⁷Moreover he put out Zedekiah's eyes, and bound him with bronze fetters to carry him off to Babylon. ⁸And the Chaldeans burned the king's house and the houses of the people with fire, and broke down the walls of Jerusalem. ⁹Then Nebuzaradan the captain of the guard carried away captive to Babylon the remnant of the people who remained in the city and those who defected to him, with the rest of the people who remained. ¹⁰But Nebuzaradan the captain of the guard left in the land of Judah the poor people, who had nothing, and gave them vineyards and fields at the same time.

¹¹Now Nebuchadnezzar king of Babylon gave charge concerning Jeremiah to Nebuzaradan the captain of the guard, saying, ¹²"Take him and look after him, and do him no harm; but do to him just as he says to you." ¹³So Nebuzaradan the captain of the guard sent Nebushasban, Rabsaris, Nergal-Sharezer, Rabmag, and all the king of Babylon's chief officers; ¹⁴then they sent *someone* to take Jeremiah

from the court of the prison, and committed him to Gedaliah the son of Ahikam, the son of Shaphan, that he should take him home. So he dwelt among the people.

15Meanwhile the word of the LORD had come to Jeremiah while he was shut up in the court of the prison, saying, 16"Go and speak to Ebed-Melech the Ethiopian, saying, 'Thus says the LORD of hosts, the God of Israel: "Behold, I will bring My words upon this city for adversity and not for good, and they shall be *performed* in that day before you. 17But I will deliver you in that day," says the LORD, "and you shall not be given into the hand of the men of whom you *are* afraid. 18For I will surely deliver you, and you shall not fall by the sword; but your life shall be as a prize to you, because you have put your trust in Me," says the LORD.' "

THE word that came to Jeremiah from the LORD after Nebuzaradan the captain of the guard had let him go from Ramah, when he had taken him bound in chains among all who were carried away captive from Jerusalem and Judah, who were carried away captive to Babylon.

2And the captain of the guard took Jeremiah and said to him: "The LORD your God has pronounced this doom on this place. 3Now the LORD has brought *it,* and has done just as He said. Because you *people* have sinned against the LORD, and not obeyed His voice, therefore this thing has come upon you. 4And now look, I free you this day from the chains that *were* on your hand. If it seems good to you to come with me to Babylon, come, and I will look after you. But if it seems wrong for you to come with me to Babylon, remain here. See, all the land *is* before you; wherever it seems good and convenient for you to go, go there."

5Now while Jeremiah had not yet gone back, *Nebuzaradan said,* "Go back to Gedaliah the son of Ahikam, the son of Shaphan, whom the king of Babylon has made governor over the cities of Judah, and dwell with him among the people. Or go wherever it seems convenient for you to go." So the captain of the guard gave him rations and a gift and let him go. 6Then Jeremiah went to Gedaliah the son of Ahikam, to Mizpah, and dwelt with him among the people who were left in the land.

7And when all the captains of the armies who *were* in the fields, they and their men, heard that the king of Babylon had made Gedaliah the son of Ahikam governor in the land, and had committed to him men, women, children, and the poorest of the land who had not been carried away captive to Babylon, 8then they came to Gedaliah at Mizpah—Ishmael the son of Nethaniah, Johanan and Jonathan the sons of Kareah, Seraiah the son of Tanhumeth, the sons of Ephai the Netophathite, and Jezaniah* the son of a Maachathite, they and their men. 9And Gedaliah the son of Ahikam, the son of Shaphan, took an oath before them and their men, saying, "Do not be afraid to serve the Chaldeans. Dwell in the land and serve the king of Babylon, and it shall be well with you. 10As for me, I will indeed dwell at Mizpah and serve the Chaldeans who come to us. But you, gather wine and summer fruit and oil, put *them* in your vessels, and dwell in your cities that you have taken." 11Likewise, when all the Jews who *were* in Moab, among the Ammonites, in Edom, and who *were* in all the countries, heard that the king of Babylon had left a remnant of Judah, and that he had set over them Gedaliah the son of Ahikam, the son of Shaphan, 12then all the Jews returned out of all places where they had been driven, and came to the land of Judah, to Gedaliah at Mizpah, and gathered wine and summer fruit in abundance.

¹³Moreover Johanan the son of Kareah and all the captains of the forces that *were* in the fields came to Gedaliah at Mizpah, ¹⁴and said to him, "Do you certainly know that Baalis the king of the Ammonites has sent Ishmael the son of Nethaniah to murder you?" But Gedaliah the son of Ahikam did not believe them.

¹⁵Then Johanan the son of Kareah spoke secretly to Gedaliah in Mizpah, saying, "Let me go, please, and I will kill Ishmael the son of Nethaniah, and no one will know *it.* Why should the murder you, so that all the Jews who are gathered to you would be scattered, and the remnant in Judah perish?"

¹⁶But Gedaliah the son of Ahikam said to Johanan the son of Kareah, "You shall not do this thing, for you speak falsely concerning Ishmael."

Now it came to pass in the seventh month *that* Ishmael the son of Nethaniah, the son of Elishama, of the royal family and of the officers of the king, came with ten men to Gedaliah the son of Ahikam, at Mizpah. And there they ate bread together in Mizpah. ²Then Ishmael the son of Nethaniah, and the ten men who were with him, arose and struck Gedaliah the son of Ahikam, the son of Shaphan, with the sword, and killed him whom the king of Babylon had made governor over the land. ³Ishmael also struck down all the Jews who were with him, *that is,* with Gedaliah at Mizpah, and the Chaldeans who were found there, the men of war.

⁴And it happened, on the second day after he had killed Gedaliah, when as yet no one knew *it,* ⁵that certain men came from Shechem, from Shiloh, and from Samaria, eighty men with their beards shaved and their clothes torn, having cut themselves, with offerings and incense in their hand, to bring *them* to the house of the LORD. ⁶Now Ishmael the son of Nethaniah went out from Mizpah to meet them, weeping as he went along; and it happened as he met them that he said to them, "Come to Gedaliah the son of Ahikam!" ⁷So it was, when they came into the midst of the city, that Ishmael the son of Nethaniah killed them *and cast them* into the midst of a pit, he and the men who were with him. ⁸But ten men were found among them who said to Ishmael, "Do not kill us, for we have treasures of wheat, barley, oil, and honey in the field." So he desisted and did not kill them among their brethren. ⁹Now the pit into which Ishmael had cast all the dead bodies of the men whom he had slain, because of Gedaliah, *was* the same one Asa the king had made for fear of Baasha king of Israel. Ishmael the son of Nethaniah filled it with *the* slain. ¹⁰Then Ishmael carried away captive all the rest of the people who *were* in Mizpah, the king's daughters and all the people who remained in Mizpah, whom Nebuzaradan the captain of the guard had committed to Gedaliah the son of Ahikam. And Ishmael the son of Nethaniah carried them away captive and departed to go over to the Ammonites.

¹¹But when Johanan the son of Kareah and all the captains of the forces that *were* with him heard of all the evil that Ishmael the son of Nethaniah had done, ¹²they took all the men and went to fight with Ishmael the son of Nethaniah; and they found him by the great pool that *is* in Gibeon. ¹³So it was, when all the people who *were* with Ishmael saw Johanan the son of Kareah, and all the captains of the forces who *were* with him, that they were glad. ¹⁴Then all the people whom Ishmael had carried away captive from Mizpah turned around and came back, and went to Johanan the son of Kareah. ¹⁵But Ishmael the son of Neth-

aniah escaped from Johanan with eight men and went to the Ammonites.

[16]Then Johanan the son of Kareah, and all the captains of the forces that were with him, took from Mizpah all the rest of the people whom he had recovered from Ishmael the son of Nethaniah after he had murdered Gedaliah the son of Ahikam—the mighty men of war and the women and the children and the eunuchs, whom he had brought back from Gibeon. [17]And they departed and dwelt in the habitation of Chimham, which is near Bethlehem, as they went on their way to Egypt, [18]because of the Chaldeans; for they were afraid of them, because Ishmael the son of Nethaniah had murdered Gedaliah the son of Ahikam, whom the king of Babylon had made governor in the land.

2 TIMOTHY 1:1-18

PAUL, an apostle of Jesus Christ* by the will of God, according to the promise of life which is in Christ Jesus,

[2]To Timothy, a beloved son:

Grace, mercy, and peace from God the Father and Christ Jesus our Lord.

[3]I thank God, whom I serve with a pure conscience, as my forefathers did, as without ceasing I remember you in my prayers night and day, [4]greatly desiring to see you, being mindful of your tears, that I may be filled with joy, [5]when I call to remembrance the genuine faith that is in you, which dwelt first in your grandmother Lois and your mother Eunice, and I am persuaded is in you also. [6]Therefore I remind you to stir up the gift of God which is in you through the laying on of my hands. [7]For God has not given us a spirit of fear, but of power and of love and of a sound mind.

[8]Therefore do not be ashamed of the testimony of our Lord, nor of me His prisoner, but share with me in the sufferings for the gospel according to the power of God, [9]who has saved us and called us with a holy calling, not according to our works, but according to His own purpose and grace which was given to us in Christ Jesus before time began, [10]but has now been revealed by the appearing of our Savior Jesus Christ, who has abolished death and brought life and immortality to light through the gospel, [11]to which I was appointed a preacher, an apostle, and a teacher of the Gentiles.* [12]For this reason I also suffer these things; nevertheless I am not ashamed, for I know whom I have believed and am persuaded that He is able to keep what I have committed to Him until that Day.

[13]Hold fast the pattern of sound words which you have heard from me, in faith and love which are in Christ Jesus. [14]That good thing which was committed to you, keep by the Holy Spirit who dwells in us.

[15]This you know, that all those in Asia have turned away from me, among whom are Phygellus and Hermogenes. [16]The Lord grant mercy to the household of Onesiphorus, for he often refreshed me, and was not ashamed of my chain; [17]but when he arrived in Rome, he sought me out very zealously and found me. [18]The Lord grant to him that he may find mercy from the Lord in that Day—and you know very well how many ways he ministered to me* at Ephesus.

PSALM 90:1–91:16

A Prayer of Moses the man of God.

LORD, You have been our dwelling place* in all generations. [2]Before the mountains were brought forth,

Or ever You had formed the
earth and the world,
Even from everlasting to
everlasting, You *are* God.

3   You turn man to destruction,
And say, "Return, O children
of men."
4   For a thousand years in Your
sight
Are like yesterday when it is
past,
And *like* a watch in the night.
5   You carry them away *like* a
flood;
They are like a sleep.
In the morning they are like
grass *which* grows up:
6   In the morning it flourishes
and grows up;
In the evening it is cut down
and withers.

7   For we have been consumed
by Your anger,
And by Your wrath we are
terrified.
8   You have set our iniquities
before You,
Our secret *sins* in the light of
Your countenance.
9   For all our days have passed
away in Your wrath;
We finish our years like a sigh.
10 The days of our lives *are*
seventy years;
And if by reason of strength
they are eighty years,
Yet their boast *is* only labor
and sorrow;
For it is soon cut off, and we
fly away.
11 Who knows the power of Your
anger?
For as the fear of You, *so is*
Your wrath.
12 So teach *us* to number our
days,
That we may gain a heart of
wisdom.

13 Return, O Lᴏʀᴅ!
How long?
And have compassion on Your
servants.
14 Oh, satisfy us early with Your
mercy,
That we may rejoice and be
glad all our days!
15 Make us glad according to
the days *in which* You have
afflicted us,
The years *in which* we have
seen evil.
16 Let Your work appear to Your
servants,
And Your glory to their
children.
17 And let the beauty of the Lᴏʀᴅ
our God be upon us,
And establish the work of our
hands for us;
Yes, establish the work of our
hands.

Hᴇ who dwells in the secret place of
the Most High
Shall abide under the shadow
of the Almighty.
2   I will say of the Lᴏʀᴅ, "*He is*
my refuge and my fortress;
My God, in Him I will trust."

3   Surely He shall deliver you
from the snare of the
fowler*
And from the perilous
pestilence.
4   He shall cover you with His
feathers,
And under His wings you
shall take refuge;
His truth *shall be your* shield
and buckler.
5   You shall not be afraid of the
terror by night,
Nor of the arrow *that* flies by
day,
6   *Nor* of the pestilence *that*
walks in darkness,

Nor of the destruction that
lays waste at noonday.
7 A thousand may fall at your
side,
And ten thousand at your
right hand;
But it shall not come near you.
8 Only with your eyes shall you
look,
And see the reward of the
wicked.

9 Because you have made the
LORD, who is my refuge,
Even the Most High, your
dwelling place,
10 No evil shall befall you,
Nor shall any plague come
near your dwelling;
11 For He shall give His angels
charge over you,
To keep you in all your ways.

12 In their hands they shall bear
you up,
Lest you dash your foot
against a stone.
13 You shall tread upon the lion
and the cobra,
The young lion and the
serpent you shall trample
underfoot.

14 "Because he has set his love
upon Me, therefore I will
deliver him;
I will set him on high,
because he has known My
name.
15 He shall call upon Me, and I
will answer him;
I will be with him in trouble;
I will deliver him and honor
him.
16 With long life I will satisfy
him,
And show him My salvation."

PROVERBS FOR TODAY/ 26:1-2

As snow in summer and rain in harvest, so honor is not fitting for a fool. Like a flitting sparrow, like a flying swallow, so a curse without cause shall not alight.

OCTOBER 23

JEREMIAH 42:1–44:23

Now all the captains of the forces, Johanan the son of Kareah, Jezaniah the son of Hoshaiah, and all the people, from the least to the greatest, came near 2and said to Jeremiah the prophet, "Please, let our petition be acceptable to you, and pray for us to the LORD your God, for all this remnant (since we are left but a few of many, as you can see), 3that

the LORD your God may show us the way in which we should walk and the thing we should do."

4Then Jeremiah the prophet said to them, "I have heard. Indeed, I will pray to the LORD your God according to your words, and it shall be, that whatever the LORD answers you, I will declare it to you. I will keep nothing back from you."

5So they said to Jeremiah, "Let the LORD be a true and faithful witness between us, if we do not do according to everything which the LORD your God sends us by you. ⁶Whether *it is* pleasing or displeasing, we will obey the voice of the LORD our God to whom we send you, that it may be well with us when we obey the voice of the LORD our God."

⁷And it happened after ten days that the word of the LORD came to Jeremiah. ⁸Then he called Johanan the son of Kareah, all the captains of the forces which *were* with him, and all the people from the least even to the greatest, ⁹and said to them, "Thus says the LORD, the God of Israel, to whom you sent me to present your petition before Him: ¹⁰'If you will still remain in this land, then I will build you and not pull *you* down, and I will plant you and not pluck *you* up. For I relent concerning the disaster that I have brought upon you. ¹¹Do not be afraid of the king of Babylon, of whom you are afraid; do not be afraid of him,' says the LORD, 'for I *am* with you, to save you and deliver you from his hand. ¹²And I will show you mercy, that he may have mercy on you and cause you to return to your own land.'

¹³"But if you say, 'We will not dwell in this land,' disobeying the voice of the LORD your God, ¹⁴saying, 'No, but we will go to the land of Egypt where we shall see no war, nor hear the sound of the trumpet, nor be hungry for bread, and there we will dwell'— ¹⁵Then hear now the word of the LORD, O remnant of Judah! Thus says the LORD of hosts, the God of Israel: 'If you wholly set your faces to enter Egypt, and go to dwell there, ¹⁶then it shall be *that* the sword which you feared shall overtake you there in the land of Egypt; the famine of which you were afraid shall follow close after you there *in* Egypt; and there you shall die. ¹⁷So shall it be with all the men who set their faces to go to Egypt to dwell there. They shall die by the sword, by famine, and by pestilence. And none of them shall remain or escape from the disaster that I will bring upon them.'

¹⁸"For thus says the LORD of hosts, the God of Israel: 'As My anger and My fury have been poured out on the inhabitants of Jerusalem, so will My fury be poured out on you when you enter Egypt. And you shall be an oath, an astonishment, a curse, and a reproach; and you shall see this place no more.'

¹⁹"The LORD has said concerning you, O remnant of Judah, 'Do not go to Egypt!' Know certainly that I have admonished you this day. ²⁰For you were hypocrites in your hearts when you sent me to the LORD your God, saying, 'Pray for us to the LORD our God, and according to all that the LORD your God says, so declare to us and we will do *it*.' ²¹And I have this day declared *it* to you, but you have not obeyed the voice of the LORD your God, or anything which He has sent you by me. ²²Now therefore, know certainly that you shall die by the sword, by famine, and by pestilence in the place where you desire to go to dwell."

Now it happened, when Jeremiah had stopped speaking to all the people all the words of the LORD their God, for which the LORD their God had sent him to them, all these words, ²that Azariah the son of Hoshaiah, Johanan the son of Kareah, and all the proud men spoke, saying to Jeremiah, "You speak falsely! The LORD our God has not sent you to say, 'Do not go to Egypt to dwell there.' ³But Baruch the son of Neriah has set you against us, to deliver us into the hand of the Chaldeans, that they may put us to death or carry us away captive to Babylon." ⁴So Johanan the son of Kareah, all the captains of the forces, and all the people would not obey the voice of the LORD, to remain in the land of Judah. ⁵But Johanan the son of Kareah and all the captains of the forces took all the remnant of Judah who had returned to dwell in the land of Judah, from all nations where they had been driven— 6men, women, children, the king's daughters, and every person whom Nebuzaradan the captain of the guard had left with Gedaliah the son of Ahikam, the son of Shaphan, and Jeremiah the prophet and Baruch the son of Neriah. 7So they went to the land of Egypt, for they did not obey the voice of the LORD. And they went as far as Tahpanhes.

8Then the word of the LORD came to Jeremiah in Tahpanhes, saying, 9"Take large stones in your hand, and hide them in the sight of the men of Judah, in the clay in the brick courtyard which *is* at the entrance to Pharaoh's house in Tahpanhes; 10and say to them, 'Thus says the LORD of hosts, the God of Israel: "Behold, I will send and bring Nebuchadnezzar the king of Babylon, My servant, and will set his throne above these stones that I have hidden. And he will spread his royal pavilion over them. 11When he comes, he shall strike the land of Egypt *and deliver* to death *those appointed* for death, and to captivity *those appointed* for captivity, and to the sword *those appointed* for the sword. 12I* will kindle a fire in the houses of the gods of Egypt, and he shall burn them and carry them away captive. And he shall array himself with the land of Egypt, as a shepherd puts on his garment, and he shall go out from there in peace. 13He shall also break the sacred pillars of Beth Shemesh* that *are* in the land of Egypt; and the houses of the gods of the Egyptians he shall burn with fire." ' "

THE word that came to Jeremiah concerning all the Jews who dwell in the land of Egypt, who dwell at Migdol, at Tahpanhes, at Noph,* and in the country of Pathros, saying, 2"Thus

says the LORD of hosts, the God of Israel: 'You have seen all the calamity that I have brought on Jerusalem and on all the cities of Judah; and behold, this day they *are* a desolation, and no one dwells in them, 3because of their wickedness which they have committed to provoke Me to anger, in that they went to burn incense *and* to serve other gods whom they did not know, they nor you nor your fathers. 4However I have sent to you all My servants the prophets, rising early and sending *them,* saying, "Oh, do not do this abominable thing that I hate!" 5But they did not listen or incline their ear to turn from their wickedness, to burn no incense to other gods. 6So My fury and My anger were poured out and kindled in the cities of Judah and in the streets of Jerusalem; and they are wasted *and* desolate, as it is this day.'

7"Now therefore, thus says the LORD, the God of hosts, the God of Israel: 'Why do you commit *this* great evil against yourselves, to cut off from you man and woman, child and infant, out of Judah, leaving none to remain, 8in that you provoke Me to wrath with the works of your hands, burning incense to other gods in the land of Egypt where you have gone to dwell, that you may cut yourselves off and be a curse and a reproach among all the nations of the earth? 9Have you forgotten the wickedness of your fathers, the wickedness of the kings of Judah, the wickedness of their wives, your own wickedness, and the wickedness of your wives, which they committed in the land of Judah and in the streets of Jerusalem? 10They have not been humbled, to this day, nor have they feared; they have not walked in My law or in My statutes that I set before you and your fathers.'

11"Therefore thus says the LORD of hosts, the God of Israel: 'Behold, I will set My face against you for catastrophe and for cutting off all Judah. 12And I will take the remnant of Judah who have set their faces to go into the land of Egypt to dwell there, and they shall all be consumed *and* fall in the land of Egypt. They shall be consumed by the sword *and* by famine. They shall die, from the least to the greatest, by the sword and by famine; and they shall be an oath, an astonishment, a curse and a reproach! 13For I will punish those who dwell in the land of Egypt, as I have punished Jerusalem, by the sword, by famine, and by pestilence, 14so that none of the remnant of Judah who have gone into the land of Egypt to dwell there shall escape or survive, lest they return to the land of Judah, to which they desire to return and dwell. For none shall return except those who escape.' "

15Then all the men who knew that their wives had burned incense to other gods, with all the women who stood by, a great multitude, and all the people who dwelt in the land of Egypt, in Pathros, answered Jeremiah, saying: 16"*As for* the word that you have spoken to us in the name of the LORD, we will not listen to you! 17But we will certainly do whatever has gone out of our own mouth, to burn incense to the queen of heaven and pour out drink offerings to her, as we have done, we and our fathers, our kings and our princes, in the cities of Judah and in the streets of Jerusalem. For *then* we had plenty of food, were well-off, and saw no trouble. 18But since we stopped burning incense to the queen of heaven and pouring out drink offerings to her, we have lacked everything and have been consumed by the sword and by famine."

19*The women also said,* "And when we burned incense to the queen of heaven and poured out drink offerings to her, did we make cakes for her, to worship her, and pour out drink offerings to her without our husbands' *permission?*"

20Then Jeremiah spoke to all the people—the men, the women, and all the people who had given him *that* answer—saying: 21"The incense that you burned in the cities of Judah and in the streets of Jerusalem, you and your fathers, your kings and your princes, and the people of the land, did not the LORD remember them, and did it *not* come into His mind? 22So the LORD could no longer bear *it,* because of the evil of your doings *and* because of the abominations which you committed. Therefore your land is a desolation, an astonishment, a curse, and without an inhabitant, as *it is* this day. 23Because you have burned incense and because you have sinned against the LORD, and have not obeyed the voice of the LORD or walked in His law, in His statutes or in His testimonies, therefore this calamity has happened to you, as *at* this day."

2 TIMOTHY 2:1-21

Y OU therefore, my son, be strong in the grace that is in Christ Jesus. 2And the things that you have heard from me among many witnesses, commit these to faithful men who will be able to teach others also. 3You therefore must endure* hardship as a good soldier of Jesus Christ. 4No one engaged in warfare entangles himself with the affairs of *this* life, that he may please him who enlisted him as a soldier. 5And also if anyone competes in athletics, he is not crowned unless he competes according to the rules. 6The hardworking farmer must be first to partake of the crops. 7Consider what I say, and may* the Lord give you understanding in all things.

8Remember that Jesus Christ, of the seed of David, was raised from the dead according to my gospel, 9for which I suffer trouble as an evildoer, *even* to the point of chains; but the word of God is not chained. 10Therefore I endure all things for the sake of the elect, that they also may obtain the salvation which is in Christ Jesus with eternal glory.

11*This is* a faithful saying:

> For if we died with *Him,*
> We shall also live with *Him.*
> 12 If we endure,
> We shall also reign with
> *Him.*
> If we deny *Him,*
> He also will deny us.
> 13 If we are faithless,
> He remains faithful;
> He cannot deny Himself.

14Remind *them* of these things, charging *them* before the Lord not to strive about words to no profit, to the ruin of the hearers. 15Be diligent to present yourself approved to God, a worker who does not need to be ashamed, rightly dividing the word of truth. 16But shun profane *and* idle babblings, for they will increase to more ungodliness. 17And their message will spread like cancer. Hymenaeus and Philetus are of this sort, 18who have strayed concerning the truth, saying that the resurrection is already past; and they overthrow the faith of some. 19Nevertheless the solid foundation of God stands, having this seal: "The Lord knows those who are His," and, "Let everyone who names the name of Christ* depart from iniquity."

20But in a great house there are not only vessels of gold and silver, but also of wood and clay, some for honor and some for dishonor. 21Therefore if anyone cleanses himself from the latter, he will be a vessel for honor, sanctified and useful for the Master, prepared for every good work.

PSALM 92:1–93:5

A Psalm. A Song for the Sabbath day.

I T *is* good to give thanks to the Lord,
And to sing praises to Your name,
O Most High;
2 To declare Your
lovingkindness in the
morning,
And Your faithfulness every
night,
3 On an instrument of ten
strings,
On the lute,
And on the harp,
With harmonious sound.
4 For You, Lord, have made me
glad through Your work;
I will triumph in the works of
Your hands.

5 O Lord, how great are Your
works!
Your thoughts are very deep.
6 A senseless man does not
know,
Nor does a fool understand
this.
7 When the wicked spring up
like grass,
And when all the workers of
iniquity flourish,
It is that they may be
destroyed forever.

8 But You, Lord, *are* on high
forevermore.
9 For behold, Your enemies,
O Lord,
For behold, Your enemies
shall perish;
All the workers of iniquity
shall be scattered.

10 But my horn You have
exalted like a wild ox;
I have been anointed with
fresh oil.
11 My eye also has seen *my
desire* on my enemies;

My ears hear *my desire* on the wicked
Who rise up against me.

12 The righteous shall flourish
like a palm tree,
He shall grow like a cedar in
Lebanon.
13 Those who are planted in the
house of the Lord
Shall flourish in the courts of
our God.
14 They shall still bear fruit in
old age;
They shall be fresh and
flourishing,
15 To declare that the Lord is
upright;
He is my rock, and *there is* no
unrighteousness in Him.

The Lord reigns, He is clothed with
majesty;
The Lord is clothed,

He has girded Himself with
strength.
Surely the world is
established, so that it
cannot be moved.
2 Your throne *is* established
from of old;
You *are* from everlasting.

3 The floods have lifted up,
O Lord,
The floods have lifted up their
voice;
The floods lift up their waves.
4 The Lord on high *is* mightier
Than the noise of many
waters,
Than the mighty waves of the
sea.

5 Your testimonies are very
sure;
Holiness adorns Your house,
O Lord, forever.

PROVERBS FOR TODAY/ 26:3-5

A whip for the horse, a bridle for the donkey, and a rod for the fool's back. Do not answer a fool according to his folly, lest you also be like him. Answer a fool according to his folly, lest he be wise in his own eyes.

OCTOBER 24

JEREMIAH 44:24–47:7

MOREOVER Jeremiah said to all the people and to all the women, "Hear the word of the Lord, all Judah who *are* in the land of Egypt! 25Thus says the Lord of hosts, the God of Israel, saying: 'You and your wives have spoken with your mouths and fulfilled with your hands, saying, "We will surely keep our vows that we have made, to burn incense to the queen of heaven and pour out

drink offerings to her." You will surely keep your vows and perform your vows!' 26Therefore hear the word of the Lord, all Judah who dwell in the land of Egypt: 'Behold, I have sworn by My great name,' says the Lord, 'that My name shall no more be named in the mouth of any man of Judah in all the land of Egypt, saying, "The Lord God lives." 27Behold, I will watch over them for adversity and not for good. And all the men of Judah who *are* in the land of Egypt shall be consumed by the sword and by famine, until there is an end to them. ²⁸Yet a small number who escape the sword shall return from the land of Egypt to the land of Judah; and all the remnant of Judah, who have gone to the land of Egypt to dwell there, shall know whose words will stand, Mine or theirs. ²⁹And this *shall be* a sign to you,' says the LORD, 'that I will punish you in this place, that you may know that My words will surely stand against you for adversity.'

³⁰"Thus says the LORD: 'Behold, I will give Pharaoh Hophra king of Egypt into the hand of his enemies and into the hand of those who seek his life, as I gave Zedekiah king of Judah into the hand of Nebuchadnezzar king of Babylon, his enemy who sought his life.' "

THE word that Jeremiah the prophet spoke to Baruch the son of Neriah, when he had written these words in a book at the instruction of Jeremiah,* in the fourth year of Jehoiakim the son of Josiah, king of Judah, saying, ²"Thus says the LORD, the God of Israel, to you, O Baruch: ³'You said, "Woe is me now! For the LORD has added grief to my sorrow. I fainted in my sighing, and I find no rest." '

⁴"Thus you shall say to him, 'Thus says the LORD: "Behold, what I have built I will break down, and what I have planted I will pluck up, that is, this whole land. ⁵And do you seek great things for yourself? Do not seek *them;* for behold, I will bring adversity on all flesh," says the LORD. "But I will give your life to you as a prize in all places, wherever you go." ' "

THE word of the LORD which came to Jeremiah the prophet against the nations. ²Against Egypt.

Concerning the army of Pharaoh Necho, king of Egypt, which was by the River Euphrates in Carchemish, and which Nebuchadnezzar king of Babylon defeated in the fourth year of Jehoiakim the son of Josiah, king of Judah:

3   "Order the buckler and shield,
    And draw near to battle!
4   Harness the horses,
    And mount up, you horsemen!
    Stand forth with *your* helmets,
    Polish the spears,
    Put on the armor!
5   Why have I seen them
      dismayed *and* turned back?
    Their mighty ones are beaten
      down;
    They have speedily fled,
    And did not look back,
    For fear *was* all around," says
      the LORD.
6   "Do not let the swift flee away,
    Nor the mighty man escape;
    They will stumble and fall
    Toward the north, by the
      River Euphrates.
7   "Who *is* this coming up like a
      flood,
    Whose waters move like the
      rivers?
8   Egypt rises up like a flood,
    And *its* waters move like the
      rivers;
    And he says, 'I will go up *and*
      cover the earth,
    I will destroy the city and its
      inhabitants.'
9   Come up, O horses, and rage,
      O chariots!
    And let the mighty men come
      forth:
    The Ethiopians and the
      Libyans who handle the
      shield,
    And the Lydians who handle
      and bend the bow.
10 For this *is* the day of the Lord
      GOD of hosts,
    A day of vengeance,
    That He may avenge Himself
      on His adversaries.
    The sword shall devour;

It shall be satiated and made drunk with their blood;
For the Lord God of hosts has a sacrifice
In the north country by the River Euphrates.

11 "Go up to Gilead and take balm, O virgin, the daughter of Egypt;
In vain you will use many medicines;
You shall not be cured.
12 The nations have heard of your shame,
And your cry has filled the land;
For the mighty man has stumbled against the mighty;
They both have fallen together."

13The word that the Lord spoke to Jeremiah the prophet, how Nebuchadnezzar king of Babylon would come *and* strike the land of Egypt.

14 "Declare in Egypt, and proclaim in Migdol;
Proclaim in Noph* and in Tahpanhes;
Say, 'Stand fast and prepare yourselves,
For the sword devours all around you.'
15 Why are your valiant *men* swept away?
They did not stand
Because the Lord drove them away.
16 He made many fall;
Yes, one fell upon another.
And they said, 'Arise!
Let us go back to our own people
And to the land of our nativity
From the oppressing sword.'
17 They cried there,

'Pharaoh, king of Egypt, *is but* a noise.
He has passed by the appointed time!'

18 "*As* I live," says the King,
Whose name *is* the Lord of hosts,
"Surely as Tabor *is* among the mountains
And as Carmel by the sea, *so* he shall come.
19 O you daughter dwelling in Egypt,
Prepare yourself to go into captivity!
For Noph* shall be waste and desolate, without inhabitant.

20 "Egypt *is* a very pretty heifer,
But destruction comes, it comes from the north.
21 Also her mercenaries are in her midst like fat bulls,
For they also are turned back,
They have fled away together.
They did not stand,
For the day of their calamity had come upon them,
The time of their punishment.
22 Her noise shall go like a serpent,
For they shall march with an army
And come against her with axes,
Like those who chop wood.

23 "They shall cut down her forest," says the Lord,
"Though it cannot be searched,
Because they *are* innumerable,
And more numerous than grasshoppers.
24 The daughter of Egypt shall be ashamed;
She shall be delivered into the hand
Of the people of the north."

25The LORD of hosts, the God of Israel, says: "Behold, I will bring punishment on Amon* of No,* and Pharaoh and Egypt, with their gods and their kings—Pharaoh and those who trust in him. 26And I will deliver them into the hand of those who seek their lives, into the hand of Nebuchadnezzar king of Babylon and the hand of his servants. Afterward it shall be inhabited as in the days of old," says the LORD.

27 "But do not fear, O My servant
Jacob,
And do not be dismayed,
O Israel!
For behold, I will save you
from afar,
And your offspring from the
land of their captivity;
Jacob shall return, have rest
and be at ease;
No one shall make *him* afraid.
28 Do not fear, O Jacob My
servant," says the LORD,
"For I *am* with you;
For I will make a complete
end of all the nations
To which I have driven you,
But I will not make a
complete end of you.
I will rightly correct you,
For I will not leave you wholly
unpunished."

THE word of the LORD that came to Jeremiah the prophet against the Philistines, before Pharaoh attacked Gaza. 2Thus says the LORD:

"Behold, waters rise out of the
north,
And shall be an overflowing
flood;
They shall overflow the land
and all that is in it,
The city and those who dwell
within;
Then the men shall cry,

And all the inhabitants of the
land shall wail.
3 At the noise of the stamping
hooves of his strong horses,
At the rushing of his chariots,
At the rumbling of his wheels,
The fathers will not look back
for *their* children,
Lacking courage,
4 Because of the day that
comes to plunder all the
Philistines,
To cut off from Tyre and
Sidon every helper who
remains;
For the LORD shall plunder the
Philistines,
The remnant of the country of
Caphtor.
5 Baldness has come upon
Gaza,
Ashkelon is cut off
With the remnant of their
valley.
How long will you cut
yourself?

6 "O you sword of the LORD,
How long until you are quiet?
Put yourself up into your
scabbard,
Rest and be still!
7 How can it be quiet,
Seeing the LORD has given it a
charge
Against Ashkelon and against
the seashore?
There He has appointed it."

2 TIMOTHY 2:22–3:17

FLEE also youthful lusts; but pursue righteousness, faith, love, peace with those who call on the Lord out of a pure heart. 23But avoid foolish and ignorant disputes, knowing that they generate strife. 24And a servant of the Lord must not quarrel but be gentle to all, able to teach, patient, 25in humility correcting those who are in opposition, if God perhaps will grant them repentance, so that they may know the truth, 26and *that* they may come to their senses *and escape* the snare of the devil, having been taken captive by him to *do* his will.

But know this, that in the last days perilous times will come: 2For men will be lovers of themselves, lovers of money, boasters, proud, blasphemers, disobedient to parents, unthankful, unholy, 3unloving, unforgiving, slanderers, without self-control, brutal, despisers of good, 4traitors, headstrong, haughty, lovers of pleasure rather than lovers of God, 5having a form of godliness but denying its power. And from such people turn away! 6For of this sort are those who creep into households and make captives of gullible women loaded down with sins, led away by various lusts, 7always learning and never able to come to the knowledge of the truth. 8Now as Jannes and Jambres resisted Moses, so do these also resist the truth: men of corrupt minds, disapproved concerning the faith; 9but they will progress no further, for their folly will be manifest to all, as theirs also was.

10But you have carefully followed my doctrine, manner of life, purpose, faith, longsuffering, love, perseverance, 11persecutions, afflictions, which happened to me at Antioch, at Iconium, at Lystra—what persecutions I endured. And out of *them* all the Lord delivered me. 12Yes, and all who desire to live godly in Christ Jesus will suffer persecution. 13But evil men and impostors will grow worse and worse, deceiving and being deceived. 14But you must continue in the things which you have learned and been assured of, knowing from whom you have learned *them,* 15and that from childhood you have known the Holy Scriptures, which are able to make you wise for

salvation through faith which is in Christ Jesus.

16All Scripture *is* given by inspiration of God, and *is* profitable for doctrine, for reproof, for correction, for instruction in righteousness, 17that the man of God may be complete, thoroughly equipped for every good work.

PSALM 94:1-23

O Lord God, to whom vengeance belongs—
O God, to whom vengeance belongs, shine forth!
2 Rise up, O Judge of the earth;
Render punishment to the proud.
3 Lord, how long will the wicked,
How long will the wicked triumph?

4 They utter speech, *and* speak insolent things;
All the workers of iniquity boast in themselves.
5 They break in pieces Your people, O Lord,
And afflict Your heritage.
6 They slay the widow and the stranger,
And murder the fatherless.
7 Yet they say, "The Lord does not see,
Nor does the God of Jacob understand."

8 Understand, you senseless among the people;
And *you* fools, when will you be wise?
9 He who planted the ear, shall He not hear?
He who formed the eye, shall He not see?
10 He who instructs the nations, shall He not correct,
He who teaches man knowledge?

11 The Lᴏʀᴅ knows the thoughts
of man,
That they *are* futile.

12 Blessed *is* the man whom You
instruct, O Lᴏʀᴅ,
And teach out of Your law,
13 That You may give him rest
from the days of adversity,
Until the pit is dug for the
wicked.
14 For the Lᴏʀᴅ will not cast off
His people,
Nor will He forsake His
inheritance.
15 But judgment will return to
righteousness,
And all the upright in heart
will follow it.

16 Who will rise up for me
against the evildoers?
Who will stand up for me
against the workers of
iniquity?
17 Unless the Lᴏʀᴅ *had been* my
help,

My soul would soon have
settled in silence.
18 If I say, "My foot slips,"
Your mercy, O Lᴏʀᴅ, will hold
me up.
19 In the multitude of my
anxieties within me,
Your comforts delight my
soul.

20 Shall the throne of iniquity,
which devises evil by law,
Have fellowship with You?
21 They gather together against
the life of the righteous,
And condemn innocent blood.
22 But the Lᴏʀᴅ has been my
defense,
And my God the rock of my
refuge.
23 He has brought on them their
own iniquity,
And shall cut them off in their
own wickedness;
The Lᴏʀᴅ our God shall cut
them off.

PROVERBS FOR TODAY / 26:6-8

He who sends a message by the hand of a fool cuts off his own *feet* and *drinks violence.* Like *the legs of the lame that hang limp* is *a proverb in the mouth of fools.* *Like one who binds a stone in a sling* is *he who gives honor to a fool.*

OCTOBER 25

JEREMIAH 48:1–49:22

AGAINST Moab.
Thus says the Lᴏʀᴅ of hosts,
the God of Israel:

"Woe to Nebo!
For it is plundered,
Kirjathaim is shamed *and*
taken;

The high stronghold* is
shamed and dismayed—
2 No more praise of Moab.
In Heshbon they have devised
evil against her:
'Come, and let us cut her off
as a nation.'
You also shall be cut down,
O Madmen!*

The sword shall pursue you;

3 A voice of crying *shall be* from
Horonaim:
'Plundering and great
destruction!'

4 "Moab is destroyed;
Her little ones have caused a
cry to be heard;*

5 For in the Ascent of Luhith
they ascend with continual
weeping;
For in the descent of
Horonaim the enemies
have heard a cry of
destruction.

6 "Flee, save your lives!
And be like the juniper* in the
wilderness.

7 For because you have trusted
in your works and your
treasures,
You also shall be taken.
And Chemosh shall go forth
into captivity,
His priests and his princes
together.

8 And the plunderer shall come
against every city;
No one shall escape.
The valley also shall perish,
And the plain shall be
destroyed,
As the Lord has spoken.

9 "Give wings to Moab,
That she may flee and get
away;
For her cities shall be
desolate,
Without any to dwell in them.

10 Cursed *is* he who does the
work of the Lord deceitfully,
And cursed *is* he who keeps
back his sword from blood.

11 "Moab has been at ease from
his* youth;
He has settled on his dregs,

And has not been emptied
from vessel to vessel,
Nor has he gone into captivity.
Therefore his taste remained
in him,
And his scent has not
changed.

12 "Therefore behold, the days
are coming," says the Lord,
"That I shall send him
wine-workers
Who will tip him over
And empty his vessels
And break the bottles.

13 Moab shall be ashamed of
Chemosh,
As the house of Israel was
ashamed of Bethel, their
confidence.

14 "How can you say, 'We *are*
mighty
And strong men for the war'?

15 Moab is plundered and gone
up *from* her cities;
Her chosen young men have
gone down to the
slaughter," says the King,
Whose name *is* the Lord of
hosts.

16 "The calamity of Moab *is* near
at hand,
And his affliction comes
quickly.

17 Bemoan him, all you who are
around him;
And all you who know his
name,
Say, 'How the strong staff is
broken,
The beautiful rod!'

18 "O daughter inhabiting Dibon,
Come down from *your* glory,
And sit in thirst;
For the plunderer of Moab
has come against you,

He has destroyed your
   strongholds.

19 O inhabitant of Aroer,
   Stand by the way and watch;
   Ask him who flees
   And her who escapes;
   Say, 'What has happened?'

20 Moab is shamed, for he is
   broken down.
   Wail and cry!
   Tell it in Arnon, that Moab is
   plundered.

21 "And judgment has come on
   the plain country:
   On Holon and Jahzah and
   Mephaath,

22 On Dibon and Nebo and Beth
   Diblathaim,

23 On Kirjathaim and Beth
   Gamul and Beth Meon,

24 On Kerioth and Bozrah,
   On all the cities of the land of
   Moab,
   Far or near.

25 The horn of Moab is cut off,
   And his arm is broken," says
   the LORD.

26 "Make him drunk,
   Because he exalted *himself*
   against the LORD.
   Moab shall wallow in his
   vomit,
   And he shall also be in
   derision.

27 For was not Israel a derision
   to you?
   Was he found among thieves?
   For whenever you speak of
   him,
   You shake *your head in scorn.*

28 You who dwell in Moab,
   Leave the cities and dwell in
   the rock,
   And be like the dove *which*
   makes her nest
   In the sides of the cave's
   mouth.

29 "We have heard the pride of
   Moab
   (He *is* exceedingly proud),
   Of his loftiness and arrogance
   and pride,
   And of the haughtiness of his
   heart."

30 "I know his wrath," says the
   LORD,
   "But it *is* not right;
   His lies have made nothing
   right.

31 Therefore I will wail for Moab,
   And I will cry out for all Moab;
   I* will mourn for the men of
   Kir Heres.

32 O vine of Sibmah! I will weep
   for you with the weeping of
   Jazer.
   Your plants have gone over
   the sea,
   They reach to the sea of Jazer.
   The plunderer has fallen on
   your summer fruit and your
   vintage.

33 Joy and gladness are taken
   From the plentiful field
   And from the land of Moab;
   I have caused wine to fail
   from the winepresses;
   No one will tread with joyous
   shouting—
   Not joyous shouting!

34 "From the cry of Heshbon to
   Elealeh and to Jahaz
   They have uttered their voice,
   From Zoar to Horonaim,
   Like a three-year-old heifer;*
   For the waters of Nimrim also
   shall be desolate.

35 "Moreover," says the LORD,
   "I will cause to cease in Moab
   The one who offers *sacrifices*
   in the high places
   And burns incense to his
   gods.

36 Therefore My heart shall wail
    like flutes for Moab,
And like flutes My heart shall
    wail
For the men of Kir Heres.
Therefore the riches they
    have acquired have
    perished.

37 "For every head *shall be* bald,
    and every beard clipped;
On all the hands *shall be* cuts,
    and on the loins sackcloth—
38 A general lamentation
On all the housetops of Moab,
And in its streets;
For I have broken Moab like
    a vessel in which *is* no
    pleasure," says the LORD.
39 "They shall wail:
'How she is broken down!
How Moab has turned her
    back with shame!'
So Moab shall be a derision
And a dismay to all those
    about her."

40 For thus says the LORD:

"Behold, one shall fly like an
    eagle,
And spread his wings over
    Moab.
41 Kerioth is taken,
And the strongholds are
    surprised;
The mighty men's hearts in
    Moab on that day shall be
Like the heart of a woman in
    birth pangs.
42 And Moab shall be destroyed
    as a people,
Because he exalted *himself*
    against the LORD.
43 Fear and the pit and the snare
    shall be upon you,
O inhabitant of Moab," says
    the LORD.
44 "He who flees from the fear
    shall fall into the pit,

And he who gets out of the pit
    shall be caught in the snare.
For upon Moab, upon it I will
    bring
The year of their punish-
    ment," says the LORD.

45 "Those who fled stood under
    the shadow of Heshbon
Because of exhaustion.
But a fire shall come out of
    Heshbon,
A flame from the midst of
    Sihon,
And shall devour the brow of
    Moab,
The crown of the head of the
    sons of tumult.
46 Woe to you, O Moab!
The people of Chemosh
    perish;
For your sons have been
    taken captive,
And your daughters captive.

47 "Yet I will bring back the
    captives of Moab
In the latter days," says the
    LORD.

Thus far *is* the judgment of Moab.

AGAINST the Ammonites.
    Thus says the LORD:

"Has Israel no sons?
Has he no heir?
Why *then* does Milcom*
    inherit Gad,
And his people dwell in its
    cities?
2 Therefore behold, the days
    are coming," says the LORD,
"That I will cause to be heard
    an alarm of war
In Rabbah of the Ammonites;
It shall be a desolate mound,
And her villages shall be
    burned with fire.
Then Israel shall take

possession of his inheritance," says the LORD.

3 "Wail, O Heshbon, for Ai is plundered!
Cry, you daughters of Rabbah,
Gird yourselves with sackcloth!
Lament and run to and fro by the walls;
For Milcom shall go into captivity
With his priests and his princes together.

4 Why do you boast in the valleys,
Your flowing valley,
   O backsliding daughter?
Who trusted in her treasures,
   saying,
'Who will come against me?'

5 Behold, I will bring fear upon you,"
Says the Lord GOD of hosts,
"From all those who are around you;
You shall be driven out, everyone headlong,
And no one will gather those who wander off.

6 But afterward I will bring back
The captives of the people of Ammon," says the LORD.

7Against Edom.
Thus says the LORD of hosts:

"*Is* wisdom no more in Teman?
Has counsel perished from the prudent?
Has their wisdom vanished?

8 Flee, turn back, dwell in the depths, O inhabitants of Dedan!
For I will bring the calamity of Esau upon him,
The time *that* I will punish him.

9 If grape gatherers came to you,
Would they not leave *some* gleaning grapes?
If thieves by night,
Would they not destroy until they have enough?

10 But I have made Esau bare;
I have uncovered his secret places,*
And he shall not be able to hide himself.
His descendants are plundered,
His brethren and his neighbors,
And he *is* no more.

11 Leave your fatherless children,
I will preserve *them* alive;
And let your widows trust in Me."

12For thus says the LORD: "Behold, those whose judgment *was* not to drink of the cup have assuredly drunk. And *are* you the one who will altogether go unpunished? You shall not go unpunished, but you shall surely drink *of it.* 13For I have sworn by Myself," says the LORD, "that Bozrah shall become a desolation, a reproach, a waste, and a curse. And all its cities shall be perpetual wastes."

14 I have heard a message from the LORD,
And an ambassador has been sent to the nations:
"Gather together, come against her,
And rise up to battle!

15 "For indeed, I will make you small among nations,
Despised among men.

16 Your fierceness has deceived you,
The pride of your heart,
O you who dwell in the clefts of the rock,

Who hold the height of the
hill!
Though you make your nest
as high as the eagle,
I will bring you down from
there," says the Lord.*

17 "Edom also shall be an
astonishment;
Everyone who goes by it will
be astonished
And will hiss at all its plagues.

18 As in the overthrow of Sodom
and Gomorrah
And their neighbors," says
the Lord,
"No one shall remain there,
Nor shall a son of man dwell
in it.

19 "Behold, he shall come up like
a lion from the floodplain*
of the Jordan
Against the dwelling place of
the strong;
But I will suddenly make him
run away from her.
And who is a chosen man that
I may appoint over her?
For who is like Me?
Who will arraign Me?
And who is that shepherd
Who will withstand Me?"

20 Therefore hear the counsel of
the Lord that He has taken
against Edom,
And His purposes that He has
proposed against the
inhabitants of Teman:
Surely the least of the flock
shall draw them out;
Surely He shall make their
dwelling places desolate
with them.

21 The earth shakes at the noise
of their fall;
At the cry its noise is heard at
the Red Sea.

22 Behold, He shall come up and
fly like the eagle,
And spread His wings over
Bozrah;
The heart of the mighty men
of Edom in that day shall be
Like the heart of a woman in
birth pangs.

2 TIMOTHY 4:1-22

I CHARGE *you* therefore before God
and the Lord Jesus Christ, who will
judge the living and the dead at*
His appearing and His kingdom:
2Preach the word! Be ready in season
and out of season. Convince, rebuke,
exhort, with all longsuffering and
teaching. 3For the time will come
when they will not endure sound doctrine, but according to their own desires, *because* they have itching ears,
they will heap up for themselves teachers; 4and they will turn *their* ears away
from the truth, and be turned aside to
fables. 5But you be watchful in all
things, endure afflictions, do the work
of an evangelist, fulfill your ministry.

6For I am already being poured out
as a drink offering, and the time of my
departure is at hand. 7I have fought the
good fight, I have finished the race, I
have kept the faith. 8Finally, there is
laid up for me the crown of righteousness, which the Lord, the righteous
Judge, will give to me on that Day, and
not to me only but also to all who have
loved His appearing.

9Be diligent to come to me quickly;
10for Demas has forsaken me, having
loved this present world, and has departed for Thessalonica—Crescens
for Galatia, Titus for Dalmatia. 11Only
Luke is with me. Get Mark and bring
him with you, for he is useful to me for
ministry. 12And Tychicus I have sent to
Ephesus. 13Bring the cloak that I left
with Carpus at Troas when you
come—and the books, especially the
parchments.

14Alexander the coppersmith did me much harm. May the Lord repay him according to his works. 15You also must beware of him, for he has greatly resisted our words.

16At my first defense no one stood with me, but all forsook me. May it not be charged against them.

17But the Lord stood with me and strengthened me, so that the message might be preached fully through me, and *that* all the Gentiles might hear. Also I was delivered out of the mouth of the lion. 18And the Lord will deliver me from every evil work and preserve *me* for His heavenly kingdom. To Him *be* glory forever and ever. Amen!

19Greet Prisca and Aquila, and the household of Onesiphorus. 20Erastus stayed in Corinth, but Trophimus I have left in Miletus sick.

21Do your utmost to come before winter.

Eubulus greets you, as well as Pudens, Linus, Claudia, and all the brethren.

22The Lord Jesus Christ* be with your spirit. Grace be with you. Amen.

PSALM 95:1–96:13

OH come, let us sing to the LORD!
Let us shout joyfully to the
Rock of our salvation.
2 Let us come before His
presence with thanksgiving;
Let us shout joyfully to Him
with psalms.
3 For the LORD *is* the great God,
And the great King above all
gods.
4 In His hand *are* the deep
places of the earth;
The heights of the hills *are*
His also.
5 The sea *is* His, for He made it;
And His hands formed the
dry *land*.

6 Oh come, let us worship and
bow down;
Let us kneel before the LORD
our Maker.
7 For He *is* our God,
And we *are* the people of His
pasture,
And the sheep of His hand.

Today, if you will hear His
voice:
8 "Do not harden your hearts, as
in the rebellion,*
As *in* the day of trial* in the
wilderness,
9 When your fathers tested Me;
They tried Me, though they
saw My work.
10 For forty years I was grieved
with *that* generation,
And said, 'It *is* a people who
go astray in their hearts,
And they do not know My
ways.'
11 So I swore in My wrath,
'They shall not enter My rest.' "

OH, sing to the LORD a new song!
Sing to the LORD, all the earth.
2 Sing to the LORD, bless His
name;
Proclaim the good news of
His salvation from day to
day.
3 Declare His glory among the
nations,
His wonders among all
peoples.

4 For the LORD *is* great and
greatly to be praised;
He *is* to be feared above all
gods.
5 For all the gods of the peoples
are idols,
But the LORD made the
heavens.
6 Honor and majesty *are* before
Him;

Strength and beauty *are* in
His sanctuary.

7 Give to the Lord, O families of
the peoples,
Give to the Lord glory and
strength.
8 Give to the Lord the glory *due*
His name;
Bring an offering, and come
into His courts.
9 Oh, worship the Lord in the
beauty of holiness!
Tremble before Him, all the
earth.

10 Say among the nations, "The
Lord reigns;
The world also is firmly
established,

It shall not be moved;
He shall judge the peoples
righteously."

11 Let the heavens rejoice, and
let the earth be glad;
Let the sea roar, and all its
fullness;
12 Let the field be joyful, and all
that *is* in it.
Then all the trees of the
woods will rejoice before
the Lord.
13 For He is coming, for He is
coming to judge the earth.
He shall judge the world with
righteousness,
And the peoples with His
truth.

PROVERBS FOR TODAY / 26:9-12

Like *a thorn* that *goes into the hand of a drunkard* is *a proverb in the mouth of fools. The great* God *who formed everything gives the fool* his *hire and the transgressor* his *wages.* * As *a dog returns to his own vomit,* so *a fool repeats his folly. Do you see a man wise in his own eyes?* There is *more hope for a fool than for him.*

OCTOBER 26

JEREMIAH 49:23–50:46

A GAINST Damascus.

"Hamath and Arpad are
shamed,
For they have heard bad news.
They are fainthearted;
There is trouble on the sea;
It cannot be quiet.
24 Damascus has grown feeble;
She turns to flee,
And fear has seized *her.*
Anguish and sorrows have
taken her like a woman in
labor.

25 Why is the city of praise not
deserted, the city of My joy?
26 Therefore her young men
shall fall in her streets,
And all the men of war shall
be cut off in that day," says
the Lord of hosts.
27 "I will kindle a fire in the wall
of Damascus,
And it shall consume the
palaces of Ben-Hadad."*

28Against Kedar and against the
kingdoms of Hazor, which Nebuchadnezzar king of Babylon shall
strike.

Thus says the LORD:

"Arise, go up to Kedar,
And devastate the men of the
East!
29 Their tents and their flocks
they shall take away.
They shall take for
themselves their curtains,
All their vessels and their
camels;
And they shall cry out to
them,
'Fear *is* on every side!'

30 "Flee, get far away! Dwell in
the depths,
O inhabitants of Hazor!" says
the LORD
"For Nebuchadnezzar king of
Babylon has taken counsel
against you,
And has conceived a plan
against you.

31 "Arise, go up to the wealthy
nation that dwells
securely," says the LORD,
"Which has neither gates nor
bars,
Dwelling alone.
32 Their camels shall be for
booty,
And the multitude of their
cattle for plunder.
I will scatter to all winds those
in the farthest corners,
And I will bring their calamity
from all its sides," says the
LORD.
33 "Hazor shall be a dwelling for
jackals, a desolation forever;
No one shall reside there,
Nor son of man dwell in it."

34The word of the LORD that came to
Jeremiah the prophet against Elam, in
the beginning of the reign of Zedekiah
king of Judah, saying, 35"Thus says the
LORD of hosts:

'Behold, I will break the bow
of Elam,
The foremost of their might.
36 Against Elam I will bring the
four winds
From the four quarters of
heaven,
And scatter them toward all
those winds;
There shall be no nations
where the outcasts of Elam
will not go.
37 For I will cause Elam to be
dismayed before their
enemies
And before those who seek
their life.
I will bring disaster upon
them,
My fierce anger,' says the
LORD;
'And I will send the sword
after them
Until I have consumed them.
38 I will set My throne in Elam,
And will destroy from there
the king and the princes,'
says the LORD.

39 'But it shall come to pass in
the latter days:
I will bring back the captives
of Elam,' says the LORD."

THE word that the LORD spoke against
Babylon *and* against the land of the
Chaldeans by Jeremiah the prophet.

2 "Declare among the nations,
Proclaim, and set up a
standard;
Proclaim—do not conceal *it*—
Say, 'Babylon is taken, Bel is
shamed.
Merodach* is broken in
pieces;
Her idols are humiliated,
Her images are broken in
pieces.'

3 For out of the north a nation
comes up against her,
Which shall make her land
desolate,
And no one shall dwell
therein.
They shall move, they shall
depart,
Both man and beast.

4 "In those days and in that
time," says the LORD,
"The children of Israel shall
come,
They and the children of
Judah together;
With continual weeping they
shall come,
And seek the LORD their God.
5 They shall ask the way to Zion,
With their faces toward it,
saying,
'Come and let us join
ourselves to the LORD
In a perpetual covenant
That will not be forgotten.'

6 "My people have been lost
sheep.
Their shepherds have led
them astray;
They have turned them away
on the mountains.
They have gone from
mountain to hill;
They have forgotten their
resting place.
7 All who found them have
devoured them;
And their adversaries said,
'We have not offended,
Because they have sinned
against the LORD, the
habitation of justice,
The LORD, the hope of their
fathers.'

8 "Move from the midst of
Babylon,

Go out of the land of the
Chaldeans;
And be like the rams before
the flocks.
9 For behold, I will raise and
cause to come up against
Babylon
An assembly of great nations
from the north country,
And they shall array
themselves against her;
From there she shall be
captured.
Their arrows *shall be* like
those of an expert warrior;*
None shall return in vain.
10 And Chaldea shall become
plunder;
All who plunder her shall be
satisfied," says the LORD.

11 "Because you were glad,
because you rejoiced,
You destroyers of My
heritage,
Because you have grown fat
like a heifer threshing grain,
And you bellow like bulls,
12 Your mother shall be deeply
ashamed;
She who bore you shall be
ashamed.
Behold, the least of the
nations *shall be* a
wilderness,
A dry land and a desert.
13 Because of the wrath of the
LORD
She shall not be inhabited,
But she shall be wholly
desolate.
Everyone who goes by
Babylon shall be horrified
And hiss at all her plagues.

14 "Put yourselves in array
against Babylon all around,
All you who bend the bow;
Shoot at her, spare no arrows,

For she has sinned against
the LORD.

15 Shout against her all around;
She has given her hand,
Her foundations have fallen,
Her walls are thrown down;
For it *is* the vengeance of the
LORD.
Take vengeance on her.
As she has done, so do to her.

16 Cut off the sower from
Babylon,
And him who handles the
sickle at harvest time.
For fear of the oppressing
sword
Everyone shall turn to his
own people,
And everyone shall flee to his
own land.

17 "Israel *is* like scattered sheep;
The lions have driven *him*
away.
First the king of Assyria
devoured him;
Now at last this
Nebuchadnezzar king of
Babylon has broken his
bones."

18 Therefore thus says the LORD of
hosts, the God of Israel:

"Behold, I will punish the king
of Babylon and his land,
As I have punished the king
of Assyria.

19 But I will bring back Israel to
his home,
And he shall feed on Carmel
and Bashan;
His soul shall be satisfied on
Mount Ephraim and Gilead.

20 In those days and in that
time," says the LORD,
"The iniquity of Israel shall be
sought, but *there shall be*
none;

And the sins of Judah, but
they shall not be found;
For I will pardon those whom
I preserve.

21 "Go up against the land of
Merathaim, against it,
And against the inhabitants of
Pekod.
Waste and utterly destroy
them," says the LORD,
"And do according to all that I
have commanded you.

22 A sound of battle *is* in the land,
And of great destruction.

23 How the hammer of the
whole earth has been cut
apart and broken!
How Babylon has become a
desolation among the
nations!
I have laid a snare for you;

24 You have indeed been
trapped, O Babylon,
And you were not aware;
You have been found and also
caught,
Because you have contended
against the LORD.

25 The LORD has opened His
armory,
And has brought out the
weapons of His indignation;
For this *is* the work of the
Lord GOD of hosts
In the land of the Chaldeans.

26 Come against her from the
farthest border;
Open her storehouses;
Cast her up as heaps of ruins,
And destroy her utterly;
Let nothing of her be left.

27 Slay all her bulls,
Let them go down to the
slaughter.
Woe to them!
For their day has come, the
time of their punishment.

28 The voice of those who flee

and escape from the land of
Babylon
Declares in Zion the
vengeance of the LORD our
God,
The vengeance of His temple.

29 "Call together the archers
against Babylon.
All you who bend the bow,
encamp against it all
around;
Let none of them escape.*
Repay her according to her
work;
According to all she has done,
do to her;
For she has been proud
against the LORD,
Against the Holy One of Israel.

30 Therefore her young men
shall fall in the streets,
And all her men of war shall
be cut off in that day," says
the LORD.

31 "Behold, I *am* against you,
O most haughty one!" says
the Lord GOD of hosts;
"For your day has come,
The time *that* I will punish
you.*

32 The most proud shall stumble
and fall,
And no one will raise him up;
I will kindle a fire in his cities,
And it will devour all around
him."

33 Thus says the LORD of hosts:

"The children of Israel *were*
oppressed,
Along with the children of
Judah;
All who took them captive
have held them fast;
They have refused to let them
go.

34 Their Redeemer *is* strong;
The LORD of hosts *is* His name.
He will thoroughly plead their
case,
That He may give rest to the
land,
And disquiet the inhabitants
of Babylon.

35 "A sword *is* against the
Chaldeans," says the LORD,
"Against the inhabitants of
Babylon,
And against her princes and
her wise men.

36 A sword *is* against the
soothsayers, and they will
be fools.
A sword *is* against her mighty
men, and they will be
dismayed.

37 A sword *is* against their
horses,
Against their chariots,
And against all the mixed
peoples who *are* in her
midst;
And they will become like
women.
A sword *is* against her
treasures, and they will be
robbed.

38 A drought* *is* against her
waters, and they will be
dried up.
For it *is* the land of carved
images,
And they are insane with *their*
idols.

39 "Therefore the wild desert
beasts shall dwell *there* with
the jackals,
And the ostriches shall dwell
in it.
It shall be inhabited no more
forever,
Nor shall it be dwelt in from
generation to generation.

40 As God overthrew Sodom and
Gomorrah

And their neighbors," says
the LORD,
"*So* no one shall reside there,
Nor son of man dwell in it.

41 "Behold, a people shall come
from the north,
And a great nation and many
kings
Shall be raised up from the
ends of the earth.
42 They shall hold the bow and
the lance;
They *are* cruel and shall not
show mercy.
Their voice shall roar like the
sea;
They shall ride on horses,
Set in array, like a man for the
battle,
Against you, O daughter of
Babylon.

43 "The king of Babylon has
heard the report about
them,
And his hands grow feeble;
Anguish has taken hold of
him,
Pangs as of a woman in
childbirth.

44 "Behold, he shall come up like
a lion from the floodplain*
of the Jordan
Against the dwelling place of
the strong;
But I will make them
suddenly run away from
her.
And who *is* a chosen *man that*
I may appoint over her?
For who *is* like Me?
Who will arraign Me?
And who *is* that shepherd
Who will withstand Me?"

45 Therefore hear the counsel of
the LORD that He has taken
against Babylon,

And His purposes that He has
proposed against the land
of the Chaldeans:
Surely the least of the flock
shall draw them out;
Surely He will make their
dwelling place desolate
with them.
46 At the noise of the taking of
Babylon
The earth trembles,
And the cry is heard among
the nations.

TITUS 1:1-16

PAUL, a bondservant of God and
an apostle of Jesus Christ, according to the faith of God's
elect and the acknowledgment of the
truth which accords with godliness,
2in hope of eternal life which God, who
cannot lie, promised before time began, 3but has in due time manifested
His word through preaching, which
was committed to me according to the
commandment of God our Savior;

4To Titus, a true son in *our* common
faith:

Grace, mercy, *and* peace from God
the Father and the Lord Jesus Christ*
our Savior.

5For this reason I left you in Crete,
that you should set in order the things
that are lacking, and appoint elders in
every city as I commanded you— 6if a
man is blameless, the husband of one
wife, having faithful children not accused of dissipation or insubordina-
tion. 7For a bishop* must be blameless, as a steward of God, not self-
willed, not quick-tempered, not given
to wine, not violent, not greedy for
money, 8but hospitable, a lover of what
is good, sober-minded, just, holy, self-
controlled, 9holding fast the faithful
word as he has been taught, that he

may be able, by sound doctrine, both to exhort and convict those who contradict.

¹⁰For there are many insubordinate, both idle talkers and deceivers, especially those of the circumcision, ¹¹whose mouths must be stopped, who subvert whole households, teaching things which they ought not, for the sake of dishonest gain. ¹²One of them, a prophet of their own, said, "Cretans *are* always liars, evil beasts, lazy gluttons." ¹³This testimony is true. Therefore rebuke them sharply, that they may be sound in the faith, ¹⁴not giving heed to Jewish fables and commandments of men who turn from the truth. ¹⁵To the pure all things are pure, but to those who are defiled and unbelieving nothing is pure; but even their mind and conscience are defiled. ¹⁶They profess to know God, but in works they deny Him, being abominable, disobedient, and disqualified for every good work.

PSALM 97:1–98:9

THE LORD reigns;
Let the earth rejoice;
Let the multitude of isles be
glad!

2   Clouds and darkness
surround Him;
Righteousness and justice *are*
the foundation of His
throne.
3   A fire goes before Him,
And burns up His enemies
round about.
4   His lightnings light the world;
The earth sees and trembles.
5   The mountains melt like wax
at the presence of the LORD,
At the presence of the Lord of
the whole earth.
6   The heavens declare His
righteousness,
And all the peoples see His
glory.

7   Let all be put to shame who
serve carved images,
Who boast of idols.
Worship Him, all *you* gods.
8   Zion hears and is glad,
And the daughters of Judah
rejoice
Because of Your judgments,
O LORD.
9   For You, LORD, *are* most high
above all the earth;
You are exalted far above all
gods.

10   You who love the LORD, hate
evil!
He preserves the souls of His
saints;
He delivers them out of the
hand of the wicked.
11   Light is sown for the
righteous,
And gladness for the upright
in heart.
12   Rejoice in the LORD, you
righteous,
And give thanks at the
remembrance of His holy
name.*

A Psalm.

OH, sing to the LORD a new song!
For He has done marvelous
things;
His right hand and His holy
arm have gained Him the
victory.
2   The LORD has made known
His salvation;
His righteousness He has
revealed in the sight of the
nations.
3   He has remembered His
mercy and His faithfulness
to the house of Israel;
All the ends of the earth have
seen the salvation of our
God.

4   Shout joyfully to the LORD, all
    the earth;
    Break forth in song, rejoice,
    and sing praises.
5   Sing to the LORD with the harp,
    With the harp and the sound
    of a psalm,
6   With trumpets and the sound
    of a horn;
    Shout joyfully before the
    LORD, the King.

7   Let the sea roar, and all its
    fullness,
    The world and those who
    dwell in it;
8   Let the rivers clap *their* hands;
    Let the hills be joyful together
    before the LORD,
9   For He is coming to judge the
    earth.
    With righteousness He shall
    judge the world,
    And the peoples with equity.

PROVERBS FOR TODAY/ 26:13-16

The lazy man says, "There is a lion in the road! A fierce lion is in the streets!" As a door turns on its hinges, so does the lazy man on his bed. The lazy man buries his hand in the bowl; * it wearies him to bring it back to his mouth. The lazy* man is *wiser in his own eyes than seven men who can answer sensibly.*

OCTOBER 27

JEREMIAH 51:1-53

THUS says the LORD:

    "Behold, I will raise up against
    Babylon,
    Against those who dwell in
    Leb Kamai,*
    A destroying wind.
2   And I will send winnowers to
    Babylon,
    Who shall winnow her and
    empty her land.
    For in the day of doom
    They shall be against her all
    around.
3   Against *her* let the archer
    bend his bow,
    And lift himself up against *her*
    in his armor.
    Do not spare her young men;
    Utterly destroy all her army.
4   Thus the slain shall fall in the
    land of the Chaldeans,

    And *those* thrust through in
    her streets.
5   For Israel is not forsaken, nor
    Judah,
    By his God, the LORD of hosts,
    Though their land was filled
    with sin against the Holy
    One of Israel."

6   Flee from the midst of
    Babylon,
    And every one save his life!
    Do not be cut off in her
    iniquity,
    For this *is* the time of the
    LORD's vengeance;
    He shall recompense her.
7   Babylon *was* a golden cup in
    the LORD's hand,
    That made all the earth drunk.
    The nations drank her wine;
    Therefore the nations are
    deranged.

8   Babylon has suddenly fallen
        and been destroyed.
    Wail for her!
    Take balm for her pain;
    Perhaps she may be healed.

9   We would have healed
        Babylon,
    But she is not healed.
    Forsake her, and let us go
        everyone to his own
        country;
    For her judgment reaches to
        heaven and is lifted up to
        the skies.

10 The Lord has revealed our
        righteousness.
    Come and let us declare in
        Zion the work of the Lord
        our God.

11 Make the arrows bright!
    Gather the shields!
    The Lord has raised up the
        spirit of the kings of the
        Medes.
    For His plan *is* against
        Babylon to destroy it,
    Because it *is* the vengeance of
        the Lord,
    The vengeance for His temple.

12 Set up the standard on the
        walls of Babylon;
    Make the guard strong,
    Set up the watchmen,
    Prepare the ambushes.
    For the Lord has both devised
        and done
    What He spoke against the
        inhabitants of Babylon.

13 O you who dwell by many
        waters,
    Abundant in treasures,
    Your end has come,
    The measure of your
        covetousness.

14 The Lord of hosts has sworn
        by Himself:
    "Surely I will fill you with men,
        as with locusts,

    And they shall lift up a shout
        against you."

15 He has made the earth by His
        power;
    He has established the world
        by His wisdom,
    And stretched out the heaven
        by His understanding.

16 When He utters *His* voice—
    There is a multitude of waters
        in the heavens:
    "He causes the vapors to
        ascend from the ends of the
        earth;
    He makes lightnings for the
        rain;
    He brings the wind out of His
        treasuries."*

17 Everyone is dull-hearted,
        without knowledge;
    Every metalsmith is put to
        shame by the carved image;
    For his molded image *is*
        falsehood,
    And *there is* no breath in them.

18 They *are* futile, a work of
        errors;
    In the time of their
        punishment they shall
        perish.

19 The Portion of Jacob *is* not
        like them,
    For He *is* the Maker of all
        things;
    And *Israel is* the tribe of His
        inheritance.
    The Lord of hosts *is* His name.

20 "You *are* My battle-ax *and*
        weapons of war:
    For with you I will break the
        nation in pieces;
    With you I will destroy
        kingdoms;

21 With you I will break in
        pieces the horse and its
        rider;
    With you I will break in

pieces the chariot and its
rider;

22 With you also I will break in
pieces man and woman;
With you I will break in
pieces old and young;
With you I will break in
pieces the young man and
the maiden;

23 With you also I will break in
pieces the shepherd and
his flock;
With you I will break in
pieces the farmer and his
yoke of oxen;
And with you I will break in
pieces governors and
rulers.

24 "And I will repay Babylon
And all the inhabitants of
Chaldea
For all the evil they have done
In Zion in your sight," says
the LORD.

25 "Behold, I *am* against you,
O destroying mountain,
Who destroys all the earth,"
says the LORD.
"And I will stretch out My
hand against you,
Roll you down from the rocks,
And make you a burnt
mountain.

26 They shall not take from you
a stone for a corner
Nor a stone for a foundation,
But you shall be desolate
forever," says the LORD.

27 Set up a banner in the land,
Blow the trumpet among the
nations!
Prepare the nations against
her,
Call the kingdoms together
against her:
Ararat, Minni, and Ashkenaz.
Appoint a general against her;

Cause the horses to come up
like the bristling locusts.

28 Prepare against her the
nations,
With the kings of the Medes,
Its governors and all its rulers,
All the land of his dominion.

29 And the land will tremble and
sorrow;
For every purpose of the LORD
shall be performed against
Babylon,
To make the land of Babylon
a desolation without
inhabitant.

30 The mighty men of Babylon
have ceased fighting,
They have remained in their
strongholds;
Their might has failed,
They became *like* women;
They have burned her
dwelling places,
The bars of her *gate* are
broken.

31 One runner will run to meet
another,
And one messenger to meet
another,
To show the king of Babylon
that his city is taken on *all*
sides;

32 The passages are blocked,
The reeds they have burned
with fire,
And the men of war are
terrified.

33For thus says the LORD of hosts,
the God of Israel:

"The daughter of Babylon *is*
like a threshing floor
When it is time to thresh her;
Yet a little while
And the time of her harvest
will come."

34 "Nebuchadnezzar the king of
Babylon

Has devoured me, he has
crushed me;
He has made me an empty
vessel,
He has swallowed me up like
a monster;
He has filled his stomach with
my delicacies,
He has spit me out.
35   Let the violence *done* to me
and my flesh *be* upon
Babylon,"
The inhabitant of Zion will say;
"And my blood be upon the
inhabitants of Chaldea!"
Jerusalem will say.

36Therefore thus says the LORD:

"Behold, I will plead your case
and take vengeance for you.
I will dry up her sea and make
her springs dry.
37   Babylon shall become a heap,
A dwelling place for jackals,
An astonishment and a
hissing,
Without an inhabitant.
38   They shall roar together like
lions,
They shall growl like lions'
whelps.
39   In their excitement I will
prepare their feasts;
I will make them drunk,
That they may rejoice,
And sleep a perpetual sleep
And not awake," says the LORD.
40   "I will bring them down
Like lambs to the slaughter,
Like rams with male goats.

41   "Oh, how Sheshach* is taken!
Oh, how the praise of the
whole earth is seized!
How Babylon has become
desolate among the nations!
42   The sea has come up over
Babylon;

She is covered with the
multitude of its waves.
43   Her cities are a desolation,
A dry land and a wilderness,
A land where no one dwells,
Through which no son of man
passes.
44   I will punish Bel in Babylon,
And I will bring out of his
mouth what he has
swallowed;
And the nations shall not
stream to him anymore.
Yes, the wall of Babylon shall
fall.

45   "My people, go out of the
midst of her!
And let everyone deliver
himself from the fierce
anger of the LORD.
46   And lest your heart faint,
And you fear for the rumor
that *will be* heard in the land
(A rumor will come *one* year,
And after that, in *another* year
A rumor *will come,*
And violence in the land,
Ruler against ruler),
47   Therefore behold, the days
are coming
That I will bring judgment on
the carved images of
Babylon;
Her whole land shall be
ashamed,
And all her slain shall fall in
her midst.
48   Then the heavens and the
earth and all that *is* in them
Shall sing joyously over
Babylon;
For the plunderers shall come
to her from the north," says
the LORD.

49   As Babylon *has caused* the
slain of Israel to fall,
So at Babylon the slain of all
the earth shall fall.

50 You who have escaped the
      sword,
    Get away! Do not stand still!
    Remember the LORD afar off,
    And let Jerusalem come to
      your mind.

51 We are ashamed because we
      have heard reproach.
    Shame has covered our faces,
    For strangers have come into
      the sanctuaries of the
      LORD'S house.

52 "Therefore behold, the days
      are coming," says the LORD,
    "That I will bring judgment on
      her carved images,
    And throughout all her land
      the wounded shall groan.
53 Though Babylon were to
      mount up to heaven,
    And though she were to
      fortify the height of her
      strength,
    Yet from Me plunderers
      would come to her," says
      the LORD.

TITUS 2:1-15

BUT as for you, speak the things which are proper for sound doctrine: ²that the older men be sober, reverent, temperate, sound in faith, in love, in patience; ³the older women likewise, that they be reverent in behavior, not slanderers, not given to much wine, teachers of good things— ⁴that they admonish the young women to love their husbands, to love their children, ⁵to be discreet, chaste, homemakers, good, obedient to their own husbands, that the word of God may not be blasphemed.

⁶Likewise, exhort the young men to be sober-minded, ⁷in all things showing yourself *to be* a pattern of good works; in doctrine *showing* integrity, reverence, incorruptibility,* ⁸sound speech that cannot be condemned, that one who is an opponent may be ashamed, having nothing evil to say of you.*

⁹*Exhort* bondservants to be obedient to their own masters, to be well pleasing in all *things,* not answering back, ¹⁰not pilfering, but showing all good fidelity, that they may adorn the doctrine of God our Savior in all things.

¹¹For the grace of God that brings salvation has appeared to all men, ¹²teaching us that, denying ungodliness and worldly lusts, we should live soberly, righteously, and godly in the present age, ¹³looking for the blessed hope and glorious appearing of our great God and Savior Jesus Christ, ¹⁴who gave Himself for us, that He might redeem us from every lawless deed and purify for Himself *His* own special people, zealous for good works.

¹⁵Speak these things, exhort, and rebuke with all authority. Let no one despise you.

PSALM 99:1-9

THE LORD reigns;
    Let the peoples tremble!
    He dwells *between* the
      cherubim;
    Let the earth be moved!
2   The LORD *is* great in Zion,
    And He *is* high above all the
      peoples.
3   Let them praise Your great
      and awesome name—
    He *is* holy.

4   The King's strength also loves
      justice;
    You have established equity;
    You have executed justice and
      righteousness in Jacob.
5   Exalt the LORD our God,
    And worship at His footstool—
    He *is* holy.

6 Moses and Aaron were
   among His priests,
   And Samuel was among those
   who called upon His name;
   They called upon the Lord,
   and He answered them.
7 He spoke to them in the
   cloudy pillar;
   They kept His testimonies
   and the ordinance He gave
   them.

8 You answered them, O Lord
   our God;
   You were to them
   God-Who-Forgives,
   Though You took vengeance
   on their deeds.
9 Exalt the Lord our God,
   And worship at His holy hill;
   For the Lord our God *is* holy.

PROVERBS FOR TODAY / 26:17

He who passes by and *meddles in a quarrel not his own* is like *one who takes a dog by the ears.*

OCTOBER 28

JEREMIAH 51:54–52:34

THE sound of a cry *comes* from
Babylon,
And great destruction from the
land of the Chaldeans,
55 Because the Lord is
   plundering Babylon
   And silencing her loud voice,
   Though her waves roar like
   great waters,
   And the noise of their voice is
   uttered,
56 Because the plunderer comes
   against her, against
   Babylon,
   And her mighty men are
   taken.
   Every one of their bows is
   broken;
   For the Lord *is* the God of
   recompense,
   He will surely repay.

57 "And I will make drunk
   Her princes and wise men,

Her governors, her deputies,
   and her mighty men.
And they shall sleep a
   perpetual sleep
And not awake," says the
   King,
Whose name *is* the Lord of
   hosts.

58Thus says the Lord of hosts:

"The broad walls of Babylon
   shall be utterly broken,
And her high gates shall be
   burned with fire;
The people will labor in vain,
And the nations, because of
   the fire;
And they shall be weary."

59The word which Jeremiah the
prophet commanded Seraiah the son
of Neriah, the son of Mahseiah, when
he went with Zedekiah the king of
Judah to Babylon in the fourth year of
his reign. And Seraiah *was* the quarter-

master. 60So Jeremiah wrote in a book all the evil that would come upon Babylon, all these words that are written against Babylon. 61And Jeremiah said to Seraiah, "When you arrive in Babylon and see it, and read all these words, 62then you shall say, 'O LORD, You have spoken against this place to cut it off, so that none shall remain in it, neither man nor beast, but it shall be desolate forever.' 63Now it shall be, when you have finished reading this book, *that* you shall tie a stone to it and throw it out into the Euphrates. 64Then you shall say, 'Thus Babylon shall sink and not rise from the catastrophe that I will bring upon her. And they shall be weary.' "

Thus far *are* the words of Jeremiah.

ZEDEKIAH *was* twenty-one years old when he became king, and he reigned eleven years in Jerusalem. His mother's name *was* Hamutal the daughter of Jeremiah of Libnah. 2He also did evil in the sight of the LORD, according to all that Jehoiakim had done. 3For because of the anger of the LORD *this* happened in Jerusalem and Judah, till He finally cast them out from His presence. Then Zedekiah rebelled against the king of Babylon.

4Now it came to pass in the ninth year of his reign, in the tenth month, on the tenth *day* of the month, *that* Nebuchadnezzar king of Babylon and all his army came against Jerusalem and encamped against it; and *they* built a siege wall against it all around. 5So the city was besieged until the eleventh year of King Zedekiah. 6By the fourth month, on the ninth day of the month, the famine had become so severe in the city that there was no food for the people of the land. 7Then the city wall was broken through, and all the men of war fled and went out of the city at night by way of the gate between the two walls, which *was* by the king's garden, even though the

Chaldeans *were* near the city all around. And they went by way of the plain.*

8But the army of the Chaldeans pursued the king, and they overtook Zedekiah in the plains of Jericho. All his army was scattered from him. 9So they took the king and brought him up to the king of Babylon at Riblah in the land of Hamath, and he pronounced judgment on him. 10Then the king of Babylon killed the sons of Zedekiah before his eyes. And he killed all the princes of Judah in Riblah. 11He also put out the eyes of Zedekiah; and the king of Babylon bound him in bronze fetters, took him to Babylon, and put him in prison till the day of his death.

12Now in the fifth month, on the tenth *day* of the month (which *was* the nineteenth year of King Nebuchadnezzar king of Babylon), Nebuzaradan, the captain of the guard, *who* served the king of Babylon, came to Jerusalem. 13He burned the house of the LORD and the king's house; all the houses of Jerusalem, that is, all the houses of the great, he burned with fire. 14And all the army of the Chaldeans who *were* with the captain of the guard broke down all the walls of Jerusalem all around. 15Then Nebuzaradan the captain of the guard carried away captive *some* of the poor people, the rest of the people who remained in the city, the defectors who had deserted to the king of Babylon, and the rest of the craftsmen. 16But Nebuzaradan the captain of the guard left *some* of the poor of the land as vinedressers and farmers.

17The bronze pillars that *were* in the house of the LORD, and the carts and the bronze Sea that *were* in the house of the LORD, the Chaldeans broke in pieces, and carried all their bronze to Babylon. 18They also took away the pots, the shovels, the trimmers, the bowls, the spoons, and all the bronze utensils with which the priests ministered. ¹⁹The basins, the firepans, the bowls, the pots, the lampstands, the spoons, and the cups, whatever *was* solid gold and whatever *was* solid silver, the captain of the guard took away. ²⁰The two pillars, one Sea, the twelve bronze bulls which *were* under *it, and* the carts, which King Solomon had made for the house of the LORD— the bronze of all these articles was beyond measure. ²¹Now *concerning* the pillars: the height of one pillar *was* eighteen cubits, a measuring line of twelve cubits could measure its circumference, and its thickness *was* four fingers; *it was* hollow. ²²A capital of bronze *was* on it; and the height of one capital *was* five cubits, with a network and pomegranates all around the capital, all of bronze. The second pillar, with pomegranates was the same. ²³There were ninety-six pomegranates on the sides; all the pomegranates, all around on the network, *were* one hundred.

²⁴The captain of the guard took Seraiah the chief priest, Zephaniah the second priest, and the three doorkeepers. ²⁵He also took out of the city an officer who had charge of the men of war, seven men of the king's close associates who were found in the city, the principal scribe of the army who mustered the people of the land, and sixty men of the people of the land who were found in the midst of the city. ²⁶And Nebuzaradan the captain of the guard took these and brought them to the king of Babylon at Riblah. ²⁷Then the king of Babylon struck them and put them to death at Riblah in the land of Hamath. Thus Judah was carried away captive from its own land.

²⁸These *are* the people whom Nebuchadnezzar carried away captive: in the seventh year, three thousand and twenty-three Jews; ²⁹in the eighteenth year of Nebuchadnezzar he carried away captive from Jerusalem eight hundred and thirty-two persons; ³⁰in the twenty-third year of Nebuchadnezzar, Nebuzaradan the captain of the guard carried away captive of the Jews seven hundred and forty-five persons. All the persons *were* four thousand six hundred.

³¹Now it came to pass in the thirty-seventh year of the captivity of Jehoiachin king of Judah, in the twelfth month, on the twenty-fifth *day* of the month, *that* Evil-Merodach* king of Babylon, in the first *year* of his reign, lifted up the head of Jehoiachin king of Judah and brought him out of prison. ³²And he spoke kindly to him and gave him a more prominent seat than those of the kings who *were* with him in Babylon. ³³So Jehoiachin changed from his prison garments, and he ate bread regularly before the king all the days of his life. ³⁴And as for his provisions, there was a regular ration given him by the king of Babylon, a portion for each day until the day of his death, all the days of his life.

TITUS 3:1-15

REMIND them to be subject to rulers and authorities, to obey, to be ready for every good work, ²to speak evil of no one, to be peaceable, gentle, showing all humility to all men. ³For we ourselves were also once foolish, disobedient, deceived, serving various lusts and pleasures, living in malice and envy, hateful and hating one another. ⁴But when the kindness and the love of God our Savior toward man appeared, ⁵not by works of righteousness which we have done, but according to His mercy He saved us, through the washing of regeneration and renewing of the Holy Spirit, ⁶whom He poured out on us abundantly through Jesus Christ our Savior, ⁷that having been justified by His grace we should become heirs according to the hope of eternal life.

⁸This is a faithful saying, and these things I want you to affirm constantly, that those who have believed in God should be careful to maintain good works. These things are good and profitable to men.

⁹But avoid foolish disputes, genealogies, contentions, and strivings about the law; for they are unprofitable and useless. ¹⁰Reject a divisive man after the first and second admonition, ¹¹knowing that such a person is warped and sinning, being self-condemned.

¹²When I send Artemas to you, or Tychicus, be diligent to come to me at Nicopolis, for I have decided to spend the winter there. ¹³Send Zenas the lawyer and Apollos on their journey with haste, that they may lack nothing. ¹⁴And let our *people* also learn to maintain good works, to *meet* urgent needs, that they may not be unfruitful.

¹⁵All who *are* with me greet you. Greet those who love us in the faith. Grace *be* with you all. Amen.

PSALM 100:1-5
A Psalm of Thanksgiving.

MAKE a joyful shout to the LORD, all you lands!
²Serve the LORD with gladness;
Come before His presence with singing.
3 Know that the LORD, He *is* God;
It is He *who* has made us, and not we ourselves;*
We are His people and the sheep of His pasture.

4 Enter into His gates with thanksgiving,
And into His courts with praise.
Be thankful to Him, *and* bless His name.
5 For the LORD *is* good;
His mercy *is* everlasting,
And His truth *endures* to all generations.

PROVERBS FOR TODAY/ 26:18-19

Like a madman who throws firebrands, arrows, and death, is the man who deceives his neighbor, and says, "I was only joking!"

OCTOBER 29

LAMENTATIONS 1:1–2:19

How lonely sits the city
That was full of people!
How like a widow is she,
Who *was* great among the nations!
The princess among the provinces
Has become a slave!

2 She weeps bitterly in the night,
Her tears *are* on her cheeks;
Among all her lovers
She has none to comfort *her.*
All her friends have dealt treacherously with her;
They have become her enemies.

3 Judah has gone into captivity,
Under affliction and hard
servitude;
She dwells among the nations,
She finds no rest;
All her persecutors overtake
her in dire straits.

4 The roads to Zion mourn
Because no one comes to the
set feasts.
All her gates are desolate;
Her priests sigh,
Her virgins are afflicted,
And she *is* in bitterness.

5 Her adversaries have become
the master,
Her enemies prosper;
For the LORD has afflicted her
Because of the multitude of
her transgressions.
Her children have gone into
captivity before the enemy.

6 And from the daughter of Zion
All her splendor has departed.
Her princes have become like
deer
That find no pasture,
That flee without strength
Before the pursuer.

7 In the days of her affliction
and roaming,
Jerusalem remembers all her
pleasant things
That she had in the days of
old.
When her people fell into the
hand of the enemy,
With no one to help her,
The adversaries saw her
And mocked at her downfall.*

8 Jerusalem has sinned gravely,
Therefore she has become
vile.*
All who honored her despise
her

Because they have seen her
nakedness;
Yes, she sighs and turns away.

9 Her uncleanness *is* in her
skirts;
She did not consider her
destiny;
Therefore her collapse was
awesome;
She had no comforter.
"O LORD, behold my affliction,
For *the* enemy is exalted!"

10 The adversary has spread his
hand
Over all her pleasant things;
For she has seen the nations
enter her sanctuary,
Those whom You commanded
Not to enter Your assembly.

11 All her people sigh,
They seek bread;
They have given their
valuables for food to
restore life.
"See, O LORD, and consider,
For I am scorned."

12 "*Is it* nothing to you, all you
who pass by?
Behold and see
If there is any sorrow like my
sorrow,
Which has been brought on
me,
Which the LORD has inflicted
In the day of His fierce anger.

13 "From above He has sent fire
into my bones,
And it overpowered them;
He has spread a net for my
feet
And turned me back;
He has made me desolate
And faint all the day.

14 "The yoke of my
    transgressions was bound;*
They were woven together by
    His hands,
And thrust upon my neck.
He made my strength fail;
The Lord delivered me into
    the hands of *those whom* I
    am not able to withstand.

15 "The Lord has trampled
    underfoot all my mighty
    men in my midst;
He has called an assembly
    against me
To crush my young men;
The Lord trampled *as* in a
    winepress
The virgin daughter of Judah.

16 "For these *things* I weep;
My eye, my eye overflows
    with water;
Because the comforter, who
    should restore my life,
Is far from me.
My children are desolate
Because the enemy
    prevailed."

17 Zion spreads out her hands,
But no one comforts her;
The LORD has commanded
    concerning Jacob
That those around him
    become his adversaries;
Jerusalem has become an
    unclean thing among them.

18 "The LORD is righteous,
For I rebelled against His
    commandment.
Hear now, all peoples,
And behold my sorrow;
My virgins and my young men
Have gone into captivity.

19 "I called for my lovers,
But they deceived me;
My priests and my elders

Breathed their last in the city,
While they sought food
To restore their life.

20 "See, O LORD, that I *am* in
    distress;
My soul is troubled;
My heart is overturned within
    me,
For I have been very
    rebellious.
Outside the sword bereaves,
At home *it is* like death.

21 "They have heard that I sigh,
But no one comforts me.
All my enemies have heard of
    my trouble;
They are glad that You have
    done *it.*
Bring on the day You have
    announced,
That they may become like
    me.

22 "Let all their wickedness come
    before You,
And do to them as You have
    done to me
For all my transgressions;
For my sighs *are* many,
And my heart *is* faint."

How the Lord has covered the
    daughter of Zion
With a cloud in His anger!
He cast down from heaven to
    the earth
The beauty of Israel,
And did not remember His
    footstool
In the day of His anger.

2 The Lord has swallowed up
    and has not pitied
All the dwelling places of
    Jacob.
He has thrown down in His
    wrath

The strongholds of the
daughter of Judah;
He has brought *them* down to
the ground;
He has profaned the kingdom
and its princes.

3 He has cut off in fierce anger
Every horn of Israel;
He has drawn back His right
hand
From before the enemy.
He has blazed against Jacob
like a flaming fire
Devouring all around.

4 Standing like an enemy, He
has bent His bow;
With His right hand, like an
adversary,
He has slain all *who were*
pleasing to His eye;
On the tent of the daughter of
Zion,
He has poured out His fury
like fire.

5 The Lord was like an enemy.
He has swallowed up Israel,
He has swallowed up all her
palaces;
He has destroyed her
strongholds,
And has increased mourning
and lamentation
In the daughter of Judah.

6 He has done violence to His
tabernacle,
As if it were a garden;
He has destroyed His place of
assembly;
The LORD has caused
The appointed feasts and
Sabbaths to be forgotten in
Zion.
In His burning indignation He
has spurned the king and
the priest.

7 The Lord has spurned His
altar,
He has abandoned His
sanctuary;
He has given up the walls of
her palaces
Into the hand of the enemy.
They have made a noise in
the house of the LORD
As on the day of a set feast.

8 The LORD has purposed to
destroy
The wall of the daughter of
Zion.
He has stretched out a line;
He has not withdrawn His
hand from destroying;
Therefore He has caused the
rampart and wall to lament;
They languished together.

9 Her gates have sunk into the
ground;
He has destroyed and broken
her bars.
Her king and her princes *are*
among the nations;
The Law *is* no *more,*
And her prophets find no
vision from the LORD.

10 The elders of the daughter of
Zion
Sit on the ground *and* keep
silence;
They throw dust on their
heads
And gird themselves with
sackcloth.
The virgins of Jerusalem
Bow their heads to the
ground.

11 My eyes fail with tears,
My heart is troubled;
My bile is poured on the
ground
Because of the destruction of
the daughter of my people,

Because the children and the infants
Faint in the streets of the city.

12 They say to their mothers,
"Where *is* grain and wine?"
As they swoon like the wounded
In the streets of the city,
As their life is poured out
In their mothers' bosom.

13 How shall I console you?
To what shall I liken you,
O daughter of Jerusalem?
What shall I compare with you, that I may comfort you,
O virgin daughter of Zion?
For your ruin *is* spread wide as the sea;
Who can heal you?

14 Your prophets have seen for you
False and deceptive visions;
They have not uncovered your iniquity,
To bring back your captives,
But have envisioned for you false prophecies and delusions.

15 All who pass by clap *their* hands at you;
They hiss and shake their heads
At the daughter of Jerusalem:
"*Is* this the city that is called
'The perfection of beauty,
The joy of the whole earth'?"

16 All your enemies have opened their mouth against you;
They hiss and gnash *their* teeth.
They say, "We have swallowed *her* up!
Surely this *is* the day we have waited for;

We have found *it,* we have seen *it!*"

17 The LORD has done what He purposed;
He has fulfilled His word
Which He commanded in days of old.
He has thrown down and has not pitied,
And He has caused an enemy to rejoice over you;
He has exalted the horn of your adversaries.

18 Their heart cried out to the Lord,
"O wall of the daughter of Zion,
Let tears run down like a river day and night;
Give yourself no relief;
Give your eyes no rest.

19 "Arise, cry out in the night,
At the beginning of the watches;
Pour out your heart like water before the face of the Lord.
Lift your hands toward Him
For the life of your young children,
Who faint from hunger at the head of every street."

PHILEMON 1-25

P AUL, a prisoner of Christ Jesus, and Timothy *our* brother,

To Philemon our beloved *friend* and fellow laborer, [2]to the beloved* Apphia, Archippus our fellow soldier, and to the church in your house:

[3]Grace to you and peace from God our Father and the Lord Jesus Christ.

[4]I thank my God, making mention of you always in my prayers, [5]hearing of your love and faith which you have to-

ward the Lord Jesus and toward all the saints, 6that the sharing of your faith may become effective by the acknowledgment of every good thing which is in you* in Christ Jesus. 7For we have* great joy* and consolation in your love, because the hearts of the saints have been refreshed by you, brother.

8Therefore, though I might be very bold in Christ to command you what is fitting, 9yet for love's sake I rather appeal to you—being such a one as Paul, the aged, and now also a prisoner of Jesus Christ— 10I appeal to you for my son Onesimus, whom I have begotten while in my chains, 11who once was unprofitable to you, but now is profitable to you and to me.

12I am sending him back.* You therefore receive him, that is, my own heart, 13whom I wished to keep with me, that on your behalf he might minister to me in my chains for the gospel. 14But without your consent I wanted to do nothing, that your good deed might not be by compulsion, as it were, but voluntary.

15For perhaps he departed for a while for this purpose, that you might receive him forever, 16no longer as a slave but more than a slave—a beloved brother, especially to me but how much more to you, both in the flesh and in the Lord.

17If then you count me as a partner, receive him as you would me. 18But if he has wronged you or owes anything, put that on my account. 19I, Paul, am writing with my own hand. I will repay—not to mention to you that you owe me even your own self besides. 20Yes, brother, let me have joy from you in the Lord; refresh my heart in the Lord.

21Having confidence in your obedience, I write to you, knowing that you will do even more than I say. 22But, meanwhile, also prepare a guest room for me, for I trust that through your prayers I shall be granted to you.

23Epaphras, my fellow prisoner in Christ Jesus, greets you, 24as do Mark, Aristarchus, Demas, Luke, my fellow laborers.

25The grace of our Lord Jesus Christ be with your spirit. Amen.

PSALM 101:1-8

A Psalm of David.

I WILL sing of mercy and justice;
To You, O LORD, I will sing praises.

2   I will behave wisely in a
       perfect way.
    Oh, when will You come to
       me?
    I will walk within my house
       with a perfect heart.

3   I will set nothing wicked
       before my eyes;
    I hate the work of those who
       fall away;
    It shall not cling to me.

4   A perverse heart shall depart
       from me;
    I will not know wickedness.

5   Whoever secretly slanders his
       neighbor,
    Him I will destroy;
    The one who has a haughty
       look and a proud heart,
    Him I will not endure.

6   My eyes *shall be* on the
       faithful of the land,
    That they may dwell with me;
    He who walks in a perfect way,
    He shall serve me.

7   He who works deceit shall not
       dwell within my house;
    He who tells lies shall not
       continue in my presence.

8   Early I will destroy all the
       wicked of the land,
    That I may cut off all the
       evildoers from the city of
       the LORD.

PROVERBS FOR TODAY/ 26:20

Where there is *no wood, the fire goes out; and where* there is *no talebearer, strife ceases.*

OCTOBER 30

LAMENTATIONS 2:20–3:66

SEE, O LORD, and consider!
To whom have You done this?
Should the women eat their
offspring,
The children they have
cuddled?*
Should the priest and prophet
be slain
In the sanctuary of the Lord?

21 "Young and old lie
On the ground in the streets;
My virgins and my young men
Have fallen by the sword;
You have slain *them* in the day
of Your anger,
You have slaughtered *and* not
pitied.

22 "You have invited as to a feast
day
The terrors that surround me.
In the day of the LORD's anger
There was no refugee or
survivor.
Those whom I have borne
and brought up
My enemies have destroyed."

I *AM* the man *who* has seen affliction by
the rod of His wrath.
2   He has led me and made *me*
walk
In darkness and not *in* light.
3   Surely He has turned His
hand against me
Time and time again
throughout the day.

4   He has aged my flesh and my
skin,
And broken my bones.
5   He has besieged me
And surrounded *me* with
bitterness and woe.
6   He has set me in dark places
Like the dead of long ago.

7   He has hedged me in so that I
cannot get out;
He has made my chain heavy.
8   Even when I cry and shout,
He shuts out my prayer.
9   He has blocked my ways with
hewn stone;
He has made my paths
crooked.

10   He *has been* to me a bear lying
in wait,
Like a lion in ambush.
11   He has turned aside my ways
and torn me in pieces;
He has made me desolate.
12   He has bent His bow
And set me up as a target for
the arrow.

13   He has caused the arrows of
His quiver
To pierce my loins.*
14   I have become the ridicule of
all my people—
Their taunting song all the
day.
15   He has filled me with
bitterness,

He has made me drink wormwood.

16 He has also broken my teeth with gravel,
And covered me with ashes.

17 You have moved my soul far from peace;
I have forgotten prosperity.

18 And I said, "My strength and my hope
Have perished from the LORD."

19 Remember my affliction and roaming,
The wormwood and the gall.

20 My soul still remembers
And sinks within me.

21 This I recall to my mind,
Therefore I have hope.

22 *Through* the LORD's mercies we are not consumed,
Because His compassions fail not.

23 *They are* new every morning;
Great *is* Your faithfulness.

24 "The LORD *is* my portion," says my soul,
"Therefore I hope in Him!"

25 The LORD *is* good to those who wait for Him,
To the soul *who* seeks Him.

26 *It is* good that *one* should hope and wait quietly
For the salvation of the LORD.

27 *It is* good for a man to bear
The yoke in his youth.

28 Let him sit alone and keep silent,
Because *God* has laid *it* on him;

29 Let him put his mouth in the dust—
There may yet be hope.

30 Let him give *his* cheek to the one who strikes him,
And be full of reproach.

31 For the Lord will not cast off forever.

32 Though He causes grief,
Yet He will show compassion
According to the multitude of His mercies.

33 For He does not afflict willingly,
Nor grieve the children of men.

34 To crush under one's feet
All the prisoners of the earth,

35 To turn aside the justice *due* a man
Before the face of the Most High,

36 Or subvert a man in his cause—
The Lord does not approve.

37 Who *is* he *who* speaks and it comes to pass,
When the Lord has not commanded *it?*

38 *Is it* not from the mouth of the Most High
That woe and well-being proceed?

39 Why should a living man complain,
A man for the punishment of his sins?

40 Let us search out and examine our ways,
And turn back to the LORD;

41 Let us lift our hearts and hands
To God in heaven.

42 We have transgressed and rebelled;
You have not pardoned.

43 You have covered *Yourself* with anger
And pursued us;
You have slain *and* not pitied.

44 You have covered Yourself with a cloud,

45 That prayer should not pass
through.
You have made us an
offscouring and refuse
In the midst of the peoples.

46 All our enemies
Have opened their mouths
against us.
47 Fear and a snare have come
upon us,
Desolation and destruction.
48 My eyes overflow with rivers
of water
For the destruction of the
daughter of my people.

49 My eyes flow and do not
cease,
Without interruption,
50 Till the LORD from heaven
Looks down and sees.
51 My eyes bring suffering to
my soul
Because of all the daughters
of my city.

52 My enemies without cause
Hunted me down like a bird.
53 They silenced* my life in the
pit
And threw stones at me.
54 The waters flowed over my
head; I said, "I am cut off!"

55 I called on Your name, O LORD,
From the lowest pit.
56 You have heard my voice:
"Do not hide Your ear
From my sighing, from my
cry for help."
57 You drew near on the day I
called on You,
And said, "Do not fear!"

58 O Lord, You have pleaded the
case for my soul;
You have redeemed my life.
59 O LORD, You have seen how I
am wronged;

Judge my case.
60 You have seen all their
vengeance,
All their schemes against me.

61 You have heard their
reproach, O LORD,
All their schemes against me,
62 The lips of my enemies
And their whispering against
me all the day.
63 Look at their sitting down and
their rising up;
I am their taunting song.

64 Repay them, O LORD,
According to the work of their
hands.
65 Give them a veiled* heart;
Your curse be upon them!
66 In Your anger,
Pursue and destroy them
From under the heavens of
the LORD.

HEBREWS 1:1-14

GOD, who at various times and in various ways spoke in time past to the fathers by the prophets, ²has in these last days spoken to us by *His* Son, whom He has appointed heir of all things, through whom also He made the worlds; ³who being the brightness of *His* glory and the express image of His person, and upholding all things by the word of His power, when He had by Himself* purged our* sins, sat down at the right hand of the Majesty on high, ⁴having become so much better than the angels, as He has by inheritance obtained a more excellent name than they.

⁵For to which of the angels did He ever say:

"You are My Son,
Today I have begotten You"?*

And again:

> "I will be to Him a Father,
> And He shall be to Me a
> Son"?*

⁶But when He again brings the first-born into the world, He says:

> "Let all the angels of God
> worship Him." *

⁷And of the angels He says:

> "Who makes His angels spirits
> And His ministers a flame of
> fire." *

⁸But to the Son He says:

> "Your throne, O God, is forever
> and ever;
> A scepter of righteousness is
> the scepter of Your
> kingdom.
> 9   You have loved righteousness
> and hated lawlessness;
> Therefore God, Your God, has
> anointed You
> With the oil of gladness more
> than Your companions." *

¹⁰And:

> "You, LORD, in the beginning
> laid the foundation of the
> earth,
> And the heavens are the work
> of Your hands.
> 11   They will perish, but You
> remain;
> And they will all grow old like
> a garment;
> 12   Like a cloak You will fold
> them up,
> And they will be changed.
> But You are the same,
> And Your years will not fail." *

¹³But to which of the angels has He ever said:

> "Sit at My right hand,
> Till I make Your enemies
> Your footstool"?*

¹⁴Are they not all ministering spirits sent forth to minister for those who will inherit salvation?

PSALM 102:1-28

A Prayer of the afflicted, when he is overwhelmed and pours out his complaint before the LORD.

HEAR my prayer, O LORD,
And let my cry come to You.
²Do not hide Your face from
me in the day of my trouble;
Incline Your ear to me;
In the day that I call, answer
me speedily.

3   For my days are consumed
like smoke,
And my bones are burned
like a hearth.
4   My heart is stricken and
withered like grass,
So that I forget to eat my
bread.
5   Because of the sound of my
groaning
My bones cling to my skin.
6   I am like a pelican of the
wilderness;
I am like an owl of the desert.
7   I lie awake,
And am like a sparrow alone
on the housetop.

8   My enemies reproach me all
day long;
Those who deride me swear
an oath against me.
9   For I have eaten ashes like
bread,
And mingled my drink with
weeping,
10   Because of Your indignation
and Your wrath;
For You have lifted me up and
cast me away.
11   My days are like a shadow
that lengthens,
And I wither away like grass.

12 But You, O LORD, shall endure forever,
And the remembrance of Your name to all generations.
13 You will arise *and* have mercy on Zion;
For the time to favor her,
Yes, the set time, has come.
14 For Your servants take pleasure in her stones,
And show favor to her dust.
15 So the nations shall fear the name of the LORD,
And all the kings of the earth Your glory.
16 For the LORD shall build up Zion;
He shall appear in His glory.
17 He shall regard the prayer of the destitute,
And shall not despise their prayer.

18 This will be written for the generation to come,
That a people yet to be created may praise the LORD.
19 For He looked down from the height of His sanctuary;
From heaven the LORD viewed the earth,
20 To hear the groaning of the prisoner,
To release those appointed to death,
21 To declare the name of the LORD in Zion,
And His praise in Jerusalem,
22 When the peoples are gathered together,
And the kingdoms, to serve the LORD.

23 He weakened my strength in the way;
He shortened my days.
24 I said, "O my God,
Do not take me away in the midst of my days;
Your years *are* throughout all generations.
25 Of old You laid the foundation of the earth,
And the heavens *are* the work of Your hands.
26 They will perish, but You will endure;
Yes, they will all grow old like a garment;
Like a cloak You will change them,
And they will be changed.
27 But You *are* the same,
And Your years will have no end.
28 The children of Your servants will continue,
And their descendants will be established before You."

PROVERBS FOR TODAY/ 26:21-22

As *charcoal* is *to burning coals, and wood to fire, so* is *a contentious man to kindle strife.* □ *The words of a talebearer* are *like tasty trifles, and they go down into the inmost body.*

OCTOBER 31

LAMENTATIONS 4:1–5:22

How the gold has become dim!
How changed the fine gold!
The stones of the sanctuary
  are scattered
At the head of every street.

2   The precious sons of Zion,
    Valuable as fine gold,
    How they are regarded as
      clay pots,
    The work of the hands of the
      potter!

3   Even the jackals present their
      breasts
    To nurse their young;
    But the daughter of my
      people *is* cruel,
    Like ostriches in the
      wilderness.

4   The tongue of the infant clings
    To the roof of its mouth for
      thirst;
    The young children ask for
      bread,
    But no one breaks *it* for them.

5   Those who ate delicacies
    Are desolate in the streets;
    Those who were brought up
      in scarlet
    Embrace ash heaps.

6   The punishment of the
      iniquity of the daughter of
      my people
    Is greater than the
      punishment of the sin of
      Sodom,
    Which was overthrown in a
      moment,
    With no hand to help her!

7   Her Nazirites* were brighter
      than snow
    And whiter than milk;
    They were more ruddy in
      body than rubies,
    Like sapphire in their
      appearance.

8   *Now* their appearance is
      blacker than soot;
    They go unrecognized in the
      streets;
    Their skin clings to their
      bones,
    It has become as dry as wood.

9   *Those* slain by the sword are
      better off
    Than *those* who die of hunger;
    For these pine away,
    Stricken *for lack* of the fruits
      of the field.

10 The hands of the
      compassionate women
    Have cooked their own
      children;
    They became food for them
    In the destruction of the
      daughter of my people.

11 The LORD has fulfilled His fury,
    He has poured out His fierce
      anger.
    He kindled a fire in Zion,
    And it has devoured its
      foundations.

12 The kings of the earth,
    And all inhabitants of the
      world,
    Would not have believed
    That the adversary and the
      enemy

Could enter the gates of
Jerusalem—

13 Because of the sins of her
prophets
And the iniquities of her
priests,
Who shed in her midst
The blood of the just.

14 They wandered blind in the
streets;
They have defiled themselves
with blood,
So that no one would touch
their garments.

15 They cried out to them,
"Go away, unclean!
Go away, go away,
Do not touch us!"
When they fled and wandered,
Those among the nations said,
"They shall no longer dwell
here."

16 The face* of the LORD
scattered them;
He no longer regards them.
The people do not respect the
priests
Nor show favor to the elders.

17 Still our eyes failed us,
Watching vainly for our help;
In our watching we watched
For a nation *that* could not
save *us.*

18 They tracked our steps
So that we could not walk in
our streets.
Our end was near;
Our days were over,
For our end had come.

19 Our pursuers were swifter
Than the eagles of the
heavens.

They pursued us on the
mountains
And lay in wait for us in the
wilderness.

20 The breath of our nostrils, the
anointed of the LORD,
Was caught in their pits,
Of whom we said, "Under his
shadow
We shall live among the
nations."

21 Rejoice and be glad,
O daughter of Edom,
You who dwell in the land of
Uz!
The cup shall also pass over
to you
And you shall become drunk
and make yourself naked.

22 *The punishment of* your
iniquity is accomplished,
O daughter of Zion;
He will no longer send you
into captivity.
He will punish your iniquity,
O daughter of Edom;
He will uncover your sins!

REMEMBER, O LORD, what has come
upon us;
Look, and behold our
reproach!

2 Our inheritance has been
turned over to aliens,
And our houses to foreigners.

3 We have become orphans and
waifs,
Our mothers *are* like widows.

4 We pay for the water we drink,
And our wood comes at a
price.

5 *They* pursue at our heels;*
We labor *and* have no rest.

6 We have given our hand *to* the
Egyptians

And the Assyrians, to be
satisfied with bread.

7 Our fathers sinned *and are* no
more,
But we bear their iniquities.
8 Servants rule over us;
There is none to deliver *us*
from their hand.
9 We get our bread *at the risk* of
our lives,
Because of the sword in the
wilderness.

10 Our skin is hot as an oven,
Because of the fever of famine.
11 They ravished the women in
Zion,
The maidens in the cities of
Judah.
12 Princes were hung up by their
hands,
And elders were not
respected.
13 Young men ground at the
millstones;
Boys staggered under *loads of*
wood.
14 The elders have ceased
gathering at the gate,
And the young men from
their music.

15 The joy of our heart has
ceased;
Our dance has turned into
mourning.
16 The crown has fallen *from* our
head.
Woe to us, for we have sinned!
17 Because of this our heart is
faint;
Because of these *things* our
eyes grow dim;
18 Because of Mount Zion which
is desolate,
With foxes walking about on
it.

19 You, O Lord, remain forever;
Your throne from generation
to generation.
20 Why do You forget us forever,
And forsake us for so long a
time?
21 Turn us back to You, O Lord,
and we will be restored;
Renew our days as of old,
22 Unless You have utterly
rejected us,
And are very angry with us!

HEBREWS 2:1-18

THEREFORE we must give the more earnest heed to the things we have heard, lest we drift away. [2]For if the word spoken through angels proved steadfast, and every transgression and disobedience received a just reward, [3]how shall we escape if we neglect so great a salvation, which at the first began to be spoken by the Lord, and was confirmed to us by those who heard *Him,* [4]God also bearing witness both with signs and wonders, with various miracles, and gifts of the Holy Spirit, according to His own will?

[5]For He has not put the world to come, of which we speak, in subjection to angels. [6]But one testified in a certain place, saying:

"*What is man that You are
mindful of him,
Or the son of man that You
take care of him?*
7 *You have made him a little
lower than the angels;
You have crowned him with
glory and honor,* *
*And set him over the works of
Your hands.*
8 *You have put all things in
subjection under his feet.*" *

For in that He put all in subjection under him, He left nothing *that is* not put under him. But now we do not yet see all things put under him. [9]But we see Jesus, who was made a little lower than the angels, for the suffering of death crowned with glory and honor, that He, by the grace of God, might taste death for everyone.

10For it was fitting for Him, for whom *are* all things and by whom *are* all things, in bringing many sons to glory, to make the captain of their salvation perfect through sufferings. 11For both He who sanctifies and those who are being sanctified *are* all of one, for which reason He is not ashamed to call them brethren, 12saying:

> "I will declare Your name to
> My brethren;
> In the midst of the assembly I
> will sing praise to You." *

13And again:

> "I will put My trust in Him." *

And again:

> "Here am I and the children
> whom God has given Me." *

14Inasmuch then as the children have partaken of flesh and blood, He Himself likewise shared in the same, that through death He might destroy him who had the power of death, that is, the devil, 15and release those who through fear of death were all their lifetime subject to bondage. 16For indeed He does not give aid to angels, but He does give aid to the seed of Abraham. 17Therefore, in all things He had to be made like *His* brethren, that He might be a merciful and faithful High Priest in things *pertaining* to God, to make propitiation for the sins of the people. 18For in that He Himself has suffered, being tempted, He is able to aid those who are tempted.

PSALM 103:1-22

A Psalm *of David.*

BLESS the LORD, O my soul;
And all that is within me, *bless* His holy name!
2   Bless the LORD, O my soul,

And forget not all His benefits:
3   Who forgives all your
      iniquities,
      Who heals all your diseases,
4   Who redeems your life from
      destruction,
      Who crowns you with
      lovingkindness and tender
      mercies,
5   Who satisfies your mouth
      with good *things,*
      So that your youth is renewed
      like the eagle's.

6   The LORD executes
      righteousness
      And justice for all who are
      oppressed.
7   He made known His ways to
      Moses,
      His acts to the children of
      Israel.
8   The LORD *is* merciful and
      gracious,
      Slow to anger, and abounding
      in mercy.
9   He will not always strive *with*
      us,
      Nor will He keep *His anger*
      forever.
10   He has not dealt with us
      according to our sins,
      Nor punished us according to
      our iniquities.

11   For as the heavens are high
      above the earth,
      So great is His mercy toward
      those who fear Him;
12   As far as the east is from the
      west,
      So far has He removed our
      transgressions from us.
13   As a father pities *his* children,
      So the LORD pities those who
      fear Him.
14   For He knows our frame;
      He remembers that we *are*
      dust.

15 *As for* man, his days *are* like grass;
As a flower of the field, so he flourishes.

16 For the wind passes over it, and it is gone,
And its place remembers it no more.*

17 But the mercy of the LORD *is* from everlasting to everlasting
On those who fear Him,
And His righteousness to children's children,

18 To such as keep His covenant,
And to those who remember His commandments to do them.

19 The LORD has established His throne in heaven,
And His kingdom rules over all.

20 Bless the LORD, you His angels,
Who excel in strength, who do His word,
Heeding the voice of His word.

21 Bless the LORD, all *you* His hosts,
You ministers of His, who do His pleasure.

22 Bless the LORD, all His works,
In all places of His dominion.

Bless the LORD, O my soul!

PROVERBS FOR TODAY/ 26:23

Fervent lips with a wicked heart are like *earthenware covered with silver dross.*

NOVEMBER 1

EZEKIEL 1:1–3:15

Now it came to pass in the thirtieth year, in the fourth *month,* on the fifth *day* of the month, as I *was* among the captives by the River Chebar, *that* the heavens were opened and I saw visions* of God. ²On the fifth *day* of the month, which *was* in the fifth year of King Jehoiachin's captivity, ³the word of the LORD came expressly to Ezekiel the priest, the son of Buzi, in the land of the Chaldeans* by the River Chebar; and the hand of the LORD was upon him there.

⁴Then I looked, and behold, a whirlwind was coming out of the north, a great cloud with raging fire engulfing itself; and brightness *was* all around it and radiating out of its midst like the color of amber, out of the midst of the fire. ⁵Also from within it *came* the likeness of four living creatures. And this *was* their appearance: they had the likeness of a man. ⁶Each one had four faces, and each one had four wings. ⁷Their legs *were* straight, and the soles of their feet *were* like the soles of calves' feet. They sparkled like the color of burnished bronze. ⁸The hands of a man *were* under their wings on their four sides; and each of the four had faces and wings. ⁹Their wings touched one another. *The creatures* did not turn when they went, but each one went straight forward.

¹⁰As for the likeness of their faces, *each* had the face of a man; each of the four had the face of a lion on the right side, each of the four had the face of an

ox on the left side, and each of the four had the face of an eagle. [11]Thus *were* their faces. Their wings stretched upward; two *wings* of each one touched one another, and two covered their bodies. [12]And each one went straight forward; they went wherever the spirit wanted to go, and they did not turn when they went.

[13]As for the likeness of the living creatures, their appearance *was* like burning coals of fire, like the appearance of torches going back and forth among the living creatures. The fire was bright, and out of the fire went lightning. [14]And the living creatures ran back and forth, in appearance like a flash of lightning.

[15]Now as I looked at the living creatures, behold, a wheel *was* on the earth beside each living creature with its four faces. [16]The appearance of the wheels and their workings *was* like the color of beryl, and all four had the same likeness. The appearance of their workings *was,* as it were, a wheel in the middle of a wheel. [17]When they moved, they went toward any one of four directions; they did not turn aside when they went. [18]As for their rims, they were so high they were awesome; and their rims *were* full of eyes, all around the four of them. [19]When the living creatures went, the wheels went beside them; and when the living creatures were lifted up from the earth, the wheels were lifted up. [20]Wherever the spirit wanted to go, they went, *because* there the spirit went; and the wheels were lifted together with them, for the spirit of the living creatures* *was* in the wheels. [21]When those went, *these* went; when those stood, *these* stood; and when those were lifted up from the earth, the wheels were lifted up together with them, for the spirit of the living creatures* *was* in the wheels.

[22]The likeness of the firmament above the heads of the living creatures* *was* like the color of an awesome crystal, stretched out over their heads. [23]And under the firmament their wings *spread out* straight, one toward another. Each one had two which covered one side, and each one had two which covered the other side of the body. [24]When they went, I heard the noise of their wings, like the noise of many waters, like the voice of the Almighty, a tumult like the noise of an army; and when they stood still, they let down their wings. [25]A voice came from above the firmament that *was* over their heads; whenever they stood, they let down their wings.

[26]And above the firmament over their heads *was* the likeness of a throne, in appearance like a sapphire stone; on the likeness of the throne *was* a likeness with the appearance of a man high above it. [27]Also from the appearance of His waist and upward I saw, as it were, the color of amber with the appearance of fire all around within it; and from the appearance of His waist and downward I saw, as it were, the appearance of fire with brightness all around. [28]Like the appearance of a rainbow in a cloud on a rainy day, so *was* the appearance of the brightness all around it. This *was* the appearance of the likeness of the glory of the LORD.

So when I saw *it,* I fell on my face, and I heard a voice of One speaking.

AND He said to me, "Son of man, stand on your feet, and I will speak to you." [2]Then the Spirit entered me when He spoke to me, and set me on my feet; and I heard Him who spoke to me. [3]And He said to me: "Son of man, I am sending you to the children of Israel, to a rebellious nation that has rebelled against Me; they and their fathers have transgressed against Me to this very day. [4]For *they are* impudent and stubborn children. I am sending you to them, and you shall say to them, 'Thus says the Lord GOD.' [5]As for them, whether they hear or whether they refuse—for they *are* a rebellious house—yet they will know that a prophet has been among them.

6"And you, son of man, do not be afraid of them nor be afraid of their words, though briers and thorns *are* with you and you dwell among scorpions; do not be afraid of their words or dismayed by their looks, though they *are* a rebellious house. 7You shall speak My words to them, whether they hear or whether they refuse, for they *are* rebellious. 8But you, son of man, hear what I say to you. Do not be rebellious like that rebellious house; open your mouth and eat what I give you."

9Now when I looked, there was a hand stretched out to me; and behold, a scroll of a book *was* in it. 10Then He spread it before me; and *there was* writing on the inside and on the outside, and written on it *were* lamentations and mourning and woe.

MOREOVER He said to me, "Son of man, eat what you find; eat this scroll, and go, speak to the house of Israel." 2So I opened my mouth, and He caused me to eat that scroll.

3And He said to me, "Son of man, feed your belly, and fill your stomach with this scroll that I give you." So I ate, and it was in my mouth like honey in sweetness.

4Then He said to me: "Son of man, go to the house of Israel and speak with My words to them. 5For you *are* not sent to a people of unfamiliar speech and of hard language, *but* to the house of Israel, 6not to many people of unfamiliar speech and of hard language, whose words you cannot understand. Surely, had I sent you to them, they would have listened to you. 7But the house of Israel will not listen to you, because they will not listen to Me; for all the house of Israel *are* impudent and hard-hearted. 8Behold, I have made your face strong against their faces, and your forehead strong against their foreheads. 9Like adamant stone, harder than flint, I have made your forehead; do not be afraid of them, nor be dismayed at their looks, though they *are* a rebellious house."

10Moreover He said to me: "Son of man, receive into your heart all My words that I speak to you, and hear with your ears. 11And go, get to the captives, to the children of your people, and speak to them and tell them, 'Thus says the Lord GOD,' whether they hear, or whether they refuse."

12Then the Spirit lifted me up, and I heard behind me a great thunderous voice: "Blessed *is* the glory of the LORD from His place!" 13*I* also *heard* the noise of the wings of the living creatures that touched one another, and the noise of the wheels beside them, and a great thunderous noise. 14So the Spirit lifted me up and took me away, and I went in bitterness, in the heat of my spirit; but the hand of the LORD was strong upon me. 15Then I came to the captives at Tel Abib, who dwelt by the River Chebar; and I sat where they sat, and remained there astonished among them seven days.

HEBREWS 3:1-19

THEREFORE, holy brethren, partakers of the heavenly calling, consider the Apostle and High Priest of our confession, Christ Jesus, 2who was faithful to Him who appointed Him, as Moses also *was faithful* in all His house. 3For this One has been counted worthy of more glory than Moses, inasmuch as He who built the house has more honor than the house. 4For every house is built by someone, but He who built all things *is* God. 5And Moses indeed *was* faithful in all His house as a servant, for a testimony of those things which would be spoken *afterward,* 6but Christ as a Son over His own house, whose house we are if we hold fast the confidence and the rejoicing of the hope firm to the end.*

7Therefore, as the Holy Spirit says:

> "Today, if you will hear His
> voice,
> 8 Do not harden your hearts as
> in the rebellion,
> In the day of trial in the
> wilderness,
> 9 Where your fathers tested
> Me, tried Me,
> And saw My works forty
> years.
> 10 Therefore I was angry with
> that generation,
> And said, 'They always go
> astray in their heart,
> And they have not known My
> ways.'
> 11 So I swore in My wrath,
> 'They shall not enter My
> rest.'"*

12Beware, brethren, lest there be in any of you an evil heart of unbelief in departing from the living God; 13but exhort one another daily, while it is called *"Today,"* lest any of you be hardened through the deceitfulness of sin. 14For we have become partakers of Christ if we hold the beginning of our confidence steadfast to the end, 15while it is said:

> "Today, if you will hear His
> voice,
> Do not harden your hearts as
> in the rebellion."*

16For who, having heard, rebelled? Indeed, *was it* not all who came out of Egypt, *led* by Moses? 17Now with whom was He angry forty years? *Was it* not with those who sinned, whose corpses fell in the wilderness? 18And to whom did He swear that they would

not enter His rest, but to those who did not obey? 19So we see that they could not enter in because of unbelief.

PSALM 104:1-23

Bless the Lord, O my soul!

> O Lord my God, You are very
> great:
> You are clothed with honor
> and majesty,
> 2 Who cover *Yourself* with light
> as *with* a garment,
> Who stretch out the heavens
> like a curtain.
>
> 3 He lays the beams of His
> upper chambers in the
> waters,
> Who makes the clouds His
> chariot,
> Who walks on the wings of
> the wind,
> 4 Who makes His angels spirits,
> His ministers a flame of fire.
>
> 5 *You who* laid the foundations
> of the earth,
> So *that* it should not be
> moved forever,
> 6 You covered it with the deep
> as *with* a garment;
> The waters stood above the
> mountains.
> 7 At Your rebuke they fled;
> At the voice of Your thunder
> they hastened away.
> 8 They went up over the
> mountains;
> They went down into the
> valleys,
> To the place which You
> founded for them.
> 9 You have set a boundary that
> they may not pass over,
> That they may not return to
> cover the earth.

10   He sends the springs into the
        valleys;
     They flow among the hills.
11   They give drink to every
        beast of the field;
     The wild donkeys quench
        their thirst.
12   By them the birds of the
        heavens have their home;
     They sing among the
        branches.
13   He waters the hills from His
        upper chambers;
     The earth is satisfied with the
        fruit of Your works.

14   He causes the grass to grow
        for the cattle,
     And vegetation for the service
        of man,
     That he may bring forth food
        from the earth,
15   And wine *that* makes glad the
        heart of man,
     Oil to make *his* face shine,
     And bread *which* strengthens
        man's heart.
16   The trees of the LORD are full
        of sap,

     The cedars of Lebanon which
        He planted,
17   Where the birds make their
        nests;
     The stork has her home in
        the fir trees.
18   The high hills *are* for the wild
        goats;
     The cliffs are a refuge for the
        rock badgers.*

19   He appointed the moon for
        seasons;
     The sun knows its going
        down.
20   You make darkness, and it is
        night,
     In which all the beasts of the
        forest creep about.
21   The young lions roar after
        their prey,
     And seek their food from God.
22   *When* the sun rises, they
        gather together
     And lie down in their dens.
23   Man goes out to his work
     And to his labor until the
        evening.

PROVERBS FOR TODAY/ 26:24-26

He who hates, disguises it *with his lips, and lays up deceit within himself; when he speaks kindly, do not believe him, for* there are *seven abominations in his heart; though his hatred is covered by deceit, his wickedness will be revealed before the assembly.*

NOVEMBER 2

EZEKIEL 3:16–6:14

Now it came to pass at the end of seven days that the word of the LORD came to me, saying, [17]"Son of man, I have made you a watchman for the house of Israel; therefore hear a word from My mouth, and give them warning from Me: [18]When I say to the wicked, 'You shall surely die,' and you give him no warning, nor speak to warn the wicked from his wicked way, to save his life, that same wicked *man* shall die in his iniquity; but his blood I will require at your hand. ¹⁹Yet, if you warn the wicked, and he does not turn from his wickedness, nor from his wicked way, he shall die in his iniquity; but you have delivered your soul.

²⁰"Again, when a righteous *man* turns from his righteousness and commits iniquity, and I lay a stumbling block before him, he shall die; because you did not give him warning, he shall die in his sin, and his righteousness which he has done shall not be remembered; but his blood I will require at your hand. ²¹Nevertheless if you warn the righteous *man* that the righteous should not sin, and he does not sin, he shall surely live because he took warning; also you will have delivered your soul."

²²Then the hand of the Lord was upon me there, and He said to me, "Arise, go out into the plain, and there I shall talk with you."

²³So I arose and went out into the plain, and behold, the glory of the Lord stood there, like the glory which I saw by the River Chebar; and I fell on my face. ²⁴Then the Spirit entered me and set me on my feet, and spoke with me and said to me: "Go, shut yourself inside your house. ²⁵And you, O son of man, surely they will put ropes on you and bind you with them, so that you cannot go out among them. ²⁶I will make your tongue cling to the roof of your mouth, so that you shall be mute and not be one to rebuke them, for they *are* a rebellious house. ²⁷But when I speak with you, I will open your mouth, and you shall say to them, 'Thus says the Lord God.' He who hears, let him hear; and he who refuses, let him refuse; for they *are* a rebellious house.

"You also, son of man, take a clay tablet and lay it before you, and portray on it a city, Jerusalem. ²Lay siege against it, build a siege wall against it, and heap up a mound against it; set camps against it also, and place battering rams against it all around. ³Moreover take for yourself an iron plate, and set it *as* an iron wall between you and the city. Set your face against it, and it shall be besieged, and you shall lay siege against it. This *will be* a sign to the house of Israel.

⁴"Lie also on your left side, and lay the iniquity of the house of Israel upon it. *According* to the number of the days that you lie on it, you shall bear their iniquity. ⁵For I have laid on you the years of their iniquity, according to the number of the days, three hundred and ninety days; so you shall bear the iniquity of the house of Israel. ⁶And when you have completed them, lie again on your right side; then you shall bear the iniquity of the house of Judah forty days. I have laid on you a day for each year.

⁷"Therefore you shall set your face toward the siege of Jerusalem; your arm *shall be* uncovered, and you shall prophesy against it. ⁸And surely I will restrain you so that you cannot turn from one side to another till you have ended the days of your siege.

⁹"Also take for yourself wheat, barley, beans, lentils, millet, and spelt; put them into one vessel, and make bread of them for yourself. *During* the number of days that you lie on your side, three hundred and ninety days, you shall eat it. ¹⁰And your food which you eat *shall be* by weight, twenty shekels a day; from time to time you shall eat it. ¹¹You shall also drink water by measure, one-sixth of a hin; from time to time you shall drink. ¹²And you shall eat it *as* barley cakes; and bake it using fuel of human waste in their sight."

¹³Then the Lord said, "So shall the children of Israel eat their defiled bread among the Gentiles, where I will drive them."

14So I said, "Ah, Lord GOD! Indeed I have never defiled myself from my youth till now; I have never eaten what died of itself or was torn by beasts, nor has abominable flesh ever come into my mouth."

15Then He said to me, "See, I am giving you cow dung instead of human waste, and you shall prepare your bread over it."

16Moreover He said to me, "Son of man, surely I will cut off the supply of bread in Jerusalem; they shall eat bread by weight and with anxiety, and shall drink water by measure and with dread, 17that they may lack bread and water, and be dismayed with one another, and waste away because of their iniquity.

"AND you, son of man, take a sharp sword, take it as a barber's razor, and pass it over your head and your beard; then take scales to weigh and divide the hair. 2You shall burn with fire one-third in the midst of the city, when the days of the siege are finished; then you shall take one-third and strike around it with the sword, and one-third you shall scatter in the wind: I will draw out a sword after them. 3You shall also take a small number of them and bind them in the edge of your garment. 4Then take some of them again and throw them into the midst of the fire, and burn them in the fire. From there a fire will go out into all the house of Israel.

5"Thus says the Lord GOD: 'This is Jerusalem; I have set her in the midst of the nations and the countries all around her. 6She has rebelled against My judgments by doing wickedness more than the nations, and against My statutes more than the countries that are all around her; for they have refused My judgments, and they have not walked in My statutes.' 7Therefore thus says the Lord GOD: 'Because you have multiplied *disobedience* more

than the nations that *are* all around you, have not walked in My statutes nor kept My judgments, nor even done* according to the judgments of the nations that *are* all around you'— 8therefore thus says the Lord GOD: 'Indeed I, even I, *am* against you and will execute judgments in your midst in the sight of the nations. 9And I will do among you what I have never done, and the like of which I will never do again, because of all your abominations. 10Therefore fathers shall eat *their* sons in your midst, and sons shall eat their fathers; and I will execute judgments among you, and all of you who remain I will scatter to all the winds.

11'Therefore, *as* I live,' says the Lord GOD, 'surely, because you have defiled My sanctuary with all your detestable things and with all your abominations, therefore I will also diminish *you;* My eye will not spare, nor will I have any pity. 12One-third of you shall die of the pestilence, and be consumed with famine in your midst; and one-third shall fall by the sword all around you; and I will scatter another third to all the winds, and I will draw out a sword after them.

13'Thus shall My anger be spent, and I will cause My fury to rest upon them, and I will be avenged; and they shall know that I, the LORD, have spoken *it* in My zeal, when I have spent My fury upon them. 14Moreover I will make you a waste and a reproach among the nations that *are* all around you, in the sight of all who pass by.

15'So it* shall be a reproach, a taunt, a lesson, and an astonishment to the nations that *are* all around you, when I execute judgments among you in anger and in fury and in furious rebukes. I, the LORD, have spoken. 16When I send against them the terrible arrows of famine which shall be for destruction, which I will send to destroy you, I will increase the famine upon you and cut off your supply of bread. [17]So I will send against you famine and wild beasts, and they will bereave you. Pestilence and blood shall pass through you, and I will bring the sword against you. I, the LORD, have spoken.' "

Now the word of the LORD came to me, saying: [2]"Son of man, set your face toward the mountains of Israel, and prophesy against them, [3]and say, 'O mountains of Israel, hear the word of the Lord GOD! Thus says the Lord GOD to the mountains, to the hills, to the ravines, and to the valleys: "Indeed I, *even* I, will bring a sword against you, and I will destroy your high places. [4]Then your altars shall be desolate, your incense altars shall be broken, and I will cast down your slain *men* before your idols. [5]And I will lay the corpses of the children of Israel before their idols, and I will scatter your bones all around your altars. [6]In all your dwelling places the cities shall be laid waste, and the high places shall be desolate, so that your altars may be laid waste and made desolate, your idols may be broken and made to cease, your incense altars may be cut down, and your works may be abolished. [7]The slain shall fall in your midst, and you shall know that I *am* the LORD.

[8]"Yet I will leave a remnant, so that you may have *some* who escape the sword among the nations, when you are scattered through the countries. [9]Then those of you who escape will remember Me among the nations where they are carried captive, because I was crushed by their adulterous heart which has departed from Me, and by their eyes which play the harlot after their idols; they will loathe themselves for the evils which they committed in all their abominations. [10]And they shall know that I *am* the LORD; I have not said in vain that I would bring this calamity upon them."

[11]"Thus says the Lord GOD: "Pound your fists and stamp your feet, and say, 'Alas, for all the evil abominations of the house of Israel! For they shall fall by the sword, by famine, and by pestilence. [12]He who is far off shall die by the pestilence, he who is near shall fall by the sword, and he who remains and is besieged shall die by the famine. Thus will I spend My fury upon them. [13]Then you shall know that I *am* the LORD, when their slain are among their idols all around their altars, on every high hill, on all the mountaintops, under every green tree, and under every thick oak, wherever they offered sweet incense to all their idols. [14]So I will stretch out My hand against them and make the land desolate, yes, more desolate than the wilderness toward Diblah, in all their dwelling places. Then they shall know that I *am* the LORD.' " ' "

HEBREWS 4:1-16

THEREFORE, since a promise remains of entering His rest, let us fear lest any of you seem to have come short of it. [2]For indeed the gospel was preached to us as well as to them; but the word which they heard did not profit them,* not being mixed with faith in those who heard *it*. [3]For we who have believed do enter that rest, as He has said:

> "So I swore in My wrath,
> 'They shall not enter My
> rest,' "*

although the works were finished from the foundation of the world. [4]For He has spoken in a certain place of the seventh *day* in this way: "And God rested on the seventh day from all His works";* [5]and again in this *place*: "They shall not enter My rest." *

[6]Since therefore it remains that

some *must* enter it, and those to whom it was first preached did not enter because of disobedience, ⁷again He designates a certain day, saying in David, *"Today,"* after such a long time, as it has been said:

> *"Today, if you will hear His voice,*
> *Do not harden your hearts."* *

⁸For if Joshua had given them rest, then He would not afterward have spoken of another day. ⁹There remains therefore a rest for the people of God. ¹⁰For he who has entered His rest has himself also ceased from his works as God *did* from His.

¹¹Let us therefore be diligent to enter that rest, lest anyone fall according to the same example of disobedience. ¹²For the word of God *is* living and powerful, and sharper than any two-edged sword, piercing even to the division of soul and spirit, and of joints and marrow, and is a discerner of the thoughts and intents of the heart. ¹³And there is no creature hidden from His sight, but all things *are* naked and open to the eyes of Him to whom we *must give* account.

¹⁴Seeing then that we have a great High Priest who has passed through the heavens, Jesus the Son of God, let us hold fast *our* confession. ¹⁵For we do not have a High Priest who cannot sympathize with our weaknesses, but was in all *points* tempted as *we are, yet* without sin. ¹⁶Let us therefore come boldly to the throne of grace, that we may obtain mercy and find grace to help in time of need.

PSALM 104:24-35

O LORD, how manifold are Your works!
In wisdom You have made them all.
The earth is full of Your possessions—

25 This great and wide sea,
In which *are* innumerable teeming things,
Living things both small and great.

26 There the ships sail about;
There is that Leviathan
Which You have made to play there.

27 These all wait for You,
That You may give *them* their food in due season.

28 *What* You give them they gather in;
You open Your hand, they are filled with good.

29 You hide Your face, they are troubled;
You take away their breath, they die and return to their dust.

30 You send forth Your Spirit, they are created;
And You renew the face of the earth.

31 May the glory of the LORD endure forever;
May the LORD rejoice in His works.

32 He looks on the earth, and it trembles;
He touches the hills, and they smoke.

33 I will sing to the LORD as long as I live;
I will sing praise to my God while I have my being.

34 May my meditation be sweet to Him;
I will be glad in the LORD.

35 May sinners be consumed from the earth,
And the wicked be no more.
Bless the LORD, O my soul!
Praise the LORD!

PROVERBS FOR TODAY/ 26:27

Whoever digs a pit will fall into it, and he who rolls a stone will have it roll back on him.

NOVEMBER 3

EZEKIEL 7:1–9:11

MOREOVER the word of the LORD came to me, saying, 2"And you, son of man, thus says the Lord GOD to the land of Israel:

'An end! The end has come
upon the four corners of
the land.

3 Now the end *has come* upon
you,
And I will send My anger
against you;
I will judge you according to
your ways,
And I will repay you for all
your abominations.

4 My eye will not spare you,
Nor will I have pity;
But I will repay your ways,
And your abominations will
be in your midst;
Then you shall know that I
am the LORD!'

5"Thus says the Lord GOD:

'A disaster, a singular disaster;
Behold, it has come!

6 An end has come,
The end has come;
It has dawned for you;
Behold, it has come!

7 Doom has come to you, you
who dwell in the land;
The time has come,
A day of trouble *is* near,
And not of rejoicing in the
mountains.

8 Now upon you I will soon
pour out My fury,
And spend My anger upon
you;
I will judge you according to
your ways,
And I will repay you for all
your abominations.

9 'My eye will not spare,
Nor will I have pity;
I will repay you according to
your ways,
And your abominations will
be in your midst.
Then you shall know that I
am the LORD who strikes.

10 'Behold, the day!
Behold, it has come!
Doom has gone out;
The rod has blossomed,
Pride has budded.

11 Violence has risen up into a
rod of wickedness;
None of them *shall remain,*
None of their multitude,
None of them;
Nor *shall there be* wailing for
them.

12 The time has come,
The day draws near.

'Let not the buyer rejoice,
Nor the seller mourn,
For wrath *is* on their whole
multitude.

13 For the seller shall not return
to what has been sold,

Though he may still be alive;
For the vision concerns the
whole multitude,
And it shall not turn back;
No one will strengthen himself
Who lives in iniquity.

14 'They have blown the trumpet
and made everyone ready,
But no one goes to battle;
For My wrath *is* on all their
multitude.
15 The sword *is* outside,
And the pestilence and famine
within.
Whoever *is* in the field
Will die by the sword;
And whoever *is* in the city,
Famine and pestilence will
devour him.

16 'Those who survive will
escape and be on the
mountains
Like doves of the valleys,
All of them mourning,
Each for his iniquity.
17 Every hand will be feeble,
And every knee will be *as*
weak *as* water.
18 They will also be girded with
sackcloth;
Horror will cover them;
Shame *will be* on every face,
Baldness on all their heads.

19 'They will throw their silver
into the streets,
And their gold will be like
refuse;
Their silver and their gold will
not be able to deliver them
In the day of the wrath of the
LORD;
They will not satisfy their
souls,
Nor fill their stomachs,
Because it became their
stumbling block of iniquity.

20 'As for the beauty of his
ornaments,
He set it in majesty;
But they made from it
The images of their
abominations—
Their detestable things;
Therefore I have made it
Like refuse to them.
21 I will give it as plunder
Into the hands of strangers,
And to the wicked of the
earth as spoil;
And they shall defile it.
22 I will turn My face from them,
And they will defile My secret
place;
For robbers shall enter it and
defile it.

23 'Make a chain,
For the land is filled with
crimes of blood,
And the city is full of violence.
24 Therefore I will bring the
worst of the Gentiles,
And they will possess their
houses;
I will cause the pomp of the
strong to cease,
And their holy places shall be
defiled.
25 Destruction comes;
They will seek peace, but
there shall be none.
26 Disaster will come upon
disaster,
And rumor will be upon
rumor.
Then they will seek a vision
from a prophet;
But the law will perish from
the priest,
And counsel from the elders.

27 'The king will mourn,
The prince will be clothed
with desolation,
And the hands of the common
people will tremble.

I will do to them according to
their way,
And according to what they
deserve I will judge them;
Then they shall know that I
am the LORD!' "

AND it came to pass in the sixth year, in the sixth *month,* on the fifth *day* of the month, as I sat in my house with the elders of Judah sitting before me, that the hand of the Lord GOD fell upon me there. ²Then I looked, and there was a likeness, like the appearance of fire— from the appearance of His waist and downward, fire; and from His waist and upward, like the appearance of brightness, like the color of amber. ³He stretched out the form of a hand, and took me by a lock of my hair; and the Spirit lifted me up between earth and heaven, and brought me in visions of God to Jerusalem, to the door of the north gate of the inner *court,* where the seat of the image of jealousy *was,* which provokes to jealousy. ⁴And behold, the glory of the God of Israel *was* there, like the vision that I saw in the plain.

⁵Then He said to me, "Son of man, lift your eyes now toward the north." So I lifted my eyes toward the north, and there, north of the altar gate, was this image of jealousy in the entrance. ⁶Furthermore He said to me, "Son of man, do you see what they are doing, the great abominations that the house of Israel commits here, to make Me go far away from My sanctuary? Now turn again, you will see greater abominations." ⁷So He brought me to the door of the court; and when I looked, there was a hole in the wall. ⁸Then He said to me, "Son of man, dig into the wall"; and when I dug into the wall, there was a door. ⁹And He said to me, "Go in, and see the wicked abominations which they are doing there." ¹⁰So I went in and saw, and there—every sort of creeping thing, abominable beasts, and all the idols of the house of Israel, portrayed all around on the walls. ¹¹And there stood before them seventy men of the elders of the house of Israel, and in their midst stood Jaazaniah the son of Shaphan. Each man had a censer in his hand, and a thick cloud of incense went up. ¹²Then He said to me, "Son of man, have you seen what the elders of the house of Israel do in the dark, every man in the room of his idols? For they say, 'The LORD does not see us, the LORD has forsaken the land.' "

¹³And He said to me, "Turn again, *and* you will see greater abominations that they are doing." ¹⁴So He brought me to the door of the north gate of the LORD's house; and to my dismay, women were sitting there weeping for Tammuz.

¹⁵Then He said to me, "Have you seen *this,* O son of man? Turn again, you will see greater abominations than these." ¹⁶So He brought me into the inner court of the LORD's house; and there, at the door of the temple of the LORD, between the porch and the altar, *were* about twenty-five men with their backs toward the temple of the LORD and their faces toward the east, and they were worshiping the sun toward the east.

¹⁷And He said to me, "Have you seen *this,* O son of man? Is it a trivial thing to the house of Judah to commit the abominations which they commit here? For they have filled the land with violence; then they have returned to provoke Me to anger. Indeed they put the branch to their nose. ¹⁸Therefore I also will act in fury. My eye will not spare nor will I have pity; and though they cry in My ears with a loud voice, I will not hear them."

THEN He called out in my hearing with a loud voice, saying, "Let those who have charge over the city draw near, each *with* a deadly weapon in his hand." ²And suddenly six men came from the direction of the upper gate, which faces north, each with his battle-ax in his hand. One man among them *was* clothed with linen and had a writer's inkhorn at his side. They went in and stood beside the bronze altar.

³Now the glory of the God of Israel had gone up from the cherub, where it had been, to the threshold of the temple.* And He called to the man clothed with linen, who *had* the writer's inkhorn at his side; ⁴and the LORD said to him, "Go through the midst of the city, through the midst of Jerusalem, and put a mark on the foreheads of the men who sigh and cry over all the abominations that are done within it."

⁵To the others He said in my hearing, "Go after him through the city and kill; do not let your eye spare, nor have any pity. ⁶Utterly slay old *and* young men, maidens and little children and women; but do not come near anyone on whom *is* the mark; and begin at My sanctuary." So they began with the elders who *were* before the temple. ⁷Then He said to them, "Defile the temple, and fill the courts with the slain. Go out!" And they went out and killed in the city.

⁸So it was, that while they were killing them, I was left *alone;* and I fell on my face and cried out, and said, "Ah, Lord GOD! Will You destroy all the remnant of Israel in pouring out Your fury on Jerusalem?"

⁹Then He said to me, "The iniquity of the house of Israel and Judah *is* exceedingly great, and the land is full of bloodshed, and the city full of perversity; for they say, 'The LORD has forsaken the land, and the LORD does not see!' ¹⁰And as for Me also, My eye will neither spare, nor will I have pity, *but* I will recompense their deeds on their own head."

¹¹Just then, the man clothed with linen, who *had* the inkhorn at his side, reported back and said, "I have done as You commanded me."

HEBREWS 5:1-14

FOR every high priest taken from among men is appointed for men in things *pertaining* to God, that he may offer both gifts and sacrifices for sins. ²He can have compassion on those who are ignorant and going astray, since he himself is also subject to weakness. ³Because of this he is required as for the people, so also for himself, to offer *sacrifices* for sins. ⁴And no man takes this honor to himself, but he who is called by God, just as Aaron *was.*

⁵So also Christ did not glorify Himself to become High Priest, *but it* was He who said to Him:

> *"You are My Son,*
> *Today I have begotten You."* *

⁶As *He* also *says* in another *place:*

> *"You are a priest forever*
> *According to the order of*
> *Melchizedek";* *

⁷who, in the days of His flesh, when He had offered up prayers and supplications, with vehement cries and tears to Him who was able to save Him from death, and was heard because of His godly fear, ⁸though He was a Son, *yet* He learned obedience by the things which He suffered. ⁹And having been perfected, He became the author of eternal salvation to all who obey Him, ¹⁰called by God as High Priest *"according to the order of Melchizedek,"* ¹¹of whom we have much to say, and hard to explain, since you have become dull of hearing.

¹²For though by this time you ought to be teachers, you need *someone* to teach you again the first principles of the oracles of God; and you have come to need milk and not solid food. ¹³For everyone who partakes *only* of milk *is*

unskilled in the word of righteousness, for he is a babe. ¹⁴But solid food belongs to those who are of full age, *that is,* those who by reason of use have their senses exercised to discern both good and evil.

PSALM 105:1-15

O, give thanks to the LORD!
Call upon His name;
Make known His deeds
among the peoples!

2   Sing to Him, sing psalms to
    Him;
    Talk of all His wondrous
    works!
3   Glory in His holy name;
    Let the hearts of those rejoice
    who seek the LORD!
4   Seek the LORD and His
    strength;
    Seek His face evermore!
5   Remember His marvelous
    works which He has done,
    His wonders, and the
    judgments of His mouth,
6   O seed of Abraham His
    servant,
    You children of Jacob, His
    chosen ones!

7   He *is* the LORD our God;
    His judgments *are* in all the
    earth.

8   He remembers His covenant
    forever,
    The word *which* He
    commanded, for a thousand
    generations,
9   *The covenant* which He made
    with Abraham,
    And His oath to Isaac,
10 And confirmed it to Jacob for
    a statute,
    To Israel *as* an everlasting
    covenant,
11 Saying, "To you I will give the
    land of Canaan
    As the allotment of your
    inheritance,"
12 When they were few in
    number,
    Indeed very few, and
    strangers in it.

13 When they went from one
    nation to another,
    From *one* kingdom to another
    people,
14 He permitted no one to do
    them wrong;
    Yes, He rebuked kings for
    their sakes,
15 *Saying,* "Do not touch My
    anointed ones,
    And do My prophets no
    harm."

PROVERBS FOR TODAY / 26:28

A lying tongue hates those who are *crushed by it, and a flattering mouth works ruin.*

NOVEMBER 4

EZEKIEL 10:1–11:25

AND I looked, and there in the firmament that was above the head of the cherubim, there appeared something like a sapphire stone, having the appearance of the likeness of a throne. 2Then He spoke to the man clothed with linen, and said, "Go in among the wheels, under the cherub, fill your hands with coals of fire from among the cherubim, and scatter *them* over the city." And he went in as I watched.

3Now the cherubim were standing on the south side of the temple* when the man went in, and the cloud filled the inner court. 4Then the glory of the LORD went up from the cherub, *and paused* over the threshold of the temple; and the house was filled with the cloud, and the court was full of the brightness of the LORD's glory. 5And the sound of the wings of the cherubim was heard *even* in the outer court, like the voice of Almighty God when He speaks.

6Then it happened, when He commanded the man clothed in linen, saying, "Take fire from among the wheels, from among the cherubim," that he went in and stood beside the wheels. 7And the cherub stretched out his hand from among the cherubim to the fire that *was* among the cherubim, and took *some of it* and put *it* into the hands of the *man* clothed with linen, who took *it* and went out. 8The cherubim appeared to have the form of a man's hand under their wings.

9And when I looked, there were four wheels by the cherubim, one wheel by one cherub and another wheel by each other cherub; the wheels appeared *to have* the color of a beryl stone. 10As for their appearance, all four looked alike—as it were, a wheel in the middle of a wheel. 11When they went, they went toward *any of* their four directions; they did not turn aside when they went, but followed in the direction the head was facing. They did not turn aside when they went. 12And their whole body, with their back, their hands, their wings, and the wheels that the four had, *were* full of eyes all around. 13As for the wheels, they were called in my hearing, "Wheel."

14Each one had four faces: the first face *was* the face of a cherub, the second face the face of a man, the third the face of a lion, and the fourth the face of an eagle. 15And the cherubim were lifted up. This *was* the living creature I saw by the River Chebar. 16When the cherubim went, the wheels went beside them; and when the cherubim lifted their wings to mount up from the earth, the same wheels also did not turn from beside them. 17When *the cherubim* stood still, *the wheels* stood still, and when *one* was lifted up, *the other* lifted itself up, for the spirit of the living creature *was* in them.

18Then the glory of the LORD departed from the threshold of the temple and stood over the cherubim. 19And the cherubim lifted their wings and mounted up from the earth in my sight. When they went out, the wheels *were* beside them; and they stood at the door of the east gate of the LORD's house, and the glory of the God of Israel *was* above them.

20This *is* the living creature I saw under the God of Israel by the River Chebar, and I knew they *were* cherubim. 21Each one had four faces and each one four wings, and the likeness of the hands of a man *was* under their wings. 22And the likeness of their faces *was* the same *as* the faces which I had seen by the River Chebar, their appearance and their persons. They each went straight forward.

THEN the Spirit lifted me up and brought me to the East Gate of the LORD's house, which faces eastward; and there at the door of the gate were twenty-five men, among whom I saw Jaazaniah the son of Azzur, and Pelatiah the son of Benaiah, princes of the people. 2And He said to me: "Son of man, these *are* the men who devise iniquity and give wicked counsel in this city, 3who say, '*The time is* not near to build houses; this *city is* the caldron, and we *are* the meat.' 4Therefore prophesy against them, prophesy, O son of man!"

5Then the Spirit of the LORD fell upon me, and said to me, "Speak! 'Thus says the LORD: "Thus you have said, O house of Israel; for I know the things that come into your mind. 6You have multiplied your slain in this city, and you have filled its streets with the slain." 7Therefore thus says the Lord GOD: "Your slain whom you have laid in its midst, they *are* the meat, and this *city is* the caldron; but I shall bring you out of the midst of it. 8You have feared the sword; and I will bring a sword upon you," says the Lord GOD. 9"And I will bring you out of its midst, and deliver you into the hands of strangers, and execute judgments on you. 10You shall fall by the sword. I will judge you at the border of Israel. Then you shall know that I *am* the LORD. 11This *city* shall not be your caldron, nor shall you be the meat in its midst. I will judge you at the border of Israel. 12And you shall know that I *am* the LORD; for you have not walked in My statutes nor executed My judgments, but have done according to the customs of the Gentiles which *are* all around you." ' "

13Now it happened, while I was prophesying, that Pelatiah the son of Benaiah died. Then I fell on my face and cried with a loud voice, and said, "Ah, Lord GOD! Will You make a complete end of the remnant of Israel?"

14Again the word of the LORD came to me, saying, 15"Son of man, your brethren, your relatives, your countrymen, and all the house of Israel in its entirety, *are* those about whom the inhabitants of Jerusalem have said, 'Get far away from the LORD; this land has been given to us as a possession.' 16Therefore say, 'Thus says the Lord GOD: "Although I have cast them far off among the Gentiles, and although I have scattered them among the countries, yet I shall be a little sanctuary for them in the countries where they have gone." ' 17Therefore say, 'Thus says the Lord GOD: "I will gather you from the peoples, assemble you from the countries where you have been scattered, and I will give you the land of Israel." ' 18And they will go there, and they will take away all its detestable things and all its abominations from there. 19Then I will give them one heart, and I will put a new spirit within them,* and take the stony heart out of their flesh, and give them a heart of flesh, 20that they may walk in My statutes and keep My judgments and do them; and they shall be My people, and I will be their God. 21But *as for those* whose hearts follow the desire for their detestable things and their abominations, I will recompense their deeds on their own heads," says the Lord GOD.

22So the cherubim lifted up their wings, with the wheels beside them, and the glory of the God of Israel *was* high above them. 23And the glory of the LORD went up from the midst of the city and stood on the mountain, which *is* on the east side of the city. 24Then the Spirit took me up and brought me in a vision by the Spirit of God into Chaldea,* to those in captivity. And the vision that I had seen went up from me. 25So I spoke to those in captivity of all the things the LORD had shown me.

HEBREWS 6:1-20

THEREFORE, leaving the discussion of the elementary *principles* of Christ, let us go on to perfection, not laying again the foundation of repentance from dead works and of faith toward God, 2of the doctrine of baptisms, of laying on of hands, of resurrection of the dead, and of eternal judgment. 3And this we will* do if God permits.

4For *it is* impossible for those who were once enlightened, and have tasted the heavenly gift, and have become partakers of the Holy Spirit, 5and have tasted the good word of God and the powers of the age to come, 6if they fall away,* to renew them again to repentance, since they crucify again for themselves the Son of God, and put *Him* to an open shame.

7For the earth which drinks in the rain that often comes upon it, and bears herbs useful for those by whom it is cultivated, receives blessing from God; 8but if it bears thorns and briers, *it is* rejected and near to being cursed, whose end *is* to be burned.

9But, beloved, we are confident of better things concerning you, yes, things that accompany salvation, though we speak in this manner. 10For God *is* not unjust to forget your work and labor of* love which you have shown toward His name, *in that* you have ministered to the saints, and do minister. 11And we desire that each one of you show the same diligence to the full assurance of hope until the end, 12that you do not become sluggish, but imitate those who through faith and patience inherit the promises.

13For when God made a promise to Abraham, because He could swear by no one greater, He swore by Himself, 14saying, *"Surely blessing I will bless you, and multiplying I will multiply you."* * 15And so, after he had patiently endured, he obtained the promise. 16For men indeed swear by the greater, and an oath for confirmation *is* for them an end of all dispute. 17Thus God, determining to show more abundantly to the heirs of promise the immutability of His counsel, confirmed *it* by an oath, 18that by two immutable things, in which it *is* impossible for God to lie, we might* have strong consolation, who have fled for refuge to lay hold of the hope set before *us.*

19This *hope* we have as an anchor of the soul, both sure and steadfast, and which enters the Presence *behind* the veil, 20where the forerunner has entered for us, *even* Jesus, having become High Priest forever according to the order of Melchizedek.

PSALM 105:16-36

MOREOVER He called for a famine in the land; He destroyed all the provision of bread.

17 He sent a man before them—
    Joseph—*who* was sold as a
    slave.
18 They hurt his feet with fetters,
    He was laid in irons.
19 Until the time that his word
    came to pass,
    The word of the LORD tested
    him.
20 The king sent and released
    him,
    The ruler of the people let
    him go free.
21 He made him lord of his
    house,
    And ruler of all his
    possessions,
22 To bind his princes at his
    pleasure,
    And teach his elders wisdom.

23 Israel also came into Egypt,
And Jacob dwelt in the land of
Ham.
24 He increased His people
greatly,
And made them stronger than
their enemies.
25 He turned their heart to hate
His people,
To deal craftily with His
servants.

26 He sent Moses His servant,
And Aaron whom He had
chosen.
27 They performed His signs
among them,
And wonders in the land of
Ham.
28 He sent darkness, and made
it dark;
And they did not rebel against
His word.
29 He turned their waters into
blood,

And killed their fish.
30 Their land abounded with
frogs,
Even in the chambers of their
kings.
31 He spoke, and there came
swarms of flies,
And lice in all their territory.
32 He gave them hail for rain,
And flaming fire in their land.
33 He struck their vines also,
and their fig trees,
And splintered the trees of
their territory.
34 He spoke, and locusts came,
Young locusts without
number,
35 And ate up all the vegetation
in their land,
And devoured the fruit of
their ground.
36 He also destroyed all the
firstborn in their land,
The first of all their strength.

PROVERBS FOR TODAY / 27:1-2

Do not boast about tomorrow, for you do not know what a day may bring forth.
□ *Let another man praise you, and not your own mouth; a stranger, and not your
own lips.*

NOVEMBER 5

EZEKIEL 12:1–14:11

Now the word of the LORD came to me, saying: 2"Son of man, you dwell in the midst of a rebellious house, which has eyes to see but does not see, and ears to hear but does not hear; for they *are* a rebellious house.

3"Therefore, son of man, prepare your belongings for captivity, and go into captivity by day in their sight. You shall go from your place into captivity to another place in their sight. It may be that they will consider, though they *are* a rebellious house. 4By day you shall bring out your belongings in their sight, as though going into captivity; and at evening you shall go in their sight, like those who go into captivity. 5Dig through the wall in their sight, and carry your belongings out through it. 6In their sight you shall bear *them* on *your* shoulders *and* carry them out at twilight; you shall cover your face, so that you cannot see the ground, for I have made you a sign to the house of Israel."

7So I did as I was commanded. I brought out my belongings by day, as though going into captivity, and at evening I dug through the wall with my hand. I brought them out at twilight, and I bore them on my shoulder in their sight.

8And in the morning the word of the LORD came to me, saying, 9"Son of man, has not the house of Israel, the rebellious house, said to you, 'What are you doing?' 10Say to them, 'Thus says the Lord GOD: "This burden concerns the prince in Jerusalem and all the house of Israel who are among them." ' 11Say, 'I am a sign to you. As I have done, so shall it be done to them; they shall be carried away into captivity.' 12And the prince who is among them shall bear his belongings on his shoulder at twilight and go out. They shall dig through the wall to carry them out through it. He shall cover his face, so that he cannot see the ground with his eyes. 13I will also spread My net over him, and he shall be caught in My snare. I will bring him to Babylon, to the land of the Chaldeans; yet he shall not see it, though he shall die there. 14I will scatter to every wind all who are around him to help him, and all his troops; and I will draw out the sword after them.

15"Then they shall know that I am the LORD, when I scatter them among the nations and disperse them throughout the countries. 16But I will spare a few of their men from the sword, from famine, and from pestilence, that they may declare all their abominations among the Gentiles wherever they go. Then they shall know that I am the LORD."

17Moreover the word of the LORD came to me, saying, 18"Son of man, eat your bread with quaking, and drink your water with trembling and anxiety. 19And say to the people of the land, 'Thus says the Lord GOD to the inhabitants of Jerusalem and to the land of Israel: "They shall eat their bread with anxiety, and drink their water with dread, so that her land may be emptied of all who are in it, because of the violence of all those who dwell in it. 20Then the cities that are inhabited shall be laid waste, and the land shall become desolate; and you shall know that I am the LORD." ' "

21And the word of the LORD came to me, saying, 22"Son of man, what is this proverb that you people have about the land of Israel, which says, 'The days are prolonged, and every vision fails'? 23Tell them therefore, 'Thus says the Lord GOD: "I will lay this proverb to rest, and they shall no more use it as a proverb in Israel." ' But say to them, "The days are at hand, and the fulfillment of every vision. 24For no more shall there be any false vision or flattering divination within the house of Israel. 25For I am the LORD. I speak, and the word which I speak will come to pass; it will no more be postponed; for in your days, O rebellious house, I will say the word and perform it," says the Lord GOD.' "

26Again the word of the LORD came to me, saying, 27"Son of man, look, the house of Israel is saying, 'The vision that he sees is for many days from now, and he prophesies of times far off.' 28Therefore say to them, 'Thus says the Lord GOD: "None of My words will be postponed any more, but the word which I speak will be done," says the Lord GOD.' "

AND the word of the LORD came to me, saying, 2"Son of man, prophesy against the prophets of Israel who prophesy, and say to those who prophesy out of their own heart, 'Hear the word of the LORD!' "

3Thus says the Lord GOD: "Woe to

the foolish prophets, who follow their own spirit and have seen nothing! ⁴O Israel, your prophets are like foxes in the deserts. ⁵You have not gone up into the gaps to build a wall for the house of Israel to stand in battle on the day of the Lord. ⁶They have envisioned futility and false divination, saying, 'Thus says the Lord!' But the Lord has not sent them; yet they hope that the word may be confirmed. ⁷Have you not seen a futile vision, and have you not spoken false divination? You say, 'The Lord says,' but I have not spoken."

⁸Therefore thus says the Lord God: "Because you have spoken nonsense and envisioned lies, therefore I *am* indeed against you," says the Lord God. ⁹"My hand will be against the prophets who envision futility and who divine lies; they shall not be in the assembly of My people, nor be written in the record of the house of Israel, nor shall they enter into the land of Israel. Then you shall know that I *am* the Lord God.

¹⁰"Because, indeed, because they have seduced My people, saying, 'Peace!' when *there is* no peace—and one builds a wall, and they plaster it with untempered *mortar*— ¹¹say to those who plaster *it* with untempered *mortar,* that it will fall. There will be flooding rain, and you, O great hailstones, shall fall; and a stormy wind shall tear *it* down. ¹²Surely, when the wall has fallen, will it not be said to you, 'Where *is* the mortar with which you plastered *it?*' "

¹³Therefore thus says the Lord God: "I will cause a stormy wind to break forth in My fury; and there shall be a flooding rain in My anger, and great hailstones in fury to consume *it.* ¹⁴So I will break down the wall you have plastered with untempered *mortar,* and bring it down to the ground, so that its foundation will be uncovered; it will fall, and you shall be consumed in the midst of it. Then you shall know that I *am* the Lord.

¹⁵"Thus will I accomplish My wrath on the wall and on those who have plastered it with untempered *mortar;* and I will say to you, 'The wall *is* no *more,* nor those who plastered it, ¹⁶*that is,* the prophets of Israel who prophesy concerning Jerusalem, and who see visions of peace for her when *there is* no peace,' " says the Lord God.

¹⁷"Likewise, son of man, set your face against the daughters of your people, who prophesy out of their own heart; prophesy against them, ¹⁸and say, 'Thus says the Lord God: "Woe to the *women* who sew *magic* charms on their sleeves* and make veils for the heads of people of every height to hunt souls! Will you hunt the souls of My people, and keep yourselves alive? ¹⁹And will you profane Me among My people for handfuls of barley and for pieces of bread, killing people who should not die, and keeping people alive who should not live, by your lying to My people who listen to lies?"

²⁰'Therefore thus says the Lord God: "Behold, I *am* against your *magic* charms by which you hunt souls there like birds. I will tear them from your arms, and let the souls go, the souls you hunt like birds. ²¹I will also tear off your veils and deliver My people out of your hand, and they shall no longer be as prey in your hand. Then you shall know that I *am* the Lord.

²²"Because with lies you have made the heart of the righteous sad, whom I have not made sad; and you have strengthened the hands of the wicked, so that he does not turn from his wicked way to save his life. ²³Therefore you shall no longer envision futility nor practice divination; for I will deliver My people out of your hand, and you shall know that I *am* the Lord." ' "

Now some of the elders of Israel came to me and sat before me. ²And the word of the Lord came to me, saying,

3"Son of man, these men have set up their idols in their hearts, and put before them that which causes them to stumble into iniquity. Should I let Myself be inquired of at all by them?

4"Therefore speak to them, and say to them, 'Thus says the Lord GOD: "Everyone of the house of Israel who sets up his idols in his heart, and puts before him what causes him to stumble into iniquity, and then comes to the prophet, I the LORD will answer him who comes, according to the multitude of his idols, 5that I may seize the house of Israel by their heart, because they are all estranged from Me by their idols." '

6"Therefore say to the house of Israel, 'Thus says the Lord GOD: "Repent, turn away from your idols, and turn your faces away from all your abominations. 7For anyone of the house of Israel, or of the strangers who dwell in Israel, who separates himself from Me and sets up his idols in his heart and puts before him what causes him to stumble into iniquity, then comes to a prophet to inquire of him concerning Me, I the LORD will answer him by Myself. 8I will set My face against that man and make him a sign and a proverb, and I will cut him off from the midst of My people. Then you shall know that I *am* the LORD.

9"And if the prophet is induced to speak anything, I the LORD have induced that prophet, and I will stretch out My hand against him and destroy him from among My people Israel. 10And they shall bear their iniquity; the punishment of the prophet shall be the same as the punishment of the one who inquired, 11that the house of Israel may no longer stray from Me, nor be profaned anymore with all their transgressions, but that they may be My people and I may be their God," says the Lord GOD.' "

HEBREWS 7:1-17

FOR this Melchizedek, king of Salem, priest of the Most High God, who met Abraham returning from the slaughter of the kings and blessed him, 2to whom also Abraham gave a tenth part of all, first being translated "king of righteousness," and then also king of Salem, meaning "king of peace," 3without father, without mother, without genealogy, having neither beginning of days nor end of life, but made like the Son of God, remains a priest continually.

4Now consider how great this man *was,* to whom even the patriarch Abraham gave a tenth of the spoils. 5And indeed those who are of the sons of Levi, who receive the priesthood, have a commandment to receive tithes from the people according to the law, that is, from their brethren, though they have come from the loins of Abraham; 6but he whose genealogy is not derived from them received tithes from Abraham and blessed him who had the promises. 7Now beyond all contradiction the lesser is blessed by the better. 8Here mortal men receive tithes, but there he *receives them,* of whom it is witnessed that he lives. 9Even Levi, who receives tithes, paid tithes through Abraham, so to speak, 10for he was still in the loins of his father when Melchizedek met him.

11Therefore, if perfection were through the Levitical priesthood (for under it the people received the law), what further need *was there* that another priest should rise according to the order of Melchizedek, and not be called according to the order of Aaron? 12For the priesthood being changed, of necessity there is also a change of the law. 13For He of whom these things are spoken belongs to another tribe, from which no man has officiated at the altar.

¹⁴For *it is* evident that our Lord arose from Judah, of which tribe Moses spoke nothing concerning priesthood.* ¹⁵And it is yet far more evident if, in the likeness of Melchizedek, there arises another priest ¹⁶who has come, not according to the law of a fleshly commandment, but according to the power of an endless life. ¹⁷For He testifies:*

> *"You are a priest forever
> According to the order of
> Melchizedek."* *

PSALM 105:37-45

H ᴇ also brought them out with silver and gold,
And *there was* none feeble among His tribes.
³⁸ Egypt was glad when they departed,
For the fear of them had fallen upon them.
³⁹ He spread a cloud for a covering,
And fire to give light in the night.
⁴⁰ *The people* asked, and He brought quail,
And satisfied them with the bread of heaven.
⁴¹ He opened the rock, and water gushed out;
It ran in the dry places *like* a river.

⁴² For He remembered His holy promise,
And Abraham His servant.
⁴³ He brought out His people with joy,
His chosen ones with gladness.
⁴⁴ He gave them the lands of the Gentiles,
And they inherited the labor of the nations,
⁴⁵ That they might observe His statutes
And keep His laws.

Praise the Lᴏʀᴅ!

PROVERBS FOR TODAY/ 27:3

A stone is *heavy and sand* is *weighty, but a fool's wrath* is *heavier than both of them.*

NOVEMBER 6

EZEKIEL 14:12–16:42

T ʜᴇ word of the Lᴏʀᴅ came again to me, saying: ¹³"Son of man, when a land sins against Me by persistent unfaithfulness, I will stretch out My hand against it; I will cut off its supply of bread, send famine on it, and cut off man and beast from it. ¹⁴Even *if* these three men, Noah, Daniel, and Job, were in it, they would deliver *only* themselves by their righteousness," says the Lord Gᴏᴅ.

¹⁵"If I cause wild beasts to pass through the land, and they empty it, and make it so desolate that no man may pass through because of the beasts, ¹⁶*even though* these three men *were* in it, *as* I live," says the Lord Gᴏᴅ, "they would deliver neither sons nor daughters; only they would be delivered, and the land would be desolate.

¹⁷"Or *if* I bring a sword on that land, and say, 'Sword, go through the land,' and I cut off man and beast from it, ¹⁸even *though* these three men *were* in it, *as* I live," says the Lord GOD, "they would deliver neither sons nor daughters, but only they themselves would be delivered.

¹⁹"Or *if* I send a pestilence into that land and pour out My fury on it in blood, and cut off from it man and beast, ²⁰even *though* Noah, Daniel, and Job *were* in it, *as* I live," says the Lord GOD, "they would deliver neither son nor daughter; they would deliver *only* themselves by their righteousness."

²¹For thus says the Lord GOD: "How much more it shall be when I send My four severe judgments on Jerusalem—the sword and famine and wild beasts and pestilence—to cut off man and beast from it? ²²Yet behold, there shall be left in it a remnant who will be brought out, *both* sons and daughters; surely they will come out to you, and you will see their ways and their doings. Then you will be comforted concerning the disaster that I have brought upon Jerusalem, all that I have brought upon it. ²³And they will comfort you, when you see their ways and their doings; and you shall know that I have done nothing without cause that I have done in it," says the Lord GOD.

THEN the word of the LORD came to me, saying: ²"Son of man, how is the wood of the vine *better* than any other wood, the vine branch which is among the trees of the forest? ³Is wood taken from it to make any object? Or can *men* make a peg from it to hang any vessel on? ⁴Instead, it is thrown into the fire for fuel; the fire devours both ends of it, and its middle is burned. Is it useful for *any* work? ⁵Indeed, when it was whole, no object could be made from it. How much less will it be useful for *any* work when the fire has devoured it, and it is burned?

⁶"Therefore thus says the Lord GOD: 'Like the wood of the vine among the trees of the forest, which I have given to the fire for fuel, so I will give up the inhabitants of Jerusalem; ⁷and I will set My face against them. They will go out from *one* fire, but *another* fire shall devour them. Then you shall know that I *am* the LORD, when I set My face against them. ⁸Thus I will make the land desolate, because they have persisted in unfaithfulness,' says the Lord GOD."

AGAIN the word of the LORD came to me, saying, ²"Son of man, cause Jerusalem to know her abominations, ³and say, 'Thus says the Lord GOD to Jerusalem: "Your birth and your nativity *are* from the land of Canaan; your father *was* an Amorite and your mother a Hittite. ⁴*As for* your nativity, on the day you were born your navel cord was not cut, nor were you washed in water to cleanse *you;* you were not rubbed with salt nor wrapped in swaddling cloths. ⁵No eye pitied you, to do any of these things for you, to have compassion on you; but you were thrown out into the open field, when you yourself were loathed on the day you were born.

⁶"And when I passed by you and saw you struggling in your own blood, I said to you in your blood, 'Live!' Yes, I said to you in your blood, 'Live!' ⁷I made you thrive like a plant in the field; and you grew, matured, and became very beautiful. *Your* breasts were formed, your hair grew, but you *were* naked and bare.

⁸"When I passed by you again and looked upon you, indeed your time *was* the time of love; so I spread My wing over you and covered your nakedness. Yes, I swore an oath to you and entered into a covenant with you, and you became Mine," says the Lord GOD.

⁹"Then I washed you in water; yes, I thoroughly washed off your blood, and I anointed you with oil. ¹⁰I clothed you in embroidered cloth and gave you sandals of badger skin; I clothed you with fine linen and covered you with silk. ¹¹I adorned you with ornaments, put bracelets on your wrists, and a chain on your neck. ¹²And I put a jewel in your nose, earrings in your ears, and a beautiful crown on your head. ¹³Thus you were adorned with gold and silver, and your clothing *was of* fine linen, silk, and embroidered cloth. You ate *pastry of* fine flour, honey, and oil. You were exceedingly beautiful, and succeeded to royalty. ¹⁴Your fame went out among the nations because of your beauty, for it *was* perfect through My splendor which I had bestowed on you," says the Lord GOD.

¹⁵"But you trusted in your own beauty, played the harlot because of your fame, and poured out your harlotry on everyone passing by who *would have* it. ¹⁶You took some of your garments and adorned multicolored high places for yourself, and played the harlot on them. *Such* things should not happen, nor be. ¹⁷You have also taken your beautiful jewelry from My gold and My silver, which I had given you, and made for yourself male images and played the harlot with them. ¹⁸You took your embroidered garments and covered them, and you set My oil and My incense before them. ¹⁹Also My food which I gave you—the pastry of fine flour, oil, and honey *which* I fed you—you set it before them as sweet incense; and *so* it was," says the Lord GOD.

²⁰"Moreover you took your sons and your daughters, whom you bore to Me, and these you sacrificed to them to be devoured. *Were* your *acts* of harlotry a small matter, ²¹that you have slain My children and offered them up to them by causing them to pass through *the fire?* ²²And in all your abominations and acts of harlotry you did not remember the days of your youth, when you were naked and bare, struggling in your blood.

²³"Then it was so, after all your wickedness—'Woe, woe to you!' says the Lord GOD— ²⁴*that* you also built for yourself a shrine, and made a high place for yourself in every street. ²⁵You built your high places at the head of every road, and made your beauty to be abhorred. You offered yourself to everyone who passed by, and multiplied your acts of harlotry. ²⁶You also committed harlotry with the Egyptians, your very fleshly neighbors, and increased your acts of harlotry to provoke Me to anger.

²⁷"Behold, therefore, I stretched out My hand against you, diminished your allotment, and gave you up to the will of those who hate you, the daughters of the Philistines, who were ashamed of your lewd behavior. ²⁸You also played the harlot with the Assyrians, because you were insatiable; indeed you played the harlot with them and still were not satisfied. ²⁹Moreover you multiplied your acts of harlotry as far as the land of the trader, Chaldea; and even then you were not satisfied.

³⁰"How degenerate is your heart!" says the Lord GOD, "seeing you do all these *things,* the deeds of a brazen harlot.

³¹"You erected your shrine at the head of every road, and built your high place in every street. Yet you were not like a harlot, because you scorned payment. ³²*You are* an adulterous wife, *who* takes strangers instead of her husband. ³³Men make payment to all harlots, but you made your payments to all your lovers, and hired them to come to you from all around for your harlotry. ³⁴You are the opposite of *other* women in your harlotry, because no one solicited you to be a harlot. In that you gave payment but no payment was

given you, therefore you are the opposite."

35"Now then, O harlot, hear the word of the LORD! 36Thus says the Lord GOD: "Because your filthiness was poured out and your nakedness uncovered in your harlotry with your lovers, and with all your abominable idols, and because of the blood of your children which you gave to them, 37surely, therefore, I will gather all your lovers with whom you took pleasure, all those you loved, *and* all those you hated; I will gather them from all around against you and will uncover your nakedness to them, that they may see all your nakedness. 38And I will judge you as women who break wedlock or shed blood are judged; I will bring blood upon you in fury and jealousy. 39I will also give you into their hand, and they shall throw down your shrines and break down your high places. They shall also strip you of your clothes, take your beautiful jewelry, and leave you naked and bare.

40"They shall also bring up an assembly against you, and they shall stone you with stones and thrust you through with their swords. 41They shall burn your houses with fire, and execute judgments on you in the sight of many women; and I will make you cease playing the harlot, and you shall no longer hire lovers. 42So I will lay to rest My fury toward you, and My jealousy shall depart from you. I will be quiet, and be angry no more."

HEBREWS 7:18-28

FOR on the one hand there is an annulling of the former commandment because of its weakness and unprofitableness, 19for the law made nothing perfect; on the other hand, *there is the* bringing in of a better hope, through which we draw near to God.

20And inasmuch as *He was* not *made*

priest without an oath 21(for they have become priests without an oath, but He with an oath by Him who said to Him:

> "The LORD has sworn
> And will not relent,
> 'You are a priest forever *
> According to the order of
> Melchizedek' "),*

22by so much more Jesus has become a surety of a better covenant.

23Also there were many priests, because they were prevented by death from continuing. 24But He, because He continues forever, has an unchangeable priesthood. 25Therefore He is also able to save to the uttermost those who come to God through Him, since He always lives to make intercession for them.

26For such a High Priest was fitting for us, *who is* holy, harmless, undefiled, separate from sinners, and has become higher than the heavens; 27who does not need daily, as those high priests, to offer up sacrifices, first for His own sins and then for the people's, for this He did once for all when He offered up Himself. 28For the law appoints as high priests men who have weakness, but the word of the oath, which came after the law, *appoints* the Son who has been perfected forever.

PSALM 106:1-12

PRAISE the LORD!

Oh, give thanks to the LORD,
for *He is* good!
For His mercy *endures* forever.

2   Who can utter the mighty acts
of the LORD?
Who can declare all His
praise?
3   Blessed *are* those who keep
justice,

And he who does*
righteousness at all times!

4 Remember me, O Lᴏʀᴅ, with
the favor *You have toward*
Your people.
Oh, visit me with Your
salvation,

5 That I may see the benefit of
Your chosen ones,
That I may rejoice in the
gladness of Your nation,
That I may glory with Your
inheritance.

6 We have sinned with our
fathers,
We have committed iniquity,
We have done wickedly.

7 Our fathers in Egypt did not
understand Your wonders;
They did not remember the
multitude of Your mercies,
But rebelled by the sea—the
Red Sea.

8 Nevertheless He saved them
for His name's sake,
That He might make His
mighty power known.

9 He rebuked the Red Sea also,
and it dried up;
So He led them through the
depths,
As through the wilderness.

10 He saved them from the hand
of him who hated *them,*
And redeemed them from the
hand of the enemy.

11 The waters covered their
enemies;
There was not one of them
left.

12 Then they believed His words;
They sang His praise.

PROVERBS FOR TODAY/ 27:4-6

Wrath is *cruel and anger a torrent, but who* is *able to stand before jealousy?*
◻ *Open rebuke* is *better than love carefully concealed. Faithful* are *the wounds of a friend, but the kisses of an enemy* are *deceitful.*

NOVEMBER 7

EZEKIEL 16:43–17:24

"**B**ᴇᴄᴀᴜsᴇ you did not remember the days of your youth, but agitated Me* with all these *things,* surely I will also recompense your deeds on *your own* head," says the Lord Gᴏᴅ. "And you shall not commit lewdness in addition to all your abominations.

44"Indeed everyone who quotes proverbs will use *this* proverb against you: 'Like mother, like daughter!' 45You *are* your mother's daughter, loathing husband and children; and you *are* the sister of your sisters, who loathed their husbands and children; your mother *was* a Hittite and your father an Amorite.

46"Your elder sister *is* Samaria, who dwells with her daughters to the north of you; and your younger sister, who dwells to the south of you, *is* Sodom and her daughters. 47You did not walk in their ways nor act according to their abominations; but, as *if that were* too little, you became more corrupt than they in all your ways.

48"*As* I live," says the Lord GOD, "neither your sister Sodom nor her daughters have done as you and your daughters have done. 49Look, this was the iniquity of your sister Sodom: She and her daughter had pride, fullness of food, and abundance of idleness; neither did she strengthen the hand of the poor and needy. 50And they were haughty and committed abomination before Me; therefore I took them away as I saw *fit.**

51"Samaria did not commit half of your sins; but you have multiplied your abominations more than they, and have justified your sisters by all the abominations which you have done. 52You who judged your sisters, bear your own shame also, because the sins which you committed were more abominable than theirs; they are more righteous than you. Yes, be disgraced also, and bear your own shame, because you justified your sisters.

53"When I bring back their captives, the captives of Sodom and her daughters, and the captives of Samaria and her daughters, then *I will also bring back* the captives of your captivity among them, 54that you may bear your own shame and be disgraced by all that you did when you comforted them. 55When your sisters, Sodom and her daughters, return to their former state, and Samaria and her daughters return to their former state, then you and your daughters will return to your former state. 56For your sister Sodom was not a byword in your mouth in the days of your pride, 57before your wickedness was uncovered. It was like the time of the reproach of the daughters of Syria* and all *those* around her, and of the daughters of the Philistines, who despise you everywhere. 58You have paid for your lewdness and your abominations," says the LORD. 59For thus says the Lord GOD: "I will deal with you as you have done, who despised the oath by breaking the covenant.

60"Nevertheless I will remember My covenant with you in the days of your youth, and I will establish an everlasting covenant with you. 61Then you will remember your ways and be ashamed, when you receive your older and your younger sisters; for I will give them to you for daughters, but not because of My covenant with you. 62And I will establish My covenant with you. Then you shall know that I *am* the LORD, 63that you may remember and be ashamed, and never open your mouth anymore because of your shame, when I provide you an atonement for all you have done," says the Lord GOD.' "

AND the word of the LORD came to me, saying, 2"Son of man, pose a riddle, and speak a parable to the house of Israel, 3and say, 'Thus says the Lord GOD:

"A great eagle with large wings
    and long pinions,
Full of feathers of various
    colors,
Came to Lebanon
And took from the cedar the
    highest branch.
4 He cropped off its topmost
    young twig
And carried it to a land of
    trade;
He set it in a city of
    merchants.
5 Then he took some of the
    seed of the land
And planted it in a fertile field;
He placed *it* by abundant
    waters
And set it like a willow tree.
6 And it grew and became a
    spreading vine of low
    stature;
Its branches turned toward
    him,
But its roots were under it.

So it became a vine,
Brought forth branches,
And put forth shoots.

7 "But there was another* great
eagle with large wings and
many feathers;
And behold, this vine bent its
roots toward him,
And stretched its branches
toward him,
From the garden terrace
where it had been planted,
That he might water it.
8 It was planted in good soil by
many waters,
To bring forth branches, bear
fruit,
And become a majestic vine." '

9 "Say, 'Thus says the Lord GOD:

"Will it thrive?
Will he not pull up its roots,
Cut off its fruit,
And leave it to wither?
All of its spring leaves will
wither,
And no great power or many
people
Will be needed to pluck it up
by its roots.
10 Behold, *it is* planted,
Will it thrive?
Will it not utterly wither when
the east wind touches it?
It will wither in the garden
terrace where it grew." ' "

11Moreover the word of the LORD
came to me, saying, 12"Say now to the
rebellious house: 'Do you not know
what these *things mean?*' Tell *them,* 'Indeed the king of Babylon went to Jerusalem and took its king and princes,
and led them with him to Babylon.
13And he took the king's offspring,
made a covenant with him, and put
him under oath. He also took away the
mighty of the land, 14that the kingdom
might be brought low and not lift itself
up, *but* that by keeping his covenant it
might stand. 15But he rebelled against
him by sending his ambassadors to
Egypt, that they might give him horses
and many people. Will he prosper?
Will he who does such *things* escape?
Can he break a covenant and still be
delivered?

16'*As* I live,' says the Lord GOD,
'surely in the place *where* the king
dwells who made him king, whose oath
he despised and whose covenant he
broke—with him in the midst of Babylon he shall die. 17Nor will Pharaoh
with *his* mighty army and great company do anything in the war, when they
heap up a siege mound and build a wall
to cut off many persons. 18Since he despised the oath by breaking the covenant, and in fact gave his hand and
still did all these *things,* he shall not
escape.' "

19Therefore thus says the Lord GOD:
"*As* I live, surely My oath which he
despised, and My covenant which he
broke, I will recompense on his own
head. 20I will spread My net over him,
and he shall be taken in My snare. I
will bring him to Babylon and try him
there for the treason which he committed against Me. 21All his fugitives*
with all his troops shall fall by the
sword, and those who remain shall be
scattered to every wind; and you shall
know that I, the LORD, have spoken."

22Thus says the Lord GOD: "I will
take also *one* of the highest branches
of the high cedar and set *it* out. I will
crop off from the topmost of its young
twigs a tender one, and will plant *it* on
a high and prominent mountain. 23On
the mountain height of Israel I will
plant it; and it will bring forth boughs,
and bear fruit, and be a majestic cedar.
Under it will dwell birds of every sort;
in the shadow of its branches they will
dwell. 24And all the trees of the field
shall know that I, the LORD, have
brought down the high tree and ex-

alted the low tree, dried up the green tree and made the dry tree flourish; I, the LORD, have spoken and have done it."

HEBREWS 8:1-13

Now *this is* the main point of the things we are saying: We have such a High Priest, who is seated at the right hand of the throne of the Majesty in the heavens, ²a Minister of the sanctuary and of the true tabernacle which the Lord erected, and not man.

³For every high priest is appointed to offer both gifts and sacrifices. Therefore *it is* necessary that this One also have something to offer. ⁴For if He were on earth, He would not be a priest, since there are priests who offer the gifts according to the law; ⁵who serve the copy and shadow of the heavenly things, as Moses was divinely instructed when he was about to make the tabernacle. For He said, *"See that you make all things according to the pattern shown you on the mountain."* * ⁶But now He has obtained a more excellent ministry, inasmuch as He is also Mediator of a better covenant, which was established on better promises.

⁷For if that first *covenant* had been faultless, then no place would have been sought for a second. ⁸Because finding fault with them, He says: *"Behold, the days are coming, says the LORD, when I will make a new covenant with the house of Israel and with the house of Judah—* ⁹ *not according to the covenant that I made with their fathers in the day when I took them by the hand to lead them out of the land of Egypt; because they did not continue in My covenant, and I disregarded them, says the LORD.* ¹⁰ *For this is the covenant that I will make with the house of Israel after those days, says the LORD: I will put My laws in their mind and write them on their hearts; and I will be their God, and they shall be My people.* ¹¹ *None of them shall teach his neighbor, and none his brother, saying, 'Know the LORD,' for all shall know Me, from the least of them to the greatest of them.* ¹² *For I will be merciful to their unrighteousness, and their sins and their lawless deeds * I will remember no more."* *

¹³In that He says, *"A new covenant, "* He has made the first obsolete. Now what is becoming obsolete and growing old is ready to vanish away.

PSALM 106:13-31

They soon forgot His works;
They did not wait for His counsel,
14 But lusted exceedingly in the wilderness,
And tested God in the desert.
15 And He gave them their request,
But sent leanness into their soul.

16 When they envied Moses in the camp,
And Aaron the saint of the LORD,
17 The earth opened up and swallowed Dathan,
And covered the faction of Abiram.
18 A fire was kindled in their company;
The flame burned up the wicked.

19 They made a calf in Horeb,
And worshiped the molded image.
20 Thus they changed their glory
Into the image of an ox that eats grass.
21 They forgot God their Savior,
Who had done great things in Egypt,

22 Wondrous works in the land
   of Ham,
   Awesome things by the Red
   Sea.
23 Therefore He said that He
   would destroy them,
   Had not Moses His chosen
   one stood before Him in
   the breach,
   To turn away His wrath, lest
   He destroy *them.*

24 Then they despised the
   pleasant land;
   They did not believe His word,
25 But complained in their tents,
   And did not heed the voice of
   the LORD.
26 Therefore He raised His hand
   in an oath against them,
   To overthrow them in the
   wilderness,

27 To overthrow their
   descendants among the
   nations,
   And to scatter them in the
   lands.

28 They joined themselves also
   to Baal of Peor,
   And ate sacrifices made to the
   dead.
29 Thus they provoked *Him* to
   anger with their deeds,
   And the plague broke out
   among them.
30 Then Phinehas stood up and
   intervened,
   And the plague was stopped.
31 And that was accounted to
   him for righteousness
   To all generations
   forevermore.

PROVERBS FOR TODAY/ 27:7-9

A satisfied soul loathes the honeycomb, but to a hungry soul every bitter thing is sweet. □ Like a bird that wanders from its nest is a man who wanders from his place. □ Ointment and perfume delight the heart, and the sweetness of a man's friend gives delight by hearty counsel.

NOVEMBER 8

EZEKIEL 18:1–19:14

THE word of the LORD came to me again, saying, 2"What do you mean when you use this proverb concerning the land of Israel, saying:

'The fathers have eaten sour
   grapes,
And the children's teeth are
   set on edge'?

3"*As* I live," says the Lord GOD, "you shall no longer use this proverb in Israel.

4 "Behold, all souls are Mine;
   The soul of the father
   As well as the soul of the son
      is Mine;
   The soul who sins shall die.
5 But if a man is just
   And does what is lawful and
      right;
6 If he has not eaten on the
      mountains,
   Nor lifted up his eyes to the
      idols of the house of Israel,
   Nor defiled his neighbor's
      wife,

Nor approached a woman
during her impurity;
7 If he has not oppressed
anyone,
But has restored to the debtor
his pledge;
Has robbed no one by
violence,
But has given his bread to the
hungry
And covered the naked with
clothing;
8 If he has not exacted usury
Nor taken any increase,
But has withdrawn his hand
from iniquity
And executed true judgment
between man and man;
9 *If* he has walked in My
statutes
And kept My judgments
faithfully—
He *is* just;
He shall surely live!"
Says the Lord GOD.

10 "If he begets a son *who is* a
robber
Or a shedder of blood,
Who does any of these *things*
11 And does none of those *duties,*
But has eaten on the
mountains
Or defiled his neighbor's wife;
12 If he has oppressed the poor
and needy,
Robbed by violence,
Not restored the pledge,
Lifted his eyes to the idols,
Or committed abomination;
13 If he has exacted usury
Or taken increase—
Shall he then live?
He shall not live!
If he has done any of these
abominations,
He shall surely die;
His blood shall be upon him.

14 "*If,* however, he begets a son

Who sees all the sins which
his father has done,
And considers but does not
do likewise;
15 *Who* has not eaten on the
mountains,
Nor lifted his eyes to the idols
of the house of Israel,
Nor defiled his neighbor's
wife;
16 Has not oppressed anyone,
Nor withheld a pledge,
Nor robbed by violence,
But has given his bread to the
hungry
And covered the naked with
clothing;
17 *Who* has withdrawn his hand
from the poor*
And not received usury or
increase,
But has executed My
judgments
And walked in My statutes—
He shall not die for the
iniquity of his father;
He shall surely live!

18 "*As for* his father,
Because he cruelly oppressed,
Robbed his brother by
violence,
And did what *is* not good
among his people,
Behold, he shall die for his
iniquity.

19"Yet you say, 'Why should the son
not bear the guilt of the father?' Because the son has done what is lawful
and right, and has kept all My statutes
and observed them, he shall surely
live. 20The soul who sins shall die. The
son shall not bear the guilt of the
father, nor the father bear the guilt of
the son. The righteousness of the righteous shall be upon himself, and the
wickedness of the wicked shall be
upon himself.
21"But if a wicked man turns from all

his sins which he has committed, keeps all My statutes, and does what is lawful and right, he shall surely live; he shall not die. ²²None of the transgressions which he has committed shall be remembered against him; because of the righteousness which he has done, he shall live. ²³Do I have any pleasure at all that the wicked should die?" says the Lord GOD, "*and* not that he should turn from his ways and live?

²⁴"But when a righteous man turns away from his righteousness and commits iniquity, and does according to all the abominations that the wicked *man* does, shall he live? All the righteousness which he has done shall not be remembered; because of the unfaithfulness of which he is guilty and the sin which he has committed, because of them he shall die.

²⁵"Yet you say, 'The way of the Lord is not fair.' Hear now, O house of Israel, is it not My way which is fair, and your ways which are not fair? ²⁶When a righteous *man* turns away from his righteousness, commits iniquity, and dies in it, it is because of the iniquity which he has done that he dies. ²⁷Again, when a wicked *man* turns away from the wickedness which he committed, and does what is lawful and right, he preserves himself alive. ²⁸Because he considers and turns away from all the transgressions which he committed, he shall surely live; he shall not die. ²⁹Yet the house of Israel says, 'The way of the Lord is not fair.' O house of Israel, is it not My ways which are fair, and your ways which are not fair?

³⁰"Therefore I will judge you, O house of Israel, every one according to his ways," says the Lord GOD. "Repent, and turn from all your transgressions, so that iniquity will not be your ruin. ³¹Cast away from you all the transgressions which you have committed, and get yourselves a new heart and a new spirit. For why should you die, O house of Israel? ³²For I have no pleasure in the death of one who dies," says the Lord GOD. "Therefore turn and live!"

"MOREOVER take up a lamentation for the princes of Israel, ²and say:

> 'What *is* your mother? A
>   lioness:
> She lay down among the lions;
> Among the young lions she
>   nourished her cubs.
> 3   She brought up one of her
>   cubs,
> And he became a young lion;
> He learned to catch prey,
> And he devoured men.
> 4   The nations also heard of him;
> He was trapped in their pit,
> And they brought him with
>   chains to the land of Egypt.
>
> 5   'When she saw that she
>   waited, *that* her hope was
>   lost,
> She took another of her cubs
>   *and* made him a young lion.
> 6   He roved among the lions,
> And became a young lion;
> He learned to catch prey;
> He devoured men.
> 7   He knew their desolate
>   places,*
> And laid waste their cities;
> The land with its fullness was
>   desolated
> By the noise of his roaring.
> 8   Then the nations set against
>   him from the provinces on
>   every side,
> And spread their net over him;
> He was trapped in their pit.
> 9   They put him in a cage with
>   chains,
> And brought him to the king
>   of Babylon;
> They brought him in nets,
> That his voice should no

longer be heard on the mountains of Israel.

10 'Your mother *was* like a vine in your bloodline,*
Planted by the waters,
Fruitful and full of branches
Because of many waters.
11 She had strong branches for scepters of rulers.
She towered in stature above the thick branches,
And was seen in her height amid the dense foliage.
12 But she was plucked up in fury,
She was cast down to the ground,
And the east wind dried her fruit.
Her strong branches were broken and withered;
The fire consumed them.
13 And now she *is* planted in the wilderness,
In a dry and thirsty land.
14 Fire has come out from a rod of her branches
And devoured her fruit,
So that she has no strong branch— a scepter for ruling.' "

This *is* a lamentation, and has become a lamentation.

HEBREWS 9:1-10

THEN indeed, even the first *covenant* had ordinances of divine service and the earthly sanctuary. ²For a tabernacle was prepared: the first *part,* in which *was* the lampstand, the table, and the showbread, which is called the sanctuary; ³and behind the second veil, the part of the tabernacle which is called the Holiest of All, ⁴which had the golden censer and the ark of the covenant overlaid on all sides with gold, in which *were* the golden pot that had the manna, Aaron's rod that budded, and the tablets of the covenant; ⁵and above it were the cherubim of glory overshadowing the mercy seat. Of these things we cannot now speak in detail.

⁶Now when these things had been thus prepared, the priests always went into the first part of the tabernacle, performing *the services.* ⁷But into the second part the high priest *went* alone once a year, not without blood, which he offered for himself and *for* the people's sins *committed* in ignorance; ⁸the Holy Spirit indicating this, that the way into the Holiest of All was not yet made manifest while the first tabernacle was still standing. ⁹It *was* symbolic for the present time in which both gifts and sacrifices are offered which cannot make him who performed the service perfect in regard to the conscience— ¹⁰*concerned* only with foods and drinks, various washings, and fleshly ordinances imposed until the time of reformation.

PSALM 106:32-48

THEY angered *Him* also at the waters of strife,*
So that it went ill with Moses on account of them;
33 Because they rebelled against His Spirit,
So that he spoke rashly with his lips.

34 They did not destroy the peoples,
Concerning whom the LORD had commanded them,
35 But they mingled with the Gentiles
And learned their works;
36 They served their idols,
Which became a snare to them.
37 They even sacrificed their sons

And their daughters to
   demons,
38 And shed innocent blood,
   The blood of their sons and
   daughters,
   Whom they sacrificed to the
   idols of Canaan;
   And the land was polluted
   with blood.
39 Thus they were defiled by
   their own works,
   And played the harlot by their
   own deeds.

40 Therefore the wrath of the
   LORD was kindled against
   His people,
   So that He abhorred His own
   inheritance
41 And He gave them into the
   hand of the Gentiles,
   And those who hated them
   ruled over them.
42 Their enemies also oppressed
   them,
   And they were brought into
   subjection under their hand.
43 Many times He delivered
   them;
   But they rebelled in their
   counsel,

And were brought low for
   their iniquity.
44 Nevertheless He regarded
   their affliction,
   When He heard their cry;
45 And for their sake He
   remembered His covenant,
   And relented according to the
   multitude of His mercies.
46 He also made them to be
   pitied
   By all those who carried them
   away captive.

47 Save us, O LORD our God,
   And gather us from among
   the Gentiles,
   To give thanks to Your holy
   name,
   To triumph in Your praise.

48 Blessed *be* the LORD God of
   Israel
   From everlasting to
   everlasting!
   And let all the people say,
   "Amen!"

   Praise the LORD!

PROVERBS FOR TODAY/ 27:10

*Do not forsake your own friend or your father's friend, nor go to your brother's house
in the day of your calamity; better* is *a neighbor nearby than a brother far away.*

NOVEMBER 9

EZEKIEL 20:1-49

IT came to pass in the seventh year, in the fifth *month,* on the tenth *day* of the month, *that* certain of the elders of Israel came to inquire of the LORD, and sat before me. ²Then the word of the LORD came to me, saying, ³"Son of man, speak to the elders of Israel, and say to them, 'Thus says the Lord GOD: "Have you come to inquire of Me? *As* I live," says the Lord GOD, "I will not be inquired of by you." ' ⁴Will you judge them, son of man, will you judge *them?* Then make known to them the abominations of their fathers.

5"Say to them, 'Thus says the Lord God: "On the day when I chose Israel and raised My hand in an oath to the descendants of the house of Jacob, and made Myself known to them in the land of Egypt, I raised My hand in an oath to them, saying, 'I *am* the Lord your God.' 6On that day I raised My hand in an oath to them, to bring them out of the land of Egypt into a land that I had searched out for them, 'flowing with milk and honey,'* the glory of all lands. 7Then I said to them, 'Each of you, throw away the abominations which are before his eyes, and do not defile yourselves with the idols of Egypt. I *am* the Lord your God.' 8But they rebelled against Me and would not obey Me. They did not all cast away the abominations which were before their eyes, nor did they forsake the idols of Egypt. Then I said, 'I will pour out My fury on them and fulfill My anger against them in the midst of the land of Egypt.' 9But I acted for My name's sake, that it should not be profaned before the Gentiles among whom they *were,* in whose sight I had made Myself known to them, to bring them out of the land of Egypt.

10"Therefore I made them go out of the land of Egypt and brought them into the wilderness. 11And I gave them My statutes and showed them My judgments, 'which, *if* a man does, he shall live by them.'* 12Moreover I also gave them My Sabbaths, to be a sign between them and Me, that they might know that I *am* the Lord who sanctifies them. 13Yet the house of Israel rebelled against Me in the wilderness; they did not walk in My statutes; they despised My judgments, 'which, *if* a man does, he shall live by them';* and they greatly defiled My Sabbaths. Then I said I would pour out My fury on them

in the wilderness, to consume them. 14But I acted for My name's sake, that it should not be profaned before the Gentiles, in whose sight I had brought them out. 15So I also raised My hand in an oath to them in the wilderness, that I would not bring them into the land which I had given *them,* 'flowing with milk and honey,'* the glory of all lands, 16because they despised My judgments and did not walk in My statutes, but profaned My Sabbaths; for their heart went after their idols. 17Nevertheless My eye spared them from destruction. I did not make an end of them in the wilderness.

18"But I said to their children in the wilderness, 'Do not walk in the statutes of your fathers, nor observe their judgments, nor defile yourselves with their idols. 19I *am* the Lord your God: Walk in My statutes, keep My judgments, and do them; 20hallow My Sabbaths, and they will be a sign between Me and you, that you may know that I *am* the Lord your God.'

21"Notwithstanding, the children rebelled against Me; they did not walk in My statutes, and were not careful to observe My judgments, 'which, *if* a man does, he shall live by them';* but they profaned My Sabbaths. Then I said I would pour out My fury on them and fulfill My anger against them in the wilderness. 22Nevertheless I withdrew My hand and acted for My name's sake, that it should not be profaned in the sight of the Gentiles, in whose sight I had brought them out. 23Also I raised My hand in an oath to those in the wilderness, that I would scatter them among the Gentiles and disperse them throughout the countries, 24because they had not executed My judgments, but had despised My statutes, profaned My Sabbaths, and their eyes were fixed on their fathers' idols.

25"Therefore I also gave them up to statutes *that were* not good, and judgments by which they could not live; 26and I pronounced them unclean because of their ritual gifts, in that they caused all their firstborn to pass through *the fire,* that I might make them desolate and that they might know that I am the LORD." '

27"Therefore, son of man, speak to the house of Israel, and say to them, 'Thus says the Lord GOD: "In this too your fathers have blasphemed Me, by being unfaithful to Me. 28When I brought them into the land *concerning* which I had raised My hand in an oath to give them, and they saw all the high hills and all the thick trees, there they offered their sacrifices and provoked Me with their offerings. There they also sent up their sweet aroma and poured out their drink offerings. 29Then I said to them, 'What *is* this high place to which you go?' So its name is called Bamah* to this day." '

30Therefore say to the house of Israel, 'Thus says the Lord GOD: "Are you defiling yourselves in the manner of your fathers, and committing harlotry according to their abominations? 31For when you offer your gifts and make your sons pass through the fire, you defile yourselves with all your idols, even to this day. So shall I be inquired of by you, O house of Israel? *As* I live," says the Lord GOD, "I will not be inquired of by you. 32What you have in your mind shall never be, when you say, 'We will be like the Gentiles, like the families in other countries, serving wood and stone.'

33"*As* I live," says the Lord GOD, "surely with a mighty hand, with an outstretched arm, and with fury poured out, I will rule over you. 34I will bring you out from the peoples and gather you out of the countries where you are scattered, with a mighty hand, with an outstretched arm, and with fury poured out. 35And I will bring you into the wilderness of the peoples, and there I will plead My case with you

face to face. 36Just as I pleaded My case with your fathers in the wilderness of the land of Egypt, so I will plead My case with you," says the Lord GOD.

37"I will make you pass under the rod, and I will bring you into the bond of the covenant; 38I will purge the rebels from among you, and those who transgress against Me; I will bring them out of the country where they dwell, but they shall not enter the land of Israel. Then you will know that I *am* the LORD.

39"As for you, O house of Israel," thus says the Lord GOD: "Go, serve every one of you his idols—and hereafter—if you will not obey Me; but profane My holy name no more with your gifts and your idols. 40For on My holy mountain, on the mountain height of Israel," says the Lord GOD, "there all the house of Israel, all of them in the land, shall serve Me; there I will accept them, and there I will require your offerings and the firstfruits of your sacrifices, together with all your holy things. 41I will accept you as a sweet aroma when I bring you out from the peoples and gather you out of the countries where you have been scattered; and I will be hallowed in you before the Gentiles. 42Then you shall know that I *am* the LORD, when I bring you into the land of Israel, into the country *for* which I raised My hand in an oath to give to your fathers. 43And there you shall remember your ways and all your doings with which you were defiled; and you shall loathe yourselves in your own sight because of all the evils that you have committed. 44Then you shall know that I *am* the LORD, when I have dealt with you for My name's sake, not according to your wicked ways nor according to your corrupt doings, O house of Israel," says the Lord GOD.' "

45Furthermore the word of the LORD came to me, saying, 46"Son of man, set your face toward the south; preach against the south and prophesy against the forest land, the South,* ⁴⁷and say to the forest of the South, 'Hear the word of the Lord! Thus says the Lord God: "Behold, I will kindle a fire in you, and it shall devour every green tree and every dry tree in you; the blazing flame shall not be quenched, and all faces from the south to the north shall be scorched by it. ⁴⁸All flesh shall see that I, the Lord, have kindled it; it shall not be quenched." ' "

⁴⁹Then I said, "Ah, Lord God! They say of me, 'Does he not speak parables?' "

HEBREWS 9:11-28

Bᴜᴛ Christ came *as* High Priest of the good things to come,* with the greater and more perfect tabernacle not made with hands, that is, not of this creation. ¹²Not with the blood of goats and calves, but with His own blood He entered the Most Holy Place once for all, having obtained eternal redemption. ¹³For if the blood of bulls and goats and the ashes of a heifer, sprinkling the unclean, sanctifies for the purifying of the flesh, ¹⁴how much more shall the blood of Christ, who through the eternal Spirit offered Himself without spot to God, cleanse your conscience from dead works to serve the living God? ¹⁵And for this reason He is the Mediator of the new covenant, by means of death, for the redemption of the transgressions under the first covenant, that those who are called may receive the promise of the eternal inheritance.

¹⁶For where there *is* a testament, there must also of necessity be the death of the testator. ¹⁷For a testament *is* in force after men are dead, since it has no power at all while the testator lives. ¹⁸Therefore not even the first *covenant* was dedicated without blood. ¹⁹For when Moses had spoken every precept to all the people according to the law, he took the blood of calves and goats, with water, scarlet wool, and hyssop, and sprinkled both the book itself and all the people, ²⁰saying, *"This is the blood of the covenant which God has commanded you."* * ²¹Then likewise he sprinkled with blood both the tabernacle and all the vessels of the ministry. ²²And according to the law almost all things are purified with blood, and without shedding of blood there is no remission.

²³Therefore *it was* necessary that the copies of the things in the heavens should be purified with these, but the heavenly things themselves with better sacrifices than these. ²⁴For Christ has not entered the holy places made with hands, *which are* copies of the true, but into heaven itself, now to appear in the presence of God for us; ²⁵not that He should offer Himself often, as the high priest enters the Most Holy Place every year with blood of another— ²⁶He then would have had to suffer often since the foundation of the world; but now, once at the end of the ages, He has appeared to put away sin by the sacrifice of Himself. ²⁷And as it is appointed for men to die once, but after this the judgment, ²⁸so Christ was offered once to bear the sins of many. To those who eagerly wait for Him He will appear a second time, apart from sin, for salvation.

PSALM 107:1-43

Oʜ, give thanks to the Lord, for *He is* good! For His mercy *endures* forever. 2 Let the redeemed of the Lord say *so,* Whom He has redeemed from the hand of the enemy, 3 And gathered out of the lands, From the east and from the west,

From the north and from the south.

4 They wandered in the wilderness in a desolate way;
They found no city to dwell in.
5 Hungry and thirsty,
Their soul fainted in them.
6 Then they cried out to the LORD in their trouble,
And He delivered them out of their distresses.
7 And He led them forth by the right way,
That they might go to a city for a dwelling place.
8 Oh, that *men* would give thanks to the LORD *for* His goodness,
And *for* His wonderful works to the children of men!
9 For He satisfies the longing soul,
And fills the hungry soul with goodness.

10 Those who sat in darkness and in the shadow of death,
Bound in affliction and irons—
11 Because they rebelled against the words of God,
And despised the counsel of the Most High,
12 Therefore He brought down their heart with labor;
They fell down, and *there was* none to help.
13 Then they cried out to the LORD in their trouble,
And He saved them out of their distresses.
14 He brought them out of darkness and the shadow of death,
And broke their chains in pieces.
15 Oh, that *men* would give thanks to the LORD *for* His goodness,

And *for* His wonderful works to the children of men!
16 For He has broken the gates of bronze,
And cut the bars of iron in two.

17 Fools, because of their transgression,
And because of their iniquities, were afflicted.
18 Their soul abhorred all manner of food,
And they drew near to the gates of death.
19 Then they cried out to the LORD in their trouble,
And He saved them out of their distresses.
20 He sent His word and healed them,
And delivered *them* from their destructions.
21 Oh, that *men* would give thanks to the LORD *for* His goodness,
And *for* His wonderful works to the children of men!
22 Let them sacrifice the sacrifices of thanksgiving,
And declare His works with rejoicing.

23 Those who go down to the sea in ships,
Who do business on great waters,
24 They see the works of the LORD,
And His wonders in the deep.
25 For He commands and raises the stormy wind,
Which lifts up the waves of the sea.
26 They mount up to the heavens,
They go down again to the depths;
Their soul melts because of trouble.

27 They reel to and fro, and
 stagger like a drunken man,
 And are at their wits' end.
28 Then they cry out to the LORD
 in their trouble,
 And He brings them out of
 their distresses.
29 He calms the storm,
 So that its waves are still.
30 Then they are glad because
 they are quiet;
 So He guides them to their
 desired haven.
31 Oh, that *men* would give
 thanks to the LORD *for* His
 goodness,
 And *for* His wonderful works
 to the children of men!
32 Let them exalt Him also in the
 assembly of the people,
 And praise Him in the
 company of the elders.

33 He turns rivers into a
 wilderness,
 And the watersprings into dry
 ground;
34 A fruitful land into barrenness,
 For the wickedness of those
 who dwell in it.
35 He turns a wilderness into
 pools of water,
 And dry land into
 watersprings.

36 There He makes the hungry
 dwell,
 That they may establish a city
 for a dwelling place,
37 And sow fields and plant
 vineyards,
 That they may yield a fruitful
 harvest.
38 He also blesses them, and
 they multiply greatly;
 And He does not let their
 cattle decrease.

39 When they are diminished
 and brought low
 Through oppression,
 affliction and sorrow,
40 He pours contempt on princes,
 And causes them to wander in
 the wilderness *where there
 is* no way;
41 Yet He sets the poor on high,
 far from affliction,
 And makes *their* families like
 a flock.
42 The righteous see *it* and
 rejoice,
 And all iniquity stops its
 mouth.

43 Whoever *is* wise will observe
 these *things,*
 And they will understand the
 lovingkindness of the LORD.

PROVERBS FOR TODAY/ 27:11

My son, be wise, and make my heart glad, that I may answer him who reproaches me.

NOVEMBER 10

EZEKIEL 21:1–22:31

AND the word of the LORD came to me, saying, [2]"Son of man, set your face toward Jerusalem, preach against the holy places, and prophesy against the land of Israel; [3]and say to the land of Israel, 'Thus says the LORD: "Behold, I *am* against you, and I will draw My sword out of its sheath and cut off both righteous and wicked from you. [4]Because I will cut off both righteous and wicked from you, therefore My sword shall go out of its sheath against all flesh from south *to* north, [5]that all flesh may know that I, the LORD, have drawn My sword out of its sheath; it shall not return anymore." ' [6]Sigh therefore, son of man, with a breaking heart, and sigh with bitterness before their eyes. [7]And it shall be when they say to you, 'Why are you sighing?' that you shall answer, 'Because of the news; when it comes, every heart will melt, all hands will be feeble, every spirit will faint, and all knees will be weak *as* water. Behold, it is coming and shall be brought to pass,' says the Lord GOD."

[8]Again the word of the LORD came to me, saying, [9]"Son of man, prophesy and say, 'Thus says the LORD!' Say:

'A sword, a sword is sharpened
  And also polished!
[10] Sharpened to make a dreadful
  slaughter,
  Polished to flash like
  lightning!
  Should we then make mirth?
  It despises the scepter of My
  son,
  As it does all wood.
[11] And He has given it to be
  polished,
  That it may be handled;

This sword is sharpened, and
  it is polished
To be given into the hand of
  the slayer.'

[12] "Cry and wail, son of man;
  For it will be against My
  people,
  Against all the princes of
  Israel.
  Terrors including the sword
  will be against My people;
  Therefore strike *your* thigh.

[13] "Because *it is* a testing,
  And what if *the sword* despises
  even the scepter?
  The scepter shall be no *more*,"

says the Lord GOD.

[14] "You therefore, son of man,
  prophesy,
  And strike *your* hands
  together.
  The third time let the sword
  do double *damage*.
  It *is* the sword *that* slays,
  The sword that slays the great
  men,
  That enters their private
  chambers.
[15] I have set the point of the
  sword against all their
  gates,
  That the heart may melt and
  many may stumble.
  Ah! *It is* made bright;
  It is grasped for slaughter:

[16] "Swords at the ready!
  Thrust right!
  Set your blade!
  Thrust left—

Wherever your edge is
ordered!

17   "I also will beat My fists
together,
And I will cause My fury to
rest;
I, the Lord, have spoken."

18The word of the Lord came to me
again, saying: 19"And son of man, appoint for yourself two ways for the
sword of the king of Babylon to go;
both of them shall go from the same
land. Make a sign; put *it* at the head of
the road to the city. 20Appoint a road for
the sword to go to Rabbah of the Ammonites, and to Judah, into fortified
Jerusalem. 21For the king of Babylon
stands at the parting of the road, at the
fork of the two roads, to use divination:
he shakes the arrows, he consults the
images, he looks at the liver. 22In his
right hand is the divination for Jerusalem: to set up battering rams, to call
for a slaughter, to lift the voice with
shouting, to set battering rams against
the gates, to heap up a *siege* mound,
and to build a wall. 23And it will be to
them like a false divination in the eyes
of those who have sworn oaths with
them; but he will bring their iniquity to
remembrance, that they may be taken.
24"Therefore thus says the Lord
God: 'Because you have made your iniquity to be remembered, in that your
transgressions are uncovered, so that
in all your doings your sins appear—
because you have come to remembrance, you shall be taken in hand.
25'Now to you, O profane, wicked
prince of Israel, whose day has come,
whose iniquity *shall* end, 26thus says
the Lord God:

"Remove the turban, and take
off the crown;
Nothing *shall remain* the
same.

Exalt the humble, and humble
the exalted.
27   Overthrown, overthrown,
I will make it overthrown!
It shall be no *longer,*
Until He comes whose right it
is,
And I will give it *to Him."*'

28"And you, son of man, prophesy
and say, 'Thus says the Lord God concerning the Ammonites and concerning their reproach,' and say:

'A sword, a sword *is* drawn,
Polished for slaughter,
For consuming, for flashing—
29   While they see false visions
for you,
While they divine a lie to you,
To bring you on the necks of
the wicked, the slain
Whose day has come,
Whose iniquity *shall* end.

30   'Return *it* to its sheath.
I will judge you
In the place where you were
created,
In the land of your nativity.
31   I will pour out My indignation
on you;
I will blow against you with
the fire of My wrath,
And deliver you into the
hands of brutal men *who
are* skillful to destroy.
32   You shall be fuel for the fire;
Your blood shall be in the
midst of the land.
You shall not be remembered,
For I the Lord have spoken.' "

Moreover the word of the Lord came to
me, saying, 2"Now, son of man, will you
judge, will you judge the bloody city?
Yes, show her all her abominations!
3Then say, 'Thus says the Lord God:
"The city sheds blood in her own
midst, that her time may come; and

she makes idols within herself to defile herself. ⁴You have become guilty by the blood which you have shed, and have defiled yourself with the idols which you have made. You have caused your days to draw near, and have come to *the end of* your years; therefore I have made you a reproach to the nations, and a mockery to all countries. ⁵*Those* near and *those* far from you will mock you as infamous *and* full of tumult.

⁶"Look, the princes of Israel: each one has used his power to shed blood in you. ⁷In you they have made light of father and mother; in your midst they have oppressed the stranger; in you they have mistreated the fatherless and the widow. ⁸You have despised My holy things and profaned My Sabbaths. ⁹In you are men who slander to cause bloodshed; in you are those who eat on the mountains; in your midst they commit lewdness. ¹⁰In you men uncover their fathers' nakedness; in you they violate women who are set apart during their impurity. ¹¹One commits abomination with his neighbor's wife; another lewdly defiles his daughter-in-law; and another in you violates his sister, his father's daughter. ¹²In you they take bribes to shed blood; you take usury and increase; you have made profit from your neighbors by extortion, and have forgotten Me," says the Lord God.

¹³"Behold, therefore, I beat My fists at the dishonest profit which you have made, and at the bloodshed which has been in your midst. ¹⁴Can your heart endure, or can your hands remain strong, in the days when I shall deal with you? I, the Lord, have spoken, and will do *it.* ¹⁵I will scatter you among the nations, disperse you throughout the countries, and remove your filthiness completely from you. ¹⁶You shall defile yourself in the sight of the nations; then you shall know that I *am* the Lord." ' "

¹⁷The word of the Lord came to me, saying, ¹⁸"Son of man, the house of Israel has become dross to Me; they *are* all bronze, tin, iron, and lead, in the midst of a furnace; they have become dross from silver. ¹⁹Therefore thus says the Lord God: 'Because you have all become dross, therefore behold, I will gather you into the midst of Jerusalem. ²⁰*As men* gather silver, bronze, iron, lead, and tin into the midst of a furnace, to blow fire on it, to melt *it;* so I will gather *you* in My anger and in My fury, and I will leave *you there* and melt you. ²¹Yes, I will gather you and blow on you with the fire of My wrath, and you shall be melted in its midst. ²²As silver is melted in the midst of a furnace, so shall you be melted in its midst; then you shall know that I, the Lord, have poured out My fury on you.' "

²³And the word of the Lord came to me, saying, ²⁴"Son of man, say to her: 'You *are* a land that is not cleansed* or rained on in the day of indignation.' ²⁵The conspiracy of her prophets* in her midst is like a roaring lion tearing the prey; they have devoured people; they have taken treasure and precious things; they have made many widows in her midst. ²⁶Her priests have violated My law and profaned My holy things; they have not distinguished between the holy and unholy, nor have they made known *the difference* between the unclean and the clean; and they have hidden their eyes from My Sabbaths, so that I am profaned among them. ²⁷Her princes in her midst *are* like wolves tearing the prey, to shed blood, to destroy people, and to get dishonest gain. ²⁸Her prophets plastered them with untempered *mortar,* seeing false visions, and divining lies for them, saying, 'Thus says the Lord God,' when the Lord had not spoken. ²⁹The people of the land have used oppressions, committed robbery, and mistreated the poor and needy; and

they wrongfully oppress the stranger. ³⁰So I sought for a man among them who would make a wall, and stand in the gap before Me on behalf of the land, that I should not destroy it; but I found no one. ³¹Therefore I have poured out My indignation on them; I have consumed them with the fire of My wrath; and I have recompensed their deeds on their own heads," says the Lord GOD.

HEBREWS 10:1-18

FOR the law, having a shadow of the good things to come, *and* not the very image of the things, can never with these same sacrifices, which they offer continually year by year, make those who approach perfect. ²For then would they not have ceased to be offered? For the worshipers, once purified, would have had no more consciousness of sins. ³But in those *sacrifices there is* a reminder of sins every year. ⁴For *it is* not possible that the blood of bulls and goats could take away sins.

⁵Therefore, when He came into the world, He said:

> "Sacrifice and offering You did
>   not desire,
>   But a body You have prepared
>   for Me.
> 6   In burnt offerings and
>   sacrifices for sin
>   You had no pleasure.
> 7   Then I said, 'Behold, I have
>   come—
>   In the volume of the book it is
>   written of Me—
>   To do Your will, O God.' " *

⁸Previously saying, "Sacrifice and offering, burnt offerings, and offerings for sin You did not desire, nor had pleasure in them" (which are offered according to the law), ⁹then He said, "Behold, I have come to do Your will, O God." * He takes away the first that

He may establish the second. ¹⁰By that will we have been sanctified through the offering of the body of Jesus Christ once *for all.*

¹¹And every priest stands ministering daily and offering repeatedly the same sacrifices, which can never take away sins. ¹²But this Man, after He had offered one sacrifice for sins forever, sat down at the right hand of God, ¹³from that time waiting till His enemies are made His footstool. ¹⁴For by one offering He has perfected forever those who are being sanctified.

¹⁵But the Holy Spirit also witnesses to us; for after He had said before,

> 16 *"This is the covenant that I will make with them after those days, says the LORD: I will put My laws into their hearts, and in their minds I will write them,"* * ¹⁷*then He adds, "Their sins and their lawless deeds I will remember no more."* * ¹⁸Now where there is remission of these, *there is* no longer an offering for sin.

PSALM 108:1-13

A Song. A Psalm of David.

O GOD, my heart is steadfast;
    I will sing and give praise, even
    with my glory.
2   Awake, lute and harp!
    I will awaken the dawn.
3   I will praise You, O LORD,
        among the peoples,
    And I will sing praises to You
        among the nations.
4   For Your mercy *is* great above
        the heavens,
    And Your truth *reaches* to the
        clouds.

5   Be exalted, O God, above the
        heavens,
    And Your glory above all the
        earth;
6   That Your beloved may be
        delivered,

Save *with* Your right hand,
and hear me.

7 God has spoken in His
holiness:
"I will rejoice;
I will divide Shechem
And measure out the Valley of
Succoth.

8 Gilead *is* Mine; Manasseh *is*
Mine;
Ephraim also *is* the helmet for
My head;
Judah *is* My lawgiver.

9 Moab *is* My washpot;
Over Edom I will cast My
shoe;

Over Philistia I will triumph."

10 Who will bring me *into* the
strong city?
Who will lead me to Edom?

11 *Is it* not *You,* O God, *who* cast
us off?
And *You,* O God, *who* did not
go out with our armies?

12 Give us help from trouble,
For the help of man is useless.

13 Through God we will do
valiantly,
For *it is* He *who* shall tread
down our enemies.*

PROVERBS FOR TODAY / 27:12

A prudent man *foresees evil* and *hides himself; the simple pass on and are punished.*

NOVEMBER 11

EZEKIEL 23:1-49

THE word of the LORD came again
to me, saying:

2 "Son of man, there were two
women,
The daughters of one mother.

3 They committed harlotry in
Egypt,
They committed harlotry in
their youth;
Their breasts were there
embraced,
Their virgin bosom was there
pressed.

4 Their names: Oholah* the
elder and Oholibah* her
sister;
They were Mine,

And they bore sons and
daughters.
As for their names,
Samaria *is* Oholah, and
Jerusalem *is* Oholibah.

5 "Oholah played the harlot even
though she was Mine;
And she lusted for her lovers,
the neighboring Assyrians,

6 *Who were* clothed in purple,
Captains and rulers,
All of them desirable young
men,
Horsemen riding on horses.

7 Thus she committed her
harlotry with them,
All of them choice men of
Assyria;
And with all for whom she
lusted,

With all their idols, she
defiled herself.
8 She has never given up her
harlotry *brought* from
Egypt,
For in her youth they had lain
with her,
Pressed her virgin bosom,
And poured out their
immorality upon her.

9 "Therefore I have delivered her
Into the hand of her lovers,
Into the hand of the Assyrians,
For whom she lusted.
10 They uncovered her
nakedness,
Took away her sons and
daughters,
And slew her with the sword;
She became a byword among
women,
For they had executed
judgment on her.

11"Now although her sister Oholibah saw *this,* she became more corrupt in her lust than she, and in her
harlotry more corrupt than her sister's harlotry.

12 "She lusted for the
neighboring Assyrians,
Captains and rulers,
Clothed most gorgeously,
Horsemen riding on horses,
All of them desirable young
men.
13 Then I saw that she was
defiled;
Both *took* the same way.
14 But she increased her
harlotry;
She looked at men portrayed
on the wall,
Images of Chaldeans
portrayed in vermilion,
15 Girded with belts around their
waists,
Flowing turbans on their
heads,
All of them looking like
captains,
In the manner of the
Babylonians of Chaldea,
The land of their nativity.
16 As soon as her eyes saw them,
She lusted for them
And sent messengers to them
in Chaldea.

17 "Then the Babylonians came
to her, into the bed of love,
And they defiled her with
their immorality;
So she was defiled by them,
and alienated herself from
them.
18 She revealed her harlotry and
uncovered her nakedness.
Then I alienated Myself from
her,
As I had alienated Myself
from her sister.

19 "Yet she multiplied her harlotry
In calling to remembrance the
days of her youth,
When she had played the
harlot in the land of Egypt.
20 For she lusted for her
paramours,
Whose flesh *is like* the flesh of
donkeys,
And whose issue *is like* the
issue of horses.
21 Thus you called to
remembrance the lewdness
of your youth,
When the Egyptians pressed
your bosom
Because of your youthful
breasts.

22"Therefore, Oholibah, thus says
the Lord God:

'Behold, I will stir up your
lovers against you,

From whom you have
alienated yourself,
And I will bring them against
you from every side:

23 The Babylonians,
All the Chaldeans,
Pekod, Shoa, Koa,
All the Assyrians with them,
All of them desirable young
men,
Governors and rulers,
Captains and men of renown,
All of them riding on horses.

24 And they shall come against
you
With chariots, wagons, and
war-horses,
With a horde of people.
They shall array against you
Buckler, shield, and helmet all
around.

'I will delegate judgment to
them,
And they shall judge you
according to their
judgments.

25 I will set My jealousy against
you,
And they shall deal furiously
with you;
They shall remove your nose
and your ears,
And your remnant shall fall by
the sword;
They shall take your sons and
your daughters,
And your remnant shall be
devoured by fire.

26 They shall also strip you of
your clothes
And take away your beautiful
jewelry.

27 'Thus I will make you cease
your lewdness and your
harlotry
Brought from the land of
Egypt,

So that you will not lift your
eyes to them,
Nor remember Egypt
anymore.'

28"For thus says the Lord GOD:
'Surely I will deliver you into the hand
of those you hate, into the hand *of those*
from whom you alienated yourself.
29They will deal hatefully with you,
take away all you have worked for, and
leave you naked and bare. The nakedness of your harlotry shall be uncovered, both your lewdness and your
harlotry. 30I will do these *things* to you
because you have gone as a harlot after the Gentiles, because you have become defiled by their idols. 31You have
walked in the way of your sister; therefore I will put her cup in your hand.'

32"Thus says the Lord GOD:

'You shall drink of your sister's
cup,
The deep and wide one;
You shall be laughed to scorn
And held in derision;
It contains much.

33 You will be filled with
drunkenness and sorrow,
The cup of horror and
desolation,
The cup of your sister
Samaria.

34 You shall drink and drain it,
You shall break its shards,
And tear at your own breasts;
For I have spoken,'
Says the Lord GOD.

35"Therefore thus says the Lord
GOD:

'Because you have forgotten
Me and cast Me behind
your back,
Therefore you shall bear the
penalty
Of your lewdness and your
harlotry.' "

36The LORD also said to me: "Son of man, will you judge Oholah and Oholibah? Then declare to them their abominations. 37For they have committed adultery, and blood *is* on their hands. They have committed adultery with their idols, and even sacrificed their sons whom they bore to Me, passing them through *the fire,* to devour *them.* 38Moreover they have done this to Me: They have defiled My sanctuary on the same day and profaned My Sabbaths. 39For after they had slain their children for their idols, on the same day they came into My sanctuary to profane it; and indeed thus they have done in the midst of My house.

40"Furthermore you sent for men to come from afar, to whom a messenger *was* sent; and there they came. And you washed yourself for them, painted your eyes, and adorned yourself with ornaments. 41You sat on a stately couch, with a table prepared before it, on which you had set My incense and My oil. 42The sound of a carefree multitude *was* with her, and Sabeans *were* brought from the wilderness with men of the common sort, who put bracelets on their wrists and beautiful crowns on their heads. 43Then I said concerning *her who had grown* old in adulteries, 'Will they commit harlotry with her now, and she *with them?'* 44Yet they went in to her, as men go in to a woman who plays the harlot; thus they went in to Oholah and Oholibah, the lewd women. 45But righteous men will judge them after the manner of adulteresses, and after the manner of women who shed blood, because they *are* adulteresses, and blood *is* on their hands.

46"For thus says the Lord GOD: 'Bring up an assembly against them, give them up to trouble and plunder. 47The assembly shall stone them with stones and execute them with their swords; they shall slay their sons and their daughters, and burn their houses

with fire. 48Thus I will cause lewdness to cease from the land, that all women may be taught not to practice your lewdness. 49They shall repay you for your lewdness, and you shall pay for your idolatrous sins. Then you shall know that I *am* the Lord GOD.' "

HEBREWS 10:19-39

THEREFORE, brethren, having boldness to enter the Holiest by the blood of Jesus, 20by a new and living way which He consecrated for us, through the veil, that is, His flesh, 21and *having* a High Priest over the house of God, 22let us draw near with a true heart in full assurance of faith, having our hearts sprinkled from an evil conscience and our bodies washed with pure water. 23Let us hold fast the confession of *our* hope without wavering, for He who promised *is* faithful. 24And let us consider one another in order to stir up love and good works, 25not forsaking the assembling of ourselves together, as *is* the manner of some, but exhorting *one another,* and so much the more as you see the Day approaching.

26For if we sin willfully after we have received the knowledge of the truth, there no longer remains a sacrifice for sins, 27but a certain fearful expectation of judgment, and fiery indignation which will devour the adversaries. 28Anyone who has rejected Moses' law dies without mercy on the testimony of two or three witnesses. 29Of how much worse punishment, do you suppose, will he be thought worthy who has trampled the Son of God underfoot, counted the blood of the covenant by which he was sanctified a common thing, and insulted the Spirit of grace? 30For we know Him who said, *"Vengeance is Mine, I will repay,"* * says the Lord.* And again, *"The LORD will judge His people."* * 31It is a fearful thing to fall into the hands of the living God.

³²But recall the former days in which, after you were illuminated, you endured a great struggle with sufferings: ³³partly while you were made a spectacle both by reproaches and tribulations, and partly while you became companions of those who were so treated; ³⁴for you had compassion on me* in my chains, and joyfully accepted the plundering of your goods, knowing that you have a better and an enduring possession for yourselves in heaven.* ³⁵Therefore do not cast away your confidence, which has great reward. ³⁶For you have need of endurance, so that after you have done the will of God, you may receive the promise:

37   "*For yet a little while,*
    And He who is coming will*
     come and will not tarry.
38   *Now the* just shall live by*
    faith;
    But if anyone draws back,
    My soul has no pleasure in
    him." *

³⁹But we are not of those who draw back to perdition, but of those who believe to the saving of the soul.

PSALM 109:1-31

To the Chief Musician. A Psalm of David.

Do not keep silent,
  O God of my praise!
²For the mouth of the wicked
  and the mouth of the
  deceitful
Have opened against me;
They have spoken against me
  with a lying tongue.
3   They have also surrounded
    me with words of hatred,
  And fought against me
    without a cause.
4   In return for my love they are
    my accusers,
  But I *give myself to* prayer.

5   Thus they have rewarded me
    evil for good,
  And hatred for my love.

6   Set a wicked man over him,
  And let an accuser* stand at
    his right hand.
7   When he is judged, let him be
    found guilty,
  And let his prayer become sin.
8   Let his days be few,
  And let another take his office.
9   Let his children be fatherless,
  And his wife a widow.
10   Let his children continually be
    vagabonds, and beg;
  Let them seek *their bread**
    also from their desolate
    places.
11   Let the creditor seize all that
    he has,
  And let strangers plunder his
    labor.
12   Let there be none to extend
    mercy to him,
  Nor let there be any to favor
    his fatherless children.
13   Let his posterity be cut off,
  And in the generation
    following let their name be
    blotted out.
14   Let the iniquity of his fathers
    be remembered before the
    Lord,
  And let not the sin of his
    mother be blotted out.
15   Let them be continually
    before the Lord,
  That He may cut off the
    memory of them from the
    earth;
16   Because he did not remember
    to show mercy,
  But persecuted the poor and
    needy man,
  That he might even slay the
    broken in heart.
17   As he loved cursing, so let it
    come to him;

As he did not delight in
blessing, so let it be far
from him.

18 As he clothed himself with
cursing as with his garment,
So let it enter his body like
water,
And like oil into his bones.

19 Let it be to him like the
garment which covers him,
And for a belt with which he
girds himself continually.

20 *Let* this *be* the LORD'S reward to
my accusers,
And to those who speak evil
against my person.

21 But You, O GOD the Lord,
Deal with me for Your name's
sake;
Because Your mercy *is* good,
deliver me.

22 For I *am* poor and needy,
And my heart is wounded
within me.

23 I am gone like a shadow when
it lengthens;
I am shaken off like a locust.

24 My knees are weak through
fasting,

And my flesh is feeble from
lack of fatness.

25 I also have become a
reproach to them;
When they look at me, they
shake their heads.

26 Help me, O LORD my God!
Oh, save me according to
Your mercy,

27 That they may know that this
is Your hand—
That You, LORD, have done it!

28 Let them curse, but You bless;
When they arise, let them be
ashamed,
But let Your servant rejoice.

29 Let my accusers be clothed
with shame,
And let them cover
themselves with their own
disgrace as with a mantle.

30 I will greatly praise the LORD
with my mouth;
Yes, I will praise Him among
the multitude.

31 For He shall stand at the right
hand of the poor,
To save *him* from those who
condemn him.

PROVERBS FOR TODAY/ 27:13

Take the garment of him who is surety for a stranger, and hold it in pledge when
he is surety for a seductress.

NOVEMBER 12

EZEKIEL 24:1–26:21

AGAIN, in the ninth year, in the
tenth month, on the tenth *day*
of the month, the word of the
LORD came to me, saying, 2"Son of man,
write down the name of the day, this

very day—the king of Babylon started
his siege against Jerusalem this very
day. 3And utter a parable to the rebellious house, and say to them, 'Thus
says the Lord GOD:

"Put on a pot, set *it* on,
And also pour water into it.
4 Gather pieces *of meat* in it,
Every good piece,
The thigh and the shoulder.
Fill *it* with choice cuts;
5 Take the choice of the flock.
Also pile *fuel* bones under it,
Make it boil well,
And let the cuts simmer in it."

6 Therefore thus says the Lord GOD:

"Woe to the bloody city,
To the pot whose scum *is* in it,
And whose scum is not gone
from it!
Bring it out piece by piece,
On which no lot has fallen.
7 For her blood is in her midst;
She set it on top of a rock;
She did not pour it on the
ground,
To cover it with dust.
8 That it may raise up fury and
take vengeance,
I have set her blood on top of
a rock,
That it may not be covered."

9 Therefore thus says the Lord GOD:

"Woe to the bloody city!
I too will make the pyre great.
10 Heap on the wood,
Kindle the fire;
Cook the meat well,
Mix in the spices,
And let the cuts be burned up.

11 "Then set the pot empty on the
coals,
That it may become hot and
its bronze may burn,
That its filthiness may be
melted in it,
That its scum may be
consumed.
12 She has grown weary with
lies,

And her great scum has not
gone from her.
Let her scum *be* in the fire!
13 In your filthiness *is* lewdness.
Because I have cleansed you,
and you were not cleansed,
You will not be cleansed of
your filthiness anymore,
Till I have caused My fury to
rest upon you.
14 I, the LORD, have spoken *it;*
It shall come to pass, and I
will do *it;*
I will not hold back,
Nor will I spare,
Nor will I relent;
According to your ways
And according to your deeds
They* will judge you,"
Says the Lord GOD.' "

15 Also the word of the LORD came to me, saying, 16 "Son of man, behold, I take away from you the desire of your eyes with one stroke; yet you shall neither mourn nor weep, nor shall your tears run down. 17 Sigh in silence, make no mourning for the dead; bind your turban on your head, and put your sandals on your feet; do not cover *your* lips, and do not eat man's bread *of sorrow.*"

18 So I spoke to the people in the morning, and at evening my wife died; and the next morning I did as I was commanded.

19 And the people said to me, "Will you not tell us what these *things signify* to us, that you behave so?"

20 Then I answered them, "The word of the LORD came to me, saying, 21 'Speak to the house of Israel, "Thus says the Lord GOD: 'Behold, I will profane My sanctuary, your arrogant boast, the desire of your eyes, the delight of your soul; and your sons and daughters whom you left behind shall fall by the sword. 22 And you shall do as I have done; you shall not cover *your* lips nor eat man's bread *of sorrow.*

23Your turbans shall be on your heads and your sandals on your feet; you shall neither mourn nor weep, but you shall pine away in your iniquities and mourn with one another. 24Thus Ezekiel is a sign to you; according to all that he has done you shall do; and when this comes, you shall know that I *am* the Lord God.' "

25'And you, son of man—*will it* not *be* in the day when I take from them their stronghold, their joy and their glory, the desire of their eyes, and that on which they set their minds, their sons and their daughters: 26on that day one who escapes will come to you to let *you* hear *it* with *your* ears; 27on that day your mouth will be opened to him who has escaped; you shall speak and no longer be mute. Thus you will be a sign to them, and they shall know that I *am* the Lord.' "

The word of the Lord came to me, saying, 2"Son of man, set your face against the Ammonites, and prophesy against them. 3Say to the Ammonites, 'Hear the word of the Lord God! Thus says the Lord God: "Because you said, 'Aha!' against My sanctuary when it was profaned, and against the land of Israel when it was desolate, and against the house of Judah when they went into captivity, 4indeed, therefore, I will deliver you as a possession to the men of the East, and they shall set their encampments among you and make their dwellings among you; they shall eat your fruit, and they shall drink your milk. 5And I will make Rabbah a stable for camels and Ammon a resting place for flocks. Then you shall know that I *am* the Lord."

6'For thus says the Lord God: "Because you clapped *your* hands, stamped your feet, and rejoiced in heart with all your disdain for the land of Israel, 7indeed, therefore, I will stretch out My hand against you, and give you as plunder to the nations; I will cut you off from the peoples, and I will cause you to perish from the countries; I will destroy you, and you shall know that I *am* the Lord."

8'Thus says the Lord God: "Because Moab and Seir say, 'Look! The house of Judah *is* like all the nations,' 9therefore, behold, I will clear the territory of Moab of cities, of the cities on its frontier, the glory of the country, Beth Jeshimoth, Baal Meon, and Kirjathaim. 10To the men of the East I will give it as a possession, together with the Ammonites, that the Ammonites may not be remembered among the nations. 11And I will execute judgments upon Moab, and they shall know that I *am* the Lord."

12'Thus says the Lord God: "Because of what Edom did against the house of Judah by taking vengeance, and has greatly offended by avenging itself on them," 13therefore thus says the Lord God: "I will also stretch out My hand against Edom, cut off man and beast from it, and make it desolate from Teman; Dedan shall fall by the sword. 14I will lay My vengeance on Edom by the hand of My people Israel, that they may do in Edom according to My anger and according to My fury; and they shall know My vengeance," says the Lord God.

15'Thus says the Lord God: "Because the Philistines dealt vengefully and took vengeance with a spiteful heart, to destroy because of the old hatred," 16therefore thus says the Lord God: "I will stretch out My hand against the Philistines, and I will cut off the Cherethites and destroy the remnant of the seacoast. 17I will execute great vengeance on them with furious rebukes; and they shall know that I *am* the Lord, when I lay My vengeance upon them." ' "

And it came to pass in the eleventh year, on the first *day* of the month, *that* the word of the Lord came to me, saying, [2]"Son of man, because Tyre has said against Jerusalem, 'Aha! She is broken who *was* the gateway of the peoples; now she is turned over to me; I shall be filled; she is laid waste.'

[3]"Therefore thus says the Lord God: 'Behold, I *am* against you, O Tyre, and will cause many nations to come up against you, as the sea causes its waves to come up. [4]And they shall destroy the walls of Tyre and break down her towers; I will also scrape her dust from her, and make her like the top of a rock. [5]It shall be *a place for* spreading nets in the midst of the sea, for I have spoken,' says the Lord God; 'it shall become plunder for the nations. [6]Also her daughter *villages* which *are* in the fields shall be slain by the sword. Then they shall know that I am the Lord.'

[7]"For thus says the Lord God: 'Behold, I will bring against Tyre from the north Nebuchadnezzar* king of Babylon, king of kings, with horses, with chariots, and with horsemen, and an army with many people. [8]He will slay with the sword your daughter *villages* in the fields; he will heap up a siege mound against you, build a wall against you, and raise a defense against you. [9]He will direct his battering rams against your walls, and with his axes he will break down your towers. [10]Because of the abundance of his horses, their dust will cover you; your walls will shake at the noise of the horsemen, the wagons, and the chariots, when he enters your gates, as men enter a city that has been breached. [11]With the hooves of his horses he will trample all your streets; he will slay your people by the sword, and your strong pillars will fall to the ground. [12]They will plunder your riches and pillage your merchandise; they will break down your walls and destroy your pleasant houses; they will lay your stones, your timber, and your soil in the midst of the water. [13]I will put an end to the sound of your songs, and the sound of your harps shall be heard no more. [14]I will make you like the top of a rock; you shall be *a place for* spreading nets, and you shall never be rebuilt, for I the Lord have spoken,' says the Lord God.

[15]"Thus says the Lord God to Tyre: 'Will the coastlands not shake at the sound of your fall, when the wounded cry, when slaughter is made in the midst of you? [16]Then all the princes of the sea will come down from their thrones, lay aside their robes, and take off their embroidered garments; they will clothe themselves with trembling; they will sit on the ground, tremble *every* moment, and be astonished at you. [17]And they will take up a lamentation for you, and say to you:

"How you have perished,
  O one inhabited by seafaring
    men,
  O renowned city,
  Who was strong at sea,
  She and her inhabitants,
  Who caused their terror *to be*
    on all her inhabitants!
18 Now the coastlands tremble
    on the day of your fall;
  Yes, the coastlands by the sea
    are troubled at your
    departure." '

[19]"For thus says the Lord God: 'When I make you a desolate city, like cities that are not inhabited, when I bring the deep upon you, and great waters cover you, [20]then I will bring you down with those who descend into the Pit, to the people of old, and I will make you dwell in the lowest part of the earth, in places desolate from antiquity, with those who go down to the Pit, so that you may never be inhabited; and I shall establish glory in the land of the living. [21]I will make you a terror, and you *shall be* no *more;* though you are sought for, you will never be found again,' says the Lord God."

HEBREWS 11:1-16

Now faith is the substance of things hoped for, the evidence of things not seen. ²For by it the elders obtained a *good* testimony.

³By faith we understand that the worlds were framed by the word of God, so that the things which are seen were not made of things which are visible.

⁴By faith Abel offered to God a more excellent sacrifice than Cain, through which he obtained witness that he was righteous, God testifying of his gifts; and through it he being dead still speaks.

⁵By faith Enoch was taken away so that he did not see death, *"and was not found, because God had taken him";** for before he was taken he had this testimony, that he pleased God. ⁶But without faith *it is* impossible to please *Him,* for he who comes to God must believe that He is, and *that* He is a rewarder of those who diligently seek Him.

⁷By faith Noah, being divinely warned of things not yet seen, moved with godly fear, prepared an ark for the saving of his household, by which he condemned the world and became heir of the righteousness which is according to faith.

⁸By faith Abraham obeyed when he was called to go out to the place which he would receive as an inheritance. And he went out, not knowing where he was going. ⁹By faith he dwelt in the land of promise as *in* a foreign country, dwelling in tents with Isaac and Jacob, the heirs with him of the same promise; ¹⁰for he waited for the city which has foundations, whose builder and maker *is* God.

¹¹By faith Sarah herself also received strength to conceive seed, and she bore a child* when she was past the age, because she judged Him faithful who had promised. ¹²Therefore from one man, and him as good as dead, were born *as many* as the stars of the sky in multitude—innumerable as the sand which is by the seashore.

¹³These all died in faith, not having received the promises, but having seen them afar off were assured of them,* embraced *them* and confessed that they were strangers and pilgrims on the earth. ¹⁴For those who say such things declare plainly that they seek a homeland. ¹⁵And truly if they had called to mind that *country* from which they had come out, they would have had opportunity to return. ¹⁶But now they desire a better, that is, a heavenly *country.* Therefore God is not ashamed to be called their God, for He has prepared a city for them.

PSALM 110:1-7

A Psalm of David.

The Lord said to my Lord,
  "Sit at My right hand,
  Till I make Your enemies Your
    footstool."
2 The Lord shall send the rod of
    Your strength out of Zion.
  Rule in the midst of Your
    enemies!

3 Your people *shall be* volunteers
  In the day of Your power;
  In the beauties of holiness,
    from the womb of the
    morning,
  You have the dew of Your
    youth.
4 The Lord has sworn
  And will not relent,
  "You *are* a priest forever
  According to the order of
    Melchizedek."

5 The Lord *is* at Your right hand;
  He shall execute kings in the
    day of His wrath.
6 He shall judge among the
    nations,

He shall fill *the places* with
dead bodies,
He shall execute the heads of
many countries.

7 He shall drink of the brook by
the wayside;
Therefore He shall lift up the
head.

PROVERBS FOR TODAY / 27:14

*He who blesses his friend with a loud voice, rising early in the morning, it will be
counted a curse to him.*

NOVEMBER 13

EZEKIEL 27:1–28:26

THE word of the LORD came again to me, saying, [2]"Now, son of man, take up a lamentation for Tyre, [3]and say to Tyre, 'You who are situated at the entrance of the sea, merchant of the peoples on many coastlands, thus says the Lord GOD:

"O Tyre, you have said,
'I *am* perfect in beauty.'
4 Your borders *are* in the midst
of the seas.
Your builders have perfected
your beauty.
5 They made all *your* planks of
fir trees from Senir;
They took a cedar from
Lebanon to make you a
mast.
6 *Of* oaks from Bashan they
made your oars;
The company of Ashurites
have inlaid your planks
With ivory from the coasts of
Cyprus.*
7 Fine embroidered linen from
Egypt was what you spread
for your sail;
Blue and purple from the
coasts of Elishah was what
covered you.

8 "Inhabitants of Sidon and
Arvad were your oarsmen;
Your wise men, O Tyre, were
in you;
They became your pilots.
9 Elders of Gebal and its wise
men
Were in you to caulk your
seams;
All the ships of the sea
And their oarsmen were in
you
To market your merchandise.

10 "Those from Persia, Lydia,*
and Libya*
Were in your army as men of
war;
They hung shield and helmet
in you;
They gave splendor to you.
11 Men of Arvad with your army
were on your walls *all*
around,
And the men of Gammad
were in your towers;
They hung their shields on
your walls *all* around;
They made your beauty
perfect.

12"Tarshish *was* your merchant because of your many luxury goods.
They gave you silver, iron, tin, and lead

for your goods. ¹³Javan, Tubal, and Meshech *were* your traders. They bartered human lives and vessels of bronze for your merchandise. ¹⁴Those from the house of Togarmah traded for your wares with horses, steeds, and mules. ¹⁵The men of Dedan *were* your traders; many isles *were* the market of your hand. They brought you ivory tusks and ebony as payment. ¹⁶Syria *was* your merchant because of the abundance of goods you made. They gave you for your wares emeralds, purple, embroidery, fine linen, corals, and rubies. ¹⁷Judah and the land of Israel *were* your traders. They traded for your merchandise wheat of Minnith, millet, honey, oil, and balm. ¹⁸Damascus *was* your merchant because of the abundance of goods you made, because of your many luxury items, with the wine of Helbon and with white wool. ¹⁹Dan and Javan paid for your wares, traversing back and forth. Wrought iron, cassia, and cane were among your merchandise. ²⁰Dedan *was* your merchant in saddlecloths for riding. ²¹Arabia and all the princes of Kedar *were* your regular merchants. They traded with you in lambs, rams, and goats. ²²The merchants of Sheba and Raamah *were* your merchants. They traded for your wares the choicest spices, all kinds of precious stones, and gold. ²³Haran, Canneh, Eden, the merchants of Sheba, Assyria, *and* Chilmad *were* your merchants. ²⁴These *were* your merchants in choice items—in purple clothes, in embroidered garments, in chests of multicolored apparel, in sturdy woven cords, which were in your marketplace.

25 "The ships of Tarshish were
    carriers of your
    merchandise.
  You were filled and very
    glorious in the midst of the
    seas.

26 Your oarsmen brought you
    into many waters,
  But the east wind broke you
    in the midst of the seas.

27 "Your riches, wares, and
    merchandise,
  Your mariners and pilots,
  Your caulkers and
    merchandisers,
  All your men of war who *are*
    in you,
  And the entire company
    which *is* in your midst,
  Will fall into the midst of the
    seas on the day of your ruin.
28 The common-land will shake
    at the sound of the cry of
    your pilots.

29 "All who handle the oar,
  The mariners,
  All the pilots of the sea
  Will come down from their
    ships *and* stand on the
    shore.
30 They will make their voice
    heard because of you;
  They will cry bitterly and cast
    dust on their heads;
  They will roll about in ashes;
31 They will shave themselves
    completely bald because of
    you,
  Gird themselves with
    sackcloth,
  And weep for you
  With bitterness of heart *and*
    bitter wailing.
32 In their wailing for you
  They will take up a
    lamentation,
  And lament for you:
  'What *city is* like Tyre,
  Destroyed in the midst of the
    sea?

33 'When your wares went out by
    sea,
  You satisfied many people;

You enriched the kings of the earth
With your many luxury goods and your merchandise.
34 But you are broken by the seas in the depths of the waters;
Your merchandise and the entire company will fall in your midst.
35 All the inhabitants of the isles will be astonished at you;
Their kings will be greatly afraid,
And *their* countenance will be troubled.
36 The merchants among the peoples will hiss at you;
You will become a horror, and *be* no more forever.' " ' "

The word of the Lord came to me again, saying, 2"Son of man, say to the prince of Tyre, 'Thus says the Lord God:

"Because your heart *is* lifted up,
And you say, 'I *am* a god,
I sit *in* the seat of gods,
In the midst of the seas,'
Yet you *are* a man, and not a god,
Though you set your heart as the heart of a god
3 (Behold, you *are* wiser than Daniel!
There is no secret that can be hidden from you!
4 With your wisdom and your understanding
You have gained riches for yourself,
And gathered gold and silver into your treasuries;
5 By your great wisdom in trade you have increased your riches,
And your heart is lifted up because of your riches),"

6"Therefore thus says the Lord God:

"Because you have set your heart as the heart of a god,
7 Behold, therefore, I will bring strangers against you,
The most terrible of the nations;
And they shall draw their swords against the beauty of your wisdom,
And defile your splendor.
8 They shall throw you down into the Pit,
And you shall die the death of the slain
In the midst of the seas.
9 "Will you still say before him who slays you,
'I *am* a god'?
But you *shall be* a man, and not a god,
In the hand of him who slays you.
10 You shall die the death of the uncircumcised
By the hand of aliens;
For I have spoken," says the Lord God.' "

11Moreover the word of the Lord came to me, saying, 12"Son of man, take up a lamentation for the king of Tyre, and say to him, 'Thus says the Lord God:

"You *were* the seal of perfection,
Full of wisdom and perfect in beauty.
13 You were in Eden, the garden of God;
Every precious stone *was* your covering:
The sardius, topaz, and diamond,
Beryl, onyx, and jasper,
Sapphire, turquoise, and emerald with gold.

The workmanship of your
timbrels and pipes
Was prepared for you on the
day you were created.

14 "You *were* the anointed cherub
who covers;
I established you;
You were on the holy
mountain of God;
You walked back and forth in
the midst of fiery stones.

15 You *were* perfect in your ways
from the day you were
created,
Till iniquity was found in you.

16 "By the abundance of your
trading
You became filled with
violence within,
And you sinned;
Therefore I cast you as a
profane thing
Out of the mountain of God;
And I destroyed you,
O covering cherub,
From the midst of the fiery
stones.

17 "Your heart was lifted up
because of your beauty;
You corrupted your wisdom
for the sake of your
splendor;
I cast you to the ground,
I laid you before kings,
That they might gaze at you.

18 "You defiled your sanctuaries
By the multitude of your
iniquities,
By the iniquity of your trading;
Therefore I brought fire from
your midst;
It devoured you,
And I turned you to ashes
upon the earth
In the sight of all who saw you.

19 All who knew you among the
peoples are astonished at
you;
You have become a horror,
And *shall be* no more
forever." ' "

20Then the word of the LORD came to
me, saying, 21"Son of man, set your
face toward Sidon, and prophesy
against her, 22and say, 'Thus says the
Lord GOD:

"Behold, I *am* against you,
O Sidon;
I will be glorified in your
midst;
And they shall know that I *am*
the LORD,
When I execute judgments in
her and am hallowed in her.

23 For I will send pestilence
upon her,
And blood in her streets;
The wounded shall be judged
in her midst
By the sword against her on
every side;
Then they shall know that I
am the LORD.

24"And there shall no longer be a
pricking brier or a painful thorn for the
house of Israel from among all *who are*
around them, who despise them. Then
they shall know that I *am* the Lord
GOD."

25'Thus says the Lord GOD: "When I
have gathered the house of Israel from
the peoples among whom they are
scattered, and am hallowed in them in
the sight of the Gentiles, then they will
dwell in their own land which I gave to
My servant Jacob. 26And they will
dwell safely there, build houses, and
plant vineyards; yes, they will dwell securely, when I execute judgments on
all those around them who despise
them. Then they shall know that I *am*
the LORD their God." ' "

HEBREWS 11:17-31

BY faith Abraham, when he was tested, offered up Isaac, and he who had received the promises offered up his only begotten *son,* ¹⁸of whom it was said, *"In Isaac your seed shall be called,"* * ¹⁹concluding that God *was* able to raise *him* up, even from the dead, from which he also received him in a figurative sense.

²⁰By faith Isaac blessed Jacob and Esau concerning things to come.

²¹By faith Jacob, when he was dying, blessed each of the sons of Joseph, and worshiped, *leaning* on the top of his staff.

²²By faith Joseph, when he was dying, made mention of the departure of the children of Israel, and gave instructions concerning his bones.

²³By faith Moses, when he was born, was hidden three months by his parents, because they saw *he was* a beautiful child; and they were not afraid of the king's command.

²⁴By faith Moses, when he became of age, refused to be called the son of Pharaoh's daughter, ²⁵choosing rather to suffer affliction with the people of God than to enjoy the passing pleasures of sin, ²⁶esteeming the reproach of Christ greater riches than the treasures in* Egypt; for he looked to the reward.

²⁷By faith he forsook Egypt, not fearing the wrath of the king; for he endured as seeing Him who is invisible. ²⁸By faith he kept the Passover and the sprinkling of blood, lest he who destroyed the firstborn should touch them.

²⁹By faith they passed through the Red Sea as by dry *land, whereas* the Egyptians, attempting *to do* so, were drowned.

³⁰By faith the walls of Jericho fell down after they were encircled for seven days. ³¹By faith the harlot Rahab did not perish with those who did not believe, when she had received the spies with peace.

PSALM 111:1-10

PRAISE the LORD!

I will praise the LORD with *my* whole heart,
In the assembly of the upright and *in* the congregation.

2   The works of the LORD *are* great,
Studied by all who have pleasure in them.

3   His work *is* honorable and glorious,
And His righteousness endures forever.

4   He has made His wonderful works to be remembered;
The LORD *is* gracious and full of compassion.

5   He has given food to those who fear Him;
He will ever be mindful of His covenant.

6   He has declared to His people the power of His works,
In giving them the heritage of the nations.

7   The works of His hands *are* verity and justice;
All His precepts *are* sure.

8   They stand fast forever and ever,
And are done in truth and uprightness.

9   He has sent redemption to His people;
He has commanded His covenant forever:
Holy and awesome *is* His name.

10   The fear of the LORD *is* the beginning of wisdom;
A good understanding have all those who do *His commandments.*
His praise endures forever.

PROVERBS FOR TODAY/ 27:15-16

A continual dripping on a very rainy day and a contentious woman are alike;
whoever restrains her restrains the wind, and grasps oil with his right hand.

NOVEMBER 14

EZEKIEL 29:1–30:26

I N the tenth year, in the tenth *month,* on the twelfth *day* of the month, the word of the LORD came to me, saying, 2"Son of man, set your face against Pharaoh king of Egypt, and prophesy against him, and against all Egypt. 3Speak, and say, 'Thus says the Lord GOD:

"Behold, I *am* against you,
O Pharaoh king of Egypt,
O great monster who lies in
the midst of his rivers,
Who has said, 'My River* *is*
my own;
I have made *it* for myself.'
4   But I will put hooks in your
jaws,
And cause the fish of your
rivers to stick to your
scales;
I will bring you up out of the
midst of your rivers,
And all the fish in your rivers
will stick to your scales.
5   I will leave you in the
wilderness,
You and all the fish of your
rivers;
You shall fall on the open field;
You shall not be picked up or
gathered.*
I have given you as food
To the beasts of the field
And to the birds of the
heavens.

6   "Then all the inhabitants of
Egypt
Shall know that I *am* the LORD,
Because they have been a
staff of reed to the house of
Israel.
7   When they took hold of you
with the hand,
You broke and tore all their
shoulders;*
When they leaned on you,
You broke and made all their
backs quiver."

8"Therefore thus says the Lord GOD: "Surely I will bring a sword upon you and cut off from you man and beast. 9And the land of Egypt shall become desolate and waste; then they will know that I *am* the LORD, because he said, 'The River *is* mine, and I have made *it.*' 10Indeed, therefore, I *am* against you and against your rivers, and I will make the land of Egypt utterly waste and desolate, from Migdol* *to* Syene, as far as the border of Ethiopia. 11Neither foot of man shall pass through it nor foot of beast pass through it, and it shall be uninhabited forty years. 12I will make the land of Egypt desolate in the midst of the countries *that are* desolate; and among the cities *that are* laid waste, her cities shall be desolate forty years; and I will scatter the Egyptians among the nations and disperse them throughout the countries."

13"Yet, thus says the Lord GOD: "At the end of forty years I will gather the

Egyptians from the peoples among whom they were scattered. ¹⁴I will bring back the captives of Egypt and cause them to return to the land of Pathros, to the land of their origin, and there they shall be a lowly kingdom. ¹⁵It shall be the lowliest of kingdoms; it shall never again exalt itself above the nations, for I will diminish them so that they will not rule over the nations anymore. ¹⁶No longer shall it be the confidence of the house of Israel, but will remind them of *their* iniquity when they turned to follow them. Then they shall know that I *am* the Lord God." ' "

¹⁷And it came to pass in the twenty-seventh year, in the first *month,* on the first *day* of the month, *that* the word of the Lord came to me, saying, ¹⁸"Son of man, Nebuchadnezzar king of Babylon caused his army to labor strenuously against Tyre; every head *was* made bald, and every shoulder rubbed raw; yet neither he nor his army received wages from Tyre, for the labor which they expended on it. ¹⁹Therefore thus says the Lord God: 'Surely I will give the land of Egypt to Nebuchadnezzar king of Babylon; he shall take away her wealth, carry off her spoil, and remove her pillage; and that will be the wages for his army. ²⁰I have given him the land of Egypt *for* his labor, because they worked for Me,' says the Lord God. ²¹'In that day I will cause the horn of the house of Israel to spring forth, and I will open your mouth to speak in their midst. Then they shall know that I *am* the Lord.' "

The word of the Lord came to me again, saying, ²"Son of man, prophesy and say, 'Thus says the Lord God:

"Wail, 'Woe to the day!'
³   For the day *is* near,
        Even the day of the Lord *is*
            near;
        It will be a day of clouds, the
            time of the Gentiles.

⁴   The sword shall come upon
        Egypt,
        And great anguish shall be in
            Ethiopia,
        When the slain fall in Egypt,
        And they take away her
            wealth,
        And her foundations are
            broken down.

⁵"Ethiopia, Libya,* Lydia,* all the mingled people, Chub, and the men of the lands who are allied, shall fall with them by the sword."
⁶'Thus says the Lord:

    "Those who uphold Egypt
        shall fall,
        And the pride of her power
            shall come down
        From Migdol *to* Syene
        Those within her shall fall by
            the sword,"
        Says the Lord God.

⁷   "They shall be desolate in the
        midst of the desolate
        countries,
        And her cities shall be in the
            midst of the cities *that are*
            laid waste.
⁸   Then they will know that I *am*
        the Lord,
        When I have set a fire in Egypt
        And all her helpers are
            destroyed.
⁹   On that day messengers shall
        go forth from Me in ships
        To make the careless
            Ethiopians afraid,
        And great anguish shall come
            upon them,
        As on the day of Egypt;
        For indeed it is coming!"

¹⁰'Thus says the Lord God:

    "I will also make a multitude of
        Egypt to cease
        By the hand of

Nebuchadnezzar king of Babylon.
11 He and his people with him,
the most terrible of the nations,
Shall be brought to destroy the land;
They shall draw their swords against Egypt,
And fill the land with the slain.
12 I will make the rivers dry,
And sell the land into the hand of the wicked;
I will make the land waste, and all that is in it,
By the hand of aliens.
I, the LORD, have spoken."

13"Thus says the Lord GOD:

"I will also destroy the idols,
And cause the images to cease from Noph;*
There shall no longer be princes from the land of Egypt;
I will put fear in the land of Egypt.
14 I will make Pathros desolate,
Set fire to Zoan,
And execute judgments in No.*
15 I will pour My fury on Sin,*
the strength of Egypt;
I will cut off the multitude of No,
16 And set a fire in Egypt;
Sin shall have great pain,
No shall be split open,
And Noph *shall be in* distress daily.
17 The young men of Aven* and Pi Beseth shall fall by the sword,
And these *cities* shall go into captivity.
18 At Tehaphnehes* the day shall also be darkened,*
When I break the yokes of Egypt there.

And her arrogant strength shall cease in her;
As for her, a cloud shall cover her,
And her daughters shall go into captivity.
19 Thus I will execute judgments on Egypt,
Then they shall know that I *am* the LORD." ' "

20And it came to pass in the eleventh year, in the first *month,* on the seventh *day* of the month, *that* the word of the LORD came to me, saying, 21"Son of man, I have broken the arm of Pharaoh king of Egypt; and see, it has not been bandaged for healing, nor a splint put on to bind it, to make it strong enough to hold a sword. 22Therefore thus says the Lord GOD: 'Surely I *am* against Pharaoh king of Egypt, and will break his arms, both the strong one and the one that was broken; and I will make the sword fall out of his hand. 23I will scatter the Egyptians among the nations, and disperse them throughout the countries. 24I will strengthen the arms of the king of Babylon and put My sword in his hand; but I will break Pharaoh's arms, and he will groan before him with the groanings of a mortally wounded *man.* 25Thus I will strengthen the arms of the king of Babylon, but the arms of Pharaoh shall fall down; they shall know that I *am* the LORD, when I put My sword into the hand of the king of Babylon and he stretches it out against the land of Egypt. 26I will scatter the Egyptians among the nations and disperse them throughout the countries. Then they shall know that I *am* the LORD.' "

HEBREWS 11:32–12:13

AND what more shall I say? For the time would fail me to tell of Gideon and Barak and Samson and Jephthah, also *of* David and

Samuel and the prophets: 33who through faith subdued kingdoms, worked righteousness, obtained promises, stopped the mouths of lions, 34quenched the violence of fire, escaped the edge of the sword, out of weakness were made strong, became valiant in battle, turned to flight the armies of the aliens. 35Women received their dead raised to life again.

Others were tortured, not accepting deliverance, that they might obtain a better resurrection. 36Still others had trial of mockings and scourgings, yes, and of chains and imprisonment. 37They were stoned, they were sawn in two, were tempted,* were slain with the sword. They wandered about in sheepskins and goatskins, being destitute, afflicted, tormented— 38of whom the world was not worthy. They wandered in deserts and mountains, *in* dens and caves of the earth.

39And all these, having obtained a good testimony through faith, did not receive the promise, 40God having provided something better for us, that they should not be made perfect apart from us.

THEREFORE we also, since we are surrounded by so great a cloud of witnesses, let us lay aside every weight, and the sin which so easily ensnares *us,* and let us run with endurance the race that is set before us, 2looking unto Jesus, the author and finisher of *our* faith, who for the joy that was set before Him endured the cross, despising the shame, and has sat down at the right hand of the throne of God.

3For consider Him who endured such hostility from sinners against Himself, lest you become weary and discouraged in your souls. 4You have not yet resisted to bloodshed, striving against sin. 5And you have forgotten the exhortation which speaks to you as to sons:

"*My son, do not despise the chastening of the LORD,
Nor be discouraged when you are rebuked by Him;*
6 *For whom the LORD loves He chastens,
And scourges every son whom He receives.*" *

7If* you endure chastening, God deals with you as with sons; for what son is there whom a father does not chasten? 8But if you are without chastening, of which all have become partakers, then you are illegitimate and not sons. 9Furthermore, we have had human fathers who corrected *us,* and we paid *them* respect. Shall we not much more readily be in subjection to the Father of spirits and live? 10For they indeed for a few days chastened *us* as seemed *best* to them, but He for *our* profit, that *we* may be partakers of His holiness. 11Now no chastening seems to be joyful for the present, but painful; nevertheless, afterward it yields the peaceable fruit of righteousness to those who have been trained by it.

12Therefore strengthen the hands which hang down, and the feeble knees, 13and make straight paths for your feet, so that what is lame may not be *dislocated,* but rather be healed.

PSALM 112:1-10

P RAISE the LORD!

Blessed *is* the man *who* fears the LORD,
Who delights greatly in His commandments.

2 His descendants will be mighty on earth;
The generation of the upright will be blessed.

3 Wealth and riches *will be* in his house,

And his righteousness
endures forever.

4 Unto the upright there arises
light in the darkness;
He is gracious, and full of
compassion, and righteous.

5 A good man deals graciously
and lends;
He will guide his affairs with
discretion.

6 Surely he will never be
shaken;
The righteous will be in
everlasting remembrance.

7 He will not be afraid of evil
tidings;
His heart is steadfast, trusting
in the LORD.

8 His heart *is* established;
He will not be afraid,
Until he sees *his desire* upon
his enemies.

9 He has dispersed abroad,
He has given to the poor;
His righteousness endures
forever;
His horn will be exalted with
honor.

10 The wicked will see *it* and be
grieved;
He will gnash his teeth and
melt away;
The desire of the wicked shall
perish.

PROVERBS FOR TODAY/ 27:17

As *iron sharpens iron, so a man sharpens the countenance of his friend.*

NOVEMBER 15

EZEKIEL 31:1–32:32

Now it came to pass in the eleventh year, in the third *month,* on the first *day* of the month, *that* the word of the LORD came to me, saying, 2"Son of man, say to Pharaoh king of Egypt and to his multitude:

'Whom are you like in your
greatness?

3 Indeed Assyria *was* a cedar in
Lebanon,
With fine branches that
shaded the forest,
And of high stature;
And its top was among the
thick boughs.

4 The waters made it grow;
Underground waters gave it
height,
With their rivers running
around the place where it
was planted,
And sent out rivulets to all the
trees of the field.

5 'Therefore its height was
exalted above all the trees
of the field;
Its boughs were multiplied,
And its branches became long
because of the abundance
of water,
As it sent them out.

6 All the birds of the heavens
made their nests in its
boughs;
Under its branches all the
beasts of the field brought
forth their young;

And in its shadow all great
  nations made their home.

7 'Thus it was beautiful in
  greatness and in the length
  of its branches,
  Because its roots reached to
  abundant waters.

8 The cedars in the garden of
  God could not hide it;
  The fir trees were not like its
  boughs,
  And the chestnut* trees were
  not like its branches;
  No tree in the garden of God
  was like it in beauty.

9 I made it beautiful with a
  multitude of branches,
  So that all the trees of Eden
  envied it,
  That *were* in the garden of
  God.'

10"Therefore thus says the Lord
GOD: 'Because you have increased in
height, and it set its top among the
thick boughs, and its heart was lifted
up in its height, 11therefore I will deliver it into the hand of the mighty one
of the nations, and he shall surely deal
with it; I have driven it out for its wickedness. 12And aliens, the most terrible
of the nations, have cut it down and left
it; its branches have fallen on the
mountains and in all the valleys; its
boughs lie broken by all the rivers of
the land; and all the peoples of the
earth have gone from under its
shadow and left it.

13 'On its ruin will remain all the
  birds of the heavens,
  And all the beasts of the field
  will come to its branches—

14'So that no trees by the waters may
ever again exalt themselves for their
height, nor set their tops among the
thick boughs, that no tree which

drinks water may ever be high enough
to reach up to them.

'For they have all been
  delivered to death,
  To the depths of the earth,
  Among the children of men
  who go down to the Pit.'

15"Thus says the Lord GOD: 'In the
day when it went down to hell, I caused
mourning. I covered the deep because
of it. I restrained its rivers, and the
great waters were held back. I caused
Lebanon to mourn for it, and all the
trees of the field wilted because of it. 16I
made the nations shake at the sound of
its fall, when I cast it down to hell together with those who descend into
the Pit; and all the trees of Eden, the
choice and best of Lebanon, all that
drink water, were comforted in the
depths of the earth. 17They also went
down to hell with it, with those *slain* by
the sword; and *those who were* its *strong*
arm dwelt in its shadows among the
nations.

18'To which of the trees in Eden will
you then be likened in glory and greatness? Yet you shall be brought down
with the trees of Eden to the depths of
the earth; you shall lie in the midst of
the uncircumcised, with *those* slain by
the sword. This *is* Pharaoh and all his
multitude,' says the Lord GOD."

AND it came to pass in the twelfth year,
in the twelfth *month,* on the first *day* of
the month, *that* the word of the LORD
came to me, saying, 2"Son of man, take
up a lamentation for Pharaoh king of
Egypt, and say to him:

'You are like a young lion
  among the nations,
  And you *are* like a monster in
  the seas,
  Bursting forth in your rivers,
  Troubling the waters with
  your feet,

And fouling their rivers.'

3"Thus says the Lord GOD:

'I will therefore spread My net
over you with a company of
many people,
And they will draw you up in
My net.
4   Then I will leave you on the
land;
I will cast you out on the open
fields,
And cause to settle on you all
the birds of the heavens.
And with you I will fill the
beasts of the whole earth.
5   I will lay your flesh on the
mountains,
And fill the valleys with your
carcass.

6   'I will also water the land with
the flow of your blood,
Even to the mountains;
And the riverbeds will be full
of you.
7   When *I* put out your light,
I will cover the heavens, and
make its stars dark;
I will cover the sun with a
cloud,
And the moon shall not give
her light.
8   All the bright lights of the
heavens I will make dark
over you,
And bring darkness upon
your land,'
Says the Lord GOD.

9'I will also trouble the hearts of
many peoples, when I bring your destruction among the nations, into the
countries which you have not known.
10Yes, I will make many peoples astonished at you, and their kings shall be
horribly afraid of you when I brandish
My sword before them; and they shall

tremble *every* moment, every man for
his own life, in the day of your fall.'
11"For thus says the Lord GOD: 'The
sword of the king of Babylon shall
come upon you. 12By the swords of the
mighty warriors, all of them the most
terrible of the nations, I will cause your
multitude to fall.

'They shall plunder the pomp
of Egypt,
And all its multitude shall be
destroyed.
13   Also I will destroy all its
animals
From beside its great waters;
The foot of man shall muddy
them no more,
Nor shall the hooves of
animals muddy them.
14   Then I will make their waters
clear,
And make their rivers run like
oil,'
Says the Lord GOD.

15   'When I make the land of
Egypt desolate,
And the country is destitute
of all that once filled it,
When I strike all who dwell in
it,
Then they shall know that I
am the LORD.

16   'This *is* the lamentation
With which they shall lament
her;
The daughters of the nations
shall lament her;
They shall lament for her, for
Egypt,
And for all her multitude,'
Says the Lord GOD."

17It came to pass also in the twelfth
year, on the fifteenth *day* of the month,
that the word of the LORD came to me,
saying:

18 "Son of man, wail over the
  multitude of Egypt,
And cast them down to the
  depths of the earth,
Her and the daughters of the
  famous nations,
With those who go down to
  the Pit:
19 'Whom do you surpass in
  beauty?
Go down, be placed with the
  uncircumcised.'

20 "They shall fall in the midst of
  those slain by the sword;
She is delivered to the sword,
Drawing her and all her
  multitudes.
21 The strong among the mighty
Shall speak to him out of the
  midst of hell
With those who help him:
'They have gone down,
They lie with the
  uncircumcised, slain by the
  sword.'

22 "Assyria *is* there, and all her
  company,
With their graves all around
  her,
All of them slain, fallen by the
  sword.
23 Her graves are set in the
  recesses of the Pit,
And her company is all
  around her grave,
All of them slain, fallen by the
  sword,
Who caused terror in the land
  of the living.

24 "There *is* Elam and all her
  multitude,
All around her grave,
All of them slain, fallen by the
  sword,
Who have gone down
  uncircumcised to the lower
  parts of the earth,

Who caused their terror in
  the land of the living;
Now they bear their shame
  with those who go down to
  the Pit.
25 They have set her bed in the
  midst of the slain,
With all her multitude,
With her graves all around it,
All of them uncircumcised,
  slain by the sword;
Though their terror was
  caused
In the land of the living,
Yet they bear their shame
With those who go down to
  the Pit;
It was put in the midst of the
  slain.

26 "There *are* Meshech and
  Tubal and all their
  multitudes,
With all their graves around it,
All of them uncircumcised,
  slain by the sword,
Though they caused their
  terror in the land of the
  living.
27 They do not lie with the
  mighty
Who are fallen of the
  uncircumcised,
Who have gone down to hell
  with their weapons of war;
They have laid their swords
  under their heads,
But their iniquities will be on
  their bones,
Because of the terror of the
  mighty in the land of the
  living.
28 Yes, you shall be broken in
  the midst of the
  uncircumcised,
And lie with *those* slain by the
  sword.

29 "There *is* Edom,
Her kings and all her princes,

Who despite their might
Are laid beside *those* slain by
   the sword;
They shall lie with the
   uncircumcised,
And with those who go down
   to the Pit.
30   There *are* the princes of the
   north,
All of them, and all the
   Sidonians,
Who have gone down with
   the slain
In shame at the terror which
   they caused by their might;
They lie uncircumcised with
   those slain by the sword,
And bear their shame with
   those who go down to the
   Pit.

31   "Pharaoh will see them
And be comforted over all his
   multitude,
Pharaoh and all his army,
Slain by the sword,"
Says the Lord GOD.

32   "For I have caused My terror
   in the land of the living;
And he shall be placed in the
   midst of the uncircumcised
With *those* slain by the sword,
Pharaoh and all his multitude,"
Says the Lord GOD.

HEBREWS 12:14-29

PURSUE peace with all *people,* and holiness, without which no one will see the Lord: ¹⁵looking carefully lest anyone fall short of the grace of God; lest any root of bitterness springing up cause trouble, and by this many become defiled; ¹⁶lest there *be* any fornicator or profane person like Esau, who for one morsel of food sold his birthright. ¹⁷For you know that afterward, when he wanted to inherit the blessing, he was rejected, for he found no place for repentance, though he sought it diligently with tears.

¹⁸For you have not come to the mountain that* may be touched and that burned with fire, and to blackness and darkness* and tempest, ¹⁹and the sound of a trumpet and the voice of words, so that those who heard *it* begged that the word should not be spoken to them anymore. ²⁰(For they could not endure what was commanded: *"And if so much as a beast touches the mountain, it shall be stoned* * or shot with an arrow."* * ²¹And so terrifying was the sight *that* Moses said, *"I am exceedingly afraid and trembling."* *)

²²But you have come to Mount Zion and to the city of the living God, the heavenly Jerusalem, to an innumerable company of angels, ²³to the general assembly and church of the firstborn *who are* registered in heaven, to God the Judge of all, to the spirits of just men made perfect, ²⁴to Jesus the Mediator of the new covenant, and to the blood of sprinkling that speaks better things than *that of* Abel.

²⁵See that you do not refuse Him who speaks. For if they did not escape who refused Him who spoke on earth, much more *shall we not escape* if we turn away from Him who *speaks* from heaven, ²⁶whose voice then shook the earth; but now He has promised, saying, *"Yet once more I shake* * not only the earth, but also heaven."* * ²⁷Now this, *"Yet once more,"* indicates the removal of those things that are being shaken, as of things that are made, that the things which cannot be shaken may remain.

²⁸Therefore, since we are receiving a kingdom which cannot be shaken, let us have grace, by which we may* serve God acceptably with reverence and godly fear. ²⁹For our God *is* a consuming fire.

PSALM 113:1–114:8

PRAISE the LORD!

Praise, O servants of the LORD,
Praise the name of the LORD!
2 Blessed be the name of the
LORD
From this time forth and
forevermore!
3 From the rising of the sun to
its going down
The LORD's name *is* to be
praised.

4 The LORD *is* high above all
nations,
His glory above the heavens.
5 Who *is* like the LORD our God,
Who dwells on high,
6 Who humbles Himself to
behold
The things that are in the
heavens and in the earth?

7 He raises the poor out of the
dust,
And lifts the needy out of the
ash heap,
8 That He may seat *him* with
princes—
With the princes of His
people.
9 He grants the barren woman
a home,

Like a joyful mother of
children.

Praise the LORD!

WHEN Israel went out of Egypt,
The house of Jacob from a
people of strange language,
2 Judah became His sanctuary,
And Israel His dominion.

3 The sea saw *it* and fled;
Jordan turned back.
4 The mountains skipped like
rams,
The little hills like lambs.
5 What ails you, O sea, that you
fled?
O Jordan, *that* you turned
back?
6 O mountains, *that* you
skipped like rams?
O little hills, like lambs?

7 Tremble, O earth, at the
presence of the Lord,
At the presence of the God of
Jacob,
8 Who turned the rock *into* a
pool of water,
The flint into a fountain of
waters.

PROVERBS FOR TODAY/ 27:18-20

*Whoever keeps the fig tree will eat its fruit; so he who waits on his master will be
honored.* □ *As in water face* reflects *face, so a man's heart* reveals *the man.*
□ *Hell* * *and Destruction* * *are never full; so the eyes of man are never satisfied.*

EZEKIEL 33:1–34:31

AGAIN the word of the LORD came to me, saying, [2]"Son of man, speak to the children of your people, and say to them: 'When I bring the sword upon a land, and the people of the land take a man from their territory and make him their watchman, [3]when he sees the sword coming upon the land, if he blows the trumpet and warns the people, [4]then whoever hears the sound of the trumpet and does not take warning, if the sword comes and takes him away, his blood shall be on his *own* head. [5]He heard the sound of the trumpet, but did not take warning; his blood shall be upon himself. But he who takes warning will save his life. [6]But if the watchman sees the sword coming and does not blow the trumpet, and the people are not warned, and the sword comes and takes *any* person from among them, he is taken away in his iniquity; but his blood I will require at the watchman's hand.'

[7]"So you, son of man: I have made you a watchman for the house of Israel; therefore you shall hear a word from My mouth and warn them for Me. [8]When I say to the wicked, 'O wicked *man,* you shall surely die!' and you do not speak to warn the wicked from his way, that wicked *man* shall die in his iniquity; but his blood I will require at your hand. [9]Nevertheless if you warn the wicked to turn from his way, and he does not turn from his way, he shall die in his iniquity; but you have delivered your soul.

[10]"Therefore you, O son of man, say to the house of Israel: 'Thus you say, "If our transgressions and our sins *lie* upon us, and we pine away in them, how can we then live?" ' [11]Say to them: '*As* I live,' says the Lord GOD, 'I have no pleasure in the death of the wicked, but that the wicked turn from his way and live. Turn, turn from your evil ways! For why should you die, O house of Israel?'

[12]"Therefore you, O son of man, say to the children of your people: 'The righteousness of the righteous man shall not deliver him in the day of his transgression; as for the wickedness of the wicked, he shall not fall because of it in the day that he turns from his wickedness; nor shall the righteous be able to live because of *his righteousness* in the day that he sins.' [13]When I say to the righteous *that* he shall surely live, but he trusts in his own righteousness and commits iniquity, none of his righteous works shall be remembered; but because of the iniquity that he has committed, he shall die. [14]Again, when I say to the wicked, 'You shall surely die,' if he turns from his sin and does what is lawful and right, [15]*if* the wicked restores the pledge, gives back what he has stolen, and walks in the statutes of life without committing iniquity, he shall surely live; he shall not die. [16]None of his sins which he has committed shall be remembered against him; he has done what is lawful and right; he shall surely live.

[17]"Yet the children of your people say, 'The way of the LORD is not fair.' But it is their way which is not fair! [18]When the righteous turns from his righteousness and commits iniquity, he shall die because of it. [19]But when the wicked turns from his wickedness and does what is lawful and right, he shall live because of it. [20]Yet you say, 'The way of the LORD is not fair.' O house of Israel, I will judge every one of you according to his own ways."

[21]And it came to pass in the twelfth

year of our captivity, in the tenth *month,* on the fifth *day* of the month, *that* one who had escaped from Jerusalem came to me and said, "The city has been captured!"

22Now the hand of the LORD had been upon me the evening before the man came who had escaped. And He had opened my mouth; so when he came to me in the morning, my mouth was opened, and I was no longer mute.

23Then the word of the LORD came to me, saying: 24"Son of man, they who inhabit those ruins in the land of Israel are saying, 'Abraham was only one, and he inherited the land. But we *are* many; the land has been given to us as a possession.'

25"Therefore say to them, 'Thus says the Lord GOD: "You eat *meat* with blood, you lift up your eyes toward your idols, and shed blood. Should you then possess the land? 26You rely on your sword, you commit abominations, and you defile one another's wives. Should you then possess the land?" '

27"Say thus to them, 'Thus says the Lord GOD: "*As* I live, surely those who *are* in the ruins shall fall by the sword, and the one who *is* in the open field I will give to the beasts to be devoured, and those who *are* in the strongholds and caves shall die of the pestilence. 28For I will make the land most desolate, her arrogant strength shall cease, and the mountains of Israel shall be so desolate that no one will pass through. 29Then they shall know that I *am* the LORD, when I have made the land most desolate because of all their abominations which they have committed." '

30"As for you, son of man, the children of your people are talking about you beside the walls and in the doors of the houses; and they speak to one another, everyone saying to his brother, 'Please come and hear what the word is that comes from the LORD.' 31So they come to you as people do, they sit before you *as* My people, and

they hear your words, but they do not do them; for with their mouth they show much love, *but* their hearts pursue their *own* gain. 32Indeed you *are* to them as a very lovely song of one who has a pleasant voice and can play well on an instrument; for they hear your words, but they do not do them. 33And when this comes to pass—surely it will come—then they will know that a prophet has been among them."

AND the word of the LORD came to me, saying, 2"Son of man, prophesy against the shepherds of Israel, prophesy and say to them, 'Thus says the Lord GOD to the shepherds: "Woe to the shepherds of Israel who feed themselves! Should not the shepherds feed the flocks? 3You eat the fat and clothe yourselves with the wool; you slaughter the fatlings, *but* you do not feed the flock. 4The weak you have not strengthened, nor have you healed those who were sick, nor bound up the broken, nor brought back what was driven away, nor sought what was lost; but with force and cruelty you have ruled them. 5So they were scattered because *there was* no shepherd; and they became food for all the beasts of the field when they were scattered. 6My sheep wandered through all the mountains, and on every high hill; yes, My flock was scattered over the whole face of the earth, and no one was seeking or searching *for them.*"

7'Therefore, you shepherds, hear the word of the LORD: 8"*As* I live," says the Lord GOD, "surely because My flock became a prey, and My flock became food for every beast of the field, because *there was* no shepherd, nor did My shepherds search for My flock, but the shepherds fed themselves and did not feed My flock"— 9therefore, O shepherds, hear the word of the LORD! 10Thus says the Lord GOD: "Behold, I *am* against the shepherds, and I will require My flock at their hand; I will cause them to cease feeding the sheep, and the shepherds shall feed themselves no more; for I will deliver My flock from their mouths, that they may no longer be food for them."

¹¹"For thus says the Lord GOD: "Indeed I Myself will search for My sheep and seek them out. ¹²As a shepherd seeks out his flock on the day he is among his scattered sheep, so will I seek out My sheep and deliver them from all the places where they were scattered on a cloudy and dark day. ¹³And I will bring them out from the peoples and gather them from the countries, and will bring them to their own land; I will feed them on the mountains of Israel, in the valleys and in all the inhabited places of the country. ¹⁴I will feed them in good pasture, and their fold shall be on the high mountains of Israel. There they shall lie down in a good fold and feed in rich pasture on the mountains of Israel. ¹⁵I will feed My flock, and I will make them lie down," says the Lord GOD. ¹⁶"I will seek what was lost and bring back what was driven away, bind up the broken and strengthen what was sick; but I will destroy the fat and the strong, and feed them in judgment."

¹⁷"And *as for* you, O My flock, thus says the Lord GOD: "Behold, I shall judge between sheep and sheep, between rams and goats. ¹⁸*Is it* too little for you to have eaten up the good pasture, that you must tread down with your feet the residue of your pasture— and to have drunk of the clear waters, that you must foul the residue with your feet? ¹⁹And *as for* My flock, they eat what you have trampled with your feet, and they drink what you have fouled with your feet."

²⁰"Therefore thus says the Lord GOD to them: "Behold, I Myself will judge between the fat and the lean sheep. ²¹Because you have pushed with side and shoulder, butted all the weak ones with your horns, and scattered them

abroad, ²²therefore I will save My flock, and they shall no longer be a prey; and I will judge between sheep and sheep. ²³I will establish one shepherd over them, and he shall feed them—My servant David. He shall feed them and be their shepherd. ²⁴And I, the LORD, will be their God, and My servant David a prince among them; I, the LORD, have spoken.

²⁵"I will make a covenant of peace with them, and cause wild beasts to cease from the land; and they will dwell safely in the wilderness and sleep in the woods. ²⁶I will make them and the places all around My hill a blessing; and I will cause showers to come down in their season; there shall be showers of blessing. ²⁷Then the trees of the field shall yield their fruit, and the earth shall yield her increase. They shall be safe in their land; and they shall know that I *am* the LORD, when I have broken the bands of their yoke and delivered them from the hand of those who enslaved them. ²⁸And they shall no longer be a prey for the nations, nor shall beasts of the land devour them; but they shall dwell safely, and no one shall make *them* afraid. ²⁹I will raise up for them a garden of renown, and they shall no longer be consumed with hunger in the land, nor bear the shame of the Gentiles anymore. ³⁰Thus they shall know that I, the LORD their God, *am* with them, and they, the house of Israel, *are* My people," says the Lord GOD.' "

³¹"You are My flock, the flock of My pasture; you *are* men, *and* I *am* your God," says the Lord GOD.

HEBREWS 13:1-25

L ET brotherly love continue. ²Do not forget to entertain strangers, for by so *doing* some have unwittingly entertained angels. ³Remember the prisoners as if chained with them—those who are mis-treated—since you yourselves are in the body also.

⁴Marriage *is* honorable among all, and the bed undefiled; but fornicators and adulterers God will judge.

⁵*Let your* conduct *be* without covet-ousness; *be* content with such things as you have. For He Himself has said, *"I will never leave you nor forsake you."* * ⁶So we may boldly say:

"The LORD is my helper;
I will not fear.
What can man do to me?" *

⁷Remember those who rule over you, who have spoken the word of God to you, whose faith follow, considering the outcome of *their* conduct. ⁸Jesus Christ *is* the same yesterday, today, and forever. ⁹Do not be carried about* with various and strange doctrines. For *it is* good that the heart be estab-lished by grace, not with foods which have not profited those who have been occupied with them.

¹⁰We have an altar from which those who serve the tabernacle have no right to eat. ¹¹For the bodies of those animals, whose blood is brought into the sanctuary by the high priest for sin, are burned outside the camp. ¹²Therefore Jesus also, that He might sanctify the people with His own blood, suffered outside the gate. ¹³Therefore let us go forth to Him, out-side the camp, bearing His reproach. ¹⁴For here we have no continuing city, but we seek the one to come. ¹⁵There-fore by Him let us continually offer the sacrifice of praise to God, that is, the fruit of *our* lips, giving thanks to His name. ¹⁶But do not forget to do good and to share, for with such sacrifices God is well pleased.

¹⁷Obey those who rule over you, and be submissive, for they watch out for your souls, as those who must give ac-count. Let them do so with joy and not

with grief, for that would be unprofit-able for you.

¹⁸Pray for us; for we are confident that we have a good conscience, in all things desiring to live honorably. ¹⁹But I especially urge *you* to do this, that I may be restored to you the sooner.

²⁰Now may the God of peace who brought up our Lord Jesus from the dead, that great Shepherd of the sheep, through the blood of the ever-lasting covenant, ²¹make you complete in every good work to do His will, working in you* what is well pleasing in His sight, through Jesus Christ, to whom *be* glory forever and ever. Amen.

²²And I appeal to you, brethren, bear with the word of exhortation, for I have written to you in few words. ²³Know that *our* brother Timothy has been set free, with whom I shall see you if he comes shortly.

²⁴Greet all those who rule over you, and all the saints. Those from Italy greet you.

²⁵Grace *be* with you all. Amen.

PSALM 115:1-18

Nᴏᴛ unto us, O LORD, not unto us, But to Your name give glory, Because of Your mercy, Because of Your truth.
2   Why should the Gentiles say, "So where *is* their God?"

3   But our God *is* in heaven; He does whatever He pleases.
4   Their idols *are* silver and gold, The work of men's hands.
5   They have mouths, but they do not speak; Eyes they have, but they do not see;
6   They have ears, but they do not hear; Noses they have, but they do not smell;

⁷ They have hands, but they do
not handle;
Feet they have, but they do
not walk;
Nor do they mutter through
their throat.
⁸ Those who make them are
like them;
So is everyone who trusts in
them.

⁹ O Israel, trust in the LORD;
He *is* their help and their
shield.
¹⁰ O house of Aaron, trust in the
LORD;
He *is* their help and their
shield.
¹¹ You who fear the LORD, trust
in the LORD;
He *is* their help and their
shield.

¹² The LORD has been mindful of
us;
He will bless us;
He will bless the house of
Israel;

He will bless the house of
Aaron.
¹³ He will bless those who fear
the LORD,
Both small and great.

¹⁴ May the LORD give you
increase more and more,
You and your children.
¹⁵ *May* you *be* blessed by the
LORD,
Who made heaven and earth.

¹⁶ The heaven, *even* the
heavens, *are* the LORD's;
But the earth He has given to
the children of men.
¹⁷ The dead do not praise the
LORD,
Nor any who go down into
silence.
¹⁸ But we will bless the LORD
From this time forth and
forevermore.

Praise the LORD!

PROVERBS FOR TODAY/ 27:21-22

The refining pot is *for silver and the furnace for gold, and a man* is valued *by what others say of him.* □ *Though you grind a fool in a mortar with a pestle along with crushed grain,* yet *his foolishness will not depart from him.*

NOVEMBER 17

EZEKIEL 35:1–36:38

MOREOVER the word of the LORD
came to me, saying, ²"Son of
man, set your face against
Mount Seir and prophesy against it,
³and say to it, 'Thus says the Lord GOD:

"Behold, O Mount Seir, I *am*
against you;
I will stretch out My hand
against you,
And make you most desolate;

"The Spirit of the LORD . . . has sent Me to heal the brokenhearted."
   Luke 4:18

"Mercy, peace, and love be multiplied to you."
Jude 2

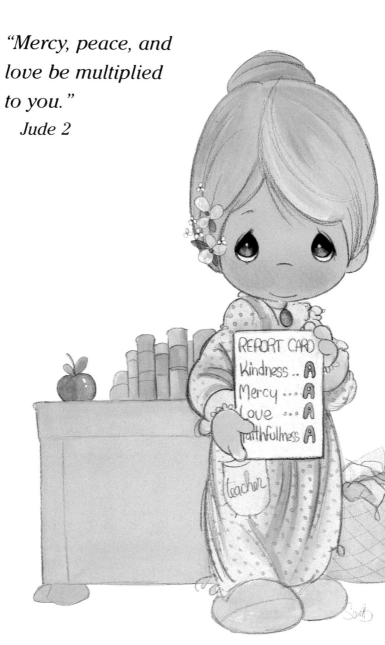

4 I shall lay your cities waste,
And you shall be desolate.
Then you shall know that I
am the LORD.

5"Because you have had an ancient hatred, and have shed *the blood of* the children of Israel by the power of the sword at the time of their calamity, *when* their iniquity *came to an* end, 6therefore, *as* I live," says the Lord GOD, "I will prepare you for blood, and blood shall pursue you; since you have not hated blood, therefore blood shall pursue you. 7Thus I will make Mount Seir most desolate, and cut off from it the one who leaves and the one who returns. 8And I will fill its mountains with the slain; on your hills and in your valleys and in all your ravines those who are slain by the sword shall fall. 9I will make you perpetually desolate, and your cities shall be uninhabited; then you shall know that I *am* the LORD.

10"Because you have said, 'These two nations and these two countries shall be mine, and we will possess them,' although the LORD was there, 11therefore, *as* I live," says the Lord GOD, "I will do according to your anger and according to the envy which you showed in your hatred against them; and I will make Myself known among them when I judge you. 12Then you shall know that I *am* the LORD. I have heard all your blasphemies which you have spoken against the mountains of Israel, saying, 'They are desolate; they are given to us to consume.' 13Thus with your mouth you have boasted against Me and multiplied your words against Me; I have heard *them*."

14"Thus says the Lord GOD: "The whole earth will rejoice when I make you desolate. 15As you rejoiced because the inheritance of the house of Israel was desolate, so I will do to you; you shall be desolate, O Mount Seir, as well as all of Edom—all of it! Then they shall know that I *am* the LORD." '

"AND you, son of man, prophesy to the mountains of Israel, and say, 'O mountains of Israel, hear the word of the LORD! 2Thus says the Lord GOD: "Because the enemy has said of you, 'Aha! The ancient heights have become our possession,' " ' 3therefore prophesy, and say, 'Thus says the Lord GOD: "Because they made *you* desolate and swallowed you up on every side, so that you became the possession of the rest of the nations, and you are taken up by the lips of talkers and slandered by the people"— 4therefore, O mountains of Israel, hear the word of the Lord GOD! Thus says the Lord GOD to the mountains, the hills, the rivers, the valleys, the desolate wastes, and the cities that have been forsaken, which became plunder and mockery to the rest of the nations all around— 5therefore thus says the Lord GOD: "Surely I have spoken in My burning jealousy against the rest of the nations and against all Edom, who gave My land to themselves as a possession, with wholehearted joy *and* spiteful minds, in order to plunder its open country." '

6"Therefore prophesy concerning the land of Israel, and say to the mountains, the hills, the rivers, and the valleys, 'Thus says the Lord GOD: "Behold, I have spoken in My jealousy and My fury, because you have borne the shame of the nations." 7Therefore thus says the Lord GOD: "I have raised My hand in an oath that surely the nations that *are* around you shall bear their own shame. 8But you, O mountains of Israel, you shall shoot forth your branches and yield your fruit to My people Israel, for they are about to come. 9For indeed I *am* for you, and I will turn to you, and you shall be tilled and sown. 10I will multiply men upon you, all the house of Israel, all of it; and the cities shall be inhabited and the ruins rebuilt. 11I will multiply upon you man and beast; and they shall increase and bear young; I will make you inhabited as in former times, and do better *for you* than at your beginnings. Then you shall know that I *am* the LORD. ¹²Yes, I will cause men to walk on you, My people Israel; they shall take possession of you, and you shall be their inheritance; no more shall you bereave them *of children*."

¹³"Thus says the Lord GOD: "Because they say to you, 'You devour men and bereave your nation *of children,*' ¹⁴therefore you shall devour men no more, nor bereave your nation anymore," says the Lord GOD. ¹⁵Nor will I let you hear the taunts of the nations anymore, nor bear the reproach of the peoples anymore, nor shall you cause your nation to stumble anymore," says the Lord GOD.' "

¹⁶Moreover the word of the LORD came to me, saying: ¹⁷"Son of man, when the house of Israel dwelt in their own land, they defiled it by their own ways and deeds; to Me their way was like the uncleanness of a woman in her customary impurity. ¹⁸Therefore I poured out My fury on them for the blood they had shed on the land, and for their idols *with which* they had defiled it. ¹⁹So I scattered them among the nations, and they were dispersed throughout the countries; I judged them according to their ways and their deeds. ²⁰When they came to the nations, wherever they went, they profaned My holy name—when they said of them, 'These *are* the people of the LORD, *and* yet they have gone out of His land.' ²¹But I had concern for My holy name, which the house of Israel had profaned among the nations wherever they went.

²²"Therefore say to the house of Israel, 'Thus says the Lord GOD: "I do not do *this* for your sake, O house of Israel, but for My holy name's sake, which you have profaned among the nations wherever you went. ²³And I will sanctify My great name, which has been profaned among the nations, which you have profaned in their midst; and the

nations shall know that I *am* the LORD," says the Lord GOD, "when I am hallowed in you before their eyes. ²⁴For I will take you from among the nations, gather you out of all countries, and bring you into your own land. ²⁵Then I will sprinkle clean water on you, and you shall be clean; I will cleanse you from all your filthiness and from all your idols. ²⁶I will give you a new heart and put a new spirit within you; I will take the heart of stone out of your flesh and give you a heart of flesh. ²⁷I will put My Spirit within you and cause you to walk in My statutes, and you will keep My judgments and do *them*. ²⁸Then you shall dwell in the land that I gave to your fathers; you shall be My people, and I will be your God. ²⁹I will deliver you from all your uncleannesses. I will call for the grain and multiply it, and bring no famine upon you. ³⁰And I will multiply the fruit of your trees and the increase of your fields, so that you need never again bear the reproach of famine among the nations. ³¹Then you will remember your evil ways and your deeds that *were* not good; and you will loathe yourselves in your own sight, for your iniquities and your abominations. ³²Not for your sake do I do *this*," says the Lord GOD, "let it be known to you. Be ashamed and confounded for your own ways, O house of Israel!"

³³"Thus says the Lord GOD: "On the day that I cleanse you from all your iniquities, I will also enable *you* to dwell in the cities, and the ruins shall be rebuilt. ³⁴The desolate land shall be tilled instead of lying desolate in the sight of all who pass by. ³⁵So they will say, 'This land that was desolate has become like the garden of Eden; and the wasted, desolate, and ruined cities *are now* fortified *and* inhabited.' ³⁶Then the nations which are left all around you shall know that I, the LORD, have rebuilt the ruined places *and* planted what was desolate. I, the LORD, have spoken *it,* and I will do *it.*"

37'Thus says the Lord GOD: "I will also let the house of Israel inquire of Me to do this for them: I will increase their men like a flock. 38Like a flock *offered as* holy *sacrifices,* like the flock at Jerusalem on its feast days, so shall the ruined cities be filled with flocks of men. Then they shall know that I *am* the LORD." ' "

JAMES 1:1-18

JAMES, a bondservant of God and of the Lord Jesus Christ,

To the twelve tribes which are scattered abroad:

Greetings.

2My brethren, count it all joy when you fall into various trials, 3knowing that the testing of your faith produces patience. 4But let patience have *its* perfect work, that you may be perfect and complete, lacking nothing. 5If any of you lacks wisdom, let him ask of God, who gives to all liberally and without reproach, and it will be given to him. 6But let him ask in faith, with no doubting, for he who doubts is like a wave of the sea driven and tossed by the wind. 7For let not that man suppose that he will receive anything from the Lord; 8*he is* a double-minded man, unstable in all his ways.

9Let the lowly brother glory in his exaltation, 10but the rich in his humiliation, because as a flower of the field he will pass away. 11For no sooner has the sun risen with a burning heat than it withers the grass; its flower falls, and its beautiful appearance perishes. So the rich man also will fade away in his pursuits.

12Blessed *is* the man who endures temptation; for when he has been approved, he will receive the crown of life which the Lord has promised to those who love Him. 13Let no one say when he is tempted, "I am tempted by God"; for God cannot be tempted by evil, nor does He Himself tempt anyone. 14But each one is tempted when he is drawn away by his own desires and enticed. 15Then, when desire has conceived, it gives birth to sin; and sin, when it is full-grown, brings forth death.

16Do not be deceived, my beloved brethren. 17Every good gift and every perfect gift is from above, and comes down from the Father of lights, with whom there is no variation or shadow of turning. 18Of His own will He brought us forth by the word of truth, that we might be a kind of firstfruits of His creatures.

PSALM 116:1-19

I LOVE the LORD, because He
  has heard
  My voice *and* my supplications.
2   Because He has inclined His
        ear to me,
      Therefore I will call *upon Him*
        as long as I live.

3   The pains of death
        surrounded me,
      And the pangs of Sheol laid
        hold of me;
      I found trouble and sorrow.
4   Then I called upon the name
        of the LORD:
      "O LORD, I implore You, deliver
        my soul!"

5   Gracious *is* the LORD, and
        righteous;
      Yes, our God *is* merciful.
6   The LORD preserves the
        simple;
      I was brought low, and He
        saved me.
7   Return to your rest, O my
        soul,
      For the LORD has dealt
        bountifully with you.

8 For You have delivered my
soul from death,
My eyes from tears,
And my feet from falling.
9 I will walk before the Lord
In the land of the living.
10 I believed, therefore I spoke,
"I am greatly afflicted."
11 I said in my haste,
"All men *are* liars."

12 What shall I render to the
Lord
For all His benefits toward
me?
13 I will take up the cup of
salvation,
And call upon the name of the
Lord.
14 I will pay my vows to the Lord
Now in the presence of all His
people.

15 Precious in the sight of the
Lord
Is the death of His saints.

16 O Lord, truly I *am* Your
servant;
I *am* Your servant, the son of
Your maidservant;
You have loosed my bonds.
17 I will offer to You the sacrifice
of thanksgiving,
And will call upon the name of
the Lord.

18 I will pay my vows to the Lord
Now in the presence of all His
people,
19 In the courts of the Lord's
house,
In the midst of you,
O Jerusalem.

Praise the Lord!

PROVERBS FOR TODAY / 27:23-27

Be diligent to know the state of your flocks, and *attend to your herds; for riches* are *not forever, nor does a crown* endure *to all generations.* When *the hay is removed, and the tender grass shows itself, and the herbs of the mountains are gathered in, the lambs* will provide *your clothing, and the goats the price of a field;* you shall have *enough goats' milk for your food, for the food of your household, and the nourishment of your maidservants.*

NOVEMBER 18

EZEKIEL 37:1–38:23

THE hand of the Lord came upon me and brought me out in the Spirit of the Lord, and set me down in the midst of the valley; and it *was* full of bones. 2Then He caused me to pass by them all around, and behold, *there were* very many in the open valley; and indeed *they were* very dry.

3And He said to me, "Son of man, can these bones live?"

So I answered, "O Lord God, You know."

4Again He said to me, "Prophesy to these bones, and say to them, 'O dry bones, hear the word of the Lord! 5Thus says the Lord God to these bones: "Surely I will cause breath to enter into you, and you shall live. 6I will put sinews on you and bring flesh upon you, cover you with skin and put breath in you; and you shall live. Then you shall know that I *am* the LORD." ' "

⁷So I prophesied as I was commanded; and as I prophesied, there was a noise, and suddenly a rattling; and the bones came together, bone to bone. ⁸Indeed, as I looked, the sinews and the flesh came upon them, and the skin covered them over; but *there was* no breath in them.

⁹Also He said to me, "Prophesy to the breath, prophesy, son of man, and say to the breath, 'Thus says the Lord GOD: "Come from the four winds, O breath, and breathe on these slain, that they may live." ' " ¹⁰So I prophesied as He commanded me, and breath came into them, and they lived, and stood upon their feet, an exceedingly great army.

¹¹Then He said to me, "Son of man, these bones are the whole house of Israel. They indeed say, 'Our bones are dry, our hope is lost, and we ourselves are cut off!' ¹²Therefore prophesy and say to them, 'Thus says the Lord GOD: "Behold, O My people, I will open your graves and cause you to come up from your graves, and bring you into the land of Israel. ¹³Then you shall know that I *am* the LORD, when I have opened your graves, O My people, and brought you up from your graves. ¹⁴I will put My Spirit in you, and you shall live, and I will place you in your own land. Then you shall know that I, the LORD, have spoken *it* and performed *it*," says the LORD.' "

¹⁵Again the word of the LORD came to me, saying, ¹⁶"As for you, son of man, take a stick for yourself and write on it: 'For Judah and for the children of Israel, his companions.' Then take another stick and write on it, 'For Joseph, the stick of Ephraim, and *for* all the house of Israel, his companions.' ¹⁷Then join them one to another for

yourself into one stick, and they will become one in your hand.

¹⁸"And when the children of your people speak to you, saying, 'Will you not show us what you *mean* by these?'— ¹⁹say to them, 'Thus says the Lord GOD: "Surely I will take the stick of Joseph, which *is* in the hand of Ephraim, and the tribes of Israel, his companions; and I will join them with it, with the stick of Judah, and make them one stick, and they will be one in My hand." ' ²⁰And the sticks on which you write will be in your hand before their eyes.

²¹"Then say to them, 'Thus says the Lord GOD: "Surely I will take the children of Israel from among the nations, wherever they have gone, and will gather them from every side and bring them into their own land; ²²and I will make them one nation in the land, on the mountains of Israel; and one king shall be king over them all; they shall no longer be two nations, nor shall they ever be divided into two kingdoms again. ²³They shall not defile themselves anymore with their idols, nor with their detestable things, nor with any of their transgressions; but I will deliver them from all their dwelling places in which they have sinned, and will cleanse them. Then they shall be My people, and I will be their God.

²⁴"David My servant *shall be* king over them, and they shall all have one shepherd; they shall also walk in My judgments and observe My statutes, and do them. ²⁵Then they shall dwell in the land that I have given to Jacob My servant, where your fathers dwelt; and they shall dwell there, they, their children, and their children's children, forever; and My servant David *shall be* their prince forever. ²⁶Moreover I will make a covenant of peace with them, and it shall be an everlasting covenant with them; I will establish them and multiply them, and I will set My sanctuary in their midst forevermore. ²⁷My

tabernacle also shall be with them; indeed I will be their God, and they shall be My people. ²⁸The nations also will know that I, the LORD, sanctify Israel, when My sanctuary is in their midst forevermore." ' "

NOW the word of the LORD came to me, saying, ²"Son of man, set your face against Gog, of the land of Magog, the prince of Rosh,* Meshech, and Tubal, and prophesy against him, ³and say, 'Thus says the Lord GOD: "Behold, I *am* against you, O Gog, the prince of Rosh, Meshech, and Tubal. ⁴I will turn you around, put hooks into your jaws, and lead you out, with all your army, horses, and horsemen, all splendidly clothed, a great company *with* bucklers and shields, all of them handling swords. ⁵Persia, Ethiopia,* and Libya* are with them, all of them *with* shield and helmet; ⁶Gomer and all its troops; the house of Togarmah *from* the far north and all its troops—many people *are* with you.

⁷"Prepare yourself and be ready, you and all your companies that are gathered about you; and be a guard for them. ⁸After many days you will be visited. In the latter years you will come into the land of those brought back from the sword *and* gathered from many people on the mountains of Israel, which had long been desolate; they were brought out of the nations, and now all of them dwell safely. ⁹You will ascend, coming like a storm, covering the land like a cloud, you and all your troops and many peoples with you."

¹⁰'Thus says the Lord GOD: "On that day it shall come to pass *that* thoughts will arise in your mind, and you will make an evil plan: ¹¹You will say, 'I will go up against a land of unwalled villages; I will go to a peaceful people, who dwell safely, all of them dwelling without walls, and having neither bars nor gates'— ¹²to take plunder and to take booty, to stretch out your hand against the waste places *that are again* inhabited, and against a people gathered from the nations, who have acquired livestock and goods, who dwell in the midst of the land. ¹³Sheba, Dedan, the merchants of Tarshish, and all their young lions will say to you, 'Have you come to take plunder? Have you gathered your army to take booty, to carry away silver and gold, to take away livestock and goods, to take great plunder?' " '

¹⁴"Therefore, son of man, prophesy and say to Gog, 'Thus says the Lord GOD: "On that day when My people Israel dwell safely, will you not know *it?* ¹⁵Then you will come from your place out of the far north, you and many peoples with you, all of them riding on horses, a great company and a mighty army. ¹⁶You will come up against My people Israel like a cloud, to cover the land. It will be in the latter days that I will bring you against My land, so that the nations may know Me, when I am hallowed in you, O Gog, before their eyes." ¹⁷Thus says the Lord GOD: "Are *you* he of whom I have spoken in former days by My servants the prophets of Israel, who prophesied for years in those days that I would bring you against them?

¹⁸"And it will come to pass at the same time, when Gog comes against the land of Israel," says the Lord GOD, "*that* My fury will show in My face. ¹⁹For in My jealousy *and* in the fire of My wrath I have spoken: 'Surely in that day there shall be a great earthquake in the land of Israel, ²⁰so that the fish of the sea, the birds of the heavens, the beasts of the field, all creeping things that creep on the earth, and all men who *are* on the face of the earth shall shake at My presence. The mountains shall be thrown down, the steep places shall fall, and every wall shall fall to the ground.' ²¹I will call for a sword against Gog throughout all My mountains,"

says the Lord God. "Every man's sword will be against his brother. 22And I will bring him to judgment with pestilence and bloodshed; I will rain down on him, on his troops, and on the many peoples who *are* with him, flooding rain, great hailstones, fire, and brimstone. 23Thus I will magnify Myself and sanctify Myself, and I will be known in the eyes of many nations. Then they shall know that I *am* the Lord." ' "

JAMES 1:19–2:17

So then,* my beloved brethren, let every man be swift to hear, slow to speak, slow to wrath; 20for the wrath of man does not produce the righteousness of God.

21Therefore lay aside all filthiness and overflow of wickedness, and receive with meekness the implanted word, which is able to save your souls.

22But be doers of the word, and not hearers only, deceiving yourselves. 23For if anyone is a hearer of the word and not a doer, he is like a man observing his natural face in a mirror; 24for he observes himself, goes away, and immediately forgets what kind of man he was. 25But he who looks into the perfect law of liberty and continues *in it,* and is not a forgetful hearer but a doer of the work, this one will be blessed in what he does.

26If anyone among you* thinks he is religious, and does not bridle his tongue but deceives his own heart, this one's religion *is* useless. 27Pure and undefiled religion before God and the Father is this: to visit orphans and widows in their trouble, *and* to keep oneself unspotted from the world.

My brethren, do not hold the faith of our Lord Jesus Christ, *the Lord* of glory, with partiality. 2For if there should come into your assembly a man with gold rings, in fine apparel, and there should also come in a poor man in filthy clothes, 3and you pay attention to the one wearing the fine clothes and say to him, "You sit here in a good place," and say to the poor man, "You stand there," or, "Sit here at my footstool," 4have you not shown partiality among yourselves, and become judges with evil thoughts?

5Listen, my beloved brethren: Has God not chosen the poor of this world *to be* rich in faith and heirs of the kingdom which He promised to those who love Him? 6But you have dishonored the poor man. Do not the rich oppress you and drag you into the courts? 7Do they not blaspheme that noble name by which you are called?

8If you really fulfill *the* royal law according to the Scripture, *"You shall love your neighbor as yourself,"* * you do well; 9but if you show partiality, you commit sin, and are convicted by the law as transgressors. 10For whoever shall keep the whole law, and yet stumble in one *point,* he is guilty of all. 11For He who said, *"Do not commit adultery,"* * also said, *"Do not murder."* * Now if you do not commit adultery, but you do murder, you have become a transgressor of the law. 12So speak and so do as those who will be judged by the law of liberty. 13For judgment is without mercy to the one who has shown no mercy. Mercy triumphs over judgment.

14What *does it* profit, my brethren, if someone says he has faith but does not have works? Can faith save him? 15If a brother or sister is naked and destitute of daily food, 16and one of you says to them, "Depart in peace, be warmed and filled," but you do not give them the things which are needed for the body, what *does it* profit? 17Thus also faith by itself, if it does not have works, is dead.

PSALM 117:1-2

PRAISE the LORD, all you Gentiles!
Laud Him, all you peoples!
²For His merciful kindness is
    great toward us,

And the truth of the LORD
    endures forever.

Praise the LORD!

PROVERBS FOR TODAY/ 28:1

The wicked flee when no one pursues, but the righteous are bold as a lion.

NOVEMBER 19

EZEKIEL 39:1–40:27

"**A**ND you, son of man, prophesy against Gog, and say, 'Thus says the Lord GOD: "Behold, I *am* against you, O Gog, the prince of Rosh,* Meshech, and Tubal; ²and I will turn you around and lead you on, bringing you up from the far north, and bring you against the mountains of Israel. ³Then I will knock the bow out of your left hand, and cause the arrows to fall out of your right hand. ⁴You shall fall upon the mountains of Israel, you and all your troops and the peoples who *are* with you; I will give you to birds of prey of every sort and *to* the beasts of the field to be devoured. ⁵You shall fall on the open field; for I have spoken," says the Lord GOD. ⁶"And I will send fire on Magog and on those who live in security in the coastlands. Then they shall know that I *am* the LORD. ⁷So I will make My holy name known in the midst of My people Israel, and I will not *let them* profane My holy name anymore. Then the nations shall know that *I am* the LORD, the Holy One in Israel. ⁸Surely it is coming, and it shall be done," says the Lord GOD. "This *is* the day of which I have spoken.

⁹"Then those who dwell in the cities of Israel will go out and set on fire and burn the weapons, both the shields and bucklers, the bows and arrows, the javelins and spears; and they will make fires with them for seven years. ¹⁰They will not take wood from the field nor cut down *any* from the forests, because they will make fires with the weapons; and they will plunder those who plundered them, and pillage those who pillaged them," says the Lord GOD.

¹¹"It will come to pass in that day *that* I will give Gog a burial place there in Israel, the valley of those who pass by east of the sea; and it will obstruct travelers, because there they will bury Gog and all his multitude. Therefore they will call *it* the Valley of Hamon Gog.* ¹²For seven months the house of Israel will be burying them, in order to cleanse the land. ¹³Indeed all the people of the land will be burying, and they will gain renown for it on the day that I am glorified," says the Lord GOD. ¹⁴"They will set apart men regularly employed, with the help of a search party,* to pass through the land and bury those bodies remaining on the ground, in order to cleanse it. At the end of seven months they will make a search. ¹⁵The search party will pass through the land; and *when anyone* sees a man's bone, he shall set up a

marker by it, till the buriers have buried it in the Valley of Hamon Gog. ¹⁶*The* name of *the* city *will* also *be* Hamonah. Thus they shall cleanse the land." '

¹⁷"And as for you, son of man, thus says the Lord God, 'Speak to every sort of bird and to every beast of the field:

> "Assemble yourselves and
>   come;
> Gather together from all sides
>   to My sacrificial meal
> Which I am sacrificing for you,
> A great sacrificial meal on the
>   mountains of Israel,
> That you may eat flesh and
>   drink blood.
> ¹⁸ You shall eat the flesh of the
>   mighty,
> Drink the blood of the princes
>   of the earth,
> Of rams and lambs,
> Of goats and bulls,
> All of them fatlings of Bashan.
> ¹⁹ You shall eat fat till you are
>   full,
> And drink blood till you are
>   drunk,
> At My sacrificial meal
> Which I am sacrificing for you.
> ²⁰ You shall be filled at My table
> With horses and riders,
> With mighty men
> And with all the men of war,"
>   says the Lord God.

²¹"I will set My glory among the nations; all the nations shall see My judgment which I have executed, and My hand which I have laid on them. ²²So the house of Israel shall know that I *am* the Lord their God from that day forward. ²³The Gentiles shall know that the house of Israel went into captivity for their iniquity; because they were unfaithful to Me, therefore I hid My face from them. I gave them into the hand of their enemies, and they all fell by the sword. ²⁴According to their uncleanness and according to their transgressions I have dealt with them, and hidden My face from them." '

²⁵"Therefore thus says the Lord God: 'Now I will bring back the captives of Jacob, and have mercy on the whole house of Israel; and I will be jealous for My holy name— ²⁶after they have borne their shame, and all their unfaithfulness in which they were unfaithful to Me, when they dwelt safely in their *own* land and no one made *them* afraid. ²⁷When I have brought them back from the peoples and gathered them out of their enemies' lands, and I am hallowed in them in the sight of many nations, ²⁸then they shall know that I *am* the Lord their God, who sent them into captivity among the nations, but also brought them back to their land, and left none of them captive any longer. ²⁹And I will not hide My face from them anymore; for I shall have poured out My Spirit on the house of Israel,' says the Lord God."

In the twenty-fifth year of our captivity, at the beginning of the year, on the tenth *day* of the month, in the fourteenth year after the city was captured, on the very same day the hand of the Lord was upon me; and He took me there. ²In the visions of God He took me into the land of Israel and set me on a very high mountain; on it toward the south *was* something like the structure of a city. ³He took me there, and behold, *there was* a man whose appearance *was* like the appearance of bronze. He had a line of flax and a measuring rod in his hand, and he stood in the gateway.

⁴And the man said to me, "Son of man, look with your eyes and hear with your ears, and fix your mind on everything I show you; for you *were* brought here so that I might show *them* to you. Declare to the house of

Israel everything you see." [5]Now there was a wall all around the outside of the temple.* In the man's hand was a measuring rod six cubits *long, each being a* cubit and a handbreadth; and he measured the width of the wall structure, one rod; and the height, one rod.

[6]Then he went to the gateway which faced east; and he went up its stairs and measured the threshold of the gateway, *which was* one rod wide, and the other threshold *was* one rod wide. [7]Each gate chamber *was* one rod long and one rod wide; between the gate chambers *was a space of* five cubits; and the threshold of the gateway by the vestibule of the inside gate *was* one rod. [8]He also measured the vestibule of the inside gate, one rod. [9]Then he measured the vestibule of the gateway, eight cubits; and the gateposts, two cubits. The vestibule of the gate *was* on the inside. [10]In the eastern gateway *were* three gate chambers on one side and three on the other; the three *were* all the same size; also the gateposts were of the same size on this side and that side.

[11]He measured the width of the entrance to the gateway, ten cubits; *and* the length of the gate, thirteen cubits. [12]*There was* a space in front of the gate chambers, one cubit *on this side* and one cubit on that side; the gate chambers *were* six cubits on this side and six cubits on that side. [13]Then he measured the gateway from the roof of *one* gate chamber to the roof of the other; the width *was* twenty-five cubits, as door faces door. [14]He measured the gateposts, sixty cubits high, and the court all around the gateway *extended* to the gatepost. [15]*From* the front of the entrance gate to the front of the vestibule of the inner gate *was* fifty cubits. [16]*There were* beveled window *frames* in the gate chambers and in their intervening archways on the inside of the gateway all around, and likewise in the vestibules. *There were* windows all around on the inside. And on each gatepost *were* palm trees.

[17]Then he brought me into the outer court; and *there were* chambers and a pavement made all around the court; thirty chambers faced the pavement. [18]The pavement was by the side of the gateways, corresponding to the length of the gateways; *this was* the lower pavement. [19]Then he measured the width from the front of the lower gateway to the front of the inner court exterior, one hundred cubits toward the east and the north.

[20]On the outer court was also a gateway facing north, and he measured its length and its width. [21]Its gate chambers, three on this side and three on that side, its gateposts and its archways, had the same measurements as the first gate; its length *was* fifty cubits and its width twenty-five cubits. [22]Its windows and those of its archways, and also its palm trees, *had* the same measurements as the gateway facing east; it was ascended by seven steps, and its archway *was* in front of it. [23]A gate of the inner court was opposite the northern gateway, just as the eastern *gateway;* and he measured from gateway to gateway, one hundred cubits.

[24]After that he brought me toward the south, and there a gateway was facing south; and he measured its gateposts and archways according to these same measurements. [25]*There were* windows in it and in its archways all around like those windows; its length *was* fifty cubits and its width twenty-five cubits. [26]Seven steps led up to it, and its archway *was* in front of them; and it had palm trees on its gateposts, one on this side and one on that side. [27]*There was* also a gateway on the inner court, facing south; and he measured from gateway to gateway toward the south, one hundred cubits.

JAMES 2:18–3:18

BUT someone will say, "You have faith, and I have works." Show me your faith without your* works, and I will show you my faith by my* works. ¹⁹You believe that there is one God. You do well. Even the demons believe—and tremble! ²⁰But do you want to know, O foolish man, that faith without works is dead?* ²¹Was not Abraham our father justified by works when he offered Isaac his son on the altar? ²²Do you see that faith was working together with his works, and by works faith was made perfect? ²³And the Scripture was fulfilled which says, *"Abraham believed God, and it was accounted to him for righteousness."* And he was called the friend of God. ²⁴You see then that a man is justified by works, and not by faith only.

²⁵Likewise, was not Rahab the harlot also justified by works when she received the messengers and sent *them* out another way?

²⁶For as the body without the spirit is dead, so faith without works is dead also.

MY brethren, let not many of you become teachers, knowing that we shall receive a stricter judgment. ²For we all stumble in many things. If anyone does not stumble in word, he *is* a perfect man, able also to bridle the whole body. ³Indeed,* we put bits in horses' mouths that they may obey us, and we turn their whole body. ⁴Look also at ships: although they are so large and are driven by fierce winds, they are turned by a very small rudder wherever the pilot desires. ⁵Even so the tongue is a little member and boasts great things.

See how great a forest a little fire kindles! ⁶And the tongue *is* a fire, a world of iniquity. The tongue is so set among our members that it defiles the whole body, and sets on fire the course of nature; and it is set on fire by hell. ⁷For every kind of beast and bird, of reptile and creature of the sea, is tamed and has been tamed by mankind. ⁸But no man can tame the tongue. *It is* an unruly evil, full of deadly poison. ⁹With it we bless our God and Father, and with it we curse men, who have been made in the similitude of God. ¹⁰Out of the same mouth proceed blessing and cursing. My brethren, these things ought not to be so. ¹¹Does a spring send forth fresh *water* and bitter from the same opening? ¹²Can a fig tree, my brethren, bear olives, or a grapevine bear figs? Thus no spring yields both salt water and fresh.*

¹³Who *is* wise and understanding among you? Let him show by good conduct *that* his works *are done* in the meekness of wisdom. ¹⁴But if you have bitter envy and self-seeking in your hearts, do not boast and lie against the truth. ¹⁵This wisdom does not descend from above, but *is* earthly, sensual, demonic. ¹⁶For where envy and self-seeking *exist,* confusion and every evil thing *are* there. ¹⁷But the wisdom that is from above is first pure, then peaceable, gentle, willing to yield, full of mercy and good fruits, without partiality and without hypocrisy. ¹⁸Now the fruit of righteousness is sown in peace by those who make peace.

PSALM 118:1-18

OH, give thanks to the LORD, for *He is* good!
For His mercy *endures* forever.

2 Let Israel now say,
"His mercy *endures* forever."
3 Let the house of Aaron now say,
"His mercy *endures* forever."
4 Let those who fear the LORD now say,

"His mercy *endures* forever."

5 I called on the Lord in distress;
The Lord answered me *and*
set me in a broad place.

6 The Lord *is* on my side;
I will not fear.
What can man do to me?

7 The Lord is for me among
those who help me;
Therefore I shall see *my*
desire on those who hate
me.

8 *It is* better to trust in the Lord
Than to put confidence in
man.

9 *It is* better to trust in the Lord
Than to put confidence in
princes.

10 All nations surrounded me,
But in the name of the Lord I
will destroy them.

11 They surrounded me,
Yes, they surrounded me;
But in the name of the Lord I
will destroy them.

12 They surrounded me like
bees;

They were quenched like a
fire of thorns;
For in the name of the Lord I
will destroy them.

13 You pushed me violently, that
I might fall,
But the Lord helped me.

14 The Lord *is* my strength and
song,
And He has become my
salvation.*

15 The voice of rejoicing and
salvation
Is in the tents of the righteous;
The right hand of the Lord
does valiantly.

16 The right hand of the Lord is
exalted;
The right hand of the Lord
does valiantly.

17 I shall not die, but live,
And declare the works of the
Lord.

18 The Lord has chastened me
severely,
But He has not given me over
to death.

PROVERBS FOR TODAY/ 28:2

Because of the transgression of a land, many are *its princes; but by a man of*
understanding and *knowledge right will be prolonged.*

NOVEMBER 20

EZEKIEL 40:28–41:26

THEN he [God's messenger]
brought me to the inner court
through the southern gateway;
he measured the southern gateway according to these same measurements.
29Also its gate chambers, its gateposts,
and its archways *were* according to

these same measurements; *there were*
windows in it and in its archways all
around; *it was* fifty cubits long and
twenty-five cubits wide. 30*There were*
archways all around, twenty-five cubits
long and five cubits wide. 31Its archways faced the outer court, palm trees
were on its gateposts, and going up to
it *were* eight steps.

32And he brought me into the inner court facing east; he measured the gateway according to these same measurements. 33Also its gate chambers, its gateposts, and its archways *were* according to these same measurements; and *there were* windows in it and in its archways all around; *it was* fifty cubits long and twenty-five cubits wide. 34Its archways faced the outer court, and palm trees *were* on its gateposts on this side and on that side; and going up to it *were* eight steps.

35Then he brought me to the north gateway and measured *it* according to these same measurements— 36also its gate chambers, its gateposts, and its archways. It had windows all around; its length *was* fifty cubits and its width twenty-five cubits. 07Its gateposts faced the outer court, palm trees *were* on its gateposts on this side and on that side, and going up to it *were* eight steps.

38*There was* a chamber and its entrance by the gateposts of the gateway, where they washed the burnt offering. 39In the vestibule of the gateway *were* two tables on this side and two tables on that side, on which to slay the burnt offering, the sin offering, and the trespass offering. 40At the outer side of the vestibule, as one goes up to the entrance of the northern gateway, *were* two tables; and on the other side of the vestibule of the gateway *were* two tables. 41Four tables *were* on this side and four tables on that side, by the side of the gateway, eight tables on which they slaughtered *the sacrifices.* 42*There were* also four tables of hewn stone for the burnt offering, one cubit and a half long, one cubit and a half wide, and one cubit high; on these they laid the instruments with which they slaughtered the burnt offering and the sacrifice. 43Inside *were* hooks, a handbreadth wide, fastened all around; and the flesh of the sacrifices *was* on the tables.

44Outside the inner gate *were* the chambers for the singers in the inner court, one facing south at the side of the northern gateway, and the other facing north at the side of the southern gateway. 45Then he said to me, "This chamber which faces south *is* for the priests who have charge of the temple. 46The chamber which faces north *is* for the priests who have charge of the altar; these *are* the sons of Zadok, from the sons of Levi, who come near the LORD to minister to Him."

47And he measured the court, one hundred cubits long and one hundred cubits wide, foursquare. The altar *was* in front of the temple. 48Then he brought me to the vestibule of the temple and measured the doorposts of the vestibule, five cubits on this side and five cubits on that side; and the width of the gateway was three cubits on this side and three cubits on that side. 49The length of the vestibule *was* twenty cubits, and the width eleven cubits; and by the steps which led up to it *there were* pillars by the doorposts, one on this side and another on that side.

THEN he brought me into the sanctuary* and measured the doorposts, six cubits wide on one side and six cubits wide on the other side—the width of the tabernacle. 2The width of the entryway *was* ten cubits, and the side walls of the entrance *were* five cubits on this side and five cubits on the other side; and he measured its length, forty cubits, and its width, twenty cubits.

3Also he went inside and measured the doorposts, two cubits; and the entrance, six cubits *high;* and the width of the entrance, seven cubits. 4He measured the length, twenty cubits; and the width, twenty cubits, beyond the sanctuary; and he said to me, "This *is* the Most Holy *Place.*"

5Next, he measured the wall of the temple, six cubits. The width of each side chamber all around the temple *was* four cubits on every side. 6The side chambers *were* in three stories, one above the other, thirty chambers in each story; they rested on ledges which *were* for the side chambers all around, that they might be supported, but not fastened to the wall of the temple. ⁷As one went up from story to story, the side chambers became wider all around, because their supporting ledges in the wall of the temple ascended like steps; therefore the width of the structure increased as one went up *from* the lowest *story* to the highest by way of the middle one. ⁸I also saw an elevation all around the temple; it was the foundation of the side chambers, a full rod, *that is,* six cubits *high*. ⁹The thickness of the outer wall of the side chambers *was* five cubits, and so also the remaining terrace by the place of the side chambers of the temple. ¹⁰And between *it and* the *wall* chambers was a width of twenty cubits all around the temple on every side. ¹¹The doors of the side chambers opened on the terrace, one door toward the north and another toward the south; and the width of the terrace *was* five cubits all around.

¹²The building that faced the separating courtyard at its western end *was* seventy cubits wide; the wall of the building *was* five cubits thick all around, and its length ninety cubits. ¹³So he measured the temple, one hundred cubits long; and the separating courtyard with the building and its walls *was* one hundred cubits long; ¹⁴also the width of the eastern face of the temple, including the separating courtyard, *was* one hundred cubits. ¹⁵He measured the length of the building behind it, facing the separating courtyard, with its galleries on the one side and on the other side, one hundred cubits, as well as the inner temple and the porches of the court, ¹⁶their doorposts and the beveled window frames. And the galleries all around their three stories opposite the threshold were paneled with wood from the ground to the windows—the windows were covered— ¹⁷from the space above the door, even to the inner room,* as well as outside, and on every wall all around, inside and outside, by measure.

¹⁸And *it was* made with cherubim and palm trees, a palm tree between cherub and cherub. *Each* cherub had two faces, ¹⁹so that the face of a man *was* toward a palm tree on one side, and the face of a young lion toward a palm tree on the other side; thus *it was* made throughout the temple all around. ²⁰From the floor to the space above the door, and on the wall of the sanctuary, cherubim and palm trees *were* carved.

²¹The doorposts of the temple *were* square, *as was* the front of the sanctuary; their appearance was similar. ²²The altar *was* of wood, three cubits high, and its length two cubits. Its corners, its length, and its sides *were* of wood; and he said to me, "This *is* the table that *is* before the Lᴏʀᴅ."

²³The temple and the sanctuary had two doors. ²⁴The doors had two panels *apiece,* two folding panels: two *panels* for one door and two panels for the other *door.* ²⁵Cherubim and palm trees *were* carved on the doors of the temple just as they *were* carved on the walls. A wooden canopy *was* on the front of the vestibule outside. ²⁶*There were* beveled window *frames* and palm trees on one side and on the other, on the sides of the vestibule—also on the side chambers of the temple and on the canopies.

JAMES 4:1-17

WHERE do wars and fights *come* from among you? Do *they* not *come* from your *desires for* pleasure that war in your members? ²You lust and do not have. You murder and covet and cannot obtain.

You fight and war. Yet* you do not have because you do not ask. ³You ask and do not receive, because you ask amiss, that you may spend *it* on your pleasures. ⁴Adulterers and* adulteresses! Do you not know that friendship with the world is enmity with God? Whoever therefore wants to be a friend of the world makes himself an enemy of God. ⁵Or do you think that the Scripture says in vain, "The Spirit who dwells in us yearns jealously"?

⁶But He gives more grace. Therefore He says:

> *"God resists the proud,*
> *But gives grace to the*
> *humble." **

⁷Therefore submit to God. Resist the devil and he will flee from you. ⁸Draw near to God and He will draw near to you. Cleanse *your* hands, *you* sinners; and purify *your* hearts, *you* double-minded. ⁹Lament and mourn and weep! Let your laughter be turned to mourning and *your* joy to gloom. ¹⁰Humble yourselves in the sight of the Lord, and He will lift you up.

¹¹Do not speak evil of one another, brethren. He who speaks evil of a brother and judges his brother, speaks evil of the law and judges the law. But if you judge the law, you are not a doer of the law but a judge. ¹²There is one Lawgiver,* who is able to save and to destroy. Who* are you to judge another?*

¹³Come now, you who say, "Today or tomorrow we will* go to such and such a city, spend a year there, buy and sell, and make a profit"; ¹⁴whereas you do not know what *will happen* tomorrow. For what *is* your life? It is even a vapor that appears for a little time and then vanishes away. ¹⁵Instead you *ought* to say, "If the Lord wills, we shall live and do this or that." ¹⁶But now you boast in your arrogance. All such boasting is evil.

¹⁷Therefore, to him who knows to do good and does not do *it,* to him it is sin.

PSALM 118:19-29

OPEN to me the gates of
righteousness;
I will go through them,
And I will praise the LORD.

20 This is the gate of the LORD,
Through which the righteous
shall enter.

21 I will praise You,
For You have answered me,
And have become my
salvation.

22 The stone *which* the builders
rejected
Has become the chief
cornerstone.

23 This was the LORD's doing;
It *is* marvelous in our eyes.

24 This *is* the day the LORD has
made;
We will rejoice and be glad in
it.

25 Save now, I pray, O LORD;
O LORD, I pray, send now
prosperity.

26 Blessed *is* he who comes in
the name of the LORD!
We have blessed you from the
house of the LORD.

27 God *is* the LORD,
And He has given us light;
Bind the sacrifice with cords
to the horns of the altar.

28 You *are* my God, and I will
praise You;
You are my God, I will exalt
You.

29 Oh, give thanks to the LORD,
for *He is* good!
For His mercy *endures* forever.

PROVERBS FOR TODAY/ 28:3-5
A poor man who oppresses the poor is like *a driving rain which leaves no food.*
□ *Those who forsake the law praise the wicked, but such as keep the law contend with them.* □ *Evil men do not understand justice, but those who seek the* LORD *understand all.*

NOVEMBER 21

EZEKIEL 42:1–43:27

THEN he [God's messenger] brought me out into the outer court, by the way toward the north; and he brought me into the chamber which *was* opposite the separating courtyard, and which *was* opposite the building toward the north. ²Facing the length, *which was* one hundred cubits (the width was fifty cubits), was the north door. ³Opposite the inner court of twenty *cubits,* and opposite the pavement of the outer court, *was* gallery against gallery in three *stories.* ⁴In front of the chambers, toward the inside, *was* a walk ten cubits wide, at a distance of one cubit; and their doors faced north. ⁵Now the upper chambers *were* shorter, because the galleries took away *space* from them more than from the lower and middle stories of the building. ⁶For they *were* in three *stories* and did not have pillars like the pillars of the courts; therefore *the upper level* was shortened more than the lower and middle levels from the ground up. ⁷And a wall which *was* outside ran parallel to the chambers, at the front of the chambers, toward the outer court; its length *was* fifty cubits. ⁸The length of the chambers toward the outer court *was* fifty cubits, whereas that facing the temple *was* one hundred cubits. ⁹At the lower chambers *was* the entrance on the east side, as one goes into them from the outer court.

¹⁰Also *there were* chambers in the thickness of the wall of the court toward the east, opposite the separating courtyard and opposite the building. ¹¹*There was* a walk in front of them also, and their appearance *was* like the chambers which *were* toward the north; they *were* as long and as wide as the others, and all their exits and entrances *were* according to plan. ¹²And corresponding to the doors of the chambers that *were* facing south, as one enters them, *there was* a door in front of the walk, the way directly in front of the wall toward the east.

¹³Then he said to me, "The north chambers *and* the south chambers, which *are* opposite the separating courtyard, *are* the holy chambers where the priests who approach the LORD shall eat the most holy offerings. There they shall lay the most holy offerings—the grain offering, the sin offering, and the trespass offering—for the place *is* holy. ¹⁴When the priests enter them, they shall not go out of the holy *chamber* into the outer court; but there they shall leave their garments in which they minister, for they *are* holy. They shall put on other garments; then they may approach *that* which *is* for the people."

¹⁵Now when he had finished measuring the inner temple, he brought me out through the gateway that faces toward the east, and measured it all around. ¹⁶He measured the east side

with the measuring rod,* five hundred rods by the measuring rod all around. ¹⁷He measured the north side, five hundred rods by the measuring rod all around. ¹⁸He measured the south side, five hundred rods by the measuring rod. ¹⁹He came around to the west side *and* measured five hundred rods by the measuring rod. ²⁰He measured it on the four sides; it had a wall all around, five hundred *cubits* long and five hundred wide, to separate the holy areas from the common.

Afterward he brought me to the gate, the gate that faces toward the east. ²And behold, the glory of the God of Israel came from the way of the east. His voice *was* like the sound of many waters; and the earth shone with His glory. ³*It was* like the appearance of the vision which I saw—like the vision which I saw when I* came to destroy the city. The visions *were* like the vision which I saw by the River Chebar; and I fell on my face. ⁴And the glory of the Lord came into the temple by way of the gate which faces toward the east. ⁵The Spirit lifted me up and brought me into the inner court; and behold, the glory of the Lord filled the temple.

⁶Then I heard *Him* speaking to me from the temple, while a man stood beside me. ⁷And He said to me, "Son of man, *this is* the place of My throne and the place of the soles of My feet, where I will dwell in the midst of the children of Israel forever. No more shall the house of Israel defile My holy name, they nor their kings, by their harlotry or with the carcasses of their kings on their high places. ⁸When they set their threshold by My threshold, and their doorpost by My doorpost, with a wall between them and Me, they defiled My holy name by the abominations which they committed; therefore I have consumed them in My anger. ⁹Now let them put their harlotry and the car-

casses of their kings far away from Me, and I will dwell in their midst forever.

¹⁰"Son of man, describe the temple to the house of Israel, that they may be ashamed of their iniquities; and let them measure the pattern. ¹¹And if they are ashamed of all that they have done, make known to them the design of the temple and its arrangement, its exits and its entrances, its entire design and all its ordinances, all its forms and all its laws. Write *it* down in their sight, so that they may keep its whole design and all its ordinances, and perform them. ¹²This *is* the law of the temple: The whole area surrounding the mountaintop *is* most holy. Behold, this *is* the law of the temple.

¹³"These are the measurements of the altar in cubits (the *cubit is* one cubit and a handbreadth): the base one cubit high and one cubit wide, with a rim all around its edge of one span. This *is* the height of the altar: ¹⁴from the base on the ground to the lower ledge, two cubits; the width of the ledge, one cubit; from the smaller ledge to the larger ledge, four cubits; and the width of the ledge, *one* cubit. ¹⁵The altar hearth *is* four cubits high, with four horns extending upward from the hearth. ¹⁶The altar hearth *is* twelve cubits long, twelve wide, square at its four corners; ¹⁷the ledge, fourteen *cubits* long and fourteen wide on its four sides, with a rim of half a cubit around it; its base, one cubit all around; and its steps face toward the east."

¹⁸And He said to me, "Son of man, thus says the Lord God: 'These *are* the ordinances for the altar on the day when it is made, for sacrificing burnt offerings on it, and for sprinkling blood on it. ¹⁹You shall give a young bull for a sin offering to the priests, the Levites, who are of the seed of Zadok, who approach Me to minister to Me,' says the Lord God. ²⁰You shall take some of its blood and put *it* on the four horns of the altar, on the four corners of the ledge, and on

the rim around it; thus you shall cleanse it and make atonement for it. ²¹Then you shall also take the bull of the sin offering, and burn it in the appointed place of the temple, outside the sanctuary. ²²On the second day you shall offer a kid of the goats without blemish for a sin offering; and they shall cleanse the altar, as they cleansed *it* with the bull. ²³When you have finished cleansing *it,* you shall offer a young bull without blemish, and a ram from the flock without blemish. ²⁴When you offer them before the Lord, the priests shall throw salt on them, and they will offer them up *as* a burnt offering to the Lord. ²⁵Every day for seven days you shall prepare a goat *for* a sin offering; they shall also prepare a young bull and a ram from the flock, both without blemish. ²⁶Seven days they shall make atonement for the altar and purify it, and so consecrate *it.* ²⁷When these days are over it shall be, on the eighth day and thereafter, that the priests shall offer your burnt offerings and your peace offerings on the altar; and I will accept you,' says the Lord God."

JAMES 5:1-20

COME now, *you* rich, weep and howl for your miseries that are coming upon *you!* ²Your riches are corrupted, and your garments are moth-eaten. ³Your gold and silver are corroded, and their corrosion will be a witness against you and will eat your flesh like fire. You have heaped up treasure in the last days. ⁴Indeed the wages of the laborers who mowed your fields, which you kept back by fraud, cry out; and the cries of the reapers have reached the ears of the Lord of Sabaoth.* ⁵You have lived on the earth in pleasure and luxury; you have fattened your hearts as* in a day of slaughter. ⁶You have condemned, you have murdered the just; he does not resist you.

⁷Therefore be patient, brethren, until the coming of the Lord. See *how* the farmer waits for the precious fruit of the earth, waiting patiently for it until it receives the early and latter rain. ⁸You also be patient. Establish your hearts, for the coming of the Lord is at hand.

⁹Do not grumble against one another, brethren, lest you be condemned.* Behold, the Judge is standing at the door! ¹⁰My brethren, take the prophets, who spoke in the name of the Lord, as an example of suffering and patience. ¹¹Indeed we count them blessed who endure. You have heard of the perseverance of Job and seen the end *intended by* the Lord—that the Lord is very compassionate and merciful.

¹²But above all, my brethren, do not swear, either by heaven or by earth or with any other oath. But let your "Yes" be "Yes," and *your* "No," "No," lest you fall into judgment.*

¹³Is anyone among you suffering? Let him pray. Is anyone cheerful? Let him sing psalms. ¹⁴Is anyone among you sick? Let him call for the elders of the church, and let them pray over him, anointing him with oil in the name of the Lord. ¹⁵And the prayer of faith will save the sick, and the Lord will raise him up. And if he has committed sins, he will be forgiven. ¹⁶Confess *your* trespasses* to one another, and pray for one another, that you may be healed. The effective, fervent prayer of a righteous man avails much. ¹⁷Elijah was a man with a nature like ours, and he prayed earnestly that it would not rain; and it did not rain on the land for three years and six months. ¹⁸And he prayed again, and the heaven gave rain, and the earth produced its fruit.

¹⁹Brethren, if anyone among you wanders from the truth, and someone turns him back, ²⁰let him know that he who turns a sinner from the error of his way will save a soul* from death and cover a multitude of sins.

PSALM 119:1-16

א ALEPH

BLESSED *are* the undefiled in
the way,
Who walk in the law of the
LORD!
2 Blessed *are* those who keep
His testimonies,
Who seek Him with the whole
heart!
3 They also do no iniquity;
They walk in His ways.
4 You have commanded *us*
To keep Your precepts
diligently.
5 Oh, that my ways were
directed
To keep Your statutes!
6 Then I would not be ashamed,
When I look into all Your
commandments.
7 I will praise You with
uprightness of heart,
When I learn Your righteous
judgments.
8 I will keep Your statutes;
Oh, do not forsake me utterly!

ב BETH

9 How can a young man cleanse
his way?
By taking heed according to
Your word.
10 With my whole heart I have
sought You;
Oh, let me not wander from
Your commandments!
11 Your word I have hidden in
my heart,
That I might not sin against
You.
12 Blessed *are* You, O LORD!
Teach me Your statutes.
13 With my lips I have declared
All the judgments of Your
mouth.
14 I have rejoiced in the way of
Your testimonies,
As *much as* in all riches.
15 I will meditate on Your
precepts,
And contemplate Your ways.
16 I will delight myself in Your
statutes;
I will not forget Your word.

PROVERBS FOR TODAY / 28:6-7

Better is *the poor who walks in his integrity than one perverse* in his *ways, though
he* be *rich.* □ *Whoever keeps the law* is *a discerning son, but a companion of
gluttons shames his father.*

NOVEMBER 22

EZEKIEL 44:1–45:12

THEN He [God's messenger]
brought me back to the outer
gate of the sanctuary which
faces toward the east, but it *was* shut.
2And the LORD said to me, "This gate
shall be shut; it shall not be opened,
and no man shall enter by it, because
the LORD God of Israel has entered by
it; therefore it shall be shut. 3*As for* the
prince, *because* he *is* the prince, he may
sit in it to eat bread before the LORD; he

shall enter by way of the vestibule of the gateway, and go out the same way."

[4]Also He brought me by way of the north gate to the front of the temple; so I looked, and behold, the glory of the LORD filled the house of the LORD; and I fell on my face. [5]And the LORD said to me, "Son of man, mark well, see with your eyes and hear with your ears, all that I say to you concerning all the ordinances of the house of the LORD and all its laws. Mark well who may enter the house and all who go out from the sanctuary.

[6]"Now say to the rebellious, to the house of Israel, 'Thus says the Lord GOD: "O house of Israel, let Us have no more of all your abominations. [7]When you brought in foreigners, uncircumcised in heart and uncircumcised in flesh, to be in My sanctuary to defile it—My house—and when you offered My food, the fat and the blood, then they broke My covenant because of all your abominations. [8]And you have not kept charge of My holy things, but you have set *others* to keep charge of My sanctuary for you." [9]Thus says the Lord GOD: "No foreigner, uncircumcised in heart or uncircumcised in flesh, shall enter My sanctuary, including any foreigner who *is* among the children of Israel.

[10]"And the Levites who went far from Me, when Israel went astray, who strayed away from Me after their idols, they shall bear their iniquity. [11]Yet they shall be ministers in My sanctuary, *as* gatekeepers of the house and ministers of the house; they shall slay the burnt offering and the sacrifice for the people, and they shall stand before them to minister to them. [12]Because they ministered to them before their idols and caused the house of Israel to fall into iniquity, therefore I have raised My hand in an oath against them," says the Lord GOD, "that they shall bear their iniquity. [13]And they shall not come near Me to minister to

Me as priest, nor come near any of My holy things, nor into the Most Holy *Place;* but they shall bear their shame and their abominations which they have committed. [14]Nevertheless I will make them keep charge of the temple, for all its work, and for all that has to be done in it.

[15]"But the priests, the Levites, the sons of Zadok, who kept charge of My sanctuary when the children of Israel went astray from Me, they shall come near Me to minister to Me; and they shall stand before Me to offer to Me the fat and the blood," says the Lord GOD. [16]"They shall enter My sanctuary, and they shall come near My table to minister to Me, and they shall keep My charge. [17]And it shall be, whenever they enter the gates of the inner court, that they shall put on linen garments; no wool shall come upon them while they minister within the gates of the inner court or within the house. [18]They shall have linen turbans on their heads and linen trousers on their bodies; they shall not clothe themselves with *anything that causes* sweat. [19]When they go out to the outer court, to the *outer* court to the people, they shall take off their garments in which they have ministered, leave them in the holy chambers, and put on other garments; and in their holy garments they shall not sanctify the people.

[20]"They shall neither shave their heads, nor let their hair grow long, but they shall keep their hair well trimmed. [21]No priest shall drink wine when he enters the inner court. [22]They shall not take as wife a widow or a divorced woman, but take virgins of the descendants of the house of Israel, or widows of priests.

[23]"And they shall teach My people *the difference* between the holy and the unholy, and cause them to discern between the unclean and the clean. [24]In controversy they shall stand as judges, *and* judge it according to My judg-

ments. They shall keep My laws and My statutes in all My appointed meetings, and they shall hallow My Sabbaths.

25"They shall not defile *themselves* by coming near a dead person. Only for father or mother, for son or daughter, for brother or unmarried sister may they defile themselves. 26After he is cleansed, they shall count seven days for him. 27And on the day that he goes to the sanctuary to minister in the sanctuary, he must offer his sin offering in the inner court," says the Lord GOD.

28"It shall be, in regard to their inheritance, *that* I *am* their inheritance. You shall give them no possession in Israel, for I *am* their possession. 29They shall eat the grain offering, the sin offering, and the trespass offering; every dedicated thing in Israel shall be theirs. 30The best of all firstfruits of any kind, and every sacrifice of any kind from all your sacrifices, shall be the priest's; also you shall give to the priest the first of your ground meal, to cause a blessing to rest on your house. 31The priests shall not eat anything, bird or beast, that died naturally or was torn *by wild beasts.*

"MOREOVER, when you divide the land by lot into inheritance, you shall set apart a district for the LORD, a holy section of the land; its length *shall be* twenty-five thousand *cubits,* and the width ten thousand. It *shall be* holy throughout its territory all around. 2Of this there shall be a square plot for the sanctuary, five hundred by five hundred *rods,* with fifty cubits around it for an open space. 3So this is the district you shall measure: twenty-five thousand *cubits* long and ten thousand wide; in it shall be the sanctuary, the Most Holy *Place.* 4It shall be a holy *section* of the land, belonging to the priests, the ministers of the sanctuary, who come near to minister to the LORD;

it shall be a place for their houses and a holy place for the sanctuary. 5*An area* twenty-five thousand *cubits* long and ten thousand wide shall belong to the Levites, the ministers of the temple; they shall have twenty chambers as a possession.*

6"You shall appoint as the property of the city *an area* five thousand *cubits* wide and twenty-five thousand long, adjacent to the district of the holy *section;* it shall belong to the whole house of Israel.

7"The prince shall have *a section* on one side and the other of the holy district and the city's property; and bordering on the holy district and the city's property, extending westward on the west side and eastward on the east side, the length *shall be* side by side with one of the *tribal* portions, from the west border to the east border. 8The land shall be his possession in Israel; and My princes shall no more oppress My people, but they shall give *the rest of* the land to the house of Israel, according to their tribes."

9Thus says the Lord GOD: "Enough, O princes of Israel! Remove violence and plundering, execute justice and righteousness, and stop dispossessing My people," says the Lord GOD. 10"You shall have honest scales, an honest ephah, and an honest bath. 11The ephah and the bath shall be of the same measure, so that the bath contains one-tenth of a homer, and the ephah one-tenth of a homer; their measure shall be according to the homer. 12The shekel *shall be* twenty gerahs; twenty shekels, twenty-five shekels, *and* fifteen shekels shall be your mina."

1 PETER 1:1-12

PETER, an apostle of Jesus Christ,

To the pilgrims of the Dispersion in Pontus, Galatia, Cappadocia,

Asia, and Bithynia, ²elect according to the foreknowledge of God the Father, in sanctification of the Spirit, for obedience and sprinkling of the blood of Jesus Christ:

Grace to you and peace be multiplied.

³Blessed *be* the God and Father of our Lord Jesus Christ, who according to His abundant mercy has begotten us again to a living hope through the resurrection of Jesus Christ from the dead, ⁴to an inheritance incorruptible and undefiled and that does not fade away, reserved in heaven for you, ⁵who are kept by the power of God through faith for salvation ready to be revealed in the last time.

⁶In this you greatly rejoice, though now for a little while, if need be, you have been grieved by various trials, ⁷that the genuineness of your faith, *being* much more precious than gold that perishes, though it is tested by fire, may be found to praise, honor, and glory at the revelation of Jesus Christ, ⁸whom having not seen* you love. Though now you do not see *Him,* yet believing, you rejoice with joy inexpressible and full of glory, ⁹receiving the end of your faith—the salvation of *your* souls.

¹⁰Of this salvation the prophets have inquired and searched carefully, who prophesied of the grace *that would come* to you, ¹¹searching what, or what manner of time, the Spirit of Christ who was in them was indicating when He testified beforehand the sufferings of Christ and the glories that would follow. ¹²To them it was revealed that, not to themselves, but to us* they were ministering the things which now have been reported to you through those who have preached the gospel to you by the Holy Spirit sent from heaven— things which angels desire to look into.

PSALM 119:17-32

ב GIMEL

DEAL bountifully with Your servant,
That I may live and keep Your word.
18 Open my eyes, that I may see Wondrous things from Your law.
19 I *am* a stranger in the earth; Do not hide Your commandments from me.
20 My soul breaks with longing For Your judgments at all times.
21 You rebuke the proud—the cursed, Who stray from Your commandments.
22 Remove from me reproach and contempt, For I have kept Your testimonies.
23 Princes also sit *and* speak against me, *But* Your servant meditates on Your statutes.
24 Your testimonies also *are* my delight *And* my counselors.

ד DALETH

25 My soul clings to the dust; Revive me according to Your word.
26 I have declared my ways, and You answered me; Teach me Your statutes.
27 Make me understand the way of Your precepts; So shall I meditate on Your wonderful works.
28 My soul melts from heaviness; Strengthen me according to Your word.
29 Remove from me the way of lying,

And grant me Your law
graciously.
30 I have chosen the way of truth;
Your judgments I have laid
before me.
31 I cling to Your testimonies;

O Lord, do not put me to
shame!
32 I will run the course of Your
commandments,
For You shall enlarge my
heart.

PROVERBS FOR TODAY / 28:8-10

One who increases his possessions by usury and extortion gathers it for him who will pity the poor. One who turns away his ear from hearing the law, even his prayer is an abomination. Whoever causes the upright to go astray in an evil way, he himself will fall into his own pit; but the blameless will inherit good.

NOVEMBER 23

EZEKIEL 45:13–46:24

"THIS *is* the offering which you shall offer: you shall give one-sixth of an ephah from a homer of wheat, and one-sixth of an ephah from a homer of barley. 14The ordinance concerning oil, the bath of oil, *is* one-tenth of a bath from a kor. A kor *is* a homer or ten baths, for ten baths *are* a homer. 15And one lamb shall be given from a flock of two hundred, from the rich pastures of Israel. These shall be for grain offerings, burnt offerings, and peace offerings, to make atonement for them," says the Lord God. 16"All the people of the land shall give this offering for the prince in Israel. 17Then it shall be the prince's part *to give* burnt offerings, grain offerings, and drink offerings, at the feasts, the New Moons, the Sabbaths, and at all the appointed seasons of the house of Israel. He shall prepare the sin offering, the grain offering, the burnt offering, and the peace offerings to make atonement for the house of Israel."

18"Thus says the Lord God: "In the first *month,* on the first *day* of the month, you shall take a young bull without blemish and cleanse the sanctuary. 19The priest shall take some of the blood of the sin offering and put *it* on the doorposts of the temple, on the four corners of the ledge of the altar, and on the gateposts of the gate of the inner court. 20And so you shall do on the seventh *day* of the month for everyone who has sinned unintentionally or in ignorance. Thus you shall make atonement for the temple.

21"In the first *month,* on the fourteenth day of the month, you shall observe the Passover, a feast of seven days; unleavened bread shall be eaten. 22And on that day the prince shall prepare for himself and for all the people of the land a bull *for* a sin offering. 23On the seven days of the feast he shall prepare a burnt offering to the Lord, seven bulls and seven rams without blemish, daily for seven days, and a kid of the goats daily *for* a sin offering. 24And he shall prepare a grain offering of one ephah for each bull and one ephah for each ram, together with a hin of oil for each ephah.

25"In the seventh *month,* on the fifteenth day of the month, at the feast, he shall do likewise for seven days, according to the sin offering, the burnt offering, the grain offering, and the oil."

'Thus says the Lord God: "The gateway of the inner court that faces toward the east shall be shut the six working days; but on the Sabbath it shall be opened, and on the day of the New Moon it shall be opened. ²The prince shall enter by way of the vestibule of the gateway from the outside, and stand by the gatepost. The priests shall prepare his burnt offering and his peace offerings. He shall worship at the threshold of the gate. Then he shall go out, but the gate shall not be shut until evening. ³Likewise the people of the land shall worship at the entrance to this gateway before the Lord on the Sabbaths and the New Moons. ⁴The burnt offering that the prince offers to the Lord on the Sabbath day *shall be* six lambs without blemish, and a ram without blemish; ⁵and the grain offering *shall be one* ephah for a ram, and the grain offering for the lambs, as much as he wants to give, as well as a hin of oil with every ephah. ⁶On the day of the New Moon *it shall be* a young bull without blemish, six lambs, and a ram; they shall be without blemish. ⁷He shall prepare a grain offering of an ephah for a bull, an ephah for a ram, as much as he wants to give for the lambs, and a hin of oil with every ephah. ⁸When the prince enters, he shall go in by way of the vestibule of the gateway, and go out the same way.

⁹"But when the people of the land come before the Lord on the appointed feast days, whoever enters by way of the north gate to worship shall go out by way of the south gate; and whoever enters by way of the south gate shall go out by way of the north gate. He shall not return by way of the gate through which he came, but shall go out through the opposite gate. ¹⁰The prince shall then be in their midst. When they go in, he shall go in; and when they go out, he shall go out. ¹¹At the festivals and the appointed feast days the grain offering shall be an ephah for a bull, an ephah for a ram, as much as he wants to give for the lambs, and a hin of oil with every ephah.

¹²"Now when the prince makes a voluntary burnt offering or voluntary peace offering to the Lord, the gate that faces toward the east shall then be opened for him; and he shall prepare his burnt offering and his peace offerings as he did on the Sabbath day. Then he shall go out, and after he goes out the gate shall be shut.

¹³"You shall daily make a burnt offering to the Lord *of* a lamb of the first year without blemish; you shall prepare it every morning. ¹⁴And you shall prepare a grain offering with it every morning, a sixth of an ephah, and a third of a hin of oil to moisten the fine flour. This grain offering is a perpetual ordinance, to be made regularly to the Lord. ¹⁵Thus they shall prepare the lamb, the grain offering, and the oil, *as* a regular burnt offering every morning."

¹⁶'Thus says the Lord God: "If the prince gives a gift *of some* of his inheritance to any of his sons, it shall belong to his sons; it is their possession by inheritance. ¹⁷But if he gives a gift of some of his inheritance to one of his servants, it shall be his until the year of liberty, after which it shall return to the prince. But his inheritance shall belong to his sons; it shall become theirs. ¹⁸Moreover the prince shall not take any of the people's inheritance by evicting them from their property; he shall provide an inheritance for his sons from his own property, so that none of My people may be scattered from his property." ' "

¹⁹Now he brought me through the entrance, which *was* at the side of the

gate, into the holy chambers of the priests which face toward the north; and there a place *was* situated at their extreme western end. 20And he said to me, "This *is* the place where the priests shall boil the trespass offering and the sin offering, *and* where they shall bake the grain offering, so that they do not bring *them* out into the outer court to sanctify the people."

21Then he brought me out into the outer court and caused me to pass by the four corners of the court; and in fact, in every corner of the court *there was another* court. 22In the four corners of the court *were* enclosed courts, forty *cubits* long and thirty wide; all four corners *were* the same size. 23*There was* a row *of building stones* all around in them, all around the four of them; and cooking hearths were made under the rows of stones all around. 24And he said to me, "These *are* the kitchens where the ministers of the temple shall boil the sacrifices of the people."

1 PETER 1:13–2:10

THEREFORE gird up the loins of your mind, be sober, and rest *your* hope fully upon the grace that is to be brought to you at the revelation of Jesus Christ; 14as obedient children, not conforming yourselves to the former lusts, *as* in your ignorance; 15but as He who called you *is* holy, you also be holy in all *your* conduct, 16because it is written, *"Be holy, for I am holy."* *

17And if you call on the Father, who without partiality judges according to each one's work, conduct yourselves throughout the time of your stay *here* in fear; 18knowing that you were not redeemed with corruptible things, *like* silver or gold, from your aimless conduct *received* by tradition from your fathers, 19but with the precious blood of Christ, as of a lamb without blemish

and without spot. 20He indeed was foreordained before the foundation of the world, but was manifest in these last times for you 21who through Him believe in God, who raised Him from the dead and gave Him glory, so that your faith and hope are in God.

22Since you have purified your souls in obeying the truth through the Spirit* in sincere love of the brethren, love one another fervently with a pure heart, 23having been born again, not of corruptible seed but incorruptible, through the word of God which lives and abides forever,* 24because

> *"All flesh is as grass,*
> *And all the glory of man * as*
> *the flower of the grass.*
> *The grass withers,*
> *And its flower falls away,*
> 25 *But the word of the LORD*
> *endures forever."* *

Now this is the word which by the gospel was preached to you.

THEREFORE, laying aside all malice, all deceit, hypocrisy, envy, and all evil speaking, 2as newborn babes, desire the pure milk of the word, that you may grow thereby,* 3if indeed you have tasted that the Lord *is* gracious.

4Coming to Him *as to* a living stone, rejected indeed by men, but chosen by God *and* precious, 5you also, as living stones, are being built up a spiritual house, a holy priesthood, to offer up spiritual sacrifices acceptable to God through Jesus Christ. 6Therefore it is also contained in the Scripture,

> *"Behold, I lay in Zion*
> *A chief cornerstone, elect,*
> *precious,*
> *And he who believes on Him*
> *will by no means be put to*
> *shame."* *

7Therefore, to you who believe, *He is* precious; but to those who are disobedient,*

*"The stone which the builders
rejected
Has become the chief
cornerstone,"* *

⁸and

*"A stone of stumbling
And a rock of offense."* *

They stumble, being disobedient to the word, to which they also were appointed.

⁹But you *are* a chosen generation, a royal priesthood, a holy nation, His own special people, that you may proclaim the praises of Him who called you out of darkness into His marvelous light; ¹⁰who once *were* not a people but *are* now the people of God, who had not obtained mercy but now have obtained mercy.

PSALM 119:33-48

ה HE

TEACH me, O LORD, the way of Your statutes,
And I shall keep it *to* the end.
34 Give me understanding, and I shall keep Your law;
Indeed, I shall observe it with *my* whole heart.
35 Make me walk in the path of Your commandments,
For I delight in it.
36 Incline my heart to Your testimonies,
And not to covetousness.
37 Turn away my eyes from looking at worthless things,
And revive me in Your way.*

38 Establish Your word to Your servant,
Who *is devoted* to fearing You.
39 Turn away my reproach which I dread,
For Your judgments *are* good.
40 Behold, I long for Your precepts;
Revive me in Your righteousness.

ו WAW

41 Let Your mercies come also to me, O LORD—
Your salvation according to Your word.
42 So shall I have an answer for him who reproaches me,
For I trust in Your word.
43 And take not the word of truth utterly out of my mouth,
For I have hoped in Your ordinances.
44 So shall I keep Your law continually,
Forever and ever.
45 And I will walk at liberty,
For I seek Your precepts.
46 I will speak of Your testimonies also before kings,
And will not be ashamed.
47 And I will delight myself in Your commandments,
Which I love.
48 My hands also I will lift up to Your commandments,
Which I love,
And I will meditate on Your statutes.

PROVERBS FOR TODAY/ 28:11
The rich man is *wise in his own eyes, but the poor who has understanding searches him out.*

EZEKIEL 47:1–48:35

THEN he [God's messenger] brought me back to the door of the temple; and there was water, flowing from under the threshold of the temple toward the east, for the front of the temple faced east; the water was flowing from under the right side of the temple, south of the altar. ²He brought me out by way of the north gate, and led me around on the outside to the outer gateway that faces east; and there was water, running out on the right side.

³And when the man went out to the east with the line in his hand, he measured one thousand cubits, and he brought me through the waters; the water *came up to my* ankles. ⁴Again he measured one thousand and brought me through the waters; the water *came up to my* knees. Again he measured one thousand and brought me through; the water *came up to my* waist. ⁵Again he measured one thousand, *and it was* a river that I could not cross; for the water was too deep, water in which one must swim, a river that could not be crossed. ⁶He said to me, "Son of man, have you seen *this?*" Then he brought me and returned me to the bank of the river.

⁷When I returned, there, along the bank of the river, *were* very many trees on one side and the other. ⁸Then he said to me: "This water flows toward the eastern region, goes down into the valley, and enters the sea. *When it* reaches the sea, *its* waters are healed. ⁹And it shall be *that* every living thing that moves, wherever the rivers go, will live. There will be a very great multitude of fish, because these waters go there; for they will be healed, and everything will live wherever the river

goes. ¹⁰It shall be *that* fishermen will stand by it from En Gedi to En Eglaim; they will be *places* for spreading their nets. Their fish will be of the same kinds as the fish of the Great Sea, exceedingly many. ¹¹But its swamps and marshes will not be healed; they will be given over to salt. ¹²Along the bank of the river, on this side and that, will grow all *kinds of* trees used for food; their leaves will not wither, and their fruit will not fail. They will bear fruit every month, because their water flows from the sanctuary. Their fruit will be for food, and their leaves for medicine."

¹³Thus says the Lord GOD: "These *are* the borders by which you shall divide the land as an inheritance among the twelve tribes of Israel. Joseph *shall have two* portions. ¹⁴You shall inherit it equally with one another; for I raised My hand in an oath to give it to your fathers, and this land shall fall to you as your inheritance.

¹⁵"This *shall be* the border of the land on the north: from the Great Sea, *by* the road to Hethlon, as one goes to Zedad, ¹⁶Hamath, Berothah, Sibraim (which *is* between the border of Damascus and the border of Hamath), to Hazar Hatticon (which *is* on the border of Hauran). ¹⁷Thus the boundary shall be from the Sea to Hazar Enan, the border of Damascus; and as for the north, northward, it is the border of Hamath. *This is* the north side.

¹⁸"On the east side you shall mark out the border from between Hauran and Damascus, and between Gilead and the land of Israel, along the Jordan, and along the eastern side of the sea. *This is* the east side.

¹⁹"The south side, toward the South,* *shall be* from Tamar to the wa-

ters of Meribah by Kadesh, along the brook to the Great Sea. *This is* the south side, toward the South.

20"The west side *shall be* the Great Sea, from the *southern* boundary until one comes to a point opposite Hamath. This *is* the west side.

21"Thus you shall divide this land among yourselves according to the tribes of Israel. 22It shall be that you will divide it by lot as an inheritance for yourselves, and for the strangers who dwell among you and who bear children among you. They shall be to you as native-born among the children of Israel; they shall have an inheritance with you among the tribes of Israel. 23And it shall be *that* in whatever tribe the stranger dwells, there you shall give *him* his inheritance," says the Lord God.

"Now these *are* the names of the tribes: From the northern border along the road to Hethlon at the entrance of Hamath, to Hazar Enan, the border of Damascus northward, in the direction of Hamath, *there shall be* one *section for* Dan from its east to its west side; 2by the border of Dan, from the east side to the west, one *section for* Asher; 3by the border of Asher, from the east side to the west, one *section for* Naphtali; 4by the border of Naphtali, from the east side to the west, one *section for* Manasseh; 5by the border of Manasseh, from the east side to the west, one *section for* Ephraim; 6by the border of Ephraim, from the east side to the west, one *section for* Reuben; 7by the border of Reuben, from the east side to the west, one *section for* Judah; 8by the border of Judah, from the east side to the west, shall be the district which you shall set apart, twenty-five thousand *cubits* in width, and *in* length the same as one of the *other* portions, from the east side to the west, with the sanctuary in the center.

9"The district that you shall set apart for the Lord *shall be* twenty-five thousand *cubits* in length and ten thousand in width. 10To these—to the priests—the holy district shall belong: on the north twenty-five thousand *cubits in length,* on the west ten thousand in width, on the east ten thousand in width, and on the south twenty-five thousand in length. The sanctuary of the Lord shall be in the center. 11*It shall be* for the priests of the sons of Zadok, who are sanctified, who have kept My charge, who did not go astray when the children of Israel went astray, as the Levites went astray. 12And *this* district of land that is set apart shall be to them a thing most holy by the border of the Levites.

13"Opposite the border of the priests, the Levites *shall have an area* twenty-five thousand *cubits* in length and ten thousand in width; its entire length *shall be* twenty-five thousand and its width ten thousand. 14And they shall not sell or exchange any of it; they may not alienate this best *part* of the land, for *it is* holy to the Lord.

15"The five thousand *cubits* in width that remain, along the edge of the twenty-five thousand, shall be for general use by the city, for dwellings and common-land; and the city shall be in the center. 16These *shall be* its measurements: the north side four thousand five hundred *cubits,* the south side four thousand five hundred, the east side four thousand five hundred, and the west side four thousand five hundred. 17The common-land of the city shall be: to the north two hundred and fifty *cubits,* to the south two hundred and fifty, to the east two hundred and fifty, and to the west two hundred and fifty. 18The rest of the length, alongside the district of the holy *section, shall be* ten thousand *cubits* to the east and ten thousand to the west. It shall be adjacent to the district of the holy *section,* and its produce shall be food for the workers of the city. 19The workers of the city, from all the tribes of Israel, shall cultivate it. 20The entire district *shall be* twenty-five thousand *cubits* by twenty-five thousand *cubits,* foursquare. You shall set apart the holy district with the property of the city.

21"The rest *shall belong* to the prince, on one side and on the other of the holy district and of the city's property, next to the twenty-five thousand *cubits* of the *holy* district as far as the eastern border, and westward next to the twenty-five thousand as far as the western border, adjacent to the *tribal* portions; *it shall belong* to the prince. It shall be the holy district, and the sanctuary of the temple *shall be* in the center. 22Moreover, apart from the possession of the Levites and the possession of the city *which are* in the midst of what *belongs* to the prince, *the area* between the border of Judah and the border of Benjamin shall belong to the prince.

23"As for the rest of the tribes, from the east side to the west, Benjamin *shall have* one *section;* 24by the border of Benjamin, from the east side to the west, Simeon *shall have* one *section;* 25by the border of Simeon, from the east side to the west, Issachar *shall have* one *section;* 26by the border of Issachar, from the east side to the west, Zebulun *shall have* one *section;* 27by the border of Zebulun, from the east side to the west, Gad *shall have* one *section;* 28by the border of Gad, on the south side, toward the South,* the border shall be from Tamar *to* the waters of Meribah *by* Kadesh, along the brook to the Great Sea. 29This *is* the land which you shall divide by lot as an inheritance among the tribes of Israel, and these *are* their portions," says the Lord GOD.

30"These *are* the exits of the city. On the north side, measuring four thousand five hundred *cubits* 31(the gates of the city *shall be* named after the tribes of Israel), the three gates northward: one gate for Reuben, one gate for Judah, and one gate for Levi; 32on the east side, four thousand five hundred *cubits,* three gates: one gate for Joseph, one gate for Benjamin, and one gate for Dan; 33on the south side, measuring four thousand five hundred *cubits,* three gates: one gate for Simeon, one gate for Issachar, and one gate for Zebulun; 34on the west side, four thousand five hundred *cubits* with their three gates: one gate for Gad, one gate for Asher, and one gate for Naphtali. 35All the way around *shall be* eighteen thousand *cubits;* and the name of the city from *that* day *shall be:* THE LORD *IS* THERE."*

1 PETER 2:11–3:7

BELOVED, I beg *you* as sojourners and pilgrims, abstain from fleshly lusts which war against the soul, 12having your conduct honorable among the Gentiles, that when they speak against you as evildoers, they may, by *your* good works which they observe, glorify God in the day of visitation.

13Therefore submit yourselves to every ordinance of man for the Lord's sake, whether to the king as supreme, 14or to governors, as to those who are sent by him for the punishment of evildoers and *for the* praise of those who do good. 15For this is the will of God, that by doing good you may put to silence the ignorance of foolish men— 16as free, yet not using liberty as a cloak for vice, but as bondservants of God. 17Honor all *people.* Love the brotherhood. Fear God. Honor the king.

18Servants, *be* submissive to *your* masters with all fear, not only to the good and gentle, but also to the harsh. 19For this *is* commendable, if because of conscience toward God one endures grief, suffering wrongfully. 20For what credit *is it* if, when you are beaten for your faults, you take it patiently? But when you do good and suffer, if you take it patiently, this *is* commendable before God. [21]For to this you were called, because Christ also suffered for us,* leaving us* an example, that you should follow His steps:

> 22 *"Who committed no sin,*
> *Nor was deceit found in His*
> *mouth";**

[23]who, when He was reviled, did not revile in return; when He suffered, He did not threaten, but committed *Himself* to Him who judges righteously; [24]who Himself bore our sins in His own body on the tree, that we, having died to sins, might live for righteousness— by whose stripes you were healed. [25]For you were like sheep going astray, but have now returned to the Shepherd and Overseer* of your souls.

W[IVES], likewise, *be* submissive to your own husbands, that even if some do not obey the word, they, without a word, may be won by the conduct of their wives, [2]when they observe your chaste conduct *accompanied* by fear. [3]Do not let your adornment be *merely* outward—arranging the hair, wearing gold, or putting on *fine* apparel— [4]rather *let it be* the hidden person of the heart, with the incorruptible *beauty* of a gentle and quiet spirit, which is very precious in the sight of God. [5]For in this manner, in former times, the holy women who trusted in God also adorned themselves, being submissive to their own husbands, [6]as Sarah obeyed Abraham, calling him lord, whose daughters you are if you do good and are not afraid with any terror. [7]Husbands, likewise, dwell with *them* with understanding, giving honor to the wife, as to the weaker vessel, and as *being* heirs together of the grace of life, that your prayers may not be hindered.

PSALM 119:49-64

> ז   ZAYIN

R[EMEMBER] the word to Your servant,
Upon which You have caused me to hope.
50   This *is* my comfort in my affliction,
For Your word has given me life.
51   The proud have me in great derision,
Yet I do not turn aside from Your law.
52   I remembered Your judgments of old, O L[ORD],
And have comforted myself.
53   Indignation has taken hold of me
Because of the wicked, who forsake Your law.
54   Your statutes have been my songs
In the house of my pilgrimage.
55   I remember Your name in the night, O L[ORD],
And I keep Your law.
56   This has become mine,
Because I kept Your precepts.

> ח   HETH

57   *You are* my portion, O L[ORD];
I have said that I would keep Your words.
58   I entreated Your favor with *my* whole heart;
Be merciful to me according to Your word.
59   I thought about my ways,
And turned my feet to Your testimonies.
60   I made haste, and did not delay
To keep Your commandments.

61 The cords of the wicked have
bound me,
But I have not forgotten Your
law.
62 At midnight I will rise to give
thanks to You,
Because of Your righteous
judgments.

63 I *am* a companion of all who
fear You,
And of those who keep Your
precepts.
64 The earth, O Lord, is full of
Your mercy;
Teach me Your statutes.

PROVERBS FOR TODAY/ 28:12-13

When the righteous rejoice, there is *great glory; but when the wicked arise, men hide themselves.* □ *He who covers his sins will not prosper, but whoever confesses and forsakes* them *will have mercy.*

NOVEMBER 25

DANIEL 1:1–2:23

In the third year of the reign of Jehoiakim king of Judah, Nebuchadnezzar king of Babylon came to Jerusalem and besieged it. 2And the Lord gave Jehoiakim king of Judah into his hand, with some of the articles of the house of God, which he carried into the land of Shinar to the house of his god; and he brought the articles into the treasure house of his god.

3Then the king instructed Ashpenaz, the master of his eunuchs, to bring some of the children of Israel and some of the king's descendants and some of the nobles, 4young men in whom *there was* no blemish, but good-looking, gifted in all wisdom, possessing knowledge and quick to understand, who *had* ability to serve in the king's palace, and whom they might teach the language and literature of the Chaldeans. 5And the king appointed for them a daily provision of the king's delicacies and of the wine which he drank, and three years of training for them, so that at the end of *that time* they might serve before the king. 6Now from among those of the sons of Judah were Daniel, Hananiah, Mishael, and Azariah. 7To them the chief of the eunuchs gave names: he gave Daniel *the name* Belteshazzar; to Hananiah, Shadrach; to Mishael, Meshach; and to Azariah, Abed-Nego.

8But Daniel purposed in his heart that he would not defile himself with the portion of the king's delicacies, nor with the wine which he drank; therefore he requested of the chief of the eunuchs that he might not defile himself. 9Now God had brought Daniel into the favor and goodwill of the chief of the eunuchs. 10And the chief of the eunuchs said to Daniel, "I fear my lord the king, who has appointed your food and drink. For why should he see your faces looking worse than the young men who *are* your age? Then you would endanger my head before the king."

11So Daniel said to the steward* whom the chief of the eunuchs had set over Daniel, Hananiah, Mishael, and Azariah, 12"Please test your servants for ten days, and let them give us vegetables to eat and water to drink.

[13]Then let our appearance be examined before you, and the appearance of the young men who eat the portion of the king's delicacies; and as you see fit, *so* deal with your servants." [14]So he consented with them in this matter, and tested them ten days.

[15]And at the end of ten days their features appeared better and fatter in flesh than all the young men who ate the portion of the king's delicacies. [16]Thus the steward took away their portion of delicacies and the wine that they were to drink, and gave them vegetables.

[17]As for these four young men, God gave them knowledge and skill in all literature and wisdom; and Daniel had understanding in all visions and dreams.

[18]Now at the end of the days, when the king had said that they should be brought in, the chief of the eunuchs brought them in before Nebuchadnezzar. [19]Then the king interviewed* them, and among them all none was found like Daniel, Hananiah, Mishael, and Azariah; therefore they served before the king. [20]And in all matters of wisdom *and* understanding about which the king examined them, he found them ten times better than all the magicians *and* astrologers who *were* in all his realm. [21]Thus Daniel continued until the first year of King Cyrus.

Now in the second year of Nebuchadnezzar's reign, Nebuchadnezzar had dreams; and his spirit was *so* troubled that his sleep left him. [2]Then the king gave the command to call the magicians, the astrologers, the sorcerers, and the Chaldeans to tell the king his dreams. So they came and stood before the king. [3]And the king said to them, "I have had a dream, and my spirit is anxious to know the dream."

[4]Then the Chaldeans spoke to the king in Aramaic,* "O king, live forever! Tell your servants the dream, and we will give the interpretation."

[5]The king answered and said to the Chaldeans, "My decision is firm: if you do not make known the dream to me, and its interpretation, you shall be cut in pieces, and your houses shall be made an ash heap. [6]However, if you tell the dream and its interpretation, you shall receive from me gifts, rewards, and great honor. Therefore tell me the dream and its interpretation."

[7]They answered again and said, "Let the king tell his servants the dream, and we will give its interpretation."

[8]The king answered and said, "I know for certain that you would gain time, because you see that my decision is firm: [9]if you do not make known the dream to me, *there is only* one decree for you! For you have agreed to speak lying and corrupt words before me till the time has changed. Therefore tell me the dream, and I shall know that you can give me its interpretation."

[10]The Chaldeans answered the king, and said, "There is not a man on earth who can tell the king's matter; therefore no king, lord, or ruler has *ever* asked such things of any magician, astrologer, or Chaldean. [11]*It is* a difficult thing that the king requests, and there is no other who can tell it to the king except the gods, whose dwelling is not with flesh."

[12]For this reason the king was angry and very furious, and gave the command to destroy all the wise *men* of Babylon. [13]So the decree went out, and they began killing the wise *men;* and they sought Daniel and his companions, to kill *them.*

[14]Then with counsel and wisdom Daniel answered Arioch, the captain of the king's guard, who had gone out to kill the wise *men* of Babylon; [15]he answered and said to Arioch the king's captain, "Why is the decree from the

king so urgent?" Then Arioch made the decision known to Daniel.

¹⁶So Daniel went in and asked the king to give him time, that he might tell the king the interpretation. ¹⁷Then Daniel went to his house, and made the decision known to Hananiah, Mishael, and Azariah, his companions, ¹⁸that they might seek mercies from the God of heaven concerning this secret, so that Daniel and his companions might not perish with the rest of the wise *men* of Babylon. ¹⁹Then the secret was revealed to Daniel in a night vision. So Daniel blessed the God of heaven.

²⁰Daniel answered and said:

"Blessed be the name of God
forever and ever,
For wisdom and might are
His.
21 And He changes the times
and the seasons;
He removes kings and raises
up kings;
He gives wisdom to the wise
And knowledge to those who
have understanding.
22 He reveals deep and secret
things;
He knows what *is* in the
darkness,
And light dwells with Him.

23 "I thank You and praise You,
O God of my fathers;
You have given me wisdom
and might,
And have now made known to
me what we asked of You,
For You have made known to
us the king's demand."

1 PETER 3:8–4:6

FINALLY, all *of you be* of one mind, having compassion for one another; love as brothers, *be* tenderhearted, *be* courteous;* ⁹not returning evil for evil or reviling for reviling, but on the contrary blessing, knowing that you were called to this, that you may inherit a blessing. ¹⁰For

"He who would love life
And see good days,
Let him refrain his tongue
from evil,
And his lips from speaking
deceit.
11 Let him turn away from evil
and do good;
Let him seek peace and
pursue it.
12 For the eyes of the LORD are
on the righteous,
And His ears are open to their
prayers;
But the face of the LORD is
against those who do evil." *

¹³And who *is* he who will harm you if you become followers of what is good? ¹⁴But even if you should suffer for righteousness' sake, *you are* blessed. *"And do not be afraid of their threats, nor be troubled."* * ¹⁵But sanctify the Lord God* in your hearts, and always *be* ready to *give* a defense to everyone who asks you a reason for the hope that is in you, with meekness and fear; ¹⁶having a good conscience, that when they defame you as evildoers, those who revile your good conduct in Christ may be ashamed. ¹⁷For *it is* better, if it is the will of God, to suffer for doing good than for doing evil.

¹⁸For Christ also suffered once for sins, the just for the unjust, that He might bring us* to God, being put to death in the flesh but made alive by the Spirit, ¹⁹by whom also He went and preached to the spirits in prison, ²⁰who formerly were disobedient, when once the Divine longsuffering waited* in the days of Noah, while *the* ark was being prepared, in which a few, that is, eight souls, were saved through water. ²¹There is also an antitype which now

saves us—baptism (not the removal of the filth of the flesh, but the answer of a good conscience toward God), through the resurrection of Jesus Christ, 22who has gone into heaven and is at the right hand of God, angels and authorities and powers having been made subject to Him.

THEREFORE, since Christ suffered for us* in the flesh, arm yourselves also with the same mind, for he who has suffered in the flesh has ceased from sin, 2that he no longer should live the rest of *his* time in the flesh for the lusts of men, but for the will of God. 3For we *have spent* enough of our past lifetime* in doing the will of the Gentiles—when we walked in lewdness, lusts, drunkenness, revelries, drinking parties, and abominable idolatries. 4In regard to these, they think it strange that you do not run with *them* in the same flood of dissipation, speaking evil of *you*. 5They will give an account to Him who is ready to judge the living and the dead. 6For this reason the gospel was preached also to those who are dead, that they might be judged according to men in the flesh, but live according to God in the spirit.

PSALM 119:65-80

ט   TETH

YOU have dealt well with Your servant,
O LORD, according to Your word.
66   Teach me good judgment and knowledge,
For I believe Your commandments.
67   Before I was afflicted I went astray,
But now I keep Your word.
68   You *are* good, and do good;

Teach me Your statutes.
69   The proud have forged a lie against me,
But I will keep Your precepts with *my* whole heart.
70   Their heart is as fat as grease,
But I delight in Your law.
71   *It is* good for me that I have been afflicted,
That I may learn Your statutes.
72   The law of Your mouth *is* better to me
Than thousands of *coins of* gold and silver.

י   YOD

73   Your hands have made me and fashioned me;
Give me understanding, that I may learn Your commandments.
74   Those who fear You will be glad when they see me,
Because I have hoped in Your word.
75   I know, O LORD, that Your judgments *are* right,
And *that* in faithfulness You have afflicted me.
76   Let, I pray, Your merciful kindness be for my comfort,
According to Your word to Your servant.
77   Let Your tender mercies come to me, that I may live;
For Your law *is* my delight.
78   Let the proud be ashamed,
For they treated me wrongfully with falsehood;
But I will meditate on Your precepts.
79   Let those who fear You turn to me,
Those who know Your testimonies.
80   Let my heart be blameless regarding Your statutes,
That I may not be ashamed.

PROVERBS FOR TODAY/ 28:14

Happy is the man who is always reverent, but he who hardens his heart will fall into calamity.

NOVEMBER 26

DANIEL 2:24–3:30

THEREFORE Daniel went to Arioch, whom the king had appointed to destroy the wise *men* of Babylon. He went and said thus to him: "Do not destroy the wise *men* of Babylon; take me before the king, and I will tell the king the interpretation."

²⁵Then Arioch quickly brought Daniel before the king, and said thus to him, "I have found a man of the captives* of Judah, who will make known to the king the interpretation."

²⁶The king answered and said to Daniel, whose name *was* Belteshazzar, "Are you able to make known to me the dream which I have seen, and its interpretation?"

²⁷Daniel answered in the presence of the king, and said, "The secret which the king has demanded, the wise *men,* the astrologers, the magicians, and the soothsayers cannot declare to the king. ²⁸But there is a God in heaven who reveals secrets, and He has made known to King Nebuchadnezzar what will be in the latter days. Your dream, and the visions of your head upon your bed, were these: ²⁹As for you, O king, thoughts came *to* your *mind while* on your bed, *about* what would come to pass after this; and He who reveals secrets has made known to you what will be. ³⁰But as for me, this secret has not been revealed to me because I have more wisdom than anyone living, but for *our* sakes who make known the interpretation to

the king, and that you may know the thoughts of your heart.

³¹"You, O king, were watching; and behold, a great image! This great image, whose splendor *was* excellent, stood before you; and its form *was* awesome. ³²This image's head *was* of fine gold, its chest and arms of silver, its belly and thighs* of bronze, ³³its legs of iron, its feet partly of iron and partly of clay.* ³⁴You watched while a stone was cut out without hands, which struck the image on its feet of iron and clay, and broke them in pieces. ³⁵Then the iron, the clay, the bronze, the silver, and the gold were crushed together, and became like chaff from the summer threshing floors; the wind carried them away so that no trace of them was found. And the stone that struck the image became a great mountain and filled the whole earth.

³⁶"This *is* the dream. Now we will tell the interpretation of it before the king. ³⁷You, O king, *are* a king of kings. For the God of heaven has given you a kingdom, power, strength, and glory; ³⁸and wherever the children of men dwell, or the beasts of the field and the birds of the heaven, He has given *them* into your hand, and has made you ruler over them all—you *are* this head of gold. ³⁹But after you shall arise another kingdom inferior to yours; then another, a third kingdom of bronze, which shall rule over all the earth. ⁴⁰And the fourth kingdom shall be as

strong as iron, inasmuch as iron breaks in pieces and shatters everything; and like iron that crushes, *that kingdom* will break in pieces and crush all the others. ⁴¹Whereas you saw the feet and toes, partly of potter's clay and partly of iron, the kingdom shall be divided; yet the strength of the iron shall be in it, just as you saw the iron mixed with ceramic clay. ⁴²And *as* the toes of the feet *were* partly of iron and partly of clay, *so* the kingdom shall be partly strong and partly fragile. ⁴³As you saw iron mixed with ceramic clay, they will mingle with the seed of men; but they will not adhere to one another, just as iron does not mix with clay. ⁴⁴And in the days of these kings the God of heaven will set up a kingdom which shall never be destroyed; and the kingdom shall not be left to other people; it shall break in pieces and consume all these kingdoms, and it shall stand forever. ⁴⁵Inasmuch as you saw that the stone was cut out of the mountain without hands, and that it broke in pieces the iron, the bronze, the clay, the silver, and the gold—the great God has made known to the king what will come to pass after this. The dream is certain, and its interpretation is sure."

⁴⁶Then King Nebuchadnezzar fell on his face, prostrate before Daniel, and commanded that they should present an offering and incense to him. ⁴⁷The king answered Daniel, and said, "Truly your God *is* the God of gods, the Lord of kings, and a revealer of secrets, since you could reveal this secret." ⁴⁸Then the king promoted Daniel and gave him many great gifts; and he made him ruler over the whole province of Babylon, and chief administrator over all the wise *men* of Babylon. ⁴⁹Also Daniel petitioned the king, and he set Shadrach, Meshach, and Abed-Nego over the affairs of the province of Babylon; but Daniel *sat* in the gate* of the king.

NEBUCHADNEZZAR the king made an image of gold, whose height *was* sixty cubits *and* its width six cubits. He set it up in the plain of Dura, in the province of Babylon. ²And King Nebuchadnezzar sent *word* to gather together the satraps, the administrators, the governors, the counselors, the treasurers, the judges, the magistrates, and all the officials of the provinces, to come to the dedication of the image which King Nebuchadnezzar had set up. ³So the satraps, the administrators, the governors, the counselors, the treasurers, the judges, the magistrates, and all the officials of the provinces gathered together for the dedication of the image that King Nebuchadnezzar had set up; and they stood before the image that Nebuchadnezzar had set up. ⁴Then a herald cried aloud: "To you it is commanded, O peoples, nations, and languages, ⁵*that* at the time you hear the sound of the horn, flute, harp, lyre, *and* psaltery, in symphony with all kinds of music, you shall fall down and worship the gold image that King Nebuchadnezzar has set up; ⁶and whoever does not fall down and worship shall be cast immediately into the midst of a burning fiery furnace."

⁷So at that time, when all the people heard the sound of the horn, flute, harp, *and* lyre, in symphony with all kinds of music, all the people, nations, and languages fell down *and* worshiped the gold image which King Nebuchadnezzar had set up.

⁸Therefore at that time certain Chaldeans came forward and accused the Jews. ⁹They spoke and said to King Nebuchadnezzar, "O king, live forever! ¹⁰You, O king, have made a decree that everyone who hears the sound of the horn, flute, harp, lyre, *and* psaltery, in symphony with all kinds of music, shall fall down and worship the gold image; ¹¹and whoever does not fall down and worship shall be cast into

the midst of a burning fiery furnace. [12]There are certain Jews whom you have set over the affairs of the province of Babylon: Shadrach, Meshach, and Abed-Nego; these men, O king, have not paid due regard to you. They do not serve your gods or worship the gold image which you have set up."

[13]Then Nebuchadnezzar, in rage and fury, gave the command to bring Shadrach, Meshach, and Abed-Nego. So they brought these men before the king. [14]Nebuchadnezzar spoke, saying to them, "*Is it* true, Shadrach, Meshach, and Abed-Nego, *that* you do not serve my gods or worship the gold image which I have set up? [15]Now if you are ready at the time you hear the sound of the horn, flute, harp, lyre, *and* psaltery, in symphony with all kinds of music, and you fall down and worship the image which I have made, *good!* But if you do not worship, you shall be cast immediately into the midst of a burning fiery furnace. And who *is* the god who will deliver you from my hands?"

[16]Shadrach, Meshach, and Abed-Nego answered and said to the king, "O Nebuchadnezzar, we have no need to answer you in this matter. [17]If that *is the case,* our God whom we serve is able to deliver us from the burning fiery furnace, and He will deliver *us* from your hand, O king. [18]But if not, let it be known to you, O king, that we do not serve your gods, nor will we worship the gold image which you have set up."

[19]Then Nebuchadnezzar was full of fury, and the expression on his face changed toward Shadrach, Meshach, and Abed-Nego. He spoke and commanded that they heat the furnace seven times more than it was usually heated. [20]And he commanded certain mighty men of valor who *were* in his army to bind Shadrach, Meshach, and Abed-Nego, *and* cast *them* into the burning fiery furnace. [21]Then these men were bound in their coats, their trousers, their turbans, and their *other* garments, and were cast into the midst of the burning fiery furnace. [22]Therefore, because the king's command was urgent, and the furnace exceedingly hot, the flame of the fire killed those men who took up Shadrach, Meshach, and Abed-Nego. [23]And these three men, Shadrach, Meshach, and Abed-Nego, fell down bound into the midst of the burning fiery furnace.

[24]Then King Nebuchadnezzar was astonished; and he rose in haste *and* spoke, saying to his counselors, "Did we not cast three men bound into the midst of the fire?"

They answered and said to the king, "True, O king."

[25]"Look!" he answered, "I see four men loose, walking in the midst of the fire; and they are not hurt, and the form of the fourth is like the Son of God."*

[26]Then Nebuchadnezzar went near the mouth of the burning fiery furnace *and* spoke, saying, "Shadrach, Meshach, and Abed-Nego, servants of the Most High God, come out, and come *here.*" Then Shadrach, Meshach, and Abed-Nego came from the midst of the fire. [27]And the satraps, administrators, governors, and the king's counselors gathered together, and they saw these men on whose bodies the fire had no power; the hair of their head was not singed nor were their garments affected, and the smell of fire was not on them.

[28]Nebuchadnezzar spoke, saying, "Blessed be the God of Shadrach, Meshach, and Abed-Nego, who sent His Angel* and delivered His servants who trusted in Him, and they have frustrated the king's word, and yielded their bodies, that they should not serve nor worship any god except their own God! [29]Therefore I make a decree that any people, nation, or language which speaks anything amiss

against the God of Shadrach, Meshach, and Abed-Nego shall be cut in pieces, and their houses shall be made an ash heap; because there is no other God who can deliver like this."

³⁰Then the king promoted Shadrach, Meshach, and Abed-Nego in the province of Babylon.

1 PETER 4:7–5:14

BUT the end of all things is at hand; therefore be serious and watchful in your prayers. ⁸And above all things have fervent love for one another, for *"love will cover a multitude of sins."* * ⁹*Be* hospitable to one another without grumbling. ¹⁰As each one has received a gift, minister it to one another, as good stewards of the manifold grace of God. ¹¹If anyone speaks, *let him speak* as the oracles of God. If anyone ministers, *let him do it* as with the ability which God supplies, that in all things God may be glorified through Jesus Christ, to whom belong the glory and the dominion forever and ever. Amen.

¹²Beloved, do not think it strange concerning the fiery trial which is to try you, as though some strange thing happened to you; ¹³but rejoice to the extent that you partake of Christ's sufferings, that when His glory is revealed, you may also be glad with exceeding joy. ¹⁴If you are reproached for the name of Christ, blessed *are you,* for the Spirit of glory and of God rests upon you.* On their part He is blasphemed, but on your part He is glorified. ¹⁵But let none of you suffer as a murderer, a thief, an evildoer, or as a busybody in other people's matters. ¹⁶Yet if *anyone suffers* as a Christian, let him not be ashamed, but let him glorify God in this matter.*

¹⁷For the time *has come* for judgment to begin at the house of God; and if *it begins* with us first, what will *be* the end of those who do not obey the gospel of God? ¹⁸Now

> *"If the righteous one is*
> *scarcely saved,*
> *Where will the ungodly and*
> *the sinner appear?"* *

¹⁹Therefore let those who suffer according to the will of God commit their souls *to Him* in doing good, as to a faithful Creator.

THE elders who are among you I exhort, I who am a fellow elder and a witness of the sufferings of Christ, and also a partaker of the glory that will be revealed: ²Shepherd the flock of God which is among you, serving as overseers, not by compulsion but willingly,* not for dishonest gain but eagerly; ³nor as being lords over those entrusted to you, but being examples to the flock; ⁴and when the Chief Shepherd appears, you will receive the crown of glory that does not fade away.

⁵Likewise you younger people, submit yourselves to *your* elders. Yes, all of *you* be submissive to one another, and be clothed with humility, for

> *"God resists the proud,*
> *But gives grace to the*
> *humble."* *

⁶Therefore humble yourselves under the mighty hand of God, that He may exalt you in due time, ⁷casting all your care upon Him, for He cares for you.

⁸Be sober, be vigilant; because* your adversary the devil walks about like a roaring lion, seeking whom he may devour. ⁹Resist him, steadfast in the faith, knowing that the same sufferings are experienced by your brotherhood in the world. ¹⁰But may* the God of all grace, who called us* to His eternal glory by Christ Jesus, after you have suffered a while, perfect, establish, strengthen, and settle *you.* ¹¹To Him *be* the glory and the dominion forever and ever. Amen.

¹²By Silvanus, our faithful brother as I consider him, I have written to you briefly, exhorting and testifying that this is the true grace of God in which you stand. ¹³She who is in Babylon, elect together with *you,* greets you; and *so does* Mark my son. ¹⁴Greet one another with a kiss of love.

Peace to you all who are in Christ Jesus. Amen.

PSALM 119:81-96

כ KAPH

M Y soul faints for Your salvation,
But I hope in Your word.
82 My eyes fail *from searching* Your word,
Saying, "When will You comfort me?"
83 For I have become like a wineskin in smoke,
Yet I do not forget Your statutes.
84 How many *are* the days of Your servant?
When will You execute judgment on those who persecute me?
85 The proud have dug pits for me,
Which *is* not according to Your law.
86 All Your commandments *are* faithful;
They persecute me wrongfully;
Help me!

87 They almost made an end of me on earth,
But I did not forsake Your precepts.
88 Revive me according to Your lovingkindness,
So that I may keep the testimony of Your mouth.

ל LAMED

89 Forever, O Lᴏʀᴅ,
Your word is settled in heaven.
90 Your faithfulness *endures* to all generations;
You established the earth, and it abides.
91 They continue this day according to Your ordinances,
For all *are* Your servants.
92 Unless Your law *had been* my delight,
I would then have perished in my affliction.
93 I will never forget Your precepts,
For by them You have given me life.
94 I *am* Yours, save me;
For I have sought Your precepts.
95 The wicked wait for me to destroy me,
But I will consider Your testimonies.
96 I have seen the consummation of all perfection,
But Your commandment *is* exceedingly broad.

PROVERBS FOR TODAY/ 28:15-16

Like *a roaring lion and a charging bear* is *a wicked ruler over poor people.* □ *A ruler who lacks understanding* is *a great oppressor,* but *he who hates covetousness will prolong* his *days.*

DANIEL 4:1-37

NEBUCHADNEZZAR the king,

To all peoples, nations, and languages that dwell in all the earth:

Peace be multiplied to you.

2 I thought it good to declare the signs and wonders that the Most High God has worked for me.

3 How great *are* His signs,
And how mighty His wonders!
His kingdom *is* an everlasting kingdom,
And His dominion *is* from generation to generation.

4 I, Nebuchadnezzar, was at rest in my house, and flourishing in my palace. 5I saw a dream which made me afraid, and the thoughts on my bed and the visions of my head troubled me. 6Therefore I issued a decree to bring in all the wise *men* of Babylon before me, that they might make known to me the interpretation of the dream. 7Then the magicians, the astrologers, the Chaldeans, and the soothsayers came in, and I told them the dream; but they did not make known to me its interpretation. 8But at last Daniel came before me (his name *is* Belteshazzar, according to the name of my god; in him *is* the Spirit of the Holy God), and I told the dream before him, *saying:*

9"Belteshazzar, chief of the magicians, because I know that the Spirit of the Holy God *is* in you, and no secret troubles you, explain to me the visions of my dream that I have seen, and its interpretation.

10 "These *were* the visions of my head *while* on my bed:

"I was looking, and behold,
A tree in the midst of the earth,
And its height was great.
11 The tree grew and became strong;
Its height reached to the heavens,
And it could be seen to the ends of all the earth.
12 Its leaves *were* lovely,
Its fruit abundant,
And in it *was* food for all.
The beasts of the field found shade under it,
The birds of the heavens dwelt in its branches,
And all flesh was fed from it.

13 "I saw in the visions of my head *while* on my bed, and there was a watcher, a holy one, coming down from heaven. 14He cried aloud and said thus:

'Chop down the tree and cut off its branches,
Strip off its leaves and scatter its fruit.
Let the beasts get out from under it,

And the birds from its branches.
15 Nevertheless leave the stump and roots in the earth,
Bound with a band of iron and bronze,
In the tender grass of the field.
Let it be wet with the dew of heaven,
And *let* him graze with the beasts
On the grass of the earth.
16 Let his heart be changed from *that of* a man,
Let him be given the heart of a beast,
And let seven times* pass over him.

17 'This decision *is* by the decree of the watchers,
And the sentence by the word of the holy ones,
In order that the living may know
That the Most High rules in the kingdom of men,
Gives it to whomever He will,
And sets over it the lowest of men.'

18 "This dream I, King Nebuchadnezzar, have seen. Now you, Belteshazzar, declare its interpretation, since all the wise *men* of my kingdom are not able to make known to me the interpretation; but you *are* able, for the Spirit of the Holy God *is* in you."

19 Then Daniel, whose name was Belteshazzar, was astonished for a time, and his thoughts troubled him. *So* the king spoke, and said, "Belteshazzar, do not let the dream or its interpretation trouble you."

Belteshazzar answered and said, "My lord, *may* the dream concern those who hate you, and its interpretation concern your enemies!

20 "The tree that you saw, which grew and became strong, whose height reached to the heavens and which *could be seen* by all the earth, 21whose leaves *were* lovely and its fruit abundant, in which *was* food for all, under which the beasts of the field dwelt, and in whose branches the birds of the heaven had their home— 22it *is* you, O king, who have grown and become strong; for your greatness has grown and reaches to the heavens, and your dominion to the end of the earth.

23 "And inasmuch as the king saw a watcher, a holy one, coming down from heaven and saying, 'Chop down the tree and destroy it, but leave its stump and roots in the earth, *bound* with a band of iron and bronze in the tender grass of the field; let it be wet with the dew of heaven, and let him graze with the beasts of the field, till seven times pass over him'; 24this is the interpretation, O king, and this is the decree of the Most High, which has come upon my lord the king: 25They shall drive you from men, your dwelling shall be with the beasts of the field, and they shall make you eat grass like oxen. They shall wet you with the dew of heaven, and seven times shall pass over you, till

you know that the Most High rules in the kingdom of men, and gives it to whomever He chooses.

26 "And inasmuch as they gave the command to leave the stump *and* roots of the tree, your kingdom shall be assured to you, after you come to know that Heaven rules. 27Therefore, O king, let my advice be acceptable to you; break off your sins by *being* righteous, and your iniquities by showing mercy to *the* poor. Perhaps there may be a lengthening of your prosperity."

28 All *this* came upon King Nebuchadnezzar. 29At the end of the twelve months he was walking about the royal palace of Babylon. 30The king spoke, saying, "Is not this great Babylon, that I have built for a royal dwelling by my mighty power and for the honor of my majesty?"

31 While the word *was still* in the king's mouth, a voice fell from heaven: "King Nebuchadnezzar, to you it is spoken: the kingdom has departed from you! 32And they shall drive you from men, and your dwelling *shall be* with the beasts of the field. They shall make you eat grass like oxen; and seven times shall pass over you, until you know that the Most High rules in the kingdom of men, and gives it to whomever He chooses."

33 That very hour the word was fulfilled concerning Nebuchadnezzar; he was driven from men and ate grass like oxen; his body was wet with the dew of heaven till his hair had grown like eagles' *feathers* and his nails like birds' *claws*.

34 And at the end of the time* I, Nebuchadnezzar, lifted my eyes to heaven, and my understanding returned to me; and I blessed the Most High and praised and honored Him who lives forever:

For His dominion *is* an everlasting dominion,
And His kingdom *is* from generation to generation.
35 All the inhabitants of the earth *are* reputed as nothing;
He does according to His will in the army of heaven
And *among* the inhabitants of the earth.
No one can restrain His hand
Or say to Him, "What have You done?"

36 At the same time my reason returned to me, and for the glory of my kingdom, my honor and splendor returned to me. My counselors and nobles resorted to me, I was restored to my kingdom, and excellent majesty was added to me. 37Now I, Nebuchadnezzar, praise and extol and honor the King of heaven, all of whose works *are* truth, and His ways justice. And those who walk in pride He is able to put down.

2 PETER 1:1-21

SIMON Peter, a bondservant and apostle of Jesus Christ,

To those who have obtained like precious faith with us by the righteousness of our God and Savior Jesus Christ:

2Grace and peace be multiplied to you in the knowledge of God and of Jesus our Lord, 3as His divine power has given to us all things that *pertain* to life and godliness, through the knowledge of Him who called us by glory and virtue, 4by which have been given to us exceedingly great and precious promises, that through these you may be partakers of the divine nature, having escaped the corruption *that is* in the world through lust.

5But also for this very reason, giving all diligence, add to your faith virtue, to virtue knowledge, 6to knowledge self-control, to self-control perseverance, to perseverance godliness, 7to godliness brotherly kindness, and to brotherly kindness love. 8For if these things are yours and abound, *you will be* neither barren nor unfruitful in the knowledge of our Lord Jesus Christ. 9For he who lacks these things is shortsighted, even to blindness, and has forgotten that he was cleansed from his old sins.

10Therefore, brethren, be even more diligent to make your call and election sure, for if you do these things you will never stumble; 11for so an entrance will be supplied to you abundantly into the everlasting kingdom of our Lord and Savior Jesus Christ.

12For this reason I will not be negligent to remind you always of these things, though you know and are established in the present truth. 13Yes, I think it is right, as long as I am in this tent, to stir you up by reminding *you,* 14knowing that shortly I *must* put off my tent, just as our Lord Jesus Christ showed me. 15Moreover I will be careful to ensure that you always have a reminder of these things after my decease.

16For we did not follow cunningly devised fables when we made known to you the power and coming of our Lord Jesus Christ, but were eyewitnesses of His majesty. 17For He received from God the Father honor and glory when such a voice came to Him from the Excellent Glory: "This is My beloved Son, in whom I am well pleased." 18And we heard this voice which came from heaven when we were with Him on the holy mountain.

19And so we have the prophetic word confirmed,* which you do well to heed as a light that shines in a dark place, until the day dawns and the morning star rises in your hearts; 20knowing this first, that no prophecy of Scripture is of any private interpretation,* 21for prophecy never came by the will of man, but holy men of God* spoke *as they were* moved by the Holy Spirit.

PSALM 119:97-112

מ   MEM

OH, how I love Your law!
It *is* my meditation all the day.
98You, through Your
    commandments, make me
    wiser than my enemies;
For they *are* ever with me.
99 I have more understanding
    than all my teachers,
For Your testimonies *are* my
    meditation.
100 I understand more than the
    ancients,
Because I keep Your precepts.
101 I have restrained my feet from
    every evil way,
That I may keep Your word.

102 I have not departed from Your judgments,
For You Yourself have taught me.
103 How sweet are Your words to my taste,
Sweeter than honey to my mouth!
104 Through Your precepts I get understanding;
Therefore I hate every false way.

נ NUN

105 Your word *is* a lamp to my feet
And a light to my path.
106 I have sworn and confirmed
That I will keep Your righteous judgments.
107 I am afflicted very much;
Revive me, O LORD, according to Your word.
108 Accept, I pray, the freewill offerings of my mouth, O LORD,
And teach me Your judgments.
109 My life *is* continually in my hand,
Yet I do not forget Your law.
110 The wicked have laid a snare for me,
Yet I have not strayed from Your precepts.
111 Your testimonies I have taken as a heritage forever,
For they *are* the rejoicing of my heart.
112 I have inclined my heart to perform Your statutes
Forever, to the very end.

PROVERBS FOR TODAY/ 28:17-18

A man burdened with bloodshed will flee into a pit; let no one help him. □ *Whoever walks blamelessly will be saved, but* he who is *perverse* in his *ways will suddenly fall.*

NOVEMBER 28

DANIEL 5:1-31

BELSHAZZAR the king made a great feast for a thousand of his lords, and drank wine in the presence of the thousand. 2While he tasted the wine, Belshazzar gave the command to bring the gold and silver vessels which his father Nebuchadnezzar had taken from the temple which *had been* in Jerusalem, that the king and his lords, his wives, and his concubines might drink from them. 3Then they brought the gold vessels that had been taken from the temple of the house of God which *had been* in Jerusalem; and the king and his lords, his wives, and his concubines drank from them. 4They drank wine, and praised the gods of gold and silver, bronze and iron, wood and stone.

5In the same hour the fingers of a man's hand appeared and wrote opposite the lampstand on the plaster of the wall of the king's palace; and the king saw the part of the hand that wrote. 6Then the king's countenance changed, and his thoughts troubled him, so that the joints of his hips were loosened and his knees knocked against each other. 7The king cried aloud to bring in the astrologers, the Chaldeans, and the soothsayers. The king spoke, saying to the wise *men* of Babylon, "Whoever reads this writing, and tells me its interpretation, shall be clothed with purple and *have* a chain of gold around his neck; and he shall be the third ruler in the kingdom." 8Now all the king's wise *men* came, but they could not read the writing, or make known to the king its interpretation. 9Then King Belshazzar was greatly troubled, his countenance was changed, and his lords were astonished.

10The queen, because of the words of the king and his lords, came to the banquet hall. The queen spoke, saying, "O king, live forever! Do not let your thoughts trouble you, nor let your countenance change. 11There is a man in your kingdom in whom *is* the Spirit of the Holy God. And in the days of your father, light and understanding and wisdom, like the wisdom of the gods, were found in him; and King Nebuchadnezzar your father—your father the king—made him chief of the magicians, astrologers, Chaldeans, *and* soothsayers. 12Inasmuch as an excellent spirit, knowledge, understanding, interpreting dreams, solving riddles, and explaining enigmas* were found in this Daniel, whom the king named Belteshazzar, now let Daniel be called, and he will give the interpretation."

13Then Daniel was brought in before the king. The king spoke, and said to Daniel, "*Are* you that Daniel who is one of the captives* from Judah, whom my father the king brought from Judah? 14I have heard of you, that the Spirit of God *is* in you, and *that* light and understanding and excellent wisdom are found in you. 15Now the wise *men,* the astrologers, have been brought in before me, that they should read this writing and make known to me its interpretation, but they could not give the interpretation of the thing. 16And I have heard of

you, that you can give interpretations and explain enigmas. Now if you can read the writing and make known to me its interpretation, you shall be clothed with purple and *have* a chain of gold around your neck, and shall be the third ruler in the kingdom."

17Then Daniel answered, and said before the king, "Let your gifts be for yourself, and give your rewards to another; yet I will read the writing to the king, and make known to him the interpretation. 18O king, the Most High God gave Nebuchadnezzar your father a kingdom and majesty, glory and honor. 19And because of the majesty that He gave him, all peoples, nations, and languages trembled and feared before him. Whomever he wished, he executed; whomever he wished, he kept alive; whomever he wished, he set up; and whomever he wished, he put down. 20But when his heart was lifted up, and his spirit was hardened in pride, he was deposed from his kingly throne, and they took his glory from him. 21Then he was driven from the sons of men, his heart was made like the beasts, and his dwelling *was* with the wild donkeys. They fed him with grass like oxen, and his body was wet with the dew of heaven, till he knew that the Most High God rules in the kingdom of men, and appoints over it whomever He chooses.

22"But you his son, Belshazzar, have not humbled your heart, although you knew all this. 23And you have lifted yourself up against the Lord of heaven. They have brought the vessels of His house before you, and you and your lords, your wives and your concubines, have drunk wine from them. And you have praised the gods of silver and gold, bronze and iron, wood and stone, which do not see or hear or know; and the God who *holds* your breath in His hand and owns all your ways, you have not glorified. 24Then the fingers* of the hand were sent from Him, and this writing was written.

25"And this is the inscription that was written:

MENE,* MENE, TEKEL,*
UPHARSIN.*

26This *is* the interpretation of *each* word. MENE: God has numbered your kingdom, and finished it; 27TEKEL: You have been weighed in the balances, and found wanting; 28PERES: Your kingdom has been divided, and given to the Medes and Persians."* 29Then Belshazzar gave the command, and they clothed Daniel with purple and *put* a chain of gold around his neck, and made a proclamation concerning him that he should be the third ruler in the kingdom.

30That very night Belshazzar, king of the Chaldeans, was slain. 31And Darius the Mede received the kingdom, *being* about sixty-two years old.

2 PETER 2:1-22

BUT there were also false prophets among the people, even as there will be false teachers among you, who will secretly bring in destructive heresies, even denying the Lord who bought them, *and* bring on themselves swift destruction. 2And many will follow their destructive ways, because of whom the way of truth will be blasphemed. 3By covetousness they will exploit you with deceptive words; for a long time their judgment has not been idle, and their destruction does* not slumber.

4For if God did not spare the angels who sinned, but cast *them* down to hell and delivered *them* into chains of darkness, to be reserved for judgment; 5and did not spare the ancient world, but saved Noah, *one of* eight *people,* a preacher of righteousness, bringing in the flood on the world of the ungodly; 6and turning the cities of Sodom and Gomorrah into ashes, condemned *them* to destruction, making *them* an example to those who afterward would live ungodly; 7and delivered righteous Lot, *who was* oppressed by the filthy conduct of the wicked 8(for that righteous man, dwelling among them, tormented *his* righteous soul from day to day by seeing and hearing *their* lawless deeds)— 9*then* the Lord knows how to deliver the godly out of temptations and to reserve the unjust under punishment for the day of judgment, 10and especially those who walk according to the flesh in the lust of uncleanness and despise authority. *They are* presumptuous, self-willed. They are not afraid to speak evil of dignitaries, 11whereas angels, who are greater in power and might, do not bring a reviling accusation against them before the Lord.

12But these, like natural brute beasts made to be caught and destroyed, speak evil of the things they do not understand, and will utterly perish in their own corruption, 13*and* will receive the wages of unrighteousness, *as* those who count it pleasure to carouse in the daytime. *They are* spots and blemishes, carousing in their own deceptions while they feast with you, 14having eyes full of adultery and that cannot cease from sin, enticing unstable souls. *They have* a heart trained in covetous practices, *and are* accursed children. 15They have forsaken the right way and gone astray, following the way of Balaam the *son* of Beor, who loved the wages of unrighteousness; 16but he was rebuked for his iniquity: a dumb donkey speaking with a man's voice restrained the madness of the prophet.

17These are wells without water, clouds* carried by a tempest, for whom is reserved the blackness of darkness forever.*

18For when they speak great swelling *words* of emptiness, they allure through the lusts of the flesh, through lewdness, the ones who have actually escaped* from those who live in error. ¹⁹While they promise them liberty, they themselves are slaves of corruption; for by whom a person is overcome, by him also he is brought into bondage. ²⁰For if, after they have escaped the pollutions of the world through the knowledge of the Lord and Savior Jesus Christ, they are again entangled in them and overcome, the latter end is worse for them than the beginning. ²¹For it would have been better for them not to have known the way of righteousness, than having known *it,* to turn from the holy commandment delivered to them. ²²But it has happened to them according to the true proverb: *"A dog returns to his own vomit,"* * and, "a sow, having washed, to her wallowing in the mire."

PSALM 119:113-128

ס SAMEK

I HATE the double-minded, But I love Your law.
¹¹⁴You *are* my hiding place and my shield; I hope in Your word.

115 Depart from me, you evildoers, For I will keep the commandments of my God!

116 Uphold me according to Your word, that I may live; And do not let me be ashamed of my hope.

117 Hold me up, and I shall be safe, And I shall observe Your statutes continually.

118 You reject all those who stray from Your statutes, For their deceit *is* falsehood.

119 You put away all the wicked of the earth *like* dross; Therefore I love Your testimonies.

120 My flesh trembles for fear of You, And I am afraid of Your judgments.

ע AYIN

121 I have done justice and righteousness; Do not leave me to my oppressors.

122 Be surety for Your servant for good; Do not let the proud oppress me.

123 My eyes fail *from seeking* Your salvation And Your righteous word.

124 Deal with Your servant according to Your mercy, And teach me Your statutes.

125 I *am* Your servant; Give me understanding, That I may know Your testimonies.

126 *It is* time for *You* to act, O LORD, *For* they have regarded Your law as void.

127 Therefore I love Your commandments More than gold, yes, than fine gold!

128 Therefore all *Your* precepts *concerning* all *things* I consider *to be* right; I hate every false way.

PROVERBS FOR TODAY / 28:19-20

He who tills his land will have plenty of bread, but he who follows frivolity will have poverty enough! A faithful man will abound with blessings, but he who hastens to be rich will not go unpunished.

NOVEMBER 29

DANIEL 6:1-28

I⟨T⟩ pleased Darius to set over the kingdom one hundred and twenty satraps, to be over the whole kingdom; ²and over these, three governors, of whom Daniel *was* one, that the satraps might give account to them, so that the king would suffer no loss. ³Then this Daniel distinguished himself above the governors and satraps, because an excellent spirit *was* in him; and the king gave thought to setting him over the whole realm. ⁴So the governors and satraps sought to find *some* charge against Daniel concerning the kingdom; but they could find no charge or fault, because he *was* faithful; nor was there any error or fault found in him. ⁵Then these men said, "We shall not find any charge against this Daniel unless we find *it* against him concerning the law of his God."

⁶So these governors and satraps thronged before the king, and said thus to him: "King Darius, live forever! ⁷All the governors of the kingdom, the administrators and satraps, the counselors and advisors, have consulted together to establish a royal statute and to make a firm decree, that whoever petitions any god or man for thirty days, except you, O king, shall be cast into the den of lions. ⁸Now, O king, establish the decree and sign the writing, so that it cannot be changed, according to the law of the Medes and Persians, which does not alter." ⁹Therefore King Darius signed the written decree.

¹⁰Now when Daniel knew that the writing was signed, he went home. And in his upper room, with his windows open toward Jerusalem, he knelt down on his knees three times that day, and prayed and gave thanks before his God, as was his custom since early days.

¹¹Then these men assembled and found Daniel praying and making supplication before his God. ¹²And they went before the king, and spoke concerning the king's decree: "Have you not signed a decree that every man who petitions any god or man within thirty days, except you, O king, shall be cast into the den of lions?"

The king answered and said, "The thing *is* true, according to the law of the Medes and Persians, which does not alter."

¹³So they answered and said before the king, "That Daniel, who is one of the captives* from Judah, does not show due regard for you, O king, or for the decree that you have signed, but makes his petition three times a day."

¹⁴And the king, when he heard *these* words, was greatly displeased with himself, and set *his* heart on Daniel to deliver him; and he labored till the going down of the sun to deliver him. ¹⁵Then these men approached the king, and said to the king, "Know, O king, that *it is* the law of the Medes and Persians that no decree or statute which the king establishes may be changed."

¹⁶So the king gave the command, and they brought Daniel and cast *him* into the den of lions. *But* the king spoke, saying to Daniel, "Your God, whom you serve continually, He will deliver you." ¹⁷Then a stone was brought and laid on the mouth of the den, and the king sealed it with his own signet ring and with the signets of his lords, that the purpose concerning Daniel might not be changed.

¹⁸Now the king went to his palace and spent the night fasting; and no mu-

sicians* were brought before him. Also his sleep went from him. ¹⁹Then the king arose very early in the morning and went in haste to the den of lions. ²⁰And when he came to the den, he cried out with a lamenting voice to Daniel. The king spoke, saying to Daniel, "Daniel, servant of the living God, has your God, whom you serve continually, been able to deliver you from the lions?"

²¹Then Daniel said to the king, "O king, live forever! ²²My God sent His angel and shut the lions' mouths, so that they have not hurt me, because I was found innocent before Him; and also, O king, I have done no wrong before you."

²³Now the king was exceedingly glad for him, and commanded that they should take Daniel up out of the den. So Daniel was taken up out of the den, and no injury whatever was found on him, because he believed in his God.

²⁴And the king gave the command, and they brought those men who had accused Daniel, and they cast *them* into the den of lions—them, their children, and their wives; and the lions overpowered them, and broke all their bones in pieces before they ever came to the bottom of the den.

²⁵Then King Darius wrote:

To all peoples, nations, and languages that dwell in all the earth:

Peace be multiplied to you.

26   I make a decree that in every dominion of my kingdom *men must* tremble and fear before the God of Daniel.

For He *is* the living God, And steadfast forever; His kingdom *is the one* which shall not be destroyed,

And His dominion *shall endure* to the end.

27   He delivers and rescues, And He works signs and wonders In heaven and on earth, Who has delivered Daniel from the power of the lions.

²⁸So this Daniel prospered in the reign of Darius and in the reign of Cyrus the Persian.

2 PETER 3:1-18

BELOVED, I [Peter] now write to you this second epistle (in *both of* which I stir up your pure minds by way of reminder), ²that you may be mindful of the words which were spoken before by the holy prophets, and of the commandment of us,* the apostles of the Lord and Savior, ³knowing this first: that scoffers will come in the last days, walking according to their own lusts, ⁴and saying, "Where is the promise of His coming? For since the fathers fell asleep, all things continue as *they were* from the beginning of creation." ⁵For this they willfully forget: that by the word of God the heavens were of old, and the earth standing out of water and in the water, ⁶by which the world *that* then existed perished, being flooded with water. ⁷But the heavens and the earth *which* are now preserved by the same word, are reserved for fire until the day of judgment and perdition of ungodly men.

⁸But, beloved, do not forget this one thing, that with the Lord one day *is* as a thousand years, and a thousand years as one day. ⁹The Lord is not slack concerning *His* promise, as some count slackness, but is longsuffering toward us,* not willing that any should perish but that all should come to repentance.

¹⁰But the day of the Lord will come

as a thief in the night, in which the heavens will pass away with a great noise, and the elements will melt with fervent heat; both the earth and the works that are in it will be burned up.* [11]Therefore, since all these things will be dissolved, what manner *of persons* ought you to be in holy conduct and godliness, [12]looking for and hastening the coming of the day of God, because of which the heavens will be dissolved, being on fire, and the elements will melt with fervent heat? [13]Nevertheless we, according to His promise, look for new heavens and a new earth in which righteousness dwells.

[14]Therefore, beloved, looking forward to these things, be diligent to be found by Him in peace, without spot and blameless; [15]and consider *that* the longsuffering of our Lord *is* salvation—as also our beloved brother Paul, according to the wisdom given to him, has written to you, [16]as also in all his epistles, speaking in them of these things, in which are some things hard to understand, which untaught and unstable *people* twist to their own destruction, as *they do* also the rest of the Scriptures.

[17]You therefore, beloved, since you know *this* beforehand, beware lest you also fall from your own steadfastness, being led away with the error of the wicked; [18]but grow in the grace and knowledge of our Lord and Savior Jesus Christ.

To Him *be* the glory both now and forever. Amen.

PSALM 119:129-152

פ PE

YOUR testimonies are wonderful; Therefore my soul keeps them. [130]The entrance of Your words gives light; It gives understanding to the simple.

[131] I opened my mouth and panted, For I longed for Your commandments.

[132] Look upon me and be merciful to me, As Your custom *is* toward those who love Your name.

[133] Direct my steps by Your word, And let no iniquity have dominion over me.

[134] Redeem me from the oppression of man, That I may keep Your precepts.

[135] Make Your face shine upon Your servant, And teach me Your statutes.

[136] Rivers of water run down from my eyes, Because *men* do not keep Your law.

צ TSADDE

[137] Righteous *are* You, O LORD, And upright *are* Your judgments.

[138] Your testimonies, *which* You have commanded, *Are* righteous and very faithful.

[139] My zeal has consumed me, Because my enemies have forgotten Your words.

[140] Your word *is* very pure; Therefore Your servant loves it.

[141] I *am* small and despised, *Yet* I do not forget Your precepts.

[142] Your righteousness *is* an everlasting righteousness, And Your law *is* truth.

[143] Trouble and anguish have overtaken me, *Yet* Your commandments *are* my delights.

[144] The righteousness of Your testimonies *is* everlasting;

Give me understanding, and I
shall live.

145 I cry out with *my* whole heart;
Hear me, O LORD!
I will keep Your statutes.
146 I cry out to You;
Save me, and I will keep Your
testimonies.
147 I rise before the dawning of
the morning,
And cry for help;
I hope in Your word.
148 My eyes are awake through
the *night* watches,

That I may meditate on Your
word.
149 Hear my voice according to
Your lovingkindness;
O LORD, revive me according
to Your justice.
150 They draw near who follow
after wickedness;
They are far from Your law.
151 You *are* near, O LORD,
And all Your commandments
are truth.
152 Concerning Your testimonies,
I have known of old that You
have founded them forever.

PROVERBS FOR TODAY / 28:21-22

To show partiality is *not good, because for a piece of bread a man will transgress.*
☐ *A man with an evil eye hastens after riches, and does not consider that poverty
will come upon him.*

NOVEMBER 30

DANIEL 7:1-28

IN the first year of Belshazzar king of Babylon, Daniel had a dream and visions of his head *while* on his bed. Then he wrote down the dream, telling the main facts.*

2Daniel spoke, saying, "I saw in my vision by night, and behold, the four winds of heaven were stirring up the Great Sea. 3And four great beasts came up from the sea, each different from the other. 4The first *was* like a lion, and had eagle's wings. I watched till its wings were plucked off; and it was lifted up from the earth and made to stand on two feet like a man, and a man's heart was given to it.

5"And suddenly another beast, a second, like a bear. It was raised up on one

side, and *had* three ribs in its mouth between its teeth. And they said thus to it: 'Arise, devour much flesh!'

6"After this I looked, and there was another, like a leopard, which had on its back four wings of a bird. The beast also had four heads, and dominion was given to it.

7"After this I saw in the night visions, and behold, a fourth beast, dreadful and terrible, exceedingly strong. It had huge iron teeth; it was devouring, breaking in pieces, and trampling the residue with its feet. It *was* different from all the beasts that *were* before it, and it had ten horns. 8I was considering the horns, and there was another horn, a little one, coming up among them, before whom three of the first horns were plucked out by the roots.

And there, in this horn, *were* eyes like the eyes of a man, and a mouth speaking pompous words.

9 "I watched till thrones were
   put in place,
   And the Ancient of Days was
   seated;
   His garment *was* white as
   snow,
   And the hair of His head *was*
   like pure wool.
   His throne *was* a fiery flame,
   Its wheels a burning fire;
10 A fiery stream issued
   And came forth from before
   Him.
   A thousand thousands
   ministered to Him;
   Ten thousand times ten
   thousand stood before Him.
   The court* was seated,
   And the books were opened.

11"I watched then because of the sound of the pompous words which the horn was speaking; I watched till the beast was slain, and its body destroyed and given to the burning flame. 12As for the rest of the beasts, they had their dominion taken away, yet their lives were prolonged for a season and a time.

13 "I was watching in the night
   visions,
   And behold, *One* like the Son
   of Man,
   Coming with the clouds of
   heaven!
   He came to the Ancient of
   Days,
   And they brought Him near
   before Him.
14 Then to Him was given
   dominion and glory and a
   kingdom,
   That all peoples, nations, and
   languages should serve
   Him.

His dominion *is* an everlasting
   dominion,
Which shall not pass away,
And His kingdom *the one*
Which shall not be destroyed.

15"I, Daniel, was grieved in my spirit within *my* body, and the visions of my head troubled me. 16I came near to one of those who stood by, and asked him the truth of all this. So he told me and made known to me the interpretation of these things: 17'Those great beasts, which are four, *are* four kings* *which* arise out of the earth. 18But the saints of the Most High shall receive the kingdom, and possess the kingdom forever, even forever and ever.'

19"Then I wished to know the truth about the fourth beast, which was different from all the others, exceedingly dreadful, *with* its teeth of iron and its nails of bronze, *which* devoured, broke in pieces, and trampled the residue with its feet; 20and the ten horns that *were* on its head, and the other *horn* which came up, before which three fell, namely, that horn which had eyes and a mouth which spoke pompous words, whose appearance *was* greater than his fellows.

21"I was watching; and the same horn was making war against the saints, and prevailing against them, 22until the Ancient of Days came, and a judgment was made *in favor* of the saints of the Most High, and the time came for the saints to possess the kingdom.

23"Thus he said:

'The fourth beast shall be
A fourth kingdom on earth,
Which shall be different from
   all *other* kingdoms,
And shall devour the whole
   earth,
Trample it and break it in
   pieces.
24 The ten horns *are* ten kings

Who shall arise from this
kingdom.
And another shall rise after
them;
He shall be different from the
first *ones,*
And shall subdue three kings.
25 He shall speak *pompous*
words against the Most
High,
Shall persecute* the saints of
the Most High,
And shall intend to change
times and law.
Then *the saints* shall be given
into his hand
For a time and times and half
a time.

26 'But the court shall be seated,
And they shall take away his
dominion,
To consume and destroy *it*
forever.
27 Then the kingdom and
dominion,
And the greatness of the
kingdoms under the whole
heaven,
Shall be given to the people,
the saints of the Most High.
His kingdom *is* an everlasting
kingdom,
And all dominions shall serve
and obey Him.'

28"This *is* the end of the account.*
As for me, Daniel, my thoughts greatly
troubled me, and my countenance
changed; but I kept the matter in my
heart."

1 JOHN 1:1-10

THAT which was from the beginning, which we have heard,
which we have seen with our
eyes, which we have looked upon, and
our hands have handled, concerning
the Word of life— ²the life was manifested, and we have seen, and bear witness, and declare to you that eternal
life which was with the Father and was
manifested to us— ³that which we
have seen and heard we declare to
you, that you also may have fellowship
with us; and truly our fellowship *is* with
the Father and with His Son Jesus
Christ. ⁴And these things we write to
you that your* joy may be full.

⁵This is the message which we have
heard from Him and declare to you,
that God is light and in Him is no darkness at all. ⁶If we say that we have fellowship with Him, and walk in
darkness, we lie and do not practice
the truth. ⁷But if we walk in the light as
He is in the light, we have fellowship
with one another, and the blood of
Jesus Christ His Son cleanses us from
all sin.

⁸If we say that we have no sin, we
deceive ourselves, and the truth is not
in us. ⁹If we confess our sins, He is
faithful and just to forgive us *our* sins
and to cleanse us from all unrighteousness. ¹⁰If we say that we have not
sinned, we make Him a liar, and His
word is not in us.

PSALM 119:153-176

ר RESH

CONSIDER my affliction and
deliver me,
For I do not forget Your law.
154 Plead my cause and redeem
me;
Revive me according to Your
word.
155 Salvation *is* far from the
wicked,
For they do not seek Your
statutes.
156 Great *are* Your tender
mercies, O LORD;
Revive me according to Your
judgments.

157 Many *are* my persecutors and
my enemies,
Yet I do not turn from Your
testimonies.

158 I see the treacherous, and am
disgusted,
Because they do not keep
Your word.

159 Consider how I love Your
precepts;
Revive me, O Lord, according
to Your lovingkindness.

160 The entirety of Your word *is*
truth,
And every one of Your
righteous judgments
endures forever.

ש SHIN

161 Princes persecute me without
a cause,
But my heart stands in awe of
Your word.

162 I rejoice at Your word
As one who finds great
treasure.

163 I hate and abhor lying,
But I love Your law.

164 Seven times a day I praise You,
Because of Your righteous
judgments.

165 Great peace have those who
love Your law,
And nothing causes them to
stumble.

166 Lord, I hope for Your salvation,
And I do Your
commandments.

167 My soul keeps Your
testimonies,

And I love them exceedingly.

168 I keep Your precepts and Your
testimonies,
For all my ways *are* before
You.

ת TAU

169 Let my cry come before You,
O Lord;
Give me understanding
according to Your word.

170 Let my supplication come
before You;
Deliver me according to Your
word.

171 My lips shall utter praise,
For You teach me Your
statutes.

172 My tongue shall speak of
Your word,
For all Your commandments
are righteousness.

173 Let Your hand become my
help,
For I have chosen Your
precepts.

174 I long for Your salvation,
O Lord,
And Your law *is* my delight.

175 Let my soul live, and it shall
praise You;
And let Your judgments help
me.

176 I have gone astray like a lost
sheep;
Seek Your servant,
For I do not forget Your
commandments.

PROVERBS FOR TODAY/ 28:23-24

He who rebukes a man will find more favor afterward than he who flatters with the tongue. □ *Whoever robs his father or his mother, and says, "It is no transgression," the same* is *companion to a destroyer.*

DECEMBER 1

DANIEL 8:1-27

In the third year of the reign of King Belshazzar a vision appeared *to* me—to me, Daniel—after the one that appeared to me the first time. ²I saw in the vision, and it so happened while I was looking, that I *was* in Shushan, the citadel, which *is* in the province of Elam; and I saw in the vision that I was by the River Ulai. ³Then I lifted my eyes and saw, and there, standing beside the river, was a ram which had two horns, and the two horns *were* high; but one *was* higher than the other, and the higher *one* came up last. ⁴I saw the ram pushing westward, northward, and southward, so that no animal could withstand him; nor *was there any* that could deliver from his hand, but he did according to his will and became great.

⁵And as I was considering, suddenly a male goat came from the west, across the surface of the whole earth, without touching the ground; and the goat *had* a notable horn between his eyes. ⁶Then he came to the ram that had two horns, which I had seen standing beside the river, and ran at him with furious power. ⁷And I saw him confronting the ram; he was moved with rage against him, attacked the ram, and broke his two horns. There was no power in the ram to withstand him, but he cast him down to the ground and trampled him; and there was no one that could deliver the ram from his hand.

⁸Therefore the male goat grew very great; but when he became strong, the large horn was broken, and in place of it four notable ones came up toward the four winds of heaven. ⁹And out of one of them came a little horn which grew exceedingly great toward the south, toward the east, and toward the Glorious *Land*. ¹⁰And it grew up to the host of heaven; and it cast down *some* of the host and *some* of the stars to the ground, and trampled them. ¹¹He even exalted *himself* as high as the Prince of the host; and by him the daily *sacrifices* were taken away, and the place of His sanctuary was cast down. ¹²Because of transgression, an army was given over *to the horn* to oppose the daily *sacrifices;* and he cast truth down to the ground. He did *all this* and prospered.

¹³Then I heard a holy one speaking; and *another* holy one said to that certain *one* who was speaking, "How long *will* the vision *be, concerning* the daily *sacrifices* and the transgression of desolation, the giving of both the sanctuary and the host to be trampled underfoot?"

¹⁴And he said to me, "For two thousand three hundred days;* then the sanctuary shall be cleansed."

¹⁵Then it happened, when I, Daniel, had seen the vision and was seeking the meaning, that suddenly there stood before me one having the appearance of a man. ¹⁶And I heard a man's voice between *the banks of* the Ulai, who called, and said, "Gabriel, make this *man* understand the vision." ¹⁷So he came near where I stood, and when he came I was afraid and fell on my face; but he said to me, "Understand, son of man, that the vision *refers* to the time of the end."

¹⁸Now, as he was speaking with me, I was in a deep sleep with my face to the ground; but he touched me, and stood me upright. ¹⁹And he said, "Look, I am making known to you what shall happen in the latter time of the indignation; for at the appointed time the end *shall be.* ²⁰The ram which you

saw, having the two horns—*they are* the kings of Media and Persia. ²¹And the male goat *is* the kingdom* of Greece. The large horn that *is* between its eyes *is* the first king. ²²As for the broken *horn* and the four that stood up in its place, four kingdoms shall arise out of that nation, but not with its power.

23   "And in the latter time of their
      kingdom,
    When the transgressors have
      reached their fullness,
    A king shall arise,
    Having fierce features,
    Who understands sinister
      schemes.
24   His power shall be mighty,
      but not by his own power;
    He shall destroy fearfully,
    And shall prosper and thrive;
    He shall destroy the mighty,
      and *also* the holy people.

25   "Through his cunning
    He shall cause deceit to
      prosper under his rule;*
    And he shall exalt *himself* in
      his heart.
    He shall destroy many in *their*
      prosperity.
    He shall even rise against the
      Prince of princes;
    But he shall be broken
      without *human* means.*

26   "And the vision of the evenings
      and mornings
    Which was told is true;
    Therefore seal up the vision,
    For *it refers* to many days *in*
      the future."

²⁷And I, Daniel, fainted and was sick for days; afterward I arose and went about the king's business. I was astonished by the vision, but no one understood it.

1 JOHN 2:1-17

MY little children, these things I write to you, so that you may not sin. And if anyone sins, we have an Advocate with the Father, Jesus Christ the righteous. ²And He Himself is the propitiation for our sins, and not for ours only but also for the whole world.

³Now by this we know that we know Him, if we keep His commandments. ⁴He who says, "I know Him," and does not keep His commandments, is a liar, and the truth is not in him. ⁵But whoever keeps His word, truly the love of God is perfected in him. By this we know that we are in Him. ⁶He who says he abides in Him ought himself also to walk just as He walked.

⁷Brethren,* I write no new commandment to you, but an old commandment which you have had from the beginning. The old commandment is the word which you heard from the beginning.* ⁸Again, a new commandment I write to you, which thing is true in Him and in you, because the darkness is passing away, and the true light is already shining.

⁹He who says he is in the light, and hates his brother, is in darkness until now. ¹⁰He who loves his brother abides in the light, and there is no cause for stumbling in him. ¹¹But he who hates his brother is in darkness and walks in darkness, and does not know where he is going, because the darkness has blinded his eyes.

12   I write to you, little children,
    Because your sins are
      forgiven you for His
      name's sake.
13   I write to you, fathers,
    Because you have known
      Him *who is* from the
      beginning.
    I write to you, young men,
    Because you have

overcome the wicked
one.
I write to you, little children,
Because you have known
the Father.

14 I have written to you, fathers,
Because you have known
Him *who is* from the
beginning.
I have written to you, young
men,
Because you are strong,
and the word of God
abides in you,
And you have overcome
the wicked one.

15Do not love the world or the things in the world. If anyone loves the world, the love of the Father is not in him. 16For all that *is* in the world—the lust of the flesh, the lust of the eyes, and the pride of life—is not of the Father but is of the world. 17And the world is passing away, and the lust of it; but he who does the will of God abides forever.

PSALM 120:1-7

A Song of Ascents.

I N my distress I cried to the LORD,
And He heard me.
2Deliver my soul, O LORD, from
lying lips
And from a deceitful tongue.

3   What shall be given to you,
Or what shall be done to you,
You false tongue?
4   Sharp arrows of the warrior,
With coals of the broom tree!

5   Woe is me, that I dwell in
Meshech,
That I dwell among the tents
of Kedar!
6   My soul has dwelt too long
With one who hates peace.
7   I *am for* peace;
But when I speak, they *are* for
war.

PROVERBS FOR TODAY / 28:25-26

He who is of a proud heart stirs up strife, but he who trusts in the LORD will be prospered. ▢ He who trusts in his own heart is a fool, but whoever walks wisely will be delivered.

DECEMBER 2

DANIEL 9:1–11:1

I N the first year of Darius the son of Ahasuerus, of the lineage of the Medes, who was made king over the realm of the Chaldeans— 2in the first year of his reign I, Daniel, understood by the books the number of the years *specified* by the word of the LORD through Jeremiah the prophet, that He would accomplish seventy years in the desolations of Jerusalem.

3Then I set my face toward the Lord God to make request by prayer and supplications, with fasting, sackcloth, and ashes. 4And I prayed to the LORD my God, and made confession, and said, "O Lord, great and awesome God, who keeps His covenant and mercy with those who love Him, and with those who keep His commandments, 5we have sinned and committed iniquity, we have done wickedly and rebelled, even by departing from Your precepts and Your judgments. 6Neither have we heeded Your servants the prophets, who spoke in Your name to our kings and our princes, to our fathers and all the people of the land. 7O Lord, righteousness *belongs* to You, but to us shame of face, as *it is* this day—to the men of Judah, to the inhabitants of Jerusalem and all Israel, those near and those far off in all the countries to which You have driven them, because of the unfaithfulness which they have committed against You.

8"O Lord, to us *belongs* shame of face, to our kings, our princes, and our fathers, because we have sinned against You. 9To the Lord our God *belong* mercy and forgiveness, though we have rebelled against Him. 10We have not obeyed the voice of the LORD our God, to walk in His laws, which He set before us by His servants the prophets. 11Yes, all Israel has transgressed Your law, and has departed so as not to obey Your voice; therefore the curse and the oath written in the Law of Moses the servant of God have been poured out on us, because we have sinned against Him. 12And He has confirmed His words, which He spoke against us and against our judges who judged us, by bringing upon us a great disaster; for under the whole heaven such has never been done as what has been done to Jerusalem.

13"As *it is* written in the Law of Moses, all this disaster has come upon us; yet we have not made our prayer before the LORD our God, that we might turn from our iniquities and understand Your truth. 14Therefore the LORD has kept the disaster in mind,

and brought it upon us; for the LORD our God *is* righteous in all the works which He does, though we have not obeyed His voice. 15And now, O Lord our God, who brought Your people out of the land of Egypt with a mighty hand, and made Yourself a name, as *it is* this day—we have sinned, we have done wickedly!

16"O Lord, according to all Your righteousness, I pray, let Your anger and Your fury be turned away from Your city Jerusalem, Your holy mountain; because for our sins, and for the iniquities of our fathers, Jerusalem and Your people *are* a reproach to all *those* around us. 17Now therefore, our God, hear the prayer of Your servant, and his supplications, and for the Lord's sake cause Your face to shine on Your sanctuary, which is desolate. 18O my God, incline Your ear and hear; open Your eyes and see our desolations, and the city which is called by Your name; for we do not present our supplications before You because of our righteous deeds, but because of Your great mercies. 19O Lord, hear! O Lord, forgive! O Lord, listen and act! Do not delay for Your own sake, my God, for Your city and Your people are called by Your name."

20Now while I *was* speaking, praying, and confessing my sin and the sin of my people Israel, and presenting my supplication before the LORD my God for the holy mountain of my God, 21yes, while I *was* speaking in prayer, the man Gabriel, whom I had seen in the vision at the beginning, being caused to fly swiftly, reached me about the time of the evening offering. 22And he informed *me,* and talked with me, and said, "O Daniel, I have now come forth to give you skill to understand. 23At the beginning of your supplications the command went out, and I have come to tell *you,* for you *are* greatly beloved; therefore consider the matter, and understand the vision:

24 "Seventy weeks* are
       determined
    For your people and for your
       holy city,
    To finish the transgression,
    To make an end of* sins,
    To make reconciliation for
       iniquity,
    To bring in everlasting
       righteousness,
    To seal up vision and
       prophecy,
    And to anoint the Most Holy.

25 "Know therefore and
       understand,
    That from the going forth of
       the command
    To restore and build
       Jerusalem
    Until Messiah the Prince,
    There shall be seven weeks
       and sixty-two weeks;
    The street* shall be built
       again, and the wall,*
    Even in troublesome times.

26 "And after the sixty-two weeks
    Messiah shall be cut off, but
       not for Himself;
    And the people of the prince
       who is to come
    Shall destroy the city and the
       sanctuary.
    The end of it *shall be* with a
       flood,
    And till the end of the war
       desolations are determined.
27 Then he shall confirm a
       covenant with many for one
       week;
    But in the middle of the week
    He shall bring an end to
       sacrifice and offering.
    And on the wing of
       abominations shall be one
       who makes desolate,
    Even until the consummation,
       which is determined,
    Is poured out on the desolate."

In the third year of Cyrus king of Persia a message was revealed to Daniel, whose name was called Belteshazzar. The message *was* true, but the appointed time *was* long;* and he understood the message, and had understanding of the vision. ²In those days I, Daniel, was mourning three full weeks. ³I ate no pleasant food, no meat or wine came into my mouth, nor did I anoint myself at all, till three whole weeks were fulfilled.

⁴Now on the twenty-fourth day of the first month, as I was by the side of the great river, that *is,* the Tigris,* ⁵I lifted my eyes and looked, and behold, a certain man clothed in linen, whose waist *was* girded with gold of Uphaz! ⁶His body *was* like beryl, his face like the appearance of lightning, his eyes like torches of fire, his arms and feet like burnished bronze in color, and the sound of his words like the voice of a multitude.

⁷And I, Daniel, alone saw the vision, for the men who were with me did not see the vision; but a great terror fell upon them, so that they fled to hide themselves. ⁸Therefore I was left alone when I saw this great vision, and no strength remained in me; for my vigor was turned to frailty in me, and I retained no strength. ⁹Yet I heard the sound of his words; and while I heard the sound of his words I was in a deep sleep on my face, with my face to the ground.

¹⁰Suddenly, a hand touched me, which made me tremble on my knees and *on* the palms of my hands. ¹¹And he said to me, "O Daniel, man greatly beloved, understand the words that I speak to you, and stand upright, for I have now been sent to you." While he was speaking this word to me, I stood trembling.

¹²Then he said to me, "Do not fear, Daniel, for from the first day that you set your heart to understand, and to humble yourself before your God,

your words were heard; and I have come because of your words. ¹³But the prince of the kingdom of Persia withstood me twenty-one days; and behold, Michael, one of the chief princes, came to help me, for I had been left alone there with the kings of Persia. ¹⁴Now I have come to make you understand what will happen to your people in the latter days, for the vision *refers* to *many* days yet *to come."*

¹⁵When he had spoken such words to me, I turned my face toward the ground and became speechless. ¹⁶And suddenly, *one* having the likeness of the sons* of men touched my lips; then I opened my mouth and spoke, saying to him who stood before me, "My lord, because of the vision my sorrows have overwhelmed me, and I have retained no strength. ¹⁷For how can this servant of my lord talk with you, my lord? As for me, no strength remains in me now, nor is any breath left in me."

¹⁸Then again, *the one* having the likeness of a man touched me and strengthened me. ¹⁹And he said, "O man greatly beloved, fear not! Peace *be* to you; be strong, yes, be strong!"

So when he spoke to me I was strengthened, and said, "Let my lord speak, for you have strengthened me."

²⁰Then he said, "Do you know why I have come to you? And now I must return to fight with the prince of Persia; and when I have gone forth, indeed the prince of Greece will come. ²¹But I will tell you what is noted in the Scripture of Truth. (No one upholds me against these, except Michael your prince.

"Also in the first year of Darius the Mede, I, *even* I, stood up to confirm and strengthen him.)"

1 JOHN 2:18–3:6

Little children, it is the last hour; and as you have heard that the* Antichrist is coming, even now many antichrists have come, by which we know that it is the last hour. ¹⁹They went out from us, but they were not of us; for if they had been of us, they would have continued with us; but *they went out* that they might be made manifest, that none of them were of us.

²⁰But you have an anointing from the Holy One, and you know all things.* ²¹I have not written to you because you do not know the truth, but because you know it, and that no lie is of the truth.

²²Who is a liar but he who denies that Jesus is the Christ? He is antichrist who denies the Father and the Son. ²³Whoever denies the Son does not have the Father either; he who acknowledges the Son has the Father also.

²⁴Therefore let that abide in you which you heard from the beginning. If what you heard from the beginning abides in you, you also will abide in the Son and in the Father. ²⁵And this is the promise that He has promised us— eternal life.

²⁶These things I have written to you concerning those who *try to* deceive you. ²⁷But the anointing which you have received from Him abides in you, and you do not need that anyone teach you; but as the same anointing teaches you concerning all things, and is true, and is not a lie, and just as it has taught you, you will* abide in Him.

²⁸And now, little children, abide in Him, that when* He appears, we may have confidence and not be ashamed before Him at His coming. ²⁹If you know that He is righteous, you know that everyone who practices righteousness is born of Him.

Behold what manner of love the Father has bestowed on us, that we should be called children of God!* Therefore the world does not know us,* because it did not know Him. ²Beloved, now we are children of God; and it has not yet been revealed what we shall be, but we know that when He is revealed, we shall be like Him, for we shall see Him as He is. ³And everyone who has this hope in Him purifies himself, just as He is pure.

⁴Whoever commits sin also commits lawlessness, and sin is lawlessness. ⁵And you know that He was manifested to take away our sins, and in Him there is no sin. ⁶Whoever abides in Him does not sin. Whoever sins has neither seen Him nor known Him.

PSALM 121:1-8

A Song of Ascents.

I WILL lift up my eyes to the hills—
From whence comes my help?
²My help *comes* from the LORD,
Who made heaven and earth.

3 He will not allow your foot to
be moved;
He who keeps you will not
slumber.
4 Behold, He who keeps Israel
Shall neither slumber nor
sleep.

5 The LORD *is* your keeper;
The LORD *is* your shade at
your right hand.
6 The sun shall not strike you
by day,
Nor the moon by night.

7 The LORD shall preserve you
from all evil;
He shall preserve your soul.
8 The LORD shall preserve your
going out and your coming
in
From this time forth, and
even forevermore.

PROVERBS FOR TODAY/ 28:27-28

He who gives to the poor will not lack, but he who hides his eyes will have many curses. □ *When the wicked arise, men hide themselves; but when they perish, the righteous increase.*

DECEMBER 3

DANIEL 11:2-35

"AND now I [God's messenger] will tell you the truth: Behold, three more kings will arise in Persia, and the fourth shall be far richer than *them* all; by his strength, through his riches, he shall stir up all against the realm of Greece. ³Then a mighty king shall arise, who shall rule with great dominion, and do according

to his will. ⁴And when he has arisen, his kingdom shall be broken up and divided toward the four winds of heaven, but not among his posterity nor according to his dominion with which he ruled; for his kingdom shall be uprooted, even for others besides these.

⁵"Also the king of the South shall become strong, as well as *one* of his princes; and he shall gain power over

him and have dominion. His dominion *shall be* a great dominion. 6And at the end of *some* years they shall join forces, for the daughter of the king of the South shall go to the king of the North to make an agreement; but she shall not retain the power of her authority, and neither he nor his authority* shall stand; but she shall be given up, with those who brought her, and with him who begot her, and with him who strengthened her in *those* times. 7But from a branch of her roots *one* shall arise in his place, who shall come with an army, enter the fortress of the king of the North, and deal with them and prevail. 8And he shall also carry their gods captive to Egypt, with their princes* *and* their precious articles of silver and gold; and he shall continue *more* years than the king of the North.

9"Also *the king of the North* shall come to the kingdom of the king of the South, but shall return to his own land. 10However his sons shall stir up strife, and assemble a multitude of great forces; and *one* shall certainly come and overwhelm and pass through; then he shall return to his fortress and stir up strife.

11"And the king of the South shall be moved with rage, and go out and fight with him, with the king of the North, who shall muster a great multitude; but the multitude shall be given into the hand of his *enemy.* 12When he has taken away the multitude, his heart will be lifted up; and he will cast down tens of thousands, but he will not prevail. 13For the king of the North will return and muster a multitude greater than the former, and shall certainly come at the end of some years with a great army and much equipment.

14"Now in those times many shall rise up against the king of the South. Also, violent men* of your people shall exalt themselves in fulfillment of the vision, but they shall fall. 15So the king of the North shall come and build a siege mound, and take a fortified city; and the forces* of the South shall not withstand *him.* Even his choice troops *shall have* no strength to resist. 16But he who comes against him shall do according to his own will, and no one shall stand against him. He shall stand in the Glorious Land with destruction in his power.*

17"He shall also set his face to enter with the strength of his whole kingdom, and upright ones* with him; thus shall he do. And he shall give him the daughter of women to destroy it; but she shall not stand *with him,* or be for him. 18After this he shall turn his face to the coastlands, and shall take many. But a ruler shall bring the reproach against them to an end; and with the reproach removed, he shall turn back on him. 19Then he shall turn his face toward the fortress of his own land; but he shall stumble and fall, and not be found.

20"There shall arise in his place one who imposes taxes *on* the glorious kingdom; but within a few days he shall be destroyed, but not in anger or in battle. 21And in his place shall arise a vile person, to whom they will not give the honor of royalty; but he shall come in peaceably, and seize the kingdom by intrigue. 22With the force* of a flood they shall be swept away from before him and be broken, and also the prince of the covenant. 23And after the league *is made* with him he shall act deceitfully, for he shall come up and become strong with a small *number of* people. 24He shall enter peaceably, even into the richest places of the province; and he shall do *what* his fathers have not done, nor his forefathers: he shall disperse among them the plunder, spoil, and riches; and he shall devise his plans against the strongholds, but *only* for a time.

25"He shall stir up his power and his courage against the king of the South with a great army. And the king of the

South shall be stirred up to battle with a very great and mighty army; but he shall not stand, for they shall devise plans against him. 26Yes, those who eat of the portion of his delicacies shall destroy him; his army shall be swept away, and many shall fall down slain. 27Both these kings' hearts *shall be* bent on evil, and they shall speak lies at the same table; but it shall not prosper, for the end *will* still *be* at the appointed time. 28While returning to his land with great riches, his heart shall be *moved* against the holy covenant; so he shall do *damage* and return to his own land.

29"At the appointed time he shall return and go toward the south; but it shall not be like the former or the latter. 30For ships from Cyprus* shall come against him; therefore he shall be grieved, and return in rage against the holy covenant, and do *damage*.

"So he shall return and show regard for those who forsake the holy covenant. 31And forces* shall be mustered by him, and they shall defile the sanctuary fortress; then they shall take away the daily *sacrifices,* and place *there* the abomination of desolation. 32Those who do wickedly against the covenant he shall corrupt with flattery; but the people who know their God shall be strong, and carry out *great exploits.* 33And those of the people who understand shall instruct many; yet *for many* days they shall fall by sword and flame, by captivity and plundering. 34Now when they fall, they shall be aided with a little help; but many shall join with them by intrigue. 35And *some* of those of understanding shall fall, to refine them, purify *them,* and make *them* white, *until* the time of the end; because *it is* still for the appointed time."

1 JOHN 3:7-24

Lɪᴛᴛʟᴇ children, let no one deceive you. He who practices righteousness is righteous, just as He is righteous. 8He who sins is of the devil, for the devil has sinned from the beginning. For this purpose the Son of God was manifested, that He might destroy the works of the devil. 9Whoever has been born of God does not sin, for His seed remains in him; and he cannot sin, because he has been born of God.

10In this the children of God and the children of the devil are manifest: Whoever does not practice righteousness is not of God, nor *is* he who does not love his brother. 11For this is the message that you heard from the beginning, that we should love one another, 12not as Cain *who* was of the wicked one and murdered his brother. And why did he murder him? Because his works were evil and his brother's righteous.

13Do not marvel, my brethren, if the world hates you. 14We know that we have passed from death to life, because we love the brethren. He who does not love *his* brother* abides in death. 15Whoever hates his brother is a murderer, and you know that no murderer has eternal life abiding in him.

16By this we know love, because He laid down His life for us. And we also ought to lay down *our* lives for the brethren. 17But whoever has this world's goods, and sees his brother in need, and shuts up his heart from him, how does the love of God abide in him?

18My little children, let us not love in word or in tongue, but in deed and in truth. 19And by this we know* that we are of the truth, and shall assure our hearts before Him. 20For if our heart condemns us, God is greater than our heart, and knows all things. 21Beloved, if our heart does not condemn us, we have confidence toward God. 22And whatever we ask we receive from Him, because we keep His commandments and do those things that are pleasing in His sight. 23And this is His commandment: that we should believe on the name of His Son Jesus Christ and love one another, as He gave us* commandment.

24Now he who keeps His commandments abides in Him, and He in him. And by this we know that He abides in us, by the Spirit whom He has given us.

PSALM 122:1-9

A Song of Ascents. Of David.

I WAS glad when they said to me, "Let us go into the house of the LORD."
2 Our feet have been standing
    Within your gates,
      O Jerusalem!

3 Jerusalem is built
    As a city that is compact
      together,

4 Where the tribes go up,
    The tribes of the LORD,
    To the Testimony of Israel,
    To give thanks to the name of
      the LORD.
5 For thrones are set there for
      judgment,
    The thrones of the house of
      David.

6 Pray for the peace of
      Jerusalem:
    "May they prosper who love
      you.
7 Peace be within your walls,
    Prosperity within your
      palaces."
8 For the sake of my brethren
      and companions,
    I will now say, "Peace *be*
      within you."
9 Because of the house of the
      LORD our God
    I will seek your good.

PROVERBS FOR TODAY/ 29:1

He who is often rebuked, and hardens his neck, will suddenly be destroyed, and that without remedy.

DECEMBER 4

DANIEL 11:36–12:13

"THEN the king shall do according to his own will: he shall exalt and magnify himself above every god, shall speak blasphemies against the God of gods, and shall prosper till the wrath has been accomplished; for what has been determined shall be done. 37He shall regard neither the God* of his fathers nor the desire of women, nor regard any god; for he shall exalt himself above *them* all. 38But in their place he shall honor a god of fortresses; and a god which his fathers did not know he shall honor with gold and silver, with precious stones and pleasant things. 39Thus he shall act against the strongest fortresses with a foreign god, which he shall acknowledge, *and* advance *its* glory; and he shall cause them to rule over many, and divide the land for gain.

40"At the time of the end the king of

the South shall attack him; and the king of the North shall come against him like a whirlwind, with chariots, horsemen, and with many ships; and he shall enter the countries, overwhelm *them,* and pass through. ⁴¹He shall also enter the Glorious Land, and many *countries* shall be overthrown; but these shall escape from his hand: Edom, Moab, and the prominent people of Ammon. ⁴²He shall stretch out his hand against the countries, and the land of Egypt shall not escape. ⁴³He shall have power over the treasures of gold and silver, and over all the precious things of Egypt; also the Libyans and Ethiopians *shall follow* at his heels. ⁴⁴But news from the east and the north shall trouble him; therefore he shall go out with great fury to destroy and annihilate many. ⁴⁵And he shall plant the tents of his palace between the seas and the glorious holy mountain; yet he shall come to his end, and no one will help him.

"At that time Michael shall stand up,
The great prince who stands *watch* over the sons of your people;
And there shall be a time of trouble,
Such as never was since there was a nation,
Even to that time.
And at that time your people shall be delivered,
Every one who is found written in the book.
2   And many of those who sleep in the dust of the earth shall awake,
Some to everlasting life,
Some to shame *and* everlasting contempt.
3   Those who are wise shall shine
Like the brightness of the firmament,
And those who turn many to righteousness

Like the stars forever and ever.

⁴"But you, Daniel, shut up the words, and seal the book until the time of the end; many shall run to and fro, and knowledge shall increase."

⁵Then I, Daniel, looked; and there stood two others, one on this riverbank and the other on that riverbank. ⁶And *one* said to the man clothed in linen, who *was* above the waters of the river, "How long shall the fulfillment of these wonders *be?*"

⁷Then I heard the man clothed in linen, who *was* above the waters of the river, when he held up his right hand and his left hand to heaven, and swore by Him who lives forever, that *it shall be* for a time, times, and half *a time;* and when the power of the holy people has been completely shattered, all these *things* shall be finished.

⁸Although I heard, I did not understand. Then I said, "My lord, what *shall be* the end of these *things?*"

⁹And he said, "Go *your way,* Daniel, for the words *are* closed up and sealed till the time of the end. ¹⁰Many shall be purified, made white, and refined, but the wicked shall do wickedly; and none of the wicked shall understand, but the wise shall understand.

¹¹"And from the time *that* the daily *sacrifice* is taken away, and the abomination of desolation is set up, *there shall be* one thousand two hundred and ninety days. ¹²Blessed *is* he who waits, and comes to the one thousand three hundred and thirty-five days.

¹³"But you, go *your way* till the end; for you shall rest, and will arise to your inheritance at the end of the days."

1 JOHN 4:1-21

Beloved, do not believe every spirit, but test the spirits, whether they are of God; because many false prophets have gone out into the world. ²By this you know the Spirit of God: Every spirit that confesses that Jesus Christ has come in the flesh is of God, ³and every spirit that does not confess that Jesus Christ has come in the flesh* is not of God. And this is the *spirit* of the Antichrist, which you have heard was coming, and is now already in the world.

⁴You are of God, little children, and have overcome them, because He who is in you is greater than he who is in the world. ⁵They are of the world. Therefore they speak *as* of the world, and the world hears them. ⁶We are of God. He who knows God hears us; he who is not of God does not hear us. By this we know the spirit of truth and the spirit of error.

⁷Beloved, let us love one another, for love is of God; and everyone who loves is born of God and knows God. ⁸He who does not love does not know God, for God is love. ⁹In this the love of God was manifested toward us, that God has sent His only begotten Son into the world, that we might live through Him. ¹⁰In this is love, not that we loved God, but that He loved us and sent His Son *to be* the propitiation for our sins. ¹¹Beloved, if God so loved us, we also ought to love one another.

¹²No one has seen God at any time. If we love one another, God abides in us, and His love has been perfected in us. ¹³By this we know that we abide in Him, and He in us, because He has given us of His Spirit. ¹⁴And we have seen and testify that the Father has sent the Son *as* Savior of the world. ¹⁵Whoever confesses that Jesus is the Son of God, God abides in him, and he in God. ¹⁶And we have known and believed the love that God has for us.

God is love, and he who abides in love abides in God, and God in him.

¹⁷Love has been perfected among us in this: that we may have boldness in the day of judgment; because as He is, so are we in this world. ¹⁸There is no fear in love; but perfect love casts out fear, because fear involves torment. But he who fears has not been made perfect in love. ¹⁹We love Him* because He first loved us.

²⁰If someone says, "I love God," and hates his brother, he is a liar; for he who does not love his brother whom he has seen, how can* he love God whom he has not seen? ²¹And this commandment we have from Him: that he who loves God *must* love his brother also.

PSALM 123:1-4

A Song of Ascents.

UNTO You I lift up my eyes,
O You who dwell in the
heavens.
2   Behold, as the eyes of
        servants *look* to the hand of
        their masters,
    As the eyes of a maid to the
        hand of her mistress,
    So our eyes *look* to the LORD
        our God,
    Until He has mercy on us.

3   Have mercy on us, O LORD,
        have mercy on us!
    For we are exceedingly filled
        with contempt.
4   Our soul is exceedingly filled
    With the scorn of those who
        are at ease,
    With the contempt of the
        proud.

PROVERBS FOR TODAY/ 29:2-4

When the righteous are in authority, the people rejoice; but when a wicked man *rules, the people groan.* ☐ *Whoever loves wisdom makes his father rejoice, but a companion of harlots wastes* his *wealth.* □ *The king establishes the land by justice,* *but he who receives bribes overthrows it.*

DECEMBER 5

HOSEA 1:1–3:5

THE word of the LORD that came to Hosea the son of Beeri, in the days of Uzziah, Jotham, Ahaz, *and* Hezekiah, kings of Judah, and in the days of Jeroboam the son of Joash, king of Israel. ²When the LORD began to speak by Hosea, the LORD said to Hosea:

"Go, take yourself a wife of
  harlotry
And children of harlotry,
For the land has committed
  great harlotry
By departing from the LORD."

³So he went and took Gomer the daughter of Diblaim, and she conceived and bore him a son. ⁴Then the LORD said to him:

"Call his name Jezreel,
For in a little *while*
I will avenge the bloodshed of
  Jezreel on the house of
  Jehu,
And bring an end to the
  kingdom of the house of
  Israel.
⁵ It shall come to pass in that
    day
That I will break the bow of
  Israel in the Valley of
  Jezreel."

⁶And she conceived again and bore a daughter. Then *God* said to him:

"Call her name Lo-Ruhamah*,

For I will no longer have
  mercy on the house of
  Israel,
But I will utterly take them
  away.*
⁷ Yet I will have mercy on the
    house of Judah,
Will save them by the LORD
  their God,
And will not save them by
  bow,
Nor by sword or battle,
By horses or horsemen."

⁸Now when she had weaned Lo-Ruhamah, she conceived and bore a son. ⁹Then *God* said:

"Call his name Lo-Ammi,*
For you *are* not My people,
And I will not be your *God*.

¹⁰ "Yet the number of the
    children of Israel
Shall be as the sand of the sea,
Which cannot be measured or
  numbered.
And it shall come to pass
In the place where it was said
  to them,
'You *are* not My people,'*
There it shall be said to them,
'*You are* sons of the living God.'
¹¹ Then the children of Judah
    and the children of Israel
Shall be gathered together,
And appoint for themselves
  one head;
And they shall come up out of
  the land,

For great *will be* the day of
    Jezreel!

"Say to your brethren, 'My people,'*
    And to your sisters, 'Mercy*
    is shown.'
2   "Bring charges against your
       mother, bring charges;
    For she *is* not My wife, nor
       am I her Husband!
    Let her put away her
       harlotries from her sight,
    And her adulteries from
       between her breasts;
3   Lest I strip her naked
    And expose her, as in the day
       she was born,
    And make her like a
       wilderness,
    And set her like a dry land,
    And slay her with thirst.

4   "I will not have mercy on her
       children,
    For they *are* the children of
       harlotry.
5   For their mother has played
       the harlot;
    She who conceived them has
       behaved shamefully.
    For she said, 'I will go after
       my lovers,
    Who give *me* my bread and
       my water,
    My wool and my linen,
    My oil and my drink.'

6   "Therefore, behold,
    I will hedge up your way with
       thorns,
    And wall her in,
    So that she cannot find her
       paths.
7   She will chase her lovers,
    But not overtake them;
    Yes, she will seek them, but
       not find *them.*
    Then she will say,
    'I will go and return to my first
       husband,

For then *it was* better for me
    than now.'
8   For she did not know
    That I gave her grain, new
       wine, and oil,
    And multiplied her silver and
       gold—
    Which they prepared for Baal.

9   "Therefore I will return and
       take away
    My grain in its time
    And My new wine in its
       season,
    And will take back My wool
       and My linen,
    Given to cover her nakedness.
10   Now I will uncover her
       lewdness in the sight of her
       lovers,
    And no one shall deliver her
       from My hand.
11   I will also cause all her mirth
       to cease,
    Her feast days,
    Her New Moons,
    Her Sabbaths—
    All her appointed feasts.

12   "And I will destroy her vines
       and her fig trees,
    Of which she has said,
    'These *are* my wages that my
       lovers have given me.'
    So I will make them a forest,
    And the beasts of the field
       shall eat them.
13   I will punish her
    For the days of the Baals to
       which she burned incense.
    She decked herself with her
       earrings and jewelry,
    And went after her lovers;
    But Me she forgot," says the
       Lord.

14   "Therefore, behold, I will
       allure her,
    Will bring her into the
       wilderness,

And speak comfort to her.
15 I will give her her vineyards
     from there,
   And the Valley of Achor as a
     door of hope;
   She shall sing there,
   As in the days of her youth,
   As in the day when she came
     up from the land of Egypt.

16 "And it shall be, in that day,"
   Says the LORD,
   "That you will call Me 'My
     Husband,'*
   And no longer call Me 'My
     Master,'*
17 For I will take from her
     mouth the names of the
     Baals,
   And they shall be
     remembered by their name
     no more.
18 In that day I will make a
     covenant for them
   With the beasts of the field,
   With the birds of the air,
   And with the creeping things
     of the ground.
   Bow and sword of battle I will
     shatter from the earth,
   To make them lie down safely.

19 "I will betroth you to Me
     forever;
   Yes, I will betroth you to Me
   In righteousness and justice,
   In lovingkindness and mercy;
20 I will betroth you to Me in
     faithfulness,
   And you shall know the LORD.

21 "It shall come to pass in that
     day
   That I will answer," says the
     LORD;
   "I will answer the heavens,
   And they shall answer the
     earth.
22 The earth shall answer
   With grain,

With new wine,
   And with oil;
   They shall answer Jezreel.*
23 Then I will sow her for Myself
     in the earth,
   And I will have mercy on her
     who had not obtained
     mercy;*
   Then I will say to those who
     were not My people,*
   'You are My people!'
   And they shall say, 'You are
     my God!' "

THEN the LORD said to me, "Go again, love a woman who is loved by a lover* and is committing adultery, just like the love of the LORD for the children of Israel, who look to other gods and love the raisin cakes of the pagans." ²So I bought her for myself for fifteen shekels of silver, and one and one-half homers of barley. ³And I said to her, "You shall stay with me many days; you shall not play the harlot, nor shall you have a man—so, too, will I be toward you."

⁴For the children of Israel shall abide many days without king or prince, without sacrifice or sacred pillar, without ephod or teraphim. ⁵Afterward the children of Israel shall return and seek the LORD their God and David their king. They shall fear the LORD and His goodness in the latter days.

1 JOHN 5:1-21

WHOEVER believes that Jesus is the Christ is born of God, and everyone who loves Him who begot also loves him who is begotten of Him. ²By this we know that we love the children of God, when we love God and keep His commandments. ³For this is the love of God, that we keep His commandments. And His commandments are not burdensome. ⁴For whatever is born of God overcomes the world. And this is the victory that has overcome the world—our* faith. 5Who is he who overcomes the world, but he who believes that Jesus is the Son of God?

6This is He who came by water and blood—Jesus Christ; not only by water, but by water and blood. And it is the Spirit who bears witness, because the Spirit is truth. 7For there are three that bear witness in heaven: the Father, the Word, and the Holy Spirit; and these three are one. 8And there are three that bear witness on earth:* the Spirit, the water, and the blood; and these three agree as one.

9If we receive the witness of men, the witness of God is greater; for this is the witness of God which* He has testified of His Son. 10He who believes in the Son of God has the witness in himself; he who does not believe God has made Him a liar, because he has not believed the testimony that God has given of His Son. 11And this is the testimony: that God has given us eternal life, and this life is in His Son. 12He who has the Son has life; he who does not have the Son of God does not have life. 13These things I have written to you who believe in the name of the Son of God, that you may know that you have eternal life,* and that you may continue to believe in the name of the Son of God.

14Now this is the confidence that we have in Him, that if we ask anything according to His will, He hears us. 15And if we know that He hears us, whatever we ask, we know that we have the petitions that we have asked of Him.

16If anyone sees his brother sinning a sin which does not lead to death, he will ask, and He will give him life for those who commit sin not leading to death. There is sin leading to death. I do not say that he should pray about that. 17All unrighteousness is sin, and there is sin not leading to death.

18We know that whoever is born of God does not sin; but he who has been born of God keeps himself,* and the wicked one does not touch him.

19We know that we are of God, and the whole world lies under the sway of the wicked one.

20And we know that the Son of God has come and has given us an understanding, that we may know Him who is true; and we are in Him who is true, in His Son Jesus Christ. This is the true God and eternal life.

21Little children, keep yourselves from idols. Amen.

PSALM 124:1-8

A Song of Ascents. Of David.

"IF it had not been the LORD who was on our side,"
Let Israel now say—
2 "If it had not been the LORD
   who was on our side,
   When men rose up against us,
3 Then they would have
   swallowed us alive,
   When their wrath was kindled
   against us;
4 Then the waters would have
   overwhelmed us,
   The stream would have gone
   over our soul;
5 Then the swollen waters
   Would have gone over our
   soul."

6 Blessed be the LORD,
   Who has not given us as prey
   to their teeth.
7 Our soul has escaped as a
   bird from the snare of the
   fowlers;*
   The snare is broken, and we
   have escaped.
8 Our help is in the name of the
   LORD,
   Who made heaven and earth.

PROVERBS FOR TODAY / 29:5-8

A man who flatters his neighbor spreads a net for his feet. □ *By transgression an evil man is snared, but the righteous sings and rejoices.* □ *The righteous considers the cause of the poor,* but *the wicked does not understand* such *know ledge.* □ *Scoffers set a city aflame, but wise* men *turn away wrath.*

DECEMBER 6

HOSEA 4:1–5:15

HEAR the word of the LORD,
You children of Israel,
For the LORD *brings* a charge
against the inhabitants of
the land:

"There is no truth or mercy
Or knowledge of God in the
land.
2   *By* swearing and lying,
Killing and stealing and
committing adultery,
They break all restraint,
With bloodshed upon
bloodshed.
3   Therefore the land will mourn;
And everyone who dwells
there will waste away
With the beasts of the field
And the birds of the air;
Even the fish of the sea will
be taken away.

4   "Now let no man contend, or
rebuke another;
For your people *are* like those
who contend with the priest.
5   Therefore you shall stumble
in the day;
The prophet also shall
stumble with you in the
night;
And I will destroy your
mother.

6   My people are destroyed for
lack of knowledge.
Because you have rejected
knowledge,
I also will reject you from
being priest for Me;
Because you have forgotten
the law of your God,
I also will forget your children.

7   "The more they increased,
The more they sinned against
Me;
I will change* their glory*
into shame.
8   They eat up the sin of My
people;
They set their heart on their
iniquity.
9   And it shall be: like people,
like priest.
So I will punish them for their
ways,
And reward them for their
deeds.
10   For they shall eat, but not
have enough;
They shall commit harlotry,
but not increase;
Because they have ceased
obeying the LORD.

11   "Harlotry, wine, and new wine
enslave the heart.
12   My people ask counsel from
their wooden *idols,*

And their staff informs them.
For the spirit of harlotry has
caused *them* to stray,
And they have played the
harlot against their God.

13 They offer sacrifices on the
mountaintops,
And burn incense on the hills,
Under oaks, poplars, and
terebinths,
Because their shade *is* good.
Therefore your daughters
commit harlotry,
And your brides commit
adultery.

14 "I will not punish your
daughters when they
commit harlotry,
Nor your brides when they
commit adultery;
For *the men* themselves go
apart with harlots,
And offer sacrifices with a
ritual harlot.*
Therefore people *who* do not
understand will be
trampled.

15 "Though you, Israel, play the
harlot,
Let not Judah offend.
Do not come up to Gilgal,
Nor go up to Beth Aven,
Nor swear an oath, *saying,* 'As
the LORD lives'—

16 "For Israel is stubborn
Like a stubborn calf;
Now the LORD will let them
forage
Like a lamb in open country.

17 "Ephraim *is* joined to idols,
Let him alone.

18 Their drink is rebellion,
They commit harlotry
continually.
Her rulers dearly love
dishonor.*

19 The wind has wrapped her up
in its wings,
And they shall be ashamed
because of their sacrifices.

"HEAR this, O priests!
Take heed, O house of Israel!
Give ear, O house of the king!
For yours *is* the judgment,
Because you have been a
snare to Mizpah
And a net spread on Tabor.

2 The revolters are deeply
involved in slaughter,
Though I rebuke them all.

3 I know Ephraim,
And Israel is not hidden from
Me;
For now, O Ephraim, you
commit harlotry;
Israel is defiled.

4 "They do not direct their deeds
Toward turning to their God,
For the spirit of harlotry is in
their midst,
And they do not know the
LORD.

5 The pride of Israel testifies to
his face;
Therefore Israel and Ephraim
stumble in their iniquity;
Judah also stumbles with
them.

6 "With their flocks and herds
They shall go to seek the
LORD,
But they will not find *Him;*
He has withdrawn Himself
from them.

7 They have dealt treacherously
with the LORD,
For they have begotten pagan
children.
Now a New Moon shall
devour them and their
heritage.

8 "Blow the ram's horn in
    Gibeah,
    The trumpet in Ramah!
    Cry aloud *at* Beth Aven,
    '*Look* behind you, O Benjamin!'
9 Ephraim shall be desolate in
    the day of rebuke;
    Among the tribes of Israel I
    make known what is sure.

10 "The princes of Judah are like
    those who remove a
    landmark;
    I will pour out my wrath on
    them like water.
11 Ephraim is oppressed *and*
    broken in judgment,
    Because he willingly walked
    by *human* precept.
12 Therefore I *will be* to Ephraim
    like a moth,
    And to the house of Judah like
    rottenness.

13 "When Ephraim saw his
    sickness,
    And Judah *saw* his wound,
    Then Ephraim went to Assyria
    And sent to King Jareb;
    Yet he cannot cure you,
    Nor heal you of your wound.
14 For I *will be* like a lion to
    Ephraim,
    And like a young lion to the
    house of Judah.
    I, *even* I, will tear *them* and go
    away;
    I will take *them* away, and no
    one shall rescue.
15 I will return again to My place
    Till they acknowledge their
    offense.
    Then they will seek My face;
    In their affliction they will
    earnestly seek Me."

2 JOHN 1-13

THE Elder,

To the elect lady and her children, whom I love in truth, and not only I, but also all those who have known the truth, [2]because of the truth which abides in us and will be with us forever:

[3]Grace, mercy, *and* peace will be with you* from God the Father and from the Lord Jesus Christ, the Son of the Father, in truth and love.

[4]I rejoiced greatly that I have found *some* of your children walking in truth, as we received commandment from the Father. [5]And now I plead with you, lady, not as though I wrote a new commandment to you, but that which we have had from the beginning: that we love one another. [6]This is love, that we walk according to His commandments. This is the commandment, that as you have heard from the beginning, you should walk in it.

[7]For many deceivers have gone out into the world who do not confess Jesus Christ *as* coming in the flesh. This is a deceiver and an antichrist. [8]Look to yourselves, that we* do not lose those things we worked for, but *that* we* may receive a full reward.

[9]Whoever transgresses* and does not abide in the doctrine of Christ does not have God. He who abides in the doctrine of Christ has both the Father and the Son. [10]If anyone comes to you and does not bring this doctrine, do not receive him into your house nor greet him; [11]for he who greets him shares in his evil deeds.

[12]Having many things to write to you, I did not wish *to do so* with paper and ink; but I hope to come to you and speak face to face, that our joy may be full. [13]The children of your elect sister greet you. Amen.

PSALM 125:1-5

A Song of Ascents.

THOSE who trust in the LORD
Are like Mount Zion,
Which cannot be moved, *but*
abides forever.
2 As the mountains surround
Jerusalem,
So the LORD surrounds His
people
From this time forth and
forever.

3 For the scepter of wickedness
shall not rest

On the land allotted to the
righteous,
Lest the righteous reach out
their hands to iniquity.

4 Do good, O LORD, to *those who
are* good,
And to *those who are* upright
in their hearts.

5 As for such as turn aside to
their crooked ways,
The LORD shall lead them away
With the workers of iniquity.

Peace *be* upon Israel!

PROVERBS FOR TODAY/ 29:9-11

If *a wise man contends with a foolish man, whether* the fool *rages or laughs,* there is *no peace.* □ *The bloodthirsty hate the blameless, but the upright seek his well-being.* * □ *A fool vents all his feelings,* * but a wise man *holds them back.*

DECEMBER 7

HOSEA 6:1–9:17

COME, and let us return to
the LORD;
For He has torn, but He will
heal us;
He has stricken, but He will
bind us up.
2 After two days He will revive
us;
On the third day He will raise
us up,
That we may live in His sight.
3 Let us know,
Let us pursue the knowledge
of the LORD.
His going forth is established
as the morning;
He will come to us like the
rain,

Like the latter *and* former
rain to the earth.

4 "O Ephraim, what shall I do to
you?
O Judah, what shall I do to
you?
For your faithfulness is like a
morning cloud,
And like the early dew it goes
away.
5 Therefore I have hewn *them*
by the prophets,
I have slain them by the
words of My mouth;
And your judgments *are like*
light *that* goes forth.
6 For I desire mercy and not
sacrifice,

And the knowledge of God
more than burnt offerings.

7 "But like men* they
transgressed the covenant;
There they dealt
treacherously with Me.
8 Gilead *is* a city of evildoers
And defiled with blood.
9 As bands of robbers lie in wait
for a man,
So the company of priests
murder on the way to
Shechem;
Surely they commit lewdness.
10 I have seen a horrible thing in
the house of Israel:
There *is* the harlotry of
Ephraim;
Israel is defiled.
11 Also, O Judah, a harvest is
appointed for you,
When I return the captives of
My people.

"WHEN I would have healed Israel,
Then the iniquity of Ephraim
was uncovered,
And the wickedness of
Samaria.
For they have committed
fraud;
A thief comes in;
A band of robbers takes spoil
outside.
2 They do not consider in their
hearts
That I remember all their
wickedness;
Now their own deeds have
surrounded them;
They are before My face.
3 They make a king glad with
their wickedness,
And princes with their lies.

4 "They *are* all adulterers.
Like an oven heated by a
baker—

He ceases stirring *the fire*
after kneading the dough,
Until it is leavened.
5 In the day of our king
Princes have made *him* sick,
inflamed with wine;
He stretched out his hand
with scoffers.
6 They prepare their heart like
an oven,
While they lie in wait;
Their baker* sleeps all night;
In the morning it burns like a
flaming fire.
7 They are all hot, like an oven,
And have devoured their
judges;
All their kings have fallen.
None among them calls upon
Me.

8 "Ephraim has mixed himself
among the peoples;
Ephraim is a cake unturned.
9 Aliens have devoured his
strength,
But he does not know *it;*
Yes, gray hairs are here and
there on him,
Yet he does not know *it.*
10 And the pride of Israel
testifies to his face,
But they do not return to the
LORD their God,
Nor seek Him for all this.

11 "Ephraim also is like a silly
dove, without sense—
They call to Egypt,
They go to Assyria.
12 Wherever they go, I will
spread My net on them;
I will bring them down like
birds of the air;
I will chastise them
According to what their
congregation has heard.

13 "Woe to them, for they have
fled from Me!

Destruction to them,
Because they have
transgressed against Me!
Though I redeemed them,
Yet they have spoken lies
against Me.

14 They did not cry out to Me
with their heart
When they wailed upon their
beds.

"They assemble together for*
grain and new wine,
They rebel against Me;*

15 Though I disciplined *and*
strengthened their arms,
Yet they devise evil against
Me;

16 They return, *but* not to the
Most High;*
They are like a treacherous
bow.
Their princes shall fall by the
sword
For the cursings of their
tongue.
This *shall be* their derision in
the land of Egypt.

"*Set* the trumpet* to your mouth!
He shall come like an eagle
against the house of the
Lord,
Because they have
transgressed My covenant
And rebelled against My law.

2 Israel will cry to Me,
'My God, we know You!'

3 Israel has rejected the good;
The enemy will pursue him.

4 "They set up kings, but not by
Me;
They made princes, but I did
not acknowledge *them.*
From their silver and gold
They made idols for
themselves—
That they might be cut off.

5 Your calf is rejected,
O Samaria!
My anger is aroused against
them—
How long until they attain to
innocence?

6 For from Israel *is* even this:
A workman made it, and it *is*
not God;
But the calf of Samaria shall
be broken to pieces.

7 "They sow the wind,
And reap the whirlwind.
The stalk has no bud;
It shall never produce meal.
If it should produce,
Aliens would swallow it up.

8 Israel is swallowed up;
Now they are among the
Gentiles
Like a vessel in which *is* no
pleasure.

9 For they have gone up to
Assyria,
Like a wild donkey alone by
itself;
Ephraim has hired lovers.

10 Yes, though they have hired
among the nations,
Now I will gather them;
And they shall sorrow a little,*
Because of the burden* of the
king of princes.

11 "Because Ephraim has made
many altars for sin,
They have become for him
altars for sinning.

12 I have written for him the
great things of My law,
But they were considered a
strange thing.

13 *For* the sacrifices of My
offerings they sacrifice
flesh and eat *it,*
But the Lord does not accept
them.
Now He will remember their

iniquity and punish their
sins.
They shall return to Egypt.

14 "For Israel has forgotten his
Maker,
And has built temples;*
Judah also has multiplied
fortified cities;
But I will send fire upon his
cities,
And it shall devour his
palaces."

Do not rejoice, O Israel, with joy like
other peoples,
For you have played the
harlot against your God.
You have made love *for* hire
on every threshing floor.
2 The threshing floor and the
winepress
Shall not feed them,
And the new wine shall fail in
her.

3 They shall not dwell in the
Lord's land,
But Ephraim shall return to
Egypt,
And shall eat unclean *things* in
Assyria.
4 They shall not offer wine
offerings to the Lord,
Nor shall their sacrifices be
pleasing to Him.
It shall be like bread of
mourners to them;
All who eat it shall be defiled.
For their bread *shall be* for
their *own* life;
It shall not come into the
house of the Lord.

5 What will you do in the
appointed day,
And in the day of the feast of
the Lord?
6 For indeed they are gone
because of destruction.

Egypt shall gather them up;
Memphis shall bury them.
Nettles shall possess their
valuables of silver;
Thorns *shall be* in their tents.

7 The days of punishment have
come;
The days of recompense have
come.
Israel knows!
The prophet *is* a fool,
The spiritual man *is* insane,
Because of the greatness of
your iniquity and great
enmity.
8 The watchman of Ephraim *is*
with my God;
But the prophet *is* a fowler's*
snare in all his ways—
Enmity in the house of his
God.
9 They are deeply corrupted,
As in the days of Gibeah.
He will remember their
iniquity;
He will punish their sins.

10 "I found Israel
Like grapes in the wilderness;
I saw your fathers
As the firstfruits on the fig
tree in its first season.
But they went to Baal Peor,
And separated themselves *to*
that shame;
They became an abomination
like the thing they loved.
11 *As for* Ephraim, their glory
shall fly away like a bird—
No birth, no pregnancy, and
no conception!
12 Though they bring up their
children,
Yet I will bereave them to the
last man.
Yes, woe to them when I
depart from them!
13 Just as I saw Ephraim like

Tyre, planted in a pleasant
place,
So Ephraim will bring out his
children to the murderer."

14 Give them, O LORD—
What will You give?
Give them a miscarrying
womb
And dry breasts!

15 "All their wickedness *is* in
Gilgal,
For there I hated them.
Because of the evil of their
deeds
I will drive them from My
house;
I will love them no more.
All their princes *are* rebellious.

16 Ephraim is stricken,
Their root is dried up;
They shall bear no fruit.
Yes, were they to bear
children,
I would kill the darlings of
their womb."

17 My God will cast them away,
Because they did not obey
Him;
And they shall be wanderers
among the nations.

3 JOHN 1-14

THE Elder,

To the beloved Gaius, whom I
love in truth:

2Beloved, I pray that you may prosper in all things and be in health, just
as your soul prospers. 3For I rejoiced
greatly when brethren came and testified of the truth *that is* in you, just as
you walk in the truth. 4I have no
greater joy than to hear that my children walk in truth.*

5Beloved, you do faithfully whatever
you do for the brethren and* for
strangers, 6who have borne witness of
your love before the church. *If* you
send them forward on their journey in
a manner worthy of God, you will do
well, 7because they went forth for His
name's sake, taking nothing from the
Gentiles. 8We therefore ought to receive* such, that we may become fellow workers for the truth.

9I wrote to the church, but Diotre-
phes, who loves to have the preeminence among them, does not receive us. 10Therefore, if I come, I will
call to mind his deeds which he does,
prating against us with malicious
words. And not content with that, he
himself does not receive the brethren,
and forbids those who wish to, putting
them out of the church.

11Beloved, do not imitate what is
evil, but what is good. He who does
good is of God, but* he who does evil
has not seen God.

12Demetrius has a *good* testimony
from all, and from the truth itself. And
we also bear witness, and you know
that our testimony is true.

13I had many things to write, but I do
not wish to write to you with pen and
ink; 14but I hope to see you shortly, and
we shall speak face to face.
Peace to you. Our friends greet you.
Greet the friends by name.

PSALM 126:1-6
A Song of Ascents.

WHEN the LORD brought back
the captivity of Zion,
We were like those who
dream.
2   Then our mouth was filled
with laughter,
And our tongue with singing.
Then they said among the
nations,

"The Lord has done great
things for them."
3 The Lord has done great
things for us,
And we are glad.

4 Bring back our captivity,
O Lord,
As the streams in the South.

5 Those who sow in tears
Shall reap in joy.
6 He who continually goes forth
weeping,
Bearing seed for sowing,
Shall doubtless come again
with rejoicing,
Bringing his sheaves *with him.*

PROVERBS FOR TODAY/ 29:12-14

If a ruler pays attention to lies, all his servants become *wicked.* □ *The poor* man
and the oppressor have this in common: the Lord *gives light to the eyes of both.*
□ *The king who judges the poor with truth, his throne will be established forever.*

DECEMBER 8

HOSEA 10:1–14:9

Israel empties *his* vine;
He brings forth fruit for himself.
According to the multitude of
his fruit
He has increased the altars;
According to the bounty of his
land
They have embellished *his*
sacred pillars.
2 Their heart is divided;
Now they are held guilty.
He will break down their
altars;
He will ruin their sacred
pillars.

3 For now they say,
"We have no king,
Because we did not fear the
Lord.
And as for a king, what would
he do for us?"
4 They have spoken words,
Swearing falsely in making a
covenant.

Thus judgment springs up
like hemlock in the furrows
of the field.

5 The inhabitants of Samaria
fear
Because of the calf* of Beth
Aven.
For its people mourn for it,
And its priests shriek for it—
Because its glory has
departed from it.
6 *The idol* also shall be carried
to Assyria
As a present for King Jareb.
Ephraim shall receive shame,
And Israel shall be ashamed
of his own counsel.

7 *As for* Samaria, her king is cut
off
Like a twig on the water.
8 Also the high places of Aven,
the sin of Israel,
Shall be destroyed.
The thorn and thistle shall
grow on their altars;

They shall say to the
mountains, "Cover us!"
And to the hills, "Fall on us!"

9 "O Israel, you have sinned
from the days of Gibeah;
There they stood.
The battle in Gibeah against
the children of iniquity*
Did not overtake them.
10 When *it is* My desire, I will
chasten them.
Peoples shall be gathered
against them
When I bind them for their
two transgressions.*
11 Ephraim *is* a trained heifer
That loves to thresh *grain;*
But I harnessed her fair neck,
I will make Ephraim pull *a
plow.*
Judah shall plow;
Jacob shall break his clods."

12 Sow for yourselves
righteousness;
Reap in mercy;
Break up your fallow ground,
For *it is* time to seek the Lord,
Till He comes and rains
righteousness on you.

13 You have plowed wickedness;
You have reaped iniquity.
You have eaten the fruit of lies,
Because you trusted in your
own way,
In the multitude of your
mighty men.
14 Therefore tumult shall arise
among your people,
And all your fortresses shall
be plundered
As Shalman plundered Beth
Arbel in the day of battle—
A mother dashed in pieces
upon *her* children.
15 Thus it shall be done to you,
O Bethel,

Because of your great
wickedness.
At dawn the king of Israel
Shall be cut off utterly.

"WHEN Israel *was* a child, I loved him,
And out of Egypt I called My
son.
2 *As* they called them,*
So they went from them;*
They sacrificed to the Baals,
And burned incense to carved
images.

3 "I taught Ephraim to walk,
Taking them by their arms;*
But they did not know that I
healed them.
4 I drew them with gentle
cords,*
With bands of love,
And I was to them as those
who take the yoke from
their neck.*
I stooped *and* fed them.

5 "He shall not return to the land
of Egypt;
But the Assyrian shall be his
king,
Because they refused to
repent.
6 And the sword shall slash in
his cities,
Devour his districts,
And consume *them,*
Because of their own
counsels.
7 My people are bent on
backsliding from Me.
Though they call to the Most
High,*
None at all exalt *Him.*

8 "How can I give you up,
Ephraim?
How can I hand you over,
Israel?
How can I make you like
Admah?

How can I set you like
  Zeboiim?
My heart churns within Me;
My sympathy is stirred.
9 I will not execute the
    fierceness of My anger;
  I will not again destroy
    Ephraim.
  For I *am* God, and not man,
  The Holy One in your midst;
  And I will not come with
    terror.*

10 "They shall walk after the LORD.
  He will roar like a lion.
  When He roars,
  Then *His* sons shall come
    trembling from the west;
11 They shall come trembling
    like a bird from Egypt,
  Like a dove from the land of
    Assyria.
  And I will let them dwell in
    their houses,"
  Says the LORD.

12 "Ephraim has encircled Me
    with lies,
  And the house of Israel with
    deceit;
  But Judah still walks with God,
  Even with the Holy One* *who*
    is faithful.

"EPHRAIM feeds on the wind,
    And pursues the east wind;
  He daily increases lies and
    desolation.
  Also they make a covenant
    with the Assyrians,
  And oil is carried to Egypt.

2 "The LORD also *brings* a charge
    against Judah,
  And will punish Jacob
    according to his ways;
  According to his deeds He
    will recompense him.
3 He took his brother by the
    heel in the womb,

And in his strength he
    struggled with God.*
4 Yes, he struggled with the
    Angel and prevailed;
  He wept, and sought favor
    from Him.
  He found Him *in* Bethel,
  And there He spoke to us—
5 That is, the LORD God of hosts.
  The LORD *is* His memorable
    name.
6 So you, by *the help of* your
    God, return;
  Observe mercy and justice,
  And wait on your God
    continually.

7 "A cunning Canaanite!
  Deceitful scales *are* in his
    hand;
  He loves to oppress.
8 And Ephraim said,
  'Surely I have become rich,
  I have found wealth for myself;
  In all my labors
  They shall find in me no
    iniquity that *is* sin.'

9 "But I *am* the LORD your God,
  Ever since the land of Egypt;
  I will again make you dwell in
    tents,
  As in the days of the
    appointed feast.
10 I have also spoken by the
    prophets,
  And have multiplied visions;
  I have given symbols through
    the witness of the
    prophets."

11 Though Gilead *has* idols—
  Surely they are vanity—
  Though they sacrifice bulls in
    Gilgal,
  Indeed their altars *shall be*
    heaps in the furrows of the
    field.

12 Jacob fled to the country of
       Syria;
   Israel served for a spouse,
   And for a wife he tended *sheep*.
13 By a prophet the Lord
       brought Israel out of Egypt,
   And by a prophet he was
       preserved.
14 Ephraim provoked *Him* to
       anger most bitterly;
   Therefore his Lord will leave
       the guilt of his bloodshed
       upon him,
   And return his reproach upon
       him.

When Ephraim spoke, trembling,
   He exalted *himself* in Israel;
   But when he offended
       through Baal *worship*, he
       died.
2 Now they sin more and more,
   And have made for
       themselves molded images,
   Idols of their silver, according
       to their skill;
   All of it *is* the work of
       craftsmen.
   They say of them,
   "Let the men who sacrifice*
       kiss the calves!"
3 Therefore they shall be like
       the morning cloud
   And like the early dew that
       passes away,
   Like chaff blown off from a
       threshing floor
   And like smoke from a
       chimney.

4 "Yet I *am* the Lord your God
   Ever since the land of Egypt,
   And you shall know no God
       but Me;
   For *there is* no savior besides
       Me.
5 I knew you in the wilderness,
   In the land of great drought.
6 When they had pasture, they
       were filled;

They were filled and their
       heart was exalted;
   Therefore they forgot Me.

7 "So I will be to them like a lion;
   Like a leopard by the road I
       will lurk;
8 I will meet them like a bear
       deprived *of her cubs;*
   I will tear open their rib cage,
   And there I will devour them
       like a lion.
   The wild beast shall tear them.

9 "O Israel, you are destroyed,*
   But your help* *is* from Me.
10 I will be your King;*
   Where *is any other,*
   That he may save you in all
       your cities?
   And your judges to whom you
       said,
   'Give me a king and princes'?
11 I gave you a king in My anger,
   And took *him* away in My
       wrath.

12 "The iniquity of Ephraim *is*
       bound up;
   His sin *is* stored up.
13 The sorrows of a woman in
       childbirth shall come upon
       him.
   He *is* an unwise son,
   For he should not stay long
       where children are born.

14 "I will ransom them from the
       power of the grave;*
   I will redeem them from
       death.
   O Death, I will be your
       plagues!*
   O Grave,* I will be your
       destruction!*
   Pity is hidden from My eyes."

15 Though he is fruitful among
       his brethren,
   An east wind shall come;

The wind of the LORD shall
come up from the
wilderness.
Then his spring shall become
dry,
And his fountain shall be
dried up.
He shall plunder the treasury
of every desirable prize.
16 Samaria is held guilty,*
For she has rebelled against
her God.
They shall fall by the sword,
Their infants shall be dashed
in pieces,
And their women with child
ripped open.

O ISRAEL, return to the LORD your God,
For you have stumbled
because of your iniquity;
2 Take words with you,
And return to the LORD.
Say to Him,
"Take away all iniquity;
Receive us graciously,
For we will offer the
sacrifices* of our lips.
3 Assyria shall not save us,
We will not ride on horses,
Nor will we say anymore to
the work of our hands, 'You
are our gods.'
For in You the fatherless finds
mercy."

4 "I will heal their backsliding,
I will love them freely,
For My anger has turned
away from him.
5 I will be like the dew to Israel;
He shall grow like the lily,
And lengthen his roots like
Lebanon.
6 His branches shall spread;
His beauty shall be like an
olive tree,
And his fragrance like
Lebanon.

7 Those who dwell under his
shadow shall return;
They shall be revived like
grain,
And grow like a vine.
Their scent* shall be like the
wine of Lebanon.

8 "Ephraim shall say, 'What have
I to do anymore with idols?'
I have heard and observed
him.
I am like a green cypress tree;
Your fruit is found in Me."

9 Who is wise?
Let him understand these
things.
Who is prudent?
Let him know them
For the ways of the LORD are
right;
The righteous walk in them,
But transgressors stumble in
them.

JUDE 1-25

JUDE, a bondservant of Jesus
Christ, and brother of James,

To those who are called, sanctified*
by God the Father, and preserved in
Jesus Christ:

2Mercy, peace, and love be multiplied to you.

3Beloved, while I was very diligent
to write to you concerning our common salvation, I found it necessary to
write to you exhorting you to contend
earnestly for the faith which was once
for all delivered to the saints. 4For certain men have crept in unnoticed, who
long ago were marked out for this condemnation, ungodly men, who turn
the grace of our God into lewdness and
deny the only Lord God* and our Lord
Jesus Christ.

⁵But I want to remind you, though you once knew this, that the Lord, having saved the people out of the land of Egypt, afterward destroyed those who did not believe. ⁶And the angels who did not keep their proper domain, but left their own abode, He has reserved in everlasting chains under darkness for the judgment of the great day; ⁷as Sodom and Gomorrah, and the cities around them in a similar manner to these, having given themselves over to sexual immorality and gone after strange flesh, are set forth as an example, suffering the vengeance of eternal fire.

⁸Likewise also these dreamers defile the flesh, reject authority, and speak evil of dignitaries. ⁹Yet Michael the archangel, in contending with the devil, when he disputed about the body of Moses, dared not bring against him a reviling accusation, but said, "The Lord rebuke you!" ¹⁰But these speak evil of whatever they do not know; and whatever they know naturally, like brute beasts, in these things they corrupt themselves. ¹¹Woe to them! For they have gone in the way of Cain, have run greedily in the error of Balaam for profit, and perished in the rebellion of Korah.

¹²These are spots in your love feasts, while they feast with you without fear, serving *only* themselves. *They are* clouds without water, carried about* by the winds; late autumn trees without fruit, twice dead, pulled up by the roots; ¹³raging waves of the sea, foaming up their own shame; wandering stars for whom is reserved the blackness of darkness forever.

¹⁴Now Enoch, the seventh from Adam, prophesied about these men also, saying, "Behold, the Lord comes with ten thousands of His saints, ¹⁵to execute judgment on all, to convict all who are ungodly among them of all their ungodly deeds which they have committed in an ungodly way, and of all the harsh things which ungodly sinners have spoken against Him."

¹⁶These are grumblers, complainers, walking according to their own lusts; and they mouth great swelling *words,* flattering people to gain advantage. ¹⁷But you, beloved, remember the words which were spoken before by the apostles of our Lord Jesus Christ: ¹⁸how they told you that there would be mockers in the last time who would walk according to their own ungodly lusts. ¹⁹These are sensual persons, who cause divisions, not having the Spirit.

²⁰But you, beloved, building yourselves up on your most holy faith, praying in the Holy Spirit, ²¹keep yourselves in the love of God, looking for the mercy of our Lord Jesus Christ unto eternal life.

²²And on some have compassion, making a distinction;* ²³but others save with fear, pulling *them* out of the fire,* hating even the garment defiled by the flesh.

24   Now to Him who is able to
       keep you* from stumbling,
    And to present *you* faultless
    Before the presence of His
       glory with exceeding joy,
25   To God our Savior,*
    Who alone is wise,*
    Be glory and majesty,
    Dominion and power,*
    Both now and forever.
    Amen.

PSALM 127:1-5

A Song of Ascents. Of Solomon.

Unless the Lord builds the house,
    They labor in vain who build it;
Unless the Lord guards the city,
    The watchman stays awake in vain.

2 *It is* vain for you to rise up
      early,
   To sit up late,
   To eat the bread of sorrows;
   For so He gives His beloved
      sleep.

3 Behold, children *are* a
      heritage from the LORD,
   The fruit of the womb *is* a
      reward.

4 Like arrows in the hand of a
      warrior,
   So *are* the children of one's
      youth.

5 Happy *is* the man who has his
      quiver full of them;
   They shall not be ashamed,
   But shall speak with their
      enemies in the gate.

PROVERBS FOR TODAY/ 29:15-17

The rod and rebuke give wisdom, but a child left to himself *brings shame to his mother.* □ *When the wicked are multiplied, transgression increases; but the righteous will see their fall.* □ *Correct your son, and he will give you rest; yes, he will give delight to your soul.*

DECEMBER 9

JOEL 1:1–3:21

THE word of the LORD that came to Joel the son of Pethuel.

2 Hear this, you elders,
   And give ear, all you
      inhabitants of the land!
   Has *anything like* this
      happened in your days,
   Or even in the days of your
      fathers?

3 Tell your children about it,
   Let your children *tell* their
      children,
   And their children another
      generation.

4 What the chewing locust* left,
      the swarming locust has
      eaten;
   What the swarming locust
      left, the crawling locust has
      eaten;
   And what the crawling locust
      left, the consuming locust
      has eaten.

5 Awake, you drunkards, and
      weep;
   And wail, all you drinkers of
      wine,
   Because of the new wine,
   For it has been cut off from
      your mouth.

6 For a nation has come up
      against My land,
   Strong, and without number;
   His teeth *are* the teeth of a
      lion,
   And he has the fangs of a
      fierce lion.

7 He has laid waste My vine,
   And ruined My fig tree;
   He has stripped it bare and
      thrown *it* away;
   Its branches are made white.

8 Lament like a virgin girded
  with sackcloth
For the husband of her youth.
9 The grain offering and the
  drink offering
Have been cut off from the
  house of the LORD;
The priests mourn, who
  minister to the LORD.
10 The field is wasted,
The land mourns;
For the grain is ruined,
The new wine is dried up,
The oil fails.

11 Be ashamed, you farmers,
Wail, you vinedressers,
For the wheat and the barley;
Because the harvest of the
  field has perished.
12 The vine has dried up,
And the fig tree has withered;
The pomegranate tree,
The palm tree also,
And the apple tree—
All the trees of the field are
  withered;
Surely joy has withered away
  from the sons of men.

13 Gird yourselves and lament,
  you priests;
Wail, you who minister before
  the altar;
Come, lie all night in
  sackcloth,
You who minister to my God;
For the grain offering and the
  drink offering
Are withheld from the house
  of your God.
14 Consecrate a fast,
Call a sacred assembly;
Gather the elders
And all the inhabitants of the
  land
Into the house of the LORD
  your God,
And cry out to the LORD.

15 Alas for the day!
For the day of the LORD *is* at
  hand;
It shall come as destruction
  from the Almighty.
16 Is not the food cut off before
  our eyes,
Joy and gladness from the
  house of our God?
17 The seed shrivels under the
  clods,
Storehouses are in shambles;
Barns are broken down,
For the grain has withered.
18 How the animals groan!
The herds of cattle are
  restless,
Because they have no pasture;
Even the flocks of sheep
  suffer punishment.*

19 O LORD, to You I cry out;
For fire has devoured the
  open pastures,
And a flame has burned all
  the trees of the field.
20 The beasts of the field also
  cry out to You,
For the water brooks are
  dried up,
And fire has devoured the
  open pastures.

BLOW the trumpet in Zion,
  And sound an alarm in My
    holy mountain!
  Let all the inhabitants of the
    land tremble;
  For the day of the LORD is
    coming,
  For it is at hand:
2 A day of darkness and
    gloominess,
  A day of clouds and thick
    darkness,
  Like the morning *clouds*
    spread over the mountains.
  A people *come,* great and
    strong,

The like of whom has never
been;
Nor will there ever be any
such after them,
Even for many successive
generations.

3 A fire devours before them,
And behind them a flame
burns;
The land *is* like the Garden of
Eden before them,
And behind them a desolate
wilderness;
Surely nothing shall escape
them.

4 Their appearance is like the
appearance of horses;
And like swift steeds, so they
run.

5 With a noise like chariots
Over mountaintops they leap,
Like the noise of a flaming fire
that devours the stubble,
Like a strong people set in
battle array.

6 Before them the people
writhe in pain;
All faces are drained of color.*

7 They run like mighty men,
They climb the wall like men
of war;
Every one marches in
formation,
And they do not break ranks.

8 They do not push one another;
Every one marches in his
own column.*
Though they lunge between
the weapons,
They are not cut down.*

9 They run to and fro in the city,
They run on the wall;
They climb into the houses,
They enter at the windows
like a thief.

10 The earth quakes before
them,

The heavens tremble;
The sun and moon grow dark,
And the stars diminish their
brightness.

11 The LORD gives voice before
His army,
For His camp is very great;
For strong *is the One* who
executes His word.
For the day of the LORD *is*
great and very terrible;
Who can endure it?

12 "Now, therefore," says the
LORD,
"Turn to Me with all your
heart,
With fasting, with weeping,
and with mourning."

13 So rend your heart, and not
your garments;
Return to the LORD your God,
For He *is* gracious and
merciful,
Slow to anger, and of great
kindness;
And He relents from doing
harm.

14 Who knows *if* He will turn
and relent,
And leave a blessing behind
Him—
A grain offering and a drink
offering
For the LORD your God?

15 Blow the trumpet in Zion,
Consecrate a fast,
Call a sacred assembly;

16 Gather the people,
Sanctify the congregation,
Assemble the elders,
Gather the children and
nursing babes;
Let the bridegroom go out
from his chamber,
And the bride from her
dressing room.

17 Let the priests, who minister
to the LORD,

Weep between the porch and
the altar;
Let them say, "Spare Your
people, O LORD,
And do not give Your heritage
to reproach,
That the nations should rule
over them.
Why should they say among
the peoples,
'Where *is* their God?' "

18 Then the LORD will be zealous
for His land,
And pity His people.
19 The LORD will answer and say
to His people,
"Behold, I will send you grain
and new wine and oil,
And you will be satisfied by
them;
I will no longer make you a
reproach among the
nations.

20 "But I will remove far from you
the northern *army,*
And will drive him away into a
barren and desolate land,
With his face toward the
eastern sea
And his back toward the
western sea;
His stench will come up,
And his foul odor will rise,
Because he has done
monstrous things."

21 Fear not, O land;
Be glad and rejoice,
For the LORD has done
marvelous things!
22 Do not be afraid, you beasts
of the field;
For the open pastures are
springing up,
And the tree bears its fruit;
The fig tree and the vine yield
their strength.

23 Be glad then, you children of
Zion,
And rejoice in the LORD your
God;
For He has given you the
former rain faithfully,*
And He will cause the rain to
come down for you—
The former rain,
And the latter rain in the first
month.
24 The threshing floors shall be
full of wheat,
And the vats shall overflow
with new wine and oil.

25 "So I will restore to you the
years that the swarming
locust has eaten,
The crawling locust,
The consuming locust,
And the chewing locust,*
My great army which I sent
among you.
26 You shall eat in plenty and be
satisfied,
And praise the name of the
LORD your God,
Who has dealt wondrously
with you;
And My people shall never be
put to shame.
27 Then you shall know that I
am in the midst of Israel:
I *am* the LORD your God
And there is no other.
My people shall never be put
to shame.

28 "And it shall come to pass
afterward
That I will pour out My Spirit
on all flesh;
Your sons and your daughters
shall prophesy,
Your old men shall dream
dreams,
Your young men shall see
visions.

29 And also on *My* menservants
and on *My* maidservants
I will pour out My Spirit in
those days.

30 "And I will show wonders in
the heavens and in the
earth:
Blood and fire and pillars of
smoke.

31 The sun shall be turned into
darkness,
And the moon into blood,
Before the coming of the
great and awesome day of
the LORD.

32 And it shall come to pass
That whoever calls on the
name of the LORD
Shall be saved.
For in Mount Zion and in
Jerusalem there shall be
deliverance,
As the LORD has said,
Among the remnant whom
the LORD calls.

"FOR behold, in those days and at that
time,
When I bring back the
captives of Judah and
Jerusalem,

2 I will also gather all nations,
And bring them down to the
Valley of Jehoshaphat;
And I will enter into judgment
with them there
On account of My people, My
heritage Israel,
Whom they have scattered
among the nations;
They have also divided up My
land.

3 They have cast lots for My
people,
Have given a boy *as payment*
for a harlot,
And sold a girl for wine, that
they may drink.

4 "Indeed, what have you to do
with Me,
O Tyre and Sidon, and all the
coasts of Philistia?
Will you retaliate against Me?
But if you retaliate against Me,
Swiftly and speedily I will
return your retaliation upon
your own head;

5 Because you have taken My
silver and My gold,
And have carried into your
temples My prized
possessions.

6 Also the people of Judah and
the people of Jerusalem
You have sold to the Greeks,
That you may remove them
far from their borders.

7 "Behold, I will raise them
Out of the place to which you
have sold them,
And will return your
retaliation upon your own
head.

8 I will sell your sons and your
daughters
Into the hand of the people of
Judah,
And they will sell them to the
Sabeans,*
To a people far off;
For the LORD has spoken."

9 Proclaim this among the
nations:
"Prepare for war!
Wake up the mighty men,
Let all the men of war draw
near,
Let them come up.

10 Beat your plowshares into
swords
And your pruning hooks into
spears;
Let the weak say, 'I *am* strong.'"

11 Assemble and come, all you
nations,

And gather together all
    around.
Cause Your mighty ones to go
    down there, O LORD.

12 "Let the nations be wakened,
    and come up to the Valley
    of Jehoshaphat;
For there I will sit to judge all
    the surrounding nations.

13 Put in the sickle, for the
    harvest is ripe.
Come, go down;
For the winepress is full,
The vats overflow—
For their wickedness *is* great."

14 Multitudes, multitudes in the
    valley of decision!
For the day of the LORD *is* near
    in the valley of decision.

15 The sun and moon will grow
    dark,
And the stars will diminish
    their brightness.

16 The LORD also will roar from
    Zion,
And utter His voice from
    Jerusalem;
The heavens and earth will
    shake;
But the LORD will be a shelter
    for His people,
And the strength of the
    children of Israel.

17 "So you shall know that I *am*
    the LORD your God,
Dwelling in Zion My holy
    mountain.
Then Jerusalem shall be holy,
And no aliens shall ever pass
    through her again."

18 And it will come to pass in
    that day
That the mountains shall drip
    with new wine,
The hills shall flow with milk,

And all the brooks of Judah
    shall be flooded with water;
A fountain shall flow from the
    house of the LORD
And water the Valley of
    Acacias.

19 "Egypt shall be a desolation,
And Edom a desolate
    wilderness,
Because of violence *against*
    the people of Judah,
For they have shed innocent
    blood in their land.

20 But Judah shall abide forever,
And Jerusalem from
    generation to generation.

21 For I will acquit them of the
    guilt of bloodshed, whom I
    had not acquitted;
For the LORD dwells in Zion."

REVELATION 1:1-20

THE Revelation of Jesus Christ,
which God gave Him to show
His servants—things which
must shortly take place. And He sent
and signified *it* by His angel to His servant John, 2who bore witness to the
word of God, and to the testimony of
Jesus Christ, to all things that he saw.
3Blessed *is* he who reads and those
who hear the words of this prophecy,
and keep those things which are written in it; for the time *is* near.

4John, to the seven churches which
are in Asia:

Grace to you and peace from Him
who is and who was and who is to
come, and from the seven Spirits who
are before His throne, 5and from Jesus
Christ, the faithful witness, the firstborn from the dead, and the ruler over
the kings of the earth.

To Him who loved us and washed*
us from our sins in His own blood, 6and
has made us kings* and priests to His

God and Father, to Him *be* glory and dominion forever and ever. Amen.

7Behold, He is coming with clouds, and every eye will see Him, even they who pierced Him. And all the tribes of the earth will mourn because of Him. Even so, Amen.

8"I am the Alpha and the Omega, *the* Beginning and *the* End,"* says the Lord,* "who is and who was and who is to come, the Almighty."

9I, John, both* your brother and companion in the tribulation and kingdom and patience of Jesus Christ, was on the island that is called Patmos for the word of God and for the testimony of Jesus Christ. 10I was in the Spirit on the Lord's Day, and I heard behind me a loud voice, as of a trumpet, 11saying, "I am the Alpha and the Omega, the First and the Last," and,* "What you see, write in a book and send *it* to the seven churches which are in Asia:* to Ephesus, to Smyrna, to Pergamos, to Thyatira, to Sardis, to Philadelphia, and to Laodicea."

12Then I turned to see the voice that spoke with me. And having turned I saw seven golden lampstands, 13and in the midst of the seven lampstands *One* like the Son of Man, clothed with a garment down to the feet and girded about the chest with a golden band. 14His head and hair *were* white like wool, as white as snow, and His eyes like a flame of fire; 15His feet *were* like fine brass, as if refined in a furnace, and His voice as the sound of many waters; 16He had in His right hand seven stars, out of His mouth went a sharp two-edged sword, and His countenance *was* like the sun shining in its strength. 17And when I saw Him, I fell at His feet as dead. But He laid His right hand on me, saying to me,* "Do not be afraid; I am the First and the Last. 18I *am* He who lives, and was dead, and behold, I am alive forevermore. Amen. And I have the keys of Hades and of Death. 19Write* the things which you have seen, and the things which are, and the things which will take place after this. 20The mystery of the seven stars which you saw in My right hand, and the seven golden lampstands: The seven stars are the angels of the seven churches, and the seven lampstands which you saw* are the seven churches."

PSALM 128:1-6

A Song of Ascents.

LESSED *is* every one who fears the LORD, Who walks in His ways.

2 When you eat the labor of your hands,
You *shall be* happy, and *it shall be* well with you.

3 Your wife *shall be* like a fruitful vine
In the very heart of your house,
Your children like olive plants All around your table.

4 Behold, thus shall the man be blessed
Who fears the LORD.

5 The LORD bless you out of Zion,
And may you see the good of Jerusalem
All the days of your life.

6 Yes, may you see your children's children.

Peace *be* upon Israel!

PROVERBS FOR TODAY/ 29:18

Where there is *no revelation,* * *the people cast off restraint; but happy* is *he who keeps the law.*

DECEMBER 10

AMOS 1:1–3:15

THE words of Amos, who was among the sheepbreeders* of Tekoa, which he saw concerning Israel in the days of Uzziah king of Judah, and in the days of Jeroboam the son of Joash, king of Israel, two years before the earthquake.

2And he said:

> "The LORD roars from Zion,
> And utters His voice from
>   Jerusalem;
> The pastures of the
>   shepherds mourn,
> And the top of Carmel
>   withers."

3Thus says the LORD:

> "For three transgressions of
>   Damascus, and for four,
> I will not turn away its
>   *punishment,*
> Because they have threshed
>   Gilead with implements of
>   iron.
> 4 But I will send a fire into the
>   house of Hazael,
> Which shall devour the
>   palaces of Ben-Hadad.
> 5 I will also break the *gate* bar
>   of Damascus,
> And cut off the inhabitant
>   from the Valley of Aven,
> And the one who holds the
>   scepter from Beth Eden.
> The people of Syria shall go
>   captive to Kir,"
> Says the LORD.

6Thus says the LORD:

> "For three transgressions of
>   Gaza, and for four,
> I will not turn away its
>   *punishment,*
> Because they took captive the
>   whole captivity
> To deliver *them* up to Edom.
> 7 But I will send a fire upon the
>   wall of Gaza,
> Which shall devour its
>   palaces.
> 8 I will cut off the inhabitant
>   from Ashdod,
> And the one who holds the
>   scepter from Ashkelon;
> I will turn My hand against
>   Ekron,
> And the remnant of the
>   Philistines shall perish,"
> Says the Lord GOD.

9Thus says the LORD:

> "For three transgressions of
>   Tyre, and for four,
> I will not turn away its
>   *punishment,*
> Because they delivered up the
>   whole captivity to Edom,
> And did not remember the
>   covenant of brotherhood.
> 10 But I will send a fire upon the
>   wall of Tyre,
> Which shall devour its
>   palaces."

11Thus says the LORD:

> "For three transgressions of
>   Edom, and for four,
> I will not turn away its
>   *punishment,*

Because he pursued his
brother with the sword,
And cast off all pity;
His anger tore perpetually,
And he kept his wrath forever.
12 But I will send a fire upon
Teman,
Which shall devour the
palaces of Bozrah."

13Thus says the LORD:

"For three transgressions of
the people of Ammon, and
for four,
I will not turn away its
punishment,
Because they ripped open the
women with child in Gilead,
That they might enlarge their
territory.
14 But I will kindle a fire in the
wall of Rabbah,
And it shall devour its palaces,
Amid shouting in the day of
battle,
And a tempest in the day of
the whirlwind.
15 Their king shall go into
captivity,
He and his princes together,"
Says the LORD.

THUS says the LORD:

"For three transgressions of
Moab, and for four,
I will not turn away its
punishment,
Because he burned the bones
of the king of Edom to lime.
2 But I will send a fire upon
Moab,
And it shall devour the
palaces of Kerioth;
Moab shall die with tumult,
With shouting *and* trumpet
sound.

3 And I will cut off the judge
from its midst,
And slay all its princes with
him,"
Says the LORD.

4Thus says the LORD:

"For three transgressions of
Judah, and for four,
I will not turn away its
punishment,
Because they have despised
the law of the LORD,
And have not kept His
commandments.
Their lies lead them astray,
Lies which their fathers
followed.
5 But I will send a fire upon
Judah,
And it shall devour the
palaces of Jerusalem."

6Thus says the LORD:

"For three transgressions of
Israel, and for four,
I will not turn away its
punishment,
Because they sell the
righteous for silver,
And the poor for a pair of
sandals.
7 They pant after* the dust of
the earth *which is* on the
head of the poor,
And pervert the way of the
humble.
A man and his father go in to
the *same* girl,
To defile My holy name.
8 They lie down by every altar
on clothes taken in pledge,
And drink the wine of the
condemned *in* the house of
their god.

9 "Yet *it was* I *who* destroyed the
Amorite before them,

Whose height *was* like the
height of the cedars,
And he *was as* strong as the
oaks;
Yet I destroyed his fruit above
And his roots beneath.

10 Also *it was* I *who* brought you
up from the land of Egypt,
And led you forty years
through the wilderness,
To possess the land of the
Amorite.

11 I raised up some of your sons
as prophets,
And some of your young men
as Nazirites.
Is it not so, O you children of
Israel?"
Says the LORD.

12 "But you gave the Nazirites
wine to drink,
And commanded the
prophets saying,
'Do not prophesy!'

13 "Behold, I am weighed down
by you,
As a cart full of sheaves is
weighed down.

14 Therefore flight shall perish
from the swift,
The strong shall not
strengthen his power,
Nor shall the mighty deliver
himself;

15 He shall not stand who
handles the bow,
The swift of foot shall not
escape,
Nor shall he who rides a
horse deliver himself.

16 The most courageous men of
might
Shall flee naked in that day,"
Says the LORD.

HEAR this word that the LORD has spoken against you, O children of Israel,
against the whole family which I
brought up from the land of Egypt, saying:

2 "You only have I known of all
the families of the earth;
Therefore I will punish you
for all your iniquities."

3 Can two walk together, unless
they are agreed?

4 Will a lion roar in the forest,
when he has no prey?
Will a young lion cry out of
his den, if he has caught
nothing?

5 Will a bird fall into a snare on
the earth, where there is no
trap for it?
Will a snare spring up from
the earth, if it has caught
nothing at all?

6 If a trumpet is blown in a city,
will not the people be afraid?
If there is calamity in a city,
will not the LORD have done
it?

7 Surely the Lord GOD does
nothing,
Unless He reveals His secret
to His servants the
prophets.

8 A lion has roared!
Who will not fear?
The Lord GOD has spoken!
Who can but prophesy?

9 "Proclaim in the palaces at
Ashdod,
And in the palaces in the land
of Egypt, and say:
'Assemble on the mountains of
Samaria;
See great tumults in her midst,
And the oppressed within her.

10 For they do not know to do
right,'
Says the LORD,
'Who store up violence and
robbery in their palaces.'"

11Therefore thus says the Lord GOD:

"An adversary *shall be* all
   around the land;
He shall sap your strength
   from you,
And your palaces shall be
   plundered."

12Thus says the LORD:

"As a shepherd takes from the
   mouth of a lion
Two legs or a piece of an ear,
So shall the children of Israel
   be taken out
Who dwell in Samaria—
In the corner of a bed and on
   the edge* of a couch!
13   Hear and testify against the
      house of Jacob,"
      Says the Lord GOD, the God of
      hosts,
14   "That in the day I punish Israel
      for their transgressions,
      I will also visit *destruction* on
      the altars of Bethel;
      And the horns of the altar
      shall be cut off
      And fall to the ground.
15   I will destroy the winter
      house along with the
      summer house;
      The houses of ivory shall
      perish,
      And the great houses shall
      have an end,"
      Says the LORD.

REVELATION 2:1-17

"To the angel of the church of
Ephesus write,
   'These things says He who
holds the seven stars in His right hand,
who walks in the midst of the seven
golden lampstands: 2"I know your
works, your labor, your patience, and
that you cannot bear those who are evil.
And you have tested those who say they
are apostles and are not, and have found
them liars; 3and you have persevered
and have patience, and have labored for
My name's sake and have not become
weary. 4Nevertheless I have *this* against
you, that you have left your first love.
5Remember therefore from where you
have fallen; repent and do the first
works, or else I will come to you quickly
and remove your lampstand from its
place—unless you repent. 6But this you
have, that you hate the deeds of the
Nicolaitans, which I also hate.

7"He who has an ear, let him hear
what the Spirit says to the churches.
To him who overcomes I will give to
eat from the tree of life, which is in the
midst of the Paradise of God." '

8"And to the angel of the church in
Smyrna write,

'These things says the First and the
Last, who was dead, and came to life:
9"I know your works, tribulation, and
poverty (but you are rich); and *I know*
the blasphemy of those who say they
are Jews and are not, but *are* a synagogue of Satan. 10Do not fear any of
those things which you are about to
suffer. Indeed, the devil is about to
throw *some* of you into prison, that you
may be tested, and you will have tribulation ten days. Be faithful until death,
and I will give you the crown of life.

11"He who has an ear, let him hear
what the Spirit says to the churches.
He who overcomes shall not be hurt
by the second death." '

12"And to the angel of the church in
Pergamos write,

'These things says He who has the
sharp two-edged sword: 13"I know your
works, and where you dwell, where
Satan's throne *is*. And you hold fast to
My name, and did not deny My faith
even in the days in which Antipas *was*
My faithful martyr, who was killed
among you, where Satan dwells. 14But I
have a few things against you, because
you have there those who hold the doctrine of Balaam, who taught Balak to put

a stumbling block before the children of Israel, to eat things sacrificed to idols, and to commit sexual immorality. [15]Thus you also have those who hold the doctrine of the Nicolaitans, which thing I hate.* [16]Repent, or else I will come to you quickly and will fight against them with the sword of My mouth.

[17]"He who has an ear, let him hear what the Spirit says to the churches. To him who overcomes I will give some of the hidden manna to eat. And I will give him a white stone, and on the stone a new name written which no one knows except him who receives it." ' "

PSALM 129:1-8

A Song of Ascents.

"ANY a time they have afflicted me from my youth,"
Let Israel now say—
2 "Many a time they have afflicted me from my youth;

Yet they have not prevailed against me.
3 The plowers plowed on my back;
They made their furrows long."
4 The LORD *is* righteous;
He has cut in pieces the cords of the wicked.

5 Let all those who hate Zion Be put to shame and turned back.
6 Let them be as the grass *on* the housetops,
Which withers before it grows up,
7 With which the reaper does not fill his hand,
Nor he who binds sheaves, his arms.
8 Neither let those who pass by them say,
"The blessing of the LORD *be* upon you;
We bless you in the name of the LORD!"

PROVERBS FOR TODAY/ 29:19-20

A servant will not be corrected by mere words; for though he understands, he will not respond. □ *Do you see a man hasty in his words? There is more hope for a fool than for him.*

DECEMBER 11

AMOS 4:1–6:14

EAR this word, you cows of Bashan, who *are* on the mountain of Samaria,
Who oppress the poor,
Who crush the needy,
Who say to your husbands,*
"Bring *wine,* let us drink!"

2 The Lord GOD has sworn by His holiness:
"Behold, the days shall come upon you
When He will take you away with fishhooks,
And your posterity with fishhooks.

3   You will go out *through*
    broken *walls,*
  Each one straight ahead of
    her,
  And you will be cast into
    Harmon,"
  Says the LORD.

4   "Come to Bethel and
    transgress,
  At Gilgal multiply
    transgression;
  Bring your sacrifices every
    morning,
  Your tithes every three days.*
5   Offer a sacrifice of
    thanksgiving with leaven,
  Proclaim *and* announce the
    freewill offerings;
  For this you love,
  You children of Israel!"
  Says the Lord GOD.
6   "Also I gave you cleanness of
    teeth in all your cities.
  And lack of bread in all your
    places;
  Yet you have not returned to
    Me,"
  Says the LORD.

7   "I also withheld rain from you,
  When *there were* still three
    months to the harvest.
  I made it rain on one city,
  I withheld rain from another
    city.
  One part was rained upon,
  And where it did not rain the
    part withered.
8   So two *or* three cities
    wandered to another city to
    drink water,
  But they were not satisfied;
  Yet you have not returned to
    Me,"
  Says the LORD.

9   "I blasted you with blight and
    mildew.
  When your gardens increased,
  Your vineyards,
  Your fig trees,
  And your olive trees,
  The locust devoured *them;*
  Yet you have not returned to
    Me,"
  Says the LORD.

10   "I sent among you a plague
    after the manner of Egypt;
  Your young men I killed with
    a sword,
  Along with your captive
    horses;
  I made the stench of your
    camps come up into your
    nostrils;
  Yet you have not returned to
    Me,"
  Says the LORD.

11   "I overthrew *some* of you,
  As God overthrew Sodom and
    Gomorrah,
  And you were like a firebrand
    plucked from the burning;
  Yet you have not returned to
    Me,"
  Says the LORD.

12   "Therefore thus will I do to
    you, O Israel;
  Because I will do this to you,
  Prepare to meet your God,
    O Israel!"

13   For behold,
  He who forms mountains,
  And creates the wind,
  Who declares to man what
    his* thought *is,*
  And makes the morning
    darkness,
  Who treads the high places of
    the earth—
  The LORD God of hosts *is* His
    name.

HEAR this word which I take up against
you, a lamentation, O house of Israel:

2 The virgin of Israel has fallen;
   She will rise no more.
   She lies forsaken on her land;
   There is no one to raise her up.

3For thus says the Lord God:

   "The city that goes out by a
       thousand
   Shall have a hundred left,
   And that which goes out by a
       hundred
   Shall have ten left to the
       house of Israel."

4For thus says the Lord to the house
of Israel:

   "Seek Me and live;
5 But do not seek Bethel,
   Nor enter Gilgal,
   Nor pass over to Beersheba;
   For Gilgal shall surely go into
       captivity,
   And Bethel shall come to
       nothing.
6 Seek the Lord and live,
   Lest He break out like fire *in*
       the house of Joseph,
   And devour *it,*
   With no one to quench *it* in
       Bethel—
7 You who turn justice to
       wormwood,
   And lay righteousness to rest
       in the earth!"

8 He made the Pleiades and
       Orion;
   He turns the shadow of death
       into morning
   And makes the day dark as
       night;
   He calls for the waters of the
       sea
   And pours them out on the
       face of the earth;
   The Lord *is* His name.
9 He rains ruin upon the strong,

   So that fury comes upon the
       fortress.
10 They hate the one who
       rebukes in the gate,
   And they abhor the one who
       speaks uprightly.
11 Therefore, because you tread
       down the poor
   And take grain taxes from
       him,
   Though you have built houses
       of hewn stone,
   Yet you shall not dwell in
       them;
   You have planted pleasant
       vineyards,
   But you shall not drink wine
       from them.
12 For I know your manifold
       transgressions
   And your mighty sins:
   Afflicting the just *and* taking
       bribes;
   Diverting the poor *from*
       justice at the gate.
13 Therefore the prudent keep
       silent at that time,
   For it *is* an evil time.

14 Seek good and not evil,
   That you may live;
   So the Lord God of hosts will
       be with you,
   As you have spoken.
15 Hate evil, love good;
   Establish justice in the gate.
   It may be that the Lord God of
       hosts
   Will be gracious to the
       remnant of Joseph.

16Therefore the Lord God of hosts,
the Lord, says this:

   "*There shall be* wailing in all
       streets,
   And they shall say in all the
       highways,
   'Alas! Alas!'

They shall call the farmer to
    mourning,
And skillful lamenters to
    wailing.
17 In all vineyards *there shall be*
    wailing,
For I will pass through you,"
Says the LORD.

18 Woe to you who desire the
    day of the LORD!
For what good *is* the day of
    the LORD to you?
It *will be* darkness, and not
    light.
19 It *will be* as though a man fled
    from a lion,
And a bear met him!
Or *as though* he went into the
    house,
Leaned his hand on the wall,
And a serpent bit him!
20 *Is* not the day of the LORD
    darkness, and not light?
Is it not very dark, with no
    brightness in it?

21 "I hate, I despise your feast
    days,
And I do not savor your
    sacred assemblies.
22 Though you offer Me burnt
    offerings and your grain
    offerings,
I will not accept *them,*
Nor will I regard your
    fattened peace offerings.
23 Take away from Me the noise
    of your songs,
For I will not hear the melody
    of your stringed
    instruments.
24 But let justice run down like
    water,
And righteousness like a
    mighty stream.

25 "Did you offer Me sacrifices
    and offerings

In the wilderness forty years,
    O house of Israel?
26 You also carried Sikkuth*
    your king*
And Chiun,* your idols,
The star of your gods,
Which you made for
    yourselves.
27 Therefore I will send you into
    captivity beyond
    Damascus,"
Says the LORD, whose name *is*
    the God of hosts.

WOE to you *who are* at ease in Zion,
    And trust in Mount Samaria,
Notable persons in the chief
    nation,
To whom the house of Israel
    comes!
2 Go over to Calneh and see;
And from there go to Hamath
    the great;
Then go down to Gath of the
    Philistines.
Are you better than these
    kingdoms?
Or is their territory greater
    than your territory?

3 *Woe to* you who put far off the
    day of doom,
Who cause the seat of
    violence to come near;
4 Who lie on beds of ivory,
Stretch out on your couches,
Eat lambs from the flock
And calves from the midst of
    the stall;
5 Who sing idly to the sound of
    stringed instruments,
And invent for yourselves
    musical instruments like
    David;
6 Who drink wine from bowls,
And anoint yourselves with
    the best ointments,
But are not grieved for the
    affliction of Joseph.
7 Therefore they shall now go

captive as the first of the
captives,
And those who recline at
banquets shall be removed.

8 The Lord God has sworn by
Himself,
The Lord God of hosts says:
"I abhor the pride of Jacob,
And hate his palaces;
Therefore I will deliver up *the*
city
And all that is in it."

9Then it shall come to pass, that if
ten men remain in one house, they
shall die. 10And when a relative *of the
dead,* with one who will burn *the bodies,*
picks up the bodies* to take them out
of the house, he will say to one inside
the house, "*Are there* any more with
you?"
Then someone will say, "None."
And he will say, "Hold your tongue!
For we dare not mention the name of
the Lord."

11 For behold, the Lord gives a
command:
He will break the great house
into bits,
And the little house into
pieces.

12 Do horses run on rocks?
Does *one* plow *there* with
oxen?
Yet you have turned justice
into gall,
And the fruit of righteousness
into wormwood,

13 You who rejoice over Lo
Debar,*
Who say, "Have we not taken
Karnaim* for ourselves
By our own strength?"

14 "But, behold, I will raise up a
nation against you,
O house of Israel,"

Says the Lord God of hosts;
"And they will afflict you from
the entrance of Hamath
To the Valley of the Arabah."

REVELATION 2:18–3:6

"AND to the angel of the church in
Thyatira write,
'These things says the Son of
God, who has eyes like a flame of fire,
and His feet like fine brass: 19I know
your works, love, service, faith,* and
your patience; and *as* for your works,
the last *are* more than the first. 20Nev-
ertheless I have a few things against
you, because you allow* that woman*
Jezebel, who calls herself a prophetess, to teach and seduce* My servants
to commit sexual immorality and eat
things sacrificed to idols. 21And I gave
her time to repent of her sexual immorality, and she did not repent.* 22In-
deed I will cast her into a sickbed, and
those who commit adultery with her
into great tribulation, unless they repent of their* deeds. 23I will kill her
children with death, and all the
churches shall know that I am He who
searches the minds and hearts. And I
will give to each one of you according
to your works.
24"Now to you I say, and* to the rest
in Thyatira, as many as do not have
this doctrine, who have not known the
depths of Satan, as they say, I will* put
on you no other burden. 25But hold fast
what you have till I come. 26And he
who overcomes, and keeps My works
until the end, to him I will give power
over the nations—

27 'He shall rule them with a rod
of iron;
They shall be dashed to
pieces like the potter's
vessels' *—

as I also have received from My
Father; 28and I will give him the morning star.

29"He who has an ear, let him hear what the Spirit says to the churches." '

"AND to the angel of the church in Sardis write,

'These things says He who has the seven Spirits of God and the seven stars: "I know your works, that you have a name that you are alive, but you are dead. 2Be watchful, and strengthen the things which remain, that are ready to die, for I have not found your works perfect before God.* 3Remember therefore how you have received and heard; hold fast and repent. Therefore if you will not watch, I will come upon you as a thief, and you will not know what hour I will come upon you. 4You* have a few names even in Sardis who have not defiled their garments; and they shall walk with Me in white, for they are worthy. 5He who overcomes shall be clothed in white garments, and I will not blot out his name from the Book of Life; but I will confess his name before My Father and before His angels.

6"He who has an ear, let him hear what the Spirit says to the churches." ' "

PSALM 130:1-8

A Song of Ascents.

OUT of the depths I have cried to You, O LORD;
2Lord, hear my voice!
Let Your ears be attentive
To the voice of my
 supplications.

3 If You, LORD, should mark
 iniquities,
 O Lord, who could stand?
4 But *there is* forgiveness with
 You,
 That You may be feared.

5 I wait for the LORD, my soul
 waits,
 And in His word I do hope.
6 My soul *waits* for the Lord
 More than those who watch
 for the morning—
 Yes, more than those who
 watch for the morning.

7 O Israel, hope in the LORD;
 For with the LORD *there is*
 mercy,
 And with Him *is* abundant
 redemption.
8 And He shall redeem Israel
 From all his iniquities.

PROVERBS FOR TODAY/ 29:21-22

He who pampers his servant from childhood will have him as a son in the end.
□ *An angry man stirs up strife, and a furious man abounds in transgression.*

DECEMBER 12

AMOS 7:1–9:15

THUS the Lord GOD showed me: Behold, He formed locust swarms at the beginning of the late crop; indeed *it was* the late crop after the king's mowings. ²And so it was, when they had finished eating the grass of the land, that I said:

> "O Lord GOD, forgive, I pray!
> Oh, that Jacob may stand,
> For he *is* small!"
> 3   *So* the LORD relented
>   concerning this.
> "It shall not be," said the LORD.

⁴Thus the Lord GOD showed me: Behold, the Lord GOD called for conflict by fire, and it consumed the great deep and devoured the territory. ⁵Then I said:

> "O Lord GOD, cease, I pray!
> Oh, that Jacob may stand,
> For he *is* small!"
> 6   *So* the LORD relented
>   concerning this.
> "This also shall not be," said
>   the Lord GOD.

⁷Thus He showed me: Behold, the Lord stood on a wall *made* with a plumb line, with a plumb line in His hand. ⁸And the LORD said to me, "Amos, what do you see?"

And I said, "A plumb line."

Then the Lord said:

> "Behold, I am setting a plumb
>   line
> In the midst of My people
>   Israel;
> I will not pass by them
>   anymore.

> 9   The high places of Isaac shall
>   be desolate,
> And the sanctuaries of Israel
>   shall be laid waste.
> I will rise with the sword
>   against the house of
>   Jeroboam."

¹⁰Then Amaziah the priest of Bethel sent to Jeroboam king of Israel, saying, "Amos has conspired against you in the midst of the house of Israel. The land is not able to bear all his words. ¹¹For thus Amos has said:

> 'Jeroboam shall die by the
>   sword,
> And Israel shall surely be led
>   away captive
> From their own land.' "

¹²Then Amaziah said to Amos:

> "Go, you seer!
> Flee to the land of Judah.
> There eat bread,
> And there prophesy.
> 13   But never again prophesy at
>   Bethel,
> For it *is* the king's sanctuary,
> And it *is* the royal residence."

¹⁴Then Amos answered, and said to Amaziah:

> "I *was* no prophet,
> Nor *was* I a son of a prophet,
> But I *was* a sheepbreeder*
> And a tender of sycamore
>   fruit.
> 15   Then the LORD took me as I
>   followed the flock,
> And the LORD said to me,
> 'Go, prophesy to My people
>   Israel.'

16 Now therefore, hear the word
of the LORD:
You say, 'Do not prophesy
against Israel,
And do not spout against the
house of Isaac.'

17"Therefore thus says the LORD:

'Your wife shall be a harlot in
the city;
Your sons and daughters shall
fall by the sword;
Your land shall be divided by
survey line;
You shall die in a defiled land;
And Israel shall surely be led
away captive
From his own land.' "

THUS the Lord GOD showed me: Be-
hold, a basket of summer fruit. 2And
He said, "Amos, what do you see?"
So I said, "A basket of summer
fruit."
Then the LORD said to me:

"The end has come upon My
people Israel;
I will not pass by them
anymore.
3 And the songs of the temple
Shall be wailing in that day,"
Says the Lord GOD—
"Many dead bodies
everywhere,
They shall be thrown out in
silence."

4 Hear this, you who swallow
up* the needy,
And make the poor of the
land fail,

5Saying:

"When will the New Moon be
past,
That we may sell grain?
And the Sabbath,

That we may trade wheat?
Making the ephah small and
the shekel large,
Falsifying the scales by deceit,
6 That we may buy the poor for
silver,
And the needy for a pair of
sandals—
Even sell the bad wheat?"

7 The LORD has sworn by the
pride of Jacob:
"Surely I will never forget any
of their works.
8 Shall the land not tremble for
this,
And everyone mourn who
dwells in it?
All of it shall swell like the
River,*
Heave and subside
Like the River of Egypt.

9 "And it shall come to pass in
that day," says the Lord
GOD,
"That I will make the sun go
down at noon,
And I will darken the earth in
broad daylight;
10 I will turn your feasts into
mourning,
And all your songs into
lamentation;
I will bring sackcloth on every
waist,
And baldness on every head;
I will make it like mourning
for an only *son,*
And its end like a bitter day.

11 "Behold, the days are coming,"
says the Lord GOD,
"That I will send a famine on
the land,
Not a famine of bread,
Nor a thirst for water,
But of hearing the words of
the LORD.

12 They shall wander from sea to
sea,
And from north to east;
They shall run to and fro,
seeking the word of the
LORD,
But shall not find *it*.

13 "In that day the fair virgins
And strong young men
Shall faint from thirst.
14 Those who swear by the sin*
of Samaria,
Who say,
'As your god lives, O Dan!'
And, 'As the way of
Beersheba lives!'
They shall fall and never rise
again."

I SAW the Lord standing by the altar,
and He said:

"Strike the doorposts, that the
thresholds may shake,
And break them on the heads
of them all.
I will slay the last of them with
the sword.
He who flees from them shall
not get away,
And he who escapes from
them shall not be delivered.

2 "Though they dig into hell,*
From there My hand shall
take them;
Though they climb up to
heaven,
From there I will bring them
down;
3 And though they hide
themselves on top of
Carmel,
From there I will search and
take them;
Though they hide from My
sight at the bottom of the
sea,
From there I will command

the serpent, and it shall bite
them;
4 Though they go into captivity
before their enemies,
From there I will command
the sword,
And it shall slay them.
I will set My eyes on them for
harm and not for good."

5 The Lord GOD of hosts,
He who touches the earth and
it melts,
And all who dwell there
mourn;
All of it shall swell like the
River,*
And subside like the River of
Egypt.
6 He who builds His layers in
the sky,
And has founded His strata in
the earth;
Who calls for the waters of
the sea,
And pours them out on the
face of the earth—
The LORD *is* His name.

7 "*Are* you not like the people of
Ethiopia to Me,
O children of Israel?" says the
LORD.
"Did I not bring up Israel from
the land of Egypt,
The Philistines from Caphtor,
And the Syrians from Kir?

8 "Behold, the eyes of the Lord
GOD *are* on the sinful
kingdom,
And I will destroy it from the
face of the earth;
Yet I will not utterly destroy
the house of Jacob,"
Says the LORD.

9 "For surely I will command,
And will sift the house of
Israel among all nations,

As *grain* is sifted in a sieve;
Yet not the smallest grain
  shall fall to the ground.
10 All the sinners of My people
  shall die by the sword,
Who say, 'The calamity shall
  not overtake nor confront
  us.'

11 "On that day I will raise up
The tabernacle* of David,
  which has fallen down,
And repair its damages;
I will raise up its ruins,
And rebuild it as in the days
  of old;
12 That they may possess the
  remnant of Edom,*
And all the Gentiles who are
  called by My name,"
Says the LORD who does this
  thing.

13 "Behold, the days are coming,"
  says the LORD,
"When the plowman shall
  overtake the reaper,
And the treader of grapes him
  who sows seed;
The mountains shall drip with
  sweet wine,
And all the hills shall flow
  with it.
14 I will bring back the captives
  of My people Israel;
They shall build the waste
  cities and inhabit *them;*
They shall plant vineyards
  and drink wine from them;
They shall also make gardens
  and eat fruit from them.
15 I will plant them in their land,
And no longer shall they be
  pulled up
From the land I have given
  them,"
Says the LORD your God.

REVELATION 3:7-22

"AND to the angel of the church in Philadelphia write,

'These things says He who is holy, He who is true, *"He who has the key of David, He who opens and no one shuts, and shuts and no one opens"*:* 8I know your works. See, I have set before you an open door, and no one can shut it;* for you have a little strength, have kept My word, and have not denied My name. 9Indeed I will make *those* of the synagogue of Satan, who say they are Jews and are not, but lie—indeed I will make them come and worship before your feet, and to know that I have loved you. 10Because you have kept My command to persevere, I also will keep you from the hour of trial which shall come upon the whole world, to test those who dwell on the earth. 11Behold,* I am coming quickly! Hold fast what you have, that no one may take your crown. 12He who overcomes, I will make him a pillar in the temple of My God, and he shall go out no more. I will write on him the name of My God and the name of the city of My God, the New Jerusalem, which comes down out of heaven from My God. And *I will write on him* My new name.

13"He who has an ear, let him hear what the Spirit says to the churches." '

14"And to the angel of the church of the Laodiceans* write,

'These things says the Amen, the Faithful and True Witness, the Beginning of the creation of God: 15"I know your works, that you are neither cold nor hot. I could wish you were cold or hot. 16So then, because you are lukewarm, and neither cold nor hot,* I will vomit you out of My mouth. 17Because you say, 'I am rich, have become wealthy, and have need of nothing'— and do not know that you are wretched, miserable, poor, blind, and naked— 18I counsel you to buy from Me gold refined in the fire, that you may be rich; and white garments, that you may be clothed, *that* the shame of your nakedness may not be revealed; and anoint your eyes with eye salve, that you may see. 19As many as I love, I rebuke and chasten. Therefore be zealous and repent. 20Behold, I stand at the door and knock. If anyone hears My voice and opens the door, I will come in to him and dine with him, and he with Me. 21To him who overcomes I will grant to sit with Me on My throne, as I also overcame and sat down with My Father on His throne. 22"He who has an ear, let him hear what the Spirit says to the churches." ' "

PSALM 131:1-3

A Song of Ascents. Of David.

LORD, my heart is not haughty,
Nor my eyes lofty.
Neither do I concern myself
with great matters,
Nor with things too profound
for me.

2   Surely I have calmed and
quieted my soul,
Like a weaned child with his
mother;
Like a weaned child *is* my
soul within me.

3   O Israel, hope in the LORD
From this time forth and
forever.

PROVERBS FOR TODAY/ 29:23

A man's pride will bring him low, but the humble in spirit will retain honor.

DECEMBER 13

OBADIAH 1-21

THE vision of Obadiah.
Thus says the Lord GOD
concerning Edom
(We have heard a report from
the LORD,
And a messenger has been
sent among the nations,
saying,
"Arise, and let us rise up
against her for battle"):

2   "Behold, I will make you small
among the nations;
You shall be greatly despised.
3   The pride of your heart has
deceived you,
You who dwell in the clefts of
the rock,

Whose habitation is high;
You who say in your heart,
'Who will bring me down to
the ground?'
4   Though you ascend *as* high
as the eagle,
And though you set your nest
among the stars,
From there I will bring you
down," says the LORD.

5   "If thieves had come to you,
If robbers by night—
Oh, how you will be cut off!—
Would they not have stolen till
they had enough?
If grape gatherers had come
to you,

Would they not have left *some* gleanings?

6 "Oh, how Esau shall be searched out!
How his hidden treasures shall be sought after!
7 All the men in your confederacy
Shall force you to the border;
The men at peace with you
Shall deceive you *and* prevail against you.
Those who eat your bread shall lay a trap* for you.
No one is aware of it.

8 "Will I not in that day," says the LORD,
"Even destroy the wise *men* from Edom,
And understanding from the mountains of Esau?
9 Then your mighty men, O Teman, shall be dismayed,
To the end that everyone from the mountains of Esau
May be cut off by slaughter.

10 "For violence against your brother Jacob,
Shame shall cover you,
And you shall be cut off forever.
11 In the day that you stood on the other side—
In the day that strangers carried captive his forces,
When foreigners entered his gates
And cast lots for Jerusalem—
Even you *were* as one of them.

12 "But you should not have gazed on the day of your brother
In the day of his captivity;*
Nor should you have rejoiced over the children of Judah

In the day of their destruction;
Nor should you have spoken proudly
In the day of distress.
13 You should not have entered the gate of My people
In the day of their calamity.
Indeed, you should not have gazed on their affliction
In the day of their calamity,
Nor laid *hands* on their substance
In the day of their calamity.
14 You should not have stood at the crossroads
To cut off those among them who escaped;
Nor should you have delivered up those among them who remained
In the day of distress.

15 "For the day of the LORD upon all the nations *is* near;
As you have done, it shall be done to you;
Your reprisal shall return upon your own head.
16 For as you drank on my holy mountain,
So shall all the nations drink continually;
Yes, they shall drink, and swallow,
And they shall be as though they had never been.

17 "But on Mount Zion there shall be deliverance,
And there shall be holiness;
The house of Jacob shall possess their possessions.
18 The house of Jacob shall be a fire,
And the house of Joseph a flame;
But the house of Esau *shall be* stubble;
They shall kindle them and devour them,

And no survivor shall *remain*
of the house of Esau,"
For the LORD has spoken.

19 The South* shall possess the
mountains of Esau,
And the Lowland shall
possess Philistia.
They shall possess the fields
of Ephraim
And the fields of Samaria.
Benjamin *shall possess* Gilead.

20 And the captives of this host
of the children of Israel
Shall possess the land of the
Canaanites
As far as Zarephath.
The captives of Jerusalem
who are in Sepharad
Shall possess the cities of the
South.*

21 Then saviors* shall come to
Mount Zion
To judge the mountains of
Esau,
And the kingdom shall be the
LORD's.

REVELATION 4:1-11

AFTER these things I looked, and
behold, a door *standing* open
in heaven. And the first voice
which I heard *was* like a trumpet
speaking with me, saying, "Come up
here, and I will show you things which
must take place after this."

²Immediately I was in the Spirit; and
behold, a throne set in heaven, and
One sat on the throne. ³And He who
sat there was* like a jasper and a sardius stone in appearance; and *there
was* a rainbow around the throne, in
appearance like an emerald. ⁴Around
the throne *were* twenty-four thrones,
and on the thrones I saw twenty-four
elders sitting, clothed in white robes;
and they had crowns* of gold on their
heads. ⁵And from the throne proceeded lightnings, thunderings, and
voices.* Seven lamps of fire *were* burning before the throne, which are the*
seven Spirits of God.

⁶Before the throne *there was* a sea
of glass, like crystal. And in the midst
of the throne, and around the throne,
were four living creatures full of eyes in
front and in back. ⁷The first living creature *was* like a lion, the second living
creature like a calf, the third living
creature had a face like a man, and the
fourth living creature *was* like a flying
eagle. ⁸*The* four living creatures, each
having six wings, were full of eyes
around and within. And they do not
rest day or night, saying:

"Holy, holy, holy,*
Lord God Almighty,
Who was and is and is to
come!"

⁹Whenever the living creatures give
glory and honor and thanks to Him
who sits on the throne, who lives forever and ever, ¹⁰the twenty-four elders
fall down before Him who sits on the
throne and worship Him who lives forever and ever, and cast their crowns
before the throne, saying:

11 "You are worthy, O Lord,*
To receive glory and honor
and power;
For You created all things,
And by Your will they exist*
and were created."

PSALM 132:1-18

A Song of Ascents.

LORD, remember David
And all his afflictions;
²How he swore to the LORD,
And vowed to the Mighty One
of Jacob:

3 "Surely I will not go into the
chamber of my house,
Or go up to the comfort of my
bed;

4 I will not give sleep to my eyes

Or slumber to my eyelids,
5 Until I find a place for the
    Lord,
    A dwelling place for the
    Mighty One of Jacob."

6 Behold, we heard of it in
    Ephrathah;
    We found it in the fields of the
    woods.*
7 Let us go into His tabernacle;
    Let us worship at His
    footstool.
8 Arise, O Lord, to Your resting
    place,
    You and the ark of Your
    strength.
9 Let Your priests be clothed
    with righteousness,
    And let Your saints shout for
    joy.

10 For Your servant David's sake,
    Do not turn away the face of
    Your Anointed.

11 The Lord has sworn *in* truth
    to David;
    He will not turn from it:
    "I will set upon your throne the
    fruit of your body.

12 If your sons will keep My
    covenant
    And My testimony which I
    shall teach them,
    Their sons also shall sit upon
    your throne forevermore."

13 For the Lord has chosen Zion;
    He has desired *it* for His
    dwelling place:
14 "This *is* My resting place
    forever;
    Here I will dwell, for I have
    desired it.
15 I will abundantly bless her
    provision;
    I will satisfy her poor with
    bread.
16 I will also clothe her priests
    with salvation,
    And her saints shall shout
    aloud for joy.
17 There I will make the horn of
    David grow;
    I will prepare a lamp for My
    Anointed.
18 His enemies I will clothe with
    shame,
    But upon Himself His crown
    shall flourish."

PROVERBS FOR TODAY/ 29:24-25

Whoever is a partner with a thief hates his own life; he swears to tell the truth, *
but reveals nothing. □ *The fear of man brings a snare, but whoever trusts in the*
Lord shall be safe.

DECEMBER 14

JONAH 1:1–4:11

Now the word of the Lord came to Jonah the son of Amittai, saying, [2]"Arise, go to Nineveh, that great city, and cry out against it; for their wickedness has come up before Me." [3]But Jonah arose to flee to Tarshish from the presence of the Lord. He went down to Joppa, and found a ship going to Tarshish; so he paid the fare, and went down into it, to go with them to Tarshish from the presence of the LORD.

4But the LORD sent out a great wind on the sea, and there was a mighty tempest on the sea, so that the ship was about to be broken up.

5Then the mariners were afraid; and every man cried out to his god, and threw the cargo that *was* in the ship into the sea, to lighten the load.* But Jonah had gone down into the lowest parts of the ship, had lain down, and was fast asleep.

6So the captain came to him, and said to him, "What do you mean, sleeper? Arise, call on your God; perhaps your God will consider us, so that we may not perish."

7And they said to one another, "Come, let us cast lots, that we may know for whose cause this trouble *has come* upon us." So they cast lots, and the lot fell on Jonah. 8Then they said to him, "Please tell us! For whose cause *is* this trouble upon us? What is your occupation? And where do you come from? What is your country? And of what people are you?"

9So he said to them, "I *am* a Hebrew; and I fear the LORD, the God of heaven, who made the sea and the dry *land*."

10Then the men were exceedingly afraid, and said to him, "Why have you done this?" For the men knew that he fled from the presence of the LORD, because he had told them. 11Then they said to him, "What shall we do to you that the sea may be calm for us?"—for the sea was growing more tempestuous.

12And he said to them, "Pick me up and throw me into the sea; then the sea will become calm for you. For I know that this great tempest *is* because of me."

13Nevertheless the men rowed hard to return to land, but they could not, for the sea continued to grow more tempestuous against them. 14There-fore they cried out to the LORD and said, "We pray, O LORD, please do not let us perish for this man's life, and do not charge us with innocent blood; for You, O LORD, have done as it pleased You." 15So they picked up Jonah and threw him into the sea, and the sea ceased from its raging. 16Then the men feared the LORD exceedingly, and offered a sacrifice to the LORD and took vows.

17Now the LORD had prepared a great fish to swallow Jonah. And Jonah was in the belly of the fish three days and three nights.

THEN Jonah prayed to the LORD his God from the fish's belly. 2And he said:

> "I cried out to the LORD
>   because of my affliction,
> And He answered me.

> "Out of the belly of Sheol I
>   cried,
> *And* You heard my voice.
> 3 For You cast me into the deep,
>   Into the heart of the seas,
>   And the floods surrounded
>   me;
>   All Your billows and Your
>   waves passed over me.
> 4 Then I said, 'I have been cast
>   out of Your sight;
>   Yet I will look again toward
>   Your holy temple.'
> 5 The waters surrounded me,
>   *even* to my soul;
>   The deep closed around me;
>   Weeds were wrapped around
>   my head.
> 6 I went down to the moorings
>   of the mountains;
>   The earth with its bars *closed*
>   behind me forever;
>   Yet You have brought up my
>   life from the pit,
>   O LORD, my God.

7 "When my soul fainted within
me,
I remembered the LORD;
And my prayer went *up* to You,
Into Your holy temple.

8 "Those who regard worthless
idols
Forsake their own Mercy.
9 But I will sacrifice to You
With the voice of
thanksgiving;
I will pay what I have vowed.
Salvation *is* of the LORD."

¹⁰So the LORD spoke to the fish, and it vomited Jonah onto dry *land.*

Now the word of the LORD came to Jonah the second time, saying, ²"Arise, go to Nineveh, that great city, and preach to it the message that I tell you." ³So Jonah arose and went to Nineveh, according to the word of the LORD. Now Nineveh was an exceedingly great city, a three-day journey* *in extent.* ⁴And Jonah began to enter the city on the first day's walk. Then he cried out and said, "Yet forty days, and Nineveh shall be overthrown!"

⁵So the people of Nineveh believed God, proclaimed a fast, and put on sackcloth, from the greatest to the least of them. ⁶Then word came to the king of Nineveh; and he arose from his throne and laid aside his robe, covered *himself* with sackcloth and sat in ashes. ⁷And he caused *it* to be proclaimed and published throughout Nineveh by the decree of the king and his nobles, saying,

Let neither man nor beast,
herd nor flock, taste anything;
do not let them eat, or drink
water. ⁸But let man and beast
be covered with sackcloth,
and cry mightily to God; yes,
let every one turn from his
evil way and from the violence

that is in his hands. ⁹Who can tell *if* God will turn and relent, and turn away from His fierce anger, so that we may not perish?

¹⁰Then God saw their works, that they turned from their evil way; and God relented from the disaster that He had said He would bring upon them, and He did not do it.

BUT it displeased Jonah exceedingly, and he became angry. ²So he prayed to the LORD, and said, "Ah, LORD, was not this what I said when I was still in my country? Therefore I fled previously to Tarshish; for I know that You *are* a gracious and merciful God, slow to anger and abundant in lovingkindness, One who relents from doing harm. ³Therefore now, O LORD, please take my life from me, for *it is* better for me to die than to live!"

⁴Then the LORD said, "*Is it* right for you to be angry?"

⁵So Jonah went out of the city and sat on the east side of the city. There he made himself a shelter and sat under it in the shade, till he might see what would become of the city. ⁶And the LORD God prepared a plant* and made it come up over Jonah, that it might be shade for his head to deliver him from his misery. So Jonah was very grateful for the plant. ⁷But as morning dawned the next day God prepared a worm, and it *so* damaged the plant that it withered. ⁸And it happened, when the sun arose, that God prepared a vehement east wind; and the sun beat on Jonah's head, so that he grew faint. Then he wished death for himself, and said, "*It is* better for me to die than to live."

⁹Then God said to Jonah, "*Is it* right for you to be angry about the plant?"

And he said, "*It is* right for me to be angry, even to death!"

¹⁰But the LORD said, "You have had

pity on the plant for which you have not labored, nor made it grow, which came up in a night and perished in a night. [11]And should I not pity Nineveh, that great city, in which are more than one hundred and twenty thousand persons who cannot discern between their right hand and their left—and much livestock?"

REVELATION 5:1-14

AND I saw in the right *hand* of Him who sat on the throne a scroll written inside and on the back, sealed with seven seals. [2]Then I saw a strong angel proclaiming with a loud voice, "Who is worthy to open the scroll and to loose its seals?" [3]And no one in heaven or on the earth or under the earth was able to open the scroll, or to look at it.

[4]So I wept much, because no one was found worthy to open and read* the scroll, or to look at it. [5]But one of the elders said to me, "Do not weep. Behold, the Lion of the tribe of Judah, the Root of David, has prevailed to open the scroll and to loose* its seven seals."

[6]And I looked, and behold,* in the midst of the throne and of the four living creatures, and in the midst of the elders, stood a Lamb as though it had been slain, having seven horns and seven eyes, which are the seven Spirits of God sent out into all the earth. [7]Then He came and took the scroll out of the right hand of Him who sat on the throne.

[8]Now when He had taken the scroll, the four living creatures and the twenty-four elders fell down before the Lamb, each having a harp, and golden bowls full of incense, which are the prayers of the saints. [9]And they sang a new song, saying:

"You are worthy to take the scroll,

And to open its seals;
For You were slain,
And have redeemed us to God by Your blood
Out of every tribe and tongue and people and nation,
10 And have made us* kings* and priests to our God;
And we* shall reign on the earth."

[11]Then I looked, and I heard the voice of many angels around the throne, the living creatures, and the elders; and the number of them was ten thousand times ten thousand, and thousands of thousands, [12]saying with a loud voice:

"Worthy is the Lamb who was slain
To receive power and riches and wisdom,
And strength and honor and glory and blessing!"

[13]And every creature which is in heaven and on the earth and under the earth and such as are in the sea, and all that are in them, I heard saying:

"Blessing and honor and glory and power
Be to Him who sits on the throne,
And to the Lamb, forever and ever!"*

[14]Then the four living creatures said, "Amen!" And the twenty-four* elders fell down and worshiped Him who lives forever and ever.*

PSALM 133:1-3

A Song of Ascents. Of David.

BEHOLD, how good and how pleasant *it is*
For brethren to dwell together in unity!

2   *It is* like the precious oil upon
         the head,
     Running down on the beard,
     The beard of Aaron,
     Running down on the edge of
         his garments.

3   *It is* like the dew of Hermon,
     Descending upon the
         mountains of Zion;
     For there the LORD
         commanded the blessing—
     Life forevermore.

PROVERBS FOR TODAY / 29:26-27

Many seek the ruler's favor, but justice for man comes *from the* LORD. □ *An unjust man* is *an abomination to the righteous, and* he who is *upright in the way* is *an abomination to the wicked.*

DECEMBER 15

MICAH 1:1–4:13

THE word of the LORD that came to Micah of Moresheth in the days of Jotham, Ahaz, *and* Hezekiah, kings of Judah, which he saw concerning Samaria and Jerusalem.

2   Hear, all you peoples!
     Listen, O earth, and all that is
         in it!
     Let the Lord GOD be a witness
         against you,
     The Lord from His holy
         temple.

3   For behold, the LORD is
         coming out of His place;
     He will come down
     And tread on the high places
         of the earth.

4   The mountains will melt
         under Him,
     And the valleys will split
     Like wax before the fire,
     Like waters poured down a
         steep place.

5   All this is for the
         transgression of Jacob
     And for the sins of the house
         of Israel.
     What *is* the transgression of
         Jacob?
     Is it not Samaria?
     And what *are* the high places
         of Judah?
     Are they not Jerusalem?

6   "Therefore I will make Samaria
         a heap of ruins in the field,
     Places for planting a vineyard;
     I will pour down her stones
         into the valley,
     And I will uncover her
         foundations.

7   All her carved images shall be
         beaten to pieces,
     And all her pay as a harlot
         shall be burned with the
         fire;
     All her idols I will lay desolate,
     For she gathered *it* from the
         pay of a harlot,
     And they shall return to the
         pay of a harlot."

8   Therefore I will wail and howl,
     I will go stripped and naked;

I will make a wailing like the
    jackals
And a mourning like the
    ostriches,
9 For her wounds *are* incurable.
For it has come to Judah;
It has come to the gate of My
    people—
To Jerusalem.

10 Tell *it* not in Gath,
Weep not at all;
In Beth Aphrah*
Roll yourself in the dust.
11 Pass by in naked shame, you
    inhabitant of Shaphir;
The inhabitant of Zaanan*
    does not go out.
Beth Ezel mourns;
Its place to stand is taken
    away from you.

12 For the inhabitant of Maroth
    pined* for good,
But disaster came down from
    the LORD
To the gate of Jerusalem.
13 O inhabitant of Lachish,
Harness the chariot to the
    swift steeds
(She *was* the beginning of sin
    to the daughter of Zion),
For the transgressions of
    Israel were found in you.

14 Therefore you shall give
    presents to Moresheth
    Gath;*
The houses of Achzib* *shall
be* a lie to the kings of Israel.
15 I will yet bring an heir to you,
    O inhabitant of Mareshah;*
The glory of Israel shall come
    to Adullam.
16 Make yourself bald and cut
    off your hair,
Because of your precious
    children;
Enlarge your baldness like an
    eagle,

For they shall go from you
    into captivity.

WOE to those who devise iniquity,
    And work out evil on their
    beds!
At morning light they practice
    it,
Because it is in the power of
    their hand.
2 They covet fields and take
    them by violence,
Also houses, and seize *them*.
So they oppress a man and
    his house,
A man and his inheritance.

3Therefore thus says the LORD:

    "Behold, against this family I
      am devising disaster,
    From which you cannot
      remove your necks;
    Nor shall you walk haughtily,
    For this *is* an evil time.
4 In that day *one* shall take up a
      proverb against you,
    And lament with a bitter
      lamentation, saying:
    'We are utterly destroyed!
    He has changed the heritage
      of my people;
    How He has removed *it* from
      me!
    To a turncoat He has divided
      our fields.' "

5 Therefore you will have no
    one to determine
    boundaries* by lot
In the assembly of the LORD.

6 "Do not prattle," *you say to
    those* who prophesy.
So they shall not prophesy to
    you;*
They shall not return insult
    for insult.*
7 *You who are* named the house
    of Jacob:

"Is the Spirit of the LORD
    restricted?
Are these His doings?
Do not My words do good
To him who walks uprightly?

8   "Lately My people have risen
        up as an enemy—
    You pull off the robe with the
        garment
    From those who trust *you,* as
        they pass by,
    Like men returned from war.
9   The women of My people you
        cast out
    From their pleasant houses;
    From their children
    You have taken away My
        glory forever.

10 "Arise and depart,
    For this *is* not *your* rest;
    Because it is defiled, it shall
        destroy,
    Yes, with utter destruction.
11 If a man should walk in a false
        spirit
    And speak a lie, *saying,*
    'I will prophesy to you of wine
        and drink,'
    Even he would be the prattler
        of this people.

12 "I will surely assemble all of
        you, O Jacob,
    I will surely gather the
        remnant of Israel;
    I will put them together like
        sheep of the fold,*
    Like a flock in the midst of
        their pasture;
    They shall make a loud noise
        because of *so many* people.
13 The one who breaks open will
        come up before them;
    They will break out,
    Pass through the gate,
    And go out by it;
    Their king will pass before
        them,

    With the LORD at their head."

AND I said:

    "Hear now, O heads of Jacob,
    And you rulers of the house
        of Israel:
    Is it not for you to know
        justice?
2   You who hate good and love
        evil;
    Who strip the skin from My
        people,*
    And the flesh from their
        bones;
3   Who also eat the flesh of My
        people,
    Flay their skin from them,
    Break their bones,
    And chop *them* in pieces
    Like *meat* for the pot,
    Like flesh in the caldron."

4   Then they will cry to the LORD,
    But He will not hear them;
    He will even hide His face
        from them at that time,
    Because they have been evil
        in their deeds.

5   Thus says the LORD
        concerning the prophets
    Who make my people stray;
    Who chant "Peace"
    While they chew with their
        teeth,
    But who prepare war against
        him
    Who puts nothing into their
        mouths:
6   "Therefore you shall have
        night without vision,
    And you shall have darkness
        without divination;
    The sun shall go down on the
        prophets,
    And the day shall be dark for
        them.
7   So the seers shall be ashamed,
    And the diviners abashed;

Indeed they shall all cover
their lips;
For *there is* no answer from
God."

8   But truly I am full of power by
the Spirit of the Lord,
And of justice and might,
To declare to Jacob his
transgression
And to Israel his sin.
9   Now hear this,
You heads of the house of
Jacob
And rulers of the house of
Israel,
Who abhor justice
And pervert all equity,
10   Who build up Zion with
bloodshed
And Jerusalem with iniquity:
11   Her heads judge for a bribe,
Her priests teach for pay,
And her prophets divine for
money.
Yet they lean on the Lord, and
say,
"Is not the Lord among us?
No harm can come upon us."
12   Therefore because of you
Zion shall be plowed *like* a
field,
Jerusalem shall become
heaps of ruins,
And the mountain of the
temple*
Like the bare hills of the
forest.

Now it shall come to pass in the latter
days
That the mountain of the
Lord's house
Shall be established on the
top of the mountains,
And shall be exalted above
the hills;
And peoples shall flow to it.
2   Many nations shall come and
say,

"Come, and let us go up to the
mountain of the Lord,
To the house of the God of
Jacob;
He will teach us His ways,
And we shall walk in His
paths."
For out of Zion the law shall
go forth,
And the word of the Lord
from Jerusalem.
3   He shall judge between many
peoples,
And rebuke strong nations
afar off;
They shall beat their swords
into plowshares,
And their spears into pruning
hooks;
Nation shall not lift up sword
against nation,
Neither shall they learn war
anymore.*

4   But everyone shall sit under
his vine and under his fig
tree,
And no one shall make *them*
afraid;
For the mouth of the Lord of
hosts has spoken.
5   For all people walk each in
the name of his god,
But we will walk in the name
of the Lord our God
Forever and ever.

6   "In that day," says the Lord,
"I will assemble the lame,
I will gather the outcast
And those whom I have
afflicted;
7   I will make the lame a
remnant,
And the outcast a strong
nation;
So the Lord will reign over
them in Mount Zion
From now on, even forever.
8   And you, O tower of the flock,

The stronghold of the
daughter of Zion,
To you shall it come,
Even the former dominion
shall come,
The kingdom of the daughter
of Jerusalem."

9   Now why do you cry aloud?
Is there no king in your midst?
Has your counselor perished?
For pangs have seized you
like a woman in labor.

10   Be in pain, and labor to bring
forth,
O daughter of Zion,
Like a woman in birth pangs.
For now you shall go forth
from the city,
You shall dwell in the field,
And to Babylon you shall go.
There you shall be delivered;
There the Lord will redeem
you
From the hand of your
enemies.

11   Now also many nations have
gathered against you,
Who say, "Let her be defiled,
And let our eye look upon
Zion."

12   But they do not know the
thoughts of the Lord,
Nor do they understand His
counsel;
For He will gather them like
sheaves to the threshing
floor.

13   "Arise and thresh, O daughter
of Zion;
For I will make your horn
iron,
And I will make your hooves
bronze;
You shall beat in pieces many
peoples;
I will consecrate their gain to
the Lord,

And their substance to the
Lord of the whole earth."

REVELATION 6:1-17

Now I saw when the Lamb opened one of the seals;* and I heard one of the four living creatures saying with a voice like thunder, "Come and see." ²And I looked, and behold, a white horse. He who sat on it had a bow; and a crown was given to him, and he went out conquering and to conquer.

³When He opened the second seal, I heard the second living creature saying, "Come and see."* ⁴Another horse, fiery red, went out. And it was granted to the one who sat on it to take peace from the earth, and that *people* should kill one another, and there was given to him a great sword.

⁵When He opened the third seal, I heard the third living creature say, "Come and see." So I looked, and behold, a black horse, and he who sat on it had a pair of scales in his hand. ⁶And I heard a voice in the midst of the four living creatures saying, "A quart* of wheat for a denarius,* and three quarts of barley for a denarius; and do not harm the oil and the wine."

⁷When He opened the fourth seal, I heard the voice of the fourth living creature saying, "Come and see." ⁸So I looked, and behold, a pale horse. And the name of him who sat on it was Death, and Hades followed with him. And power was given to them over a fourth of the earth, to kill with sword, with hunger, with death, and by the beasts of the earth.

⁹When He opened the fifth seal, I saw under the altar the souls of those who had been slain for the word of God and for the testimony which they held. ¹⁰And they cried with a loud voice, saying, "How long, O Lord, holy and true, until You judge and avenge our blood on those who dwell on the

earth?" ¹¹Then a white robe was given to each of them; and it was said to them that they should rest a little while longer, until both *the number of* their fellow servants and their brethren, who would be killed as they *were,* was completed.

¹²I looked when He opened the sixth seal, and behold,* there was a great earthquake; and the sun became black as sackcloth of hair, and the moon* became like blood. ¹³And the stars of heaven fell to the earth, as a fig tree drops its late figs when it is shaken by a mighty wind. ¹⁴Then the sky receded as a scroll when it is rolled up, and every mountain and island was moved out of its place. ¹⁵And the kings of the earth, the great men, the rich men, the commanders,* the mighty men, every slave and every free man, hid themselves in the caves and in the rocks of the mountains, ¹⁶and said to the mountains and rocks, "Fall on us and hide us from the face of Him who sits on the throne and from the wrath of the Lamb! ¹⁷For the great day of His wrath has come, and who is able to stand?"

PSALM 134:1-3

A Song of Ascents.

BEHOLD, bless the LORD,
All *you* servants of the LORD,
Who by night stand in the
house of the LORD!

2 Lift up your hands *in the* sanctuary,
And bless the LORD.

3 The LORD who made heaven
and earth
Bless you from Zion!

PROVERBS FOR TODAY/ 30:1-4

The words of Agur the son of Jakeh, his *utterance. This man declared to Ithiel—to Ithiel and Ucal: surely I* am *more stupid than* any *man, and do not have the understanding of a man. I neither learned wisdom nor have knowledge of the Holy One. Who has ascended into heaven, or descended? Who has gathered the wind in His fists? Who has bound the waters in a garment? Who has established all the ends of the earth? What* is *His name, and what* is *His Son's name, if you know?*

DECEMBER 16

MICAH 5:1–7:20

Now gather yourself in troops,
O daughter of troops;
He has laid siege against us;
They will strike the judge of
Israel with a rod on the
cheek.

2 "But you, Bethlehem
Ephrathah,

Though you are little among
the thousands of Judah,
Yet out of you shall come
forth to Me
The One to be Ruler in Israel,
Whose goings forth *are* from
of old,
From everlasting."

3 Therefore He shall give them
up,

Until the time *that* she who is
in labor has given birth;
Then the remnant of His
brethren
Shall return to the children of
Israel.
4 And He shall stand and feed
His flock
In the strength of the Lord,
In the majesty of the name of
the Lord His God;
And they shall abide,
For now He shall be great
To the ends of the earth;
5 And this *One* shall be peace.

When the Assyrian comes
into our land,
And when he treads in our
palaces,
Then we will raise against him
Seven shepherds and eight
princely men.
6 They shall waste with the
sword the land of Assyria,
And the land of Nimrod at its
entrances;
Thus He shall deliver *us* from
the Assyrian,
When he comes into our land
And when he treads within
our borders.

7 Then the remnant of Jacob
Shall be in the midst of many
peoples,
Like dew from the Lord,
Like showers on the grass,
That tarry for no man
Nor wait for the sons of men.
8 And the remnant of Jacob
Shall be among the Gentiles,
In the midst of many peoples,
Like a lion among the beasts
of the forest,
Like a young lion among
flocks of sheep,
Who, if he passes through,
Both treads down and tears in
pieces,

And none can deliver.
9 Your hand shall be lifted
against your adversaries,
And all your enemies shall be
cut off.

10 "And it shall be in that day,"
says the Lord,
"That I will cut off your horses
from your midst
And destroy your chariots.
11 I will cut off the cities of your
land
And throw down all your
strongholds.
12 I will cut off sorceries from
your hand,
And you shall have no
soothsayers.
13 Your carved images I will also
cut off,
And your sacred pillars from
your midst;
You shall no more worship
the work of your hands;
14 I will pluck your wooden
images* from your midst;
Thus I will destroy your cities.
15 And I will execute vengeance
in anger and fury
On the nations that have not
heard."*

Hear now what the Lord says:

"Arise, plead your case before
the mountains,
And let the hills hear your
voice.
2 Hear, O you mountains, the
Lord's complaint,
And you strong foundations of
the earth;
For the Lord has a complaint
against His people,
And He will contend with
Israel.

3 "O My people, what have I
done to you?

And how have I wearied you?
Testify against Me.
4 For I brought you up from the
land of Egypt,
I redeemed you from the
house of bondage;
And I sent before you Moses,
Aaron, and Miriam.
5 O My people, remember now
What Balak king of Moab
counseled,
And what Balaam the son of
Beor answered him,
From Acacia Grove* to Gilgal,
That you may know the
righteousness of the LORD."

6 With what shall I come before
the LORD,
And bow myself before the
High God?
Shall I come before Him with
burnt offerings,
With calves a year old?
7 Will the LORD be pleased with
thousands of rams,
Ten thousand rivers of oil?
Shall I give my firstborn *for*
my transgression,
The fruit of my body *for* the
sin of my soul?

8 He has shown you, O man,
what *is* good;
And what does the LORD
require of you
But to do justly,
To love mercy,
And to walk humbly with your
God?

9 The LORD's voice cries to the
city—
Wisdom shall see Your name:

"Hear the rod!
Who has appointed it?
10 Are there yet the treasures of
wickedness
In the house of the wicked,

And the short measure *that is*
an abomination?
11 Shall I count pure *those* with
the wicked scales,
And with the bag of deceitful
weights?
12 For her rich men are full of
violence,
Her inhabitants have spoken
lies,
And their tongue is deceitful
in their mouth.

13 "Therefore I will also make *you*
sick by striking you,
By making *you* desolate
because of your sins.
14 You shall eat, but not be
satisfied;
Hunger* *shall be* in your
midst.
You may carry *some* away,*
but shall not save *them;*
And what you do rescue I will
give over to the sword.

15 "You shall sow, but not reap;
You shall tread the olives, but
not anoint yourselves with
oil;
And *make* sweet wine, but not
drink wine.
16 For the statutes of Omri are
kept;
All the works of Ahab's house
are done;
And you walk in their
counsels,
That I may make you a
desolation,
And your inhabitants a
hissing.
Therefore you shall bear the
reproach of My people."*

WOE is me!
For I am like those who
gather summer fruits,
Like those who glean vintage
grapes;

There is no cluster to eat
Of the first-ripe fruit which my
soul desires.
2 The faithful man has perished
from the earth,
And there is no one upright
among men.
They all lie in wait for blood;
Every man hunts his brother
with a net.

3 That they may successfully do
evil with both hands—
The prince asks for gifts,
The judge seeks a bribe,
And the great man utters his
evil desire;
So they scheme together.
4 The best of them is like a
brier;
The most upright is sharper
than a thorn hedge;
The day of your watchman
and your punishment
comes;
Now shall be their perplexity.

5 Do not trust in a friend;
Do not put your confidence in
a companion;
Guard the doors of your
mouth
From her who lies in your
bosom.
6 For son dishonors father,
Daughter rises against her
mother,
Daughter-in-law against her
mother-in-law;
A man's enemies are the men
of his own household.
7 Therefore I will look to the
LORD;
I will wait for the God of my
salvation;
My God will hear me.

8 Do not rejoice over me, my
enemy;
When I fall, I will arise;

When I sit in darkness,
The LORD will be a light to me.
9 I will bear the indignation of
the LORD,
Because I have sinned against
Him,
Until He pleads my case
And executes justice for me.
He will bring me forth to the
light;
I will see His righteousness.
10 Then she who is my enemy
will see,
And shame will cover her who
said to me,
"Where is the LORD your God?"
My eyes will see her;
Now she will be trampled
down
Like mud in the streets.

11 In the day when your walls
are to be built,
In that day the decree shall go
far and wide.*
12 In that day they* shall come
to you
From Assyria and the fortified
cities,*
From the fortress* to the
River,*
From sea to sea,
And mountain to mountain.
13 Yet the land shall be desolate
Because of those who dwell in
it,
And for the fruit of their
deeds.

14 Shepherd Your people with
Your staff,
The flock of Your heritage,
Who dwell solitarily in a
woodland,
In the midst of Carmel;
Let them feed in Bashan and
Gilead,
As in days of old.

15 "As in the days when you came
   out of the land of Egypt,
   I will show them* wonders."

16 The nations shall see and be
   ashamed of all their might;
   They shall put *their* hand over
   their mouth;
   Their ears shall be deaf.
17 They shall lick the dust like a
   serpent;
   They shall crawl from their
   holes like snakes of the
   earth.
   They shall be afraid of the
   LORD our God,
   And shall fear because of You.
18 Who *is* a God like You,
   Pardoning iniquity
   And passing over the
   transgression of the
   remnant of His heritage?
   He does not retain His anger
   forever,
   Because He delights *in* mercy.
19 He will again have
   compassion on us,
   And will subdue our iniquities.

   You will cast all our* sins
   Into the depths of the sea.
20 You will give truth to Jacob
   And mercy to Abraham,
   Which You have sworn to our
   fathers
   From days of old.

REVELATION 7:1-17

AFTER these things I saw four angels standing at the four corners of the earth, holding the
four winds of the earth, that the wind
should not blow on the earth, on the
sea, or on any tree. ²Then I saw another angel ascending from the east,
having the seal of the living God. And
he cried with a loud voice to the four
angels to whom it was granted to harm
the earth and the sea, ³saying, "Do not

harm the earth, the sea, or the trees till
we have sealed the servants of our
God on their foreheads." ⁴And I heard
the number of those who were sealed.
One hundred *and* forty-four thousand
of all the tribes of the children of Israel
were sealed:

5 of the tribe of Judah twelve
   thousand *were* sealed;*
   of the tribe of Reuben twelve
   thousand *were* sealed;
   of the tribe of Gad twelve
   thousand *were* sealed;
6 of the tribe of Asher twelve
   thousand *were* sealed;
   of the tribe of Naphtali twelve
   thousand *were* sealed;
   of the tribe of Manasseh
   twelve thousand *were*
   sealed;
7 of the tribe of Simeon twelve
   thousand *were* sealed;
   of the tribe of Levi twelve
   thousand *were* sealed;
   of the tribe of Issachar twelve
   thousand *were* sealed;
8 of the tribe of Zebulun twelve
   thousand *were* sealed;
   of the tribe of Joseph twelve
   thousand *were* sealed;
   of the tribe of Benjamin
   twelve thousand *were*
   sealed.

⁹After these things I looked, and behold, a great multitude which no one
could number, of all nations, tribes,
peoples, and tongues, standing before
the throne and before the Lamb,
clothed with white robes, with palm
branches in their hands, ¹⁰and crying
out with a loud voice, saying, "Salvation *belongs* to our God who sits on the
throne, and to the Lamb!" ¹¹All the angels stood around the throne and the
elders and the four living creatures,
and fell on their faces before the
throne and worshiped God, ¹²saying:

"Amen! Blessing and glory and
wisdom,
Thanksgiving and honor and
power and might,
Be to our God forever and
ever.
Amen."

¹³Then one of the elders answered, saying to me, "Who are these arrayed in white robes, and where did they come from?"

¹⁴And I said to him, "Sir,* you know."

So he said to me, "These are the ones who come out of the great tribulation, and washed their robes and made them white in the blood of the Lamb. ¹⁵Therefore they are before the throne of God, and serve Him day and night in His temple. And He who sits on the throne will dwell among them. ¹⁶They shall neither hunger anymore nor thirst anymore; the sun shall not strike them, nor any heat; ¹⁷for the Lamb who is in the midst of the throne will shepherd them and lead them to living fountains of waters.* And God will wipe away every tear from their eyes."

PSALM 135:1-21

Praise the Lord!
Praise the name of the Lord;
Praise *Him,* O you servants of
the Lord!

2   You who stand in the house of
the Lord,
In the courts of the house of
our God,

3   Praise the Lord, for the Lord
is good;
Sing praises to His name, for
it is pleasant.

4   For the Lord has chosen
Jacob for Himself,
Israel for His special treasure.

5   For I know that the Lord *is*
great,

And our Lord *is* above all
gods.

6   Whatever the Lord pleases
He does,
In heaven and in earth,
In the seas and in all deep
places.

7   He causes the vapors to
ascend from the ends of the
earth;
He makes lightning for the
rain;
He brings the wind out of His
treasuries.

8   He destroyed the firstborn of
Egypt,
Both of man and beast.

9   He sent signs and wonders
into the midst of you,
O Egypt,
Upon Pharaoh and all his
servants.

10   He defeated many nations
And slew mighty kings—

11   Sihon king of the Amorites,
Og king of Bashan,
And all the kingdoms of
Canaan—

12   And gave their land *as* a
heritage,
A heritage to Israel His
people.

13   Your name, O Lord, *endures*
forever,
Your fame, O Lord,
throughout all generations.

14   For the Lord will judge His
people,
And He will have compassion
on His servants.

15   The idols of the nations *are*
silver and gold,
The work of men's hands.

16   They have mouths, but they
do not speak;
Eyes they have, but they do
not see;

17 They have ears, but they do
  not hear;
  Nor is there *any* breath in
  their mouths.
18 Those who make them are
  like them;
  So is everyone who trusts in
  them.

19 Bless the LORD, O house of
  Israel!

Bless the LORD, O house of
  Aaron!
20 Bless the LORD, O house of
  Levi!
  You who fear the LORD, bless
  the LORD!
21 Blessed be the LORD out of
  Zion,
  Who dwells in Jerusalem!

Praise the LORD!

PROVERBS FOR TODAY/ 30:5-6

Every word of God is *pure; He* is *a shield to those who put their trust in Him. Do not add to His words, lest He rebuke you, and you be found a liar.*

DECEMBER 17

NAHUM 1:1–3:19

THE burden* against Nineveh. The book of the vision of Nahum the Elkoshite.

2 God *is* jealous, and the LORD
  avenges;
  The LORD avenges and *is*
  furious.
  The LORD will take vengeance
  on His adversaries,
  And He reserves *wrath* for
  His enemies;
3 The LORD *is* slow to anger and
  great in power,
  And will not at all acquit *the
  wicked.*

  The LORD has His way
  In the whirlwind and in the
  storm,
  And the clouds *are* the dust of
  His feet.
4 He rebukes the sea and
  makes it dry,
  And dries up all the rivers.

Bashan and Carmel wither,
  And the flower of Lebanon
  wilts.
5 The mountains quake before
  Him,
  The hills melt,
  And the earth heaves* at His
  presence,
  Yes, the world and all who
  dwell in it.

6 Who can stand before His
  indignation?
  And who can endure the
  fierceness of His anger?
  His fury is poured out like fire,
  And the rocks are thrown
  down by Him.

7 The LORD *is* good,
  A stronghold in the day of
  trouble;
  And He knows those who
  trust in Him.
8 But with an overflowing flood
  He will make an utter end of
  its place,

And darkness will pursue His
    enemies.

9 What do you conspire against
    the LORD?
He will make an utter end *of it.*
Affliction will not rise up a
    second time.
10 For while tangled *like* thorns,
And while drunken *like*
    drunkards,
They shall be devoured like
    stubble fully dried.
11 From you comes forth *one*
Who plots evil against the
    LORD,
A wicked counselor.

12 Thus says the LORD:

"Though *they are* safe, and
    likewise many,
Yet in this manner they will be
    cut down
When he passes through.
Though I have afflicted you,
I will afflict you no more;
13 For now I will break off his
    yoke from you,
And burst your bonds apart."

14 The LORD has given a
    command concerning you:
"Your name shall be
    perpetuated no longer.
Out of the house of your gods
I will cut off the carved image
    and the molded image.
I will dig your grave,
For you are vile."

15 Behold, on the mountains
The feet of him who brings
    good tidings,
Who proclaims peace!
O Judah, keep your appointed
    feasts,
Perform your vows.
For the wicked one shall no
    more pass through you;

He is utterly cut off.

HE who scatters* has come up before
your face. Man the fort!
    Watch the road!
Strengthen *your* flanks!
Fortify *your* power mightily.

2 For the LORD will restore the
    excellence of Jacob
Like the excellence of Israel,
For the emptiers have
    emptied them out
And ruined their vine
    branches.

3 The shields of his mighty
    men *are* made red,
The valiant men *are* in scarlet.
The chariots *come* with
    flaming torches
In the day of his preparation,
And the spears are
    brandished.*
4 The chariots rage in the
    streets,
They jostle one another in the
    broad roads;
They seem like torches,
They run like lightning.

5 He remembers his nobles;
They stumble in their walk;
They make haste to her walls,
And the defense is prepared.
6 The gates of the rivers are
    opened,
And the palace is dissolved.
7 It is decreed:*
She shall be led away captive,
She shall be brought up;
And her maidservants shall
    lead *her* as with the voice of
    doves,
Beating their breasts.

8 Though Nineveh of old *was*
    like a pool of water,
Now they flee away.
"Halt! Halt!" *they cry;*

But no one turns back.

9 Take spoil of silver!
Take spoil of gold!
There is no end of treasure,
Or wealth of every desirable
prize.

10 She is empty, desolate, and
waste!
The heart melts, and the
knees shake;
Much pain *is* in every side,
And all their faces are drained
of color.*

11 Where *is* the dwelling of the
lions,
And the feeding place of the
young lions,
Where the lion walked, the
lioness *and* lion's cub,
And no one made *them* afraid?

12 The lion tore in pieces
enough for his cubs,
Killed for his lionesses,
Filled his caves with prey,
And his dens with flesh.

13 "Behold, I *am* against you," says
the LORD of hosts, "I will burn your*
chariots in smoke, and the sword shall
devour your young lions; I will cut off
your prey from the earth, and the
voice of your messengers shall be
heard no more."

WOE to the bloody city!
It *is* all full of lies *and* robbery.
Its victim never departs.

2 The noise of a whip
And the noise of rattling
wheels,
Of galloping horses,
Of clattering chariots!

3 Horsemen charge with bright
sword and glittering spear.
There is a multitude of slain,
A great number of bodies,
Countless corpses—
They stumble over the
corpses—

4 Because of the multitude of

harlotries of the seductive
harlot,
The mistress of sorceries,
Who sells nations through
her harlotries,
And families through her
sorceries.

5 "Behold, I *am* against you,"
says the LORD of hosts;
"I will lift your skirts over your
face,
I will show the nations your
nakedness,
And the kingdoms your
shame.

6 I will cast abominable filth
upon you,
Make you vile,
And make you a spectacle.

7 It shall come to pass *that* all
who look upon you
Will flee from you, and say,
'Nineveh is laid waste!
Who will bemoan her?'
Where shall I seek
comforters for you?"

8 Are you better than No Amon*
That was situated by the
River,*
That had the waters around
her,
Whose rampart *was* the sea,
Whose wall *was* the sea?

9 Ethiopia and Egypt *were* her
strength,
And *it was* boundless;
Put and Lubim were your*
helpers.

10 Yet she *was* carried away,
She went into captivity;
Her young children also were
dashed to pieces
At the head of every street;
They cast lots for her
honorable men,
And all her great men were
bound in chains.

11 You also will be drunk;

You will be hidden;
You also will seek refuge from
the enemy.

12 All your strongholds *are* fig
trees with ripened figs:
If they are shaken,
They fall into the mouth of the
eater.

13 Surely, your people in your
midst *are* women!
The gates of your land are
wide open for your enemies;
Fire shall devour the bars of
your *gates.*

14 Draw your water for the siege!
Fortify your strongholds!
Go into the clay and tread the
mortar!
Make strong the brick kiln!

15 There the fire will devour you,
The sword will cut you off;
It will eat you up like a locust.

Make yourself many—like
the locust!
Make yourself many— like
the *swarming* locusts!

16 You have multiplied your
merchants more than the
stars of heaven.
The locust plunders and flies
away.

17 Your commanders *are* like
swarming locusts,
And your generals like great
grasshoppers,
Which camp in the hedges on
a cold day;
When the sun rises they flee
away,
And the place where they *are*
is not known.

18 Your shepherds slumber,
O king of Assyria;
Your nobles rest *in the dust.*
Your people are scattered on
the mountains,
And no one gathers them.

19 Your injury *has* no healing,
Your wound is severe.
All who hear news of you
Will clap *their* hands over you,
For upon whom has not your
wickedness passed
continually?

REVELATION 8:1-13

WHEN He [the Lamb] opened
the seventh seal, there was
silence in heaven for about
half an hour. [2]And I saw the seven angels who stand before God, and to
them were given seven trumpets.
[3]Then another angel, having a golden
censer, came and stood at the altar. He
was given much incense, that he
should offer *it* with the prayers of all
the saints upon the golden altar which
was before the throne. [4]And the smoke
of the incense, with the prayers of the
saints, ascended before God from the
angel's hand. [5]Then the angel took the
censer, filled it with fire from the altar,
and threw *it* to the earth. And there
were noises, thunderings, lightnings,
and an earthquake.

[6]So the seven angels who had the
seven trumpets prepared themselves
to sound.

[7]The first angel sounded: And hail
and fire followed, mingled with blood,
and they were thrown to the earth.*
And a third of the trees were burned
up, and all green grass was burned up.

[8]Then the second angel sounded:
And *something* like a great mountain
burning with fire was thrown into the
sea, and a third of the sea became
blood. [9]And a third of the living creatures in the sea died, and a third of the
ships were destroyed.

[10]Then the third angel sounded:
And a great star fell from heaven,
burning like a torch, and it fell on a
third of the rivers and on the springs of
water. [11]The name of the star is Worm-

wood. A third of the waters became wormwood, and many men died from the water, because it was made bitter.

12Then the fourth angel sounded: And a third of the sun was struck, a third of the moon, and a third of the stars, so that a third of them were darkened. A third of the day did not shine, and likewise the night.

13And I looked, and I heard an angel* flying through the midst of heaven, saying with a loud voice, "Woe, woe, woe to the inhabitants of the earth, because of the remaining blasts of the trumpet of the three angels who are about to sound!"

PSALM 136:1-26

O H, give thanks to the LORD, for *He is* good!
For His mercy *endures* forever.
2 Oh, give thanks to the God of gods!
For His mercy *endures* forever.
3 Oh, give thanks to the Lord of lords!
For His mercy *endures* forever:

4 To Him who alone does great wonders,
For His mercy *endures* forever;
5 To Him who by wisdom made the heavens,
For His mercy *endures* forever;
6 To Him who laid out the earth above the waters,
For His mercy *endures* forever;
7 To Him who made great lights,
For His mercy *endures* forever—
8 The sun to rule by day,

For His mercy *endures* forever;
9 The moon and stars to rule by night,
For His mercy *endures* forever.

10 To Him who struck Egypt in their firstborn,
For His mercy *endures* forever;
11 And brought out Israel from among them,
For His mercy *endures* forever;
12 With a strong hand, and with an outstretched arm,
For His mercy *endures* forever;
13 To Him who divided the Red Sea in two,
For His mercy *endures* forever;
14 And made Israel pass through the midst of it,
For His mercy *endures* forever;
15 But overthrew Pharaoh and his army in the Red Sea,
For His mercy *endures* forever;
16 To Him who led His people through the wilderness,
For His mercy *endures* forever;
17 To Him who struck down great kings,
For His mercy *endures* forever;
18 And slew famous kings,
For His mercy *endures* forever—
19 Sihon king of the Amorites,
For His mercy *endures* forever;
20 And Og king of Bashan,
For His mercy *endures* forever—
21 And gave their land as a heritage,

"There is born to you this day in the city of David a Savior, who is Christ the Lord."
    Luke 2:11

"Let the heavens rejoice, and let the earth be glad."
Psalm 96:11

*"Great is the LORD,
and greatly to be
praised."*
Psalm 145:3

For His mercy *endures* forever;

22 A heritage to Israel His servant,
For His mercy *endures* forever.

23 Who remembered us in our lowly state,
For His mercy *endures* forever;

24 And rescued us from our enemies,
For His mercy *endures* forever;

25 Who gives food to all flesh,
For His mercy *endures* forever.

26 Oh, give thanks to the God of heaven!
For His mercy *endures* forever.

PROVERBS FOR TODAY/ 30:7-9

Two things *I request of You (deprive me not before I die): remove falsehood and lies far from me; give me neither poverty nor riches—feed me with the food allotted to me; lest I be full and deny You, and say, "Who is the LORD?" Or lest I be poor and steal, and profane the name of my God.*

DECEMBER 18

HABAKKUK 1:1–3:19

THE burden* which the prophet Habakkuk saw.

2 O LORD, how long shall I cry,
And You will not hear?
Even cry out to You,
"Violence!"
And You will not save.

3 Why do You show me iniquity,
And cause *me* to see trouble?
For plundering and violence *are* before me;
There is strife, and contention arises.

4 Therefore the law is powerless,
And justice never goes forth.
For the wicked surround the righteous;
Therefore perverse judgment proceeds.

5 "Look among the nations and watch—
Be utterly astounded!
For *I will* work a work in your days
Which you would not believe,
though it were told *you*.

6 For indeed I am raising up the Chaldeans,
A bitter and hasty nation
Which marches through the breadth of the earth,
To possess dwelling places *that are* not theirs.

7 They are terrible and dreadful;
Their judgment and their dignity proceed from themselves.

8 Their horses also are swifter than leopards,
And more fierce than evening wolves.
Their chargers charge ahead;
Their cavalry comes from afar;

They fly as the eagle *that*
hastens to eat.

9 "They all come for violence;
Their faces are set *like* the
east wind.
They gather captives like
sand.
10 They scoff at kings,
And princes are scorned by
them.
They deride every stronghold,
For they heap up earthen
mounds and seize it.
11 Then *his* mind* changes, and
he transgresses;
He commits offense,
Ascribing this power to his
god."

12 Are You not from everlasting,
O LORD my God, my Holy
One?
We shall not die.
O LORD, You have appointed
them for judgment;
O Rock, You have marked
them for correction.
13 *You are* of purer eyes than to
behold evil,
And cannot look on
wickedness.
Why do You look on those
who deal treacherously,
And hold Your tongue when
the wicked devours
A *person* more righteous than
he?
14 *Why* do You make men like
fish of the sea,
Like creeping things *that have*
no ruler over them?

15 They take up all of them with
a hook,
They catch them in their net,
And gather them in their
dragnet.
Therefore they rejoice and
are glad.

16 Therefore they sacrifice to
their net,
And burn incense to their
dragnet;
Because by them their share
is sumptuous
And their food plentiful.
17 Shall they therefore empty
their net,
And continue to slay nations
without pity?

I WILL stand my watch
And set myself on the
rampart,
And watch to see what He will
say to me,
And what I will answer when I
am corrected.

²Then the LORD answered me and
said:

"Write the vision
And make *it* plain on tablets,
That he may run who reads it.
3 For the vision *is* yet for an
appointed time;
But at the end it will speak,
and it will not lie.
Though it tarries, wait for it;
Because it will surely come,
It will not tarry.

4 "Behold the proud,
His soul is not upright in him;
But the just shall live by his
faith.

5 "Indeed, because he
transgresses by wine,
He is a proud man,
And he does not stay at home.
Because he enlarges his
desire as hell,*
And he *is* like death, and
cannot be satisfied,
He gathers to himself all
nations

And heaps up for himself all peoples.

6 "Will not all these take up a proverb against him,
And a taunting riddle against him, and say,
'Woe to him who increases
What is not his—how long?
And to him who loads himself with many pledges'?*

7 Will not your creditors* rise up suddenly?
Will they not awaken who oppress you?
And you will become their booty.

8 Because you have plundered many nations,
All the remnant of the people shall plunder you,
Because of men's blood
And the violence of the land *and* the city,
And of all who dwell in it.

9 "Woe to him who covets evil gain for his house,
That he may set his nest on high,
That he may be delivered from the power of disaster!

10 You give shameful counsel to your house,
Cutting off many peoples,
And sin *against* your soul.

11 For the stone will cry out from the wall,
And the beam from the timbers will answer it.

12 "Woe to him who builds a town with bloodshed,
Who establishes a city by iniquity!

13 Behold, *is it* not of the LORD of hosts
That the peoples labor to feed the fire,*

And nations weary themselves in vain?

14 For the earth will be filled
With the knowledge of the glory of the LORD,
As the waters cover the sea.

15 "Woe to him who gives drink to his neighbor,
Pressing* *him to* your bottle,
Even to make *him* drunk,
That you may look on his nakedness!

16 You are filled with shame instead of glory.
You also—drink!
And be exposed as uncircumcised!*
The cup of the LORD's right hand *will be* turned against you,
And utter shame will be on your glory.

17 For the violence *done to* Lebanon will cover you,
And the plunder of beasts *which* made them afraid,
Because of men's blood
And the violence of the land *and* the city,
And of all who dwell in it.

18 "What profit is the image, that its maker should carve it,
The molded image, a teacher of lies,
That the maker of its mold should trust in it,
To make mute idols?

19 Woe to him who says to wood, 'Awake!'
To silent stone, 'Arise! It shall teach!'
Behold, it is overlaid with gold and silver,
Yet in it there is no breath at all.

20 "But the LORD is in His holy temple.

Let all the earth keep silence
before Him."

A PRAYER of Habakkuk the prophet, on
Shigionoth.*

2 O LORD, I have heard Your
speech *and* was afraid;
O LORD, revive Your work in
the midst of the years!
In the midst of the years
make *it* known;
In wrath remember mercy.

3 God came from Teman,
The Holy One from Mount
Paran.   Selah

His glory covered the
heavens,
And the earth was full of His
praise.
4 *His* brightness was like the
light;
He had rays *flashing* from His
hand,
And there His power *was*
hidden.
5 Before Him went pestilence,
And fever followed at His feet.

6 He stood and measured the
earth;
He looked and startled the
nations.
And the everlasting
mountains were scattered,
The perpetual hills bowed.
His ways *are* everlasting.
7 I saw the tents of Cushan in
affliction;
The curtains of the land of
Midian trembled.

8 O LORD, were *You* displeased
with the rivers,
Was Your anger against the
rivers,
Was Your wrath against the
sea,

That You rode on Your horses,
Your chariots of salvation?
9 Your bow was made quite
ready;
Oaths were sworn over *Your*
arrows.*   Selah

You divided the earth with
rivers.
10 The mountains saw You *and*
trembled;
The overflowing of the water
passed by.
The deep uttered its voice,
And lifted its hands on high.
11 The sun and moon stood still
in their habitation;
At the light of Your arrows
they went,
At the shining of Your
glittering spear.

12 You marched through the
land in indignation;
You trampled the nations in
anger.
13 You went forth for the
salvation of Your people,
For salvation with Your
Anointed.
You struck the head from the
house of the wicked,
By laying bare from
foundation to neck.   Selah

14 You thrust through with his
own arrows
The head of his villages.
They came out like a
whirlwind to scatter me;
Their rejoicing was like
feasting on the poor in
secret.
15 You walked through the sea
with Your horses,
Through the heap of great
waters.

16 When I heard, my body
trembled;

My lips quivered at *the* voice;
Rottenness entered my bones;
And I trembled in myself,
That I might rest in the day of
   trouble.
When he comes up to the
   people,
He will invade them with his
   troops.

17 Though the fig tree may not
      blossom,
   Nor fruit be on the vines;
   Though the labor of the olive
      may fail,
   And the fields yield no food;
   Though the flock may be cut
      off from the fold,
   And there be no herd in the
      stalls—
18 Yet I will rejoice in the LORD,
   I will joy in the God of my
      salvation.

19 The LORD God* is my strength;
   He will make my feet like
      deer's *feet,*
   And He will make me walk on
      my high hills.

To the Chief Musician. With my
stringed instruments.

REVELATION 9:1-21

THEN the fifth angel sounded: And
I saw a star fallen from heaven to
the earth. To him was given the
key to the bottomless pit. ²And he
opened the bottomless pit, and smoke
arose out of the pit like the smoke of a
great furnace. So the sun and the air
were darkened because of the smoke
of the pit. ³Then out of the smoke locusts came upon the earth. And to
them was given power, as the scorpions of the earth have power. ⁴They
were commanded not to harm the
grass of the earth, or any green thing,
or any tree, but only those men who do

not have the seal of God on their foreheads. ⁵And they were not given *authority* to kill them, but to torment
them *for* five months. Their torment
was like the torment of a scorpion
when it strikes a man. ⁶In those days
men will seek death and will not find it;
they will desire to die, and death will
flee from them.

⁷The shape of the locusts was like
horses prepared for battle. On their
heads were crowns of something like
gold, and their faces *were* like the faces
of men. ⁸They had hair like women's
hair, and their teeth were like lions'
teeth. ⁹And they had breastplates like
breastplates of iron, and the sound of
their wings *was* like the sound of chariots with many horses running into
battle. ¹⁰They had tails like scorpions,
and there were stings in their tails.
Their power *was* to hurt men five
months. ¹¹And they had as king over
them the angel of the bottomless pit,
whose name in Hebrew *is* Abaddon,
but in Greek he has the name Apol-
lyon.

¹²One woe is past. Behold, still two
more woes are coming after these
things.

¹³Then the sixth angel sounded:
And I heard a voice from the four
horns of the golden altar which is before God, ¹⁴saying to the sixth angel
who had the trumpet, "Release the
four angels who are bound at the
great river Euphrates." ¹⁵So the four
angels, who had been prepared for
the hour and day and month and year,
were released to kill a third of mankind. ¹⁶Now the number of the army
of the horsemen *was* two hundred
million; I heard the number of them.
¹⁷And thus I saw the horses in the
vision: those who sat on them had
breastplates of fiery red, hyacinth
blue, and sulfur yellow; and the heads
of the horses *were* like the heads of
lions; and out of their mouths came
fire, smoke, and brimstone. ¹⁸By

these three *plagues* a third of mankind was killed—by the fire and the smoke and the brimstone which came out of their mouths. ¹⁹For their power* is in their mouth and in their tails; for their tails *are* like serpents, having heads; and with them they do harm.

²⁰But the rest of mankind, who were not killed by these plagues, did not repent of the works of their hands, that they should not worship demons, and idols of gold, silver, brass, stone, and wood, which can neither see nor hear nor walk. ²¹And they did not repent of their murders or their sorceries* or their sexual immorality or their thefts.

PSALM 137:1-9

B^y the rivers of Babylon,
There we sat down, yea,
we wept
When we remembered Zion.
2   We hung our harps
Upon the willows in the midst
of it.
3   For there those who carried
us away captive asked of us
a song,

And those who plundered us
requested mirth,
Saying, "Sing us *one* of the
songs of Zion!"

4   How shall we sing the LORD's
song
In a foreign land?
5   If I forget you, O Jerusalem,
Let my right hand forget *its*
skill!
6   If I do not remember you,
Let my tongue cling to the
roof of my mouth—
If I do not exalt Jerusalem
Above my chief joy.

7   Remember, O LORD, against
the sons of Edom
The day of Jerusalem,
Who said, "Raze *it,* raze *it,*
To its very foundation!"

8   O daughter of Babylon, who
are to be destroyed,
Happy the one who repays
you as you have served us!
9   Happy the one who takes and
dashes
Your little ones against the
rock!

PROVERBS FOR TODAY/ 30:10

Do not malign a servant to his master, lest he curse you, and you be found guilty.

DECEMBER 19

ZEPHANIAH 1:1–3:20

T^{HE} word of the LORD which came
to Zephaniah the son of Cushi,
the son of Gedaliah, the son of
Amariah, the son of Hezekiah, in the

days of Josiah the son of Amon, king of
Judah.

2   "I will utterly consume
everything

From the face of the land,"
Says the LORD;

3 "I will consume man and beast;
I will consume the birds of the
heavens,
The fish of the sea,
And the stumbling blocks*
along with the wicked.
I will cut off man from the
face of the land,"
Says the LORD.

4 "I will stretch out My hand
against Judah,
And against all the inhabitants
of Jerusalem.
I will cut off every trace of
Baal from this place,
The names of the idolatrous
priests* with the *pagan
priests*—

5 Those who worship the host
of heaven on the housetops;
Those who worship and
swear *oaths* by the LORD,
But who *also* swear by
Milcom;*

6 Those who have turned back
from *following* the LORD,
And have not sought the
LORD, nor inquired of Him."

7 Be silent in the presence of
the Lord GOD;
For the day of the LORD *is* at
hand,
For the LORD has prepared a
sacrifice;
He has invited* His guests.

8 "And it shall be,
In the day of the LORD'S
sacrifice,
That I will punish the princes
and the king's children,
And all such as are clothed
with foreign apparel.

9 In the same day I will punish
All those who leap over the
threshold,*

Who fill their masters' houses
with violence and deceit.

10 "And there shall be on that
day," says the LORD,
"The sound of a mournful cry
from the Fish Gate,
A wailing from the Second
Quarter,
And a loud crashing from the
hills.

11 Wail, you inhabitants of
Maktesh!*
For all the merchant people
are cut down;
All those who handle money
are cut off.

12 "And it shall come to pass at
that time
That I will search Jerusalem
with lamps,
And punish the men
Who are settled in
complacency,*
Who say in their heart,
'The LORD will not do good,
Nor will He do evil.'

13 Therefore their goods shall
become booty,
And their houses a desolation;
They shall build houses, but
not inhabit *them;*
They shall plant vineyards,
but not drink their wine."

14 The great day of the LORD *is*
near;
It is near and hastens quickly.
The noise of the day of the
LORD is bitter;
There the mighty men shall
cry out.

15 That day *is* a day of wrath,
A day of trouble and distress,
A day of devastation and
desolation,
A day of darkness and
gloominess,

A day of clouds and thick
    darkness,
16 A day of trumpet and alarm
    Against the fortified cities
    And against the high towers.

17 "I will bring distress upon men,
    And they shall walk like blind
      men,
    Because they have sinned
      against the LORD;
    Their blood shall be poured
      out like dust,
    And their flesh like refuse."

18 Neither their silver nor their
      gold
    Shall be able to deliver them
    In the day of the LORD's wrath;
    But the whole land shall be
      devoured
    By the fire of His jealousy,
    For He will make speedy
      riddance
    Of all those who dwell in the
      land.

GATHER yourselves together, yes,
    gather together,
    O undesirable* nation,
2 Before the decree is issued,
    Or the day passes like chaff,
    Before the LORD's fierce anger
      comes upon you,
    Before the day of the LORD's
      anger comes upon you!
3 Seek the LORD, all you meek
      of the earth,
    Who have upheld His justice.
    Seek righteousness, seek
      humility.
    It may be that you will be
      hidden
    In the day of the LORD's anger.

4 For Gaza shall be forsaken,
    And Ashkelon desolate;
    They shall drive out Ashdod
      at noonday,
    And Ekron shall be uprooted.

5 Woe to the inhabitants of the
      seacoast,
    The nation of the Cherethites!
    The word of the LORD *is*
      against you,
    O Canaan, land of the
      Philistines:
    "I will destroy you;
    So there shall be no
      inhabitant."

6 The seacoast shall be
      pastures,
    With shelters* for shepherds
      and folds for flocks.
7 The coast shall be for the
      remnant of the house of
      Judah;
    They shall feed *their* flocks
      there;
    In the houses of Ashkelon
      they shall lie down at
      evening.
    For the LORD their God will
      intervene for them,
    And return their captives.

8 "I have heard the reproach of
      Moab,
    And the insults of the people
      of Ammon,
    With which they have
      reproached My people,
    And made arrogant threats
      against their borders.
9 Therefore, as I live,"
    Says the LORD of hosts, the
      God of Israel,
    "Surely Moab shall be like
      Sodom,
    And the people of Ammon
      like Gomorrah—
    Overrun with weeds and
      saltpits,
    And a perpetual desolation.
    The residue of My people
      shall plunder them,
    And the remnant of My
      people shall possess them."

10 This they shall have for their
pride,
Because they have
reproached and made
arrogant threats
Against the people of the LORD
of hosts.

11 The LORD *will be* awesome to
them,
For He will reduce to nothing
all the gods of the earth;
People shall worship Him,
Each one from his place,
Indeed all the shores of the
nations.

12 "You Ethiopians also,
You shall be slain by My
sword."

13 And He will stretch out His
hand against the north,
Destroy Assyria,
And make Nineveh a
desolation,
As dry as the wilderness.

14 The herds shall lie down in
her midst,
Every beast of the nation.
Both the pelican and the
bittern
Shall lodge on the capitals *of*
her *pillars;*
Their voice shall sing in the
windows;
Desolation *shall be* at the
threshold;
For He will lay bare the cedar
work.

15 This is the rejoicing city
That dwelt securely,
That said in her heart,
"I *am it,* and *there is* none
besides me."
How has she become a
desolation,
A place for beasts to lie down!
Everyone who passes by her
Shall hiss and shake his fist.

WOE to her who is rebellious and
polluted,
To the oppressing city!

2 She has not obeyed *His* voice,
She has not received
correction;
She has not trusted in the
LORD,
She has not drawn near to her
God.

3 Her princes in her midst *are*
roaring lions;
Her judges *are* evening wolves
That leave not a bone till
morning.

4 Her prophets are insolent,
treacherous people;
Her priests have polluted the
sanctuary,
They have done violence to
the law.

5 The LORD *is* righteous in her
midst,
He will do no
unrighteousness.
Every morning He brings His
justice to light;
He never fails,
But the unjust knows no
shame.

6 "I have cut off nations,
Their fortresses are
devastated;
I have made their streets
desolate,
With none passing by.
Their cities are destroyed;
There is no one, no inhabitant.

7 I said, 'Surely you will fear Me,
You will receive instruction'—
So that her dwelling would
not be cut off,
Despite everything for which I
punished her.
But they rose early and
corrupted all their deeds.

8 "Therefore wait for Me," says
    the Lord,
"Until the day I rise up for
    plunder;*
My determination *is* to gather
    the nations
To My assembly of kingdoms,
To pour on them My
    indignation,
All My fierce anger;
All the earth shall be devoured
With the fire of My jealousy.

9 "For then I will restore to the
    peoples a pure language,
That they all may call on the
    name of the Lord,
To serve Him with one accord.
10 From beyond the rivers of
    Ethiopia
My worshipers,
The daughter of My
    dispersed ones,
Shall bring My offering.
11 In that day you shall not be
    shamed for any of your
    deeds
In which you transgress
    against Me;
For then I will take away from
    your midst
Those who rejoice in your
    pride,
And you shall no longer be
    haughty
In My holy mountain.
12 I will leave in your midst
A meek and humble people,
And they shall trust in the
    name of the Lord.
13 The remnant of Israel shall do
    no unrighteousness
And speak no lies,
Nor shall a deceitful tongue
    be found in their mouth;
For they shall feed *their* flocks
    and lie down,
And no one shall make *them*
    afraid."

14 Sing, O daughter of Zion!
Shout, O Israel!
Be glad and rejoice with all
    your heart,
O daughter of Jerusalem!
15 The Lord has taken away your
    judgments,
He has cast out your enemy.
The King of Israel, the Lord,
    is in your midst;
You shall see* disaster no
    more.

16 In that day it shall be said to
    Jerusalem:
"Do not fear;
Zion, let not your hands be
    weak.
17 The Lord your God in your
    midst,
The Mighty One, will save;
He will rejoice over you with
    gladness,
He will quiet *you* with His love,
He will rejoice over you with
    singing."

18 "I will gather those who
    sorrow over the appointed
    assembly,
Who are among you,
To whom its reproach *is* a
    burden.
19 Behold, at that time
I will deal with all who afflict
    you;
I will save the lame,
And gather those who were
    driven out;
I will appoint them for praise
    and fame
In every land where they
    were put to shame.
20 At that time I will bring you
    back,
Even at the time I gather you;
For I will give you fame and
    praise
Among all the peoples of the
    earth,

When I return your captives
before your eyes,"
Says the LORD.

REVELATION 10:1-11

I SAW still another mighty angel coming down from heaven, clothed with a cloud. And a rainbow *was* on his head, his face *was* like the sun, and his feet like pillars of fire. ²He had a little book open in his hand. And he set his right foot on the sea and *his* left *foot* on the land, ³and cried with a loud voice, as *when* a lion roars. When he cried out, seven thunders uttered their voices. ⁴Now when the seven thunders uttered their voices,* I was about to write; but I heard a voice from heaven saying to me,* "Seal up the things which the seven thunders uttered, and do not write them."

⁵The angel whom I saw standing on the sea and on the land raised up his hand* to heaven ⁶and swore by Him who lives forever and ever, who created heaven and the things that are in it, the earth and the things that are in it, and the sea and the things that are in it, that there should be delay no longer, ⁷but in the days of the sounding of the seventh angel, when he is about to sound, the mystery of God would be finished, as He declared to His servants the prophets.

⁸Then the voice which I heard from heaven spoke to me again and said, "Go, take the little book which is open in the hand of the angel who stands on the sea and on the earth."

⁹So I went to the angel and said to him, "Give me the little book."

And he said to me, "Take and eat it; and it will make your stomach bitter, but it will be as sweet as honey in your mouth."

¹⁰Then I took the little book out of the angel's hand and ate it, and it was as sweet as honey in my mouth. But when I had eaten it, my stomach became bitter. ¹¹And he* said to me, "You must prophesy again about many peoples, nations, tongues, and kings."

PSALM 138:1-8

A Psalm *of David.*

I WILL praise You with my whole heart;
Before the gods I will sing praises to You.
2 I will worship toward Your holy temple,
And praise Your name
For Your lovingkindness and Your truth;
For You have magnified Your word above all Your name.
3 In the day when I cried out,
You answered me,
And made me bold *with* strength in my soul.

4 All the kings of the earth shall praise You, O LORD,
When they hear the words of Your mouth.
5 Yes, they shall sing of the ways of the LORD,
For great *is* the glory of the LORD.
6 Though the LORD *is* on high,
Yet He regards the lowly;
But the proud He knows from afar.

7 Though I walk in the midst of trouble, You will revive me;
You will stretch out Your hand
Against the wrath of my enemies,
And Your right hand will save me.
8 The LORD will perfect *that which* concerns me;
Your mercy, O LORD, *endures* forever;
Do not forsake the works of Your hands.

PROVERBS FOR TODAY/ 30:11-14

There is *a generation* that *curses its father, and does not bless its mother.* There is *a generation* that is *pure in its own eyes,* yet *is not washed from its filthiness.* There is *a generation—oh, how lofty are their eyes! And their eyelids are lifted up.* There is *a generation whose teeth* are like *swords, and whose fangs* are like *knives, to devour the poor from off the earth, and the needy from* among *men.*

DECEMBER 20

HAGGAI 1:1–2:23

Iɴ the second year of King Darius, in the sixth month, on the first day of the month, the word of the Lᴏʀᴅ came by Haggai the prophet to Zerubbabel the son of Shealtiel, governor of Judah, and to Joshua the son of Jehozadak, the high priest, saying, ²"Thus speaks the Lᴏʀᴅ of hosts, saying: 'This people says, "The time has not come, the time that the Lᴏʀᴅ's house should be built." ' "

³Then the word of the Lᴏʀᴅ came by Haggai the prophet, saying, ⁴*"Is it* time for you yourselves to dwell in your paneled houses, and this temple* *to lie* in ruins?" ⁵Now therefore, thus says the Lᴏʀᴅ of hosts: "Consider your ways!

6 "You have sown much, and
   bring in little;
You eat, but do not have
   enough;
You drink, but you are not
   filled with drink;
You clothe yourselves, but no
   one is warm;
And he who earns wages,
Earns wages *to put* into a bag
   with holes."

⁷Thus says the Lᴏʀᴅ of hosts: "Consider your ways! ⁸Go up to the mountains and bring wood and build the temple, that I may take pleasure in it and be glorified," says the Lᴏʀᴅ. ⁹*"You*

looked for much, but indeed *it came to* little; and when you brought it home, I blew it away. Why?" says the Lᴏʀᴅ of hosts. "Because of My house that *is in* ruins, while every one of you runs to his own house. ¹⁰Therefore the heavens above you withhold the dew, and the earth withholds its fruit. ¹¹For I called for a drought on the land and the mountains, on the grain and the new wine and the oil, on whatever the ground brings forth, on men and livestock, and on all the labor of *your* hands."

¹²Then Zerubbabel the son of Shealtiel, and Joshua the son of Jehozadak, the high priest, with all the remnant of the people, obeyed the voice of the Lᴏʀᴅ their God, and the words of Haggai the prophet, as the Lᴏʀᴅ their God had sent him; and the people feared the presence of the Lᴏʀᴅ. ¹³Then Haggai, the Lᴏʀᴅ's messenger, spoke the Lᴏʀᴅ's message to the people, saying, "I *am* with you, says the Lᴏʀᴅ." ¹⁴So the Lᴏʀᴅ stirred up the spirit of Zerubbabel the son of Shealtiel, governor of Judah, and the spirit of Joshua the son of Jehozadak, the high priest, and the spirit of all the remnant of the people; and they came and worked on the house of the Lᴏʀᴅ of hosts, their God, ¹⁵on the twenty-fourth day of the sixth month, in the second year of King Darius.

In the seventh *month,* on the twenty-first of the month, the word of the LORD came by Haggai the prophet, saying: 2"Speak now to Zerubbabel the son of Shealtiel, governor of Judah, and to Joshua the son of Jehozadak, the high priest, and to the remnant of the people, saying: 3'Who is left among you who saw this temple* in its former glory? And how do you see it now? In comparison with it, *is this* not in your eyes as nothing? 4Yet now be strong, Zerubbabel,' says the LORD; 'and be strong, Joshua, son of Jehozadak, the high priest; and be strong, all you people of the land,' says the LORD, 'and work; for I *am* with you,' says the LORD of hosts. 5'*According to* the word that I covenanted with you when you came out of Egypt, so My Spirit remains among you; do not fear!'

6"For thus says the LORD of hosts: 'Once more (it *is* a little while) I will shake heaven and earth, the sea and dry land; 7and I will shake all nations, and they shall come to the Desire of All Nations,* and I will fill this temple with glory,' says the LORD of hosts. 8'The silver *is* Mine, and the gold *is* Mine,' says the LORD of hosts. 9'The glory of this latter temple shall be greater than the former,' says the LORD of hosts. 'And in this place I will give peace,' says the LORD of hosts."

10On the twenty-fourth *day* of the ninth *month,* in the second year of Darius, the word of the LORD came by Haggai the prophet, saying, 11"Thus says the LORD of hosts: 'Now, ask the priests *concerning the* law, saying, 12"If one carries holy meat in the fold of his garment, and with the edge he touches bread or stew, wine or oil, or any food, will it become holy?" ' "

Then the priests answered and said, "No."

13And Haggai said, "If *one who is* unclean *because* of a dead body touches any of these, will it be unclean?"

So the priests answered and said, "It shall be unclean."

14Then Haggai answered and said, "'So is this people, and so is this nation before Me,' says the LORD, 'and so is every work of their hands; and what they offer there is unclean.

15'And now, carefully consider from this day forward: from before stone was laid upon stone in the temple of the LORD— 16since those *days,* when *one* came to a heap of twenty ephahs, there were *but* ten; when *one* came to the wine vat to draw out fifty baths from the press, there were *but* twenty. 17I struck you with blight and mildew and hail in all the labors of your hands; yet you did not *turn* to Me,' says the LORD. 18'Consider now from this day forward, from the twenty-fourth day of the ninth month, from the day that the foundation of the LORD's temple was laid—consider it: 19Is the seed still in the barn? As yet the vine, the fig tree, the pomegranate, and the olive tree have not yielded *fruit.* But from this day I will bless *you.'* "

20And again the word of the LORD came to Haggai on the twenty-fourth day of the month, saying, 21"Speak to Zerubbabel, governor of Judah, saying:

'I will shake heaven and earth.
22   I will overthrow the throne of
      kingdoms;
   I will destroy the strength of
      the Gentile kingdoms.
   I will overthrow the chariots
   And those who ride in them;
   The horses and their riders
      shall come down,
   Every one by the sword of his
      brother.

23'In that day,' says the LORD of hosts, 'I will take you, Zerubbabel My servant, the son of Shealtiel,' says the LORD, 'and will make you like a signet *ring;* for I have chosen you,' says the LORD of hosts."

REVELATION 11:1-19

THEN I was given a reed like a measuring rod. And the angel stood,* saying, "Rise and measure the temple of God, the altar, and those who worship there. ²But leave out the court which is outside the temple, and do not measure it, for it has been given to the Gentiles. And they will tread the holy city underfoot *for* forty-two months. ³And I will give *power* to my two witnesses, and they will prophesy one thousand two hundred and sixty days, clothed in sackcloth."

⁴These are the two olive trees and the two lampstands standing before the God* of the earth. ⁵And if anyone wants to harm them, fire proceeds from their mouth and devours their enemies. And if anyone wants to harm them, he must be killed in this manner. ⁶These have power to shut heaven, so that no rain falls in the days of their prophecy; and they have power over waters to turn them to blood, and to strike the earth with all plagues, as often as they desire.

⁷When they finish their testimony, the beast that ascends out of the bottomless pit will make war against them, overcome them, and kill them. ⁸And their dead bodies *will lie* in the street of the great city which spiritually is called Sodom and Egypt, where also our* Lord was crucified. ⁹Then *those* from the peoples, tribes, tongues, and nations will see their dead bodies three-and-a-half days, and not allow* their dead bodies to be put into graves. ¹⁰And those who dwell on the earth will rejoice over them, make merry, and send gifts to one another, because these two prophets tormented those who dwell on the earth. ¹¹Now after the three-and-a-half

days the breath of life from God entered them, and they stood on their feet, and great fear fell on those who saw them. ¹²And they* heard a loud voice from heaven saying to them, "Come up here." And they ascended to heaven in a cloud, and their enemies saw them. ¹³In the same hour there was a great earthquake, and a tenth of the city fell. In the earthquake seven thousand people were killed, and the rest were afraid and gave glory to the God of heaven.

¹⁴The second woe is past. Behold, the third woe is coming quickly.

¹⁵Then the seventh angel sounded: And there were loud voices in heaven, saying, "The kingdoms* of this world have become *the kingdoms* of our Lord and of His Christ, and He shall reign forever and ever!" ¹⁶And the twenty-four elders who sat before God on their thrones fell on their faces and worshiped God, ¹⁷saying:

"We give You thanks, O Lord
    God Almighty,
The One who is and who was
    and who is to come,*
Because You have taken Your
    great power and reigned.
18 The nations were angry, and
    Your wrath has come,
And the time of the dead, that
    they should be judged,
And that You should reward
    Your servants the prophets
    and the saints,
And those who fear Your
    name, small and great,
And should destroy those
    who destroy the earth."

¹⁹Then the temple of God was opened in heaven, and the ark of His covenant* was seen in His temple. And there were lightnings, noises, thunderings, an earthquake, and great hail.

PSALM 139:1-24

For the Chief Musician. A Psalm of David.

O LORD, You have searched me and known *me.*
²You know my sitting down and my rising up;
You understand my thought afar off.

3 You comprehend my path and my lying down,
And are acquainted with all my ways.

4 For *there is* not a word on my tongue,
But behold, O LORD, You know it altogether.

5 You have hedged me behind and before,
And laid Your hand upon me.

6 *Such* knowledge *is* too wonderful for me;
It is high, I cannot *attain* it.

7 Where can I go from Your Spirit?
Or where can I flee from Your presence?

8 If I ascend into heaven, You *are* there;
If I make my bed in hell, behold, You *are there.*

9 *If* I take the wings of the morning,
And dwell in the uttermost parts of the sea,

10 Even there Your hand shall lead me,
And Your right hand shall hold me.

11 If I say, "Surely the darkness shall fall* on me,"
Even the night shall be light about me;

12 Indeed, the darkness shall not hide from You,
But the night shines as the day;
The darkness and the light *are* both alike *to You.*

13 For You formed my inward parts;
You covered me in my mother's womb.

14 I will praise You, for I am fearfully *and* wonderfully made;*
Marvelous are Your works,
And *that* my soul knows very well.

15 My frame was not hidden from You,
When I was made in secret,
And skillfully wrought in the lowest parts of the earth.

16 Your eyes saw my substance, being yet unformed.
And in Your book they all were written,
The days fashioned for me,
When *as yet there were* none of them.

17 How precious also are Your thoughts to me, O God!
How great is the sum of them!

18 *If* I should count them, they would be more in number than the sand;
When I awake, I am still with You.

19 Oh, that You would slay the wicked, O God!
Depart from me, therefore, you bloodthirsty men.

20 For they speak against You wickedly;
Your enemies take *Your name* in vain.*

21 Do I not hate them, O LORD, who hate You?
And do I not loathe those who rise up against You?

22 I hate them with perfect hatred;
I count them my enemies.

23 Search me, O God, and know my heart;

Try me, and know my
anxieties;
24 And see if *there is any* wicked
way in me,

And lead me in the way
everlasting.

PROVERBS FOR TODAY / 30:15-16

The leech has two daughters—Give and *Give! There are three* things that *are never satisfied, four never say, "Enough!": the grave,* * *the barren womb, the earth* that *is not satisfied with water—and the fire never says, "Enough!"*

DECEMBER 21

ZECHARIAH 1:1-21

In the eighth month of the second year of Darius, the word of the LORD came to Zechariah the son of Berechiah, the son of Iddo the prophet, saying, 2"The LORD has been very angry with your fathers. 3Therefore say to them, 'Thus says the LORD of hosts: "Return to Me," says the LORD of hosts, "and I will return to you," says the LORD of hosts. 4"Do not be like your fathers, to whom the former prophets preached, saying, 'Thus says the LORD of hosts: "Turn now from your evil ways and your evil deeds." ' But they did not hear nor heed Me," says the LORD.

5 "Your fathers, where *are* they?
    And the prophets, do they live
       forever?
6 Yet surely My words and My
       statutes,
    Which I commanded My
       servants the prophets,
    Did they not overtake your
       fathers?

"So they returned and said:

'Just as the LORD of hosts
    determined to do to us,

According to our ways and
    according to our deeds,
So He has dealt with us.' " ' "

7On the twenty-fourth day of the eleventh month, which is the month Shebat, in the second year of Darius, the word of the LORD came to Zechariah the son of Berechiah, the son of Iddo the prophet: 8I saw by night, and behold, a man riding on a red horse, and it stood among the myrtle trees in the hollow; and behind him *were* horses: red, sorrel, and white. 9Then I said, "My lord, what *are* these?" So the angel who talked with me said to me, "I will show you what they *are.*"

10And the man who stood among the myrtle trees answered and said, "These *are the ones* whom the LORD has sent to walk to and fro throughout the earth."

11So they answered the Angel of the LORD, who stood among the myrtle trees, and said, "We have walked to and fro throughout the earth, and behold, all the earth is resting quietly."

12Then the Angel of the LORD answered and said, "O LORD of hosts, how long will You not have mercy on Jerusalem and on the cities of Judah, against which You were angry these seventy years?"

¹³And the Lord answered the angel who talked to me, *with* good *and* comforting words. ¹⁴So the angel who spoke with me said to me, "Proclaim, saying, 'Thus says the Lord of hosts:

"I am zealous for Jerusalem
And for Zion with great zeal.
¹⁵ I am exceedingly angry with the nations at ease;
For I was a little angry,
And they helped—*but* with evil *intent.*"

¹⁶'Therefore thus says the Lord:

"I am returning to Jerusalem with mercy;
My house shall be built in it,"
says the Lord of hosts,
"And a *surveyor's* line shall be stretched out over Jerusalem." '

¹⁷"Again proclaim, saying, 'Thus says the Lord of hosts:

"My cities shall again spread out through prosperity;
The Lord will again comfort Zion,
And will again choose Jerusalem." ' "

¹⁸Then I raised my eyes and looked, and there *were* four horns. ¹⁹And I said to the angel who talked with me, "What *are* these?"

So he answered me, "These *are* the horns that have scattered Judah, Israel, and Jerusalem."

²⁰Then the Lord showed me four craftsmen. ²¹And I said, "What are these coming to do?"

So he said, "These *are* the horns that scattered Judah, so that no one could lift up his head; but the craftsmen* are coming to terrify them, to cast out the horns of the nations that lifted up *their* horn against the land of Judah to scatter it."

REVELATION 12:1–13:1a

Now a great sign appeared in heaven: a woman clothed with the sun, with the moon under her feet, and on her head a garland of twelve stars. ²Then being with child, she cried out in labor and in pain to give birth.

³And another sign appeared in heaven: behold, a great, fiery red dragon having seven heads and ten horns, and seven diadems on his heads. ⁴His tail drew a third of the stars of heaven and threw them to the earth. And the dragon stood before the woman who was ready to give birth, to devour her Child as soon as it was born. ⁵She bore a male Child who was to rule all nations with a rod of iron. And her Child was caught up to God and His throne. ⁶Then the woman fled into the wilderness, where she has a place prepared by God, that they should feed her there one thousand two hundred and sixty days.

⁷And war broke out in heaven: Michael and his angels fought with the dragon; and the dragon and his angels fought, ⁸but they did not prevail, nor was a place found for them* in heaven any longer. ⁹So the great dragon was cast out, that serpent of old, called the Devil and Satan, who deceives the whole world; he was cast to the earth, and his angels were cast out with him.

¹⁰Then I heard a loud voice saying in heaven, "Now salvation, and strength, and the kingdom of our God, and the power of His Christ have come, for the accuser of our brethren, who accused them before our God day and night, has been cast

down. ¹¹And they overcame him by the blood of the Lamb and by the word of their testimony, and they did not love their lives to the death. ¹²Therefore rejoice, O heavens, and you who dwell in them! Woe to the inhabitants of the earth and the sea! For the devil has come down to you, having great wrath, because he knows that he has a short time."

¹³Now when the dragon saw that he had been cast to the earth, he persecuted the woman who gave birth to the male *Child.* ¹⁴But the woman was given two wings of a great eagle, that she might fly into the wilderness to her place, where she is nourished for a time and times and half a time, from the presence of the serpent. ¹⁵So the serpent spewed water out of his mouth like a flood after the woman, that he might cause her to be carried away by the flood. ¹⁶But the earth helped the woman, and the earth opened its mouth and swallowed up the flood which the dragon had spewed out of his mouth. ¹⁷And the dragon was enraged with the woman, and he went to make war with the rest of her offspring, who keep the commandments of God and have the testimony of Jesus Christ.*

THEN I* stood on the sand of the sea.

PSALM 140:1-13

To the Chief Musician. A Psalm of David.

DELIVER me, O LORD, from evil men;
Preserve me from violent men,
2 Who plan evil things in *their* hearts;
They continually gather together *for* war.
3 They sharpen their tongues like a serpent;
The poison of asps *is* under their lips. Selah

4 Keep me, O LORD, from the hands of the wicked;
Preserve me from violent men,
Who have purposed to make my steps stumble.
5 The proud have hidden a snare for me, and cords;
They have spread a net by the wayside;
They have set traps for me.
Selah

6 I said to the LORD: "You *are* my God;
Hear the voice of my supplications, O LORD.
7 O GOD the Lord, the strength of my salvation,
You have covered my head in the day of battle.
8 Do not grant, O LORD, the desires of the wicked;
Do not further his *wicked* scheme,
Lest they be exalted. Selah

9 "*As for* the head of those who surround me,
Let the evil of their lips cover them;
10 Let burning coals fall upon them;
Let them be cast into the fire,
Into deep pits, that they rise not up again.
11 Let not a slanderer be established in the earth;
Let evil hunt the violent man to overthrow *him.*"

12 I know that the LORD will maintain
The cause of the afflicted,
And justice for the poor.
13 Surely the righteous shall give thanks to Your name;
The upright shall dwell in Your presence.

PROVERBS FOR TODAY / 30:17

The eye that mocks his father, and scorns obedience to his mother, the ravens of the valley will pick it out, and the young eagles will eat it.

DECEMBER 22

ZECHARIAH 2:1–3:10

THEN I raised my eyes and looked, and behold, a man with a measuring line in his hand. ²So I said, "Where are you going?"

And he said to me, "To measure Jerusalem, to see what *is* its width and what *is* its length."

³And there *was* the angel who talked with me, going out; and another angel was coming out to meet him, ⁴who said to him, "Run, speak to this young man, saying: 'Jerusalem shall be inhabited *as* towns without walls, because of the multitude of men and livestock in it. ⁵For I,' says the LORD, 'will be a wall of fire all around her, and I will be the glory in her midst.' "

⁶"Up, up! Flee from the land of the north," says the LORD; "for I have spread you abroad like the four winds of heaven," says the LORD. ⁷Up, Zion! Escape, you who dwell with the daughter of Babylon."

⁸For thus says the LORD of hosts: "He sent Me after glory, to the nations which plunder you; for he who touches you touches the apple of His eye. ⁹For surely I will shake My hand against them, and they shall become spoil for their servants. Then you will know that the LORD of hosts has sent Me.

¹⁰"Sing and rejoice, O daughter of Zion! For behold, I am coming and I will dwell in your midst," says the LORD. ¹¹"Many nations shall be joined to the LORD in that day, and they shall become My people. And I will dwell in your midst. Then you will know that the LORD of hosts has sent Me to you. ¹²And the LORD will take possession of Judah as His inheritance in the Holy Land, and will again choose Jerusalem. ¹³Be silent, all flesh, before the LORD, for He is aroused from His holy habitation!"

THEN he showed me Joshua the high priest standing before the Angel of the LORD, and Satan standing at his right hand to oppose him. ²And the LORD said to Satan, "The LORD rebuke you, Satan! The LORD who has chosen Jerusalem rebuke you! *Is* this not a brand plucked from the fire?"

³Now Joshua was clothed with filthy garments, and was standing before the Angel.

⁴Then He answered and spoke to those who stood before Him, saying, "Take away the filthy garments from him." And to him He said, "See, I have removed your iniquity from you, and I will clothe you with rich robes."

⁵And I said, "Let them put a clean turban on his head."

So they put a clean turban on his head, and they put the clothes on him. And the Angel of the LORD stood by.

⁶Then the Angel of the LORD admonished Joshua, saying, ⁷"Thus says the LORD of hosts:

'If you will walk in My ways,
And if you will keep My
command,
Then you shall also judge My
house,

And likewise have charge of
My courts;
I will give you places to walk
Among these who stand here.

8 'Hear, O Joshua, the high
priest,
You and your companions
who sit before you,
For they are a wondrous sign;
For behold, I am bringing
forth My Servant the
BRANCH.

9 For behold, the stone
That I have laid before Joshua:
Upon the stone *are* seven
eyes.
Behold, I will engrave its
inscription,'
Says the LORD of hosts,
'And I will remove the iniquity
of that land in one day.

10 In that day,' says the LORD of
hosts,
'Everyone will invite his
neighbor
Under his vine and under his
fig tree.' "

REVELATION 13:1b-18

A ND I saw a beast rising up out of
the sea, having seven heads
and ten horns,* and on his
horns ten crowns, and on his heads a
blasphemous name. ²Now the beast
which I saw was like a leopard, his feet
were like *the feet of* a bear, and his
mouth like the mouth of a lion. The
dragon gave him his power, his throne,
and great authority. ³And *I saw* one of
his heads as if it had been mortally
wounded, and his deadly wound was
healed. And all the world marveled
and followed the beast. ⁴So they worshiped the dragon who gave authority
to the beast; and they worshiped the
beast, saying, "Who *is* like the beast?
Who is able to make war with him?"
⁵And he was given a mouth speak-

ing great things and blasphemies, and
he was given authority to continue* for
forty-two months. ⁶Then he opened
his mouth in blasphemy against God,
to blaspheme His name, His tabernacle, and those who dwell in heaven. ⁷It
was granted to him to make war with
the saints and to overcome them. And
authority was given him over every
tribe,* tongue, and nation. ⁸All who
dwell on the earth will worship him,
whose names have not been written in
the Book of Life of the Lamb slain from
the foundation of the world.

⁹If anyone has an ear, let him hear.
¹⁰He who leads into captivity shall go
into captivity; he who kills with the
sword must be killed with the sword.
Here is the patience and the faith of the
saints.

¹¹Then I saw another beast coming
up out of the earth, and he had two
horns like a lamb and spoke like a
dragon. ¹²And he exercises all the authority of the first beast in his presence, and causes the earth and those
who dwell in it to worship the first
beast, whose deadly wound was
healed. ¹³He performs great signs, so
that he even makes fire come down
from heaven on the earth in the sight
of men. ¹⁴And he deceives those* who
dwell on the earth by those signs
which he was granted to do in the sight
of the beast, telling those who dwell on
the earth to make an image to the
beast who was wounded by the sword
and lived. ¹⁵He was granted *power* to
give breath to the image of the beast,
that the image of the beast should both
speak and cause as many as would not
worship the image of the beast to be
killed. ¹⁶He causes all, both small and
great, rich and poor, free and slave, to
receive a mark on their right hand or
on their foreheads, ¹⁷and that no one
may buy or sell except one who has
the mark or* the name of the beast, or
the number of his name.

¹⁸Here is wisdom. Let him who has

understanding calculate the number of the beast, for it is the number of a man: His number *is* 666.

PSALM 141:1-10

A Psalm of David.

Lord, I cry out to You; Make haste to me! Give ear to my voice when I cry out to You.
2 Let my prayer be set before You *as* incense, The lifting up of my hands *as* the evening sacrifice.

3 Set a guard, O Lord, over my mouth; Keep watch over the door of my lips.
4 Do not incline my heart to any evil thing, To practice wicked works With men who work iniquity; And do not let me eat of their delicacies.

5 Let the righteous strike me;

It shall be a kindness. And let him rebuke me; *It shall be* as excellent oil; Let my head not refuse it. For still my prayer *is* against the deeds of the wicked.
6 Their judges are overthrown by the sides of the cliff, And they hear my words, for they are sweet.
7 Our bones are scattered at the mouth of the grave, As when one plows and breaks up the earth.

8 But my eyes *are* upon You, O God the Lord; In You I take refuge; Do not leave my soul destitute.
9 Keep me from the snares they have laid for me, And from the traps of the workers of iniquity.
10 Let the wicked fall into their own nets, While I escape safely.

PROVERBS FOR TODAY/ 30:18-20

There are three things which *are too wonderful for me, yes, four* which *I do not understand: the way of an eagle in the air, the way of a serpent on a rock, the way of a ship in the midst of the sea, and the way of a man with a virgin.* □ *This* is *the way of an adulterous woman: She eats and wipes her mouth, and says, "I have done no wickedness."*

DECEMBER 23

ZECHARIAH 4:1–5:11

Now the angel who talked with me came back and wakened me, as a man who is wakened out of his sleep. 2And he said to me, "What do you see?"

So I said, "I am looking, and there *is* a lampstand of solid gold with a bowl on top of it, and on the *stand* seven lamps with seven pipes to the seven lamps. 3Two olive trees *are* by it, one at the right of the bowl and the other at its left." 4So I answered and spoke to the angel who talked with me, saying, "What *are* these, my lord?"

⁵Then the angel who talked with me answered and said to me, "Do you not know what these are?"

And I said, "No, my lord."

⁶So he answered and said to me:

> "This *is* the word of the LORD to
>   Zerubbabel:
> 'Not by might nor by power,
>   but by My Spirit,'
> Says the LORD of hosts.
> ⁷ 'Who *are* you, O great
>   mountain?
> Before Zerubbabel *you shall
>   become* a plain!
> And he shall bring forth the
>   capstone
> With shouts of
> "Grace, grace to it!" ' "

⁸Moreover the word of the LORD came to me, saying:

> ⁹ "The hands of Zerubbabel
>   Have laid the foundation of
>   this temple;*
> His hands shall also finish *it.*
> Then you will know
> That the LORD of hosts has
>   sent Me to you.
> ¹⁰ For who has despised the day
>   of small things?
> For these seven rejoice to see
> The plumb line in the hand of
>   Zerubbabel.
> They are the eyes of the LORD,
> Which scan to and fro
>   throughout the whole
>   earth."

¹¹Then I answered and said to him, "What *are* these two olive trees—at the right of the lampstand and at its left?" ¹²And I further answered and said to him, "What *are these* two olive branches that *drip* into the receptacles* of the two gold pipes from which the golden *oil* drains?"

¹³Then he answered me and said, "Do you not know what these *are?*"

And I said, "No, my lord."

¹⁴So he said, "These *are* the two anointed ones, who stand beside the Lord of the whole earth."

THEN I turned and raised my eyes, and saw there a flying scroll.

²And he said to me, "What do you see?"

So I answered, "I see a flying scroll. Its length *is* twenty cubits and its width ten cubits."

³Then he said to me, "This *is* the curse that goes out over the face of the whole earth: 'Every thief shall be expelled,' according *to* this side of *the scroll;* and, 'Every perjurer shall be expelled,' according *to* that side of it."

> ⁴ "I will send out *the curse,*" says
>   the LORD of hosts;
> "It shall enter the house of the
>   thief
> And the house of the one who
>   swears falsely by My name.
> It shall remain in the midst of
>   his house
> And consume it, with its
>   timber and stones."

⁵Then the angel who talked with me came out and said to me, "Lift your eyes now, and see what this *is* that goes forth."

⁶So I asked, "What *is* it?" And he said, "It *is* a basket* that is going forth."

He also said, "This *is* their resemblance throughout the earth: ⁷Here *is* a lead disc lifted up, and this *is* a woman sitting inside the basket"; ⁸then he said, "This *is* Wickedness!" And he thrust her down into the basket, and threw the lead cover* over its mouth. ⁹Then I raised my eyes and looked, and there *were* two women, coming with the wind in their wings; for they had wings like the wings of a stork, and they lifted up the basket between earth and heaven.

¹⁰So I said to the angel who talked with me, "Where are they carrying the basket?"

¹¹And he said to me, "To build a house for it in the land of Shinar;* when it is ready, *the basket* will be set there on its base."

REVELATION 14:1-20

THEN I looked, and behold, a* Lamb standing on Mount Zion, and with Him one hundred *and* forty-four thousand, having* His Father's name written on their foreheads. ²And I heard a voice from heaven, like the voice of many waters, and like the voice of loud thunder. And I heard the sound of harpists playing their harps. ³They sang as it were a new song before the throne, before the four living creatures, and the elders; and no one could learn that song except the hundred *and* forty-four thousand who were redeemed from the earth. ⁴These are the ones who were not defiled with women, for they are virgins. These are the ones who follow the Lamb wherever He goes. These were redeemed* from *among* men, *being* firstfruits to God and to the Lamb. ⁵And in their mouth was found no deceit,* for they are without fault before the throne of God.*

⁶Then I saw another angel flying in the midst of heaven, having the everlasting gospel to preach to those who dwell on the earth—to every nation, tribe, tongue, and people— ⁷saying with a loud voice, "Fear God and give glory to Him, for the hour of His judgment has come; and worship Him who made heaven and earth, the sea and springs of water."

⁸And another angel followed, saying, "Babylon* is fallen, is fallen, that great city, because she has made all nations drink of the wine of the wrath of her fornication."

⁹Then a third angel followed them, saying with a loud voice, "If anyone worships the beast and his image, and receives *his* mark on his forehead or on his hand, ¹⁰he himself shall also drink of the wine of the wrath of God, which is poured out full strength into the cup of His indignation. He shall be tormented with fire and brimstone in the presence of the holy angels and in the presence of the Lamb. ¹¹And the smoke of their torment ascends forever and ever; and they have no rest day or night, who worship the beast and his image, and whoever receives the mark of his name."

¹²Here is the patience of the saints; here *are* those* who keep the commandments of God and the faith of Jesus.

¹³Then I heard a voice from heaven saying to me,* "Write: 'Blessed *are* the dead who die in the Lord from now on.' "

"Yes," says the Spirit, "that they may rest from their labors, and their works follow them."

¹⁴Then I looked, and behold, a white cloud, and on the cloud sat *One* like the Son of Man, having on His head a golden crown, and in His hand a sharp sickle. ¹⁵And another angel came out of the temple, crying with a loud voice to Him who sat on the cloud, "Thrust in Your sickle and reap, for the time has come for You* to reap, for the harvest of the earth is ripe." ¹⁶So He who sat on the cloud thrust in His sickle on the earth, and the earth was reaped.

¹⁷Then another angel came out of the temple which is in heaven, he also having a sharp sickle.

¹⁸And another angel came out from the altar, who had power over fire, and he cried with a loud cry to him who had the sharp sickle, saying, "Thrust in your sharp sickle and gather the clusters of the vine of the earth, for her grapes are fully ripe." ¹⁹So the angel

thrust his sickle into the earth and gathered the vine of the earth, and threw *it* into the great winepress of the wrath of God. 20And the winepress was trampled outside the city, and blood came out of the winepress, up to the horses' bridles, for one thousand six hundred furlongs.

PSALM 142:1-7

A Contemplation* of David. A Prayer when he was in the cave.

I CRY out to the LORD with my voice; With my voice to the LORD I make my supplication.
2 I pour out my complaint before Him;
I declare before Him my trouble.

3 When my spirit was overwhelmed within me,
Then You knew my path.
In the way in which I walk

They have secretly set a snare for me.
4 Look on *my* right hand and see,
For *there is* no one who acknowledges me;
Refuge has failed me;
No one cares for my soul.

5 I cried out to You, O LORD:
I said, "You *are* my refuge,
My portion in the land of the living.
6 Attend to my cry,
For I am brought very low;
Deliver me from my persecutors,
For they are stronger than I.
7 Bring my soul out of prison,
That I may praise Your name;
The righteous shall surround me,
For You shall deal bountifully with me."

PROVERBS FOR TODAY/ 30:21-23

For three things *the earth is perturbed, yes, for four it cannot bear up: for a servant when he reigns, a fool when he is filled with food, a hateful* woman *when she is married, and a maidservant who succeeds her mistress.*

DECEMBER 24

ZECHARIAH 6:1–7:14

THEN I turned and raised my eyes and looked, and behold, four chariots *were* coming from between two mountains, and the mountains *were* mountains of bronze. 2With the first chariot *were* red horses, with the second chariot black horses, 3with the third chariot white horses, and with the fourth chariot dappled horses—strong *steeds*. 4Then I answered and said to the angel who

talked with me, "What *are* these, my lord?"
5And the angel answered and said to me, "These *are* four spirits of heaven, who go out from *their* station before the Lord of all the earth. 6The one with the black horses is going to the north country, the white are going after them, and the dappled are going toward the south country." 7Then the strong *steeds* went out, eager to go, that they might walk to and

fro throughout the earth. And He said, "Go, walk to and fro throughout the earth." So they walked to and fro throughout the earth. 8And He called to me, and spoke to me, saying, "See, those who go toward the north country have given rest to My Spirit in the north country."

9Then the word of the LORD came to me, saying: 10"Receive *the gift* from the captives—from Heldai, Tobijah, and Jedaiah, who have come from Babylon—and go the same day and enter the house of Josiah the son of Zephaniah. 11Take the silver and gold, make an elaborate crown, and set *it* on the head of Joshua the son of Jehozadak, the high priest. 12Then speak to him, saying, 'Thus says the LORD of hosts, saying:

> "Behold, the Man whose name
> *is* the BRANCH!
> From His place He shall
> branch out,
> And He shall build the temple
> of the LORD;
> 13 Yes, He shall build the temple
> of the LORD.
> He shall bear the glory,
> And shall sit and rule on His
> throne;
> So He shall be a priest on His
> throne,
> And the counsel of peace shall
> be between them both." '

14"Now the elaborate crown shall be for a memorial in the temple of the LORD for Helem,* Tobijah, Jedaiah, and Hen the son of Zephaniah. 15Even those from afar shall come and build the temple of the LORD. Then you shall know that the LORD of hosts has sent Me to you. And *this* shall come to pass if you diligently obey the voice of the LORD your God."

Now in the fourth year of King Darius it came to pass *that* the word of the LORD came to Zechariah, on the fourth day of the ninth month, Chislev, 2when *the people** sent Sherezer,* with Regem-Melech and his men, *to* the house of God,* to pray before the LORD, 3*and* to ask the priests who *were* in the house of the LORD of hosts, and the prophets, saying, "Should I weep in the fifth month and fast as I have done for so many years?"

4Then the word of the LORD of hosts came to me, saying, 5"Say to all the people of the land, and to the priests: 'When you fasted and mourned in the fifth and seventh *months* during those seventy years, did you really fast for Me—for Me? 6When you eat and when you drink, do you not eat and drink *for yourselves?* 7*Should you* not *have obeyed* the words which the LORD proclaimed through the former prophets when Jerusalem and the cities around it were inhabited and prosperous, and the South* and the Lowland were inhabited?' "

8Then the word of the LORD came to Zechariah, saying, 9"Thus says the LORD of hosts:

> 'Execute true justice,
> Show mercy and compassion
> Everyone to his brother.
> 10 Do not oppress the widow or
> the fatherless,
> The alien or the poor.
> Let none of you plan evil in
> his heart
> Against his brother.'

11But they refused to heed, shrugged their shoulders, and stopped their ears so that they could not hear. 12Yes, they made their hearts like flint, refusing to hear the law and the words which the LORD of hosts had sent by His Spirit through the former prophets. Thus great wrath came from the LORD of hosts. 13Therefore it happened, *that* just as He proclaimed and they would not hear, so they called out and I would not listen," says the LORD of hosts. [14]"But I scattered them with a whirlwind among all the nations which they had not known. Thus the land became desolate after them, so that no one passed through or returned; for they made the pleasant land desolate."

REVELATION 15:1-8

THEN I saw another sign in heaven, great and marvelous: seven angels having the seven last plagues, for in them the wrath of God is complete.

[2]And I saw *something* like a sea of glass mingled with fire, and those who have the victory over the beast, over his image and over his mark* *and* over the number of his name, standing on the sea of glass, having harps of God. [3]They sing the song of Moses, the servant of God, and the song of the Lamb, saying:

> "Great and marvelous *are* Your works,
> Lord God Almighty!
> Just and true *are* Your ways,
> O King of the saints!*
> [4] Who shall not fear You,
> O Lord, and glorify Your name?
> For *You* alone *are* holy.
> For all nations shall come and worship before You,
> For Your judgments have been manifested."

[5]After these things I looked, and behold,* the temple of the tabernacle of the testimony in heaven was opened. [6]And out of the temple came the seven angels having the seven plagues, clothed in pure bright linen, and having their chests girded with golden bands. [7]Then one of the four living creatures gave to the seven angels seven golden bowls full of the wrath of God who lives forever and ever. [8]The temple was filled with smoke from the glory of God and from His power, and no one was able to enter the temple till the seven plagues of the seven angels were completed.

PSALM 143:1-12

A Psalm of David.

HEAR my prayer, O LORD,
Give ear to my supplications!
In Your faithfulness answer me,
And in Your righteousness.
[2] Do not enter into judgment with Your servant,
For in Your sight no one living is righteous.

[3] For the enemy has persecuted my soul;
He has crushed my life to the ground;
He has made me dwell in darkness,
Like those who have long been dead.
[4] Therefore my spirit is overwhelmed within me;
My heart within me is distressed.

[5] I remember the days of old;
I meditate on all Your works;
I muse on the work of Your hands.
[6] I spread out my hands to You;
My soul *longs* for You like a thirsty land.   Selah

[7] Answer me speedily, O LORD;
My spirit fails!
Do not hide Your face from me,
Lest I be like those who go down into the pit.
[8] Cause me to hear Your lovingkindness in the morning,

For in You do I trust;
Cause me to know the way in
   which I should walk,
For I lift up my soul to You.

9 Deliver me, O Lord, from my
   enemies;
In You I take shelter.*
10 Teach me to do Your will,
For You *are* my God;
Your Spirit *is* good.

Lead me in the land of
   uprightness.
11 Revive me, O Lord, for Your
   name's sake!
For Your righteousness' sake
   bring my soul out of trouble.
12 In Your mercy cut off my
   enemies,
And destroy all those who
   afflict my soul;
For I *am* Your servant.

PROVERBS FOR TODAY / 30:24-28

There are four things which *are little on the earth, but they* are *exceedingly wise: the ants* are *a people not strong, yet they prepare their food in the summer; the rock badgers* * are *a feeble folk, yet they make their homes in the crags; the locusts have no king, yet they all advance in ranks; the spider* * *skillfully grasps with its hands, and it is in kings' palaces.*

DECEMBER 25

ZECHARIAH 8:1-23

A GAIN the word of the Lord of hosts came, saying, 2"Thus says the Lord of hosts:

'I am zealous for Zion with
   great zeal;
With great fervor I am
   zealous for her.'

3"Thus says the Lord:

'I will return to Zion,
And dwell in the midst of
   Jerusalem.
Jerusalem shall be called the
   City of Truth,
The Mountain of the Lord of
   hosts,
The Holy Mountain.'

4"Thus says the Lord of hosts:

'Old men and old women shall
   again sit
In the streets of Jerusalem,
Each one with his staff in his
   hand
Because of great age.
5 The streets of the city
Shall be full of boys and girls
Playing in its streets.'

6"Thus says the Lord of hosts:

'If it is marvelous in the eyes
   of the remnant of this
   people in these days,
Will it also be marvelous in
   My eyes?'
Says the Lord of hosts.

7"Thus says the Lord of hosts:

'Behold, I will save My people
    from the land of the east
And from the land of the west;
8   I will bring them *back,*
And they shall dwell in the
    midst of Jerusalem.
They shall be My people
And I will be their God,
In truth and righteousness.'

9"Thus says the Lord of hosts:

'Let your hands be strong,
You who have been hearing in
    these days
These words by the mouth of
    the prophets,
Who *spoke* in the day the
    foundation was laid
For the house of the Lord of
    hosts,
That the temple might be
    built.
10 For before these days
There were no wages for man
    nor any hire for beast;
There was no peace from the
    enemy for whoever went
    out or came in;
For I set all men, everyone,
    against his neighbor.

11But now I *will* not *treat* the remnant
of this people as in the former days,'
says the Lord of hosts.

12 'For the seed *shall be*
    prosperous,
The vine shall give its fruit,
The ground shall give her
    increase,
And the heavens shall give
    their dew—
I will cause the remnant of
    this people
To possess all these.
13 And it shall come to pass

That just as you were a curse
    among the nations,
O house of Judah and house
    of Israel,
So I will save you, and you
    shall be a blessing.
Do not fear,
Let your hands be strong.'

14"For thus says the Lord of hosts:

'Just as I determined to punish
    you
When your fathers provoked
    Me to wrath,'
Says the Lord of hosts,
'And I would not relent,
15 So again in these days
I am determined to do good
To Jerusalem and to the
    house of Judah.
Do not fear.
16 These *are* the things you shall
    do:
Speak each man the truth to
    his neighbor;
Give judgment in your gates
    for truth, justice, and peace;
17 Let none of you think evil in
    your* heart against your
    neighbor;
And do not love a false oath.
For all these *are things* that I
    hate,'
Says the Lord."

18Then the word of the Lord of hosts
came to me, saying, 19"Thus says the
Lord of hosts:

'The fast of the fourth *month,*
The fast of the fifth,
The fast of the seventh,
And the fast of the tenth,
Shall be joy and gladness and
    cheerful feasts
For the house of Judah.
Therefore love truth and
    peace.'

20"Thus says the LORD of hosts:

'Peoples shall yet come,
Inhabitants of many cities;
21 The inhabitants of one *city*
shall go to another, saying,
"Let us continue to go and pray
before the LORD,
And seek the LORD of hosts.
I myself will go also."
22 Yes, many peoples and strong
nations
Shall come to seek the LORD of
hosts in Jerusalem,
And to pray before the LORD.'

23"Thus says the LORD of hosts: 'In those days ten men from every language of the nations shall grasp the sleeve of a Jewish man, saying, "Let us go with you, for we have heard *that* God *is* with you." ' "

REVELATION 16:1-21

THEN I heard a loud voice from the temple saying to the seven angels, "Go and pour out the bowls* of the wrath of God on the earth."
²So the first went and poured out his bowl upon the earth, and a foul and loathsome sore came upon the men who had the mark of the beast and those who worshiped his image.
³Then the second angel poured out his bowl on the sea, and it became blood as of a dead *man;* and every living creature in the sea died.
⁴Then the third angel poured out his bowl on the rivers and springs of water, and they became blood. ⁵And I heard the angel of the waters saying:

"You are righteous, O Lord,*
The One who is and who was
and who is to be,*
Because You have judged
these things.

6 For they have shed the blood
of saints and prophets,
And You have given them
blood to drink.
For* it is their just due."

⁷And I heard another from* the altar saying, "Even so, Lord God Almighty, true and righteous *are* Your judgments."

⁸Then the fourth angel poured out his bowl on the sun, and power was given to him to scorch men with fire. ⁹And men were scorched with great heat, and they blasphemed the name of God who has power over these plagues; and they did not repent and give Him glory.

¹⁰Then the fifth angel poured out his bowl on the throne of the beast, and his kingdom became full of darkness; and they gnawed their tongues because of the pain. ¹¹They blasphemed the God of heaven because of their pains and their sores, and did not repent of their deeds.

¹²Then the sixth angel poured out his bowl on the great river Euphrates, and its water was dried up, so that the way of the kings from the east might be prepared. ¹³And I saw three unclean spirits like frogs *coming* out of the mouth of the dragon, out of the mouth of the beast, and out of the mouth of the false prophet. ¹⁴For they are spirits of demons, performing signs, *which* go out to the kings of the earth and* of the whole world, to gather them to the battle of that great day of God Almighty.

¹⁵"Behold, I am coming as a thief. Blessed *is* he who watches, and keeps his garments, lest he walk naked and they see his shame."

¹⁶And they gathered them together to the place called in Hebrew, Armageddon.*

¹⁷Then the seventh angel poured out his bowl into the air, and a loud voice came out of the temple of

heaven, from the throne, saying, "It is done!" 18And there were noises and thunderings and lightnings; and there was a great earthquake, such a mighty and great earthquake as had not occurred since men were on the earth. 19Now the great city was divided into three parts, and the cities of the nations fell. And great Babylon was remembered before God, to give her the cup of the wine of the fierceness of His wrath. 20Then every island fled away, and the mountains were not found. 21And great hail from heaven fell upon men, *each hailstone* about the weight of a talent. Men blasphemed God because of the plague of the hail, since that plague was exceedingly great.

PSALM 144:1-15

A Psalm of David.

B LESSED *be* the LORD my Rock,
Who trains my hands for war,
And my fingers for battle—
2 My lovingkindness and my
fortress,
My high tower and my
deliverer,
My shield and *the One* in
whom I take refuge,
Who subdues my people*
under me.

3 LORD, what *is* man, that You
take knowledge of him?
Or the son of man, that You
are mindful of him?
4 Man is like a breath;
His days *are* like a passing
shadow.

5 Bow down Your heavens,
O LORD, and come down;
Touch the mountains, and
they shall smoke.
6 Flash forth lightning and
scatter them;

Shoot out Your arrows and
destroy them.
7 Stretch out Your hand from
above;
Rescue me and deliver me out
of great waters,
From the hand of foreigners,
8 Whose mouth speaks lying
words,
And whose right hand *is* a
right hand of falsehood.

9 I will sing a new song to You,
O God;
On a harp of ten strings I will
sing praises to You,
10 *The One* who gives salvation
to kings,
Who delivers David His
servant
From the deadly sword.

11 Rescue me and deliver me
from the hand of foreigners,
Whose mouth speaks lying
words,
And whose right hand *is* a
right hand of falsehood—
12 That our sons *may be* as
plants grown up in their
youth;
That our daughters *may be* as
pillars,
Sculptured in palace style;
13 *That* our barns *may be* full,
Supplying all kinds of produce;
That our sheep may bring
forth thousands
And ten thousands in our
fields;
14 *That* our oxen *may be*
well-laden;
That there be no breaking in
or going out;
That there be no outcry in our
streets.
15 Happy *are* the people who are
in such a state;
Happy *are* the people whose
God *is* the LORD!

PROVERBS FOR TODAY/ 30:29-31

There are three things which *are majestic in pace, yes, four* which *are stately in walk: a lion,* which is *mighty among beasts and does not turn away from any; a greyhound,* * *a male goat also, and a king* whose *troops* are *with him.* *

DECEMBER 26

ZECHARIAH 9:1-17

THE burden* of the word of the LORD
Against the land of Hadrach,
And Damascus its resting place
(For the eyes of men
And all the tribes of Israel
Are on the LORD);

2   Also *against* Hamath, *which borders on it,*
And *against* Tyre and Sidon,
though they are very wise.

3   For Tyre built herself a tower,
Heaped up silver like the dust,
And gold like the mire of the streets.

4   Behold, the LORD will cast her out;
He will destroy her power in the sea,
And she will be devoured by fire.

5   Ashkelon shall see *it* and fear;
Gaza also shall be very sorrowful;
And Ekron, for He dried up her expectation.
The king shall perish from Gaza,
And Ashkelon shall not be inhabited.

6   "A mixed race shall settle in Ashdod,

And I will cut off the pride of the Philistines.
7   I will take away the blood from his mouth,
And the abominations from between his teeth.
But he who remains, even he *shall be* for our God,
And shall be like a leader in Judah,
And Ekron like a Jebusite.
8   I will camp around My house Because of the army,
Because of him who passes by and him who returns.
No more shall an oppressor pass through them,
For now I have seen with My eyes.

9   "Rejoice greatly, O daughter of Zion!
Shout, O daughter of Jerusalem!
Behold, your King is coming to you;
He *is* just and having salvation,
Lowly and riding on a donkey,
A colt, the foal of a donkey.
10   I will cut off the chariot from Ephraim
And the horse from Jerusalem;
The battle bow shall be cut off.
He shall speak peace to the nations;
His dominion *shall be* 'from sea to sea,

And from the River to the
ends of the earth.'*

11 "As for you also,
Because of the blood of your
covenant,
I will set your prisoners free
from the waterless pit.
12 Return to the stronghold,
You prisoners of hope.
Even today I declare
That I will restore double to
you.
13 For I have bent Judah, My
bow,
Fitted the bow with Ephraim,
And raised up your sons,
O Zion,
Against your sons, O Greece,
And made you like the sword
of a mighty man."

14 Then the LORD will be seen
over them,
And His arrow will go forth
like lightning.
The Lord GOD will blow the
trumpet,
And go with whirlwinds from
the south.
15 The LORD of hosts will defend
them;
They shall devour and subdue
with slingstones.
They shall drink *and* roar as if
with wine;
They shall be filled *with blood*
like basins,
Like the corners of the altar.
16 The LORD their God will save
them in that day,
As the flock of His people.
For they *shall be like* the
jewels of a crown,
Lifted like a banner over His
land—
17 For how great is its* goodness
And how great its* beauty!
Grain shall make the young
men thrive,

And new wine the young
women.

REVELATION 17:1-18

THEN one of the seven angels who
had the seven bowls came and
talked with me, saying to me,*
"Come, I will show you the judgment
of the great harlot who sits on many
waters, ²with whom the kings of the
earth committed fornication, and the
inhabitants of the earth were made
drunk with the wine of her fornication."

³So he carried me away in the Spirit
into the wilderness. And I saw a
woman sitting on a scarlet beast *which
was* full of names of blasphemy, having
seven heads and ten horns. ⁴The
woman was arrayed in purple and scarlet, and adorned with gold and precious stones and pearls, having in her
hand a golden cup full of abominations
and the filthiness of her fornication.*
⁵And on her forehead a name *was* written:

MYSTERY,
BABYLON THE GREAT,
THE MOTHER OF HARLOTS
AND OF THE ABOMINATIONS
OF THE EARTH.

⁶I saw the woman, drunk with the
blood of the saints and with the blood
of the martyrs of Jesus. And when I
saw her, I marveled with great amazement.

⁷But the angel said to me, "Why did
you marvel? I will tell you the mystery
of the woman and of the beast that carries her, which has the seven heads
and the ten horns. ⁸The beast that you
saw was, and is not, and will ascend out
of the bottomless pit and go to perdition. And those who dwell on the earth
will marvel, whose names are not written in the Book of Life from the foundation of the world, when they see the
beast that was, and is not, and yet is.*

9"Here *is* the mind which has wisdom: The seven heads are seven mountains on which the woman sits. 10There are also seven kings. Five have fallen, one is, *and* the other has not yet come. And when he comes, he must continue a short time. 11The beast that was, and is not, is himself also the eighth, and is of the seven, and is going to perdition.

12"The ten horns which you saw are ten kings who have received no kingdom as yet, but they receive authority for one hour as kings with the beast. 13These are of one mind, and they will give their power and authority to the beast. 14These will make war with the Lamb, and the Lamb will overcome them, for He is Lord of lords and King of kings; and those *who are* with Him *are* called, chosen, and faithful."

15Then he said to me, "The waters which you saw, where the harlot sits, are peoples, multitudes, nations, and tongues. 16And the ten horns which you saw on* the beast, these will hate the harlot, make her desolate and naked, eat her flesh and burn her with fire. 17For God has put it into their hearts to fulfill His purpose, to be of one mind, and to give their kingdom to the beast, until the words of God are fulfilled. 18And the woman whom you saw is that great city which reigns over the kings of the earth."

PSALM 145:1-21

A Praise of David.

I WILL extol You, my God, O King; And I will bless Your name forever and ever.
2 Every day I will bless You, And I will praise Your name forever and ever.
3 Great *is* the LORD, and greatly to be praised; And His greatness *is* unsearchable.

4 One generation shall praise Your works to another, And shall declare Your mighty acts.
5 I* will meditate on the glorious splendor of Your majesty, And on Your wondrous works.*
6 *Men* shall speak of the might of Your awesome acts, And I will declare Your greatness.
7 They shall utter the memory of Your great goodness, And shall sing of Your righteousness.

8 The LORD *is* gracious and full of compassion, Slow to anger and great in mercy.
9 The LORD *is* good to all, And His tender mercies *are* over all His works.

10 All Your works shall praise You, O LORD, And Your saints shall bless You.
11 They shall speak of the glory of Your kingdom, And talk of Your power,
12 To make known to the sons of men His mighty acts, And the glorious majesty of His kingdom.
13 Your kingdom *is* an everlasting kingdom, And Your dominion *endures* throughout all generations.*

14 The LORD upholds all who fall, And raises up all *who are* bowed down.
15 The eyes of all look expectantly to You, And You give them their food in due season.
16 You open Your hand

And satisfy the desire of
every living thing.

17 The LORD *is* righteous in all
His ways,
Gracious in all His works.
18 The LORD *is* near to all who
call upon Him,
To all who call upon Him in
truth.
19 He will fulfill the desire of
those who fear Him;

He also will hear their cry and
save them.
20 The LORD preserves all who
love Him,
But all the wicked He will
destroy.
21 My mouth shall speak the
praise of the LORD,
And all flesh shall bless His
holy name
Forever and ever.

PROVERBS FOR TODAY/ 30:32

If you have been foolish in exalting yourself, or if you have devised evil, put your
hand on your *mouth.*

DECEMBER 27

ZECHARIAH 10:1–11:17

Ask the LORD for rain
In the time of the latter rain.*
The LORD will make flashing
clouds;
He will give them showers of
rain,
Grass in the field for
everyone.

2 For the idols* speak delusion;
The diviners envision lies,
And tell false dreams;
They comfort in vain.
Therefore *the people* wend
their way like sheep;
They are in trouble because
there is no shepherd.

3 "My anger is kindled against
the shepherds,
And I will punish the
goatherds.

For the LORD of hosts will visit
His flock,
The house of Judah,
And will make them as His
royal horse in the battle.
4 From him comes the
cornerstone,
From him the tent peg,
From him the battle bow,
From him every ruler*
together.
5 They shall be like mighty
men,
Who tread down *their enemies*
In the mire of the streets in
the battle.
They shall fight because the
LORD is with them,
And the riders on horses shall
be put to shame.

6 "I will strengthen the house of
Judah,
And I will save the house of
Joseph.

I will bring them back,
Because I have mercy on
them.
They shall be as though I had
not cast them aside;
For I *am* the Lord their God,
And I will hear them.
7 *Those of* Ephraim shall be like
a mighty man,
And their heart shall rejoice
as if with wine.
Yes, their children shall see *it*
and be glad;
Their heart shall rejoice in
the Lord.
8 I will whistle for them and
gather them,
For I will redeem them;
And they shall increase as
they once increased.

9 "I will sow them among the
peoples,
And they shall remember Me
in far countries;
They shall live, together with
their children,
And they shall return.
10 I will also bring them back
from the land of Egypt,
And gather them from
Assyria.
I will bring them into the land
of Gilead and Lebanon,
Until no *more room* is found
for them.
11 He shall pass through the sea
with affliction,
And strike the waves of the
sea:
All the depths of the River*
shall dry up.
Then the pride of Assyria
shall be brought down,
And the scepter of Egypt shall
depart.

12 "So I will strengthen them in
the Lord,

And they shall walk up and
down in His name,"
Says the Lord.

Open your doors, O Lebanon,
That fire may devour your
cedars.
2 Wail, O cypress, for the cedar
has fallen,
Because the mighty *trees* are
ruined.
Wail, O oaks of Bashan,
For the thick forest has come
down.
3 *There is* the sound of wailing
shepherds!
For their glory is in ruins.
There is the sound of roaring
lions!
For the pride* of the Jordan is
in ruins.

4Thus says the Lord my God,
"Feed the flock for slaughter, 5whose
owners slaughter them and feel no
guilt; those who sell them say,
'Blessed be the Lord, for I am rich';
and their shepherds do not pity
them. 6For I will no longer pity the
inhabitants of the land," says the
Lord. "But indeed I will give everyone into his neighbor's hand and into
the hand of his king. They shall attack the land, and I will not deliver
them from their hand."

7So I fed the flock for slaughter, in
particular the poor of the flock.* I
took for myself two staffs: the one I
called Beauty,* and the other I called
Bonds;* and I fed the flock. 8I dismissed the three shepherds in one
month. My soul loathed them, and
their soul also abhorred me. 9Then I
said, "I will not feed you. Let what is
dying die, and what is perishing perish. Let those that are left eat each
other's flesh." 10And I took my staff,
Beauty, and cut it in two, that I might
break the covenant which I had made
with all the peoples. 11So it was bro-

ken on that day. Thus the poor* of the flock, who were watching me, knew that it *was* the word of the LORD. [12]Then I said to them, "If it is agreeable to you, give *me* my wages; and if not, refrain." So they weighed out for my wages thirty *pieces* of silver.

[13]And the LORD said to me, "Throw it to the potter"—that princely price they set on me. So I took the thirty *pieces* of silver and threw them into the house of the LORD for the potter. [14]Then I cut in two my other staff, Bonds, that I might break the brotherhood between Judah and Israel.

[15]And the LORD said to me, "Next, take for yourself the implements of a foolish shepherd. [16]For indeed I will raise up a shepherd in the land *who* will not care for those who are cut off, nor seek the young, nor heal those that are broken, nor feed those that still stand. But he will eat the flesh of the fat and tear their hooves in pieces.

[17]   "Woe to the worthless
            shepherd,
        Who leaves the flock!
        A sword *shall be* against his
            arm
        And against his right eye;
        His arm shall completely
            wither,
        And his right eye shall be
            totally blinded."

REVELATION 18:1-24

AFTER these things I saw another angel coming down from heaven, having great authority, and the earth was illuminated with his glory. [2]And he cried mightily* with a loud voice, saying, "Babylon the great is fallen, is fallen, and has become a dwelling place of demons, a prison for every foul spirit, and a cage for every unclean and hated bird! [3]For all the nations have drunk of the wine of the wrath of her fornication, the kings of the earth have committed fornication with her, and the merchants of the earth have become rich through the abundance of her luxury."

[4]And I heard another voice from heaven saying, "Come out of her, my people, lest you share in her sins, and lest you receive of her plagues. [5]For her sins have reached* to heaven, and God has remembered her iniquities. [6]Render to her just as she rendered to you,* and repay her double according to her works; in the cup which she has mixed, mix double for her. [7]In the measure that she glorified herself and lived luxuriously, in the same measure give her torment and sorrow; for she says in her heart, 'I sit *as* queen, and am no widow, and will not see sorrow.' [8]Therefore her plagues will come in one day—death and mourning and famine. And she will be utterly burned with fire, for strong *is* the Lord God who judges* her.

[9]"The kings of the earth who committed fornication and lived luxuriously with her will weep and lament for her, when they see the smoke of her burning, [10]standing at a distance for fear of her torment, saying, 'Alas, alas, that great city Babylon, that mighty city! For in one hour your judgment has come.'

[11]"And the merchants of the earth will weep and mourn over her, for no one buys their merchandise anymore: [12]merchandise of gold and silver, precious stones and pearls, fine linen and purple, silk and scarlet, every kind of citron wood, every kind of object of ivory, every kind of object of most precious wood, bronze, iron, and marble; [13]and cinnamon and incense, fragrant oil and frankincense, wine and oil, fine flour and wheat, cattle and sheep, horses and chariots, and bodies and souls of men. [14]The

fruit that your soul longed for has gone from you, and all the things which are rich and splendid have gone from you,* and you shall find them no more at all. ¹⁵The merchants of these things, who became rich by her, will stand at a distance for fear of her torment, weeping and wailing, ¹⁶and saying, 'Alas, alas, that great city that was clothed in fine linen, purple, and scarlet, and adorned with gold and precious stones and pearls! ¹⁷For in one hour such great riches came to nothing.' Every shipmaster, all who travel by ship, sailors, and as many as trade on the sea, stood at a distance ¹⁸and cried out when they saw the smoke of her burning, saying, 'What is like this great city?' ¹⁹"They threw dust on their heads and cried out, weeping and wailing, and saying, 'Alas, alas, that great city, in which all who had ships on the sea became rich by her wealth! For in one hour she is made desolate.' ²⁰"Rejoice over her, O heaven, and you holy apostles* and prophets, for God has avenged you on her!" ²¹Then a mighty angel took up a stone like a great millstone and threw it into the sea, saying, "Thus with violence the great city Babylon shall be thrown down, and shall not be found anymore. ²²The sound of harpists, musicians, flutists, and trumpeters shall not be heard in you anymore. No craftsman of any craft shall be found in you anymore, and the sound of a millstone shall not be heard in you anymore. ²³The light of a lamp shall not shine in you anymore, and the voice of bridegroom and bride shall not be heard in you anymore. For your merchants were the great men of the earth, for by your sorcery all the nations were deceived. ²⁴And in her was found the blood of prophets and saints, and of all who were slain on the earth."

PSALM 146:1-10

Praise the LORD!

Praise the LORD, O my soul!
2 While I live I will praise the LORD;
I will sing praises to my God while I have my being.

3 Do not put your trust in princes,
Nor in a son of man, in whom *there is* no help.
4 His spirit departs, he returns to his earth;
In that very day his plans perish.

5 Happy *is he* who *has* the God of Jacob for his help,
Whose hope *is* in the LORD his God,
6 Who made heaven and earth,
The sea, and all that *is* in them;
Who keeps truth forever,
7 Who executes justice for the oppressed,
Who gives food to the hungry.
The LORD gives freedom to the prisoners.

8 The LORD opens *the eyes of* the blind;
The LORD raises those who are bowed down;
The LORD loves the righteous.
9 The LORD watches over the strangers;
He relieves the fatherless and widow;
But the way of the wicked He turns upside down.

10 The LORD shall reign forever—
Your God, O Zion, to all generations.

Praise the LORD!

For as *the churning of milk produces butter, and wringing the nose produces blood,
so the forcing of wrath produces strife.*

DECEMBER 28

ZECHARIAH 12:1–13:9

THE burden* of the word of the LORD against Israel. Thus says the LORD, who stretches out the heavens, lays the foundation of the earth, and forms the spirit of man within him: 2"Behold, I will make Jerusalem a cup of drunkenness to all the surrounding peoples, when they lay siege against Judah and Jerusalem. 3And it shall happen in that day that I will make Jerusalem a very heavy stone for all peoples; all who would heave it away will surely be cut in pieces, though all nations of the earth are gathered against it. 4In that day," says the LORD, "I will strike every horse with confusion, and its rider with madness; I will open My eyes on the house of Judah, and will strike every horse of the peoples with blindness. 5And the governors of Judah shall say in their heart, 'The inhabitants of Jerusalem *are* my strength in the LORD of hosts, their God.' 6In that day I will make the governors of Judah like a firepan in the woodpile, and like a fiery torch in the sheaves; they shall devour all the surrounding peoples on the right hand and on the left, but Jerusalem shall be inhabited again in her own place—Jerusalem.

7"The LORD will save the tents of Judah first, so that the glory of the house of David and the glory of the inhabitants of Jerusalem shall not become greater than that of Judah. 8In that day the LORD will defend the inhabitants of Jerusalem; the one who is fee-

ble among them in that day shall be like David, and the house of David *shall be* like God, like the Angel of the LORD before them. 9It shall be in that day *that* I will seek to destroy all the nations that come against Jerusalem.

10"And I will pour on the house of David and on the inhabitants of Jerusalem the Spirit of grace and supplication; then they will look on Me whom they pierced. Yes, they will mourn for Him as one mourns for *his* only *son,* and grieve for Him as one grieves for a firstborn. 11In that day there shall be a great mourning in Jerusalem, like the mourning at Hadad Rimmon in the plain of Megiddo.* 12And the land shall mourn, every family by itself: the family of the house of David by itself, and their wives by themselves; the family of the house of Nathan by itself, and their wives by themselves; 13the family of the house of Levi by itself, and their wives by themselves; the family of Shimei by itself, and their wives by themselves; 14all the families that remain, every family by itself, and their wives by themselves.

"IN that day a fountain shall be opened for the house of David and for the inhabitants of Jerusalem, for sin and for uncleanness.

2"It shall be in that day," says the LORD of hosts, "*that* I will cut off the names of the idols from the land, and they shall no longer be remembered. I will also cause the prophets and the unclean spirit to depart from the land.

3It shall come to pass *that* if anyone still prophesies, then his father and mother who begot him will say to him, 'You shall not live, because you have spoken lies in the name of the LORD.' And his father and mother who begot him shall thrust him through when he prophesies. 4"And it shall be in that day *that* every prophet will be ashamed of his vision when he prophesies; they will not wear a robe of coarse hair to deceive. 5But he will say, 'I *am* no prophet, I *am* a farmer; for a man taught me to keep cattle from my youth.' 6And *one* will say to him, 'What are these wounds between your arms?'* Then he will answer, '*Those* with which I was wounded in the house of my friends.'

7   "Awake, O sword, against My Shepherd,
    Against the Man who is My Companion,"
    Says the LORD of hosts.
  "Strike the Shepherd,
  And the sheep will be scattered;
  Then I will turn My hand against the little ones.

8   And it shall come to pass in all the land,"
    Says the LORD,
  "*That* two-thirds in it shall be cut off *and* die,
  But *one*-third shall be left in it:

9   I will bring the *one*-third through the fire,
  Will refine them as silver is refined,
  And test them as gold is tested.
  They will call on My name,
  And I will answer them.
  I will say, 'This *is* My people';
  And each one will say, 'The LORD *is* my God.' "

REVELATION 19:1-21

AFTER these things I heard* a loud voice of a great multitude in heaven, saying, "Alleluia! Salvation and glory and honor and power *belong* to the Lord* our God! 2For true and righteous *are* His judgments, because He has judged the great harlot who corrupted the earth with her fornication; and He has avenged on her the blood of His servants *shed* by her." 3Again they said, "Alleluia! Her smoke rises up forever and ever!" 4And the twenty-four elders and the four living creatures fell down and worshiped God who sat on the throne, saying, "Amen! Alleluia!" 5Then a voice came from the throne, saying, "Praise our God, all you His servants and those who fear Him, both* small and great!"

6And I heard, as it were, the voice of a great multitude, as the sound of many waters and as the sound of mighty thunderings, saying, "Alleluia! For the* Lord God Omnipotent reigns! 7Let us be glad and rejoice and give Him glory, for the marriage of the Lamb has come, and His wife has made herself ready." 8And to her it was granted to be arrayed in fine linen, clean and bright, for the fine linen is the righteous acts of the saints.

9Then he said to me, "Write: 'Blessed *are* those who are called to the marriage supper of the Lamb!' " And he said to me, "These are the true sayings of God." 10And I fell at his feet to worship him. But he said to me, "See *that you do* not *do that!* I am your fellow servant, and of your brethren who have the testimony of Jesus. Worship God! For the testimony of Jesus is the spirit of prophecy."

11Now I saw heaven opened, and behold, a white horse. And He who sat on him *was* called Faithful and True, and in righteousness He judges and makes war. 12His eyes *were* like a flame of fire, and on His head *were* many crowns. He had* a name written that no one knew except Himself. ¹³He *was* clothed with a robe dipped in blood, and His name is called The Word of God. ¹⁴And the armies in heaven, clothed in fine linen, white and clean,* followed Him on white horses. ¹⁵Now out of His mouth goes a sharp* sword, that with it He should strike the nations. And He Himself will rule them with a rod of iron. He Himself treads the winepress of the fierceness and wrath of Almighty God. ¹⁶And He has on *His* robe and on His thigh a name written:

KING OF KINGS
AND LORD OF LORDS.

¹⁷Then I saw an angel standing in the sun; and he cried with a loud voice, saying to all the birds that fly in the midst of heaven, "Come and gather together for the supper of the great God,* ¹⁸that you may eat the flesh of kings, the flesh of captains, the flesh of mighty men, the flesh of horses and of those who sit on them, and the flesh of all *people,* free* and slave, both small and great."

¹⁹And I saw the beast, the kings of the earth, and their armies, gathered together to make war against Him who sat on the horse and against His army. ²⁰Then the beast was captured, and with him the false prophet who worked signs in his presence, by which he deceived those who received the mark of the beast and those who worshiped his image. These two were cast alive into the lake of fire burning with brimstone. ²¹And the rest were killed with the sword which proceeded from the mouth of Him who sat on the horse. And all the birds were filled with their flesh.

PSALM 147:1-20

PRAISE the LORD!
For *it is* good to sing praises to our God;
For *it is* pleasant, *and* praise is beautiful.

2 The LORD builds up Jerusalem;
He gathers together the outcasts of Israel.

3 He heals the brokenhearted
And binds up their wounds.

4 He counts the number of the stars;
He calls them all by name.

5 Great *is* our Lord, and mighty in power;
His understanding *is* infinite.

6 The LORD lifts up the humble;
He casts the wicked down to the ground.

7 Sing to the LORD with thanksgiving;
Sing praises on the harp to our God,

8 Who covers the heavens with clouds,
Who prepares rain for the earth,
Who makes grass to grow on the mountains.

9 He gives to the beast its food,
And to the young ravens that cry.

10 He does not delight in the strength of the horse;
He takes no pleasure in the legs of a man.

11 The LORD takes pleasure in those who fear Him,
In those who hope in His mercy.

12 Praise the LORD, O Jerusalem!
Praise your God, O Zion!

13 For He has strengthened the bars of your gates;

He has blessed your children
within you.

14 He makes peace *in* your
borders,
And fills you with the finest
wheat.

15 He sends out His command *to
the* earth;
His word runs very swiftly.

16 He gives snow like wool;
He scatters the frost like
ashes;

17 He casts out His hail like
morsels;
Who can stand before His
cold?

18 He sends out His word and
melts them;
He causes His wind to blow,
and the waters flow.

19 He declares His word to
Jacob,
His statutes and His
judgments to Israel.

20 He has not dealt thus with any
nation;
And *as for His* judgments,
they have not known them.

Praise the LORD!

PROVERBS FOR TODAY/ 31:1-7

The words of King Lemuel, the utterance which his mother taught him; What, my son? And what, son of my womb? And what, son of my vows? Do not give your strength to women, nor your ways to that which destroys kings. It is not for kings, O Lemuel, it is not for kings to drink wine, nor for princes intoxicating drink; lest they drink and forget the law, and pervert the justice of all the afflicted. Give strong drink to him who is perishing, and wine to those who are bitter of heart. Let him drink and forget his poverty, and remember his misery no more.

DECEMBER 29

ZECHARIAH 14:1-21

B EHOLD, the day of the LORD
is coming,
And your spoil will be divided
in your midst.

2 For I will gather all the
nations to battle against
Jerusalem;
The city shall be taken,
The houses rifled,
And the women ravished.
Half of the city shall go into
captivity,
But the remnant of the people
shall not be cut off from the
city.

3 Then the LORD will go forth
And fight against those
nations,
As He fights in the day of
battle.

4 And in that day His feet will
stand on the Mount of
Olives,
Which faces Jerusalem on the
east.
And the Mount of Olives shall
be split in two,
From east to west,

Making a very large valley;
Half of the mountain shall
move toward the north
And half of it toward the south.

5 Then you shall flee *through*
My mountain valley,
For the mountain valley shall
reach to Azal.
Yes, you shall flee
As you fled from the
earthquake
In the days of Uzziah king of
Judah.

Thus the LORD my God will
come,
And all the saints with You.*

6 It shall come to pass in that
day
That there will be no light;
The lights will diminish.
7 It shall be one day
Which is known to the LORD—
Neither day nor night.
But at evening time it shall
happen
That it will be light.

8 And in that day it shall be
That living waters shall flow
from Jerusalem,
Half of them toward the
eastern sea
And half of them toward the
western sea;
In both summer and winter it
shall occur.
9 And the LORD shall be King
over all the earth.
In that day it shall be—
"The LORD *is* one,"*
And His name one.

10All the land shall be turned into a
plain from Geba to Rimmon south of
Jerusalem. *Jerusalem** shall be raised
up and inhabited in her place from
Benjamin's Gate to the place of the

First Gate and the Corner Gate, and
from the Tower of Hananel to the
king's winepresses.

11 *The people* shall dwell in it;
And no longer shall there be
utter destruction,
But Jerusalem shall be safely
inhabited.

12And this shall be the plague with
which the LORD will strike all the
people who fought against Jerusalem:

Their flesh shall dissolve
while they stand on their
feet,
Their eyes shall dissolve in
their sockets,
And their tongues shall
dissolve in their mouths.
13 It shall come to pass in that
day
That a great panic from the
LORD will be among them.
Everyone will seize the hand
of his neighbor,
And raise his hand against his
neighbor's hand;
14 Judah also will fight at
Jerusalem.
And the wealth of all the
surrounding nations
Shall be gathered together:
Gold, silver, and apparel in
great abundance.

15 Such also shall be the plague
On the horse *and* the mule,
On the camel and the donkey,
And on all the cattle that will
be in those camps.
So *shall* this plague *be*.

16And it shall come to pass *that* everyone who is left of all the nations
which came against Jerusalem shall
go up from year to year to worship the
King, the LORD of hosts, and to keep

the Feast of Tabernacles. [17]And it shall be *that* whichever of the families of the earth do not come up to Jerusalem to worship the King, the LORD of hosts, on them there will be no rain. [18]If the family of Egypt will not come up and enter in, they *shall have* no *rain;* they shall receive the plague with which the LORD strikes the nations who do not come up to keep the Feast of Tabernacles. [19]This shall be the punishment of Egypt and the punishment of all the nations that do not come up to keep the Feast of Tabernacles.

[20]In that day "HOLINESS TO THE LORD" shall be *engraved* on the bells of the horses. The pots in the LORD's house shall be like the bowls before the altar. [21]Yes, every pot in Jerusalem and Judah shall be holiness to the LORD of hosts.* Everyone who sacrifices shall come and take them and cook in them. In that day there shall no longer be a Canaanite in the house of the LORD of hosts.

REVELATION 20:1-15

THEN I saw an angel coming down from heaven, having the key to the bottomless pit and a great chain in his hand. [2]He laid hold of the dragon, that serpent of old, who is *the* Devil and Satan, and bound him for a thousand years; [3]and he cast him into the bottomless pit, and shut him up, and set a seal on him, so that he should deceive the nations no more till the thousand years were finished. But after these things he must be released for a little while.

[4]And I saw thrones, and they sat on them, and judgment was committed to them. Then *I saw* the souls of those who had been beheaded for their witness to Jesus and for the word of God, who had not worshiped the beast or his image, and had not received *his* mark on their foreheads or on their hands. And they lived and reigned with Christ for a* thousand years. [5]But the rest of the dead did not live again until the thousand years were finished. This *is* the first resurrection. [6]Blessed and holy *is* he who has part in the first resurrection. Over such the second death has no power, but they shall be priests of God and of Christ, and shall reign with Him a thousand years.

[7]Now when the thousand years have expired, Satan will be released from his prison [8]and will go out to deceive the nations which are in the four corners of the earth, Gog and Magog, to gather them together to battle, whose number *is* as the sand of the sea. [9]They went up on the breadth of the earth and surrounded the camp of the saints and the beloved city. And fire came down from God out of heaven and devoured them. [10]The devil, who deceived them, was cast into the lake of fire and brimstone where* the beast and the false prophet *are.* And they will be tormented day and night forever and ever.

[11]Then I saw a great white throne and Him who sat on it, from whose face the earth and the heaven fled away. And there was found no place for them. [12]And I saw the dead, small and great, standing before God,* and books were opened. And another book was opened, which is *the Book* of Life. And the dead were judged according to their works, by the things which were written in the books. [13]The sea gave up the dead who were in it, and Death and Hades delivered up the dead who were in them. And they were judged, each one according to his works. [14]Then Death and Hades were cast into the lake of fire. This is the second death.* [15]And anyone not found written in the Book of Life was cast into the lake of fire.

PSALM 148:1-14

PRAISE the LORD!

Praise the LORD from the
heavens;
Praise Him in the heights!
2 Praise Him, all His angels;
Praise Him, all His hosts!
3 Praise Him, sun and moon;
Praise Him, all you stars of
light!
4 Praise Him, you heavens of
heavens,
And you waters above the
heavens!

5 Let them praise the name of
the LORD,
For He commanded and they
were created.
6 He also established them
forever and ever;
He made a decree which shall
not pass away.

7 Praise the LORD from the
earth,
You great sea creatures and
all the depths;

8 Fire and hail, snow and
clouds;
Stormy wind, fulfilling His
word;
9 Mountains and all hills;
Fruitful trees and all cedars;
10 Beasts and all cattle;
Creeping things and flying
fowl;
11 Kings of the earth and all
peoples;
Princes and all judges of the
earth;
12 Both young men and maidens;
Old men and children.

13 Let them praise the name of
the LORD,
For His name alone is exalted;
His glory *is* above the earth
and heaven.
14 And He has exalted the horn
of His people,
The praise of all His saints—
Of the children of Israel,
A people near to Him.

Praise the LORD!

PROVERBS FOR TODAY/ 31:8-9

Open your mouth for the speechless, in the cause of all who are *appointed to die.* *
Open your mouth, judge righteously, and plead the cause of the poor and needy.

DECEMBER 30

MALACHI 1:1–2:17

THE burden* of the word of the
LORD to Israel by Malachi.

2 "I have loved you," says the
LORD.
"Yet you say, 'In what way have
You loved us?'

Was not Esau Jacob's
brother?"
Says the LORD.
"Yet Jacob I have loved;
3 But Esau I have hated,
And laid waste his mountains
and his heritage

For the jackals of the
wilderness."

4 Even though Edom has said,
"We have been impoverished,
But we will return and build
the desolate places,"

Thus says the LORD of hosts:

"They may build, but I will
throw down;
They shall be called the
Territory of Wickedness,
And the people against whom
the LORD will have
indignation forever.
5 Your eyes shall see,
And you shall say,
'The LORD is magnified beyond
the border of Israel.'

6 "A son honors *his* father,
And a servant *his* master.
If then I am the Father,
Where *is* My honor?
And if I *am* a Master,
Where *is* My reverence?
Says the LORD of hosts
To you priests who despise
My name.
Yet you say, 'In what way have
we despised Your name?'

7 "You offer defiled food on My
altar,
But say,
'In what way have we defiled
You?'
By saying,
'The table of the LORD is
contemptible.'
8 And when you offer the blind
as a sacrifice,
Is it not evil?
And when you offer the lame
and sick,
Is it not evil?
Offer it then to your governor!
Would he be pleased with you?

Would he accept you
favorably?"
Says the LORD of hosts.

9 "But now entreat God's favor,
That He may be gracious to
us.
While this is being *done* by
your hands,
Will He accept you favorably?"
Says the LORD of hosts.
10 "Who *is there* even among you
who would shut the doors,
So that you would not kindle
fire *on* My altar in vain?
I have no pleasure in you,"
Says the LORD of hosts,
"Nor will I accept an offering
from your hands.
11 For from the rising of the sun,
even to its going down,
My name *shall be* great
among the Gentiles;
In every place incense *shall be*
offered to My name,
And a pure offering;
For My name shall be great
among the nations,"
Says the LORD of hosts.

12 "But you profane it,
In that you say,
'The table of the LORD* is
defiled;
And its fruit, its food, *is*
contemptible.'
13 You also say,
'Oh, what a weariness!'
And you sneer at it,"
Says the LORD of hosts.
"And you bring the stolen, the
lame, and the sick;
Thus you bring an offering!
Should I accept this from your
hand?"
Says the LORD.
14 "But cursed *be* the deceiver
Who has in his flock a male,
And takes a vow,

But sacrifices to the Lord
what is blemished—
For I *am* a great King,"
Says the LORD of hosts,
"And My name *is to be* feared
among the nations.

"AND now, O priests, this commandment is for you.
2   If you will not hear,
And if you will not take *it* to
heart,
To give glory to My name,"
Says the LORD of hosts,
"I will send a curse upon you,
And I will curse your
blessings.
Yes, I have cursed them
already,
Because you do not take *it* to
heart.

3   "Behold, I will rebuke your
descendants
And spread refuse on your
faces,
The refuse of your solemn
feasts;
And *one* will take you away
with it.
4   Then you shall know that I
have sent this
commandment to you,
That My covenant with Levi
may continue,"
Says the LORD of hosts.
5   "My covenant was with him,
one of life and peace,
And I gave them to him *that
he might* fear *Me;*
So he feared Me
And was reverent before My
name.
6   The law of truth* was in his
mouth,
And injustice was not found
on his lips.
He walked with Me in peace
and equity,

And turned many away from
iniquity.
7   "For the lips of a priest should
keep knowledge,
And *people* should seek the
law from his mouth;
For he is the messenger of
the LORD of hosts.
8   But you have departed from
the way;
You have caused many to
stumble at the law.
You have corrupted the
covenant of Levi,"
Says the LORD of hosts.
9   "Therefore I also have made
you contemptible and base
Before all the people,
Because you have not kept
My ways
But have shown partiality in
the law."

10   Have we not all one Father?
Has not one God created us?
Why do we deal
treacherously with one
another
By profaning the covenant of
the fathers?
11   Judah has dealt treacherously,
And an abomination has been
committed in Israel and in
Jerusalem,
For Judah has profaned
The LORD's holy *institution*
which He loves:
He has married the daughter
of a foreign god.
12   May the LORD cut off from the
tents of Jacob
The man who does this, being
awake and aware,*
Yet who brings an offering to
the LORD of hosts!

13   And this is the second thing
you do:

You cover the altar of the Lord
with tears,
With weeping and crying;
So He does not regard the
offering anymore,
Nor receive *it* with goodwill
from your hands.
14 Yet you say, "For what
reason?"
Because the Lord has been
witness
Between you and the wife of
your youth,
With whom you have dealt
treacherously;
Yet she is your companion
And your wife by covenant.
15 But did He not make *them*
one,
Having a remnant of the
Spirit?
And why one?
He seeks godly offspring.
Therefore take heed to your
spirit,
And let none deal
treacherously with the wife
of his youth.

16 "For the Lord God of Israel
says
That He hates divorce,
For it covers one's garment
with violence,"
Says the Lord of hosts.
"Therefore take heed to your
spirit,
That you do not deal
treacherously."

17 You have wearied the Lord
with your words;
Yet you say,
"In what way have we wearied
Him?"
In that you say,
"Everyone who does evil
Is good in the sight of the
Lord,
And He delights in them,"

Or, "Where *is* the God of
justice?"

REVELATION 21:1-27

Now I saw a new heaven and a new earth, for the first heaven and the first earth had passed away. Also there was no more sea. [2]Then I, John,* saw the holy city, New Jerusalem, coming down out of heaven from God, prepared as a bride adorned for her husband. [3]And I heard a loud voice from heaven saying, "Behold, the tabernacle of God *is* with men, and He will dwell with them, and they shall be His people. God Himself will be with them *and be* their God. [4]And God will wipe away every tear from their eyes; there shall be no more death, nor sorrow, nor crying. There shall be no more pain, for the former things have passed away."

[5]Then He who sat on the throne said, "Behold, I make all things new." And He said to me,* "Write, for these words are true and faithful."

[6]And He said to me, "It is done!* I am the Alpha and the Omega, the Beginning and the End. I will give of the fountain of the water of life freely to him who thirsts. [7]He who overcomes shall inherit all things,* and I will be his God and he shall be My son. [8]But the cowardly, unbelieving,* abominable, murderers, sexually immoral, sorcerers, idolaters, and all liars shall have their part in the lake which burns with fire and brimstone, which is the second death."

[9]Then one of the seven angels who had the seven bowls filled with the seven last plagues came to me* and talked with me, saying, "Come, I will show you the bride, the Lamb's wife."* [10]And he carried me away in the Spirit to a great and high mountain, and showed me the great city, the holy* Jerusalem, descending out of heaven from God, [11]having the glory of God.

Her light *was* like a most precious stone, like a jasper stone, clear as crystal. ¹²Also she had a great and high wall with twelve gates, and twelve angels at the gates, and names written on them, which are *the names* of the twelve tribes of the children of Israel: ¹³three gates on the east, three gates on the north, three gates on the south, and three gates on the west.

¹⁴Now the wall of the city had twelve foundations, and on them were the names* of the twelve apostles of the Lamb. ¹⁵And he who talked with me had a gold reed to measure the city, its gates, and its wall. ¹⁶The city is laid out as a square; its length is as great as its breadth. And he measured the city with the reed: twelve thousand furlongs. Its length, breadth, and height are equal. ¹⁷Then he measured its wall: one hundred *and* forty-four cubits, *according* to the measure of a man, that is, of an angel. ¹⁸The construction of its wall was *of* jasper; and the city *was* pure gold, like clear glass. ¹⁹The foundations of the wall of the city *were* adorned with all kinds of precious stones: the first foundation *was* jasper, the second sapphire, the third chalcedony, the fourth emerald, ²⁰the fifth sardonyx, the sixth sardius, the seventh chrysolite, the eighth beryl, the ninth topaz, the tenth chrysoprase, the eleventh jacinth, and the twelfth amethyst. ²¹The twelve gates *were* twelve pearls: each individual gate was of one pearl. And the street of the city *was* pure gold, like transparent glass.

²²But I saw no temple in it, for the Lord God Almighty and the Lamb are its temple. ²³The city had no need of the sun or of the moon to shine in it,* for the glory* of God illuminated it. The Lamb *is* its light. ²⁴And the nations of those who are saved* shall walk in its light, and the kings of the earth bring their glory and honor into it.* ²⁵Its gates shall not be shut at all by day (there shall be no night there). ²⁶And they shall bring the glory and the honor of the nations into it.* ²⁷But there shall by no means enter it anything that defiles, or causes* an abomination or a lie, but only those who are written in the Lamb's Book of Life.

PSALM 149:1-9

P RAISE the LORD!

Sing to the LORD a new song,
And His praise in the
assembly of saints.

2 Let Israel rejoice in their
Maker;
Let the children of Zion be
joyful in their King.

3 Let them praise His name
with the dance;
Let them sing praises to Him
with the timbrel and harp.

4 For the LORD takes pleasure in
His people;
He will beautify the humble
with salvation.

5 Let the saints be joyful in
glory;
Let them sing aloud on their
beds.

6 *Let* the high praises of God *be*
in their mouth,
And a two-edged sword in
their hand,

7 To execute vengeance on the
nations,
And punishments on the
peoples;

8 To bind their kings with
chains,
And their nobles with fetters
of iron;

9 To execute on them the
written judgment—
This honor have all His saints.

Praise the LORD!

PROVERBS FOR TODAY / 31:10-24

Who* can find a virtuous* wife? For her worth is far above rubies. The heart of her husband safely trusts her; so he will have no lack of gain. She does him good and not evil all the days of her life. She seeks wool and flax, and willingly works with her hands. She is like the merchant ships, she brings her food from afar. She also rises while it is yet night, and provides food for her household, and a portion for her maidservants. She considers a field and buys it; from her profits she plants a vineyard. She girds herself with strength, and strengthens her arms. She perceives that her merchandise is good, and her lamp does not go out by night. She stretches out her hands to the distaff, and her hand holds the spindle. She extends her hand to the poor, yes, she reaches out her hands to the needy. She is not afraid of snow for her household, for all her household is clothed with scarlet. She makes tapestry for herself; her clothing is fine linen and purple. Her husband is known in the gates, when he sits among the elders of the land. She makes linen garments and sells them, and supplies sashes for the merchants.

DECEMBER 31

MALACHI 3:1–4:6

"BEHOLD, I send My messenger,
And he will prepare the way
before Me.
And the Lord, whom you seek,
Will suddenly come to His
temple,
Even the Messenger of the
covenant,
In whom you delight.
Behold, He is coming,"
Says the LORD of hosts.

2 "But who can endure the day
of His coming?
And who can stand when He
appears?
For He *is* like a refiner's fire
And like launderers' soap.

3 He will sit as a refiner and a
purifier of silver;
He will purify the sons of Levi,
And purge them as gold and
silver,
That they may offer to the
LORD
An offering in righteousness.

4 "Then the offering of Judah
and Jerusalem
Will be pleasant to the LORD,
As in the days of old,
As in former years.

5 And I will come near you for
judgment;
I will be a swift witness
Against sorcerers,
Against adulterers,
Against perjurers,
Against those who exploit
wage earners and widows
and orphans,
And against those who turn
away an alien—
Because they do not fear Me,"
Says the LORD of hosts.

6 "For I *am* the LORD, I do not
change;
Therefore you are not
consumed, O sons of Jacob.

7 Yet from the days of your
fathers
You have gone away from My
ordinances

And have not kept *them.*
Return to Me, and I will
return to you,"
Says the LORD of hosts.
"But you said,
'In what way shall we return?'

8 "Will a man rob God?
Yet you have robbed Me!
But you say,
'In what way have we robbed
You?'
In tithes and offerings.

9 You are cursed with a curse,
For you have robbed Me,
Even this whole nation.

10 Bring all the tithes into the
storehouse,
That there may be food in My
house,
And try Me now in this,"
Says the LORD of hosts,
"If I will not open for you the
windows of heaven
And pour out for you *such*
blessing
That *there will* not *be room*
enough *to receive it.*

11 "And I will rebuke the
devourer for your sakes,
So that he will not destroy the
fruit of your ground,
Nor shall the vine fail to bear
fruit for you in the field,"
Says the LORD of hosts;

12 And all nations will call you
blessed,
For you will be a delightful
land,"
Says the LORD of hosts.

13 "Your words have been harsh
against Me,"
Says the LORD,
"Yet you say,
'What have we spoken against
You?'

14 You have said,
'It is useless to serve God;

What profit *is it* that we have
kept His ordinance,
And that we have walked as
mourners
Before the LORD of hosts?

15 So now we call the proud
blessed,
For those who do wickedness
are raised up;
They even tempt God and go
free.' "

16 Then those who feared the
LORD spoke to one another,
And the LORD listened and
heard *them;*
So a book of remembrance
was written before Him
For those who fear the LORD
And who meditate on His
name.

17 "They shall be Mine," says the
LORD of hosts,
"On the day that I make them
My jewels.*
And I will spare them
As a man spares his own son
who serves him."

18 Then you shall again discern
Between the righteous and
the wicked,
Between one who serves God
And one who does not serve
Him.

"FOR behold, the day is coming,
Burning like an oven,
And all the proud, yes, all who
do wickedly will be stubble.
And the day which is coming
shall burn them up,"
Says the LORD of hosts,
"That will leave them neither
root nor branch.

2 But to you who fear My name
The Sun of Righteousness
shall arise
With healing in His wings;
And you shall go out

And grow fat like stall-fed calves.

3 You shall trample the wicked,
For they shall be ashes under the soles of your feet
On the day that I do *this*,"
Says the LORD of hosts.

4 "Remember the Law of Moses,
My servant,
Which I commanded him in Horeb for all Israel,
With the statutes and judgments.

5 Behold, I will send you Elijah the prophet
Before the coming of the great and dreadful day of the LORD.

6 And he will turn
The hearts of the fathers to the children,
And the hearts of the children to their fathers,
Lest I come and strike the earth with a curse."

REVELATION 22:1-21

A ND he [the angel] showed me a pure* river of water of life, clear as crystal, proceeding from the throne of God and of the Lamb. ²In the middle of its street, and on either side of the river, *was* the tree of life, which bore twelve fruits, each *tree* yielding its fruit every month. The leaves of the tree *were* for the healing of the nations. ³And there shall be no more curse, but the throne of God and of the Lamb shall be in it, and His servants shall serve Him. ⁴They shall see His face, and His name *shall be* on their foreheads. ⁵There shall be no night there: They need no lamp nor light of the sun, for the Lord God gives them light. And they shall reign forever and ever.

⁶Then he said to me, "These words *are* faithful and true." And the Lord God of the holy* prophets sent His angel to show His servants the things which must shortly take place.

⁷"Behold, I am coming quickly! Blessed *is* he who keeps the words of the prophecy of this book."

⁸Now I, John, saw and heard* these things. And when I heard and saw, I fell down to worship before the feet of the angel who showed me these things. ⁹Then he said to me, "See *that you do not do that.* For* I am your fellow servant, and of your brethren the prophets, and of those who keep the words of this book. Worship God." ¹⁰And he said to me, "Do not seal the words of the prophecy of this book, for the time is at hand. ¹¹He who is unjust, let him be unjust still; he who is filthy, let him be filthy still; he who is righteous, let him be righteous* still; he who is holy, let him be holy still."

¹²"And behold, I am coming quickly, and My reward *is* with Me, to give to every one according to his work. ¹³I am the Alpha and the Omega, *the* Beginning and *the* End, the First and the Last."*

¹⁴Blessed *are* those who do His commandments,* that they may have the right to the tree of life, and may enter through the gates into the city. ¹⁵But* outside *are* dogs and sorcerers and sexually immoral and murderers and idolaters, and whoever loves and practices a lie.

¹⁶"I, Jesus, have sent My angel to testify to you these things in the churches. I am the Root and the Offspring of David, the Bright and Morning Star."

¹⁷And the Spirit and the bride say, "Come!" And let him who hears say, "Come!" And let him who thirsts come. Whoever desires, let him take the water of life freely.

¹⁸For* I testify to everyone who hears the words of the prophecy of this book: If anyone adds to these things, God will add* to him the plagues that

are written in this book; [19]and if anyone takes away from the words of the book of this prophecy, God shall take away* his part from the Book* of Life, from the holy city, and *from* the things which are written in this book.

[20]He who testifies to these things says, "Surely I am coming quickly."

Amen. Even so, come, Lord Jesus!

[21]The grace of our Lord Jesus Christ *be* with you all.* Amen.

PSALM 150:1-6

PRAISE the LORD!

Praise God in His sanctuary;
Praise Him in His mighty
firmament!

2 Praise Him for His mighty acts;
Praise Him according to His excellent greatness!

3 Praise Him with the sound of the trumpet;
Praise Him with the lute and harp!

4 Praise Him with the timbrel and dance;
Praise Him with stringed instruments and flutes!

5 Praise Him with loud cymbals;
Praise Him with clashing cymbals!

6 Let everything that has breath praise the LORD.

Praise the LORD!

PROVERBS FOR TODAY/ 31:25-31

Strength and honor are *her clothing; she shall rejoice in time to come. She opens her mouth with wisdom, and on her tongue* is *the law of kindness. She watches over the ways of her household, and does not eat the bread of idleness. Her children rise up and call her blessed; her husband* also, *and he praises her: "Many daughters have done well, but you excel them all." Charm* is *deceitful and beauty* is *passing, but a woman* who *fears the LORD, she shall be praised. Give her of the fruit of her hands, and let her own works praise her in the gates.*

Textual Notes

JANUARY 1

Gen. 1:2 Words in italic type have been added for clarity. They are not found in the original Hebrew or Aramaic. **1:26** Syriac reads *all the wild animals of.* **2:4** Hebrew *toledoth,* literally *generations* **2:14** Or *Tigris*

Matt. 1:6 Words in italic type have been added for clarity. They are not found in the original Greek. **1:7** NU-Text reads *Asaph.* **1:10** NU-Text reads *Amos.* **1:23** Isaiah 7:14. Words in oblique type in the New Testament are quoted from the Old Testament. **1:25** NU-Text reads *a Son.* **2:6** Micah 5:2

JANUARY 2

Gen. 4:8 Samaritan Pentateuch, Septuagint, Syriac, and Vulgate add *"Let us go out to the field."* **4:15** Following Masoretic Text and Targum; Septuagint, Syriac, and Vulgate read *Not so.* **4:26** Greek *Enos*

Matt. 2:15 Hosea 11:1 **2:18** Jeremiah 31:15 **3:3** Isaiah 40:3

Ps. 2:9 Following Masoretic Text and Targum; Septuagint, Syriac, and Vulgate read *rule* (compare Revelation 2:27). **2:12** Septuagint and Vulgate read *Embrace discipline;* Targum reads *Receive instruction.* / Septuagint reads *the LORD.*

JANUARY 3

Gen. 5:9 Hebrew *Qenan* **6:3** Septuagint, Syriac, Targum, and Vulgate read *abide.* **6:5** Following Masoretic Text and Targum; Vulgate reads *God;* Septuagint reads *LORD God.* **7:22** Septuagint and Vulgate omit *of the spirit.*

Matt. 3:11 M-Text omits *and fire.* **3:16** Or *he* **4:4** Deuteronomy 8:3 **4:6** Psalm 91:11, 12 **4:7** Deuteronomy 6:16 **4:10** M-Text reads *Get behind Me.* / Deuteronomy 6:13

Prov. 1:12 Or *the grave*

JANUARY 4

Gen. 9:1 Compare Genesis 1:28 **9:9** Literally *seed* **10:3** Spelled *Diphath* in 1 Chronicles 1:6 **10:4** Spelled *Rodanim* in Samaritan Pentateuch and 1 Chronicles 1:7 **10:6** Or *Phut* **10:23** Called *Meshech* in Septuagint and 1 Chronicles 1:17 **10:24** Following Masoretic Text, Vulgate, and Targum; Septuagint reads *Arphaxad begot Cainan, and Cainan begot Salah* (compare Luke 3:35, 36). **10:28** Spelled *Ebal* in 1 Chronicles 1:22

Matt. 4:16 Isaiah 9:1, 2

Ps. 4:3 Many Hebrew manuscripts, Septuagint, Targum, and Vulgate read *made wonderful.*

Prov. 1:21 Septuagint, Syriac, and Targum read *top of the walls;* Vulgate reads *the head of multitudes.*

JANUARY 5

Gen. 12:6 Hebrew *Alon Moreh* **12:9** Hebrew *Negev* **12:13** Literally *my soul* **13:1** Hebrew *Negev*

Matt. 5:21 Exodus 20:13; Deuteronomy 5:17 **5:22** NU-Text omits *without a cause.*

Ps. 5:title Hebrew *nehiloth*

JANUARY 6

Gen. 13:15 Literally *seed,* and so throughout the book **13:18** Hebrew *Alon Mamre* **14:1** Hebrew *goyim* **14:9** Hebrew *goyim* **14:13** Hebrew *Alon Mamre*

Matt. 5:27 NU-Text and M-Text omit *to those of old.* / Exodus 20:14; Deuteronomy 5:18 **5:32** Or *fornication* **5:38** Exodus 21:24; Leviticus 24:20; Deuteronomy 19:21 **5:43** Compare Leviticus 19:18 **5:44** NU-Text omits three clauses from this verse, leaving, *"But I say to you, love your enemies and pray for those who persecute you."* **5:47** M-Text reads *friends.* / NU-Text reads *Gentiles.*

Ps. 6:title Hebrew *sheminith*

JANUARY 7

Gen. 16:14 Literally *Well of the One Who Lives and Sees Me* **18:1** Hebrew *Alon Mamre* **18:11** Literally *the manner of women had ceased to be with Sarah*

Matt. 6:4 NU-Text omits *openly.* **6:6** NU-Text omits *openly.* **6:13** NU-Text omits *For Yours* through *Amen.* **6:18** NU-Text and M-Text omit *openly.*

Ps. 7:title Hebrew *Shiggaion* **7:6** Following Masoretic Text, Targum, and Vulgate; Septuagint reads *O LORD my God.*

JANUARY 8

Gen. 19:17 Septuagint, Syriac, and Vulgate read *they.*

Matt. 7:14 NU-Text and M-Text read *How . . . !*

Ps. 8:title Hebrew *Al Gittith* **8:5** Hebrew *Elohim, God;* Septuagint, Syriac, Targum, and Jewish tradition translate as *angels.*

JANUARY 9

Gen. 20:16 Literally *it is a covering of the eyes for you* **21:31** Literally *Well of the Oath* or *Well of the Seven* **22:5** Or *young man* **22:14** Hebrew *YHWH Yireh* **22:23** Spelled *Rebecca* in Romans 9:10

Ps. 9:title Hebrew *Muth Labben*

JANUARY 10

Gen. 24:7 Literally *seed*

Matt. 8:15 NU-Text and M-Text read *Him.* **8:17** Isaiah 53:4

Ps. 9:16 Hebrew *Higgaion*

Prov. 3:6 Or *make smooth* or *straight*

JANUARY 11

Gen. 25:15 Masoretic Text reads *Hadad.* **25:25** Literally *Hairy* **25:26** Literally *Supplanter* **25:30** Literally *Red*
Matt. 8:28 NU-Text reads *Gadarenes.* **8:31** NU-Text reads *send us.*
Prov. 3:8 Literally *navel,* figurative of the body / Literally *drink* or *refreshment*

JANUARY 12

Gen. 26:20 Literally *Quarrel* **26:21** Literally *Enmity* **26:22** Literally *Spaciousness* **26:33** Literally *Oath* or *Seven* / Literally *Well of the Oath* or *Well of the Seven*
Matt. 9:8 / NU-Text reads *were afraid.* **9:13** Hosea 6:6 / NU-Text omits *to repentance.* **9:14** NU-Text brackets *often* as disputed.

JANUARY 13

Gen. 28:19 Or *House of God* **29:32** Literally *See, a Son* **29:33** Literally *Heard* **29:34** Literally *Attached* **29:35** Literally *Praise*
Matt. 9:35 NU-Text omits *among the people.* **9:36** NU-Text and M-Text read *harassed.*
Ps. 11:7 Or *The upright beholds His countenance*

JANUARY 14

Gen. 30:6 Literally *Judge* **30:8** Literally *My Wrestling* **30:11** Following Qere, Syriac, and Targum; Kethib, Septuagint, and Vulgate read *in fortune.* / Literally *Troop* or *Fortune* **30:13** Literally *Happy* **30:18** Literally *Wages* **30:20** Literally *Dwelling* **30:24** Literally *He Will Add*
Matt. 10:3 NU-Text omits *Lebbaeus, whose surname was.* **10:4** NU-Text reads *Cananaean.* **10:8** NU-Text reads *raise the dead, cleanse the lepers;* M-Text omits *raise the dead.* **10:25** NU-Text and M-Text read *Beelzebul.*
Ps. 12:title Hebrew *sheminith*

JANUARY 15

Gen. 31:47 Literally, in Aramaic, *Heap of Witness* / Literally, in Hebrew, *Heap of Witness* **31:49** Literally *Watch* **32:2** Literally *Double Camp*
Matt. 10:36 Micah 7:6 **11:2** NU-Text reads *by* for *two of.*

JANUARY 16

Gen. 32:28 Literally *Prince with God* **32:30** Literally *Face of God* **32:31** Same as *Peniel,* verse 30 **33:17** Literally *Booths* **33:20** Literally *God, the God of Israel*
Matt. 11:10 Malachi 3:1 **11:19** NU-Text reads *works.* **11:23** NU-Text reads *will you be exalted to heaven? No, you will be.*

JANUARY 17

Gen. 35:7 Literally *God of the House of God* **35:8** Literally *Terebinth of Weeping* **35:18** Literally *Son of My Sorrow* / Literally *Son of the Right Hand* **35:27** Literally *Town of Arba* **36:11** Spelled *Zephi* in 1 Chronicles 1:36 **36:16** Samaritan Pentateuch omits *Chief Korah.* **36:22** Spelled *Homam* in 1 Chronicles 1:39 **36:23** Spelled *Alian* in 1 Chronicles 1:40 / Spelled *Shephi* in 1 Chronicles 1:40 **36:24** Following Masoretic Text and Vulgate (*hot springs*); Septuagint reads *Jamin;* Targum reads *mighty men;* Talmud interprets as

mules. **36:26** Hebrew *Dishan* / Spelled *Hamran* in 1 Chronicles 1:41 **36:27** Spelled *Jaakan* in 1 Chronicles 1:42 **36:39** Spelled *Hadad* in Samaritan Pentateuch, Syriac, and 1 Chronicles 1:50 / Spelled *Pai* in 1 Chronicles 1.50 **36:40** Spelled *Aliah* in 1 Chronicles 1:51
Matt. 12:7 Hosea 6:6 **12:8** NU-Text and M-Text omit *even.* **12:15** NU-Text brackets *multitudes* as disputed. **12:21** Isaiah 42:1-4

JANUARY 18

Gen. 37:36 Masoretic Text reads *Medanites.* **38:29** Literally *Breach* or *Breakthrough*
Matt. 12:22 NU-Text omits *blind and.* **12:24** NU-Text and M-Text read *Beelzebul.* **12:35** NU-Text and M-Text omit *of his heart.*

JANUARY 19

Gen. 39:23 Literally *his hand*
Matt. 13:15 NU-Text and M-Text read *would.* / Isaiah 6:9, 10

JANUARY 20

Gen. 41:51 Literally *Making Forgetful* **41:52** Literally *Fruitfulness* **41:56** Literally *all that was in them*
Matt. 13:33 Greek *sata,* approximately two pecks in all **13:35** Psalm 78:2
Ps. 18:13 Following Masoretic Text, Targum, and Vulgate; a few Hebrew manuscripts and Septuagint omit *Hailstones and coals of fire.*

JANUARY 21

Matt. 13:51 NU-Text omits *Jesus said to them.* / NU-Text omits *Lord.* **13:52** Or *for.* **13:55** NU-Text reads *Joseph.*

JANUARY 22

Matt. 14:24 NU-Text reads *many furlongs away from the land.* **14:30** NU-Text brackets *that* and *boisterous* as disputed. **14:33** NU-Text omits *came and.* **14:34** NU-Text reads *came to land at.*

JANUARY 23

Gen. 46:10 Spelled *Nemuel* in 1 Chronicles 4:24 / Called *Jarib* in 1 Chronicles 4:24 / Called *Zerah* in 1 Chronicles 4:24 **46:13** Spelled *Puah* in 1 Chronicles 7:1 / Same as *Jashub* in Numbers 26:24 and 1 Chronicles 7:1 **46:16** Spelled *Zephon* in Samaritan Pentateuch, Septuagint, and Numbers 26:15 / Called *Ozni* in Numbers 26:16 / Spelled *Arod* in Numbers 26:17 **46:21** Called *Hupham* in Numbers 26:39 **46:23** Called *Shuham* in Numbers 26:42 **46:24** Spelled *Jahziel* in 1 Chronicles 7:13 / Spelled *Shallum* in 1 Chronicles 7:13 **47:21** Following Masoretic Text and Targum; Samaritan Pentateuch, Septuagint, and Vulgate read *made the people virtual slaves.*
Matt. 15:4 Exodus 20:12; Deuteronomy 5:16 / Exodus 21:17 **15:6** NU-Text omits *or mother.* / NU-Text omits *word.* **15:8** NU-Text omits *draw near to Me with their mouth, And.* **15:9** Isaiah 29:13
Ps. 19:4 Septuagint, Syriac, and Vulgate read *sound;* Targum reads *business.*
Prov. 4:18 Literally *light*

JANUARY 24

Matt. 15:39 NU-Text reads *Magadan.* **16:3** NU-Text omits *Hypocrites.* **16:4** NU-Text omits *the prophet.* **16:8** NU-Text reads *you have no bread.*

JANUARY 25

Gen. 50:11 Literally *Mourning of Egypt* **Exod. 1:5** Literally *who came from the loins of* / Dead Sea Scrolls and Septuagint read *seventy-five* (compare Acts 7:14). **1:22** Samaritan Pentateuch, Septuagint, and Targum add *to the Hebrews.* **2:10** Literally *Drawn Out* **Matt. 16:19** Or *will have been bound . . . will have been loosed* **17:4** NU-Text reads *I will.*
Prov. 5:5 Or *Sheol*

JANUARY 26

Exod. 2:22 Literally *Stranger There*
Matt. 17:11 NU-Text omits *first.* **17:15** Literally *moonstruck* **17:20** NU-Text reads *little faith.* **17:21** NU-Text omits this verse. **17:22** NU-Text reads *gathering together.* **17:24** NU-Text reads *Capharnaum* (here and elsewhere). **17:27** Greek *stater,* the exact amount to pay the temple tax (didrachma) for two.
Ps. 22:title Hebrew *Aijeleth Hashahar* **22:8** Septuagint, Syriac, and Vulgate read *hoped;* Targum reads *praised.* **22:16** Following some Hebrew manuscripts, Septuagint, Syriac, Vulgate, Masoretic Text reads *Like a lion.*

JANUARY 27

Exod. 4:9 That is, the Nile **4:25** Literally *his*
Matt. 18:11 NU-Text omits this verse. **18:16** Deuteronomy 19:15 **18:19** NU-Text and M-Text read *Again, assuredly, I say.*
Ps. 22:27 Following Masoretic Text, Septuagint, and Targum; Arabic, Syriac, and Vulgate read *Him.*

JANUARY 28

Exod. 6:3 Hebrew *YHWH,* traditionally *Jehovah* **6:15** Spelled *Nemuel* in Numbers 26:12
Matt. 18:29 NU-Text omits *at his feet.* / NU-Text and M-Text omit *all.* **10:35** NU-Text omits *his trespasses.* **19:4** NU-Text reads *created.* / Genesis 1:27; 5:2 **19:5** Genesis 2:24 **19:9** Or *fornication*
Ps. 23:6 Following Septuagint, Syriac, Targum, and Vulgate; Masoretic Text reads *return.*

JANUARY 29

Exod. 8:23 Literally *set a ransom* (compare Exodus 9:4 and 11:7)
Matt. 19:16 NU-Text omits *Good.* **19:17** NU-Text reads *Why do you ask Me about what is good?* / NU-Text reads *There is One who is good.* **19:19** Exodus 20:12-16; Deuteronomy 5:16-20 / Leviticus 19:18 **19:20** NU-Text omits *from my youth.* **19:29** NU-Text omits *or wife.*
Prov. 6:5 That is, one who catches birds in a trap or snare

JANUARY 30

Matt. 20:6 NU-Text omits *idle.* **20:7** NU-Text omits the last clause of this verse. **20:16** NU-Text omits the last sentence of this verse. **20:22** NU-Text omits *and be baptized with the baptism that I am baptized with.*

20:23 NU-Text omits *and be baptized with the baptism that I am baptized with.*

JANUARY 31

Exod. 12:40 Samaritan Pentateuch and Septuagint read *Egypt and Canaan.*
Matt. 21:1 M-Text reads *Bethsphage.* **21:4** NU-Text omits *All.* **21:5** Zechariah 9:9 **21:7** NU-Text reads *and He sat.* **21:9** Psalm 118:26 **21:12** NU-Text omits *of God.* **21:13** Isaiah 56:7 / Jeremiah 7:11 **21:16** Psalm 8:2
Ps. 25:12 Or *he* / Or *he*

FEBRUARY 1

Exod. 13:19 Genesis 50:25 **14:25** Samaritan Pentateuch, Septuagint, and Syriac read *bound.*
Matt. 21:42 Psalm 118:22, 23

FEBRUARY 2

Exod. 15:23 Literally *Bitter* **16:31** Literally *What?* (compare Exodus 16:15) **17:7** Literally *Tempted* / Literally *Contention*
Matt. 22:13 NU-Text omits *take him away, and.* **22:30** NU-Text omits *of God.* **22:32** Exodus 3:6, 15
Prov. 6:22 Literally *it* **6:26** Literally *a man's wife, that is, of another*

FEBRUARY 3

Exod. 17:15 Hebrew *YHWH Nissi* **18:3** Compare Exodus 2:22 **18:4** Literally *My God Is Help* **18:12** Following Masoretic Text and Septuagint; Syriac, Targum, and Vulgate read *offered.*
Matt. 22:37 Deuteronomy 6:5 **22:39** Leviticus 19:18 **22:44** Psalm 110:1 **23:3** NU-Text omits *to observe.* **23:8** NU-Text omits *the Christ.*

FEBRUARY 4

Exod. 19:18 Septuagint reads *all the people.*
Matt. 23:14 NU-Text omits this verse. **23:17** NU-Text reads *sanctified.* **23:21** M-Text reads *dwelt.* **23:25** M-Text reads *unrighteousness.* **23:39** Psalm 118:26
Ps. 28:8 Following Masoretic Text and Targum; Septuagint, Syriac, and Vulgate read *the strength of His people.*

FEBRUARY 5

Matt. 24:6 NU-Text omits *all.* **24:7** NU-Text omits *pestilences.* **24:15** Daniel 11:31; 12:11
Prov. 7:22 Septuagint, Syriac, and Targum read *as a dog to bonds;* Vulgate reads *as a lamb . . . to bonds.*

FEBRUARY 6

Exod. 23:17 Hebrew *YHWH,* usually translated *LORD* **23:31** Hebrew *Nahar,* the Euphrates
Matt. 24:33 Or *He* **24:36** NU-Text adds *nor the Son.* **24:42** NU-Text reads *day.* **24:48** NU-Text omits *his coming.*
Ps. 30:3 Following Qere and Targum; Kethib, Septuagint, Syriac, and Vulgate read *from those who descend to the pit.* **30:4** Or *His holiness*
Prov. 7:27 Or *Sheol*

FEBRUARY 7
Matt. 25:6 NU-Text omits *is coming.* **25:13** NU-Text omits the rest of this verse.

FEBRUARY 8
Exod. 28:4 That is, an ornamented vest **28:30** Literally *the Lights and the Perfections* (compare Leviticus 8:8)
Matt. 25:31 NU-Text omits *holy.* **25:44** NU-Text and M-Text omit *Him.* **26:3** NU-Text omits *the scribes.*

FEBRUARY 9
Exod. 29:37 Compare Numbers 4:15 and Haggai 2:11-13
Matt. 26:26 M-Text reads *gave thanks for.* **26:28** NU-Text omits *new.* **26:31** Zechariah 13:7 **26:42** NU-Text reads *if this may not pass away unless.*
Prov. 8:16 Masoretic Text, Syriac, Targum, and Vulgate read *righteousness;* Septuagint, Bomberg, and some manuscripts and editions read *earth.*

FEBRUARY 10
Exod. 30:29 Compare Numbers 4:15 and Haggai 2:11-13 **31:10** Or *woven garments*
Matt. 26:52 M-Text reads *die.* **26:59** NU-Text omits *the elders.* **26:60** NU-Text puts a comma after *but found none,* does not capitalize *Even,* and omits *they found none.* / NU-Text omits *false witnesses.*
Ps. 32:title Hebrew *Maschil*
Prov. 8:30 A Jewish tradition reads *one brought up.*

FEBRUARY 11
Exod. 32:13 Genesis 13:15 and 22:17
Matt. 27:2 NU-Text omits *Pontius.* **27:10** Jeremiah 32:6-9
Ps. 33:7 Septuagint, Targum, and Vulgate read *in a vessel.*

FEBRUARY 12
Exod. 34:28 Literally *Ten Words*
Matt. 27:16 NU-Text reads *Jesus Barabbas.* **27:24** NU-Text omits *just.*

FEBRUARY 13
Exod. 35:19 Or *woven garments*
Matt. 27:34 NU-Text omits *sour.* **27:35** NU-Text and M-Text omit the rest of this verse. / Psalm 22:18 **27:41** M-Text reads *with the scribes, the Pharisees, and the elders.* **27:42** NU-Text reads *He is the King of Israel!* / NU-Text and M-Text read *we will believe in Him.* **27:46** Psalm 22:1 **27:56** NU-Text reads *Joseph.* **27:64** NU-Text omits *by night.*
Ps. 34:7 Or *Angel*

FEBRUARY 14
Matt. 28:2 NU-Text omits *from the door.* **28:9** NU-Text omits the first clause of this verse. **28:19** M-Text omits *therefore.* **28:20** NU-Text omits *Amen.*

FEBRUARY 15
Exod. 39:1 Or *woven garments* **39:41** Or *woven garments*
Mark 1:2 NU-Text reads *Isaiah the prophet.* / Malachi 3:1 **1:3** Isaiah 40:3 **1:10** NU-Text reads *out of.* **1:14** NU-Text omits *of the kingdom.* **1:27** NU-Text reads *What is this? A new doctrine with authority.*
Ps. 35:5 Or *Angel*

FEBRUARY 16
Mark 2:2 NU-Text omits *Immediately.*
Prov. 9:18 Or *Sheol*

FEBRUARY 17
Mark 2:16 NU-Text reads *of the.* **2:17** NU-Text omits *to repentance.* **3:5** NU-Text omits *as whole as the other.*

FEBRUARY 18
Lev. 6:18 Compare Numbers 4:15 and Haggai 2:11-13 **6:27** Compare Numbers 4:15 and Haggai 2:11-13 **6:30** The Most Holy Place when capitalized **7:21** Following Masoretic Text, Septuagint, and Vulgate; Samaritan Pentateuch, Syriac, and Targum read *swarming thing* (compare 5:2).
Mark 3:14 NU-Text adds *whom He also named apostles.* **3:15** NU-Text omits *to heal sicknesses and.* **3:16** NU-Text reads *and He appointed the twelve: Simon . . . .*

FEBRUARY 19
Lev. 8:8 Literally *the Lights and the Perfections* (compare Exodus 28:30)
Mark 3:32 NU-Text and M-Text add *and Your sisters.* **4:4** NU-Text and M-Text omit *of the air.* **4:9** NU-Text and M-Text omit *to them.* **4:12** Isaiah 6:9, 10

FEBRUARY 20
Lev. 10:18 The Most Holy Place when capitalized
Mark 4:40 NU-Text reads *Have you still no faith?* **5:1** NU-Text reads *Gerasenes.* **5:3** NU-Text adds *anymore.* **5:13** NU-Text reads *And He gave.*
Ps. 37:36 Following Masoretic Text, Septuagint, and Targum; Syriac and Vulgate read *I passed by.*

FEBRUARY 22
Lev. 13:2 Hebrew *saraath,* disfiguring skin diseases, including leprosy, and so in verses 2-46 and 14:1-32 **13:47** A mold, fungus, or similar infestation, and so in verses 47-59
Mark 6:11 NU-Text reads *whatever place.* / NU-Text omits the rest of this verse. **6:15** / NU-Text and M-Text omit *or.*

FEBRUARY 23
Lev. 14:34 Decomposition by mildew, mold, dry rot, etc., and so in verses 34-53
Mark 6:33 NU-Text and M-Text read *they.* **6:36** NU-Text reads *something to eat* and omits the rest of verse. **6:44** NU-Text and M-Text omit *about.*

FEBRUARY 24
Mark 7:2 NU-Text omits *when* and *they found fault.* **7:7** Isaiah 29:13 **7:8** NU-Text omits the rest of this verse. **7:10** Exodus 20:12; Deuteronomy 5:16 / Exodus 21:17 **7:16** NU-Text omits this verse. **7:19** NU-Text ends quotation with *eliminated,* setting off the final clause as Mark's comment that Jesus has declared all foods clean.

FEBRUARY 25
Lev. 16:33 That is, the Most Holy Place
Mark 7:24 NU-Text omits *and Sidon.*

FEBRUARY 26
Mark 8:14 NU-Text and M-Text read *they.* **8:17** NU-Text

omits *still.* **8:26** NU-Text reads *"Do not even go into the town."*

Ps. 42:title Hebrew *Maschil* **42:2** Following Masoretic Text and Vulgate; some Hebrew manuscripts, Septuagint, Syriac, and Targum read *I see the face of God.* **42:5** Following Masoretic Text and Targum; a few Hebrew manuscripts, Septuagint, Syriac, and Vulgate read *The help of my countenance, my God.* **42:6** Following Masoretic Text and Targum; a few Hebrew manuscripts, Septuagint, Syriac, and Vulgate put *my God* at the end of verse 5.

FEBRUARY 27
Lev. 21:7 Literally *he*
Mark 9:23 NU-Text reads *"If You can! All things. . . ."* **9:29** NU-Text omits *and fasting.*

FEBRUARY 28
Mark 9:40 M-Text reads *against you is on your side.* **9:44** NU-Text omits this verse. **9:46** NU-Text omits the last clause of verse 45 and all of verse 46. **9:48** Isaiah 66:24 **9:49** NU-Text omits the rest of this verse. **10:6** Genesis 1:27; 5:2 **10:8** Genesis 2:24
Ps. 44:title Hebrew *Maschil* **44:4** Following Masoretic Text and Targum; Septuagint and Vulgate read *and my God.* / Following Masoretic Text and Targum; Septuagint, Syriac, and Vulgate read *who commands.*

MARCH 1
Mark 10:19 Exodus 20:12-16; Deuteronomy 5:16-20 **10:24** NU-Text omits *for those who trust in riches.* **10:29** NU-Text omits *or wife.*
Prov. 10:21 Literally *heart*

MARCH 2
Ps. 45:title Hebrew *Shoshannim* / Hebrew *Maschil*

MARCH 3
Num. 1:14 Spelled *Reuel* in 2:14
Mark 11:1 M-Text reads *Bethsphage.* **11:4** NU-Text and M-Text read *a.* **11:9** Psalm 118:26 **11:10** NU-Text omits *in the name of the Lord.* **11:17** Isaiah 56:7 / Jeremiah 7:11 **11:26** NU-Text omits this verse.

MARCH 4
Num. 2:14 Spelled *Deuel* in 1:14 and 7:42 **3:9** Samaritan Pentateuch and Septuagint read *Me.* **3:28** Some manuscripts of the Septuagint read *three.*
Mark 12:4 NU-Text omits *and at him they threw stones.* **12:11** Psalm 118:22, 23

MARCH 5
Num. 4:7 Literally *the continual bread* **4:28** Literally *hand* **4:33** Literally *hand*
Mark 12:26 Exodus 3:6, 15 **12:28** / NU-Text reads *seeing.* **12:30** Deuteronomy 6:4, 5 / NU-Text omits this sentence. **12:31** Leviticus 19:18 **12:33** NU-Text omits *with all the soul.* **12:36** Psalm 110:1
Ps. 48:14 Following Masoretic Text and Syriac; Septuagint and Vulgate read *Forever.*

MARCH 6
Num. 7:8 Literally *hand* **7:42** Spelled *Reuel* in 2:14
Mark 12:42 Greek *lepta,* very small copper coins worth a fraction of a penny **13:8** NU-Text omits *and troubles.*

13:9 NU-Text and M-Text read *will stand.* **13:11** NU-Text omits *or premeditate.*
Ps. 49:11 Septuagint, Syriac, Targum, and Vulgate read *Their graves shall be their houses forever.* **49:12** Following Masoretic Text and Targum; Septuagint, Syriac, and Vulgate read *understand* (compare verse 20).

MARCH 7
Mark 13:14 Daniel 11:31; 12:11 / NU-Text omits *spoken of by Daniel the prophet.* **13:29** Or *He*
Ps. 50:18 Septuagint, Syriac, Targum, and Vulgate read *run.*

MARCH 8
Num. 10:29 Septuagint reads *Raguel* (compare Exodus 2:18). **11:3** Literally *Burning*
Mark 14:19 NU-Text omits this sentence.
Ps. 51:4 Septuagint, Targum, and Vulgate read *in Your words.*

MARCH 9
Num. 11:25 Targum and Vulgate read *did not cease.* **11:34** Literally *Graves of Craving* **13:8** Septuagint and Vulgate read *Oshea.* **13:16** Septuagint and Vulgate read *Oshea.* **13:24** Literally *Cluster* **13:33** Hebrew *nephilim*
Mark 14:22 NU-Text omits *eat.* **14:24** NU-Text omits *new.* **14:27** NU-Text omits *because of Me this night.* / Zechariah 13:7
Ps. 52:title Hebrew *Maschil*

MARCH 10
Num. 14:8 Exodus 3:8 **14:18** Exodus 34:6, 7 **15:16** Compare Exodus 12:49
Mark 14:65 NU-Text reads *received Him with slaps.* **14:70** NU-Text omits *and your speech shows it.*
Ps. 53:title Hebrew *Maschil*

MARCH 11
Mark 15:4 NU-Text reads *of which they accuse You.* **15:8** NU-Text reads *going up.* **15:28** Isaiah 53:12 / NU-Text omits this verse. **15:32** M-Text reads *believe Him.* **15:34** Psalm 22:1 **15:39** NU-Text reads *that He thus breathed His last.*
Ps. 54:title Hebrew *neginoth* / Hebrew *Maschil*
Prov. 11:5 Or *make smooth* or *straight*

MARCH 12
Mark 16:8 NU-Text and M-Text omit *quickly.* **16:18** NU-Text reads *and in their hands they will.* **16:20** Verses 9-20 are bracketed in NU-Text as not original. They are lacking in Codex Sinaiticus and Codex Vaticanus, although nearly all other manuscripts of Mark contain them.
Ps. 55:title Hebrew *neginoth* / Hebrew *Maschil*

MARCH 13
Num. 19:9 Literally *impurity* **20:13** Literally *Contention*
Luke 1:1 Or *are most surely believed* **1:17** Malachi 4:5, 6
Ps. 56:title Hebrew *Jonath Elem Rechokim*

MARCH 14
Num. 21:3 Literally *Utter Destruction* **21:14** Ancient unknown places; Vulgate reads *What He did in the Red*

Sea. **21:20** Hebrew *Jeshimon* **22:5** That is, the Euphrates / Or *the people of Amau*
Luke 1:28 NU-Text omits *blessed are you among women.*
1:29 NU-Text omits *when she saw him.*
Ps. 57:title Hebrew *Al Tashcheth*

MARCH 15

Num. 23:10 Or *dust cloud* **23:15** Following Masoretic Text, Targum, and Vulgate; Syriac reads *call;* Septuagint reads *go and ask God.* **23:28** Hebrew *Jeshimon*
Luke 1:78 NU-Text reads *shall visit.*
Ps. 58:title Hebrew *Al Tashcheth*

MARCH 16

Num. 24:9 Genesis 49:9 **24:17** Hebrew *Sheth* (compare Jeremiah 48:45) **24:24** Hebrew *Kittim /* Literally *he or that one* **25:1** Hebrew *Shittim*
Luke 2:5 NU-Text omits *wife.* **2:9** NU-Text omits *behold.* **2:14** NU-Text reads *toward men of goodwill.* **2:17** NU-Text omits *widely.* **2:21** NU-Text reads *for His circumcision.* **2:23** Exodus 13:2, 12, 15 **2:24** Leviticus 12:8 **2:33** NU-Text reads *And His father and mother.*
Ps. 59:title Hebrew *Al Tashcheth* **59:9** Following Masoretic Text and Syriac; some Hebrew manuscripts, Septuagint, Targum, and Vulgate read *my Strength.* **59:10** Following Qere; some Hebrew manuscripts, Septuagint, and Vulgate read *My God, His mercy;* Kethib, some Hebrew manuscripts and Targum read *O God, my mercy;* Syriac reads *O God, Your mercy.* **59:15** Following Septuagint and Vulgate; Masoretic Text, Syriac, and Targum read *spend the night.*

MARCH 17

Num. 26:12 Spelled *Jemuel* in Genesis 46:10 and Exodus 6:15 / Called *Jarib* in 1 Chronicles 4:24 **26:13** Called *Zohar* in Genesis 46:10 **26:15** Called *Ziphion* in Genesis 46:16 **26:16** Called *Ezbon* in Genesis 46:16 **26:17** Spelled *Arodi* in Samaritan Pentateuch, Syriac, and Genesis 46:16 **26:23** Hebrew *Puvah* (compare Genesis 46:13 and 1 Chronicles 7:1); Samaritan Pentateuch, Septuagint, Syriac, and Vulgate read *Puah.* / Samaritan Pentateuch, Septuagint, Syriac, and Vulgate read *Puaites.* **26:30** Called *Abiezer* in Joshua 17:2 **26:35** Called *Bered* in 1 Chronicles 7:20 **26:39** Masoretic Text reads *Shephupham,* spelled *Shephuphan* in 1 Chronicles 8:5. / Called *Huppim* in Genesis 46:21 **26:40** Called *Addar* in 1 Chronicles 8:3 **26:42** Called *Hushim* in Genesis 46:23 **26:48** Spelled *Jahziel* in 1 Chronicles 7:13
Luke 2:37 NU-Text reads *a widow until she was eighty-four.* **2:38** NU-Text reads *to God.* **2:40** NU-Text omits *in spirit.* **2:43** NU-Text reads *And His parents.*
Ps. 60:title Hebrew *Shushan Eduth* **60:12** Compare verses 5-12 with 108:6-13

MARCH 18

Luke 3:2 NU-Text and M-Text read *in the high priesthood of Annas and Caiaphas.* **3:6** Isaiah 40:3-5 **3:19** NU-Text reads *his brother's wife.*
Ps. 61:title Hebrew *neginah*

MARCH 19

Luke 3:24 This and several other names in the genealogy

are spelled somewhat differently in the NU-Text. Since the New King James Version uses the Old Testament spelling for persons mentioned in the New Testament, these variations, which come from the Greek, have not been footnoted.

MARCH 20

Luke 4:1 NU-Text reads *in.* **4:4** Deuteronomy 8:3 / NU-Text omits *but by every word of God.* **4:5** NU-Text reads *And taking Him up, he showed Him.* **4:8** NU-Text omits *Get behind Me, Satan.* / NU-Text and M-Text omit *For.* / Deuteronomy 6:13 **4:11** Psalm 91:11, 12 **4:12** Deuteronomy 6:16 **4:18** NU-Text omits *to heal the brokenhearted.* **4:19** Isaiah 61:1, 2 **4:23** Here and elsewhere the NU-Text spelling is *Capharnaum.* **4:26** Greek *Sarepta*
Prov. 11:21 Literally *hand to hand*

MARCH 21

Num. 32:41 Literally *Towns of Jair* **33:8** Many Hebrew manuscripts, Samaritan Pentateuch, Syriac, Targum, and Vulgate read *from Pi Hahiroth* (compare verse 7).
Luke 4:41 NU-Text omits *the Christ.* **4:44** NU-Text reads *Judea.*

MARCH 22

Num. 33:45 Same as *Ije Abarim,* verse 44 **33:49** Hebrew *Abel Shittim*
Luke 5:17 NU-Text reads *present with Him to heal.*

MARCH 23

Deut. 1:1 Hebrew *arabah* / One manuscript of the Septuagint, also Targum and Vulgate, read *Red Sea.* **1:4** Septuagint, Syriac, and Vulgate read *and* (compare Joshua 12:4). **1:7** Hebrew *arabah*
Luke 5:30 NU-Text reads *But the Pharisees and their scribes.* **5:33** NU-Text omits *Why do,* making the verse a statement. **5:36** NU-Text reads *No one tears a piece from a new garment and puts it on an old one.* **5:38** NU-Text omits *and both are preserved.* **5:39** NU-Text omits *immediately.* / NU-Text reads *good.* **6:1** NU-Text reads *on a Sabbath.* **6:9** M-Text reads *to kill.* **6:10** NU-Text and M-Text read *to him.* / NU-Text omits *as whole as the other.*

MARCH 24

Deut. 2:11 Hebrew *rephaim* **2:20** Hebrew *rephaim* **3:11** Hebrew *rephaim* **3:13** Hebrew *rephaim* **3:14** Literally *Towns of Jair*
Luke 6:26 NU-Text and M-Text omit *to you.* / M-Text omits *all.*
Ps. 67:title Hebrew *neginoth*

MARCH 25

Deut. 4:48 Syriac reads *Sirion* (compare 3:9).
Luke 6:45 NU-Text omits *treasure of his heart.* **6:48** NU-Text reads *for it was well built.* **6:49** NU-Text reads *collapsed.* **7:10** NU-Text omits *who had been sick.*
Ps. 68:4 Masoretic Text reads *deserts;* Targum reads *heavens* (compare verse 34 and Isaiah 19:1).

MARCH 26

Deut. 6:3 Exodus 3:8 **6:4** Or *The Lord is our God, the Lord alone* (that is, the only one)
Luke 7:19 NU-Text reads *the Lord.* **7:27** Malachi 3:1

7:28 NU-Text reads *there is none greater than John.*
7:31 NU-Text and M-Text omit *And the Lord said.*
Ps. 68:23 Septuagint, Syriac, Targum, and Vulgate read *you may dip your foot.* **68:28** Septuagint, Syriac, Targum, and Vulgate read *Command, O God.*

MARCH 27
Deut. 7:5 Hebrew *Asherim,* Canaanite deities
Luke 8:3 NU-Text and M-Text read *them.*
Ps. 69:title Hebrew *Shoshannim*

MARCH 28
Luke 8:10 Isaiah 6:9

MARCH 29
Deut. 11:9 Exodus 3:8 **11:14** Following Masoretic Text and Targum; Samaritan Pentateuch, Septuagint, and Vulgate read *He.* **11:24** That is, the Mediterranean
Luke 8:26 NU-Text reads *Gerasenes.* **8:27** NU-Text reads *who had demons and for a long time wore no clothes.* **8:37** NU-Text reads *Gerasenes.*
Ps. 70:2 Following Masoretic Text, Septuagint, Targum, and Vulgate; some Hebrew manuscripts and Syriac read *be appalled* (compare 40:15).
Prov. 12:4 Literally *A wife of valor*

MARCH 30
Deut. 14:5 Or *addax*
Luke 8:45 NU-Text omits *and those with him.* / NU-Text omits *and You say, "Who touched Me?'* **8:48** NU-Text omits *be of good cheer.* **8:40** NU-Text adds *anymore.* **8:51** NU-Text adds *with Him.* / NU-Text and M-Text read *Peter, John, and James.* **8:54** NU-Text omits *put them all outside.*

MARCH 31
Luke 9:23 M-Text omits *daily.*
Ps. 72:5 Following Masoretic Text and Targum; Septuagint and Vulgate read *They shall continue.*

APRIL 1
Deut. 20:8 Following Masoretic Text and Targum; Samaritan Pentateuch, Septuagint, Syriac, and Vulgate read *lest he make his brother's heart faint.*
Luke 9:35 NU-Text reads *This is My Son, the Chosen One.* **9:50** NU-Text reads *you.* / NU-Text reads *your.*
Ps. 73:7 Targum reads *face bulges;* Septuagint, Syriac, and Vulgate read *iniquity bulges.*

APRIL 2
Luke 9:54 NU-Text omits *just as Elijah did.* **9:55** NU-Text omits the rest of this verse. **9:56** NU-Text omits the first sentence of this verse. **10:1** NU-Text reads *seventy-two others.* **10:11** NU-Text reads *our feet.* **10:12** NU-Text and M-Text omit *But.*
Ps. 74:title Hebrew *Maschil*
Prov. 12:11 Literally *heart*

APRIL 3
Deut. 23:4 Hebrew *Aram Naharaim* **23:17** Hebrew *qedeshah,* feminine of *qadesh* (see following note) / Hebrew *qadesh,* that is, one practicing sodomy and prostitution in religious rituals
Luke 10:15 NU-Text reads *will you be exalted to heaven? You will be thrust down to Hades!* **10:17** NU-

reads *seventy-two.* **10:20** NU-Text and M-Text omit *rather.* **10:22** M-Text reads *And turning to the disciples He said, "All . . . .* **10:27** Deuteronomy 6:5 / Leviticus 19:18 **10:35** NU-Text omits *when he departed.*
Ps. 75:title Hebrew *Al Tashcheth*

APRIL 4
Deut. 26:3 Septuagint reads *my.* **26:5** Or *Aramean* **26:9** Exodus 3:8 **26:15** Exodus 3:8 **27:3** Exodus 3:8
Luke 10:39 NU-Text reads *the Lord's.* **10:41** NU-Text reads *the Lord.* **11:2** NU-Text omits *Our* and *in heaven.* / NU-Text omits the rest of this verse. **11:4** NU-Text omits *But deliver us from the evil one.* **11:11** NU-Text omits the words from *bread* through *for* in the next sentence.
Ps. 76:title Hebrew *neginoth* **76:2** That is, Jerusalem

APRIL 5
Deut. 28:56 Literally *her eye shall be evil toward*
Luke 11:15 NU-Text and M-Text read *Beelzebul.* **11:29** NU-Text omits *the prophet.*

APRIL 6
Deut. 29:19 Or *stubbornness*
Luke 11:44 NU-Text omits *scribes and Pharisees, hypocrites.* **11:53** NU-Text reads *And when He left there.* **11:54** NU-Text omits *and seeking* and *that they might accuse Him.* **12:6** Greek *assarion,* a coin of very small value
Ps. 78:title Hebrew *Maschil*

APRIL 7
Luke 12:15 NU-Text reads *all covetousness.* **12:31** NU-Text reads *His kingdom, and these things.*

APRIL 8
Deut. 32:43 A Dead Sea Scroll fragment adds *And let all the gods (angels) worship Him* (compare Septuagint and Hebrews 1:6). **32:44** Hebrew *Hoshea* (compare Numbers 13:8, 16)
Luke 12:39 NU-Text reads *he would not have allowed.*

APRIL 9
Deut. 33:16 Genesis 49:26
Luke 13:9 NU-Text reads *And if it bears fruit after that, well. But if not, you can cut it down.* **13:15** NU-Text and M-Text read *Hypocrites.* **13:19** NU-Text omits *large.* **13:21** Greek *sata,* approximately two pecks in all

APRIL 10
Deut. 34:2 That is, the Mediterranean **Josh. 2:1** Hebrew *Shittim*
Luke 13:31 NU-Text reads *In that very hour.* **13:35** NU-Text and M-Text omit *assuredly.* / Psalm 118:26 **14:3** NU-Text adds *or not.* **14:5** NU-Text and M-Text read *son.*

APRIL 11
Josh. 3:1 Hebrew *Shittim*
Luke 14:15 M-Text reads *dinner.*
Ps. 80:title Hebrew *Shoshannim* / Hebrew *Eduth* **80:11** That is, the Mediterranean / That is, the Euphrates

APRIL 12
Josh. 5:1 Following Kethib; Qere, some Hebrew manu-

scripts and editions, Septuagint, Syriac, Targum, and Vulgate read *they.* **5:3** Hebrew *Gibeath Haaraloth*
5:6 Exodus 3:8 **5:9** Literally *Rolling* **7:1** Called *Zimri* in 1 Chronicles 2:6
Luke 15:8 Greek *drachma,* a valuable coin often worn in a ten-piece garland by married women **15:22** NU-Text reads *Quickly bring.*
Ps. 81:title Hebrew *Al Gittith*

APRIL 13
Josh. 7:26 Literally *Trouble* **8:31** Deuteronomy 27:5, 6
Luke 16:6 Greek *batos,* eight or nine gallons each (Old Testament *bath*) **16:7** Greek *koros,* ten or twelve bushels each (Old Testament *kor*) **16:9** NU-Text reads *it fails.*
Ps. 82:1 Hebrew *elohim, mighty ones;* that is, the judges
82:6 Hebrew *elohim, mighty ones;* that is, the judges

APRIL 14
Josh. 10:28 Following Masoretic Text and most authorities; many Hebrew manuscripts, some manuscripts of the Septuagint, and some manuscripts of the Targum read *it.* **10:40** Hebrew *Negev,* and so throughout this book
Luke 16:21 NU-Text reads *with what fell.* **17:3** NU-Text omits *against you.* **17:4** M-Text omits *to you.*
17:9 NU-Text ends verse with *commanded;* M-Text omits *him.*

APRIL 15
Josh. 11:8 Hebrew *Misrephoth Maim* **11:13** Hebrew *tel,* a heap of successive city ruins **11:16** Hebrew *arabah*
Luke 17:21 NU-Text reverses *here* and *there.* **17:23** NU-Text reverses *here* and *there.* **17:36** NU-Text and M-Text omit verse 36.
Ps. 84:title Hebrew *Al Gittith* **84:7** Septuagint, Syriac, and Vulgate read *The God of gods shall be seen.*

APRIL 16
Josh. 13:5 Or *Giblites* **13:6** Hebrew *Misrephoth Maim*

APRIL 17
Josh. 15:8 Literally *Giants* **15:40** Or *Lahmam*
Luke 18:20 Exodus 20:12-16; Deuteronomy 5:16-20
18:28 NU-Text reads *our own.*

APRIL 18
Josh. 16:2 Septuagint reads *Bethel* (that is, Luz).
16:7 Or *Naaran* (compare 1 Chronicles 7:28)
17:2 Called *Jeezer* in Numbers 26:30 **18:16** Literally *Giants* **18:18** Or *Beth Arabah* (compare 15:6 and 18:22)
Luke 19:5 NU-Text omits *and saw him.* **19:13** The *mina* (Greek *mna,* Hebrew *minah*) was worth about three months' salary.

APRIL 19
Josh. 19:28 Following Masoretic Text, Targum, and Vulgate; a few Hebrew manuscripts read *Abdon* (compare 21:30 and 1 Chronicles 6:74).
Luke 19:29 M-Text reads *Bethsphage.* **19:38** Psalm 118:26 **19:45** NU-Text reads *those who were selling.*
19:46 NU-Text reads *shall be.* / Isaiah 56:7 / Jeremiah 7:11
Ps. 88:title Hebrew *Maschil*

APRIL 20
Josh. 21:37 Following Septuagint and Vulgate (compare 1 Chronicles 6:78, 79); Masoretic Text, Bomberg, and Targum omit verses 36 and 37. **22:14** Literally *thousands*
Luke 20:5 NU-Text and M-Text omit *then.* **20:17** Psalm 118:22 **20:19** M-Text reads *but they were afraid.*
20:23 NU-Text omits *Why do you test Me?*
Ps. 89:title Hebrew *Maschil*

APRIL 21
Josh. 22:21 Literally *thousands* **22:30** Literally *thousands* **22:34** Septuagint adds *and half the tribe of Manasseh*
Luke 20:30 NU-Text ends verse 30 here. **20:31** NU-Text and M-Text read *the seven also left no children.*
20:37 Exodus 3:6, 15 **20:43** Psalm 110:1
Ps. 89:19 Following many Hebrew manuscripts; Masoretic Text, Septuagint, Targum, and Vulgate read *holy ones.*

APRIL 22
Josh. 24:2 Hebrew *Nahar,* the Euphrates, and so in verses 3, 14, and 15
Luke 21:4 NU-Text omits *for God.* **21:8** NU-Text omits *Therefore.*
Prov. 13:23 Literally *what is swept away*

APRIL 23
Judg. 1:9 Hebrew *Negev,* and so throughout this book
1:14 Septuagint and Vulgate read *he urged her.*
1:35 Spelled *Shaalabbin* in Joshua 19:42
2:3 Septuagint, Targum, and Vulgate read *enemies to you.* **2:5** Literally *Weeping*
Luke 21:36 NU-Text reads *may have strength.*
Ps. 90:1 Septuagint, Targum, and Vulgate read *refuge.*
91:3 That is, one who catches birds in a trap or snare

APRIL 24
Judg. 2:13 Canaanite goddesses **3:7** Name or symbol for Canaanite goddesses **3:24** Literally *his*
Luke 22:14 NU-Text omits *twelve.* **22:18** NU-Text adds *from now on.* **22:31** NU-Text omits *And the Lord said.*

APRIL 25
Judg. 4:10 Literally *at his feet* **5:15** Following Septuagint, Syriac, Targum, and Vulgate; Masoretic Text reads *And my princes in Issachar.* / Literally *at his feet* **5:17** Or *at ease* **5:23** Or *Angel*
Luke 22:37 Isaiah 53:12 **22:44** NU-Text brackets verses 43 and 44 as not in the original text.

APRIL 26
Judg. 6:13 Hebrew *adoni,* used of man **6:15** Hebrew *Adonai,* used of God **6:24** Hebrew *YHWH Shalom*
6:25 Hebrew *Asherah,* a Canaanite goddess **6:32** Literally *Let Baal Plead*
Luke 22:57 NU-Text reads *denied it.* **22:60** NU-Text and M-Text read *a rooster.* **22:61** NU-Text adds *today.*
22:64 NU-Text reads *And having blindfolded Him, they asked Him.* **22:68** NU-Text omits *also* and *Me or let Me go.* **23:2** NU-Text omits *our.* **23:6** NU-Text omits *of Galilee.*
Ps. 95:8 Or *Meribah* / Or *Massah*

APRIL 27

Judg. 7:22 Hebrew *Beth Shittah*
Luke 23:15 NU-Text reads *for he sent Him back to us.*
23:17 NU-Text omits verse 17.   **23:23** NU-Text omits
and of the chief priests.   **23:25** NU-Text and M-Text
omit *to them.*   **23:30** Hosea 10:8   **23:34** NU-Text
brackets the first sentence as a later addition.
23:38 NU-Text omits *written* and *in letters of Greek,
Latin, and Hebrew.*   **23:39** NU-Text reads *Are You not
the Christ?*   **23:42** NU-Text reads *And he said, "Jesus,
remember me.*
Ps. 97:12 Or *His holiness*

APRIL 28

Luke 23:44 NU-Text adds *already.*   **23:45** NU-Text reads
obscured.   **23:46** Psalm 31:5   **23:51** NU-Text reads
who was waiting.   **24:1** NU-Text omits *and certain other
women with them.*   **24:4** NU-Text omits *greatly.*
24:12 NU-Text omits *lying.*

APRIL 29

Judg. 9:29 Literally *hand* / Following Masoretic Text and
Targum; Dead Sea Scrolls read *they;* Septuagint reads *I.*
9:37 Hebrew *Meonenim*   **10:4** Literally *Towns of Jair*
(compare Numbers 32:41 and Deuteronomy 3.14)
10:12 Some Septuagint manuscripts read *Midianites.*
Luke 24:13 Literally *sixty stadia*   **24:17** NU-Text reads
as you walk? And they stood still, looking sad.
24:40 Some printed New Testaments omit this verse. It
is found in nearly all Greek manuscripts.   **24:42** NU-
Text omits *and some honeycomb.*   **24:46** NU-Text
reads *written, that the Christ should suffer and rise.*
24:49 NU-Text omits *of Jerusalem.*   **24:53** NU-Text
omits *praising and.* / NU-Text omits *Amen.*
Ps. 100:3 Following Kethib, Septuagint, and Vulgate;
Qere, many Hebrew manuscripts, and Targum read *we
are His.*

APRIL 30

Judg. 11:33 Literally *Plain of Vineyards*
John 1:5 Or *overcome*   **1:9** Or *That was the true Light
which, coming into the world, gives light to every man.*
1:11 That is, His own things or domain / That is, His
own people   **1:16** NU-Text reads *For.*   **1:18** NU-Text
reads *only begotten God.*   **1:23** Isaiah 40.3   **1:28** NU-
Text and M-Text read *Bethany.*
Prov. 14:14 Literally *from above himself*

MAY 1

Judg. 13:25 Literally *Camp of Dan* (compare 18:12)
14:15 Following Masoretic Text, Targum, and Vulgate;
Septuagint and Syriac read *fourth.*
John 1:42 NU-Text reads *John.*   **1:51** NU-Text omits
hereafter.

MAY 2

Judg. 15:17 Literally *Jawbone Height*   **15:19** Literally
Jawbone (compare verse 14) / Literally *Spring of the
Caller*   **16:19** Following Masoretic Text, Targum, and
Vulgate; Septuagint reads *he began to be weak.*
John 2:17 NU-Text and M-Text read *will eat.* / Psalm 69:9
2:22 NU-Text and M-Text omit *to them.*
Ps. 103:16 Compare Job 7:10

MAY 3

Judg. 17:5 Hebrew *teraphim*   **18:7** Following Masoretic
Text, Targum, and Vulgate; Septuagint reads *with Syria.*
18:12 Literally *Camp of Dan*   **18:30** Septuagint and
Vulgate read *Moses.*
John 3:13 NU-Text omits *who is in heaven.*   **3:15** NU-
Text omits *not perish but.*
Ps. 104:18 Or *rock hyrax* (compare Leviticus 11:5)

MAY 4

Judg. 19:22 Literally *sons of Belial*   **19:24** Literally *his*
19:29 Literally *with her bones*   **20:13** Literally *sons of
Belial*   **20:18** Or *Bethel*   **20:26** Or *Bethel*   **20:34** Literally *they*   **20:45** Septuagint reads *the rest.*
Prov. 14:23 Literally *talk of the lips*

MAY 5

Judg. 21:2 Or *Bethel*   **Ruth 1:20** Literally *Pleasant* / Literally *Bitter*
John 4:42 NU-Text omits *the Christ.*

MAY 6

Ruth 3:9 Or *Spread the corner of your garment over your
maidservant*   **3:15** Many Hebrew manuscripts, Syriac,
and Vulgate read *she;* Masoretic Text, Septuagint, and
Targum read *he.*   **4:1** Hebrew *peloni almoni;* literally *so
and so*   **4:4** Following many Hebrew manuscripts,
Septuagint, Syriac, Targum, and Vulgate; Masoretic Text
reads *he.*   **4:5** Literally *raise up*   **4:10** Probably his
civic office   **4:20** Hebrew *Salmah*

MAY 7

1 Sam. 1:1 Spelled *Eliel* in 1 Chronicles 6:34 / Spelled
Toah in 1 Chronicles 6:34   **1:9** Hebrew *heykal,* palace
or temple   **1:16** Literally *daughter of Belial*   **1:20** Literally *Heard by God*   **1:23** Following Masoretic Text,
Targum, and Vulgate; Dead Sea Scrolls, Septuagint, and
Syriac read *your.*   **1:24** Dead Sea Scrolls, Septuagint,
and Syriac read *a three-year-old bull.*   **2:1** That is,
strength   **2:12** Literally *sons of Belial*
John 5:2 NU-Text reads *Bethzatha.*   **5:4** NU-Text omits
waiting for the moving of the water at the end of verse 3,
and all of verse 4.   **5:16** NU-Text omits *and sought to
kill Him.*
Prov. 14:29 Literally *short of spirit*

MAY 8

1 Sam. 2:22 Following Masoretic Text, Targum, and Vulgate; Dead Sea Scrolls and Septuagint omit the rest of
this verse.   **3:3** Hebrew *heykal,* palace or temple
3:15 Following Masoretic Text, Targum, and Vulgate;
Septuagint adds *and he arose in the morning.*   **4:1** Following Masoretic Text and Targum; Septuagint and Vulgate add *And it came to pass in those days that the
Philistines gathered themselves together to fight;*
Septuagint adds further *against Israel.*   **4:13** Following
Masoretic Text and Vulgate; Septuagint reads *beside the
gate watching the road.*   **4:21** Literally *Inglorious*
Ps. 106:3 Septuagint, Syriac, Targum, and Vulgate read
those who do.

MAY 9

1 Sam. 5:2 A Philistine idol   **5:4** Following Septuagint,
Syriac, Targum, and Vulgate; Masoretic Text reads

Dagon. **5:6** Probably bubonic plague. Septuagint and Vulgate add here *And in the midst of their land rats sprang up, and there was a great death panic in the city.* **6:19** Or *He struck seventy men of the people and fifty oxen of a man* **7:3** Canaanite goddesses **7:4** Canaanite goddesses **7:12** Literally *Stone of Help*

John 6:11 NU-Text omits *to the disciples, and the disciples.* **6:19** Literally *twenty-five or thirty stadia*

MAY 10

1 Sam. 8:16 Septuagint reads *cattle.* **9:21** Literally *tribes* **9:25** Following Masoretic Text and Targum; Septuagint omits *He spoke with Saul on top of the house;* Septuagint and Vulgate add ' *And he prepared a bed for Saul on top of the house, and he slept.*

John 6:22 NU-Text omits *that* and *which His disciples had entered.* **6:31** Exodus 16:4; Nehemiah 9:15; Psalm 78:24

Ps. 106:32 Or *Meribah*

MAY 11

1 Sam. 10:1 Following Masoretic Text, Targum, and Vulgate; Septuagint reads *His people Israel; and you shall rule the people of the Lord;* Septuagint and Vulgate add *And you shall deliver His people from the hands of their enemies all around them. And this shall be a sign to you, that God has anointed you to be a prince.* **10:19** Literally *thousands*

John 6:45 Isaiah 54:13 / M-Text reads *hears and has learned.* **6:47** NU-Text omits *in Me.* **6:55** NU-Text reads *true food* and *true drink.* **6:69** NU-Text reads *You are the Holy One of God.*

MAY 12

1 Sam. 12:8 Following Masoretic Text, Targum, and Vulgate; Septuagint adds *and the Egyptians afflicted them.* **12:10** Canaanite goddesses **12:11** Syriac reads *Deborah,* Targum reads *Gideon.* / Septuagint and Syriac read *Barak;* Targum reads *Simson.* / Syriac reads *Simson.* **13:1** The Hebrew is difficult (compare 2 Samuel 5:4; 2 Kings 14:2; see also 2 Samuel 2:10; Acts 13:21). **13:5** Following Masoretic Text, Septuagint, Targum, and Vulgate; Syriac and some manuscripts of the Septuagint read *three.* **13:15** Following Masoretic Text and Targum; Septuagint and Vulgate add *And the rest of the people went up after Saul to meet the people who fought against them, going from Gilgal to Gibeah in the hill of Benjamin.* **13:21** About two-thirds shekel weight

John 7:1 That is, the ruling authorities **7:8** NU-Text omits *yet.* **7:16** NU-Text and M-Text read *So Jesus.* **7:26** NU-Text omits *truly.* **7:29** NU-Text and M-Text omit *But.*

Ps. 108:13 Compare verses 6–13 with 60:5–12

MAY 13

1 Sam. 14:14 Literally *half the area plowed by a yoke* (of oxen in a day) **14:18** Following Masoretic Text, Targum, and Vulgate; Septuagint reads *ephod.* / Following Masoretic Text, Targum, and Vulgate; Septuagint reads *ephod.* **14:41** Following Masoretic Text and Targum; Septuagint and Vulgate read *Why do You not answer Your servant today? If the injustice is with me or Jonathan my son, O LORD God of Israel, give proof; and if You say it is with Your people Israel, give holiness.*

14:47 Septuagint and Vulgate read *prospered.* **14:49** Called *Abinadab* in 1 Chronicles 8:33 and 9:39

John 7:33 NU-Text and M-Text omit *to them.* **7:39** NU-Text reads *who believed.* / NU-Text omits *Holy.* **7:40** NU-Text reads *some.* **7:50** NU-Text reads *hebore.* **7:52** NU-Text reads *is to rise.* **7:53** The words *And everyone* through *sin no more* (8:11) are bracketed by NU-Text as not original. They are present in over 900 manuscripts.

Ps. 109:6 Hebrew *satan* **109:10** Following Masoretic Text and Targum; Septuagint and Vulgate read *be cast out.*

MAY 14

1 Sam. 16:7 Septuagint reads *For God does not see as man sees;* Targum reads *It is not by the appearance of a man;* Vulgate reads *Nor do I judge according to the looks of a man.* **16:11** Following Septuagint and Vulgate; Masoretic Text reads *turn around;* Targum and Syriac read *turn away.*

John 8:2 M-Text reads *very early.* **8:4** M-Text reads *we found this woman.* **8:5** M-Text reads *in our law Moses commanded.* / NU-Text and M-Text read *to stone such.* / M-Text adds *about her.* **8:6** NU-Text and M-Text omit *as though He did not hear.* **8:7** M-Text reads *He looked up.* **8:9** NU-Text and M-Text omit *being convicted by their conscience.* **8:10** NU-Text omits *and saw no one but the woman;* M-Text reads *He saw her and said.* / NU-Text and M-Text omit *of yours.* **8:11** NU-Text and M-Text add *from now on.*

MAY 15

1 Sam. 17:52 Following Masoretic Text, Syriac, Targum, and Vulgate; Septuagint reads *Gath.*

Prov. 15:11 Or *Sheol* / Hebrew *Abaddon*

MAY 16

1 Sam. 19:24 Compare 1 Samuel 10:12

John 8:38 NU-Text reads *heard from.* **8:54** NU-Text and M-Text read *our.* **8:59** NU-Text omits the rest of this verse.

MAY 17

1 Sam. 20:25 Following Masoretic Text, Syriac, Targum, and Vulgate; Septuagint reads *he sat across from Jonathan.* **21:11** Compare 1 Samuel 18:7

John 9:4 NU-Text reads *We.* **9:8** NU-Text reads *a beggar.* **9:9** NU-Text reads *"No, but he is like him."* **9:11** NU-Text omits *the pool of.* **9:35** NU-Text reads *Son of Man.*

Prov. 15:17 Or *vegetables*

MAY 18

1 Sam. 23:15 Or *in Horesh* **23:23** Literally *thousands* **23:28** Hebrew *Sela Hammahlekoth*

John 10:8 M-Text omits *before Me.*

MAY 19

1 Sam. 25:1 Following Masoretic Text, Syriac, Targum, and Vulgate; Septuagint reads *Maon.* **25:17** Literally *son of Belial* **25:25** Literally *Fool* **25:44** Spelled *Paltiel* in 2 Samuel 3:15

John 10:26 NU-Text omits *as I said to you.* **10:34** Psalm 82:6 **10:38** NU-Text reads *understand.*

MAY 20

1 Sam. 27:8 Or *Gezrites* **28:13** Hebrew *elohim*
28:17 Or *him*, that is, David
John 11:18 Literally *fifteen stadia* **11:30** NU-Text adds
still. **11:31** NU-Text reads *supposing that she was going to the tomb to weep there*. **11:41** NU-Text omits
from the place where the dead man was lying.
11:50 NU-Text reads *you*.

MAY 21

1 Sam. 29:5 Compare 1 Samuel 18:7 **29:10** Following
Masoretic Text, Targum, and Vulgate; Septuagint adds
*and go to the place which I have selected for you there;
and set no bothersome word in your heart, for you are
good before me. And rise on your way*. **30:22** Literally
men of Belial **30:30** Or *Borashan* **31:10** Spelled *Beth
Shean* in Joshua 17:11 and elsewhere
John 12:1 NU-Text omits *who had been dead*.
12:5 About one year's wages for a worker. **12:7** NU-
Text reads *that she may keep*. **12:13** Psalm 118:26
12:15 Zechariah 9:9
Ps. 118:14 Compare Exodus 15:2
Prov. 15:24 Or *Sheol*

MAY 22

2 Sam. 2:8 Called *Esh-Baal* in 1 Chronicles 8:33 and 9:39
John 12:38 Isaiah 53:1 **12:40** Isaiah 6:10 **12:41** NU-
Text reads *because*. **12:47** NU-Text reads *keep them*.

MAY 23

2 Sam. 2:16 Hebrew *Helkath Hazzurim* **3:15** Spelled
Palti in 1 Samuel 25:44 **3:18** Following many Hebrew
manuscripts, Septuagint, Syriac, and Targum; Masoretic
Text reads *he*.
John 13:2 NU-Text reads *And during supper*. **13:18** NU-
Text reads *My bread*. / Psalm 41:9 **13:25** NU-Text and
M-Text add *thus*.
Prov. 15:30 Literally *fat*

MAY 24

2 Sam. 4:1 That is, Ishbosheth **4:4** Called *Merib-Baal* in
1 Chronicles 8:34 and 9:40 **5:8** Compare 1 Chronicles
11:6 **5:9** Literally *The Landfill* **5:14** Spelled *Shimea*
in 1 Chronicles 3:5 **5:15** Spelled *Elishama* in 1 Chronicles 3:6 **5:20** Literally *Master of Breakthroughs*
5:25 Following Masoretic Text, Targum, and Vulgate;
Septuagint reads *Gibeon*. **6:2** Septuagint, Targum, and
Vulgate omit *by the Name;* many Hebrew manuscripts
and Syriac read *there*. **6:3** Septuagint adds *with the
ark*. **6:8** Literally *Outburst Against Uzzah*
John 14:2 Literally *dwellings* / NU-Text adds a word
which would cause the text to read either *if it were not
so, would I have told you that I go to prepare a place for
you?* or *if it were not so I would have told you; for I go to
prepare a place for you*. **14:14** NU-Text adds *Me*.

MAY 25

2 Sam. 7:11 That is, a royal dynasty **7:16** Septuagint
reads *Me*. **7:22** Targum and Syriac read *O Lord God*.
8:4 Or *seven thousand* (compare 1 Chronicles 18:4)
8:8 Spelled *Tibhath* in 1 Chronicles 18:8 **8:9** Spelled
Tou in 1 Chronicles 18:9 **8:10** Spelled *Hadoram* in
1 Chronicles 18:10 **8:12** Septuagint, Syriac, and some
Hebrew manuscripts read *Edom*. **8:13** Septuagint,

Syriac, and some Hebrew manuscripts read *Edomites*
(compare 1 Chronicles 18:12). **8:17** Spelled *Shavsha*
in 1 Chronicles 18:16
John 14:15 NU-Text reads *you will keep*. **14:28** NU-Text
omits *I said*.
Ps. 119:37 Following Masoretic Text, Septuagint, and Vulgate; Targum reads *Your words*.

MAY 26

2 Sam. 9:11 Septuagint reads *David's table*. **10:16** Hebrew *Hadarezer* / That is, the Euphrates **10:19** Hebrew
Hadarezer **11:21** Same as *Jerubbaal* (Gideon), Judges
6:32ff.
John 15:2 Or *lifts up* **15:7** NU-Text omits *you will*.
15:25 Psalm 69:4

MAY 27

2 Sam. 12:22 A few Hebrew manuscripts and Syriac read
God. **12:24** Following Kethib, Septuagint, and Vulgate;
Qere, a few Hebrew manuscripts, Syriac, and Targum
read *she*. **12:25** Qere, some Hebrew manuscripts,
Syriac, and Targum read *she*. / Literally *Beloved of the
Lord*
John 16:3 NU-Text and M-Text omit *to you*. **16:4** NU-
Text reads *their*. **16:15** NU-Text and M-Text read *He
takes of Mine and will declare it to you*. **16:33** NU-Text
and M-Text omit *will*.
Prov. 16:5 Literally *hand to hand*

MAY 28

2 Sam. 13:34 Septuagint adds *And the watchman went
and told the king, and said, "I see men from the way of
Horonaim, from the regions of the mountains."*
13:39 Following Masoretic Text, Syriac, and Vulgate;
Septuagint reads *the spirit of the king;* Targum reads *the
soul of King David*. / Following Masoretic Text and
Targum; Septuagint and Vulgate read *ceased to pursue
after*.
John 17:2 M-Text reads *shall*. **17:11** NU-Text and M-
Text read *keep them through Your name which You have
given Me*. **17:12** NU-Text omits *in the world*. / NU-
Text reads *in Your name which You gave Me. And I
guarded them;* (or *it;*). **17:20** NU-Text and M-Text omit
will.

MAY 29

2 Sam. 14:4 Many Hebrew manuscripts, Septuagint,
Syriac, and Vulgate read *came*. **15:7** Septuagint manuscripts, Syriac, and Josephus read *four*.
John 18:15 M-Text reads *the other*. **18:20** NU-Text
reads *where all the Jews meet*.

MAY 30

2 Sam. 16:12 Following Kethib, Septuagint, Syriac, and
Vulgate; Qere reads *my eyes;* Targum reads *tears of my
eyes*.
John 19:3 NU-Text reads *And they came up to Him and
said*. **19:7** NU-Text reads *the law*. **19:16** NU-Text
omits *and led Him away*.

MAY 31

2 Sam. 17:25 Spelled *Jether* in 1 Chronicles 2:17 and
elsewhere / Following Masoretic Text, some manuscripts of the Septuagint, and Targum; some manu-

scripts of the Septuagint read *Ishmaelite* (compare 1 Chronicles 2:17); Vulgate reads *of Jezrael.*
John 19:24 Psalm 22:18   **19:28** M-Text reads *seeing.*
19:36 Exodus 12:46; Numbers 9:12; Psalm 34:20
19:37 Zechariah 12:10

JUNE 1

2 Sam. 18:12 The ancient versions read *'Protect the young man Absalom for me!'*
John 20:16 NU-Text adds *in Hebrew.*   **20:18** NU-Text reads *disciples, "I have seen the Lord,"* . . .   **20:19** NU-Text omits *assembled.*   **20:29** NU-Text and M-Text omit *Thomas.*

JUNE 2

2 Sam. 19:40 Masoretic Text reads *Chimham.*   **20:1** Literally *man of Belial*
John 21:3 NU-Text omits *immediately.*   **21:15** NU-Text reads *John.*   **21:16** NU-Text reads *John.*   **21:17** NU-Text reads *John.*

JUNE 3

2 Sam. 20:14 Literally *him*   **21:8** Or *Merab* (compare 1 Samuel 18:19 and 25:44; 2 Samuel 3:14 and 6:23)   **21:12** Spelled *Beth Shean* in Joshua 17:11 and elsewhere   **21:18** Spelled *Sippai* in 1 Chronicles 20:4   **21:19** Spelled *Jair* in 1 Chronicles 20:5   **21:21** Spelled *Shammah* in 1 Samuel 16:9 and elsewhere   **22:2** Compare Psalm 18   **22:8** Following Masoretic Text, Septuagint, and Targum; Syriac and Vulgate read *hills* (compare Psalm 18:7).   **22:11** Following Masoretic Text and Septuagint; many Hebrew manuscripts, Syriac, and Vulgate read *He flew* (compare Psalm 18:10); Targum reads *He spoke with power.*
Acts 1:8 NU-Text reads *My witnesses.*   **1:14** NU-Text omits *and supplication.*   **1:15** NU-Text reads *brethren.*   **1:20** Psalm 69:25 / Psalm 109:8 / Greek *episkopen*

JUNE 4

2 Sam. 22:25 Septuagint, Syriac, and Vulgate read *the cleanness of my hands in His sight* (compare Psalm 18:24); Targum reads *my cleanness before His word.*   **22:33** Dead Sea Scrolls, Septuagint, Syriac, and Vulgate read *It is God who arms me with strength* (compare Psalm 18:32); Targum reads *It is God who sustains me with strength.* / Following Qere, Septuagint, Syriac, Targum, and Vulgate (compare Psalm 18:32); Kethib reads *His.*   **22:34** Following Qere, Septuagint, Syriac, Targum, and Vulgate (compare Psalm 18:33); Kethib reads *His.*   **22:46** Following Septuagint, Targum, and Vulgate (compare Psalm 18:45); Masoretic Text reads *gird themselves.*   **23:8** Literally *One Who Sits in the Seat* (compare 1 Chronicles 11:11) / Following Masoretic Text and Targum; Septuagint and Vulgate read *the three.*   **23:9** Spelled *Dodai* in 1 Chronicles 27:4   **23:18** Following Masoretic Text, Septuagint, and Vulgate; some Hebrew manuscripts and Syriac read *thirty;* Targum reads *the mighty men.*
Acts 2:1 NU-Text reads *together.*   **2:21** Joel 2:28-32   **2:23** NU-Text omits *have taken.*   **2:28** Psalm 16:8-11   **2:30** NU-Text omits *according to the flesh, He would raise up the Christ* and completes the verse with *He would seat one on his throne.*   **2:35** Psalm 110:1

2:41 NU-Text omits *gladly.*   **2:47** NU-Text omits *to the church.*

JUNE 5

2 Sam. 23:35 Spelled *Hezro* in 1 Chronicles 11:37   **24:13** Following Masoretic Text, Syriac, Targum, and Vulgate; Septuagint reads *three* (compare 1 Chronicles 21:12).   **24:16** Or *Angel* / Spelled *Ornan* in 1 Chronicles 21:15
Acts 3:20 NU-Text and M-Text read *Christ Jesus, who was ordained for you before.*   **3:23** Deuteronomy 18:15, 18, 19   **3:24** NU-Text and M-Text read *proclaimed.*   **3:25** Genesis 22:18; 26:4; 28:14

JUNE 6

Acts 4:11 Psalm 118:22   **4:25** NU-Text reads *who through the Holy Spirit, by the mouth of our father, Your servant David.*   **4:26** Psalm 2:1, 2   **4:36** NU-Text reads *Joseph.*
Ps. 124:7 That is, persons who catch birds in a trap or snare

JUNE 7

1 Kings 2:24 That is, a royal dynasty
Acts 5:23 NU-Text and M-Text omit *outside.*   **5:24** NU-Text omits *the high priest.*   **5:25** NU-Text and M-Text omit *saying.*   **5:41** NU-Text reads *the name;* M-Text reads *the name of Jesus.*

JUNE 8

1 Kings 4:8 Literally *Son of Hur*   **4:9** Literally *Son of Deker*   **4:10** Literally *Son of Hesed*   **4:11** Literally *Son of Abinadab*   **4:13** Literally *Son of Geber*   **4:21** That is, the Euphrates   **4:24** That is, the Euphrates   **4:26** Following Masoretic Text and most other authorities; some manuscripts of the Septuagint read *four* (compare 2 Chronicles 9:25).
Acts 6:1 That is, Greek-speaking Jews.   **6:8** NU-Text reads *grace.*   **6:13** NU-Text omits *blasphemous.*

JUNE 9

1 Kings 5:3 Literally *them*   **5:11** Following Masoretic Text, Targum, and Vulgate; Septuagint and Syriac read *twenty thousand.*   **5:16** Following Masoretic Text, Targum, and Vulgate; Septuagint reads *three thousand six hundred.*   **5:17** Literally *house,* and so frequently throughout this book   **6:1** Following Masoretic Text, Targum, and Vulgate; Septuagint reads *fortieth.*   **6:3** Hebrew *heykal;* here the main room of the temple, elsewhere called the holy place (compare Exodus 26:33 and Ezekiel 41:1) / Literally *it*   **6:5** Hebrew *debir;* here the inner room of the temple, elsewhere called the Most Holy Place (compare verse 16)   **6:8** Following Masoretic Text and Vulgate; Septuagint reads *upper story;* Targum reads *ground story.*   **6:27** Literally *house*
Acts 7:3 Genesis 12:1   **7:7** Genesis 15:14 / Exodus 3:12   **7:14** Or *seventy* (compare Exodus 1:5)   **7:28** Exodus 2:14

JUNE 10

1 Kings 7:7 Literally *floor,* that is, of the upper level   **7:13** Hebrew *Hiram* (compare 2 Chronicles 2:13, 14)   **7:26** Or *three thousand* (compare 2 Chronicles 4:5)

7:40 Hebrew *Hiram* (compare 2 Chronicles 2:13, 14)
7:45 Hebrew *Hiram* (compare 2 Chronicles 2:13, 14)
Acts 7:30 NU-Text omits *of the Lord.* **7:32** Exodus 3:6, 15 **7:34** Exodus 3:5, 7, 8, 10 **7:35** Exodus 2:14 **7:37** Deuteronomy 18:15 / NU-Text and M-Text omit *Him you shall hear.* **7:40** Exodus 32:1, 23 **7:43** Amos 5:25-27 **7:50** Isaiah 66:1, 2

JUNE 11
1 Kings 8:17 Literally *house*, and so in verses 18-20
Acts 8:5 Or *a*
Prov. 17:1 Or *sacrificial meals*

JUNE 12
1 Kings 9:13 Literally *Good for Nothing* **9:15** Literally *The Landfill* **9:24** Literally *he* (compare 2 Chronicles 8:11) **9:26** Hebrew *Eloth* (compare 2 Kings 14:22) **10:11** Or *algum* (compare 2 Chronicles 9:10, 11) **10:22** Literally *ships of Tarshish*, deep-sea vessels / Or *peacocks* **10:26** Following Septuagint, Syriac, Targum, and Vulgate (compare 2 Chronicles 9:25); Masoretic Text reads *led.* **10:29** Literally *by their hands*
Acts 8:33 Isaiah 53:7, 8 **8:37** NU-Text and M-Text omit this verse. It is found in Western texts, including the Latin tradition.

JUNE 13
1 Kings 11:33 Following Masoretic Text and Targum; Septuagint, Syriac, and Vulgate read *he has* **12:11** Literally *scorpions* **12:14** Literally *scorpions*
Acts 9:5 NU-Text and M-Text omit the last sentence of verse 5 and begin verse 6 with *But arise and go.* **9:17** M-Text omits *Jesus.* **9:20** NU-Text reads *Jesus.*

JUNE 14
1 Kings 12:31 Literally *a house* **13:12** Septuagint, Syriac, Targum, and Vulgate read *showed him.* **13:32** Literally *houses*
Acts 9:31 NU-Text reads *church . . . was edified.*
Ps. 132:6 Hebrew *Jaar*

JUNE 15
1 Kings 14:15 That is, the Euphrates / Hebrew *Asherim*, Canaanite deities **14:24** Hebrew *qadesh*, that is, one practicing sodomy and prostitution in religious rituals **14:31** Spelled *Abijah* in 2 Chronicles 12:16ff **15:6** Following Masoretic Text, Septuagint, Targum, and Vulgate; some Hebrew manuscripts and Syriac read *Abijam.* **15:12** Hebrew *qedeshim*, that is, those practicing sodomy and prostitution in religious rituals **15:13** A Canaanite goddess
Acts 10:6 NU-Text and M-Text omit the last sentence of this verse. **10:21** NU-Text and M-Text omit *who had been sent to him from Cornelius.*

JUNE 16
1 Kings 16:33 Hebrew *Asherah*, a Canaanite goddess **16:34** Compare Joshua 6:26
Acts 10:30 NU-Text reads *Four days ago to this hour, at the ninth hour.* **10:32** NU-Text omits the last sentence of this verse. **10:39** NU-Text and M-Text add *also.*

JUNE 17
1 Kings 18:19 A Canaanite goddess **18:31** Genesis 32:28

JUNE 18
1 Kings 19:5 Or *Angel* **19:7** Or *Angel*
Acts 12:5 NU-Text reads *constantly* (or *earnestly*).

JUNE 19
1 Kings 21:23 Following Masoretic Text and Septuagint; some Hebrew manuscripts, Syriac, Targum, and Vulgate read *plot of ground* (compare 2 Kings 9:36).
Acts 12:25 NU-Text and M-Text read *to.* **13:6** NU-Text reads *the whole island.*

JUNE 20
1 Kings 22:7 Or *him* **22:38** Syriac and Targum read *they washed his armor.* **22:46** Hebrew *qadesh*, that is, one practicing sodomy and prostitution in religious rituals **22:48** Or *ships of Tarshish*
Acts 13:17 M-Text omits *Israel.* **13:22** Psalm 89:20 / 1 Samuel 13:14 **13:23** M-Text reads *for Israel salvation.* **13:33** Psalm 2:7 **13:34** Isaiah 55:3 **13:35** Psalm 16:10 **13:41** Habakkuk 1:5

JUNE 21
2 Kings 1:3 Or *Angel* **1:15** Or *Angel* **1:17** The son of Ahab king of Israel (compare 3:1)
Acts 13:42 Or *And when they went out of the synagogue of the Jews;* NU-Text reads *And when they went out of the synagogue, they begged.* **13:47** Isaiah 49:6
Ps. 139:11 Vulgate and Symmachus read *cover.* **139:14** Following Masoretic Text and Targum; Septuagint, Syriac, and Vulgate read *You are fearfully wonderful.* **139:20** Septuagint and Vulgate read *They take your cities in vain.*

JUNE 22
Prov. 17:22 Or *makes medicine even better*

JUNE 23
2 Kings 5:12 Following Kethib, Septuagint, and Vulgate; Qere, Syriac, and Targum read *Amanah.*
Acts 15:11 NU-Text and M-Text omit *Christ.* **15:17** Amos 9:11, 12 **15:18** NU-Text (combining with v. 17) reads *Says the Lord, who makes these things known from eternity (of old).* **15:20** Or *fornication* **15:22** NU-Text and M-Text read *Barsabbas.* **15:24** NU-Text omits *saying, "You must be circumcised and keep the law".* **15:29** Or *fornication* **15:33** NU-Text reads *to those who had sent them.* **15:34** NU-Text and M-Text omit this verse.
Prov. 17:23 Literally *from the bosom*

JUNE 24
Acts 16:7 NU-Text adds *of Jesus.*
Ps. 142:title Hebrew *Maschil*

JUNE 25
2 Kings 8:21 Spelled *Jehoram* in verse 16
Ps. 143:9 Septuagint and Vulgate read *To You I flee.*

JUNE 26
2 Kings 9:27 Literally *The Garden House* **9:36** 1 Kings 21:23 **10:1** Following Masoretic Text, Syriac, and Targum; Septuagint reads *Samaria;* Vulgate reads *city.* **10:12** Or *The Shearing House* **10:21** Literally *house*, and so elsewhere in this chapter
Acts 17:5 NU-Text omits *who were not persuaded;* M-Text

omits *becoming envious.* **17:18** NU-Text and M-Text add *also.* **17:26** NU-Text omits *blood.*
Ps. 144:2 Following Masoretic Text, Septuagint, and Vulgate; Syriac and Targum read *the peoples* (compare 18:47).

JUNE 27

2 Kings 11:12 That is, the Law (compare Exodus 25:16, 21 and Deuteronomy 31:9) **12:1** Spelled *Joash* in 11:2ff **12:4** Compare Leviticus 27:2ff **12:19** Spelled *Jehoash* in 12:1ff **12:20** Literally *The Landfill* **12:21** Called *Zabad* in 2 Chronicles 24:26 / Called *Shimrith* in 2 Chronicles 24:26
Acts 18:7 NU-Text reads *Titius Justus.* **18:17** NU-Text reads *they all.* **18:21** NU-Text omits *I must* through *Jerusalem.*
Ps. 145:5 Following Masoretic Text and Targum; Dead Sea Scrolls, Septuagint, Syriac, and Vulgate read *They.* / Literally *on the words of Your wondrous works* **145:13** Following Masoretic Text and Targum; Dead Sea Scrolls, Septuagint, Syriac, and Vulgate add *The Lord is faithful in all His words, and holy in all His works.*

JUNE 28

2 Kings 13:1 Spelled *Jehoash* in 12:1ff **13:6** Hebrew *Asherah,* a Canaanite goddess **13:10** Spelled *Joash* in verse 9 **13:25** Spelled *Joash* in verses 12-14, 25 **14:6** Deuteronomy 24:16 **14:8** Spelled *Joash* in 13:12ff and 2 Chronicles 25:17ff **14:21** Called *Uzziah* in 2 Chronicles 26:1ff, Isaiah 6:1, and elsewhere

JUNE 29

2 Kings 15:12 2 Kings 10:30 **15:13** Called *Azariah* in 14:21ff and 15:1ff **15:19** That is, Tiglath-Pileser III (compare verse 29) **15:33** Spelled *Jerushah* in 2 Chronicles 27:1 **16:6** Some ancient authorities read *Syrians.*
Acts 19:13 NU-Text reads *I.* **19:16** M-Text reads *and they overpowered.* / NU-Text reads *both of them.* **19:24** Greek *Artemis* **19:27** NU-Text reads *she be deposed from her magnificence.* **19:37** NU-Text reads *our.*

JUNE 30

2 Kings 17:10 Hebrew *Asherim,* Canaanite deities **18:2** Called *Abijah* in 2 Chronicles 29:1ff **18:4** Hebrew *Asherah,* a Canaanite goddess / Literally *Bronze Thing*
Acts 20:8 NU-Text and M-Text read *we.* **20:24** NU-Text reads *But I do not count my life of any value or dear to myself.* **20:28** M-Text reads *of the Lord and God.* **20:34** NU-Text and M-Text omit *Yes.*

JULY 1

2 Kings 18:17 A title, probably *Commander in Chief* / A title, probably *Chief Officer* / A title, probably *Chief of Staff* or *Governor* **18:26** Literally *Judean* **19:31** Following many Hebrew manuscripts and ancient versions (compare Isaiah 37:32); Masoretic Text omits *of hosts.* **19:35** Or *Angel*
Acts 21:4 NU-Text reads *the disciples.* **21:8** NU-Text omits *who were Paul's companions.*
Prov. 18:8 A Jewish tradition reads *wounds.*

JULY 2

2 Kings 20:12 Spelled *Merodach-Baladan* in Isaiah 39:1 **20:13** Following many Hebrew manuscripts, Syriac, and Targum; Masoretic Text omits *all.* **21:3** Hebrew *Asherah,* a Canaanite goddess / The gods of the Assyrians **21:7** A Canaanite goddess
Acts 21:22 NU-Text reads *What then is to be done? They will certainly.* **21:25** NU-Text omits *that they should observe no such thing, except.* **21:29** M-Text omits *previously.*

JULY 3

2 Kings 22:12 *Abdon the son of Micah* in 2 Chronicles 34:20 **23:4** A Canaanite goddess / The gods of the Assyrians **23:6** Hebrew *Asherah,* a Canaanite goddess **23:7** Hebrew *qedeshim,* that is, those practicing sodomy and prostitution in religious rituals **23:10** Kethib reads *Sons.* **23:19** Following Septuagint, Syriac, and Vulgate; Masoretic Text and Targum omit *the Lord.* **23:27** 1 Kings 8:29
Acts 22:9 NU-Text omits *and were afraid.*

JULY 4

2 Kings 23:34 That is, Jehoahaz **24:17** Literally *his* **25:4** Literally *he* / Or *Arabah,* that is, the Jordan Valley **25:23** Spelled *Jezaniah* in Jeremiah 40:8 **25:27** Literally *Man of Marduk*
Acts 22:20 NU-Text omits *to his death.* **23:5** Exodus 22:28 **23:9** NU-Text omits last clause and reads *what if a spirit or an angel has spoken to him?*
Ps. 2:9 Following Masoretic Text and Targum; Septuagint, Syriac, and Vulgate read *rule* (compare Revelation 2:27). **2:12** Septuagint and Vulgate read *Embrace discipline;* Targum reads *Receive instruction.* / Septuagint reads *the Lord.*

JULY 5

1 Chron. 1:2 Hebrew *Qenan* **1:4** Following Masoretic Text and Vulgate; Septuagint adds *the sons of Noah.* **1:6** Spelled *Riphath* in Genesis 10:3 **1:7** Spelled *Tarshish* in Genesis 10:4 / Spelled *Dodanim* in Genesis 10:4 **1:9** Spelled *Sabtah* in Genesis 10:7 / Spelled *Raamah* in Genesis 10:7 **1:17** Spelled *Mash* in Genesis 10:23 **1:19** Literally *Division* **1:22** Spelled *Obal* in Genesis 10:28 **1:30** Spelled *Hadar* in Genesis 25:15 **1:36** Spelled *Zepho* in Genesis 36:11 / Compare Genesis 36:12 **1:40** Spelled *Alvan* in Genesis 36:23 / Spelled *Shepho* in Genesis 36:23 **1:41** Spelled *Hemdan* in Genesis 36:26 **1:42** Spelled *Akan* in Genesis 36:27 **1:50** Spelled *Hadar* in Genesis 36:39 / Spelled *Pau* in Genesis 36:39 **1:51** Spelled *Alvah* in Genesis 36:40 **2:7** Spelled *Achan* in Joshua 7:1 and elsewhere **2:9** Spelled *Caleb* in 2:18, 42 **2:11** Spelled *Salmon* in Ruth 4:21 and Luke 3:32 **2:13** Spelled *Shammah* in 1 Samuel 16:9 and elsewhere **2:17** Compare 2 Samuel 17:25
Acts 23:15 NU-Text omits *tomorrow.* **23:30** NU-Text reads *there would be a plot against the man.*

JULY 6

1 Chron. 2:19 Spelled *Ephrathah* elsewhere **2:52** Same as the *Manahethites,* verse 54 **3:1** Called *Chileab* in 2 Samuel 3:3 **3:5** Spelled *Shammua* in 14:4 and 2 Samuel 5:14 / Spelled *Bathsheba* in 2 Samuel 11:3 / Called *Eliam* in 2 Samuel 11:3   **3:6** Spelled *Elishua* in 14:5 and 2 Samuel 5:15 / Spelled *Elpelet* in 14:5   **3:8** Spelled *Beeliada* in 14:7   **3:10** Spelled *Abijam* in 1 Kings 15:1   **3:11** Spelled *Jehoram* in 2 Kings 1:17 and 8:16 / Spelled *Jehoash* in 2 Kings 12:1   **3:12** Called *Uzziah* in Isaiah 6:1   **3:15** Called *Jehoahaz* in 2 Kings 23:31   **3:16** Compare 2 Kings 24:17   **3:17** Also called *Coniah* in Jeremiah 22:24 and *Jehoiachin* in 2 Kings 24:8 / Or *Jeconiah the captive were*

Acts 24:6 NU-Text ends the sentence here and omits the rest of verse 6, all of verse 7, and the first clause of verse 8.   **24:9** NU-Text and M-Text read *joined the attack.*   **24:15** NU-Text omits *of the dead.*   **24:20** NU-Text and M-Text read *say what wrongdoing they found.*   **24:26** NU-Text omits *that he might release him.*

Ps. 4:3 Many Hebrew manuscripts, Septuagint, Targum, and Vulgate read *made wonderful.*

JULY 7

1 Chron. 4:9 Literally *He Will Cause Pain*   **4:13** Septuagint and Vulgate add *and Meonothai.*   **4:14** Literally *Valley of Craftsmen*   **4:17** Literally *she*   **4:18** Or *His Judean wife*   **4:23** Literally *Plants* / Literally *Hedges*   **4:24** Called *Jachin* in Genesis 46:10 / Called *Zohar* in Genesis 46:10   **4:33** Or *Baalath Beer* (compare Joshua 19:8)   **5:6** Hebrew *Tilgath-Pilneser*

Acts 25:2 NU-Text reads *chief priests.*   **26:10** NU-Text omits *to destruction,* although it is implied.

Ps. 5:title Hebrew *nehiloth*

JULY 8

1 Chron. 5:26 Hebrew *Tilgath-Pilneser*   **6:16** Hebrew *Gershom* (alternate spelling of *Gershon,* as in verses 1, 17, 20, 43, 62, and 71)   **6:26** Compare verses 35 / Spelled *Zuph* in verse 35 and 1 Samuel 1:1 / Compare verse 34   **6:27** Compare verse 34   **6:28** Following Septuagint, Syriac, and Arabic (compare verse 33 and 1 Samuel 8:2) / Hebrew *Vashent*   **6:34** Spelled *Elihu* in 1 Samuel 1:1 / Spelled *Tohu* in 1 Samuel 1:1   **6:58** Spelled *Holon* in Joshua 21:15   **6:59** Spelled *Ain* in Joshua 21:16   **6:60** Spelled *Almon* in Joshua 21:18   **6:77** Hebrew *Rimmono,* alternate spelling of *Rimmon;* see 4:32

Acts 26:17 NU-Text and M-Text omit *now.*

Ps. 6:title Hebrew *sheminith*

JULY 9

1 Chron. 7:1 Spelled *Puvah* in Genesis 46:13   **7:12** Called *Hupham* in Numbers 26:39   **7:13** Spelled *Jahzeel* in Genesis 46:24 / Spelled *Shillem* in Genesis 46:24   **7:14** The son of Gilead (compare Numbers 26:30, 31)   **7:15** Compare verse 12 / Literally *the second* / Compare Numbers 26:30-33   **7:23** Literally *In Tragedy*   **7:27** Hebrew *Non*   **7:28** Many Hebrew manuscripts, Bomberg, Septuagint, Targum, and Vulgate read *Gazza.*   **7:31** Or *Birzavith* or *Birzoth*   **7:32** Spelled *Shemer* in verse 34 / Spelled *Helem* in verse 35   **7:37** Spelled *Jether* in verse 38   **8:1** Spelled *Ahiram* in Numbers 26:38   **8:3** Called *Ard* in Numbers 26:40   **8:32** Spelled *Shimeam* in 9:38   **8:33** Also the son of Gibeon (compare 9:36, 39) / Called *Jishui* in 1 Samuel 14:49 / Called *Ishbosheth* in 2 Samuel 2:8 and else-

where   **8:34** Called *Mephibosheth* in 2 Samuel 4:4   **8:36** Spelled *Jarah* in 9:42   **8:37** Spelled *Rephaiah* in 9:43

Acts 27:14 NU-Text reads *Euraquilon.*   **27:16** NU-Text reads *Cauda.*   **27:17** M-Text reads *Syrtes.*

Ps. 7:title Hebrew *Shiggaion*   **7:6** Following Masoretic Text, Targum, and Vulgate; Septuagint reads *O Lord my God.*

JULY 10

1 Chron. 9:37 Called *Zecher* in 8:31   **9:38** Spelled *Shimeah* in 8:32   **9:41** Spelled *Tarea* in 8:35 / Following Arabic, Syriac, Targum, and Vulgate (compare 8:35); Masoretic Text and Septuagint omit *and Ahaz.*   **9:42** Spelled *Jehoaddah* in 8:36   **9:43** Spelled *Raphah* in 8:37

Ps. 8:title Hebrew *Al Gittith*   **8:5** Hebrew *Elohim, God;* Septuagint, Syriac, Targum, and Jewish tradition translate as *angels.*

Prov. 18:24 Following Greek manuscripts, Targum, Syriac, and Vulgate; Masoretic Text reads *may come to ruin*

JULY 11

1 Chron. 11:8 Literally *The Landfill*   **11:11** Following Qere; Kethib, Septuagint, and Vulgate read *the thirty* (compare 2 Samuel 23:8)   **11:20** Following Masoretic Text, Septuagint, and Vulgate; Syriac reads *thirty.*   **11:27** Spelled *Harodite* in 2 Samuel 23:25 / Called *Paltite* in 2 Samuel 23:26   **11:30** Spelled *Heleb* in 2 Samuel 23:29 and *Heldai* in 1 Chronicles 27:15   **11:31** Spelled *Ittai* in 2 Samuel 23:29   **11:32** Spelled *Hiddai* in 2 Samuel 23:30 / Spelled *Abi-Albon* in 2 Samuel 23:31   **11:33** Spelled *Barhumite* in 2 Samuel 23:31   **11:39** Spelled *Beerothite* in 2 Samuel 23:37

Acts 28:19 That is, the ruling authorities   **28:25** NU-Text reads *your.*   **28:27** Isaiah 6:9, 10   **28:29** NU-Text omits this verse.

Ps. 9:title Hebrew *Muth Labben*

JULY 12

1 Chron. 13:6 Called *Baale Judah* in 2 Samuel 6:2   **13:9** Called *Nachon* in 2 Samuel 6:6   **13:11** Literally *Outburst Against Uzza*   **14:4** Spelled *Shimea* in 3:5   **14:5** Spelled *Elishama* in 3:6 / Spelled *Eliphelet* in 3:6   **14:7** Spelled *Eliada* in 3:8   **14:11** Literally *Master of Breakthroughs*

Rom. 1:16 NU-Text omits *of Christ.*   **1:17** Habakkuk 2:4

Ps. 9:16 Hebrew *Higgaion*

JULY 13

1 Chron. 15:18 Following Masoretic Text and Vulgate; Septuagint omits *Ben.*   **16:22** Compare verses 8-22 with Psalm 105:1-15   **16:33** Compare verses 23-33 with Psalm 96:1-13   **16:34** Compare verse 34 with Psalm 106:1   **16:36** Compare verses 35, 36 with Psalm 106:47, 48

Rom. 1:29 NU-Text omits *sexual immorality.*   **1:31** NU-Text omits *unforgiving.*

JULY 14

1 Chron. 17:10 That is, a royal dynasty   **18:3** Hebrew *Hadarezer,* and so throughout chapters 18 and 19   **18:4** Or *seven hundred* (compare 2 Samuel 8:4)

18:8 Spelled *Betah* in 2 Samuel 8:8　**18:9** Spelled *Toi* in 2 Samuel 8:9, 10　**18:10** Spelled *Joram* in 2 Samuel 8:10　**18:12** Or *Syrians* (compare 2 Samuel 8:13)　**18:16** Spelled *Seraiah* in 2 Samuel 8:17
Rom. 2:6 Psalm 62:12; Proverbs 24:12　**2:17** NU-Text reads *But if.*　**2:24** Isaiah 52:5; Ezekiel 36:22

JULY 15

1 Chron. 19:6 Hebrew *Aram Naharaim* / Spelled *Zoba* in 2 Samuel 10:6　**19:16** That is, the Euphrates / Spelled *Shobach* in 2 Samuel 10:16　**19:18** Or *seven hundred* (compare 2 Samuel 10:18) / Or *horsemen* (compare 2 Samuel 10:18)　**20:3** Septuagint reads *cut them.*　**20:4** Spelled *Saph* in 2 Samuel 21:18　**20:5** Spelled *Jaare-Oregim* in 2 Samuel 21:19　**20:7** Spelled *Shimeah* in 2 Samuel 21:21 and *Shammah* in 1 Samuel 16:9　**21:12** Or *seven* (compare 2 Samuel 24:13) / Or *Angel*, and so elsewhere in this chapter　**21:15** Or *He* / Or *Your* / Spelled *Araunah* in 2 Samuel 24:16
Rom. 3:4 Psalm 51:4
Ps. 11:7 Or *The upright beholds His countenance*

JULY 16

1 Chron. 22:9 Literally *Peaceful*　**23:7** Spelled *Libni* in Exodus 6:17　**23:10** Septuagint and Vulgate read *Zizah* (compare verse 11).　**23:15** Hebrew *Gershom* (compare 6:16)　**23:16** Spelled *Shubael* in 24:20
Rom. 3:12 Psalms 14:1-3; 53:1-3; Ecclesiastes 7:20　**3:13** Psalm 5:9 / Psalm 140:3　**3:14** Psalm 10:7　**3:17** Isaiah 59:7, 8　**3:18** Psalm 36:1　**3:22** NU-Text omits *and on all.*
Ps. 12:title Hebrew *sheminith*

JULY 17

1 Chron. 24:15 Septuagint and Vulgate read *Aphses.*　**24:16** Masoretic Text reads *Jehezkel.*　**24:20** Spelled *Shebuel* in 23:16　**24:22** Spelled *Shelomith* in 23:18　**24:23** Supplied from 23:19 (following some Hebrew manuscripts and Septuagint manuscripts) / Supplied from 23:19 (following some Hebrew manuscripts and Septuagint manuscripts)　**25:2** Spelled *Jesharelah* in verse 14　**25:3** Spelled *Jizri* in verse 11 / *Shimei*, appearing in one Hebrew and several Septuagint manuscripts, completes the total of six sons (compare verse 17).　**25:4** Spelled *Azarel* in verse 18 / Spelled *Shubael* in verse 20 / Spelled *Jeremoth* in verse 22　**25:5** That is, to increase his power or influence　**25:11** Spelled *Zeri* in verse 3　**25:14** Spelled *Asharelah* in verse 2　**25:18** Spelled *Uzziel* in verse 4　**25:20** Spelled *Shebuel* in verse 4　**25:22** Spelled *Jerimoth* in verse 4
Rom. 4:1 Or *Abraham our (fore)father according to the flesh has found?*　**4:3** Genesis 15:6　**4:8** Psalm 32:1, 2
Prov. 19:16 Literally *despises*, figurative of recklessness or carelessness

JULY 18

1 Chron. 26:15 Hebrew *asuppim*　**26:17** Hebrew *asuppim*　**26:18** Probably a court or colonnade extending west of the temple　**27:4** Hebrew *Dodai*, usually spelled *Dodo* (compare 2 Samuel 23:9)　**27:8** Spelled *Shammoth* in 11:27 and *Shammah* in 2 Samuel 23:11　**27:15** Spelled *Heled* in 11:30 and *Heleb* in 2 Samuel 23:29
Rom. 4:17 Genesis 17:5　**4:18** Genesis 15:5　**4:22** Gen-

esis 15:6　**5:1** Another ancient reading is, *let us have peace.*

JULY 19

1 Chron. 29:1 Literally *palace*　**29:8** Possibly the same as *Jehieli* (compare 26:21, 22)　**29:19** Literally *palace*
Prov. 19:18 Literally *to put him to death;* a Jewish tradition reads *on his crying.*

JULY 20

2 Chron. 1:5 Some authorities read *it was there.*　**1:17** Literally *by their hands*　**2:3** Hebrew *Huram* (compare 1 Kings 5:1)　**2:12** Hebrew *Huram* (compare 1 Kings 5:1)　**2:13** Spelled *Hiram* in 1 Kings 7:13 / Literally *father* (compare 1 Kings 7:13, 14)　**3:1** Literally *He*, following Masoretic Text and Vulgate; Septuagint reads *the Lord*; Targum reads *the Angel of the Lord*. / Spelled *Araunah* in 2 Samuel 24:16ff　**3:4** The main room of the temple; elsewhere called the holy place (compare 1 Kings 6:3) / Following Masoretic Text, Septuagint, and Vulgate; Arabic, some manuscripts of the Septuagint, and Syriac omit *one hundred and.*　**3:5** Literally *house*　**3:15** Literally *house* / Or *eighteen* (compare 1 Kings 7:15; 2 Kings 25:17; and Jeremiah 52:21)

JULY 21

2 Chron. 4:5 Or *two thousand* (compare 1 Kings 7:26)　**4:16** Literally *father*　**4:17** Spelled *Zaretan* in 1 Kings 7:46　**5:7** Literally *house*　**5:13** Compare Psalm 106:1　**6:7** Literally *house*, and so in verses 8-10
Rom. 7:7 Exodus 20:17; Deuteronomy 5:21

JULY 22

2 Chron. 6:12 Literally *he* (compare 1 Kings 8:22)　**6:18** Literally *house*　**6:42** Compare Psalm 132:8-10　**7:1** Literally *house*　**7:3** Compare Psalm 106:1　**7:6** Compare Psalm 106:1　**7:8** That is, the Shihor (compare 1 Chronicles 13:5)　**8:2** Hebrew *Huram* (compare 2 Chronicles 2:3)
Rom. 8:1 NU-Text omits the rest of this verse.
Ps. 18:13 Following Masoretic Text, Targum, and Vulgate; a few Hebrew manuscripts and Septuagint omit *Hailstones and coals of fire.*
Prov. 19:24 Septuagint and Syriac read *bosom;* Targum and Vulgate read *armpit.*

JULY 23

2 Chron. 8:16 Following Septuagint, Syriac, and Vulgate; Masoretic Text reads *as far as.*　**8:17** Hebrew *Eloth* (compare 2 Kings 14:22)　**9:10** Or *almug* (compare 1 Kings 10:11, 12)　**9:11** Or *almug* (compare 1 Kings 10:11, 12)　**9:16** Or *three minas* (compare 1 Kings 10:17)　**9:21** Hebrew *Huram* (compare 1 Kings 10:22) / Literally *ships of Tarshish* (deep-sea vessels) / Or *peacocks*　**9:26** That is, the Euphrates　**10:11** Literally *scorpions*　**10:14** Following many Hebrew manuscripts, Septuagint, Syriac, and Vulgate (compare verse 10 and 1 Kings 12:14); Masoretic Text reads *I.* / Literally *scorpions*

JULY 24

2 Chron. 11:16 Literally *after them*　**11:20** Literally *daughter*, but in the broader sense of granddaughter

(compare 2 Chronicles 13:2) **12:16** Spelled *Abijam* in 1 Kings 14:31 **13:2** Spelled *Maachah* in 11:20, 21 and 1 Kings 15:2 **13:19** Or *Ephron*
Rom. 8:26 NU-Text omits *for us.* **8:36** Psalm 44:22

JULY 25

2 Chron. 15:8 Following Masoretic Text and Septuagint; Syriac and Vulgate read *Azariah the son of Oded* (compare verse 1). **15:16** A Canaanite deity
Rom. 9:3 Or *relatives* **9:7** Genesis 21:12 **9:9** Genesis 18:10, 14 **9:12** Genesis 25:23 **9:13** Malachi 1:2, 3 **9:15** Exodus 33:19 **9:17** Exodus 9:16
Ps. 19:4 Septuagint, Syriac, and Vulgate read *sound;* Targum reads *business.*

JULY 26

2 Chron. 17:4 Septuagint reads *LORD God.* **18:6** Or *him*
Rom. 9:25 Hosca 2:23 **9:26** Hosea 1:10 **9:27** Isaiah 10:22, 23 **9:28** NU-Text reads *For the Lord will finish the work and cut it short upon the earth.* **9:29** Literally, in Hebrew, *Hosts* / Isaiah 1:9 **9:31** NU-Text omits *of righteousness.* **9:32** NU-Text reads *by works.* **9:33** Isaiah 8:14; 28:16 **10:1** NU-Text reads *them.* **10:5** Leviticus 18:5 **10:6** Deuteronomy 30:12 **10:7** Deuteronomy 30:13 **10:8** Deuteronomy 30:14 **10:11** Isaiah 28:16 **10:13** Joel 2:32
Prov. 20:2 Literally *fear* or *terror* which is produced by the king's wrath

JULY 27

2 Chron. 19:8 Septuagint and Vulgate read *for the inhabitants of Jerusalem.* **20:1** Following Masoretic Text and Vulgate; Septuagint reads *Meunites* (compare 26:7). **20:2** Following Masoretic Text, Septuagint, and Vulgate; some Hebrew manuscripts and Old Latin read *Edom.* **20:21** Compare Psalm 106:1 **20:25** A few Hebrew manuscripts, Old Latin, and Vulgate read *garments;* Septuagint reads *armor.* **20:26** Literally *Blessing*
Rom. 10:15 NU-Text omits *preach the gospel of peace, Who.* / Isaiah 52:7; Nahum 1:15 **10:16** Isaiah 53:1 **10:18** Psalm 19:4 **10:19** Deuteronomy 32:21 **10:20** Isaiah 65:1 **10:21** Isaiah 65:2 **11:3** 1 Kings 19:10, 14 **11:4** 1 Kings 19:18 **11:6** NU-Text omits the rest of this verse. **11:8** Deuteronomy 29:4; Isaiah 29:10 **11:10** Psalm 69:22, 23

JULY 28

2 Chron. 21:17 Elsewhere called *Ahaziah* (compare 2 Chronicles 22:1) **22:2** Or *twenty-two* (compare 2 Kings 8:26) **22:5** Also spelled *Joram* (compare verses 5 and 7; 2 Kings 8:28; and elsewhere) **22:6** Some Hebrew manuscripts, Septuagint, Syriac, Vulgate, and 2 Kings 8:29 read *Ahaziah.* **22:11** Spelled *Jehosheba* in 2 Kings 11:2 **23:11** That is, the Law (compare Exodus 25:16, 21; 31:18) **23:17** Literally *house*
Rom. 11:22 NU-Text adds *of God.* **11:26** Or *delivered* **11:27** Isaiah 59:20, 21 **11:34** Isaiah 40:13; Jeremiah 23:18 **11:35** Job 41:11
Ps. 22:title Hebrew *Aijeleth Hashahar* **22:8** Septuagint, Syriac, and Vulgate read *hoped;* Targum reads *praised.* **22:16** Following some Hebrew manuscripts, Septuagint, Syriac, Vulgate; Masoretic Text reads *Like a lion.*

JULY 29

2 Chron. 24:25 Septuagint and Vulgate read *son* (compare verses 20-22). **24:26** Or *Jozachar* (compare 2 Kings 12:21) / Or *Shomer* (compare 2 Kings 12:21) **25:4** Deuteronomy 24:16 **25:17** Spelled *Jehoash* in 2 Kings 14:8ff
Rom. 12:19 Deuteronomy 32:35 **12:20** Proverbs 25:21, 22
Ps. 22:27 Following Masoretic Text, Septuagint, and Targum; Arabic, Syriac, and Vulgate read *Him.*

JULY 30

2 Chron. 26:1 Called *Azariah* in 2 Kings 14:21ff **26:2** Hebrew *Eloth* **26:5** Several Hebrew manuscripts, Septuagint, Syriac, Targum, and Arabic read *fear.* **26:12** Literally *chief fathers* **27:1** Spelled *Jerusha* in 2 Kings 15:33 **28:16** Septuagint, Syriac, and Vulgate read *king* (compare verse 20). **28:20** Hebrew *Tilgath-Pilneser*
Rom. 13:9 NU-Text omits *"You shall not bear false witness."* / Exodus 20:13-15, 17; Deuteronomy 5:17-19, 21 / Leviticus 19:18
Ps. 23:6 Following Septuagint, Syriac, Targum, and Vulgate; Masoretic Text reads *return.*

JULY 31

2 Chron. 29:1 Spelled *Abi* in 2 Kings 18:2
Rom. 14:6 NU-Text omits the rest of this sentence. **14:9** NU-Text omits *and rose.* **14:10** NU-Text reads *of God.* **14:11** Isaiah 45:23 **14:18** NU-Text reads *this.* **14:21** NU-Text omits *or is offended or is made weak.* **14:22** NU-Text reads *The faith which you have—have.* **14:23** M-Text puts Romans 16:25-27 here.

AUGUST 1

2 Chron. 30:3 That is, the first month (compare Leviticus 23:5); literally *at that time* **31:2** That is, the temple
Rom. 15:3 Psalm 69:9 **15:7** NU-Text and M-Text read *you.* **15:9** 2 Samuel 22:50; Psalm 18:49 **15:10** Deuteronomy 32:43 **15:11** Psalm 117:1 **15:12** Isaiah 11:10 **15:14** M-Text reads *others.* **15:21** Isaiah 52:15
Ps. 25:12 Or *he* / Or *he*
Prov. 20:14 Literally *evil, evil*

AUGUST 2

2 Chron. 32:3 Literally *mighty men* **32:4** Following Masoretic Text and Vulgate; Arabic, Septuagint, and Syriac read *king.* **32:5** Literally *The Landfill* **32:18** Literally *Judean* **32:22** Septuagint reads *gave them rest;* Vulgate reads *gave them treasures.* **32:28** Following Septuagint and Vulgate; Arabic and Syriac omit *folds for flocks;* Masoretic Text reads *flocks for sheepfolds.* **32:30** Literally *brought it straight* (compare 2 Kings 20:20) **33:3** The gods of the Assyrians **33:11** That is, nose hooks (compare 2 Kings 19:28)
Rom. 15:24 NU-Text omits *I shall come to you* (and joins Spain with the next sentence). **15:29** NU-Text omits *of the gospel.* **16:5** NU-Text reads *Asia.*

AUGUST 3

2 Chron. 33:18 Literally *words* **33:19** Septuagint reads *the seers.* **34:6** Literally *swords* **34:8** Literally *house* **34:20** *Achbor the son of Michaiah* in 2 Kings 22:12

34:22 Spelled *Tikvah* in 2 Kings 22:14 / Spelled *Harhas* in 2 Kings 22:14
Rom. 16:11 Or *relative*   **16:16** NU-Text reads *All the churches.*   **16:18** NU-Text and M-Text omit *Jesus.*   **16:24** NU-Text omits this verse.   **16:27** M-Text puts Romans 16:25-27 after Romans 14:23.

AUGUST 4

2 Chron. 36:2 Masoretic Text reads *Joahaz.*   **36:4** Literally *his* / Masoretic Text reads *Joahaz.*   **36:9** Some Hebrew manuscripts, Septuagint, Syriac, and 2 Kings 24:8 read *eighteen.*   **36:10** Literally *his* (compare 2 Kings 24:17)

AUGUST 5

Ezra 2:1 Compare this chapter with Nehemiah 7:6-73.   **2:2** Spelled *Mispereth* in Nehemiah 7:7 / Spelled *Nehum* in Nehemiah 7:7   **2:10** Spelled *Binnui* in Nehemiah 7:15   **2:18** Called *Hariph* in Nehemiah 7:24   **2:20** Called *Gibeon* in Nehemiah 7:25   **2:24** Called *Beth Azmaveth* in Nehemiah 7:28   **2:25** Called *Kirjath Jearim* in Nehemiah 7:29   **2:40** Spelled *Hodevah* in Nehemiah 7:43   **2:44** Spelled *Sia* in Nehemiah 7:47   **2:50** Spelled *Nephishesim* in Nehemiah 7:52   **2:52** Spelled *Bazlith* in Nehemiah 7:54   **2:55** Spelled *Perida* in Nehemiah 7:57   **2:57** Spelled *Amon* in Nehemiah 7:59   **2:59** Spelled *Addon* in Nehemiah 7:61 / Literally *seed*   **2:61** Or *Hakkoz*   **2:63** Hebrew *Tirshatha*
1 Cor. 1:19 Isaiah 29:14   **1:23** NU-Text reads *Gentiles.*   **1:31** Jeremiah 9:24   **2:1** NU-Text reads *mystery.*   **2:4** NU-Text omits *human.*

AUGUST 6

Ezra 3:2 Spelled *Jehozadak* in 1 Chronicles 6:14   **3:8** Spelled *Jehozadak* in 1 Chronicles 6:14   **3:9** Or *Hodaviah* (compare 2:40)   **3:10** Following Septuagint, Syriac, and Vulgate; Masoretic Text reads *they stationed the priests.*   **3:11** Compare Psalm 136:1   **4:8** The original language of Ezra 4:8 through 6:18 is Aramaic.   **4:9** Literally *Then* / Or *Susa*   **4:10** That is, the Euphrates / Literally *and now*   **4:11** Literally *and now*   **4:17** Literally *and now*
1 Cor. 2:9 Isaiah 64:4   **2:13** NU-Text omits *Holy.*   **2:16** Isaiah 40:13
Ps. 28:8 Following Masoretic Text and Targum; Septuagint, Syriac, and Vulgate read *the strength of His people.*

AUGUST 7

Ezra 5:2 Spelled *Jehozadak* in 1 Chronicles 6:14   **5:3** That is, the Euphrates   **6:1** Literally *house of the scrolls*   **6:2** Probably *Ecbatana,* the ancient capital of Media
1 Cor. 3:19 Job 5:13   **3:20** Psalm 94:11
Prov. 20:27 Literally *the rooms of the belly*

AUGUST 8

Ezra 7:12 The original language of Ezra 7:12-26 is Aramaic. / Literally *and now*   **8:5** Following Masoretic Text and Vulgate; Septuagint reads *the sons of Zatho, Shechaniah.*   **8:10** Following Masoretic Text and Vulgate; Septuagint reads *the sons of Banni, Shelomith.*   **8:17** Following Vulgate; Masoretic Text reads *to Iddo his brother;* Septuagint reads *to their brethren.*

1 Cor. 4:3 Literally *day*
Ps. 30:3 Following Qere and Targum; Kethib, Septuagint, Syriac, and Vulgate read *from those who descend to the pit.*   **30:4** Or *His holiness*
Prov. 20:30 Literally *the rooms of the belly*

AUGUST 9

1 Cor. 5:1 NU-Text omits *named.*   **5:5** NU-Text omits *Jesus.*   **5:7** NU-Text omits *for us.*   **5:13** Deuteronomy 17:7; 19:19; 22:21, 24; 24:7

AUGUST 10

Ezra 10:18 Spelled *Jehozadak* in 1 Chronicles 6:14   **10:29** Or *Jeremoth*   **10:35** Or *Cheluhi,* or *Cheluhu*   **10:37** Or *Jaasu*   **10:43** Or *Jaddu*
1 Cor. 6:9 That is, catamites   **6:16** Genesis 2:24   **6:20** NU-Text ends the verse at *body.*

AUGUST 11

Neh. 1:1 Or *Susa*   **1:5** Literally *Him* / Literally *His*   **1:8** Leviticus 26:33   **1:9** Deuteronomy 30:2-5   **2:7** That is, the Euphrates, and so elsewhere in this book   **2:8** Literally *house*   **2:10** Literally *servant,* and so elsewhere in this book   **3:1** Hebrew *Hammeah,* also at 12:39   **3:2** Literally *On his hand*   **3:4** Or *Hakkoz*   **3:5** Literally *necks*   **3:7** Literally *throne*   **3:8** Literally *the son*
Prov. 21:4 Or *lamp*

AUGUST 12

Neh. 3:16 Septuagint, Syriac, and Vulgate read *tomb.*   **3:18** Following Masoretic Text and Vulgate; some Hebrew manuscripts, Septuagint, and Syriac read *Binnui* (compare verse 24).   **3:20** A few Hebrew manuscripts, Syriac, and Vulgate read *Zaccai.*   **3:21** Or *Hakkoz*   **3:31** Literally *Inspection* or *Recruiting*   **4:21** Literally *them*   **5:13** Literally *my lap*
1 Cor. 7:34 M-Text adds *also.*   **7:37** Or *virgin daughter*   **7:38** NU-Text reads *his own virgin.*
Ps. 32:title Hebrew *Maschil*
Prov. 21:6 Septuagint reads *Pursue vanity on the snares of death;* Vulgate reads *Is vain and foolish, and shall stumble on the snares of death;* Targum reads *They shall be destroyed, and they shall fall who seek death.*   **21:7** Literally *drag them away*

AUGUST 13

Neh. 5:16 Following Masoretic Text; Septuagint, Syriac, and Vulgate read *I.*   **6:6** Hebrew *Gashmu*   **7:6** Compare verses 6-72 with Ezra 2:1-70   **7:7** Spelled *Mispar* in Ezra 2:2   **7:15** Spelled *Bani* in Ezra 2:10   **7:24** Called *Jorah* in Ezra 2:18   **7:25** Called *Gibbar* in Ezra 2:20   **7:28** Called *Azmaveth* in Ezra 2:24   **7:43** Spelled *Hodaviah* in Ezra 2:40   **7:47** Spelled *Siaha* in Ezra 2:44   **7:48** Masoretic Text reads *Lebanah.* / Masoretic Text reads *Hagabah.* / Or *Shalmai,* or *Shamlai*   **7:52** Spelled *Nephusim* in Ezra 2:50   **7:54** Spelled *Bazluth* in Ezra 2:52   **7:57** Spelled *Peruda* in Ezra 2:55   **7:59** Spelled *Ami* in Ezra 2:57
Ps. 33:7 Septuagint, Targum, and Vulgate read *in a vessel.*
Prov. 21:8 Or *The way of a man is perverse and strange*

AUGUST 14

Neh. 7:61 Spelled *Addan* in Ezra 2:59   **7:63** Or *Hakkoz*

7:65 Hebrew *Tirshatha* **7:70** Hebrew *Tirshatha* **8:9** Hebrew *Tirshatha* **9:1** Literally *earth on them* **9:17** Following Masoretic Text and Vulgate; Septuagint reads *in Egypt.* **9:21** Compare Deuteronomy 29:5

1 Cor. 9:9 Deuteronomy 25:4 **9:18** NU-Text omits *of Christ.*

AUGUST 15

Neh. 9:22 Literally *corners* / Following Masoretic Text and Vulgate; Septuagint omits *The land of.* **9:29** Leviticus 18:5

1 Cor. 9:20 NU-Text adds *though not being myself under the law.* **9:21** NU-Text reads *God's law.* / NU-Text reads *Christ's law.* **9:22** NU-Text omits *as.* **10:7** Exodus 32:6 **10:11** NU-Text omits *all.*

Ps. 34:7 Or *Angel*

AUGUST 16

Neh. 11:9 Or *Hassenuah* **11:14** Or *the son of Haggedolim* **11:17** Or *Michah* **11:24** Literally *at the king's hand* **12:4** Or *Ginnethon* (compare verse 16) **12:14** Or *Malluch* (compare verse 2) / Or *Shechaniah* (compare verse 3) **12:15** Or *Rehum* (compare verse 3) / Or *Meremoth* (compare verse 3) **12:17** Or *Mijamin* (compare verse 5) / Or *Maadiah* (compare verse 5) **12:20** Or *Sallu* (compare verse 7) **12:26** Spelled *Jehozadak* in 1 Chronicles 6:14

1 Cor. 10:23 NU-Text omits *for me.* / NU-Text omits *for me.* **10:26** Psalm 24:1 **10:28** NU-Text omits the rest of this verse. / Psalm 24:1

Prov. 21:14 Literally *in the bosom*

AUGUST 17

Neh. 12:41 Or *Mijamin* (compare verse 5) **1 Cor. 11:15** M-Text omits *to her.* **Ps. 35:5** Or *Angel*

AUGUST 18

Esther 1:1 Generally identified with Xerxes I (485-464 B.C.) **1:2** Or *Susa,* and so throughout this book **2:3** Hebrew *Hege* **2:6** Literally *Who* / Same as *Jehoiachin,* 2 Kings 24:6 and elsewhere **3:7** Septuagint adds *to destroy the people of Mordecai in one day;* Vulgate adds *the nation of the Jews should be destroyed.* / Following Masoretic Text and Vulgate; Septuagint reads *and the lot fell on the fourteenth of the month.* **3:13** Septuagint adds the text of the letter here.

1 Cor. 11:24 NU-Text omits *Take, eat.* / NU-Text omits *broken.* **11:27** NU-Text and M-Text read *the blood.* **11:29** NU-Text omits *in an unworthy manner.* / NU-Text omits *Lord's.*

AUGUST 19

Esther 4:17 Septuagint adds a prayer of Mordecai here. **5:1** Septuagint adds many extra details in verses 1 and 2.

1 Cor. 12:2 NU-Text and M-Text add *when.* **12:9** NU-Text reads *one.* **12:13** NU-Text omits *into.*

AUGUST 20

Esther 8:10 Literally *sons of the swift horses* **8:12** Septuagint adds the text of the letter here. **9:17** Literally *it* **9:18** Literally *it* **9:25** Literally *she* or *it* / Literally *his* **10:3** Literally *seed.* Septuagint and Vul-

gate add a dream of Mordecai here; Vulgate adds six more chapters.

1 Cor. 12:31 NU-Text reads *greater.* **13:3** NU-Text reads *so I may boast.*

AUGUST 21

Job 1:5 Literally *blessed,* but used here in the evil sense, and so in verse 11 and 2:5, 9 **1:6** Literally *the Adversary,* and so throughout this book **1:15** Literally *Sheba* (compare 6:19) **1:19** Septuagint omits *across.* **3:6** Septuagint, Syriac, Targum, and Vulgate read *be joined.* **3:24** Literally *my bread*

1 Cor. 14:5 NU-Text reads *and.*

AUGUST 22

Job 5:5 Septuagint reads *They shall not be taken from evil men;* Vulgate reads *And the armed man shall take him by violence.* / Septuagint reads *The might shall draw them off;* Vulgate reads *And the thirsty shall drink up their riches.* **7:15** Literally *my bones* **7:20** Following Masoretic Text, Targum, and Vulgate; Septuagint and Jewish tradition read *to You.*

1 Cor. 14:21 Isaiah 28:11, 12 **14:25** NU-Text omits *And thus.* **14:34** NU-Text omits *your.* **14:38** NU-Text reads *if anyone does not recognize this, he is not recognized.*

Ps. 37.36 Following Masoretic Text, Septuagint, and Targum; Syriac and Vulgate read *I passed by.*

AUGUST 23

Job 8:22 Literally *will not be* **9:13** Hebrew *rahab* **1 Cor. 15:27** Psalm 8:6 **Prov. 21:29** Qere and Septuagint read *understands.*

AUGUST 24

Job 12:5 Or *disaster* **12:19** Literally *priests,* but not in a technical sense **12:24** Literally *heart* **13:27** Literally *inscribe a print* **13:28** Literally *He* **14:3** Septuagint, Syriac, and Vulgate read *him.* **14:17** Literally *plaster over* **15:11** Septuagint reads *a secret thing.*

1 Cor. 15:32 Isaiah 22:13 **15:39** NU-Text and M-Text omit *of flesh.* **15:45** Genesis 2:7 **15:47** NU-Text omits *the Lord.* **15:49** M-Text reads *let us also bear.* **15:54** Isaiah 25:8 **15:55** Hosea 13:14 / NU-Text reads *O Death, where is your victory? O Death, where is your sting?*

AUGUST 25

Job 16:13 Literally *kidneys* **16:14** Vulgate reads *giant.* **16:15** Literally *horn* **17:10** Following some Hebrew manuscripts, Septuagint, Syriac, and Vulgate; Masoretic Text and Targum read *all of them.* **18:17** Literally *before the outside,* meaning distinguished, famous **19:3** A Jewish tradition reads *make yourselves strange to me.*

1 Cor. 16:22 Greek *anathema* / Aramaic *Maranatha*

AUGUST 26

Job 20:20 Literally *belly* **21:13** Or *Sheol* **21:19** Literally *his* **21:24** Septuagint and Vulgate read *bowels;* Syriac reads *sides;* Targum reads *breasts.* **21:28** Vulgate omits *the tent.* **22:17** Septuagint and Syriac read *us.* **22:20** Septuagint reads *substance.* **22:25** The an-

cient versions suggest *defense;* Hebrew reads *gold* as in verse 24.
2 Cor. 1:10 NU-Text reads *shall.* **1:11** M-Text reads *your behalf.*

AUGUST 27

Job 23:2 Following Masoretic Text, Targum, and Vulgate; Septuagint and Syriac read *His.* **24:19** Or *Sheol* **27:15** Literally *his* **27:18** Following Masoretic Text and Vulgate; Septuagint and Syriac read *spider* (compare 8:14); Targum reads *decay.* **27:19** Following Masoretic Text and Targum; Septuagint and Syriac read *But shall not add* (that is, do it again); Vulgate reads *But take away nothing.*
2 Cor. 2:10 NU-Text reads indeed, *what I have forgiven, if I have forgiven anything, I did it for your sakes.*

AUGUST 28

Job 28:8 Literally *sons of pride,* figurative of the great lions **28:27** Literally *it* **29:6** Masoretic Text reads *wrath;* ancient versions and some Hebrew manuscripts read *cream* (compare 20:17). **30:11** Following Masoretic Text, Syriac, and Targum; Septuagint and Vulgate read *His.*
2 Cor. 2:17 M-Text reads *the rest.*
Ps. 42:title Hebrew *Maschil* **42:2** Following Masoretic Text and Vulgate; some Hebrew manuscripts, Septuagint, Syriac, and Targum read *I see the face of God.* **42:5** Following Masoretic Text and Targum; a few Hebrew manuscripts, Septuagint, Syriac, and Vulgate read *The help of my countenance, my God.* **42:6** Following Masoretic Text and Targum; a few Hebrew manuscripts, Septuagint, Syriac, and Vulgate put *my God* at the end of verse 5.

AUGUST 29

Job 31:18 Literally *her* (compare verse 16) **31:20** Literally *loins* **31:26** Literally *light* **31:32** Following Septuagint, Syriac, Targum, and Vulgate; Masoretic Text reads *road.* **31:39** Literally *its strength* **32:4** Vulgate reads *till Job had spoken.* **32:7** Literally *Days,* that is, years **32:9** Or *Men of many years* **33:6** Literally *as your mouth* **33:28** Or *my* (Kethib) / Or *my* (Kethib)
2 Cor. 3:6 Or *spirit*

AUGUST 30

Job 36:12 Masoretic Text reads *as one without knowledge.* **36:14** Hebrew *qedeshim,* that is, those practicing sodomy and prostitution in religious rituals
Ps. 44:title Hebrew *Maschil* **44:4** Following Masoretic Text and Targum; Septuagint and Vulgate read *and my God.* / Following Masoretic Text and Targum; Septuagint, Syriac, and Vulgate read *who commands.*

AUGUST 31

Job 37:12 Literally *the world of the earth* **38:32** Literally *Constellations* **38:36** Literally *inward parts* **39:3** Literally *pangs,* figurative of offspring **39:19** Or *a mane*
2 Cor. 4:13 Psalm 116:10

SEPTEMBER 1

Job 40:15 A large animal, exact identity unknown **41:1** A large sea creature, exact identity unknown **41:6** Or *bargain over him* **41:12** Literally *keep silent*

about **41:25** Or *purify themselves* **42:10** Literally *Job's captivity;* that is, what was captured from Job
Ps. 45:title Hebrew *Shoshannim* / Hebrew *Maschil*

SEPTEMBER 2

Eccles. 1:2 Or *Absurdity, Frustration, Futility, Nonsense;* and so throughout this book **2:8** Exact meaning unknown **2:25** Following Masoretic Text, Targum, and Vulgate; some Hebrew manuscripts, Septuagint, and Syriac read *without Him.* **3:21** Septuagint, Syriac, Targum, and Vulgate read *Who knows whether the spirit . . . goes upward, and whether . . . goes downward to the earth?*
2 Cor. 6:2 Isaiah 49:8

SEPTEMBER 3

Eccles. 5:6 Literally *voice*
2 Cor. 6:16 NU-Text reads *we.* / Leviticus 26:12; Jeremiah 32:38; Ezekiel 37:27 **6:17** Isaiah 52:11; Ezekiel 20:34, 41 **6:18** 2 Samuel 7:14

SEPTEMBER 4

Eccles. 8:10 Some Hebrew manuscripts, Septuagint, and Vulgate read *praised.* **9:2** Septuagint, Syriac, and Vulgate read *good and bad.* **9:14** Septuagint, Syriac, and Vulgate read *bulwarks.*
Ps. 48:14 Following Masoretic Text and Syriac; Septuagint and Vulgate read *Forever.*

SEPTEMBER 5

Eccles. 10:1 Targum and Vulgate omit *putrefy.* **11:5** Or *spirit* **12:6** Following Qere and Targum; Kethib reads *removed;* Septuagint and Vulgate read *broken.* **12:11** Literally *masters of the assemblies*
2 Cor. 8:4 NU-Text and M-Text omit *that we would receive,* thus changing text to *urgency for the favor and fellowship . . .* **8:15** Exodus 16:18
Ps. 49:11 Septuagint, Syriac, Targum, and Vulgate read *Their graves shall be their houses forever.* **49:12** Following Masoretic Text and Targum; Septuagint, Syriac, and Vulgate read *understand* (compare verse 20).

SEPTEMBER 6

Song of Sol. 1:2 A Palestinian young woman (compare 6:13). The speaker and audience are identified according to the number, gender, and person of the Hebrew words. Occasionally the identity is not certain. / Masculine singular, that is, the Beloved **1:4** Masculine singular, that is, the Beloved / Feminine singular, that is, the Shulamite / Masculine singular, that is, the Beloved / Masculine singular, that is, the Beloved **1:7** Septuagint, Syriac, and Vulgate read *wanders.* **1:11** Feminine singular, that is, the Shulamite **2:17** Literally *Separation* **3:9** A portable enclosed chair
2 Cor. 8:16 NU-Text reads *has put.* **8:24** NU-Text and M-Text omit *and.*
Ps. 50:18 Septuagint, Syriac, Targum, and Vulgate read *run.*

SEPTEMBER 7

Song of Sol. 6:12 Hebrew *Ammi Nadib* **6:13** Hebrew *Mahanaim* **7:9** Septuagint, Syriac, and Vulgate read *lips and teeth.* **8:6** Or *Sheol* / Literally *A flame of Yah* (a poetic form of *YHWH, the Lord*)

2 Cor. 9:4 NU-Text reads *this confidence*. **9:9** Psalm 112:9 **9:10** NU-Text reads *Now He who supplies . . . will supply. . . .*
Ps. 51:4 Septuagint, Targum, and Vulgate read *in Your words*.

SEPTEMBER 8

Isa. 1:17 Some ancient versions read *the oppressed*.
1:29 Following Masoretic Text, Septuagint, and Vulgate; some Hebrew manuscripts and Targum read *you*.
2 Cor. 10:7 NU-Text reads *even as we are*. **10:8** NU-Text omits *us*. **10:17** Jeremiah 9:24
Ps. 52:title Hebrew *Maschil*

SEPTEMBER 9

Isa. 3:6 Literally *hand*
2 Cor. 11:3 NU-Text adds *and purity*. **11:6** NU-Text omits *been*.
Ps. 53:title Hebrew *Maschil*

SEPTEMBER 10

Isa. 7:3 Literally *A Remnant Shall Return* **7:14** Literally *God-With-Us* **7:20** That is, the Euphrates
Ps. 54:title Hebrew *neginoth* / Hebrew *Maschil*

SEPTEMBER 11

Isa. 8:1 Literally *Speed the Spoil, Hasten the Booty*
8:7 That is, the Euphrates **8:8** Literally *God-With-Us*
8:10 Hebrew *Immanuel* **9:3** Following Qere and Targum; Kethib and Vulgate read *not increased joy;* Septuagint reads *Most of the people You brought down in Your joy*.
2 Cor. 12:1 NU-Text reads *necessary, though not profitable, to boast*.
Ps. 55:title Hebrew *neginoth* / Hebrew *Maschil*

SEPTEMBER 12

Isa. 10:16 Following Bomberg; Masoretic Text and Dead Sea Scrolls read *YHWH* (*the LORD*). **10:30** Following Masoretic Text, Targum, and Vulgate; Septuagint and Syriac read *Listen to her, O Anathoth* **11:15** Following Masoretic Text and Vulgate; Septuagint, Syriac, and Targum read *dry up*. / That is, the Euphrates
2 Cor. 12:11 NU-Text omits *in boasting*. **12:19** NU-Text reads *You have been thinking for a long time. . . .*
Ps. 56:title Hebrew *Jonath Elem Rechokim*
Prov. 23:6 Literally *one who has an evil eye*

SEPTEMBER 13

Isa. 12:2 Exodus 15:2 **14:4** Or *insolent* **14:12** Literally *Day Star*
2 Cor. 13:1 Deuteronomy 19:15 **13:2** NU-Text omits *I write*. **13:7** NU-Text reads *we*.
Ps. 57:title Hebrew *Al Tashcheth*

SEPTEMBER 14

Isa. 15:2 Hebrew *bayith* (*house*) **15:4** Following Masoretic Text, Targum, and Vulgate; Septuagint and Syriac read *loins*. **15:5** Or *The Third Eglath*, an unknown city (compare Jeremiah 48:34) **15:9** Following Masoretic Text and Targum; Dead Sea Scrolls and Vulgate read *Dibon;* Septuagint reads *Rimon*. / Following Masoretic Text and Targum; Dead Sea Scrolls and Vulgate read *Dibon;* Septuagint reads *Rimon*. **17:2** Following Masoretic Text and Vulgate; Septuagint reads *It shall be for-*

saken forever; Targum reads *Its cities shall be forsaken and desolate*. **17:8** Hebrew *Asherah*, a Canaanite goddess **17:9** Septuagint reads *Hivites;* Targum reads *laid waste;* Vulgate reads *as the plows*. / Septuagint reads *Amorites;* Targum reads *in ruins;* Vulgate reads *corn*.
18:7 Following Dead Sea Scrolls, Septuagint, and Vulgate; Masoretic Text omits *From;* Targum reads *To*.
Gal. 1:18 NU-Text reads *Cephas*.
Ps. 58:title Hebrew *Al Tashcheth*

SEPTEMBER 15

Isa. 19:7 That is, the Nile **19:13** That is, ancient Memphis **19:15** Compare Isaiah 9:14-16 **19:18** Some Hebrew manuscripts, Arabic, Dead Sea Scrolls, Targum, and Vulgate read *Sun;* Septuagint reads *Asedek* (literally *Righteousness*). **20:1** Or *the Commander in Chief* **21:8** Dead Sea Scrolls read *Then the observer cried*.
Gal. 2:11 NU-Text reads *Cephas*. **2:14** NU-Text reads *how can you*. / Some interpreters stop the quotation here.
Ps. 59:title Hebrew *Al Tashcheth* **59:9** Following Masoretic Text and Syriac; some Hebrew manuscripts, Septuagint, Targum, and Vulgate read *my Strength*. **59:10** Following Qere; some Hebrew manuscripts, Septuagint, and Vulgate read *My God, His mercy;* Kethib, some Hebrew manuscripts and Targum read *O God, my mercy;* Syriac reads *O God, Your mercy*. **59:15** Following Septuagint and Vulgate; Masoretic Text, Syriac, and Targum read *spend the night*.
Prov. 23:14 Or *Sheol*

SEPTEMBER 16

Isa. 22:19 Septuagint omits *he will pull you down;* Syriac, Targum, and Vulgate read *I will pull you down*.
23:1 Hebrew *Kittim*, western lands, especially Cyprus **23:2** Following Masoretic Text and Vulgate; Septuagint and Targum read *passing over the water;* Dead Sea Scrolls read *your messengers passing over the sea*. **23:3** That is, the Nile **23:10** That is, the Nile
Gal. 3:1 NU-Text omits *that you should not obey the truth*. / NU-Text omits *among you*. **3:6** Genesis 15:6 **3:8** Genesis 12:3; 18:18; 22:18; 26:4; 28:14
Ps. 60:title Hebrew *Shushan Eduth* **60:12** Compare verses 5-12 with 108:6-13

SEPTEMBER 17

Isa. 26:4 Or *Rock of Ages* **26:19** Following Masoretic Text and Vulgate; Syriac and Targum read *their dead bodies;* Septuagint reads *those in the tombs*. **27:2** Following Masoretic Text (Kittel's *Biblia Hebraica*), Bomberg, and Vulgate; Masoretic Text (*Biblia Hebraica Stuttgartensia*), some Hebrew manuscripts, and Septuagint read *delight;* Targum reads *choice vineyard*. **27:9** Hebrew *Asherim*, Canaanite deities **27:12** That is, the Euphrates
Gal. 3:10 Deuteronomy 27:26 **3:11** Habakkuk 2:4 **3:12** Leviticus 18:5 **3:13** Deuteronomy 21:23 **3:16** Genesis 12:7; 13:15; 24:7 **3:17** NU-Text omits *in Christ*.
Ps. 61:title Hebrew *neginah*

SEPTEMBER 18

Isa. 29:1 That is, Jerusalem **30:7** Literally *Rahab Sits Idle*

Gal. 4:4 Or *made* **4:7** NU-Text reads *through God* and omits *through Christ.* **4:15** NU-Text reads *Where.* **4:24** NU-Text and M-Text omit *the.* **4:27** Isaiah 54:1 **4:30** Genesis 21:10

SEPTEMBER 19

Isa. 33:2 Septuagint omits *their;* Syriac, Targum, and Vulgate read *our.* **33:8** Following Masoretic Text and Vulgate; Dead Sea Scrolls read *witnesses;* Septuagint omits *cities;* Targum reads *They have been removed from their cities.*
Gal. 5:1 NU-Text reads *For freedom Christ has made us free; stand fast therefore.*

SEPTEMBER 20

Isa. 36:2 A title, probably *Chief of Staff* or *Governor* **36:11** Literally *Judean*
Gal. 5:14 Leviticus 19:18 **5:19** NU-Text omits *adultery.* **5:21** NU-Text omits *murders.*

SEPTEMBER 21

Isa. 37:36 Or *Angel* **38:11** Hebrew *YAH, YAH* / Following some Hebrew manuscripts; Masoretic Text and Vulgate read *rest;* Septuagint omits *among the inhabitants of the world;* Targum reads *land.* **38:14** Following Bomberg; Masoretic Text and Dead Sea Scrolls read *Lord.* **38:15** Following Masoretic Text and Vulgate; Dead Sea Scrolls and Targum read *And shall I say to Him;* Septuagint omits first half of this verse.
Gal. 6:14 Or *by which* (the cross)

SEPTEMBER 22

Isa. 39:1 Spelled *Berodach-Baladan* in 2 Kings 20:12 **40:3** Following Masoretic Text, Targum, and Vulgate; Septuagint omits *in the desert.* **40:6** Following Masoretic Text and Targum; Dead Sea Scrolls, Septuagint, and Vulgate read *I.* **40:12** Following Masoretic Text, Septuagint, and Vulgate; Dead Sea Scrolls read *waters of the sea;* Targum reads *waters of the world.*
Eph. 1:10 NU-Text and M-Text omit *both.* **1:14** NU-Text reads *which.* **1:18** NU-Text and M-Text read *hearts.*

SEPTEMBER 23

Isa. 41:29 Following Masoretic Text and Vulgate; Dead Sea Scrolls, Syriac, and Targum read *nothing;* Septuagint omits the first line.
Ps. 67:title Hebrew *neginoth*

SEPTEMBER 24

Isa. 45:2 Dead Sea Scrolls and Septuagint read *mountains;* Targum reads *I will trample down the walls;* Vulgate reads *I will humble the great ones of the earth.*
Eph. 3:9 NU-Text and M-Text read *stewardship (dispensation).* / NU-Text omits *through Jesus Christ.* **3:14** NU-Text omits *of our Lord Jesus Christ.*
Ps. 68:4 Masoretic Text reads *deserts;* Targum reads *heavens* (compare verse 34 and Isaiah 19:1).

SEPTEMBER 25

Eph. 4:6 NU-Text omits *you;* M-Text reads *us.* **4:8** Psalm 68:18 **4:9** NU-Text omits *first.*
Ps. 68:23 Septuagint, Syriac, Targum, and Vulgate read *you may dip your foot.* **68:28** Septuagint, Syriac, Targum, and Vulgate read *Command, O God.*

SEPTEMBER 26

Isa. 48:16 The Hebrew verb is singular. **49:5** Qere, Dead Sea Scrolls, and Septuagint read *is gathered to Him;* Kethib reads *is not gathered.* **49:17** Dead Sea Scrolls, Septuagint, Targum, and Vulgate read *builders.* **49:24** Following Masoretic Text and Targum; Dead Sea Scrolls, Syriac, and Vulgate read *the mighty;* Septuagint reads *unjustly.*
Eph. 4:17 NU-Text omits *the rest of the.* **4:25** Zechariah 8:16 **4:26** Psalm 4:4
Ps. 69:title Hebrew *Shoshannim*

SEPTEMBER 27

Isa. 51:23 Literally *your soul* **52:5** Dead Sea Scrolls read *Mock;* Septuagint reads *Marvel and wail;* Targum reads *Boast themselves;* Vulgate reads *Treat them unjustly.* **52:15** Or *startle* **53:9** Literally *he* or *He* **53:11** Following Masoretic Text, Targum, and Vulgate; Dead Sea Scrolls and Septuagint read *From the labor of His soul He shall see light.*
Eph. 5:5 NU-Text reads *For know this.* **5:9** NU-Text reads *light.* **5:21** NU-Text reads *Christ.* **5:30** NU-Text omits the rest of this verse. **5:31** Genesis 2:24

SEPTEMBER 28

Isa. 56:5 Literally *him* **57:8** Literally *hand,* a euphemism
Eph. 6:2 Deuteronomy 5:16 **6:9** NU-Text reads *He who is both their Master and yours.* **6:12** NU-Text reads *rulers of this darkness.*
Ps. 70:2 Following Masoretic Text, Septuagint, Targum, and Vulgate; some Hebrew manuscripts and Syriac read *be appalled* (compare 40:15).

SEPTEMBER 29

Phil. 1:1 Literally *overseers* **1:16** NU-Text reverses the contents of verses 16 and 17. **1:23** NU-Text and M-Text read *But.*

SEPTEMBER 30

Isa. 62:4 Literally *My Delight Is in Her* / Literally *Married*
Phil. 1:28 NU-Text reads *of your salvation.*
Ps. 72:5 Following Masoretic Text and Targum; Septuagint and Vulgate read *They shall continue.*

OCTOBER 1

Isa. 65:11 Literally *Troop* or *Fortune,* a pagan deity / Literally *Number* or *Destiny,* a pagan deity
Phil. 3:3 NU-Text and M-Text read *who worship in the Spirit of God.*
Ps. 73:7 Targum reads *face bulges;* Septuagint, Syriac, and Vulgate read *iniquity bulges.*

OCTOBER 2

Isa. 66:19 Following Masoretic Text and Targum; Septuagint reads *Put* (compare Jeremiah 46:9).
Phil. 3:16 NU-Text omits *rule* and the rest of the verse.
Ps. 74:title Hebrew *Maschil*

OCTOBER 3

Jer. 2:10 Hebrew *Kittim,* western lands, especially Cyprus / In the northern Arabian desert, representative of the eastern cultures **2:16** That is, Memphis in ancient Egypt **2:18** That is, the Euphrates

Phil. 4:3 NU-Text and M-Text read *Yes.* **4:13** NU-Text reads *Him who.* **4:23** NU-Text reads *your spirit.*
Ps. 75:title Hebrew *Al Tashcheth*

OCTOBER 4

Col. 1:2 NU-Text omits *and the Lord Jesus Christ.*
1:6 NU-Text and M-Text add *and growing.* **1:14** NU-Text and M-Text omit *through His blood.*
Ps. 76:title Hebrew *neginoth* **76:2** That is, Jerusalem

OCTOBER 5

Col. 1:27 M-Text reads *who.* **2:2** NU-Text omits *both of the Father and.* **2:7** NU-Text omits *in it.*

OCTOBER 6

Col. 2:11 NU-Text omits *of the sins.* **2:18** NU-Text omits *not.* **2:20** NU-Text and M-Text omit *Therefore.*
Ps. 78:title Hebrew *Maschil*

OCTOBER 8

Jer. 10:13 Psalm 135:7 **11:5** Exodus 3:8
Col. 3:24 NU-Text omits *for.* **4:8** NU-Text reads *you may know our circumstances and he may.* **4:12** NU-Text reads *fully assured.* **4:13** NU Text reads *concern.* **4:15** NU-Text reads *Nympha . . . her house.*
Prov. 24:28 Septuagint and Vulgate read *Do not deceive.*

OCTOBER 9

Jer. 12:5 Or *thicket* **12:10** Literally *shepherds* or *pastors* **13:4** Hebrew *Perath*
1 Thess. 1:1 NU-Text omits *from God our Father and the Lord Jesus Christ.* **2:2** NU-Text and M-Text omit *even.*

OCTOBER 10

Jer. 15:14 Following Masoretic Text and Vulgate; Septuagint, Syriac, and Targum read *cause you to serve* (compare 17:4).
1 Thess. 2:11 NU-Text and M-Text read *implored.*
Ps. 80:title Hebrew *Shoshannim* / Hebrew *Eduth* **80:11** That is, the Mediterranean / That is, the Euphrates

OCTOBER 11

Jer. 17:2 Hebrew *Asherim,* Canaanite deities **17:8** Qere and Targum read *see.* **18:17** Following Septuagint, Syriac, Targum, and Vulgate; Masoretic Text reads *look them in.*
1 Thess. 4:8 NU-Text reads *who also gives.* **4:14** Or *those who through Jesus sleep*
Ps. 81:title Hebrew *Al Gittith*

OCTOBER 12

Jer. 20:3 Literally *Fear on Every Side* **21:2** Hebrew *Nebuchadrezzar,* and so elsewhere **21:4** Or *Babylonians*
1 Thess. 5:27 NU-Text omits *holy.*
Ps. 82:1 Hebrew *elohim, mighty ones;* that is, the judges **82:6** Hebrew *elohim, mighty ones;* that is, the judges

OCTOBER 13

Jer. 22:11 Also called *Jehoahaz* **22:24** Also called *Jeconiah* and *Jehoiachin* **23:6** Hebrew *YHWH Tsidkenu*
2 Thess. 1:10 NU-Text and M-Text read *have believed.*

OCTOBER 14

Jer. 23:33 Septuagint, Targum, and Vulgate read '*You are the burden.*' **25:26** A code word for *Babylon* (compare 51:41)

2 Thess. 2:2 NU-Text reads *the Lord.* **2:3** NU-Text reads *lawlessness.* **2:4** NU-Text omits *as God.* **2:7** Or *he* / Or *he*
Ps. 84:title Hebrew *Al Gittith* **84:7** Septuagint, Syriac, and Vulgate read *The God of gods shall be seen.*

OCTOBER 15

Jer. 26:18 Literally *house* / Compare Micah 3:12 **27:1** Following Masoretic Text, Targum, and Vulgate; some Hebrew manuscripts, Arabic, and Syriac read *Zedekiah* (compare 27:3, 12; 28:1). / Septuagint omits verse 1.
2 Thess. 3:6 NU-Text and M-Text read *they.*

OCTOBER 16

1 Tim. 1:17 NU-Text reads *to the only God.*

OCTOBER 17

1 Tim. 2:7 NU-Text omits *in Christ.*

OCTOBER 18

Jer. 31:32 Following Masoretic Text, Targum, and Vulgate; Septuagint and Syriac read *and I turned away from them.* **32:4** Literally *mouth to mouth* **32:22** Exodus 3:8
1 Tim. 3:1 Literally *overseer* **3:3** NU-Text omits *not greedy for money.* **3:16** NU-Text reads *Who.*
Ps. 88:title Hebrew *Maschil*

OCTOBER 19

Jer. 33:4 Compare Isaiah 22:10 **33:5** Compare 2 Kings 23:14 **33:16** Compare 23:5, 6 **34:3** Literally *mouth to mouth*
1 Tim. 4:10 NU-Text reads *we labor and strive.* **4:12** NU-Text omits *in spirit.*
Ps. 89:title Hebrew *Maschil*

OCTOBER 20

Jer. 36:4 Literally *from Jeremiah's mouth* **36:6** Literally *from my mouth* **36:17** Literally *with his mouth* **36:26** Hebrew *Hammelech* **36:27** Literally *from Jeremiah's mouth* **36:32** Literally *from Jeremiah's mouth*
1 Tim. 5:4 NU-Text and M-Text omit *good and.* **5:16** NU-Text omits *man or.* **5:18** Deuteronomy 25:4 / Luke 10:7
Ps. 89:19 Following many Hebrew manuscripts; Masoretic Text, Septuagint, Targum, and Vulgate read *holy ones.*

OCTOBER 21

Jer. 38:1 Same as *Jehucal* (compare 37:3) **38:2** Compare 21:9 **38:6** Hebrew *Hammelech*
1 Tim. 6:5 NU-Text and M-Text read *constant friction.* / NU-Text omits this sentence. **6:7** NU-Text omits *and it is certain.*

OCTOBER 22

Jer. 39:3 A title, probably *Chief Officer;* also verse 13 / A title, probably *Troop Commander;* also verse 13 **39:4** Or *the arabah,* that is, the Jordan Valley **40:8** Spelled *Jaazaniah* in 2 Kings 25:23
2 Tim. 1:1 NU-Text and M-Text read *Christ Jesus.* **1:11** NU-Text omits *of the Gentiles.* **1:18** *To me* is from the Vulgate and a few Greek manuscripts.

Ps. 90:1 Septuagint, Targum, and Vulgate read *refuge.*
91:3 That is, one who catches birds in a trap or snare

OCTOBER 23

Jer. 43:12 Following Masoretic Text and Targum;
Septuagint, Syriac, and Vulgate read *He.* **43:13** Literally *House of the Sun,* ancient On; later called Heliopolis **44:1** That is, ancient Memphis
2 Tim. 2:3 NU-Text reads *You must share.* **2:7** NU-Text reads *the Lord will give you.* **2:19** NU-Text and M-Text read *the Lord.*

OCTOBER 24

Jer. 45:1 Literally *from Jeremiah's mouth* **46:14** That is, ancient Memphis **46:19** That is, ancient Memphis **46:25** A sun god / That is, ancient Thebes

OCTOBER 25

Jer. 48:1 Hebrew *Misgab* **48:2** A city of Moab
48:4 Following Masoretic Text, Targum, and Vulgate; Septuagint reads *Proclaim it in Zoar.* **48:6** Or *Aroer,* a city of Moab **48:11** The Hebrew uses masculine and feminine pronouns interchangeably in this chapter.
48:31 Following Dead Sea Scrolls, Septuagint, and Vulgate; Masoretic Text reads *He.* **48:34** Or *The Third Eglath,* an unknown city (compare Isaiah 15:5)
49:1 Hebrew *Malcam,* literally *their king,* a god of the Ammonites; also called *Molech* (compare verse 3)
49:10 Compare Obadiah 5, 6 **49:16** Compare Obadiah 3, 4 **49:19** Or *thicket*
2 Tim. 4:1 NU-Text omits *therefore* and reads *and by* for *at.* **4:22** NU-Text omits *Jesus Christ.*
Ps. 95:8 Or *Meribah* / Or *Massah*
Prov. 26:10 The Hebrew is difficult; ancient and modern translators differ greatly.

OCTOBER 26

Jer. 49:27 Compare Amos 1:4 **50:2** A Babylonian god; sometimes spelled *Marduk* **50:9** Following some Hebrew manuscripts, Septuagint, and Syriac; Masoretic Text, Targum, and Vulgate read *a warrior who makes childless.* **50:29** Qere, some Hebrew manuscripts, Septuagint, and Targum add *to her.* **50:31** Following Masoretic Text and Targum; Septuagint and Vulgate read *The time of your punishment.* **50:38** Following Masoretic Text, Targum, and Vulgate; Syriac reads *sword;* Septuagint omits *A drought is.* **50:44** Or *thicket*
Titus 1:4 NU-Text reads *and Christ Jesus.* **1:7** Literally *overseer*
Ps. 97:12 Or *His holiness*
Prov. 26:15 Compare 19:24

OCTOBER 27

Jer. 51:1 A code word for Chaldea (Babylonia); may be translated *The Midst of Those Who Rise Up Against Me* **51:16** Psalm 135:7 **51:41** A code word for Babylon (compare Jeremiah 25:26)
Titus 2:7 NU-Text omits *incorruptibility.* **2:8** NU-Text and M-Text read *us.*

OCTOBER 28

Jer. 52:7 Or *the arabah,* that is, the Jordan Valley
52:31 Or *Awil-Marduk*
Ps. 100:3 Following Kethib, Septuagint, and Vulgate;

Qere, many Hebrew manuscripts, and Targum read *we are His.*

OCTOBER 29

Lam. 1:7 Vulgate reads *her Sabbaths.* **1:8** Septuagint and Vulgate read *moved* or *removed.* **1:14** Following Masoretic Text and Targum; Septuagint, Syriac, and Vulgate read *watched over.*
Philem. 2 NU-Text reads *to our sister Apphia.* **6** NU-Text and M-Text read *us.* **7** NU-Text reads *had.* / M-Text reads *thanksgiving.* **12** NU-Text reads *back to you in person, that is, my own heart.*

OCTOBER 30

Lam. 2:20 Vulgate reads *a span long.* **3:13** Literally *kidneys* **3:53** Septuagint reads *put to death.* **3:65** A Jewish tradition reads *sorrow of.*
Heb. 1:3 NU-Text omits *by Himself.* / NU-Text omits *our.* **1:5** Psalm 2:7 / 2 Samuel 7:14 **1:6** Deuteronomy 32:43 (Septuagint, Dead Sea Scrolls); Psalm 97:7 **1:7** Psalm 104:4 **1:9** Psalm 45:6, 7 **1:12** Psalm 102:25-27 **1:13** Psalm 110:1

OCTOBER 31

Lam. 4:7 Or *nobles* **4:16** Targum reads *anger.* **5:5** Literally *necks*
Heb. 2:7 NU-Text and M-Text omit the rest of verse 7. **2:8** Psalm 8:4-6 **2:12** Psalm 22:22 **2:13** 2 Samuel 22:3; Isaiah 8:17 / Isaiah 8:18
Ps. 103:16 Compare Job 7:10

NOVEMBER 1

Ezek. 1:1 Following Masoretic Text, Septuagint, and Vulgate; Syriac and Targum read *a vision.* **1:3** Or *Babylonians,* and so elsewhere in this book **1:20** Literally *living creature;* Septuagint and Vulgate read *spirit of life;* Targum reads *creatures.* **1:21** Literally *living creature;* Septuagint and Vulgate read *spirit of life;* Targum reads *creatures.* **1:22** Following Septuagint, Targum, and Vulgate; Masoretic Text reads *living creature.*
Heb. 3:6 NU-Text omits *firm to the end.* **3:11** Psalm 95:7-11 **3:15** Psalm 95:7, 8
Ps. 104:18 Or *rock hyrax* (compare Leviticus 11:5)

NOVEMBER 2

Ezek. 5:7 Following Masoretic Text, Septuagint, Targum, and Vulgate; many Hebrew manuscripts and Syriac read *but have done* (compare 11:12). **5:15** Septuagint, Syriac, Targum, and Vulgate read *you.*
Heb. 4:2 NU-Text and M-Text read *profit them, since they were not united by faith with those who heeded it.* **4:3** Psalm 95:11 **4:4** Genesis 2:2 **4:5** Psalm 95:11 **4:7** Psalm 95:7, 8

NOVEMBER 3

Ezek. 9:3 Literally *house*
Heb. 5:5 Psalm 2:7 **5:6** Psalm 110:4

NOVEMBER 4

Ezek. 10:3 Literally *house,* also in verses 4 and 18 **10:17** Literally *they* / Literally *they* / Literally *they* **11:19** Literally *you* **11:24** Or *Babylon,* and so elsewhere in this book
Heb. 6:3 M-Text reads *let us do.* **6:6** Or *and have fallen*

away. **6:10** NU-Text omits *labor of.* **6:14** Genesis 22:17 **6:18** M-Text omits *might.*

NOVEMBER 5

Ezek. 13:18 Literally *over all the joints of My hands;* Vulgate reads *under every elbow;* Septuagint and Targum read *on all elbows of the hands.*
Heb. 7:14 NU-Text reads *priests.* **7:17** NU-Text reads *it is testified.* / Psalm 110:4

NOVEMBER 6

Heb. 7:21 NU-Text ends the quotation here. / Psalm 110:4
Ps. 106:3 Septuagint, Syriac, Targum, and Vulgate read *those who do.*

NOVEMBER 7

Ezek. 16:43 Following Septuagint, Syriac, Targum, and Vulgate; Masoretic Text reads *were agitated with Me.* **16:50** Vulgate reads *you saw;* Septuagint reads *he saw;* Targum reads *as was revealed to Me.* **16:57** Following Masoretic Text, Septuagint, Targum, and Vulgate; many Hebrew manuscripts and Syriac read *Edom.* **17:7** Following Septuagint, Syriac, and Vulgate; Masoretic Text and Targum read *one.* **17:21** Following Masoretic Text and Vulgate; many Hebrew manuscripts and Syriac read *choice men;* Targum reads *mighty men;* Septuagint omits *All his fugitives.*
Heb. 8:5 Exodus 25:40 **8:12** NU-Text omits *and their lawless deeds.* / Jeremiah 31:31-34

NOVEMBER 8

Ezek. 18:17 Following Masoretic Text, Targum, and Vulgate; Septuagint reads *iniquity* (compare verse 8). **19:7** Septuagint reads *He stood in insolence;* Targum reads *He destroyed its palaces;* Vulgate reads *He learned to make widows.* **19:10** Literally *blood.* Following Masoretic Text, Syriac, and Vulgate; Septuagint reads *like a flower on a pomegranate tree;* Targum reads *in your likeness.*
Ps. 106:32 Or *Meribah*

NOVEMBER 9

Ezek. 20:6 Exodus 3:8 **20:11** Leviticus 18:5 **20:13** Leviticus 18:5 **20:15** Exodus 3:8 **20:21** Leviticus 18:5 **20:29** Literally *High Place* **20:46** Hebrew *Negev*
Heb. 9:11 NU-Text reads *that have come.* **9:20** Exodus 24:8

NOVEMBER 10

Ezek. 22:24 Following Masoretic Text, Syriac, and Vulgate; Septuagint reads *showered upon.* **22:25** Following Masoretic Text and Vulgate; Septuagint reads *princes;* Targum reads *scribes.*
Heb. 10:7 Psalm 40:6-8 **10:9** NU-Text and M-Text omit *O God.* **10:16** Jeremiah 31:33 **10:17** Jeremiah 31:34
Ps. 108:13 Compare verses 6-13 with 60:5-12

NOVEMBER 11

Ezek. 23:4 Literally *Her Own Tabernacle* / Literally *My Tabernacle Is in Her*
Heb. 10:30 Deuteronomy 32:35 / NU-Text omits *says the Lord.* / Deuteronomy 32:36 **10:34** NU-Text reads *the prisoners* instead of *me in my chains.* / NU-Text omits *in heaven.* **10:37** Or *that which* **10:38** NU-Text reads *my just one.* / Habakkuk 2:3, 4

NOVEMBER 12

Ezek. 24:14 Septuagint, Syriac, Targum, and Vulgate read *I.* **26:7** Hebrew *Nebuchadrezzar,* and so elsewhere in this book
Heb. 11:5 Genesis 5:24 **11:11** NU-Text omits *she bore a child.* **11:13** NU-Text and M-Text omit *were assured of them.*

NOVEMBER 13

Ezek. 27:6 Hebrew *Kittim,* western lands, especially Cyprus **27:10** Hebrew *Lud* / Hebrew *Put*
Heb. 11:18 Genesis 21:12 **11:26** NU-Text and M-Text read *of.*

NOVEMBER 14

Ezek. 29:3 That is, the Nile **29:5** Following Masoretic Text, Septuagint, and Vulgate; some Hebrew manuscripts and Targum read *buried.* **29:7** Following Masoretic Text and Vulgate; Septuagint and Syriac read *hand.* **29:10** Or *tower* **30:5** Hebrew *Put* / Hebrew *Lud* **30:13** That is, ancient Memphis **30:14** That is, ancient Thebes **30:15** That is, ancient Pelusium **30:17** That is, ancient On (Heliopolis) **30:18** Spelled *Tahpanhes* in Jeremiah 43:7 and elsewhere / Following many Hebrew manuscripts, Bomberg, Septuagint, Syriac, Targum, and Vulgate; Masoretic Text reads *refrained.*
Heb. 11:37 NU-Text omits *were tempted.* **12:6** Proverbs 3:11, 12 **12:7** NU-Text and M-Text read *It is for discipline that you endure; God.*

NOVEMBER 15

Ezek. 31:8 Hebrew *armon*
Heb. 12:18 NU-Text reads *to that which.* / NU-Text reads *gloom.* **12:20** NU-Text and M-Text omit the rest of this verse. / Exodus 19:12, 13 **12:21** Deuteronomy 9:19 **12:26** NU-Text reads *will shake.* / Haggai 2:6 **12:28** M-Text omits *may.*
Prov. 27:20 Or *Sheol* / Hebrew *Abaddon*

NOVEMBER 16

Heb. 13:5 Deuteronomy 31:6, 8; Joshua 1:5 **13:6** Psalm 118:6 **13:9** NU-Text and M-Text read *away.* **13:21** NU-Text and M-Text read *us.*

NOVEMBER 18

Ezek. 38:2 Targum, Vulgate, and Aquila read *chief prince of* (also verse 3). **38:5** Hebrew *Cush* / Hebrew *Put*
James 1:19 NU-Text reads *Know this* or *This you know.* **1:26** NU-Text omits *among you.* **2:8** Leviticus 19:18 **2:11** Exodus 20:14; Deuteronomy 5:18 / Exodus 20:13; Deuteronomy 5:17

NOVEMBER 19

Ezek. 39:1 Targum, Vulgate and Aquila read *chief prince of.* **39:11** Literally *The Multitude of Gog* **39:14** Literally *those who pass through* **40:5** Literally *house,* and so elsewhere in this book
James 2:18 NU-Text omits *your.* / NU-Text omits *my.* **2:20** NU-Text reads *useless.* **2:23** Genesis 15:6

3:3 NU-Text reads *Now if.* **3:12** NU-Text reads *Neither can a salty spring produce fresh water.*
Ps. 118:14 Compare Exodus 15:2

NOVEMBER 20

Ezek. 41:1 Hebrew *heykal*, here the main room of the temple, sometimes called the *holy place* (compare Exodus 26:33) **41:17** Literally *house*, here *the Most Holy Place*
James 4:2 NU-Text and M-Text omit *Yet.* **4:4** NU-Text omits *Adulterers and.* **4:6** Proverbs 3:34 **4:12** NU-Text adds *and Judge.* / NU-Text and M-Text read *But who.* / NU-Text reads *a neighbor.* **4:13** M-Text reads *let us.*

NOVEMBER 21

Ezek. 42:16 Compare 40:5 **43:3** Some Hebrew manuscripts and Vulgate read *He.*
James 5:4 Literally, in Hebrew, *Hosts* **5:5** NU-Text omits *as.* **5:9** NU-Text and M-Text read *judged.* **5:12** M-Text reads *hypocrisy.* **5:16** NU-Text reads *Therefore confess your sins.* **5:20** NU-Text reads *his soul.*

NOVEMBER 22

Ezek. 45:5 Following Masoretic Text, Targum, and Vulgate; Septuagint reads *a possession, cities of dwelling.*
1 Pet. 1:8 M-Text reads *known.* **1:12** NU-Text and M-Text read *you.*

NOVEMBER 23

1 Pet. 1:16 Leviticus 11:44, 45; 19:2; 20:7 **1:22** NU-Text omits *through the Spirit.* **1:23** NU-Text omits *forever.* **1:24** NU-Text reads *all its glory.* **1:25** Isaiah 40:6-8 **2:2** NU-Text adds *up to salvation.* **2:6** Isaiah 28:16 **2:7** NU-Text reads *to those who disbelieve.* / Psalm 118:22 **2:8** Isaiah 8:14
Ps. 119:37 Following Masoretic Text, Septuagint, and Vulgate; Targum reads *Your words.*

NOVEMBER 24

Ezek. 47:19 Hebrew *Negev* **48:28** Hebrew *Negev* **48:35** Hebrew *YHWH Shammah*
1 Pet. 2:21 NU-Text reads *you.* / NU-Text and M-Text read *you.* **2:22** Isaiah 53:9 **2:25** Greek *Episkopos*

NOVEMBER 25

Dan. 1:11 Hebrew *Melzar*, also in verse 16 **1:19** Literally *talked with them* **2:4** The original language of Daniel 2:4b through 7:28 is Aramaic.
1 Pet. 3:8 NU-Text reads *humble.* **3:12** Psalm 34:12-16 **3:14** Isaiah 8:12 **3:15** NU-Text reads *Christ as Lord.* **3:18** NU-Text and M-Text read *you.* **3:20** NU-Text and M-Text read *when the longsuffering of God waited patiently.* **4:1** NU-Text omits *for us.* **4:3** NU-Text reads *time.*

NOVEMBER 26

Dan. 2:25 Literally *of the sons of the captivity* **2:32** Or *sides* **2:33** Or *baked clay*, and so in verses 34, 35, and 42 **2:49** That is, the king's court **3:25** Or *a son of the gods* **3:28** Or *angel*
1 Pet. 4:8 Proverbs 10:12 **4:14** NU-Text omits the rest of this verse. **4:16** NU-Text reads *name.* **4:18** Proverbs 11:31 **5:2** NU-Text adds *according to God.* **5:5** Proverbs 3:34 **5:8** NU-Text and M-Text omit *because.* **5:10** NU-Text reads *But the God of all grace . . . will perfect, establish, strengthen, and settle you.* / NU-Text and M-Text read *you.*

NOVEMBER 27

Dan. 4:16 Possibly *seven years*, and so in verses 23, 25, and 32 **4:34** Literally *days*
2 Pet. 1:19 Or *We also have the more sure prophetic word.* **1:20** Or *origin* **1:21** NU-Text reads *but men spoke from God.*

NOVEMBER 28

Dan. 5:12 Literally *untying knots*, and so in verse 16 **5:13** Literally *of the sons of the captivity* **5:24** Literally *palm* **5:25** Literally *a mina* (50 shekels) from the verb "to number" / Literally *a shekel* from the verb "to weigh" / Literally *and half-shekels* from the verb "to divide" **5:28** Aramaic *Paras*, consonant with *Peres*
2 Pet. 2:3 M-Text reads *will not.* **2:17** NU-Text reads *and mists.* / NU-Text omits *forever.* **2:18** NU-Text reads *are barely escaping.* **2:22** Proverbs 26:11

NOVEMBER 29

Dan. 6:13 Literally *of the sons of the captivity* **6:18** Exact meaning unknown
2 Pet. 3:2 NU-Text and M-Text read *commandment of the apostles of your Lord and Savior* or *commandment of your apostles of the Lord and Savior.* **3:9** NU-Text reads *you.* **3:10** NU-Text reads *laid bare* (literally *found*).

NOVEMBER 30

Dan. 7:1 Literally *the head* (or *chief*) *of the words* **7:10** Or *judgment* **7:17** Representing their kingdoms (compare verse 23) **7:25** Literally *wear out* **7:28** Literally *the word*
1 John 1:4 NU-Text and M-Text read *our.*

DECEMBER 1

Dan. 8:14 Literally *evening-mornings* **8:21** Literally *king*, representing his kingdom (compare 7:17, 23) **8:25** Literally *hand* / Literally *hand*
1 John 2:7 NU-Text reads *Beloved.* / NU-Text omits *from the beginning.*

DECEMBER 2

Dan. 9:24 Literally *sevens*, and so throughout the chapter / Following Qere, Septuagint, Syriac, and Vulgate; Kethib and Theodotion read *To seal up.* **9:25** Or *open square* / Or *moat* **10:1** Or *and of great conflict* **10:4** Hebrew *Hiddekel.* **10:16** Theodotion and Vulgate read *the son;* Septuagint reads *a hand.*
1 John 2:18 NU-Text omits *the.* **2:20** NU-Text reads *you all know.* **2:27** NU-Text reads *you abide.* **2:28** NU-Text reads *if.* **3:1** NU-Text adds *And we are.* / M-Text reads *you.*

DECEMBER 3

Dan. 11:6 Literally *arm* **11:8** Or *molded images* **11:14** Or *robbers*, literally *sons of breakage* **11:15** Literally *arms* **11:16** Literally *hand* **11:17** Or *bring equitable terms* **11:22** Literally *arms* **11:30** Hebrew *Kittim*, western lands, especially Cyprus **11:31** Literally *arms*

1 John 3:14 NU-Text omits *his brother.* **3:19** NU-Text reads *we shall know.* **3:23** M-Text omits *us.*

DECEMBER 4

Dan. 11:37 Or *gods*
1 John 4:3 NU-Text omits *that* and *Christ has come in the flesh.* **4:19** NU-Text omits *Him.* **4:20** NU-Text reads *he cannot.*

DECEMBER 5

Hos. 1:6 Literally *No-Mercy* / Or *That I may forgive them at all* **1:9** Literally *Not-My-People* **1:10** Hebrew *Io-ammi* (compare verse 9) **2:1** Hebrew *Ammi* (compare 1:9, 10) / Hebrew *Ruhamah* (compare 1:6) **2:16** Hebrew *Ishi* / Hebrew *Baali* **2:22** Literally *God Will Sow* **2:23** Hebrew *Io-ruhamah* / Hebrew *Io-ammi* **3:1** Literally *friend* or *husband*
1 John 5:4 M-Text reads *your.* **5:8** NU-Text and M-Text omit the words from *in heaven* (verse 7) through *on earth* (verse 8). Only four or five very late manuscripts contain these words in Greek. **5:9** NU-Text reads *God, that.* **5:13** NU-Text omits the rest of this verse. **5:18** NU-Text reads *him.*
Ps. 124:7 That is, persons who catch birds in a trap or snare

DECEMBER 6

Hos. 4:7 Following Masoretic Text, Septuagint, and Vulgate; scribal tradition, Syriac, and Targum read *They will change.* / Following Masoretic Text, Septuagint, Syriac, Targum, and Vulgate; scribal tradition reads *My glory.* **4:14** Compare Deuteronomy 23:18 **4:18** Hebrew is difficult; a Jewish tradition reads *Her rulers shamefully love, 'Give!'*
2 John 3 NU-Text and M-Text read *us.* **8** NU-Text reads *you.* / NU-Text reads *you.* **9** NU-Text reads *goes ahead.*
Prov. 29:10 Literally *soul* **29:11** Literally *spirit*

DECEMBER 7

Hos. 6:7 Or *like Adam* **7:6** Following Masoretic Text and Vulgate; Syriac and Targum read *Their anger;* Septuagint reads *Ephraim* **7:14** Following Masoretic Text and Targum; Vulgate reads *thought upon;* Septuagint reads *slashed themselves for* (compare 1 Kings 18:28). / Following Masoretic Text, Syriac, and Targum; Septuagint omits *They rebel against Me;* Vulgate reads *They departed from Me.* **7:16** Or *upward* **8:1** Hebrew *shophar,* ram's horn **8:10** Or *begin to diminish* / Or *oracle* **8:14** Or *palaces* **9:8** That is, one who catches birds in a trap or snare
3 John 4 NU-Text reads *the truth.* **5** NU-Text adds *especially.* **8** NU-Text reads *support.* **11** NU-Text and M-Text omit *but.*

DECEMBER 8

Hos. 10:5 Literally *calves* **10:9** So read many Hebrew manuscripts, Septuagint, and Vulgate; Masoretic Text reads *unruliness.* **10:10** Or *in their two habitations* **11:2** Following Masoretic Text and Vulgate; Septuagint reads *Just as I called them;* Targum interprets as *I sent prophets to a thousand of them.* / Following Masoretic Text, Targum, and Vulgate; Septuagint reads *from My face.* **11:3** Some Hebrew manuscripts, Septuagint, Syriac, and Vulgate read *My arms.* **11:4** Literally *cords*

of a man / Literally *jaws* **11:7** Or *upward* **11:9** Or *I will not enter a city* **11:12** Or *holy ones* **12:3** Compare Genesis 32:28 **13:2** Or *those who offer human sacrifice* **13:9** Literally *it* or *he destroyed you* / Literally *in your help* **13:10** Septuagint, Syriac, Targum, and Vulgate read *Where is your king?* **13:14** Or *Sheol* / Septuagint reads *where is your punishment?* / Or *Sheol* / Septuagint reads *where is your sting?* **13:16** Septuagint reads *shall be disfigured* **14:2** Literally *bull calves;* Septuagint reads *fruit.* **14:7** Literally *remembrance*
Jude 1 NU-Text reads *beloved.* **4** NU-Text omits *God.* **12** NU-Text and M-Text read *along.* **22** NU-Text reads *who are doubting* (or *making distinctions*). **23** NU-Text adds *and on some have mercy with fear* and omits *with fear* in first clause. **24** M-Text reads *them.* **25** NU-Text reads *To the only God our Savior.* / NU-Text omits *Who . . . is wise* and adds *through Jesus Christ our Lord.* / NU-Text adds *Before all time.*

DECEMBER 9

Joel 1:4 Exact identity of these locusts is unknown. **1:18** Septuagint and Vulgate read *are made desolate.* **2:6** Septuagint, Targum, and Vulgate read *gather blackness.* **2:8** Literally *his own highway* / That is, they are not halted by losses **2:23** Or *the teacher of righteousness* **2:26** Compare 1:4 **3:8** Literally *Shebaites* (compare Isaiah 60:6 and Ezekiel 27:22)
Rev. 1:5 NU-Text reads *loves us and freed;* M-Text reads *loves us and washed.* **1:6** NU-Text and M-Text read *a kingdom.* **1:8** NU-Text and M-Text omit *the Beginning and the End.* / NU-Text and M-Text add *God.* **1:9** NU-Text and M-Text omit *both.* **1:11** NU-Text and M-Text omit *I am* through third *and.* / NU-Text and M-Text omit *which are in Asia.* **1:17** NU-Text and M-Text omit *to me.* **1:19** NU-Text and M-Text read *Therefore, write.* **1:20** NU-Text and M-Text omit *which you saw.*
Prov. 29:18 Or *prophetic vision*

DECEMBER 10

Amos 1:1 Compare 2 Kings 3:4 **2:7** Or *trample on* **3:12** The Hebrew is uncertain.
Rev. 2:15 NU-Text and M-Text read *likewise* for *which thing I hate.*

DECEMBER 11

Amos 4:1 Literally *their lords* or *their masters* **4:4** Or *years* (compare Deuteronomy 14:28) **4:13** Or *His* **5:26** A pagan deity / Septuagint and Vulgate read *tabernacle of Moloch.* / A pagan deity **6:10** Literally *bones* **6:13** Literally *Nothing* / Literally *Horns,* symbol of strength
Rev. 2:19 NU-Text and M-Text read *faith, service.* **2:20** NU-Text and M-Text read *I have against you that you tolerate.* / M-Text reads *your wife Jezebel.* / NU-Text and M-Text read *and teaches and seduces.* **2:21** NU-Text and M-Text read *time to repent, and she does not want to repent of her sexual immorality.* **2:22** NU-Text and M-Text read *her.* **2:24** NU-Text and M-Text omit *and.* / NU-Text and M-Text omit *will.* **2:27** Psalm 2:9 **3:2** NU-Text and M-Text read *My God.* **3:4** NU-Text and M-Text read *Nevertheless you have a few names in Sardis.*

DECEMBER 12

Amos 7:14 Compare 2 Kings 3:4   **8:4** Or *trample on* (compare 2:7)   **8:8** That is, the Nile; some Hebrew manuscripts, Septuagint, Syriac, Targum, and Vulgate read *River* (compare 9:5); Masoretic Text reads *the light*.   **8:14** Or *Ashima,* a Syrian goddess   **9:2** Or *Sheol*   **9:5** That is, the Nile   **9:11** Literally *booth,* figure of a deposed dynasty   **9:12** Septuagint reads *mankind.*

Rev. 3:7 Isaiah 22:22   **3:8** NU-Text and M-Text read *which no one can shut.*   **3:11** NU-Text and M-Text omit *Behold.*   **3:14** NU-Text and M-Text read *in Laodicea.*   **3:16** NU-Text and M-Text read *hot nor cold.*

DECEMBER 13

Obad. 7 Or *wound,* or *plot*   **12** Literally *on the day he became a foreigner*   **19** Hebrew *Negev*   **20** Hebrew *Negev*   **21** Or *deliverers*

Rev. 4:3 M-Text omits *And He who sat there was* (which makes the description in verse 3 modify the throne rather than God).   **4:4** NU-Text and M-Text read *robes, with crowns.*   **4:5** NU-Text and M-Text read *voices, and thunderings. /* M-Text omits *the.*   **4:6** NU-Text and M-Text add *something like.*   **4:8** M-Text has *holy* nine times.   **4:11** NU-Text and M-Text read *our Lord and God. /* NU-Text and M-Text read *existed.*

Ps. 132:6 Hebrew *Jaar*

Prov. 29:24 Literally *hears the adjuration*

DECEMBER 14

Jon. 1:5 Literally *from upon them*   **3:3** Exact meaning unknown   **4:6** Hebrew *kikayon,* exact identity unknown

Rev. 5:4 NU-Text and M-Text omit *and read.*   **5:5** NU-Text and M-Text omit *to loose.*   **5:6** NU-Text and M-Text read *I saw in the midst . . . a Lamb standing.*   **5:10** NU-Text and M-Text read *them. /* NU-Text reads *a kingdom. /* NU-Text and M-Text read *they.*   **5:13** M-Text adds *Amen.*   **5:14** NU-Text and M-Text omit *twenty-four. /* NU-Text and M-Text omit *Him who lives forever and ever.*

DECEMBER 15

Mic. 1:10 Literally *House of Dust*   **1:11** Literally *Going Out*   **1:12** Literally *was sick*   **1:14** Literally *Possession of Gath /* Literally *Lie*   **1:15** Literally *Inheritance*   **2:5** Literally *one casting a surveyor's line*   **2:6** Literally *to these /* Vulgate reads *He shall not take shame.*   **2:12** Hebrew *Bozrah*   **3:2** Literally *them*   **3:12** Literally *house*   **4:3** Compare Isaiah 2:2-4

Rev. 6:1 NU-Text and M-Text read *seven seals.*   **6:3** NU-Text and M-Text omit *and see.*   **6:6** Greek *choinix;* that is, approximately one quart / This was approximately one day's wage for a worker.   **6:12** NU-Text and M-Text omit *behold. /* NU-Text and M-Text read *the whole moon.*   **6:15** NU-Text and M-Text read *the commanders, the rich men.*

DECEMBER 16

Mic. 5:14 Hebrew *Asherim,* Canaanite deities   **5:15** Or *obeyed*   **6:5** Hebrew *Shittim* (compare Numbers 25:1; Joshua 2:1, 3:1)   **6:14** Or *Emptiness* or *Humiliation /* Targum and Vulgate read *You shall take hold.*   **6:16** Following Masoretic Text, Targum, and Vulgate; Septuagint reads *of nations.*   **7:11** Or *the boundary shall be ex-*

tended   **7:12** Literally *he,* collective of the captives / Hebrew *arey mazor,* possibly *cities of Egypt /* Hebrew *mazor,* possibly *Egypt /* That is, the Euphrates   **7:15** Literally *him,* collective for the captives   **7:19** Literally *their*

Rev. 7:5 In NU-Text and M-Text *were sealed* is stated only in verses 5a and 8c; the words are understood in the remainder of the passage.   **7:14** NU-Text and M-Text read *My lord.*   **7:17** NU-Text and M-Text read *to fountains of the waters of life.*

DECEMBER 17

Nah. 1:1 Or *oracle*   **1:5** Targum reads *burns.*   **2:1** Vulgate reads *he who destroys.*   **2:3** Literally *the cypresses are shaken;* Septuagint and Syriac read *the horses rush about;* Vulgate reads *the drivers are stupefied.*   **2:7** Hebrew *Huzzab*   **2:10** Compare Joel 2:6   **2:13** Literally *her*   **3:8** That is, ancient Thebes; Targum and Vulgate read *populous Alexandria. /* Literally *rivers,* that is, the Nile and the surrounding canals   **3:9** Septuagint reads *her.*

Rev. 8:7 NU-Text and M-Text add *and a third of the earth was burned up.*   **8:13** NU-Text and M-Text read *eagle.*

DECEMBER 18

Hab. 1:1 Or *oracle*   **1:11** Literally *spirit* or *wind*   **2:5** Or *Sheol*   **2:6** Syriac and Vulgate read *thick clay.*   **2:7** Literally *those who bite you*   **2:13** Literally *for what satisfies fire,* that is, for what is of no lasting value   **2:15** Literally *Attaching* or *Joining*   **2:16** Dead Sea Scrolls and Septuagint read *And reel!;* Syriac and Vulgate read *And fall fast asleep!*   **3:1** Exact meaning unknown   **3:9** Literally *rods* or *tribes* (compare verse 14)   **3:19** Hebrew *YHWH Adonai*

Rev. 9:19 NU-Text and M-Text read *the power of the horses.*   **9:21** NU-Text and M-Text read *drugs.*

DECEMBER 19

Zeph. 1:3 Figurative of idols   **1:4** Hebrew *chemarim*   **1:5** Or *Malcam,* an Ammonite god, also called *Molech* (compare Leviticus 18:21)   **1:7** Literally *set apart, consecrated*   **1:9** Compare 1 Samuel 5:5   **1:11** Literally *Mortar,* a market district of Jerusalem   **1:12** Literally *on their lees,* that is, settled like the dregs of wine   **2:1** Or *shameless*   **2:6** Literally *excavations,* either underground huts or cisterns   **3:8** Septuagint and Syriac read *for witness;* Targum reads *for the day of My revelation* for judgment; Vulgate reads *for the day of My resurrection that is to come.*   **3:15** Some Hebrew manuscripts, Septuagint, and Bomberg read *see;* Masoretic Text and Vulgate read *fear.*

Rev. 10:4 NU-Text and M-Text read *sounded. /* NU-Text and M-Text omit *to me.*   **10:5** NU-Text and M-Text read *right hand.*   **10:11** NU-Text and M-Text read *they.*

DECEMBER 20

Hag. 1:4 Literally *house,* and so in verse 8   **2:3** Literally *house,* and so in verses 7 and 9   **2:7** Or *the desire of all nations*

Rev. 11:1 NU-Text and M-Text omit *And the angel stood.*   **11:4** NU-Text and M-Text read *Lord.*   **11:8** NU-Text and M-Text read *their.*   **11:9** NU-Text and M-Text read *nations see . . . and will not allow.*   **11:12** M-Text reads *I.*   **11:15** NU-Text and M-Text read *kingdom . . . has become.*   **11:17** NU-Text and M-Text omit

and who is to come. **11:19** M-Text reads *the covenant of the Lord.*
Ps. 139:11 Vulgate and Symmachus read *cover.*
139:14 Following Masoretic Text and Targum; Septuagint, Syriac, and Vulgate read *You are fearfully wonderful.* **139:20** Septuagint and Vulgate read *They take your cities in vain.*
Prov. 30:16 Or *Sheol*

DECEMBER 21

Zech. 1:21 Literally *these*
Rev. 12:8 M-Text reads *him.* **12:17** NU-Text and M-Text omit *Christ.* **13:1** NU-Text reads *he.*

DECEMBER 22

Rev. 13:1 NU-Text and M-Text read *ten horns and seven heads.* **13:5** M-Text reads *make war.* **13:7** NU-Text and M-Text add *and people.* **13:14** M-Text reads *my own people.* **13:17** NU-Text and M-Text omit *or.*

DECEMBER 23

Zech. 4:9 Literally *house* **4:12** Literally *into the hands of* **5:6** Hebrew *ephah,* a measuring container, and so elsewhere **5:8** Literally *stone* **5:11** That is, Babylon
Rev. 14:1 NU-Text and M-Text read *the.* / NU-Text and M-Text add *His name and.* **14:4** M-Text adds *by Jesus.* **14:5** NU-Text and M-Text read *falsehood.* / NU-Text and M-Text omit *before the throne of God.* **14:8** NU-Text reads *Babylon the great is fallen, is fallen, which has made;* M-Text reads *Babylon the great is fallen. She has made.* **14:12** NU-Text and M-Text omit *here are those.* **14:13** NU-Text and M-Text omit *to me.* **14:15** NU-Text and M-Text omit *for You.*
Ps. 142:title Hebrew *Maschil*

DECEMBER 24

Zech. 6:14 Following Masoretic Text, Targum, and Vulgate; Syriac reads *for Heldai* (compare verse 10); Septuagint reads *for the patient ones.* **7:2** Literally *they* (compare verse 5) / Or *Sar-Ezer* / Hebrew *Bethel* **7:7** Hebrew *Negev*
Rev. 15:2 NU-Text and M-Text omit *over his mark.* **15:3** NU-text and M-Text read *nations.* **15:5** NU-Text and M-Text omit *behold.*
Ps. 143:9 Septuagint and Vulgate read *To You I flee.*
Prov. 30:26 Or *hyraxes* **30:28** Or *lizard*

DECEMBER 25

Zech. 8:17 Literally *his*
Rev. 16:1 NU-Text and M-Text read *seven bowls.* **16:5** NU-Text and M-Text omit *O Lord.* / NU-Text and M-Text read *who was, the Holy One.* **16:6** NU-Text and M-Text omit *For.* **16:7** NU-Text and M-Text omit *another from.* **16:14** NU-Text and M-Text omit *of the earth and.* **16:16** M-Text reads *Megiddo.*
Ps. 144:2 Following Masoretic Text, Septuagint, and Vulgate; Syriac and Targum read *the peoples* (compare 18:47).
Prov. 30:31 Exact identity unknown / A Jewish tradition reads *a king against whom there is no uprising.*

DECEMBER 26

Zech. 9:1 Or *oracle* **9:10** Psalm 72:8 **9:17** Or *His* / Or *His*

Rev. 17:1 NU-Text and M-Text omit *to me.* **17:4** M-Text reads *the filthiness of the fornication of the earth.* **17:8** NU-Text and M-Text read *and shall be present.* **17:16** NU-Text and M-Text read *saw, and the beast.*
Ps. 145:5 Following Masoretic Text and Targum; Dead Sea Scrolls, Septuagint, Syriac, and Vulgate read *They.* / Literally *on the words of Your wondrous works* **145:13** Following Masoretic Text and Targum; Dead Sea Scrolls, Septuagint, Syriac, and Vulgate add *The Lord is faithful in all His words, and holy in all His works.*

DECEMBER 27

Zech. 10:1 That is, spring rain **10:2** Hebrew *teraphim* **10:4** Or *despot* **10:11** That is, the Nile **11:3** Or *floodplain, thicket* **11:7** Following Masoretic Text, Targum, and Vulgate; Septuagint reads *for the Canaanites.* / Or *Grace,* and so in verse 10 / Or *Unity,* and so in verse 14 **11:11** Following Masoretic Text, Targum, and Vulgate; Septuagint reads *the Canaanites.*
Rev. 18:2 NU-Text and M-Text omit *mightily.* **18:5** NU-Text and M-Text read *have been heaped up.* **18:6** NU-Text and M-Text omit *to you.* **18:8** NU-Text and M-Text read *has judged.* **18:14** NU-Text and M-Text read *been lost to you.* **18:20** NU-Text and M-Text read *saints and apostles.*

DECEMBER 28

Zech. 12:1 Or *oracle* **12:11** Hebrew *Megiddon* **13:6** Or *hands*
Rev. 19:1 NU-Text and M-Text add *something like.* / NU-Text and M-Text omit *the Lord.* **19:5** NU-Text and M-Text omit *both.* **19:6** NU-Text and M-Text read *our.* **19:12** M-Text adds *names written, and.* **19:14** NU-Text and M-Text read *pure white linen.* **19:15** M-Text adds *two-edged.* **19:17** NU-Text and M-Text read *the great supper of God.* **19:18** NU-Text and M-Text read *both free.*

DECEMBER 29

Zech. 14:5 Or *you;* Septuagint, Targum, and Vulgate read *Him.* **14:9** Compare Deuteronomy 6:4 **14:10** Literally *She* **14:21** Or *on every pot . . . , shall be (engraved) "HOLINESS TO THE LORD OF HOSTS"*
Rev. 20:4 M-Text reads *the.* **20:10** NU-Text and M-Text add *also.* **20:12** NU-Text and M-Text read *the throne.* **20:14** NU-text and M-Text add *the lake of fire.*
Prov. 31:8 Literally *sons of passing away*

DECEMBER 30

Mal. 1:1 Or *oracle* **1:12** Following Bomberg; Masoretic Text reads *Lord.* **2:6** Or *true instruction* **2:12** Talmud and Vulgate read *teacher and student.*
Rev. 21:2 NU-Text and M-Text omit *John.* **21:5** NU-Text and M-Text omit *to me.* **21:6** M-Text omits *It is done.* **21:7** M-Text reads *overcomes, I shall give him these things.* **21:8** M-Text adds *and sinners.* **21:9** NU-Text and M-Text omit *to me.* / M-Text reads *I will show you the woman, the Lamb's bride.* **21:10** NU-Text and M-Text omit *the great* and read *the holy city, Jerusalem.* **21:14** NU-Text and M-Text read *twelve names.* **21:23** NU-Text and M-Text omit *in it.* / M-Text reads *the very glory.* **21:24** NU-Text and M-Text omit *of those who are saved.* / M-Text reads *the glory and honor of the*

nations to Him. **21:26** M-Text adds *that they may enter in.* **21:27** NU-Text and M-Text read *anything profane, nor one who causes.*

Prov. 31:10 Verses 10 through 31 are an alphabetic acrostic in Hebrew (compare Psalm 119). / Literally *a wife of valor,* in the sense of all forms of excellence

DECEMBER 31

Mal. 3:17 Literally *special treasure*

Rev. 22:1 NU-Text and M-Text omit *pure.* **22:6** NU-Text and M-Text read *spirits of the prophets.* **22:8** NU-Text and M-Text read *am the one who heard and saw.* **22:9** NU-Text and M-Text omit *For.* **22:11** NU-Text and M-Text read *do right.* **22:13** NU-Text and M-Text read *the First and the Last, the Beginning and the End.* **22:14** NU-Text reads *wash their robes.* **22:15** NU-Text and M-Text omit *But.* **22:18** NU-Text and M-Text omit *For.* / M-Text reads *may God add.* **22:19** M-Text reads *may God take away.* / NU-Text and M-Text read *tree of life.* **22:21** NU-Text reads *with all;* M-Text reads *with all the saints.*

Where Can I Find It?

Great Passages from the Bible

Great Stories from the Bible